ALL GLORY TO ŚRĪ GURU AND GAURĀṄGA

ŚRĪMAD BHĀGAVATAM

of

KṚṢṆA-DVAIPĀYANA VYĀSA

पुंसां स्वकामाय विविक्तमार्गै-
रभ्यर्चतां कामदुघाङ्घ्रिपद्मम् ।
प्रदर्शयन्तं कृपया नखेन्दु-
मयूखभिन्नाङ्गुलिचारुपत्रम् ॥

puṁsāṁ sva-kāmāya vivikta-mārgair
abhyarcatāṁ kāma-dughāṅghri-padmam
pradarśayantaṁ kṛpayā nakhendu-
mayūkha-bhinnāṅguli-cāru-patram

(p. 315)

BOOKS by
His Divine Grace A. C. Bhaktivedanta Swami Prabhupāda

Bhagavad-gītā As It Is
Śrīmad-Bhāgavatam
Śrī Caitanya-caritāmṛta (17 vols.)
Teachings of Lord Caitanya
The Nectar of Devotion
The Nectar of Instruction
Śrī Īśopaniṣad
Easy Journey to Other Planets
Kṛṣṇa Consciousness: The Topmost Yoga System
Kṛṣṇa, The Supreme Personality of Godhead (3 vols.)
Perfect Questions, Perfect Answers
Dialectic Spiritualism – A Vedic View of Western Philosophy
Teachings of Lord Kapila, the Son of Devahūti
Transcendental Teachings of Prahlād Mahārāja
Kṛṣṇa, the Reservoir of Pleasure
The Science of Self-Realization
Life Comes from Life
The Perfection of Yoga
Beyond Birth and Death
On the Way to Kṛṣṇa
Geetār-gan (Bengali)
Rāja-vidyā: The King of Knowledge
Elevation to Kṛṣṇa Consciousness
Kṛṣṇa Consciousness: The Matchless Gift
Back to Godhead Magazine (Founder)

Endpapers: On the bank of the Ganges, Śukadeva Gosvāmī speaks *Śrīmad-Bhāgavatam* for the first time. Mahārāja Parīkṣit and other exalted saints and sages listen with rapt attention.

ŚRĪMAD BHĀGAVATAM

Third Canto
"The Status Quo"

With the Original Sanskrit Text,
Its Roman Transliteration, Synonyms,
Translation and Elaborate Purports

by

His Divine Grace
A. C. Bhaktivedanta Swami Prabhupāda
Founder-*Ācārya* of the International Society for Krishna Consciousness

Published by
Krishna Books Inc
English Edition

This classic edition of

ŚRĪMAD BHĀGAVATAM

Third Canto
"The Status Quo"

is the English edition published by
the Bhaktivedanta Book Trust in 1972

Krishna Books Inc is licensed by the Bhaktivedanta Book Trust
to print and publish the pre-1978 literary works of
His Divine Grace A. C. Bhaktivedanta Swami Prabhupāda

To obtain further information contact Krishna Books Inc
On the Internet at http://www.krishnabooks.org
By email at info@krishnabooks.org

Krishna Books Inc
578 Washington Blvd., Suite 808
Marina del Rey, CA 90292, USA

Published by
Krishna Books Inc
English Edition

ISBN: 978-1-60293-303-3
ISBN: 978-1-60293-300-2 (10 volume set)

Table of Contents

Preface *xix*
Introduction *xxiii*

CHAPTER ONE
Questions by Vidura **1**
Vidura Questions Maitreya Ṛṣi 1
Dhṛtarāṣṭra Sets Fire to the House of the Pāṇḍavas 5
Yudhiṣṭhira Unfairly Defeated in Gambling 6
Political Suggestions by Vidura 9
Vidura Insulted by Duryodhana 12
Vidura the Pilgrim 18
The Yadus Die Due to Violent Passion 21
Vidura Meets Uddhava 24
Vidura Questions Uddhava 26
How Akrura Fell on Kṛṣṇa's Footsteps 32
How Arjuna Satisfied Lord Śiva 37
Vidura Laments for Dhṛtarāṣṭra 40
Why Kṛṣṇa Refrained from Killing the Kurus 42
Kṛṣṇa Appears for the Sake of the Yadus 46

CHAPTER TWO
Remembrance of Lord Kṛṣṇa **47**
Uddhava in His Childhood 48
Uddhava's Ecstatic Changes 51
The Sun of the World Has Set 53
The Yadus Unable to Know Kṛṣṇa as Supreme 56
Kṛṣṇa's Body the Ornament of All Ornaments 60
The *Gopīs'* Anguish when Kṛṣṇa Left 63
Kṛṣṇa's Behavior Pains Vidura 66
Śiśupāla's Merging into the Body of Kṛṣṇa 70
Pūtanā Granted the Position of Kṛṣṇa's Mother 75

Kṛṣṇa Dispatched to the House of Nanda Mahārāja 78
Child Kṛṣṇa Appeared Like a Lion Cub 79
Great Wizards Killed by Kṛṣṇa 83
Kṛṣṇa Enjoyed the *Rāsa* Dance 86

CHAPTER THREE
The Lord's Pastimes Out of Vṛndāvana **89**
Kaṁsa Killed by Kṛṣṇa and Balarāma 89
Rukmiṇī Swept Away by Kṛṣṇa 91
Kṛṣṇa Marries the Kidnapped Princesses 96
Kṛṣṇa Exhibits the Powers of His Devotees 97
The Great Burden of Earth Abated 100
The Yadus Quarrel Among Themselves 102
Horse Sacrifices Performed by Yudhiṣṭhira 105
Kṛṣṇa Enjoys Conjugal Love 108
The Yadus Visit Places of Pilgrimage 112

CHAPTER FOUR
Vidura Approaches Maitreya **117**
The Yadus Destroyed by the Will of Kṛṣṇa 118
Kṛṣṇa's Eyes Reddish Like the Sunrise 122
Uddhava Awarded Kṛṣṇa's Ultimate Favor 126
Although Unborn, Kṛṣṇa Takes Birth 130
Pure Devotees Have No Material Afflictions 133
Nara-Nārāyaṇa Still in the Himalayas 137
Devotees Are Servants of Society 140
Vidura Afflicted by Kṛṣṇa's Departure 142
Kṛṣṇa Leaves the Vision of the Mundane World 147
Uddhava Reaches Badarikāśrama 149
Envious Beasts Cannot Know Kṛṣṇa 152

CHAPTER FIVE
Vidura's Talks With Maitreya **155**
Vidura Satisfied in Transcendence 155
Great Philanthropic Souls 158
The Independent, Desireless Lord 160

A Civilized Man Must Be Twice-born 162
The Nectar of Topics of Kṛṣṇa 167
Topics of Kṛṣṇa the Only Remedy 169
Materialists Pitied by the Pitiable 172
The All-Inclusive Service 176
Vidura Formerly the Controller Yamarāja 178
Compassion of the Lord for the Sleeping Energy 182
The Reservoir of Would-be Entities 186
The Chief Function of False Ego is Godlessness 189
Controlling Deities of Physical Elements 194
The Shade of Kṛṣṇa's Lotus Feet 197
Brahmā, Viṣṇu and Maheśvara 201
The Kingdom of All Pleasures 205
Lumps of Sin in the Shape of Foodstuffs 209
Implication in Conditions of Cosmic Creation 212

CHAPTER SIX
Creation of the Universal Form 215
The Supreme Lord Enters the Twenty-three Elements 216
The Gigantic Universal Form Manifested 219
The Aggregate Creation Rests in Viṣṇu 222
Demigods Construct the Cosmos 225
The Mouth of the Universal Form Manifested 228
His Eyes Manifested 229
His Ears Manifested 230
His Skin Manifested 231
His Hands and Legs Manifested 232
His Heart Manifested 234
His Ego Manifested 234
Planets Manifested from the Universal Form 236
Vedic Wisdom Manifested 238
Service Manifested from the Legs of Viṣṇu 243
The Creation of the Social Divisions 244
Glorification of Kṛṣṇa by Pure Speech 247
Kṛṣṇa's Bewildering Potency 251
Obeisances to Kṛṣṇa a Matter of Sanity 252

CHAPTER SEVEN
Further Inquiries by Vidura 255
Kṛṣṇa, Master of All Energies 256
Pure Soul Is Pure Consciousness 260
Maitreya Agitated by the Inquisitive Vidura 262
The Bewilderment of Mischievous Living Beings 266
Cessation of Unlimited Miserable Conditions 271
The Lowest of Fools Live Merrily 274
Questions by Vidura 279
Contradictions of Faithless Atheists 284
Spiritual Masters Are Kind to the Needy 288
Spotless Devotees of the Lord 291
Maitreya Ṛṣi Immortal 293

CHAPTER EIGHT
Manifestation of Brahmā From Garbhodakaśāyī Viṣṇu 295
The Book *Bhagāvatam* and Devotee *Bhāgavata* 297
Great Sages Travel Via the Ganges 299
The Brahminical Power of Forgiveness 303
The Subtle Subject of Creation 306
Lord Brahmā Born of the Lotus Flower 308
The Eternal Wheel in the Hand of Viṣṇu 311
Brahmā Developed Required Knowledge 312
The Lord Shows His Lotus Feet 316
Viṣṇu, the Self-Situated Tree 318
Brahmā Inclined to Create 321

CHAPTER NINE
Brahmā's Prayers for Creative Energy 323
Brahmā Born From the Lotus Flower 325
Those Who Neglect the Lord's Personal Form 327
The Perplexities of the Conditioned Souls 332
Devotees See Through the Ears 337
Acts of Religion Never Go in Vain 342

The Tree of the Cosmic Manifestation 345
Brahmā Prays for the Lord's Protection 354
The Lord Instructs the Devotee From Within 361
Transcendental Vision Frees One From Illusion 362
The Lord Pleased With the Prayers of Brahmā 369
The Dearmost Object Is the Lord 371

CHAPTER TEN
Divisions of the Creation 375
Penances of Brahmā 377
Fourteen Planetary Divisions Created 381
Unchangeable and Limitless Eternal Time 383
Nine Kinds of Creation 386
Creation of Human Beings 393
Creation of the Demigods 395

CHAPTER ELEVEN
Calculation of Time, From the Atom 397
The Ultimate Particle Is the Atom 397
Division of Gross Time 400
Duration of Life of the Human Being 404
The Sun Enlivens All Living Beings 407
Duration of the Four Millenniums 409
Duration of Life of the Manus 413
Brahmā's Night 415
Radius of the Material World 424

CHAPTER TWELVE
Creation of the Kumāras and Others 427
Creation of the Nescient Engagements 428
Creation of the Four Kumāras 430
Creation of Rudra 433
The Sons and Grandsons of Rudra 438
Narada Born From the Deliberation of Brahmā 443
Brahmā Attracted to His Daughter 447

Brahmā Gives Up His Body 452
Manifestation of the Four *Vedas* 455
Varṇāśrama-dharma Established by Brahmā 460
Brahmā As the Complete Form of the Absolute Truth 463
Creation of Svāyambhuva Manu 466

CHAPTER THIRTEEN
The Appearance of Lord Varāha 469
Hearing From the Mouths of Pure Devotees 471
Brahmā Pleased With Manu 475
Devotional Service As One's Own Self-interest 479
Small Boar Comes Out of Brahmā's Nostril 483
The Tumultuous Voice of Lord Boar 487
Lord Boar Lifts the Earth 492
Prayers of the Sages to Lord Boar 495
The Lord Is Bound by Sacrifice Only 499
The Earth As the Wife of the Lord 503
Hearing the Auspicious Narration of Lord Boar 508

CHAPTER FOURTEEN
Pregnancy of Diti in the Evening 513
Two Different Boar Incarnations 514
Diti Afflicted With Sex Desire 518
Kaśyapa Marries Thirteen Daughters of Dakṣa 522
Taking Shelter of a Wife 527
Lord Śiva, the King of the Ghosts 530
Kaśyapa Obliged to Perform a Forbidden Act 537
Śiva As the Worshipable Lord of All Women 541
Sons Born of Diti's Condemned Womb 543
Prahlāda as the Would-be Grandson of Diti 548
Satisfaction of Diti 553

CHAPTER FIFTEEN
Description of the Kingdom of God 555
The Force of the Pregnancy of Diti 556

Living Entities Conducted by the Vedic Directions 561
The Lord and His Devotees Reside in Vaikuṇṭha 566
The Inhabitants of Vaikuṇṭha 571
Importance of the Human Form of Life 576
The Four Kumāras Reach Vaikuṇṭha 580
The Doormen Block the Kumāras' Way 584
There Is Complete Harmony in Vaikuṇṭha 589
A *Brāhmaṇa*'s Curse Cannot Be Counteracted 592
The Lord Is the Reservoir of All Pleasure 596
The Kumāras Smell the Aroma of *Tulasī* Leaves 601
Prayers of the Kumāras 608

CHAPTER SIXTEEN
The Two Doorkeepers of Vaikuṇṭha, Jaya and Vijaya, Cursed by the Sages 617
The Lord Always Favors the Brāhmaṇas 620
The Brāhmaṇas Are Ever Satisfied With the Lord's *Prasāda* 624
The Lord's Lovely and Illuminating Speech 630
Prayers of the Sages 632
Lakṣmī Waits Upon the Lord 636
Kṛṣṇa's Pastimes Exhibited by Submission 642
The Sages Leave the Transcendental Abode 646
The Gatekeepers Fall From Vaikuṇṭha 651

CHAPTER SEVENTEEN
Victory of Hiraṇyākṣa Over All the Directions of the Universe 657
The Birth of the Two Demons 659
Omens of Evil Times 665
The Benediction of Hiraṇyakaśipu 669
Hiraṇyākṣa Shows His Splendor 673
Varuṇa Waxes Angry 676

CHAPTER EIGHTEEN
The Battle Between Lord Boar and the Demon Hiraṇyākṣa **679**
The Lord in His Boar Incarnation 680
The Abusive Words of the Demon 685
The Lord Expresses His Terrible Anger 688
Hiraṇyākṣa and the Lord Strike Each Other 694
Brahmā Addresses Nārāyaṇa 697

CHAPTER NINETEEN
The Killing of the Demon Hiraṇyākṣa **703**
The Lord Accepts Brahmā's Prayer 703
The Lord Invokes His Sudarśana Discus 706
The Great Demon's Valor Frustrated 710
The Demon Employs Many Conjuring Tricks 713
Diti Recalls the Words of Her Husband 717
Brahmā Arrives on the Spot 720
Lord Hari Returns to His Own Abode 724
Hearing the Works and Deeds of Devotees 728

CHAPTER TWENTY
Conversation Between Maitreya and Vidura **733**
Vidura Born From the Body of Vedavyāsa 735
Hearing the Magnanimous Activities of the Lord 738
Questions by Vidura 740
Production of the Total Material Elements 742
Brahmā Born From the Lotus Flower 746
Brahmā Throws Off the Body of Ignorance 749
Demons Born From the Buttocks of Brahmā 752
The Demons Take Twilight for a Damsel 757
Brahmā Gives Up His Form of Moonlight 764
Creation of the Siddhas and Vidyādharas 768
Brahmā Evolves Great Sages as His Sons 772

CHAPTER TWENTY-ONE

Conversation Between Manu and Kardama 775

Priyavrata and Uttānapāda Rule the World 776
Penance Practiced by Kardama Muni 779
Description of the Form of the Lord 783
Prayers by Kardama Muni 787
The Umbrella of the Lord's Lotus Feet 793
The Lord Creates Just Like a Spider 796
Viṣṇu's Words as Sweet as Nectar 799
Svāyambhuva Manu's Daughter Promised to Kardama 804
The Lord to Appear as the Son of Devahūti 810
Sāma Veda Vibrated by the Wings of Garuḍa 813
The Holy Lake Bindu-sarovara Described 816
Kardama Delights the King With Sweet Accents 822

CHAPTER TWENTY-TWO

The Marriage of Kardama Muni and Devahūti 829

The Emperor Addresses Kardama 829
The *Brāhmaṇas* and *Kṣatriyas* Protect Each Other 832
Devahūti Desires a Suitable Husband 838
Kardama Is Offered Devahūti's Hand 842
The Captivating Beauty of Devahūti 846
Kardama's Face Captures Devahūti's Mind 851
Śatarūpā Gives a Dowry to the Bride 852
The Citizens of Brahmāvarta Greet the Emperor 856
Svāyambhuva Manu as a Saintly King 860

CHAPTER TWENTY-THREE

Devahūti's Lamentation 869

Devahūti Serves Kardama With Intimacy and Respect 870
Kardama Blesses Devahūti 875
Devahūti Desires a Child by Bodily Union 879
Kardama Creates an Aerial Mansion 882
Devahūti's Heart Displeased 888
One Thousand Maidservants Serve Devahūti 891

Devahūti Appears Before Kardama 895
Kardama Enjoys for Many, Many Years 899
Kardama Returns to His Hermitage 902
Devahūti Gives Birth to Nine Daughters 906
Devahūti Laments 909
The Value of Association With a Saintly Person 912

CHAPTER TWENTY-FOUR
Renunciation of Kardama Muni 917
Devahūti Worships the Master of the Universe 920
The Supreme Lord Appears in Devahūti 922
Lord Brahmā Praises Kardama 927
Description of Kapila Muni's Bodily Features 932
Kardama Gives His Daughters in Marriage 937
Kardama's Prayers to Kapila 940
The Lord Has Innumerable Forms 944
Kardama Desires to Renounce Family Life 948
Kapila Appears to Explain Sāṅkhya Philosophy 951
Kardama Leaves for the Forest 957
Kardama Becomes Situated in Devotional Service 961

CHAPTER TWENTY-FIVE
The Gories of Devotional Service 965
The Lord Takes Birth as Kapila Muni 965
Devahūti Questions Her Son 970
The Lord Explains the Path of the Transcendentalists 977
Conditional Life and Liberation 980
Devotional Service Is the Only Auspicious Path 984
The Symptoms of a *Sādhu* 987
The Value of Attachment to Devotees 991
The Easiest Process of Mystic Power 994
Devahūti Inquires About Devotional Service 997
The Senses Represent the Demigods 1001
Devotional Service Dissolves the Subtle Body 1002
Devotees Like to See the Forms of the Lord 1003

Devotees Enjoy All Offered Benedictions 1009
Unflinching Devotional Service Described 1013
The Wind Blows Out of Fear of the Lord 1017

CHAPTER TWENTY-SIX
Fundamental Principles of Material Nature 1023
Knowledge Is the Ultimate Perfection 1024
The Lord Accepts the Subtle Material Energy 1028
Material Consciousness Causes Conditional Life 1033
The Aggregate Elements Are Known as the *Pradhāna* 1038
Time Is the Twenty-fifth Element 1041
The Lord Impregnates Material Nature 1045
The Characteristics of Pure Consciousness 1049
The Mind Is Known as Lord Aniruddha 1053
The Characteristics of Intelligence 1055
Manifestation of the Sound Element 1058
The Characteristics of the Ethereal Element 1061
The Characteristics of Form 1065
The Characteristics of Water 1067
The Earth Sustains All Elements 1069
Appearance of the Celebrated Cosmic Being 1073
Division of the Universe 1076
The Demigods Try to Awaken the Universal Form 1083
The Cosmic Being Arises From the Causal Waters 1087

CHAPTER TWENTY-SEVEN
Understanding Material Nature 1091
Transmigration of the Conditioned Soul 1094
The Controlling Process of the *Yoga* System 1098
The Qualities of a Devotee 1101
A Liberated Soul Realizes the Lord 1105
A Devotee Is Freed From False Ego 1108
Devahūti Makes Her First Inquiry 1112
Devotional Service Performed in Knowledge 1118
Material Nature Cannot Harm an Enlightened Soul 1123
The Devotee Goes to the Transcendental Abode 1126

CHAPTER TWENTY-EIGHT
Kapila's Instructions on the Execution of Devotional Service **1129**
Kapila Explains the System of *Yoga* 1129
One Should Eat Very Frugally 1132
One Must Control the Unbridled Mind 1136
The *Yogīs* Are Freed From Mental Disturbances 1139
Description of the Form of the Lord 1142
The Lord Is Eternally Very Beautiful 1146
The Pastimes of the Lord Are Always Attractive 1148
The Lord's Lotus Feet Act Like Thunderbolts 1151
The Moonlike Navel of the Lord 1156
The Lord's Club Smashes Demons 1159
The Benevolent Smile of Lord Śrī Hari 1164
The *Yogī* Develops Pure Love of God 1166
The Liberated Soul Forgets His Bodily Demands 1171
The Supreme Lord Is the Seer 1174
The Spirit Soul Manifests in Different Bodies 1177

CHAPTER TWENTY-NINE
Explanation of Devotional Service by Lord Kapila **1181**
The Ultimate End of All Philosophical Systems 1181
Lord Kapila Speaks 1186
Devotion in the Mode of Passion 1189
Unadulterated Devotional Service 1191
A Devotee Must Execute Prescribed Duties 1196
Temple Worship Is the Duty of a Devotee 1198
A Devotee Avoids the Company of Nondevotees 1202
The Supreme Soul Is Present Everywhere 1204
A Separatist Never Attains Peace of Mind 1207
Different Grades of Living Entities 1213
Different Grades of Human Beings 1216
A Devotee Offers Respect to All Living Beings 1220
Lord Viṣṇu Is the Time Factor 1224
Expansion of the Total Universal Body 1229

CHAPTER THIRTY

Description by Lord Kapila of Adverse Fruitive Activities **1233**

The Powerful Strength of the Time Factor 1233
Conditioned Souls Delight in Hellish Enjoyment 1237
The Attached Householder Remains in Family Life 1240
The Foolish Family Man Prepares for Death 1244
The Materialist Dies Most Pathetically 1247
The Criminal Is Brought Before Yamarāja 1252
Hellish Punishments on This Planet 1255

CHAPTER THIRTY-ONE

Lord Kapila's Instructions on the Movements of the Living Entities **1263**

Development of the Material Body 1264
Agony of the Child in the Womb 1267
Prayers of the Child in the Womb 1273
One Must Surrender to Paramātmā 1278
The Human Form of Life Is the Highest 1282
The Pangs of Birth 1288
The Distresses of Boyhood 1291
The Conditioned Soul Again Goes to Hell 1295
Dangers of Association With Women 1298
The Woman Is the Representation of *Māyā* 1304
The Materialist Involves Himself in Fruitive Activities 1307
One Should Not View Death With Horror 1311

CHAPTER THIRTY-TWO

Entanglement in Fruitive Activities **1315**

Materialists Can Be Elevated to the Moon 1318
The Path of Illumination 1322
Lord Brahmā Closes the Material Universe 1324
Materialists Work With Attachment to the Result 1329
Materialists Are Compared to Hogs 1332

The Devotee's Mind Becomes Equipoised 1337
The Greatest Common Understanding for All *Yogīs* 1341
The Entire Universe Has Come From the Lord 1344
The Supreme Personality of Godhead Is One 1348
Kapila's Instruction Is Not Meant for the Envious 1355

CHAPTER THIRTY-THREE
Activities of Kapila **1361**
Prayers of Devahūti 1362
The Lord Assumes Many Incarnations 1366
Those Who Chant the Holy Names Are Glorious 1370
Kapila Replies to His Mother 1374
Devahūti Begins to Practice *Bhakti-yoga* 1377
The Opulence of Kardama Muni's Household 1380
Devahūti Aggrieved at the Loss of Her Son 1384
Devahūti Attains Transcendental Bliss 1387
Devahūti Appears Like Fire Surrounded by Smoke 1391
The Ocean Offers Kapila a Place of Residence 1396

Appendixes
The Author 1401
References 1403
Glossary of Personal Names 1405
Glossary 1413
Sanskrit Pronunciation Guide 1421
Index of Sanskrit Verses 1425
General Index 1465

Preface

We must know the present need of human society. And what is that need? Human society is no longer bounded by geographical limits to particular countries or communities. Human society is broader than in the Middle Ages, and the world tendency is toward one state or one human society. The ideals of spiritual communism, according to *Śrīmad-Bhāgavatam,* are based more or less on the oneness of the entire human society, nay, of the entire energy of living beings. The need is felt by great thinkers to make this a successful ideology. *Śrīmad-Bhāgavatam* will fill this need in human society. It begins, therefore, with the aphorism of Vedānta philosophy *janmādy asya yataḥ* to establish the ideal of a common cause.

Human society, at the present moment, is not in the darkness of oblivion. It has made rapid progress in the field of material comforts, education and economic development throughout the entire world. But there is a pinprick somewhere in the social body at large, and therefore there are large-scale quarrels, even over less important issues. There is need of a clue as to how humanity can become one in peace, friendship and prosperity with a common cause. *Śrīmad-Bhāgavatam* will fill this need, for it is a cultural presentation for the respiritualization of the entire human society.

Śrīmad-Bhāgavatam should be introduced also in the schools and colleges, for it is recommended by the great student-devotee Prahlāda Mahārāja in order to change the demoniac face of society.

kaumāra ācaret prājño
dharmān bhāgavatān iha
durlabhaṁ mānuṣaṁ janma
tad apy adhruvam arthadam

(*Bhāg.* 7.6.1)

Disparity in human society is due to lack of principles in a godless civilization. There is God, or the Almighty One, from whom everything emanates, by whom everything is maintained and in whom everything is merged to rest. Material science has tried to find the ultimate source of creation very insufficiently, but it is a fact that there is one ultimate source of everything that be. This ultimate source is explained rationally and authoritatively in the beautiful *Bhāgavatam*, or *Śrīmad-Bhāgavatam*.

Śrīmad-Bhāgavatam is the transcendental science not only for knowing the ultimate source of everything but also for knowing our relation with Him and our duty toward perfection of the human society on the basis of this perfect knowledge. It is powerful reading matter in the Sanskrit language, and it is now rendered into English elaborately so that simply by a careful reading one will know God perfectly well, so much so that the reader will be sufficiently educated to defend himself from the onslaught of atheists. Over and above this, the reader will be able to convert others to accepting God as a concrete principle.

Śrīmad-Bhāgavatam begins with the definition of the ultimate source. It is a bona fide commentary on the *Vedānta-sūtra* by the same author, Śrīla Vyāsadeva, and gradually it develops into nine cantos up to the highest state of God realization. The only qualification one needs to study this great book of transcendental knowledge is to proceed step by step cautiously and not jump forward haphazardly like with an ordinary book. It should be gone through chapter by chapter, one after another. The reading matter is so arranged with its original Sanskrit text, its English transliteration, synonyms, translation and purports so that one is sure to become a God-realized soul at the end of finishing the first nine cantos.

The Tenth Canto is distinct from the first nine cantos because it deals directly with the transcendental activities of the Personality of Godhead Śrī Kṛṣṇa. One will be unable to capture the effects of the Tenth Canto without going through the first nine cantos. The book is complete in twelve cantos, each independent, but it is good for all to read them in small installments one after another.

I must admit my frailties in presenting *Śrīmad-Bhāgavatam*, but still I am hopeful of its good reception by the thinkers and leaders of society on the strength of the following statement of *Śrīmad-Bhāgavatam* (1.5.11):

tad-vāg-visargo janatāgha-viplavo
yasmin prati-ślokam abaddhavaty api
nāmāny anantasya yaśo 'ṅkitāni yac
chṛṇvanti gāyanti gṛṇanti sādhavaḥ

"On the other hand, that literature which is full with descriptions of the transcendental glories of the name, fame, form and pastimes of the unlimited Supreme Lord is a transcendental creation meant to bring about a revolution in the impious life of a misdirected civilization. Such transcendental literatures, even though irregularly composed, are heard, sung and accepted by purified men who are thoroughly honest."

Oṁ tat sat

A.C. Bhaktivedanta Swami
Dated at Delhi
December 15, 1962

Introduction

"This *Bhāgavata Purāṇa* is as brilliant as the sun, and it has arisen just after the departure of Lord Kṛṣṇa to His own abode, accompanied by religion, knowledge, etc. Persons who have lost their vision due to the dense darkness of ignorance in the age of Kali shall get light from this *Purāṇa*." (*Śrīmad- Bhāgavatam* 1.3.43)

The timeless wisdom of India is expressed in the *Vedas*, ancient Sanskrit texts that touch upon all fields of human knowledge. Originally preserved through oral tradition, the *Vedas* were first put into writing five thousand years ago by Śrīla Vyāsadeva, the "literary incarnation of God." After compiling the *Vedas*, Vyāsadeva set forth their essence in the aphorisms known as *Vedānta-sūtras*. *Śrīmad-Bhāgavatam* (*Bhāgavata Purāṇa*) is Vyasadeva's commentary on his own *Vedānta-sūtras*. It was written in the maturity of his spiritual life under the direction of Nārada Muni, his spiritual master. Referred to as "the ripened fruit of the tree of Vedic literature," *Śrīmad-Bhāgavatam* is the most complete and authoritative exposition of Vedic knowledge.

After compiling the *Bhāgavatam*, Vyāsa imparted the synopsis of it to his son, the sage Śukadeva Gosvāmī. Śukadeva Gosvāmī subsequently recited the entire *Bhāgavatam* to Mahārāja Parīkṣit in an assembly of learned saints on the bank of the Ganges at Hastināpura (now Delhi). Mahārāja Parīkṣit was the emperor of the world and was a great *rājarṣi* (saintly king). Having received a warning that he would die within a week, he renounced his entire kingdom and retired to the bank of the Ganges to fast until death and receive spiritual enlightenment. The *Bhāgavatam* begins with Emperor Parīkṣit's sober inquiry to Śukadeva Gosvāmī: "You are the spiritual master of great saints and devotees. I am therefore begging you to show the way of perfection for all persons, and especially for one who is about to die. Please let me know what a man should hear, chant, remember and worship, and also what he should not do. Please explain all this to me."

Śukadeva Gosvāmī's answer to this question, and numerous other questions posed by Mahārāja Parīkṣit, concerning everything from the nature of the self to the origin of the universe, held the assembled sages in rapt attention continuously for the seven days leading up to the king's death. The sage Sūta Gosvāmī, who was present in that assembly when Śukadeva Gosvāmī first recited *Śrīmad-Bhāgavatam*, later repeated the *Bhāgavatam* before a gathering of sages in the forest of Naimiṣāraṇya. Those sages, concerned about the spiritual welfare of the people in general, had gathered to perform a long, continuous chain of sacrifices to counteract the degrading influence of the incipient age of Kali. In response to the sages' request that he speak the essence of Vedic wisdom, Sūta Gosvāmī repeated from memory the entire eighteen thousand verses of *Śrīmad-Bhāgavatam*, as spoken by Śukadeva Gosvāmī to Mahārāja Parīkṣit.

The reader of *Śrīmad-Bhāgavatam* hears Sūta Gosvāmī relate the questions of Mahārāja Parīkṣit and the answers of Śukadeva Gosvāmī. Also, Sūta Gosvāmī sometimes responds directly to the questions put by Śaunaka Ṛṣi, the spokesman for the sages gathered at Naimisaranya. One therefore simultaneously hears two dialogues: one between Mahārāja Parīkṣit and Śukadeva Gosvāmī on the bank of the Ganges, and another at Naimisaranya between Sūta Gosvāmī and the sages at Naimiṣāraṇya forest, headed by Śaunaka Ṛṣi. Furthermore, while instructing King Parīkṣit, Śukadeva Gosvāmī often relates historical episodes and gives accounts of lengthy philosophical discussions between such great souls as the saint Maitreya and his disciple Vidura. With this understanding of the history of the *Bhāgavatam*, the reader will easily be able to follow its intermingling of dialogues and events from various sources. Since philosophical wisdom, not chronological order, is most important in the text, one need only be attentive to the subject matter of *Śrīmad-Bhāgavatam* to appreciate fully its profound message.

The translator of this edition compare the *Bhāgavatam* to sugar candy— wherever you taste it, you will find it equally sweet and relishable. Therefore, to taste the sweetness of the *Bhāgavatam*, one may begin by reading any of its volumes. After such an introductory taste, however, the serious reader is best advised to go back to the First Canto and then proceed through the *Bhāgavatam*, canto after canto, in its natural order.

This edition of the *Bhāgavatam* is the first complete English translation of this important text with an elaborate commentary, and it is the first widely available to the English-speaking public. The first twelve volumes (Canto One through Canto Ten, Part One) are the product of the scholarly and devotional effort of His Divine Grace A.C.Bhaktivedanta Swami Prabhupāda, the founder-*ācārya* of the International Society for Krishna Consciousness and the world's most distinguished teacher of Indian religious and philosophical thought. His consummate Sanskrit scholarship and intimate familiarity with Vedic culture and thought as well as the modern way of life combine to reveal to the West a magnificent exposition of this important classic.

Readers will find this work of value for many reasons. For those interested in the classical roots of Indian civilization, it serves as a vast reservoir of detailed information on virtually every one of its aspects. For students of comparative philosophy and religion, the *Bhāgavatam* offers a penetrating view into the meaning of India's profound spiritual heritage. To sociologists and anthropologists, the *Bhāgavatam* reveals the practical workings of a peaceful and scientifically organized Vedic culture, whose institutions were integrated on the basis of a highly developed spiritual world view.

Students of literature will discover the *Bhāgavatam* to be a master piece of majestic poetry. For students of psychology, the text provides important perspectives on the nature of consciousness, human behavior and the philosophical study of identity. Finally, to those seeking spiritual insight, the *Bhāgavatam* offers simple and practical guidance for attainment of the highest self-knowledge and realization of the Absolute Truth. The entire multivolume text, presented by the Bhaktivedanta Book Trust, promises to occupy a significant place in the intellectual, cultural and spiritual life of modern man for a long time to come.

—The Publishers

CHAPTER ONE

Questions by Vidura

TEXT 1

श्रीशुक उवाच
एवमेतत्पुरा पृष्टो मैत्रेयो भगवान् किल ।
क्षत्त्रा वनं प्रविष्टेन त्यक्त्वा स्वगृहमृद्धिमत् ॥ १ ॥

śrī-śuka uvāca
evam etat purā pṛṣṭo
maitreyo bhagavān kila
kṣattrā vanaṁ praviṣṭena
tyaktvā sva-gṛham ṛddhimat

śrī-śukaḥ uvāca—Śrī Śukadeva Gosvāmī said; *evam*—thus; *etat*—this; *purā*—formerly; *pṛṣṭaḥ*—being asked; *maitreyaḥ*—the great sage Maitreya; *bhagavān*—His Grace; *kila*—certainly; *kṣattrā*—by Vidura; *vanam*—forest; *praviṣṭena*—entering; *tyaktvā*—renouncing; *sva-gṛham*—own house; *ṛddhimat*—prosperous.

TRANSLATION

Śukadeva Gosvāmī said: After renouncing his prosperous home and entering the forest, King Vidura, the great devotee, asked this question of His Grace Maitreya Ṛṣi.

TEXT 2

यद्वा अयं मन्त्रकृद्वो भगवानखिलेश्वरः ।
पौरवेन्द्रगृहं हित्वा प्रविवेशात्मसात्कृतम् ॥ २ ॥

yad vā ayaṁ mantra-kṛd vo
bhagavān akhileśvaraḥ
pauravendra-gṛhaṁ hitvā
praviveśātmasāt kṛtam

yat—the house; *vai*—what else is there to say; *ayam*—Śrī Kṛṣṇa; *mantra-kṛt*—minister; *vaḥ*—you people; *bhagavān*—the Personality of Godhead; *akhila-īśvaraḥ*—the Lord of everything; *pauravendra*—Duryodhana; *gṛham*—house; *hitvā*—giving up; *praviveśa*—entered; *ātmasāt*—identify with oneself; *kṛtam*—so accepted.

TRANSLATION

What else is there to say about the residential house of the Pāṇḍavas? Śrī Kṛṣṇa, the Lord of everything, acted as your minister. He used to enter that house as if it were His own, and He did not take any care of Duryodhana's house.

PURPORT

According to the Gauḍīya *acintya-bhedābheda-tattva* philosophy, anything which satisfies the senses of the Supreme Lord, Śrī Kṛṣṇa, is also Śrī Kṛṣṇa. For example, Śrī Vṛndāvana-dhāma is nondifferent from Śrī Kṛṣṇa (*tad-dhāma vṛndāvanam*) because at Vṛndāvana the Lord enjoys the transcendental bliss of His internal potency. Similarly, the house of the Pāṇḍavas was also the source of transcendental bliss for the Lord. It is mentioned here that the Lord identified the house with His own Self. Thus the house of the Pāṇḍavas was as good as Vṛndāvana, and Vidura should not have given up that place of transcendental bliss. Therefore the reason for his quitting the house was not exactly family misunderstanding; rather, Vidura took the opportunity to meet Ṛṣi Maitreya and discuss transcendental knowledge. For a saintly person like Vidura, any disturbance due to worldly affairs is insignificant. Such disturbances, however, are sometimes favorable for higher realization, and therefore Vidura took advantage of a family misunderstanding in order to meet Maitreya Ṛṣi.

TEXT 3

राजोवाच
कुत्र क्षत्तुर्भगवता मैत्रेयेणास सङ्गमः ।
कदा वा सह संवाद एतद्वर्णय नः प्रभो ॥ ३ ॥

rājovāca
kutra kṣattur bhagavatā
maitreyeṇāsa saṅgamaḥ
kadā vā saha-saṁvāda
etad varṇaya naḥ prabho

rājā uvāca—the King said; *kutra*—wherein; *kṣattuḥ*—with Vidura; *bhagavatā*—and with His Grace; *maitreyeṇa*—with Maitreya; *āsa*—there was; *saṅgamaḥ*—meeting; *kadā*—when;

vā—also; *saha*—with; *saṁvādaḥ*—discussion; *etat*—this; *varṇaya*—describe; *naḥ*—unto me; *prabho*—O my lord.

TRANSLATION

The King asked Śukadeva Gosvāmī: Where and when did the meeting and discussion take place between Saint Vidura and His Grace Maitreya Muni? Kindly oblige, my lord, and describe this to us.

PURPORT

Exactly as Śaunaka Ṛṣi inquired of Sūta Gosvāmī and Sūta Gosvāmī replied, so Śrīla Śukadeva Gosvāmī replied to King Parīkṣit's inquiries. The King was very anxious to understand the meaningful discussion that took place between the two great souls.

TEXT 4

न ह्यल्पार्थोदयस्तस्य विदुरस्यामलात्मनः ।
तस्मिन् वरीयसि प्रश्नः साधुवादोपबृंहितः ॥ ४ ॥

na hy alpārthodayas tasya
vidurasyāmalātmanaḥ
tasmin varīyasi praśnaḥ
sādhu-vādopabṛṁhitaḥ

na—never; *hi*—certainly; *alpa-artha*—small (unimportant) purpose; *udayaḥ*—raised; *tasya*—his; *vidurasya*—of Vidura; *amala-ātmanaḥ*—of the saintly man; *tasmin*—in that; *varīyasi*—highly purposeful; *praśnaḥ*—question; *sādhu-vāda*—things approved by saints and sages; *upabṛṁhitaḥ*—full with.

TRANSLATION

Saint Vidura was a great and pure devotee of the Lord, and therefore his questions to His Grace Ṛṣi Maitreya must have been very purposeful, on the highest level, and approved by learned circles.

PURPORT

Questions and answers among different classes of men have different value. Inquiries by mercantile men in a business exchange cannot be expected to be highly purposeful in spiritual values. Questions and answers by different classes of men can be guessed by the caliber of the persons concerned. In *Bhagavad-gītā*, the discussion was between

Lord Śrī Kṛṣṇa and Arjuna, the Supreme Person and the supreme devotee respectively. The Lord admitted Arjuna to be His devotee and friend (Bg. 4.3), and therefore any sane man can guess that the discussion was on the topic of the *bhakti-yoga* system. Actually the whole *Bhagavad-gītā* is based on the principle of *bhakti-yoga.* There is a difference between *karma* and *karma-yoga. Karma* is regulated action for the enjoyment of the fruit by the performer, but *karma-yoga* is action performed by the devotee for the satisfaction of the Lord. *Karma-yoga* is based on *bhakti,* or pleasing the Lord, whereas *karma* is based on pleasing the senses of the performer himself. According to *Śrīmad-Bhāgavatam,* one is advised to approach a bona fide spiritual master when one is actually inclined to question from an elevated level of spiritual understanding. A common man who has no interest in spiritual values has no need to approach a spiritual master just as a matter of following fashion.

As a student, Mahārāja Parīkṣit was serious about learning the science of God, and Śukadeva Gosvāmī was a bona fide spiritual master in the transcendental science. Both of them knew that the topics discussed by Vidura and Ṛṣi Maitreya were elevated, and thus Mahārāja Parīkṣit was very interested in learning from the bona fide spiritual master.

TEXT 5

सूत उवाच
स एवमृषिवर्योऽयं पृष्टो राज्ञा परीक्षिता ।
प्रत्याह तं सुबहुवित्प्रीतात्मा श्रूयतामिति ॥ ५ ॥

sūta uvāca
sa evam ṛṣi-varyo 'yaṁ
pṛṣṭo rājñā parīkṣitā
praty āha taṁ subahu-vit
prītātmā śrūyatām iti

sūtaḥ uvāca—Śrī Sūta Gosvāmī said; *saḥ*—he; *evam*—thus; *ṛṣi-varyaḥ*—the great *ṛṣi;* *ayam*—Śukadeva Gosvāmī; *pṛṣṭaḥ*—being questioned; *rājñā*—by the King; *parīkṣitā*—Mahārāja Parīkṣit; *prati*—to; *āha*—replied; *tam*—unto the King; *su-bahu-vit*—highly experienced; *prīta-ātmā*—fully satisfied; *śrūyatām*—please hear me; *iti*—thus.

TRANSLATION

Śrī Suta Gosvāmī said: The great sage Śukadeva Gosvāmī was highly experienced and was pleased with the King. Thus being questioned by the King, he said to him, "Please hear the topics attentively."

TEXT 6

श्रीशुक उवाच
यदा तु राजा स्वसुतानसाधून्
पुष्णन्नधर्मेण विनष्टदृष्टिः ।
भ्रातुर्यविष्ठस्य सुतान् विबन्धून्
प्रवेश्य लाक्षाभवने ददाह ॥ ६ ॥

śrī-śuka uvāca
yadā tu rājā sva-sutān asādhūn
puṣṇan na dharmeṇa vinaṣṭa-dṛṣṭiḥ
bhrātur yaviṣṭhasya sutān vibandhūn
praveśya lākṣā-bhavane dadāha

śrī-śukaḥ uvāca—Śrī Śukadeva Gosvāmī said; *yadā*—when; *tu*—but; *rājā*—King Dhṛtarāṣṭra; *sva-sutān*—his own sons; *asādhūn*—dishonest; *puṣṇan*—nourishing; *na*—never; *dharmeṇa*—on the right path; *vinaṣṭa-dṛṣṭiḥ*—one who has lost his insight; *bhrātuḥ*—of his brother; *yaviṣṭhasya*—younger; *sutān*—sons; *vibandhūn*—having no guardian (father); *praveśya*—made to enter; *lākṣā*—lacquer; *bhavane*—in the house; *dadāha*—set on fire.

TRANSLATION

Śrī Śukadeva Gosvāmī said: King Dhṛtarāṣṭra became blind under the influence of impious desires to nourish his dishonest sons, and thus he set fire to the lacquer house to burn his fatherless nephews, the Pāṇḍavas.

PURPORT

Dhṛtarāṣṭra was blind from birth, but his blindness in committing impious activities to support his dishonest sons was a greater blindness than his physical lack of eyesight. The physical lack of sight does not bar one from spiritual progress. But when one is blind spiritually, even though physically fit, that blindness is dangerously detrimental to the progressive path of human life.

TEXT 7

यदा सभायां कुरुदेवदेव्याः
केशाभिमर्शं सुतकर्म गर्ह्यम् ।
न वारयामास नृपः स्नुषायाः
स्वास्रैर्हरन्त्याः कुचकुङ्कुमानि ॥ ७ ॥

yadā sabhāyāṁ kuru-deva-devyāḥ
keśābhimarśaṁ suta-karma garhyam
na vārayām āsa nṛpaḥ snuṣāyāḥ
svāsrair harantyāḥ kuca-kuṅkumāni

yadā—when; *sabhāyām*—the assembly; *kuru-deva-devyāḥ*—of Draupadī, the wife of godly Yudhiṣṭhira; *keśa-abhimarśam*—insult by grabbing her hair; *suta-karma*—action taken by his son; *garhyam*—which was abominable; *na*—did not; *vārayām āsa*—forbid; *nṛpaḥ*—the King; *snuṣāyāḥ*—of his daughter-in-law; *svāsraiḥ*—by her tears; *harantyāḥ*—of she who was washing; *kuca-kuṅkumāni*—red dust on her breast.

TRANSLATION

The King did not forbid his son Duḥśāsana's abominable action of grabbing the hair of Draupadī, the wife of the godly King Yudhiṣṭhira, even though her tears washed the red dust on her breast.

TEXT 8

द्यूते त्वधर्मेण जितस्य साधोः
सत्यावलम्बस्य वनं गतस्य ।
न याचतोऽदात्समयेन दायं
तमोजुषाणो यदजातशत्रोः ॥ ८ ॥

dyūte tv adharmeṇa jitasya sādhoḥ
satyāvalambasya vanaṁ gatasya
na yācato 'dāt samayena dāyaṁ
tamo-juṣāṇo yad ajāta-śatroḥ

dyūte—by means of gambling; *tu*—but; *adharmeṇa*—by unfair tricks; *jitasya*—of the vanquished; *sādhoḥ*—a saintly person; *satya-avalambasya*—one who embraced truth as shelter; *vanam*—forest; *gatasya*—of the goer; *na*—never; *yācataḥ*—when asked for; *adāt*—delivered; *samayena*—in due course; *dāyam*—right share; *tamaḥ-juṣāṇaḥ*—overwhelmed by illusion; *yat*—as much as; *ajāta-śatroḥ*—of one who had no enemy.

TRANSLATION

Yudhiṣṭhira, who was born without any enemy, was unfairly defeated in gambling. But because he had taken the vow of truthfulness, he went off to the forest. When he came back in due course and begged the return of his rightful share of the kingdom, he was refused by Dhṛtarāṣṭra, who was overwhelmed by illusion.

His Divine Grace
A. C. Bhaktivedanta Swami Prabhupāda
Founder-Ācārya of International Society for Krishna Consciousness

PLATE ONE Vidura, his ears pierced by the arrows of Duryodhana's sharp words, felt afflicted to the core of his heart. Placing his bow on the door, he quit his brother's palace. He was not sorry, for he considered the acts of the Lord's external energy to be supreme. (*pp.* 8-14)

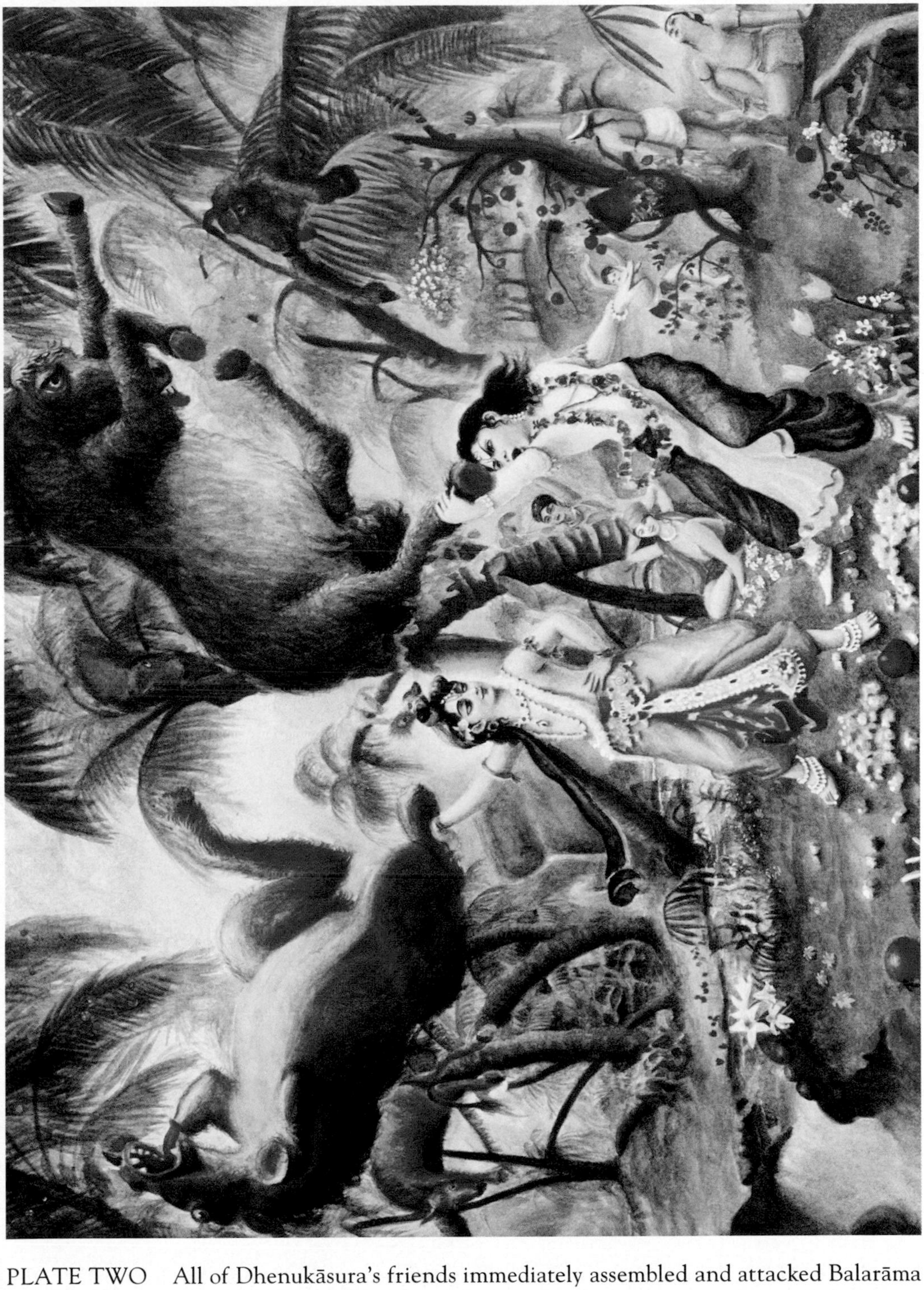

PLATE TWO All of Dhenukāsura's friends immediately assembled and attacked Balarāma and Kṛṣṇa with great force. But Kṛṣṇa and Balarāma caught each of the asses by the hind legs and wheeled them around. Thus They killed all of them by throwing them into the palm trees. (*p.83*)

PLATE THREE   When Kṛṣṇa entered the courtyard of the demon Naraka's palace, the 16,100 princesses came forward excitedly, captivated by the Lord's beauty. (*pp.* 94-95)

PLATE FOUR Kālayavana got down from his chariot and ran after Kṛṣṇa, but the Lord stayed just out of reach. (*p.* 97)

PLATE FIVE Foreseeing the end of His family (the Yadu dynasty), and desiring to bring to a close His earthly pastimes, Lord Śrī Kṛṣṇa went to a secluded spot on the bank of the River Sarasvatī and sat down beneath a young banyan tree. (*pp. 119-127*)

PLATE SIX After talking with Uddhava on the bank of the River Yamunā, Vidura went to Hardwar, at the source of the celestial Ganges, to meet Maitreya Muni. *(pp. 154-176)*

PLATE SEVEN After sitting in meditation on his lotus seat for more than three hundred trillion years, Lord Brahmā developed the knowledge with which to see the Supreme Lord within his heart. Brahmā could see on the cosmic water a gigantic lotuslike bedstead, the body of Śeṣa-nāga, on which the Personality of Godhead was lying alone. (*pp. 312-314*)

PLATE EIGHT Lord Śrī Kṛṣṇa performed the *rāsa* dance, a completely spiritual pastime, in the company of the *gopīs*, the cowherd damsels of Vṛndāvana. (*p. 343*)

PLATE NINE When the Lord appeared as Lord Kṛṣṇa, He lifted the Govardhana Hill as an umbrella to protect His devotees from a torrential downpour of rain. (*p. 344*)

PLATE TEN At the time of the devastation…a great fire emanates from the mouths of Saṅkarṣaṇa, Ananta, the serpent bed of the Personality of Godhead. (*pp. 415-417*)

PLATE ELEVEN Due to the sages' disobedience, Lord Brahmā's anger came out from between his eyebrows as a child of mixed blue and red. This child was Rudra (Lord Śiva), the incarnation of anger. (*pp. 430-433*)

PLATE TWELVE The post of Brahmā, the first created living being, the engineer of the universal creation, is the highest responsible post in the universe, and it is offered to the most perfect personality in the universe. (*pp. 417-463*)

PLATE THIRTEEN While the sage Kaśyapa was meditating in trance, his wife Diti, afflicted by sexual desire, begged him for sexual intercourse. (*pp.* 518-536)

PLATE FOURTEEN The four Kumāras, great sages appearing as children, directly saw the Supreme Personality of Godhead in the spiritual world, the kingdom of God. (*pp.* 595-602)

By his acts of penance, Lord Brahmā was able to see Garbhodakaśāyī Viṣṇu.

PURPORT

Mahārāja Yudhiṣṭhira was the rightful heir to his father's kingdom. But just to favor his own sons, headed by Duryodhana, Dhṛtarāṣṭra, Mahārāja Yudhiṣṭhira's uncle, adopted various unfair means to cheat his nephews of their rightful share of the kingdom. At last the Pāṇḍavas demanded only five villages, one for each of the five brothers, but that was also refused by the usurpers. This incident led to the War of Kurukṣetra. The Battle of Kurukṣetra, therefore, was induced by the Kurus, and not the Pāṇḍavas.

As *kṣatriyas,* the proper livelihood of the Pāṇḍavas was only to rule, and not to accept any other occupation. A *brāhmaṇa, kṣatriya* or *vaiśya* will not accept employment for his livelihood under any circumstances.

TEXT 9

यदा च पार्थप्रहितः सभायां
जगद्गुरुर्यानि जगाद कृष्णः ।
न तानि पुंसाममृतायनानि
राजोरु मेने क्षतपुण्यलेशः ॥ ९ ॥

yadā ca pārtha-prahitaḥ sabhāyāṁ
jagad-gurur yāni jagāda kṛṣṇaḥ
na tāni puṁsām amṛtāyanāni
rājoru mene kṣata-puṇya-leśaḥ

yadā—when; *ca*—also; *pārtha-prahitaḥ*—being advised by Arjuna; *sabhāyām*—in the assembly; *jagat-guruḥ*—of the teacher of the world; *yāni*—those; *jagāda*—went; *kṛṣṇaḥ*—Lord Kṛṣṇa; *na*—never; *tāni*—such words; *puṁsām*—of all men of sense; *amṛta-ayanāni*—as good as nectar; *rājā*—the King (Dhṛtarāṣṭra or Duryodhana); *uru*—very important; *mene*—did consider; *kṣata*—dwindling; *puṇya-leśaḥ*—fragment of pious acts.

TRANSLATION

Lord Kṛṣṇa was sent by Arjuna into the assembly as the spiritual master of the whole world, and although His words were heard by some [like Bhīṣma] as pure nectar, it was not so for the others, who were completely bereft of the last farthing of past pious works. The King [Dhṛtarāṣṭra or Duryodhana] did not take the words of Lord Kṛṣṇa very seriously.

PURPORT

Lord Kṛṣṇa, who is the spiritual master of the entire universe, accepted the duty of a messenger, and, deputed by Arjuna, went to the assembly of King Dhṛtarāṣṭra on a peace mission. Kṛṣṇa is everyone's Lord, yet because He was the transcendental friend of Arjuna, He gladly accepted the role of messenger, exactly like an ordinary friend. That is the beauty of the Lord's behavior with His pure devotees. He reached the assembly and spoke about peace, and the message was relished by Bhīṣma and other great leaders because it was spoken by the Lord Himself. But due to the exhaustion of the pious results of their past deeds, Duryodhana, or his father, Dhṛtarāṣṭra, did not take the message very seriously. That is the way of persons who have no credit of pious deeds. By past pious deeds, one may become the king of a country, but because the results of the pious acts of Duryodhana and company were dwindling, it became evident from their actions that they were sure to lose the kingdom to the Pāṇḍavas. The message of Godhead is always like nectar to the devotees, but it is just the opposite to the nondevotees. Sugar candy is always sweet to a healthy man, but it tastes very bitter to persons suffering from jaundice.

TEXT 10

यदोपहूतो भवनं प्रविष्टो
मन्त्राय पृष्टः किल पूर्वजेन ।
अथाह तन्मन्त्रदृशां वरीयान्
यन्मन्त्रिणो वैदुरिकं वदन्ति ॥१०॥

yadopahūto bhavanaṁ praviṣṭo
mantrāya pṛṣṭaḥ kila pūrvajena
athāha tan mantra-dṛśāṁ varīyān
yan mantriṇo vaidurikaṁ vadanti

yadā—when; *upahūtaḥ*—was called by; *bhavanam*—the palace; *praviṣṭaḥ*—entered; *mantrāya*—for consultation; *pṛṣṭaḥ*—asked by; *kila*—of course; *pūrvajena*—by the elder brother; *atha*—thus; *āha*—said; *tat*—that; *mantra*—advice; *dṛśām*—just suitable; *varīyān*—excellent; *yat*—that which; *mantriṇaḥ*—the ministers of state, or expert politicians; *vaidurikam*—instructions by Vidura; *vadanti*—do they say.

TRANSLATION

When Vidura was invited by his elder brother [Dhṛtarāṣṭra] for consultation, he entered the house and gave instructions which were exactly to the point.

His advice is well known, and instructions by Vidura are approved by expert ministers of state.

PURPORT

Political suggestions by Vidura are known as expert, just as, in modern times, Paṇḍita Cāṇakya is considered the authority in good counsel in both political and moral instructions.

TEXT 11

अजातशत्रोः प्रतियच्छ दायं
तितिक्षतो दुर्विषहं तवागः ।
सहानुजो यत्र वृकोदराहिः
श्वसन् रुषा यत्त्वमलं बिभेषि ॥११॥

ajāta-śatroḥ pratiyaccha dāyaṁ
titikṣato durviṣahaṁ tavāgaḥ
sahānujo yatra vṛkodarāhiḥ
śvasan ruṣā yat tvam alaṁ bibheṣi

ajāta-śatroḥ—of Yudhiṣṭhira, who has no enemy; *pratiyaccha*—return; *dāyam*—legitimate share; *titikṣataḥ*—of he who is so forbearing; *durviṣaham*—unbearable; *tava*—your; *āgaḥ*—offense; *saha*—along with; *anujaḥ*—younger brothers; *yatra*—wherein; *vṛkodara*—Bhīma; *ahiḥ*—revenging snake; *śvasan*—breathing heavily; *ruṣā*—in anger; *yat*—whom; *tvam*—you; *alam*—verily; *bibheṣi*—do fear.

TRANSLATION

[Vidura said:] You must now return the legitimate share to Yudhiṣṭhira, who has no enemies and who has been forbearing through untold sufferings due to your offenses. He is waiting with his younger brothers, among whom is the revengeful Bhīma, breathing heavily like a snake. Surely you are afraid of him.

TEXT 12

पार्थांस्तु देवो भगवान्मुकुन्दो
गृहीतवान् सक्षितिदेवदेवः ।

आस्ते स्वपुर्यां यदुदेवदेवो
विनिर्जिताशेषनृदेवदेवः ॥१२॥

pārthāṁs tu devo bhagavān mukundo
gṛhītavān sakṣiti-deva-devaḥ
āste sva-puryāṁ yadu-deva-devo
vinirjitāśeṣa-nṛdeva-devaḥ

pārthān—the sons of Pṛthā (Kuntī); *tu*—but; *devaḥ*—the Lord; *bhagavān*—the Personality of Godhead; *mukundaḥ*—Śrī Kṛṣṇa, who awards liberation; *gṛhītavān*—has taken up; *sa*—with; *kṣiti-deva-devaḥ*—the *brāhmaṇas* and the demigods; *āste*—is present; *sva-puryām*—along with His family; *yadu-deva-devaḥ*—worshiped by the royal order of the Yadu dynasty; *vinirjita*—who have been conquered; *aśeṣa*—unlimited; *nṛdeva*—kings; *devaḥ*—Lord.

TRANSLATION

Lord Kṛṣṇa, the Personality of Godhead, has accepted the sons of Pṛthā as His kinsmen, and all the kings of the world are with Lord Śrī Kṛṣṇa. He is present in His home with all His family members, the kings and princes of the Yadu dynasty, who have conquered an unlimited number of rulers, and He is their Lord.

PURPORT

Vidura gave Dhṛtarāṣṭra very good counsel regarding political alliance with the sons of Pṛthā, the Pāṇḍavas. The first thing he said was that Lord Kṛṣṇa was intimately related with them as their cousin. Because Lord Kṛṣṇa is the Supreme Personality of Godhead, He is worshipable by all *brāhmaṇas* and demigods, who are the controllers of the universal affairs. Besides that, Lord Kṛṣṇa and His family members, the royal order of the Yadu dynasty, were the conquerors of all kings of the world.

The *kṣatriyas* used to fight the kings of various dominions and kidnap their beautiful princess-daughters, after conquering their relatives. This system was laudable because the *kṣatriyas* and the princesses would be married only on the basis of the chivalry of the conquering *kṣatriya*. All the young princes of the Yadu dynasty married the daughters of other kings in this way, by chivalrous force, and thus they were conquerors of all the kings of the world. Vidura wanted to impress upon his elder brother that fighting with the Pāṇḍavas was fraught with many dangers because they were supported by Lord Kṛṣṇa, who had conquered, even in His childhood, demons like Kaṁsa and Jarāsandha and demigods like Brahmā and Indra. Therefore all universal power was behind the Pāṇḍavas.

TEXT 13

स एष दोषः पुरुषद्विडास्ते
गृहान् प्रविष्टो यमपत्यमत्या ।
पुष्णासि कृष्णाद्विमुखो गतश्री-
स्त्यजाश्वशैवं कुलकौशलाय ॥१३॥

sa eṣa doṣaḥ puruṣa-dviḍ āste
gṛhān praviṣṭo yam apatya-matyā
puṣṇāsi kṛṣṇād vimukho gata-śrīs
tyajāśv aśaivaṁ kula-kauśalāya

saḥ—he; *eṣaḥ*—this; *doṣaḥ*—offense personified; *puruṣa-dviṭ*—envious of Lord Kṛṣṇa; *āste*—exists; *gṛhān*—household; *praviṣṭaḥ*—entered; *yam*—whom; *apatya-matyā*—thinking to be your son; *puṣṇāsi*—maintaining; *kṛṣṇāt*—from Kṛṣṇa; *vimukhaḥ*—in opposition; *gata-śrīḥ*—devoid of everything auspicious; *tyaja*—give up; *āśu*—as soon as possible; *aśaivam*—inauspicious; *kula*—family; *kauśalāya*—for the sake of.

TRANSLATION

You are maintaining offense personified, Duryodhana, as your infallible son, but he is envious of Lord Kṛṣṇa. And because you are thus maintaining a nondevotee of Kṛṣṇa, you are devoid of all auspicious qualities. Relieve yourself of this ill fortune as soon as possible and do good to the whole family!

PURPORT

A good son is called *apatya,* one who does not allow his father to fall down. The son can protect the father's soul when the father is dead by offering sacrifices to please the Supreme Lord, Viṣṇu. This system is still prevalent in India. After the death of his father, a son goes to offer sacrifices at the lotus feet of Viṣṇu at Gayā and thus delivers the father's soul if the father is fallen. But if the son is already an enemy of Viṣṇu, how, in such an inimical mood, can he offer sacrifice unto Lord Viṣṇu's lotus feet? Lord Kṛṣṇa is directly the Personality of Godhead, Viṣṇu, and Duryodhana was inimical to Him. He would therefore be unable to protect his father, Dhṛtarāṣṭra, after his death. He himself was to fall down because of his faithlessness towards Viṣṇu. How, then, could he protect his father? Vidura advised Dhṛtarāṣṭra to get rid of such an unworthy son as Duryodhana as soon as possible if he was at all anxious to see to the good of his family.

According to the moral instructions of Cāṇakya Paṇḍita, "What is the use of a son who is neither a learned man nor a devotee of the Lord?" If a son is not a devotee of the Supreme Lord, he is just like blind eyes—a source of trouble. A physician may sometimes advise the extrication of such useless eyes from their sockets so that one can be relieved of the constant trouble. Duryodhana was exactly like blind, troubling eyes; he would be a source of great trouble to the family of Dhṛtarāṣṭra, as foreseen by Vidura. Vidura therefore rightly advised his eldest brother to get rid of this source of trouble. Dhṛtarāṣṭra was wrongly maintaining such personified offense under the mistaken impression that Duryodhana was a good son, able to liberate his father.

TEXT 14

इत्यूचिवांस्तत्र सुयोधनेन
प्रवृद्धकोपस्फुरिताधरेण ।
असत्कृतः सत्स्पृहणीयशीलः
क्षत्ता सकर्णानुजसौबलेन ॥१४॥

ity ūcivāṁs tatra suyodhanena
pravṛddha-kopa-sphuritādhareṇa
asat-kṛtaḥ sat-spṛhaṇīya-śīlaḥ
kṣattā sakarṇānuja-saubalena

iti—thus; *ūcivān*—while speaking; *tatra*—there; *suyodhanena*—by Duryodhana; *pravṛddha*—swollen with; *kopa*—anger; *sphurita*—flapping; *adhareṇa*—lips; *asat-kṛtaḥ*—insulted; *sat*—respectable; *spṛhaṇīya-śīlaḥ*—desirable qualities; *kṣattā*—Vidura; *sa*—with; *karṇa*—Karṇa; *anuja*—younger brothers; *saubalena*—with Śakuni.

TRANSLATION

While speaking thus, Vidura, whose personal character was esteemed by respectable persons, was insulted by Duryodhana, who was swollen with anger and whose lips were trembling. Duryodhana was in company with Karṇa, his younger brothers and his maternal uncle Śakuni.

PURPORT

It is said that giving good counsel to a foolish person causes the fool to become angry, just as feeding milk to a snake only increases its venomous poison. Saint Vidura was so honorable that his character was looked up to by all respectable persons. But

Duryodhana was so foolish that he dared to insult Vidura. This was due to his bad association with Śakuni, his maternal uncle, as well as with his friend Karṇa, who always encouraged Duryodhana in his nefarious acts.

TEXT 15

क एनमत्रोपजुहाव जिह्मं
दास्याः सुतं यद्बलिनैव पुष्टः ।
तस्मिन् प्रतीपः परकृत्य आस्ते
निर्वास्यतामाशु पुराच्छ्वसानः ॥१५॥

ka enam atropajuhāva jihmaṁ
dāsyāḥ sutaṁ yad-balinaiva puṣṭaḥ
tasmin pratīpaḥ parakṛtya āste
nirvāsyatām āśu purāc chvasānaḥ

kaḥ—who; *enam*—this; *atra*—here; *upajuhāva*—called for; *jihmam*—crooked; *dāsyāḥ*—of a kept mistress; *sutam*—son; *yat*—whose; *balina*—by whose subsistence; *eva*—certainly; *puṣṭaḥ*—grown up; *tasmin*—unto him; *pratīpaḥ*—enmity; *para-kṛtya*—enemy's interest; *āste*—situated; *nirvāsyatām*—get him out; *āśu*—immediately; *purāt*—from the palace; *śvasānaḥ*—let him breathe only.

TRANSLATION

Who asked him to come here, this son of a kept mistress? He is so crooked that he spies in the interest of the enemy against those on whose support he has grown up. Toss him out of the palace immediately and leave him with only his breath.

PURPORT

When getting married, the *kṣatriya* kings would take on several other youthful girls along with the married princess. These girl attendants of the king were known as *dāsīs*, or attendant mistresses. By intimate association with the king, the *dāsīs* would get sons. Such sons were called *dāsī-putras*. They had no claim to a royal position, but they would get maintenance and other facilities just like princes. Vidura was the son of such a *dāsī*, and he was thus not counted amongst the *kṣatriyas*. King Dhṛtarāṣṭra was very affectionate toward his younger *dāsī-putra* brother, Vidura, and Vidura was a great friend and philosophical advisor to Dhṛtarāṣṭra. Duryodhana knew very well that Vidura was a great soul and well-wisher, but unfortunately he used strong words to hurt his innocent uncle. Duryodhana not only attacked Vidura's birth, but also called him an infidel because he seemed to support the cause of Yudhiṣṭhira, whom Duryodhana considered his enemy. He desired that Vidura be immediately put out of the palace and deprived of all his possessions. If possible, he would have liked him caned until he was left with nothing but his breath. He charged that Vidura was a spy of the Pāṇḍavas because he advised King Dhṛtarāṣṭra in their favor. Such is the situation of palace life and the intricacies of diplomacy that even a faultless person like Vidura could be charged with something abominable and punished. Vidura was struck with wonder at such unexpected behavior from his nephew Duryodhana, and before anything actually happened, he decided to leave the palace for good.

TEXT 16

स्वयं धनुर्द्वारि निधाय मायां
भ्रातुः पुरो मर्मसु ताडितोऽपि ।
स इत्यमत्युल्बणकर्णबाणै-
र्गतव्यथोऽयादुरु मानयानः ॥१६॥

svayaṁ dhanur dvāri nidhāya māyāṁ
bhrātuḥ puro marmasu tāḍito 'pi
sa ittham atyulbaṇa-karṇa-bāṇair
gata-vyatho 'yād uru mānayānaḥ

svayam—he himself; *dhanuḥ dvāri*—bow on the door; *nidhāya*—keeping; *māyām*—the external nature; *bhrātuḥ*—brother's; *puraḥ*—from the palace; *marmasu*—in the core of the heart; *tāḍitaḥ*—being afflicted; *api*—in spite of; *saḥ*—he (Vidura); *ittham*—like this; *ati-ulbaṇa*—severely; *karṇa*—ear; *bāṇaiḥ*—by the arrows; *gata-vyathaḥ*—without being sorry; *ayāt*—exited; *uru*—great; *māna-yānaḥ*—so thinking.

TRANSLATION

Thus being pierced by arrows through his ears and afflicted to the core of his heart, Vidura placed his bow on the door and quit his brother's palace. He was not sorry, for he considered the acts of the external energy to be supreme.

PURPORT

A pure devotee of the Lord is never perturbed by an awkward position created by the external energy of the Lord. In *Bhagavad-gītā* (3.27) it is stated:

prakṛteḥ kriyamāṇāni
guṇaiḥ karmāṇi sarvaśaḥ
ahaṅkāra-vimūḍhātmā
kartāham iti manyate

A conditioned soul is absorbed in material existence under the influence of different modes of external energy. Absorbed in the false ego, he thinks that he is doing everything by himself. The external energy of the Lord, the material nature, is fully under the control of the Supreme Lord, and the conditioned soul is fully under the grip of the external energy. Therefore, the conditioned soul is fully under the control of the law of the Lord. But, due to illusion only, he thinks himself independent in his activities. Duryodhana was acting under such influence of the external nature, by which he would be vanquished at the ultimate end. He could not accept the sound advice of Vidura, but on the contrary he insulted that great soul, who was the well-wisher of his whole family. Vidura could understand this because he was a pure devotee of the Lord. In spite of being very strongly insulted by Duryodhana's words, Vidura could see that Duryodhana, under the influence of *māyā,* the external energy, was making progress on the path toward his own ruination. He therefore considered the acts of the external energy to be supreme, yet he also saw how the internal energy of the Lord helped him in that particular situation. A devotee is always in a renounced temperament because the worldly attractions can never satisfy him. Vidura was never attracted by the royal palace of his brother. He was always ready to leave the place and devote himself completely to the transcendental loving service of the Lord. Now he got the opportunity by the grace of Duryodhana, and instead of being sorry at the strong words of insult, he thanked him from within because it gave him the chance to live alone in a holy place and fully engage in the devotional service of the Lord. The word *gata-vyathaḥ* (without being sorry) is significant here because Vidura was relieved from the tribulations which trouble every man entangled in material activities. He therefore thought that there was no need to defend his brother with his bow because his brother was meant for ruination. Thus he left the palace before Duryodhana could act. *Māyā,* the supreme energy of the Lord, acted here both internally and externally.

TEXT 17

स निर्गतः कौरवपुण्यलब्धो
गजाह्वयात्तीर्थपदः पदानि ।

अन्वाक्रमत्पुण्यचिकीर्षयोर्व्यां
अधिष्ठितो यानि सहस्रमूर्तिः ॥१७॥

sa nirgataḥ kaurava-puṇya-labdho
gajāhvayāt tīrtha-padaḥ padāni
anvākramat puṇya-cikīrṣayorvyām
adhiṣṭhito yāni sahasra-mūrtiḥ

saḥ—he (Vidura); *nirgataḥ*—after having quit; *kaurava*—the Kuru dynasty; *puṇya*—piety; *labdhaḥ*—so achieved; *gaja-āhvayāt*—from Hastināpura; *tīrtha-padaḥ*—of the Supreme Lord; *padāni*—pilgrimages; *anvākramat*—took shelter; *puṇya*—piety; *cikīrṣayā*—desiring so; *urvyām*—of high grade; *adhiṣṭhitaḥ*—situated; *yāni*—all those; *sahasra*—thousands; *mūrtiḥ*—forms.

TRANSLATION

By his piety, Vidura achieved the advantages of the pious Kauravas. After leaving Hastināpura, he took shelter of many places of pilgrimages, which are the Lord's lotus feet. With a desire to gain a high order of pious life, he traveled to holy places where thousands of transcendental forms of the Lord are situated.

PURPORT

Vidura was undoubtedly a highly elevated and pious soul, otherwise he would not have taken his birth in the Kaurava family. To have high parentage, to possess wealth, to be highly learned and to have great personal beauty are all due to past pious acts. But such pious possessions are not sufficient for obtaining the grace of the Lord and being engaged in His transcendental loving service. Vidura considered himself less pious, and therefore he decided to travel to all the great places of pilgrimage in the world in order to achieve greater piety and advance nearer to the Lord. At that time, Lord Kṛṣṇa was personally present in the world, and Vidura could have at once approached Him directly, but he did not do so because he was not sufficiently freed from sin. One cannot be one hundred percent devoted to the Lord unless and until he is completely free from all effects of sin. Vidura was conscious that by the association of the diplomatic Dhṛtarāṣṭra and Duryodhana he had lost his piety and was therefore not fit to associate at once with the Lord. In *Bhagavad-gītā* (7.28) this is confirmed in the following verse:

yeṣāṁ tv anta-gataṁ pāpaṁ
janānāṁ puṇya-karmaṇām
te dvandva-moha-nirmuktā
bhajante māṁ dṛḍha-vratāḥ

Persons who are sinful *asuras* like Kaṁsa and Jarāsandha cannot think of Lord Kṛṣṇa as the Supreme Personality of Godhead, the Absolute Truth. Only those who are pure devotees, those who follow the regulative principles of religious life as prescribed in the scriptures, are able to engage themselves in *karma-yoga* and then *jñāna-yoga* and thereafter, by pure meditation, can understand pure consciousness. When God consciousness is developed, one can take advantage of the association of pure devotees. *Syān mahat-sevayā viprāḥ puṇya-tīrtha-niṣevaṇāt:* one is able to associate with the Lord even during the existence of this life.

Places of pilgrimages are meant for eradicating the sins of the pilgrims, and they are distributed all over the universe just to give facility to all concerned for attaining pure existence and God realization. One should not be satisfied, however, merely by visiting the places of pilgrimage and performing one's prescribed duties; he should be eager to meet the great souls who are already there, engaged in the service of the Lord. In each and every place of pilgrimage, the Lord is present in His various transcendental forms.

These forms are called *arcā-mūrtis,* or forms of the Lord which can be easily appreciated by the common man. The Lord is transcendental to our mundane senses. He cannot be seen with our present eyes, nor can He be heard with our present ears. To the degree that we have entered into the service of the Lord or to the proportion to which our lives are freed from sins, we can perceive the Lord. But even though we are not free from sins, the Lord is kind enough to allow us the facility of seeing Him in His *arcā-mūrtis* in the temple. The Lord is all-powerful, and therefore He is able to accept our service by presentation of His *arcā* form. No one, therefore, should foolishly think the *arcā* in the temple to be an idol. Such an *arcā-mūrti* is not an idol but the Lord Himself, and to the proportion to which one is free from sins, he is able to know the significance of the *arcā-mūrti.* The guidance of a pure devotee is therefore always required.

In the land of Bhāratavarṣa there are many hundreds and thousands of places of pilgrimage distributed all over the country, and by traditional practice the common man visits such holy places during all seasons of the year. Some of the *arcā* representations of the Lord situated in different places of pilgrimage are mentioned herewith. The Lord is present at Mathurā (the birthplace of Lord Kṛṣṇa) as Ādi-keśava; the Lord is present at Purī (Orissa) as Lord Jagannātha (also known as Puruṣottama); He is present at Allahabad (Prayāga) as Bindu-mādhava; at Mandara Hill He is present as

Madhusūdana. In the Ānandāraṇya, He is known as Vāsudeva, Padmanābha and Janārdana; at Viṣṇukāñcī, He is known as Viṣṇu; and at Māyāpur, He is known as Hari. There are millions and billions of such *arcā* forms of the Lord distributed all over the universe. All these *arcā-mūrtis* are summarized in the *Caitanya-caritāmṛta* in the following words:

sarvatra prakāśa tāṅra—bhakte sukha dite
jagatera adharma nāśi' dharma sthāpite

"The Lord has so distributed Himself all over the universe just to give pleasure to the devotees, to give the common man facility to eradicate his sins, and to establish religious principles in the world."

TEXT 18

पुरेषु पुण्योपवनाद्रिकुञ्जे-
ष्वपङ्कतोयेषु सरित्सरःसु ।
अनन्तलिङ्गैः समलङ्कृतेषु
चचार तीर्थायतनेष्वनन्यः ॥१८॥

pureṣu puṇyopavanādri-kuñjeṣv
apaṅka-toyeṣu sarit-saraḥsu
ananta-liṅgaiḥ samalaṅkṛteṣu
cacāra tīrthāyataneṣv ananyaḥ

pureṣu—holy places like Ayodhyā, Dvārakā and Mathurā; *puṇya*—piety; *upavana*—the air; *adri*—hill; *kuñjeṣu*—in the orchards; *apaṅka*—without sin; *toyeṣu*—in the water; *sarit*—river; *saraḥsu*—lakes; *ananta-liṅgaiḥ*—the forms of the Unlimited; *samalaṅkṛteṣu*—being so decorated; *cacāra*—executed; *tīrtha*—places of pilgrimage; *āyataneṣu*—holy lands; *ananyaḥ*—alone or seeing Kṛṣṇa alone.

TRANSLATION

He began to travel alone, thinking only of Kṛṣṇa, through various holy places like Ayodhyā, Dvārakā and Mathurā. He traveled where the air, hill, orchard, river and lake are all pure and sinless and where the forms of the Unlimited decorate the temples. Thus he performed the pilgrim's progress.

PURPORT

These *arcā* forms of the Lord may be considered idols by the atheists, but that does not matter for persons like Vidura or His many other servants. The forms of the Lord are mentioned here as *ananta-liṅga.* Such forms of the Lord have unlimited potency, the same as that of the Lord Himself. There is no difference between the potencies of the *arcā* and those of the personal forms of the Lord. The example of the postbox and post office may be applied here. The little postboxes distributed all over the city have the same potency as the postal system in general. The duty of the post office is to carry letters from one place to another. If one puts letters in postboxes authorized by the general post office, the function of carrying letters is performed without a doubt. Similarly, the *arcā-mūrti* can also deliver the same unlimited potency of the Lord as when He is personally present. Vidura, therefore, could see nothing but Kṛṣṇa in the different *arcā* forms, and ultimately he was able to realize Kṛṣṇa alone and nothing else.

TEXT 19

गां पर्यटन्मेध्यविविक्तवृत्तिः
सदाप्लुतोऽधःशयनोऽवधूतः ।
अलक्षितः स्वैरवधूतवेषो
व्रतानि चेरे हरितोषणानि ॥१९॥

gāṁ paryaṭan medhya-vivikta-vṛttiḥ
sadāpluto 'dhaḥ śayano 'vadhūtaḥ
alakṣitaḥ svair avadhūta-veṣo
vratāni cere hari-toṣaṇāni

gām—earth; *paryaṭan*—traversing; *medhya*—pure; *vivikta-vṛttiḥ*—independent occupation for living; *sadā*—always; *āplutaḥ*—sanctified; *adhaḥ*—on the earth; *śayanaḥ*—lying; *avadhūtaḥ*—without dressing (of the hair, etc.); *alakṣitaḥ*—without being seen; *svaiḥ*—alone; *avadhūta-veṣaḥ*—dressed like a mendicant; *vratāni*—vows; *cere*—performed; *hari-toṣaṇāni*—that pleased the Lord.

TRANSLATION

While so traversing the earth, he simply performed duties to please the Supreme Lord Hari. His occupation was pure and independent. He was constantly sanctified by taking his bath in holy places, although he was in the dress of a mendicant and had no hair dressing nor a bed on which to lie. Thus he was always unseen by his various relatives.

PURPORT

The first and foremost duty of a pilgrim is to satisfy the Supreme Lord Hari. While traveling as a pilgrim, one should not be worried about pleasing society. There is no need to depend on social formalities or occupation or dress. One should remain always absorbed in the function of pleasing the Lord. Thus sanctified by thought and action, one is able to realize the Supreme Lord by the process of a pilgrim's journey.

TEXT 20

इत्थं व्रजन् भारतमेव वर्षं
कालेन यावद्गतवान् प्रभासम् ।
तावच्छशास क्षितिमेकचक्रा-
मेकातपत्रामजितेन पार्थः ॥२०॥

itthaṁ vrajan bhāratam eva varṣaṁ
kālena yāvad gatavān prabhāsam
tāvac chaśāsa kṣitim eka cakrām
ekātapatrām ajitena pārthaḥ

ittham—like this; *vrajan*—while traveling; *bhāratam*—India; *eva*—only; *varṣam*—the tract of land; *kālena*—in due course of time; *yāvat*—when; *gatavān*—visited; *prabhāsam*—the Prabhāsa pilgrimage site; *tāvat*—at that time; *śaśāsa*—ruled; *kṣitim*—the world; *eka-cakrām*—by one military force; *eka*—one; *ātapatrām*—flag; *ajitena*—by the mercy of the unconquerable Kṛṣṇa; *pārthaḥ*—Mahārāja Yudhiṣṭhira.

TRANSLATION

Thus, when he was in the land of Bhāratavarṣa traveling to all the places of pilgrimage, he visited Prabhāsakṣetra. At that time Mahārāja Yudhiṣṭhira was the emperor and held the world under one military strength and one flag.

PURPORT

More than five thousand years ago, while Saint Vidura was traveling the earth as a pilgrim, India was known as Bhāratavarṣa, as it is known even today. The history of the world cannot give any systematic account for more than three thousand years into the past, but before that the whole world was under the flag and military strength of Mahārāja Yudhiṣṭhira, who was the emperor of the world. At present there are hundreds and thousands of flags flapping in the United Nations, but during the time of Vidura there was, by the grace of Ajita, Lord Kṛṣṇa, only one flag. The nations of the world are very eager to again have one state under one flag, but for this they must seek the favor of Lord Kṛṣṇa, who alone can help us become one worldwide nation.

TEXT 21

तत्राथ शुश्राव सुहृद्विनष्टिं
वनं यथा वेणुजवह्निसंश्रयम् ।
संस्पर्धया दग्धमथानुशोचन्
सरस्वतीं प्रत्यगियाय तूष्णीम् ॥२१॥

tatrātha śuśrāva suhṛd-vinaṣṭiṁ
vanaṁ yathā veṇuja-vahni-saṁśrayam
saṁspardhayā dagdham athānuśocan
sarasvatīṁ pratyag iyāya tūṣṇīm

tatra—there; *atha*—thereafter; *śuśrāva*—heard; *suhṛt*—kinsmen; *vinaṣṭim*—all dead; *vanam*—forest; *yathā*—as much as; *veṇuja-vahni*—fire due to the bamboos; *saṁśrayam*—friction with one another; *saṁspardhayā*—by violent passion; *dagdham*—burnt; *atha*—thus; *anuśocan*—thinking; *sarasvatīm*—the River Sarasvatī; *pratyak*—westward; *iyāya*—went; *tūṣṇīm*—silently.

TRANSLATION

At the place of pilgrimage at Prabhāsa, it came to his knowledge that all his relatives had died due to violent passion, just as an entire forest burns due to fire produced by the friction of bamboos. After this he proceeded west, where the River Sarasvatī flows.

PURPORT

Both the Kauravas and the Yādavas were relatives of Vidura, and Vidura heard of their extinction due to fratricidal war. The comparison of the friction of forest bamboos to that of passionate human societies is appropriate. The whole world is compared to a forest. At any moment there may be a flare-up of fire in the forest due to friction. No one goes to the forest to set it on fire, but due only to friction between bamboos, fire takes place and burns an entire forest. Similarly, in the greater forest of worldly transaction, the fire of war takes place because of the violent passion of the conditioned souls illusioned by the external energy. Such a worldly fire can be extinguished only by the water of the mercy cloud of saints, just as a forest fire can be extinguished only by rains falling from a cloud.

TEXT 22

तस्यां त्रितस्योशनसो मनोश्च
पृथोरथाग्नेरसितस्य वायोः ।

तीर्थं सुदासस्य गवां गुहस्य
यच्छ्राद्धदेवस्य स आसिषेवे ॥२२॥

tasyāṁ tritasyośanaso manoś ca
pṛthor athāgner asitasya vāyoḥ
tīrthaṁ sudāsasya gavāṁ guhasya
yac chrāddhadevasya sa āsiṣeve

tasyām—on the bank of the River Sarasvatī; *tritasya*—the pilgrimage site named Trita; *uśanasaḥ*—the pilgrimage site named Uśanā; *manoḥ ca*—as also of the pilgrimage site named Manu; *pṛthoḥ*—that of Pṛthu; *atha*—thereafter; *agneḥ*—that of Agni; *asitasya*—that of Asita; *vāyoḥ*—that of Vāyu; *tīrtham*—places of pilgrimages; *sudāsasya*—of the name Sudāsa; *gavām*—that of Go; *guhasya*—that of Guha; *yat*—thereupon; *śrāddhadevasya*—of the name Śrāddhadeva; *saḥ*—Vidura; *āsiṣeve*—duly visited and performed the rituals.

TRANSLATION

On the bank of the River Sarasvatī there were eleven places of pilgrimage, namely, (1) Trita, (2) Uśanā, (3) Manu, (4) Pṛthu, (5) Agni, (6) Asita, (7) Vāyu, (8) Sudāsa, (9) Go, (10) Guha and (11) Śrāddhadeva. Vidura visited all of them and duly performed rituals.

TEXT 23

अन्यानि चेह द्विजदेवदेवैः
कृतानि नानायतनानि विष्णोः ।
प्रत्यङ्गमुख्याङ्कितमन्दिराणि
यद्दर्शनात्कृष्णमनुस्मरन्ति ॥२३॥

anyāni ceha dvija-deva-devaiḥ
kṛtāni nānāyatanāni viṣṇoḥ
pratyaṅga-mukhyāṅkita-mandirāṇi
yad-darśanāt kṛṣṇam anusmaranti

anyāni—others; *ca*—also; *iha*—here; *dvija-deva*—by the great sages; *devaiḥ*—and the demigods; *kṛtāni*—established by; *nānā*—various; *āyatanāni*—various forms; *viṣṇoḥ*—of the Supreme Personality of Godhead; *prati*—each and every; *aṅga*—part; *mukhya*—the chief; *aṅkita*—marked; *mandirāṇi*—temples; *yat*—which; *darśanāt*—by seeing from a distance; *kṛṣṇam*—the original Personality of Godhead; *anusmaranti*—constantly remembers.

TRANSLATION

There were also many other temples of various forms of the Supreme Personality of Godhead Viṣṇu, established by great sages and demigods. These temples were marked with the chief emblems of the Lord, and they reminded one always of the original Personality of Godhead, Lord Kṛṣṇa.

PURPORT

Human society is divided into four social orders of life and four spiritual divisions, applying to each and every individual person. This system is called *varṇāśrama-dharma* and has already been discussed in many places in this great literature. The sages, or persons who completely devoted themselves to the spiritual upliftment of the entire human society, were known as *dvija-deva,* the best amongst the twice-born. The denizens of superior planets, from the moon planet and upwards, were known as *devas.* Both the *dvija-devas* and the *devas* always establish temples of Lord Viṣṇu in His various forms, such as Govinda, Madhusūdana, Nṛsiṁha, Mādhava, Keśava, Nārāyaṇa, Padmanābha, Pārtha-sārathi and many others. The Lord expands Himself in innumerable forms, but all of them are nondifferent from one another. Lord Viṣṇu has four hands, and each hand holds a particular item—either a conchshell, wheel, club or lotus flower. Of these four emblems, the *cakra,* or wheel, is the chief. Lord Kṛṣṇa, being the original Viṣṇu form, has only one emblem, namely the wheel, and therefore He is sometimes called the Cakrī. The Lord's *cakra* is the symbol of the power by which the Lord controls the whole manifestation. The tops of Viṣṇu temples are marked with the symbol of the wheel so that people may have the chance to see the symbol from a very long distance and at once remember Lord Kṛṣṇa. The purpose of building very high temples is to give people a chance to see them from a distant place. This system is carried on in India whenever a new temple is constructed, and it appears that it is coming down from a time before recorded history. The foolish propaganda by atheists that temples were constructed only in later days is refuted here because Vidura visited these temples at least five thousand years ago, and the temples of Viṣṇu were in existence long, long before Vidura visited them. The great sages and demigods never established statues of men or demigods, but they established temples of Viṣṇu for the benefit of common men, to raise them to the platform of God consciousness.

TEXT 24

ततस्त्वतिव्रज्य सुराष्ट्रमृद्धं
सौवीरमत्स्यान् कुरुजाङ्गलांश्च ।

कालेन तावद्यमुनामुपेत्य
तत्रोद्धवं भागवतं ददर्श ॥२४॥

tatas tv ativrajya surāṣṭram ṛddhaṁ
sauvīra-matsyān kurujāṅgalāṁś ca
kālena tāvad yamunām upetya
tatroddhavaṁ bhāgavataṁ dadarśa

tataḥ—from there; *tu*—but; *ativrajya*—by passing over; *surāṣṭram*—the kingdom of Surat; *ṛddham*—very wealthy; *sauvīra*—the kingdom of Sauvīra; *matsyān*—the kingdom of Matsya; *kurujāṅgalān*—the kingdom of western India up to the Delhi province; *ca*—also; *kālena*—in course of time; *tāvat*—as soon as; *yamunām*—bank of the River Yamunā; *upetya*—reaching; *tatra*—there; *uddhavam*—Uddhava, one of the prominent Yadus; *bhāgavatam*—the great devotee of Lord Kṛṣṇa; *dadarśa*—happened to see.

TRANSLATION

Thereafter he passed through very wealthy provinces like Surat, Sauvīra and Matsya and through western India, known as Kurujāṅgala. At last he reached the bank of the Yamunā, where he happened to meet Uddhava, the great devotee of Lord Kṛṣṇa.

PURPORT

The tract of land comprising about one hundred square miles from modern Delhi to the Mathurā district in Uttar Pradesh, including a portion of the Gurgaon district in Punjab (East India), is considered to be the topmost place of pilgrimage in all of India. This land is sacred because Lord Kṛṣṇa traveled through it many times. From the very beginning of His appearance, He was at Mathurā in the house of His maternal uncle Kaṁsa, and He was reared by His foster father Mahārāja Nanda at Vṛndāvana. There are still many devotees of the Lord lingering there in ecstasy in search of Kṛṣṇa and His childhood associates, the *gopīs*. It is not that such devotees meet Kṛṣṇa face to face in that tract of land, but a devotee's eagerly searching after Kṛṣṇa is as good as his seeing Him personally. How this is so cannot be explained, but it is factually realized by those who are pure devotees of the Lord. Philosophically, one can understand that Lord Kṛṣṇa and His remembrance are on the absolute plane and that the very idea of searching for Him at Vṛndāvana in pure God consciousness gives more pleasure to the devotee than seeing Him face to face. Such devotees of the Lord see Him face to face at every moment, as confirmed in the *Brahma-saṁhitā* (5.38):

premāñjana-cchurita-bhakti-vilocanena
santaḥ sadaiva hṛdayeṣu vilokayanti
yaṁ śyāmasundaram acintya-guṇa-svarūpaṁ
govindam ādi-puruṣaṁ tam ahaṁ bhajāmi

"Those who are in ecstasy of love with the Supreme Personality of Godhead, Lord Śyāmasundara [Kṛṣṇa], see Him always in their hearts due to love and devotional service rendered to the Lord." Both Vidura and Uddhava were such elevated devotees, and therefore they both came to the bank of the Yamunā and met each other.

TEXT 25

स वासुदेवानुचरं प्रशान्तं
बृहस्पतेः प्राक् तनयं प्रतीतम् ।
आलिंग्य गाढं प्रणयेन भद्रं
स्वानामपृच्छद्भगवत्प्रजानाम् ॥२५॥

sa vāsudevānucaraṁ praśāntaṁ
bṛhaspateḥ prāk tanayaṁ pratītam
āliṅgya gāḍhaṁ praṇayena bhadraṁ
svānām apṛcchad bhagavat-prajānām

saḥ—he, Vidura; *vāsudeva*—Lord Kṛṣṇa; *anucaram*—constant companion; *praśāntam*—very sober and gentle; *bṛhaspateḥ*—of Bṛhaspati, the learned spiritual master of the demigods; *prāk*—formerly; *tanayam*—son or disciple; *pratītam*—acknowledged; *āliṅgya*—embracing; *gāḍham*—very feelingly; *praṇayena*—in love; *bhadram*—auspicious; *svānām*—his own; *apṛcchat*—asked; *bhagavat*—of the Personality of Godhead; *prajānām*—family.

TRANSLATION

Then, due to his great love and feeling, Vidura embraced him [Uddhava], who was a constant companion of Lord Kṛṣṇa and formerly a great student of Bṛhaspati's. Vidura then asked him for news of the family of Lord Kṛṣṇa, the Personality of Godhead.

PURPORT

Vidura was older than Uddhava, like a father, and therefore when the two met, Uddhava bowed down before Vidura, and Vidura embraced him because Uddhava was younger, like a son. Vidura's brother Pāṇḍu was Lord Kṛṣṇa's uncle, and Uddhava was a cousin to Lord Kṛṣṇa. According to social custom, therefore, Vidura was to be respected by Uddhava on the level of his father. Uddhava was a great scholar in logic, and he was known to be a son or disciple of Bṛhaspati, the greatly learned priest and spiritual master of the demigods. Vidura asked Uddhava about the welfare of his relatives, although he already knew that they were no longer in the world. This inquiry appears to be very queer, but Śrīla Jīva Gosvāmī states that the news was shocking to Vidura, who therefore inquired again due to great curiosity. Thus his inquiry was psychological and not practical.

TEXT 26

कच्चित्पुराणौ पुरुषौ स्वनाभ्य-
पाद्मानुवृत्त्येह किलावतीर्णौ ।
आसात उर्व्याः कुशलं विधाय
कृतक्षणौ कुशलं शूरगेहे ॥२६॥

kaccit purāṇau puruṣau svanābhya-
pādmānuvṛttyeha kilāvatīrṇau
āsāta urvyāḥ kuśalaṁ vidhāya
kṛta-kṣaṇau kuśalaṁ śūra-gehe

kaccit—whether; *purāṇau*—the original; *puruṣau*—Personalities of Godhead (Kṛṣṇa and Balarāma); *svanābhya*—Brahmā; *pādma-anuvṛttyā*—by the request of the one who is born from the lotus; *iha*—here; *kila*—certainly; *avatīrṇau*—incarnated; *āsāte*—are; *urvyāḥ*—in the world; *kuśalam*—well-being; *vidhāya*—for doing so; *kṛta-kṣaṇau*—the elevators of everyone's prosperity; *kuśalam*—all well; *śūra-gehe*—in the house of Śūrasena.

TRANSLATION

[Please tell me] whether the original Personalities of Godhead, who incarnated Themselves at the request of Brahmā [who is born out of the lotus flower from the Lord] and who have increased the prosperity of the world by elevating everyone, are doing well in the house of Śūrasena.

PURPORT

Lord Kṛṣṇa and Balarāma are not two different Personalities of Godhead. God is one without a second, but He expands Himself in many forms without their being separate from one another. They are all plenary expansions. The immediate expansion of Lord Kṛṣṇa is Baladeva, and Brahmā, born from the lotus flower from Garbhodakaśāyī Viṣṇu, is an expansion of Baladeva. This indicates that Kṛṣṇa and

Baladeva are not subjected to the regulations of the universe; on the contrary, the whole universe is under Their subjugation. They appeared at the request of Brahmā to liberate the burden of the world, and They relieved the world by many superhuman activities so that everyone became happy and prosperous. Without the grace of the Lord, no one can become happy and prosperous. Because the happiness of the family of the Lord's devotees depends on the happiness of the Lord, Vidura first of all inquired about the well-being of the Lord.

TEXT 27

कच्चित्कुरूणां परमः सुहृन्नो
भामः स आस्ते सुखमङ्ग शौरिः ।
यो वै स्वसॄणां पितृवद्ददाति
वरान् वदान्यो वरतर्पणेन ॥२७॥

kaccit kurūṇāṁ paramaḥ suhṛn no
bhāmaḥ sa āste sukham aṅga śauriḥ
yo vai svasṝṇāṁ pitṛvad dadāti
varān vadānyo vara-tarpaṇena

kaccit—whether; *kurūṇām*—of the Kurus; *paramaḥ*—greatest; *suhṛt*—well-wisher; *naḥ*—our; *bhāmaḥ*—brother-in-law; *saḥ*—he; *āste*—is; *sukham*—happy; *aṅga*—O Uddhava; *śauriḥ*—Vasudeva; *yaḥ*—one who; *vai*—certainly; *svasṝṇām*—of the sisters; *pitṛ-vat*—like a father; *dadāti*—gives; *varān*—everything desirable; *vadānyaḥ*—munificent; *vara*—wife; *tarpaṇena*—by pleasing.

TRANSLATION

[Please tell me] whether the best friend of the Kurus, our brother-in-law Vasudeva, is doing well. He is very munificent. He is like a father to his sisters, and he is always pleasing to his wives.

PURPORT

Lord Kṛṣṇa's father, Vasudeva, had sixteen wives, and one of them, named Pauravī or Rohiṇī, the mother of Baladeva, was the sister of Vidura. Vasudeva, therefore, was the husband of Vidura's sister, and thus they were brothers-in-law. Vasudeva's sister Kuntī was the wife of Pāṇḍu, Vidura's elder brother, and in that sense also, Vasudeva was brother-in-law to Vidura. Kuntī was younger than Vasudeva, and it was the duty of the elder brother to treat younger sisters as daughters. Whenever anything was needed by Kuntī, it was munificently delivered by Vasudeva, due to his great love for his younger sister. Vasudeva never dissatisfied his wives, and at the same time he supplied the objects desired by his sister. He had special attention for Kuntī because she became a widow at an early age. While inquiring about Vasudeva's welfare, Vidura remembered all about him and the family relationship.

TEXT 28

कच्चिद्वरूथाधिपतिर्यदूनां
प्रद्युम्न आस्ते सुखमङ्ग वीरः ।
यं रुक्मिणी भगवतोऽभिलेभे
आराध्य विप्रान् स्मरमादिसर्गे ॥२८॥

kaccid varūthādhipatir yadūnāṁ
pradyumna āste sukham aṅga vīraḥ
yaṁ rukmiṇī bhagavato 'bhilebhe
ārādhya viprān smaram ādi-sarge

kaccit—whether; *varūtha*—of the military; *adhipatiḥ*—commander-in-chief; *yadūnām*—of the Yadus; *pradyumnaḥ*—the son of Kṛṣṇa named Pradyumna; *āste*—is; *sukham*—happy; *aṅga*—O Uddhava; *vīraḥ*—the great warrior; *yam*—whom; *rukmiṇī*—the wife of Kṛṣṇa named Rukmiṇī; *bhagavataḥ*—from the Personality of Godhead; *abhilebhe*—got as a prize; *ārādhya*—pleasing; *viprān*—*brāhmaṇas*; *smaram*—Cupid (Kāmadeva); *ādi-sarge*—in his previous life.

TRANSLATION

O Uddhava, please tell me how is Pradyumna, the commander-in-chief of the Yadus, who was Cupid in a former life? Rukmiṇī bore him as her son from Lord Kṛṣṇa, by the grace of brāhmaṇas whom she pleased.

PURPORT

According to Śrīla Jīva Gosvāmī, Smara (Cupid, or Kāmadeva) is one of the eternal associates of Lord Kṛṣṇa. Jīva Gosvāmī has explained this very elaborately in his treatise *Kṛṣṇa-sandarbha.*

TEXT 29

कच्चित्सुखं सात्वतवृष्णिभोज-
दाशार्हकाणामधिपः स आस्ते ।

यमभ्यषिञ्चच्छतपत्रनेत्रो
नृपासनाशां परिहृत्य दूरात् ॥२९॥

kaccit sukhaṁ sātvata-vṛṣṇi-bhoja-
dāśārhakāṇām adhipaḥ sa āste
yam abhyaṣiñcac chata-patra-netro
nṛpāsanāśāṁ parihṛtya dūrāt

kaccit—whether; *sukham*—is all well; *sātvata*—the Sātvata race; *vṛṣṇi*—the Vṛṣṇi dynasty; *bhoja*—the Bhoja dynasty; *dāśārhakāṇām*—the Dāśārha race; *adhipaḥ*—King Ugrasena; *saḥ*—he; *āste*—does exist; *yam*—whom; *abhyaṣiñcat*—installed; *śata-patra-netraḥ*—Lord Śrī Kṛṣṇa; *nṛpa-āsana-āśām*—hope of the royal throne; *parihṛtya*—giving up; *dūrāt*—at a distant place.

TRANSLATION

O my friend, [tell me] whether Ugrasena, the King of the Sātvatas, Vṛṣṇis, Bhojas and Dāśārhas, is now doing well. He went far away from his kingdom, leaving aside all hopes of his royal throne, but Lord Kṛṣṇa again installed him.

TEXT 30

कच्चिद्धरेः सौम्य सुतः सदृक्ष
आस्तेऽग्रणी रथिनां साधु साम्बः ।
असूत यं जाम्बवती व्रताढ्या
देवं गुहं योऽम्बिकया धृतोऽग्रे ॥३०॥

kaccid dhareḥ saumya sutaḥ sadṛkṣa
āste 'graṇī rathināṁ sādhu sāmbaḥ
asūta yaṁ jāmbavatī vratāḍhyā
devaṁ guhaṁ yo 'mbikayā dhṛto 'gre

kaccit—whether; *hareḥ*—of the Personality of Godhead; *saumya*—O grave one; *sutaḥ*—son; *sadṛkṣaḥ*—similar; *āste*—fares well; *agraṇīḥ*—foremost; *rathinām*—of the warriors; *sādhu*—well behaved; *sāmbaḥ*—Sāmba; *asūta*—gave birth; *yam*—whom; *jāmbavatī*—Jāmbavatī, a queen of Lord Kṛṣṇa's; *vratāḍhyā*—enriched by vows; *devam*—the demigod; *guham*—of the name Kārttikeya; *yaḥ*—whom; *ambikayā*—unto the wife of Śiva; *dhṛtaḥ*—born; *agre*—in the previous birth.

TRANSLATION

O gentle one, does Sāmba fare well? He exactly resembles the son of the Personality of Godhead. In a previous birth he was born as Kārttikeya in the

womb of the wife of Lord Śiva, and now he has been born in the womb of Jāmbavatī, the most enriched wife of Kṛṣṇa.

PURPORT

Lord Śiva, one of the three qualitative incarnations of the Personality of Godhead, is the plenary expansion of the Lord. Kārttikeya, born of him, is on the level of Pradyumna, another son of Lord Kṛṣṇa. When Lord Śrī Kṛṣṇa descends into the material world, all His plenary portions also appear with Him to exhibit different functions of the Lord. But for the pastimes at Vṛndāvana, all functions are performed by the Lord's different plenary expansions. Vāsudeva is a plenary expansion of Nārāyaṇa. When the Lord appeared as Vāsudeva before Devakī and Vasudeva, He appeared in His capacity as Nārāyaṇa. Similarly, all the demigods of the heavenly kingdom appeared as associates of the Lord in the forms of Pradyumna, Sāmba, Uddhava, etc. It is learned here that Kāmadeva appeared as Pradyumna, Kārttikeya as Sāmba, and one of the Vasus as Uddhava. All of them served in their different capacities in order to enrich the pastimes of Kṛṣṇa.

TEXT 31

क्षेमं स कच्चिद्युयुधान आस्ते
यः फाल्गुनाल्लब्धधनूरहस्यः ।
लेभेऽञ्जसाधोक्षजसेवयैव
गतिं तदीयां यतिभिर्दुरापाम् ॥३१॥

kṣemaṁ sa kaccid yuyudhāna āste
yaḥ phālgunāl labdha-dhanū-rahasyaḥ
lebhe 'ñjasādhokṣaja-sevayaiva
gatiṁ tadīyāṁ yatibhir durāpām

kṣemam—all good; *saḥ*—he; *kaccit*—whether; *yuyudhānaḥ*—Sātyaki; *āste*—is there; *yaḥ*—one who; *phālgunāt*—from Arjuna; *labdha*—has achieved; *dhanuḥ-rahasyaḥ*—one who understands the intricacies of military art; *lebhe*—also achieved; *añjasā*—summarily; *adhokṣaja*—of the Transcendence; *sevayā*—by service; *eva*—certainly; *gatim*—destination; *tadīyām*—transcendental; *yatibhiḥ*—by great renouncers; *durāpām*—very difficult to achieve.

TRANSLATION

O Uddhava, does Yuyudhāna fare well? He learned the intricacies of the military art from Arjuna and attained the transcendental destination which is very difficult to reach even for great renouncers.

PURPORT

The destination of transcendence is to become the personal associate of the Personality of Godhead, who is known as *adhokṣaja,* He who is beyond the reach of the senses. The renouncers of the world, the *sannyāsīs*, give up all worldly connections, namely, family, wife, children, friends, home, wealth—everything—to attain the transcendental bliss of Brahman happiness. But *adhokṣaja* happiness is beyond Brahman happiness. The empiric philosophers enjoy a transcendental quality of bliss by philosophical speculation on the Supreme Truth, but beyond that pleasure is the pleasure enjoyed by Brahman in His eternal form of the Personality of Godhead. Brahman bliss is enjoyed by living entities after liberation from material bondage. But Parabrahman, the Personality of Godhead, enjoys eternally a bliss of His own potency, which is called the *hlādinī* potency. The empiric philosopher who studies Brahman by negation of the external features has not yet learned the quality of the *hlādinī* potency of Brahman. Out of many potencies of the Omnipotent, there are three features of His internal potency—namely *saṁvit, sandhinī* and *hlādinī.* And in spite of their strict adherence to the principles of *yama, niyama, āsana, dhyāna, dhāraṇā* and *prāṇāyāma*, the great *yogīs* and *jñānīs* are unable to enter into the internal potency of the Lord. This internal potency is, however, easily realized by the devotees of the Lord by dint of devotional service. Yuyudhāna achieved this stage of life, just as he achieved expert knowledge in military science from Arjuna. Thus his life was successful to the fullest extent from both the material and spiritual angles of vision. That is the way of devotional service to the Lord.

TEXT 32

कच्चिद् बुधः स्वस्त्यनमीव आस्ते
श्वफल्कपुत्रो भगवत्प्रपन्नः ।
यः कृष्णपादाङ्कितमार्गपांसु-
ष्वचेष्टत प्रेमविभिन्नधैर्यः ॥३२॥

kaccid budhaḥ svasty anamīva āste
śvaphalka-putro bhagavat-prapannaḥ
yaḥ kṛṣṇa-pādāṅkita-mārga-pāṁsuṣv
aceṣṭata prema-vibhinna-dhairyaḥ

kaccit—whether; *budhaḥ*—very learned; *svasti*—well; *anamīvaḥ*—faultless; *āste*—does exist; *śvaphalka-putraḥ*—the son of Śvaphalka, Akrūra; *bhagavat*—regarding the Personality of Godhead; *prapannaḥ*—surrendered; *yaḥ*—one who; *kṛṣṇa*—the Lord; *pāda-aṅkita*—marked with footprints; *mārga*—path; *pāṁsuṣu*—in the dust; *aceṣṭata*—exhibited; *prema-vibhinna*—lost in transcendental love; *dhairyaḥ*—mental equilibrium.

TRANSLATION

Please tell me whether Akrūra, the son of Śvaphalka, is doing well. He is a faultless soul surrendered unto the Personality of Godhead. He once lost his mental equilibrium due to his ecstasy of transcendental love and fell down on the dust of a road which was marked with the footprints of Lord Kṛṣṇa.

PURPORT

When Akrūra came to Vṛndāvana in search of Kṛṣṇa, he saw the footprints of the Lord on the dust of Nanda-grāma and at once fell on them in ecstasy of transcendental love. This ecstasy is possible for a devotee who is fully absorbed in incessant thoughts of Kṛṣṇa. Such a pure devotee of the Lord is naturally faultless because he is always associated with the supremely pure Personality of Godhead. Constant thought of the Lord is the antiseptic method for keeping oneself free from the infectious contamination of the material qualities. The pure devotee of the Lord is always in company with the Lord by thinking of Him. Yet, in the particular context of time and place, the transcendental emotions take a different turn, and this breaks the mental equilibrium of the devotee. Lord Caitanya displayed the typical example of transcendental ecstasy, as we can understand from the life of this incarnation of God.

TEXT 33

कच्चिच्छिवं देवकभोजपुत्र्या
विष्णुप्रजाया इव देवमातुः ।
या वै स्वगर्भेण दधार देवं
त्रयी यथा यज्ञवितानमर्थम् ॥३३॥

kaccic chivaṁ devaka-bhoja-putryā
viṣṇu-prajāyā iva deva-mātuḥ
yā vai sva-garbheṇa dadhāra devaṁ
trayī yathā yajña-vitānam artham

kaccit—whether; *śivam*—everything well; *devaka-bhoja-putryāḥ*—of the daughter of King Devaka-bhoja; *viṣṇu-prajāyāḥ*—of she who gave birth to the Personality of Godhead; *iva*—like that of; *deva-mātuḥ*—of the mother of the demigods (Aditi); *yā*—one who; *vai*—indeed; *sva-garbheṇa*—by her own womb; *dadhāra*—conceived; *devam*—the Supreme Lord; *trayī*—the *Vedas*; *yathā*—as much as; *yajña-vitānam*—of spreading the sacrifice; *artham*—purpose.

TRANSLATION

As the Vedas are the reservoir of sacrificial purposes, so the daughter of King Devaka-bhoja conceived the Supreme Personality of Godhead in her womb, as did the mother of the demigods. Is she [Devakī] doing well?

PURPORT

The *Vedas* are full of transcendental knowledge and spiritual values, and thus Devakī, the mother of Lord Kṛṣṇa, conceived the Lord in her womb as the personified meaning of the *Vedas*. There is no difference between the *Vedas* and the Lord. The *Vedas* aim at the understanding of the Lord, and the Lord is the *Vedas* personified. Devakī is compared to the meaningful *Vedas* and the Lord to their purpose personified.

TEXT 34

अपिस्विदास्ते भगवान् सुखं वो
यः सात्वतां कामदुघोऽनिरुद्धः ।
यमामनन्ति स्म हि शब्दयोनिं
मनोमयं सत्त्वतुरीयतत्त्वम् ॥३४॥

apisvid āste bhagavān sukhaṁ vo
yaḥ sātvatāṁ kāma-dugho 'niruddhaḥ
yam āmananti sma hi śabda-yoniṁ
mano-mayaṁ sattva-turīya-tattvam

api—as also; *svit*—whether; *āste*—does He; *bhagavān*—the Personality of Godhead; *sukham*—all happiness; *vaḥ*—of you; *yaḥ*—one who; *sātvatām*—of the devotees; *kāma-dughaḥ*—source of all desires; *aniruddhaḥ*—the plenary expansion Aniruddha; *yam*—whom; *āmananti*—they accept; *sma*—from yore; *hi*—certainly; *śabda-yonim*—the cause of the *Ṛg Veda; manaḥ-mayam*—creator of the mind; *sattva*—transcendental; *turīya*—the fourth expansion; *tattvam*—principle.

TRANSLATION

May I inquire whether Aniruddha is doing well? He is the fulfiller of all the desires of the pure devotees and has been considered from yore to be the cause of the Ṛg Veda, the creator of the mind and the fourth Plenary expansion of Viṣṇu.

PURPORT

Ādi-caturbhuja, the original expansions from Baladeva, are Vāsudeva, Saṅkarṣaṇa, Pradyumna and Aniruddha. All of Them are *viṣṇu-tattvas,* or nondifferent Personalities of Godhead. In the incarnation of Śrī Rāma, all these different expansions appeared for particular pastimes. Lord Rāma is the original Vāsudeva, and His brothers were Saṅkarṣaṇa, Pradyumna and Aniruddha. Aniruddha is also the cause of Mahā-Viṣṇu, from whose breathing the *Ṛg Veda* appeared. All this is nicely explained in the *Mārkaṇḍeya Purāṇa.* In the incarnation of Lord Kṛṣṇa, Aniruddha appeared as the son of the Lord. Lord Kṛṣṇa in Dvārakā is the Vāsudeva expansion of the original group. The original Lord Kṛṣṇa never leaves Goloka Vṛndāvana. All the plenary expansions are one and the same *viṣṇu-tattva,* and there is no difference in Their potency.

TEXT 35

अपिस्विदन्ये च निजात्मदैव-
मनन्यवृत्त्या समनुव्रता ये ।
हृदीकसत्यात्मजचारुदेष्ण-
गदादयः स्वस्ति चरन्ति सौम्य ॥३५॥

apisvid anye ca nijātma-daivam
ananya-vṛttyā samanuvratā ye
hṛdīka-satyātmaja-cārudeṣṇa-
gadādayaḥ svasti caranti saumya

api—as also; *svit*—whether; *anye*—others; *ca*—and; *nija-ātma*—of one's own self; *daivam*—Śrī Kṛṣṇa; *ananya*—absolutely; *vṛttyā*—faith; *samanuvratāḥ*—followers; *ye*—all those who; *hṛdīka*—Hṛdīka; *satya-ātmaja*—the son of Satyabhāmā; *cārudeṣṇa*—Cārudeṣṇa; *gada*—Gada; *ādayaḥ*—and others; *svasti*—all well; *caranti*—pass time; *saumya*—O sober one.

TRANSLATION

O sober one, others, such as Hṛdīka, Cārudeṣṇa, Gada and the son of Satyabhāmā, who accept Lord Śrī Kṛṣṇa as the soul of the self and thus follow His path without deviation—are they well?

TEXT 36

अपि स्वदोर्भ्यां विजयाच्युताभ्यां
धर्मेण धर्मः परिपाति सेतुम् ।

दुर्योधनोऽतप्यत यत्सभायां
साम्राज्यलक्ष्म्या विजयानुवृत्त्या ॥३६॥

api sva-dorbhyāṁ vijayācyutābhyāṁ
dharmeṇa dharmaḥ paripāti setum
duryodhano 'tapyata yat-sabhāyāṁ
sāmrājya-lakṣmyā vijayānuvṛttyā

api—as also; *sva-dorbhyām*—own arms; *vijaya*—Arjuna; *acyutā-bhyām*—along with Śrī Kṛṣṇa; *dharmeṇa*—on religious principles; *dharmaḥ*—King Yudhiṣṭhira; *paripāti*—maintains; *setum*—the respect of religion; *duryodhanaḥ*—Duryodhana; *atapyata*—envied; *yat*—whose; *sabhāyām*—royal assembly; *sāmrājya*—imperial; *lakṣmyā*—opulence; *vijaya-anuvṛttyā*—by the service of Arjuna.

TRANSLATION

Also let me inquire whether Mahārāja Yudhiṣṭhira is now maintaining the kingdom according to religious principles and with respect for the path of religion. Formerly Duryodhana was burning with envy because Yudhiṣṭhira was being protected by the arms of Kṛṣṇa and Arjuna as if they were his own arms.

PURPORT

Mahārāja Yudhiṣṭhira was the emblem of religion. When he was ruling his kingdom with the help of Lord Kṛṣṇa and Arjuna, the opulence of his kingdom surpassed all imaginations of the opulence of the kingdom of heaven. His actual arms were Lord Kṛṣṇa and Arjuna, and thus he surpassed everyone's opulence. Duryodhana, being envious of this opulence, planned so many schemes to put Yudhiṣṭhira into difficulty, and at last the Battle of Kurukṣetra was brought about. After the Battle of Kurukṣetra, Mahārāja Yudhiṣṭhira was again able to rule his legitimate kingdom, and he reinstated the principles of honor and respect for religion. That is the beauty of a kingdom ruled by a pious king like Mahārāja Yudhiṣṭhira.

TEXT 37

किं वा कृताघेष्वघमत्यमर्षी
भीमोऽहिवद्दीर्घतमं व्यमुञ्चत् ।
यस्याङ्घ्रिपातं रणभूर्न सेहे
मार्गं गदायाश्चरतो विचित्रम् ॥३७॥

kiṁ vā kṛtāgheṣv agham atyamarṣī
bhīmo 'hivad dīrghatamaṁ vyamuñcat
yasyāṅghri-pātaṁ raṇa-bhūr na sehe
mārgaṁ gadāyāś carato vicitram

kim—whether; *vā*—either; *kṛta*—performed; *agheṣu*—unto the sinners; *agham*—angry; *ati-amarṣī*—unconquerable; *bhīmaḥ*—Bhīma; *ahi-vat*—like a cobra; *dīrgha-tamam*—long-cherished; *vyamuñcat*—has released; *yasya*—whose; *aṅghri-pātam*—putting on the steps; *raṇa-bhūḥ*—the field of battle; *na*—could not; *sehe*—tolerate; *mārgam*—the path; *gadāyāḥ*—by the clubs; *carataḥ*—playing; *vicitram*—wonderful.

TRANSLATION

[Please tell me] whether the unconquerable Bhīma, who is like a cobra, has released his long-cherished anger upon the sinners? The field of battle could not tolerate even the wonderful playing of his club when he stepped on the path.

PURPORT

Vidura knew the strength of Bhīma. Whenever Bhīma was on the battlefield, his steps on the path and the wonderful playing of his club were unbearable for the enemy. Powerful Bhīma did not take steps against the sons of Dhṛtarāṣṭra for a long time. Vidura's inquiry was whether he had yet released his anger, which was like that of a suffering cobra. When a cobra releases its venom after long-cherished anger, its victim cannot survive.

TEXT 38

कच्चिद्यशोधा रथयूथपानां
गाण्डीवधन्वोपरतारिरास्ते ।
अलक्षितो यच्छरकूटगूढो
मायाकिरातो गिरिशस्तुतोष ॥३८॥

kaccid yaśodhā ratha-yūthapānāṁ
gāṇḍīva-dhanvoparatārir āste
alakṣito yac-chara-kūṭa-gūḍho
māyā-kirāto giriśas tutoṣa

kaccit—whether; *yaśaḥ-dhā*—famous; *ratha-yūthapānām*—amongst the great chariot warriors; *gāṇḍīva*—Gandiva; *dhanvā*—bow; *uparata-ariḥ*—one who has vanquished the enemies; *āste*—doing well; *alakṣitaḥ*—without being identified; *yat*—whose; *śara-kūṭa-gūḍhaḥ*—being covered by arrows; *māyā-kirātaḥ*—false hunter; *giriśaḥ*—Lord Śiva; *tutoṣa*—was satisfied.

TRANSLATION

[Please tell me] whether Arjuna, whose bow bears the name Gāṇḍīva and who is always famous amongst the chariot warriors for vanquishing his enemies, is doing well. He once satisfied Lord Śiva by covering him with arrows when Śiva came as an unidentified false hunter.

PURPORT

Lord Śiva tested Arjuna's strength by picking a quarrel with him over a hunted boar. He confronted Arjuna in the false dress of a hunter, and Arjuna covered him with arrows until Lord Śiva was satisfied with Arjuna's fighting. He offered Arjuna the Pāśupati weapon and blessed him. Here Vidura inquired about the great warrior's well-being.

TEXT 39

यमावुतस्वित्तनयौ पृथायाः
पार्थैर्वृतौ पक्ष्मभिरक्षिणीव ।
रेमात उद्दाय मृधे स्वरिक्थं
परात्सुपर्णाविव वज्रिवक्त्रात् ॥३९॥

yamāv utasvit tanayau pṛthāyāḥ
pārthair vṛtau pakṣmabhir akṣiṇīva
remāta uddaya mṛdhe sva-riktham
parāt suparṇāv iva vajri-vaktrāt

yamau—twins (Nakula and Sahadeva); *utasvit*—whether; *tanayau*—sons; *pṛthāyāḥ*—of Pṛthā; *pārthaiḥ*—by the sons of Pṛthā; *vṛtau*—protected; *pakṣmabhiḥ*—by shields; *akṣiṇī*—of the eyes; *iva*—like; *remāte*—playing carelessly; *uddāya*—snatching; *mṛdhe*—in the fight; *sva-riktham*—own property; *parāt*—from the enemy Duryodhana; *suparṇau*—Garuḍa, the carrier of Lord Viṣṇu; *iva*—like; *vajri-vaktrāt*—from the mouth of Indra.

TRANSLATION

Are the twin brothers who are protected by their brothers doing well? Just as the eye is always protected by the eyelid, they are protected by the sons of

Pṛthā, who snatched back their rightful kingdom from the hands of their enemy Duryodhana, just as Garuḍa snatched nectar from the mouth of Indra, the thunderbolt carrier.

PURPORT

Indra, the King of heaven, carries a thunderbolt in his hand and is very strong, yet Garuḍa, the carrier of Lord Viṣṇu, was able to snatch nectar from his mouth. Similarly, Duryodhana was as strong as the King of heaven, and still the sons of Pṛthā, the Pāṇḍavas, were able to snatch away their kingdom from Duryodhana. Both Garuḍa and the Pārthas are pet devotees of the Lord, and thus it was possible for them to face such strong enemies.

Vidura's inquiry was about the youngest brothers of the Pāṇḍavas, namely Nakula and Sahadeva. These twin brothers were sons of Mādrī, the stepmother of the other Pāṇḍavas. But although they were stepbrothers, because Kuntī took charge of them after the departure of Mādrī with her husband Mahārāja Pāṇḍu, Nakula and Sahadeva were as good as the other three Pāṇḍavas, Yudhiṣṭhira, Bhīma and Arjuna. The five brothers are known in the world as regular brothers. The three elder Pāṇḍavas took care of the younger brothers, just as the eyelid takes care of the eye. Vidura was anxious to know whether, after winning back their own kingdom from the hands of Duryodhana, the younger brothers were still living happily under the care of the elder brothers.

TEXT 40

अहो पृथापि ध्रियतेऽर्भकार्थे
राजर्षिवर्येण विनापि तेन ।
यस्त्वेकवीरोऽधिरथो विजिग्ये
धनुर्द्वितीयः ककुभश्चतस्रः ॥४०॥

aho pṛthāpi dhriyate 'rbhakārthe
rājarṣi-varyeṇa vināpi tena
yas tv eka-vīro 'dhiratho vijigye
dhanur dvitīyaḥ kakubhaś catasraḥ

aho—O my lord; *pṛthā*—Kuntī; *api*—also; *dhriyate*—bears her life; *arbhaka-arthe*—for the sake of fatherless children; *rājarṣi*—King Pāṇḍu; *varyeṇa*—the best; *vinā api*—without him; *tena*—him; *yaḥ*—one who; *tu*—but; *eka*—alone; *vīraḥ*—the warrior; *adhirathaḥ*—commander; *vijigye*—could conquer; *dhanuḥ*—the bow; *dvitīyaḥ*—the second; *kakubhaḥ*—directions; *catasraḥ*—four.

TRANSLATION

O my lord, is Pṛthā still living? She lived only for the sake of her fatherless children; otherwise it was impossible for her to live without King Pāṇḍu, who was the greatest commander and who alone conquered the four directions simply with the help of a second bow.

PURPORT

A faithful wife cannot live without her lord, the husband, and therefore all widows used to voluntarily embrace the burning fire which consumed the dead husband. This system was very common in India because all the wives were chaste and faithful to their husbands. Later on, with the advent of the age of Kali, the wives gradually began to be less adherent to their husbands, and the voluntary embrace of the fire by the widows became a thing of the past. Very recently the system was abolished, since the voluntary system had become a forcible social custom.

When Mahārāja Pāndu died, both his wives, namely Kuntī and Mādrī, were prepared to embrace the fire, but Mādrī requested Kuntī to live for the sake of the younger children, the five Pāṇdavas. This was agreed upon by Kuntī at the added request of Vyāsadeva. In spite of her great bereavement, Kuntī decided to live, not to enjoy life in the absence of her husband, but only to give protection to the children. This incident is referred to here by Vidura because he knew all the facts about his sister-in-law Kuntīdevī. It is understood that Mahārāja Pāndu was a great warrior and that he alone, with the help of bow and arrow, could conquer the world's four directions. In the absence of such a husband, it was almost impossible for Kuntī to live on even as a widow, but she had to do it for the sake of the five children.

TEXT 41

सौम्यानुशोचे तमधःपतन्तं
भ्रात्रे परेताय विदुद्रुहे यः ।
निर्यापितो येन सुहृत्स्वपुर्या
अहं स्वपुत्रान् समनुव्रतेन ॥४१॥

saumyānuśoce tam adhaḥ-patantaṁ
bhrātre paretāya vidudruhe yaḥ
niryāpito yena suhṛt sva-puryā
ahaṁ sva-putrān samanuvratena

saumya—O gentle one; *anuśoce*—just lamenting; *tam*—him; *adhaḥ-patantam*—gliding down; *bhrātre*—on his brother's; *paretāya*—death; *vidudruhe*—revolted against; *yaḥ*—one who; *niryāpitaḥ*—driven out; *yena*—by whom; *suhṛt*—well-wisher; *sva-puryāḥ*—from his own house; *aham*—myself; *sva-putrān*—with his own sons; *samanu-vratena*—accepting the same line of action.

TRANSLATION

O gentle one, I simply lament for he [Dhṛtarāṣṭra] who rebelled against his brother after death. By him I was driven out of my own house, although I am his sincere well-wisher, because he accepted the line of action adopted by his own sons.

PURPORT

Vidura did not ask about the welfare of his elder brother because there was no chance of his well-being, only news of his gliding down to hell. Vidura was a sincere well-wisher for Dhṛtarāṣṭra, and he had a thought about him in the corner of his heart. He lamented that Dhṛtarāṣṭra could rebel against the sons of his dead brother Pāṇḍu and that he could drive him (Vidura) out of his own house on the dictation of his crooked sons. In spite of these actions, Vidura never became an enemy of Dhṛtarāṣṭra but continued to be his well-wisher, and at the last stage of Dhṛtarāṣṭra's life, it was Vidura only who proved to be his real friend. Such is the behavior of a Vaiṣṇava like Vidura: he desires all good, even for his enemies.

TEXT 42

सोऽहं हरेर्मर्त्यविडम्बनेन
दृशो नृणां चालयतो विधातुः ।
नान्योपलक्ष्यः पदवीं प्रसादा-
च्चरामि पश्यन् गतविस्मयोऽत्र ॥४२॥

so 'haṁ harer martya-viḍambanena
dṛśo nṛṇāṁ cālayato vidhātuḥ
nānyopalakṣyaḥ padavīṁ prasādāc
carāmi paśyan gata-vismayo 'tra

saḥ aham—therefore, I; *hareḥ*—of the Personality of Godhead; *martya*—in this mortal world; *viḍambanena*—without being recognized; *dṛśaḥ*—on sight; *nṛṇām*—of the people in general; *cālayataḥ*—bewildering; *vidhātuḥ*—in order to do it; *na*—not; *anya*—other;

upalakṣyaḥ—seen by others; *padavīm*—glories; *prasādāt*—by the grace of; *carāmi*—do travel; *paśyan*—by seeing; *gata-vismayaḥ*—without doubt; *atra*—in this matter.

TRANSLATION

I am not astonished at this, having traveled over the world without being seen by others. The activities of the Personality of Godhead, which are like those of a man in this mortal world, are bewildering to others, but I know of His greatness by His grace, and thus I am happy in all respects.

PURPORT

Although he was the brother of Dhṛtarāṣṭra, Vidura was completely different. By the grace of Lord Kṛṣṇa, he was not foolish like his brother, and thus his brother's association could not influence him. Dhṛtarāṣṭra and his materialistic sons wanted to falsely lord it over the world by dint of their own strength. The Lord encouraged them in this, and thus they became more and more bewildered. But Vidura wanted to achieve sincere devotional service of the Lord and therefore became a soul absolutely surrendered to the Absolute Personality of Godhead. He could realize this in the progress of his pilgrim's journey, and thus he was freed from all doubts. He was not at all sorry to be bereft of his hearth and home because he now had experience that dependence on the mercy of the Lord is a greater freedom than so-called freedom at home. A person should not be in the renounced order of life unless he is firmly convinced of being protected by the Lord. This stage of life is explained in *Bhagavad-gītā* as *abhayaṁ sattva-saṁśuddhiḥ:* every living entity is factually completely dependent on the mercy of the Lord, but unless one is in the pure state of existence, he cannot be established in this position. This stage of dependence is called *sattva-saṁśuddhiḥ,* or purification of one's existence. The result of such purification is exhibited in fearlessness. A devotee of the Lord, who is called *nārāyaṇa-para,* is never afraid of anything because he is always aware of the fact that the Lord protects him in all circumstances. With this conviction, Vidura traveled alone, and he was not seen or recognized by any friend or foe. Thus he enjoyed freedom of life without obligation to the many duties of the world.

When Lord Śrī Kṛṣṇa was personally present in the mortal world in His eternal, blissful form of Śyāmasundara, those who were not pure devotees of the Lord could not recognize Him or know His glories. *Avajānānti māṁ mūḍhā mānuṣīṁ tanum āśritam* (Bg. 9.11): He is always bewildering to the nondevotees, but He is always seen by the devotees by dint of their pure devotional service to Him.

TEXT 43

नूनं नृपाणां त्रिमदोत्पथानां
महीं मुहुश्चालयतां चमूभिः ।
वधात्प्रपन्नार्तिजिहीर्षयेशो-
ऽप्युपैक्षताघं भगवान् कुरूणाम् ॥४३॥

nūnaṁ nṛpāṇāṁ tri-madotpathānāṁ
mahīṁ muhuś cālayatāṁ camūbhiḥ
vadhāt prapannārti-jihīrṣayeśo
'py upaikṣatāghaṁ bhagavān kurūṇām

nūnam—of course; *nṛpāṇām*—of the kings; *tri*—three; *mada-utpathānām*—going astray out of false pride; *mahīm*—earth; *muhuḥ*—constantly; *cālayatām*—agitating; *camūbhiḥ*—by movement of soldiers; *vadhāt*—from the act of killing; *prapanna*—surrendered; *ārti-jihīrṣaya*—willing to relieve the distress of the sufferers; *īśaḥ*—the Lord; *api*—in spite of; *upaikṣata*—waited; *agham*—offenses; *bhagavān*—the Supreme Lord; *kurūṇām*—of the Kurus.

TRANSLATION

Despite His being the Lord and being always willing to relieve the distress of sufferers, He [Kṛṣṇa] refrained from killing the Kurus, although they committed all sorts of sins and although He saw other kings constantly agitating the earth by their strong military movements carried out under the dictation of three kinds of false pride.

PURPORT

As declared in *Bhagavad-gītā,* the Lord appears in the mortal world to execute His much-needed mission of killing the miscreants and giving protection to the suffering faithful. In spite of that mission, Lord Kṛṣṇa tolerated the insult to Draupadī by the Kurus and the injustices perpetrated against the Pāṇḍavas, as well as insults to Himself. The question may be raised, "Why did He tolerate such injustices and insults in His presence? Why did He not chastise the Kurus immediately?" When Draupadī was insulted in the assembly by the Kurus by their attempt to see her naked in the presence of all, the Lord protected Draupadī by supplying an unlimited length of clothing. But He did not chastise the insulting party immediately. This silence of the Lord did not mean, however, that He excused the offenses of the Kurus. There were many other kings on earth who had become very proud of three kinds of possessions—wealth, education and followers—and they were constantly agitating the earth by movements of military strength. The Lord was just waiting to get them together on the Battlefield of Kurukṣetra and kill them all at one time, just to make a short-cut in His killing mission. Godless kings or heads of state, when puffed up by advancement of material wealth, education and increase of population, always make a show of military strength and give trouble to the innocent. When Lord Kṛṣṇa was personally present, there were many such kings all over the world, and He thus arranged for the Battle of Kurukṣetra. In His manifestation of *viśva-rūpa,* the Lord expressed His mission of killing as follows: "I have willingly descended on the earth in My capacity of inexorable Time in order to decrease the unwanted population. I shall finish all those who have assembled here except you, the Pāṇḍavas. This killing does not wait for you to take part in it. It is already arranged: all will be killed by Me. If you want to become famous as the hero of the battlefield and thus enjoy the booty of war, then, O Savyasācī, just become the immediate cause of this killing and thus take the credit. I have already killed all the great warriors—Bhīṣma, Droṇa, Jayadratha, Karṇa and many other great generals. Do not worry. Fight the battle and be famous as a great hero." (Bg. 11.32-34)

The Lord always wants to see His devotee as the hero of some episode which He Himself performs. He wanted to see His devotee and friend Arjuna as the hero of the Battle of Kurukṣetra, and thus He waited for all the miscreants of the world to assemble. That, and nothing else, is the explanation of His waiting.

TEXT 44

अजस्य जन्मोत्पथनाशनाय
कर्माण्यकर्तुर्ग्रहणाय पुंसाम् ।
नन्वन्यथा कोऽर्हति देहयोगं
परो गुणानामुत कर्मतन्त्रम् ॥४४॥

ajasya janmotpatha-nāśanāya
karmāṇy akartur grahaṇāya puṁsām
nanv anyathā ko 'rhati deha-yogaṁ
paro guṇānām uta karma-tantram

ajasya—of the unborn; *janma*—appearance; *utpatha-nāśanāya*—for the sake of annihilating the upstarts; *karmāṇi*—works; *akartuḥ*—of one who has nothing to do; *grahaṇāya*—to take up; *puṁsām*—of all persons; *nanu anyathā*—otherwise; *kaḥ*—who; *arhati*—may deserve; *deha-yogam*—contact of the body; *paraḥ*—transcendental; *guṇānām*—of the three modes of nature; *uta*—what to speak of; *karma-tantram*—the law of action and reaction.

TRANSLATION

The appearance of the Lord is manifested for the annihilation of the upstarts. His activities are transcendental and are enacted for the understanding of all persons. Otherwise, since the Lord is transcendental to all material modes, what purpose could He serve by coming to earth?

PURPORT

Īśvaraḥ paramaḥ kṛṣṇaḥ sac-cid-ānanda-vigrahaḥ (*Bs.* 5.1): the form of the Lord is eternal, blissful, and all-knowing. His so-called birth is therefore an appearance only, like the birth of the sun on the horizon. His birth does not, like that of the living entities, take place under the influence of material nature and the bondage of the reactions of past deeds. His works and activities are independent pastimes and are not subject to the reactions of material nature. In *Bhagavad-gītā* (4.14) it is said:

na māṁ karmāṇi limpanti
na me karma-phale spṛhā
iti māṁ yo 'bhijānāti
karmabhir na sa badhyate

The law of *karma* enacted by the Supreme Lord for the living entities cannot be applicable to Him, nor has the Lord any desire to improve Himself by activities like those of ordinary living beings. Ordinary living beings work for the improvement of their conditional lives. But the Lord is already full of all opulence, all strength, all fame, all beauty, all knowledge and all renunciation. Why should He desire improvement? No one can excel Him in any opulence, and therefore the desire for improvement is absolutely useless for Him. One should always discriminate between the activities of the Lord and those of ordinary living beings. Thus one may come to the right conclusion regarding the Lord's transcendental position. One who can come to the conclusion of the Lord's transcendence can become a devotee of the Lord and can at once be free from all reactions of past deeds. It is said, *karmāṇi nirdahati kintu ca bhakti-bhājām:* the Lord minimizes or nullifies the reactionary influence of the devotee's past deeds. (*Bs.* 5.54)

The activities of the Lord are to be accepted and relished by all living entities. His activities are to attract the ordinary man towards the Lord. The Lord always acts in favor of the devotees, and therefore ordinary men who are fruitive actors or seekers of salvation may be attracted to the Lord when He acts as protector of the devotees. The fruitive actors can attain their goals by devotional service, and the salvationists can also attain their goal in life by devotional service to the Lord. The devotees do not want the fruitive results of their work, nor do they want any kind of salvation. They relish the glorious superhuman activities of the Lord, such as His lifting Govardhana Hill and His killing the demon Pūtanā in infancy. His activities are enacted to attract all kinds of men—*karmīs, jñānīs* and *bhaktas.* Because He is transcendental to all laws of *karma,* there is no possibility of His accepting a form of *māyā* as is forced on the ordinary living entities who are bound by the actions and reactions of their own deeds.

The secondary purpose of His appearance is to annihilate the upstart *asuras* and to stop the nonsense of atheistic propaganda by less intelligent persons. By the Lord's causeless mercy, the *asuras* who are killed personally by the Personality of Godhead get salvation. The meaningful appearance of the Lord is always distinct from ordinary birth. Even the pure devotees have no connection with the material body, and certainly the Lord, who appears as He is, in His *sac-cid-ānanda* [Bs. 5.1] form, is not limited by a material form.

TEXT 45

तस्य प्रपन्नाखिललोकपाना-
मवस्थितानामनुशासने स्वे ।
अर्थाय जातस्य यदुष्वजस्य
वार्तां सखे कीर्तय तीर्थकीर्तेः ॥४५॥

tasya prapannākhila-lokapānām
avasthitānām anuśāsane sve
arthāya jātasya yaduṣv ajasya
vārtām sakhe kīrtaya tīrtha-kīrteḥ

tasya—His; *prapanna*—surrendered; *akhila-loka-pānām*—all rulers of the entire universe; *avasthitānām*—situated in; *anuśāsane*—under the control of; *sve*—own self; *arthāya*—for the interest of; *jātasya*—of the born; *yaduṣu*—in the family of the Yadus; *ajasya*—of the unborn; *vārtām*—topics; *sakhe*—O my friend; *kīrtaya*—please narrate; *tīrtha-kīrteḥ*—of the Lord, whose glories are chanted in the places of pilgrimage.

TRANSLATION

O my friend, please, therefore, chant the glories of the Lord, who is meant to be glorified in the places of pilgrimage. He is unborn, and yet He appears by His causeless mercy upon the surrendered rulers of all parts of the universe. Only for their interest did He appear in the family of His unalloyed devotees the Yadus.

PURPORT

There are innumerable rulers all over the universe in different varieties of planets: the sun-god in the sun planet, the moon-god in the moon planet, Indra in the heavenly planet, Vāyu, Varuṇa, and those in the Brahmaloka planet, where Lord Brahmā is living. All are obedient servants of the Lord. Whenever there is any trouble in the administration of the innumerable planets in different universes, the rulers pray for an appearance, and the Lord appears. The *Bhāgavatam* (1.3.28) has already confirmed this in the following verse:

ete cāṁśa-kalāḥ puṁsaḥ
kṛṣṇas tu bhagavān svayam
indrāri-vyākulaṁ lokaṁ
mṛḍayanti yuge yuge

In every millennium, whenever there is any trouble for the obedient rulers, the Lord appears. He also appears for the sake of His pure unalloyed devotees. The surrendered rulers and the pure devotees are always strictly under the control of the Lord, and they are never disobedient to the desires of the Lord. The Lord is therefore always attentive to them.

The purpose of pilgrimages is to remember the Lord constantly, and therefore the Lord is known as *tīrtha-kīrti.* The purpose of going to a place of pilgrimage is to get the chance to glorify the Lord. Even today, although times have changed, there are still pilgrimage sites in India. For example, in Mathurā and Vṛndāvana, where we had a chance to stay, people are awake from early in the morning at 4 A.M. up until nighttime and are constantly engaged, some way or other, in chanting the holy glories of the Lord. The beauty of such a pilgrimage site is that automatically one remembers the holy glories of the Lord. His name, fame, quality, form, pastimes and entourage are all identical to the Lord, and therefore chanting the glories of the Lord invokes the personal presence of the Lord. Anytime or anywhere pure devotees meet and chant the glories of the Lord, the Lord is present without any doubt. It is said by the Lord Himself that He always stays where His pure devotees chant His glories.

Thus end the Bhaktivedanta purports of the Third Canto, First Chapter, of the Śrīmad-Bhāgavatam, *entitled "Questions by Vidura."*

CHAPTER TWO

Remembrance of Lord Kṛṣṇa

TEXT 1

श्रीशुक उवाच
इति भागवतः पृष्टः क्षत्त्रा वार्तां प्रियाश्रयाम् ।
प्रतिवक्तुं न चोत्सेह औत्कण्ठ्यात्स्मारितेश्वरः ॥ १ ॥

śrī-śuka uvāca
iti bhāgavataḥ pṛṣṭaḥ
kṣattrā vārtāṁ priyāśrayām
prativaktuṁ na cotseha
autkaṇṭhyāt smāriteśvaraḥ

śrī-śukaḥ uvāca—Śrī Śukadeva said; *iti*—thus; *bhāgavataḥ*—the great devotee; *pṛṣṭaḥ*—being asked; *kṣattrā*—by Vidura; *vārtām*—message; *priya-āśrayām*—regarding the dearest; *prativaktum*—to reply; *na*—not; *ca*—also; *utsehe*—became eager; *autkaṇṭhyāt*—by excessive anxiety; *smārita*—remembrance; *īśvaraḥ*—the Lord.

TRANSLATION

Śrī Śukadeva Gosvāmī said: When the great devotee Uddhava was asked by Vidura to speak on the messages of the dearest [Lord Kṛṣṇa], Uddhava was unable to answer immediately due to excessive anxiety at the remembrance of the Lord.

TEXT 2

यः पञ्चहायनो मात्रा प्रातराशाय याचितः ।
तन्नैच्छद्रचयन् यस्य सपर्यां बाललीलया ॥ २ ॥

yaḥ pañca-hāyano mātrā
prātar-āśāya yācitaḥ
tan naicchad racayan yasya
saparyāṁ bāla-līlayā

yaḥ—one who; *pañca*—five; *hāyanaḥ*—years old; *mātrā*—by his mother; *prātaḥ-āśāya*—for breakfast; *yācitaḥ*—called for; *tat*—that; *na*—not; *aicchat*—liked; *racayan*—playing; *yasya*—whose; *saparyām*—service; *bāla-līlayā*—childhood.

TRANSLATION

He was one who even in his childhood, at the age of five years, was so absorbed in the service of Lord Kṛṣṇa that when he was called by his mother for morning breakfast, he did not wish to have it.

PURPORT

From his very birth, Uddhava was a natural devotee of Lord Kṛṣṇa, or a *nitya-siddha*, a liberated soul. From natural instinct he used to serve Lord Kṛṣṇa, even in his childhood. He used to play with dolls in the form of Kṛṣṇa, he would serve the dolls by dressing, feeding and worshiping them, and thus he was constantly absorbed in the play of transcendental realization. These are the signs of an eternally liberated soul. An eternally liberated soul is a devotee of the Lord who never forgets Him. Human life is meant for reviving one's eternal relation with the Lord, and all religious injunctions are meant for awakening this dormant instinct of the living entity. The sooner this awakening is brought about, the quicker the mission of human life is fulfilled. In a good family of devotees, the child gets the opportunity to serve the Lord in many ways. A soul who is already advanced in devotional service has the opportunity to take birth in such an enlightened family. This is confirmed in the *Bhagavad-gītā* (6.41). *Śucīnāṁ śrīmatāṁ gehe yoga-bhraṣṭo 'bhijāyate:* even the fallen devotee gets the opportunity to take his birth in the family of a well-situated *brāhmaṇa* or in a rich, well-to-do mercantile family. In both these families there is a good opportunity to revive one's sense of God consciousness automatically because particularly in these families the worship of Lord Kṛṣṇa is regularly performed and the child gets the opportunity to imitate the process of worship called *arcanā*.

The *pāñcarātrikī* formula for training persons in devotional service is temple worship, whereby the neophytes get the opportunity to learn devotional service to the Lord. Mahārāja Parīkṣit also used to play with Kṛṣṇa dolls in his childhood. In India the children in good families are still given dolls of the Lord like Rāma and Kṛṣṇa, or sometimes the demigods, so that they may develop the aptitude of service to the Lord. By the grace of the Lord we were given the same opportunity by our parents, and the beginning of our life was based on this principle.

TEXT 3

स कथं सेवया तस्य कालेन जरसं गतः ।
पृष्टो वार्तां प्रतिब्रूयाद्भर्तुः पादावनुस्मरन् ॥ ३ ॥

sa kathaṁ sevayā tasya
kālena jarasaṁ gataḥ
pṛṣṭo vārtāṁ pratibrūyād
bhartuḥ pādāv anusmaran

saḥ—Uddhava; *katham*—how; *sevayā*—by such service; *tasya*—his; *kālena*—in course of time; *jarasam*—invalidity; *gataḥ*—undergone; *pṛṣṭaḥ*—asked for; *vārtām*—message; *pratibrūyāt*—just to reply; *bhartuḥ*—of the Lord; *pādau*—His lotus feet; *anusmaran*—remembering.

TRANSLATION

Uddhava thus served the Lord continually from childhood, and in his old age that attitude of service never slackened. As soon as he was asked about the message of the Lord, he at once remembered all about Him.

PURPORT

Transcendental service to the Lord is not mundane. The service attitude of the devotee gradually increases and never becomes slackened. Generally, in old age a person is allowed retirement from mundane service. But in the transcendental service of the Lord there is no retirement at all; on the contrary, the service attitude increases more and more with the progress of age. In the transcendental service there is no satiation, and therefore there is no retirement. Materially, when a man becomes tired by rendering service in his physical body, he is allowed retirement, but in the transcendental service there is no feeling of fatigue because it is spiritual service and is not on the bodily plane. Service on the bodily plane dwindles as the body grows older, but the spirit is never old, and therefore on the spiritual plane the service is never tiresome.

Uddhava undoubtedly became old, but that does not mean that his spirit became old. His service attitude matured on the transcendental plane, and therefore as soon as he was questioned by Vidura about Lord Kṛṣṇa, he at once remembered his Lord by reference to the context and forgot himself on the physical plane. That is the sign of pure devotional service to the Lord, as will be explained later on (*lakṣaṇaṁ bhakti-yogasya*, etc.) in Lord Kapila's instructions to His mother, Devahūti.

TEXT 4

स मुहूर्तमभूत्तूष्णीं कृष्णाङ्घ्रिसुधया भृशम् ।
तीव्रेण भक्तियोगेन निमग्नः साधु निर्वृतः ॥ ४ ॥

sa muhūrtam abhūt tūṣṇīṁ
kṛṣṇāṅghri-sudhayā bhṛśam
tīvreṇa bhakti-yogena
nimagnaḥ sādhu nirvṛtaḥ

saḥ—Uddhava; *muhūrtam*—for a moment; *abhūt*—became; *tūṣṇīm*—dead silent; *kṛṣṇa-aṅghri*—the lotus feet of the Lord; *sudhayā*—by the nectar; *bhṛśam*—well matured; *tīvreṇa*—by very strong; *bhakti-yogena*—devotional service; *nimagnaḥ*—absorbed in; *sādhu*—good; *nirvṛtaḥ*—fully in love.

TRANSLATION

For a moment he remained dead silent, and his body did not move. He became absorbed in the nectar of remembering the Lord's lotus feet in devotional ecstasy, and he appeared to be going increasingly deeper into that ecstasy.

PURPORT

On the inquiry by Vidura about Kṛṣṇa, Uddhava appeared to be awakened from slumber. He appeared to regret that he had forgotten the lotus feet of the Lord. Thus he again remembered the lotus feet of the Lord and remembered all his transcendental loving service unto Him, and by so doing he felt the same ecstasy that he used to feel in the presence of the Lord. Because the Lord is absolute, there is no difference between His remembrance and His personal presence. Thus Uddhava remained completely silent for a moment, but then he appeared to be going deeper and deeper into ecstasy. Feelings of ecstasy are displayed by highly advanced devotees of the Lord. There are eight kinds of transcendental changes in the body—tears, shivering of the body, perspiration, restlessness, throbbing, choking of the throat, etc.—and all were manifested by Uddhava in the presence of Vidura.

TEXT 5

पुलकोद्भिन्नसर्वाङ्गो मुञ्चन्मीलद्दृशा शुचः ।
पूर्णार्थो लक्षितस्तेन स्नेहप्रसरसम्प्लुतः ॥ ५ ॥

pulakodbhinna-sarvāṅgo
muñcan mīlad-dṛśā śucaḥ

pūrṇārtho lakṣitas tena
sneha-prasara-samplutaḥ

pulaka-udbhinna—bodily changes of transcendental ecstasy; *sarva-aṅgaḥ*—every part of the body; *muñcan*—smearing; *mīlat*—opening; *dṛśā*—by the eyes; *śucaḥ*—tears of grief; *pūrṇa-arthaḥ*—complete achievement; *lakṣitaḥ*—thus observed; *tena*—by Vidura; *sneha-prasara*—extensive love; *samplutaḥ*—thoroughly assimilated.

TRANSLATION

It was so observed by Vidura that Uddhava had all the transcendental bodily changes due to total ecstasy, and he was trying to wipe away tears of separation from his eyes. Thus Vidura could understand that Uddhava had completely assimilated extensive love for the Lord.

PURPORT

The symptoms of the highest order of devotional life were observed by Vidura, an experienced devotee of the Lord, and he confirmed Uddhava's perfectional stage of love of Godhead. Ecstatic bodily changes are manifested from the spiritual plane and are not artificial expressions developed by practice. There are three different stages of development in devotional service. The first stage is that of following the regulative principles prescribed in the codes of devotional service, the second stage is that of assimilation and realization of the steady condition of devotional service, and the last stage is that of ecstasy symptomized by transcendental bodily expression. The nine different modes of devotional service, such as hearing, chanting and remembering, are the beginning of the process. By regular hearing of the glories and pastimes of the Lord, the impurities in the student's heart begin to be washed off. The more one is cleansed of impurities, the more one becomes fixed in devotional service. Gradually the activities take the forms of steadiness, firm faith, taste, realization and assimilation, one after another. These different stages of gradual development increase love of God to the highest stage, and in the highest stage there are still more symptoms, such as affection, anger and attachment, gradually rising in exceptional cases to the *mahā-bhāva* stage, which is generally not possible for the living entities. All these were manifested by Lord Śrī Caitanya Mahāprabhu, the personification of love of God.

In the *Bhakti-rasāmṛta-sindhu* by Śrīla Rūpa Gosvāmī, the chief disciple of Lord Śrī Caitanya Mahāprabhu, these transcendental symptoms displayed by pure devotees like Uddhava are systematically described. We have written a summary study of *Bhakti-*

rasāmṛta-sindhu entitled *The Nectar of Devotion,* and one may consult this book for more detailed information on the science of devotional service.

TEXT 6

शनकैर्भगवल्लोकान्नृलोकं पुनरागतः ।
विमृज्य नेत्रे विदुरं प्रीत्याहोद्धव उत्स्मयन् ॥ ६ ॥

śanakair bhagaval-lokān
nṛlokaṁ punar āgataḥ
vimṛjya netre viduraṁ
prītyāhoddhava utsmayan

śanakaiḥ—gradually; *bhagavat*—the Lord; *lokāt*—from the abode; *nṛlokam*—the planet of the human beings; *punaḥ āgataḥ*—coming again; *vimṛjya*—wiping; *netre*—eyes; *viduram*—unto Vidura; *prītyā*—in affection; *āha*—said; *uddhavaḥ*—Uddhava; *utsmayan*—by all those remembrances.

TRANSLATION

The great devotee Uddhava soon came back from the abode of the Lord to the human plane, and wiping his eyes, he awakened his reminiscence of the past and spoke to Vidura in a pleasing mood.

PURPORT

When Uddhava was fully absorbed in the transcendental ecstasy of love of God, he actually forgot all about the external world. The pure devotee lives constantly in the abode of the Supreme Lord, even in the present body, which apparently belongs to this world. The pure devotee is not exactly on the bodily plane, since he is absorbed in the transcendental thought of the Supreme. When Uddhava wanted to speak to Vidura, he came down from the abode of the Lord, Dvārakā, to the material plane of human beings. Even though a pure devotee is present on this mortal planet, he is here in relation to the Lord for engagement in transcendental loving service, and not for any material cause. A living entity can live either on the material plane or in the transcendental abode of the Lord, in accordance with his existential condition. The conditional changes of the living entity are explained in the *Caitanya-caritāmṛta* in the instructions given to Śrīla Rūpa Gosvāmī by Lord Śrī Caitanya: "The living entities all over the universes are enjoying the effects of the respective fruitive results of their own work, life after life. Out of all of them, some may be influenced by the association of pure devotees and thus get the chance to execute devotional service by attainment of taste. This taste is the seed of devotional service, and one who is fortunate enough to have received such a seed is advised to sow it in the core of his heart. As one cultivates a seed by pouring water to fructify it, the seed of devotional service sown in the heart of the devotee may be cultured by pouring water in the form of hearing and chanting of the holy name and pastimes of the Lord. The creeper of devotional service, so nourished, gradually grows, and the devotee, acting as a gardener, goes on pouring the water of constant hearing and chanting. The creeper of devotional service gradually grows so high that it passes through the entire material universe and enters into the spiritual sky, growing still higher and higher until it reaches the planet Goloka Vṛndāvana. The devotee-gardener is in touch with the abode of the Lord even from the material plane by dint of performing devotional service to the Lord simply by hearing and chanting. As a creeper takes shelter of another, stronger tree, similarly the creeper of devotional service, nourished by the devotee, takes shelter of the lotus feet of the Lord and thus becomes fixed. When the creeper is fixed, then the fruit of the creeper comes into existence, and the gardener who nourished it is able to enjoy this fruit of love, and his life becomes successful." That Uddhava attained this stage is evident from his dealings. He could simultaneously reach the supreme planet and still appear in this world.

TEXT 7

उद्धव उवाच

कृष्णद्युमणिनिम्लोचे गीर्णेष्वजगरेण ह ।
किं नु नः कुशलं ब्रूयां गतश्रीषु गृहेष्वहम् ॥ ७ ॥

uddhava uvāca
kṛṣṇa-dyumaṇi nimloce
gīrṇeṣv ajagareṇa ha
kiṁ nu naḥ kuśalaṁ brūyāṁ
gata-śrīṣu gṛheṣv aham

uddhavaḥ uvāca—Śrī Uddhava said; *kṛṣṇa-dyumaṇi*—the Kṛṣṇa sun; *nimloce*—having set; *gīrṇeṣu*—being swallowed; *ajagareṇa*—by the great snake; *ha*—in the past; *kim*—what; *nu*—else; *naḥ*—our; *kuśalam*—welfare; *brūyām*—may I say; *gata*—gone away; *śrīṣu gṛheṣu*—in the house; *aham*—I.

TRANSLATION

Śrī Uddhava said: My dear Vidura, the sun of the world, Lord Kṛṣṇa, has set, and our house has now been swallowed by the great snake of time. What can I say to you about our welfare?

PURPORT

The disappearance of the Kṛṣṇa sun may be explained as follows, according to the commentary of Śrīla Viśvanātha Cakravartī Ṭhākura. Vidura was struck with great sorrow when he got the hint of the annihilation of the great Yadu dynasty as well as of his own family, the Kuru dynasty. Uddhava could understand the grief of Vidura, and therefore he first of all wanted to sympathize with him by saying that after the sunset everyone is in darkness. Since the entire world was merged in the darkness of grief, neither Vidura nor Uddhava nor anyone else could be happy. Uddhava was as much aggrieved as Vidura, and there was nothing further to be said about their welfare.

The comparison of Kṛṣṇa to the sun is very appropriate. As soon as the sun sets, darkness automatically appears. But the darkness experienced by the common man does not affect the sun itself either at the time of sunrise or of sunset. Lord Kṛṣṇa's appearance and disappearance are exactly like that of the sun. He appears and disappears in innumerable universes, and as long as He is present in a particular universe there is all transcendental light in that universe, but the universe from which He passes away is put into darkness. His pastimes, however, are everlasting. The Lord is always present in some universe, just as the sun is present in either the eastern or the western hemisphere. The sun is always present either in India or in America, but when the sun is present in India, the American land is in darkness, and when the sun is present in America, the Indian hemisphere is in darkness.

As the sun appears in the morning and gradually rises to the meridian and then again sets in one hemisphere while simultaneously rising in the other, so Lord Kṛṣṇa's disappearance in one universe and the beginning of His different pastimes in another take place simultaneously. As soon as one pastime is finished here, it is manifested in another universe. And thus His *nitya-līlā,* or eternal pastimes, are going on without ending. As the sunrise takes place once in twenty-four hours, similarly the pastimes of Lord Kṛṣṇa take place in a universe once in a daytime of Brahmā, the account of which is given in the *Bhagavad-gītā* as 4,300,000,000 solar years. But wherever the Lord is present, all His different pastimes as described in the revealed scriptures take place at regular intervals.

As at sunset the snakes become powerful, thieves are encouraged, ghosts become active, the lotus becomes disfigured and the *cakravākī* laments, so with the disappearance of Lord Kṛṣṇa, the atheists feel enlivened, and the devotees become sorry.

TEXT 8

दुर्भगो बत लोकोऽयं यदवो नितरामपि ।
ये संवसन्तो न विदुर्हरिं मीना इवोडुपम् ॥ ८ ॥

durbhago bata loko 'yaṁ
yadavo nitarām api
ye saṁvasanto na vidur
hariṁ mīnā ivoḍupam

durbhagaḥ—unfortunate; *bata*—certainly; *lokaḥ*—universe; *ayam*—this; *yadavaḥ*—the Yadu dynasty; *nitarām*—more specifically; *api*—also; *ye*—those; *saṁvasantaḥ*—living together; *na*—did not; *viduḥ*—understand; *harim*—the Personality of Godhead; *mīnāḥ*—the fishes; *iva uḍupam*—like the moon.

TRANSLATION

This universe with all its planets is most unfortunate. And even more unfortunate are the members of the Yadu dynasty because they could not identify Lord Hari as the Personality of Godhead, any more than the fish could identify the moon.

PURPORT

Uddhava lamented for the unfortunate persons of the world who could not recognize Lord Śrī Kṛṣṇa in spite of seeing all His transcendental godly qualities. From the very beginning of His appearance within the prison bars of King Kaṁsa up to His *mausala-līlā,* although He exhibited His potencies as the Personality of Godhead in the six opulences of wealth, strength, fame, beauty, knowledge and renunciation, the foolish persons of the world could not understand that He was the Supreme Lord. Foolish persons might have thought Him an extraordinary historic figure because they had no intimate touch with the Lord, but more unfortunate were the family members of the Lord, the members of the Yadu dynasty, who were always in company with the Lord but were unable to recognize Him as the Supreme Personality of Godhead. Uddhava lamented his own fortune also because although he knew Kṛṣṇa to be the Supreme Personality of Godhead, he could not properly use the opportunity to render devotional service to the Lord. He regretted everyone's misfortune, including his own. The pure devotee of the Lord thinks himself most unfortunate. That is due to excessive love for the Lord and is one of the transcendental perceptions of *viraha,* the suffering of separation.

It is learned from the revealed scriptures that the moon was born from the milk ocean. There is a milk ocean in the upper planets, and there Lord Viṣṇu, who controls the heart of every living being as Paramātmā (the Supersoul), resides as the Kṣīrodakaśāyī Viṣṇu. Those who do not believe in the existence of the ocean of milk because they have experience only of the salty water in the ocean should know that the world is also called the *go*, which means the cow. The urine of a cow is salty, and according to Āyur-vedic medicine the cow's urine is very effective in treating patients suffering from liver trouble. Such patients may not have any experience of the cow's milk because milk is never given to liver patients. But the liver patient may know that the cow has milk also, although he has never tasted it. Similarly, men who have experience only of this tiny planet where the saltwater ocean exists may take information from the revealed scriptures that there is also an ocean of milk, although we have never seen it. From this ocean of milk the moon was born, but the fish in the milk ocean could not recognize that the moon was not another fish and was different from them. The fish took the moon to be one of them or maybe something illuminating, but nothing more. The unfortunate persons who do not recognize Lord Kṛṣṇa are like such fish. They take Him to be one of them, although a little extraordinary in opulence, strength, etc. The *Bhagavad-gītā* (9.11) confirms such foolish persons to be most unfortunate: *avajānanti māṁ mūḍhā mānuṣīṁ tanum āśritam.*

TEXT 9

इङ्गितज्ञाः पुरुप्रौढा एकारामाश्च सात्वताः ।
सात्वतामृषभं सर्वे भूतावासममंसत ॥ ९ ॥

iṅgita-jñāḥ puru-prauḍhā
ekārāmāś ca sātvatāḥ
sātvatām ṛṣabhaṁ sarve
bhūtāvāsam amaṁsata

iṅgita-jñāḥ—expert in psychic study; *puru-prauḍhāḥ*—highly experienced; *eka*—one; *ārāmāḥ*—relaxation; *ca*—also; *sātvatāḥ*—devotees, or own men; *sātvatām ṛṣabham*—head of the family; *sarve*—all; *bhūta-āvāsam*—all-pervading; *amaṁsata*—could think.

TRANSLATION

The Yadus were all experienced devotees, learned and expert in psychic study. Over and above this, they were always with the Lord in all kinds of relaxations, and still they were only able to know Him as the one Supreme who dwells everywhere.

PURPORT

In the *Vedas* it is said that the Supreme Lord or the Paramātmā cannot be understood simply by the strength of one's erudition or power of mental speculation: *nāyam ātmā pravacanena labhyo na medhayā na bahunā śrutena* (*Kaṭha Upaniṣad* 1.2.23). He can be known only by one who has the mercy of the Lord. The Yādavas were all exceptionally learned and experienced, but in spite of their knowing the Lord as the one who lives in everyone's heart, they could not understand that He is the original Personality of Godhead. This lack of knowledge was not due to their insufficient erudition; it was due to their misfortune. In Vṛndāvana, however, the Lord was not even known as the Paramātmā because the residents of Vṛndāvana were pure unconventional devotees of the Lord and could think of Him only as their object of love. They did not know that He is the Personality of Godhead. The Yadus, or the residents of Dvārakā, however, could know Lord Kṛṣṇa as Vāsudeva, or the Supersoul living everywhere, but not as the Supreme Lord. As scholars of the *Vedas*, they verified the Vedic hymns: *eko devaḥ. .. sarva-bhūtādhivāsaḥ... antaryāmī...* and *vṛṣṇīnāṁ para-devatā. ...* The Yadus, therefore, accepted Lord Kṛṣṇa as the Supersoul incarnated in their family, and not more than that.

TEXT 10

देवस्य मायया स्पृष्टा ये चान्यदसदाश्रिताः ।
भ्राम्यते धीर्न तद्वाक्यैरात्मन्युप्तात्मनो हरौ ॥१०॥

devasya māyayā spṛṣṭā
ye cānyad asad-āśritāḥ
bhrāmyate dhīr na tad-vākyair
ātmany uptātmano harau

devasya—of the Personality of Godhead; *māyayā*—by the influence of external energy; *spṛṣṭāḥ*—infected; *ye*—all those; *ca*—and; *anyat*—others; *asat*—illusory; *āśritāḥ*—being taken to; *bhrāmyate*—bewilder; *dhīḥ*—intelligence; *na*—not; *tat*—of them; *vākyaiḥ*—by those words; *ātmani*—in the Supreme Self; *upta-ātmanaḥ*—surrendered souls; *harau*—unto the Lord.

TRANSLATION

Under no circumstances can the words of persons bewildered by the illusory energy of the Lord deviate the intelligence of those who are completely surrendered souls.

PURPORT

Lord Śrī Kṛṣṇa is the Supreme Personality of Godhead according to all the evidences of the *Vedas.* He is accepted by all *ācāryas,* including Śrīpāda Śaṅkarācārya. But when He was present in the world, different classes of men accepted Him differently, and therefore their calculations of the Lord were also different. Generally, persons who had faith in the revealed scriptures accepted the Lord as He is, and all of them merged into great bereavement when the Lord disappeared from the world. In the First Canto we have already discussed the lamentation of Arjuna and Yudhiṣṭhira, to whom the disappearance of Lord Kṛṣṇa was almost intolerable up to the end of their lives.

The Yādavas were only partially cognizant of the Lord, but they are also glorious because they had the opportunity to associate with the Lord, who acted as the head of their family, and they also rendered the Lord intimate service. The Yādavas and other devotees of the Lord are different from those who wrongly calculated Him to be an ordinary human personality. Such persons are certainly bewildered by the illusory energy. They are hellish and are envious of the Supreme Lord. The illusory energy acts very powerfully on them because in spite of their elevated mundane education, such persons are faithless and are infected by the mentality of atheism. They are always very eager to establish that Lord Kṛṣṇa was an ordinary man who was killed by a hunter due to His many impious acts in plotting to kill the sons of Dhṛtarāṣṭra and Jarāsandha, the demoniac kings of the earth. Such persons have no faith in the statement of the *Bhagavad-gītā* that the Lord is unaffected by the reactions of work: *na māṁ karmāṇi limpanti.* According to the atheistic point of view, Lord Kṛṣṇa's family, the Yadu dynasty, was vanquished due to being cursed by the *brāhmaṇas* for the sins committed by Kṛṣṇa in killing the sons of Dhṛtarāṣṭra, etc. All these blasphemies do not touch the heart of the devotees of the Lord because they know perfectly well what is what. Their intelligence regarding the Lord is never disturbed. But those who are disturbed by the statements of the *asuras* are also condemned. That is what Uddhava meant in this verse.

TEXT 11

प्रदर्श्यातप्ततपसामवितृप्तदृशां नृणाम् ।
आदायान्तरधाद्यस्तु स्वबिम्बं लोकलोचनम् ॥११॥

pradarśyātapta-tapasām
avitṛpta-dṛśāṁ nṛṇām

ādāyāntar adhād yas tu
sva-bimbaṁ loka-locanam

pradarśya—by exhibiting; *atapta*—without undergoing; *tapasām*—penances; *avitṛpta-dṛśām*—without fulfillment of vision; *nṛṇām*—of persons; *ādāya*—taking; *antaḥ*—disappearance; *adhāt*—performed; *yaḥ*—He who; *tu*—but; *sva-bimbam*—His own form; *loka-locanam*—public vision.

TRANSLATION

Lord Śrī Kṛṣṇa, who manifested His eternal form before the vision of all on the earth, performed His disappearance by removing His form from the sight of those who were unable to see Him [as He is] due to not executing required penance.

PURPORT

In this verse the word *avitṛpta-dṛśām* is most significant. The conditioned souls in the material world are all trying to satisfy their senses in various ways, but they have failed to do so because it is impossible to be satisfied by such efforts. The example of the fish on land is very appropriate. If one takes a fish from the water and puts it on the land, it cannot be made happy by any amount of offered pleasure. The spirit soul can be happy only in the association of the supreme living being, the Personality of Godhead, and nowhere else. The Lord, by His unlimited causeless mercy, has innumerable Vaikuṇṭha planets in the *brahmajyoti* sphere of the spiritual world, and in that transcendental world there is an unlimited arrangement for the unlimited pleasure of the living entities.

The Lord Himself comes to display His transcendental pastimes, typically represented at Vṛndāvana, Mathurā and Dvārakā. He appears just to attract the conditioned souls back to Godhead, back home to the eternal world. But for want of sufficient piety, the onlookers are not attracted by such pastimes of the Lord. In *Bhagavad-gītā* it is said that only those who have completely surpassed the way of sinful reaction can engage themselves in the transcendental loving service of the Lord. The entire Vedic way of ritualistic performances is to put every conditioned soul on the path of piety. By strict adherence to the prescribed principles for all orders of social life, one can attain the qualities of truthfulness, control of the mind, control of the senses, forbearance, etc., and can be elevated to the plane of rendering pure devotional service to the Lord. Only by such a transcendental vision are one's material hankerings fully satisfied.

When the Lord was present, persons who were able to satisfy their material hankerings by seeing Him in true perspective were thus able to go back with Him to His kingdom. But those persons who were unable to see the Lord as He is remained attached to material hankerings and were not able to go back home, back to Godhead. When the Lord passed beyond the vision of all, He did so in His original eternal form, as stated in this verse. The Lord left in His own body; He did not leave His body as is generally misunderstood by the conditioned souls. This statement defeats the false propaganda of the faithless nondevotees that the Lord passed away like an ordinary conditioned soul. The Lord appeared in order to release the world from the undue burden of the nonbelieving *asuras,* and after doing this, He disappeared from the world's eyes.

TEXT 12

यन्मर्त्यलीलौपयिकं स्वयोग-
मायाबलं दर्शयता गृहीतम् ।
विस्मापनं स्वस्य च सौभगर्द्धेः
परं पदं भूषणभूषणाङ्गम् ॥१२॥

yan martya-līlaupayikaṁ sva-yoga-
māyā-balaṁ darśayatā gṛhītam
vismāpanaṁ svasya ca saubhagarddheḥ
paraṁ padaṁ bhūṣaṇa-bhūṣaṇāṅgam

yat—His eternal form which; *martya*—mortal world; *līlā-upayikam*—just suitable for the pastimes; *sva-yoga-māyā-balam*—potency of the internal energy; *darśayatā*—for manifestation; *gṛhītam*—discovered; *vismāpanam*—wonderful; *svasya*—of His own; *ca*—and; *saubhaga-ṛddheḥ*—of the opulent; *param*—supreme; *padam*—ultimate stand; *bhūṣaṇa*—ornament; *bhūṣaṇa-aṅgam*—of the ornaments.

TRANSLATION

The Lord appeared in the mortal world by His internal potency, yoga-māyā. He came in His eternal form, which is just suitable for His pastimes. These pastimes were wonderful for everyone, even for those proud of their own opulence, including the Lord Himself in His form as the Lord of Vaikuṇṭha. Thus His [Śrī Kṛṣṇa's] transcendental body is the ornament of all ornaments.

PURPORT

In conformity with the Vedic hymns (*nityo nityānāṁ cetanaś cetanānām*), the Personality of Godhead is more excellent than all other living beings within all the universes in the material world. He is the chief of all living entities; no one can surpass Him or be equal to Him in wealth, strength, fame, beauty, knowledge or renunciation. When Lord Kṛṣṇa was within this universe, He seemed to be a human being because He appeared in a manner just suitable for His pastimes in the mortal world. He did not appear in human society in His Vaikuṇṭha feature with four hands because that would not have been suitable for His pastimes. But in spite of His appearing as a human being, no one was or is equal to Him in any respect in any of the six different opulences. Everyone is more or less proud of his opulence in this world, but when Lord Kṛṣṇa was in human society, He excelled all His contemporaries within the universe.

When the Lord's pastimes are visible to the human eye, they are called *prakaṭa*, and when they are not visible they are called *aprakaṭa*. In fact, the Lord's pastimes never stop, just as the sun never leaves the sky. The sun is always in its right orbit in the sky, but it is sometimes visible and sometimes invisible to our limited vision. Similarly, the pastimes of the Lord are always current in one universe or another, and when Lord Kṛṣṇa disappeared from the transcendental abode of Dvārakā, it was simply a disappearance from the eyes of the people there. It should not be misunderstood that His transcendental body, which is just suitable for the pastimes in the mortal world, is in any way inferior to His different expansions in the Vaikuṇṭhalokas. His body manifested in the material world is transcendental par excellence in the sense that His pastimes in the mortal world excel His mercy displayed in the Vaikuṇṭhalokas. In the Vaikuṇṭhalokas the Lord is merciful toward the liberated or *nitya-mukta* living entities, but in His pastimes in the mortal world He is merciful even to the fallen souls who are *nitya-baddha*, or conditioned forever. The six excellent opulences which He displayed in the mortal world by the agency of His internal potency, *yoga-māyā*, are rare even in the Vaikuṇṭhalokas. All His pastimes were manifested not by the material energy but by His spiritual energy. The excellence of His *rāsa-līlā* at Vṛndāvana and His householder life with sixteen thousand wives is wonderful even for Nārāyaṇa in Vaikuṇṭha and is certainly so for other living entities within this mortal world. His pastimes are wonderful even for other incarnations of the Lord, such as Śrī Rāma, Nṛsiṁha and Varāha. His opulence was so superexcellent that His pastimes were adored even by the Lord of Vaikuṇṭha, who is not different from Lord Kṛṣṇa Himself.

TEXT 13

यद्धर्मसूनोर्बत राजसूये
निरीक्ष्य दृक्स्वस्त्ययनं त्रिलोकः ।
कार्त्स्न्येन चाद्येह गतं विधातु-
रर्वाक्सृतौ कौशलमित्यमन्यत ॥१३॥

yad dharma-sūnor bata rājasūye
nirīkṣya dṛk-svastyayanaṁ tri-lokaḥ
kārtsnyena cādyeha gataṁ vidhātur
arvāk-sṛtau kauśalam ity amanyata

yat—the form which; *dharma-sūnoḥ*—of Mahārāja Yudhiṣṭhira; *bata*—certainly; *rājasūye*—in the arena of the *rājasūya* sacrifice; *nirīkṣya*—by observing; *dṛk*—sight; *svastyayanam*—pleasing; *tri-lokaḥ*—the three worlds; *kārtsnyena*—in sum total; *ca*—thus; *adya*—today; *iha*—within the universe; *gatam*—surpassed; *vidhātuḥ*—of the creator (Brahmā); *arvāk*—recent mankind; *sṛtau*—in the material world; *kauśalam*—dexterity; *iti*—thus; *amanyata*—contemplated.

TRANSLATION

All the demigods from the upper, lower and middle universal planetary systems assembled at the altar of the rājasūya sacrifice performed by Mahārāja Yudhiṣṭhira. After seeing the beautiful bodily features of Lord Kṛṣṇa, they all contemplated that He was the ultimate dexterous creation of Brahmā, the creator of human beings.

PURPORT

There was nothing comparable to the bodily features of Lord Kṛṣṇa when He was present in this world. The most beautiful object in the material world may be compared to the blue lotus flower or the full moon in the sky, but even the lotus flower and the moon were defeated by the beauty of the bodily features of Lord Kṛṣṇa, and this was certified by the demigods, the most beautiful living creatures in the universe. The demigods thought that Lord Kṛṣṇa, like themselves, was also created by Lord Brahmā, but in fact Brahmā was created by Lord Kṛṣṇa. It was not within the power of Brahmā to create the transcendental beauty of the Supreme Lord. No one is the creator of Kṛṣṇa; rather, He is the creator of everyone. As He says in *Bhagavad-gītā* (10.8), *ahaṁ sarvasya prabhavo mattaḥ sarvaṁ pravartate.*

TEXT 14

यस्यानुरागप्लुतहासरास-
लीलावलोकप्रतिलब्धमानाः ।
व्रजस्त्रियो दृग्भिरनुप्रवृत्त-
धियोऽवतस्थुः किल कृत्यशेषाः ॥१४॥

yasyānurāga-pluta-hāsa-rāsa-
līlāvaloka-pratilabdha-mānāḥ
vraja-striyo dṛgbhir anupravṛtta-
dhiyo 'vatasthuḥ kila kṛtya-śeṣāḥ

yasya—whose; *anurāga*—attachment; *pluta*—enhanced by; *hāsa*—laughter; *rāsa*—humors; *līlā*—pastimes; *avaloka*—glancing; *pratilabdha*—obtained thereof; *mānāḥ*—anguished; *vraja-striyaḥ*—damsels of Vraja; *dṛgbhiḥ*—with the eyes; *anupravṛtta*—following; *dhiyaḥ*—by intelligence; *avatasthuḥ*—sat silently; *kila*—indeed; *kṛtya-śeṣāḥ*—without finishing household duties.

TRANSLATION

The damsels of Vraja, after pastimes of laughter, humor and exchanges of glances, were anguished when Kṛṣṇa left them. They used to follow Him with their eyes, and thus they sat down with stunned intelligence and could not finish their household duties.

PURPORT

In His boyhood at Vṛndāvana, Lord Kṛṣṇa was notorious as a teasing friend in transcendental love to all the girls His age. His love for them was so intense that there is no comparison to that ecstasy, and the damsels of Vraja were so much attached to Him that their affection excelled that of the great demigods like Brahmā and Śiva. Lord Kṛṣṇa finally admitted His defeat before the transcendental affection of the *gopīs* and declared that He was unable to repay them for their unalloyed affection. Although the *gopīs* were seemingly anguished by the Lord's teasing behavior, when Kṛṣṇa would leave them they could not tolerate the separation and used to follow Him with their eyes and minds. They were so stunned by the situation that they could not finish their household duties. No one could excel Him even in the dealing of love exchanged between boys and girls. It is said in the revealed scriptures that Lord Kṛṣṇa personally never goes beyond the boundary of Vṛndāvana. He remains there eternally because of the transcendental love of the inhabitants. Thus even though He is not visible at present, He is not away from Vṛndāvana for a moment.

TEXT 15

स्वशान्तरूपेष्वितरैः स्वरूपै-
रभ्यर्द्यमानेष्वनुकम्पितात्मा ।
परावरेशो महदंशयुक्तो
ह्यजोऽपि जातो भगवान् यथाग्निः ॥१५॥

sva-śānta-rūpeṣv itaraiḥ sva-rūpair
abhyardyamāneṣv anukampitātmā
parāvareśo mahad-aṁśa-yukto
hy ajo 'pi jāto bhagavān yathāgniḥ

sva-śānta-rūpeṣu—unto the peaceful devotees of the Lord; *itaraiḥ*—others, nondevotees; *sva-rūpaiḥ*—according to their own modes of nature; *abhyardyamāneṣu*—being harassed by; *anukampita-ātmā*—the all-compassionate Lord; *para-avara*—spiritual and material; *īśaḥ*—controller; *mahat-aṁśa-yuktaḥ*—accompanied by the plenary portion of *mahat-tattva; hi*—certainly; *ajaḥ*—the unborn; *api*—although; *jātaḥ*—is born; *bhagavān*—the Personality of Godhead; *yathā*—as if; *agniḥ*—the fire.

TRANSLATION

The Personality of Godhead, the all-compassionate controller of both the spiritual and material creations, is unborn, but when there is friction between His peaceful devotees and persons who are in the material modes of nature, He takes birth just like fire, accompanied by the mahat-tattva.

PURPORT

The devotees of the Lord are by nature peaceful because they have no material hankering. A liberated soul has no hankering, and therefore he has no lamentation. One who wants to possess also laments when he loses his possession. Devotees have no hankerings for material possessions and no hankerings for spiritual salvation. They are situated in the transcendental loving service of the Lord as a matter of duty, and they do not mind where they are or how they have to act. *Karmīs*, *jñānīs* and *yogīs* all hanker to possess some material or spiritual assets. *Karmīs* want material possessions, *jñānīs* and *yogīs* want spiritual possessions, but devotees do not want any material or spiritual assets. They want only to serve the Lord anywhere in the material or spiritual worlds that the Lord desires, and the Lord is always specifically compassionate towards such devotees.

The *karmīs, jñānīs* and *yogīs* have their particular mentalities in the modes of nature, and therefore they are called *itara* or nondevotees. These *itaras,* including even the *yogīs,* sometimes harass the devotees of the Lord. Durvāsā Muni, a great *yogī,* harassed Mahārāja Ambarīṣa because the latter was a great devotee of the Lord. And the great *karmī* and *jñānī* Hiraṇyakaśipu even harassed his own Vaiṣṇava son, Prahlāda Mahārāja. There are many instances of such harassment of the peaceful devotees of the Lord by the *itaras.* When such friction takes place, the Lord, out of His great compassion towards His pure devotees, appears in person, accompanied by His plenary portions controlling the *mahat-tattva.*

The Lord is everywhere, in both the material and spiritual domains, and He appears for the sake of His devotees when there is friction between His devotee and the non-devotee. As electricity is generated by friction of matter anywhere and everywhere, the Lord, being all-pervading, appears because of the friction of devotees and non-devotees. When Lord Kṛṣṇa appears on a mission, all His plenary portions accompany Him. When He appeared as the son of Vasudeva, there were differences of opinion about His incarnation. Some said, "He is the Supreme Personality of Godhead." Some said, "He is an incarnation of Nārāyaṇa," and others said, "He is the incarnation of Kṣīrodakaśāyī Viṣṇu." But actually He is the original Supreme Personality of Godhead—*kṛṣṇas tu bhagavān svayam*—and Nārāyaṇa, the *puruṣas* and all other incarnations accompany Him to function as different parts of His pastimes. *Mahad-aṁśa-yuktaḥ* indicates that He is accompanied by the *puruṣas,* who create the *mahat-tanva.* It is confirmed in the Vedic hymns, *mahāntaṁ vibhum ātmānam.*

Lord Kṛṣṇa appeared, just like electricity, when there was friction between Kaṁsa and Vasudeva and Ugrasena. Vasudeva and Ugrasena were the Lord's devotees, and Kaṁsa, a representative of the *karmīs* and *jñānīs,* was a nondevotee. Kṛṣṇa, as He is, is compared to the sun. He first appeared from the ocean of the womb of Devakī, and gradually He satisfied the inhabitants of the places surrounding Mathurā, just as the sun enlivens the lotus flower in the morning. After gradually rising to the meridian of Dvārakā, the Lord set like the sun, placing everything in darkness, as described by Uddhava.

TEXT 16

मां खेदयत्येतदजस्य जन्म-
विडम्बनं यद्वसुदेवगेहे ।

व्रजे च वासोऽरिभयादिव स्वयं
पुराद् व्यवात्सीद्यदनन्तवीर्यः ॥१६॥

mām khedayaty etad ajasya janma-
viḍambanaṁ yad vasudeva-gehe
vraje ca vāso 'ri-bhayād iva svayaṁ
purād vyavātsīd yad-ananta-vīryaḥ

mām—to me; *khedayati*—gives me distress; *etat*—this; *ajasya*—of the unborn; *janma*—birth; *viḍambanam*—bewildering; *yat*—that; *vasudeva-gehe*—in the home of Vasudeva; *vraje*—in Vṛndāvana; *ca*—also; *vāsaḥ*—inhabitation; *ari*—enemy; *bhayāt*—because of fear; *iva*—as if; *svayam*—Himself; *purāt*—from Mathurā Purī; *vyavātsīt*—fled; *yat*—one who is; *ananta-vīryaḥ*—unlimitedly powerful.

TRANSLATION

When I think of Lord Kṛṣṇa—how He was born in the prison house of Vasudeva although He is unborn, how He went away from His father's protection to Vraja and lived there incognito out of fear of the enemy, and how, although unlimitedly powerful, He fled from Mathurā in fear—all these bewildering incidents give me distress.

PURPORT

Because Lord Śrī Kṛṣṇa is the original person from whom everything and everyone has emanated—*ahaṁ sarvasya prabhavaḥ* (Bg. 10.8), *janmādy asya yataḥ* (Vs. 1.1.2)—nothing can be equal to or greater than Him. The Lord is supremely perfect, and whenever He enacts His transcendental pastimes as a son, a rival or an object of enmity, He plays the part so perfectly that even pure devotees like Uddhava are bewildered. For example, Uddhava knew perfectly well that Lord Śrī Kṛṣṇa is eternally existent and can neither die nor disappear for good, yet he lamented for Lord Kṛṣṇa. All these events are perfect arrangements to give perfection to His supreme glories. It is for enjoyment's sake. When a father plays with his little son and the father lies down on the floor as if defeated by the son, it is just to give the little son pleasure, and nothing more. Because the Lord is all-powerful, it is possible for Him to adjust opposites such as birth and no birth, power and defeat, fear and fearlessness. A pure devotee knows very well how it is possible for the Lord to adjust opposite things, but he laments for the nondevotees who, not knowing the supreme glories of the Lord, think of Him as imaginary simply because there are so many apparently contradictory statements in the scriptures. Factually there is nothing contradictory; everything is possible when we understand the Lord as the Lord and not as one of us, with all our imperfection.

TEXT 17

दुनोति चेतः स्मरतो ममैतद्
यदाह पादावभिवन्द्य पित्रोः ।
तताम्ब कंसादुरुशङ्कितानां
प्रसीदतं नोऽकृतनिष्कृतीनाम् ॥१७॥

dunoti cetaḥ smarato mamaitad
yad āha pādāv abhivandya pitroḥ
tātāmba kaṁsād uru-śaṅkitānām
prasīdataṁ no 'kṛta-niṣkṛtīnām

dunoti—it gives me pain; *cetaḥ*—heart; *smarataḥ*—while thinking of; *mama*—my; *etat*—this; *yat*—as much as; *āha*—said; *pādau*—feet; *abhivandya*—worshiping; *pitroḥ*—of the parents; *tāta*—My dear father; *amba*—My dear mother; *kaṁsāt*—out of Kaṁsa's; *uru*—great; *śaṅkitānām*—of those who are afraid; *prasīdatam*—be pleased with; *naḥ*—Our; *akṛta*—not executed; *niṣkṛtīnām*—duties to serve you.

TRANSLATION

Lord Kṛṣṇa begged pardon from His parents for Their [Kṛṣṇa's and Balarāma's] inability to serve their feet, due to being away from home because of great fear of Kaṁsa. He said, "O mother, O father, please excuse Us for this inability." All this behavior of the Lord gives me pain at heart.

PURPORT

It appears that Lord Kṛṣṇa and Baladeva were both very greatly afraid of Kaṁsa, and therefore They had to hide Themselves. But if Lord Kṛṣṇa and Baladeva are the Supreme Personality of Godhead, how was it possible that They were afraid of Kaṁsa? Is there any contradiction in such statements? Vasudeva, due to his great appreciation for Kṛṣṇa, wanted to give Him protection. He never thought that Kṛṣṇa was the Supreme Lord and could protect Himself; he thought of Kṛṣṇa as his son. Because Vasudeva was a great devotee of the Lord, he did not like to think that Kṛṣṇa might be killed like his other children. Morally, Vasudeva was bound to deliver Kṛṣṇa to the hands of Kaṁsa because he had promised to turn over all his children. But out of his great love for Kṛṣṇa he broke his promise, and the Lord was very pleased with Vasudeva for his transcendental mentality. He did not want to disturb the intense affection of Vasudeva, and thus He agreed to be carried by His father to the house of Nanda and Yaśodā. And just to test the intense love of Vasudeva, Lord Kṛṣṇa fell down in the waters of the Yamunā while His father was crossing the river. Vasudeva became mad after his child as he tried to recover Him in the midst of the rising river.

These are all glorified pastimes of the Lord, and there is no contradiction in such manifestations. Since Kṛṣṇa is the Supreme Lord, He was never afraid of Kaṁsa, but to please His father He agreed to be so. And the most brilliant part of His supreme character was that He begged pardon from His parents for being unable to serve their feet while absent from home because of fear of Kaṁsa. The Lord, whose lotus feet are worshiped by demigods like Brahmā and Śiva, wanted to worship the feet of Vasudeva. Such instruction by the Lord to the world is quite appropriate. Even if one is the Supreme Lord, one must serve his parents. A son is indebted to his parents in so many ways, and it is the duty of the son to serve his parents, however great the son may be. Indirectly, Kṛṣṇa wanted to teach the atheists who do not accept the supreme fatherhood of God, and they may learn from this action how much the Supreme Father has to be respected. Uddhava was simply struck with wonder by such glorious behavior of the Lord, and he was very sorry that he was unable to go with Him.

TEXT 18

को वा अमुष्याङ्घ्रिसरोजरेणुं
विस्मर्तुमीशीत पुमान् विजिघ्रन् ।
यो विस्फुरद्भ्रूविटपेन भूमे-
र्भारं कृतान्तेन तिरश्चकार ॥१८॥

ko vā amuṣyāṅghri-saroja-reṇuṁ
vismartum īśīta pumān vijighran
yo visphurad-bhrū-viṭapena bhūmer
bhāraṁ kṛtāntena tiraścakāra

kaḥ—who else; *vā*—either; *amuṣya*—the Lord's; *aṅghri*—feet; *saroja-reṇum*—dust of the lotus; *vismartum*—to forget; *īśīta*—may be able; *pumān*—person; *vijighran*—smelling; *yaḥ*—one who; *visphurat*—expanding; *bhrū-viṭapena*—by the leaves of the eyebrows; *bhūmeḥ*—of the earth; *bhāram*—burden; *kṛta-antena*—by death-blows; *tiraścakāra*—executed.

TRANSLATION

Who, after smelling the dust of His lotus feet even once, could ever forget it? Simply by expanding the leaves of His eyebrows, Kṛṣṇa has given the deathblow to those who were burdening the earth.

PURPORT

Lord Kṛṣṇa cannot be accepted as one of the human beings, even though He played the role of an obedient son. His actions were so extraordinary that by the simple raising of His eyebrows He could deliver death-blows to those who were burdening the earth.

TEXT 19

दृष्टा भवद्भिर्ननु राजसूये
चैद्यस्य कृष्णं द्विषतोऽपि सिद्धिः ।
यां योगिनः संस्पृहयन्ति सम्यग्
योगेन कस्तद्विरहं सहेत ॥१९॥

dṛṣṭā bhavadbhir nanu rājasūye
caidyasya kṛṣṇaṁ dviṣato 'pi siddhiḥ
yāṁ yoginaḥ saṁspṛhayanti samyag
yogena kas tad-virahaṁ saheta

dṛṣṭā—it has been seen; *bhavadbhiḥ*—by your good self; *nanu*—of course; *rājasūye*—in the assembly of the *rājasūya* sacrifice performed by Mahārāja Yudhiṣṭhira; *caidyasya*—of the King of Cedi (Śiśupāla); *kṛṣṇam*—unto Kṛṣṇa; *dviṣataḥ*—envying; *api*—in spite of; *siddhiḥ*—success; *yām*—which; *yoginaḥ*—the *yogīs*; *saṁspṛhayanti*—verily desire; *samyak*—fully; *yogena*—by performance of *yoga*; *kaḥ*—who; *tat*—His; *viraham*—separation; *saheta*—can tolerate.

TRANSLATION

You have personally seen how the King of Cedi [Śiśupāla] achieved success in yoga practice, although he hated Lord Kṛṣṇa. Even the actual yogīs aspire after such success with great interest by performance of their various practices. Who can tolerate separation from Him?

PURPORT

Lord Kṛṣṇa's causeless mercy was exhibited in the great assembly of Mahārāja Yudhiṣṭhira. He was merciful even to His enemy the King of Cedi, who always tried to be an envious rival of the Lord. Because it is not possible to be a bona fide rival of the Lord, the King of Cedi was extremely malicious toward Lord Kṛṣṇa. In this he was like many other *asuras,* such as Kaṁsa and Jarāsandha. In the open assembly of the *rājasūya* sacrifice performed by Mahārāja Yudhiṣṭhira, Śiśupāla insulted Lord Kṛṣṇa, and he was finally killed by the Lord. But it was seen by everyone in the assembly that a light flashed out of the body of the King of Cedi and merged into the body of Lord Kṛṣṇa. This means that Cedirāja achieved the salvation of attaining oneness with the Supreme, which is a perfection most desired by the *jñānīs* and *yogīs* and for which they execute their different types of transcendental activities.

It is a fact that persons who are trying to understand the Supreme Truth by their personal endeavors of mental speculation or mystic powers of *yoga* achieve the same goal as others who are personally killed by the Lord. Both achieve the salvation of merging in the *brahmajyoti* rays of the transcendental body of the Lord. The Lord was merciful even to His enemy, and the success of the King of Cedi was observed by everyone who was present in the assembly. Vidura was also present there, and therefore Uddhava referred the incident to his memory.

TEXT 20

तथैव चान्ये नरलोकवीरा
य आहवे कृष्णमुखारविन्दम् ।
नेत्रैः पिबन्तो नयनाभिरामं
पार्थास्त्रपूतः पदमापुरस्य ॥२०॥

tathaiva cānye nara-loka-vīrā
ya āhave kṛṣṇa-mukhāravindam
netraiḥ pibanto nayanābhirāmaṁ
pārthāstra-pūtaḥ padam āpur asya

tathā—as also; *eva ca*—and certainly; *anye*—others; *nara-loka*—human society; *vīrāḥ*—fighters; *ye*—those; *āhave*—on the battlefield (of Kurukṣetra); *kṛṣṇa*—Lord Kṛṣṇa's; *mukha-aravindam*—face like a lotus flower; *netraiḥ*—with the eyes; *pibantaḥ*—while seeing; *nayana-abhirāmam*—very pleasing to the eyes; *pārtha*—Arjuna; *astra-pūtaḥ*—purified by arrows; *padam*—abode; *āpuḥ*—achieved; *asya*—of Him.

TRANSLATION

Certainly others who were fighters on the Battlefield of Kurukṣetra were purified by the onslaught of Arjuna's arrows, and while seeing the lotuslike face of Kṛṣṇa, so pleasing to the eyes, they achieved the abode of the Lord.

PURPORT

The Supreme Personality of Godhead, Lord Śrī Kṛṣṇa, appears in this world for two missionary purposes: to deliver the faithful and to annihilate the miscreants. But because the Lord is absolute, His two different kinds of actions, although apparently different, are ultimately one and the same. His annihilation of a person like Śiśupāla is as auspicious as His actions for the protection of the faithful. All the warriors who fought against Arjuna but who were able to see the lotuslike face of the Lord on the battlefront achieved the abode of the Lord, exactly as the devotees of the Lord do. The words "pleasing to the eyes of the seer" are very significant. When the warriors from the other side of the battlefield saw Lord Kṛṣṇa at the front, they appreciated His beauty, and their dormant instinct of love of God was awakened. Śiśupāla saw the Lord also, but he saw Him as his enemy, and his love was not awakened. Therefore Śiśupāla achieved oneness with the Lord by merging in the impersonal glare of His body, called the *brahmajyoti*. Others, who were in the marginal position, being neither friends nor enemies but slightly in love of Godhead by appreciating the beauty of His face, were at once promoted to the spiritual planets, the Vaikuṇṭhas. The Lord's personal abode is called Goloka Vṛndāvana, and the abodes where His plenary expansions reside are called the Vaikuṇṭhas, where the Lord is present as Nārāyaṇa. Love of Godhead is dormant in every living entity, and the entire process of devotional service unto the Lord is meant for awakening this dormant, eternal love of Godhead. But there are degrees of such transcendental awakening. Those whose love of God is awakened to the fullest extent go back to the Goloka Vṛndāvana planet in the spiritual sky, whereas persons who have just awakened to love of Godhead by accident or association are transferred to the Vaikuṇṭha planets. Essentially there is no material difference between Goloka and Vaikuṇṭha, but in the Vaikuṇṭhas the Lord is served in unlimited opulence, whereas in Goloka the Lord is served in natural affection.

This love of God is awakened by the association of pure devotees of the Lord. Here the word *pārthāstra-pūtaḥ* is significant. Those who saw the beautiful face of the Lord on the Battlefield of Kurukṣetra were purified first by Arjuna when he made his onslaught with arrows. The Lord appeared for the mission of diminishing the burden of the world, and Arjuna was assisting the Lord by fighting on His behalf. Arjuna personally declined to fight, and the whole instruction of the *Bhagavad-gītā* was given to Arjuna to engage him in the fight. As a pure devotee of the Lord, Arjuna agreed to fight in preference to his own decision, and thus Arjuna fought to assist the Lord in His mission of diminishing the burden of the world. All the activities of a pure devotee are executed on behalf of the Lord because a pure devotee of the Lord has nothing to do for his personal interest. Arjuna's killing was as good as killing by the Lord Himself. As soon as Arjuna shot an arrow at an enemy, that enemy became purified of all material contaminations and became eligible to be transferred to the spiritual sky. Those warriors who appreciated the lotus feet of the Lord and saw His face at the front had their dormant love of God awakened, and thus they were transferred at once to Vaikuṇṭhaloka not to the impersonal state of *brahmajyoti* as was Śiśupāla. Śiśupāla died without appreciating the Lord, while others died with appreciation of the Lord. Both were transferred to the spiritual sky, but those who awakened to love of God were transferred to the planets of the transcendental sky.

Uddhava seemingly lamented that his own position was less than that of the warriors on the Battlefield of Kurukṣetra because they had attained to Vaikuṇṭha whereas he remained to lament the disappearance of the Lord.

TEXT 21

स्वयं त्वसाम्यातिशयस्त्र्यधीशः
स्वाराज्यलक्ष्म्याप्तसमस्तकामः ।
बलिं हरद्भिश्चिरलोकपालैः
किरीटकोट्येडितपादपीठः ॥२१॥

svayaṁ tv asāmyātiśayas tryadhīśaḥ
svārājya-lakṣmy-āpta-samasta-kāmaḥ
baliṁ haradbhiś cira-loka-pālaiḥ
kirīṭa-koṭyeḍita-pāda-pīṭhaḥ

svayam—Himself; *tu*—but; *asāmya*—unique; *atiśayaḥ*—greater; *tri-adhīśaḥ*—Lord of the three; *svārājya*—independent supremacy; *lakṣmī*—fortune; *āpta*—achieved; *samasta-kāmaḥ*—all desires; *balim*—worshiping paraphernalia; *haradbhiḥ*—offered by; *cira-loka-pālaiḥ*—by the eternal maintainers of the order of creation; *kirīṭa-koṭya*—millions of helmets; *īḍita-pāda-pīṭhaḥ*—feet honored by prayers.

TRANSLATION

Lord Śrī Kṛṣṇa is the Lord of all kinds of threes and is independently supreme by achievement of all kinds of fortune. He is worshiped by the eternal maintainers of the creation, who offer Him the paraphernalia of worship by touching their millions of helmets to His feet.

PURPORT

Lord Śrī Kṛṣṇa is so mild and merciful, as described in the above verses, and yet He is the Lord of all kinds of threes. He is the Supreme Lord of the three worlds, the three qualities of material nature and the three *puruṣas* (Kāraṇodakaśāyī, Garbhodakaśāyī and Kṣīrodakaśāyī Viṣṇu). There are innumerable universes, and in each and every universe there are different manifestations of Brahmā, Viṣṇu and Rudra. Besides that, there is the Śeṣa-mūrti who bears all the universes on His hoods. And Lord Kṛṣṇa is the Lord of all of them. As the incarnation of Manu, He is the original source of all Manus in innumerable universes. Each universe has manifestations of 504,000 Manus. He is the Lord of the three principal potencies, namely *cit-śakti, māyā-śakti* and *taṭastha-śakti,* and He is the complete master of six kinds of fortune—wealth, strength, fame, beauty, knowledge and renunciation. There is none who can excel Him in any matter of enjoyment, and certainly there is no one greater than Him. No one is equal to or greater than Him. It is the duty of everyone, whoever and wherever one may be, to surrender completely unto Him. It is not wonderful, therefore, that all the transcendental controllers surrender to Him and make all offerings of worship.

TEXT 22

तत्तस्य कैङ्कर्यमलं भृतान्नो
विग्लापयत्यङ्ग यदुग्रसेनम् ।
तिष्ठन्निषण्णं परमेष्ठिधिष्ण्ये
न्यबोधयद्देव निधारयेति ॥२२॥

tat tasya kaiṅkaryam alaṁ bhṛtān no
viglāpayaty aṅga yad ugrasenam
tiṣṭhan niṣaṇṇaṁ parameṣṭhi-dhiṣṇye
nyabodhayad deva nidhārayeti

tat—therefore; *tasya*—His; *kaiṅkaryam*—service; *alam*—of course; *bhṛtān*—the servitors; *naḥ*—us; *viglāpayati*—gives pain; *aṅga*—O Vidura; *yat*—as much as; *ugrasenam*—unto King Ugrasena; *tiṣṭhan*—being seated; *niṣaṇṇam*—waiting upon Him; *parameṣṭhi-dhiṣṇye*—on the royal throne; *nyabodhayat*—submitted; *deva*—addressing my Lord; *nidhāraya*—please know it; *iti*—thus.

TRANSLATION

Therefore, O Vidura, does it not pain us, His servitors, when we remember that He [Lord Kṛṣṇa] used to stand before King Ugrasena, who

was sitting on the royal throne, and used to submit explanations before him, saying, "O My lord, please let it be known to you"?

PURPORT

Lord Kṛṣṇa's gentle behavior before His so-called superiors such as His father, grandfather and elder brother, His amiable behavior with His so-called wives, friends and contemporaries, His behavior as a child before His mother Yaśodā, and His naughty dealings with His young girl friends cannot bewilder a pure devotee like Uddhava. Others, who are not devotees, are bewildered by such behavior of the Lord, who acted just like a human being. This bewilderment is explained by the Lord Himself in the *Bhagavad-gītā* (9.11) as follows:

avajānanti māṁ mūḍhā
mānuṣīṁ tanum āśritam
paraṁ bhāvam ajānanto
mama bhūta-maheśvaram

Persons with a poor fund of knowledge belittle the Personality of Godhead, Lord Kṛṣṇa, not knowing His exalted position as the Lord of everything. In *Bhagavad-gītā* the Lord has explained His position clearly, but the demoniac atheistic student squeezes out an interpretation to suit his own purpose and misleads unfortunate followers into the same mentality. Such unfortunate persons merely pick up some slogans from the great book of knowledge, but are unable to estimate the Lord as the Supreme Personality of Godhead. Pure devotees like Uddhava, however, are never misled by such atheistic opportunists.

TEXT 23

अहो बकी यं स्तनकालकूटं
जिघांसयापाययदप्यसाध्वी ।
लेभे गतिं धात्र्युचितां ततोऽन्यं
कं वा दयालुं शरणं व्रजेम ॥२३॥

aho bakī yaṁ stana-kāla-kūṭaṁ
jighāṁsayāpāyayad apy asādhvī
lebhe gatiṁ dhātry-ucitāṁ tato 'nyaṁ
kaṁ vā dayāluṁ śaraṇaṁ vrajema

aho—alas; *bakī*—the she-demon (Pūtanā); *yam*—whom; *stana*—of her breast; *kāla*—deadly; *kūṭam*—poison; *jighāṁsayā*—out of envy; *apāyayat*—nourished; *api*—although; *asādhvī*—unfaithful; *lebhe*—achieved; *gatim*—destination; *dhātrī-ucitām*—just suitable for the nurse; *tataḥ*—beyond whom; *anyam*—other; *kam*—who else; *vā*—certainly; *dayālum*—merciful; *śaraṇam*—shelter; *vrajema*—shall I take.

TRANSLATION

Alas, how shall I take shelter of one more merciful than He who granted the position of mother to a she-demon [Pūtanā] although she was unfaithful and she prepared deadly poison to be sucked from her breast?

PURPORT

Here is an example of the extreme mercy of the Lord, even to His enemy. It is said that a noble man accepts the good qualities of a person of doubtful character, just as one accepts nectar from a stock of poison. In His babyhood, He was administered deadly poison by Pūtanā, a she-demon who tried to kill the wonderful baby. And because she was a demon, it was impossible for her to know that the Supreme Lord, even though playing the part of a baby, was no one less than the same Supreme Personality of Godhead. His value as the Supreme Lord did not diminish upon His becoming a baby to please His devotee Yaśodā. The Lord may assume the form of a baby or a shape other than that of a human being, but it doesn't make the slightest difference; He is always the same Supreme. A living creature, however powerful he may become by dint of severe penance, can never become equal to the Supreme Lord.

Lord Kṛṣṇa accepted the motherhood of Pūtanā because she pretended to be an affectionate mother, allowing Kṛṣṇa to suck her breast. The Lord accepts the least qualification of the living entity and awards him the highest reward. That is the standard of His character. Therefore, who but the Lord can be the ultimate shelter?

TEXT 24

मन्येऽसुरान् भागवतांस्त्र्यधीशे
संरम्भमार्गाभिनिविष्टचित्तान् ।
ये संयुगेऽचक्षत तार्क्ष्यपुत्र-
मंसे सुनाभायुधमापतन्तम् ॥२४॥

manye 'surān bhāgavatāṁs tryadhīśe
saṁrambha-mārgābhiniviṣṭa-cittān

ye saṁyuge 'cakṣata tārkṣya-putram
aṁse sunābhāyudham āpatantam

manye—I think; *asurān*—the demons; *bhāgavatān*—great devotees; *tri-adhīśe*—unto the Lord of the threes; *saṁrambha*—enmity; *mārga*—by the way of; *abhiniviṣṭa-cittān*—absorbed in thought; *ye*—those; *saṁyuge*—in the fight; *acakṣata*—could see; *tārkṣya-putram*—Garuḍa, the carrier of the Lord; *aṁse*—on the shoulder; *sunābha*—the wheel; *āyudham*—one who carries the weapon; *āpatantam*—coming forward.

TRANSLATION

I consider the demons, who are inimical toward the Lord, to be more than the devotees because while fighting with the Lord, absorbed in thoughts of enmity, they are able to see the Lord carried on the shoulder of Garuḍa, the son of Tārkṣya [Kaśyapa], and carrying the wheel weapon in His hand.

PURPORT

The *asuras* who fought against the Lord face to face got salvation due to their being killed by the Lord. This salvation of the demons is not due to their being devotees of the Lord; it is because of the Lord's causeless mercy. Anyone who is slightly in touch with the Lord, somehow or other, is greatly benefited, even to the point of salvation, due to the excellence of the Lord. He is so kind that He awards salvation even to His enemies because they come into contact with Him and are indirectly absorbed in Him by their inimical thoughts. Actually, the demons can never be equal to the pure devotees, but Uddhava was thinking in that way because of his feelings of separation. He was thinking that at the last stage of his life he might not be able to see the Lord face to face as did the demons. The fact is that the devotees who are always engaged in the devotional service of the Lord in transcendental love are rewarded many hundreds and thousands of times more than the demons by being elevated to the spiritual planets, where they remain with the Lord in eternal, blissful existence. The demons and impersonalists are awarded the facility of merging in the *brahmajyoti* effulgence of the Lord, whereas the devotees are admitted into the spiritual planets. For comparison, one can just imagine the difference between floating in space and residing in one of the planets in the sky. The pleasure of the living entities on the planets is greater than that of those who have no body and who merge with the molecules of the sun's rays. The impersonalists, therefore, are no more favored than the enemies of the Lord; rather, they are both on the same level of spiritual salvation.

TEXT 25

वसुदेवस्य देवक्यां जातो भोजेन्द्रबन्धने ।
चिकीर्षुर्भगवानस्याः शमजेनाभियाचितः ॥२५॥

vasudevasya devakyāṁ
jāto bhojendra-bandhane
cikīrṣur bhagavān asyāḥ
śam ajenābhiyācitaḥ

vasudevasya—of the wife of Vasudeva; *devakyām*—in the womb of Devakī; *jātaḥ*—born of; *bhoja-indra*—of the King of the Bhojas; *bandhane*—in the prison house; *cikīrṣuḥ*—for doing; *bhagavān*—the Personality of Godhead; *asyāḥ*—of the earth; *śam*—welfare; *ajena*—by Brahmā; *abhiyācitaḥ*—being prayed for.

TRANSLATION

The Personality of Godhead, Lord Śrī Kṛṣṇa, being prayed to by Brahmā to bring welfare to the earth, was begotten by Vasudeva in the womb of his wife Devakī in the prison of the King of Bhoja.

PURPORT

Although there is no difference between the Lord's pastimes of appearance and disappearance, the devotees of the Lord do not generally discuss the subject matter of His disappearance. Vidura inquired indirectly from Uddhava about the incident of the Lord's disappearance by asking him to relate *krsna kathā*, or topics on the history of Lord Kṛṣṇa. Thus Uddhava began the topics from the very beginning of His appearance as the son of Vasudeva and Devakī in the prison of Kaṁsa, the King of the Bhojas, at Mathurā. The Lord has no business in this world, but when He is so requested by devotees like Brahmā, He descends on the earth for the welfare of the entire universe. This is stated in *Bhagavad-gītā* (4.8): *paritrāṇāya sādhūnāṁ vināśāya ca duṣkṛtām/ dharma-saṁsthāpanārthāya sambhavāmi yuge yuge.*

TEXT 26

ततो नन्दव्रजमितः पित्रा कंसाद्विबिभ्यता ।
एकादश समास्तत्र गूढार्चिः सबलोऽवसत् ॥२६॥

tato nanda-vrajam itaḥ
pitrā kaṁsād vibibhyatā
ekādaśa samās tatra
gūḍhārciḥ sa-balo 'vasat

tataḥ—thereafter; *nanda-vrajam*—cow pastures of Nanda Mahārāja; *itaḥ*—being brought up; *pitrā*—by His father; *kaṁsāt*—from Kaṁsa; *vibibhyatā*—being afraid of; *ekādaśa*—eleven; *samāḥ*—years; *tatra*—therein; *gūḍha-arciḥ*—covered fire; *sa-balaḥ*—with Baladeva; *avasat*—resided.

TRANSLATION

Thereafter, His father, being afraid of Kaṁsa, brought Him to the cow pastures of Mahārāja Nanda, and there He lived for eleven years like a covered flame with His elder brother, Baladeva.

PURPORT

There was no necessity of the Lord's being dispatched to the house of Nanda Mahārāja out of fear of Kaṁsa's determination to kill Him as soon as He appeared. It is the business of the *asuras* to try to kill the Supreme Personality of Godhead or to prove by all means that there is no God or that Kṛṣṇa is an ordinary human being and not God. Lord Kṛṣṇa is not affected by such determination of men of Kaṁsa's class, but in order to play the role of a child He agreed to be carried by His father to the cow pastures of Nanda Mahārāja because Vasudeva was afraid of Kaṁsa. Nanda Mahārāja was due to receive Him as his child, and Yaśodāmayī was also to enjoy the childhood pastimes of the Lord, and therefore to fulfill everyone's desire, He was carried from Mathurā to Vṛndāvana just after His appearance in the prison house of Kaṁsa. He lived there for eleven years and completed all His fascinating pastimes of childhood, boyhood and adolescence with His elder brother, Lord Baladeva, His first expansion. Vasudeva's thought of protecting Kṛṣṇa from the wrath of Kaṁsa is part of a transcendental relationship. The Lord enjoys more when someone takes Him as his subordinate son who needs the protection of a father than He does when someone accepts Him as the Supreme Lord. He is the father of everyone, and He protects everyone, but when His devotee takes it for granted that the Lord is to be protected by the devotee's care, it is a transcendental joy for the Lord. Thus when Vasudeva, out of fear of Kaṁsa, carried Him to Vṛndāvana, the Lord enjoyed it; otherwise, He had no fear from Kaṁsa or anyone else.

TEXT 27

परीतो वत्सपैर्वत्सांश्चारयन् व्यहरद्विभुः ।
यमुनोपवने कूजद्द्विजसङ्कुलिताङ्घ्रिपे ॥२७॥

parīto vatsapair vatsāṁś
cārayan vyaharad vibhuḥ
yamunopavane kūjad-
dvija-saṅkulitāṅghripe

parītaḥ—surrounded by; *vatsapaiḥ*—cowherd boys; *vatsān*—calves; *cārayan*—herding, tending; *vyaharat*—enjoyed by traveling; *vibhuḥ*—the Almighty; *yamunā*—the Yamunā River; *upavane*—gardens on the shore; *kūjat*—vibrated by the voice; *dvija*—the twice-born birds; *saṅkulita*—densely situated; *aṅghripe*—in the trees.

TRANSLATION

In His childhood, the Almighty Lord was surrounded by cowherd boys and calves, and thus He traveled on the shore of the Yamunā River, through gardens densely covered with trees and filled with vibrations of chirping birds.

PURPORT

Nanda Mahārāja was a landholder for King Kaṁsa, but because by caste he was a *vaiśya,* a member of the mercantile and agricultural community, he maintained thousands of cows. It is the duty of the *vaiśyas* to give protection to the cows, just as the *kṣatriyas* are to give protection to the human beings. Because the Lord was a child, He was put in charge of the calves with His cowherd boy friends. These cowherd boys were great *ṛṣis* and *yogīs* in their previous births, and after many such pious births, they gained the association of the Lord and could play with Him on equal terms. Such cowherd boys never cared to know who Kṛṣṇa was, but they played with Him as a most intimate and lovable friend. They were so fond of the Lord that at night they would only think of the next morning when they would be able to meet the Lord and go together to the forests for cowherding.

The forests on the shore of the Yamunā are all beautiful gardens full of trees of mango, jackfruit, apples, guava, oranges, grapes, berries, palmfruit and so many other plants and fragrant flowers. And because the forest was on the bank of the Yamunā, naturally there were ducks, cranes and peacocks on the branches of the trees. All these trees and birds and beasts were pious living entities born in the transcendental abode of Vṛndāvana just to give pleasure to the Lord and His eternal associates, the cowherd boys.

While playing like a small child with His associates, the Lord killed many demons, including Aghāsura, Bakāsura, Pralambāsura and Gardabhāsura. Although He appeared at Vṛndāvana just as a boy, He was actually like the covered flames of a fire. As a small particle of fire can kindle a great fire with fuel, so the Lord killed all these great demons, beginning from His babyhood in the house of Nanda Mahārāja. The land of Vṛndāvana, the Lord's childhood playground, still remains today, and anyone who visits these places enjoys the same transcendental bliss, although the Lord is not physically visible to our imperfect eyes. Lord Caitanya recommended this land of the Lord as identical with the Lord and therefore worshipable by the devotees. This instruction is taken up especially by the followers of Lord Caitanya known as the Gauḍīya Vaiṣṇavas. And because the land is identical with the Lord, devotees like Uddhava and Vidura visited these places five thousand years ago in order to have direct contact with the Lord, visible or not visible. Thousands of devotees of the Lord are still wandering in these sacred places of Vṛndāvana, and all of them are preparing themselves to go back home, back to Godhead.

TEXT 28

कौमारीं दर्शयंश्चेष्टां प्रेक्षणीयां व्रजौकसाम् ।
रुदन्निव हसन्मुग्धबालसिंहावलोकनः ॥२८॥

kaumārīṁ darśayaṁś ceṣṭāṁ
prekṣaṇīyāṁ vrajaukasām
rudann iva hasan mugdha-
bāla-siṁhāvalokanaḥ

kaumārīm—just suitable to childhood; *darśayan*—while showing; *ceṣṭām*—activities; *prekṣaṇīyām*—worthy to be seen; *vraja-okasām*—by the inhabitants of the land of Vṛndāvana; *rudan*—crying; *iva*—just like; *hasan*—laughing; *mugdha*—struck with wonder; *bāla-siṁha*—lion cub; *avalokanaḥ*—looking like that.

TRANSLATION

When the Lord displayed His activities just suitable for childhood, He was visible only to the residents of Vṛndāvana. Sometimes He would cry and sometimes laugh, just like a child, and while so doing He would appear like a lion cub.

PURPORT

If anyone wants to enjoy the childhood pastimes of the Lord, then he has to follow in the footsteps of the residents of Vraja like Nanda, Upananda and other parental inhabitants. A child may insist on having something and cry like anything to get it, disturbing the whole neighborhood, and then immediately after achieving the desired thing, he laughs. Such crying and laughing is enjoyable to the parents and elderly members of the family, so the Lord would simultaneously cry and laugh in this way and merge His devotee-parents in the humor of transcendental pleasure. These incidents are enjoyable only by the residents of Vraja like Nanda Mahārāja, and not by the impersonalist worshipers of Brahman or Paramātmā. Sometimes when attacked in the forest by demons, Kṛṣṇa would appear struck with wonder, but He looked on them like the cub of a lion and killed them. His childhood companions would also be struck with wonder, and when they came back home they would narrate the story to their parents, and everyone would appreciate the qualities of their Kṛṣṇa. Child Kṛṣṇa did not belong only to His parents, Nanda and Yaśodā; He was the son of all the elderly inhabitants of Vṛndāvana and the friend of all contemporary boys and girls. Everyone loved Kṛṣṇa. He was the life and soul of everyone, including the animals, the cows and the calves.

TEXT 29

स एव गोधनं लक्ष्म्या निकेतं सितगोवृषम् ।
चारयन्ननुगान् गोपान् रणद्वेणुररीरमत् ॥२९॥

sa eva go-dhanaṁ lakṣmyā
niketaṁ sita-go-vṛṣam
cārayann anugān gopān
raṇad-veṇur arīramat

saḥ—He (Lord Kṛṣṇa); *eva*—certainly; *go-dhanam*—the treasure of cows; *lakṣmyāḥ*—by opulence; *niketam*—reservoir; *sita-go-vṛṣam*—beautiful cows and bulls; *cārayan*—herding; *anugān*—the followers; *gopān*—cowherd boys; *raṇat*—blowing; *veṇuḥ*—flute; *arīramat*—enlivened.

TRANSLATION

While herding the very beautiful bulls, the Lord, who was the reservoir of all opulence and fortune, used to blow His flute, and thus He enlivened His faithful followers, the cowherd boys.

PURPORT

As He grew to six and seven years old, the Lord was given charge of looking after the cows and bulls in the grazing grounds. He was the son of a well-to-do landholder who owned hundreds and thousands of cows, and according to Vedic economics, one is considered to be a rich man by the strength of his store of grains and cows. With only these two things, cows and grain, humanity can solve its eating problem. Human society needs only sufficient grain and sufficient cows to solve its economic problems. All other things but these two are artificial necessities created by man to kill his valuable life at the human level and waste his time in things which are not needed. Lord Kṛṣṇa, as the teacher of human society, personally showed by His acts that the mercantile community, or the *vaiśyas,* should herd cows and bulls and thus give protection to the valuable animals. According to *smṛti* regulation, the cow is the mother and the bull the father of the human being. The cow is the mother because just as one sucks the breast of one's mother, human society takes cow's milk. Similarly, the bull is the father of human society because the father earns for the children just as the bull tills the ground to produce food grains. Human society will kill its spirit of life by killing the father and the mother. It is mentioned herein that the beautiful cows and bulls were of various checkered colors—red, black, green, yellow, ash, etc. And because of their colors and healthy smiling features, the atmosphere was enlivening.

Over and above all, the Lord used to play His celebrated flute. The sound vibrated by His flute would give His friends such transcendental pleasure that they would forget all the talks of the *brahmānanda* which is so praised by the impersonalists. These cowherd boys, as will be explained by Śukadeva Gosvāmī, were living entities who had accumulated heaps of pious acts and thus were enjoying with the Lord in person and were hearing His transcendental flute. The *Brahma-saṁhitā* (5.30) confirms the Lord's blowing His transcendental flute.

veṇuṁ kvaṇantam aravinda-dalāyatākṣaṁ
barhāvataṁsam asitāmbuda-sundarāṅgam
kandarpa-koṭi-kaminīya-viśeṣa-śobhaṁ
govindam ādi-puruṣaṁ tam ahaṁ bhajāmi

Brahmājī said, "I worship Govinda, the primeval Lord, who plays on His transcendental flute. His eyes are like lotus flowers, He is decorated with peacock plumes, and His bodily color resembles a fresh black cloud although His bodily features are more beautiful than millions of cupids." These are the special features of the Lord.

TEXT 30

प्रयुक्तान् भोजराजेन मायिनः कामरूपिणः ।
लीलया व्यनुदत्तांस्तान् बालः क्रीडनकानिव ॥३०॥

prayuktān bhoja-rājena
māyinaḥ kāma-rūpiṇaḥ
līlayā vyanudat tāṁs tān
bālaḥ krīḍanakān iva

prayuktān—engaged; *bhoja-rājena*—by King Kaṁsa; *māyinaḥ*—great wizards; *kāma-rūpiṇaḥ*—who could assume any form they liked; *līlayā*—in the course of the pastimes; *vyanudat*—killed; *tān*—them; *tān*—as they came there; *bālaḥ*—the child; *krīḍanakān*—dolls; *iva*—like that.

TRANSLATION

The great wizards who were able to assume any form were engaged by the King of Bhoja, Kaṁsa, to kill Kṛṣṇa, but in the course of His pastimes the Lord killed them as easily as a child breaks dolls.

PURPORT

The atheist Kaṁsa wanted to kill Kṛṣṇa just after His birth. He failed to do so, but later on he got information that Kṛṣṇa was living in Vṛndāvana at the house of Nanda Mahārāja. He therefore engaged many wizards who could perform wonderful acts and assume any form they liked. All of them appeared before the child-Lord in various forms, like Agha, Baka, Pūtanā, Śakaṭa, Tṛṇāvarta, Dhenuka and Gardabha, and they tried to kill the Lord at every opportunity. But one after another, all of them were killed by the Lord as if He were only playing with dolls. Children play with toy lions, elephants, boars and many similar dolls, which are broken by the children in the course of their playing with them. Before the Almighty Lord, any powerful living being is just like a toy lion in the hands of a playing child. No one can excel God in any capacity, and therefore no one can be equal to or greater than Him, nor can anyone attain the stage of equality with God by any kind of endeavor. *Jñāna, yoga* and *bhakti* are three recognized processes of spiritual realization. The perfection of such processes can lead one to the desired goal of life in spiritual value, but that does not mean that one can attain a perfection equal to the Lord's by such endeavors. The Lord is the Lord at every stage. When He was playing just like a child on the lap of His mother Yaśodāmayī or just like a cowherd boy with His transcendental friends, He continued to remain God, without the slightest diminution of His six opulences. Thus He is always unrivaled.

TEXT 31

विपन्नान् विषपानेन निगृह्य भुजगाधिपम् ।
उत्थाप्यापाययद्गावस्तत्तोयं प्रकृतिस्थितम् ॥३१॥

vipannān viṣa-pānena
nigṛhya bhujagādhipam
utthāpyāpāyayad gāvas
tat toyaṁ prakṛti-sthitam

vipannān—perplexed in great difficulties; *viṣa-pānena*—by drinking poison; *nigṛhya*—subduing; *bhujaga-adhipam*—the chief of the reptiles; *utthāpya*—after coming out; *apāyayat*—caused to drink; *gāvaḥ*—the cows; *tat*—that; *toyam*—water; *prakṛti*—natural; *sthitam*—situated.

TRANSLATION

The inhabitants of Vṛndāvana were perplexed by great difficulties because a certain portion of the Yamunā was poisoned by the chief of the reptiles [Kāliya]. The Lord chastised the snake-king within the water and drove him away, and after coming out of the river, He caused the cows to drink the water and proved that the water was again in its natural state.

TEXT 32

अयाजयद्गोसवेन गोपराजं द्विजोत्तमैः ।
वित्तस्य चोरुभारस्य चिकीर्षन् सद्व्ययं विभुः ॥३२॥

ayājayad go-savena
gopa-rājaṁ dvijottamaiḥ
vittasya coru-bhārasya
cikīrṣan sad-vyayaṁ vibhuḥ

ayājayat—made to perform; *go-savena*—by worship of the cows; *gopa-rājam*—the king of the cowherds; *dvija-uttamaiḥ*—by the learned *brāhmaṇas; vittasya*—of the wealth; *ca*—also; *uru-bhārasya*—great opulence; *cikīrṣan*—desiring to act; *sat-vyayam*—proper utilization; *vibhuḥ*—the great.

TRANSLATION

The Supreme Lord, Kṛṣṇa, desired to utilize the opulent financial strength of Mahārāja Nanda for worship of the cows, and also He wanted to give a lesson to Indra, the King of heaven. Thus He advised His father to perform worship of go, or the pasturing land and the cows, with the help of learned brāhmaṇas.

PURPORT

Since He is the teacher of everyone, the Lord also taught His father, Nanda Mahārāja. Nanda Mahārāja was a well-to-do landholder and owner of many cows, and, as was the custom, he used to perform yearly worship of Indra, the King of heaven, with great opulence. This worship of demigods by the general populace is also advised in the Vedic literature just so people can accept the superior power of the Lord. The demigods are servants of the Lord deputed to look after the management of various activities of universal affairs. Therefore it is advised in the Vedic scriptures that one should perform *yajñas* to appease the demigods. But one who is devoted to the Supreme Lord has no need to appease the demigods. Worship of the demigods by common people is an arrangement for acknowledging the supremacy of the Supreme Lord, but it is not necessary. Such appeasement is generally recommended for material gains only. As we have already discussed in the Second Canto of this literature, one who admits the supremacy of the Supreme Personality of Godhead does not need to worship the secondary demigods. Sometimes, being worshiped and adored by less intelligent living beings, the demigods become puffed up with power and forget the supremacy of the Lord. This happened when Lord Kṛṣṇa was present in the universe, and thus the Lord wanted to give a lesson to the King of heaven, Indra. He therefore asked Mahārāja Nanda to stop the sacrifice offered to Indra and to use the money properly by performing a ceremony worshiping the cows and the pasturing ground on the hill of Govardhana. By this act Lord Kṛṣṇa taught human society, as He has instructed in the *Bhagavad-gītā* also, that one should worship the Supreme Lord by all acts and by all their results. That will bring about the desired success. The *vaiśyas* are specifically advised to give protection to the cows and their pasturing ground or agricultural land instead of squandering their hard-earned money. That will satisfy the Lord. The perfection of one's occupational duty, whether in the sphere of duty to oneself, one's community or one's nation, is judged by the degree to which the Lord is satisfied.

TEXT 33

वर्षतीन्द्रे व्रजः कोपाद्भग्नमानेऽतिविह्वलः ।
गोत्रलीलातपत्रेण त्रातो भद्रानुगृह्णता ॥३३॥

varṣatīndre vrajaḥ kopād
bhagnamāne 'tivihvalaḥ
gotra-līlātapatreṇa
trāto bhadrānugṛhṇatā

varṣati—in pouring water; *indre*—by the King of heaven, Indra; *vrajaḥ*—the land of cows (Vṛndāvana); *kopāt bhagnamāne*—having been in anger on being insulted; *ati*—highly; *vihvalaḥ*—perturbed; *gotra*—the hill for the cows; *līlā-ātapatreṇa*—by the pastime umbrella; *trātaḥ*—were protected; *bhadra*—O sober one; *anugṛhṇatā*—by the merciful Lord.

TRANSLATION

O sober Vidura, King Indra, his honor having been insulted, poured water incessantly on Vṛndāvana, and thus the inhabitants of Vraja, the land of cows, were greatly distressed. But the compassionate Lord Kṛṣṇa saved them from danger with His pastime umbrella, the Govardhana Hill.

TEXT 34

शरच्छशिकरैर्मृष्टं मानयन् रजनीमुखम् ।
गायन् कलपदं रेमे स्त्रीणां मण्डलमण्डनः ॥३४॥

śarac-chaśi-karair mṛṣṭaṁ
mānayan rajanī-mukham
gāyan kala-padaṁ reme
strīṇāṁ maṇḍala-maṇḍanaḥ

śarat—autumn; *śaśi*—of the moon; *karaiḥ*—by the shining; *mṛṣṭam*—brightened; *mānayan*—thinking so; *rajanī-mukham*—the face of the night; *gāyan*—singing; *kala-padam*—pleasing songs; *reme*—enjoyed; *strīṇām*—of the women; *maṇḍala-maṇḍanaḥ*—as the central beauty of the assembly of women.

TRANSLATION

In the third season of the year, the Lord enjoyed as the central beauty of the assembly of women by attracting them with His pleasing songs in an autumn night brightened by moonshine.

PURPORT

Before leaving the land of cows, Vṛndāvana, the Lord pleased His young girl friends, the transcendental *gopīs,* in His *rāsa-līlā* pastimes. Here Uddhava stopped his description of the Lord's activities.

Thus end the Bhaktivedanta purports of the Third Canto, Second Chapter, of the Śrīmad-Bhāgavatam, *entitled "Remembrance of Lord Kṛṣṇa."*

CHAPTER THREE

The Lord's Pastimes Out of Vṛndāvana

TEXT 1

उद्धव उवाच
ततः स आगत्य पुरं स्वपित्रो-
श्चिकीर्षया शं बलदेवसंयुतः ।
निपात्य तुङ्गाद्रिपुयूथनाथं
हतं व्यकर्षद् व्यसुमोजसोर्व्याम् ॥ १ ॥

uddhava uvāca
tataḥ sa āgatya puraṁ sva-pitroś
cikīrṣayā śaṁ baladeva-saṁyutaḥ
nipātya tuṅgād ripu-yūtha-nāthaṁ
hataṁ vyakarṣad vyasum ojasorvyām

uddhavaḥ uvāca—Śrī Uddhava said; *tataḥ*—thereafter; *saḥ*—the Lord; *āgatya*—coming; *puram*—to the city of Mathurā; *sva-pitroḥ*—own parents; *cikīrṣayā*—wishing well; *śam*—well-being; *baladeva-saṁyutaḥ*—with Lord Baladeva; *nipātya*—dragging down; *tuṅgāt*—from the throne; *ripu-yūtha-nātham*—leader of public enemies; *hatam*—killed; *vyakarṣat*—pulled; *vyasum*—dead; *ojasā*—by strength; *urvyām*—on the ground.

TRANSLATION

Śrī Uddhava said: Thereafter Lord Kṛṣṇa went to Mathurā City with Śrī Baladeva, and to please Their parents They dragged Kaṁsa, the leader of public enemies, down from his throne and killed him, pulling him along the ground with great strength.

PURPORT

King Kaṁsa's death is only briefly described here because such pastimes are vividly and elaborately described in the Tenth Canto. The Lord proved to be a worthy son of His parents even at the age of sixteen years. Both brothers, Lord Kṛṣṇa and Lord Baladeva, went to Mathurā from Vṛndāvana and killed Their maternal uncle, who had given so much trouble to Their parents, Vasudeva and Devakī. Kaṁsa was a great giant, and Vasudeva and Devakī never thought that Kṛṣṇa and Balarāma (Baladeva) would be able to kill such a great and strong enemy. When the two brothers attacked Kaṁsa on the throne, Their parents feared that now Kaṁsa would finally get the opportunity to kill their sons, whom they had hidden for so long in the house of Nanda Mahārāja. The parents of the Lord, due to parental affection, felt extreme danger, and they almost fainted. Just to convince them that They had actually killed Kaṁsa, Kṛṣṇa and Baladeva pulled Kaṁsa's dead body along the ground to encourage them.

TEXT 2

सान्दीपनेः सकृत्प्रोक्तं ब्रह्माधीत्य सविस्तरम् ।
तस्मै प्रादाद्वरं पुत्रं मृतं पञ्चजनोदरात् ॥ २ ॥

sāndīpaneḥ sakṛt proktaṁ
brahmādhītya sa-vistaram
tasmai prādād varaṁ putraṁ
mṛtaṁ pañca-janodarāt

sāndīpaneḥ—of Sāndīpani Muni; *sakṛt*—once only; *proktam*—instructed; *brahma*—all the *Vedas* with their different branches of knowledge; *adhītya*—after studying; *sa-vistaram*—in all details; *tasmai*—unto him; *prādāt*—rewarded; *varam*—a benediction; *putram*—his son; *mṛtam*—who was already dead; *pañca-jana*—the region of the departed souls; *udarāt*—from within.

TRANSLATION

The Lord learned all the Vedas with their different branches simply by hearing them once from His teacher, Sāndīpani Muni, whom He rewarded by bringing back his dead son from the region of Yamaloka.

PURPORT

No one but the Supreme Lord can become well versed in all the branches of Vedic wisdom simply by hearing once from his teacher. Nor can anyone bring a dead body back to life after the soul has already gone to the region of Yamarāja. But Lord Kṛṣṇa ventured to the planet of Yamaloka and found the dead son of His teacher and brought him back to his father as a reward for the instructions received. The Lord is constitutionally well versed in all the *Vedas*, and yet to teach by example that everyone must go to learn the *Vedas* from an authorized teacher and must satisfy the teacher by service and reward, He Himself adopted this system. The Lord offered His services to His teacher, Sāndīpani Muni, and the *muni,* knowing the power of the Lord, asked something which was impossible to be done by anyone else. The teacher asked that his beloved son, who had died, be brought back to him, and the Lord fulfilled the request. The Lord is not, therefore, an ingrate to anyone who renders Him some sort of service. The devotees of the Lord who always engage in His loving service are never to be disappointed in the progressive march of devotional service.

TEXT 3

समाहुता भीष्मककन्यया ये
श्रियः सवर्णेन बुभूषयैषाम् ।
गान्धर्ववृत्त्या मिषतां स्वभागं
जह्रे पदं मूर्ध्नि दधत्सुपर्णः ॥ ३ ॥

samāhutā bhīṣmaka-kanyayā ye
śriyaḥ savarṇena bubhūṣayaiṣām
gāndharva-vṛttyā miṣatāṁ sva-bhāgaṁ
jahre padaṁ mūrdhni dadhat suparṇaḥ

samāhutāḥ—invited; *bhīṣmaka*—of King Bhīṣmaka; *kanyayā*—by the daughter; *ye*—all those; *śriyaḥ*—fortune; *sa-varṇena*—by a similar sequence; *bubhūṣayā*—expecting to be so; *eṣām*—of them; *gāndharva*—in marrying; *vṛttyā*—by such a custom; *miṣatām*—carrying so; *sva-bhāgam*—own share; *jahre*—took away; *padam*—feet; *mūrdhni*—on the head; *dadhat*—placed; *suparṇaḥ*—Garuḍa.

TRANSLATION

Attracted by the beauty and fortune of Rukmiṇī, the daughter of King Bhīṣmaka, many great princes and kings assembled to marry her. But Lord Kṛṣṇa, stepping over the other hopeful candidates, carried her away as His own share, as Garuḍa carried away nectar.

PURPORT

Princess Rukmiṇī, the daughter of King Bhīṣmaka, was actually as attractive as fortune itself because she was as valuable as gold both in color and in value. Since the goddess of fortune, Lakṣmī, is the property of the Supreme Lord, Rukmiṇī was actually meant for Lord Kṛṣṇa. But Śiśupāla was selected as her bridegroom by Rukmiṇī's elder brother, although King Bhīṣmaka wanted his daughter to be married to Kṛṣṇa. Rukmiṇī invited Kṛṣṇa to take her away from the clutches of Śiśupāla, so when the bridegroom, Śiśupāla, came there with his party with the desire to marry Rukmiṇī, Kṛṣṇa all of a sudden swept her from the scene, stepping over the heads of all the princes there, just as Garuḍa carried away nectar from the hands of the demons. This incident will be clearly explained in the Tenth Canto.

TEXT 4

ककुद्मिनोऽविद्धनसो दमित्वा
स्वयंवरे नाग्नजितीमुवाह ।
तद्भग्नमानानपि गृध्यतोऽज्ञा-
ञ्जघ्नेऽक्षतः शस्त्रभृतः स्वशस्त्रैः ॥ ४ ॥

kakudmino 'viddha-naso damitvā
svayaṁvare nāgnajitīm uvāha
tad-bhagnamānān api gṛdhyato 'jñāñ
jaghne 'kṣataḥ śastra-bhṛtaḥ sva-śastraiḥ

kakudminaḥ—bulls whose noses were not pierced; *aviddha-nasaḥ*—pierced by the nose; *damitvā*—subduing; *svayaṁvare*—in the open competition to select the bridegroom; *nāgnajitīm*—Princess Nāgnajitī; *uvāha*—married; *tat-bhagnamānān*—in that way all who were disappointed; *api*—even though; *gṛdhyataḥ*—wanted; *ajñān*—the fools; *jaghne*—killed and wounded; *akṣataḥ*—without being wounded; *śastra-bhṛtaḥ*—equipped with all weapons; *sva-śastraiḥ*—by His own weapons.

TRANSLATION

By subduing seven bulls whose noses were not pierced, the Lord achieved the hand of Princess Nāgnajitī in the open competition to select her bridegroom. Although the Lord was victorious, His competitors asked the hand of the princess, and thus there was a fight. Well equipped with weapons, the Lord killed or wounded all of them, but He was not hurt Himself.

TEXT 5

प्रियं प्रभुर्ग्राम्य इव प्रियाया
विधित्सुराच्छैद् द्युतरुं यदर्थे ।
वज्र्याद्रवत्तं सगणो रुषान्धः
क्रीडामृगो नूनमयं वधूनाम् ॥ ५ ॥

priyaṁ prabhur grāmya iva priyāyā
vidhitsur ārcchad dyutaruṁ yad-arthe
vajry ādravat taṁ sa-gaṇo ruṣāndhaḥ
krīḍā-mṛgo nūnam ayaṁ vadhūnām

priyam—of the dear wife; *prabhuḥ*—the Lord; *grāmyaḥ*—ordinary living being; *iva*—in the manner of; *priyāyāḥ*—just to please; *vidhitsuḥ*—wishing; *ārcchat*—brought about; *dyutarum*—the *pārijāta* flower tree; *yat*—for which; *arthe*—in the matter of; *vajrī*—Indra, the King of heaven; *ādravat tam*—went forward to fight with Him; *sa-gaṇaḥ*—with full strength; *ruṣā*—in anger; *andhaḥ*—blind; *krīḍā-mṛgaḥ*—henpecked; *nūnam*—of course; *ayam*—this; *vadhūnām*—of the wives.

TRANSLATION

Just to please His dear wife, the Lord brought back the pārijāta tree from heaven, just as an ordinary husband would do. But Indra, the King of heaven, induced by his wives (henpecked as he was), ran after the Lord with full force to fight Him.

PURPORT

The Lord once went to the heavenly planet to present an earring to Aditi, the mother of the demigods, and His wife Satyabhāma also went with Him. There is a special flowering tree called the *pārijāta,* which grows only in the heavenly planets, and Satyabhāmā wanted this tree. Just to please His wife, like an ordinary husband, the Lord brought back the tree, and this enraged Vajrī, or the controller of the thunderbolt. Indra's wives inspired him to run after the Lord to fight, and Indra, because he was a henpecked husband and also a fool, listened to them and dared to fight with Kṛṣṇa. He was a fool on this occasion because he forgot that everything belongs to the Lord.

There was no fault on the part of the Lord, even though He took away the tree from the heavenly kingdom, but because Indra was henpecked, dominated by his beautiful wives like Śacī, he became a fool, just as all persons who are dominated by their wives are generally foolish. Indra thought that Kṛṣṇa was a henpecked husband who only by the will of His wife Satyabhāmā took away the property of heaven, and therefore he thought that Kṛṣṇa could be punished. He forgot that the Lord is the proprietor of everything and cannot be henpecked. The Lord is fully independent, and by His will only He can have hundreds and thousands of wives like Satyabhāmā. He was not, therefore, attached to Satyabhāmā because she was a beautiful wife, but He was pleased with her devotional service and thus wanted to reciprocate the unalloyed devotion of His devotee.

TEXT 6

सुतं मृधे खं वपुषा ग्रसन्तं
दृष्ट्वा सुनाभोन्मथितं धरित्र्या ।
आमन्त्रितस्तत्तनयाय शेषं
दत्त्वा तदन्तःपुरमाविवेश ॥ ६ ॥

sutaṁ mṛdhe khaṁ vapuṣā grasantaṁ
dṛṣṭvā sunābhonmathitaṁ dharitryā
āmantritas tat-tanayāya śeṣaṁ
dattvā tad-antaḥ-puram āviveśa

sutam—son; *mṛdhe*—in the fight; *kham*—the sky; *vapuṣā*—by his body; *grasantam*—while devouring; *dṛṣṭvā*—seeing; *sunābha*—by the Sudarśana wheel; *unmathitam*—killed; *dharitryā*—by the earth; *āmantritaḥ*—being prayed for; *tat-tanayāya*—to the son of Narakāsura; *śeṣam*—that which was taken from; *dattvā*—returning it; *tat*—his; *antaḥ-puram*—inside the house; *āviveśa*—entered.

TRANSLATION

Narakāsura, the son of Dharitrī, the earth, tried to grasp the whole sky, and for this he was killed by the Lord in a fight. His mother then prayed to the Lord. This led to the return of the kingdom to the son of Narakāsura, and thus the Lord entered the house of the demon.

PURPORT

It is said in other *purāṇas* that Narakāsura was the son of Dharitrī, the earth, by the Lord Himself. But he became a demon due to the bad association of Bāṇa, another demon. An atheist is called a demon, and it is a fact that even a person born of good parents can turn into a demon by bad association. Birth is not always the criterion of goodness; unless and until one is trained in the culture of good association, one cannot become good.

TEXT 7

तत्राहृतास्ता नरदेवकन्याः
कुजेन दृष्ट्वा हरिमार्तबन्धुम् ।
उत्थाय सद्यो जगृहुः प्रहर्ष-
व्रीडानुरागप्रहितावलोकैः ॥ ७ ॥

tatrāhṛtās tā nara-deva-kanyāḥ
kujena dṛṣṭvā harim ārta-bandhum
utthāya sadyo jagṛhuḥ praharṣa-
vrīḍānurāga-prahitāvalokaiḥ

tatra—inside the house of Narakāsura; *āhṛtāḥ*—kidnapped; *tāḥ*—all those; *nara-deva-kanyāḥ*—daughters of many kings; *kujena*—by the demon; *dṛṣṭvā*—by seeing; *harim*—the Lord; *ārta-bandhum*—the friend of the distressed; *utthāya*—at once got up; *sadyaḥ*—then and there; *jagṛhuḥ*—accepted; *praharṣa*—joyfully; *vrīḍa*—shyness; *anurāga*—attachment; *prahita-avalokaiḥ*—by eager glances.

TRANSLATION

There in the house of the demon, all the princesses kidnapped by Narakāsura at once became alert upon seeing the Lord, the friend of the distressed. They looked upon Him with eagerness, joy and shyness and offered to be His wives.

PURPORT

Narakāsura kidnapped many daughters of great kings and kept them imprisoned in his palace. But when he was killed by the Lord and the Lord entered the house of the demon, all the princesses were enlivened with joy and offered to become His wives because the Lord is the only friend of the distressed. Unless the Lord accepted them, there would be no chance of their being married because the demon kidnapped them from their fathers' custody and therefore no one would agree to marry them. According to Vedic society, girls are transferred from the custody of the father to the custody of the husband. Since these princesses had already been taken away from the custody of their fathers, it would have been difficult for them to have any husband other than the Lord Himself.

TEXT 8

आसां मुहूर्त एकस्मिन्नानागारेषु योषिताम् ।
सविधं जगृहे पाणीननुरूपः स्वमायया ॥ ८ ॥

āsāṁ muhūrta ekasmin
nānāgāreṣu yoṣitām
sa-vidhaṁ jagṛhe pāṇīn
anurūpaḥ sva-māyayā

āsām—all those; *muhūrte*—at one time; *ekasmin*—simultaneously; *nānā-āgāreṣu*—in different compartments; *yoṣitām*—of the women; *sa-vidham*—with perfect rituals; *jagṛhe*—accepted; *pāṇīn*—hands; *anurūpaḥ*—exactly to match; *sva-māyayā*—by His internal potency.

TRANSLATION

All those princesses were lodged in different apartments, and the Lord simultaneously assumed different bodily expansions exactly matching each and every princess. He accepted their hands in perfect rituals by His internal potency.

PURPORT

In the *Brahma-saṁhitā* (5.33) the Lord is described as follows in regard to His innumerable plenary expansions:

advaitam acyutam anādim ananta-rūpam
ādyaṁ purāṇa-puruṣaṁ nava-yauvanaṁ ca
vedeṣu durlabham adurlabham ātma-bhaktau
govindam ādi-puruṣaṁ tam ahaṁ bhajāmi

"The Lord, Govinda, whom I worship, is the original Personality of Godhead. He is nondifferent from His innumerable plenary expansions, who are all infallible, original and unlimited and who have eternal forms. Although He is primeval, the oldest personality, He is always fresh and young." By His internal potency the Lord can expand Himself into various personalities of *svayaṁ-prakāśa* and again into *prābhava* and *vaibhava* forms, and all of them are nondifferent from one another. The forms into which the Lord expanded to marry the princesses in different apartments were all slightly different just to match each and every one of them. They are called *vaibhava-vilāsa* forms of the Lord and are effected by His internal potency, *yoga-māyā*.

TEXT 9

तास्वपत्यान्यजनयदात्मतुल्यानि सर्वतः ।
एकैकस्यां दश दश प्रकृतेर्विबुभूषया ॥ ९ ॥

tāsv apatyāny ajanayad
ātma-tulyāni sarvataḥ
ekaikasyāṁ daśa daśa
prakṛter vibubhūṣayā

tāsu—unto them; *apatyāni*—offspring; *ajanayat*—begot; *ātma-tulyāni*—all like Himself; *sarvataḥ*—in all respects; *eka-ekasyām*—in each and every one of them; *daśa*—ten; *daśa*—ten; *prakṛteḥ*—for expanding Himself; *vibubhūṣayā*—so desiring.

TRANSLATION

Just to expand Himself according to His transcendental features, the Lord begot in each and every one of them ten offspring with exactly His own qualities.

TEXT 10

कालमागधशाल्वादीननीकै रुन्धतः पुरम् ।
अजीघनत्स्वयं दिव्यं स्वपुंसां तेज आदिशत् ॥१०॥

kāla-māgadha-śālvādīn
anīkai rundhataḥ puram
ajīghanat svayaṁ divyaṁ
sva-puṁsāṁ teja ādiśat

kāla—Kālayavana; *māgadha*—the King of Magadha (Jarāsandha); *śālva*—King Śālva; *ādīn*—and others; *anīkaiḥ*—by the soldiers; *rundhataḥ*—being encircled; *puram*—the city of Mathurā; *ajīghanat*—killed; *svayam*—personally; *divyam*—transcendental; *sva-puṁsām*—of His own men; *tejaḥ*—prowess; *ādiśat*—exhibited.

TRANSLATION

Kālayavana, the King of Magadha and Sālva attacked the city of Mathurā, but when the city was encircled by their soldiers, the Lord refrained from killing them personally, just to show the power of His own men.

PURPORT

After the death of Kaṁsa, when Mathurā was encircled by the soldiers of Kālayavana, Jarāsandha and Sālva, the Lord seemingly fled from the city, and thus He is known as Ranchor, or one who fled from fighting. Actually, the fact was that the Lord wanted to kill them through the agency of His own men, devotees like Mucukunda and Bhīma. Kālayavana and the King of Magadha were killed by Mucukunda and Bhīma respectively, who acted as agents of the Lord. By such acts the Lord wanted to exhibit the prowess of His devotees, as if He were personally unable to fight but His devotees could kill them. The relationship of the Lord with His devotees is a very happy one. Actually, the Lord descended at the request of Brahmā in order to kill all the undesirables of the world, but to divide the share of glory He sometimes engaged His devotees to take the credit. The Battle of Kurukṣetra was designed by the Lord Himself, but just to give credit to His devotee Arjuna (*nimitta-mātraṁ bhava savyasācin*), He played the part of the charioteer, while Arjuna was given the chance to play the fighter and thus become the hero of the Battle of Kurukṣetra. What He wants to do Himself by His transcendental plans, He executes through His confidential devotees. That is the way of the Lord's mercy towards His pure unalloyed devotees.

TEXT 11

शम्बरं द्विविदं बाणं मुरं बल्वलमेव च ।
अन्यांश्च दन्तवक्रादीनवधीत्कांश्च घातयत् ॥११॥

śambaraṁ dvividaṁ bāṇaṁ
muraṁ balvalam eva ca
anyāṁś ca dantavakrādīn
avadhīt kāṁś ca ghātayat

śambaram—Śambara; *dvividam*—Dvivida; *bāṇam*—Bāṇa; *muram*—Mura; *balvalam*—Balvala; *eva ca*—as also; *anyān*—others; *ca*—also; *dantavakra-ādīn*—like Dantavakra and others; *avadhīt*—killed; *kān ca*—and many others; *ghātayat*—caused to be killed.

TRANSLATION

Of kings like Śambara, Dvivida, Bāṇa, Mura, Balvala and many other demons, such as Dantavakra, some He killed Himself, and some He caused to be killed by others [Śrī Baladeva, etc.].

TEXT 12

अथ ते भ्रातृपुत्राणां पक्षयोः पतितान्नृपान् ।
चचाल भूः कुरुक्षेत्रं येषामापततां बलैः ॥१२॥

atha te bhrātṛ-putrāṇāṁ
pakṣayoḥ patitān nṛpān
cacāla bhūḥ kurukṣetraṁ
yeṣām āpatatāṁ balaiḥ

atha—thereafter; *te*—your; *bhrātṛ-putrāṇām*—of the nephews; *pakṣayoḥ*—of both sides; *patitān*—killed; *nṛpān*—kings; *cacāla*—shook; *bhūḥ*—the earth; *kurukṣetram*—the Battle of Kurukṣetra; *yeṣām*—of whom; *āpatatām*—traversing; *balaiḥ*—by strength.

TRANSLATION

Then, O Vidura, the Lord caused all the kings, both the enemies and those on the side of your fighting nephews, to be killed in the Battle of Kurukṣetra. All those kings were so great and strong that the earth seemed to shake as they traversed the warfield.

TEXT 13

सकर्णदुःशासनसौबलानां
कुमन्त्रपाकेन हतश्रियायुषम् ।
सुयोधनं सानुचरं शयानं
भग्नोरुमूर्व्यां न ननन्द पश्यन् ॥१३॥

sa karṇa-duḥśāsana-saubalānāṁ
kumantra-pākena hata-śriyāyuṣam
suyodhanaṁ sānucaraṁ śayānaṁ
bhagnorum ūrvyāṁ na nananda paśyan

saḥ—He (the Lord); *karṇa*—Karṇa; *duḥśāsana*—Duḥśāsana; *saubalānām*—Saubala; *kumantra-pākena*—by the intricacy of ill advice; *hata-śriya*—bereft of fortune; *āyuṣam*—duration of life; *suyodhanam*—Duryodhana; *sa-anucaram*—with followers; *śayānam*—lying down; *bhagna*—broken; *ūrum*—thighs; *ūrvyām*—very powerful; *na*—did not; *nananda*—take pleasure; *paśyan*—seeing like that.

TRANSLATION

Duryodhana was bereft of his fortune and duration of life because of the intricacy of ill advice given by Karṇa, Duḥśāsana and Saubala. When he lay on the ground with his followers, his thighs broken although he was powerful, the Lord was not happy to see the scene.

PURPORT

The fall of Duryodhana, the leading son of Dhṛtarāṣṭra, was not pleasing to the Lord, although He was on the side of Arjuna and it was He who advised Bhīma how to break the thighs of Duryodhana while the fight was going on. The Lord is constrained to award punishment upon the wrongdoer, but He is not happy to award such punishments because the living entities are originally His parts and parcels. He is harder than the thunderbolt for the wrongdoer and softer than the rose for the faithful. The wrongdoer is misled by bad associates and by ill advice, which is against the established principles of the Lord's order, and thus he becomes subject to punishment. The surest path to happiness is to live by the principles laid down by the Lord and not disobey His established laws, which are enacted in the *Vedas* and the *Purāṇas* for the forgetful living entities.

TEXT 14

कियान् भुवोऽयं क्षपितोरुभारो
यद्द्रोणभीष्मार्जुनभीममूलैः ।
अष्टादशाक्षौहिणिको मदंशै-
रास्ते बलं दुर्विषहं यदूनाम् ॥१४॥

kiyān bhuvo 'yaṁ kṣapitoru-bhāro
yad droṇa-bhīṣmārjuna-bhīma-mūlaiḥ
aṣṭādaśākṣauhiṇiko mad-aṁśair
āste balaṁ durviṣahaṁ yadūnām

kiyān—what is this; *bhuvaḥ*—of the earth; *ayam*—this; *kṣapita*—abated; *uru*—very great; *bhāraḥ*—burden; *yat*—which; *droṇa*—Droṇa; *bhīṣma*—Bhīṣma; *arjuna*—Arjuna; *bhīma*—Bhīma; *mūlaiḥ*—with the help; *aṣṭādaśa*—eighteen; *akṣauhiṇikaḥ*—phalanxes of military strength (*vide Bhāg.* 1.16.34); *mat-aṁśaiḥ*—with My descendants; *āste*—are still there; *balam*—great strength; *durviṣaham*—unbearable; *yadūnām*—of the Yadu dynasty.

TRANSLATION

[After the end of the Battle of Kurukṣetra, the Lord said:] The abatement of the earth's great burden, eighteen akṣauhiṇīs, has now been effected with the help of Droṇa, Bhīṣma, Arjuna and Bhīma. But what is this? There is still the great strength of the Yadu dynasty, born of Myself, which may be a more unbearable burden.

PURPORT

It is a wrong theory that due to an increase in population the world becomes overburdened and therefore there are wars and other annihilating processes. The earth is never overburdened. The heaviest mountains and oceans on the face of the earth hold more living entities than there are human beings, and they are not overburdened. If a census were taken of all the living beings on the surface of the earth, certainly it would be found that the number of humans is not even five percent of the total number of living beings. If the birthrate of human beings is increasing, then the birthrate of other living beings is increasing proportionately. The birthrate of lower animals-beasts, aquatics, birds, etc.-is far greater than that of human beings. There is an adequate arrangement for food for all the living beings all over the earth by the order of the Supreme Lord, and He can arrange more and more if there is actually a disproportionate increase of living beings.

Therefore, there is no question of an increase in population causing a burden. The earth became overburdened due to *dharma-glāni*, or irregular discharge of the Lord's desire. The Lord appeared on the earth to curb the increase in miscreants, and not the increase in population, as is wrongly put forward by the mundane economist. When Lord Kṛṣṇa appeared, there had been a sufficient increase in miscreants who had violated the desire of the Lord. The material creation is meant for fulfilling the desire of the Lord, and His desire is that the conditioned souls who are unfit to enter into the kingdom of God have a chance to improve their conditions for entering. The entire process of cosmic arrangement is intended just to give a chance to the conditioned souls to enter the kingdom of God, and there is an adequate arrangement for their maintenance by the nature of the Lord.

Therefore, although there may be a great increase in population on the surface of the earth, if the people are exactly in line with God consciousness and are not miscreants, such a burden on the earth is a source of pleasure for her. There are two kinds of burdens. There is the burden of the beast and the burden of love. The burden of the beast is unbearable, but the burden of love is a source of pleasure. Śrīla Viśvanātha Cakravartī describes the burden of love very practically. He says that the burden of the husband on the young wife, the burden of the child on the lap of the mother, and the burden of wealth on the businessman, although actually burdens from the viewpoint of heaviness, are sources of pleasure, and in the absence of such burdensome objects, one may feel the burden of separation, which is heavier to bear than the actual burden of love. When Lord Kṛṣṇa referred to the burden of the Yadu dynasty on the earth, He referred to something different than the burden of the beast. The large numbers of family members born of Lord Kṛṣṇa counted to some millions and were certainly a great increase in the population of the earth, but because all of them were expansions of the Lord Himself by His transcendental plenary expansions, they were a source of great pleasure for the earth. When the Lord referred to them in connection with the burden on the earth, He had in mind their imminent disappearance from the earth. All the members of the family of Lord Kṛṣṇa were incarnations of different demigods, and they were to disappear from the surface of the earth along with the Lord. When He referred to the unbearable heaviness on the earth in connection with the Yadu dynasty, He was referring to the burden of their separation. Śrīla Jīva Gosvāmī confirms this inference.

TEXT 15

मिथो यदैषां भविता विवादो
मध्वामदाताम्रविलोचनानाम् ।
नैषां वधोपाय इयानतोऽन्यो
मय्युद्यतेऽन्तर्दधते स्वयं स्म ॥१५॥

mitho yadaiṣāṁ bhavitā vivādo
madhv-āmadātāmra-vilocanānām
naiṣāṁ vadhopāya iyān ato 'nyo
mayy udyate 'ntardadhate svayaṁ sma

mithaḥ—one another; *yadā*—when; *eṣām*—of them; *bhavitā*—will take place; *vivādaḥ*—quarrel; *madhu-āmada*—intoxication by drinking; *ātāmra-vilocanānām*—of their eyes being copper-red; *na*—not; *eṣām*—of them; *vadha-upāyaḥ*—means of disappearance; *iyān*—like this; *ataḥ*—besides this; *anyaḥ*—alternative; *mayi*—on My; *udyate*—disappearance; *antaḥ-dadhate*—will disappear; *svayam*—themselves; *sma*—certainly.

TRANSLATION

When they quarrel among themselves, influenced by intoxication, with their eyes red like copper because of drinking [madhu], then only will they disappear; otherwise, it will not be possible. On My disappearance, this incident will take place.

PURPORT

The Lord and His associates appear and disappear by the will of the Lord. They are not subjected to the laws of material nature. No one was able to kill the family of the Lord, nor was there any possibility of their natural death by the laws of nature. The only means, therefore, for their disappearance was the make-show of a fight amongst themselves, as if brawling in intoxication due to drinking. That so-called fighting would also take place by the will of the Lord, otherwise there would be no cause for their fighting. Just as Arjuna was made to be illusioned by family affection and thus the *Bhagavad-gītā* was spoken, so the Yadu dynasty was made to be intoxicated by the will of the Lord, and nothing more. The devotees and associates of the Lord are completely surrendered souls. Thus they are transcendental instruments in the hands of the Lord and can be used in any way the Lord desires. The pure devotees also enjoy such pastimes of the Lord because they want to see Him happy. Devotees of the Lord never assert independent individuality; on the contrary, they utilize their individuality in pursuit of the desires of the Lord, and this cooperation of the devotees with the Lord makes a perfect scene of the Lord's pastimes.

TEXT 16

एवं सञ्चिन्त्य भगवान् स्वराज्ये स्थाप्य धर्मजम् ।
नन्दयामास सुहृदः साधूनां वर्त्म दर्शयन् ॥१६॥

evaṁ sañcintya bhagavān
sva-rājye sthāpya dharmajam
nandayām āsa suhṛdaḥ
sādhūnāṁ vartma darśayan

evam—thus; *sañcintya*—thinking within Himself; *bhagavān*—the Personality of Godhead; *sva-rājye*—in his own kingdom; *sthāpya*—installing; *dharmajam*—Mahārāja Yudhiṣṭhira; *nandayām āsa*—gladdened; *suhṛdaḥ*—the friends; *sādhūnām*—of the saints; *vartma*—the path; *darśayan*—by indicating.

TRANSLATION

Lord Śrī Kṛṣṇa, thus thinking to Himself, established Mahārāja Yudhiṣṭhira in the position of supreme control of the world in order to show the ideal of administration on the path of piety.

TEXT 17

उत्तरायां धृतः पूरोर्वंशः साध्वभिमन्युना ।
स वै द्रौण्यस्त्रसम्प्लुष्टः पुनर्भगवता धृतः ॥१७॥

uttarāyāṁ dhṛtaḥ pūror
vaṁśaḥ sādhv-abhimanyunā
sa vai drauṇy-astra-sampluṣṭaḥ
punar bhagavatā dhṛtaḥ

uttarāyām—unto Uttarā; *dhṛtaḥ*—conceived; *pūroḥ*—of Pūru; *vaṁśaḥ*—descendant; *sādhu-abhimanyunā*—by the hero Abhimanyu; *saḥ*—he; *vai*—certainly; *drauṇi-astra*—by the weapon of Drauṇi, the son of Droṇa; *sampluṣṭaḥ*—being burnt; *punaḥ*—again, for the second time; *bhagavatā*—by the Personality of Godhead; *dhṛtaḥ*—was protected.

TRANSLATION

The embryo of Pūru's descendant begotten by the great hero Abhimanyu in the womb of Uttarā, his wife, was burnt by the weapon of the son of Droṇa, but later he was again protected by the Lord.

PURPORT

The embryonic body of Parīkṣit which was in formation after Uttarā's pregnancy by Abhimanyu, the great hero, was burned by the *brahmāstra* of Aśvatthāmā, but a second body was given by the Lord within the womb, and thus the descendant of Pūru was saved. This incident is the direct proof that the body and the living entity, the spiritual spark, are different. When the living entity takes shelter in the womb of a woman through the injection of the semen of a man, there is an emulsification of the man's and woman's discharges, and thus a body is formed the size of a pea, gradually developing into a complete body. But if the developing embryo is destroyed in some way or other, the living entity has to take shelter in another body or in the womb of another woman. The particular living entity who was selected to be the descendant of Mahārāja Pūru, or the Pāṇḍavas, was not an ordinary living entity, and by the superior will of the Lord he was destined to be the successor to Mahārāja Yudhiṣṭhira. Therefore, when Aśvatthāmā destroyed the embryo of Mahārāja Parīkṣit, the Lord, by His own internal potency, entered into the womb of Uttarā by His plenary portion just to give audience to the would-be Mahārāja Parīkṣit, who was in great danger. By His appearance within the womb, the Lord encouraged the child and gave him complete protection in a new body by His omnipotency. By His power of omnipresence He was present both inside and outside of Uttarā and other members of the Pāṇḍava family.

TEXT 18

अयाजयद्धर्मसुतमश्वमेधैस्त्रिभिर्विभुः ।
सोऽपि क्ष्मामनुजै रक्षन् रेमे कृष्णमनुव्रतः ॥१८॥

ayājayad dharma-sutam
aśvamedhais tribhir vibhuḥ

so 'pi kṣmām anujai rakṣan
reme kṛṣṇam anuvrataḥ

ayājayat—made to perform; *dharma-sutam*—by the son of Dharma (Mahārāja Yudhiṣṭhira); *aśvamedhaiḥ*—by horse sacrifices; *tribhiḥ*—three; *vibhuḥ*—the Supreme Lord; *saḥ*—Mahārāja Yudhiṣṭhira; *api*—also; *kṣmām*—the earth; *anujaiḥ*—assisted by his younger brothers; *rakṣan*—protecting; *reme*—enjoyed; *kṛṣṇam*—Kṛṣṇa, the Personality of Godhead; *anuvrataḥ*—constant follower.

TRANSLATION

The Supreme Lord induced the son of Dharma to perform three horse sacrifices, and Mahārāja Yudhiṣṭhira, constantly following Kṛṣṇa, the Personality of Godhead, protected and enjoyed the earth, assisted by his younger brothers.

PURPORT

Mahārāja Yudhiṣṭhira was the ideal monarchical representative on the earth because he was a constant follower of the Supreme Lord, Śrī Kṛṣṇa. As stated in the *Vedas* (*Īśopaniṣad*), the Lord is the proprietor of the entire manifested cosmic creation, which presents a chance for the conditioned souls to revive their eternal relationship with the Lord and thus go back to Godhead, back home. The whole system of the material world is arranged with that program and plan. Anyone who violates the plan is punished by the law of nature, which is acting by the direction of the Supreme Lord. Mahārāja Yudhiṣṭhira was installed on the throne of the earth as a representative of the Lord. The king is always expected to be the representative of the Lord. Perfect monarchy necessitates representation of the supreme will of the Lord, and Mahārāja Yudhiṣṭhira was the ideal monarch on this supreme principle. Both the King and the subjects were happy in the discharge of worldly duties, and thus protection of the citizens and enjoyment of natural life, with full cooperation of material nature, followed in the reign of Mahārāja Yudhiṣṭhira and his worthy descendants like Mahārāja Parīkṣit.

TEXT 19

भगवानपि विश्वात्मा लोकवेदपथानुगः ।
कामान् सिषेवे द्वार्वत्यामसक्तः सांख्यमास्थितः ॥१९॥

bhagavān api viśvātmā
loka-veda-pathānugaḥ

kāmān siṣeve dvārvatyām
asaktaḥ sāṅkhyam āsthitaḥ

bhagavān—the Personality of Godhead; *api*—also; *viśva-ātmā*—the Supersoul of the universe; *loka*—customary; *veda*—Vedic principles; *patha-anugaḥ*—follower of the path; *kāmān*—the necessities of life; *siṣeve*—enjoyed; *dvārvatyām*—in the city of Dvārakā; *asaktaḥ*—without being attached; *sāṅkhyam*—knowledge in Sāṅkhya philosophy; *āsthitaḥ*—being situated.

TRANSLATION

Simultaneously, the Personality of Godhead enjoyed life in the city of Dvārakā, strictly in conformity with the Vedic customs of society. He was situated in detachment and knowledge, as enunciated by the Sāṅkhya system of philosophy.

PURPORT

While Mahārāja Yudhiṣṭhira was the Emperor of the earth, Lord Śrī Kṛṣṇa was the King of Dvārakā and was known as Dvārakādhīśa. Like other subordinate kings, He was under the regime of Mahārāja Yudhiṣṭhira. Although Lord Śrī Kṛṣṇa is the supreme emperor of the entire creation, while He was on this earth He never violated the principles of the Vedic injunctions because they are the guide for human life. Regulated human life according to the Vedic principles, which are based on the system of knowledge called Sāṅkhya philosophy, is the real way of enjoyment of the necessities of life. Without such knowledge, detachment and custom, the so-called human civilization is no more than an animal society of eat, drink, be merry and enjoy. The Lord was acting freely, as He willed, yet by His practical example He taught not to lead a life which goes against the principles of detachment and knowledge. Attainment of knowledge and detachment, as very elaborately discussed in Sāṅkhya philosophy, is the real perfection of life. Knowledge means to know that the mission of the human form of life is to end all the miseries of material existence and that in spite of having to fulfill the bodily necessities in a regulated way, one must be detached from such animal life. Fulfilling the demands of the body is animal life, and fulfilling the mission of spirit soul is the human mission.

TEXT 20

स्निग्धस्मितावलोकेन वाचा पीयूषकल्पया ।
चरित्रेणानवद्येन श्रीनिकेतेन चात्मना ॥२०॥

snigdha-smitāvalokena
vācā pīyūṣa-kalpayā
caritreṇānavadyena
śrī-niketena cātmanā

snigdha—gentle; *smita-avalokena*—by a glance with a sweet smile; *vācā*—by words; *pīyūṣa-kalpayā*—compared to nectar; *caritreṇa*—by character; *anavadyena*—without flaw; *śrī*—fortune; *niketena*—residence; *ca*—and; *ātmanā*—by His transcendental body.

TRANSLATION

He was there in His transcendental body, the residence of the goddess of fortune, with His usual gentle and sweetly smiling face, His nectarean words and His flawless character.

PURPORT

In the previous verse it is described that Lord Kṛṣṇa, being situated in the truths of Sāṅkhya philosophy, is detached from all kinds of matter. In the present verse it is described that He is the residence of the goddess of fortune. These two things are not at all contradictory. Lord Kṛṣṇa is detached from the variegatedness of the inferior nature, but He is in eternal, blissful enjoyment of the spiritual nature, or His internal potency. One who has a poor fund of knowledge cannot understand this distinction between the external and internal potencies. In *Bhagavad-gītā,* the internal potency is described as the *parā prakṛti.* In the *Viṣṇu Purāṇa* also, the internal potency of Viṣṇu is described as *parā śakti.* The Lord is never detached from the association of *parā śakti.* This *parā śakti* and her manifestations are described in the *Brahma-saṁhitā* (5.37) as *ānanda-cinmaya-rasa-pratibhāvitābhiḥ.* The Lord is eternally joyful and cognizant in the taste derived from such transcendental bliss. Negation of the variegatedness of the inferior energy does not necessitate negation of the positive transcendental bliss of the spiritual world. Therefore the Lord's gentleness, His smile, His character and everything related to Him are all transcendental. Such manifestations of the internal potency are the reality, of which the material shadow is only a temporary representation from which everyone with proper knowledge must be detached.

TEXT 21

इमं लोकममुं चैव रमयन् सुतरां यदून् ।
रेमे क्षणदया दत्तक्षणस्त्रीक्षणसौहृदः ॥२१॥

imaṁ lokam amuṁ caiva
ramayan sutarāṁ yadūn
reme kṣaṇadayā datta-
kṣaṇa-strī-kṣaṇa-sauhṛdaḥ

imam—this; *lokam*—earth; *amum*—and the other worlds; *ca*—also; *eva*—certainly; *ramayan*—pleasing; *sutarām*—specifically; *yadūn*—the Yadus; *reme*—enjoyed; *kṣaṇadayā*—by night; *datta*—given by; *kṣaṇa*—leisure; *strī*—with women; *kṣaṇa*—conjugal love; *sauhṛdaḥ*—friendship.

TRANSLATION

The Lord enjoyed His pastimes, both in this world and in other worlds [higher planets], specifically in the association of the Yadu dynasty. At leisure hours offered by night, He enjoyed the friendship of conjugal love with women.

PURPORT

The Lord enjoyed in this world with His pure devotees. Although He is the Personality of Godhead and is transcendental to all material attachment, He nevertheless exhibited much attachment for His pure devotees on the earth, as well as for the demigods who engage in His service in the heavenly planets as powerful delegated directors in the management of all material activities. He displayed special attachment for His family members, the Yadus, as well as for His sixteen thousand wives, who had the opportunity to meet Him in the leisure hours of night. All these attachments of the Lord are manifestations of His internal potency, of which the external potency is only a shadow representation. In the *Skanda Purāṇa, Prabhāsa-khaṇḍa,* in the topics between Lord Śiva and Gaurī, there is confirmation of His internal potential manifestations. There is mention of the Lord's meeting with sixteen thousand cowherd damsels although He is the Haṁsa (transcendental) Supersoul and maintainer of all living entities. The sixteen thousand cowherd damsels are a display of sixteen varieties of internal potencies. This will be more elaborately explained in the Tenth Canto. It is said there that Lord Kṛṣṇa is just like the moon and the internal potential damsels are like the stars around the moon.

TEXT 22

तस्यैवं रममाणस्य संवत्सरगणान् बहून् ।
गृहमेधेषु योगेषु विरागः समजायत ॥२२॥

tasyaivaṁ ramamāṇasya
saṁvatsara-gaṇān bahūn
gṛhamedheṣu yogeṣu
virāgaḥ samajāyata

tasya—His; *evam*—thus; *ramamāṇasya*—enjoying; *saṁvatsara*—years; *gaṇān*—many; *bahūn*—great many; *gṛhamedheṣu*—in household life; *yogeṣu*—in sex life; *virāgaḥ*—detachment; *samajāyata*—awakened.

TRANSLATION

The Lord was thus engaged in household life for many, many years, but at last His detachment from ephemeral sex life was fully manifested.

PURPORT

Even though the Lord is never attached to any kind of material sex life, as the universal teacher He remained a householder for many, many years, just to teach others how one should live in householder life. Śrīla Viśvanātha Cakravartī Ṭhākura explains that the word *samajāyata* means "fully exhibited." In all His activities while present on the earth, the Lord exhibited detachment. This was fully displayed when He wanted to teach by example that one should not remain attached to household life for all the days of one's life. One should naturally develop detachment as a matter of course. The Lord's detachment from household life does not indicate detachment from His eternal associates, the transcendental cowherd damsels. But the Lord desired to end His so-called attachment to the three modes of material nature. He can never be detached from the service of His transcendental associates like Rukmiṇī and other goddesses of fortune, as described in the *Brahma-saṁhitā* (5.29): *lakṣmī-sahasra-śata-sambhrama-sevyamānam.*

TEXT 23

दैवाधीनेषु कामेषु दैवाधीनः स्वयं पुमान् ।
को विश्रम्भेत योगेन योगेश्वरमनुव्रतः ॥२३॥

daivādhīneṣu kāmeṣu
daivādhīnaḥ svayaṁ pumān
ko viśrambheta yogena
yogeśvaram anuvrataḥ

daiva—supernatural; *adhīneṣu*—being controlled; *kāmeṣu*—in sense enjoyment; *daiva-adhīnaḥ*—controlled by supernatural force; *svayam*—himself; *pumān*—living entity; *kaḥ*—whoever; *viśrambheta*—can have faith in; *yogena*—by devotional service; *yogeśvaram*—the Supreme Lord; *anuvrataḥ*—serving.

TRANSLATION

Every living entity is controlled by a supernatural force, and thus his sense enjoyment is also under the control of that supernatural force. No one, therefore, can put his faith in Lord Kṛṣṇa's transcendental sense activities but one who has become a devotee of the Lord by rendering devotional service.

PURPORT

As stated in *Bhagavad-gītā*, no one can understand the transcendental birth and activities of the Lord. The same fact is herein corroborated: no one but one who is enlightened by the devotional service of the Lord can understand the difference between the Lord's activities and those of others, who are controlled by the supernatural force. The sense enjoyment of all animals, men and demigods within the purview of the material universe is controlled by the supernatural force called the *prakṛti*, or *daivī-māyā*. No one is independent in obtaining sense enjoyment, and everyone in this material world is after sense enjoyment. Persons who are themselves under the control of supernatural power cannot believe that Lord Kṛṣṇa is not under any control beyond Himself in the matter of sense enjoyment. They cannot understand that His senses are transcendental. In the *Brahma-saṁhitā* the Lord's senses are described as omnipotent; i.e., with any sense He can perform the activities of the other senses. One who has limited senses cannot believe that the Lord can eat by His transcendental power of hearing and can perform the act of sex life simply by seeing. The controlled living entity cannot even dream of such sense activities in his conditional life. But simply by the activities of *bhakti-yoga*, he can understand that the Lord and His activities are always transcendental. As the Lord says in *Bhagavad-gītā* (18.55), *bhaktyā mām abhijānāti yāvān yaś cāsmi tattvataḥ:* one cannot know even a fraction of the activities of the Lord if he is not a pure devotee of the Lord.

TEXT 24

पुर्यां कदाचित्क्रीडद्भिर्यदुभोजकुमारकैः ।
कोपिता मुनयः शेपुर्भगवन्मतकोविदाः ॥२४॥

puryāṁ kadācit krīḍadbhir
yadu-bhoja-kumārakaiḥ
kopitā munayaḥ śepur
bhagavan-mata-kovidāḥ

puryām—in the city of Dvārakā; *kadācit*—once upon a time; *krīḍadbhiḥ*—by sporting activities; *yadu*—the descendants of Yadu; *bhoja*—the descendants of Bhoja; *kumārakaiḥ*—princes; *kopitāḥ*—became angry; *munayaḥ*—the great sages; *śepuḥ*—cursed; *bhagavat*—the Personality of Godhead; *mata*—desire; *kovidāḥ*—cognizant.

TRANSLATION

Once upon a time, great sages were made angry by the sporting activities of the princely descendants of the Yadu and Bhoja dynasties, and thus, as desired by the Lord, the sages cursed them.

PURPORT

The associates of the Lord who were playing the part of princely descendants of the Yadu and Bhoja dynasties were not ordinary living entities. It is not possible that they could offend any saintly man or sage, nor could the sages, who were all pure devotees of the Lord, be influenced to anger by any of the sporting activities of the princes born in the holy dynasties of Yadu or Bhoja, wherein the Lord Himself appeared as a descendant. The cursing of the princes by the sages was another transcendental pastime of the Lord to make a show of anger. The princes were cursed in order that one may know that even the descendants of the Lord, who could never be vanquished by any act of material nature, were subjected to the reactions of anger by great devotees of the Lord. One should therefore take great care and attention not to commit an offense at the feet of a devotee of the Lord.

TEXT 25

ततः कतिपयैर्मासैर्वृष्णिभोजान्धकादयः ।
ययुः प्रभासं संहृष्टा रथैर्देवविमोहिताः ॥२५॥

tataḥ katipayair māsair
vṛṣṇi-bhojāndhakādayaḥ
yayuḥ prabhāsaṁ saṁhṛṣṭā
rathair deva-vimohitāḥ

tataḥ—thereafter; *katipayaiḥ*—a few; *māsaiḥ*—months passing; *vṛṣṇi*—the descendants of Vṛṣṇi; *bhoja*—the descendants of Bhoja; *andhaka-ādayaḥ*—and others, like the sons of Andhaka; *yayuḥ*—went; *prabhāsam*—the place of pilgrimage named Prabhāsa; *saṁhṛṣṭāḥ*—with great pleasure; *rathaiḥ*—on their chariots; *deva*—by Kṛṣṇa; *vimohitāḥ*—bewildered.

TRANSLATION

A few months passed, and then, bewildered by Kṛṣṇa, all the descendants of Vṛṣṇi, Bhoja and Andhaka who were incarnations of demigods went to Prabhāsa, while those who were eternal devotees of the Lord did not leave but remained in Dvārakā.

TEXT 26

तत्र स्नात्वा पितॄन्देवानृषींश्चैव तदम्भसा ।
तर्पयित्वाथ विप्रेभ्यो गावो बहुगुणा ददुः ॥२६॥

tatra snātvā pitṝn devān
ṛṣīṁś caiva tad-ambhasā
tarpayitvātha viprebhyo
gāvo bahu-guṇā daduḥ

tatra—there; *snātvā*—by taking bath; *pitṝn*—forefathers; *devān*—demigods; *ṛṣīn*—great sages; *ca*—also; *eva*—certainly; *tat*—of that; *ambhasā*—by the water; *tarpayitvā*—by pleasing; *atha*—thereupon; *viprebhyaḥ*—unto the *brāhmaṇas; gāvaḥ*—cows; *bahu-guṇāḥ*—greatly useful; *daduḥ*—gave in charity.

TRANSLATION

After arriving there, all of them took bath, and with the water of this place of pilgrimage they offered their respects to the forefathers, demigods and great sages and thus satisfied them. They gave cows to the brāhmaṇas in royal charity.

PURPORT

Amongst the devotees of the Lord there are several divisions, mainly *nitya-siddhas* and *sādhana-siddhas.* The *nitya-siddha* devotees never fall down to the region of the material atmosphere, even though they sometimes come onto the material plane to execute the mission of the Lord. The *sādhana-siddha* devotees are chosen from the conditioned souls. Out of the *sādhana* devotees, there are mixed and pure devotees.

The mixed devotees are sometimes enthusiastic about fruitive activities and are habituated to philosophical speculation. The pure devotees are free from all these mixtures and are completely absorbed in the service of the Lord, regardless of how and where they are situated. Pure devotees of the Lord are not enthusiastic to put aside their service to the Lord in order to go visit holy places of pilgrimage. A great devotee of the Lord in modern times, Śrī Narottama dāsa Ṭhākura, has sung like this: "To visit holy places of pilgrimage is another bewilderment of the mind because devotional service to the Lord at any place is the last word in spiritual perfection."

For pure devotees of the Lord who are completely satisfied with the transcendental loving service of the Lord, there is hardly any necessity to visit the various places of pilgrimage. But those who are not so advanced have the prescribed duties of visiting pilgrimage sites and regularly performing the rituals. The part of the princely order of the Yadu dynasty who went to Prabhāsa performed all duties to be done in a place of pilgrimage and offered their pious actions to their forefathers and others.

As a rule, every human being is indebted to God, the demigods, great sages, other living entities, people in general, forefathers, etc., for various contributions received from them. Thus everyone is obliged to repay the debt of gratitude. The Yadus who went to the Prabhāsa pilgrimage site performed their duties by distributing land, gold, and well-nourished cows in royal charity, as described in the following verse.

TEXT 27

हिरण्यं रजतं शय्यां वासांस्यजिनकम्बलान् ।
यानं रथानिभान् कन्या धरां वृत्तिकरीमपि ॥२७॥

hiraṇyaṁ rajataṁ śayyāṁ
vāsāṁsy ajina-kambalān
yānaṁ rathān ibhān kanyā
dharāṁ vṛtti-karīm api

hiraṇyam—gold; *rajatam*—gold coins; *śayyām*—bedding; *vāsāṁsi*—clothing; *ajina*—animal skin for seats; *kambalān*—blankets; *yānam*—horses; *rathān*—chariots; *ibhān*—elephants; *kanyāḥ*—girls; *dharām*—land; *vṛtti-karīm*—to provide livelihood; *api*—also.

TRANSLATION

The brāhmaṇas were not only given well-fed cows in charity, but also gold, gold coins, bedding, clothing, animal-skin seats, blankets, horses, elephants, girls and sufficient land for maintenance.

PURPORT

All these charities were meant for the *brāhmaṇas,* whose lives were devoted entirely to the welfare of society, both spiritually and materially. The *brāhmaṇas* were not giving their services as paid servants, but the society provided them with all necessities. It was arranged for some of the *brāhmaṇas,* who were in difficulty for marriage, to be given girls. The *brāhmaṇas,* therefore, had no economic problems. The *kṣatriya* kings and rich mercantile men would provide them with all that they needed, and in exchange the *brāhmaṇas* were completely devoted to the elevation of society. That was the way of social cooperation between the different castes. When the *brāhmaṇa* class or caste gradually became easygoing, being fed by the society although they had no brahminical qualifications, they degraded themselves into *brahma-bandhus,* or disqualified *brāhmaṇas,* and thus other members of society also gradually fell down from the social standard of progressive life. As described in *Bhagavad-gītā,* the caste system is the creation of the Lord and is arranged according to the quality of work rendered to society and not in terms of birthright, as falsely claimed in the present degraded society.

TEXT 28

अन्नं चोरुरसं तेभ्यो दत्त्वा भगवदर्पणम् ।
गोविप्रार्थासवः शूराः प्रणेमुर्भुवि मूर्धभिः ॥२८॥

annaṁ coru-rasaṁ tebhyo
dattvā bhagavad-arpaṇam
go-viprārthāsavaḥ śūrāḥ
praṇemur bhuvi mūrdhabhiḥ

annam—foodstuff; *ca*—also; *uru-rasam*—highly delicious; *tebhyaḥ*—unto the *brāhmaṇas; dattvā*—after supplying; *bhagavat-arpaṇam*—which was first offered to the Personality of Godhead; *go*—cows; *vipra*—*brāhmaṇas; artha*—purpose; *asavaḥ*—purpose of living; *śūrāḥ*—all the valiant *kṣatriyas; praṇemuḥ*—offered obeisances; *bhuvi*—touching the ground; *mūrdhabhiḥ*—with their heads.

TRANSLATION

Thereafter they offered the brāhmaṇas highly delicious foodstuffs first offered to the Personality of Godhead and offered their respectful obeisances by touching their heads to the ground. They lived perfectly by protecting the cows and the brāhmaṇas.

PURPORT

The behavior exhibited by the descendants of Yadu in the pilgrimage site of Prabhāsa was highly cultured and exactly to the point of human perfection. The perfection of human life is attained by following three principles of civilization: protecting the cows, maintaining the brahminical culture and, above all, becoming a pure devotee of the Lord. Without becoming a devotee of the Lord, one cannot perfect one's human life. The perfection of human life is to be elevated to the spiritual world, where there is no birth, no death, no disease and no old age. That is the highest perfectional aim of human life. Without this aim, any amount of material advancement in so-called comforts can only bring the defeat of the human form of life.

Brāhmaṇas and Vaiṣṇavas do not accept any foodstuff which is not first offered to the Personality of Godhead. Foodstuff offered to the Lord is accepted by the devotees as the mercy of the Lord. After all, the Lord supplies all kinds of foodstuff, both to the human being and to other animals. A human being must be conscious of the fact that all foodstuffs, namely grains, vegetables, milk, water, etc.—the prime necessities of life—are supplied for mankind by the Lord, and such foodstuffs cannot be manufactured by any scientist or materialist in a laboratory or factory established by human effort. The intelligent class of men are called *brāhmaṇas,* and those who have realized the Absolute Truth in His supreme personal feature are called Vaiṣṇavas. But both of them accept foodstuffs which are the remnants of sacrifice. Sacrifice is ultimately meant to satisfy the *yajña-puruṣa,* Viṣṇu. In *Bhagavad-gītā* (3.13) it is said that one who accepts foodstuffs as the remnants of sacrifice is freed from all sinful reactions, and one who cooks foodstuffs for maintenance of his body takes in all kinds of sins, which lead only to suffering. The foodstuffs prepared by the Yadus at the Prabhāsa pilgrimage site to offer to the bona fide *brāhmaṇas* there were all offered to the Personality of Godhead, Viṣṇu. The Yadus offered their sincere obeisances by touching their heads to the ground. The Yadus or any enlightened family in Vedic culture are trained for attainment of human perfection by total cooperation of service between the different divisions of social orders.

The word *uru-rasam* is also significant here. Hundreds of delicacies can be prepared simply by the combination of grains, vegetables and milk. All such preparations are in the mode of goodness and therefore may be offered to the Personality of Godhead. As stated in *Bhagavad-gītā* (9.26), the Lord accepts only foodstuffs which are within the range of fruits, flowers, leaves and liquids, provided they are offered in complete devotional service. Devotional service is the only criterion for a bona fide offering to the Lord. The Lord assures that He positively eats such foodstuffs offered by the devotees.

So, judging from all sides, the Yadus were perfectly trained civilized persons, and their being cursed by the *brāhmaṇa* sages was only by the desire of the Lord; the whole incident was a warning to all concerned that no one should behave lightly with *brāhmaṇas* and Vaiṣṇavas.

Thus end the Bhaktivedanta purports of the Third Canto, Third Chapter, of the Śrīmad-Bhāgavatam, *entitled "The Lord's pastimes Out of Vṛndāvana."*

CHAPTER FOUR

Vidura Approaches Maitreya

TEXT 1

उद्धव उवाच

अथ ते तदनुज्ञाता भुक्त्वा पीत्वा च वारुणीम् ।
तया विभ्रंशितज्ञाना दुरुक्तैर्मर्म पस्पृशुः ॥ १ ॥

uddhava uvāca

atha te tad-anujñātā
bhuktvā pītvā ca vāruṇīm
tayā vibhraṁśita-jñānā
duruktair marma paspṛśuḥ

uddhavaḥ uvāca—Uddhava said; *atha*—thereafter; *te*—they (the Yādavas); *tat*—by the *brahmaṇas*; *anujñātāḥ*—being permitted; *bhuktvā*—after partaking; *pītvā*—drinking; *ca*—and; *vāruṇīm*—liquor; *tayā*—by that; *vibhraṁśita-jñānāḥ*—being bereft of knowledge; *duruktaiḥ*—with harsh words; *marma*—the core of the heart; *paspṛśuḥ*—touched.

TRANSLATION

Thereafter, all of them [the descendants of Vṛṣṇi and Bhoja], being permitted by the brāhmaṇas, partook of the remnants of prasāda and also drank liquor made of rice. By drinking they all became delirious, and, bereft of knowledge, they touched the cores of each other's hearts with harsh words.

PURPORT

In ceremonies when *brāhmaṇas* and Vaiṣṇavas are sumptuously fed, the host partakes of the remnants of foodstuff after the guest has given permission. So the descendants of Vṛṣṇi and Bhoja formally took permission from the *brāhmaṇas* and ate the prepared foodstuff. *Kṣatriyas* are permitted to drink at certain occasions, so they all drank a kind of light liquor made of rice. By such drinking they became delirious and bereft of sense, so much so that they forgot their relationship with one another and used harsh words which touched the cores of each other's hearts. Drinking is so harmful that even such a highly cultured family becomes affected by intoxication and can forget themselves in a drunken state. The descendants of Vṛṣṇi and Bhoja were not expected to forget themselves in this way, but by the will of the Supreme it happened, and thus they became harsh towards one another.

TEXT 2

तेषां मैरेयदोषेण विषमीकृतचेतसाम् ।
निम्लोचति रवावासीद्वेणूनामिव मर्दनम् ॥ २ ॥

teṣāṁ maireya-doṣeṇa
viṣamīkṛta-cetasām
nimlocati ravāv āsīd
veṇūnām iva mardanam

teṣām—of them; *maireya*—of intoxication; *doṣeṇa*—by the faults; *viṣamīkṛta*—became unbalanced; *cetasām*—of those of whom the minds; *nimlocati*—sets; *ravau*—the sun; *āsīt*—takes place; *veṇūnām*—of the bamboos; *iva*—as; *mardanam*—destruction.

TRANSLATION

As by the friction of bamboos destruction takes place, so also, at sunset, by the interaction of the faults of intoxication, all their minds became unbalanced, and destruction took place.

PURPORT

When there is need of fire in the forest, by the will of the Supreme it takes place due to friction among the bamboos. Similarly, the descendants of Yadu were all destroyed by the will of the Lord by the process of self-destruction. Just as there is no possibility of a fire's occurring deep in the forest due to human effort, so also there was no power in the universe which could vanquish the descendants of Yadu, who were protected by the Lord. The Lord wanted them to be so destroyed, and thus they obeyed His order, as indicated by the word *tad-anujñāta.*

TEXT 3

भगवान् स्वात्ममायाया गतिं तामवलोक्य सः ।
सरस्वतीमुपस्पृश्य वृक्षमूलमुपाविशत् ॥ ३ ॥

bhagavān svātma-māyāyā
gatiṁ tām avalokya saḥ

sarasvatīm upaspṛśya
vṛkṣa-mūlam upāviśat

bhagavān—the Personality of Godhead; *sva-ātma-māyāyā*—by His internal potency; *gatim*—the end; *tām*—that; *avalokya*—foreseeing; *saḥ*—He (Kṛṣṇa); *sarasvatīm*—the River Sarasvatī; *upaspṛśya*—after sipping water; *vṛkṣa-mūlam*—at the foot of a tree; *upāviśat*—sat down.

TRANSLATION

The Personality of Godhead, Lord Śrī Kṛṣṇa, after foreseeing the end [of His family] by His internal potency, went to the bank of the River Sarasvatī, sipped water, and sat down underneath a tree.

PURPORT

All the above-mentioned activities of the Yadus and Bhojas were executed by the internal potency of the Lord because He wanted them to be dispatched to their respective abodes after He had finished His mission of descent. They were all His sons and grandsons and were given complete protection by the paternal affection of the Lord. How they could be vanquished in the presence of the Lord is answered in this verse: everything was done by the Lord Himself (*svātma-māyāyāḥ*). The Lord's family members were either incarnations of His plenary expansions or demigods from the heavenly planets, and thus before His departure He separated them by His internal potency. Before being dispatched to their respective abodes, they were sent to the holy place of Prabhāsa, where they performed pious activities and took food and drink to their heart's content. It was then arranged for them to be sent back to their abodes so that others could see that the powerful Yadu dynasty was no longer in the world. In the previous verse, the word *anujñāta,* indicating that the whole sequence of events was arranged by the Lord, is significant. These particular pastimes of the Lord are not a manifestation of His external energy, or material nature. Such an exhibition of His internal potency is eternal, and therefore one should not conclude that the Yadus and Bhojas died in a drunken state in an ordinary fratricidal war. Śrī Jīva Gosvāmī comments on these incidents as magical performances.

TEXT 4

अहं चोक्तो भगवता प्रपन्नार्तिहरेण ह ।
बदरीं त्वं प्रयाहीति स्वकुलं सञ्जिहीर्षुणा ॥ ४ ॥

ahaṁ cokto bhagavatā
prapannārti-hareṇa ha
badarīṁ tvaṁ prayāhīti
sva-kulaṁ sañjihīrṣuṇā

aham—I; *ca*—and; *uktaḥ*—was told; *bhagavatā*—by the Supreme Lord; *prapanna*—of the surrendered; *ārti-hareṇa*—by He who is the vanquisher of the distresses; *ha*—indeed; *badarīm*—to Badarī; *tvam*—you; *prayāhi*—should go; *iti*—thus; *sva-kulam*—His own family; *sañjihīrṣuṇā*—who desired to destroy.

TRANSLATION

The Lord is the vanquisher of the distresses of one who is surrendered unto Him. Thus He who desired to destroy His family told me previously to go to Badarikāśrama.

PURPORT

While at Dvārakā, Uddhava was warned to avoid the distresses which were to follow the disappearance of the Lord and the destruction of the Yadu dynasty. He was advised to proceed to Badarikāśrama because there he could associate with the devotees of Nara-Nārāyaṇa, and in their association of devotional service he could increase his eagerness for chanting, hearing, knowledge and detachment.

TEXT 5

तथापि तदभिप्रेतं जानन्नहमरिन्दम ।
पृष्ठतोऽन्वगमं भर्तुः पादविश्लेषणाक्षमः ॥ ५ ॥

tathāpi tad-abhipretaṁ
jānann aham arindama
pṛṣṭhato 'nvagamaṁ bhartuḥ
pāda-viśleṣaṇākṣamaḥ

tathā api—yet, in spite of; *tat-abhipretam*—His desire; *jānan*—knowing; *aham*—I; *arimdama*—O subduer of the enemy (Vidura); *pṛṣṭhataḥ*—behind; *anvagamam*—followed; *bhartuḥ*—of the master; *pāda-viśleṣaṇa*—separation from His lotus feet; *akṣamaḥ*—not being able.

TRANSLATION

Yet in spite of my knowing His desire [to destroy the dynasty], O Arindama [Vidura], I followed Him because it was impossible for me to bear separation from the lotus feet of the master.

TEXT 6

अद्राक्षमेकमासीनं विचिन्वन् दयितं पतिम् ।
श्रीनिकेतं सरस्वत्यां कृतकेतमकेतनम् ॥ ६ ॥

adrākṣam ekam āsīnaṁ
vicinvan dayitaṁ patim
śrī-niketaṁ sarasvatyāṁ
kṛta-ketam aketanam

adrākṣam—I saw; *ekam*—alone; *āsīnam*—sitting; *vicinvan*—deeply thinking; *dayitam*—patron; *patim*—master; *śrī-niketam*—the shelter of the goddess of fortune; *sarasvatyām*—on the bank of the Sarasvatī; *kṛta-ketam*—taking shelter; *aketanam*—being situated without a shelter.

TRANSLATION

Thus following, I saw my patron and master [Lord Śrī Kṛṣṇa] sitting alone and deeply thinking, taking shelter on the bank of the River Sarasvatī although He is the shelter of the goddess of fortune.

PURPORT

Those who are in the renounced order of life often take shelter underneath a tree. The Lord was found by Uddhava in that condition of taking shelter as do persons who have no shelter. Because He is the proprietor of everything, everywhere is His shelter, and everywhere is under His shelter. The entire material and spiritual cosmic manifestation is sustained by Him, and therefore He is the shelter of everything. So there was nothing astonishing in His taking shelter in the way of the unsheltered who are in the renounced order of life.

TEXT 7

श्यामावदातं विरजं प्रशान्तारुणलोचनम् ।
दोर्भिश्चतुर्भिर्विदितं पीतकौशाम्बरेण च ॥ ७ ॥

śyāmāvadātaṁ virajaṁ
praśāntāruṇa-locanam
dorbhiś caturbhir viditaṁ
pīta-kauśāmbareṇa ca

śyāma-avadātam—beautiful with black color; *virajam*—formed of pure goodness; *praśānta*—peaceful; *aruṇa*—reddish; *locanam*—eyes; *dorbhiḥ*—by the arms; *caturbhiḥ*—four; *viditam*—being recognized; *pīta*—yellow; *kauśa*—silken; *ambareṇa*—with garments; *ca*—and.

TRANSLATION

The Lord's body is blackish, but is eternal, full of bliss and knowledge, and very, very beautiful. His eyes are always peaceful, and they are reddish like the rising morning sun. I could immediately recognize Him as the Supreme Personality of Godhead by His four hands, different symbolic representations, and yellow silk garments.

TEXT 8

वाम ऊरावधिश्रित्य दक्षिणाङ्घ्रिसरोरुहम् ।
अपाश्रितार्भकाश्वत्थमकृशं त्यक्तपिप्पलम् ॥ ८ ॥

vāma ūrāv adhiśritya
dakṣiṇāṅghri-saroruham
apāśritārbhakāśvattham
akṛśaṁ tyakta-pippalam

vāme—on the left; *ūrau*—thigh; *adhiśritya*—placed on; *dakṣiṇa-aṅghri-saroruham*—the right lotus foot; *apāśrita*—taking rest against; *arbhaka*—young; *aśvattham*—banyan tree; *akṛśam*—cheerful; *tyakta*—having left; *pippalam*—household comforts.

TRANSLATION

The Lord was sitting, taking rest against a young banyan tree, with His right lotus foot on His left thigh, and although He had left all household comforts, He looked quite cheerful in that posture.

PURPORT

According to Śrīla Viśvanātha Cakravartī Ṭhākura, the Lord's sitting posture—keeping His back against the newly grown banyan tree—is also meaningful. *Aśvattha,* the banyan tree, is so called because the tree does not die very quickly; it continues to live for many, many years. His legs and their energies are the material ingredients, which are five in all: earth, water, fire, air and sky. The material energies represented by the banyan tree are all products of His external potency and are therefore kept to His back. And because this particular universe is the smallest of all, the banyan tree is therefore designated as small, or as a child. *Tyakta-pippalam* indicates that He had now finished His pastimes in this particular small universe, but since the Lord is absolute and eternally blissful, there is no difference between His leaving or accepting something. The Lord was now prepared to leave this particular universe and go into another, just as the sun rises on one particular planet and sets in another simultaneously but does not change its own situation.

TEXT 9

तस्मिन्महाभागवतो द्वैपायनसुहृत्सखा ।
लोकाननुचरन् सिद्ध आससाद यदृच्छया ॥ ९ ॥

tasmin mahā-bhāgavato
dvaipāyana-suhṛt-sakhā
lokān anucaran siddha
āsasāda yadṛcchayā

tasmin—then; *mahā-bhāgavataḥ*—a great devotee of the Lord; *dvaipāyana*—of Kṛṣṇa-dvaipāyana Vyāsa; *suhṛt*—a well-wisher; *sakhā*—a friend; *lokān*—the three worlds; *anucaran*—traveling; *siddhe*—in that *āśrama;* *āsasāda*—arrived; *yadṛcchayā*—by his own perfect accord.

TRANSLATION

At that time, after traveling in many parts of the world, Maitreya, a great devotee of the Lord and a friend and well-wisher of the great sage Kṛṣṇa-dvaipāyana Vyāsa, reached that spot out of his own perfect accord.

PURPORT

Maitreya was one of the disciples of Maharṣi Parāśara, the father of Vyāsadeva. Thus Vyāsadeva and Maitreya were friends and mutual well-wishers. By some fortunate accident, Maitreya reached the place where Lord Śrī Kṛṣṇa was resting. To meet the Lord is not an ordinary incident. Maitreya was a great sage and a learned scholar-philosopher but not a pure devotee of the Lord, and therefore his meeting with the Lord at that time may have been due to *ajñāta-sukṛti,* or some unknown devotional service. Pure devotees always engage in pure devotional activities, and therefore their meeting with the Lord is natural. But when those who are not up to that standard meet the Lord, it is due to the unforeseen fortune of accidental devotional service.

TEXT 10

तस्यानुरक्तस्य मुनेर्मुकुन्दः
प्रमोदभावानतकन्धरस्य ।
आश्रृण्वतो मामनुरागहास-
समीक्षया विश्रमयन्नुवाच ॥१०॥

tasyānuraktasya muner mukundaḥ
pramoda-bhāvānata-kandharasya
āśṛṇvato mām anurāga-hāsa-
samīkṣayā viśramayann uvāca

tasya—his (Maitreya's); *anuraktasya*—although attached; *muneḥ*—of the sage; *mukundaḥ*—the Lord who awards salvation; *pramoda-bhāva*—in a pleasing attitude; *ānata*—lowered; *kandharasya*—of the shoulder; *āśṛṇvataḥ*—while thus hearing; *mām*—unto me; *anurāga-hāsa*—with kind smiling; *samīkṣayā*—particularly seeing me; *viśra-mayan*—allowing me complete rest; *uvāca*—said.

TRANSLATION

Maitreya Muni was greatly attached to Him [the Lord], and he was listening in a pleasing attitude, with his shoulder lowered. With a smile and a particular glance upon me, having allowed me to rest, the Lord spoke as follows.

PURPORT

Although both Uddhava and Maitreya were great souls, the Lord's attention was more on Uddhava because he was a spotlessly pure devotee. A *jñāna-bhakta,* or one whose devotion is mixed with the monistic viewpoint, is not a pure devotee. Although Maitreya was a devotee, his devotion was mixed. The Lord reciprocates with His devotees on the basis of transcendental love and not on the basis of philosophical knowledge or fruitive activities. In the transcendental loving service of the Lord, there is no place for monistic knowledge or fruitive activities. The *gopīs* in Vṛndāvana were neither highly learned scholars nor mystic *yogīs.* They had spontaneous love for the Lord, and thus He became their heart and soul, and the *gopīs* also became the heart and soul of the Lord. Lord Caitanya approved the relationship of the *gopīs* with the Lord as supreme. Herein the Lord's attitude towards Uddhava was more intimate than with Maitreya Muni.

TEXT 11

श्रीभगवानुवाच
वेदाहमन्तर्मनसीप्सितं ते
ददामि यत्तद् दुरवापमन्यैः ।
सत्रे पुरा विश्वसृजां वसूनां
मत्सिद्धिकामेन वसो त्वयेष्टः ॥११॥

śrī-bhagavān uvāca
vedāham antar manasīpsitaṁ te
dadāmi yat tad duravāpam anyaiḥ
satre purā viśva-sṛjāṁ vasūnāṁ
mat-siddhi-kāmena vaso tvayeṣṭaḥ

śrī-bhagavān uvāca—the Personality of Godhead said; *veda*—know; *aham*—I; *antaḥ*—within; *manasi*—the mind; *īpsitam*—what you desired; *te*—your; *dadāmi*—I give you; *yat*—which is; *tat*—that; *duravāpam*—very difficult to achieve; *anyaiḥ*—by others; *satre*—in the sacrifice; *purā*—in the days of yore; *viśva-sṛjām*—of those who expanded this creation; *vasūnām*—of the Vasus; *mat-siddhi-kāmena*—with a desire to achieve My association; *vaso*—O Vasu; *tvayā*—by you; *iṣṭaḥ*—ultimate goal of life.

TRANSLATION

O Vasu, I know from within your mind what you desired in the days of yore when the Vasus and other demigods responsible for expanding the universal affairs performed sacrifices. You particularly desired to achieve My association. This is very difficult to obtain for others, but I award it unto you.

PURPORT

Uddhava is one of the eternal associates of the Lord, and a plenary portion of Uddhava was one of the eight Vasus in the days of yore. The eight Vasus and the demigods in the upper planetary system, who are responsible for the management of the universal affairs, performed a sacrifice in the days of yore, desiring to fulfill their respective ultimate goals in life. At that time an expansion of Uddhava, acting as one of the Vasus, desired to become an associate of the Lord. The Lord knew this because He is present in the heart of every living entity as Paramātmā, the Superconsciousness. In everyone's heart there is the representation of the Superconsciousness, who gives memory to the partial consciousness of every living entity. The living entity, as partial consciousness, forgets incidents of his past life, but the Superconsciousness reminds him how to act in terms of his past cultivation of knowledge. *Bhagavad-gītā* confirms this fact in various ways: *ye yathā māṁ prapadyante tāṁs tathaiva bhajāmy aham* (Bg. 4.11), *sarvasya cāhaṁ hṛdi sanniviṣṭo mattaḥ smṛtir jñānam apohanaṁ ca* (Bg. 15.15).

Everyone is at liberty to desire as he likes, but the desire is fulfilled by the Supreme Lord. Everyone is independent to think or desire, but the fulfillment of one's desire depends on the supreme will. This law is expressed as "Man proposes, God disposes." In the days of yore, when the demigods and Vasus performed sacrifice, Uddhava, as one of the Vasus, desired to enter into the association of the Lord, which is very difficult for those busy in empiric philosophical speculation or fruitive activities. Such persons have practically no information of the facts about becoming an associate of the Lord. Only the pure devotees can know, by the mercy of the Lord, that the personal association of the Lord is the highest perfection of life. The Lord assured Uddhava that He would fulfill his desire. It appears that when the Lord informed him by His indication to Uddhava, the great sage Maitreya finally became aware of the importance of entering into the association of the Lord.

TEXT 12

स एष साधो चरमो भवाना-
मासादितस्ते मदनुग्रहो यत् ।
यन्मां नृलोकान् रह उत्सृजन्तं
दिष्ट्या ददृश्वान् विशदानुवृत्त्या ॥१२॥

sa eṣa sādho caramo bhavānām
āsāditas te mad-anugraho yat
yan māṁ nṛlokān raha utsṛjantaṁ
diṣṭyā dadṛśvān viśadānuvṛttyā

saḥ—that; *eṣaḥ*—of those; *sādho*—O honest one; *caramaḥ*—the ultimate; *bhavānām*—of all your incarnations (as Vasu); *āsāditaḥ*—now achieved; *te*—unto you; *mat*—My; *anugrahaḥ*—mercy; *yat*—as it is; *yat*—because; *mām*—Me; *nṛ-lokān*—the planets of the conditioned souls; *rahaḥ*—in seclusion; *utsṛjantam*—while quitting; *diṣṭyā*—by seeing; *dadṛśvān*—what you have seen; *viśada-anuvṛttyā*—by unflinching devotion.

TRANSLATION

O honest one, your present life is the last and the supermost because in this term of life you have been awarded My ultimate favor. Now you can go to My transcendental abode, Vaikuṇṭha, by leaving this universe of conditioned

living entities. Your visit to Me in this lonely place because of your pure and unflinching devotional service is a great boon for you.

PURPORT

When a person is fully conversant with knowledge of the Lord as far as can be known by a perfect living entity in the liberated state, he is allowed to enter into the spiritual sky, where the Vaikuṇṭha planets exist. The Lord was sitting in a lonely place just about to disappear from the vision of the inhabitants of this universe, and Uddhava was fortunate to see Him even at that time and thus receive the Lord's permission to enter Vaikuṇṭha. The Lord is everywhere at all times, and His appearance and disappearance are merely the experience of the inhabitants of a particular universe. He is just like the sun. The sun does not appear or disappear in the sky; it is only in the experience of men that in the morning the sun rises and in the evening the sun sets. The Lord is simultaneously both in Vaikuṇṭha and everywhere within and without Vaikuṇṭha.

TEXT 13

पुरा मया प्रोक्तमजाय नाभ्ये
पद्मे निषण्णाय ममादिसर्गे ।
ज्ञानं परं मन्महिमावभासं
यत्सूरयो भागवतं वदन्ति ॥१३॥

purā mayā proktam ajāya nābhye
padme niṣaṇṇāya mamādi-sarge
jñānaṁ paraṁ man-mahimāvabhāsam
yat sūrayo bhāgavataṁ vadanti

purā—in the days of yore; *mayā*—by Me; *proktam*—was said; *ajāya*—unto Brahmā; *nābhye*—out of the navel; *padme*—on the lotus; *niṣaṇṇāya*—unto the one situated on; *mama*—My; *ādi-sarge*—in the beginning of creation; *jñānam*—knowledge; *param*—sublime; *mat-mahimā*—My transcendental glories; *avabhāsam*—that which clarifies; *yat*—which; *sūrayaḥ*—the great learned sages; *bhāgavatam*—*Śrīmad-Bhāgavatam*; *vadanti*—do say.

TRANSLATION

O Uddhava, in the lotus millennium in the days of yore, at the beginning of the creation, I spoke unto Brahmā, who is situated on the lotus that grows out of My navel, about My transcendental glories, which the great sages describe as Śrīmad-Bhāgavatam.

PURPORT

The explanation of the Supreme Self, as given to Brahmā and already explained in the Second Canto of this great literature, is further clarified herein. The Lord said that the concise form of *Śrīmad-Bhāgavatam* as explained to Brahmā was meant to elucidate His personality. The impersonal explanation of those four verses in the Second Canto is nullified herewith. Śrīdhara Svāmī also explains in this connection that the same concise form of the *Bhāgavatam* concerned the pastimes of Lord Kṛṣṇa and was never meant for impersonal indulgence.

TEXT 14

इत्यादृतोक्तः परमस्य पुंसः
प्रतिक्षणानुग्रहभाजनोऽहम् ।
स्नेहोत्थरोमा स्खलिताक्षरस्तं
मुञ्चञ्छुचः प्राञ्जलिराबभाषे ॥१४॥

ity ādṛtoktaḥ paramasya puṁsaḥ
pratikṣaṇānugraha-bhājano 'ham
snehottha-romā skhalitākṣaras taṁ
muñcañ chucaḥ prāñjalir ābabhāṣe

iti—thus; *ādṛta*—being favored; *uktaḥ*—addressed; *paramasya*—of the Supreme; *puṁsaḥ*—Personality of Godhead; *pratikṣaṇa*—every moment; *anugraha-bhājanaḥ*—object of favor; *aham*—myself; *sneha*—affection; *uttha*—eruption; *romā*—hairs on the body; *skhalita*—slackened; *akṣaraḥ*—of the eyes; *tam*—that; *muñcan*—smearing; *śucaḥ*—tears; *prāñjaliḥ*—with folded hands; *ābabhāṣe*—said.

TRANSLATION

Uddhava said: O Vidura, when I was thus favored at every moment by the Supreme Personality of Godhead and addressed by Him with great affection, my words failed in tears, and the hairs on my body erupted. After smearing my tears, I, with folded hands, spoke like this.

TEXT 15

को न्वीश ते पादसरोजभाजां
सुदुर्लभोऽर्थेषु चतुर्ष्वपीह ।
तथापि नाहं प्रवृणोमि भूमन्
भवत्पदाम्भोजनिषेवणोत्सुकः ॥१५॥

ko nv īśa te pāda-saroja-bhājāṁ
sudurlabho 'rtheṣu caturṣv apīha
tathāpi nāhaṁ pravṛṇomi bhūman
bhavat-padāmbhoja-niṣevaṇotsukaḥ

kaḥ nu īśa—O my Lord; *te*—Your; *pāda-saroja-bhājām*—of the devotees engaged in the transcendental loving service of Your lotus feet; *su-durlabhaḥ*—very difficult to obtain; *artheṣu*—in the matter of; *caturṣu*—in the four objectives; *api*—in spite of; *iha*—in this world; *tathā api*—yet; *na*—do not; *aham*—I; *pravṛṇomi*—prefer; *bhūman*—O great one; *bhavat*—Your; *pada-ambhoja*—lotus feet; *niṣevaṇa-utsukaḥ*—anxious to serve.

TRANSLATION

O my Lord, devotees who engage in the transcendental loving service of Your lotus feet have no difficulty in achieving anything within the realm of the four principles of religiosity, economic development, sense gratification and liberation. But, O great one, as far as I am concerned, I have preferred only to engage in the loving service of Your lotus feet.

PURPORT

Those who are associated with the Lord in the Vaikuṇṭha planets achieve all the bodily features of the Lord and appear to be the same as Lord Viṣṇu. Such liberation is called *sārūpya-mukti,* which is one of the five kinds of liberation. The devotees engaged in the transcendental loving service of the Lord never accept the *sāyujya-mukti,* or merging in the rays of the Lord called the *brahmajyoti.* The devotees can achieve not only liberation but any success in the realm of religiosity, economic development or sense gratification up to the standard of the demigods in the heavenly planets. But such a pure devotee as Uddhava refuses to accept all such facilities. A pure devotee wants simply to engage in the service of the Lord and does not consider his own personal benefit.

TEXT 16

कर्माण्यनीहस्य भवोऽभवस्य ते
दुर्गाश्रयोऽथारिभयात्पलायनम् ।
कालात्मनो यत्प्रमदायुताश्रमः
स्वात्मन्रतेः खिद्यति धीर्विदामिह ॥१६॥

karmāṇy anīhasya bhavo 'bhavasya te
durgāśrayo 'thāri-bhayāt palāyanam

kālātmano yat pramadā-yutāśramaḥ
svātman-rateḥ khidyati dhīr vidām iha

karmāṇi—activities; *anīhasya*—of one who has no desire; *bhavaḥ*—birth; *abhavasya*—of one who is never born; *te*—your; *durga-āśrayaḥ*—taking shelter of the fort; *atha*—thereafter; *ari-bhayāt*—out of fear of the enemies; *palāyanam*—flee; *kāla-ātmanaḥ*—of He who is the controller of eternal time; *yat*—that; *pramadā-āyuta*—in the association of women; *āśramaḥ*—household life; *sva-ātman*—in Your own Self; *rateḥ*—one who enjoys; *khidyati*—is disturbed; *dhīḥ*—intelligence; *vidām*—of the learned; *iha*—in this world.

TRANSLATION

My Lord, even the learned sages become disturbed in their intelligence when they see that Your Greatness engages in fruitive work although You are free from all desires, that You take birth although You are unborn, that You flee out of fear of the enemy and take shelter in a fort although You are the controller of invincible time, and that You enjoy householder life surrounded by many women although You enjoy in Your Self.

PURPORT

Pure devotees of the Lord are not very much concerned with philosophical speculation in regard to transcendental knowledge of the Lord. Nor is it possible to acquire complete knowledge of the Lord. Whatever little knowledge they have about the Lord is sufficient for them because devotees are simply satisfied in hearing and chanting about the transcendental pastimes of the Lord. This gives them all transcendental bliss. But some of the pastimes of the Lord appear contradictory, even to such pure devotees, and thus Uddhava asked the Lord about some of the contradictory incidents in His pastimes. The Lord is described as having nothing to do personally, and it is actually so because even in the creation and sustenance of the material world, the Lord has nothing to do. It seems contradictory, then, to hear that the Lord personally lifts the Govardhana Hill for the protection of His unalloyed devotees. The Lord is the Supreme Brahman, the Absolute Truth, the Personality of Godhead appearing like a man, but Uddhava had doubts whether He could have so many transcendental activities.

There is no difference between the Personality of Godhead and the impersonal Brahman. How then can the Lord have so many things to do, whereas the impersonal Brahman is stated to have nothing to do either materially or spiritually? If the Lord is ever unborn, how then is He born as the son of Vasudeva and Devakī? He is fearful even to *kāla*, the supreme fear, and yet the Lord is afraid of fighting Jarāsandha and takes shelter in a fort. How can one who is full in Himself take pleasure in the association of many women? How can He take wives and, just like a householder, take pleasure in the association of family members, children, relatives and parents? All these apparently contradictory happenings bewilder even the greatest learned scholars, who, thus bewildered, cannot understand whether inactivity is a fact or whether His activities are only imitations.

The solution is that the Lord has nothing to do with anything mundane. All His activities are transcendental. This cannot be understood by the mundane speculators. For the mundane speculators there is certainly a kind of bewilderment, but for the transcendental devotees there is nothing astonishing in this. The Brahman conception of the Absolute Truth is certainly the negation of all mundane activities, but the Para-brahman conception is full with transcendental activities. One who knows the distinctions between the conception of Brahman and the conception of Supreme Brahman is certainly the real transcendentalist. There is no bewilderment for such transcendentalists. The Lord Himself also declares in *Bhagavad-gītā* (10.2), "Even the great sages and demigods can know hardly anything about My activities and transcendental potencies." The right explanation of the Lord's activities is given by Grandfather Bhīṣmadeva (*Bhāg.* 1.9.16) as follows:

na hy asya karhicid rājan
pumān veda vidhitsitam
yad-vijijñāsayā yuktā
muhyanti kavayo 'pi hi

TEXT 17

मन्त्रेषु मां वा उपहूय यत्त्व-
मकुण्ठिताखण्डसदात्मबोधः ।
पृच्छेः प्रभो मुग्ध इवाप्रमत्त-
स्तन्नो मनो मोहयतीव देव ॥१७॥

mantreṣu māṁ vā upahūya yat tvam
akuṇṭhitākhaṇḍa-sadātma-bodhaḥ
pṛccheḥ prabho mugdha ivāpramattas
tan no mano mohayatīva deva

mantreṣu—in consultations; *mām*—unto me; *vai*—as either; *upahūya*—by calling; *yat*—as much as; *tvam*—Your Lordship; *akuṇṭhita*—without hesitation; *akhaṇḍa*—without being separated; *sadā*—eternally; *ātma*—self; *bodhaḥ*—intelligent; *pṛccheḥ*—asked; *prabho*—O my Lord; *mugdhaḥ*—bewildered; *iva*—as if it were so; *apramattaḥ*—although never bewildered; *tat*—that; *naḥ*—our; *manaḥ*—mind; *mohayati*—bewilders; *iva*—as it is so; *deva*—O my Lord.

TRANSLATION

O my Lord, Your eternal Self is never divided by the influence of time, and there is no limitation to Your perfect knowledge. Thus You were sufficiently able to consult with Yourself, yet You called upon me for consultation, as if bewildered, although You are never bewildered. And this act of Yours bewilders me.

PURPORT

Uddhava was never actually bewildered, but he says that all these contradictions appear to be bewildering. The whole discussion between Kṛṣṇa and Uddhava was meant for the benefit of Maitreya, who was sitting nearby. The Lord used to call Uddhava for consultation when the city was attacked by Jarāsandha and others and when He executed great sacrifices as part of His routine royal work as Lord of Dvārakā. The Lord has no past, present and future because He is unhampered by the influence of eternal time and thus nothing is hidden from Him. He is eternally self-intelligent. Therefore His calling for Uddhava to give Him enlightenment is certainly astonishing. All these actions of the Lord appear to be contradictory, although there is no contradiction in the routine activities of the Lord. Therefore it is better to see them as they are and not attempt to explain them.

TEXT 18

ज्ञानं परं स्वात्मरहःप्रकाशं
प्रोवाच कस्मै भगवान् समग्रम् ।
अपि क्षमं नो ग्रहणाय भर्त-
र्वदाञ्जसा यद् वृजिनं तरेम ॥१८॥

jñānaṁ paraṁ svātma-rahaḥ-prakāśaṁ
provāca kasmai bhagavān samagram
api kṣamaṁ no grahaṇāya bhartar
vadāñjasā yad vṛjinaṁ tarema

jñānam—knowledge; *param*—supreme; *sva-ātma*—own self; *rahaḥ*—mystery; *prakāśam*—enlightening; *provāca*—said; *kasmai*—unto Ka (Brahmājī); *bhagavān*—the Personality of

Godhead; *samagram*—in sum total; *api*—if so; *kṣamam*—able; *naḥ*—unto me; *grahaṇāya*—acceptable; *bhartaḥ*—O my Lord; *vada*—say; *añjasā*—in detail; *yat*—that which; *vṛjinam*—miseries; *tarema*—can cross over.

TRANSLATION

My Lord, kindly explain to us, if You think us competent to receive it, that transcendental knowledge which gives enlightenment about Yourself and which You explained before to Brahmājī.

PURPORT

A pure devotee like Uddhava has no material afflictions because he engages constantly in the transcendental loving service of the Lord. A devotee feels afflicted without the association of the Lord. Constant remembrance of the Lord's activities keeps the devotee alive, and therefore Uddhava requested that the Lord please enlighten him with the knowledge of *Śrīmad-Bhāgavatam,* as previously instructed to Brahmājī.

TEXT 19

इत्यावेदितहार्दाय मह्यं स भगवान् परः ।
आदिदेशारविन्दाक्ष आत्मनः परमां स्थितिम् ॥१९॥

ity āvedita-hārdāya
mahyaṁ sa bhagavān paraḥ
ādideśāravindākṣa
ātmanaḥ paramāṁ sthitim

iti āvedita—thus being prayed to by me; *hārdāya*—from the core of my heart; *mahyam*—unto me; *saḥ*—He; *bhagavān*—the Personality of Godhead; *paraḥ*—Supreme; *ādideśa*—instructed; *aravinda-akṣaḥ*—the lotus-eyed; *ātmanaḥ*—of Himself; *paramām*—transcendental; *sthitim*—situation.

TRANSLATION

When I thus expressed my heartfelt desires unto the Supreme Personality of Godhead, the lotus-eyed Lord instructed me about His transcendental situation.

PURPORT

The words *paramāṁ sthitim* are significant in this verse. The Lord's transcendental situation was not even spoken of to Brahmā when the four verses of *Śrīmad-*

Bhāgavatam (2.9.33-36) were explained. This transcendental situation comprises His dealings with devotees engaged in transcendental loving service, as exhibited at Dvārakā and Vṛndāvana. When the Lord explained His specific transcendental situation, it was meant for Uddhava only, and therefore Uddhava particularly said *mahyam* ("unto me"), although the great sage Maitreya was also sitting there. Such a transcendental situation is hardly understood by those whose devotion is mixed with speculative knowledge or fruitive activities. The Lord's activities in confidential love are very rarely disclosed to the general devotees who are attracted by devotion mixed with knowledge and mysticism. Such activities are the inconceivable pastimes of the Lord.

TEXT 20

स एवमाराधितपादतीर्था-
दधीततत्त्वात्मविबोधमार्गः ।
प्रणम्य पादौ परिवृत्य देव-
मिहागतोऽहं विरहातुरात्मा ॥२०॥

sa evam ārādhita-pāda-tīrthād
adhīta-tattvātma-vibodha-mārgaḥ
praṇamya pādau parivṛtya devam
ihāgato 'haṁ virahāturātmā

saḥ—so myself; *evam*—thus; *ārādhita*—worshiped; *pāda-tīrthāt*—from the Personality of Godhead; *adhīta*—studied; *tattva-ātma*—self-knowledge; *vibodha*—understanding; *mārgaḥ*—path; *praṇamya*—after saluting; *pādau*—at His lotus feet; *parivṛtya*—after circumambulating; *devam*—the Lord; *iha*—at this place; *āgataḥ*—reached; *aham*—I; *viraha*—separation; *ātura-ātmā*—aggrieved in self.

TRANSLATION

I have studied the path of understanding self-knowledge from my spiritual master, the Personality of Godhead, and thus after circumambulating Him I have come to this place, very much aggrieved due to separation.

PURPORT

Śrī Uddhava's actual life is the direct symbol of the *catuḥ-ślokī Bhāgavatam* enunciated first to Brahmājī by the Personality of Godhead. These four very great and important verses from *Śrīmad-Bhāgavatam* are particularly taken out by the Māyāvādī speculators, who construe a different purport to suit their impersonal view of monism. Here is the proper answer to such unauthorized speculators. The verses of *Śrīmad-*

Bhāgavatam are purely theistic science understandable by the postgraduate students of *Bhagavad-gītā*. The unauthorized dry speculators are offenders at the lotus feet of the Lord Śrī Kṛṣṇa because they distort the purports of *Bhagavad-gītā* and *Śrīmad-Bhāgavatam* to mislead the public and prepare a direct path to the hell known as Andhatāmisra. As confirmed in *Bhagavad-gītā* (16.20) such envious speculators are without knowledge and are surely condemned life after life. They unnecessarily take shelter of Śrīpāda Śaṅkarācārya, but he was not so drastic as to commit an offense at the lotus feet of Lord Kṛṣṇa. According to Lord Śrī Caitanya Mahāprabhu, Śrīpāda Śaṅkarācārya preached the Māyāvāda philosophy for a particular purpose. Such a philosophy was necessary to defeat the Buddhist philosophy of the nonexistence of the spirit soul, but it was never meant for perpetual acceptance. It was an emergency. Thus Lord Kṛṣṇa was accepted by Śaṅkarācārya as the Supreme Personality of Godhead in his commentation on *Bhagavad-gītā*. Since he was a great devotee of Lord Kṛṣṇa, he did not dare write any commentary on *Śrīmad-Bhāgavatam* because that would have been a direct offense at the lotus feet of the Lord. But later speculators, in the name of Māyāvāda philosophy, unnecessarily make their commentary on the *catuḥ-ślokī Bhāgavatam* without any bona fide intent.

The monistic dry speculators have no business in the *Śrīmad-Bhāgavatam* because this particular Vedic literature is forbidden for them by the great author himself. Śrīla Vyāsadeva has definitely forbidden persons engaged in religiosity, economic development, sense gratification and, finally, salvation, from trying to understand *Śrīmad-Bhāgavatam*, which is not meant for them (*Bhāg.* 1.1.2). Śrīpāda Śrīdhara Svāmī, the great commentator on *Śrīmad-Bhāgavatam*, has definitely forbidden the salvationists or monists to deal in *Śrīmad-Bhāgavatam*. It is not for them. Yet such unauthorized persons perversely try to understand *Śrīmad-Bhāgavatam*, and thus they commit offenses at the feet of the Lord, which even Śrīpāda Śaṅkarācārya dared not do. Thus they prepare for their continuation of miserable life. It should be particularly noted herein that Uddhava studied the *catuḥ-ślokī Bhāgavatam* directly from the Lord, who spoke them first to Brahmājī, and this time the Lord explained more confidentially the self-knowledge mentioned as the *paramāṁ sthitim*. Upon learning such self-knowledge of love, Uddhava felt very much aggrieved by feelings of separation from the Lord. Unless one is awakened to the stage of Uddhava—everlastingly feeling the separation of the Lord in transcendental love, as exhibited by Lord Caitanya also—one cannot understand the real import of the four essential verses of *Śrīmad-Bhāgavatam*. One should not indulge in the unauthorized act of twisting the meaning and thereby putting himself on the dangerous path of offense.

TEXT 21

सोऽहं तद्दर्शनाह्लादवियोगार्तियुतः प्रभो ।
गमिष्ये दयितं तस्य बदर्याश्रममण्डलम् ॥२१॥

so 'haṁ tad-darśanāhlāda-
viyogārti-yutaḥ prabho
gamiṣye dayitaṁ tasya
badaryāśrama-maṇḍalam

saḥ aham—thus myself; *tat*—His; *darśana*—audience; *āhlāda*—pleasure; *viyoga*—without that; *ārti-yutaḥ*—afflicted by distress; *prabho*—my dear sir; *gamiṣye*—shall go; *dayitam*—so instructed; *tasya*—His; *badaryāśrama*—Badarikāśrama, in the Himalayas; *maṇḍalam*—association.

TRANSLATION

My dear Vidura, now I am mad for want of the pleasure of seeing Him, and just to mitigate this I am now proceeding to Badarikāśrama in the Himalayas for association, as I have been instructed by Him.

PURPORT

A pure devotee of the Lord of the standard of Uddhava constantly associates with the Lord in the double perception of simultaneous separation and meeting. The pure devotee is not for a moment unengaged in the transcendental service of the Lord. Execution of the Lord's service is the main occupation of the pure devotee. Uddhava's separation from the Lord was unbearable, and therefore he started to Badarikāśrama in obedience to the Lord's order because the order of the Lord and the Lord Himself are identical. As long as one is engaged in the execution of the order of the Lord, there is no factual separation from Him.

TEXT 22

यत्र नारायणो देवो नरश्च भगवानृषिः ।
मृदु तीव्रं तपो दीर्घं तेपाते लोकभावनौ ॥२२॥

yatra nārāyaṇo devo
naraś ca bhagavān ṛṣiḥ
mṛdu tīvraṁ tapo dīrghaṁ
tepāte loka-bhāvanau

yatra—where; *nārāyaṇaḥ*—the Personality of Godhead; *devaḥ*—by incarnation; *naraḥ*—human being; *ca*—also; *bhagavān*—the Lord; *ṛṣiḥ*—great sage; *mṛdu*—amiable to everyone; *tīvram*—severe; *tapaḥ*—penance; *dīrgham*—very long; *tepāte*—performing; *loka-bhāvanau*—welfare of all living entities.

TRANSLATION

There in Badarikāśrama the Personality of Godhead, in His incarnation as the sages Nara and Nārāyaṇa, has been undergoing great penance since time immemorial for the welfare of all amiable living entities.

PURPORT

Badarikāśrama in the Himalayas, the abode of the Nara-Nārāyaṇa sages, is a great place of pilgrimage for the Hindus. Even up to the present, hundreds and thousands of pious Hindus go to pay respects to the incarnation of Godhead Nara-Nārāyaṇa. It appears that even five thousand years ago this holy place was being visited by such a holy being as Uddhava, and even at that time the place was known to be very, very old. This particular pilgrimage site is very difficult to visit for ordinary men because of its difficult situation in the Himalayas in a place which is covered by ice almost all year. A few months during the summer season people can visit this place at great personal inconvenience. There are four *dhāmas,* or kingdoms of God, which represent the planets of the spiritual sky, which consists of the *brahma-jyotir* and the Vaikuṇṭhas. These are Badarikāśrama, Rameśvara, Jagannātha Purī and Dvārakā. Faithful Hindus still visit all these holy places for perfection of spiritual realization, following in the footsteps of devotees like Uddhava.

TEXT 23

श्रीशुक उवाच
इत्युद्धवादुपाकर्ण्य सुहृदां दुःसहं वधम् ।
ज्ञानेनाशमयत्क्षत्ता शोकमुत्पतितं बुधः ॥२३॥

śrī-śuka uvāca
ity uddhavād upākarṇya
suhṛdāṁ duḥsahaṁ vadham
jñānenāśamayat kṣattā
śokam utpatitaṁ budhaḥ

śrī-śukaḥ uvāca—Śrī Śuka Gosvāmī said; *iti*—thus; *uddhavāt*—from Uddhava; *upākarṇya*—hearing; *suhṛdām*—of friends and relatives; *duḥsaham*—unbearable; *vadham*—annihilation; *jñānena*—by transcendental knowledge; *aśamayat*—pacified himself; *kṣattā*—Vidura; *śokam*—bereavement; *utpatitam*—arisen; *budhaḥ*—the learned.

TRANSLATION

Śrī Śukadeva Gosvāmī said: After hearing from Uddhava all about the annihilation of his friends and relatives, the learned Vidura pacified his overwhelming bereavement by dint of his transcendental knowledge.

PURPORT

Vidura was informed that the result of the Battle of Kuruksetra was the annihilation of his friends and relatives as well as the destruction of the Yadu dynasty and also the passing away of the Lord. All these hurled him into bereavement for the time being, but because he was highly advanced in transcendental knowledge, he was quite competent to pacify himself by enlightenment. As it is stated in *Bhagavad-gītā* due to our long association with bodily relationships, bereavement on account of the annihilation of friends and relatives is not at all astonishing, but one has to learn the art of subduing such bereavement with higher, transcendental knowledge. The talks between Uddhava and Vidura on the topic of Kṛṣṇa began at sunset, and Vidura was now further advanced in knowledge due to his association with Uddhava.

TEXT 24

स तं महाभागवतं व्रजन्तं कौरवर्षभः ।
विश्रम्भादभ्यधत्तेदं मुख्यं कृष्णपरिग्रहे ॥२४॥

sa taṁ mahā-bhāgavataṁ
vrajantaṁ kauravarṣabhaḥ
viśrambhād abhyadhattedaṁ
mukhyaṁ kṛṣṇa-parigrahe

saḥ—Vidura; *tam*—unto Uddhava; *mahā-bhāgavatam*—the great devotee of the Lord; *vrajantam*—while going; *kaurava-ṛṣabhaḥ*—the best amongst the Kauravas; *viśrambhāt*—out of confidence; *abhyadhatta*—submitted; *idam*—this; *mukhyam*—unto the chief; *kṛṣṇa*—Lord Kṛṣṇa; *parigrahe*—in devotional service to the Lord.

TRANSLATION

While Uddhava, the chief and most confidential amongst the devotees of the Lord, was going away, Vidura, in affection and confidence, questioned him.

PURPORT

Vidura was much older than Uddhava. By family relationship Uddhava was a contemporary brother of Kṛṣṇa's, while Vidura was as elderly as Kṛṣṇa's father Vasudeva. But although junior by age, Uddhava was much advanced in the devotional service of the Lord, and therefore he is described herein as the chief amongst the devotees of the Lord. Vidura was confident about this, and thus he addressed Uddhava in that higher category. That is the way of courteous dealings between two devotees.

TEXT 25

विदुर उवाच
ज्ञानं परं स्वात्मरहःप्रकाशं
यदाह योगेश्वर ईश्वरस्ते ।
वक्तुं भवान्नोऽर्हति यद्धि विष्णो-
र्भृत्याः स्वभृत्यार्थकृतश्चरन्ति ॥२५॥

vidura uvāca
jñānaṁ paraṁ svātma-rahaḥ-prakāśaṁ
yad āha yogeśvara īśvaras te
vaktuṁ bhavān no 'rhati yad dhi viṣnor
bhṛtyāḥ sva-bhṛtyārtha-kṛtaś caranti

viduraḥ uvāca—Vidura said; *jñānam*—knowledge; *param*—transcendental; *sva-ātma*—regarding the self; *rahaḥ*—mystery; *prakāśam*—enlightening; *yat*—that which; *āha*—said; *yoga-īśvaraḥ*—the master of all mystics; *īśvaraḥ*—the Lord; *te*—unto you; *vaktum*—to narrate; *bhavān*—your good self; *naḥ*—unto me; *arhati*—deserve; *yat*—for; *hi*—reason of; *viṣṇoḥ*—of Lord Viṣṇu; *bhṛtyāḥ*—servants; *sva-bhṛtya-artha-kṛtaḥ*—for the interest of their servants; *caranti*—do wander.

TRANSLATION

Vidura said: O Uddhava, because the servants of Viṣṇu, the Lord, wander in the interest of serving others, it is quite fit that you kindly describe the self-knowledge with which you have been enlightened by the Lord Himself.

PURPORT

The servants of the Lord are actually the servants of society. They have no interest in human society other than to enlighten it in transcendental knowledge; they are interested in imparting knowledge of the relationship of the living being with the Supreme Lord, the activities in that transcendental relationship, and the ultimate goal of human life. That is the real knowledge which can help society achieve the real aim of human welfare. Knowledge in the matter of the bodily necessities of eating, sleeping, mating and fearing, transformed into various branches of advancement of knowledge, is all temporary. A living being is not the material body but an eternal part and parcel of the Supreme Being, and thus revival of his self-knowledge is essential. Without this knowledge, the human life is baffled. The servants of the Lord, Viṣṇu, are entrusted with this responsible work, and so they wander over the earth and to all other planets in the universe. Thus the knowledge which was received by Uddhava directly from the Lord deserves to be distributed in human society, especially to persons like Vidura, who are highly advanced in the devotional service of the Lord.

Real transcendental knowledge descends in the disciplic succession from the Lord to Uddhava, from Uddhava to Vidura and so on. Such supreme transcendental knowledge is not possible to achieve by the process of imperfect speculation as performed by the so-called learned mundane wranglers. Vidura was anxious to know from Uddhava that confidential knowledge known as *paramāṁ sthitim,* in which the Lord is known by His transcendental pastimes. Although Vidura was older than Uddhava, he was anxious to become a servant of Uddhava in the transcendental relationship. This formula of transcendental disciplic succession is taught by Lord Caitanya also. Lord Caitanya advises that one receive transcendental knowledge from anyone—whether a *brāhmaṇa* or a *śūdra,* a householder or a *sannyāsī*—provided that person is factually conversant with the science of Kṛṣṇa. A person who knows the science of Kṛṣṇa is factually a bona fide spiritual master.

TEXT 26

उद्धव उवाच

ननु ते तत्त्वसंराध्य ऋषिः कौषारवोऽन्तिके ।
साक्षाद्भगवतादिष्टो मर्त्यलोकं जिहासता ॥२६॥

uddhava uvāca
nanu te tattva-saṁrādhya
ṛṣiḥ kauṣāravo 'ntike

sākṣād bhagavatādiṣṭo
martya-lokaṁ jihāsatā

uddhavaḥ uvāca—Uddhava said; *nanu*—however; *te*—of yourself; *tattva-saṁrādhyaḥ*—one who is worshipable for reception of transcendental knowledge; *ṛṣiḥ*—learned scholar; *kauṣāravaḥ*—unto the son of Kuṣāru (Maitreya); *antike*—staying nearby; *sākṣāt*—directly; *bhagavatā*—by the Personality of Godhead; *ādiṣṭaḥ*—instructed; *martya-lokam*—mortal world; *jihāsatā*—while quitting.

TRANSLATION

Śrī Uddhava said: You may take lessons from the great learned sage Maitreya, who is nearby and who is worshipable for reception of transcendental knowledge. He was directly instructed by the Personality of Godhead while He was about to quit this mortal world.

PURPORT

Although one may be well versed in the transcendental science, one should be careful about the offense of *maryādā-vyatikrama*, or impertinently surpassing a greater personality. According to scriptural injunction one should be very careful of transgressing the law of *maryādā-vyatikrama* because by so doing one loses his duration of life, his opulence, fame and piety and the blessings of all the world. To be well versed in the transcendental science necessitates awareness of the techniques of spiritual science. Uddhava, being well aware of all these technicalities of transcendental science, advised Vidura to approach Maitreya Ṛṣi to receive transcendental knowledge. Vidura wanted to accept Uddhava as his spiritual master, but Uddhava did not accept the post because Vidura was as old as Uddhava's father and therefore Uddhava could not accept him as his disciple, especially when Maitreya was present nearby. The rule is that in the presence of a higher personality one should not be very eager to impart instructions, even if one is competent and well versed. So Uddhava decided to send an elderly person like Vidura to Maitreya, another elderly person, but he was well versed also because he was directly instructed by the Lord while He was about to quit this mortal world. Since both Uddhava and Maitreya were directly instructed by the Lord, both had the authority to become the spiritual master of Vidura or anyone else, but Maitreya, being elderly, had the first claim to becoming the spiritual master, especially for Vidura, who was much older than Uddhava. One should not be eager to become a spiritual master cheaply for the sake of profit and fame, but should become a spiritual master only for the service of the Lord. The Lord never tolerates the impertinence of *maryādā-vyatikrama.* One should never pass over the honor due to an elderly spiritual master in the interests of one's own personal gain and fame. Impertinence on the part of the pseudo spiritual master is very risky to progressive spiritual realization.

TEXT 27

श्रीशुक उवाच

इति सह विदुरेण विश्वमूर्ते-
गुणकथया सुधया प्लावितोरुतापः ।
क्षणमिव पुलिने यमस्वसुस्तां
समुषित औपगविर्निशां ततोऽगात् ॥२७॥

śrī-śuka uvāca

iti saha vidureṇa viśva-mūrter
guṇa-kathayā sudhayā plāvitorutāpaḥ
kṣaṇam iva puline yamasvasus tāṁ
samuṣita aupagavir niśāṁ tato 'gāt

śrī-śukaḥ uvāca—Śrī Śukadeva Gosvāmī said; *iti*—thus; *saha*—along with; *vidureṇa*—Vidura; *viśva-mūrteḥ*—of the Universal Person; *guṇa-kathayā*—in the discourse of transcendental qualities; *sudhayā*—nectarean; *plāvita-uru-tāpaḥ*—overwhelmed by great affliction; *kṣaṇam*—moment; *iva*—like that; *puline*—on the bank of; *yamasvasuḥ tām*—River Yamunā; *samuṣitaḥ*—passed on; *aupagaviḥ*—the son of Aupagava (Uddhava); *niśām*—the night; *tataḥ*—thereafter; *agāt*—went away.

TRANSLATION

Śukadeva Gosvāmī said: O King, after thus discussing with Vidura the transcendental name, fame, qualities, etc., on the bank of the Yamunā, Uddhava was overwhelmed with great affliction. He passed the night as if it were a moment, and thereafter he went away.

PURPORT

The word used here for Kṛṣṇa is *viśva-mūrti.* Both Uddhava and Vidura were in great affliction because of Lord Kṛṣṇa's departure, and the more they discussed the transcendental name, fame and qualities of the Lord, the more the picture of the Lord became visible to them everywhere. Such visualization of the transcendental form of the Lord is neither false nor imaginary but is factual Absolute Truth. When the Lord is perceived as *viśva-mūrti,* it is not that He loses His personality or transcendental eternal form, but He becomes visible in the same form everywhere.

TEXT 28

राजोवाच
निधनमुपगतेषु वृष्णिभोजे-
ष्वधिरथयूथपयूथपेषु मुख्यः ।
स तु कथमवशिष्ट उद्धवो यद्धरि-
रपि तत्यज आकृतिं त्र्यधीशः ॥२८॥

rājovāca
nidhanam upagateṣu vṛṣṇi-bhojeṣv
adhiratha-yūthapa-yūthapeṣu mukhyaḥ
sa tu katham avaśiṣṭa uddhavo yad
dharir api tatyaja ākṛtiṁ tryadhīśaḥ

rājā uvāca—the King inquired; *nidhanam*—destruction; *upagateṣu*—having overtaken; *vṛṣṇi*—of the Vṛṣṇi dynasty; *bhojeṣu*—the Bhoja dynasty; *adhiratha*—great commander; *yūtha-pa*—commander in chief; *yūtha-peṣu*—amongst them; *mukhyaḥ*—prominent; *saḥ*—he; *tu*—only; *katham*—how; *avaśiṣṭaḥ*—remained; *uddhavaḥ*—Uddhava; *yat*—whereas; *hariḥ*—the Personality of Godhead; *api*—also; *tatyaje*—finished; *ākṛtim*—complete pastimes; *tri-adhīśaḥ*—the Lord of the three worlds.

TRANSLATION

The King inquired: At the end of the pastimes of the Lord of the three worlds, Śrī Kṛṣṇa, and after the disappearance of the members of the Vṛṣṇi and Bhoja dynasties, who were the best of the great commanders, why did Uddhava alone remain?

PURPORT

According to Śrī Jīva Gosvāmī, *nidhanam* means the transcendental abode of the Lord. *Ni* means the highest, and *dhanam* means opulence. And because the abode of the Lord is the highest manifestation of transcendental opulence, His abode can therefore be called *nidhanam.* Apart from the grammatical elucidation, the real purpose of the word *nidhanam* is to indicate that all the members of the Vṛṣṇi and Bhoja dynasties were direct associates of the Lord, and after the end of His pastimes, all the associates were dispatched to their respective positions in the transcendental abode.

Śrīla Viśvanātha Cakravartī Ṭhākura elucidates the meaning of *ākṛtim* as pastimes. Ā means complete, and *kṛtim* means transcendental pastimes. Since the Lord is identical with His transcendental body, there is no question of His changing or quitting His body. To act in accordance with the rules and customs of the material world, the Lord seems to take His birth or leave His body, but the pure devotees of the Lord know well the actual fact. It is necessary, therefore, for the serious students of *Śrīmad-Bhāgavatam* to follow the notes and comments of the great *ācāryas* like Jīva Gosvāmī and Viśvanātha Cakravartī. To others, who are not devotees of the Lord, the comments and explanations of such *ācāryas* may appear to be grammatical jugglery, but to the students who are in the line of disciplic succession, the explanations of the great *ācāryas* are quite fit.

The word *upagateṣu* is also significant. All the members of Vṛṣṇi and Bhoja directly reached the abode of the Lord. Other devotees do not reach the abode of the Lord directly, but the pure associates of the Lord have no attraction for the opulence of any planets of the material world. Sometimes, due to inquisitiveness, devotees who are to be promoted to the abode of the Lord have some attraction for the opulence of the higher material planets above the earth, and thus they desire to see them while going up to the perfection. But the Vṛṣṇis and Bhojas were directly dispatched because they had no attraction for material planets. Śrīla Viśvanātha Cakravartī Ṭhākura also suggests that according to the *Amara-kośa* dictionary, *ākṛti* also means "signal." Lord Kṛṣṇa ordered Uddhava by signal to go to Badarikāśrama after His departure, and Uddhava, as a pure devotee of the Lord, carried out the order more faithfully than going back to Godhead, or the abode of the Lord. That was the cause of his remaining alone even after the departure of the Lord from the face of the earth.

TEXT 29

श्रीशुक उवाच

ब्रह्मशापापदेशेन कालेनामोघवाञ्छितः ।
संहृत्य स्वकुलं स्फीतं त्यक्ष्यन्देहमचिन्तयत् ॥२९॥

śrī-śuka uvāca
brahma-śāpāpadeśena
kālenāmogha-vāñchitaḥ
saṁhṛtya sva-kulaṁ sphītaṁ
tyakṣyan deham acintayat

śrī-śukaḥ uvāca—Śrī Śukadeva Gosvāmī said; *brahma-śāpa*—cursing by the *brāhmaṇas; apadeśena*—on the plea, by such a show; *kālena*—by the eternal time; *amogha*—unfailing; *vāñchitaḥ*—one who so desires; *saṁhṛtya*—closing; *sva-kulam*—own family; *sphītam*—excessively numerous; *tyakṣyan*—after giving up; *deham*—the universal form; *acintayat*—thought to Himself.

TRANSLATION

Śukadeva Gosvāmī replied: My dear King, the cursing of the brāhmaṇas was only a plea, but the actual fact was the supreme desire of the Lord. He wanted to disappear from the face of the earth after dispatching His excessively numerous family members. He thought to Himself as follows.

PURPORT

In this verse the word *tyakṣyan* is very significant in relation to Lord Śrī Kṛṣṇa's leaving His body. Since He is the eternal form of existence, knowledge and bliss, His body and His Self are identical. Therefore how is it possible that He would leave His body and then disappear from the vision of the world? There is a great controversy amongst the nondevotees or Māyāvādīs about the mysterious disappearance of the Lord, and the doubts of those men with a poor fund of knowledge have been very elaborately cleared by Śrīla Jīva Gosvāmī in his *Kṛṣṇa-sandarbha.*

According to *Brahma-saṁhitā,* the Lord has many forms. It is stated therein that the Lord has innumerable forms, and when He appears within the vision of the living entities, as Lord Kṛṣṇa actually appeared, all such forms amalgamate with Him. Besides all these infallible forms, He has His universal form, as manifested before Arjuna on the Battlefield of Kurukṣetra. Here in this verse the word *sphītam* is also used, which indicates that He left His gigantic universal form called the *virāṭ-rūpa,* not His primeval, eternal form, because there is hardly any possibility of His changing His form of *sac-cid-ānanda.* This simple understanding is at once realized by the devotees of the Lord, but those who are nondevotees, who perform hardly any devotional service to the Lord, either do not understand this simple fact or purposely raise a controversy to defeat the eternity of the transcendental body of the Lord. This is due to the defect called the cheating propensity of the imperfect living entities.

By practical experience also, it is seen, up to the present day, that the Lord's transcendental form is worshiped by devotees in different temples, and all the devotees of the Lord factually realize that the form of the Deity in the temple is nondifferent from the form of the Lord. This inconceivable performance of the internal potency of the

Lord is described in *Bhagavad-gītā* (7.25): *nāhaṁ prakāśaḥ sarvasya yoga-māyā-samāvṛtaḥ.* The Lord reserves the right of not being exposed to everyone. In the *Padma Purāṇa* it is said, *ataḥ śrī-kṛṣṇa-nāmādi na bhaved grāhyam indriyaiḥ.* The name and form of the Lord cannot be perceived by the material senses, but when He appears within the vision of the mundane people He assumes the form of the *virāṭ-rūpa.* This is an additional material exhibition of form and is supported by the logic of a subject and its adjectives. In grammar, when an adjective is taken away from the subject, the subject it modifies does not change. Similarly, when the Lord quits His *virāṭ-rūpa,* His eternal form does not change, although there is no material difference between Himself and any one of His innumerable forms. In the Fifth Canto it will be seen how the Lord is worshiped in different planets in His different forms, even now, and how He is worshiped in different temples of this earth also.

Śrīla Jīva Gosvāmī and Śrīla Viśvanātha Cakravartī Ṭhākura have very elaborately explained this incident of the Lord's disappearance in their commentaries, quoting various authentic versions of Vedic literatures. We purposely do not include them all here to avoid an increase in the volume of this book. The entire matter is explained in *Bhagavad-gītā,* as quoted above: the Lord reserves the right of not being exposed to everyone. He always keeps Himself out of the vision of the nondevotees, who are devoid of love and devotion, and thus He puts them still further away from the Lord. The Lord appeared on the invitation of Brahmā, who prayed before the Kṣīrodakaśāyī Viṣṇu, and therefore when the Lord appeared, all the forms of Viṣṇu amalgamated with Him, and when the mission was fulfilled, all of them disintegrated from Him in the usual course.

TEXT 30

अस्माल्लोकादुपरते मयि ज्ञानं मदाश्रयम् ।
अर्हत्युद्धव एवाद्धा सम्प्रत्यात्मवतां वरः ॥३०॥

asmāl lokād uparate
mayi jñānaṁ mad-āśrayam
arhaty uddhava evāddhā
sampraty ātmavatāṁ varaḥ

asmāt—from this (universe); *lokāt*—earth; *uparate*—having disappeared; *mayi*—of Myself; *jñānam*—knowledge; *mat-āśrayam*—concerning Myself; *arhati*—deserves; *uddhavaḥ*—Uddhava; *eva*—certainly; *addhā*—directly; *samprati*—at the present moment; *ātmavatām*—of the devotees; *varaḥ*—foremost.

TRANSLATION

Now I shall leave the vision of this mundane world, and I see that Uddhava, the foremost of My devotees, is the only one who can be directly entrusted with knowledge about Me.

PURPORT

Jñānaṁ mad-āśrayam is significant in this verse. Transcendental knowledge has three departmental divisions, namely knowledge of impersonal Brahman, knowledge of the all-pervading Supersoul and knowledge of the Personality of Godhead. Out of the three, transcendental knowledge of the Personality of Godhead has special significance and is known as *bhagavat-tattva-vijñāna*, specific knowledge of the Personality of Godhead. This specific knowledge is realized by pure devotional service and no other means. *Bhagavad-gītā* (18.55) confirms this: *bhaktyā mām abhijānāti yāvān yaś cāsmi tattvataḥ*. "Only persons engaged in devotional service can factually know the transcendental position of the Lord." Uddhava was considered to be the best amongst all devotees of that time, and therefore he was directly instructed by the Lord's grace, so that people might take advantage of Uddhava's knowledge after the disappearance of the Lord from the vision of the world. This is one of the reasons why Uddhava was advised to go to Badarikāśrama, where the Lord is personally represented by the Nara-Nārāyaṇa Deity. One who is transcendentally advanced can gain direct inspiration from the temple Deity, and thus a devotee of the Lord always takes shelter of a recognized temple of the Lord in order to make tangible advancement in transcendental knowledge by the grace of the Lord.

TEXT 31

नोद्धवोऽण्वपि मन्न्यूनो यद्गुणैर्नार्दितः प्रभुः ।
अतो मद्वयुनं लोकं ग्राहयन्निह तिष्ठतु ॥३१॥

noddhavo 'ṇv api man-nyūno
yad guṇair nārditaḥ prabhuḥ
ato mad-vayunaṁ lokaṁ
grāhayann iha tiṣṭhatu

na—not; *uddhavaḥ*—Uddhava; *aṇu*—slightly; *api*—also; *mat*—to Myself; *nyūnaḥ*—inferior; *yat*—because; *guṇaiḥ*—by the modes of material nature; *na*—nor; *arditaḥ*—affected; *prabhuḥ*—master; *ataḥ*—therefore; *mat-vayunam*—knowledge of Me (the Personality of

Godhead); *lokam*—the world; *grāhayan*—just to disseminate; *iha*—in this world; *tiṣṭhatu*—may remain.

TRANSLATION

Uddhava is not inferior to Me in any way because he is never affected by the modes of material nature. Therefore he may remain in this world in order to disseminate specific knowledge of the Personality of Godhead.

PURPORT

The specific qualification for becoming the representative of the Lord is to be unaffected by the material modes of nature. The highest qualification of a person in the material world is to be a *brāhmaṇa.* But since a *brāhmaṇa* is in the mode of goodness, to be a *brāhmaṇa* is not sufficient for becoming a representative of the Lord. One has to transcend the mode of goodness also and be situated in unalloyed goodness, unaffected by any of the qualities of material nature. This stage of transcendental qualification is called *śuddha-sattva,* or *vasudeva,* and in this stage the science of God can be realized. As the Lord is not affected by the modes of material nature, so a pure devotee of the Lord is also not affected by the modes of nature. That is the primary qualification for being one with the Lord. A person who is able to attain this transcendental qualification is called *jīvan-mukta*, or liberated, even though he is apparently in material conditions. This liberation is achieved by one who constantly engages in the transcendental loving service of the Lord. In *Bhakti-rasāmṛta-sindhu* (1.2.187) it is stated:

īhā yasya harer dāsye
karmaṇā manasā girā
nikhilāsv apy avasthāsu
jīvan-muktaḥ sa ucyate

"Anyone who, by his actions, mind and words, lives only for the transcendental loving service of the Lord, is certainly a liberated soul, even though he may appear to be in a condition of material existence." Uddhava was in such a transcendental position, and thus he was selected to be the factual representative of the Lord in His bodily absence from the vision of the world. Such a devotee of the Lord is never affected by material strength, intelligence or even renunciation. Such a devotee of the Lord can withstand all onslaughts of material nature, and therefore he is known as *gosvāmī.* Only such *gosvāmīs* can penetrate the mysteries of the Lord's transcendental loving relationships.

TEXT 32

एवं त्रिलोकगुरुणा सन्दिष्टः शब्दयोनिना ।
बदर्याश्रममासाद्य हरिमीजे समाधिना ॥३२॥

evaṁ tri-loka-guruṇā
sandiṣṭaḥ śabda-yoninā
badaryāśramam āsādya
harim īje samādhinā

evam—thus; *tri-loka*—three worlds; *guruṇā*—by the spiritual master; *sandiṣṭaḥ*—being perfectly taught; *śabda-yoninā*—by one who is the source of all Vedic knowledge; *badaryāśramam*—in the pilgrimage site of Badarikāśrama; *āsādya*—reaching; *harim*—unto the Lord; *īje*—satisfied; *samādhinā*—by trance.

TRANSLATION

Śukadeva Gosvāmī informed the King that Uddhava, being thus instructed by the Supreme Personality of Godhead, who is the source of all Vedic knowledge and the spiritual master of the three worlds, reached the pilgrimage site of Badarikāśrama and engaged himself there in trance to satisfy the Lord.

PURPORT

Lord Śrī Kṛṣṇa is factually the spiritual master of the three worlds, and He is the original source of all Vedic knowledge. It is very difficult, however, to understand the personal feature of the Absolute Truth, even from the *Vedas.* His personal instructions are needed in order to understand the Personality of Godhead as the Supreme Absolute Truth. *Bhagavad-gītā* is the evidence of such transcendental knowledge in gist. One cannot know the Supreme Lord unless one is graced by the Lord Himself. Lord Kṛṣṇa exhibited this specific mercy towards Arjuna and Uddhava while He was in the material world.

Undoubtedly *Bhagavad-gītā* was spoken by the Lord on the Battlefield of Kurukṣetra just to encourage Arjuna to fight, and yet to complete the transcendental knowledge of *Bhagavad-gītā,* the Lord instructed Uddhava. The Lord wanted Uddhava to fulfill His mission and disseminate knowledge which He had not spoken even in *Bhagavad-gītā.* Persons who are attached to the words of the *Vedas* may also know from this verse that the Lord is the source of all Vedic knowledge. One who is unable to understand the Supreme Personality of Godhead by going through the pages of the *Vedas* may take shelter of one of the Lord's devotees, such as Uddhava, in order to advance further in knowledge of the Supreme Personality of Godhead. The *Brahma-saṁhitā* says that it is very difficult to understand the Supreme Personality of Godhead from the *Vedas*, but He is easily understood from a pure devotee like Uddhava. Taking mercy on the great sages who lived at Badarikāśrama, the Lord authorized Uddhava to speak on His behalf. Unless one has such authorization, one cannot understand or preach the devotional service of the Lord.

While present on this earth, the Lord executed many uncommon activities, even traveling in space to bring down the *pārijāta* from heaven and recovering the son of His teacher (Sāndīpani Muni) from the regions of death. Uddhava was certainly informed of the conditions of life on other planets, and all the sages were anxious to know of them, just as we are anxious to know about the planets in space. Uddhava was particularly deputed to carry a message to Badarikāśrama, not only to the sages of that place of pilgrimage but also to the Nara-Nārāyaṇa Deities. Such a message must have been more confidential than the knowledge described in the pages of the *Vedas*.

The Lord is undoubtedly the source of all knowledge, and the messages dispatched through Uddhava to Nara-Nārāyaṇa and other sages were also part of the Vedic knowledge, but they were more confidential and could be sent or understood only through such a pure devotee as Uddhava. Since such confidential knowledge was known only to the Lord and Uddhava, it is said that Uddhava was as good as the Lord Himself. Every living entity can, like Uddhava, also become a confidential messenger on the same level as the Lord, provided he becomes confidential himself by dint of loving devotional service. Such confidential knowledge is entrusted, as confirmed in *Bhagavad-gītā* only to pure devotees like Uddhava and Arjuna, and one has to learn the mystery through them, and not otherwise. One cannot understand *Bhagavad-gītā* or *Śrīmad-Bhāgavatam* without the help of such confidential devotees of the Lord. According to Śrīla Viśvanātha Cakravartī Ṭhākura, that confidential message must have concerned the mystery of His departure and the annihilation of His dynasty after the end of His appearance in the mundane world for one hundred years. Everyone must have been very anxious to know about the mystery of the annihilation of the Yadu dynasty, and that message must have been explained by the Lord to Uddhava and dispatched to Badarikāśrama for the information of Nara-Nārāyaṇa and other pure devotees of the Lord.

TEXT 33

विदु रोऽप्युद्धवाच्छ्रुत्वा कृष्णस्य परमात्मनः ।
क्रीडयोपात्तदेहस्य कर्माणि श्लाघितानि च ॥३३॥

viduro 'py uddhavāc chrutvā
kṛṣṇasya paramātmanaḥ
krīḍayopātta-dehasya
karmāṇi ślāghitāni ca

viduraḥ—Vidura; *api*—also; *uddhavāt*—from the source of Uddhava; *śrutvā*—having heard; *kṛṣṇasya*—of Lord Kṛṣṇa; *parama-ātmanaḥ*—of the Supersoul; *krīḍayā*—for the sake of pastimes in the mortal world; *upātta*—extraordinarily accepted; *dehasya*—of the body; *karmāṇi*—transcendental activities; *ślāghitāni*—most glorious; *ca*—also.

TRANSLATION

Vidura also heard from Uddhava about the appearance and disappearance of Lord Kṛṣṇa, the Supersoul, in the mortal world, which is a subject matter sought after with great perseverance by the great sages.

PURPORT

The subject matter of the appearance and disappearance of the Supersoul, Lord Śrī Kṛṣṇa, is a mystery even for the great sages. The word *paramātmanaḥ* is significant in this verse. An ordinary living being is generally called the *ātmā,* but Lord Kṛṣṇa is never an ordinary living being because He is *paramātmā,* the Supersoul. Yet His appearance as one of the human beings and His disappearance again from the mortal world are subject matters for the research workers who execute research work with great perseverance. Such subject matters are certainly of increasing interest because the researchers have to search out the transcendental abode of the Lord, which He enters after finishing His pastimes in the mortal world. But even the great sages have no information that beyond the material sky is the spiritual sky where Śrī Kṛṣṇa eternally resides with His associates, although at the same time He exhibits His pastimes in the mortal world in all the universes one after another. This fact is confirmed in *Brahma-saṁhitā* (5.37): *goloka eva nivasaty akhilātma-bhūtaḥ.* "The Lord, by His inconceivable potency, resides in His eternal abode, Goloka, yet at the same time, as the Supersoul, He is present everywhere—in both the spiritual and material skies—by His multivarieties of manifestation." Therefore His appearance and disappearance are simultaneously going on, and no one can say definitely which of them is the beginning and which is the end. His eternal pastimes have no beginning or end, and one has to learn of them from the pure devotee only and not waste valuable time in so-called research work.

TEXT 34

देहन्यासं च तस्यैवं धीराणां धैर्यवर्धनम् ।
अन्येषां दुष्करतरं पशूनां विक्लवात्मनाम् ॥३४॥

deha-nyāsaṁ ca tasyaivaṁ
dhīrāṇāṁ dhairya-vardhanam
anyeṣāṁ duṣkarataraṁ
paśūnāṁ viklavātmanām

deha-nyāsam—entering the body; *ca*—also; *tasya*—His; *evam*—also; *dhīrāṇām*—of great sages; *dhairya*—perseverance; *vardhanam*—increasing; *anyeṣām*—for others; *duṣkara-taram*—very difficult to ascertain; *paśūnām*—of the beasts; *viklava*—disturbed; *ātmanām*—of such a mind.

TRANSLATION

The Lord's glorious acts and His acceptance of various transcendental forms for the performance of extraordinary pastimes in the mortal world are very difficult for anyone other than His devotees to understand, and for the beasts they are simply a mental disturbance.

PURPORT

The transcendental forms and pastimes of the Lord, as described in *Bhagavad-gītā,* are difficult subject matters for those who are not devotees to understand. The Lord never reveals Himself to persons like the *jñānīs* and *yogīs.* And there are others who, because of their envying the Lord from the bottom of their hearts, are classified amongst the beasts, and for such envious beasts the subject matter of the Lord's appearance and disappearance is simply a mental disturbance. As confirmed in *Bhagavad-gītā* (7.15), the miscreants who are simply concerned with material enjoyment, who work very hard like beasts of burden, can hardly know the Personality of Godhead at any stage due to *āsurika-bhāva,* or a spirit of revolt against the Supreme Lord.

The transcendental bodily expansions manifested by the Lord for His pastimes in the mortal world, and the appearance and disappearance of such transcendental expansions, are difficult subject matters, and those who are not devotees are advised not to discuss the Lord's appearance and disappearance, lest they commit further offenses at the lotus feet of the Lord. The more they discuss the transcendental appearance and disappearance of the Lord in the asuric spirit, the more they enter into the darkest region of hell, as stated in *Bhagavad-gītā* (16.20). Anyone who is against the transcendental loving service of the Lord is more or less a beastly creature, as confirmed in this verse of *Śrīmad-Bhāgavatam.*

TEXT 35

आत्मानं च कुरुश्रेष्ठ कृष्णेन मनसेक्षितम् ।
ध्यायन् गते भागवते रुरोद प्रेमविह्वलः ॥३५॥

ātmānaṁ ca kuru-śreṣṭha
kṛṣṇena manasekṣitam
dhyāyan gate bhāgavate
ruroda prema-vihvalaḥ

ātmānam—himself; *ca*—also; *kuru-śreṣṭha*—O best amongst the Kurus; *kṛṣṇena*—by Kṛṣṇa; *manasā*—by the mind; *īkṣitam*—remembered; *dhyāyan*—thus thinking of; *gate*—having gone; *bhāgavate*—of the devotee; *ruroda*—cried loudly; *prema-vihvalaḥ*—overwhelmed by the ecstasy of love.

TRANSLATION

Understanding that he was remembered by Lord Kṛṣṇa [while quitting this world], Vidura began to cry loudly, overwhelmed by the ecstasy of love.

PURPORT

Vidura was overwhelmed by the ecstasy of love when he understood that Lord Kṛṣṇa, the Supreme Personality of Godhead, thought of him at the last moment. Although he thought of himself as insignificant, he was remembered by the Lord, by His causeless mercy. Vidura accepted this as a great favor, and thus he cried. This crying is the last word in the progressive path of devotional service. One who can cry for the Lord in love is certainly successful in the line of devotional service.

TEXT 36

कालिन्द्याः कतिभिः सिद्ध अहोभिर्भरतर्षभ ।
प्रापद्यत स्वःसरितं यत्र मित्रासुतो मुनिः ॥३६॥

kālindyāḥ katibhiḥ siddha
ahobhir bharatarṣabha
prāpadyata svaḥ-saritaṁ
yatra mitrā-suto muniḥ

kālindyāḥ—on the bank of the Yamunā; *katibhiḥ*—a few; *siddhe*—being so passed; *ahobhiḥ*—days; *bharata-ṛṣabha*—O best of the Bharata dynasty; *prāpadyata*—reached; *svaḥ-saritam*—the celestial water of the Ganges; *yatra*—where; *mitrā-sutaḥ*—the son of Mitra-; *muniḥ*—sage.

TRANSLATION

After passing a few days on the bank of the River Yamunā, Vidura, the self-realized soul, reached the bank of the Ganges, where the great sage Maitreya was situated.

Thus end the Bhaktivedanta purports of the Fourth Chapter, Third Canto, of the Śrīmad-Bhāgavatam, *entitled "Vidura Approaches Maitreya."*

CHAPTER FIVE

Vidura's Talks with Maitreya

TEXT 1

श्रीशुक उवाच
द्वारि द्युनद्या ऋषभः कुरूणां
मैत्रेयमासीनमगाधबोधम् ।
क्षत्तोपसृत्याच्युतभावसिद्धः
पप्रच्छ सौशील्यगुणाभितृप्तः ॥ १ ॥

śrī-śuka uvāca
dvāri dyu-nadyā ṛsabhaḥ kurūṇāṁ
maitreyam āsīnam agādha-bodham
kṣattopasṛtyācyuta-bhāva-siddhaḥ
papraccha sauśīlya-guṇābhitṛptaḥ

śrī-śukaḥ uvāca—Śukadeva Gosvāmī said; *dvāri*—at the source of; *dyu-nadyāḥ*—the celestial River Ganges; *ṛṣabhaḥ*—the best of the Kurus; *kurūṇām*—of the Kurus; *maitreyam*—unto Maitreya; *āsīnam*—sitting; *agādha-bodham*—of unfathomed knowledge; *kṣattā*—Vidura; *upasṛtya*—having approached nearer; *acyuta*—the infallible Lord; *bhāva*—character; *siddhaḥ*—perfect; *papraccha*—inquired; *sauśīlya*—gentleness; *guṇa-abhitṛptaḥ*—satisfied in transcendental qualities.

TRANSLATION

Śukadeva Gosvāmī said: Vidura, the best amongst the Kuru dynasty, who was perfect in devotional service to the Lord, thus reached the source of the celestial Ganges River [Hardwar], where Maitreya, the great, fathomless learned sage of the world, was seated. Vidura, who was perfect in gentleness and satisfied in transcendence, inquired from him.

PURPORT

Vidura was already perfect due to his unalloyed devotion to the infallible Lord. The Lord and the living entities are all qualitatively the same by nature, but the Lord is quantitatively much greater than any individual living entity. He is ever infallible, whereas the living entities are prone to fall under the illusory energy. Vidura had already surpassed the fallible nature of the living entity in conditional life due to his being *acyuta-bhāva,* or legitimately absorbed in the devotional service of the Lord. This stage of life is called *acyuta-bhāva-siddha,* or perfection by dint of devotional service. Anyone, therefore, who is absorbed in the devotional service of the Lord is a liberated soul and has all admirable qualities. The learned sage Maitreya was sitting in a solitary place on the bank of the Ganges at Hardwar, and Vidura, who was a perfect devotee of the Lord and possessed all good transcendental qualities, approached him for inquiry.

TEXT 2

विदुर उवाच

सुखाय कर्माणि करोति लोको
न तैः सुखं वान्यदुपारमं वा ।
विन्देत भूयस्तत एव दुःखं
यदत्र युक्तं भगवान् वदेन्नः ॥ २ ॥

vidura uvāca
sukhāya karmāṇi karoti loko
na taiḥ sukhaṁ vānyad-upāramaṁ vā
vindeta bhūyas tata eva duḥkhaṁ
yad atra yuktaṁ bhagavān vaden naḥ

viduraḥ uvāca—Vidura said; *sukhāya*—for attaining happiness; *karmāṇi*—fruitive activities; *karoti*—everyone does so; *lokaḥ*—in this world; *na*—never; *taiḥ*—by those activities; *sukham*—any happiness; *vā*—or; *anyat*—differently; *upāramam*—satiation; *vā*—either; *vindeta*—achieves; *bhūyaḥ*—on the contrary; *tataḥ*—by such activities; *eva*—certainly; *duḥkham*—miseries; *yat*—that which; *atra*—under the circumstances; *yuktam*—right course; *bhagavān*—O great one; *vadet*—may kindly enlighten; *naḥ*—us.

TRANSLATION

Vidura said: O great sage, everyone in this world engages in fruitive activities to attain happiness, but one finds neither satiation nor the mitigation of distress. On the contrary, one is only aggravated by such activities. Please, therefore, give us directions on how one should live for real happiness.

PURPORT

Vidura asked Maitreya some common questions, which was not originally his intention. Uddhava asked Vidura to approach Maitreya Muni and inquire into all the truths concerning the Lord, His name, fame, quality, form, pastimes, entourage, etc., and thus when Vidura approached Maitreya, he should have asked only about the Lord. But out of natural humility he did not immediately ask about the Lord, but inquired into a subject which would be of great importance to the common man. A common man cannot understand the Lord. He must first know the real position of his life under the influence of the illusory energy. In illusion one thinks that he can be happy only by fruitive activities, but what actually happens is that one becomes more and more entangled in the network of action and reaction and does not find any solution to the problem of life. There is a nice song in this connection: "Because of a great desire to have all happiness in life, I built this house. But unfortunately the whole scheme has turned to ashes because the house was unexpectedly set on fire." The law of nature is like that. Everyone tries to become happy by planning in the material world, but the law of nature is so cruel that it sets fire to one's schemes; the fruitive worker is not happy in his schemes, nor is there any satiation of his continuous hankering for happiness.

TEXT 3

जनस्य कृष्णाद्विमुखस्य दैवा-
दधर्मशीलस्य सुदुःखितस्य ।
अनुग्रहायेह चरन्ति नूनं
भूतानि भव्यानि जनार्दनस्य ॥ ३ ॥

janasya kṛṣṇād vimukhasya daivād
adharma-śīlasya suduḥkhitasya
anugrahāyeha caranti nūnaṁ
bhūtāni bhavyāni janārdanasya

janasya—of the common man; *kṛṣṇāt*—from the Supreme Lord, Kṛṣṇa; *vimukhasya*—of the one who has turned his face against the Lord; *daivāt*—by the influence of external energy; *adharma-śīlasya*—of one who is engaged in irreligion; *su-duḥkhitasya*—of one who is always unhappy; *anugrahāya*—due to being compassionate towards them; *iha*—in this world; *caranti*—wander; *nūnam*—certainly; *bhūtāni*—persons; *bhavyāni*—great philanthropic souls; *janārdanasya*—of the Supreme Personality of Godhead.

TRANSLATION

O my lord, great philanthropic souls travel on the earth on behalf of the Supreme Personality of Godhead to show compassion to the fallen souls who are averse to the sense of subordination to the Lord.

PURPORT

To be obedient to the wishes of the Supreme Lord is the natural position of every living entity. But due only to past misdeeds, a living being becomes averse to the sense of subordination to the Lord and suffers all the miseries of material existence. No one has anything to do but render devotional service to the Supreme Lord, Śrī Kṛṣṇa. Therefore any activity other than transcendental loving service to the Lord is more or less a rebellious action against the supreme will. All fruitive activity, empirical philosophy and mysticism are more or less against the sense of subordination to the Lord, and any living entity engaged in such rebellious activity is more or less condemned by the laws of material nature, which work under the subordination of the Lord. Great unalloyed devotees of the Lord are compassionate towards the fallen, and therefore they travel all over the world with the mission of bringing souls back to Godhead, back to home. Such pure devotees of the Lord carry the message of Godhead in order to deliver the fallen souls, and therefore the common man who is bewildered by the influence of the external energy of the Lord should avail himself of their association.

TEXT 4

तत्साधुवर्यादिश वर्त्म शं नः
संराधितो भगवान् येन पुंसाम् ।
हृदि स्थितो यच्छति भक्तिपूते
ज्ञानं सतत्त्वाधिगमं पुराणम् ॥ ४ ॥

tat sādhu-varyādiśa vartma śaṁ naḥ
saṁrādhito bhagavān yena puṁsām
hṛdi sthito yacchati bhakti-pūte
jñānaṁ sa-tattvādhigamaṁ purāṇam

tat—therefore; *sādhu-varya*—O great one amongst the saints; *ādiśa*—please instruct; *vartma*—the path; *śam*—auspicious; *naḥ*—for us; *saṁrādhitaḥ*—being perfectly served; *bhagavān*—the Personality of Godhead; *yena*—by which; *puṁsām*—of the living entity; *hṛdi sthitaḥ*—residing in the heart; *yacchati*—awards; *bhakti-pūte*—unto the unalloyed devotee;

jñānam—knowledge; *sa*—that; *tattva*—truth; *adhigamam*—by which one learns; *purāṇam*—authorized, old.

TRANSLATION

Therefore, O great sage, please give me instruction on the transcendental devotional service of the Lord, so that He who is situated in the heart of everyone can be pleased to impart, from within, knowledge of the Absolute Truth in terms of the ancient Vedic principles delivered only to those who are purified by the process of devotional service.

PURPORT

As already explained in the First Canto of *Śrīmad-Bhāgavatam,* the Absolute Truth is realized in three different phases—although they are one and the same—in terms of the knower's capacity to understand. The most capable transcendentalist is the pure devotee of the Lord, who is without any tinge of fruitive actions or philosophical speculation. By devotional service only does one's heart become completely purified from all material coverings like *karma, jñāna* and *yoga.* Only in such a purified stage does the Lord, who is seated in everyone's heart with the individual soul, give instruction so that the devotee can reach the ultimate destination of going back home, back to Godhead. This is confirmed in *Bhagavad-gītā* (10.10): *teṣāṁ satata-yuktānāṁ bhajatām.* Only when the Lord is satisfied with the devotional service of the devotee does He impart knowledge, as He did for Arjuna and Uddhava.

The *jñānīs, yogīs* and *karmīs* cannot expect this direct cooperation of the Lord. They are not able to satisfy the Lord by transcendental loving service, nor do they believe in such service to the Lord. The *bhakti* process, as performed under the regulative principles of *vaidhī-bhakti,* or devotional service following the prescribed rules and regulations, is defined by the revealed scriptures and confirmed by great *ācāryas.* This practice can help the neophyte devotee to rise to the stage of *rāga-bhakti,* in which the Lord responds from within as the *caitya-guru,* or the spiritual master as Superconsciousness. All transcendentalists other than devotees make no distinction between the individual soul and the Supersoul because they miscalculate the Superconsciousness and the individual consciousness to be one and the same. Such miscalculation by the nondevotees makes them unfit to receive any direction from within, and therefore they are bereft of the direct cooperation of the Lord. After many, many births, when such a nondualist comes to sense that the Lord is worshipable and that the devotee is simultaneously one with and different from the Lord, then only can he surrender unto the Lord, Vāsudeva. Pure devotional service begins from that point. The process of understanding the Absolute Truth adopted by the misguided nondualist is very difficult, whereas the devotee's way of understanding the Absolute Truth comes directly from the Lord, who is pleased by devotional service. On behalf of many neophyte devotees, Vidura, at the very first instance, inquired from Maitreya about the path of devotional service, by which the Lord, who is seated within the heart, can be pleased.

TEXT 5

करोति कर्माणि कृतावतारो
यान्यात्मतन्त्रो भगवांस्त्र्यधीशः ।
यथा ससर्जाग्र इदं निरीहः
संस्थाप्य वृत्तिं जगतो विधत्ते ॥ ५ ॥

karoti karmāṇi kṛtāvatāro
yāny ātma-tantro bhagavāṁs tryadhīśaḥ
yathā sasarjāgra idaṁ nirīhaḥ
saṁsthāpya vṛttiṁ jagato vidhatte

karoti—does them; *karmāṇi*—transcendental activities; *kṛta*—by accepting; *avatāraḥ*—incarnations; *yāni*—all those; *ātma-tantraḥ*—Self-independent; *bhagavān*—the Personality of Godhead; *tri-adhīśaḥ*—the Lord of the three worlds; *yathā*—as much as; *sasarja*—created; *agre*—at first; *idam*—this cosmic manifestation; *nirīhaḥ*—although desireless; *saṁsthāpya*—by establishing; *vṛttim*—means of livelihood; *jagataḥ*—of the universes; *vidhatte*—as He regulates.

TRANSLATION

O great sage, kindly narrate how the Supreme Personality of Godhead, who is the independent, desireless Lord of the three worlds and the controller of all energies, accepts incarnations and creates the cosmic manifestation with perfectly arranged regulative principles for its maintenance.

PURPORT

Lord Kṛṣṇa is the original Personality of Godhead from whom the three creative incarnations, namely the *puruṣa-avatāras*—Kāraṇārṇavaśāyī Viṣṇu, Garbhodakaśāyī Viṣṇu and Kṣīrodakaśāyī Viṣṇu—expand. The whole material creation is conducted by the three *puruṣas* in successive stages under the external energy of the Lord, and thus material nature is controlled by Him. Thinking material nature to be independent is like seeking milk from the nipplelike bags on the neck of a goat. The

Lord is independent and desireless. He does not create the material world for His own satisfaction as we create our household affairs to fulfill our material desires. Actually the material world is created for the illusory enjoyment of the conditioned souls, who have been against the transcendental service of the Lord since time immemorial. But the material universes are full in themselves. There is no scarcity for maintenance in the material world. Because of their poor fund of knowledge, the materialists are disturbed when there is an apparent increase of population on the earth. Whenever there is a living being on the earth, however, his subsistence is immediately arranged by the Lord. The other species of living entities, who far outnumber human society, are never disturbed for maintenance; they are never seen dying of starvation. It is only human society that is disturbed about the food situation and, to cover up the real fact of administrative mismanagement, takes shelter in the plea that the population is excessively increasing. If there is any scarcity in the world, it is the scarcity of God consciousness, otherwise, by the grace of the Lord, there is no scarcity of anything.

TEXT 6

यथा पुनः स्वे ख इदं निवेश्य
शेते गुहायां स निवृत्तवृत्तिः ।
योगेश्वराधीश्वर एक एत-
दनुप्रविष्टो बहुधा यथासीत् ॥ ६ ॥

yathā punaḥ sve kha idaṁ niveśya
śete guhāyāṁ sa nivṛtta-vṛttiḥ
yogeśvarādhīśvara eka etad
anupraviṣṭo bahudhā yathāsīt

yathā—as much as; *punaḥ*—again; *sve*—in His; *khe*—form of space (*virāṭ-rūpa*); *idam*—this; *niveśya*—entering into; *śete*—lies down; *guhāyām*—within the universe; *saḥ*—He (the Personality of Godhead); *nivṛtta*—without endeavor; *vṛttiḥ*—means of livelihood; *yoga-īśvara*—the master of all mystic powers; *adhīśvaraḥ*—proprietor of everything; *ekaḥ*—one without a second; *etat*—this; *anupraviṣṭaḥ*—entering afterwards; *bahudhā*—by innumerable; *yathā*—as much as; *āsīt*—exists.

TRANSLATION

He lies down on His own heart spread in the form of the sky, and thus placing the whole creation in that space, He expands Himself into many living entities, which are manifested as different species of life. He does not have to

endeavor for His maintenance, because He is the master of all mystic powers and the proprietor of everything. Thus He is distinct from the living entities.

PURPORT

The questions regarding creation, maintenance and destruction, which are mentioned in many parts of the *Śrīmad-Bhāgavatam,* are in relation to different millenniums (*kalpas*), and therefore they are differently described by different authorities when questioned by different students. There is no difference regarding the creative principles and the Lord's control over them, yet there are some differences in the minute details because of different *kalpas.* The gigantic sky is the material body of the Lord, called the *virāṭ-rūpa,* and all material creations are resting on the sky, or the heart of the Lord. Therefore, beginning from the sky, the first material manifestation to the gross vision, down to the earth, everything is called Brahman. *Sarvaṁ khalv idaṁ brahma:* "There is nothing but the Lord, and He is one without a second." The living entities are the superior energies, whereas matter is the inferior energy, and the combination of these energies brings about the manifestation of this material world, which is in the heart of the Lord.

TEXT 7

क्रीडन् विधत्ते द्विजगोसुराणां
क्षेमाय कर्माण्यवतारभेदैः ।
मनो न तृप्यत्यपि शृण्वतां नः
सुश्लोकमौलेश्चरितामृतानि ॥ ७ ॥

krīḍan vidhatte dvija-go-surāṇāṁ
kṣemāya karmāṇy avatāra-bhedaiḥ
mano na tṛpyaty api śṛṇvatāṁ naḥ
suśloka-mauleś caritāmṛtāni

krīḍan—manifesting pastimes; *vidhatte*—He performs; *dvija*—twice-born; *go*—cows; *surāṇām*—of the demigods; *kṣemāya*—welfare; *karmāṇi*—transcendental activities; *avatāra*—incarnations; *bhedaiḥ*—differently; *manaḥ*—mind; *na*—never; *tṛpyati*—satisfies; *api*—in spite of; *śṛṇvatām*—continuously hearing; *naḥ*—our; *su-śloka*—auspicious; *mauleḥ*—of the Lord; *carita*—characteristics; *amṛtāni*—undying.

TRANSLATION

You may narrate also about the auspicious characteristics of the Lord in His different incarnations for the welfare of the twice-born, the cows and the

demigods. Our minds are never satisfied completely, although we continuously hear of His transcendental activities.

PURPORT

The Lord appears in this universe in different incarnations like Matsya, Kūrma, Varāha and Nṛsiṁha, and He manifests His different transcendental activities for the welfare of the twice-born, the cows and the demigods. The Lord is directly concerned with the twice-born or civilized men. A civilized man is one who has taken his birth twice. A living entity takes birth in this mundane world due to the union of male and female. A human being is born due to union of the father and mother, but a civilized human being has another birth by contact with a spiritual master, who becomes the actual father. The father and mother of the material body are so only in one birth, and in the next birth the father and mother may be a different couple. But the bona fide spiritual master, as the representative of the Lord, is the eternal father because the spiritual master has the responsibility to lead the disciple to spiritual salvation, or the ultimate goal of life. Therefore, a civilized man must be twice-born, otherwise he is no more than the lower animals.

The cow is the most important animal for developing the human body to perfection. The body can be maintained by any kind of foodstuff, but cow's milk is particularly essential for developing the finer tissues of the human brain so that one can understand the intricacies of transcendental knowledge. A civilized man is expected to live on foodstuffs comprising fruits, vegetables, grains, sugar and milk. The bull helps in the agricultural process of producing grain, etc., and thus in one sense the bull is the father of humankind, whereas the cow is the mother, for she supplies milk to human society. A civilized man is therefore expected to give all protection to the bulls and cows.

The demigods, or the living entities who live in the higher planets, are far superior to human beings. Since they have better arrangements for living conditions, they live far more luxuriously than human beings, yet they are all devotees of the Lord. The Lord incarnates in different forms, such as those of a fish, a tortoise, a hog, and a combined lion and man, just to give protection to civilized man, the cow and the demigods, who are directly responsible for the regulative life of progressive self-realization. The whole system of the material creation is planned so that the conditioned souls may have the opportunity for self-realization. One who takes advantage of such an arrangement is called a demigod or civilized man. The cow is meant to help maintain such a high standard of living.

The Lord's pastimes for the protection of the twice-born civilized men, the cows and the demigods are all transcendental. A human being is inclined to hear good narrations and stories, and therefore there are so many books, magazines and newspapers on the market to satisfy the interests of the developed soul. But the pleasure in such literature, after it is read once, becomes stale, and people do not take any interest in reading such literature repeatedly. In fact, newspapers are read for less than an hour and then thrown in the dustbins as rubbish. The case is similar with all other mundane literatures. But the beauty of transcendental literatures like *Bhagavad-gītā* and *Śrīmad-Bhāgavatam* is that they never become old. They have been read in the world by civilized man for the last five thousand years, and they have never become old. They are ever fresh to the learned scholars and devotees, and even by daily repetition of the verses of *Bhagavad-gītā* and *Śrīmad-Bhāgavatam*, there is no satiation for devotees like Vidura. Vidura might have heard the pastimes of the Lord many, many times before he met Maitreya, but still he wanted the same narrations to be repeated because he was never satiated by hearing them. That is the transcendental nature of the Lord's glorious pastimes.

TEXT 8

यैस्तत्त्वभेदैरधिलोकनाथो
लोकानलोकान् सह लोकपालान् ।
अचीक्लृपद्यत्र हि सर्वसत्त्व-
निकायभेदोऽधिकृतः प्रतीतः ॥ ८ ॥

yais tattva-bhedair adhiloka-nātho
lokān alokān saha lokapālān
acīkḷpad yatra hi sarva-sattva-
nikāya-bhedo 'dhikṛtaḥ pratītaḥ

yaiḥ—by whom; *tattva*—truth; *bhedaiḥ*—by differentiation; *adhiloka-nāthaḥ*—the King of the kings; *lokān*—planets; *alokān*—planets of the lower region; *saha*—along with; *loka-pālān*—respective kings; *acīkḷpat*—planned; *yatra*—wherein; *hi*—certainly; *sarva*—all; *sattva*—existence; *nikāya*—living entities; *bhedaḥ*—difference; *adhikṛtaḥ*—occupied; *pratītaḥ*—it so appears.

TRANSLATION

The Supreme King of all kings has created different planets and places of habitation where living entities are situated in terms of the modes of nature and work, and He has created their different kings and rulers.

PURPORT

Lord Kṛṣṇa is the chief King of all kings, and He has created different planets for all kinds of living entities. Even on this planet there are different places for inhabitation by different types of men. There are places like deserts, ice lands, and valleys in mountainous countries, and in each of them there are different kinds of men born of different modes of nature according to their past deeds. There are people in the Arabian deserts and in the valleys of the Himalayan Mountains, and the inhabitants of these two places differ from one another, just as the inhabitants of the ice lands also differ from them. Similarly, there are also different planets. The planets below the earth down to the Pātāla planet are full of various kinds of living beings; no planet is vacant, as wrongly imagined by the modern so-called scientist. In *Bhagavad-gītā* we find it said by the Lord that the living entities are *sarva-gata,* or present in every sphere of life. So there is no doubt that on other planets there are also inhabitants like us, sometimes with greater intelligence and greater opulence. The living conditions for those of greater intelligence are more luxurious than on this earth. There are also planets where no sunlight reaches, and there are living entities who must live there due to their past deeds. All such plans for living conditions are made by the Supreme Lord, and Vidura requested Maitreya to describe this for the sake of further enlightenment.

TEXT 9

येन प्रजानामुत आत्मकर्म-
रूपाभिधानां च भिदां व्यधत्त ।
नारायणो विश्वसृगात्मयोनि-
रेतच्च नो वर्णय विप्रवर्य ॥ ९ ॥

yena prajānām uta ātma-karma-
rūpābhidhānāṁ ca bhidāṁ vyadhatta
nārāyaṇo viśvasṛg ātma-yonir
etac ca no varṇaya vipra-varya

yena—by which; *prajānām*—of those who are born; *uta*—as also; *ātma-karma*—destined engagement; *rūpa*—form and feature; *abhidhānām*—endeavors; *ca*—also; *bhidām*—differentiation; *vyadhatta*—dispersed; *nārāyaṇaḥ*—the Supreme Personality of Godhead; *viśvasṛk*—the creator of the universe; *ātma-yoniḥ*—self-sufficient; *etat*—all these; *ca*—also; *naḥ*—unto us; *varṇaya*—describe; *vipra-varya*—O chief amongst the *brāhmaṇas.*

TRANSLATION

O chief amongst the brāhmaṇas, please also describe how Nārāyaṇa, the creator of the universe and the self-sufficient Lord, has differently created the natures, activities, forms, features and names of the different living creatures.

PURPORT

Every living being is under the plan of his natural inclinations in terms of the modes of material nature. His work is manifested in terms of the nature of the three modes, his form and bodily features are designed according to his work, and his name is designated according to his bodily features. For example, the higher classes of men are white (*śukla*), and the lower classes of men are black. This division of white and black is in terms of one's white and black duties of life. Pious acts lead one to take birth in a good and highly placed family, to become rich, to become learned, and to acquire beautiful bodily features. Impious acts lead one to become poor by parentage, to be always in want, to become a fool or illiterate and to acquire ugly bodily features. Vidura requested Maitreya to explain these differences between all the living creatures made by Nārāyaṇa, the Supreme Personality of Godhead.

TEXT 10

परावरेषां भगवन् व्रतानि
श्रुतानि मे व्यासमुखादभीक्ष्णम् ।
अतृप्नुम क्षुल्लसुखावहानां
तेषामृते कृष्णकथामृतौघात् ॥१०॥

parāvareṣāṁ bhagavan vratāni
śrutāni me vyāsa-mukhād abhīkṣṇam
atṛpnuma kṣulla-sukhāvahānāṁ
teṣām ṛte kṛṣṇa-kathāmṛtaughāt

para—higher; *avareṣām*—of these lower; *bhagavan*—O my lord, O great one; *vratāni*—occupations; *śrutāni*—heard; *me*—by me; *vyāsa*—Vyāsa; *mukhāt*—from the mouth; *abhīkṣṇam*—repeatedly; *atṛpnuma*—I am satisfied; *kṣulla*—little; *sukha-āvahānām*—that which causes happiness; *teṣām*—out of that; *ṛte*—without; *kṛṣṇa-kathā*—talks about the Personality of Godhead, Lord Kṛṣṇa; *amṛta-oghāt*—from the nectar.

TRANSLATION

O my lord, I have repeatedly heard about these higher and lower statuses of human society from the mouth of Vyāsadeva, and I am quite satiated with

all these lesser subject matters and their happiness. They have not satisfied me with the nectar of topics about Kṛṣṇa.

PURPORT

Because people are very much interested in hearing social and historical presentations, Śrīla Vyāsadeva has compiled many books such as the *Purāṇas* and *Mahābhārata.* These books are reading matter for the mass of people, and they were compiled with a view to reviving their God consciousness, now forgotten in the conditional life of material existence. The real purpose of such literatures is not so much to present topics of historical references, but to revive the people's sense of God consciousness. For example, *Mahābhārata* is the history of the Battle of Kurukṣetra, and common people read it because it is full of topics regarding the social, political and economic problems of human society. But factually the most important part of *Mahābhārata* is *Bhagavad-gītā,* which is automatically taught to readers along with the historical narrations of the Battle of Kurukṣetra.

Vidura explained to Maitreya his position of being fully satiated with the knowledge of mundane social and political topics and having no more interest in them. He was anxious to hear transcendental topics regarding Lord Śrī Kṛṣṇa. Because there were insufficient topics directly concerning Kṛṣṇa in the *Purāṇas, Mahābhārata,* etc., he was not satisfied and wanted to know more about Kṛṣṇa. *Kṛṣṇa-kathā,* or topics regarding Kṛṣṇa, are transcendental, and there is no satiation in hearing such topics. *Bhagavad-gītā* is important on account of its being *kṛṣṇa-kathā,* or speeches delivered by Lord Kṛṣṇa. The story of the Battle of Kurukṣetra may be interesting for the mass of people, but to a person like Vidura, who is highly advanced in devotional service, only *kṛṣṇa-kathā* and that which is dovetailed with *kṛṣṇa-kathā* is interesting. Vidura wanted to hear of everything from Maitreya, and so he inquired from him, but he desired that all the topics be in relationship with Kṛṣṇa. As fire is never satisfied in its consumption of firewood, so a pure devotee of the Lord never hears enough about Kṛṣṇa. Historical events and other narrations concerning social and political incidents all become transcendental as soon as they are in relationship with Kṛṣṇa. That is the way to transform mundane things into spiritual identity. The whole world can be transformed into Vaikuṇṭha if all worldly activities are dovetailed with *kṛṣṇa-kathā.*

There are two important *kṛṣṇa-kathās* current in the world—*Bhagavad-gītā* and *Śrīmad-Bhāgavatam. Bhagavad-gītā* is *kṛṣṇa-kathā* because it is spoken by Kṛṣṇa, whereas *Śrīmad-Bhāgavatam* is *kṛṣṇa-kathā* because it narrates about Kṛṣṇa. Lord Caitanya advised all His disciples to preach *kṛṣṇa-kathā* all over the world without discrimination because the transcendental value of *kṛṣṇa-kathā* can purify one and all from material contamination.

TEXT 11

कस्तृप्नुयात्तीर्थपदोऽभिधानात्
सत्रेषु वः सूरिभिरीड्यमानात् ।
यः कर्णनाडीं पुरुषस्य यातो
भवप्रदां गेहरतिं छिनत्ति ॥११॥

kas tṛpnuyāt tīrtha-pado 'bhidhānāt
satreṣu vaḥ sūribhir īḍyamānāt
yaḥ karṇa-nāḍīṁ puruṣasya yāto
bhava-pradāṁ geha-ratiṁ chinatti

kaḥ—who is that man; *tṛpnuyāt*—that can be satisfied; *tīrtha-padaḥ*—whose lotus feet are all the places of pilgrimage; *abhidhānāt*—from the talks of; *satreṣu*—in human society; *vaḥ*—one who is; *sūribhiḥ*—by great devotees; *īḍyamānāt*—one who is so worshiped; *yaḥ*—who; *karṇa-nāḍīm*—in the holes of the ears; *puruṣasya*—of a man; *yātaḥ*—entering; *bhava-pradām*—that which awards births and deaths; *geha-ratim*—family affection; *chinatti*—is cut off.

TRANSLATION

Who in human society can be satisfied without hearing sufficient talk of the Lord, whose lotus feet are the sum total of all places of pilgrimage and who is worshiped by great sages and devotees? Such topics can cut off one's bondage to family affection simply by entering the holes of one's ears.

PURPORT

Kṛṣṇa-kathā is so powerful that simply by entering into a person's ear it can at once give deliverance from the bondage of family affection. Family affection is an illusory manifestation of the external energy, and it is the only impetus for all mundane activities. As long as there is mundane activity and the mind is absorbed in such engagement, one has to undergo the repetition of birth and death in the current material nescience. People are most influenced by the mode of ignorance, and some are influenced by the passionate mode of material nature, and under the spell of these two modes a living being is actuated by the material conception of life. The mundane qualities do not allow a living entity to understand his real position. The qualities of both ignorance and passion strongly bind one to the illusory bodily conception of the self. The best among the fools who are thus deluded are those who engage in altruistic activities under the spell of the material mode of passion. *Bhagavad-gītā*, which is direct *kṛṣṇa-kathā*, gives humanity the elementary lesson that the body is perishable and that the consciousness which is spread throughout the body is imperishable. The conscious being, the imperishable self, is eternally existent and cannot be killed under any circumstances, even after the dissolution of the body. Anyone who misunderstands this perishable body to be the self and who works for it in the name of sociology, politics, philanthropy, altruism, nationalism or internationalism, under the false plea of the bodily conception of life, is certainly a fool and does not know the implications of reality and unreality. Some of them are above the modes of ignorance and passion and are situated in the mode of goodness, but mundane goodness is always contaminated by tinges of ignorance and passion. Mundane goodness can enlighten one that the body and the self are different, and one in goodness is concerned with the self and not the body. But due to being contaminated, those in mundane goodness cannot understand the real nature of the self as a person. Their impersonal conception of the self as distinct from the body keeps them in the mode of goodness within material nature, and unless they are attracted by *kṛṣṇa-kathā*, they will never be liberated from the bondage of material existence. *Kṛṣṇa-kathā* is the only remedy for all people of the world because it can situate one in pure consciousness of the self and liberate one from material bondage. To preach *kṛṣṇa-kathā* all over the world, as recommended by Lord Caitanya, is the greatest missionary activity, and all sensible men and women of the world may join in this great movement started by Lord Caitanya.

TEXT 12

मुनिर्विवक्षुर्भगवद्गुणानां
सखापि ते भारतमाह कृष्णः ।
यस्मिन्नृणां ग्राम्यसुखानुवादै-
र्मतिर्गृहीता नु हरेः कथायाम् ॥१२॥

munir vivakṣur bhagavad-guṇānāṁ
sakhāpi te bhāratam āha kṛṣṇaḥ
yasmin nṛṇāṁ grāmya-sukhānuvādair
matir gṛhītā nu hareḥ kathāyām

muniḥ—the sage; *vivakṣuḥ*—described; *bhagavat*—of the Personality of Godhead; *guṇānām*—transcendental qualities; *sakhā*—friend; *api*—also; *te*—your; *bhāratam*—the

Mahābhārata; āha—has described; *kṛṣṇaḥ*—Kṛṣṇa-dvaipāyana Vyāsa; *yasmin*—in which; *nṛṇām*—of the people; *grāmya*—worldly; *sukha-anuvādaiḥ*—pleasure derived from mundane topics; *matiḥ*—attention; *gṛhītā nu*—just to draw towards; *hareḥ*—of the Lord; *kathāyām*—speeches of (*Bhagavad-gītā*).

TRANSLATION

Your friend the great sage Kṛṣṇa-dvaipāyana Vyāsa has already described the transcendental qualities of the Lord in his great work the Mahābhārata. But the whole idea is to draw the attention of the mass of people to kṛṣṇa-kathā [Bhagavad-gītā] through their strong affinity for hearing mundane topics.

PURPORT

The great sage Kṛṣṇa-dvaipāyana Vyāsa is the author of all Vedic literature, of which his works *Vedānta-sūtra, Śrīmad-Bhāgavatam* and *Mahābhārata* are very popular readings. As stated in *Bhāgavatam* (1.4.25), Śrīla Vyāsadeva compiled the *Mahābhārata* for the less intelligent class of men, who take more interest in mundane topics than in the philosophy of life. The *Vedānta-sūtra* was compiled for persons already above the mundane topics, who might already have tasted the bitterness of the so-called happiness of mundane affairs. The first aphorism of *Vedānta-sūtra* is *athāto brahma jijñāsā*, i.e., only when one has finished the business of mundane inquiries in the marketplace of sense gratification can one make relevant inquiries regarding Brahman, the Transcendence. Those persons who are busy with the mundane inquiries which fill the newspapers and other such literatures are classified as *strī-śūdra-dvija-bandhus*, or women, the laborer class and unworthy sons of the higher classes (*brāhmaṇa, kṣatriya* and *vaiśya*). Such less intelligent men cannot understand the purpose of *Vedānta-sūtra*, although they may make a show of studying the *sūtras* in a perverted way. The real purpose of *Vedānta-sūtra* is explained by the author himself in the *Śrīmad-Bhāgavatam*, and anyone trying to understand *Vedānta-sūtra* without reference to *Śrīmad-Bhāgavatam* is certainly misguided. Such misguided persons, who are interested in the mundane affairs of philanthropic and altruistic work under the misconception of the body as the self, could better take advantage of the *Mahābhārata*, which was specifically compiled by Śrīla Vyāsadeva for their benefit. The great author has compiled the *Mahābhārata* in such a way that the less intelligent class of men, who are more interested in mundane topics, may read the *Mahābhārata* with great relish and in the course of such mundane happiness can also take advantage of *Bhagavad-gītā*, the preliminary study of *Śrīmad-Bhāgavatam* or the *Vedānta-sūtra*. Śrīla Vyāsadeva had no interest in writing a history of mundane activities other than to give less intelligent persons a chance for transcendental realization through *Bhagavad-gītā.* Vidura's reference to the *Mahābhārata* indicates that he had heard of the *Mahābhārata* from Vyāsadeva, his real father, while he was away from home and was touring the places of pilgrimage.

TEXT 13

सा श्रद्दधानस्य विवर्धमाना
विरक्तिमन्यत्र करोति पुंसः ।
हरेः पदानुस्मृतिनिर्वृतस्य
समस्तदुःखाप्ययमाशु धत्ते ॥१३॥

sā śraddadhānasya vivardhamānā
viraktim anyatra karoti puṁsaḥ
hareḥ padānusmṛti-nirvṛtasya
samasta-duḥkhāpyayam āśu dhatte

sā—those topics of Kṛṣṇa, or *kṛṣṇa-kathā; śraddadhānasya* of one who is anxious to hear; *vivardhamānā*—gradually increasing; *viraktim*—indifference; *anyatra*—in other things (than such topics); *karoti*—does; *puṁsaḥ*—of one who is so engaged; *hareḥ*—of the Lord; *pada-anusmṛti*—constant remembrance of the lotus feet of the Lord; *nirvṛtasya*—one who has achieved such transcendental bliss; *samasta-duḥkha*—all miseries; *apyayam*—vanquished; *āśu*—without delay; *dhatte*—executes.

TRANSLATION

For one who is anxious to engage constantly in hearing such topics, kṛṣṇa-kathā gradually increases his indifference towards all other things. Such constant remembrance of the lotus feet of Lord Kṛṣṇa by the devotee who has achieved transcendental bliss vanquishes all his miseries without delay.

PURPORT

We must certainly know that on the absolute plane *kṛṣṇa-kathā* and Kṛṣṇa are one and the same. The Lord is the Absolute Truth, and therefore His name, form, quality, etc., which are all understood to be *kṛṣṇa-kathā,* are nondifferent from Him. *Bhagavad-gītā,* being spoken by the Lord, is as good as the Lord Himself. When a sincere devotee reads *Bhagavad-gītā,* this is as good as seeing the Lord face to face in his personal presence, but this is not so for the mundane wrangler. All the potencies of the Lord are there when one reads *Bhagavad-gītā*, provided it is read in the way recommended in the *Gītā* by the Lord Himself. One cannot foolishly manufacture an interpretation of *Bhagavad-gītā* and still bring about transcendental benefit. Anyone who tries to squeeze some artificial meaning or interpretation from *Bhagavad-gītā* for an ulterior motive is not *śraddadhāna-puṁsaḥ* (one engaged anxiously in bona fide hearing of *kṛṣṇa-kathā*). Such a person cannot derive any benefit from reading *Bhagavad-gīta*, however great a scholar he may be in the estimation of a layman. The *śraddadhāna*, or faithful devotee, can actually derive all the benefits of *Bhagavad-gītā* because by the omnipotency of the Lord he achieves the transcendental bliss which vanquishes attachment and nullifies all concomitant material miseries. Only the devotee, by his factual experience, can understand the import of this verse spoken by Vidura. The pure devotee of the Lord enjoys life by constantly remembering the lotus feet of the Lord by hearing *kṛṣṇa-kathā*. For such a devotee there is no such thing as material existence, and the much advertised bliss of *brahmānanda* is like a fig for the devotee who is in the midst of the transcendental ocean of bliss.

TEXT 14

तान्छोच्यशोच्यानविदोऽनुशोचे
हरेः कथायां विमुखानघेन ।
क्षिणोति देवोऽनिमिषस्तु येषा-
मायुर्वृथावादगतिस्मृतीनाम् ॥१४॥

tāñ chocya-śocyān avido 'nuśoce
hareḥ kathāyāṁ vimukhān aghena
kṣiṇoti devo 'nimiṣas tu yeṣām
āyur vṛthā-vāda-gati-smṛtīnām

tān—all those; *śocya*—pitiable; *śocyān*—of the pitiable; *avidaḥ*—ignorant; *anuśoce*—I pity; *hareḥ*—of the Lord; *kathāyām*—to the topics of; *vimukhān*—averse; *aghena*—because of sinful activities; *kṣiṇoti*—decaying; *devaḥ*—the Lord; *animiṣaḥ*—eternal time; *tu*—but; *yeṣām*—of whom; *āyuḥ*—duration of life; *vṛthā*—uselessly; *vāda*—philosophical speculations; *gati*—ultimate goal; *smṛtīnām*—of those following different rituals.

TRANSLATION

O sage, persons who because of their sinful activities are averse to the topics of Transcendence and thus ignorant of the purpose of the Mahābhārata [Bhagavad-gītā] are pitied by the pitiable. I also pity them because I see how

their duration of life is spoiled by eternal time while they involve themselves in presentations of philosophical speculation, theoretical ultimate goals of life, and different modes of ritual.

PURPORT

According to the modes of material nature, there are three kinds of relationships between human beings and the Supreme Personality of Godhead. Those who are in the modes of ignorance and passion are averse to the existence of God, or else they formally accept the existence of God in the capacity of an order supplier. Above them are those who are in the mode of goodness. This second class of men believe the Supreme Brahman to be impersonal. They accept the cult of *bhakti,* in which hearing of *kṛṣṇa-kathā* is the first item, as a means and not the end. Above them are those who are pure devotees. They are situated in the transcendental stage above the mode of material goodness. Such persons are decidedly convinced that the name, form, fame, qualities, etc., of the Personality of Godhead are nondifferent from one another on the absolute plane. For them, hearing of the topics of Kṛṣṇa is equal to meeting with Him face to face. According to this class of men, who are situated in pure devotional service to the Lord, the highest goal of human life is *puruṣārtha,* devotional service to the Lord, the real mission of life. The impersonalists, because they engage in mental speculation and have no faith in the Personality of Godhead, have no business hearing the topics of Kṛṣṇa. Such persons are pitiable for the first-class pure devotees of the Lord. The pitiable impersonalists pity those who are influenced by the modes of ignorance and passion, but the pure devotees of the Lord take pity on them both because both waste their most valuable time in the human form of life in false pursuits, sense enjoyment and mental speculative presentations of different theories and goals of life.

TEXT 15

तदस्य कौषारव शर्मदातु-
हरेः कथामेव कथासु सारम् ।
उद्धृत्य पुष्पेभ्य इवार्तबन्धो
शिवाय नः कीर्तय तीर्थकीर्तेः ॥१५॥

tad asya kauṣārava śarma-dātur
hareḥ kathām eva kathāsu sāram
uddhṛtya puṣpebhya ivārta-bandho
śivāya naḥ kīrtaya tīrtha-kīrteḥ

tat—therefore; *asya*—His; *kauṣārava*—O Maitreya; *śarma-dātuḥ*—of one who awards good fortune; *hareḥ*—of the Lord; *kathām*—topics; *eva*—only; *kathāsu*—of all topics; *sāram*—the essence; *uddhṛtya*—by quoting; *puṣpebhyaḥ*—from the flowers; *iva*—like that; *ārta-bandho*—O friend of the distressed; *śivāya*—for welfare; *naḥ*—of us; *kīrtaya*—kindly describe; *tīrtha*—pilgrimage; *kīrteḥ*—of glorious.

TRANSLATION

O Maitreya, O friend of the distressed, the glories of the Supreme Lord can alone do good for people all over the world. Therefore, just as bees collect honey from flowers, kindly describe the essence of all topics—the topics of the Lord.

PURPORT

There are many topics for different persons in different modes of material nature, but the essential topics are those in relationship with the Supreme Lord. Unfortunately, materially affected conditioned souls are all more or less averse to topics of the Supreme Lord because some of them do not believe in the existence of God and some of them believe only in the impersonal feature of the Lord. In both cases there is nothing for them to say of God. Both the nonbelievers and the impersonalists deny the essence of all topics; therefore, they engage in topics of relativity in various ways, either in sense gratification or in mental speculation. For the pure devotees like Vidura, the topics of both the mundaners and the mental speculators are useless in all respects. Thus Vidura requested Maitreya to talk of the essence only, the talks of Kṛṣṇa, and nothing else.

TEXT 16

स विश्वजन्मस्थितिसंयमार्थे
कृतावतारः प्रगृहीतशक्तिः ।
चकार कर्माण्यतिपूरुषाणि
यानीश्वरः कीर्तय तानि मह्यम् ॥१६॥

sa viśva-janma-sthiti-saṁyamārthe
kṛtāvatāraḥ pragṛhīta-śaktiḥ
cakāra karmāṇy atipūruṣāṇi
yānīśvaraḥ kīrtaya tāni mahyam

saḥ—the Personality of Godhead; *viśva*—universe; *janma*—creation; *sthiti*—maintenance; *saṁyama-arthe*—with a view to perfect control; *kṛta*—accepted; *avatāraḥ*—incarnation; *pragṛhīta*—accomplished with; *śaktiḥ*—potency; *cakāra*—performed; *karmāṇi*—transcendental activities; *ati-pūruṣāṇi*—superhuman; *yāni*—all those; *īśvaraḥ*—the Lord; *kīrtaya*—please chant; *tāni*—all those; *mahyam*—unto me.

TRANSLATION

Kindly chant all those superhuman transcendental activities of the supreme controller, the Personality of Godhead, who accepted incarnations fully equipped with all potency for the full manifestation and maintenance of the cosmic creation.

PURPORT

Vidura was undoubtedly very eager to hear about Lord Kṛṣṇa in particular, but he was overwhelmed because Lord Kṛṣṇa had just passed away from the visible world. He therefore wanted to hear about Him in His *puruṣa* incarnations, which He manifests with full potencies for the creation and maintenance of the cosmic world. The activities of the *puruṣa* incarnations are but an extension of the activities of the Lord. This hint was given by Vidura to Maitreya because Maitreya could not decide which part of the activities of Lord Kṛṣṇa should be chanted.

TEXT 17

श्रीशुक उवाच
स एवं भगवान् पृष्टः क्षत्त्रा कौषारवो मुनिः ।
पुंसां निःश्रेयसार्थेन तमाह बहुमानयन् ॥१७॥

śrī-śuka uvāca
sa evaṁ bhagavān pṛṣṭaḥ
kṣattrā kauṣāravo muniḥ
puṁsāṁ niḥśreyasārthena
tam āha bahu-mānayan

śrī-śukaḥ uvāca—Śrī Śukadeva Gosvāmī said; *saḥ*—he; *evam*—thus; *bhagavān*—the great sage; *pṛṣṭaḥ*—being requested; *kṣattrā*—by Vidura; *kauṣāravaḥ*—Maitreya; *muniḥ*—the great sage; *puṁsām*—for all people; *niḥśreyasa*—for the greatest welfare; *arthena*—for that; *tam*—unto him; *āha*—narrated; *bahu*—greatly; *mānayan*—honoring.

TRANSLATION

Śukadeva Gosvāmī said: The great sage Maitreya Muni, after honoring Vidura very greatly, began to speak, at Vidura's request, for the greatest welfare of all people.

PURPORT

The great sage Maitreya Muni is described here as *bhagavān* because he surpassed all ordinary human beings in learning and experience. Thus his selection of the greatest welfare service for the world is considered authoritative. The all-inclusive welfare service for the entire human society is devotional service to the Lord, and, as requested by Vidura, the sage described the same very appropriately.

TEXT 18

मैत्रेय उवाच
साधु पृष्टं त्वया साधो लोकान् साध्वनुगृह्णता ।
कीर्तिं वितन्वता लोके आत्मनोऽधोक्षजात्मनः ॥१८॥

maitreya uvāca
sādhu pṛṣṭaṁ tvayā sādho
lokān sādhv anugṛhṇatā
kīrtiṁ vitanvatā loke
ātmano 'dhokṣajātmanaḥ

maitreyaḥ uvāca—Śrī Maitreya said; *sādhu*—all good; *pṛṣṭam*—I am asked; *tvayā*—by you; *sādho*—O good one; *lokān*—all the people; *sādhu anugṛhṇatā*—showing mercy in goodness; *kīrtim*—glories; *vitanvatā*—broadcasting; *loke*—in the world; *ātmanaḥ*—of the self; *adhokṣaja*—the Transcendence; *ātmanaḥ*—mind.

TRANSLATION

Śrī Maitreya said: O Vidura, all glory unto you. You have inquired from me of the greatest of all goodness, and thus you have shown your mercy both to the world and to me because your mind is always absorbed in thoughts of the Transcendence.

PURPORT

Maitreya Muni, who was experienced in the science of Transcendence, could understand that Vidura's mind was fully absorbed in Transcendence. *Adhokṣaja* means that which transcends the limits of sense perception or sensuous experience. The Lord is transcendental to our sense experience, but He reveals Himself to the sincere devotee. Because Vidura was always absorbed in thought of the Lord, Maitreya could estimate Vidura's transcendental value. He appreciated the valuable inquiries of Vidura and thus thanked him with great honor.

TEXT 19

नैतच्चित्रं त्वयि क्षत्तर्बादरायणवीर्यजे ।
गृहीतोऽनन्यभावेन यत्त्वया हरिरीश्वरः ॥१९॥

naitac citraṁ tvayi kṣattar
bādarāyaṇa-vīryaje
gṛhīto 'nanya-bhāvena
yat tvayā harir īśvaraḥ

na—never; *etat*—such inquiries; *citram*—very wonderful; *tvayi*—in you; *kṣattaḥ*—O Vidura; *bādarāyaṇa*—of Vyāsadeva; *vīrya-je*—born from the semen; *gṛhītaḥ*—accepted; *ananya-bhāvena*—without deviation from the thought; *yat*—because; *tvayā*—by you; *hariḥ*—the Personality of Godhead; *īśvaraḥ*—the Lord.

TRANSLATION

O Vidura, it is not at all wonderful that you have so accepted the Lord without deviation of thought, for you were born from the semen of Vyāsadeva.

PURPORT

The value of great parentage and noble birth is evaluated here in connection with the birth of Vidura. The culture of a human being begins when the father invests his semen in the womb of the mother. According to his status of work, a living entity is placed in a particular father's semen, and because Vidura was not an ordinary living entity, he was given the chance to be born from the semen of Vyāsa. The birth of a human being is a great science, and therefore reformation of the act of impregnation according to the Vedic ritual called *Garbhādhāna-saṁskāra* is very important for generating good population. The problem is not to check the growth of the population, but to generate good population on the level of Vidura, Vyāsa and Maitreya. There is no need to check the growth of population if the children are born as human beings with all precautions regarding their birth. So-called birth control is not only vicious but also useless.

TEXT 20

माण्डव्यशापाद्भगवान् प्रजासंयमनो यमः ।
भ्रातुः क्षेत्रे भुजिष्यायां जातः सत्यवतीसुतात् ॥२०॥

māṇḍavya-śāpād bhagavān
prajā-saṁyamano yamaḥ
bhrātuḥ kṣetre bhujiṣyāyāṁ
jātaḥ satyavatī-sutāt

māṇḍavya—the great *ṛṣi* Māṇḍavya Muni; *śāpāt*—by his curse; *bhagavān*—the greatly powerful; *prajā*—one who is born; *saṁyamanaḥ*—controller of death; *yamaḥ*—known as Yamarāja; *bhrātuḥ*—of the brother; *kṣetre*—in the wife; *bhujiṣyāyām*—kept; *jātaḥ*—born; *satyavatī*—Satyavatī (the mother of both Vicitravīrya and Vyāsadeva); *sutāt*—by the son (Vyāsadeva).

TRANSLATION

I know that you are now Vidura due to the cursing of Māṇḍavya Muni and that formerly you were King Yamarāja, the great controller of living entities after their death. You were begotten by the son of Satyavatī, Vyāsadeva, in the kept wife of his brother.

PURPORT

Māṇḍavya Muni was a great sage (cf. *Bhāg.* 1.13.1), and Vidura was formerly the controller Yamarāja, who takes charge of the living entities after death. Birth, maintenance and death are three conditional states of the living entities who are within the material world. As the appointed controller after death, Yamarāja once tried Māṇḍavya Muni for his childhood profligacy and ordered him to be pierced with a lance. Māṇḍavya, being angry at Yamarāja for awarding him undue punishment, cursed him to become a *śūdra* (member of the less intelligent laborer class). Thus Yamarāja took birth in the womb of the kept wife of Vicitravīrya from the semen of Vicitravīrya's brother, Vyāsadeva. Vyāsadeva is the son of Satyavatī by the great King Śāntanu, the father of Bhīṣmadeva. This mysterious history of Vidura was known to Maitreya Muni because he happened to be a contemporary friend of Vyāsadeva's. In spite of Vidura's birth from the womb of a kept wife, because he had otherwise high parentage and great connection he inherited the highest talent of becoming a great devotee of the Lord. To take birth in such a great family is understood to be an advantage for attaining devotional life. Vidura was given this chance due to his previous greatness.

TEXT 21

भवान् भगवतो नित्यं सम्मतः सानुगस्य ह ।
यस्य ज्ञानोपदेशाय मादिशद्भगवान् व्रजन् ॥२१॥

bhavān bhagavato nityaṁ
sammataḥ sānugasya ha
yasya jñānopadeśāya
mādiśad bhagavān vrajan

bhavān—your good self; *bhagavataḥ*—of the Personality of Godhead; *nityam*—eternal; *sammataḥ*—recognized; *sa-anugasya*—one of the associates; *ha*—have been; *yasya*—of whom; *jñāna*—knowledge; *upadeśāya*—for instructing; *mā*—unto me; *ādiśat*—so ordered; *bhagavān*—the Personality of Godhead; *vrajan*—while returning to His abode.

TRANSLATION

Your good self is one of the eternal associates of the Supreme Personality of Godhead for whose sake the Lord, while going back to His abode, left instructions with me.

PURPORT

Yamarāja, the great controller of life after death, decides the living entities' destinies in their next lives. He is surely among the most confidential representatives of the Lord. Such confidential posts are offered to great devotees of the Lord who are as good as His eternal associates in the spiritual sky. And because Vidura happened to be among them, the Lord, while returning to Vaikuṇṭha, left instructions for Vidura with Maitreya Muni. Generally the eternal associates of the Lord in the spiritual sky do not come to the material world. Sometimes they come, however, by the order of the Lord—not to hold any administrative post, but to associate with the Lord in person or to propagate the message of God in human society. Such empowered representatives are called *śaktyāveśa-avatāras,* or incarnations invested with transcendental power of attorney.

TEXT 22

अथ ते भगवल्लीला योगमायोरुबृंहिताः ।
विश्वस्थित्युद्भवान्तार्था वर्णयाम्यनुपूर्वशः ॥२२॥

atha te bhagaval-līlā
yoga-māyorubṛṁhitāḥ
viśva-sthity-udbhavāntārthā
varṇayāmy anupūrvaśaḥ

atha—therefore; *te*—unto you; *bhagavat*—pertaining to the Personality of Godhead; *līlāḥ*—pastimes; *yoga-māyā*—energy of the Lord; *uru*—greatly; *bṛṁhitāḥ*—extended by; *viśva*—of the cosmic world; *sthiti*—maintenance; *udbhava*—creation; *anta*—dissolution; *arthāḥ*—purpose; *varṇayāmi*—I shall describe; *anupūrvaśaḥ*—systematically.

TRANSLATION

I shall therefore describe to you the pastimes by which the Personality of Godhead extends His transcendental potency for the creation, maintenance and dissolution of the cosmic world as they occur one after another.

PURPORT

The omnipotent Lord, by His different energies, can perform anything and everything He likes. The creation of the cosmic world is done by His *yogamāyā* energy.

TEXT 23

भगवानेक आसेदमग्र आत्मात्मनां विभुः ।
आत्मेच्छानुगतावात्मा नानामत्युपलक्षणः ॥२३॥

bhagavān eka āsedam
agra ātmātmanāṁ vibhuḥ
ātmecchānugatāv ātmā
nānā-maty-upalakṣaṇaḥ

bhagavān—the Personality of Godhead; *ekaḥ*—one without a second; *āsa*—was there; *idam*—this creation; *agre*—prior to the creation; *ātmā*—in His own form; *ātmanām*—of the living entities; *vibhuḥ*—master; *ātmā*—Self; *icchā*—desire; *anugatau*—being merged in; *ātmā*—Self; *nānā-mati*—different vision; *upalakṣaṇaḥ*—symptoms.

TRANSLATION

The Personality of Godhead, the master of all living entities, existed prior to the creation as one without a second. It is by His will only that creation is made possible and again everything merges in Him. This Supreme Self is symptomized by different names.

PURPORT

The great sage here begins to explain the purpose of the four original verses of the *Śrīmad-Bhāgavatam.* Although they have no access to the *Śrīmad-Bhāgavatam,* the followers of the Māyāvāda (impersonalist) school sometimes screw out an imaginary explanation of the original four verses, but we must accept the actual explanation given herein by Maitreya Muni because he, along with Uddhava, personally heard it directly from the Lord. The first line of the original four verses runs, *aham evāsam evāgre.* The word *aham* is misinterpreted by the Māyāvāda school into meanings which no one but the interpreter can understand. Here *aham* is explained as the Supreme Personality of Godhead, not the individual living entities. Before the creation, there was only the Personality of Godhead; there were no *puruṣa* incarnations and certainly no living entities, nor was there the material energy, by which the manifested creation is effected. The *puruṣa* incarnations and all the different energies of the Supreme Lord were merged in Him only.

The Personality of Godhead is described herein as the master of all other living entities. He is like the sun disc, and the living entities are like the molecules of the sun's rays. This existence of the Lord before the creation is confirmed by the *śrutis: vāsudevo vā idaṁ agra āsīt na brahmā na ca śaṅkaraḥ, eko vai nārāyaṇa āsīn na brahmā neśanaḥ.* Because everything that be is an emanation from the Personality of Godhead, He always exists alone without a second. He can so exist because He is all-perfect and omnipotent. Everything other than Him, including His plenary expansions, the *viṣṇu-tattvas,* is His part and parcel. Before the creation there were no Kāraṇārṇavaśāyī or Garbhodakaśāyī or Kṣīrodakaśāyī Viṣṇus, or was there Brahmā nor Śaṅkara. The Viṣṇu plenary expansion and the living entities beginning from Brahmā are separated parts and parcels. Although the spiritual existence was there with the Lord, the material existence was dormant in Him. By His will only is the material manifestation done and undone. The diversity of the Vaikuṇṭhaloka is one with the Lord, just as the diversity of soldiers is one with and the same as the king. As explained in *Bhagavad-gītā* (9.7), the material creation takes place at intervals by the will of the Lord, and in the periods between dissolution and creation, the living entities and the material energy remain dormant in Him.

TEXT 24

स वा एष तदा द्रष्टा नापश्यद् दृश्यमेकराट् ।
मेनेऽसन्तमिवात्मानं सुप्तशक्तिरसुप्तदृक् ॥२४॥

sa vā eṣa tadā draṣṭā
nāpaśyad dṛśyam ekarāṭ
mene 'santam ivātmānaṁ
supta-śaktir asupta-dṛk

saḥ—the Personality of Godhead; *vā*—either; *eṣaḥ*—all these; *tadā*—at that time; *draṣṭā*—the seer; *na*—did not; *apaśyat*—see; *dṛśyam*—the cosmic creation; *eka-rāṭ*—undisputed proprietor; *mene*—thought like this; *asantam*—nonexistent; *iva*—like that; *ātmānam*—plenary manifestations; *supta*—unmanifested; *śaktiḥ*—material energy; *asupta*—manifested; *dṛk*—internal potency.

TRANSLATION

The Lord, the undisputed proprietor of everything, was the only seer. The cosmic manifestation was not present at that time, and thus He felt imperfect without His plenary and separated parts and parcels. The material energy was dormant, whereas the internal potency was manifested.

PURPORT

The Lord is the supreme seer because only by His glance did the material energy become active for cosmic manifestation. At that time the seer was there, but the external energy, over which the glance of the Lord is cast, was not present. He felt somewhat insufficient, like a husband feeling lonely in the absence of his wife. This is a poetic simile. The Lord wanted to create the cosmic manifestation to give another chance to the conditioned souls who were dormant in forgetfulness. The cosmic manifestation gives the conditioned souls a chance to go back home, back to Godhead, and that is its main purpose. The Lord is so kind that in the absence of such a manifestation He feels something wanting, and thus the creation takes place. Although the creation of the internal potency was manifested, the other potency appeared to be sleeping, and the Lord wanted to awaken her to activity, just as a husband wants to awaken his wife from the sleeping state for enjoyment. It is the compassion of the Lord for the sleeping energy that He wants to see her awaken for enjoyment like the other wives who are awake. The whole process is to enliven the sleeping conditioned souls to the real life of spiritual consciousness so that they may thus become as perfect as the ever-liberated souls in the Vaikuṇṭhalokas. Since the Lord is *sac-cid-ānanda-vigraha,* He likes every part and parcel of His different potencies to take part in the blissful *rasa* because participation with the Lord in His eternal *rāsa-līlā* is the highest living condition, perfect in spiritual bliss and eternal knowledge.

TEXT 25

सा वा एतस्य संद्रष्टुः शक्तिः सदसदात्मिका ।
माया नाम महाभाग ययेदं निर्ममे विभुः ॥२५॥

sā vā etasya saṁdraṣṭuḥ
śaktiḥ sad-asad-ātmikā
māyā nāma mahā-bhāga
yayedaṁ nirmame vibhuḥ

sā—that external energy; *vā*—is either; *etasya*—of the Lord; *saṁdraṣṭuḥ*—of the perfect seer; *śaktiḥ*—energy; *sat-asat-ātmikā*—as both the cause and the effect; *māyā nāma*—called by the name *māyā; mahā-bhāga*—O fortunate one; *yayā*—by which; *idam*—this material world; *nirmame*—constructed; *vibhuḥ*—the Almighty.

TRANSLATION

The Lord is the seer, and the external energy, which is seen, works as both cause and effect in the cosmic manifestation. O greatly fortunate Vidura, this external energy is known as māyā or illusion, and through her agency only is the entire material manifestation made possible.

PURPORT

The material nature, known as *māyā*, is both the material and efficient cause of the cosmos, but in the background the Lord is the consciousness for all activities. As in the individual body the consciousness is the source of all energies of the body, so the supreme consciousness of the Lord is the source of all energies in material nature. This is confirmed in *Bhagavad-gītā* (9.10) as follows:

mayādhyakṣeṇa prakṛtiḥ
sūyate sa-carācaram
hetunānena kaunteya
jagad viparivartate

"Throughout all the energies of material nature there is the hand of the Supreme Lord as the final superintendent. Due to this supreme cause only, the activities of material nature appear planned and systematic, and all thing regularly evolve."

TEXT 26

कालवृत्त्या तु मायायां गुणमय्यामधोक्षजः ।
पुरुषेणात्मभूतेन वीर्यमाधत्त वीर्यवान् ॥२६॥

kāla-vṛttyā tu māyāyāṁ
guṇa-mayyām adhokṣajaḥ
puruṣeṇātma-bhūtena
vīryam ādhatta vīryavān

kāla—the eternal time; *vṛttyā*—by the influence of; *tu*—but; *māyāyām*—in the external energy; *guṇa-mayyām*—in the qualitative modes of nature; *adhokṣajaḥ*—the Transcendence; *puruṣeṇa*—by the *puruṣa* incarnation; *ātma-bhūtena*—who is the plenary expansion of the Lord; *vīryam*—the seeds of the living entities; *ādhatta*—impregnated; *vīryavān*—the Supreme Living Being.

TRANSLATION

The Supreme Living Being in His feature as the transcendental puruṣa incarnation, who is the Lord's plenary expansion, impregnates the material nature of three modes, and thus by the influence of eternal time the living entities appear.

PURPORT

The offspring of any living being is born after the father impregnates the mother with semen, and the living entity floating in the semen of the father takes the shape of the mother's form. Similarly, mother material nature cannot produce any living entity from her material elements unless and until she is impregnated with living entities by the Lord Himself. That is the mystery of the generation of the living entities. This impregnating process is performed by the first *puruṣa* incarnation, Kāraṇārṇavaśāyī Viṣṇu. Simply by His glance over material nature, the whole matter is accomplished.

We should not understand the process of impregnation by the Personality of Godhead in terms of our conception of sex. The omnipotent Lord can impregnate just by His eyes, and therefore He is called all-potent. Each and every part of His transcendental body can perform each and every function of the other parts. This is confirmed in the *Brahma-saṁhitā* (5.32): *aṅgāni yasya sakalendriya-vṛttimanti.* In *Bhagavad-gītā* (14.3) also, the same principle is confirmed: *mama yonir mahad-brahma tasmin garbhaṁ dadhāmy aham.* When the cosmic creation is manifested, the living entities are directly supplied from the Lord; they are never products of material nature. Thus, no scientific advancement of material science can ever produce a living being. That is the whole mystery of the material creation. The living entities are foreign to matter, and thus they cannot be happy unless they are situated in the same spiritual life as the Lord. The mistaken living being, out of forgetfulness of this original condition of life, unnecessarily wastes time trying to become happy in the material world. The whole Vedic process is to remind one of this essential feature of life. The Lord offers the conditioned soul a material body for his so-called enjoyment, but if one does not come to his senses and enter into spiritual consciousness, the Lord again puts him in the unmanifested condition as it existed in the beginning of the creation. The Lord is described here as *vīryavān*, or the greatest potent being, because He impregnates material nature with innumerable living entities who are conditioned from time immemorial.

TEXT 27

ततोऽभवन् महत्तत्त्वमव्यक्तात्कालचोदितात् ।
विज्ञानात्मात्मदेहस्थं विश्वं व्यञ्जंस्तमोनुदः ॥२७॥

tato 'bhavan mahat-tattvam
avyaktāt kāla-coditāt
vijñānātmātma-deha-sthaṁ
viśvaṁ vyañjaṁs tamo-nudaḥ

tataḥ—thereafter; *abhavat*—came into existence; *mahat*—supreme; *tattvam*—sum total; *avyaktāt*—from the unmanifested; *kāla-coditāt*—by the interaction of time; *vijñāna-ātmā*—unalloyed goodness; *ātma-deha-stham*—situated on the bodily self; *viśvam*—complete universes; *vyañjan*—manifesting; *tamaḥ-nudaḥ*—the supreme light.

TRANSLATION

Thereafter, influenced by the interactions of eternal time, the supreme sum total of matter called the mahat-tattva became manifested, and in this mahat-tattva the unalloyed goodness, the Supreme Lord, sowed the seeds of universal manifestation out of His own body.

PURPORT

In due course of time, the impregnated material energy was manifested first as the total material ingredients. Everything takes its own time to fructify, and therefore the word *kāla-coditāt*, "influenced by time," is used herein. The *mahat-tattva* is the total consciousness because a portion of it is represented in everyone as the intellect. The *mahat-tattva* is directly connected with the supreme consciousness of the Supreme Being, but still it appears as matter. The *mahat-tattva*, or shadow of pure consciousness, is the germinating place of all creation. It is pure goodness with the slight addition of the material mode of passion, and therefore activity is generated from this point.

TEXT 28

सोऽप्यंशगुणकालात्मा भगवद्दृष्टिगोचरः ।
आत्मानं व्यकरोदात्मा विश्वस्यास्य सिसृक्षया ॥२८॥

so 'py aṁśa-guṇa-kālātmā
bhagavad-dṛṣṭi-gocaraḥ
ātmānaṁ vyakarod ātmā
viśvasyāsya sisṛkṣayā

saḥ—*mahat-tattva; api*—also; *aṁśa*—*puruṣa* plenary expansion; *guṇa*—chiefly the quality of ignorance; *kāla*—the duration of time; *ātmā*—full consciousness; *bhagavat*—the Personality of Godhead; *dṛṣṭi-gocaraḥ*—range of sight; *ātmānam*—many different forms; *vyakarot*—differentiated; *ātmā*—reservoir; *viśvasya*—the would-be entities; *asya*—of this; *sisṛkṣayā*—generates the false ego.

TRANSLATION

Thereafter the mahat-tattva differentiated itself into many different forms as the reservoir of the would-be entities. The mahat-tattva is chiefly in the mode of ignorance, and it generates the false ego. It is a plenary expansion of the Personality of Godhead, with full consciousness of creative principles and time for fructification.

PURPORT

The *mahat-tattva* is the via medium between pure spirit and material existence. It is the junction of matter and spirit wherefrom the false ego of the living entity is generated. All living entities are differentiated parts and parcels of the Personality of Godhead. Under the pressure of false ego, the conditioned souls, although parts and parcels of the Supreme Personality of Godhead, claim to be the enjoyers of material nature. This false ego is the binding force of material existence. The Lord again and again gives a chance to the bewildered conditioned souls to get free from this false ego, and that is why the material creation takes place at intervals. He gives the conditioned souls all facilities for rectifying the activities of the false ego, but He does not interfere with their small independence as parts and parcels of the Lord.

TEXT 29

महत्तत्त्वाद्विकुर्वाणादहंतत्त्वं व्यजायत ।
कार्यकारणकर्त्रात्मा भूतेन्द्रियमनोमयः ।
वैकारिकस्तैजसश्च तामसश्चेत्यहं त्रिधा ॥२९॥

mahat-tattvād vikurvāṇād
ahaṁ-tattvaṁ vyajāyata
kārya-kāraṇa-kartrātmā
bhūtendriya-mano-mayaḥ
vaikārikas taijasaś ca
tāmasaś cety ahaṁ tridhā

mahat—the great; *tattvāt*—from the causal truth; *vikurvāṇāt*—being transformed; *aham*—false ego; *tattvam*—material truth; *vyajāyata*—became manifested; *kārya*—effects; *kāraṇa*—cause; *kartṛ*—doer; *ātmā*—soul or source; *bhūta*—material ingredients; *indriya*—senses; *manaḥ-mayaḥ*—hovering on the mental plane; *vaikārikaḥ*—the mode of goodness; *taijasaḥ*—the mode of passion; *ca*—and; *tāmasaḥ*—the mode of ignorance; *ca*—and; *iti*—thus; *aham*—false ego; *tridhā*—three kinds.

TRANSLATION

Mahat-tattva, or the great causal truth, transforms into false ego, which is manifested in three phases—cause, effect and the doer. All such activities are on the mental plane and are based on the material elements, gross senses and mental speculation. The false ego is represented in three different modes—goodness, passion and ignorance.

PURPORT

A pure living entity in his original spiritual existence is fully conscious of his constitutional position as an eternal servitor of the Lord. All souls who are situated in such pure consciousness are liberated, and therefore they eternally live in bliss and knowledge in the various Vaikuṇṭha planets in the spiritual sky. When the material creation is manifested, it is not meant for them. The eternally liberated souls are called *nitya-muktas*, and they have nothing to do with the material creation. The material creation is meant for rebellious souls who are not prepared to accept subordination under the Supreme Lord. This spirit of false lordship is called false ego. It is manifested in three modes of material nature, and it exists in mental speculation only. Those who are in the mode of goodness think that each and every person is God, and thus they laugh at the pure devotees, who try to engage in the transcendental loving service of the Lord. Those who are puffed up by the mode of passion try to lord it over material nature in various ways. Some of them engage in altruistic activities as if they were agents appointed to do good to others by their mental speculative plans. Such men accept the standard ways of mundane altruism, but their plans are made on the basis of false ego. This false ego extends to the limit of becoming one with the Lord. The last class of egoistic conditioned souls—those in the mode of ignorance—are misguided by identification of the gross body with the self. Thus, all their activities are centered around the body only. All these persons are given the chance to play with false egoistic ideas, but at the same time the Lord is kind enough to give them a chance to take help from scriptures like *Bhagavad-gītā* and *Śrīmad-Bhāgavatam* so that they may understand the science of Kṛṣṇa and thus make their lives successful. The entire material creation, therefore, is meant for the falsely egoistic living entities hovering on the mental plane under different illusions in the modes of material nature.

TEXT 30

अहंतत्त्वाद्विकुर्वाणान्मनो वैकारिकादभूत् ।
वैकारिकाश्च ये देवा अर्थाभिव्यञ्जनं यतः ॥३०॥

ahaṁ-tattvād vikurvāṇān
mano vaikārikād abhūt
vaikārikāś ca ye devā
arthābhivyañjanaṁ yataḥ

aham-tattvāt—from the principle of false ego; *vikurvāṇāt*—by transformation; *manaḥ*—the mind; *vaikārikāt*—by interaction with the mode of goodness; *abhūt*—generated; *vaikārikāḥ*—by interaction with goodness; *ca*—also; *ye*—all these; *devāḥ*—demigods; *artha*—the phenomenon; *abhivyañjanam*—physical knowledge; *yataḥ*—the source.

TRANSLATION

The false ego is transformed into mind by interaction with the mode of goodness. All the demigods who control the phenomenal world are also products of the same principle, namely the interaction of false ego and the mode of goodness.

PURPORT

False ego interacting with the different modes of material nature is the source of all materials in the phenomenal world.

TEXT 31

तैजसानीन्द्रियाण्येव ज्ञानकर्ममयानि च ॥३१॥

taijasānīndriyāṇy eva
jñāna-karma-mayāni ca

taijasāni—the mode of passion; *indriyāṇi*—the senses; *eva*—certainly; *jñāna*—knowledge, philosophical speculations; *karma*—fruitive activities; *mayāni*—predominating; *ca*—also.

TRANSLATION

The senses are certainly products of the mode of passion in false ego, and therefore philosophical speculative knowledge and fruitive activities are predominantly products of the mode of passion.

PURPORT

The chief function of the false ego is godlessness. When a person forgets his constitutional position as an eternally subordinate part and parcel of the Supreme Personality of Godhead and wants to be happy independently, he functions mainly in two ways. He first attempts to act fruitively for personal gain or sense gratification, and after attempting such fruitive activities for a considerable time, when he is frustrated he becomes a philosophical speculator and thinks himself to be on the same level as God. This false idea of becoming one with the Lord is the last snare of the illusory energy, which traps a living entity into the bondage of forgetfulness under the spell of false ego.

The best means of liberation from the clutches of false ego is to give up the habit of philosophical speculation regarding the Absolute Truth. One should know definitely that the Absolute Truth is never realized by the philosophical speculations of the imperfect egoistic person. The Absolute Truth, or the Supreme Personality of Godhead, is realized by hearing about Him in all submission and love from a bona fide authority who is a representative of the twelve great authorities mentioned in the *Śrīmad-Bhāgavatam.* By such an attempt only can one conquer the illusory energy of the Lord, although for others she is unsurpassable, as confirmed in *Bhagavad-gītā* (7.14).

TEXT 32

तामसो भूतसूक्ष्मादिर्यतः खं लिङ्गमात्मनः ॥३२॥

tāmaso bhūta-sūkṣmādir
yataḥ khaṁ liṅgam ātmanaḥ

tāmasaḥ—from the mode of passion; *bhūta-sūkṣma-ādiḥ*—subtle sense objects; *yataḥ*—from which; *kham*—the sky; *liṅgam*—symbolic representation; *ātmanaḥ*—of the Supreme Soul.

TRANSLATION

The sky is a product of sound, and sound is the transformation of egoistic passion. In other words, the sky is the symbolic representation of the Supreme Soul.

PURPORT

In the Vedic hymns it is said, *etasmād ātmanaḥ ākāśaḥ sambhūtaḥ.* The sky is the symbolic representation of the Supreme Soul. Those who are egoistic in passion and ignorance cannot conceive of the Personality of Godhead. For them the sky is the symbolic representation of the Supreme Soul.

TEXT 33

कालमायांशयोगेन भगवद्वीक्षितं नभः ।
नभसोऽनुसृतं स्पर्शं विकुर्वन्निर्ममेऽनिलम् ॥३३॥

kāla-māyāṁśa-yogena
bhagavad-vīkṣitaṁ nabhaḥ
nabhaso 'nusṛtaṁ sparśaṁ
vikurvan nirmame 'nilam

kāla—time; *māyā*—external energy; *aṁśa-yogena*—partly mixed; *bhagavat*—the Personality of Godhead; *vīkṣitam*—glanced over; *nabhaḥ*—the sky; *nabhasaḥ*—from the sky; *anusṛtam*—being so contacted; *sparśam*—touch; *vikurvat*—being transformed; *nirmame*—was created; *anilam*—the air.

TRANSLATION

Thereafter the Personality of Godhead glanced over the sky, partly mixed with eternal time and external energy, and thus developed the touch sensation, from which the air in the sky was produced.

PURPORT

All material creations take place from subtle to gross. The entire universe has developed in that manner. From the sky developed the touch sensation, which is a mixture of eternal time, the external energy and the glance of the Personality of Godhead. The touch sensation developed into the air in the sky. Similarly, all other gross matter also developed from subtle to gross: sound developed into sky, touch developed into air, form developed into fire, taste developed into water, and smell developed into earth.

TEXT 34

अनिलोऽपि विकुर्वाणो नभसोरुबलान्वितः ।
ससर्ज रूपतन्मात्रं ज्योतिर्लोकस्य लोचनम् ॥३४॥

anilo 'pi vikurvāṇo
nabhasoru-balānvitaḥ
sasarja rūpa-tanmātraṁ
jyotir lokasya locanam

anilaḥ—air; *api*—also; *vikurvāṇaḥ*—being transformed; *nabhasā*—sky; *uru-bala-anvitaḥ*—extremely powerful; *sasarja*—created; *rūpa*—form; *tat-mātram*—sense perception; *jyotiḥ*—electricity; *lokasya*—of the world; *locanam*—light to see.

TRANSLATION

Thereafter the extremely powerful air, interacting with the sky, generated the form of sense perception, and the perception of form transformed into electricity, the light to see the world.

TEXT 35

अनिलेनान्वितं ज्योतिर्विकुर्वत्परवीक्षितम् ।
आधत्ताम्भो रसमयं कालमायांशयोगतः ॥३५॥

anilenānvitaṁ jyotir
vikurvat paravīkṣitam
ādhattāmbho rasa-mayaṁ
kāla-māyāṁśa-yogataḥ

anilena—by the air; *anvitam*—interacted; *jyotiḥ*—electricity; *vikurvat*—being transformed; *paravīkṣitam*—being glanced over by the Supreme; *ādhatta*—created; *ambhaḥ rasa-mayam*—water with taste; *kāla*—of eternal time; *māyā-aṁśa*—and external energy; *yogataḥ*—by a mixture.

TRANSLATION

When electricity was surcharged in the air and was glanced over by the Supreme, at that time, by a mixture of eternal time and external energy, there occurred the creation of water and taste.

TEXT 36

ज्योतिषाम्भोऽनुसंसृष्टं विकुर्वद्ब्रह्मवीक्षितम् ।
महीं गन्धगुणामाधात्कालमायांशयोगतः ॥३६॥

jyotiṣāmbho 'nusaṁsṛṣṭaṁ
vikurvad brahma-vīkṣitam
mahīṁ gandha-guṇām ādhāt
kāla-māyāṁśa-yogataḥ

jyotiṣā—electricity; *ambhaḥ*—water; *anusaṁsṛṣṭam*—thus created; *vikurvat*—due to transformation; *brahma*—the Supreme; *vīkṣitam*—so glanced over; *mahīm*—the earth; *gandha*—smell; *guṇām*—qualification; *ādhāt*—was created; *kāla*—eternal time; *māyā*—external energy; *aṁśa*—partially; *yogataḥ*—by intermixture.

TRANSLATION

Thereafter the water produced from electricity was glanced over by the Supreme Personality of Godhead and mixed with eternal time and external energy. Thus it was transformed into the earth, which is qualified primarily by smell.

PURPORT

From the descriptions of the physical elements in the above verses it is clear that in all stages the glance of the Supreme is needed with the other additions and alterations. In every transformation, the last finishing touch is the glance of the Lord, who acts as a painter does when he mixes different colors to transform them into a particular color. When one element mixes with another, the number of its qualities increases. For example, the sky is the cause of air. The sky has only one quality, namely sound, but by the interaction of the sky with the glance of the Lord, mixed with eternal time and external nature, the air is produced, which has two qualities—sound and touch. Similarly after the air is created, interaction of sky and air, touched by time and the external energy of the Lord, produces electricity. And after the interaction of electricity with air and sky, mixed with time, external energy and the Lord's glance over them, the water is produced. In the final stage of sky there is one quality, namely sound; in the air two qualities, sound and touch; in the electricity three qualities, namely sound, touch and form; in the water four qualities, sound, touch, form and taste; and in the last stage of physical development the result is earth, which has all five qualities—sound, touch, form, taste and smell. Although they are different mixtures of different materials, such mixtures do not take place automatically, just as a mixture of colors does not take place automatically without the touch of the living painter. The automatic system is factually activated by the glancing touch of the Lord. Living consciousness is the final word in all physical changes. This fact is mentioned in *Bhagavad-gītā* (9.10) as follows:

mayādhyakṣeṇa prakṛtiḥ
sūyate sa-carācaram
hetunānena kaunteya
jagad viparivartate

The conclusion is that the physical elements may work very wonderfully to the laymen's eyes, but their workings actually take place under the supervision of the Lord. Those who can mark only the changes of the physical elements and cannot perceive the hidden hands of the Lord behind them are certainly less intelligent persons, although they may be advertised as great material scientists.

TEXT 37

भूतानां नभ आदीनां यद्यद्भव्यावरावरम् ।
तेषां परानुसंसर्गाद्यथासंख्यं गुणान् विदुः ॥३७॥

bhūtānāṁ nabha-ādīnāṁ
yad yad bhavyāvarāvaram
teṣāṁ parānusaṁsargād
yathā saṅkhyaṁ guṇān viduḥ

bhūtānām—of all the physical elements; *nabhaḥ*—the sky; *ādīnām*—beginning from; *yat*—as; *yat*—and as; *bhavya*—O gentle one; *avara*—inferior; *varam*—superior; *teṣām*—all of them; *para*—the Supreme; *anusaṁsargāt*—last touch; *yathā*—as many; *saṅkhyam*—number; *guṇān*—qualities; *viduḥ*—you may understand.

TRANSLATION

O gentle one, of all the physical elements, beginning from the sky down to the earth, all the inferior and superior qualities are due only to the final touch of the glance of the Supreme Personality of Godhead.

TEXT 38

एते देवाः कला विष्णोः कालमायांशलिङ्गिनः ।
नानात्वात्स्वक्रियानीशाः प्रोचुः प्राञ्जलयो विभुम् ॥३८॥

ete devāḥ kalā viṣṇoḥ
kāla-māyāṁśa-liṅginaḥ
nānātvāt sva-kriyānīśāḥ
procuḥ prāñjalayo vibhum

ete—of all these physical elements; *devāḥ*—the controlling demigods; *kalāḥ*—parts and parcels; *viṣṇoḥ*—of the Supreme Personality of Godhead; *kāla*—time; *māyā*—external energy; *aṁśa*—part and parcel; *liṅginaḥ*—so embodied; *nānātvāt*—because of various; *sva-kriyā*—personal duties; *anīśāḥ*—not being able to perform; *procuḥ*—uttered; *prāñjalayaḥ*—fascinating; *vibhum*—unto the Lord.

TRANSLATION

The controlling deities of all the above-mentioned physical elements are empowered expansions of Lord Viṣṇu. They are embodied by eternal time under the external energy, and they are His parts and parcels. Because they were entrusted with different functions of universal duties and were unable to perform them, they offered fascinating prayers to the Lord as follows.

PURPORT

The conception of various controlling demigods who inhabit the higher planetary systems for the management of universal affairs is not imaginary, as proposed by persons with a poor fund of knowledge. The demigods are expanded parts and parcels of the Supreme Lord Viṣṇu, and they are embodied by time, external energy and partial consciousness of the Supreme. Human beings, animals, birds, etc., are also parts and parcels of the Lord and have different material bodies, but they are not the controlling deities of material affairs. They are, rather, controlled by such demigods. Such control is not superfluous; it is as necessary as the controlling departments in the affairs of a modern state. The demigods should not be despised by the controlled living beings. They are all great devotees of the Lord entrusted to execute certain functions of universal affairs. One may be angry with Yamarāja for his thankless task of punishing sinful souls, but Yamarāja is one of the authorized devotees of the Lord, and so are all the other demigods. A devotee of the Lord is never controlled by such deputed demigods, who function as assistants of the Lord, but he shows them all respects on account of the responsible positions to which they have been appointed by the Lord. At the same time, a devotee of the Lord does not foolishly mistake them to be the Supreme Lord. Only foolish persons accept the demigods as being on the same level as Viṣṇu; actually they are all appointed as servants of Viṣṇu.

Anyone who places the Lord and the demigods on the same level is called a *pāṣaṇḍī*, or atheist. The demigods are worshiped by persons who are more or less adherents of the processes of *jñāna, yoga* and *karma*, i.e., the impersonalists, meditators and fruitive workers. The devotees, however, worship only the Supreme Lord Viṣṇu. This worship is not for any material benefit, as desired by all the materialists, even up to the salvationists, mystics and fruitive workers. Devotees worship the Supreme Lord to attain unalloyed devotion to the Lord. The Lord, however, is not worshiped by others, who have no program for attaining love of God, which is the essential aim of human life. Persons averse to a loving relationship with God are more or less condemned by their own actions.

The Lord is equal to every living entity, just like the flowing Ganges. The Ganges water is meant for the purification of everyone, yet the trees on the banks of the Ganges have different values. A mango tree on the bank of the Ganges drinks the water, and the *nimba* tree also drinks the same water. But the fruits of both trees are different. One is celestially sweet, and the other is hellishly bitter. The condemned bitterness of the *nimba* is due to its own past work, just as the sweetness of the mango is also due to its own *karma*. The Lord says in *Bhagavad-gītā* (16.19):

tān ahaṁ dviṣataḥ krūrān
saṁsāreṣu narādhamān
kṣipāmy ajasram aśubhān
āsurīṣv eva yoniṣu

"The envious, the mischievous, the lowest of mankind, these do I ever put back into the ocean of material existence, into various demoniac species of life." Demigods like Yamarāja and other controllers are there for the unwanted conditioned souls who always engage in threatening the tranquillity of the kingdom of God. Since all the demigods are confidential devotee-servitors of the Lord, they are never to be condemned.

TEXT 39

देवा ऊचुः

नमाम ते देव पदारविन्दं
प्रपन्नतापोपशमातपत्रम् ।
यन्मूलकेता यतयोऽञ्जसोरु-
संसारदुःखं बहिरुत्क्षिपन्ति ॥३९॥

devā ūcuḥ
namāma te deva padāravindaṁ
prapanna-tāpopaśamātapatram
yan-mūla-ketā yatayo 'ñjasoru-
saṁsāra-duḥkhaṁ bahir utkṣipanti

devāḥ ūcuḥ—the demigods said; *namāma*—we offer our respectful obeisances; *te*—Your; *deva*—O Lord; *pada-aravindam*—lotus feet; *prapanna*—surrendered; *tāpa*—distress; *upaśama*—suppresses; *ātapatram*—umbrella; *yat-mūla-ketāḥ*—shelter of the lotus feet; *yatayaḥ*—great sages; *añjasā*—totally; *uru*—great; *saṁsāra-duḥkham*—miseries of material existence; *bahiḥ*—out; *utkṣipanti*—forcibly throw.

TRANSLATION

The demigods said: O Lord, Your lotus feet are like an umbrella for the surrendered souls, protecting them from all the miseries of material existence. All the sages under that shelter throw off all material miseries. We therefore offer our respectful obeisances unto Your lotus feet.

PURPORT

There are many sages and saints who engage in trying to conquer rebirth and all other material miseries. But of all of them, those who take shelter under the lotus feet of the Lord can completely throw off all such miseries without difficulty. Others, who are engaged in transcendental activities in different ways, cannot do so. For them it is very difficult. They may artificially think of becoming liberated without accepting the shelter of the lotus feet of the Lord, but that is not possible. One is sure to fall again to material existence from such false liberation, even though one may have undergone severe penances and austerities. This is the opinion of the demigods, who are not only well versed in Vedic knowledge but are also seers of the past, present and future. The opinions of the demigods are valuable because the demigods are authorized to hold positions in the affairs of universal management. They are appointed by the Lord as His confidential servants.

TEXT 40

धातर्यदस्मिन् भव ईश जीवा-
स्तापत्रयेणाभिहता न शर्म ।
आत्मन्लभन्ते भगवंस्तवाङ्घ्रि-
च्छायां सविद्यामत आश्रयेम ॥४०॥

dhātar yad asmin bhava īśa jīvās
tāpa-trayeṇābhihatā na śarma
ātman labhante bhagavaṁs tavāṅghri-
cchāyāṁ sa-vidyām ata āśrayema

dhātaḥ—O father; *yat*—because; *asmin*—in this; *bhave*—material world; *īśa*—O Lord; *jīvāḥ*—the living entities; *tāpa*—miseries; *trayeṇa*—by the three; *abhihatāḥ*—always embarrassed; *na*—never; *śarma*—in happiness; *ātman*—self; *labhante*—do gain; *bhagavan*—O Personality of Godhead; *tava*—Your; *aṅghri-chāyām*—shade of Your feet; *sa-vidyām*—full of knowledge; *ataḥ*—obtain; *āśrayema*—shelter.

TRANSLATION

O Father, O Lord, O Personality of Godhead, the living entities in the material world can never have any happiness because they are overwhelmed by the three kinds of miseries. Therefore they take shelter of the shade of Your lotus feet, which are full of knowledge, and we also thus take shelter of them.

PURPORT

The way of devotional service is neither sentimental nor mundane. It is the path of reality by which the living entity can attain the transcendental happiness of being freed from the three kinds of material miseries—miseries arising from the body and mind, from other living entities and from natural disturbances. Everyone who is conditioned by material existence—whether he be a man or beast or demigod or bird—must suffer from *ādhyātmika* (bodily or mental) pains, *ādhibhautika* pains (those offered by living creatures), and *ādhidaivika* pains (those due to supernatural disturbances). His happiness is nothing but a hard struggle to get free from the miseries of conditional life. But there is only one way he can be rescued, and that is by accepting the shelter of the lotus feet of the Supreme Personality of Godhead.

The argument that unless one has proper knowledge one cannot be freed from material miseries is undoubtedly true. But because the lotus feet of the Lord are full of transcendental knowledge, acceptance of His lotus feet completes that necessity. We have already discussed this point in the First Canto (1.2.7):

vāsudeve bhagavati
bhakti-yogaḥ prayojitaḥ
janayaty āśu vairāgyaṁ
jñānaṁ ca yad ahaitukam

There is no want of knowledge in the devotional service of Vāsudeva, the Personality of Godhead. He, the Lord, personally takes charge of dissipating the darkness of ignorance from the heart of a devotee. He confirms this in *Bhagavad-gītā* (10.10):

teṣāṁ satata-yuktānāṁ
bhajatāṁ prīti-pūrvakam
dadāmi buddhi-yogaṁ taṁ
yena mām upayānti te

Empiric philosophical speculation cannot give one relief from the threefold miseries of material existence. Simply to endeavor for knowledge without devoting oneself to the Lord is a waste of valuable time.

TEXT 41

मार्गन्ति यत्ते मुखपद्मनीडै-
श्छन्दःसुपर्णैर्ऋषयो विविक्ते ।
यस्याघमर्षोदसरिद्वरायाः
पदं पदं तीर्थपदः प्रपन्नाः ॥४१॥

mārganti yat te mukha-padma-nīḍaiś
chandaḥ-suparṇair ṛṣayo vivikte
yasyāgha-marṣoda-sarid-varāyāḥ
padaṁ padaṁ tīrtha-padaḥ prapannāḥ

mārganti—searching after; *yat*—as; *te*—Your; *mukha-padma*—lotuslike face; *nīḍaiḥ*—by those who have taken shelter of such a lotus flower; *chandaḥ*—Vedic hymns; *suparṇaiḥ*—by the wings; *ṛṣayaḥ*—the sages; *vivikte*—in clear mind; *yasya*—whose; *agha-marṣa-uda*—that which offers freedom from all reactions to sin; *sarit*—rivers; *varāyāḥ*—in the best; *padam padam*—in every step; *tīrtha-padaḥ*—one whose lotus feet are as good as a place of pilgrimage; *prapannāḥ*—taking shelter.

TRANSLATION

The lotus feet of the Lord are by themselves the shelter of all places of pilgrimage. The great clear-minded sages, carried by the wings of the Vedas, always search after the nest of Your lotuslike face. Some of them surrender to Your lotus feet at every step by taking shelter of the best of rivers [the Ganges], which can deliver one from all sinful reactions.

PURPORT

The *paramahaṁsas* are compared to royal swans who make their nests on the petals of the lotus flower. The Lord's transcendental bodily parts are always compared to the lotus flower because in the material world the lotus flower is the last word in beauty. The most beautiful thing in the world is the *Vedas*, or *Bhagavad-gītā*, because therein knowledge is imparted by the Personality of Godhead Himself. The *paramahaṁsa* makes his nest in the lotuslike face of the Lord and always seeks shelter at His lotus feet, which are reached by the wings of Vedic wisdom. Since the Lord is the original source of all emanations, intelligent persons, enlightened by Vedic knowledge, seek the shelter of the Lord, just as birds who leave the nest again search out the nest to take complete rest. All Vedic knowledge is meant for understanding the Supreme Lord, as stated by the Lord in *Bhagavad-gītā* (15.15): *vedaiś ca sarvair aham eva vedyaḥ.* Intelligent persons, who are like swans, take shelter of the Lord by all means and do not hover on the mental plane by fruitlessly speculating on different philosophies.

The Lord is so kind that He has spread the River Ganges throughout the universe so that by taking bath in that holy river everyone can get release from the reactions of sins, which occur at every step. There are many rivers in the world which are able to evoke one's sense of God consciousness simply by one's bathing in them, and the River Ganges is chief amongst them. In India there are five sacred rivers, but the Ganges is the most sacred. The River Ganges and *Bhagavad-gītā* are chief sources of transcendental happiness for mankind, and intelligent persons can take shelter of them to go back home, back to Godhead. Even Śrīpāda Śaṅkarācārya recommends that a little knowledge in *Bhagavad-gītā* and the drinking of a little quantity of Ganges water can save one from the punishment of Yamarāja.

TEXT 42

यच्छ्रद्धया श्रुतवत्या च भक्त्या
सम्मृज्यमाने हृदयेऽवधाय ।
ज्ञानेन वैराग्यबलेन धीरा
व्रजेम तत्तेऽङ्घ्रिसरोजपीठम् ॥४२॥

yac chraddhayā śrutavatyā ca bhaktyā
sammṛjyamāne hṛdaye 'vadhāya
jñānena vairāgya-balena dhīrā
vrajema tat te 'ṅghri-saroja-pīṭham

yat—that which; *śraddhayā*—by eagerness; *śrutavatyā*—simply by hearing; *ca*—also; *bhaktyā*—in devotion; *sammṛjyamāne*—being cleansed; *hṛdaye*—in the heart; *avadhāya*—meditation; *jñānena*—by knowledge; *vairāgya*—detachment; *balena*—by the strength of; *dhīrāḥ*—the pacified; *vrajema*—must go to; *tat*—that; *te*—Your; *aṅghri*—feet; *saroja-pīṭham*—lotus sanctuary.

TRANSLATION

Simply by hearing about Your lotus feet with eagerness and devotion and by meditating upon them within the heart, one at once becomes enlightened with knowledge, and on the strength of detachment one becomes pacified. We must therefore take shelter of the sanctuary of Your lotus feet.

PURPORT

The miracles of meditating on the lotus feet of the Lord with eagerness and devotion are so great that no other process can compare to it. The minds of materialistic persons are so disturbed that it is almost impossible for them to search after the Supreme Truth by personal regulative endeavors. But even such materialistic men, with a little eagerness for hearing about the transcendental name, fame, qualities, etc., can surpass all other methods of attaining knowledge and detachment. The conditioned soul is attached to the bodily conception of the self, and therefore he is in ignorance. Culture of self-knowledge can bring about detachment from material affection, and without such detachment there is no meaning to knowledge. The most stubborn attachment for material enjoyment is sex life. One who is attached to sex life is to be understood as devoid of knowledge. Knowledge must be followed by detachment. That is the way of self-realization. These two essentials for self-realization—knowledge and detachment—become manifest very quickly if one performs devotional service to the lotus feet of the Lord. The word *dhīra* is very significant in this connection. A person who is not disturbed even in the presence of cause of disturbance is called *dhīra.* Śrī Yāmunācārya says, "Since my heart has been overwhelmed by the devotional service of Lord Kṛṣṇa, I cannot even think of sex life, and if thoughts of sex come upon me I at once feel disgust." A devotee of the Lord becomes an elevated *dhīra* by the simple process of meditating in eagerness on the lotus feet of the Lord.

Devotional service entails being initiated by a bona fide spiritual master and following his instruction in regard to hearing about the Lord. Such a bona fide spiritual master is accepted by regularly hearing from him about the Lord. The improvement in knowledge and detachment can be perceived by devotees as an actual experience.

Lord Śrī Caitanya Mahāprabhu strongly recommended this process of hearing from a bona fide devotee, and by following this process one can achieve the highest result, conquering all other methods.

TEXT 43

विश्वस्य जन्मस्थितिसंयमार्थे
कृतावतारस्य पदाम्बुजं ते ।
व्रजेम सर्वे शरणं यदीश
स्मृतं प्रयच्छत्यभयं स्वपुंसाम् ॥४३॥

viśvasya janma-sthiti-saṁyamārthe
kṛtāvatārasya padāmbujaṁ te
vrajema sarve śaraṇaṁ yad īśa
smṛtaṁ prayacchaty abhayaṁ sva-puṁsām

viśvasya—of the cosmic universe; *janma*—creation; *sthiti*—maintenance; *saṁyama-arthe*—for the dissolution also; *kṛta*—accepted or assumed; *avatārasya*—of the incarnations; *pada-ambujam*—lotus feet; *te*—Your; *vrajema*—let us take shelter of; *sarve*—all of us; *śaraṇam*—shelter; *yat*—that which; *īśa*—O Lord; *smṛtam*—remembrance; *prayacchati*—awarding; *abhayam*—courage; *sva-puṁsām*—of the devotees.

TRANSLATION

O Lord, You assume incarnations for the creation, maintenance and dissolution of the cosmic manifestation, and therefore we all take shelter of Your lotus feet because they always award remembrance and courage to Your devotees.

PURPORT

For the creation, maintenance and dissolution of the cosmic manifestations there are three incarnations: Brahmā, Viṣṇu and Maheśvara (Lord Śiva). They are the controllers or masters of the three modes of material nature, which cause the phenomenal manifestation. Viṣṇu is the master of the mode of goodness, Brahmā is the master of the mode of passion, and Maheśvara is the master of the mode of ignorance. There are different kinds of devotees according to the modes of nature. Persons in the mode of goodness worship Lord Viṣṇu, those in the mode of passion worship Lord Brahmā, and those in the mode of ignorance worship Lord Śiva. All three of these deities are incarnations of the Supreme Lord Kṛṣṇa because He is the original Supreme Personality of Godhead. The demigods directly refer to the lotus feet of the Supreme Lord and not to the different incarnations. The incarnation of Viṣṇu in the material world is, however, directly worshiped by the demigods. It is learned from various scriptures that the demigods approach Lord Viṣṇu in the ocean of milk and submit their grievances whenever there is some difficulty in the administration of universal affairs. Although they are incarnations of the Lord, Lord Brahmā and Lord Śiva worship Lord Viṣṇu, and thus they are also counted amongst the demigods and not as the Supreme Personality of Godhead. Persons who worship Lord Viṣṇu are called demigods, and persons who do not do so are called *asuras*, or demons. Viṣṇu always takes the part of the demigods, but Brahmā and Śiva sometimes take the side of the demons; it is not that they become one in interest with them, but sometimes they do something in order to gain control over the demons.

TEXT 44

यत्सानुबन्धेऽसति देहगेहे
ममाहमित्यूढदुराग्रहाणाम् ।
पुंसां सुदूरं वसतोऽपि पुर्यां
भजेम तत्ते भगवन् पदाब्जम् ॥४४॥

yat sānubandhe 'sati deha-gehe
mamāham ity ūḍha-durāgrahāṇām
puṁsāṁ sudūraṁ vasato 'pi puryāṁ
bhajema tat te bhagavan padābjam

yat—because; *sa-anubandhe*—due to becoming entangled; *asati*—thus being; *deha*—the gross material body; *gehe*—in the home; *mama*—mine; *aham*—I; *iti*—thus; *ūḍha*—great, deep; *durāgrahāṇām*—undesirable eagerness; *puṁsām*—of persons; *su-dūram*—far away; *vasataḥ*—dwelling; *api*—although; *puryām*—within the body; *bhajema*—let us worship; *tat*—therefore; *te*—Your; *bhagavan*—O Lord; *pada-abjam*—lotus feet.

TRANSLATION

O Lord, persons who are entangled by undesirable eagerness for the temporary body and kinsmen, and who are bound by thoughts of "mine" and "I," are unable to see Your lotus feet, although Your lotus feet are situated within their own bodies. But let us take shelter of Your lotus feet.

PURPORT

The whole Vedic philosophy of life is that one should get rid of the material encagement of gross and subtle bodies, which only cause one to continue in a condemned life of miseries. This material body continues as long as one is not detached from the false conception of lording it over material nature. The impetus for lording it over material nature is the sense of "mine" and "I." "I am the lord of all that I survey. So many things I possess, and I shall possess more and more. Who can be richer than I in wealth and education? I am the master, and I am God. Who else is there but me?" All these ideas reflect the philosophy of *ahaṁ mama,* the conception that "I am everything." Persons conducted by such a conception of life can never get liberation from material bondage. But even a person perpetually condemned to the miseries of material existence can get relief from bondage if he simply agrees to hear only *kṛṣṇa-kathā.* In this age of Kali, the process of hearing *kṛṣṇa-kathā* is the most effective means to gain release from unwanted family affection and thus find permanent freedom in life. The age of Kali is full of sinful reactions, and people are more and more addicted to the qualities of this age, but simply by hearing and chanting of *kṛṣṇa-kathā* one is sure to go back to Godhead. Therefore, people should be trained to hear only *kṛṣṇa-kathā*—by all means—in order to get relief from all miseries.

TEXT 45

तान् वै ह्यसद्‌वृत्तिभिरक्षिभिर्ये
परहृतान्तर्मनसः परेश ।
अथो न पश्यन्त्युरुगाय नूनं
ये ते पदन्यासविलासलक्ष्याः ॥४५॥

tān vai hy asad-vṛttibhir akṣibhir ye
parāhṛtāntar-manasaḥ pareśa
atho na paśyanty urugāya nūnaṁ
ye te padanyāsa-vilāsa-lakṣyāḥ

tān—the lotus feet of the Lord; *vai*—certainly; *hi*—for; *asat*—materialistic; *vṛttibhiḥ*—by those who are influenced by external energy; *akṣibhiḥ*—by the senses; *ye*—those; *parāhṛta*—missing at a distance; *antaḥ-manasaḥ*—of the internal mind; *pareśa*—O Supreme; *atho*—therefore; *na*—never; *paśyanti*—can see; *urugāya*—O great; *nūnam*—but; *ye*—those who; *te*—Your; *padanyāsa*—activities; *vilāsa*—transcendental enjoyment; *lakṣyāḥ*—those who see.

TRANSLATION

O great Supreme Lord, offensive persons whose internal vision has been too affected by external materialistic activities cannot see Your lotus feet, but they are seen by Your pure devotees, whose one and only aim is to transcendentally enjoy Your activities.

PURPORT

As stated in *Bhagavad-gītā* (18.61), the Lord is situated in everyone's heart. It is natural that one should he able to see the Lord at least within himself. But that is not possible for those whose internal vision has been covered by external activities. The pure soul, which is symptomized by consciousness, can be easily perceived even by a common man because consciousness is spread all over the body. The *yoga* system as recommended in *Bhagavad-gītā* is to concentrate the mental activities internally and thus see the lotus feet of the Lord within oneself. But there are many so-called *yogīs* who have no concern with the Lord but are only concerned with consciousness, which they accept as the final realization. Such realization of consciousness is taught by *Bhagavad-gītā* within only a few minutes, whereas the so-called *yogīs* take continuous years to realize it because of their offenses at the lotus feet of the Lord. The greatest offense is to deny the existence of the Lord as separate from the individual souls or to accept the Lord and the individual soul as one and the same. The impersonalists misinterpret the theory of reflection, and thus they wrongly accept the individual consciousness as the supreme consciousness.

The theory of the reflection of the Supreme can be clearly understood without difficulty by any sincere common man. When there is a reflection of the sky on the water, both the sky and the stars are seen within the water, but it is understood that the sky and the stars are not to be accepted on the same level. The stars are parts of the sky, and therefore they cannot be equal to the whole. The sky is the whole, and the stars are parts. They cannot be one and the same. Transcendentalists who do not accept the supreme consciousness as separate from the individual consciousness are as offensive as the materialists who deny even the existence of the Lord.

Such offenders cannot actually see the lotus feet of the Lord within themselves, nor are they even able to see the devotees of the Lord. The devotees of the Lord are so kind that they roam to all places to enlighten people in God consciousness. The offenders, however, lose the chance to receive the Lord's devotees, although the offenseless common man is at once influenced by the devotees' presence. In this connection there is an interesting story of a hunter and Devarṣi Nārada. A hunter in the forest, although a great sinner, was not an intentional offender. He was at once influenced by the presence of Nārada, and he agreed to take the path of devotion, leaving aside his hearth and home. But the offenders Nalakūvara and Maṇigrīva, even though living amongst the demigods, had to undergo the punishment of becoming trees in their next lives, although by the grace of a devotee they were later delivered by the Lord. Offenders have to wait until they receive the mercy of devotees, and then they can become eligible to see the lotus feet of the Lord within themselves. But due to their offenses and their extreme materialism, they cannot see even the devotees of the Lord. Engaged in external activities, they kill the internal vision. The Lord's devotees, however, do not mind the offenses of the foolish in their many gross and subtle bodily endeavors. The Lord's devotees continue to bestow the blessings of devotion upon all such offenders without hesitation. That is the nature of devotees.

TEXT 46

पानेन ते देव कथासुधायाः
प्रवृद्धभक्त्या विशदाशया ये ।
वैराग्यसारं प्रतिलभ्य बोधं
यथाञ्जसान्वीयुरकुण्ठधिष्ण्यम् ॥४६॥

pānena te deva kathā-sudhāyāḥ
pravṛddha-bhaktyā viśadāśayā ye
vairāgya-sāraṁ pratilabhya bodhaṁ
yathāñjasānvīyur akuṇṭha-dhiṣṇyam

pānena—by drinking; *te*—of You; *deva*—O Lord; *kathā*—topics; *sudhāyāḥ*—of the nectar; *pravṛddha*—highly enlightened; *bhaktyā*—by devotional service; *viśada-āśayāḥ*—with a greatly serious attitude; *ye*—those who; *vairāgya-sāram*—the entire purport of renunciation; *pratilabhya*—achieving; *bodham*—intelligence; *yathā*—as much as; *añjasā*—quickly; *anvīyuḥ*—achieve; *akuṇṭha-dhiṣṇyam*—Vaikuṇṭhaloka in the spiritual sky.

TRANSLATION

O Lord, persons who, because of their serious attitude, attain the stage of enlightened devotional service achieve the complete meaning of renunciation and knowledge and attain the Vaikuṇṭhaloka in the spiritual sky simply by drinking the nectar of Your topics.

PURPORT

The difference between the impersonalistic mental speculators and the pure devotees of the Lord is that the former pass through a miserable understanding of the Absolute Truth at every stage, whereas the devotees enter into the kingdom of all pleasures even from the beginning of their attempt. The devotee has only to hear about devotional activities, which are as simple as anything in ordinary life, and he also acts very simply, whereas the mental speculator has to pass through a jugglery of words, which are partially facts and partially a make-show for the maintenance of an artificial impersonal status. In spite of his strenuous efforts to attain perfect knowledge, the impersonalist attains merging into the impersonal oneness of the *brahma-jyotir* of the Lord, which is also attained by the enemies of the Lord simply because of their being killed by Him. The devotees, however, attain to the highest stage of knowledge and renunciation and achieve the Vaikuṇṭhalokas, the planets in the spiritual sky. The impersonalist attains only the sky, and does not achieve any tangible transcendental bliss, whereas the devotee attains to the planets where real spiritual life prevails. With a serious attitude, the devotee throws away all achievements like so much dust, and he accepts only devotional service, the transcendental culmination.

TEXT 47

तथापरे चात्मसमाधियोग-
बलेन जित्वा प्रकृतिं बलिष्ठाम् ।
त्वामेव धीराः पुरुषं विशन्ति
तेषां श्रमः स्यान्न तु सेवया ते ॥४७॥

tathāpare cātma-samādhi-yoga-
balena jitvā prakṛtiṁ baliṣṭhām
tvām eva dhīrāḥ puruṣaṁ viśanti
teṣāṁ śramaḥ syān na tu sevayā te

tathā—as far as; *apare*—others; *ca*—also; *ātma-samādhi*—transcendental self-realization; *yoga*—means; *balena*—by the strength of; *jitvā*—conquering; *prakṛtim*—acquired nature or modes of nature; *baliṣṭhām*—very powerful; *tvām*—You; *eva*—only; *dhīrāḥ*—pacified; *puruṣam*—person; *viśanti*—enters into; *teṣām*—for them; *śramaḥ*—much labor; *syāt*—has to be taken; *na*—never; *tu*—but; *sevayā*—by serving; *te*—of You.

TRANSLATION

Others, who are pacified by means of transcendental self-realization and have conquered over the modes of nature by dint of strong power and knowledge, also enter into You, but for them there is much pain, whereas the devotee simply discharges devotional service and thus feels no such pain.

PURPORT

In terms of a labor of love and its returns, the *bhaktas,* or devotees of the Lord, always have priority over persons who are addicted to the association of *jñānīs,* or impersonalists, and *yogīs*, or mystics. The word *apare* (others) is very significant in this connection. "Others" refers to the *jñānīs* and the *yogīs*, whose only hope is to merge into the existence of the impersonal *brahmajyoti*. Although their destination is not so important in comparison to the destination of the devotees, the labor of the nondevotees is far greater than that of the *bhaktas*. One may suggest that there is sufficient labor for the devotees also in the matter of discharging devotional service. But that labor is compensated by the enhancement of transcendental pleasure. The devotees derive more transcendental pleasure while engaged continuously in the service of the Lord than when they have no such engagement. In the family combination of a man and a woman there is much labor and responsibility for both of them, yet when they are single they feel more trouble for want of their united activities.

The union of the impersonalists and the union of the devotees are not on a par. The impersonalists try to fully stop their individuality by attaining *sāyujya-mukti*, or unification by merging into oneness, whereas the devotees keep their individuality to exchange feelings in relationship with the supreme individual Lord. Such reciprocation of feelings takes place in the transcendental Vaikuṇṭha planets, and therefore the liberation sought by the impersonalists is already achieved in devotional service. The devotees attain *mukti* automatically, while continuing the transcendental pleasure of maintaining individuality. As explained in the previous verse, the destination of the devotees is Vaikuṇṭha, or *akuṇṭha-dhiṣṇya*, the place where anxieties are completely eradicated. One should not mistake the destination of the devotees and that of the impersonalists to be one and the same. The destinations are distinctly different, and the transcendental pleasure derived by the devotee is also distinct from *cin-mātra*, or spiritual feelings alone.

TEXT 48

तत्ते वयं लोकसिसृक्षयाद्य
त्वयानुसृष्टास्त्रिभिरात्मभिः स्म ।
सर्वे वियुक्ताः स्वविहारतन्त्रं
न शक्नुमस्तत्प्रतिहर्तवे ते ॥४८॥

tat te vayaṁ loka-sisṛkṣayādya
tvayānusṛṣṭās tribhir ātmabhiḥ sma
sarve viyuktāḥ sva-vihāra-tantraṁ
na śaknumas tat pratihartave te

tat—therefore; *te*—Your; *vayam*—all of us; *loka*—world; *sisṛkṣayā*—for the sake of creation; *ādya*—O Original person; *tvayā*—by You; *anusṛṣṭāḥ*—being created one after another; *tribhiḥ*—by the three modes of nature; *ātmabhiḥ*—by one's own; *sma*—in the past; *sarve*—all; *viyuktāḥ*—separated; *sva-vihāra-tantram*—the network of activities for one's own pleasure; *na*—not; *śaknumaḥ*—could do it; *tat*—that; *pratihartave*—to award; *te*—unto Your.

TRANSLATION

O Original Person, we are therefore but Yours only. Although we are Your creatures, we are born one after another under the influence of the three modes of nature, and for this reason we are separated in action. Therefore, after the creation we could not act concertedly for Your transcendental pleasure.

PURPORT

The cosmic creation is working under the influence of the three modes of the external potency of the Lord. Different creatures are also under the same influence, and therefore they cannot act concertedly in satisfying the Lord. Because of this diverse activity, there cannot be any harmony in the material world. The best policy, therefore, is to act for the sake of the Lord. That will bring about the desired harmony.

TEXT 49

यावद्बलिं तेऽज हराम काले
यथा वयं चान्नमदाम यत्र ।
यथोभयेषां त इमे हि लोका
बलिं हरन्तोऽन्नमदन्त्यनूहाः ॥४९॥

yāvad baliṁ te 'ja harāma kāle
yathā vayaṁ cānnam adāma yatra
yathobhayeṣāṁ ta ime hi lokā
baliṁ haranto 'nnam adanty anūhāḥ

yāvat—as it may be; *balim*—offerings; *te*—Your; *aja*—O unborn one; *harāma*—shall offer; *kāle*—at the right time; *yathā*—as much as; *vayam*—we; *ca*—also; *annam*—food grains; *adāma*—shall partake; *yatra*—whereupon; *yathā*—as much as; *ubhayeṣām*—both for You and for us; *te*—all; *ime*—these; *hi*—certainly; *lokāḥ*—living entities; *balim*—offerings; *harantaḥ*—while offering; *annam*—grains; *adanti*—eat; *anūhāḥ*—without disturbance.

TRANSLATION

O unborn one, please enlighten us regarding the ways and means by which we can offer You all enjoyable grains and commodities so that both we and all

other living entities in this world can maintain ourselves without disturbance and can easily accumulate the necessities of life both for You and for ourselves.

PURPORT

Developed consciousness begins from the human form of life and further increases in the forms of the demigods living in higher planets. The earth is situated almost in the middle of the universe, and the human form of life is the via medium between the life of the demigods and that of the demons. The planetary systems above the earth are especially meant for the higher intellectuals, called demigods. They are called demigods because although their standard of life is far more advanced in culture, enjoyment, luxury, beauty, education and duration of life, they are always fully God conscious. Such demigods are always ready to render service to the Supreme Lord because they are perfectly aware of the fact that every living entity is constitutionally an eternal subordinate servitor of the Lord. They also know that it is the Lord only who can maintain all living entities with all the necessities of life. The Vedic hymns, *eko bahūnāṁ yo vidadhāti kāmān, tā enam abruvann āyatanaṁ naḥ prajānīhi yasmin pratiṣṭhitā annam adāme*, etc., confirm this truth. In *Bhagavad-gītā* also, the Lord is mentioned as *bhūta-bhṛt*, or the maintainer of all living creatures.

The modern theory that starvation is due to an increase in population is not accepted by the demigods or the devotees of the Lord. The devotees or demigods are fully aware that the Lord can maintain any number of living entities, provided they are conscious of how to eat. If they want to eat like ordinary animals, who have no God consciousness, then they must live in starvation, poverty and want, like the jungle animals in the forest. The jungle animals are also maintained by the Lord with their respective foodstuffs, but they are not advanced in God consciousness. Similarly, human beings are provided with food grains, vegetables, fruits and milk by the grace of the Lord, but it is the duty of human beings to acknowledge the mercy of the Lord. As a matter of gratitude, they should feel obliged to the Lord for their supply of foodstuff, and they must first offer Him food in sacrifice and then partake of the remnants.

In *Bhagavad-gītā* (3.13) it is confirmed that one who takes foodstuff after a performance of sacrifice eats real food for proper maintenance of the body and soul, but one who cooks for himself and does not perform any sacrifice eats only lumps of sin in the shape of foodstuffs. Such sinful eating can never make one happy or free from scarcity. Famine is not due to an increase in population, as less intelligent economists think. When human society is grateful to the Lord for all His gifts for the maintenance of the living entities, then there is certainly no scarcity or want in society. But when men are unaware of the intrinsic value of such gifts from the Lord, surely they are in want. A person who has no God consciousness may live in opulence for the time being due to his past virtuous acts, but if one forgets his relationship with the Lord, certainly he must await the stage of starvation by the law of the powerful material nature. One cannot escape the vigilance of the powerful material nature unless he leads a God conscious or devotional life.

TEXT 50

त्वं नः सुराणामसि सान्वयानां
कूटस्थ आद्यः पुरुषः पुराणः ।
त्वं देव शक्त्यां गुणकर्मयोनौ
रेतस्त्वजायां कविमादधेऽजः ॥५०॥

tvaṁ naḥ surāṇām asi sānvayānām
kūṭa-stha ādyaḥ puruṣaḥ purāṇaḥ
tvaṁ deva śaktyāṁ guṇa-karma-yonau
retas tv ajāyāṁ kavim ādadhe 'jaḥ

tvam—Your Lordship; *naḥ*—of us; *surāṇām*—of the demigods; *asi*—You are; *sa-anvayānām*—with different gradations; *kūṭa-sthaḥ*—one who is unchanged; *ādyaḥ*—without any superior; *puruṣaḥ*—the founder person; *purāṇaḥ*—the oldest, who has no other founder; *tvam*—You; *deva*—O Lord; *śaktyām*—unto the energy; *guṇa-karma-yonau*—unto the cause of the material modes and activities; *retaḥ*—semen of birth; *tu*—indeed; *ajāyām*—for begetting; *kavim*—the total living entities; *ādadhe*—initiated; *ajaḥ*—one who is unborn.

TRANSLATION

You are the original personal founder of all the demigods and the orders of different gradations, yet You are the oldest and are unchanged. O Lord, You have no source or superior. You have impregnated the external energy with the semen of the total living entities, yet You are unborn.

PURPORT

The Lord, the Original Person, is the father of all other living entities, beginning from Brahmā, the personality from whom all other living entities in different gradations of species are generated. Yet the supreme father has no other father. Every one of the living entities of all grades, up to Brahmā, the original creature of the universe, is begotten by a father, but He, the Lord, has no father. When He descends on the material plane, out of His causeless mercy He accepts one of His great devotees as His father to keep pace with the rules of the material world. But since He is the Lord, He is always independent in choosing who will become His father. For example, the Lord came out of a pillar in His incarnation as Nṛsiṁhadeva, and by the Lord's causeless mercy, Ahalyā came out of a stone by the touch of the lotus feet of His incarnation as Lord Śrī Rāma. He is also the companion of every living entity as the Supersoul, but He is unchanged. The living entity changes his body in the material world, but even when the Lord is in the material world, He is ever unchanged. That is His prerogative.

As confirmed in *Bhagavad-gītā* (14.3), the Lord impregnates the external or material energy, and thus the total living entities later come out in different gradations, beginning from Brahmā, the first demigod, down to the insignificant ant. All gradations of living entities are manifested by Brahmā and the external energy, but the Lord is the original father of everyone. The relationship of every living being with the Supreme Lord is certainly one of son and father and not one of equality. Sometimes in love the son is more than the father, but the relationship of father and son is one of the superior and the subordinate. Every living entity, however great he may be, even up to demigods like Brahmā and Indra, is an eternally subordinate servitor of the supreme father. The *mahat-tattva* principle is the generating source of all the modes of material nature, and the living entities take birth in the material world in bodies supplied by the mother, material nature, in terms of their previous work. The body is a gift of material nature, but the soul is originally part and parcel of the Supreme Lord.

TEXT 51

ततो वयं मत्प्रमुखा यदर्थे
बभूविमात्मन् करवाम किं ते ।
त्वं नः स्वचक्षुः परिदेहि शक्त्या
देव क्रियार्थे यदनुग्रहाणाम् ॥५१॥

tato vayaṁ mat-pramukhā yad-arthe
babhūvimātman karavāma kiṁ te
tvaṁ naḥ sva-cakṣuḥ paridehi śaktyā
deva kriyārthe yad-anugrahāṇām

tataḥ—therefore; *vayam*—all of us; *mat-pramukhāḥ*—coming from the total cosmos, the *mahat-tattva; yat-arthe*—for the purpose of which; *babhūvima*—created; *ātman*—O Supreme Self; *karavāma*—shall do; *kim*—what; *te*—Your service; *tvam*—Yourself; *naḥ*—to us; *sva-cakṣuḥ*—personal plan; *paridehi*—specifically grant us; *śaktyā*—with potency to work; *deva*—

O Lord; *kriyā-arthe*—for acting; *yat*—from which; *anugrahāṇām*—of those who are specifically favored.

TRANSLATION

O Supreme Self, please give us, who are created in the beginning from the mahat-tattva, the total cosmic energy, Your kind directions on how we shall act. Kindly award us Your perfect knowledge and potency so that we can render You service in the different departments of subsequent creation.

PURPORT

The Lord creates this material world and impregnates the material energy with the living entities who will act in the material world. All these actions have a divine plan behind them. The plan is to give the conditioned souls who so desire a chance to enjoy sense gratification. But there is another plan behind the creation: to help the living entities realize that they are created for the transcendental sense gratification of the Lord and not for their individual sense gratification. This is the constitutional position of the living entities. The Lord is one without a second, and He expands Himself into many for His transcendental pleasure. All the expansions—the *viṣṇu-tattvas,* the *jīva-tattvas* and the *śakti-tattvas* (the Personalities of Godhead, the living entities and the different potential energies)—are different offshoots from the same one Supreme Lord. The *jīva-tattvas* are separated expansions of the *viṣṇu-tattvas,* and although there are potential differences between them, they are all meant for the transcendental sense gratification of the Supreme Lord. Some of the *jīvas,* however, wanted to lord it over material nature in imitation of the lordship of the Personality of Godhead. Regarding when and why such propensities overcame the pure living entities, it can only be explained that the *jīva-tattvas* have infinitesimal independence and that due to misuse of this independence some of the living entities have become implicated in the conditions of cosmic creation and are therefore called *nitya-baddhas,* or eternally conditioned souls.

The expansions of Vedic wisdom also give the *nitya-baddhas,* the conditioned living entities, a chance to improve, and those who take advantage of such transcendental knowledge gradually regain their lost consciousness of rendering transcendental loving service to the Lord. The demigods are amongst the conditioned souls who have developed this pure consciousness of service to the Lord but who at the same time continue to desire to lord it over the material energy. Such mixed consciousness puts a conditioned soul in the position of managing the affairs of this creation. The demigods are entrusted leaders of the conditioned souls. As some of the old prisoners in government jails are entrusted with some responsible work of prison management, so the demigods are improved conditioned souls acting as representatives of the Lord in the material creation. Such demigods are devotees of the Lord in the material world, and when completely free from all material desire to lord it over the material energy they become pure devotees and have no desire but to serve the Lord. Therefore any living entity who desires a position in the material world may desire so in the service of the Lord and may seek power and intelligence from the Lord, as exemplified by the demigods in this particular verse. One cannot do anything unless he is enlightened and empowered by the Lord. The Lord says in *Bhagavad-gītā* (15.15), *mattaḥ smṛtir jñānam apohanaṁ ca.* All recollections, knowledge, etc., as well as all forgetfulness, are engineered by the Lord, who is sitting within the heart of everyone. The intelligent man seeks the help of the Lord, and the Lord helps the sincere devotees engaged in His multifarious services.

The demigods are entrusted by the Lord to create different species of living entities according to their past deeds. They are herein asking the favor of the Lord for the intelligence and power to carry out their task. Similarly, any conditioned soul may also engage in the service of the Lord under the guidance of an expert spiritual master and thus gradually become freed from the entanglement of material existence. The spiritual master is the manifested representative of the Lord, and anyone who puts himself under the guidance of a spiritual master and acts accordingly is said to be acting in terms of *buddhi-yoga,* as explained in *Bhagavad-gītā* (2.41):

vyavasāyātmikā buddhir
ekeha kuru-nandana
bahu-śākhā hy anantāś ca
buddhayo 'vyavasāyinām

Thus end the Bhaktivedanta purports of the Third Canto, Fifth Chapter, of the Śrīmad-Bhāgavatam, *entitled "Vidura's Talks with Maitreya."*

CHAPTER SIX

Creation of the Universal Form

TEXT 1

ऋषिरुवाच
इति तासां स्वशक्तीनां सतीनामसमेत्य सः ।
प्रसुप्तलोकतन्त्राणां निशाम्य गतिमीश्वरः ॥ १ ॥

ṛṣir uvāca
iti tāsāṁ sva-śaktīnāṁ
satīnām asametya saḥ
prasupta-loka-tantrāṇāṁ
niśāmya gatim īśvaraḥ

ṛṣiḥ uvāca—the Ṛṣi Maitreya said; *iti*—thus; *tāsām*—their; *sva śaktīnām*—own potency; *satīnām*—so situated; *asametya*—without combination; *saḥ*—He (the Lord); *prasupta*—suspended; *loka-tantrāṇām*—in the universal creations; *niśāmya*—hearing; *gatim*—progress; *īśvaraḥ*—the Lord.

TRANSLATION

The Ṛṣi Maitreya said: The Lord thus heard about the suspension of the progressive creative functions of the universe due to the noncombination of His potencies, such as the mahat-tattva.

PURPORT

There is nothing wanting in the creation of the Lord; all the potencies are there in a dormant state. But unless they are combined by the will of the Lord, nothing can progress. The suspended progressive work of creation can only be revived by the direction of the Lord.

TEXT 2

कालसंज्ञां तदा देवीं बिभ्रच्छक्तिमुरुक्रमः ।
त्रयोविंशतितत्त्वानां गणं युगपदाविशत् ॥ २ ॥

kāla-sañjñāṁ tadā devīṁ
bibhrac-chaktim urukramaḥ
trayoviṁśati tattvānāṁ
gaṇaṁ yugapad āviśat

kāla-sañjñām—known as Kālī; *tadā*—at that time; *devīm*—the goddess; *bibhrat*—destructive; *śaktim*—potency; *urukramaḥ*—the supreme powerful; *trayaḥ-viṁśati*—twenty-three; *tattvānām*—of the elements; *gaṇam*—all of them; *yugapat*—simultaneously; *āviśat*—entered.

TRANSLATION

The Supreme Powerful Lord then simultaneously entered into the twenty-three elements with the goddess Kālī, His external energy, who alone amalgamates all the different elements.

PURPORT

The ingredients of matter are counted as twenty-three: the total material energy, false ego, sound, touch, form, taste, smell, earth, water, fire, air, sky, eye, ear, nose, tongue, skin, hand, leg, evacuating organ, genitals, speech and mind. All are combined together by the influence of time and are again dissolved in the course of time. Time, therefore, is the energy of the Lord and acts in her own way by the direction of the Lord. This energy is called Kālī and is represented by the dark destructive goddess generally worshiped by persons influenced by the mode of darkness or ignorance in material existence. In the Vedic hymn this process is described as *mūla-prakṛtir avikṛtir mahadādyāḥ prakṛti-vikṛtayaḥ sapta ṣoḍaśakas tu vikāro na prakṛtir na vikṛtiḥ puruṣaḥ*. The energy which acts as material nature in a combination of twenty-three ingredients is not the final source of creation. The Lord enters into the elements and applies His energy, called Kālī. In all other Vedic scriptures the same principle is accepted. In *Brahma-saṁhitā* (5.35) it is stated:

eko 'py asau racayituṁ jagad-aṇḍa-koṭiṁ
yac-chaktir asti jagad-aṇḍa-cayā yad-antaḥ
aṇḍāntara-stha-paramāṇu-cayāntara-sthaṁ
govindam ādi-puruṣaṁ tam ahaṁ bhajāmi

"I worship the primeval Lord, Govinda, who is the original Personality of Godhead. By His partial plenary expansion [Mahā-viṣṇu], He enters into material nature, and then into each and every universe [as Garbhodakaśāyī Viṣṇu], and then [as Kṣīrodakaśāyī

Viṣṇu] into all the elements, including every atom of matter. Such manifestations of cosmic creation are innumerable, both in the universes and in the individual atoms."

Similarly, this is confirmed in *Bhagavad-gītā* (10.42):

athavā bahunaitena
kiṁ jñātena tavārjuna
viṣṭabhyāham idaṁ kṛtsnam
ekāṁśena sthito jagat

"O Arjuna, there is no necessity of your knowing about My innumerable energies, which act in various ways. I enter into the material creation by My partial plenary expansion [Paramātmā, or the Supersoul] in all the universes and in all the elements thereof, and thus the work of creation goes on." The wonderful activities of material nature are due to Lord Kṛṣṇa, and thus He is the final cause, or the ultimate cause of all causes.

TEXT 3

सोऽनुप्रविष्टो भगवांश्चेष्टारूपेण तं गणम् ।
भिन्नं संयोजयामास सुप्तं कर्म प्रबोधयन् ॥ ३ ॥

so 'nupraviṣṭo bhagavāṁś
ceṣṭārūpeṇa taṁ gaṇam
bhinnaṁ saṁyojayām āsa
suptaṁ karma prabodhayan

saḥ—that; *anupraviṣṭaḥ*—thus entering later on; *bhagavān*—the Personality of Godhead; *ceṣṭā-rūpeṇa*—by His representation of attempt, Kālī; *tam*—them; *gaṇam*—all the living entities, including the demigods; *bhinnam*—separately; *saṁyojayām āsa*—engaged to work; *suptam*—sleeping; *karma*—work; *prabodhayan*—enlightening.

TRANSLATION

Thus when the Personality of Godhead entered into the elements by His energy, all the living entities were enlivened into different activities, just as one is engaged in his work after awakening from sleep.

PURPORT

Every individual soul remains unconscious after the dissolution of the creation and thus enters into the Lord with His material energy. These individual living entities are conditioned souls everlastingly, but in each and every material creation they are given a chance to liberate themselves and become free souls. They are all given a chance to take advantage of the Vedic wisdom and find out what is their relationship with the Supreme Lord, how they can be liberated, and what the ultimate profit is in such liberation. By properly studying the *Vedas* one becomes conscious of his position and thus takes to the transcendental devotional service of the Lord and is gradually promoted to the spiritual sky. The individual souls in the material world engage in different activities according to their past unfinished desires. After the dissolution of a particular body, the individual soul forgets everything, but the all-merciful Lord, who is situated in everyone's heart as the witness, the Supersoul, awakens him and reminds him of his past desires, and thus he begins to act accordingly in his next life. This unseen guidance is described as fate, and a sensible man can understand that this continues his material bondage in the three modes of nature.

The unconscious sleeping stage of the living entity just after the partial or total dissolution of the creation is wrongly accepted as the final stage of life by some less intelligent philosophers. After the dissolution of the partial material body, a living entity remains unconscious for only a few months, and after the total dissolution of the material creation, he remains unconscious for many millions of years. But when the creation is again revived, he is awakened to his work by the Lord. The living entity is eternal, and the wakeful state of his consciousness, manifested by activities, is his natural condition of life. He cannot stop acting while awake, and thus he acts according to his diverse desires. When his desires are trained in the transcendental service of the Lord, his life becomes perfect, and he is promoted to the spiritual sky to enjoy eternal awakened life.

TEXT 4

प्रबुद्धकर्मा दैवेन त्रयोविंशतिको गणः ।
प्रेरितोऽजनयत्स्वाभिर्मात्राभिरधिपूरुषम् ॥ ४ ॥

prabuddha-karmā daivena
trayoviṁśatiko gaṇaḥ
prerito 'janayat svābhir
mātrābhir adhipūruṣam

prabuddha—awakened; *karmā*—activities; *daivena*—by the will of the Supreme; *trayaḥ-viṁśatikaḥ*—by the twenty-three principal ingredients; *gaṇaḥ*—the combination; *preritaḥ*—induced by; *ajanayat*—manifested; *svābhiḥ*—by His personal; *mātrābhiḥ*—plenary expansion; *adhipūruṣam*—the gigantic universal form (*viśva-rūpa*).

TRANSLATION

When the twenty-three principal elements were set in action by the will of the Supreme, the gigantic universal form, or the viśvarūpa body of the Lord, came into existence.

PURPORT

The *virāṭ-rūpa* or *viśva-rūpa,* the gigantic universal form of the Lord, which is very much appreciated by the impersonalist, is not an eternal form of the Lord. It is manifested by the supreme will of the Lord after the ingredients of material creation. Lord Kṛṣṇa exhibited this *virāṭ* or *viśva-rūpa* to Arjuna just to convince the impersonalists that He is the original Personality of Godhead. Kṛṣṇa exhibited the *virāṭ-rūpa;* it is not that Kṛṣṇa was exhibited by the *virāṭ-rūpa.* The *virāṭ-rūpa* is not, therefore, an eternal form of the Lord exhibited in the spiritual sky; it is a material manifestation of the Lord. The *arcā-vigraha,* or the worshipable Deity in the temple, is a similar manifestation of the Lord for the neophytes. But in spite of their material touch, such forms of the Lord as the *virāṭ* and *arcā* are all nondifferent from His eternal form as Lord Kṛṣṇa.

TEXT 5

परेण विशता स्वस्मिन्मात्रया विश्वसृग्गणः ।
चुक्षोभान्योन्यमासाद्य यस्मिन्लोकाश्चराचराः ॥ ५ ॥

pareṇa viśatā svasmin
mātrayā viśva-sṛg-gaṇaḥ
cukṣobhānyonyam āsādya
yasmin lokāś carācarāḥ

pareṇa—by the Lord; *viśatā*—thus entering; *svasmin*—by His own self; *mātrayā*—by a plenary portion; *viśva-sṛk*—the elements of universal creation; *gaṇaḥ*—all; *cukṣobha*—transformed; *anyonyam*—one another; *āsādya*—having obtained; *yasmin*—in which; *lokāḥ*—the planets; *cara-acarāḥ*—movable and immovable.

TRANSLATION

As the Lord, in His plenary portion, entered into the elements of the universal creation, they transformed into the gigantic form in which all the planetary systems and all movable and immovable creations rest.

PURPORT

The elements of cosmic creation are all matter and have no potency to increase in volume unless entered into by the Lord in His plenary portion. This means that matter does not increase or decrease unless it is spiritually touched. Matter is a product of spirit and increases only by the touch of spirit. The entire cosmic manifestation has not assumed its gigantic form by itself, as wrongly calculated by less intelligent persons. As long as spirit is within matter, matter can increase as needed; but without the spirit, matter stops increasing. For example, as long as there is spiritual consciousness within the material body of a living entity, the body increases to the required size, but a dead material body, which has no spiritual consciousness, stops increasing. In *Bhagavad-gītā* (Chapter Two) importance is given to the spiritual consciousness, not the body. The entire cosmic body increased by the same process that we experience in our small bodies. One should not, however, foolishly think that the individual infinitesimal soul is the cause of the gigantic manifestation of the universal form. The universal form is called the *virāṭ-rūpa* because the Supreme Lord is within it in His plenary portion.

TEXT 6

हिरण्मयः स पुरुषः सहस्रपरिवत्सरान् ।
आण्डकोश उवासाप्सु सर्वसत्त्वोपबृंहितः ॥ ६ ॥

hiraṇmayaḥ sa puruṣaḥ
sahasra-parivatsarān
āṇḍa-kośa uvāsāpsu
sarva-sattvopabṛṁhitaḥ

hiraṇmayaḥ—the Garbhodakaśāyī Viṣṇu, who also assumes the *virāṭ-rūpa; saḥ*—He; *puruṣaḥ*—incarnation of Godhead; *sahasra*—one thousand; *parivatsarān*—celestial years; *āṇḍa-kośe*—within the global universe; *uvāsa*—resided; *apsu*—on the water; *sarva-sattva*—all living entities lying with Him; *upabṛṁhitaḥ*—so spread.

TRANSLATION

The gigantic virāṭ-puruṣa, known as Hiraṇmaya, lived for one thousand celestial years on the water of the universe, and all the living entities lay with Him.

PURPORT

After the Lord entered each and every universe as the Garbhodakaśāyī Viṣṇu, half of the universe was filled with water. The cosmic manifestation of the planetary systems, outer space, etc., which are visible to us, is only one half of the complete universe. Before the manifestation takes place and after the entrance of Viṣṇu within the universe, there is a period of one thousand celestial years. All the living entities injected within the womb of the *mahat-tattva* are divided in all universes with the incarnation of Garbhodakaśāyī Viṣṇu, and all of them lie down with the Lord until Brahmā is born. Brahmā is the first living being within the universe, and from him all other demigods and living creatures are born. Manu is the original father of mankind, and therefore, in Sanskrit, mankind is called *mānuṣya.* Humanity in different bodily qualities is distributed throughout the various planetary systems.

TEXT 7

स वै विश्वसृजां गर्भो देवकर्मात्मशक्तिमान् ।
विबभाजात्मनात्मानमेकधा दशधा त्रिधा ॥ ७ ॥

sa vai viśva-sṛjāṁ garbho
deva-karmatma-śaktimān
vibabhājātmanātmānam
ekadhā daśadhā tridha

saḥ—that; *vai*—certainly; *viśva-sṛjām*—of the gigantic *virāṭ* form; *garbhah*—total energy; *deva*—living energy; *karma*—activity of life; *ātma*—self; *śaktimān*—full with potencies; *vibabhāja*—divided; *ātmanā*—by Himself; *ātmānam*—Himself; *ekadhā*—in oneness; *daśadhā*—in ten; *tridhā*—and in three.

TRANSLATION

The total energy of the mahat-tattva, in the form of the gigantic virāṭ-rūpa, divided Himself by Himself into the consciousness of the living entitics, the life of activity, and self-identification, which are subdivided into one, ten and three respectively.

PURPORT

Consciousness is the sign of the living entity, or the soul. The existence of the soul is manifest in the form of consciousness, called *jñāna-śakti.* The total consciousness is that of the gigantic *virāṭ-rūpa,* and the same consciousness is exhibited in individual persons. The activity of consciousness is performed through the air of life, which is of ten divisions. The airs of life are called *prāṇa, apāna, udāna, vyāna* and *samāna* and are also differently qualified as *nāga, kūrma, kṛkara, devadatta* and *dhanañjaya.* The consciousness of the soul becomes polluted by the material atmosphere, and thus various activities are exhibited in the false ego of bodily identification. These various activities are described in *Bhagavad-gītā* (2.41) as *bahu-śākhā hy anantāś ca buddhayo 'vyavasāyinām.* The conditioned soul is bewildered into various activities for want of pure consciousness. In pure consciousness the activity is one. The consciousness of the individual soul becomes one with the supreme consciousness when there is complete synthesis between the two.

The monist believes that there is only one consciousness, whereas the *sātvatas,* or the devotees, believe that although there is undoubtedly one consciousness, they are one because there is agreement. The individual consciousness is advised to dovetail with the supreme consciousness, as instructed by the Lord in *Bhagavad-gītā* (18.66): *sarva-dharmān parityajya mām ekaṁ śaraṇaṁ vraja.* The individual consciousness (Arjuna) is advised to dovetail with the supreme consciousness and thus maintain his conscious purity. It is foolish to try to stop the activities of consciousness, but they can be purified when they are dovetailed with the Supreme. This consciousness is divided into three modes of self-identification according to the proportion of purity: *ādhyātmika,* or self-identification with the body and mind, *ādhibhautika,* or self-identification with the material products, and *ādhidaivika,* or self-identification as a servant of the Lord. Of the three, *ādhidaivika* self-identification is the beginning of purity of consciousness in pursuance of the desire of the Lord.

TEXT 8

एष ह्यशेषसत्त्वानामात्मांशः परमात्मनः ।
आद्योऽवतारो यत्रासौ भूतग्रामो विभाव्यते ॥ ८ ॥

eṣa hy aśeṣa-sattvānām
ātmāṁśaḥ paramātmanaḥ
ādyo 'vatāro yatrāsau
bhūta-grāmo vibhāvyate

eṣaḥ—this; *hi*—certainly; *aśeṣa*—unlimited; *sattvānām*—living entities; *ātmā*—Self; *aṁśaḥ*—part; *parama-ātmanaḥ*—of the Supersoul; *ādyaḥ*—the first; *avatāraḥ*—incarnation; *yatra*—whereupon; *asau*—all those; *bhūta-grāmaḥ*—the aggregate creations; *vibhāvyate*—flourish.

TRANSLATION

The gigantic universal form of the Supreme Lord is the first incarnation and plenary portion of the Supersoul. He is the Self of an unlimited number of living entities, and in Him rests the aggregate creation, which thus flourishes.

PURPORT

The Supreme Lord expands Himself in two ways, by personal plenary expansions and separated minute expansions. The personal plenary expansions are *viṣṇu-tattvas*, and the separated expansions are living entities. Since the living entities are very small, they are sometimes described as the marginal energy of the Lord. But the mystic *yogīs* consider the living entities and the Supersoul, Paramātmā, to be one and the same. It is, however, a minor point of controversy; after all, everything created rests on the gigantic *virāṭ* or universal form of the Lord.

TEXT 9

साध्यात्मः साधिदैवश्च साधिभूत इति त्रिधा ।
विराट् प्राणो दशविध एकधा हृदयेन च ॥ ९ ॥

sādhyātmaḥ sādhidaivaś ca
sādhibhūta iti tridhā
virāṭ prāṇo daśa-vidha
ekadhā hṛdayena ca

sa-ādhyātmaḥ—the body and mind with all the senses; *sa-ādhidaivaḥ*—and the controlling demigods of the senses; *ca*—and; *sa-ādhibhūtah*—the present objectives; *iti*—thus; *tridhā*—three; *virāṭ*—gigantic; *prāṇaḥ*—moving force; *daśa-vidhaḥ*—ten kinds; *ekadhā*—one only; *hṛdayena*—living energy; *ca*—also.

TRANSLATION

The gigantic universal form is represented by three, ten and one in the sense that He is the body and the mind and the senses, He is the dynamic force for all movements by ten kinds of life energy, and He is the one heart where life energy is generated.

PURPORT

In *Bhagavad-gītā* (7.4-5) it is stated that the eight elements earth, water, fire, air, sky, mind, intelligence and false ego are all products of the Lord's inferior energy, whereas the living entities, who are seen to utilize the inferior energy, originally belong to the superior energy, the internal potency of the Lord. The eight inferior energies work grossly and subtly, whereas the superior energy works as the central generating force. This is experienced in the human body. The gross elements, namely, earth, etc., form the external gross body and are like a coat, whereas the subtle mind and false ego act like the inner clothing of the body.

The movements of the body are first generated from the heart, and all the activities of the body are made possible by the senses, powered by the ten kinds of air within the body. The ten kinds of air are described as follows: The main air passing through the nose in breathing is called *prāṇa.* The air which passes through the rectum as evacuated bodily air is called *apāna.* The air which adjusts the foodstuff within the stomach and which sometimes sounds as belching is called *samāna.* The air which passes through the throat and the stoppage of which constitutes suffocation is called the *udāna* air. And the total air which circulates throughout the entire body is called the *vyāna* air. Subtler than these five airs, there are others also. That which facilitates the opening of the eyes, mouth, etc., is called *nāga* air. The air which increases appetite is called *kṛkara* air. The air which helps contraction is called *kūrma* air. The air which helps relaxation by opening the mouth wide (in yawning) is called *devadatta* air, and the air which helps sustenance is called *dhanañjaya* air.

All these airs are generated from the center of the heart, which is one only. This central energy is superior energy of the Lord, who is seated within the heart with the soul of the body, who acts under the guidance of the Lord. This is explained in *Bhagavad-gītā* (15.15) as follows:

sarvasya cāhaṁ hṛdi sanniviṣṭo
mattaḥ smṛtir jñānam apohanaṁ ca
vedaiś ca sarvair aham eva vedyo
vedānta-kṛd veda-vid eva cāham

The complete central force is generated from the heart by the Lord, who is seated there and who helps the conditioned soul in remembering and forgetting. The conditioned state is due to the soul's forgetfulness of his relationship of subordination to the Lord. One who wants to continue to forget the Lord is helped by the Lord to forget Him birth after birth, but one who remembers Him, by dint of association with a devotee of the Lord, is helped to remember Him more and more. Thus the conditioned soul can ultimately go back home, back to Godhead.

This process of transcendental help by the Lord is described in *Bhagavad-gītā* (10.10) as follows:

teṣāṁ satata-yuktānāṁ
bhajatāṁ prīti-pūrvakam
dadāmi buddhi-yogaṁ taṁ
yena mām upayānti te

The *buddhi-yoga* process of self-realization with intelligence transcendental to the mind (devotional service) can alone elevate one from the conditioned state of material entanglement in the cosmic construction. The conditioned state of the living entity is like that of a person who is within the depths of a huge mechanical arrangement. The mental speculators can reach the point of *buddhi-yoga* after many, many lifetimes of speculation, but the intelligent person who begins from the platform of intelligence above the mind makes rapid progress in self-realization. Because the *buddhi-yoga* process entails no fear of deterioration or retrogression at any time, it is the guaranteed path to self-realization, as confirmed in *Bhagavad-gītā* (2.40). The mental speculators cannot understand that the two birds (*Śvetāśvatara Upaniṣad*) sitting in one tree are the soul and the Supersoul. The individual soul eats the fruit of the tree, while the other bird does not eat the fruit but only observes the activities of the eating bird. Without attachment, the witnessing bird helps the fruit-eating bird perform fruitful activities. One who cannot understand this difference between the soul and the Supersoul, or God and the living entities, is certainly still in the entanglement of the cosmic machinery and thus must still await the time when he will be free from bondage.

TEXT 10

स्मरन् विश्वसृजामीशो विज्ञापितमधोक्षजः ।
विराजमतपत्स्वेन तेजसैषां विवृत्तये ॥१०॥

smaran viśva-sṛjām īśo
vijñāpitam adhokṣajaḥ
virājam atapat svena
tejasaiṣāṁ vivṛttaye

smaran—remembering; *viśva-sṛjām*—of the demigods entrusted with the task of cosmic construction; *īśaḥ*—the Supreme Lord; *vijñāpitam*—as He was prayed for; *adhokṣajaḥ*—the Transcendence; *virājam*—the gigantic universal form; *atapat*—considered thus; *svena*—by His own; *tejasā*—energy; *eṣām*—for them; *vivṛttaye*—for understanding.

TRANSLATION

The Supreme Lord is the Supersoul of all the demigods entrusted with the task of constructing the cosmic manifestation. Being thus prayed to [by the demigods], He thought to Himself and thus manifested the gigantic form for their understanding.

PURPORT

The impersonalists are captivated by the gigantic universal form of the Supreme. They think that the control behind this gigantic manifestation is imagination. Intelligent persons, however, can estimate the value of the cause by observing the wonders of the effects. For example, the individual human body does not develop from the womb of the mother independently but because the living entity, the soul, is within the body. Without the living entity, a material body cannot automatically take shape or develop. When any material object displays development, it must be understood that there is a spiritual soul within the manifestation. The gigantic universe has developed gradually, just as the body of a child develops. The conception that the Transcendence enters within the universe is, therefore, logical. As the materialists cannot find the soul and the Supersoul within the heart, similarly, for want of sufficient knowledge, they cannot see that the Supreme Soul is the cause of the universe. The Lord is therefore described in the Vedic language as *avāṅ-mānasa-gocaraḥ,* beyond the conception of words and minds.

Due to a poor fund of knowledge, the mental speculators try to bring the Supreme within the purview of words and minds, but the Lord refuses to be so intelligible; the speculator has no adequate words or mind to gauge the infinity of the Lord. The Lord is called *adhokṣaja,* or the person who is beyond perception by the blunt, limited potency of our senses. One cannot perceive the transcendental name or form of the Lord by mental speculation. The mundane Ph.D.'s are completely unable to speculate on the Supreme with their limited senses. Such attempts by the puffed up Ph.D's are compared to the philosophy of the frog in the well. A frog in a well was informed of the gigantic Pacific Ocean, and he began to puff himself up in order to understand or measure the length and breadth of the Pacific Ocean. Ultimately the frog burst and died. The title Ph.D. can also be interpreted as Plough Department, a title meant for the tillers in the paddy field. The attempt of the tillers in the paddy field to understand the cosmic manifestation and the cause behind such wonderful work can be compared to the endeavor of the frog in the well to calculate the measurement of the Pacific Ocean.

The Lord can reveal Himself only to a person who is submissive and who engages in His transcendental loving service. The demigods controlling the elements and ingredients of universal affairs prayed to the Lord for guidance, and thus He manifested His gigantic form, as He did at the request of Arjuna.

TEXT 11

अथ तस्याभितप्तस्य कतिधायतनानि ह ।
निरभिद्यन्त देवानां तानि मे गदतः शृणु ॥११॥

atha tasyābhitaptasya
katidhāyatanāni ha
nirabhidyanta devānāṁ
tāni me gadataḥ śṛṇu

atha—therefore; *tasya*—His; *abhitaptasya*—in terms of His contemplation; *katidhā*—how many; *āyatanāni*—embodiments; *ha*—there were; *nirabhidyanta*—by separated parts; *devānām*—of the demigods; *tāni*—all those; *me gadataḥ*—described by me; *śṛṇu*—just hear.

TRANSLATION

Maitreya said: You may now hear from me how the Supreme Lord separated Himself into the diverse forms of the demigods after the manifestation of the gigantic universal form.

PURPORT

The demigods are separated parts and parcels of the Supreme Lord, as are all other living entities. The only difference between the demigods and the ordinary living entities is that when the living entities are rich in pious acts of devotional service to the Lord, and when their desire to lord it over material energy has vanished, they are promoted to the posts of demigods, who are entrusted by the Lord with executing the management of the universal affairs.

TEXT 12

तस्याग्निरास्यं निर्भिन्नं लोकपालोऽविशत्पदम् ।
वाचा स्वांशेन वक्तव्यं ययासौ प्रतिपद्यते ॥१२॥

tasyāgnir āsyaṁ nirbhinnaṁ
loka-pālo 'viśat padam
vācā svāṁśena vaktavyaṁ
yayāsau pratipadyate

tasya—His; *agniḥ*—fire; *āsyam*—mouth; *nirbhinnam*—thus separated; *loka-pālaḥ*—the directors of material affairs; *aviśat*—entered; *padam*—respective positions; *vācā*—by words; *sva-aṁśena*—by one's own part; *vaktavyam*—speeches; *yayā*—by which; *asau*—they; *pratipadyate*—express.

TRANSLATION

Agni, or heat, separated from His mouth, and all the directors of material affairs entered into it in their respective positions. By that energy the living entity expresses himself in words.

PURPORT

The mouth of the gigantic universal form of the Lord is the source of the speaking power. The director of the fire element is the controlling deity, or the *ādhidaiva.* The speeches delivered are *ādhyātma,* or bodily functions, and the subject matter of the speeches is material productions, or the *ādhibhūta* principle.

TEXT 13

निर्भिन्नं तालु वरुणो लोकपालोऽविशद्धरेः ।
जिह्वयांशेन च रसं ययासौ प्रतिपद्यते ॥१३॥

nirbhinnaṁ tālu varuṇo
loka-pālo 'viśad dhareḥ
jihvayāṁśena ca rasaṁ
yayāsau pratipadyate

nirbhinnam—separated; *tālu*—palate; *varuṇaḥ*—the deity controlling air; *loka-pālaḥ*—director of the planets; *aviśat*—entered; *hareḥ*—of the Lord; *jihvayā aṁśena*—with the part of the tongue; *ca*—also; *rasam*—tastes; *yayā*—by which; *asau*—the living entity; *pratipadyate*—expresses.

TRANSLATION

When the palate of the gigantic form was separately manifested, Varuṇa, the director of air in the planetary systems, entered therein, and thus the living entity has the facility to taste everything with his tongue.

TEXT 14

निर्भिन्ने अश्विनौ नासे विष्णोराविशतां पदम् ।
घ्राणेनांशेन गन्धस्य प्रतिपत्तिर्यतो भवेत् ॥१४॥

nirbhinne aśvinau nāse
viṣṇor āviśatāṁ padam

ghrāṇenāṁśena gandhasya
pratipattir yato bhavet

nirbhinne—thus being separated; *aśvinau*—the dual Aśvinīs; *nāse*—of the two nostrils; *viṣṇoḥ*—of the Lord; *āviśatām*—entering; *padam*—post; *ghrāṇena aṁśena*—by partially smelling; *gandhasya*—aroma; *pratipattiḥ*—experience; *yataḥ*—whereupon; *bhavet*—becomes.

TRANSLATION

When the Lord's two nostrils separately manifested themselves, the dual Aśvinī-kumāras entered them in their proper positions, and because of this the living entities can smell the aromas of everything.

TEXT 15

निर्भिन्ने अक्षिणी त्वष्टा लोकपालोऽविशद्विभोः ।
चक्षुषांशेन रूपाणां प्रतिपत्तिर्यतो भवेत् ॥१५॥

nirbhinne akṣiṇī tvaṣṭā
loka-pālo 'viśad vibhoḥ
cakṣuṣāṁśena rūpāṇāṁ
pratipattir yato bhavet

nirbhinne—thus being separated; *akṣiṇī*—the eyes; *tvaṣṭā*—the sun; *loka-pālaḥ*—director of light; *aviśat*—entered; *vibhoḥ*—of the great; *cakṣuṣā aṁśena*—by the part of the eyesight; *rūpāṇām*—of the forms; *pratipattiḥ*—experience; *yataḥ*—by which; *bhavet*—becomes.

TRANSLATION

Thereafter, the two eyes of the gigantic form of the Lord were separately manifested. The sun, the director of light, entered them with the partial representation of eyesight, and thus the living entities can have vision of forms.

TEXT 16

निर्भिन्नान्यस्य चर्माणि लोकपालोऽनिलोऽविशत् ।
प्राणेनांशेन संस्पर्शं येनासौ प्रतिपद्यते ॥१६॥

nirbhinnāny asya carmāṇi
loka-pālo 'nilo 'viśat
prāṇenāṁśena saṁsparśaṁ
yenāsau pratipadyate

nirbhinnāni—being separated; *asya*—of the gigantic form; *carmāṇi*—skin; *loka-pālaḥ*—the director; *anilaḥ*—air; *aviśat*—entered; *prāṇena aṁśena*—the part of the breathing; *saṁsparśam*—touch; *yena*—by which; *asau*—the living entity; *pratipadyate*—can experience.

TRANSLATION

When there was a manifestation of skin separated from the gigantic form, Anila, the deity directing the wind, entered with partial touch, and thus the living entities can realize tactile knowledge.

TEXT 17

कर्णावस्य विनिर्भिन्नौ धिष्ण्यं स्वं विविशुर्दिशः ।
श्रोत्रेणांशेन शब्दस्य सिद्धिं येन प्रपद्यते ॥१७॥

karṇāv asya vinirbhinnau
dhiṣṇyaṁ svaṁ viviśur diśaḥ
śrotreṇāṁśena śabdasya
siddhiṁ yena prapadyate

karṇau—the ears; *asya*—of the gigantic form; *vinirbhinnau*—being thus separated; *dhiṣṇyam*—the controlling deity; *svam*—own; *viviśuḥ*—entered; *diśaḥ*—of the directions; *śrotreṇa aṁśena*—with the hearing principles; *śabdasya*—of the sound; *siddhim*—perfection; *yena*—by which; *prapadyate*—is experienced.

TRANSLATION

When the ears of the gigantic form became manifested, all the controlling deities of the directions entered into them with the hearing principles, by which all the living entities hear and take advantage of sound.

PURPORT

The ear is the most important instrument in the body of the living entity. Sound is the most important medium for carrying the message of distant and unknown things. The perfection of all sound or knowledge enters through the ear and makes one's life perfect. The entire Vedic system of knowledge is received by aural reception only, and thus sound is the most important source of knowledge.

TEXT 18

त्वचमस्य विनिर्भिन्नां विविशुर्धिष्ण्यमोषधीः ।
अंशेन रोमभिः कण्डूं यैरसौ प्रतिपद्यते ॥१८॥

tvacam asya vinirbhinnāṁ
viviśur dhiṣṇyam oṣadhīḥ
aṁśena romabhiḥ kaṇḍūṁ
yair asau pratipadyate

tvacam—skin; *asya*—of the gigantic form; *vinirbhinnām*—being separately manifested; *viviśuḥ*—entered; *dhiṣṇyam*—the controlling deity; *oṣadhīḥ*—sensations; *aṁśena*—with parts; *romabhiḥ*—through the hairs on the body; *kaṇḍūm*—itching; *yaiḥ*—by which; *asau*—the living entity; *pratipadyate*—experiences.

TRANSLATION

When there was a separate manifestation of skin, the controlling deities of sensations and their different parts entered into it, and thus the living entities feel itching and happiness due to touch.

PURPORT

For sense perception there are two principal items, touch and itching, and both of them are controlled by the skin and hairs on the body. According to Śrī Viśvanātha Cakravartī, the controlling deity of touch is the air passing within the body, and the controlling deity of the hairs on the body is Oṣadhya. For the skin the object of perception is touch, and for the hairs on the body the object of perception is itching.

TEXT 19

मेढ्रं तस्य विनिर्भिन्नं स्वधिष्ण्यं क उपाविशत् ।
रेतसांशेन येनासावानन्दं प्रतिपद्यते ॥१९॥

meḍhraṁ tasya vinirbhinnaṁ
sva-dhiṣṇyaṁ ka upāviśat
retasāṁśena yenāsāv
ānandaṁ pratipadyate

meḍhram—genitals; *tasya*—of the gigantic form; *vinirbhinnam*—being separated; *sva-dhiṣṇyam*—own position; *kaḥ*—Brahmā, the original living creature; *upāviśat*—entered; *retasā aṁśena*—with the part of the semen; *yena*—by which; *asau*—the living entity; *ānandam*—sex pleasure; *pratipadyate*—experiences.

TRANSLATION

When the genitals of the gigantic form separately became manifest, then Prajāpati, the original living creature, entered into them with his partial semen, and thus the living entities can enjoy sex pleasure.

TEXT 20

गुदं पुंसो विनिर्भिन्नं मित्रो लोकेश आविशत् ।
पायुनांशेन येनासौ विसर्गं प्रतिपद्यते ॥२०॥

gudaṁ puṁso vinirbhinnaṁ
mitro lokeśa āviśat
pāyunāṁśena yenāsau
visargaṁ pratipadyate

gudam—evacuating outlet; *puṁsaḥ*—of the gigantic form; *vinirbhinnam*—being separately manifested; *mitraḥ*—the sun-god; *loka-īśaḥ*—the director named Mitra; *āviśat*—entered; *pāyunā aṁśena*—with the partial evacuation process; *yena*—by which; *asau*—the living entity; *visargam*—evacuation; *pratipadyate*—performs.

TRANSLATION

The evacuating channel separately became manifest, and the director named Mitra entered into it with partial organs of evacuation. Thus the living entities are able to pass stool and urine.

TEXT 21

हस्तावस्य विनिर्भिन्नाविन्द्रः स्वर्पतिराविशत् ।
वार्तयांशेन पुरुषो यया वृत्तिं प्रपद्यते ॥२१॥

hastāv asya vinirbhinnāv
indraḥ svar-patir āviśat
vārtayāṁśena puruṣo
yayā vṛttiṁ prapadyate

hastau—hands; *asya*—of the gigantic form; *vinirbhinnau*—being separately manifested; *indraḥ*—the King of heaven; *svaḥ-patiḥ*—the ruler of heavenly planets; *āviśat*—entered into it; *vārtayā aṁśena*—with partial mercantile principles; *puruṣaḥ*—the living entity; *yayā*—by which; *vṛttim*—business of livelihood; *prapadyate*—transacts.

TRANSLATION

Thereafter, when the hands of the gigantic form separately became manifested, Indra, the ruler of the heavenly planets, entered into them, and thus the living entity is able to transact business for his livelihood.

TEXT 22

पादावस्य विनिर्भिन्नौ लोकेशो विष्णुराविशत् ।
गत्या स्वांशेन पुरुषो यया प्राप्यं प्रपद्यते ॥२२॥

pādāv asya vinirbhinnau
lokeśo viṣṇur āviśat
gatyā svāṁśena puruṣo
yayā prāpyaṁ prapadyate

pādau—the legs; *asya*—of the gigantic form; *vinirbhinnau*—being manifested separately; *loka-īśaḥ viṣṇuḥ*—the demigod Viṣṇu (not the Personality of Godhead); *āviśat*—entered; *gatyā*—by the power of movement; *sva-aṁśena*—with his own parts; *puruṣaḥ*—living entity; *yayā*—by which; *prāpyam*—destination; *prapadyate*—reaches.

TRANSLATION

Thereafter the legs of the gigantic form separately became manifest, and the demigod named Viṣṇu [not the Personality of Godhead] entered with partial movement. This helps the living entity move to his destination.

TEXT 23

बुद्धिं चास्य विनिर्भिन्नां वागीशो धिष्ण्यमाविशत् ।
बोधेनांशेन बोद्धव्यम् प्रतिपत्तिर्यतो भवेत् ॥२३॥

buddhiṁ cāsya vinirbhinnāṁ
vāg-īśo dhiṣṇyam āviśat
bodhenāṁśena boddhavyam
pratipattir yato bhavet

buddhim—intelligence; *ca*—also; *asya*—of the gigantic form; *vinirbhinnām*—being separately manifested; *vāk-īśaḥ*—Brahmā, lord of the *Vedas; dhiṣṇyam*—the controlling power; *āviśat*—entered in; *bodhena aṁśena*—with his part of intelligence; *boddhavyam*—the matter of understanding; *pratipattiḥ*—understood; *yataḥ*—by which; *bhavet*—so becomes.

TRANSLATION

When the intelligence of the gigantic form separately became manifest, Brahmā, the lord of the Vedas, entered into it with the partial power of understanding, and thus an object of understanding is experienced by the living entities.

TEXT 24

हृदयं चास्य निर्भिन्नं चन्द्रमा धिष्ण्यमाविशत् ।
मनसांशेन येनासौ विक्रियां प्रतिपद्यते ॥२४॥

hṛdayaṁ cāsya nirbhinnaṁ
candramā dhiṣṇyam āviśat
manasāṁśena yenāsau
vikriyāṁ pratipadyate

hṛdayam—heart; *ca*—also; *asya*—of the gigantic form; *nirbhinnam*—being manifested separately; *candramā*—the moon demigod; *dhiṣṇyam*—with controlling power; *āviśat*—entered into; *manasā aṁśena*—partly with mental activity; *yena*—by which; *asau*—the living entity; *vikriyām*—resolution; *pratipadyate*—transacts.

TRANSLATION

After that, the heart of the gigantic form separately manifested itself, and into it entered the moon demigod with partial mental activity. Thus the living entity can conduct his mental speculations.

TEXT 25

आत्मानं चास्य निर्भिन्नमभिमानोऽविशत्पदम् ।
कर्मणांशेन येनासौ कर्तव्यं प्रतिपद्यते ॥२५॥

ātmānaṁ cāsya nirbhinnam
abhimāno 'viśat padam
karmaṇāṁśena yenāsau
kartavyaṁ pratipadyate

ātmānam—false ego; *ca*—also; *asya*—of the gigantic form; *nirbhinnam*—being separately manifested; *abhimānaḥ*—false identification; *aviśat*—entered; *padam*—in position; *karmaṇā*—activities; *aṁśena*—by the part; *yena*—by which; *asau*—the living entity; *kartavyam*—objective activities; *pratipadyate*—takes in.

TRANSLATION

Thereafter the materialistic ego of the gigantic form separately manifested itself, and into it entered Rudra, the controller of false ego, with his own partial activities, by which the living entity transacts his objective actions.

PURPORT

The false ego of materialistic identity is controlled by the demigod Rudra, an incarnation of Lord Śiva. Rudra is the incarnation of the Supreme Lord who controls the mode of ignorance within material nature. The activities of the false ego are based on the objective of the body and mind. Most persons conducted by the false ego are controlled by Lord Śiva. When one reaches a finer version of ignorance, he falsely thinks of himself as the Supreme Lord. That egoistic conviction of the conditioned soul is the last snare of the illusory energy which controls the entire material world.

TEXT 26

सत्त्वं चास्य विनिर्भिन्नं महान्धिष्ण्यमुपाविशत् ।
चित्तेनांशेन येनासौ विज्ञानं प्रतिपद्यते ॥२६॥

sattvaṁ cāsya vinirbhinnaṁ
mahān dhiṣṇyam upāviśat
cittenāṁśena yenāsau
vijñānaṁ pratipadyate

sattvam—consciousness; *ca*—also; *asya*—of the gigantic form; *vinirbhinnam*—being separately manifested; *mahān*—the total energy, *mahat-tattva; dhiṣṇyam*—with control; *upāviśat*—entered into; *cittena aṁśena*—along with His part of consciousness; *yena*—by which; *asau*—the living entity; *vijñānam*—specific knowledge; *pratipadyate*—cultivates.

TRANSLATION

Thereafter, when His consciousness separately manifested itself, the total energy, mahat-tattva, entered with His conscious part. Thus the living entity is able to conceive specific knowledge.

TEXT 27

शीर्ष्णोऽस्य द्यौर्धरा पद्भ्यां खं नाभेरुदपद्यत ।
गुणानां वृत्तयो येषु प्रतीयन्ते सुरादयः ॥२७॥

śīrṣṇo 'sya dyaur dharā padbhyāṁ
khaṁ nābher udapadyata
guṇānāṁ vṛttayo yeṣu
pratīyante surādayaḥ

śīrṣṇaḥ—head; *asya*—of the gigantic form; *dyauḥ*—the heavenly planets; *dharā*—earthly planets; *padbhyām*—on His legs; *kham*—the sky; *nābheḥ*—from the abdomen; *udapadyata*—became manifested; *guṇānām*—of the three modes of nature; *vṛttayaḥ*—reactions; *yeṣu*—in which; *pratīyante*—manifest; *sura-ādayaḥ*—the demigods and others.

TRANSLATION

Thereafter, from the head of the gigantic form, the heavenly planets were manifested, and from His legs the earthly planets and from His abdomen the sky separately manifested themselves. Within them the demigods and others also were manifested in terms of the modes of material nature.

TEXT 28

आत्यन्तिकेन सत्त्वेन दिवं देवाः प्रपेदिरे ।
धरां रजःस्वभावेन पणयो ये च ताननु ॥२८॥

ātyantikena sattvena
divaṁ devāḥ prapedire
dharāṁ rajaḥ-svabhāvena
paṇayo ye ca tān anu

ātyantikena—excessive; *sattvena*—by the mode of goodness; *divam*—in the higher planets; *devāḥ*—the demigods; *prapedire*—have been situated; *dharām*—on the earth; *rajaḥ*—the mode of passion; *svabhāvena*—by nature; *paṇayaḥ*—the human being; *ye*—all those; *ca*—also; *tān*—their; *anu*—subordinate.

TRANSLATION

The demigods, qualified by the superexcellent quality of the mode of goodness, are situated in the heavenly planets, whereas the human beings, because of their nature in the mode of passion, live on the earth in company with their subordinates.

PURPORT

In *Bhagavad-gītā* (14.14-15) it is said that those who are highly developed in the mode of goodness are promoted to the higher, heavenly planetary system, and those who are overpowered by the mode of passion are situated in the middle planetary systems—the earth and similar planets. But those who are surcharged with the mode of ignorance are degraded to the lower planetary systems or to the animal kingdom.

The demigods are highly developed in the mode of goodness, and thus they are situated in the heavenly planets. Below human beings are the animals, although some of them mingle with human society; cows, horses, dogs, etc., are habituated to living under the protection of human beings.

The word *ātyantikena* is very significant in this verse. By development of the mode of goodness of material nature one can become situated in the heavenly planets. But by excessive development of the modes of passion and ignorance, the human being indulges in killing the animals who are meant to be protected by mankind. Persons who indulge in unnecessary animal killing have excessively developed in the modes of passion and ignorance and have no hope of advancing to the mode of goodness; they are destined to be degraded to lower statuses of life. The planetary systems are calculated as upper and lower in terms of the classes of living entities who live there.

TEXT 29

तार्तीयेन स्वभावेन भगवन्नाभिमाश्रिताः ।
उभयोरन्तरं व्योम ये रुद्रपार्षदां गणाः ॥२९॥

tārtīyena svabhāvena
bhagavan-nābhim āśritāḥ
ubhayor antaraṁ vyoma
ye rudra-pārṣadāṁ gaṇāḥ

tārtīyena—by excessive development of the third mode of material nature, the mode of ignorance; *svabhāvena*—by such nature; *bhagavat-nābhim*—the abdominal navel of the gigantic form of the Personality of Godhead; *āśritāḥ*—those who are so situated; *ubhayoḥ*—between the two; *antaram*—in between; *vyoma*—the sky; *ye*—all of whom; *rudra-pārṣadām*—associates of Rudra; *gaṇāḥ*—population.

TRANSLATION

Living entities who are associates of Rudra develop in the third mode of material nature, or ignorance. They are situated in the sky between the earthly planets and the heavenly planets.

PURPORT

This middle portion of the sky is called Bhuvarloka, as confirmed by both Śrīla Viśvanātha Cakravartī and Śrīla Jīva Gosvāmī. In *Bhagavad-gītā* it is stated that those who develop in the mode of passion are situated in the middle region. Those who are situated in the mode of goodness are promoted to the regions of the demigods, those who are situated in the mode of passion are placed in human society, and those who are situated in the mode of ignorance are placed in the society of animals or ghosts. There are no contradictions in this conclusion. Numerous living entities are distributed all over the universe in different planets and are so situated in terms of their own qualities in the modes of material nature.

TEXT 30

मुखतोऽवर्तत ब्रह्म पुरुषस्य कुरूद्वह ।
यस्तून्मुखत्वाद्वर्णानां मुख्योऽभूद्ब्राह्मणो गुरुः ॥३०॥

mukhato 'vartata brahma
puruṣasya kurūdvaha
yas tūnmukhatvād varṇānāṁ
mukhyo 'bhūd brāhmaṇo guruḥ

mukhataḥ—from the mouth; *avartata*—generated; *brahma*—the Vedic wisdom; *puruṣasya*—of the *virāṭ-puruṣa,* the gigantic form; *kuru-udvaha*—O chief of the Kuru dynasty; *yaḥ*—who are; *tu*—due to; *unmukhatvāt*—inclined to; *varṇānām*—of the orders of society; *mukhyaḥ*—the chief; *abhūt*—so became; *brāhmaṇaḥ*—called the *brāhmaṇas; guruḥ*—the recognized teacher or spiritual master.

TRANSLATION

O chief of the Kuru dynasty, the Vedic wisdom became manifested from the mouth of the virāṭ, the gigantic form. Those who are inclined to this Vedic knowledge are called brāhmaṇas, and they are the natural teachers and spiritual masters of all the orders of society.

PURPORT

As confirmed in *Bhagavad-gītā* (4.13), the four orders of human society developed with the order of the body of the gigantic form. The bodily divisions are the mouth, arms, waist and legs. Those who are situated on the mouth are called *brāhmaṇas,* those who are situated on the arms are called *kṣatriyas,* those who are situated on the waist are called *vaiśyas,* and those who are situated on the legs are called *śūdras.* Everyone is situated in the body of the Supreme in His gigantic *viśva-rūpa* form. In terms of the four orders, therefore, no caste is to be considered degraded because of being situated on a particular part of the body. In our own bodies we do not show any actual difference in our treatment towards the hands or legs. Each and every part of the body is important, although the mouth is the most important of the bodily parts. If other parts are cut off from the body, a man can continue his life, but if the mouth is cut off, one cannot live. Therefore, this most important part of the body of the Lord is called the sitting place of the *brāhmaṇas*, who are inclined to the Vedic wisdom. One who is not inclined to the Vedic wisdom but to mundane affairs cannot be called a *brāhmaṇa*, even if he is born of a *brāhmaṇa* family or father. To have a *brāhmaṇa* father does not qualify one as a *brāhmaṇa*. The main qualification of a *brāhmaṇa* is to be inclined to the Vedic wisdom. The *Vedas* are situated on the mouth of the Lord, and therefore anyone who is inclined to the Vedic wisdom is certainly situated on the mouth of the Lord, and he is a *brāhmaṇa*. This inclination towards Vedic wisdom is also not restricted to any particular caste or community. Anyone from any family and from any part of the world may become inclined to the Vedic wisdom, and that will qualify him as a real *brāhmaṇa*.

A real *brāhmaṇa* is the natural teacher or spiritual master. Unless one has Vedic knowledge, one cannot become a spiritual master. The perfect knowledge of the *Vedas* is to know the Lord, the Personality of Godhead, and that is the end of Vedic knowledge, or Vedānta. One who is situated in the impersonal Brahman and has no information of the Supreme Personality of Godhead may become a *brāhmaṇa*, but he cannot become a spiritual master. It is said in the *Padma Purāṇa:*

ṣaṭ-karma-nipuṇo vipro
mantra-tantra-viśāradaḥ
avaiṣṇavo gurur na syād
vaiṣṇavaḥ śva-paco guruḥ

An impersonalist can become a qualified *brāhmaṇa*, but he cannot become a spiritual master unless and until he is promoted to the stage of a Vaiṣṇava, or a devotee of the Personality of Godhead. Lord Caitanya, the great authority of Vedic wisdom in the modern age, stated:

kibā vipra, kibā nyāsī, śūdra kene naya
yei kṛṣṇa-tattva-vettā, sei 'guru' haya

A person may be a *brāhmaṇa* or a *śūdra* or a *sannyāsī*, but if he happens to be well versed in the science of Kṛṣṇa, then he is fit to become a spiritual master. (Cc. *Madhya* 8.128) The qualification, then, of a spiritual master is not to be a qualified *brāhmaṇa*, but to be well versed in the science of Kṛṣṇa.

One who is conversant with Vedic wisdom is a *brāhmaṇa.* And only a *brāhmaṇa* who is a pure Vaiṣṇava and knows all the intricacies of the science of Kṛṣṇa can become a spiritual master.

TEXT 31

बाहुभ्योऽवर्तत क्षत्रं क्षत्रियस्तदनुव्रतः ।
यो जातस्त्रायते वर्णान् पौरुषः कण्टकक्षतात् ॥३१॥

bāhubhyo 'vartata kṣatraṁ
kṣatriyas tad anuvrataḥ
yo jātas trāyate varṇān
pauruṣaḥ kaṇṭaka-kṣatāt

bāhubhyaḥ—from the arms; *avartata*—generated; *kṣatram*—the power of protection; *kṣatriyaḥ*—in relation to the power of protection; *tat*—that; *anuvrataḥ*—followers; *yaḥ*—one who; *jātaḥ*—so becomes; *trāyate*—delivers; *varṇān*—the other occupations; *pauruṣaḥ*—representative of the Personality of Godhead; *kaṇṭaka*—of disturbing elements like thieves and debauchees; *kṣatāt*—from the mischief.

TRANSLATION

Thereafter the power of protection was generated from the arms of the gigantic virāṭ form, and in relation to such power the kṣatriyas also came into existence by following the kṣatriya principle of protecting society from the disturbance of thieves and miscreants.

PURPORT

As the *brāhmaṇas* are recognized by their particular qualification of inclination towards the transcendental knowledge of Vedic wisdom, so also the *kṣatriyas* are recognized by the power to protect society from the disturbing elements of thieves and miscreants. The word *anuvrataḥ* is significant. A person who follows the *kṣatriya* principles by protecting society from thieves and miscreants is called a *kṣatriya,* not the one who is simply born a *kṣatriya.* The conception of the caste system is always based on quality and not on the qualification of birth. Birth is an extraneous consideration; it is not the main feature of the orders and divisions. In *Bhagavad-gītā* (18.41-44) the qualifications of the *brāhmaṇas, kṣatriyas, vaiśyas* and *śūdras* are specifically mentioned, and it is understood that all such qualifications are needed before one can be designated as belonging to a particular group.

Lord Viṣṇu is always mentioned as the *puruṣa* in all Vedic scriptures. Sometimes the living entities are also mentioned as *puruṣas*, although they are essentially *puruṣa-śakti* (*parā śakti* or *parā prakṛti*), the superior energy of the *puruṣa*. Illusioned by the external potency of the *puruṣa* (the Lord), the living entities falsely think of themselves as the *puruṣa* although they actually have no qualifications. The Lord has the power to protect. Of the three deities Brahmā, Viṣṇu and Maheśvara, the first has the power to create, the second has the power to protect, and the third has the power to destroy. The word *puruṣa* is significant in this verse because the *kṣatriyas* are expected to represent the *puruṣa* Lord in giving protection to the *prajās*, or all those who are born in the land and water. Protection is therefore meant for both man and the animals. in modern society the *prajās* are not protected from the hands of thieves and miscreants. The modern democratic state, which has no *kṣatriyas*, is a government of the *vaiśyas* and *śūdras*, and not of *brāhmaṇas* and *kṣatriyas* as formerly. Mahārāja Yudhiṣṭhira and his grandson, Mahārāja Parīkṣit, were typical *kṣatriya* kings, for they gave protection to all men and animals. When the personification of Kali attempted to kill a cow, Mahārāja Parīkṣit at once prepared himself to kill the miscreant, and the personification of Kali was banished from his kingdom. That is the sign of *puruṣa*, or the representative of Lord Viṣṇu. According to Vedic civilization, a qualified *kṣatriya* monarch is given the respect of the Lord because he represents the Lord by giving protection to the *prajās*. Modern elected presidents cannot even give protection from theft cases, and therefore one has to take protection from an insurance company. The problems of modern human society are due to the lack of qualified *brāhmaṇas* and *kṣatriyas* and the overinfluence of the *vaiśyas* and *śūdras* by so-called general franchise.

TEXT 32

विशोऽवर्तन्त तस्योर्वोर्लोकवृत्तिकरीर्विभोः ।
वैश्यस्तदुद्भवो वार्तां नृणां यः समवर्तयत् ॥३२॥

viśo 'vartanta tasyorvor
loka-vṛttikarīr vibhoḥ
vaiśyas tad-udbhavo vārtāṁ
nṛṇāṁ yaḥ samavartayat

viśaḥ—means of living by production and distribution; *avartanta*—generated; *tasya*—His (the gigantic form's); *ūrvoḥ*—from the thighs; *loka-vṛttikarīḥ*—means of livelihood; *vibhoḥ*—of the Lord; *vaiśyaḥ*—the mercantile community; *tat*—their; *udbhavaḥ*—orientation; *vārtām*—means of living; *nṛṇām*—of all men; *yaḥ*—one who; *samavartayat*—executed.

TRANSLATION

The means of livelihood of all persons, namely production of grains and their distribution to the prajās, was generated from the thighs of the Lord's gigantic form. The mercantile men who take charge of such execution are called vaiśyas.

PURPORT

Human society's means of living is clearly mentioned here as *viśa,* or agriculture and the business of distributing agricultural products, which involves transport, banking, etc. Industry is an artificial means of livelihood, and large-scale industry especially is the source of all the problems of society. In *Bhagavad-gītā* also the duties of the *vaiśyas,* who are engaged in *viśa,* are stated as cow protection, agriculture and business. We have already discussed that the human being can safely depend on the cow and agricultural land for his livelihood.

The exchange of produce by banking and transportation is a branch of this type of living. The *vaiśyas* are divided into many subsections: some of them are called *kṣetrī,* or landowners, some are called *kṛṣaṇa,* or land tillers, some of them are called *tila-vaṇik,* or grain raisers, some are called *gandha-vaṇik,* or merchants in spices, and some are called *suvarṇa-vaṇik,* or merchants in gold and banking. The *brāhmaṇas* are the teachers and spiritual masters, the *kṣatriyas* protect the citizens from the hands of thieves and miscreants, and the *vaiśyas* are in charge of production and distribution. The *śūdras,* the unintelligent class of men who cannot act independently in any of the above-mentioned activities, are meant for serving the three higher classes for their livelihood.

Formerly, the *brāhmaṇas* were given all the necessities of life by the *kṣatriyas* and *vaiśyas* because they had no time to spend making a living. The *kṣatriyas* would collect taxes from the *vaiśyas* and *śūdras,* but the *brāhmaṇas* were exempt from paying income tax or land revenue. That system of human society was so nice that there were no political, social and economic upheavals. The different castes, or *varṇa* classifications, are therefore essential for maintaining a peaceful human society.

TEXT 33

पद्भ्यां भगवतो जज्ञे शुश्रूषा धर्मसिद्धये ।
तस्यां जातः पुरा शूद्रो यद्वृत्त्या तुष्यते हरिः ॥३३॥

padbhyāṁ bhagavato jajñe
śuśrūṣā dharma-siddhaye
tasyāṁ jātaḥ purā śūdro
yad-vṛttyā tuṣyate hariḥ

padbhyām—from the legs; *bhagavataḥ*—of the Personality of Godhead; *jajñe*—became manifested; *śuśrūṣā*—service; *dharma*—occupational duty; *siddhaye*—for the matter of; *tasyām*—in that; *jātaḥ*—being generated; *purā*—formerly; *śūdraḥ*—the servitors; *yat-vṛttyā*—the occupation by which; *tuṣyate*—becomes satisfied; *hariḥ*—the Supreme Personality of Godhead.

TRANSLATION

Thereafter, service was manifested from the legs of the Personality of Godhead for the sake of perfecting the religious function. Situated on the legs are the śūdras, who satisfy the Lord by service.

PURPORT

Service is the real constitutional occupation of all living entities. The living entities are meant to render service to the Lord, and they can attain religious perfection by this service attitude. One cannot attain religious perfection simply by speculating to attain theoretical knowledge. The *jñānī* division of spiritualists go on speculating only to distinguish the soul from matter, but they have no information of the activities of the soul after being liberated by knowledge. It is said that persons who only mentally speculate to know things as they are and who do not engage in the transcendental loving service of the Lord are simply wasting their time.

It is clearly said here that the principle of service was generated from the legs of the Lord for the sake of perfecting the religious process, but this transcendental service is different from the idea of service in the material world. In the material world, no one wants to be a servant; everyone wants to become the master because false mastership is the basic disease of the conditioned soul. The conditioned soul in the material world wants to lord it over others. Illusioned by the external energy of the Lord, he is forced to become a servant of the material world. That is the real position of the conditioned soul. The last snare of the illusory, external energy is the conception of becoming one with the Lord, and due to this conception the illusioned soul remains in the bondage of material energy, falsely thinking himself a liberated soul and "as good as Nārāyaṇa."

It is actually better to be a *śūdra* than to be a *brāhmaṇa* and not develop the service attitude, because that attitude alone satisfies the Lord. Every living being—even if he be a *brāhmaṇa* by qualification—must take to the transcendental service of the Lord. Both *Bhagavad-gītā* and the *Śrīmad-Bhāgavatam* support that this service attitude is the perfection of the living entity. A *brāhmaṇa, kṣatriya, vaiśya* or *śūdra* can perfect his occupational duties only by rendering service unto the Lord. A *brāhmaṇa* is supposed to know this fact due to his perfection in Vedic wisdom. The other sections are supposed to follow the direction of the *brāhmaṇa* Vaiṣṇava (one who is a *brāhmaṇa* by qualification and a Vaiṣṇava by action). That will make the entire society perfect in regard to the order of its social construction. A disordered society cannot satisfy either the members of the society or the Lord. Even if one is not a perfect *brāhmaṇa, kṣatriya, vaiśya* or *śūdra* but takes to the service of the Lord, not caring for the perfection of his social position, he becomes a perfect human being simply by developing the attitude of service to the Supreme Lord.

TEXT 34

एते वर्णाः स्वधर्मेण यजन्ति स्वगुरुं हरिम् ।
श्रद्धयात्मविशुद्ध्यर्थं यज्जाताः सह वृत्तिभिः ॥३४॥

ete varṇāḥ sva-dharmeṇa
yajanti sva-guruṁ harim
śraddhayātma-viśuddhy-arthaṁ
yaj-jātāḥ saha vṛttibhiḥ

ete—all these; *varṇāḥ*—orders of society; *sva-dharmeṇa*—by one's own occupational duties; *yajanti*—worship; *sva-gurum*—with the spiritual master; *harim*—the Supreme Personality of Godhead; *śraddhayā*—with faith and devotion; *ātma*—self; *viśuddhi-artham*—for purifying; *yat*—from whom; *jātāḥ*—born; *saha*—along with; *vṛttibhiḥ*—occupational duty.

TRANSLATION

All these different social divisions are born, with their occupational duties and living conditions, from the Supreme Personality of Godhead. Thus for unconditional life and self-realization one has to worship the Supreme Lord under the direction of the spiritual master.

PURPORT

Since they are born from different parts of the body of the Supreme Lord in His gigantic form, all living entities in all parts of the entire universe are supposed to be eternal servitors of the supreme body. Every part of our own body, such as the mouth, hands, thighs and legs, is meant to render service to the whole. That is their constitutional position. In subhuman life the living entities are not conscious of this constitutional position, but in the human form of life they are supposed to know this through the system of the *varṇas,* the social orders. As above mentioned, the *brāhmaṇa* is the spiritual master of all the orders of society, and thus brahminical culture, culminating in the transcendental service of the Lord, is the basic principle for purifying the soul.

In conditioned life the soul is under the impression that he can become the lord of the universe, and the last point of this misconception is to think oneself the Supreme. The foolish conditioned soul does not take into account that the Supreme cannot be conditioned by *māyā,* or illusion. If the Supreme were to become conditioned by illusion, where would be His supremacy? In that case, *māyā,* or illusion, would be the Supreme. Therefore, because the living entities are conditioned, they cannot be supreme. The actual position of the conditioned soul is explained in this verse: all the conditioned souls are impure due to contact with the material energy in three modes of nature. Therefore it is necessary that they purify themselves under the guidance of the bona fide spiritual master, who not only is a *brāhmaṇa* by qualification but must also be a Vaiṣṇava. The only self-purifying process mentioned herein is to worship the Lord under the recognized method—under the guidance of the bona fide spiritual master. That is the natural way of purification, and no other method is recommended as bona fide. The other methods of purification may be helpful to come to this stage of life, but ultimately one has to come to this last point before he attains actual perfection. *Bhagavad-gītā* (7.19) confirms this truth as follows:

bahūnāṁ janmanām ante
jñānavān māṁ prapadyate
vāsudevaḥ sarvam iti
sa mahātmā sudurlabhaḥ

TEXT 35

एतत्क्षत्तर्भगवतो दैवकर्मात्मरूपिणः ।
कः श्रद्दध्यादुपाकर्तुं योगमायाबलोदयम् ॥३५॥

etat kṣattar bhagavato
daiva-karmātma-rūpiṇaḥ
kaḥ śraddadhyād upākartuṁ
yogamāyā-balodayam

etat—this; *kṣattaḥ*—O Vidura; *bhagavataḥ*—of the Supreme Personality of Godhead; *daiva-karma-ātma-rūpiṇaḥ*—of the gigantic form of transcendental work, time and nature; *kaḥ*—who else; *śraddadhyāt*—can aspire; *upākartum*—measure in totality; *yogamāyā*—internal potency; *bala-udayam*—manifested by the strength of.

TRANSLATION

O Vidura, who can estimate or measure the transcendental time, work and potency of the gigantic form manifested by the internal potency of the Supreme Personality of Godhead?

PURPORT

The froggish philosophers may go on with their mental speculations on the subject matter of the *virāṭ*, the gigantic form exhibited by the *yogamāyā* internal potency of the Supreme Personality of Godhead, but factually no one can measure such a vast exhibition. In *Bhagavad-gītā* (11.16), Arjuna, the recognized devotee of the Lord, says:

aneka-bāhūdara-vaktra-netraṁ
paśyāmi tvāṁ sarvato 'nanta-rūpam
nāntaṁ na madhyaṁ na punas tavādiṁ
paśyāmi viśveśvara viśva-rūpa

"O my Lord, O gigantic *viśva-rūpa* form, O master of the universe, I see innumerable hands, bodies, mouths and eyes in all directions, and they are all unlimited. I cannot find the end of this manifestation, nor do I see the middle, nor the beginning."

Bhagavad-gītā was specifically spoken to Arjuna, and the *viśva-rūpa* was exhibited before him at his request. He was awarded the specific eyes to see this *viśva-rūpa*, yet although he was able to see the Lord's innumerable hands and mouths, he was unable to see Him completely. Since Arjuna was unable to estimate the length and breadth of the potency of the Lord, who else would be able to do so? One may only indulge in miscalculation like the frog-philosopher. The frog-philosopher wanted to estimate the length and breadth of the Pacific Ocean by his experience of a well three cubic feet large, and thus he began to puff himself up to become as big as the Pacific Ocean, but at last he burst and died by this process. This story is applicable to the mental philosophers who, under the illusion of the Lord's external energy, indulge in estimating the length and breadth of the Supreme Lord. The best path is to become a coolheaded, submissive devotee of the Lord, try to hear about the Lord from the bona fide spiritual master, and thus serve the Lord in transcendental loving service, as suggested in the previous verse.

TEXT 36

तथापि कीर्तयाम्यङ्ग यथामति यथाश्रुतम् ।
कीर्तिं हरेः स्वां सत्कर्तुं गिरमन्याभिधासतीम् ॥३६॥

tathāpi kīrtayāmy aṅga
yathā-mati yathā-śrutam
kīrtiṁ hareḥ svāṁ sat-kartuṁ
giram anyābhidhāsatīm

tathā—therefore; *api*—although it is so; *kīrtayāmi*—I do describe; *aṅga*—O Vidura; *yathā*—as much as; *mati*—intelligence; *yathā*—as much as; *śrutam*—heard; *kīrtim*—glories; *hareḥ*—of the Lord; *svām*—own; *sat-kartum*—just purify; *giram*—speeches; *anyābhidhā*—otherwise; *asatīm*—unchaste.

TRANSLATION

In spite of my inability, whatever I have been able to hear [from the spiritual master] and whatever I could assimilate I am now describing in glorification of the Lord by pure speech, for otherwise my power of speaking would remain unchaste.

PURPORT

The purification of the conditioned soul necessitates purification of his consciousness. By the presence of consciousness, the presence of the transcendental soul is verified, and as soon as consciousness leaves the body, the material body is not active. Consciousness is perceived, therefore, by activities. The theory put forward by empiric philosophers that consciousness can remain in an inactive state is the proof of their poor fund of knowledge. One should not become unchaste by stopping the activities of pure consciousness. If the activities of pure consciousness are stopped, certainly the conscious living force will be otherwise engaged because unless engaged the consciousness has no standing. Consciousness cannot be silent, even for a moment. When the body does not act, the consciousness acts in the form of dreams. Unconsciousness is artificial; by induced extraneous help it remains for a limited period, but when the intoxication of the drug is finished or when one is awake, the consciousness again acts earnestly.

Maitreya's statement is that in order to avoid unchaste conscious activities, he was trying to describe the unlimited glories of the Lord, although he did not have the ability to describe them perfectly. This glorification of the Lord is not a product of research, but the result of hearing submissively from the authority of the spiritual master. It is also not possible to repeat all that one has heard from his spiritual master, but one can narrate as far as possible by one's honest endeavor. It does not matter whether the Lord's glories are fully explained or not. One must attempt to engage one's bodily, mental and verbal activities in the transcendental glorification of the Lord, otherwise such activities will remain unchaste and impure. The existence of the conditioned soul can be purified only by the method of engaging mind and speech in the service of the Lord. The *tridaṇḍi-sannyāsī* of the Vaiṣṇava school accepts three rods, representing the vow to engage in the service of the Lord with body, mind and speech, whereas the *ekadaṇḍi-sannyāsī* takes the vow to become one with the Supreme. Since the Lord is the Absolute, there is no distinction between Him and His glories. The glories of the Lord as chanted by the Vaiṣṇava *sannyāsī* are as substantial as the Lord Himself, and thus while glorifying the Lord the devotee becomes one with Him in transcendental interest, although he remains eternally a transcendental servitor. This simultaneously one and different position of the devotee makes him eternally purified, and thus his life becomes a complete success.

TEXT 37

एकान्तलाभं वचसो नु पुंसां
सुश्लोकमौलेर्गुणवादमाहुः ।
श्रुतेश्च विद्वद्भिरुपाकृतायां
कथासुधायामुपसम्प्रयोगम् ॥३७॥

ekānta-lābhaṁ vacaso nu puṁsāṁ
suśloka-mauler guṇa-vādam āhuḥ
śruteś ca vidvadbhir upākṛtāyāṁ
kathā-sudhāyām upasamprayogam

eka-anta—the one which has no comparison; *lābham*—gain; *vacasaḥ*—by discussions; *nu puṁsām*—after the Supreme Person; *suśloka*—pious; *mauleḥ*—activities; *guṇa-vādam*—glorification; *āhuḥ*—it is so said; *śruteḥ*—of the ear; *ca*—also; *vidvadbhiḥ*—by the learned; *upākṛtāyām*—being so edited; *kathā-sudhāyām*—in the nectar of such a transcendental message; *upasamprayogam*—serves the real purpose, being nearer to.

TRANSLATION

The highest perfectional gain of humanity is to engage in discussions of the activities and glories of the Pious Actor. Such activities are so nicely

arranged in writing by the greatly learned sages that the actual purpose of the ear is served just by being near them.

PURPORT

The impersonalists are very much afraid of hearing the activities of the Lord because they think that the happiness derived from the transcendental situation of Brahman is the ultimate goal of life; they think that anyone's activity, even that of the Personality of Godhead, is mundane. But the idea of happiness indicated in this verse is different because it relates to the activities of the Supreme Personality, who has transcendental qualities. The word *guṇa-vādam* is significant because the qualities of the Lord and His activities and pastimes are the subject matter for the discussions of devotees. A *ṛṣi* like Maitreya is certainly not interested in discussing anything pertaining to mundane qualities, yet he says that the highest perfectional stage of transcendental realization is to discuss the Lord's activities. Śrīla Jīva Gosvāmī, therefore, concludes that topics regarding the transcendental activities of the Lord are far beyond the transcendental realization of *kaivalya* happiness. These transcendental activities of the Lord are so arranged in writing by the great sages that simply by hearing of those narrations one becomes perfectly self-realized, and the proper use of the ear and the tongue is also achieved. *Śrīmad-Bhāgavatam* is one of such great literatures, and the highest perfectional state of life is attained simply by hearing and reciting its contents.

TEXT 38

आत्मनोऽवसितो वत्स महिमा कविनादिना ।
संवत्सरसहस्रान्ते धिया योगविपक्कया ॥३८॥

ātmano 'vasito vatsa
mahimā kavinādinā
saṁvatsara-sahasrānte
dhiyā yoga-vipakkayā

ātmanaḥ—of the Supreme Soul; *avasitaḥ*—known; *vatsa*—O my dear son; *mahimā*—glories; *kavinā*—by the poet Brahmā; *ādinā*—original; *saṁvatsara*—celestial years; *sahasra-ante*—at the end of one thousand; *dhiyā*—by intelligence; *yoga-vipakkayā*—by matured meditation.

TRANSLATION

O my son, the original poet, Brahmā, after mature meditation for one thousand celestial years, could know only that the glories of the Supreme Soul are inconceivable.

PURPORT

There are some froggish philosophers who want to know the Supreme Soul by means of philosophy and mental speculation. And when the devotees, who are to some extent in knowledge of the Supreme Lord, admit that the glories of the Lord are inestimable or inconceivable, the froggish philosophers adversely criticize them. These philosophers, like the frog in the well who tried to estimate the measurement of the Pacific Ocean, like to take trouble over fruitless mental speculation instead of taking instructions from devotees like the original poet, namely, Brahmā. Lord Brahmā underwent a severe type of meditation for one thousand celestial years, yet he said that the glories of the Lord are inconceivable. Therefore what can the froggish philosophers hope to gain from their mental speculations?

It is said in the *Brahma-saṁhitā* that the mental speculator may fly through the sky of speculation with the velocity of the mind or the wind for thousands of millions of years, and still he will find it inconceivable. The devotees, however, do not waste time in such vain searching after knowledge of the Supreme, but they submissively hear the glories of the Lord from bona fide devotees. Thus they transcendentally enjoy the process of hearing and chanting. The Lord approves of the devotional activities of the devotees or *mahātmās*, and He says:

mahātmānas tu māṁ pārtha
daivīṁ prakṛtim āśritāḥ
bhajanty ananya-manaso
jñātvā bhūtādim avyayam

satataṁ kīrtayanto māṁ
yatantaś ca dṛḍha-vratāḥ
namasyantaś ca māṁ bhaktyā
nitya-yuktā upāsate

(*Bg.* 9.13-14)

The pure devotees of the Lord take shelter of the *parā prakṛti*, the internal potency of the Lord called Lakṣmīdevī, Sītādevī, Śrīmatī Rādhārāṇī or Śrīmatī Rukmiṇīdevī, and thus they become actual *mahātmās*, or great souls. *Mahātmās* are not fond of indulging in mental speculations, but they actually take to the devotional service of the Lord, without the slightest deviation. Devotional service is manifested by the primary process of hearing and chanting about the activities of the Lord. This transcendental method practiced by the *mahātmās* gives them sufficient knowledge of the Lord because if the Lord can at all be known to some extent, it is only through the means of devotional service and no other way. One may go on speculating and waste the valuable time of his human life, but that will not help anyone to enter into the precincts of the Lord. The *mahātmās*, however, are not concerned with knowing the Lord by mental speculation because they enjoy hearing about His glorious activities in His transcendental dealings with His devotees or with the demons. The devotees take pleasure in both and are happy in this life and the life after.

TEXT 39

अतो भगवतो माया मायिनामपि मोहिनी ।
यत्स्वयं चात्मवर्त्मात्मा न वेद किमुतापरे ॥३९॥

ato bhagavato māyā
māyinām api mohinī
yat svayaṁ cātma-vartmātmā
na veda kim utāpare

ataḥ—therefore; *bhagavataḥ*—godly; *māyā*—potencies; *māyinām*—of the jugglers; *api*—even; *mohinī*—enchanting; *yat*—that which; *svayam*—personally; *ca*—also; *ātma-vartma*—self-sufficient; *ātmā*—self; *na*—does not; *veda*—know; *kim*—what; *uta*—to speak of; *apare*—others.

TRANSLATION

The wonderful potency of the Supreme Personality of Godhead is bewildering even to the jugglers. That potential power is unknown even to the self-sufficient Lord, so it is certainly unknown to others.

PURPORT

The froggish philosophers and mundane wranglers in science and mathematical calculation may not believe in the inconceivable potency of the Supreme Personality of Godhead, but they are sometimes puzzled by the wonderful jugglery of man and nature. Such jugglers and magicians of the mundane world are actually puzzled by the jugglery of the Lord in His transcendental activities, but they try to adjust their bewilderment by saying that it is all mythology. There is, however, nothing impossible or mythological in the Supreme Omnipotent Person. The most wonderful puzzle for the mundane wranglers is that while they remain calculating the length and breadth of the unlimited potency of the Supreme Person, His faithful devotees are set free from the bondage of material encagement simply by appreciating the wonderful jugglery of the Supreme in the practical field. The devotees of the Lord see the wonderful dexterity in everything with which they come in contact in all circumstances of eating, sleeping, working, etc. A small banyan fruit contains thousands of small seeds, and each seed holds the potency of another tree, which again holds the potency of many millions of such fruits as causes and effects. So the trees and seeds engage the devotees in meditation about the activities of the Lord, while the mundane wranglers waste time in dry speculation and mental concoction, which are fruitless in both this life and the next. In spite of their pride in speculation, they can never appreciate the simple potential activities of the banyan tree. Such speculators are poor souls destined to remain in matter perpetually.

TEXT 40

यतोऽप्राप्य न्यवर्तन्त वाचश्च मनसा सह ।
अहं चान्य इमे देवास्तस्मै भगवते नमः ॥४०॥

yato 'prāpya nyavartanta
vācaś ca manasā saha
ahaṁ cānya ime devās
tasmai bhagavate namaḥ

yataḥ—from whom; *aprāpya*—being unable to measure; *nyavartanta*—cease to try; *vācaḥ*—words; *ca*—also; *manasā*—with the mind; *saha*—with; *aham ca*—also the ego; *anye*—other; *ime*—all these; *devāḥ*—demigods; *tasmai*—unto Him; *bhagavate*—unto the Personality of Godhead; *namaḥ*—offer obeisances.

TRANSLATION

Words, mind and ego, with their respective controlling demigods, have failed to achieve success in knowing the Supreme Personality of Godhead. Therefore, we simply have to offer our respectful obeisances unto Him as a matter of sanity.

PURPORT

The froggish calculator may raise the objection that if the Absolute is unknowable even by the controlling deities of speech, mind and ego, namely the *Vedas*, Brahmā, Rudra and all the demigods headed by Bṛhaspati, then why should the devotees be so interested in this unknown object? The answer is that the transcendental ecstasy enjoyed by the devotees in delineating the pastimes of the Lord is certainly unknown to nondevotees and mental speculators. Unless one relishes transcendental joy, naturally one will come back from his speculations and concocted conclusions because he will see them as neither factual nor enjoyable. The devotees can at least know that the Absolute Truth is the Supreme Personality of Godhead Viṣṇu, as the Vedic hymns confirm: *oṁ tad viṣṇoḥ paramaṁ padaṁ sadā paśyanti sūrayaḥ*. *Bhagavad-gītā* (15.15) also confirms this fact: *vedaiś ca sarvair aham eva vedyaḥ*. By culture of Vedic knowledge one must know Lord Kṛṣṇa and should not falsely speculate on the word *aham*, or "I." The only method for understanding the Supreme Truth is devotional service, as stated in *Bhagavad-gītā* (18.55): *bhaktyā mām abhijānāti yāvān yaś cāsmi tattvataḥ*. Only by devotional service can one know that the ultimate truth is the Personality of Godhead and that Brahman and Paramātmā are only His partial features. This is confirmed in this verse by the great sage Maitreya. With devotion he offers his sincere surrender, *namaḥ*, to the Supreme Personality of Godhead, *bhagavate*. One has to follow in the footsteps of great sages and devotees like Maitreya and Vidura, Mahārāja Parīkṣit and Śukadeva Gosvāmī, and engage in the transcendental devotional service of the Lord if one would know His ultimate feature, which is above Brahman and Paramātmā.

Thus end the Bhaktivedanta purports of the Third Canto, Sixth Chapter, of the Śrīmad-Bhāgavatam, *entitled "Creation of the Universal Form."*

CHAPTER SEVEN

Further Inquires by Vidura

TEXT 1

श्रीशुक उवाच

एवं ब्रुवाणं मैत्रेयं द्वैपायनसुतो बुधः ।
प्रीणयन्निव भारत्या विदुरः प्रत्यभाषत ॥ १ ॥

śrī-śuka uvāca
evaṁ bruvāṇaṁ maitreyaṁ
dvaipāyana-suto budhaḥ
prīṇayann iva bhāratyā
viduraḥ pratyabhāṣata

śrī-śukaḥ uvāca—Śrī Śukadeva Gosvāmī said; *evam*—thus; *bruvāṇam*—speaking; *maitreyam*—unto the sage. Maitreya; *dvaipāyana-sutaḥ*—the son of Dvaipāyana; *budhaḥ*—learned; *prīṇayan*—in a pleasing manner; *iva*—as it was; *bharatyā*—in the manner of a request; *viduraḥ*—Vidura; *pratyabhāṣata*—expressed.

TRANSLATION

Śrī Śukadeva Gosvāmī said: O King, while Maitreya, the great sage, was thus speaking, Vidura, the learned son of Dvaipāyana Vyāsa, exprcssed a request in a pleasing manner by asking this question.

TEXT 2

विदुर उवाच

ब्रह्मन् कथं भगवतश्चिन्मात्रस्याविकारिणः ।
लीलया चापि युज्येरन्निर्गुणस्य गुणाः क्रियाः ॥ २ ॥

vidura uvāca
brahman kathaṁ bhagavataś
cin-mātrasyāvikāriṇaḥ
līlayā cāpi yujyeran
nirguṇasya guṇāḥ kriyāḥ

viduraḥ uvāca—Vidura said; *brahman*—O *brāhmaṇa; katham*—how; *bhagavataḥ*—of the Personality of Godhead; *cit-mātrasya*—of the complete spiritual whole; *avikāriṇaḥ*—of the unchangeable; *līlayā*—by His pastime; *ca*—either; *api*—even though it is so; *yujyeran*—take place; *nirguṇasya*—who is without the modes of nature; *guṇāḥ*—modes of nature; *kriyāḥ*—activities.

TRANSLATION

Śrī Vidura said: O great brāhmaṇa, since the Supreme Personality of Godhead is the complete spiritual whole and is unchangeable, how is He connected with the material modes of nature and their activities? If this is His pastime, how do the activities of the unchangeable take place and exhibit qualities without the modes of nature?

PURPORT

As described in the previous chapter, the difference between the Supersoul, the Supreme Lord, and the living entities is that the activities of the Lord in creating the cosmic manifestation are performed by the Lord through the agency of His multifarious energies, but this manifestation is bewildering to the living entities. The Lord is therefore the master of the energies, whereas the living entities are subjugated by them. By asking various questions about transcendental activities, Vidura is clearing the misconception that when the Lord either descends on the earth in His incarnation or appears Himself with all His potencies, He too is subjected to the influence of *māyā*, just like an ordinary living entity. This is generally the calculation of less intelligent philosophers who consider the position of the Lord and that of the living entities to be on the same level. Vidura is hearing the great sage Maitreya refute these arguments. The Lord is described in this verse as *cin-mātra,* or completely spiritual. The Personality of Godhead has unlimited potencies to create and manifest many wonderful things, both temporary and permanent. Because this material world is the creation of His external energy, it thus appears to be temporary; it is manifested at certain intervals, maintained for some time, and again dissolved and conserved in His own energy. As described in *Bhagavad-gītā* (8.19), *bhūtvā bhūtvā pralīyate.* But the creation of His internal potency, the spiritual world, is not a temporary manifestation like the material world, but is eternal and full of transcendental knowledge, opulence, energy, strength, beauties and glories. Such manifestations of the Lord's potencies are eternal and are therefore called *nirguṇa,* or free from all tinges of the modes of material nature, even up to the mode of material goodness. The spiritual world is transcendental even to material goodness and thus is unchangeable. Since the Supreme Lord of such eternal and unchangeable qualities is never subjugated by anything like material influence, how can His activities and form be conceived to be under the influence of illusory *māyā*, as is the case with the living entities?

A juggler or magician displays many wonders with his acts and arts. He can become a cow by his magical tactics, and yet he is not that cow; but at the same time, the cow displayed by the magician is not different from him. Similarly, the material potency is not different from the Lord because it is an emanation from Him, but at the same time, that manifestation of potency is not the Supreme Lord. The Lord's transcendental knowledge and potency always remain the same; they do not change, even when displayed in the material world. As stated in *Bhagavad-gītā,* the Lord descends on the earth by His own internal potency, and therefore there is no question of His becoming materially contaminated, changed or otherwise affected by the modes of material nature. The Lord is *saguṇa* by His own internal potency, but at the same time He is *nirguṇa,* since He is not in touch with the material energy. The restrictions of the prison house are applicable to prisoners who are condemned by the king's law, but the king is never affected by such implications, although he may visit the prison house out of his good will. In the *Viṣṇu Purāṇa* the six opulences of the Lord are stated to be nondifferent from Him. The opulences of transcendental knowledge, strength, opulence, potency, beauty and renunciation are all identical with the Personality of Godhead. When He personally displays such opulences in the material world, they have no connection with the modes of material nature. The very word *cin-mātratva* is the guarantee that the Lord's activities are always transcendental, even when displayed in the material world. His activities are as good as the Supreme Personality Himself, otherwise liberated devotees like Śukadeva Gosvāmī would not have been attracted by them. Vidura inquired how the Lord's activities can be in the modes of material nature, as is sometimes miscalculated by persons with a poor fund of knowledge. The inebriety of the material qualities is due to the difference between the material body and the spirit soul. The conditioned soul's activities are displayed through the medium of the modes of material nature and are therefore perverted in appearance. However, the Lord's body and the Lord Himself are one and the same, and when the Lord's activities are displayed, they are certainly nondifferent from the Lord in all respects. The conclusion is that persons who consider the Lord's activities material are certainly mistaken.

TEXT 3

क्रीडायामुद्यमोऽर्भस्य कामश्चिक्रीडिषान्यतः ।
स्वतस्तृप्तस्य च कथं निवृत्तस्य सदान्यतः ॥ ३ ॥

krīḍāyām udyamo 'rbhasya
kāmaś cikrīḍiṣānyataḥ
svatas-tṛptasya ca kathaṁ
nivṛttasya sadānyataḥ

krīḍāyām—in the matter of playing; *udyamaḥ*—enthusiasm; *arbhasya*—of the boys; *kāmaḥ*—desire; *cikrīḍiṣā*—willingness to play; *anyataḥ*—with other boys; *svataḥ-tṛptasya*—for one who is self-satisfied; *ca*—also; *katham*—what for; *nivṛttasya*—one who is detached; *sadā*—at all times; *anyataḥ*—otherwise.

TRANSLATION

Boys are enthusiastic to play with other boys or with various diversions because they are encouraged by desire. But there is no possibility of such desire for the Lord because He is self-satisfied and detached from everything at all times.

PURPORT

Since the Supreme Personality of Godhead is one without a second, there is no possibility that anything besides Him can exist. He expands Himself by His energies in multiforms of self-expansions and separated expansions as well, just as fire expands itself by heat and light. Since there is no other existence besides the Lord Himself, the Lord's association with anything manifests His association with Himself. In *Bhagavad-gītā* (9.4) the Lord says:

mayā tatam idaṁ sarvaṁ
jagad avyakta-mūrtinā
mat-sthāni sarva-bhūtāni
na cāhaṁ teṣv avasthitaḥ

"The complete manifestation of the cosmic situation is an expansion of the Lord Himself in His impersonal feature. All things are situated in Him only, yet He is not in them." That is the opulence of the Lord's attachment and detachment. He is attached to everything, yet He is detached from all.

TEXT 4

अस्राक्षीद्भगवान् विश्वं गुणमय्यात्ममायया ।
तया संस्थापयत्येतद्भूयः प्रत्यपिधास्यति ॥ ४ ॥

asrākṣīd bhagavān viśvaṁ
guṇa-mayyātma-māyayā
tayā saṁsthāpayaty etad
bhūyaḥ pratyapidhāsyati

asrākṣīt—caused to create; *bhagavān*—the Personality of Godhead; *viśvam*—the universe; *guṇa-mayyā*—endowed with three modes of material nature; *ātma*—self; *māyayā*—by the potency; *tayā*—by her; *saṁsthāpayati*—maintains; *etat*—all these; *bhūyaḥ*—then again; *pratyapidhāsyati*—conversely dissolves also.

TRANSLATION

By His self-sheltered potency of the three modes of material nature, the Lord has caused the creation of this universe. By her He maintains the creation and conversely dissolves it, again and again.

PURPORT

This cosmic universe is created by the Lord for those living entities who are carried away by the illusory thought of becoming one with Him by imitation. The three modes of material nature are for the further bewilderment of the conditioned souls. The conditioned living entity, bewildered by the illusory energy, considers himself a part of the material creation due to forgetfulness of his spiritual identity, and thus he becomes entangled in material activities life after life. This material world is not for the purpose of the Lord Himself, but is for the conditioned souls who wanted to be controllers due to misuse of their God-gifted minute independence. Thus the conditioned souls are subjected to repeated birth and death.

TEXT 5

देशतः कालतो योऽसाववस्थातः स्वतोऽन्यतः ।
अविलुप्तावबोधात्मा स युज्येताजया कथम् ॥ ५ ॥

deśataḥ kālato yo 'sāv
avasthātaḥ svato 'nyataḥ
aviluptāvabodhātmā
sa yujyetājayā katham

deśataḥ—circumstantial; *kālataḥ*—by the influence of time; *yaḥ*—one who; *asau*—the living entity; *avasthātaḥ*—by situation; *svataḥ*—by dream; *anyataḥ*—by others; *avilupta*—extinct; *avabodha*—consciousness; *ātmā*—pure self; *saḥ*—he; *yujyeta*—engaged; *ajayā*—with nescience; *katham*—how is it so.

TRANSLATION

The pure soul is pure consciousness and is never out of consciousness, either due to circumstances, time, situations, dreams or other causes. How then does he become engaged in nescience?

PURPORT

The consciousness of the living being is always present and never changes under any circumstances, as above mentioned. When a living man moves from one place to another, he is conscious that he has changed his position. He is always present in the past, present and future, like electricity. One can remember incidents from his past and can conjecture about his future also on the basis of past experience. He never forgets his personal identity, even though he is placed in awkward circumstances. How then can the living entity become forgetful of his real identity as pure spirit soul and identify with matter unless influenced by something beyond himself? The conclusion is that the living entity is influenced by the *avidyā* potency, as confirmed in both the *Viṣṇu Purāṇa* and the beginning of *Śrīmad-Bhāgavatam.* The living entity is mentioned in *Bhagavad-gītā* (7.5) as *parā prakṛti,* and in the *Viṣṇu Purāṇa* he is mentioned as the *parā śakti.* He is part and parcel of the Supreme Lord as potency and not as the potent. The potent can exhibit many potencies, but the potency cannot equal the potent at any stage. One potency may be overcome by another potency, but to the potent, all potencies are under control. The *jīva* potency, or the *kṣetrajña-śakti* of the Lord, has the tendency to be overpowered by the external potency, *avidyā-karma-saṁjñā,* and in this way he is placed in the awkward circumstances of material existence. The living entity cannot be forgetful of his real identity unless influenced by the *avidyā* potency. Because the living entity is prone to the influence of the *avidyā* potency, he can never equal the supreme potent.

TEXT 6

भगवानेक एवैष सर्वक्षेत्रेष्ववस्थितः ।
अमुष्य दुर्भगत्वं वा क्लेशो वा कर्मभिः कुतः ॥ ६ ॥

bhagavān eka evaiṣa
sarva-kṣetreṣv avasthitaḥ
amuṣya durbhagatvaṁ vā
kleśo vā karmabhiḥ kutaḥ

bhagavān—the Supreme Personality of Godhead; *ekaḥ*—alone; *eva eṣaḥ*—all these; *sarva*—all; *kṣetreṣu*—in the living entities; *avasthitaḥ*—situated; *amuṣya*—of the living entities;

durbhagatvam—misfortune; *vā*—either; *kleśaḥ*—miseries; *vā*—or; *karmabhiḥ*—by activities; *kutaḥ*—what for.

TRANSLATION

The Lord, as the Supersoul, is situated in every living being's heart. Why then do the living entities' activities result in misfortune and misery?

PURPORT

The next question put forward by Vidura to Maitreya is, "Why are the living entities subjected to so many miseries and misfortunes in spite of the Lord's presence in their hearts as the Supersoul?" The body is considered a fruitful tree, and the living entity and the Lord as Supersoul are like two birds seated in that tree. The individual soul is eating the fruit of the tree, but the Supersoul, the Lord, is witnessing the activities of the other bird. A citizen of the state may be in miseries for want of sufficient supervision by the state authority, but how can it be possible that a citizen suffers from other citizens while the chief of the state is personally present? From another point of view, it is understood that the *jīva* living entity is qualitatively one with the Lord, and thus his knowledge in the pure state of life cannot be covered by nescience, especially in the presence of the Supreme Lord. How then does the living entity become subjected to ignorance and covered by the influence of *māyā*? The Lord is the father and protector of every living entity, and He is known as the *bhūta-bhṛt*, or the maintainer of the living entities. Why then should the living entity he subjected to so many sufferings and misfortunes? It should not be so, but actually we see that it happens everywhere. This question is therefore put forward by Vidura for solution.

TEXT 7

एतस्मिन्मे मनो विद्वन् खिद्यतेऽज्ञानसङ्कटे ।
तन्नः पराणुद विभो कश्मलं मानसं महत् ॥ ७ ॥

etasmin me mano vidvan
khidyate 'jñāna-saṅkaṭe
tan naḥ parāṇuda vibho
kaśmalaṁ mānasaṁ mahat

etasmin—in this; *me*—my; *manaḥ*—mind; *vidvan*—O learned one; *khidyate*—is troubling; *ajñāna*—nescience; *saṅkaṭe*—in distress; *tat*—therefore; *naḥ*—my; *parāṇuda*—clear up; *vibho*—O great one; *kaśmalam*—illusion; *mānasam*—relating to the mind; *mahat*—great.

TRANSLATION

O great and learned one, my mind is greatly illusioned by the distress of this nescience, and I therefore request you to clear it up.

PURPORT

Such mental bewilderment as represented here by Vidura takes place for some living entities, but not for everyone, for if everyone were bewildered there would be no possibility of a solution by higher personalities.

TEXT 8

श्रीशुक उवाच
स इत्थं चोदितः क्षत्त्रा तत्त्वजिज्ञासुना मुनिः ।
प्रत्याह भगवच्चित्तः स्मयन्निव गतस्मयः ॥ ८ ॥

śrī-śuka uvāca
sa ittham coditaḥ kṣattrā
tattva-jijñāsunā muniḥ
pratyāha bhagavac-cittaḥ
smayann iva gata-smayaḥ

śrī-śukaḥ uvāca—Śrī Śukadeva Gosvāmī said; *saḥ*—he (Maitreya Muni); *ittham*—in this way; *coditaḥ*—being agitated; *kṣattrā*—by Vidura; *tattva-jijñāsunā*—by one who was anxious to inquire to know the truth; *muniḥ*—the great sage; *pratyāha*—replied; *bhagavat-cittaḥ*—God conscious; *smayan*—wondering; *iva*—as if; *gata-smayaḥ*—without hesitation.

TRANSLATION

Śrī Śukadeva Gosvāmī said: O King, Maitreya, being thus agitated by the inquisitive Vidura, at first seemed astonished, but then he replied to him without hesitation, since he was fully God conscious.

PURPORT

Since the great sage Maitreya was filled with God consciousness, he had no reason to be astonished at such contradictory questions by Vidura. Therefore, although as a devotee he externally expressed surprise, as if he did not know how to reply to those questions, he immediately became perfectly settled and properly replied to Vidura. *Yasmin vijñāte sarvam evaṁ vijñātaṁ bhavati.* Anyone who is a devotee of the Lord knows about the Lord to some extent, and devotional service to the Lord makes him able to know everything by the grace of the Lord. Although a devotee may apparently express himself to be ignorant, he is full of knowledge in every intricate matter.

TEXT 9

मैत्रेय उवाच
सेयं भगवतो माया यन्नयेन विरुध्यते ।
ईश्वरस्य विमुक्तस्य कार्पण्यमुत बन्धनम् ॥ ९ ॥

maitreya uvāca
seyaṁ bhagavato māyā
yan nayena virudhyate
īśvarasya vimuktasya
kārpaṇyam uta bandhanam

maitreyaḥ uvāca—Maitreya said; *sā iyam*—such a statement; *bhagavataḥ*—of the Personality of Godhead; *māyā*—illusion; *yat*—that which; *nayena*—by logic; *virudhyate*—becomes contradictory; *īśvarasya*—of the Supreme Personality of Godhead; *vimuktasya*—of the ever liberated; *kārpaṇyam*—insufficiency; *uta*—as also, what to speak of; *bandhanam*—bondage.

TRANSLATION

Śrī Maitreya said: Certain conditioned souls put forward the theory that the Supreme Brahman, or the Personality of Godhead, is overcome by illusion, or māyā, and at the same time thcy maintain that He is unconditioned. This is against all logic.

PURPORT

Sometimes it appears that the Supreme Personality of Godhead, who is one hundred percent spiritual, cannot be the cause of the illusory potency which covers the knowledge of the individual soul. But factually there is no doubt that the illusory, external energy is also part and parcel of the Supreme Lord. When Vyāsadeva realized the Supreme Personality of Godhead, he saw the Lord along with His external potency, which covers the pure knowledge of the individual living entities. Why the external energy acts in this way may be considered as follows, as analyzed by great commentators like Viśvanātha Cakravartī Ṭhākura and Śrīla Jīva Gosvāmī. Although the material, illusory energy is distinct from the spiritual energy, it is one of the many energies of the Lord, and thus the material modes of nature (the mode of goodness, etc.)

are surely qualities of the Lord. The energy and the energetic Personality of Godhead are not different, and although such energy is one with the Lord, He is never overpowered by it. Although the living entities are also parts and parcels of the Lord, they are overcome by the material energy. The inconceivable *yogam aiśvaram* of the Lord, as mentioned in *Bhagavad-gītā* (9.5), is misunderstood by the froggish philosophers. In order to support a theory that Nārāyaṇa (the Lord Himself) becomes a *daridra-nārāyaṇa*, a poor man, they propose that the material energy overcomes the Supreme Lord. Śrīla Jīva Gosvāmī and Śrīla Viśvanātha Cakravartī Ṭhākura, however, offer a very nice example in explanation. They say that although the sun is all light, the clouds, darkness and snowfall are all part and parcel of the sun. Without the sun there is no possibility of the sky's being overcast with clouds or darkness, nor can there be snowfall on the earth. Although life is sustained by the sun, life is also disturbed by darkness and snowfall produced by the sun. But it is also a fact that the sun itself is never overcome by darkness, clouds or snowfall; the sun is far, far away from such disturbances. Only those who have a poor fund of knowledge say that the sun is covered by a cloud or by darkness. Similarly, the Supreme Brahman, or the Parabrahman, the Personality of Godhead, is always unaffected by the influence of the material energy, although it is one of His energies (*parāsya śaktir vividhaiva śrūyate*.

There is no reason to assert that the Supreme Brahman is overpowered by the illusory energy. The clouds, darkness and snowfall can cover only a very insignificant portion of the sun's rays. Similarly, the modes of material nature may react upon the raylike living entities. It is the misfortune of the living entity, certainly not without reason, that the influence of the material energy acts on his pure consciousness and eternal bliss. This covering up of pure consciousness and eternal bliss is due to *avidyā-karmā-saṁjñā,* the energy which acts on the infinitesimal living entities who misuse their minute independence. According to *Viṣṇu Purāṇa, Bhagavad-gītā* and all other Vedic literatures, the living entities are generated from the *taṭasthā* energy of the Lord, and thus they are always the energy of the Lord and are not the energetic. The living entities are like the sun's rays. Although, as explained above, there is no qualitative difference between the sun and its rays, the sun's rays are sometimes overpowered by another energy of the sun, namely by clouds or by snowfall. Similarly, although the living entities are qualitatively one with the superior energy of the Lord, they have the tendency to be overpowered by the inferior, material energy. In the Vedic hymns it is said that the living entities are like the sparks of a fire. The sparks of fire also are fire, but the burning potency of the sparks is different from that of the original fire. When the sparks fly out of touch with the original fire, they come under the influence of a nonfiery atmosphere; thus they maintain the potency to be again one with the fire as sparks, but not as the original fire. The sparks can everlastingly remain within the original fire as its parts and parcels, but the moment the sparks become separated from the original fire, their misfortunes and miseries begin. The clear conclusion is that the Supreme Lord, who is the original fire, is never overpowered, but the infinitesimal sparks of the fire can become overpowered by the illusory effect of *māyā.* It is a most ludicrous argument to say that the Supreme Lord is overpowered by His own material energy. The Lord is the master of the material energy, but the living entities are in the conditioned state, controlled by the material energy. That is the version of *Bhagavad-gītā.* The froggish philosophers who put forward the argument that the Supreme Lord is overpowered by the material mode of goodness are themselves illusioned by the same material energy, although they think of themselves as liberated souls. They support their arguments by a false and laborious jugglery of words, which is a gift of the same illusory energy of the Lord. But the poor froggish philosophers, due to a false sense of knowledge, cannot understand the situation.

In the Sixth Canto, Ninth Chapter, thirty-fourth verse, of the *Śrīmad-Bhāgavatam* it is stated:

duravabodha iva tavāyaṁ vihāra-yogo yad aśaraṇo 'śarīra idam anavekṣitāsmat-samavāya ātmanaivāvikriyamāṇena saguṇam aguṇaḥ sṛjasi pāsi harasi.

Thus the demigods prayed to the Supreme Lord that although His activities are very difficult to understand, they can still be understood to some extent by those who sincerely engage in the transcendental loving service of the Lord. The demigods admitted that although the Lord is apart from the material influence or creation, He nevertheless creates, maintains and annihilates the complete cosmic manifestation by the agency of the demigods.

TEXT 10

यदर्थेन विनामुष्य पुंस आत्मविपर्ययः ।
प्रतीयत उपद्रष्टुः स्वशिरश्छेदनादिकः ॥१०॥

yad arthena vināmuṣya
puṁsa ātma-viparyayaḥ
pratīyata upadraṣṭuḥ
sva-śiraś chedanādikaḥ

yat—thus; *arthena*—a purpose or meaning; *vinā*—without; *amuṣya*—of such a one; *puṁsaḥ*—of the living entity; *ātma-viparyayaḥ*—upset about self-identification; *pratīyate*—so appear; *upadraṣṭuḥ*—of the superficial onlooker; *sva-śiraḥ*—own head; *chedana-ādikaḥ*—cutting off.

TRANSLATION

The living entity is in distress regarding his self-identity. He has no factual background, like a man who dreams that he sees his head cut off.

PURPORT

A teacher in school once threatened his pupil that he would cut off the pupil's head and hang it on the wall so that the child could see how his head had been cut off. The child became frightened and stopped his mischief. Similarly, the miseries of the pure soul and the disruption of his self-identification are managed by the external energy of the Lord, which controls those mischievous living entities who want to go against the will of the Lord. Actually there is no bondage or misery for the living entity, nor does he ever lose his pure knowledge. In his pure consciousness, when he thinks a little seriously about his position, he can understand that he is eternally subordinate to the mercy of the Supreme and that his attempt to become one with the Supreme Lord is a false illusion. Life after life the living entity falsely tries to lord it over material nature and become the lord of the material world, but there is no tangible result. At last, when frustrated, he gives up his material activities and tries to become one with the Lord and speculate with much jugglery of words, but without success.

These activities are performed under the dictation of the illusory energy. The experience is compared to the experience of one's having his head cut off in a dream. The man whose head has been cut off also *sees* that his head has been cut off. If a person's head is severed he loses his power to see. Therefore if a man sees that his head has been cut off, it means that he thinks like that in hallucination. Similarly a living entity is eternally subordinate to the Supreme Lord, and he has this knowledge with him, but, artificially, he thinks that he is God himself and that although he is God he has lost his knowledge due to *māyā*. This conception has no meaning, just as there is no meaning to seeing one's head being cut off. This is the process by which knowledge is covered. And because this artificial rebellious condition of the living entity gives him all troubles, it is to be understood that he should take to his normal life as a devotee of the Lord and be relieved from the misconception of being God. The so-called liberation of thinking oneself God is that last reaction of *avidyā* by which the living entity is entrapped. The conclusion is that a living entity deprived of eternal transcendental service to the Lord becomes illusioned in many ways. Even in his conditional life he is the eternal servant of the Lord. His servitude under the spell of illusory *māyā* is also a manifestation of his eternal condition of service. Because he has rebelled against the service of the Lord, he is therefore put in the service of the *māyā*. He is still serving, but in a perverted manner. When he wants to get out of service under material bondage, he next desires to become one with the Lord. This is another illusion. The best course, therefore, is to surrender unto the Lord and thus get rid of the illusory *māyā* for good, as confirmed in *Bhagavad-gītā* (7.14):

daivī hy eṣā guṇamayī
mama māyā duratyayā
mām eva ye prapadyante
māyām etāṁ taranti te

TEXT 11

यथा जले चन्द्रमसः कम्पादिस्तत्कृतो गुणः ।
दृश्यतेऽसन्नपि द्रष्टुरात्मनोऽनात्मनो गुणः ॥११॥

yathā jale candramasaḥ
kampādis tat-kṛto guṇaḥ
dṛśyate 'sann api draṣṭur
ātmano 'nātmano guṇaḥ

yathā—as; *jale*—in the water; *candramasaḥ*—of the moon; *kampa-ādiḥ*—quivering, etc.; *tat-kṛtaḥ*—done by the water; *guṇaḥ*—quality; *dṛśyate*—it is so seen; *asan api*—without existence; *draṣṭuḥ*—of the seer; *ātmanaḥ*—of the self; *anātmanaḥ*—of other than the self; *guṇaḥ*—quality.

TRANSLATION

As the moon reflected on water appears to the seer to tremble due to being associated with the quality of the water, so the self associated with matter appears to be qualified as matter.

PURPORT

The Supreme Soul, the Personality of Godhead, is compared to the moon in the sky, and the living entities are compared to the reflection of the moon on water. The moon in the sky is fixed and does not appear to quiver like the moon on the water. Actually, like the original moon in the sky, the moon reflected on the water should also not quiver, but because of being associated with water, the reflection appears to be quivering, although in actual fact the moon is fixed. The water moves, but the moon does not move. Similarly, the living entities appear to be tainted by material qualities like illusion, lamentation and miseries, although in the pure soul such qualities are completely absent. The word *pratīyate,* which means "apparently" and "not actually" (like the experience of having one's head cut off in a dream), is significant here. The reflection of the moon on the water is the separated rays of the moon and not the actual moon. The separated parts and parcels of the Lord entangled in the water of material existence have the quivering quality, whereas the Lord is like the actual moon in the sky, which is not at all in touch with water. The light of the sun and moon reflected on matter makes the matter bright and praiseworthy. The living symptoms are compared to the light of the sun and the moon illuminating material manifestations like trees and mountains. The reflection of the sun or moon is accepted as the real sun or moon by less intelligent men, and the pure monistic philosophy develops from these ideas. In fact, the light of the sun and the moon are actually different from the sun and moon themselves, although they are always connected. The light of the moon spread throughout the sky appears to be impersonal, but the moon planet, as it is, is personal, and the living entities on the moon planet are also personal. In the rays of the moon, different material entities appear to be comparatively more or less important. The light of the moon on the Taj Mahal appears to be more beautiful than the same light in the wilderness. Although the light of the moon is the same everywhere, due to being differently appreciated it appears different. Similarly, the light of the Lord is equally distributed everywhere, but due to being differently received, it appears to be different. One should not, therefore, accept the reflection of the moon on the water as actual and misunderstand the whole situation through monistic philosophy. The quivering quality of the moon is also variable. When the water is standing still, there is no quivering. A more settled conditioned soul quivers less, but due to material connection the quivering quality is more or less present everywhere.

TEXT 12

स वै निवृत्तिधर्मेण वासुदेवानुकम्पया ।
भगवद्भक्तियोगेन तिरोधत्ते शनैरिह ॥१२॥

sa vai nivṛtti-dharmeṇa
vāsudevānukampayā
bhagavad-bhakti-yogena
tirodhatte śanair iha

saḥ—that; *vai*—also; *nivṛtti*—detachment; *dharmeṇa*—by engagement; *vāsudeva*—the Supreme Personality of Godhead; *anukampayā*—by the mercy of; *bhagavat*—in relation with the Personality of Godhead; *bhakti-yogena*—by linking up; *tirodhatte*—diminishes; *śanaiḥ*—gradually; *iha*—in this existence.

TRANSLATION

But that misconception of self-identity can be diminished gradually by the mercy of the Personality of Godhead, Vāsudeva, through the process of devotional service to the Lord in the mode of detachment.

PURPORT

The quivering quality of material existence, which comes from identification with matter or from thinking oneself, under the material influence of philosophical speculation, to be God, can be eradicated by devotional service to the Lord, by the mercy of the Personality of Godhead, Vāsudeva. As discussed in the First Canto, because the application of devotional service to Lord Vāsudeva invites pure knowledge, it quickly detaches one from the material conception of life and thus revives one's normal condition of spiritual existence, even in this life, and frees one from the material winds which cause one to quiver. Only knowledge in devotional service can elevate one towards the path of liberation. The development of knowledge for the purpose of knowing everything, without rendering devotional service, is considered fruitless labor, and one cannot get the desired result by such labor of love. Lord Vāsudeva is pleased by devotional service only, and thus His mercy is realized by association with pure devotees of the Lord. Pure devotees of the Lord are transcendental to all material desires, including the desire for the results of fruitive activities and philosophical speculation. If one wants to acquire the mercy of the Lord, he has to associate with pure devotees. Such association alone can, by degrees, release one from the quivering elements.

TEXT 13

यदेन्द्रियोपरामोऽथ द्रष्ट्रात्मनि परे हरौ ।
विलीयन्ते तदा क्लेशाः संसुप्तस्येव कृत्स्नशः ॥१३॥

yadendriyoparāmo 'tha
draṣṭrātmani pare harau

vilīyante tadā kleśāḥ
saṁsuptasyeva kṛtsnaśaḥ

yadā—when; *indriya*—senses; *uparāmaḥ*—satiated; *atha*—thus; *draṣṭṛ-ātmani*—unto the seer, the Supersoul; *pare*—in the Transcendence; *harau*—unto the Supreme Personality of Godhead; *vilīyante*—become merged in; *tadā*—at that time; *kleśāḥ*—miseries; *saṁsuptasya*—one who has enjoyed sound sleep; *iva*—like; *kṛtsnaśaḥ*—completely.

TRANSLATION

When the senses are satisfied in the seer-Supersoul, the Personality of Godhead, and merge in Him, all miseries are completely vanquished, as after a sound sleep.

PURPORT

The quivering of the living entity as described above is due to the senses. Since the entire material existence is meant for sense gratification, the senses are the medium of material activities, and they cause the quivering of the steady soul. Therefore, these senses are to be detached from all such material activities. According to the impersonalists the senses are stopped from work by merging the soul in the Supersoul Brahman. The devotees, however, do not stop the material senses from acting, but they engage their transcendental senses in the service of the Transcendence, the Supreme Personality of Godhead. In either case, the activities of the senses in the material field are to be stopped by cultivation of knowledge, and, if possible, they can be engaged in the service of the Lord. The senses are transcendental in nature, but their activities become polluted when contaminated by matter. We have to treat the senses to cure them of the material disease, not stop them from acting, as suggested by the impersonalist. In *Bhagavad-gītā* (2.59) it is said that one ceases all material activities only when satisfied by contact with a better engagement. Consciousness is active by nature and cannot be stopped from working. Artificially stopping a mischievous child is not the real remedy. The child must be given some better engagement so that he will automatically stop causing mischief. In the same way, the mischievous activities of the senses can be stopped only by better engagement in relation with the Supreme Personality of Godhead. When the eyes are engaged in seeing the beautiful form of the Lord, the tongue engaged in tasting *prasāda,* or remnants of foodstuff offered to the Lord, the ears are engaged in hearing His glories, the hands engaged in cleaning the temple of the Lord, the legs engaged in visiting His temples—or when all the senses are engaged in transcendental variegatedness—then only can the transcendental senses become satiated and eternally free from material engagement. The Lord, as the Supersoul residing in everyone's heart and as the Supreme Personality of Godhead in the transcendental world far beyond the material creation, is the seer of all our activities. Our activities must be so transcendentally saturated that the Lord will be kind enough to look upon us favorably and engage us in His transcendental service; then only can the senses be satisfied completely and be no longer troubled by material attraction.

TEXT 14

अशेषसंक्लेशशमं विधत्ते गुणानुवादश्रवणं मुरारेः ।
किं वा पुनस्तच्चरणारविन्द परागसेवारतिरात्मलब्धा ॥१४॥

aśeṣa-saṅkleśa-śamaṁ vidhatte
guṇānuvāda-śravaṇaṁ murāreḥ
kiṁ vā punas tac-caraṇāravinda-
parāga-sevā-ratir ātma-labdhā

aśeṣa—unlimited; *saṅkleśa*—miserable conditions; *śamam*—cessation; *vidhatte*—can perform; *guṇa-anuvāda*—of the transcendental name, form, qualities, pastimes, entourage and paraphernalia, etc.; *śravaṇam*—hearing and chanting; *murāreḥ*—of Murāri (Śrī Kṛṣṇa), the Personality of Godhead; *kim vā*—what to speak of; *punaḥ*—again; *tat*—His; *caraṇa-aravinda*—lotus feet; *parāga-sevā*—to the service of the flavorful dust; *ratiḥ*—attraction; *ātma-labdhā*—those who have gained such self-achievement.

TRANSLATION

Simply by chanting and hearing of the transcendental name, form, etc., of the Personality of Godhead, Śrī Kṛṣṇa, one can achieve the cessation of unlimited miserable conditions. Therefore what to speak of those who have attained attraction for serving the flavor of the dust of the Lord's lotus feet?

PURPORT

Two different methods for controlling the material senses are recommended in the Vedic scriptural wisdom. One of them is the process of *jñāna*, or the path of philosophical understanding of the Supreme—Brahma, Paramātmā and Bhagavān. The other is that of direct engagement in the transcendental loving devotional service of the Lord. Of these two most popular methods, the path of devotional service is recommended here as the best because one on the path of devotional service does not have to wait for the attainment of the fruitive results of pious activities or for the results of knowledge. The two stages of executing devotional service are, first, the stage of practicing devotional service with our present senses under the regulations of the recognized scriptures and, second, attaining sincere attachment for serving the particles of the dust of the lotus feet of the Lord. The first stage is called *sādhana-bhakti*, or devotional service for the neophyte, which is rendered under the direction of a pure devotee, and the second stage is called *rāga-bhakti*, in which the mature devotee automatically takes to the various services of the Lord out of sincere attachment. The great sage Maitreya now gives the final answer to all the questions of Vidura: devotional service to the Lord is the ultimate means to mitigate all the miserable conditions of material existence. The path of knowledge or that of mystic gymnastics may be adopted as a means for the purpose, but unless mixed with *bhakti*, or devotional service, they are unable to award the desired result. By practicing *sādhana-bhakti* one may gradually rise to the point of *rāga-bhakti*, and by performing *rāga-bhakti* in loving transcendental service one can even control the Supreme Powerful Lord.

TEXT 15

विदुर उवाच
संञ्छिन्नः संशयो मह्यं तव सूक्तासिना विभो ।
उभयत्रापि भगवन्मनो मे सम्प्रधावति ॥१५॥

vidura uvāca
sañchinnaḥ saṁśayo mahyaṁ
tava sūktāsinā vibho
ubhayatrāpi bhagavan
mano me sampradhāvati

viduraḥ uvāca—Vidura said; *sañchinnaḥ*—cut off; *saṁśayaḥ*—doubts; *mahyam*—unto me; *tava*—your; *sūkta-asinā*—by the weapon of convincing words; *vibho*—O my lord; *ubhayatra api*—both in God and in the living entity; *bhagavan*—O powerful one; *manaḥ*—mind; *me*—my; *sampradhāvati*—perfectly entering.

TRANSLATION

Vidura said: O powerful sage, my lord, all my doubts about the Supreme Personality of Godhead and the living entities have now been removed by your convincing words. My mind is now perfectly entering into them.

PURPORT

The science of Kṛṣṇa, or the science of God and the living entities, is so subtle that even a personality like Vidura has to consult persons like the sage Maitreya. Doubts about the eternal relationship of the Lord and the living entity are created by mental speculators in different ways, but the conclusive fact is that the relationship of God and the living entity is one of the predominator and the predominated. The Lord is the eternal predominator, and the living entities are eternally predominated. Real knowledge of this relationship entails reviving the lost consciousness to this standard, and the process for such revival is devotional service to the Lord. By clearly understanding from authorities like the sage Maitreya, one can become situated in real knowledge, and the disturbed mind can thus be fixed on the progressive path.

TEXT 16

साध्वेतद् व्याहृतं विद्वन्नात्ममायायनं हरेः ।
आभात्यपार्थं निर्मूलं विश्वमूलं न यद्बहिः ॥१६॥

sādhv etad vyāhṛtaṁ vidvan
nātma-māyāyanaṁ hareḥ
ābhāty apārthaṁ nirmūlaṁ
viśva-mūlaṁ na yad bahiḥ

sādhu—as good as it should be; *etat*—all these explanations; *vyāhṛtam*—thus spoken; *vidvan*—O learned one; *na*—not; *ātma*—the self; *māyā*—energy; *ayanam*—movement; *hareḥ*—of the Personality of Godhead; *ābhāti*—appears; *apārtham*—without meaning; *nirmūlam*—without basis; *viśva-mūlam*—the origin is the Supreme; *na*—not; *yat*—which; *bahiḥ*—outside.

TRANSLATION

O learned sage, your explanations are very good, as they should be. Disturbances to the conditioned soul have no other basis than the movement of the external energy of the Lord.

PURPORT

A living entity's unlawful desire to become one with the Lord in every respect is the root cause of the entire material manifestation, for otherwise the Lord has no need to create such a manifestation, even for His pastimes. The conditioned soul, under the spell of the external energy of the Lord, falsely suffers many unfortunate incidents in material life. The Lord is the predominator of the external energy, *māyā,* whereas the living entity is predominated by the same *māyā* under the material condition. The false attempt of the living entity to occupy the predominating post of the Lord is the cause of his material bondage, and the conditioned soul's attempt to become one with the Lord is the last snare of *māyā.*

TEXT 17

यश्च मूढतमो लोके यश्च बुद्धेः परं गतः ।
तावुभौ सुखमेधेते क्लिश्यत्यन्तरितो जनः ॥१७॥

yaś ca mūḍhatamo loke
yaś ca buddheḥ paraṁ gataḥ
tāv ubhau sukham edhete
kliśyaty antarito janaḥ

yaḥ—one who is; *ca*—also; *mūḍha-tamaḥ*—the lowest of the fools; *loke*—in the world; *yaḥ ca*—and one who is; *buddheḥ*—of intelligence; *param*—transcendental; *gataḥ*—gone; *tau*—of them; *ubhau*—both; *sukham*—happiness; *edhete*—enjoy; *kliśyati*—suffer; *antaritaḥ*—situated between; *janaḥ*—persons.

TRANSLATION

Both the lowest of fools and he who is transcendental to all intelligence enjoy happiness, whereas persons between them suffer the material pangs.

PURPORT

The lowest of fools do not understand material miseries; they pass their lives merrily and do not inquire into the miseries of life. Such persons are almost on the level of the animals, who, although in the eyes of superiors are always miserable in life, are unaware of material distresses. A hog's life is degraded in its standard of happiness, which entails living in a filthy place, engaging in sex enjoyment at every opportune moment, and laboring hard in a struggle for existence, but this is unknown to the hog. Similarly, human beings who are unaware of the miseries of material existence and are happy in sex life and hard labor are the lowest of fools. Yet because they have no sense of miseries, they supposedly enjoy so-called happiness. The other class of men, those who are liberated and are situated in the transcendental position above intelligence, are really happy and are called *paramahaṁsas.* But persons who are neither like hogs and dogs nor on the level of the *paramahaṁsas* feel the material pangs, and for them inquiry about the Supreme Truth is necessary. The *Vedānta-sūtra* states, *athāto brahma-jijñāsā:* "Now one should inquire about Brahman." This inquiry is necessary for those who are between the *paramahaṁsas* and the fools who have forgotten the question of self-realization in the midst of life in sense gratification.

TEXT 18

अर्थाभावं विनिश्चित्य प्रतीतस्यापि नात्मनः ।
तां चापि युष्मच्चरणसेवयाहं पराणुदे ॥१८॥

arthābhāvaṁ viniścitya
pratītasyāpi nātmanaḥ
tāṁ cāpi yuṣmac-caraṇa-
sevayāhaṁ parāṇude

artha-abhāvam—without substance; *viniścitya*—being ascertained; *pratītasya*—of the apparent values; *api*—also; *na*—never; *ātmanaḥ*—of the self; *tām*—that; *ca*—also; *api*—thus; *yuṣmat*—your; *caraṇa*—feet; *sevayā*—by service; *aham*—myself; *parāṇude*—shall be able to give up.

TRANSLATION

But, my dear sir, I am obliged to you because now I can understand that this material manifestation is without substance, although it appears real. I am confident that by serving your feet it will be possible for me to give up the false idea.

PURPORT

The sufferings of the conditioned soul are superficial and have no intrinsic value, like the cutting off of one's head in a dream. Yet although this statement is theoretically very true, it is very difficult for the common man or the neophyte on the transcendental path to realize practically. However, by serving the feet of great transcendentalists like Maitreya Muni and by constantly associating with them, one is enabled to give up the false idea that the soul suffers from material pangs.

TEXT 19

यत्सेवया भगवतः कूटस्थस्य मधुद्विषः ।
रतिरासो भवेत्तीव्रः पादयोर्व्यसनार्दनः ॥१९॥

yat-sevayā bhagavataḥ
kūṭa-sthasya madhu-dviṣaḥ
rati-rāso bhavet tīvraḥ
pādayor vyasanārdanaḥ

yat—to whom; *sevayā*—by service; *bhagavataḥ*—of the Personality of Godhead; *kūṭa-sthasya*—of the unchangeable; *madhu-dviṣaḥ*—the enemy of the Madhu *asura*; *rati-rāsaḥ*—attachment in different relationships; *bhavet*—develops; *tīvraḥ*—highly ecstatic; *pādayoḥ*—of the feet; *vyasana*—distresses; *ardanaḥ*—vanquishing.

TRANSLATION

By serving the feet of the spiritual master, one is enabled to develop transcendental ecstasy in the service of the Personality of Godhead, who is the unchangeable enemy of the Madhu demon and whose service vanquishes one's material distresses.

PURPORT

The association of a bona fide spiritual master like the sage Maitreya can be of absolute help in achieving transcendental attachment for the direct service of the Lord. The Lord is the enemy of the Madhu demon, or in other words He is the enemy of the suffering of His pure devotee. The word *rati-rāsaḥ* is significant in this verse. Service to the Lord is rendered in different transcendental mellows (relationships): neutral, active, friendly, parental and nuptial. A living entity in the liberated position of transcendental service to the Lord becomes attracted to one of the above-mentioned mellows, and when one is engaged in transcendental loving service to the Lord, one's service attachment in the material world is automatically vanquished. As stated in *Bhagavad-gītā* (2.59), *rasa-varjaṁ raso 'py asya paraṁ dṛṣṭvā nivartate.*

TEXT 20

दुरापा ह्यल्पतपसः सेवा वैकुण्ठवर्त्मसु ।
यत्रोपगीयते नित्यं देवदेवो जनार्दनः ॥२०॥

durāpā hy alpa-tapasaḥ
sevā vaikuṇṭha-vartmasu
yatropagīyate nityaṁ
deva-devo janārdanaḥ

durāpā—rarely obtainable; *hi*—certainly; *alpa-tapasaḥ*—of one whose austerity is meager; *sevā*—service; *vaikuntha*—the transcendental kingdom of God; *vartmasu*—on the path of; *yatra*—wherein; *upagīyate*—is glorified; *nityam*—always; *deva*—of the demigods; *devaḥ*—the Lord; *jana-ardanaḥ*—the controller of the living entities.

TRANSLATION

Persons whose austerity is meager can hardly obtain the service of the pure devotees who are progressing on the path back to the kingdom of Godhead, the Vaikuṇṭhas. Pure devotees engage one hundred percent in glorifying the Supreme Lord, who is the Lord of the demigods and the controller of all living entities.

PURPORT

The path of liberation, as recommended by all authorities, is to serve the *mahātmā* transcendentalists. As far as *Bhagavad-gītā* is concerned, the *mahātmās* are the pure devotees who are on the path to Vaikuṇṭha, the kingdom of God, and who always chant and hear the glories of the Lord rather than talk of dry, profitless philosophy. This system of association has been recommended since time immemorial, but in this age of quarrel and hypocrisy it is especially recommended by Lord Śrī Caitanya Mahāprabhu. Even if one has no assets of favorable austerity, if he nevertheless takes shelter of the *mahātmās*, who are engaged in chanting and hearing the glories of the Lord, he is sure to make progress on the path back home, back to Godhead.

TEXT 21

सृष्ट्वाग्रे महदादीनि सविकाराण्यनुक्रमात् ।
तेभ्यो विराजमुद्धृत्य तमनु प्राविशद्विभुः ॥२१॥

sṛṣṭvāgre mahad-ādīni
sa-vikārāṇy anukramāt
tebhyo virājam uddhṛtya
tam anu prāviśad vibhuḥ

sṛṣṭvā—after creating; *agre*—in the beginning; *mahat-ādīni*—the total material energy; *sa-vikārāṇi*—along with the sense organs; *anukramāt*—by a gradual process of differentiation; *tebhyaḥ*—out of that; *virājam*—the gigantic universal form; *uddhṛtya*—manifesting; *tam*—unto that; *anu*—later; *prāviśat*—entered; *vibhuḥ*—the Supreme.

TRANSLATION

After creating the total material energy, the mahat-tattva, and thereby manifesting the gigantic universal form with senses and sense organs, the Supreme Lord entered within it.

PURPORT

Fully satisfied by the answers of the sage Maitreya, Vidura wanted to understand the remaining portions of the creative function of the Lord, and he took the clue from the previous topics.

TEXT 22

यमाहुराद्यं पुरुषं सहस्राङ्घ्र्यूरुबाहुकम् ।
यत्र विश्व इमे लोकाः सविकाशं त आसते ॥२२॥

yam āhur ādyaṁ puruṣaṁ
sahasrāṅghry-ūru-bāhukam
yatra viśva ime lokāḥ
sa-vikāśaṁ ta āsate

yam—who; *āhuḥ*—is called; *ādyam*—original; *puruṣam*—incarnation for cosmic manifestation; *sahasra*—thousand; *aṅghri*—legs; *ūru*—thighs; *bāhukam*—hands; *yatra*—wherein; *viśvaḥ*—the universe; *ime*—all these; *lokāḥ*—planets; *sa-vikāśam*—with respective developments; *te*—all of them; *āsate*—living.

TRANSLATION

The puruṣa incarnation lying on the Causal Ocean is called the original puruṣa in the material creations, and in His virāṭ form, in whom all the planets and their inhabitants live, He has many thousands of legs and hands.

PURPORT

The first *puruṣa* is Kāraṇodakaśāyī Viṣṇu, the second *puruṣa* is Garbhodakaśāyī Viṣṇu, and the third *puruṣa* is Kṣīrodakaśāyī Viṣṇu, in whom is contemplated the *virāṭ-puruṣa*, the gigantic form in which all the planets with their different developments and inhabitants are floating.

TEXT 23

यस्मिन् दशविधः प्राणः सेन्द्रियार्थेन्द्रियस्त्रिवृत् ।
त्वयेरितो यतो वर्णास्तद्विभूतीर्वदस्व नः ॥२३॥

yasmin daśa-vidhaḥ prāṇaḥ
sendriyārthendriyas tri-vṛt
tvayerito yato varṇās
tad-vibhūtīr vadasva naḥ

yasmin—in which; *daśa-vidhaḥ*—ten kinds of; *prāṇaḥ*—air of life; *sa*—with; *indriya*—senses; *artha*—interest; *indriyaḥ*—of the senses; *tri-vṛt*—three kinds of life vigor; *tvayā*—by you; *īritaḥ*—explained; *yataḥ*—wherefrom; *varṇāḥ*—four specific divisions; *tat-vibhūtīḥ*—prowess; *vadasva*—please describe; *naḥ*—unto me.

TRANSLATION

O great brāhmaṇa, you have told me that the gigantic virāṭ form and His senses, sense objects and ten kinds of life air exist with three kinds of life vigor. Now, if you will, kindly explain to me the different powers of the specific divisions.

TEXT 24

यत्र पुत्रैश्च पौत्रैश्च नप्तृभिः सह गोत्रजैः ।
प्रजा विचित्राकृतय आसन् याभिरिदं ततम् ॥२४॥

yatra putraiś ca pautraiś ca
naptṛbhiḥ saha gotrajaiḥ
prajā vicitrākṛtaya
āsan yābhir idaṁ tatam

yatra—wherein; *putraiḥ*—along with sons; *ca*—and; *pautraiḥ*—along with grandsons; *ca*—also; *naptṛbhiḥ*—with grandsons from daughters; *saha*—along with; *gotra-jaiḥ*—of the same family; *prajāḥ*—generations; *vicitra*—of different kinds; *ākṛtayaḥ*—so done; *āsan*—exist; *yābhiḥ*—by whom; *idam*—all these planets; *tatam*—spread.

TRANSLATION

O my lord, I think that the process manifest in the forms of sons, grandsons and family members has spread all over the universe in different varieties and species.

TEXT 25

प्रजापतीनां स पतिश्चक्लृपे कान् प्रजापतीन् ।
सर्गांश्चैवानुसर्गांश्च मनून्मन्वन्तराधिपान् ॥२५॥

prajāpatīnāṁ sa patiś
cakḷpe kān prajāpatīn
sargāṁś caivānusargāṁś ca
manūn manvantarādhipān

prajā-patīnām—of the demigods like Brahmā and others; *saḥ*—he; *patiḥ*—leader; *cakḷpe*—decided; *kān*—whomsoever; *prajāpatīn*—fathers of the living entities; *sargān*—generations; *ca*—also; *eva*—certainly; *anusargān*—later generations; *ca*—and; *manūn*—the Manus; *manvantara-adhipān*—and the changes of such.

TRANSLATION

O learned brāhmaṇa, please describe how the leader of all the demigods, namely Prajāpati, Brahmā, decided to establish the various Manus, the heads of the ages. Please describe the Manus also, and please describe the descendants of those Manus.

PURPORT

The human race, or *manuṣya-sara,* descends from the Manus, sons and grandsons of the Prajāpati, Brahmā. The descendants of Manu reside in all the different planets and rule all the universe.

TEXT 26

उपर्यधश्च ये लोका भूमेर्मित्रात्मजासते ।
तेषां संस्थां प्रमाणं च भूर्लोकस्य च वर्णय ॥२६॥

upary adhaś ca ye lokā
bhūmer mitrātmajāsate
teṣāṁ saṁsthāṁ pramāṇaṁ ca
bhūr-lokasya ca varṇaya

upari—on the head; *adhaḥ*—underneath; *ca*—also; *ye*—which; *lokāḥ*—planets; *bhūmeḥ*—of the earth; *mitra-ātmaja*—O son of Mitrā (Maitreya Muni); *āsate*—do exist; *teṣām*—their; *saṁsthām*—situation; *pramāṇam ca*—also their measurement; *bhūḥ-lokasya*—of the earthly planets; *ca*—also; *varṇaya*—please describe.

TRANSLATION

O son of Mitrā, kindly describe how the planets are situated above the earth as well as underneath it, and also please mention their measurement as well as that of the earthly planets.

PURPORT

Yasmin vijñāte sarvam evaṁ vijñātaṁ bhavati. This Vedic hymn declares emphatically that the devotee of the Lord knows everything material and spiritual in relationship with the Lord. Devotees are not simply emotional, as is ill conceived by certain less intelligent men. Their direction is practical. They know everything that is and all the details of the Lord's domination over the different creations.

TEXT 27

तिर्यङ्मानुषदेवानां सरीसृपपतत्त्रिणाम् ।
वद नः सर्गसंव्यूहं गार्भस्वेदद्विजोद्भिदाम् ॥२७॥

tiryaṅ-mānuṣa-devānām
sarīsṛpa-patattriṇām
vada naḥ sarga-saṁvyūhaṁ
gārbha-sveda-dvijodbhidām

tiryak—subhuman; *mānuṣa*—human beings; *devānām*—of the superhuman beings, or demigods; *sarīsṛpa*—reptiles; *patattriṇām*—of the birds; *vada*—kindly describe; *naḥ*—unto me; *sarga*—generation; *saṁvyūham*—specific divisions; *gārbha*—embryonic; *sveda*—perspiration; *dvija*—twice-born; *udbhidām*—of the planets, etc.

TRANSLATION

Also please describe the living beings under different classifications: subhumans, humans, those born of the embryo, those born of perspiration, those who are twice-born [birds], and the plants and vegetables. Kindly describe their generations and subdivisions also.

TEXT 28

गुणावतारैर्विश्वस्य सर्गस्थित्यप्ययाश्रयम् ।
सृजतः श्रीनिवासस्य व्याचक्ष्वोदारविक्रमम् ॥२८॥

guṇāvatārair viśvasya
sarga-sthity-apyayāśrayam
sṛjataḥ śrīnivāsasya
vyācakṣvodāra-vikramam

guṇa—modes of material nature; *avatāraiḥ*—of the incarnations; *viśvasya*—of the universe; *sarga*—creation; *sthiti*—maintenance; *apyaya*—destruction; *āśrayam*—and ultimate rest; *sṛjataḥ*—of the one who creates; *śrīnivāsasya*—of the Personality of Godhead; *vyācakṣva*—kindly describe; *udāra*—magnanimous; *vikramam*—specific activities.

TRANSLATION

Please also describe the incarnations of the material modes of nature—Brahmā, Viṣṇu and Maheśvara—and please describe the incarnation of the Supreme Personality of Godhead and His magnanimous activities.

PURPORT

Although Brahmā, Viṣṇu and Maheśvara, the three incarnations of the material modes of nature, are the principal deities for the creation, maintenance and destruction of the cosmic manifestation, they are not the final authority. The Supreme Personality of Godhead Lord Kṛṣṇa is the ultimate goal, the cause of all causes. He is the *āśraya,* or the final rest of everything.

TEXT 29

वर्णाश्रमविभागांश्च रूपशीलस्वभावतः ।
ऋषीणां जन्मकर्माणि वेदस्य च विकर्षणम् ॥२९॥

varṇāśrama-vibhāgāṁś ca
rūpa-śīla-svabhāvataḥ
ṛṣīṇāṁ janma-karmāṇi
vedasya ca vikarṣaṇam

varṇa-āśrama—the four divisions of social statuses and orders of spiritual culture; *vibhāgān*—respective divisions; *ca*—also; *rūpa*—personal feature s; *śīla-svabhāvataḥ*—personal character; *ṛṣīṇām*—of the sages; *janma*—birth; *karmāṇi*—activities; *vedasya*—of the *Vedas; ca*—and; *vikarṣaṇam*—categorical divisions.

TRANSLATION

O great sage, kindly describe the divisions and orders of human society in terms of symptoms, behavior and the characteristics of mental equilibrium

and sense control. Also please describe the births of the great sages and the categorical divisions of the Vedas.

PURPORT

The four statuses and orders of human society—*brāhmaṇas, kṣatriyas, vaiśyas* and *śūdras*, as well as *brahmacārīs, gṛhasthas, vānaprasthas* and *sannyāsīs*—are all divisions of quality, education, culture and spiritual advancement attained by practicing control of the mind and the senses. All these divisions are based on the particular nature of each individual person, not on the principle of birth. Birth is not mentioned in this verse because birth is immaterial. Vidura is famous in history as born of a *śūdrāṇī* mother, yet he is more than a *brāhmaṇa* by qualification because he is seen here to be the disciple of a great sage, Maitreya Muni. Unless one achieves at least the brahminical qualifications, one cannot understand the Vedic hymns. *Mahābhārata* is also a division of the *Vedas,* but it is meant for women, *śūdras* and *dvija-bandhus,* the worthless children of the higher section. The less intelligent section of society can avail themselves of the Vedic instructions simply by studying the *Mahābhārata.*

TEXT 30

यज्ञस्य च वितानानि योगस्य च पथः प्रभो ।
नैष्कर्म्यस्य च सांख्यस्य तन्त्रं वा भगवत्स्मृतम् ॥३०॥

yajñasya ca vitānāni
yogasya ca pathaḥ prabho
naiṣkarmyasya ca sāṅkhyasya
tantraṁ vā bhagavat-smṛtam

yajñasya—of sacrifices; *ca*—also; *vitānāni*—expansions; *yogasya*—of the mystic powers; *ca*—also; *pathaḥ*—ways; *prabho*—O my lord; *naiṣkarmyasya*—of knowledge; *ca*—and; *sāṅkhyasya*—of analytical studies; *tantram*—the path of devotional service; *vā*—as well as; *bhagavat*—in relation with the Personality of Godhead; *smṛtam*—regulative principles.

TRANSLATION

Please also describe the expansions of different sacrifices and the paths of mystic powers, analytical study of knowledge, and devotional service, all with their respective regulations.

PURPORT

The word *tantram* is significant herein. Sometimes *tantram* is misunderstood to be the black spiritual science of materialistic persons engaged in sense gratification, but here *tantram* means the science of devotional service compiled by Śrīla Nārada Muni. One can take advantage of such regulative explanations of the path of devotional service and make progressive advancement in the devotional service of the Lord. Sāṅkhya philosophy is the basic principle of acquiring knowledge, as will be explained by the sage Maitreya. The Sāṅkhya philosophy enunciated by Kapiladeva, the son of Devahūti, is the real source of knowledge about the Supreme Truth. Knowledge not based on the Sāṅkhya philosophy is mental speculation and can yield no tangible profit.

TEXT 31

पाषण्डपथवैषम्यं प्रतिलोमनिवेशनम् ।
जीवस्य गतयो याश्च यावतीर्गुणकर्मजाः ॥३१॥

pāṣaṇḍa-patha-vaiṣamyaṁ
pratiloma-niveśanam
jīvasya gatayo yāś ca
yāvatīr guṇa-karmajāḥ

pāṣaṇḍa-patha—the path of the faithless; *vaiṣamyam*—imperfection by contradiction; *pratiloma*—crossbreeding; *niveśanam*—situation; *jīvasya*—of the living entities; *gatayaḥ*—movements; *yāḥ*—as they are; *ca*—also; *yāvatīḥ*—as many as; *guṇa*—modes of material nature; *karma-jāḥ*—generated by different work.

TRANSLATION

Please also describe the imperfections and contradictions of the faithless atheists, the situation of crossbreeding, and the movements of the living entities in various species of life according to their particular modes of nature and work.

PURPORT

The combination of living entities in different modes of material nature is called crossbreeding. The faithless atheists do not believe in the existence of God, and thus their paths of philosophy are contradictory. Atheistic philosophies never agree with one another. Different species of life are evidence of varieties of mixtures of the modes of material nature.

TEXT 32

धर्मार्थकाममोक्षाणां निमित्तान्यविरोधतः ।
वार्तायां दण्डनीतेश्च श्रुतस्य च विधिं पृथक् ॥३२॥

dharmārtha-kāma-mokṣāṇāṁ
nimittāny avirodhataḥ
vārtāyā daṇḍa-nīteś ca
śrutasya ca vidhiṁ pṛthak

dharma—religiosity; *artha*—economic development; *kāma*—sense gratification; *mokṣāṇām*—salvation; *nimittāni*—causes; *avirodhataḥ*—without being contradictory; *vārtāyāḥ*—on the principles of the means of livelihood; *daṇḍa-nīteḥ*—of law and order; *ca*—also; *śrutasya*—of the codes of scriptures; *ca*—also; *vidhim*—regulations; *pṛthak*—different.

TRANSLATION

You may also describe the noncontradictory causes of religiosity, economic development, sense gratification and salvation and also the different means of livelihood and different processes of law and order as mentioned in the revealed scriptures.

TEXT 33

श्राद्धस्य च विधिं ब्रह्मन् पितृणां सर्गमेव च ।
ग्रहनक्षत्रताराणां कालावयवसंस्थितिम् ॥३३॥

śrāddhasya ca vidhiṁ brahman
pitṝṇāṁ sargam eva ca
graha-nakṣatra tārāṇāṁ
kālāvayava-saṁsthitim

śrāddhasya—of the periodical offerings of respects; *ca*—also; *vidhim*—regulations; *brahman*—O *brāhmaṇa; pitṝṇām*—of the forefathers; *sargam*—creation; *eva*—as; *ca*—also; *graha*—planetary system; *nakṣatra*—the stars; *tārāṇām*—luminaries; *kāla*—time; *avayava*—duration; *saṁsthitim*—situations.

TRANSLATION

Please also explain the regulations for offering respects to the forefathers, the creation of the Pitṛloka, the time schedule in the planets, stars and luminaries, and their respective situations.

PURPORT

The time durations of day and night as well as months and years are different in the different planets, stars and luminaries. The higher planets like the moon and Venus have time measurements different from those of the earth. It is said that six months of this planet earth equal one day of the higher planets. In *Bhagavad-gītā* the duration of one day in Brahmaloka is measured to be 1,000 times the four *yugas*, or 4,300,000 years multiplied by 1,000. And the month and year in Brahmaloka are calculated in that measure.

TEXT 34

दानस्य तपसो वापि यच्चेष्टापूर्तयोः फलम् ।
प्रवासस्थस्य यो धर्मो यश्च पुंस उतापदि ॥३४॥

dānasya tapaso vāpi
yac ceṣṭā-pūrtayoḥ phalam
pravāsa-sthasya yo dharmo
yaś ca puṁsa utāpadi

dānasya—of charity; *tapasaḥ*—of penance; *vāpi*—lake; *yat*—that which; *ca*—and; *iṣṭā*—endeavor; *pūrtayoḥ*—of reservoirs of water; *phalam*—fruitive result; *pravāsa-sthasya*—one who is away from home; *yaḥ*—that which; *dharmaḥ*—duty; *yaḥ ca*—and which; *puṁsaḥ*—of man; *uta*—described; *āpadi*—in danger.

TRANSLATION

Please also describe the fruitive results of charity and penance and of digging reservoirs of water. Please describe the situation of persons who are away from home and also the duty of a man in an awkward position.

PURPORT

The digging of reservoirs of water for public use is a great work of charity, and retiring from family life after fifty years of age is a great act of penance performed by the sober human being.

TEXT 35

येन वा भगवांस्तुष्येद्धर्मयोनिर्जनार्दनः ।
सम्प्रसीदति वा येषामेतदाख्याहि मेऽनघ ॥३५॥

yena vā bhagavāṁs tuṣyed
dharma-yonir janārdanaḥ
samprasīdati vā yeṣām
etad ākhyāhi me 'nagha

yena—by which; *vā*—either; *bhagavān*—the Personality of Godhead; *tuṣyet*—is satisfied; *dharma-yoniḥ*—the father of all religion; *janārdanaḥ*—the controller of all living being; *samprasīdati*—completely satisfied; *vā*—either, or; *yeṣām*—of those; *etat*—all these; *ākhyāhi*—kindly describe; *me*—unto me; *anagha*—O sinless one.

TRANSLATION

O sinless one, because the Personality of Godhead, the controller of all living entities, is the father of all religion and all those who are candidates for religious activities, kindly describe how He can be completely satisfied.

PURPORT

All religious activities are meant ultimately to satisfy the Supreme Personality of Godhead. The Lord is the father of all religious principles. As stated in *Bhagavad-gītā* (7.16), four kinds of pious men—the needy, the distressed, the enlightened and the inquisitive—approach the Lord in devotional service, and their devotion is mixed with material affection. But above them are the pure devotees, whose devotion is not tainted by any material tinges of fruitive work or speculative knowledge. Those who are only miscreants throughout their lives are compared to demons (Bg. 7.15). They are bereft of all knowledge, in spite of any academic educational career they may pursue. Such miscreants are never candidates for satisfying the Lord.

TEXT 36

अनुव्रतानां शिष्याणां पुत्राणां च द्विजोत्तम ।
अनापृष्टमपि ब्रूयुर्गुरवो दीनवत्सलाः ॥३६॥

anuvratānāṁ śiṣyāṇāṁ
putrāṇāṁ ca dvijottama
anāpṛṣṭam api brūyur
guravo dīna-vatsalāḥ

anuvratānām—the followers; *śiṣyāṇām*—of the disciples; *putrāṇām*—of the sons; *ca*—also; *dvija-uttama*—O best amongst the *brāhmaṇas*; *anāpṛṣṭam*—that which is not asked for; *api*—

in spite of; *brūyuḥ*—please describe; *guravaḥ*—the spiritual masters; *dīna-vatsalāḥ*—who are kind to the needy.

TRANSLATION

O best among the brāhmaṇas, those who are spiritual masters are very kind to the needy. They are always kind to their followers, disciples and sons, and without being asked by them, the spiritual master describes all that is knowledge.

PURPORT

There are many subjects to be known from the bona fide spiritual master. The followers, disciples and sons are all on one level for the bona fide spiritual master, and he is always kind to them and always speaks to them on transcendental subjects, even though he is not asked by them. That is the nature of the bona fide spiritual master. Vidura appealed to Maitreya Muni to speak on subjects about which he might not have asked.

TEXT 37

तत्त्वानां भगवंस्तेषां कतिधा प्रतिसङ्क्रमः ।
तत्रेमं क उपासीरन् क उ स्विदनुशेरते ॥३७॥

tattvānāṁ bhagavaṁs teṣāṁ
katidhā pratisaṅkramaḥ
tatremaṁ ka upāsīran
ka u svid anuśerate

tattvānām—of the elements of nature; *bhagavan*—O great sage; *teṣām*—of them; *katidhā*—how many; *pratisaṅkramaḥ*—dissolutions; *tatra*—thereupon; *imam*—unto the Supreme Lord; *ke*—who are they; *upāsīran*—being saved; *ke*—who are they; *u*—who; *svit*—may; *anuśerate*—serve the Lord while He sleeps.

TRANSLATION

Please describe how many dissolutions there are for the elements of material nature and who survives after the dissolutions to serve the Lord while He is asleep.

PURPORT

In the *Brahma-saṁhitā* (5.47-48) it is said that all the material manifestations with innumerable universes appear and disappear with the breathing of Mahā-viṣṇu lying in *yoga-nidrā*, or mystic sleep.

yaḥ kāraṇārṇava-jale bhajati sma yoga-
nidrām ananta-jagad-aṇḍa-saroma-kūpaḥ
ādhāra-śaktim avalambya parāṁ sva-mūrtiṁ
govindam ādi-puruṣaṁ tam ahaṁ bhajāmi

yasyaika-niśvasita-kālam athāvalambya
jīvanti loma-vilajā jagad-aṇḍa-nāthāḥ
viṣṇur mahān sa iha yasya kalā-viśeṣo
govindam ādi-puruṣaṁ tam ahaṁ bhajāmi

"Govinda, the ultimate and Supreme Personality of Godhead [Lord Kṛṣṇa], lies sleeping unlimitedly on the Causal Ocean in order to create unlimited numbers of universes during that sleep. He lies on the water by His own internal potency, and I worship that original Supreme Godhead.

"Due to His breathing, innumerable universes come into existence, and when He withdraws His breath there occurs the dissolution of all the lords of the universes. That plenary portion of the Supreme Lord is called Mahā-viṣṇu, and He is a part of the part of Lord Kṛṣṇa. I worship Govinda, the original Lord."

After the dissolution of the material manifestations, the Lord and His kingdom beyond the Causal Ocean do not disappear, nor do the inhabitants, the Lord's associates. The associates of the Lord are far more numerous than the living entities who have forgotten the Lord due to material association. The impersonalist's explanation of the word *aham* in the four verses of the original *Bhāgavatam—aham evāsam evāgre* etc.—is refuted here. The Lord and His eternal associates remain after the dissolution. Vidura's inquiry about such persons is a clear indication of the existence of all the paraphernalia of the Lord. This is also confirmed in the *Kāśī-khaṇḍa*, as quoted by both Jīva Gosvāmī and Śrīla Viśvanātha Cakravartī, who follow in the footsteps of Śrīla Śrīdhara Svāmī.

na cyavante hi yad-bhaktā
mahatyāṁ pralayāpadi
ato 'cyuto 'khile loke
sa ekaḥ sarva-go 'vyayaḥ

"The devotees of the Lord never annihilate their individual existences even after the dissolution of the entire cosmic manifestation. The Lord and the devotees who associate with Him are always eternal, in both the material and spiritual worlds."

TEXT 38

पुरुषस्य च संस्थानं स्वरूपं वा परस्य च ।
ज्ञानं च नैगमं यत्तद्गुरुशिष्यप्रयोजनम् ॥३८॥

puruṣasya ca saṁsthānaṁ
svarūpaṁ vā parasya ca
jñānaṁ ca naigamaṁ yat tad
guru-śiṣya-prayojanam

puruṣasya—of the living entity; *ca*—also; *saṁsthānam*—existence; *svarūpam*—identity; *vā*—either, or; *parasya*—of the Supreme; *ca*—also; *jñānam*—knowledge; *ca*—also; *naigamam*—in the matter of the *Upaniṣads; yat*—that; *tat*—the same; *guru*—spiritual master; *śiṣya*—disciple; *prayojanam*—necessity.

TRANSLATION

What are the truths regarding the living entities and the Supreme Personality of Godhead? What are their identities? What are the specific values in the knowledge in the Vedas, and what are the necessities for the spiritual master and his disciples?

PURPORT

The living entities are constitutionally servitors of the Lord, who can accept all kinds of service from everyone. It is clearly declared (Bg. 5.29) that the Lord is the supreme enjoyer of the benefits of all sacrifices and penances, the proprietor of all that is manifested and the friend of all living entities. That is His real identity. Therefore, when the living entity accepts this supreme proprietorship of the Lord and acts in that attitude, he resumes his real identity. In order to elevate the living entity to this standard of knowledge, there is the necessity of spiritual association. The bona fide spiritual master desires that his disciples know the process of rendering transcendental service to the Lord, and the disciples also know that they have to learn about the eternal relationship between God and the living entity from a self-realized soul. To disseminate transcendental knowledge one must retire from mundane activities on the strength of enlightenment in knowledge in terms of Vedic wisdom. That is the sum and substance of all the questions in this verse.

TEXT 39

निमित्तानि च तस्येह प्रोक्तान्यनघसूरिभिः ।
स्वतो ज्ञानं कुतः पुंसां भक्तिर्वैराग्यमेव वा ॥३९॥

nimittāni ca tasyeha
proktāny anagha-sūribhiḥ
svato jñānaṁ kutaḥ puṁsāṁ
bhaktir vairāgyam eva vā

nimittāni—the source of knowledge; *ca*—also; *tasya*—of such knowledge; *iha*—in this world; *proktāni*—mentioned; *anagha*—spotless; *sūribhiḥ*—by devotees; *svataḥ*—self-sufficient; *jñānam*—knowledge; *kutaḥ*—how; *puṁsām*—of the living entity; *bhaktiḥ*—devotional service; *vairāgyam*—detachment; *eva*—certainly; *vā*—also.

TRANSLATION

Spotless devotees of the Lord have mentioned the source of such knowledge. How could one have knowledge of devotional service and detachment without the help of such devotees?

PURPORT

There are many inexperienced persons who advocate self-realization without the help of a spiritual master. They decry the necessity of the spiritual master and try themselves to take his place by propagating the theory that a spiritual master is not necessary. *Śrīmad-Bhāgavatam,* however, does not approve this viewpoint. Even the great transcendental scholar Vyāsadeva had need of a spiritual master, and under the instruction of his spiritual master, Nārada, he prepared this sublime literature, *Śrīmad-Bhāgavatam.* Even Lord Caitanya, although He is Kṛṣṇa Himself, accepted a spiritual master; even Lord Kṛṣṇa accepted a spiritual master, Sāndīpani Muni, in order to be enlightened; and all the *ācāryas* and saints of the world had spiritual masters. In *Bhagavad-gītā* Arjuna accepted Lord Kṛṣṇa as his spiritual master, although there was no necessity of such a formal declaration. So, in all cases, there is no question about the necessity of accepting a spiritual master. The only stipulation is that the spiritual master should be bona fide; i.e., the spiritual master must be in the proper chain of disciplic succession, called the *paramparā* system.

Sūris are great scholars, but they may not always be *anagha,* or spotless. The *anagha-sūri* is one who is a pure devotee of the Lord. Those who are not pure devotees of the Lord, or who want to be on an equal level with Him, are not *anagha-sūri.* Pure devotees have prepared many books of knowledge on the basis of authorized scriptures. Śrīla Rūpa Gosvāmī and his assistants, under the instructions of Lord Śrī Caitanya Mahāprabhu, have all written various literatures for the guidance of prospective devotees, and anyone who is very serious about raising himself to the standard of a pure devotee of the Lord must take advantage of those literatures.

TEXT 40

एतान्मे पृच्छतः प्रश्नान् हरेः कर्मविवित्सया ।
ब्रूहि मेऽज्ञस्य मित्रत्वादजया नष्टचक्षुषः ॥४०॥

etān me pṛcchataḥ praśnān
hareḥ karma-vivitsayā
brūhi me 'jñasya mitratvād
ajayā naṣṭa-cakṣuṣaḥ

etān—all these; *me*—my; *pṛcchataḥ*—of one who inquires; *praśnān*—questions; *hareḥ*—of the Supreme Lord; *karma*—pastimes; *vivitsayā*—desiring to know; *brūhi*—kindly describe; *me*—unto me; *ajñasya*—of one who is ignorant; *mitratvāt*—because of friendship; *ajayā*—by the external energy; *naṣṭa-cakṣuṣaḥ*—those who have lost their vision.

TRANSLATION

My dear sage, I have put all these questions before you with a view to knowing the pastimes of Hari, the Supreme Personality of Godhead. You are the friend of all, so kindly describe them for all those who have lost their vision.

PURPORT

Vidura put forward many varieties of questions with a view to understanding the principles of transcendental loving service to the Lord. As stated in *Bhagavad-gītā* (2.41), devotional service to the Lord is one, and the mind of the devotee is not diverted to the many branches of uncertainties. Vidura's purpose was to be situated in that service to the Lord, wherein one merges undivertedly. He claimed the friendship of Maitreya Muni, not because he was Maitreya's son but because Maitreya was actually the friend of all who have lost their spiritual vision due to material influence.

TEXT 41

सर्वे वेदाश्च यज्ञाश्च तपो दानानि चानघ ।
जीवाभयप्रदानस्य न कुर्वीरन् कलामपि ॥४१॥

sarve vedāś ca yajñāś ca
tapo dānāni cānagha
jīvābhaya-pradānasya
na kurvīran kalām api

sarve—all kinds of; *vedāḥ*—divisions of the *Vedas; ca*—also; *yajñāḥ*—sacrifices; *ca*—also; *tapaḥ*—penances; *dānāni*—charities; *ca*—and; *anagha*—O spotless one; *jīva*—the living entity; *abhaya*—immunity from material pangs; *pradānasya*—of one who gives such assurance; *na*—not; *kurvīran*—can be equalized; *kalām*—even partially; *api*—certainly.

TRANSLATION

O spotless one, your answers to all these questions will grant immunity from all material miseries. Such charity is greater than all Vedic charities, sacrifices, penances, etc.

PURPORT

The highest perfectional work of charity is to give people in general immunity from the anxieties of material existence. This can be done only by performing activities in devotional service to the Lord. Such knowledge is incomparable. Cultivation of the knowledge in the *Vedas,* performance of sacrifice, and distribution of munificent charities all together cannot form even a part of the immunity from the pangs of material existence that is gained from devotional service. The charity of Maitreya not only will help Vidura, but, due to its universal nature, will deliver all others in all times. Thus Maitreya is immortal.

TEXT 42

श्रीशुक उवाच
स इत्थमापृष्टपुराणकल्पः कुरुप्रधानेन मुनिप्रधानः ।
प्रवृद्धहर्षो भगवत्कथायां सञ्चोदितस्तं प्रहसन्निवाह ॥४२॥

śrī-śuka uvāca
sa ittham āpṛṣṭa-purāṇa-kalpaḥ
kuru-pradhānena muni-pradhānaḥ
pravṛddha-harṣo bhagavat-kathāyāṁ
sañcoditas taṁ prahasann ivāha

śrī-śukaḥ uvāca—Śrī Śukadeva Gosvāmī said; *saḥ*—he; *ittham*—thus; *āpṛṣṭa*—being questioned; *purāṇa-kalpaḥ*—one who knows how to explain the supplements of the *Vedas* (the *Purāṇas*); *kuru-pradhānena*—by the chief of the Kurus; *muni-pradhānaḥ*—the chief amongst the sages; *pravṛddha*—sufficiently enriched; *harṣaḥ*—satisfaction; *bhagavat*—the Personality of Godhead; *kathāyām*—in the topics of; *sañcoditaḥ*—being so infused; *tam*—unto Vidura; *prahasan*—with smiles; *iva*—like that; *āha*—replied.

TRANSLATION

Śrī Śukadeva Gosvāmī said: Thus the chief of the sages, who was always enthusiastic about describing topics regarding the Personality of Godhead, began to narrate the descriptive explanation of the Purāṇas, being so infused by Vidura. He was very much enlivened by speaking on the transcendental activities of the Lord.

PURPORT

Great learned sages like Maitreya Muni are always very enthusiastic about describing the transcendental activities of the Lord. Maitreya Muni, being thus invited by Vidura to speak, appeared to be smiling because he actually felt transcendental bliss.

Thus end the Bhaktivedanta purports of the Third Canto, Seventh Chapter, of the Śrīmad-Bhāgavatam, *entitled "Further Inquiries by Vidura."*

CHAPTER EIGHT

Manifestation of Brahmā from Garbhodakaśāyī Viṣṇu

TEXT 1

मैत्रेय उवाच
सत्सेवनीयो बत पूरुवंशो
यल्लोकपालो भगवत्प्रधानः ।
बभूविथेहाजितकीर्तिमालां
पदे पदे नूतनयस्यभीक्ष्णम् ॥ १ ॥

maitreya uvāca
sat-sevanīyo bata pūru-vaṁśo
yal loka-pālo bhagavat-pradhānaḥ
babhūvithehājita-kīrti-mālāṁ
pade pade nūtanayasy abhīkṣṇam

maitreyaḥ uvāca—Śrī Maitreya Muni said; *sat-sevanīyaḥ*—worthy to serve the pure devotees; *bata*—oh, certainly; *pūru-vaṁśaḥ*—the descendants of King Pūru; *yat*—because; *loka-pālaḥ*—the kings are; *bhagavat-pradhānaḥ*—chiefly devoted to the Personality of Godhead; *babhūvitha*—you are also born; *iha*—in this; *ajita*—the Lord, who is unconquerable; *kīrti-mālām*—chain of transcendental activities; *pade pade*—step by step; *nūtanayasi*—becoming newer and newer; *abhīkṣṇam*—always.

TRANSLATION

The great sage Maitreya Muni said to Vidura: The royal dynasty of King Pūru is worthy to serve the pure devotees because all the descendants of that family are devoted to the Personality of Godhead. You are also born in that family, and it is wonderful that because of your attempt the transcendental pastimes of the Lord are becoming newer and newer at every moment.

PURPORT

The great sage Maitreya thanked Vidura and praised him by reference to his family glories. The Pūru dynasty was full of devotees of the Personality of Godhead and was therefore glorious. Because they were not attached to impersonal Brahman or to the localized Paramātmā but were directly attached to Bhagavān, the Personality of Godhead, they were worthy to render service to the Lord and His pure devotees. Because Vidura was one of the descendants of that family, naturally he engaged in spreading wide the ever-new glories of the Lord. Maitreya felt happy to have such glorious company as Vidura. He considered the company of Vidura most desirable because such association can accelerate one's dormant propensities for devotional service.

TEXT 2

सोऽहं नृणां क्षुल्लसुखाय दुःखं
महद्गतानां विरमाय तस्य ।
प्रवर्तये भागवतं पुराणं
यदाह साक्षाद्भगवानृषिभ्यः ॥ २ ॥

so 'haṁ nṛṇāṁ kṣulla-sukhāya duḥkhaṁ
mahad gatānāṁ viramāya tasya
pravartaye bhāgavataṁ purāṇaṁ
yad āha sākṣād bhagavān ṛṣibhyaḥ

saḥ—that; *aham*—I; *nṛṇām*—of the human being; *kṣulla*—very little; *sukhāya*—for happiness; *duḥkham*—distress; *mahat*—great; *gatānām*—entered into; *viramāya*—for mitigation; *tasya*—his; *pravartaye*—in beginning; *bhāgavatam*—*Śrīmad-Bhāgavatam*; *purāṇam*—Vedic supplement; *yat*—which; *āha*—said; *sākṣāt*—directly; *bhagavān*—the Personality of Godhead; *ṛṣibhyaḥ*—unto the sages.

TRANSLATION

Let me now begin speaking on the Bhāgavata Purāṇa, which was directly spoken to the great sages by the Personality of Godhead for the benefit of those who are entangled in extreme miseries for the sake of very little pleasure.

PURPORT

The sage Maitreya proposed to speak on *Śrīmad-Bhāgavatam* because it was especially compiled, and traditionally comes down in the disciplic succession, for the solution of all the problems of human society. Only one who is fortunate can have the opportunity to hear *Śrīmad-Bhāgavatam* in the association of pure devotees of the Lord. Under the spell of material energy, the living entities are entrapped in the bondage of many difficulties simply for the sake of a little bit of material happiness. They engage in fruitive activities, not knowing the implications. Under the false impression that the body is the self, the living entities foolishly relate to so many false attachments. They think that they can engage with materialistic paraphernalia forever. This gross misconception of life is so strong that a person suffers continually, life after life, under the external energy of the Lord. If one comes in contact with the book *Bhāgavatam* as well as with the devotee *bhāgavata,* who knows what the *Bhāgavatam* is, then such a fortunate man gets out of the material entanglement. Therefore Śrī Maitreya Muni, out of compassion for the suffering men in the world, proposes to speak on the *Śrīmad-Bhāgavatam* first and last.

TEXT 3

आसीनमुर्व्यां भगवन्तमाद्यं
सङ्कर्षणं देवमकुण्ठसत्त्वम् ।
विवित्सवस्तत्त्वमतः परस्य
कुमारमुख्या मुनयोऽन्वपृच्छन् ॥ ३ ॥

āsīnam urvyāṁ bhagavantam ādyaṁ
saṅkarṣaṇaṁ devam akuṇṭha-sattvam
vivitsavas tattvam ataḥ parasya
kumāra-mukhyā munayo 'nvapṛcchan

āsīnam—seated; *urvyām*—in the bottom of the universe; *bhagavantam*—unto the Lord; *ādyam*—the original; *saṅkarṣaṇam*—Saṅkarṣaṇa; *devam*—the Personality of Godhead; *akuṇṭha-sattvam*—undeterred knowledge; *vivitsavaḥ*—being inquisitive to know; *tattvam ataḥ*—truth like this; *parasya*—regarding the Supreme Personality of Godhead; *kumāra*—the boy-saint; *mukhyāḥ*—headed by; *munayaḥ*—great sages; *anvapṛcchan*—inquired like this.

TRANSLATION

Some time ago, being inquisitive to know, Sanat-kumāra, the chief of the boy-saints, accompanied by other great sages, inquired exactly like you about the truths regarding Vāsudeva, the Supreme, from Lord Saṅkarṣaṇa, who is seated at the bottom of the universe.

PURPORT

This is in clarification of the statement that the Lord spoke directly on the *Śrīmad-Bhāgavatam.* When and unto whom the *Bhāgavatam* was spoken is explained herewith.

Questions similar to those put forward by Vidura were asked by great sages like Sanat-kumāra, and Lord Saṅkarṣaṇa, the plenary expansion of the Supreme Lord Vāsudeva, answered them.

TEXT 4

स्वमेव धिष्ण्यं बहु मानयन्तं
यद्वासुदेवाभिधमामनन्ति ।
प्रत्यग्धृताक्षाम्बुजकोशमीष-
दुन्मीलयन्तं विबुधोदयाय ॥ ४ ॥

svam eva dhiṣṇyaṁ bahu mānayantaṁ
yad vāsudevābhidham āmananti
pratyag-dhṛtākṣāmbuja-kośam īṣad
unmīlayantaṁ vibudhodayāya

svam—Himself; *eva*—thus; *dhiṣṇyam*—situated; *bahu*—greatly; *mānayantam*—esteemed; *yat*—that which; *vāsudeva*—Lord Vāsudeva; *abhidham*—by the name; *āmananti*—acknowledge; *pratyak-dhṛta-akṣa*—eyes settled for introspection; *ambuja-kośam*—lotuslike eye; *īṣat*—slightly; *unmīlayantam*—opened; *vibudha*—of the greatly learned sages; *udayāya*—for the sake of advancement.

TRANSLATION

At that time Lord Saṅkarṣaṇa was meditating upon His Supreme Lord, whom the learned esteem as Lord Vāsudeva, but for the sake of the advancement of the great learned sages He slightly opened His lotus like eyes and began to speak.

TEXT 5

स्वर्धुन्युदार्द्रैः स्वजटाकलापै-
रुपस्पृशन्तश्चरणोपधानम् ।
पद्मं यदर्चन्त्यहिराजकन्याः
सप्रेमनानाबलिभिर्वरार्थाः ॥ ५ ॥

svardhuny-udārdraiḥ sva-jaṭā-kalāpair
upaspṛśantaś caraṇopadhānam
padmaṁ yad arcanty ahi-rāja-kanyāḥ
sa-prema nānā-balibhir varārthāḥ

svardhunī-uda—by the water of the Ganges; *ārdraiḥ*—being moistened; *sva-jaṭā*—bunch of hairs; *kalāpaiḥ*—situated on the head; *upaspṛśantaḥ*—by so touching; *caraṇa-upadhānam*—the shelter of His feet; *padmam*—the lotus shelter; *yat*—that which; *arcanti*—worships; *ahi-rāja*—the serpent-king; *kanyāḥ*—daughters; *sa-prema*—with great devotion; *nānā*—various; *balibhiḥ*—paraphernalia; *vara-arthāḥ*—being desirous of husbands.

TRANSLATION

The sages came from the highest planets down to the lower region through the water of the Ganges, and therefore the hair on their heads was wet. They touched the lotus feet of the Lord, which are worshiped with various paraphernalia by the daughters of the serpent-king when they desire good husbands.

PURPORT

The Ganges water flows directly from the lotus feet of Viṣṇu, and its course runs from the highest planet of the universe down to the lowest. The sages came down from Satyaloka by taking advantage of the flowing water, a process of transportation made possible by the power of mystic *yoga*. If a river flows thousands and thousands of miles, a perfect *yogī* can at once transport himself from one place to another simply by dipping in its water. The Ganges is the only celestial river which flows throughout the universe, and great sages travel all over the universe via this sacred river. The statement that their hair was wet indicates that it was directly moistened by the water originating from the lotus feet of Viṣṇu (the Ganges). Whoever touches the water of the Ganges to his head surely touches the lotus feet of the Lord directly and can become free from all effects of sinful acts. If after taking a bath in the Ganges or being washed of all sins, a man guards himself against committing further sinful acts, then certainly he is delivered. But if he again takes up sinful activities, his bath in the Ganges is as good as that of the elephant, who nicely takes his bath in a river but later spoils the whole thing by covering himself with dust on the land.

TEXT 6

मुहुर्गृणन्तो वचसानुराग-
स्खलत्पदेनास्य कृतानि तज्ज्ञाः ।
किरीटसाहस्रमणिप्रवेक-
प्रद्योतितोद्दामफणासहस्रम् ॥ ६ ॥

muhur gṛṇanto vacasānurāga-
skhalat-padenāsya kṛtāni taj-jñāḥ
kirīṭa-sāhasra-maṇi-praveka-
pradyotitoddāma-phaṇā-sahasram

muhuḥ—again and again; *gṛṇantaḥ*—glorifying; *vacasā*—by words; *anurāga*—with great affection; *skhalat-padena*—with symmetrical rhythm; *asya*—of the Lord; *kṛtāni*—activities; *tat-jñāḥ*—those who know the pastimes; *kirīṭa*—helmets; *sāhasra*—thousands; *maṇi-praveka*—glowing effulgence of the valuable stones; *pradyotita*—emanating from; *uddāma*—raised; *phaṇā*—hoods; *sahasram*—thousands.

TRANSLATION

The four Kumāras, headed by Sanat-kumāra, who all knew the transcendental pastimes of the Lord, glorified the Lord in rhythmic accents with selected words full of affection and love. At that time Lord Saṅkarṣaṇa, with His thousands of raised hoods, began to radiate an effulgence from the glowing stones on His head.

PURPORT

The Lord is sometimes addressed as *uttamaśloka,* which means "one who is worshiped with selected words by devotees." A profusion of such selected words comes from a devotee who is fully absorbed in affection and love for the devotional service of the Lord. There are many instances in which even a small boy who was a great devotee of the Lord could offer excellent prayers in the choicest words for glorification of the pastimes of the Lord. In other words, without the development of fine affection and love, one cannot offer prayers to the Lord very suitably.

TEXT 7

प्रोक्तं किलैतद्भगवत्तमेन
निवृत्तिधर्माभिरताय तेन ।
सनत्कुमाराय स चाह पृष्टः
सांख्यायनायाङ्ग धृतव्रताय ॥ ७ ॥

proktaṁ kilaitad bhagavattamena
nivṛtti-dharmābhiratāya tena
sanat-kumārāya sa cāha pṛṣṭaḥ
sāṅkhyāyanāyāṅga dhṛta-vratāya

proktam—was said; *kila*—certainly; *etat*—this; *bhagavattamena*—by Lord Saṅkarṣaṇa; *nivṛtti*—renunciation; *dharma-abhiratāya*—unto one who has taken this religious vow; *tena*—by Him; *sanat-kumārāya*—unto Sanat-kumāra; *saḥ*—he; *ca*—also; *āha*—said; *pṛṣṭaḥ*—when inquired of; *sāṅkhyāyanāya*—unto the great sage Sāṅkhyāyana; *aṅga*—my dear Vidura; *dhṛta-vratāya*—unto one who has taken such a vow.

TRANSLATION

Lord Saṅkarṣaṇa thus spoke the purport of Śrīmad-Bhāgavatam to the great sage Sanat-kumāra, who had already taken the vow of renunciation. Sanat-kumāra also, in his turn, when inquired of by Sāṅkhyāyana Muni, explained Śrīmad-Bhāgavatam as he had heard it from Saṅkarṣaṇa.

PURPORT

This is the way of the *paramparā* system. Although Sanat-kumāra, the well-known great saintly Kumāra, was in the perfect stage of life, still he heard the message of *Śrīmad-Bhāgavatam* from Lord Saṅkarṣaṇa. Similarly, when he was questioned by Sāṅkhyāyana Ṛṣi, he spoke to him the same message he had heard from Lord Saṅkarṣaṇa. In other words, unless one hears from the proper authority one cannot become a preacher. In devotional service, therefore, two items out of the nine, namely hearing and chanting, are most important. Without hearing nicely, one cannot preach the message of Vedic knowledge.

TEXT 8

सांख्यायनः पारमहंस्यमुख्यो
विवक्षमाणो भगवद्विभूतीः ।
जगाद सोऽस्मद्गुरवेऽन्विताय
पराशरायाथ बृहस्पतेश्च ॥ ८ ॥

sāṅkhyāyanaḥ pāramahaṁsya-mukhyo
vivakṣamāṇo bhagavad-vibhūtīḥ
jagāda so 'smad-gurave 'nvitāya
parāśarāyātha bṛhaspateś ca

sāṅkhyāyanaḥ—the great sage Sāṅkhyāyana; *pāramahaṁsya-mukhyaḥ*—the chief of all transcendentalists; *vivakṣamāṇaḥ*—while reciting; *bhagavat-vibhūtīḥ*—the glories of the Lord; *jagāda*—explained; *saḥ*—he; *asmat*—of me; *gurave*—unto the spiritual master; *anvitāya*—followed; *parāśarāya*—unto the sage Parāśara; *atha bṛhaspateḥ ca*—also to Bṛhaspati.

TRANSLATION

The great sage Sāṅkhyāyana was the chief amongst the transcendentalists, and when he was describing the glories of the Lord in terms of Śrīmad-Bhāgavatam, it so happened that my spiritual master, Parāśara, and Bṛhaspati both heard him.

TEXT 9

प्रोवाच मह्यं स दयालुरुक्तो
मुनिः पुलस्त्येन पुराणमाद्यम् ।
सोऽहं तवैतत्कथयामि वत्स
श्रद्धालवे नित्यमनुव्रताय ॥ ९ ॥

provāca mahyaṁ sa dayālur ukto
muniḥ pulastyena purāṇam ādyam
so 'haṁ tavaitat kathayāmi vatsa
śraddhālave nityam anuvratāya

provāca—said; *mahyam*—unto me; *saḥ*—he; *dayāluḥ*—kindhearted; *uktaḥ*—aforementioned; *muniḥ*—sage; *pulastyena*—by the sage Pulastya; *purāṇam ādyam*—the foremost of all the *Purāṇas*; *saḥ aham*—that also I; *tava*—unto you; *etat*—this; *kathayāmi*—shall speak; *vatsa*—my dear son; *śraddhālave*—unto one who is faithful; *nityam*—always; *anuvratāya*—unto one who is a follower.

TRANSLATION

The great sage Parāśara, as aforementioned, being so advised by the great sage Pulastya, spoke unto me the foremost of the Purāṇas [Bhāgavatam]. I shall also describe this before you, my dear son, in terms of my hearing, because you are always my faithful follower.

PURPORT

The great sage of the name Pulastya is the father of all demoniac descendants. Once upon a time Parāśara began a sacrifice in which all the demons were to be burnt to death because his father had been killed and devoured by one of them. The great sage Vasiṣṭha Muni arrived at the sacrifice and requested Parāśara to stop the deadly action, and because of Vasiṣṭha's position and respect in the community of sages, Parāśara could not deny the request. Parāśara having stopped the sacrifice, Pulastya, the father of the demons, appreciated his brahminical temperament and gave the blessing that in the future he would be a great speaker on the Vedic literatures called the *Purāṇas*, the supplements of the *Vedas*. Parāśara's action was appreciated by Pulastya because Parāśara had forgiven the demons out of his brahminical power of forgiveness. Parāśara was able to demolish all the demons in the sacrifice, but he considered, "Demons are so made that they devour living creatures, men and animals, but why on that account should I withdraw my brahminical qualification of forgiveness?" As the great speaker of the *Purāṇas*, Parāśara first of all spoke on the *Śrīmad-Bhāgavata Purāṇa* because it is the foremost of all the *Purāṇas*. Maitreya Muni desired to narrate the same *Bhāgavatam* be had heard from Parāśara, and Vidura was qualified to hear it because of his faithfulness and his following the instructions received from superiors. So *Śrīmad-Bhāgavatam* was being narrated from time immemorial by the disciplic succession, even before the time of Vyāsadeva. The so-called historians calculate the *Purāṇas* to be only a few hundred years old, but factually the *Purāṇas* existed from time immemorial, before all historical calculations by the mundaners and speculative philosophers.

TEXT 10

उदाप्लुतं विश्वमिदं तदासीद्
यन्निद्रयामीलितदृङ् न्यमीलयत् ।
अहीन्द्रतल्पेऽधिशयान एकः
कृतक्षणः स्वात्मरतौ निरीहः ॥१०॥

udaplutaṁ viśvam idaṁ tadāsīd
yan nidrayāmīlita-dṛṅ nyamīlayat
ahīndra-talpe 'dhiśayāna ekaḥ
kṛta-kṣaṇaḥ svātma-ratau nirīhaḥ

uda—water; *āplutam*—submerged in; *viśvam*—the three worlds; *idam*—this; *tadā*—at that time; *āsīt*—it so remained; *yat*—in which; *nidrayā*—in slumber; *amīlita*—closed; *dṛk*—eyes; *nyamīlayat*—not completely closed; *ahi-indra*—the great snake Ananta; *talpe*—on the bed of; *adhiśayānaḥ*—lying on; *ekaḥ*—alone; *kṛta-kṣaṇaḥ*—being engaged; *sva-ātma-ratau*—enjoying in His internal potency; *nirīhaḥ*—without any part of external energy.

TRANSLATION

At that time when the three worlds were submerged in water, Garbhodakaśāyī Viṣṇu was alone, lying on His bedstead, the great snake Ananta, and although He appeared to be in slumber in His own internal

potency, free from the action of the external energy, His eyes were not completely closed.

PURPORT

The Lord is eternally enjoying transcendental bliss by His internal potency, whereas the external potency is suspended during the time of the dissolution of the cosmic manifestation.

TEXT 11

सोऽन्तःशरीरेऽर्पितभूतसूक्ष्मः
कालात्मिकां शक्तिमुदीरयाणः ।
उवास तस्मिन् सलिले पदे स्वे
यथानलो दारुणि रुद्धवीर्यः ॥११॥

so 'ntaḥ śarīre 'rpita-bhūta-sūkṣmaḥ
kālātmikāṁ śaktim udīrayāṇaḥ
uvāsa tasmin salile pade sve
yathānalo dāruṇi ruddha-vīryaḥ

saḥ—the Supreme Lord; *antaḥ*—within; *śarīre*—in the transcendental body; *arpita*—kept; *bhūta*—material elements; *sūkṣmaḥ*—subtle; *kāla-ātmikām*—the form of time; *śaktim*—energy; *udīrayāṇaḥ*—invigorating; *uvāsa*—resided; *tasmin*—therein; *salile*—in the water; *pade*—in the place; *sve*—His own; *yathā*—as much as; *analaḥ*—fire; *dāruṇi*—in the fuel wood; *ruddha-vīryaḥ*—submerged strength.

TRANSLATION

Just like the strength of fire within fuel wood, the Lord remained within the water of dissolution, submerging all the living entities in their subtle bodies. He lay in the self-invigorated energy called kāla.

PURPORT

After the three worlds—the upper, lower and middle planetary systems—merged into the water of dissolution, the living entities of all the three worlds remained in their subtle bodies by dint of the energy called *kāla*. In this dissolution, the gross bodies became unmanifest, but the subtle bodies existed, just like the water of the material creation. Thus the material energy was not completely wound up, as is the case in the full dissolution of the material world.

TEXT 12

चतुर्युगानां च सहस्रमप्सु
स्वपन् स्वयोदीरितया स्वशक्त्या ।
कालाख्ययासादितकर्मतन्त्रो
लोकानपीतान्ददृशे स्वदेहे ॥१२॥

catur-yugānāṁ ca sahasram apsu
svapan svayodīritayā sva-śaktyā
kālākhyayāsādita-karma-tantro
lokān apītān dadṛśe sva-dehe

catuḥ—four; *yugānām*—of the millenniums; *ca*—also; *sahasram*—one thousand; *apsu*—in the water; *svapan*—dreaming in sleep; *svayā*—with His internal potency; *udīritayā*—for further development; *sva-śaktyā*—by His own energy; *kāla-ākhyayā*—by the name *kāla; āsādita*—being so engaged; *karma-tantraḥ*—in the matter of fruitive activities; *lokān*—the total living entities; *apītān*—bluish; *dadṛśe*—saw it so; *sva-dehe*—in His own body.

TRANSLATION

The Lord lay down for four thousand yuga cycles in His internal potency, and by His external energy He appeared to be sleeping within the water. When the living entities were coming out for further development of their fruitive activities, actuated by the energy called kāla-śakti, He saw His transcendental body as bluish.

PURPORT

In the *Viṣṇu Purāṇa, kāla-śakti* is mentioned as *avidyā.* The symptom of the influence of the *kāla-śakti* is that one has to work in the material world for fruitive results. The fruitive workers are described in *Bhagavad-gītā* as *mūḍhas,* or foolish. Such foolish living entities are very enthusiastic to work for some temporary benefit within perpetual bondage. One thinks himself very clever throughout his life if he is able to leave behind him a great asset of wealth for his children, and to achieve this temporary benefit he takes the risk of all sinful activities, without knowledge that such activities will keep him perpetually bound by the shackles of material bondage. Due to this polluted mentality and due to material sins, the aggregate combination of living entities appeared to be bluish. Such an impetus of activity for fruitive result is made possible by the dictation of the external energy of the Lord, *kāla.*

TEXT 13

तस्यार्थसूक्ष्माभिनिविष्टदृष्टे-
रन्तर्गतोऽर्थो रजसा तनीयान् ।
गुणेन कालानुगतेन विद्धः
सूष्यंस्तदाभिद्यत नाभिदेशात् ॥१३॥

tasyārtha-sūkṣmābhiniviṣṭa-dṛṣṭer
antar-gato 'rtho rajasā tanīyān
guṇena kālānugatena viddhaḥ
sūṣyaṁs tadābhidyata nābhi-deśāt

tasya—His; *artha*—subject; *sūkṣma*—subtle; *abhiniviṣṭa-dṛṣṭeḥ*—of one whose attention was fixed; *antaḥ-gataḥ*—internal; *arthaḥ*—purpose; *rajasā*—by the mode of passion of material nature; *tanīyān*—very subtle; *guṇena*—by the qualities; *kāla-anugatena*—in due course of time; *viddhaḥ*—agitated; *sūṣyan*—generating; *tadā*—then; *abhidyata*—pierced through; *nābhi-deśāt*—from the abdomen.

TRANSLATION

The subtle subject matter of creation, on which the Lord's attention was fixed, was agitated by the material mode of passion, and thus the subtle form of creation pierced through His abdomen.

TEXT 14

स पद्मकोशः सहसोदतिष्ठत्
कालेन कर्मप्रतिबोधनेन ।
स्वरोचिषा तत्सलिलं विशालं
विद्योतयन्नर्क इवात्मयोनिः ॥१४॥

sa padma-kośaḥ sahasodatiṣṭhat
kālena karma-pratibodhanena
sva-rociṣā tat salilaṁ viśālaṁ
vidyotayann arka ivātma-yoniḥ

saḥ—that; *padma-kośaḥ*—bud of a lotus flower; *sahasā*—suddenly; *udatiṣṭhat*—appeared; *kālena*—by time; *karma*—fruitive activities; *pratibodhanena*—awakening; *sva-rociṣā*—by its own effulgence; *tat*—that; *salilam*—water of devastation; *viśālam*—vast; *vidyotayan*—illuminating; *arkaḥ*—the sun; *iva*—like; *ātma-yoniḥ*—generating from the Personality of Viṣṇu.

TRANSLATION

Piercing through, this sum total form of the fruitive activity of the living entities took the shape of the bud of a lotus flower generated from the Personality of Viṣṇu, and by His supreme will it illuminated everything, like the sun, and dried up the vast waters of devastation.

TEXT 15

तल्लोकपद्मं स उ एव विष्णुः
प्रावीविशत्सर्वगुणावभासम् ।
तस्मिन् स्वयं वेदमयो विधाता
स्वयम्भुवं यं स्म वदन्ति सोऽभूत् ॥१५॥

tal loka-padmaṁ sa u eva viṣṇuḥ
prāvīviśat sarva-guṇāvabhāsam
tasmin svayaṁ vedamayo vidhātā
svayambhuvaṁ yaṁ sma vadanti so 'bhūt

tat—that; *loka*—universal; *padmam*—lotus flower; *saḥ*—He; *u*—certainly; *eva*—factually; *viṣṇuḥ*—the Lord; *prāvīviśat*—entered into; *sarva*—all; *guṇa-avabhāsam*—reservoir of all modes of nature; *tasmin*—in which; *svayam*—in person; *veda-mayaḥ*—the personality of Vedic wisdom; *vidhātā*—controller of the universe; *svayam-bhuvam*—self-born; *yam*—whom; *sma*—in the past; *vadanti*—do say; *saḥ*—he; *abhūt*—generated.

TRANSLATION

Into that universal lotus flower Lord Viṣṇu personally entered as the Supersoul, and when it was thus impregnated with all the modes of material nature, the personality of Vedic wisdom, whom we call the self-born, was generated.

PURPORT

This lotus flower is the universal *virāṭ* form, or the gigantic form of the Lord in the material world. It becomes amalgamated in the Personality of Godhead Viṣṇu, in His abdomen, at the time of dissolution, and it becomes manifest at the time of creation. This is due to Garbhodakaśāyī Viṣṇu, who enters into each of the universes. In this form is the sum total of all the fruitive activities of the living entities conditioned by material nature, and the first of them, namely Brahmā, or the controller of the universe, is generated from this lotus flower. This first-born living being, unlike all the others, has no material father, and thus he is called self-born, or *svayambhū*. He goes to sleep with Nārāyaṇa at the time of devastation, and when there is another creation, he is born in this way. From this description we have the conception of three—the gross *virāṭ* form, the subtle Hiraṇyagarbha and the material creative force, Brahmā.

TEXT 16

तस्यां स चाम्भोरुहकर्णिकाया-
मवस्थितो लोकमपश्यमानः ।
परिक्रमन् व्योम्नि विवृत्तनेत्र-
श्चत्वारि लेभेऽनुदिशं मुखानि ॥१६॥

tasyāṁ sa cāmbho-ruha-karṇikāyām
avasthito lokam apaśyamānaḥ
parikraman vyomni vivṛtta-netraś
catvāri lebhe 'nudiśaṁ mukhāni

tasyām—in that; *saḥ*—Brahmā; *ca*—and; *ambhaḥ*—water; *ruha-karṇikāyām*—whorl of the lotus; *avasthitaḥ*—being situated; *lokam*—the world; *apaśyamānaḥ*—without being able to see; *parikraman*—circumambulating; *vyomni*—in space; *vivṛtta-netraḥ*—while moving the eyes; *catvāri*—four; *lebhe*—achieved; *anudiśam*—in terms of direction; *mukhāni*—heads.

TRANSLATION

Brahmā, born out of the lotus flower, could not see the world, although he was situated in the whorl. He therefore circumambulated all of space, and while moving his eyes in all directions he achieved four heads in terms of the four directions.

TEXT 17

तस्माद्युगान्तश्वसनावघूर्ण-
जलोर्मिचक्रात्सलिलाद्विरूढम् ।
उपाश्रितः कञ्जमु लोकतत्त्वं
नात्मानमद्धाविददादिदेवः ॥१७॥

tasmād yugānta-śvasanāvaghūrṇa-
jalormi-cakrāt salilād virūḍham
upāśritaḥ kañjam u loka-tattvaṁ
nātmānam addhāvidad ādi-devaḥ

tasmāt—from there; *yuga-anta*—at the end of the millennium; *śvasana*—the air of devastation; *avaghūrṇa*—because of movement; *jala*—water; *ūrmi-cakrāt*—out of the circle of waves; *salilāt*—from the water; *virūḍham*—situated on them; *upāśritaḥ*—having the shelter of; *kañjam*—lotus flower; *u*—in astonishment; *loka-tattvam*—the mystery of creation; *na*—not; *ātmānam*—himself; *addhā*—perfectly; *avidat*—could understand; *ādi-devaḥ*—the first demigod.

TRANSLATION

Lord Brahmā, situated in that lotus, could not perfectly understand the creation, the lotus or himself. At the end of the millennium the air of devastation began to move the water and the lotus in great circular waves.

PURPORT

Lord Brahmā was perplexed about his creation, the lotus and the world, even though he tried to understand them for one millennium, which is beyond calculation in the solar years of human beings. No one, therefore, can know the mystery of the creation and cosmic manifestation simply by mental speculation. The human being is so limited in his capacity that without the help of the Supreme he can hardly understand the mystery of the will of the Lord in terms of creation, continuance and destruction.

TEXT 18

क एष योऽसावहमब्जपृष्ठ
एतत्कुतो वाब्जमनन्यदप्सु ।
अस्ति ह्यधस्तादिह किञ्चनैत-
दधिष्ठितं यत्र सता नु भाव्यम् ॥१८॥

ka eṣa yo 'sāv aham abja-pṛṣṭha
etat kuto vābjam ananyad apsu
asti hy adhastād iha kiñcanaitad
adhiṣṭhitaṁ yatra satā nu bhāvyam

kaḥ—who; *eṣaḥ*—this; *yaḥ asau aham*—that I am; *abja-pṛṣṭhe*—on top of the lotus; *etat*—this; *kutaḥ*—wherefrom; *vā*—either; *abjam*—lotus flower; *ananyat*—otherwise; *apsu*—in the water; *asti*—there is; *hi*—certainly; *adhastāt*—from below; *iha*—in this; *kiñcana*—anything; *etat*—this; *adhiṣṭhitam*—situated; *yatra*—wherein; *satā*—automatically; *nu*—or not; *bhāvyam*—must be.

TRANSLATION

Lord Brahmā, in his ignorance, contemplated: Who am I that am situated on the top of this lotus? Wherefrom has it sprouted? There must be something downwards, and that from which this lotus has grown must be within the water.

PURPORT

The subject matter of the speculations of Brahmā in the beginning regarding the creation of the cosmic manifestation is still a subject matter for mental speculators. The most intelligent man is he who tries to find the cause of his personal existence and that of the whole cosmic creation and thus tries to find the ultimate cause. If his attempt is properly executed with penances and perseverance, it is sure to be crowned with success.

TEXT 19

स इत्थमुद्वीक्ष्य तदब्जनाल-
नाडीभिरन्तर्जलमाविवेश ।
नार्वाग्गतस्तत्खरनालनाल-
नाभिं विचिन्वंस्तदविन्दताजः ॥१९॥

sa ittham udvīkṣya tad-abja-nāla-
nāḍībhir antar-jalam āviveśa
nārvāg-gatas tat-khara-nāla-nāla-
nābhiṁ vicinvaṁs tad avindatājaḥ

saḥ—he (Brahmā); *ittham*—in this way; *udvīkṣya*—contemplating; *tat*—that; *abja*—lotus; *nāla*—stem; *nāḍībhiḥ*—by the pipe; *antaḥ-jalam*—within the water; *āviveśa*—entered into; *na*—not; *arvāk-gataḥ*—in spite of going inside; *tat-khara-nāla*—the stem of the lotus; *nāla*—pipe; *nābhim*—of the navel; *vicinvan*—thinking much of it; *tat*—that; *avindata*—understood; *ajaḥ*—the self-born.

TRANSLATION

Lord Brahmā, thus contemplating, entered the water through the channel of the stem of the lotus. But in spite of entering the stem and going nearer to the navel of Viṣṇu, he could not trace out the root.

PURPORT

By dint of one's personal endeavor one may go nearer to the Lord, but without the Lord's mercy one cannot reach the ultimate point. Such understanding of the Lord is possible only by devotional service, as confirmed in *Bhagavad-gītā* (18.55): *bhaktyā mām abhijānāti yāvān yaś cāsmi tattvataḥ.*

TEXT 20

तमस्यपारे विदुरात्मसर्गं
विचिन्वतोऽभूत्सुमहांस्त्रिणेमिः ।
यो देहभाजां भयमीरयाणः
परिक्षिणोत्यायुरजस्य हेतिः ॥२०॥

tamasy apāre vidurātma-sargaṁ
vicinvato 'bhūt sumahāṁs tri-ṇemiḥ
yo deha-bhājāṁ bhayam īrayāṇaḥ
parikṣiṇoty āyur ajasya hetiḥ

tamasi apāre—because of an ignorant way of searching; *vidura*—O Vidura; *ātma-sargam*—the cause of his creation; *vicinvataḥ*—while contemplating; *abhūt*—it so became; *su-mahān*—very great; *tri-nemiḥ*—time of three dimensions; *yaḥ*—which; *deha-bhājām*—of the embodied; *bhayam*—fearfulness; *īrayāṇaḥ*—generating; *parikṣiṇoti*—diminishing the one hundred years; *āyuḥ*—duration of life; *ajasya*—of the self-born; *hetiḥ*—the wheel of eternal time.

TRANSLATION

O Vidura, while searching in that way about his existence, Brahmā reached his ultimate time, which is the eternal wheel in the hand of Viṣṇu and which generates fear in the mind of the living entity like the fear of death.

TEXT 21

ततो निवृत्तोऽप्रतिलब्धकामः
स्वधिष्ण्यमासाद्य पुनः स देवः ।
शनैर्जितश्वासनिवृत्तचित्तो
न्यषीददारूढसमाधियोगः ॥२१॥

tato nivṛtto 'pratilabdha-kāmaḥ
sva-dhiṣṇyam āsādya punaḥ sa devaḥ
śanair jita-śvāsa-nivṛtta-citto
nyaṣīdad ārūḍha-samādhi-yogaḥ

tataḥ—thereafter; *nivṛttaḥ*—retired from that endeavor; *apratilabdha-kāmaḥ*—without achievement of the desired destination; *sva-dhiṣṇyam*—own seat; *āsādya*—reaching; *punaḥ*—

again; *saḥ*—he; *devaḥ*—the demigod; *śanaiḥ*—without delay; *jita-śvāsa*—controlling the breathing; *nivṛtta*—retired; *cittaḥ*—intelligence; *nyaṣīdat*—sat down; *ārūḍha*—in confidence; *samādhi-yogaḥ*—in meditation on the Lord.

TRANSLATION

Thereafter, being unable to achieve the desired destination, he retired from such searching and came back again to the top of the lotus. Thus, controlling all objectives, he concentrated his mind on the Supreme Lord.

PURPORT

Samādhi involves concentrating the mind upon the supreme cause of all, even if one is unaware of whether His actual nature is personal, impersonal or localized. Concentration of the mind on the Supreme is certainly a form of devotional service. To cease from personal sense endeavors and to concentrate on the supreme cause is a sign of self-surrender, and when self-surrender is present, that is a sure sign of devotional service. Each and every living entity needs to engage in devotional service to the Lord if he wishes to understand the ultimate cause of his existence.

TEXT 22

कालेन सोऽजः पुरुषायुषाभि-
प्रवृत्तयोगेन विरूढबोधः ।
स्वयं तदन्तर्हृदयेऽवभात-
मपश्यतापश्यत यन्न पूर्वम् ॥२२॥

kālena so 'jaḥ puruṣāyuṣābhi-
pravṛtta-yogena virūḍha-bodhaḥ
svayaṁ tad antar-hṛdaye 'vabhātam
apaśyatāpaśyata yan na pūrvam

kālena—in due course of time; *saḥ*—he; *ajaḥ*—the self-born Brahmā; *puruṣa-āyuṣā*—by the duration of his age; *abhipravṛtta*—being engaged; *yogena*—in meditation; *virūḍha*—developed; *bodhaḥ*—intelligence; *svayam*—automatically; *tat antaḥ-hṛdaye*—in the heart; *avabhātam*—manifested; *apaśyata*—saw; *apaśyata*—did see; *yat*—which; *na*—not; *pūrvam*—before.

TRANSLATION

At the end of Brahmā's one hundred years, when his meditation was complete, he developed the required knowledge, and as a result he could see

in his heart the Supreme within himself, whom he could not see before with the greatest endeavor.

PURPORT

The Supreme Lord can be experienced only through the process of devotional service and not by one's personal endeavor in mental speculation. The age of Brahmā is calculated in terms of *divya* years, which are distinct from the solar years of human beings. The *divya* years are calculated in *Bhagavad-gītā* (8.17): *sahasra-yuga-paryantam ahar yad brahmaṇo viduḥ.* Brahmā's one day is equal to one thousand times the aggregate of the four *yugas* (calculated to be 4,300,000 years). On that basis, Brahmā meditated for one hundred years before he could understand the supreme cause of all causes, and then he wrote the *Brahma-saṁhitā,* which is approved and recognized by Lord Caitanya and in which he sings, *govindam ādi-puruṣaṁ tam ahaṁ bhajāmi.* One has to wait for the mercy of the Lord before one can either render service unto Him or know Him as He is.

TEXT 23

मृणालगौरायतशेषभोग-
पर्यङ्क एकं पुरुषं शयानम् ।
फणातपत्रायुतमूर्धरत्न-
द्युभिर्हतध्वान्तयुगान्ततोये ॥२३॥

mṛṇāla-gaurāyata-śeṣa-bhoga-
paryaṅka ekaṁ puruṣaṁ śayānam
phaṇātapatrāyuta-mūrdha-ratna-
dyubhir hata-dhvānta-yugānta-toye

mṛṇāla—lotus flower; *gaura*—white all over; *āyata*—gigantic; *śeṣa-bhoga*—body of Śeṣa-nāga; *paryaṅke*—on the bed; *ekam*—alone; *puruṣam*—the Supreme Person; *śayānam*—was lying; *phaṇa-ātapatra*—umbrella of a serpent hood; *āyuta*—bedecked with; *mūrdha*—head; *ratna*—jewels; *dyubhiḥ*—by the rays; *hata-dhvānta*—darkness dissipated; *yuga-anta*—devastation; *toye*—in the water.

TRANSLATION

Brahmā could see that on the water there was a gigantic lotuslike white bedstead, the body of Śeṣa-nāga, on which the Personality of Godhead was lying alone. The whole atmosphere was illuminated by the rays of the jewels

bedecking the hood of Śeṣa-nāga, and that illumination dissipated all the darkness of those regions.

TEXT 24

प्रेक्षां क्षिपन्तं हरितोपलाद्रेः
सन्ध्याभ्रनीवेरुरुरुक्ममूर्ध्नः ।
रत्नोदधारौषधिसौमनस्य
वनस्रजो वेणुभुजाङ्घ्रिपाङ्घ्रेः ॥२४॥

prekṣāṁ kṣipantaṁ haritopalādreḥ
sandhyābhra-nīver uru-rukma-mūrdhnaḥ
ratnodadhārauṣadhi-saumanasya
vana-srajo veṇu-bhujāṅghripāṅghreḥ

prekṣām—the panorama; *kṣipantam*—deriding; *harita*—green; *upala*—coral; *adreḥ*—of the hell; *sandhyā-abhra-nīveḥ*—of the dress of the evening sky; *uru*—great; *rukma*—gold; *mūrdhnaḥ*—on the summit; *ratna*—jewels; *udadhāra*—waterfalls; *auṣadhi*—herbs; *saumanasya*—of the scenery; *vana-srajaḥ*—flower garland; *veṇu*—dress; *bhuja*—hands; *aṅghripa*—trees; *aṅghreḥ*—legs.

TRANSLATION

The luster of the transcendental body of the Lord mocked the beauty of the coral mountain. The coral mountain is very beautifully dressed by the evening sky, but the yellow dress of the Lord mocked its beauty. There is gold on the summit of the mountain, but the Lord's helmet, bedecked with jewels, mocked it. The mountain's waterfalls, herbs, etc., with a panorama of flowers, seem like garlands, but the Lord's gigantic body, and His hands and legs, decorated with jewels, pearls, tulasī leaves and flower garlands, mocked the scene on the mountain.

PURPORT

The panoramic beauty of nature, which strikes one with wonder, may be taken as a perverted reflection of the transcendental body of the Lord. One who is therefore attracted by the beauty of the Lord is no longer attracted by the beauty of material nature, although he does not minimize its beauty. In *Bhagavad-gītā* (2.59) it is described that one who is attracted by *param*, the Supreme, is no longer attracted by anything inferior.

TEXT 25

आयामतो विस्तरतः स्वमान-
देहेन लोकत्रयसङ्ग्रहेण ।
विचित्रदिव्याभरणांशुकानां
कृतश्रियापाश्रितवेषदेहम् ॥२५॥

āyāmato vistarataḥ sva-māna-
dehena loka-traya-saṅgraheṇa
vicitra-divyābharaṇāṁśukānāṁ
kṛta-śriyāpāśrita-veṣa-deham

āyāmataḥ—by length; *vistarataḥ*—by breadth; *sva-māna*—by His own measurement; *dehena*—by the transcendental body; *loka-traya*—the three (upper, middle and lower) planetary systems; *saṅgraheṇa*—by total absorption; *vicitra*—variegated; *divya*—transcendental; *ābharaṇa-aṁśukānām*—rays of the ornaments; *kṛta-śriyā apāśrita*—beauty created by those dresses and ornaments; *veṣa*—dressed; *deham*—transcendental body.

TRANSLATION

His transcendental body, unlimited in length and breadth, occupied the three planetary systems, upper, middle and lower. His body was self-illuminated by unparalleled dress and variegatedness and was properly ornamented.

PURPORT

The length and breadth of the transcendental body of the Supreme Personality of Godhead could only be measured by His own measurement because He is all-pervading throughout the complete cosmic manifestation. The beauty of material nature is due to His personal beauty, yet He is always magnificently dressed and ornamented to prove His transcendental variegatedness, which is so important in the advancement of spiritual knowledge.

TEXT 26

पुंसां स्वकामाय विविक्तमार्गै-
रभ्यर्चतां कामदुघाङ्घ्रिपद्मम् ।
प्रदर्शयन्तं कृपया नखेन्दु-
मयूखभिन्नाङ्गुलिचारुपत्रम् ॥२६॥

puṁsāṁ sva-kāmāya vivikta-mārgair
abhyarcatāṁ kāma-dughāṅghri-padmam
pradarśayantaṁ kṛpayā nakhendu-
mayūkha-bhinnāṅguli-cāru-patram

puṁsām—of the human being; *sva-kāmāya*—according to the desire; *vivikta-mārgaiḥ*—by the path of devotional service; *abhyarcatām*—worshiped; *kāma-dugha-aṅghri-padmam*—the lotus feet of the Lord, which can award all desired fruits; *pradarśayantam*—while showing them; *kṛpayā*—by causeless mercy; *nakha*—nails; *indu*—moonlike; *mayūkha*—rays; *bhinna*—divided; *aṅguli*—figures; *cāru-patram*—very beautiful.

TRANSLATION

The Lord showed His lotus feet by raising them. His lotus feet are the source of all awards achieved by devotional service free from material contamination. Such awards are for those who worship Him in pure devotion. The splendor of the transcendental rays from His moonlike toenails and fingernails appeared like the petals of a flower.

PURPORT

The Lord fulfills the desires of everyone just as one desires. Pure devotees are interested in achieving the transcendental service of the Lord, which is nondifferent from Him. Therefore, the Lord is the only desire of the pure devotees, and devotional service is the only spotless process for achieving His favor. Śrīla Rūpa Gosvāmī says in his *Bhakti-rasāmṛta-sindhu* (1.1.11) that pure devotional service is *jñāna-karmādy-anāvṛtam:* pure devotional service is without any tinge of speculative knowledge and fruitive activities. Such devotional service is able to award the pure devotee the highest result, namely direct association with the Supreme Personality of Godhead, Lord Kṛṣṇa. According to the *Gopāla-tāpanī Upaniṣad,* the Lord showed one of the many thousands of petals of His lotus feet. It is said: *brāhmaṇo'sāv anavaratam me dhyātaḥ stutaḥ parārdhānte so 'budhyata gopa-veśo me purastāt āvirbabhūva.* After penetrating for millions of years, Lord Brahmā could understand the transcendental form of the Lord as Śrī Kṛṣṇa, in the dress of a cowherd boy, and thus he recorded his experience in the *Brahma-saṁhitā* in the famous prayer, *govindam ādi-puruṣaṁ tam ahaṁ bhajāmi.*

TEXT 27

मुखेन लोकार्तिहरस्मितेन
परिस्फुरत्कुण्डलमण्डितेन ।

शोणायितेनाधरबिम्बभासा
प्रत्यर्हयन्तं सुनसेन सुभ्र्वा ॥२७॥

mukhena lokārti-hara-smitena
parisphurat-kuṇḍala-maṇḍitena
śoṇāyitenādhara-bimba-bhāsā
pratyarhayantaṁ sunasena subhrvā

mukhena—by a gesture of the face; *loka-ārti-hara*—vanquisher of the distress of the devotees; *smitena*—by smiling; *parisphurat*—dazzling; *kuṇḍala*—earrings; *maṇḍitena*—decorated with; *śoṇāyitena*—acknowledging; *adhara*—of His lips; *bimba*—reflection; *bhāsā*—rays; *pratyarhayantam*—reciprocating; *su-nasena*—by His pleasing nose; *su-bhrvā*—and pleasing eyebrows.

TRANSLATION

He also acknowledged the service of the devotees and vanquished their distress by His beautiful smile. The reflection of His face, decorated with earrings, was so pleasing because it dazzled with the rays from His lips and the beauty of His nose and eyebrows.

PURPORT

Devotional service to the Lord is very much obliging to Him. There are many transcendentalists in different fields of spiritual activities, but devotional service to the Lord is unique. Devotees do not ask anything from the Lord in exchange for their service. Even the most desirable liberation is refused by devotees, although offered by the Lord. Thus the Lord becomes a kind of debtor to the devotees, and He can only try to repay the devotees' service with His ever-enchanting smile. The devotees are ever satisfied by the smiling face of the Lord, and they become enlivened. And by seeing the devotees so enlivened, the Lord Himself is further satisfied. So there is continuous transcendental competition between the Lord and His devotees by such reciprocation of service and acknowledgment.

TEXT 28

कदम्बकिञ्जल्कपिशङ्गवाससा
स्वलङ्कृतं मेखलया नितम्बे ।
हारेण चानन्तधनेन वत्स
श्रीवत्सवक्षःस्थलवल्लभेन ॥२८॥

kadamba-kiñjalka-piśaṅga-vāsasā
svalaṅkṛtaṁ mekhalayā nitambe
hāreṇa cānanta-dhanena vatsa
śrīvatsa-vakṣaḥ-sthala-vallabhena

kadamba-kiñjalka—saffron dust of the *kadamba* flower; *piśaṅga*—dress of the color; *vāsasā*—by clothing; *su-alaṅkṛtam*—well decorated; *mekhalayā*—by the belt; *nitambe*—on the waist; *hāreṇa*—by the garland; *ca*—also; *ananta*—highly; *dhanena*—valuable; *vatsa*—my dear Vidura; *śrīvatsa*—of the transcendental marking; *vakṣaḥ-sthala*—on the chest; *vallabhena*—very pleasing.

TRANSLATION

O my dear Vidura, the Lord's waist was covered with yellow cloth resembling the saffron dust of the kadamba flower, and it was encircled by a well-decorated belt. His chest was decorated with the śrīvatsa marking and a necklace of unlimited value.

TEXT 29

परार्ध्यकेयूरमणिप्रवेक-
पर्यस्तदोर्दण्डसहस्रशाखम् ।
अव्यक्तमूलं भुवनाङ्घ्रिपेन्द्र-
महीन्द्रभोगैरधिवीतवल्शम् ॥२९॥

parārdhya-keyūra-maṇi-praveka-
paryasta-dordaṇḍa-sahasra-śākham
avyakta-mūlaṁ bhuvanāṅghripendram
ahīndra-bhogair adhivīta-valśam

parārdhya—very valuable; *keyūra*—ornaments; *maṇi-praveka*—highly valuable jewels; *paryasta*—disseminating; *dordaṇḍa*—arms; *sahasra-śākham*—with thousands of branches; *avyakta-mūlam*—self-situated; *bhuvana*—universal; *aṅghripa*—trees; *indram*—the Lord; *ahi-indra*—Anantadeva; *bhogaiḥ*—by hoods; *adhivīta*—surrounded; *valśam*—shoulders.

TRANSLATION

As a sandalwood tree is decorated with fragrant flowers and branches, the Lord's body was decorated with valuable jewels and pearls. He was the self-situated tree, the Lord of all others in the universe. And as a sandalwood tree is covered with many snakes, so the Lord's body was also covered by the hoods of Ananta.

PURPORT

The word *avyakta-mūlam* is significant here. Generally, no one can see the roots of a tree. But as far as the Lord is concerned, He is the root of Himself because there is no other separate cause of His standing but He Himself. In the *Vedas* it is said that the Lord is *svāśrayāśraya*; He is His own support, and there is no other support for Him. Therefore, *avyakta* means the Supreme Lord Himself and no one else.

TEXT 30

चराचरौको भगवन्महीध्र-
महीन्द्रबन्धुं सलिलोपगूढम् ।
किरीटसाहस्रहिरण्यशृङ्गा-
माविर्भवत्कौस्तुभरत्नगर्भम् ॥३०॥

carācarauko bhagavan-mahīdhram
ahīndra-bandhuṁ salilopagūḍham
kirīṭa-sāhasra-hiraṇya-śṛṅgam
āvirbhavat kaustubha-ratna-garbham

cara—moving animals; *acara*—nonmoving trees; *okaḥ*—the place or situation; *bhagavat*—the Personality of Godhead; *mahīdhram*—the mountain; *ahi-indra*—Śrī Anantadeva; *bandhum*—friend; *salila*—water; *upagūḍham*—submerged; *kirīṭa*—helmets; *sāhasra*—thousands; *hiraṇya*—gold; *śṛṅgam*—peaks; *āvirbhavat*—manifested; *kaustubha*—the Kaustubha jewel; *ratna-garbham*—ocean.

TRANSLATION

Like a great mountain, the Lord stands as the abode for all moving and nonmoving living entities. He is the friend of the snakes because Lord Ananta is His friend. As a mountain has thousands of golden peaks, so the Lord was seen with the thousands of golden-helmeted hoods of Ananta-nāga; and as a mountain is sometimes filled with jewels, so also His transcendental body was fully decorated with valuable jewels. As a mountains is sometimes submerged in the ocean water, so the Lord is sometimes submerged in the water of devastation.

TEXT 31

निवीतमाम्नायमधुव्रतश्रिया
स्वकीर्तिमय्या वनमालया हरिम् ।

सूर्येन्दुवाय्वग्न्यगमं त्रिधामभिः
परिक्रमत्प्राधनिकैर्दुरासदम् ॥३१॥

nivītam āmnāya-madhu-vrata-śriyā
sva-kīrti-mayyā vana-mālayā harim
sūryendu-vāyv-agny-agamaṁ tri-dhāmabhiḥ
parikramat-prādhanikair durāsadam

nivītam—so being enclosed; *āmnāya*—Vedic wisdom; *madhu-vrata-śriyā*—sweet sound in beauty; *sva-kīrti-mayyā*—by His own glories; *vana-mālayā*—flower garland; *harim*—unto the Lord; *sūrya*—the sun; *indu*—the moon; *vāyu*—the air; *agni*—the fire; *agamam*—unapproachable; *tri-dhāmabhiḥ*—by the three planetary systems; *parikramat*—circumambulating; *prādhanikaiḥ*—for fighting; *durāsadam*—very difficult to reach.

TRANSLATION

Lord Brahmā, thus looking upon the Lord in the shape of a mountain, concluded that He was Hari, the Personality of Godhead. He saw that the garland of flowers on His chest glorified Him with Vedic wisdom in sweet songs and looked very beautiful. He was protected by the Sudarśana wheel for fighting, and even the sun, moon, air, fire, etc., could not have access to Him.

TEXT 32

तर्ह्येव तन्नाभिसरःसरोज-
मात्मानमम्भः श्वसनं वियच्च ।
ददर्श देवो जगतो विधाता
नातः परं लोकविसर्गदृष्टिः ॥३२॥

tarhy eva tan-nābhi-saraḥ-sarojam
ātmānam ambhaḥ śvasanaṁ viyac ca
dadarśa devo jagato vidhātā
nātaḥ paraṁ loka-visarga-dṛṣṭiḥ

tarhi—therefore; *eva*—certainly; *tat*—His; *nābhi*—navel; *saraḥ*—lake; *sarojam*—lotus flower; *ātmānam*—Brahmā; *ambhaḥ*—the devastating water; *śvasanam*—the drying air; *viyat*—the sky; *ca*—also; *dadarśa*—looked upon; *devaḥ*—demigod; *jagataḥ*—of the universe; *vidhātā*—maker of the destination; *na*—not; *ataḥ param*—beyond; *loka-visarga*—creation of the cosmic manifestation; *dṛṣṭiḥ*—glance.

TRANSLATION

When Lord Brahmā, the maker of the universal destination, thus saw the Lord, he simultaneously glanced over creation. Lord Brahmā saw the lake in Lord Viṣṇu's navel, and the lotus flower, as well as the devastating water, the drying air and the sky. All became visible to him.

TEXT 33

स कर्मबीजं रजसोपरक्तः
प्रजाः सिसृक्षन्नियदेव दृष्ट्वा ।
अस्तौद्विसर्गाभिमुखस्तमीड्य-
मव्यक्तवर्त्मन्यभिवेशितात्मा ॥३३॥

sa karma-bījaṁ rajasoparaktaḥ
prajāḥ sisṛkṣann iyad eva dṛṣṭvā
astaud visargābhimukhas tam īḍyam
avyakta-vartmany abhiveśitātmā

saḥ—he (Brahmā); *karma-bījam*—seed of worldly activities; *rajasā uparaktaḥ*—initiated by the mode of passion; *prajāḥ*—living entities; *sisṛkṣan*—willing to create progeny; *iyat*—all the five causes of creation; *eva*—thus; *dṛṣṭvā*—looking on; *astaut*—prayed for; *visarga*—creation after the creation by the Lord; *abhimukhaḥ*—towards; *tam*—that; *īḍyam*—worshipable; *avyakta*—transcendental; *vartmani*—on the path of; *abhiveśita*—fixed; *ātmā*—mind.

TRANSLATION

Lord Brahmā, thus being surcharged with the mode of passion, became inclined to create, and after seeing the five causes of creation indicated by the Personality of Godhead, he began to offer his respectful prayers on the path of the creative mentality.

PURPORT

Even if one is in the material mode of passion, to create something in the world he has to take shelter of the Supreme for the necessary energy. That is the path of the successful termination of any attempt.

Thus end the Bhaktivedanta purports of the Third Canto, Eighth Chapter, of the Śrīmad-Bhāgavatam, *entitled "Manifestation of Brahmā from Garbhodakaśāyī Viṣṇu."*

CHAPTER NINE

Brahmā's Prayers for Creative Energy

TEXT 1

ब्रह्मोवाच
ज्ञातोऽसि मेऽद्य सुचिरान्ननु देहभाजां
न ज्ञायते भगवतो गतिरित्यवद्यम् ।
नान्यत्त्वदस्ति भगवन्नपि तन्न शुद्धं
मायागुणव्यतिकराद्यदुरुर्विभासि ॥ १ ॥

brahmovāca
jñāto 'si me 'dya sucirān nanu deha-bhājāṁ
na jñāyate bhagavato gatir ity avadyam
nānyat tvad asti bhagavann api tan na śuddhaṁ
māyā-guṇa-vyatikarād yad urur vibhāsi

brahmā uvāca—Lord Brahmā said; *jñātaḥ*—known; *asi*—You are; *me*—by me; *adya*—today; *sucirāt*—after a long time; *nanu*—but; *deha-bhājām*—of one who has a material body; *na*—not; *jñāyate*—is known; *bhagavataḥ*—of the Personality of Godhead; *gatiḥ*—course; *iti*—so it is; *avadyam*—great offense; *na anyat*—none beyond; *tvat*—You; *asti*—there is; *bhagavan*—O my Lord; *api*—even though there is; *tat*—anything that may be; *na*—never; *śuddham*—absolute; *māyā*—material energy; *guṇa-vyatikarāt*—because of the mixture of the modes of; *yat*—to which; *uruḥ* transcendental; *vibhāsi*—You are.

TRANSLATION

Lord Brahmā said: O my Lord, today, after many, many years of penance, I have come to know about You. Oh, how unfortunate the embodied living entities are that they are unable to know Your personality! My Lord, You are the only knowable object because there is nothing supreme beyond You. If there is anything supposedly superior to You, it is not the Absolute. You exist as the Supreme by exhibiting the creative energy of matter.

PURPORT

The highest peak of the ignorance of the living entities who are conditioned by material bodies is that they are unaware of the supreme cause of the cosmic manifestation. Different people have different theories regarding the supreme cause, but none of them are genuine. The only supreme cause is Viṣṇu, and the intervening impediment is the illusory energy of the Lord. The Lord has employed His wonderful material energy in manifesting many, many wonderful distractions in the material world, and the conditioned souls, illusioned by the same energy, are thus unable to know the supreme cause. The most stalwart scientists and philosophers, therefore, cannot be accepted as wonderful. They only appear wonderful because they are instruments in the hands of the illusory energy of the Lord. Under illusion, the general mass of people deny the existence of the Supreme Lord and accept the foolish products of illusory energy as supreme.

One can know the supreme cause, the Personality of Godhead, by the causeless mercy of the Lord, which is bestowed upon the Lord's pure devotees like Brahmā and those in his disciplic succession. By acts of penance only was Lord Brahmā able to see the Garbhodakaśāyī Viṣṇu, and by realization only could he understand the Lord as He is. Brahmā was extremely satisfied upon observing the magnificent beauty and opulence of the Lord, and he admitted that nothing can be comparable to Him. Only by penance can one appreciate the beauty and opulence of the Lord, and when one is acquainted with that beauty and opulence, he is no longer attracted by any other. This is confirmed in *Bhagavad-gītā* (2.59): *paraṁ dṛṣṭvā nivartate.*

Foolish human beings who do not endeavor to investigate the supreme beauty and opulence of the Lord are here condemned by Brahmā. It is imperative that every human being try for such knowledge, and if anyone does not do so, his life is spoiled. Anything that is beautiful and opulent in the material sense is enjoyed by those living entities who are like crows. Crows always engage in picking at rejected garbage, whereas the white ducks do not mix with the crows. Rather, they take pleasure in transparent lakes with lotus flowers, surrounded by beautiful orchards. Both crows and ducks are undoubtedly birds by birth, but they are not of the same feather.

TEXT 2

रूपं यदेतदवबोधरसोदयेन
शश्वन्निवृत्ततमसः सदनुग्रहाय ।
आदौ गृहीतमवतारशतैकबीजं
यन्नाभिपद्मभवनादहमाविरासम् ॥ २ ॥

rūpaṁ yad etad avabodha-rasodayena
śaśvan-nivṛtta-tamasaḥ sad-anugrahāya

ādau gṛhītam avatāra-śataika-bījaṁ
yan-nābhi-padma-bhavanād aham āvirāsam

rūpam—form; *yat*—which; *etat*—that; *avabodha-rasa*—of Your internal potency; *udayena*—with the manifestation; *śaśvat*—forever; *nivṛtta*—freed from; *tamasaḥ*—material contamination; *sat-anugrahāya*—for the sake of the devotees; *ādau*—original in the creative energy of matter; *gṛhītam*—accepted; *avatāra*—of incarnations; *śata-eka-bījam*—the root cause of hundreds; *yat*—that which; *nābhi-padma*—the navel lotus flower; *bhavanāt*—from the home; *aham*—myself; *āvirāsam*—generated.

TRANSLATION

The form which I see is eternally freed from material contamination and has advented to show mercy to the devotees as a manifestation of internal potency. This incarnation is the origin of many other incarnations, and I am born from the lotus flower grown from Your navel home.

PURPORT

The three deities Brahmā, Viṣṇu and Maheśvara (Śiva), the executive heads of the three modes of material nature (passion, goodness and ignorance), are all generated from Garbhodakaśāyī Viṣṇu, who is described herein by Brahmā. From the Kṣīrodakaśāyī Viṣṇu, many Viṣṇu incarnations expand at different ages in the duration of the cosmic manifestation. They are expanded only for the transcendental happiness of the pure devotees. The incarnations of Viṣṇu, who appear at different ages and times, are never to be compared to the conditioned souls. The *viṣṇu-tattvas* are not to be compared to deities like Brahmā and Śiva, nor are they on the same level. Anyone who compares them is called a *pāṣaṇḍī*, or infidel. *Tamasaḥ*, mentioned herein, is the material nature, and the spiritual nature has a completely separate existence from *tamaḥ*. Therefore, spiritual nature is called *avabodha-rasa*, or *avarodha-rasa*. *Avarodha* means "that which completely nullifies." In the Transcendence there is no chance of material contact by any means. Brahmā is the first living being, and therefore he mentions his birth from the lotus flower generated from the abdomen of Garbhodakaśāyī Viṣṇu.

TEXT 3

नातः परं परम यद्भवतः स्वरूप-
मानन्दमात्रमविकल्पमविद्धवर्चः ।
पश्यामि विश्वसृजमेकमविश्वमात्मन्
भूतेन्द्रियात्मकमदस्त उपाश्रितोऽस्मि ॥३॥

nātaḥ paraṁ parama yad bhavataḥ svarūpam
ānanda-mātram avikalpam aviddha-varcaḥ
paśyāmi viśva-sṛjam ekam aviśvam ātman
bhūtendriyātmaka-madas ta upāśrito 'smi

na—do not; *ataḥ param*—hereafter; *parama*—O Supreme; *yat*—that which; *bhavataḥ*—of Your Lordship; *svarūpam*—eternal form; *ānanda-mātram*—impersonal Brahman effulgence; *avikalpam*—without changes; *aviddha-varcaḥ*—without deterioration of potency; *paśyāmi*—do I see; *viśva-sṛjam*—creator of the cosmic manifestation; *ekam*—one without a second; *aviśvam*—and yet not of matter; *ātman*—O Supreme Cause; *bhūta*—body; *indriya*—senses; *ātmaka*—on such identification; *madaḥ*—pride; *te*—unto You; *upāśritaḥ*—surrendered; *asmi*—I am.

TRANSLATION

O my Lord, I do not see a form superior to Your present form of eternal bliss and knowledge. In Your impersonal Brahman effulgence in the spiritual sky, there is no occasional change and no deterioration of internal potency. I surrender unto You because whereas I am proud of my material body and senses, Your Lordship is the cause of the cosmic manifestation and yet You are untouched by matter.

PURPORT

As stated in *Bhagavad-gītā* (18.55), *bhaktyā mām abhijānāti yāvān yaś cāsmi tattvatah:* the Supreme Personality of Godhead can only be partially known, and only by the process of devotional service to the Lord. Lord Brahmā became aware that the Supreme Lord Kṛṣṇa has many, many eternal, blissful forms of knowledge. He has described such expansions of the Supreme Lord, Govinda, in his *Brahma-saṁhitā* (5.33), as follows:

advaitam acyutam anādim ananta-rūpam
ādyaṁ purāṇa-puruṣaṁ nava-yauvanaṁ ca
vedeṣu durlabham adurlabham ātma-bhaktau
govindam ādi-puruṣaṁ tam ahaṁ bhajāmi

"I worship Govinda, the primeval Lord, who is nondual and infallible. He is the original cause of all causes, even though He expands in many, many forms. Although He is the oldest personality, He is ever youthful, unaffected by old age. The Supreme Personality of Godhead cannot be known by the academic wisdom of the *Vedas*; one has to approach the devotee of the Lord to understand Him."

The only way to understand the Lord as He is, is by devotional service to the Lord, or by approaching the devotee of the Lord who always has the Lord in his heart. By devotional perfection one can understand that the impersonal *brahmajyoti* is only a partial representation of the Supreme Personality of Godhead, Lord Kṛṣṇa, and that the three *puruṣa* expansions in the material creation are His plenary portions. In the spiritual sky of the *brahmajyoti* there is no change of various *kalpas* or millenniums, and there are no creative activities in the Vaikuṇṭha worlds. The influence of time is conspicuous by its absence. The rays of the transcendental body of the Lord, the unlimited *brahmajyoti,* are undeterred by the influence of material energy. In the material world also, the initial creator is the Lord Himself. He brings about the creation of Brahmā, who becomes the subsequent creator, empowered by the Lord.

TEXT 4

तद्वा इदं भुवनमङ्गल मङ्गलाय
ध्याने स्म नो दर्शितं त उपासकानाम् ।
तस्मै नमो भगवतेऽनुविधेम तुभ्यं
योऽनादृतो नरकभाग्भिरसत्प्रसङ्गैः ॥ ४ ॥

tad vā idaṁ bhuvana-maṅgala maṅgalāya
dhyāne sma no darśitaṁ ta upāsakānām
tasmai namo bhagavate 'nuvidhema tubhyaṁ
yo 'nādṛto naraka-bhāgbhir asat-prasaṅgaiḥ

tat—the Supreme Personality of Godhead, Śrī Kṛṣṇa; *vā*—or; *idam*—this present form; *bhuvana-maṅgala*—O You who are all-auspicious for all the universes; *maṅgalāya*—for the sake of all prosperity; *dhyāne*—in meditation; *sma*—as it were; *naḥ*—unto us; *darśitam*—manifested; *te*—Your; *upāsakānām*—of the devotees; *tasmai*—unto Him; *namaḥ*—my respectful obeisances; *bhagavate*—unto the Personality of Godhead; *anuvidhema*—I perform; *tubhyam*—unto You; *yaḥ*—which; *anādṛtaḥ*—is neglected; *naraka-bhāgbhiḥ*—by persons destined for hell; *asat-prasaṅgaiḥ*—by material topics.

TRANSLATION

This present form, or any transcendental form expanded by the Supreme Personality of Godhead, Śrī Kṛṣṇa, is equally auspicious for all the universes. Since You have manifested this eternal personal form upon whom Your devotees meditate, I therefore offer my respectful obeisances unto You. Those

who are destined to be dispatched to the path of hell neglect Your personal form because of speculating on material topics.

PURPORT

Regarding the personal and impersonal features of the Supreme Absolute Truth, the personal forms exhibited by the Lord in His different plenary expansions are all for the benediction of all the universes. The personal form of the Lord is also worshiped in meditation as Supersoul, Paramātmā, but the impersonal *brahmajyoti* is not worshiped. Persons who are addicted to the impersonal feature of the Lord, whether in meditation or otherwise, are all pilgrims to hell because, as stated in *Bhagavad-gītā* (12.5), impersonalists simply waste their time in mundane mental speculation because they are addicted more to false arguments than to reality. Therefore, the association of the impersonalists is condemned herewith by Brahmā.

All the plenary expansions of the Personality of Godhead are equally potent, as confirmed in the *Brahma-saṁhitā* (5.46):

dīpārcir eva hi daśāntaram abhyupetya
dīpāyate vivṛta-hetu-samāna-dharmā
yas tādṛg eva hi ca viṣṇutayā vibhāti
govindam ādi-puruṣaṁ tam ahaṁ bhajāmi

The Lord expands Himself as the flames of a fire expand one after another. Although the original flame, or Śrī Kṛṣṇa, is accepted as Govinda, the Supreme Person, all other expansions, such as Rāma, Nṛsiṁha and Varāha, are as potent as the original Lord. All such expanded forms are transcendental. In the beginning of *Śrīmad-Bhāgavatam* it is made clear that the Supreme Truth is eternally uncontaminated by material touch. There is no jugglery of words and activities in the transcendental kingdom of the Lord. All the Lord's forms are transcendental, and such manifestations are ever identical. The particular form of the Lord exhibited to a devotee is not mundane, even though the devotee may retain material desire, nor is it manifest under the influence of material energy, as is foolishly considered by the impersonalists. Impersonalists who consider the transcendental forms of the Lord to be products of the material world are surely destined for hell.

TEXT 5

ये तु त्वदीयचरणाम्बुजकोशगन्धं
जिघ्रन्ति कर्णविवरैः श्रुतिवातनीतम् ।

भक्त्या गृहीतचरणः परया च तेषां
नापैषि नाथ हृदयाम्बुरुहात्स्वपुंसाम् ॥५॥

ye tu tvadīya-caraṇāmbuja-kośa-gandhaṁ
jighranti karṇa-vivaraiḥ śruti-vāta-nītam
bhaktyā gṛhīta-caraṇaḥ parayā ca teṣāṁ
nāpaiṣi nātha hṛdayāmburuhāt sva-puṁsām

ye—those who; *tu*—but; *tvadīya*—Your; *caraṇa-ambuja*—lotus feet; *kośa*—inside; *gandham*—flavor; *jighranti*—smell; *karṇa-vivaraiḥ*—through the channel of the ears; *śruti-vāta-nītam*—carried by the air of Vedic sound; *bhaktyā*—by devotional service; *gṛhīta-caraṇaḥ*—accepting the lotus feet; *parayā*—transcendental; *ca*—also; *teṣām*—for them; *na*—never; *apaiṣi*—separate; *nātha*—O my Lord; *hṛdaya*—heart; *ambu-ruhāt*—from the lotus of; *sva-puṁsām*—of Your own devotees.

TRANSLATION

O my Lord, persons who smell the aroma of Your lotus feet, carried by the air of Vedic sound through the holes of the ears, accept Your devotional service. For them You are never separated from the lotus of their hearts.

PURPORT

For the pure devotee of the Lord there is nothing beyond the lotus feet of the Lord, and the Lord knows that such devotees do not wish anything more than that. The word *tu* specifically establishes this fact. The Lord also does not wish to be separated from the lotus hearts of those pure devotees. That is the transcendental relationship between the pure devotees and the Personality of Godhead. Because the Lord does not wish to separate Himself from the hearts of such pure devotees, it is understood that they are specifically dearer than the impersonalists. The relationship of the pure devotees with the Lord develops because of devotional service to the Lord on the authentic basis of Vedic authority. Such pure devotees are not mundane sentimentalists, but are factually realists because their activities are supported by the Vedic authorities who have given aural reception to the facts mentioned in the Vedic literatures.

The word *parayā* is very significant. *Parā bhakti,* or spontaneous love of God, is the basis of an intimate relationship with the Lord. This highest stage of relationship with the Lord can be attained simply by hearing about Him (His name, form, quality, etc.) from authentic sources like *Bhagavad-gītā* and *Śrīmad-Bhāgavatam,* recited by pure, unalloyed devotees of the Lord.

TEXT 6

तावद्भयं द्रविणदेहसुहृन्निमित्तं
शोकः स्पृहा परिभवो विपुलश्च लोभः ।
तावन्ममेत्यसदवग्रह आर्तिमूलं
यावन्न तेऽङ्घ्रिमभयं प्रवृणीत लोकः ॥६॥

tāvad bhayaṁ draviṇa-deha-suhṛn-nimittaṁ
śokaḥ spṛhā paribhavo vipulaś ca lobhaḥ
tāvan mamety asad-avagraha ārti-mūlaṁ
yāvan na te 'ṅghrim abhayaṁ pravṛṇīta lokaḥ

tāvat—until then; *bhayam*—fear; *draviṇa*—wealth; *deha*—body; *suhṛt*—relatives; *nimittam*—for the matter of; *śokaḥ*—lamentation; *spṛhā*—desire; *paribhavaḥ*—paraphernalia; *vipulaḥ*—very great; *ca*—also; *lobhaḥ*—avarice; *tāvat*—up to that time; *mama*—mine; *iti*—thus; *asat*—perishable; *avagrahaḥ*—undertaking; *ārti-mūlam*—full of anxieties; *yāvat*—as long as; *na*—do not; *te*—Your; *aṅghrim abhayam*—safe lotus feet; *pravṛṇīta*—take shelter; *lokaḥ*—the people of the world.

TRANSLATION

O my Lord, the people of the world are embarrassed by all material anxieties—they are always afraid. They always try to protect wealth, body and friends, they are filled with lamentation and unlawful desires and paraphernalia, and they avariciously base their undertakings on the perishable conceptions of "my" and "mine." As long as they do not take shelter of Your safe lotus feet, they are full of such anxieties.

PURPORT

One may question how one can always think of the Lord in regard to His name, fame, quality, etc., if one is embarrassed by thoughts of family affairs. Everyone in the material world is full of thoughts about how to maintain his family, how to protect his wealth, how to keep pace with friends and relatives, etc. Thus he is always in fear and lamentation, trying to keep up with the status quo. In answer to this question, this verse spoken by Brahmā is very appropriate.

A pure devotee of the Lord never thinks of himself as the proprietor of his home. He surrenders everything unto the supreme control of the Lord, and thus he has no fear for maintaining his family or protecting the interests of his family. Because of this surrender, he no longer has any attraction for wealth. Even if there is attraction for wealth, it is not for sense enjoyment, but for the service of the Lord. A pure devotee may be attracted to accumulating wealth just like an ordinary man, but the difference is that a devotee acquires money for the service of the Lord, whereas the ordinary man acquires money for his sense enjoyment. Thus the acquisition of wealth by a devotee is not a source of anxieties, as is the case for a worldly man. And because a pure devotee accepts everything in the sense of serving the Lord, the poisonous teeth of accumulation of wealth are extracted. If a snake has its poison removed and bites a man, there is no fatal effect. Similarly, wealth accumulated in the cause of the Lord has no poisonous teeth, and the effect is not fatal. A pure devotee is never entangled in material worldly affairs even though he may remain in the world like an ordinary man.

TEXT 7

दैवेन ते हतधियो भवतः प्रसङ्गा-
त्सर्वाशुभोपशमनाद्विमुखेन्द्रिया ये ।
कुर्वन्ति कामसुखलेशलवाय दीना
लोभाभिभूतमनसोऽकुशलानि शश्वत् ॥७॥

daivena te hata-dhiyo bhavataḥ prasaṅgāt
sarvāśubhopaśamanād vimukhendriya ye
kurvanti kāma-sukha-leśa-lavāya dīnā
lobhābhibhūta-manaso 'kuśalāni śaśvat

daivena—by fate of misfortune; *te*—they; *hata-dhiyaḥ*—bereft of memory; *bhavataḥ*—of You; *prasaṅgāt*—from the topics; *sarva*—all; *aśubha*—inauspiciousness; *upaśamanāt*—curbing down; *vimukha*—turned against; *indriyāḥ*—senses; *ye*—those; *kurvanti*—act; *kāma*—sense gratification; *sukha*—happiness; *leśa*—brief; *lavāya*—for a moment only; *dīnāḥ*—poor fellows; *lobha-abhibhūta*—overwhelmed by greed; *manasaḥ*—of one whose mind; *akuśalāni*—inauspicious activities; *śaśvat*—always.

TRANSLATION

O my Lord, persons who are bereft of the all-auspicious performance of chanting and hearing about Your transcendental activities are certainly unfortunate and are also bereft of good sense. They engage in inauspicious activities, enjoying sense gratification for a very little while.

PURPORT

The next question is why people are against such auspicious activities as chanting and hearing the glories and pastimes of the Lord, which can bring total freedom from the cares and anxieties of material existence. The only answer to this question is that they are unfortunate because of supernatural control due to their offensive activities performed simply for the sake of sense gratification. The Lord's pure devotees, however, take compassion upon such unfortunate persons and, in a missionary spirit, try to persuade them into the line of devotional service. Only by the grace of pure devotees can such unfortunate men be elevated to the position of transcendental service.

TEXT 8

क्षुत्तृट्त्रिधातुभिरिमा मुहुरर्द्यमानाः
शीतोष्णवातवरषैरितरेतराच्च ।
कामाग्निनाच्युत रुषा च सुदुर्भरेण
सम्पश्यतो मन उरुक्रम सीदते मे ॥ ८ ॥

kṣut-tṛṭ-tridhātubhir imā muhur ardyamānāḥ
śītoṣṇa-vāta-varaṣair itaretarāc ca
kāmāgninācyuta-ruṣā ca sudurbhareṇa
sampaśyato mana urukrama sīdate me

kṣut—hunger; *tṛṭ*—thirst; *tri-dhātubhiḥ*—three humors, namely mucus, bile and wind; *imāḥ*—all of them; *muhuḥ*—always; *ardyamānāḥ*—perplexed; *śīta*—winter; *uṣṇa*—summer; *vāta*—wind; *varaṣaiḥ*—by rains; *itara-itarāt*—and many other disturbances; *ca*—also; *kāma-agninā*—by strong sex urges; *acyuta-ruṣā*—indefatigable anger; *ca*—also; *sudurbhareṇa*—most unbearable; *sampaśyataḥ*—so observing; *manaḥ*—mind; *urukrama*—O great actor; *sīdate*—becomes despondent; *me*—my.

TRANSLATION

O great actor, my Lord, all these poor creatures are constantly perplexed by hunger, thirst, severe cold, secretion and bile, attacked by coughing winter, blasting summer, rains and many other disturbing elements, and overwhelmed by strong sex urges and indefatigable anger. I take pity on them, and I am very much aggrieved for them.

PURPORT

A pure devotee of the Lord like Brahmā and persons in his disciplic succession are always unhappy to see the perplexities of the conditioned souls, who are suffering the onslaughts of the threefold miseries which pertain to the body and mind, to the disturbances of material nature, and to many other such material disadvantages. Not knowing adequate measures for relieving such difficulties, suffering persons sometimes pose themselves as leaders of the people, and the unfortunate followers are put into further disadvantages under such so-called leadership. This is like a blind man's leading another blind man to fall into a ditch. Therefore, unless the devotees of the Lord take pity on them and teach them the right path, their lives are hopeless failures. The devotees of the Lord who voluntarily take the responsibility of raising the foolish materialistic sense enjoyers are as confidential to the Lord as Lord Brahmā.

TEXT 9

यावत्पृथक्त्वमिदमात्मन इन्द्रियार्थ-
मायाबलं भगवतो जन ईश पश्येत् ।
तावन्न संसृतिरसौ प्रतिसङ्क्रमेत
व्यर्थापि दुःखनिवहं वहती क्रियार्था ॥९॥

yāvat pṛthaktvam idam ātmana indriyārtha-
māyā-balaṁ bhagavato jana īśa paśyet
tāvan na saṁsṛtir asau pratisaṅkrameta
vyarthāpi duḥkha-nivahaṁ vahatī kriyārthā

yāvat—as long as; *pṛthaktvam*—separatism; *idam*—this; *ātmanaḥ*—of the body; *indriya-artha*—for sense gratification; *māyā-balam*—influence of external energy; *bhagavataḥ*—of the Personality of Godhead; *janaḥ*—a person; *īśa*—O my Lord; *paśyet*—sees; *tāvat*—so long; *na*—not; *saṁsṛtiḥ*—the influence of material existence; *asau*—that man; *pratisaṅkrameta*—can overcome; *vyarthā api*—although without meaning; *duḥkha-nivaham*—multiple miseries; *vahatī*—bringing; *kriyā-arthā*—for fruitive activities.

TRANSLATION

O my Lord, the material miseries are without factual existence for the soul. Yet as long as the conditioned soul sees the body as meant for sense enjoyment, he cannot get out of the entanglement of material miseries, being influenced by Your external energy.

PURPORT

The whole trouble of the living entity in material existence is that he has an independent conception of life. He is always dependent on the rules of the Supreme Lord, in both the conditioned and liberated states, but by the influence of the external energy the conditioned soul thinks himself independent of the supremacy of the Personality of Godhead. His constitutional position is to dovetail himself with the desire of the supreme will, but as long as he does not do so, he is sure to drag on in the shackles of material bondage. As stated in *Bhagavad-gītā* (2.55), *prajahāti yadā kāmān sarvān pārtha mano-gatān:* he has to give up all sorts of plans manufactured by mental concoction. The living entity has to dovetail himself with the supreme will. That will help him to get out of the entanglement of material existence.

TEXT 10

अह्न्यापृतार्तकरणा निशि निःशयाना
नानामनोरथधिया क्षणभग्ननिद्राः ।
दैवाहतार्थरचना ऋषयोऽपि देव
युष्मत्प्रसङ्गविमुखा इह संसरन्ति ॥१०॥

ahny āpṛtārta-karaṇā niśi niḥśayānā
nānā-manoratha-dhiyā kṣaṇa-bhagna-nidrāḥ
daivāhatārtha-racanā ṛṣayo 'pi deva
yuṣmat-prasaṅga-vimukhā iha saṁsaranti

ahni—during the daytime; *āpṛta*—engaged; *ārta*—distressing engagement; *karaṇāḥ*—senses; *niśi*—at night; *niḥśayānāḥ*—insomnia; *nānā*—various; *manoratha*—mental speculations; *dhiyā*—by intelligence; *kṣaṇa*—constantly; *bhagna*—broken; *nidrāḥ*—sleep; *daiva*—superhuman; *āhata-artha*—frustrated; *racanāḥ*—plans; *ṛṣayaḥ*—great sages; *api*—also; *deva*—O my Lord; *yuṣmat*—Your Lordship's; *prasaṅga*—topic; *vimukhāḥ*—turned against; *iha*—in this (material world); *saṁsaranti*—do rotate.

TRANSLATION

Such nondevotees engage their senses in very troublesome and extensive work, and they suffer insomnia at night because their intelligence constantly breaks their sleep with various mental speculations. They are frustrated in all their various plans by supernatural power. Even great sages, if they are against Your transcendental topics, must rotate in this material world.

PURPORT

As described in the previous verse, people who have no taste for the devotional service of the Lord are occupied in material engagements. Most of them engage during the daytime in hard physical labor; their senses are engaged very extensively in troublesome duties in the gigantic plants of heavy industrial enterprise. The owners of such factories are engaged in finding a market for their industrial products, and the laborers are engaged in extensive production involving huge mechanical arrangements. "Factory" is another name for hell. At night, hellishly engaged persons take advantage of wine and women to satisfy their tired senses, but they are not even able to have sound sleep because their various mental speculative plans constantly interrupt their sleep. Because they suffer from insomnia sometimes they feel sleepy in the morning for lack of sufficient rest. By the arrangement of supernatural power, even the great scientists and thinkers of the world suffer frustration of their various plans and thus rot in the material world birth after birth. A great scientist may make discoveries in atomic energy for the quick destruction of the world and may be awarded the best prize in recognition of his service (or disservice), but he also has to undergo the reactions of his work by rotating in the cycle of repeated births and deaths under the superhuman law of material nature. All these people who are against the principle of devotional service are destined to rotate in this material world without fail.

This verse particularly mentions that even sages who are averse to the principles of devotional service to the Lord are also condemned to undergo the terms of material existence. Not only in this age, but formerly also, there were many sages who tried to invent their own systems of religion without reference to devotional service to the Supreme Lord, but there cannot be any religious principle without devotional service to the Lord. The Supreme Lord is the leader of the entire range of living entities, and no one can be equal to or greater than Him. Even the Lord's impersonal feature and all-pervading localized feature cannot be on an equal level with the Supreme Personality of Godhead. Therefore, there cannot be any religion or system of genuine philosophy for the advancement of the living entities without the principle of devotional service.

The impersonalists, who take much trouble in penance and austerity for self-liberation, may approach the impersonal *brahmajyoti*, but ultimately, because of not being situated in devotional service, they glide down again to the material world to undergo another term of material existence. This is confirmed as follows:

ye 'nye 'ravindākṣa vimukta-māninas
tvayy asta-bhāvād aviśuddha-buddhayaḥ
āruhya kṛcchreṇa paraṁ padaṁ tataḥ
patanty adho 'nādṛta-yuṣmad-aṅghrayaḥ

"Persons who are falsely under the impression of being liberated, without devotional service to the Lord, may reach the goal of the *brahmajyoti*, but because of their impure consciousness and for want of shelter in the Vaikuṇṭhalokas, such so-called liberated persons again fall down into material existence." (*Bhag.* 10.2.32)

Therefore, no one can manufacture any system of religion without the principle of devotional service to the Lord. As we find in the Sixth Canto of *Śrīmad-Bhāgavatam*, the initiator of religious principles is the Lord Himself. In *Bhagavad-gītā* also we find that the Lord condemns all forms of religion other than that which entails the process of surrendering unto the Supreme. Any system which leads one to the devotional service of the Lord, and nothing else, is actually religion or philosophy. In the Sixth Canto we find the following statements of Yamarāja, the controller of all unfaithful living entities:

dharmaṁ tu sākṣād bhagavat-praṇītaṁ
na vai vidur ṛṣayo nāpi devāḥ
na siddha-mukhyā asurā manuṣyāḥ
kuto nu vidyādhara-cāraṇādayaḥ

svayambhūr nāradaḥ śambhuḥ
kumāraḥ kapilo manuḥ
prahlādo janako bhīṣmo
balir vaiyāsakir vayam

dvādaśaite vijānīmo
dharmaṁ bhāgavataṁ bhaṭāḥ
guhyaṁ viśuddhaṁ durbodhaṁ
yaṁ jñātvāmṛtam aśnute

"The principles of religion are initiated by the Supreme Personality of Godhead, and no one else, including the sages and demigods, can manufacture any such principles. Since even great sages and demigods are unauthorized to inaugurate such principles of religion, what to speak of others—the so-called mystics, demons, human beings, Vidyādharas and Cāraṇas living in the lower planets? Twelve personalities—Brahmā, Nārada, Lord Śiva, Kumāra, Kapila, Manu, Prahlāda Mahārāja, Janaka Mahārāja, Bhīṣma, Bali, Śukadeva Gosvāmī and Yamarāja—are agents of the Lord authorized to speak and propagate the principles of religion." (*Bhag.* 6.3.19-21)

The principles of religion are not open to any ordinary living entity. They are just to bring the human being onto the platform of morality. Nonviolence, etc., are necessary for misguided persons because unless one is moral and nonviolent one cannot understand the principles of religion. To understand what is actually religion is very difficult even if one is situated in the principles of morality and nonviolence. It is very confidential because as soon as one is conversant with the real principles of religion, he is at once liberated to the eternal life of bliss and knowledge. Therefore, one who is not situated in the principles of devotional service to the Lord should not pose himself as a religious leader of the innocent public. The *Īśopaniṣad* emphatically forbids this nonsense in the following *mantra:*

andhaṁ tamaḥ praviśanti
ye 'sambhūtim upāsate
tato bhūya iva te tamo
ya u sambhūtyāṁ ratāḥ
(*Īśopaniṣad 12*)

A person in ignorance of the principles of religion who therefore does nothing in the matter of religion is far better than a person who misguides others in the name of religion without reference to the factual religious principles of devotional service. Such so-called leaders of religion are sure to be condemned by Brahmā and other great authorities.

TEXT 11

त्वं भक्तियोगपरिभावितहृत्सरोज
आस्से श्रुतेक्षितपथो ननु नाथ पुंसाम् ।
यद्यद्धिया त उरुगाय विभावयन्ति
तत्तद्वपुः प्रणयसे सदनुग्रहाय ॥११॥

tvaṁ bhakti-yoga-paribhāvita-hṛt-saroja
āsse śruteksita-patho nanu nātha puṁsām
yad-yad-dhiyā ta urugāya vibhāvayanti
tat-tad-vapuḥ praṇayase sad-anugrahāya

tvam—unto You; *bhakti-yoga*—in devotional service; *paribhāvita*—being one hundred percent engaged; *hṛt*—of the heart; *saroje*—on the lotus; *āsse*—You reside; *śruta-ikṣita*—seen through the ear; *pathaḥ*—the path; *nanu*—now; *nātha*—O my Lord; *puṁsām*—of the devotees; *yat-yat*—whichever; *dhiyā*—by meditating; *te*—Your; *urugāya*—O multiglorious; *vibhāvayanti*—they specifically think of; *tat-tat*—the very same; *vapuḥ*—transcendental form; *praṇayase*—do You manifest; *sat-anugrahāya*—to show Your causeless mercy.

TRANSLATION

O my Lord, Your devotees can see You through the ears by the process of bona fide hearing, and thus their hearts become cleansed, and You take Your

seat there. You are so merciful to Your devotees that You manifest Yourself in the particular eternal form of transcendence in which they always think of You.

PURPORT

The statement here that the Lord manifests Himself before the devotee in the form in which the devotee likes to worship Him indicates that the Lord becomes subordinate to the desire of the devotee—so much so that He manifests His particular form as the devotee demands. This demand of the devotee is satisfied by the Lord because He is pliable in terms of the transcendental loving service of the devotee. This is also confirmed in *Bhagavad-gītā* (4.11): *ye yathā māṁ prapadyante tāṁs tathaiva bhajāmy aham.* We should note, however, that the Lord is never the order supplier of the devotee. Here in this verse it is particularly mentioned: *tvaṁ bhakti-yoga-paribhāvita.* This indicates the efficiency achieved through execution of matured devotional service, or *premā,* love of Godhead. This state of *premā* is achieved by the gradual process of development from faith to love. On faith one associates with bona fide devotees, and by such association one can become engaged in bona fide devotional service, which includes proper initiation and the execution of the primary devotional duties prescribed in the revealed scriptures. This is clearly indicated herein by the word *śrutekṣita.* The *śrutekṣita* path is to hear from bona fide devotees who are conversant with Vedic wisdom, free from mundane sentiment. By this bona fide hearing process, the neophyte devotee becomes cleansed of all material rubbish, and thus he becomes attached to one of the many transcendental forms of the Lord, as described in the *Vedas.*

This attachment of the devotee to a particular form of the Lord is due to natural inclination. Each and every living entity is originally attached to a particular type of transcendental service because he is eternally the servitor of the Lord. Lord Caitanya says that the living entity is eternally a servitor of the Supreme Personality of Godhead, Śrī Kṛṣṇa. Therefore, every living entity has a particular type of service relationship with the Lord, eternally. This particular attachment is invoked by practice of regulative devotional service to the Lord, and thus the devotee becomes attached to the eternal form of the Lord, exactly like one who is already eternally attached. This attachment for a particular form of the Lord is called *svarūpa-siddhi.* The Lord sits on the lotus heart of the devotee in the eternal form the pure devotee desires, and thus the Lord does not part from the devotee, as confirmed in the previous verse. The Lord, however, does not disclose Himself to a casual or inauthentic worshiper to be exploited.

This is confirmed in *Bhagavad-gītā* (7.25): *nāhaṁ prakāśaḥ sarvasya yoga-māyā-samāvṛtaḥ.* Rather, by *yoga-māyā,* the Lord remains concealed to the nondevotees or casual devotees who are serving their sense gratification. The Lord is never visible to the pseudodevotees who worship the demigods in charge of universal affairs. The conclusion is that the Lord cannot become the order supplier of a pseudodevotee, but He is always prepared to respond to the desires of a pure, unconditional devotee, who is free from all tinges of material infection.

TEXT 12

नातिप्रसीदति तथोपचितोपचारै-
राराधितः सुरगणैर्हृदिबद्धकामैः ।
यत्सर्वभूतदययासदलभ्ययैको
नानाजनेष्ववहितः सुहृदन्तरात्मा ॥१२॥

nātiprasīdati tathopacitopacārair
ārādhitaḥ sura-gaṇair hṛdi baddha-kāmaiḥ
yat sarva-bhūta-dayayāsad-alabhyayaiko
nānā-janeṣv avahitaḥ suhṛd antar-ātmā

na—never; *ati*—very much; *prasīdati*—become satisfied; *tathā*—as much as; *upacita*—by pompous arrangement; *upacāraiḥ*—with much worshipable paraphernalia; *ārādhitaḥ*—being worshiped; *sura-gaṇaiḥ*—by the celestial demigods; *hṛdi baddha-kāmaiḥ*—with hearts full of all sorts of material desires; *yat*—that which; *sarva*—all; *bhūta*—living entities; *dayayā*—to show them causeless mercy; *asat*—nondevotee; *alabhyayā*—not being achieved; *ekaḥ*—one without a second; *nānā*—various; *janeṣu*—in living entities; *avahitaḥ*—perceived; *suhṛt*—well-wishing friend; *antaḥ*—within; *ātmā*—Supersoul.

TRANSLATION

My Lord, You are not very much satisfied by the worship of the demigods, who arrange for Your worship very pompously, with various paraphernalia, but who are full of material hankerings. You are situated in everyone's heart as the Supersoul just to show Your causeless mercy, and You are the eternal well-wisher, but You are unavailable for the nondevotee.

PURPORT

The demigods in the celestial heavenly planets, who are appointed administrators of the material affairs, are also devotees of the Lord. But, at the same time, they have desires for material opulence and sense gratification. The Lord is so kind that He awards them all sorts of material happiness, more than they can desire, but He is not satisfied with them because they are not pure devotees. The Lord does not want any one of His innumerable sons (the living entities) to remain in the material world of threefold miseries to perpetually suffer the material pangs of birth, death, old age and disease. The demigods in the heavenly planets, and many devotees on this planet also, want to remain in the material world as devotees of the Lord and take advantage of material happiness. They do so at a risk of falling down to the lower status of existence, and this makes the Lord dissatisfied with them.

Pure devotees are not desirous of any material enjoyment, nor are they averse to it. They completely dovetail their desires with the desires of the Lord and perform nothing on their personal account. Arjuna is a good example. On his own sentiment, due to family affection, Arjuna did not want to fight, but finally, after hearing *Śrīmad Bhagavad-gītā,* he agreed to fight in the interests of the Lord. Therefore, the Lord is very much satisfied with pure devotees because they do not act for sense gratification but only in terms of the Lord's desire. As Paramātmā, or Supersoul, He is situated in everyone's heart, always giving everyone the chance of good counsel. Thus everyone should take the opportunity and render transcendental loving service to Him wholly and solely.

The nondevotees, however, are neither like the demigods nor like the pure devotees, but are averse to the transcendental relationship with the Lord. They have revolted against the Lord and must perpetually undergo the reactions of their own activities.

Bhagavad-gītā (4.11) states: *ye yathā māṁ prapadyante tāṁs tathaiva bhajāmy aham.* "Although the Lord is equally kind to every living being, the living beings, for their own part, are able to please the Lord to either a greater or lesser extent." The demigods are called *sakāma* devotees, or devotees with material desires in mind, while the pure devotees are called *niṣkāma* devotees because they have no desires for their personal interests. The *sakāma* devotees are self-interested because they do not think of others, and therefore they are not able to satisfy the Lord perfectly, whereas the pure devotees take the missionary responsibility of turning nondevotees into devotees, and they are therefore able to satisfy the Lord more than the demigods. The Lord is unmindful of the nondevotees, although He is sitting within everyone's heart as well-wisher and Supersoul. However, He also gives them the chance to receive His mercy through His pure devotees who are engaged in missionary activities. Sometimes the Lord Himself descends for missionary activities, as He did in the form of Lord Caitanya, but mostly He sends His bona fide representatives, and thus He shows His causeless mercy towards the nondevotees. The Lord is so satisfied with His pure devotees that He wants to give them the credit for missionary success, although He could do the work personally. This is the sign of His satisfaction with His pure, *niṣkāma* devotees, compared to the *sakāma* devotees. By such transcendental activities the Lord simultaneously becomes free from the charge of partiality and exhibits His pleasure with the devotees.

Now a question arises: If the Lord is sitting in the hearts of nondevotees, why are they not moved to become devotees? It may be answered that the stubborn nondevotees are like the barren land or alkaline field, where no agricultural activities can be successful. As part and parcel of the Lord, every individual living entity has a minute quantity of independence, and by misuse of this minute independence, the nondevotees commit offense after offense, to both the Lord and His pure devotees engaged in missionary work. As a result of such acts, they become as barren as an alkaline field, where there is no strength to produce.

TEXT 13

पुंसामतो विविधकर्मभिरध्वराद्यै-
दार्नेन चोग्रतपसा परिचर्यया च ।
आराधनं भगवतस्तव सत्क्रियार्थो
धर्मोऽर्पितः कर्हिचिद्म्रियते न यत्र ॥१३॥

puṁsam ato vividha-karmabhir adhvarādyair
dānena cogra-tapasā paricaryayā ca
ārādhanaṁ bhagavatas tava sat-kriyārtho
dharmo 'rpitaḥ karhicid mriyate na yatra

puṁsām—of the people; *ataḥ*—therefore; *vividha-karmabhiḥ*—by various fruitive activities; *adhvara-ādyaiḥ*—by performance of Vedic rituals; *dānena*—by charities; *ca*—and; *ugra*—very hard; *tapasā*—austerity; *paricaryayā*—by transcendental service; *ca*—also; *ārādhanam*—worship; *bhagavataḥ*—of the Personality of Godhead; *tava*—Your; *sat-kriyā-arthaḥ*—simply for pleasing Your Lordship; *dharmaḥ*—religion; *arpitaḥ*—so offered; *karhicit*—at any time; *mriyate*—vanquishes; *na*—never; *yatra*—there.

TRANSLATION

But the pious activities of the people, such as performance of Vedic rituals, charity, austere penances, and transcendental service, performed with a view

to worship You and satisfy You by offering You the fruitive results, are also beneficial. Such acts of religion never go in vain.

PURPORT

Absolute devotional service, conducted in nine different spiritual activities—hearing, chanting, remembering, worshiping, praying, etc.—does not always appeal to people with a pompous nature; they are more attracted by the Vedic superficial rituals and other costly performances of social religious shows. But the process according to the Vedic injunctions is that the fruits of all pious activities should be offered to the Supreme Lord. In *Bhagavad-gītā* (9.27), the Lord demands that whatever one may do in one's daily activities, such as worship, sacrifice, and offering charity, all the results should be offered to Him only. This offering of the results of pious acts unto the Supreme Lord is a sign of devotional service to the Lord and is of permanent value, whereas enjoying the same results for oneself is only temporary. Anything done on account of the Lord is a permanent asset and accumulates in the form of unseen piety for gradual promotion to the unalloyed devotional service of the Lord. These undetected pious activities will one day result in full-fledged devotional service by the grace of the Supreme Lord. Therefore, any pious act done on account of the Supreme Lord is also recommended here for those who are not pure devotees.

TEXT 14

शश्वत्स्वरूपमहसैव निपीतभेद-
मोहाय बोधधिषणाय नमः परस्मै ।
विश्वोद्भवस्थितिलयेषु निमित्तलीला-
रासाय ते नम इदं चकृमेश्वराय ॥१४॥

śaśvat svarūpa-mahasaiva nipīta-bheda-
mohāya bodha-dhiṣaṇāya namaḥ parasmai
viśvodbhava-sthiti-layeṣu nimitta-līlā-
rāsāya te nama idaṁ cakṛmeśvarāya

śaśvat—eternally; *svarūpa*—transcendental form; *mahasā*—by the glories; *eva*—certainly; *nipīta*—distinguished; *bheda*—differentiation; *mohāya*—unto the illusory conception; *bodha*—self-knowledge; *dhiṣaṇāya*—intelligence; *namaḥ*—obeisances; *parasmai*—unto the Transcendence; *viśva-udbhava*—creation of the cosmic manifestation; *sthiti*—maintenance; *layeṣu*—also destruction; *nimitta*—for the matter of; *līlā*—by such pastimes; *rāsāya*—for enjoyment; *te*—unto You; *namaḥ*—obeisances; *idam*—this; *cakṛma*—do I perform; *īśvarāya*—unto the Supreme.

TRANSLATION

Let me offer my obeisances unto the Supreme Transcendence, who is eternally distinguished by His internal potency. His indistinguishable impersonal feature is realized by intelligence for self-realization. I offer my obeisances unto Him who by His pastimes enjoys the creation, maintenance and dissolution of the cosmic manifestation.

PURPORT

The Supreme Lord is eternally distinguished from the living entities by His internal potency, although He is also understood in His impersonal feature by self-realized intelligence. Devotees of the Lord, therefore, offer all respectful obeisances unto the impersonal feature of the Lord. The word *rāsa* is significant herein. The *rāsa* dance is performed by Lord Kṛṣṇa in the company of the cowherd damsels at Vṛndāvana, and the Personality of Godhead Garbhodakaśāyī Viṣṇu is also engaged in *rāsa* enjoyment with His external potency, by which He creates, maintains and dissolves the entire material manifestation. Indirectly, Lord Brahmā offers his respectful obeisances unto Lord Śrī Kṛṣṇa, who is factually ever engaged in *rāsa* enjoyment with the *gopīs,* as confirmed in the *Gopāla-tāpanī Upaniṣad* in the following words: *parārdhānte so 'budhyata gopa-veśo me puruṣaḥ purastād āvirbabhūva.* The distinction between the Lord and the living entity is definitely experienced when there is sufficient intelligence to understand His internal potency, as distinguished from the external potency by which He makes possible the material manifestation.

TEXT 15

यस्यावतारगुणकर्मविडम्बनानि
नामानि येऽसुविगमे विवशा गृणन्ति ।
तेऽनैकजन्मशमलं सहसैव हित्वा
संयान्त्यपावृतामृतं तमजं प्रपद्ये ॥१५॥

yasyāvatāra-guṇa-karma-viḍambanāni
nāmāni ye 'su-vigame vivaśā gṛṇanti
te 'naika-janma-śamalaṁ sahasaiva hitvā
saṁyānty apāvṛtāmṛtaṁ tam ajaṁ prapadye

yasya—whose; *avatāra*—incarnations; *guṇa*—transcendental qualities; *karma*—activities; *viḍambanāni*—all mysterious; *nāmāni*—transcendental names; *ye*—those; *asu-vigame*—while quitting this life; *vivaśāḥ*—automatically; *gṛṇanti*—invoke; *te*—they; *anaika*—many; *janma*—births; *śamalam*—accumulated sins; *sahasā*—immediately; *eva*—certainly; *hitvā*—giving up; *saṁyānti*—obtain; *apāvṛta*—open; *amṛtam*—immortality; *tam*—Him; *ajam*—the unborn; *prapadye*—I take shelter.

TRANSLATION

Let me take shelter of the lotus feet of Him whose incarnations, qualities and activities are mysterious imitations of worldly affairs. One who invokes His transcendental names, even unconsciously, at the time he quits this life, is certainly washed immediately of the sins of many, many births and attains Him without fail.

PURPORT

The activities of the incarnations of the Supreme Personality of Godhead are a kind of imitation of the activities going on in the material world. He is just like an actor on a stage. An actor imitates the activities of a king on stage, although actually he is not the king. Similarly, when the Lord incarnates, He imitates parts with which He has nothing to do. In *Bhagavad-gītā* (4.14), it is said that the Lord has nothing to do with the activities in which He is supposedly engaged: *na māṁ karmāṇi limpanti na me karma-phale spṛhā.* The Lord is omnipotent; simply by His will He can perform anything and everything. When the Lord appeared as Lord Kṛṣṇa, He played the part of the son of Yaśodā and Nanda, and He lifted the Govardhana Hill, although lifting a hill is not His concern. He can lift millions of Govardhana Hills by His simple desire; He does not need to lift it with His hand. But He imitates the ordinary living entity by this lifting, and at the same time He exhibits His supernatural power. Thus His name is chanted as the lifter of Govardhana Hill, or Śrī Govardhanadhārī. Therefore, His acts in His incarnations and His partiality to the devotees are all imitations only, just like the stage makeup of an expert dramatical player. His acts in that capacity, however, are all omnipotent, and the remembrance of such activities of the incarnations of the Supreme Personality of Godhead is as powerful as the Lord Himself. Ajāmila remembered the holy name of the Lord, Nārāyaṇa, by merely calling the name of his son Nārāyaṇa, and that gave him a complete opportunity to achieve the highest perfection of life.

TEXT 16

यो वा अहं च गिरिशश्च विभुः स्वयं च
स्थित्युद्भवप्रलयहेतव आत्ममूलम् ।
भित्त्वा त्रिपाद्ववृध एक उरुप्ररोह-
स्तस्मै नमो भगवते भुवनद्रुमाय ॥१६॥

yo vā ahaṁ ca giriśaś ca vibhuḥ svayaṁ ca
sthity-udbhava-pralaya-hetava ātma-mūlam
bhittvā tri-pād vavṛdha eka uru-prarohas
tasmai namo bhagavate bhuvana-drumāya

yaḥ—one who; *vai*—certainly; *aham ca*—also I; *giriśaḥ ca*—also Śiva; *vibhuḥ*—the Almighty; *svayam*—personality (as Viṣṇu); *ca*—and; *sthiti*—maintenance; *udbhava*—creation; *pralaya*—dissolution; *hetavaḥ*—the causes; *ātma-mūlam*—self-rooted; *bhittvā*—having penetrated; *tri-pāt*—three trunks; *vavṛdhe*—grew; *ekaḥ*—one without a second; *uru*—many; *prarohaḥ*—branches; *tasmai*—unto Him; *namaḥ*—obeisances; *bhagavate*—unto the Personality of Godhead; *bhuvana-drumāya*—unto the tree of the planetary system.

TRANSLATION

Your Lordship is the prime root of the tree of the planetary systems. This tree has grown by first penetrating the material nature in three trunks—as me, Śiva and You, the Almighty—for creation, maintenance and dissolution, and we three have grown with many branches. Therefore I offer my obeisances unto You, the tree of the cosmic manifestation.

PURPORT

The cosmic manifestation is grossly divided into three worlds, the upper, lower and middle planetary systems, and then it broadens into the cosmos of fourteen planetary systems, with the manifestation of the Supreme Personality of Godhead as the supreme root. Material nature, which appears to be the cause of the cosmic manifestation, is only the agency or energy of the Lord. This is confirmed in *Bhagavad-gītā* (9.10): *mayādhyakṣeṇa prakṛtiḥ sūyate sa-carācaram.* "Only under the superintendence of the Supreme Lord does material nature appear to be the cause of all creation, maintenance and dissolution." The Lord expands Himself into three—Viṣṇu, Brahmā and Śiva—for maintenance, creation and destruction respectively. Of the three principal agents controlling the three modes of material nature, Viṣṇu is the Almighty; even though He is within material nature for the purpose of maintenance, He is not controlled by the laws of material nature. The other two, Brahmā and Śiva, although almost as greatly powerful as Viṣṇu, are within the control of the material energy of the Supreme Lord. The conception of many gods controlling the many departments of material nature is ill conceived of by the foolish pantheist. God is one without a second, and He is the primal cause of all causes. As there are many departmental heads of governmental affairs, so there are many heads of management of the universal affairs.

Due to a poor fund of knowledge, the impersonalist does not believe in the personal management of things as they are. But in this verse it is clearly explained that everything is personal and nothing is impersonal. We have already discussed this point in the Introduction, and it is confirmed here in this verse. The tree of the material manifestation is described in the Fifteenth Chapter of *Bhagavad-gītā* as an *aśvattha* tree whose root is upward. We have actual experience of such a tree when we see the shadow of a tree on the bank of a reservoir of water. The reflection of the tree on the water appears to hang down from its upward roots. The tree of creation described here is only a shadow of the reality which is Parabrahman, Viṣṇu. In the internal potential manifestation of the Vaikuṇṭhalokas, the actual tree exists, and the tree reflected in the material nature is only the shadow of this actual tree. The impersonalists' theory that Brahman is void of all variegatedness is false because the shadow-tree described in *Bhagavad-gītā* cannot exist without being the reflection of a real tree. The real tree is situated in the eternal existence of spiritual nature, full of transcendental varieties, and Lord Viṣṇu is the root of that tree also. The root is the same—the Lord—both for the real tree and the false, but the false tree is only the perverted reflection of the real tree. The Lord, being the real tree, is here offered obeisances by Brahmā on his own behalf and also on behalf of Lord Śiva.

TEXT 17

लोको विकर्मनिरतः कुशले प्रमत्तः
कर्मण्ययं त्वदुदिते भवदर्चने स्वे ।
यस्तावदस्य बलवानिह जीविताशां
सद्यश्छिनत्त्यनिमिषाय नमोऽस्तु तस्मै ॥१७॥

loko vikarma-nirataḥ kuśale pramattaḥ
karmaṇy ayaṁ tvad-udite bhavad-arcane sve
yas tāvad asya balavān iha jivitāśāṁ
sadyaś chinatty animiṣāya namo 'stu tasmai

lokaḥ—people in general; *vikarma*—work without sense; *nirataḥ*—engaged in; *kuśale*—in beneficial activity; *pramattaḥ*—negligent; *karmaṇi*—in activity; *ayam*—this; *tvat*—by You; *udite*—enunciated; *bhavat*—of You; *arcane*—in worship; *sve*—their own; *yaḥ*—who; *tāvat*—as long as; *asya*—of the people in general; *balavān*—very strong; *iha*—this; *jīvita-āśām*—struggle for existence; *sadyaḥ*—directly; *chinatti*—is cut to pieces; *animiṣāya*—by the eternal time; *namaḥ*—my obeisances; *astu*—let there be; *tasmai*—unto Him.

TRANSLATION

People in general all engage in foolish acts, not in the really beneficial activities enunciated directly by You for their guidance. As long as their tendency for foolish work remains powerful, all their plans in the struggle for existence will be cut to pieces. I therefore offer my obeisances unto Him who acts as eternal time.

PURPORT

People in general are all engaged in senseless work. They are systematically unmindful of the real beneficial work, which is the devotional service of the Lord, technically called the *arcanā* regulations. The *arcanā* regulations are directly instructed by the Lord in the *Nārada-Pañcarātra* and are strictly followed by the intelligent men, who know well that the highest perfectional goal of life is to reach Lord Viṣṇu, who is the root of the tree called the cosmic manifestation. Also, in the *Bhāgavatam* and in *Bhagavad-gītā* such regulative activities are clearly mentioned. Foolish people do not know that their self-interest is in realization of Viṣṇu. The *Bhāgavatam* (7.5.30-32) says:

matir na kṛṣṇe parataḥ svato vā
mitho 'bhipadyeta gṛha-vratānām
adānta-gobhir viśatāṁ tamisraṁ
punaḥ punaś carvita-carvaṇānām

na te viduḥ svārtha-gatiṁ hi viṣṇuṁ
durāśayā ye bahir-artha-māninaḥ
andhā yathāndhair upanīyamānās
te 'pīśa-tantryām uru-dāmni baddhāḥ

naiṣāṁ matis tāvad urukramāṅghriṁ
spṛśaty anarthāpagamo yad-arthaḥ
mahīyasāṁ pāda-rajo-'bhiṣekaṁ
niṣkiñcanānāṁ na vṛṇīta yāvat

"Persons who are determined to totally rot in false, material happiness cannot become Kṛṣṇa-minded either by instructions from teachers, by self-realization or by parliamentary discussions. They are dragged by the unbridled senses into the darkest region of ignorance, and thus they madly engage in what is called 'chewing the chewed.'

"Because of their foolish activities, they are unaware that the ultimate goal of human life is to achieve Viṣṇu, the Lord of the cosmic manifestation, and so their struggle for existence is in the wrong direction of material civilization, which is under the external energy. They are led by similar foolish persons, just as one blind man is led by another blind man and both fall in the ditch.

"Such foolish men cannot be attracted towards the activities of the Supreme Powerful, who is actually the neutralizing measure for their foolish activities, unless and until they have the good sense to be guided by the great souls who are completely freed from material attachment."

In *Bhagavad-gītā* the Lord asks everyone to give up all other occupational duties and absolutely engage in *arcanā* activities, or in pleasing the Lord. But almost no one is attracted to such *arcanā* activity. Everyone is more or less attracted by activities which are conditions of rebellion against the Supreme Lord. The systems of *jñāna* and *yoga* are also indirectly rebellious acts against the Lord. There is no auspicious activity except *arcanā* of the Lord. *Jñāna* and *yoga* are sometimes accepted within the purview of *arcanā* when the ultimate aim is Viṣṇu, and not otherwise. The conclusion is that only the devotees of the Lord are bona fide human beings eligible for salvation. Others are vainly struggling for existence without any actual benefit.

TEXT 18

यस्माद्बिभेम्यहमपि द्विपरार्धधिष्ण्य-
मध्यासितः सकललोकनमस्कृतं यत् ।
तेपे तपो बहुसवोऽवरुरुत्समान-
स्तस्मै नमो भगवतेऽधिमखाय तुभ्यम् ॥१८॥

yasmād bibhemy aham api dviparārdha-dhiṣṇyam
adhyāsitaḥ sakala-loka-namaskṛtaṁ yat
tepe tapo bahu-savo 'varurutsamānas
tasmai namo bhagavate 'dhimakhāya tubhyam

yasmāt—from whom; *bibhemi*—fear; *aham*—I; *api*—also; *dvi-para-ardha*—up to the limit of 4,300,000,000 × 2 × 30 × 12 × 100 solar years; *dhiṣṇyam*—place; *adhyāsitaḥ*—situated in;

sakala-loka—all other planets; *namaskṛtam*—honored by; *yat*—that; *tepe*—underwent; *tapaḥ*—penances; *bahu-savaḥ*—many, many years; *avarurutsamānaḥ*—desiring to obtain You; *tasmai*—unto Him; *namaḥ*—I do offer my obeisances; *bhagavate*—unto the Supreme Personality of Godhead; *adhimakhāya*—unto Him who is the enjoyer of all sacrifices; *tubhyam*—unto Your Lordship.

TRANSLATION

Your Lordship, I offer my respectful obeisances unto You who are indefatigable time and the enjoyer of all sacrifices. Although I am situated in an abode which will continue to exist for a time duration of two parārdhas, although I am the leader of all other planets in the universe, and although I have undergone many, many years of penance for self-realization, still I offer my respects unto You.

PURPORT

Brahmā is the greatest personality in the universe because he has the longest duration of life. He is the most respectable personality because of his penance, influence, prestige, etc., and still he has to offer his respectful obeisances unto the Lord. Therefore, it is incumbent upon all others, who are far, far below the standard of Brahmā, to do as he did and offer respects as a matter of duty.

TEXT 19

तिर्यङ्मनुष्यविबुधादिषु जीवयोनि-
ष्वात्मेच्छयात्मकृतसेतुपरीप्सया यः ।
रेमे निरस्तविषयोऽप्यवरुद्धदेह-
स्तस्मै नमो भगवते पुरुषोत्तमाय ॥१९॥

tiryaṅ-manuṣya-vibudhādiṣu jīva-yoniṣv
ātmecchayātma-kṛta-setu-parīpsayā yaḥ
reme nirasta-viṣayo 'py avaruddha-dehas
tasmai namo bhagavate puruṣottamāya

tiryak—animals lower than human beings; *manuṣya*—human beings, etc.; *vibudha-ādiṣu*—amongst the demigods; *jīva-yoniṣu*—in different species of life; *ātma*—self; *icchayā*—by the will; *ātma-kṛta*—self-created; *setu*—obligations; *parīpsayā*—desiring to preserve; *yaḥ*—who; *reme*—performing transcendental pastimes; *nirasta*—not being affected; *viṣayaḥ*—material contamination; *api*—certainly; *avaruddha*—manifested; *dehaḥ*—transcendental body;

tasmai—unto Him; *namaḥ*—my obeisances; *bhagavate*—unto the Personality of Godhead; *puruṣottamāya*—the primeval Lord.

TRANSLATION

O my Lord, by Your own will You appear in the various species of living entities, among animals lower than human beings as well as among the demigods, to perform Your transcendental pastimes. You are not affected by material contamination. You come just to fulfill the obligations of Your own principles of religion, and therefore, O Supreme Personality, I offer my obeisances unto You for manifesting such different forms.

PURPORT

The Lord's incarnations in different species of life are all transcendental. He appears as a human being in His incarnations of Kṛṣṇa, Rāma, etc., but He is not a human being. Anyone who mistakes Him for an ordinary human being is certainly not very intelligent, as confirmed in *Bhagavad-gītā* (9.11): *avajānanti māṁ mūḍhā mānuṣīṁ tanum āśritam.* The same principle is applicable when He appears as the hog or fish incarnations. They are transcendental forms of the Lord and are manifested under certain necessities of His own pleasure and pastimes. Such manifestations of the transcendental forms of the Lord are accepted by Him mostly to enliven His devotees. All His incarnations are manifested whenever there is a need to deliver His devotees and maintain His own principles.

TEXT 20

योऽविद्ययानुपहतोऽपि दशार्धवृत्त्या
निद्रामुवाह जठरीकृतलोकयात्रः ।
अन्तर्जलेऽहिकशिपुस्पर्शानुकूलां
भीमोर्मिमालिनि जनस्य सुखं विवृण्वन् ॥२०॥

yo 'vidyayānupahato 'pi daśārdha-vṛttyā
nidrām uvāha jaṭharī-kṛta-loka-yātraḥ
antar-jale 'hi-kaśipu-sparśānukūlāṁ
bhīmormi-mālini janasya sukhaṁ vivṛṇvan

yaḥ—one; *avidyayā*—influenced by nescience; *anupahataḥ*—without being affected; *api*—in spite of; *daśa-ardha*—five; *vṛttyā*—interaction; *nidrām*—sleep; *uvāha*—accepted; *jaṭharī*—within the abdomen; *kṛta*—doing so; *loka-yātraḥ*—maintenance of the different entities;

antaḥ-jale—within the water of devastation; *ahi-kaśipu*—on the snake bed; *sparśa-anukūlām*—happy for the touch; *bhīma-ūrmi*—violent waves; *mālini*—chain of; *janasya*—of the intelligent person; *sukham*—happiness; *vivṛṇvan*—showing.

TRANSLATION

My Lord, You accept the pleasure of sleeping in the water of devastation, where there are violent waves, and You enjoy pleasure on the bed of snakes, showing the happiness of Your sleep to intelligent persons. At that time, all the universal planets are stationed within Your abdomen.

PURPORT

Persons who cannot think of anything beyond the limit of their own power are like frogs in a well who cannot imagine the length and breadth of the great Pacific Ocean. Such people take it as legendary when they hear that the Supreme Lord is lying on His bed within the great ocean of the universe. They are surprised that one can lie down within water and sleep very happily. But a little intelligence can mitigate this foolish astonishment. There are many living entities within the bed of the ocean who also enjoy the material bodily activities of eating, sleeping, defending and mating. If such insignificant living entities can enjoy life within the water, why can't the Supreme Lord, who is all-powerful, sleep on the cool body of a serpent and enjoy in the turmoil of violent ocean waves? The distinction of the Lord is that His activities are all transcendental, and He is able to do anything and everything without being deterred by limitations of time and space. He can enjoy His transcendental happiness regardless of material considerations.

TEXT 21

यन्नाभिपद्मभवनादहमासमीड्य
लोकत्रयोपकरणो यदनुग्रहेण ।
तस्मै नमस्त उदरस्थभवाय योग-
निद्रावसानविकसन्नलिनेक्षणाय ॥२१॥

yan-nābhi-padma-bhavanād aham āsam īḍya
loka-trayopakaraṇo yad-anugraheṇa
tasmai namas ta udara-stha-bhavāya yoga-
nidrāvasāna-vikasan-nalinekṣaṇāya

yat—whose; *nābhi*—navel; *padma*—lotus; *bhavanāt*—from the house of; *aham*—I; *āsam*—became manifested; *īḍya*—O worshipable one; *loka-traya*—the three worlds; *upakaraṇaḥ*—

helping in the creation of; *yat*—whose; *anugraheṇa*—by the mercy; *tasmai*—unto Him; *namaḥ*—my obeisances; *te*—unto You; *udara-stha*—situated within the abdomen; *bhavāya*—having the universe; *yoga-nidrā-avasāna*—after the end of that transcendental sleep; *vikasat*—blossoming; *nalina-īkṣaṇāya*—unto Him whose opening eyes are like lotuses.

TRANSLATION

O object of my worship, I am born from the house of Your lotus navel for the purpose of creating the universe by Your mercy. All these planets of the universe were stationed within Your transcendental abdomen while You were enjoying sleep. Now, Your sleep having ended, Your eyes are open like blossoming lotuses in the morning.

PURPORT

Brahmā is teaching us the beginning of *arcanā* regulations from morning (four o'clock) to night (ten o'clock). Early in the morning, the devotee has to rise from his bed and pray to the Lord, and there are other regulative principles for offering *maṅgala-ārati* early in the morning. Foolish nondevotees, not understanding the importance of *arcanā,* criticize the regulative principles, but they have no eyes to see that the Lord also sleeps, by His own will. The impersonal conception of the Supreme is so detrimental to the path of devotional service that it is very difficult to associate with the stubborn nondevotees, who always think in terms of material conceptions.

Impersonalists always think backwards. They think that because there is form in matter, spirit should be formless; because in matter there is sleep, in spirit there cannot be sleep; and because the sleeping of the Deity is accepted in *arcanā* worship, the *arcanā* is *māyā.* All these thoughts are basically material. To think either positively or negatively is still thinking materially. Knowledge accepted from the superior source of the *Vedas* is standard. Here in these verses of the *Śrīmad-Bhāgavatam,* we find that *arcanā* is recommended. Before Brahmā took up the task of creation, he found the Lord sleeping on the serpent bed in the waves of the water of devastation. Therefore, sleeping exists in the internal potency of the Lord, and this is not denied by pure devotees of the Lord like Brahmā and his disciplic succession. It is clearly said here that the Lord slept very happily within the violent waves of the water, manifesting thereby that He is able to do anything and everything by His transcendental will and not be hampered by any circumstances. The Māyāvādī cannot think beyond this material experience, and thus he denies the Lord's ability to sleep within the water. His mistake is that he compares the Lord to himself—and that comparison is also a material thought. The whole philosophy of the Māyāvāda school, based on "not this, not that" (*neti, neti*), is basically material. Such thought cannot give one the chance to know the Supreme Personality of Godhead as He is.

TEXT 22

सोऽयं समस्तजगतां सुहृदेक आत्मा
सत्त्वेन यन्मृडयते भगवान् भगेन ।
तेनैव मे दृशमनुस्पृशताद्यथाहं
स्रक्ष्यामि पूर्ववदिदं प्रणतप्रियोऽसौ ॥२२॥

so 'yaṁ samasta-jagatāṁ suhṛd eka ātmā
sattvena yan mṛḍayate bhagavān bhagena
tenaiva me dṛśam anuspṛśatād yathāhaṁ
srakṣyāmi pūrvavad idaṁ praṇata-priyo 'sau

saḥ—He; *ayam*—the Lord; *samasta-jagatām*—of all the universes; *suhṛt ekaḥ*—the one friend and philosopher; *ātmā*—the Supersoul; *sattvena*—by the mode of goodness; *yat*—one who; *mṛḍayate*—causes happiness; *bhagavān*—the Personality of Godhead; *bhagena*—with six opulences; *tena*—by Him; *eva*—certainly; *me*—to me; *dṛśam*—power of introspection; *anuspṛśatāt*—let Him give; *yathā*—as; *aham*—I; *srakṣyāmi*—will be able to create; *pūrva-vat*—as before; *idam*—this universe; *praṇata*—surrendered; *priyaḥ*—dear; *asau*—He (the Lord).

TRANSLATION

Let the Supreme Lord be merciful towards me. He is the one friend and soul of all living entities in the world, and He maintains all, for their ultimate happiness, by His six transcendental opulences. May He be merciful towards me so that I, as before, may be empowered with the introspection to create, for I am also one of the surrendered souls who are dear to the Lord.

PURPORT

The Supreme Lord, Puruṣottama, or Śrī Kṛṣṇa, is the maintainer of all, in both the transcendental and material worlds. He is the life and friend of all because there is eternally natural affection and love between the living entities and the Lord. He is the one friend and well-wisher for all, and He is one without a second. The Lord maintains all the living entities everywhere by His six transcendental opulences, for which He is known as *bhagavān,* or the Supreme Personality of Godhead. Lord Brahmā prayed for His mercy so that he might be able to create the universal affairs as he did before; only by the Lord's causeless mercy could he create both material and spiritual personalities like Marīci and Nārada respectively. Brahmā prayed to the Lord because He is very much dear to the surrendered soul. The surrendered soul knows nothing but the Lord, and therefore the Lord is very affectionate towards him.

TEXT 23

एष प्रपन्नवरदो रमयात्मशक्त्या
यद्यत्करिष्यति गृहीतगुणावतारः ।
तस्मिन् स्वविक्रममिदं सृजतोऽपि चेतो
युञ्जीत कर्मशमलं च यथा विजह्याम् ॥२३॥

eṣa prapanna-varado ramayātma-śaktyā
yad yat kariṣyati gṛhīta-guṇāvatāraḥ
tasmin sva-vikramam idaṁ sṛjato 'pi ceto
yuñjīta karma-śamalaṁ ca yathā vijahyām

eṣaḥ—this; *prapanna*—one who is surrendered; *vara-daḥ*—benefactor; *ramayā*—enjoying always with the goddess of fortune (Lakṣmī); *ātma-śaktyā*—with His internal potency; *yat yat*—whatever; *kariṣyati*—He may act; *gṛhīta*—accepting; *guṇa-avatāraḥ*—incarnation of the mode of goodness; *tasmin*—unto Him; *sva-vikramam*—with omnipotency; *idam*—this cosmic manifestation; *sṛjataḥ*—creating; *api*—in spite of; *cetaḥ*—heart; *yuñjīta*—be engaged; *karma*—work; *śamalam*—material affection; *ca*—also; *yathā*—as much as; *vijahyām*—I can give up.

TRANSLATION

The Supreme Lord, the Personality of Godhead, is always the benefactor of the surrendered souls. His activities are always enacted through His internal potency, Ramā, or the goddess of fortune. I pray only to engage in His service in the creation of the material world, and I pray that I not be materially affected by my works, for thus I may be able to give up the false prestige of being the creator.

PURPORT

In the matter of material creation, maintenance and destruction, there are three incarnations of the material modes of nature—Brahmā, Viṣṇu and Maheśvara. But the Lord's incarnation as Viṣṇu, in His internal potency, is the supreme energy for the total activities. Brahmā, who is only an assistant in the modes of creation, wanted to remain in his actual position as an instrument of the Lord instead of becoming puffed up by the false prestige of thinking himself the creator. That is the way of becoming dear to the Supreme Lord and receiving His benediction. Foolish men want to take credit for all creations made by them, but intelligent persons know very well that not a blade of grass can move without the will of the Lord; thus all the credit for wonderful creations must go to Him. By spiritual consciousness only can one be free from the contamination of material affection and receive the benedictions offered by the Lord.

TEXT 24

नाभिहसतोऽम्भसि यस्य पुंसो
विज्ञानशक्तिरहमासमनन्तशक्तेः ।
रूपं विचित्रमिदमस्य विवृण्वतो मे
मा रीरिषीष्ट निगमस्य गिरां विसर्गः ॥२४॥

nābhi-hradād iha sato 'mbhasi yasya puṁso
vijñāna-śaktir aham āsam ananta-śakteḥ
rūpaṁ vicitram idam asya vivṛṇvato me
mā rīriṣīṣṭa nigamasya girāṁ visargaḥ

nābhi-hradāt—from the navel lake; *iha*—in this millennium; *sataḥ*—lying; *ambhasi*—in the water; *yasya*—one whose; *puṁsaḥ*—of the Personality of Godhead; *vijñāna*—of the total universe; *śaktiḥ*—energy; *aham*—I; *āsam*—was born; *ananta*—unlimited; *śakteḥ*—of the powerful; *rūpam*—form; *vicitram*—variegated; *idam*—this; *asya*—His; *vivṛṇvataḥ*—manifesting; *me*—unto me; *mā*—may not; *rīriṣīṣṭa*—vanish; *nigamasya*—of the *Vedas; girām*—of the sounds; *visargaḥ*—vibration.

TRANSLATION

The Lord's potencies arc innumerable. As He lies down in the water of devastation, I am born as the total universal energy from the navel lake in which the lotus sprouts. I am now engaged in manifesting His diverse energies in the form of the cosmic manifestation. I therefore pray that in the course of my material activities I may not be deviated from the vibration of the Vedic hymns.

PURPORT

Every person engaged in the transcendental loving service of the Lord in this material world is prone to so many material activities, and if one is not strong enough to protect himself against the onslaught of material affection, he may be diverted from the spiritual energy. In the material creation Brahmā has to create all kinds of living entities with bodies suitable to their material conditions. Brahmā wants to be protected by the Lord because he has to contact many, many vicious living entities. An ordinary *brāhmaṇa* may fall from the *brahma-tejas,* or the power of brahminical excellence, due to his association with many fallen, conditioned souls. Brahmā, as the supermost *brāhmaṇa,* is afraid of such a falldown, and therefore he prays to the Lord for protection. This is a warning for one and all in the spiritual advancement of life. Unless one is sufficiently protected by the Lord, he may fall down from his spiritual position; therefore one has to pray constantly to the Lord for protection and the blessing to carry out one's duty. Lord Caitanya also entrusted His missionary work to His devotees and assured them of His protection against the onslaught of material affection. The path of spiritual life is stated in the *Vedas* to be like the edge of a sharpened razor. A little inattentiveness may at once create havoc and bloodshed, but one who is a completely surrendered soul, always seeking protection from the Lord in the discharge of his entrusted duties, has no fear of falling into material contamination.

TEXT 25

सोऽसावदभ्रकरुणो भगवान् विवृद्ध-
प्रेमस्मितेन नयनाम्बुरुहं विजृम्भन् ।
उत्थाय विश्वविजयाय च नो विषादं
माध्व्या गिरापनयतात्पुरुषः पुराणः ॥२५॥

so 'sāv adabhra-karuṇo bhagavān vivṛddha-
prema-smitena nayanāmburuhaṁ vijṛmbhan
utthāya viśva-vijayāya ca no viṣādaṁ
mādhvyā girāpanayatāt puruṣaḥ purāṇaḥ

saḥ—He (the Lord); *asau*—that; *adabhra*—unlimited; *karuṇaḥ*—merciful; *bhagavān*—the Personality of Godhead; *vivṛddha*—excessive; *prema*—love; *smitena*—by smiling; *nayana-amburuham*—the lotus eyes; *vijṛmbhan*—by opening; *utthāya*—for flourishing; *viśva-vijayāya*—for glorifying the cosmic creation; *ca*—as also; *naḥ*—our; *viṣādam*—dejection; *mādhvyā*—by sweet; *girā*—words; *apanayatāt*—let Him kindly remove; *puruṣaḥ*—the Supreme; *purāṇaḥ*—oldest.

TRANSLATION

The Lord, who is supreme and is the oldest of all, is unlimitedly merciful. I wish that He may smilingly bestow His benediction upon me by opening His lotus eyes. He can uplift the entire cosmic creation and remove our dejection by kindly speaking His directions.

PURPORT

The Lord is ever increasingly merciful upon the fallen souls of this material world. The whole cosmic manifestation is a chance for all to improve themselves in devotional service to the Lord, and everyone is meant for that purpose. The Lord expands Himself into many personalities who are either self-expansions or separated expansions. The personalities of the individual souls are His separated expansions, whereas the self-expansions are the Lord Himself. The self-expansions are predominators, and the separated expansions are predominated for reciprocation of transcendental bliss with the supreme form of bliss and knowledge. The liberated souls can join in this blissful reciprocation of predominator and predominated without materially concocted ideas. The typical example of such a transcendental exchange between the predominator and the predominated is the Lord's *rāsa-līlā* with the *gopīs*. The *gopīs* are predominated expansions of the internal potency, and therefore the Lord's participation in the *rāsa-līlā* dance is never to be considered like the mundane relationship of man and woman. It is, rather, the highest perfectional stage of the exchange of feelings between the Lord and the living entities. The Lord gives the fallen souls the chance for this highest perfection of life. Lord Brahmā is entrusted with the management of the complete cosmic show, and therefore he prays that the Lord bestow His blessings upon him so that he may execute its purpose.

TEXT 26

मैत्रेय उवाच
स्वसम्भवं निशाम्यैवं तपोविद्यासमाधिभिः ।
यावन्मनोवचः स्तुत्वा विरराम स खिन्नवत् ॥२६॥

maitreya uvāca
sva-sambhavaṁ niśāmyaivaṁ
tapo-vidyā-samādhibhiḥ
yāvan mano-vacaḥ stutvā
virarāma sa khinnavat

maitreyaḥ uvāca—the great sage Maitreya said; *sva-sambhavam*—the source of his appearance; *niśāmya*—by seeing; *evam*—thus; *tapaḥ*—penance; *vidyā*—knowledge; *samādhibhiḥ*—as also by concentration of the mind; *yāvat*—as far as possible; *manaḥ*—mind; *vacaḥ*—words; *stutvā*—having prayed; *virarāma*—became silent; *saḥ*—he (Brahmā); *khinna-vat*—as if tired.

TRANSLATION

The sage Maitreya said: O Vidura, after observing the source of his appearance, namely the Personality of Godhead, Brahmā prayed for His mercy as far as his mind and words would permit him. Thus having prayed, he became silent, as if tired from his activities of penance, knowledge and mental concentration.

PURPORT

Brahmā's enlightenment in knowledge was due to the Lord sitting within his heart. After being created, Brahmā could not ascertain the source of his appearance, but after penance and mental concentration he could see the source of his birth, and thus he became enlightened through his heart. The spiritual master outside and the spiritual master within are both representations of the Lord. Unless one has contact with such bona fide representations, one cannot claim to be a spiritual master. Lord Brahmā had no opportunity to take the help of a spiritual master from outside because at that time Brahmā himself was the only creature in the universe. Therefore, on becoming satisfied by the prayers of Brahmā, the Lord enlightened him about everything from within.

TEXTS 27-28

अथाभिप्रेतमन्वीक्ष्य ब्रह्मणो मधुसूदनः ।
विषण्णचेतसं तेन कल्पव्यतिकराम्भसा ॥२७॥
लोकसंस्थानविज्ञान आत्मनः परिखिद्यतः ।
तमाहागाधया वाचा कश्मलं शमयन्निव ॥२८॥

athābhipretam anvīkṣya
brahmaṇo madhusūdanaḥ
viṣaṇṇa-cetasaṁ tena
kalpa-vyatikarāmbhasā

loka-saṁsthāna-vijñāna
ātmanaḥ parikhidyataḥ
tam āhāgādhayā vācā
kaśmalaṁ śamayann iva

atha—thereupon; *abhipretam*—intention; *anvīkṣya*—observing; *brahmaṇaḥ*—of Brahmā; *madhusūdanaḥ*—the killer of the Madhu demon; *viṣaṇṇa*—depressed; *cetasam*—of the heart; *tena*—by him; *kalpa*—millennium; *vyatikara-ambhasā*—devastating water; *loka-saṁsthāna*—

situation of the planetary system; *vijñāne*—in the science; *ātmanaḥ*—of himself; *parikhidyataḥ*—sufficiently anxious; *tam*—unto him; *āha*—said; *agādhayā*—deeply thoughtful; *vācā*—by words; *kaśmalam*—impurities; *śamayan*—removing; *iva*—like that.

TRANSLATION

The Lord saw that Brahmā was very anxious about the planning and construction of the different planetary systems and was depressed upon seeing the devastating water. He could understand the intention of Brahmā, and thus He spoke in deep, thoughtful words, removing all the illusion that had arisen.

PURPORT

The devastating water was so fearful that even Brahmā was perturbed at its appearance and became very anxious about how to situate the different planetary systems in outer space to accommodate the different kinds of living entities, such as the human beings, those lower than the human beings, and the superhuman beings. All the planets in the universe are situated according to the different grades of living entities under the influence of the modes of material nature. There are three modes of material nature, and when they are mixed with one another they become nine. When the nine are mixed they become eighty one, and the eighty-one also become mixed, and thus we ultimately do not know how the delusion increases and increases. Lord Brahmā had to accommodate different places and situations for the requisite bodies of the conditioned souls. The task was meant only for Brahmā, and no one in the universe can even understand how difficult it was. But by the grace of the Lord, Brahmā was able to execute the tremendous task so perfectly that everyone is amazed to see the workmanship of the *vidhātā*, or the regulator.

TEXT 29

श्रीभगवानुवाच
मा वेदगर्भ गास्तन्द्रीं सर्गं उद्यममावह ।
तन्मयापादितं ह्यग्रे यन्मां प्रार्थयते भवान् ॥२९॥

śrī-bhagavān uvāca
mā veda-garbha gās tandrīṁ
sarga udyamam āvaha
tan mayāpāditaṁ hy agre
yan māṁ prārthayate bhavān

śrī-bhagavān uvāca—the Lord, the Personality of Godhead, said; *mā*—do not; *veda-garbha*—O You who have the depth of all Vedic wisdom; *gāḥ tandrīm*—become dejected; *sarge*—for creation; *udyamam*—enterprises; *āvaha*—you just undertake; *tat*—that (which you want); *mayā*—by Me; *āpāditam*—executed; *hi*—certainly; *agre*—previously; *yat*—which; *mām*—from Me; *prārthayate*—begging; *bhavān*—you.

TRANSLATION

The Supreme Personality of Godhead then said: O Brahmā, O depth of Vedic wisdom, be neither depressed nor anxious about the execution of creation. What you are begging from Me has already been granted before.

PURPORT

Any person authorized by either the Lord or by His bona fide representative is already blessed, as is the work entrusted to him. Of course, the person entrusted with such a responsibility should always be aware of his incapability and must always look for the mercy of the Lord for the successful execution of his duty. One should not be puffed up because he is entrusted with certain executive work. Fortunate is he who is so entrusted, and if he is always fixed in the sense of being subordinate to the will of the Supreme, he is sure to come out successful in the discharge of his work. Arjuna was entrusted with the work of fighting on the Battlefield of Kurukṣetra, and before he was so entrusted, the Lord had already arranged for his victory. But Arjuna was always conscious of his position as subordinate to the Lord, and thus he accepted Him as the supreme guide in his responsibility. Anyone who takes pride in doing responsible work but does not give credit to the Supreme Lord is certainly falsely proud and cannot execute anything nicely. Brahmā and persons in the line of his disciplic succession who follow in his footsteps are always successful in the discharge of loving transcendental service to the Supreme Lord.

TEXT 30

भूयस्त्वं तप आतिष्ठ विद्यां चैव मदाश्रयाम् ।
ताभ्यामन्तर्हृदि ब्रह्मन् लोकान्द्रक्ष्यस्यपावृतान् ॥३०॥

bhūyas tvaṁ tapa ātiṣṭha
vidyāṁ caiva mad-āśrayām
tābhyām antar-hṛdi brahman
lokān drakṣyasy apāvṛtān

bhūyaḥ—again; *tvam*—yourself; *tapaḥ*—penance; *ātiṣṭha*—be situated; *vidyām*—in the knowledge; *ca*—also; *eva*—certainly; *mat*—My; *āśrayām*—under the protection; *tābhyām*—by those qualifications; *antaḥ*—within; *hṛdi*—in the heart; *brahman*—O *brāhmaṇa; lokān*—all the worlds; *drakṣyasi*—you will see; *apāvṛtān*—all disclosed.

TRANSLATION

O Brahmā, situate yourself in penance and meditation and follow the principles of knowledge to receive My favor. By these actions you will be able to understand everything from within your heart.

PURPORT

The mercy the Lord bestows upon a particular person engaged in executing the responsible work entrusted unto him is beyond imagination. But His mercy is received due to our penance and perseverance in executing devotional service. Brahmā was entrusted with the work of creating the planetary systems. The Lord instructed him that when he meditated he would very easily know where and how the planetary systems must be arranged. The directions were to come from within, and there was no necessity for anxiety in that task. Such instructions of *buddhi-yoga* are directly imparted by the Lord from within, as confirmed in *Bhagavad-gītā* (10.10).

TEXT 31

तत आत्मनि लोके च भक्तियुक्तः समाहितः ।
द्रष्टासि मां ततं ब्रह्मन्मयि लोकांस्त्वमात्मनः ॥३१॥

tata ātmani loke ca
bhakti-yuktaḥ samāhitaḥ
draṣṭāsi māṁ tataṁ brahman
mayi lokāṁs tvam ātmanaḥ

tataḥ—thereafter; *ātmani*—in yourself; *loke*—in the universe; *ca*—also; *bhakti-yuktaḥ*—being situated in devotional service; *samāhitaḥ*—being completely absorbed; *draṣṭā asi*—you shall see; *mām*—Me; *tatam*—spread throughout; *brahman*—O Brahmā; *mayi*—in Me; *lokān*—all the universe; *tvam*—you; *ātmanaḥ*—the living entities.

TRANSLATION

O Brahmā, when you are absorbed in devotional service, in the course of your creative activities, you will see Me in you and throughout the universe,

and you will see that you yourself, the universe and the living entities are all in Me.

PURPORT

It is cited herein by the Lord that during his daytime Brahmā would see Him as Lord Śrī Kṛṣṇa. He would appreciate how the Lord expanded Himself into all the calves during His childhood at Vṛndāvana, he would know how Yaśodāmayī saw all the universes and planetary systems within the mouth of Kṛṣṇa during His playful childhood pastimes, and he would also see that there are many millions of Brahmās during the appearance of Lord Kṛṣṇa in Brahmā's daytime. But all these manifestations of the Lord, appearing everywhere in His eternal, transcendental forms, cannot be understood by anyone but the pure devotees, who are always engaged in devotional service to the Lord and are fully absorbed in the Lord. The high qualifications of Brahmā are also indicated herein.

TEXT 32

यदा तु सर्वभूतेषु दारुष्वग्निमिव स्थितम् ।
प्रतिचक्षीत मां लोको जह्यात्तर्ह्येव कश्मलम् ॥३२॥

yadā tu sarva-bhūteṣu
dāruṣv agnim iva sthitam
praticakṣīta māṁ loko
jahyāt tarhy eva kaśmalam

yadā—when; *tu*—but; *sarva*—all; *bhūteṣu*—in the living entities; *dāruṣu*—in wood; *agnim*—fire; *iva*—like; *sthitam*—situated; *praticakṣīta*—you shall see; *mām*—Me; *lokaḥ*—and the universe; *jahyāt*—can give up; *tarhi*—then at once; *eva*—certainly; *kaśmalam*—illusion.

TRANSLATION

You will see Me in all living entities as well as all over the universe, just as fire is situated in wood. Only in that state of transcendental vision will you be able to be free from all kinds of illusion.

PURPORT

Brahmā prayed that he might not forget his eternal relationship with the Lord during the course of his material activities. In answer to that prayer, the Lord said that he should not think of existing without a relationship with His omnipotency. The example is given of the fire in wood. The fire kindled in wood is always the same, although the wood may be of different types. Similarly, the bodies within the material creation may be specifically different according to shape and quality, but the spirit souls within them are not different from one another. The quality of fire, warmth, is the same everywhere, and the spiritual spark, or part and parcel of the Supreme Spirit, is the same in every living being; thus the potency of the Lord is distributed all over His creation. This transcendental knowledge alone can save one from the contamination of material illusion. Since the Lord's potency is distributed everywhere, a pure soul, or devotee of the Lord, can see everything in relationship with the Lord, and therefore he has no affection for the outer coverings. That pure spiritual conception makes him immune to all contamination of material association. The pure devotee never forgets the touch of the Lord in all circumstances.

TEXT 33

यदा रहितमात्मानं भूतेन्द्रियगुणाशयैः ।
स्वरूपेण मयोपेतं पश्यन् स्वाराज्यमृच्छति ॥३३॥

yadā rahitam ātmānaṁ
bhūtendriya-guṇāśayaiḥ
svarūpeṇa mayopetaṁ
paśyan svārājyam ṛcchati

yadā—when; *rahitam*—freed from; *ātmānam*—self; *bhūta*—material elements; *indriya*—material senses; *guṇa-āśayaiḥ*—under the influence of the material modes of nature; *svarūpeṇa*—in pure existence; *mayā*—by Me; *upetam*—approaching; *paśyan*—by seeing; *svārājyam*—spiritual kingdom; *ṛcchati*—enjoy.

TRANSLATION

When you are free from the conception of gross and subtle bodies and when your senses are free from all influences of the modes of material nature, you will realize your pure form in My association. At that time you will be situated in pure consciousness.

PURPORT

In the *Bhakti-rasāmṛta-sindhu* it is said that a person whose only desire is to render transcendental loving service to the Lord is a free person in any condition of material existence. That service attitude is the *svarūpa,* or real form, of the living entity. Lord Śrī Caitanya Mahāprabhu, in the *Caitanya-caritāmṛta,* also confirms this statement by declaring that the real, spiritual form of the living entity is eternal servitorship to the Supreme Lord. The Māyāvāda school shudders at the thought of a service attitude in the living entity, not knowing that in the transcendental world the service of the Lord is based on transcendental love. Transcendental loving service is never to be compared to the forced service of the material world. In the material world, even if one is under the conception that he is no one's servant, he is still the servant of his senses, under the dictation of the material modes. Factually no one is master here in the material world, and therefore the servants of the senses have a very bad experience of servitude. They shudder at the thought of service because they have no knowledge of the transcendental position. In transcendental loving service, the servitor is as free as the Lord. The Lord is *svarāṭ*, or fully independent, and the servant is also fully independent, or *svarāṭ*, in the spiritual atmosphere because there is no forced service. There the transcendental loving service is due to spontaneous love. A reflected glimpse of such service is experienced in the service of the mother unto the son, the friend's service unto the friend, or the wife's service unto the husband. These reflections of service by friends, parents or wives are not forced, but are due only to love. Here in this material world, however, the loving service is only a reflection. The real service, or service in *svarūpa*, is present in the transcendental world, in association with the Lord. The very same service in transcendental love can be practiced in devotion here.

This verse is also applicable to the *jñānī* school. The enlightened *jñānī*, when free from all material contaminations, namely the gross and subtle bodies together with the senses of the material modes of nature, is placed in the Supreme and is thus liberated from material bondage. The *jñānīs* and the devotees are actually in agreement up to the point of liberation from material contamination. But whereas the *jñānīs* remain pacified on the platform of simple understanding, the devotees develop further spiritual advancement in loving service. The devotees develop a spiritual individuality in their spontaneous service attitude, which is enhanced on and on, up to the point of *mādhurya-rasa*, or transcendental loving service reciprocated between the lover and the beloved.

TEXT 34

नानाकर्मवितानेन प्रजा बह्वीः सिसृक्षतः ।
नात्मावसीदत्यस्मिंस्ते वर्षीयान्मदनुग्रहः ॥३४॥

nānā-karma-vitānena
prajā bahvīḥ sisṛkṣataḥ

nātmāvasīdaty asmiṁs te
varṣīyān mad-anugrahaḥ

nānā-karma—varieties of service; *vitānena*—by expansion of; *prajāḥ*—population; *bahvīḥ*—innumerable; *sisṛkṣataḥ*—desiring to increase; *na*—never; *ātmā*—self; *avasīdati*—will be bereaved; *asmin*—in the matter; *te*—of you; *varṣīyān*—always increasing; *mat*—My; *anugrahaḥ*—causeless mercy.

TRANSLATION

Since you have desired to increase the population innumerably and expand your varieties of service, you shall never be deprived in this matter because My causeless mercy upon you will always increase for all time.

PURPORT

A pure devotee of the Lord, being cognizant of the facts of the particular time, object and circumstances, always desires to expand the number of devotees of the Lord in various ways. Such expansions of transcendental service may appear to be material to the materialist, but factually they are expansions of the causeless mercy of the Lord towards the devotee. Plans for such activities may appear to be material activities, but they are different in potency, being engaged in the satisfaction of the transcendental senses of the Supreme.

TEXT 35

ऋषिमाद्यं न बध्नाति पापीयांस्त्वां रजोगुणः ।
यन्मनो मयि निर्बद्धं प्रजाः संसृजतोऽपि ते ॥३५॥

ṛṣim ādyaṁ na badhnāti
pāpīyāṁs tvāṁ rajo-guṇaḥ
yan mano mayi nirbaddhaṁ
prajāḥ saṁsṛjato 'pi te

ṛṣim—unto the great sage; *ādyam*—the first of the kind; *na*—never; *badhnāti*—encroaches; *pāpīyān*—vicious; *tvām*—you; *rajaḥ-guṇaḥ*—the material mode of passion; *yat*—because; *manaḥ*—mind; *mayi*—in Me; *nirbaddham*—compact in; *prajāḥ*—progeny; *saṁsṛjataḥ*—generating; *api*—in spite of; *te*—your.

TRANSLATION

You are the original ṛṣi, and because your mind is always fixed on Me, even though you will be engaged in generating various progeny, the vicious mode of passion will never encroach upon you.

PURPORT

The same assurance is given to Brahmā in the Second Canto, Chapter Nine, verse 36. Being so favored by the Lord, Brahmā's schemes and plans are all infallible. If sometimes Brahmā is seen to be bewildered, as, in the Tenth Canto, he is bewildered by seeing the action of the internal potency, that is also for his further advancement in transcendental service. Arjuna is found to be similarly bewildered. All such bewilderment of the pure devotees of the Lord is specifically meant for their further advancement in knowledge of the Lord.

TEXT 36

ज्ञातोऽहं भवता त्वद्य दुर्विज्ञेयोऽपि देहिनाम् ।
यन्मां त्वं मन्यसेऽयुक्तं भूतेन्द्रियगुणात्मभिः ॥३६॥

jñāto 'haṁ bhavatā tv adya
durvijñeyo 'pi dehinām
yan māṁ tvaṁ manyase 'yuktaṁ
bhūtendriya-guṇātmabhiḥ

jñātaḥ—known; *aham*—Myself; *bhavatā*—by you; *tu*—but; *adya*—today; *duḥ*—difficult; *vijñeyaḥ*—to be known; *api*—in spite of; *dehinām*—for the conditioned soul; *yat*—because; *mām*—Me; *tvam*—you; *manyase*—understand; *ayuktam*—without being made of; *bhūta*—material elements; *indriya*—material senses; *guṇa*—material modes; *ātmabhiḥ*—and false ego like the conditioned soul.

TRANSLATION

Although I am not easily knowable by the conditioned soul, you have known Me today because you know that My personality is not constituted of anything material, and specifically not of the five gross and three subtle elements.

PURPORT

Knowledge of the Supreme Absolute Truth does not necessitate negation of the material manifestation but understanding of spiritual existence as it is. To think that because material existence is realized in forms therefore spiritual existence must be formless is only a negative material conception of spirit. The real spiritual conception is that spiritual form is not material form. Brahmā appreciated the eternal form of the Lord in that way, and the Personality of Godhead approved of Brahmā's spiritual conception. In *Bhagavad-gītā* the Lord condemned the material conception of Kṛṣṇa's body which arises because He is apparently present like a man. The Lord may appear in any of His many, many spiritual forms, but He is not materially composed, nor has He any difference between body and self. That is the way of conceiving the spiritual form of the Lord.

TEXT 37

तुभ्यं मद्विचिकित्सायामात्मा मे दर्शितोऽबहिः ।
नालेन सलिले मूलं पुष्करस्य विचिन्वतः ॥३७॥

tubhyaṁ mad-vicikitsāyām
ātmā me darśito 'bahiḥ
nālena salile mūlaṁ
puṣkarasya vicinvataḥ

tubhyam—unto you; *mat*—Me; *vicikitsāyām*—on your trying to know; *ātmā*—self; *me*—of Myself; *darśitaḥ*—exhibited; *abahiḥ*—from within; *nālena*—through the stem; *salile*—in the water; *mūlam*—root; *puṣkarasya*—of the lotus, the primeval source; *vicinvataḥ*—contemplating.

TRANSLATION

When you were contemplating whether there was a source to the stem of the lotus of your birth and you even entered into that stem, you could not trace out anything. But at that time I manifested My form from within.

PURPORT

The Personality of Godhead can be experienced only by His causeless mercy, not by mental speculation or with the help of the material senses. Material senses cannot approach the transcendental understanding of the Supreme Personality of Godhead. He can be appreciated only by submissive devotional service when He reveals Himself before the devotee. Only by love of Godhead can one know God, and not otherwise. The Personality of Godhead cannot be seen with the material eyes, but He can be seen from within by spiritual eyes opened by the ointment of love of Godhead. As long as one's spiritual eyes are closed due to the dirty covering of matter, one cannot see the Lord. But when the dirt is removed by the process of devotional service, one can see the Lord, without a doubt. Brahmā's personal endeavor to see the root of the lotus pipe failed, but when the Lord was satisfied by his penance and devotion, He revealed Himself from within with no external endeavor.

TEXT 38

यच्चकर्थाङ्ग मत्स्तोत्रं मत्कथाभ्युदयाङ्कितम् ।
यद्वा तपसि ते निष्ठा स एष मदनुग्रहः ॥३८॥

yac cakarthāṅga mat-stotraṁ
mat-kathābhyudayāṅkitam
yad vā tapasi te niṣṭhā
sa eṣa mad-anugrahaḥ

yat—that which; *cakartha*—performed; *aṅga*—O Brahmā; *mat-stotram*—prayers for Me; *mat-kathā*—words regarding My activities; *abhyudaya-aṅkitam*—enumerating My transcendental glories; *yat*—or that; *vā*—either; *tapasi*—in penance; *te*—your; *niṣṭhā*—faith; *saḥ*—that; *eṣaḥ*—all these; *mat*—My; *anugrahaḥ*—causeless mercy.

TRANSLATION

O Brahmā, the prayers that you have chanted praising the glories of My transcendental activities, the penances you have undertaken to understand Me, and your firm faith in Me—all these are to be considered My causeless mercy.

PURPORT

When a living entity desires to serve the Lord in transcendental loving service, the Lord helps the devotee in so many ways as the *caitya-guru,* or the spiritual master within, and thus the devotee can perform many wonderful activities beyond material estimation. By the mercy of the Lord even a layman can compose prayers of the highest spiritual perfection. Such spiritual perfection is not limited by material qualifications but is developed by dint of one's sincere endeavor to render transcendental service. Voluntary endeavor is the only qualification for spiritual perfection. Material acquisitions of wealth or education are not considered.

TEXT 39

प्रीतोऽहमस्तु भद्रं ते लोकानां विजयेच्छया ।
यदस्तौषीर्गुणमयं निर्गुणं मानुवर्णयन् ॥३९॥

prīto 'ham astu bhadraṁ te
lokānām vijayecchayā
yad astauṣīr guṇamayaṁ
nirguṇaṁ mānuvarṇayan

prītaḥ—pleased; *aham*—Myself; *astu*—let it be so; *bhadram*—all benediction; *te*—unto you; *lokānām*—of the planets; *vijaya*—for glorification; *icchayā*—by your desire; *yat*—that which; *astauṣīḥ*—you prayed for; *guṇa-mayam*—describing all transcendental qualities; *nirguṇam*—although I am free from all material qualities; *mā*—Me; *anuvarṇayan*—nicely describing.

TRANSLATION

I am very much pleased by your description of Me in terms of My transcendental qualities, which appear mundane to the mundaners. I grant you all benedictions in your desire to glorify all the planets by your activities.

PURPORT

A pure devotee of the Lord like Brahmā and those in his line of disciplic succession always desire that the Lord be known all over the universe by each and every one of the living entities. That desire of the devotee is always blessed by the Lord. The impersonalist sometimes prays for the mercy of the Personality of Godhead Nārāyaṇa as the embodiment of material goodness, but such prayers do not satisfy the Lord because He is not thereby glorified in terms of His actual transcendental qualities. The pure devotees of the Lord are always most dear to Him, although He is always kind and merciful to all living entities. Here the word *guṇamayam* is significant because it indicates the Lord's possessing transcendental qualities.

TEXT 40

य एतेन पुमान्नित्यं स्तुत्वा स्तोत्रेण मां भजेत् ।
तस्याशु सम्प्रसीदेयं सर्वकामवरेश्वरः ॥४०॥

ya etena pumān nityaṁ
stutvā stotreṇa māṁ bhajet
tasyāśu samprasīdeyaṁ
sarva-kāma-vareśvarah

yaḥ—anyone who; *etena*—by this; *pumān*—human being; *nityam*—regularly; *stutvā*—praying; *stotreṇa*—by the verses; *mām*—Me; *bhajet*—may worship; *tasya*—his; *āśu*—very soon; *samprasīdeyam*—I shall fulfill; *sarva*—all; *kāma*—desires; *vara-īśvaraḥ*—the Lord of all benediction.

TRANSLATION

Any human being who prays like Brahmā, and who thus worships Me, shall very soon be blessed with the fulfillment of all his desires, for I am the Lord of all benediction.

PURPORT

The prayers offered by Brahmā cannot be chanted by anyone who desires to fulfill his own sense gratification. Such prayers can be selected only by a person who wants to satisfy the Lord in His service. The Lord certainly fulfills all desires in regard to transcendental loving service, but He cannot fulfill the whims of nondevotees, even when such casual devotees offer Him the best of prayers.

TEXT 41

पूर्तेन तपसा यज्ञैर्दानैर्योगसमाधिना ।
राद्धं निःश्रेयसं पुंसां मत्प्रीतिस्तत्त्वविन्मतम् ॥४१॥

pūrtena tapasā yajñair
dānair yoga-samādhinā
rāddhaṁ niḥśreyasaṁ puṁsāṁ
mat-prītis tattvavin-matam

pūrtena—by traditional good work; *tapasā*—by penances; *yajñaiḥ*—by sacrifices; *dānaiḥ*—by charities; *yoga*—by mysticism; *samādhinā*—by trance; *rāddham*—success; *niḥśreyasam*—ultimately beneficial; *puṁsām*—of the human being; *mat*—of Me; *prītiḥ*—satisfaction; *tattva-vit*—expert transcendentalist; *matam*—opinion.

TRANSLATION

It is the opinion of expert transcendentalists that the ultimate goal of performing all traditional good works, penances, sacrifices, charities, mystic activities, trances, etc., is to invoke My satisfaction.

PURPORT

There are many traditionally pious activities in human society, such as altruism, philanthropy, nationalism, internationalism, charity, sacrifice, penance, and even meditation in trance, and all of them can be fully beneficial only when they lead to the satisfaction of the Supreme Personality of Godhead. The perfection of any activity—social, political, religious or philanthropic—is to satisfy the Supreme Lord. This secret of success is known to the devotee of the Lord, as exemplified by Arjuna on the Battlefield of Kurukṣetra. As a good, nonviolent man, Arjuna did not want to fight with his kinsmen, but when he understood that Kṛṣṇa wanted the fight and had arranged it at Kurukṣetra, he gave up his own satisfaction and fought for the satisfaction of the Lord. That is the right decision for all intelligent men. One's only concern should be to satisfy the Lord by one's activities. If the Lord is satisfied by an action, whatever it may be, then it is successful. Otherwise, it is simply a waste of time. That is the standard of all sacrifice, penance, austerity, mystic trance and other good and pious work.

TEXT 42

अहमात्मात्मनां धातः प्रेष्ठः सन् प्रेयसामपि ।
अतो मयि रतिं कुर्याद्देहादिर्यत्कृते प्रियः ॥४२॥

aham ātmātmanāṁ dhātaḥ
preṣṭhaḥ san preyasām api
ato mayi ratiṁ kuryād
dehādir yat-kṛte priyaḥ

aham—I am; *ātmā*—the Supersoul; *ātmanām*—of all other souls; *dhātaḥ*—director; *preṣṭhaḥ*—the dearest; *san*—being; *preyasām*—of all dear things; *api*—certainly; *ataḥ*—therefore; *mayi*—unto Me; *ratim*—attachment; *kuryāt*—one should do; *deha-ādiḥ*—the body and mind; *yat-kṛte*—on whose account; *priyaḥ*—very dear.

TRANSLATION

I am the Supersoul of every individual. I am the supreme director and the dearest. People are wrongly attached to the gross and subtle bodies, but they should be attached to Me only.

PURPORT

The Supreme Lord, the Personality of Godhead, is the dearest in both the conditioned and liberated states. When a person does not know that the Lord is the only dearmost object, then he is in the conditioned state of life, and when one knows perfectly well that the Lord is the only dearmost object, he is considered to be liberated. There are degrees of knowing one's relationship with the Lord, depending on the degree of realization as to why the Supreme Lord is the dearmost object of every living being. The real reason is clearly stated in *Bhagavad-gītā* (15.7). *Mamaivāṁśo jīva-loke jīva-bhūtaḥ sanātanaḥ*: the living entities are eternally parts and parcels of the Supreme Lord. The living entity is called the *ātmā*, and the Lord is called the Paramātmā. The living entity is called Brahman, and the Lord is called the Para-brahman, or the Parameśvara. *Īśvaraḥ paramaḥ kṛṣṇaḥ*. The conditioned souls, who do not have self-realization, accept the material body as the dearmost. The idea of the dearmost is then spread all over the body, both concentrated and extended. The attachment for one's own body and its extensions like children and relatives is actually developed on the basis of the real living entity. As soon as the real living entity is out of the body, even the body of the most dear son is no longer attractive. Therefore the living spark, or eternal part of the Supreme, is the real basis of affection, and not the body. Because the living entities are also parts of the whole living entity, that supreme living entity is the factual basis of affection for all. One who has forgotten the basic principle of his love for everything has only flickering love because he is in *māyā*. The more one is affected by the principle of *māyā*, the more he is detached from the basic principle of love. One cannot factually love anything unless he is fully developed in the loving service of the Lord.

In the present verse, stress is given to focusing love upon the Supreme Personality of Godhead. The word *kuryāt* is significant here. This means "one must have it." It is just to stress that we must have more and more attachment to the principle of love. The influence of *māyā* is experienced by the part and parcel spiritual entity, but it cannot influence the Supersoul, the Paramātmā. The Māyāvādī philosophers, accepting the influence of *māyā* on the living entity, want to become one with the Paramātmā. But because they have no actual love for Paramātmā, they remain ever entrapped by the influence of *māyā* and are unable to approach the vicinity of Paramātmā. This inability is due to their lack of affection for the Paramātmā. A rich miser does not know how to utilize his wealth, and therefore, in spite of his being very rich, his miserly behavior keeps him everlastingly a poor man. On the other hand, a person who knows how to utilize wealth can quickly become a rich man, even with a small credit balance.

The eyes and the sun are very intimately related because without sunlight the eyes are unable to see. But the other parts of the body, being attached to the sun as a source of warmth, take more advantage of the sun than do the eyes. Without possessing affection for the sun, the eyes cannot bear the rays of the sun; or, in other words, such eyes have no capacity to understand the utility of the sun's rays. Similarly, the empiric philosophers, despite their theoretical knowledge of Brahman, cannot utilize the mercy of the Supreme Brahman because they lack affection. So many impersonal philosophers remain everlastingly under the influence of *māyā* Because, although they indulge in theoretical knowledge of Brahman, they do not develop affection for Brahman nor do they have any scope for development of affection because of their defective method. A devotee of the sun-god, even though devoid of eyesight, can see the sun-god as he is even from this planet, whereas one who is not a devotee of the sun cannot even bear the glaring sunlight. Similarly, by devotional service, even though one is not on the level of a *jñānī*, one can see the Personality of Godhead within himself due to his development of pure love. In all circumstances one should try to develop love of Godhead, and that will solve all contending problems.

TEXT 43

सर्ववेदमयेनेदमात्मनात्मात्मयोनिना ।
प्रजाः सृज यथापूर्वं याश्च मय्यनुशेरते ॥४३॥

sarva-veda-mayenedam
ātmanātmātma-yoninā
prajāḥ sṛja yathā-pūrvaṁ
yāś ca mayy anuśerate

sarva—all; *veda-mayena*—under complete Vedic wisdom; *idam*—this; *ātmanā*—by the body; *ātmā*—you; *ātma-yoninā*—directly born of the Lord; *prajāḥ*—living entities; *sṛja*—generate; *yathā-pūrvam*—as it was hereinbefore; *yāḥ*—which; *ca*—also; *mayi*—in Me; *anuśerate*—lie.

TRANSLATION

By following My instructions you can now generate the living entities as before, by dint of your complete Vedic wisdom and the body you have directly received from Me, the supreme cause of everything.

TEXT 44

मैत्रेय उवाच
तस्मा एवं जगत्स्रष्ट्रे प्रधानपुरुषेश्वरः ।
व्यज्येदं स्वेन रूपेण कञ्जनाभस्तिरोदधे ॥४४॥

maitreya uvāca
tasmā evaṁ jagat-sraṣṭre
pradhāna-puruṣeśvaraḥ
vyajyedaṁ svena rūpeṇa
kañja-nābhas tirodadhe

maitreyaḥ uvāca—the sage Maitreya said; *tasmai*—unto him; *evam*—thus; *jagat-sraṣṭre*—unto the creator of the universe; *pradhāna-puruṣa-īśvaraḥ*—the primeval Lord, the Personality of Godhead; *vyajya idam*—after instructing this; *svena*—in His person; *rūpeṇa*—by the form; *kañja-nābhaḥ*—the Personality of Godhead Nārāyaṇa; *tirodadhe*—disappeared.

TRANSLATION

The sage Maitreya said: After instructing Brahmā, the creator of the universe, to expand, the primeval Lord, the Personality of Godhead in His personal form as Nārāyaṇa, disappeared.

PURPORT

Before his activity in creating the universe, Brahmā saw the Lord. That is the explanation of the *catuḥ-ślokī Bhāgavatam.* When the creation awaited Brahmā's activity, Brahmā saw the Lord, and therefore the Lord existed in His personal form before the creation. His eternal form is not created by the attempt of Brahmā, as imagined by less intelligent men. The Personality of Godhead appeared as He is before Brahmā, and He disappeared from him in the same form, which is not materially tinged.

Thus end the Bhaktivedanta purports of the Third Canto, Ninth Chapter, of the Śrīmad-Bhāgavatam, *entitled "Brahmā's prayers for Creative Energy."*

CHAPTER TEN

Divisions of the Creation

TEXT 1

विदुर उवाच
अन्तर्हिते भगवति ब्रह्मा लोकपितामहः ।
प्रजाः ससर्ज कतिधा दैहिकीर्मानसीर्विभुः ॥ १ ॥

vidura uvāca
antarhite bhagavati
brahmā loka-pitāmahaḥ
prajāḥ sasarja katidhā
daihikīr mānasīr vibhuḥ

viduraḥ uvāca—Śrī Vidura said; *antarhite*—after the disappearance; *bhagavati*—of the Personality of Godhead; *brahmā*—the first created living being; *loka-pitāmahaḥ*—the grandfather of all planetary inhabitants; *prajāḥ*—generations; *sasarja*—created; *katidhāḥ*—how many; *daihikīḥ*—from his body; *mānasīḥ*—from his mind; *vibhuḥ*—the great.

TRANSLATION

Śrī Vidura said: O great sage, please let me know how Brahmā, the grandfather of the planetary inhabitants, created the bodies of the living entities from his own body and mind after the disappearance of the Supreme Personality of Godhead.

TEXT 2

ये च मे भगवन् पृष्टास्त्वय्यर्था बहुवित्तम ।
तान् वदस्वानुपूर्व्येण छिन्धि नः सर्वसंशयान् ॥ २ ॥

ye ca me bhagavan pṛṣṭās
tvayy arthā bahuvittama
tān vadasvānupūrvyeṇa
chindhi naḥ sarva-saṁśayān

ye—all those; *ca*—also; *me*—by me; *bhagavan*—O powerful one; *pṛṣṭāḥ*—inquired; *tvayi*—unto you; *arthāḥ*—purpose; *bahu-vit-tama*—O greatly learned one; *tān*—all of them; *vadasva*—kindly describe; *ānupūrvyeṇa*—from beginning to end; *chindhi*—kindly eradicate; *naḥ*—my; *sarva*—all; *saṁśayān*—doubts.

TRANSLATION

O greatly learned one, kindly eradicate all my doubts, and let me know of all that I have inquired from you from the beginning to the end.

PURPORT

Vidura asked all relevant questions of Maitreya because he knew well that Maitreya was the right person to reply to all the points of his inquiries. One must be confident about the qualifications of his teacher; one should not approach a layman for replies to specific spiritual inquiries. Such inquiries, when replied to with imaginative answers by the teacher, are a program for wasting time.

TEXT 3

सूत उवाच
एवं सञ्चोदितस्तेन क्षत्त्रा कौषारविर्मुनिः ।
प्रीतः प्रत्याह तान् प्रश्नान् हृदिस्थानथ भार्गव ॥ ३ ॥

sūta uvāca
evaṁ sañcoditas tena
kṣattrā kauṣāravir muniḥ
prītaḥ pratyāha tān praśnān
hṛdi-sthān atha bhārgava

sūtaḥ uvāca—Śrī Sūta Gosvāmī said; *evam*—thus; *sañcoditaḥ*—being enlivened; *tena*—by him; *kṣattrā*—by Vidura; *kauṣāraviḥ*—the son of Kuṣāra; *muniḥ*—great sage; *prītaḥ*—being pleased; *pratyāha*—replied; *tān*—those; *praśnān*—questions; *hṛdi-sthān*—from the core of his heart; *atha*—thus; *bhārgava*—O son of Bhṛgu.

TRANSLATION

Sūta Gosvāmī said: O son of Bhṛgu, the great sage Maitreya Muni, thus hearing from Vidura, felt very much enlivened. Everything was in his heart, and thus he began to reply to the questions one after another.

PURPORT

The phrase *sūta uvāca* ("Sūta Gosvāmī said") appears to indicate a break in the discourse between Mahārāja Parīkṣit and Śukadeva Gosvāmī. While Śukadeva Gosvāmī was speaking to Mahārāja Parīkṣit, Sūta Gosvāmī was only one member of a large audience. But Sūta Gosvāmī was speaking to the sages of Naimiṣāraṇya, headed by the sage Śaunaka, a descendant of Śukadeva Gosvāmī. This, however, does not make any substantial difference in the topics under discussion.

TEXT 4

मैत्रेय उवाच
विरिञ्चोऽपि तथा चक्रे दिव्यं वर्षशतं तपः ।
आत्मन्यात्मानमावेश्य यथाह भगवानजः ॥ ४ ॥

maitreya uvāca
viriñco 'pi tathā cakre
divyaṁ varṣa-śataṁ tapaḥ
ātmany ātmānam āveśya
yathāha bhagavān ajaḥ

maitreyaḥ uvāca—the great sage Maitreya said; *viriñcaḥ*—Brahmā; *api*—also; *tathā*—in that manner; *cakre*—performed; *divyam*—celestial; *varṣa-śatam*—one hundred years; *tapaḥ*—penances; *ātmani*—unto the Lord; *ātmānam*—his own self; *āveśya*—engaging; *yathā āha*—as it was spoken; *bhagavān*—the Personality of Godhead; *ajaḥ*—the unborn.

TRANSLATION

The greatly learned sage Maitreya said: O Vidura, Brahmā thus engaged himself in penances for one hundred celestial years, as advised by the Personality of Godhead, and applied himself in devotional service to the Lord.

PURPORT

That Brahmā engaged himself for the Personality of Godhead, Nārāyaṇa, means that he engaged himself in the service of the Lord; that is the highest penance one can perform for any number of years. There is no retirement from such service, which is eternal and ever encouraging.

TEXT 5

तद्विलोक्याब्जसम्भूतो वायुना यदधिष्ठितः ।
पद्ममम्भश्च तत्कालकृतवीर्येण कम्पितम् ॥ ५ ॥

tad vilokyābja-sambhūto
vāyunā yad-adhiṣṭhitaḥ
padmam ambhaś ca tat-kāla-
kṛta-vīryeṇa kampitam

tat vilokya—looking into that; *abja-sambhūtaḥ*—whose source of birth was a lotus; *vāyunā*—by the air; *yat*—that; *adhiṣṭhitaḥ*—on which he was situated; *padmam*—lotus; *ambhaḥ*—water; *ca*—also; *tat-kāla-kṛta*—which was effected by eternal time; *vīryeṇa*—by its inherent force; *kampitam*—trembling.

TRANSLATION

Thereafter Brahmā saw that both the lotus on which he was situated and the water on which the lotus was growing were trembling due to a strong, violent wind.

PURPORT

The material world is called illusory because it is a place of forgetfulness of the transcendental service of the Lord. Thus one engaged in the the Lord's devotional service in the material world may sometimes be very much disturbed by awkward circumstances. There is a declaration of war between the two parties, the illusory energy and the devotee, and sometimes the weak devotees fall victim to the onslaught of the powerful illusory energy. Lord Brahmā, however, was sufficiently strong, by the causeless mercy of the Lord, and he could not be victimized by the material energy, although it gave him cause for anxiety when it managed to totter the existence of his position.

TEXT 6

तपसा ह्येधमानेन विद्यया चात्मसंस्थया ।
विवृद्धविज्ञानबलो न्यपाद् वायुं सहाम्भसा ॥ ६ ॥

tapasā hy edhamānena
vidyayā cātma-saṁsthayā
vivṛddha-vijñāna-balo
nyapād vāyuṁ sahāmbhasā

tapasā—by penance; *hi*—certainly; *edhamānena*—increasing; *vidyayā*—by transcendental knowledge; *ca*—also; *ātma*—self; *saṁsthayā*—situated in the self; *vivṛddha*—matured; *vijñāna*—practical knowledge; *balaḥ*—power; *nyapāt*—drank; *vāyum*—the wind; *saha ambhasā*—along with the water.

TRANSLATION

Long penance and transcendental knowledge of self-realization had matured Brahmā in practical knowledge, and thus he drank the wind completely, along with the water.

PURPORT

Lord Brahmā's struggle for existence is a personal example of the continued fight between the living entities in the material world and the illusory energy called *māyā*. Beginning from Brahmā down to this age, the living entities are struggling with the forces of material nature. By advanced knowledge in science and transcendental realization, one can try to control the material energy, which works against our endeavors, and in the modern age advanced material scientific knowledge and penance have played very wonderful roles in controlling the powers of the material energy. Such control of the material energy, however, can be most successfully carried out if one is a soul surrendered unto the Supreme Personality of Godhead and carries out His order in the spirit of loving transcendental service.

TEXT 7

तद्विलोक्य वियद्व्यापि पुष्करं यदधिष्ठितम् ।
अनेन लोकान् प्राग्लीनान् कल्पितास्मीत्यचिन्तयत् ॥ ७ ॥

tad vilokya viyad-vyāpi
puṣkaraṁ yad-adhiṣṭhitam
anena lokān prāg-līnān
kalpitāsmīty acintayat

tat vilokya—looking into that; *viyat-vyāpi*—extensively widespread; *puṣkaram*—the lotus; *yat*—that which; *adhiṣṭhitam*—he was situated; *anena*—by this; *lokān*—all the planets; *prāk-līnān*—previously merged in dissolution; *kalpitā asmi*—I shall create; *iti*—thus; *acintayat*—he thought.

TRANSLATION

Thereafter he saw that the lotus on which he was situated was spread throughout the universe, and he contemplated how to create all the planets, which were previously merged in that very same lotus.

PURPORT

The seeds of all the planets in the universe were impregnated in the lotus on which Brahmā was situated. All the planets were already generated by the Lord, and all the living entities were also born in Brahmā. The material world and the living entities were all already generated in seedling forms by the Supreme Personality of Godhead, and Brahmā was to disseminate the same seedlings all over the universe. The real creation is therefore called *sarga,* and, later on, the manifestation by Brahmā is called *visarga.*

TEXT 8

पद्मकोशं तदाविश्य भगवत्कर्मचोदितः ।
एकं व्यभाङ्क्षीदुरुधा त्रिधा भाव्यं द्विसप्तधा ॥ ८ ॥

padma-kośaṁ tadāviśya
bhagavat-karma-coditaḥ
ekaṁ vyabhāṅkṣīd urudhā
tridhā bhāvyaṁ dvi-saptadhā

padma-kośam—the whorl of the lotus; *tadā*—then; *āviśya*—entering into; *bhagavat*—by the Supreme Personality of Godhead; *karma*—in activities; *coditaḥ*—being encouraged by; *ekam*—one; *vyabhāṅkṣīt*—divided into; *urudhā*—great division; *tridhā*—three divisions; *bhāvyam*—capable of further creation; *dvi-saptadhā*—fourteen divisions.

TRANSLATION

Thus engaged in the service of the Supreme Personality of Godhead, Lord Brahmā entered into the whorl of the lotus, and as it spread all over the universe he divided it into three divisions of worlds and later into fourteen divisions.

TEXT 9

एतावाञ्जीवलोकस्य संस्थाभेदः समाहृतः ।
धर्मस्य ह्यनिमित्तस्य विपाकः परमेष्ठ्यसौ ॥ ९ ॥

etāvāñ jīva-lokasya
saṁsthā-bhedaḥ samāhṛtaḥ
dharmasya hy animittasya
vipākaḥ parameṣṭhy asau

etāvān—up to this; *jīva-lokasya*—of the planets inhabited by the living entities; *saṁsthā-bhedaḥ*—different situations of habitation; *samāhṛtaḥ*—performed completely; *dharmasya*—of religion; *hi*—certainly; *animittasya*—of causelessness; *vipākaḥ*—mature stage; *parameṣṭhī*—the highest personality in the universe; *asau*—that.

TRANSLATION

Lord Brahmā is the most exalted personality in the universe because of his causeless devotional service unto the Lord in mature transcendental knowledge. He therefore created all the fourteen planetary divisions for inhabitation by the different types of living entities.

PURPORT

The Supreme Lord is the reservoir of all the qualities of the living entities. The conditioned souls in the material world reflect only part of those qualities, and therefore they are sometimes called *pratibimbas.* These *pratibimba* living entities, as parts and parcels of the Supreme Lord, have inherited different proportions of His original qualities, and in terms of their inheritance of these qualities, they appear as different species of life and are accommodated in different planets according to the plan of Brahmā. Brahmā is the creator of the three worlds, namely the lower planets, called the Pātālalokas, the middle planets, called the Bhūrlokas, and the upper planets, called the Svarlokas. Still higher planets, such as Maharloka, Tapoloka, Satyaloka and Brahmaloka, do not dissolve in the devastating water. This is because of the causeless devotional service rendered unto the Lord by their inhabitants, whose existence continues up to the end of *dvi-parārdha* time, when they are generally liberated from the chain of birth and death in the material world.

TEXT 10

विदुर उवाच

यथात्थ बहुरूपस्य हरेरद्भुतकर्मणः ।
कालाख्यं लक्षणं ब्रह्मन् यथा वर्णय नः प्रभो ॥१०॥

vidura uvāca
yathāttha bahu-rūpasya
harer adbhuta-karmaṇaḥ
kālākhyaṁ lakṣaṇaṁ brahman
yathā varṇaya naḥ prabho

viduraḥ uvāca—Vidura said; *yathā*—as; *āttha*—you have said; *bahu-rūpasya*—having varieties of forms; *hareḥ*—of the Lord; *adbhuta*—wonderful; *karmaṇaḥ*—of the actor; *kāla*—time; *ākhyam*—of the name; *lakṣaṇam*—symptoms; *brahman*—O learned *brāhmaṇa; yathā*—as it is; *varṇaya*—please describe; *naḥ*—unto us; *prabho*—O lord.

TRANSLATION

Vidura inquired from Maitreya: O my lord, O greatly learned sage, kindly describe eternal time, which is another form of the Supreme Lord, the wonderful actor. What are the symptoms of that eternal time? Please describe them to us in detail.

PURPORT

The complete universe is a manifestation of varieties of entities, beginning from the atoms up to the gigantic universe itself, and all is under the control of the Supreme Lord in His form of *kāla,* or eternal time. The controlling time has different dimensions in relation to particular physical embodiments. There is a time for atomic dissolution and a time for the universal dissolution. There is a time for the annihilation of the body of the human being, and there is a time for the annihilation of the universal body. Also, growth, development and resultant actions all depend on the time factor. Vidura wanted to know in detail the different physical manifestations and their times of annihilation.

TEXT 11

मैत्रेय उवाच
गुणव्यतिकराकारो निर्विशेषोऽप्रतिष्ठितः ।
पुरुषस्तदुपादानमात्मानं लीलयासृजत् ॥११॥

maitreya uvāca
guṇa-vyatikarākāro
nirviśeṣo 'pratiṣṭhitaḥ
puruṣas tad-upādānam
ātmānaṁ līlayāsṛjat

maitreyaḥ uvāca—Maitreya said; *guṇa-vyatikara*—of the interactions of the modes of material nature; *ākāraḥ*—source; *nirviśeṣaḥ*—without diversity; *apratiṣṭhitaḥ*—unlimited; *puruṣaḥ*—of the Supreme Person; *tat*—that; *upādānam*—instrument; *ātmānam*—the material creation; *līlayā*—by pastimes; *asṛjat*—created.

TRANSLATION

Maitreya said: Eternal time is the primeval source of the interactions of the three modes of material nature. It is unchangeable and limitless, and it works as the instrument of the Supreme Personality of Godhead for His pastimes in the material creation.

PURPORT

The impersonal time factor is the background of the material manifestation as the instrument of the Supreme Lord. It is the ingredient of assistance offered to material nature. No one knows where time began and where it ends, and it is time only which can keep a record of the creation, maintenance and destruction of the material manifestation. This time factor is the material cause of creation and is therefore a self expansion of the Personality of Godhead. Time is considered the impersonal feature of the Lord.

The time factor is also explained by modern men in various ways. Some accept it almost as it is explained in the *Śrīmad-Bhāgavatam.* For example, in Hebrew literature time is accepted, in the same spirit, as a representation of God. It is stated therein: "God, who at sundry times and in diverse manners spake in time past unto the fathers by the prophets...." Metaphysically, time is distinguished as absolute and real. Absolute time is continuous and is unaffected by the speed or slowness of material things. Time is astronomically and mathematically calculated in relation to the speed, change and life of a particular object. Factually, however, time has nothing to do with the relativities of things; rather, everything is shaped and calculated in terms of the facility offered by time. Time is the basic measurement of the activity of our senses, by which we calculate past, present and future; but in factual calculation, time has no beginning and no end. Paṇḍita Cāṇakya says that even a slight fraction of time cannot be purchased with millions of dollars, and therefore even a moment of time lost without profit must be calculated as the greatest loss in life. Time is not subject to any form of psychology, nor are the moments objective realities in themselves, but they are dependent on particular experiences.

Therefore, Śrīla Jīva Gosvāmī concludes that the time factor is intermixed with the activities—actions and reactions—of the external energy of the Lord. The external energy, or material nature, works under the superintendence of the time factor as the Lord Himself, and that is why material nature appears to have produced so many wonderful things in the cosmic manifestation. *Bhagavad-gītā* (9.10) confirms this conclusion as follows:

mayādhyakṣeṇa prakṛtiḥ
sūyate sa-carācaram
hetunānena kaunteya
jagad viparivartate

TEXT 12

विश्वं वै ब्रह्मतन्मात्रं संस्थितं विष्णुमायया ।
ईश्वरेण परिच्छिन्नं कालेनाव्यक्तमूर्तिना ॥१२॥

viśvaṁ vai brahma-tan-mātraṁ
saṁsthitaṁ viṣṇu-māyayā
īśvareṇa paricchinnaṁ
kālenāvyakta-mūrtinā

viśvam—the material phenomenon; *vai*—certainly; *brahma*—the Supreme; *tat-mātram*—the same as; *saṁsthitam*—situated; *viṣṇu-māyayā*—by the energy of Viṣṇu; *īśvareṇa*—by the Personality of Godhead; *paricchinnam*—separated; *kālena*—by the eternal time; *avyakta*—unmanifested; *mūrtinā*—by such a feature.

TRANSLATION

This cosmic manifestation is separated from the Supreme Lord as material energy by means of kāla, which is the unmanifested, impersonal feature of the Lord. It is situated as the objective manifestation of the Lord under the influence of the same material energy of Viṣṇu.

PURPORT

As stated previously by Nārada before Vyāsadeva (*Bhag.* 1.5.20), *idaṁ hi viśvaṁ bhagavān ivetaraḥ*: this manifested world is the self-same Personality of Godhead, but it appears to be something else beyond or besides the Lord. It appears so because of its being separated from the Lord by means of *kāla*. It is something like the tape-recorded voice of a person who is now separated from the voice. As the tape recording is situated on the tape, so the whole cosmic manifestation is situated on the material energy and appears separate by means of *kāla*. The material manifestation is therefore the objective manifestation of the Supreme Lord and exhibits His impersonal feature so much adored by impersonalist philosophers.

TEXT 13

यथेदानीं तथाग्रे च पश्चादप्येतदीदृशम् ॥१३॥

yathedānīṁ tathāgre ca
paścād apy etad īdṛśam

yathā—as it is; *idānīm*—at present; *tathā*—so it was; *agre*—in the beginning; *ca*—and; *paścāt*—at the end; *api*—also; *etat īdṛśam*—it continues to be the same.

TRANSLATION

This cosmic manifestation is as it is now, it was the same in the past, and it will continue in the same way in the future.

PURPORT

There is a systematic schedule for the perpetual manifestation, maintenance and annihilation of the material world, as stated in *Bhagavad-gītā* (9.8): *bhūta-grāmam imaṁ kṛtsnam avaśaṁ prakṛter vaśāt*. As it is created now and as it will be destroyed later on, so also it existed in the past and again will be created, maintained and destroyed in due course of time. Therefore, the systematic activities of the time factor are perpetual and eternal and cannot be stated to be false. The manifestation is temporary and occasional, but it is not false as claimed by the Māyāvādī philosophers.

TEXT 14

सर्गो नवविधस्तस्य प्राकृतो वैकृतस्तु यः ।
कालद्रव्यगुणैरस्य त्रिविधः प्रतिसंक्रमः ॥१४॥

sargo nava-vidhas tasya
prākṛto vaikṛtas tu yaḥ
kāla-dravya-guṇair asya
tri-vidhaḥ pratisaṅkramaḥ

sargaḥ—creation; *nava-vidhaḥ*—of nine different kinds; *tasya*—its; *prākṛtaḥ*—material; *vaikṛtaḥ*—by the modes of material nature; *tu*—but; *yaḥ*—that which; *kāla*—eternal time;

dravya—matter; *guṇaiḥ*—qualities; *asya*—its; *tri-vidhaḥ*—three kinds; *pratisaṅkramaḥ*—annihilation.

TRANSLATION

There are nine different kinds of creations besides the one which naturally occurs due to the interactions of the modes. There are three kinds of annihilations due to eternal time, the material elements and the quality of one's work.

PURPORT

The scheduled creations and annihilations take place in terms of the supreme will. There are other creations due to interactions of material elements which take place by the intelligence of Brahmā. Later these will be more explicitly explained. At present, only preliminary information is given. The three kinds of annihilations are (1) due to the scheduled time of the annihilation of the entire universe, (2) due to a fire which emanates from the mouth of Ananta, and (3) due to one's qualitative actions and reactions.

TEXT 15

आद्यस्तु महतः सर्गो गुणवैषम्यमात्मनः ।
द्वितीयस्त्वहमो यत्र द्रव्यज्ञानक्रियोदयः ॥१५॥

ādyas tu mahataḥ sargo
guṇa-vaiṣamyam ātmanaḥ
dvitīyas tv ahamo yatra
dravya-jñāna-kriyodayaḥ

ādyaḥ—the first; *tu*—but; *mahataḥ*—of the total emanation from the Lord; *sargaḥ*—creation; *guṇa-vaiṣamyam*—interaction of the material modes; *ātmanaḥ*—of the Supreme; *dvitīyaḥ*—the second; *tu*—but; *ahamaḥ*—false ego; *yatra*—wherein; *dravya*—material ingredients; *jñāna*—material knowledge; *kriyā-udayaḥ*—awakening of activities (work).

TRANSLATION

Of the nine creations, the first one is the creation of the mahat-tattva, or the sum total of the material ingredients, wherein the modes interact due to the presence of the Supreme Lord. In the second, the false ego is generated in which the material ingredients, material knowledge and material activities arise.

PURPORT

The first emanation from the Supreme Lord for material creation is called the *mahat-tattva.* The interaction of the material modes is the cause of false identification, or the sense that a living being is made of material elements. This false ego is the cause of identifying the body and mind with the soul proper. Material resources and the capacity and knowledge to work are all generated in the second term of creation, after the *mahat-tattva. Jñāna* indicates the senses which are sources of knowledge, and their controlling deities. Work entails the working organs and their controlling deities. All these are generated in the second creation.

TEXT 16

भूतसर्गस्तृतीयस्तु तन्मात्रो द्रव्यशक्तिमान् ।
चतुर्थ ऐन्द्रियः सर्गो यस्तु ज्ञानक्रियात्मकः ॥१६॥

bhūta-sargas tṛtīyas tu
tan-mātro dravya-śaktimān
caturtha aindriyaḥ sargo
yas tu jñāna-kriyātmakaḥ

bhūta-sargaḥ—creation of matter; *tṛtīyaḥ*—is the third; *tu*—but; *tat-mātraḥ*—sense perception; *dravya*—of the elements; *śaktimān*—generator; *caturthaḥ*—the fourth; *aindriyaḥ*—in the matter of the senses; *sargaḥ*—creation; *yaḥ*—that which; *tu*—but; *jñāna*—knowledge-acquiring; *kriyā*—working; *ātmakaḥ*—basically.

TRANSLATION

The sense perceptions are created in the third creation, and from these the elements are generated. The fourth creation is the creation of knowledge and of working capacity.

TEXT 17

वैकारिको देवसर्गः पञ्चमो यन्मयं मनः ।
षष्ठस्तु तमसः सर्गो यस्त्वबुद्धिकृतः प्रभोः ॥१७॥

vaikāriko deva-sargaḥ
pañcamo yan-mayaṁ manaḥ
ṣaṣṭhas tu tamasaḥ sargo
yas tv abuddhi-kṛtaḥ prabhoḥ

vaikārikaḥ—interaction of the mode of goodness; *deva*—the demigods, or controlling deities; *sargaḥ*—creation; *pañcamaḥ*—fifth; *yat*—that which; *mayam*—sum total; *manaḥ*—mind; *ṣaṣṭhaḥ*—sixth; *tu*—but; *tamasaḥ*—of darkness; *sargaḥ*—creation; *yaḥ*—that which; *tu*—expletive; *abuddhi-kṛtaḥ*—made foolish; *prabhoḥ*—of the master.

TRANSLATION

The fifth creation is that of the controlling deities by the interaction of the mode of goodness, of which the mind is the sum total. The sixth creation is the ignorant darkness of the living entity, by which the master acts as a fool.

PURPORT

The demigods in the higher planets are called *devas* because they are all devotees of Lord Viṣṇu. *Viṣṇu-bhaktaḥ smṛto daiva āsuras tad-viparyayaḥ:* all the devotees of Lord Viṣṇu are *devas,* or demigods, whereas all others are *asuras.* That is the division of the *devas* and the *asuras. Devas* are situated in the mode of goodness of material nature, whereas the *asuras* are situated in the modes of passion or ignorance. The demigods, or controlling deities, are entrusted with departmental management of all the different functions of the material world. For example, one of our sense organs, the eye, is controlled by light, light is distributed by the sun rays, and their controlling deity is the sun. Similarly, mind is controlled by the moon. All other senses, both for working and for acquiring knowledge, are controlled by the different demigods. The demigods are assistants of the Lord in the management of material affairs.

After the creation of the demigods, all entities are covered by the darkness of ignorance. Each and every living being in the material world is conditioned by his mentality of lording it over the resources of material nature. Although a living entity is the master of the material world, he is conditioned by ignorance, by the false impression of being the proprietor of material things.

The energy of the Lord called *avidyā* is the bewildering factor of the conditioned souls. The material nature is called *avidyā,* or ignorance, but to the devotees of the Lord engaged in pure devotional service, this energy becomes *vidyā,* or pure knowledge. This is confirmed in *Bhagavad-gītā.* The energy of the Lord transforms from *mahāmāyā* to *yogamāyā* and appears to pure devotees in her real feature. The material nature therefore appears to function in three phases: as the creative principle of the material world, as ignorance and as knowledge. As disclosed in the previous verse, in the fourth creation the power of knowledge is also created. The conditioned souls are not originally fools, but by the influence of the *avidyā* function of material nature they are made fools, and thus they are unable to utilize knowledge in the proper channel.

By the influence of darkness, the conditioned soul forgets his relationship with the Supreme Lord and is overwhelmed by attachment, hatred, pride, ignorance and false identification, the five kinds of illusion that cause material bondage.

TEXT 18

षडिमे प्राकृताः सर्गा वैकृतानपि मे शृणु ।
रजोभाजो भगवतो लीलेयं हरिमेधसः ॥१८॥

ṣaḍ ime prākṛtāḥ sargā
vaikṛtān api me śṛṇu
rajo-bhājo bhagavato
līleyaṁ hari-medhasaḥ

ṣaṭ—six; *ime*—all these; *prākṛtāḥ*—of the material energy; *sargāḥ*—creations; *vaikṛtān*—secondary creations by Brahmā; *api*—also; *me*—from me; *śṛṇu*—just hear; *rajaḥ-bhājaḥ*—of the incarnation of the mode of passion (Brahmā); *bhagavataḥ*—of the greatly powerful; *līlā*—pastime; *iyam*—this; *hari*—the Supreme Personality of Godhead; *medhasaḥ*—of one who has such a brain.

TRANSLATION

All the above are natural creations by the external energy of the Lord. Now hear from me about the creations by Brahmā, who is an incarnation of the mode of passion and who, in the matter of creation, has a brain like that of the Personality of Godhead.

TEXT 19

सप्तमो मुख्यसर्गस्तु षड्विधस्तस्थुषां च यः ।
वनस्पत्योषधिलतात्वक्सारा वीरुधो द्रुमाः ॥१९॥

saptamo mukhya-sargas tu
ṣaḍ-vidhas tasthuṣāṁ ca yaḥ
vanaspaty-oṣadhi-latā-
tvaksārā vīrudho drumāḥ

saptamaḥ—the seventh; *mukhya*—principle; *sargaḥ*—creation; *tu*—indeed; *ṣaṭ-vidhaḥ*—six kinds of; *tasthuṣām*—of those who do not move; *ca*—also; *yaḥ*—those; *vanaspati*—fruit trees without flowers; *oṣadhi*—trees and plants existing until the fruit is ripe; *latā*—creepers;

tvaksārāḥ—pipe plants; *vīrudhaḥ*—creepers without support; *drumāḥ*—trees with flowers and fruits.

TRANSLATION

The seventh creation is that of the immovable entities, which are of six kinds: the fruit trees without flowers, trees and plants which exist until the fruit is ripe, creepers, pipe plants, creepers which have no support, and trees with flowers and fruits.

TEXT 20

उत्स्रोतसस्तमःप्राया अन्तःस्पर्शा विशेषिणः ॥२०॥

utsrotasas tamaḥ-prāyā
antaḥ-sparśā viśeṣiṇaḥ

utsrotasaḥ—they seek their subsistence upwards; *tamaḥ-prāyāḥ*—almost unconscious; *antaḥ-sparśāḥ*—slightly feeling within; *viśeṣiṇaḥ*—with varieties of manifestation.

TRANSLATION

All the immovable trees and plants seek their subsistence upwards. They are almost unconscious but have feelings of pain within. They are manifested in variegatedness.

TEXT 21

तिरश्चामष्टमः सर्गः सोऽष्टाविंशद्विधो मतः ।
अविदो भूरितमसो घ्राणज्ञा हृद्यवेदिनः ॥२१॥

tiraścām aṣṭamaḥ sargaḥ
so 'ṣṭāviṁśad-vidho mataḥ
avido bhūri-tamaso
ghrāṇa-jñā hṛdy avedinaḥ

tiraścām—species of lower animals; *aṣṭamaḥ*—the eighth; *sargaḥ*—creation; *saḥ*—they are; *aṣṭāviṁśat*—twenty-eight; *vidhaḥ*—varieties; *mataḥ*—considered; *avidaḥ*—without knowledge of tomorrow; *bhūri*—extensively; *tamasaḥ*—ignorant; *ghrāṇa-jñāḥ*—can know desirables by smell; *hṛdi avedinaḥ*—can remember very little in the heart.

TRANSLATION

The eighth creation is that of the lower species of life, and they are of different varieties, numbering twenty-eight. They are all extensively foolish and ignorant. They know their desirables by smell, but are unable to remember anything within the heart.

PURPORT

In the Vedas the symptoms of the lower animals are described as follows: *athetareṣāṁ paśūnāḥ aśanāpipāse evābhivijñānaṁ na vijñātaṁ vadanti na vijñātaṁ paśyanti na viduḥ śvastanaṁ na lokālokāv iti; yad vā, bhūri-tamaso bahu-ruṣaḥ ghrāṇenaiva jānanti hṛdyaṁ prati svapriyaṁ vastv eva vindanti bhojana-śayanādy-arthaṁ gṛhṇanti.* "Lower animals have knowledge only of their hunger and thirst. They have no acquired knowledge, no vision. Their behavior exhibits no dependence on formalities. Extensively ignorant, they can know their desirables only by smell, and by such intelligence only can they understand what is favorablc and unfavorable. Their knowledge is concerned only with eating and sleeping." Therefore, even the most ferocious lower animals, such as tigers, can bc tamed simply by regularly supplying meals and accommodations for sleeping. Only snakes cannot be tamed by such an arrangement.

TEXT 22

गौरजो महिषः कृष्णः सूकरो गवयो रुरुः ।
द्विशफाः पशवश्चेमे अविरुष्ट्रश्च सत्तम ॥२२॥

gaur ajo mahiṣaḥ kṛṣṇaḥ
sūkaro gavayo ruruḥ
dvi-śaphāḥ paśavaś ceme
avir uṣṭraś ca sattama

gauḥ—the cow; *ajaḥ*—the goat; *mahiṣaḥ*—the buffalo; *kṛṣṇaḥ*—a kind of stag; *sūkaraḥ*—hog; *gavayaḥ*—a species of animal; *ruruḥ*—deer; *dvi-śaphāḥ*—having two hooves; *paśavaḥ*—animals; *ca*—also; *ime*—all these; *aviḥ*—lamb; *uṣṭraḥ*—camel; *ca*—and; *sattama*—O purest.

TRANSLATION

O purest Vidura, of the lower animals the cow, goat, buffalo, kṛṣṇa-stag, hog, gavaya animal, deer, lamb and camel all have two hooves.

TEXT 23

खरोऽश्वोऽश्वतरो गौरः शरभश्चमरी तथा ।
एते चैकशफाः क्षत्तः शृणु पञ्चनखान् पशून् ॥२३॥

kharo 'śvo 'śvataro gauraḥ
śarabhaś camarī tathā
ete caika-śaphāḥ kṣattaḥ
śṛṇu pañca-nakhān paśūn

kharaḥ—ass; *aśvaḥ*—horse; *aśvataraḥ*—mule; *gauraḥ*—white deer; *śarabhaḥ*—bison; *camarī*—wild cow; *tathā*—thus; *ete*—all these; *ca*—and; *eka*—only one; *śaphāḥ*—hoof; *kṣattaḥ*—O Vidura; *śṛṇu*—just hear now; *pañca*—five; *nakhān*—nails; *paśūn*—animals.

TRANSLATION

The horse, mule, ass, gaura, śarabha bison and wild cow all have only one hoof. Now you may hear from me about the animals who have five nails.

TEXT 24

श्वा सृगालो वृको व्याघ्रो मार्जारः शशशल्लकौ ।
सिंहः कपिर्गजः कूर्मो गोधा च मकरादयः ॥२४॥

śvā sṛgālo vṛko vyāghro
mārjāraḥ śaśa-śallakau
siṁhaḥ kapir gajaḥ kūrmo
godhā ca makarādayaḥ

śvā—dog; *sṛgālaḥ*—jackal; *vṛkaḥ*—fox; *vyāghraḥ*—tiger; *mārjāraḥ*—cat; *śaśa*—rabbit; *śallakau*—*sajāru* (with thorns on the body); *siṁhaḥ*—lion; *kapiḥ*—monkey; *gajaḥ*—elephant; *kūrmaḥ*—tortoise; *godhā*—*gosāpa* (snake with four legs); *ca*—also; *makara-ādayaḥ*—the alligator and others.

TRANSLATION

The dog, jackal, tiger, fox, cat, rabbit, sajāru, lion, monkey, elephant, tortoise, alligator, gosāpa, etc., all have five nails in their claws. They are known as pañca-nakhas, or animals having five nails.

TEXT 25

कङ्कगृध्रबकश्येनभासभल्लूकबर्हिणः ।
हंससारसचक्राह्वकाकोलूकादयः खगाः ॥२५॥

kaṅka-gṛdhra-baka-śyena-
bhāsa-bhallūka-barhiṇaḥ
haṁsa-sārasa-cakrāhva-
kākolūkādayaḥ khagāḥ

kaṅka—heron; *gṛdhra*—vulture; *baka*—crane; *śyena*—hawk; *bhāsa*—the *bhāsa; bhallūka*—the *bhallūka; barhiṇaḥ*—the peacock; *haṁsa*—swan; *sārasa*—the *sārasa; cakrāhva*—the *cakravāka; kāka*—crow; *ulūka*—owl; *ādayaḥ*—and others; *khagāḥ*—the birds.

TRANSLATION

The heron, vulture, crane, hawk, bhāsa, bhallūka, peacock, swan, sārasa, cakravāka, crow, owl and others are the birds.

TEXT 26

अर्वाक्स्रोतस्तु नवमः क्षत्तरेकविधो नृणाम् ।
रजोऽधिकाः कर्मपरा दुःखे च सुखमानिनः ॥२६॥

arvāk-srotas tu navamaḥ
kṣattar eka-vidho nṛṇām
rajo 'dhikāḥ karma-parā
duḥkhe ca sukha-māninaḥ

arvāk—downwards; *srotaḥ*—passage of food; *tu*—but; *navamaḥ*—the ninth; *kṣattaḥ*—O Vidura; *eka-vidhaḥ*—one species; *nṛṇām*—of human beings; *rajaḥ*—the mode of passion; *adhikāḥ*—very prominent; *karma-parāḥ*—interested in working; *duḥkhe*—in misery; *ca*—but; *sukha*—happiness; *māninaḥ*—thinking.

TRANSLATION

The creation of the human beings, who are of one species only and who stock their eatables in the belly, is the ninth in the rotation. In the human race, the mode of passion is very prominent. Humans are always busy in the midst of miserable life, but they think themselves happy in all respects.

PURPORT

The human being is more passionate than the animals, and thus the sex life of the human being is more irregular. The animals have their due time for sexual intercourse, but the human being has no regular time for such activities. The human being is endowed with a higher, advanced stage of consciousness for getting relief from the existence of material miseries, but due to his ignorance he thinks that his higher consciousness is meant for advancing in the material comforts of life. Thus his intelligence is misused in the animal propensities—eating, sleeping, defending and mating—instead of spiritual realization. By advancing in material comforts the human being puts himself into a more miserable condition, but, illusioned by the material energy, he always thinks himself happy, even while in the midst of misery. Such misery of human life is distinct from the natural comfortable life enjoyed even by the animals.

TEXT 27

वैकृतास्त्रय एवैते देवसर्गश्च सत्तम ।
वैकारिकस्तु यः प्रोक्तः कौमारस्तूभयात्मकः ॥२७॥

vaikṛtās traya evaite
deva-sargaś ca sattama
vaikārikas tu yaḥ proktaḥ
kaumāras tūbhayātmakaḥ

vaikṛtāḥ—creations of Brahmā; *trayaḥ*—three kinds; *eva*—certainly; *ete*—all these; *deva-sargaḥ*—appearance of the demigods; *ca*—also; *sattama*—O good Vidura; *vaikārikaḥ*—creation of demigods by nature; *tu*—but; *yaḥ*—which; *proktaḥ*—described before; *kaumāraḥ*—the four Kumāras; *tu*—but; *ubhaya-ātmakaḥ*—both ways (namely *vaikṛta* and *prākṛta*).

TRANSLATION

O good Vidura, these last three creations and the creation of demigods (the tenth creation) are vaikṛta creations, which are different from the previously described prākṛta (natural) creations. The appearance of the Kumāras is both.

TEXTS 28-29

देवसर्गश्चाष्टविधो विबुधाः पितरोऽसुराः ।
गन्धर्वाप्सरसः सिद्धा यक्षरक्षांसि चारणाः ॥२८॥
भूतप्रेतपिशाचाश्च विद्याध्राः किन्नरादयः ।
दशैते विदुराख्याताः सर्गास्ते विश्वसृक्कृताः ॥२९॥

deva-sargaś cāṣṭa-vidho
vibudhāḥ pitaro 'surāḥ
gandharvāpsarasaḥ siddhā
yakṣa-rakṣāṁsi cāraṇāḥ

bhūta-preta-piśācāś ca
vidyādhrāḥ kinnarādayaḥ
daśaite vidurākhyātāḥ
sargās te viśva-sṛk-kṛtāḥ

deva-sargaḥ—creation of the demigods; *ca*—also; *aṣṭa-vidhaḥ*—eight kinds; *vibudhāḥ*—the demigods; *pitaraḥ*—the forefathers; *asurāḥ*—the demons; *gandharva*—the expert artisans in the higher planets; *apsarasaḥ*—the angels; *siddhāḥ*—persons who are perfect in mystic powers; *yakṣa*—the superprotectors; *rakṣāṁsi*—giants; *cāraṇāḥ*—the celestial singers; *bhūta*—jinn; *preta*—evil spirits; *piśācāḥ*—attendant spirits; *ca*—also; *vidyādhrāḥ*—the celestial denizens named Vidyādharas; *kinnara*—superhuman beings; *ādayaḥ*—and others; *daśa ete*—all these ten (creations); *vidura*—O Vidura; *ākhyātāḥ*—described; *sargāḥ*—creations; *te*—unto you; *viśva-sṛk*—the creator of the universe (Brahmā); *kṛtāḥ*—done by him.

TRANSLATION

The creation of the demigods is of eight varieties: (1) the demigods, (2) the forefathers, (3) the asuras, or demons, (4) the Gandharvas and Apsarās, or angels, (5) the Yakṣas and Rākṣasas, (6) the Siddhas, Cāraṇas and Vidyādharas, (7) the Bhūtas, Pretas and Piśācas, and (8) the superhuman beings, celestial singers, etc. All are created by Brahmā, the creator of the universe.

PURPORT

As explained in the Second Canto of *Śrīmad-Bhāgavatam*, the Siddhas are inhabitants of Siddhaloka, where the residents travel in space without vehicles. At their mere will they can pass from one planet to another without difficulty. Therefore, in the upper planets the inhabitants are far superior to the inhabitants of this planet in all matters of art, culture and science, since they possess brains superior to those of human beings. The spirits and jinn mentioned in this connection are also counted among the demigods because they are able to perform uncommon functions not possible for men.

TEXT 30

अतः परं प्रवक्ष्यामि वंशान्मन्वन्तराणि च ।
एवं रजःप्लुतः स्रष्टा कल्पादिष्वात्मभूर्हरिः ।
सृजत्यमोघसङ्कल्प आत्मैवात्मानमात्मना ॥३०॥

ataḥ paraṁ pravakṣyāmi
vaṁśān manvantarāṇi ca
evaṁ rajaḥ-plutaḥ sraṣṭā
kalpādiṣv ātmabhūr hariḥ
sṛjaty amogha-saṅkalpa
ātmaivātmānam ātmanā

ataḥ—here; *param*—after; *pravakṣyāmi*—I shall explain; *vaṁśān*—descendants; *manvantarāṇi*—different advents of Manus; *ca*—and; *evam*—thus; *rajaḥ-plutaḥ*—infused with the mode of passion; *sraṣṭā*—the creator; *kalpa-ādiṣu*—in different millenniums; *ātma-bhūḥ*—self-advent; *hariḥ*—the Personality of Godhead; *sṛjati*—creates; *amogha*—unfailing; *saṅkalpaḥ*—determination; *ātmā eva*—He Himself; *ātmānam*—Himself; *ātmanā*—by His own energy.

TRANSLATION

Now I shall describe the descendants of the Manus. The creator, Brahmā, as the incarnation of the passion mode of the Personality of Godhead, creates the universal affairs with unfailing desires in every millennium by the force of the Lord's energy.

PURPORT

The cosmic manifestation is an expansion of one of the many energies of the Supreme Personality of Godhead; the creator and the created are both emanations of the same Supreme Truth, as stated in the beginning of the *Bhāgavatam: janmādy asya yataḥ.*

Thus end the Bhaktivedanta purports of the Third Canto, Tenth Chapter, of the Śrīmad-Bhāgavatam, *entitled "Divisions of the Creation."*

CHAPTER ELEVEN

Calculation of Time, from the Atom

TEXT 1

मैत्रेय उवाच

चरमः सद्विशेषाणामनेकोऽसंयुतः सदा ।
परमाणुः स विज्ञेयो नृणामैक्यभ्रमो यतः

maitreya uvāca
caramaḥ sad-viśeṣāṇām
aneko 'saṁyutaḥ sadā
paramāṇuḥ sa vijñeyo
nṛṇām aikya-bhramo yataḥ

maitreyaḥ uvāca—Maitreya said; *caramaḥ*—ultimate; *sat*—effect; *viśeṣāṇām*—symptoms; *anekaḥ*—innumerable; *asaṁyutaḥ*—unmixed; *sada*—always; *parama-aṇuḥ*—atoms; *saḥ*—that; *vijñeyaḥ*—should be understood; *nṛṇām*—of men; *aikya*—oneness; *bhramaḥ*—mistaken; *yataḥ*—from which.

TRANSLATION

The material manifestation's ultimate particle, which is indivisible and not formed into a body, is called the atom. It exists always as an invisible identity, even after the dissolution of all forms. The material body is but a combination of such atoms, but it is misunderstood by the common man.

PURPORT

The atomic description of the *Śrīmad-Bhāgavatam* is almost the same as the modern science of atomism, and this is further described in the Paramāṇu-vāda of Kaṇāda. In modern science also, the atom is accepted as the ultimate indivisible particle of which the universe is composed. *Śrīmad-Bhāgavatam* is the full text of all descriptions of knowledge, including the theory of atomism. The atom is the minute subtle form of eternal time.

TEXT 2

सत एव पदार्थस्य स्वरूपावस्थितस्य यत् ।
कैवल्यं परममहानविशेषो निरन्तरः ॥ २ ॥

sata eva padārthasya
svarūpāvasthitasya yat
kaivalyaṁ parama-mahān
aviśeṣo nirantaraḥ

sataḥ—of the effective manifestation; *eva*—certainly; *pada-arthasya*—of physical bodies; *svarūpa-avasthitasya*—staying in the same form even to the time of dissolution; *yat*—that which; *kaivalyam*—oneness; *parama*—the supreme; *mahān*—unlimited; *aviśeṣaḥ*—forms; *nirantaraḥ*—eternally.

TRANSLATION

Atoms are the ultimate state of the manifest universe. When they stay in their own forms without forming different bodies, they are called the unlimited oneness. There are certainly different bodies in physical forms, but the atoms themselves form the complete manifestation.

TEXT 3

एवं कालोऽप्यनुमितः सौक्ष्म्ये स्थौल्ये च सत्तम ।
संस्थानभुक्त्या भगवानव्यक्तो व्यक्तभुग्विभुः ॥ ३ ॥

evaṁ kālo 'py anumitaḥ
saukṣmye sthaulye ca sattama
saṁsthāna-bhuktyā bhagavān
avyakto vyakta-bhug vibhuḥ

evam—thus; *kālaḥ*—time; *api*—also; *anumitaḥ*—measured; *saukṣmye*—in the subtle; *sthaulye*—in the gross forms; *ca*—also; *sattama*—O best; *saṁsthāna*—combinations of the atoms; *bhuktyā*—by the motion; *bhagavān*—the Supreme Personality of Godhead; *avyaktaḥ*—unmanifested; *vyakta-bhuk*—controlling all physical movement; *vibhuḥ*—the great potential.

TRANSLATION

One can estimate time by measuring the movement of the atomic combination of bodies. Time is the potency of the almighty Personality of

Godhead, Hari, who controls all physical movement although He is not visible in the physical world.

TEXT 4

स कालः परमाणुर्वै यो भुङ्क्ते परमाणुताम् ।
सतोऽविशेषभुग्यस्तु स कालः परमो महान् ॥ ४ ॥

sa kālaḥ paramāṇur vai
yo bhuṅkte paramāṇutām
sato 'viśeṣa-bhug yas tu
sa kālaḥ paramo mahān

saḥ—that; *kālaḥ*—eternal time; *parama-aṇuḥ*—atomic; *vai*—certainly; *yaḥ*—which; *bhuṅkte*—passes through; *parama-aṇutām*—the space of an atom; *sataḥ*—of the entire aggregate; *aviśeṣa-bhuk*—passing through the nondual exhibition; *yaḥ tu*—which; *saḥ*—that; *kālaḥ*—time; *paramaḥ*—the supreme; *mahān*—the great.

TRANSLATION

Atomic time is measured according to its covering a particular atomic space. That time which covers the unmanifest aggregate of atoms is called the great time.

PURPORT

Time and space are two correlative terms. Time is measured in terms of its covering a certain space of atoms. Standard time is calculated in terms of the movement of the sun. The time covered by the sun in passing over an atom is calculated as atomic time. The greatest time of all covers the entire existence of the nondual manifestation. All the planets rotate and cover space, and space is calculated in terms of atoms. Each planet has its particular orbit for rotating, in which it moves without deviation, and similarly the sun has its orbit. The complete calculation of the time of creation, maintenance and dissolution, measured in terms of the circulation of the total planetary systems until the end of creation, is known as the supreme *kāla*.

TEXT 5

अणुर्द्वौ परमाणू स्यात्त्रसरेणुस्त्रयः स्मृतः ।
जालार्करश्म्यवगतः खमेवानुपतन्नगात् ॥ ५ ॥

aṇur dvau paramāṇū syāt
trasareṇus trayaḥ smṛtaḥ
jālārka-raśmy-avagataḥ
kham evānupatann agāt

aṇuḥ—double atom; *dvau*—two; *parama-aṇu*—atoms; *syāt*—become; *trasareṇuḥ*—hexatom; *trayaḥ*—three; *smṛtaḥ*—considered; *jāla-arka*—of sunshine through the holes of a window screen; *raśmi*—by the rays; *avagataḥ*—can be known; *kham eva*—towards the sky; *anupatan agāt*—going up.

TRANSLATION

The division of gross time is calculated as follows: two atoms make one double atom, and three double atoms make one hexatom. This hexatom is visible in the sunshine which enters through the holes of a window screen. One can clearly see that the hexatom goes up towards the sky.

PURPORT

The atom is described as an invisible particle, but when six such atoms combine together, they are called a *trasareṇu*, and this is visible in the sunshine pouring through the holes of a window screen.

TEXT 6

त्रसरेणुत्रिकं भुङ्क्ते यः कालः स त्रुटिः स्मृतः ।
शतभागस्तु वेधः स्यात्तैस्त्रिभिस्तु लवः स्मृतः ॥ ६ ॥

trasareṇu-trikaṁ bhuṅkte
yaḥ kālaḥ sa truṭiḥ smṛtaḥ
śata-bhāgas tu vedhaḥ syāt
tais tribhis tu lavaḥ smṛtaḥ

trasareṇu-trikam—combination of three hexatoms; *bhuṅkte*—as they take time to integrate; *yaḥ*—that which; *kālaḥ*—duration of time; *saḥ*—that; *truṭiḥ*—by the name *truṭi*; *smṛtaḥ*—is called; *śata-bhāgaḥ*—one hundred *truṭis*; *tu*—but; *vedhaḥ*—called a *vedha*; *syāt*—it so happens; *taiḥ*—by them; *tribhiḥ*—three times; *tu*—but; *lavaḥ*—*lava*; *smṛtaḥ*—so called.

TRANSLATION

The time duration needed for the integration of three trasareṇus is called a truṭi, and one hundred truṭis make one vedha. Three vedhas make one lava.

PURPORT

It is calculated that if a second is divided into 1687.5 parts, each part is the duration of a *truṭi,* which is the time occupied in the integration of eighteen atomic particles. Such a combination of atoms into different bodies creates the calculation of material time. The sun is the central point for calculating all different durations.

TEXT 7

निमेषस्त्रिलवो ज्ञेय आम्नातस्ते त्रयः क्षणः ।
क्षणान् पञ्च विदुः काष्ठां लघु ता दश पञ्च च ॥ ७ ॥

nimeṣas tri-lavo jñeya
āmnātas te trayaḥ kṣaṇaḥ
kṣaṇān pañca viduḥ kāṣṭhāṁ
laghu tā daśa pañca ca

nimeṣaḥ—the duration of time called a *nimeṣa; tri-lavaḥ*—the duration of three *lavas; jñeyaḥ*—is to be known; *āmnātaḥ*—it is so called; *te*—they; *trayaḥ*—three; *kṣaṇaḥ*—the duration of time called a *kṣaṇa; kṣaṇān*—such *kṣaṇas; pañca*—five; *viduḥ*—one should understand; *kāṣṭhām*—the duration of time called a *kāṣṭhā; laghu*—the duration of time called a *laghu; tāḥ*—those; *daśa pañca*—fifteen; *ca*—also.

TRANSLATION

The duration of time of three lavas is equal to one nimeṣa, the combination of three nimeṣas makes one kṣaṇa, five kṣaṇas combined together make one kāṣṭhā, and fifteen kāṣṭhās make one laghu.

PURPORT

By calculation it is found that one *laghu* is equal to two minutes. The atomic calculation of time in terms of Vedic wisdom may be converted into present time with this understanding.

TEXT 8

लघूनि वै समाम्नाता दश पञ्च च नाडिका ।
ते द्वे मुहूर्तः प्रहरः षड्यामः सप्त वा नृणाम् ॥ ८ ॥

laghūni vai samāmnātā
daśa pañca ca nāḍikā

te dve muhūrtaḥ praharaḥ
ṣaḍ yāmaḥ sapta vā nṛṇām

laghūni—such *laghus* (each of two minutes); *vai*—exactly; *samāmnātā*—is called; *daśa pañca*—fifteen; *ca*—also; *nāḍikā*—a *nāḍikā; te*—of them; *dve*—two; *muhūrtaḥ*—a moment; *praharaḥ*—three hours; *ṣaṭ*—six; *yāmaḥ*—one fourth of a day or night; *sapta*—seven; *vā*—or; *nṛṇām*—of human calculation.

TRANSLATION

Fifteen laghus make one nāḍikā, which is also called a daṇḍa. Two daṇḍas make one muhūrta, and six or seven daṇḍas make one fourth of a day or night, according to human calculation.

TEXT 9

द्वादशार्धपलोन्मानं चतुर्भिश्चतुरङ्गुलैः ।
स्वर्णमाषैः कृतच्छिद्रं यावत्प्रस्थजलप्लुतम् ॥ ९ ॥

dvādaśārdha-palonmānaṁ
caturbhiś catur-aṅgulaiḥ
svarṇa-māṣaiḥ kṛta-cchidraṁ
yāvat prastha-jala-plutam

dvādaśa-ardha—six; *pala*—of the scale of weight; *unmānam*—measuring pot; *caturbhiḥ*—by weight of four; *catuḥ-aṅgulaiḥ*—four fingers by measure; *svarṇa*—of gold; *māṣaiḥ*—of the weight; *kṛta-chidram*—making a hole; *yāvat*—as long as; *prastha*—measuring one *prastha; jala-plutam*—filled by water.

TRANSLATION

The measuring pot for one nāḍikā, or daṇḍa, can be prepared with a six-pala-weight [fourteen ounce] pot of copper, in which a hole is bored with a gold probe weighing four māṣa and measuring four fingers long. When the pot is placed on water, the time before the water overflows in the pot is called one daṇḍa.

PURPORT

It is advised herein that the bore in the copper measuring pot must be made with a probe weighing not more than four *māṣa* and measuring not longer than four fingers. This regulates the diameter of the hole. The pot is submerged in water, and the overflooding time is called a *daṇḍa.* This is another way of measuring the duration of a *daṇḍa,* just as time is measured by sand in a glass. It appears that in the days of Vedic civilization there was no dearth of knowledge in physics, chemistry or higher mathematics. Measurements were calculated in different ways, as simply as could be done.

TEXT 10

यामाश्चत्वारश्चत्वारो मर्त्यानामहनी उभे ।
पक्षः पञ्चदशाहानि शुक्लः कृष्णश्च मानद ॥१०॥

yāmāś catvāraś catvāro
martyānām ahanī ubhe
pakṣaḥ pañca-daśāhāni
śuklaḥ kṛṣṇaś ca mānada

yāmāḥ—three hours; *catvāraḥ*—four; *catvāraḥ*—and four; *martyānām*—of the human beings; *ahanī*—duration of day; *ubhe*—both day and night; *pakṣaḥ*—fortnight; *pañca-daśa*—fifteen; *ahāni*—days; *śuklaḥ*—white; *kṛṣṇaḥ*—black; *ca*—also; *mānada*—measured.

TRANSLATION

It is calculated that there are four praharas, which are also called yāmas, in the day and four in the night of the human being. Similarly, fifteen days and nights are a fortnight, and there are two fortnights, white and black, in a month.

TEXT 11

तयोः समुच्चयो मासः पितॄणां तदहर्निशम् ।
द्वौ तावृतुः षडयनं दक्षिणं चोत्तरं दिवि ॥११॥

tayoḥ samuccayo māsaḥ
pitṝṇāṁ tad ahar-niśam
dvau tāv ṛtuḥ ṣaḍ ayanaṁ
dakṣiṇaṁ cottaraṁ divi

tayoḥ—of them; *samuccayaḥ*—aggregate; *māsaḥ*—month; *pitṝṇām*—of the Pitā planets; *tat*—that (month); *ahaḥ-niśam*—day and night; *dvau*—two; *tau*—months; *ṛtuḥ*—a season; *ṣaṭ*—six; *ayanam*—the movement of the sun in six months; *dakṣiṇam*—southern; *ca*—also; *uttaram*—northern; *divi*—in the heavens.

TRANSLATION

The aggregate of two fortnights is one month, and that period is one complete day and night for the Pitā planets. Two of such months comprise one season, and six months comprise one complete movement of the sun from south to north.

TEXT 12

अयने चाहनी प्राहुर्वत्सरो द्वादश स्मृतः ।
संवत्सरशतं नृणां परमायुर्निरूपितम् ॥१२॥

ayane cāhanī prāhur
vatsaro dvādaśa smṛtaḥ
saṁvatsara-śataṁ nṛṇāṁ
paramāyur nirūpitam

ayane—in the solar movement (of six months); *ca*—and; *ahanī*—a day of the demigods; *prāhuḥ*—it is said; *vatsaraḥ*—one calendar year; *dvādaśa*—twelve months; *smṛtaḥ*—is so called; *saṁvatsara-śatam*—one hundred years; *nṛṇām*—of human beings; *parama-āyuḥ*—duration of life; *nirūpitam*—is estimated.

TRANSLATION

Two solar movements make one day and night of the demigods, and that combination of day and night is one complete calendar year for the human being. The human being has a duration of life of one hundred years.

TEXT 13

ग्रहर्क्षताराचक्रस्थः परमाण्वादिना जगत् ।
संवत्सरावसानेन पर्येत्यनिमिषो विभुः ॥१३॥

graharkṣa-tārā-cakra-sthaḥ
paramāṇv-ādinā jagat
saṁvatsarāvasānena
paryety animiṣo vibhuḥ

graha—influential planets like the moon; *ṛkṣa*—luminaries like Aśvinī; *tārā*—stars; *cakra-sthaḥ*—in the orbit; *parama-aṇu-ādinā*—along with the atoms; *jagat*—the entire universe; *saṁvatsara-avasānena*—by the end of one year; *paryeti*—completes its orbit; *animiṣaḥ*—the eternal time; *vibhuḥ*—the Almighty.

TRANSLATION

Influential stars, planets, luminaries and atoms all over the universe are rotating in their respective orbits under the direction of the Supreme, represented by eternal kāla.

PURPORT

In the *Brahma-saṁhitā* it is stated that the sun is the eye of the Supreme and it rotates in its particular orbit of time. Similarly, beginning from the sun down to the atom, all bodies are under the influence of the *kāla-cakra,* or the orbit of eternal time, and each of them has a scheduled orbital time of one *saṁvatsara.*

TEXT 14

संवत्सरः परिवत्सर इडावत्सर एव च ।
अनुवत्सरो वत्सरश्च विदुरैवं प्रभाष्यते ॥१४॥

saṁvatsaraḥ parivatsara
iḍā-vatsara eva ca
anuvatsaro vatsaraś ca
viduraivaṁ prabhāṣyate

saṁvatsaraḥ—orbit of the sun; *parivatsaraḥ*—circumambulation of Bṛhaspati; *iḍā-vatsaraḥ*—orbit of the stars; *eva*—as they are; *ca*—also; *anuvatsarah*—orbit of the moon; *vatsaraḥ*—one calendar year; *ca*—also; *vidura*—O Vidura; *evam*—thus; *prabhāṣyate*—they are so told.

TRANSLATION

There are five different names for the orbits of the sun, moon, stars and luminaries in the firmament, and they each have their own saṁvatsara.

PURPORT

The subject matters of physics, chemistry, mathematics, astronomy, time and space dealt with in the above verses of *Śrīmad-Bhāgavatam* are certainly very interesting to students of the particular subject, but as far as we are concerned, we cannot explain them very thoroughly in terms of technical knowledge. The subject is summarized by the statement that above all the different branches of knowledge is the supreme control of *kāla,* the plenary representation of the Supreme Personality of Godhead.

Nothing exists without Him, and therefore everything, however wonderful it may appear to our meager knowledge, is but the work of the magical wand of the Supreme Lord. As far as time is concerned, we beg to subjoin herewith a table of timings in terms of the modern clock.

One *truṭi*	-	8/13,500	second		One *laghu*	-	2	minutes
One *vedha*	-	8/135	second		One *daṇḍa*	-	30	minutes
One *lava*	-	8/45	second		One *prahara*	-	3	hours
One *nimeṣa*	-	8/15	second		One day	-	12	hours
One *kṣaṇa*	-	8/5	second		One night	-	12	hours
One *kāṣṭhā*	-	8	seconds		One *pakṣa*	-	15	days

Two *pakṣas* comprise one month, and twelve months comprise one calendar year, or one full orbit of the sun. A human being is expected to live up to one hundred years. That is the way of the controlling measure of eternal time.

The *Brahma-saṁhitā* (5.52) affirms this control in this way:

yac-cakṣur eṣa savitā sakala-grahāṇāṁ
rājā samasta-sura-mūrtir aśeṣa-tejāḥ
yasyājñayā bhramati saṁbhṛta-kāla-cakro
govindam ādi-puruṣaṁ tam ahaṁ bhajāmi

"I worship Govinda, the primeval Lord, the Supreme Personality of Godhead, under whose control even the sun, which is considered to be the eye of the Lord, rotates within the fixed orbit of eternal time. The sun is the king of all planetary systems and has unlimited potency in heat and light."

TEXT 15

यः सृज्यशक्तिमुरुधोच्छ्वसयन् स्वशक्त्या
पुंसोऽभ्रमाय दिवि धावति भूतभेदः ।
कालाख्यया गुणमयं क्रतुभिर्वितन्वं-
स्तस्मै बलिं हरत वत्सरपञ्चकाय ॥१५॥

yaḥ sṛjya-śaktim urudhocchvasayan sva-śaktyā
puṁso 'bhramāya divi dhāvati bhūta-bhedaḥ
kālākhyayā guṇamayaṁ kratubhir vitanvaṁs
tasmai baliṁ harata vatsara-pañcakāya

yaḥ—one who; *sṛjya*—of creation; *śaktim*—the seeds; *urudhā*—in various ways; *ucchvasayan*—invigorating; *sva-śaktyā*—by his own energy; *puṁsaḥ*—of the living entity; *abhramāya*—to dissipate darkness; *divi*—during the daytime; *dhāvati*—moves; *bhūta-bhedaḥ*—distinct from all other material form; *kāla-ākhyayā*—by the name eternal time; *guṇa-mayam*—the material results; *kratubhiḥ*—by offerings; *vitanvan*—enlarging; *tasmai*—unto him; *balim*—ingredients of offerings; *harata*—one should offer; *vatsara-pañcakāya*—offerings every five years.

TRANSLATION

O Vidura, the sun enlivens all living entities with his unlimited heat and light. He diminishes the duration of life of all living entities in order to release them from their illusion of material attachment, and he enlarges the path of elevation to the heavenly kingdom. He thus moves in the firmament with great velocity, and therefore everyone should offer him respects once every five years with all ingredients of worship.

TEXT 16

विदुर उवाच
पितृदेवमनुष्याणामायुः परमिदं स्मृतम् ।
परेषां गतिमाचक्ष्व ये स्युः कल्पाद् बहिर्विदः ॥१८॥

vidura uvāca
pitṛ-deva-manuṣyāṇām
āyuḥ param idaṁ smṛtam
pareṣāṁ gatim ācakṣva
ye syuḥ kalpād bahir vidaḥ

viduraḥ uvāca—Vidura said; *pitṛ*—the Pitā planets; *deva*—the heavenly planets; *manuṣyāṇām*—and that of the human beings; *āyuḥ*—duration of life; *param*—final; *idam*—in their own measurement; *smṛtam*—calculated; *pareṣām*—of the superior living entities; *gatim*—duration of life; *ācakṣva*—kindly calculate; *ye*—all those who; *syuḥ*—are; *kalpāt*—from the millennium; *bahiḥ*—outside; *vidaḥ*—greatly learned.

TRANSLATION

Vidura said: I now understand the life durations of the residents of the Pitā planets and heavenly planets as well as that of the human beings. Now kindly inform me of the durations of life of those greatly learned living entities who are beyond the range of a kalpa.

PURPORT

The partial dissolution of the universe that takes place at the end of Brahmā's day does not affect all the planetary systems. The planets of highly learned living entities like the sages Sanaka and Bhṛgu are not affected by the dissolutions of the millenniums. All the planets are of different types, and each is controlled by a different *kāla-cakra,* or schedule of eternal time. The time of the earth planet is not applicable to other, more elevated planets. Therefore, Vidura herein inquires about the duration of life on other planets.

TEXT 17

भगवान् वेद कालस्य गतिं भगवतो ननु ।
विश्वं विचक्षते धीरा योगराद्धेन चक्षुषा ॥१७॥

bhagavān veda kālasya
gatiṁ bhagavato nanu
viśvaṁ vicakṣate dhīrā
yoga-rāddhena cakṣuṣā

bhagavān—O spiritually powerful one; *veda*—you know; *kālasya*—of the eternal time; *gatim*—movements; *bhagavataḥ*—of the Supreme Personality of Godhead; *nanu*—as a matter of course; *viśvam*—the whole universe; *vicakṣate*—see; *dhīrāḥ*—those who are self-realized; *yoga-rāddhena*—by dint of mystic vision; *cakṣuṣā*—by the eyes.

TRANSLATION

O spiritually powerful one, you can understand the movements of eternal time, which is the controlling form of the Supreme Personality of Godhead. Because you are a self-realized person, you can see everything by the power of mystic vision.

PURPORT

Those who have reached the highest perfectional stage of mystic power and can see everything in the past, present and future are called *tri-kāla-jñas.* Similarly, the devotees of the Lord can see everything clearly that is in the revealed scriptures. The devotees of Lord Śrī Kṛṣṇa can very easily understand the science of Kṛṣṇa, as well as the situation of the material and spiritual creations, without difficulty. Devotees do not have to endeavor for any *yoga-siddhi,* or perfection in mystic powers. They are competent to understand everything by the grace of the Lord, who is sitting in everyone's heart.

TEXT 18

मैत्रेय उवाच
कृतं त्रेता द्वापरं च कलिश्चेति चतुर्युगम् ।
दिव्यैर्द्वादशभिर्वर्षैः सावधानं निरूपितम् ॥१८॥

maitreya uvāca
kṛtaṁ tretā dvāparaṁ ca
kaliś ceti catur-yugam
divyair dvādaśabhir varṣaiḥ
sāvadhānaṁ nirūpitam

maitreyaḥ uvāca—Maitreya said; *kṛtam*—the age of Satya; *tretā*—the age of Tretā; *dvāparam*—the age of Dvāpara; *ca*—also; *kaliḥ*—the age of Kali; *ca*—and; *iti*—thus; *catuḥ-yugam*—four millenniums; *divyaiḥ*—of the demigods; *dvādaśabhiḥ*—twelve; *varṣaiḥ*—thousands of years; *sa-avadhānam*—approximately; *nirūpitam*—ascertained.

TRANSLATION

Maitreya said: O Vidura, the four millenniums are called the Satya, Tretā, Dvāpara and Kali yugas. The aggregate number of years of all of these combined is equal to twelve thousand years of the demigods.

PURPORT

The years of the demigods are equal to 360 years of humankind. As will be clarified in the subsequent verses, 12,000 of the demigods' years, including the transitional periods which are called *yuga-sandhyās*, comprise the total of the aforementioned four millenniums. Thus the aggregate of the above-mentioned four millenniums is 4,320,000 years.

TEXT 19

चत्वारि त्रीणि द्वे चैकं कृतादिषु यथाक्रमम् ।
संख्यातानि सहस्राणि द्विगुणानि शतानि च ॥१९॥

catvāri trīṇi dve caikaṁ
kṛtādiṣu yathā-kramam

saṅkhyātāni sahasrāṇi
dvi-guṇāni śatāni ca

catvāri—four; *trīṇi*—three; *dve*—two; *ca*—also; *ekam*—one; *kṛta-ādiṣu*—in the Satya-yuga; *yathā-kramam*—and subsequently others; *saṅkhyātāni*—numbering; *sahasrāṇi*—thousands; *dvi-guṇāni*—twice; *śatāni*—hundreds; *ca*—also.

TRANSLATION

The duration of the Satya millennium equals 4,800 years of the years of the demigods; the duration of the Tretā millennium equals 3,600 years of the demigods; the duration of the Dvāpara millennium equals 2,400 years; and that of the Kali millennium is 1,200 years of the demigods.

PURPORT

As aforementioned, one year of the demigods is equal to 360 years of the human beings. The duration of the Satya-yuga is therefore 4,800 × 360, or 1,728,000 years. The duration of the Tretā-yuga is 3,600 × 360, or 1,296,000 years. The duration of the Dvāpara-yuga is 2,400 × 360, or 864,000 years. And the last, the Kali-yuga, is 1,200 × 360, or 432,000 years.

TEXT 20

संध्यासंध्यांशयोरन्तर्यः कालः शतसंख्ययोः ।
तमेवाहुर्युगं तज्ज्ञा यत्र धर्मो विधीयते ॥२०॥

sandhyā-sandhyāṁśayor antar
yaḥ kālaḥ śata-saṅkhyayoḥ
tam evāhur yugaṁ taj-jñā
yatra dharmo vidhīyate

sandhyā—transitional period before; *sandhyā-aṁśayoḥ*—and transitional period after; *antaḥ*—within; *yaḥ*—that which; *kālaḥ*—duration of time; *śata-saṅkhyayoḥ*—hundreds of years; *tam eva*—that period; *āhuḥ*—they call; *yugam*—millennium; *tat-jñāḥ*—the expert astronomers; *yatra*—wherein; *dharmaḥ*—religion; *vidhīyate*—is performed.

TRANSLATION

The transitional periods before and after every millennium, which are a few hundred years as aforementioned, are known as yuga-sandhyās, or the

conjunctions of two millenniums, according to the expert astronomers. In those periods all kinds of religious activities are performed.

TEXT 21

धर्मश्चतुष्पान्मनुजान् कृते समनुवर्तते ।
स एवान्येष्वधर्मेण व्येति पादेन वर्धता ॥२१॥

dharmaś catuṣ-pān manujān
kṛte samanuvartate
sa evānyeṣv adharmeṇa
vyeti pādena vardhatā

dharmaḥ—religion; *catuḥ-pāt*—complete four dimensions; *manujān*—mankind; *kṛte*—in the Satya-yuga; *samanuvartate*—properly maintained; *saḥ*—that; *eva*—certainly; *anyeṣu*—in other; *adharmeṇa*—by the influence of irreligion; *vyeti*—declined; *pādena*—by one part; *vardhatā*—gradually increasing proportionately.

TRANSLATION

O Vidura, in the Satya millennium mankind properly and completely maintained the principles of religion, but in other millenniums religion gradually decreased by one part as irreligion was proportionately admitted.

PURPORT

In the Satya millennium, complete execution of religious principles prevailed. Gradually, the principles of religion decreased by one part in each of the subsequent millenniums. In other words, at present there is one part religion and three parts irreligion. Therefore people in this age are not very happy.

TEXT 22

त्रिलोक्या युगसाहस्रं बहिराब्रह्मणो दिनम् ।
तावत्येव निशा तात यन्निमीलति विश्वसृक् ॥२२॥

tri-lokyā yuga-sāhasraṁ
bahir ābrahmaṇo dinam
tāvaty eva niśā tāta
yan nimīlati viśva-sṛk

tri-lokyāḥ—of the three worlds; *yuga*—the four *yugas*; *sāhasram*—one thousand; *bahiḥ*—outside of; *ābrahmaṇaḥ*—up to Brahmaloka; *dinam*—is a day; *tāvatī*—a similar (period); *eva*—certainly; *niśā*—is night; *tāta*—O dear one; *yat*—because; *nimīlati*—goes to sleep; *viśva-sṛk*—Brahmā.

TRANSLATION

Outside of the three planetary systems [Svarga, Martya and Pātāla], the four yugas multiplied by one thousand comprise one day on the planet of Brahmā. A similar period comprises a night of Brahmā, in which the creator of the universe goes to sleep.

PURPORT

When Brahmā goes to sleep in his nighttime, the three planetary systems below Brahmaloka are all submerged in the water of devastation. In his sleeping condition, Brahmā dreams about the Garbhodakaśāyī Viṣṇu and takes instruction from the Lord for the rehabilitation of the devastated area of space.

TEXT 23

निशावसान आरब्धो लोककल्पोऽनुवर्तते ।
यावद्दिनं भगवतो मनून् भुञ्जंश्चतुर्दश ॥२३॥

niśāvasāna ārabdho
loka-kalpo 'nuvartate
yāvad dinaṁ bhagavato
manūn bhuñjaṁś catur-daśa

niśā—night; *avasāne*—termination; *ārabdhaḥ*—beginning from; *loka-kalpaḥ*—further creation of the three worlds; *anuvartate*—follows; *yāvat*—until; *dinam*—the daytime; *bhagavataḥ*—of the lord (Brahmā); *manūn*—the Manus; *bhuñjan*—existing through; *catuḥ-daśa*—fourteen.

TRANSLATION

After the end of Brahmā's night, the creation of the three worlds begins again in the daytime of Brahmā, and they continue to exist through the life durations of fourteen consecutive Manus, or fathers of mankind.

PURPORT

At the end of the life of each Manu there are shorter dissolutions also.

TEXT 24

स्वं स्वं कालं मनुर्भुङ्क्ते साधिकां ह्येकसप्ततिम् ॥२४॥

svaṁ svaṁ kālaṁ manur bhuṅkte
sādhikāṁ hy eka-saptatim

svam—own; *svam*—accordingly; *kālam*—duration of life; *manuḥ*—Manu; *bhuṅkte*—enjoys; *sa-adhikām*—a little more than; *hi*—certainly; *eka-saptatim*—seventy-one.

TRANSLATION

Each and every Manu enjoys a life of a little more than seventy-one sets of four millenniums.

PURPORT

The duration of life of a Manu comprises seventy-one sets of four millenniums, as described in the *Viṣṇu Purāṇa.* The duration of life of one Manu is about 852,000 years in the calculation of the demigods, or, in the calculation of human beings, 306,720,000 years.

TEXT 25

मन्वन्तरेषु मनवस्तद्वंश्या ऋषयः सुराः ।
भवन्ति चैव युगपत्सुरेशाश्चानु ये च तान् ॥२५॥

manvantareṣu manavas
tad-vaṁśyā ṛṣayaḥ surāḥ
bhavanti caiva yugapat
sureśāś cānu ye ca tān

manu-antareṣu—after the dissolution of each and every Manu; *manavaḥ*—other Manus; *tat-vaṁśyāḥ*—and their descendants; *ṛṣayaḥ*—the seven famous sages; *surāḥ*—devotees of the Lord; *bhavanti*—flourish; *ca eva*—also all of them; *yugapat*—simultaneously; *sura-īśāḥ*—demigods like Indra; *ca*—and; *anu*—followers; *ye*—all; *ca*—also; *tān*—them.

TRANSLATION

After the dissolution of each and every Manu, the next Manu comes in order, along with his descendants, who rule over the different planets; but the seven famous sages, and demigods like Indra and their followers, such as the Gandharvas, all appear simultaneously with Manu.

PURPORT

There are fourteen Manus in one day of Brahmā, and each of them has different descendants.

TEXT 26

एष दैनन्दिनः सर्गो ब्राह्मस्त्रैलोक्यवर्तनः ।
तिर्यङ्नृपितृदेवानां सम्भवो यत्र कर्मभिः ॥२६॥

eṣa dainan-dinaḥ sargo
brāhmas trailokya-vartanaḥ
tiryaṅ-nṛ-pitṛ-devānāṁ
sambhavo yatra karmabhiḥ

eṣaḥ—all these creations; *dainam-dinaḥ*—daily; *sargaḥ*—creation; *brāhmaḥ*—in terms of the days of Brahmā; *trailokya-vartanaḥ*—revolution of the three worlds; *tiryak*—animals lower than the human beings; *nṛ*—human beings; *pitṛ*—of the Pitā planets; *devānām*—of the demigods; *sambhavaḥ*—appearance; *yatra*—wherein; *karmabhiḥ*—in the cycle of fruitive activities.

TRANSLATION

In the creation, during Brahmā's day, the three planetary systems—Svarga, Martya and Pātāla—revolve, and the inhabitants, including the lower animals, human beings, demigods and Pitās, appear and disappear in terms of their fruitive activities.

TEXT 27

मन्वन्तरेषु भगवान् बिभ्रत्सत्त्वं स्वमूर्तिभिः ।
मन्वादिभिरिदं विश्वमवत्युदितपौरुषः ॥२७॥

manvantareṣu bhagavān
bibhrat sattvaṁ sva-mūrtibhiḥ
manv-ādibhir idaṁ viśvam
avaty udita-pauruṣaḥ

manu-antareṣu—in each change of Manu; *bhagavān*—the Personality of Godhead; *bibhrat*—manifesting; *sattvam*—His internal potency; *sva-mūrtibhiḥ*—by His different incarnations; *manu-ādibhiḥ*—as Manus; *idam*—this; *viśvam*—the universe; *avati*—maintains; *udita*—discovering; *pauruṣaḥ*—divine potencies.

TRANSLATION

In each and every change of Manu, the Supreme Personality of Godhead appears by manifesting His internal potency in different incarnations, as Manu and others. Thus He maintains the universe by discovered power.

TEXT 28

तमोमात्रामुपादाय प्रतिसंरुद्धविक्रमः ।
कालेनानुगताशेष आस्ते तूष्णीं दिनात्यये ॥२८॥

tamo-mātrām upādāya
pratisaṁruddha-vikramaḥ
kālenānugatāśeṣa
āste tūṣṇīṁ dinātyaye

tamaḥ—the mode of ignorance, or the darkness of night; *mātrām*—an insignificant portion only; *upādāya*—accepting; *pratisaṁruddha-vikramaḥ*—suspending all power of manifestation; *kālena*—by means of the eternal *kāla; anugata*—merged in; *aśeṣaḥ*—innumerable living entities; *āste*—remains; *tūṣṇīm*—silent; *dina-atyaye*—at the end of the day.

TRANSLATION

At the end of the day, under the insignificant portion of the mode of darkness, the powerful manifestation of the universe merges in the darkness of night. By the influence of eternal time, the innumerable living entities remain merged in that dissolution, and everything is silent.

PURPORT

This verse is an explanation of the night of Brahmā, which is the effect of the influence of time in touch with an insignificant portion of the modes of material nature in darkness. The dissolution of the three worlds is effected by the incarnation of darkness, Rudra, represented by the fire of eternal time which blazes over the three worlds. These three worlds are known as Bhūḥ, Bhuvaḥ and Svaḥ (Pātāla, Martya and Svarga). The innumerable living entities merge into that dissolution, which appears to be the dropping of the curtain of the scene of the Supreme Lord's energy, and so everything becomes silent.

TEXT 29

तमेवान्वपिधीयन्ते लोका भूरादयस्त्रयः ।
निशायामनुवृत्तायां निर्मुक्तशशिभास्करम् ॥२९॥

tam evānv api dhīyante
lokā bhūr-ādayas trayaḥ
niśāyām anuvṛttāyāṁ
nirmukta-śaśi-bhāskaram

tam—that; *eva*—certainly; *anu*—after; *api dhīyante*—are out of sight; *lokāḥ*—the planets; *bhūḥ-ādayaḥ*—the three worlds, Bhūḥ, Bhuvaḥ and Svaḥ; *trayaḥ*—three; *niśāyām*—in the night; *anuvṛttāyām*—ordinary; *nirmukta*—without glare; *śaśi*—the moon; *bhāskaram*—the sun.

TRANSLATION

When the night of Brahmā ensues, all the three worlds are out of sight, and the sun and the moon are without glare, just as in the due course of an ordinary night.

PURPORT

It is understood that the glare of the sun and moon disappear from the sphere of the three worlds, but the sun and the moon themselves do not vanish. They appear in the remaining portion of the universe, which is beyond the sphere of the three worlds. The portion in dissolution remains without sunrays or moonglow. It all remains dark and full of water, and there are indefatigable winds, as explained in the following verses.

TEXT 30

त्रिलोक्यां दह्यमानायां शक्त्या सङ्कर्षणाग्निना ।
यान्त्यूष्मणा महर्लोकाज्जनं भृग्वादयोऽर्दिताः ॥३०॥

tri-lokyāṁ dahyamānāyāṁ
śaktyā saṅkarṣaṇāgninā
yānty ūṣmaṇā maharlokāj
janaṁ bhṛgv-ādayo 'rditāḥ

tri-lokyām—when the spheres of the three worlds; *dahyamānāyām*—being set ablaze; *śaktyā*—by the potency; *saṅkarṣaṇa*—from the mouth of Saṅkarṣaṇa; *agninā*—by the fire; *yānti*—they go; *ūṣmaṇā*—heated by the warmth; *mahaḥ-lokāt*—from Maharloka; *janam*—to Janaloka; *bhṛgu*—the sage Bhṛgu; *ādayaḥ*—and others; *arditāḥ*—being so distressed.

TRANSLATION

The devastation takes place due to the fire emanating from the mouth of Saṅkarṣaṇa, and thus great sages like Bhṛgu and other inhabitants of

Maharloka transport themselves to Janaloka, being distressed by the warmth of the blazing fire which rages through the three worlds below.

TEXT 31

तावत्त्रिभुवनं सद्यः कल्पान्तैधितसिन्धवः ।
प्लावयन्त्युत्कटाटोपचण्डवातेरितोर्मयः ॥३१॥

tāvat tri-bhuvanaṁ sadyaḥ
kalpāntaidhita-sindhavaḥ
plāvayanty utkaṭāṭopa-
caṇḍa-vāteritormayaḥ

tāvat—then; *tri-bhuvanam*—all the three worlds; *sadyaḥ*—immediately after; *kalpa-anta*—in the beginning of the devastation; *edhita*—inflated; *sindhavaḥ*—all the oceans; *plāvayanti*—inundate; *utkaṭa*—violent; *āṭopa*—agitation; *caṇḍa*—hurricane; *vāta*—by winds; *irita*—blown; *ūrmayaḥ*—waves.

TRANSLATION

At the beginning of the devastation all the seas overflow, and hurricane winds blow very violently. Thus the waves of the seas become ferocious, and in no time at all the three worlds are full of water.

PURPORT

It is said that the blazing fire from the mouth of Saṅkarṣaṇa rages for one hundred years of the demigods, or 36,000 human years. Then for another 36,000 years there are torrents of rain, accompanied by violent winds and waves, and the seas and oceans overflow. These reactions of 72,000 years are the beginning of the partial devastation of the three worlds. People forget all these devastations of the worlds and think themselves happy in the material progress of civilization. This is called *māyā*, or "that which is not."

TEXT 32

अन्तः स तस्मिन् सलिल आस्तेऽनन्तासनो हरिः ।
योगनिद्रानिमीलाक्षः स्तूयमानो जनालयैः ॥३२॥

antaḥ sa tasmin salila
āste 'nantāsano hariḥ

yoga-nidrā-nimīlākṣaḥ
stūyamāno janālayaiḥ

antaḥ—within; *saḥ*—that; *tasmin*—in that; *salile*—water; *āste*—there is; *ananta*—Ananta; *āsanaḥ*—on the seat of; *hariḥ*—the Lord; *yoga*—mystic; *nidrā*—sleep; *nimīla-akṣaḥ*—eyes closed; *stūya-mānaḥ*—being glorified; *jana-ālayaiḥ*—by the inhabitants of the Janaloka planets.

TRANSLATION

The Supreme Lord, the Personality of Godhead, lies down in the water on the seat of Ananta, with His eyes closed, and the inhabitants of the Janaloka planets offer their glorious prayers unto the Lord with folded hands.

PURPORT

We should not understand the sleeping condition of the Lord to be the same as our sleep. Here the word *yoga-nidrā* is specifically mentioned, which indicates that the Lord's sleeping condition is also a manifestation of His internal potency. Whenever the word *yoga* is used it should be understood to refer to that which is transcendental. In the transcendental stage all activities are always present, and they are glorified by prayers of great sages like Bhṛgu.

TEXT 33

एवंविधैरहोरात्रैः कालगत्योपलक्षितैः ।
अपक्षितमिवास्यापि परमायुर्वयःशतम् ॥३३॥

evaṁ-vidhair aho-rātraiḥ
kāla-gatyopalakṣitaiḥ
apakṣitam ivāsyāpi
paramāyur vayaḥ-śatam

evam—thus; *vidhaiḥ*—by the process of; *ahaḥ*—days; *rātraiḥ*—by nights; *kāla-gatyā*—advancement of time; *upalakṣitaiḥ*—by such symptoms; *apakṣitam*—declined; *iva*—just like; *asya*—his; *api*—although; *parama-āyuḥ*—duration of life; *vayaḥ*—years; *śatam*—one hundred.

TRANSLATION

Thus the process of the exhaustion of the duration of life exists for every one of the living beings, including Lord Brahmā. One's life endures for only one hundred years, in terms of the times in the different planets.

PURPORT

Every living being lives for one hundred years in terms of the times in different planets for different entities. These one hundred years of life are not equal in every case. The longest duration of one hundred years belongs to Brahmā, but although the life of Brahmā is very long, it expires in the course of time. Brahmā is also afraid of his death, and thus he performs devotional service to the Lord, just to release himself from the clutches of illusory energy. Animals, of course, have no sense of responsibility, but even humans, who have developed a sense of responsibility, while away their valuable time without engaging in devotional service to the Lord; they live merrily, unafraid of impending death. This is the madness of human society. The madman has no responsibility in life. Similarly, a human being who does not develop a sense of responsibility before he dies is no better than the madman who tries to enjoy material life very happily without concern for the future. It is necessary that every human being be responsible in preparing himself for the next life, even if he has a duration of life like that of Brahmā, the greatest of all living creatures within the universe.

TEXT 34

यदर्धमायुषस्तस्य परार्धमभिधीयते ।
पूर्वः परार्धोऽपक्रान्तो ह्यपरोऽद्य प्रवर्तते ॥३४॥

yad ardham āyuṣas tasya
parārdham abhidhīyate
pūrvaḥ parārdho 'pakrānto
hy aparo 'dya pravartate

yat—that which; *ardham*—half; *āyuṣaḥ*—of the duration of life; *tasya*—his; *parārdham*—a *parārdha; abhidhīyate*—is called; *pūrvaḥ*—the former; *para-ardhaḥ*—half of the duration of life; *apakrāntaḥ*—having passed; *hi*—certainly; *aparaḥ*—the latter; *adya*—in this millennium; *pravartate*—shall begin.

TRANSLATION

The one hundred years of Brahmā's life are divided into two parts, the first half and the second half. The first half of the duration of Brahmā's life is already over, and the second half is now current.

PURPORT

The duration of one hundred years in the life of Brahmā has already been discussed in many places in this work, and it is described in *Bhagavad-gītā* (8.17) also. Fifty years of the life of Brahmā are already over, and fifty years are yet to be completed; then, for Brahmā also, death is inevitable.

TEXT 35

पूर्वस्यादौ परार्धस्य ब्राह्मो नाम महानभूत् ।
कल्पो यत्राभवद्ब्रह्मा शब्दब्रह्मेति यं विदुः ॥३५॥

pūrvasyādau parārdhasya
brāhmo nāma mahān abhūt
kalpo yatrābhavad brahmā
śabda-brahmeti yaṁ viduḥ

pūrvasya—of the first half; *ādau*—in the beginning; *para-ardhasya*—of the superior half; *brāhmaḥ*—Brāhma-kalpa; *nāma*—of the name; *mahān*—very great; *abhūt*—was manifest; *kalpaḥ*—millennium; *yatra*—whereupon; *abhavat*—appeared; *brahmā*—Lord Brahmā; *śabda-brahma iti*—the sounds of the *Vedas*; *yam*—which; *viduḥ*—they know.

TRANSLATION

In the beginning of the first half of Brahmā's life, there was a millennium called Brāhma-kalpa, wherein Lord Brahmā appeared. The birth of the Vedas was simultaneous with Brahmā's birth.

PURPORT

According to *Padma Purāṇa* (*Prabhāsa-khaṇḍa*), in thirty days of Brahmā many *kalpas* take place, such as the Varāha-kalpa and Pitṛ-kalpa. Thirty days make one month of Brahmā, beginning from the full moon to the disappearance of the moon. Twelve such months complete one year, and fifty years complete one *parārdha*, or one half the duration of the life of Brahmā. The Śveta-varāha appearance of the Lord is the first birthday of Brahmā. The birth date of Brahmā is in the month of March, according to Hindu astronomical calculation. This statement is reproduced from the explanation of Śrīla Viśvanātha Cakravartī Ṭhākura.

TEXT 36

तस्यैव चान्ते कल्पोऽभूद् यं पाद्ममभिचक्षते ।
यद्धरेर्नाभिसरस आसील्लोकसरोरुहम् ॥३६॥

tasyaiva cānte kalpo 'bhūd
yaṁ pādmam abhicakṣate
yad dharer nābhi-sarasa
āsīl loka-saroruham

tasya—of the Brāhma-kalpa; *eva*—certainly; *ca*—also; *ante*—at the end of; *kalpaḥ*—millennium; *abhūt*—came into existence; *yam*—which; *pādmam*—Pādma; *abhicakṣate*—is called; *yat*—in which; *hareḥ*—of the Personality of Godhead; *nābhi*—in the navel; *sarasaḥ*—from the reservoir of water; *āsīt*—there was; *loka*—of the universe; *saroruham*—lotus.

TRANSLATION

The millennium which followed the first Brāhma millennium is known as the Pādma-kalpa because in that millennium the universal lotus flower grew out of the navel reservoir of water of the Personality of Godhead, Hari.

PURPORT

The millennium following the Brāhma-kalpa is known as the Pādma-kalpa because the universal lotus grows in that millennium. The Pādma kalpa is also called the Pitṛ-kalpa in certain *Purāṇas.*

TEXT 37

अयं तु कथितः कल्पो द्वितीयस्यापि भारत ।
वाराह इति विख्यातो यत्रासीच्छूकरो हरिः ॥३७॥

ayaṁ tu kathitaḥ kalpo
dvitīyasyāpi bhārata
vārāha iti vikhyāto
yatrāsīc chūkaro hariḥ

ayam—this; *tu*—but; *kathitaḥ*—known as; *kalpaḥ*—the current millennium; *dvitīyasya*—of the second half; *api*—certainly; *bhārata*—O descendant of Bharata; *vārāhaḥ*—Vārāha; *iti*—thus; *vikhyātaḥ*—is celebrated; *yatra*—in which; *āsīt*—appeared; *śūkaraḥ*—hog shape; *hariḥ*—the Personality of Godhead.

TRANSLATION

O descendant of Bharata, the first millennium in the second half of the life of Brahmā is also known as the Vārāha millennium because the Personality of Godhead appeared in that millennium as the hog incarnation.

PURPORT

The different millenniums known as the Brāhma, Pādma and Vārāha *kalpas* appear a little puzzling for the layman. There are some scholars who think these *kalpas* to be one and the same. According to Śrīla Viśvanātha Cakravartī, the Brāhma-kalpa in the beginning of the first half appears to be the Pādma-kalpa. We can, however, simply abide by the text and understand that the present millennium is in the second half of the duration of the life of Brahmā.

TEXT 38

कालोऽयं द्विपरार्धाख्यो निमेष उपचर्यते ।
अव्याकृतस्यानन्तस्य ह्यनादेर्जगदात्मनः ॥३८॥

kālo 'yaṁ dvi-parārdhākhyo
nimeṣa upacaryate
avyākṛtasyānantasya
hy anāder jagad-ātmanaḥ

kālaḥ—eternal time; *ayam*—this (as measured by Brahmā's duration of life); *dvi-parārdha-ākhyaḥ*—measured by the two halves of Brahmā's life; *nimeṣaḥ*—less than a second; *upacaryate*—is so measured; *avyākṛtasya*—of one who is unchanged; *anantasya*—of the unlimited; *hi*—certainly; *anādeḥ*—of the beginningless; *jagat-ātmanaḥ*—of the soul of the universe.

TRANSLATION

The duration of the two parts of Brahmā's life, as above mentioned, is calculated to be equal to one nimeṣa [less than a second] for the Supreme Personality of Godhead, who is unchanging and unlimited and is the cause of all causes of the universe.

PURPORT

The great sage Maitreya has given a considerable description of the time of different dimensions, beginning from the atom up to the duration of the life of Brahmā. Now he attempts to give some idea of the time of the unlimited Personality of Godhead. He just gives a hint of His unlimited time by the standard of the life of Brahmā. The entire duration of the life of Brahmā is calculated to be less than a second of the Lord's time, and it is explained in the *Brahma-saṁhitā* (5.48) as follows:

yasyaika-niśvasita-kālam athāvalambya
jīvanti loma-vilajā jagad-aṇḍa-nāthāḥ
viṣṇur mahān sa iha yasya kalā-viśeṣo
govindam ādi-puruṣaṁ tam ahaṁ bhajāmi

"I worship Govinda, the Supreme Personality of Godhead, the cause of all causes, whose plenary portion is Mahā-viṣṇu. All the heads of the innumerable universes [the Brahmās] live only by taking shelter of the time occupied by one of His breaths." The impersonalists do not believe in the form of the Lord, and thus they would hardly believe in the Lord's sleeping. Their idea is obtained by a poor fund of knowledge; they calculate everything in terms of man's capacity. They think that the existence of the Supreme is just the opposite of active human existence; because the human being has senses, the Supreme must be without sense perception; because the human being has a form, the Supreme must be formless; and because the human being sleeps, the Supreme must not sleep. *Śrīmad-Bhāgavatam,* however, does not agree with such impersonalists. It is clearly stated herein that the Supreme Lord rests in *yoga-nidrā,* as previously discussed. And because He sleeps, naturally He must breathe, and the *Brahma-saṁhitā* confirms that within His breathing period innumerable Brahmās take birth and die.

There is complete agreement between *Śrīmad-Bhāgavatam* and the *Brahma-saṁhitā.* Eternal time is never lost along with the life of Brahmā. It continues, but it has no ability to control the Supreme Personality of Godhead because the Lord is the controller of time. In the spiritual world there is undoubtedly time, but it has no control over activities. Time is unlimited, and the spiritual world is also unlimited, since everything there exists on the absolute plane.

TEXT 39

कालोऽयं परमाण्वादिर्द्विपरार्धान्त ईश्वरः ।
नैवेशितुं प्रभुर्भूम्न ईश्वरो धाममानिनाम् ॥३९॥

kālo 'yaṁ paramāṇv-ādir
dvi-parārdhānta īśvaraḥ
naiveśituṁ prabhur bhūmna
īśvaro dhāma-māninām

kālaḥ—the eternal time; *ayam*—this; *parama-aṇu*—atom; *ādiḥ*—beginning from; *dvi-parārdha*—two superdurations of time; *antaḥ*—to the end; *īśvaraḥ*—controller; *na*—never; *eva*—certainly; *īśitum*—to control; *prabhuḥ*—capable; *bhūmnaḥ*—of the Supreme; *īśvaraḥ*—controller; *dhāma-māninām*—of those who are body conscious.

TRANSLATION

Eternal time is certainly the controller of different dimensions, from that of the atom up to the superdivisions of the duration of Brahmā's life; but, nevertheless, it is controlled by the Supreme. Time can control only those who are body conscious, even up to the Satyaloka or the other higher planets of the universe.

TEXT 40

विकारैः सहितो युक्तैर्विशेषादिभिरावृतः ।
आण्डकोशो बहिरयं पञ्चाशत्कोटिविस्तृतः ॥४०॥

vikāraiḥ sahito yuktair
viśeṣādibhir āvṛtaḥ
āṇḍakośo bahir ayaṁ
pañcāśat-koṭi-vistṛtaḥ

vikāraiḥ—by the transformation of the elements; *sahitaḥ*—along with; *yuktaiḥ*—being so amalgamated; *viśeṣa*—manifestations; *ādibhiḥ*—by them; *āvṛtaḥ*—covered; *āṇḍa-kośaḥ*—the universe; *bahiḥ*—outside; *ayam*—this; *pañcāśat*—fifty; *koṭi*—ten million; *vistṛtaḥ*—widespread.

TRANSLATION

This phenomenal material world is expanded to a diameter of four billion miles, as a combination of eight material elements transformed into sixteen further categories, within and without, as follows.

PURPORT

As explained before, the entire material world is a display of sixteen diversities and eight material elements. The analytical studies of the material world are the subject matter of Sāṅkhya philosophy. The first sixteen diversities are the eleven senses and five sense objects, and the eight elements are the gross and subtle matter, namely earth, water, fire, air, sky, mind, intelligence and ego. All these combined together are distributed throughout the entire universe, which extends diametrically to four billion miles. Besides this universe of our experience, there are innumerable other universes. Some of them are bigger than the present one, and all of them are clustered together under similar material elements as described below.

TEXT 41

दशोत्तराधिकैर्यत्र प्रविष्टः परमाणुवत् ।
लक्ष्यतेऽन्तर्गताश्चान्ये कोटिशो ह्यण्डराशयः ॥४१॥

daśottarādhikair yatra
praviṣṭaḥ paramāṇuvat
lakṣyate 'ntar-gatāś cānye
koṭiśo hy aṇḍa-rāśayaḥ

daśa-uttara-adhikaiḥ—with ten times greater thickness; *yatra*—in which; *praviṣṭaḥ*—entered; *parama-aṇu-vat*—like atoms; *lakṣyate*—it (the mass of universes) appears; *antaḥ-gatāḥ*—come together; *ca*—and; *anye*—in the other; *koṭiśaḥ*—clustered; *hi*—for; *aṇḍa-rāśayaḥ*—huge combination of universes.

TRANSLATION

The layers or elements covering the universes are each ten times thicker than the one before, and all the universes clustered together appear like atoms in a huge combination.

PURPORT

The coverings of the universes are also constituted of the elements of earth, water, fire, air and ether, and each is ten times thicker than the one before. The first covering of the universe is earth, and it is ten times thicker than the universe itself. If the universe is four billion miles in size, then the size of the earthly covering of the universe is four billion times ten. The covering of water is ten times greater than the earthly covering, the covering of fire is ten times greater than the watery covering, the covering of air is ten times greater than that of the fire, the covering of ether is ten times greater still than that of air, and so on. The universe within the coverings of matter appears to be like an atom in comparison to the coverings, and the number of universes is unknown even to those who can estimate the coverings of the universes.

TEXT 42

तदाहुरक्षरं ब्रह्म सर्वकारणकारणम् ।
विष्णोर्धाम परं साक्षात्पुरुषस्य महात्मनः ॥४२॥

tad āhur akṣaraṁ brahma
sarva-kāraṇa-kāraṇam

viṣṇor dhāma paraṁ sākṣāt
puruṣasya mahātmanaḥ

tat—that; *āhuḥ*—is said; *akṣaram*—infallible; *brahma*—the supreme; *sarva-kāraṇa*—all causes; *kāraṇam*—the supreme cause; *viṣṇoḥ dhāma*—the spiritual abode of Viṣṇu; *param*—the supreme; *sākṣāt*—without doubt; *puruṣasya*—of the *puruṣa* incarnation; *mahātmanaḥ*—of the Mahā-Viṣṇu.

TRANSLATION

The Supreme Personality of Godhead, Śrī Kṛṣṇa, is therefore said to be the original cause of all causes. Thus the spiritual abode of Viṣṇu is eternal without a doubt, and it is also the abode of Mahā-Viṣṇu, the origin of all manifestations.

PURPORT

Lord Mahā-Viṣṇu, who is resting in *yoga-nidrā* on the Causal Ocean and creating innumerable universes by His breathing process, only temporarily appears in the *mahat-tattva* for the temporary manifestation of the material worlds. He is a plenary portion of Lord Śrī Kṛṣṇa, and thus although He is nondifferent from Lord Kṛṣṇa, His formal appearance in the material world as an incarnation is temporary. The original form of the Personality of Godhead is actually the *svarūpa,* or real form, and He eternally resides in the Vaikuṇṭha world (Viṣṇuloka). The word *mahātmanaḥ* is used here to indicate Mahā-Viṣṇu, and His real manifestation is Lord Kṛṣṇa, who is called *parama,* as confirmed in the *Brahma-saṁhitā:*

īśvaraḥ paramaḥ kṛṣṇaḥ
sac-cid-ānanda-vigrahaḥ
anādir ādir govindaḥ
sarva-kāraṇa-kāraṇam
[Bs. 5.1]

"The Supreme Lord is Kṛṣṇa, the original Personality of Godhead known as Govinda. His form is eternal, full of bliss and knowledge, and He is the original cause of all causes."

Thus end the Bhaktivedanta purports of the Third Canto, Eleventh Chapter, of the Śrīmad-Bhāgavatam, *entitled "Calculation of Time, From the Atom."*

CHAPTER TWELVE

Creation of the Kumāras and Others

TEXT 1

मैत्रेय उवाच
इति ते वर्णितः क्षत्तः कालाख्यः परमात्मनः ।
महिमा वेदगर्भोऽथ यथास्राक्षीन्निबोध मे ॥ १ ॥

maitreya uvāca
iti te varṇitaḥ kṣattaḥ
kālākhyaḥ paramātmanaḥ
mahimā veda-garbho 'tha
yathāsrākṣīn nibodha me

maitreyaḥ uvāca—Śrī Maitreya said; *iti*—thus; *te*—unto you; *varṇitaḥ*—described; *kṣattaḥ*—O Vidura; *kāla-ākhyaḥ*—by the name eternal time; *paramātmanaḥ*—of the Supersoul; *mahimā*—glories; *veda-garbhaḥ*—Lord Brahmā, the reservoir of the *Vedas; atha*—hereafter; *yathā*—as it is; *asrākṣīt*—did create; *nibodha*—just try to understand; *me*—from me.

TRANSLATION

Śrī Maitreya said: O learned Vidura, so far I have explained to you the glories of the form of the Supreme Personality of Godhead in His feature of kāla. Now you can hear from me about the creation of Brahmā, the reservoir of all Vedic knowledge.

TEXT 2

ससर्जाग्रेऽन्धतामिस्रमथ तामिस्रमादिकृत् ।
महामोहं च मोहं च तमश्चाज्ञानवृत्तयः ॥ २ ॥

sasarjāgre 'ndha-tāmisram
atha tāmisram ādi-kṛt
mahāmohaṁ ca mohaṁ ca
tamaś cājñāna-vṛttayaḥ

sasarja—created; *agre*—at first; *andha-tāmisram*—the sense of death; *atha*—then; *tāmisram*—anger upon frustration; *ādi-kṛt*—all these; *mahā-moham*—ownership of enjoyable objects; *ca*—also; *moham*—illusory conception; *ca*—also; *tamaḥ*—darkness in self-knowledge; *ca*—as well as; *ajñāna*—nescience; *vṛttayaḥ*—engagements.

TRANSLATION

Brahmā first created the nescient engagements like self-deception, the sense of death, anger after frustration, the sense of false ownership, and the illusory bodily conception, or forgetfulness of one's real identity.

PURPORT

Before the factual creation of the living entities in different varieties of species, the conditions under which a living being in the material world has to live were created by Brahmā. Unless a living entity forgets his real identity, it is impossible for him to live in the material conditions of life. Therefore the first condition of material existence is forgetfulness of one's real identity. And by forgetting one's real identity, one is sure to be afraid of death, although a pure living soul is deathless and birthless. This false identification with material nature is the cause of false ownership of things which are offered by the arrangement of superior control. All material resources are offered to the living entity for his peaceful living and for the discharge of the duties of self-realization in conditioned life. But due to false identification, the conditioned soul becomes entrapped by the sense of false ownership of the property of the Supreme Lord. It is evident from this verse that Brahmā himself is a creation of the Supreme Lord, and the five kinds of nescience which condition the living entities in material existence are creations of Brahmā. It is simply ludicrous to think the living entity to be equal with the Supreme Being when one can understand that the conditioned souls are under the influence of Brahmā's magic wand. Patañjali also accepts that there are five kinds of nescience, as mentioned herein.

TEXT 3

दृष्ट्वा पापीयसीं सृष्टिं नात्मानं बह्वमन्यत ।
भगवद्ध्यानपूतेन मनसान्यां ततोऽसृजत् ॥ ३ ॥

dṛṣṭvā pāpīyasīṁ sṛṣṭiṁ
nātmānaṁ bahv amanyata
bhagavad-dhyāna-pūtena
manasānyāṁ tato 'sṛjat

dṛṣṭvā—by seeing; *pāpīyasīm*—sinful; *sṛṣṭim*—creation; *na*—did not; *ātmānam*—unto himself; *bahu*—much pleasure; *amanyata*—felt; *bhagavat*—on the Personality of Godhead; *dhyāna*—meditation; *pūtena*—purified by that; *manasā*—by such a mentality; *anyām*—another; *tataḥ*—thereafter; *asṛjat*—created.

TRANSLATION

Seeing such a misleading creation as a sinful task, Brahmā did not feel much pleasure in his activity, and therefore he purified himself by meditation on the Personality of Godhead. Then he began another term of creation.

PURPORT

Although he created the different influences of nescience, Lord Brahmā was not satisfied in performing such a thankless task, but he had to do it because most of the conditioned souls wanted it to be so. Lord Kṛṣṇa says in *Bhagavad-gītā* (15.15) that He is present in everyone's heart and is helping everyone to either remember of forget. The question may be raised why the Lord, who is all-merciful, helps one to remember and another to forget. Actually, His mercy is not exhibited in partiality towards one and enmity towards another. The living entity, as part and parcel of the Lord, is partially independent because he partially possesses all the qualities of the Lord. Anyone who has some independence may sometimes misuse it due to ignorance. When the living entity prefers to misuse his independence and glide down towards nescience, the all-merciful Lord first of all tries to protect him from the trap, but when the living entity persists in gliding down to hell, the Lord helps him to forget his real position. The Lord helps the falling living entity glide down to the lowest point, just to give him the chance to see if he is happy by misusing his independence.

Almost all the conditioned souls who are rotting in the material world are misusing their independence, and therefore five kinds of nescience are imposed upon them. As an obedient servitor of the Lord, Brahmā creates all these as a matter of necessity, but he is not happy in doing so because a devotee of the Lord naturally does not like to see anyone falling down from his real position. Persons who do not care for the path of realization get full facilities from the Lord for executing their proclivities to the fullest extent, and Brahmā helps in that procedure without fail.

TEXT 4

सनकं च सनन्दं च सनातनमथात्मभूः ।
सनत्कुमारं च मुनीन्निष्क्रियानूर्ध्वरेतसः ॥ ४ ॥

sanakaṁ ca sanandaṁ ca
sanātanam athātmabhūḥ
sanat-kumāraṁ ca munīn
niṣkriyān ūrdhva-retasaḥ

sanakam—Sanaka; *ca*—also; *sanandam*—Sananda; *ca*—and; *sanātanam*—Sanātana; *atha*—thereafter; *ātma-bhūḥ*—Brahmā, who is self-born; *sanat-kumāram*—Sanat-kumāra; *ca*—also; *munīn*—the great sages; *niṣkriyān*—free from all fruitive action; *ūrdhva-retasaḥ*—those whose semen flows upwards.

TRANSLATION

In the beginning, Brahmā created four great sages named Sanaka, Sananda, Sanātana and Sanat-kumāra. All of them were unwilling to adopt materialistic activities because they were highly elevated due to their semen's flowing upwards.

PURPORT

Although Brahmā created the principles of nescience as a matter of necessity for those living entities who were destined to ignorance by the will of the Lord, he was not satisfied in performing such a thankless task. He therefore created four principles of knowledge: *sāṅkhya,* or empirical philosophy for the analytical study of material conditions; *yoga,* or mysticism for liberation of the pure soul from material bondage; *vairāgya,* the acceptance of complete detachment from material enjoyment in life to elevate oneself to the highest spiritual understanding; and *tapas,* or the various kinds of voluntary austerities performed for spiritual perfection. Brahmā created the four great sages Sanaka, Sananda, Sanātana and Sanat to entrust them with these four principles of spiritual advancement, and they inaugurated their own spiritual party, or *sampradāya,* known as the Kumāra-sampradāya, or later on as the Nimbārka-sampradāya, for the advancement of *bhakti.* All of these great sages became great devotees, for without devotional service to the Personality of Godhead one cannot achieve success in any activity of spiritual value.

TEXT 5

तान् बभाषे स्वभूः पुत्रान् प्रजाः सृजत पुत्रकाः ।
तन्नैच्छन्मोक्षधर्माणो वासुदेवपरायणाः ॥ ५ ॥

tān babhāṣe svabhūḥ putrān
prajāḥ sṛjata putrakāḥ
tan naicchan mokṣa-dharmāṇo
vāsudeva-parāyaṇāḥ

tān—unto the Kumāras, as above mentioned; *babhāṣe*—addressed; *svabhūḥ*—Brahmā; *putrān*—unto the sons; *prajāḥ*—generations; *sṛjata*—to create; *putrakāḥ*—O my sons; *tat*—that; *na*—not; *aicchan*—desired; *mokṣa-dharmāṇaḥ*—pledged to the principles of liberation; *vāsudeva*—the Personality of Godhead; *parāyaṇāḥ*—who are so devoted.

TRANSLATION

Brahmā spoke to his sons after generating them. "My dear sons," he said, "now generate progeny." But due to their being attached to Vāsudeva, the Supreme Personality of Godhead, they aimed at liberation, and therefore they expressed their unwillingness.

PURPORT

The four sons of Brahmā, the Kumāras, declined to become family men even on the request of their great father, Brahmā. Those who are serious about gaining release from material bondage should not be entangled in the false relationship of family bondage. People may ask how the Kumāras could refuse the orders of Brahmā, who was their father and above all the creator of the universe. The reply is that one who is *vāsudeva-parāyaṇa*, or seriously engaged in the devotional service of the Personality of Godhead, Vāsudeva, need not care for any other obligation. It is enjoined in the *Bhāgavatam* (11.5.41):

devarṣi-bhūtāpta-nṛṇāṁ pitṝṇāṁ
na kiṅkaro nāyam ṛṇī ca rājan
sarvātmanā yaḥ śaraṇaṁ śaraṇyaṁ
gato mukundaṁ parihṛtya kartam

"Anyone who has completely given up all worldly relationships and has taken absolute shelter of the lotus feet of the Lord, who gives us salvation and who alone is fit to be taken shelter of, is no longer a debtor or servant of anyone, including the demigods, forefathers, sages, other living entities, relatives and members of human society." Thus there was nothing wrong in the acts of the Kumāras when they refused their great father's request that they become family men.

TEXT 6

सोऽवध्यातः सुतैरेवं प्रत्याख्यातानुशासनैः ।
क्रोधं दुर्विषहं जातं नियन्तुमुपचक्रमे ॥ ६ ॥

so 'vadhyātaḥ sutair evaṁ
pratyākhyātānuśāsanaiḥ
krodhaṁ durviṣahaṁ jātaṁ
niyantum upacakrame

saḥ—he (Brahmā); *avadhyātaḥ*—thus being disrespected; *sutaiḥ*—by the sons; *evam*—thus; *pratyākhyāta*—refusing to obey; *anuśāsanaiḥ*—the order of their father; *krodham*—anger; *durviṣaham*—too much to be tolerated; *jātam*—thus generated; *niyantum*—to control; *upacakrame*—tried his best.

TRANSLATION

On the refusal of the sons to obey the order of their father, there was much anger generated in the mind of Brahmā, which he tried to control and not express.

PURPORT

Brahmā is the director in charge of the mode of passion of material nature. Therefore it was natural for him to become angry on the refusal of his sons to obey his order. Although the Kumāras were right in such acts of refusal, Brahmā, being absorbed in the mode of passion, could not check his passionate anger. He did not express it, however, because he knew that his sons were far enlightened in spiritual advancement and thus he should not express his anger before them.

TEXT 7

धिया निगृह्यमाणोऽपि भ्रुवोर्मध्यात्प्रजापतेः ।
सद्योऽजायत तन्मन्युः कुमारो नीललोहितः ॥ ७ ॥

dhiyā nigṛhyamāṇo 'pi
bhruvor madhyāt prajāpateḥ
sadyo 'jāyata tan-manyuḥ
kumāro nīla-lohitaḥ

dhiyā—by intelligence; *nigṛhyamāṇaḥ*—being controlled; *api*—in spite of; *bhruvoḥ*—of the eyebrows; *madhyāt*—from between; *prajāpateḥ*—of Brahmā; *sadyaḥ*—at once; *ajāyata*—generated; *tat*—his; *manyuḥ*—anger; *kumāraḥ*—a child; *nīla-lohitaḥ*—mixture of blue and red.

TRANSLATION

Although he tried to curb his anger, it came out from between his eyebrows, and a child mixed blue and red was immediately generated.

PURPORT

The face of anger is the same whether exhibited due to ignorance or knowledge. Although Brahmā tried to curb his anger, he could not do so, even though he is the supreme being. Such anger in its true color came from between the eyebrows of Brahmā as Rudra, in a mixed color of blue (ignorance) and red (passion), because anger is the product of passion and ignorance.

TEXT 8

स वै रुरोद देवानां पूर्वजो भगवान् भवः ।
नामानि कुरु मे धातः स्थानानि च जगद्गुरो ॥ ८ ॥

sa vai ruroda devānāṁ
pūrvajo bhagavān bhavaḥ
nāmāni kuru me dhātaḥ
sthānāni ca jagad-guro

saḥ—he; *vai*—certainly; *ruroda*—cried loudly; *devānām pūrvajaḥ*—the eldest of all demigods; *bhagavān*—the most powerful; *bhavaḥ*—Lord Śiva; *nāmāni*—different names; *kuru*—designate; *me*—my; *dhātaḥ*—O destiny maker; *sthānāni*—places; *ca*—also; *jagat guro*—O teacher of the universe.

TRANSLATION

After his birth he began to cry: O destiny maker, teacher of the universe, kindly designate my name and place.

TEXT 9

इति तस्य वचः पाद्मो भगवान् परिपालयन् ।
अभ्यधाद्भद्रया वाचा मा रोदीस्तत्करोमि ते ॥ ९ ॥

iti tasya vacaḥ pādmo
bhagavān paripālayan
abhyadhād bhadrayā vācā
mā rodīs tat karomi te

iti—thus; *tasya*—his; *vacaḥ*—request; *pādmaḥ*—one who is born from the lotus flower; *bhagavān*—the powerful; *paripālayan*—accepting the request; *abhyadhāt*—pacified; *bhadrayā*—by gentle; *vācā*—words; *mā*—do not; *rodīḥ*—cry; *tat*—that; *karomi*—I shall do it; *te*—as desired by you.

TRANSLATION

The all-powerful Brahmā, who was born from the lotus flower, pacified the boy with gentle words, accepting his request, and said: Do not cry. I shall certainly do as you desire.

TEXT 10

यदरोदीः सुरश्रेष्ठ सोद्वेग इव बालकः ।
ततस्त्वामभिधास्यन्ति नाम्ना रुद्र इति प्रजाः ॥१०॥

yad arodīḥ sura-śreṣṭha
sodvega iva bālakaḥ
tatas tvām abhidhāsyanti
nāmnā rudra iti prajāḥ

yat—as much as; *arodīḥ*—cried loudly; *sura-śreṣṭha*—O chief of the demigods; *sa-udvegaḥ*—with great anxiety; *iva*—like; *bālakaḥ*—a boy; *tataḥ*—therefore; *tvām*—you; *abhidhāsyanti*—will call; *nāmnā*—by the name; *rudraḥ*—Rudra; *iti*—thus; *prajāḥ*—people.

TRANSLATION

Thereafter Brahmā said: O chief of the demigods, you shall be called by the name Rudra by all people because you have so anxiously cried.

TEXT 11

हृदिन्द्रियाण्यसुर्व्योम वायुरग्निर्जलं मही ।
सूर्यश्चन्द्रस्तपश्चैव स्थानान्यग्रे कृतानि ते ॥११॥

hṛd indriyāṇy asur vyoma
vāyur agnir jalaṁ mahī
sūryaś candras tapaś caiva
sthānāny agre kṛtāni te

hṛt—the heart; *indriyāṇi*—the senses; *asuḥ*—life air; *vyoma*—the sky; *vāyuḥ*—the air; *agniḥ*—fire; *jalam*—water; *mahī*—the earth; *sūryaḥ*—the sun; *candraḥ*—the moon; *tapaḥ*—

austerity; *ca*—as well as; *eva*—certainly; *sthānāni*—all these places; *agre*—hereinbefore; *kṛtāni*—already made; *te*—for you.

TRANSLATION

My dear boy, I have already selected the following places for your residence: the heart, the senses, the air of life, the sky, the air, the fire, the water, the earth, the sun, the moon and austerity.

PURPORT

The creation of Rudra from between the eyebrows of Brahmā as the result of his anger, generated from the mode of passion partly touched by ignorance, is very significant. In *Bhagavad-gītā* (3.37) the principle of Rudra is described. *Krodha* (anger) is the product of *kāma* (lust), which is the result of the mode of passion. When lust and hankering are unsatisfied, the element of *krodha* appears, which is the formidable enemy of the conditioned soul. This most sinful and inimical passion is represented as *ahaṅkāra,* or the false egocentric attitude of thinking oneself to be all in all. Such an egocentric attitude on the part of the conditioned soul, who is completely under the control of material nature, is described in *Bhagavad-gītā* as foolish. The egocentric attitude is a manifestation of the Rudra principle in the heart, wherein *krodha* (anger) is generated. This anger develops in the heart and is further manifested through various senses, like the eyes, hands and legs. When a man is angry he expresses such anger with red-hot eyes and sometimes makes a display of clenching his fists or kicking his legs. This exhibition of the Rudra principle is the proof of Rudra's presence in such places. When a man is angry he breathes very rapidly, and thus Rudra is represented in the air of life, or in the activities of breathing. When the sky is overcast with dense clouds and roars in anger, and when the wind blows very fiercely, the Rudra principle is manifested, and so also when the seawater is infuriated by the wind it appears in a gloomy feature of Rudra, which is very fearful to the common man. When fire is ablaze we can also experience the presence of Rudra, and when there is an inundation over the earth we can understand that this is also the representation of Rudra.

There are many earthly creatures who constantly represent the Rudra element. The snake, tiger and lion are always representations of Rudra. Sometimes, because of the extreme heat of the sun, there are cases of heatstroke, and due to the extreme coldness created by the moon there are cases of collapse. There are many sages empowered with the influence of austerity and many *yogīs,* philosophers and renouncers who sometimes exhibit their acquired power under the influence of the Rudra principle of anger and passion. The great *yogī* Durvāsā, under the influence of this Rudra principle, picked a quarrel with Mahārāja Ambarīṣa, and a *brāhmaṇa* boy exhibited the Rudra principle by cursing the great King Parīkṣit. When the Rudra principle is exhibited by persons who are not engaged in the devotional service of the Supreme Personality of Godhead, the angry person falls down from the peak of his improved position. This is confirmed as follows:

ye 'nye 'ravindākṣa vimukta-māninas
tvayy asta-bhāvād aviśuddha-buddhayaḥ
āruhya kṛcchreṇa paraṁ padaṁ tataḥ
patanty adho 'nādṛta-yuṣmad-aṅghrayaḥ
(*Bhāg.* 10.2.32)

The most lamentable falldown of the impersonalist is due to his false and unreasonable claim of being one with the Supreme.

TEXT 12

मन्युर्मनुर्महिनसो महाञ्छिव ऋतध्वजः ।
उग्ररेता भवः कालो वामदेवो धृतव्रतः ॥१२॥

manyur manur mahinaso
mahāñ chiva ṛtadhvajaḥ
ugraretā bhavaḥ kālo
vāmadevo dhṛtavrataḥ

manyuḥ, manuḥ, mahinasaḥ, mahān, śivaḥ, ṛtadhvajaḥ, ugaretāḥ, bhavaḥ, kālaḥ, vāmadevaḥ, dhṛtavrataḥ—all names of Rudra.

TRANSLATION

Lord Brahmā said: My dear boy Rudra, you have eleven other names: Manyu, Manu, Mahinasa, Mahān, Śiva, Ṛtadhvaja, Ugraretā, Bhava, Kāla, Vāmadeva and Dhṛtavrata.

TEXT 13

धीर्धृतिरसलोमा च नियुत्सर्पिरिलाम्बिका ।
इरावती स्वधा दीक्षा रुद्राण्यो रुद्र ते स्त्रियः ॥१३॥

dhīr dhṛti-rasalomā ca
niyut sarpir ilāmbikā

irāvatī svadhā dīkṣā
rudrāṇyo rudra te striyaḥ

dhīḥ, dhṛti, rasalā, umā, niyut, sarpiḥ, ilā, ambikā, irāvatī, svadhā, dīkṣā rudrāṇyaḥ—the eleven Rudrāṇīs; *rudra*—O Rudra; *te*—unto you; *striyaḥ*—wives.

TRANSLATION

O Rudra, you also have eleven wives, called the Rudrāṇīs, and they are as follows: Dhī, Dhṛti, Rasalā, Umā, Niyut, Sarpi, Ilā, Ambikā, Irāvatī, Svadhā and Dīkṣā.

TEXT 14

गृहाणैतानि नामानि स्थानानि च सयोषणः ।
एभिः सृज प्रजा बह्वीः प्रजानामसि यत्पतिः ॥१४॥

gṛhāṇaitāni nāmāni
sthānāni ca sa-yoṣaṇaḥ
ebhiḥ sṛja prajā bahvīḥ
prajānām asi yat patiḥ

gṛhāṇa—just accept; *etāni*—all these; *nāmāni*—different names; *sthānāni*—as well as places; *ca*—also; *sa-yoṣaṇaḥ*—along with wives; *ebhiḥ*—with them; *sṛja*—just generate; *prajāḥ*—progeny; *bahvīḥ*—on a large scale; *prajānām*—of the living entities; *asi*—you are; *yat*—since; *patiḥ*—the master.

TRANSLATION

My dear boy, you may now accept all the names and places designated for you and your different wives, and since you are now one of the masters of the living entities, you may increase the population on a large scale.

PURPORT

Brahmā, as the father of Rudra, selected the wives of his son, his living places, and his names as well. It is natural that one should accept the wife selected by one's father, just as a son accepts the name given by the father or as he accepts the property offered by the father. That is the general course in increasing the population of the world. On the other hand, the Kumāras did not accept the offering of their father because they were elevated far beyond the business of generating a great number of sons. As the son can refuse the order of the father for higher purposes, so the father can refuse to maintain his sons in increasing population because of higher purposes.

TEXT 15

इत्यादिष्टः स्वगुरुणा भगवान्नीललोहितः ।
सत्त्वाकृतिस्वभावेन ससर्जात्मसमाः प्रजाः ॥१५॥

ity ādiṣṭaḥ sva-guruṇā
bhagavān nīla-lohitaḥ
sattvākṛti-svabhāvena
sasarjātma-samāḥ prajāḥ

iti—thus; *ādiṣṭaḥ*—being ordered; *sva-guruṇā*—by his own spiritual master; *bhagavān*—the most powerful; *nīla-lohitaḥ*—Rudra, whose color is mixed blue and red; *sattva*—power; *ākṛti*—bodily features; *svabhāvena*—and with a very furious mode of nature; *sasarja*—created; *ātma-samāḥ*—like his own prototype; *prajāḥ*—generations.

TRANSLATION

The most powerful Rudra, whose bodily color was blue mixed with red, created many offspring exactly resembling him in features, strength and furious nature.

TEXT 16

रुद्राणां रुद्रसृष्टानां समन्ताद् ग्रसतां जगत् ।
निशाम्यासंख्यशो यूथान् प्रजापतिरशङ्कत ॥१६॥

rudrāṇāṁ rudra-sṛṣṭānāṁ
samantād grasatāṁ jagat
niśāmyāsaṅkhyaśo yūthān
prajāpatir aśaṅkata

rudrāṇām—of the sons of Rudra; *rudra-sṛṣṭānām*—who were generated by Rudra; *samantāt*—being assembled together; *grasatām*—while devouring; *jagat*—the universe; *niśāmya*—by observing their activities; *asaṅkhyaśaḥ*—unlimited; *yūthān*—assembly; *prajā-patiḥ*—the father of the living entities; *aśaṅkata*—became afraid of.

TRANSLATION

The sons and grandsons generated by Rudra were unlimited in number, and when they assembled together they attempted to devour the entire

universe. When Brahmā, the father of the living entities, saw this, he became afraid of the situation.

PURPORT

The generations of Rudra, the incarnation of anger, were so dangerous to the maintenance of universal affairs that even Brahmā, the father of the living entities, became afraid of them. The so-called devotees or followers of Rudra are also a menace. They are sometimes dangerous even to Rudra himself. Descendants of Rudra sometimes make plans to kill Rudra—by the grace of Rudra. That is the nature of his devotees.

TEXT 17

अलं प्रजाभिः सृष्टाभिरीदृशीभिः सुरोत्तम ।
मया सह दहन्तीभिर्दिशश्चक्षुर्भिरुल्बणैः ॥१७॥

alaṁ prajābhiḥ sṛṣṭābhir
īdṛśībhiḥ surottama
mayā saha dahantībhir
diśaś cakṣurbhir ulbaṇaiḥ

alam—unnecessary; *prajābhiḥ*—by such living entities; *sṛṣṭābhiḥ*—generated; *īdṛśībhiḥ*—of this type; *sura-uttama*—O best among the demigods; *mayā*—me; *saha*—along with; *dahantībhiḥ*—who are burning; *diśaḥ*—all sides; *cakṣurbhiḥ*—by the eyes; *ulbaṇaiḥ*—fiery flames.

TRANSLATION

Brahmā told Rudra: O best among the demigods, there is no need for you to generate living entities of this nature. They have begun to devastate everything on all sides with the fiery flames from their eyes, and they have even attacked me.

TEXT 18

तप आतिष्ठ भद्रं ते सर्वभूतसुखावहम् ।
तपसैव यथापूर्वं स्रष्टा विश्वमिदं भवान् ॥१८॥

tapa ātiṣṭha bhadraṁ te
sarva-bhūta-sukhāvaham

tapasaiva yathā pūrvaṁ
sraṣṭā viśvam idaṁ bhavān

tapaḥ—penance; *ātiṣṭha*—be situated; *bhadram*—auspicious; *te*—unto you; *sarva*—all; *bhūta*—living entities; *sukha-āvaham*—bringing happiness; *tapasā*—by penance; *eva*—only; *yathā*—as much as; *pūrvam*—before; *sraṣṭā*—will create; *viśvam*—the universe; *idam*—this; *bhavān*—yourself.

TRANSLATION

My dear son, you had better situate yourself in penance, which is auspicious for all living entities and which will bring all benediction upon you. By penance only shall you be able to create the universe as it was before.

PURPORT

In the creation, maintenance and dissolution of the cosmic manifestation, the three deities Brahmā, Viṣṇu and Maheśvara, or Śiva, are respectively in charge. Rudra was advised not to destroy while the period of creation and maintenance was going on, but to situate himself in penance and wait for the time of dissolution, when his services would be called for.

TEXT 19

तपसैव परं ज्योतिर्भगवन्तमधोक्षजम् ।
सर्वभूतगुहावासमञ्जसा विन्दते पुमान् ॥१९॥

tapasaiva paraṁ jyotir
bhagavantam adhokṣajam
sarva-bhūta-guhāvāsam
añjasā vindate pumān

tapasā—by penance; *eva*—only; *param*—the supreme; *jyotiḥ*—light; *bhagavantam*—unto the Personality of Godhead; *adhokṣajam*—He who is beyond the approach of the senses; *sarva-bhūta-guhā-āvāsam*—residing in the heart of all living entities; *añjasā*—completely; *vindate*—can know; *pumān*—a person.

TRANSLATION

By penance only can one even approach the Personality of Godhead, who is within the heart of every living entity and at the same time beyond the reach of all senses.

PURPORT

Rudra was advised by Brahmā to perform penance as an example to his sons and followers that penance is necessary for attaining the favor of the Supreme Personality of Godhead. In *Bhagavad-gītā* it is said that the common mass of people follow the path shown by an authority. Thus Brahmā, disgusted with the Rudra generations and afraid of being devoured by the increase of population, asked Rudra to stop producing such an unwanted generation and take to penance for attaining the favor of the Supreme Lord. We find, therefore, in pictures, that Rudra is always sitting in meditation for the attainment of the favor of the Lord. Indirectly, the sons and followers of Rudra are advised to stop the business of annihilation, following the Rudra principle while the peaceful creation of Brahmā is going on.

TEXT 20

मैत्रेय उवाच
एवमात्मभुवादिष्टः परिक्रम्य गिरां पतिम् ।
बाढमित्यमुमामन्त्र्य विवेश तपसे वनम् ॥२०॥

maitreya uvāca
evam ātmabhuvādiṣṭaḥ
parikramya girāṁ patim
bāḍham ity amum āmantrya
viveśa tapase vanam

maitreyaḥ uvāca—Śrī Maitreya said; *evam*—thus; *ātma-bhuvā*—by Brahmā; *ādiṣṭaḥ*—being so requested; *parikramya*—by circumambulating; *girām*—of the *Vedas*; *patim*—unto the master; *bāḍham*—that is right; *iti*—thus; *amum*—unto Brahmā; *āmantrya*—thus addressing; *viveśa*—entered into; *tapase*—for the matter of penance; *vanam*—into the forest.

TRANSLATION

Śrī Maitreya said: Thus Rudra, having been ordered by Brahmā, circumambulated his father, the master of the Vedas. Addressing him with words of assent, he entered the forest to perform austere penances.

TEXT 21

अथाभिध्यायतः सर्गं दश पुत्राः प्रजज्ञिरे ।
भगवच्छक्तियुक्तस्य लोकसन्तानहेतवः ॥२१॥

athābhidhyāyataḥ sargaṁ
daśa putrāḥ prajajñire
bhagavac-chakti-yuktasya
loka-santāna-hetavaḥ

atha—thus; *abhidhyāyataḥ*—while thinking of; *sargam*—creation; *daśa*—ten; *putrāḥ*—sons; *prajajñire*—were begotten; *bhagavat*—regarding the Personality of Godhead; *śakti*—potency; *yuktasya*—empowered with; *loka*—the world; *santāna*—generation; *hetavaḥ*—the causes.

TRANSLATION

Brahmā, who was empowered by the Supreme Personality of Godhead, thought of generating living entities and begot ten sons for the extension of the generations.

TEXT 22

मरीचिरत्र्यङ्गिरसौ पुलस्त्यः पुलहः क्रतुः ।
भृगुर्वसिष्ठो दक्षश्च दशमस्तत्र नारदः ॥२२॥

marīcir atry-aṅgirasau
pulastyaḥ pulahaḥ kratuḥ
bhṛgur vasiṣṭho dakṣaś ca
daśamas tatra nāradaḥ

marīciḥ, atri, aṅgirasau, pulastyaḥ, pulahaḥ, kratuḥ, bhṛguḥ, vasiṣṭhaḥ, dakṣaḥ—names of sons of Brahmā; *ca*—and; *daśamaḥ*—the tenth; *tatra*—there; *nāradaḥ*—Nārada.

TRANSLATION

Marīci, Atri, Aṅgirā, Pulastya, Pulaha, Kratu, Bhṛgu, Vasiṣṭha, Dakṣa, and the tenth son, Nārada, were thus born.

PURPORT

The whole process of the creation, maintenance and dissolution of the cosmic manifestation is meant to give the conditioned souls a chance to go back home, back to Godhead. Brahmā created Rudra to help him in his creative endeavor, but from the very beginning Rudra began to devour the whole creation, and thus he had to be stopped from such devastating activities. Brahmā therefore created another set of good children, who were mostly in favor of worldly fruitive activities. He knew very well, however, that without devotional service to the Lord there is hardly any benefit for the conditioned souls, and therefore he at last created his worthy son Nārada, who is the supreme spiritual master of all transcendentalists. Without devotional service to the Lord one cannot make progress in any department of activity, although the path of devotional service is always independent of anything material. Only the transcendental loving service of the Lord can deliver the real goal of life, and thus the service rendered by Śrīman Nārada Muni is the highest among all the sons of Brahmā.

TEXT 23

उत्सङ्गान्नारदो जज्ञे दक्षोऽङ्गुष्ठात्स्वयम्भुवः ।
प्राणाद्वसिष्ठः सञ्जातो भृगुस्त्वचि करात्क्रतुः ॥२३॥

utsaṅgān nārado jajñe
dakṣo 'ṅguṣṭhāt svayambhuvaḥ
prāṇād vasiṣṭhaḥ sañjāto
bhṛgus tvaci karāt kratuḥ

utsaṅgāt—by transcendental deliberation; *nāradaḥ*—Mahāmuni Nārada; *jajñe*—was generated; *dakṣaḥ* Dakṣa; *aṅguṣṭhāt*—from the thumb; *svayambhuvaḥ*—of Brahmā; *prāṇāt*—from the life air, or breathing; *vasiṣṭhaḥ*—Vasiṣtha; *sañjātaḥ*—was born; *bhṛguḥ*—the sage Bhṛgu; *tvaci*—from the touch; *karat*—from the hand; *kratuḥ*—the sage Kratu.

TRANSLATION

Nārada was born from the deliberation of Brahmā, which is the best part of the body. Vasiṣṭha was born from his breathing, Dakṣa from a thumb, Bhṛgu from his touch, and Kratu from his hand.

PURPORT

Nārada was born from the best deliberation of Brahmā because Nārada was able to deliver the Supreme Lord to anyone he liked. The Supreme Personality of Godhead cannot be realized by any amount of Vedic knowledge or by any number of penances. But a pure devotee of the Lord like Nārada can deliver the Supreme Lord by his good will. The very name Nārada suggests that he can deliver the Supreme Lord. *Nāra* means the "Supreme Lord," and *da* means "one who can deliver." That he can deliver the Supreme Lord does not mean that the Lord is like a commodity that can be delivered to any person. But Nārada can deliver to anyone the transcendental loving service of the Lord as a servitor, friend, parent or lover, as one may desire out of one's own transcendental love for the Lord. In other words, it is Nārada only who can deliver the path of *bhakti-yoga,* the highest mystic means for attainment of the Supreme Lord.

TEXT 24

पुलहो नाभितो जज्ञे पुलस्त्यः कर्णयोर्ऋषिः ।
अङ्गिरा मुखतोऽक्ष्णोऽत्रिर्मरीचिर्मनसोऽभवत् ॥२४॥

pulaho nābhito jajñe
pulastyaḥ karṇayor ṛṣiḥ
aṅgirā mukhato 'kṣṇo 'trir
marīcir manaso 'bhavat

pulahaḥ—the sage Pulaha; *nābhitaḥ*—from the navel; *jajñe*—generated; *pulastyaḥ*—the sage Pulastya; *karṇayoḥ*—from the ears; *ṛṣiḥ*—the great sage; *aṅgirāḥ*—the sage Aṅgirā; *mukhataḥ*—from the mouth; *akṣṇaḥ*—from the eyes; *atriḥ*—the sage Atri; *marīciḥ*—the sage Marīci; *manasaḥ*—from the mind; *abhavat*—appeared.

TRANSLATION

Pulastya was generated from the ears, Aṅgirā from the mouth, Atri from the eyes, Marīci from the mind and Pulaha from the navel of Brahmā.

TEXT 25

धर्मः स्तनाद्दक्षिणतो यत्र नारायणः स्वयम् ।
अधर्मः पृष्ठतो यस्मान्मृत्युर्लोकभयङ्करः ॥२५॥

dharmaḥ stanād dakṣiṇato
yatra nārāyaṇaḥ svayam
adharmaḥ pṛṣṭhato yasmān
mṛtyur loka-bhayaṅkaraḥ

dharmaḥ—religion; *stanāt*—from the breast; *dakṣiṇataḥ*—on the right side; *yatra*—wherein; *nārāyaṇaḥ*—the Supreme Lord; *svayam*—personally; *adharmaḥ*—irreligion; *pṛṣṭhataḥ*—from the back; *yasmāt*—from which; *mṛtyuḥ*—death; *loka*—to the living entity; *bhayam-karaḥ*—horrible.

TRANSLATION

Religion was manifested from the breast of Brahmā, wherein is seated the Supreme Personality of Godhead Nārāyaṇa, and irreligion appeared from his back, where horrible death takes place for the living entity.

PURPORT

That religion was manifested from the place where the Personality of Godhead is personally situated is very significant because religion means devotional service to the Personality of Godhead, as confirmed in *Bhagavad-gītā* as well as the *Bhāgavatam.* In *Bhagavad-gītā* the last instruction is to give up all other engagements in the name of religion and take shelter of the Personality of Godhead. *Śrīmad-Bhāgavatam* also confirms that the highest perfection of religion is that which leads to the devotional service of the Lord, unmotivated and unhampered by material impediments. Religion in its perfect form is the devotional service of the Lord, and irreligion is just the opposite. The heart is the most important part of the body, whereas the back is the most neglected part. When one is attacked by an enemy one is apt to endure attacks from the back and protect himself carefully from all attacks on the chest. All types of irreligion spring from the back of Brahmā, whereas real religion, the devotional service of the Lord, is generated from the chest, the seat of Nārāyaṇa. Anything which does not lead to the devotional service of the Lord is irreligion, and anything which leads to the devotional service of the Lord is called religion.

TEXT 26

हृदि कामो भ्रुवः क्रोधो लोभश्चाधरदच्छदात् ।
आस्याद्वाक्सिन्धवो मेढ्रान्निर्ऋतिः पायोरघाश्रयः ॥२६॥

hṛdi kāmo bhruvaḥ krodho
lobhaś cādhara-dacchadāt
āsyād vāk sindhavo meḍhrān
nirṛtiḥ pāyor aghāśrayaḥ

hṛdi—from the heart; *kāmaḥ*—lust; *bhruvaḥ*—from the eyebrows; *krodhaḥ*—anger; *lobhaḥ*—greed; *ca*—also; *adhara-dacchadāt*—from between the lips; *āsyāt*—from the mouth; *vāk*—speaking; *sindhavaḥ*—the seas; *meḍhrāt*—from the penis; *nirṛtiḥ*—low activities; *pāyoḥ*—from the anus; *agha-āśrayaḥ*—reservoir of all vices.

TRANSLATION

Lust and desire became manifested from the heart of Brahmā, anger from between his eyebrows, greed from between his lips, the power of speaking from his mouth, the ocean from his penis, and low and abominable activities from his anus, the source of all sins.

PURPORT

A conditioned soul is under the influence of mental speculation. However great one may be in the estimation of mundane education and learning, he cannot be free from the influence of psychic activities. Therefore it is very difficult to give up lust and the desires for low activities until one is in the line of devotional service to the Lord. When one is frustrated in lust and low desires, anger is generated from the mind and expressed from between the eyebrows. Ordinary men are therefore advised to concentrate the mind by focusing on the place between the eyebrows, whereas the devotees of the Lord are already practiced to place the Supreme Personality of Godhead on the seat of their minds. The theory of becoming desireless is untenable because the mind cannot be made desireless. When it is recommended that one be desireless, it is understood that one should not desire things which are destructive to spiritual values. A devotee of the Lord always has the Lord in his mind, and thus he does not need to be desireless because all his desires are in relationship with the service of the Lord. The power of speaking is called Sarasvatī, or the goddess of learning, and the birthplace of the goddess of learning is the mouth of Brahmā. Even if a man is endowed with the favor of the goddess of learning, it is quite possible for his heart to be full of lust and material desire and his eyebrows to display symptoms of anger. One may be very learned in the mundane estimation, but that does not mean that he is free from all low activities of lust and anger. Good qualifications can be expected only from a pure devotee, who is always engaged in the thought of the Lord, or in *samādhi,* with faith.

TEXT 27

छायायाः कर्दमो जज्ञे देवहूत्याः पतिः प्रभुः ।
मनसो देहतश्चेदं जज्ञे विश्वकृतो जगत् ॥२७॥

chāyāyāḥ kardamo jajñe
devahūtyāḥ patiḥ prabhuḥ
manaso dehataś cedaṁ
jajñe viśva-kṛto jagat

chāyāyāḥ—by the shadow; *kardamaḥ*—Kardama Muni; *jajñe*—became manifested; *devahūtyāḥ*—of Devahūti; *patiḥ*—husband; *prabhuḥ*—the master; *manasaḥ*—from the mind; *dehataḥ*—from the body; *ca*—also; *idam*—this; *jajñe*—developed; *viśva*—the universe; *kṛtaḥ*—of the creator; *jagat*—cosmic manifestation.

TRANSLATION

Sage Kardama, husband of the great Devahūti, was manifested from the shadow of Brahmā. Thus all became manifested from either the body or the mind of Brahmā.

PURPORT

Although one of the three modes of material nature is always prominent, they are never represented unalloyed by one another. Even in the most prominent existence of the two lower qualities, the modes of passion and ignorance, there is sometimes a tinge of the mode of goodness. Therefore all the sons generated from the body or the mind of Brahmā were in the modes of passion and ignorance, but some of them, like Kardama, were born in the mode of goodness. Nārada was born in the transcendental state of Brahmā.

TEXT 28

वाचं दुहितरं तन्वीं स्वयम्भूर्हरतीं मनः ।
अकामां चकमे क्षत्तः सकाम इति नः श्रुतम् ॥२८॥

vācaṁ duhitaraṁ tanvīṁ
svayambhūr haratīṁ manaḥ
akāmāṁ cakame kṣattaḥ
sa-kāma iti naḥ śrutam

vācam—Vāk; *duhitaram*—unto the daughter; *tanvīm*—born of his body; *svayambhūḥ*—Brahmā; *haratīm*—attracting; *manaḥ*—his mind; *akāmām*—without being sexually inclined; *cakame*—desired; *kṣattaḥ*—O Vidura; *sa-kāmaḥ*—being sexually inclined; *iti*—thus; *naḥ*—we; *śrutam*—have heard.

TRANSLATION

O Vidura, we have heard that Brahmā had a daughter named Vāk who was born from his body and who attracted his mind toward sex, although she was not sexually inclined towards him.

PURPORT

Balavān indriya-grāmo vidvāṁsam api karṣati (*Bhāg.* 9.19.17). It is said that the senses are so mad and strong that they can bewilder even the most sensible and

Therefore it is advised that one should not indulge in living alone even with one's mother, sister or daughter. *Vidvāṁsam api karṣati* means that even the most learned also become victims of the sensuous urge. Maitreya hesitated to state this anomaly on the part of Brahmā, who was sexually inclined to his own daughter, but still he mentioned it because sometimes it so happens, and the living example is Brahmā himself, although he is the primeval living being and the most learned within the whole universe. If Brahmā could be a victim of the sexual urge, then what of others, who are prone to so many mundane frailties? This extraordinary immorality on the part of Brahmā was heard to have occurred in some particular *kalpa,* but it could not have happened in the *kalpa* in which Brahmā heard directly from the Lord the four essential verses of *Śrīmad-Bhāgavatam* because the Lord benedicted Brahmā, after giving him lessons on the *Bhāgavatam,* that he would never be bewildered in any *kalpa* whatsoever. This indicates that before the hearing of *Śrīmad-Bhāgavatam* he might have fallen a victim to such sensuality, but after hearing *Śrīmad-Bhāgavatam* directly from the Lord, there was no possibility of such failures.

One should, however, take serious note of this incident. The human being is a social animal, and his unrestricted mixing with the fair sex leads to downfall. Such social freedom of man and woman, especially among the younger section, is certainly a great stumbling block on the path of spiritual progress. Material bondage is due only to sexual bondage, and therefore unrestricted association of man and woman is surely a great impediment. Maitreya cited this example on the part of Brahmā just to bring to our notice this great danger.

TEXT 29

तमधर्मे कृतमतिं विलोक्य पितरं सुताः ।
मरीचिमुख्या मुनयो विश्रम्भात्प्रत्यबोधयन् ॥२९॥

tam adharme kṛta-matiṁ
vilokya pitaraṁ sutāḥ
marīci-mukhyā munayo
viśrambhāt pratyabodhayan

tam—unto him; *adharme*—in the matter of immortality; *kṛta-matim*—the mind being so given; *vilokya*—seeing thus; *pitaram*—unto the father; *sutāḥ*—sons; *marīci-mukhyāḥ*—headed by Marīci; *munayaḥ*—sages; *viśrambhāt*—with due respect; *pratyabodhayan*—submitted as follows.

TRANSLATION

Thus, finding their father so deluded in an act of immorality, the sages headed by Marīci, all sons of Brahmā, spoke as follows with great respect.

PURPORT

The sages like Marīci were not in the wrong in submitting their protests against the acts of their great father. They knew very well that even though their father committed a mistake, there must have been some great purpose behind the show, otherwise such a great personality could not have committed such a mistake. It might be that Brahmā wanted to warn his subordinates about human frailties in their dealings with women. This is always very dangerous for persons who are on the path of self-realization. Therefore, great personalities like Brahmā, even when in the wrong, should not be neglected, nor could the great sages headed by Marīci show any disrespect because of his extraordinary behavior.

TEXT 30

नैतत्पूर्वैः कृतं त्वद्ये न करिष्यन्ति चापरे ।
यस्त्वं दुहितरं गच्छेरनिगृह्याङ्गजं प्रभुः ॥३०॥

naitat pūrvaiḥ kṛtaṁ tvad ye
na kariṣyanti cāpare
yas tvaṁ duhitaraṁ gaccher
anigṛhyāṅgajaṁ prabhuḥ

na—never; *etat*—such a thing; *pūrvaiḥ*—by any other Brahmā, or yourself in any previous *kalpa; kṛtam*—performed; *tvat*—by you; *ye*—that which; *na*—nor; *kariṣyanti*—will do; *ca*—also; *apare*—anyone else; *yaḥ*—that which; *tvam*—you; *duhitaram*—unto the daughter; *gaccheḥ*—would go; *anigṛhya*—without controlling; *aṅgajam*—sex desire; *prabhuḥ*—O father.

TRANSLATION

O father, this performance in which you are endeavoring to complicate yourself was never attempted by any other Brahmā, nor by anyone else, nor by you in previous kalpas, nor will anyone dare to attempt it in the future. You are the supreme being in the universe, so how is it that you want to have sex with your daughter and cannot control your desire?

PURPORT

The post of Brahmā is the supermost post in the universe, and it appears that there are many Brahmās and many universes besides the one in which we are situated. One who fills this post must be ideal in behavior, for Brahmā sets the example for all living entities. Brahmā, the living entity who is the most pious and spiritually elevated, is entrusted with a post next to that of the Personality of Godhead.

TEXT 31

तेजीयसामपि ह्येतन्न सुश्लोक्यं जगद्गुरो ।
यद्वृत्तमनुतिष्ठन् वै लोकः क्षेमाय कल्पते ॥३१॥

tejīyasām api hy etan
na suślokyaṁ jagad-guro
yad-vṛttam anutiṣṭhan vai
lokaḥ kṣemāya kalpate

tejīyasām—of the most powerful; *api*—also; *hi*—certainly; *etat*—such an act; *na*—not suitable; *su-ślokyam*—good behavior; *jagat-guro*—O spiritual master of the universe; *yat*—whose; *vṛttam*—character; *anutiṣṭhan*—following; *vai*—certainly; *lokaḥ*—the world; *kṣemāya*—for prosperity; *kalpate*—becomes eligible.

TRANSLATION

Even though you are the most powerful being, this act does not suit you because your character is followed for spiritual improvement by people in general.

PURPORT

It is said that a supremely powerful living entity can do anything and everything he likes and such acts do not affect him in any way. For example, the sun, the most powerful fiery planet in the universe, can evaporate water from anywhere and still remain as powerful. The sun evaporates water from filthy places and yet is not infected with the quality of the filth. Similarly, Brahmā remains unimpeachable in all conditions. But still, since he is the spiritual master of all living entities, his behavior and character should be so ideal that people will follow such sublime behavior and derive the highest spiritual benefit. Therefore, he should not have acted as he did.

TEXT 32

तस्मै नमो भगवते य इदं स्वेन रोचिषा ।
आत्मस्थं व्यञ्जयामास स धर्मं पातुमर्हति ॥३२॥

tasmai namo bhagavate
ya idaṁ svena rociṣā
ātma-sthaṁ vyañjayām āsa
sa dharmaṁ pātum arhati

tasmai—unto Him; *namaḥ*—obeisances; *bhagavate*—unto the Personality of Godhead; *yaḥ*—who; *idam*—this; *svena*—by His own; *rociṣā*—effulgence; *ātma-stham*—situated in Himself; *vyañjayām āsa*—has manifested; *saḥ*—He; *dharmam*—religion; *pātum*—for protection; *arhati*—may kindly do so.

TRANSLATION

Let us offer our respectful obeisances unto the Personality of Godhead, who, by His own effulgence, while situated in Himself, has manifested this cosmos. May He also protect religion for all goodness.

PURPORT

Lust for sexual intercourse is so strong that it appears herein that Brahmā could not be dissuaded from his determination in spite of the appeal by his great sons like Marīci. Therefore, the great sons began to pray to the Supreme Lord for the good sense of Brahmā. It is only by the grace of the Supreme Lord that one can be protected from the allurement of lusty material desires. The Lord gives protection to devotees who are always engaged in His transcendental loving service, and by His causeless mercy He forgives the accidental fall of a devotee. Therefore, sages like Marīci prayed for the mercy of the Lord, and their prayer was fruitful.

TEXT 33

स इत्थं गृणतः पुत्रान् पुरो दृष्ट्वा प्रजापतीन् ।
प्रजापतिपतिस्तन्वं तत्याज व्रीडितस्तदा ।
तां दिशो जगृहुर्घोरां नीहारं यद्विदुस्तमः ॥३३॥

sa itthaṁ gṛṇataḥ putrān
puro dṛṣṭvā prajāpatīn

prajāpati-patis tanvaṁ
tatyāja vrīḍitas tadā
tāṁ diśo jagṛhur ghorāṁ
nīhāraṁ yad vidus tamaḥ

saḥ—he (Brahmā); *ittham*—thus; *gṛṇataḥ*—speaking; *putrān*—sons; *puraḥ*—before; *dṛṣṭvā*—seeing; *prajā-patīn*—all the progenitors of living entities; *prajāpati-patiḥ*—the father of them (Brahmā); *tanvam*—body; *tatyāja*—quit; *vrīḍitaḥ*—ashamed; *tadā*—at that time; *tām*—that body; *diśaḥ*—all directions; *jagṛhuḥ*—accepted; *ghorām*—blamable; *nīhāram*—fog; *yat*—which; *viduḥ*—they know as; *tamaḥ*—darkness.

TRANSLATION

The father of all Prajāpatis, Brahmā, thus seeing all his Prajāpati sons speaking in that way, became very much ashamed and at once gave up the body he had accepted. Later that body appeared in all directions as the dangerous fog in darkness.

PURPORT

The best way to compensate for one's sinful acts is to give up one's body at once, and Brahmā, the leader of the living entities, showed this by his personal example. Brahmā has a fabulous duration of life, but he was obliged to give up his body due to his grievous sin, even though he had merely contemplated it in his mind without having actually done it.

This is a lesson for the living entities, showing how sinful an act it is to indulge in unrestricted sex life. Even to think of abominable sex life is sinful, and to compensate for such acts, one has to give up his body. In other words, one's duration of life, blessings, opulence, etc., are decreased by sinful acts, and the most dangerous type of sinful act is unrestricted sex.

Ignorance is the cause of sinful life, or sinful life is the cause of gross ignorance. The feature of ignorance is darkness or fog. Darkness or fog still covers the whole universe, and the sun is the only counteracting principle. One who takes shelter of the Lord, the perpetual light, has no fear of being annihilated in the darkness of fog or ignorance.

TEXT 34

कदाचिद् ध्यायतः स्रष्टुर्वेदा आसंश्चतुर्मुखात् ।
कथं स्रक्ष्याम्यहं लोकान् समवेतान् यथा पुरा ॥३४॥

kadācid dhyāyataḥ sraṣṭur
vedā āsaṁś catur-mukhāt
kathaṁ srakṣyāmy ahaṁ lokān
samavetān yathā purā

kadācit—once upon a time; *dhyāyataḥ*—while contemplating; *sraṣṭuḥ*—of Brahmā; *vedāḥ*—the Vedic literature; *āsan*—became manifested; *catuḥ-mukhāt*—from the four mouths; *katham srakṣyāmi*—how shall I create; *aham*—myself; *lokān*—all these worlds; *samavetān*—assembled; *yathā*—as they were; *purā*—in the past.

TRANSLATION

Once upon a time, when Brahmā was thinking of how to create the worlds as in the past millennium, the four Vedas, which contain all varieties of knowledge, became manifested from his four mouths.

PURPORT

As a fire can consume anything and everything without being contaminated, so, by the grace of the Lord, the fire of Brahmā's greatness consumed his desire for the sinful act of sex with his daughter. The *Vedas* are the source of all knowledge, and they were first revealed to Brahmā by the mercy of the Supreme Personality of Godhead while Brahmā was thinking of re-creating the material world. Brahmā is powerful by dint of his devotional service unto the Lord, and the Lord is always ready to forgive His devotee if by chance he falls down from the noble path of devotional service. The *Śrīmad-Bhāgavatam* (11.5.42) confirms this as follows:

sva-pāda-mūlaṁ bhajataḥ priyasya
tyaktvānya-bhāvasya hariḥ pareśaḥ
vikarma yac cotpatitaṁ kathañ-cid
dhunoti sarvaṁ hṛdi sannviṣṭaḥ

"Any person who is engaged one hundred percent in the transcendental loving service of the Lord, at His lotus feet, is very dear to the Personality of Godhead Hari, and the Lord, being situated in the heart of the devotee, excuses all kinds of sins committed by chance." It was never expected that a great personality like Brahmā would ever think of sex indulgence with his daughter. The example shown by Brahmā only suggests that the power of material nature is so strong that it can act upon everyone, even Brahmā. Brahmā was saved by the mercy of the Lord with a little punishment, but by the grace of the Lord he did not lose his prestige as the great Brahmā.

TEXT 35

चातुर्होत्रं कर्मतन्त्रमुपवेदनयैः सह ।
धर्मस्य पादाश्चत्वारस्तथैवाश्रमवृत्तयः ॥३५॥

cātur-hotraṁ karma-tantram
upaveda-nayaiḥ saha
dharmasya pādāś catvāras
tathaivāśrama-vṛttayaḥ

cātuḥ—four; *hotram*—paraphernalia for sacrifice; *karma*—action; *tantram*—expansions of such activities; *upaveda*—supplementary to the *Vedas*; *nayaiḥ*—by logical conclusions; *saha*—along with; *dharmasya*—of religiosity; *pādāḥ*—principles; *catvāraḥ*—four; *tathā eva*—in the same way; *āśrama*—social orders; *vṛttayaḥ*—occupations.

TRANSLATION

The four kinds of paraphernalia for conducting the fire sacrifice became manifest: the performer [the chanter], the offerer, the fire, and the action performed in terms of the supplementary Vedas. Also the four principles of religiosity [truth, austerity, mercy and cleanliness] and the duties in the four social orders all became manifest.

PURPORT

Eating, sleeping, defending and mating are the four principles of material bodily demands which are common to both the animals and human society. To distinguish human society from the animals there is the performance of religious activities in terms of the social statuses and orders of life. They are all clearly mentioned in the Vedic literatures and were manifested by Brahmā when the four *Vedas* were generated from his four mouths. Thus the duties of humankind in terms of the statuses and social orders were established to be observed by the civilized man. Those who traditionally follow these principles are called Āryans, or progressive human beings.

TEXT 36

विदुर उवाच
स वै विश्वसृजामीशो वेदादीन् मुखतोऽसृजत् ।
यद् यद् येनासृजद् देवस्तन्मे ब्रूहि तपोधन ॥३६॥

vidura uvāca
sa vai viśva-sṛjām īśo
vedādīn mukhato 'sṛjat
yad yad yenāsṛjad devas
tan me brūhi tapo-dhana

viduraḥ uvāca—Vidura said; *saḥ*—he (Brahmā); *vai*—certainly; *viśva*—the universe; *sṛjām*—of those who created; *īśaḥ*—the controller; *veda-ādīn*—the *Vedas*, etc.; *mukhataḥ*—from the mouth; *asṛjat*—established; *yat*—that; *yat*—which; *yena*—by which; *asṛjat*—created; *devaḥ*—the god; *tat*—that; *me*—unto me; *brūhi*—please explain; *tapaḥ-dhana*—O sage whose only wealth is penance.

TRANSLATION

Vidura said: O great sage whose only wealth is penance, kindly explain to me how and with whose help Brahmā established the Vedic knowledge which emanated from his mouth.

TEXT 37

मैत्रेय उवाच
ऋग्यजुःसामाथर्वाख्यान् वेदान् पूर्वादिभिर्मुखैः ।
शास्त्रमिज्यां स्तुतिस्तोमं प्रायश्चित्तं व्यधात्क्रमात् ॥३७॥

maitreya uvāca
ṛg-yajuḥ-sāmātharvākhyan
vedān pūrvādibhir mukhaiḥ
śāstram ijyāṁ stuti-stomaṁ
prāyaścittaṁ vyadhāt kramāt

maitreyaḥ uvāca—Maitreya said; *ṛk-yajuḥ-sāma-atharva*—the four *Vedas*; *ākhyān*—of the name; *vedān*—Vedic literatures; *pūrva-ādibhiḥ*—beginning with the front; *mukhaiḥ*—by the mouths; *śāstram*—Vedic hymns not pronounced before; *ijyām*—priestly rituals; *stuti-stomam*—the subject matter of the reciters; *prāyaścittam*—transcendental activities; *vyadhāt*—established; *kramāt*—one after another.

TRANSLATION

Maitreya said: Beginning from the front face of Brahmā, gradually the four Vedas—Ṛk, Yajur, Sāma and Atharva—became manifest. Thereafter, Vedic hymns which had not been pronounced before, priestly rituals, the subject

matters of the recitation, and transcendental activities were all established, one after another.

TEXT 38

आयुर्वेदं धनुर्वेदं गान्धर्वं वेदमात्मनः ।
स्थापत्यं चासृजद् वेदं क्रमात्पूर्वादिभिर्मुखैः ॥३८॥

āyur-vedaṁ dhanur-vedaṁ
gāndharvaṁ vedam ātmanaḥ
sthāpatyaṁ cāsṛjad vedaṁ
kramāt pūrvādibhir mukhaiḥ

āyuḥ-vedam—medical science; *dhanuḥ-vedam*—military science; *gāndharvam*—musical art; *vedam*—they are all Vedic knowledge; *ātmanaḥ*—of his own; *sthāpatyam*—architectural; *ca*—also; *asṛjat*—created; *vedam*—knowledge; *kramāt*—respectively; *pūrva-ādibhiḥ*—beginning from the front face; *mukhaiḥ*—by the mouths.

TRANSLATION

He also created the medical science, military art, musical art and architectural science, all from the Vedas. They all emanated one after another, beginning from the front face.

PURPORT

The *Vedas* contain perfect knowledge, which includes all kinds of knowledge necessary for the human society, not only on this particular planet but on other planets as well. It is understood that military art is also necessary knowledge for the upkeep of social order, as is the art of music. All these groups of knowledge are called the *Upapurāṇa*, or supplements of the *Vedas*. Spiritual knowledge is the main topic of the *Vedas,* but to help the human being's spiritual pursuit of knowledge, the other information, as above mentioned, forms necessary branches of the Vedic knowledge.

TEXT 39

इतिहासपुराणानि पञ्चमं वेदमीश्वरः ।
सर्वेभ्य एव वक्त्रेभ्यः ससृजे सर्वदर्शनः ॥३९॥

itihāsa-purāṇāni
pañcamaṁ vedam īśvaraḥ

sarvebhya eva vaktrebhyaḥ
sasṛje sarva-darśanaḥ

itihāsa—histories; *purāṇāni*—the *Purāṇas* (supplementary *Vedas*); *pañcamam*—the fifth; *vedam*—the Vedic literature; *īśvaraḥ*—the Lord; *sarvebhyaḥ*—all together; *eva*—certainly; *vaktrebhyaḥ*—from his mouths; *sasṛje*—created; *sarva*—all around; *darśanaḥ*—one who can see all time.

TRANSLATION

Then he created the fifth Veda—the Purāṇas and the histories—from all his mouths, since he could see all the past, present and future.

PURPORT

There are histories of particular countries and nations and of the world, but the *Purāṇas* are the histories of the universe, not only in one millennium, but in many *kalpas.* Brahmā has knowledge of those historical facts, and therefore all the *Purāṇas* are histories. As originally composed by Brahmā, they are part of the *Vedas* and are called the fifth *Veda.*

TEXT 40

षोडश्युक्थौ पूर्ववक्त्रात्पुरीष्यग्निष्टुतावथ ।
आप्तोर्यामातिरात्रौ च वाजपेयं सगोसवम् ॥४०॥

ṣoḍaśy-ukthau pūrva-vaktrāt
purīṣy-agniṣṭutāv atha
āptoryāmātirātrau ca
vājapeyaṁ sagosavam

ṣoḍaśī-ukthau—types of sacrifice; *pūrva-vaktrāt*—from the eastern mouth; *purīṣi-agniṣṭutau*—types of sacrifice; *atha*—then; *āptoryāma-atirātrau*—types of sacrifice; *ca*—and; *vājapeyam*—type of sacrifice; *sa-gosavam*—type of sacrifice.

TRANSLATION

All the different varieties of fire sacrifices [ṣoḍaśī, uktha, purīṣi, agniṣṭoma, āptoryāma, atirātra, vājapeya and gosava] became manifested from the eastern mouth of Brahmā.

TEXT 41

विद्या दानं तपः सत्यं धर्मस्येति पदानि च ।
आश्रमांश्च यथासंख्यमसृजत्सह वृत्तिभिः ॥४१॥

vidyā dānaṁ tapaḥ satyaṁ
dharmasyeti padāni ca
āśramāṁś ca yathā-saṅkhyam
asṛjat saha vṛttibhiḥ

vidyā—education; *dānam*—charity; *tapaḥ*—penance; *satyam*—truth; *dharmasya*—of religion; *iti*—thus; *padāni*—four legs; *ca*—also; *āśramān*—orders of life; *ca*—also; *yathā*—as they are; *saṅkhyam*—in number; *asṛjat*—created; *saha*—along with; *vṛttibhiḥ*—by vocations.

TRANSLATION

Education, charity, penance and truth are said to be the four legs of religion, and to learn this there are four orders of life with different classifications of castes according to vocation. Brahmā created all these in systematic order.

PURPORT

The nucleus of the four social orders—*brahmacarya,* or student life, *gṛhastha,* or householder family life, *vānaprastha,* or retired life for practicing penance, and *sannyāsa,* or renounced life for preaching the truth—is the four legs of religion. The vocational divisions are the *brāhmaṇas,* or the intelligent class, the *kṣatriyas,* or administrative class, the *vaiśyas,* or mercantile productive class, and the *śūdras,* or general laborer class who have no specific qualifications. All were systematically planned and created by Brahmā for the regular promotion of self-realization. Student life is meant for acquiring the best education; household family life is meant for gratifying the senses, provided it is performed with a charitable disposition of mind, retirement from household life is meant for penance, for advancement in spiritual life, and renounced life is meant for preaching the Absolute Truth to the people in general. The combined actions of all members of society make the whole situation favorable for the upliftment of the mission of human life. The beginning of this social institution is based on education meant for purifying the animal propensities of the human being. The highest purificatory process is knowledge of the Supreme Personality of Godhead, the purest of the pure.

TEXT 42

सावित्रं प्राजापत्यं च ब्राह्मं चाथ बृहत्तथा ।
वार्तासञ्चयशालीनशिलोञ्छ इति वै गृहे ॥४२॥

sāvitraṁ prājāpatyaṁ ca
brāhmaṁ cātha bṛhat tathā
vārtā sañcaya-śālīna-
śiloñcha iti vai gṛhe

sāvitram—the thread ceremony of the twice-born; *prājāpatyam*—to execute the vow for one year; *ca*—and; *brāhmam*—acceptance of the *Vedas; ca*—and; *atha*—also; *bṛhat*—complete abstinence from sex life; *tathā*—then; *vārtā*—vocation in terms of Vedic sanction; *sañcaya*—professional duty; *śālīnā*—livelihood without asking anyone for cooperation; *śila-uñchaḥ*—picking up rejected grains; *iti*—thus; *vai*—even though; *gṛhe*—in household life.

TRANSLATION

Then the thread ceremony for the twice-born was inaugurated, as were the rules to be followed for at least one year after acceptance of the Vedas, rules for observing complete abstinence from sex life, vocations in terms of Vedic injunctions, various professional duties in household life, and the method of maintaining a livelihood without anyone's cooperation by picking up rejected grains.

PURPORT

During student life the *brahmacārīs* were given full instructions about the importance of the human form of life. Thus the basic education was designed to encourage the student in becoming free from family encumbrances. Only students unable to accept such a vow in life were allowed to go home and marry a suitable wife. Otherwise, the student would remain a permanent *brahmacārī,* observing complete abstinence from sex life for his whole life. It all depended on the quality of the student's training. We had the opportunity to meet an avowed *brahmacārī* in the personality of our spiritual master, Oṁ Viṣṇupāda Śrī Śrīmad Bhaktisiddhānta Gosvāmī Mahārāja. Such a great soul is called a *naiṣṭhika-brahmacārī.*

TEXT 43

वैखानसा वालखिल्यौदुम्बराः फेनपा वने ।
न्यासे कुटीचकः पूर्वं बह्वोदो हंसनिष्क्रियौ ॥४३॥

vaikhānasā vālakhilyau-
dumbarāḥ phenapā vane
nyāse kuṭīcakaḥ pūrvaṁ
bahvodo haṁsa-niṣkriyau

vaikhānasāḥ—the section of men who retire from active life and live on half-boiled meals; *vālakhilya*—one who quits his former stock of grains on receipt of more; *audumbarāḥ*—one who lives on what he gets from the direction towards which he starts after rising from bed; *phenapāḥ*—one who lives on the fruits which automatically fall from the tree; *vane*—in the forest; *nyāse*—in the order of renunciation; *kuṭīcakaḥ*—life in the family without attachment; *pūrvam*—in the beginning; *bahvodaḥ*—giving up all material activities and engaging fully in transcendental service; *haṁsa*—fully engaged in transcendental knowledge; *niṣkriyau*—stopping all kinds of activities.

TRANSLATION

The four divisions of retired life are the vaikhānasas, vālakhilyas, audumbaras and phenapas. The four divisions of the renounced order of life are the kuṭīcakas, bahvodas, haṁsas and niṣkriyas. All these were manifested from Brahmā.

PURPORT

The *varṇāśrama-dharma*, or the institution of the four divisions and orders of social and spiritual life, is not a new invention of the modern age, as proposed by the less intelligent. It is an institution established by Brahmā from the beginning of the creation. This is also confirmed in the *Bhagavad-gītā* (4.13): *cātur-varṇyaṁ mayā sṛṣṭam.*

TEXT 44

आन्वीक्षिकी त्रयी वार्ता दण्डनीतिस्तथैव च ।
एवं व्याहृतयश्चासन् प्रणवो ह्यस्य दह्रतः ॥४४॥

ānvīkṣikī trayī vārtā
daṇḍa-nītis tathaiva ca
evaṁ vyāhṛtayaś cāsan
praṇavo hy asya dahrataḥ

ānvīkṣikī—logic; *trayī*—the three goals, namely religion, economy and salvation; *vārtā*—sense gratification; *daṇḍa*—law and order; *nītiḥ*—moral codes; *tathā*—as also; *eva ca*—

respectively; *evam*—thus; *vyāhṛtayaḥ*—the celebrated hymns *bhūḥ, bhuvaḥ* and *svaḥ*; *ca*—also; *āsan*—came into existence; *praṇavaḥ*—the *oṁkāra; hi*—certainly; *asya*—of him (Brahmā); *dahrataḥ*—from the heart.

TRANSLATION

The science of logical argument, the Vedic goals of life, and also law and order, moral codes, and the celebrated hymns bhūḥ, bhuvaḥ and svaḥ all became manifested from the mouths of Brahmā, and the praṇava oṁkāra was manifested from his heart.

TEXT 45

तस्योष्णिगासील्लोमभ्यो गायत्री च त्वचो विभोः ।
त्रिष्टुम्मांसात्स्नुतोऽनुष्टुब्जगत्यस्थ्नः प्रजापतेः ॥४५॥

tasyoṣṇig āsīl lomabhyo
gāyatrī ca tvaco vibhoḥ
triṣṭum māṁsāt snuto 'nuṣṭub
jagaty asthnaḥ prajāpateḥ

tasya—his; *uṣṇik* one of the Vedic meters; *āsīt*—generated; *lomabhyaḥ*—from the hairs on the body; *gāyatrī*—the principal Vedic hymn; *ca*—also; *tvacaḥ*—from the skin; *vibhoḥ*—of the Lord; *triṣṭup*—a particular type of poetic meter; *māṁsāt*—from the flesh; *snutaḥ*—from the sinews; *anuṣṭup*—another type of poetic meter; *jagatī*—another type of poetic meter; *asthnaḥ*—from the bones; *prajāpateḥ*—of the father of the living entities.

TRANSLATION

Thereafter the art of literary expression, uṣṇik, was generated from the hairs on the body of the almighty Prajāpati. The principal Vedic hymn, gāyatrī, was generated from the skin, triṣṭup from the flesh, anuṣṭup from the veins, and jagatī from the bones of the lord of the living entities.

TEXT 46

मज्जायाः पङ्क्तिरुत्पन्ना बृहती प्राणतोऽभवत् ॥४६॥

majjāyāḥ paṅktir utpannā
bṛhatī prāṇato 'bhavat

majjāyāḥ—from the bone marrow; *paṅktiḥ*—a particular type of verse; *utpannā*—became manifested; *bṛhatī*—another type of verse; *prāṇataḥ*—out of the life-breathing; *abhavat*—generated.

TRANSLATION

The art of writing verse, paṅkti, became manifested from the bone marrow, and that of bṛhatī, another type of verse, was generated from the life-breath of the lord of the living entities.

TEXT 47

स्पर्शस्तस्याभवज्जीवः स्वरो देह उदाहृत ।
ऊष्माणमिन्द्रियाण्याहुरन्तःस्था बलमात्मनः ।
स्वराः सप्त विहारेण भवन्ति स्म प्रजापतेः ॥४७॥

sparśas tasyābhavaj jīvaḥ
svaro deha udāhṛta
ūṣmāṇam indriyāṇy āhur
antaḥ-sthā balam ātmanaḥ
svarāḥ sapta vihāreṇa
bhavanti sma prajāpateḥ

sparśaḥ—the set of letters from *ka* to *ma; tasya*—his; *abhavat*—became; *jīvaḥ*—the soul; *svaraḥ*—vowels; *dehaḥ*—his body; *udāhṛtaḥ*—are expressed; *ūṣmāṇam*—the letters *śa, ṣa, sa* and *ha; indriyāṇi*—the senses; *āhuḥ*—are called; *antaḥ-sthāḥ*—the set of letters so known (*ya, ra, la* and *va*); *balam*—energy; *ātmanaḥ*—of his self; *svarāḥ*—music; *sapta*—seven; *vihāreṇa*—by the sensual activities; *bhavanti sma*—became manifested; *prajāpateḥ*—of the lord of the living entities.

TRANSLATION

Brahmā's soul was manifested as the touch alphabets, his body as the vowels, his senses as the sibilant alphabets, his strength as the intermediate alphabets and his sensual activities as the seven notes of music.

PURPORT

In Sanskrit there are thirteen vowels and thirty-five consonants. The vowels are *a, ā, i, ī, u, ū, ṛ, ṝ, ḷ, e, ai, o, au*, and the consonants are *ka, kha, ga, gha*, etc. Amongst the consonants, the first twenty-five letters are called the *sparśas.* There are also four *antaḥ-sthas.* Of the *ūṣmas* there are three *s*'s, called *tālavya, mūrdhanya* and *dantya.* The musical notes are *ṣa, ṛ, gā, ma, dha*, and *ni.* All these sound vibrations are originally called *śabda-brahma*, or spiritual sound. It is said, therefore, that Brahmā was created in the Mahā-kalpa as the incarnation of spiritual sound. The *Vedas* are spiritual sound, and therefore there is no need of material interpretation for the sound vibration of the Vedic literature. The *Vedas* should be vibrated as they are, although they are symbolically represented with letters which are known to us materially. In the ultimate issue there is nothing material because everything has its origin in the spiritual world. The material manifestation is therefore called illusion in the proper sense of the term. For those who are realized souls there is nothing but spirit.

TEXT 48

शब्दब्रह्मात्मनस्तस्य व्यक्ताव्यक्तात्मनः परः ।
ब्रह्मावभाति विततो नानाशक्त्युपबृंहितः ॥४८॥

śabda-brahmātmanas tasya
vyaktāvyaktātmanaḥ paraḥ
brahmāvabhāti vitato
nānā-śakty-upabṛṁhitaḥ

śabda-brahma—transcendental sound; *ātmanaḥ*—of the Supreme Lord; *tasya*—His; *vyakta*—manifested; *avyakta-ātmanaḥ*—of the unmanifested; *paraḥ*—transcendental; *brahmā*—the Absolute; *avabhāti*—completely manifested; *vitataḥ*—distributing; *nānā*—multifarious; *śakti*—energies; *upabṛṁhitaḥ*—invested with.

TRANSLATION

Brahmā is the personal representation of the Supreme Personality of Godhead as the source of transcendental sound and is therefore above the conception of manifested and unmanifested. Brahmā is thc complete form of the Absolute Truth and is invested with multifarious energies.

PURPORT

The post of Brahmā is the highest responsible post within the universe, and it is offered to the most perfect personality of the universe. Sometimes the Supreme Personality of Godhead has to become Brahmā when there is no suitable living being to occupy the post. In the material world, Brahmā is the complete representation of the Supreme Personality of Godhead, and transcendental sound, *praṇava*, comes from him. He is therefore invested with multifarious energies, from which all the demigods like Indra, Candra and Varuṇa are manifested. His transcendental value is not to be minimized, even though he exhibited a tendency to enjoy his own daughter. There is a purpose for the exhibition of such a tendency by Brahmā, and he is not to be condemned like an ordinary living entity.

TEXT 49

ततोऽपरामुपादाय स सर्गाय मनो दधे ॥४९॥

tato 'parām upādāya
sa sargāya mano dadhe

tataḥ—thereafter; *aparām*—another; *upādāya*—having accepted; *saḥ*—he; *sargāya*—in the matter of creation; *manaḥ*—mind; *dadhe*—gave attention.

TRANSLATION

Thereafter Brahmā accepted another body, in which sex life was not forbidden, and thus he engaged himself in the matter of further creation.

PURPORT

In his former body, which was transcendental, affection for sex life was forbidden, and Brahmā therefore had to accept another body to allow himself to be connected with sex. He thus engaged himself in the matter of creation. His former body transformed into fog, as previously described.

TEXT 50

ऋषीणां भूरिवीर्याणामपि सर्गमविस्तृतम् ।
ज्ञात्वा तद्धृदये भूयश्चिन्तयामास कौरव ॥५०॥

ṛṣīṇāṁ bhūri-vīryāṇām
api sargam avistṛtam
jñātvā tad dhṛdaye bhūyaś
cintayām āsa kaurava

ṛsīṇām—of the great sages; *bhūri-vīryāṇām*—with great potential power; *api*—in spite of; *sargam*—the creation; *avistṛtam*—not extended; *jñātvā*—knowing; *tat*—that; *hṛdaye*—in his heart; *bhūyaḥ*—again; *cintayām āsa*—he began to consider; *kaurava*—O son of the Kurus.

TRANSLATION

O son of the Kurus, when Brahmā saw that in spite of the presence of sages of great potency there was no sufficient increase in population, he seriously began to consider how the population could be increased.

TEXT 51

अहो अद्भुतमेतन्मे व्यापृतस्यापि नित्यदा ।
न ह्येधन्ते प्रजा नूनं दैवमत्र विघातकम् ॥५१॥

aho adbhutam etan me
vyāpṛtasyāpi nityadā
na hy edhante prajā nūnaṁ
daivam atra vighātakam

aho—alas; *adbhutam*—it is wonderful; *etat*—this; *me*—for me; *vyāpṛtasya*—being busy; *api*—although; *nityadā*—always; *na*—does not; *hi*—certainly; *edhante*—generate; *prajāḥ*—living entities; *nūnam*—however; *daivam*—destiny; *atra*—herein; *vighātakam*—against.

TRANSLATION

Brahmā thought to himself: Alas, it is wonderful that in spite of my being scattered all over, there is still insufficient population throughout the universe. There is no other cause for this misfortune but destiny.

TEXT 52

एवं युक्तकृतस्तस्य दैवं चावेक्षतस्तदा ।
कस्य रूपमभूद् द्वेधा यत्कायमभिचक्षते ॥५२॥

evaṁ yukta-kṛtas tasya
daivaṁ cāvekṣatas tadā
kasya rūpam abhud dvedhā
yat kāyam abhicakṣate

evam—thus; *yukta*—contemplating; *kṛtaḥ*—while doing so; *tasya*—his; *daivam*—supernatural power; *ca*—also; *avekṣataḥ*—observing; *tadā*—at that time; *kasya*—of Brahmā; *rūpam*—form; *abhūt*—became manifested; *dvedhā*—twofold; *yat*—which is; *kāyam*—his body; *abhicakṣate*—is said to be.

TRANSLATION

While he was thus absorbed in contemplation and was observing the supernatural power, two other forms were generated from his body. They are still celebrated as the body of Brahmā.

PURPORT

Two bodies came out from the body of Brahmā. One had a mustache, and the other had swollen breasts. No one can explain the source of their manifestation, and therefore until today they are known as the *kāyam,* or the body of Brahmā, with no indication of their relationship as his son or daughter.

TEXT 53

ताभ्यां रूपविभागाभ्यां मिथुनं समपद्यत ॥५३॥

tābhyāṁ rūpa-vibhāgābhyāṁ
mithunaṁ samapadyata

tābhyām—of them; *rūpa*—form; *vibhāgābhyām*—thus being divided; *mithunam*—sex relation; *samapadyata*—perfectly executed.

TRANSLATION

The two newly separated bodies united together in a sexual relationship.

TEXT 54

यस्तु तत्र पुमान् सोऽभून्मनुः स्वायम्भुवः स्वराट् ।
स्त्री यासीच्छतरूपाख्या महिष्यस्य महात्मनः ॥५४॥

yas tu tatra pumān so 'bhūn
manuḥ svāyambhuvaḥ svarāṭ
strī yāsīc chatarūpākhyā
mahiṣy asya mahātmanaḥ

yaḥ—one who; *tu*—but; *tatra*—there; *pumān*—the male; *saḥ*—he; *abhūt*—became; *manuḥ*—the father of mankind; *svāyambhuvah*—of the name Svāyambhuva; *sva-rāṭ*—fully independent; *strī*—the woman; *yā*—one who; *āsīt*—there was; *śatarūpā*—of the name Śatarūpā; *ākhyā*—known as; *mahiṣī*—the queen; *asya*—of him; *mahātmanaḥ*—the great soul.

TRANSLATION

Out of them, the one who had the male form became known as the Manu named Svāyambhuva, and the woman became known as Śatarūpā, the queen of the great soul Manu.

TEXT 55

तदा मिथुनधर्मेण प्रजा ह्येधाम्बभूविरे ॥५५॥

tadā mithuna-dharmeṇa
prajā hy edhām babhūvire

tadā—at that time; *mithuna*—sex life; *dharmeṇa*—according to regulative principles; *prajāḥ*—generations; *hi*—certainly; *edhām*—increased; *babhūvire*—took place.

TRANSLATION

Thereafter, by sex indulgence, they gradually increased generations of population one after another.

TEXT 56

स चापि शतरूपायां पञ्चापत्यान्यजीजनत् ।
प्रियव्रतोत्तानपादौ तिस्रः कन्याश्च भारत ।
आकूतिर्देवहूतिश्च प्रसूतिरिति सत्तम ॥५६॥

sa cāpi śatarūpāyāṁ
pañcāpatyany ajījanat
priyavratottānapādau
tisraḥ kanyāś ca bhārata
ākūtir devahūtiś ca
prasūtir iti sattama

saḥ—he (Manu); *ca*—also; *api*—in due course; *śatarūpāyām*—unto Śatarūpā; *pañca*—five; *apatyāni*—children; *ajījanat*—begot; *priyavrata*—Priyavrata; *uttānapādau*—Uttānapāda; *tisraḥ*—three in number; *kanyāḥ*—daughters; *ca*—also; *bhārata*—O son of Bharata; *ākūtiḥ*—Ākūti; *devahūtiḥ*—Devahūti; *ca*—and; *prasūtiḥ*—Prasūti; *iti*—thus; *sattama*—O best of all.

TRANSLATION

O son of Bharata, in due course of time he [Manu] begot in Śatarūpā five children—two sons, Priyavrata and Uttānapāda, and three daughters, Ākūti, Devahūti and Prasūti.

TEXT 57

आकूतिं रुचये प्रादात्कर्दमाय तु मध्यमाम् ।
दक्षायादात्प्रसूतिं च यत आपूरितं जगत् ॥५७॥

ākūtiṁ rucaye prādāt
kardamāya tu madhyamām
dakṣāyādāt prasūtiṁ ca
yata āpūritaṁ jagat

ākūtim—the daughter named Ākūti; *rucaye*—unto the sage Ruci; *prādāt*—handed over; *kardamāya*—unto the sage Kardama; *tu*—but; *madhyamām*—the middle one (Devahūti); *dakṣāya*—unto Dakṣa; *adāt*—handed over; *prasūtim*—the youngest daughter; *ca*—also; *yataḥ*—wherefrom; *āpūritam*—is fulfilled; *jagat*—the whole world.

TRANSLATION

The father, Manu, handed over his first daughter, Ākūti, to the sage Ruci, the middle daughter, Devahūti, to the sage Kardama, and the youngest, Prasūti, to Dakṣa. From them, all the world filled with population.

PURPORT

The history of the creation of the population of the universe is given herewith. Brahmā is the original living creature in the universe, from whom were generated the Manu Svāyambhuva and his wife Śatarūpā. From Manu, two sons and three daughters were born, and from them all the population in different planets has sprung up until now. Therefore, Brahmā is known as the grandfather of everyone, and the Personality of Godhead, being the father of Brahmā, is known as the great-grandfather of all living beings. This is confirmed in *Bhagavad-gītā* (11.39) as follows:

vāyur yamo 'gnir varuṇaḥ śaśāṅkaḥ
prajāpatis tvaṁ prapitāmahaś ca
namo namas te 'stu sahasra-kṛtvaḥ
punaś ca bhūyo 'pi namo namas te

"You are the Lord of air, the supreme justice Yama, the fire, and the Lord of rains. You are the moon, and You are the great-grandfather. Therefore I offer my respectful obeisances unto You again and again."

Thus end the Bhaktivedanta purports of the Third Canto, Twelfth Chapter, of the Śrīmad-Bhāgavatam, *entitled "Creation of the Kumāras and Others."*

CHAPTER THIRTEEN

The Appearance of Lord Varāha

TEXT 1

श्रीशुक उवाच
निशम्य वाचं वदतो मुनेः पुण्यतमां नृप ।
भूयः पप्रच्छ कौरव्यो वासुदेवकथादृतः ॥ १ ॥

śrī-śuka uvāca
niśamya vācaṁ vadato
muneḥ puṇyatamāṁ nṛpa
bhūyaḥ papraccha kauravyo
vāsudeva-kathādṛtaḥ

śrī-śukaḥ uvāca—Śrī Śukadeva Gosvāmī said; *niśamya*—after hearing; *vācam*—talks; *vadataḥ*—while speaking; *muneḥ*—of Maitreya Muni; *puṇya-tamām*—the most virtuous; *nṛpa*—O King; *bhūyaḥ*—then again; *papraccha*—inquired; *kauravyaḥ*—the best amongst the Kurus (Vidura); *vāsudeva-kathā*—topics on the subject of the Personality of Godhead, Vāsudeva; *ādṛtaḥ*—one who so adores.

TRANSLATION

Śrī Śukadeva Gosvāmī said: O King, after hearing all these most virtuous topics from the sage Maitreya, Vidura inquired further on the topics of the Supreme Personality of Godhead, which he adored to hear.

PURPORT

The word *ādṛtaḥ* is significant because it indicates that Vidura had a natural inclination for hearing the transcendental message of the Supreme Personality of Godhead, and he was never fully satisfied though continuing to hear those topics. He wanted to hear more and more so that he could be more and more blessed by the transcendental message.

TEXT 2

विदुर उवाच
स वै स्वायम्भुवः सम्राट् प्रियः पुत्रः स्वयम्भुवः ।
प्रतिलभ्य प्रियां पत्नीं किं चकार ततो मुने ॥ २ ॥

vidura uvāca
sa vai svāyambhuvaḥ samrāṭ
priyaḥ putraḥ svayambhuvaḥ
pratilabhya priyāṁ patnīṁ
kiṁ cakāra tato mune

viduraḥ uvāca—Vidura said; *saḥ*—he; *vai*—easily; *svāyambhuvaḥ*—Svāyambhuva Manu; *samrāṭ*—the king of all kings; *priyaḥ*—dear; *putraḥ*—son; *svayambhuvaḥ*—of Brahmā; *pratilabhya*—after obtaining; *priyām*—most loving; *patnīm*—wife; *kim*—what; *cakāra*—did; *tataḥ*—thereafter; *mune*—O great sage.

TRANSLATION

Vidura said: O great sage, what did Svāyambhuva, the dear son of Brahmā, do after obtaining his very loving wife?

TEXT 3

चरितं तस्य राजर्षेरादिराजस्य सत्तम ।
ब्रूहि मे श्रद्दधानाय विष्वक्सेनाश्रयो ह्यसौ ॥ ३ ॥

caritaṁ tasya rājarṣer
ādi-rājasya sattama
brūhi me śraddadhānāya
viṣvaksenāśrayo hy asau

caritam—character; *tasya*—his; *rājarṣeḥ*—of the saintly king; *ādi-rājasya*—of the original king; *sattama*—O most pious one; *brūhi*—kindly speak; *me*—unto me; *śraddadhānāya*—unto one eager to receive; *viṣvaksena*—of the Personality of Godhead; *āśrayaḥ*—one who has taken shelter; *hi*—certainly; *asau*—that king.

TRANSLATION

O best of the virtuous, the original king of kings [Manu] was a great devotee of the Personality of Godhead Hari, and thus it is worth hearing of his sublime character and activities. Please describe them. I am very eager to hear.

PURPORT

Śrīmad-Bhāgavatam is full of the transcendental topics of the Personality of Godhead and His pure devotees. In the absolute world there is no difference in quality between the Supreme Lord and His pure devotee. Therefore, hearing the topics of the Lord and hearing of the character and activities of the pure devotee have the same result, namely, the development of devotional service.

TEXT 4

श्रुतस्य पुंसां सुचिरश्रमस्य
नन्वञ्जसा सूरिभिरीडितोऽर्थः ।
तत्तद्‌गुणानुश्रवणं मुकुन्द-
पादारविन्दं हृदयेषु येषाम् ॥ ४ ॥

śrutasya puṁsāṁ sucira-śramasya
nanv añjasā sūribhir īḍito 'rthaḥ
tat-tad-guṇānuśravaṇaṁ mukunda-
pādāravindaṁ hṛdayeṣu yeṣām

śrutasya—of persons who are in the process of hearing; *puṁsām*—of such persons; *sucira*—for a long time; *śramasya*—laboring very hard; *nanu*—certainly; *añjasā*—elaborately; *sūribhiḥ*—by pure devotees; *īḍitaḥ*—explained by; *arthaḥ*—statements; *tat*—that; *tat*—that; *guṇa*—transcendental qualities; *anuśravaṇam*—thinking; *mukunda*—the Personality of Godhead, who awards liberation; *pāda-aravindam*—the lotus feet; *hṛdayeṣu*—within the heart; *yeṣām*—of them.

TRANSLATION

Persons who hear from a spiritual master with great labor and for a long time must hear from the mouths of pure devotees about the character and activities of pure devotees. Pure devotees always think within their hearts of the lotus feet of the Personality of Godhead, who awards His devotees liberation.

PURPORT

Transcendental students are those who undergo great penance in being trained by hearing the *Vedas* from a bona fide spiritual master. Not only must they hear about the activities of the Lord, but they must also hear about the transcendental qualities of the devotees who are constantly thinking of the lotus feet of the Lord within their hearts. A pure devotee of the Lord cannot be separated from the lotus feet of the Lord for even a moment. Undoubtedly the Lord is always within the hearts of all living creatures, but they hardly know about it because they are deluded by the illusory material energy. The devotees, however, realize the presence of the Lord, and therefore they can always see the lotus feet of the Lord within their hearts. Such pure devotees of the Lord are as glorious as the Lord; they are, in fact, recommended by the Lord as more worshipable than He Himself. Worship of the devotee is more potent than worship of the Lord. It is therefore the duty of the transcendental students to hear of pure devotees, as explained by similar devotees of the Lord, because one cannot explain about the Lord or His devotee unless one happens to be a pure devotee himself.

TEXT 5

श्रीशुक उवाच
इति ब्रुवाणं विदुरं विनीतं
सहस्रशीर्ष्णश्चरणोपधानम् ।
प्रहृष्टरोमा भगवत्कथायां
प्रणीयमानो मुनिरभ्यचष्ट ॥ ५ ॥

śrī-śuka uvāca
iti bruvāṇaṁ viduraṁ vinītaṁ
sahasra-śīrṣṇaś caraṇopadhānam
prahṛṣṭa-romā bhagavat-kathāyāṁ
praṇīyamāno munir abhyacaṣṭa

śrī-śukaḥ uvāca—Śrī Śukadeva Gosvāmī said; *iti*—thus; *bruvāṇam*—speaking; *viduram*—unto Vidura; *vinītam*—very gentle; *sahasra-śīrṣṇaḥ*—the Personality of Godhead Kṛṣṇa; *caraṇa*—lotus feet; *upadhānam*—pillow; *prahṛṣṭa-romā*—hairs standing in ecstasy; *bhagavat*—in relationship with the Personality of Godhead; *kathāyām*—in the words; *praṇīyamānaḥ*—being influenced by such spirit; *muniḥ*—the sage; *abhyacaṣṭa*—attempted to speak.

TRANSLATION

Śrī Śukadeva Gosvāmī said: The Personality of Godhead Śrī Kṛṣṇa was pleased to place His lotus feet on the lap of Vidura because Vidura was very meek and gentle. The sage Maitreya was very pleased with Vidura's words, and, being influenced by his spirit, he attempted to speak.

PURPORT

The word *sahasra-śīrṣṇaḥ* is very significant. One who has diverse energies and activities and a wonderful brain is known as the *sahasra-śīrṣṇaḥ*. This qualification is applicable only to the Personality of Godhead, Śrī Kṛṣṇa, and no one else. The Personality of Godhead was pleased to dine sometimes with Vidura at his home, and while resting He placed His lotus feet on the lap of Vidura. Maitreya was inspired by the thought of Vidura's wonderful fortune. The hairs of his body stood on end, and he was pleased to narrate the topics of the Personality of Godhead with great delight.

TEXT 6

मैत्रेय उवाच
यदा स्वभार्यया सार्धं जातः स्वायम्भुवो मनुः ।
प्राञ्जलिः प्रणतश्चेदं वेदगर्भमभाषत ॥ ६ ॥

maitreya uvāca
yadā sva-bhāryayā sārdhaṁ
jātaḥ svāyambhuvo manuḥ
prāñjaliḥ praṇataś cedaṁ
veda-garbham abhāṣata

maitreyaḥ uvāca—Maitreya said; *yadā*—when; *sva-bhāryayā*—along with his wife; *sārdham*—accompanied by; *jātaḥ*—appeared; *svāyambhuvaḥ*—Svayambhuva Manu; *manuḥ*—the father of mankind; *prāñjaliḥ*—with folded hands; *praṇataḥ*—in obeisances; *ca*—also; *idam*—this; *veda-garbham*—unto the reservoir of Vedic wisdom; *abhāṣata*—addressed.

TRANSLATION

The sage Maitreya said to Vidura: After his appearance, Manu, the father of mankind, along with his wife, thus addressed the reservoir of Vedic wisdom, Brahmā, with obeisances and folded hands.

TEXT 7

त्वमेकः सर्वभूतानां जन्मकृद् वृत्तिदः पिता ।
तथापि नः प्रजानां ते शुश्रूषा केन वा भवेत् ॥ ७ ॥

tvam ekaḥ sarva-bhūtānāṁ
janma-kṛd vṛttidaḥ pitā
tathāpi naḥ prajānāṁ te
śuśrūṣā kena vā bhavet

tvam—you; *ekaḥ*—one; *sarva*—all; *bhūtānām*—living entities; *janma-kṛt*—progenitor; *vṛtti-daḥ*—source of subsistence; *pitā*—the father; *tathā api*—yet; *naḥ*—ourselves; *prajānām*—of all who are born; *te*—of you; *śuśrūṣā*—service; *kena*—how; *vā*—either; *bhavet*—may be possible.

TRANSLATION

You are the father of all living entities and the source of their subsistence because they are all born of you. Please order us how we may be able to render service unto you.

PURPORT

A son's duty is not only to make the father the source of supply for all his needs, but also, when he is grown up, to render service unto him. That is the law of creation beginning from the time of Brahmā. A father's duty is to bring up the son until he is grown, and when the son is grown up, it is his duty to render service unto the father.

TEXT 8

तद्विधेहि नमस्तुभ्यं कर्मस्वीड्यात्मशक्तिषु ।
यत्कृत्वेह यशो विष्वगमुत्र च भवेद्गतिः ॥ ८ ॥

tad vidhehi namas tubhyaṁ
karmasv īdyātma-śaktiṣu
yat kṛtveha yaśo viṣvag
amutra ca bhaved gatiḥ

tat—that; *vidhehi*—give direction; *namaḥ*—my obeisances; *tubhyam*—unto you; *karmasu*—in duties; *īdya*—O worshipful one; *ātma-śaktiṣu*—within our working capacity; *yat*—which; *kṛtvā*—doing; *iha*—in this world; *yaśaḥ*—fame; *viṣvak*—everywhere; *amutra*—in the next world; *ca*—and; *bhavet*—it should be; *gatiḥ*—progress.

TRANSLATION

O worshipful one, please give us your direction for the execution of duty within our working capacity so that we can follow it for fame in this life and progress in the next.

PURPORT

Brahmā is the direct recipient of Vedic knowledge from the Personality of Godhead, and anyone discharging his entrusted duties in disciplic succession from Brahmā is sure to gain fame in this life and salvation in the next. The disciplic succession from Brahmā is called the Brahma-sampradāya, and it descends as follows: Brahmā, Nārada, Vyāsa, Madhva Muni (Pūrṇaprajña), Padmanābha, Nṛhari, Mādhava, Akṣobhya,

Jayatīrtha, Jñānasindhu, Dayānidhi, Vidyānidhi, Rājendra, Jayadharma, Puruṣottama, Brahmaṇyatīrtha, Vyāsatīrtha, Lakṣmīpati, Mādhavendra Purī, Īśvara Purī, Śrī Caitanya Mahāprabhu, Svarūpa Dāmodara and Śrī Rūpa Gosvāmī and others, Śrī Raghunātha dāsa Gosvāmī, Kṛṣṇadāsa Gosvāmī, Narottama dāsa Ṭhākura, Viśvanātha Cakravartī, Jagannātha dāsa Bābājī, Bhaktivinoda Ṭhākura, Gaurakiśora dāsa Bābājī, Śrīmad Bhaktisiddhānta Sarasvatī, A. C. Bhaktivedanta Swami.

This line of disciplic succession from Brahmā is spiritual, whereas the genealogical succession from Manu is material, but both are on the progressive march towards the same goal of Kṛṣṇa consciousness.

TEXT 9

ब्रह्मोवाच
प्रीतस्तुभ्यमहं तात स्वस्ति स्ताद्वां क्षितीश्वर ।
यन्निर्व्यलीकेन हृदा शाधि मेत्यात्मनार्पितम् ॥ ९ ॥

brahmovāca
prītas tubhyam ahaṁ tāta
svasti stād vāṁ kṣitīśvara
yan nirvyalīkena hṛdā
śādhi mety ātmanārpitam

brahmā uvāca—Brahmā said; *prītaḥ*—pleased; *tubhyam*—unto you; *aham*—I; *tāta*—my dear son; *svasti*—all blessings; *stāt*—let there be; *vām*—unto you both; *kṣiti-īśvara*—O lord of the world; *yat*—because; *nirvyalīkena*—without reservation; *hṛdā*—by the heart; *śādhi*—give instruction; *mā*—unto me; *iti*—thus; *ātmanā*—by self; *arpitam*—surrendered.

TRANSLATION

Lord Brahmā said: My dear son, O lord of the world, I am very pleased with you, and I desire all blessings for both you and your wife. You have without reservation surrendered yourself unto me with your heart for my instructions.

PURPORT

The relationship between the father and the son is always sublime. The father is naturally disposed with good will towards the son, and he is always ready to help the son in his progress in life. But in spite of the father's good will, the son is sometimes misguided because of his misuse of personal independence. Every living entity, however small or big he may be, has the choice of independence. If the son is unreservedly willing to be guided by the father, the father is ten times more eager to instruct and guide him by all means. The father and son relationship as exhibited here in the dealings of Brahmā and Manu is excellent. Both the father and the son are well qualified, and their example should be followed by all humankind. Manu, the son, unreservedly asked the father, Brahmā, to instruct him, and the father, who was full of Vedic wisdom, was very glad to instruct. The example of the father of mankind may be rigidly followed by mankind, and that will advance the cause of the relationship of fathers and sons.

TEXT 10

एतावत्यात्मजैर्वीर कार्या ह्यपचितिर्गुरौ ।
शक्त्याप्रमत्तैर्गृह्येत सादरं गतमत्सरैः ॥१०॥

etāvaty ātmajair vīra
kāryā hy apacitir gurau
śaktyāpramattair gṛhyeta
sādaraṁ gata-matsaraiḥ

etāvatī—just exactly like this; *ātmajaiḥ*—by the offspring; *vīra*—O hero; *kāryā*—should be performed; *hi*—certainly; *apacitiḥ*—worship; *gurau*—unto the superior; *śaktyā*—with full capacity; *apramattaiḥ*—by the sane; *gṛhyeta*—should be accepted; *sa-ādaram*—with great delight; *gata-matsaraiḥ*—by those who are beyond the limit of envy.

TRANSLATION

O hero, your example is quite befitting a son in relationship with his father. This sort of adoration for the superior is required. One who is beyond the limit of envy and who is sane accepts the order of his father with great delight and executes it to his full capacity.

PURPORT

When the four previous sons of Brahmā, the sages Sanaka, Sanātana, Sanandana and Sanat-kumāra, refused to obey their father, Brahmā was mortified, and his anger was manifested in the shape of Rudra. That incident was not forgotten by Brahmā, and therefore the obedience of Manu Svāyambhuva was very encouraging. From the material point of view, the four sages' disobedience to the order of their father was certainly abominable, but because such disobedience was for a higher purpose, they were free from the reaction of disobedience. Those who disobey their fathers on material grounds, however, are surely subjected to disciplinary reaction for such disobedience. Manu's obedience to his father on material grounds was certainly free from envy, and in the material world it is imperative for ordinary men to follow the example of Manu.

TEXT 11

स त्वमस्यामपत्यानि सदृशान्यात्मनो गुणैः ।
उत्पाद्य शास धर्मेण गां यज्ञैः पुरुषं यज ॥११॥

sa tvam asyām apatyāni
sadṛśāny ātmano guṇaiḥ
utpādya śāsa dharmeṇa
gāṁ yajñaiḥ puruṣaṁ yaja

saḥ—therefore that obedient son; *tvam*—as you are; *asyām*—in her; *apatyāni*—children; *sadṛśāni*—equally qualified; *ātmanaḥ*—of yourself; *guṇaiḥ*—with the characteristics; *utpādya*—having begotten; *śāsa*—rule; *dharmeṇa*—on the principles of devotional service; *gām*—the world; *yajñaiḥ*—by sacrifices; *puruṣam*—the Supreme Personality of Godhead; *yaja*—worship.

TRANSLATION

Since you are my very obedient son, I ask you to beget children qualified like yourself in the womb of your wife. Rule the world in pursuance of the principles of devotional service unto the Supreme Personality of Godhead, and thus worship the Lord by performances of yajña.

PURPORT

The purpose of the material creation by Brahmā is clearly described herein. Every human being should beget nice children in the womb of his wife, as a sacrifice for the purpose of worshiping the Supreme Personality of Godhead in devotional service. In the *Viṣṇu Purāṇa* (3.8.9) it is stated:

varṇāśramācāravatā
puruṣeṇa paraḥ pumān
viṣṇur ārādhyate panthā
nānyat tat-toṣa-kāraṇam

"One can worship the Supreme Personality of Godhead, Viṣṇu, by proper discharge of the principles of *varṇa* and *āśrama*. There is no alternative to pacifying the Lord by execution of the principles of the *varṇāśrama* system."

Viṣṇu worship is the ultimate aim of human life. Those who take the license of married life for sense enjoyment must also take the responsibility to satisfy the Supreme Personality of Godhead, Viṣṇu, and the first stepping-stone is the *varṇāśrama-dharma* system. *Varṇāśrama-dharma* is the systematic institution for advancing in worship of Viṣṇu. However, if one directly engages in the process of devotional service to the Supreme Personality of Godhead, it may not be necessary to undergo the disciplinary system of *varṇāśrama-dharma*. The other sons of Brahmā, the Kumāras, directly engaged in devotional service, and thus they had no need to execute the principles of *varṇāśrama-dharma*.

TEXT 12

परं शुश्रूषणं मह्यं स्यात्प्रजारक्षया नृप ।
भगवांस्ते प्रजाभर्तुर्हृषीकेशोऽनुतुष्यति ॥१२॥

paraṁ śuśrūṣaṇaṁ mahyaṁ
syāt prajā-rakṣayā nṛpa
bhagavāṁs te prajā-bhartur
hṛṣīkeśo 'nutuṣyati

param—the greatest; *śuśrūṣaṇam*—devotional service; *mahyam*—unto me; *syāt*—should be; *prajā*—the living entities born in the material world; *rakṣayā*—by saving them from being spoiled; *nṛpa*—O King; *bhagavān*—the Personality of Godhead; *te*—with you; *prajā-bhartuḥ*—with the protector of the living beings; *hṛṣīkeśaḥ*—the Lord of the senses; *anutuṣyati*—is satisfied.

TRANSLATION

O King, if you can give proper protection to the living beings in the material world, that will be the best service for me. When the Supreme Lord sees you to be a good protector of the conditioned souls, certainly the master of the senses will be very pleased with you.

PURPORT

The whole administrative system is arranged for the purpose of going back home, back to Godhead. Brahmā is the representative of the Supreme Personality of Godhead, and Manu is the representative of Brahmā. Similarly, all other kings on different planets of the universe are representatives of Manu. The lawbook for the entire human society is the *Manu-saṁhitā,* which directs all activities towards the transcendental service of the Lord. Every king, therefore, must know that his responsibility in administration is not merely to exact taxes from the citizens but to see personally that the citizens under him are being trained in Viṣṇu worship. Everyone must be educated in Viṣṇu worship and engaged in the devotional service of Hṛṣīkeśa, the owner of the senses. The conditioned souls are meant not to satisfy their material senses but to satisfy the senses of Hṛṣīkeśa, the Supreme Personality of Godhead. That is the purpose of the complete administrative system. One who knows this secret, as disclosed here in the version of Brahmā, is the perfect administrative head. One who does not know this is a show-bottle administrator. By training the citizens in the devotional service of the Lord, the head of a state can be free in his responsibility, otherwise he will fail in the onerous duty entrusted to him and thus be punishable by the supreme authority. There is no other alternative in the discharge of administrative duty.

TEXT 13

येषां न तुष्टो भगवान् यज्ञलिङ्गो जनार्दनः ।
तेषां श्रमो ह्यपार्थाय यदात्मा नादृतः स्वयम् ॥१३॥

yeṣāṁ na tuṣṭo bhagavān
yajña-liṅgo janārdanaḥ
teṣāṁ śramo hy apārthāya
yad ātmā nādṛtaḥ svayam

yeṣām—of those with whom; *na*—never; *tuṣṭaḥ*—satisfied; *bhagavān*—the Personality of Godhead; *yajña-liṅgaḥ*—the form of sacrifice; *janārdanaḥ*—Lord Kṛṣṇa, or the *viṣṇu-tattva; teṣām*—of them; *śramaḥ*—labor; *hi*—certainly; *apārthāya*—without profit; *yat*—because; *ātmā*—the Supreme Soul; *na*—not; *ādṛtaḥ*—respected; *svayam*—his own self.

TRANSLATION

The Supreme Personality of Godhead, Janārdana [Lord Kṛṣṇa], is the form to accept all the results of sacrifice. If He is not satisfied, then one's labor for advancement is futile. He is the ultimate Self, and therefore one who does not satisfy Him certainly neglects his own interests.

PURPORT

Brahmā is deputed as the supreme head of universal affairs, and he in his turn deputes Manu and others as *charges d'affaires* of the material manifestation, but the whole show is for the satisfaction of the Supreme Personality of Godhead. Brahmā knows how to satisfy the Lord, and similarly persons engaged in the line of Brahmā's plan of activities also know how to satisfy the Lord. The Lord is satisfied by the process of devotional service, consisting of the ninefold process of hearing, chanting, etc. It is in one's own sell-interest to execute prescribed devotional service, and anyone who neglects this process neglects his own self-interest. Everyone wants to satisfy his senses, but above the senses is the mind, above the mind is the intelligence, above the intelligence is the individual self, and above the individual self is the Superself. Above even the Superself is the Supreme Personality of Godhead, *viṣṇu-tattva.* The primeval Lord and the cause of all causes is Śrī Kṛṣṇa. The complete process of perfectional service is to render service for the satisfaction of the transcendental senses of Lord Kṛṣṇa, who is known as Janārdana.

TEXT 14

मनुरुवाच
आदेशेऽहं भगवतो वर्तेयामीवसूदन ।
स्थानं त्विहानुजानीहि प्रजानां मम च प्रभो ॥१४॥

manur uvāca
ādeśe 'haṁ bhagavato
varteyāmīva-sūdana
sthānaṁ tv ihānujānīhi
prajānāṁ mama ca prabho

manuḥ uvāca—Śrī Manu said; *ādeśe*—under the order; *aham*—I; *bhagavataḥ*—of your powerful self; *varteya*—shall stay; *amīva-sūdana*—O killer of all sins; *sthānam*—the place; *tu*—but; *iha*—in this world; *anujānīhi*—please let me know; *prajānām*—of the living entities born from me; *mama*—my; *ca*—also; *prabho*—O lord.

TRANSLATION

Śrī Manu said: O all-powerful lord, O killer of all sins, I shall abide by your order. Now please let me know my place and that of the living entities born of me.

TEXT 15

यदोकः सर्वभूतानां मही मग्ना महाम्भसि ।
अस्या उद्धरणे यत्नो देव देव्या विधीयताम् ॥१५॥

yad okaḥ sarva-bhūtānāṁ
mahī magnā mahāmbhasi
asyā uddharaṇe yatno
deva devyā vidhīyatām

yat—because; *okaḥ*—the dwelling place; *sarva*—for all; *bhūtānām*—living entities; *mahī*—the earth; *magnā*—merged; *mahā-ambhasi*—in the great water; *asyāḥ*—of this; *uddharaṇe*—in the lifting; *yatnaḥ*—attempt; *deva*—O master of the demigods; *devyāḥ*—of this earth; *vidhīyatām*—let it be done.

TRANSLATION

O master of the demigods, please attempt to lift the earth, which is merged in the great water, because it is the dwelling place for all the living entities. It can be done by your endeavor and by the mercy of the Lord.

PURPORT

The great water mentioned in this connection is the Garbhodaka Ocean, which fills half of the universe.

TEXT 16

मैत्रेय उवाच
परमेष्ठी त्वपां मध्ये तथा सन्नामवेक्ष्य गाम् ।
कथमेनां समुन्नेष्य इति दध्यौ धिया चिरम् ॥१६॥

maitreya uvāca
parameṣṭhī tv apāṁ madhye
tathā sannām avekṣya gām
katham enāṁ samunneṣya
iti dadhyau dhiyā ciram

maitreyaḥ uvāca—Śrī Maitreya Muni said; *parameṣṭhī*—Brahmā; *tu*—also; *apām*—the water; *madhye*—within; *tathā*—thus; *sannām*—situated; *avekṣya*—seeing; *gām*—the earth; *katham*—how; *enām*—this; *samunnesye*—I shall lift; *iti*—thus; *dadhyau*—gave attention; *dhiyā*—by intelligence; *ciram*—for a long time.

TRANSLATION

Śrī Maitreya said: Thus, seeing the earth merged in the water, Brahmā gave his attention for a long time to how it could be lifted.

PURPORT

According to Jīva Gosvāmī, the topics delineated here are of different millenniums. The present topics are of the Śveta-varāha millennium, and topics regarding the Cākṣuṣa millennium will also be discussed in this chapter.

TEXT 17

सृजतो मे क्षितिर्वार्भिः प्लाव्यमाना रसां गता ।
अथात्र किमनुष्ठेयमस्माभिः सर्गयोजितैः ।
यस्याहं हृदयादासं स ईशो विदधातु मे ॥१७॥

sṛjato me kṣitir vārbhiḥ
plāvyamānā rasāṁ gatā
athātra kim anuṣṭheyam
asmābhiḥ sarga-yojitaiḥ
yasyāhaṁ hṛdayād āsaṁ
sa īśo vidadhātu me

sṛjataḥ—while engaged in creation; *me*—of me; *kṣitiḥ*—the earth; *vārbhiḥ*—by the water; *plāvyamānā*—being inundated; *rasām*—depth of water; *gatā*—gone down; *atha*—therefore; *atra*—in this matter; *kim*—what; *anuṣṭheyam*—is right to be attempted; *asmābhiḥ*—by us; *sarga*—creation; *yojitaiḥ*—engaged in; *yasya*—the one from whose; *aham*—I; *hṛdayāt*—from the heart; *āsam*—born; *saḥ*—He; *īśaḥ*—the Lord; *vidadhātu*—may direct; *me*—unto me.

TRANSLATION

Brahmā thought: While I have been engaged in the process of creation, the earth has been inundated by a deluge and has gone down into the depths of the ocean. What can we do who are engaged in this matter of creation? It is best to let the Almighty Lord direct us.

PURPORT

The devotees of the Lord, who are all confidential servitors, are sometimes perplexed in the discharge of their respective duties, but they are never discouraged. They have full faith in the Lord, and He paves the way for the smooth progress of the devotee's duty.

TEXT 18

इत्यभिध्यायतो नासाविवरात्सहसानघ ।
वराहतोको निरगादङ्गुष्ठपरिमाणकः ॥१८॥

ity abhidhyāyato nāsā-
vivarāt sahasānagha
varāha-toko niragād
aṅguṣṭha-parimāṇakaḥ

iti—thus; *abhidhyāyataḥ*—while thinking; *nāsā-vivarāt*—from the nostrils; *sahasā*—all of a sudden; *anagha*—O sinless one; *varāha-tokaḥ*—a minute form of Varāha (a boar); *niragāt*—came out; *aṅguṣṭha*—the upper portion of the thumb; *parimāṇakaḥ*—of the measurement.

TRANSLATION

O sinless Vidura, all of a sudden, while Brahmā was engaged in thinking, a small form of a boar came out of his nostril. The measurement of the creature was not more than the upper portion of a thumb.

TEXT 19

तस्याभिपश्यतः खस्थः क्षणेन किल भारत ।
गजमात्रः प्रववृधे तदद्भुतमभून्महत् ॥१९॥

tasyābhipaśyataḥ kha-sthaḥ
kṣaṇena kila bhārata
gaja-mātraḥ pravavṛdhe
tad adbhutam abhūn mahat

tasya—his; *abhipaśyataḥ*—while thus observing; *kha-sthaḥ*—situated in the sky; *kṣaṇena*—suddenly; *kila*—verily; *bhārata*—O descendant of Bharata; *gaja-mātraḥ*—just like an elephant; *pravavṛdhe*—thoroughly expanded; *tat*—that; *adbhutam*—extraordinary; *abhūt*—transformed; *mahat*—into a gigantic body.

TRANSLATION

O descendant of Bharata, while Brahmā was observing Him, that boar became situated in the sky in a wonderful manifestation as gigantic as a great elephant.

TEXT 20

मरीचिप्रमुखैर्विप्रैः कुमारैर्मनुना सह ।
दृष्ट्वा तत्सौकरं रूपं तर्कयामास चित्रधा ॥२०॥

marīci-pramukhair vipraiḥ
kumārair manunā saha

dṛṣṭvā tat saukaraṁ rūpaṁ
tarkayām āsa citradhā

marīci—the great sage Marīci; *pramukhaiḥ*—headed by; *vipraiḥ*—all *brāhmaṇas; kumāraiḥ*—with the four Kumāras; *manunā*—and with Manu; *saha*—with; *dṛṣṭvā*—seeing; *tat*—that; *saukaram*—appearance like a boar; *rūpam*—form; *tarkayām āsa*—argued among themselves; *citradhā*—in various ways.

TRANSLATION

Struck with wonder at observing the wonderful boarlike form in the sky, Brahmā, with great brāhmaṇas like Marīci, as well as the Kumāras and Manu, began to argue in various ways.

TEXT 21

किमेतत्सूकरव्याजं सत्त्वं दिव्यमवस्थितम् ।
अहो बताश्चर्यमिदं नासाया मे विनिःसृतम् ॥२१॥

kim etat sūkara-vyājaṁ
sattvaṁ divyam avasthitam
aho batāścaryam idaṁ
nāsāyā me viniḥsṛtam

kim—what; *etat*—this; *sūkara*—boar; *vyājam*—pretention; *sattvam*—entity; *divyam*—extraordinary; *avasthitam*—situated; *aho bata*—oh, it is; *āścaryam*—very wonderful; *idam*—this; *nāsāyāḥ*—from the nose; *me*—my; *viniḥsṛtam*—came out.

TRANSLATION

Is this some extraordinary entity come in the pretense of a boar? It is very wonderful that He has come from my nose.

TEXT 22

दृष्टोऽङ्गुष्ठशिरोमात्रः क्षणाद्गण्डशिलासमः ।
अपि स्विद्भगवानेष यज्ञो मे खेदयन्मनः ॥२२॥

dṛṣṭo 'ṅguṣṭha-śiro-mātraḥ
kṣaṇād gaṇḍa-śilā-samaḥ
api svid bhagavān eṣa
yajño me khedayan manaḥ

dṛṣṭaḥ—just seen; *aṅguṣṭha*—thumb; *śiraḥ*—tip; *mātraḥ*—only; *kṣaṇāt*—immediately; *gaṇḍa-śilā*—large stone; *samaḥ*—like; *api svit*—whether; *bhagavān*—the Personality of Godhead; *eṣaḥ*—this; *yajñaḥ*—Viṣṇu; *me*—my; *khedayan*—perturbing; *manaḥ*—mind.

TRANSLATION

First of all this boar was seen no bigger than the tip of a thumb, and within a moment He was as large as a stone. My mind is perturbed. Is He the Supreme Personality of Godhead, Viṣṇu?

PURPORT

Since Brahmā is the supermost person in the universe and he had never before experienced such a form, he could guess that the wonderful appearance of the boar was an incarnation of Viṣṇu. The uncommon features symptomatic of the incarnation of Godhead can bewilder even the mind of Brahmā.

TEXT 23

इति मीमांसतस्तस्य ब्रह्मणः सह सूनुभिः ।
भगवान् यज्ञपुरुषो जगर्जागेन्द्रसन्निभः ॥२३॥

iti mīmāṁsatas tasya
brahmaṇaḥ saha sūnubhiḥ
bhagavān yajña-puruṣo
jagarjāgendra-sannibhaḥ

iti—thus; *mīmāṁsataḥ*—while deliberating; *tasya*—his; *brahmaṇaḥ*—of Brahmā; *saha*—along with; *sūnubhiḥ*—his sons; *bhagavān*—the Personality of Godhead; *yajña*—Lord Viṣṇu; *puruṣaḥ*—the Supreme Person; *jagarja*—resounded; *aga-indra*—great mountain; *sannibhaḥ*—like.

TRANSLATION

While Brahmā was deliberating with his sons, the Supreme Personality of Godhead, Viṣṇu, roared tumultuously like a great mountain.

PURPORT

It appears that great hills and mountains also have their roaring power because they are also living entities. The volume of the sound vibrated is in proportion to the size of the material body. While Brahmā was guessing about the appearance of the Lord's incarnation as a boar, the Lord confirmed Brahmā's contemplation by roaring with His gorgeous voice.

TEXT 24

ब्रह्माणं हर्षयामास हरिस्तांश्च द्विजोत्तमान् ।
स्वगर्जितेन ककुभः प्रतिस्वनयता विभुः ॥२४॥

brahmāṇaṁ harṣayām āsa
haris tāṁś ca dvijottamān
sva-garjitena kakubhaḥ
pratisvanayatā vibhuḥ

brahmāṇam—unto Brahmā; *harṣayām āsa*—enlivened; *hariḥ*—the Personality of Godhead; *tān*—all of them; *ca*—also; *dvija-uttamān*—highly elevated *brāhmaṇas; sva-garjitena*—by His uncommon voice; *kakubhaḥ*—all directions; *pratisvanayatā*—which echoed; *vibhuḥ*—the omnipotent.

TRANSLATION

The omnipotent Supreme Personality of Godhead enlivened Brahmā and the other highly elevated brāhmaṇas by again roaring with His uncommon voice, which echoed in all directions.

PURPORT

Brahmā and other enlightened *brāhmaṇas* who know the Supreme Personality of Godhead are enlivened by the appearance of the Lord in any of His multi-incarnations. The appearance of the wonderful and gigantic incarnation of Viṣṇu as the mountainlike boar did not fill them with any kind of fear, although the Lord's resounding voice was tumultuous and echoed horribly in all directions as an open threat to all demons who might challenge His omnipotency.

TEXT 25

निशम्य ते घर्घरितं स्वखेद-
क्षयिष्णु मायामयसूकरस्य ।
जनस्तपःसत्यनिवासिनस्ते
त्रिभिः पवित्रैर्मुनयोऽगृणन् स्म ॥२५॥

niśamya te ghargharitaṁ sva-kheda-
kṣayiṣṇu māyāmaya-sūkarasya

janas-tapaḥ-satya-nivāsinas te
tribhiḥ pavitrair munayo 'gṛṇan sma

niśamya—just after hearing; *te*—those; *gharghharitam*—the tumultuous sound; *sva-kheda*—personal lamentation; *kṣayiṣṇu*—destroying; *māyā-maya*—all-merciful; *sūkarasya*—of Lord Boar; *janaḥ*—the Janaloka planet; *tapaḥ*—the Tapoloka planet; *satya*—the Satyaloka planet; *nivāsinaḥ*—residents; *te*—all of them; *tribhiḥ*—from the three *Vedas; pavitraiḥ*—by the all-auspicious *mantras; munayaḥ*—great thinkers and sages; *agṛṇan sma*—chanted.

TRANSLATION

When the great sages and thinkers who are residents of Janaloka, Tapoloka and Satyaloka heard the tumultuous voice of Lord Boar, which was the all-auspicious sound of the all-merciful Lord, they chanted auspicious chants from the three Vedas.

PURPRT

The word *māyāmaya* is very significant in this verse. *Māyā* means "mercy," "specific knowledge" and also "illusion." Therefore Lord Boar is everything; He is merciful, He is all knowledge, and He is illusion also. The sound which He vibrated as the boar incarnation was answered by the Vedic hymns of the great sages in the planets Janaloka, Tapoloka and Satyaloka. The highest intellectual and pious living entities live in those planets, and when they heard the extraordinary voice of the boar, they could understand that the specific sound was vibrated by the Lord and no one else. Therefore they replied by praying to the Lord with Vedic hymns. The earth planet was submerged in the mire, but on hearing the sound of the Lord, the inhabitants of the higher planets were all jubilant because they knew that the Lord was there to deliver the earth. Therefore Brahmā and all the sages, such as Bhṛgu, Brahmā's other sons, and learned *brāhmaṇas,* were enlivened, and they concertedly joined in praising the Lord with the transcendental vibrations of the Vedic hymns. The most important is the *Bṛhan-nāradīya Purāṇa* verse Hare Kṛṣṇa, Hare Kṛṣṇa, Kṛṣṇa Kṛṣṇa, Hare Hare/ Hare Rāma, Hare Rāma, Rāma Rāma, Hare Hare.

TEXT 26

तेषां सतां वेदवितानमूर्ति-
ब्रह्मावधार्यात्मगुणानुवादम् ।
विनद्य भूयो विबुधोदयाय
गजेन्द्रलीलो जलमाविवेश ॥२६॥

teṣāṁ satāṁ veda-vitāna-mūrtir
brahmāvadhāryātma-guṇānuvādam
vinadya bhūyo vibudhodayāya
gajendra-līlo jalam āviveśa

teṣām—of them; *satām*—of the great devotees; *veda*—all knowledge; *vitāna-mūrtiḥ*—the form of expansion; *brahma*—Vedic sound; *avadhārya*—knowing it well; *ātma*—of Himself; *guṇa-anuvādam*—transcendental glorification; *vinadya*—resounding; *bhūyaḥ*—again; *vibudha*—of the transcendentally learned; *udayāya*—for the elevation or benefit; *gajendra-līlaḥ*—playing like an elephant; *jalam*—the water; *āviveśa*—entered.

TRANSLATION

Playing like an elephant, He entered into the water after roaring again in reply to the Vedic prayers by the great devotees. The Lord is the object of the Vedic prayers, and thus He understood that the devotees' prayers were meant for Him.

PURPORT

The form of the Lord in any shape is always transcendental and full of knowledge and mercy. The Lord is the destroyer of all material contamination because His form is personified Vedic knowledge. All the *Vedas* worship the transcendental form of the Lord. In the Vedic *mantras* the devotees request the Lord to remove the glaring effulgence because it covers His real face. That is the version of the *Īśopaniṣad.* The Lord has no material form, but His form is always understood in terms of the *Vedas.* The *Vedas* are said to be the breath of the Lord, and that breath was inhaled by Brahmā, the original student of the *Vedas.* The breathing from the nostril of Brahmā caused the appearance of Lord Boar, and therefore the boar incarnation of the Lord is the personified *Vedas.* The glorification of the incarnation by the sages on the higher planets consisted of factual Vedic hymns. Whenever there is glorification of the Lord, it is to be understood that Vedic *mantras* are being rightly vibrated. The Lord was therefore pleased when such Vedic *mantras* were chanted, and to encourage His pure devotees, He roared once more and entered the water to rescue the submerged earth.

TEXT 27

उत्क्षिप्तवालः खचरः कठोरः
सटा विधुन्वन् खररोमशत्वक् ।

खुराहताभ्रः सितदंष्ट्र ईक्षा-
ज्योतिर्बभासे भगवान्महीध्रः ॥२७॥

utkṣipta-vālaḥ kha-caraḥ kaṭhoraḥ
saṭā vidhunvan khara-romaśa-tvak
khurāhatābhraḥ sita-daṁṣṭra īkṣā-
jyotir babhāse bhagavān mahīdhraḥ

utkṣipta-vālaḥ—slashing with the tail; *kha-caraḥ*—in the sky; *kaṭhoraḥ*—very hard; *saṭāḥ*—hairs on the shoulder; *vidhunvan*—quivering; *khara*—sharp; *romaśa-tvak*—skin full of hairs; *khura-āhata*—struck by the hooves; *abhraḥ*—the clouds; *sita-daṁṣṭraḥ*—white tusks; *īkṣā*—glance; *jyotiḥ*—luminous; *babhāse*—began to emit an effulgence; *bhagavān*—the Personality of Godhead; *mahī-dhraḥ*—the supporter of the world.

TRANSLATION

Before entering the water to rescue the earth, Lord Boar flew in the sky, slashing His tail, His hard hairs quivering. His very glance was luminous, and He scattered the clouds in the sky with His hooves and His glittering white tusks.

PURPORT

When the Lord is offered prayers by His devotees, His transcendental activities are described. Here are some of the transcendental features of Lord Boar. As the residents of the upper three planetary systems offered their prayers to the Lord, it is understood that His body expanded throughout the sky, beginning from the topmost planet, Brahmaloka, or Satyaloka. It is stated in the *Brahma-saṁhitā* that His eyes are the sun and the moon; therefore His very glance over the sky was as illuminating as the sun or the moon. The Lord is described herein as *mahīdhraḥ*, which means either a "big mountain" or the "sustainer of the earth." In other words, the Lord's body was as big and hard as the Himalayan Mountains; otherwise how was it possible that He kept the entire earth on the support of His white tusks? The poet Jayadeva, a great devotee of the Lord, has sung of the incident in his prayers for the incarnations:

vasati daśana-śikhare dharaṇī tava lagnā
śaśini kalaṅka-kaleva nimagnā
keśava dhṛta-śūkara-rūpa jaya jagadīśa hare

"All glories to Lord Keśava [Kṛṣṇa], who appeared as the boar. The earth was held between His tusks, which appeared like the scars on the moon."

TEXT 28

घ्राणेन पृथ्व्याः पदवीं विजिघ्रन्
क्रोडापदेशः स्वयमध्वराङ्गः ।
करालदंष्ट्रोऽप्यकरालदृग्भ्या-
मुद्वीक्ष्य विप्रान् गृणतोऽविशत्कम् ॥२८॥

ghrāṇena pṛthvyāḥ padavīṁ vijighran
kroḍāpadeśaḥ svayam adhvarāṅgaḥ
karāla-daṁṣṭro 'py akarāla-dṛgbhyām
udvīkṣya viprān gṛṇato 'viśat kam

ghrāṇena—by smelling; *pṛthvyāḥ*—of the earth; *padavīm*—situation; *vijighran*—searching after the earth; *kroḍa-apadeśaḥ*—assuming the body of a hog; *svayam*—personally; *adhvara*—transcendental; *aṅgaḥ*—body; *karāla*—fearful; *daṁṣṭraḥ*—teeth (tusks); *api*—in spite of; *akarāla*—not fearful; *dṛgbhyām*—by His glance; *udvīkṣya*—glancing over; *viprān*—all the *brāhmaṇa*—devotees; *gṛṇataḥ*—who were engaged in prayers; *aviśat*—entered; *kam*—the water.

TRANSLATION

He was personally the Supreme Lord Viṣṇu and was therefore transcendental, yet because He had the body of a hog, He searched after the earth by smell. His tusks were fearful, and He glanced over the devotee-brāhmaṇas engaged in offering prayers. Thus He entered the water.

PURPORT

We should always remember that although the body of a hog is material, the hog form of the Lord was not materially contaminated. It is not possible for an earthly hog to assume a gigantic form spreading throughout the sky, beginning from the Satyaloka. His body is always transcendental in all circumstances; therefore, the assumption of the form of a boar is only His pastime. His body is all *Vedas*, or transcendental. But since He had assumed the form of a boar, He began to search out the earth by smelling, just like a hog. The Lord can perfectly play the part of any living entity. The gigantic feature of the boar was certainly very fearful for all nondevotees, but to the pure devotees of the Lord He was not at all fearful; on the contrary, He was so pleasingly glancing upon His devotees that all of them felt transcendental happiness.

TEXT 29

स वज्रकूटाङ्गनिपातवेग-
विशीर्णकुक्षिः स्तनयन्नुदन्वान् ।
उत्सृष्टदीर्घोर्मिभुजैरिवार्त-
श्चुक्रोश यज्ञेश्वर पाहि मेति ॥२९॥

sa vajra-kūṭāṅga-nipāta-vega-
viśīrṇa-kukṣiḥ stanayann udanvān
utsṛṣṭa-dīrghormi-bhujair ivārtaś
cukrośa yajñeśvara pāhi meti

saḥ—that; *vajra-kūṭa-aṅga*—body like a great mountain; *nipāta-vega*—the force of diving; *viśīrṇa*—bifurcating; *kukṣiḥ*—the middle portion; *stanayan*—resounding like; *udanvān*—the ocean; *utsṛṣṭa*—creating; *dīrgha*—high; *ūrmi*—waves; *bhujaiḥ*—by the arms; *iva ārtaḥ*—like a distressed person; *cukrośa*—prayed loudly; *yajña-īśvara*—O master of all sacrifices; *pāhi*—please protect; *mā*—unto me; *iti*—thus.

TRANSLATION

Diving into the water like a giant mountain, Lord Boar divided the middle of the ocean, and two high waves appeared as the arms of the ocean, which cried loudly as if praying to the Lord, "O Lord of all sacrifices, please do not cut me in two! Kindly give me protection!"

PURPORT

Even the great ocean was perturbed by the falling of the mountainlike body of the transcendental boar, and it appeared to be frightened, as if death were imminent.

TEXT 30

खुरैः क्षुरप्रैर्दरयंस्तदाप
उत्पारपारं त्रिपरू रसायाम् ।
ददर्श गां तत्र सुषुप्सुरग्रे
यां जीवधानीं स्वयमभ्यधत्त ॥३०॥

khuraiḥ kṣuraprair darayaṁs tad āpa
utpāra-pāraṁ tri-parū rasāyām
dadarśa gāṁ tatra suṣupsur agre
yāṁ jīva-dhānīṁ svayam abhyadhatta

khuraiḥ—by the hooves; *kṣurapraiḥ*—compared to a sharp weapon; *darayan*—penetrating; *tat*—that; *āpaḥ*—water; *utpāra-pāram*—found the limitation of the unlimited; *tri-paruḥ*—the master of all sacrifices; *rasāyām*—within the water; *dadarśa*—found; *gām*—the earth; *tatra*—there; *suṣupsuḥ*—lying; *agre*—in the beginning; *yām*—whom; *jīva-dhānīm*—the resting place for all living entities; *svayam*—personally; *abhyadhatta*—uplifted.

TRANSLATION

Lord Boar penetrated the water with His hooves, which were like sharp arrows, and found the limits of the ocean, although it was unlimited. He saw the earth, the resting place for all living beings, lying as it was in the beginning of creation, and He personally lifted it.

PURPORT

The word *rasāyām* is sometimes interpreted to mean Rasātala, the lowest planetary system, but that is not applicable in this connection, according to Viśvanātha Cakravartī Ṭhākura. The earth is seven times superior to the other planetary systems, namely Tala, Atala, Talātala, Vitala, Rasātala, Pātāla, etc. Therefore the earth cannot be situated in the Rasātala planetary system. It is described in the *Viṣṇu-dharma*:

pātāla-mūleśvara-bhoga-saṁhatau
vinyasya pādau pṛthivīṁ ca bibhrataḥ
yasyopamāno na babhūva so 'cyuto
mamāstu māṅgalya-vivṛddhaye hariḥ

Therefore the Lord found the earth on the bottom of the Garbhodaka Ocean, where the planets rest during the devastation at the end of Brahmā's day.

TEXT 31

स्वदंष्ट्रयोद्धृत्य महीं निमग्नां
स उत्थितः संरुरुचे रसायाः ।
तत्रापि दैत्यं गदयापतन्तं
सुनाभसन्दीपिततीव्रमन्युः ॥३१॥

sva-daṁṣṭrayoddhṛtya mahīṁ nimagnāṁ
sa utthitaḥ saṁruruce rasāyāḥ
tatrāpi daityaṁ gadayāpatantaṁ
sunābha-sandīpita-tīvra-manyuḥ

sva-daṁṣṭrayā—by His own tusks; *uddhṛtya*—raising; *mahīm*—the earth; *nimagnām*—submerged; *saḥ*—He; *utthitaḥ*—getting up; *saṁruruce*—appeared very splendid; *rasāyāḥ*—from the water; *tatra*—there; *api*—also; *daityam*—unto the demon; *gadayā*—with the club; *āpatantam*—rushing towards Him; *sunābha*—the wheel of Kṛṣṇa; *sandīpita*—glowing; *tīvra*—fierce; *manyuḥ*—anger.

TRANSLATION

Lord Boar very easily took the earth on His tusks and got it out of the water. Thus He appeared very splendid. Then, His anger glowing like the Sudarśana wheel, He immediately killed the demon [Hiraṇyākṣa], although he tried to fight with the Lord.

PURPORT

According to Śrīla Jīva Gosvāmī, the Vedic literatures describe the incarnation of Lord Varāha (Boar) in two different devastations, namely the Cākṣuṣa devastation and the Svāyambhuva devastation. This particular appearance of the boar incarnation actually took place in the Svāyambhuva devastation, when all planets other than the higher ones—Jana, Mahar and Satya—merged in the water of devastation. This particular incarnation of the boar was seen by the inhabitants of the planets mentioned above. Śrīla Viśvanātha Cakravartī suggests that the sage Maitreya amalgamated both the boar incarnations in different devastations and summarized them in his description to Vidura.

TEXT 32

जघान रुन्धानमसह्यविक्रमं
स लीलयेभं मृगराडिवाम्भसि ।
तद्रक्तपङ्काङ्कितगण्डतुण्डो
यथा गजेन्द्रो जगतीं विभिन्दन् ॥३२॥

jaghāna rundhānam asahya-vikramaṁ
sa līlayebhaṁ mṛgarāḍ ivāmbhasi
tad-rakta-paṅkāṅkita-gaṇḍa-tuṇḍo
yathā gajendro jagatīṁ vibhindan

jaghāna—killed; *rundhānam*—the obstructive enemy; *asahya*—unbearable; *vikramam*—prowess; *saḥ*—He; *līlayā*—easily; *ibham*—the elephant; *mṛga-rāṭ*—the lion; *iva*—like; *ambhasi*—in the water; *tat-rakta*—of his blood; *paṅka-aṅkita*—smeared by the pool; *gaṇḍa*—

cheeks; *tuṇḍaḥ*—tongue; *yathā*—as if; *gajendraḥ*—the elephant; *jagatīm*—earth; *vibhindan*—digging.

TRANSLATION

Thereupon Lord Boar killed the demon within the water, just as a lion kills an elephant. The cheeks and tongue of the Lord became smeared with the blood of the demon, just as an elephant becomes reddish from digging in the purple earth.

TEXT 33

तमालनीलं सितदन्तकोट्या
क्ष्मामुत्क्षिपन्तं गजलीलयाङ्ग ।
प्रज्ञाय बद्धाञ्जलयोऽनुवाकै-
र्विरिञ्चिमुख्या उपतस्थुरीशम् ॥३३॥

tamāla-nīlaṁ sita-danta-koṭyā
kṣmām utkṣipantaṁ gaja-līlayāṅga
prajñāya baddhāñjalayo 'nuvākair
viriñci-mukhyā upatasthur īśam

tamāla—a blue tree named the *tamāla; nīlam*—bluish; *sita*—white; *danta*—tusks; *koṭyā*—with the curved edge; *kṣmām*—the earth; *utkṣipantam*—while suspending; *gaja-līlayā*—playing like an elephant; *aṅga*—O Vidura; *prajñāya*—after knowing it well; *baddha*—folded; *añjalayaḥ*—hands; *anuvākaiḥ*—by Vedic hymns; *viriñci*—Brahmā; *mukhyāḥ*—headed by; *upatasthuḥ*—offered prayers; *īśam*—unto the Supreme Lord.

TRANSLATION

Then the Lord, playing like an elephant, suspended the earth on the edge of His curved white tusks. He assumed a bluish complexion like that of a tamāla tree, and thus the sages, headed by Brahmā, could understand Him to be the Supreme Personality of Godhead and offered respectful obeisances unto the Lord.

TEXT 34

ऋषय ऊचुः
जितं जितं तेऽजित यज्ञभावन
त्रयीं तनुं स्वां परिधुन्वते नमः ।

यद्रोमगर्तेषु निलिल्युरद्धय-
स्तस्मै नमः कारणसूकराय ते ॥३४॥

ṛṣaya ūcuḥ
jitaṁ jitaṁ te 'jita yajña-bhāvana
trayīṁ tanuṁ svāṁ paridhunvate namaḥ
yad-roma-garteṣu nililyur addhayas
tasmai namaḥ kāraṇa-sūkarāya te

ṛṣayaḥ ūcuḥ—the glorified sages uttered; *jitam*—all glories; *jitam*—all victories; *te*—unto You; *ajita*—O unconquerable one; *yajña-bhāvana*—one who is understood by performances of sacrifice; *trayīm*—personified *Vedas; tanum*—such a body; *svām*—own; *paridhunvate*—shaking; *namaḥ*—all obeisances; *yat*—whose; *roma*—hairs; *garteṣu*—in the holes; *nililyuḥ*—submerged; *addhayaḥ*—the oceans; *tasmai*—unto Him; *namaḥ*—offering obeisances; *kāraṇa-sūkarāya*—unto the hog form assumed for reasons; *te*—unto You.

TRANSLATION

All the sages uttered with great respect: O unconquerable enjoyer of all sacrifices, all glories and all victories unto You! You are moving in Your form of the personified Vedas, and in the hair holes of Your body the oceans are submerged. For certain reasons [to uplift the earth] You have now assumed the form of a boar.

PURPORT

The Lord can assume any form He likes, and in all circumstances He is the cause of all causes. Since His form is transcendental, He is always the Supreme Personality of Godhead, as He is in the Causal Ocean in the form of Mahā-Viṣṇu. Innumerable universes generate from the holes of His bodily hairs, and thus His transcendental body is the *Vedas* personified. He is the enjoyer of all sacrifices, and He is the unconquerable Supreme Personality of Godhead. He is never to be misunderstood to be other than the Supreme Lord because of His assuming the form of a boar to lift the earth. That is the clear understanding of sages and great personalities like Brahmā and other residents of the higher planetary systems.

TEXT 35

रूपं तवैतन्ननु दुष्कृतात्मनां
दुर्दर्शनं देव यदध्वरात्मकम् ।

छन्दांसि यस्य त्वचि बर्हिरोम-
स्वाज्यं दृशि त्वङ्घ्रिषु चातुर्होत्रम् ॥३५॥

rūpaṁ tavaitan nanu duṣkṛtātmanāṁ
durdarśanaṁ deva yad adhvarātmakam
chandāṁsi yasya tvaci barhi-romasv
ājyaṁ dṛśi tv aṅghriṣu cātur-hotram

rūpam—form; *tava*—Your; *etat*—this; *nanu*—but; *duṣkṛta-ātmanām*—of souls who are simply miscreants; *durdarśanam*—very difficult to see; *deva*—O Lord; *yat*—that; *adhvara-ātmakam*—worshipable by performances of sacrifice; *chandāṁsi*—the Gāyatrī *mantra* and others; *yasya*—whose; *tvaci*—touch of the skin; *barhiḥ*—sacred grass called *kuśa; romasu*—hairs on the body; *ājyam*—clarified butter; *dṛśi*—in the eyes; *tu*—also; *aṅghriṣu*—on the four legs; *cātuḥ-hotram*—four kinds of fruitive activities.

TRANSLATION

O Lord, Your form is worshipable by performances of sacrifice, but souls who are simply miscreants are unable to see it. All the Vedic hymns, Gāyatrī and others, are in the touch of Your skin. In Your bodily hairs is the kuśa grass, in Your eyes is the clarified butter, and in Your four legs are the four kinds of fruitive activities.

PURPORT

There is a class of miscreants who are known in the words of *Bhagavad-gītā* as *veda-vādī,* or so-called strict followers of the *Vedas.* They do not believe in the incarnation of the Lord, what to speak of the Lord's incarnation as the worshipable hog. They describe worship of the different forms or incarnations of the Lord as anthropomorphism. In the estimation of *Śrīmad-Bhāgavatam* these men are miscreants, and in *Bhagavad-gītā* (7.15) they are called not only miscreants but also fools and the lowest of mankind, and it is said that their knowledge has been plundered by illusion due to their atheistic temperament. For such condemned persons, the Lord's incarnation as the gigantic hog is invisible. These strict followers of the *Vedas* who despise the eternal forms of the Lord may know from *Śrīmad-Bhāgavatam* that such incarnations are personified forms of the *Vedas.* Lord Boar's skin, His eyes and His bodily hair holes are all described here as different parts of the *Vedas.* He is therefore the personified form of the Vedic hymns, and specifically the Gāyatrī *mantra.*

TEXT 36

स्रक्तुण्ड आसीत्स्रुव ईश नासयो-
रिडोदरे चमसाः कर्णरन्ध्रे ।
प्राशित्रमास्ये ग्रसने ग्रहास्तु ते
यच्चर्वणं ते भगवन्नग्निहोत्रम् ॥३६॥

srak tuṇḍa āsīt sruva īśa nāsayor
iḍodare camasāḥ karṇa-randhre
prāśitram āsye grasane grahās tu te
yac carvaṇaṁ te bhagavann agni-hotram

srak—the plate for sacrifice; *tuṇḍe*—on the tongue; *āsīt*—there is; *sruvaḥ*—another plate for sacrifice; *īśa*—O Lord; *nāsayoḥ*—of the nostrils; *iḍā*—the plate for eating; *udare*—in the belly; *camasāḥ*—another plate for sacrifices; *karṇa-randhre*—in the holes of the ears; *prāśitram*—the plate called the Brahmā plate; *āsye*—in the mouth; *grasane*—in the throat; *grahāḥ*—the plates known as *soma* plates; *tu*—but; *te*—Your; *yat*—that which; *carvaṇam*—chewing; *te*—Your; *bhagavan*—O my Lord; *agni-hotram*—is Your eating through Your sacrificial fire.

TRANSLATION

O Lord, Your tongue is a plate of sacrifice, Your nostril is another plate of sacrifice, in Your belly is the eating plate of sacrifice, and another plate of sacrifice is the holes of Your ears. In Your mouth is the Brahmā plate of sacrifice, Your throat is the plate of sacrifice known as soma, and whatever You chew is known as agni-hotra.

PURPORT

The *veda-vādīs* say that there is nothing more than the *Vedas* and the performances of sacrifice mentioned in the *Vedas.* They have recently made a rule in their group to formally observe daily sacrifice; they simply ignite a small fire and offer something whimsically, but they do not strictly follow the sacrificial rules and regulations mentioned in the *Vedas.* It is understood that by regulation there are different plates of sacrifice required, such as *srak, sruvā, barhis, cātur-hotra, iḍā, camasa, prāśitra, graha* and *agni-hotra.* One cannot achieve the results of sacrifice unless one observes the strict regulations. In this age there is practically no facility for performing sacrifices in strict discipline. Therefore, in this age of Kali there is a stricture regarding such sacrifices: it is explicitly directed that one should perform *saṅkīrtana-yajña* and nothing more. The incarnation of the Supreme Lord is Yajñeśvara, and unless one has respect for the incarnation of the Lord, he cannot perfectly perform sacrifice. In other words, taking shelter of the Lord and rendering service unto Him is the factual performance of all sacrifices, as explained herein. Different plates of sacrifice correspond to the different parts of the body of the Lord's incarnation. In the *Śrīmad-Bhāgavatam*, Eleventh Canto, it is explicitly directed that one should perform *saṅkīrtana-yajña* to please the Lord's incarnation as Śrī Caitanya Mahāprabhu. This should be rigidly followed in order to achieve the result of *yajña* performance.

TEXT 37

दीक्षानुजन्मोपसदः शिरोधरं
त्वं प्रायणीयोदयनीयदंष्ट्रः ।
जिह्वा प्रवर्ग्यस्तव शीर्षकं क्रतोः
सत्यावसथ्यं चितयोऽसवो हि ते ॥३७॥

dīkṣānujanmopasadaḥ śirodharaṁ
tvaṁ prāyaṇīyodayanīya-daṁṣṭraḥ
jihvā pravargyas tava śīrṣakaṁ kratoḥ
satyāvasathyaṁ citayo 'savo hi te

dīkṣā—initiation; *anujanma*—spiritual birth, or repeated incarnations; *upasadaḥ*—three kinds of desires (relationship, activities and ultimate goal); *śiraḥ-dharam*—the neck; *tvam*—You; *prāyaṇīya*—after the result of initiation; *udayanīya*—the last rites of desires; *daṁṣṭraḥ*—the tusks; *jihvā*—the tongue; *pravargyaḥ*—prior activities; *tava*—Your; *śīrṣakam*—head; *kratoḥ*—of the sacrifice; *satya*—fire without sacrifice; *āvasathyam*—fire of worship; *citayaḥ*—aggregate of all desires; *asavaḥ*—life breath; *hi*—certainly; *te*—Your.

TRANSLATION

Moreover, O Lord, the repetition of Your appearance is the desire for all kinds of initiation. Your neck is the place for three desires, and Your tusks are the result of initiation and the end of all desires. Your tongue is the prior activities of initiation, Your head is the fire without sacrifice as well as the fire of worship, and Your living forces are the aggregate of all desires.

TEXT 38

सोमस्तु रेतः सवनान्यवस्थितिः
संस्थाविभेदास्तव देव धातवः ।

सत्राणि सर्वाणि शरीरसन्धि-
स्त्वं सर्वयज्ञक्रतुरिष्टिबन्धनः ॥३८॥

somas tu retaḥ savanāny avasthitiḥ
saṁsthā-vibhedās tava deva dhātavaḥ
satrāṇi sarvāṇi śarīra-sandhis
tvaṁ sarva-yajña-kratur iṣṭi-bandhanaḥ

somaḥ tu retaḥ—Your semen is the sacrifice called *soma; savanāni*—ritualistic performances of the morning; *avasthitiḥ*—different statuses of bodily growth; *saṁsthā-vibhedāḥ*—seven varieties of sacrifices; *tava*—Your; *deva*—O Lord; *dhātavaḥ*—ingredients of the body such as skin and flesh; *satrāṇi*—sacrifices performed over twelve days; *sarvāṇi*—all of them; *śarīra*—the bodily; *sandhiḥ*—joints; *tvam*—Your Lordship; *sarva*—all; *yajña—asoma* sacrifices; *kratuḥ—soma* sacrifices; *iṣṭi*—the ultimate desire; *bandhanaḥ*—attachment.

TRANSLATION

O Lord, Your semen is the sacrifice called soma-yajña. Your growth is the ritualistic performances of the morning. Your skin and touch sensations are the seven elements of the agniṣṭoma sacrifice. Your bodily joints are symbols of various other sacrifices performed in twelve days. Therefore You are the object of all sacrifices called soma and asoma, and You are bound by yajñas only.

PURPORT

There are seven kinds of routine *yajñas* performed by all followers of the Vedic rituals, and they are called *agniṣṭoma, atyagniṣṭoma, uktha, ṣoḍaśī, vājapeya, atirātra* and *āptoryāma*. Anyone performing such *yajñas* regularly is supposed to be situated with the Lord. But anyone who is in contact with the Supreme Lord by discharging devotional service is understood to have performed all different varieties of *yajñas*.

TEXT 39

नमो नमस्तेऽखिलमन्त्रदेवता-
द्रव्याय सर्वक्रतवे क्रियात्मने ।
वैराग्यभक्त्यात्मजयानुभावित-
ज्ञानाय विद्यागुरवे नमो नमः ॥३९॥

namo namas te 'khila-mantra-devatā-
dravyāya sarva-kratave kriyātmane

vairāgya-bhaktyātmajayānubhāvita-
jñānāya vidyā-gurave namo namaḥ

namaḥ namaḥ—obeisances unto You; *te*—unto You, who are worshipable; *akhila*—all-inclusive; *mantra*—hymns; *devatā*—the Supreme Lord; *dravyāya*—unto all ingredients for performing sacrifices; *sarva-kratave*—unto all kinds of sacrifices; *kriyā-ātmane*—unto You, the supreme form of all sacrifices; *vairāgya*—renunciation; *bhaktyā*—by devotional service; *ātma-jaya-anubhāvita*—perceivable by conquering the mind; *jñānāya*—such knowledge; *vidyā-gurave*—the supreme spiritual master of all knowledge; *namaḥ namaḥ*—again I offer my respectful obeisances.

TRANSLATION

O Lord, You are the Supreme Personality of Godhead and are worshipable by universal prayers, Vedic hymns and sacrificial ingredients. We offer our obeisances unto You. You can be realized by the pure mind freed from all visible and invisible material contamination. We offer our respectful obeisances to You as the supreme spiritual master of knowledge in devotional service.

PURPORT

The qualification of *bhakti,* or devotional service to the Lord, is that the devotee should be free from all material contaminations and desires. This freedom is called *vairāgya,* or renouncement of material desires. One who engages in devotional service to the Lord according to regulative principles is automatically freed from material desires, and in that pure state of mind one can realize the Personality of Godhead. The Personality of Godhead, being situated in everyone's heart, instructs the devotee regarding pure devotional service so that he may ultimately achieve the association of the Lord. This is confirmed in *Bhagavad-gītā* (10.10) as follows:

teṣāṁ satata-yuktānāṁ
bhajatāṁ prīti-pūrvakam
dadāmi buddhi-yogaṁ taṁ
yena mām upayānti te

"To one who constantly engages in the devotional service of the Lord with faith and love, the Lord certainly gives the intelligence to achieve Him at the ultimate end."

One has to conquer the mind, and one may do it by following the Vedic rituals and by performing different types of sacrifice. The ultimate end of all those performances is to attain *bhakti*, or the devotional service of the Lord. Without *bhakti* one cannot understand the Supreme Personality of Godhead. The original Personality of Godhead or His innumerable expansions of Viṣṇu are the only objects of worship by all the Vedic rituals and sacrificial performances.

TEXT 40

दंष्ट्राग्रकोट्या भगवंस्त्वया धृता
विराजते भूधर भूः सभूधरा ।
यथा वनान्निःसरतो दता धृता
मतङ्गजेन्द्रस्य सपत्रपद्मिनी ॥४०॥

daṁṣṭrāgra-koṭyā bhagavaṁs tvayā dhṛtā
virājate bhūdhara bhūḥ sa-bhūdharā
yathā vanān niḥsarato datā dhṛtā
mataṅ-gajendrasya sa-patra-padminī

daṁṣṭra-agra—the tips of the tusks; *koṭyā*—by the edges; *bhagavan*—O Personality of Godhead; *tvayā*—by You; *dhṛtā*—sustained; *virājate*—is so beautifully situated; *bhū-dhara*—O lifter of the earth; *bhūḥ*—the earth; *sa-bhūdharā*—with mountains; *yathā*—as much as; *vanāt*—from the water; *niḥsarataḥ*—coming out; *datā*—by the tusk; *dhṛtā*—captured; *matam-gajendrasya*—infuriated elephant; *sa-patra*—with leaves; *padminī*—the lotus flower.

TRANSLATION

O lifter of the earth, the earth with its mountains, which You have lifted with Your tusks, is situated as beautifully as a lotus flower with leaves sustained by an infuriated elephant just coming out of the water.

PURPORT

The fortune of the earth planet is praised because of its being specifically sustained by the Lord; its beauty is appreciated and compared to that of a lotus flower situated on the trunk of an elephant. As a lotus flower with leaves is very beautifully situated, so the world, with its many beautiful mountains, appeared on the tusks of the Lord Boar.

TEXT 41

त्रयीमयं रूपमिदं च सौकरं
भूमण्डलेनाथ दता धृतेन ते ।

चकास्ति शृङ्गोढघनेन भूयसा
कुलाचलेन्द्रस्य यथैव विभ्रमः ॥४१॥

trayīmayaṁ rūpam idaṁ ca saukaraṁ
bhū-maṇḍalenātha datā dhṛtena te
cakāsti śṛṅgoḍha-ghanena bhūyasā
kulācalendrasya yathaiva vibhramaḥ

trayī-mayam—*Vedas* personified; *rūpam*—form; *idam*—this; *ca*—also; *saukaram*—the boar; *bhū-maṇḍalena*—by the earth planet; *atha*—now; *datā*—by the tusk; *dhṛtena*—sustained by; *te*—Your; *cakāsti*—is glowing; *śṛṅga-ūḍha*—sustained by the peaks; *ghanena*—by the clouds; *bhūyasā*—more glorified; *kula-acala-indrasya*—of the great mountains; *yathā*—as much as; *eva*—certainly; *vibhramaḥ*—decoration.

TRANSLATION

O Lord, as the peaks of great mountains become beautiful when decorated with clouds, Your transcendental body has become beautiful because of Your lifting the earth on the edge of Your tusks.

PURPORT

The word *vibhramaḥ* is significant. *Vibhramaḥ* means "illusion" as well as "beauty." When a cloud rests on the peak of a great mountain, it appears to be sustained by the mountain, and at the same time it looks very beautiful. Similarly, the Lord has no need to sustain the earth on His tusks, but when He does so the world becomes beautiful, just as the Lord becomes more beautiful because of His pure devotees on the earth. Although the Lord is the transcendental personification of the Vedic hymns, He has become more beautiful because of His appearance to sustain the earth.

TEXT 42

संस्थापयैनां जगतां सतस्थुषां
लोकाय पत्नीमसि मातरं पिता ।
विधेम चास्यै नमसा सह त्वया
यस्यां स्वतेजोऽग्निमिवारणावधाः ॥४२॥

saṁsthāpayaināṁ jagatāṁ sa-tasthuṣāṁ
lokāya patnīm asi mātaraṁ pitā
vidhema cāsyai namasā saha tvayā
yasyāṁ sva-tejo 'gnim ivāraṇāv adhāḥ

saṁsthāpaya enām—raise this earth; *jagatām*—both the moving and; *sa-tasthuṣām*—nonmoving; *lokāya*—for their residence; *patnīm*—wife; *asi*—You are; *mātaram*—the mother; *pitā*—the father; *vidhema*—do we offer; *ca*—also; *asyai*—unto the mother; *namasā*—with all obeisances; *saha*—along with; *tvayā*—with You; *yasyām*—in whom; *sva-tejaḥ*—by Your own potency; *agnim*—fire; *iva*—likened; *araṇau*—in the *araṇi* wood; *adhāḥ*—invested.

TRANSLATION

O Lord, for the residential purposes of all inhabitants, both moving and nonmoving, this earth is Your wife, and You are the supreme father. We offer our respectful obeisances unto You, along with mother earth, in whom You have invested Your own potency, just as an expert sacrificer puts fire in the araṇi wood.

PURPORT

The so-called law of gravitation which sustains the planets is described herein as the potency of the Lord. This potency is invested by the Lord in the way that an expert sacrificial *brāhmaṇa* puts fire in the *araṇi* wood by the potency of Vedic *mantras.* By this arrangement the world becomes habitable for both the moving and nonmoving creatures. The conditioned souls, who are residents of the material world, are put in the womb of mother earth in the same way the seed of a child is put by the father in the womb of the mother. This conception of the Lord and the earth as father and mother is explained in *Bhagavad-gītā* (14.4). Conditioned souls are devoted to the motherland in which they take their birth, but they do not know their father. The mother is not independent in producing children. Similarly, material nature cannot produce living creatures unless in contact with the supreme father, the Supreme Personality of Godhead. *Śrīmad-Bhāgavatam* teaches us to offer obeisances unto the mother along with the Father, the Supreme Lord, because it is the Father only who impregnates the mother with all energies for the sustenance and maintenance of all living beings, both moving and nonmoving.

TEXT 43

कः श्रद्दधीतान्यतमस्तव प्रभो
रसां गताया भुव उद्विबर्हणम् ।
न विस्मयोऽसौ त्वयि विश्वविस्मये
यो माययेदं ससृजेऽतिविस्मयम् ॥४३॥

kaḥ śraddadhītānyatamas tava prabho
rasāṁ gatāyā bhuva udvibarhaṇam
na vismayo 'sau tvayi viśva-vismaye
yo māyayedaṁ sasṛje 'tivismayam

kaḥ—who else; *śraddadhīta*—can endeavor; *anyatamaḥ*—anyone besides Yourself; *tava*—Your; *prabho*—O Lord; *rasām*—in the water; *gatāyāḥ*—while lying in; *bhuvaḥ*—of the earth; *udvibarhaṇam*—deliverance; *na*—never; *vismayaḥ*—wonderful; *asau*—such an act; *tvayi*—unto You; *viśva*—universal; *vismaye*—full of wonders; *yaḥ*—one who; *māyayā*—by potencies; *idam*—this; *sasṛje*—created; *ativismayam*—surpassing all wonders.

TRANSLATION

Who else but You, the Supreme Personality of Godhead, could deliver the earth from within the water? It is not very wonderful for You, however, because You acted most wonderfully in the creation of the universe. By Your energy You have created this wonderful cosmic manifestation.

PURPORT

When a scientist discovers something impressive to the ignorant mass of people, the common man, without inquiry, accepts such a discovery as wonderful. But the intelligent man is not struck with wonder by such discoveries. He gives all credit to the person who created the wonderful brain of the scientist. A common man is also struck with wonder by the wonderful action of material nature, and he gives all credit to the cosmic manifestation. The learned Kṛṣṇa conscious person, however, knows well that behind the cosmic manifestation is the brain of Kṛṣṇa, as confirmed in *Bhagavad-gītā* (9.10): *mayādhyakṣeṇa prakṛtiḥ sūyate sa-carācaram.* Since Kṛṣṇa can direct the wonderful cosmic manifestation, it is not at all wonderful for Him to assume the gigantic form of a boar and thus deliver the earth from the mire of the water. A devotee is therefore not astonished to see the wonderful boar because he knows that the Lord is able to act far more wonderfully by His potencies, which are inconceivable to the brain of even the most erudite scientist.

TEXT 44

विधुन्वता वेदमयं निजं वपु-
र्जनस्तपःसत्यनिवासिनो वयम् ।
सटाशिखोद्धूतशिवाम्बुबिन्दुभि-
र्विमृज्यमाना भृशमीश पाविताः ॥४४॥

vidhunvatā vedamayaṁ nijaṁ vapur
janas-tapaḥ-satya-nivāsino vayam
saṭā-śikhoddhūta-śivāmbu-bindubhir
vimṛjyamānā bhṛśam īśa pāvitāḥ

vidhunvatā—while shaking; *veda-mayam*—personified *Vedas;* *nijam*—own; *vapuḥ*—body; *janaḥ*—the Janaloka planetary system; *tapaḥ*—the Tapoloka planetary system; *satya*—the Satyaloka planetary system; *nivāsinaḥ*—the inhabitants; *vayam*—we; *saṭā*—hairs on the shoulder; *śikha-uddhūta*—sustained by the tip of the hair; *śiva*—auspicious; *ambu*—water; *bindubhiḥ*—by the particles; *vimṛjyamānāḥ*—we are thus sprinkled by; *bhṛśam*—highly; *īśa*—O Supreme Lord; *pāvitāḥ*—purified.

TRANSLATION

O Supreme Lord, undoubtedly we are inhabitants of the most pious planets—the Jana, Tapas and Satya lokas—but still we have been purified by the drops of water sprinkled from Your shoulder hairs by the shaking of Your body.

PURPORT

Ordinarily the body of a hog is considered impure, but one should not consider that the hog incarnation assumed by the Lord is also impure. That form of the Lord is the personified *Vedas* and is transcendental. The inhabitants of the Jana, Tapas and Satya *lokas* are the most pious persons in the material world, but because those planets are situated in the material world, there are so many material impurities there also. Therefore, when the drops of water from the tips of the Lord's shoulder hairs were sprinkled upon the bodies of the inhabitants of the higher planets, they felt purified. The Ganges water is pure because of its emanating from the toe of the Lord, and there is no difference between the water emanating from the toe and that from the tips of the hair on the shoulder of Lord Boar. They are both absolute and transcendental.

TEXT 45

स वै बत भ्रष्टमतिस्तवैषते
यः कर्मणां पारमपारकर्मणः ।
यद्योगमायागुणयोगमोहितं
विश्वं समस्तं भगवन् विधेहि शम् ॥४५॥

sa vai bata bhraṣṭa-matis tavaiṣate
yaḥ karmaṇāṁ pāram apāra-karmaṇaḥ

yad-yogamāyā-guṇa-yoga-mohitaṁ
viśvaṁ samastaṁ bhagavan vidhehi śam

saḥ—he; *vai*—certainly; *bata*—alas; *bhraṣṭa-matiḥ*—nonsense; *tava*—Your; *eṣate*—desires; *yaḥ*—one who; *karmaṇām*—of activities; *pāram*—limit; *apāra-karmaṇaḥ*—of one who has unlimited activities; *yat*—by whom; *yoga*—mystic power; *māyā*—potency; *guṇa*—modes of material nature; *yoga*—mystic power; *mohitam*—bewildered; *viśvam*—the universe; *samastam*—in total; *bhagavan*—O Supreme Personality of Godhead; *vidhehi*—just be pleased to bestow; *śam*—good fortune.

TRANSLATION

O Lord, there is no limit to Your wonderful activities. Anyone who desires to know the limit of Your activities is certainly nonsensical. Everyone in this world is conditioned by the powerful mystic potencies. Please bestow Your causeless mercy upon these conditioned souls.

PURPORT

Mental speculators who want to understand the limit of the Unlimited are certainly nonsensical. Every one of them is captivated by the external potencies of the Lord. The best thing for them is to surrender unto Him, knowing Him to be inconceivable, for thus they can receive His causeless mercy. This prayer was offered by the inhabitants of the higher planetary systems, namely the Jana, Tapas and Satya *lokas*, who are far more intelligent and powerful than humans.

Viśvaṁ samastam is very significant here. There are the material world and the spiritual world. The sages pray: "Both worlds are bewildered by Your different energies. Those who are in the spiritual world are absorbed in Your loving service, forgetting themselves and You also, and those in the material world are absorbed in material sense gratification and therefore also forget You. No one can know You, because You are unlimited. It is best not to try to know You by unnecessary mental speculation. Rather, kindly bless us so that we can worship You with causeless devotional service."

TEXT 46

मैत्रेय उवाच
इत्युपस्थीयमानोऽसौ मुनिभिर्ब्रह्मवादिभिः ।
सलिले स्वखुराक्रान्त उपाधत्तावितावनिम् ॥४६॥

maitreya uvāca
ity upasthīyamāno 'sau
munibhir brahma-vādibhiḥ
salile sva-khurākrānta
upādhattāvitāvanim

maitreyaḥ uvāca—the sage Maitreya said; *iti*—thus; *upasthīyamānaḥ*—being praised by; *asau*—Lord Boar; *munibhiḥ*—by the great sages; *brahma-vādibhiḥ*—by the transcendentalists; *salile*—on the water; *sva-khura-ākrānte*—touched by His own hooves; *upādhatta*—placed; *avitā*—the maintainer; *avanim*—the earth.

TRANSLATION

The sage Maitreya said: The Lord, being thus worshiped by all the great sages and transcendentalists, touched the earth with His hooves and placed it on the water.

PURPORT

The earth was placed on the water by His inconceivable potency. The Lord is all-powerful, and therefore He can sustain the huge planets either on the water or in the air, as He likes. The tiny human brain cannot conceive how these potencies of the Lord can act. Man can give some vague explanation of the laws by which such phenomena are made possible, but actually the tiny human brain is unable to conceive of the activities of the Lord, which are therefore called inconceivable. Yet the frog-philosophers still try to give some imaginary explanation.

TEXT 47

स इत्थं भगवानुर्वीं विष्वक्सेनः प्रजापतिः ।
रसाया लीलयोन्नीतामप्सु न्यस्य ययौ हरिः ॥४७॥

sa itthaṁ bhagavān urvīṁ
viṣvaksenaḥ prajāpatiḥ
rasāyā līlayonnītām
apsu nyasya yayau hariḥ

saḥ—He; *ittham*—in this manner; *bhagavān*—the Personality of Godhead; *urvīm*—the earth; *viṣvaksenaḥ*—another name of Viṣṇu; *prajā-patiḥ*—the Lord of the living entities; *rasāyāḥ*—from within the water; *līlayā*—very easily; *unnītām*—raised; *apsu*—on the water; *nyasya*—placing; *yayau*—returned to His own abode; *hariḥ*—the Personality of Godhead.

TRANSLATION

In this manner the Personality of Godhead, Lord Viṣṇu, the maintainer of all living entities, raised the earth from within the water, and having placed it afloat on the water, He returned to His own abode.

PURPORT

The Personality of Godhead Lord Viṣṇu descends by His will to the material planets in His innumerable incarnations for particular purposes, and again He goes back to His own abode. When He descends He is called an *avatāra* because *avatāra* means "one who descends." Neither the Lord Himself nor His specific devotees who come to this earth are ordinary living entities like us.

TEXT 48

य एवमेतां हरिमेधसो हरेः
कथां सुभद्रां कथनीयमायिनः ।
शृण्वीत भक्त्या श्रवयेत वोशतीं
जनार्दनोऽस्याशु हृदि प्रसीदति ॥४८॥

ya evam etāṁ hari-medhaso hareḥ
kathāṁ subhadrāṁ kathanīya-māyinaḥ
śṛṇvīta bhaktyā śravayeta vośatīṁ
janārdano 'syāśu hṛdi prasīdati

yaḥ—one who; *evam*—thus; *etām*—this; *hari-medhasaḥ*—who destroys the material existence of the devotee; *hareḥ*—of the Personality of Godhead; *kathām*—narration; *subhadrām*—auspicious; *kathanīya*—worthy to narrate; *māyinaḥ*—of the merciful by His internal potency; *śṛṇvīta*—hears; *bhaktyā*—in devotion; *śravayeta*—also allows others to hear; *vā*—either; *uśatīm*—very pleasing; *janārdanaḥ*—the Lord; *asya*—his; *āśu*—very soon; *hṛdi*—within the heart; *prasīdati*—becomes very pleased.

TRANSLATION

If one hears and describes in a devotional service attitude this auspicious narration of Lord Boar, which is worthy of description, the Lord, who is within the heart of everyone, is very pleased.

PURPORT

In His various incarnations, the Lord appears, acts and leaves behind Him a narrative history which is as transcendental as He Himself. Every one of us is fond of hearing some wonderful narration, but most stories are neither auspicious nor worth hearing because they are of the inferior quality of material nature. Every living entity is of superior quality, spirit soul, and nothing material can be auspicious for him. Intelligent persons should therefore hear personally and cause others to hear the descriptive narrations of the Lord's activities, for that will destroy the pangs of material existence. Out of His causeless mercy only, the Lord comes to this earth and leaves behind His merciful activities so that the devotees may derive transcendental benefit.

TEXT 49

तस्मिन् प्रसन्ने सकलाशिषां प्रभौ
किं दुर्लभं ताभिरलं लवात्मभिः ।
अनन्यदृष्ट्या भजतां गुहाशयः
स्वयं विधत्ते स्वगतिं परः पराम् ॥४९॥

tasmin prasanne sakalāśiṣāṁ prabhau
kiṁ durlabhaṁ tābhir alaṁ lavātmabhiḥ
ananya-dṛṣṭyā bhajatāṁ guhāśayaḥ
svayaṁ vidhatte sva-gatiṁ paraḥ parām

tasmin—unto Him; *prasanne*—being pleased; *sakala-āśiṣām*—of all benediction; *prabhau*—unto the Lord; *kim*—what is that; *durlabham*—very difficult to obtain; *tābhiḥ*—with them; *alam*—away; *lava-ātmabhiḥ*—with insignificant gains; *ananya-dṛṣṭyā*—by nothing but devotional service; *bhajatām*—of those who are engaged in devotional service; *guhā-āśayaḥ*—residing within the heart; *svayam*—personally; *vidhatte*—executes; *sva-gatim*—in His own abode; *paraḥ*—the supreme; *parām*—transcendental.

TRANSLATION

Nothing remains unachieved when the Supreme Personality of Godhead is pleased with someone. By transcendental achievement one understands everything else to be insignificant. One who engages in transcendental loving service is elevated to the highest perfectional stage by the Lord Himself, who is seated in everyone's heart.

PURPORT

As stated in *Bhagavad-gītā* (10.10), the Lord gives intelligence to the pure devotees so that they may be elevated to the highest perfectional stage. It is confirmed herein that a pure devotee, who constantly engages in the loving service of the Lord, is awarded all knowledge necessary to reach the Supreme Personality of Godhead. For such a devotee there is nothing valuable to be achieved but the Lord's service. If one serves faithfully, there is no possibility of frustration because the Lord Himself takes charge of the devotee's advancement. The Lord is seated in everyone's heart, and He knows the devotee's motive and arranges everything achievable. In other words, the pseudo devotee, who is anxious to achieve material gains, cannot attain the highest perfectional stage because the Lord is in knowledge of his motive. One merely has to become sincere in his purpose, and then the Lord is there to help in every way.

TEXT 50

को नाम लोके पुरुषार्थसारवित्
पुराकथानां भगवत्कथासुधाम् ।
आपीय कर्णाञ्जलिभिर्भवापहा-
महो विरज्येत विना नरेतरम् ॥५०॥

ko nāma loke puruṣārtha-sāravit
purā-kathānāṁ bhagavat-kathā-sudhām
āpīya karṇāñjalibhir bhavāpahām
aho virajyeta vinā naretaram

kaḥ—who; *nāma*—indeed; *loke*—in the world; *puruṣa-artha*—goal of life; *sāra-vit*—one who knows the essence of; *purā-kathānām*—of all past histories; *bhagavat*—regarding the Personality of Godhead; *kathā-sudhām*—the nectar of the narrations about the Personality of Godhead; *āpīya*—by drinking; *karṇa-añjalibhiḥ*—by aural reception; *bhava-apahām*—that which kills all material pangs; *aho*—alas; *virajyeta*—could refuse; *vinā*—except; *nara-itaram*—other than the human being. being.

TRANSLATION

Who, other than one who is not a human being, can exist in this world and not be interested in the ultimate goal of life? Who can refuse the nectar of narrations about the Personality of Godhead's activities, which by itself can deliver one from all material pangs?

PURPORT

The narration of the activities of the Personality of Godhead is like a constant flow of nectar. No one can refuse to drink such nectar except one who is not a human being. Devotional service to the Lord is the highest goal of life for every human being, and such devotional service begins by hearing about the transcendental activities of the Personality of Godhead. Only an animal, or a man who is almost an animal in behavior, can refuse to take an interest in hearing the transcendental message of the Lord. There are many books of stories and histories in the world, but except for the histories or narrations on the topics of the Personality of Godhead, none are capable of diminishing the burden of material pangs. Therefore one who is serious about eliminating material existence must chant and hear of the transcendental activities of the Personality of Godhead. Otherwise one must be compared to the nonhumans.

Thus end the Bhaktivedanta purports of the Third Canto, Thirteenth Chapter, of the Śrīmad-Bhāgavatam, *entitled "The Appearance of Lord Varāha."*

CHAPTER FOURTEEN

Pregnancy of Diti in the Evening

TEXT 1

श्रीशुक उवाच

निशम्य कौषारविणोपवर्णितां
हरेः कथां कारणसूकरात्मनः ।
पुनः स पप्रच्छ तमुद्यताञ्जलि-
र्न चातितृप्तो विदुरो धृतव्रतः ॥ १ ॥

śrī-śuka uvāca
niśamya kauṣāraviṇopavarṇitāṁ
hareḥ kathāṁ kāraṇa-sūkarātmanaḥ
punaḥ sa papraccha tam udyatāñjalir
na cātitṛpto viduro dhṛta-vrataḥ

śrī-śukaḥ uvāca—Śrī Śukadeva Gosvāmī said; *niśamya*—after hearing; *kauṣāraviṇā*—by the sage Maitreya; *upavarṇitām*—described; *hareḥ*—of the Personality of Godhead; *kathām*—narrations; *kāraṇa*—for the reason of lifting the earth; *sūkara-ātmanaḥ*—of the boar incarnation; *punaḥ*—again; *saḥ*—he; *papraccha*—inquired; *tam*—from him (Maitreya); *udyata-añjaliḥ* with folded hands; *na*—never; *ca*—also; *ati-tṛptaḥ*—very much satisfied; *viduraḥ*—Vidura; *dhṛta-vrataḥ*—taken to a vow.

TRANSLATION

Śukadeva Gosvāmī said: After hearing from the great sage Maitreya about the Lord's incarnation as Varāha, Vidura, who had taken a vow, begged him with folded hands to please narrate further transcendental activities of the Lord, since he [Vidura] did not yet feel satisfied.

TEXT 2

विदुर उवाच

तेनैव तु मुनिश्रेष्ठ हरिणा यज्ञमूर्तिना ।
आदिदैत्यो हिरण्याक्षो हत इत्यनुशुश्रुम ॥ २ ॥

vidura uvāca
tenaiva tu muni-śreṣṭha
hariṇā yajña-mūrtinā
ādi-daityo hiraṇyākṣo
hata ity anuśuśruma

viduraḥ uvāca—Śrī Vidura said; *tena*—by Him; *eva*—certainly; *tu*—but; *muni-śreṣṭha*—O chief among the sages; *hariṇā*—by the Personality of Godhead; *yajña-mūrtinā*—the form of sacrifices; *ādi*—original; *daityaḥ*—demon; *hiraṇyākṣaḥ*—by the name Hiraṇyākṣa; *hataḥ*—slain; *iti*—thus; *anuśuśruma*—heard in succession.

TRANSLATION

Śrī Vidura said: O chief amongst the great sages, I have heard by disciplic succession that Hiraṇyākṣa, the original demon, was slain by the same form of sacrifices, the Personality of Godhead [Lord Boar].

PURPORT

As referred to previously, the boar incarnation was manifested in two millenniums—namely Svāyambhuva and Cākṣuṣa. In both millenniums there was a boar incarnation of the Lord, but in the Svāyambhuva millennium He lifted the earth from within the water of the universe, whereas in the Cākṣuṣa millennium He killed the first demon, Hiraṇyākṣa. In the Svāyambhuva millennium He assumed the color white, and in the Cākṣuṣa millennium He assumed the color red. Vidura had already heard about one of them, and he proposed to hear about the other. The two different boar incarnations described are the one Supreme Personality of Godhead.

TEXT 3

तस्य चोद्धरतः क्षौणीं स्वदंष्ट्राग्रेण लीलया ।
दैत्यराजस्य च ब्रह्मन् कस्माद्धेतोरभून्मृधः ॥ ३ ॥

tasya coddharataḥ kṣauṇīṁ
sva-daṁṣṭrāgreṇa līlayā
daitya-rājasya ca brahman
kasmād dhetor abhūn mṛdhaḥ

tasya—His; *ca*—also; *uddharataḥ*—while lifting; *kṣauṇīm*—the earth planet; *sva-daṁṣṭra-agreṇa*—by the edge of His tusks; *līlayā*—in His pastimes; *daitya-rājasya*—of the king of demons; *ca*—and; *brahman*—O brāhmaṇa; *kasmāt*—from what; *hetoḥ*—reason; *abhūt*—there was; *mṛdhaḥ*—fight.

TRANSLATION

What was the reason, O brāhmaṇa, for the fight between the demon king and Lord Boar while the Lord was lifting the earth as His pastime?

TEXT 4

श्रद्दधानाय भक्ताय ब्रूहि तज्जन्मविस्तरम् ।
ऋषे न तृप्यति मनः परं कौतूहलं हि मे ॥ ४ ॥

śraddadhānāya bhaktāya
brūhi taj-janma-vistaram
ṛṣe na tṛpyati manaḥ
paraṁ kautūhalaṁ hi me

śraddadhānāya—unto a faithful person; *bhaktāya*—unto a devotee; *brūhi*—please narrate; *tat*—His; *janma*—appearance; *vistaram*—in detail; *ṛṣe*—O great sage; *na*—not; *tṛpyati*—become satisfied; *manaḥ*—mind; *param*—very much; *kautūhalam*—inquisitive; *hi*—certainly; *me*—my.

TRANSLATION

My mind has become very inquisitive, and therefore I am not satisfied with hearing the narration of the Lord's appearance. Please, therefore, speak more and more to a devotee who is faithful.

PURPORT

One who is actually faithful and inquisitive is qualified to hear the transcendental pastimes of the appearance and disappearance of the Supreme Personality of Godhead. Vidura was a suitable candidate to receive such transcendental messages.

TEXT 5

मैत्रेय उवाच
साधु वीर त्वया पृष्टमवतारकथां हरेः ।
यत्त्वं पृच्छसि मर्त्यानां मृत्युपाशविशातनीम् ॥ ५ ॥

maitreya uvāca
sādhu vīra tvayā pṛṣṭam
avatāra-kathāṁ hareḥ
yat tvaṁ pṛcchasi martyānām
mṛtyu-pāśa-viśātanīm

maitreyaḥ uvāca—Maitreya said; *sādhu*—devotee; *vīra*—O warrior; *tvayā*—by you; *pṛṣṭam*—inquired; *avatāra-kathām*—topics on the incarnation of the Lord; *hareḥ*—of the Personality of Godhead; *yat*—that which; *tvam*—your good self; *pṛcchasi*—asking me; *martyānām*—of those who are destined for death; *mṛtyu-pāśa*—the chain of birth and death; *viśātanīm*—source of liberation.

TRANSLATION

The great sage Maitreya said: O warrior, the inquiry made by you is just befitting a devotee because it concerns the incarnation of the Personality of Godhead. He is the source of liberation from the chain of birth and death for all those who are otherwise destined to die.

PURPORT

The great sage Maitreya addressed Vidura as a warrior not only because Vidura belonged to the Kuru family but because he was anxious to hear about the chivalrous activities of the Lord in His incarnations of Varāha and Nṛsiṁha. Because the inquiries concerned the Lord, they were perfectly befitting a devotee. A devotee has no taste for hearing anything mundane. There are many topics of mundane warfare, but a devotee is not inclined to hear them. The topics of the warfare in which the Lord engages do not concern the war of death but the war against the chain of *māyā* which obliges one to accept repeated birth and death. In other words, one who takes delight in hearing the war topics of the Lord is relieved from the chains of birth and death. Foolish people are suspicious of Kṛṣṇa's taking part in the Battle of Kurukṣetra, not knowing that His taking part insured liberation for all who were present on the battlefield. It is said by Bhīṣmadeva that all who were present on the Battlefield of Kurukṣetra attained their original spiritual existences after death. Therefore, hearing the war topics of the Lord is as good as any other devotional service.

TEXT 6

ययोत्तानपदः पुत्रो मुनिना गीतयार्भकः ।
मृत्योः कृत्वैव मूर्ध्न्यङ्घ्रिमारुरोह हरेः पदम् ॥ ६ ॥

yayottānapadaḥ putro
muninā gītayārbhakaḥ
mṛtyoḥ kṛtvaiva mūrdhny aṅghrim
āruroha hareḥ padam

yayā—by which; *uttānapadaḥ*—of King Uttānapāda; *putraḥ*—son; *muninā*—by the sage; *gītayā*—being sung; *arbhakaḥ*—a child; *mṛtyoḥ*—of death; *kṛtvā*—placing; *eva*—certainly; *mūrdhni*—on the head; *aṅghrim*—feet; *āruroha*—ascended; *hareḥ*—of the Personality of Godhead; *padam*—to the abode.

TRANSLATION

By hearing these topics from the sage [Nārada], the son of King Uttānapāda [Dhruva] was enlightened regarding the Personality of Godhead, and he ascended to the abode of the Lord, placing his feet over the head of death.

PURPORT

While quitting his body, Mahārāja Dhruva, the son of King Uttānapāda, was attended by personalities like Sunanda and others, who received him in the kingdom of God. He left this world at an early age, as a young boy, although he had attained the throne of his father and had several children of his own. Because he was due to quit this world, death was waiting for him. He did not care for death, however, and even with his present body he boarded a spiritual airplane and went directly to the planet of Viṣṇu because of his association with the great sage Nārada, who had spoken to him the narration of the pastimes of the Lord.

TEXT 7

अथात्रापीतिहासोऽयं श्रुतो मे वर्णितः पुरा ।
ब्रह्मणा देवदेवेन देवानामनुपृच्छताम् ॥ ७ ॥

athātrāpītihāso 'yaṁ
śruto me varṇitaḥ purā
brahmaṇā deva-devena
devānām anupṛcchatām

atha—now; *atra*—in this matter; *api*—also; *itihāsaḥ*—history; *ayam*—this; *śrutaḥ*—heard; *me*—by me; *varṇitaḥ*—described; *purā*—years ago; *brahmaṇā*—by Brahmā; *deva-devena*—the foremost of the demigods; *devānām*—by the demigods; *anupṛcchatām*—asking.

TRANSLATION

This history of the fight between the Lord as a boar and the demon Hiraṇyākṣa was heard by me in a year long ago as it was described by the foremost of the demigods, Brahmā, when he was questioned by the other demigods.

TEXT 8

दितिर्दाक्षायणी क्षत्तर्मारीचं कश्यपं पतिम् ।
अपत्यकामा चकमे सन्ध्यायां हृच्छयार्दिता ॥ ८ ॥

ditir dākṣāyaṇī kṣattar
mārīcaṁ kaśyapaṁ patim
apatya-kāmā cakame
sandhyāyāṁ hṛc-chayārditā

ditiḥ—Diti; *dākṣāyaṇī*—the daughter of Dakṣa; *kṣattaḥ*—O Vidura; *mārīcam*—the son of Marīci; *kaśyapam*—Kaśyapa; *patim*—her husband; *apatya-kāmā*—desirous of having a child; *cakame*—longed for; *sandhyāyām*—in the evening; *hṛt-śaya*—by sex desires; *arditā*—distressed.

TRANSLATION

Diti, daughter of Dakṣa, being afflicted with sex desire, begged her husband, Kaśyapa, the son of Marīci, to have intercourse with her in the evening in order to beget a child.

TEXT 9

इष्ट्वाग्निजिह्वं पयसा पुरुषं यजुषां पतिम् ।
निम्लोचत्यर्क आसीनमग्न्यगारे समाहितम् ॥ ९ ॥

iṣṭvāgni-jihvaṁ payasā
puruṣaṁ yajuṣāṁ patim
nimlocaty arka āsīnam
agny-agāre samāhitam

iṣṭvā—after worshiping; *agni*—fire; *jihvam*—tongue; *payasā*—by oblation; *puruṣam*—unto the Supreme Person; *yajuṣām*—of all sacrifices; *patim*—master; *nimlocati*—while setting; *arke*—the sun; *āsīnam*—sitting; *agni-agāre*—in the sacrificial hall; *samāhitam*—completely in trance.

TRANSLATION

The sun was setting, and the sage was sitting in trance after offering oblations to the Supreme Personality of Godhead, Viṣṇu, whose tongue is the sacrificial fire.

PURPORT

Fire is considered to be the tongue of the Personality of Godhead Viṣṇu, and oblations of grains and clarified butter offered to the fire are thus accepted by Him.

That is the principle of all sacrifices, of which Lord Viṣṇu is the master. In other words, the satisfaction of Lord Viṣṇu includes the satisfaction of all demigods and other living beings.

TEXT 10

दितिरुवाच
एष मां त्वत्कृते विद्वन् काम आत्तशरासनः ।
दुनोति दीनां विक्रम्य रम्भामिव मतङ्गजः ॥१०॥

ditir uvāca
eṣa māṁ tvat-kṛte vidvan
kāma ātta-śarāsanaḥ
dunoti dīnāṁ vikramya
rambhām iva mataṅgajaḥ

ditiḥ uvāca—beautiful Diti said; *eṣaḥ*—all these; *mām*—unto me; *tvat-kṛte*—for you; *vidvan*—O learned one; *kāmaḥ*—Cupid; *ātta-śarāsanaḥ*—taking his arrows; *dunoti*—distresses; *dīnām*—poor me; *vikramya*—attacking; *rambhām*—banana tree; *iva*—like; *matam-gajaḥ*—mad elephant.

TRANSLATION

In that place the beautiful Diti expressed her desire: O learned one, Cupid is taking his arrows and distressing me forcibly, as a mad elephant troubles a banana tree.

PURPORT

Beautiful Diti, seeing her husband absorbed in trance, began to speak loudly, not attempting to attract him by bodily expressions. She frankly said that her whole body was distressed by sex desire because of her husband's presence, just as a banana tree is troubled by a mad elephant. It was not natural for her to agitate her husband when he was in trance, but she could not control her strong sexual appetite. Her sex desire was like a mad elephant, and therefore it was the prime duty of her husband to give her all protection by fulfilling her desire.

TEXT 11

तद्भवान्दह्यमानायां सपत्नीनां समृद्धिभिः ।
प्रजावतीनां भद्रं ते मय्यायुङ्क्तामनुग्रहम् ॥११॥

tad bhavān dahyamānāyāṁ
sa-patnīnāṁ samṛddhibhiḥ
prajāvatīnāṁ bhadraṁ te
mayy āyuṅktām anugraham

tat—therefore; *bhavān*—your good self; *dahyamānāyām*—being distressed; *sa-patnīnām*—of the co-wives; *samṛddhibhiḥ*—by the prosperity; *prajā-vatīnām*—of those who have children; *bhadram*—all prosperity; *te*—unto you; *mayi*—unto me; *āyuṅktām*—do unto me, in all respects; *anugraham*—favor.

TRANSLATION

Therefore you should be kind towards me by showing me complete mercy. I desire to have sons, and I am much distressed by seeing the opulence of my co-wives. By performing this act, you will become happy.

PURPORT

In *Bhagavad-gītā* sexual intercourse for begetting children is accepted as righteous. A person sexually inclined for simple sense gratification, however, is unrighteous. In Diti's appeal to her husband for sex, it was not exactly that she was afflicted by sex desires, but she desired sons. Since she had no sons, she felt poorer than her co-wives. Therefore Kaśyapa was supposed to satisfy his bona fide wife.

TEXT 12

भर्तर्याप्तोरुमानानां लोकानाविशते यशः ।
पतिर्भवद्विधो यासां प्रजया ननु जायते ॥१२॥

bhartary āptorumānānāṁ
lokān āviśate yaśaḥ
patir bhavad-vidho yāsāṁ
prajayā nanu jāyate

bhartari—by the husband; *āpta-urumānānām*—of those who are beloved; *lokān*—in the world; *āviśate*—spreads; *yaśaḥ*—fame; *patiḥ*—husband; *bhavat-vidhaḥ*—like your good self; *yāsām*—of those whose; *prajayā*—by children; *nanu*—certainly; *jāyate*—expands.

TRANSLATION

A woman is honored in the world by the benediction of her husband, and a husband like you will become famous by having children because you are meant for the expansion of living entities.

PURPORT

According to Ṛṣabhadeva, one should not become a father or mother unless one is confident that he can beget children whom he can deliver from the clutches of birth and death. Human life is the only opportunity to get out of the material scene, which is full of the miseries of birth, death, old age and diseases. Every human being should be given the opportunity to take advantage of his human form of life, and a father like Kaśyapa is supposed to beget good children for the purpose of liberation.

TEXT 13

पुरा पिता नो भगवान्दक्षो दुहितृवत्सलः ।
कं वृणीत वरं वत्सा इत्यपृच्छत नः पृथक् ॥१३॥

purā pitā no bhagavān
dakṣo duhitṛ-vatsalaḥ
kaṁ vṛṇīta varaṁ vatsā
ity apṛcchata naḥ pṛthak

purā—in days long ago; *pitā*—father; *naḥ*—our; *bhagavān*—the most opulent; *dakṣaḥ*—Dakṣa; *duhitṛ-vatsalaḥ*—affectionate to his daughters; *kam*—unto whom; *vṛṇīta*—you want to accept; *varam*—your husband; *vatsāḥ*—O my children; *iti*—thus; *apṛcchata*—inquired; *naḥ*—us; *pṛthak*—separately.

TRANSLATION

In days long ago, our father, the most opulent Dakṣa, who was affectionate to his daughters, asked each of us separately whom we would prefer to select as our husband.

PURPORT

It appears from this verse that free selection of a husband was allowed by the father, but not by free association. The daughters were asked separately to submit their selection of a husband who was famous for his acts and personality. The ultimate selection depended on the choice of the father.

TEXT 14

स विदित्वात्मजानां नो भावं सन्तानभावनः ।
त्रयोदशाददात्तासां यास्ते शीलमनुव्रताः ॥१४॥

sa viditvātmajānāṁ no
bhāvaṁ santāna-bhāvanaḥ
trayodaśādadāt tāsāṁ
yās te śīlam anuvratāḥ

saḥ—Dakṣa; *viditvā*—understanding; *ātma-jānām*—of the daughters; *naḥ*—our; *bhāvam*—indication; *santāna*—children; *bhāvanaḥ*—well-wisher; *trayodaśa*—thirteen; *adadāt*—handed over; *tāsām*—of all of them; *yāḥ*—those who are; *te*—your; *śīlam*—behavior; *anuvratāḥ*—all faithful.

TRANSLATION

Our well-wishing father, Dakṣa, after knowing our intentions, handed over thirteen of his daughters unto you, and since then we have all been faithful.

PURPORT

Generally the daughters were too shy to express their opinions before their father, but the father would accept the daughters' intentions through someone else, such as a grandmother to whom the grandchildren had free access. King Dakṣa collected the opinions of his daughters and thus handed over thirteen to Kaśyapa. Every one of Diti's sisters was a mother of children. Therefore, since she was equally faithful to the same husband, why should she remain without children?

TEXT 15

अथ मे कुरु कल्याणं कामं कमललोचन ।
आर्तोपसर्पणं भूमन्नमोघं हि महीयसि ॥१५॥

atha me kuru kalyāṇaṁ
kāmaṁ kamala-locana
ārtopasarpaṇaṁ bhūmann
amoghaṁ hi mahīyasi

atha—therefore; *me*—unto me; *kuru*—kindly do; *kalyāṇam*—benediction; *kāmam*—desire; *kamala-locana*—O lotus-eyed one; *ārta*—of the distressed; *upasarpaṇam*—the approaching; *bhūman*—O great one; *amogham*—without failure; *hi*—certainly; *mahīyasi*—to a great person.

TRANSLATION

O lotus-eyed one, kindly bless me by fulfilling my desire. When someone in distress approaches a great person, his pleas should never go in vain.

PURPORT

Diti knew well that her request might be rejected because of the untimely situation, but she pleaded that when there is an emergency or a distressful condition, there is no consideration of time or situation.

TEXT 16

इति तां वीर मारीचः कृपणां बहुभाषिणीम् ।
प्रत्याहानुनयन् वाचा प्रवृद्धानङ्गकश्मलाम् ॥१६॥

iti tāṁ vīra mārīcaḥ
kṛpaṇāṁ bahu-bhāṣiṇīm
pratyāhānunayan vācā
pravṛddhānaṅga-kaśmalām

iti—thus; *tām*—unto her; *vīra*—O hero; *mārīcaḥ*—the son of Marīci (Kaśyapa); *kṛpaṇām*—unto the poor; *bahu-bhāṣiṇīm*—too talkative; *pratyāha*—replied; *anunayan*—pacifying; *vācā*—by words; *pravṛddha*—highly agitated; *anaṅga*—lust; *kaśmalām*—contaminated.

TRANSLATION

O hero [Vidura], Diti, being thus afflicted by the contamination of lust, and therefore poor and talkative, was pacified by the son of Marīci in suitable words.

PURPORT

When a man or woman is afflicted by the lust of sex desire, it is to be understood as sinful contamination. Kaśyapa was engaged in his spiritual activities, but he did not have sufficient strength to refuse his wife, who was thus afflicted. He could have refused her with strong words expressing impossibility, but he was not as spiritually strong as Vidura. Vidura is addressed here as a hero because no one is stronger in self-control than a devotee of the Lord. It appears that Kaśyapa was already inclined to have sexual enjoyment with his wife, and because he was not a strong man he tried to dissuade her only with pacifying words.

TEXT 17

एष तेऽहं विधास्यामि प्रियं भीरु यदिच्छसि ।
तस्याः कामं न कः कुर्यात्सिद्धिस्त्रैवर्गिकी यतः ॥१७॥

eṣa te 'haṁ vidhāsyāmi
priyaṁ bhīru yad icchasi
tasyāḥ kāmaṁ na kaḥ kuryāt
siddhis traivargikī yataḥ

eṣaḥ—this; *te*—your request; *aham*—I; *vidhāsyāmi*—shall execute; *priyam*—very dear; *bhīru*—O afflicted one; *yat*—what; *icchasi*—you are desiring; *tasyāḥ*—her; *kāmam*—desires; *na*—not; *kaḥ*—who; *kuryāt*—would perform; *siddhiḥ*—perfection of liberation; *traivargikī*—three; *yataḥ*—from whom.

TRANSLATION

O afflicted one, I shall forthwith gratify whatever desire is dear to you, for who else but you is the source of the three perfections of liberation?

PURPORT

The three perfections of liberation are religiosity, economic development and sense gratification: For a conditioned soul, the wife is considered to be the source of liberation because she offers her service to the husband for his ultimate liberation. Conditional material existence is based on sense gratification, and if someone has the good fortune to get a good wife, he is helped by the wife in all respects. If one is disturbed in his conditional life, he becomes more and more entangled in material contamination. A faithful wife is supposed to cooperate with her husband in fulfilling all material desires so that he can then become comfortable and execute spiritual activities for the perfection of life. If, however, the husband is progressive in spiritual advancement, the wife undoubtedly shares in his activities, and thus both the wife and the husband profit in spiritual perfection. It is essential, therefore, that girls as well as boys be trained to discharge spiritual duties so that at the time of cooperation both will be benefited. The training of the boy is *brahmacarya,* and the training of the girl is chastity. A faithful wife and spiritually trained *brahmacārī* are a good combination for advancement of the human mission.

TEXT 18

सर्वाश्रमानुपादाय स्वाश्रमेण कलत्रवान् ।
व्यसनार्णवमत्येति जलयानैर्यथार्णवम् ॥१८॥

sarvāśramān upādāya
svāśrameṇa kalatravān

vyasanārṇavam atyeti
jala-yānair yathārṇavam

sarva—all; *āśramān*—social orders; *upādāya*—completing; *sva*—own; *āśrameṇa*—by the social orders; *kalatra-vān*—a person living with a wife; *vyasana-arṇavam*—the dangerous ocean of material existence; *atyeti*—one can cross over; *jala-yānaiḥ*—with seagoing vessels; *yathā*—as; *arṇavam*—the ocean.

TRANSLATION

As one can cross over the ocean with seagoing vessels, one can cross the dangerous situation of the material ocean by living with a wife.

PURPORT

There are four social orders for cooperation in the endeavor for liberation from material existence. The orders of *brahmacarya,* or pious student life, household life with a wife, retired life and renounced life all depend for successful advancement on the householder who lives with a wife. This cooperation is essential for the proper functioning of the institution of the four social orders and the four spiritual orders of life. This Vedic *varṇāśrama* system is generally known as the caste system. The man who lives with a wife has a great responsibility in maintaining the members of the other social orders—the *brahmacārīs, vānaprasthas* and *sannyāsīs.* Except for the *gṛhasthas,* or the householders, everyone is supposed to engage in the spiritual advancement of life, and therefore the *brahmacārī,* the *vānaprastha* and the *sannyāsī* have very little time to earn a livelihood. They therefore collect alms from the *gṛhasthas,* and thus they secure the bare necessities of life and cultivate spiritual understanding. By helping the other three sections of society cultivate spiritual values, the householder also makes advancement in spiritual life. Ultimately every member of society automatically becomes spiritually advanced and easily crosses the ocean of nescience.

TEXT 19

यामाहुरात्मनो ह्यर्धं श्रेयस्कामस्य मानिनि ।
यस्यां स्वधुरमध्यस्य पुमांश्चरति विज्वरः ॥१९॥

yām āhur ātmano hy ardhaṁ
śreyas-kāmasya mānini
yasyāṁ sva-dhuram adhyasya
pumāṁś carati vijvaraḥ

yām—the wife who; *āhuḥ*—is said; *ātmanaḥ*—of the body; *hi*—thus; *ardham*—half; *śreyaḥ*—welfare; *kāmasya*—of all desires; *mānini*—O respectful one; *yasyām*—in whom; *sva-dhuram*—all responsibilities; *adhyasya*—entrusting; *pumān*—a man; *carati*—moves; *vijvaraḥ*—without anxiety.

TRANSLATION

O respectful one, a wife is so helpful that she is called the better half of a man's body because of her sharing in all auspicious activities. A man can move without anxiety entrusting all responsibilities to his wife.

PURPORT

By the Vedic injunction, the wife is accepted as the better half of a man's body because she is supposed to be responsible for discharging half of the duties of the husband. A family man has a responsibility to perform five kinds of sacrifices, called *pañca-yajña,* in order to get relief from all kinds of unavoidable sinful reaction incurred in the course of his affairs. When a man becomes qualitatively like the cats and dogs, he forgets his duties in cultivating spiritual values, and thus he accepts his wife as a sense gratificatory agency. When the wife is accepted as a sense gratificatory agency, personal beauty is the main consideration, and as soon as there is a break in personal sense gratification, there is disruption or divorce. But when husband and wife aim at spiritual advancement by mutual cooperation, there is no consideration of personal beauty or the disruption of so-called love. In the material world there is no question of love. Marriage is actually a duty performed in mutual cooperation as directed in the authoritative scriptures for spiritual advancement. Therefore marriage is essential in order to avoid the life of cats and dogs, who are not meant for spiritual enlightenment.

TEXT 20

यामाश्रित्येन्द्रियारातीन्दुर्जयानितराश्रमैः ।
वयं जयेम हेलाभिर्दस्यून्दुर्गपतिर्यथा ॥२०॥

yām āśrityendriyārātīn
durjayān itarāśramaiḥ
vayaṁ jayema helābhir
dasyūn durga-patir yathā

yām—whom; *āśritya*—taking shelter of; *indriya*—senses; *arātīn*—enemies; *durjayān*—difficult to conquer; *itara*—other than the householders; *āśramaiḥ*—by orders of society;

vayam—we; *jayema*—can conquer; *helābhiḥ*—easily; *dasyūn*—invading plunderers; *durga-patiḥ*—a fort commander; *yathā*—as.

TRANSLATION

As a fort commander very easily conquers invading plunderers, by taking shelter of a wife one can conquer the senses, which are unconquerable in the other social orders.

PURPORT

Of the four orders of human society—the student, or *brahmacārī* order, the householder, or *gṛhastha* order, the retired, or *vānaprastha* order, and the renounced, or *sannyāsī* order—the householder is on the safe side. The bodily senses are considered plunderers of the fort of the body. The wife is supposed to be the commander of the fort, and therefore whenever there is an attack on the body by the senses, it is the wife who protects the body from being smashed. The sex demand is inevitable for everyone, but one who has a fixed wife is saved from the onslaught of the sense enemies. A man who possesses a good wife does not create a disturbance in society by corrupting virgin girls. Without a fixed wife, a man becomes a debauchee of the first order and is a nuisance in society—unless he is a trained *brahmacārī, vānaprastha* or *sannyāsī.* Unless there is rigid and systematic training of the *brahmacārī* by the expert spiritual master, and unless the student is obedient, it is sure that the so-called *brahmacārī* will fall prey to the attack of sex. There are so many instances of falldown, even for great *yogīs* like Viśvāmitra. A *gṛhastha* is saved, however, because of his faithful wife. Sex life is the cause of material bondage, and therefore it is prohibited in three *āśramas* and is allowed only in the *gṛhastha-āśrama.* The *gṛhastha* is responsible for producing first-quality *brahmacārīs, vānaprasthas* and *sannyāsīs.*

TEXT 21

न वयं प्रभवस्तां त्वामनुकर्तुं गृहेश्वरि ।
अप्यायुषा वा कार्त्स्न्येन ये चान्ये गुणगृध्नवः ॥२१॥

na vayaṁ prabhavas tāṁ tvām
anukartuṁ gṛheśvari
apy āyuṣā vā kārtsnyena
ye cānye guṇa-gṛdhnavaḥ

na—never; *vayam*—we; *prabhavaḥ*—are able; *tām*—that; *tvām*—unto you; *anukartum*—do the same; *gṛha-īśvari*—O queen of the home; *api*—in spite of; *āyuṣā*—by duration of life;

vā—or (in the next life); *kārtsnyena*—entire; *ye*—who; *ca*—also; *anye*—others; *guṇa-gṛdhnavaḥ*—those who are able to appreciate qualities.

TRANSLATION

O queen of the home, we are not able to act like you, nor could we repay you for what you have done, even if we worked for our entire life or even after death. To repay you is not possible, even for those who are admirers of personal qualities.

PURPORT

So much glorification of a woman by her husband indicates that he is henpecked or is talking lightly in joke. Kaśyapa meant that householders living with wives enjoy the heavenly blessings of sense enjoyment and at the same time have no fear of going down to hell. The man in the renounced order of life has no wife and may be driven by sex desire to seek another woman or another's wife and thus go to hell. In other words, the so-called man of the renounced order, who has left his house and wife, goes to hell if he again desires sexual pleasure, knowingly or unknowingly. In that way the householders are on the side of safety. Therefore husbands as a class cannot repay their debt to women either in this life or in the next. Even if they engage themselves in repaying the women throughout their whole lives, it is still not possible. Not all husbands are as able to appreciate the good qualities of their wives, but even though one is able to appreciate these qualities, it is still not possible to repay the debt to the wife. Such extraordinary praises by a husband for his wife are certainly in the mode of joking.

TEXT 22

अथापि काममेतं ते प्रजात्यै करवाण्यलम् ।
यथा मां नातिरोचन्ति मुहूर्तं प्रतिपालय ॥२२॥

athāpi kāmam etaṁ te
prajātyai karavāṇy alam
yathā māṁ nātirocanti
muhūrtaṁ pratipālaya

atha api—even though (it is not possible); *kāmam*—this sex desire; *etam*—as it is; *te*—your; *prajātyai*—for the sake of children; *karavāṇi*—let me do; *alam*—without delay; *yathā*—as;

mām—unto me; *na*—may not; *atirocanti*—reproach; *muhūrtam*—a few seconds; *pratipālaya*—wait for.

TRANSLATION

Even though it is not possible to repay you, I shall satisfy your sex desire immediately for the sake of begetting children. But you must wait for only a few seconds so that others may not reproach me.

PURPORT

The henpecked husband may not be able to repay his wife for all the benefits that he derives from her, but as for begetting children by fulfilling sexual desire, it is not at all difficult for any husband unless he is thoroughly impotent. This is a very easy task for a husband under normal conditions. In spite of Kaśyapa's being very eager, he requested her to wait for a few seconds so that others might not reproach him. He explains his position as follows.

TEXT 23

एषा घोरतमा वेला घोराणां घोरदर्शना ।
चरन्ति यस्यां भूतानि भूतेशानुचराणि ह ॥२३॥

eṣā ghoratamā velā
ghorāṇāṁ ghora-darśanā
caranti yasyāṁ bhūtāni
bhūteśānucarāṇi ha

eṣā—this time; *ghora-tamā*—most horrible; *velā*—period; *ghorāṇām*—of the horrible; *ghora-darśanā*—horrible looking; *caranti*—move; *yasyām*—in which; *bhūtāni*—ghosts; *bhūta-īśa*—the lord of the ghosts; *anucarāṇi*—constant companions; *ha*—indeed.

TRANSLATION

This particular time is most inauspicious because at this time the horrible-looking ghosts and constant companions of the lord of the ghosts are visible.

PURPORT

Kaśyapa has already told his wife Diti to wait for a while, and now he warns her that failure to consider the particular time will result in punishment from the ghosts and evil spirits who move during this time, along with their master, Lord Rudra.

TEXT 24

एतस्यां साध्वि सन्ध्यायां भगवान् भूतभावनः ।
परीतो भूतपर्षद्भिर्वृषेणाटति भूतराट् ॥२४॥

etasyāṁ sādhvi sandhyāyāṁ
bhagavān bhūta-bhāvanaḥ
parīto bhūta-parṣadbhir
vṛṣeṇāṭati bhūtarāṭ

etasyām—in this period; *sādhvi*—O chaste one; *sandhyāyām*—at the junction of day and night (evening); *bhagavān*—the Personality of God; *bhūta-bhāvanaḥ*—the well-wisher of the ghostly characters; *parītaḥ*—surrounded by; *bhūta-parṣadbhiḥ*—by ghostly companions; *vṛṣeṇa*—on the back of the bull carrier; *aṭati*—travels; *bhūta-rāṭ*—the king of the ghosts.

TRANSLATION

Lord Śiva, the king of the ghosts, sitting on the back of his bull carrier, travels at this time, accompanied by ghosts who follow him for their welfare.

PURPORT

Lord Śiva, or Rudra, is the king of the ghosts. Ghostly characters worship Lord Śiva to be gradually guided toward a path of self-realization. Māyāvādī philosophers are mostly worshipers of Lord Śiva, and Śrīpāda Śaṅkarācārya is considered to be the incarnation of Lord Śiva for preaching godlessness to the Māyāvādī philosophers. Ghosts are bereft of a physical body because of their grievously sinful acts, such as suicide. The last resort of the ghostly characters in human society is to take shelter of suicide, either material or spiritual. Material suicide causes loss of the physical body, and spiritual suicide causes loss of the individual identity. Māyāvādī philosophers desire to lose their individuality and merge into the impersonal spiritual *brahmajyoti* existence. Lord Śiva, being very kind to the ghosts, sees that although they are condemned, they get physical bodies. He places them into the wombs of women who indulge in sexual intercourse regardless of the restrictions on time and circumstance. Kaśyapa wanted to impress this fact upon Diti so that she might wait for a while.

TEXT 25

श्मशानचक्रानिलधूलिधूम्र-
विकीर्णविद्योतजटाकलापः ।

भस्मावगुण्ठामलरुक्मदेहो
देवस्त्रिभिः पश्यति देवरस्ते ॥२५॥

śmaśāna-cakrānila-dhūli-dhūmra-
vikīrṇa-vidyota-jaṭā-kalāpaḥ
bhasmāvaguṇṭhāmala-rukma-deho
devas tribhiḥ paśyati devaras te

śmaśāna—burning crematorium; *cakra-anila*—whirlwind; *dhūli*—dust; *dhūmra*—smoky; *vikīrṇa-vidyota*—thus smeared over beauty; *jaṭā-kalāpaḥ*—bunches of matted hair; *bhasma*—ashes; *avaguṇṭha*—covered by; *amala*—stainless; *rukma*—reddish; *dehaḥ*—body; *devaḥ*—the demigod; *tribhiḥ*—with three eyes; *paśyati*—sees; *devaraḥ*—younger brother of the husband; *te*—your.

TRANSLATION

Lord Śiva's body is reddish, and he is unstained, but he is covered with ashes. His hair is dusty from the whirlwind dust of the burning crematorium. He is the younger brother of your husband, and he sees with his three eyes.

PURPORT

Lord Śiva is not an ordinary living entity, nor is he in the category of Viṣṇu, or the Supreme Personality of Godhead. He is far more powerful than any living entity up to the standard of Brahmā, yet he is not on an equal level with Viṣṇu. Since he is almost like Lord Viṣṇu, Śiva can see past, present and future. One of his eyes is like the sun, another is like the moon, and his third eye, which is between his eyebrows, is like fire. He can generate fire from his middle eye, and he is able to vanquish any powerful living entity, including Brahmā, yet he does not live pompously in a nice house, etc., nor does he possess any material properties, although he is master of the material world. He lives mostly in the crematorium, where dead bodies are burnt, and the whirlwind dust of the crematorium is his bodily dress. He is unstained by material contamination. Kaśyapa took him as his younger brother because the youngest sister of Diti (Kaśyapa's wife) was married to Lord Śiva. The husband of one's sister is considered one's brother. By that social relationship, Lord Śiva happened to be the younger brother of Kaśyapa. Kaśyapa warned his wife that because Lord Śiva would see their sex indulgence, the time was not appropriate. Diti might argue that they would enjoy sex life in a private place, but Kaśyapa reminded her that Lord Śiva has three eyes, called the sun, moon and fire, and one cannot escape his vigilance any more than one can escape Viṣṇu. Although seen by the police, a criminal is sometimes not immediately punished; the police wait for the proper time to apprehend him. The forbidden time for sexual intercourse would be noted by Lord Śiva, and Diti would meet with proper punishment by giving birth to a child of ghostly character or a godless impersonalist. Kaśyapa foresaw this, and thus he warned his wife Diti.

TEXT 26

न यस्य लोके स्वजनः परो वा
नात्यादृतो नोत कश्चिद्विगर्ह्यः ।
वयं व्रतैर्यच्चरणापविद्धा-
माशास्महेऽजां बत भुक्तभोगाम् ॥२६॥

na yasya loke sva-janaḥ paro vā
nātyādṛto nota kaścid vigarhyaḥ
vayaṁ vratair yac-caraṇāpaviddhām
āśāsmahe 'jāṁ bata bhukta-bhogām

na—never; *yasya*—of whom; *loke*—in the world; *sva-janaḥ*—kinsman; *paraḥ*—unconnected; *vā*—nor; *na*—neither; *ati*—greater; *ādṛtaḥ*—favorable; *na*—not; *uta*—or; *kaścit*—anyone; *vigarhyaḥ*—criminal; *vayam*—we; *vrataiḥ*—by vows; *yat*—whose; *caraṇa*—feet; *apaviddhām*—rejected; *āśāsmahe*—respectfully worship; *ajām*—*mahā-prasāda*; *bata*—certainly; *bhukta-bhogām*—remnants of foodstuff.

TRANSLATION

Lord Śiva regards no one as his relative, yet there is no one who is not connected with him; he does not regard anyone as very favorable or abominable. We respectfully worship the remnants of his foodstuff, and we vow to accept what is rejected by him.

PURPORT

Kaśyapa informed his wife that just because Lord Śiva happened to be his brother-in-law, that should not encourage her in her offense towards him. Kaśyapa warned her that actually Lord Śiva is not connected with anyone, nor is anyone his enemy. Since he is one of the three controllers of the universal affairs, he is equal to everyone. His greatness is incomparable because he is a great devotee of the Supreme Personality of Godhead. It is said that among all the devotees of the Personality of Godhead, Lord Śiva is the greatest. Thus the remnants of foodstuff left by him are accepted by other devotees as *mahā-prasāda*, or great spiritual foodstuff. The remnants of foodstuff offered to Lord Kṛṣṇa are called *prasāda,* but when the same *prasāda* is eaten by a great devotee like Lord Śiva, it is called *mahā-prasāda.* Lord Śiva is so great that he does not care for the material prosperity for which every one of us is so eager. Pārvatī, who is the powerful material nature personified, is under his full control as his wife, yet he does not use her even to build a residential house. He prefers to remain without shelter, and his great wife also agrees to live with him humbly. People in general worship goddess Durgā, the wife of Lord Śiva, for material prosperity, but Lord Śiva engages her in his service without material desire. He simply advises his great wife that of all kinds of worship, the worship of Viṣṇu is the highest, and greater than that is the worship of a great devotee or anything in relation with Viṣṇu.

TEXT 27

यस्यानवद्याचरितं मनीषिणो
गृणन्त्यविद्यापटलं बिभित्सवः ।
निरस्तसाम्यातिशयोऽपि यत्स्वयं
पिशाचचर्यामचरद्गतिः सताम् ॥२७॥

yasyānavadyācaritaṁ manīṣiṇo
gṛṇanty avidyā-paṭalaṁ bibhitsavaḥ
nirasta-sāmyātiśayo 'pi yat svayaṁ
piśāca-caryām acarad gatiḥ satām

yasya—whose; *anavadya*—unimpeachable; *ācaritam*—character; *manīṣiṇaḥ*—great sages; *gṛṇanti*—follow; *avidyā*—nescience; *paṭalam*—mass; *bibhitsavaḥ*—desiring to dismantle; *nirasta*—nullified; *sāmya*—equality; *atiśayaḥ*—greatness; *api*—in spite of; *yat*—as; *svayam*—personally; *piśāca*—devil; *caryām*—activities; *acarat*—performed; *gatiḥ*—destination; *satām*—of the devotees of the Lord.

TRANSLATION

Although no one in the material world is equal to or greater than Lord Śiva, and although his unimpeachable character is followed by great souls to dismantle the mass of nescience, he nevertheless remains as if a devil to give salvation to all devotees of the Lord.

PURPORT

Lord Śiva's uncivilized, devilish characteristics are never abominable because he teaches the sincere devotees of the Lord how to practice detachment from material enjoyment. He is called Mahādeva, or the greatest of all demigods, and no one is equal to or greater than him in the material world. He is almost equal with Lord Viṣṇu. Although he always associates with Māyā, Durgā, he is above the reactionary stage of the three modes of material nature, and although he is in charge of devilish characters in the mode of ignorance, he is not affected by such association.

TEXT 28

हसन्ति यस्याचरितं हि दुर्भगाः
स्वात्मन्-रतस्याविदुषः समीहितम् ।
यैर्वस्त्रमाल्याभरणानुलेपनैः
श्वभोजनं स्वात्मतयोपलालितम् ॥२८॥

hasanti yasyācaritaṁ hi durbhagāḥ
svātman-ratasyāviduṣaḥ samīhitam
yair vastra-mālyābharaṇānulepanaiḥ
śva-bhojanaṁ svātmatayopalālitam

hasanti—laugh at; *yasya*—whose; *ācaritam*—activity; *hi*—certainly; *durbhagāḥ*—the unfortunate; *sva-ātman*—in the self; *ratasya*—of one engaged; *aviduṣaḥ*—not knowing; *samīhitam*—his purpose; *yaiḥ*—by whom; *vastra*—clothing; *mālya*—garlands; *ābharaṇa*—ornaments; *anu*—such luxurious; *lepanaiḥ*—with ointments; *śva-bhojanam*—eatable by the dogs; *sva-ātmatayā*—as if the self; *upalālitam*—fondled.

TRANSLATION

Unfortunate, foolish persons, not knowing that he is engaged in his own self, laugh at him. Such foolish persons engage in maintaining the body—which is eatable by dogs—with dresses, ornaments, garlands and ointments.

PURPORT

Lord Śiva never accepts any luxurious dress, garland, ornament or ointment. But those who are addicted to the decoration of the body, which is finally eatable by dogs, very luxuriously maintain it as the self. Such persons do not understand Lord Śiva, but they approach him for luxurious material comforts. There are two kinds of devotees of Lord Śiva. One class is the gross materialist seeking only bodily comforts from Lord Śiva, and the other class desires to become one with him. They are mostly impersonalists and prefer to chant *śivo 'ham,* "I am Śiva," or "After liberation I shall become one with Lord Śiva." In other words, the *karmīs* and *jñānīs* are generally devotees of Lord Śiva, but they do not properly understand his real purpose in life. Sometimes so-called devotees of Lord Śiva imitate him in using poisonous intoxicants. Lord Śiva once swallowed an ocean of poison, and thus his throat became blue. The imitation Śivas try to follow him by indulging in poisons, and thus they are ruined. The real purpose of Lord Śiva is to serve the Soul of the soul, Lord Kṛṣṇa. He desires that all luxurious articles, such as nice garments, garlands, ornaments and cosmetics, be given to Lord Kṛṣṇa only, because Kṛṣṇa is the real enjoyer. He refuses to accept such luxurious items himself because they are only meant for Kṛṣṇa. However, since they do not know this purpose of Lord Śiva, foolish persons either laugh at him or profitlessly try to imitate him.

TEXT 29

ब्रह्मादयो यत्कृतसेतुपाला
यत्कारणं विश्वमिदं च माया ।
आज्ञाकरी यस्य पिशाचचर्या
अहो विभूम्नश्चरितं विडम्बनम् ॥२९॥

brahmādayo yat-kṛta-setu-pālā
yat-kāraṇaṁ viśvam idaṁ ca māyā
ājñā-karī yasya piśāca-caryā
aho vibhūmnaś caritaṁ viḍambanam

brahma-ādayaḥ—demigods like Brahmā; *yat*—whose; *kṛta*—activities; *setu*—religious rites; *pālāḥ*—observers; *yat*—one who is; *kāraṇam*—the origin of; *viśvam*—the universe; *idam*—this; *ca*—also; *māyā*—material energy; *ājñā-karī*—order carrier; *yasya*—whose; *piśāca*—devilish; *caryā*—activity; *aho*—O my lord; *vibhūmnaḥ*—of the great; *caritam*—character; *viḍambanam*—simply imitation.

TRANSLATION

Demigods like Brahmā also follow the religious rites observed by him. He is the controller of the material energy, which causes the creation of the material world. He is great, and therefore his devilish characteristics are simply imitation.

PURPORT

Lord Śiva is the husband of Durgā, the controller of the material energy. Durgā is personified material energy, and Lord Śiva, being her husband, is the controller of the material energy. He is also the incarnation of the mode of ignorance and one of the three deities representing the Supreme Lord. As His representative, Lord Śiva is identical with the Supreme Personality of Godhead. He is very great, and his renunciation of all material enjoyment is an ideal example of how one should be materially unattached. One should therefore follow in his footsteps and be unattached to matter, not imitate his uncommon acts like drinking poison.

TEXT 30

मैत्रेय उवाच

सैवं संविदिते भर्त्रा मन्मथोन्मथितेन्द्रिया ।
जग्राह वासो ब्रह्मर्षेर्वृषलीव गतत्रपा ॥३०॥

maitreya uvāca
saivaṁ saṁvidite bhartrā
manmathonmathitendriyā
jagrāha vāso brahmarṣer
vṛṣalīva gata-trapā

maitreyaḥ uvāca—Maitreya said; *sā*—she; *evam*—thus; *saṁvidite*—in spite of being informed; *bhartrā*—by her husband; *manmatha*—by Cupid; *unmathita*—being pressed; *indriyā*—senses; *jagrāha*—caught hold of; *vāsaḥ*—clothing; *brahma-ṛṣeḥ*—of the great *brāhmaṇa*—sage; *vṛṣalī*—public prostitute; *iva*—like; *gata-trapā*—without shame.

TRANSLATION

Maitreya said: Diti was thus informed by her husband, but she was pressed by Cupid for sexual satisfaction. She caught hold of the clothing of the great brāhmaṇa sage, just like a shameless public prostitute.

PURPORT

The difference between a married wife and a public prostitute is that one is restrained in sex life by the rules and regulations of the scriptures, whereas the other is unrestricted in sex life and is conducted solely by the strong sex urge. Although very enlightened, Kaśyapa, the great sage, became a victim of his prostitute wife. Such is the strong force of material energy.

TEXT 31

स विदित्वाथ भार्यायास्तं निर्बन्धं विकर्मणि ।
नत्वा दिष्टाय रहसि तयाथोपविवेश हि ॥३१॥

sa viditvātha bhāryāyās
taṁ nirbandhaṁ vikarmaṇi
natvā diṣṭāya rahasi
tayāthopaviveśa hi

saḥ—he; *viditvā*—understanding; *atha*—thereupon; *bhāryāyāḥ*—of the wife; *tam*—that; *nirbandham*—obstinacy; *vikarmaṇi*—in the forbidden act; *natvā*—offering obeisances; *diṣṭāya*—unto worshipable fate; *rahasi*—in a secluded place; *tayā*—with her; *atha*—thus; *upaviveśa*—lay; *hi*—certainly.

TRANSLATION

Understanding his wife's purpose, he was obliged to perform the forbidden act, and thus after offering his obeisances unto worshipable fate, he lay with her in a secluded place.

PURPORT

It appears from the talks of Kaśyapa with his wife that he was a worshiper of Lord Śiva, and although he knew that Lord Śiva would not be pleased with him for such a forbidden act, he was obliged to act by his wife's desire, and thus he offered his obeisances unto fate. He knew that the child born of such untimely sexual intercourse would certainly not be a good child, but could not protect himself because he was too obligated to his wife. In a similar case, however, when Ṭhākura Haridāsa was tempted by a public prostitute at the dead of night, he avoided the allurement because of his perfection in Kṛṣṇa consciousness. That is the difference between a Kṛṣṇa conscious person and others. Kaśyapa Muni was greatly learned and enlightened, and he knew all the rules and regulations of systematic life, yet he failed to protect himself from the attack of sex desire. Ṭhākura Haridāsa was not born of a *brāhmaṇa* family, nor was he himself *brāhmaṇa*, yet he could protect himself from such an attack due to his being Kṛṣṇa conscious. Ṭhākura Haridāsa used to chant the holy name of the Lord three hundred thousand times daily.

TEXT 32

अथोपस्पृश्य सलिलं प्राणानायम्य वाग्यतः ।
ध्यायञ्जजाप विरजं ब्रह्म ज्योतिः सनातनम् ॥३२॥

athopaspṛśya salilaṁ
prāṇān āyamya vāg-yataḥ
dhyāyañ jajāpa virajaṁ
brahma jyotiḥ sanātanam

atha—thereafter; *upaspṛśya*—touching or taking bath in water; *salilam*—water; *prāṇān āyamya*—practicing trance; *vāk-yataḥ*—controlling speech; *dhyāyan*—meditating; *jajāpa*—chanted within the mouth; *virajam*—pure; *brahma*—Gāyatrī hymns; *jyotiḥ*—effulgence; *sanātanam*—eternal.

TRANSLATION

Thereafter the brāhmaṇa took his bath in the water and controlled his speech by practicing trance, meditating on the eternal effulgence and chanting the holy Gāyatrī hymns within his mouth.

PURPORT

As one has to take bath after using the toilet, so one has to wash himself with water after sexual intercourse, especially when at a forbidden time. Kaśyapa Muni meditated on the impersonal *brahmajyoti* by chanting the Gāyatrī *mantra* within his mouth. When a Vedic *mantra* is chanted within the mouth so that only the chanter can hear, the chanting is called *japa.* But when such *mantras* are chanted loudly, it is called *kīrtana.* The Vedic hymn Hare Kṛṣṇa, Hare Kṛṣṇa, Kṛṣṇa Kṛṣṇa, Hare Hare/ Hare Rāma, Hare Rāma, Rāma Rāma, Hare Hare can be chanted both softly to oneself or loudly; therefore it is called the *mahā-mantra,* or the great hymn.

Kaśyapa Muni appears to be an impersonalist. Comparing his character with that of Ṭhākura Haridāsa as referred to above, it is clear that the personalist is stronger in sense control than the impersonalist. This is explained in *Bhagavad-gītā* as *paraṁ dṛṣṭvā nivartate*; i.e., one ceases to accept lower grade things when one is situated in a superior condition. One is supposed to be purified after taking bath and chanting Gāyatrī, but the *mahā-mantra* is so powerful that one can chant loudly or softly, in any condition, and he is protected from all the evils of material existence.

TEXT 33

दितिस्तु व्रीडिता तेन कर्मावद्येन भारत ।
उपसङ्गम्य विप्रर्षिमधोमुख्यभ्यभाषत ॥३३॥

ditis tu vrīḍitā tena
karmāvadyena bhārata
upasaṅgamya viprarṣim
adho-mukhy abhyabhāṣata

ditiḥ—Diti, the wife of Kaśyapa; *tu*—but; *vrīḍitā*—ashamed; *tena*—by that; *karma*—act; *avadyena*—faulty; *bhārata*—O son of the Bharata family; *upasaṅgamya*—going nearer to;

vipra-ṛṣim—the *brāhmaṇa*—sage; *adhaḥ-mukhī*—with her face lowered; *abhyabhāṣata*—politely said.

TRANSLATION

O son of the Bharata family, Diti, after this, went nearer to her husband, her face lowered because of her faulty action. She spoke as follows.

PURPORT

When one is ashamed of an abominable action, one naturally becomes down-faced. Diti came to her senses after the abominable sexual intercourse with her husband. Such sexual intercourse is condemned as prostitution. In other words, sex life with one's wife is equal to prostitution if the regulations are not properly followed.

TEXT 34

दितिरुवाच
न मे गर्भमिमं ब्रह्मन् भूतानामृषभोऽवधीत् ।
रुद्रः पतिर्हि भूतानां यस्याकरवमंहसम् ॥३४॥

ditir uvāca
na me garbham imaṁ brahman
bhūtānām ṛṣabho 'vadhīt
rudraḥ patir hi bhūtānāṁ
yasyākaravam aṁhasam

ditiḥ uvāca—the beautiful Diti said; *na*—not; *me*—my; *garbham*—pregnancy; *imam*—this; *brahman*—O *brāhmaṇa*; *bhūtānām*—of all living entities; *ṛṣabhaḥ*—the noblest of all living entities; *avadhīt*—let him kill; *rudraḥ*—Lord Śiva; *patiḥ*—master; *hi*—certainly; *bhūtānām*—of all living entities; *yasya*—whose; *akaravam*—I have done; *aṁhasam*—offense.

TRANSLATION

The beautiful Diti said: My dear brāhmaṇa, kindly see that my embryo is not killed by Lord Śiva, the lord of all living entities, because of the great offense I have committed against him.

PURPORT

Diti was conscious of her offense and was anxious to be excused by Lord Śiva. Lord Śiva has two popular names, Rudra and Āśutoṣa. He is very prone to anger as well as quickly pacified. Diti knew that because of his being quickly angered he might spoil the pregnancy she had so unlawfully achieved. But because he was also Āśutoṣa, she implored her *brāhmaṇa*-husband to help her in pacifying Lord Śiva, for her husband was a great devotee of Lord Śiva. In other words, Lord Śiva might have been angry with Diti because she obliged her husband to transgress the law, but he would not refuse her husband's prayer. Therefore the application for excuse was submitted through her husband. She prayed to Lord Śiva as follows.

TEXT 35

नमो रुद्राय महते देवायोग्राय मीढुषे ।
शिवाय न्यस्तदण्डाय धृतदण्डाय मन्यवे ॥३५॥

namo rudrāya mahate
devāyogrāya mīḍhuṣe
śivāya nyasta-daṇḍāya
dhṛta-daṇḍāya manyave

namaḥ—all obeisances unto; *rudrāya*—unto the angry Lord Śiva; *mahate*—unto the great; *devāya*—unto the demigod; *ugrāya*—unto the ferocious; *mīḍhuṣe*—unto the fulfiller of all material desires; *śivāya*—unto the all-auspicious; *nyasta-daṇḍāya*—unto the forgiving; *dhṛta-daṇḍāya*—unto the immediate chastiser; *manyave*—unto the angry.

TRANSLATION

Let me offer my obeisances unto the angry Lord Śiva, who is simultaneously the very ferocious great demigod and the fulfiller of all material desires. He is all-auspicious and forgiving, but his anger can immediately move him to chastise.

PURPORT

Diti prayed for the mercy of Lord Śiva very cleverly. She prayed: "The lord can cause me to cry, but if he likes he can also stop my crying because he is Āśutoṣa. He is so great that if he likes he can immediately destroy my pregnancy, but by his mercy he can also fulfill my desire that my pregnancy not be spoiled. Because he is all-auspicious, it is not difficult for him to excuse me from being punished, although he is now ready to punish me because I have moved his great anger. He appears like a man, but he is the lord of all men."

TEXT 36

स नः प्रसीदतां भामो भगवानुर्वनुग्रहः ।
व्याधस्याप्यनुकम्प्यानां स्त्रीणां देवः सतीपतिः ॥३६॥

sa naḥ prasīdatāṁ bhāmo
bhagavān urv-anugrahaḥ
vyādhasyāpy anukampyānāṁ
strīṇāṁ devaḥ satī-patiḥ

saḥ—he; *naḥ*—with us; *prasīdatām*—be pleased; *bhāmaḥ*—brother-in-law; *bhagavān*—the personality of all opulences; *uru*—very great; *anugrahaḥ*—merciful; *vyādhasya*—of the hunter; *api*—also; *anukampyānām*—of the objects of mercy; *strīṇām*—of the women; *devaḥ*—the worshipable lord; *satī-patiḥ*—the husband of Satī (the chaste).

TRANSLATION

Let him be pleased with us, since he is my brother-in-law, the husband of my sister Satī. He is also the worshipable lord of all women. He is the personality of all opulences and can show mercy towards women, who are excused even by the uncivilized hunters.

PURPORT

Lord Śiva is the husband of Satī, one of the sisters of Diti. Diti invoked the pleasure of her sister Satī so that Satī would request her husband to excuse her. Besides that, Lord Śiva is the worshipable lord of all women. He is naturally very kind towards women, on whom even the uncivilized hunters also show their mercy. Since Lord Śiva is himself associated with women, he knows very well their defective nature, and he might not take very seriously Diti's unavoidable offense, which occurred due to her faulty nature. Every virgin girl is supposed to be a devotee of Lord Śiva. Diti remembered her childhood worship of Lord Śiva and begged his mercy.

TEXT 37

मैत्रेय उवाच
स्वसर्गस्याशिषं लोक्यामाशासानां प्रवेपतीम् ।
निवृत्तसन्ध्यानियमो भार्यामाह प्रजापतिः ॥३७॥

maitreya uvāca
sva-sargasyāśiṣaṁ lokyām
āśāsānāṁ pravepatīm

nivṛtta-sandhyā-niyamo
bhāryām āha prajāpatiḥ

maitreyaḥ uvāca—the great sage Maitreya said; *sva-sargasya*—of her own children; *āśiṣam*—welfare; *lokyām*—in the world; *āśāsānām*—desiring; *pravepatīm*—while trembling; *nivṛtta*—averted from; *sandhyā-niyamaḥ*—the rules and regulations of evening; *bhāryām*—unto the wife; *āha*—said; *prajāpatiḥ*—the progenitor.

TRANSLATION

Maitreya said: The great sage Kaśyapa thus addressed his wife, who was trembling because of fear that her husband was offended. She understood that he had been dissuaded from his daily duties of offering evening prayers, yet she desired the welfare of her children in the world.

TEXT 38

कश्यप उवाच
अप्रायत्यादात्मनस्ते दोषान्मौहूर्तिकादुत ।
मन्निदेशातिचारेण देवानां चातिहेलनात् ॥३८॥

kaśyapa uvāca
aprāyatyād ātmanas te
doṣān mauhūrtikād uta
man-nideśāticāreṇa
devānāṁ cātihelanāt

kaśyapaḥ uvāca—the learned *brāhmaṇa* Kaśyapa said; *aprāyatyāt*—because of the pollution; *ātmanaḥ*—of the mind; *te*—your; *doṣāt*—because of defilement; *mauhūrtikāt*—in terms of the moment; *uta*—also; *mat*—my; *nideśa*—direction; *aticāreṇa*—being too neglectful; *devānām*—of the demigods; *ca*—also; *atihelanāt*—being too apathetic.

TRANSLATION

The learned Kaśyapa said: Because of your mind's being polluted, because of defilement of the particular time, because of your negligence of my directions, and because of your being apathetic to the demigods, everything was inauspicious.

PURPORT

The conditions for having good progeny in society are that the husband should be disciplined in religious and regulative principles and the wife should be faithful to the husband. In *Bhagavad-gītā* (7.11) it is said that sexual intercourse according to religious principles is a representation of Kṛṣṇa consciousness. Before engaging in sexual intercourse, both the husband and the wife must consider their mental condition, the particular time, the husband's direction, and obedience to the demigods. According to Vedic society, there is a suitable auspicious time for sex life, which is called the time for *garbhādhāna.* Diti neglected all the principles of scriptural injunction, and therefore, although she was very anxious for auspicious children, she was informed that her children would not be worthy to be the sons of a *brāhmaṇa.* There is a clear indication herein that a *brāhmaṇa's* son is not always a *brāhmaṇa.* Personalities like Rāvaṇa and Hiraṇyakaśipu were actually born of *brāhmaṇas,* but they were not accepted as *brāhmaṇas* because their fathers did not follow the regulative principles for their birth. Such children are called demons, or Rākṣasas. There were only one or two Rākṣasas in the previous ages due to negligence of the disciplinary methods, but during the age of Kali there is no discipline in sex life. How, then, can one expect good children? Certainly unwanted children cannot be a source of happiness in society, but through the Kṛṣṇa consciousness movement they can be raised to the human standard by chanting the holy name of God. That is the unique contribution of Lord Caitanya to human society.

TEXT 39

भविष्यतस्तवाभद्रावभद्रे जाठराधमौ ।
लोकान् सपालांस्त्रींश्चण्डि मुहुराक्रन्दयिष्यतः ॥३९॥

bhaviṣyatas tavābhadrāv
abhadre jāṭharādhamau
lokān sa-pālāṁs trīṁś caṇḍi
muhur ākrandayiṣyataḥ

bhaviṣyataḥ—will take birth; *tava*—your; *abhadrau*—two contemptuous sons; *abhadre*—O unlucky one; *jāṭhara-adhamau*—born of a condemned womb; *lokān*—all planets; *sa-pālān*—with their rulers; *trīn*—three; *caṇḍi*—haughty one; *muhuḥ*—constantly; *ākran-dayiṣyataḥ*—will cause lamentation.

TRANSLATION

O haughty one, you will have two contemptuous sons born of your condemned womb. Unlucky woman, they will cause constant lamentation to all the three worlds!

PURPORT

Contemptuous sons are born of the condemned womb of their mother. In *Bhagavad-gītā* (1.40) it is said, "When there is deliberate negligence of the regulative principles of religious life, the women as a class become polluted, and as a result there are unwanted children." This is especially true for boys; if the mother is not good, there cannot be good sons. The learned Kaśyapa could foresee the character of the sons who would be born of the condemned womb of Diti. The womb was condemned because of the mother's being too sexually inclined and thus transgressing all the laws and injunctions of the scriptures. In a society where such women are predominant, one should not expect good children.

TEXT 40

प्राणिनां हन्यमानानां दीनानामकृतागसाम् ।
स्त्रीणां निगृह्यमाणानां कोपितेषु महात्मसु ॥४०॥

prāṇinām̐ hanyamānānām
dīnānām akṛtāgasām
strīṇām̐ nigṛhyamāṇānām
kopiteṣu mahātmasu

prāṇinām—when the living entities; *hanyamānānām*—being killed; *dīnānām*—of the poor; *akṛta-āgasām*—of the faultless; *strīṇām*—of the women; *nigṛhyamāṇānām*—being tortured; *kopiteṣu*—being enraged; *mahātmasu*—when the great souls.

TRANSLATION

They will kill poor, faultless living entities, torture women and enrage the great souls.

PURPORT

Demoniac activities are predominant when innocent, faultless living entities are killed, women are tortured, and the great souls engaged in Kṛṣṇa consciousness are enraged. In a demoniac society, innocent animals are killed to satisfy the tongue, and women are tortured by unnecessary sexual indulgence. Where there are women and meat, there must be liquor and sex indulgence. When these are prominent in society, by God's grace one can expect a change in the social order by the Lord Himself or by His bona fide representative.

TEXT 41

तदा विश्वेश्वरः क्रुद्धो भगवाल्लोकभावनः ।
हनिष्यत्यवतीर्यासौ यथाद्रीन् शतपर्वधृक् ॥४१॥

tadā viśveśvaraḥ kruddho
bhagavāl loka-bhāvanaḥ
haniṣyaty avatīryāsau
yathādrīn śataparva-dhṛk

tadā—at that time; *viśva-īśvaraḥ*—the Lord of the universe; *kruddhaḥ*—in great anger; *bhagavān*—the Supreme Personality of Godhead; *loka-bhāvanaḥ*—desiring the welfare of the people in general; *haniṣyati*—will kill; *avatīrya*—descending Himself; *asau*—He; *yathā*—as if; *adrīn*—the mountains; *śata-parva-dhṛk*—the controller of the thunderbolt (Indra).

TRANSLATION

At that time the Lord of the universe, the Supreme Personality of Godhead, who is the well-wisher of all living entities, will descend and kill them, just as Indra smashes the mountains with his thunderbolts.

PURPORT

As stated in *Bhagavad-gītā* (4.8), the Lord descends as an incarnation to deliver the devotees and kill the miscreants. The Lord of the universe and of everything would appear to kill the sons of Diti because of their offending the devotees of the Lord. There are many agents of the Lord, such as Indra, Candra, Varuṇa, goddess Durgā, and Kālī, who can chastise any formidable miscreants in the world. The example of mountains being smashed by a thunderbolt is very appropriate. The mountain is considered the most strongly built body within the universe, yet it can be easily smashed by the arrangement of the Supreme Lord. The Supreme Personality of Godhead does not need to descend in order to kill any strongly built body; He comes down just for the sake of His devotees. Everyone is subject to the miseries offered by material nature, but because the activities of miscreants, such as killing innocent people and animals or torturing women, are harmful to everyone and are therefore a source of pain for the devotees, the Lord comes down. He descends only to give relief to His ardent devotees. The killing of the miscreant by the Lord is also the mercy of the Lord towards the miscreant, although apparently the Lord takes the side of the devotee. Since the Lord is absolute, there is no difference between His activities of killing the miscreants and favoring the devotees.

TEXT 42

दितिरुवाच
वधं भगवता साक्षात्सुनाभोदारबाहुना ।
आशासे पुत्रयोर्मह्यं मा क्रुद्धाद्ब्राह्मणादप्रभो ॥४२॥

ditir uvāca
vadhaṁ bhagavatā sākṣāt
sunābhodāra-bāhunā
āśāse putrayor mahyaṁ
mā kruddhād brāhmaṇād prabho

ditiḥ uvāca—Diti said; *vadham*—the killing; *bhagavatā*—by the Supreme Personality of Godhead; *sākṣāt*—directly; *sunābha*—with His Sudarśana weapon; *udāra*—very magnanimous; *bāhunā*—by the arms; *āśāse*—I desire; *putrayoḥ*—of the sons; *mahyam*—of mine; *mā*—never be it so; *kruddhāt*—by the rage; *brāhmaṇāt*—of the *brāhmaṇas; prabho*—O my husband.

TRANSLATION

Diti said: It is very good that my sons will be magnanimously killed by the arms of the Personality of Godhead with His Sudarśana weapon. O my husband, may they never be killed by the wrath of the brāhmaṇa-devotees.

PURPORT

When Diti heard from her husband that the great souls would be angered by the activities of her sons, she was very anxious. She thought that her sons might be killed by the wrath of the *brāhmaṇas.* The Lord does not appear when the *brāhmaṇas* become angry at someone, because the wrath of a *brāhmaṇa* is sufficient in itself. He certainly appears, however, when His devotee simply becomes sorry. A devotee of the Lord never prays to the Lord to appear for the sake of the troubles the miscreants cause for him, and he never bothers Him by asking for protection. Rather, the Lord is anxious to give protection to the devotees. Diti knew well that the killing of her sons by the Lord would also be His mercy, and therefore she says that the wheel and arms of the Lord are magnanimous. If someone is killed by the wheel of the Lord and is thus fortunate enough to see the arms of the Lord, that is sufficient for his liberation. Such good fortune is not achieved even by the great sages.

TEXT 43

न ब्रह्मदण्डदग्धस्य न भूतभयदस्य च ।
नारकाश्चानुगृह्णन्ति यां यां योनिमसौ गतः ॥४३॥

na brahma-daṇḍa-dagdhasya
na bhūta-bhayadasya ca
nārakāś cānugṛhṇanti
yāṁ yāṁ yonim asau gataḥ

na—never; *brahma-daṇḍa*—punishment by a *brāhmaṇa; dagdhasya*—of one who is so punished; *na*—neither; *bhūta-bhaya-dasya*—of one who is always fearful to the living entities; *ca*—also; *nārakāḥ*—those condemned to hell; *ca*—also; *anugṛhṇanti*—do any favor; *yām yām*—whichever; *yonim*—species of life; *asau*—the offender; *gataḥ*—goes.

TRANSLATION

A person who is condemned by a brāhmaṇa or is always fearful to other living entities is not favored either by those who are already in hell or by those in the species in which he is born.

PURPORT

A practical example of a condemned species of life is the dog. Dogs are so condemned that they never show any sympathy to their contemporaries.

TEXTS 44-45

कश्यप उवाच
कृतशोकानुतापेन सद्यः प्रत्यवमर्शनात् ।
भगवत्युरुमानाच्च भवे मय्यपि चादरात् ॥४४॥
पुत्रस्यैव च पुत्राणां भवितैकः सतां मतः ।
गास्यन्ति यद्यशः शुद्धं भगवद्यशसा समम् ॥४५॥

kaśyapa uvāca
kṛta-śokānutāpena
sadyaḥ pratyavamarśanāt
bhagavaty uru-mānāc ca
bhave mayy api cādarāt

putrasyaiva ca putrāṇāṁ
bhavitaikaḥ satāṁ mataḥ
gāsyanti yad-yaśaḥ śuddhaṁ
bhagavad-yaśasā samam

kaśyapaḥ uvāca—the learned Kaśyapa said; *kṛta-śoka*—having lamented; *anutāpena*—by penitence; *sadyaḥ*—immediately; *pratyavamarśanāt*—by proper deliberation; *bhagavati*—unto the Supreme Personality of Godhead; *uru*—great; *mānāt*—adoration; *ca*—and; *bhave*—unto Lord Śiva; *mayi api*—unto me also; *ca*—and; *ādarāt*—by respect; *putrasya*—of the son; *eva*—certainly; *ca*—and; *putrāṇām*—of the sons; *bhavitā*—shall be born; *ekaḥ*—one; *satām*—of the devotees; *mataḥ*—approved; *gāsyanti*—will broadcast; *yat*—of whom; *yaśaḥ*—recognition; *śuddham*—transcendental; *bhagavat*—of the Personality of Godhead; *yaśasā*—with recognition; *samam*—equally.

TRANSLATION

The learned Kaśyapa said: Because of your lamentation, penitence and proper deliberation, and also because of your unflinching faith in the Supreme Personality of Godhead and your adoration for Lord Śiva and me, one of the sons [Prahlāda] of your son [Hiraṇyakaśipu] will be an approved devotee of the Lord, and his fame will be broadcast equally with that of the Personality of Godhead.

TEXT 46

योगैर्हेमेव दुर्वर्णं भावयिष्यन्ति साधवः ।
निर्वैरादिभिरात्मानं यच्छीलमनुवर्तितुम् ॥४६॥

yogair hemeva durvarṇaṁ
bhāvayiṣyanti sādhavaḥ
nirvairādibhir ātmānaṁ
yac-chīlam anuvartitum

yogaiḥ—by the rectifying processes; *hema*—gold; *iva*—like; *durvarṇam*—inferior quality; *bhāvayiṣyanti*—will purify; *sādhavaḥ*—saintly persons; *nirvaira-ādibhiḥ*—by practice of freedom from animosity, etc.; *ātmānam*—the self; *yat*—whose; *śīlam*—character; *anuvartitum*—to follow in the footsteps.

TRANSLATION

In order to follow in his footsteps, saintly persons will try to emulate his character by practicing freedom from animosity, just as the purifying processes rectify gold of inferior quality.

PURPORT

Yoga practice, the process of purifying one's existential identity, is based mainly on self-control. Without self-control one cannot practice freedom from animosity. In the conditional state, every living being is envious of another living being, but in the liberated state there is an absence of animosity. Prahlāda Mahārāja was tortured by his father in so many ways, yet after the death of his father he prayed for his father's liberation by the Supreme Personality of Godhead. He did not ask any benediction that he might have asked, but he prayed that his atheistic father might be liberated. He never cursed any of the persons who engaged in torturing him at the instigation of his father.

TEXT 47

यत्प्रसादादिदं विश्वं प्रसीदति यदात्मकम् ।
स स्वदृग्भगवान् यस्य तोष्यतेऽनन्यया दृशा ॥४७॥

yat-prasādād idaṁ viśvaṁ
prasīdati yad-ātmakam
sa sva-dṛg bhagavān yasya
toṣyate 'nanyayā dṛśā

yat—by whose; *prasādāt*—mercy of; *idam*—this; *viśvam*—universe; *prasīdati*—becomes happy; *yat*—whose; *ātmakam*—because of His omnipotence; *saḥ*—He; *sva-dṛk*—taking special care for His devotees; *bhagavān*—the Supreme Personality of Godhead; *yasya*—whose; *toṣyate*—becomes pleased; *ananyayā*—without deviation; *dṛśā*—by intelligence.

TRANSLATION

Everyone will be pleased with him because the Personality of Godhead, the supreme controller of the universe, is always satisfied with a devotee who does not wish for anything beyond Him.

PURPORT

The Supreme Personality of Godhead is situated everywhere as the Supersoul, and He can dictate to anyone and everyone as He likes. The would-be grandson of Diti, who was predicted to be a great devotee, would be liked by everyone, even by the enemies of his father, because he would have no other vision besides the Supreme Personality of Godhead. A pure devotee of the Lord sees the presence of his worshipable Lord everywhere. The Lord reciprocates in such a way that all living entities in whom the Lord is dwelling as the Supersoul also like a pure devotee because the Lord is present in their hearts and can dictate to them to be friendly to His devotee. There are many instances in history wherein even the most ferocious animal became friendly to a pure devotee of the Lord.

TEXT 48

स वै महाभागवतो महात्मा
महानुभावो महतां महिष्ठः ।
प्रवृद्धभक्त्या ह्यनुभाविताशये
निवेश्य वैकुण्ठमिमं विहास्यति ॥४८॥

sa vai mahā-bhāgavato mahātmā
mahānubhāvo mahatāṁ mahiṣṭhaḥ
pravṛddha-bhaktyā hy anubhāvitāśaye
niveśya vaikuṇṭham imaṁ vihāsyati

saḥ—he; *vai*—certainly; *mahā-bhāgavataḥ*—the topmost devotee; *mahā-ātmā*—expanded intelligence; *mahā-anubhāvaḥ*—expanded influence; *mahatām*—of the great souls; *mahiṣṭhaḥ*—the greatest; *pravṛddha*—well matured; *bhaktyā*—by devotional service; *hi*—certainly; *anubhāvita*—being situated in the *anubhāva* stage of ecstasy; *āśaye*—in the mind; *niveśya*—entering; *vaikuṇṭham*—in the spiritual sky; *imam*—this (material world); *vihāsyati*—will quit.

TRANSLATION

That topmost devotee of the Lord will have expanded intelligence and expanded influence and will be the greatest of the great souls. Due to matured devotional service, he will certainly be situated in transcendental ecstasy and will enter the spiritual sky after quitting this material world.

PURPORT

There are three stages of transcendental development in devotional service, which are technically called *sthāyi-bhāva, anubhāva* and *mahābhāva.* Continual perfect love of Godhead is called *sthāyi-bhāva,* and when it is performed in a particular type of transcendental relationship it is called *anubhāva.* But the stage of *mahābhāva* is visible amongst the personal pleasure potential energies of the Lord. It is understood that the grandson of Diti, namely Prahlāda Mahārāja, would constantly meditate on the Lord and reiterate His activities. Because he would constantly remain in meditation, he would easily transfer himself to the spiritual world after quitting his material body. Such meditation is still more conveniently performed by chanting and hearing the holy name of the Lord. This is especially recommended in this age of Kali.

TEXT 49

अलम्पटः शीलधरो गुणाकरो
हृष्टः परर्द्ध्या व्यथितो दुःखितेषु ।
अभूतशत्रुर्जगतः शोकहर्ता
नैदाघिकं तापमिवोडुराजः ॥४९॥

alampaṭaḥ śīla-dharo guṇākaro
hṛṣṭaḥ pararddhyā vyathito duḥkhiteṣu
abhūta-śatrur jagataḥ śoka-hartā
naidāghikaṁ tāpam ivoḍurājaḥ

alampaṭaḥ—virtuous; *śīla-dharaḥ*—qualified; *guṇa-ākaraḥ*—reservoir of all good qualities; *hṛṣṭaḥ*—jolly; *para-ṛddhyā*—by others' happiness; *vyathitaḥ*—distressed; *duḥkhiteṣu*—in others' unhappiness; *abhūta-śatruḥ*—without enemies; *jagataḥ*—of all the universe; *śoka-hartā*—destroyer of lamentation; *naidāghikam*—due to the summer sun; *tāpam*—distress; *iva*—likened; *uḍu-rājaḥ*—the moon.

TRANSLATION

He will be a virtuously qualified reservoir of all good qualities; he will be jolly and happy in others' happiness, distressed in others' distress, and will have no enemies. He will be a destroyer of the lamentation of all the universes, like the pleasant moon after the summer sun.

PURPORT

Prahlāda Mahārāja, the exemplary devotee of the Lord, had all the good qualities humanly possible. Although he was the emperor of this world, he was not profligate. Beginning from his childhood he was the reservoir of all good qualities. Without enumerating those qualities, it is said here summarily that he was endowed with all good qualities. That is the sign of a pure devotee. The most important characteristic of a pure devotee is that he is not *lampaṭa,* or licentious, and another quality is that he is always eager to mitigate the miseries of suffering humanity. The most obnoxious misery of a living entity is his forgetfulness of Kṛṣṇa. A pure devotee, therefore, always tries to evoke everyone's Kṛṣṇa consciousness. This is the panacea for all miseries.

TEXT 50

अन्तर्बहिश्चामलमब्जनेत्रं
स्वपूरुषेच्छानुगृहीतरूपम् ।

पौत्रस्तव श्रीललनाललामं
द्रष्टा स्फुरत्कुण्डलमण्डिताननम् ॥५०॥

antar bahiś cāmalam abja-netraṁ
sva-pūruṣecchānugṛhīta-rūpam
pautras tava śrī-lalanā-lalāmaṁ
draṣṭā sphurat-kuṇḍala-maṇḍitānanam

antaḥ—within; *bahiḥ*—without; *ca*—also; *amalam*—spotless; *abja-netram*—lotus eyes; *sva-pūruṣa*—own devotee; *icchā-anugṛhīta-rūpam*—accepting form according to desire; *pautraḥ*—grandchild; *tava*—your; *śrī-lalanā*—beautiful goddess of fortune; *lalāmam*—decorated; *draṣṭā*—will see; *sphurat-kuṇḍala*—with brilliant earrings; *maṇḍita*—decorated; *ānanam*—face.

TRANSLATION

Your grandson will be able to see, inside and outside, the Supreme Personality of Godhead, whose wife is the beautiful goddess of fortune. The Lord can assume the form desired by the devotee, and His face is always beautifully decorated with earrings.

PURPORT

It is predicted herewith that the grandson of Diti, Prahlāda Mahārāja, would not only see the Personality of Godhead within himself by meditation but would also be able to see Him personally with his eyes. This direct vision is possible only for one who is highly elevated in Kṛṣṇa consciousness, for the Lord is not possible to see with material eyes. The Supreme Personality of Godhead has multifarious eternal forms such as Kṛṣṇa, Baladeva, Saṅkarṣaṇa, Aniruddha, Pradyumna, Vāsudeva, Nārāyaṇa, Rāma, Nṛsiṁha, Varāha and Vāmana, and the devotee of the Lord knows all those Viṣṇu forms. A pure devotee becomes attached to one of the eternal forms of the Lord, and the Lord is pleased to appear before him in the form desired. A devotee does not imagine something whimsical about the form of the Lord, nor does he ever think that the Lord is impersonal and can assume a form desired by the nondevotee. The nondevotee has no idea of the form of the Lord, and thus he cannot think of any one of the above-mentioned forms. But whenever a devotee sees the Lord, he sees Him in a most beautifully decorated form, accompanied by His constant companion the goddess of fortune, who is eternally beautiful.

TEXT 51

मैत्रेय उवाच
श्रुत्वा भागवतं पौत्रममोदत दितिर्भृशम् ।
पुत्रयोश्च वधं कृष्णाद्विदित्वासीन्महामनाः ॥५१॥

maitreya uvāca
śrutvā bhāgavataṁ pautram
amodata ditir bhṛśam
putrayoś ca vadhaṁ kṛṣṇād
viditvāsīn mahā-manāḥ

maitreyaḥ uvāca—the sage Maitreya said; *śrutvā*—by hearing; *bhāgavatam*—to be a great devotee of the Lord; *pautram*—grandson; *amodata*—took pleasure; *ditiḥ*—Diti; *bhṛśam*—very greatly; *putrayoḥ*—of two sons; *ca*—also; *vadham*—the killing; *kṛṣṇāt*—by Kṛṣṇa; *viditvā*—knowing this; *āsīt*—became; *mahā-manāḥ*—highly pleased in mind.

TRANSLATION

The sage Maitreya said: Hearing that her grandson would be a great devotee and that her sons would be killed by Kṛṣṇa, Diti was highly pleased in mind.

PURPORT

Diti was very aggrieved to learn that because of her untimely pregnancy her sons would be demons and would fight with the Lord. But when she heard that her grandson would be a great devotee and that her two sons would be killed by the Lord, she was very satisfied. As the wife of a great sage and the daughter of a great Prajāpati, Dakṣa, she knew that being killed by the Personality of Godhead is a great fortune. Since the Lord is absolute, His acts of violence and nonviolence are both on the absolute platform. There is no difference in such acts of the Lord. Mundane violence and nonviolence have nothing to do with the Lord's acts. A demon killed by Him attains the same result as one who attains liberation after many, many births of penance and austerity. The word *bhṛśam* is significant herein because it indicates that Diti was pleased beyond her expectations.

Thus end the Bhaktivedanta purports of the Third Canto, Fourteenth Chapter, of the Śrīmad-Bhāgavatam, *entitled "Pregnancy of Diti in the Evening."*

CHAPTER FIFTEEN

Description of the Kingdom of God

TEXT 1

मैत्रेय उवाच
प्राजापत्यं तु तत्तेजः परतेजोहनं दितिः ।
दधार वर्षाणि शतं शङ्कमाना सुरार्दनात् ॥ १ ॥

maitreya uvāca
prājāpatyaṁ tu tat tejaḥ
para-tejo-hanaṁ ditiḥ
dadhāra varṣāṇi śataṁ
śaṅkamānā surārdanāt

maitreyaḥ uvāca—the sage Maitreya said; *prājāpatyam*—of the great Prajāpati; *tu*—but; *tat tejaḥ* his powerful semen; *para-tejaḥ*—others' prowess; *hanam*—troubling; *ditiḥ*—Diti (Kaśyapa's wife); *dadhāra*—bore; *varṣāṇi*—years; *śatam*—hundred; *śaṅkamānā*—being doubtful; *sura-ardanāt*—disturbing to the demigods.

TRANSLATION

Śrī Maitreya said: My dear Vidura, Diti, the wife of the sage Kaśyapa, could understand that the sons within her womb would be a cause of disturbance to the demigods. As such, she continuously bore the powerful semen of Kaśyapa Muni, which was meant to give trouble to others, for one hundred years.

PURPORT

The great sage Śrī Maitreya was explaining to Vidura the activities of the demigods, including Lord Brahmā. When Diti heard from her husband that the sons she bore within her abdomen would be causes of disturbances to the demigods, she was not very happy. There are two classes of men—devotees and nondevotees. Nondevotees are called demons, and devotees are called demigods. No sane man or woman can tolerate the nondevotees' giving trouble to devotees. Diti, therefore, was reluctant to give birth to her babies; she waited for one hundred years so that at least she could save the demigods from the disturbance for that period.

TEXT 2

लोके तेनाहतालोके लोकपाला हतौजसः ।
न्यवेदयन् विश्वसृजे ध्वान्तव्यतिकरं दिशाम् ॥ २ ॥

loke tenāhatāloke
loka-pālā hataujasaḥ
nyavedayan viśva-sṛje
dhvānta-vyatikaraṁ diśām

loke—within this universe; *tena*—by the force of the pregnancy of Diti; *āhata*—being devoid of; *āloke*—light; *loka-pālāḥ*—the demigods of various planets; *hata-ojasaḥ*—whose prowess was diminished; *nyavedayan*—asked; *viśva-sṛje*—Brahmā; *dhvānta-vyatikaram*—expansion of darkness; *diśām*—in all directions.

TRANSLATION

By the force of the pregnancy of Diti, the light of the sun and moon was impaired in all the planets, and the demigods of various planets, being disturbed by that force, asked the creator of the universe, Brahmā, "What is this expansion of darkness in all directions?"

PURPORT

It appears from this verse of *Śrīmad-Bhāgavatam* that the sun is the source of light for all the planets in the universe. The modern scientific theory which states that there are many suns in each universe is not supported by this verse. It is understood that in each universe there is only one sun, which supplies light to all the planets. In *Bhagavad-gītā* the moon is also stated to be one of the stars. There are many stars, and when we see them glittering at night we can understand that they are reflectors of light; just as moonlight is a reflection of sunlight, other planets also reflect sunlight, and there are many other planets which cannot be seen by our naked eyes. The demoniac influence of the sons in the womb of Diti expanded darkness throughout the universe.

TEXT 3

देवा ऊचुः
तम एतद्विभो वेत्थ संविग्ना यद्वयं भृशम् ।
न ह्यव्यक्तं भगवतः कालेनास्पृष्टवर्त्मनः ॥ ३ ॥

devā ūcuḥ
tama etad vibho vettha
saṁvignā yad vayaṁ bhṛśam
na hy avyaktaṁ bhagavataḥ
kālenāspṛṣṭa-vartmanaḥ

devāḥ ūcuḥ—the demigods said; *tamaḥ*—darkness; *etat*—this; *vibho*—O great one; *vettha*—you know; *saṁvignāḥ*—very anxious; *yat*—because; *vayam*—we; *bhṛśam*—very much; *na*—not; *hi*—because; *avyaktam*—unmanifest; *bhagavataḥ*—of You (the Supreme Personality of Godhead); *kālena*—by time; *aspṛṣṭa*—untouched; *vartmanaḥ*—whose way.

TRANSLATION

The fortunate demigods said: O great one, just see this darkness, which you know very well and which is causing us anxieties. Because the influence of time cannot touch you, there is nothing unmanifest before you.

PURPORT

Brahmā is addressed herein as Vibhu and as the Personality of Godhead. He is the Supreme Personality of Godhead's incarnation of the mode of passion in the material world. He is nondifferent, in the representative sense, from the Supreme Personality of Godhead, and therefore the influence of time cannot affect him. The influence of time, which manifests as past, present and future, cannot touch higher personalities like Brahmā and other demigods. Sometimes demigods and great sages who have attained such perfection are called *tri-kāla-jña.*

TEXT 4

देवदेव जगद्धातर्लोकनाथशिखामणे ।
परेषामपरेषां त्वं भूतानामसि भाववित् ॥ ४ ॥

deva-deva jagad-dhātar
lokanātha-śikhāmaṇe
pareṣām apareṣāṁ tvaṁ
bhūtānām asi bhāva-vit

deva-deva—O god of the demigods; *jagat-dhātaḥ*—O sustainer of the universe; *lokanātha-śikhāmaṇe*—O head jewel of all the demigods in other planets; *pareṣām*—of the spiritual world; *apareṣām*—of the material world; *tvam*—you; *bhūtānām*—of all living entities; *asi*—are; *bhāva-vit*—knowing the intentions.

TRANSLATION

O god of the demigods, sustainer of the universe, head jewel of all the demigods in other planets, you know the intentions of all living entities, in both the spiritual and material worlds.

PURPORT

Because Brahmā is almost on an equal footing with the Personality of Godhead, he is addressed here as the god of the demigods, and because he is the secondary creator of this universe, he is addressed as the sustainer of the universe. He is the head of all the demigods, and therefore he is addressed here as the head jewel of the demigods. It is not difficult for him to understand everything which is happening in both the spiritual and material worlds. He knows everyone's heart and everyone's intentions. Therefore he was requested to explain this incident. Why was the pregnancy of Diti causing such anxieties all over the universe?

TEXT 5

नमो विज्ञानवीर्याय माययेदमुपेयुषे ।
गृहीतगुणभेदाय नमस्तेऽव्यक्तयोनये ॥ ५ ॥

namo vijñāna-vīryāya
māyayedam upeyuṣe
gṛhīta-guṇa-bhedāya
namas te 'vyakta-yonaye

namaḥ—respectful obeisances; *vijñāna-vīryāya*—O original source of strength and scientific knowledge; *māyayā*—by the external energy; *idam*—this body of Brahmā; *upeyuṣe*—having obtained; *gṛhīta*—accepting; *guṇa-bhedāya*—the differentiated mode of passion; *namaḥ te*—offering obeisances unto you; *avyakta*—unmanifested; *yonaye*—source.

TRANSLATION

O original source of strength and scientific knowledge, all obeisances unto you! You have accepted the differentiated mode of passion from the Supreme Personality of Godhead. With the help of external energy you are born of the unmanifested source. All obeisances unto you!

PURPORT

The *Vedas* are the original scientific knowledge for all departments of understanding, and this knowledge of the *Vedas* was first impregnated into the heart of Brahmā by the Supreme Personality of Godhead. Therefore Brahmā is the original source of all scientific knowledge. He is born directly from the transcendental body of Garbhodakaśāyī Viṣṇu, who is never seen by any creature of this material universe and therefore always remains unmanifested. Brahmā is stated here to be born of the unmanifested. He is the incarnation of the mode of passion in material nature, which is the separated, external energy of the Supreme Lord.

TEXT 6

ये त्वानन्येन भावेन भावयन्त्यात्मभावनम् ।
आत्मनि प्रोतभुवनं परं सदसदात्मकम् ॥ ६ ॥

ye tvānanyena bhāvena
bhāvayanty ātma-bhāvanam
ātmani prota-bhuvanaṁ
paraṁ sad-asad-ātmakam

ye—those who; *tvā*—on you; *ananyena*—without deviation; *bhāvena*—with devotion; *bhāvayanti*—meditate; *ātma-bhāvanam*—who generates all living entities; *ātmani*—within your self; *prota*—linked; *bhuvanam*—all the planets; *param*—the supreme; *sat*—effect; *asat*—cause; *ātmakam*—generator.

TRANSLATION

O lord, all these planets exist within your self, and all the living entities are generated from you. Therefore you are the cause of this universe, and anyone who meditates upon you without deviation attains devotional service.

TEXT 7

तेषां सुपक्वयोगानां जितश्वासेन्द्रियात्मनाम् ।
लब्धयुष्मत्प्रसादानां न कुतश्चित्पराभवः ॥ ७ ॥

teṣāṁ supakva-yogānāṁ
jita-śvāsendriyātmanām
labdha-yuṣmat-prasādānāṁ
na kutaścit parābhavaḥ

teṣām—of them; *su-pakva-yogānām*—who are mature mystics; *jita*—controlled; *śvāsa*—breath; *indriya*—the senses; *ātmanām*—the mind; *labdha*—attained; *yuṣmat*—your; *prasādānām*—mercy; *na*—not; *kutaścit*—anywhere; *parābhavaḥ*—defeat.

TRANSLATION

There is no defeat in this material world for persons who control the mind and senses by controlling the breathing process and who are therefore experienced, mature mystics. This is because by such perfection in yoga they have attained your mercy.

PURPORT

The purpose of yogic performances is explained here. It is said that an experienced mystic attains full control of the senses and the mind by controlling the breathing process. Therefore, controlling the breathing process is not the ultimate aim of *yoga.* The real purpose of yogic performances is to control the mind and the senses. Anyone who has such control is to be understood to be an experienced, mature mystic *yogī*. It is indicated herein that a *yogī* who has control over the mind and senses has the actual benediction of the Lord, and he has no fear. In other words, one cannot attain the mercy and benediction of the Supreme Lord until one is able to control the mind and the senses. This is actually possible when one fully engages in Kṛṣṇa consciousness. A person whose senses and mind are always engaged in the transcendental service of the Lord has no possibility of engaging in material activities. The devotees of the Lord are not defeated anywhere in the universe. It is stated, *nārāyaṇa-parāḥ sarve:* one who is *nārāyaṇa-para,* or a devotee of the Supreme Personality of Godhead, is not afraid anywhere, whether he is sent to hell or promoted to heaven (*Bhāg.* 6.17.28).

TEXT 8

यस्य वाचा प्रजाः सर्वा गावस्तन्त्येव यन्त्रिताः ।
हरन्ति बलिमायत्तास्तस्मै मुख्याय ते नमः ॥ ८ ॥

yasya vācā prajāḥ sarvā
gāvas tantyeva yantritāḥ
haranti balim āyattās
tasmai mukhyāya te namaḥ

yasya—of whom; *vācā*—by the Vedic directions; *prajāḥ*—living entities; *sarvāḥ*—all; *gāvaḥ*—bulls; *tantyā*—by a rope; *iva*—as; *yantritāḥ*—are directed; *haranti*—offer, take away; *balim*—presentation, ingredients for worship; *āyattāḥ*—under control; *tasmai*—unto him; *mukhyāya*—unto the chief person; *te*—unto you; *namaḥ*—respectful obeisances.

TRANSLATION

All the living entities within the universe are conducted by the Vedic directions, as a bull is directed by the rope attached to its nose. No one can violate the rules laid down in the Vedic literatures. To the chief person, who has contributed the Vedas, we offer our respect!

PURPORT

The Vedic literatures are the laws of the Supreme Personality of Godhead. One cannot violate the injunctions given in the Vedic literatures any more than one can violate the state laws. Any living creature who wants real benefit in life must act according to the direction of the Vedic literature. The conditioned souls who have come to this material world for material sense gratification are regulated by the injunctions of the Vedic literature. Sense gratification is just like salt. One cannot take too much or too little, but one must take some salt in order to make one's foodstuff palatable. Those conditioned souls who have come to this material world should utilize their senses according to the direction of the Vedic literature, otherwise they will be put into a more miserable condition of life. No human being or demigod can enact laws like those of the Vedic literature because the Vedic regulations are prescribed by the Supreme Lord.

TEXT 9

स त्वं विधत्स्व शं भूमंस्तमसा लुप्तकर्मणाम् ।
अदभ्रदयया दृष्ट्या आपन्नानर्हसीक्षितुम् ॥ ९ ॥

sa tvaṁ vidhatsva śaṁ bhūmaṁs
tamasā lupta-karmaṇām
adabhra-dayayā dṛṣṭyā
āpannān arhasīkṣitum

saḥ—he; *tvam*—you; *vidhatsva*—perform; *śam*—good fortune; *bhūman*—O great lord; *tamasā*—by the darkness; *lupta*—have been suspended; *karmaṇām*—of prescribed duties; *adabhra*—magnanimous, without reservation; *dayayā*—mercy; *dṛṣṭyā*—by your glance; *āpannān*—us, the surrendered; *arhasi*—are able; *īkṣitum*—to see.

TRANSLATION

The demigods prayed to Brahmā: Please look upon us mercifully, for we have fallen into a miserable condition; because of the darkness, all our work has been suspended.

PURPORT

Because of complete darkness throughout the universe, the regular activities and engagements of all the different planets were suspended. In the North and South Poles of this planet there are sometimes no divisions of day and night; similarly, when the sunlight does not approach the different planets within the universe, there is no distinction between day and night.

TEXT 10

एष देव दितेर्गर्भ ओजः काश्यपमर्पितम् ।
दिशस्तिमिरयन् सर्वा वर्धतेऽग्निरिवैधसि ॥१०॥

esa deva diter garbha
ojaḥ kāśyapam arpitam
diśas timirayan sarvā
vardhate 'gnir ivaidhasi

eṣaḥ—this; *deva*—O lord; *diteḥ*—of Diti; *garbhaḥ*—womb; *ojaḥ*—semen; *kāśyapam*—of Kaśyapa; *arpitam*—deposited; *diśaḥ*—directions; *timirayan*—causing complete darkness; *sarvāḥ*—all; *vardhate*—overloads; *agniḥ*—fire; *iva*—as; *edhasi*—fuel.

TRANSLATION

As fuel overloads a fire, so the embryo created by the semen of Kaśyapa in the womb of Diti has caused complete darkness throughout the universe.

PURPORT

The darkness throughout the universe is explained herewith as being caused by the embryo created in the womb of Diti by the semen of Kaśyapa.

TEXT 11

मैत्रेय उवाच

स प्रहस्य महाबाहो भगवान् शब्दगोचरः ।
प्रत्याचष्टात्मभूर्देवान् प्रीणन् रुचिरया गिरा ॥११॥

maitreya uvāca
sa prahasya mahā-bāho
bhagavān śabda-gocaraḥ

pratyācaṣṭātma-bhūr devān
prīṇan ruciraya girā

maitreyaḥ uvāca—Maitreya said; *saḥ*—he; *prahasya*—smiling; *mahā-bāho*—O mighty-armed (Vidura); *bhagavān*—the possessor of all opulences; *śabda-gocaraḥ*—who is understood by transcendental sound vibration; *pratyācaṣṭa*—replied; *ātma-bhūḥ*—Lord Brahmā; *devān*—the demigods; *prīṇan*—satisfying; *rucirayā*—with sweet; *girā*—words.

TRANSLATION

Śrī Maitreya said: Thus Lord Brahmā, who is understood by transcendental vibration, tried to satisfy the demigods, being pleased with their words of prayer.

PURPORT

Brahmā could understand the misdeeds of Diti, and therefore he smiled at the whole situation. He replied to the demigods present there in words they could understand.

TEXT 12

ब्रह्मोवाच
मानसा मे सुता युष्मत्पूर्वजाः सनकादयः ।
चेरुर्विहायसा लोकाल्लोकेषु विगतस्पृहाः ॥१२॥

brahmovāca
mānasā me sutā yuṣmat-
pūrvajāḥ sanakādayaḥ
cerur vihāyasā lokāl
lokeṣu vigata-spṛhāḥ

brahmā uvāca—Lord Brahmā said; *mānasāḥ*—born from the mind; *me*—my; *sutāḥ*—sons; *yuṣmat*—than you; *pūrva-jāḥ*—born previously; *sanaka-ādayaḥ*—headed by Sanaka; *ceruḥ*—traveled; *vihāyasā*—by traveling in outer space or flying in the sky; *lokān*—to the material and spiritual worlds; *lokeṣu*—among the people; *vigata-spṛhāḥ*—without any desire.

TRANSLATION

Lord Brahmā said: My four sons Sanaka, Sanātana, Sanandana and Sanat-kumāra, who were born from my mind, are your predecessors. Sometimes they travel throughout the material and spiritual skies without any definite desire.

PURPORT

When we speak of desire we refer to desire for material sense gratification. Saintly persons like Sanaka, Sanātana, Sanandana and Sanat-kumāra have no material desire, but sometimes they travel all over the universe, out of their own accord, to preach devotional service.

TEXT 13

त एकदा भगवतो वैकुण्ठस्यामलात्मनः ।
ययुर्वैकुण्ठनिलयं सर्वलोकनमस्कृतम् ॥१३॥

ta ekadā bhagavato
vaikuṇṭhasyāmalātmanaḥ
yayur vaikuṇṭha-nilayaṁ
sarva-loka-namaskṛtam

te—they; *ekadā*—once upon a time; *bhagavataḥ*—of the Supreme Personality of Godhead; *vaikuṇṭhasya*—of Lord Viṣṇu; *amala-ātmanaḥ*—being freed from all material contamination; *yayuḥ*—entered; *vaikuṇṭha-nilayam*—the abode named Vaikuṇṭha; *sarva-loka*—by the residents of all the material planets; *namaskṛtam*—worshiped.

TRANSLATION

After thus traveling all over the universes, they also entered into the spiritual sky, for they were freed from all material contamination. In the spiritual sky there are spiritual planets known as Vaikuṇṭhas, which are the residence of the Supreme Personality of Godhead and His pure devotees and are worshiped by the residents of all the material planets.

PURPORT

The material world is full of cares and anxieties. In any one of the planets, beginning from the highest down to the lowest, Pātāla, every living creature must be full of cares and anxieties because in the material planets one cannot live eternally. The living entities, however, are actually eternal. They want an eternal home, an eternal residence, but because of accepting a temporal abode in the material world, they are naturally full of anxiety. In the spiritual sky the planets are called Vaikuṇṭha because the residents of these planets are free from all anxieties. For them there is no question of birth, death, old age and diseases, and therefore they are not anxious. On the other hand, the residents of the material planets are always afraid of birth, death, disease and old age, and therefore they are full of anxieties.

TEXT 14

वसन्ति यत्र पुरुषाः सर्वे वैकुण्ठमूर्तयः ।
येऽनिमित्तनिमित्तेन धर्मेणाराधयन् हरिम् ॥१४॥

vasanti yatra puruṣāḥ
sarve vaikuṇṭha-mūrtayaḥ
ye 'nimitta-nimittena
dharmeṇārādhayan harim

vasanti—they live; *yatra*—where; *puruṣāḥ*—persons; *sarve*—all; *vaikuṇṭha-mūrtayaḥ*—having a four-handed form similar to that of the Supreme Lord, Viṣṇu; *ye*—those Vaikuṇṭha persons; *animitta*—without desire for sense gratification; *nimittena*—caused by; *dharmeṇa*—by devotional service; *ārādhayan*—continuously worshiping; *harim*—unto the Supreme Personality of Godhead.

TRANSLATION

In the Vaikuṇṭha planets all the residents are similar in form to the Supreme Personality of Godhead. They all engage in devotional service to the Lord without desires for sense gratification.

PURPORT

The residents and the form of living in Vaikuṇṭha are described in this verse. The residents are all like the Supreme Personality of Godhead Nārāyaṇa. In the Vaikuṇṭha planets Kṛṣṇa's plenary feature as four-handed Nārāyaṇa is the predominating Deity, and the residents of Vaikuṇṭhaloka are also four-handed, just contrary to our conception here in the material world. Nowhere in the material world do we find a human being with four hands. In Vaikuṇṭhaloka there is no occupation but the service of the Lord, and this service is not rendered with a purpose. Although every service has a particular result, the devotees never aspire for the fulfillment of their own desires; their desires are fulfilled by rendering transcendental loving service to the Lord.

TEXT 15

यत्र चाद्यः पुमानास्ते भगवान् शब्दगोचरः ।
सत्त्वं विष्टभ्य विरजं स्वानां नो मृडयन् वृषः ॥१५॥

yatra cādyaḥ pumān āste
bhagavān śabda-gocaraḥ
sattvaṁ viṣṭabhya virajaṁ
svānāṁ no mṛḍayan vṛṣaḥ

yatra—in the Vaikuṇṭha planets; *ca*—and; *ādyaḥ*—original; *pumān*—person; *āste*—is there; *bhagavān*—the Supreme Personality of Godhead; *śabda-gocaraḥ*—understood through the Vedic literature; *sattvam*—the mode of goodness; *viṣṭabhya*—accepting; *virajam*—uncontaminated; *svānām*—of His own associates; *naḥ*—us; *mṛḍayan*—increasing happiness; *vṛṣaḥ*—the personification of religious principles.

TRANSLATION

In the Vaikuṇṭha planets is the Supreme Personality of Godhead, who is the original person and who can be understood through the Vedic literature. He is full of the uncontaminated mode of goodness, with no place for passion or ignorance. He contributes religious progress for the devotees.

PURPORT

The kingdom of the Supreme Personality of Godhead in the spiritual sky cannot be understood by any process other than hearing from the description of the *Vedas.* No one can go see it. In this material world also, one who is unable to pay to go to a far distant place by motorized conveyances can only understand about that place from authentic books. Similarly, the Vaikuntha planets in the spiritual sky are beyond this material sky. The modern scientists who are trying to travel in space are having difficulty going even to the nearest planet, the moon, to say nothing of the highest planets within the universe. There is no possibility that they can go beyond the material sky, enter the spiritual sky and see for themselves the spiritual planets, Vaikuṇṭha. Therefore, the kingdom of God in the spiritual sky can be understood only through the authentic descriptions of the *Vedas* and *Purāṇas.*

In the material world there are three modes of material qualities—goodness, passion and ignorance—but in the spiritual world there is no trace of the modes of passion and ignorance; there is only the mode of goodness, which is uncontaminated by any tinge of ignorance or passion. In the material world, even if a person is completely in goodness, he is sometimes subject to be polluted by tinges of the modes of ignorance and passion. But in the Vaikuṇṭha world, the spiritual sky, only the mode of goodness in its pure form exists. The Lord and His devotees reside in the Vaikuṇṭha planets, and they are of the same transcendental quality, namely, *śuddha-sattva,* the mode of pure goodness. The Vaikuṇṭha planets are very dear to the Vaiṣṇavas, and for the progressive march of the Vaiṣṇavas toward the kingdom of God, the Lord Himself helps His devotees.

TEXT 16

यत्र नैःश्रेयसं नाम वनं कामदुघैर्द्रुमैः ।
सर्वर्तुश्रीभिर्विभ्राजत्कैवल्यमिव मूर्तिमत् ॥१६॥

yatra naiḥśreyasaṁ nāma
vanaṁ kāma-dughair drumaiḥ
sarvartu-śrībhir vibhrājat
kaivalyam iva mūrtimat

yatra—in the Vaikuṇṭha planets; *naiḥśreyasam*—auspicious; *nāma*—named; *vanam*—forests; *kāma-dughaiḥ*—yielding desire; *drumaiḥ*—with trees; *sarva*—all; *ṛtu*—seasons; *śrībhiḥ*—with flowers and fruits; *vibhrājat*—splendid; *kaivalyam*—spiritual; *iva*—as; *mūrtimat*—personal.

TRANSLATION

In those Vaikuṇṭha planets there are many forests which are very auspicious. In those forests the trees are desire trees, and in all seasons they are filled with flowers and fruits because everything in the Vaikuṇṭha planets is spiritual and personal.

PURPORT

In the Vaikuṇṭha planets the land, the trees, the fruits and flowers and the cows—everything—is completely spiritual and personal. The trees are desire trees. On this material planet the trees can produce fruits and flowers according to the order of material energy, but in the Vaikuṇṭha planets the trees, the land, the residents and the animals are all spiritual. There is no difference between the tree and the animal or the animal and the man. Here the word *mūrtimat* indicates that everything has a spiritual form. Formlessness, as conceived by the impersonalists, is refuted in this verse; in the Vaikuṇṭha planets, although everything is spiritual, everything has a particular form. The trees and the men have form, and because all of them, although differently formed, are spiritual, there is no difference between them.

TEXT 17

वैमानिकाः सललनाश्चरितानि शश्वद्
गायन्ति यत्र शमलक्षपणानि भर्तुः ।
अन्तर्जलेऽनुविकसन्मधुमाधवीनां
गन्धेन खण्डितधियोऽप्यनिलं क्षिपन्तः ॥१७॥

vaimānikāḥ sa-lalanāś caritāni śaśvad
gāyanti yatra śamala-kṣapaṇāni bhartuḥ
antar-jale 'nuvikasan-madhu-mādhavīnāṁ
gandhena khaṇḍita-dhiyo 'py anilaṁ kṣipantaḥ

vaimānikāḥ—flying in their airplanes; *sa-lalanāḥ*—along with their wives; *caritāni*—activities; *śaśvat*—eternally; *gāyanti*—sing; *yatra*—in those Vaikuṇṭha planets; *śamala*—all inauspicious qualities; *kṣapaṇāni*—devoid of; *bhartuḥ*—of the Supreme Lord; *antaḥ-jale*—in the midst of the water; *anuvikasat*—blossoming; *madhu*—fragrant, laden with honey; *mādhavīnām*—of the *mādhavī* flowers; *gandhena*—by the fragrance; *khaṇḍita*—disturbed; *dhiyaḥ*—minds; *api*—even though; *anilam*—breeze; *kṣipantaḥ*—deriding.

TRANSLATION

In the Vaikuṇṭha planets the inhabitants fly in their airplanes, accompanied by their wives and consorts, and eternally sing of the character and activities of the Lord, which are always devoid of all inauspicious qualities. While singing the glories of the Lord, they deride even the presence of the blossoming mādhavī flowers, which are fragrant and laden with honey.

PURPORT

It appears from this verse that the Vaikuṇṭha planets are full of all opulences. There are airplanes in which the inhabitants travel in the spiritual sky with their sweethearts. There is a breeze carrying the fragrance of blossoming flowers, and this breeze is so nice that it also carries the honey of the flowers. The inhabitants of Vaikuṇṭha, however, are so interested in glorifying the Lord that they do not like the disturbance of such a nice breeze while they are chanting the Lord's glories. In other words, they are pure devotees. They consider glorification of the Lord more important than their own sense gratification. In the Vaikuṇṭha planets there is no question of sense gratification. To smell the fragrance of a blossoming flower is certainly very nice, but it is simply for sense gratification. The inhabitants of Vaikuṇṭha give first preference to the service of the Lord, not their own sense gratification. Serving the

Lord in transcendental love yields such transcendental pleasure that, in comparison, sense gratification is counted as insignificant.

TEXT 18

पारावतान्यभृतसारसचक्रवाक-
दात्यूहहंसशुकतित्तिरिबर्हिणां यः ।
कोलाहलो विरमतेऽचिरमात्रमुच्चै-
र्भृङ्गाधिपे हरिकथामिव गायमाने ॥१८॥

pārāvatānyabhṛta-sārasa-cakravāka-
dātyūha-haṁsa-śuka-tittiri-barhiṇāṁ yaḥ
kolāhalo viramate 'cira-mātram uccair
bhṛṅgādhipe hari-kathām iva gāyamāne

pārāvata—pigeons; *anyabhṛta*—cuckoo; *sārasa*—crane; *cakravāka*—*cakravāka*; *dātyūha*—gallinule; *haṁsa*—swan; *śuka*—parrot; *tittiri*—partridge; *barhiṇam*—of the peacock; *yaḥ*—which; *kolāhalaḥ*—tumult; *viramate*—stops; *acira-mātram*—temporarily; *uccaiḥ*—loudly; *bhṛṅga-adhipe*—king of the bumblebees; *hari-kathām*—the glories of the Lord; *iva*—as; *gāyamāne*—while singing.

TRANSLATION

When the king of bees hums in a high pitch, singing the glories of the Lord, there is a temporary lull in the noise of the pigeon, the cuckoo, the crane, the cakravāka, the swan, the parrot, the partridge and the peacock. Such transcendental birds stop their own singing simply to hear the glories of the Lord.

PURPORT

This verse reveals the absolute nature of Vaikuṇṭha. There is no difference between the birds there and the human residents. The situation in the spiritual sky is that everything is spiritual and variegated. Spiritual variegatedness means that everything is animate. There is nothing inanimate. Even the trees, the ground, the plants, the flowers, the birds and the beasts are all on the level of Kṛṣṇa consciousness. The special feature of Vaikuṇṭhaloka is that there is no question of sense gratification. In the material world even an ass enjoys his sound vibration, but in the Vaikuṇṭhas such nice birds as the peacock, the *cakravāka* and the cuckoo prefer to hear the vibration of the glories of the Lord from the bees. The principles of devotional service, beginning with hearing and chanting, are very prominent in the Vaikuṇṭha world.

TEXT 19

मन्दारकुन्दकुरबोत्पलचम्पकार्ण-
पुन्नागनागबकुलाम्बुजपारिजाताः ।
गन्धे ऽर्चिते तुलसिकाभरणेन तस्या
यस्मिंस्तपः सुमनसो बहु मानयन्ति ॥१९॥

mandāra-kunda-kurabotpala-campakārṇa-
punnāga-nāga-bakulāmbuja-pārijātāḥ
gandhe 'rcite tulasikābharaṇena tasyā
yasmiṁs tapaḥ sumanaso bahu mānayanti

mandāra—mandāra; kunda-kunda; kuraba-kuraba; utpala-utpala; campaka-campaka; arṇa-arṇa flower; *punnāga—punnāga; nāga-nāgakeśara; bakula-bakula; ambuja*—lily; *pārijātāḥ—pārijāta; gandhe*—fragrance; *arcite*—being worshiped; *tulasikā—tulasi; ābharaṇena*—with a garland; *tasyāḥ*—of her; *yasmin*—in which Vaikuṇṭha; *tapaḥ*—austerity; *su-manasaḥ*—good minded, Vaikuṇṭha minded; *bahu*—very much; *mānayanti*—glorify.

TRANSLATION

Although flowering plants like the mandāra, kunda, kurabaka, utpala, campaka, arṇa, punnāga, nāgakeśara, bakula, lily and pārijāta are full of transcendental fragrance, they are still conscious of the austerities performed by tulasī, for tulasī is given special preference by the Lord, who garlands Himself with tulasī leaves.

PURPORT

The importance of *tulasī* leaves is very clearly mentioned here. *Tulasī* plants and their leaves are very important in devotional service. Devotees are recommended to water the *tulasī* tree every day and collect the leaves to worship the Lord. One time an atheistic *svāmī* remarked, "What is the use of watering the *tulasī* plant? It is better to water eggplant. By watering the eggplant one can get some fruits, but what is the use of watering the *tulasī*?" These foolish creatures, unacquainted with devotional service, sometimes play havoc with the education of people in general.

The most important thing about the spiritual world is that there is no envy among the devotees there. This is true even among the flowers, which are all conscious of the greatness of *tulasī*. In the Vaikuṇṭha world entered by the four Kumāras, even the birds and flowers are conscious of service to the Lord.

TEXT 20

यत्संकुलं हरिपदानतिमात्रदृष्टै-
वैदूर्यमारकतहेममयैर्विमानैः ।
येषां बृहत्कटितटाः स्मितशोभिमुख्यः
कृष्णात्मनां न रज आदधुरुत्स्मयाद्यैः ॥२०॥

yat saṅkulaṁ hari-padānati-mātra-dṛṣṭair
vaidūrya-mārakata-hema-mayair vimānaiḥ
yeṣāṁ bṛhat-kaṭi-taṭāḥ smita-śobhi-mukhyaḥ
kṛṣṇātmanāṁ na raja ādadhur utsmayādyaiḥ

yat—that Vaikuṇṭha abode; *saṅkulam*—is pervaded; *hari-pada*—at the two lotus feet of Hari, the Supreme Personality of Godhead; *ānati*—by obeisances; *mātra*—simply; *dṛṣṭaiḥ*—are obtained; *vaidūrya*—lapis lazuli; *mārakata*—emeralds; *hema*—gold; *mayaiḥ*—made of; *vimānaiḥ*—with airplanes; *yeṣām*—of those passengers; *bṛhat*—large; *kaṭi-taṭāḥ*—hips; *smita*—smiling; *śobhi*—beautiful; *mukhyaḥ*—faces; *kṛṣṇa*—in Kṛṣṇa; *ātmanām*—whose minds are absorbed; *na*—not; *rajaḥ*—sex desire; *ādadhuḥ*—stimulate; *utsmaya-ādyaiḥ*—by intimate friendly dealings, laughing and joking.

TRANSLATION

The inhabitants of Vaikuṇṭha travel in their airplanes made of lapis lazuli, emerald and gold. Although crowded by their consorts, who have large hips and beautiful smiling faces, they cannot be stimulated to passion by their mirth and beautiful charms.

PURPORT

In the material world, opulences are achieved by materialistic persons by dint of their labor. One cannot enjoy material prosperity unless he works very hard to achieve it. But the devotees of the Lord who are residents of Vaikuṇṭha have the opportunity to enjoy a transcendental situation of jewels and emeralds. Ornaments made of gold bedecked with jewels are achieved not by working hard but by the benediction of the Lord. In other words, devotees in the Vaikuṇṭha world, or even in this material world, cannot be poverty-stricken, as is sometimes supposed. They have ample opulences for enjoyment, but they need not labor to achieve them. It is also stated that in the Vaikuṇṭha world the consorts of the residents are many, many times more beautiful than we can find in this material world, even in the higher planets. It is specifically mentioned here that a woman's large hips are very attractive and they stimulate man's passion, but the wonderful feature of Vaikuṇṭha is that although the women have large hips and beautiful faces and are decorated with ornaments of emeralds and jewels, the men are so absorbed in Kṛṣṇa consciousness that the beautiful bodies of the women cannot attract them. In other words, there is enjoyment of the association of the opposite sex, but there is no sexual relationship. The residents of Vaikuṇṭha have a better standard of pleasure, so there is no need of sex pleasure.

TEXT 21

श्री रूपिणी क्वणयती चरणारविन्दं
लीलाम्बुजेन हरिसद्मनि मुक्तदोषा ।
संलक्ष्यते स्फटिककुड्य उपेतहेम्नि
सम्मार्जतीव यदनुग्रहणेऽन्ययत्नः ॥२१॥

śrī rūpiṇī kvaṇayatī caraṇāravindaṁ
līlāmbujena hari-sadmani mukta-doṣā
saṁlakṣyate sphaṭika-kuḍya upeta-hemni
sammārjatīva yad-anugrahaṇe 'nya-yatnaḥ

śrī—Lakṣmī, the goddess of fortune; *rūpiṇī*—assuming a beautiful form; *kvaṇayatī*—tinkling; *caraṇa-aravindam*—lotus feet; *līlā-ambujena*—playing with a lotus flower; *hari-sadmani*—the house of the Supreme Personality; *mukta-doṣā*—freed from all faults; *saṁlakṣyate*—becomes visible; *sphaṭika*—crystal; *kuḍye*—walls; *upeta*—mixed; *hemni*—gold; *sammārjatī iva*—appearing like a sweeper; *yat-anugrahaṇe*—to receive her favor; *anya*—others'; *yatnaḥ*—very much careful.

TRANSLATION

The ladies in the Vaikuṇṭha planets are as beautiful as the goddess of fortune herself. Such transcendentally beautiful ladies, their hands playing with lotuses and their leg bangles tinkling, are sometimes seen sweeping the marble walls, which are bedecked at intervals with golden borders, in order to receive the grace of the Supreme Personality of Godhead.

PURPORT

In the *Brahma-saṁhitā* it is stated that the Supreme Lord, Govinda, is always served in His abode by many, many millions of goddesses of fortune. *Lakṣmī-sahasra-śata-sambhrama-sevyamānam.* These millions and trillions of goddesses of fortune who reside in the Vaikuṇṭha planets are not exactly consorts of the Supreme Personality of Godhead, but are the wives of the devotees of the Lord and also engage in the service of the Supreme Personality of Godhead. It is stated here that in the Vaikuṇṭha planets the houses are made of marble. Similarly, in the *Brahma-saṁhitā* it is stated that the ground on the Vaikuṇṭha planets is made of touchstone. Thus there is no need to sweep the stone in Vaikuṇṭha, for there is hardly any dust on it, but still, in order to satisfy the Lord, the ladies there always engage in dusting the marble walls. Why? The reason is that they are eager to achieve the grace of the Lord by doing so.

It is also stated here that in the Vaikuṇṭha planets the goddesses of fortune are faultless. Generally the goddess of fortune does not remain steadily in one place. Her name is Cañcalā, which means "one who is not steady." We find, therefore, that a man who is very rich may become the poorest of the poor. Another example is Rāvaṇa. Rāvaṇa took away Lakṣmī, Sītājī, to his kingdom, and instead of being happy by the grace of Lakṣmī, his family and his kingdom were vanquished. Thus Lakṣmī in the house of Rāvaṇa is Cañcalā, or unsteady. Men of Rāvaṇa's class want Lakṣmī only, without her husband, Nārāyaṇa; therefore they become unsteady due to Lakṣmījī. Materialistic persons find fault on the part of Lakṣmī, but in Vaikuṇṭha Lakṣmījī is fixed in the service of the Lord. In spite of her being the goddess of fortune, she cannot be happy without the grace of the Lord. Even the goddess of fortune needs the Lord's grace in order to be happy, yet in the material world even Brahmā, the highest created being, seeks the favor of Lakṣmī for happiness.

TEXT 22

वापीषु विद्रुमतटास्वमलामृताप्सु
प्रेष्यान्विता निजवने तुलसीभिरीशम् ।
अभ्यर्चती स्वलकमुन्नसमीक्ष्य वक्त्र-
मुच्छेषितं भगवतेत्यमताङ्ग यच्छ्रीः ॥२२॥

vāpīṣu vidruma-taṭāsv amalāmṛtāpsu
preṣyānvitā nija-vane tulasībhir īśam
abhyarcatī svalakam unnasam īkṣya vaktram
ucchesitaṁ bhagavatety amatāṅga yac-chrīḥ

vāpīṣu—in the ponds; *vidruma*—made of coral; *taṭāsu*—banks; *amala*—transparent; *amṛta*—nectarean; *apsu*—water; *preṣyā-anvitā*—surrounded by maidservants; *nija-vane*—in her own garden; *tulasībhiḥ*—with *tulasī; īśam*—the Supreme Lord; *abhyarcatī*—worship; *su-alakam*—with her face decorated with *tilaka; unnasam*—raised nose; *īkṣya*—by seeing; *vaktram*—face; *ucchesitam*—being kissed; *bhagavatā*—by the Supreme Lord; *iti*—thus; *amata*—thought; *aṅga*—O demigods; *yat-śrīḥ*—whose beauty.

TRANSLATION

The goddesses of fortune worship the Lord in their own gardens by offering tulasī leaves on the coral-paved banks of transcendental reservoirs of water. While offering worship to the Lord, they can see on the water the reflection of their beautiful faces with raised noses, and it appears that they have become more beautiful because of the Lord's kissing their faces.

PURPORT

Generally, when a woman is kissed by her husband, her face becomes more beautiful. In Vaikuṇṭha also, although the goddess of fortune is naturally as beautiful as can be imagined, she nevertheless awaits the kissing of the Lord to make her face more beautiful. The beautiful face of the goddess of fortune appears in ponds of transcendental crystal water when she worships the Lord with *tulasī* leaves in her garden.

TEXT 23

यन्न व्रजन्त्यघभिदो रचनानुवादा-
च्छृण्वन्ति येऽन्यविषयाः कुकथा मतिघ्नीः ।
यास्तु श्रुता हतभगैर्नृभिरात्तसारा-
स्तांस्तान् क्षिपन्त्यशरणेषु तमःसु हन्त ॥२३॥

yan na vrajanty agha-bhido racanānuvādāc
chṛṇvanti ye 'nya-viṣayāḥ kukathā mati-ghnīḥ
yās tu śrutā hata-bhagair nṛbhir ātta-sārās
tāṁs tān kṣipanty aśaraṇeṣu tamaḥsu hanta

yat—Vaikuṇṭha; *na*—never; *vrajanti*—approach; *agha-bhidaḥ*—of the vanquisher of all kinds of sins; *racanā*—of the creation; *anuvādāt*—than narrations; *śṛṇvanti*—hear; *ye*—those who; *anya*—other; *viṣayāḥ*—subject matter; *ku-kathāḥ*—bad words; *mati-ghnīḥ*—killing intelligence; *yāḥ*—which; *tu*—but; *śrutāḥ*—are heard; *hata-bhagaiḥ*—unfortunate; *nṛbhiḥ*—by men; *ātta*—taken away; *sārāḥ*—values of life; *tān tān*—such persons; *kṣipanti*—are thrown; *aśaraṇeṣu*—devoid of all shelter; *tamaḥsu*—in the darkest part of material existence; *hanta*—alas.

TRANSLATION

It is very much regrettable that unfortunate people do not discuss the description of the Vaikuṇṭha planets but engage in topics which are unworthy to hear and which bewilder one's intelligence. Those who give up the topics of

Vaikuṇṭha and take to talk of the material world are thrown into the darkest region of ignorance.

PURPORT

The most unfortunate persons are the impersonalists, who cannot understand the transcendental variegatedness of the spiritual world. They are afraid to talk about the beauty of the Vaikuṇṭha planets because they think that variegatedness must be material. Such impersonalists think that the spiritual world is completely void, or, in other words, that there is no variegatedness. This mentality is described here as *ku-kathā mati-ghnīḥ,* "intelligence bewildered by unworthy words." The philosophies of voidness and of the impersonal situation of the spiritual world are condemned here because they bewilder one's intelligence. How can the impersonalist and the void philosopher think of this material world, which is full of variegatedness, and then say that there is no variegatedness in the spiritual world? It is said that this material world is the perverted reflection of the spiritual world, so unless there is variegatedness in the spiritual world, how can there be temporary variegatedness in the material world? That one can transcend this material world does not imply that there is no transcendental variegatedness.

Here in the *Bhāgavatam,* in this verse particularly, it is stressed that people who try to discuss and understand the real spiritual nature of the spiritual sky and the Vaikuṇṭhas are fortunate. The variegatedness of the Vaikuṇṭha planets is described in relation to the transcendental pastimes of the Lord. But instead of trying to understand the spiritual abode and the spiritual activities of the Lord, people are more interested in politics and economic developments. They hold many conventions, meetings and discussions to solve the problems of this worldly situation, where they can remain for only a few years, but they are not interested in understanding the spiritual situation of the Vaikuṇṭha world. If they are at all fortunate, they become interested in going back home, back to Godhead, but unless they understand the spiritual world, they rot in this material darkness continuously.

TEXT 24

येऽभ्यर्थितामपि च नो नृगतिं प्रपन्ना
ज्ञानं च तत्त्वविषयं सहधर्म यत्र ।
नाराधनं भगवतो वितरन्त्यमुष्य
सम्मोहिता विततया बत मायया ते ॥२४॥

ye 'bhyarthitām api ca no nṛ-gatiṁ prapannā
jñānaṁ ca tattva-viṣayaṁ saha-dharmaṁ yatra
nārādhanaṁ bhagavato vitaranty amuṣya
sammohitā vitatayā bata māyayā te

ye—those persons; *abhyarthitām*—desired; *api*—certainly; *ca*—and; *naḥ*—by us (Brahmā and the other demigods); *nṛ-gatim*—the human form of life; *prapannāḥ*—have attained; *jñānam*—knowledge; *ca*—and; *tattva-viṣayam*—subject matter about the Absolute Truth; *saha-dharmam*—along with religious principles; *yatra*—where; *na*—not; *ārādhanam*—worship; *bhagavataḥ*—of the Supreme Personality of Godhead; *vitaranti*—perform; *amuṣya*—of the Supreme Lord; *sammohitāḥ*—being bewildered; *vitatayā*—all-pervading; *bata*—alas; *māyayā*—by the influence of the illusory energy; *te*—they.

TRANSLATION

Lord Brahmā said: My dear demigods, the human form of life is of such importance that we also desire to have such life, for in the human form one can attain perfect religious truth and knowledge. If one in this human form of life does not understand the Supreme Personality of Godhead and His abode, it is to be understood that he is very much affected by the influence of external nature.

PURPORT

Brahmājī condemns very vehemently the condition of the human being who does not take interest in the Personality of Godhead and His transcendental abode, Vaikuṇṭha. The human form of life is desired even by Brahmājī. Brahmā and other demigods have much better material bodies than human beings, yet the demigods, including Brahmā, nevertheless desire to attain the human form of life because it is specifically meant for the living entity who can attain transcendental knowledge and religious perfection. It is not possible to go back to Godhead in one life, but in the human form one should at least understand the goal of life and begin Kṛṣṇa consciousness. It is said that the human form is a great boon because it is the most suitable boat for crossing over the nescience ocean. The spiritual master is considered to be the most able captain in that boat, and the information from the scriptures is the favorable wind for floating over the ocean of nescience. The human being who does not take advantage of all these facilities in this life is committing suicide. Therefore one who does not begin Kṛṣṇa consciousness in the human form of life loses his life to the influence of the illusory energy. Brahmā regrets the situation of such a human being.

TEXT 25

यच्च व्रजन्त्यनिमिषामृषभानुवृत्त्या
दूरेयमा ह्युपरि नः स्पृहणीयशीलाः ।
भर्तुर्मिथः सुयशसः कथनानुराग-
वैक्लव्यबाष्पकलया पुलकीकृताङ्गाः ॥२५॥

yac ca vrajanty animiṣām ṛṣabhānuvṛttyā
dūre yamā hy upari naḥ spṛhaṇīya-śīlāḥ
bhartur mithaḥ suyaśasaḥ kathanānurāga-
vaiklavya-bāṣpa-kalayā pulakī-kṛtāṅgāḥ

yat—Vaikuṇṭha; *ca*—and; *vrajanti*—go; *animiṣām*—of the demigods; *ṛṣabha*—chief; *anuvṛttyā*—following in the footsteps; *dūre*—keeping at a distance; *yamāḥ*—regulative principles; *hi*—certainly; *upari*—above; *naḥ*—us; *spṛhaṇīya*—to be desired; *śīlāḥ*—good qualities; *bhartuḥ*—of the Supreme Lord; *mithaḥ*—for one another; *suyaśasaḥ*—glories; *kathana*—by discussions, discourses; *anurāga*—attraction; *vaiklavya*—ecstasy; *bāṣpa-kalayā*—tears in the eyes; *pulakī-kṛta*—shivering; *aṅgāḥ*—bodies.

TRANSLATION

Persons whose bodily features change in ecstasy and who breathe heavily and perspire due to hearing the glories of the Lord are promoted to the kingdom of God, even though they do not care for meditation and other austerities. The kingdom of God is above the material universes, and it is desired by Brahmā and other demigods.

PURPORT

It is clearly stated herein that the kingdom of God is above the material universes. Just as there are many hundreds of thousands of higher planets above this earth, so there are many millions and billions of spiritual planets belonging to the spiritual sky. Brahmājī states herein that the spiritual kingdom is above the kingdom of the demigods. One can enter the kingdom of the Supreme Lord only when one is highly developed in desirable qualities. All good qualities develop in the person of a devotee. It is stated in *Śrīmad-Bhāgavatam*, Fifth Canto, Eighteenth Chapter, verse 12, that anyone who is Kṛṣṇa conscious is endowed with all the good qualities of the demigods. In the material world the qualities of the demigods are highly appreciated, just as, even in our experience, the qualities of a gentleman are more highly appreciated than the qualities of a man in ignorance or in a lower condition of life. The qualities of the demigods in the higher planets are far superior to the qualities of the inhabitants of this earth.

Brahmājī confirms herewith that only persons who have developed the desirable qualities can enter into the kingdom of God. In the *Caitanya-caritāmṛta,* the devotee's desirable qualities are described to be twenty-six in number. They are stated as follows: He is very kind; he does not quarrel with anyone; he accepts Kṛṣṇa consciousness as the highest goal of life; he is equal to everyone; no one can find fault in his character; he is magnanimous, mild and always clean, internally and externally; he does not profess to possess anything in this material world; he is a benefactor to all living entities; he is peaceful and is a soul completely surrendered to Kṛṣṇa; he has no material desire to fulfill; he is meek and humble, always steady, and has conquered the sensual activities; he does not eat more than required to maintain body and soul together; he is never mad after material identity; he is respectful to all others and does not demand respect for himself; he is very grave, very compassionate and very friendly; he is poetic; he is expert in all activities, and he is silent in nonsense. Similarly, in *Śrīmad-Bhāgavatam,* Third Canto, Twenty-fifth Chapter, verse 21, the qualifications of a saintly person are mentioned. It is said there that a saintly person eligible to enter into the kingdom of God is very tolerant and very kind to all living entities. He is not partial; he is kind both to human beings and to animals. He is not such a fool that he will kill a goat Nārāyaṇa to feed a human Nārāyaṇa, or *daridra-nārāyaṇa.* He is very kind to all living entities; therefore he has no enemy. He is very peaceful. These are the qualities of persons who are eligible to enter into the kingdom of God. That such a person gradually becomes liberated and enters the kingdom of God is confirmed in *Śrīmad-Bhāgavatam,* Fifth Canto, Fifth Chapter, verse 2. The *Śrīmad-Bhāgavatam,* Second Canto, Third Chapter, verse 24, also states that if a person does not cry or exhibit bodily changes after chanting the holy name of God without offense, it is to be understood that he is hardhearted and that therefore his heart does not change even after he chants the holy name of God, Hare Kṛṣṇa. These bodily changes can take place due to ecstasy when we offenselessly chant the holy names of God: Hare Kṛṣṇa, Hare Kṛṣṇa, Kṛṣṇa Kṛṣṇa, Hare Hare/ Hare Rāma, Hare Rāma, Rāma Rāma, Hare Hare.

It may be noted that there are ten offenses we should avoid. The first offense is to decry persons who try in their lives to broadcast the glories of the Lord. People must be educated in understanding the glories of the Supreme; therefore the devotees who engage in preaching the glories of the Lord are never to be decried. It is the greatest offense. Furthermore, the holy name of Viṣṇu is the most auspicious name, and His pastimes are also nondifferent from the holy name of the Lord. There are many foolish persons who say that one can chant Hare Kṛṣṇa or chant the name of Kālī or Durgā or Śiva because they are all the same. If one thinks that the holy name of the Supreme Personality of Godhead and the names and activities of the demigods are on the same level, or if one accepts the holy name of Viṣṇu to be a material sound vibration, that is also an offense. The third offense is to think of the spiritual master who spreads the glories of the Lord as an ordinary human being. The fourth offense is to consider the Vedic literatures, such as the *Purāṇas* or other transcendentally revealed scriptures, to be ordinary books of knowledge. The fifth offense is to think that devotees have given artificial importance to the holy name of God. The actual fact is that the Lord is nondifferent from His name. The highest realization of spiritual value is to chant the holy name of God, as prescribed for the age—Hare Kṛṣṇa, Hare Kṛṣṇa, Kṛṣṇa Kṛṣṇa, Hare Hare/ Hare Rāma, Hare Rāma, Rāma Rāma, Hare Hare. The sixth offense is to give some interpretation on the holy name of God. The seventh offense is to act sinfully on the strength of chanting the holy name of God. It is understood that one can be freed from all sinful reaction simply by chanting the holy name of God, but if one thinks that he is therefore at liberty to commit all kinds of sinful acts, that is a symptom of offense. The eighth offense is to equate the chanting of Hare Kṛṣṇa with other spiritual activities, such as meditation, austerity, penance or sacrifice. They cannot be equated at any level. The ninth offense is to specifically glorify the importance of the holy name before persons who have no interest. The tenth offense is to be attached to the misconception of possessing something, or to accept the body as one's self, while executing the process of spiritual cultivation.

When one is free from all ten of these offenses in chanting the holy name of God, he develops the ecstatic bodily features called *pulakāśru. Pulaka* means "symptoms of happiness," and *aśru* means "tears in the eyes." The symptoms of happiness and tears in the eyes must appear in a person who has chanted the holy name offenselessly. Here in this verse it is stated that those who have actually developed the symptoms of happiness and tears in the eyes by chanting the glories of the Lord are eligible to enter the kingdom of God. In the *Caitanya-caritāmṛta* it is said that if one does not develop these symptoms while chanting Hare Kṛṣṇa, it is to be understood that he is still offensive. *Caitanya-caritāmṛta* suggests a nice remedy in this connection. There it is said in verse 31, Chapter Eight, of *Ādi-līlā,* that if anyone takes shelter of Lord Caitanya and just chants the holy name of the Lord, Hare Kṛṣṇa, he becomes freed from all offenses.

TEXT 26

तद्विश्वगुर्वधिकृतं भुवनैकवन्द्यं
दिव्यं विचित्रविबुधाग्र्यविमानशोचिः ।
आपुः परां मुदमपूर्वमुपेत्य योग-
मायाबलेन मुनयस्तदथो विकुण्ठम् ॥२६॥

tad viśva-gurv-adhikṛtaṁ bhuvanaika-vandyam
divyaṁ vicitra-vibudhāgrya-vimāna-śociḥ
āpuḥ parāṁ mudam apūrvam upetya yoga-
māyā-balena munayas tad atho vikuṇṭham

tat—then; *viśva-guru*—by the teacher of the universe, the Supreme Personality of Godhead; *adhikṛtam*—predominated; *bhuvana*—of the planets; *eka*—alone; *vandyam*—worthy to be worshiped; *divyam*—spiritual; *vicitra*—highly decorated; *vibudha-agrya*—of the devotees (who are the best of the learned); *vimāna*—of the airplanes; *śociḥ*—illuminated; *āpuḥ*—attained; *parām*—the highest; *mudam*—happiness; *apūrvam*—unprecedented; *upetya*—having attained; *yoga-māyā*—by spiritual potency; *balena*—by the influence; *munayaḥ*—the sages; *tat*—Vaikuṇṭha; *atho*—that; *vikuṇṭham*—Viṣṇu.

TRANSLATION

Thus the great sages, Sanaka, Sanātana, Sanandana and Sanat-kumāra, upon reaching the above-mentioned Vaikuṇṭha in the spiritual world by dint of their mystic yoga performance, perceived unprecedented happiness. They found that the spiritual sky was illuminated by highly decorated airplanes piloted by the best devotees of Vaikuṇṭha and was predominated by the Supreme Personality of Godhead.

PURPORT

The Supreme Personality of Godhead is one without a second. He is above everyone. No one is equal to Him, nor is anyone greater than Him. Therefore He is described here as *viśva-guru.* He is the prime living entity of the entire material and spiritual creation and is *bhuvanaika-vandyam,* the only worshipable personality in the three worlds. The airplanes in the spiritual sky are self-illuminated and are piloted by great devotees of the Lord. In other words, in the Vaikuṇṭha planets there is no scarcity of the things which are available in the material world; they are available, but they are more valuable because they are spiritual and therefore eternal and blissful. The sages felt an unprecedented happiness because Vaikuṇṭha was not predominated by an ordinary man. The Vaikuṇṭha planets are predominated by expansions of Kṛṣṇa, who are differently named as Madhusūdana, Mādhava, Nārāyaṇa, Pradyumna, etc. These transcendental planets are worshipable because the Personality of Godhead personally rules them. It is said here that the sages reached the transcendental spiritual sky by dint of their mystic power. That is the perfection of the *yoga* system. The breathing exercises and disciplines to keep health in proper order are not the ultimate goals of *yoga* perfection. The *yoga* system as generally understood is *aṣṭāṅga-yoga,* or *siddhi,* eightfold perfection in *yoga.* By dint of perfection in *yoga* one can become lighter than the lightest and heavier than the heaviest; one can go wherever he likes and can achieve opulences as he likes. There are eight such perfections. The *ṛṣis,* the four Kumāras, reached Vaikuṇṭha by becoming lighter than the lightest and thus passing over the space of the material world. Modern mechanical space vehicles are unsuccessful because they cannot go to the highest region of this material creation, and they certainly cannot enter the spiritual sky. But by perfection of the *yoga* system one not only can travel through material space, but can surpass material space and enter the spiritual sky. We learn this fact also from an incident concerning Durvāsā Muni and Mahārāja Ambarīṣa. It is understood that in one year Durvāsā Muni traveled everywhere and went into the spiritual sky to meet the Supreme Personality of Godhead, Nārāyaṇa. By present standards, scientists calculate that if one could travel at the speed of light, it would take forty thousand years to reach the highest planet of this material world. But the *yoga* system can carry one without limitation or difficulty. The word *yogamāyā* is used in this verse. *Yoga-māyā-balena vikuṇṭham.* The transcendental happiness exhibited in the spiritual world and all other spiritual manifestations there are made possible by the influence of *yogamāyā,* the internal potency of the Supreme Personality of Godhead.

TEXT 27

तस्मिन्नतीत्य मुनयः षडसज्जमानाः
कक्षाः समानवयसावथ सप्तमायाम् ।
देवावचक्षत गृहीतगदौ परार्ध्य-
केयूरकुण्डलकिरीटविटङ्कवेषौ ॥२७॥

tasminn atītya munayaḥ ṣaḍ asajjamānāḥ
kakṣāḥ samāna-vayasāv atha saptamāyām
devāv acakṣata gṛhīta-gadau parārdhya-
keyūra-kuṇḍala-kirīṭa-viṭaṅka-veṣau

tasmin—in that Vaikuṇṭha; *atītya*—after passing through; *munayaḥ*—the great sages; *ṣaṭ*—six; *asajja mānāḥ*—without being much attracted; *kakṣāḥ*—walls; *samāna*—equal; *vayasau*—age; *atha*—thereafter; *saptamāyām*—at the seventh gate; *devau*—two Vaikuṇṭha doormen; *acakṣata*—saw; *gṛhīta*—carrying; *gadau*—maces; *para-ardhya*—most valuable; *keyūra*—bracelets; *kuṇḍala*—earrings; *kirīṭa*—helmets; *viṭaṅka*—beautiful; *veṣau*—garments.

TRANSLATION

After passing through the six entrances of Vaikuṇṭha-purī, the Lord's residence, without feeling astonishment at all the decorations, they saw at the seventh gate two shining beings of the same age, armed with maces and adorned with most valuable jewelry, earrings, diamonds, helmets, garments, etc.

PURPORT

The sages were so eager to see the Lord within Vaikuṇṭha-purī that they did not care to see the transcendental decorations of the six gates which they passed by one after another. But at the seventh door they found two doormen of the same age. The significance of the doormen's being of the same age is that in the Vaikuṇṭha planets there is no old age, so one cannot distinguish who is older than whom. The inhabitants of Vaikuṇṭha are decorated like the Supreme Personality of Godhead, Nārāyaṇa, with *śaṅkha, cakra, gadā* and *padma* (conch, wheel, club and lotus).

TEXT 28

मत्तद्विरेफवनमालिकया निवीतौ
विन्यस्तयासितचतुष्टयबाहुमध्ये ।
वक्त्रं भ्रुवा कुटिलया स्फुटनिर्गमाभ्यां
रक्तेक्षणेन च मनाग्रभसं दधानौ ॥२८॥

matta-dvirepha-vanamālikayā nivītau
vinyastayāsita-catuṣṭaya-bāhu-madhye
vaktraṁ bhruvā kuṭilayā sphuṭa-nirgamābhyāṁ
raktekṣaṇena ca manāg rabhasaṁ dadhānau

matta—intoxicated; *dvi-repha*—bees; *vana-mālikayā*—with a garland of fresh flowers; *nivītau*—hanging on the neck; *vinyastayā*—placed around; *asita*—blue; *catuṣṭaya*—four; *bāhu*—hands; *madhye*—between; *vaktram*—face; *bhruvā*—with their eyebrows; *kuṭilayā*—arched; *sphuṭa*—snorting; *nirgamābhyām*—breathing; *rakta*—reddish; *īkṣaṇena*—with eyes; *ca*—and; *manāk*—somewhat; *rabhasam*—agitated; *dadhānau*—glanced over.

TRANSLATION

The two doormen were garlanded with fresh flowers which attracted intoxicated bees and which were placed around their necks and between their four blue arms. From their arched eyebrows, discontented nostrils and reddish eyes, they appeared somewhat agitated.

PURPORT

Their garlands attracted swarms of bees because they were garlands of fresh flowers. In the Vaikuṇṭha world everything is fresh, new and transcendental. The inhabitants of Vaikuṇṭha have bodies of bluish color and four hands like Nārāyaṇa.

TEXT 29

द्वार्येतयोर्निविविशुर्मिषतोरपृष्ट्वा
पूर्वा यथा पुरटवज्रकपाटिका याः ।
सर्वत्र तेऽविषमया मुनयः स्वदृष्ट्या
ये सञ्चरन्त्यविहता विगताभिशङ्काः ॥२९॥

dvāry etayor nivivišur miṣator apṛṣṭvā
pūrvā yathā puraṭa-vajra-kapāṭikā yāḥ
sarvatra te 'viṣamayā munayaḥ sva-dṛṣṭyā
ye sañcaranty avihatā vigatābhiśaṅkāḥ

dvāri—in the door; *etayoḥ*—both doorkeepers; *nivivišuḥ*—entered; *miṣatoḥ*—while seeing; *apṛṣṭvā* without asking; *pūrvāḥ*—as before; *yathā*—as; *puraṭa*—made of gold; *vajra*—and diamond; *kapāṭikāḥ*—the doors; *yāḥ*—which; *sarvatra*—everywhere; *te*—they; *aviṣa-mayā*—without any sense of discrimination; *munayaḥ*—the great sages; *sva-dṛṣṭyā*—out of their own will; *ye*—who; *sañcaranti*—move; *avihatāḥ*—without being checked; *vigata*—without; *abhiśaṅkāḥ*—doubt.

TRANSLATION

The great sages, headed by Sanaka, had opened doors everywhere. They had no idea of "ours" and "theirs." With open minds, they entered the seventh door out of their own will, just as they had passed through the six other doors, which were made of gold and diamonds.

PURPORT

The great sages—namely, Sanaka, Sanātana, Sanandana and Sanat-kumāra—although very old in years, maintained themselves eternally as small children. They were not at all duplicitous, and they entered the doors exactly as little children enter places without any idea of what it is to trespass. That is a child's nature. A child can enter any place, and no one checks him. Indeed, a child is generally welcome in his attempts to go places, but if it so happens that a child is checked from entering a door, he naturally becomes very sorry and angry. That is the nature of a child. In this case, the same thing happened. The childlike saintly personalities entered all the six doors of the palace, and no one checked them; therefore when they attempted to enter the seventh door and were forbidden by the doormen, who checked them with their sticks, they naturally became very angry and sorrowful. An ordinary child would cry, but because these were not ordinary children, they immediately made preparations to punish the doormen, for the doormen had committed a great offense. Even to this day a saintly person is never checked from entering anyone's door in India.

TEXT 30

तान् वीक्ष्य वातरशनांश्चतुरः कुमारान्
वृद्धान्दशार्धवयसो विदितात्मतत्त्वान् ।
वेत्रेण चास्खलयतामतदर्हणांस्तौ
तेजो विहस्य भगवत्प्रतिकूलशीलौ ॥३०॥

tān vīkṣya vāta-raśanāṁś caturaḥ kumārān
vṛddhān daśārdha-vayaso viditātma-tattvān
vetreṇa cāskhalayatām atad-arhaṇāṁs tau
tejo vihasya bhagavat-pratikūla-śīlau

tān—them; *vīkṣya*—after seeing; *vāta-raśanān*—naked; *caturaḥ*—four; *kumārān*—boys; *vṛddhān*—aged; *daśa-ardha*—five years; *vayasaḥ*—appearing as of the age; *vidita*—had realized; *ātma-tattvān*—the truth of the self; *vetreṇa*—with their staffs; *ca*—also; *askhalayatām*—forbade; *a-tat-arhaṇān*—not deserving such from them; *tau*—those two porters; *tejaḥ*—glories; *vihasya*—disregarding the etiquette; *bhagavat-pratikūla-śīlau*—having a nature displeasing to the Lord.

TRANSLATION

The four boy-sages, who had nothing to cover their bodies but the atmosphere, looked only five years old, even though they were the oldest of all living creatures and had realized the truth of the self. But when the porters, who happened to possess a disposition quite unpalatable to the Lord, saw the sages, they blocked their way with their staffs, despising their glories, although the sages did not deserve such treatment at their hands.

PURPORT

The four sages were the first-born sons of Brahmā. Therefore all other living entities, including Lord Śiva, are born later and are therefore younger than the four Kumāras. Although they looked like five-year-old boys and traveled naked, the Kumāras were older than all other living creatures and had realized the truth of the self. Such saints were not to be forbidden to enter the kingdom of Vaikuṇṭha, but by chance the doormen objected to their entrance. This was not fitting. The Lord is always anxious to serve sages like the Kumāras, but in spite of knowing this fact, the doormen, astonishingly and outrageously, prohibited them from entering.

TEXT 31

ताभ्यां मिषत्स्वनिमिषेषु निषिध्यमानाः
स्वर्हत्तमा ह्यपि हरेः प्रतिहारपाभ्याम् ।
ऊचुः सुहृत्तमदिदृक्षितभङ्ग ईष-
त्कामानुजेन सहसा त उपप्लुताक्षाः ॥३१॥

tābhyāṁ miṣatsv animiṣeṣu niṣidhyamānāḥ
svarhattamā hy api hareḥ pratihāra-pābhyām
ūcuḥ suhṛttama-didṛkṣita-bhaṅga īṣat
kāmānujena sahasā ta upaplutākṣāḥ

tābhyām—by those two porters; *miṣatsu*—while looking on; *animiṣeṣu*—demigods living in Vaikuṇṭha; *niṣidhyamānāḥ*—being forbidden; *su-arhattamāḥ*—by far the fittest persons; *hi api*—although; *hareḥ*—of Hari, the Supreme Personality of Godhead; *pratihāra-pābhyām*—by the two doorkeepers; *ūcuḥ*—said; *suhṛt-tama*—most beloved; *didṛkṣita*—eagerness to see; *bhaṅge*—hindrance; *īṣat*—slight; *kāma-anujena*—by the younger brother of lust (anger); *sahasā*—suddenly; *te*—those great sages; *upapluta*—agitated; *akṣāḥ*—eyes.

TRANSLATION

When the Kumāras, although by far the fittest persons, were thus forbidden entrance by the two chief doorkeepers of Śrī Hari while other divinities looked on, their eyes suddenly turned red because of anger due to their great eagerness to see their most beloved master, Śrī Hari, the Personality of Godhead.

PURPORT

According to the Vedic system, a *sannyāsī*, a person in the renounced order of life, is dressed in saffron-colored garments. This saffron dress is practically a passport for the mendicant and *sannyāsī* to go anywhere. The *sannyāsī's* duty is to enlighten people in Kṛṣṇa consciousness. Those in the renounced order of life have no other business but preaching the glories and supremacy of the Supreme Personality of Godhead. Therefore the Vedic sociological conception is that a *sannyāsī* should not be restricted; he is allowed to go anywhere and everywhere he wants, and he is not refused any gift he might demand from a householder. The four Kumāras came to see the Supreme Personality of Godhead Nārāyaṇa. The word *suhṛttama,* "best of all friends," is important. As Lord Kṛṣṇa states in the *Bhagavad-gītā,* He is the best friend of all living entities. *Suhṛdaṁ sarva-bhūtānām.* No one can be a greater well-wishing friend to any living entity than the Supreme Personality of Godhead. He is so kindly disposed towards everyone that in spite of our completely forgetting our relationship with the Supreme Lord, He comes Himself—sometimes personally, as Lord Kṛṣṇa appeared on this earth, and sometimes as His devotee, as did Lord Caitanya Mahāprabhu—and sometimes He sends His bona fide devotees to reclaim all the fallen souls. Therefore, He is the greatest well-wishing friend of everyone, and the Kumāras wanted to see Him. The doorkeepers should have known that the four sages had no other business, and therefore to restrict them from entering the palace was not apt.

In this verse it is figuratively stated that the younger brother of desire suddenly appeared in person when the sages were forbidden to see their most beloved Personality of Godhead. The younger brother of desire is anger. If one's desire is not fulfilled, the younger brother, anger, follows. Here we can mark that even great saintly persons like the Kumāras were also angry, but they were not angry for their personal interests. They were angry because they were forbidden to enter the palace to see the Personality of Godhead. Therefore the theory that in the perfectional stage one should not have anger is not supported in this verse. Anger will continue even in the liberated stage. These four mendicant brothers, the Kumāras, were considered liberated persons, but still they were angry because they were restricted in their service to the Lord. The difference between the anger of an ordinary person and that of a liberated person is that an ordinary person becomes angry because his sense desires are not being fulfilled, whereas a liberated person like the Kumāras becomes angry when restricted in the discharge of duties for serving the Supreme Personality of Godhead.

In the previous verse it has been clearly mentioned that the Kumāras were liberated persons. *Viditātma-tattva* means "one who understands the truth of self-realization." One who does not understand the truth of self-realization is called ignorant, but one who understands the self, the Superself, their interrelation, and activities in self-realization is called *viditātma-tattva.* Although the Kumāras were already liberated persons, they nevertheless became angry. This point is very important. Becoming liberated does not necessitate losing one's sensual activities. Sense activities continue even in the liberated stage. The difference is, however, that sense activities in liberation are accepted only in connection with Kṛṣṇa consciousness, whereas sense activities in the conditioned stage are enacted for personal sense gratification.

TEXT 32

मुनय ऊचुः
को वामिहैत्य भगवत्परिचर्ययोच्चै-
स्तद्धर्मिणां निवसतां विषमः स्वभावः ।
तस्मिन् प्रशान्तपुरुषे गतविग्रहे वां
को वात्मवत्कुहकयोः परिशङ्कनीयः ॥३२॥

munaya ūcuḥ
ko vām ihaitya bhagavat-paricaryayoccais
tad-dharmiṇāṁ nivasatāṁ viṣamaḥ svabhāvaḥ
tasmin praśānta-puruṣe gata-vigrahe vāṁ
ko vātmavat kuhakayoḥ pariśaṅkanīyaḥ

munayaḥ—the great sages; *ūcuḥ*—said; *kaḥ*—who; *vām*—you two; *iha*—in Vaikuṇṭha; *etya*—having attained; *bhagavat*—of the Supreme Personality of Godhead; *paricaryayā*—by the service; *uccaiḥ*—having been developed by past pious actions; *tat-dharmiṇām*—of the devotees; *nivasatām*—dwelling in Vaikuṇtha; *viṣamaḥ*—discordant; *svabhāvaḥ*—mentality; *tasmin*—in the Supreme Lord; *praśānta-puruṣe*—without anxieties; *gata-vigrahe*—without any enemy; *vām*—of you two; *kaḥ*—who; *vā*—or; *ātma-vat*—like yourselves; *kuhakayoḥ*—maintaining duplicity; *pariśaṅkanīyaḥ*—not becoming trustworthy.

TRANSLATION

The sages said: Who are these two persons who have developed such a discordant mentality even though they are posted in the service of the Lord in the highest position and are expected to have developed the same qualities as the Lord? How are these two persons living in Vaikuṇṭha? Where is the possibility of an enemy's coming into this kingdom of God? The Supreme Personality of Godhead has no enemy. Who could be envious of Him? Probably these two persons are imposters; therefore they suspect others to be like themselves.

PURPORT

The difference between the inhabitants of a Vaikuṇṭha planet and those of a material planet is that in Vaikuṇṭha all the residents engage in the service of the Lord Himself and are equipped with all His good qualities. It has been analyzed by great personalities that when a conditioned soul is liberated and becomes a devotee, about seventy-nine percent of all the good qualities of the Lord develop in his person. Therefore in the Vaikuṇṭha world there is no question of enmity between the Lord and the residents. Here in this material world the citizens may be inimical to the chief executives or heads of state, but in Vaikuṇṭha there is no such mentality. One is not allowed to enter Vaikuṇṭha unless he has completely developed the good qualities. The basic principle of goodness is to accept subordination to the Supreme Personality of Godhead. The sages, therefore, were surprised to see that the two doormen who checked them from entering the palace were not exactly like the residents of Vaikuṇṭhaloka. It may be said that a doorman's duty is to determine who should be allowed to enter the palace and who should not. But that is not relevant in this matter because no one is allowed to enter the Vaikuṇṭha planets unless he has developed one hundred percent his mentality of devotional service to the Supreme Lord. No enemy of the Lord can enter Vaikuṇṭhaloka. The Kumāras concluded that the only reason for the doormen's checking them was that the doormen themselves were imposters.

TEXT 33

न ह्यन्तरं भगवतीह समस्तकुक्षा-
वात्मानमात्मनि नभो नभसीव धीराः ।
पश्यन्ति यत्र युवयोः सुरलिङ्गिनोः किं
व्युत्पादितं ह्युदरभेदि भयं यतोऽस्य ॥३३॥

na hy antaraṁ bhagavatīha samasta-kukṣāv
ātmānam ātmani nabho nabhasīva dhīrāḥ
paśyanti yatra yuvayoḥ sura-liṅginoḥ kiṁ
vyutpāditaṁ hy udara-bhedi bhayaṁ yato 'sya

na—not; *hi*—because; *antaram*—distinction; *bhagavati*—in the Supreme Personality of Godhead; *iha*—here; *samasta-kukṣau*—everything is within the abdomen; *ātmānam*—the living entity; *ātmani*—in the Supersoul; *nabhaḥ*—the small quantity of air; *nabhasi*—within the whole air; *iva*—as; *dhīrāḥ*—the learned; *paśyanti*—see; *yatra*—in whom; *yuvayoḥ*—of you two; *sura-liṅginoḥ*—dressed like inhabitants of Vaikuṇṭha; *kim*—how; *vyutpāditam*—

awakened, developed; *hi*—certainly; *udara-bhedi*—distinction between the body and the soul; *bhayam*—fearfulness; *yataḥ*—wherefrom; *asya*—of the Supreme Lord.

TRANSLATION

In the Vaikuṇṭha world there is complete harmony between the residents and the Supreme Personality of Godhead, just as there is complete harmony within space between the big and the small skies. Why then is there a seed of fear in this field of harmony? These two persons are dressed like inhabitants of Vaikuṇṭha, but wherefrom can their disharmony come into existence?

PURPORT

Just as there are different departments in each state in this material world—the civil department and the criminal department—so, in God's creation, there are two departments of existence. As in the material world we find that the criminal department is far, far smaller than the civil department, so this material world, which is considered the criminal department, is one fourth of the entire creation of the Lord. All living entities who are residents of the material universes are considered to be more or less criminals because they do not wish to abide by the order of the Lord or they are against the harmonious activities of God's will. The principle of creation is that the Supreme Lord, the Personality of Godhead, is by nature joyful, and He becomes many in order to enhance His transcendental joy. The living entities like ourselves, being part and parcel of the Supreme Lord, are meant to satisfy the senses of the Lord. Thus, whenever there is a discrepancy in that harmony, immediately the living entity is entrapped by *māyā,* or illusion.

The external energy of the Lord is called the material world, and the kingdom of the internal energy of the Lord is called Vaikuṇṭha, or the kingdom of God. In the Vaikuṇṭha world there is no disharmony between the Lord and the residents. Therefore God's creation in the Vaikuṇṭha world is perfect. There is no cause of fear. The entire kingdom of God is such a completely harmonious unit that there is no possibility of enmity. Everything there is absolute. Just as there are many physiological constructions within the body yet they work in one order for the satisfaction of the stomach, and just as in a machine there are hundreds and thousands of parts yet they run in harmony to fulfill the function of the machine, in the Vaikuṇṭha planets the Lord is perfect, and the inhabitants also perfectly engage in the service of the Lord.

The Māyāvādī philosophers, the impersonalists, interpret this verse of *Śrīmad-Bhāgavatam* to mean that the small sky and the big sky are one, but this idea cannot stand. The example of the big sky and the small skies is also applicable within a person's body. The big sky is the body itself, and the intestines and other parts of the body occupy the small sky. Each and every part of the body has individuality, even though occupying a small part of the total body. Similarly, the whole creation is the body of the Supreme Lord, and we created beings, or anything that is created, are but a small part of that body. The parts of the body are never equal to the whole. This is never possible. In *Bhagavad-gītā* it is said that the living entities, who are parts and parcels of the Supreme Lord, are eternally parts and parcels. According to the Māyāvādī philosophers, the living entity in illusion considers himself part and parcel although he is actually one and the same as the supreme whole. This theory is not valid. The oneness of the whole and the part is in their quality. The qualitative oneness of the small and large portions of the sky does not imply that the small sky becomes the big sky.

There is no cause for the politics of divide and rule in the Vaikuṇṭha planets; there is no fear, because of the united interests of the Lord and the residents. *Māyā* means disharmony between the living entities and the Supreme Lord, and Vaikuṇṭha means harmony between them. Actually all living entities are provided for and maintained by the Lord because He is the supreme living entity. But foolish creatures, although actually under the control of the supreme living entity, defy His existence, and that state is called *māyā*. Sometimes they deny that there is such a being as God. They say, "Everything is void." And sometimes they deny Him in a different way: "There may be a God, but He has no form." Both these conceptions arise from the rebellious condition of the living entity. As long as this rebellious condition prevails, the material world will continue in disharmony.

Harmony or disharmony is realized because of the law and order of a particular place. Religion is the law and order of the Supreme Lord. In the *Śrīmad Bhagavad-gītā* we find that religion means devotional service, or Kṛṣṇa consciousness. Kṛṣṇa says, "Give up all other religious principles and simply become a soul surrendered unto Me." This is religion. When one is fully conscious that Kṛṣṇa is the supreme enjoyer and Supreme Lord and one acts accordingly, that is real religion. Anything which goes against this principle is not religion. Kṛṣṇa therefore says: "Just give up all other religious principles." In the spiritual world this religious principle of Kṛṣṇa consciousness is maintained in harmony, and therefore that world is called Vaikuṇṭha. If the same principles can be adopted here, wholly or partially, then it is also Vaikuṇṭha. So it is with any society, such as the International Society for Krishna Consciousness: If the members of the International Society for Krishna Consciousness, putting faith in

Kṛṣṇa as the center, live in harmony according to the order and principles of *Bhagavad-gītā*, then they are living in Vaikuṇṭha, not in this material world.

TEXT 34

तद्वाममुष्य परमस्य विकुण्ठभर्तुः
कर्तुं प्रकृष्टमिह धीमहि मन्दधीभ्याम् ।
लोकानितो व्रजतमन्तरभावदृष्ट्या
पापीयसस्त्रय इमे रिपवोऽस्य यत्र ॥३४॥

tad vām amuṣya paramasya vikuṇṭha-bhartuḥ
kartuṁ prakṛṣṭam iha dhīmahi manda-dhībhyām
lokān ito vrajatam antara-bhāva-dṛṣṭyā
pāpīyasas traya ime ripavo 'sya yatra

tat—therefore; *vām*—unto these two; *amuṣya*—of Him; *paramasya*—the Supreme; *vikuṇṭha-bhartuḥ*—the Lord of Vaikuṇṭha; *kartum*—to bestow; *prakṛṣṭam*—benefit; *iha*—in the matter of this offense; *dhīmahi*—let us consider; *manda-dhībhyām*—those whose intelligence is not very nice; *lokān*—to the material world; *itaḥ*—from this place (Vaikuṇṭha); *vrajatam*—go; *antara-bhāva*—duality; *dṛṣṭyā*—on account of seeing; *pāpīyasaḥ*—sinful; *trayaḥ*—three; *ime*—these; *ripavaḥ*—enemies; *asya*—of a living entity; *yatra*—where.

TRANSLATION

Therefore let us consider how these two contaminated persons should be punished. The punishment should be apt, for thus benefit can eventually be bestowed upon them. Since they find duality in the existence of Vaikuṇṭha life, they are contaminated and should be removed from this place to the material world, where the living entities have three kinds of enemies.

PURPORT

The reason why pure souls come into the existential circumstances of the material world, which is considered to be the criminal department of the Supreme Lord, is stated in *Bhagavad-gītā*, Seventh Chapter, verse 27. It is stated that as long as a living entity is pure, he is in complete harmony with the desires of the Supreme Lord, but as soon as he becomes impure he is in disharmony with the desires of the Lord. By contamination he is forced to transfer to this material world, where the living entities have three enemies, namely desire, anger and lust. These three enemies force the living entities to continue material existence, and when one is free from them he is eligible to enter the kingdom of God. One should not, therefore, be angry in the absence of an opportunity for sense gratification, and one should not be lusty to acquire more than necessary. In this verse it is clearly stated that the two doormen should be sent into the material world, where criminals are allowed to reside. Since the basic principles of criminality are sense gratification, anger and unnecessary lust, persons conducted by these three enemies of the living entity are never promoted to Vaikuṇṭhaloka. People should learn *Bhagavad-gītā* and accept the Supreme Personality of Godhead, Kṛṣṇa, as the Lord of everything; they should practice satisfying the senses of the Supreme Lord instead of trying to satisfy their own senses. Training in Kṛṣṇa consciousness will help one be promoted to Vaikuṇṭha.

TEXT 35

तेषामितीरितमुभाववधार्य घोरं
तं ब्रह्मदण्डमनिवारणमस्त्रपूगैः ।
सद्यो हरेरनुचरावुरु बिभ्यतस्तत्-
पादग्रहावपततामतिकातरेण ॥३५॥

teṣām itīritam ubhāv avadhārya ghoraṁ
taṁ brahma-daṇḍam anivāraṇam astra-pūgaiḥ
sadyo harer anucarāv uru bibhyatas tat-
pāda-grahāv apatatām atikātareṇa

teṣām—of the four Kumāras; *iti*—thus; *īritam*—uttered; *ubhau*—both doorkeepers; *avadhārya*—understanding; *ghoram*—terrible; *tam*—that; *brahma-daṇḍam*—curse of a *brāhmaṇa; anivāraṇam*—not able to be counteracted; *astra-pūgaiḥ*—by any kind of weapon; *sadyaḥ*—at once; *hareḥ*—of the Supreme Lord; *anucarau*—devotees; *uru*—very much; *bibhyataḥ*—became fearful; *tat-pāda-grahau*—grasping their feet; *apatatām*—fell down; *atikātareṇa*—in great anxiety.

TRANSLATION

When the doormen of Vaikuṇṭhaloka, who were certainly devotees of the Lord, found that they were going to be cursed by the brāhmaṇas, they at once became very much afraid and fell down at the feet of the brāhmaṇas in great anxiety, for a brāhmaṇa's curse cannot be counteracted by any kind of weapon.

PURPORT

Although, by chance, the doormen committed a mistake by checking the *brāhmaṇas* from entering the gate of Vaikuṇṭha, they were at once aware of the gravity of the curse. There are many kinds of offenses, but the greatest offense is to offend a devotee of the Lord. Because the doormen were also devotees of the Lord, they were able to understand their mistake and were terrified when the four Kumāras were ready to curse them.

TEXT 36

भूयादघोनि भगवद्भिरकारि दण्डो
यो नौ हरेत सुरहेलनमप्यशेषम् ।
मा वोऽनुतापकलया भगवत्स्मृतिघ्नो
मोहो भवेदिह तु नौ व्रजतोरधोऽधः ॥३६॥

bhūyād aghoni bhagavadbhir akāri daṇḍo
yo nau hareta sura-helanam apy aśeṣam
mā vo 'nutāpa-kalayā bhagavat-smṛti-ghno
moho bhaved iha tu nau vrajator adho 'dhaḥ

bhūyāt—let it be; *aghoni*—for the sinful; *bhagavadbhiḥ*—by you; *akāri*—was done; *daṇḍaḥ*—punishment; *yaḥ*—that which; *nau*—in relation to us; *hareta*—should destroy; *sura-helanam*—disobeying great demigods; *api*—certainly; *aśeṣam*—unlimited; *mā*—not; *vaḥ*—of you; *anutāpa*—repentance; *kalayā*—by a little; *bhagavat*—of the Supreme Personality of Godhead; *smṛti-ghnaḥ*—destroying the memory of; *mohaḥ*—illusion; *bhavet*—should be; *iha*—in the foolish species of life; *tu*—but; *nau*—of us; *vrajatoḥ*—who are going; *adhaḥ adhaḥ*—down to the material world.

TRANSLATION

After being cursed by the sages, the doormen said: It is quite apt that you have punished us for neglecting to respect sages like you. But we pray that due to your compassion at our repentance, the illusion of forgetting the Supreme Personality of Godhead will not come upon us as we go progressively downward.

PURPORT

To a devotee, any heavy punishment is tolerable but the one which effects forgetfulness of the Supreme Lord. The doormen, who were also devotees, could understand the punishment meted out to them, for they were conscious of the great offense they had committed by not allowing the sages to enter Vaikuṇṭhaloka. In the lowest species of life, including the animal species, forgetfulness of the Lord is very prominent. The doormen were aware that they were going to the criminal department of the material world, and they expected that they might go to the lowest species and forget the Supreme Lord. They prayed, therefore, that this might not happen in the lives they were going to accept because of the curse. In *Bhagavad-gītā*, Sixteenth Chapter, verses 19 and 20, it is said that those who are envious of the Lord and His devotees are thrown into the species of abominable life; life after life such fools are unable to remember the Supreme Personality of Godhead, and therefore they continue going down and down.

TEXT 37

एवं तदैव भगवानरविन्दनाभः
स्वानां विबुध्य सदतिक्रममार्यहृद्यः ।
तस्मिन् ययौ परमहंसमहामुनीना-
मन्वेषणीयचरणौ चलयन् सहश्रीः ॥३७॥

evaṁ tadaiva bhagavān aravinda-nābhaḥ
svānāṁ vibudhya sad-atikramam ārya-hṛdyaḥ
tasmin yayau paramahaṁsa-mahā-munīnām
anveṣaṇīya-caraṇau calayan saha-śrīḥ

evam—thus; *tadā eva*—at that very moment; *bhagavān*—the Supreme Personality of Godhead; *aravinda-nābhaḥ*—with a lotus growing from His navel; *svānām*—of His own servants; *vibudhya*—learned about; *sat*—to the great sages; *atikramam*—the insult; *ārya*—of the righteous; *hṛdyaḥ*—the delight; *tasmin*—there; *yayau*—went; *paramahaṁsa*—recluses; *mahā-munīnām*—by the great sages; *anveṣaṇīya*—which are worthy to be sought; *caraṇau*—the two lotus feet; *calayan*—walking; *saha-śrīḥ*—with the goddess of fortune.

TRANSLATION

At that very moment, the Lord, who is called Padmanābha because of the lotus grown from His navel and who is the delight of the righteous, learned about the insult offered by His own servants to the saints. Accompanied by His spouse, the goddess of fortune, He went to the spot on those very feet sought for by recluses and great sages.

PURPORT

In *Bhagavad-gītā* the Lord declares that His devotees cannot be vanquished at any time. The Lord could understand that the quarrel between the doormen and the sages was taking a different turn, and therefore He instantly came out of His place and went to the spot to stop further aggravation so that His devotees, the doormen, might not be vanquished for good.

TEXT 38

तं त्वागतं प्रतिहृतौपयिकं स्वपुम्भि-
स्तेऽचक्षताक्षविषयं स्वसमाधिभाग्यम् ।
हंसश्रियोर्व्यजनयोः शिववायुलोल-
च्छुभ्रातपत्रशशिकेसरशीकराम्बुम् ॥३८॥

taṁ tv āgataṁ pratihṛtaupayikaṁ sva-pumbhis
te 'cakṣatākṣa-viṣayaṁ sva-samādhi-bhāgyam
haṁsa-śriyor vyajanayoḥ śiva-vāyu-lolac-
chubhrātapatra-śaśi-kesara-śīkarāmbum

tam—Him; *tu*—but; *āgatam*—coming forward; *pratihṛta*—carried; *aupayikam*—the paraphernalia; *sva-pumbhiḥ*—by His own associates; *te*—the great sages (the Kumāras); *acakṣata*—saw; *akṣa-viṣayam*—now a subject matter for seeing; *sva-samādhi-bhāgyam*—visible simply by ecstatic trance; *haṁsa-śriyoḥ*—as beautiful as white swans; *vyajanayoḥ*—the *cāmaras* (bunches of white hair); *śiva-vāyu*—favorable winds; *lolat*—moving; *śubhra-ātapatra*—the white umbrella; *śaśi*—the moon; *kesara*—pearls; *śīkara*—drops; *ambum*—water.

TRANSLATION

The sages, headed by Sanaka Ṛṣi, saw that the Supreme Personality of Godhead, Viṣṇu, who was formerly visible only within their hearts in ecstatic trance, had now actually become visible to their eyes. As He came forward, accompanied by His own associates bearing all paraphernalia, such as an umbrella and a cāmara fan, the white bunches of hair moved very gently, like two swans, and due to their favorable breeze the pearls garlanding the umbrella also moved, like drops of nectar falling from the white full moon or ice melting due to a gust of wind.

PURPORT

In this verse we find the word *acakṣatākṣa-viṣayam.* The Supreme Lord cannot be seen by ordinary eyes, but He now became visible to the eyesight of the Kumāras. Another significant word is *samādhi-bhāgyam.* Meditators who are very fortunate can see the Viṣṇu form of the Lord within their hearts by following the yogic process. But to see Him face to face is a different matter. This is only possible for pure devotees. The Kumāras, therefore, upon seeing the Lord coming forward with His associates, who were holding an umbrella and a *cāmara* fan, were struck with wonder that they were seeing the Lord face to face. It is said in the *Brahma-saṁhitā* that devotees, being elevated in love of God, always see Śyāmasundara, the Supreme Personality of Godhead, within their hearts. But when they are mature, the same God is visible before them face to face. For ordinary persons the Lord is not visible; however, when one can understand the significance of His holy name and one engages himself in the devotional service of the Lord, beginning with the tongue, by chanting and tasting *prasāda,* then gradually the Lord reveals Himself. Thus the devotee constantly sees the Lord within his heart, and, in a more mature stage, one can see the same Lord directly, as we see everything else.

TEXT 39

कृत्स्नप्रसादसुमुखं स्पृहणीयधाम
स्नेहावलोककलया हृदि संस्पृशन्तम् ।
श्यामे पृथावुरसि शोभितया श्रिया स्व-
श्चूडामणिं सुभगयन्तमिवात्मधिष्ण्यम् ॥३९॥

kṛtsna-prasāda-sumukhaṁ spṛhaṇīya-dhāma
snehāvaloka-kalayā hṛdi saṁspṛśantam
śyāme pṛthāv urasi śobhitayā śriyā svaś-
cūḍāmaṇiṁ subhagayantam ivātma-dhiṣṇyam

kṛtsna-prasāda—blessing everyone; *su-mukham*—auspicious face; *spṛhaṇīya*—desirable; *dhāma*—shelter; *sneha*—affection; *avaloka*—looking upon; *kalayā*—by expansion; *hṛdi*—within the heart; *saṁspṛśantam*—touching; *śyāme*—unto the Lord with blackish color; *pṛthau*—broad; *urasi*—chest; *śobhitayā*—being decorated; *śriyā*—goddess of fortune; *svaḥ*—heavenly planets; *cūḍā-maṇim*—summit; *subhagayantam*—spreading good fortune; *iva*—like; *ātma*—the Supreme Personality of Godhead; *dhiṣṇyam*—abode.

TRANSLATION

The Lord is the reservoir of all pleasure. His auspicious presence is meant for everyone's benediction, and His affectionate smiling and glancing touch the core of the heart. The Lord's beautiful bodily color is blackish, and His broad chest is the resting place of the goddess of fortune, who glorifies the entire spiritual world, the summit of all heavenly planets. Thus it appeared

that the Lord was personally spreading the beauty and good fortune of the spiritual world.

PURPORT

When the Lord came, He was pleased with everyone; therefore it is stated here, *kṛtsna-prasāda-sumukham.* The Lord knew that even the offensive doormen were His pure devotees, although by chance they committed an offense at the feet of other devotees. To commit an offense against a devotee is very dangerous in devotional service. Lord Caitanya therefore said that an offense to a devotee is just like a mad elephant run loose; when a mad elephant enters a garden, it tramples all the plants. Similarly, an offense unto the feet of a pure devotee murders one's position in devotional service. On the part of the Lord there was no offended mood because He does not accept any offense created by His sincere devotee. But a devotee should be very cautious of committing offenses at the feet of another devotee. The Lord, being equal to all, and being especially inclined to His devotee, looked as mercifully at the offenders as at the offended. This attitude of the Lord was due to His unlimited quantity of transcendental qualities. His cheerful attitude towards the devotees was so pleasing and heart-touching that His very smile was attractive for them. That attraction was glorious not only for all the higher planets of this material world, but beyond, for the spiritual world also. Generally a human being has no idea of what the constitutional position is in the higher material planets, which are far better constituted in regard to all paraphernalia, yet the Vaikuṇṭha planet is so pleasing and so celestial that it is compared to the middle jewel or locket in a necklace of jewels.

In this verse the words *spṛhaṇīya-dhāma* indicate that the Lord is the reservoir of all pleasure because He has all the transcendental qualities. Although only some of these are aspired for by persons who hanker after the pleasure of merging in the impersonal Brahman, there are other aspirants who want to associate with the Lord personally as His servants. The Lord is so kind that He gives shelter to everyone—both impersonalists and devotees. He gives shelter to the impersonalists in His impersonal Brahman effulgence, whereas He gives shelter to the devotees in His personal abodes known as the Vaikuṇṭhalokas. He is especially inclined to His devotee; He touches the core of the heart of the devotee simply by smiling and glancing over him. The Lord is always served in the Vaikuṇṭhaloka by many hundreds and thousands of goddesses of fortune, as stated by the *Brahma-saṁhitā* (*lakṣmī-sahasra-śata-sambhrama-sevyamānam*). In this material world, one is glorified if he is favored even a pinch by the goddess of fortune, so we can simply imagine how glorified is the kingdom of God in the spiritual world, where many hundreds and thousands of goddesses of fortune engage in the direct service of the Lord. Another feature of this verse is that it openly declares where the Vaikuṇṭhalokas are situated. They are situated as the summit of all the heavenly planets, which are above the sun globe, at the upper limit of the universe, and are known as Satyaloka, or Brahmaloka. The spiritual world is situated beyond the universe. Therefore it is stated here that the spiritual world, Vaikuṇṭhaloka, is the summit of all planetary systems.

TEXT 40

पीतांशुके पृथुनितम्बिनि विस्फुरन्त्या
काञ्च्यालिभिर्विरुतया वनमालया च ।
वल्गुप्रकोष्ठवलयं विनतासुतांसे
विन्यस्तहस्तमितरेण धुनानमब्जम् ॥४०॥

pītāṁśuke pṛthu-nitambini visphurantyā
kāñcyālibhir virutayā vana-mālayā ca
valgu-prakoṣṭha-valayaṁ vinatā-sutāṁse
vinyasta-hastam itareṇa dhunānam abjam

pīta-aṁśuke—covered with a yellow cloth; *pṛthu-nitambini*—on His large hips; *visphurantyā*—shining brightly; *kāñcyā*—with a girdle; *alibhiḥ*—by the bees; *virutayā*—humming; *vana-mālayā*—with a garland of fresh flowers; *ca*—and; *valgu*—lovely; *prakoṣṭha*—wrists; *valayam*—bracelets; *vinatā-suta*—of Garuḍa, the son of Vinatā; *aṁse*—on the shoulder; *vinyasta*—rested; *hastam*—one hand; *itareṇa*—with another hand; *dhunānam*—being twirled; *abjam*—a lotus flower.

TRANSLATION

He was adorned with a girdle that shone brightly on the yellow cloth covering His large hips, and He wore a garland of fresh flowers which was distinguished by humming bees. His lovely wrists were graced with bracelets, and He rested one of His hands on the shoulder of Garuḍa, His carrier, and twirled a lotus with another hand.

PURPORT

Here is a full description of the Personality of Godhead as personally experienced by the sages. The Lord's personal body was covered with yellow robes, and His waist was thin. In Vaikuṇṭha, whenever there is a flower garland on the chest of the Personality of Godhead or any one of His associates, it is described that the humming bees are there. All these features were very beautiful and attractive for the devotees. One of the Lord's hands rested on His carrier, Garuḍa, and in another hand He twirled a lotus flower. These are personal characteristics of the Personality of Godhead, Nārāyaṇa.

TEXT 41

विद्युत्क्षिपन्मकरकुण्डलमण्डनार्ह-
गण्डस्थलोन्नसमुखं मणिमत्किरीटम् ।
दोर्दण्डषण्डविवरे हरता परार्ध्य-
हारेण कन्धरगतेन च कौस्तुभेन ॥४१॥

vidyut-kṣipan-makara-kuṇḍala-maṇḍanārha-
gaṇḍa-sthalonnasa-mukhaṁ maṇimat-kirīṭam
dor-daṇḍa-ṣaṇḍa-vivare haratā parārdhya-
hāreṇa kandhara-gatena ca kaustubhena

vidyut—lightning; *kṣipat*—outshining; *makara*—alligator shaped; *kuṇḍala*—earrings; *maṇḍana*—decoration; *arha*—as it fits; *gaṇḍa-sthala*—cheeks; *unnasa*—prominent nose; *mukham*—countenance; *maṇi-mat*—gem-studded; *kirīṭam*—crown; *doḥ-daṇḍa*—of His four stout arms; *ṣaṇḍa*—group; *vivare*—between; *haratā*—charming; *para-ardhya*—by the most precious; *hāreṇa*—necklace; *kandhara-gatena*—adorning His neck; *ca*—and; *kaustubhena*—by the Kaustubha jewel.

TRANSLATION

His countenance was distinguished by cheeks that enhanced the beauty of His alligator-shaped pendants, which outshone lightning. His nose was prominent, and His head was covered with a gem-studded crown. A charming necklace hung between His stout arms, and His neck was adorned with the gem known by the name Kaustubha.

TEXT 42

अत्रोपसृष्टमिति चोत्स्मितमिन्दिरायाः
स्वानां धिया विरचितं बहुसौष्ठवाढ्यम् ।
मह्यं भवस्य भवतां च भजन्तमङ्गं
नेमुर्निरीक्ष्य नवितृप्तदृशो मुदा कैः ॥४२॥

atropasṛṣṭam iti cotsmitam indirāyāḥ
svānāṁ dhiyā viracitaṁ bahu-sauṣṭhavāḍhyam
mahyaṁ bhavasya bhavatāṁ ca bhajantam aṅgaṁ
nemur nirīkṣya na vitṛpta-dṛśo mudā kaiḥ

atra—here, in the matter of the beauty; *upasṛṣṭam*—curbed down; *iti*—thus; *ca*—and; *utsmitam*—the pride of her beauty; *indirāyāḥ*—of the goddess of fortune; *svānām*—of His own devotees; *dhiyā*—by intelligence; *viracitam*—meditated on; *bahu-sauṣṭhava-ādhyam*—very beautifully decorated; *mahyam*—of me; *bhavasya*—of Lord Śiva; *bhavatām*—of all of you; *ca*—and; *bhajantam*—worshiped; *aṅgam*—the figure; *nemuḥ*—bowed down; *nirīkṣya*—after seeing; *na*—not; *vitṛpta*—satiated; *dṛśaḥ*—eyes; *mudā*—joyously; *kaiḥ*—by their heads.

TRANSLATION

The exquisite beauty of Nārāyaṇa, being many times magnified by the intelligence of His devotees, was so attractive that it defeated the pride of the goddess of fortune in being the most beautiful. My dear demigods, the Lord who thus manifested Himself is worshipable by me, by Lord Śiva and by all of you. The sages regarded Him with unsated eyes and joyously bowed their heads at His lotus feet.

PURPORT

The beauty of the Lord was so enchanting that it could not be sufficiently described. The goddess of fortune is supposed to be the most beautiful sight within the spiritual and material creations of the Lord; she has a sense of being the most beautiful, yet her beauty was defeated when the Lord appeared. In other words, the beauty of the goddess of fortune is secondary in the presence of the Lord. In the words of Vaiṣṇava poets, it is said that the Lord's beauty is so enchanting that it defeats hundreds of thousands of Cupids. He is therefore called Madana-mohana. It is also described that the Lord sometimes becomes mad after the beauty of Rādhārāṇī. Poets describe that under those circumstances, although Lord Kṛṣṇa is Madana-mohana, He becomes Madana-dāha, or enchanted by the beauty of Rādhārāṇī. Actually the Lord's beauty is superexcellent, surpassing even the beauty of Lakṣmī in Vaikuṇṭha. The devotees of the Lord in the Vaikuṇṭha planets want to see the Lord as the most beautiful, but the devotees in Gokula or Kṛṣṇaloka want to see Rādhārāṇī as more beautiful than Kṛṣṇa. The adjustment is that the Lord, being *bhakta-vatsala,* or one who wants to please His devotees, assumes such features so that devotees like Lord Brahmā, Lord Śiva and other demigods may be pleased. Here also, for the devotee-sages, the Kumāras, the

Lord appeared in His most beautiful feature, and they continued to see Him without satiation and wanted to continue seeing Him more and more.

TEXT 43

तस्यारविन्दनयनस्य पदारविन्द-
किञ्जल्कमिश्रतुलसीमकरन्दवायुः ।
अन्तर्गतः स्वविवरेण चकार तेषां
सङ्क्षोभमक्षरजुषामपि चित्ततन्वोः ॥४३॥

tasyāravinda-nayanasya padāravinda-
kiñjalka-miśra-tulasī-makaranda-vāyuḥ
antar-gataḥ sva-vivareṇa cakāra teṣāṁ
saṅkṣobham akṣara-juṣām api citta-tanvoḥ

tasya—of Him; *aravinda-nayanasya*—of the lotus-eyed Lord; *pada-aravinda*—of the lotus feet; *kiñjalka*—with the toes; *miśra*—mixed; *tulasī*—the *tulasī* leaves; *makaranda*—fragrance; *vāyuḥ*—breeze; *antaḥ-gataḥ*—entered within; *sva-vivareṇa*—through their nostrils; *cakāra*—made; *teṣām*—of the Kumāras; *saṅkṣobham*—agitation for change; *akṣara-juṣām*—attached to impersonal Brahman realization; *api*—even though; *citta-tanvoḥ*—in both mind and body.

TRANSLATION

When the breeze carrying the aroma of tulasī leaves from the toes of the lotus feet of the Personality of Godhead entered the nostrils of those sages, they experienced a change both in body and in mind, even though they were attached to the impersonal Brahman understanding.

PURPORT

It appears from this verse that the four Kumāras were impersonalists or protagonists of the philosophy of monism, becoming one with the Lord. But as soon as they saw the Lord's features, their minds changed. In other words, the impersonalist who feels transcendental pleasure in striving to become one with the Lord is defeated when he sees the beautiful transcendental features of the Lord. Because of the fragrance of His lotus feet, carried by the air and mixed with the aroma of *tulasī*, their minds changed; instead of becoming one with the Supreme Lord, they thought it wise to be devotees. Becoming a servitor of the lotus feet of the Lord is better than becoming one with the Lord.

TEXT 44

ते वा अमुष्य वदनासितपद्मकोश-
मुद्वीक्ष्य सुन्दरतराधरकुन्दहासम् ।
लब्धाशिषः पुनरवेक्ष्य तदीयमङ्घ्रि-
द्वन्द्वं नखारुणमणिश्रयणं निदध्युः ॥४४॥

te vā amuṣya vadanāsita-padma-kośam
udvīkṣya sundaratarādhara-kunda-hāsam
labdhāśiṣaḥ punar avekṣya tadīyam aṅghri-
dvandvaṁ nakhāruṇa-maṇi-śrayaṇaṁ nidadhyuḥ

te—those sages; *vai*—certainly; *amuṣya*—of the Supreme Personality of Godhead; *vadana*—face; *asita*—blue; *padma*—lotus; *kośam*—inside; *udvīkṣya*—after looking up; *sundara-tara*—more beautiful; *adhara*—lips; *kunda*—jasmine flower; *hāsam*—smiling; *labdha*—achieved; *āśiṣaḥ*—aims of life; *punaḥ*—again; *avekṣya*—looking down; *tadīyam*—His; *aṅghri-dvandvam*—pair of lotus feet; *nakha*—nails; *aruṇa*—red; *maṇi*—rubies; *śrayaṇam*—shelter; *nidadhyuḥ*—meditated.

TRANSLATION

The Lord's beautiful face appeared to them like the inside of a blue lotus, and the Lord's smile appeared to be a blossoming jasmine flower. After seeing the face of the Lord, the sages were fully satisfied, and when they wanted to see Him further, they looked upon the nails of His lotus feet, which resembled rubies. Thus they viewed the Lord's transcendental body again and again, and so they finally achieved meditation on the Lord's personal feature.

TEXT 45

पुंसां गतिं मृगयतामिह योगमार्गै-
र्ध्यानास्पदं बहु मतं नयनाभिरामम् ।
पौंस्नं वपुर्दर्शयानमनन्यसिद्धै-
रौत्पत्तिकैः समगृणन् युतमष्टभोगैः ॥४५॥

puṁsāṁ gatiṁ mṛgayatām iha yoga-mārgair
dhyānāspadaṁ bahu-mataṁ nayanābhirāmam
pauṁsnaṁ vapur darśayānam ananya-siddhair
autpattikaiḥ samagṛṇan yutam aṣṭa-bhogaiḥ

puṁsām—of those persons; *gatim*—liberation; *mṛgayatām*—who are searching; *iha*—here in this world; *yoga-mārgaiḥ*—by the process of *aṣṭāṅga-yoga; dhyāna-āspadam*—object of meditation; *bahu*—by the great *yogis; matam*—approved; *nayana*—eyes; *abhirāmam*—pleasing; *pauṁsnam*—human; *vapuḥ*—form; *darśayānam*—displaying; *ananya*—not by others; *siddhaiḥ*—perfected; *autpattikaiḥ*—eternally present; *samagṛṇan*—praised; *yutam*—the Supreme Personality of Godhead, who is endowed; *aṣṭa-bhogaiḥ*—with eight kinds of achievement.

TRANSLATION

This is the form of the Lord which is meditated upon by the followers of the yoga process, and it is pleasing to the yogīs in meditation. It is not imaginary but factual, as proved by great yogīs. The Lord is full in eight kinds of achievement, but for others these achievements are not possible in full perfection.

PURPORT

The success of the *yoga* process is very nicely described here. It is specifically mentioned that the form of the Lord as four-handed Nārāyaṇa is the object of meditation for the followers of *yoga-mārga*. In the modern age there are so many so-called *yogīs* who do not target their meditation on the four-handed Nārāyaṇa form. Some of them try to meditate on something impersonal or void, but that is not approved by the great *yogīs* who follow the standard method. The real *yoga-mārga* process is to control the senses, sit in a solitary and sanctified place and meditate on the four-handed form of Nārāyaṇa, decorated as described in this chapter as He appeared before the four sages. This Nārāyaṇa form is Kṛṣṇa's expansion; therefore the Kṛṣṇa consciousness movement which is now spreading is the real, topmost process of *yoga* practice.

Kṛṣṇa consciousness is the highest *yoga* performance by trained devotional *yogīs*. Despite all the allurement of *yoga* practice, the eight kinds of yogic perfections are hardly achievable by the common man. But here it is described that the Lord, who appeared before the four sages, is Himself full of all eight of those perfections. The highest *yoga-mārga* process is to concentrate the mind twenty-four hours a day on Kṛṣṇa. This is called Kṛṣṇa consciousness. The *yoga* system, as described in *Śrīmad-Bhāgavatam* and *Bhagavad-gītā* or as recommended in the Patañjali *yoga* process, is different from the nowadays—practiced *haṭha-yoga* as it is generally understood in the Western countries. Real *yoga* practice is to control the senses and, after such control is established, to concentrate the mind on the Nārāyaṇa form of the Supreme Personality of Godhead, Śrī Kṛṣṇa. Lord Kṛṣṇa is the original Personality of Godhead, and all the other Viṣṇu forms—with four hands decorated with conch, lotus, club and wheel—are plenary expansions of Kṛṣṇa. In *Bhagavad-gītā* it is recommended that one meditate upon the form of the Lord. To practice concentration of the mind, one has to sit with the head and the back in a straight line, and one must practice in a secluded place, sanctified by a sacred atmosphere. The *yogī* should observe the rules and regulations of *brahmacarya*—to strictly live a life of self-restraint and celibacy. One cannot practice *yoga* in a congested city, living a life of extravagancy, including unrestricted sex indulgence and adultery of the tongue. *Yoga* practice necessitates controlling the senses, and the beginning of sense control is to control the tongue. One who can control the tongue can also have control over the other senses. One cannot allow the tongue to take all kinds of forbidden food and drink and at the same time advance in the practice of *yoga*. It is a very regrettable fact that many unauthorized so-called *yogīs* come to the Western countries and exploit people's inclination towards *yoga* practice. Such unauthorized *yogīs* even dare to say publicly that one can indulge in the habit of drinking and at the same time practice meditation.

Five thousand years ago Lord Kṛṣṇa recommended *yoga* practice to Arjuna, but Arjuna frankly expressed his inability to follow the stringent rules and regulations of the *yoga* system. One should be very practical in every field of activities and should not waste his valuable time in practicing useless gymnastic feats in the name of *yoga*. Real *yoga* is to search out the four-handed Supersoul within one's heart and see Him perpetually in meditation. Such continued meditation is called *samādhi,* and the object of this meditation is the four-handed Nārāyaṇa, with bodily decorations as described in this chapter of *Śrīmad-Bhāgavatam*. If, however, one wants to meditate upon something void or impersonal, it will take a very long time before he achieves success in *yoga* practice. We cannot concentrate our mind on something void or impersonal. Real *yoga* is to fix the mind on the form of the Lord, the four-handed Nārāyaṇa who is sitting in everyone's heart.

By meditation one can understand that God is seated within one's heart. Even if one does not know it, God is seated within the heart of everyone. Not only is He seated in the heart of the human being, but He is also within the hearts of cats and dogs. *Bhagavad-gītā* certifies this fact by the declaration of the Lord, *īśvaraḥ sarva-bhūtānāṁ hṛd-deśe*. The *īśvara,* the supreme controller of the world, is seated in the heart of everyone. Not only is He in everyone's heart, but He is also present within the atom. No place is vacant or devoid of the presence of the Lord. That is the statement of *Īśopaniṣad.* God is present everywhere, and His right of proprietorship applies to everything. The feature of the Lord by which He is present everywhere is called Paramātmā. *Ātmā* means the individual soul, and Paramātmā means the individual Supersoul; both *ātmā* and Paramātmā are individual persons. The difference between *ātmā* and Paramātmā is that the *ātmā,* or the soul, is present only in a particular body, whereas the Paramātmā is present everywhere. In this connection, the example of the sun is very nice. An individual person may be situated in one place, but the sun, even though a similar individual entity, is present on the head of every individual person. In *Bhagavad-gītā* this is explained. Therefore even though the qualities of all entities, including the Lord, are equal, the Supersoul is different from the individual soul by quantitative power of expansion. The Lord, or the Supersoul, can expand Himself into millions of different forms, whereas the individual soul cannot do so.

The Supersoul, being seated in everyone's heart, can witness everyone's activities—past, present and future. In the *Upaniṣads* the Supersoul is described as being seated with the individual soul as friend and witness. As a friend, the Lord is always anxious to get back His friend, the individual soul, and bring him back home, back to Godhead. As a witness He is the bestower of all benedictions, and He endows each individual with the result of his actions. The Supersoul gives the individual soul all facilities to achieve whatever he desires to enjoy in this material world. Suffering is a reaction to the living entity's propensity to try to lord it over the material world. But the Lord instructs His friend, the individual soul, who is also His son, to give up all other engagements and simply surrender unto Him for perpetual bliss and an eternal life full of knowledge. This is the last instruction of *Bhagavad-gītā,* the most authorized and widely read book on all varieties of *yoga.* Thus the last word of *Bhagavad-gītā* is the last word in the perfection of *yoga.*

It is stated in *Bhagavad-gītā* that a person who is always absorbed in Kṛṣṇa consciousness is the topmost *yogī.* What is Kṛṣṇa consciousness? As the individual soul is present by his consciousness throughout his entire body, so the Supersoul, or Paramātmā, is present throughout the whole creation by superconsciousness. This superconscious energy is imitated by the individual soul, who has limited consciousness. I can understand what is going on within my limited body, but I cannot feel what is going on in another's body. I am present throughout my body by my consciousness, but my consciousness is not present in another's body. The Supersoul, or Paramātmā, however, being present everywhere and within everyone, is also conscious of everyone's existence. The theory that the soul and the Supersoul are one is not acceptable because it is not confirmed by authoritative Vedic literature. The individual soul's consciousness cannot act in superconsciousness. This superconsciousness can be achieved, however, by dovetailing individual consciousness with the consciousness of the Supreme. This dovetailing process is called surrender, or Kṛṣṇa consciousness. From the teachings of *Bhagavad-gītā* we learn very clearly that Arjuna, in the beginning, did not want to fight with his brothers and relatives, but after understanding *Bhagavad-gītā* he dovetailed his consciousness with the superconsciousness of Kṛṣṇa. He was then in Kṛṣṇa consciousness.

A person in full Kṛṣṇa consciousness acts by the dictation of Kṛṣṇa. In the beginning of Kṛṣṇa consciousness, dictation is received through the transparent medium of the spiritual master. When one is sufficiently trained and acts in submissive faith and love for Kṛṣṇa under the direction of the bona fide spiritual master, the dovetailing process becomes more firm and accurate. This stage of devotional service by the devotee in Kṛṣṇa consciousness is the most perfect stage of the *yoga* system. At this stage, Kṛṣṇa, or the Supersoul, dictates from within, while from without the devotee is helped by the spiritual master, who is the bona fide representative of Kṛṣṇa. From within He helps the devotee as *caitya,* for He is seated within the heart of everyone. Understanding that God is seated within everyone's heart is not, however, sufficient. One has to be acquainted with God from both within and without, and one must take dictation from within and without to act in Kṛṣṇa consciousness. This is the highest perfectional stage of the human form of life and the topmost perfection of all *yoga.*

For a perfect *yogī,* there are eight kinds of superachievements: one can become lighter than air, one can become smaller than the atom, one can become bigger than a mountain, one can achieve whatever he desires, one can control like the Lord, and so on. But when one rises to the perfectional stage of receiving dictation from the Lord, that is greater than any stage of material achievements above mentioned. The breathing exercise of the *yoga* system which is generally practiced is just the beginning. Meditation on the Supersoul is just another step forward. But to obtain direct contact with the Supersoul and take dictation from Him is the highest perfectional stage. The breathing exercises of meditation practice were very difficult even five thousand years ago, otherwise Arjuna would not have rejected the proposal of Kṛṣṇa that he adopt this system. This age of Kali is called the fallen age. In this age, people in general are short-living and very slow to understand self-realization or spiritual life; they are mostly unfortunate, and therefore if someone is a little bit interested in self-realization he is likely to be misguided by so many frauds. The only way to realize the perfect stage of *yoga* is to follow the principles of *Bhagavad-gītā* as practiced by Lord Caitanya. This is the simplest and highest perfection of *yoga* practice. Lord Caitanya demonstrated this

Kṛṣṇa consciousness *yoga* system in a practical manner simply by chanting the holy name of Kṛṣṇa, as prescribed in the *Vedānta, Śrīmad-Bhāgavatam, Bhagavad-gītā,* and many important *Purāṇas.*

The largest number of Indians follow this *yoga* process, and in the United States it is gradually spreading in many cities. It is very easy and practical for this age, especially for those who are serious about success in *yoga.* No other process of *yoga* can be successful in this age. The meditation process was possible in the golden age, Satya-yuga, because people in that age used to live for hundreds of thousands of years. If one wants success in practical *yoga* practice, it is advised that he take to the chanting of Hare Kṛṣṇa, Hare Kṛṣṇa, Kṛṣṇa Kṛṣṇa, Hare Hare/ Hare Rāma, Hare Rāma, Rāma Rāma, Hare Hare, and he will actually feel himself making progress. In *Bhagavad-gītā* this practice of Kṛṣṇa consciousness is prescribed as *rāja-vidyā,* or the king of all erudition.

Those who have taken to this most sublime *bhakti-yoga* system, who practice devotional service in transcendental love of Kṛṣṇa, can testify to its happy and easy execution. The four sages Sanaka, Sanātana, Sanandana and Sanat-kumāra also became attracted by the features of the Lord and the transcendental aroma of the dust of His lotus feet, as already described in verse 43.

Yoga necessitates controlling the senses, and *bhakti-yoga,* or Kṛṣṇa consciousness, is the process of purifying the senses. When the senses are purified, they are automatically controlled. One cannot stop the activities of the senses by artificial means, but if one purifies the senses by engaging in the service of the Lord, the senses not only can be controlled from rubbish engagement, but can be engaged in the Lord's transcendental service, as aspired to by the four sages Sanaka, Sanātana, Sanandana and Sanat-kumāra. Kṛṣṇa consciousness is not, therefore, a manufactured concoction of the speculative mind. It is the process enjoined in *Bhagavad-gītā* (9.34): *man-manā bhava mad-bhakto mad-yājī māṁ namaskuru.*

TEXT 46

कुमारा ऊचुः

योऽन्तर्हितो हृदि गतोऽपि दुरात्मनां त्वं
सोऽद्यैव नो नयनमूलमनन्त राद्धः ।
यर्ह्येव कर्णविवरेण गुहां गतो नः
पित्रानुवर्णितरहा भवदुद्भवेन ॥४६॥

kumārā ūcuḥ
yo 'ntarhito hṛdi gato 'pi durātmanāṁ tvaṁ
so 'dyaiva no nayana-mūlam ananta rāddhaḥ
yarhy eva karṇa-vivareṇa guhāṁ gato naḥ
pitrānuvarṇita-rahā bhavad-udbhavena

kumārāḥ ūcuḥ—the Kumāras said; *yaḥ*—He who; *antarhitaḥ*—not manifested; *hṛdi*—in the heart; *gataḥ*—is seated; *api*—even though; *durātmanām*—to the rascals; *tvam*—You; *saḥ*—He; *adya*—today; *eva*—certainly; *naḥ*—of us; *nayana-mūlam*—face to face; *ananta*—O unlimited one; *rāddhaḥ*—attained; *yarhi*—when; *eva*—certainly; *karṇa-vivareṇa*—through the ears; *guhām*—intelligence; *gataḥ*—have attained; *naḥ*—our; *pitrā*—by our father; *anuvarṇita*—described; *rahāḥ*—mysteries; *bhavat-udbhavena*—by Your appearance.

TRANSLATION

The Kumāras said: Our dear Lord, You are not manifested to rascals, even though You are seated within the heart of everyone. But as far as we are concerned, we see You face to face, although You are unlimited. The statements we have heard about You from our father, Brahmā, through the ears have now been actually realized by Your kind appearance.

PURPORT

The so-called *yogīs* who concentrate their mind or meditate upon the impersonal or void are described here. This verse of *Śrīmad-Bhāgavatam* describes persons who are expected to be very expert *yogīs* engaged in meditation but who do not find the Supreme Personality of Godhead seated within the heart. These persons are described here as *durātmā,* which means a person who has a very crooked heart, or a less intelligent person, just opposite to a *mahātmā,* which means one who has a broad heart. Those so-called *yogīs* who, although engaged in meditation, are not broad hearted cannot find the four-handed Nārāyaṇa form, even though He is seated within their heart. Although the first realization of the Supreme Absolute Truth is impersonal Brahman, one should not remain satisfied with experiencing the impersonal effulgence of the Supreme Lord. In the *Īśopaniṣad* also, the devotee prays that the glaring effulgence of Brahman may be removed from his eyes so that he can see the real, personal feature of the Lord and thus satisfy himself fully. Similarly, although the Lord is not visible in the beginning because of His glaring bodily effulgence, if a devotee sincerely wants to see Him, the Lord is revealed to him. It is said in *Bhagavad-gītā* that the Lord cannot be seen by our imperfect eyes, He cannot be heard by our imperfect ears, and He cannot be experienced by our imperfect senses; but if one engages in devotional service with faith and devotion, then God reveals Himself.

Here the four sages Sanat-kumāra, Sanātana, Sanandana and Sanaka are described as actually sincere devotees. Although they had heard from their father, Brahmā, about the personal feature of the Lord, only the impersonal feature—Brahman—was revealed to them. But because they were sincerely searching for the Lord, they finally saw His personal feature directly, which corresponded with the description given by their father. They thus became fully satisfied. Here they express their gratitude because although they were foolish impersonalists in the beginning, by the grace of the Lord they could now have the good fortune to see His personal feature. Another significant aspect of this verse is that the sages describe their experience of hearing from their father, Brahmā, who was born of the Lord directly. In other words, the disciplic succession from the Lord to Brahmā and from Brahmā to Nārada and from Nārada to Vyāsa, and so on, is accepted here. Because the Kumāras were sons of Brahmā, they had the opportunity to learn Vedic knowledge from the disciplic succession of Brahmā, and therefore, in spite of their impersonalist beginnings, they became, in the end, direct seers of the personal feature of the Lord.

TEXT 47

तं त्वां विदाम भगवन् परमात्मतत्त्वं
सत्त्वेन सम्प्रति रतिं रचयन्तमेषाम् ।
यत्तेऽनुतापविदितैर्दृढभक्तियोगै-
रुद्ग्रन्थयो हृदि विदुर्मुनयो विरागाः ॥४७॥

taṁ tvāṁ vidāma bhagavan param ātma-tattvaṁ
sattvena samprati ratiṁ racayantam eṣām
yat te 'nutāpa-viditair dṛḍha-bhakti-yogair
udgranthayo hṛdi vidur munayo virāgāḥ

tam—Him; *tvām*—You; *vidāma*—we know; *bhagavan*—O Supreme Personality of Godhead; *param*—the Supreme; *ātma-tattvam*—Absolute Truth; *sattvena*—by Your form of pure goodness; *samprati*—now; *ratim*—love of God; *racayantam*—creating; *eṣām*—of all of them; *yat*—which; *te*—Your; *anutāpa*—mercy; *viditaiḥ*—understood; *dṛḍha*—unflinching; *bhakti-yogaiḥ*—through devotional service; *udgranthayaḥ*—without attachment, free from material bondage; *hṛdi*—in the heart; *viduḥ*—understood; *munayaḥ*—great sages; *virāgāḥ*—not interested in material life.

TRANSLATION

We know that You are the Supreme Absolute Truth, the Personality of Godhead, who manifests His transcendental form in the uncontaminated mode of pure goodness. This transcendental, eternal form of Your personality can be understood only by Your mercy, through unflinching devotional service, by great sages whose hearts have been purified in the devotional way.

PURPORT

The Absolute Truth can be understood in three features—impersonal Brahman, localized Paramātmā, and Bhagavān, the Supreme Personality of Godhead. Here it is admitted that the Supreme Personality of Godhead is the last word in understanding the Absolute Truth. Even though the four Kumāras were instructed by their great learned father, Brahmā, they could not actually understand the Absolute Truth. They could only understand the Supreme Absolute Truth when they personally saw the Personality of Godhead with their own eyes. In other words, if one sees or understands the Supreme Personality of Godhead, the other two features of the Absolute Truth—namely impersonal Brahman and localized Paramātmā—are also automatically understood. Therefore the Kumāras confirm: "You are the ultimate Absolute Truth." The impersonalist may argue that since the Supreme Personality of Godhead was so nicely decorated, He was therefore not the Absolute Truth. But here it is confirmed that all the variegatedness of the absolute platform is constituted of *śuddha-sattva,* pure goodness. In the material world, any quality—goodness, passion or ignorance—is contaminated. Even the quality of goodness here in the material world is not free from tinges of passion and ignorance. But in the transcendental world, only pure goodness, without any tinge of passion or ignorance, exists; therefore the form of the Supreme Personality of Godhead and His variegated pastimes and paraphernalia are all pure *sattva-guṇa.* Such variegatedness in pure goodness is exhibited eternally by the Lord for the satisfaction of the devotee. The devotee does not want to see the Supreme Personality of Absolute Truth in voidness or impersonalism. In one sense, absolute transcendental variegatedness is meant only for the devotees, not for others, because this distinct feature of transcendental variegatedness can be understood only by the mercy of the Supreme Lord and not by mental speculation or the ascending process. It is said that one can understand the Supreme Personality of Godhead when one is even slightly favored by Him; otherwise, without His mercy, a man may speculate for thousands of years and not understand what is actually the Absolute Truth. This mercy can be perceived by the devotee when he is completely freed from contamination. It is stated, therefore, that only when all contamination is rooted out and the devotee is completely detached from material attractions can he receive this mercy of the Lord.

TEXT 48

नात्यन्तिकं विगणयन्त्यपि ते प्रसादं
किम्वन्यदर्पितभयं भ्रुव उन्नयैस्ते ।
येऽङ्ग त्वदङ्घ्रिशरणा भवतः कथायाः
कीर्तन्यतीर्थयशसः कुशला रसज्ञाः ॥४८॥

nātyantikaṁ vigaṇayanty api te prasādaṁ
kimv anyad arpita-bhayaṁ bhruva unnayais te
ye 'ṅga tvad-aṅghri-śaraṇā bhavataḥ kathāyāḥ
kīrtanya-tīrtha-yaśasaḥ kuśalā rasa-jñāḥ

na—not; *ātyantikam*—liberation; *vigaṇayanti*—care for; *api*—even; *te*—those; *prasādam*—benedictions; *kim u*—what to speak; *anyat*—other material happinesses; *arpita*—given; *bhayam*—fearfulness; *bhruvaḥ*—of the eyebrows; *unnayaiḥ*—by the raising; *te*—Your; *ye*—those devotees; *aṅga*—O Supreme Personality of Godhead; *tvat*—Your; *aṅghri*—lotus feet; *śaraṇāḥ*—who have taken shelter; *bhavataḥ*—Your; *kathāyāḥ*—narrations; *kīrtanya*—worth chanting; *tīrtha*—pure; *yaśasaḥ*—glories; *kuśalāḥ*—very expert; *rasa-jñāḥ*—knowers of the mellows or humors.

TRANSLATION

Persons who are very expert and most intelligent in understanding things as they are engage in hearing narrations of the auspicious activities and pastimes of the Lord, which are worth chanting and worth hearing. Such persons do not care even for the highest material benediction, namely liberation, to say nothing of other less important benedictions like the material happiness of the heavenly kingdom.

PURPORT

The transcendental bliss enjoyed by the devotees of the Lord is completely different from the material happiness enjoyed by less intelligent persons. The less intelligent persons in the material world are engaged by the four principles of benediction called *dharma, artha, kāma* and *mokṣa.* Generally they prefer to take to religious life to achieve some material benediction, the purpose of which is to satisfy the senses. When, by that process, they become confused or frustrated in fulfilling the maximum amount of sense enjoyment, they try to become one with the Supreme, which is, according to their conception, *mukti,* or liberation. There are five kinds of liberation, the least important of which is called *sāyujya,* to become one with the Supreme. Devotees don't care for such liberation because they are actually intelligent. Nor are they inclined to accept any of the other four kinds of liberation, namely to live on the same planet as the Lord, to live with Him side by side as an associate, to have the same opulence, and to attain the same bodily features. They are concerned only with glorifying the Supreme Lord and His auspicious activities. Pure devotional service is *śravaṇaṁ kīrtanam.* Pure devotees, who take transcendental pleasure in hearing and chanting the glories of the Lord, do not care for any kind of liberation; even if they are offered the five liberations, they refuse to accept them, as stated in the *Bhāgavatam* in the Third Canto. Materialistic persons aspire for the sense enjoyment of heavenly pleasure in the heavenly kingdom, but devotees reject such material pleasure at once. The devotee does not even care for the post of Indra. A devotee knows that any pleasurable material position is subject to be annihilated at a certain point. Even if one reaches the post of Indra, Candra, or any other demigod, he must be dissolved at a certain stage. A devotee is never interested in such temporary pleasure. From Vedic scriptures it is understood that sometimes even Brahmā and Indra fall down, but a devotee in the transcendental abode of the Lord never falls. This transcendental stage of life, in which one feels transcendental pleasure in hearing the Lord's pastimes, is also recommended by Lord Caitanya. When Lord Caitanya was talking with Rāmānanda Rāya, there were varieties of suggestions offered by Rāmānanda regarding spiritual realization, but Lord Caitanya rejected all but one—that one should hear the glories of the Lord in association with pure devotees. That is acceptable for everyone, especially in this age. One should engage himself in hearing from pure devotees about the activities of the Lord. That is considered the supreme benediction for mankind.

TEXT 49

कामं भवः स्ववृजिनैर्निरयेषु नः स्ता-
च्चेतोऽलिवद्यदि नु ते पदयो रमेत ।
वाचश्च नस्तुलसिवद्यदि तेऽङ्घ्रिशोभाः
पूर्येत ते गुणगणैर्यदि कर्णरन्ध्रः ॥४९॥

kāmaṁ bhavaḥ sva-vṛjinair nirayeṣu naḥ stāc
ceto 'livad yadi nu te padayo rameta
vācaś ca nas tulasivad yadi te 'ṅghri-śobhāḥ
pūryeta te guṇa-gaṇair yadi karṇa-randhraḥ

kāmam—as much as deserved; *bhavaḥ*—birth; *sva-vṛjinaiḥ*—by our own sinful activities; *nirayeṣu*—in low births; *naḥ*—our; *stāt*—let it be; *cetaḥ*—minds; *ali-vat*—like bees; *yadi*—if; *nu*—may be; *te*—Your; *padayoḥ*—at Your lotus feet; *rameta*—are engaged; *vācaḥ*—words; *ca*—and; *naḥ*—our; *tulasi-vat*—like the *tulasī* leaves; *yadi*—if; *te*—Your; *aṅghri*—at Your lotus feet; *śobhāḥ*—beautified; *pūryeta*—are filled; *te*—Your; *guṇa-gaṇaiḥ*—by transcendental qualities; *yadi*—if; *karṇa-randhraḥ*—the holes of the ears.

TRANSLATION

O Lord, we pray that You let us be born in any hellish condition of life, just as long as our hearts and minds are always engaged in the service of Your lotus feet, our words are made beautiful [by speaking of Your activities] just as tulasī leaves are beautified when offered unto Your lotus feet, and as long as our ears are always filled with the chanting of Your transcendental qualities.

PURPORT

The four sages now offer their humility to the Personality of Godhead because of their having been haughty in cursing two other devotees of the Lord. Jaya and Vijaya, the two doorkeepers who checked them from entering the Vaikuṇṭha planet, were certainly offenders, but as Vaiṣṇavas, the four sages should not have cursed them in anger. After the incident, they became conscious that they had done wrong by cursing the devotees of the Lord, and they prayed to the Lord that even in the hellish condition of life their minds might not be distracted from the engagement of service to the lotus feet of Lord Nārāyaṇa. Those who are devotees of the Lord are not afraid of any condition of life, provided there is constant engagement in the service of the Lord. It is said of the *nārāyaṇa-para,* or those who are devotees of Nārāyaṇa, the Supreme Personality of Godhead, *na kutaścana bibhyati* (*Bhāg.* 6.17.28). They are not afraid of entering a hellish condition, for since they are engaged in the transcendental loving service of the Lord, heaven or hell is the same for them. In material life both heaven and hell are one and the same because they are material; in either place there is no engagement in the Lord's service. Therefore those who are engaged in the service of the Lord see no distinction between heaven and hell; it is only the materialists who prefer one to the other.

These four devotees prayed to the Lord that although they might go to hell because they had cursed devotees, they might not forget the service of the Lord. The transcendental loving service of the Lord is performed in three ways—with the body, with the mind and with words. Here the sages pray that their words may always be engaged in glorifying the Supreme Lord. One may speak very nicely with ornamental language or one may be expert at controlled grammatical presentation, but if one's words are not engaged in the service of the Lord, they have no flavor and no actual use. The example is given here of *tulasī* leaves. The *tulasī* leaf is very useful even from the medicinal or antiseptic point of view. It is considered sacred and is offered to the lotus feet of the Lord. The *tulasī* leaf has numerous good qualities, but if it were not offered to the lotus feet of the Lord, *tulasī* could not be of much value or importance. Similarly, one may speak very nicely from the rhetorical or grammatical point of view, which may be very much appreciated by a materialistic audience, but if one's words are not offered to the service of the Lord, they are useless. The holes of the ears are very small and can be filled with any insignificant sound, so how can they receive as great a vibration as the glorification of the Lord? The answer is that the holes of the ears are like the sky. As the sky can never be filled up, the quality of the ear is such that one may go on pouring in vibrations of various kinds, yet it is capable of receiving more and more vibrations. A devotee is not afraid of going to hell if he has the opportunity to hear the glories of the Lord constantly. This is the advantage of chanting Hare Kṛṣṇa, Hare Kṛṣṇa, Kṛṣṇa Kṛṣṇa, Hare Hare/ Hare Rāma, Hare Rāma, Rāma Rāma, Hare Hare. One may be put in any condition, but God gives him the prerogative to chant Hare Kṛṣṇa. In any condition of life, if one goes on chanting he will never be unhappy.

TEXT 50

प्रादुश्चकर्थ यदिदं पुरुहूत रूपं
तेनेश निर्वृतिमवापुरलं दृशो नः ।
तस्मा इदं भगवते नम इद्विधेम
योऽनात्मनां दुरुदयो भगवान् प्रतीतः ॥५०॥

prāduścakartha yad idaṁ puruhūta rūpaṁ
teneśa nirvṛtim avāpur alaṁ dṛśo naḥ
tasmā idaṁ bhagavate nama id vidhema
yo 'nātmanāṁ durudayo bhagavān pratītaḥ

prāduścakartha—You have manifested; *yat*—which; *idam*—this; *puruhūta*—O greatly worshiped; *rūpam*—eternal form; *tena*—by that form; *īśa*—O Lord; *nirvṛtim*—satisfaction; *avāpuḥ*—obtained; *alam*—so much; *dṛśaḥ*—vision; *naḥ*—our; *tasmai*—unto Him; *idam*—this; *bhagavate*—unto the Supreme Personality of Godhead; *namaḥ*—obeisances; *it*—only; *vidhema*—let us offer; *yaḥ*—who; *anātmanām*—of those who are less intelligent; *durudayaḥ*—cannot be seen; *bhagavān*—the Supreme Personality of Godhead; *pratītaḥ*—has been seen by us.

TRANSLATION

O Lord, we therefore offer our respectful obeisances unto Your eternal form as the Personality of Godhead, which You have so kindly manifested before us. Your supreme, eternal form cannot be seen by unfortunate, less intelligent persons, but we are so much satisfied in our mind and vision to see it.

PURPORT

The four sages were impersonalists in the beginning of their spiritual life, but afterwards, by the grace of their father and spiritual master, Brahmā, they understood the eternal, spiritual form of the Lord and felt completely satisfied. In other words, the transcendentalists who aspire to the impersonal Brahman or localized Paramātmā are not fully satisfied and still hanker for more. Even if they are satisfied in their minds, still, transcendentally, their eyes are not satisfied. But as soon as such persons come to realize the Supreme Personality of Godhead, they are satisfied in all respects. In other words, they become devotees and want to see the form of the Lord continually. It is confirmed in the *Brahma-saṁhitā* that one who has developed transcendental love of Kṛṣṇa by smearing his eyes with the ointment of love sees constantly the eternal form of the Lord. The particular word used in this connection, *anātmanām,* signifies those who have no control over the mind and senses and who therefore speculate and want to become one with the Lord. Such persons cannot have the pleasure of seeing the eternal form of the Lord. For the impersonalists and the so-called *yogīs,* the Lord is always hidden by the curtain of *yogamāyā. Bhagavad-gītā* says that even when Lord Kṛṣṇa was seen by everyone while He was present on the surface of the earth, the impersonalists and the so-called *yogīs* could not see Him because they were devoid of devotional eyesight. The theory of the impersonalists and so-called *yogīs* is that the Supreme Lord assumes a particular form when He comes in touch with *māyā,* although actually He has no form. This very conception of the impersonalists and so-called *yogīs* checks them from seeing the Supreme Personality of Godhead as He is. The Lord, therefore, is always beyond the sight of such nondevotees. The four sages felt so much obliged to the Lord that they offered their respectful obeisances unto Him again and again.

Thus end the Bhaktivedanta purports of the Third Canto, Fifteenth Chapter, of the Śrīmad-Bhāgavatam, *entitled "Description of the Kingdom of God."*

CHAPTER SIXTEEN

The Two Doorkeepers of Vaikuṇṭha, Jaya and Vijaya, Cursed by the Sages

TEXT 1

ब्रह्मोवाच
इति तद् गृणतां तेषां मुनीनां योगधर्मिणाम् ।
प्रतिनन्द्य जगादेदं विकुण्ठनिलयो विभुः ॥ १ ॥

brahmovāca
iti tad gṛṇatāṁ teṣāṁ
munīnāṁ yoga-dharmiṇām
pratinandya jagādedaṁ
vikuṇṭha-nilayo vibhuḥ

brahmā uvāca—Lord Brahmā said; *iti*—thus; *tat*—speech; *gṛṇatām*—praising; *teṣām*—of them; *munīnām*—those four sages; *yoga-dharmiṇām*—engaged in linking with the Supreme; *pratinandya*—after congratulating; *jagāda*—said; *idam*—these words; *vikuṇṭha-nilayaḥ*—whose abode is bereft of anxiety; *vibhuḥ*—the Supreme Personality of Godhead.

TRANSLATION

Lord Brahmā said: After thus congratulating the sages for their nice words, the Supreme Personality of Godhead, whose abode is in the kingdom of God, spoke as follows.

TEXT 2

श्रीभगवानुवाच
एतौ तौ पार्षदौ मह्यं जयो विजय एव च ।
कदर्थीकृत्य मां यद्वो बह्वक्रातामतिक्रमम् ॥ २ ॥

śrī-bhagavān uvāca
etau tau pārṣadau mahyaṁ
jayo vijaya eva ca

kadarthī-kṛtya māṁ yad vo
bahv akrātām atikramam

śrī-bhagavān uvāca—the Supreme Personality of Godhead said; *etau*—these two; *tau*—they; *pārṣadau*—attendants; *mahyam*—of Mine; *jayaḥ*—named Jaya; *vijayaḥ*—named Vijaya; *eva*—certainly; *ca*—and; *kadarthī-kṛtya*—by ignoring; *mām*—Me; *yat*—which; *vaḥ*—against you; *bahu*—great; *akrātām*—have committed; *atikramam*—offense.

TRANSLATION

The Personality of Godhead said: These attendants of Mine, Jaya and Vijaya by name, have committed a great offense against you because of ignoring Me.

PURPORT

To commit an offense at the feet of a devotee of the Lord is a great wrong. Even when a living entity is promoted to Vaikuṇtha, there is still the chance that he may commit offenses, but the difference is that when one is in a Vaikuṇṭha planet, even if by chance one commits an offense, he is protected by the Lord. This is the remarkable fact in the dealings of the Lord and the servitor, as seen in the present incident concerning Jaya and Vijaya. The word *atikramam* used herein indicates that in offending a devotee one neglects the Supreme Lord Himself.

By mistake the doormen held the sages from entering Vaikuṇṭhaloka, but because they were engaged in the transcendental service of the Lord, their annihilation was not expected by advanced devotees. The Lord's presence on the spot was very pleasing to the hearts of the devotees. The Lord understood that the trouble was due to His lotus feet not being seen by the sages, and therefore He wanted to please them by personally going there. The Lord is so merciful that even if there is some impediment for the devotee, He Himself manages matters in such a way that the devotee is not bereft of having audience at His lotus feet. There is a very good example in the life of Haridāsa Ṭhākura. When Caitanya Mahāprabhu was residing at Jagannātha Purī, Haridāsa Ṭhākura, who happened to be Muhammadan by birth, was with Him. In Hindu temples, especially in those days, no one but a Hindu was allowed to enter. Although Haridāsa Ṭhākura was the greatest of all Hindus in his behavior, he considered himself a Muhammadan and did not enter the temple. Lord Caitanya could understand his humility, and since he did not go to see the temple, Lord Caitanya Himself, who is nondifferent from Jagannātha, used to come and sit with Haridāsa Ṭhākura daily. Here in *Śrīmad-Bhāgavatam* we also find this same behavior of the Lord.

His devotees were prevented from seeing His lotus feet, but the Lord Himself came to see them on the same lotus feet for which they aspired. It is also significant that He was accompanied by the goddess of fortune. The goddess of fortune is not to be seen by ordinary persons, but the Lord was so kind that although the devotees did not aspire for such an honor, He appeared before them with the goddess of fortune.

TEXT 3

यस्त्वेतयोर्धृतो दण्डो भवद्भिर्मामनुव्रतैः ।
स एवानुमतोऽस्माभिर्मुनयो देवहेलनात् ॥ ३ ॥

yas tv etayor dhṛto daṇḍo
bhavadbhir mām anuvrataiḥ
sa evānumato 'smābhir
munayo deva-helanāt

yaḥ—which; *tu*—but; *etayoḥ*—regarding both Jaya and Vijaya; *dhṛtaḥ*—has been given; *daṇḍaḥ*—punishment; *bhavadbhiḥ*—by you; *mām*—Me; *anuvrataiḥ*—devoted to; *saḥ*—that; *eva*—certainly; *anumataḥ*—is approved; *asmābhiḥ*—by Me; *munayaḥ* O great sages; *deva*—against you; *helanāt*—because of an offense.

TRANSLATION

O great sages, I approve of the punishment that you who are devoted to Me have meted out to them.

TEXT 4

तद्वः प्रसादयाम्यद्य ब्रह्म दैवं परं हि मे ।
तद्धीत्यात्मकृतं मन्ये यत्स्वपुम्भिरसत्कृताः ॥ ४ ॥

tad vaḥ prasādayāmy adya
brahma daivaṁ paraṁ hi me
tad dhīty ātma-kṛtaṁ manye
yat sva-pumbhir asat-kṛtāḥ

tat—therefore; *vaḥ*—you sages; *prasādayāmi*—I am seeking your forgiveness; *adya*—just now; *brahma*—the *brāhmaṇas; daivam*—most beloved personalities; *param*—highest; *hi*—because; *me*—My; *tat*—that offense; *hi*—because; *iti*—thus; *ātma-kṛtam*—done by Me; *manye*—I consider; *yat*—which; *sva-pumbhiḥ*—by My own attendants; *asat-kṛtāḥ*—having been disrespected.

TRANSLATION

To Me, the brāhmaṇa is the highest and most beloved personality. The disrespect shown by My attendants has actually been displayed by Me because the doormen are My servitors. I take this to be an offense by Myself; therefore I seek your forgiveness for the incident that has arisen.

PURPORT

The Lord is always in favor of the *brāhmaṇas* and the cows, and therefore it is said, *go-brāhmaṇa-hitāya ca.* Lord Kṛṣṇa, or Viṣṇu, the Supreme Personality of Godhead, is also the worshipable Deity of the *brāhmaṇas.* In the Vedic literature, in the *ṛg-mantra* hymns of the *Ṛg Veda,* it is stated that those who are actually *brāhmaṇas* always look to the lotus feet of Viṣṇu: *oṁ tad viṣṇoḥ paramaṁ padaṁ sadā paśyanti sūrayaḥ.* Those who are qualified *brāhmaṇas* worship only the Viṣṇu form of the Supreme Personality of Godhead, which means Kṛṣṇa, Rāma and all Viṣṇu expansions. A so-called *brāhmaṇa* who is born in the family of *brāhmaṇas* but performs activities aimed against the Vaiṣṇavas cannot be accepted as a *brāhmaṇa,* because *brāhmaṇa* means Vaiṣṇava and Vaiṣṇava means *brāhmaṇa.* One who has become a devotee of the Lord is also a *brāhmaṇa.* The formula is *brahma jānātīti brāhmaṇaḥ.* A *brāhmaṇa* is one who has understood Brahman, and a Vaiṣṇava is one who has understood the Personality of Godhead. Brahman realization is the beginning of realization of the Personality of Godhead. One who understands the Personality of Godhead also knows the impersonal feature of the Supreme, which is Brahman. Therefore one who becomes a Vaiṣṇava is already a *brāhmaṇa.* It should be noted that the glories of the *brāhmaṇa* described in this chapter by the Lord Himself refer to His devotee-*brāhmaṇa,* or the Vaiṣṇava. It should never be misunderstood that the so-called *brāhmaṇas* who are born in *brāhmaṇa* families but have no brahminical qualifications are referred to in this connection.

TEXT 5

यन्नामानि च गृह्णाति लोको भृत्ये कृतागसि ।
सोऽसाधुवादस्तत्कीर्तिं हन्ति त्वचमिवामयः ॥ ५ ॥

yan-nāmāni ca gṛhṇāti
loko bhṛtye kṛtāgasi
so 'sādhu-vādas tat-kīrtiṁ
hanti tvacam ivāmayaḥ

yat—of whom; *nāmāni*—the names; *ca*—and; *gṛhṇāti*—take; *lokaḥ*—people in general; *bhṛtye*—when a servant; *kṛta-āgasi*—has committed something wrong; *saḥ*—that; *asādhu-vādaḥ*—blame; *tat*—of that person; *kīrtim*—the reputation; *hanti*—destroys; *tvacam*—the skin; *iva*—as; *āmayaḥ*—leprosy.

TRANSLATION

A wrong act committed by a servant leads people in general to blame his master, just as a spot of white leprosy on any part of the body pollutes all of the skin.

PURPORT

A Vaiṣṇava, therefore, should be fully qualified. As stated in the *Bhāgavatam*, anyone who has become a Vaiṣṇava has developed all the good qualities of the demigods. There are twenty-six qualifications mentioned in the *Caitanya-caritāmṛta*. A devotee should always see that his Vaiṣṇava qualities increase with the advancement of his Kṛṣṇa consciousness. A devotee should be blameless because any offense by the devotee is a scar on the Supreme Personality of Godhead. The devotee's duty is to be always conscious in his dealings with others, especially with another devotee of the Lord.

TEXT 6

यस्यामृतामलयशःश्रवणावगाहः
सद्यः पुनाति जगदाश्वपचाद्विकुण्ठः ।
सोऽहं भवद्भ्य उपलब्धसुतीर्थकीर्ति-
श्छिन्द्यां स्वबाहुमपि वः प्रतिकूलवृत्तिम् ॥ ६ ॥

yasyāmṛtāmala-yaśaḥ-śravaṇāvagāhaḥ
sadyaḥ punāti jagad āśvapacād vikuṇṭhaḥ
so 'haṁ bhavadbhya upalabdha-sutīrtha-kīrtiś
chindyāṁ sva-bāhum api vaḥ pratikūla-vṛttim

yasya—of whom; *amṛta*—nectar; *amala*—uncontaminated; *yaśaḥ*—glories; *śravaṇa*—hearing; *avagāhaḥ*—entering into; *sadyaḥ*—immediately; *punāti*—purifies; *jagat*—the universe; *āśva-pacāt*—including even the dog-eaters; *vikuṇṭhaḥ*—without anxiety; *saḥ*—that person; *aham*—I am; *bhavadbhyaḥ*—from you; *upalabdha*—obtained; *su-tīrtha*—the best place of pilgrimage; *kīrtiḥ*—the fame; *chindyām*—would cut off; *sva-bāhum*—My own arm; *api*—even; *vaḥ*—towards you; *pratikūla-vṛttim*—acting inimically.

TRANSLATION

Anyone in the entire world, even down to the caṇḍāla, who lives by cooking and eating the flesh of the dog, is immediately purified if he takes bath in hearing through the ear the glorification of My name, fame, etc. Now you have realized Me without doubt; therefore I will not hesitate to lop off My own arm if its conduct is found hostile to you.

PURPORT

Real purification can take place in human society if its members take to Kṛṣṇa consciousness. This is clearly stated in all Vedic literature. Anyone who takes to Kṛṣṇa consciousness in all sincerity, even if he is not very advanced in good behavior, is purified. A devotee can be recruited from any section of human society, although it is not expected that everyone in all segments of society is well behaved. As stated in this verse and in many places in *Bhagavad-gītā,* even if one is not born in a *brāhmaṇa* family, or even if he is born in a family of *caṇḍālas,* if he simply takes to Kṛṣṇa consciousness he is immediately purified. In *Bhagavad-gītā,* Ninth Chapter, verses 30-32, it is clearly stated that even though a man is not well behaved, if he simply takes to Kṛṣṇa consciousness he is understood to be a saintly person. As long as a person is in this material world he has two different relationships in his dealings with others—one relationship pertains to the body, and the other pertains to the spirit. As far as bodily affairs or social activities are concerned, although a person is purified on the spiritual platform, it is sometimes seen that he acts in terms of his bodily relationships. If a devotee born in the family of a *caṇḍāla* (the lowest caste) is sometimes found engaged in his habitual activities, he is not to be considered a *caṇḍāla.* In other words, a Vaiṣṇava should not be evaluated in terms of his body. The *śāstra* states that no one should think the Deity in the temple to be made of wood or stone, and no one should think that a person coming from a lower-caste family who has taken to Kṛṣṇa consciousness is still of the same low caste. These attitudes are forbidden because anyone who takes to Kṛṣṇa consciousness is understood to be fully purified. He is at least engaged in the process of purification, and if he sticks to the principle of Kṛṣṇa consciousness he will very soon be fully purified. The conclusion is that if one takes to Kṛṣṇa consciousness with all seriousness, he is to be understood as already purified, and Kṛṣṇa is ready to give him protection by all means. The Lord assures herein that He is ready to give protection to His devotee even if there is need to cut off part of His own body.

TEXT 7

यत्सेवया चरणपद्मपवित्ररेणुं
सद्यःक्षताखिलमलं प्रतिलब्धशीलम् ।
न श्रीर्विरक्तमपि मां विजहाति यस्याः
प्रेक्षालवार्थ इतरे नियमान् वहन्ति ॥ ७ ॥

yat-sevayā caraṇa-padma-pavitra-reṇuṁ
sadyaḥ kṣatākhila-malaṁ pratilabdha-śīlam
na śrīr viraktam api māṁ vijahāti yasyāḥ
prekṣā-lavārtha itare niyamān vahanti

yat—of whom; *sevayā*—by the service; *caraṇa*—feet; *padma*—lotus; *pavitra*—sacred; *reṇum*—the dust; *sadyaḥ*—immediately; *kṣata*—wiped out; *akhila*—all; *malam*—sins; *pratilabdha*—acquired; *śīlam*—disposition; *na*—not; *śrīḥ*—the goddess of fortune; *viraktam*—have no attachment; *api*—even though; *mām*—Me; *vijahāti*—leave; *yasyāḥ*—of the goddess of fortune; *prekṣā-lava-arthaḥ*—for obtaining a slight favor; *itare*—others, like Lord Brahmā; *niyamān*—sacred vows; *vahanti*—observe.

TRANSLATION

The Lord continued: Because I am the servitor of My devotees, My lotus feet have become so sacred that they immediately wipe out all sin, and I have acquired such a disposition that the goddess of fortune does not leave Me, even though I have no attachment for her and others praise her beauty and observe sacred vows to secure from her even a slight favor.

PURPORT

The relationship between the Lord and His devotee is transcendentally beautiful. As the devotee thinks that it is due to being a devotee of the Lord that he is elevated in all good qualities, so the Lord also thinks that it is because of His devotion to the servitor that all His transcendental glories have increased. In other words, as the devotee is always anxious to render service to the Lord, so the Lord is ever anxious to render service to the devotee. The Lord admits herein that although He certainly has the quality that anyone who receives a slight particle of the dust of His lotus feet becomes at once a great personality, this greatness is due to His affection for His devotee. It is because of this affection that the goddess of fortune does not leave Him and that not only one but many thousands of goddesses of fortune engage in His service. In the material world, simply to get a little favor from the goddess of fortune, people observe many rigid regulations of austerity and penance. The Lord cannot tolerate any inconvenience on the part of the devotee. He is therefore famous as *bhakta-vatsala.*

TEXT 8

नाहं तथाद्मि यजमानहविर्वितानेश्च्योतद्घृतप्लुतमदन् हुतभुङ्मुखेन ।
यद्ब्राह्मणस्य मुखतश्चरतोऽनुघासं
तुष्टस्य मय्यवहितैर्निजकर्मपाकैः ॥ ८ ॥

nāhaṁ tathādmi yajamāna-havir vitāne
ścyotad-ghṛta-plutam adan huta-bhuṅ-mukhena
yad brāhmaṇasya mukhataś carato 'nughāsaṁ
tuṣṭasya mayy avahitair nija-karma-pākaiḥ

na—not; *aham*—I; *tathā*—on the other hand; *admi*—I eat; *yajamāna*—by the sacrificer; *haviḥ*—the oblations; *vitāne*—in the sacrificial fire; *ścyotat*—pouring; *ghṛta*—ghee; *plutam*—mixed; *adan*—eating; *huta-bhuk*—the sacrificial fire; *mukhena*—by the mouth; *yat*—as; *brāhmaṇasya*—of the *brāhmaṇa; mukhataḥ*—from the mouth; *carataḥ*—acting; *anughāsam*—morsels; *tuṣṭasya*—satisfied; *mayi*—to Me; *avahitaiḥ*—offered; *nija*—own; *karma*—activities; *pākaiḥ*—by the results.

TRANSLATION

I do not enjoy the oblations offered by the sacrificers in the sacrificial fire, which is one of My own mouths, with the same relish as I do the delicacies overflowing with ghee which are offered to the mouths of the brāhmaṇas who have dedicated to Me the results of their activities and who are ever satisfied with My prasāda.

PURPORT

The devotee of the Lord, or the Vaiṣṇava, does not take anything without offering it to the Lord. Since a Vaiṣṇava dedicates all the results of his activities to the Lord, he does not taste anything eatable which is not first offered to Him. The Lord also relishes giving to the Vaiṣṇava's mouth all eatables offered to Him. It is clear from this verse that the Lord eats through the sacrificial fire and the *brāhmaṇa's* mouth. So many articles—grains, ghee, etc.—are offered in sacrifice for the satisfaction of the Lord. The Lord accepts sacrificial offerings from the *brāhmaṇas* and devotees, and elsewhere it is stated that whatever is given for the *brāhmaṇas* and Vaiṣṇavas to eat is also accepted by the Lord. But here it is said that He accepts offerings to the mouths of *brāhmaṇas* and Vaiṣṇavas with even greater relish. The best example of this is found in the life of Advaita Prabhu in his dealings with Haridāsa Ṭhākura. Even though Haridāsa was born of a Muhammadan family, Advaita Prabhu offered him the first dish of *prasāda* after the performance of a sacred fire ceremony. Haridāsa Ṭhākura informed him that he was born of a Muhammadan family and asked why Advaita Prabhu was offering the first dish to a Muhammadan instead of an elevated *brāhmaṇa*. Out of his humbleness, Haridāsa condemned himself a Muhammadan, but Advaita Prabhu, being an experienced devotee, accepted him as a real *brāhmaṇa*. Advaita Prabhu asserted that by offering the first dish to Haridāsa Ṭhākura, he was getting the result of feeding one hundred thousand *brāhmaṇas*. The conclusion is that if one can feed a *brāhmaṇa* or Vaiṣṇava, it is better than performing hundreds of thousands of sacrifices. In this age, therefore, it is recommended that *harer nāma*—chanting the holy name of God—and pleasing the Vaiṣṇava are the only means to elevate oneself to spiritual life.

TEXT 9

येषां बिभर्म्यहमखण्डविकुण्ठयोग-
मायाविभूतिरमलाङ्घ्रिरजः किरीटैः ।
विप्रांस्तु को न विषहेत यदर्हणाम्भः
सद्यः पुनाति सहचन्द्रललामलोकान् ॥९॥

yeṣāṁ bibharmy aham akhaṇḍa-vikuṇṭha-yoga-
māyā-vibhūtir amalāṅghri-rajaḥ kirīṭaiḥ
viprāṁs tu ko na viṣaheta yad-arhaṇāmbhaḥ
sadyaḥ punāti saha-candra-lalāma-lokān

yeṣām—of the *brāhmaṇas; bibharmi*—I bear; *aham*—I; *akhaṇḍa*—unbroken; *vikuṇṭha*—unobstructed; *yoga-māyā*—internal energy; *vibhūtiḥ*—opulence; *amala*—pure; *aṅghri*—of the feet; *rajaḥ*—the dust; *kirīṭaiḥ*—on My helmet; *viprān*—the *brāhmaṇas; tu*—then; *kaḥ*—who; *na*—not; *viṣaheta*—carry; *yat*—of the Supreme Lord; *arhaṇa-ambhaḥ*—water which has washed the feet; *sadyaḥ*—at once; *punāti*—sanctifies; *saha*—along with; *candra-lalāma*—Lord Śiva; *lokān*—the three worlds.

TRANSLATION

I am the master of My unobstructed internal energy, and the water of the Ganges is the remnant left after My feet are washed. That water sanctifies the three worlds, along with Lord Śiva, who bears it on his head. If I can take the dust of the feet of the Vaiṣṇava on My head, who will refuse to do the same?

PURPORT

The difference between the internal and external energies of the Supreme Personality of Godhead is that in the internal energy, or in the spiritual world, all the opulences are undisturbed, whereas in the external or material energy, all the opulences are temporary manifestations. The Lord's supremacy is equal in both the spiritual and material worlds, but the spiritual world is called the kingdom of God, and the material world is called the kingdom of *māyā. Māyā* refers to that which is not actually fact. The opulence of the material world is a reflection. It is stated in *Bhagavad-gītā* that this material world is just like a tree whose roots are up and branches down. This means that the material world is the shadow of the spiritual world. Real opulence is in the spiritual world. In the spiritual world the predominating Deity is the Lord Himself, whereas in the material world there are many lords. That is the difference between the internal and external energies. The Lord says that although He is the predominating factor of the internal energy and although the material world is sanctified just by the water that has washed His feet, He has the greatest respect for the *brāhmaṇa* and the Vaiṣṇava. When the Lord Himself offers so much respect to the Vaiṣṇava and the *brāhmaṇa*, how can one deny such respect to such personalities?

TEXT 10

ये मे तनूर्द्विजवरान्दुहतीर्मदीया
भूतान्यलब्धशरणानि च भेदबुद्ध्या ।
द्रक्ष्यन्त्यघक्षतदृशो ह्यहिमन्यवस्तान्
गृध्रा रुषा मम कुषन्त्यधिदण्डनेतुः ॥१०॥

ye me tanūr dvija-varān duhatīr madīyā
bhūtāny alabdha-śaraṇāni ca bheda-buddhyā
drakṣyanty agha-kṣata-dṛśo hy ahi-manyavas tān
gṛdhrā ruṣā mama kuṣanty adhidaṇḍa-netuḥ

ye—which persons; *me*—My; *tanūḥ*—body; *dvija-varān*—the best of the *brāhmaṇas; duhatīḥ*—cows; *madīyāḥ*—relating to Me; *bhūtāni*—living entities; *alabdha-śaraṇāni*—defenseless; *ca*—and; *bheda-buddhyā*—considering as different; *drakṣyanti*—see; *agha*—by sin; *kṣata*—is impaired; *dṛśaḥ*—whose faculty of judgment; *hi*—because; *ahi*—like a snake; *manyavaḥ*—angry; *tān*—those same persons; *gṛdhrāḥ*—the vulturelike messengers; *ruṣā*—angrily; *mama*—My; *kuṣanti*—tear; *adhidaṇḍa-netuḥ*—of the superintendent of punishment, Yamarāja.

TRANSLATION

The brāhmaṇas, the cows and the defenseless creatures are My own body. Those whose faculty of judgment has been impaired by their own sin look upon these as distinct from Me. They are just like furious serpents, and they are angrily torn apart by the bills of the vulturelike messengers of Yamarāja, the superintendent of sinful persons.

PURPORT

The defenseless creatures, according to *Brahma-saṁhitā*, are the cows, *brāhmaṇas*, women, children and old men. Of these five, the *brāhmaṇas* and cows are especially mentioned in this verse because the Lord is always anxious about the benefit of the *brāhmaṇas* and the cows and is prayed to in this way. The Lord especially instructs, therefore, that no one should be envious of these five, especially the cows and *brāhmaṇas*. In some of the *Bhāgavatam* readings, the word *duhitṝḥ* is used instead of *duhatīḥ*. But in either case, the meaning is the same. *Duhatīḥ* means "cow," and *duhitṝḥ* can also be used to mean "cow" because the cow is supposed to be the daughter of the sun-god. Just as children are taken care of by the parents, women as a class should be taken care of by the father, husband or grown-up son. Those who are helpless must be taken care of by their respective guardians, otherwise the guardians will be subjected to the punishment of Yamarāja, who is appointed by the Lord to supervise the activities of sinful living creatures. The assistants, or messengers, of Yamarāja are likened here to vultures, and those who do not execute their respective duties in protecting their wards are compared to serpents. Vultures deal very seriously with serpents, and similarly the messengers will deal very seriously with neglectful guardians.

TEXT 11

ये ब्राह्मणान्मयि धिया क्षिपतोऽर्चयन्त-
स्तुष्यद्धृदः स्मितसुधोक्षितपद्मवक्त्राः ।
वाण्यानुरागकलयात्मजवद् गृणन्तः
सम्बोधयन्त्यहमिवाहमुपाहृतस्तैः ॥११॥

ye brāhmaṇān mayi dhiyā kṣipato 'rcayantas
tuṣyad-dhṛdaḥ smita-sudhokṣita-padma-vaktrāḥ
vāṇyānurāga-kalayātmajavad gṛṇantaḥ
sambodhayanty aham ivāham upāhṛtas taiḥ

ye—which persons; *brāhmaṇān*—the *brāhmaṇas; mayi*—in Me; *dhiyā*—with intelligence; *kṣipataḥ*—uttering harsh words; *arcayantaḥ*—respecting; *tuṣyat*—gladdened; *hṛdaḥ*—hearts; *smita*—smiling; *sudhā*—nectar; *ukṣita*—wet; *padma*—lotuslike; *vaktrāḥ*—faces; *vāṇyā*—with words; *anurāga-kalayā*—loving; *ātmaja-vat*—like a son; *gṛṇantaḥ*—praising; *sambodhayanti*—pacify; *aham*—I; *iva*—as; *aham*—I; *upāhṛtaḥ*—being controlled; *taiḥ*—by them.

TRANSLATION

On the other hand, they captivate My heart who are gladdened in heart and who, their lotus faces enlightened by nectarean smiles, respect the brāhmaṇas, even though the brāhmaṇas utter harsh words. They look upon the brāhmaṇas as My own Self and pacify them by praising them in loving words, even as a son would appease an angry father or as I am pacifying you.

PURPORT

It has been observed in many instances in the Vedic scriptures that when the *brāhmaṇas* or Vaiṣṇavas curse someone in an angry mood, the person who is cursed does not take it upon himself to treat the *brāhmaṇas* or Vaiṣṇavas in the same way. There are many examples of this. For instance, the sons of Kuvera, when cursed by the great sage Nārada, did not seek revenge in the same harsh way, but submitted. Here also, when Jaya and Vijaya were cursed by the four Kumāras, they did not become harsh towards them; rather, they submitted. That should be the way of treating *brāhmaṇas* and Vaiṣṇavas. One may sometimes be faced with a grievous situation created by a *brāhmaṇa,* but instead of meeting him with a similar mood, one should try to pacify him with a smiling face and mild treatment. *Brāhmaṇas* and Vaiṣṇavas should be accepted as earthly representatives of Nārāyaṇa. Nowadays some foolish persons have manufactured the term *daridra-nārāyaṇa,* indicating that the poor man should be accepted as the representative of Nārāyaṇa. But in Vedic literature we do not find that poor men should be treated as representatives of Nārāyaṇa. Of course, "those who are unprotected" are mentioned here, but the definition of this phrase is clear from the *śāstras.* The poor man should not be unprotected, but the *brāhmaṇa* should especially be treated as the representative of Nārāyaṇa and should be worshiped like Him. It is specifically said that to pacify the *brāhmaṇas,* one's face should be lotuslike. A lotuslike face is exhibited when one is adorned with love and affection. In this respect, the example of the father's being angry at the son and the son's trying to pacify the father with smiling and sweet words is very appropriate.

TEXT 12

तन्मे स्वभर्तुरवसायमलक्षमाणौ
युष्मद्व्यतिक्रमगतिं प्रतिपद्य सद्यः ।
भूयो ममान्तिकमितां तदनुग्रहो मे
यत्कल्पतामचिरतो भृतयोर्विवासः ॥१२॥

tan me sva-bhartur avasāyam alakṣamāṇau
yuṣmad-vyatikrama-gatiṁ pratipadya sadyaḥ
bhūyo mamāntikam itāṁ tad anugraho me
yat kalpatām acirato bhṛtayor vivāsaḥ

tat—therefore; *me*—My; *sva-bhartuḥ*—of their master; *avasāyam*—the intention; *alakṣamāṇau*—not knowing; *yuṣmat*—against you; *vyatikrama*—offense; *gatim*—result; *pratipadya*—reaping; *sadyaḥ*—immediately; *bhūyaḥ*—again; *mama antikam*—near Me; *itām*—obtain; *tat*—that; *anugrahaḥ*—a favor; *me*—to Me; *yat*—which; *kalpatām*—let it be arranged; *aciratah*—not long; *bhṛtayoḥ*—of these two servants; *vivāsaḥ*—exile.

TRANSLATION

These servants of Mine have transgressed against you, not knowing the mind of their master. I shall therefore deem it a favor done to Me if you order that, although reaping the fruit of their transgression, they may return to My presence soon and the time of their exile from My abode may expire before long.

PURPORT

From this statement we can understand how anxious the Lord is to get his servitor back into Vaikuṇṭha. This incident, therefore, proves that those who have once entered a Vaikuṇṭha planet can never fall down. The case of Jaya and Vijaya is not a falldown; it is just an accident. The Lord is always anxious to get such devotees back again to the Vaikuṇṭha planets as soon as possible. It is to be assumed that there is no possibility of a misunderstanding between the Lord and the devotees, but when there are discrepancies or disruptions between one devotee and another, one has to suffer the consequences, although that suffering is temporary. The Lord is so kind to His devotees that He took all the responsibility for the doormen's offense and requested the sages to give them facilities to return to Vaikuṇṭha as soon as possible.

TEXT 13

ब्रह्मोवाच
अथ तस्योशतीं देवीमृषिकुल्यां सरस्वतीम् ।
नास्वाद्य मन्युदष्टानां तेषामात्माप्यतृप्यत ॥१३॥

brahmovāca

atha tasyośatīṁ devīm
ṛṣi-kulyāṁ sarasvatīm
nāsvādya manyu-daṣṭānāṁ
teṣām ātmāpy atṛpyata

brahmā—Lord Brahmā; *uvāca*—said; *atha*—now; *tasya*—of the Supreme Lord; *uśatīm*—lovely; *devīm*—shining; *ṛṣi-kulyām*—like a series of Vedic hymns; *sarasvatīm*—speech; *na*—not; *āsvādya*—hearing; *manyu*—anger; *daṣṭānām*—bitten; *teṣām*—of those sages; *ātmā*—the mind; *api*—even though; *atṛpyata*—satiated.

TRANSLATION

Brahmā continued: Even though the sages had been bitten by the serpent of anger, their souls were not satiated with hearing the Lord's lovely and illuminating speech, which was like a series of Vedic hymns.

TEXT 14

सतीं व्यादाय शृण्वन्तो लघ्वीं गुर्वर्थगह्वराम् ।
विगाह्यागाधगम्भीरां न विदुस्तच्चिकीर्षितम् ॥१४॥

satīṁ vyādāya śṛṇvanto
laghvīṁ gurv-artha-gahvarām
vigāhyāgādha-gambhīrāṁ
na vidus tac-cikīrṣitam

satīm—excellent; *vyādāya*—with attentive aural reception; *śṛṇvantaḥ*—hearing; *laghvīm*—properly composed; *guru*—momentous; *artha*—import; *gahvarām*—difficult to understand; *vigāhya*—pondering; *agādha*—deep; *gambhīrām*—grave; *na*—not; *viduḥ*—understand; *tat*—of the Supreme Lord; *cikīrṣitam*—the intention.

TRANSLATION

The Lord's excellent speech was difficult to comprehend because of its momentous import and its most profound significance. The sages heard it

with wide-open ears and pondered it as well. But although hearing, they could not understand what He intended to do.

PURPORT

It should be understood that no one can surpass the Supreme Personality of Godhead in speaking. There is no difference between the Supreme Person and His speeches, for He stands on the absolute platform. The sages tried with wide open ears to understand the words from the lips of the Supreme Lord, but although His speech was very concise and meaningful, the sages could not completely comprehend what He was saying. They could not even comprehend the purport of the speech or what the Supreme Lord wanted to do. Nor could they understand whether the Lord was angry or pleased with them.

TEXT 15

ते योगमाययारब्धपारमेष्ठ्यमहोदयम् ।
प्रोचुः प्राञ्जलयो विप्राः प्रहृष्टाः क्षुभितत्वचः ॥१५॥

te yoga-māyayārabdha-
pārameṣṭhya-mahodayam
procuḥ prāñjalayo viprāḥ
prahṛṣṭāḥ kṣubhita-tvacaḥ

te—those; *yoga-māyayā*—through His internal potency; *ārabdha*—had been revealed; *pārameṣṭhya*—of the Supreme Personality of Godhead; *mahā-udayam*—multiglories; *procuḥ*—spoke; *prāñjalayaḥ*—with folded hands; *viprāḥ*—the four *brāhmaṇas; prahṛṣṭāḥ*—extremely delighted; *kṣubhita-tvacaḥ*—hair standing on end.

TRANSLATION

The four brāhmaṇa-sages were nevertheless extremely delighted to behold Him, and they experienced a thrill throughout their bodies. They then spoke as follows to the Lord, who had revealed the multiglories of the Supreme Personality through His internal potency, yogamāyā.

PURPORT

The sages were almost too puzzled to speak before the Supreme Personality of Godhead for the first time, and the hairs of their bodies stood erect due to their extreme joy. The highest opulence in the material world is called *pārameṣṭhya*, the opulence of Brahmā. But that material opulence of Brahmā, who lives on the topmost planet within this material world, cannot compare to the opulence of the Supreme Lord because the transcendental opulence in the spiritual world is caused by *yogamāyā*, whereas the opulence in the material world is caused by *mahāmāyā*.

TEXT 16

ऋषय ऊचुः
न वयं भगवन् विद्मस्तव देव चिकीर्षितम् ।
कृतो मेऽनुग्रहश्चेति यदध्यक्षः प्रभाषसे ॥१६॥

ṛṣaya ūcuḥ
na vayaṁ bhagavan vidmas
tava deva cikīrṣitam
kṛto me 'nugrahaś ceti
yad adhyakṣaḥ prabhāṣase

ṛṣayaḥ—the sages; *ūcuḥ*—said; *na*—not; *vayam*—we; *bhagavan*—O Supreme Personality of Godhead; *vidmaḥ*—did know; *tava*—Your; *deva*—O Lord; *cikīrṣitam*—wish for us to do; *kṛtaḥ*—has been done; *me*—unto Me; *anugrahaḥ*—favor; *ca*—and; *iti*—thus; *yat*—which; *adhyakṣaḥ*—the supreme ruler; *prabhāṣase*—You say.

TRANSLATION

The sages said: O Supreme Personality of Godhead, we are unable to know what You intend for us to do, for even though You are the supreme ruler of all, You speak in our favor as if we had done something good for You.

PURPORT

The sages could understand that the Supreme Personality of Godhead, who is above everyone, was speaking as if He were in the wrong; therefore it was difficult for them to understand the words of the Lord. They could understand, however, that the Lord was speaking in such a humble way just to show them His all-merciful favor.

TEXT 17

ब्रह्मण्यस्य परं दैवं ब्राह्मणाः किल ते प्रभो ।
विप्राणां देवदेवानां भगवानात्मदैवतम् ॥१७॥

brahmaṇyasya paraṁ daivaṁ
brāhmaṇāḥ kila te prabho
viprāṇāṁ deva-devānāṁ
bhagavān ātma-daivatam

brahmaṇyasya—of the supreme director of the brahminical culture; *param*—the highest; *daivam*—position; *brāhmaṇāḥ*—the *brāhmaṇas; kila*—for the teaching of others; *te*—Your; *prabho*—O Lord; *viprāṇām*—of the *brāhmaṇas; deva-devānām*—to be worshiped by the demigods; *bhagavān*—the Supreme Personality of Godhead; *ātma*—the self; *daivatam*—worshipable Deity.

TRANSLATION

O Lord, You are the supreme director of the brahminical culture. Your considering the brāhmaṇas to be in the highest position is Your example for teaching others. Actually You are the supreme worshipable Deity, not only for the gods but for the brāhmaṇas also.

PURPORT

In the *Brahma-saṁhitā* it is clearly stated that the Supreme Personality of Godhead is the cause of all causes. There are undoubtedly many demigods, the chiefs of whom are Brahmā and Śiva. Lord Viṣṇu is the Lord of Brahmā and Śiva, not to speak of the *brāhmaṇas* in this material world. As mentioned in *Bhagavad-gītā,* the Supreme Lord is very favorable towards all activities performed according to brahminical culture, or the qualities of control of the senses and mind, cleanliness, forbearance, faith in scripture, and practical and theoretical knowledge. The Lord is the Supersoul of everyone. In *Bhagavad-gītā* it is said that the Lord is the source of all emanations; thus He is also the source of Brahmā and Śiva.

TEXT 18

त्वत्तः सनातनो धर्मो रक्ष्यते तनुभिस्तव ।
धर्मस्य परमो गुह्यो निर्विकारो भवान्मतः ॥१८॥

tvattaḥ sanātano dharmo
rakṣyate tanubhis tava
dharmasya paramo guhyo
nirvikāro bhavān mataḥ

tvattaḥ—from You; *sanātanaḥ*—eternal; *dharmaḥ*—occupation; *rakṣyate*—is protected; *tanubhiḥ*—by multimanifestations; *tava*—Your; *dharmasya*—of religious principles;

paramaḥ—the supreme; *guhyaḥ*—objective; *nirvikāraḥ*—unchangeable; *bhavān*—You; *mataḥ*—in our opinion.

TRANSLATION

You are the source of the eternal occupation of all living entities, and by Your multimanifestations of Personalities of Godhead, You have always protected religion. You are the supreme objective of religious principles, and in our opinion You are inexhaustible and unchangeable eternally.

PURPORT

The statement in this verse *dharmasya paramo guhyaḥ* refers to the most confidential part of all religious principles. This is confirmed in *Bhagavad-gītā.* The conclusion of Lord Kṛṣṇa in His advice to Arjuna is: "Give up all other religious engagement and just surrender unto Me." This is the most confidential knowledge in executing religious principles. In the *Bhāgavatam* also it is stated that if one does not become Kṛṣṇa conscious after very rigidly executing one's specified religious duties, all his labor in following so-called religious principles is simply a waste of time. Here also the sages confirm the statement that the Supreme Lord, not the demigods, is the ultimate goal of all religious principles. There are many foolish propagandists who say that worship of the demigods is also a way to reach the supreme goal, but in the authorized statements of *Śrīmad-Bhāgavatam* and *Bhagavad-gītā* this is not accepted. *Bhagavad-gītā* says that one who worships a particular demigod can reach the demigod's planet, but one who worships the Supreme Personality of Godhead can enter into Vaikuṇṭha. Some propagandists say that regardless of what one does he will ultimately reach the supreme abode of the Personality of Godhead, but this is not valid. The Lord is eternal, the Lord's servitor is eternal, and the Lord's abode is also eternal. They are all described here as *sanātana*, or eternal. The result of devotional service, therefore, is not temporary, as is the achievement of heavenly planets by worshiping the demigods. The sages wanted to stress that although the Lord, out of His causeless mercy, says that He worships the *brāhmaṇas* and Vaiṣṇavas, actually the Lord is worshipable not only by the *brāhmaṇas* and Vaiṣṇavas but also by the demigods.

TEXT 19

तरन्ति ह्यञ्जसा मृत्युं निवृत्ता यदनुग्रहात् ।
योगिनः स भवान् किं स्विदनुगृह्येत यत्परैः ॥१९॥

taranti hy añjasā mṛtyuṁ
nivṛttā yad-anugrahāt
yoginaḥ sa bhavān kiṁ svid
anugṛhyeta yat paraiḥ

taranti—cross over; *hi*—because; *añjasā*—easily; *mṛtyum*—birth and death; *nivṛttāḥ*—ceasing all material desires; *yat*—Your; *anugrahāt*—by mercy; *yoginaḥ*—transcendentalists; *saḥ*—the Supreme Lord; *bhavān*—You; *kim svit*—never possible; *anugṛhyeta*—may be favored; *yat*—which; *paraiḥ*—by others.

TRANSLATION

Mystics and transcendentalists, by the mercy of the Lord, cross beyond nescience by ceasing all material desires. It is not possible, therefore, that the Supreme Lord can be favored by others.

PURPORT

Unless one is favored by the Supreme Lord, one cannot cross over the ocean of the nescience of repeated birth and death. Here it is stated that *yogīs* or mystics cross beyond nescience by the mercy of the Supreme Personality of Godhead. There are many kinds of mystics, such as the *karma-yogī, jñāna-yogī, dhyāna-yogī* and *bhakti-yogī*. The *karmīs* particularly search after the favor of the demigods, the *jñānīs* want to become one with the Supreme Absolute Truth, and the *yogīs* are satisfied simply by partial vision of the Supreme Personality of Godhead, Paramātmā, and ultimately by oneness with Him. But the *bhaktas,* the devotees, want to associate with the Supreme Personality of Godhead eternally and serve Him. It has already been admitted that the Lord is eternal, and those who want the favor of the Supreme Lord perpetually are also eternal. Therefore *yogīs* here means devotees. By the mercy of the Lord, devotees can easily pass beyond the nescience of birth and death and attain the eternal abode of the Lord. The Lord is therefore not in need of another's favor because no one is equal to or greater than Him. Actually, everyone needs the favor of the Lord for successful understanding of his human mission.

TEXT 20

यं वै विभूतिरुपयात्यनुवेलमन्यै-
रर्थार्थिभिः स्वशिरसा धृतपादरेणुः ।
धन्यार्पिताङ्घ्रितुलसीनवदामधाम्नो
लोकं मधुव्रतपतेरिव कामयाना ॥२०॥

yaṁ vai vibhūtir upayāty anuvelam anyair
arthārthibhiḥ sva-śirasā dhṛta-pāda-reṇuḥ
dhanyārpitāṅghri-tulasī-nava-dāma-dhāmno
lokaṁ madhuvrata-pater iva kāma-yānā

yam—whom; *vai*—certainly; *vibhūtiḥ*—Lakṣmī, the goddess of fortune; *upayāti*—waits upon; *anuvelam*—occasionally; *anyaiḥ*—by others; *artha*—material facility; *arthibhiḥ*—by those who desire; *sva-śirasā*—on their own heads; *dhṛta*—accepting; *pāda*—of the feet; *reṇuḥ*—the dust; *dhanya*—by the devotees; *arpita*—offered; *aṅghri*—at Your feet; *tulasī*—of *tulasī* leaves; *nava*—fresh; *dāma*—on the garland; *dhāmnaḥ*—having a place; *lokam*—the place; *madhu-vrata-pateḥ*—of the king of the bees; *iva*—like; *kāma-yānā*—is anxious to secure.

TRANSLATION

The goddess of fortune, Lakṣmī, the dust of whose feet is worn on the head by others, waits upon You, as appointed, for she is anxious to secure a place in the abode of the king of bees, who hovers on the fresh wreath of tulasī leaves offered at Your feet by some blessed devotee.

PURPORT

As previously described, *tulasī* has attained all superior qualities due to being placed at the lotus feet of the Lord. The comparison made here is very nice. As the king of bees hovers over the *tulasī leaves* offered to the lotus feet of the Lord, so Lakṣmī, the goddess who is sought by the demigods, *brāhmaṇas,* Vaiṣṇavas and everyone else, always engages in rendering service to the lotus feet of the Lord. The conclusion is that no one can be the benefactor of the Lord; everyone is actually the servant of the servant of the Lord.

TEXT 21

यस्तां विविक्तचरितैरनुवर्तमानां
नात्याद्रियत्परमभागवतप्रसङ्गः ।
स त्वं द्विजानुपथपुण्यरजःपुनीतः
श्रीवत्सलक्ष्म किमगा भगभाजनस्त्वम् ॥२१॥

yas tāṁ vivikta-caritair anuvartamānāṁ
nātyādriyat parama-bhāgavata-prasaṅgaḥ
sa tvaṁ dvijānupatha-puṇya-rajaḥ-punītaḥ
śrīvatsa-lakṣma kim agā bhaga-bhājanas tvam

yaḥ—who; *tām*—Lakṣmī; *vivikta*—completely pure; *caritaiḥ*—devotional services; *anuvartamānām*—serving; *na*—not; *atyādriyat*—attached; *parama*—the highest; *bhāgavata*—devotees; *prasaṅgaḥ*—attached; *saḥ*—the Supreme Lord; *tvam*—You; *dvija*—of the *brāhmaṇas; anupatha*—on the path; *puṇya*—sanctified; *rajaḥ*—dust; *punītaḥ*—purified; *śrīvatsa*—of Śrīvatsa; *lakṣma*—the mark; *kim*—what; *agāḥ*—You obtained; *bhaga*—all opulences or all good qualities; *bhājanaḥ*—the reservoir; *tvam*—You.

TRANSLATION

O Lord, You are exceedingly attached to the activities of Your pure devotees, yet You are never attached to the goddesses of fortune who constantly engage in Your transcendental loving service. How can You be purified, therefore, by the dust of the path traversed by the brāhmaṇas, and how can You be glorified or made fortunate by the marks of Śrīvatsa on Your chest?

PURPORT

It is said in the *Brahma-saṁhitā* that the Lord is always served by many hundreds of thousands of goddesses of fortune in His Vaikuṇṭha planet, yet because of His attitude of renunciation of all opulences, He is not attached to any one of them. The Lord has six opulences—unlimited wealth, unlimited fame, unlimited strength, unlimited beauty, unlimited knowledge and unlimited renunciation. All the demigods and other living entities worship Lakṣmī, the goddess of fortune, just to get her favor, yet the Lord is never attached to her because He can create an unlimited number of such goddesses for His transcendental service. The goddess of fortune, Lakṣmī, is sometimes envious of the *tulasī* leaves which are placed at the lotus feet of the Lord, for they remain fixed there and do not move, whereas Lakṣmījī, although stationed by the chest of the Lord, sometimes has to please other devotees who pray for her favor. Lakṣmījī sometimes has to go to satisfy her numerous devotees, but *tulasī* leaves never forsake their position, and the Lord therefore appreciates the service of the *tulasī* more than the service of Lakṣmī. When the Lord says, therefore, that it is due to the causeless mercy of the *brāhmaṇas* that Lakṣmījī does not leave Him, we can understand that Lakṣmījī is attracted by the opulence of the Lord, not by the *brāhmaṇas'* benedictions upon Him. The Lord is not dependent on anyone's mercy for His opulence; He is always self-sufficient. The Lord's statement that His opulence is due to the benediction of the *brāhmaṇas* and Vaiṣṇavas is only to teach others that they should offer respect to the *brāhmaṇas* and Vaiṣṇavas, the devotees of the Lord.

TEXT 22

धर्मस्य ते भगवतस्त्रियुग त्रिभिः स्वैः
पद्भिश्चराचरमिदं द्विजदेवतार्थम् ।
नूनं भृतं तदभिघाति रजस्तमश्च
सत्त्वेन नो वरदया तनुवा निरस्य ॥२२॥

dharmasya te bhagavatas tri-yuga tribhiḥ svaiḥ
padbhiś carācaram idaṁ dvija-devatārtham
nūnaṁ bhṛtaṁ tad-abhighāti rajas tamaś ca
sattvena no varadayā tanuvā nirasya

dharmasya—of the personification of all religion; *te*—of You; *bhagavataḥ*—of the Supreme Personality of Godhead; *tri-yuga*—You who are manifest in all three millenniums; *tribhiḥ*—by three; *svaiḥ*—Your own; *padbhiḥ*—feet; *cara-acaram*—animate and inanimate; *idam*—this universe; *dvija*—the twice-born; *devatā*—the demigods; *artham*—for the sake of; *nūnam*—however; *bhṛtam*—protected; *tat*—those feet; *abhighāti*—destroying; *rajaḥ*—the mode of passion; *tamaḥ*—the mode of ignorance; *ca*—and; *sattvena*—of pure goodness; *naḥ*—unto us; *vara-dayā*—bestowing all blessings; *tanuvā*—by Your transcendental form; *nirasya*—driving away.

TRANSLATION

O Lord, You are the personification of all religion. Therefore You manifest Yourself in three millenniums, and thus You protect this universe, which consists of animate and inanimate beings. By Your grace, which is of pure goodness and is the bestower of all blessings, kindly drive away the elements of rajas and tamas for the sake of the demigods and twice-born.

PURPORT

The Lord is addressed in this verse as *tri-yuga,* or one who appears in three millenniums—namely the Satya, Dvāpara and Tretā *yugas.* He is not mentioned as appearing in the fourth millennium, or Kali-yuga. It is described in Vedic literature that in Kali-yuga He comes as *channa-avatāra,* or an incarnation, but He does not appear as a manifest incarnation. In the other *yugas,* however, the Lord is a manifest incarnation, and therefore he is addressed as *tri-yuga,* or the Lord who appears in three *yugas.*

Śrīdhara Svāmī describes *tri-yuga* as follows: *yuga* means "couple," and *tri* means "three." The Lord is manifested as three couples by His six opulences, or three couples of opulences. In that way He can be addressed as *tri-yuga.* The Lord is the personality of religious principles. In three millenniums religious principles are protected by three kinds of spiritual culture, namely austerity, cleanliness and mercy. The Lord is called *tri-yuga* in that way also. In the age of Kali these three requisites to spiritual culture are almost absent, but the Lord is so kind that in spite of Kali-yuga's being devoid of these three spiritual qualities, He comes and protects the people of this age in His covered incarnation as Lord Caitanya. Lord Caitanya is called "covered" because although He is Kṛṣṇa Himself, He presents Himself as a devotee of Kṛṣṇa, not directly Kṛṣṇa. The devotees pray to Lord Caitanya, therefore, to eliminate their stock of passion and ignorance, the most conspicuous assets of this *yuga*. In the Kṛṣṇa consciousness movement one cleanses himself of the modes of passion and ignorance by chanting the holy name of the Lord, Hare Kṛṣṇa, Hare Kṛṣṇa, as introduced by Lord Caitanya.

The four Kumāras were cognizant of their situation in the modes of passion and ignorance because, although in Vaikuṇṭha, they wanted to curse devotees of the Lord. Since they were conscious of their own weakness, they prayed to the Lord to remove their still-existing passion and ignorance. The three transcendental qualifications—cleanliness, austerity and mercy—are the qualifications of the twice-born and the demigods. Those who are not situated in the quality of goodness cannot accept these three principles of spiritual culture. For the Kṛṣṇa consciousness movement, therefore, there are three sinful activities which are prohibited—namely illicit sex, intoxication, and eating food other than the *prasāda* offered to Kṛṣṇa. These three prohibitions are based on the principles of austerity, cleanliness and mercy. Devotees are merciful because they spare the poor animals, and they are clean because they are free of contamination from unwanted foodstuff and unwanted habits. Austerity is represented by restricted sex life. These principles, indicated by the prayers of the four Kumāras, should be followed by the devotees who are engaged in Kṛṣṇa consciousness.

TEXT 23

न त्वं द्विजोत्तमकुलं यदिहात्मगोपं
गोप्ता वृषः स्वर्हणेन ससूनृतेन ।
तर्ह्येव नङ्‌क्ष्यति शिवस्तव देव पन्था
लोकोऽग्रहीष्यदृषभस्य हि तत्प्रमाणम् ॥२३॥

na tvaṁ dvijottama-kulaṁ yadi hātma-gopaṁ
goptā vṛṣaḥ svarhaṇena sa-sūnṛtena
tarhy eva naṅkṣyati śivas tava deva panthā
loko 'grahīṣyad ṛṣabhasya hi tat pramāṇam

na—not; *tvam*—You; *dvija*—of the twice-born; *uttama-kulam*—the highest class; *yadi*—if; *ha*—indeed; *ātma-gopam*—worthy to be protected by You; *goptā*—the protector; *vṛṣaḥ*—the best; *su-arhaṇena*—by worship; *sa-sūnṛtena*—along with mild words; *tarhi*—then; *eva*—certainly; *naṅkṣyati*—will be lost; *śivaḥ*—auspicious; *tava*—Your; *deva*—O Lord; *panthāḥ*—the path; *lokaḥ*—the people in general; *agrahīṣyat*—would accept; *ṛṣabhasya*—of the best; *hi*—because; *tat*—that; *pramāṇam*—authority.

TRANSLATION

O Lord, You are the protector of the highest of the twice-born. If You do not protect them by offering worship and mild words, then certainly the auspicious path of worship will be rejected by people in general, who act on the strength and authority of Your Lordship.

PURPORT

In *Bhagavad-gītā* it is stated by the Lord Himself that the acts and character of great authorities are followed by people in general. Leaders of ideal character are therefore needed in society. Kṛṣṇa, the Supreme Personality of Godhead, appeared in this material world just to show the example of perfect authority, and people have to follow His path. The Vedic injunction is that one cannot understand the Absolute Truth simply by mental speculation or logical argument. One has to follow the authorities. *Mahājano yena gataḥ sa panthāḥ.* Great authorities should be followed; otherwise, if we simply depend on the scriptures, we are sometimes misled by rascals, or else we cannot understand or follow the different spiritual injunctions. The best path is to follow the authorities. The four *brāhmaṇa*-sages stated that Kṛṣṇa is naturally the protector of the cows and *brāhmaṇas: go-brāhmaṇa-hitāya ca.* When Kṛṣṇa was on this planet, He set a practical example. He was a cowherd boy, and He was very respectful to the *brāhmaṇas* and devotees.

It is also affirmed herein that the *brāhmaṇas* are the best of the twice-born. *Brāhmaṇas, kṣatriyas* and *vaiśyas* are all twice-born, but the *brāhmaṇas* are the best. When there is a fight between two persons, each of them protects the upper part of his body—the head, the arms and the belly. Similarly, for the actual advancement of human civilization, the best part of the social body, namely the *brāhmaṇas,* the *kṣatriyas* and *vaiśyas* (the intelligent class of men, the military class and the mercantile men) should be given special protection. Protection of the laborers should not be neglected, but special protection should be given to the upper orders. Of all classes of men, the *brāhmaṇas* and the Vaiṣṇavas should be given special protection. They should be worshiped. When their protection is performed, it is just like worshiping God. That is not exactly protection; it is a duty. One should worship the *brāhmaṇas* and Vaiṣṇavas by offering them all kinds of endowments and sweet words, and if one has no means to offer anything, he must at least use sweet words to pacify them. The Lord personally exhibited this behavior towards the Kumāras.

If this system is not introduced by the leaders, then human civilization will be lost. When there is no protection and special treatment for persons who are devotees of the Lord, who are highly intelligent in spiritual life, then the whole society is lost. The word *naṅkṣyati* indicates that such a civilization becomes spoiled and is annihilated. The kind of civilization recommended is called *deva-patha,* which means the "royal road of the demigods." Demigods are supposed to be fully fixed in devotional service, or Kṛṣṇa consciousness; that is the auspicious path that should be protected. If the authorities or the leaders of society do not give special respect to the *brāhmaṇas* and Vaiṣṇavas and do not offer them not only sweet words but all facilities, then the path of progress will be lost to human civilization. The Lord personally wanted to teach this, and therefore He offered so much praise to the Kumāras.

TEXT 24

तत्तेऽनभीष्टमिव सत्त्वनिधेर्विधित्सोः
क्षेमं जनाय निजशक्तिभिरुद्धृतारेः ।
नैतावता त्र्यधिपतेर्बत विश्वभर्तु-
स्तेजः क्षतं त्ववनतस्य स ते विनोदः ॥२४॥

tat te 'nabhīṣṭam iva sattva-nidher vidhitsoḥ
kṣemaṁ janāya nija-śaktibhir uddhṛtāreḥ
naitāvatā try-adhipater bata viśva-bhartus
tejaḥ kṣataṁ tv avanatasya sa te vinodaḥ

tat—that destruction of the path of auspiciousness; *te*—by You; *anabhīṣṭam*—is not liked; *iva*—as; *sattva-nidheḥ*—the reservoir of all goodness; *vidhitsoḥ*—desiring to do; *kṣemam*—good; *janāya*—for the people in general; *nija-śaktibhiḥ*—by Your own potencies; *uddhṛta*—destroyed; *areḥ*—the opposite element; *na*—not; *etāvatā*—by this; *tri-adhipateḥ*—of the proprietor of the three kinds of creations; *bata*—O Lord; *viśva-bhartuḥ*—the maintainer of the universe; *tejaḥ*—potency; *kṣatam*—reduced; *tu*—but; *avanatasya*—submissive; *saḥ*—that; *te*—Your; *vinodaḥ*—pleasure.

TRANSLATION

Dear Lord, You never want the auspicious path to be destroyed, for You are the reservoir of all goodness. Just to benefit people in general, You destroy the evil element by Your mighty potency. You are the proprietor of the three creations and the maintainer of the entire universe. Therefore Your potency is not reduced by Your submissive behavior. Rather, by submission You exhibit Your transcendental pastimes.

PURPORT

Lord Kṛṣṇa was never reduced in His position by becoming a cowherd boy or by offering respect to Sudāmā Brāhmaṇa or His other devotees like Nanda Mahārāja, Vasudeva, Mahārāja Yudhiṣṭhira and the Pāṇḍavas' mother, Kuntī. Everyone knew that He was the Supreme Personality of Godhead, Kṛṣṇa, yet His behavior was exemplary. The Supreme Personality of Godhead is *sac-cid-ānanda-vigraha;* His form is completely spiritual, full of bliss and knowledge, and it is eternal. Because the living entities are His parts and parcels, originally they also belong to the same quality of eternal form as the Lord, but when they come in contact with *māyā,* the material potency, due to their forgetfulness their existential constitution is covered. We should try to understand the appearance of Lord Kṛṣṇa in this spirit, as the Kumāras pray to Him. He is eternally a cowherd boy at Vṛndāvana, He is eternally the leader of the Battle of Kurukṣetra, and He is eternally the opulent prince of Dvārakā and the lover of the damsels of Vṛndāvana; all His appearances are meaningful because they show His real characteristics to the conditioned souls, who have forgotten their relationship with the Supreme Lord. He does everything for their benefit. The force exhibited in the Battle of Kurukṣetra by the desire of Kṛṣṇa and through the agency of Arjuna was also necessary because when people become too irreligious, force is required. Nonviolence in this respect is rascaldom.

TEXT 25

यं वानयोर्दममधीश भवान् विधत्ते
वृत्तिं नु वा तदनुमन्महि निर्व्यलीकम् ।
अस्मासु वा य उचितो ध्रियतां स दण्डो
येऽनागसौ वयमयुंक्ष्महि किल्बिषेण ॥२५॥

yaṁ vānayor damam adhīśa bhavān vidhatte
vṛttiṁ nu vā tad anumanmahi nirvyalīkam

asmāsu vā ya ucito dhriyatāṁ sa daṇḍo
ye 'nāgasau vayam ayuṅkṣmahi kilbiṣeṇa

yam—which; *vā*—or; *anayoḥ*—of both of them; *damam*—punishment; *adhīśa*—O Lord; *bhavān*—Your Lordship; *vidhatte*—awards; *vṛttim*—better existence; *nu*—certainly; *vā*—or; *tat*—that; *anumanmahi*—we accept; *nirvyalīkam*—without duplicity; *asmāsu*—to us; *vā*—or; *yaḥ*—whichever; *ucitaḥ*—is proper; *dhriyatām*—may be awarded; *saḥ*—that; *daṇḍaḥ*—punishment; *ye*—who; *anāgasau*—sinless; *vayam*—we; *ayuṅkṣmahi*—allotted; *kilbiṣeṇa*—with a curse.

TRANSLATION

O Lord, whatever punishment You wish to award to these two innocent persons or also to us we shall accept without duplicity. We understand that we have cursed two faultless persons.

PURPORT

The sages, the four Kumāras, now reject their cursing of the two doorkeepers, Jaya and Vijaya, because they are now conscious that persons who engage in the service of the Lord cannot be at fault at any stage. It is said that anyone who has implicit faith in the service of the Lord, or who actually engages in transcendental loving service, has all the good qualities of the demigods. Therefore, a devotee cannot be at fault. If sometimes it is found that he is in error by accident or by some temporary arrangement, that should not be taken very seriously. The cursing of Jaya and Vijaya is here repented. Now the Kumāras are thinking in terms of their position in the modes of passion and ignorance, and they are prepared to accept any kind of punishment from the Lord. In general, when dealing with devotees, we should not try to find faults. In *Bhagavad-gītā* also it is confirmed that the devotee who faithfully serves the Supreme Lord, even if found to commit a gross mistake, should be considered a *sādhu*, or saintly person. Due to former habits he may commit some wrong, but because he is engaged in the service of the Lord, that wrong should not be taken very seriously.

TEXT 26

श्रीभगवानुवाच
एतौ सुरेतरगतिं प्रतिपद्य सद्यः
संरम्भसम्भृतसमाध्यनुबद्धयोगौ ।
भूयः सकाशमुपयास्यत आशु यो वः
शापो मयैव निमितस्तदवेत विप्राः ॥२६॥

śrī-bhagavān uvāca
etau suretara-gatiṁ pratipadya sadyaḥ
saṁrambha-sambhṛta-samādhy-anubaddha-yogau
bhūyaḥ sakāśam upayāsyata āśu yo vaḥ
śāpo mayaiva nimitas tad aveta viprāḥ

śrī-bhagavān uvāca—the Supreme Personality of Godhead replied; *etau*—these two doorkeepers; *sura-itara*—demoniac; *gatim*—the womb; *pratipadya*—obtaining; *sadyaḥ*—quickly; *saṁrambha*—by anger; *sambhṛta*—intensified; *samādhi*—concentration of mind; *anubaddha*—firmly; *yogau*—united with Me; *bhūyaḥ*—again; *sakāśam*—to My presence; *upayāsyataḥ*—shall return; *āśu*—shortly; *yaḥ*—which; *vaḥ*—of you; *śāpaḥ*—curse; *mayā*—by Me; *eva*—alone; *nimitaḥ*—ordained; *tat*—that; *aveta*—know; *viprāḥ*—O *brāhmaṇas.*

TRANSLATION

The Lord replied: O brāhmaṇas, know that the punishment you inflicted on them was originally ordained by Me, and therefore they will fall to a birth in a demoniac family. But they will be firmly united with Me in thought through mental concentration intensified by anger, and they will return to My presence shortly.

PURPORT

The Lord stated that the punishment inflicted by the sages upon the doorkeepers Jaya and Vijaya was conceived by the Lord Himself. Without the Lord's sanction, nothing can happen. It is to be understood that there was a plan in the cursing of the Lord's devotees in Vaikuṇṭha, and His plan is explained by many stalwart authorities. The Lord sometimes desires to fight. The fighting spirit also exists in the Supreme Lord, otherwise how could fighting be manifested at all? Because the Lord is the source of everything, anger and fighting are also inherent in His personality. When He desires to fight with someone, He has to find an enemy, but in the Vaikuṇṭha world there is no enemy because everyone is engaged fully in His service. Therefore He sometimes comes to the material world as an incarnation in order to manifest His fighting spirit.

In *Bhagavad-gītā* (4.8) also it is said that the Lord appears just to give protection to the devotees and to annihilate the nondevotees. The nondevotees are found in the material world, not in the spiritual world; therefore, when the Lord wants to fight, He has to come to this world. But who will fight with the Supreme Lord? No one is able to fight with Him! Therefore, because the Lord's pastimes in the material world are always performed with His associates, not with others, He has to find some devotee who will play the part of an enemy. In *Bhagavad-gītā* the Lord says to Arjuna, "My dear Arjuna, both you and I have appeared many, many times in this material world, but you have forgotten, whereas I remember." Thus Jaya and Vijaya were selected by the Lord to fight with Him in the material world, and that was the reason the sages came to see Him and accidentally the doorkeepers were cursed. It was the Lord's desire to send them to the material world, not perpetually, but for some time. Therefore, just as on a theatrical stage someone takes the part of enemy to the proprietor of the stage, although the play is for a short time and there is no permanent enmity between the servant and the proprietor, so the *sura janas* (devotees) were cursed by the sages to go to the *asura jana,* or atheistic families. That a devotee should come into an atheistic family is surprising, but it is simply a show. After finishing their mock fighting, both the devotee and the Lord are again associated in the spiritual planets. That is very explicitly explained here. The conclusion is that no one falls from the spiritual world, or Vaikuṇṭha planet, for it is the eternal abode. But sometimes, as the Lord desires, devotees come into this material world as preachers or as atheists. In each case we must understand that there is a plan of the Lord. Lord Buddha, for example, was an incarnation, yet he preached atheism: "There is no God." But actually there was a plan behind this, as explained in the *Bhāgavatam.*

TEXT 27

ब्रह्मोवाच
अथ ते मुनयो दृष्ट्वा नयनानन्दभाजनम् ।
वैकुण्ठं तदधिष्ठानं विकुण्ठं च स्वयंप्रभम् ॥२७॥

brahmovāca
atha te munayo dṛṣṭvā
nayanānanda-bhājanam
vaikuṇṭhaṁ tad-adhiṣṭhānaṁ
vikuṇṭhaṁ ca svayaṁ-prabham

brahmā uvāca—Lord Brahmā said; *atha*—now; *te*—those; *munayaḥ*—sages; *dṛṣṭvā*—after seeing; *nayana*—of the eyes; *ānanda*—pleasure; *bhājanam*—producing; *vaikuṇṭham*—the Vaikuṇṭha planet; *tat*—of Him; *adhiṣṭhānam*—the abode; *vikuṇṭham*—the Supreme Personality of Godhead; *ca*—and; *svayam-prabham*—self-illuminating.

TRANSLATION

Lord Brahmā said: After seeing the Lord of Vaikuṇṭha, the Supreme Personality of Godhead, in the self-illuminated Vaikuṇṭha planet, the sages left that transcendental abode.

PURPORT

The transcendental abode of the Supreme Personality of Godhead, as stated in *Bhagavad-gītā* and confirmed in this verse, is self-illuminated. In *Bhagavad-gītā* it is said that in the spiritual world there is no need of sun, moon or electricity. This indicates that all the planets there are self-illuminated, self-sufficient and independent; everything there is complete. Lord Kṛṣṇa says that once one goes to that Vaikuṇṭha planet, he never returns. The inhabitants of Vaikuṇṭha never return to the material world, but the incident of Jaya and Vijaya was a different case. They came to the material world for some time, and then they returned to Vaikuṇṭha.

TEXT 28

भगवन्तं परिक्रम्य प्रणिपत्यानुमान्य च ।
प्रतिजग्मुः प्रमुदिताः शंसन्तो वैष्णवीं श्रियम् ॥२८॥

bhagavantaṁ parikramya
praṇipatyānumānya ca
pratijagmuḥ pramuditāḥ
śaṁsanto vaiṣṇavīṁ śriyam

bhagavantam—the Supreme Personality of Godhead; *parikramya*—after circumambulating; *praṇipatya*—after offering obeisances; *anumānya*—after learning; *ca*—and; *pratijagmuḥ*—returned; *pramuditāḥ*—extremely delighted; *śaṁsantaḥ*—glorifying; *vaiṣṇavīm*—of the Vaiṣṇavas; *śriyam*—opulence.

TRANSLATION

The sages circumambulated the Supreme Lord, offered their obeisances and returned, extremely delighted at learning of the divine opulences of the Vaiṣṇava.

PURPORT

It is still a respectful practice to circumambulate the Lord in Hindu temples. Especially in Vaiṣṇava temples there is an arrangement for people to offer their respects to the Deity and circumambulate the temple at least three times.

TEXT 29

भगवाननुगावाह यातं मा भैष्टमस्तु शम् ।
ब्रह्मतेजः समर्थोऽपि हन्तुं नेच्छे मतं तु मे ॥२९॥

bhagavān anugāv āha
yātaṁ mā bhaiṣṭam astu śam
brahma-tejaḥ samartho 'pi
hantuṁ necche mataṁ tu me

bhagavān—the Supreme Personality of Godhead; *anugau*—to His two attendants; *āha*—said; *yātam*—depart from this place; *mā*—let there not be; *bhaiṣṭam*—fear; *astu*—let there be; *śam*—happiness; *brahma*—of a *brāhmaṇa; tejaḥ*—the curse; *samarthaḥ*—being able; *api*—even; *hantum*—to nullify; *na icche*—do not desire; *matam*—approved; *tu*—on the contrary; *me*—by Me.

TRANSLATION

The Lord then said to His attendants, Jaya and Vijaya: Depart this place, but fear not. All glories unto you. Though I am capable of nullifying the brāhmaṇas' curse, I would not do so. On the contrary, it has My approval.

PURPORT

As explained in connection with text 26, all the incidents that took place had the approval of the Lord. Ordinarily, there is no possibility that the four sages could be so angry with the doorkeepers, nor could the Supreme Lord neglect His two doorkeepers, nor can one come back from Vaikuṇṭha after once taking birth there. All these incidents, therefore, were designed by the Lord Himself for the sake of His pastimes in the material world. Thus He plainly says that it was done with His approval. Otherwise, it would have been impossible for inhabitants of Vaikuṇṭha to come back to this material world simply because of a brahminical curse. The Lord especially blesses the so-called culprits: "All glories unto you." A devotee, once accepted by the Lord, can never fall down. That is the conclusion of this incident.

TEXT 30

एतत्पुरैव निर्दिष्टं रमया क्रुद्धया यदा ।
पुरापवारिता द्वारि विशन्ती मय्युपारते ॥३०॥

etat puraiva nirdiṣṭaṁ
ramayā kruddhayā yadā
purāpavāritā dvāri
viśantī mayy upārate

etat—this departure; *purā*—formerly; *eva*—certainly; *nirdiṣṭam*—foretold; *ramayā*—by Lakṣmī; *kruddhayā*—furious; *yadā*—when; *purā*—previously; *apavāritā*—prevented; *dvāri*—at the gate; *viśantī*—entering; *mayi*—as I; *upārate*—was resting.

TRANSLATION

This departure from Vaikuṇṭha was foretold by Lakṣmī, the goddess of fortune. She was very angry because when she left My abode and then returned, you stopped her at the gate while I was sleeping.

TEXT 31

मयि संरम्भयोगेन निस्तीर्य ब्रह्महेलनम् ।
प्रत्येष्यतं निकाशं मे कालेनाल्पीयसा पुनः ॥३१॥

mayi saṁrambha-yogena
nistīrya brahma-helanam
pratyeṣyataṁ nikāśaṁ me
kālenālpīyasā punaḥ

mayi—unto Me; *saṁrambha-yogena*—by practice of mystic *yoga* in anger; *nistīrya*—being liberated from; *brahma-helanam*—the result of disobedience to the *brāhmaṇas*; *pratyeṣyatam*—will come back; *nikāśam*—near; *me*—Me; *kālena*—in due course of time; *alpīyasā*—very short; *punaḥ*—again.

TRANSLATION

The Lord assured the two Vaikuṇṭha inhabitants, Jaya and Vijaya: By practicing the mystic yoga system in anger, you will be cleansed of the sin of disobeying the brāhmaṇas and within a very short time return to Me.

PURPORT

The Supreme Personality of Godhead advised the two doorkeepers, Jaya and Vijaya, that by dint of *bhakti-yoga* in anger they would be delivered from the curses of the *brāhmaṇas.* Śrīla Madhva Muni remarks in this connection that by practicing *bhakti-yoga* one can become free from all sinful reactions. Even a *brahma-śāpa,* or curse by a *brāhmaṇa,* which cannot be overcome by any other means, can be overcome by *bhakti-yoga.*

One can practice *bhakti-yoga* in many *rasas.* There are twelve *rasas,* five primary and seven secondary. The five primary *rasas* constitute direct *bhakti-yoga,* but although the seven secondary *rasas* are indirect, they are also counted within *bhakti-yoga* if they are used in the service of the Lord. In other words, *bhakti-yoga* is all-inclusive. If one somehow or other becomes attached to the Supreme Personality of Godhead, he becomes engaged in *bhakti-yoga,* as described in *Śrīmad-Bhāgavatam* (10.29.15): *kāmaṁ krodhaṁ bhayam.* The *gopīs* were attracted to Kṛṣṇa by *bhakti-yoga* in a relationship of lusty desire (*kāma*). Similarly, Kaṁsa was attached to *bhakti-yoga* by dint of fear of his death. Thus *bhakti-yoga* is so powerful that even becoming an enemy of the Lord and always thinking of Him can deliver one very quickly. It is said, *viṣṇu-bhaktaḥ smṛto daiva āsuras tad-vipanyayaḥ:* "Devotees of Lord Viṣṇu are called demigods, whereas nondevotees are called *asuras.*" But *bhakti-yoga* is so powerful that both demigods and *asuras* can derive its benefits if they always think of the Personality of Godhead. The basic principle of *bhakti-yoga* is to think of the Supreme Lord always. The Lord says in *Bhagavad-gītā* (18.65), *man-manā bhava mad-bhaktaḥ:* "Always think of Me." It doesn't matter which way one thinks; the very thought of the Personality of Godhead is the basic principle of *bhakti-yoga.*

In the material planets there are different grades of sinful activities, of which disrespecting a *brāhmaṇa* or a Vaiṣṇava is the most sinful. Here it is clearly stated that one can overcome even that grave sin simply by thinking of Viṣṇu, not even favorably but in anger. Thus even if those who are not devotees always think of Viṣṇu, they become free from all sinful activities. Kṛṣṇa consciousness is the highest form of thought. Lord Viṣṇu is thought of in this age by chanting Hare Kṛṣṇa, Hare Kṛṣṇa, Kṛṣṇa Kṛṣṇa, Hare Hare/ Hare Rāma, Hare Rāma, Rāma Rāma, Hare Hare. From the statements of the *Bhāgavatam* it appears that if one thinks of Kṛṣṇa, even as an enemy, that particular qualification—*thinking of Viṣṇu, or Kṛṣṇa*—cleanses one of all sins.

TEXT 32

द्वाःस्थावादिश्य भगवान् विमानश्रेणिभूषणम् ।
सर्वातिशयया लक्ष्म्या जुष्टं स्वं धिष्ण्यमाविशत् ॥३२॥

dvāḥsthāv ādiśya bhagavān
vimāna-śreṇi-bhūṣaṇam
sarvātiśayayā lakṣmyā
juṣṭaṁ svaṁ dhiṣṇyam āviśat

dvāḥ-sthau—to the doorkeepers; *ādiśya*—just directing them; *bhagavān*—the Supreme Personality of Godhead; *vimāna-śreṇi-bhūṣaṇam*—always decorated with first-class airplanes; *sarva-atiśayayā*—in every respect extensively opulent; *lakṣmyā*—opulences; *juṣṭam*—bedecked with; *svam*—His own; *dhiṣṇyam*—abode; *āviśat*—went back.

TRANSLATION

After thus speaking at the door of Vaikuṇṭha, the Lord returned to His abode, where there are many celestial airplanes and all-surpassing wealth and splendor.

PURPORT

It is clear from this verse that all the incidents took place at the entrance of Vaikuṇṭhaloka. In other words, the sages were not actually within Vaikuṇṭhaloka, but were at the gate. It could be asked, "How could they return to the material world if they entered Vaikuṇṭhaloka?" But factually they did not enter, and therefore they returned. There are many similar incidents where great *yogīs* and *brāhmaṇas*, by dint of their *yoga* practice, have gone from this material world to Vaikuṇṭhaloka—but they were not meant to stay there. They came back. It is also confirmed here that the Lord was surrounded by many Vaikuṇṭha airplanes. Vaikuṇṭhaloka is described here as having splendid opulence, far surpassing the splendor of this material world.

All other living creatures, including the demigods, are born of Brahmā, and Brahmā is born of Lord Viṣṇu. Kṛṣṇa states in *Bhagavad-gītā,* in the Tenth Chapter, *ahaṁ sarvasya prabhavaḥ:* Lord Viṣṇu is the origin of all manifestations in the material world. Those who know that Lord Viṣṇu is the origin of everything, who are conversant with the process of creation and who understand that Viṣṇu, or Kṛṣṇa, is the most worshipable object of all living entities, engage themselves in Viṣṇu worship as Vaiṣṇavas. The Vedic hymns also confirm this: *oṁ tad viṣṇoḥ paramaṁ padam.* The goal of life is to understand Viṣṇu. The *Bhāgavatam* also confirms this elsewhere. Foolish people, not knowing that Viṣṇu is the supreme worshipable object, create so many worshipable objects in this material world, and therefore they fall down.

TEXT 33

तौ तु गीर्वाणऋषभौ दुस्तराद्धरिलोकतः ।
हतश्रियौ ब्रह्मशापादभूतां विगतस्मयौ ॥३३॥

tau tu gīrvāṇa-ṛṣabhau
dustarād dhari-lokataḥ
hata-śriyau brahma-śāpād
abhūtāṁ vigata-smayau

tau—those two gatekeepers; *tu*—but; *gīrvāṇa-ṛṣabhau*—the best of the demigods; *dustarāt*—unable to be avoided; *hari-lokataḥ*—from Vaikuṇṭha, the abode of Lord Hari; *hata-śriyau*—diminished in beauty and luster; *brahma-śāpāt*—from the curse of a *brāhmaṇa*; *abhūtām*—became; *vigata-smayau*—morose.

TRANSLATION

But those two gatekeepers, the best of the demigods, their beauty and luster diminished by the curse of the brāhmaṇas, became morose and fell from Vaikuṇṭha, the abode of the Supreme Lord.

TEXT 34

तदा विकुण्ठधिषणात्तयोर्निपतमानयोः ।
हाहाकारो महानासीद्विमानाग्र्येषु पुत्रकाः ॥३४॥

tadā vikuṇṭha-dhiṣaṇāt
tayor nipatamānayoḥ
hāhā-kāro mahān āsīd
vimānāgryeṣu putrakāḥ

tadā—then; *vikuṇṭha*—of the Supreme Lord; *dhiṣaṇāt*—from the abode; *tayoḥ*—as both of them; *nipatamānayoḥ*—were falling; *hāhā-kāraḥ*—roaring in disappointment; *mahān*—great; *āsīt*—occurred; *vimāna-agryeṣu*—in the best of airplanes; *putrakāḥ*—O demigods.

TRANSLATION

Then, as Jaya and Vijaya fell from the Lord's abode, a great roar of disappointment arose from all the demigods, who were sitting in their splendid airplanes.

TEXT 35

तावेव ह्यधुना प्राप्तौ पार्षदप्रवरौ हरेः ।
दितेर्जठरनिर्विष्टं काश्यपं तेज उल्बणम् ॥३५॥

tāv eva hy adhunā prāptau
pārṣada-pravarau hareḥ
diter jaṭhara-nirviṣṭaṁ
kāśyapaṁ teja ulbaṇam

tau—those two doorkeepers; *eva*—certainly; *hi*—addressed; *adhunā*—now; *prāptau*—having gotten; *pārṣada-pravarau*—important associates; *hareḥ*—of the Supreme Personality of Godhead; *diteḥ*—of Diti; *jaṭhara*—womb; *nirviṣṭam*—entering; *kāśyapam*—of Kaśyapa Muni; *tejaḥ*—semen; *ulbaṇam*—very strong.

TRANSLATION

Lord Brahmā continued: Those two principal doorkeepers of the Personality of Godhead have now entered the womb of Diti, the powerful semen of Kaśyapa Muni having covered them.

PURPORT

Here is clear proof of how a living entity coming originally from Vaikuṇṭhaloka is encaged in material elements. The living entity takes shelter within the semen of a father, which is injected within the womb of a mother, and with the help of the mother's emulsified ovum the living entity grows a particular type of a body. In this connection it is to be remembered that the mind of Kaśyapa Muni was not in order when he conceived the two sons, Hiraṇyākṣa and Hiraṇyakaśipu. Therefore the semen he discharged was simultaneously extremely powerful and mixed with the quality of anger. It is to be concluded that while conceiving a child one's mind must be very sober and devotional. For this purpose the *Garbhādhāna-saṁskāra* is recommended in the Vedic scriptures. If the mind of the father is not sober, the semen discharged will not be very good. Thus the living entity, wrapped in the matter produced from the father and mother, will be demoniac like Hiraṇyākṣa and Hiraṇyakaśipu. The conditions of conception are to be carefully studied. This is a very great science.

TEXT 36

तयोरसुरयोरद्य तेजसा यमयोर्हि वः ।
आक्षिप्तं तेज एतर्हि भगवांस्तद्विधित्सति ॥३६॥

tayor asurayor adya
tejasā yamayor hi vaḥ
ākṣiptaṁ teja etarhi
bhagavāṁs tad vidhitsati

tayoḥ—of them; *asurayoḥ*—of the two *asuras; adya*—today; *tejasā*—by the prowess; *yamayoḥ*—of the twins; *hi*—certainly; *vaḥ*—of all you demigods; *ākṣiptam*—agitated; *tejaḥ*—power; *etarhi*—thus certainly; *bhagavān*—the Supreme Personality of Godhead; *tat*—that; *vidhitsati*—desires to do.

TRANSLATION

It is the prowess of these twin asuras [demons] that has disturbed you, for it has minimized your power. There is no remedy within my power, however, for it is the Lord Himself who desires to do all this.

PURPORT

Although Hiraṇyakaśipu and Hiraṇyākṣa, formerly Jaya and Vijaya, became *asuras,* the demigods of this material world could not control them, and therefore Lord Brahmā said that neither he nor all the demigods could counteract the disturbance they created. They came within the material world by the order of the Supreme Personality of Godhead, and He alone could counteract such disturbances. In other words, although Jaya and Vijaya assumed the bodies of *asuras,* they remained more powerful than anyone, thus proving that the Supreme Personality of Godhead desired to fight because the fighting spirit is also within Him. He is the original in everything, but when He desires to fight He must fight with a devotee. Therefore by His desire only were Jaya and Vijaya cursed by the Kumāras. The Lord ordered the gatekeepers to go down to the material world to become His enemies so that He could fight with them and His fighting desires would be satisfied by the service of His personal devotees.

Brahmā showed the demigods that the situation created by the darkness, for which they were disturbed, was the desire of the Supreme Lord. He wanted to show that even though these two attendants were coming in the forms of demons, they were very powerful, greater than the demigods, who could not control them. No one can surpass the acts of the Supreme Lord. The demigods were also advised not to try to counteract this incident, because it was ordered by the Lord. Similarly, anyone who is ordered by the Lord to perform some action in this material world, especially preaching His glories, cannot be counteracted by anyone; the will of the Lord is executed under all circumstances.

TEXT 37

विश्वस्य यः स्थितिलयोद्भवहेतुराद्यो
योगेश्वरैरपि दुरत्यययोगमायः ।
क्षेमं विधास्यति स नो भगवांस्त्र्यधीश-
स्तत्रास्मदीयविमृशेन कियानिहार्थः ॥३७॥

viśvasya yaḥ sthiti-layodbhava-hetur ādyo
yogeśvarair api duratyaya-yogamāyaḥ
kṣemaṁ vidhāsyati sa no bhagavāṁs tryadhīśas
tatrāsmadīya-vimṛśena kiyān ihārthaḥ

viśvasya—of the universe; *yaḥ*—who; *sthiti*—maintenance; *laya*—destruction; *udbhava*—creation; *hetuḥ*—the cause; *ādyaḥ*—the most ancient person; *yoga-īśvaraiḥ*—by the masters of *yoga; api*—even; *duratyaya*—cannot be easily understood; *yoga-māyaḥ*—His *yogamāyā* potency; *kṣemam*—good; *vidhāsyati*—will do; *saḥ*—He; *naḥ*—of us; *bhagavān*—the Supreme Personality of Godhead; *tri-adhīśaḥ*—the controller of the three modes of material nature; *tatra*—there; *asmadīya*—by our; *vimṛśena*—deliberation; *kiyān*—what; *iha*—on this subject; *arthaḥ*—purpose.

TRANSLATION

My dear sons, the Lord is the controller of the three modes of nature and is responsible for the creation, preservation and dissolution of the universe. His wonderful creative power, yogamāyā, cannot be easily understood even by the masters of yoga. That most ancient person, the Personality of Godhead, will alone come to our rescue. What purpose can we serve on His behalf by deliberating on the subject?

PURPORT

When something is arranged by the Supreme Personality of Godhead, one should not be disturbed by it, even if it appears to be a reverse according to one's calculations. For example, sometimes we see that a powerful preacher is killed, or sometimes he is put into difficulty, just as Haridāsa Ṭhākura was. He was a great devotee who came into this material world to execute the will of the Lord by preaching the Lord's glories. But Haridāsa was punished at the hands of the Kazi by being beaten in twenty-two marketplaces. Similarly, Lord Jesus Christ was crucified, and Prahlāda Mahārāja was put through so many tribulations. The Pāṇḍavas, who were direct friends of Kṛṣṇa, lost their kingdom, their wife was insulted, and they had to undergo many severe tribulations. Seeing all these reverses affect devotees, one should not be disturbed; one should simply understand that in these matters there must be some plan of the Supreme Personality of Godhead. The *Bhāgavatam's* conclusion is that a devotee is never disturbed by such reverses. He accepts even reverse conditions as the grace of the Lord. One who continues to serve the Lord even in reverse conditions is assured that he will go back to Godhead, back to the Vaikuṇṭha planets. Lord Brahmā assured the demigods that there was no use in talking about how the disturbing situation of darkness was taking place, since the actual fact was that it was ordered by the Supreme Lord. Brahmā knew this because he was a great devotee; it was possible for him to understand the plan of the Lord.

Thus end the Bhaktivedanta purports of the Third Canto, Sixteenth Chapter, of the Śrīmad-Bhāgavatam, *entitled "The Two Doorkeepers of Vaikuṇṭha, Jaya and Vijaya, Cursed by the Sages.*

CHAPTER SEVENTEEN

Victory of Hiraṇyākṣa Over All the Directions of the Universe

TEXT 1

मैत्रेय उवाच
निशम्यात्मभुवा गीतं कारणं शङ्कयोज्झिताः ।
ततः सर्वे न्यवर्तन्त त्रिदिवाय दिवौकसः ॥ १ ॥

maitreya uvāca
niśamyātma-bhuvā gītaṁ
kāraṇaṁ śaṅkayojjhitāḥ
tataḥ sarve nyavartanta
tridivāya divaukasaḥ

maitreyaḥ—the sage Maitreya; *uvāca*—said; *niśamya*—upon hearing; *ātma-bhuvā*—by Brahmā; *gītam*—explanation; *kāraṇam*—the cause; *śaṅkayā*—from fear; *ujjhitāḥ*—freed; *tataḥ*—then; *sarve*—all; *nyavartanta*—returned; *tri-divāya*—to the heavenly planets; *diva-okasaḥ*—the demigods (who inhabit the higher planets).

TRANSLATION

Śrī Maitreya said: The demigods, the inhabitants of the higher planets, were freed from all fear upon hearing the cause of the darkness explained by Brahmā, who was born from Viṣṇu. Thus they all returned to their respective planets.

PURPORT

The demigods, who are denizens of higher planets, are also very much afraid of incidents such as the universe's becoming dark, and so they consulted Brahmā. This indicates that the quality of fear exists for every living entity in the material world. The four principal activities of material existence are eating, sleeping, fearing and mating. The fear element exists also in the demigods. On every planet, even in the higher planetary systems, including the moon and the sun, as well as on this earth, the same principles of animal life exist. Otherwise, why are the demigods also afraid of the darkness? The difference between the demigods and ordinary human beings is that the demigods approach authority, whereas the inhabitants of this earth defy authority. If people would only approach the authority, then every adverse condition in this universe could be rectified. Arjuna was also disturbed on the Battlefield of Kurukṣetra, but he approached the authority, Kṛṣṇa, and his problem was solved. The conclusive instruction of this incident is that we may be disturbed by some material condition, but if we approach the authority who can actually explain the matter, then our problem is solved. The demigods approached Brahmā for the meaning of the disturbance, and after hearing from him they were satisfied and returned home peacefully.

TEXT 2

दितिस्तु भर्तुरादेशादपत्यपरिशङ्किनी ।
पूर्णे वर्षशते साध्वी पुत्रौ प्रसुषुवे यमौ ॥ २ ॥

ditis tu bhartur ādeśād
apatya-pariśaṅkinī
pūrṇe varṣa-śate sādhvī
putrau prasuṣuve yamau

ditiḥ—Diti; *tu*—but; *bhartuḥ*—of her husband; *ādeśāt*—by the order; *apatya*—from her children; *pariśaṅkinī*—being apprehensive of trouble; *pūrṇe*—full; *varṣa-śate*—after one hundred years; *sādhvī*—the virtuous lady; *putrau*—two sons; *prasuṣuve*—begot; *yamau*—twins.

TRANSLATION

The virtuous lady Diti had been very apprehensive of trouble to the gods from the children in her womb, and her husband predicted the same. She brought forth twin sons after a full one hundred years of pregnancy.

TEXT 3

उत्पाता बहवस्तत्र निपेतुर्जायमानयोः ।
दिवि भुव्यन्तरिक्षे च लोकस्योरुभयावहाः ॥ ३ ॥

utpātā bahavas tatra
nipetur jāyamānayoḥ
divi bhuvy antarikṣe ca
lokasyoru-bhayāvahāḥ

utpātāḥ—natural disturbances; *bahavaḥ*—many; *tatra*—there; *nipetuḥ*—occurred; *jāyamānayoḥ*—on their birth; *divi*—in the heavenly planets; *bhuvi*—on the earth; *antarikṣe*—in outer space; *ca*—and; *lokasya*—to the world; *uru*—greatly; *bhaya-āvahāḥ*—causing fear.

TRANSLATION

On the birth of the two demons there were many natural disturbances, all very fearful and wonderful, in the heavenly planets, the earthly planets and in between them.

TEXT 4

सहाचला भुवश्चेलुर्दिशः सर्वाः प्रजज्वलुः ।
सोल्काश्चाशनयः पेतुः केतवश्चार्तिहेतवः ॥ ४ ॥

sahācalā bhuvaś celur
diśaḥ sarvāḥ prajajvaluḥ
solkāś cāśanayaḥ petuḥ
ketavaś cārti-hetavaḥ

saha—along with; *acalāḥ*—the mountains; *bhuvaḥ*—of the earth; *celuḥ*—shook; *diśaḥ*—directions; *sarvāḥ*—all; *prajajvaluḥ*—blazed like fire; *sa*—with; *ulkāḥ*—meteors; *ca*—and; *aśanayaḥ*—thunderbolts; *petuḥ*—fell; *ketavaḥ*—comets; *ca*—and; *ārti-hetavaḥ*—the cause of all inauspiciousness.

TRANSLATION

There were earthquakes along the mountains on the earth, and it appeared that there was fire everywhere. Many inauspicious planets like Saturn appeared, along with comets, meteors and thunderbolts.

PURPORT

When natural disturbances occur on a planet, one should understand that a demon must have taken birth there. In the present age the number of demoniac people is increasing; therefore natural disturbances are also increasing. There is no doubt about this, as we can understand from the statements of the *Bhāgavatam*.

TEXT 5

ववौ वायुः सुदुःस्पर्शः फूत्कारानीरयन्मुहुः ।
उन्मूलयन्नगपतीन्वात्यानीको रजोध्वजः ॥ ५ ॥

vavau vāyuḥ suduḥsparśaḥ
phūt-kārān īrayan muhuḥ
unmūlayan naga-patīn
vātyāniko rajo-dhvajaḥ

vavau—blew; *vāyuḥ*—the winds; *su-duḥsparśaḥ*—unpleasant to touch; *phūt-kārān*—hissing sounds; *īrayan*—giving out; *muhuḥ*—again and again; *unmūlayan*—uprooting; *naga-patīn*—gigantic trees; *vātyā*—cyclonic air; *anīkaḥ*—armies; *rajaḥ*—dust; *dhvajaḥ*—ensigns.

TRANSLATION

There blew winds which were most uninviting to the touch, hissing again and again and uprooting gigantic trees. They had storms for their armies and clouds of dust for their ensigns.

PURPORT

When there are natural disturbances like blowing cyclones, too much heat or snowfall, and uprooting of trees by hurricanes, it is to be understood that the demoniac population is increasing and so the natural disturbance is also taking place. There are many countries on the globe, even at the present moment, where all these disturbances are current. This is true all over the world. There is insufficient sunshine, and there are always clouds in the sky, snowfall and severe cold. These assure that such places are inhabited by demoniac people who are accustomed to all kinds of forbidden, sinful activity.

TEXT 6

उद्धसत्तडिदम्भोदघटया नष्टभागणे ।
व्योम्नि प्रविष्टतमसा न स्म व्यादृश्यते पदम् ॥ ६ ॥

uddhasat-taḍid-ambhoda-
ghaṭayā naṣṭa-bhāgaṇe
vyomni praviṣṭa-tamasā
na sma vyādṛśyate padam

uddhasat—laughing loudly; *taḍit*—lightning; *ambhoda*—of clouds; *ghaṭayā*—by masses; *naṣṭa*—lost; *bhā-gaṇe*—the luminaries; *vyomni*—in the sky; *praviṣṭa*—enveloped; *tamasā*—by darkness; *na*—not; *sma vyādṛśyate*—could be seen; *padam*—any place.

TRANSLATION

The luminaries in the heavens were screened by masses of clouds, in which lightning sometimes flashed as though laughing. Darkness reigned everywhere, and nothing could be seen.

TEXT 7

चुक्रोश विमना वार्धिरुदूर्मिः क्षुभितोदरः ।
सोदपानाश्च सरितश्चुक्षुभुः शुष्कपङ्कजाः ॥ ७ ॥

cukrośa vimanā vārdhir
udūrmiḥ kṣubhitodaraḥ
sodapānāś ca saritaś
cukṣubhuḥ śuṣka-paṅkajāḥ

cukrośa—wailed aloud; *vimanāḥ*—stricken with sorrow; *vārdhiḥ*—the ocean; *udūrmiḥ*—high waves; *kṣubhita*—agitated; *udaraḥ*—the creatures inside; *sa-udapānāḥ*—with the drinking water of the lakes and the wells; *ca*—and; *saritaḥ*—the rivers; *cukṣubhuḥ*—were agitated; *śuṣka*—withered; *paṅkajāḥ*—lotus flowers.

TRANSLATION

The ocean with its high waves wailed aloud as if stricken with sorrow, and there was a commotion among the creatures inhabiting the ocean. The rivers and lakes were also agitated, and lotuses withered.

TEXT 8

मुहुः परिधयोऽभूवन् सराह्वोः शशिसूर्ययोः ।
निर्घाता रथनिर्ह्रादा विवरेभ्यः प्रजज्ञिरे ॥ ८ ॥

muhuḥ paridhayo 'bhūvan
sarāhvoḥ śaśi-sūryayoḥ
nirghātā ratha-nirhrādā
vivarebhyaḥ prajajñire

muhuḥ—again and again; *paridhayaḥ*—misty halos; *abhūvan*—appeared; *sa-rāhvoḥ*—during eclipses; *śaśi*—of the moon; *sūryayoḥ*—of the sun; *nirghātāḥ*—claps of thunder; *ratha-nirhrādāḥ*—sounds like those of rattling chariots; *vivarebhyaḥ*—from the mountain caves; *prajajñire*—were produced.

TRANSLATION

Misty halos appeared around the sun and the moon during solar and lunar eclipses again and again. Claps of thunder were heard even without clouds, and sounds like those of rattling chariots emerged from the mountain caves.

TEXT 9

अन्तर्ग्रामेषु मुखतो वमन्त्यो वह्निमुल्बणम् ।
सृगालोलूकटङ्कारैः प्रणेदुरशिवं शिवाः ॥ ९ ॥

antar-grāmeṣu mukhato
vamantyo vahnim ulbaṇam
sṛgālolūka-ṭaṅkāraiḥ
praṇedur aśivaṁ śivāḥ

antaḥ—in the interior; *grāmeṣu*—in the villages; *mukhataḥ*—from their mouths; *vamantyaḥ*—vomiting; *vahnim*—fire; *ulbaṇam*—fearful; *sṛgāla*—jackals; *ulūka*—owls; *ṭaṅkāraiḥ*—with their cries; *praṇeduḥ*—created their respective vibrations; *aśivam*—portentously; *śivāḥ*—the she-jackals.

TRANSLATION

In the interior of the villages she-jackals yelled portentously, vomiting strong fire from their mouths, and jackals and owls also joined them with their cries.

TEXT 10

स्रीतवद्रोदनवदुन्नमय्य शिरोधराम् ।
व्यमुञ्चन् विविधा वाचो ग्रामसिंहास्ततस्ततः ॥१०॥

saṅgītavad rodanavad
unnamayya śirodharām
vyamuñcan vividhā vāco
grāma-siṁhās tatas tataḥ

saṅgīta-vat—like singing; *rodana-vat*—like wailing; *unnamayya*—raising; *śirodharām*—the neck; *vyamuñcan*—uttered; *vividhāḥ*—various; *vācaḥ*—cries; *grāma-siṁhāḥ*—the dogs; *tataḥ tataḥ*—here and there.

TRANSLATION

Raising their necks, dogs cried here and there, now in the manner of singing and now of wailing.

TEXT 11

खराश्च कर्कशैः क्षत्तः खुरैर्घ्नन्तो धरातलम् ।
खार्काररभसा मत्ताः पर्यधावन् वरूथशः ॥११॥

kharāś ca karkaśaiḥ kṣattaḥ
khurair ghnanto dharā-talam
khārkāra-rabhasā mattāḥ
paryadhāvan varūthaśaḥ

kharāḥ—asses; *ca*—and; *karkaśaiḥ*—hard; *kṣattaḥ*—O Vidura; *khuraiḥ*—with their hooves; *ghnantaḥ*—striking; *dharā-talam*—the surface of the earth; *khāḥ-kāra*—braying; *rabhasāḥ*—wildly engaged in; *mattāḥ*—mad; *paryadhāvan*—ran hither and thither; *varūthaśaḥ*—in herds.

TRANSLATION

O Vidura, the asses ran hither and thither in herds, striking the earth with their hard hooves and wildly braying.

PURPORT

Asses also feel very respectable as a race, and when they run in flocks hither and thither in so-called jollity, it is understood to be a bad sign for human society.

TEXT 12

रुदन्तो रासभत्रस्ता नीडादुदपतन् खगाः ।
घोषेऽरण्ये च पशवः शकृन्मूत्रमकुर्वत ॥१२॥

rudanto rāsabha-trastā
nīḍād udapatan khagāḥ
ghoṣe 'raṇye ca paśavaḥ
śakṛn-mūtram akurvata

rudantaḥ—shrieking; *rāsabha*—by the asses; *trastāḥ*—frightened; *nīḍāt*—from the nest; *udapatan*—flew up; *khagāḥ*—birds; *ghoṣe*—in the cowshed; *araṇye*—in the woods; *ca*—and; *paśavaḥ*—the cattle; *śakṛt*—dung; *mūtram*—urine; *akurvata*—passed.

TRANSLATION

Frightened by the braying of the asses, birds flew shrieking from their nests, while cattle in the cowsheds as well as in the woods passed dung and urine.

TEXT 13

गावोऽत्रसन्नसृग्दोहास्तोयदाः पूयवर्षिणः ।
व्यरुदन्देवलिङ्गानि द्रुमाः पेतुर्विनानिलम् ॥१३॥

gāvo 'trasann asṛg-dohās
toyadāḥ pūya-varṣiṇaḥ
vyarudan deva-liṅgāni
drumāḥ petur vinānilam

gāvaḥ—the cows; *atrasan*—were frightened; *asṛk*—blood; *dohāḥ*—yielding; *toyadāḥ*—clouds; *pūya*—pus; *varṣiṇaḥ*—raining; *vyarudan*—shed tears; *deva-liṅgāni*—the images of the gods; *drumāḥ*—trees; *petuḥ*—fell down; *vinā*—without; *anilam*—a blast of wind.

TRANSLATION

Cows, terrified, yielded blood in place of milk, clouds rained pus, the images of the gods in the temples shed tears, and trees fell down without a blast of wind.

TEXT 14

ग्रहान् पुण्यतमानन्ये भगणांश्चापि दीपिताः ।
अतिचेरुर्वक्रगत्या युयुधुश्च परस्परम् ॥१४॥

grahān puṇyatamān anye
bhagaṇāṁś cāpi dīpitāḥ
aticerur vakra-gatyā
yuyudhuś ca parasparam

grahān—planets; *puṇya-tamān*—most auspicious; *anye*—others (the ominous planets); *bhagaṇān*—luminaries; *ca*—and; *api*—also; *dīpitāḥ*—illuminating; *aticeruḥ*—overlapped; *vakra-gatyā*—taking retrograde courses; *yuyudhuḥ*—came into conflict; *ca*—and; *paraḥ-param*—with one another.

TRANSLATION

Ominous planets such as Mars and Saturn shone brighter and surpassed the auspicious ones such as Mercury, Jupiter and Venus as well as a number of lunar mansions. Taking seemingly retrograde courses, the planets came in conflict with one another.

PURPORT

The entire universe is moving under the three modes of material nature. Those living entities who are in goodness are called the pious species—pious lands, pious trees, etc. It is similar with the planets also; many planets are considered pious, and others are considered impious. Saturn and Mars are considered impious. When the pious planets shine very brightly, it is an auspicious sign, but when the inauspicious planets shine very brightly, this is not a very good sign.

TEXT 15

दृष्ट्वान्यांश्च महोत्पातानतत्तत्त्वविदः प्रजाः ।
ब्रह्मपुत्रानृते भीता मेनिरे विश्वसम्प्लवम् ॥१५॥

dṛṣṭvānyāṁś ca mahotpātān
atat-tattva-vidaḥ prajāḥ
brahma-putrān ṛte bhītā
menire viśva-samplavam

dṛṣṭvā—having seen; *anyān*—others; *ca*—and; *mahā*—great; *utpātān*—evil omens; *a-tat-tattva-vidaḥ*—not knowing the secret (of the portents); *prajāḥ*—people; *brahma-putrān*—the sons of Brahmā (the four Kumāras); *ṛte*—except; *bhītāḥ*—being fearful; *menire*—thought; *viśva-samplavam*—the dissolution of the universe.

TRANSLATION

Marking these and many other omens of evil times, everyone but the four sage—sons of Brahmā, who were aware of the fall of Jaya and Vijaya and of their birth as Diti's sons, was seized with fear. They did not know the secrets of these portents and thought that the dissolution of the universe was at hand.

PURPORT

According to *Bhagavad-gītā*, Seventh Chapter, the laws of nature are so stringent that it is impossible for the living entity to surpass their enforcement. It is also explained that only those who are fully surrendered to Kṛṣṇa in Kṛṣṇa consciousness can be saved. We can learn from the description of the *Śrīmad-Bhāgavatam* that it is because of the birth of two great demons that there were so many natural disturbances. It is to be indirectly understood, as previously described, that when there are constant disturbances on the earth, that is an omen that some demoniac people have been born or that the demoniac population has increased. In former days there were only two demons—those born of Diti—yet there were so many disturbances. At the present day, especially in this age of Kali, these disturbances are always visible, which indicates that the demoniac population has certainly increased.

To check the increase of demoniac population, the Vedic civilization enacted so many rules and regulations of social life, the most important of which is the *garbhādhāna* process for begetting good children. In *Bhagavad-gītā* Arjuna informed Kṛṣṇa that if there is unwanted population (*varṇa-saṅkara*), the entire world will appear to be hell. People are very anxious for peace in the world, but there are so many unwanted children born without the benefit of the *garbhādhāna* ceremony, just like the demons born from Diti. Diti was so lusty that she forced her husband to copulate at a time which was inauspicious, and therefore the demons were born to create disturbances. In having sex life to beget children, one should observe the process for begetting nice children; if each and every householder in every family observes the Vedic system, then there are nice children, not demons, and automatically there is peace in the world. If we do not follow regulations in life for social tranquillity, we cannot expect peace. Rather, we will have to undergo the stringent reactions of natural laws.

TEXT 16

तावादिदैत्यौ सहसा व्यज्यमानात्मपौरुषौ ।
ववृधातेऽश्मसारेण कायेनाद्रिपती इव ॥१६॥

tāv ādi-daityau sahasā
vyajyamānātma-pauruṣau
vavṛdhāte 'śma-sāreṇa
kāyenādri-patī iva

tau—those two; *ādi-daityau*—demons in the beginning of creation; *sahasā*—quickly; *vyajyamāna*—being manifest; *ātma*—own; *pauruṣau*—prowess; *vavṛdhāte*—grew; *aśma-sāreṇa*—steellike; *kāyena*—with bodily frames; *adri-patī*—two great mountains; *iva*—like.

TRANSLATION

These two demons who appeared in ancient times soon began to exhibit uncommon bodily features; they had steellike frames which began to grow just like two great mountains.

PURPORT

There are two classes of men in the world; one is called the demon, and the other is called the demigod. The demigods concern themselves with the spiritual upliftment of human society, whereas the demons are concerned with physical and material upliftment. The two demons born of Diti began to make their bodies as strong as iron frames, and they were so tall that they seemed to touch outer space. They were decorated with valuable ornaments, and they thought that this was success in life. Originally it was planned that Jaya and Vijaya, the two doorkeepers of Vaikuṇṭha, were to take birth in this material world, where, by the curse of the sages, they were to play the part of always being angry with the Supreme Personality of Godhead. As demoniac persons, they became so angry that they were not concerned with the Supreme Personality of Godhead, but simply with physical comforts and physical upliftment.

TEXT 17

दिविस्पृशौ हेमकिरीटकोटिभि-
निरुद्धकाष्ठौ स्फुरदङ्गदाभुजौ ।
गां कम्पयन्तौ चरणैः पदे पदे
कट्या सुकाञ्च्यार्कमतीत्य तस्थतुः ॥१७॥

divi-spṛśau hema-kirīṭa-koṭibhir
niruddha-kāṣṭhau sphurad-aṅgadā-bhujau
gāṁ kampayantau caraṇaiḥ pade pade
kaṭyā sukāñcyārkam atītya tasthatuḥ

divi-spṛśau—touching the sky; *hema*—golden; *kirīṭa*—of their helmets; *koṭibhiḥ*—with the crests; *niruddha*—blocked; *kāṣṭhau*—the directions; *sphurat*—brilliant; *aṅgadā*—bracelets; *bhujau*—on whose arms; *gām*—the earth; *kampayantau*—shaking; *caraṇaiḥ*—with their feet; *pade pade*—at every step; *kaṭyā*—with their waists; *su-kāñcyā*—with beautiful decorated belts; *arkam*—the sun; *atītya*—surpassing; *tasthatuḥ*—they stood.

TRANSLATION

Their bodies became so tall that they seemed to kiss the sky with the crests of their gold crowns. They blocked the view of all directions and while walking shook the earth at every step. Their arms were adorned with brilliant bracelets, and they stood as if covering the sun with their waists, which were bound with excellent and beautiful girdles.

PURPORT

In the demoniac way of civilization, people are interested in getting a body constructed in such a way that when they walk on the street the earth will tremble and when they stand it will appear that they cover the sun and the vision of the four directions. If a race appears strong in body, their country is materially considered to be among the highly advanced nations of the world.

TEXT 18

प्रजापतिर्नाम तयोरकार्षीद्
यः प्राक् स्वदेहाद्यमयोरजायत ।
तं वै हिरण्यकशिपुं विदुः प्रजा
यं तं हिरण्याक्षमसूत साग्रतः ॥१८॥

prajāpatir nāma tayor akārṣīd
yaḥ prāk sva-dehād yamayor ajāyata
taṁ vai hiraṇyakaśipuṁ viduḥ prajā
yaṁ taṁ hiraṇyākṣam asūta sāgrataḥ

prajāpatiḥ—Kaśyapa; *nāma*—names; *tayoḥ*—of the two; *akārṣīt*—gave; *yaḥ*—who; *prāk*—first; *sva-dehāt*—from his body; *yamayoḥ*—of the twins; *ajāyata*—was delivered; *tam*—him; *vai*—indeed; *hiraṇyakaśipum*—Hiraṇyakaśipu; *viduḥ*—know; *prajāḥ*—people; *yam*—whom; *tam*—him; *hiraṇyākṣam*—Hiraṇyākṣa; *asūta*—gave birth to; *sā*—she (Diti); *agrataḥ*—first.

TRANSLATION

Kaśyapa, Prajāpati, the creator of the living entities, gave his twin sons their names; the one who was born first he named Hiraṇyākṣa, and the one who was first conceived by Diti he named Hiraṇyakaśipu.

PURPORT

There is an authoritative Vedic literature called *Piṇḍa-siddhi* in which the scientific understanding of pregnancy is very nicely described. It is stated that when the male secretion enters the menstrual flux in the uterus in two successive drops, the mother develops two embryos in her womb, and she brings forth twins in a reverse order to that in which they were first conceived; the child conceived first is born later, and the one conceived later is brought forth first. The first child conceived in the womb lives behind the second child, so when birth takes place the second child appears first, and the first child appears second. In this case it is understood that Hiraṇyākṣa, the second child conceived, was delivered first, whereas Hiraṇyakaśipu, the child who was behind him, having been conceived first, was born second.

TEXT 19

चक्रे हिरण्यकशिपुर्दोर्भ्यां ब्रह्मवरेण च ।
वशे सपालाँल्लोकांस्त्रीनकुतोमृत्युरुद्धतः ॥१९॥

cakre hiraṇyakaśipur
dorbhyāṁ brahma-vareṇa ca
vaśe sa-pālāl̐ lokāṁs trīn
akuto-mṛtyur uddhataḥ

cakre—made; *hiraṇyakaśipuḥ*—Hiraṇyakaśipu; *dorbhyām*—by his two arms; *brahma-vareṇa*—by the benediction of Brahmā; *ca*—and; *vaśe*—under his control; *sa-pālān*—along with their protectors; *lokān*—the worlds; *trīn*—three; *akutaḥ-mṛtyuḥ*—fearing death from no one; *uddhataḥ*—puffed up.

TRANSLATION

The elder child, Hiraṇyakaśipu, was unafraid of death from anyone within the three worlds because he received a benediction from Lord Brahmā. He was proud and puffed up due to this benediction and was able to bring all three planetary systems under his control.

PURPORT

As will be revealed in later chapters, Hiraṇyakaśipu underwent severe austerity and penance to satisfy Brahmā and thus receive a benediction of immortality. Actually, it is impossible even for Lord Brahmā to give anyone the benediction of becoming immortal, but indirectly Hiraṇyakaśipu received the benediction that no one within this material world would be able to kill him. In other words, because he originally came from the abode of Vaikuṇṭha, he was not to be killed by anyone within this material world. The Lord desired to appear Himself to kill him. One may be very proud of his material advancement in knowledge, but he cannot be immune to the four principles of material existence, namely birth, death, old age and disease. It was the Lord's plan to teach people that even Hiraṇyakaśipu, who was so powerful and strongly built, could not live more than his destined duration of life. One may become as strong and puffed up as Hiraṇyakaśipu and bring under his control all the three worlds, but there is no possibility of continuing life eternally or keeping the conquered booty forever. So many emperors have ascended to power, and they are now lost in oblivion; that is the history of the world.

TEXT 20

हिरण्याक्षोऽनुजस्तस्य प्रियः प्रीतिकृदन्वहम् ।
गदापाणिर्दिवं यातो युयुत्सुर्मृगयन् रणम् ॥२०॥

hiraṇyākṣo 'nujas tasya
priyaḥ prīti-kṛd anvaham
gadā-pāṇir divaṁ yāto
yuyutsur mṛgayan raṇam

hiraṇyākṣaḥ—Hiraṇyākṣa; *anujaḥ*—younger brother; *tasya*—his; *priyaḥ*—beloved; *prīti-kṛt*—ready to please; *anu-aham*—every day; *gadā-pāṇiḥ*—with a club in hand; *divam*—to the higher planets; *yātaḥ*—traveled; *yuyutsuḥ*—desirous to fight; *mṛgayan*—seeking; *raṇam*—combat.

TRANSLATION

His younger brother, Hiraṇyākṣa, was always ready to satisfy his elder brother by his activities. Hiraṇyākṣa took a club on his shoulder and traveled all over the universe with a fighting spirit just to satisfy Hiraṇyakaśipu.

PURPORT

The demoniac spirit is to train all family members to exploit the resources of this universe for personal sense gratification, whereas the godly spirit is to engage everything in the service of the Lord. Hiraṇyakaśipu was himself very powerful, and he made his younger brother, Hiraṇyākṣa, powerful to assist him in fighting with everyone and lording it over material nature as long as possible. If possible, he wanted to rule the universe eternally. These are demonstrations of the spirit of the demoniac living entity.

TEXT 21

तं वीक्ष्य दुःसहजवं रणत्काञ्चननूपुरम् ।
वैजयन्त्या स्रजा जुष्टमंसन्यस्तमहागदम् ॥२१॥

taṁ vīkṣya duḥsaha-javaṁ
raṇat-kāñcana-nūpuram

vaijayantyā srajā juṣṭam
aṁsa-nyasta-mahā-gadam

tam—him; *vīkṣya*—having seen; *duḥsaha*—difficult to control; *javam*—temper; *raṇat*—tinkling; *kāñcana*—gold; *nūpuram*—anklets; *vaijayantyā srajā*—with a *vaijayantī* garland; *juṣṭam*—adorned; *aṁsa*—on his shoulder; *nyasta*—rested; *mahā-gadam*—a huge mace.

TRANSLATION

Hiraṇyākṣa's temper was difficult to control. He had anklets of gold tinkling about his feet, he was adorned with a gigantic garland, and he rested his huge mace on one of his shoulders.

TEXT 22

मनोवीर्यवरोत्सिक्तमसृण्यमकुतोभयम् ।
भीता निलिल्यिरे देवास्तार्क्ष्यत्रस्ता इवाहयः ॥२२॥

mano-vīrya-varotsiktam
asṛṇyam akuto-bhayam
bhītā nililyire devās
tārkṣya-trastā ivāhayaḥ

manaḥ-vīrya—by mental and bodily strength; *vara*—by the boon; *utsiktam*—proud; *asṛṇyam*—not able to be checked; *akutaḥ-bhayam*—fearing no one; *bhītāḥ*—frightened; *nililyire*—hid themselves; *devāḥ*—the demigods; *tārkṣya*—Garuḍa; *trastāḥ*—frightened of; *iva*—like; *ahayaḥ*—snakes.

TRANSLATION

His mental and bodily strength as well as the boon conferred upon him had made him proud. He feared death at the hands of no one, and there was no checking him. The gods, therefore, were seized with fear at his very sight, and they hid themselves even as snakes hide themselves for fear of Garuḍa.

PURPORT

The *asuras* are generally strongly built, as described here, and therefore their mental condition is very sound, and their prowess is also extraordinary. Hiraṇyākṣa and Hiraṇyakaśipu, having received the boon that they would not be killed by any other living entity within this universe, were almost immortal, and thus they were completely fearless.

TEXT 23

स वै तिरोहितान् दृष्ट्वा महसा स्वेन दैत्यराट् ।
सेन्द्रान्देवगणान् क्षीबानपश्यन् व्यनदद् भृशम् ॥२३॥

sa vai tirohitān dṛṣṭvā
mahasā svena daitya-rāṭ
sendrān deva-gaṇān kṣībān
apaśyan vyanadad bhṛśam

saḥ—he; *vai*—indeed; *tirohitān*—vanished; *dṛṣṭvā*—having seen; *mahasā*—by might; *svena*—his own; *daitya-rāṭ*—the chief of the Daityas (demons); *sa-indrān*—along with Indra; *deva-gaṇān*—the demigods; *kṣībān*—intoxicated; *apaśyan*—not finding; *vyanadat*—roared; *bhṛśam*—loudly.

TRANSLATION

On not finding Indra and the other demigods, who had previously been intoxicated with power, the chief of the Daityas, seeing that they had all vanished before his might, roared loudly.

TEXT 24

ततो निवृत्तः क्रीडिष्यन् गम्भीरं भीमनिस्वनम् ।
विजगाहे महासत्त्वो वार्धिं मत्त इव द्विपः ॥२४॥

tato nivṛttaḥ krīḍiṣyan
gambhīraṁ bhīma-nisvanam
vijagāhe mahā-sattvo
vārdhiṁ matta iva dvipaḥ

tataḥ—then; *nivṛttaḥ*—returned; *krīḍiṣyan*—for the sake of sport; *gambhīram*—deep; *bhīma-nisvanam*—making a terrible sound; *vijagāhe*—dived; *mahā-sattvaḥ*—the mighty being; *vārdhim*—in the ocean; *mattaḥ*—in wrath; *iva*—like; *dvipaḥ*—an elephant.

TRANSLATION

After returning from the heavenly kingdom, the mighty demon, who was like an elephant in wrath, for the sake of sport dived into the deep ocean, which was roaring terribly.

TEXT 25

तस्मिन् प्रविष्टे वरुणस्य सैनिका
यादोगणाः सन्नधियः ससाध्वसाः ।
अहन्यमाना अपि तस्य वर्चसा
प्रधर्षिता दूरतरं प्रदुद्रुवुः ॥२५॥

tasmin praviṣṭe varuṇasya sainikā
yādo-gaṇāḥ sanna-dhiyaḥ sasādhvasāḥ
ahanyamānā api tasya varcasā
pradharṣitā dūrataraṁ pradudruvuḥ

tasmin praviṣṭe—when he entered the ocean; *varuṇasya*—of Varuṇa; *sainikāḥ*—the defenders; *yādaḥ-gaṇāḥ*—the aquatic animals; *sanna-dhiyaḥ*—depressed; *sa-sādhvasāḥ*—with fear; *ahanyamānāḥ*—not being hit; *api*—even; *tasya*—his; *varcasā*—by splendor; *pradharṣitāḥ*—stricken; *dūra-taram*—far away; *pradudruvuḥ*—they ran fast.

TRANSLATION

On his entering the ocean, the aquatic animals who formed the host of Varuṇa were stricken with fear and ran far away. Thus Hiraṇyākṣa showed his splendor without dealing a blow.

PURPORT

Materialistic demons sometimes appear to be very powerful and are seen to establish their supremacy throughout the world. Here also it appears that Hiraṇyākṣa, by his demoniac strength, actually established his supremacy throughout the universe, and the demigods were afraid of his uncommon power. Not only were the demigods in space afraid of the demons Hiraṇyakaśipu and Hiraṇyākṣa, but so also were the aquatic animals within the sea.

TEXT 26

स वर्षपूगानुदधौ महाबल-
श्चरन्महोर्मीञ्छ्वसनेरितान्मुहुः ।
मौर्व्याभिजघ्ने गदया विभावरी-
मासेदिवांस्तात पुरीं प्रचेतसः ॥२६॥

sa varṣa-pūgān udadhau mahā-balaś
caran mahormīñ chvasaneritān muhuḥ

maurvyābhijaghne gadayā vibhāvarīm
āsedivāṁs tāta purīṁ pracetasaḥ

saḥ—he; *varṣa-pūgān*—for many years; *udadhau*—in the ocean; *mahā-balaḥ*—mighty; *caran*—moving; *mahā-ūrmīn*—gigantic waves; *śvasana*—by the wind; *īritān*—tossed; *muhuḥ*—again and again; *maurvyā*—iron; *abhijaghne*—he struck; *gadayā*—with his mace; *vibhāvarīm*—Vibhāvarī; *āsedivān*—reached; *tāta*—O dear Vidura; *purīm*—the capital; *pracetasaḥ*—of Varuṇa.

TRANSLATION

Moving about in the ocean for many, many years, the mighty Hiraṇyākṣa smote the gigantic wind-tossed waves again and again with his iron mace and reached Vibhāvarī, the capital of Varuṇa.

PURPORT

Varuṇa is supposed to be the predominating deity of the waters, and his capital, which is known as Vibhāvarī, is within the watery kingdom.

TEXT 27

तत्रोपलभ्यासुरलोकपालकं
यादोगणानामृषभं प्रचेतसम् ।
स्मयन् प्रलब्धुं प्रणिपत्य नीचव-
ज्जगाद मे देह्यधिराज संयुगम् ॥२७॥

tatropalabhyāsura-loka-pālakaṁ
yādo-gaṇānām ṛṣabhaṁ pracetasam
smayan pralabdhuṁ praṇipatya nīcavaj
jagāda me dehy adhirāja saṁyugam

tatra—there; *upalabhya*—having reached; *asura-loka*—of the regions where the demons reside; *pālakam*—the guardian; *yādaḥ-gaṇānām*—of the aquatic creatures; *ṛṣabham*—the lord; *pracetasam*—Varuṇa; *smayan*—smiling; *pralabdhum*—to make fun; *praṇipatya*—having bowed down; *nīca-vat*—like a lowborn man; *jagāda*—he said; *me*—to me; *dehi*—give; *adhirāja*—O great lord; *saṁyugam*—battle.

TRANSLATION

Vibhāvarī is the home of Varuṇa, lord of the aquatic creatures and guardian of the lower regions of the universe, where the demons generally

reside. There Hiraṇyākṣa fell at Varuṇa's feet like a lowborn man, and to make fun of him he said with a smile, "Give me battle, O Supreme Lord!"

PURPORT

The demoniac person always challenges others and tries to occupy others' property by force. Here these symptoms are fully displayed by Hiraṇyākṣa, who begged war from a person who had no desire to fight.

TEXT 28

त्वं लोकपालोऽधिपतिर्बृहच्छ्रवा
वीर्यापहो दुर्मदवीरमानिनाम् ।
विजित्य लोकेऽखिलदैत्यदानवान्
यद्राजसूयेन पुरायजत्प्रभो ॥२८॥

tvaṁ loka-pālo 'dhipatir bṛhac-chravā
vīryāpaho durmada-vīra-māninām
vijitya loke 'khila-daitya-dānavān
yad rājasūyena purāyajat prabho

tvam—you (Varuṇa); *loka-pālaḥ*—guardian of the planet; *adhipatiḥ*—a ruler; *bṛhat-śravāḥ*—of wide fame; *vīrya*—the power; *apahaḥ*—diminished; *durmada*—of the proud; *vīra-māninām*—thinking themselves very big heroes; *vijitya*—having conquered; *loke*—in the world; *akhila*—all; *daitya*—the demons; *dānavān*—the Dānavas; *yat*—whence; *rāja-sūyena*—with a Rājasūya sacrifice; *purā*—formerly; *ayajat*—worshiped; *prabho*—O lord.

TRANSLATION

You are the guardian of an entire sphere and a ruler of wide fame. Having crushed the might of arrogant and conceited warriors and having conquered all the Daityas and Dānavas in the world, you once performed a Rājasūya sacrifice to the Lord.

TEXT 29

स एवमुत्सिक्तमदेन विद्विषा
दृढं प्रलब्धो भगवानपां पतिः ।
रोषं समुत्थं शमयन् स्वया धिया
व्यवोचदङ्गोपशमं गता वयम् ॥२९॥

sa evaṁ utsikta-madena vidviṣā
dṛḍhaṁ pralabdho bhagavān apāṁ patiḥ
roṣaṁ samutthaṁ śamayan svayā dhiyā
vyavocad aṅgopaśamaṁ gatā vayam

saḥ—Varuṇa; *evam*—thus; *utsikta*—puffed up; *madena*—with vanity; *vidviṣā*—by the enemy; *dṛḍham*—deeply; *pralabdhaḥ*—mocked; *bhagavān*—worshipful; *apām*—of the waters; *patiḥ*—the lord; *roṣam*—anger; *samuttham*—sprung up; *śamayan*—controlling; *svayā dhiyā*—by his reason; *vyavocat*—he replied; *aṅga*—O dear one; *upaśamam*—desisting from warfare; *gatāḥ*—gone; *vayam*—we.

TRANSLATION

Thus mocked by an enemy whose vanity knew no bounds, the worshipful lord of the waters waxed angry, but by dint of his reason he managed to curb the anger that had sprung up in him, and he replied: O dear one, we have now desisted from warfare, having grown too old for combat.

PURPORT

As we see, warmongering materialists always create fighting without reason.

TEXT 30

पश्यामि नान्यं पुरुषात्पुरातनाद्
यः संयुगे त्वां रणमार्गकोविदम् ।
आराधयिष्यत्यसुरर्षभेहि तं
मनस्विनो यं गृणते भवादृशाः ॥३०॥

paśyāmi nānyaṁ puruṣāt purātanād
yaḥ saṁyuge tvāṁ raṇa-mārga-kovidam
ārādhayiṣyaty asurarṣabhehi taṁ
manasvino yaṁ gṛṇate bhavādṛśāḥ

paśyāmi—I see; *na*—not; *anyam*—other; *puruṣāt*—than the person; *purātanāt*—most ancient; *yaḥ*—who; *saṁyuge*—in battle; *tvām*—to you; *raṇa-mārga*—in the tactics of war; *kovidam*—very much skilled; *ārādhayiṣyati*—will give satisfaction; *asura-ṛṣabha*—O chief of the *asuras; ihi*—approach; *tam*—Him; *manasvinaḥ*—heroes; *yam*—whom; *gṛṇate*—praise; *bhavādṛśāḥ*—like you.

TRANSLATION

You are so skilled in war that I do not see anyone else but the most ancient person, Lord Viṣṇu, who can give satisfaction in battle to you. Therefore, O chief of the asuras, approach Him, whom even heroes like you mention with praise.

PURPORT

Aggressive materialistic warriors are actually punished by the Supreme Lord for their policy of unnecessarily disturbing world peace. Therefore Varuṇa advised Hiraṇyākṣa that the right course to satisfy his fighting spirit would be to seek to fight with Viṣṇu.

TEXT 31

तं वीरमारादभिपद्य विस्मयः
शयिष्यसे वीरशये श्वभिर्वृतः ।
यस्त्वद्विधानामसतां प्रशान्तये
रूपाणि धत्ते सदनुग्रहेच्छया ॥३१॥

taṁ vīram ārād abhipadya vismayaḥ
śayiṣyase vīra-śaye śvabhir vṛtaḥ
yas tvad-vidhānām asatāṁ praśāntaye
rūpāṇi dhatte sad-anugrahecchayā

tam—Him; *vīram*—the great hero; *ārāt*—quickly; *abhipadya*—on reaching; *vismayaḥ*—rid of pride; *śayiṣyase*—you will lie down; *vīraśaye*—on the battlefield; *śvabhiḥ*—by dogs; *vṛtaḥ*—surrounded; *yaḥ*—He who; *tvat-vidhānām*—like you; *asatām*—of wicked persons; *praśāntaye*—for the extermination; *rūpāṇi*—forms; *dhatte*—He assumes; *sat*—to the virtuous; *anugraha*—to show His grace; *icchayā*—with a desire.

TRANSLATION

Varuṇa continued: On reaching Him you will be rid of your pride at once and will lie down on the field of battle, surrounded by dogs, for eternal sleep. It is in order to exterminate wicked fellows like you and to show His grace to the virtuous that He assumes His various incarnations like Varāha.

PURPORT

Asuras do not know that their bodies consist of the five elements of material nature and that when they fall they become objects of pastimes for dogs and vultures. Varuṇa advised Hiraṇyākṣa to meet Viṣṇu in His boar incarnation so that his hankering for aggressive war would be satisfied and his powerful body would be vanquished.

Thus end the Bhaktivedanta purports of the Third Canto, Seventeenth Chapter, of the Śrīmad-Bhāgavatam, *entitled "Victory of Hiraṇyākṣa Over All the Directions of the Universe."*

PLATE FIFTEEN Being challenged by the Personality of Godhead in the form of a boar, the demon Hiraṇyākṣa became angry and agitated, and he trembled like a challenged cobra. (*pp. 691-694*)

PLATE SIXTEEN   Under the guidance of Lord Viṣṇu, Brahmā brought his intelligence to bear and began to create the universe. (*pp. 746-770*)

PLATE SEVENTEEN After ten thousand years, the lotus-eyed Supreme Personality of Godhead became pleased with Kardama Muni and showed him His transcendental form. (*pp. 779-784*)

PLATE EIGHTEEN Seeking to please his beloved wife, the sage Kardama exercised his yogic power and instantly produced an aerial mansion that could travel at his will. (*pp.* 882-887)

PLATE NINETEEN Following the order of Kardama Muni, Devahūti entered Lake Bindu-sarovara. In a house inside the lake she saw one thousand girls, all in the prime of youth and fragrant as lotuses. (*pp. 890-895*)

PLATE TWENTY After thus speaking to Kardama Muni's wife Devahūti, Lord Brahmā, accompanied by the four Kumāras and Nārada, went back to the highest of the three planetary systems on his swan carrier. (*pp.* 929-936)

PLATE TWENTY-ONE Thereupon Kardama Muni, the progenitor of human society, circumambulated his son, Kapila, and with a pacified mind, he at once left for the forest. (*pp.* 948-957)

PLATE TWENTY-TWO After hearing of Devahūti's uncontaminated desire for transcendental realization, Kapiladeva thanked her within Himself for her questions, and thus, His face smiling, He explained the path of *sāṅkhya-yoga* for the transcendentalists, who are interested in self-realization. (*pp.* 969-980)

PLATE TWENTY-THREE Because our eyes and other senses are imperfect, we cannot see Lord Kṛṣṇa present everywhere in His original, spiritual form. But since Kṛṣṇa is omnipotent, out of His mercy He agrees to appear before us in a stone form called the *arcā-vigraha*, the Deity. (*pp. 1006-1007*)

PLATE TWENTY-FOUR "That primeval Lord is expert in playing His flute, His eyes are like the petals of blooming lotuses, His head is bedecked with a peacock feather, His figure is tinged with the bluish hue of fresh rainclouds, and His unique loveliness is more charming than that of millions of Cupids." (*p. 1026*)

PLATE TWENTY-FIVE The Supreme Personality of Godhead is most charming to look at, for His serene aspect gladdens the eyes and souls of those who behold Him in the ecstatic trance of meditation. (*pp. 1137-1146*)

PLATE TWENTY-SIX With her lustrous fingers, Lakṣmī always carefully massages the feet, legs and thighs of Lord Nārāyaṇa, who reclines on the thousand-headed serpent Śeṣa Nāga in the Garbha Ocean. (*p. 1153*)

PLATE TWENTY-SEVEN The man who engaged with uncontrolled senses in maintaining his family dies in great grief, seeing his relatives crying. He dies most pathetically, in great pain and without consciousness. At that time the wrathful Yamadūtas (the messengers of the lord of death) come before him, and in great fear he passes stool and urine. (*pp. 1247-1249*)

PLATE TWENTY-EIGHT After judgment, the sinner is at once engaged in the torturous punishment he is destined to suffer. He is placed in the midst of burning pieces of wood, and his limbs are set on fire. In some cases he is made to eat his own flesh or have it eaten by others. His entrails are pulled out by the hounds and vultures of hell, even though he is still alive to see it, and he is subjected to torment by the bites of serpents, scorpions, gnats and other creatures. (*pp. 1250-1254*)

PLATE TWENTY-NINE The first step in Kapiladeva's *sāṅkhya-yoga* system is to understand the difference between the soul and the body, and how the soul passes through various bodies by the process of reincarnation. (*pp. 1263-1272*)

PLATE THIRTY Sometimes the Supreme Personality of Godhead wonders how much transcendental pleasure is within Himself, and He wants to taste His own potency. Thus at the end of the millennium the Lord licks His own toe to taste the nectar for which the devotees always aspire. (*p. 1365*)

CHAPTER EIGHTEEN

The Battle Between Lord Boar and the Demon Hiraṇyākṣa

TEXT 1

मैत्रेय उवाच
तदेवमाकर्ण्य जलेशभाषितं
महामनास्तद्विगणय्य दुर्मदः ।
हरेर्विदित्वा गतिमङ्ग नारदाद्
रसातलं निर्विविशे त्वरान्वितः ॥ १ ॥

maitreya uvāca
tad evam ākarṇya jaleśa-bhāṣitaṁ
mahā-manās tad vigaṇayya durmadaḥ
harer viditvā gatim aṅga nāradād
rasātalaṁ nirviviśe tvarānvitaḥ

maitreyaḥ—the great sage Maitreya; *uvāca*—said; *tat*—that; *evam*—thus; *ākarṇya*—hearing; *jala-īśa*—of the controller of water, Varuṇa; *bhāṣitam*—words; *mahā-manāḥ*—proud; *tat*—those words; *vigaṇayya*—having paid little heed to; *durmadaḥ*—vainglorious; *hareḥ*—of the Supreme Personality of Godhead; *viditvā*—having learned; *gatim*—the whereabouts; *aṅga*—O dear Vidura; *nāradāt*—from Nārada; *rasātalam*—to the depths of the ocean; *nirviviśe*—entered; *tvarā-anvitaḥ*—with great speed.

TRANSLATION

Maitreya continued: The proud and falsely glorious Daitya paid little heed to the words of Varuṇa. O dear Vidura, he learned from Nārada the whereabouts of the Supreme Personality of Godhead and hurriedly betook himself to the depths of the ocean.

PURPORT

Materialistic warmongers are not even afraid to fight with their mightiest enemy, the Personality of Godhead. The demon was very encouraged to learn from Varuṇa that there was one fighter who could actually combat him, and he was very enthusiastic to search out the Supreme Personality of Godhead just to give Him a fight, even though it was predicted by Varuṇa that by fighting with Viṣṇu he would become prey for dogs, jackals and vultures. Since demoniac persons are less intelligent, they dare to fight with Viṣṇu, who is known as Ajita, or one who has never been conquered.

TEXT 2

ददर्श तत्राभिजितं धराधरं
प्रोन्नीयमानावनिमग्रदंष्ट्रया ।
मुष्णन्तमक्ष्णा स्वरुचोऽरुणश्रिया
जहास चाहो वनगोचरो मृगः ॥ २ ॥

dadarśa tatrābhijitaṁ dharā-dharaṁ
pronnīyamānāvanim agra-daṁṣṭrayā
muṣṇantam akṣṇā sva-ruco 'ruṇa-śriyā
jahāsa cāho vana-gocaro mṛgaḥ

dadarśa—he saw; *tatra*—there; *abhijitam*—the victorious; *dharā*—the earth; *dharam*—bearing; *pronnīyamāna*—being raised upward; *avanim*—the earth; *agra-daṁṣṭrayā*—by the tip of His tusk; *muṣṇantam*—who was diminishing; *akṣṇā*—with His eyes; *sva-rucaḥ*—Hiraṇyākṣa's own splendor; *aruṇa*—reddish; *śriyā*—radiant; *jahāsa*—he laughed; *ca*—and; *aho*—oh; *vana-gocaraḥ*—amphibious; *mṛgaḥ*—beast.

TRANSLATION

He saw there the all-powerful Personality of Godhead in His boar incarnation, bearing the earth upward on the ends of His tusks and robbing him of his splendor with His reddish eyes. The demon laughed: Oh, an amphibious beast!

PURPORT

In a previous chapter we have discussed the incarnation of the Supreme Personality of Godhead as Varāha, the boar. While Varāha, with His tusks, engaged in uplifting the submerged earth from the depths of the waters, this great demon Hiraṇyākṣa met Him and challenged Him, calling Him a beast. Demons cannot understand the incarnations of the Lord; they think that His incarnations as a fish or boar or tortoise are big beasts only. They misunderstand the body of the Supreme Personality of Godhead, even in His human form, and they deride His descent. In the Caitanya-sampradāya there is sometimes a demoniac misconception about the descent of

Nityānanda Prabhu. Nityānanda Prabhu's body is spiritual, but demoniac persons consider the body of the Supreme Personality to be material, just like ours. *Avajānanti māṁ mūḍhāḥ*: persons who have no intelligence deride the transcendental form of the Lord as material.

TEXT 3

आहैनमेह्यज्ञ महीं विमुञ्च नो
रसौकसां विश्वसृजेयमर्पिता ।
न स्वस्ति यास्यस्यनया ममेक्षतः
सुराधमासादितसूकराकृते ॥ ३ ॥

āhainam ehy ajña mahīṁ vimuñca no
rasaukasāṁ viśva-sṛjeyam arpitā
na svasti yāsyasy anayā mamekṣataḥ
surādhamāsādita-sūkarākṛte

āha—Hiraṇyākṣa said; *enam*—to the Lord; *ehi*—come and fight; *ajña*—O fool; *mahīm*—the earth; *vimuñca*—give up; *naḥ*—to us; *rasā-okasām*—of the inhabitants of the lower regions; *viśva-sṛja*—by the creator of the universe; *iyam*—this earth; *arpitā*—entrusted; *na*—not; *svasti*—well-being; *yāsyasi*—You will go; *anayā*—with this; *mama īkṣataḥ*—while I am seeing; *sura-adhama*—O lowest of the demigods; *āsādita*—having taken; *sūkara-ākṛte*—the form of a boar.

TRANSLATION

The demon addressed the Lord: O best of the demigods, dressed in the form of a boar, just hear me. This earth is entrusted to us, the inhabitants of the lower regions, and You cannot take it from my presence and not be hurt by me.

PURPORT

Śrīdhara Svāmī, commenting on this verse, states that although the demon wanted to deride the Personality of Godhead in the form of a boar, actually he worshiped Him in several words. For example, he addressed Him as *vana-gocaraḥ*, which means "one who is a resident of the forest," but another meaning of *vana-gocaraḥ* is "one who lies on the water." Viṣṇu lies on the water, so the Supreme Personality of Godhead can be properly addressed in this way. The demon also addressed Him as *mṛgaḥ*, indicating, unintentionally, that the Supreme Personality is sought after by great sages, saintly persons and transcendentalists. He also addressed Him as *ajña*. Śrīdhara Svāmī says that *jña* means "knowledge," and there is no knowledge which is unknown to the Supreme Personality of Godhead. Indirectly, therefore, the demon said that Viṣṇu knows everything. The demon addressed Him as *surādhama. Sura* means "the demigods," and *adhama* means "Lord of all there is." He is Lord of all the demigods; therefore He is the best of all demigods, or God. When the demon used the phrase "in my presence," the implied meaning was, "In spite of my presence, You are completely able to take away the earth." *Na svasti yāsyasi:* "unless You kindly take this earth from our custody, there can be no good fortune for us."

TEXT 4

त्वं नः सपत्नैरभवाय किं भृतो
यो मायया हन्त्यसुरान् परोक्षजित् ।
त्वां योगमायाबलमल्पपौरुषं
संस्थाप्य मूढ प्रमृजे सुहृच्छुचः ॥ ४ ॥

tvaṁ naḥ sapatnair abhavāya kiṁ bhṛto
yo māyayā hanty asurān parokṣa-jit
tvāṁ yogamāyā-balam alpa-pauruṣaṁ
saṁsthāpya mūḍha pramṛje suhṛc-chucaḥ

tvam—You; *naḥ*—us; *sapatnaiḥ*—by our enemies; *abhavāya*—for killing; *kim*—is it that; *bhṛtaḥ*—maintained; *yaḥ*—He who; *māyayā*—by deception; *hanti*—kills; *asurān*—the demons; *parokṣa-jit*—who conquered by remaining invisible; *tvām*—You; *yogamāyā-balam*—whose strength is bewildering power; *alpa-pauruṣam*—whose power is meager; *saṁsthāpya*—after killing; *mūḍha*—fool; *pramṛje*—I shall wipe out; *suhṛt-śucaḥ*—the grief of my kinsmen.

TRANSLATION

You rascal, You have been nourished by our enemies to kill us, and You have killed some demons by remaining invisible. O fool, Your power is only mystic, so today I shall enliven my kinsmen by killing You.

PURPORT

The demon used the word *abhavāya,* which means "for killing." Śrīdhara Svāmī comments that this "killing" means liberating, or, in other words, killing the process of continued birth and death. The Lord kills the process of birth and death and keeps Himself invisible. The activities of the Lord's internal potency are inconceivable, but by a slight exhibition of this potency, the Lord, by His grace, can deliver one from nescience. *Śucaḥ* means "miseries"; the miseries of material existence can be extinguished by the Lord by His potential energy of internal *yogamāyā*. In the *Upaniṣads* (*Śvetāśvatara Up.* 6.8) it is stated, *parāsya śaktir vividhaiva śrūyate.* The Lord is invisible to the eyes of the common man, but His energies act in various ways. When demons are in adversity, they think that God is hiding Himself and is working by His mystic potency. They think that if they can find God they can kill Him just by seeing Him. Hiraṇyākṣa thought that way, and he challenged the Lord: "You have done tremendous harm to our community, taking the part of the demigods, and You have killed our kinsmen in so many ways, always keeping Yourself hidden. Now I see You face to face, and I am not going to let You go. I shall kill You and save my kinsmen from Your mystic misdeeds."

Not only are demons always anxious to kill God with words and philosophy, but they think that if one is materially powerful he can kill God with materially fatal weapons. Demons like Kaṁsa, Rāvaṇa and Hiraṇyakaśipu thought themselves powerful enough to kill even God. Demons cannot understand that God, by His multifarious potencies, can work so wonderfully that He can be present everywhere and still remain in His eternal abode, Goloka Vṛndāvana.

TEXT 5

त्वयि संस्थिते गदया शीर्णशीर्ष-
ण्यस्मद्भुजच्युतया ये च तुभ्यम् ।
बलिं हरन्त्यृषयो ये च देवाः
स्वयं सर्वे न भविष्यन्त्यमूलाः ॥ ५ ॥

tvayi saṁsthite gadayā śīrṇa-śīrṣaṇy
asmad-bhuja-cyutayā ye ca tubhyam
baliṁ haranty ṛṣayo ye ca devāḥ
svayaṁ sarve na bhaviṣyanty amūlāḥ

tvayi—when You; *saṁsthite*—are killed; *gadayā*—by the mace; *śīrṇa*—smashed; *śīrṣaṇi*—skull; *asmat-bhuja*—from my hand; *cyutayā*—released; *ye*—those who; *ca*—and; *tubhyam*—to You; *balim*—presentations; *haranti*—offer; *ṛṣayaḥ*—sages; *ye*—those who; *ca*—and; *devāḥ*—demigods; *svayam*—automatically; *sarve*—all; *na*—not; *bhaviṣyanti*—will exist; *amūlāḥ*—without roots.

TRANSLATION

The demon continued: When You fall dead with Your skull smashed by the mace hurled by my arms, the demigods and sages who offer You oblations and

sacrifice in devotional service will also automatically cease to exist, like trees without roots.

PURPORT

Demons are very much disturbed when devotees worship the Lord in the prescribed ways recommended in the scriptures. In the Vedic scriptures, the neophyte devotees are advised to engage in nine kinds of devotional service, such as to hear and chant the holy name of God, to remember Him always, to chant on beads Hare Kṛṣṇa, Hare Kṛṣṇa, Kṛṣṇa Kṛṣṇa, Hare Hare/ Hare Rāma, Hare Rāma, Rāma Rāma, Hare Hare, to worship the Lord in the form of His Deity incarnation in the temples, and to engage in various activities of Kṛṣṇa consciousness to increase the number of godly persons for perfect peace in the world. Demons do not like such activity. They are always envious of God and His devotees. Their propaganda not to worship in the temple or church but simply to make material advancement for satisfaction of the senses is always current. The demon Hiraṇyākṣa, upon seeing the Lord face to face, wanted to make a permanent solution by killing the Personality of Godhead with his powerful mace. The example of an uprooted tree mentioned here by the demon is very significant. Devotees accept that God is the root of everything. Their example is that just as the stomach is the source of energy of all the limbs of the body, God is the original source of all energy manifested in the material and spiritual worlds; therefore, as supplying food to the stomach is the process to satisfy all the limbs of the body, Kṛṣṇa consciousness, or developing love of Kṛṣṇa, is the sublime method for satisfying the source of all happiness. The demon wants to uproot this source because if the root, God, were to be checked, the activities of the Lord and the devotees would automatically stop. The demon would be very much satisfied by such a situation in society. Demons are always anxious to have a godless society for their sense gratification. According to Śrīdhara Svāmī, this verse means that when the demon would be deprived of his mace by the Supreme Personality of Godhead, not only the neophyte devotees but also the ancient sagacious devotees of the Lord would be very much satisfied.

TEXT 6

स तुद्यमानोऽरिदुरुक्ततोमरै-
दंष्ट्राग्रगां गामुपलक्ष्य भीताम् ।
तोदं मृषन्निरगादम्बुमध्याद्
ग्राहाहतः सकरेणुर्यथेभः ॥ ६ ॥

sa tudyamāno 'ri-durukta-tomarair
daṁṣṭrāgra-gāṁ gām upalakṣya bhītām
todaṁ mṛṣan niragād ambu-madhyād
grāhāhataḥ sa-kareṇur yathebhaḥ

saḥ—He; *tudyamānaḥ*—being pained; *ari*—of the enemy; *durukta*—by the abusive words; *tomaraiḥ*—by the weapons; *daṁṣṭra-agra*—on the ends of His tusks; *gām*—situated; *gām*—the earth; *upalakṣya*—seeing; *bhītām*—frightened; *todam*—the pain; *mṛṣan*—bearing; *niragāt*—He came out; *ambu-madhyāt*—from the midst of the water; *grāha*—by a crocodile; *āhataḥ*—attacked; *sa-kareṇuḥ*—along with a she-elephant; *yathā*—as; *ibhaḥ*—an elephant.

TRANSLATION

Although the Lord was pained by the shaftlike abusive words of the demon, He bore the pain. But seeing that the earth on the ends of His tusks was frightened, He rose out of the water just as an elephant emerges with its female companion when assailed by an alligator.

PURPORT

The Māyāvādī philosopher cannot understand that the Lord has feelings. The Lord is satisfied if someone offers Him a nice prayer, and similarly, if someone decries His existence or calls Him by ill names, God is dissatisfied. The Supreme Personality of Godhead is decried by the Māyāvādī philosophers, who are almost demons. They say that God has no head, no form, no existence and no legs, hands or other bodily limbs. In other words, they say that He is dead or lame. All these misconceptions of the Supreme Lord are a source of dissatisfaction to Him; He is never pleased with such atheistic descriptions. In this case, although the Lord felt sorrow from the piercing words of the demon, He delivered the earth for the satisfaction of the demigods, who are ever His devotees. The conclusion is that God is as sentient as we are. He is satisfied by our prayers and dissatisfied by our harsh words against Him. In order to give protection to His devotee, He is always ready to tolerate insulting words from the atheists.

TEXT 7

तं निःसरन्तं सलिलादनुद्रुतो
हिरण्यकेशो द्विरदं यथा झषः ।
करालदंष्ट्रोऽशनिनिस्वनोऽब्रवीद्
गतह्रियां किं त्वसतां विगर्हितम् ॥ ७ ॥

taṁ niḥsarantaṁ salilād anudruto
hiraṇya-keśo dviradaṁ yathā jhaṣaḥ
karāla-daṁṣṭro 'śani-nisvano 'bravīd
gata-hriyāṁ kiṁ tv asatāṁ vigarhitam

tam—Him; *niḥsarantam*—coming out; *salilāt*—from the water; *anudrutaḥ*—chased; *hiraṇya-keśaḥ*—having golden hair; *dviradam*—an elephant; *yathā*—as; *jhaṣaḥ*—a crocodile; *karāla-daṁṣṭraḥ*—having fearful teeth; *aśani-nisvanaḥ*—roaring like thunder; *abravīt*—he said; *gata-hriyām*—for those who are shameless; *kim*—what; *tu*—indeed; *asatām*—for the wretches; *vigarhitam*—reproachable.

TRANSLATION

The demon, who had golden hair on his head and fearful tusks, gave chase to the Lord while He was rising from the water, even as an alligator would chase an elephant. Roaring like thunder, he said: Are You not ashamed of running away before a challenging adversary? There is nothing reproachable for shameless creatures!

PURPORT

When the Lord was coming out of the water, taking the earth in His arms to deliver it, the demon derided Him with insulting words, but the Lord did not care because He was very conscious of His duty. For a dutiful man there is nothing to fear. Similarly, those who are powerful have no fear of derision or unkind words from an enemy. The Lord had nothing to fear from anyone, yet He was merciful to His enemy by neglecting him. Although apparently He fled from the challenge, it was just to protect the earth from calamity that He tolerated Hiraṇyākṣa's deriding words.

TEXT 8

स गामुदस्तात्सलिलस्य गोचरे
विन्यस्य तस्यामदधात्स्वसत्त्वम् ।
अभिष्टुतो विश्वसृजा प्रसूनै-
रापूर्यमाणो विबुधैः पश्यतोऽरेः ॥ ८ ॥

sa gām udastāt salilasya gocare
vinyasya tasyām adadhāt sva-sattvam
abhiṣṭuto viśva-sṛjā prasūnair
āpūryamāṇo vibudhaiḥ paśyato 'reḥ

saḥ—the Lord; *gām*—the earth; *udastāt*—on the surface; *salilasya*—of the water; *gocare*—within His sight; *vinyasya*—having placed; *tasyām*—to the earth; *adadhāt*—He invested; *sva*—His own; *sattvam*—existence; *abhiṣṭutaḥ*—praised; *viśva-sṛjā*—by Brahmā (the creator of the universe); *prasūnaiḥ*—by flowers; *āpūryamāṇaḥ*—becoming satisfied; *vibudhaiḥ*—by the demigods; *paśyataḥ*—while looking on; *areḥ*—the enemy.

TRANSLATION

The Lord placed the earth within His sight on the surface of the water and transferred to her His own energy in the form of the ability to float on the water. While the enemy stood looking on, Brahmā, the creator of the universe, extolled the Lord, and the other demigods rained flowers on Him.

PURPORT

Those who are demons cannot understand how the Supreme Personality of Godhead floated the earth on water, but to devotees of the Lord this is not a very wonderful act. Not only the earth but many, many millions of planets are floating in the air, and this floating power is endowed upon them by the Lord; there is no other possible explanation. The materialists can explain that the planets are floating by the law of gravitation, but the law of gravitation works under the control or direction of the Supreme Lord. That is the version of *Bhagavad-gītā,* which confirms, by the Lord's statement, that behind the material laws or nature's laws and behind the growth, maintenance, production and evolution of all the planetary systems—behind everything—is the Lord's direction. The Lord's activities could be appreciated only by the demigods, headed by Brahmā, and therefore when they saw the uncommon prowess of the Lord in keeping the earth on the surface of the water, they showered flowers on Him in appreciation of His transcendental activity.

TEXT 9

परानुषक्तं तपनीयोपकल्पं
महागदं काञ्चनचित्रदंशम् ।
मर्माण्यभीक्ष्णं प्रतुदन्तं दुरुक्तैः
प्रचण्डमन्युः प्रहसंस्तं बभाषे ॥ ९ ॥

parānuṣaktaṁ tapanīyopakalpaṁ
mahā-gadaṁ kāñcana-citra-daṁśam
marmāṇy abhīkṣṇaṁ pratudantaṁ duruktaiḥ
pracaṇḍa-manyuḥ prahasaṁs taṁ babhāṣe

parā—from behind; *anuṣaktam*—who followed very closely; *tapanīya-upakalpam*—who had a considerable amount of gold ornaments; *mahā-gadam*—with a great mace; *kāñcana*—golden; *citra*—beautiful; *daṁśam*—armor; *marmāṇi*—the core of the heart; *abhīkṣṇam*—constantly; *pratudantam*—piercing; *duruktaiḥ*—by abusive words; *pracaṇḍa*—terrible; *manyuḥ*—anger; *prahasan*—laughing; *tam*—to him; *babhāṣe*—He said.

TRANSLATION

The demon, who had a wealth of ornaments, bangles and beautiful golden armor on his body, chased the Lord from behind with a great mace. The Lord tolerated his piercing ill words, but in order to reply to him, He expressed His terrible anger.

PURPORT

The Lord could have chastised the demon immediately while the demon was deriding the Lord with ill words, but the Lord tolerated him to please the demigods and to show that they should not be afraid of demons while discharging their duties. Therefore His toleration was displayed mainly to drive away the fears of the demigods, who should know that the Lord is always present to protect them. The demon's derision of the Lord was just like the barking of dogs; the Lord did not care about it, since He was doing His own work in delivering the earth from the midst of the water. Materialistic demons always possess large amounts of gold in various shapes, and they think that a large amount of gold, physical strength and popularity can save them from the wrath of the Supreme Personality of Godhead.

TEXT 10

श्रीभगवानुवाच
सत्यं वयं भो वनगोचरा मृगा
युष्मद्विधान्मृगये ग्रामसिंहान् ।
न मृत्युपाशैः प्रतिमुक्तस्य वीरा
विकत्थनं तव गृह्णन्त्यभद्र ॥१०॥

śrī-bhagavān uvāca
satyaṁ vayaṁ bho vana-gocarā mṛgā
yuṣmad-vidhān mṛgaye grāma-siṁhān
na mṛtyu-pāśaiḥ pratimuktasya vīrā
vikatthanaṁ tava gṛhṇanty abhadra

śrī-bhagavān uvāca—the Supreme Personality of Godhead said; *satyam*—indeed; *vayam*—We; *bhoḥ*—O; *vana-gocarāḥ*—dwelling in the forest; *mṛgāḥ*—creatures; *yuṣmat-vidhān*—like you; *mṛgaye*—I am searching to kill; *grāma-siṁhān*—dogs; *na*—not; *mṛtyu-pāśaiḥ*—by the bonds of death; *pratimuktasya*—of one who is bound; *vīrāḥ*—the heroes; *vikatthanam*—loose talk; *tava*—your; *gṛhṇanti*—take notice of; *abhadra*—O mischievous one.

TRANSLATION

The Personality of Godhead said: Indeed, We are creatures of the jungle, and We are searching after hunting dogs like you. One who is freed from the entanglement of death has no fear from the loose talk in which you are indulging, for you are bound up by the laws of death.

PURPORT

Demons and atheistic persons can go on insulting the Supreme Personality of Godhead, but they forget that they are subjected to the laws of birth and death. They think that simply by decrying the existence of the Supreme Lord or defying His stringent laws of nature, one can be freed from the clutches of birth and death. In *Bhagavad-gītā* it is said that simply by understanding the transcendental nature of God one can go back home, back to Godhead. But demons and atheistic persons do not try to understand the nature of the Supreme Lord; therefore they remain in the entanglement of birth and death.

TEXT 11

एते वयं न्यासहरा रसौकसां
गतह्रियो गदया द्राविातास्ते ।
तिष्ठामहेऽथापि कथञ्चिदाजौ
स्थेयं क्व यामो बलिनोत्पाद्य वैरम् ॥११॥

ete vayaṁ nyāsa-harā rasaukasāṁ
gata-hriyo gadayā drāvitās te
tiṣṭhāmahe 'thāpi kathañcid ājau
stheyaṁ kva yāmo balinotpādya vairam

ete—Ourselves; *vayam*—We; *nyāsa*—of the charge; *harāḥ*—thieves; *rasā-okasām*—of the inhabitants of Rasātala; *gata-hriyaḥ*—shameless; *gadayā*—by the mace; *drāvitāḥ*—chased; *te*—your; *tiṣṭhāmahe*—We shall stay; *atha api*—nevertheless; *kathañcit*—somehow; *ājau*—on the battlefield; *stheyam*—We must stay; *kva*—where; *yāmaḥ*—can We go; *balinā*—with a powerful enemy; *utpādya*—having created; *vairam*—enmity.

TRANSLATION

Certainly We have stolen the charge of the inhabitants of Rasātala and have lost all shame. Although bitten by your powerful mace, I shall stay here in the water for some time because, having created enmity with a powerful enemy, I now have no place to go.

PURPORT

The demon should have known that God cannot be driven out of any place, for He is all-pervading. Demons think of their possessions as their property, but actually everything belongs to the Supreme Personality of Godhead, who can take anything at any time He likes.

TEXT 12

त्वं पद्रथानां किल यूथपाधिपो
घटस्व नोऽस्वस्तय आश्वनूहः ।
संस्थाप्य चास्मान् प्रमृजाश्रु स्वकानां
यः स्वां प्रतिज्ञां नातिपिपर्त्यसभ्यः ॥१२॥

tvaṁ pad-rathānāṁ kila yūthapādhipo
ghaṭasva no 'svastaya āśv anūhaḥ
saṁsthāpya cāsmān pramṛjāśru svakānāṁ
yaḥ svāṁ pratijñāṁ nātipiparty asabhyaḥ

tvam—you; *pad-rathānām*—of foot soldiers; *kila*—indeed; *yūthapa*—of the leaders; *adhipaḥ*—the commander; *ghaṭasva*—take steps; *naḥ*—Our; *asvastaye*—for defeat; *āśu*—promptly; *anūhaḥ*—without consideration; *saṁsthāpya*—having killed; *ca*—and; *asmān*—Us; *pramṛja*—wipe away; *aśru*—tears; *svakānām*—of your kith and kin; *yaḥ*—he who; *svām*—his own; *pratijñām*—promised word; *na*—not; *atipiparti*—fulfills; *asabhyaḥ*—not fit to sit in an assembly.

TRANSLATION

You are supposed to be the commander of many foot soldiers, and now you may take prompt steps to overthrow Us. Give up all your foolish talk and wipe out the cares of your kith and kin by slaying Us. One may be proud, yet he does not deserve a seat in an assembly if he fails to fulfill his promised word.

PURPORT

A demon may be a great soldier and commander of a large number of infantry, but in the presence of the Supreme Personality of Godhead he is powerless and is destined to die. The Lord, therefore, challenged the demon not to go away, but to fulfill his promised word to kill Him.

TEXT 13

मैत्रेय उवाच
सोऽधिक्षिप्तो भगवता प्रलब्धश्च रुषा भृशम् ।
आजहारोल्बणं क्रोधं क्रीड्यमानोऽहिराडिव ॥१३॥

maitreya uvāca
so 'dhikṣipto bhagavatā
pralabdhaś ca ruṣā bhṛśam
ājahārolbaṇaṁ krodhaṁ
krīḍyamāno 'hi-rāḍ iva

maitreyaḥ—the great sage Maitreya; *uvāca*—said; *saḥ*—the demon; *adhikṣiptaḥ*—having been insulted; *bhagavatā*—by the Personality of Godhead; *pralabdhaḥ*—ridiculed; *ca*—and; *ruṣā*—angry; *bhṛśam*—greatly; *ājahāra*—collected; *ulbaṇam*—great; *krodham*—anger; *krīḍyamānaḥ*—being played with; *ahi-rāṭ*—a great cobra; *iva*—like.

TRANSLATION

Śrī Maitreya said: The demon, being thus challenged by the Personality of Godhead, became angry and agitated, and he trembled in anger like a challenged cobra.

PURPORT

A cobra is very fierce before ordinary persons, but before an enchanter who can play with him, he is a plaything. Similarly, a demon may be very powerful in his own domain, but before the Lord he is insignificant. The demon Rāvaṇa was a fierce figure before the demigods, but when he was before Lord Rāmacandra he trembled and prayed to his deity, Lord Śiva, but to no avail.

TEXT 14

सृजन्नमर्षितः श्वासान्मन्युप्रचलितेन्द्रियः ।
आसाद्य तरसा दैत्यो गदयान्यहनद्धरिम् ॥१४॥

sṛjann amarṣitaḥ śvāsān
manyu-pracalitendriyaḥ
āsādya tarasā daityo
gadayā nyahanad dharim

sṛjan—giving out; *amarṣitaḥ*—being angry; *śvāsān*—breaths; *manyu*—by wrath; *pracalita*—agitated; *indriyaḥ*—whose senses; *āsādya*—attacking; *tarasā*—quickly; *daityaḥ*—the demon; *gadayā*—with his mace; *nyahanat*—struck; *harim*—Lord Hari.

TRANSLATION

Hissing indignantly, all his senses shaken by wrath, the demon quickly sprang upon the Lord and dealt Him a blow with his powerful mace.

TEXT 15

भगवांस्तु गदावेगं विसृष्टं रिपुणोरसि ।
अवञ्चयत्तिरश्चीनो योगारूढ इवान्तकम् ॥१५॥

bhagavāṁs tu gadā-vegaṁ
visṛṣṭaṁ ripuṇorasi
avañcayat tiraścīno
yogārūḍha ivāntakam

bhagavān—the Lord; *tu*—however; *gadā-vegam*—the blow of the mace; *visṛṣṭam*—thrown; *ripuṇā*—by the enemy; *urasi*—at His breast; *avañcayat*—dodged; *tiraścīnaḥ*—aside; *yoga-ārūḍhaḥ*—an accomplished *yogī*; *iva*—like; *antakam*—death.

TRANSLATION

The Lord, however, by moving slightly aside, dodged the violent mace-blow aimed at His breast by the enemy, just as an accomplished yogī would elude death.

PURPORT

The example is given herein that the perfect *yogī* can overcome a deathblow although it is offered by the laws of nature. It is useless for a demon to beat the transcendental body of the Lord with a powerful mace, for no one can surpass His prowess. Those who are advanced transcendentalists are freed from the laws of nature, and even a deathblow cannot act on them. Superficially it may be seen that a *yogī* is attacked by a deathblow, but by the grace of the Lord he can overcome many such attacks for the service of the Lord. As the Lord exists by His own independent prowess, by the grace of the Lord the devotees also exist for His service.

TEXT 16

पुनर्गदां स्वामादाय भ्रामयन्तमभीक्ष्णशः ।
अभ्यधावद्धरिः क्रुद्धः संरम्भाद्दष्टदच्छदम् ॥१६॥

punar gadāṁ svām ādāya
bhrāmayantam abhīkṣṇaśaḥ
abhyadhāvad dhariḥ kruddhaḥ
saṁrambhād daṣṭa-dacchadam

punaḥ—again; *gadām*—mace; *svām*—his; *ādāya*—having taken; *bhrāmayantam*—brandishing; *abhīkṣṇaśaḥ*—repeatedly; *abhyadhāvat*—rushed to meet; *hariḥ*—the Personality of Godhead; *kruddhaḥ*—angry; *saṁrambhāt*—in rage; *daṣṭa*—bitten; *dacchadam*—his lip.

TRANSLATION

The Personality of Godhead now exhibited His anger and rushed to meet the demon, who bit his lip in rage, took up his mace again and began to repeatedly brandish it about.

TEXT 17

ततश्च गदयारातिं दक्षिणस्यां भ्रुवि प्रभुः ।
आजघ्ने स तु तां सौम्य गदया कोविदोऽहनत् ॥१७॥

tataś ca gadayārātiṁ
dakṣiṇasyāṁ bhruvi prabhuḥ
ājaghne sa tu tāṁ saumya
gadayā kovido 'hanat

tataḥ—then; *ca*—and; *gadayā*—with His mace; *arātim*—the enemy; *dakṣiṇasyām*—on the right; *bhruvi*—on the brow; *prabhuḥ*—the Lord; *ājaghne*—struck; *saḥ*—the Lord; *tu*—but; *tām*—the mace; *saumya*—O gentle Vidura; *gadayā*—with his mace; *kovidaḥ*—expert; *ahanat*—he saved himself.

TRANSLATION

Then with His mace the Lord struck the enemy on the right of his brow, but since the demon was expert in fighting, O gentle Vidura, he protected himself by a maneuver of his own mace.

TEXT 18

एवं गदाभ्यां गुर्वीभ्यां हर्यक्षो हरिरेव च ।
जिगीषया सुसंरब्धावन्योन्यमभिजघ्नतुः ॥१८॥

evaṁ gadābhyāṁ gurvībhyāṁ
haryakṣo harir eva ca
jigīṣayā susaṁrabdhāv
anyonyam abhijaghnatuḥ

evam—in this way; *gadābhyām*—with their maces; *gurvībhyām*—huge; *haryakṣaḥ*—the demon Haryakṣa (Hiraṇyākṣa); *hariḥ*—Lord Hari; *eva*—certainly; *ca*—and; *jigīṣayā*—with a desire for victory; *susaṁrabdhau*—enraged; *anyonyam*—each other; *abhijaghnatuḥ*—they struck.

TRANSLATION

In this way, the demon Haryakṣa and the Lord, the Personality of Godhead, struck each other with their huge maces, each enraged and seeking his own victory.

PURPORT

Haryakṣa is another name for Hiraṇyākṣa, the demon.

TEXT 19

तयोः स्पृधोस्तिग्मगदाहताङ्गयोः
क्षतास्रवघ्राणविवृद्धमन्व्योः ।
विचित्रमार्गांश्चरतोर्जिगीषया
व्यभादिलायामिव शुष्मिणोर्मृधः ॥१९॥

tayoḥ spṛdhos tigma-gadāhatāṅgayoḥ
kṣatāsrava-ghrāṇa-vivṛddha-manyvoḥ
vicitra-mārgāṁś carator jigīṣayā
vyabhād ilāyām iva śuṣmiṇor mṛdhaḥ

tayoḥ—them; *spṛdhoḥ*—the two combatants; *tigma*—pointed; *gadā*—by the maces; *āhata*—injured; *aṅgayoḥ*—their bodies; *kṣata-āsrava*—blood coming out from the injuries; *ghrāṇa*—smell; *vivṛddha*—increased; *manyvoḥ*—anger; *vicitra*—of various kinds; *mārgān*—maneuvers; *caratoḥ*—performing; *jigīṣayā*—with a desire to win; *vyabhāt*—it looked like; *ilāyām*—for the sake of a cow (or the earth); *iva*—like; *śuṣmiṇoḥ*—of two bulls; *mṛdhaḥ*—an encounter.

TRANSLATION

There was keen rivalry between the two combatants; both had sustained injuries on their bodies from the blows of each other's pointed maces, and each grew more and more enraged at the smell of blood on his person. In their eagerness to win, they performed maneuvers of various kinds, and their contest looked like an encounter between two forceful bulls for the sake of a cow.

PURPORT

Here the earth planet is called *ilā*. This earth was formerly known as Ilāvṛta-varṣa, and when Mahārāja Parīkṣit ruled the earth it was called Bhārata-varṣa. Actually, Bhārata-varṣa is the name for the entire planet, but gradually Bhārata-varṣa has come to mean India. As India has recently been divided into Pakistan and Hindustan, similarly the earth was formerly called Ilāvṛta-varṣa, but gradually as time passed it was divided by national boundaries.

TEXT 20

दैत्यस्य यज्ञावयवस्य माया-
गृहीतवाराहतनोर्महात्मनः ।
कौरव्य मह्यां द्विषतोर्विमर्दनं
दिदृक्षुरागादृषिभिर्वृतः स्वराट् ॥२०॥

daityasya yajñāvayavasya māyā-
gṛhīta-vārāha-tanor mahātmanaḥ
kauravya mahyāṁ dviṣator vimardanaṁ
didṛkṣur āgād ṛṣibhir vṛtaḥ svarāṭ

daityasya—of the demon; *yajña-avayavasya*—of the Personality of Godhead (of whose body *yajña* is a part); *māyā*—through His potency; *gṛhīta*—was assumed; *vārāha*—of a boar; *tanoḥ*—whose form; *mahā-ātmanaḥ*—of the Supreme Lord; *kauravya*—O Vidura (descendant of Kuru); *mahyām*—for the sake of the world; *dviṣatoḥ*—of the two enemies; *vimardanam*—the fight; *didṛkṣuḥ*—desirous to see; *āgāt*—came; *ṛṣibhiḥ*—by the sages; *vṛtaḥ*—accompanied; *svarāṭ*—Brahmā.

TRANSLATION

O descendant of Kuru, Brahmā, the most independent demigod of the universe, accompanied by his followers, came to see the terrible fight for the

sake of the world between the demon and the Personality of Godhead, who appeared in the form of a boar.

PURPORT

The fight between the Lord, the Supreme Personality of Godhead, and the demon is compared to a fight between bulls for the sake of a cow. The earth planet is also called *go*, or cow. As bulls fight between themselves to ascertain who will have union with a cow, there is always a constant fight between the demons and the Supreme Lord or His representative for supremacy over the earth. Here the Lord is significantly described as *yajñāvayava*. One should not consider the Lord to have the body of an ordinary boar. He can assume any form, and He possesses all such forms eternally. It is from Him that all other forms have emanated. This boar form is not to be considered the form of an ordinary hog; His body is actually full of *yajña*, or worshipful offerings. *Yajña* (sacrifices) are offered to Viṣṇu. *Yajña* means the body of Viṣṇu. His body is not material; therefore He should not be taken to be an ordinary boar.

Brahmā is described in this verse as *svarāṭ*. Actually, full independence is exclusive to the Lord Himself, but as part and parcel of the Supreme Lord, every living entity has a minute quantity of independence. Each and every one of the living entities within this universe has this minute independence, but Brahmā, being the chief of all living entities, has a greater potential of independence than any other. He is the representative of Kṛṣṇa, the Supreme Personality of Godhead, and has been assigned to preside over universal affairs. All other demigods work for him; therefore he is described here as *svarāṭ*. He is always accompanied by great sages and transcendentalists, all of whom came to see the bullfight between the demon and the Lord.

TEXT 21

आसन्नशौण्डीरमपेतसाध्वसं
कृतप्रतीकारमहार्यविक्रमम् ।
विलक्ष्य दैत्यं भगवान् सहस्रणी-
र्जगाद नारायणमादिसूकरम् ॥२१॥

āsanna-śauṇḍīram apeta-sādhvasaṁ
kṛta-pratīkāram ahārya-vikramam
vilakṣya daityaṁ bhagavān sahasra-ṇīr
jagāda nārāyaṇam ādi-sūkaram

āsanna—attained; *śauṇḍīram*—power; *apeta*—devoid of; *sādhvasam*—fear; *kṛta*—making; *pratīkāram*—opposition; *ahārya*—unopposable; *vikramam*—having power; *vilakṣya*—having seen; *daityam*—the demon; *bhagavān*—the worshipful Brahmā; *sahasra-nīḥ*—the leader of thousands of sages; *jagāda*—addressed; *nārāyaṇam*—Lord Nārāyaṇa; *ādi*—the original; *sūkaram*—having the form of a boar.

TRANSLATION

After arriving at the place of combat, Brahmā, the leader of thousands of sages and transcendentalists, saw the demon, who had attained such unprecedented power that no one could fight with him. Brahmā then addressed Nārāyaṇa, who was assuming the form of a boar for the first time.

TEXTS 22-23

ब्रह्मोवाच
एष ते देव देवानामङ्घ्रिमूलमुपेयुषाम् ।
विप्राणां सौरभेयीणां भूतानामप्यनागसाम् ॥२२॥
आगस्कृद्भयकृद्दुष्कृदस्मद्राद्धवरोऽसुरः ।
अन्वेषन्नप्रतिरथो लोकानटति कण्टकः ॥२३॥

brahmovāca
eṣa te deva devānām
aṅghri-mūlam upeyuṣām
viprāṇāṁ saurabheyīṇāṁ
bhūtānām apy anāgasām

āgas-kṛd bhaya-kṛd duṣkṛd
asmad-rāddha-varo 'surah
anveṣann apratiratho
lokān aṭati kaṇṭakaḥ

brahmā uvāca—Lord Brahmā said; *eṣaḥ*—this demon; *te*—Your; *deva*—O Lord; *devānām*—to the demigods; *aṅghri-mūlam*—Your feet; *upeyuṣām*—to those having obtained; *viprāṇām*—to the *brāhmaṇas; saurabheyīṇām*—to the cows; *bhūtānām*—to ordinary living entities; *api*—also; *anāgasām*—innocent; *āgaḥ-kṛt*—an offender; *bhaya-kṛt*—a source of fear; *duṣkṛt*—wrongdoer; *asmat*—from me; *rāddha-varaḥ*—having attained a boon; *asuraḥ*—a demon; *anveṣan*—searching; *apratirathaḥ*—having no proper combatant; *lokān*—all over the universe; *aṭati*—he wanders; *kaṇṭakaḥ*—being a pinprick for everyone.

TRANSLATION

Lord Brahmā said: My dear Lord, this demon has proved to be a constant pinprick to the demigods, the brāhmaṇas, the cows and innocent persons who are spotless and always dependent upon worshiping Your lotus feet. He has become a source of fear by unnecessarily harassing them. Since he has attained a boon from me, he has become a demon, always searching for a proper combatant, wandering all over the universe for this infamous purpose.

PURPORT

There are two classes of living entities; one is called *sura,* or the demigods, and the other is called *asura,* or the demons. Demons are generally fond of worshiping the demigods, and there are evidences that by such worship they get extensive power for their sense gratification. This later proves to be a cause of trouble to the *brāhmaṇas,* demigods and other innocent living entities. Demons habitually find fault with the demigods, *brāhmaṇas* and innocent, to whom they are a constant source of fear. The way of the demon is to take power from the demigods and then tease the demigods themselves. There is an instance of a great devotee of Lord Śiva who obtained a boon from Lord Śiva that the head of whomever he touched with his hand would come off its trunk. As soon as the boon was offered to him, the demon wanted to touch the very head of Lord Śiva. That is their way. The devotees of the Supreme Personality of Godhead do not, however, ask any favor for sense gratification. Even if they are offered liberation, they refuse it. They are happy simply engaging in the transcendental loving service of the Lord.

TEXT 24

मैनं मायाविनं दृप्तं निरङ्कुशमसत्तमम् ।
आक्रीड बालवद्देव यथाशीविषमुत्थितम् ॥२४॥

mainaṁ māyāvinaṁ dṛptaṁ
niraṅkuśam asattamam
ākrīḍa bālavad deva
yathāśīviṣam utthitam

mā—do not; *enam*—him; *māyā-vinam*—skilled in conjuring tricks; *dṛptam*—arrogant; *niraṅkuśam*—self-sufficient; *asat-tamam*—most wicked; *ākrīḍa*—play with; *bāla-vat*—like a child; *deva*—O Lord; *yathā*—as; *āśīviṣam*—a serpent; *utthitam*—aroused.

TRANSLATION

Lord Brahmā continued: My dear Lord, there is no need to play with this serpentine demon, who is always very skilled in conjuring tricks and is arrogant, self-sufficient and most wicked.

PURPORT

No one is unhappy when a serpent is killed. It is a practice among village boys to catch a serpent by the tail and play with it for some time and then kill it. Similarly, the Lord could have killed the demon at once, but He played with him in the same way as a child plays with a snake before killing it. Brahmā requested, however, that since the demon was more wicked and undesirable than a serpent, there was no need to play with him. It was his wish that he be killed at once, without delay.

TEXT 25

न यावदेष वर्धेत स्वां वेलां प्राप्य दारुणः ।
स्वां देव मायामास्थाय तावज्जह्यघमच्युत ॥२५॥

na yāvad eṣa vardheta
svāṁ velāṁ prāpya dāruṇaḥ
svāṁ deva māyām āsthāya
tāvaj jahy agham acyuta

na yāvat—before; *eṣaḥ*—this demon; *vardheta*—may increase; *svām*—his own; *velām*—demoniac hour; *prāpya*—having reached; *dāruṇaḥ*—formidable; *svām*—Your own; *deva*—O Lord; *māyām*—internal potency; *āsthāya*—using; *tāvat*—at once; *jahi*—kill; *agham*—the sinful one; *acyuta*—O infallible one.

TRANSLATION

Brahmā continued: My dear Lord, You are infallible. Please kill this sinful demon before the demoniac hour arrives and he presents another formidable approach favorable to him. You can kill him by Your internal potency without doubt.

TEXT 26

एषा घोरतमा सन्ध्या लोकच्छम्बट्करी प्रभो ।
उपसर्पति सर्वात्मन् सुराणां जयमावह ॥२६॥

eṣā ghoratamā sandhyā
loka-cchambaṭ-karī prabho
upasarpati sarvātman
surāṇāṁ jayam āvaha

eṣā—this; *ghora-tamā*—darkest; *sandhyā*—evening time; *loka*—the world; *chambaṭ-karī*—destroying; *prabho*—O Lord; *upasarpati*—is approaching; *sarva-ātman*—O Soul of all souls; *surāṇām*—to the demigods; *jayam*—victory; *āvaha*—bring.

TRANSLATION

My Lord, the darkest evening, which covers the world, is fast approaching. Since You are the Soul of all souls, kindly kill him and win victory for the demigods.

TEXT 27

अधुनैषोऽभिजिन्नाम योगो मौहूर्तिको ह्यगात् ।
शिवाय नस्त्वं सुहृदामाशु निस्तर दुस्तरम् ॥२७॥

adhunaiṣo 'bhijin nāma
yogo mauhūrtiko hy agāt
śivāya nas tvaṁ suhṛdām
āśu nistara dustaram

adhunā—now; *eṣaḥ*—this; *abhijit nāma*—called *abhijit*; *yogaḥ*—auspicious; *mauhūrtikaḥ*—moment; *hi*—indeed; *agāt*—has almost passed; *śivāya*—for the welfare; *naḥ*—of us; *tvam*—You; *suhṛdām*—of Your friends; *āśu*—quickly; *nistara*—dispose of; *dustaram*—the formidable foe.

TRANSLATION

The auspicious period known as abhijit, which is most opportune for victory, commenced at midday and has all but passed; therefore, in the interest of Your friends, please dispose of this formidable foe quickly.

TEXT 28

दिष्ट्या त्वां विहितं मृत्युमयमासादितः स्वयम् ।
विक्रम्यैनं मृधे हत्वा लोकानाधेहि शर्मणि ॥२८॥

diṣṭyā tvāṁ vihitaṁ mṛtyum
ayam āsāditaḥ svayam
vikramyainaṁ mṛdhe hatvā
lokān ādhehi śarmaṇi

diṣṭyā—by fortune; *tvām*—to You; *vihitam*—ordained; *mṛtyum*—death; *ayam*—this demon; *āsāditaḥ*—has come; *svayam*—of his own accord; *vikramya*—exhibiting Your prowess; *enam*—him; *mṛdhe*—in the duel; *hatvā*—killing; *lokān*—the worlds; *ādhehi*—establish; *śarmaṇi*—in peace.

TRANSLATION

This demon, luckily for us, has come of his own accord to You, his death ordained by You; therefore, exhibiting Your ways, kill him in the duel and establish the worlds in peace.

Thus end the Bhaktivedanta purports of the Third Canto, Eighteenth Chapter, of the Śrīmad-Bhāgavatam, *entitled "The Battle Between Lord Boar and the Demon Hiraṇyākṣa."*

CHAPTER NINETEEN

The Killing of the Demon Hiraṇyākṣa

TEXT 1

मैत्रेय उवाच
अवधार्य विरिञ्चस्य निर्व्यलीकामृतं वचः ।
प्रहस्य प्रेमगर्भेण तदपाङ्गेन सोऽग्रहीत् ॥ १ ॥

maitreya uvāca
avadhārya viriñcasya
nirvyalīkāmṛtaṁ vacaḥ
prahasya prema-garbheṇa
tad apāṅgena so 'grahīt

maitreyaḥ uvāca—Maitreya said; *avadhārya*—after hearing; *viriñcasya*—of Lord Brahmā; *nirvyalīka*—free from all sinful purposes; *amṛtam*—nectarean; *vacaḥ*—words; *prahasya*—heartily laughing; *prema-garbheṇa*—laden with love; *tat*—those words; *apāṅgena*—with a glance; *saḥ*—the Supreme Personality of Godhead; *agrahīt*—accepted.

TRANSLATION

Śrī Maitreya said: After hearing the words of Brahmā, the creator, which were free from all sinful purposes and as sweet as nectar, the Lord heartily laughed and accepted his prayer with a glance laden with love.

PURPORT

The word *nirvyalīka* is very significant. The prayers of the demigods or devotees of the Lord are free from all sinful purposes, but the prayers of demons are always filled with sinful purposes. The demon Hiraṇyākṣa became powerful by deriving a boon from Brahmā, and after attaining that boon he created a disturbance because of his sinful intentions. The prayers of Brahmā and other demigods are not to be compared to the prayers of the demons. Their purpose is to please the Supreme Lord; therefore the Lord smiled and accepted the prayer to kill the demon. Demons, who are never interested in praising the Supreme Personality of Godhead because they have no information of Him, go to the demigods, and in *Bhagavad-gītā* this is condemned. Persons who go to the demigods and pray for advancement in sinful activities are considered to be bereft of all intelligence. Demons have lost all intelligence because they do not know what is actually their self-interest. Even if they have information of the Supreme Personality of Godhead, they decline to approach Him; it is not possible for them to get their desired boons from the Supreme Lord because their purposes are always sinful. It is said that the dacoits in Bengal used to worship the goddess Kālī for fulfillment of their sinful desires to plunder others' property, but they never went to a Viṣṇu temple because they might have been unsuccessful in praying to Viṣṇu. Therefore the prayers of the demigods or the devotees of the Supreme Personality of Godhead are always untinged by sinful purposes.

TEXT 2

ततः सपत्नं मुखतश्चरन्तमकुतोभयम् ।
जघानोत्पत्य गदया हनावसुरमक्षजः ॥ २ ॥

tataḥ sapatnaṁ mukhataś
carantam akuto-bhayam
jaghānotpatya gadayā
hanāv asuram akṣajaḥ

tataḥ—then; *sapatnam*—enemy; *mukhataḥ*—in front of Him; *carantam*—stalking; *akutaḥ-bhayam*—fearlessly; *jaghāna*—struck; *utpatya*—after springing up; *gadayā*—with His mace; *hanau*—at the chin; *asuram*—the demon; *akṣa-jaḥ*—the Lord, who was born from the nostril of Brahmā.

TRANSLATION

The Lord, who had appeared from the nostril of Brahmā, sprang and aimed His mace at the chin of His enemy, the Hiraṇyākṣa demon, who was stalking fearlessly before Him.

TEXT 3

सा हता तेन गदया विहता भगवत्करात् ।
विघूर्णितापतद्रेजे तदद्भुतमिवाभवत् ॥ ३ ॥

sā hatā tena gadayā
vihatā bhagavat-karāt
vighūrṇitāpatad reje
tad adbhutam ivābhavat

sā—that mace; *hatā*—struck; *tena*—by Hiraṇyākṣa; *gadayā*—with his mace; *vihatā*—slipped; *bhagavat*—of the Supreme Personality of Godhead; *karāt*—from the hand; *vighūrṇitā*—whirling; *apatat*—fell down; *reje*—was shining; *tat*—that; *adbhutam*—miraculous; *iva*—indeed; *abhavat*—was.

TRANSLATION

Struck by the demon's mace, however, the Lord's mace slipped from His hand and looked splendid as it fell down whirling. This was miraculous, for the mace was blazing wonderfully.

TEXT 4

स तदा लब्धतीर्थोऽपि न बबाधे निरायुधम् ।
मानयन् स मृधे धर्मं विष्वक्सेनं प्रकोपयन् ॥ ४ ॥

sa tadā labdha-tīrtho 'pi
na babādhe nirāyudham
mānayan sa mṛdhe dharmaṁ
viṣvaksenaṁ prakopayan

saḥ—that Hiraṇyākṣa; *tadā*—then; *labdha-tīrthaḥ*—having gained an excellent opportunity; *api*—although; *na*—not; *babādhe*—attacked; *nirāyudham*—having no weapon; *mānayan*—respecting; *saḥ*—Hiraṇyākṣa; *mṛdhe*—in battle; *dharmam*—the code of combat; *viṣvaksenam*—the Supreme Personality of Godhead; *prakopayan*—making angry.

TRANSLATION

Even though the demon had an excellent opportunity to strike his unarmed foe without obstruction, he respected the law of single combat, thereby kindling the fury of the Supreme Lord.

TEXT 5

गदायामपविद्धायां हाहाकारे विनिर्गते ।
मानयामास तद्धर्मं सुनाभं चास्मरद्विभुः ॥ ५ ॥

gadāyām apaviddhāyāṁ
hāhā-kāre vinirgate

mānayām āsa tad-dharmaṁ
sunābhaṁ cāsmarad vibhuḥ

gadāyām—as His mace; *apaviddhāyām*—fell; *hāhā-kāre*—a cry of alarm; *vinirgate*—arose; *mānayām āsa*—acknowledged; *tat*—of Hiraṇyākṣa; *dharmam*—righteousness; *sunābham*—the Sudarśana *cakra;* *ca*—and; *asmarat*—remembered; *vibhuḥ*—the Supreme Personality of Godhead.

TRANSLATION

As the Lord's mace fell to the ground and a cry of alarm arose from the witnessing crowd of gods and ṛṣis, the Personality of Godhead acknowledged the demon's love of righteousness and therefore invoked His Sudarśana discus.

TEXT 6

तं व्यग्रचक्रं दितिपुत्राधमेन
स्वपार्षदमुख्येन विषज्जमानम् ।
चित्रा वाचोऽतद्विदां खेचराणां
तत्र स्मासन् स्वस्ति तेऽमुं जहीति ॥ ६ ॥

taṁ vyagra-cakraṁ diti-putrādhamena
sva-pārṣada-mukhyena viṣajjamānam
citrā vāco 'tad-vidāṁ khe-carāṇāṁ
tatra smāsan svasti te 'muṁ jahīti

tam—unto the Personality of Godhead; *vyagra*—revolving; *cakram*—whose discus; *diti-putra*—son of Diti; *adhamena*—vile; *sva-pārṣada*—of His associates; *mukhyena*—with the chief; *viṣajjamānam*—playing; *citrāḥ*—various; *vācaḥ*—expressions; *a-tat-vidām*—of those who did not know; *khe-carāṇām*—flying in the sky; *tatra*—there; *sma āsan*—occurred; *svasti*—fortune; *te*—unto You; *amum*—him; *jahi*—please kill; *iti*—thus.

TRANSLATION

As the discus began to revolve in the Lord's hands and the Lord contended at close quarters with the chief of His Vaikuṇṭha attendants, who had been born as Hiraṇyākṣa, a vile son of Diti, there issued from every direction strange expressions uttered by those who were witnessing from airplanes. They had no knowledge of the Lord's reality, and they cried, "May victory attend You! Pray dispatch him. Play no more with him."

TEXT 7

स तं निशाम्यात्तरथाङ्गमग्रतो
व्यवस्थितं पद्मपलाशलोचनम् ।
विलोक्य चामर्षपरिप्लुतेन्द्रियो
रुषा स्वदन्तच्छदमादशच्छ्वसन् ॥ ७ ॥

sa taṁ niśāmyātta-rathāṅgam agrato
vyavasthitaṁ padma-palāśa-locanam
vilokya cāmarṣa-pariplutendriyo
ruṣā sva-danta-cchadam ādaśac chvasan

saḥ—that demon; *tam*—the Supreme Personality of Godhead; *niśāmya*—after seeing; *ātta-rathāṅgam*—armed with the Sudarśana disc; *agrataḥ*—before him; *vyavasthitam*—standing in position; *padma*—lotus flower; *palāśa*—petals; *locanam*—eyes; *vilokya*—after seeing; *ca*—and; *amarṣa*—by indignation; *paripluta*—overpowered; *indriyaḥ*—his senses; *ruṣā*—with great resentment; *sva-danta-chadam*—his own lip; *ādaśat*—bit; *śvasan*—hissing.

TRANSLATION

When the demon saw the Personality of Godhead, who had eyes just like lotus petals, standing in position before him, armed with His Sudarśana discus, his senses were overpowered by indignation. He began to hiss like a serpent, and he bit his lip in great resentment.

TEXT 8

करालदंष्ट्रश्चक्षुर्भ्यां सञ्चक्षाणो दहन्निव ।
अभिप्लुत्य स्वगदया हतोऽसीत्याहनद्धरिम् ॥ ८ ॥

karāla-daṁṣṭraś cakṣurbhyāṁ
sañcakṣāṇo dahann iva
abhiplutya sva-gadayā
hato 'sīty āhanad dharim

karāla—fearful; *daṁṣṭraḥ*—having tusks; *cakṣurbhyām*—with both eyes; *sañcakṣāṇaḥ*—staring; *dahan*—burning; *iva*—as if; *abhiplutya*—attacking; *sva-gadayā*—with his own club; *hataḥ*—slain; *asi*—You are; *iti*—thus; *āhanat*—struck; *harim*—at Hari.

TRANSLATION

The demon, who had fearful tusks, stared at the Personality of Godhead as though to burn Him. Springing into the air, he aimed his mace at the Lord, exclaiming at the same time, "You are slain!"

TEXT 9

पदा सव्येन तां साधो भगवान् यज्ञसूकरः ।
लीलया मिषतः शत्रोः प्राहरद्वातरंहसम् ॥ ९ ॥

padā savyena tāṁ sādho
bhagavān yajña-sūkaraḥ
līlayā miṣataḥ śatroḥ
prāharad vāta-raṁhasam

padā—with His foot; *savyena*—left; *tām*—that mace; *sādho*—O Vidura; *bhagavān*—the Supreme Personality of Godhead; *yajña-sūkaraḥ*—in His boar form, the enjoyer of all sacrifices; *līlayā*—playfully; *miṣataḥ*—looking on; *śatroḥ*—of His enemy (Hiraṇyākṣa); *prāharat*—knocked down; *vāta-raṁhasam*—having the force of a tempest.

TRANSLATION

O saintly Vidura, while His enemy looked on, the Lord in His boar form, the enjoyer of all sacrificial offerings, playfully knocked down the mace with His left foot, even as it came upon Him with the force of a tempest.

TEXT 10

आह चायुधमाधत्स्व घटस्व त्वं जिगीषसि ।
इत्युक्तः स तदा भूयस्ताडयन् व्यनदद् भृशम् ॥१०॥

āha cāyudham ādhatsva
ghaṭasva tvaṁ jigīṣasi
ity uktaḥ sa tadā bhūyas
tāḍayan vyanadad bhṛśam

āha—He said; *ca*—and; *āyudham*—weapon; *ādhatsva*—take up; *ghaṭasva*—try; *tvam*—you; *jigīṣasi*—are eager to conquer; *iti*—thus; *uktaḥ*—challenged; *saḥ*—Hiraṇyākṣa; *tadā*—at that time; *bhūyaḥ*—again; *tāḍayan*—striking at; *vyanadat*—roared; *bhṛśam*—loudly.

TRANSLATION

The Lord then said: "Take up your weapon and try again, eager as you are to conquer Me." Challenged in these words, the demon aimed his mace at the Lord and once more loudly roared.

TEXT 11

तां स आपतर्ती वीक्ष्य भगवान् समवस्थितः ।
जग्राह लीलया प्राप्तां गरुत्मानिव पन्नगीम् ॥११॥

tāṁ sa āpatatīṁ vīkṣya
bhagavān samavasthitaḥ
jagrāha līlayā prāptāṁ
garutmān iva pannagīm

tām—that mace; *saḥ*—He; *āpatatīm*—flying toward; *vīkṣya*—after seeing; *bhagavān*—the Supreme Personality of Godhead; *samavasthitaḥ*—stood firmly; *jagrāha*—caught; *līlayā*—easily; *prāptām*—entered into His presence; *garutmān*—Garuḍa; *iva*—as; *pannagīm*—a serpent.

TRANSLATION

When the Lord saw the mace flying toward Him, He stood firmly where He was and caught it with the same ease as Garuḍa, the king of birds, would seize a serpent.

TEXT 12

स्वपौरुषे प्रतिहते हतमानो महासुरः ।
नैच्छद्गदां दीयमानां हरिणा विगतप्रभः ॥१२॥

sva-pauruṣe pratihate
hata-māno mahāsuraḥ
naicchad gadāṁ dīyamānāṁ
hariṇā vigata-prabhaḥ

sva-pauruṣe—his valor; *pratihate*—frustrated; *hata*—destroyed; *mānaḥ*—pride; *mahā-asuraḥ*—the great demon; *na aicchat*—desired not (to take); *gadām*—the mace; *dīyamānām*—being offered; *hariṇā*—by Hari; *vigata-prabhaḥ*—reduced in splendor.

TRANSLATION

His valor thus frustrated, the great demon felt humiliated and was put out of countenance. He was reluctant to take back the mace when it was offered by the Personality of Godhead.

TEXT 13

जग्राह त्रिशिखं शूलं ज्वलज्ज्वलनलोलुपम् ।
यज्ञाय धृतरूपाय विप्रायाभिचरन् यथा ॥१३॥

jagrāha tri-śikhaṁ śūlaṁ
jvalaj-jvalana-lolupam
yajñāya dhṛta-rūpāya
viprāyābhicaran yathā

jagrāha—took up; *tri-śikham*—three-pointed; *śūlam*—trident; *jvalat*—flaming; *jvalana*—fire; *lolupam*—rapacious; *yajñāya*—at the enjoyer of all sacrifices; *dhṛta-rūpāya*—in the form of Varāha; *viprāya*—unto a *brāhmaṇa;* *abhicaran*—acting malevolently; *yathā*—as.

TRANSLATION

He now took a trident which was as rapacious as a flaming fire and hurled it against the Lord, the enjoyer of all sacrifices, even as one would use penance for a malevolent purpose against a holy brāhmaṇa.

TEXT 14

तदोजसा दैत्यमहाभटार्पितं
चकासदन्तःख उदीर्णदीधिति ।
चक्रेण चिच्छेद निशातनेमिना
हरिर्यथा तार्क्ष्यपतत्रमुज्झितम् ॥१४॥

tad ojasā daitya-mahā-bhaṭārpitaṁ
cakāsad antaḥ-kha udīrṇa-dīdhiti
cakreṇa ciccheda niśāta-neminā
harir yathā tārkṣya-patatram ujjhitam

tat—that trident; *ojasā*—with all his strength; *daitya*—among the demons; *mahā-bhaṭa*—by the mighty fighter; *arpitam*—hurled; *cakāsat*—shining; *antaḥ-khe*—in the middle of the sky; *udīrṇa*—increased; *dīdhiti*—illumination; *cakreṇa*—by the Sudarśana disc; *ciccheda*—He cut to pieces; *niśāta*—sharpened; *neminā*—rim; *hariḥ*—Indra; *yathā*—as; *tārkṣya*—of Garuḍa; *patatram*—the wing; *ujjhitam*—abandoned.

TRANSLATION

Hurled by the mighty demon with all his strength, the flying trident shone brightly in the sky. The Personality of Godhead, however, tore it to pieces with His discus Sudarśana, which had a sharp-edged rim, even as Indra cut off a wing of Garuḍa.

PURPORT

The context of the reference given herein regarding Garuḍa and Indra is this. Once upon a time, Garuḍa, the carrier of the Lord, snatched away a nectar pot from the hands of the demigods in heaven in order to liberate his mother, Vinatā, from the clutches of his stepmother, Kadrū, the mother of the serpents. On learning of this, Indra, the King of heaven, hurled his thunderbolt against Garuḍa. With a view to respect the infallibility of Indra's weapon, Garuḍa, though otherwise invincible, being the Lord's own mount, dropped one of his wings, which was shattered to pieces by the thunderbolt. The inhabitants of higher planets are so sensible that even in the process of fighting they observe the preliminary rules and regulations of gentleness. In this case, Garuḍa wanted to show respect for Indra; since he knew that Indra's weapon must destroy something, he offered his wing.

TEXT 15

वृक्णे स्वशूले बहुधारिणा हरेः
प्रत्येत्य विस्तीर्णमुरो विभूतिमत् ।
प्रवृद्धरोषः स कठोरमुष्टिना
नदन् प्रहृत्यान्तरधीयतासुरः ॥१५॥

vṛkṇe sva-śūle bahudhāriṇā hareḥ
pratyetya vistīrṇam uro vibhūtimat
pravṛddha-roṣaḥ sa kaṭhora-muṣṭinā
nadan prahṛtyāntaradhīyatāsuraḥ

vṛkṇe—when cut; *sva-śūle*—his trident; *bahudhā*—to many pieces; *ariṇā*—by the Sudarśana *cakra; hareḥ*—of the Supreme Personality of Godhead; *pratyetya*—after advancing toward; *vistīrṇam*—broad; *uraḥ*—chest; *vibhūti-mat*—the abode of the goddess of fortune; *pravṛddha*—having been increased; *roṣaḥ*—anger; *saḥ*—Hiraṇyākṣa; *kaṭhora*—hard; *muṣṭinā*—with his fist; *nadan*—roaring; *prahṛtya*—after striking; *antaradhīyata*—disappeared; *asuraḥ*—the demon.

TRANSLATION

The demon was enraged when his trident was cut to pieces by the discus of the Personality of Godhead. He therefore advanced toward the Lord and, roaring aloud, struck his hard fist against the Lord's broad chest, which bore the mark of Śrīvatsa. Then he went out of sight.

PURPORT

Śrīvatsa is a curl of white hair on the chest of the Lord which is a special sign of His being the Supreme Personality of Godhead. In Vaikuṇṭhaloka or in Goloka Vṛndāvana, the inhabitants are exactly of the same form as the Personality of Godhead, but by this Śrīvatsa mark on the chest of the Lord He is distinguished from all others.

TEXT 16

तेनेत्थमाहतः क्षत्तर्भगवानादिसूकरः ।
नाकम्पत मनाक् क्वापि स्रजा हत इव द्विपः ॥१६॥

tenettham āhataḥ kṣattar
bhagavān ādi-sūkaraḥ
nākampata manāk kvāpi
srajā hata iva dvipaḥ

tena—by Hiraṇyākṣa; *ittham*—thus; *āhataḥ*—struck; *kṣattaḥ*—O Vidura; *bhagavān*—the Supreme Personality of Godhead; *ādi-sūkaraḥ*—the first boar; *na akampata*—did not feel quaking; *manāk*—even slightly; *kva api*—anywhere; *srajā*—by a garland of flowers; *hataḥ*—struck; *iva*—as; *dvipaḥ*—an elephant.

TRANSLATION

Hit in this manner by the demon, O Vidura, the Lord, who had appeared as the first boar, did not feel the least quaking in any part of His body, any more than an elephant would when struck with a wreath of flowers.

PURPORT

As previously explained, the demon was originally a servitor of the Lord in Vaikuṇṭha, but somehow or other he fell as a demon. His fight with the Supreme Lord was meant for his liberation. The Lord enjoyed the striking on His transcendental body, just like a fully grown-up father fighting with his child. Sometimes a father takes pleasure in having a mock fight with his small child, and similarly the Lord felt Hiraṇyākṣa's striking on His body to be like flowers offered for worship. In other words, the Lord desired to fight in order to enjoy His transcendental bliss; therefore He enjoyed the attack.

TEXT 17

अथोरुधासृजन्मायां योगमायेश्वरे हरौ ।
यां विलोक्य प्रजास्त्रस्ता मेनिरेऽस्योपसंयमम् ॥१७॥

athorudhāsṛjan māyāṁ
yoga-māyeśvare harau
yāṁ vilokya prajās trastā
menire 'syopasaṁyamam

atha—then; *urudhā*—in many ways; *asṛjat*—he cast; *māyām*—conjuring tricks; *yoga-māyā-īśvare*—the Lord of *yogamāyā; harau*—at Hari; *yām*—which; *vilokya*—after seeing; *prajāḥ*—the people; *trastāḥ*—fearful; *menire*—thought; *asya*—of this universe; *upasaṁyamam*—the dissolution.

TRANSLATION

The demon, however, employed many conjuring tricks against the Personality of Godhead, who is the Lord of yogamāyā. At the sight of this the people were filled with alarm and thought that the dissolution of the universe was near.

PURPORT

The fighting enjoyment of the Supreme Lord with His devotee, who had been converted into a demon, appeared severe enough to bring about the dissolution of the universe. This is the greatness of the Supreme Personality of Godhead; even the wavering of His little finger appears to be a great and very dangerous movement in the eyes of the inhabitants of the universe.

TEXT 18

प्रववुर्वायवश्चण्डास्तमः पांसवमैरयन् ।
दिग्भ्यो निपेतुर्ग्रावाणः क्षेपणैः प्रहिता इव ॥१८॥

pravavur vāyavaś caṇḍās
tamaḥ pāṁsavam airayan
digbhyo nipetur grāvāṇaḥ
kṣepaṇaiḥ prahitā iva

pravavuḥ—were blowing; *vāyavaḥ*—winds; *caṇḍāḥ*—fierce; *tamaḥ*—darkness; *pāṁsavam*—caused by dust; *airayan*—were spreading; *digbhyaḥ*—from every direction; *nipetuḥ*—came down; *grāvāṇaḥ*—stones; *kṣepaṇaiḥ*—by machine guns; *prahitāḥ*—thrown; *iva*—as if.

TRANSLATION

Fierce winds began to blow from all directions, spreading darkness occasioned by dust and hail storms; stones came in volleys from every corner, as if thrown by machine guns.

TEXT 19

द्यौर्नष्टभगणाभ्रौघैः सविद्युत्स्तनयित्नुभिः ।
वर्षद्भिः पूयकेशासृग्विण्मूत्रास्थीनि चासकृत् ॥१९॥

dyaur naṣṭa-bhagaṇābhraughaiḥ
sa-vidyut-stanayitnubhiḥ
varṣadbhiḥ pūya-keśāsṛg-
viṇ-mūtrāsthīni cāsakṛt

dyauḥ—the sky; *naṣṭa*—having disappeared; *bha-gaṇa*—luminaries; *abhra*—of clouds; *oghaiḥ*—by masses; *sa*—accompanied by; *vidyut*—lightning; *stanayitnubhiḥ*—and thunder; *varṣadbhiḥ*—raining; *pūya*—pus; *keśa*—hair; *asṛk*—blood; *viṭ*—stool; *mūtra*—urine; *asthīni*—bones; *ca*—and; *asakṛt*—again and again.

TRANSLATION

The luminaries in outer space disappeared due to the sky's being overcast with masses of clouds, which were accompanied by lightning and thunder. The sky rained pus, hair, blood, stool, urine and bones.

TEXT 20

गिरयः प्रत्यदृश्यन्त नानायुधमुचोऽनघ ।
दिग्वाससो यातुधान्यः शूलिन्यो मुक्तमूर्धजाः॥२०॥

girayaḥ pratyadṛśyanta
nānāyudha-muco 'nagha
dig-vāsaso yātudhānyaḥ
śūlinyo mukta-mūrdhajāḥ

girayaḥ—mountains; *pratyadṛśyanta*—appeared; *nānā*—various; *āyudha*—weapons; *mucaḥ*—discharging; *anagha*—O sinless Vidura; *dik-vāsasaḥ*—naked; *yātudhānyaḥ*—demonesses; *śūlinyaḥ*—armed with tridents; *mukta*—hanging loose; *mūrdhajāḥ*—hair.

TRANSLATION

O sinless Vidura, mountains discharged weapons of various kinds, and naked demonesses armed with tridents appeared with their hair hanging loose.

TEXT 21

बहुभिर्यक्षरक्षोभिः पत्त्यश्वरथकुञ्जरैः
आततायिभिरुत्सृष्टा हिंस्रा वाचोऽतिवैशसाः ॥२१॥

bahubhir yakṣa-rakṣobhiḥ
patty-aśva-ratha-kuñjaraiḥ
ātatāyibhir utsṛṣṭā
hiṁsrā vāco 'tivaiśasāḥ

bahubhiḥ—by many; *yakṣa-rakṣobhiḥ*—Yakṣas and Rākṣasas; *patti*—marching on foot; *aśva*—on horses; *ratha*—on chariots; *kuñjaraiḥ*—or on elephants; *ātatāyibhiḥ*—ruffians; *utsṛṣṭāḥ*—were uttered; *hiṁsrāḥ*—cruel; *vācaḥ*—words; *ati-vaiśasāḥ*—murderous.

TRANSLATION

Cruel and savage slogans were uttered by hosts of ruffian Yakṣas and Rākṣasas, who all either marched on foot or rode on horses, elephants or chariots.

TEXT 22

प्रादुष्कृतानां मायानामासुरीणां विनाशयत् ।
सुदर्शनास्त्रं भगवान् प्रायुङ्क्त दयितं त्रिपात् ॥२२॥

prāduṣkṛtānāṁ māyānām
āsurīṇāṁ vināśayat
sudarśanāstraṁ bhagavān
prāyuṅkta dayitaṁ tri-pāt

prāduṣkṛtānām—displayed; *māyānām*—the magical forces; *āsurīṇām*—displayed by the demon; *vināśayat*—desiring to destroy; *sudarśana-astram*—the Sudarśana weapon; *bhagavān*—the Supreme Personality of Godhead; *prāyuṅkta*—threw; *dayitam*—beloved; *tri-pāt*—the enjoyer of all sacrifices.

TRANSLATION

The Lord, the personal enjoyer of all sacrifices, now discharged His beloved Sudarśana, which was capable of dispersing the magical forces displayed by the demon.

PURPORT

Even famous *yogīs* and demons can sometimes enact very magical feats by their mystic power, but in the presence of the Sudarśana *cakra*, when it is let loose by the Lord, all such magical jugglery is dispersed. The instance of the quarrel between Durvāsā Muni and Mahārāja Ambarīṣa is a practical example in this matter. Durvāsā Muni wanted to display many magical wonders, but when the Sudarśana *cakra* appeared, Durvāsā himself was afraid and fled to various planets for his personal protection. The Lord is described here as *tri-pāt*, which means that He is the enjoyer of three kinds of sacrifices. In *Bhagavad-gītā* the Lord confirms that He is the beneficiary and enjoyer of all sacrifices, penances and austerities. The Lord is the enjoyer of three kinds of *yajña*. As further described in *Bhagavad-gītā*, there are sacrifices of goods, sacrifices of meditation and sacrifices of philosophical speculation. Those on the paths of *jñāna*, *yoga* and *karma* all have to come in the end to the Supreme Lord because *vāsudevaḥ sarvam iti* —the Supreme Lord is the ultimate enjoyer of everything. That is the perfection of all sacrifice.

TEXT 23

तदा दितेः समभवत्सहसा हृदि वेपथुः ।
स्मरन्त्या भर्तुरादेशं स्तनाच्चासृक् प्रसुस्रुवे ॥२३॥

tadā diteḥ samabhavat
sahasā hṛdi vepathuḥ
smarantyā bhartur ādeśam
stanāc cāsṛk prasusruve

tadā—at that moment; *diteḥ*—of Diti; *samabhavat*—occurred; *sahasā*—suddenly; *hṛdi*—in the heart; *vepathuḥ*—a shudder; *smarantyāḥ*—recalling; *bhartuḥ*—of her husband, Kaśyapa; *ādeśam*—the words; *stanāt*—from her breast; *ca*—and; *asṛk*—blood; *prasusruve*—flowed.

TRANSLATION

At that very moment, a shudder suddenly ran through the heart of Diti, the mother of Hiraṇyākṣa. She recalled the words of her husband, Kaśyapa, and blood flowed from her breasts.

PURPORT

At Hiraṇyākṣa's last moment, his mother, Diti, remembered what her husband had said. Although her sons would be demons, they would have the advantage of being killed by the Personality of Godhead Himself. She remembered this incident by the grace of the Lord, and her breasts flowed blood instead of milk. In many instances we find that when a mother is moved by affection for her sons, milk flows from her breasts. In the case of the demon's mother, the blood could not transform into milk, but it flowed down her breasts as it was. Blood transforms into milk. To drink milk is auspicious, but to drink blood is inauspicious, although they are one and the same thing. This formula is applicable in the case of cow's milk also.

TEXT 24

विनष्टासु स्वमायासु भूयश्चाव्रज्य केशवम् ।
रुषोपगूहमानोऽमुं ददृशेऽवस्थितं बहिः ॥२४॥

vinaṣṭāsu sva-māyāsu
bhūyaś cāvrajya keśavam
ruṣopagūhamāno 'muṁ
dadṛśe 'vasthitaṁ bahiḥ

vinaṣṭāsu—when dispelled; *sva-māyāsu*—his magic forces; *bhūyaḥ*—again; *ca*—and; *āvrajya*—after coming into the presence; *keśavam*—the Supreme Personality of Godhead; *ruṣā*—full of rage; *upagūhamānaḥ*—embracing; *amum*—the Lord; *dadṛśe*—saw; *avasthitam*—standing; *bahiḥ*—outside.

TRANSLATION

When the demon saw his magic forces dispelled, he once again came into the presence of the Personality of Godhead, Keśava, and, full of rage, tried to embrace Him within his arms to crush Him. But to his great amazement he found the Lord standing outside the circle of his arms.

PURPORT

In this verse the Lord is addressed as Keśava because He killed the demon Keśī in the beginning of creation. Keśava is also a name of Kṛṣṇa. Kṛṣṇa is the origin of all incarnations, and it is confirmed in *Brahma-saṁhitā* that Govinda, the Supreme Personality of Godhead, the cause of all causes, exists simultaneously in His different incarnations and expansions. The demon's attempt to measure the Supreme Personality of Godhead is significant. The demon wanted to embrace Him with his arms, thinking that with his limited arms he could capture the Absolute by material power. He did not know that God is the greatest of the great and the smallest of the small. No one can capture the Supreme Lord or bring Him under his control. But the demoniac person always attempts to measure the length and breadth of the Supreme Lord. By His inconceivable potency the Lord can become the universal form, as explained in *Bhagavad-gītā,* and at the same time He can remain within the box of His devotees as their worshipable Deity. There are many devotees who keep a statue of the Lord in a small box and carry it with them everywhere; every morning they worship the Lord in the box. The Supreme Lord, Keśava, or the Personality of Godhead, Kṛṣṇa, is not bound by any measurement of our calculation. He can remain with His devotee in any suitable form, yet He is unapproachable by any amount of demoniac activities.

TEXT 25

तं मुष्टिभिर्विनिघ्नन्तं वज्रसारैरधोक्षजः ।
करेण कर्णमूलेऽहन् यथा त्वाष्ट्रं मरुत्पतिः ॥२५॥

taṁ muṣṭibhir vinighnantaṁ
vajra-sārair adhokṣajaḥ
kareṇa karṇa-mūle 'han
yathā tvāṣṭraṁ marut-patiḥ

tam—Hiraṇyākṣa; *muṣṭibhiḥ*—with his fists; *vinighnantam*—striking; *vajra-sāraiḥ*—as hard as a thunderbolt; *adhokṣajaḥ*—Lord Adhokṣaja; *kareṇa*—with the hand; *karṇa-mūle*—at the root of the ear; *ahan*—struck; *yathā*—as; *tvāṣṭram*—the demon Vṛtra (son of Tvaṣṭā); *marut-patiḥ*—Indra (lord of the Maruts).

TRANSLATION

The demon now began to strike the Lord with his hard fists, but Lord Adhokṣaja slapped him in the root of the ear, even as Indra, the lord of the Maruts, hit the demon Vṛtra.

PURPORT

The Lord is explained here to be *adhokṣaja,* beyond the reach of all material calculation. *Akṣaja* means "the measurement of our senses," and *adhokṣaja* means "that which is beyond the measurement of our senses."

TEXT 26

स आहतो विश्वजिता ह्यवज्ञया
परिभ्रमद्गात्र उदस्तलोचनः ।
विशीर्णबाह्वङ्घ्रिशिरोरुहोऽपतद्
यथा नगेन्द्रो लुलितो नभस्वता ॥२६॥

sa āhato viśva-jitā hy avajñayā
paribhramad-gātra udasta-locanaḥ
viśīrṇa-bāhv-aṅghri-śiroruho 'patad
yathā nagendro lulito nabhasvatā

saḥ—he; *āhataḥ*—having been struck; *viśva-jitā*—by the Supreme Personality of Godhead; *hi*—though; *avajñayā*—indifferently; *paribhramat*—wheeling; *gātraḥ*—body; *udasta*—bulged out; *locanaḥ*—eyes; *viśīrṇa*—broken; *bāhu*—arms; *aṅghri*—legs; *śiraḥ-ruhaḥ*—hair; *apatat*—fell down; *yathā*—like; *naga-indraḥ*—a gigantic tree; *lulitaḥ*—uprooted; *nabhasvatā*—by the wind.

TRANSLATION

Though struck indifferently by the Lord, the conqueror of all, the demon's body began to wheel. His eyeballs bulged out of their sockets. His arms and legs broken and the hair on his head scattered, he fell down dead, like a gigantic tree uprooted by the wind.

PURPORT

It does not take even a moment for the Lord to kill any powerful demon, including Hiraṇyākṣa. The Lord could have killed him long before, but He allowed the demon to display the full extent of his magical feats. One may know that by magical feats, by scientific advancement of knowledge or by material power one cannot become the equal of the Supreme Personality of Godhead. His one signal is sufficient to destroy all our attempts. His inconceivable power, as displayed here, is so strong that the demon, despite all his demoniac maneuvers, was killed by the Lord when the Lord desired, simply by one slap.

TEXT 27

क्षितौ शयानं तमकुण्ठवर्चसं
करालदंष्ट्रं परिदष्टदच्छदम् ।
अजादयो वीक्ष्य शशंसुरागता
अहो इमां को नु लभेत संस्थितिम् ॥२७॥

kṣitau śayānaṁ tam akuṇṭha-varcasaṁ
karāla-daṁṣṭraṁ paridaṣṭa-dacchadam
ajādayo vīkṣya śaśaṁsur āgatā
aho imaṁ ko nu labheta saṁsthitim

kṣitau—on the ground; *śayānam*—lying; *tam*—Hiraṇyākṣa; *akuṇṭha*—unfaded; *varcasam*—glow; *karāla*—fearful; *daṁṣṭram*—teeth; *paridaṣṭa*—bitten; *dat-chadam*—lip; *aja-ādayaḥ*—Brahmā and others; *vīkṣya*—having seen; *śaśaṁsuḥ*—admiringly said; *āgatāḥ*—arrived; *aho*—oh; *imam*—this; *kaḥ*—who; *nu*—indeed; *labheta*—could meet; *saṁsthitim*—death.

TRANSLATION

Aja [Brahmā] and others arrived on the spot to see the fearfully tusked demon lying on the ground, biting his lip. The glow of his face was yet unfaded, and Brahmā admiringly said: Oh, who could meet such blessed death?

PURPORT

Although the demon was dead, his bodily luster was unfaded. This is very peculiar because when a man or animal is dead, the body immediately becomes pale, the luster gradually fades, and decomposition takes place. But here, although Hiraṇyākṣa lay dead, his bodily luster was unfaded because the Lord, the Supreme Spirit, was touching his body. One's bodily luster remains fresh only as long as the spirit soul is present. Although the demon's soul had departed his body, the Supreme Spirit touched the body, and therefore his bodily luster did not fade. The individual soul is different from the Supreme Personality of Godhead. One who sees the Supreme Personality of Godhead when he quits his body is certainly very fortunate, and therefore personalities like Brahmā and the other demigods eulogized the death of the demon.

TEXT 28

यं योगिनो योगसमाधिना रहो
ध्यायन्ति लिङ्गादसतो मुमुक्षया ।

तस्यैष दैत्यऋषभः पदाहतो
मुखं प्रपश्यंस्तनुमुत्ससर्ज ह ॥२८॥

yaṁ yogino yoga-samādhinā raho
dhyāyanti liṅgād asato mumukṣayā
tasyaiṣa daitya-ṛṣabhaḥ padāhato
mukhaṁ prapaśyaṁs tanum utsasarja ha

yam—whom; *yoginaḥ*—the *yogīs*; *yoga-samādhinā*—in mystic trance; *rahaḥ*—in seclusion; *dhyāyanti*—meditate upon; *liṅgāt*—from the body; *asataḥ*—unreal; *mumukṣayā*—seeking freedom; *tasya*—of Him; *eṣaḥ*—this; *daitya*—son of Diti; *ṛṣabhaḥ*—the crest jewel; *padā*—by a foot; *āhataḥ*—struck; *mukham*—countenance; *prapaśyan*—while gazing on; *tanum*—the body; *utsasarja*—he cast off; *ha*—indeed.

TRANSLATION

Brahmā continued: He was struck by a forefoot of the Lord, whom yogīs, seeking freedom from their unreal material bodies, meditate upon in seclusion in mystic trance. While gazing on His countenance, this crest jewel of Diti's sons has cast off his mortal coil.

PURPORT

The process of *yoga* is very clearly described in this verse of *Śrīmad-Bhāgavatam.* It is said here that the ultimate end of the *yogīs* and mystics who perform meditation is to get rid of this material body. Therefore they meditate in secluded places to attain yogic trance. *Yoga* has to be performed in a secluded place, not in public or in a demonstration on stage, as nowadays practiced by many so-called *yogīs.* Real *yoga* aims at ridding one of the material body. *Yoga* practice is not intended to keep the body fit and young. Such advertisements of so-called *yoga* are not approved by any standard method. Particularly mentioned in this verse is the word *yam,* or "unto whom," indicating that meditation should be targeted on the Personality of Godhead. Even if one concentrates his mind on the boar form of the Lord, that is also *yoga.* As confirmed in *Bhagavad-gītā,* one who concentrates his mind constantly in meditation upon the Personality of Godhead in one of His many varieties of forms is the first-class *yogī,* and he can very easily attain trance simply by meditating upon the form of the Lord. If one is able to continue such meditation on the Lord's form at the time of one's death, one is liberated from this mortal body and is transferred to the kingdom of God. This opportunity was given to the demon by the Lord, and therefore Brahmā and other demigods were astonished. In other words, the perfection of *yoga* practice can be attained by a demon also if he is simply kicked by the Lord.

TEXT 29

एतौ तौ पार्षदावस्य शापाद्यातावसद्गतिम् ।
पुनः कतिपयैः स्थानं प्रपत्स्येते ह जन्मभिः ॥२९॥

etau tau pārṣadāv asya
śāpād yātāv asad-gatim
punaḥ katipayaiḥ sthānaṁ
prapatsyete ha janmabhiḥ

etau—these two; *tau*—both; *pārṣadau*—personal assistants; *asya*—of the Personality of Godhead; *śāpāt*—because of being cursed; *yātau*—have gone; *asat-gatim*—to take birth in a demoniac family; *punaḥ*—again; *katipayaiḥ*—a few; *sthānam*—own place; *prapatsyete*—will get back; *ha*—indeed; *janmabhiḥ*—after births.

TRANSLATION

These two personal assistants of the Supreme Lord, having been cursed, have been destined to take birth in demoniac families. After a few such births, they will return to their own positions.

TEXT 30

देवा ऊचुः
नमो नमस्तेऽखिलयज्ञतन्तवे
स्थितौ गृहीतामलसत्त्वमूर्तये ।
दिष्ट्या हतोऽयं जगतामरुन्तुद-
स्त्वत्पादभक्त्या वयमीश निर्वृताः ॥३०॥

devā ūcuḥ
namo namas te 'khila-yajña-tantave
sthitau gṛhītāmala-sattva-mūrtaye
diṣṭyā hato 'yaṁ jagatām aruntudas
tvat-pāda-bhaktyā vayam īśa nirvṛtāḥ

devāḥ—the demigods; *ūcuḥ*—said; *namaḥ*—obeisances; *namaḥ*—obeisances; *te*—unto You; *akhila-yajña-tantave*—the enjoyer of all sacrifices; *sthitau*—for the purpose of maintaining; *gṛhīta*—assumed; *amala*—pure; *sattva*—goodness; *mūrtaye*—form; *diṣṭyā*—fortunately; *hataḥ*—slain; *ayam*—this; *jagatām*—to the worlds; *aruntudaḥ*—causing torment; *tvat-pāda*—to Your feet; *bhaktyā*—with devotion; *vayam*—we; *īśa*—O Lord; *nirvṛtāḥ*—have attained happiness.

TRANSLATION

The demigods addressed the Lord: All obeisances unto You! You are the enjoyer of all sacrifices, and You have assumed the form of a boar, in pure goodness, for the purpose of maintaining the world. Fortunately for us, this demon, who was a torment to the worlds, has been slain by You, and we too, O Lord, are now at ease, in devotion to Your lotus feet.

PURPORT

The material world consists of three modes—goodness, passion and ignorance—but the spiritual world is pure goodness. It is said here that the form of the Lord is pure goodness, which means that it is not material. In the material world there is no pure goodness. In the *Bhāgavatam* the stage of pure goodness is called *sattvaṁ viśuddham. Viśuddham* means "pure." In pure goodness there is no contamination by the two inferior qualities, namely passion and ignorance. The form of the boar, therefore, in which the Lord appeared, is nothing of the material world. There are many other forms of the Lord, but none of them belong to the material qualities. Such forms are nondifferent from the Viṣṇu form, and Viṣṇu is the enjoyer of all sacrifices.

The sacrifices which are recommended in the *Vedas* are meant to please the Supreme Personality of Godhead. In ignorance only, people try to satisfy many other agents, but the real purpose of life is to satisfy the Supreme Lord, Viṣṇu. All sacrifices are meant to please the Supreme Lord. The living entities who know this perfectly well are called demigods, godly or almost God. Since the living entity is part and parcel of the Supreme Lord, it is his duty to serve the Lord and please Him. The demigods are all attached to the Personality of Godhead, and for their pleasure the demon, who was a source of trouble to the world, was killed. Purified life is meant to please the Lord, and all sacrifices performed in purified life are called Kṛṣṇa consciousness. This Kṛṣṇa consciousness is developed by devotional service, as clearly mentioned here.

TEXT 31

मैत्रेय उवाच

एवं हिरण्याक्षमसह्यविक्रमं
स सादयित्वा हरिरादिसूकरः ।
जगाम लोकं स्वमखण्डितोत्सवं
समीडितः पुष्करविष्टरादिभिः ॥३१॥

maitreya uvāca

evaṁ hiraṇyākṣam asahya-vikramaṁ
sa sādayitvā harir ādi-sūkaraḥ
jagāma lokaṁ svam akhaṇḍitotsavaṁ
samīḍitaḥ puṣkara-viṣṭarādibhiḥ

maitreyaḥ uvāca—Śrī Maitreya said; *evam*—thus; *hiraṇyākṣam*—Hiraṇyākṣa; *asahya-vikramam*—very powerful; *saḥ*—the Lord; *sādayitvā*—after killing; *hariḥ*—the Supreme Personality of Godhead; *ādi-sūkaraḥ*—the origin of the boar species; *jagāma*—returned; *lokam*—to His abode; *svam*—own; *akhaṇḍita*—uninterrupted; *utsavam*—festival; *samīḍitaḥ*—being praised; *puṣkara-viṣṭara*—lotus seat (by Lord Brahmā, whose seat is a lotus); *ādibhiḥ*—and the others.

TRANSLATION

Śrī Maitreya continued: After thus killing the most formidable demon Hiraṇyākṣa, the Supreme Lord Hari, the origin of the boar species, returned to His own abode, where there is always an uninterrupted festival. The Lord was praised by all the demigods, headed by Brahmā.

PURPORT

The Lord is spoken of herewith as the origin of the boar species. As stated in the *Vedānta-sūtra* (1.1.2), the Absolute Truth is the origin of everything. Therefore it is to be understood that all 8,400,000 species of bodily forms originate from the Lord, who is always *ādi,* or the beginning. In *Bhagavad-gītā* Arjuna addresses the Lord as *ādyam,* or the original. Similarly, in the *Brahma-saṁhitā* the Lord is addressed as *ādi-puruṣam,* the original person. Indeed, in *Bhagavad-gītā* (10.8) the Lord Himself declares, *mattaḥ sarvaṁ pravartate:* "From Me everything proceeds."

In this situation the Lord assumed the shape of a boar to kill the demon Hiraṇyākṣa and pick up the earth from the Garbha Ocean. Thus He became *ādi-sūkara,* the original boar. In the material world a boar or pig is considered most abominable, but the *ādi-sūkara,* the Supreme Personality of Godhead, was not treated as an ordinary boar. Even Lord Brahmā and the other demigods praised the Lord's form as a boar.

This verse confirms the statement in *Bhagavad-gītā* that the Lord appears as He is from His transcendental abode for the sake of killing the miscreants and saving the devotees. By killing the demon Hiraṇyākṣa He fulfilled His promise to kill the demons and always protect the demigods headed by Brahmā. The statement that the Lord returned to His own abode indicates that He has His own particular transcendental residence. Since He is full of all energies, He is all-pervasive in spite of His residing in

Goloka Vṛndāvana, just as the sun, although situated in a particular place within the universe, is present by its sunshine throughout the universe.

Although the Lord has His particular abode in which to reside, He is all-pervasive. The impersonalists accept one aspect of the Lord's features, the all-pervasive aspect, but they cannot understand His localized situation in His transcendental abode, where He always engages in fully transcendental pastimes. Especially mentioned in this verse is the word *akhaṇḍitotsavam. Utsava* means "pleasure." Whenever some function takes place to express happiness, it is called *utsava. Utsava,* the expression of complete happiness, is always present in the Vaikuṇṭhalokas, the abode of the Lord, who is worshipable even by demigods like Brahmā, to say nothing of other, less important entities such as human beings.

The Lord descends from His abode to this world, and therefore He is called *avatāra,* which means "one who descends." Sometimes *avatāra* is understood to refer to an incarnation who assumes a material form of flesh and bone, but actually *avatāra* refers to one who descends from higher regions. The Lord's abode is situated far above this material sky, and He descends from that higher position; thus He is called *avatāra.*

TEXT 32

मया यथानूक्तमवादि ते हरेः
कृतावतारस्य सुमित्र चेष्टितम् ।
यथा हिरण्याक्ष उदारविक्रमो
महामृधे क्रीडनवन्निराकृतः ॥३२॥

mayā yathānūktam avādi te hareḥ
kṛtāvatārasya sumitra ceṣṭitam
yathā hiraṇyākṣa udāra-vikramo
mahā-mṛdhe krīḍanavan nirākṛtaḥ

mayā—by me; *yathā*—as; *anūktam*—told; *avādi*—was explained; *te*—to you; *hareḥ*—of the Supreme Personality of Godhead; *kṛta-avatārasya*—who assumed the incarnation; *sumitra*—O dear Vidura; *ceṣṭitam*—the activities; *yathā*—as; *hiraṇyākṣaḥ*—Hiraṇyākṣa; *udāra*—very extensive; *vikramaḥ*—prowess; *mahā-mṛdhe*—in a great fight; *krīḍana-vat*—like a plaything; *nirākṛtaḥ*—was killed.

TRANSLATION

Maitreya continued: My dear Vidura, I have explained to you the Personality of Godhead's coming down as the first boar incarnation and

killing in a great fight a demon of unprecedented prowess as if he were just a plaything. This has been narrated by me as I heard it from my predecessor spiritual master.

PURPORT

Here the sage Maitreya admits that he explained the incident of the killing of Hiraṇyākṣa by the Supreme Personality of Godhead as a straight narration; he did not manufacture anything or add interpretation, but explained whatever he had heard from his spiritual master. Thus he accepted as bona fide the system of *paramparā,* or receiving the transcendental message in disciplic succession. Unless received by this bona fide process of hearing from a spiritual master, the statement of an *ācārya* or preceptor cannot be valid.

It is also stated here that although the demon Hiraṇyākṣa was unlimited in prowess, he was just like a doll for the Lord. A child breaks so many dolls without real endeavor. Similarly, although a demon may be very powerful and extraordinary in the eyes of an ordinary man in the material world, to the Lord, killing such a demon is no difficulty. He can kill millions of demons as simply as a child plays with dolls and breaks them.

TEXT 33

सूत उवाच
इति कौषारवाख्यातामाश्रुत्य भगवत्कथाम् ।
क्षत्तानन्दं परं लेभे महाभागवतो द्विज ॥३३॥

sūta uvāca
iti kauṣāravākhyātām
āśrutya bhagavat-kathām
kṣattānandaṁ paraṁ lebhe
mahā-bhāgavato dvija

sūtaḥ—Sūta Gosvāmī; *uvāca*—said; *iti*—thus; *kauṣārava*—from Maitreya (son of Kuṣāru); *ākhyātām*—told; *āśrutya*—having heard; *bhagavat-kathām*—the narration about the Lord; *kṣattā*—Vidura; *ānandam*—bliss; *param*—transcendental; *lebhe*—achieved; *mahā-bhāgavataḥ*—the great devotee; *dvija*—O *brāhmaṇa* (Śaunaka).

TRANSLATION

Śrī Sūta Gosvāmī continued: My dear brāhmaṇa, Kṣattā [Vidura] the great devotee of the Lord achieved transcendental bliss by hearing the narration of

the pastimes of the Supreme Personality of Godhead from the authoritative source of the sage Kauṣārava [Maitreya], and he was very pleased.

PURPORT

If anyone wants to derive transcendental pleasure by hearing the pastimes of the Lord, he must hear from the authoritative source, as explained here. Maitreya heard the narration from his bona fide spiritual master, and Vidura also heard from Maitreya. One becomes an authority simply by presenting whatever he has heard from his spiritual master, and one who does not accept a bona fide spiritual master cannot be an authority. This is clearly explained here. If one wants to have transcendental pleasure, he must find a person with authority. It is also stated in the *Bhāgavatam* that simply by hearing from an authoritative source, with the ear and the heart, one can relish the pastimes of the Lord, otherwise it is not possible. Sanātana Gosvāmī, therefore, has especially warned that one should not hear anything about the personality of the Lord from the lips of a nondevotee. Nondevotees are considered to be like serpents; as milk is poisoned by a serpent's touch, so, although the narration of the pastimes of the Lord is as pure as milk, when administered by serpentlike nondevotees it becomes poisonous. Not only does it have no effect in transcendental pleasure, but it is dangerous also. Lord Caitanya Mahāprabhu has warned that no description of the pastimes of the Lord should be heard from the Māyāvāda, or impersonalist, school. He has clearly said, *māyāvādi-bhāṣya śunile haya sarva nāśa:* if anyone hears the Māyāvādīs' interpretation of the pastimes of the Lord, or their interpretation of *Bhagavad-gītā, Śrīmad-Bhāgavatam* or any other Vedic literature, then he is doomed. Once one is associated with impersonalists, he can never understand the personal feature of the Lord and His transcendental pastimes.

Sūta Gosvāmī was speaking to the sages headed by Śaunaka, and therefore he addressed them in this verse as *dvija,* twice-born. The sages assembled in Naimiṣāraṇya hearing *Śrīmad-Bhāgavatam* from Sūta Gosvāmī were all *brāhmaṇas,* but to acquire the qualifications of a *brāhmaṇa* is not everything. Merely to be twice-born is not perfection. Perfection is attained when one hears the pastimes and activities of the Lord from a bona fide source.

TEXT 34

अन्येषां पुण्यश्लोकानामुद्दामयशसां सताम् ।
उपश्रुत्य भवेन्मोदः श्रीवत्साङ्कस्य किं पुनः ॥३४॥

anyeṣāṁ puṇya-ślokānām
uddāma-yaśasāṁ satām
upaśrutya bhaven modaḥ
śrīvatsāṅkasya kiṁ punaḥ

anyeṣām—of others; *puṇya-ślokānām*—of pious reputation; *uddāma-yaśasām*—whose fame is spread everywhere; *satām*—of the devotees; *upaśrutya*—by hearing; *bhavet*—may arise; *modaḥ*—pleasure; *śrīvatsa-aṅkasya*—of the Lord, who bears the mark Śrīvatsa; *kim punaḥ*—what to speak of.

TRANSLATION

What to speak of hearing the pastimes of the Lord, whose chest is marked with Śrīvatsa, people may take transcendental pleasure even in hearing of the works and deeds of the devotees, whose fame is immortal.

PURPORT

Bhāgavatam literally means the pastimes of the Lord and the Lord's devotees. For example, there are pastimes of Lord Kṛṣṇa and narrations of devotees like Prahlāda, Dhruva and Mahārāja Ambarīṣa. Both pastimes pertain to the Supreme Personality of Godhead because the devotees' pastimes are in relation with Him. The *Mahābhārata*, for example, the history of the Pāṇḍavas and their activities, is sacred because the Pāṇḍavas had a direct relationship with the Supreme Personality of Godhead.

TEXT 35

यो गजेन्द्रं झषग्रस्तं ध्यायन्तं चरणाम्बुजम् ।
क्रोशन्तीनां करेणूनां कृच्छ्रतोऽमोचयद् द्रुतम् ॥३५॥

yo gajendraṁ jhaṣa-grastaṁ
dhyāyantaṁ caraṇāmbujam
krośantīnāṁ kareṇūnāṁ
kṛcchrato 'mocayad drutam

yaḥ—He who; *gaja-indram*—the king of elephants; *jhaṣa*—an alligator; *grastam*—attacked by; *dhyāyantam*—meditating upon; *caraṇa*—feet; *ambujam*—lotus; *krośantīnām*—while crying; *kareṇūnām*—the female elephants; *kṛcchrataḥ*—from danger; *amocayat*—delivered; *drutam*—quickly.

TRANSLATION

The Personality of Godhead delivered the king of the elephants, who was attacked by an alligator and who meditated upon the lotus feet of the Lord. At that time the female elephants who accompanied him were crying, and the Lord saved them from the impending danger.

PURPORT

The example of the elephant in danger who was saved by the Supreme Lord is especially cited here because even if one is an animal he can approach the Personality of Godhead in devotional service, whereas even a demigod cannot approach the Supreme Person unless he is a devotee.

TEXT 36

तं सुखाराध्यमृजुभिरनन्यशरणैर्नृभिः ।
कृतज्ञः को न सेवेत दुराराध्यमसाधुभिः ॥३६॥

taṁ sukhārādhyam ṛjubhir
ananya-śaraṇair nṛbhiḥ
kṛtajñaḥ ko na seveta
durārādhyam asādhubhiḥ

tam—unto Him; *sukha*—easily; *ārādhyam*—worshiped; *ṛjubhiḥ*—by the unpretentious; *ananya*—no other; *śaraṇaiḥ*—who take shelter; *nṛbhiḥ*—by men; *kṛta-jñaḥ*—grateful soul; *kaḥ*—what; *na*—not; *seveta*—would render service; *durārādhyam*—impossible to be worshiped; *asādhubhiḥ*—by the nondevotees.

TRANSLATION

What grateful soul is there who would not render his loving service to such a great master as the Personality of Godhead? The Lord can be easily pleased by spotless devotees who resort exclusively to Him for protection, though the unrighteous man finds it difficult to propitiate Him.

PURPORT

Every living entity, especially persons in the human race, must feel grateful for the benedictions offered by the grace of the Supreme Lord. Anyone, therefore, with a simple heart of gratefulness must be Kṛṣṇa conscious and offer devotional service to the Lord. Those who are actually thieves and rogues do not recognize or acknowledge the benedictions offered to them by the Supreme Lord, and they cannot render Him devotional service. Ungrateful persons are those who do not understand how much benefit they are deriving by the arrangement of the Lord. They enjoy the sunshine and moonshine, and they get water free of charge, yet they do not feel grateful, but simply go on enjoying these gifts of the Lord. Therefore, they must be called thieves and rogues.

TEXT 37

यो वै हिरण्याक्षवधं महाद्भुतं
विक्रीडितं कारणसूकरात्मनः ।
शृणोति गायत्यनुमोदतेऽञ्जसा
विमुच्यते ब्रह्मवधादपि द्विजाः ॥३७॥

yo vai hiraṇyākṣa-vadhaṁ mahādbhutaṁ
vikrīḍitaṁ kāraṇa-sūkarātmanaḥ
śṛṇoti gāyaty anumodate 'ñjasā
vimucyate brahma-vadhād api dvijāḥ

yaḥ—he who; *vai*—indeed; *hiraṇyākṣa-vadham*—of the killing of Hiraṇyākṣa; *mahā-adbhutam*—most wonderful; *vikrīḍitam*—pastime; *kāraṇa*—for reasons like raising the earth from the ocean; *sūkara*—appearing in the form of a boar; *ātmanaḥ*—of the Supreme Personality of Godhead; *śṛṇoti*—hears; *gāyati*—chants; *anumodate*—takes pleasure; *añjasā*—at once; *vimucyate*—becomes freed; *brahma-vadhāt*—from the sin of killing a *brāhmaṇa*; *api*—even; *dvijāḥ*—O *brāhmaṇas.*

TRANSLATION

O brāhmaṇas, anyone who hears, chants, or takes pleasure in the wonderful narration of the killing of the Hiraṇyākṣa demon by the Lord, who appeared as the first boar in order to deliver the world, is at once relieved of the results of sinful activities, even the killing of a brāhmaṇa.

PURPORT

Since the Personality of Godhead is in the absolute position, there is no difference between His pastimes and His personality. Anyone who hears about the pastimes of the Lord associates with the Lord directly, and one who associates directly with the Lord is certainly freed from all sinful activities, even to the extent of the killing of a *brāhmaṇa*, which is considered the most sinful activity in the material world. One should be very eager to hear about the activities of the Lord from the bona fide source, the pure devotee. If one simply gives aural reception to the narration and accepts the glories of the Lord, then he is qualified. The impersonalist philosophers cannot understand the activities of the Lord. They think that all His activities are *māyā*; therefore they are called Māyāvādīs. Since everything to them is *māyā*, these narrations are not for them. Some impersonalists are reluctant to hear *Śrīmad-Bhāgavatam*, although many of them are now taking an interest in it just for monetary gain. Actually, however, they have no faith. On the contrary, they describe it in their own way. We should not hear, therefore, from the Māyāvādīs. We have to hear from Sūta Gosvāmī or Maitreya, who actually present the narrations as they are, and only then can we relish the pastimes of the Lord; otherwise the effects on the neophyte audience will be poisonous.

TEXT 38

एतन्महापुण्यमलं पवित्रं
धन्यं यशस्यं पदमायुराशिषाम् ।
प्राणेन्द्रियाणां युधि शौर्यवर्धनं
नारायणोऽन्ते गतिरङ्ग शृण्वताम् ॥३८॥

etan mahā-puṇyam alaṁ pavitraṁ
dhanyaṁ yaśasyaṁ padam āyur-āśiṣām
prāṇendriyāṇāṁ yudhi śaurya-vardhanaṁ
nārāyaṇo 'nte gatir aṅga śṛṇvatām

etat—this narrative; *mahā-puṇyam*—conferring great merit; *alam*—very; *pavitram*—sacred; *dhanyam*—conferring wealth; *yaśasyam*—bearing fame; *padam*—the receptacle; *āyuḥ*—of longevity; *āśiṣām*—of the objects of one's desire; *prāṇa*—of the vital organs; *indriyāṇām*—of the organs of action; *yudhi*—on the field of battle; *śaurya*—the strength; *vardhanam*—increasing; *nārāyaṇaḥ*—Lord Nārāyaṇa; *ante*—at the end of life; *gatiḥ*—shelter; *aṅga*—O dear Śaunaka; *śṛṇvatām*—of those who listen.

TRANSLATION

This most sacred narrative confers extraordinary merit, wealth, fame, longevity, and all the objects of one's desire. On the field of battle it promotes the strength of one's vital organs and organs of action. One who listens to it at the last moment of his life is transferred to the supreme abode of the Lord, O dear Śaunaka.

PURPORT

Devotees are generally attracted by the narratives of the pastimes of the Lord, and even though they do not prosecute austerities or meditation, this very process of *hearing* attentively about the pastimes of the Lord will endow them with innumerable benefits, such as wealth, fame, longevity and other desirable aims of life. If one continues to hear *Śrīmad-Bhāgavatam,* which is full of narratives of the pastimes of the Lord, at the end of this life, one is sure to be transferred to the eternal, transcendental abode of the Lord. Thus hearers are benefited both ultimately and for as long as they are in the material world. That is the supreme, sublime result of engaging in devotional service. The beginning of devotional service is to spare some time and listen to *Śrīmad-Bhāgavatam* from the right source. Lord Caitanya Mahāprabhu also recommended five items of devotional service, namely to serve the devotees of the Lord, to chant Hare Kṛṣṇa, to hear *Śrīmad-Bhāgavatam,* to worship the Deity of the Lord and to live in a place of pilgrimage. Just performing these five activities can deliver one from the miserable condition of material life.

Thus end the Bhaktivedanta purports of the Third Canto, Nineteenth Chapter, of the Śrīmad-Bhāgavatam, *entitled "The Killing of the Demon Hiraṇyākṣa."*

CHAPTER TWENTY

Conversation Between Maitreya and Vidura

TEXT 1

शौनक उवाच
महीं प्रतिष्ठामध्यस्य सौते स्वायम्भुवो मनुः ।
कान्यन्वतिष्ठद् द्वाराणि मार्गायावरजन्मनाम् ॥ १ ॥

śaunaka uvāca
mahīṁ pratiṣṭhām adhyasya
saute svāyambhuvo manuḥ
kāny anvatiṣṭhad dvārāṇi
mārgāyāvara-janmanām

śaunakaḥ—Śaunaka; *uvāca*—said; *mahīm*—the earth; *pratiṣṭhām*—situated; *adhyasya*—having secured; *saute*—O Sūta Gosvāmī; *svāyambhuvaḥ*—Svāyambhuva; *manuḥ*—Manu; *kāni*—what; *anvatiṣṭhat*—performed; *dvārāṇi*—ways; *mārgāya*—to get out; *avara*—later; *janmanām*—of those to be born.

TRANSLATION

Śrī Śaunaka inquired: O Sūta Gosvāmī, after the earth was again situated in its orbit, what did Svāyambhuva Manu do to show the path of liberation to persons who were to take birth later on?

PURPORT

The appearance of the Lord as the first boar incarnation occurred during the time of Svāyambhuva Manu, whereas the present age is in the period of Vaivasvata Manu. Each Manu's period lasts seventy-two times the cycle of four ages, and one cycle of ages equals 4,320,000 solar years. Thus 4,320,000 × 72 solar years is the reign of one Manu. In each Manu's period there are many changes in many ways, and there are fourteen Manus within one day of Brahmā. It is understood here that Manu creates scriptural regulations for the salvation of the conditioned souls, who come to the material world for material enjoyment. The Lord is so kind that any soul who wants to enjoy in this material world is given full facility for enjoyment, and at the same time he is shown the path of salvation. Śaunaka Ṛṣi, therefore, inquired from Sūta Gosvāmī: "What did Svāyambhuva Manu do after the reinstatement of the earth in its orbital situation?"

TEXT 2

क्षत्ता महाभागवतः कृष्णस्यैकान्तिकः सुहृत् ।
यस्तत्याजाग्रजं कृष्णे सापत्यमघवानिति ॥ २ ॥

kṣattā mahā-bhāgavataḥ
kṛṣṇasyaikāntikaḥ suhṛt
yas tatyājāgrajaṁ kṛṣṇe
sāpatyam aghavān iti

kṣattā—Vidura; *mahā-bhāgavataḥ*—a great devotee of the Lord; *kṛṣṇasya*—of Lord Kṛṣṇa; *ekāntikaḥ*—unalloyed devotee; *suhṛt*—intimate friend; *yaḥ*—he who; *tatyāja*—abandoned; *agra-jam*—his elder brother (King Dhṛtarāṣṭra); *kṛṣṇe*—toward Kṛṣṇa; *sa-apatyam*—along with his one hundred sons; *agha-vān*—offender; *iti*—thus.

TRANSLATION

Śaunaka Ṛṣi inquired about Vidura, who was a great devotee and friend of Lord Kṛṣṇa and who gave up the company of his elder brother because the latter, along with his sons, played tricks against the desires of the Lord.

PURPORT

The incident referred to here is that Vidura left the protection of his elder brother Dhṛtarāṣṭra, went traveling everywhere to sacred places and met Maitreya at Hardwar. Śaunaka Ṛṣi here inquires about the topics of the conversation between Maitreya Ṛṣi and Vidura. Vidura's qualification was that he was not only a friend of the Lord but also a great devotee. When Kṛṣṇa tried to stop the war and mitigate the misunderstanding between the cousin-brothers, they refused to accept His counsel; therefore Kṣattā, or Vidura, was unsatisfied with them, and he left the palace. As a devotee, Vidura showed by example that anywhere that Kṛṣṇa is not honored is a place unfit for human habitation. A devotee may be tolerant regarding his own interests, but he should not be tolerant when there is misbehavior toward the Lord or the Lord's devotee. Here the word *aghavān* is very significant, for it indicates that the Kauravas, Dhṛtarāṣṭra's sons, lost the war because of being sinful in disobeying the instructions of Kṛṣṇa.

TEXT 3

द्वैपायनादनवरो महित्वे तस्य देहजः ।
सर्वात्मना श्रितः कृष्णं तत्परांश्चाप्यनुव्रतः ॥ ३ ॥

dvaipāyanād anavaro
mahitve tasya dehajaḥ
sarvātmanā śritaḥ kṛṣṇaṁ
tat-parāṁś cāpy anuvratah

dvaipāyanāt—from Vyāsadeva; *anavaraḥ*—in no way inferior; *mahitve*—in greatness; *tasya*—his (Vyāsa's); *deha-jaḥ*—born of his body; *sarva-ātmanā*—with all his heart; *śritaḥ*—took shelter; *kṛṣṇam*—Lord Kṛṣṇa; *tat-parān*—those devoted to Him; *ca*—and; *api*—also; *anuvrataḥ*—followed.

TRANSLATION

Vidura was born from the body of Vedavyāsa and was not less than he. Thus he accepted the lotus feet of Kṛṣṇa wholeheartedly and was attached to His devotees.

PURPORT

The history of Vidura is that he was born of a *śūdra* mother, but his seminal father was Vyāsadeva; thus he was not less than Vyāsadeva in any respect. Since he was born of a great father, who was supposed to be an incarnation of Nārāyaṇa and who composed all the Vedic literatures, Vidura was also a great personality. He accepted Kṛṣṇa as his worshipable Lord and followed His instructions wholeheartedly.

TEXT 4

किमन्वपृच्छन्मैत्रेयं विरजास्तीर्थसेवया ।
उपगम्य कुशावर्त आसीनं तत्त्ववित्तमम् ॥ ४ ॥

kim anvapṛcchan maitreyaṁ
virajās tīrtha-sevayā
upagamya kuśāvarta
āsīnaṁ tattva-vittamam

kim—what; *anvapṛcchat*—inquired; *maitreyam*—from the sage Maitreya; *virajāḥ*—Vidura, who was without material contamination; *tīrtha-sevayā*—by visiting sacred places; *upagamya*—having met; *kuśāvarte*—at Kuśāvarta (Haridvāra, or Hardwar); *āsīnam*—who was abiding; *tattva-vit-tamam*—the foremost knower of the science of spiritual life.

TRANSLATION

Vidura was purified of all passion by wandering in sacred places, and at last he reached Hardwar, where he met the great sage who knew the science of spiritual life, and he inquired from him. Śaunaka Ṛṣi therefore asked: What more did Vidura inquire from Maitreya?

PURPORT

Here the words *virajās tīrtha-sevayā* refer to Vidura, who was completely cleansed of all contamination by traveling to places of pilgrimage. In India there are hundreds of sacred places of pilgrimage, of which Prayāga, Hardwar, Vṛndāvana and Rāmeśvaram are considered principal. After leaving his home, which was full of politics and diplomacy, Vidura wanted to purify himself by traveling to all the sacred places, which are so situated that anyone who goes there automatically becomes purified. This is especially true in Vṛndāvana; any person may go there, and even if he is sinful he will at once contact an atmosphere of spiritual life and will automatically chant the names of Kṛṣṇa and Rādhā. That we have actually seen and experienced. It is recommended in the *śāstras* that after retiring from active life and accepting the *vānaprastha* (retired) order, one should travel everywhere to places of pilgrimage in order to purify himself. Vidura completely discharged this duty, and at last he reached Kuśāvarta, or Hardwar, where the sage Maitreya was sitting.

Another significant point is that one must go to sacred places not only to take bath there but to search out great sages like Maitreya and take instructions from them. If one does not do so, his traveling to places of pilgrimage is simply a waste of time. Narottama dāsa Ṭhākura, a great *ācārya* of the Vaiṣṇava sect, has, for the present, forbidden us to go to such places of pilgrimage because in this age, the times having so changed, a sincere person may have a different impression on seeing the behavior of the present residents of the pilgrimage sites. He has recommended that instead of taking the trouble to travel to such places, one should concentrate his mind on Govinda, and that will help him. Of course, to concentrate one's mind on Govinda in any place is a path meant for those who are the most spiritually advanced; it is not for ordinary persons. Ordinary persons may still derive benefit from traveling to holy places like Prayāga, Mathurā, Vṛndāvana and Hardwar.

It is recommended in this verse that one find a person who knows the science of God, or a *tattva-vit*. *Tattva-vit* means "one who knows the Absolute Truth." There are many pseudotranscendentalists, even at places of pilgrimage. Such men are always present, and one has to be intelligent enough to find the actual person to be consulted;

then one's attempt to progress by traveling to different holy places will be successful. One has to be freed from all contamination, and at the same time he has to find a person who knows the science of Kṛṣṇa. Kṛṣṇa helps a sincere person; as stated in the *Caitanya-caritāmṛta, guru-kṛṣṇa-prasāde:* by the mercy of the spiritual master and Kṛṣṇa, one attains the path of salvation, devotional service. If one sincerely searches for spiritual salvation, then Kṛṣṇa, being situated in everyone's heart, gives him the intelligence to find a suitable spiritual master. By the grace of a spiritual master like Maitreya, one gets the proper instruction and advances in his spiritual life.

TEXT 5

तयोः संवदतोः सूत प्रवृत्ता ह्यमलाः कथाः ।
आपो गाङ्गा इवाघघ्नीर्हरेः पादाम्बुजाश्रयाः ॥ ५ ॥

tayoḥ saṁvadatoḥ sūta
pravṛttā hy amalāḥ kathāḥ
āpo gāṅgā ivāgha-ghnīr
hareḥ pādāmbujāśrayāḥ

tayoḥ—while the two (Maitreya and Vidura); *saṁvadatoḥ*—were conversing; *sūta*—O Sūta; *pravṛttāḥ*—arose; *hi*—certainly; *amalāḥ*—spotless; *kathāḥ*—narrations; *āpaḥ*—waters; *gāṅgāḥ*—of the River Ganges; *iva*—like; *agha-ghnīḥ*—vanquishing all sins; *hareḥ*—of the Lord; *pāda-ambuja*—the lotus feet; *āśrayāḥ*—taking shelter.

TRANSLATION

Śaunaka inquired about the conversation between Vidura and Maitreya: There must have been many narrations of the spotless pastimes of the Lord. The hearing of such narrations is exactly like bathing in the water of the Ganges, for it can free one from all sinful reactions.

PURPORT

The water of the Ganges is purified because it pours forth from the lotus feet of the Lord. Similarly, *Bhagavad-gītā* is as good as the water of the Ganges because it is spoken from the mouth of the Supreme Lord. So it is with any topic on the pastimes of the Lord or the characteristics of His transcendental activities. The Lord is absolute; there is no difference between His words, His perspiration or His pastimes. The water of the Ganges, the narrations of His pastimes and the words spoken by Him are all on the absolute platform, and thus taking shelter of any one of them is equally good. Śrīla

Rūpa Gosvāmī has enunciated that anything in relationship with Kṛṣṇa is on the transcendental platform. If we can dovetail all our activities in relationship with Kṛṣṇa, then we do not stand on the material platform, but always on the spiritual platform.

TEXT 6

ता नः कीर्तय भद्रं ते कीर्तन्योदारकर्मणः ।
रसज्ञः को नु तृप्येत हरिलीलामृतं पिबन् ॥ ६ ॥

tā naḥ kīrtaya bhadraṁ te
kīrtanyodāra-karmaṇaḥ
rasajñaḥ ko nu tṛpyeta
hari-līlāmṛtaṁ piban

tāḥ—those talks; *naḥ*—to us; *kīrtaya*—narrate; *bhadram te*—may all good come unto you; *kīrtanya*—should be chanted; *udāra*—liberal; *karmaṇaḥ*—activities; *rasa-jñaḥ*—a devotee who can appreciate mellow tastes; *kaḥ*—who; *nu*—indeed; *tṛpyeta*—would feel satisfied; *hari-līlā-amṛtam*—the nectar of the pastimes of the Lord; *piban*—drinking.

TRANSLATION

O Sūta Gosvāmī, all good fortune to you! Please narrate the activities of the Lord, which are all magnanimous and worth glorifying. What sort of devotee can be satiated by hearing the nectarean pastimes of the Lord?

PURPORT

The narration of the pastimes of the Lord, which are always enacted on the transcendental platform, should be received with all respect by devotees. Those who are actually on the transcendental platform are never satiated by hearing the continuous narration of the pastimes of the Lord. For example, if any self-realized soul reads from *Bhagavad-gītā,* he will never feel satiated. The narrations of *Bhagavad-gītā* and *Śrīmad-Bhāgavatam* may be read thousands and thousands of times, and still, without fail, new aspects of the subject matter will be relished by the devotee.

TEXT 7

एवमुग्रश्रवाः पृष्ट ऋषिभिर्नैमिषायनैः ।
भगवत्यर्पिताध्यात्मस्तानाह श्रूयतामिति ॥ ७ ॥

evam ugraśravāḥ pṛṣṭa
ṛṣibhir naimiṣāyanaiḥ

bhagavaty arpitādhyātmas
tān āha śrūyatām iti

evam—thus; *ugraśravāḥ*—Sūta Gosvāmī; *pṛṣṭaḥ*—being asked; *ṛṣibhiḥ*—by the sages; *naimiṣa-ayanaiḥ*—who were assembled in the forest of Naimiṣa; *bhagavati*—unto the Lord; *arpita*—dedicated; *adhyātmaḥ*—his mind; *tān*—to them; *āha*—said; *śrūyatām*—just hear; *iti*—thus.

TRANSLATION

On being asked to speak by the great sages of Naimiṣāraṇya, the son of Romaharṣaṇa, Sūta Gosvāmī, whose mind was absorbed in the transcendental pastimes of the Lord, said: Please hear what I shall now speak.

TEXT 8

सूत उवाच
हरेर्धृतक्रोडतनोः स्वमायया
निशम्य गोरुद्धरणं रसातलात् ।
लीलां हिरण्याक्षमवज्ञया हतं
सञ्जातहर्षो मुनिमाह भारतः ॥ ८ ॥

sūta uvāca
harer dhṛta-kroḍa-tanoḥ sva-māyayā
niśamya gor uddharaṇaṁ rasātalāt
līlāṁ hiraṇyākṣam avajñayā hataṁ
sañjāta-harṣo munim āha bhārataḥ

sūtaḥ uvāca—Sūta said; *hareḥ*—of the Lord; *dhṛta*—who had assumed; *kroḍa*—of a boar; *tanoḥ*—body; *sva-māyayā*—by His divine potency; *niśamya*—having heard; *goḥ*—of the earth; *uddharaṇam*—uplifting; *rasātalāt*—from the bottom of the ocean; *līlām*—sport; *hiraṇyākṣam*—the demon Hiraṇyākṣa; *avajñayā*—neglectfully; *hatam*—killed; *sañjāta-harṣaḥ*—being overjoyed; *munim*—to the sage (Maitreya); *āha*—said; *bhārataḥ*—Vidura.

TRANSLATION

Sūta Gosvāmī continued: Vidura, the descendant of Bharata, was delighted to hear the story of the Lord, who, having assumed by His own divine potency the form of a boar, had enacted the sport of lifting the earth from the bottom of the ocean and indifferently killing the demon Hiraṇyākṣa. Vidura then spoke to the sage as follows.

PURPORT

It is stated here that the Lord assumed the form of a boar by His own potency. His form is not actually the form of a conditioned soul. A conditioned soul is forced to accept a particular type of body by the higher authority of material laws, but here it is clearly said that the Lord was not forced to accept the form of a boar by the external power. In *Bhagavad-gītā* the same fact is confirmed; when the Lord descends to this earth, He assumes a form by His own internal potency. The form of the Lord, therefore, can never consist of material energy. The Māyāvāda version that when Brahman assumes a form the form is accepted from *māyā* is not acceptable, because although *māyā* is superior to the conditioned soul, she is not superior to the Supreme Personality of Godhead; she is under the control of the Supreme Godhead, as confirmed in *Bhagavad-gītā. Māyā* is under His superintendence; *māyā* cannot overcome the Lord. The Māyāvāda idea that the living entity is the Supreme Absolute Truth but has become covered by *māyā* is invalid, because *māyā* cannot be so great that it can cover the Supreme. The covering capacity can be employed on the part and parcel of Brahman, not on the Supreme Brahman.

TEXT 9

विदुर उवाच

प्रजापतिपतिः सृष्ट्वा प्रजासर्गे प्रजापतीन् ।
किमारभत मे ब्रह्मन् प्रब्रूह्यव्यक्तमार्गवित् ॥ ९ ॥

vidura uvaca
prajāpati-patiḥ sṛṣṭvā
prajā-sarge prajāpatīn
kim ārabhata me brahman
prabrūhy avyakta-mārga-vit

viduraḥ uvāca—Vidura said; *prajāpati-patiḥ*—Lord Brahmā; *sṛṣṭvā*—after creating; *prajā-sarge*—for the purpose of creating living beings; *prajāpatīn*—the Prajāpatis; *kim*—what; *ārabhata*—started; *me*—to me; *brahman*—O holy sage; *prabrūhi*—tell; *avyakta-mārga-vit*—knower of that which we do not know.

TRANSLATION

Vidura said: Since you know of matters inconceivable to us, tell me, O holy sage, what did Brahmā do to create living beings after evolving the Prajāpatis, the progenitors of living beings?

PURPORT

Significant here is the word *avyakta-mārga-vit,* "one who knows that which is beyond our perception." To know matters beyond one's perception, one has to learn from a superior authority in the line of disciplic succession. Just to know who is our father is beyond our perception. For that, the mother is the authority. Similarly, we have to understand everything beyond our perception from the authority who actually knows. The first *avyakta-mārga-vit,* or authority, is Brahmā, and the next authority in disciplic succession is Nārada. Maitreya Ṛṣi belongs to that disciplic succession, so he also is *avyakta-mārga-vit.* Anyone in the bona fide line of disciplic succession is *avyakta-mārga-vit,* a personality who knows that which is beyond ordinary perception.

TEXT 10

ये मरीच्यादयो विप्रा यस्तु स्वायम्भुवो मनुः ।
ते वै ब्रह्मण आदेशात्कथमेतदभावयन् ॥१०॥

ye marīcy-ādayo viprā
yas tu svāyambhuvo manuḥ
te vai brahmaṇa ādeśāt
katham etad abhāvayan

ye—those; *marīci-ādayaḥ*—great sages headed by Marīci; *viprāḥ*—*brāhmaṇas*; *yaḥ*—who; *tu*—indeed; *svāyambhuvaḥ manuḥ*—and Svāyambhuva Manu; *te*—they; *vai*—indeed; *brahmaṇaḥ*—of Lord Brahmā; *ādeśāt*—by the order; *katham*—how; *etat*—this universe; *abhāvayan*—evolved.

TRANSLATION

Vidura inquired: How did the Prajāpatis [such progenitors of living entities as Marīci and Svāyambhuva Manu] create according to the instruction of Brahmā, and how did they evolve this manifested universe?

TEXT 11

सद्वितीयाः किमसृजन् स्वतन्त्रा उत कर्मसु ।
आहोस्वित्संहताः सर्व इदं स्म समकल्पयन् ॥११॥

sa-dvitīyāḥ kim asṛjan
svatantrā uta karmasu

āho svit saṁhatāḥ sarva
idaṁ sma samakalpayan

sa-dvitīyāḥ—with their wives; *kim*—whether; *asṛjan*—created; *sva-tantrāḥ*—remaining independent; *uta*—or; *karmasu*—in their actions; *āho svit*—or else; *saṁhatāḥ*—jointly; *sarve*—all the Prajāpatis; *idam*—this; *sma samakalpayan*—produced.

TRANSLATION

Did they evolve the creation in conjunction with their respective wives, did they remain independent in their action, or did they all jointly produce it?

TEXT 12

मैत्रेय उवाच
दैवेन दुर्वितर्क्येण परेणानिमिषेण च ।
जातक्षोभाद्भगवतो महानासीद् गुणत्रयात् ॥१२॥

maitreya uvāca
daivena durvitarkyeṇa
pareṇānimiṣeṇa ca
jāta-kṣobhād bhagavato
mahān āsīd guṇa-trayāt

maitreyaḥ uvāca—Maitreya said; *daivena*—by superior management known as destiny; *durvitarkyeṇa*—beyond empiric speculation; *pareṇa*—by Mahā-viṣṇu; *animiṣeṇa*—by the potency of eternal time; *ca*—and; *jāta-kṣobhāt*—the equilibrium was agitated; *bhagavataḥ*—of the Personality of Godhead; *mahān*—the total material elements (the *mahat-tattva*); *āsīt*—were produced; *guṇa-trayāt*—from the three modes of nature.

TRANSLATION

Maitreya said: When the equilibrium of the combination of the three modes of nature was agitated by the unseen activity of the living entity, by Mahā-viṣṇu and by the force of time, the total material elements were produced.

PURPORT

The cause of the material creation is described here very lucidly. The first cause is *daiva*, or the destiny of the conditioned soul. The material creation exists for the conditioned soul who wanted to become a false lord for sense enjoyment. One cannot trace out the history of when the conditioned soul first desired to lord it over material nature, but in Vedic literature we always find that the material creation is meant for the sense enjoyment of the conditioned soul. There is a nice verse which says that the sum and substance of the conditioned soul's sense enjoyment is that as soon as he forgets his primary duty, to render service to the Lord, he creates an atmosphere of sense enjoyment, which is called *māyā;* that is the cause of material creation.

Another word used here is *durvitarkyeṇa.* No one can argue about when and how the conditioned soul became desirous of sense enjoyment, but the cause is there. Material nature is an atmosphere meant only for the sense enjoyment of the conditioned soul, and it is created by the Personality of Godhead. It is mentioned here that in the beginning of the creation the material nature, or *prakṛti,* is agitated by the Personality of Godhead, Viṣṇu. There are three Viṣṇus mentioned. One is Mahā-viṣṇu, another is Garbhodakaśāyī Viṣṇu, and the third is Kṣīrodakaśāyī Viṣṇu. The First Canto of *Śrīmad-Bhāgavatam* discusses all these three Viṣṇus, and here also it is confirmed that Viṣṇu is the cause of creation. From *Bhagavad-gītā* also we learn that *prakṛti* begins to work and is still working under Kṛṣṇa's, or Viṣṇu's, glance of superintendence, but the Supreme Personality of Godhead is unchangeable. One should not mistakenly think that because the creation emanates from the Supreme Personality of Godhead, He has therefore transformed into this material cosmic manifestation. He exists in His personal form always, but the cosmic manifestation takes place by His inconceivable potency. The workings of that energy are difficult to comprehend, but it is understood from Vedic literature that the conditioned soul creates his own destiny and is offered a particular body by the laws of nature under the superintendence of the Supreme Personality of Godhead, who always accompanies him as Paramatmā.

TEXT 13

रजःप्रधानान्महतस्त्रिलिङ्गो दैवचोदितात् ।
जातः ससर्ज भूतादिर्वियदादीनि पञ्चशः ॥१३॥

rajaḥ-pradhānān mahatas
tri-liṅgo daiva-coditāt
jātaḥ sasarja bhūtādir
viyad-ādīni pañcaśaḥ

rajaḥ-pradhānāt—in which the element of *rajas,* or passion, predominates; *mahataḥ*—from the *mahat-tattva; tri-liṅgaḥ*—of three kinds; *daiva-coditāt*—impelled by superior authority; *jātaḥ*—was born; *sasarja*—evolved; *bhūta-ādiḥ*—the false ego (origin of the material elements); *viyat*—the ether; *ādīni*—beginning with; *pañcaśaḥ*—in groups of five.

TRANSLATION

As impelled by the destiny of the jīva, the false ego, which is of three kinds, evolved from the mahat-tattva, in which the element of rajas predominates. From the ego, in turn, evolved many groups of five principles.

PURPORT

The primordial matter, or *prakṛti,* material nature, consisting of three modes, generates four groups of five. The first group is called elementary and consists of earth, water, fire, air and ether. The second group of five is called *tan-mātra,* referring to the subtle elements (sense objects): sound, touch, form, taste and smell. The third group is the five sense organs for acquiring knowledge: eyes, ears, nose, tongue and skin. The fourth group is the five working senses: speech, hands, feet, anus and genitals. Some say that there are five groups of five. One group is the sense objects, one is the five elements, one is the five sense organs for acquiring knowledge, another is the senses for working, and the fifth group is the five deities who control these divisions.

TEXT 14

तानि चैकैकशः स्रष्टुमसमर्थानि भौतिकम् ।
संहत्य दैवयोगेन हैममण्डमवासृजन् ॥१४॥

tāni caikaikaśaḥ sraṣṭum
asamarthāni bhautikam
saṁhatya daiva-yogena
haimam aṇḍam avāsṛjan

tāni—those elements; *ca*—and; *eka-ekaśaḥ*—separately; *sraṣṭum*—to produce; *asamarthāni*—unable; *bhautikam*—the material universe; *saṁhatya*—having combined; *daiva-yogena*—with the energy of the Supreme Lord; *haimam*—shining like gold; *aṇḍam*—globe; *avāsṛjan*—produced.

TRANSLATION

Separately unable to produce the material universe, they combined with the help of the energy of the Supreme Lord and were able to produce a shining egg.

TEXT 15

सोऽशयिष्टाब्धिसलिले आण्डकोशो निरात्मकः ।
साग्रं वै वर्षसाहस्रमन्ववात्सीत्तमीश्वरः ॥१५॥

so 'śayiṣṭābdhi-salile
āṇḍakośo nirātmakaḥ
sāgraṁ vai varṣa-sāhasram
anvavātsīt tam īśvaraḥ

saḥ—it; *aśayiṣṭa*—lay; *abdhi-salile*—on the waters of the Causal Ocean; *āṇḍa-kośaḥ*—egg; *nirātmakaḥ*—in an unconscious state; *sāgram*—a little more than; *vai*—in fact; *varṣa-sāhasram*—a thousand years; *anvavātsīt*—became situated; *tam*—in the egg; *īśvaraḥ*—the Lord.

TRANSLATION

For over one thousand years the shiny egg lay on the waters of the Causal Ocean in the lifeless state. Then the Lord entered it as Garbhodakaśāyī Viṣṇu.

PURPORT

From this verse it appears that all the universes are floating in the Causal Ocean.

TEXT 16

तस्य नाभेरभूत्पद्मं सहस्रार्कोरुदीधिति ।
सर्वजीवनिकायौको यत्र स्वयमभूत्स्वराट् ॥१६॥

tasya nābher abhut padmaṁ
sahasrārkoru-dīdhiti
sarva-jīvanikāyauko
yatra svayam abhūt svarāṭ

tasya—of the Lord; *nābheḥ*—from the navel; *abhūt*—sprouted up; *padmam*—a lotus; *sahasra-arka*—a thousand suns; *uru*—more; *dīdhiti*—with dazzling splendor; *sarva*—all; *jīva-nikāya*—resting place of conditioned souls; *okaḥ*—place; *yatra*—where; *svayam*—himself; *abhūt*—emanated; *sva-rāṭ*—the omnipotent (Lord Brahmā).

TRANSLATION

From the navel of the Personality of Godhead Garbhodakaśāyī Viṣṇu sprouted a lotus flower effulgent like a thousand blazing suns. This lotus flower is the reservoir of all conditioned souls, and the first living entity who came out of the lotus flower was the omnipotent Brahmā

PURPORT

It appears from this verse that the conditioned souls who rested within the body of the Personality of Godhead after the dissolution of the last creation came out in the sum total form of the lotus. This is called *hiraṇyagarbha.* The first living entity to come out was Lord Brahmā, who is independently able to create the rest of the manifested universe. The lotus is described here as effulgent as the glare of a thousand suns. This indicates that the living entities, as parts and parcels of the Supreme Lord, are also of the same quality, since the Lord also diffuses His bodily glare, known as *brahmajyotir.* The description of Vaikuṇṭhaloka, as stated in *Bhagavad-gītā* and other Vedic literatures, is confirmed herewith. In Vaikuṇṭha, the spiritual sky, there is no need of sunshine, moonshine, electricity or fire. Every planet there is self-effulgent like the sun.

TEXT 17

सोऽनुविष्टो भगवता यः शेते सलिलाशये ।
लोकसंस्थां यथापूर्वं निर्ममे संस्थया स्वया ॥१७॥

so 'nuviṣṭo bhagavatā
yaḥ śete salilāśaye
loka-saṁsthāṁ yathā pūrvaṁ
nirmame saṁsthayā svayā

saḥ—Lord Brahmā; *anuviṣṭaḥ*—was entered; *bhagavatā*—by the Lord; *yaḥ*—who; *śete*—sleeps; *salila-āśaye*—on the Garbhodaka Ocean; *loka-saṁsthām*—the universe; *yathā pūrvam*—as previously; *nirmame*—created; *saṁsthayā*—by intelligence; *svayā*—his own.

TRANSLATION

When that Supreme Personality of Godhead who is lying on the Garbhodaka Ocean entered the heart of Brahmā, Brahmā brought his intelligence to bear, and with the intelligence invoked he began to create the universe as it was before.

PURPORT

At a certain time, the Personality of Godhead, Kāraṇodakaśāyī Viṣṇu, lies in the Kāraṇa Ocean and produces many thousands of universes from His breathing; then He enters again into each and every universe as Garbhodakaśāyī Viṣṇu and fills up half of each universe with His own perspiration. The other half of the universe remains vacant, and that vacant region is called outer space. Then the lotus flower sprouts from His abdomen and produces the first living creature, Brahmā. Then again, as

Kṣīrodakaśāyī Viṣṇu, the Lord enters into the heart of every living entity, including Brahmā. This is confirmed in *Bhagavad-gītā,* Fifteenth Chapter. The Lord says, "I am seated in everyone's heart, and by Me are remembrance and forgetfulness made possible." As the witness of the activities of the individual entities, the Lord gives each one remembrance and intelligence to act according to his desire at the time he was annihilated in his last birth in the last millennium. This intelligence is invoked according to one's own capacity, or by the law of *karma.*

Brahmā was the first living entity, and he was empowered by the Supreme Lord to act in charge of the mode of passion; therefore, he was given the required intelligence, which is so powerful and extensive that he is almost independent of the control of the Supreme Personality of Godhead. Just as a highly posted manager is almost as independent as the owner of a firm, Brahmā is described here as independent because, as the Lord's representative to control the universe, he is almost as powerful and independent as the Supreme Personality of Godhead. The Lord, as the Supersoul within Brahmā, gave him the intelligence to create. The creative power, therefore, of every living entity is not his own; it is by the grace of the Lord that one can create. There are many scientists and great workers in this material world who have wonderful creative force, but they act and create only according to the direction of the Supreme Lord. A scientist may create many wonderful inventions by the direction of the Lord, but it is not possible for him to overcome the stringent laws of material nature by his intelligence, nor is it possible to acquire such intelligence from the Lord, for the Lord's supremacy would then be hampered. It is stated in this verse that Brahmā created the universe as it was before. This means that he created everything by the same name and form as in the previous cosmic manifestation.

TEXT 18

ससर्ज च्छाययाविद्यां पञ्चपर्वाणमग्रतः ।
तामिस्रमन्धतामिस्रं तमो मोहो महातमः ॥१८॥

sasarja cchāyayāvidyāṁ
pañca-parvāṇam agrataḥ
tāmisram andha-tāmisraṁ
tamo moho mahā-tamaḥ

sasarja—created; chāyayā—with his shadow; avidyām—ignorance; pañca-parvāṇam—five varieties; agrataḥ—first of all; tāmisram—tāmisra; andha-tāmisram-andha-tāmisra; tamaḥ-tamas; mohaḥ-moha; mahā-tamaḥ-mahā-tamas, or mahā-moha.

TRANSLATION

First of all, Brahmā created from his shadow the coverings of ignorance of the conditioned souls. They are five in number and are called tāmisra, andha-tāmisra, tamas, moha and mahā-moha.

PURPORT

The conditioned souls, or living entities who come to the material world to enjoy sense gratification, are covered in the beginning by five different conditions. The first condition is a covering of *tāmisra,* or anger. Constitutionally, each and every living entity has minute independence; it is misuse of that minute independence for the conditioned soul to think that he can also enjoy like the Supreme Lord or to think, "Why shall I not be a free enjoyer like the Supreme Lord?" This forgetfulness of his constitutional position is due to anger or envy. The living entity, being eternally a part-and-parcel servitor of the Supreme Lord, can never, by constitution, be an equal enjoyer with the Lord. When he forgets this, however, and tries to be one with Him, his condition is called *tāmisra.* Even in the field of spiritual realization, this *tāmisra* mentality of the living entity is hard to overcome. In trying to get out of the entanglement of material life, there are many who want to be one with the Supreme. Even in their transcendental activities, this lower-grade mentality of *tāmisra* continues.

Andha-tāmisra involves considering death to be the ultimate end. The atheists generally think that the body is the self and that everything is therefore ended with the end of the body. Thus they want to enjoy material life as far as possible during the existence of the body. Their theory is: "As long as you live, you should live prosperously. Never mind whether you commit all kinds of so-called sins. You must eat sumptuously. Beg, borrow and steal, and if you think that by stealing and borrowing you are being entangled in sinful activities for which you will have to pay, then just forget that misconception because after death everything is finished. No one is responsible for anything he does during his life." This atheistic conception of life is killing human civilization, for it is without knowledge of the continuation of eternal life.

This *andha-tāmisra* ignorance is due to *tamas.* The condition of not knowing anything about the spirit soul is called *tamas.* This material world is also generally called *tamas* because ninety-nine percent of its living entities are ignorant of their identity as soul. Almost everyone is thinking that he is this body; he has no information of the spirit soul. Guided by this misconception, one always thinks, "This is my body, and anything in relationship with this body is mine." For such misguided living entities, sex life is the background of material existence. Actually, the conditioned souls, in ignorance in this material world, are simply guided by sex life, and as soon as they get the opportunity for sex life, they become attached to so-called home, motherland, children, wealth and opulence. As these attachments increase, *moha,* or the illusion of the bodily concept of life, also increases. Thus the idea that "I am this body, and everything belonging to this body is mine" also increases, and as the whole world is put into *moha*, sectarian societies, families and nationalities are created, and they fight with one another. *Mahā-moha* means to be mad after material enjoyment. Especially in this age of Kali, everyone is overwhelmed by the madness to accumulate paraphernalia for material enjoyment. These definitions are very nicely given in *Viṣṇu Purāṇa*, wherein it is said:

tamo 'viveko mohaḥ syād
antaḥ-karaṇa-vibhramaḥ
mahā-mohas tu vijñeyo
grāmya-bhoga-sukhaiṣaṇā

maraṇaṁ hy andha-tāmisraṁ
tāmisraṁ krodha ucyate
avidyā pañca-parvaiṣā
prādurbhūtā mahātmanaḥ

TEXT 19

विससर्जात्मनः कायं नाभिनन्दंस्तमोमयम् ।
जगृहुर्यक्षरक्षांसि रात्रिं क्षुत्तृट्समुद्भवाम् ॥१९॥

visasarjātmanaḥ kāyaṁ
nābhinandaṁs tamomayam
jagṛhur yakṣa-rakṣāṁsi
rātriṁ kṣut-tṛṭ-samudbhavām

visasarja—threw off; *ātmanaḥ*—his own; *kāyam*—body; *na*—not; *abhinandan*—being pleased; *tamaḥ-mayam*—made of ignorance; *jagṛhuḥ*—took possession; *yakṣa-rakṣāṁsi*—the Yakṣas and Rākṣasas; *rātrim*—night; *kṣut*—hunger; *tṛṭ*—thirst; *samudbhavām*—the source.

TRANSLATION

Out of disgust, Brahmā threw off the body of ignorance, and taking this opportunity, Yakṣas and Rākṣasas sprang for possession of the body, which continued to exist in the form of night. Night is the source of hunger and thirst.

TEXT 20

क्षुत्तृड्भ्यामुपसृष्टास्ते तं जग्धुमभिदुद्रुवुः ।
मा रक्षतैनं जक्षध्वमित्यूचुः क्षुत्तृडर्दिताः ॥२०॥

kṣut-tṛḍbhyām upasṛṣṭās te
taṁ jagdhum abhidudruvuḥ
mā rakṣatainaṁ jakṣadhvam
ity ūcuḥ kṣut-tṛd-arditāḥ

kṣut-tṛḍbhyām—by hunger and thirst; *upasṛṣṭāḥ*—were overcome; *te*—the demons (Yakṣas and Rākṣasas); *tam*—Lord Brahmā; *jagdhum*—to eat; *abhidudruvuḥ*—ran toward; *mā*—do not; *rakṣata*—spare; *enam*—him; *jakṣadhvam*—eat; *iti*—thus; *ūcuḥ*—said; *kṣut-tṛṭ-arditāḥ*—afflicted by hunger and thirst.

TRANSLATION

Overpowered by hunger and thirst, they ran to devour Brahmā from all sides and cried, "Spare him not! Eat him up!"

PURPORT

The representatives of the Yakṣas and Rākṣasas still exist in some countries of the world. It is understood that such uncivilized men take pleasure in killing their own grandfathers and holding a "love feast" by roasting the bodies.

TEXT 21

देवस्तानाह संविग्नो मा मां जक्षत रक्षत ।
अहो मे यक्षरक्षांसि प्रजा यूयं बभूविथ ॥२१॥

devas tān āha saṁvigno
mā māṁ jakṣata rakṣata
aho me yakṣa-rakṣāṁsi
prajā yūyaṁ babhūvitha

devaḥ—Lord Brahmā; *tān*—to them; *āha*—said; *saṁvignaḥ*—being anxious; *mā*—do not; *mām*—me; *jakṣata*—eat; *rakṣata*—protect; *aho*—oh; *me*—my; *yakṣa-rakṣāṁsi*—O Yakṣas and Rākṣasas; *prajāḥ*—sons; *yūyam*—you; *babhūvitha*—were born.

TRANSLATION

Brahmā, the head of the demigods, full of anxiety, asked them, "Do not eat me, but protect me. You are born from me and have become my sons. Therefore you are Yakṣas and Rākṣasas."

PURPORT

The demons who were born from the body of Brahmā were called Yakṣas and Rākṣasas because some of them cried that Brahmā should be eaten and the others cried that he should not be protected. The ones who said that he should be eaten were called Yakṣas, and the ones who said that he should not be protected became Rākṣasas, man-eaters. The two, Yakṣas and Rākṣasas, are the original creation by Brahmā and are represented even until today in the uncivilized men who are scattered all over the universe. They are born of the mode of ignorance, and therefore, because of their behavior, they are called Rākṣasas, or man-eaters.

TEXT 22

देवताः प्रभया या या दीव्यन् प्रमुखतोऽसृजत् ।
ते अहार्षुर्देवयन्तो विसृष्टां तां प्रभामहः ॥२२॥

devatāḥ prabhayā yā yā
dīvyan pramukhato 'sṛjat
te ahārṣur devayanto
visṛṣṭāṁ tāṁ prabhām ahaḥ

devatāḥ—the demigods; *prabhayā*—with the glory of light; *yāḥ yāḥ*—those who; *dīvyan*—shining; *pramukhataḥ*—chiefly; *asṛjat*—created; *te*—they; *ahārṣuḥ*—took possession of; *devayantaḥ*—being active; *visṛṣṭām*—separated; *tām*—that; *prabhām*—effulgent form; *ahaḥ*—daytime.

TRANSLATION

He then created the chief demigods, who were shining with the glory of goodness. He dropped before them the effulgent form of daytime, and the demigods sportingly took possession of it.

PURPORT

Demons were born from the creation of night, and the demigods were born from the creation of day. In other words, demons like the Yakṣas and Rākṣasas are born of the quality of ignorance, and demigods are born of the quality of goodness.

TEXT 23

देवोऽदेवाञ्जघनतः सृजति स्मातिलोलुपान् ।
त एनं लोलुपतया मैथुनायाभिपेदिरे ॥२३॥

devo 'devāñ jaghanataḥ
sṛjati smātilolupān
ta enaṁ lolupatayā
maithunāyābhipedire

devaḥ—Lord Brahmā; *adevān*—demons; *jaghanataḥ*—from his buttocks; *sṛjati sma*—gave birth; *ati-lolupān*—excessively fond of sex; *te*—they; *enam*—Lord Brahmā; *lolupatayā*—with lust; *maithunāya*—for copulation; *abhipedire*—approached.

TRANSLATION

Lord Brahmā then gave birth to the demons from his buttocks, and they were very fond of sex. Because they were too lustful, they approached him for copulation.

PURPORT

Sex life is the background of material existence. Here also it is repeated that demons are very fond of sex life. The more one is free from the desires for sex, the more he is promoted to the level of the demigods; the more one is inclined to enjoy sex, the more he is degraded to the level of demoniac life.

TEXT 24

ततो हसन् स भगवानसुरैर्निरपत्रपैः ।
अन्वीयमानस्तरसा क्रुद्धो भीतः परापतत् ॥२४॥

tato hasan sa bhagavān
asurair nirapatrapaiḥ
anvīyamānas tarasā
kruddho bhītaḥ parāpatat

tataḥ—then; *hasan*—laughing; *saḥ bhagavān*—the worshipful Lord Brahmā; *asuraiḥ*—by the demons; *nirapatrapaiḥ*—shameless; *anvīyamānaḥ*—being followed; *tarasā*—in great haste; *kruddhaḥ*—angry; *bhītaḥ*—being afraid; *parāpatat*—ran away.

TRANSLATION

The worshipful Brahmā first laughed at their stupidity, but finding the shameless asuras close upon him, he grew indignant and ran in great haste out of fear.

PURPORT

Sexually inclined demons have no respect even for their father, and the best policy for a saintly father like Brahmā is to leave such demoniac sons.

TEXT 25

स उपव्रज्य वरदं प्रपन्नार्तिहरं हरिम् ।
अनुग्रहाय भक्तानामनुरूपात्मदर्शनम् ॥२५॥

sa upavrajya varadaṁ
prapannārti-haraṁ harim
anugrahāya bhaktānām
anurūpātma-darśanam

saḥ—Lord Brahmā; *upavrajya*—approaching; *vara-dam*—the bestower of all boons; *prapanna*—of those taking shelter at His lotus feet; *ārti*—distress; *haram*—who dispels; *harim*—Lord Śrī Hari; *anugrahāya*—for showing mercy; *bhaktānām*—to His devotees; *anurūpa*—in suitable forms; *ātma-darśanam*—who manifests Himself.

TRANSLATION

He approached the Personality of Godhead, who bestows all boons and who dispels the agony of His devotees and of those who take shelter of His lotus feet. He manifests His innumerable transcendental forms for the satisfaction of His devotees.

PURPORT

Here the words *bhaktānām anurūpātma-darśanam* mean that the Personality of Godhead manifests His multiforms according to the desires of the devotees. For example, Hanumānjī (Vajrāṅgajī) wanted to see the form of the Lord as the Personality of Godhead Rāmacandra, whereas other Vaiṣṇavas want to see the form of Rādhā-Kṛṣṇa, and still other devotees want to see the Lord in the form of Lakṣmī-Nārāyaṇa. The Māyāvādī philosophers think that although all these forms are assumed by the Lord just as the devotees desire to see Him, actually He is impersonal. From *Brahma-saṁhitā,* however, we can understand that this is not so, for the Lord has multiforms. It is said in the *Brahma-saṁhitā, advaitam acyutam.* The Lord does not appear before the devotee because of the devotee's imagination. *Brahma-saṁhitā* further explains that the Lord has innumerable forms: *rāmādi-mūrtiṣu kalā-niyamena tiṣṭhan.* He exists in millions and millions of forms. There are 8,400,000 spieces of living entities, but the incarnations of the Supreme Lord are innumerable. In the *Bhāgavatam* it is stated that as the waves in the sea cannot be counted but appear and disappear continually, the incarnations and forms of the Lord are innumerable. A devotee is attached to a particular form, and it is that form which he worships. We have just described the first appearance of the boar within this universe. There are innumerable universes, and somewhere or other the boar form is now existing. All the forms of the Lord are eternal. It is the devotee's inclination to worship a particular form, and he engages in devotional service to that form. In a verse in the *Rāmāyaṇa,* Hanumān, the great devotee of Rāma, said, "I know that there is no difference between the Sītā-Rāma and Lakṣmī-Nārāyaṇa forms of the Supreme Personality of Godhead, but nevertheless, the form of Rāma and Sītā has absorbed my affection and love. Therefore I want to see the Lord in the forms of Rāma and Sītā." Similarly, the Gauḍīya Vaiṣṇava loves the forms of Rādhā and Kṛṣṇa, and Kṛṣṇa and Rukmiṇī at Dvārakā. The words *bhaktānām anurūpātma-darśanam* mean that the Lord is always pleased to favor the devotee in the particular form in which the devotee wants to worship and render service unto Him. In this verse it is stated that Brahmā approached Hari, the Supreme Personality of Godhead. This form of the Lord is Kṣīrodakaśāyī Viṣṇu. Whenever there is some trouble and Brahmā has to approach the Lord, he can approach Kṣīrodakaśāyī Viṣṇu, and it is the grace of the Lord that whenever Brahmā approaches about disturbances in the universe, the Lord gives him relief in so many ways.

TEXT 26

पाहि मां परमात्मंस्ते प्रेषणेनासृजं प्रजाः ।
ता इमा यभितुं पापा उपाक्रामन्ति मां प्रभो ॥२६॥

pāhi māṁ paramātmaṁs te
preṣaṇenāsṛjaṁ prajāḥ
tā imā yabhituṁ pāpā
upākrāmanti māṁ prabho

pāhi—protect; *mām*—me; *parama-ātman*—O Supreme Lord; *te*—Your; *preṣaṇena*—by order; *asṛjam*—I created; *prajāḥ*—living beings; *tāḥ imāḥ*—those very persons; *yabhitum*—to have sex; *pāpāḥ*—sinful beings; *upākrāmanti*—are approaching; *mām*—me; *prabho*—O Lord.

TRANSLATION

Lord Brahmā, approaching the Lord, addressed Him thus: My Lord, please protect me from these sinful demons, who were created by me under Your order. They are infuriated by an appetite for sex and have come to attack me.

PURPORT

It appears here that the homosexual appetite of males for each other is created in this episode of the creation of the demons by Brahmā. In other words, the homosexual appetite of a man for another man is demoniac and is not for any sane male in the ordinary course of life.

TEXT 27

त्वमेकः किल लोकानां क्लिष्टानां क्लेशनाशनः ।
त्वमेकः क्लेशदस्तेषामनासन्नपदां तव ॥२७॥

tvam ekaḥ kila lokānāṁ
kliṣṭānāṁ kleśa-nāśanaḥ
tvam ekaḥ kleśadas teṣām
anāsanna-padāṁ tava

tvam—You; *ekaḥ*—alone; *kila*—indeed; *lokānām*—of the people; *kliṣṭānām*—afflicted with miseries; *kleśa*—the distresses; *nāśanaḥ*—relieving; *tvam ekaḥ*—You alone; *kleśa-daḥ*—inflicting distress; *teṣām*—on those; *anāsanna*—not taken shelter; *padām*—feet; *tava*—Your.

TRANSLATION

My Lord, You are the only one capable of ending the affliction of the distressed and inflicting agony on those who never resort to Your feet.

PURPORT

The words *kleśadas teṣām anāsanna-padāṁ tava* indicate that the Lord has two concerns. The first is to give protection to persons who take shelter of His lotus feet, and the second is to give trouble to those who are always demoniac and who are inimical toward the Lord. *Māyā's* function is to give afflictions to the nondevotees. Here Brahmā said, "You are the protector of the surrendered souls; therefore I surrender unto Your lotus feet. Please give me protection from these demons."

TEXT 28

सोऽवधार्यास्य कार्पण्यं विविक्ताध्यात्मदर्शनः ।
विमुञ्चात्मतनुं घोरामित्युक्तो विमुमोच ह ॥२८॥

so 'vadhāryāsya kārpaṇyaṁ
viviktādhyātma-darśanaḥ

vimuñcātma-tanuṁ ghorām
ity ukto vimumoca ha

saḥ—the Supreme Lord, Hari; *avadhārya*—perceiving; *asya*—of Lord Brahmā; *kārpaṇyam*—the distress; *vivikta*—without a doubt; *adhyātma*—minds of others; *darśanaḥ*—one who can see; *vimuñca*—cast off; *ātma-tanum*—your body; *ghorām*—impure; *iti uktaḥ*—thus commanded; *vimumoca ha*—Lord Brahmā threw it off.

TRANSLATION

The Lord, who can distinctly see the minds of others, perceived Brahmā's distress and said to him: "Cast off this impure body of yours." Thus commanded by the Lord, Brahmā cast off his body.

PURPORT

The Lord is described here by the word *viviktādhyātma-darśanaḥ.* If anyone can completely perceive another's distress without doubt, it is the Lord Himself. If someone is in distress and wants to get relief from his friend, sometimes it so happens that his friend does not appreciate the volume of distress he is suffering. But for the Supreme Lord it is not difficult. The Supreme Lord, as Paramātmā, is sitting within the heart of every living entity, and He directly perceives the exact causes of distress. In *Bhagavad-gītā* the Lord says, *sarvasya cāhaṁ hṛdi sanniviṣṭaḥ:* "I am sitting in everyone's heart, and because of Me one's remembrance and forgetfulness occur." Thus whenever one fully surrenders unto the Supreme Lord, one finds that He is sitting within one's heart. He can give us direction how to get out of dangers or how to approach Him in devotional service. The Lord, however, asked Brahmā to give up his present body because it had created the demoniac principle. According to Śrīdhara Svāmī, Brahmā's constant dropping of his body does not refer to his actually giving up his body. Rather, he suggests that Brahmā gave up a particular mentality. Mind is the subtle body of the living entity. We may sometimes be absorbed in some thought which is sinful, but if we give up the sinful thought, it may be said that we give up the body. Brahmā's mind was not in correct order when he created the demons. It must have been full of passion because the entire creation was passionate; therefore such passionate sons were born. It follows that any father and mother should also be careful while begetting children. The mental condition of a child depends upon the mental status of his parents at the time he is conceived. According to the Vedic system, therefore, the *garbhādhāna-saṁskāra,* or the ceremony for giving birth to a child, is observed. Before begetting a child, one has to sanctify his perplexed mind. When the parents engage their minds in the lotus feet of the Lord and in such a state the child is born, naturally good devotee children come; when the society is full of such good population, there is no trouble from demoniac mentalities.

TEXT 29

तां क्वणच्चरणाम्भोजां मदविह्वललोचनाम् ।
काञ्चीकलापविलसद्दुकूलच्छन्नरोधसम् ॥२९॥

tāṁ kvaṇac-caraṇāmbhojāṁ
mada-vihvala-locanām
kāñcī-kalāpa-vilasad-
dukūla-cchanna-rodhasam

tām—that body; *kvaṇat*—tinkling with ankle bells; *caraṇa-ambhojām*—with lotus feet; *mada*—intoxication; *vihvala*—overwhelmed; *locanām*—with eyes; *kāñcī-kalāpa*—with a girdle made of golden ornaments; *vilasat*—shining; *dukūla*—by fine cloth; *channa*—covered; *rodhasam*—having hips.

TRANSLATION

The body given up by Brahmā took the form of the evening twilight, when the day and night meet, a time which kindles passion. The asuras, who are passionate by nature, dominated as they are by the element of rajas, took it for a damsel, whose lotus feet resounded with the tinkling of anklets, whose eyes were wide with intoxication and whose hips were covered by fine cloth, over which shone a girdle.

PURPORT

As early morning is the period for spiritual cultivation, the beginning of evening is the period for passion. Demoniac men are generally very fond of sex enjoyment; therefore they very much appreciate the approach of evening. The demons took the approach of the evening twilight to be a beautiful woman, and they began to adore her in various ways. They imagined the twilight to be a very beautiful woman with tinkling bangles on her feet, a girdle on her hips, and beautiful breasts, and for their sexual satisfaction they imagined the appearance of this beautiful girl before them.

TEXT 30

अन्योन्यश्लेषयोत्तुङ्गनिरन्तरपयोधराम् ।
सुनासां सुद्विजां स्निग्धहासलीलावलोकनाम् ॥३०॥

anyonya-śleṣayottuṅga-
nirantara-payodharām
sunāsāṁ sudvijāṁ snigdha-
hāsa-līlāvalokanām

anyonya—to each other; *śleṣayā*—because of clinging; *uttuṅga*—raised; *nirantara*—without intervening space; *payaḥ-dharām*—breasts; *su-nāsām*—shapely nose; *su-dvijām*—beautiful teeth; *snigdha*—lovely; *hāsa*—smile; *līlā-avalokanām*—sportful glance.

TRANSLATION

Her breasts projected upward because of their clinging to each other, and they were too contiguous to admit any intervening space. She had a shapely nose and beautiful teeth; a lovely smile played on her lips, and she cast a sportful glance at the asuras.

TEXT 31

गूहन्तीं व्रीडयात्मानं नीलालकवरूथिनीम् ।
उपलभ्यासुरा धर्म सर्वे सम्मुमुहुः स्त्रियम् ॥३१॥

gūhantīṁ vrīḍayātmānaṁ
nīlālaka-varūthinīm
upalabhyāsurā dharma
sarve sammumuhuḥ striyam

gūhantīm—hiding; *vrīḍayā*—out of shyness; *ātmānam*—herself; *nīla*—dark; *alaka*—hair; *varūthinīm*—a bunch; *upalabhya*—upon imagining; *asurāḥ*—the demons; *dharma*—O Vidura; *sarve*—all; *sammumuhuḥ*—were captivated; *striyam*—woman.

TRANSLATION

Adorned with dark tresses, she hid herself, as it were, out of shyness. Upon seeing that girl, the asuras were all infatuated with an appetite for sex.

PURPORT

The difference between demons and demigods is that a beautiful woman very easily attracts the minds of demons, but she cannot attract the mind of a godly person. A godly person is full of knowledge, and a demoniac person is full of ignorance. Just as a child is attracted by a beautiful doll, similarly a demon, who is less intelligent and full of ignorance, is attracted by material beauty and an appetite for sex. The godly person knows that this nicely dressed and ornamented attraction of high breasts, high hips, beautiful nose and fair complexion is *māyā*. All the beauty a woman can display is only a combination of flesh and blood. Śrī Śaṅkarācārya has advised all persons not to be attracted by the interaction of flesh and blood; they should be attracted by the real beauty In spiritual life. The real beauty is Kṛṣṇa and Rādhā. One who is attracted by the beauty of Rādhā and Kṛṣṇa cannot be attracted by the false beauty of this material world. That is the difference between a demon and a godly person or devotee.

TEXT 32

अहो रूपमहो धैर्यमहो अस्या नवं वयः ।
मध्ये कामयमानानामकामेव विसर्पति ॥३२॥

aho rūpam aho dhairyam
aho asyā navaṁ vayaḥ
madhye kāmayamānānām
akāmeva visarpati

aho—oh; *rūpam*—what beauty; *aho*—oh; *dhairyam*—what self-control; *aho*—oh; *asyāḥ*—her; *navam*—budding; *vayaḥ*—youth; *madhye*—in the midst; *kāmayamānānām*—of those passionately longing for; *akāmā*—free from passion; *iva*—like; *visarpati*—walking with us.

TRANSLATION

The demons praised her: Oh, what a beauty! What rare self-control! What a budding youth! In the midst of us all, who are passionately longing for her, she is moving about like one absolutely free from passion.

TEXT 33

वितर्कयन्तो बहुधा तां सन्ध्यां प्रमदाकृतिम् ।
अभिसम्भाव्य विश्रम्भात्पर्यपृच्छन् कुमेधसः ॥३३॥

vitarkayanto bahudhā
tāṁ sandhyāṁ pramadākṛtim
abhisambhāvya viśrambhāt
paryapṛcchan kumedhasaḥ

vitarkayantaḥ—indulging in speculations; *bahudhā*—various kinds; *tām*—her; *sandhyām*—the evening twilight; *pramadā*—a young woman; *ākṛtim*—in the form of; *abhisambhāvya*—treating with great respect; *viśrambhāt*—fondly; *paryapṛcchan*—questioned; *ku-medhasaḥ*—wicked-minded.

TRANSLATION

Indulging in various speculations about the evening twilight, which appeared to them endowed with the form of a young woman, the wicked-minded asuras treated her with respect and fondly spoke to her as follows.

TEXT 34

कासि कस्यासि रम्भोरु को वार्थस्तेऽत्र भामिनि ।
रूपद्रविणपण्येन दुर्भगान्नो विबाधसे ॥३४॥

kāsi kasyāsi rambhoru
ko vārthas te 'tra bhāmini
rūpa-draviṇa-paṇyena
durbhagān no vibādhase

kā—who; *asi*—are you; *kasya*—belonging to whom; *asi*—are you; *rambhoru*—O pretty one; *kaḥ*—what; *vā*—or; *arthaḥ*—object; *te*—your; *atra*—here; *bhāmini*—O passionate lady; *rūpa*—beauty; *draviṇa*—priceless; *paṇyena*—with the commodity; *durbhagān*—unfortunate; *naḥ*—us; *vibādhase*—you tantalize.

TRANSLATION

Who are you, O pretty girl? Whose wife or daughter are you, and what can be the object of your appearing before us? Why do you tantalize us, unfortunate as we are, with the priceless commodity of your beauty?

PURPORT

The mentality of the demons in being enamored by the false beauty of this material world is expressed herein. The demoniac can pay any price for the skin beauty of this material world. They work very hard all day and night, but the purpose of their hard work is to enjoy sex life. Sometimes they misrepresent themselves as *karma-yogīs*, not knowing the meaning of the word *yoga*. *Yoga* means to link up with the Supreme Personality of Godhead, or to act in Kṛṣṇa consciousness. A person who works very hard, no matter in what occupation, and who offers the result of the work to the service of the Supreme Personality of Godhead, Kṛṣṇa, is called a *karma-yogī*.

TEXT 35

या वा काचित्त्वमबले दिष्ट्या सन्दर्शनं तव ।
उत्सुनोषीक्षमाणानां कन्दुकक्रीडया मनः ॥३५॥

yā vā kācit tvam abale
diṣṭyā sandarśanaṁ tava
utsunoṣīkṣamāṇānāṁ
kanduka-krīḍayā manaḥ

yā—whosoever; *vā*—or; *kācit*—anyone; *tvam*—you; *abale*—O beautiful girl; *diṣṭyā*—by fortune; *sandarśanam*—seeing; *tava*—of you; *utsunoṣi*—you agitate; *īkṣamāṇānām*—of the onlookers; *kanduka*—with a ball; *krīḍayā*—by play; *manaḥ*—the mind.

TRANSLATION

Whosoever you may be, O beautiful girl, we are fortunate in being able to see you. While playing with a ball, you have agitated the minds of all onlookers.

PURPORT

Demons arrange many kinds of performances to see the glaring beauty of a beautiful woman. Here it is stated that they saw the girl playing with a ball. Sometimes the demoniac arrange for so-called sports, like tennis, with the opposite sex. The purpose of such sporting is to see the bodily construction of the beautiful girl and enjoy a subtle sex mentality. This demoniac sex mentality of material enjoyment is sometimes encouraged by so-called *yogīs* who encourage the public to enjoy sex life in different varieties and at the same time advertise that if one meditates on a certain manufactured *mantra* one can become God within six months. The public wants to be cheated, and Kṛṣṇa therefore creates such cheaters to misrepresent and delude. These so-called *yogīs* are actually enjoyers of the world garbed as *yogīs*. *Bhagavad-gītā*, however, recommends that if one wants to enjoy life, then it cannot be with these gross senses. A patient is advised by the experienced physician to refrain from ordinary enjoyment while in the diseased condition. A diseased person cannot enjoy anything; he has to restrain his enjoyment in order to get rid of the disease. Similarly, our material condition is a diseased condition. If one wants to enjoy real sense enjoyment, then one must get free of the entanglement of material existence. In spiritual life we can enjoy sense enjoyment which has no end. The difference between material and spiritual enjoyment is that material enjoyment is limited. Even if a man engages in material sex enjoyment, he cannot enjoy it for long. But when the sex enjoyment is given up, then one can enter spiritual life, which is unending. In the *Bhāgavatam* (5.5.1) it is stated that *brahma-saukhya*, spiritual happiness, is *ananta*, unending. Foolish creatures are enamored by the beauty of matter and think that the enjoyment it offers is real, but actually that is not real enjoyment.

TEXT 36

नैकत्र ते जयति शालिनि पादपद्मं
घ्नन्त्या मुहुः करतलेन पततपतङ्गम् ।
मध्यं विषीदति बृहत्स्तनभारभीतं
शान्तेव दृष्टिरमला सुशिखासमूहः ॥३६॥

naikatra te jayati śālini pāda-padmaṁ
ghnantyā muhuḥ kara-talena patat-pataṅgam
madhyaṁ viṣīdati bṛhat-stana-bhāra-bhītaṁ
śānteva dṛṣṭir amalā suśikhā-samūhaḥ

na—not; *ekatra*—in one place; *te*—your; *jayati*—stay; *śālini*—O beautiful woman; *pāda-padmam*—lotus feet; *ghnantyāḥ*—striking; *muhuḥ*—again and again; *kara-talena*—by the palm of the hand; *patat*—bouncing; *pataṅgam*—the ball; *madhyam*—waist; *viṣīdati*—gets fatigued; *bṛhat*—full grown; *stana*—of your breasts; *bhāra*—by the weight; *bhītam*—oppressed; *śāntā iva*—as if fatigued; *dṛṣṭiḥ*—vision; *amalā*—clear; *su*—beautiful; *śikhā*—your hair; *samūhaḥ*—bunch.

TRANSLATION

O beautiful woman, when you strike the bouncing ball against the ground with your hand again and again, your lotus feet do not stay in one place. Oppressed by the weight of your full-grown breasts, your waist becomes fatigued, and your clear vision grows dull, as it were. Pray braid your comely hair.

PURPORT

The demons observed beautiful gestures in the woman's every step. Here they praise her full-grown breasts, her scattered hair and her movements in stepping forward and backward while playing with the ball. In every step they enjoy her womanly beauty, and while they enjoy her beauty their minds become agitated by sex desire. As moths at night surround a fire and are killed, so the demons become victims of the movements of the ball-like breasts of a beautiful woman. The scattered hair of a beautiful woman also afflicts the heart of a lusty demon.

TEXT 37

इति सायन्तनीं सन्ध्यामसुराः प्रमदायतीम् ।
प्रलोभयन्तीं जगृहुर्मत्वा मूढधियः स्त्रियम् ॥३७॥

iti sāyantanīṁ sandhyām
asurāḥ pramadāyatīm
pralobhayantīṁ jagṛhur
matvā mūḍha-dhiyaḥ striyam

iti—in this way; *sāyantanīm*—the evening; *sandhyām*—twilight; *asurāḥ*—the demons; *pramadāyatīm*—behaving like a wanton woman; *pralobhayantīm*—alluring; *jagṛhuḥ*—seized; *matvā*—thinking to be; *mūḍha-dhiyaḥ*—unintelligent; *striyam*—a woman.

TRANSLATION

The asuras, clouded in their understanding, took the evening twilight to be a beautiful woman showing herself in her alluring form, and they seized her.

PURPORT

The *asuras* are described here as *mūḍha-dhiyaḥ*, meaning that they are captivated by ignorance, just like the ass. The demons were captivated by the false, glaring beauty of this material form, and thus they embraced her.

TEXT 38

प्रहस्य भावगम्भीरं जिघ्रन्त्यात्मानमात्मना ।
कान्त्या ससर्ज भगवान् गन्धर्वाप्सरसां गणान् ॥३८॥

prahasya bhāva-gambhīraṁ
jighrantyātmānam ātmanā
kāntyā sasarja bhagavān
gandharvāpsarasāṁ gaṇān

prahasya—smiling; *bhāva-gambhīram*—with a deep purpose; *jighrantyā*—understanding; *ātmānam*—himself; *ātmanā*—by himself; *kāntyā*—by his loveliness; *sasarja*—created; *bhagavān*—the worshipful Lord Brahmā; *gandharva*—the celestial musicians; *apsarasām*—and of the heavenly dancing girls; *gaṇān*—the hosts of.

TRANSLATION

With a laugh full of deep significance, the worshipful Brahmā then evolved by his own loveliness, which seemed to enjoy itself by itself, the hosts of Gandharvas and Apsarās.

PURPORT

The musicians in the upper planetary systems are called Gandharvas, and the dancing girls are called Apsarās. After being attacked by the demons and evolving a form of a beautiful woman in the twilight, Brahmā next created Gandharvas and Apsarās. Music and dancing employed in sense gratification are to be accepted as demoniac, but the same music and dancing, when employed in glorifying the Supreme Lord as *kīrtana,* are transcendental, and they bring about a life completely fit for spiritual enjoyment.

TEXT 39

विससर्ज तनुं तां वै ज्योत्स्नां कान्तिमतीं प्रियाम् ।
त एव चाददुः प्रीत्या विश्वावसुपुरोगमाः ॥३९॥

visasarja tanuṁ tāṁ vai
jyotsnāṁ kāntimatīṁ priyām
ta eva cādaduḥ prītyā
viśvāvasu-purogamāḥ

visasarja—gave up; *tanum*—form; *tām*—that; *vai*—in fact; *jyotsnām*—moonlight; *kānti-matīm*—shining; *priyām*—beloved; *te*—the Gandharvas; *eva*—certainly; *ca*—and; *ādaduḥ*—took possession; *prītyā*—gladly; *viśvāvasu-puraḥ-gamāḥ*—headed by Viśvāvasu.

TRANSLATION

After that, Brahmā gave up that shining and beloved form of moonlight. Viśvāvasu and other Gandharvas gladly took possession of it.

TEXT 40

सृष्ट्वा भूतपिशाचांश्च भगवानात्मतन्द्रिणा ।
दिग्वाससो मुक्तकेशान् वीक्ष्य चामीलयद् दृशौ ॥४०॥

sṛṣṭvā bhūta-piśācāṁś ca
bhagavān ātma-tandriṇā
dig-vāsaso mukta-keśān
vīkṣya cāmīlayad dṛśau

sṛṣṭvā—having created; *bhūta*—ghosts; *piśācān*—fiends; *ca*—and; *bhagavān*—Lord Brahmā; *ātma*—his; *tandriṇā*—from laziness; *dik-vāsasaḥ*—naked; *mukta*—disheveled; *keśān*—hair; *vīkṣya*—seeing; *ca*—and; *amīlayat*—closed; *dṛśau*—two eyes.

TRANSLATION

The glorious Brahmā next evolved from his sloth the ghosts and fiends, but he closed his eyes when he saw them stand naked with their hair scattered.

PURPORT

Ghosts and mischievous hobgoblins are also the creation of Brahmā; they are not false. All of them are meant for putting the conditioned soul into various miseries. They are understood to be the creation of Brahmā under the direction of the Supreme Lord.

TEXT 41

जगृहुस्तद्विसृष्टां तां जृम्भणाख्यां तनुं प्रभोः ।
निद्रामिन्द्रियविक्लेदो यया भूतेषु दृश्यते ।
येनोच्छिष्टान्धर्षयन्ति तमुन्मादं प्रचक्षते ॥४१॥

jagṛhus tad-visṛṣṭāṁ tāṁ
jṛmbhaṇākhyāṁ tanuṁ prabhoḥ
nidrām indriya-vikledo
yayā bhūteṣu dṛśyate
yenocchiṣṭān dharṣayanti
tam unmādaṁ pracakṣate

jagṛhuḥ—took possession; *tat-visṛṣṭām*—thrown off by him; *tām*—that; *jṛmbhaṇa-ākhyām*—known as yawning; *tanum*—the body; *prabhoḥ*—of Lord Brahmā; *nidrām*—sleep; *indriya-vikledaḥ*—drooling; *yayā*—by which; *bhūteṣu*—among the living beings; *dṛśyate*—is observed; *yena*—by which; *ucchiṣṭān*—smeared with stool and urine; *dharṣayanti*—bewilder; *tam*—that; *unmādam*—madness; *pracakṣate*—is spoken of.

TRANSLATION

The ghosts and hobgoblins took possession of the body thrown off in the form of yawning by Brahmā, the creator of the living entities. This is also known as the sleep which causes drooling. The hobgoblins and ghosts attack men who are impure, and their attack is spoken of as insanity.

PURPORT

The disease of insanity or being haunted by ghosts takes place in an unclean state of existence. Here it is clearly stated that when a man is fast asleep and saliva flows from his mouth and he remains unclean, ghosts then take advantage of his unclean state and haunt his body. In other words, those who drool while sleeping are considered unclean and are subject to be haunted by ghosts or to go insane.

TEXT 42

ऊर्जस्वन्तं मन्यमान आत्मानं भगवानजः ।
साध्यान् गणान् पितृगणान् परोक्षेणासृजत्प्रभुः ॥४२॥

ūrjasvantaṁ manyamāna
ātmānaṁ bhagavān ajaḥ
sādhyān gaṇān pitṛ-gaṇān
parokṣeṇāsṛjat prabhuḥ

ūrjaḥ-vantam—full of energy; *manyamānaḥ*—recognizing; *ātmānam*—himself; *bhagavān*—the most worshipful; *ajaḥ*—Brahmā; *sādhyān*—the demigods; *gaṇān*—hosts; *pitṛ-gaṇān*—and the Pitās; *parokṣeṇa*—from his invisible form; *asṛjat*—created; *prabhuḥ*—the lord of beings.

TRANSLATION

Recognizing himself to be full of desire and energy, the worshipful Brahmā, the creator of the living entities, evolved from his own invisible form, from his navel, the hosts of Sādhyas and Pitās.

PURPORT

The Sādhyas and Pitās are invisible forms of departed souls, and they are also created by Brahmā.

TEXT 43

त आत्मसर्गं तं कायं पितरः प्रतिपेदिरे ।
साध्येभ्यश्च पितृभ्यश्च कवयो यद्वितन्वते ॥४३॥

ta ātma-sargaṁ taṁ kāyaṁ
pitaraḥ pratipedire
sādhyebhyaś ca pitṛbhyaś ca
kavayo yad vitanvate

te—they; *ātma-sargam*—source of their existence; *tam*—that; *kāyam*—body; *pitaraḥ*—the Pitās; *pratipedire*—accepted; *sādhyebhyaḥ*—to the Sādhyas; *ca*—and; *pitṛbhyaḥ*—to the Pitās; *ca*—also; *kavayaḥ*—those well versed in rituals; *yat*—through which; *vitanvate*—offer oblations.

TRANSLATION

The Pitās themselves took possession of the invisible body, the source of their existence. It is through the medium of this invisible body that those well versed in the rituals offer oblations to the Sādhyas and Pitās [in the form of their departed ancestors] on the occasion of śrāddha.

PURPORT

Śrāddha is a ritualistic performance observed by the followers of the *Vedas.* There is a yearly occasion of fifteen days when ritualistic religionists follow the principle of offering oblations to departed souls. Thus those fathers and ancestors who, by freaks of nature, might not have a gross body for material enjoyment can again gain such bodies due to the offering of *śrāddha* oblations by their descendants. The performance of *śrāddha,* or offering oblations with *prasāda,* is still current in India, especially at Gayā, where oblations are offered at the lotus feet of Viṣṇu in a celebrated temple. Because the Lord is thus pleased with the devotional service of the descendants, by His grace He liberates the condemned souls of forefathers who do not have gross bodies, and He favors them to again receive a gross body for development of spiritual advancement.

Unfortunately, by the influence of *māyā,* the conditioned soul employs the body he gets for sense gratification, forgetting that such an occupation may lead him to return to an invisible body. The devotee of the Lord, or one who is in Kṛṣṇa consciousness, however, does not need to perform such ritualistic ceremonies as *śrāddha* because he is always pleasing the Supreme Lord; therefore his fathers and ancestors who might have been in difficulty are automatically relieved. The vivid example is Prahlāda Mahārāja. Prahlāda Mahārāja requested Lord Nṛsiṁhadeva to deliver his sinful father, who had so many times offended the lotus feet of the Lord. The Lord replied that in a family where a Vaiṣṇava like Prahlāda is born, not only his father but his father's father and their fathers—up to the fourteenth father back—are all automatically delivered. The conclusion, therefore, is that Kṛṣṇa consciousness is the sum total of all good work for the family, for society and for all living entities. In the *Caitanya-caritāmṛta* the author says that a person fully conversant with Kṛṣṇa consciousness does not perform any rituals because he knows that simply by serving Kṛṣṇa in full Kṛṣṇa consciousness, all rituals are automatically performed.

TEXT 44

सिद्धान् विद्याधरांश्चैव तिरोधानेन सोऽसृजत् ।
तेभ्योऽददात्तमात्मानमन्तर्धानाख्यमद्भुतम् ॥४४॥

siddhān vidyādharāṁś caiva
tirodhānena so 'sṛjat
tebhyo 'dadāt tam ātmānam
antardhānākhyam adbhutam

siddhān—the Siddhas; *vidyādharān*—Vidyādharas; *ca eva*—and also; *tirodhānena*—by the faculty of remaining hidden from vision; *saḥ*—Lord Brahmā; *asṛjat*—created; *tebhyaḥ*—to them; *adadāt*—gave; *tam ātmānam*—that form of his; *antardhāna-ākhyam*—known as the Antardhāna; *adbhutam*—wonderful.

TRANSLATION

Then Lord Brahmā, by his ability to be hidden from vision, created the Siddhas and Vidyādharas and gave them that wonderful form of his known as the Antardhāna.

PURPORT

Antardhāna means that these living creatures can be perceived to be present, but they cannot be seen by vision.

TEXT 45

स किन्नरान् किम्पुरुषान् प्रत्यात्म्येनासृजत्प्रभुः ।
मानयन्नात्मनात्मानमात्माभासं विलोकयन् ॥४५॥

sa kinnarān kimpuruṣān
pratyātmyenāsṛjat prabhuḥ
mānayann ātmanātmānam
ātmābhāsaṁ vilokayan

saḥ—Lord Brahmā; *kinnarān*—the Kinnaras; *kimpuruṣān*—the Kimpuruṣas; *pratyātmyena*—from his reflection (in water); *asṛjat*—created; *prabhuḥ*—the lord of the living beings (Brahmā); *mānayan*—admiring; *ātmanā ātmānam*—himself by himself; *ātma-ābhāsam*—his reflection; *vilokayan*—seeing.

TRANSLATION

One day, Brahmā, the creator of the living entities, beheld his own reflection in the water, and admiring himself, he evolved Kimpuruṣas as well as Kinnaras out of that reflection.

TEXT 46

ते तु तज्जगृहू रूपं त्यक्तं यत्परमेष्ठिना ।
मिथुनीभूय गायन्तस्तमेवोषसि कर्मभिः ॥४६॥

te tu taj jagṛhū rūpaṁ
tyaktaṁ yat parameṣṭhinā
mithunī-bhūya gāyantas
tam evoṣasi karmabhiḥ

te—they (the Kinnaras and Kimpuruṣas); *tu*—but; *tat*—that; *jagṛhuḥ*—took possession of; *rūpam*—that shadowy form; *tyaktam*—given up; *yat*—which; *parameṣṭhinā*—by Brahmā; *mithunī-bhūya*—coming together with their spouses; *gāyantaḥ*—praise in song; *tam*—him; *eva*—only; *uṣasi*—at daybreak; *karmabhiḥ*—with his exploits.

TRANSLATION

The Kimpuruṣas and Kinnaras took possession of that shadowy form left by Brahmā. That is why they and their spouses sing his praises by recounting his exploits at every daybreak.

PURPORT

The time early in the morning, one and a half hours before sunrise, is called *brāhma-muhūrta.* During this *brāhma-muhūrta,* spiritual activities are recommended. Spiritual activities performed early in the morning have a greater effect than in any other part of the day.

TEXT 47

देहेन वै भोगवता शयानो बहुचिन्तया ।
सर्गेऽनुपचिते क्रोधादुत्ससर्ज ह तद्वपुः ॥४७॥

dehena vai bhogavatā
śayāno bahu-cintayā
sarge 'nupacite krodhād
utsasarja ha tad vapuḥ

dehena—with his body; *vai*—indeed; *bhogavatā*—stretching out full length; *śayānaḥ*—lying fully stretched; *bahu*—great; *cintayā*—with concern; *sarge*—the creation; *anupacite*—not proceeded; *krodhāt*—out of anger; *utsasarja*—gave up; *ha*—in fact; *tat*—that; *vapuḥ*—body.

TRANSLATION

Once Brahmā lay down with his body stretched at full length. He was very concerned that the work of creation had not proceeded apace, and in a sullen mood he gave up that body too.

TEXT 48

येऽहीयन्तामुतः केशा अहयस्तेऽङ्ग जज्ञिरे ।
सर्पाः प्रसर्पतः क्रूरा नागा भोगोरुकन्धराः ॥४८॥

ye 'hīyantāmutaḥ keśā
ahayas te 'ṅga jajñire
sarpāḥ prasarpataḥ krūrā
nāgā bhogoru-kandharāḥ

ye—which; *ahīyanta*—dropped out; *amutaḥ*—from that; *keśāḥ*—hairs; *ahayaḥ*—snakes; *te*—they; *aṅga*—O dear Vidura; *jajñire*—took birth as; *sarpāḥ*—snakes; *prasarpataḥ*—from the crawling body; *krūrāḥ*—envious; *nāgāḥ*—cobras; *bhoga*—with hoods; *uru*—big; *kandharāḥ*—whose necks.

TRANSLATION

O dear Vidura, the hair that dropped from that body transformed into snakes, and even while the body crawled along with its hands and feet contracted, there sprang from it ferocious serpents and Nāgas with their hoods expanded.

TEXT 49

स आत्मानं मन्यमानः कृतकृत्यमिवात्मभूः ।
तदा मनून् ससर्जान्ते मनसा लोकभावनान् ॥४९॥

sa ātmānaṁ manyamānaḥ
kṛta-kṛtyam ivātmabhūḥ
tadā manūn sasarjānte
manasā loka-bhāvanān

saḥ—Lord Brahmā; *ātmānam*—himself; *manyamānaḥ*—considering; *kṛta-kṛtyam*—had accomplished the object of life; *iva*—as if; *ātmabhūḥ*—born from the Supreme; *tadā*—then; *manūn*—the Manus; *sasarja*—created; *ante*—at the end; *manasā*—from his mind; *loka*—of the world; *bhāvanān*—promoting the welfare.

TRANSLATION

One day Brahmā, the self-born, the first living creature, felt as if the object of his life had been accomplished. At that time he evolved from his mind the Manus, who promote the welfare activities or the universe.

TEXT 50

तेभ्यः सोऽसृजत्स्वीयं पुरं पुरुषमात्मवान् ।
तान् दृष्ट्वा ये पुरा सृष्टाः प्रशशंसुः प्रजापतिम् ॥५०॥

tebhyaḥ so 'sṛjat svīyaṁ
puraṁ puruṣam ātmavān
tān dṛṣṭvā ye purā sṛṣṭāḥ
praśaśaṁsuḥ prajāpatim

tebhyaḥ—to them; *saḥ*—Lord Brahmā; *asṛjat*—gave; *svīyam*—his own; *puram*—body; *puruṣam*—human; *ātma-vān*—self-possessed; *tān*—them; *dṛṣṭvā*—on seeing; *ye*—those who; *purā*—earlier; *sṛṣṭāḥ*—were created (the demigods, Gandharvas, etc., who were created earlier); *praśaśaṁsuḥ*—applauded; *prajāpatim*—Brahmā (the lord of created beings).

TRANSLATION

The self-possessed creator gave them his own human form. On seeing the Manus, those who had been created earlier—the demigods, the Gandharvas and so on—applauded Brahmā, the lord of the universe.

TEXT 51

अहो एतज्जगत्स्रष्टः सुकृतं बत ते कृतम् ।
प्रतिष्ठिताः क्रिया यस्मिन् साकमन्नमदामहे ॥५१॥

aho etaj jagat-sraṣṭaḥ
sukṛtaṁ bata te kṛtam
pratiṣṭhitāḥ kriyā yasmin
sākam annam adāma he

aho—oh; *etat*—this; *jagat-sraṣṭaḥ*—O creator of the universe; *sukṛtam*—well done; *bata*—indeed; *te*—by you; *kṛtam*—produced; *pratiṣṭhitāḥ*—established soundly; *kriyāḥ*—all ritualistic performances; *yasmin*—in which; *sākam*—along with this; *annam*—the sacrificial oblations; *adāma*—we shall share; *he*—O.

TRANSLATION

They prayed: O creator of the universe, we are glad; what you have produced is well done. Since ritualistic acts have now been established soundly in this human form, we shall all share the sacrificial oblations.

PURPORT

The importance of sacrifice is also mentioned in *Bhagavad-gītā,* Third Chapter, verse 10. The Lord confirms there that in the beginning of creation Brahmā created the Manus, along with the ritualistic sacrificial method, and blessed them: "Continue these sacrificial rites, and you will be gradually elevated to your proper position of self-realization and will also enjoy material happiness." All the living entities created by Brahmā are conditioned souls and are inclined to lord it over material nature. The purpose of sacrificial rituals is to revive, gradually, the spiritual realization of the living entities. That is the beginning of life within this universe. These sacrificial rituals, however, are intended to please the Supreme Lord. Unless one pleases the Supreme Lord, or unless one is Kṛṣṇa conscious, one cannot be happy either in material enjoyment or in spiritual realization.

TEXT 52

तपसा विद्यया युक्तो योगेन सुसमाधिना ।
ऋषीनृषिर्हृषीकेशः ससर्जाभिमताः प्रजाः ॥५२॥

tapasā vidyayā yukto
yogena susamādhinā
ṛṣīn ṛṣir hṛṣīkeśaḥ
sasarjābhimatāḥ prajāḥ

tapasā—by penance; *vidyayā*—by worship; *yuktaḥ*—being engaged; *yogena*—by concentration of the mind in devotion; *su-samādhinā*—by nice meditation; *ṛṣīn*—the sages; *ṛṣiḥ*—the first seer (Brahmā); *hṛṣīkeśaḥ*—the controller of his senses; *sasarja*—created; *abhimatāḥ*—beloved; *prajāḥ*—sons.

TRANSLATION

Having equipped himself with austere penance, adoration, mental concentration and absorption in devotion, accompanied by dispassion, and having controlled his senses, Brahmā, the self-born living creature, evolved great sages as his beloved sons.

PURPORT

The ritualistic performances of sacrifice are meant for material economic development; in other words, they are meant to keep the body in good condition for cultivation of spiritual knowledge. But for actual attainment of spiritual knowledge, other qualifications are needed. What is essential is *vidyā,* or worship of the Supreme Lord. Sometimes the word *yoga* is used to refer to the gymnastic performances of different bodily postures which help mental concentration. Generally, the different bodily postures in the *yoga* system are accepted by less intelligent men to be the end of *yoga,* but actually they are meant to concentrate the mind upon the Supersoul. After creating persons for economic development, Brahmā created sages who would set the example for spiritual realization.

TEXT 53

तेभ्यश्चैकैकशः स्वस्य देहस्यांशमदादजः ।
यत्तत्समाधियोगर्द्धितपोविद्याविरक्तिमत् ॥५३॥

tebhyaś caikaikaśaḥ svasya
dehasyāṁśam adād ajaḥ
yat tat samādhi-yogarddhi-
tapo-vidyā-viraktimat

tebhyaḥ—to them; *ca*—and; *ekaikaśaḥ*—each one; *svasya*—of his own; *dehasya*—body; *aṁśam*—part; *adāt*—gave; *ajaḥ*—the unborn Brahmā; *yat*—which; *tat*—that; *samādhi*—deep meditation; *yoga*—concentration of the mind; *ṛddhi*—supernatural power; *tapaḥ*—austerity; *vidyā*—knowledge; *virakti*—renunciation; *mat*—possessing.

TRANSLATION

To each one of these sons the unborn creator of the universe gave a part of his own body, which was characterized by deep meditation, mental concentration, supernatural power, austerity, adoration and renunciation.

PURPORT

The word *viraktimat* in this verse means "possessed of the qualification of renunciation." Spiritual realization cannot be attained by materialistic persons. For those who are addicted to sense enjoyment, spiritual realization is not possible. In *Bhagavad-gītā* it is stated that those who are too attached to seeking material possessions and material enjoyment cannot reach *yoga-samādhi,* absorption in Kṛṣṇa consciousness. Propaganda that one can enjoy this life materially and at the same time spiritually advance is simply bogus. The principles of renunciation are four: (1) to avoid illicit sex life, (2) to avoid meat-eating, (3) to avoid intoxication and (4) to avoid gambling. These four principles are called *tapasya,* or austerity. To absorb the mind in the Supreme in Kṛṣṇa consciousness is the process of spiritual realization.

Thus end the Bhaktivedanta purports of the Third Canto, Twentieth Chapter, of the Śrīmad-Bhāgavatam, *entitled "Conversation Between Maitreya and Vidura."*

CHAPTER TWENTY-ONE

Conversation Between Manu and Kardama

TEXT 1

विदुर उवाच
स्वायम्भुवस्य च मनोर्वंशः परमसम्मतः ।
कथ्यतां भगवन् यत्र मैथुनेनैधिरे प्रजाः ॥ १ ॥

vidura uvāca
svāyambhuvasya ca manor
vaṁśaḥ parama-sammataḥ
kathyatām bhagavan yatra
maithunenaidhire prajāḥ

viduraḥ uvāca—Vidura said; *svāyambhuvasya*—of Svāyambhuva; *ca*—and; *manoḥ*—of Manu; *vaṁśaḥ*—the dynasty; *parama*—most; *sammataḥ*—esteemed; *kathyatām*—kindly describe; *bhagavan*—O worshipful sage; *yatra*—in which; *maithunena*—through sexual intercourse; *edhire*—multiplied; *prajāḥ*—the progeny.

TRANSLATION

Vidura said: The line of Svāyambhuva Manu was most esteemed. O worshipful sage, I beg you—give me an account of this race, whose progeny multiplied through sexual intercourse.

PURPORT

Regulated sex life to generate good population is worth accepting. Actually, Vidura was not interested in hearing the history of persons who merely engaged in sex life, but he was interested in the progeny of Svāyambhuva Manu because in that dynasty, good devotee kings appeared who protected their subjects very carefully with spiritual knowledge. By hearing the history of their activities, therefore, one becomes more enlightened. An important word used in this connection is *parama-sammataḥ*, which indicates that the progeny created by Svāyambhuva Manu and his sons was approved of by great authorities. In other words, sex life for creating exemplary population is acceptable to all sages and authorities of Vedic scripture.

TEXT 2

प्रियव्रतोत्तानपादौ सुतौ स्वायम्भुवस्य वै ।
यथाधर्मं जुगुपतुः सप्तद्वीपवतीं महीम् ॥ २ ॥

priyavratottānapādau
sutau svāyambhuvasya vai
yathā-dharmaṁ jugupatuḥ
sapta-dvīpavatīṁ mahīm

priyavrata—Mahārāja Priyavrata; *uttānapādau*—and Mahārāja Uttānapāda; *sutau*—the two sons; *svāyambhuvasya*—of Svāyambhuva Manu; *vai*—indeed; *yathā*—according to; *dharmam*—religious principles; *jugupatuḥ*—ruled; *sapta-dvīpa-vatīm*—consisting of seven islands; *mahīm*—the world.

TRANSLATION

The two great sons of Svāyambhuva Manu—Priyavrata and Uttānapāda—ruled the world, consisting of seven islands, just according to religious principles.

PURPORT

Śrīmad-Bhāgavatam is also a history of the great rulers of different parts of the universe. In this verse the names of Priyavrata and Uttānapāda, sons of Svāyambhuva, are mentioned. They ruled this earth, which is divided into seven islands. These seven islands are still current, as Asia, Europe, Africa, America, Australia and the North and South Poles. There is no chronological history of all the Indian kings in *Śrīmad-Bhāgavatam*, but the deeds of the most important kings, such as Priyavrata and Uttānapāda, and many others, like Lord Rāmacandra and Mahārāja Yudhiṣṭhira, are recorded because the activities of such pious kings are worth hearing; people may benefit by studying their histories.

TEXT 3

तस्य वै दुहिता ब्रह्मन्देवहूतीति विश्रुता ।
पत्नी प्रजापतेरुक्ता कर्दमस्य त्वयानघ ॥ ३ ॥

tasya vai duhitā brahman
devahūtīti viśrutā
patnī prajāpater uktā
kardamasya tvayānagha

tasya—of that Manu; *vai*—indeed; *duhitā*—the daughter; *brahman*—O holy *brāhmaṇa*; *devahūti*—named Devahūti; *iti*—thus; *viśrutā*—was known; *patnī*—wife; *prajāpateḥ*—of the lord of created beings; *uktā*—has been spoken of; *kardamasya*—of Kardama Muni; *tvayā*—by you; *anagha*—O sinless one.

TRANSLATION

O holy brāhmaṇa, O sinless one, you have spoken of his daughter, known by the name Devahūti, as the wife of the sage Kardama, the lord of created beings.

PURPORT

Here we are speaking of Svāyambhuva Manu, but in *Bhagavad-gītā* we hear about Vaivasvata Manu. The present age belongs to the Vaivasvata Manu. Svāyambhuva Manu was previously ruling, and his history begins from the Varāha age, or the millennium when the Lord appeared as the boar. There are fourteen Manus in one day of the life of Brahmā, and in the life of each Manu there are particular incidents. The Vaivasvata Manu of *Bhagavad-gītā* is different from Svāyambhuva Manu.

TEXT 4

तस्यां स वै महायोगी युक्तायां योगलक्षणैः ।
ससर्ज कतिधा वीर्यं तन्मे शुश्रूषवे वद ॥ ४ ॥

tasyāṁ sa vai mahā-yogī
yuktāyāṁ yoga-lakṣaṇaiḥ
sasarja katidhā vīryaṁ
tan me śuśrūṣave vada

tasyām—in her; *saḥ*—Kardama Muni; *vai*—in fact; *mahā-yogī*—great mystic *yogī*; *yuktāyām*—endowed; *yoga-lakṣaṇaiḥ*—with the eightfold symptoms of yogic perfection; *sasarja*—propagated; *katidhā*—how many times; *vīryam*—offspring; *tat*—that narration; *me*—to me; *śuśrūṣave*—who am eager to hear; *vada*—tell.

TRANSLATION

How many offspring did that great yogī beget through the princess, who was endowed with eightfold perfection in the yoga principles? Oh, pray tell me this, for I am eager to hear it.

PURPORT

Here Vidura inquired about Kardama Muni and his wife, Devahūti, and about their children. It is described here that Devahūti was very much advanced in the performance of eightfold *yoga*. The eight divisions of *yoga* performance are described as (1) control of the senses, (2) strict following of the rules and regulations, (3) practice of the different sitting postures, (4) control of the breath, (5) withdrawing the senses from sense objects, (6) concentration of the mind, (7) meditation and (8) self-realization. After self-realization there are eight further perfectional stages, which are called *yoga-siddhis*. The husband and wife, Kardama and Devahūti, were advanced in *yoga* practice; the husband was a *mahā-yogī*, great mystic, and the wife was a *yoga-lakṣaṇa*, or one advanced in *yoga*. They united and produced children. Formerly, after making their lives perfect, great sages and saintly persons used to beget children, otherwise they strictly observed the rules and regulations of celibacy. *Brahmacarya* (following the rules and regulations of celibacy) is required for perfection of self-realization and mystic power. There is no recommendation in the Vedic scriptures that one can go on enjoying material sense gratification at one's whims, as one likes, and at the same time become a great meditator by paying a rascal some money.

TEXT 5

रुचिर्यो भगवान् ब्रह्मन्दक्षो वा ब्रह्मणः सुतः ।
यथा ससर्ज भूतानि लब्ध्वा भार्यां च मानवीम् ॥ ५ ॥

rucir yo bhagavān brahman
dakṣo vā brahmaṇaḥ sutaḥ
yathā sasarja bhūtāni
labdhvā bhāryāṁ ca mānavīm

ruciḥ—Ruci; *yaḥ*—who; *bhagavān*—worshipful; *brahman*—O holy sage; *dakṣaḥ*—Dakṣa; *vā*—and; *brahmaṇaḥ*—of Lord Brahmā; *sutaḥ*—the son; *yathā*—in what way; *sasarja*—generated; *bhūtāni*—offspring; *labdhvā*—after securing; *bhāryām*—as their wives; *ca*—and; *mānavīm*—the daughters of Svāyambhuva Manu.

TRANSLATION

O holy sage, tell me how the worshipful Ruci and Dakṣa, the son of Brahmā, generated children after securing as their wives the other two daughters of Svāyambhuva Manu.

PURPORT

All the great personalities who increased the population in the beginning of the creation are called Prajāpatis. Brahmā is also known as Prajāpati, as were some of his later sons. Svāyambhuva Manu is also known as Prajāpati, as is Dakṣa, another son of Brahmā. Svāyambhuva had two daughters, Ākūti and Prasūti. The Prajāpati Ruci married Ākūti, and Dakṣa married Prasūti. These couples and their children produced immense numbers of children to populate the entire universe. Vidura's inquiry was, "How did they beget the population in the beginning?"

TEXT 6

मैत्रेय उवाच
प्रजाः सृजेति भगवान् कर्दमो ब्रह्मणोदितः ।
सरस्वत्यां तपस्तेपे सहस्राणां समा दश ॥ ६ ॥

maitreya uvāca
prajāḥ sṛjeti bhagavān
kardamo brahmaṇoditaḥ
sarasvatyāṁ tapas tepe
sahasrāṇāṁ samā daśa

maitreyaḥ uvāca—the great sage Maitreya said; *prajāḥ*—children; *sṛja*—beget; *iti*—thus; *bhagavān*—the worshipful; *kardamaḥ*—Kardama Muni; *brahmaṇā*—by Lord Brahmā; *uditaḥ*—commanded; *sarasvatyām*—on the bank of the River Sarasvatī; *tapaḥ*—penance; *tepe*—practiced; *sahasrāṇām*—of thousands; *samāḥ*—years; *daśa*—ten.

TRANSLATION

The great sage Maitreya replied: Commanded by Lord Brahmā to beget children in the worlds, the worshipful Kardama Muni practiced penance on the bank of the River Sarasvatī for a period of ten thousand years.

PURPORT

It is understood herein that Kardama Muni meditated in *yoga* for ten thousand years before attaining perfection. Similarly, we have information that Vālmīki Muni also practiced *yoga* meditation for sixty thousand years before attaining perfection. Therefore, *yoga* practice can be successfully performed by persons who have a very long duration of life, such as one hundred thousand years; in that way it is possible to have perfection in *yoga*. Otherwise, there is no possibility of attaining the real perfection. Following the regulations, controlling the senses and practicing the different sitting postures are merely the preliminary practices. We do not know how people can be captivated by the bogus *yoga* system in which it is stated that simply by meditating fifteen minutes daily one can attain the perfection of becoming one with God. This age (Kali-yuga) is the age of bluffing and quarrel. Actually there is no possibility of attaining *yoga* perfection by such paltry proposals. The Vedic literature, for emphasis, clearly states three times that in this age of Kali-*kalau nāsty eva nāsty eva nāsty eva*—there is no other alternative, no other alternative, no other alternative than *harer nāma*, chanting the holy name of the Lord.

TEXT 7

ततः समाधियुक्तेन क्रियायोगेन कर्दमः ।
सम्प्रपेदे हरिं भक्त्या प्रपन्नवरदाशुषम् ॥ ७ ॥

tataḥ samādhi-yuktena
kriyā-yogena kardamaḥ
samprapede hariṁ bhaktyā
prapanna-varadāśuṣam

tataḥ—then, in that penance; *samādhi-yuktena*—in trance; *kriyā-yogena*—by *bhakti-yoga* worship; *kardamaḥ*—the sage Kardama; *samprapede*—served; *harim*—the Personality of Godhead; *bhaktyā*—in devotional service; *prapanna*—to the surrendered souls; *varadāśuṣam*—the bestower of all blessings.

TRANSLATION

During that period of penance, the sage Kardama, by worship through devotional service in trance, propitiated the Personality of Godhead, who is the quick bestower of all blessings upon those who flee to Him for protection.

PURPORT

The significance of meditation is described here. Kardama Muni practiced mystic *yoga* meditation for ten thousand years just to please the Supreme Personality of Godhead, Hari. Therefore, whether one practices *yoga* or speculates and does research to find God, one's efforts must be mixed with the process of devotion. Without devotion, nothing can be perfect. The target of perfection and realization is the Supreme Personality of Godhead. In the Sixth Chapter of *Bhagavad-gītā* it is clearly said that one who constantly engages in Kṛṣṇa consciousness is the topmost *yogī*. The Personality of Godhead, Hari, also fulfills the desires of His surrendered devotee. One has to surrender unto the lotus feet of the Personality of Godhead, Hari, or Kṛṣṇa, in order to achieve real success. Devotional service, or engagement in Kṛṣṇa consciousness, is the direct method, and all other methods, although recommended, are indirect. In this age of Kali the direct method is especially more feasible than the indirect because people are short-living, their intelligence is poor, and they are poverty-stricken and embarrassed by so many miserable disturbances. Lord Caitanya, therefore, has given the greatest boon: in this age one simply has to chant the holy name of God to attain perfection in spiritual life.

The words *samprapede harim* mean that in various ways Kardama Muni satisfied the Supreme Personality of Godhead, Hari, by his devotional service. Devotional service is also expressed by the word *kriyā-yogena.* Kardama Muni not only meditated but also engaged in devotional service; to attain perfection in *yoga* practice or meditation, one must act in devotional service by hearing, chanting, remembering, etc. Remembering is meditation also. But who is to be remembered? One should remember the Supreme Personality of Godhead. Not only must one remember the Supreme Person; one must hear about the activities of the Lord and chant His glories. This information is in the authoritative scriptures. After engaging himself for ten thousand years in performing different types of devotional service, Kardama Muni attained the perfection of meditation, but that is not possible in this age of Kali, wherein it is very difficult to live for as much as one hundred years. At the present moment, who will be successful in the rigid performance of the many *yoga* rules and regulations? Moreover, perfection is attained only by those who are surrendered souls. Where there is no mention of the Personality of Godhead, where is there surrender? And where there is no meditation upon the Personality of Godhead, where is the *yoga* practice? Unfortunately, people in this age, especially persons who are of a demoniac nature, want to be cheated. Thus the Supreme Personality of Godhead sends great cheaters who mislead them in the name of *yoga* and render their lives useless and doomed. In *Bhagavad-gītā,* therefore, it is clearly stated, in the Sixteenth Chapter, verse 17, that rascals of self-made authority, being puffed up by illegally collected money, perform *yoga* without following the authoritative books. They are very proud of the money they have plundered from innocent persons who wanted to be cheated.

TEXT 8

तावत्प्रसन्नो भगवान् पुष्कराक्षः कृते युगे ।
दर्शयामास तं क्षत्तः शाब्दं ब्रह्म दधद्वपुः ॥ ८ ॥

tāvat prasanno bhagavān
puṣkarākṣaḥ kṛte yuge

darśayām āsa taṁ kṣattaḥ
śābdaṁ brahma dadhad vapuḥ

tāvat—then; *prasannaḥ*—being pleased; *bhagavān*—the Supreme Personality of Godhead; *puṣkara-akṣaḥ*—lotus-eyed; *kṛte yuge*—in the Satya-yuga; *darśayām āsa*—showed; *tam*—to that Kardama Muni; *kṣattaḥ*—O Vidura; *śābdam*—which is to be understood only through the *Vedas; brahma*—the Absolute Truth; *dadhat*—exhibiting; *vapuḥ*—His transcendental body.

TRANSLATION

Then, in the Satya-yuga, the lotus-eyed Supreme Personality of Godhead, being pleased, showed Himself to that Kardama Muni and displayed His transcendental form, which can be understood only through the Vedas.

PURPORT

Here two points are very significant. The first is that Kardama Muni attained success by *yoga* practice in the beginning of Satya-yuga, when people used to live for one hundred thousand years. Kardama Muni attained success, and the Lord, being pleased with him, showed him His form, which is not imaginary. Sometimes the impersonalists recommend that one can arbitrarily concentrate one's mind on some form he imagines or which pleases him. But here it is very clearly said that the form which the Lord showed to Kardama Muni by His divine grace is described in the Vedic literature. *Śābdaṁ brahma:* the forms of the Lord are clearly indicated in the Vedic literature. Kardama Muni did not discover any imaginary form of God, as alleged by rascals; he actually saw the eternal, blissful and transcendental form of the Lord.

TEXT 9

स तं विरजमर्काभं सितपद्मोत्पलस्रजम् ।
स्निग्धनीलालकव्रातवक्त्राब्जं विरजोऽम्बरम् ॥ ९ ॥

sa taṁ virajam arkābhaṁ
sita-padmotpala-srajam
snigdha-nīlālaka-vrāta-
vaktrābjaṁ virajo 'mbaram

saḥ—that Kardama Muni; *tam*—Him; *virajam*—without contamination; *arka-ābham*—effulgent like the sun; *sita*—white; *padma*—lotuses; *utpala*—water lilies; *srajam*—garland; *snigdha*—slick; *nīla*—blackish-blue; *alaka*—of locks of hair; *vrāta*—an abundance; *vaktra*—face; *abjam*—lotuslike; *virajaḥ*—spotless; *ambaram*—clothing.

TRANSLATION

Kardama Muni saw the Supreme Personality of Godhead, who is free from material contamination, in His eternal form, effulgent like the sun, wearing a garland of white lotuses and water lilies. The Lord was clad in spotless yellow silk, and His lotus face was fringed with slick dark locks of curly hair.

TEXT 10

किरीटिनं कुण्डलिनं शङ्खचक्रगदाधरम् ।
श्वेतोत्पलक्रीडनकं मनःस्पर्शस्मितेक्षणम् ॥१०॥

kirīṭinaṁ kuṇḍalinaṁ
śaṅkha-cakra-gadā-dharam
śvetotpala-krīḍanakaṁ
manaḥ-sparśa-smitekṣaṇam

kirīṭinam—adorned with a crown; *kuṇḍalinam*—wearing earrings; *śaṅkha*—conch; *cakra*—disc; *gadā*—mace; *dharam*—holding; *śveta*—white; *utpala*—lily; *krīḍanakam*—plaything; *manaḥ*—heart; *sparśa*—touching; *smita*—smiling; *īkṣaṇam*—and glancing.

TRANSLATION

Adorned with a crown and earrings, He held His characteristic conch, disc and mace in three of His hands and a white lily in the fourth. He glanced about in a happy, smiling mood whose sight captivates the hearts of all devotees.

TEXT 11

विन्यस्तचरणाम्भोजमंसदेशे गरुत्मतः ।
दृष्ट्वा खेऽवस्थितं वक्षःश्रियं कौस्तुभकन्धरम् ॥११॥

vinyasta-caraṇāmbhojam
aṁsa-deśe garutmataḥ
dṛṣṭvā khe 'vasthitaṁ vakṣaḥ-
śriyaṁ kaustubha-kandharam

vinyasta—having been placed; *caraṇa-ambhojam*—lotus feet; *aṁsa-deśe*—on the shoulders; *garutmataḥ*—of Garuḍa; *dṛṣṭvā*—having seen; *khe*—in the air; *avasthitam*—standing; *vakṣaḥ*—on His chest; *śriyam*—auspicious mark; *kaustubha*—the Kaustubha gem; *kandharam*—neck.

TRANSLATION

A golden streak on His chest, the famous Kaustubha gem suspended from His neck, He stood in the air with His lotus feet placed on the shoulders of Garuḍa.

PURPORT

The descriptions in verses 9-11 of the Lord in His transcendental, eternal form are understood to be descriptions from the authoritative Vedic version. These descriptions are certainly not the imagination of Kardama Muni. The decorations of the Lord are beyond material conception, as admitted even by impersonalists like Śaṅkarācārya: Nārāyaṇa, the Supreme Personality of Godhead, has nothing to do with the material creation. The varieties of the transcendental Lord—His body, His form, His dress, His instruction, His words—are not manufactured by the material energy, but are all confirmed in the Vedic literature. By performance of *yoga* Kardama Muni actually saw the Supreme Lord as He is. There was no point in seeing an imagined form of God after practicing *yoga* for ten thousand years. The perfection of *yoga*, therefore, does not terminate in voidness or impersonalism; on the contrary, the perfection of *yoga* is attained when one actually sees the Personality of Godhead in His eternal form. The process of Kṛṣṇa consciousness is to deliver the form of Kṛṣṇa directly. The form of Kṛṣṇa is described in the authoritative Vedic literature *Brahma-saṁhitā:* His abode is made of *cintāmaṇi* stone, and the Lord plays there as a cowherd boy and is served by many thousands of *gopīs.* These descriptions are authoritative, and a Kṛṣṇa conscious person takes them directly, acts on them, preaches them and practices devotional service as enjoined in the authoritative scriptures.

TEXT 12

जातहर्षोऽपतन्मूर्ध्ना क्षितौ लब्धमनोरथः ।
गीर्भिस्त्वभ्यगृणात्प्रीतिस्वभावात्मा कृताञ्जलिः ॥१२॥

jāta-harṣo 'patan mūrdhnā
kṣitau labdha-manorathaḥ
gīrbhis tv abhyagṛṇāt prīti-
svabhāvātmā kṛtāñjaliḥ

jāta-harṣaḥ—naturally jubilant; *apatat*—he fell down; *mūrdhnā*—with his head; *kṣitau*—on the ground; *labdha*—having been achieved; *manaḥ-rathaḥ*—his desire; *gīrbhiḥ*—with prayers; *tu*—and; *abhyagṛṇāt*—he satisfied; *prīti-svabhāva-ātmā*—whose heart is by nature always full of love; *kṛta-añjaliḥ*—with folded hands.

TRANSLATION

When Kardama Muni actually realized the Supreme Personality of Godhead in person, he was greatly satisfied because his transcendental desire was fulfilled. He fell on the ground with his head bowed to offer obeisances unto the lotus feet of the Lord. His heart naturally full of love of God, with folded hands he satisfied the Lord with prayers.

PURPORT

The realization of the personal form of the Lord is the highest perfectional stage of *yoga.* In the Sixth Chapter of *Bhagavad-gītā,* where *yoga* practice is described, this realization of the personal form of the Lord is called the perfection of *yoga.* After practicing the sitting postures and other regulative principles of the system, one finally reaches the stage of *samādhi*—absorption in the Supreme. In the *samādhi* stage one can see the Supreme Personality of Godhead in His partial form as Paramātmā, or as He is. *Samādhi* is described in authoritative *yoga* scriptures, such as the *Patañjali-sūtras,* to be a transcendental pleasure. The *yoga* system described in the books of Patañjali is authoritative, and the modern so-called *yogīs* who have manufactured their own ways, not consulting the authorities, are simply ludicrous. The Patañjali *yoga* system is called *aṣṭāṅga-yoga.* Sometimes impersonalists pollute the Patañjali *yoga* system because they are monists. Patañjali describes that the soul is transcendentally pleased when he meets the Supersoul and sees Him. If the existence of the Supersoul and the individual is admitted, then the impersonalist theory of monism is nullified. Therefore some impersonalists and void philosophers twist the Patañjali system in their own way and pollute the whole *yoga* process.

According to Patañjali, when one becomes free from all material desires he attains his real, transcendental situation, and realization of that stage is called spiritual power. In material activities a person engages in the modes of material nature. The aspirations of such people are (1) to be religious, (2) to be economically enriched, (3) to be able to gratify the senses and, at last, (4) to become one with the Supreme. According to the monists, when a *yogī* becomes one with the Supreme and loses his individual existence, he attains the highest stage, called *kaivalya.* But actually, the stage of realization of the Personality of Godhead is *kaivalya.* The oneness of understanding that the Supreme Lord is fully spiritual and that in full spiritual realization one can understand what He is—the Supreme Personality of Godhead—is called *kaivalya,* or, in the language of Patañjali, realization of spiritual power. His proposal is that when one is freed from material desires and fixed in spiritual realization of the self and the Superself, that is called *cit-śakti.* In full spiritual realization there is a perception of spiritual happiness, and that happiness is described in *Bhagavad-gītā* as the supreme happiness, which is beyond the material senses. Trance is described to be of two kinds, *samprajñāta* and *asamprajñāta,* or mental speculation and self-realization. In *samādhi* or *asamprajñāta* one can realize, by his spiritual senses, the spiritual form of the Lord. That is the ultimate goal of spiritual realization.

According to Patañjali, when one is fixed in constant realization of the supreme form of the Lord, one has attained the perfectional stage, as attained by Kardama Muni. Unless one attains this stage of perfection—beyond the perfection of the preliminaries of the *yoga* system—there is no ultimate realization. There are eight perfections in the *aṣṭāṅga-yoga* system. One who has attained them can become lighter than the lightest and greater than the greatest, and he can achieve whatever he likes. But even achieving such material success in *yoga* is not the perfection or the ultimate goal. The ultimate goal is described here: Kardama Muni saw the Supreme Personality of Godhead in His eternal form. Devotional service begins with the relationship of the individual soul and the Supreme Soul, or Kṛṣṇa and Kṛṣṇa's devotees, and when one attains it there is no question of falling down. If, through the *yoga* system, one wants to attain the stage of seeing the Supreme Personality of Godhead face to face, but is attracted instead to attainment of some material power, then he is detoured from proceeding further. Material enjoyment, as encouraged by bogus *yogīs,* has nothing to do with the transcendental realization of spiritual happiness. Real devotees of *bhakti-yoga* accept only the material necessities of life absolutely needed to maintain the body and soul together; they refrain completely from all exaggerated material sense gratification. They are prepared to undergo all kinds of tribulation, provided they can make progress in the realization of the Personality of Godhead.

TEXT 13

ऋषिरुवाच
जुष्टं बताद्याखिलसत्त्वराशेः
सांसिद्ध्यमक्ष्णोस्तव दर्शनान्नः ।
यद्दर्शनं जन्मभिरीड्य सद्भि-
राशासते योगिनो रूढयोगाः ॥१३॥

ṛṣir uvāca
juṣṭaṁ batādyākhila-sattva-rāśeḥ
sāṁsiddhyam akṣṇos tava darśanān naḥ

yad-darśanaṁ janmabhir īḍya sadbhir
āśāsate yogino rūḍha-yogāḥ

ṛṣiḥ uvāca—the great sage said; *juṣṭam*—is attained; *bata*—ah; *adya*—now; *akhila*—all; *sattva*—of goodness; *rāśeḥ*—who are the reservoir; *sāṁsiddhyam*—the complete success; *akṣṇoḥ*—of the two eyes; *tava*—of You; *darśanāt*—from the sight; *naḥ*—by us; *yat*—of whom; *darśanam*—sight; *janmabhiḥ*—through births; *īḍya*—O worshipable Lord; *sadbhiḥ*—gradually elevated in position; *āśāsate*—aspire; *yoginaḥ*—*yogīs;* *rūḍha-yogāḥ*—having obtained perfection in *yoga.*

TRANSLATION

The great sage Kardama said: O supreme worshipful Lord, my power of sight is now fulfilled, having attained the greatest perfection of the sight of You, who are the reservoir of all existences. Through many successive births of deep meditation, advanced yogīs aspire to see Your transcendental form.

PURPORT

The Supreme Personality of Godhead is described here as the reservoir of all goodness and all pleasure. Unless one is situated in the mode of goodness, there is no real pleasure. When, therefore, one's body, mind and activities are situated in the service of the Lord, one is on the highest perfectional stage of goodness. Kardama Muni says, "Your Lordship is the reservoir of all that can be understood by the nomenclature of goodness, and by experiencing You face to face, eye to eye, the perfection of sight has now been attained." These statements are the pure devotional situation; for a devotee, the perfection of the senses is to engage in the service of the Lord. The sense of sight, when engaged in seeing the beauty of the Lord, is perfected; the power to hear, when engaged in hearing the glories of the Lord, is perfected; the power to taste, when one enjoys by eating *prasāda,* is perfected. When all the senses engage in relationship with the Personality of Godhead, one's perfection is technically called *bhakti-yoga,* which entails detaching the senses from material indulgence and attaching them to the service of the Lord. When one is freed from all designated conditional life and fully engages in the service of the Lord, one's service is called *bhakti-yoga.* Kardama Muni admits that seeing the Lord personally in *bhakti-yoga* is the perfection of sight. The exalted perfection of seeing the Lord is not exaggerated by Kardama Muni. He gives evidence that those who are actually elevated in *yoga* aspire in life after life to see this form of the Personality of Godhead. He was not a fictitious *yogī.* Those who are actually on the advanced path aspire only to see the eternal form of the Lord.

TEXT 14

ये मायया ते हतमेधसस्त्वत्-
पादारविन्दं भवसिन्धुपोतम् ।
उपासते कामलवाय तेषां
रासीश कामान्निरयेऽपि ये स्युः ॥१४॥

ye māyayā te hata-medhasas tvat-
pādāravindaṁ bhava-sindhu-potam
upāsate kāma-lavāya teṣāṁ
rāsīśa kāmān niraye 'pi ye syuḥ

ye—those persons; *māyayā*—by the deluding energy; *te*—of You; *hata*—has been lost; *medhasaḥ*—whose intelligence; *tvat*—Your; *pāda-aravindam*—lotus feet; *bhava*—of mundane existence; *sindhu*—the ocean; *potam*—the boat for crossing; *upāsate*—worship; *kāma-lavāya*—for obtaining trivial pleasures; *teṣām*—their; *rāsi*—You bestow; *īśa*—O Lord; *kāmān*—desires; *niraye*—in hell; *api*—even; *ye*—which desires; *syuḥ*—can be available.

TRANSLATION

Your lotus feet are the true vessel to take one across the ocean of mundane nescience. Only persons deprived of their intelligence by the spell of the deluding energy will worship those feet with a view to attain the trivial and momentary pleasures of the senses, which even persons rotting in hell can attain. However, O my Lord, You are so kind that You bestow mercy even upon them.

PURPORT

As stated in *Bhagavad-gītā,* Seventh Chapter, there are two kinds of devotees—those who desire material pleasures and those who desire nothing but service to the Lord. Material pleasures can be attained even by hogs and dogs, whose condition of life is hellish. The hog also eats, sleeps and enjoys sex life to the full extent, and it is also very satisfied with such hellish enjoyment of material existence. Modern *yogīs* advise that because one has senses, one must enjoy to the fullest extent like cats and dogs, yet one can go on and practice *yoga.* This is condemned here by Kardama Muni; he says that such material pleasures are available for cats and dogs in a hellish condition. The Lord is so kind that if so-called *yogīs* are satisfied by hellish pleasures, He can give them facilities to attain all the material pleasures they desire, but they cannot attain the perfectional stage attained by Kardama Muni.

Hellish and demoniac persons do not actually know what is the ultimate attainment in perfection, and therefore they think that sense gratification is the highest goal of life. They advise that one can satisfy the senses and at the same time, by reciting some *mantra* and by some practice, can cheaply aspire for perfection. Such persons are described here as *hata-medhasaḥ,* which means "those whose brains are spoiled." They aspire for material enjoyment by perfection of *yoga* or meditation. In *Bhagavad-gītā* it is stated by the Lord that the intelligence of those who worship the demigods has been spoiled. Similarly, here too it is stated by Kardama Muni that one who aspires after material enjoyment by practice of *yoga* has spoiled his brain substance and is fool number one. Actually, the intelligent practitioner of *yoga* should aspire for nothing else but to cross over the ocean of nescience by worshiping the Personality of Godhead and to see the lotus feet of the Lord. The Lord is so kind, however, that even today persons whose brain substance is spoiled are given the benediction to become cats, dogs or hogs and enjoy material happiness from sex life and sense gratification. The Lord confirms this benediction in *Bhagavad-gītā:* "Whatever a person aspires to receive from Me, I offer him as he desires."

TEXT 15

तथा स चाहं परिवोढुकामः
समानशीलां गृहमेधधेनुम् ।
उपेयिवान्मूलमशेषमूलं
दुराशयः कामदुघाङ्घ्रिपस्य ॥१५॥

tathā sa cāhaṁ parivoḍhu-kāmaḥ
samāna-śīlāṁ gṛhamedha-dhenum
upeyivān mūlam aśeṣa-mūlaṁ
durāśayaḥ kāma-dughāṅghripasya

tathā—similarly; *saḥ*—myself; *ca*—also; *aham*—I; *parivoḍhu-kāmaḥ*—desiring to marry; *samāna-śīlām*—a girl of like disposition; *gṛha-medha*—in married life; *dhenum*—a cow of plenty; *upeyivān*—have approached; *mūlam*—the root (lotus feet); *aśeṣa*—of everything; *mūlam*—the source; *durāśayaḥ*—with lustful desire; *kāma-dugha*—yielding all desires; *aṅghripasya*—(of You) who are the tree.

TRANSLATION

Therefore, desiring to marry a girl of like disposition who may prove to be a veritable cow of plenty in my married life, to satisfy my lustful desire I too

have sought the shelter of Your lotus feet, which are the source of everything, for You are like a desire tree.

PURPORT

In spite of his condemning persons who approach the Lord for material advantages, Kardama Muni expressed his material inability and desire before the Lord by saying, "Although I know that nothing material should be asked from You, I nevertheless desire to marry a girl of like disposition." The phrase "like disposition" is very significant. Formerly, boys and girls of similar dispositions were married; the similar natures of the boy and girl were united in order to make them happy. Not more than twenty-five years ago, and perhaps it is still current, parents in India used to consult the horoscope of the boy and girl to see whether there would be factual union in their psychological conditions. These considerations are very important. Nowadays marriage takes place without such consultation, and therefore, soon after the marriage, there is divorce and separation. Formerly husband and wife used to live together peacefully throughout their whole lives, but nowadays it is a very difficult task.

Kardama Muni wanted to have a wife of like disposition because a wife is necessary to assist in spiritual and material advancement. It is said that a wife yields the fulfillment of all desires in religion, economic development and sense gratification. If one has a nice wife, he is to be considered a most fortunate man. In astrology, a man is considered fortunate who has great wealth, very good sons or a very good wife. Of these three, one who has a very good wife is considered the most fortunate. Before marrying, one should select a wife of like disposition and not be enamored by so-called beauty or other attractive features for sense gratification. In the *Bhāgavatam*, Twelfth Canto, it is said that in the Kali-yuga marriage will be based on the consideration of sex life; as soon as there is deficiency in sex life, the question of divorce will arise.

Kardama Muni could have asked his benediction from Umā, for it is recommended in the scriptures that if anyone wants a good wife, he should worship Umā. But he preferred to worship the Supreme Personality of Godhead because it is recommended in the *Bhāgavatam* that everyone, whether he is full of desires, has no desire or desires liberation, should worship the Supreme Lord. Of these three classes of men, one tries to be happy by fulfillment of material desires, another wants to be happy by becoming one with the Supreme, and another, the perfect man, is a devotee. He does not want anything in return from the Personality of Godhead; he only wants to render transcendental loving service. In any case, everyone should worship the Supreme Personality of Godhead, for He will fulfill everyone's desire. The advantage of worshiping the Supreme Person is that even if one has desires for material enjoyment, if he worships Kṛṣṇa he will gradually become a pure devotee and have no more material hankering.

TEXT 16

प्रजापतेस्ते वचसाधीश तन्त्या
लोकः किलायं कामहतोऽनुबद्धः ।
अहं च लोकानुगतो वहामि
बलिं च शुक्लानिमिषाय तुभ्यम् ॥१६॥

prajāpates te vacasādhīśa tantyā
lokaḥ kilāyaṁ kāma-hato 'nubaddhaḥ
ahaṁ ca lokānugato vahāmi
baliṁ ca śuklānimiṣāya tubhyam

prajāpateḥ—who are the master of all living entities; *te*—of You; *vacasā*—under the direction; *adhīśa*—O my Lord; *tantyā*—by a rope; *lokaḥ*—conditioned souls; *kila*—indeed; *ayam*—these; *kāma-hataḥ*—conquered by lusty desires; *anubaddhaḥ*—are bound; *aham*—I; *ca*—and; *loka-anugataḥ*—following the conditioned souls; *vahāmi*—offer; *balim*—oblations; *ca*—and; *śukla*—O embodiment of religion; *animiṣāya*—existing as eternal time; *tubhyam*—to You.

TRANSLATION

O my Lord, You are the master and leader of all living entities. Under Your direction, all conditioned souls, as if bound by rope, are constantly engaged in satisfying their desires. Following them, O embodiment of religion, I also bear oblations for You, who are eternal time.

PURPORT

In the *Kaṭha Upaniṣad* it is stated that the Supreme Lord is the leader of all living entities. He is their sustainer and the awarder of all their necessities and desires. No living entity is independent; all are dependent on the mercy of the Supreme Lord. Therefore the Vedic instruction is that one should enjoy life under the direction of the supreme leader, the Personality of Godhead. Vedic literatures like *Īśopaniṣad* direct that since everything belongs to the Supreme Personality of Godhead, one should not encroach upon another's property, but should enjoy one's individual allotment. The best program for every living entity is to take direction from the Supreme Lord and enjoy material or spiritual life.

A question may be raised: Since Kardama Muni was advanced in spiritual life, why then did he not ask the Lord for liberation? Why did he want to enjoy material life in spite of his personally seeing and experiencing the Supreme Lord? The answer is that not everyone is competent to be liberated from material bondage. It is everyone's duty, therefore, to enjoy according to his present position, but under the direction of the Lord or the *Vedas.* The *Vedas* are considered to be the direct words of the Lord. The Lord gives us the opportunity to enjoy material life as we want, and at the same time He gives directions for the modes and processes of abiding by the *Vedas* so that gradually one may be elevated to liberation from material bondage. The conditioned souls who have come to the material world to fulfill their desires to lord it over material nature are bound by the laws of nature. The best course is to abide by the Vedic rules; that will help one to be gradually elevated to liberation.

Kardama Muni addresses the Lord as *śukla,* which means "the leader of religion." One who is pious should follow the rules of religion, for such rules are prescribed by the Lord Himself. No one can manufacture or concoct a religion; "religion" refers to the injunctions or laws of the Lord. In *Bhagavad-gītā* the Lord says that religion means to surrender unto Him. Therefore one should follow the Vedic regulations and surrender unto the Supreme Lord because that is the ultimate goal of perfection in human life. One should live a life of piety, follow the religious rules and regulations, marry and live peacefully for elevation to the higher status of spiritual realization.

TEXT 17

लोकांश्च लोकानुगतान् पशूंश्च
हित्वा श्रितास्ते चरणातपत्रम् ।
परस्परं त्वद्गुणवादसीधु-
पीयूषनिर्यापितदेहधर्माः ॥१७॥

lokāṁś ca lokānugatān paśūṁś ca
hitvā śritās te caraṇātapatram
parasparaṁ tvad-guṇa-vāda-sīdhu-
pīyūṣa-niryāpita-deha-dharmāḥ

lokān—worldly affairs; *ca*—and; *loka-anugatān*—the followers of worldly affairs; *paśūn*—beastly; *ca*—and; *hitvā*—having given up; *śritāḥ*—taken shelter; *te*—Your; *caraṇa*—of lotus feet; *ātapatram*—the umbrella; *parasparam*—with one another; *tvat*—Your; *guṇa*—of qualities; *vāda*—by discussion; *sīdhu*—intoxicating; *pīyūṣa*—by the nectar; *niryāpita*—extinguished; *deha-dharmāḥ*—the primary necessities of the body.

TRANSLATION

However, persons who have given up stereotyped worldly affairs and the beastly followers of these affairs, and who have taken shelter of the umbrella of Your lotus feet by drinking the intoxicating nectar of Your qualities and activities in discussions with one another, can be freed from the primary necessities of the material body.

PURPORT

After describing the necessity of married life, Kardama Muni asserts that marriage and other social affairs are stereotyped regulations for persons who are addicted to material sense enjoyment. The principles of animal life—eating, sleeping, mating and defending—are actually necessities of the body, but those who engage in transcendental Kṛṣṇa consciousness, giving up all the stereotyped activities of this material world, are freed from social conventions. Conditioned souls are under the spell of material energy, or eternal time—past, present and future—but as soon as one engages in Kṛṣṇa consciousness, he transcends the limits of past and present and becomes situated in the eternal activities of the soul. One has to act in terms of the Vedic injunctions in order to enjoy material life, but those who have taken to the devotional service of the Lord are not afraid of the regulations of this material world. Such devotees do not care for the conventions of material activities; they boldly take to that shelter which is like an umbrella against the sun of repeated birth and death.

Constant transmigration of the soul from one body to another is the cause of suffering in material existence. This conditional life in material existence is called *saṁsāra.* One may perform good work and take his birth in a very nice material condition, but the process under which birth and death take place is like a terrible fire. Śrī Viśvanātha Cakravartī Ṭhākura, in his prayer to the spiritual master, has described this. *Saṁsāra,* or the repetition of birth and death, is compared to a forest fire. A forest fire takes place automatically, without anyone's endeavor, by the friction of dried wood, and no fire department or sympathetic person can extinguish it. The raging forest fire can be extinguished only when there is a constant downpour of water from a cloud. The cloud is compared to the mercy of the spiritual master. By the grace of the spiritual master the cloud of the mercy of the Personality of Godhead is brought in, and then only, when the rains of Kṛṣṇa consciousness fall, can the fire of material existence be extinguished. This is also explained here. In order to find freedom from the stereotyped conditional life of material existence, one has to take shelter of the lotus feet of the Lord, not in the manner in which the impersonalists indulge, but in devotional service, chanting and hearing of the activities of the Lord. Only then can one be freed from the actions and reactions of material existence. It is recommended here that one should give up the conditional life of this material world and the association of so-called civilized human beings who are simply following, in a polished way, the same stereotyped principles of eating, sleeping, defending and mating. Chanting and hearing of the glories of the Lord is described here as *tvad-guṇa-vāda-sīdhu.* Only by drinking the nectar of chanting and hearing the pastimes of the Lord can one forget the intoxication of material existence.

TEXT 18

न तेऽजराक्षभ्रमिरायुरेषां
त्रयोदशारं त्रिशतं षष्टिपर्व ।
षण्नेम्यनन्तच्छदि यत्त्रिणाभि
करालस्रोतो जगदाच्छिद्य धावत् ॥१८॥

na te 'jarākṣa-bhramir āyur eṣāṁ
trayodaśāraṁ tri-śataṁ ṣaṣṭi-parva
ṣaṇ-nemy ananta-cchadi yat tri-ṇābhi
karāla-sroto jagad ācchidya dhāvat

na—not; *te*—Your; *ajara*—of imperishable Brahman; *akṣa*—on the axle; *bhramiḥ*—rotating; *āyuḥ*—span of life; *eṣām*—of the devotees; *trayodaśa*—thirteen; *aram*—spokes; *tri-śatam*—three hundred; *ṣaṣṭi*—sixty; *parva*—functions; *ṣaṭ*—six; *nemi*—rims; *ananta*—innumerable; *chadi*—leaves; *yat*—which; *tri*—three; *nābhi*—naves; *karāla-srotaḥ*—with tremendous velocity; *jagat*—the universe; *ācchidya*—cutting short; *dhāvat*—running.

TRANSLATION

Your wheel, which has three naves, rotates around the axis of the imperishable Brahman. It has thirteen spokes, 360 joints, six rims and numberless leaves carved upon it. Though its revolution cuts short the life-span of the entire creation, this wheel of tremendous velocity cannot touch the life-span of the devotees of the Lord.

PURPORT

The time factor cannot affect the span of life of the devotees. In *Bhagavad-gītā* it is stated that a little execution of devotional service saves one from the greatest danger. The greatest danger is transmigration of the soul from one body to another, and only devotional service to the Lord can stop this process. It is stated in the Vedic literatures, *harim vinā na mṛtim taranti:* without the mercy of the Lord, one cannot stop the cycle of birth and death. In *Bhagavad-gītā* it is stated that only by understanding the transcendental nature of the Lord and His activities, His appearance and disappearance, can one stop the cycle of death and go back to Him. The time factor is divided into many fractions of moments, hours, months, years, periods, seasons, etc. All the divisions in this verse are determined according to the astronomical calculations of Vedic literature. There are six seasons, called *ṛtus,* and there is the period of four months called *cāturmāsya.* Three periods of four months complete one year. According to Vedic astronomical calculations, there are thirteen months. The thirteenth month is called *adhi-māsa* or *mala-māsa* and is added every third year. The time factor, however, cannot touch the lifespan of the devotees. In another verse it is stated that when the sun rises and sets it takes away the life of all living entities, but it cannot take away the life of those who are engaged in devotional service. Time is compared here to a big wheel which has 360 joints, six rims in the shape of seasons, and numberless leaves in the shape of moments. It rotates on the eternal existence, Brahman.

TEXT 19

एकः स्वयं सञ्जगतः सिसृक्षया-
द्वितीययात्मन्नधियोगमायया ।
सृजस्यदः पासि पुनर्ग्रसिष्यसे
यथोर्णनाभिर्भगवन् स्वशक्तिभिः ॥१९॥

ekaḥ svayaṁ sañ jagataḥ sisṛkṣayā-
dvitīyayātmann adhi-yogamāyayā
sṛjasy adaḥ pāsi punar grasiṣyase
yathorṇa-nābhir bhagavan sva-śaktibhiḥ

ekaḥ—one; *svayam*—Yourself; *san*—being; *jagataḥ*—the universes; *sisṛkṣayā*—with a desire to create; *advitīyayā*—without a second; *ātman*—in Yourself; *adhi*—controlling; *yoga-māyayā*—by *yogamāyā; sṛjasi*—You create; *adaḥ*—those universes; *pāsi*—You maintain; *punaḥ*—again; *grasiṣyase*—You will wind up; *yathā*—like; *ūrṇa-nābhiḥ*—a spider; *bhagavan*—O Lord; *sva-śaktibhiḥ*—by its own energy.

TRANSLATION

My dear Lord, You alone create the universes. O Personality of Godhead, desiring to create these universes, You create them, maintain them and again wind them up by Your own energies, which are under the control of Your second energy, called yogamāyā, just as a spider creates a cobweb by its own energy and again winds it up.

PURPORT

In this verse two important words nullify the impersonalist theory that everything is God. Here Kardama says, "O Personality of Godhead, You are alone, but You have various energies." The example of the spider is very significant also. The spider is an individual living entity, and by its energy it creates a cobweb and plays on it, and whenever it likes it winds up the cobweb, thus ending the play. When the cobweb is manufactured by the saliva of the spider, the spider does not become impersonal. Similarly, the creation and manifestation of the material or spiritual energy does not render the creator impersonal. Here the very prayer suggests that God is sentient and can hear the prayers and fulfill the desires of the devotee. Therefore, He is *sac-cid-ānanda-vigraha,* the form of bliss, knowledge and eternity.

TEXT 20

नैतद्बताधीश पदं तवेप्सितं
यन्मायया नस्तनुषे भूतसूक्ष्मम् ।
अनुग्रहायास्त्वपि यर्हि मायया
लसत्तुलस्या भगवान् विलक्षितः ॥२०॥

naitad batādhīśa padaṁ tavepsitaṁ
yan māyayā nas tanuṣe bhūta-sūkṣmam
anugrahāyāstv api yarhi māyayā
lasat-tulasyā bhagavān vilakṣitaḥ

na—not; *etat*—this; *bata*—indeed; *adhīśa*—O Lord; *padam*—material world; *tava*—Your; *īpsitam*—desire; *yat*—which; *māyayā*—by Your external energy; *naḥ*—for us; *tanuṣe*—You manifest; *bhūta-sūkṣmam*—the elements, gross and subtle; *anugrahāya*—for bestowing mercy; *astu*—let it be; *api*—also; *yarhi*—when; *māyayā*—through Your causeless mercy; *lasat*—splendid; *tulasyā*—with a wreath of *tulasī* leaves; *bhagavān*—the Supreme Personality of Godhead; *vilakṣitaḥ*—is perceived.

TRANSLATION

My dear Lord, although it is not Your desire, You manifest this creation of gross and subtle elements just for our sensual satisfaction. Let Your causeless mercy be upon us, for You have appeared before us in Your eternal form, adorned with a splendid wreath of tulasī leaves.

PURPORT

It is clearly stated here that the material world is not created by the personal will of the Supreme Lord; it is created by His external energy because the living entities want to enjoy it. This material world is not created for those who do not want to enjoy sense gratification, who constantly remain in transcendental loving service and who are eternally Kṛṣṇa conscious. For them, the spiritual world is eternally existing, and they enjoy there. Elsewhere in the *Śrīmad-Bhāgavatam* it is stated that for those who have taken shelter of the lotus feet of the Supreme Personality of Godhead, this material world is useless; because this material world is full of danger at every step, it is not meant for the devotees but for living entities who want to lord it over the material energy at their own risk. Kṛṣṇa is so kind that He allows the sense-enjoying living entities a separate world created by Him to enjoy as they like, yet at the same time He appears in His personal form. The Lord unwillingly creates this material world, but He descends in His personal form or sends one of His reliable sons or a servant or a reliable author like Vyāsadeva to give instruction. He Himself also instructs in His speeches of *Bhagavad-gītā*. This propaganda work goes on side by side with the creation to convince the misguided living entities who are rotting in this material world to come back to Him and surrender unto Him. Therefore the last instruction of *Bhagavad-gītā* is this: "Give up all your manufactured engagements in the material world and just surrender unto Me. I shall protect you from all sinful reactions."

TEXT 21

तं त्वानुभूत्योपरतक्रियार्थं
स्वमायया वर्तितलोकतन्त्रम् ।
नमाम्यभीक्ष्णं नमनीयपाद-
सरोजमल्पीयसि कामवर्षम् ॥२१॥

taṁ tvānubhūtyoparata-kriyārthaṁ
sva-māyayā vartita-loka-tantram

namāmy abhīkṣṇaṁ namanīya-pāda-
sarojam alpīyasi kāma-varṣam

tam—that; *tvā*—You; *anubhūtyā*—by realizing; *uparata*—disregarded; *kriyā*—enjoyment of fruitive activities; *artham*—in order that; *sva-māyayā*—by Your own energy; *vartita*—brought about; *loka-tantram*—the material worlds; *namāmi*—I offer obeisances; *abhīkṣṇam*—continuously; *namanīya*—worshipable; *pāda-sarojam*—lotus feet; *alpīyasi*—on the insignificant; *kāma*—desires; *varṣam*—showering.

TRANSLATION

I continuously offer my respectful obeisances unto Your lotus feet, of which it is worthy to take shelter, because You shower all benedictions on the insignificant. To give all living entities detachment from fruitive activity by realizing You, You have expanded these material worlds by Your own energy.

PURPORT

Everyone, therefore, whether he desires material enjoyment, liberation or the transcendental loving service of the Lord, should engage himself, offering obeisances unto the Supreme Lord, because the Lord can award everyone his desired benediction. In *Bhagavad-gītā* the Lord affirms, *ye yathā māṁ prapadyante:* anyone who desires to be a successful enjoyer in this material world is awarded that benediction by the Lord, anyone who wants to be liberated from the entanglement of this material world is given liberation by the Lord, and anyone who desires to constantly engage in His service in full Kṛṣṇa consciousness is awarded that benediction by the Lord. For material enjoyment He has prescribed so many ritualistic sacrificial performances in the *Vedas*, and thus people may take advantage of those instructions and enjoy material life in higher planets or in a noble aristocratic family. These processes are mentioned in the *Vedas*, and one can take advantage of them. It is similar with those who want to be liberated from this material world.

Unless one is disgusted with the enjoyment of this material world, he cannot aspire for liberation. Liberation is for one who is disgusted with material enjoyment. *Vedānta-sūtra* says, therefore, *athāto brahma jijñāsā:* those who have given up the attempt to be happy in this material world can inquire about the Absolute Truth. For those who want to know the Absolute Truth, the *Vedānta-sūtra* is available, as is *Śrīmad-Bhāgavatam*, the actual explanation of *Vedānta-sūtra*. Since *Bhagavad-gītā* is also *Vedānta-sūtra*, by understanding *Śrīmad-Bhāgavatam*, *Vedānta-sūtra* or *Bhagavad-gītā* one can obtain real knowledge. When one obtains real knowledge, he becomes theoretically one with the Supreme, and when he actually begins the service of Brahman, or Kṛṣṇa consciousness, he is not only liberated but situated in his spiritual life. Similarly, for those who want to lord it over material nature, there are so many departments of material enjoyment; material knowledge and material science are available, and the Lord provides for persons who want to enjoy them. The conclusion is that one should worship the Supreme Personality of Godhead for any benediction. The word *kāma-varṣam* is very significant, for it indicates that He satisfies the desires of anyone who approaches Him. But one who sincerely loves Kṛṣṇa and yet wants material enjoyment is in perplexity. Kṛṣṇa, being very kind toward him, gives him an opportunity to engage in the transcendental loving service of the Lord, and so he gradually forgets the hallucination.

TEXT 22

ऋषिरुवाच
इत्यव्यलीकं प्रणुतोऽब्जनाभ-
स्तमाबभाषे वचसामृतेन ।
सुपर्णपक्षोपरि रोचमानः
प्रेमस्मितोद्वीक्षणविभ्रमद्भ्रूः ॥२२॥

ṛṣir uvāca
ity avyalīkaṁ praṇuto 'bja-nābhas
tam ābabhāṣe vacasāmṛtena
suparṇa-pakṣopari rocamānaḥ
prema-smitodvīkṣaṇa-vibhramad-bhrūḥ

ṛṣiḥ uvāca—the great sage Maitreya said; *iti*—thus; *avyalīkam*—sincerely; *praṇutaḥ*—having been praised; *abja-nābhaḥ*—Lord Viṣṇu; *tam*—to Kardama Muni; *ābabhāṣe*—replied; *vacasā*—with words; *amṛtena*—as sweet as nectar; *suparṇa*—of Garuḍa; *pakṣa*—the shoulders; *upari*—upon; *rocamānaḥ*—shining; *prema*—of affection; *smita*—with a smile; *udvīkṣaṇa*—looking; *vibhramat*—gracefully moving; *bhrūḥ*—eyebrows.

TRANSLATION

Maitreya resumed: Sincerely extolled in these words, Lord Viṣṇu, shining very beautifully on the shoulders of Garuḍa, replied with words as sweet as nectar. His eyebrows moved gracefully as He looked at the sage with a smile full of affection.

PURPORT

The word *vacasāmṛtena* is significant. Whenever the Lord speaks, He speaks from the transcendental world. He does not speak from the material world. Since He is transcendental, His speech is also transcendental, as is His activity; everything in relation to Him is transcendental. The word *amṛta* refers to one who does not meet with death. The words and activities of the Lord are deathless; therefore they are not manufactured of this material world. The sound of this material world and that of the spiritual world are completely different. The sound of the spiritual world is nectarean and eternal, whereas the sound of the material world is hackneyed and subject to end. The sound of the holy name—Hare Kṛṣṇa, Hare Kṛṣṇa, Kṛṣṇa Kṛṣṇa, Hare Hare—everlastingly increases the enthusiasm of the chanter. If one repeats monotonous material words, he will feel exhausted, but if he chants Hare Kṛṣṇa twenty-four hours a day, he will never feel exhausted; rather, he will feel encouraged to continue chanting more and more. When the Lord replied to the sage Kardama, the word *vacasāmṛtena* is specifically mentioned, since He spoke from the transcendental world. He replied in transcendental words, and when He spoke His eyebrows moved with great affection. When a devotee praises the glories of the Lord, the Lord is very satisfied, and He bestows His transcendental benediction upon the devotee without reservation because He is always causelessly merciful toward His devotee.

TEXT 23

श्रीभगवानुवाच

विदित्वा तव चैत्यं मे पुरैव समयोजि तत् ।
यदर्थमात्मनियमैस्त्वयैवाहं समर्चितः ॥२३॥

śrī-bhagavān uvāca
viditvā tava caityaṁ me
puraiva samayoji tat
yad-artham ātma-niyamais
tvayaivāhaṁ samarcitaḥ

śrī-bhagavān uvāca—the Supreme Lord said; *viditvā*—understanding; *tava*—your; *caityam*—mental condition; *me*—by Me; *purā*—previously; *eva*—certainly; *samayoji*—was arranged; *tat*—that; *yat-artham*—for the sake of which; *ātma*—of the mind and senses; *niyamaiḥ*—by discipline; *tvayā*—by you; *eva*—only; *aham*—I; *samarcitaḥ*—have been worshiped.

TRANSLATION

The Supreme Lord said: Having come to know what was in your mind, I have already arranged for that for which you have worshiped Me well through your mental and sensory discipline.

PURPORT

The Supreme Personality of Godhead in His Paramātmā feature is situated in everyone's heart. He knows, therefore, the past, present and future of every individual person as well as his desires, activities and everything about him. It is stated in *Bhagavad-gītā* that He is seated in the heart as a witness. The Personality of Godhead knew the heart's desire of Kardama Muni, and He had already arranged for the fulfillment of his desires. He never disappoints a sincere devotee, regardless of what he wants, but He never allows anything which will be detrimental to the individual's devotional service.

TEXT 24

न वै जातु मृषैव स्यात्प्रजाध्यक्ष मदर्हणम् ।
भवद्विधेष्वतितरां मयि सङ्गृभितात्मनाम् ॥२४॥

na vai jātu mṛṣaiva syāt
prajādhyakṣa mad-arhaṇam
bhavad-vidheṣv atitarāṁ
mayi saṅgṛbhitātmanām

na—not; *vai*—indeed; *jātu*—ever; *mṛṣā*—useless; *eva*—only; *syāt*—it may be; *prajā*—of the living entities; *adhyakṣa*—O leader; *mat-arhaṇam*—worship of Me; *bhavat-vidheṣu*—unto persons like you; *atitarām*—entirely; *mayi*—on Me; *saṅgṛbhita*—are fixed; *ātmanām*—of those whose minds.

TRANSLATION

The Lord continued: My dear ṛṣi, O leader of the living entities, for those who serve Me in devotion by worshiping Me, especially persons like you who have given up everything unto Me, there is never any question of frustration.

PURPORT

Even if he has some desires, one engaged in the service of the Lord is never frustrated. Those engaged in His service are called *sakāma* and *akāma*. Those who approach the Supreme Personality of Godhead with desires for material enjoyment are called *sakāma,* and those devotees who have no material desires for sense gratification but serve the Supreme Lord out of spontaneous love for Him are called *akāma. Sakāma* devotees are divided into four classes—those in distress, those in need of money, the inquisitive and the wise. Someone worships the Supreme Lord because of bodily or mental distress, someone else worships the Supreme Lord because he is in need of money, someone else worships the Lord out of inquisitiveness to know Him as He is, and someone wants to know the Lord as a philosopher can know Him, by the research work of his wisdom. There is no frustration for any of these four classes of men; each is endowed with the desired result of his worship.

TEXT 25

प्रजापतिसुतः सम्राण्मनुर्विख्यातमङ्गलः ।
ब्रह्मावर्तं योऽधिवसन् शास्ति सप्तार्णवां महीम् ॥२५॥

prajāpati-sutaḥ samrāṇ
manur vikhyāta-maṅgalaḥ
brahmāvartaṁ yo 'dhivasan
śāsti saptārṇavāṁ mahīm

prajāpati-sutaḥ—the son of Lord Brahmā; *samrāṭ*—the Emperor; *manuḥ*—Svāyambhuva Manu; *vikhyāta*—well known; *maṅgalaḥ*—whose righteous acts; *brahmāvartam*—Brahmāvarta; *yaḥ*—he who; *adhivasan*—living in; *śāsti*—rules; *sapta*—seven; *arṇavām*—oceans; *mahīm*—the earth.

TRANSLATION

The Emperor Svāyambhuva Manu, the son of Lord Brahmā, who is well known for his righteous acts, has his seat in Brahmāvarta and rules over the earth with its seven oceans.

PURPORT

Sometimes it is stated that Brahmāvarta is a part of Kurukṣetra or that Kurukṣetra itself is situated in Brahmāvarta, because the demigods are recommended to perform spiritual ritualistic performances in Kurukṣetra. But in others' opinion, Brahmāvarta is a place in Brahmaloka, where Svāyambhuva ruled. There are many places on the surface of this earth which are also known in the higher planetary systems; we have places on this planet like Vṛndāvana, Dvārakā and Mathurā, but they are also eternally situated in Kṛṣṇaloka. There are many similar names on the surface of the earth, and it may be that in the Boar age Svāyambhuva Manu ruled this planet, as stated here. The word *maṅgalaḥ* is significant. *Maṅgala* means one who is elevated in every respect in the opulences of religious performances, ruling power, cleanliness and all other good qualities. *Vikhyāta* means "celebrated." Svāyambhuva Manu was celebrated for all good qualities and opulences.

TEXT 26

स चेह विप्र राजर्षिर्महिष्या शतरूपया ।
आयास्यति दिदृक्षुस्त्वां परश्वो धर्मकोविदः ॥२६॥

sa ceha vipra rājarṣir
mahiṣyā śatarūpayā
āyāsyati didṛkṣus tvāṁ
paraśvo dharma-kovidaḥ

saḥ—Svāyambhuva Manu; *ca*—and; *iha*—here; *vipra*—O holy *brāhmaṇa; rāja-ṛṣiḥ*—the saintly king; *mahiṣyā*—along with his queen; *śatarūpayā*—called Śatarūpā; *āyāsyati*—will come; *didṛkṣuḥ*—desiring to see; *tvām*—you; *paraśvaḥ*—the day after tomorrow; *dharma*—in religious activities; *kovidaḥ*—expert.

TRANSLATION

The day after tomorrow, O brāhmaṇa, that celebrated emperor, who is expert in religious activities, will come here with his queen, Śatarūpā, wishing to see you.

TEXT 27

आत्मजामसितापाङ्गीं वयःशीलगुणान्विताम् ।
मृगयन्तीं पतिं दास्यत्यनुरूपाय ते प्रभो ॥२७॥

ātmajām asitāpāṅgīṁ
vayaḥ-śīla-guṇānvitām
mṛgayantīṁ patiṁ dāsyaty
anurūpāya te prabho

ātma-jām—his own daughter; *asita*—black; *apāṅgīm*—eyes; *vayaḥ*—grown-up age; *śīla*—with character; *guṇa*—with good qualities; *anvitām*—endowed; *mṛgayantīm*—searching for;

patim—a husband; *dāsyati*—he will give; *anurūpāya*—who are suitable; *te*—unto you; *prabho*—My dear sir.

TRANSLATION

He has a grown-up daughter whose eyes are black. She is ready for marriage, and she has good character and all good qualities. She is also searching for a good husband. My dear sir, her parents will come to see you, who are exactly suitable for her, just to deliver their daughter as your wife.

PURPORT

The selection of a good husband for a good girl was always entrusted to the parents. Here it is clearly stated that Manu and his wife were coming to see Kardama Muni to offer their daughter because the daughter was well qualified and the parents were searching out a similarly qualified man. This is the duty of parents. Girls are never thrown into the public street to search out their husband, for when girls are grown up and are searching after a boy, they forget to consider whether the boy they select is actually suitable for them. Out of the urge of sex desire, a girl may accept anyone, but if the husband is chosen by the parents, they can consider who is to be selected and who is not. According to the Vedic system, therefore, the girl is given over to a suitable boy by the parents; she is never allowed to select her own husband independently.

TEXT 28

समाहितं ते हृदयं यत्रेमान् परिवत्सरान् ।
सा त्वां ब्रह्मन्नृपवधूः काममाशु भजिष्यति ॥२८॥

samāhitaṁ te hṛdayaṁ
yatremān parivatsarān
sā tvāṁ brahman nṛpa-vadhūḥ
kāmam āśu bhajiṣyati

samāhitam—has been fixed; *te*—your; *hṛdayam*—heart; *yatra*—on whom; *imān*—for all these; *parivatsarān*—years; *sā*—she; *tvām*—you; *brahman*—O *brāhmaṇa; nṛpa-vadhūḥ*—the princess; *kāmam*—as you desire; *āśu*—very soon; *bhajiṣyati*—will serve.

TRANSLATION

That princess, O holy sage, will be just the type you have been thinking of in your heart for all these long years. She will soon be yours and will serve you to your heart's content.

PURPORT

The Lord awards all benedictions according to the heart's desire of a devotee, so the Lord informed Kardama Muni, "The girl who is coming to be married with you is a princess, the daughter of Emperor Svāyambhuva, and so just suitable for your purpose." Only by God's grace can one get a nice wife just as he desires. Similarly, it is only by God's grace that a girl gets a husband suitable to her heart. Thus it is said that if we pray to the Supreme Lord in every transaction of our material existence, everything will be done very nicely and just suitable to our heart's desire. In other words, in all circumstances we must take shelter of the Supreme Personality of Godhead and depend completely on His decision. Man proposes, God disposes. The fulfillment of desires, therefore, should be entrusted to the Supreme Personality of Godhead; that is the nicest solution. Kardama Muni desired only a wife, but because he was a devotee of the Lord, the Lord selected a wife for him who was the Emperor's daughter, a princess. Thus Kardama Muni got a wife beyond his expectation. If we depend on the choice of the Supreme Personality of Godhead, we will receive benedictions in greater opulence than we desire.

It is also significantly noted here that Kardama Muni was a *brāhmaṇa*, whereas Emperor Svāyambhuva was a *kṣatriya*. Therefore, intercaste marriage was current even in those days. The system was that a *brāhmaṇa* could marry the daughter of a *kṣatriya*, but a *kṣatriya* could not marry the daughter of a *brāhmaṇa*. We have evidences from the history of the Vedic age that Śukrācārya offered his daughter to Mahārāja Yayāti, but the King had to refuse to marry the daughter of a *brāhmaṇa*; only with the special permission of the *brāhmaṇa* could they marry. Intercaste marriage, therefore, was not prohibited in the olden days, many millions of years ago, but there was a regular system of social behavior.

TEXT 29

या त आत्मभृतं वीर्यं नवधा प्रसविष्यति ।
वीर्ये त्वदीये ऋषय आधास्यन्त्यञ्जसात्मनः ॥२९॥

yā ta ātma-bhṛtaṁ vīryaṁ
navadhā prasaviṣyati
vīrye tvadīye ṛṣaya
ādhāsyanty añjasātmanaḥ

yā—she; *te*—by you; *ātma-bhṛtam*—sown in her; *vīryam*—the seed; *nava-dhā*—nine daughters; *prasaviṣyati*—will bring forth; *vīrye tvadīye*—in the daughters begotten by you; *ṛṣayaḥ*—the sages; *ādhāsyanti*—will beget; *añjasā*—in total; *ātmanaḥ*—children.

TRANSLATION

She will bring forth nine daughters from the seed sown in her by you, and through the daughters you beget, the sages will duly beget children.

TEXT 30

त्वं च सम्यगनुष्ठाय निदेशं म उशत्तमः ।
मयि तीर्थीकृताशेषक्रियार्थो मां प्रपत्स्यसे ॥३०॥

tvaṁ ca samyag anuṣṭhāya
nideśaṁ ma uśattamaḥ
mayi tīrthī-kṛtāśeṣa-
kriyārtho māṁ prapatsyase

tvam—you; *ca*—and; *samyak*—properly; *anuṣṭhāya*—having carried out; *nideśam*—command; *me*—My; *uśattamaḥ*—completely cleansed; *mayi*—unto Me; *tīrthī-kṛta*—having resigned; *aśeṣa*—all; *kriyā*—of actions; *arthaḥ*—the fruits; *mām*—to Me; *prapatsyase*—you will attain.

TRANSLATION

With your heart cleansed by properly carrying out My command, resigning to Me the fruits of all your acts, you will finally attain to Me.

PURPORT

Here the words *tīrthī-kṛtāśeṣa-kriyārthaḥ* are significant. *Tīrtha* means a sanctified place where charity is given. People used to go to places of pilgrimage and give munificently in charity. This system is still current. Therefore the Lord said, "In order to sanctify your activities and the results of your actions, you will offer everything unto Me." This is also confirmed in *Bhagavad-gītā:* "Whatever you do, whatever you eat, whatever you sacrifice, the result should be given to Me only." In another place in *Bhagavad-gītā* the Lord said, "I am the enjoyer of all sacrifices, all penances and everything done for the welfare of mankind or society." All activities, therefore, whether for the welfare of family, society, country or humanity at large, must be performed in Kṛṣṇa consciousness. That is the instruction given by the Lord to Kardama Muni. Mahārāja Yudhiṣṭhira welcomed Nārada Muni: "Wherever you are present, that place becomes sanctified because the Lord Himself is always seated in your heart." Similarly, if we act in Kṛṣṇa consciousness under the direction of the Lord and His representative, then everything is sanctified. This is the indication given to

Kardama Muni, who acted on it and therefore received the most excellent wife and child, as will be disclosed in later verses.

TEXT 31

कृत्वा दयां च जीवेषु दत्त्वा चाभयमात्मवान् ।
मय्यात्मानं सह जगद् द्रक्ष्यस्यात्मनि चापि माम् ॥३१॥

kṛtvā dayāṁ ca jīveṣu
dattvā cābhayam ātmavān
mayy ātmānaṁ saha jagad
drakṣyasy ātmani cāpi mām

kṛtvā—having shown; *dayām*—compassion; *ca*—and; *jīveṣu*—toward living beings; *dattvā*—having given; *ca*—and; *abhayam*—assurance of safety; *ātma-vān*—self-realized; *mayi*—in Me; *ātmānam*—yourself; *saha jagat*—along with the universe; *drakṣyasi*—you will perceive; *ātmani*—in yourself; *ca*—and; *api*—also; *mām*—Me.

TRANSLATION

Showing compassion to all living entities, you will attain self-realization. Giving assurance of safety to all, you will perceive your own self as well as all the universes in Me, and Myself in you.

PURPORT

The simple process of self-realization for every living entity is described here. The first principle to be understood is that this world is a product of the supreme will. There is an identity of this world with the Supreme Lord. This identity is accepted in a misconceived way by the impersonalists; they say that the Supreme Absolute Truth, transforming Himself into the universe, loses His separate existence. Thus they accept the world and everything in it to be the Lord. That is pantheism, wherein everything is considered to be the Lord. This is the view of the impersonalist. But those who are personal devotees of the Lord take everything to be the property of the Supreme Lord. Everything, whatever we see, is the manifestation of the Supreme Lord; therefore, everything should be engaged in the service of the Lord. This is oneness. The difference between the impersonalist and the personalist is that the impersonalist does not accept the separate existence of the Lord, but the personalist accepts the Lord; he understands that although He distributes Himself in so many ways, He has His separate personal existence. This is described in *Bhagavad-gītā*: "I am spread all over the universe in My impersonal form. Everything is resting on Me, but I am not present." There is a nice example regarding the sun and the sunshine. The sun, by its sunshine, is spread all over the universe, and all the planets rest on the sunshine. But all the planets are different from the sun planet; one cannot say that because the planets are resting on the sunshine, these planets are also the sun. Similarly, the impersonal or pantheistic view that everything is God is not a very intelligent proposal. The real position, as explained by the Lord Himself, is that although nothing can exist without Him, it is not a fact that everything *is* Him. He is different from everything. So here also the Lord says: "You will see everything in the world to be nondifferent from Me." This means that everything should be considered a product of the Lord's energy, and therefore everything should be employed in the service of the Lord. One's energy should be utilized for one's self-interest. That is the perfection of the energy.

This energy can be utilized for real self-interest if one is compassionate. A person in Kṛṣṇa consciousness, a devotee of the Lord, is always compassionate. He is not satisfied that only he himself is a devotee, but he tries to distribute the knowledge of devotional service to everyone. There are many devotees of the Lord who faced many risks in distributing the devotional service of the Lord to people in general. That should be done.

It is also said that a person who goes to the temple of the Lord and worships with great devotion, but who does not show sympathy to people in general or show respect to other devotees, is considered to be a third-class devotee. The second-class devotee is he who is merciful and compassionate to the fallen soul. The second-class devotee is always cognizant of his position as an eternal servant of the Lord; he therefore makes friendships with devotees of the Lord, acts compassionately toward the general public in teaching them devotional service, and refuses to cooperate or associate with nondevotees. As long as one is not compassionate to people in general in his devotional service to the Lord, he is a third-class devotee. The first-class devotee gives assurance to every living being that there is no fear of this material existence: "Let us live in Kṛṣṇa consciousness and conquer the nescience of material existence."

It is indicated here that Kardama Muni was directed by the Lord to be very compassionate and liberal in his householder life and to give assurance to the people in his renounced life. A *sannyāsī,* one in the renounced order of life, is meant to give enlightenment to the people. He should travel, going from home to home to enlighten. The householder, by the spell of *māyā,* becomes absorbed in family affairs and forgets his relationship with Kṛṣṇa. If he dies in forgetfulness, like the cats and dogs, then his life is spoiled. It is the duty of a *sannyāsī,* therefore, to go and awaken the forgetful souls with enlightenment of their eternal relationship with the Lord and to engage them in devotional service. The devotee should show mercy to the fallen souls and also give them the assurance of fearlessness. As soon as one becomes a devotee of the Lord, he is convinced that he is protected by the Lord. Fear itself is afraid of the Lord; therefore, what has he to do with fearfulness?

To award fearlessness to the common man is the greatest act of charity. A *sannyāsī*, or one who is in the renounced order of life, should wander from door to door, from village to village, from town to town and from country to country, all over the world as far as he is able to travel, and enlighten the householders about Kṛṣṇa consciousness. A person who is a householder but is initiated by a *sannyāsī* has the duty to spread Kṛṣṇa consciousness at home; as far as possible, he should call his friends and neighbors to his house and hold classes in Kṛṣṇa consciousness. Holding a class means chanting the holy name of Kṛṣṇa and speaking from *Bhagavad-gītā* or *Śrīmad-Bhāgavatam*. There are immense literatures for spreading Kṛṣṇa consciousness, and it is the duty of each and every householder to learn about Kṛṣṇa from his *sannyāsī* spiritual master. There is a division of labor in the Lord's service. The householder's duty is to earn money because a *sannyāsī* is not supposed to earn money but is completely dependent on the householder. The householder should earn money by business or by profession and spend at least fifty percent of his income to spread Kṛṣṇa consciousness; twenty-five percent he can spend for his family, and twenty-five percent he should save to meet emergencies. This example was shown by Rūpa Gosvāmī, so devotees should follow it.

Actually, to be one with the Supreme Lord means to be one with the interest of the Lord. Becoming one with the Supreme Lord does not imply becoming as great as the Supreme Lord. It is impossible. The part is never equal to the whole. The living entity is always a minute part. Therefore his oneness with the Lord is that he is interested in the one interest of the Lord. The Lord wants every living entity to always think about Him, to be His devotee and always worship Him. This is clearly stated in *Bhagavad-gītā: man-manā bhava mad-bhaktaḥ*. Kṛṣṇa wants everyone always to think of Him. Everyone should always offer obeisances to Kṛṣṇa. This is the will of the Supreme Lord, and devotees should try to fulfill His desire. Since the Lord is unlimited, His desire is also unlimited. There is no stoppage, and therefore the service of the devotee is also unlimited. In the transcendental world there is unlimited competition between the Lord and the servitor. The Lord wants to fulfill His desires unlimitedly, and the devotee also serves Him to fulfill His unlimited desires. There is an unlimited oneness of interest between the Lord and His devotee.

TEXT 32

सहाहं स्वांशकलया त्वद्वीर्येण महामुने ।
तव क्षेत्रे देवहूत्यां प्रणेष्ये तत्त्वसंहिताम् ॥३२॥

sahāhaṁ svāṁśa-kalayā
tvad-vīryeṇa mahā-mune
tava kṣetre devahūtyāṁ
praṇeṣye tattva-saṁhitām

saha—with; *aham*—I; *sva-aṁśa-kalayā*—My own plenary portion; *tvat-vīryeṇa*—by your semen; *mahā-mune*—O great sage; *tava kṣetre*—in your wife; *devahūtyām*—in Devahūti; *praṇeṣye*—I shall instruct; *tattva*—of the ultimate principles; *saṁhitām*—the doctrine.

TRANSLATION

O great sage, I shall manifest My own plenary portion through your wife, Devahūti, along with your nine daughters, and I shall instruct her in the system of philosophy that deals with the ultimate principles or categories.

PURPORT

Herein the word *svāṁśa-kalayā* indicates that the Lord would appear as the son of Devahūti and Kardama Muni as Kapiladeva, the first propounder of the Sāṅkhya philosophy, which is mentioned here as *tattva-saṁhitā.* The Lord foretold to Kardama Muni that He would appear in His incarnation Kapiladeva and would propagate the philosophy of Sāṅkhya. Sāṅkhya philosophy is very well known in the world as propagated by another Kapiladeva, but that Sāṅkhya philosophy is different from the Sāṅkhya which was propounded by the Lord Himself. There are two kinds of Sāṅkhya philosophy: one is godless Sāṅkhya philosophy, and the other is godly Sāṅkhya philosophy. The Sāṅkhya propagated by Kapiladeva, son of Devahūti, is godly philosophy.

There are different manifestations of the Lord. He is one, but He has become many. He divides Himself into two different expansions, one called *kalā* and the other *vibhinnāṁśa.* Ordinary living entities are called *vibhinnāṁśa* expansions, and the unlimited expansions of *viṣṇu-tattva*, such as Vāmana, Govinda, Nārāyaṇa, Pradyumna, Vāsudeva and Ananta, are called *svāṁśa-kalā. Svāṁśa* refers to a direct expansion, and *kalā* denotes an expansion from the expansion of the original Lord. Baladeva is an expansion of Kṛṣṇa, and from Baladeva the next expansion is Saṅkarṣaṇa; thus Saṅkarṣaṇa is *kalā*, but Baladeva is *svāṁśa.* There is no difference, however, among

Them. This is very nicely explained in the *Brahma-saṁhitā* (5.46): *dīpārcir eva hi daśāntaram abhyupetya.* With one candle one may light a second candle, with the second a third and then a fourth, and in this way one can light up thousands of candles, and no candle is inferior to another in distributing light. Every candle has the full potential candlepower, but there is still the distinction that one candle is the first, another the second, another the third and another the fourth. Similarly, there is no difference between the immediate expansion of the Lord and His secondary expansion. The Lord's names are considered in exactly the same way; since the Lord is absolute, His name, His form, His pastimes, His paraphernalia and His quality all have the same potency. In the absolute world, the name Kṛṣṇa is the transcendental sound representation of the Lord. There is no potential difference between His quality, name, form, etc. If we chant the name of the Lord, Hare Kṛṣṇa, that has as much potency as the Lord Himself. There is no potential difference between the form of the Lord whom we worship and the form of the Lord in the temple. One should not think that one is worshiping a doll or statue of the Lord, even if others consider it to be a statue. Because there is not potential difference, one gets the same result by worshiping the statue of the Lord or the Lord Himself. This is the science of Kṛṣṇa consciousness.

TEXT 33

मैत्रेय उवाच
एवं तमनुभाष्याथ भगवान् प्रत्यगक्षजः ।
जगाम बिन्दुसरसः सरस्वत्या परिश्रितात् ॥३३॥

maitreya uvāca
evaṁ tam anubhāṣyātha
bhagavān pratyag-akṣajaḥ
jagāma bindusarasaḥ
sarasvatyā pariśritāt

maitreyaḥ uvāca—the great sage Maitreya said; *evam*—thus; *tam*—to him; *anubhāṣya*—having spoken; *atha*—then; *bhagavān*—the Lord; *pratyak*—directly; *akṣa*—by senses; *jaḥ*—who is perceived; *jagāma*—went away; *bindu-sarasaḥ*—from Lake Bindu-sarovara; *sarasvatyā*—by the River Sarasvatī; *pariśritāt*—encircled.

TRANSLATION

Maitreya went on: Thus having spoken to Kardama Muni, the Lord, who reveals Himself only when the senses are in Kṛṣṇa consciousness, departed

from that lake called Bindu-sarovara, which was encircled by the River Sarasvatī.

PURPORT

One word in this verse is very significant. The Lord is stated here to be *pratyag-akṣaja.* He is imperceptible to material senses, but still He can be seen. This appears to be contradictory. We have material senses, but how can we see the Supreme Lord? He is called *adhokṣaja,* which means that He cannot be seen by the material senses. *Akṣaja* means "knowledge perceived by material senses." Because the Lord is not an object that can be understood by speculation with our material senses, He is also called *ajita;* He will conquer, but no one can conquer Him. What does it mean, then, that still He can be seen? It is explained that no one can hear the transcendental name of Kṛṣṇa, no one can understand His transcendental form, and no one can assimilate His transcendental pastimes. It is not possible. Then how is it possible that He can be seen and understood? When one is trained in devotional service and renders service unto Him, gradually one's senses are purified of material contamination. When one's senses are thus purified, then one can see, one can understand, one can hear and so on. The purification of the material senses and perception of the transcendental form, name and quality of Kṛṣṇa are combined together in one word, *pratyag-akṣaja,* which is used here.

TEXT 34

निरीक्षतस्तस्य ययावशेष-
सिद्धेश्वराभिष्टुतसिद्धमार्गः ।
आकर्णयन् पत्ररथेन्द्रपक्षै-
रुच्चारितं स्तोममुदीर्णसाम ॥३४॥

nirīkṣatas tasya yayāv aśeṣa-
siddheśvarābhiṣṭuta-siddha-mārgaḥ
ākarṇayan patra-rathendra-pakṣair
uccāritaṁ stomam udīrṇa-sāma

nirīkṣataḥ tasya—while he was looking on; *yayau*—He left; *aśeṣa*—all; *siddha-īśvara*—by liberated souls; *abhiṣṭuta*—is praised; *siddha-mārgaḥ*—the way to the spiritual world; *ākarṇayan*—hearing; *patra-ratha-indra*—of Garuḍa (king of birds); *pakṣaiḥ*—by the wings; *uccāritam*—vibrated; *stomam*—hymns; *udīrṇa-sāma*—forming the *Sāma Veda.*

TRANSLATION

While the sage stood looking on, the Lord left by the pathway leading to Vaikuṇṭha, a path extolled by all great liberated souls. The sage stood listening as the hymns forming the basis of the Sāma Veda were vibrated by the flapping wings of the Lord's carrier, Garuḍa.

PURPORT

In the Vedic literature it is stated that the two wings of the transcendental bird Garuḍa, who carries the Lord everywhere, are two divisions of the *Sāma Veda* known as *bṛhat* and *rathāntara.* Garuḍa works as the carrier of the Lord; therefore he is considered the transcendental prince of all carriers. With his two wings Garuḍa began to vibrate the *Sāma Veda,* which is chanted by great sages to pacify the Lord. The Lord is worshiped by Brahmā, by Lord Śiva, by Garuḍa and other demigods with selected poems, and great sages worship Him with the hymns of Vedic literatures, such as the *Upaniṣads* and *Sāma Veda.* These *Sāma Veda* utterances are automatically heard by the devotee when another great devotee of the Lord, Garuḍa, flaps his wings.

It is clearly stated here that the sage Kardama began to look to the path by which the Lord was being carried to Vaikuṇṭha. It is thus confirmed that the Lord descends from His abode, Vaikuṇṭha, in the spiritual sky, and is carried by Garuḍa. The path which leads to Vaikuṇṭha is not worshiped by the ordinary class of transcendentalists. Only those who are already liberated from material bondage can become devotees of the Lord. Those who are not liberated from material bondage cannot understand transcendental devotional service. In *Bhagavad-gītā* it is clearly stated, *yatatām api siddhānām.* There are many persons who are trying to attain perfection by striving for liberation from material bondage, and those who are actually liberated are called *brahma-bhūta* or *siddha.* Only the *siddhas,* or persons liberated from material bondage, can become devotees. This is also confirmed in *Bhagavad-gītā:* anyone who is engaged in Kṛṣṇa consciousness, or devotional service, is already liberated from the influence of the modes of material nature. Here it is also confirmed that the path of devotional service is worshiped by liberated persons, not the conditioned souls. The conditioned soul cannot understand the devotional service of the Lord. Kardama Muni was a liberated soul who saw the Supreme Lord in person, face to face. There was no doubt that he was liberated, and thus he could see Garuḍa carrying the Lord on the way to Vaikuṇṭha and hear the flapping of his wings vibrating the sound of Hare Kṛṣṇa, the essence of the *Sāma Veda.*

TEXT 35

अथ सम्प्रस्थिते शुक्ले कर्दमो भगवानृषिः ।
आस्ते स्म बिन्दुसरसि तं कालं प्रतिपालयन् ॥३५॥

atha samprasthite śukle
kardamo bhagavān ṛṣiḥ
āste sma bindusarasi
taṁ kālaṁ pratipālayan

atha—then; *samprasthite śukle*—when the Lord had gone; *kardamaḥ*—Kardama Muni; *bhagavān*—the greatly powerful; *ṛṣiḥ*—sage; *āste sma*—stayed; *bindu-sarasi*—on the bank of Lake Bindu-sarovara; *tam*—that; *kālam*—time; *pratipālayan*—awaiting.

TRANSLATION

Then, after the departure of the Lord, the worshipful sage Kardama stayed on the bank of Bindu-sarovara, awaiting the time of which the Lord had spoken.

TEXT 36

मनुः स्यन्दनमास्थाय शातकौम्भपरिच्छदम् ।
आरोप्य स्वां दुहितरं सभार्यः पर्यटन्महीम् ॥३६॥

manuḥ syandanam āsthāya
śātakaumbha-paricchadam
āropya svāṁ duhitaraṁ
sa-bhāryaḥ paryaṭan mahīm

manuḥ—Svāyambhuva Manu; *syandanam*—the chariot; *āsthāya*—having mounted; *śātakaumbha*—made of gold; *paricchadam*—the outer cover; *āropya*—putting on; *svām*—his own; *duhitaram*—daughter; *sa-bhāryaḥ*—along with his wife; *paryaṭan*—traveling all over; *mahīm*—the globe.

TRANSLATION

Svāyambhuva Manu, with his wife, mounted his chariot, which was decorated with golden ornaments. Placing his daughter on it with them, he began traveling all over the earth.

PURPORT

The Emperor Manu, as the great ruler of the world, could have engaged an agent to find a suitable husband for his daughter, but because he loved her just as a father should, he himself left his state on a golden chariot, with only his wife, to find her a suitable husband.

TEXT 37

तस्मिन् सुधन्वन्नहनि भगवान् यत्समादिशत् ।
उपायादाश्रमपदं मुनेः शान्तव्रतस्य तत् ॥३७॥

tasmin sudhanvann ahani
bhagavān yat samādiśat
upāyād āśrama-padaṁ
muneḥ śānta-vratasya tat

tasmin—on that; *su-dhanvan*—O great bowman Vidura; *ahani*—on the day; *bhagavān*—the Lord; *yat*—which; *samādiśat*—foretold; *upāyāt*—he reached; *āśrama-padam*—the holy hermitage; *muneḥ*—of the sage; *śānta*—completed; *vratasya*—whose vows of austerity; *tat*—that.

TRANSLATION

O Vidura, they reached the hermitage of the sage, who had just completed his vows of austerity on the very day foretold by the Lord.

TEXTS 38-39

यस्मिन् भगवतो नेत्रान्न्यपतन्नश्रुबिन्दवः ।
कृपया सम्परीतस्य प्रपन्नेऽर्पितया भृशम् ॥३८॥
तद्वै बिन्दुसरो नाम सरस्वत्या परिप्लुतम् ।
पुण्यं शिवामृतजलं महर्षिगणसेवितम् ॥३९॥

yasmin bhagavato netrān
nyapatann aśru-bindavaḥ
kṛpayā samparītasya
prapanne 'rpitayā bhṛśam

tad vai bindusaro nāma
sarasvatyā pariplutam
puṇyaṁ śivāmṛta-jalaṁ
maharṣi-gaṇa-sevitam

yasmin—in which; *bhagavataḥ*—of the Lord; *netrāt*—from the eye; *nyapatan*—fell down; *aśru-bindavaḥ*—teardrops; *kṛpayā*—by compassion; *samparītasya*—who was overwhelmed; *prapanne*—on the surrendered soul (Kardama); *arpitayā*—placed upon; *bhṛśam*—extremely;

tat—that; *vai*—indeed; *bindu-saraḥ*—lake of tears; *nāma*—called; *sarasvatyā*—by the River Sarasvatī; *pariplutam*—overflowed; *puṇyam*—holy; *śiva*—auspicious; *amṛta*—nectar; *jalam*—water; *mahā-ṛṣi*—of great sages; *gaṇa*—by hosts; *sevitam*—served.

TRANSLATION

The holy Lake Bindu-sarovara, flooded by the waters of the River Sarasvatī, was resorted to by hosts of eminent sages. Its holy water was not only auspicious but as sweet as nectar. It was called Bindu-sarovara because drops of tears had fallen there from the eyes of the Lord, who was overwhelmed by extreme compassion for the sage who had sought His protection.

PURPORT

Kardama underwent austerities to gain the causeless mercy of the Lord, and when the Lord arrived there He was so compassionate that in pleasure He shed tears, which became Bindu-sarovara. Bindu-sarovara, therefore, is worshiped by great sages and learned scholars because, according to the philosophy of the Absolute Truth, the Lord and the tears from His eyes are not different. Just as drops of perspiration which fell from the toe of the Lord became the sacred Ganges, so teardrops from the transcendental eyes of the Lord became Bindu-sarovara. Both are transcendental entities and are worshiped by great sages and scholars. The water of Bindu-sarovara is described here as *śivāmṛta jala. Śiva* means "curing." Anyone who drinks the water of Bindu-sarovara is cured of all material diseases; similarly, anyone who takes his bath in the Ganges also is relieved of all material diseases. These claims are accepted by great scholars and authorities and are still being acted upon even in this fallen age of Kali.

TEXT 40

पुण्यद्रुमलताजालैः कूजत्पुण्यमृगद्विजैः ।
सर्वर्तुफलपुष्पाढ्यं वनराजिश्रियान्वितम् ॥४०॥

puṇya-druma-latā-jālaiḥ
kūjat-puṇya-mṛga-dvijaiḥ
sarvartu-phala-puṣpāḍhyaṁ
vana-rāji-śriyānvitam

puṇya—pious; *druma*—of trees; *latā*—of creepers; *jālaiḥ*—with clusters; *kūjat*—uttering cries; *puṇya*—pious; *mṛga*—animals; *dvijaiḥ*—with birds; *sarva*—in all; *ṛtu*—seasons; *phala*—in fruits; *puṣpa*—in flowers; *āḍhyam*—rich; *vana-rāji*—of groves of trees; *śriyā*—by the beauty; *anvitam*—adorned.

TRANSLATION

The shore of the lake was surrounded by clusters of pious trees and creepers, rich in fruits and flowers of all seasons, that afforded shelter to pious animals and birds, which uttered various cries. It was adorned by the beauty of groves of forest trees.

PURPORT

It is stated here that Bindu-sarovara was surrounded by pious trees and birds. As there are different classes of men in human society, some pious and virtuous and some impious and sinful, so also among trees and birds there are the pious and the impious. Trees which do not bear nice fruit or flowers are considered impious, and birds which are very nasty, such as crows, are considered impious. In the land surrounding Bindu-sarovara there was not a single impious bird or tree. Every tree bore fruits and flowers, and every bird sang the glories of the Lord—Hare Kṛṣṇa, Hare Kṛṣṇa, Kṛṣṇa Kṛṣṇa, Hare Hare/ Hare Rāma, Hare Rāma, Rāma Rāma, Hare Hare.

TEXT 41

मत्तद्विजगणैर्घुष्टं मत्तभ्रमरविभ्रमम् ।
मत्तबर्हिनटाटोपमाह्वयन्मत्तकोकिलम् ॥४१॥

matta-dvija-gaṇair ghuṣṭaṁ
matta-bhramara-vibhramam
matta-barhi-naṭāṭopam
āhvayan-matta-kokilam

matta—overjoyed; *dvija*—of birds; *gaṇaiḥ*—by flocks; *ghuṣṭam*—resounded; *matta*—intoxicated; *bhramara*—of bees; *vibhramam*—wandering; *matta*—maddened; *barhi*—of peacocks; *naṭa*—of dancers; *āṭopam*—pride; *āhvayat*—calling one another; *matta*—merry; *kokilam*—cuckoos.

TRANSLATION

The area resounded with the notes of overjoyed birds. Intoxicated bees wandered there, intoxicated peacocks proudly danced, and merry cuckoos called one another.

PURPORT

The beauty of the pleasant sounds heard in the area surrounding Lake Bindu-sarovara is described here. After drinking honey, the black bees became maddened, and they hummed in intoxication. Merry peacocks danced just like actors and actresses, and merry cuckoos called their mates very nicely.

TEXTS 42-43

कदम्बचम्पकाशोककरञ्जबकुलासनैः ।
कुन्दमन्दारकुटजैश्चूतपोतैरलङ्कृतम् ॥४२॥
कारण्डवैः प्लवैर्हंसैः कुररैर्जलकुक्कुटैः ।
सारसैश्चक्रवाकैश्च चकोरैर्वल्गु कूजितम् ॥४३॥

kadamba-campakāśoka-
karañja-bakulāsanaiḥ
kunda-mandāra-kuṭajaiś
cūta-potair alaṅkṛtam

kāraṇḍavaiḥ plavair haṁsaiḥ
kurarair jala-kukkuṭaiḥ
sārasaiś cakravākaiś ca
cakorair valgu kūjitam

kadamba—kadamba flowers; campaka—campaka flowers; aśoka—aśoka flowers; karañja—karañja flowers; bakula—bakula flowers; āsanaiḥ—by āsana trees; kunda—kunda; mandāra—mandāra; kuṭajaiḥ—and by kuṭaja trees; cūta-potaiḥ—by young mango trees; alaṅkṛtam—adorned; kāraṇḍavaiḥ—by kāraṇḍava ducks; plavaiḥ—by plavas; haṁsaiḥ—by swans; kuraraiḥ—by ospreys; jala-kukkuṭaiḥ—by waterfowl; sārasaiḥ—by cranes; cakravākaiḥ—by cakravāka birds; ca—and; cakoraiḥ—by cakora birds; valgu—pleasing; kūjitam—vibration of birds' sounds.

TRANSLATION

Lake Bindu-sarovara was adorned by flowering trees such as kadamba, campaka, aśoka, karañja, bakula, āsana, kunda, mandāra, kuṭaja and young mango trees. The air was filled with the pleasing notes of kāraṇḍava ducks, plavas, swans, ospreys, waterfowl, cranes, cakravākas and cakoras.

PURPORT

For most of the trees, flowers, fruits and birds mentioned here as surrounding Bindu-sarovara Lake, English synonyms cannot be found. All the trees mentioned are very pious in that they produce a nice aromatic flower, such as the *campaka, kadamba* and *bakula.* The sweet sounds of waterfowl and cranes made the surrounding area as pleasant as possible and created a very suitable spiritual atmosphere.

TEXT 44

तथैव हरिणैः क्रोडैः श्वाविद्गवयकुञ्जरैः ।
गोपुच्छैर्हरिभिर्मर्कैर्नकुलैर्नाभिभिर्वृतम् ॥४४॥

tathaiva hariṇaiḥ kroḍaiḥ
śvāvid-gavaya-kuñjaraiḥ
gopucchair haribhir markair
nakulair nābhibhir vṛtam

tathā eva—likewise; *hariṇaiḥ*—by deer; *kroḍaiḥ*—by boars; *śvāvit*—porcupines; *gavaya*—a wild animal closely resembling the cow; *kuñjaraiḥ*—by elephants; *gopucchaiḥ*—by baboons; *haribhiḥ*—by lions; *markaiḥ*—by monkeys; *nakulaiḥ*—by mongooses; *nābhibhiḥ*—by musk deer; *vṛtam*—surrounded.

TRANSLATION

Its shores abounded with deer, boars, porcupines, gavayas, elephants, baboons, lions, monkeys, mongooses and musk deer.

PURPORT

Musk deer are not found in every forest, but only in places like Bindu-sarovara. They are always intoxicated by the aroma of musk secreted from their navels. *Gavayas*, the species of cow mentioned herein, bear a bunch of hair at the end of their tails. This bunch of hair is used in temple worship to fan the Deities. *Gavayas* are sometimes called *camarīs*, and they are considered very sacred. In India there are still gypsies or forest mercantile people who flourish by trading *kastūrī*, or musk, and the bunches of hair from the *camarīs*. These are always in great demand for the higher classes of Hindu population, and such business still goes on in large cities and villages in India.

TEXTS 45-47

प्रविश्य तत्तीर्थवरमादिराजः सहात्मजः ।
ददर्श मुनिमासीनं तस्मिन् हुतहुताशनम् ॥४५॥
विद्योतमानं वपुषा तपस्युग्रयुजा चिरम् ।
नातिक्षामं भगवतः स्निग्धापाङ्गावलोकनात् ।
तद्व्याहृतामृतकलापीयूषश्रवणेन च ॥४६॥
प्रांशुं पद्मपलाशाक्षं जटिलं चीरवाससम् ।
उपसंश्रित्य मलिनं यथार्हणमसंस्कृतम् ॥४७॥

praviśya tat tīrtha-varam
ādi-rājaḥ sahātmajaḥ
dadarśa munim āsīnaṁ
tasmin huta-hutāśanam

vidyotamānaṁ vapuṣā
tapasy ugra-yujā ciram
nātikṣāmaṁ bhagavataḥ
snigdhāpāṅgāvalokanāt

tad-vyāhṛtāmṛta-kalā-
pīyūṣa-śravaṇena ca

prāṁśuṁ padma-palāśākṣaṁ
jaṭilaṁ cīra-vāsasam
upasaṁśritya malinaṁ
yathārhaṇam asaṁskṛtam

praviśya—entering; *tat*—that; *tīrtha-varam*—best of sacred places; *ādi-rājaḥ*—the first monarch (Svāyambhuva Manu); *saha-ātmajaḥ*—along with his daughter; *dadarśa*—saw; *munim*—the sage; *āsīnam*—sitting; *tasmin*—in the hermitage; *huta*—being offered oblations; *huta-aśanam*—the sacred fire; *vidyotamānam*—shining brilliantly; *vapuṣā*—by his body; *tapasi*—in penance; *ugra*—terribly; *yujā*—engaged in *yoga; ciram*—for a long time; *na*—not; *atikṣāmam*—very emaciated; *bhagavataḥ*—of the Lord; *snigdha*—affectionate; *apāṅga*—sidelong; *avalokanāt*—from the glance; *tat*—of Him; *vyāhṛta*—from the words; *amṛta-kalā*—moonlike; *pīyūṣa*—the nectar; *śravaṇena*—by hearing; *ca*—and; *prāṁśum*—tall; *padma*—lotus flower; *palāśa*—petal; *akṣam*—eyes; *jaṭilam*—matted locks; *cīra-vāsasam*—having rags for clothes; *upasaṁśritya*—having approached; *malinam*—soiled; *yathā*—like; *arhaṇam*—gem; *asaṁskṛtam*—unpolished.

TRANSLATION

Entering that most sacred spot with his daughter and going near the sage, the first monarch, Svāyambhuva Manu, saw the sage sitting in his hermitage, having just propitiated the sacred fire by pouring oblations into it. His body shone most brilliantly; though he had engaged in austere penance for a long time, he was not emaciated, for the Lord had cast His affectionate sidelong glance upon him and he had also heard the nectar flowing from the moonlike words of the Lord. The sage was tall, his eyes were large, like the petals of a lotus, and he had matted locks on his head. He was clad in rags. Svāyambhuva Manu approached and saw him to be somewhat soiled, like an unpolished gem.

PURPORT

Here are some descriptions of a *brahmacārī-yogī.* In the morning, the first duty of a *brahmacārī* seeking spiritual elevation is *huta-hutāśana,* to offer sacrificial oblations to the Supreme Lord. Those engaged in *brahmacarya* cannot sleep until seven or nine o'clock in the morning. They must rise early in the morning, at least one and a half hours before the sun rises, and offer oblations, or in this age, they must chant the holy name of the Lord, Hare Kṛṣṇa. As referred to by Lord Caitanya, *kalau nāsty eva nāsty eva nāsty eva gatir anyathā:* there is no other alternative, no other alternative, no other alternative, in this age, to chanting the holy name of the Lord. The *brahmacārī* must rise early in the morning and, after placing himself, should chant the holy name of the Lord. From the very features of the sage, it appeared that he had undergone great austerities; that is the sign of one observing *brahmacarya,* the vow of celibacy. If one lives otherwise, it will be manifest in the lust visible in his face and body. The word *vidyotamānam* indicates that the *brahmacārī* feature showed in his body. That is the certificate that one has undergone great austerity in *yoga.* A drunkard or smoker or sex-monger can never be eligible to practice *yoga.* Generally *yogīs* look very skinny because of their not being comfortably situated, but Kardama Muni was not emaciated, for he had seen the Supreme Personality of Godhead face to face. Here the word *snigdhāpāṅgāvalokanāt* means that he was fortunate enough to see the Supreme Lord face to face. He looked healthy because he had directly received the nectarean sound vibrations from the lotus lips of the Personality of Godhead. Similarly, one who hears the transcendental sound vibration of the holy name of the Lord, Hare Kṛṣṇa, also improves in health. We have actually seen that many *brahmacārīs* and *gṛhasthas* connected with the International Society for Krishna Consciousness have improved in health, and a luster has come to their faces. It is essential that a *brahmacārī* engaged in spiritual advancement look very healthy and lustrous. The comparison of the sage to an unpolished gem is very appropriate. Even if a gem just taken from a mine looks unpolished, the luster of the gem cannot be stopped. Similarly, although Kardama was not properly dressed and his body was not properly cleansed, his overall appearance was gemlike.

TEXT 48

अथोटजमुपायातं नृदेवं प्रणतं पुरः ।
सपर्यया पर्यगृह्णात्प्रतिनन्द्यानुरूपया ॥४८॥

athoṭajam upāyātaṁ
nṛdevaṁ praṇataṁ puraḥ

saparyayā paryagṛhṇāt
pratinandyānurūpayā

atha—then; *uṭajam*—the hermitage; *upāyātam*—approached; *nṛdevam*—the monarch; *praṇatam*—bowed down; *puraḥ*—in front; *saparyayā*—with honor; *paryagṛhṇāt*—received him; *pratinandya*—greeting him; *anurūpayā*—befitting the King's position.

TRANSLATION

Seeing that the monarch had come to his hermitage and was bowing before him, the sage greeted him with benediction and received him with due honor.

PURPORT

Emperor Svāyambhuva Manu not only approached the cottage of dried leaves possessed by the hermit Kardama but also offered respectful obeisances unto him. Similarly, it was the duty of the hermit to offer blessings to kings who used to approach his hermitage in the jungle.

TEXT 49

गृहीतार्हणमासीनं संयतं प्रीणयन्मुनिः ।
स्मरन् भगवदादेशमित्याह श्लक्ष्णया गिरा ॥४९॥

gṛhītārhaṇam āsīnaṁ
saṁyataṁ prīṇayan muniḥ
smaran bhagavad-ādeśam
ity āha ślakṣṇayā girā

gṛhīta—received; *arhaṇam*—honor; *āsīnam*—seated; *saṁyatam*—remained silent; *prīṇayan*—delighting; *muniḥ*—the sage; *smaran*—remembering; *bhagavat*—of the Lord; *ādeśam*—the order; *iti*—thus; *āha*—spoke; *ślakṣṇayā*—sweet; *girā*—with a voice.

TRANSLATION

After receiving the sage's attention, the King sat down and was silent. Recalling the instructions of the Lord, Kardama then spoke to the King as follows, delighting him with his sweet accents.

TEXT 50

नूनं चङ्क्रमणं देव सतां संरक्षणाय ते ।
वधाय चासतां यस्त्वं हरेः शक्तिर्हि पालिनी ॥५०॥

nūnaṁ caṅkramaṇaṁ deva
satāṁ saṁrakṣaṇāya te
vadhāya cāsatāṁ yas tvaṁ
hareḥ śaktir hi pālinī

nūnam—surely; *caṅkramaṇam*—the tour; *deva*—O lord; *satām*—of the virtuous; *saṁrakṣaṇāya*—for the protection; *te*—your; *vadhāya*—for killing; *ca*—and; *asatām*—of the demons; *yaḥ*—the person who; *tvam*—you; *hareḥ*—of the Supreme Personality of Godhead; *śaktiḥ*—the energy; *hi*—since; *pālinī*—protecting.

TRANSLATION

The tour you have undertaken, O lord, is surely intended to protect the virtuous and kill the demons, since you embody the protecting energy of Śrī Hari.

PURPORT

It appears from many Vedic literatures, especially histories like *Śrīmad-Bhāgavatam* and the *Purāṇas*, that the pious kings of old used to tour their kingdoms in order to give protection to the pious citizens and to chastise or kill the impious. Sometimes they used to kill animals in the forests to practice the killing art because without such practice they would not be able to kill the undesirable elements. *Kṣatriyas* are allowed to commit violence in that way because violence for a good purpose is a part of their duty. Here two terms are clearly mentioned: *vadhāya*, "for the purpose of killing," and *asatām*, "those who are undesirable." The protecting energy of the king is supposed to be the energy of the Supreme Lord. In *Bhagavad-gītā* (4.8) the Lord says, *paritrāṇāya sādhūnāṁ vināśāya ca duṣkṛtām.* The Lord descends to give protection to the pious and to kill the demons. The potency, therefore, to give protection to the pious and kill the demons or undesirables is directly an energy from the Supreme Lord, and the king or the chief executive of the state is supposed to possess such energy. In this age it is very difficult to find such a head of state who is expert in killing the undesirables. Modern heads of state sit very nicely in their palaces and try without reason to kill innocent persons.

TEXT 51

योऽर्केन्द्वग्नीन्द्रवायूनां यमधर्मप्रचेतसाम् ।
रूपाणि स्थान आधत्से तस्मै शुक्लाय ते नमः ॥५१॥

yo 'rkendv-agnīndra-vāyūnāṁ
yama-dharma-pracetasām
rūpāṇi sthāna ādhatse
tasmai śuklāya te namaḥ

yaḥ—you who; *arka*—of the sun; *indu*—of the moon; *agni*—of Agni, the fire-god; *indra*—of Indra, the lord of heaven; *vāyūnām*—of Vāyu, the wind-god; *yama*—of Yama, the god of punishment; *dharma*—of Dharma, the god of piety; *pracetasām*—and of Varuṇa, the god of the waters; *rūpāṇi*—the forms; *sthāne*—when necessary; *ādhatse*—you assume; *tasmai*—unto Him; *śuklāya*—unto Lord Viṣṇu; *te*—unto you; *namaḥ*—obeisances.

TRANSLATION

You assume, when necessary, the part of the sun-god; the moon-god; Agni, the god of fire; Indra, the lord of paradise; Vāyu, the wind-god; Yama, the god of punishment; Dharma, the god of piety; and Varuṇa, the god presiding over the waters. All obeisances to you, who are none other than Lord Viṣṇu!

PURPORT

Since the sage Kardama was a *brāhmaṇa* and Svāyambhuva was a *kṣatriya*, the sage was not supposed to offer obeisances to the King because socially his position was greater than the King's. But he offered his obeisances to Svāyambhuva Manu because as Manu, king and emperor, he was the representative of the Supreme Lord. The Supreme Lord is always worshipable, regardless of whether one is a *brāhmaṇa*, a *kṣatriya* or a *śūdra*. As the representative of the Supreme Lord, the King deserved respectful obeisances from everyone.

TEXTS 52-54

न यदा रथमास्थाय जैत्रं मणिगणार्पितम् ।
विस्फूर्जच्चण्डकोदण्डो रथेन त्रासयन्नघान् ॥५२॥
स्वसैन्यचरणक्षुण्णं वेपयन्मण्डलं भुवः ।
विकर्षन् बृहतीं सेनां पर्यटस्यंशुमानिव ॥५३॥
तदैव सेतवः सर्वे वर्णाश्रमनिबन्धनाः ।
भगवद्रचिता राजन् भिद्येरन् बत दस्युभिः ॥५४॥

na yadā ratham āsthāya
jaitraṁ maṇi-gaṇārpitam
visphūrjac-caṇḍa-kodaṇḍo
rathena trāsayann aghān

sva-sainya-caraṇa-kṣuṇṇaṁ
vepayan maṇḍalaṁ bhuvaḥ
vikarṣan bṛhatīṁ senāṁ
paryaṭasy aṁśumān iva

tadaiva setavaḥ sarve
varṇāśrama-nibandhanāḥ
bhagavad-racitā rājan
bhidyeran bata dasyubhiḥ

na—not; *yadā*—when; *ratham*—the chariot; *āsthāya*—having mounted; *jaitram*—victorious; *maṇi*—of jewels; *gaṇa*—with clusters; *arpitam*—bedecked; *visphūrjat*—twanging; *caṇḍa*—a fearful sound just to punish the criminals; *kodaṇḍaḥ*—bow; *rathena*—by the presence of such a chariot; *trāsayan*—threatening; *aghān*—all the culprits; *sva-sainya*—of your soldiers; *caraṇa*—by the feet; *kṣuṇṇam*—trampled; *vepayan*—causing to tremble; *maṇḍalam*—the globe; *bhuvaḥ*—of the earth; *vikarṣan*—leading; *bṛhatīm*—huge; *senām*—army; *paryaṭasi*—you roam about; *aṁśumān*—the brilliant sun; *iva*—like; *tadā*—then; *eva*—certainly; *setavaḥ*—religious codes; *sarve*—all; *varṇa*—of *varṇas; āśrama*—of *āśramas; nibandhanāḥ*—obligations; *bhagavat*—by the Lord; *racitāḥ*—created; *rājan*—O King; *bhidyeran*—they would be broken; *bata*—alas; *dasyubhiḥ*—by rogues.

TRANSLATION

If you did not mount your victorious jeweled chariot, whose mere presence threatens culprits, if you did not produce fierce sounds by the twanging of your bow, and if you did not roam about the world like the brilliant sun, leading a huge army whose trampling feet cause the globe of the earth to tremble, then all the moral laws governing the varṇas and āśramas created by the Lord Himself would be broken by the rogues and rascals.

PURPORT

It is the duty of a responsible king to protect the social and spiritual orders in human society. The spiritual orders are divided into four *āśramas-brahmacarya, gṛhastha, vānaprastha* and *sannyāsa*—and the social orders, according to work and qualification, are made up of the *brāhmaṇas,* the *kṣatriyas,* the *vaiśyas* and the *śūdras.* These social orders, according to the different grades of work and qualification, are described in *Bhagavad-gītā.* Unfortunately, for want of proper protection by responsible kings, the system of social and spiritual orders has now become a hereditary caste system. But this is not the actual system. Human society means that society which is making progress toward spiritual realization. The most advanced human society was known as *ārya; ārya* refers to those who are advancing. So the question is, "Which society is advancing?" Advancement does not mean creating material "necessities" unnecessarily and thus wasting human energy in aggravation over so-called material comforts. Real advancement is advancement toward spiritual realization, and the community which acted toward this end was known as the Āryan civilization. The intelligent men, the *brāhmaṇas,* as exemplified by Kardama Muni, were engaged in advancing the spiritual cause, and *kṣatriyas* like Emperor Svāyambhuva used to rule the country and insure that all facilities for spiritual realization were nicely provided. It is the duty of the king to travel all over the country and see that everything is in order. Indian civilization on the basis of the four *varṇas* and *āśramas* deteriorated because of her dependency on foreigners, or those who did not follow the civilization of *varṇāśrama.* Thus the *varṇāśrama* system has now been degraded into the caste system.

The institution of four *varṇas* and four *āśramas* is confirmed herewith to be *bhagavad-racita,* which means "designed by the Supreme Personality of Godhead." In *Bhagavad-gītā* this is also confirmed: *cātur-varṇyaṁ mayā sṛṣṭam.* The Lord says that the institution of four *varṇas* and four *āśramas* "is created by Me." Anything created by the Lord cannot be closed or covered. The divisions of *varṇas* and *āśramas* will continue to exist, either in their original form or in degraded form, but because they are created by the Lord, the Supreme Personality of Godhead, they cannot be extinguished. They are like the sun, a creation of God, and therefore will remain. Either covered by clouds or in a clear sky, the sun will continue to exist. Similarly, when the *varṇāśrama* system becomes degraded, it appears as a hereditary caste system, but in every society there is an intelligent class of men, a martial class, a mercantile class and a laborer class. When they are regulated for cooperation among communities according to the Vedic principles, then there is peace and spiritual advancement. But when there is hatred and malpractice and mutual mistrust in the caste system, the whole system becomes degraded, and as stated herein, it creates a deplorable state. At the present moment, the entire world is in this deplorable condition because of giving rights to so many interests. This is due to the degradation of the four castes of *varṇas* and *āśramas.*

TEXT 55

अधर्मश्च समेधेत लोलुपैर्व्यङ्कुशैर्नृभिः ।
शयाने त्वयि लोकोऽयं दस्युग्रस्तो विनङ्क्ष्यति ॥५५॥

adharmaś ca samedheta
lolupair vyaṅkuśair nṛbhiḥ
śayāne tvayi loko 'yaṁ
dasyu-grasto vinaṅkṣyati

adharmaḥ—unrighteousness; *ca*—and; *samedheta*—would flourish; *lolupaiḥ*—simply hankering after money; *vyaṅkuśaiḥ*—uncontrolled; *nṛbhiḥ*—by men; *śayāne tvayi*—when you lie down for rest; *lokaḥ*—world; *ayam*—this; *dasyu*—by the miscreants; *grastaḥ*—attacked; *vinaṅkṣyati*—it will perish.

TRANSLATION

If you gave up all thought of the world's situation, unrighteousness would flourish, for men who hanker only after money would be unopposed. Such miscreants would attack, and the world would perish.

PURPORT

Because the scientific division of four *varṇas* and four *āśramas* is now being extinguished, the entire world is being governed by unwanted men who have no training in religion, politics or social order, and it is in a very deplorable condition. In the institution of four *varṇas* and four *āśramas* there are regular training principles for the different classes of men. Just as, in the modern age, there is a necessity for engineers, medical practitioners and electricians, and they are properly trained in different scientific institutions, similarly, in former times, the higher social orders, namely the intelligent class (the *brāhmaṇas*), the ruling class (the *kṣatriyas*) and the mercantile class (the *vaiśyas*), were properly trained. *Bhagavad-gītā* describes the duties of the *brāhmaṇas, kṣatriyas, vaiśyas* and *śūdras.* When there is no such training, one simply claims that because he is born in a *brāhmaṇa* or *kṣatriya* family, he is therefore a *brāhmaṇa* or a *kṣatriya,* even though he performs the duties of a *śūdra.* Such undue claims to being a higher-caste man make the system of scientific social orders into a caste system, completely degrading the original system. Thus society is now in chaos, and there is neither peace nor prosperity. It is clearly stated herein that unless there is the vigilance of a strong king, impious, unqualified men will claim a certain status in society, and that will make the social order perish.

TEXT 56

अथापि पृच्छे त्वां वीर यदर्थं त्वमिहागतः ।
तद्वयं निर्व्यलीकेन प्रतिपद्यामहे हृदा ॥५६॥

athāpi pṛcche tvāṁ vīra
yad-arthaṁ tvam ihāgataḥ
tad vayaṁ nirvyalīkena
pratipadyāmahe hṛdā

atha api—in spite of all this; *pṛcche*—I ask; *tvām*—you; *vīra*—O valiant King; *yat-artham*—the purpose; *tvam*—you; *iha*—here; *āgataḥ*—have come; *tat*—that; *vayam*—we; *nirvyalīkena*—without reservation; *pratipadyāmahe*—we shall carry out; *hṛdā*—with heart and soul.

TRANSLATION

In spite of all this, I ask you, O valiant King, the purpose for which you have come here. Whatever it may be, we shall carry it out without reservation.

PURPORT

When a guest comes to a friend's house, it is understood that there is some special purpose. Kardama Muni could understand that such a great king as Svāyambhuva, although traveling to inspect the condition of his kingdom, must have had some special purpose to come to his hermitage. Thus he prepared himself to fulfill the King's desire. Formerly it was customary that the sages used to go to the kings and the kings used to visit the sages in their hermitages; each was glad to fulfill the other's purpose. This reciprocal relationship is called *bhakti-kārya*. There is a nice verse describing the relationship of mutual beneficial interest between the *brāhmaṇa* and the *kṣatriya* (*kṣatraṁ dvijatvam*). *Kṣatram* means "the royal order," and *dvijatvam* means "the brahminical order." The two were meant for mutual interest. The royal order would give protection to the *brāhmaṇas* for the cultivation of spiritual advancement in society, and the *brāhmaṇas* would give their valuable instruction to the royal order on how the state and the citizens can gradually be elevated in spiritual perfection.

Thus end the Bhaktivedanta purports of the Third Canto, Twenty-first Chapter, of the Śrīmad-Bhāgavatam, *entitled "Conversation Between Manu and Kardama."*

CHAPTER TWENTY-TWO

The Marriage of Kardama Muni and Devahūti

TEXT 1

मैत्रेय उवाच
एवमाविष्कृताशेषगुणकर्मोदयो मुनिम् ।
सव्रीड इव तं सम्राडुपारतमुवाच ह ॥ १ ॥

maitreya uvāca
evam āviṣkṛtāśeṣa-
guṇa-karmodayo munim
savrīḍa iva taṁ samrāḍ
upāratam uvāca ha

maitreyaḥ—the great sage Maitreya; *uvāca*—said; *evam*—thus; *āviṣkṛta*—having been described; *aśeṣa*—all; *guṇa*—of the virtues; *karma*—of the activities; *udayaḥ*—the greatness; *munim*—the great sage; *sa-vrīḍaḥ*—feeling modest; *iva*—as though; *tam*—him (Kardama); *samrāṭ*—Emperor Manu; *upāratam*—silent; *uvāca ha*—addressed.

TRANSLATION

Śrī Maitreya said: After describing the greatness of the Emperor's manifold qualities and activities, the sage became silent, and the Emperor, feeling modesty, addressed him as follows.

TEXT 2

मनुरुवाच
ब्रह्मासृजत्स्वमुखतो युष्मानात्मपरीप्सया ।
छन्दोमयस्तपोविद्यायोगयुक्तानलम्पटान् ॥ २ ॥

manur uvāca
brahmāsṛjat sva-mukhato
yuṣmān ātma-parīpsayā
chandomayas tapo-vidyā-
yoga-yuktān alampaṭān

manuḥ—Manu; *uvāca*—said; *brahmā*—Lord Brahmā; *asṛjat*—created; *sva-mukhataḥ*—from his face; *yuṣmān*—you (*brāhmaṇas*); *ātma-parīpsayā*—to protect himself by expanding; *chandaḥ-mayaḥ*—the form of the *Vedas; tapaḥ-vidyā-yoga-yuktān*—full of austerity, knowledge and mystic power; *alampaṭān*—averse to sense gratification.

TRANSLATION

Manu replied: To expand himself in Vedic knowledge, Lord Brahmā, the personified Veda, from his face created you, the brāhmaṇas, who are full of austerity, knowledge and mystic power and are averse to sense gratification.

PURPORT

The purpose of the *Vedas* is to propagate the transcendental knowledge of the Absolute Truth. The *brāhmaṇas* were created from the mouth of the Supreme Person, and therefore they are meant to spread the knowledge of the *Vedas* in order to spread the glories of the Lord. In *Bhagavad-gītā* also Lord Kṛṣṇa says that all the *Vedas* are meant for understanding the Supreme Personality of Godhead. It is especially mentioned here (*yoga-yuktān alampaṭān*) that *brāhmaṇas* are full of mystic power and are completely averse to sense gratification. Actually there are two kinds of occupations. One occupation, in the material world, is sense gratification, and the other occupation is spiritual activity—to satisfy the Lord by His glorification. Those who engage in sense gratification are called demons, and those who spread the glorification of the Lord or satisfy the transcendental senses of the Lord are called demigods. It is specifically mentioned here that the *brāhmaṇas* are created from the face of the cosmic personality, or *virāṭ-puruṣa;* similarly the *kṣatriyas* are said to be created from His arms, the *vaiśyas* are created from His waist, and the *śūdras* are created from His legs. *Brāhmaṇas* are especially meant for austerity, learning and knowledge and are averse to all kinds of sense gratification.

TEXT 3

तत्त्राणायासृजच्चास्मान्दोःसहस्रात्सहस्रपात् ।
हृदयं तस्य हि ब्रह्म क्षत्रमङ्गं प्रचक्षते ॥ ३ ॥

tat-trāṇāyāsṛjac cāsmān
doḥ-sahasrāt sahasra-pāt
hṛdayaṁ tasya hi brahma
kṣatram aṅgaṁ pracakṣate

tat-trāṇāya—for the protection of the *brāhmaṇas; asṛjat*—created; *ca*—and; *asmān*—us (*kṣatriyas*); *doḥ-sahasrāt*—from His thousand arms; *sahasra-pāt*—the thousand-legged Supreme Being (the universal form); *hṛdayam*—heart; *tasya*—His; *hi*—for; *brahma*—*brāhmaṇas; kṣatram*—the *kṣatriyas; aṅgam*—arms; *pracakṣate*—are spoken of.

TRANSLATION

For the protection of the brāhmaṇas, the thousand-legged Supreme Being created us, the kṣatriyas, from His thousand arms. Hence the brāhmaṇas are said to be His heart and the kṣatriyas His arms.

PURPORT

Kṣatriyas are specifically meant to maintain the *brāhmaṇas* because if the *brāhmaṇas* are protected, then the head of civilization is protected. *Brāhmaṇas* are supposed to be the head of the social body; if the head is clear and has not gone mad, then everything is in proper position. The Lord is described thus: *namo brahmaṇya-devāya go-brāhmaṇa-hitāya ca.* The purport of this prayer is that the Lord specifically protects the *brāhmaṇas* and the cows, and then He protects all other members of society (*jagad-dhitāya*). It is His will that universal welfare work depends on the protection of cows and *brāhmaṇas*; thus brahminical culture and cow protection are the basic principles for human civilization. *Kṣatriyas* are especially meant to protect the *brāhmaṇas,* as is the supreme will of the Lord: *go-brāhmaṇa-hitāya ca.* As, within the body, the heart is a very important part, so the *brāhmaṇas* are also the important element in human society. The *kṣatriyas* are more like the whole body; even though the whole body is bigger than the heart, the heart is more important.

TEXT 4

अतो ह्यन्योन्यमात्मानं ब्रह्म क्षत्रं च रक्षतः ।
रक्षति स्माव्ययो देवः स यः सदसदात्मकः ॥ ४ ॥

ato hy anyonyam ātmānaṁ
brahma kṣatraṁ ca rakṣataḥ
rakṣati smāvyayo devaḥ
sa yaḥ sad-asad-ātmakaḥ

ataḥ—hence; *hi*—certainly; *anyonyam*—each other; *ātmānam*—the self; *brahma*—the *brāhmaṇas; kṣatram*—the *kṣatriyas; ca*—and; *rakṣataḥ*—protect; *rakṣati sma*—protects; *avyayaḥ*—immutable; *devaḥ*—the Lord; *saḥ*—He; *yaḥ*—who; *sat-asat-ātmakaḥ*—the form of the cause and effect.

TRANSLATION

That is why the brāhmaṇas and kṣatriyas protect each other, as well as themselves; and the Lord Himself, who is both the cause and effect and is yet immutable, protects them through each other.

PURPORT

The entire social structure of *varṇa* and *āśrama* is a cooperative system meant to uplift all to the highest platform of spiritual realization. The *brāhmaṇas* are intended to be protected by the *kṣatriyas,* and the *kṣatriyas* also are intended to be enlightened by the *brāhmaṇas.* When the *brāhmaṇas* and *kṣatriyas* cooperate nicely, the other subordinate divisions, the *vaiśyas,* or mercantile people, and the *śūdras,* or laborer class, automatically flourish. The entire elaborate system of Vedic society was therefore based on the importance of the *brāhmaṇas* and *kṣatriyas.* The Lord is the real protector, but He is unattached to the affairs of protection. He creates *brāhmaṇas* for the protection of the *kṣatriyas,* and *kṣatriyas* for the protection of the *brāhmaṇas.* He remains aloof from all activities; therefore, He is called *nirvikāra,* "without activity." He has nothing to do. He is so great that He does not perform action personally, but His energies act. The *brāhmaṇas* and *kṣatriyas,* and anything that we see, are different energies acting upon one another.

Although individual souls are all different, the Superself, or Supersoul, is the Supreme Personality of Godhead. Individually one's self may differ from others in certain qualities and may engage in different activities, such as those of a *brāhmaṇa, kṣatriya* or *vaiśya,* but when there is complete cooperation among different individual souls, the Supreme Personality of Godhead as Supersoul, Paramātmā, being one in every individual soul, is pleased and gives them all protection. As stated before, the *brāhmaṇas* are produced from the mouth of the Lord, and the *kṣatriyas* are produced from the chest or arms of the Lord. If the different castes or social sections, although apparently differently occupied in different activities, nevertheless act in full cooperation, then the Lord is pleased. This is the idea of the institution of four *varṇas* and four *āśramas.* If the members of different *āśramas* and *varṇas* cooperate fully in Kṛṣṇa consciousness, then society is well protected by the Lord, without doubt.

In *Bhagavad-gītā* it is stated that the Lord is the proprietor of all different bodies. The individual soul is the proprietor of his individual body, but the Lord clearly states, "My dear Bhārata, you must know that I am also *kṣetra jña.*" *Kṣetra jña* means "the knower or proprietor of the body." The individual soul is the proprietor of the individual body, but the Supersoul, the Personality of Godhead, Kṛṣṇa, is the proprietor of all bodies everywhere. He is the proprietor not only of human bodies but of birds, beasts and all other entities, not only on this planet but on other planets also. He is the supreme proprietor; therefore He does not become divided by protecting the different individual souls. He remains one and the same. That the sun appears on top of everyone's head when at the meridian does not imply that the sun becomes divided. One man thinks that the sun is on his head only, whereas five thousand miles away another man is thinking that the sun is only on his head. Similarly, the Supersoul, the Supreme Personality of Godhead, is one, but He appears to individually oversee each individual soul. This does not mean that the individual soul and the Supersoul are one. They are one in quality, as spirit soul, but the individual soul and Supersoul are different.

TEXT 5

तव सन्दर्शनादेवच्छिन्ना मे सर्वसंशयाः ।
यत्स्वयं भगवान् प्रीत्या धर्ममाह रिरक्षिषोः ॥ ५ ॥

tava sandarśanād eva
cchinnā me sarva-saṁśayāḥ
yat svayaṁ bhagavān prītyā
dharmam āha rirakṣiṣoḥ

tava—your; *sandarśanāt*—by sight; *eva*—only; *chinnāḥ*—resolved; *me*—my; *sarva-saṁśayāḥ*—all doubts; *yat*—inasmuch as; *svayam*—personally; *bhagavān*—Your Lordship; *prītyā*—lovingly; *dharmam*—duty; *āha*—explained; *rirakṣiṣoḥ*—of a king anxious to protect his subjects.

TRANSLATION

Now I have resolved all my doubts simply by meeting you, for Your Lordship has very kindly and clearly explained the duty of a king who desires to protect his subjects.

PURPORT

Manu described herewith the result of seeing a great saintly person. Lord Caitanya says that one should always try to associate with saintly persons because if one establishes a proper association with a saintly person, even for a moment, one attains all perfection. Somehow or other, if one meets a saintly person and achieves his favor, then the entire mission of one's human life is fulfilled. In our personal experience we have actual proof of this statement of Manu. Once we had the opportunity to meet Viṣṇupāda Śrī Śrīmad Bhaktisiddhānta Sarasvatī Gosvāmī Mahārāja, and on first sight he requested this humble self to preach his message in the Western countries. There was no preparation for this, but somehow or other he desired it, and by his grace we are now engaged in executing his order, which has given us a transcendental occupation and has saved and liberated us from the occupation of material activities. Thus it is actually a fact that if one meets a saintly person completely engaged in transcendental duties and achieves his favor, then one's life mission becomes complete. What is not possible to achieve in thousands of lives can be achieved in one moment if there is an opportunity to meet a saintly person. It is therefore enjoined in Vedic literature that one should always try to associate with saintly persons and try to disassociate oneself from the common man, because by one word of a saintly person one can be liberated from material entanglement. A saintly person has the power, because of his spiritual advancement, to give immediate liberation to the conditioned soul. Here Manu admits that all his doubts are now over because Kardama has very kindly described the different duties of individual souls.

TEXT 6

दिष्ट्या मे भगवान् दृष्टो दुर्दर्शो योऽकृतात्मनाम् ।
दिष्ट्या पादरजः स्पृष्टं शीर्ष्णा मे भवतः शिवम् ॥ ६ ॥

diṣṭyā me bhagavān dṛṣṭo
durdarśo yo 'kṛtātmanām
diṣṭyā pāda-rajaḥ spṛṣṭaṁ
śīrṣṇā me bhavataḥ śivam

diṣṭyā—by good fortune; *me*—my; *bhagavān*—all-powerful; *dṛṣṭaḥ*—is seen; *durdarśaḥ*—not easily seen; *yaḥ*—who; *akṛta-ātmanām*—of those who have not controlled the mind and senses; *diṣṭyā*—by my good fortune; *pāda-rajaḥ*—the dust of the feet; *spṛṣṭam*—is touched; *śīrṣṇā*—by the head; *me*—my; *bhavataḥ*—your; *śivam*—causing all auspiciousness.

TRANSLATION

It is my good fortune that I have been able to see you, for you cannot easily be seen by persons who have not subdued the mind or controlled the senses. I am all the more fortunate to have touched with my head the blessed dust of your feet.

PURPORT

The perfection of transcendental life can be achieved simply by touching the holy dust of the lotus feet of a holy man. In the *Bhāgavatam* it is said, *mahat-pāda-rajo-'bhiṣekam,* which means to be blessed by the holy dust of the lotus feet of a *mahat,* a great devotee. As stated in *Bhagavad-gītā, mahātmānas tu:* those who are great souls are under the spell of spiritual energy, and their symptom is that they fully engage in Kṛṣṇa consciousness for the service of the Lord. Therefore they are called *mahat.* Unless one is fortunate enough to have the dust of the lotus feet of a *mahātmā* on one's head, there is no possibility of perfection in spiritual life.

The *paramparā* system of disciplic succession is very important as a means of spiritual success. One becomes a *mahat* by the grace of his *mahat* spiritual master. If one takes shelter of the lotus feet of a great soul, there is every possibility of one's also becoming a great soul. When Mahārāja Rahūgaṇa asked Jaḍa Bharata about his wonderful achievement of spiritual success, he replied to the King that spiritual success is not possible simply by following the rituals of religion or simply by converting oneself into a *sannyāsī* or offering sacrifices as recommended in the scriptures. These methods are undoubtedly helpful for spiritual realization, but the real effect is brought about by the grace of a *mahātmā.* In Viśvanātha Cakravartī Ṭhākura's eight stanzas of prayer to the spiritual master, it is clearly stated that simply by satisfying the spiritual master one can achieve the supreme success in life, and in spite of executing all ritualistic performances, if one cannot satisfy the spiritual master, one has no access to spiritual perfection. Here the word *akṛtātmanām* is very significant. *Ātmā* means "body," "soul," or "mind," and *akṛtātmā* means the common man, who cannot control the senses or the mind. Because the common man is unable to control the senses and the mind, it is his duty to seek the shelter of a great soul or a great devotee of the Lord and just try to please him. That will make his life perfect. A common man cannot rise to the topmost stage of spiritual perfection simply by following the rituals and religious principles. He has to take shelter of a bona fide spiritual master and work under his direction faithfully and sincerely; then he becomes perfect, without a doubt.

TEXT 7

दिष्ट्या त्वयानुशिष्टोऽहं कृतश्चानुग्रहो महान् ।
अपावृतैः कर्णरन्ध्रैर्जुष्टा दिष्ट्योशतीर्गिरः ॥ ७ ॥

diṣṭyā tvayānuśiṣṭo 'haṁ
kṛtaś cānugraho mahān

apāvṛtaiḥ karṇa-randhrair
juṣṭā diṣṭyośatīr girah

diṣṭyā—luckily; *tvayā*—by you; *anuśiṣṭaḥ*—instructed; *aham*—I; *kṛtaḥ*—bestowed; *ca*—and; *anugrahaḥ*—favor; *mahān*—great; *apāvṛtaiḥ*—open; *karṇa-randhraiḥ*—with the holes of the ears; *juṣṭāḥ*—received; *diṣṭyā*—by good fortune; *uśatīḥ*—pure; *giraḥ*—words.

TRANSLATION

I have fortunately been instructed by you, and thus great favor has been bestowed upon me. I thank God that I have listened with open ears to your pure words.

PURPORT

Śrīla Rūpa Gosvāmī has given directions, in his *Bhakti-rasāmṛta-sindhu,* on how to accept a bona fide spiritual master and how to deal with him. First, the desiring candidate must find a bona fide spiritual master, and then he must very eagerly receive instructions from him and execute them. This is reciprocal service. A bona fide spiritual master or saintly person always desires to elevate a common man who comes to him. Because everyone is under the delusion of *māyā* and is forgetful of his prime duty, Kṛṣṇa consciousness, a saintly person always desires that everyone become a saintly person. It is the function of a saintly person to invoke Kṛṣṇa consciousness in every forgetful common man.

Manu said that since he was advised and instructed by Kardama Muni, he was very much favored. He considered himself lucky to receive the message by aural reception. It is especially mentioned here that one should be very inquisitive to hear with open ears from the authorized source of the bona fide spiritual master. How is one to receive? One should receive the transcendental message by aural reception. The word *karṇa-randhraiḥ* means "through the holes of the ears." The favor of the spiritual master is not received through any other part of the body but the ears. This does not mean, however, that the spiritual master gives a particular type of *mantra* through the ears in exchange for some dollars and if the man meditates on that he achieves perfection and becomes God within six months. Such reception through the ears is bogus. The real fact is that a bona fide spiritual master knows the nature of a particular man and what sort of duties he can perform in Kṛṣṇa consciousness, and he instructs him in that way. He instructs him through the ear, not privately, but publicly. "You are fit for such and such work in Kṛṣṇa consciousness. You can act in this way." One person is advised to act in Kṛṣṇa consciousness by working in the Deities' room, another is advised to act in Kṛṣṇa consciousness by performing editorial work, another is advised to do preaching work, and another is advised to carry out Kṛṣṇa consciousness in the cooking department. There are different departments of activity in Kṛṣṇa consciousness, and a spiritual master, knowing the particular ability of a particular man, trains him in such a way that by his tendency to act he becomes perfect. *Bhagavad-gītā* makes it clear that one can attain the highest perfection of spiritual life simply by offering service according to his ability, just as Arjuna served Kṛṣṇa by his ability in the military art. Arjuna offered his service fully as a military man, and he became perfect. Similarly, an artist can attain perfection simply by performing artistic work under the direction of the spiritual master. If one is a literary man, he can write articles and poetry for the service of the Lord under the direction of the spiritual master. One has to receive the message of the spiritual master regarding how to act in one's capacity, for the spiritual master is expert in giving such instructions.

This combination, the instruction of the spiritual master and the faithful execution of the instruction by the disciple, makes the entire process perfect. Śrīla Viśvanātha Cakravartī Ṭhākura describes in his explanation of the verse in *Bhagavad-gītā, vyavasāyātmikā buddhiḥ,* that one who wants to be certain to achieve spiritual success must take the instruction from the spiritual master as to what his particular function is. He should faithfully try to execute that particular instruction and should consider that his life and soul. The faithful execution of the instruction which he receives from the spiritual master is the only duty of a disciple, and that will bring him perfection. One should be very careful to receive the message from the spiritual master through the ears and execute it faithfully. That will make one's life successful.

TEXT 8

स भवान्दुहितृस्नेहपरिक्लिष्टात्मनो मम ।
श्रोतुमर्हसि दीनस्य श्रावितं कृपया मुने ॥ ८ ॥

sa bhavān duhitṛ-sneha-
parikliṣṭātmano mama
śrotum arhasi dīnasya
śrāvitaṁ kṛpayā mune

saḥ—yourself; *bhavān*—Your Honor; *duhitṛ-sneha*—by affection for my daughter; *parikliṣṭa-ātmanaḥ*—whose mind is agitated; *mama*—my; *śrotum*—to listen; *arhasi*—be pleased; *dīnasya*—of my humble self; *śrāvitam*—to the prayer; *kṛpayā*—graciously; *mune*—O sage.

TRANSLATION

O great sage, graciously be pleased to listen to the prayer of my humble self, for my mind is troubled by affection for my daughter.

PURPORT

When a disciple is perfectly in consonance with the spiritual master, having received his message and executed it perfectly and sincerely, he has a right to ask a particular favor from the spiritual master. Generally a pure devotee of the Lord or a pure disciple of a bona fide spiritual master does not ask any favor either from the Lord or the spiritual master, but even if there is a need to ask a favor from the spiritual master, one cannot ask that favor without satisfying him fully. Svāyambhuva Manu wanted to disclose his mind regarding the function he wanted to execute due to affection for his daughter.

TEXT 9

प्रियव्रतोत्तानपदोः स्वसेयं दुहिता मम ।
अन्विच्छति पतिं युक्तं वयःशीलगुणादिभिः ॥ ९ ॥

priyavratottānapadoḥ
svaseyaṁ duhitā mama
anvicchati patiṁ yuktaṁ
vayaḥ-śīla-guṇādibhiḥ

priyavrata-uttānapadoḥ—of Priyavrata and Uttānapāda; *svasā*—sister; *iyam*—this; *duhitā*—daughter; *mama*—my; *anvicchati*—is seeking; *patim*—husband; *yuktam*—suited; *vayaḥ-śīla-guṇa-ādibhiḥ*—by age, character, good qualities, etc.

TRANSLATION

My daughter is the sister of Priyavrata and Uttānapāda. She is seeking a suitable husband in terms of age, character and good qualities.

PURPORT

The grown-up daughter of Svāyambhuva Manu, Devahūti, had good character and was well qualified; therefore she was searching for a suitable husband just befitting her age, qualities and character. The purpose of Manu's introducing his daughter as the sister of Priyavrata and Uttānapāda, two great kings, was to convince the sage that the girl came from a great family. She was his daughter and at the same time the sister of *kṣatriyas*; she did not come from a lower-class family. Manu therefore offered her to

Kardama as just suitable for his purpose. It is clear that although the daughter was mature in age and qualities, she did not go out and find her husband independently. She expressed her desire for a suitable husband corresponding to her character, age and quality, and the father himself, out of affection for his daughter, took charge of finding such a husband.

TEXT 10

यदा तु भवतः शीलश्रुतरूपवयोगुणान् ।
अशृणोन्नारदादेषा त्वय्यासीत्कृतनिश्चया ॥१०॥

yadā tu bhavataḥ śīla-
śruta-rūpa-vayo-guṇān
aśṛṇon nāradād eṣā
tvayy āsīt kṛta-niścayā

yadā—when; *tu*—but; *bhavataḥ*—your; *śīla*—noble character; *śruta*—learning; *rūpa*—beautiful appearance; *vayaḥ*—youth; *guṇān*—virtues; *aśṛnot*—heard; *nāradāt*—from Nārada Muni; *eṣā*—Devahūti; *tvayi*—in you; *āsīt*—became; *kṛta-niścayā*—fixed in determination.

TRANSLATION

The moment she heard from the sage Nārada of your noble character, learning, beautiful appearance, youth and other virtues, she fixed her mind upon you.

PURPORT

The girl Devahūti did not personally see Kardama Muni, nor did she personally experience his character or qualities, since there was no social intercourse by which she could gain such understanding. But she heard about Kardama Muni from the authority of Nārada Muni. Hearing from an authority is a better experience than gaining personal understanding. She heard from Nārada Muni that Kardama Muni was just fit to be her husband; therefore she became fixed in her heart that she would marry him, and she expressed her desire to her father, who therefore brought her before him.

TEXT 11

तत्प्रतीच्छ द्विजाग्र्येमां श्रद्धयोपहृतां मया ।
सर्वात्मनानुरूपां ते गृहमेधिषु कर्मसु ॥११॥

tat pratīccha dvijāgryemāṁ
śraddhayopahṛtāṁ mayā
sarvātmanānurūpāṁ te
gṛhamedhiṣu karmasu

tat—therefore; *pratīccha*—please accept; *dvija-agrya*—O best of the *brāhmaṇas; imām*—her; *śraddhayā*—with faith; *upahṛtām*—offered as a presentation; *mayā*—by me; *sarva-ātmanā*—in every way; *anurūpām*—suitable; *te*—for you; *gṛha-medhiṣu*—in the household; *karmasu*—duties.

TRANSLATION

Therefore please accept her, O chief of the brāhmaṇas, for I offer her with faith and she is in every respect fit to be your wife and take charge of your household duties.

PURPORT

The words *gṛhamedhiṣu karmasu* mean "in household duties." Another word is also used here: *sarvātmanānurūpām*. The purport is that a wife should not only be equal to her husband in age, character and qualities, but must be helpful to him in his household duties. The household duty of a man is not to satisfy his sense gratification, but to remain with a wife and children and at the same time attain advancement in spiritual life. One who does not do so is not a householder but a *gṛhamedhī*. Two words are used in Sanskrit literature; one is *gṛhastha*, and the other is *gṛhamedhī*. The difference between *gṛhamedhī* and *gṛhastha* is that *gṛhastha* is also an *āśrama*, or spiritual order, but if one simply satisfies his senses as a householder, then he is a *gṛhamedhī*. For a *gṛhamedhī*, to accept a wife means to satisfy the senses, but for a *gṛhastha* a qualified wife is an assistant in every respect for advancement in spiritual activities. It is the duty of the wife to take charge of household affairs and not to compete with the husband. A wife is meant to help, but she cannot help her husband unless he is completely equal to her in age, character and quality.

TEXT 12

उद्यतस्य हि कामस्य प्रतिवादो न शस्यते ।
अपि निर्मुक्तसङ्गस्य कामरक्तस्य किं पुनः ॥१२॥

udyatasya hi kāmasya
prativādo na śasyate
api nirmukta-saṅgasya
kāma-raktasya kiṁ punaḥ

udyatasya—which has come of itself; *hi*—in fact; *kāmasya*—of material desire; *prativādaḥ*—the denial; *na*—not; *śasyate*—to be praised; *api*—even; *nirmukta*—of one who is free; *saṅgasya*—from attachment; *kāma*—to sensual pleasures; *raktasya*—of one addicted; *kim punaḥ*—how much less.

TRANSLATION

To deny an offering that has come of itself is not commendable even for one absolutely free from all attachment, much less one addicted to sensual pleasure.

PURPORT

In material life everyone is desirous of sense gratification; therefore, a person who gets an object of sense gratification without endeavor should not refuse to accept it. Kardama Muni was not meant for sense gratification, yet he aspired to marry and prayed to the Lord for a suitable wife. This was known to Svāyambhuva Manu. He indirectly convinced Kardama Muni: "You desire a suitable wife like my daughter, and she is now present before you. You should not reject the fulfillment of your prayer; you should accept my daughter."

TEXT 13

य उद्यतमनादृत्य कीनाशमभियाचते ।
क्षीयते तद्यशः स्फीतं मानश्चावज्ञया हतः ॥१३॥

ya udyatam anādṛtya
kīnāśam abhiyācate
kṣīyate tad-yaśaḥ sphītaṁ
mānaś cāvajñayā hataḥ

yaḥ—who; *udyatam*—an offering; *anādṛtya*—rejecting; *kīnāśam*—from a miser; *abhiyācate*—begs; *kṣīyate*—is lost; *tat*—his; *yaśaḥ*—reputation; *sphītam*—widespread; *mānaḥ*—honor; *ca*—and; *avajñayā*—by neglectful behavior; *hataḥ*—destroyed.

TRANSLATION

One who rejects an offering that comes of its own accord but later begs a boon from a miser thus loses his widespread reputation, and his pride is humbled by the neglectful behavior of others.

PURPORT

The general procedure of Vedic marriage is that a father offers his daughter to a suitable boy. That is a very respectable marriage. A boy should not go to the girl's father and ask for the hand of his daughter in marriage. That is considered to be humbling one's respectable position. Svāyambhuva Manu wanted to convince Kardama Muni, since he knew that the sage wanted to marry a suitable girl: "I am offering just such a suitable wife. Do not reject the offer, or else, because you are in need of a wife, you will have to ask for such a wife from someone else, who may not behave with you so well. In that case your position will be humbled."

Another feature of this incident is that Svāyambhuva Manu was the emperor, but he went to offer his qualified daughter to a poor *brāhmaṇa.* Kardama Muni had no worldly possessions—he was a hermit living in the forest—but he was advanced in culture. Therefore, in offering one's daughter to a person, the culture and quality are counted as prominent, not wealth or any other material consideration.

TEXT 14

अहं त्वाशृणवं विद्वन् विवाहार्थं समुद्यतम् ।
अतस्त्वमुपकुर्वाणः प्रत्तां प्रतिगृहाण मे ॥१४॥

ahaṁ tvāśṛṇavaṁ vidvan
vivāhārthaṁ samudyatam
atas tvam upakurvāṇaḥ
prattāṁ pratigṛhāṇa me

aham—I; *tvā*—you; *aśṛṇavam*—heard; *vidvan*—O wise man; *vivāha-artham*—for the sake of marriage; *samudyatam*—prepared; *ataḥ*—hence; *tvam*—you; *upakurvāṇaḥ*—not taken a vow of perpetual celibacy; *prattām*—offered; *pratigṛhāṇa*—please accept; *me*—of me.

TRANSLATION

Svāyambhuva Manu continued: O wise man, I heard that you were prepared to marry. Please accept her hand, which is being offered to you by me, since you have not taken a vow of perpetual celibacy.

PURPORT

The principle of *brahmacarya* is celibacy. There are two kinds of *brahmacārīs.* One is called *naiṣṭhika-brahmacārī,* which means one who takes a vow of celibacy for his whole life, whereas the other, the *upakurvāṇa-brahmacārī,* is a *brahmacārī* who takes the vow of celibacy up to a certain age. For example, he may take the vow to remain celibate up to twenty-five years of age; then, with the permission of his spiritual master, he enters married life. *Brahmacarya* is student life, the beginning of life in the spiritual orders, and the principle of *brahmacarya* is celibacy. Only a householder can indulge in sense gratification or sex life, not a *brahmacārī*. Svāyambhuva Manu requested Kardama Muni to accept his daughter, since Kardama had not taken the vow of *naiṣṭhika-brahmacarya.* He was willing to marry, and the suitable daughter of a high royal family was presented.

TEXT 15

ऋषिरुवाच
बाढमुद्वोढुकामोऽहमप्रत्ता च तवात्मजा ।
आवयोरनुरूपोऽसावाद्यो वैवाहिको विधिः ॥१५॥

ṛṣir uvāca
bāḍham udvoḍhu-kāmo 'ham
apratta ca tavātmajā
āvayor anurūpo 'sāv
ādyo vaivāhiko vidhiḥ

ṛṣiḥ—the great sage Kardama; *uvāca*—said; *bāḍham*—very well; *udvoḍhu-kāmaḥ*—desirous to marry; *aham*—I; *aprattā*—not promised to anyone else; *ca*—and; *tava*—your; *ātma-jā*—daughter; *āvayoḥ*—of us two; *anurūpaḥ*—proper; *asau*—this; *ādyaḥ*—first; *vaivahikaḥ*—of marriage; *vidhiḥ*—ritualistic ceremony.

TRANSLATION

The great sage replied: Certainly I have a desire to marry, and your daughter has not yet married or given her word to anyone. Therefore our marriage according to the Vedic system can take place.

PURPORT

There were many considerations by Kardama Muni before accepting the daughter of Svāyambhuva Manu. Most important is that Devahūti had first of all fixed her mind on marrying him. She did not choose to have any other man as her husband. That is a great consideration because female psychology dictates that when a woman offers her heart to a man for the first time, it is very difficult for her to take it back. Also, she had not married before; she was a virgin girl. All these considerations convinced Kardama Muni to accept her. Therefore he said, "Yes, I shall accept your daughter under religious regulations of marriage." There are different kinds of marriages, of which the first-class marriage is held by inviting a suitable bridegroom for the daughter and giving her in charity, well dressed and well decorated with ornaments, along with a dowry according to the means of the father. There are other kinds of marriage, such as *gāndharva* marriage and marriage by love, which are also accepted as marriage. Even if one is forcibly kidnapped and later on accepted as a wife, that is also accepted. But Kardama Muni accepted the first-class way of marriage because the father was willing and the daughter was qualified. She had never offered her heart to anyone else. All these considerations made Kardama Muni agree to accept the daughter of Svāyambhuva Manu.

TEXT 16

कामः स भूयान्नरदेव तेऽस्याः
पुत्र्याः समाम्नायविधौ प्रतीतः ।
क एव ते तनयां नाद्रियेत
स्वयैव कान्त्या क्षिपतीमिव श्रियम् ॥१६॥

kāmaḥ sa bhūyān naradeva te 'syāḥ
putryāḥ samāmnāya-vidhau pratītaḥ
ka eva te tanayāṁ nādriyeta
svayaiva kāntyā kṣipatīm iva śriyam

kāmaḥ—desire; *saḥ*—that; *bhūyāt*—let it be fulfilled; *nara-deva*—O King; *te*—your; *asyāḥ*—this; *putryāḥ*—of the daughter; *samāmnāya-vidhau*—in the process of the Vedic scriptures; *pratītaḥ*—recognized; *kaḥ*—who; *eva*—in fact; *te*—your; *tanayām*—daughter; *na ādriyeta*—would not adore; *svayā*—by her own; *eva*—alone; *kāntyā*—bodily luster; *kṣipatīm*—excelling; *iva*—as if; *śriyam*—ornaments.

TRANSLATION

Let your daughter's desire for marriage, which is recognized in the Vedic scriptures, be fulfilled. Who would not accept her hand? She is so beautiful that by her bodily luster alone she excels the beauty of her ornaments.

PURPORT

Kardama Muni wanted to marry Devahūti in the recognized manner of marriage prescribed in the scriptures. As stated in the Vedic scriptures, the first-class process is to call the bridegroom to the home of the bride and hand her to him in charity with a dowry of necessary ornaments, gold, furniture and other household paraphernalia. This form of marriage is prevalent among higher-class Hindus even today and is declared in the *śāstras* to confer great religious merit on the bride's father. To give a daughter in charity to a suitable son-in-law is considered to be one of the pious activities of a householder. There are eight forms of marriage mentioned in the scripture *Manu-smṛti*, but only one process of marriage, *brāhma* or *rājasika* marriage, is now current. Other kinds of marriage-by love, by exchange of garlands or by kidnapping the bride-are now forbidden in this Kali age. Formerly, *kṣatriyas* would, at their pleasure, kidnap a princess from another royal house, and there would he a fight between the *kṣatriya* and the girl's family; then, if the kidnapper was the winner, the girl would be offered to him for marriage. Even Kṛṣṇa married Rukmiṇī by that process, and some of His sons and grandsons also married by kidnapping. Kṛṣṇa's grandsons kidnapped Duryodhana's daughter, which caused a fight between the Kuru and Yadu families. Afterward, an adjustment was made by the elderly members of the Kuru family. Such marriages were current in bygone ages, but at the present moment they are impossible because the strict principles of *kṣatriya* life have practically been abolished. Since India has become dependent on foreign countries, the particular influences of her social orders have been lost; now, according to the scriptures, everyone is a *śūdra*. The so-called *brāhmaṇas, kṣatriyas* and *vaiśyas* have forgotten their traditional activities, and in the absence of these activities they are called *śūdras*. It is said in the scriptures, *kalau śūdra-sambhavaḥ*. In the age of Kali everyone will be like *śūdras*. The traditional social customs are not followed in this age, although formerly they were followed strictly.

TEXT 17

यां हर्म्यपृष्ठे क्वणदङ्घ्रिशोभां
विक्रीडतीं कन्दुकविह्वलाक्षीम् ।
विश्वावसुर्न्यपतत्स्वाद्विमाना-
द्विलोक्य सम्मोहविमूढचेताः ॥१७॥

yāṁ harmya-pṛṣṭhe kvaṇad-aṅghri-śobhāṁ
vikrīḍatīṁ kanduka-vihvalākṣīm
viśvāvasur nyapatat svād vimānād
vilokya sammoha-vimūḍha-cetāḥ

yām—whom; *harmya-pṛṣṭhe*—on the roof of the palace; *kvaṇat-aṅghri-śobhām*—whose beauty was heightened by the tinkling ornaments on her feet; *vikrīḍatīm*—playing; *kanduka-vihvala-akṣīm*—with eyes bewildered, following her ball; *viśvāvasuḥ*—Viśvāvasu; *nyapatat*—fell down; *svāt*—from his own; *vimānāt*—from the airplane; *vilokya*—seeing; *sammoha-vimūḍha-cetāḥ*—whose mind was stupefied.

TRANSLATION

I have heard that Viśvāvasu, the great Gandharva, his mind stupefied with infatuation, fell from his airplane after seeing your daughter playing with a ball on the roof of the palace, for she was indeed beautiful with her tinkling ankle bells and her eyes moving to and fro.

PURPORT

It is understood that not only at the present moment but in those days also there were skyscrapers. Herein we find the word *harmya-pṛṣṭhe. Harmya* means "a very big palatial building." *Svād vimānāt* means "from his own airplane." It is suggested that private airplanes or helicopters were also current in those days. The Gandharva Viśvāvasu, while flying in the sky, could see Devahūti playing ball on the roof of the palace. Ball playing was also current, but aristocratic girls would not play in a public place. Ball playing and other such pleasures were not meant for ordinary women and girls; only princesses like Devahūti could indulge in such sports. It is described here that she was seen from the flying airplane. This indicates that the palace was very high, otherwise how could one see her from an airplane? The vision was so distinct that the Gandharva Viśvāvasu was bewildered by her beauty and by hearing the sound of her ankle bangles, and being captivated by the sound and beauty, he fell down. Kardama Muni mentioned the incident as he had heard it.

TEXT 18

तां प्रार्थयन्तीं ललनाललाम-
मसेवितश्रीचरणैरदृष्टाम् ।
वत्सां मनोरुच्चपदः स्वसारं
को नानुमन्येत बुधोऽभियाताम् ॥१८॥

tāṁ prārthayantīṁ lalanā-lalāmam
asevita-śrī-caraṇair adṛṣṭām
vatsāṁ manor uccapadaḥ svasāraṁ
ko nānumanyeta budho 'bhiyātām

tām—her; *prārthayantīm*—seeking; *lalanā-lalāmam*—the ornament of women; *asevita-śrī-caraṇaiḥ*—by those who have not worshiped the feet of Lakṣmī; *adṛṣṭām*—not seen; *vatsām*—beloved daughter; *manoḥ*—of Svāyambhuva Manu; *uccapadaḥ*—of Uttānapāda; *svasāram*—sister; *kaḥ*—what; *na anumanyeta*—would not welcome; *budhaḥ*—wise man; *abhiyātām*—who has come of her own accord.

TRANSLATION

What wise man would not welcome her, the very ornament of womanhood, the beloved daughter of Svāyambhuva Manu and sister of Uttānapāda? Those who have not worshiped the gracious feet of the goddess of fortune cannot even perceive her, yet she has come of her own accord to seek my hand.

PURPORT

Kardama Muni praised the beauty and qualification of Devahūti in different ways. Devahūti was actually the ornament of all ornamented beautiful girls. A girl becomes beautiful by putting ornaments on her body, but Devahūti was more beautiful than the ornaments; she was considered the ornament of the ornamented beautiful girls. Demigods and Gandharvas were attracted by her beauty. Kardama Muni, although a great sage, was not a denizen of the heavenly planets, but it is mentioned in the previous verse that Viśvāvasu, who came from heaven, was also attracted by the beauty of Devahūti. Besides her personal beauty, she was the daughter of Emperor Svāyambhuva and sister of King Uttānapāda. Who could refuse the hand of such a girl?

TEXT 19

अतो भजिष्ये समयेन साध्वीं
यावत्तेजो बिभृयादात्मनो मे ।
अतो धर्मान् पारमहंस्यमुख्यान्
शुक्लप्रोक्तान् बहु मन्येऽविहिंस्रान् ॥१९॥

ato bhajiṣye samayena sādhvīṁ
yāvat tejo bibhṛyād ātmano me
ato dharmān pāramahaṁsya-mukhyān
śukla-proktān bahu manye 'vihiṁsrān

ataḥ—therefore; *bhajiṣye*—I shall accept; *samayena*—on the conditions; *sādhvīm*—the chaste girl; *yāvat*—until; *tejaḥ*—semen; *bibhṛyāt*—may bear; *ātmanaḥ*—from my body; *me*—my; *ataḥ*—thereafter; *dharmān*—the duties; *pāramahaṁsya-mukhyān*—of the best of the *paramahaṁsas*; *śukla-proktān*—spoken by Lord Viṣṇu; *bahu*—much; *manye*—I shall consider; *avihiṁsrān*—free from envy.

TRANSLATION

Therefore I shall accept this chaste girl as my wife, on the condition that after she bears semen from my body, I shall accept the life of devotional

service accepted by the most perfect human beings. That process was described by Lord Viṣṇu. It is free from envy.

PURPORT

Kardama Muni expressed his desire for a very beautiful wife to Emperor Svāyambhuva and accepted the Emperor's daughter for marriage. Kardama Muni was in the hermitage practicing complete celibacy as a *brahmacārī,* and although he had the desire to marry, he did not want to be a householder for the whole span of his life because he was conversant with the Vedic principles of human life. According to Vedic principles, the first part of life should be utilized in *brahmacarya* for the development of character and spiritual qualities. In the next part of life, one may accept a wife and beget children, but one should not beget children like cats and dogs.

Kardama Muni desired to beget a child who would be a ray of the Supreme Personality of Godhead. One should beget a child who can perform the duties of Viṣṇu, otherwise there is no need to produce children. There are two kinds of children born of good fathers: one is educated in Kṛṣṇa consciousness so that he can be delivered from the clutches of *māyā* in that very life, and the other is a ray of the Supreme Personality of Godhead and teaches the world the ultimate goal of life. As will be described in later chapters, Kardama Muni begot such a child-Kapila, the incarnation of the Personality of Godhead who enunciated the philosophy of Sāṅkhya. Great householders pray to God to send His representative so that there may be an auspicious movement in human society. This is one reason to beget a child. Another reason is that a highly enlightened parent can train a child in Kṛṣṇa consciousness so that the child will not have to come back again to this miserable world. Parents should see to it that the child born of them does not enter the womb of a mother again. Unless one can train a child for liberation in that life, there is no need to marry or produce children. If human society produces children like cats and dogs for the disturbance of social order, then the world becomes hellish, as it has in this age of Kali. In this age, neither parents nor their children are trained; both are animalistic and simply eat, sleep, mate, defend, and gratify their senses. This disorder in social life cannot bring peace to human society. Kardama Muni explains beforehand that he would not associate with the girl Devahūti for the whole duration of his life. He would simply associate with her until she had a child. In other words, sex life should be utilized only to produce a nice child, not for any other purpose. Human life is especially meant for complete devotion to the service of the Lord. That is the philosophy of Lord Caitanya.

After fulfilling his responsibility to produce a nice child, one should take *sannyāsa* and engage in the perfectional *paramahaṁsa* stage. *Paramahaṁsa* refers to the most highly elevated perfectional stage of life. There are four stages within *sannyāsa* life, and *paramahaṁsa* is the highest order. The *Śrīmad-Bhāgavatam* is called the *paramahaṁsa-saṁhitā,* the treatise for the highest class of human beings. The *paramahaṁsa* is free from envy. In other stages, even in the householder stage of life, there is competition and envy, but since the activities of the human being in the *paramahaṁsa* stage are completely engaged in Kṛṣṇa consciousness, or devotional service, there is no scope for envy. In the same order as Kardama Muni, about one hundred years ago, Ṭhākura Bhaktivinoda also wanted to beget a child who could preach the philosophy and teachings of Lord Caitanya to the fullest extent. By his prayers to the Lord he had as his child Bhaktisiddhānta Sarasvatī Gosvāmī Mahārāja, who at the present moment is preaching the philosophy of Lord Caitanya throughout the entire world through his bona fide disciples.

TEXT 20

यतोऽभवद्विश्वमिदं विचित्रं
संस्थास्यते यत्र च वावतिष्ठते ।
प्रजापतीनां पतिरेष मह्यं
परं प्रमाणं भगवाननन्तः ॥२०॥

yato 'bhavad viśvam idaṁ vicitraṁ
saṁsthāsyate yatra ca vāvatiṣṭhate
prajāpatīnāṁ patir eṣa mahyaṁ
paraṁ pramāṇaṁ bhagavān anantaḥ

yataḥ—from whom; *abhavat*—emanated; *viśvam*—creation; *idam*—this; *vicitram*—wonderful; *saṁsthāsyate*—will dissolve; *yatra*—in whom; *ca*—and; *vā*—or; *avatiṣṭhate*—presently exists; *prajā-patīnām*—of the Prajāpatis; *patiḥ*—the Lord; *eṣaḥ*—this; *mahyam*—to me; *param*—highest; *pramāṇam*—authority; *bhagavān*—Supreme Lord; *anantaḥ*—unlimited.

TRANSLATION

The highest authority for me is the unlimited Supreme Personality of Godhead, from whom this wonderful creation emanates and in whom its sustenance and dissolution rest. He is the origin of all Prajāpatis, the personalities meant to produce living entities in this world.

PURPORT

Kardama Muni was ordered by his father, Prajāpati, to produce children. In the beginning of creation the Prajāpatis were meant to produce the large population which was to reside in the planets of the gigantic universe. But Kardama Muni said that although his father was Prajāpati, who desired him to produce children, actually his origin was the Supreme Personality of Godhead, Viṣṇu, because Viṣṇu is the origin of everything; He is the actual creator of this universe, He is the actual maintainer, and when everything is annihilated, it rests in Him only. That is the conclusion of *Śrīmad-Bhāgavatam.* For creation, maintenance and annihilation there are the three deities Brahmā, Viṣṇu and Maheśvara (Śiva), but Brahmā and Maheśvara are qualitative expansions of Viṣṇu. Viṣṇu is the central figure. Viṣṇu, therefore, takes charge of maintenance. No one can maintain the whole creation but He. There are innumerable entities, and they have innumerable demands; no one but Viṣṇu can fulfill the innumerable demands of all the innumerable living entities. Brahmā is ordered to create, and Śiva is ordered to annihilate. The middle function, maintenance, is taken charge of by Viṣṇu. Kardama Muni knew very well, by his power in progressive spiritual life, that Viṣṇu, the Personality of Godhead, was his worshipable Deity. Whatever Viṣṇu desired was his duty, and nothing else. He was not prepared to beget a number of children. He would beget only one child, who would help the mission of Viṣṇu. As stated in *Bhagavad-gītā,* whenever there is a discrepancy in the discharge of religious principles, the Lord descends on the surface of the earth to protect religious principles and to annihilate the miscreants.

Marrying and begetting a child is considered to liquidate one's debts to the family in which one is born. There are many debts which are imposed upon a child just after his birth. There are debts to the family in which one is born, debts to the demigods, debts to the Pitās, debts to the *ṛṣis,* etc. But if someone engages only in the service of the Supreme Lord, the Personality of Godhead, who is actually worshipable, then even without trying to liquidate other debts, one becomes free from all obligations. Kardama Muni preferred to devote his life as a servant of the Lord in *paramahaṁsa* knowledge and to beget a child only for that purpose, not to beget numberless children to fill up the vacancies in the universe.

TEXT 21

मैत्रेय उवाच

स उग्रधन्वन्नियदेवाबभाषे
आसीच्च तूष्णीमरविन्दनाभम् ।

धियोपगृह्णन् स्मितशोभितेन
मुखेन चेतो लुलुभे देवहूत्याः ॥२१॥

maitreya uvāca
sa ugra-dhanvann iyad evābabhāṣe
āsīc ca tūṣṇīm aravinda-nābham
dhiyopagṛhṇan smita-śobhitena
mukhena ceto lulubhe devahūtyāḥ

maitreyaḥ—the great sage Maitreya; *uvāca*—said; *saḥ*—he (Kardama); *ugra-dhanvan*—O great warrior Vidura; *iyat*—this much; *eva*—only; *ābabhāṣe*—spoke; *āsīt*—became; *ca*—and; *tūṣṇīm*—silent; *aravinda-nābham*—Lord Viṣṇu (whose navel is adorned by a lotus); *dhiyā*—by thought; *upagṛhṇan*—seizing; *smita-śobhitena*—beautified by his smile; *mukhena*—by his face; *cetaḥ*—the mind; *lulubhe*—was captivated; *devahūtyāḥ*—of Devahūti.

TRANSLATION

Śrī Maitreya said: O great warrior Vidura, the sage Kardama said this much only and then became silent, thinking of his worshipable Lord Viṣṇu, who has a lotus on His navel. As he silently smiled, his face captured the mind of Devahūti, who began to meditate upon the great sage.

PURPORT

It appears that Kardama Muni was fully absorbed in Kṛṣṇa consciousness because as soon as he became silent, he at once began to think of Lord Viṣṇu. That is the way of Kṛṣṇa consciousness. Pure devotees are so absorbed in thought of Kṛṣṇa that they have no other engagement; although they may seem to think or act otherwise, they are always thinking of Kṛṣṇa. The smile of such a Kṛṣṇa conscious person is so attractive that simply by smiling he wins so many admirers, disciples and followers.

TEXT 22

सोऽनु ज्ञात्वा व्यवसितं महिष्या दुहितुः स्फुटम् ।
तस्मै गुणगणाढ्याय ददौ तुल्यां प्रहर्षितः ॥२२॥

so 'nu jñātvā vyavasitaṁ
mahiṣyā duhituḥ sphuṭam
tasmai guṇa-gaṇāḍhyāya
dadau tulyāṁ praharṣitaḥ

saḥ—he (Emperor Manu); *anu*—afterward; *jñātvā*—having known; *vyavasitam*—the fixed decision; *mahiṣyāḥ*—of the Queen; *duhituḥ*—of his daughter; *sphuṭam*—clearly; *tasmai*—to him; *guṇa-gaṇa-āḍhyāya*—who was endowed with a host of virtues; *dadau*—gave away; *tulyām*—who was equal (in good qualities); *praharṣitaḥ*—extremely pleased.

TRANSLATION

After having unmistakably known the decision of the Queen, as well as that of Devahūti, the Emperor most gladly gave his daughter to the sage, whose host of virtues was equaled by hers.

TEXT 23

शतरूपा महाराज्ञी पारिबर्हान्महाधनान् ।
दम्पत्योः पर्यदात्प्रीत्या भूषावासः परिच्छदान् ॥२३॥

śatarūpā mahā-rājñī
pāribarhān mahā-dhanān
dampatyoḥ paryadāt prītyā
bhūṣā-vāsaḥ paricchadān

śatarūpā—Empress Śatarūpā; *mahā-rājñī*—the Empress; *pāribarhān*—dowry; *mahā-dhanān*—valuable presents; *dam-patyoḥ*—to the bride and bridegroom; *paryadāt*—gave; *prītyā*—out of affection; *bhūṣā*—ornaments; *vāsaḥ*—clothes; *paricchadān*—articles for household use.

TRANSLATION

Empress Śatarūpā lovingly gave most valuable presents, suitable for the occasion, such as jewelry, clothes and household articles, in dowry to the bride and bridegroom.

PURPORT

The custom of giving one's daughter in charity with a dowry is still current in India. The gifts are given according to the position of the father of the bride. *Pāribarhān mahā-dhanān* means the dowry which must be awarded to the bridegroom at the time of marriage. Here *mahā-dhanān* means greatly valuable gifts befitting the dowry of an empress. The words *bhūṣā-vāsaḥ paricchadān* also appear here. *Bhūṣā* means "ornaments," *vāsaḥ* means "clothing," and *paricchadān* means "various household articles." All things befitting the marriage ceremony of an emperor's daughter were awarded to Kardama Muni, who was until now observing celibacy as a *brahmacārī*. The bride, Devahūti, was very richly dressed with ornaments and clothing.

In this way Kardama Muni was married with full opulence to a qualified wife and was endowed with the necessary paraphernalia for household life. In the Vedic way of marriage such a dowry is still given to the bridegroom by the father of the bride; even in poverty-stricken India there are marriages where hundreds and thousands of rupees are spent for a dowry. The dowry system is not illegal, as some have tried to prove. The dowry is a gift given to the daughter by the father to show good will, and it is compulsory. In rare cases where the father is completely unable to give a dowry, it is enjoined that he must at least give a fruit and a flower. As stated in *Bhagavad-gītā*, God can also be pleased even by a fruit and a flower. When there is financial inability and no question of accumulating a dowry by another means, one can give a fruit and flower for the satisfaction of the bridegroom.

TEXT 24

प्रत्तां दुहितरं सम्राट् सदृक्षाय गतव्यथः ।
उपगुह्य च बाहुभ्यामौत्कण्ठ्योन्मथिताशयः ॥२४॥

prattāṁ duhitaraṁ samrāṭ
sadṛkṣāya gata-vyathaḥ
upaguhya ca bāhubhyām
autkaṇṭhyonmathitāśayaḥ

prattām—who was given; *duhitaram*—daughter; *samrāṭ*—the Emperor (Manu); *sadṛkṣāya*—unto a suitable person; *gata-vyathaḥ*—relieved of his responsibility; *upaguhya*—embracing; *ca*—and; *bāhubhyām*—with his two arms; *autkaṇṭhya-unmathita-āśayaḥ*—having an anxious and agitated mind.

TRANSLATION

Thus relieved of his responsibility by handing over his daughter to a suitable man, Svāyambhuva Manu, his mind agitated by feelings of separation, embraced his affectionate daughter with both his arms.

PURPORT

A father always remains in anxiety until he can hand over his grownup daughter to a suitable boy. A father and mother's responsibility for children continues until they marry them to suitable spouses; when the father is able to perform that duty, he is relieved of his responsibility.

TEXT 25

अशक्नुवंस्तद्विरहं मुञ्चन् बाष्पकलां मुहुः ।
आसिञ्चदम्ब वत्सेति नेत्रोदैर्दुहितुः शिखाः ॥२५॥

aśaknuvaṁs tad-virahaṁ
muñcan bāṣpa-kalāṁ muhuḥ
āsiñcad amba vatseti
netrodair duhituḥ śikhāḥ

aśaknuvan—being unable to bear; *tat-viraham*—separation from her; *muñcan*—shedding; *bāṣpa-kalām*—tears; *muhuḥ*—again and again; *āsiñcat*—he drenched; *amba*—my dear mother; *vatsa*—my dear daughter; *iti*—thus; *netra-udaiḥ*—by the water from his eyes; *duhituḥ*—of his daughter; *śikhāḥ*—the locks of hair.

TRANSLATION

The Emperor was unable to bear the separation of his daughter. Therefore tears poured from his eyes again and again, drenching his daughter's head as he cried, "My dear mother! My dear daughter!"

PURPORT

The word *amba* is significant. A father sometimes addresses his daughter in affection as "mother" and sometimes as "my darling." The feeling of separation occurs because until the daughter is married she remains the daughter of the father, but after her marriage she is no longer claimed as a daughter in the family; she must go to the husband's house, for after marriage she becomes the property of the husband. According to *Manu-saṁhitā*, a woman is never independent. She must remain the property of the father while she is not married, and she must remain the property of the husband until she is elderly and has grown-up children of her own. In old age, when the husband has taken *sannyāsa* and left home, she remains the property of the sons. A woman is always dependent, either upon the father, husband or elderly sons. That will be exhibited in the life of Devahūti. Devahūti's father handed over responsibility for her to the husband, Kardama Muni, and in the same way, Kardama Muni also left home, giving the responsibility to his son, Kapiladeva. This narration will describe these events one after another.

TEXTS 26-27

आमन्त्र्य तं मुनिवरमनुज्ञातः सहानुगः ।
प्रतस्थे रथमारुह्य सभार्यः स्वपुरं नृपः ॥२६॥
उभयोर्ऋषिकुल्यायाः सरस्वत्याः सुरोधसोः ।
ऋषीणामुपशान्तानां पश्यन्नाश्रमसम्पदः ॥२७॥

āmantrya taṁ muni-varam
anujñātaḥ sahānugaḥ
pratasthe ratham āruhya
sabhāryaḥ sva-puraṁ nṛpaḥ

ubhayor ṛṣi-kulyāyāḥ
sarasvatyāḥ surodhasoḥ
ṛṣīṇām upaśāntānāṁ
paśyann āśrama-sampadaḥ

āmantrya—taking permission to go; *tam*—from him (Kardama); *muni-varam*—from the best of sages; *anujñātaḥ*—being permitted to leave; *saha-anugaḥ*—along with his retinue; *pratasthe*—started for; *ratham āruhya*—mounting his chariot; *sa-bhāryaḥ*—along with his wife; *sva-puram*—his own capital; *nṛpaḥ*—the Emperor; *ubhayoḥ*—on both; *ṛṣi-kulyāyāḥ*—agreeable to the sages; *sarasvatyāḥ*—of the River Sarasvatī; *su-rodhasoḥ*—the charming banks; *ṛṣīṇām*—of the great sages; *upaśāntānām*—tranquil; *paśyan*—seeing; *āśrama-sampadaḥ*—the prosperity of the beautiful hermitages.

TRANSLATION

After asking and obtaining the great sage's permission to leave, the monarch mounted his chariot with his wife and started for his capital, followed by his retinue. Along the way he saw the prosperity of the tranquil seers' beautiful hermitages on both the charming banks of the Sarasvatī, the river so agreeable to saintly persons.

PURPORT

As cities are constructed in the modern age with great engineering and architectural craftsmanship, so in days gone by there were neighborhoods called *ṛṣi-kulas*, where great saintly persons resided. In India there are still many magnificent places for spiritual understanding; there are many *ṛṣis* and saintly persons living in nice cottages on the banks of the Ganges and Yamunā for purposes of spiritual cultivation. While passing through the *ṛṣi-kulas* the King and his party were very much satisfied with the beauty of the cottages and hermitages. It is stated here, *paśyann āśrama-sampadaḥ*. The great sages had no skyscrapers, but the hermitages were so beautiful that the King was very much pleased at the sight.

TEXT 28

तमायान्तमभिप्रेत्य ब्रह्मावर्तात्प्रजाः पतिम् ।
गीतसंस्तुतिवादित्रैः प्रत्युदीयुः प्रहर्षिताः ॥२८॥

tam āyāntam abhipretya
brahmāvartāt prajāḥ patim
gīta-saṁstuti-vāditraiḥ
pratyudīyuḥ praharṣitāḥ

tam—him; *āyāntam*—who was arriving; *abhipretya*—knowing of; *brahmāvartāt*—from Brahmāvarta; *prajāḥ*—his subjects; *patim*—their lord; *gīta-saṁstuti-vāditraiḥ*—with songs, praise and instrumental music; *pratyudīyuḥ*—came forward to greet; *praharṣitāḥ*—overjoyed.

TRANSLATION

Overjoyed to know of his arrival, his subjects came forth from Brahmāvarta to greet their returning lord with songs, prayers and musical instruments.

PURPORT

It is the custom of the citizens of a kingdom's capital to receive the king when he returns from a tour. There is a similar description when Kṛṣṇa returned to Dvārakā after the Battle of Kurukṣetra. At that time He was received by all classes of citizens at the gate of the city. Formerly, capital cities were surrounded by walls, and there were different gates for regular entrance. Even in Delhi today there are old gates, and some other old cities have such gates where citizens would gather to receive the king. Here also the citizens of Barhiṣmatī, the capital of Brahmāvarta, the kingdom of Svāyambhuva, came nicely dressed to receive the Emperor with decorations and musical instruments.

TEXTS 29-30

बर्हिष्मती नाम पुरी सर्वसम्पत्समन्विता ।
न्यपतन् यत्र रोमाणि यज्ञस्याङ्गं विधुन्वतः ॥२९॥
कुशाः काशास्त एवासन् शश्वद्धरितवर्चसः ।
ऋषयो यैः पराभाव्य यज्ञघ्नान् यज्ञमीजिरे ॥३०॥

barhiṣmatī nāma purī
sarva-sampat-samanvitā
nyapatan yatra romāṇi
yajñasyāṅgaṁ vidhunvataḥ

kuśāḥ kāśās ta evāsan
śaśvad-dharita-varcasaḥ
ṛṣayo yaiḥ parābhāvya
yajña-ghnān yajñam ījire

barhiṣmatī—Barhiṣmatī; *nāma*—named; *purī*—city; *sarva-sampat*—all kinds of wealth; *samanvitā*—full of; *nyapatan*—fell down; *yatra*—where; *romāṇi*—the hairs; *yajñasya*—of Lord Boar; *aṅgam*—His body; *vidhunvataḥ*—shaking; *kuśāḥ*—*kuśa* grass; *kāśāḥ*—*kāśa* grass; *te*—they; *eva*—certainly; *āsan*—became; *śaśvat-harita*—of evergreen; *varcasaḥ*—having the color; *ṛṣayaḥ*—the sages; *yaiḥ*—by which; *parābhāvya*—defeating; *yajña-ghnān*—the disturbers of the sacrificial performances; *yajñam*—Lord Viṣṇu; *ījire*—they worshiped.

TRANSLATION

The city of Barhiṣmatī, rich in all kinds of wealth, was so called because Lord Viṣṇu's hair dropped there from His body when He manifested Himself as Lord Boar. As He shook His body, this very hair fell and turned into blades of evergreen kuśa grass and kāśa [another kind of grass used for mats], by means of which the sages worshiped Lord Viṣṇu after defeating the demons who had interfered with the performance of their sacrifices.

PURPORT

Any place directly connected with the Supreme Lord is called *pīṭha-sthāna.* Barhiṣmatī, the capital of Svāyambhuva Manu, was exalted not because the city was very rich in wealth and opulence, but because the hairs of Lord Varāha fell at this very spot. These hairs of the Lord later grew as green grass, and the sages used to worship the Lord with that grass after the time when the Lord killed the demon Hiraṇyākṣa. *Yajña* means Viṣṇu, the Supreme Personality of Godhead. In *Bhagavad-gītā, karma* is described as *yajñārtha. Yajñārtha-karma* means "work done only for the satisfaction of Viṣṇu." If something is done for sense gratification or any other purpose, it will be binding upon the worker. If one wants to be freed from the reaction of his work, he must perform everything for the satisfaction of Viṣṇu, or Yajña. In the capital of Svāyambhuva Manu, Barhiṣmatī, these particular functions were being performed by the great sages and saintly persons.

TEXT 31

कुशकाशमयं बर्हिरास्तीर्य भगवान्मनुः ।
अयजद्यज्ञपुरुषं लब्धा स्थानं यतो भुवम् ॥३१॥

kuśa-kāśamayaṁ barhir
āstīrya bhagavān manuḥ
ayajad yajña-puruṣaṁ
labdhā sthānaṁ yato bhuvam

kuśa—of *kuśa* grass; *kāśa*—and of *kāśa* grass; *mayam*—made; *barhiḥ*—a seat; *āstīrya*—having spread; *bhagavān*—the greatly fortunate; *manuḥ*—Svāyambhuva Manu; *ayajat*—worshiped; *yajña-puruṣam*—Lord Viṣṇu; *labdhā*—had achieved; *sthānam*—the abode; *yataḥ*—from whom; *bhuvam*—the earth.

TRANSLATION

Manu spread a seat of kuśas and kāśas and worshiped the Lord, the Personality of Godhead, by whose grace he had obtained the rule of the terrestrial globe.

PURPORT

Manu is the father of mankind, and therefore from *Manu* comes the word *man,* or, in Sanskrit, *manuṣya.* Those who are in a better position in the world, having sufficient wealth, should especially take lessons from Manu, who acknowledged his kingdom and opulence to be gifts from the Supreme Personality of Godhead and thus always engaged in devotional service. Similarly, the descendants of Manu, or human beings, especially those who are situated in a well-to-do condition, must consider that whatever riches they have are gifts from the Supreme Personality of Godhead. Those riches should be utilized for the service of the Lord in sacrifices performed to please Him. That is the way of utilizing wealth and opulence. No one can achieve wealth, opulence, good birth, a beautiful body or nice education without the mercy of the Supreme Lord. Therefore, those who are in possession of such valuable facilities must acknowledge their gratefulness to the Lord by worshiping Him and offering what they have received from Him. When such acknowledgement is given, either by a family, nation or society, their abode becomes almost like Vaikuṇṭha, and it becomes free from the operation of the threefold miseries of this material world. In the modern age the mission of Kṛṣṇa consciousness is for everyone to acknowledge the supremacy of Lord Kṛṣṇa; whatever one has in his possession must be considered a gift by the grace of the

Lord. Everyone, therefore, should engage in devotional service through Kṛṣṇa consciousness. If one wants to be happy and peaceful in his position, either as a householder or citizen or member of human society, one must promote devotional service for the pleasure of the Lord.

TEXT 32

बर्हिष्मतीं नाम विभुर्यां निर्विश्य समावसत् ।
तस्यां प्रविष्टो भवनं तापत्रयविनाशनम् ॥३२॥

barhiṣmatīṁ nāma vibhur
yāṁ nirviśya samāvasat
tasyāṁ praviṣṭo bhavanaṁ
tāpa-traya-vināśanam

barhiṣmatīm—the city Barhiṣmatī; *nāma*—named; *vibhuḥ*—the very powerful Svāyambhuva Manu; *yām*—which; *nirviśya*—having entered; *samāvasat*—he lived in previously; *tasyām*—in that city; *praviṣṭaḥ*—entered; *bhavanam*—the palace; *tāpa-traya*—the threefold miseries; *vināśanam*—destroying.

TRANSLATION

Having entered the city of Barhiṣmatī, in which he had previously lived, Manu entered his palace, which was filled with an atmosphere that eradicated the three miseries of material existence.

PURPORT

The material world, or material existential life, is filled with threefold miseries: miseries pertaining to the body and mind, miseries pertaining to natural disturbances and miseries inflicted by other living entities. Human society is meant to create a spiritual atmosphere by spreading the spirit of Kṛṣṇa consciousness. The miseries of material existence cannot affect the status of Kṛṣṇa consciousness. It is not that the miseries of the material world completely vanish when one takes to Kṛṣṇa consciousness, but for one who is Kṛṣṇa conscious the miseries of material existence have no effect. We cannot stop the miseries of the material atmosphere, but Kṛṣṇa consciousness is the antiseptic method to protect us from being affected by the miseries of material existence. For a Kṛṣṇa conscious person, both living in heaven and living in hell are equal. How Svāyambhuva Manu created an atmosphere wherein he was not affected by material miseries is explained in the following verses.

TEXT 33

सभार्यः सप्रजः कामान् बुभुजेऽन्याविरोधतः ।
सङ्गीयमानसत्कीर्तिः सस्त्रीभिः सुरगायकैः ।
प्रत्यूषेष्वनुबद्धेन हृदा शृण्वन् हरेः कथाः ॥३३॥

sabhāryaḥ saprajaḥ kāmān
bubhuje 'nyāvirodhataḥ
saṅgīyamāna-sat-kīrtiḥ
sastrībhiḥ sura-gāyakaiḥ
praty-ūṣeṣv anubaddhena
hṛdā śṛṇvan hareḥ kathāḥ

sa-bhāryaḥ—along with his wife; *sa-prajaḥ*—along with his subjects; *kāmān*—the necessities of life; *bubhuje*—he enjoyed; *anya*—from others; *avirodhataḥ*—without disturbance; *saṅgīyamāna*—being praised; *sat-kīrtiḥ*—reputation for pious activities; *sa-strībhiḥ*—along with their wives; *sura-gāyakaiḥ*—by celestial musicians; *prati-ūṣeṣu*—at every dawn; *anubaddhena*—being attached; *hṛdā*—with the heart; *śṛṇvan*—listening to; *hareḥ*—of Lord Hari; *kathāḥ*—the topics.

TRANSLATION

Emperor Svāyambhuva Manu enjoyed life with his wife and subjects and fulfilled his desires without being disturbed by unwanted principles contrary to the process of religion. Celestial musicians and their wives sang in chorus about the pure reputation of the Emperor, and early in the morning, every day, he used to listen to the pastimes of the Supreme Personality of Godhead with a loving heart.

PURPORT

Human society is actually meant for realization of perfection in Kṛṣṇa consciousness. There is no restriction against living with a wife and children, but life should be so conducted that one may not go against the principles of religion, economic development, regulated sense enjoyment and, ultimately, liberation from material existence. The Vedic principles are designed in such a way that the conditioned souls who have come to this material existence may be guided in fulfilling their material desires and at the same time be liberated and go back to Godhead, back home.

It is understood that Emperor Svāyambhuva Manu enjoyed his household life by following these principles. It is stated here that early in the morning there were musicians who used to sing with musical instruments about the glories of the Lord, and the Emperor, with his family, personally used to hear about the pastimes of the Supreme Person. This custom is still prevalent in India in some of the royal families and temples. Professional musicians sing with *śahnāīs,* and the sleeping members of the house gradually get up from their beds in a pleasing atmosphere. During bedtime also the singers sing songs in relationship with the pastimes of the Lord, with *śahnāī* accompaniment, and the householders gradually fall asleep remembering the glories of the Lord. In every house, in addition to the singing program, there is an arrangement for *Bhāgavatam* lectures in the evening; family members sit down, hold Hare Kṛṣṇa *kīrtana,* hear narrations from *Śrīmad-Bhāgavatam* and *Bhagavad-gītā* and enjoy music before going to bed. The atmosphere created by this *saṅkīrtana* movement lives in their hearts, and while sleeping they also dream of the singing and glorification of the Lord. In such a way, perfection of Kṛṣṇa consciousness can be attained. This practice is very old, as learned from this verse of *Śrīmad-Bhāgavatam;* millions of years ago, Svāyambhuva Manu used to avail himself of this opportunity to live householder life in the peace and prosperity of a Kṛṣṇa consciousness atmosphere.

As far as temples are concerned, in each and every royal palace or rich man's house, inevitably there is a nice temple, and the members of the household rise early in the morning and go to the temple to see the *maṅgalārātrika* ceremony. The *maṅgalārātrika* ceremony is the first worship of the morning. In the *ārātrika* ceremony a light is offered in circles before the Deities, as are a conchshell and flowers and a fan. The Lord is supposed to rise early in the morning and take some light refreshment and give audience to the devotees. The devotees then go back to the house or sing the glories of the Lord in the temple. The early morning ceremony still takes place in Indian temples and palaces. Temples are meant for the assembly of the general public. Temples within palaces are especially for the royal families, but in many of these palace temples the public is also allowed to visit. The temple of the King of Jaipur is situated within the palace, but the public is allowed to assemble; if one goes there, he will see that the temple is always crowded with at least five hundred devotees. After the *maṅgalārātrika* ceremony they sit down together and sing the glories of the Lord with musical instruments and thus enjoy life. Temple worship by the royal family is also mentioned in *Bhagavad-gītā,* where it is stated that those who fail to achieve success in the *bhakti-yoga* principles within one life are given a chance to take birth in the next life in a family of rich men or in a royal family or family of learned *brāhmaṇas* or devotees. If one gets the opportunity to take birth in these families, he can achieve the facilities of a Kṛṣṇa conscious atmosphere without difficulty. A child born in that Kṛṣṇa atmosphere is sure to develop Kṛṣṇa consciousness. The perfection which he failed to attain in his last life is again offered in this life, and he can make himself perfect without fail.

TEXT 34

निष्णातं योगमायासु मुनिं स्वायम्भुवं मनुम् ।
यदाभ्रंशयितुं भोगा न शेकुर्भगवत्परम् ॥३४॥

niṣṇātaṁ yogamāyāsu
muniṁ svāyambhuvaṁ manum
yad ābhraṁśayituṁ bhogā
na śekur bhagavat-param

niṣṇātam—absorbed; *yoga-māyāsu*—in temporary enjoyment; *munim*—who was equal to a saint; *svāyambhuvam*—Svāyambhuva; *manum*—Manu; *yat*—from which; *ābhraṁśayitum*—to cause to deviate; *bhogāḥ*—material enjoyments; *na*—not; *śekuḥ*—were able; *bhagavat-param*—who was a great devotee of the Supreme Personality of Godhead.

TRANSLATION

Thus Svāyambhuva Manu was a saintly king. Although absorbed in material happiness, he was not dragged to the lowest grade of life, for he always enjoyed his material happiness in a Kṛṣṇa conscious atmosphere.

PURPORT

The kingly happiness of material enjoyment generally drags one to the lowest grade of life, namely degradation to animal life, because of unrestricted sense enjoyment. But Svāyambhuva Manu was considered as good as a saintly sage because the atmosphere created in his kingdom and home was completely Kṛṣṇa conscious. The case is similar with the conditioned souls in general; they have come into this material life for sense gratification, but if they are able to create a Kṛṣṇa conscious atmosphere, as depicted here or as prescribed in revealed scriptures, by temple worship and household Deity worship, then in spite of their material enjoyment they can make advancement in pure Kṛṣṇa consciousness without a doubt. At the present moment, modern civilization is too much attached to the material way of life, or sense gratification. Therefore, the Kṛṣṇa consciousness movement can give the people in general the best opportunity to utilize their human life in the midst of material enjoyment. Kṛṣṇa consciousness does not stop them in their propensity for material enjoyment, but simply regulates their habits in the life of sense enjoyment. In spite of their enjoying the material advantages, they can be liberated in this very life by practicing Kṛṣṇa consciousness by the simple method of chanting the holy names of the Lord—Hare Kṛṣṇa, Hare Kṛṣṇa, Kṛṣṇa Kṛṣṇa, Hare Hare/ Hare Rāma, Hare Rāma, Rāma Rāma, Hare Hare.

TEXT 35

अयातयामास्तस्यासन् यामाः स्वान्तरयापनाः ।
शृण्वतो ध्यायतो विष्णोःकुर्वतो ब्रुवतःकथाः ॥३५॥

ayāta-yāmās tasyāsan
yāmāḥ svāntara-yāpanāḥ
śṛṇvato dhyāyato viṣṇoḥ
kurvato bruvataḥ kathāḥ

ayāta-yāmāḥ—time never lost; *tasya*—of Manu; *āsan*—were; *yāmāḥ*—the hours; *sva-antara*—his duration of life; *yāpanāḥ*—bringing to an end; *śṛṇvataḥ*—hearing; *dhyāyataḥ*—contemplating; *viṣṇoḥ*—of Lord Viṣṇu; *kurvataḥ*—acting; *bruvataḥ*—speaking; *kathāḥ*—the topics.

TRANSLATION

Consequently, although his duration of life gradually came to an end, his long life, consisting of a Manvantara era, was not spent in vain, since he ever engaged in hearing, contemplating, writing down and chanting the pastimes of the Lord.

PURPORT

As freshly prepared food is very tasteful but if kept for three or four hours becomes stale and tasteless, so the existence of material enjoyment can endure as long as life is fresh, but at the fag end of life everything becomes tasteless, and everything appears to be vain and painful. The life of Emperor Svāyambhuva Manu, however, was not tasteless; as he grew older, his life remained as fresh as in the beginning because of his continued Kṛṣṇa consciousness. The life of a man in Kṛṣṇa consciousness is always fresh. It is said that the sun rises in the morning and sets in the evening and its business is to reduce the duration of everyone's life. But the sunrise and sunset cannot diminish the life of one who engages in Kṛṣṇa consciousness. Svāyambhuva Manu's life did not become stale after some time, for he engaged himself always in chanting about and meditating upon Lord Viṣṇu. He was the greatest *yogī* because he never wasted his time. It is especially mentioned here, *viṣṇoḥ kurvato bruvataḥ kathāḥ*. When he talked, he talked only of Kṛṣṇa and Viṣṇu, the Personality of Godhead; when he heard something, it was about Kṛṣṇa; when he meditated, it was upon Kṛṣṇa and His activities.

It is stated that his life was very long, seventy-one *yugas*. One *yuga* is completed in 4,320,000 years, seventy-one of such *yugas* is the duration of the life of a Manu, and fourteen such Manus come and go in one day of Brahma. For the entire duration of his life—4,320,000 × 71 years—Manu engaged in Krsna consciousness by chanting, hearing, talking about and meditating upon Kṛṣṇa. Therefore, his life was not wasted, nor did it become stale.

TEXT 36

स एवं स्वान्तरं निन्ये युगानामेकसप्ततिम् ।
वासुदेवप्रसङ्गेन परिभूतगतित्रयः ॥३६॥

sa evaṁ svāntaraṁ ninye
yugānām eka-saptatim
vāsudeva-prasaṅgena
paribhūta-gati-trayaḥ

saḥ—he (Svāyambhuva Manu); *evam*—thus; *sva-antaram*—his own period; *ninye*—passed; *yugānām*—of the cycles of four ages; *eka-saptatim*—seventy-one; *vāsudeva*—with Vāsudeva; *prasaṅgena*—by topics connected; *paribhūta*—transcended; *gati-trayaḥ*—the three destinations.

TRANSLATION

He passed his time, which lasted seventy-one cycles of the four ages [71 x 4,320,000 years], always thinking of Vāsudeva and always engaged in matters regarding Vāsudeva. Thus he transcended the three destinations.

PURPORT

The three destinations are meant for persons who are under the control of the three modes of material nature. These destinations are sometimes described as the awakened, dreaming and unconscious stages. In *Bhagavad-gītā* the three destinations are described as the destinations of persons in the modes of goodness, passion and ignorance. It is stated in the *Gītā* that those who are in the mode of goodness are promoted to better living conditions in higher planets, and those who are in the mode of passion remain within this material world on the earth or on heavenly planets, but those who are in the mode of ignorance are degraded to an animal life on planets where life is lower than human. But one who is Kṛṣṇa conscious is above these three modes of material nature. It is stated in *Bhagavad-gītā* that anyone who engages in devotional service to the Lord automatically becomes transcendental to the three destinations of material nature and is situated in the *brahma-bhūta,* or self-realized, stage. Although Svāyambhuva Manu, the ruler of this material world, appeared to be absorbed in material happiness, he was neither in the mode of goodness nor in the modes of passion or ignorance, but in the transcendental stage.

Therefore, one who fully engages in devotional service is always liberated. Bilvamaṅgala Ṭhākura, a great devotee of the Lord, stated: "If I have unflinching devotion to the lotus feet of Kṛṣṇa, then Mother Liberation is always engaged in my service. The complete perfection of material enjoyment, religion and economic development is at my command." People are after *dharma, artha, kāma* and *mokṣa.* Generally they perform religious activities to achieve some material gain, and they engage in material activity for sense gratification. After being frustrated in material sense gratification, one wants to be liberated and become one with the Absolute Truth. These four principles form the transcendental path for the less intelligent. Those who are actually intelligent engage in Kṛṣṇa consciousness, not caring for these four principles of the transcendental method. They at once elevate themselves to the transcendental platform which is above liberation. Liberation is not a very great achievement for a devotee, to say nothing of the results of ritualistic performances in religion, economic development or the materialistic life of sense gratification. Devotees do not care for these. They are situated always on the transcendental platform of the *brahma-bhūta* stage of self-realization.

TEXT 37

शारीरा मानसा दिव्या वैयासे ये च मानुषाः ।
भौतिकाश्च कथं क्लेशा बाधन्ते हरिसंश्रयम् ॥३७॥

śārīrā mānasā divyā
vaiyāse ye ca mānuṣāḥ
bhautikāś ca kathaṁ kleśā
bādhante hari-saṁśrayam

śārīrāḥ—pertaining to the body; *mānasāḥ*—pertaining to the mind; *divyāḥ*—pertaining to supernatural powers (demigods); *vaiyāse*—O Vidura; *ye*—those; *ca*—and; *mānuṣāḥ*—

pertaining to other men; *bhautikāḥ*—pertaining to other living beings; *ca*—and; *katham*—how; *kleśāḥ*—miseries; *bādhante*—can trouble; *hari-saṁśrayam*—one who has taken shelter of Lord Kṛṣṇa.

TRANSLATION

Therefore, O Vidura, how can persons completely under the shelter of Lord Kṛṣṇa in devotional service be put into miseries pertaining to the body, the mind, nature, and other men and living creatures?

PURPORT

Every living entity within this material world is always afflicted by some kind of miseries, pertaining either to the body, the mind or natural disturbances. Distresses due to cold in winter and severe heat in summer always inflict miseries on the living entities in this material world, but one who has completely taken shelter of the lotus feet of the Lord in Kṛṣṇa consciousness is in the transcendental stage; he is not disturbed by any miseries, either due to the body, the mind, or natural disturbances of summer and winter. He is transcendental to all these miseries.

TEXT 38

यः पृष्टो मुनिभिः प्राह धर्मान्नानाविधाञ्छुभान् ।
नृणां वर्णाश्रमाणां च सर्वभूतहितः सदा ॥३८॥

yaḥ pṛṣṭo munibhiḥ prāha
dharmān nānā-vidhāñ chubhān
nṛṇāṁ varṇāśramāṇāṁ ca
sarva-bhūta-hitaḥ sadā

yaḥ—who; *pṛṣṭaḥ*—being questioned; *munibhiḥ*—by the sages; *prāha*—spoke; *dharmān*—the duties; *nānā-vidhān*—many varieties; *śubhān*—auspicious; *nṛṇām*—of human society; *varṇa-āśramāṇām*—of the *varṇas* and *āśramas; ca*—and; *sarva-bhūta*—for all living beings; *hitaḥ*—who does welfare; *sadā*—always.

TRANSLATION

In reply to questions asked by certain sages, he [Svāyambhuva Manu], out of compassion for all living entities, taught the diverse sacred duties of men in general and the different varṇas and āśramas.

TEXT 39

एतत्त आदिराजस्य मनोश्चरितमद्भुतम् ।
वर्णितं वर्णनीयस्य तदपत्योदयं शृणु ॥३९॥

etat ta ādi-rājasya
manoś caritam adbhutam
varṇitaṁ varṇanīyasya
tad-apatyodayaṁ śṛṇu

etat—this; *te*—unto you; *ādi-rājasya*—of the first emperor; *manoḥ*—of Svāyambhuva Manu; *caritam*—the character; *adbhutam*—wonderful; *varṇitam*—described; *varṇanīyasya*—whose reputation is worthy of description; *tat-apatya*—of his daughter; *udayam*—to the flourishing; *śṛṇu*—please listen.

TRANSLATION

I have spoken to you of the wonderful character of Svāyambhuva Manu, the original king, whose reputation is worthy of description. Please hear as I speak of the flourishing of his daughter Devahūti.

Thus end the Bhaktivedanta purports of the Third Canto, Twenty-second Chapter, of the Śrīmad-Bhāgavatam, *entitled "The Marriage of Kardama Muni and Devahūti."*

CHAPTER TWENTY-THREE

Devahūti's Lamentation

TEXT 1

मैत्रेय उवाच
पितृभ्यां प्रस्थिते साध्वी पतिमिङ्गितकोविदा ।
नित्यं पर्यचरत्प्रीत्या भवानीव भवं प्रभुम् ॥ १ ॥

maitreya uvāca
pitṛbhyāṁ prasthite sādhvī
patim iṅgita-kovidā
nityaṁ paryacarat prītyā
bhavānīva bhavaṁ prabhum

maitreyaḥ uvāca—Maitreya said; *pitṛbhyām*—by the parents; *prasthite*—at the departure; *sādhvī*—the chaste woman; *patim*—her husband; *iṅgita-kovidā*—understanding the desires; *nityam*—constantly; *paryacarat*—she served; *prītyā*—with great love; *bhavānī*—the goddess Pārvatī; *iva*—like; *bhavam*—Lord Śiva; *prabhum*—her lord.

TRANSLATION

Maitreya continued: After the departure of her parents, the chaste woman Devahūti, who could understand the desires of her husband, served him constantly with great love, as Bhavānī, the wife of Lord Śiva, serves her husband.

PURPORT

The specific example of Bhavānī is very significant. *Bhavānī* means the wife of Bhava, or Lord Śiva. Bhavānī, or Pārvatī, the daughter of the King of the Himalayas, selected Lord Śiva, who appears to be just like a beggar, as her husband. In spite of her being a princess, she undertook all kinds of tribulations to associate with Lord Śiva, who did not even have a house, but was sitting underneath the trees and passing his time in meditation. Although Bhavānī was the daughter of a very great king, she used to serve Lord Śiva just like a poor woman. Similarly, Devahūti was the daughter of an emperor, Svāyambhuva Manu, yet she preferred to accept Kardama Muni as her husband. She served him with great love and affection, and she knew how to please him. Therefore, she is designated here as *sādhvī,* which means "a chaste, faithful wife." Her rare example is the ideal of Vedic civilization. Every woman is expected to be as good and chaste as Devahūti or Bhavānī. Today in Hindu society, unmarried girls are still taught to worship Lord Śiva with the idea that they may get husbands like him. Lord Śiva is the ideal husband, not in the sense of riches or sense gratification, but because he is the greatest of all devotees. *Vaiṣṇavānāṁ yathā śambhuḥ:* Śambhu, or Lord Śiva, is the ideal Vaiṣṇava. He constantly meditates upon Lord Rāma and chants Hare Rāma, Hare Rāma, Rāma Rāma, Hare Hare. Lord Śiva has a Vaiṣṇava *sampradāya,* which is called the Viṣṇusvāmī-sampradāya. Unmarried girls worship Lord Śiva so that they can expect a husband who is as good a Vaiṣṇava as he. The girls are not taught to select a husband who is very rich or very opulent for material sense gratification; rather, if a girl is fortunate enough to get a husband as good as Lord Śiva in devotional service, then her life becomes perfect. The wife is dependent on the husband, and if the husband is a Vaiṣṇava, then naturally she shares the devotional service of the husband because she renders him service. This reciprocation of service and love between husband and wife is the ideal of a householder's life.

TEXT 2

विश्रम्भेणात्मशौचेन गौरवेण दमेन च ।
शुश्रूषया सौहृदेन वाचा मधुरया च भोः ॥ २ ॥

viśrambheṇātma-śaucena
gauraveṇa damena ca
śuśrūṣayā sauhṛdena
vācā madhurayā ca bhoḥ

viśrambheṇa—with intimacy; *ātma-śaucena*—with purity of mind and body; *gauraveṇa*—with great respect; *damena*—with control of the senses; *ca*—and; *śuśrūṣayā*—with service; *sauhṛdena*—with love; *vācā*—with words; *madhurayā*—sweet; *ca*—and; *bhoḥ*—O Vidura.

TRANSLATION

O Vidura, Devahūti served her husband with intimacy and great respect, with control of the senses, with love and with sweet words.

PURPORT

Here two words are very significant. Devahūti served her husband in two ways, *viśrambheṇa* and *gauraveṇa.* These are two important processes in serving the husband or the Supreme Personality of Godhead. *Viśrambheṇa* means "with intimacy," and *gauraveṇa* means "with great reverence." The husband is a very intimate friend; therefore, the wife must render service just like an intimate friend, and at the same time she must understand that the husband is superior in position, and thus she must offer him all respect. A man's psychology and woman's psychology are different. As constituted by bodily frame, a man always wants to be superior to his wife, and a woman, as bodily constituted, is naturally inferior to her husband. Thus the natural instinct is that the husband wants to post himself as superior to the wife, and this must be observed. Even if there is some wrong on the part of the husband, the wife must tolerate it, and thus there will be no misunderstanding between husband and wife. *Viśrambheṇa* means "with intimacy," but it must not be familiarity that breeds contempt. According to the Vedic civilization, a wife cannot call her husband by name. In the present civilization the wife calls her husband by name, but in Hindu civilization she does not. Thus the inferiority and superiority complexes are recognized. *Damena ca:* a wife has to learn to control herself even if there is a misunderstanding. *Sauhṛdena vācā madhurayā* means always desiring good for the husband and speaking to him with sweet words. A person becomes agitated by so many material contacts in the outside world; therefore, in his home life he must be treated by his wife with sweet words.

TEXT 3

विसृज्य कामं दम्भं च द्वेषं लोभमघं मदम् ।
अप्रमत्तोद्यता नित्यं तेजीयांसमतोषयत् ॥ ३ ॥

visṛjya kāmaṁ dambhaṁ ca
dveṣaṁ lobham aghaṁ madam
apramattodyatā nityaṁ
tejīyāṁsam atoṣayat

visṛjya—giving up; *kāmam*—lust; *dambham*—pride; *ca*—and; *dveṣam*—envy; *lobham*—greed; *agham*—sinful activities; *madam*—vanity; *apramattā*—sane; *udyatā*—laboring diligently; *nityam*—always; *tejīyāṁsam*—her very powerful husband; *atoṣayat*—she pleased.

TRANSLATION

Working sanely and diligently, she pleased her very powerful husband, giving up all lust, pride, envy, greed, sinful activities and vanity.

PURPORT

Here are some of the qualities of a great husband's great wife. Kardama Muni is great by spiritual qualification. Such a husband is called *tejīyāṁsam,* most powerful. Although a wife may be equal to her husband in advancement in spiritual consciousness, she should not be vainly proud. Sometimes it happens that the wife comes from a very rich family, as did Devahūti, the daughter of Emperor Svāyambhuva Manu. She could have been very proud of her parentage, but that is forbidden. The wife should not be proud of her parental position. She must always be submissive to the husband and must give up all vanity. As soon as the wife becomes proud of her parentage, her pride creates great misunderstanding between the husband and wife, and their nuptial life is ruined. Devahūti was very careful about that, and therefore it is said here that she gave up pride completely. Devahūti was not unfaithful. The most sinful activity for a wife is to accept another husband or another lover. Cāṇakya Paṇḍita has described four kinds of enemies at home. If the father is in debt he is considered to be an enemy; if the mother has selected another husband in the presence of her grown-up children, she is considered to be an enemy; if a wife does not live well with her husband but deals very roughly, then she is an enemy; and if a son is a fool, he is also an enemy. In family life, father, mother, wife and children are assets, but if the wife or mother accepts another husband in the presence of her husband or son, then, according to Vedic civilization, she is considered an enemy. A chaste and faithful woman must not practice adultery—that is a greatly sinful act.

TEXTS 4-5

स वै देवर्षिवर्यस्तां मानवीं समनुव्रताम् ।
दैवाद्गरीयसः पत्युराशासानां महाशिषः ॥ ४ ॥
कालेन भूयसा क्षामां कर्शितां व्रतचर्यया ।
प्रेमगद्गदया वाचा पीडितः कृपयाब्रवीत् ॥ ५ ॥

sa vai devarṣi-varyas tāṁ
mānavīṁ samanuvratām
daivād garīyasaḥ patyur
āśāsānāṁ mahāśiṣaḥ

kālena bhūyasā kṣāmāṁ
karśitāṁ vrata-caryayā
prema-gadgadayā vācā
pīḍitaḥ kṛpayābravīt

saḥ—he (Kardama); *vai*—certainly; *deva-ṛṣi*—of the celestial sages; *varyaḥ*—the foremost; *tām*—her; *mānavīm*—the daughter of Manu; *samanuvratām*—fully devoted; *daivāt*—than providence; *garīyasaḥ*—who was greater; *patyuḥ*—from her husband; *āśāsānām*—expecting; *mahā-āśiṣaḥ*—great blessings; *kālena bhūyasā*—for a long time; *kṣāmām*—weak; *karśitām*—emaciated; *vrata-caryayā*—by religious observances; *prema*—with love; *gadgadayā*—stammering; *vācā*—with a voice; *pīḍitaḥ*—overcome; *kṛpayā*—with compassion; *abravīt*—he said.

TRANSLATION

The daughter of Manu, who was fully devoted to her husband, looked upon him as greater even than providence. Thus she expected great blessings from him. Having served him for a long time, she grew weak and emaciated due to her religious observances. Seeing her condition, Kardama, the foremost of celestial sages, was overcome with compassion and spoke to her in a voice choked with great love.

PURPORT

The wife is expected to be of the same category as the husband. She must be prepared to follow the principles of the husband, and then there will be happy life. If the husband is a devotee and the wife is materialistic, there cannot be any peace in the home. The wife must see the tendencies of the husband and must be prepared to follow him. From *Mahābhārata* we learn that when Gāndhārī understood that her would-be husband, Dhṛtarāṣṭra, was blind, she immediately began to practice blindness herself. Thus she covered her eyes and played the part of a blind woman. She decided that since her husband was blind, she must also act like a blind woman, otherwise she would be proud of her eyes, and her husband would be seen as inferior. The word *samanuvrata* indicates that it is the duty of a wife to adopt the special circumstances in which the husband is situated. Of course, if the husband is as great as Kardama Muni, then a very good result accrues from following him. But even if the husband is not a great devotee like Kardama Muni, it is the wife's duty to adapt herself according to his mentality. That makes married life very happy. It is also mentioned herein that by following the strict vows of a chaste woman, Princess Devahūti became very skinny, and therefore her husband became compassionate. He knew that she was the daughter of a great king and yet was serving him just like an ordinary woman. She was reduced in health by such activities, and he became compassionate and addressed her as follows.

TEXT 6

कर्दम उवाच
तुष्टोऽहमद्य तव मानवि मानदायाः
शुश्रूषया परमया परया च भक्त्या ।
यो देहिनामयमतीव सुहृत्स देहो
नावेक्षितः समुचितः क्षपितुं मदर्थे ॥ ६ ॥

kardama uvāca
tuṣṭo 'ham adya tava mānavi mānadāyāḥ
śuśrūṣayā paramayā parayā ca bhaktyā
yo dehinām ayam atīva suhṛt sa deho
nāvekṣitaḥ samucitaḥ kṣapituṁ mad-arthe

kardamaḥ uvāca—the great sage Kardama said; *tuṣṭaḥ*—pleased; *aham*—I am; *adya*—today; *tava*—with you; *mānavi*—O daughter of Manu; *māna-dāyāḥ*—who are respectful; *śuśrūṣayā*—by the service; *paramayā*—most excellent; *parayā*—highest; *ca*—and; *bhaktyā*—by the devotion; *yaḥ*—that which; *dehinām*—to the embodied; *ayam*—this; *atīva*—extremely; *suhṛt*—dear; *saḥ*—that; *dehaḥ*—body; *na*—not; *avekṣitaḥ*—taken care of; *samucitaḥ*—properly; *kṣapitum*—to expend; *mat-arthe*—on my account.

TRANSLATION

Kardama Muni said: O respectful daughter of Svāyambhuva Manu, today I am very much pleased with you for your great devotion and most excellent loving service. Since the body is so dear to embodied beings, I am astonished that you have neglected your own body to use it on my behalf.

PURPORT

It is indicated here that one's body is very dear, yet Devahūti was so faithful to her husband that not only did she serve him with great devotion, service and respect, but she did not even care for her own health. That is called selfless service. It appears that Devahūti had no sense pleasure, even with her husband, otherwise she would not have deteriorated in health. Acting to facilitate Kardama Muni's engagement in spiritual elevation, she continually assisted him, not caring for bodily comfort. It is the duty of a faithful and chaste wife to help her husband in every respect, especially when the husband is engaged in Kṛṣṇa consciousness. In this case, the husband also amply rewarded the wife. This is not to be expected by a woman who is the wife of an ordinary person.

TEXT 7

ये मे स्वधर्मनिरतस्य तपःसमाधि-
विद्यात्मयोगविजिता भगवत्प्रसादाः ।
तानेव ते मदनुसेवनयावरुद्धान्
दृष्टिं प्रपश्य वितराम्यभयानशोकान् ॥ ७ ॥

ye me sva-dharma-niratasya tapaḥ-samādhi-
vidyātma-yoga-vijitā bhagavat-prasādāḥ
tān eva te mad-anusevanayāvaruddhān
dṛṣṭiṁ prapaśya vitarāmy abhayān aśokān

ye—those which; *me*—by me; *sva-dharma*—own religious life; *niratasya*—fully occupied with; *tapaḥ*—in austerity; *samādhi*—in meditation; *vidyā*—in Kṛṣṇa consciousness; *ātma-yoga*—by fixing the mind; *vijitāḥ*—achieved; *bhagavat-prasādāḥ*—the blessings of the Lord; *tān*—them; *eva*—even; *te*—by you; *mat*—to me; *anusevanayā*—by devoted service; *avaruddhān*—obtained; *dṛṣṭim*—transcendental vision; *prapaśya*—just see; *vitarāmi*—I am giving; *abhayān*—which are free from fear; *aśokān*—which are free from lamentation.

TRANSLATION

Kardama Muni continued: I have achieved the blessings of the Lord in discharging my own religious life of austerity, meditation and Kṛṣṇa consciousness. Although you have not yet experienced these achievements, which are free from fear and lamentation, I shall offer them all to you because you are engaged in my service. Now just look at them. I am giving you the transcendental vision to see how nice they are.

PURPORT

Devahūti engaged only in the service of Kardama Muni. She was not supposed to be so advanced in austerity, ecstasy, meditation or Kṛṣṇa consciousness, but, imperceptibly, she was sharing her husband's achievements, which she could neither see nor experience. Automatically she achieved these graces of the Lord.

What are the graces of the Lord? It is stated here that the graces of the Lord are *abhaya*, free from fearfulness. In the material world, if someone accumulates a million dollars, he is always full of fear because he is always thinking, "What if the money is lost?" But the benediction of the Lord, *bhagavat-prasāda*, is never to be lost. It is simply to be enjoyed. There is no question of loss. One simply gains and enjoys gaining. *Bhagavad-gītā* also confirms this: when one achieves the grace of the Lord, the result is that *sarva-duḥkhāni,* all distresses, are destroyed. When situated in the transcendental position, one is freed from the two kinds of material diseases—hankering and lamentation. This is also stated in *Bhagavad-gītā.* After devotional life begins, we can achieve the full result of love of Godhead. Love of Kṛṣṇa is the highest perfection of *bhagavat-prasāda,* or divine mercy. This transcendental achievement is so greatly valuable that no material happiness can compare to it. Prabodhānanda Sarasvatī said that if one achieves the grace of Lord Caitanya he becomes so great that he does not care a fig even for the demigods, he thinks of monism as hellish, and for him the perfection of controlling the senses is as easy as anything. Heavenly pleasures become to him no more than stories. Actually, there is no comparison between material happiness and transcendental happiness.

By the grace of Kardama Muni, Devahūti experienced actual realization simply by serving. We get a similar example in the life of Nārada Muni. In his previous life, Nārada was a maidservant's son, but his mother was engaged in the service of great devotees. He got the opportunity to serve the devotees, and simply by eating the remnants of their foodstuff and carrying out their orders he became so elevated that in his next life he became the great personality Nārada. For spiritual achievement the easiest path is to take shelter of a bona fide spiritual master and to serve him with heart and soul. That is the secret of success. As stated by Viśvanātha Cakravartī Ṭhākura in his eight stanzas of prayer to the spiritual master, *yasya prasādād bhagavat-prasādaḥ:* by serving or receiving the grace of the spiritual master, one receives the grace of the Supreme Lord. By serving her devotee husband, Kardama Muni, Devahūti shared in his achievements. Similarly, a sincere disciple, simply by serving a bona fide spiritual master, can achieve all the mercy of the Lord and the spiritual master simultaneously.

TEXT 8

अन्ये पुनर्भगवतो भ्रुव उद्विजृम्भ-
विभ्रंशितार्थरचनाः किमुरुक्रमस्य ।
सिद्धासि भुङ्क्ष्व विभवान्निजधर्मदोहान्
दिव्यान्नरैर्दुरधिगान्नृपविक्रियाभिः ॥ ८ ॥

anye punar bhagavato bhruva udvijṛmbha-
vibhraṁśitārtha-racanāḥ kim urukramasya
siddhāsi bhuṅkṣva vibhavān nija-dharma-dohān
divyān narair duradhigān nṛpa-vikriyābhiḥ

anye—others; *punaḥ*—again; *bhagavataḥ*—of the Lord; *bhruvaḥ*—of the eyebrows; *udvijṛmbha*—by the movement; *vibhraṁśita*—annihilated; *artha-racanāḥ*—material achievements; *kim*—what use; *urukramasya*—of Lord Viṣṇu (far-stepping); *siddhā*—successful; *asi*—you are; *bhuṅkṣva*—enjoy; *vibhavān*—the gifts; *nija-dharma*—by your own principles of devotion; *dohān*—gained; *divyān*—transcendental; *naraiḥ*—by persons; *duradhigān*—difficult to obtain; *nṛpa-vikriyābhiḥ*—proud of aristocracy.

TRANSLATION

Kardama Muni continued: What is the use of enjoyments other than the Lord's grace? All material achievements are subject to be annihilated simply by a movement of the eyebrows of Lord Viṣṇu, the Supreme Personality of Godhead. By your principles of devotion to your husband, you have achieved and can enjoy transcendental gifts very rarely obtained by persons proud of aristocracy and material possessions.

PURPORT

Lord Caitanya recommended that the greatest achievement of human life is to achieve the grace of the Lord, love of God. He said, *premā pumartho mahān:* to achieve love of Godhead is the highest perfection of life. The same perfection is recommended by Kardama Muni to his wife. His wife belonged to a very aristocratic royal family. Generally, those who are very materialistic or who possess material wealth and prosperity are unable to appreciate the value of transcendental love of God. Although Devahūti was a princess coming from a very great royal family, fortunately she was under the supervision of her great husband, Kardama Muni, who offered her the best gift which can be bestowed in human life—the grace of the Lord, or love of God. This grace of the Lord was achieved by Devahūti by the good will and satisfaction of her husband. She served her husband, who was a great devotee and saintly person, with great sincerity, love, affection and service, and Kardama Muni was satisfied. He willingly gave love of God, and he recommended that she accept it and enjoy it because he had already achieved it.

Love of God is not an ordinary commodity. Caitanya Mahāprabhu was worshiped by Rūpa Gosvāmī because He distributed love of God, *kṛṣṇa-premā,* to everyone. Rūpa Gosvāmī praised Him as *mahā-vadānya,* a greatly munificent personality, because He was freely distributing to everyone love of Godhead, which is achieved by wise men only after many, many births. *Kṛṣṇa-premā,* Kṛṣṇa consciousness, is the highest gift which can be bestowed on anyone whom we presume to love.

One word used in this verse, *nija-dharma-dohān*, is very significant. Devahūti, as the wife of Kardama Muni, achieved an invaluable gift from her husband because she was very faithful to him. For a woman the first principle of religion is to be faithful to her husband. If, fortunately, the husband is a great personality, then the combination is perfect, and the lives of both the wife and the husband are at once fulfilled.

TEXT 9

एवं ब्रुवाणमबलाखिलयोगमाया-
विद्याविचक्षणमवेक्ष्य गताधिरासीत् ।
सम्प्रश्रयप्रणयविह्वलया गिरेषद्-
व्रीडावलोकविलसद्धसिताननाह ॥ ९ ॥

evaṁ bruvāṇam abalākhila-yogamāyā-
vidyā-vicakṣaṇam avekṣya gatādhir āsīt
sampraśraya-praṇaya-vihvalayā gireṣad-
vrīḍāvaloka-vilasad-dhasitānanāha

evam—thus; *bruvāṇam*—speaking; *abalā*—the woman; *akhila*—all; *yoga-māyā*—of transcendental science; *vidyā-vicakṣaṇam*—excelling in knowledge; *avekṣya*—after hearing; *gata-ādhiḥ*—satisfied; *āsīt*—she became; *sampraśraya*—with humility; *praṇaya*—and with love; *vihvalayā*—choked up; *girā*—with a voice; *īṣat*—slightly; *vrīḍā*—bashful; *avaloka*—with a glance; *vilasat*—shining; *hasita*—smiling; *ānanā*—her face; *āha*—she spoke.

TRANSLATION

Upon hearing the speaking of her husband, who excelled in knowledge of all kinds of transcendental science, innocent Devahūti was very satisfied. Her smiling face shining with a slightly bashful glance, she spoke in a choked voice because of great humility and love.

PURPORT

It is said that if one is already engaged in Kṛṣṇa consciousness and is rendering transcendental loving service to the Lord, then it can be supposed that he has finished all the recommended courses of austerity, penance, religion, sacrifice, mystic *yoga* and meditation. Devahūti's husband was so expert in the transcendental science that there was nothing for him to argue about, and when she heard him speak she was confident that since he was very much advanced in devotional service he had already surpassed all transcendental educational activities. She had no doubt about the gifts offered by her husband; she knew that he was expert in offering such gifts, and when she understood that he was offering the greatest gift, she was very satisfied. She was overwhelmed with ecstatic love, and therefore she could not reply; then, with faltering language, just like an attractive wife, she spoke the following words.

TEXT 10

देवहूतिरुवाच

राद्धं बत द्विजवृषैतदमोघयोग-
मायाधिपे त्वयि विभो तदवैमि भर्तः ।
यस्तेऽभ्यधायि समयः सकृदङ्गसङ्गो
भूयाद्गरीयसि गुणः प्रसवः सतीनाम् ॥१०॥

devahūtir uvāca
rāddhaṁ bata dvija-vṛṣaitad amogha-yoga-
māyādhipe tvayi vibho tad avaimi bhartaḥ
yas te 'bhyadhāyi samayaḥ sakṛd aṅga-saṅgo
bhūyād garīyasi guṇaḥ prasavaḥ satīnām

devahūtiḥ uvāca—Devahūti said; *rāddham*—it has been achieved; *bata*—indeed; *dvija-vṛṣa*—O best of the *brāhmaṇas; etat*—this; *amogha*—infallible; *yoga-māyā*—of mystic powers; *adhipe*—the master; *tvayi*—in you; *vibho*—O great one; *tat*—that; *avaimi*—I know; *bhartaḥ*—O husband; *yaḥ*—that which; *te*—by you; *abhyadhāyi*—was given; *samayaḥ*—promise; *sakṛt*—once; *aṅga-saṅgaḥ*—bodily union; *bhūyāt*—may be; *garīyasi*—when very glorious; *guṇaḥ*—a great quality; *prasavaḥ*—progeny; *satīnām*—of chaste women.

TRANSLATION

Śrī Devahūti said: My dear husband, O best of brāhmaṇas, I know that you have achieved perfection and are the master of all the infallible mystic powers because you are under the protection of yogamāyā, the transcendental nature. But you once made a promise that our bodily union should now fulfill, since children are a great quality for a chaste woman who has a glorious husband.

PURPORT

Devahūti expressed her happiness by uttering the word *bata*, for she knew that her husband was in a highly elevated, transcendental position and was under the shelter of *yogamāyā.* As stated in *Bhagavad-gītā,* those who are great souls, *mahātmās*, are not under the control of the material energy. The Supreme Lord has two energies, material and spiritual. The living entities are marginal energy. As marginal energy, a person may be under the control of the material energy or the spiritual energy (*yogamāyā*).

Kardama Muni was a great soul, and therefore he was under the spiritual energy, which means that he was directly connected with the Supreme Lord. The symptom of this is Kṛṣṇa consciousness, constant engagement in devotional service. This was known to Devahūti, yet she was anxious to have a son by bodily union with the sage. She reminded her husband of his promise to her parents: "I will remain only until the time of Devahūti's pregnancy." She reminded him that for a chaste woman to have a child by a great personality is most glorious. She wanted to be pregnant, and she prayed for that. The word *strī* means "expansion." By bodily union of the husband and wife their qualities are expanded: children born of good parents are expansions of the parents' personal qualifications. Both Kardama Muni and Devahūti were spiritually enlightened; therefore she desired from the beginning that first she be pregnant and then she be empowered with the achievement of God's grace and love of God. For a woman it is a great ambition to have a son of the same quality as a highly qualified husband. Since she had the opportunity to have Kardama Muni as her husband, she also desired to have a child by bodily union.

TEXT 11

तत्रेतिकृत्यमुपशिक्ष यथोपदेशं
येनैष मे कर्शितोऽतिरिरंसयात्मा ।
सिद्ध्येत ते कृतमनोभवधर्षिताया
दीनस्तदीश भवनं सदृशं विचक्ष्व ॥११॥

tatreti-kṛtyam upaśikṣa yathopadeśaṁ
yenaiṣa me karśito 'tiriraṁsayātmā
siddhyeta te kṛta-manobhava-dharṣitāyā
dīnas tad īśa bhavanaṁ sadṛśaṁ vicakṣva

tatra—in that; *iti-kṛtyam*—what is necessary to be done; *upaśikṣa*—perform; *yathā*—according to; *upadeśam*—instruction in scripture; *yena*—by which; *eṣaḥ*—this; *me*—my; *karśitaḥ*—emaciated; *atiriraṁ-sayā*—due to intense passion not being satisfied; *ātmā*—body; *siddhyeta*—it may he rendered fit; *te*—for you; *kṛta*—excited; *manaḥ-bhava*—by emotion; *dharṣitāyāḥ*—who am struck; *dīnaḥ*—poor; *tat*—therefore; *īśa*—O my dear lord; *bhavanam*—house; *sadṛśam*—suitable; *vicakṣva*—please think of.

TRANSLATION

Devahūti continued: My dear lord, I am struck by excited emotion for you. Therefore kindly make what arrangements must be made according to the

scriptures so that my skinny body, emaciated through unsatisfied passion, may be rendered fit for you. Also, my lord, please think of a suitable house for this purpose.

PURPORT

The Vedic literatures are not only full of spiritual instruction but are also instructive in how to prosecute material existence very nicely, with the ultimate aim of spiritual perfection. Devahūti asked her husband, therefore, how to prepare herself for sex life according to the Vedic instructions. Sex life is especially meant for having good children. The circumstances for creating good children are mentioned in *kāma-śāstra,* the scripture in which suitable arrangements are prescribed for factually glorious sex life. Everything needed is mentioned in the scriptures—what sort of house and decorations there should be, what sort of dress the wife should have, how she should be decorated with ointments, scents and other attractive features, etc. With these requisites fulfilled, the husband will be attracted by her beauty, and a favorable mental situation will be created. The mental situation at the time of sex life may then be transferred into the womb of the wife, and good children can come out of that pregnancy. Here is a special reference to Devahūti's bodily features. Because she had become skinny, she feared that her body might have no attraction for Kardama. She wanted to be instructed how to improve her bodily condition in order to attract her husband. Sexual intercourse in which the husband is attracted to the wife is sure to produce a male child, but sexual intercourse based on attraction of the wife for the husband may produce a girl. That is mentioned in the *Āyur-veda.* When the passion of the woman is greater, there is a chance of a girl's being born. When the passion of the man is greater, then there is the possibility of a son. Devahūti wanted the passion of her husband to be increased by the arrangement mentioned in the *kāma-śāstra.* She wanted him to instruct her in that way, and she also requested that he arrange for a suitable house because the hermitage in which Kardama Muni was living was very simple and completely in the mode of goodness, and there was less possibility of passion's being aroused in his heart.

TEXT 12

मैत्रेय उवाच

प्रियायाः प्रियमन्विच्छन् कर्दमो योगमास्थितः ।
विमानं कामगं क्षत्तस्तर्ह्येवाविरचीकरत् ॥१२॥

maitreya uvāca
priyāyāḥ priyam anvicchan
kardamo yogam āsthitaḥ
vimānaṁ kāma-gaṁ kṣattas
tarhy evāviracīkarat

maitreyaḥ—the great sage Maitreya; *uvāca*—said; *priyāyāḥ*—of his beloved wife; *priyam*—the pleasure; *anvicchan*—seeking; *kardamaḥ*—the sage Kardama; *yogam*—yogic power; *āsthitaḥ*—exercised; *vimānam*—an airplane; *kāma-gam*—moving at will; *kṣattaḥ*—O Vidura; *tarhi*—instantly; *eva*—quite; *āviracīkarat*—he produced.

TRANSLATION

Maitreya continued: O Vidura, seeking to please his beloved wife, the sage Kardama exercised his yogic power and instantly produced an aerial mansion that could travel at his will.

PURPORT

Here the words *yogam āsthitaḥ* are significant. The sage Kardama was completely perfect in *yoga.* As the result of real *yoga* practice there are eight kinds of perfection: the *yogī* can become smaller than the smallest, greater than the greatest or lighter than the lightest, he can achieve anything he likes, he can create even a planet, he can establish influence over anyone, etc. In this way yogic perfection is achieved, and after this one can achieve the perfection of spiritual life. Thus it was not very wonderful for Kardama Muni to create a mansion in the air, according to his own desire, to fulfill the desire of his beloved wife. He at once created the palace, which is described in the following verses.

TEXT 13

सर्वकामदुघं दिव्यं सर्वरत्नसमन्वितम् ।
सर्वर्द्ध्युपचयोदर्कं मणिस्तम्भैरुपस्कृतम् ॥१३॥

sarva-kāma-dughaṁ divyaṁ
sarva-ratna-samanvitam
sarvarddhy-upacayodarkaṁ
maṇi-stambhair upaskṛtam

sarva—all; *kāma*—desires; *dugham*—yielding; *divyam*—wonderful; *sarva-ratna*—all sorts of jewels; *samanvitam*—bedecked with; *sarva*—all; *ṛddhi*—of wealth; *upacaya*—increase; *udarkam*—gradual; *maṇi*—of precious stones; *stambhaiḥ*—with pillars; *upaskṛtam*—adorned.

TRANSLATION

It was a wonderful structure, bedecked with all sorts of jewels, adorned with pillars of precious stones, and capable of yielding whatever one desired. It was equipped with every form of furniture and wealth, which tended to increase in the course of time.

PURPORT

The castle created in the sky by Kardama Muni may be called "a castle in the air," but by his mystic power of *yoga* Kardama Muni actually constructed a huge castle in the air. To our feeble imagination, a castle in the sky is an impossibility, but if we scrutinizingly consider the matter we can understand that it is not impossible at all. If the Supreme Personality of Godhead can create so many planets, carrying millions of castles in the air, a perfect *yogī* like Kardama Muni can easily construct one castle in the air. The castle is described as *sarva-kāma-dugham*, "yielding whatever one desired." It was full of jewels. Even the pillars were made of pearls and valuable stones. These valuable jewels and stones were not subject to deterioration, but were everlastingly and increasingly opulent. We sometimes hear of castles thus bedecked on the surface of this earth also. The castles constructed by Lord Kṛṣṇa for His 16,108 wives were so bedecked with jewels that there was no need of lamplight during the night.

TEXTS 14-15

दिव्योपकरणोपेतं सर्वकालसुखावहम् ।
पट्टिकाभिः पताकाभिर्विचित्राभिरलङ्कृतम् ॥१४॥
स्रग्भिर्विचित्रमाल्याभिर्मञ्जुशिञ्जत्षडङ्घ्रिभिः ।
दुकूलक्षौमकौशेयैर्नानावस्त्रैर्विराजितम् ॥१५॥

divyopakaraṇopetaṁ
sarva-kāla-sukhāvaham
paṭṭikābhiḥ patākābhir
vicitrābhir alaṅkṛtam

sragbhir vicitra-mālyābhir
mañju-śiñjat-ṣaḍ-aṅghribhiḥ
dukūla-kṣauma-kauśeyair
nānā-vastrair virājitam

divya—wonderful; *upakaraṇa*—with paraphernalia; *upetam*—equipped; *sarva-kāla*—in all seasons; *sukha-āvaham*—bringing happiness; *paṭṭikābhiḥ*—with festoons; *patākābhiḥ*—with flags; *vicitrābhiḥ*—of various colors and fabrics; *alaṅkṛtam*—decorated; *sragbhiḥ*—with wreaths; *vicitra-mālyābhiḥ*—with charming flowers; *mañju*—sweet; *śiñjat*—humming; *ṣaṭ-aṅghribhiḥ*—with bees; *dukūla*—fine cloth; *kṣauma*—linen; *kauśeyaiḥ*—of silk cloth; *nānā*—various; *vastraiḥ*—with tapestries; *virājitam*—embellished.

TRANSLATION

The castle was fully equipped with all necessary paraphernalia, and it was pleasing in all seasons. It was decorated all around with flags, festoons and artistic work of variegated colors. It was further embellished with wreaths of charming flowers that attracted sweetly humming bees and with tapestries of linen, silk and various other fabrics.

TEXT 16

उपर्युपरि विन्यस्तनिलयेषु पृथक्पृथक् ।
क्षिप्तैः कशिपुभिः कान्तं पर्यङ्कव्यजनासनैः ॥१६॥

upary upari vinyasta-
nilayeṣu pṛthak pṛthak
kṣiptaiḥ kaśipubhiḥ kāntaṁ
paryaṅka-vyajanāsanaiḥ

upari upari—one upon another; *vinyasta*—placed; *nilayeṣu*—in stories; *pṛthak pṛthak*—separately; *kṣiptaiḥ*—arranged; *kaśipubhiḥ*—with beds; *kāntam*—charming; *paryaṅka*—couches; *vyajana*—fans; *āsanaiḥ*—with seats.

TRANSLATION

The palace looked charming, with beds, couches, fans and seats, all separately arranged in seven stories.

PURPORT

It is understood from this verse that the castle had many stories. The words *upary upari vinyasta* indicate that skyscrapers are not newly invented. Even in those days, millions of years ago, the idea of building many-storied houses was current. They contained not merely one or two rooms, but many different apartments, and each was completely decorated with cushions, bedsteads, sitting places and carpets.

TEXT 17

तत्र तत्र विनिक्षिप्तनानाशिल्पोपशोभितम् ।
महामरकतस्थल्या जुष्टं विद्रुमवेदिभिः ॥१७॥

tatra tatra vinikṣipta-
nānā-śilpopaśobhitam
mahā-marakata-sthalyā
juṣṭaṁ vidruma-vedibhiḥ

tatra tatra—here and there; *vinikṣipta*—placed; *nānā*—various; *śilpa*—by artistic engravings; *upaśobhitam*—extraordinarily beautiful; *mahā-marakata*—of great emeralds; *sthalyā*—with a floor; *juṣṭam*—furnished; *vidruma*—of coral; *vedibhiḥ*—with raised platforms (daises).

TRANSLATION

Its beauty was enhanced by artistic engravings here and there on the walls. The floor was of emerald, with coral daises.

PURPORT

At the present moment people are very proud of their architectural art, yet floors are generally decorated with colored cement. It appears, however, that the castle constructed by the yogic powers of Kardama Muni had floors of emerald with coral daises.

TEXT 18

द्वाःसु विद्रुमदेहल्या भातं वज्रकपाटवत् ।
शिखरेष्विन्द्रनीलेषु हेमकुम्भैरधिश्रितम् ॥१८॥

dvāḥsu vidruma-dehalyā
bhātaṁ vajra-kapāṭavat
śikhareṣv indranīleṣu
hema-kumbhair adhiśritam

dvāḥsu—in the entrances; *vidruma*—of coral; *dehalyā*—with a threshold; *bhātam*—beautiful; *vajra*—bedecked with diamonds; *kapāṭa-vat*—having doors; *śikhareṣu*—on the domes; *indra-nīleṣu*—of sapphires; *hema-kumbhaiḥ*—with gold pinnacles; *adhiśritam*—crowned.

TRANSLATION

The palace was very beautiful, with its coral thresholds at the entrances and its doors bedecked with diamonds. Gold pinnacles crowned its domes of sapphire.

TEXT 19

चक्षुष्मत्पद्मरागाग्र्यैर्वज्रभित्तिषु निर्मितैः ।
जुष्टं विचित्रवैतानैर्महार्हैर्हेमतोरणैः ॥१९॥

cakṣuṣmat padmarāgāgryair
vajra-bhittiṣu nirmitaiḥ
juṣṭaṁ vicitra-vaitānair
mahārhair hema-toraṇaiḥ

cakṣuḥ-mat—as if possessed of eyes; *padma-rāga*—with rubies; *agryaiḥ*—choicest; *vajra*—of diamond; *bhittiṣu*—on the walls; *nirmitaiḥ*—set; *juṣṭam*—furnished; *vicitra*—various; *vaitānaiḥ*—with canopies; *mahā-arhaiḥ*—greatly valuable; *hema-toraṇaiḥ*—with gates of gold.

TRANSLATION

With the choicest rubies set in its diamond walls, it appeared as though possessed of eyes. It was furnished with wonderful canopies and greatly valuable gates of gold.

PURPORT

Artistic jewelry and decorations giving the appearance of eyes are not imaginary. Even in recent times the Mogul emperors constructed their palaces with decorations of jeweled birds with eyes made of valuable stones. The stones have been taken away by the authorities, but the decorations are still present in some of the castles constructed by the Mogul emperors in New Delhi. The royal palaces were built with jewels and rare stones resembling eyes, and thus at night they would give off reflective light without need of lamps.

TEXT 20

हंसपारावतव्रातैस्तत्र तत्र निकूजितम् ।
कृत्रिमान् मन्यमानैः स्वानधिरुह्याधिरुह्य च ॥२०॥

haṁsa-pārāvata-vrātais
tatra tatra nikūjitam
kṛtrimān manyamānaiḥ svān
adhiruhyādhiruhya ca

haṁsa—of swans; *pārāvata*—of pigeons; *vrātaiḥ*—with multitudes; *tatra tatra*—here and there; *nikūjitam*—vibrated; *kṛtrimān*—artificial; *manyamānaiḥ*—thinking; *svān*—belonging to their own kind; *adhiruhya adhiruhya*—rising repeatedly; *ca*—and.

TRANSLATION

Here and there in that palace were multitudes of live swans and pigeons, as well as artificial swans and pigeons so lifelike that the real swans rose above them again and again, thinking them live birds like themselves. Thus the palace vibrated with the sounds of these birds.

TEXT 21

विहारस्थानविश्रामसंवेशप्राङ्गणाजिरैः ।
यथोपजोषं रचितैर्विस्मापनमिवात्मनः ॥२१॥

vihāra-sthāna-viśrāma-
saṁveśa-prāṅgaṇājiraiḥ
yathopajoṣaṁ racitair
vismāpanam ivātmanaḥ

vihāra-sthāna—pleasure grounds; *viśrāma*—resting chambers; *saṁveśa*—bedrooms; *prāṅgaṇa*—inner yards; *ajiraiḥ*—with outer yards; *yathā-upajoṣam*—according to comfort; *racitaiḥ*—which were designed; *vismāpanam*—causing astonishment; *iva*—indeed; *ātmanaḥ*—to himself (Kardama).

TRANSLATION

The castle had pleasure grounds, resting chambers, bedrooms and inner and outer yards designed with an eye to comfort. All this caused astonishment to the sage himself.

PURPORT

Kardama Muni, being a saintly person, was living in a humble hermitage, but when he saw the palace constructed by his yogic powers, which was full of resting rooms, rooms for sex enjoyment, and inner and outer yards, he himself was astonished. That is the way of a God-gifted person. A devotee like Kardama Muni exhibited such opulence by his yogic power at the request of his wife, but when the opulence was produced, he himself could not understand how such manifestations could be possible. When a *yogī's* power is exhibited, the *yogī* himself is sometimes astonished.

TEXT 22

ईदृग्गृहं तत्पश्यन्तीं नातिप्रीतेन चेतसा ।
सर्वभूताशयाभिज्ञः प्रावोचत्कर्दमः स्वयम् ॥२२॥

īdṛg gṛhaṁ tat paśyantīṁ
nātiprītena cetasā
sarva-bhūtāśayābhijñah
prāvocat kardamaḥ svayam

īdṛk—such; *gṛham*—house; *tat*—that; *paśyantīm*—looking at; *na atiprītena*—not much pleased; *cetasā*—with a heart; *sarva-bhūta*—of everyone; *āśaya-abhijñaḥ*—understanding the heart; *prāvocat*—he addressed; *kardamaḥ*—Kardama; *svayam*—personally.

TRANSLATION

When he saw Devahūti looking at the gigantic, opulent palace with a displeased heart, Kardama Muni could understand her feelings because he could study the heart of anyone. Thus he personally addressed his wife as follows.

PURPORT

Devahūti had spent a long time in the hermitage, not taking much care of her body. She was covered with dirt, and her clothing was not very nice. Kardama Muni was surprised that he could produce such a palace, and similarly his wife, Devahūti, was also astonished. How could she live in that opulent palace? Kardama Muni could understand her astonishment, and thus he spoke as follows.

TEXT 23

निमज्ज्यास्मिन् ह्रदे भीरु विमानमिदमारुह ।
इदं शुक्लकृतं तीर्थमाशिषां यापकं नृणाम् ॥२३॥

nimajjyāsmin hrade bhīru
vimānam idam āruha

idaṁ śukla-kṛtaṁ tīrtham
āśiṣāṁ yāpakaṁ nṛṇām

nimajjya—after bathing; *asmin*—in this; *hrade*—in the lake; *bhīru*—O fearful one; *vimānam*—airplane; *idam*—this; *āruha*—ascend; *idam*—this; *śukla-kṛtam*—created by Lord Viṣṇu; *tīrtham*—sacred lake; *āśiṣām*—the desires; *yāpakam*—bestowing; *nṛṇām*—of human beings.

TRANSLATION

My dear Devahūti, you look very much afraid. First bathe in Lake Bindu-sarovara, created by Lord Viṣṇu Himself, which can grant all the desires of a human being, and then mount this airplane.

PURPORT

It is still the system to go to places of pilgrimage and take a bath in the water there. In Vṛndāvana the people take baths in the River Yamunā. In other places, such as Prayāga, they take baths in the River Ganges. The words *tīrtham āśiṣāṁ yāpakam* refer to the fulfillment of desires by bathing in a place of pilgrimage. Kardama Muni advised his good wife to bathe in Lake Bindu-sarovara so that she could revive the former beauty and luster of her body.

TEXT 24

सा तद्भर्तुः समादाय वचः कुवलयेक्षणा ।
सरजं बिभ्रती वासो वेणीभूतांश्च मूर्धजान् ॥२४॥

sā tad bhartuḥ samādāya
vacaḥ kuvalayekṣaṇā
sarajaṁ bibhratī vāso
veṇī-bhūtāṁś ca mūrdhajān

sā—she; *tat*—then; *bhartuḥ*—of her husband; *samādāya*—accepting; *vacaḥ*—the words; *kuvalaya-īkṣaṇā*—the lotus-eyed; *sa-rajam*—dirty; *bibhratī*—wearing; *vāsaḥ*—clothing; *veṇī-bhūtān*—matted; *ca*—and; *mūrdha-jān*—hair.

TRANSLATION

The lotus-eyed Devahūti accepted the order of her husband. Because of her dirty dress and the locks of matted hair on her head, she did not look very attractive.

PURPORT

It appears that Devahūti's hair had remained uncombed for many years and had become complicated in tangles. In other words, she neglected her bodily dress and comforts to engage in the service of her husband.

TEXT 25

अङ्गं च मलपङ्केन सञ्छन्नं शबलस्तनम् ।
आविवेश सरस्वत्याः सरः शिवजलाशयम् ॥२५॥

aṅgaṁ ca mala-paṅkena
sañchannaṁ śabala-stanam
āviveśa sarasvatyāḥ
saraḥ śiva-jalāśayam

aṅgam—body; *ca*—and; *mala-paṅkena*—with dirt; *sañchannam*—covered; *śabala*—discolored; *stanam*—breasts; *āviveśa*—she entered; *sarasvatyāḥ*—of the River Sarasvatī; *saraḥ*—the lake; *śiva*—sacred; *jala*—waters; *āśayam*—containing.

TRANSLATION

Her body was coated with a thick layer of dirt, and her breasts were discolored. She dove, however, into the lake, which contained the sacred waters of the Sarasvatī.

TEXT 26

सान्तःसरसि वेश्मस्थाः शतानि दश कन्यकाः ।
सर्वाः किशोरवयसो ददर्शोत्पलगन्धयः ॥२६॥

sāntaḥ sarasi veśma-sthāḥ
śatāni daśa kanyakāḥ
sarvāḥ kiśora-vayaso
dadarśotpala-gandhayaḥ

sā—she; *antaḥ*—inside; *sarasi*—in the lake; *veśma-sthāḥ*—situated in a house; *śatāni daśa*—ten hundred; *kanyakāḥ*—girls; *sarvāḥ*—all; *kiśora-vayasaḥ*—in the prime of youth; *dadarśa*—she saw; *utpala*—like lotuses; *gandhayaḥ*—fragrant.

TRANSLATION

In a house inside the lake she saw one thousand girls, all in the prime of youth and fragrant like lotuses.

TEXT 27

तां दृष्ट्वा सहसोत्थाय प्रोचुः प्राञ्जलयः स्त्रियः ।
वयं कर्मकरीस्तुभ्यं शाधि नः करवाम किम् ॥२७॥

tāṁ dṛṣṭvā sahasotthāya
procuḥ prāñjalayaḥ striyaḥ
vayaṁ karma-karīs tubhyaṁ
śādhi naḥ karavāma kim

tām—her; *dṛṣṭvā*—seeing; *sahasā*—suddenly; *utthāya*—rising; *procuḥ*—they said; *prāñjalayaḥ*—with folded hands; *striyaḥ*—the damsels; *vayam*—we; *karma-karīḥ*—maidservants; *tubhyam*—for you; *śādhi*—please tell; *naḥ*—us; *karavāma*—we can do; *kim*—what.

TRANSLATION

Seeing her, the damsels suddenly rose and said with folded hands, "We are your maidservants. Tell us what we can do for you."

PURPORT

While Devahūti was thinking of what to do in that great palace in her dirty clothes, there were at once, by the yogic powers of Kardama Muni, one thousand maidservants prepared to serve her. They appeared before Devahūti within the water and presented themselves as her maidservants, simply awaiting her orders.

TEXT 28

स्नानेन तां महार्हेण स्नापयित्वा मनस्विनीम् ।
दुकूले निर्मले नूत्ने ददुरस्यै च मानदाः ॥२८॥

snānena tāṁ mahārheṇa
snāpayitvā manasvinīm
dukūle nirmale nūtne
dadur asyai ca mānadāḥ

snānena—with bathing oils; *tām*—her; *mahā-arheṇa*—very costly; *snāpayitvā*—after bathing; *manasvinīm*—the virtuous wife; *dukūle*—in fine cloth; *nirmale*—spotless; *nūtne*—new; *daduḥ*—they gave; *asyai*—to her; *ca*—and; *māna-dāḥ*—the respectful girls.

TRANSLATION

The girls, being very respectful to Devahūti, brought her forth, and after bathing her with valuable oils and ointments, they gave her fine, new, spotless cloth to cover her body.

TEXT 29

भूषणानि परार्ध्यानि वरीयांसि द्युमन्ति च ।
अन्नं सर्वगुणोपेतं पानं चैवामृतासवम् ॥२९॥

bhūṣaṇāni parārdhyāni
varīyāṁsi dyumanti ca
annaṁ sarva-guṇopetaṁ
pānaṁ caivāmṛtāsavam

bhūṣaṇāni—ornaments; *para-ardhyāni*—most valuable; *varīyāṁsi*—very excellent; *dyumanti*—splendid; *ca*—and; *annam*—food; *sarva-guṇa*—all good qualities; *upetam*—containing; *pānam*—beverages; *ca*—and; *eva*—also; *amṛta*—sweet; *āsavam*—intoxicating.

TRANSLATION

They then decorated her with very excellent and valuable jewels, which shone brightly. Next they offered her food containing all good qualities, and a sweet, inebriating drink called āsavam.

PURPORT

Āsavam is an Āyur-vedic medical preparation; it is not a liquor. It is especially made from drugs and is meant to improve metabolism for the healthy condition of the body.

TEXT 30

अथादर्शे स्वमात्मानं स्रग्विणं विरजाम्बरम् ।
विरजं कृतस्वस्त्ययनं कन्याभिर्बहुमानितम् ॥३०॥

athādarśe svam ātmānaṁ
sragviṇaṁ virajāmbaram
virajaṁ kṛta-svastyayanaṁ
kanyābhir bahu-mānitam

atha—then; *ādarśe*—in a mirror; *svam ātmānam*—her own reflection; *srak-viṇam*—adorned with a garland; *viraja*—unsullied; *ambaram*—robes; *virajam*—freed from all bodily dirt; *kṛta-svasti-ayanam*—decorated with auspicious marks; *kanyābhiḥ*—by the maids; *bahu-mānitam*—very respectfully served.

TRANSLATION

Then in a mirror she beheld her own reflection. Her body was completely freed from all dirt, and she was adorned with a garland. Dressed in unsullied robes and decorated with auspicious marks of tilaka, she was served very respectfully by the maids.

TEXT 31

स्नातं कृतशिरःस्नानं सर्वाभरणभूषितम् ।
निष्कग्रीवं वलयिनं कूजत्काञ्चननूपुरम् ॥३१॥

snātaṁ kṛta-śiraḥ-snānaṁ
sarvābharaṇa-bhūṣitam
niṣka-grīvaṁ valayinaṁ
kūjat-kāñcana-nūpuram

snātam—bathed; *kṛta-śiraḥ*—including the head; *snānam*—bathing; *sarva*—all over; *ābharaṇa*—with ornaments; *bhūṣitam*—decorated; *niṣka*—a gold necklace with a locket; *grīvam*—on the neck; *valayinam*—with bangles; *kūjat*—tinkling; *kāñcana*—made of gold; *nūpuram*—ankle bells.

TRANSLATION

Her entire body, including her head, was completely bathed, and she was decorated all over with ornaments. She wore a special necklace with a locket. There were bangles on her wrists and tinkling anklets of gold about her ankles.

PURPORT

The word *kṛta-śiraḥ-snānam* appears here. According to the *smṛti-śāstra's* directions for daily duties, ladies are allowed to bathe daily up to the neck. The hair on the head does not necessarily have to be washed daily because the mass of wet hair may cause a cold. For ladies, therefore, taking a bath up to the neck is ordinarily prescribed, and they take a full bath only on certain occasions. On this occasion Devahūti took a full bath and washed her hair very nicely. When a lady takes an ordinary bath it is called *mala-snāna*, and when she takes a full bath, including the head, it is called *śiraḥ-snāna*.

At this time she needs sufficient oil to smear on her head. That is the direction of the commentators of *smṛti-śāstra.*

TEXT 32

श्रोण्योरध्यस्तया काञ्च्या काञ्चन्या बहुरत्नया ।
हारेण च महार्हेण रुचकेन च भूषितम् ॥३२॥

śroṇyor adhyastayā kāñcyā
kāñcanyā bahu-ratnayā
hāreṇa ca mahārheṇa
rucakena ca bhūṣitam

śroṇyoḥ—on the hips; *adhyastayā*—worn; *kāñcyā*—with a girdle; *kāñcanyā*—made of gold; *bahu-ratnayā*—decorated with numerous jewels; *hāreṇa*—with a pearl necklace; *ca*—and; *mahā-arheṇa*—precious; *rucakena*—with auspicious substances; *ca*—and; *bhūṣitam*—adorned.

TRANSLATION

About her hips she wore a girdle of gold, set with numerous jewels, and she was further adorned with a precious pearl necklace and auspicious substances.

PURPORT

Auspicious substances include saffron, *kuṅkuma* and sandalwood pulp. Before taking a bath there are other auspicious substances, such as turmeric mixed with mustard seed oil, which are smeared all over the body. All kinds of auspicious substances were used to bathe Devahūti from top to toe.

TEXT 33

सुदता सुभ्रुवा श्लक्ष्णस्निग्धापाङ्गेन चक्षुषा ।
पद्मकोशस्पृधा नीलैरलकैश्च लसन्मुखम् ॥३३॥

sudatā subhruvā ślakṣṇa-
snigdhāpāṅgena cakṣuṣā
padma-kośa-spṛdhā nīlair
alakaiś ca lasan-mukham

su-datā—with beautiful teeth; *su-bhruvā*—with charming eyebrows; *ślakṣṇa*—lovely; *snigdha*—moist; *apāṅgena*—corners of eyes; *cakṣuṣā*—with eyes; *padma-kośa*—lotus buds;

spṛdhā—defeating; *nīlaiḥ*—bluish; *alakaiḥ*—with curling hair; *ca*—and; *lasat*—shining; *mukham*—countenance.

TRANSLATION

Her countenance shone, with beautiful teeth and charming eyebrows. Her eyes, distinguished by lovely moist corners, defeated the beauty of lotus buds. Her face was surrounded by dark curling tresses.

PURPORT

According to Vedic culture, white teeth are very much appreciated. Devahūti's white teeth increased the beauty of her face and made it look like a lotus flower. When a face looks very attractive, the eyes are generally compared to lotus petals and the face to a lotus flower.

TEXT 34

यदा सस्मार ऋषभमृषीणां दयितं पतिम् ।
तत्र चास्ते सह स्त्रीभिर्यत्रास्ते स प्रजापतिः ॥३४॥

yadā sasmāra ṛṣabham
ṛṣīṇāṁ dayitaṁ patim
tatra cāste saha strībhir
yatrāste sa prajāpatiḥ

yadā—when; *sasmāra*—she thought of; *ṛṣabham*—the foremost; *ṛṣīṇām*—among the *ṛṣis*; *dayitam*—dear; *patim*—husband; *tatra*—there; *ca*—and; *āste*—she was present; *saha*—along with; *strībhiḥ*—the maidservants; *yatra*—where; *āste*—was present; *saḥ*—he; *prajāpatiḥ*—the Prajāpati (Kardama).

TRANSLATION

When she thought of her great husband, the best of the sages, Kardama Muni, who was very dear to her, she, along with all the maidservants, at once appeared where he was.

PURPORT

It appears from this verse that in the beginning Devahūti thought herself to be dirty and dressed in a very niggardly way. When her husband asked her to enter the lake, she saw the maidservants, and they took care of her. Everything was done within the water, and as soon as she thought of her beloved husband, Kardama, she was brought before him without delay. These are some of the powers attained by perfect *yogīs;* they can immediately execute anything they desire.

TEXT 35

भर्तुः पुरस्तादात्मानं स्त्रीसहस्रवृतं तदा ।
निशाम्य तद्योगगतिं संशयं प्रत्यपद्यत ॥३५॥

bhartuḥ purastād ātmānaṁ
strī-sahasra-vṛtaṁ tadā
niśāmya tad-yoga-gatiṁ
saṁśayaṁ pratyapadyata

bhartuḥ—of her husband; *purastāt*—in the presence; *ātmānam*—herself; *strī-sahasra*—by a thousand maids; *vṛtam*—surrounded; *tadā*—then; *niśāmya*—seeing; *tat*—his; *yoga-gatim*—yogic power; *saṁśayam pratyapadyata*—she was amazed.

TRANSLATION

She was amazed to find herself surrounded by a thousand maids in the presence of her husband and to witness his yogic power.

PURPORT

Devahūti saw everything miraculously done, yet when brought before her husband she could understand that it was all due to his great yogic mystic power. She understood that nothing was impossible for a *yogī* like Kardama Muni.

TEXTS 36-37

स तां कृतमलस्नानां विभ्राजन्तीमपूर्ववत् ।
आत्मनो बिभ्रतीं रूपं संवीतरुचिरस्तनीम् ॥३६॥
विद्याधरीसहस्रेण सेव्यमानां सुवाससम् ।
जातभावो विमानं तदारोहयदमित्रहन् ॥३७॥

sa tāṁ kṛta-mala-snānāṁ
vibhrājantīm apūrvavat
ātmano bibhratīṁ rūpaṁ
saṁvīta-rucira-stanīm

vidyādharī-sahasreṇa
sevyamānāṁ suvāsasam
jāta-bhāvo vimānaṁ tad
ārohayad amitra-han

saḥ—the sage; *tām*—her (Devahūti); *kṛta-mala-snānām*—bathed clean; *vibhrājantīm*—shining forth; *apūrva-vat*—unprecedentedly; *ātmanaḥ*—her own; *bibhratīm*—possessing; *rūpam*—beauty; *saṁvīta*—girded; *rucira*—charming; *stanīm*—with breasts; *vidyādharī*—of Gandharva girls; *sahasreṇa*—by a thousand; *sevyamānām*—being waited upon; *su-vāsasam*—dressed in excellent robes; *jāta-bhāvaḥ*—struck with fondness; *vimānam*—airplane like a mansion; *tat*—that; *ārohayat*—he put her on board; *amitra-han*—O destroyer of the enemy.

TRANSLATION

The sage could see that Devahūti had washed herself clean and was shining forth as though no longer his former wife. She had regained her own original beauty as the daughter of a prince. Dressed in excellent robes, her charming breasts duly girded, she was waited upon by a thousand Gandharva girls. O destroyer of the enemy, his fondness for her grew, and he placed her on the aerial mansion.

PURPORT

Before her marriage, when Devahūti was brought by her parents before the sage Kardama, she was the perfectly beautiful princess, and Kardama Muni remembered her former beauty. But after her marriage, when she was engaged in the service of Kardama Muni, she neglected to care for her body like a princess, since there was no means for such care; her husband was living in a cottage, and since she was always engaged in serving him, her royal beauty disappeared, and she became just like an ordinary maidservant. Now, after being bathed by the Gandharva girls by the order of Kardama Muni's yogic power, she regained her beauty, and Kardama Muni felt attracted to the beauty she had shown before the marriage. The real beauty of a young woman is her breasts. When Kardama Muni saw the breasts of his wife so nicely decorated, increasing her beauty many times, he was attracted, even though he was a great sage. Śrīpāda Śaṅkarācārya has therefore warned the transcendentalists that one who is after transcendental realization should not be attracted by the raised breasts of a woman because they are nothing but an interaction of fat and blood within the body.

TEXT 38

तस्मिन्नलुप्तमहिमा प्रिययानुरक्तो
विद्याधरीभिरुपचीर्णवपुर्विमाने ।
बभ्राज उत्कचकुमुद्गणवानपीच्य-
स्ताराभिरावृत इवोडुपतिर्नभःस्थः ॥३८॥

tasminn alupta-mahimā priyayānurakto
vidyādharībhir upacīrṇa-vapur vimāne
babhrāja utkaca-kumud-gaṇavān apīcyas
tārābhir āvṛta ivoḍu-patir nabhaḥ-sthaḥ

tasmin—in that; *alupta*—not lost; *mahimā*—glory; *priyayā*—with his beloved consort; *anuraktaḥ*—attached; *vidyādharībhiḥ*—by the Gandharva girls; *upacīrṇa*—waited upon; *vapuḥ*—his person; *vimāne*—on the airplane; *babhrāja*—he shone; *utkaca*—open; *kumut-gaṇavān*—the moon, which is followed by rows of lilies; *apīcyaḥ*—very charming; *tārābhiḥ*—by stars; *āvṛtaḥ*—surrounded; *iva*—as; *uḍu-patiḥ*—the moon (the chief of the stars); *nabhaḥ-sthaḥ*—in the sky.

TRANSLATION

Though seemingly attached to his beloved consort while served by the Gandharva girls, the sage did not lose his glory, which was mastery over his self. In the aerial mansion Kardama Muni with his consort shone as charmingly as the moon in the midst of the stars in the sky, which causes rows of lilies to open in ponds at night.

PURPORT

The mansion was in the sky, and therefore the comparison to the full moon and stars is very beautifully composed in this verse. Kardama Muni looked like the full moon, and the girls who surrounded his wife, Devahūti, seemed just like the stars. On a full-moon night the stars and the moon together form a beautiful constellation; similarly, in that aerial mansion in the sky, Kardama Muni with his beautiful wife and the damsels surrounding them appeared like the moon and stars on a full-moon night.

TEXT 39

तेनाष्टलोकपविहारकुलाचलेन्द्र-
द्रोणीष्वनङ्गसखमारुतसौभगासु ।

सिद्धैर्नुतो द्युधुनिपातशिवस्वनासु
रेमे चिरं धनदवल्ललनावरूथी ॥३९॥

tenāṣṭa-lokapa-vihāra-kulācalendra-
droṇīṣv anaṅga-sakha-māruta-saubhagāsu
siddhair nuto dyudhuni-pāta-śiva-svanāsu
reme ciraṁ dhanadaval-lalanā-varūthī

tena—by that airplane; *aṣṭa-loka-pa*—of the predominating deities of the eight heavenly planets; *vihāra*—the pleasure grounds; *kula-acala-indra*—of the king of the mountains (Meru); *droṇīṣu*—in the valleys; *anaṅga*—of passion; *sakha*—the companions; *māruta*—with breezes; *saubhagāsu*—beautiful; *siddhaiḥ*—by the Siddhas; *nutaḥ*—being praised; *dyu-dhuni*—of the Ganges; *pāta*—of the downfall; *śiva-svanāsu*—vibrating with auspicious sounds; *reme*—he enjoyed; *ciram*—for a long time; *dhanada-vat*—like Kuvera; *lalanā*—by damsels; *varūthī*—surrounded.

TRANSLATION

In that aerial mansion he traveled to the pleasure valleys of Mount Meru, which were rendered all the more beautiful by cool, gentle, fragrant breezes that stimulated passion. In these valleys, the treasurer of the gods, Kuvera, surrounded by beautiful women and praised by the Siddhas, generally enjoys pleasure. Kardama Muni also, surrounded by the beautiful damsels and his wife, went there and enjoyed for many, many years.

PURPORT

Kuvera is one of the eight demigods who are in charge of different directions of the universe. It is said that Indra is in charge of the eastern side of the universe, where the heavenly planet, or paradise, is situated. Similarly, Agni is in charge of the southeastern portion of the universe; Yama, the demigod who punishes sinners, is in charge of the southern portion; Nirṛti is in charge of the southwestern part of the universe; Varuṇa, the demigod in charge of the waters, is in charge of the western portion; Vāyu, who controls the air and who has wings to travel in the air, is in charge of the northwestern part of the universe; and Kuvera, the treasurer of the demigods, is in charge of the northern part of the universe. All these demigods take pleasure in the valleys of Mount Meru, which is situated somewhere between the sun and the earth. In the aerial mansion, Kardama Muni traveled throughout the eight directions controlled by the different demigods described above, and as the demigods go to Mount Meru, he also went there to enjoy life. When one is surrounded by young, beautiful girls, sex stimulation naturally becomes prominent. Kardama Muni was sexually stimulated, and he enjoyed his wife for many, many years in that part of Mount Meru. But his sex indulgence was praised by many, many Siddhas, beings who have attained perfection, because it was intended to produce good progeny for the good of universal affairs.

TEXT 40

वैश्रम्भके सुरसने नन्दने पुष्पभद्रके ।
मानसे चैत्ररथ्ये च स रेमे रामया रतः ॥४०॥

vaiśrambhake surasane
nandane puṣpabhadrake
mānase caitrarathye ca
sa reme rāmayā rataḥ

vaiśrambhake—in the Vaiśrambhaka garden; *surasane*—in Surasana; *nandane*—in Nandana; *puṣpabhadrake*—in Puṣpabhadraka; *mānase*—by the Mānasa-sarovara Lake; *caitrarathye*—in Caitrarathya; *ca*—and; *saḥ*—he; *reme*—enjoyed; *rāmayā*—by his wife; *rataḥ*—satisfied.

TRANSLATION

Satisfied by his wife, he enjoyed in that aerial mansion not only on Mount Meru but in different gardens known as Vaiśrambhaka, Surasana, Nandana, Puṣpabhadraka and Caitrarathya, and by the Mānasa-sarovara Lake.

TEXT 41

भ्राजिष्णुना विमानेन कामगेन महीयसा ।
वैमानिकानत्यशेत चरँल्लोकान् यथानिलः ॥४१॥

bhrājiṣṇunā vimānena
kāma-gena mahīyasā
vaimānikān atyaśeta
caral̐ lokān yathānilaḥ

bhrājiṣṇunā—splendid; *vimānena*—with the airplane; *kāma-gena*—which flew according to his desire; *mahīyasā*—very great; *vaimānikān*—the demigods in their airplanes; *atyaśeta*—he surpassed; *caran*—traveling; *lokān*—through the planets; *yathā*—like; *anilaḥ*—the air.

TRANSLATION

He traveled in that way through the various planets, as the air passes uncontrolled in every direction. Coursing through the air in that great and splendid aerial mansion, which could fly at his will, he surpassed even the demigods.

PURPORT

The planets occupied by the demigods are restricted to their own orbits, but Kardama Muni, by his yogic power, could travel all over the different directions of the universe without restriction. The living entities who are within the universe are called conditioned souls; that is, they are not free to move everywhere. We are inhabitants of this earthly globe; we cannot move freely to other planets. In the modern age, man is trying to go to other planets, but so far he has been unsuccessful. It is not possible to travel to any other planets because by the laws of nature even the demigods cannot move from one planet to another. But Kardama Muni, by his yogic power, could surpass the strength of the demigods and travel in space in all directions. The comparison here is very suitable. The words *yathā anilaḥ* indicate that as the air is free to move anywhere without restriction, so Kardama Muni unrestrictedly traveled in all directions of the universe.

TEXT 42

किं दुरापादनं तेषां पुंसामुद्दामचेतसाम् ।
यैराश्रितस्तीर्थपदश्चरणो व्यसनात्ययः ॥४२॥

kiṁ durāpādanaṁ teṣāṁ
puṁsām uddāma-cetasām
yair āśritas tīrtha-padaś
caraṇo vyasanātyayaḥ

kim—what; *durāpādanam*—difficult to achieve; *teṣām*—for those; *puṁsām*—men; *uddāma-cetasām*—who are determined; *yaiḥ*—by whom; *āśritaḥ*—taken refuge; *tīrtha-padaḥ*—of the Supreme Personality of Godhead; *caraṇaḥ*—feet; *vyasana-atyayaḥ*—which vanquish dangers.

TRANSLATION

What is difficult to achieve for determined men who have taken refuge of the Supreme Personality of Godhead's lotus feet? His feet are the source of sacred rivers like the Ganges, which put an end to the dangers of mundane life.

PURPORT

The words *yair āśritas tīrtha-padaś caraṇaḥ* are significant here. The Supreme Personality of Godhead is known as *tīrtha-pāda.* The Ganges is called a sacred river because it emanates from the toe of Viṣṇu. The Ganges is meant to eradicate all the material distresses of the conditioned souls. For any living entity, therefore, who has taken shelter of the holy lotus feet of the Lord, nothing is impossible. Kardama Muni is special not because he was a great mystic, but because he was a great devotee. Therefore it is said here that for a great devotee like Kardama Muni, nothing is impossible. Although *yogīs* can perform wonderful feats, as Kardama has already displayed, Kardama was more than a *yogī* because he was a great devotee of the Lord; therefore he was more glorious than an ordinary *yogī.* As it is confirmed in *Bhagavad-gītā,* "Out of the many *yogīs,* he who is a devotee of the Lord is first class." For a person like Kardama Muni there is no question of being conditioned; he was already a liberated soul and better than the demigods, who are also conditioned. Although he was enjoying with his wife and many other women, he was above material, conditional life. Therefore the word *vyasanātyayaḥ* is used to indicate that he was beyond the position of a conditioned soul. He was transcendental to all material limitations.

TEXT 43

प्रेक्षयित्वा भुवो गोलं पत्न्यै यावान् स्वसंस्थया ।
बह्वाश्चर्यं महायोगी स्वाश्रमाय न्यवर्तत ॥४३॥

prekṣayitvā bhuvo golaṁ
patnyai yāvān sva-saṁsthayā
bahv-āścaryaṁ mahā-yogī
svāśramāya nyavartata

prekṣayitvā—after showing; *bhuvaḥ*—of the universe; *golam*—the globe; *patnyai*—to his wife; *yāvān*—as much; *sva-saṁsthayā*—with its arrangements; *bahu-āścaryam*—full of many wonders; *mahā-yogī*—the great *yogī* (Kardama); *sva-āśramāya*—to his own hermitage; *nyavartata*—returned.

TRANSLATION

After showing his wife the globe of the universe and its different arrangements, full of many wonders, the great yogī Kardama Muni returned to his own hermitage.

PURPORT

All the planets are here described as *gola,* round. Every planet is round, and each planet is a different shelter, just like islands in the great ocean. Planets are sometimes called *dvīpa* or *varṣa.* This earth planet is called Bhārata-varṣa because it was ruled by King Bharata. Another significant word used in this verse is *bahv-āścaryam,* "many wonderful things." This indicates that the different planets are distributed all over the universe in the eight directions, and each and every one of them is wonderful in itself. Each planet has its particular climatic influences and particular types of inhabitants and is completely equipped with everything, including the beauty of the seasons. In the *Brahma-saṁhitā* (5.40) it is similarly stated, *vibhūti-bhinnam:* on each and every planet there are different opulences. It cannot be expected that one planet is exactly like another. By God's grace, by nature's law, each and every planet is made differently and has different wonderful features. All such wonders were personally experienced by Kardama Muni while he traveled with his wife, yet he could return again to his humble hermitage. He showed his princess-wife that although he was living in the hermitage, he had the power to go everywhere and do anything by mystic *yoga.* That is the perfection of *yoga.* One cannot become a perfect *yogī* simply by showing some sitting postures, nor by such sitting postures or so-called meditation can one become God, as is being advertised. Foolish persons are misled into believing that simply by some caricature of meditation and sitting postures one can become God within six months.

Here is the example of a perfect *yogī;* he could travel all over the universe. Similarly, there is a description of Durvāsā Muni, who also traveled in space. Actually, the perfect *yogī* can do that. But even if one can travel all over the universe and show wonderful feats like Kardama Muni, he cannot be compared to the Supreme Personality of Godhead, whose power and inconceivable energy can never be attained by any conditioned or liberated soul. By the actions of Kardama Muni we can understand that in spite of his immense mystic power, he remained a devotee of the Lord. That is the real position of every living entity.

TEXT 44

विभज्य नवधात्मानं मानवीं सुरतोत्सुकाम् ।
रामां निरमयन् रेमे वर्षपूगान्मुहूर्तवत् ॥४४॥

vibhajya navadhātmānaṁ
mānavīṁ suratotsukām
rāmāṁ niramayan reme
varṣa-pūgān muhūrtavat

vibhajya—having divided; *nava-dhā*—into nine; *ātmānam*—himself; *mānavīm*—the daughter of Manu (Devahūti); *surata*—for sex life; *utsukām*—who was eager; *rāmām*—to his wife; *niramayan*—giving pleasure; *reme*—he enjoyed; *varṣa-pūgān*—for many years; *muhūrtavat*—like a moment.

TRANSLATION

After coming back to his hermitage, he divided himself into nine personalities just to give pleasure to Devahūti, the daughter of Manu, who was eager for sex life. In that way he enjoyed with her for many, many years, which passed just like a moment.

PURPORT

Here the daughter of Svāyambhuva Manu, Devahūti, is described as *suratotsuka.* After traveling with her husband all over the universe, in Mount Meru and the beautiful gardens of the heavenly kingdoms, she naturally became sexually stimulated, and in order to satisfy her sexual desire, Kardama Muni expanded himself into nine forms. Instead of one, he became nine, and nine persons had sexual intercourse with Devahūti for many, many years. It is understood that the sexual appetite of a woman is nine times greater than that of a man. That is clearly indicated here. Otherwise, Kardama Muni would have had no reason to expand himself into nine. Here is another example of yogic power. As the Supreme Personality of Godhead can expand Himself in millions of forms, a *yogī* can also expand up to nine forms, but not more than that. Another example is that of Saubhari Muni; he also expanded himself into eight forms. But however powerful a *yogī* may be, he cannot expand himself into more than eight or nine forms. The Supreme Personality of Godhead, however, can expand Himself into millions of forms, *ananta-rūpa*—innumerable, countless forms—as stated in the *Brahma-saṁhitā.* No one can compare to the Supreme Personality of Godhead by any conceivable energetic manifestation of power.

TEXT 45

तस्मिन् विमान उत्कृष्टां शय्यां रतिकरीं श्रिता ।
न चाबुध्यत तं कालं पत्यापीच्येन सङ्गता ॥४५॥

tasmin vimāna utkṛṣṭāṁ
śayyāṁ rati-karīṁ śritā
na cābudhyata taṁ kālaṁ
patyāpīcyena saṅgatā

tasmin—in that; *vimāne*—airplane; *utkṛṣṭām*—excellent; *śayyām*—a bed; *rati-karīm*—increasing sexual desires; *śritā*—situated on; *na*—not; *ca*—and; *abudhyata*—she noticed; *tam*—that; *kālam*—time; *patyā*—with her husband; *apīcyena*—most handsome; *saṅgatā*—in company.

TRANSLATION

In that aerial mansion, Devahūti, in the company of her handsome husband, situated on an excellent bed that increased sexual desires, could not realize how much time was passing.

PURPORT

Sex indulgence is so enjoyable for materialistic people that when they engage in such activities they forget how time is passing. Saint Kardama and Devahūti, in their sex indulgence, also forgot how time was passing by.

TEXT 46

एवं योगानुभावेन दम्पत्यो रममाणयोः ।
शतं व्यतीयुः शरदः कामलालसयोर्मनाक् ॥४६॥

evaṁ yogānubhāvena
dam-patyo ramamāṇayoḥ
śataṁ vyatīyuḥ śaradaḥ
kāma-lālasayor manak

evam—thus; *yoga-anubhāvena*—by yogic powers; *dam-patyoḥ*—the couple; *ramamāṇayoḥ*—while enjoying themselves; *śatam*—a hundred; *vyatīyuḥ*—passed; *śaradaḥ*—autumns; *kāma*—sexual pleasure; *lālasayoḥ*—who were eagerly longing for; *manāk*—like a short time.

TRANSLATION

While the couple, who eagerly longed for sexual pleasure, were thus enjoying themselves by virtue of mystic powers, a hundred autumns passed like a brief span of time.

TEXT 47

तस्यामाधत्त रेतस्तां भावयन्नात्मनात्मवित् ।
नोधा विधाय रूपं स्वं सर्वसङ्कल्पविद्विभुः ॥४७॥

tasyām ādhatta retas tāṁ
bhāvayann ātmanātma-vit
nodhā vidhāya rūpaṁ svaṁ
sarva-saṅkalpa-vid vibhuḥ

tasyām—in her; *ādhatta*—he deposited; *retaḥ*—semen; *tām*—her; *bhāvayan*—regarding; *ātmanā*—as half of himself; *ātma-vit*—a knower of spirit soul; *nodhā*—into nine; *vidhāya*—having divided; *rūpam*—body; *svam*—his own; *sarva-saṅkalpa-vit*—the knower of all desires; *vibhuḥ*—the powerful Kardama.

TRANSLATION

The powerful Kardama Muni was the knower of everyone's heart, and he could grant whatever one desired. Knowing the spiritual soul, he regarded her as half of his body. Dividing himself into nine forms, he impregnated Devahūti with nine discharges of semen.

PURPORT

Since Kardama Muni could understand that Devahūti wanted many children, at the first chance he begot nine children at one time. He is described here as *vibhu*, the most powerful master. By his yogic power he could at once produce nine daughters in the womb of Devahūti.

TEXT 48

अतः सा सुषुवे सद्यो देवहूतिः स्त्रियः प्रजाः ।
सर्वास्ताश्चारुसर्वाङ्ग्यो लोहितोत्पलगन्धयः ॥४८॥

ataḥ sā suṣuve sadyo
devahūtiḥ striyaḥ prajāḥ
sarvās tāś cāru-sarvāṅgyo
lohitotpala-gandhayaḥ

ataḥ—then; *sā*—she; *suṣuve*—gave birth; *sadyaḥ*—on the same day; *devahūtiḥ*—Devahūti; *striyaḥ*—females; *prajāḥ*—progeny; *sarvāḥ*—all; *tāḥ*—they; *cāru-sarva-aṅgyaḥ*—charming in every limb; *lohita*—red; *utpala*—like the lotus; *gandhayaḥ*—fragrant.

TRANSLATION

Immediately afterward, on the same day, Devahūti gave birth to nine female children, all charming in every limb and fragrant with the scent of the red lotus flower.

PURPORT

Devahūti was too sexually excited, and therefore she discharged more ova, and nine daughters were born. It is said in the *smṛti-śāstra* as well as in the *Āyur-veda* that when the discharge of the male is greater, male children are begotten, but when the discharge of the female is greater, female children are begotten. It appears from the circumstances that Devahūti was more sexually excited, and therefore she had nine daughters at once. All the daughters, however, were very beautiful, and their bodies were nicely formed; each resembled a lotus flower and was fragrant like a lotus.

TEXT 49

पतिं सा प्रव्रजिष्यन्तं तदालक्ष्योशतीबहिः ।
स्मयमाना विक्लवेन हृदयेन विदूयता ॥४९॥

patiṁ sā pravrajiṣyantaṁ
tadālakṣyośatī bahiḥ
smayamānā viklavena
hṛdayena vidūyatā

patim—her husband; *sā*—she; *pravrajiṣyantam*—going to leave home; *tadā*—then; *ālakṣya*—after seeing; *uśatī*—beautiful; *bahiḥ*—outwardly; *smayamānā*—smiling; *viklavena*—agitated; *hṛdayena*—with a heart; *vidūyatā*—being distressed.

TRANSLATION

When she saw her husband about to leave home, she smiled externally, but at heart she was agitated and distressed.

PURPORT

Kardama Muni finished his household affairs quickly by his mystic power. The building of the castle in the air, traveling all over the universe with his wife in the company of beautiful girls, and begetting of children were finished, and now, according to his promise to leave home for his real concern of spiritual realization after impregnating his wife, he was about to go away. Seeing her husband about to leave, Devahūti was very disturbed, but to satisfy her husband she was smiling. The example of Kardama Muni should be understood very clearly; a person whose main concern is Kṛṣṇa consciousness, even if he is entrapped in household life, should always be ready to leave household enticement as soon as possible.

TEXT 50

लिखन्त्यधोमुखी भूमिं पदा नखमणिश्रिया ।
उवाच ललितां वाचं निरुध्याश्रुकलां शनैः ॥५०॥

likhanty adho-mukhī bhūmiṁ
padā nakha-maṇi-śriyā
uvāca lalitāṁ vācaṁ
nirudhyāśru-kalāṁ śanaiḥ

likhantī—scratching; *adhaḥ-mukhī*—her head bent down; *bhūmim*—the ground; *padā*—with her foot; *nakha*—nails; *maṇi*—gemlike; *śriyā*—with radiant; *uvāca*—she spoke; *lalitām*—charming; *vācam*—accents; *nirudhya*—suppressing; *aśru-kalām*—tears; *śanaiḥ*—slowly.

TRANSLATION

She stood and scratched the ground with her foot, which was radiant with the luster of her gemlike nails. Her head bent down, she spoke in slow yet charming accents, suppressing her tears.

PURPORT

Devahūti was so beautiful that her toenails appeared just like pearls, and as she scratched the ground it appeared as if pearls had been thrown on the ground. When a woman scratches the ground with her foot, it is a sign that her mind is very disturbed. These signs were sometimes exhibited by the *gopīs* before Kṛṣṇa. When the *gopīs* came in the dead of night and Kṛṣṇa asked them to return to their homes, the *gopīs* also scratched the ground like this because their minds were very disturbed.

TEXT 51

देवहूतिरुवाच
सर्वं तद्भगवान्मह्यमुपोवाह प्रतिश्रुतम् ।
अथापि मे प्रपन्नाया अभयं दातुमर्हसि ॥५१॥

devahūtir uvāca
sarvaṁ tad bhagavān mahyam
upovāha pratiśrutam
athāpi me prapannāyā
abhayaṁ dātum arhasi

devahūtiḥ—Devahūti; *uvāca*—said; *sarvam*—all; *tat*—that; *bhagavān*—Your Lordship; *mahyam*—for me; *upovāha*—has been fulfilled; *pratiśrutam*—promised; *atha api*—yet; *me*—unto me; *prapannāyai*—unto one who has surrendered; *abhayam*—fearlessness; *dātum*—to give; *arhasi*—you deserve.

TRANSLATION

Śrī Devahūti said: My lord, you have fulfilled all the promises you gave me, yet because I am your surrendered soul, you should give me fearlessness too.

PURPORT

Devahūti requested her husband to grant her something without fear. As a wife, she was a fully surrendered soul to her husband, and it is the responsibility of the husband to give his wife fearlessness. How one awards fearlessness to his subordinate is mentioned in the Fifth Canto of *Śrīmad-Bhāgavatam.* One who cannot get free from the clutches of death is dependent, and he should not become a spiritual master, nor a husband, nor a kinsman, nor a father, nor a mother, etc. It is the duty of the superior to give fearlessness to the subordinate. To take charge of someone, therefore, either as father, mother, spiritual master, relative or husband, one must accept the responsibility to give his ward freedom from the fearful situation of material existence. Material existence is always fearful and full of anxiety. Devahūti is saying, "You have given me all sorts of material comforts by your yogic power, and since you are now prepared to go away, you must give me your last award so that I may get free from this material, conditional life."

TEXT 52

ब्रह्मन्दुहितृभिस्तुभ्यं विमृग्याः पतयः समाः ।
कश्चित्स्यान्मे विशोकाय त्वयि प्रव्रजिते वनम् ॥५२॥

brahman duhitṛbhis tubhyaṁ
vimṛgyāḥ patayaḥ samāḥ
kaścit syān me viśokāya
tvayi pravrajite vanam

brahman—my dear *brāhmaṇa; duhitṛbhiḥ*—by the daughters themselves; *tubhyam*—for you; *vimṛgyāḥ*—to be found out; *patayaḥ*—husbands; *samāḥ*—suitable; *kaścit*—someone; *syāt*—there should be; *me*—my; *viśokāya*—for solace; *tvayi*—when you; *pravrajite*—departed; *vanam*—to the forest.

TRANSLATION

My dear brāhmaṇa, as far as your daughters are concerned, they will find their own suitable husbands and go away to their respective homes. But who will give me solace after your departure as a sannyāsī?

PURPORT

It is said that the father himself becomes the son in another form. The father and son are therefore considered to be nondifferent. A widow who has her son is actually not a widow, because she has the representative of her husband. Similarly, Devahūti is indirectly asking Kardama Muni to leave a representative so that in his absence she might be relieved of her anxieties by a suitable son. A householder is not expected to remain at home for all his days. After getting his sons and daughters married, a householder can retire from household life, leaving his wife in the charge of the grown-up sons. That is the social convention of the Vedic system. Devahūti is indirectly asking that in his absence from home there be at least one male child to give her relief from her anxieties. This relief means spiritual instruction. Relief does not mean material comforts. Material comforts will end with the end of the body, but spiritual instruction will not end; it will go on with the spirit soul. Instruction in spiritual advancement is necessary, but without having a worthy son, how could Devahūti advance in spiritual knowledge? It is the duty of the husband to liquidate his debt to his wife. The wife gives her sincere service to the husband, and he becomes indebted to her because one cannot accept service from his subordinate without giving him something in exchange. The spiritual master cannot accept service from a disciple without awarding him spiritual instruction. That is the reciprocation of love and duty. Thus Devahūti reminds her husband, Kardama Muni, that she has rendered him faithful service. Even considering the situation on the basis of liquidating his debt toward his wife, he must give a male child before he leaves. Indirectly, Devahūti requests her husband to remain at home a few days more, or at least until a male child is born.

TEXT 53

एतावतालं कालेन व्यतिक्रान्तेन मे प्रभो ।
इन्द्रियार्थप्रसङ्गेन परित्यक्तपरात्मनः ॥५३॥

etāvatālaṁ kālena
vyatikrāntena me prabho

indriyārtha-prasaṅgena
parityakta-parātmanaḥ

etāvatā—so much; *alam*—for nothing; *kālena*—time; *vyatikrāntena*—passed by; *me*—my; *prabho*—O my lord; *indriya-artha*—sense gratification; *prasaṅgena*—in the matter of indulging; *parityakta*—disregarding; *para-ātmanaḥ*—knowledge of the Supreme Lord.

TRANSLATION

Until now we have simply wasted so much of our time in sense gratification, neglecting to cultivate knowledge of the Supreme Lord.

PURPORT

Human life is not meant to be wasted, like that of the animals, in sense gratificatory activities. Animals always engage in sense gratification-eating, sleeping, fearing and mating—but that is not the engagement of the human being, although, because of the material body, there is need of sense gratification according to a regulative principle. So, in effect, Devahūti said to her husband: "So far we have these daughters, and we have enjoyed material life in the aerial mansion, traveling all over the universe. These boons have come by your grace, but they have all been for sense gratification. Now there must be something for my spiritual advancement."

TEXT 54

इन्द्रियार्थेषु सज्जन्त्या प्रसङ्गस्त्वयि मे कृतः ।
अजानन्त्या परं भावं तथाप्यस्त्वभयाय मे ॥५४॥

indriyārtheṣu sajjantyā
prasaṅgas tvayi me kṛtaḥ
ajānantyā paraṁ bhāvaṁ
tathāpy astv abhayāya me

indriya-artheṣu—to sense gratification; *sajjantyā*—being attached; *prasaṅgaḥ*—affinity; *tvayi*—for you; *me*—by me; *kṛtaḥ*—was done; *ajānantyā*—not knowing; *param bhāvam*—your transcendent situation; *tathā api*—nonetheless; *astu*—let it be; *abhayāya*—for fearlessness; *me*—my.

TRANSLATION

Not knowing your transcendental situation, I have loved you while remaining attached to the objects of the senses. Nonetheless, let the affinity I have developed for you rid me of all fear.

PURPORT

Devahūti is lamenting her position. As a woman, she had to love someone. Somehow or other, she came to love Kardama Muni, but without knowing of his spiritual advancement. Kardama Muni could understand Devahūti's heart; generally all women desire material enjoyment. They are called less intelligent because they are mostly prone to material enjoyment. Devahūti laments because her husband had given her the best kind of material enjoyment, but she did not know that he was so advanced in spiritual realization. Her plea was that even though she did not know the glories of her great husband, because she had taken shelter of him she must be delivered from material entanglement. Association with a great personality is most important. In *Caitanya-caritāmṛta* Lord Caitanya says that *sādhu-saṅga,* the association of a great saintly person, is very important, because even if one is not advanced in knowledge, simply by association with a great saintly person one can immediately make considerable advancement in spiritual life. As a woman, as an ordinary wife, Devahūti became attached to Kardama Muni in order to satisfy her sense enjoyment and other material necessities, but actually she associated with a great personality. Now she understood this, and she wanted to utilize the advantage of the association of her great husband.

TEXT 55

सङ्गो यः संसृतेर्हेतुरसत्सु विहितोऽधिया ।
स एव साधुषु कृतो निःसङ्गत्वाय कल्पते ॥५५॥

saṅgo yaḥ saṁsṛter hetur
asatsu vihito 'dhiyā
sa eva sādhuṣu kṛto
niḥsaṅgatvāya kalpate

saṅgaḥ—association; *yaḥ*—which; *saṁsṛteḥ*—of the cycle of birth and death; *hetuḥ*—the cause; *asatsu*—with those engaged in sense gratification; *vihitaḥ*—done; *adhiyā*—through ignorance; *saḥ*—the same thing; *eva*—certainly; *sādhuṣu*—with saintly persons; *kṛtaḥ*—performed; *niḥsaṅgatvāya*—to liberation; *kalpate*—leads.

TRANSLATION

Association for sense gratification is certainly the path of bondage. But the same type of association, performed with a saintly person, leads to the path of liberation, even if performed without knowledge.

PURPORT

The association of a saintly person in any way bears the same result. For example, Lord Kṛṣṇa met many kinds of living entities, and some treated Him as an enemy, and some treated Him as an agent for sense gratification. It is generally said that the *gopīs* were attached to Kṛṣṇa for sense attractions, and yet they became first-class devotees of the Lord. Kaṁsa, Śiśupāla, Dantavakra and other demons, however, were related to Kṛṣṇa as enemies. But whether they associated with Kṛṣṇa as enemies or for sense gratification, out of fear or as pure devotees, they all got liberation. That is the result of association with the Lord. Even if one does not understand who He is, the results have the same efficacy. Association with a great saintly person also results in liberation, just as whether one goes toward fire knowingly or unknowingly, the fire will make one warm. Devahūti expressed her gratefulness, for although she wanted to associate with Kardama Muni only for sense gratification, because he was spiritually great she was sure to be liberated by his benediction.

TEXT 56

नेह यत्कर्म धर्माय न विरागाय कल्पते ।
न तीर्थपदसेवायै जीवन्नपि मृतो हि सः ॥५६॥

neha yat karma dharmāya
na virāgāya kalpate
na tīrtha-pada-sevāyai
jīvann api mṛto hi saḥ

na—not; *iha*—here; *yat*—which; *karma*—work; *dharmāya*—for perfection of religious life; *na*—not; *virāgāya*—for detachment; *kalpate*—leads; *na*—not; *tīrtha-pada*—of the Lord's lotus feet; *sevāyai*—to devotional service; *jīvan*—living; *api*—although; *mṛtaḥ*—dead; *hi*—indeed; *saḥ*—he.

TRANSLATION

Anyone whose work is not meant to elevate him to religious life, anyone whose religious ritualistic performances do not raise him to renunciation, and anyone situated in renunciation that does not lead him to devotional service to the Supreme Personality of Godhead, must be considered dead, although he is breathing.

PURPORT

Devahūti's statement is that since she was attached to living with her husband for sense gratification, which does not lead to liberation from material entanglement, her life was simply a waste of time. Any work one performs that does not lead to the state of religious life is useless activity. Everyone is by nature inclined to some sort of work, and when that work leads one to religious life and religious life leads one to renunciation and renunciation leads one to devotional service, one attains the perfection of work. As stated in *Bhagavad-gītā*, any work that does not lead ultimately to the standard of devotional service is a cause of bondage in the material world. *Yajñārthāt karmaṇo 'nyatra loko 'yaṁ karma-bandhanaḥ.* Unless one is gradually elevated to the position of devotional service, beginning from his natural activity, he is to be considered a dead body. Work which does not lead one to the understanding of Kṛṣṇa consciousness is considered useless.

TEXT 57

साहं भगवतो नूनं वञ्चिता मायया दृढम् ।
यत्त्वां विमुक्तिदं प्राप्य न मुमुक्षेय बन्धनात् ॥५७॥

sāhaṁ bhagavato nūnaṁ
vañcitā māyayā dṛḍham
yat tvāṁ vimuktidaṁ prāpya
na mumukṣeya bandhanāt

sā—that very person; *aham*—I am; *bhagavataḥ*—of the Lord; *nūnam*—surely; *vañcitā*—cheated; *māyayā*—by the illusory energy; *dṛḍham*—solidly; *yat*—because; *tvām*—you; *vimukti-dam*—who gives liberation; *prāpya*—having attained; *na mumukṣeya*—I have not sought liberation; *bandhanāt*—from material bondage.

TRANSLATION

My lord, surely I have been solidly cheated by the insurmountable illusory energy of the Supreme Personality of Godhead, for in spite of having obtained your association, which gives liberation from material bondage, I did not seek such liberation.

PURPORT

An intelligent man should utilize good opportunities. The first opportunity is the human form of life, and the second opportunity is to take birth in a suitable family where there is cultivation of spiritual knowledge; this is rarely obtained. The greatest opportunity is to have the association of a saintly person. Devahūti was conscious that she was born as the daughter of an emperor. She was sufficiently educated and cultured, and at last she got Kardama Muni, a saintly person and a great *yogī*, as her husband. Still, if she did not get liberation from the entanglement of material energy, then certainly she would be cheated by the insurmountable illusory energy. Actually, the illusory, material energy is cheating everyone. People do not know what they are doing when they worship the material energy in the form of goddess Kālī or Durgā for material boons. They ask, "Mother, give me great riches, give me a good wife, give me fame, give me victory." But such devotees of the goddess Māyā, or Durgā, do not know that they are being cheated by that goddess. Material achievement is actually no achievement because as soon as one is illusioned by the material gifts, he becomes more and more entangled, and there is no question of liberation. One should be intelligent enough to know how to utilize material assets for the purpose of spiritual realization. That is called *karma-yoga* or *jñāna-yoga.* Whatever we have we should use as service to the Supreme Person. It is advised in *Bhagavad-gītā sva-karmaṇā tam abhyarcya:* one should try to worship the Supreme Personality of Godhead by one's assets. There are many forms of service to the Supreme Lord, and anyone can render service unto Him according to the best of his ability.

Thus end the Bhaktivedanta purports of the Third Canto, Twenty-third Chapter, of the Śrīmad-Bhāgavatam, *entitled "Devahūti's Lamentation."*

CHAPTER TWENTY-FOUR

The Renunciation of Kardama Muni

TEXT 1

मैत्रेय उवाच
निर्वेदवादिनीमेवं मनोर्दुहितरं मुनिः ।
दयालुः शालिनीमाह शुक्लाभिव्याहृतं स्मरन् ॥ १ ॥

maitreya uvāca
nirveda-vādinīm evaṁ
manor duhitaraṁ muniḥ
dayāluḥ śālinīm āha
śuklābhivyāhṛtaṁ smaran

maitreyaḥ—the great sage Maitreya; *uvāca*—said; *nirveda-vādinīm*—who was speaking words full of renunciation; *evam*—thus; *manoḥ*—of Svāyambhuva Manu; *duhitaram*—to the daughter; *muniḥ*—the sage Kardama; *dayāluḥ*—merciful; *śālinīm*—who was worthy of praise; *āha*—replied; *śukla*—by Lord Viṣṇu; *abhivyāhṛtam*—what was said; *smaran*—recalling.

TRANSLATION

Recalling the words of Lord Viṣṇu, the merciful sage Kardama replied as follows to Svāyambhuva Manu's praiseworthy daughter, Devahūti, who was speaking words full of renunciation.

TEXT 2

ऋषिरुवाच
मा खिदो राजपुत्रीत्थमात्मानं प्रत्यनिन्दिते ।
भगवांस्तेऽक्षरो गर्भमदूरात्सम्प्रपत्स्यते ॥ २ ॥

ṛṣir uvāca
mā khido rāja-putrīttham
ātmānaṁ praty anindite
bhagavāṁs te 'kṣaro garbham
adūrāt samprapatsyate

ṛṣiḥ uvāca—the sage said; *mā khidaḥ*—do not be disappointed; *rāja-putri*—O princess; *ittham*—in this way; *ātmānam*—yourself; *prati*—toward; *anindite*—O praiseworthy Devahūti; *bhagavān*—the Supreme Personality of Godhead; *te*—your; *akṣaraḥ*—infallible; *garbham*—womb; *adūrāt*—without delay; *samprapatsyate*—will enter.

TRANSLATION

The sage said: Do not be disappointed with yourself, O princess. You are actually praiseworthy. The infallible Supreme Personality of Godhead will shortly enter your womb as your son.

PURPORT

Kardama Muni encouraged his wife not to be sorry, thinking herself unfortunate, because the Supreme Personality of Godhead, by His incarnation, was going to come from her body.

TEXT 3

धृतव्रतासि भद्रं ते दमेन नियमेन च ।
तपोद्रविणदानैश्च श्रद्धया चेश्वरं भज ॥ ३ ॥

dhṛta-vratāsi bhadraṁ te
damena niyamena ca
tapo-draviṇa-dānaiś ca
śraddhayā ceśvaraṁ bhaja

dhṛta-vratā asi—you have undertaken sacred vows; *bhadram te*—may God bless you; *damena*—by control of the senses; *niyamena*—by religious observances; *ca*—and; *tapaḥ*—austerities; *draviṇa*—of money; *dānaiḥ*—by giving in charity; *ca*—and; *śraddhayā*—with great faith; *ca*—and; *īśvaram*—the Supreme Lord; *bhaja*—worship.

TRANSLATION

You have undertaken sacred vows. God will bless you. Hence you should worship the Lord with great faith, through sensory control, religious observances, austerities and gifts of your money in charity.

PURPORT

In order to spiritually advance or to achieve the mercy of the Lord, one must be self-controlled in the following manner: he must be restrained in sense gratification and must follow the rules and regulations of religious principles. Without austerity and penance and without sacrificing one's riches, one cannot achieve the mercy of the Supreme Lord. Kardama Muni advised his wife: "You have to factually engage in devotional service with austerity and penance, following the religious principles and giving charity. Then the Supreme Lord will be pleased with you, and He will come as your son."

TEXT 4

स त्वयाराधितः शुक्लो वितन्वन्मामकंयशः ।
छेत्ता ते हृदयग्रन्थिमौदर्यो ब्रह्मभावनः ॥ ४ ॥

sa tvayārādhitaḥ śuklo
vitanvan māmakaṁ yaśaḥ
chettā te hṛdaya-granthim
audaryo brahma-bhāvanaḥ

saḥ—He; *tvayā*—by you; *ārādhitaḥ*—being worshiped; *śuklaḥ*—the Personality of Godhead; *vitanvan*—spreading; *māmakam*—my; *yaśaḥ*—fame; *chettā*—He will cut; *te*—your; *hṛdaya*—of the heart; *granthim*—knot; *audaryaḥ*—your son; *brahma*—knowledge of Brahman; *bhāvanaḥ*—teaching.

TRANSLATION

The Personality of Godhead, being worshiped by you, will spread my name and fame. He will vanquish the knot of your heart by becoming your son and teaching knowledge of Brahman.

PURPORT

When the Supreme Personality of Godhead comes to disseminate spiritual knowledge for the benefit of all people, He generally descends as the son of a devotee, being pleased by the devotee's devotional service. The Supreme Personality of Godhead is the father of everyone. No one, therefore, is His father, but by His inconceivable energy He accepts some of the devotees as His parents and descendants. It is explained here that spiritual knowledge vanquishes the knot of the heart. Matter and spirit are knotted by false ego. This identification of oneself with matter, which is called *hṛdaya-granthi,* exists for all conditioned souls, and it becomes more and more tightened when there is too much affection for sex life. The explanation was given by Lord Ṛṣabha to His sons that this material world is an atmosphere of attraction between male and female. That attraction takes the shape of a knot in the heart, and by material affection it becomes still more tight. For people who hanker after material possessions, society, friendship and love, this knot of affection becomes very strong. It is only by *brahma-bhāvana*—the instruction by which spiritual knowledge is enhanced—that the knot in the heart is cut to pieces. No material weapon is needed to cut this knot, but it requires bona fide spiritual instruction. Kardama Muni instructed his wife, Devahūti, that the Lord would appear as her son and disseminate spiritual knowledge to cut the knot of material identification.

TEXT 5

मैत्रेय उवाच
देवहूत्यपि सन्देशं गौरवेण प्रजापतेः ।
सम्यक् श्रद्धाय पुरुषं कूटस्थमभजद्गुरुम् ॥ ५ ॥

maitreya uvāca
devahūty api sandeśaṁ
gauraveṇa prajāpateḥ
samyak śraddhāya puruṣaṁ
kūṭa-stham abhajad gurum

maitreyaḥ uvāca—Maitreya said; *devahūtī*—Devahūti; *api*—also; *sandeśam*—the direction; *gauraveṇa*—with great respect; *prajāpateḥ*—of Kardama; *samyak*—complete; *śraddhāya*—having faith in; *puruṣam*—the Supreme Personality of Godhead; *kūṭa-stham*—situated in everyone's heart; *abhajat*—worshiped; *gurum*—most worshipable.

TRANSLATION

Śrī Maitreya said: Devahūti was fully faithful and respectful toward the direction of her husband, Kardama, who was one of the Prajāpatis, or generators of human beings in the universe. O great sage, she thus began to worship the master of the universe, the Supreme Personality of Godhead, who is situated in everyone's heart.

PURPORT

This is the process of spiritual realization; one has to receive instruction from a bona fide spiritual master. Kardama Muni was Devahūti's husband, but because he instructed her on how to achieve spiritual perfection, he naturally became her spiritual master also. There are many instances wherein the husband becomes the spiritual master. Lord Śiva also is the spiritual master of his consort, Pārvatī. A husband should be so enlightened that he should become the spiritual master of his wife in order to enlighten her in the advancement of Kṛṣṇa consciousness. Generally *strī*, or woman, is less intelligent than man; therefore, if the husband is intelligent enough, the woman gets a great opportunity for spiritual enlightenment.

Here it is clearly said (*samyak śraddhāya*) that with great faith one should receive knowledge from the spiritual master and with great faith execute the performance of service. Śrīla Viśvanātha Cakravartī Ṭhākura, in his commentary on *Bhagavad-gītā*, has especially stressed the instruction of the spiritual master. One should accept the instruction of the spiritual master as one's life and soul. Whether one is liberated or not liberated, one should execute the instruction of the spiritual master with great faith. It is also stated that the Lord is situated in everyone's heart. One does not have to seek the Lord outside; He is already there. One simply has to concentrate on one's worship in good faith, as instructed by the bona fide spiritual master, and one's efforts will come out successfully. It is also clear that the Supreme Personality of Godhead does not appear as an ordinary child; He appears as He is. As stated in *Bhagavad-gītā*, He appears by His own internal potency, *ātmā-māyā*. And how does He appear? He appears when pleased by the worship of a devotee. A devotee may ask the Lord to appear as her son. The Lord is already sitting within the heart, and if He comes out from the body of a devotee it does not mean that the particular woman becomes His mother in the material sense. He is always there, but in order to please His devotee, He appears as her son.

TEXT 6

तस्यां बहुतिथे काले भगवान्मधुसूदनः ।
कार्दमं वीर्यमापन्नो जज्ञेऽग्निरिव दारुणि ॥ ६ ॥

tasyāṁ bahu-tithe kāle
bhagavān madhusūdanaḥ
kārdamaṁ vīryam āpanno
jajñe 'gnir iva dāruṇi

tasyām—in Devahūti; *bahu-tithe kāle*—after many years; *bhagavān*—the Supreme Personality of Godhead; *madhu-sūdanaḥ*—the killer of the demon Madhu; *kārdamam*—of Kardama; *vīryam*—the semen; *āpannaḥ*—entered; *jajñe*—He appeared; *agniḥ*—fire; *iva*—like; *dāruṇi*—in wood.

TRANSLATION

After many, many years, the Supreme Personality of Godhead, Madhusūdana, the killer of the demon Madhu, having entered the semen of Kardama, appeared in Devahūti just as fire comes from wood in a sacrifice.

PURPORT

It is clearly stated here that the Lord is always the Supreme Personality of Godhead, although He appeared as the son of Kardama Muni. Fire is already present in wood, but by a certain process, fire is kindled. Similarly, God is all-pervading. He is everywhere, and since He may come out from everything, He appeared in His devotee's semen. Just as an ordinary living entity takes his birth by taking shelter of the semen of a certain living entity, the Supreme Personality of Godhead accepts the shelter of the semen of His devotee and comes out as His son. This manifests His full independence to act in any way, and it does not mean that He is an ordinary living entity forced to take birth in a certain type of womb. Lord Nṛsiṁha appeared from the pillar of Hiraṇyakaśipu's palace, Lord Varāha appeared from the nostril of Brahmā, and Lord Kapila appeared from the semen of Kardama, but this does not mean that the nostril of Brahmā or the pillar of Hiraṇyakaśipu's palace or the semen of Kardama Muni is the source of the appearance of the Lord. The Lord is always the Lord. *Bhagavān madhusūdanaḥ*—He is the killer of all kinds of demons, and He always remains the Lord, even if He appears as the son of a particular devotee. The word *kārdamam* is significant, for it indicates that the Lord had some devotional affection or relationship in devotional service with Kardama and Devahūti. But we should not mistakenly understand that He was born just like an ordinary living entity from the semen of Kardama Muni in the womb of Devahūti.

TEXT 7

अवादयंस्तदा व्योम्नि वादित्राणि घनाघनाः ।
गायन्ति तं स्म गन्धर्वा नृत्यन्त्यप्सरसो मुदा ॥ ७ ॥

avādayaṁs tadā vyomni
vāditrāṇi ghanāghanāḥ
gāyanti taṁ sma gandharvā
nṛtyanty apsaraso mudā

avādayan—sounded; *tadā*—at that time; *vyomni*—in the sky; *vāditrāṇi*—musical instruments; *ghanāghanāḥ*—the rain clouds; *gāyanti*—sang; *tam*—to Him; *sma*—certainly;

gandharvāḥ—the Gandharvas; *nṛtyanti*—danced; *apsarasaḥ*—the Apsarās; *mudā*—in joyful ecstasy.

TRANSLATION

At the time of His descent on earth, demigods in the form of raining clouds sounded musical instruments in the sky. The celestial musicians, the Gandharvas, sang the glories of the Lord, while celestial dancing girls known as Apsarās danced in joyful ecstasy.

TEXT 8

पेतुः सुमनसो दिव्याः खेचरैरपवर्जिताः ।
प्रसेदुश्च दिशः सर्वा अम्भांसि च मनांसि च ॥ ८ ॥

petuḥ sumanaso divyāḥ
khe-carair apavarjitāḥ
praseduś ca diśah sarvā
ambhāṁsi ca manāṁsi ca

petuḥ—fell; *sumanasaḥ*—flowers; *divyāḥ*—beautiful; *khe-caraiḥ*—by the demigods who fly in the sky; *apavarjitāḥ*—dropped; *praseduḥ*—became satisfied; *ca*—and; *diśaḥ*—directions; *sarvāḥ*—all; *ambhāṁsi*—waters; *ca*—and; *manāṁsi*—minds; *ca*—and.

TRANSLATION

At the time of the Lord's appearance, the demigods flying freely in the sky showered flowers. All the directions, all the waters and everyone's mind became very satisfied.

PURPORT

It is learned herewith that in the higher sky there are living entities who can travel through the air without being hampered. Although we can travel in outer space, we are hampered by so many impediments, but they are not. We learn from the pages of *Śrīmad-Bhāgavatam* that the inhabitants of the planet called Siddhaloka can travel in space from one planet to another without impediment. They showered flowers on the earth when Lord Kapila, the son of Kardama, appeared.

TEXT 9

तत्कर्दमाश्रमपदं सरस्वत्या परिश्रितम् ।
स्वयम्भूः साकमृषिभिर्मरीच्यादिभिरभ्ययात् ॥ ९ ॥

tat kardamāśrama-padaṁ
sarasvatyā pariśritam
svayambhūḥ sākam ṛṣibhir
marīcy-ādibhir abhyayāt

tat—that; *kardama*—of Kardama; *āśrama-padam*—to the place of the hermitage; *sarasvatyā*—by the River Sarasvatī; *pariśritam*—surrounded; *svayambhūḥ*—Brahmā (the self-born); *sākam*—along with; *ṛṣibhiḥ*—the sages; *marīci*—the great sage Marīci; *ādibhiḥ*—and others; *abhyayāt*—he came there.

TRANSLATION

Brahmā, the first-born living being, went along with Marīci and other sages to the place of Kardama's hermitage, which was surrounded by the River Sarasvatī.

PURPORT

Brahmā is called Svayambhū because he is not born of any material father and mother. He is the first living creature and is born from the lotus which grows from the abdomen of the Supreme Personality of Godhead Garbhodakaśāyī Viṣṇu. Therefore he is called Svayambhū, self-born.

TEXT 10

भगवन्तं परं ब्रह्म सत्त्वेनांशेन शत्रुहन् ।
तत्त्वसंख्यानविज्ञप्त्यै जातं विद्वानजः स्वराट् ॥१०॥

bhagavantaṁ paraṁ brahma
sattvenāṁśena śatru-han
tattva-saṅkhyāna-vijñaptyai
jātaṁ vidvān ajaḥ svarāṭ

bhagavantam—the Lord; *param*—supreme; *brahma*—Brahman; *sattvena*—having an uncontaminated existence; *aṁśena*—by a plenary portion; *śatru-han*—O killer of the enemy, Vidura; *tattva-saṅkhyāna*—the philosophy of the twenty-four material elements; *vijñaptyai*—for explaining; *jātam*—appeared; *vidvān*—knowing; *ajaḥ*—the unborn (Lord Brahmā); *svarāṭ*—independent.

TRANSLATION

Maitreya continued: O killer of the enemy, the unborn Lord Brahmā, who is almost independent in acquiring knowledge, could understand that a portion

of the Supreme Personality of Godhead, in His quality of pure existence, had appeared in the womb of Devahūti just to explain the complete state of knowledge known as sāṅkhya-yoga.

PURPORT

In *Bhagavad-gītā,* Fifteenth Chapter, it is stated that the Lord Himself is the compiler of *Vedānta-sūtra,* and He is the perfect knower of *Vedānta-sūtra.* Similarly, the Sāṅkhya philosophy is compiled by the Supreme Personality of Godhead in His appearance as Kapila. There is an imitation Kapila who has a Sāṅkhya philosophical system, but Kapila the incarnation of God is different from that Kapila. Kapila the son of Kardama Muni, in His system of Sāṅkhya philosophy, very explicitly explained not only the material world but also the spiritual world. Brahmā could understand this fact because he is *svarāṭ,* almost independent in receiving knowledge. He is called *svarāṭ* because he did not go to any school or college to learn but learned everything from within. Because Brahmā is the first living creature within this universe, he had no teacher; his teacher was the Supreme Personality of Godhead Himself, who is seated in the heart of every living creature. Brahmā acquired knowledge directly from the Supreme Lord within the heart; therefore he is sometimes called *svarāṭ* and *aja.*

Another important point is stated here. *Sattvenāṁśena:* when the Supreme Personality of Godhead appears, He brings with Him all His paraphernalia of Vaikuṇṭha; therefore His name, His form, His quality, His paraphernalia and His entourage all belong to the transcendental world. Real goodness is in the transcendental world. Here in the material world, the quality of goodness is not pure. Goodness may exist, but there must also be some tinges of passion and ignorance. In the spiritual world the unalloyed quality of goodness prevails; there the quality of goodness is called *śuddha-sattva,* pure goodness. Another name for *śuddha-sattva* is *vasudeva* because God is born from Vasudeva. Another meaning is that when one is purely situated in the qualities of goodness, he can understand the form, name, quality, paraphernalia and entourage of the Supreme Personality of Godhead. The word *aṁśena* also indicates that the Supreme Personality of Godhead, Kṛṣṇa, appeared as Kapiladeva in a portion of His portion. God expands either as *kalā* or as *aṁśa. Aṁśa* means "direct expansion," and *kalā* means "expansion of the expansion." There is no difference between the expansion, the expansion of the expansion, and the Supreme Personality of Godhead directly, as there is no difference between one candle and another—but still the candle from which the others are lit is called the original. Kṛṣṇa, therefore, is called the Parabrahman, or the ultimate Godhead and cause of all causes.

TEXT 11

सभाजयन् विशुद्धेन चेतसा तच्चिकीर्षितम् ।
प्रहृष्यमाणैरसुभिः कर्दमं चेदमभ्यधात् ॥११॥

sabhājayan viśuddhena
cetasā tac-cikīrṣitam
prahṛṣyamāṇair asubhiḥ
kardamaṁ cedam abhyadhāt

sabhājayan—worshiping; *viśuddhena*—pure; *cetasā*—with a heart; *tat*—of the Supreme Personality of Godhead; *cikīrṣitam*—the intended activities; *prahṛṣyamāṇaiḥ*—gladdened; *asubhiḥ*—with senses; *kardamam*—to Kardama Muni; *ca*—and Devahūti; *idam*—this; *abhyadhāt*—spoke.

TRANSLATION

After worshiping the Supreme Lord with gladdened senses and a pure heart for His intended activities as an incarnation, Brahmā spoke as follows to Kardama and Devahūti.

PURPORT

As explained in *Bhagavad-gītā*, Fourth Chapter, anyone who understands the transcendental activities, the appearance and the disappearance of the Supreme Personality of Godhead is to be considered liberated. Brahmā, therefore, is a liberated soul. Although he is in charge of this material world, he is not exactly like the common living entity. Since he is liberated from the majority of the follies of the common living entities, he was in knowledge of the appearance of the Supreme Personality of Godhead, and he therefore worshiped the Lord's activities, and with a glad heart he also praised Kardama Muni because the Supreme Personality of Godhead, as Kapila, had appeared as his son. One who can become the father of the Supreme Personality of Godhead is certainly a great devotee. There is a verse spoken by a *brāhmaṇa* in which he says that he does not know what the *Vedas* and what the *Purāṇas* are, but while others might be interested in the *Vedas* or *Purāṇas*, he is interested in Nanda Mahārāja, who appeared as the father of Kṛṣṇa. The *brāhmaṇa* wanted to worship Nanda Mahārāja because the Supreme Personality of Godhead, as a child, crawled in the yard of his house. These are some of the good sentiments of devotees. If a recognized devotee brings forth the Supreme Personality of Godhead as his son, how he should be praised! Brahmā, therefore, not only worshiped the incarnation of Godhead Kapila but also praised His so-called father, Kardama Muni.

TEXT 12

ब्रह्मोवाच
त्वया मेऽपचितिस्तात कल्पिता निर्व्यलीकतः ।
यन्मे सञ्जगृहे वाक्यं भवान्मानद मानयन् ॥१२॥

brahmovāca
tvayā me 'pacitis tāta
kalpitā nirvyalīkataḥ
yan me sañjagṛhe vākyaṁ
bhavān mānada mānayan

brahmā—Lord Brahmā; *uvāca*—said; *tvayā*—by you; *me*—my; *apacitiḥ*—worship; *tāta*—O son; *kalpitā*—is accomplished; *nirvyalīkataḥ*—without duplicity; *yat*—since; *me*—my; *sañjagṛhe*—have completely accepted; *vākyam*—instructions; *bhavān*—you; *māna-da*—O Kardama (one who offers honor to others); *mānayan*—respecting.

TRANSLATION

Lord Brahmā said: My dear son Kardama, since you have completely accepted my instructions without duplicity, showing them proper respect, you have worshiped me properly. Whatever instructions you took from me you have carried out, and thereby you have honored me.

PURPORT

Lord Brahmā, as the first living entity within the universe, is supposed to be the spiritual master of everyone, and he is also the father, the creator, of all beings. Kardama Muni is one of the Prajāpatis, or creators of the living entities, and he is also a son of Brahmā. Brahmā praises Kardama because he carried out the orders of the spiritual master *in toto* and without cheating. A conditioned soul in the material world has the disqualification of cheating. He has four disqualifications: he is sure to commit mistakes, he is sure to be illusioned, he is prone to cheat others, and his senses are imperfect. But if one carries out the order of the spiritual master by disciplic succession, or the *paramparā* system, he overcomes the four defects. Therefore, knowledge received from the bona fide spiritual master is not cheating. Any other knowledge which is manufactured by the conditioned soul is cheating only. Brahmā knew well that Kardama Muni exactly carried out the instructions received from him and that he actually honored his spiritual master. To honor the spiritual master means to carry out his instructions word for word.

TEXT 13

एतावत्येव शुश्रूषा कार्या पितरि पुत्रकैः ।
बाढमित्यनुमन्येत गौरवेण गुरोर्वचः ॥१३॥

etāvaty eva śuśrūṣā
kāryā pitari putrakaiḥ
bāḍham ity anumanyeta
gauraveṇa guror vacaḥ

etāvatī—to this extent; *eva*—exactly; *śuśrūṣā*—service; *kāryā*—ought to be rendered; *pitari*—to the father; *putrakaiḥ*—by the sons; *bāḍham iti*—accepting, "Yes, sir"; *anumanyeta*—he should obey; *gauraveṇa*—with due deference; *guroḥ*—of the *guru*; *vacaḥ*—commands.

TRANSLATION

Sons ought to render service to their father exactly to this extent. One should obey the command of his father or spiritual master with due deference, saying, "Yes, sir."

PURPORT

Two words in this verse are very important; one word is *pitari*, and another word is *guroḥ*. The son or disciple should accept the words of his spiritual master and father without hesitation. Whatever the father and the spiritual master order should be taken without argument: "Yes." There should be no instance in which the disciple or the son says, "This is not correct. I cannot carry it out." When he says that, he is fallen. The father and the spiritual master are on the same platform because a spiritual master is the second father. The higher classes are called *dvija*, twice-born. Whenever there is a question of birth, there must be a father. The first birth is made possible by the actual father, and the second birth is made possible by the spiritual master. Sometimes the father and the spiritual master may be the same man, and sometimes they are different men. In any case, the order of the father or the order of the spiritual master must be carried out without hesitation, with an immediate yes. There should be no argument. That is real service to the father and to the spiritual master. Viśvanātha Cakravartī Ṭhākura has stated that the order of the spiritual master is the life and soul of the disciples. As a man cannot separate his life from his body, a disciple cannot separate the order of the spiritual master from his life. If a disciple follows the instruction of the spiritual master in that way, he is sure to become perfect. This is confirmed in the *Upaniṣads:* the import of Vedic instruction is revealed automatically only to one who has implicit faith in the Supreme Personality of Godhead and in his spiritual master. One may be materially considered an illiterate man, but if he has faith in the spiritual master as well as in the Supreme Personality of Godhead, then the meaning of scriptural revelation is immediately manifested before him.

TEXT 14

इमा दुहितरः सत्यस्तव वत्स सुमध्यमाः ।
सर्गमेतं प्रभावैः स्वैर्बृंहयिष्यन्त्यनेकधा ॥१४॥

imā duhitaraḥ satyas
tava vatsa sumadhyamāḥ
sargam etaṁ prabhāvaiḥ svair
bṛṁhayiṣyanty anekadhā

imāḥ—these; *duhitaraḥ*—daughters; *satyaḥ*—chaste; *tava*—your; *vatsa*—O my dear son; *sumadhyamāḥ*—thin-waisted; *sargam*—creation; *etam*—this; *prabhāvaiḥ*—by descendants; *svaiḥ*—their own; *bṛṁhayiṣyanti*—they will increase; *aneka-dhā*—in various ways.

TRANSLATION

Lord Brahmā then praised Kardama Muni's nine daughters, saying: All your thin-waisted daughters are certainly very chaste. I am sure they will increase this creation by their own descendants in various ways.

PURPORT

In the beginning of creation, Brahmā was concerned more or less with increasing the population, and when he saw that Kardama Muni had already begotten nine nice daughters, he was hopeful that through the daughters many children would come who would take charge of the creative principle of the material world. He was therefore happy to see them. The word *sumadhyamā* means "a good daughter of a beautiful woman." If she has a thin waist, a woman is considered very beautiful. All the daughters of Kardama Muni were of the same beautiful feature.

TEXT 15

अतस्त्वमृषिमुख्येभ्यो यथाशीलं यथारुचि ।
आत्मजाः परिदेह्यद्य विस्तृणीहि यशो भुवि ॥१५॥

atas tvam ṛṣi-mukhyebhyo
yathā-śīlaṁ yathā-ruci
ātmajāḥ paridehy adya
vistṛṇīhi yaśo bhuvi

ataḥ—therefore; *tvam*—you; *ṛṣi-mukhyebhyaḥ*—unto the foremost sages; *yathā-śīlam*—according to temperament; *yathā-ruci*—according to taste; *ātma-jāḥ*—your daughters; *paridehi*—please give away; *adya*—today; *vistṛṇīhi*—spread; *yaśaḥ*—fame; *bhuvi*—over the universe.

TRANSLATION

Therefore, today please give away your daughters to the foremost of the sages, with due regard for the girls' temperaments and likings, and thereby spread your fame all over the universe.

PURPORT

The nine principal *ṛṣis,* or sages, are Marīci, Atri, Aṅgirā, Pulastya, Pulaha, Kratu, Bhṛgu, Vasiṣṭha and Atharvā. All these *ṛṣis* are most important, and Brahmā desired that the nine daughters already born of Kardama Muni be handed over to them. Here two words are used very significantly-*yathā-śīlam* and *yathā-ruci.* The daughters should be handed over to the respective *ṛṣis,* not blindly, but according to the combination of character and taste. That is the art of combining a man and woman. Man and woman should not be united simply on the consideration of sex life. There are many other considerations, especially character and taste. If the taste and character differ between the man and woman, their combination will be unhappy. Even about forty years ago, in Indian marriages, the taste and character of the boy and girl were first of all matched, and then they were allowed to marry. This was done under the direction of the respective parents. The parents used to astrologically determine the character and tastes of the boy and girl, and when they corresponded, the match was selected: "This girl and this boy are just suitable, and they should be married." Other considerations were less important. The same system was also advised in the beginning of the creation by Brahmā: "Your daughters should be handed over to the *ṛṣis* according to taste and character."

According to astrological calculation, a person is classified according to whether he belongs to the godly or demoniac quality. In that way the spouse was selected. A girl of godly quality should be handed over to a boy of godly quality. A girl of demoniac quality should be handed over to a boy of demoniac quality. Then they will be happy. But if the girl is demoniac and the boy is godly, then the combination is incompatible; they cannot be happy in such a marriage. At the present moment, because boys and girls are not married according to quality and character, most marriages are unhappy, and there is divorce.

It is foretold in the Twelfth Canto of the *Bhāgavatam* that in this age of Kali married life will be accepted on the consideration of sex only; when the boy and girl are pleased in sex, they get married, and when there is deficiency in sex, they separate. That is not actual marriage, but a combination of men and women like cats and dogs. Therefore, the children produced in the modern age are not exactly human beings. Human beings must be twice-born. A child is first born of a good father and mother, and then he is born again of the spiritual master and the *Vedas*. The first mother and father bring about his birth into the world; then the spiritual master and the *Vedas* become his second father and mother. According to the Vedic system of marriage for producing children, every man and woman was enlightened in spiritual knowledge, and at the time of their combination to produce a child, everything was scrutinizingly and scientifically done.

TEXT 16

वेदाहमाद्यं पुरुषमवतीर्णं स्वमायया ।
भूतानां शेवधिं देहं बिभ्राणं कपिलं मुने ॥१६॥

vedāham ādyaṁ puruṣam
avatīrṇaṁ sva-māyayā
bhūtānāṁ śevadhiṁ dehaṁ
bibhrāṇaṁ kapilaṁ mune

veda—know; *aham*—I; *ādyam*—the original; *puruṣam*—enjoyer; *avatīrṇam*—incarnated; *sva-māyayā*—by His own internal energy; *bhūtānām*—of all the living entities; *śevadhim*—the bestower of all desired, who is just like a vast treasure; *deham*—the body; *bibhrāṇam*—assuming; *kapilam*—Kapila Muni; *mune*—O sage Kardama.

TRANSLATION

O Kardama, I know that the original Supreme Personality of Godhead has now appeared as an incarnation by His internal energy. He is the bestower of

all desired by the living entities, and He has now assumed the body of Kapila Muni.

PURPORT

In this verse we find the words *puruṣam avatīrṇaṁ sva-māyayā.* The Supreme Personality of Godhead is everlastingly, eternally the form of *puruṣa,* the predominator or enjoyer, and when He appears He never accepts anything of this material energy. The spiritual world is a manifestation of His personal, internal potency, whereas the material world is a manifestation of His material, or differentiated, energy. The word *sva-māyayā,* "by His own internal potency," indicates that whenever the Supreme Personality of Godhead descends, He comes in His own energy. He may assume the body of a human being, but that body is not material. In *Bhagavad-gītā,* therefore, it is clearly stated that only fools and rascals, *mūḍhas,* consider the body of Kṛṣṇa to be the body of a common human being. The word *śevadhim* means that He is the original bestower of all the necessities of life upon the living entities. In the *Vedas* also it is stated that He is the chief living entity and that He bestows all the desired necessities of other living entities. Because He is the bestower of the necessities of all others, He is called God. The Supreme is also a living entity; He is not impersonal. As we are individual, the Supreme Personality of Godhead is also individual—but He is the supreme individual. That is the difference between God and the ordinary living entities.

TEXT 17

ज्ञानविज्ञानयोगेन कर्मणामुद्धरन् जटाः ।
हिरण्यकेशः पद्माक्षः पद्ममुद्रापदाम्बुजः ॥१७॥

jñāna-vijñāna-yogena
karmaṇām uddharan jaṭāḥ
hiraṇya-keśaḥ padmākṣaḥ
padma-mudrā-padāmbujaḥ

jñāna—of scriptural knowledge; *vijñāna*—and application; *yogena*—by means of mystic *yoga; karmaṇām*—of material actions; *uddharan*—uprooting; *jaṭāḥ*—the roots; *hiraṇya-keśaḥ*—golden hair; *padma-akṣaḥ*—lotus-eyed; *padma-mudrā*—marked with the sign of the lotus; *pada-ambujaḥ*—having lotus feet.

TRANSLATION

By mystic yoga and the practical application of knowledge from the scriptures, Kapila Muni, who is characterized by His golden hair, His eyes

just like lotus petals and His lotus feet, which bear the marks of lotus flowers, will uproot the deep-rooted desire for work in this material world.

PURPORT

In this verse the activities and bodily features of Kapila Muni are very nicely described. The activities of Kapila Muni are forecast herein: He will present the philosophy of Sāṅkhya in such a way that by studying His philosophy people will be able to uproot the deep-rooted desire for *karma*, fruitive activities. Everyone in this material world engages in achieving the fruits of his labor. A man tries to be happy by achieving the fruits of his own honest labor, but actually he becomes more and more entangled. One cannot get out of this entanglement unless he has perfect knowledge, or devotional service.

Those who are trying to get out of the entanglement by speculation are also doing their best, but in the Vedic scriptures we find that if one has taken to the devotional service of the Lord in Kṛṣṇa consciousness, he can very easily uproot the deep-rooted desire for fruitive activities. Sāṅkhya philosophy will be broadcast by Kapila Muni for that purpose. His bodily features are also described herein. *Jñāna* does not refer to ordinary research work. *Jñāna* entails receiving knowledge from the scriptures through the spiritual master by disciplic succession. In the modern age there is a tendency to do research by mental speculation and concoction. But the man who speculates forgets that he himself is subject to the four defects of nature: he is sure to commit mistakes, his senses are imperfect, he is sure to fall into illusion, and he is cheating. Unless one has perfect knowledge from disciplic succession, he simply puts forth some theories of his own creation; therefore he is cheating people. *Jñāna* means knowledge received through disciplic succession from the scriptures, and *vijñāna* means practical application of such knowledge. Kapila Muni's Sāṅkhya system of philosophy is based on *jñāna* and *vijñāna*.

TEXT 18

एष मानवि ते गर्भं प्रविष्टः कैटभार्दनः ।
अविद्यासंशयग्रन्थिं छित्त्वा गां विचरिष्यति ॥१८॥

eṣa mānavi te garbhaṁ
praviṣṭaḥ kaiṭabhārdanaḥ
avidyā-saṁśaya-granthiṁ
chittvā gāṁ vicariṣyati

eṣaḥ—the same Supreme Personality of Godhead; *mānavi*—O daughter of Manu; *te*—your; *garbham*—womb; *praviṣṭaḥ*—has entered; *kaiṭabha-ardanaḥ*—the killer of the demon Kaiṭabha; *avidyā*—of ignorance; *saṁśaya*—and of doubt; *granthim*—the knot; *chittvā*—cutting off; *gām*—the world; *vicariṣyati*—He will travel over.

TRANSLATION

Lord Brahmā then told Devahūti: My dear daughter of Manu, the same Supreme Personality of Godhead who killed the demon Kaiṭabha is now within your womb. He will cut off all the knots of your ignorance and doubt. Then He will travel all over the world.

PURPORT

Here the word *avidyā* is very significant. *Avidyā* means forgetfulness of one's identity. Every one of us is a spirit soul, but we have forgotten. We think, "I am this body." This is called *avidyā. Saṁśaya-granthi* means "doubtfulness." The knot of doubtfulness is tied when the soul identifies with the material world. That knot is also called *ahaṅkāra,* the junction of matter and spirit. By proper knowledge received from the scriptures in disciplic succession and by proper application of that knowledge, one can free himself from this binding combination of matter and spirit. Brahmā assures Devahūti that her son will enlighten her, and after enlightening her He will travel all over the world, distributing the system of Sāṅkhya philosophy.

The word *saṁśaya* means "doubtful knowledge." Speculative and pseudo yogic knowledge is all doubtful. At the present moment the so-called *yoga* system is prosecuted on the understanding that by agitation of the different stations of the bodily construction one can find that he is God. The mental speculators think similarly, but they are all doubtful. Real knowledge is expounded in *Bhagavad-gītā:* "Just become Kṛṣṇa conscious. Just worship Kṛṣṇa and become a devotee of Kṛṣṇa." That is real knowledge, and anyone who follows that system becomes perfect without a doubt.

TEXT 19

अयं सिद्धगणाधीशः सांख्याचार्यैः सुसम्मतः ।
लोके कपिल इत्याख्यां गन्ता ते कीर्तिवर्धनः ॥१९॥

ayaṁ siddha-gaṇādhīśaḥ
sāṅkhyācāryaiḥ susammataḥ

loke kapila ity ākhyāṁ
gantā te kīrti-vardhanaḥ

ayam—this Personality of Godhead; *siddha-gaṇa*—of the perfected sages; *adhīśaḥ*—the head; *sāṅkhya-ācāryaiḥ*—by *ācāryas* expert in Sāṅkhya philosophy; *su-sammataḥ*—approved according to Vedic principles; *loke*—in the world; *kapilaḥ iti*—as Kapila; *ākhyām*—celebrated; *gantā*—He will go about; *te*—your; *kīrti*—fame; *vardhanaḥ*—increasing.

TRANSLATION

Your son will be the head of all the perfected souls. He will be approved by the ācāryas expert in disseminating real knowledge, and among the people He will be celebrated by the name Kapila. As the son of Devahūti, He will increase your fame.

PURPORT

Sāṅkhya philosophy is the philosophical system enunciated by Kapila, the son of Devahūti. The other Kapila, who is not the son of Devahūti, is an imitation. This is the statement of Brahmā, and because we belong to Brahmā's disciplic succession we should accept his statement that the real Kapila is the son of Devahūti and that real Sāṅkhya philosophy is the system of philosophy which He introduced and which will be accepted by the *ācāryas*, the directors of spiritual discipline. The word *susammata* means "accepted by persons who are counted upon to give their good opinion."

TEXT 20

मैत्रेय उवाच
तावाश्वास्य जगत्स्रष्टा कुमारैः सहनारदः ।
हंसो हंसेन यानेन त्रिधामपरमं ययौ ॥२०॥

maitreya uvāca
tāv āśvāsya jagat-sraṣṭā
kumāraiḥ saha-nāradaḥ
haṁso haṁsena yānena
tri-dhāma-paramaṁ yayau

maitreyaḥ uvāca—Maitreya said; *tau*—the couple; *āśvāsya*—having reassured; *jagat-sraṣṭā*—the creator of the universe; *kumāraiḥ*—along with the Kumāras; *saha-nāradaḥ*—with Nārada; *haṁsaḥ*—Lord Brahmā; *haṁsena yānena*—by his swan carrier; *tri-dhāma-paramam*—to the highest planetary system; *yayau*—went.

TRANSLATION

Śrī Maitreya said: After thus speaking to Kardama Muni and his wife Devahūti, Lord Brahmā, the creator of the universe, who is also known as Haṁsa, went back to the highest of the three planetary systems on his swan carrier with the four Kumāras and Nārada.

PURPORT

The words *haṁsena yānena* are very significant here. *Haṁsa-yāna,* the airplane by which Brahmā travels all over outer space, resembles a swan. Brahmā is also known as Haṁsa because he can grasp the essence of everything. His abode is called *tri-dhāma-paramam.* There are three divisions of the universe—the upper planetary system, the middle planetary system and the lower planetary system—but his abode is above even Siddhaloka, the upper planetary system. He returned to his own planet with the four Kumāras and Nārada because they were not going to be married. The other *ṛṣis* who came with him, such as Marīci and Atri, remained there because they were to be married to the daughters of Kardama, but his other sons—Sanat, Sanaka, Sanandana, Sanātana and Nārada—went back with him in his swan-shaped airplane. The four Kumāras and Nārada are *naiṣṭhika-brahmacārīs. Naiṣṭhika-brahmacārī* refers to one who never wastes his semen at any time. They were not to attend the marriage ceremony of their other brothers, Marīci and the other sages, and therefore they went back with their father, Haṁsa.

TEXT 21

गते शतधृतौ क्षत्तः कर्दमस्तेन चोदितः ।
यथोदितं स्वदुहितॄः प्रादाद्विश्वसृजां ततः ॥२१॥

gate śata-dhṛtau kṣattaḥ
kardamas tena coditaḥ
yathoditaṁ sva-duhitṝḥ
prādād viśva-sṛjāṁ tataḥ

gate—after he departed; *śata-dhṛtau*—Lord Brahmā; *kṣattaḥ*—O Vidura; *kardamaḥ*—Kardama Muni; *tena*—by him; *coditaḥ*—ordered; *yathā-uditam*—as told; *sva-duhitṝḥ*—his own daughters; *prādāt*—handed over; *viśva-sṛjām*—to the creators of the world's population; *tataḥ*—thereafter.

TRANSLATION

O Vidura, after the departure of Brahmā, Kardama Muni, having been ordered by Brahmā, handed over his nine daughters, as instructed, to the nine great sages who created the population of the world.

TEXTS 22-23

मरीचये कलां प्रादादनसूयामथात्रये ।
श्रद्धामङ्गिरसेऽयच्छत्पुलस्त्याय हविर्भुवम् ॥२२॥
पुलहाय गतिं युक्तां क्रतवे च क्रियां सतीम् ।
ख्यातिं च भृगवेऽयच्छद्वसिष्ठायाप्यरुन्धतीम् ॥२३॥

marīcaye kalāṁ prādād
anasūyām athātraye
śraddhām aṅgirase 'yacchat
pulastyāya havirbhuvam
pulahāya gatiṁ yuktām
kratave ca kriyāṁ satīm
khyātiṁ ca bhṛgave 'yacchad
vasiṣṭhāyāpy arundhatīm

marīcaye—unto Marīci; *kalām*—Kalā; *prādāt*—he handed over; *anasūyām*—Anasūyā; *atha*—then; *atraye*—unto Atri; *śraddhām*—Śraddhā; *aṅgirase*—unto Aṅgirā; *ayacchat*—he gave away; *pulastyāya*—unto Pulastya; *havirbhuvam*—Havirbhū; *pulahāya*—unto Pulaha; *gatim*—Gati; *yuktām*—suitable; *kratave*—unto Kratu; *ca*—and; *kriyām*—Kriyā; *satīm*—virtuous; *khyātim*—Khyāti; *ca*—and; *bhṛgave*—unto Bhṛgu; *ayacchat*—he gave away; *vasiṣṭhāya*—unto the sage Vasiṣṭha; *api*—also; *arundhatīm*—Arundhatī.

TRANSLATION

Kardama Muni handed over his daughter Kalā to Marīci, and another daughter, Anasūyā, to Atri. He delivered Śraddhā to Aṅgirā, and Havirbhū to Pulastya. He delivered Gati to Pulaha, the chaste Kriyā to Kratu, Khyāti to Bhṛgu, and Arundhatī to Vasiṣṭha.

TEXT 24

अथर्वणेऽददाच्छान्तिं यया यज्ञो वितन्यते ।
विप्रर्षभान् कृतोद्वाहान् सदारान् समलालयत् ॥२४॥

atharvaṇe 'dadāc chāntiṁ
yayā yajño vitanyate
viprarṣabhān kṛtodvāhān
sadārān samalālayat

atharvaṇe—to Atharvā; *adadāt*—he gave away; *śāntim*—Śānti; *yayā*—by whom; *yajñaḥ*—sacrifice; *vitanyate*—is performed; *vipra-ṛṣabhān*—the foremost *brāhmaṇas; kṛta-udvāhān*—married; *sa-dārān*—with their wives; *samalālayat*—maintained them.

TRANSLATION

He delivered Śānti to Atharvā. Because of Śānti, sacrificial ceremonies are well performed. Thus he got the foremost brāhmaṇas married, and he maintained them along with their wives.

TEXT 25

ततस्त ऋषयः क्षत्तः कृतदारा निमन्त्र्य तम् ।
प्रातिष्ठन्नन्दिमापन्नाः स्वं स्वमाश्रममण्डलम् ॥२५॥

tatas ta ṛṣayaḥ kṣattaḥ
kṛta-dārā nimantrya tam
prātiṣṭhan nandim āpannāḥ
svaṁ svam āśrama-maṇḍalam

tataḥ—then; *te*—they; *ṛṣayaḥ*—the sages; *kṣattaḥ*—O Vidura; *kṛta-dārāḥ*—thus married; *nimantrya*—taking leave of; *tam*—Kardama; *prātiṣṭhan*—they departed; *nandim*—joy; *āpannāḥ*—obtained; *svam svam*—each to his own; *āśrama-maṇḍalam*—hermitage.

TRANSLATION

Thus married, the sages took leave of Kardama and departed full of joy, each for his own hermitage, O Vidura.

TEXT 26

स चावतीर्णं त्रियुगमाज्ञाय विबुधर्षभम् ।
विविक्त उपसङ्गम्य प्रणम्य समभाषत ॥२६॥

sa cāvatīrṇaṁ tri-yugam
ājñāya vibudharṣabham

vivikta upasaṅgamya
praṇamya samabhāṣata

saḥ—the sage Kardama; *ca*—and; *avatīrṇam*—descended; *tri-yugam*—Viṣṇu; *ājñāya*—having understood; *vibudha-ṛṣabham*—the chief of the demigods; *vivikte*—in a secluded place; *upasaṅgamya*—having approached; *praṇamya*—offering obeisances; *samabhāṣata*—he spoke.

TRANSLATION

When Kardama Muni understood that the Supreme Personality of Godhead, the chief of all the demigods, Viṣṇu, had descended, Kardama approached Him in a secluded place, offered obeisances and spoke as follows.

PURPORT

Lord Viṣṇu is called *tri-yuga.* He appears in three *yugas*-Satya, Tretā and Dvāpara—but in Kali-yuga He does not appear. From the prayers of Prahlāda Mahārāja, however, we understand that He appears garbed as a devotee in Kali-yuga. Lord Caitanya is that devotee. Kṛṣṇa appeared in the form of a devotee, but although He never disclosed Himself, Rūpa Gosvāmī could understand His identity, for the Lord cannot hide Himself from a pure devotee. Rūpa Gosvāmī detected Him when he offered his first obeisances to Lord Caitanya. He knew that Lord Caitanya was Kṛṣṇa Himself and therefore offered his obeisances with the following words: "I offer my respects to Kṛṣṇa, who has now appeared as Lord Caitanya." This is also confirmed in the prayers of Prahlāda Mahārāja: in Kali-yuga He does not directly appear, but He appears as a devotee. Viṣṇu, therefore, is known as *tri-yuga.* Another explanation of *tri-yuga* is that He has three pairs of divine attributes, namely power and affluence, piety and renown, and wisdom and dispassion. According to Śrīdhara Svāmī, His three pairs of opulences are complete riches and complete strength, complete fame and complete beauty, and complete wisdom and complete renunciation. There are different interpretations of *tri-yuga,* but it is accepted by all learned scholars that *tri-yuga* means Viṣṇu. When Kardama Muni understood that his son, Kapila, was Viṣṇu Himself, he wanted to offer his obeisances. Therefore, when Kapila was alone he offered his respects and expressed his mind as follows.

TEXT 27

अहो पापच्यमानानां निरये स्वैरमङ्गलैः ।
कालेन भूयसा नूनं प्रसीदन्तीह देवताः ॥२७॥

aho pāpacyamānānāṁ
niraye svair amaṅgalaiḥ
kālena bhūyasā nūnaṁ
prasīdantīha devatāḥ

aho—oh; *pāpacyamānānām*—with those being much afflicted; *niraye*—in the hellish material entanglement; *svaiḥ*—their own; *amaṅgalaiḥ*—by misdeeds; *kālena bhūyasā*—after a long time; *nūnam*—indeed; *prasīdanti*—they are pleased; *iha*—in this world; *devatāḥ*—the demigods.

TRANSLATION

Kardama Muni said: Oh, after a long time the demigods of this universe have become pleased with the suffering souls who are in material entanglement because of their own misdeeds.

PURPORT

This material world is a place for suffering, which is due to the misdeeds of the inhabitants, the conditioned souls themselves. The sufferings are not extraneously imposed upon them; rather, the conditioned souls create their own suffering by their own acts. In the forest, fire takes place automatically. It is not that someone has to go there and set a fire; because of friction among various trees, fire occurs automatically. When there is too much heat from the forest fire of this material world, the demigods, including Brahmā himself, being harassed, approach the Supreme Lord, the Supreme Personality of Godhead, and appeal to Him to alleviate the condition. Then the Supreme Personality of Godhead descends. In other words, when the demigods become distressed by the sufferings of the conditioned souls, they approach the Lord to remedy the suffering, and the Personality of Godhead descends. When the Lord descends, all the demigods become enlivened. Therefore Kardama Muni said, "After many, many years of human suffering, all the demigods are now satisfied because Kapiladeva, the incarnation of Godhead, has appeared."

TEXT 28

बहुजन्मविपक्वेन सम्यग्योगसमाधिना ।
द्रष्टुं यतन्ते यतयः शून्यागारेषु यत्पदम् ॥२८॥

bahu-janma-vipakvena
samyag-yoga-samādhinā
draṣṭuṁ yatante yatayaḥ
śūnyāgāreṣu yat-padam

bahu—many; *janma*—after births; *vipakvena*—which is mature; *samyak*—perfect; *yoga-samādhinā*—by trance in *yoga; draṣṭum*—to see; *yatante*—they endeavor; *yatayaḥ*—the *yogīs; śūnya-agāreṣu*—in secluded places; *yat*—whose; *padam*—feet.

TRANSLATION

After many births, mature yogīs, by complete trance in yoga, endeavor in secluded places to see the lotus feet of the Supreme Personality of Godhead.

PURPORT

Some important things are mentioned here about *yoga.* The word *bahu janma-vipakvena* means "after many, many births of mature *yoga* practice." And another word, *samyag-yoga-samādhinā,* means "by complete practice of the *yoga* system." Complete practice of *yoga* means *bhakti-yoga;* unless one comes to the point of *bhakti-yoga,* or surrender unto the Supreme Personality of Godhead, one's *yoga* practice is not complete. This same point is corroborated in the *Śrīmad Bhagavad-gītā. Bahūnāṁ janmanām ante:* after many, many births, the *jñānī* who has matured in transcendental knowledge surrenders unto the Supreme Personality of Godhead. Kardama Muni repeats the same statement. After many, many years and many, many births of complete practice of *yoga,* one can see the lotus feet of the Supreme Lord in a secluded place. It is not that after one practices some sitting postures he immediately becomes perfect. One has to perform *yoga* a long time—"many, many births"—to become mature, and a *yogī* has to practice in a secluded place. One cannot practice *yoga* in a city or in a public park and declare that he has become God simply by some exchange of dollars. This is all bogus propaganda. Those who are actually *yogīs* practice in a secluded place, and after many, many births they become successful, provided they surrender unto the Supreme Personality of Godhead. This is the completion of *yoga.*

TEXT 29

स एव भगवानद्य हेलनं नगणय्य नः ।
गृहेषु जातो ग्राम्याणां यः स्वानां पक्षपोषणः ॥२९॥

sa eva bhagavān adya
helanaṁ na gaṇayya naḥ
gṛheṣu jāto grāmyāṇām
yaḥ svānāṁ pakṣa-poṣaṇaḥ

saḥ eva—that very same; *bhagavān*—Supreme Personality of Godhead; *adya*—today; *helanam*—negligence; *na*—not; *gaṇayya*—considering high and low; *naḥ*—our; *gṛheṣu*—in the houses; *jātaḥ*—appeared; *grāmyāṇām*—of ordinary householders; *yaḥ*—He who; *svānām*—of His own devotees; *pakṣa-poṣaṇaḥ*—who supports the party.

TRANSLATION

Not considering the negligence of ordinary householders like us, that very same Supreme Personality of Godhead appears in our homes just to support His devotees.

PURPORT

Devotees are so affectionate toward the Personality of Godhead that although He does not appear before those who practice *yoga* in a secluded place even for many, many births, He agrees to appear in a householder's home where devotees engage in devotional service without material *yoga* practice. In other words, devotional service to the Lord is so easy that even a householder can see the Supreme Personality of Godhead as one of the members of his household, as his son, as Kardama Muni experienced. He was a householder, although a *yogī*, but he had the incarnation of the Supreme Personality of Godhead Kapila Muni as his son.

Devotional service is such a powerful transcendental method that it surpasses all other methods of transcendental realization. The Lord says, therefore, that He lives neither in Vaikuṇṭha nor in the heart of a *yogī*, but He lives where His pure devotees are always chanting and glorifying Him. The Supreme Personality of Godhead is known as *bhakta-vatsala.* He is never described as *jñānī-vatsala* or *yogī-vatsala.* He is always described as *bhakta-vatsala* because He is more inclined toward His devotees than toward other transcendentalists. In *Bhagavad-gītā* it is confirmed that only a devotee can understand Him as He is. *Bhaktyā mām abhijānāti:* "One can understand Me only by devotional service, not otherwise." That understanding alone is real because although *jñānīs,* mental speculators, can realize only the effulgence, or the bodily luster, of the Supreme Personality of Godhead, and *yogīs* can realize only the partial representation of the Supreme Personality of Godhead, a *bhakta* not only realizes Him as He is but also associates with the Personality of Godhead face to face.

TEXT 30

स्वीयं वाक्यमृतं कर्तुमवतीर्णोऽसि मे गृहे ।
चिकीर्षुर्भगवान् ज्ञानं भक्तानां मानवर्धनः ॥३०॥

svīyaṁ vākyam ṛtaṁ kartum
avatīrṇo 'si me gṛhe
cikīrṣur bhagavān jñānaṁ
bhaktānāṁ māna-vardhanaḥ

svīyam—Your own; *vākyam*—words; *ṛtam*—true; *kartum*—to make; *avatīrṇaḥ*—descended; *asi*—You are; *me gṛhe*—in my house; *cikīrṣuḥ*—desirous of disseminating; *bhagavān*—the Personality of Godhead; *jñānam*—knowledge; *bhaktānām*—of the devotees; *māna*—the honor; *vardhanaḥ*—who increases.

TRANSLATION

Kardama Muni said: You, my dear Lord, who are always increasing the honor of Your devotees, have descended in my home just to fulfill Your word and disseminate the process of real knowledge.

PURPORT

When the Lord appeared before Kardama Muni after his mature *yoga* practice, He promised that He would become Kardama's son. He descended as the son of Kardama Muni in order to fulfill that promise. Another purpose of His appearance is *cikīrṣur bhagavān jñānam,* to distribute knowledge. Therefore, He is called *bhaktānāṁ māna-vardhanaḥ,* "He who increases the honor of His devotees." By distributing Sāṅkhya He would increase the honor of the devotees; therefore, Sāṅkhya philosophy is not dry mental speculation. Sāṅkhya philosophy means devotional service. How could the honor of the devotees be increased unless Sāṅkhya were meant for devotional service? Devotees are not interested in speculative knowledge; therefore, the Sāṅkhya enunciated by Kapila Muni is meant to establish one firmly in devotional service. Real knowledge and real liberation is to surrender unto the Supreme Personality of Godhead and engage in devotional service.

TEXT 31

तान्येव तेऽभिरूपाणि रूपाणि भगवंस्तव ।
यानि यानि च रोचन्ते स्वजनानामरूपिणः ॥३१॥

tāny eva te 'bhirūpāṇi
rūpāṇi bhagavaṁs tava
yāni yāni ca rocante
sva-janānām arūpiṇaḥ

tāni—those; *eva*—truly; *te*—Your; *abhirūpāṇi*—suitable; *rūpāṇi*—forms; *bhagavan*—O Lord; *tava*—Your; *yāni yāni*—whichever; *ca*—and; *rocante*—are pleasing; *sva-janānām*—to Your own devotees; *arūpiṇaḥ*—of one with no material form.

TRANSLATION

My dear Lord, although You have no material form, You have Your own innumerable forms. They truly are Your transcendental forms, which are pleasing to Your devotees.

PURPORT

In the *Brahma-saṁhitā* it is stated that the Lord is one Absolute, but He has *ananta,* or innumerable, forms. *Advaitam acyutam anādim ananta-rūpam.* The Lord is the original form, but still He has multiforms. Those multiforms are manifested by Him transcendentally, according to the tastes of His multidevotees. It is understood that once Hanumān, the great devotee of Lord Rāmacandra, said that he knew that Nārāyaṇa, the husband of Lakṣmī, and Rāma, the husband of Sītā, are one and the same, and that there is no difference between Lakṣmī and Sītā, but as for himself, he liked the form of Lord Rāma. In a similar way, some devotees worship the original form of Kṛṣṇa. When we say "Kṛṣṇa" we refer to all forms of the Lord—not only Kṛṣṇa, but Rāma, Nṛsiṁha, Varāha, Nārāyaṇa, etc. The varieties of transcendental forms exist simultaneously. That is also stated in the *Brahma-saṁhitā: rāmādi-mūrtiṣu. .. nānāvatāram.* He already exists in multiforms, but none of the forms are material. Śrīdhara Svāmī has commented that *arūpiṇaḥ,* "without form," means without material form. The Lord has form, otherwise how can it be stated here, *tāny eva te 'bhirūpāṇi rūpāṇi bhagavaṁs tava:* "You have Your forms, but they are not material. Materially You have no form, but spiritually, transcendentally, You have multiforms"? Māyāvādī philosophers cannot understand these transcendental forms of the Lord, and being disappointed, they say that the Supreme Lord is impersonal. But that is not a fact; whenever there is form there is a person. Many times in many Vedic literatures the Lord is described as *puruṣa,* which means "the original form, the original enjoyer." The conclusion is that the Lord has no material form, and yet, according to the liking of different grades of devotees, He simultaneously exists in multiforms, such as Rāma, Nṛsiṁha, Varāha, Nārāyaṇa and Mukunda. There are many thousands and thousands of forms, but they are all *viṣṇu-tattva,* Kṛṣṇa.

TEXT 32

त्वां सूरिभिस्तत्त्वबुभुत्सयाद्धा
सदाभिवादार्हणपादपीठम् ।
ऐश्वर्यवैराग्ययशोऽवबोध-
वीर्यश्रिया पूर्तमहं प्रपद्ये ॥३२॥

tvāṁ sūribhis tattva-bubhutsayāddhā
sadābhivādārhaṇa-pāda-pīṭham
aiśvarya-vairāgya-yaśo-'vabodha-
vīrya-śriyā pūrtam ahaṁ prapadye

tvām—unto You; *sūribhiḥ*—by the great sages; *tattva*—the Absolute Truth; *bubhutsayā*—with a desire to understand; *addhā*—certainly; *sadā*—always; *abhivāda*—of worshipful respects; *arhaṇa*—which are worthy; *pāda*—of Your feet; *pīṭham*—to the seat; *aiśvarya*—opulence; *vairāgya*—renunciation; *yaśaḥ*—fame; *avabodha*—knowledge; *vīrya*—strength; *śriyā*—with beauty; *pūrtam*—who are full; *aham*—I; *prapadye*—surrender.

TRANSLATION

My dear Lord, Your lotus feet are the reservoir that always deserves to receive worshipful homage from all great sages eager to understand the Absolute Truth. You are full in opulence, renunciation, transcendental fame, knowledge, strength and beauty, and therefore I surrender myself unto Your lotus feet.

PURPORT

Actually, those who are searching after the Absolute Truth must take shelter of the lotus feet of the Supreme Personality of Godhead and worship Him. In *Bhagavad-gītā* Lord Kṛṣṇa advised Arjuna many times to surrender unto Him, especially at the end of the Ninth Chapter—*man-manā bhava mad-bhaktaḥ*: "If you want to be perfect, just always think of Me, become My devotee, worship Me and offer your obeisances to Me. In this way you will understand Me, the Personality of Godhead, and ultimately you will come back to Me, back to Godhead, back home." Why is it so? The Lord is always full in six opulences, as mentioned herein: wealth, renunciation, fame, knowledge, strength and beauty. The word *pūrtam* means "in full." No one can claim that all wealth belongs to him, but Kṛṣṇa can claim it, since He has full wealth. Similarly, He is full in knowledge, renunciation, strength and beauty. He is full in everything, and no one can surpass Him. Another one of Kṛṣṇa's names is *asamaurdhva,* which means that no one is equal to or greater than Him.

TEXT 33

परं प्रधानं पुरुषं महान्तं
कालं कविं त्रिवृतं लोकपालम् ।
आत्मानुभूत्यानुगतप्रपञ्चं
स्वच्छन्दशक्तिं कपिलं प्रपद्ये ॥३३॥

paraṁ pradhānaṁ puruṣaṁ mahāntaṁ
kālaṁ kaviṁ tri-vṛtaṁ loka-pālam
ātmānubhūtyānugata-prapañcaṁ
svacchanda-śaktiṁ kapilaṁ prapadye

param—transcendental; *pradhānam*—supreme; *puruṣam*—person; *mahāntam*—who is the origin of the material world; *kālam*—who is time; *kavim*—fully cognizant; *tri-vṛtam*—three modes of material nature; *loka-pālam*—who is the maintainer of all the universes; *ātma*—in Himself; *anubhūtya*—by internal potency; *anugata*—dissolved; *prapañcam*—whose material manifestations; *sva-chanda*—independently; *śaktim*—who is powerful; *kapilam*—to Lord Kapila; *prapadye*—I surrender.

TRANSLATION

I surrender unto the Supreme Personality of Godhead, descended in the form of Kapila, who is independently powerful and transcendental, who is the Supreme Person and the Lord of the sum total of matter and the element of time, who is the fully cognizant maintainer of all the universes under the three modes of material nature, and who absorbs the material manifestations after their dissolution.

PURPORT

The six opulences—wealth, strength, fame, beauty, knowledge and renunciation—are indicated here by Kardama Muni, who addresses Kapila Muni, his son, as *param.* The word *param* is used in the beginning of *Śrīmad-Bhāgavatam,* in the phrase *paraṁ satyam,* to refer to the *summum bonum,* or the Supreme Personality of Godhead. *Param* is explained further by the next word, *pradhānam,* which means the chief, the origin, the source of everything—*sarva-kāraṇa-kāraṇam*—the cause of all causes. The Supreme Personality of Godhead is not formless; He is *puruṣam,* or the enjoyer, the original person. He is the time element and is all-cognizant. He knows everything—

past, present and future—as confirmed in *Bhagavad-gītā.* The Lord says, "I know everything—present, past and future—in every corner of the universe." The material world, which is moving under the spell of the three modes of nature, is also a manifestation of His energy. *Parāsya śaktir vividhaiva śrūyate:* everything that we see is an interaction of His energies (*Śvetāśvatara Up.* 6.8). *Parasya brahmaṇaḥ śaktis tathedam akhilaṁ jagat.* This is the version of the *Viṣṇu Purāṇa.* We can understand that whatever we see is an interaction of the three modes of material nature, but actually it is all an interaction of the Lord's energy. *Loka-pālam:* He is actually the maintainer of all living entities. *Nityo nityānām:* He is the chief of all living entities; He is one, but He maintains many, many living entities. God maintains all other living entities, but no one can maintain God. That is His *svacchanda-śakti;* He is not dependent on others. Someone may call himself independent, but he is still dependent on someone higher. The Personality of Godhead, however, is absolute; there is no one higher than or equal to Him.

Kapila Muni appeared as the son of Kardama Muni, but because Kapila is an incarnation of the Supreme Personality of Godhead, Kardama Muni offered respectful obeisances unto Him with full surrender. Another word in this verse is very important: *ātmānubhūtyānugata-prapañcam.* The Lord descends either as Kapila or Rāma, Nṛsiṁha or Varāha, and whatever forms He assumes in the material world are all manifestations of His own personal internal energy. They are never forms of the material energy. The ordinary living entities who are manifested in this material world have bodies created by the material energy, but when Kṛṣṇa or any one of His expansions or parts of the expansions descends on this material world, although He appears to have a material body, His body is not material. He always has a transcendental body. But fools and rascals, who are called *mūḍhas,* consider Him one of them, and therefore they deride Him. They refuse to accept Kṛṣṇa as the Supreme Personality of Godhead because they cannot understand Him. In *Bhagavad-gītā* Kṛṣṇa says, *avajānanti māṁ mūḍhāḥ:* "Those who are rascals and fools deride Me." When God descends in a form, this does not mean that He assumes His form with the help of the material energy. He manifests His spiritual form as He exists in His spiritual kingdom.

TEXT 34

आ स्माभिपृच्छेऽद्य पतिं प्रजानां
त्वयावतीर्णर्ण उतासकामः ।
परिव्रजत्पदवीमास्थितोऽहं
चरिष्ये त्वां हृदि युञ्जन् विशोकः ॥३४॥

ā smābhipṛcche 'dya patiṁ prajānāṁ
tvayāvatīrṇarṇa utāpta-kāmaḥ
parivrajat-padavīm āsthito 'haṁ
cariṣye tvāṁ hṛdi yuñjan viśokaḥ

ā sma abhipṛcche—I am inquiring; *adya*—now; *patim*—the Lord; *prajānām*—of all created beings; *tvayā*—by You; *avatīrṇa-ṛṇaḥ*—free from debts; *uta*—and; *āpta*—fulfilled; *kāmaḥ*—desires; *parivrajat*—of an itinerant mendicant; *padavīm*—the path; *āsthitaḥ*—accepting; *aham*—I; *cariṣye*—I shall wander; *tvām*—You; *hṛdi*—in my heart; *yuñjan*—keeping; *viśokaḥ*—free from lamentation.

TRANSLATION

Today I have something to ask from You, who are the Lord of all living entities. Since I have now been liberated by You from my debts to my father, and since all my desires are fulfilled, I wish to accept the order of an itinerant mendicant. Renouncing this family life, I wish to wander about, free from lamentation, thinking always of You in my heart.

PURPORT

Actually, *sannyāsa,* or renunciation of material household life, necessitates complete absorption in Kṛṣṇa consciousness and immersion in the self. One does not take *sannyāsa,* freedom from family responsibility in the renounced order of life, to make another family or to create an embarrassing transcendental fraud in the name of *sannyāsa.* The *sannyāsī's* business is not to become proprietor of so many things and amass money from the innocent public. A *sannyāsī* is proud that he is always thinking of Kṛṣṇa within himself. Of course, there are two kinds of devotees of the Lord. One is called *goṣṭhy-ānandī,* which means those who are preachers and have many followers for preaching the glories of the Lord and who live among those many, many followers just to organize missionary activities. Other devotees are *ātmānandī,* or self-satisfied, and do not take the risk of preaching work. They remain, therefore, alone with God. In this classification was Kardama Muni. He wanted to be free from all anxieties and remain alone within his heart with the Supreme Personality of Godhead. *Parivrāja* means "an itinerant mendicant." A mendicant *sannyāsī* should not live anywhere for more than three days. He must be always moving because his duty is to move from door to door and enlighten people about Kṛṣṇa consciousness.

TEXT 35

श्रीभगवानुवाच
मया प्रोक्तं हि लोकस्य प्रमाणं सत्यलौकिके ।
अथाजनि मया तुभ्यं यदवोचमृतं मुने ॥३५॥

śrī-bhagavān uvāca
mayā proktaṁ hi lokasya
pramāṇaṁ satya-laukike
athājani mayā tubhyaṁ
yad avocam ṛtaṁ mune

śrī-bhagavān uvāca—the Supreme Personality of Godhead said; *mayā*—by Me; *proktam*—spoken; *hi*—in fact; *lokasya*—for the people; *pramāṇam*—authority; *satya*—spoken in scripture; *laukike*—and in ordinary speech; *atha*—therefore; *ajani*—there was birth; *mayā*—by Me; *tubhyam*—to you; *yat*—that which; *avocam*—I said; *ṛtam*—true; *mune*—O sage.

TRANSLATION

The Personality of Godhead Kapila said: Whatever I speak, whether directly or in the scriptures, is authoritative in all respects for the people of the world. O Muni, because I told you before that I would become your son, I have descended to fulfill this truth.

PURPORT

Kardama Muni was to leave his family life to completely engage in the service of the Lord. But since he knew that the Lord Himself, as Kapila, had taken birth in his home as his own son, why was he preparing to leave home to search out self-realization or God realization? God Himself was present in his home—why should he leave home? Such a question may certainly arise. But here it is said that whatever is spoken in the *Vedas* and whatever is practiced in accordance with the injunctions of the *Vedas* is to be accepted as authoritative in society. Vedic authority says that a householder must leave home after his fiftieth year. *Pañcāśordhvaṁ vanaṁ vrajet:* one must leave his family life and enter the forest after the age of fifty. This is an authoritative statement of the *Vedas*, based on the division of social life into four departments of activity—*brahmacarya, gṛhastha, vānaprastha* and *sannyāsa.*

Kardama Muni practiced *yoga* very rigidly as a *brahmacārī* before his marriage, and he became so powerful and attained so much mystic power that his father, Brahmā, ordered him to marry and beget children as a householder. Kardama did that also; he begot nine good daughters and one son, Kapila Muni, and thus his householder duty was also performed nicely, and now his duty was to leave. Even though he had the Supreme Personality of Godhead as his son, he had to respect the authority of the *Vedas.* This is a very important lesson. Even if one has God in his home as his son, one should still follow the Vedic injunctions. It is stated, *mahājano yena gataḥ sa panthāḥ:* one should traverse the path which is followed by great personalities.

Kardama Muni's example is very instructive, for in spite of having the Supreme Personality of Godhead as his son, he left home just to obey the authority of the Vedic injunction. Kardama Muni states here the main purpose of his leaving home: while traveling all over the world as a mendicant, he would always remember the Supreme Personality of Godhead within his heart and thereby be freed from all the anxieties of material existence. In this age of Kali-yuga *sannyāsa* is prohibited because persons in this age are all *śūdras* and cannot follow the rules and regulations of *sannyāsa* life. It is very commonly found that so-called *sannyāsīs* are addicted to nonsense—even to having private relationships with women. This is the abominable situation in this age. Although they dress themselves as *sannyāsīs,* they still cannot free themselves from the four principles of sinful life, namely illicit sex life, meat-eating, intoxication and gambling. Since they are not freed from these four principles, they are cheating the public by posing as *svāmīs.*

In Kali-yuga the injunction is that no one should accept *sannyāsa.* Of course, those who actually follow the rules and regulations must take *sannyāsa.* Generally, however, people are unable to accept *sannyāsa* life, and therefore Caitanya Mahāprabhu stressed, *kalau nāsty eva nāsty eva na-sty eva gatir anyathā.* In this age there is no other alternative, no other alternative, no other alternative than to chant the holy name of the Lord: Hare Kṛṣṇa, Hare Kṛṣṇa, Kṛṣṇa Kṛṣṇa, Hare Hare. The main purpose of *sannyāsa* life is to be in constant companionship with the Supreme Lord, either by thinking of Him within the heart or hearing of Him through aural reception. In this age, hearing is more important than thinking because one's thinking may be disturbed by mental agitation, but if one concentrates on hearing, he will be forced to associate with the sound vibration of Kṛṣṇa. Kṛṣṇa and the sound vibration "Kṛṣṇa" are nondifferent, so if one loudly vibrates Hare Kṛṣṇa, he will be able to think of Kṛṣṇa immediately. This process of chanting is the best process of self-realization in this age; therefore Lord Caitanya preached it so nicely for the benefit of all humanity.

TEXT 36

एतन्मे जन्म लोकेऽस्मिन्मुमुक्षूणां दुराशयात् ।
प्रसंख्यानाय तत्त्वानां सम्मतायात्मदर्शने ॥३६॥

etan me janma loke 'smin
mumukṣūṇāṁ durāśayāt
prasaṅkhyānāya tattvānāṁ
sammatāyātma-darśane

etat—this; *me*—My; *janma*—birth; *loke*—in the world; *asmin*—in this; *mumukṣūṇām*—by those great sages seeking liberation; *durāśayāt*—from unnecessary material desires; *prasaṅkhyānāya*—for explaining; *tattvānām*—of the truths; *sammatāya*—which is highly esteemed; *ātma-darśane*—in self-realization.

TRANSLATION

My appearance in this world is especially to explain the philosophy of Sāṅkhya, which is highly esteemed for self-realization by those desiring freedom from the entanglement of unnecessary material desires.

PURPORT

Here the word *durāśayāt* is very significant. *Dur* refers to trouble or *duḥkha*, miseries. *Āśayāt* means "from the shelter." We conditioned souls have taken shelter of the material body, which is full of troubles and miseries. Foolish people cannot understand the situation, and this is called ignorance, illusion, or the spell of *māyā*. Human society should very seriously understand that the body itself is the source of all miserable life. Modern civilization is supposed to be making advancement in scientific knowledge, but what is this scientific knowledge? It is based on bodily comforts only, without knowledge that however comfortably one maintains his body, the body is destructible. As stated in *Bhagavad-gītā*, *antavanta ime dehāḥ:* these bodies are destined to be destroyed. *Nityasyoktāḥ śarīriṇaḥ* refers to the living soul, or the living spark, within the body. That soul is eternal, but the body is not eternal. For our activity we must have a body; without a body, without sense organs, there is no activity. But people are not inquiring whether it is possible to have an eternal body. Actually they aspire for an eternal body because even though they engage in sense enjoyment, that sense enjoyment is not eternal. They are therefore in want of something which they can enjoy eternally, but they do not understand how to attain that perfection. Sāṅkhya philosophy, therefore, as stated herein by Kapiladeva, is *tattvānām*. The Sāṅkhya philosophy system is designed to afford understanding of the real truth. What is that real truth? The real truth is knowledge of how to get out of the material body, which is the source of all trouble. Lord Kapila's incarnation, or descent, is especially meant for this purpose. That is clearly stated here.

TEXT 37

एष आत्मपथोऽव्यक्तो नष्टः कालेन भूयसा ।
तं प्रवर्तयितुं देहमिमं विद्धि मया भृतम् ॥३७॥

eṣa ātma-patho 'vyakto
naṣṭaḥ kālena bhūyasā
taṁ pravartayituṁ deham
imaṁ viddhi mayā bhṛtam

eṣaḥ—this; *ātma-pathaḥ*—path of self-realization; *avyaktaḥ*—difficult to be known; *naṣṭaḥ*—lost; *kālena bhūyasā*—in the course of time; *tam*—this; *pravartayitum*—to introduce again; *deham*—body; *imam*—this; *viddhi*—please know; *mayā*—by Me; *bhṛtam*—assumed.

TRANSLATION

This path of self-realization, which is difficult to understand, has now been lost in the course of time. Please know that I have assumed this body of Kapila to introduce and explain this philosophy to human society again.

PURPORT

It is not true that Sāṅkhya philosophy is a new system of philosophy introduced by Kapila as material philosophers introduce new kinds of mental speculative thought to supersede that of another philosopher. On the material platform, everyone, especially the mental speculator, tries to be more prominent than others. The field of activity of the speculators is the mind; there is no limit to the different ways in which one can agitate the mind. The mind can be unlimitedly agitated, and thus one can put forward an unlimited number of theories. Sāṅkhya philosophy is not like that; it is not mental speculation. It is factual, but at the time of Kapila it was lost.

In due course of time, a particular type of knowledge may be lost or may be covered for the time being; that is the nature of this material world. A similar statement was made by Lord Kṛṣṇa in *Bhagavad-gītā. Sa kāleneha mahatā yogo naṣṭaḥ:* "In course of time the *yoga* system as stated in *Bhagavad-gītā* was lost." It was coming in *paramparā*, in disciplic succession, but due to the passage of time it was lost. The time factor is so pressing that in the course of time everything within this material world is spoiled or lost. The *yoga* system of *Bhagavad-gītā* was lost before the meeting of Kṛṣṇa and Arjuna. Therefore Kṛṣṇa again enunciated the same ancient *yoga* system to Arjuna, who could actually understand *Bhagavad-gītā*. Similarly, Kapila also said that the system of Sāṅkhya philosophy was not exactly being introduced by Him; it was already current, but in course of time it was mysteriously lost, and therefore He appeared to reintroduce it. That is the purpose of the incarnation of Godhead. *Yadā yadā hi dharmasya glānir bhavati bhārata. Dharma* means the real occupation of the living entity. When there is a discrepancy in the eternal occupation of the living entity, the Lord comes and introduces the real occupation of life. Any so-called religious system that is not in the line of devotional service is called *adharma-saṁsthāpana.* When people forget their eternal relationship with God and engage in something other than devotional service, their engagement is called irreligion. How one can get out of the miserable condition of material life is stated in Sāṅkhya philosophy, and the Lord Himself is explaining this sublime system.

TEXT 38

गच्छ कामं मयापृष्टो मयि संन्यस्तकर्मणा ।
जित्वा सुदुर्जयं मृत्युममृतत्वाय मां भज ॥३८॥

gaccha kāmaṁ mayāpṛṣṭo
mayi sannyasta-karmaṇā
jitvā sudurjayaṁ mṛtyum
amṛtatvāya māṁ bhaja

gaccha—go; *kāmam*—as you wish; *mayā*—by Me; *āpṛṣṭaḥ*—sanctioned; *mayi*—to Me; *sannyasta*—completely surrendered; *karmaṇā*—with your activities; *jitvā*—having conquered; *sudurjayam*—insurmountable; *mṛtyum*—death; *amṛtatvāya*—for eternal life; *mām*—unto Me; *bhaja*—engage in devotional service.

TRANSLATION

Now, being sanctioned by Me, go as you desire, surrendering all your activities to Me. Conquering insurmountable death, worship Me for eternal life.

PURPORT

The purpose of Sāṅkhya philosophy is stated herein. If anyone wants real, eternal life, he has to engage himself in devotional service, or Kṛṣṇa consciousness. To become free from birth and death is not an easy task. Birth and death are natural to this material body. *Sudurjayam* means "very, very difficult to overcome." The modern so-called scientists do not have sufficient means to understand the process of victory over birth and death. Therefore, they set aside the question of birth and death; they do not consider it. They simply engage in the problems of the material body, which is transient and sure to end.

Actually, human life is meant for conquering the insurmountable process of birth and death. That can be done as stated here. *Māṁ bhaja:* one must engage in the devotional service of the Lord. In *Bhagavad-gītā* also the Lord says, *man-manā bhava mad-bhaktaḥ:* "Just become My devotee. Just worship Me." But foolish so-called scholars say that it is not Kṛṣṇa whom we must worship and to whom we must surrender; it is something else. Without Kṛṣṇa's mercy, therefore, no one can understand the Sāṅkhya philosophy or any philosophy which is especially meant for liberation. Vedic knowledge confirms that one becomes entangled in this material life because of ignorance and that one can become free from material embarrassment by becoming situated in factual knowledge. Sāṅkhya means that factual knowledge by which one can get out of the material entanglement.

TEXT 39

मामात्मानं स्वयंज्योतिः सर्वभूतगुहाशयम् ।
आत्मन्येवात्मना वीक्ष्य विशोकोऽभयमृच्छसि ॥३९॥

māṁ ātmānaṁ svayaṁ-jyotiḥ
sarva-bhūta-guhāśayam
ātmany evātmanā vīkṣya
viśoko 'bhayam ṛcchasi

mām—Me; *ātmānam*—the Supreme Soul, or Paramātmā; *svayam-jyotiḥ*—self-effulgent; *sarva-bhūta*—of all beings; *guhā*—in the hearts; *āśayam*—dwelling; *ātmani*—in your own heart; *eva*—indeed; *ātmanā*—through your intellect; *vīkṣya*—always seeing, always thinking; *viśokaḥ*—free from lamentation; *abhayam*—fearlessness; *ṛcchasi*—you will achieve.

TRANSLATION

In your own heart, through your intellect, you will always see Me, the supreme self-effulgent soul dwelling within the hearts of all living entities. Thus you will achieve the state of eternal life, free from all lamentation and fear.

PURPORT

People are very anxious to understand the Absolute Truth in various ways, especially by experiencing the *brahmajyotir,* or Brahman effulgence, by meditation and by mental speculation. But Kapiladeva uses the word *mām* to emphasize that the Personality of Godhead is the ultimate feature of the Absolute Truth. In *Bhagavad-gītā* the Personality of Godhead always says *mām*, "unto Me," but the rascals misinterpret the clear meaning. *Mām* is the Supreme Personality of Godhead. If one can see the Supreme Personality of Godhead as He appears in different incarnations and understand that He has not assumed a material body but is present in His own eternal, spiritual form, then one can understand the nature of the Personality of Godhead. Since the less intelligent cannot understand this point, it is stressed everywhere again and again. Simply by seeing the form of the Lord as He presents Himself by His own internal potency as Kṛṣṇa or Rāma or Kapila, one can directly see the *brahmajyotir*, because the *brahmajyotir* is no more than the effulgence of His bodily luster. Since the sunshine is the luster of the sun planet, by seeing the sun one automatically sees the sunshine; similarly, by seeing the Supreme Personality of Godhead one simultaneously sees and experiences the Paramātmā feature as well as the impersonal Brahman feature of the Supreme.

The *Bhāgavatam* has already enunciated that the Absolute Truth is present in three features—in the beginning as the impersonal Brahman, in the next stage as the Paramātmā in everyone's heart, and, at last, as the ultimate realization of the Absolute Truth, Bhagavān, the Supreme Personality of Godhead. One who sees the Supreme Person can automatically realize the other features, namely the Paramātmā and Brahman features of the Lord. The words used here are *viśoko 'bhayam ṛcchasi.* Simply by seeing the Personality of Godhead one realizes everything, and the result is that one becomes situated on the platform where there is no lamentation and no fear. This can be attained simply by devotional service to the Personality of Godhead.

TEXT 40

मात्र आध्यात्मिकीं विद्यां शमनीं सर्वकर्मणाम् ।
वितरिष्ये यया चासौ भयं चातितरिष्यति ॥४०॥

mātra ādhyātmikīṁ vidyāṁ
śamanīṁ sarva-karmaṇām
vitariṣye yayā cāsau
bhayaṁ cātitariṣyati

mātre—to My mother; *ādhyātmikīm*—which opens the door of spiritual life; *vidyām*—knowledge; *śamanīm*—ending; *sarva-karmaṇām*—all fruitive activities; *vitariṣye*—I shall give; *yayā*—by which; *ca*—also; *asau*—she; *bhayam*—fear; *ca*—also; *atitariṣyati*—will overcome.

TRANSLATION

I shall also describe this sublime knowledge, which is the door to spiritual life, to My mother, so that she also can attain perfection and self-realization, ending all reactions to fruitive activities. Thus she also will be freed from all material fear.

PURPORT

Kardama Muni was anxious about his good wife, Devahūti, while leaving home, and so the worthy son promised that not only would Kardama Muni be freed from the material entanglement, but Devahūti would also be freed by receiving instruction from her son. A very good example is set here: the husband goes away, taking the *sannyāsa* order for self-realization, but his representative, the son, who is equally educated, remains at home to deliver the mother. A *sannyāsī* is not supposed to take his wife with him. At the *vānaprastha* stage of retired life, or the stage midway between householder life and renounced life, one may keep his wife as an assistant without sex relations, but in the *sannyāsa* order of life one cannot keep his wife with him. Otherwise, a person like Kardama Muni could have kept his wife with him, and there would have been no hindrance to his prosecution of self-realization.

Kardama Muni followed the Vedic injunction that no one in *sannyāsa* life can have any kind of relationship with women. But what is the position of a woman who is left by her husband? She is entrusted to the son, and the son promises that he will deliver his mother from entanglement. A woman is not supposed to take *sannyāsa*. So-called spiritual societies concocted in modern times give *sannyāsa* even to women, although there is no sanction in the Vedic literature for a woman's accepting *sannyāsa*. Otherwise, if it were sanctioned, Kardama Muni could have taken his wife and given her *sannyāsa*. The woman must remain at home. She has only three stages of life: dependency on the father in childhood, dependency on the husband in youth and, in old age, dependency on the grown-up son, such as Kapila. In old age the progress of woman depends on the grown-up son. The ideal son, Kapila Muni, is assuring His father of the deliverance of His mother so that His father may go peacefully without anxiety for his good wife.

TEXT 41

मैत्रेय उवाच

एवं समुदितस्तेन कपिलेन प्रजापतिः ।
दक्षिणीकृत्य तं प्रीतो वनमेव जगाम ह ॥४१॥

maitreya uvāca
evaṁ samuditas tena
kapilena prajāpatiḥ
dakṣiṇī-kṛtya taṁ prīto
vanam eva jagāma ha

maitreyaḥ uvāca—the great sage Maitreya said; *evam*—thus; *samuditaḥ*—addressed; *tena*—by Him; *kapilena*—by Kapila; *prajāpatiḥ*—the progenitor of human society; *dakṣiṇī-kṛtya*—having circumambulated; *tam*—Him; *prītaḥ*—being pacified; *vanam*—to the forest; *eva*—indeed; *jagāma*—he left; *ha*—then.

TRANSLATION

Śrī Maitreya said: Thus when Kardama Muni, the progenitor of human society, was spoken to in fullness by his son, Kapila, he circumambulated Him, and with a good, pacified mind he at once left for the forest.

PURPORT

Going to the forest is compulsory for everyone. It is not a mental excursion upon which one person goes and another does not. Everyone should go to the forest at least as a *vānaprastha*. Forest—going means to take one-hundred—percent shelter of the Supreme Lord, as explained by Prahlāda Mahārāja in his talks with his father. *Sadā samudvigna-dhiyām* (*Bhāg.* 7.5.5). People who have accepted a temporary, material body are always full of anxieties. One should not, therefore, be very much affected by this material body, but should try to be freed. The preliminary process to become freed is to go to the forest or give up family relationships and exclusively engage in Kṛṣṇa consciousness. That is the purpose of going to the forest. Otherwise, the forest is only a place of monkeys and wild animals. To go to the forest does not mean to become a monkey or a ferocious animal. It means to accept exclusively the shelter of the Supreme Personality of Godhead and engage oneself in full service. One does not actually have to go to the forest. At the present moment this is not at all advisable for a man who has spent his life all along in big cities. As explained by Prahlāda Mahārāja (*hitvātma-pātaṁ gṛham andha-kūpam*), one should not remain always engaged in the responsibilities of family life because family life without Kṛṣṇa consciousness is just like a blind well. Alone in a field, if one falls into a blind well and no one is there to save him, he may cry for years, and no one will see or hear where the crying is coming from. Death is sure. Similarly, those who are forgetful of their eternal relationship with the Supreme Lord are in the blind well of family life; their position is very ominous. Prahlāda Mahārāja advised that one should give up this well somehow or other and take to Kṛṣṇa consciousness and thus be freed from material entanglement, which is full of anxieties.

TEXT 42

व्रतं स आस्थितो मौनमात्मैकशरणो मुनिः ।
निःसङ्गो व्यचरत्क्षोणीमनग्निरनिकेतनः ॥४२॥

vrataṁ sa āsthito maunam
ātmaika-śaraṇo muniḥ
niḥsaṅgo vyacarat kṣoṇīm
anagnir aniketanaḥ

vratam—vow; *saḥ*—he (Kardama); *āsthitaḥ*—accepted; *maunam*—silence; *ātma*—by the Supreme Personality of Godhead; *eka*—exclusively; *śaraṇaḥ*—being sheltered; *muniḥ*—the sage; *niḥsaṅgaḥ*—without association; *vyacarat*—he traveled; *kṣoṇīm*—the earth; *anagniḥ*—without fire; *aniketanaḥ*—without shelter.

TRANSLATION

The sage Kardama accepted silence as a vow in order to think of the Supreme Personality of Godhead and take shelter of Him exclusively. Without association, he traveled over the surface of the globe as a sannyāsī, devoid of any relationship with fire or shelter.

PURPORT

Here the words *anagnir aniketanaḥ* are very significant. A *sannyāsī* should be completely detached from fire and any residential quarters. A *gṛhastha* has a relationship with fire, either for offering sacrifices or for cooking, but a *sannyāsī* is freed from these two responsibilities. He does not have to cook or offer fire for sacrifice because he is always engaged in Kṛṣṇa consciousness; therefore he has already accomplished all ritualistic performances of religion. *Aniketanaḥ* means "without lodging." He should not have his own house, but should depend completely on the Supreme Lord for his food and lodging. He should travel.

Mauna means "silence." Unless one becomes silent, he cannot think completely about the pastimes and activities of the Lord. It is not that because one is a fool and cannot speak nicely he therefore takes the vow of *mauna*. Rather, one becomes silent so that people will not disturb him. It is said by Cāṇakya Paṇḍita that a rascal appears very intelligent as long as he does not speak. But speaking is the test. The so-called silence of a silent impersonalist *svāmī* indicates that he has nothing to say; he simply wants to beg. But the silence adopted by Kardama Muni was not like that. He became silent for relief from nonsensical talk. One is called a *muni* when he remains grave and does not talk nonsense. Mahārāja Ambarīṣa set a very good example; whenever he spoke, he spoke about the pastimes of the Lord. *Mauna* necessitates refraining from nonsensical talking, and engaging the talking facility in the pastimes of the Lord. In that way one can chant and hear about the Lord in order to perfect his life. *Vratam* means that one should take a vow as explained in *Bhagavad-gītā, amānitvam adambhitvam,* without hankering for personal respect and without being proud of one's material position. *Ahiṁsā* means not being violent. There are eighteen processes for attaining knowledge and perfection, and by his vow, Kardama Muni adopted all the principles of self-realization.

TEXT 43

मनो ब्रह्मणि युञ्जानो यत्तत्सदसतः परम् ।
गुणावभासे विगुण एकभक्त्यानुभाविते ॥४३॥

mano brahmaṇi yuñjāno
yat tat sad-asataḥ param
guṇāvabhāse viguṇa
eka-bhaktyānubhāvite

manaḥ—mind; *brahmaṇi*—on the Supreme; *yuñjānaḥ*—fixing; *yat*—which; *tat*—that; *sat-asataḥ*—cause and effect; *param*—beyond; *guṇa-avabhāse*—who manifests the three modes of material nature; *viguṇe*—who is beyond the material modes; *eka-bhaktyā*—by exclusive devotion; *anubhāvite*—who is perceived.

TRANSLATION

He fixed his mind upon the Supreme Personality of Godhead, Parabrahman, who is beyond cause and effect, who manifests the three modes of material nature, who is beyond those three modes, and who is perceived only through unfailing devotional service.

PURPORT

Whenever there is *bhakti,* there must be three things present—the devotee, the devotion and the Lord. Without these three—*bhakta, bhakti* and Bhagavān—there is no meaning to the word *bhakti.* Kardama Muni fixed his mind on the Supreme Brahman and realized Him through *bhakti,* or devotional service. This indicates that he fixed his mind on the personal feature of the Lord because *bhakti* cannot be executed unless one has realization of the personal feature of the Absolute Truth. *Guṇāvabhāse:* He is beyond the three modes of material nature, but it is due to Him that the three modes of material nature are manifested. In other words, although the material energy is an emanation of the Supreme Lord, He is not affected, as we are, by the modes of material nature. We are conditioned souls, but He is not affected, although the material nature has emanated from Him. He is the supreme living entity and is never affected by *māyā,* but we are subordinate, minute living entities, prone to be affected by the limitations of *māyā.* If he is in constant contact with the Supreme Lord by devotional service, the conditioned living entity also becomes freed from the infection of *māyā.* This is confirmed in *Bhagavad-gītā: sa guṇān samatītyaitān.* A person engaged in Kṛṣṇa consciousness is at once liberated from the influence of the three modes of material nature. In other words, once the conditioned soul engages himself in devotional service, he also becomes liberated like the Lord.

TEXT 44

निरहङ्कृतिर्निर्ममश्च निर्द्वन्द्वः समदृक् स्वदृक् ।
प्रत्यक्प्रशान्तधीर्धीरः प्रशान्तोर्मिरिवोदधिः ॥४४॥

nirahaṅkṛtir nirmamaś ca
nirdvandvaḥ sama-dṛk sva-dṛk
pratyak-praśānta-dhīr dhīraḥ
praśāntormir ivodadhiḥ

nirahaṅkṛtiḥ—without false ego; *nirmamaḥ*—without material affection; *ca*—and; *nirdvandvaḥ*—without duality; *sama-dṛk*—seeing equality; *sva-dṛk*—seeing himself; *pratyak*—turned inward; *praśānta*—perfectly composed; *dhīḥ*—mind; *dhīraḥ*—sober, not disturbed; *praśānta*—calmed; *ūrmiḥ*—whose waves; *iva*—like; *udadhiḥ*—the ocean.

TRANSLATION

Thus he gradually became unaffected by the false ego of material identity and became free from material affection. Undisturbed, equal to everyone and without duality, he could indeed see himself also. His mind was turned inward and was perfectly calm, like an ocean unagitated by waves.

PURPORT

When one's mind is in full Kṛṣṇa consciousness and one fully engages in rendering devotional service to the Lord, he becomes just like an ocean unagitated by waves. This very example is also cited in *Bhagavad-gītā:* one should become like the ocean. The ocean is filled by many thousands of rivers, and millions of tons of its water evaporates into clouds, yet the ocean is the same unagitated ocean. The laws of nature may work, but if one is fixed in devotional service at the lotus feet of the Lord, he is not agitated, for he is introspective. He does not look outside to material nature, but he looks in to the spiritual nature of his existence; with a sober mind, he simply engages in the service of the Lord. Thus he realizes his own self without false identification with matter and without affection for material possessions. Such a great devotee is never in trouble with others because he sees everyone from the platform of spiritual understanding; he sees himself and others in the right perspective.

TEXT 45

वासुदेवे भगवति सर्वज्ञे प्रत्यगात्मनि ।
परेण भक्तिभावेन लब्धात्मा मुक्तबन्धनः ॥४५॥

vāsudeve bhagavati
sarva-jñe pratyag-ātmani
pareṇa bhakti-bhāvena
labdhātmā mukta-bandhanaḥ

vāsudeve—to Vāsudeva; *bhagavati*—the Personality of Godhead; *sarva-jñe*—omniscient; *pratyak-ātmani*—the Supersoul within everyone; *pareṇa*—transcendental; *bhakti-bhāvena*—by devotional service; *labdha-ātmā*—being situated in himself; *mukta-bandhanaḥ*—liberated from material bondage.

TRANSLATION

He thus became liberated from conditioned life and became self-situated in transcendental devotional service to the Personality of Godhead, Vāsudeva, the omniscient Supersoul within everyone.

PURPORT

When one engages in the transcendental devotional service of the Lord one becomes aware that his constitutional position, as an individual soul, is to be eternally a servitor of the Supreme Lord, Vāsudeva. Self-realization does not mean that because the Supreme Soul and the individual soul are both souls they are equal in every respect. The individual soul is prone to be conditioned, and the Supreme Soul is never conditioned. When the conditioned soul realizes that he is subordinate to the Supreme Soul, his position is called *labdhātmā,* self-realization, or *mukta-bandhana,* freedom from material contamination. Material contamination continues as long as one thinks that he is as good as the Supreme Lord or is equal with Him. This condition is the last snare of *māyā. Māyā* always influences the conditioned soul. Even after much meditation and speculation, if one continues to think himself one with the Supreme Lord, it is to be understood that he is still in the last snares of the spell of *māyā.*

The word *pareṇa* is very significant. *Para* means "transcendental, untinged by material contamination." Full consciousness that one is an eternal servant of the Lord is called *parā bhakti.* If one has any identification with material things and executes devotional service for attainment of some material gain, that is *viddhā bhakti,* contaminated *bhakti.* One can actually become liberated by execution of *parā bhakti.*

Another word mentioned here is *sarva jñe.* The Supersoul sitting within the heart is all-cognizant. He knows. I may forget my past activities due to the change of body, but because the Supreme Lord as Paramātmā is sitting within me, He knows everything; therefore the result of my past *karma,* or past activities, is awarded to me. I may forget, but He awards me suffering or enjoyment for the misdeeds or good deeds of my past life. One should not think that he is freed from reaction because he has forgotten the actions of his past life. Reactions will take place, and what kind of reactions there will be is judged by the Supersoul, the witness.

TEXT 46

आत्मानं सर्वभूतेषु भगवन्तमवस्थितम् ।
अपश्यत्सर्वभूतानि भगवत्यपि चात्मनि ॥४६॥

ātmānaṁ sarva-bhūteṣu
bhagavantam avasthitam
apaśyat sarva-bhūtāni
bhagavaty api cātmani

ātmānam—the Supersoul; *sarva-bhūteṣu*—in all living beings; *bhagavantam*—the Supreme Personality of Godhead; *avasthitam*—situated; *apaśyat*—he saw; *sarva-bhūtāni*—all living beings; *bhagavati*—in the Supreme Personality of Godhead; *api*—moreover; *ca*—and; *ātmani*—on the Supersoul.

TRANSLATION

He began to see that the Supreme Personality of Godhead is seated in everyone's heart, and that everyone is existing on Him, because He is the Supersoul of everyone.

PURPORT

That everyone is existing on the Supreme Personality of Godhead does not mean that everyone is also Godhead. This is also explained in *Bhagavad-gītā:* everything is resting on Him, the Supreme Lord, but that does not mean that the Supreme Lord is also everywhere. This mysterious position has to be understood by highly advanced devotees. There are three kinds of devotees—the neophyte devotee, the intermediate devotee and the advanced devotee. The neophyte devotee does not understand the techniques of devotional science, but simply offers devotional service to the Deity in the temple; the intermediate devotee understands who God is, who is a devotee, who is a nondevotee and who is innocent, and he deals with such persons differently. But a person who sees that the Lord is sitting as Paramātmā in everyone's heart and that everything is depending or existing on the transcendental energy of the Supreme Lord is in the highest devotional position.

TEXT 47

इच्छाद्वेषविहीनेन सर्वत्र समचेतसा ।
भगवद्भक्तियुक्तेन प्राप्ता भागवती गतिः ॥४७॥

icchā-dveṣa-vihīnena
sarvatra sama-cetasā
bhagavad-bhakti-yuktena
prāptā bhāgavatī gatiḥ

icchā—desire; *dveṣa*—and hatred; *vihīnena*—freed from; *sarvatra*—everywhere; *sama*—equal; *cetasā*—with the mind; *bhagavat*—unto the Personality of Godhead; *bhakti-yuktena*—by discharging devotional service; *prāptā*—was attained; *bhāgavatī gatiḥ*—the destination of the devotee (going back home, back to Godhead).

TRANSLATION

Freed from all hatred and desire, Kardama Muni, being equal to everyone because of discharging uncontaminated devotional service, ultimately attained the path back to Godhead.

PURPORT

As stated in *Bhagavad-gītā,* only by devotional service can one understand the transcendental nature of the Supreme Lord and, after understanding Him perfectly in His transcendental position, enter into the kingdom of God. The process of entering into the kingdom of God is *tri-pāda-bhūti-gati,* or the path back home, back to Godhead, by which one can attain the ultimate goal of life. Kardama Muni, by his perfect devotional knowledge and service, achieved this ultimate goal, which is known as *bhāgavatī gatiḥ.*

Thus end the Bhaktivedanta purports of the Third Canto, Twenty-fourth Chapter, of the Śrīmad-Bhāgavatam, *entitled "The Renunciation of Kardama Muni."*

CHAPTER TWENTY-FIVE

The Glories of Devotional Service

TEXT 1

शौनक उवाच
कपिलस्तत्त्वसंख्याता भगवानात्ममायया ।
जातः स्वयमजः साक्षादात्मप्रज्ञप्तये नृणाम् ॥ १ ॥

śaunaka uvāca
kapilas tattva-saṅkhyātā
bhagavān ātma-māyayā
jātaḥ svayam ajaḥ sākṣād
ātma-prajñaptaye nṛṇām

śaunakaḥ uvāca—Śrī Śaunaka said; *kapilaḥ*—Lord Kapila; *tattva*—of the truth; *saṅkhyātā*—the expounder; *bhagavān*—the Supreme Personality of Godhead; *ātma-māyayā*—by His internal potency; *jātaḥ*—took birth; *svayam*—Himself; *ajaḥ*—unborn; *sākṣat*—in person; *ātma-prajñaptaye*—to disseminate transcendental knowledge; *nṛṇām*—for the human race.

TRANSLATION

Śrī Śaunaka said: Although He is unborn, the Supreme Personality of Godhead took birth as Kapila Muni by His internal potency. He descended to disseminate transcendental knowledge for the benefit of the whole human race.

PURPORT

The word *ātma-prajñaptaye* indicates that the Lord descends for the benefit of the human race to give transcendental knowledge. Material necessities are quite sufficiently provided for in the Vedic knowledge, which offers a program for good living conditions and gradual elevation to the platform of goodness. In the mode of goodness one's knowledge expands. On the platform of passion there is no knowledge, for passion is simply an impetus to enjoy material benefits. On the platform of ignorance there is no knowledge and no enjoyment, but simply life almost like that of animals.

The *Vedas* are meant to elevate one from the mode of ignorance to the platform of goodness. When one is situated in the mode of goodness he is able to understand knowledge of the self, or transcendental knowledge. This knowledge cannot be appreciated by any ordinary man. Therefore, since a disciplic succession is required, this knowledge is expounded either by the Supreme Personality of Godhead Himself or by His bona fide devotee. Śaunaka Muni also states here that Kapila, the incarnation of the Supreme Personality of Godhead, took birth, or appeared, simply to appreciate and disseminate transcendental knowledge. Simply to understand that one is not matter but spirit soul (*ahaṁ brahmāsmi:* "I am by nature Brahman") is not sufficient knowledge for understanding the self and his activities. One must be situated in the activities of Brahman. Knowledge of those activities is explained by the Supreme Personality of Godhead Himself. Such transcendental knowledge can be appreciated in human society but not in animal society, as clearly indicated here by the word *nṛṇām,* "for the human beings." Human beings are meant for regulated life. By nature, there is regulation in animal life also, but that is not like the regulative life as described in the scriptures or by the authorities. Human life is regulated life, not animal life. In regulated life only can one understand transcendental knowledge.

TEXT 2

न ह्यस्य वर्ष्मणः पुंसां वरिम्णः सर्वयोगिनाम् ।
विश्रुतौ श्रुतदेवस्य भूरि तृप्यन्ति मेऽसवः ॥ २ ॥

na hy asya varṣmaṇaḥ puṁsāṁ
varimṇaḥ sarva-yoginām
viśrutau śruta-devasya
bhūri tṛpyanti me 'savaḥ

na—not; *hi*—indeed; *asya*—about Him; *varṣmaṇaḥ*—the greatest; *puṁsām*—among men; *varimṇaḥ*—the foremost; *sarva*—all; *yoginām*—of *yogīs;* *viśrutau*—in hearing; *śruta-devasya*—the master of the *Vedas;* *bhūri*—repeatedly; *tṛpyanti*—are sated; *me*—my; *asavaḥ*—senses.

TRANSLATION

Śaunaka continued: There is no one who knows more than the Lord Himself. No one is more worshipable or more mature a yogī than He. He is therefore the master of the Vedas, and to hear about Him always is the actual pleasure of the senses.

PURPORT

In *Bhagavad-gītā* it is stated that no one can be equal to or greater than the Supreme Personality of Godhead. This is confirmed in the *Vedas* also: *eko bahūnāṁ yo vidadhāti kāmān.* He is the supreme living entity and is supplying the necessities of all other living entities. Thus all other living entities, both *viṣṇu-tattva* and *jīva-tattva,* are subordinate to the Supreme Personality of Godhead, Kṛṣṇa. The same concept is confirmed here. *Na hy asya varṣmaṇaḥ puṁsām:* amongst the living entities, no one can surpass the Supreme Person because no one is richer, more famous, stronger, more beautiful, wiser or more renounced than He. These qualifications make Him the Supreme Godhead, the cause of all causes. *Yogīs* are very proud of performing wonderful feats, but no one can compare to the Supreme Personality of Godhead.

Anyone who is associated with the Supreme Lord is accepted as a first-class *yogī.* Devotees may not be as powerful as the Supreme Lord, but by constant association with the Lord they become as good as the Lord Himself. Sometimes the devotees act more powerfully than the Lord. Of course, that is the Lord's concession.

Also used here is the word *varimṇaḥ,* meaning "the most worshipful of all *yogīs.*" To hear from Kṛṣṇa is the real pleasure of the senses; therefore He is known as Govinda, for by His words, by His teachings, by His instruction—by everything connected with Him—He enlivens the senses. Whatever He instructs is from the transcendental platform, and His instructions, being absolute, are nondifferent from Him. Hearing from Kṛṣṇa or His expansion or plenary expansion like Kapila is very pleasing to the senses. *Bhagavad-gītā* can be read or heard many times, but because it gives great pleasure, the more one reads *Bhagavad-gītā* the more he gets the appetite to read and understand it, and each time he gets new enlightenment. That is the nature of the transcendental message. Similarly, we find that transcendental happiness in the *Śrīmad-Bhāgavatam.* The more we hear and chant the glories of the Lord, the more we become happy.

TEXT 3

यद्यद्विधत्ते भगवान् स्वच्छन्दात्मात्ममायया ।
तानि मे श्रद्दधानस्य कीर्तन्यान्यनुकीर्तय ॥ ३ ॥

yad yad vidhatte bhagavān
svacchandātmātma-māyayā
tāni me śraddadhānasya
kīrtanyāny anukīrtaya

yat yat—whatever; *vidhatte*—He performs; *bhagavān*—the Personality of Godhead; *sva-chanda-ātmā*—full of self-desire; *ātma-māyayā*—by His internal potency; *tāni*—all of them; *me*—to me; *śraddadhānasya*—faithful; *kīrtanyāni*—worthy of praise; *anukīrtaya*—please describe.

TRANSLATION

Therefore please precisely describe all the activities and pastimes of the Personality of Godhead, who is full of self-desire and who assumes all these activities by His internal potency.

PURPORT

The word *anukīrtaya* is very significant. *Anukīrtaya* means to follow the description—not to create a concocted mental description, but to follow. Śaunaka Ṛṣi requested Sūta Gosvāmī to describe what he had actually heard from his spiritual master, Śukadeva Gosvāmī, about the transcendental pastimes the Lord manifested by His internal energy. Bhagavān, the Supreme Personality of Godhead, has no material body, but He can assume any kind of body by His supreme will. That is made possible by His internal energy.

TEXT 4

सूत उवाच
द्वैपायनसखस्त्वेवं मैत्रेयो भगवांस्तथा ।
प्राहेदं विदुरं प्रीत आन्वीक्षिक्यां प्रचोदितः ॥ ४ ॥

sūta uvāca
dvaipāyana-sakhas tv evaṁ
maitreyo bhagavāṁs tathā
prāhedaṁ viduraṁ prīta
ānvīkṣikyāṁ pracoditaḥ

sūtaḥ uvāca—Sūta Gosvāmī said; *dvaipāyana-sakhaḥ*—friend of Vyāsadeva; *tu*—then; *evam*—thus; *maitreyaḥ*—Maitreya; *bhagavān*—worshipful; *tathā*—in that way; *prāha*—spoke; *idam*—this; *viduram*—to Vidura; *prītaḥ*—being pleased; *ānvīkṣikyām*—about transcendental knowledge; *pracoditaḥ*—being asked.

TRANSLATION

Śrī Sūta Gosvāmī said: The most powerful sage Maitreya was a friend of Vyāsadeva. Being encouraged and pleased by Vidura's inquiry about transcendental knowledge, Maitreya spoke as follows.

PURPORT

Questions and answers are very satisfactorily dealt with when the inquirer is bona fide and the speaker is also authorized. Here Maitreya is considered a powerful sage, and therefore he is also described as *bhagavān.* This word can be used not only for the Supreme Personality of Godhead but for anyone who is almost as powerful as the Supreme Lord. Maitreya is addressed as *bhagavān* because he was spiritually far advanced. He was a personal friend of Dvaipāyana Vyāsadeva, a literary incarnation of the Lord. Maitreya was very pleased with the inquiries of Vidura because they were the inquiries of a bona fide, advanced devotee. Thus Maitreya was encouraged to answer. When there are discourses on transcendental topics between devotees of equal mentality, the questions and answers are very fruitful and encouraging.

TEXT 5

मैत्रेय उवाच

पितरि प्रस्थितेऽरण्यं मातुः प्रियचिकीर्षया ।
तस्मिन् बिन्दुसरेऽवात्सीद्भगवान् कपिलः किल ॥ ५ ॥

maitreya uvāca
pitari prasthite 'raṇyaṁ
mātuḥ priya-cikīrṣayā
tasmin bindusare 'vātsīd
bhagavān kapilaḥ kila

maitreyaḥ uvāca—Maitreya said; *pitari*—when the father; *prasthite*—left; *araṇyam*—for the forest; *mātuḥ*—His mother; *priya-cikīrṣayā*—with a desire to please; *tasmin*—on that; *bindusare*—Lake Bindu-sarovara; *avātsīt*—He stayed; *bhagavān*—the Lord; *kapilaḥ*—Kapila; *kila*—indeed.

TRANSLATION

Maitreya said: When Kardama left for the forest, Lord Kapila stayed on the strand of the Bindu-sarovara to please His mother, Devahūti.

PURPORT

In the absence of the father it is the duty of the grown son to take charge of his mother and serve her to the best of his ability so that she will not feel separation from her husband, and it is the duty of the husband to leave home as soon as there is a grown son to take charge of his wife and family affairs. That is the Vedic system of household life. One should not remain continually implicated in household affairs up to the time of death. He must leave. Family affairs and the wife may be taken charge of by a grown son.

TEXT 6

तमासीनमकर्माणं तत्त्वमार्गाग्रदर्शनम् ।
स्वसुतं देवहूत्याह धातुः संस्मरती वचः ॥ ६ ॥

tam āsīnam akarmāṇaṁ
tattva-mārgāgra-darśanam
sva-sutaṁ devahūty āha
dhātuḥ saṁsmaratī vacaḥ

tam—to Him (Kapila); *āsīnam*—seated; *akarmāṇam*—at leisure; *tattva*—of the Absolute Truth; *mārga-agra*—the ultimate goal; *darśanam*—who could show; *sva-sutam*—her son; *devahūtiḥ*—Devahūti; *āha*—said; *dhātuḥ*—of Brahmā; *saṁsmaratī*—remembering; *vacaḥ*—the words.

TRANSLATION

When Kapila, who could show her the ultimate goal of the Absolute Truth, was sitting leisurely before her, Devahūti remembered the words Brahmā had spoken to her, and she therefore began to question Kapila as follows.

TEXT 7

देवहूतिरुवाच
निर्विण्णा नितरां भूमन्नसदिन्द्रियतर्षणात् ।
येन सम्भाव्यमानेन प्रपन्नान्धं तमः प्रभो ॥ ७ ॥

devahūtir uvāca
nirviṇṇā nitarāṁ bhūmann
asad-indriya-tarṣaṇāt
yena sambhāvyamānena
prapannāndhaṁ tamaḥ prabho

devahūtiḥ uvāca—Devahūti said; *nirviṇṇā*—disgusted; *nitarām*—very; *bhūman*—O my Lord; *asat*—impermanent; *indriya*—of the senses; *tarṣaṇāt*—from agitation; *yena*—by which; *sambhāvyamānena*—being prevalent; *prapannā*—I have fallen; *andham tamaḥ*—into the abyss of ignorance; *prabho*—O my Lord.

TRANSLATION

Devahūti said: I am very sick of the disturbance caused by my material senses, for because of this sense disturbance, my Lord, I have fallen into the abyss of ignorance.

PURPORT

Here the word *asad-indriya-tarṣaṇāt* is significant. *Asat* means "impermanent," "temporary," and *indriya* means "senses." Thus *asad-indriya-tarṣaṇāt* means "from being agitated by the temporarily manifest senses of the material body." We are evolving through different statuses of material bodily existence—sometimes in a human body, sometimes in an animal body—and therefore the engagements of our material senses are also changing. Anything which changes is called temporary, or *asat.* We should know that beyond these temporary senses are our permanent senses, which are now covered by the material body. The permanent senses, being contaminated by matter, are not acting properly. Devotional service, therefore, involves freeing the senses from this contamination. When the contamination is completely removed and the senses act in the purity of unalloyed Kṛṣṇa consciousness, we have reached *sad-indriya,* or eternal sensory activities. Eternal sensory activities are called devotional service, whereas temporary sensory activities are called sense gratification. Unless one becomes tired of material sense gratification, there is no opportunity to hear transcendental messages from a person like Kapila. Devahūti expressed that she was tired. Now that her husband had left home, she wanted to get relief by hearing the instructions of Lord Kapila.

TEXT 8

तस्य त्वं तमसोऽन्धस्य दुष्पारस्याद्य पारगम् ।
सच्चक्षुर्जन्मनामन्ते लब्धं मे त्वदनुग्रहात् ॥ ८ ॥

tasya tvaṁ tamaso 'ndhasya
duṣpārasyādya pāragam
sac-cakṣur janmanām ante
labdhaṁ me tvad-anugrahāt

tasya—that; *tvam*—You; *tamasaḥ*—ignorance; *andhasya*—darkness; *duṣpārasya*—difficult to cross; *adya*—now; *pāra-gam*—crossing over; *sat*—transcendental; *cakṣuḥ*—eye; *janmanām*—of births; *ante*—at the end; *labdham*—attained; *me*—my; *tvat-anugrahāt*—by Your mercy.

TRANSLATION

Your Lordship is my only means of getting out of this darkest region of ignorance because You are my transcendental eye, which, by Your mercy only, I have attained after many, many births.

PURPORT

This verse is very instructive, since it indicates the relationship between the spiritual master and the disciple. The disciple or conditioned soul is put into this darkest region of ignorance and therefore is entangled in the material existence of sense gratification. It is very difficult to get out of this entanglement and attain freedom, but if one is fortunate enough to get the association of a spiritual master like Kapila Muni or His representative, then by his grace one can be delivered from the mire of ignorance. The spiritual master is therefore worshiped as one who delivers the disciple from the mire of ignorance with the light of the torch of knowledge. The word *pāragam* is very significant. *Pāragam* refers to one who can take the disciple to the other side. This side is conditioned life; the other side is the life of freedom. The spiritual master takes the disciple to the other side by opening his eyes with knowledge. We are suffering simply because of ignorance. By the instruction of the spiritual master, the darkness of ignorance is removed, and thus the disciple is enabled to go to the side of freedom. It is stated in *Bhagavad-gītā* that after many, many births one surrenders to the Supreme Personality of Godhead. Similarly, if, after many, many births, one is able to find a bona fide spiritual master and surrender to such a bona fide representative of Kṛṣṇa, one can be taken to the side of light.

TEXT 9

य आद्यो भगवान् पुंसामीश्वरो वै भवान् किल ।
लोकस्य तमसान्धस्य चक्षुः सूर्य इवोदितः ॥ ९ ॥

ya ādyo bhagavān puṁsām
īśvaro vai bhavān kila
lokasya tamasāndhasya
cakṣuḥ sūrya ivoditaḥ

yaḥ—He who; *ādyaḥ*—the origin; *bhagavān*—the Supreme Personality of Godhead; *puṁsām*—of all living entities; *īśvaraḥ*—the Lord; *vai*—in fact; *bhavān*—You; *kila*—indeed; *lokasya*—of the universe; *tamasā*—by the darkness of ignorance; *andhasya*—blinded; *cakṣuḥ*—eye; *sūryaḥ*—the sun; *iva*—like; *uditaḥ*—risen.

TRANSLATION

You are the Supreme Personality of Godhead, the origin and Supreme Lord of all living entities. You have arisen to disseminate the rays of the sun in order to dissipate the darkness of the ignorance of the universe.

PURPORT

Kapila Muni is accepted as an incarnation of the Supreme Personality of Godhead, Kṛṣṇa. Here the word *ādyaḥ* means "the origin of all living entities," and *puṁsām īśvaraḥ* means "the Lord (*īśvara*) of the living entities" (*īśvaraḥ paramaḥ kṛṣṇaḥ*). Kapila Muni is the direct expansion of Kṛṣṇa, who is the sun of spiritual knowledge. As the sun dissipates the darkness of the universe, so when the light of the Supreme Personality of Godhead comes down, it at once dissipates the darkness of *māyā*. We have our eyes, but without the light of the sun our eyes are of no value. Similarly, without the light of the Supreme Lord, or without the divine grace of the spiritual master, one cannot see things as they are.

TEXT 10

अथ मे देव सम्मोहमपाक्रष्टुं त्वमर्हसि ।
योऽवग्रहोऽहंममेतीत्येतस्मिन् योजितस्त्वया ॥१०॥

atha me deva sammoham
apākraṣṭuṁ tvam arhasi
yo 'vagraho 'haṁ mametīty
etasmin yojitas tvayā

atha—now; *me*—my; *deva*—O Lord; *sammoham*—delusion; *apākraṣṭum*—to dispel; *tvam*—You; *arhasi*—be pleased; *yaḥ*—which; *avagrahaḥ*—misconception; *aham*—I; *mama*—mine; *iti*—thus; *iti*—thus; *etasmin*—in this; *yojitaḥ*—engaged; *tvayā*—by You.

TRANSLATION

Now be pleased, my Lord, to dispel my great delusion. Due to my feeling of false ego, I have been engaged by Your māyā and have identified myself with the body and consequent bodily relations.

PURPORT

The false ego of identifying one's body as one's self and of claiming things possessed in relationship with this body is called *māyā*. In *Bhagavad-gītā*, Fifteenth Chapter, the

Lord says, "I am sitting in everyone's heart, and from Me come everyone's remembrance and forgetfulness." Devahūti has stated that false identification of the body with the self and attachment for possessions in relation to the body are also under the direction of the Lord. Does this mean that the Lord discriminates by engaging one in His devotional service and another in sense gratification? If that were true, it would be an incongruity on the part of the Supreme Lord, but that is not the actual fact. As soon as the living entity forgets his real, constitutional position of eternal servitorship to the Lord and wants instead to enjoy himself by sense gratification, he is captured by *māyā*. This capture by *māyā* is the consciousness of false identification with the body and attachment for the possessions of the body. These are the activities of *māyā*, and since *māyā* is also an agent of the Lord, it is indirectly the action of the Lord. The Lord is merciful; if anyone wants to forget Him and enjoy this material world, He gives him full facility, not directly but through the agency of His material potency. Therefore, since the material potency is the Lord's energy, indirectly it is the Lord who gives the facility to forget Him. Devahūti therefore said, "My engagement in sense gratification was also due to You. Now kindly get me free from this entanglement."

By the grace of the Lord one is allowed to enjoy this material world, but when one is disgusted with material enjoyment and is frustrated, and when one sincerely surrenders unto the lotus feet of the Lord, then the Lord is so kind that He frees one from entanglement. Kṛṣṇa says, therefore, in *Bhagavad-gītā*, "First of all surrender, and then I will take charge of you and free you from all reactions of sinful activities." Sinful activities are those activities performed in forgetfulness of our relationship with the Lord. In this material world, activities for material enjoyment which are considered to be pious are also sinful. For example, one sometimes gives something in charity to a needy person with a view to getting back the money four times increased. Giving with the purpose of gaining something is called charity in the mode of passion. Everything done here is done in the modes of material nature, and therefore all activities but service to the Lord are sinful. Because of sinful activities we become attracted by the illusion of material attachment, and we think, "I am this body." I think of the body as myself and of bodily possessions as "mine." Devahūti requested Lord Kapila to free her from that entanglement of false identification and false possession.

TEXT 11

तं त्वा गताहं शरणं शरण्यं
स्वभृत्यसंसारतरोः कुठारम् ।

जिज्ञासयाहं प्रकृतेः पूरुषस्य
नमामि सद्धर्मविदां वरिष्ठम् ॥११॥

taṁ tvā gatāhaṁ śaraṇaṁ śaraṇyaṁ
sva-bhṛtya-saṁsāra-taroḥ kuṭhāram
jijñāsayāhaṁ prakṛteḥ pūruṣasya
namāmi sad-dharma-vidāṁ variṣṭham

tam—that person; *tvā*—unto You; *gatā*—have gone; *aham*—I; *śaraṇam*—shelter; *śaraṇyam*—worth taking shelter of; *sva-bhṛtya*—for Your dependents; *saṁsāra*—of material existence; *taroḥ*—of the tree; *kuṭhāram*—the ax; *jijñāsayā*—with the desire to know; *aham*—I; *prakṛteḥ*—of matter (woman); *pūruṣasya*—of spirit (man); *namāmi*—I offer obeisances; *sat-dharma*—of the eternal occupation; *vidām*—of the knowers; *variṣṭham*—unto the greatest.

TRANSLATION

Devahūti continued: I have taken shelter of Your lotus feet because You are the only person of whom to take shelter. You are the ax which can cut the tree of material existence. I therefore offer my obeisances unto You, who are the greatest of all transcendentalists, and I inquire from You as to the relationship between man and woman and between spirit and matter.

PURPORT

Sāṅkhya philosophy, as is well known, deals with *prakṛti* and *puruṣa. Puruṣa* is the Supreme Personality of Godhead or anyone who imitates the Supreme Personality of Godhead as an enjoyer, and *prakṛti* means "nature." In this material world, material nature is being exploited by the *puruṣas,* or the living entities. The intricacies in the material world of the relationship of the *prakṛti* and *puruṣa*, or the enjoyed and the enjoyer, is called *saṁsāra,* or material entanglement. Devahūti wanted to cut the tree of material entanglement, and she found the suitable weapon in Kapila Muni. The tree of material existence is explained in the Fifteenth Chapter of *Bhagavad-gītā* as an *aśvattha* tree whose root is upwards and whose branches are downwards. It is recommended there that one has to cut the root of this material existential tree with the ax of detachment. What is the attachment? The attachment involves *prakṛti* and *puruṣa.* The living entities are trying to lord it over material nature. Since the conditioned soul takes material nature to be the object of his enjoyment and he takes the position of the enjoyer, he is therefore called *puruṣa.*

Devahūti questioned Kapila Muni, for she knew that only He could cut her attachment to this material world. The living entities, in the guises of men and women, are trying to enjoy the material energy; therefore in one sense everyone is *puruṣa* because *puruṣa* means "enjoyer" and *prakṛti* means "enjoyed." In this material world both the so-called man and so-called woman are imitating the real *puruṣa;* the Supreme Personality of Godhead is actually the enjoyer in the transcendental sense, whereas all others are *prakṛti.* The living entities are considered *prakṛti.* In *Bhagavad-gītā,* matter is analyzed as *aparā,* or inferior nature, whereas beyond this inferior nature there is another, superior nature—the living entities. Living entities are also *prakṛti,* or enjoyed, but under the spell of *māyā,* the living entities are falsely trying to take the position of enjoyers. That is the cause of *saṁsāra-bandha,* or conditional life. Devahūti wanted to get out of conditional life and place herself in full surrender. The Lord is *śaraṇya,* which means "the only worthy personality to whom one can fully surrender," because He is full of all opulences. If anyone actually wants relief, the best course is to surrender unto the Supreme Personality of Godhead. The Lord is also described here as *sad-dharma-vidāṁ variṣṭham.* This indicates that of all transcendental occupations the best occupation is eternal loving service unto the Supreme Personality of Godhead. *Dharma* is sometimes translated as "religion," but that is not exactly the meaning. *Dharma* actually means "that which one cannot give up," "that which is inseparable from oneself." The warmth of fire is inseparable from fire; therefore warmth is called the *dharma,* or nature, of fire. Similarly, *sad-dharma* means "eternal occupation." That eternal occupation is engagement in the transcendental loving service of the Lord. The purpose of Kapiladeva's Sāṅkhya philosophy is to propagate pure, uncontaminated devotional service, and therefore He is addressed here as the most important personality amongst those who know the transcendental occupation of the living entity.

TEXT 12

मैत्रेय उवाच

इति स्वमातुर्निरवद्यमीप्सितं
निशम्य पुंसामपवर्गवर्धनम् ।
धियाभिनन्द्यात्मवतां सतां गति-
र्बभाष ईषत्स्मितशोभिताननः ॥१२॥

maitreya uvāca
iti sva-mātur niravadyam īpsitaṁ
niśamya puṁsām apavarga-vardhanam

dhiyābhinandyātmavatāṁ satāṁ gatir
babhāṣa īṣat-smita-śobhitānanaḥ

maitreyaḥ uvāca—Maitreya said; *iti*—thus; *sva-mātuḥ*—of His mother; *niravadyam*—uncontaminated; *īpsitam*—desire; *niśamya*—after hearing; *puṁsām*—of people; *apavarga*—cessation of bodily existence; *vardhanam*—increasing; *dhiyā*—mentally; *abhinandya*—having thanked; *ātma-vatām*—interested in self-realization; *satām*—of the transcendentalists; *gatiḥ*—the path; *babhāṣe*—He explained; *īṣat*—slightly; *smita*—smiling; *śobhita*—beautiful; *ānanaḥ*—His face.

TRANSLATION

Maitreya said: After hearing of His mother's uncontaminated desire for transcendental realization, the Lord thanked her within Himself for her questions, and thus, His face smiling, He explained the path of the transcendentalists, who are interested in self-realization.

PURPORT

Devahūti has surrendered her confession of material entanglement and her desire to gain release. Her questions to Lord Kapila are very interesting for persons who are actually trying to get liberation from material entanglement and attain the perfectional stage of human life. Unless one is interested in understanding his spiritual life, or his constitutional position, and unless he also feels inconvenience in material existence, his human form of life is spoiled. One who does not care for these transcendental necessities of life and simply engages like an animal in eating, sleeping, fearing and mating has spoiled his life. Lord Kapila was very much satisfied by His mother's questions because the answers stimulate one's desire for liberation from the conditional life of material existence. Such questions are called *apavarga-vardhanam.* Those who have actual spiritual interest are called *sat,* or devotees. *Satām prasaṅgāt. Sat* means "that which eternally exists," and *asat* means "that which is not eternal." Unless one is situated on the spiritual platform, he is not *sat;* he is *asat.* The *asat* stands on a platform which will not exist, but anyone who stands on the spiritual platform will exist eternally. As spirit soul, everyone exists eternally, but the *asat* has accepted the material world as his shelter, and therefore he is full of anxiety. *Asad-grāhān,* the incompatible situation of the spirit soul who has the false idea of enjoying matter, is the cause of the soul's being *asat.* Actually, the spirit soul is not *asat.* As soon as one is conscious of this fact and takes to Kṛṣṇa consciousness, he becomes *sat.*

Satāṁ gatiḥ, the path of the eternal, is very interesting to persons who are after liberation, and His Lordship Kapila began to speak about that path.

TEXT 13

श्रीभगवानुवाच
योग आध्यात्मिकः पुंसां मतो निःश्रेयसाय मे ।
अत्यन्तोपरतिर्यत्र दुःखस्य च सुखस्य च ॥१३॥

śrī-bhagavān uvāca
yoga ādhyātmikaḥ puṁsām
mato niḥśreyasāya me
atyantoparatir yatra
duḥkhasya ca sukhasya ca

śrī-bhagavān uvāca—the Personality of Godhead said; *yogaḥ*—the *yoga* system; *ādhyātmikaḥ*—relating to the soul; *puṁsām*—of living entities; *mataḥ*—is approved; *niḥśreyasāya*—for the ultimate benefit; *me*—by Me; *atyanta*—complete; *uparatiḥ*—detachment; *yatra*—where; *duḥkhasya*—from distress; *ca*—and; *sukhasya*—from happiness; *ca*—and.

TRANSLATION

The Personality of Godhead answered: The yoga system which relates to the Lord and the individual soul, which is meant for the ultimate benefit of the living entity, and which causes detachment from all happiness and distress in the material world, is the highest yoga system.

PURPORT

In the material world, everyone is trying to get some material happiness, but as soon as we get some material happiness, there is also material distress. In the material world one cannot have unadulterated happiness. Any kind of happiness one has is contaminated by distress also. For example, if we want to drink milk then we have to bother to maintain a cow and keep her fit to supply milk. Drinking milk is very nice; it is also pleasure. But for the sake of drinking milk one has to accept so much trouble. The *yoga* system, as here stated by the Lord, is meant to end all material happiness and material distress. The best *yoga,* as taught in *Bhagavad-gītā* by Kṛṣṇa, is *bhakti-yoga.* It is also mentioned in the *Gītā* that one should try to be tolerant and not be disturbed by material happiness or distress. Of course, one may say that he is not disturbed by material happiness, but he does not know that just after one enjoys so-called material happiness, material distress will follow. This is the law of the material world. Lord Kapila states that the *yoga* system is the science of the spirit. One practices *yoga* in order to attain perfection on the spiritual platform. There is no question of material happiness or distress. It is transcendental. Lord Kapila will eventually explain how it is transcendental, but the preliminary introduction is given here.

TEXT 14

तमिमं ते प्रवक्ष्यामि यमवोचं पुरानघे ।
ऋषीणां श्रोतुकामानां योगं सर्वाङ्गनैपुणम् ॥१४॥

tam imaṁ te pravakṣyāmi
yam avocaṁ purānaghe
ṛṣīṇāṁ śrotu-kāmānāṁ
yogaṁ sarvāṅga-naipuṇam

tam imam—that very; *te*—to you; *pravakṣyāmi*—I shall explain; *yam*—which; *avocam*—I explained; *purā*—formerly; *anaghe*—O pious mother; *ṛṣiṇām*—to the sages; *śrotu-kāmānām*—eager to hear; *yogam*—*yoga* system; *sarva-aṅga*—in all respects; *naipuṇam*—serviceable and practical.

TRANSLATION

O most pious mother, I shall now explain unto you the ancient yoga system, which I explained formerly to the great sages. It is serviceable and practical in every way.

PURPORT

The Lord does not manufacture a new system of *yoga*. Sometimes it is claimed that someone has become an incarnation of God and is expounding a new theological aspect of the Absolute Truth. But here we find that although Kapila Muni is the Lord Himself and is capable of manufacturing a new doctrine for His mother, He nevertheless says, "I shall just explain the ancient system which I once explained to the great sages because they were also anxious to hear about it." When we have a superexcellent process already present in Vedic scriptures, there is no need to concoct a new system, to mislead the innocent public. At present it has become a fashion to reject the standard system and present something bogus in the name of a newly invented process of *yoga*.

TEXT 15

चेतः खल्वस्य बन्धाय मुक्तये चात्मनो मतम् ।
गुणेषु सक्तं बन्धाय रतं वा पुंसि मुक्तये ॥१५॥

cetaḥ khalv asya bandhāya
muktaye cātmano matam
guṇeṣu saktaṁ bandhāya
rataṁ vā puṁsi muktaye

cetaḥ—consciousness; *khalu*—indeed; *asya*—of him; *bandhāya*—for bondage; *muktaye*—for liberation; *ca*—and; *ātmanaḥ*—of the living entity; *matam*—is considered; *guṇeṣu*—in the three modes of nature; *saktam*—attracted; *bandhāya*—for conditional life; *ratam*—attached; *vā*—or; *puṁsi*—in the Supreme Personality of Godhead; *muktaye*—for liberation.

TRANSLATION

The stage in which the consciousness of the living entity is attracted by the three modes of material nature is called conditional life. But when that same consciousness is attached to the Supreme Personality of Godhead, one is situated in the consciousness of liberation.

PURPORT

There is a distinction here between Kṛṣṇa consciousness and *māyā* consciousness. *Guṇeṣu,* or *māyā* consciousness, involves attachment to the three material modes of nature, under which one works sometimes in goodness and knowledge, sometimes in passion and sometimes in ignorance. These different qualitative activities, with the central attachment for material enjoyment, are the cause of one's conditional life. When the same *cetaḥ,* or consciousness, is transferred to the Supreme Personality of Godhead, Kṛṣṇa, or when one becomes Kṛṣṇa conscious, he is on the path of liberation.

TEXT 16

अहं ममाभिमानोत्थैः कामलोभादिभिर्मलैः ।
वीतं यदा मनः शुद्धमदुःखमसुखं समम् ॥१६॥

ahaṁ mamābhimānotthaiḥ
kāma-lobhādibhir malaiḥ
vītaṁ yadā manaḥ śuddham
aduḥkham asukhaṁ samam

aham—I; *mama*—mine; *abhimāna*—from the misconception; *utthaiḥ*—produced; *kāma*—lust; *lobha*—greed; *ādibhiḥ*—and so on; *malaiḥ*—from the impurities; *vītam*—freed; *yadā*—when; *manaḥ*—the mind; *śuddham*—pure; *aduḥkham*—without distress; *asukham*—without happiness; *samam*—equipoised.

TRANSLATION

When one is completely cleansed of the impurities of lust and greed produced from the false identification of the body as "I" and bodily possessions as "mine," one's mind becomes purified. In that pure state he transcends the stage of so-called material happiness and distress.

PURPORT

Kāma and *lobha* are the symptoms of material existence. Everyone always desires to possess something. It is said here that desire and greed are the products of false identification of oneself with the body. When one becomes free from this contamination, then his mind and consciousness also become freed and attain their original state. Mind, consciousness and the living entity exist. Whenever we speak of the living entity, this includes the mind and consciousness. The difference between conditional life and liberated life occurs when we purify the mind and the consciousness. When they are purified, one becomes transcendental to material happiness and distress.

In the beginning Lord Kapila has said that perfect *yoga* enables one to transcend the platform of material distress and happiness. How this can be done is explained here: one has to purify his mind and consciousness. This can be done by the *bhakti-yoga* system. As explained in the *Nārada Pañcarātra,* one's mind and senses should be purified (*tat-paratvena nirmalam*). One's senses must be engaged in devotional service to the Lord. That is the process. The mind must have some engagement. One cannot make the mind vacant. Of course there are some foolish attempts to try to make the mind vacant or void, but that is not possible. The only process that will purify the mind is to engage it in Kṛṣṇa. The mind must be engaged. If we engage our mind in Kṛṣṇa, naturally the consciousness becomes fully purified, and there is no chance of the entrance of material desire and greed.

TEXT 17

तदा पुरुष आत्मानं केवलं प्रकृतेः परम् ।
निरन्तरं स्वयंज्योतिरणिमानमखण्डितम् ॥१७॥

tadā puruṣa ātmānaṁ
kevalaṁ prakṛteḥ param
nirantaraṁ svayaṁ-jyotir
aṇimānam akhaṇḍitam

tadā—then; *puruṣaḥ*—the individual soul; *ātmānam*—himself; *kevalam*—pure; *prakṛteḥ param*—transcendental to material existence; *nirantaram*—nondifferent; *svayam-jyotiḥ*—self-effulgent; *aṇimānam*—infinitesimal; *akhaṇḍitam*—not fragmented.

TRANSLATION

At that time the soul can see himself to be transcendental to material existence and always self-effulgent, never fragmented, although very minute in size.

PURPORT

In the state of pure consciousness, or Kṛṣṇa consciousness, one can see himself as a minute particle nondifferent from the Supreme Lord. As stated in *Bhagavad-gītā*, the *jīva*, or the individual soul, is eternally part and parcel of the Supreme Lord. Just as the sun's rays are minute particles of the brilliant constitution of the sun, so a living entity is a minute particle of the Supreme Spirit. The individual soul and the Supreme Lord are not separated as in material differentiation. The individual soul is a particle from the very beginning. One should not think that because the individual soul is a particle, it is fragmented from the whole spirit. Māyāvāda philosophy enunciates that the whole spirit exists, but a part of it, which is called the *jīva*, is entrapped by illusion. This philosophy, however, is unacceptable because spirit cannot be divided like a fragment of matter. That part, the *jīva*, is eternally a part. As long as the Supreme Spirit exists, His part and parcel also exists. As long as the sun exists, the molecules of the sun's rays also exist.

The *jīva* particle is estimated in the Vedic literature to be one ten-thousandth the size of the upper portion of a hair. It is therefore infinitesimal. The Supreme Spirit is infinite, but the living entity, or the individual soul, is infinitesimal, although it is not different in quality from the Supreme Spirit. Two words in this verse are to be particularly noted. One is *nirantaram*, which means "nondifferent," or "of the same quality." The individual soul is also expressed here as *aṇimānam. Aṇimānam* means "infinitesimal." The Supreme Spirit is all-pervading, but the very small spirit is the individual soul. *Akhaṇḍitam* means not exactly "fragmented" but "constitutionally always infinitesimal." No one can separate the molecular parts of the sunshine from the sun, but at the same time the molecular part of the sunshine is not as expansive as the sun itself. Similarly, the living entity, by his constitutional position, is qualitatively the same as the Supreme Spirit, but he is infinitesimal.

TEXT 18

ज्ञानवैराग्ययुक्तेन भक्तियुक्तेन चात्मना ।
परिपश्यत्युदासीनं प्रकृतिं च हतौजसम् ॥१८॥

jñāna-vairāgya-yuktena
bhakti-yuktena cātmanā
paripaśyaty udāsīnaṁ
prakṛtiṁ ca hataujasam

jñāna—knowledge; *vairāgya*—renunciation; *yuktena*—equipped with; *bhakti*—devotional service; *yuktena*—equipped with; *ca*—and; *ātmanā*—by the mind; *paripaśyati*—one sees; *udāsīnam*—indifferent; *prakṛtim*—material existence; *ca*—and; *hata-ojasam*—reduced in strength.

TRANSLATION

In that position of self-realization, by practice of knowledge and renunciation in devotional service, one sees everything in the right perspective; he becomes indifferent to material existence, and the material influence acts less powerfully upon him.

PURPORT

As the contamination of the germs of a particular disease can influence a weaker person, similarly the influence of material nature, or illusory energy, can act on the weaker, or conditioned, soul but not on the liberated soul. Self-realization is the position of the liberated state. One understands his constitutional position by knowledge and *vairāgya,* renunciation. Without knowledge, one cannot have realization. The realization that one is the infinitesimal part and parcel of the Supreme Spirit makes him unattached to material, conditional life. That is the beginning of devotional service. Unless one is liberated from material contamination, one cannot engage himself in the devotional service of the Lord. In this verse, therefore, it is stated, *jñāna-vairāgya-yuktena:* when one is in full knowledge of one's constitutional position and is in the renounced order of life, detached from material attraction, then, by pure devotional service, *bhakti-yuktena,* he can engage himself as a loving servant of the Lord. *Paripaśyati* means that he can see everything in its right perspective. Then the influence of material nature becomes almost nil. This is also confirmed in *Bhagavad-gītā. Brahma-bhūtaḥ prasannātmā:* when one is self-realized he becomes happy and free from the influence of material nature, and at that time he is freed from lamentation and hankering. The Lord states that position as *mad-bhaktiṁ labhate parām,* the real state of beginning devotional service. Similarly, it is confirmed in the *Nārada-pañcarātra* that when the senses are purified they can then be engaged in the devotional service of the Lord. One who is attached to material contamination cannot be a devotee.

TEXT 19

न युज्यमानया भक्त्या भगवत्यखिलात्मनि ।
सदृशोऽस्ति शिवः पन्था योगिनां ब्रह्मसिद्धये ॥१९॥

na yujyamānayā bhaktyā
bhagavaty akhilātmani
sadṛśo 'sti śivaḥ panthā
yogināṁ brahma-siddhaye

na—not; *yujyamānayā*—being performed; *bhaktyā*—devotional service; *bhagavati*—towards the Supreme Personality of Godhead; *akhila-ātmani*—the Supersoul; *sadṛśaḥ*—like; *asti*—there is; *śivaḥ*—auspicious; *panthāḥ*—path; *yoginām*—of the *yogīs; brahma-siddhaye*—for perfection in self-realization.

TRANSLATION

Perfection in self-realization cannot be attained by any kind of yogī unless he engages in devotional service to the Supreme Personality of Godhead, for that is the only auspicious path.

PURPORT

That knowledge and renunciation are never perfect unless joined by devotional service is explicitly explained here. *Na yujyamānayā* means "without being dovetailed." When there is devotional service, then the question is where to offer that service. Devotional service is to be offered to the Supreme Personality of Godhead, who is the Supersoul of everything, for that is the only reliable path of self-realization, or Brahman realization. The word *brahma-siddhaye* means to understand oneself to be different from matter, to understand oneself to be Brahman. The Vedic words are *ahaṁ brahmāsmi. Brahma-siddhi* means that one should know that he is not matter; he is pure soul. There are different kinds of *yogīs*, but every *yogī* is supposed to engage in self-realization, or Brahman realization. It is clearly stated here that unless one is fully engaged in the devotional service of the Supreme Personality of Godhead one cannot have easy approach to the path of *brahma-siddhi.*

In the beginning of the Second Chapter of *Śrīmad-Bhāgavatam* it is stated that when one engages himself in the devotional service of Vāsudeva, spiritual knowledge and renunciation of the material world automatically become manifest. Thus a devotee does not have to try separately for renunciation or knowledge. Devotional service itself is so powerful that by one's service attitude, everything is revealed. It is stated here, *śivaḥ panthāḥ:* this is the only auspicious path for self-realization. The path of devotional service is the most confidential means for attaining Brahman realization. That perfection in Brahman realization is attained through the auspicious path of devotional service indicates that the so-called Brahman realization, or realization of the *brahmajyotir* effulgence, is not *brahma-siddhi.* Beyond that *brahmajyotir* there is the Supreme Personality of Godhead. In the *Upaniṣads* a devotee prays to the Lord to kindly put aside the effulgence, *brahmajyotir,* so that the devotee may see within the *brahmajyotir* the actual, eternal form of the Lord. Unless one attains realization of the transcendental form of the Lord, there is no question of *bhakti. Bhakti* necessitates the existence of the recipient of devotional service and the devotee who renders devotional service. *Brahma-siddhi* through devotional service is realization of the Supreme Personality of Godhead. The understanding of the effulgent rays of the body of the Supreme Godhead is not the perfect stage of *brahma-siddhi,* or Brahman realization. Nor is the realization of the Paramātmā feature of the Supreme Person perfect, for Bhagavān, the Supreme Personality of Godhead, is *akhilātmā*-He is the Supersoul. One who realizes the Supreme Personality realizes the other features, namely the Paramātmā feature and the Brahman feature, and that total realization is *brahma-siddhi.*

TEXT 20

प्रसङ्गमजरं पाशमात्मनः कवयो विदुः ।
स एव साधुषु कृतो मोक्षद्वारमपावृतम् ॥२०॥

prasaṅgam ajaraṁ pāśam
ātmanaḥ kavayo viduḥ
sa eva sādhuṣu kṛto
mokṣa-dvāram apāvṛtam

prasaṅgam—attachment; *ajaram*—strong; *pāśam*—entanglement; *ātmanaḥ*—of the soul; *kavayaḥ*—learned men; *viduḥ*—know; *saḥ eva*—that same; *sādhuṣu*—to the devotees; *kṛtaḥ*—applied; *mokṣa-dvāram*—the door of liberation; *apāvṛtam*—opened.

TRANSLATION

Every learned man knows very well that attachment for the material is the greatest entanglement of the spirit soul. But that same attachment, when applied to the self-realized devotees, opens the door of liberation.

PURPORT

Here it is clearly stated that attachment for one thing is the cause of bondage in conditioned life, and the same attachment, when applied to something else, opens the door of liberation. Attachment cannot be killed; it has simply to be transferred. Attachment for material things is called material consciousness, and attachment for Kṛṣṇa or His devotee is called Kṛṣṇa consciousness. Consciousness, therefore, is the platform of attachment. It is clearly stated here that when we simply purify the consciousness from material consciousness to Kṛṣṇa consciousness, we attain liberation. Despite the statement that one should give up attachment, desirelessness is not possible for a living entity. A living entity, by constitution, has the propensity to be attached to something. We see that if someone has no object of attachment, if he has no children, then he transfers his attachment to cats and dogs. This indicates that the propensity for attachment cannot be stopped; it must be utilized for the best purpose. Our attachment for material things perpetuates our conditional state, but the same attachment, when transferred to the Supreme Personality of Godhead or His devotee, is the source of liberation.

Here it is recommended that attachment should be transferred to the self-realized devotees, the *sādhus.* And who is a *sādhu*? A *sādhu* is not just an ordinary man with a saffron robe or long beard. A *sādhu* is described in *Bhagavad-gītā* as one who unflinchingly engages in devotional service. Even though one is found not to be following the strict rules and regulations of devotional service, if one simply has unflinching faith in Kṛṣṇa, the Supreme Person, he is understood to be a *sādhu. Sādhur eva sa mantavyaḥ.* A *sādhu* is a strict follower of devotional service. It is recommended here that if one at all wants to realize Brahman, or spiritual perfection, his attachment should be transferred to the *sādhu,* or devotee. Lord Caitanya also confirmed this. *Lava-mātra sādhu-saṅge sarva-siddhi haya:* simply by a moment's association with a *sādhu,* one can attain perfection.

Mahātmā is a synonym of *sādhu*. It is said that service to a *mahātmā*, or elevated devotee of the Lord, is *dvāram āhur vimukteḥ*, the royal road of liberation. *Mahat-sevāṁ dvāram āhur vimuktes tamo-dvāraṁ yoṣitāṁ saṅgi-saṅgam* (*Bhāg.* 5.5.2). Rendering service to the materialists has the opposite effect. If anyone offers service to a gross materialist, or a person engaged only in sense enjoyment, then by association with such a person the door to hell is opened. The same principle is confirmed here. Attachment to a devotee is attachment to the service of the Lord because if one associates with a *sādhu*, the result will be that the *sādhu* will teach him how to become a devotee, a worshiper and a sincere servitor of the Lord. These are the gifts of a *sādhu*. If we want to associate with a *sādhu*, we cannot expect him to give us instructions on how to improve our material condition, but he will give us instructions on how to cut the knot of the contamination of material attraction and how to elevate ourselves in devotional service. That is the result of associating with a *sādhu*. Kapila Muni first of all instructs that the path of liberation begins with such association.

TEXT 21

तितिक्षवः कारुणिकाः सुहृदः सर्वदेहिनाम् ।
अजातशत्रवः शान्ताः साधवः साधुभूषणाः ॥२१॥

titikṣavaḥ kāruṇikāḥ
suhṛdaḥ sarva-dehinām
ajāta-śatravaḥ śāntāḥ
sādhavaḥ sādhu-bhūṣaṇāḥ

titikṣavaḥ—tolerant; *kāruṇikāḥ*—merciful; *suhṛdaḥ*—friendly; *sarva-dehinām*—to all living entities; *ajāta-śatravaḥ*—inimical to none; *śāntāḥ*—peaceful; *sādhavaḥ*—abiding by scriptures; *sādhu-bhūṣaṇāḥ*—adorned with sublime characteristics.

TRANSLATION

The symptoms of a sādhu are that he is tolerant, merciful and friendly to all living entities. He has no enemies, he is peaceful, he abides by the scriptures, and all his characteristics are sublime.

PURPORT

A *sādhu*, as described above, is a devotee of the Lord. His concern, therefore, is to enlighten people in devotional service to the Lord. That is his mercy. He knows that without devotional service to the Lord, human life is spoiled. A devotee travels all over the country, from door to door, preaching, "Be Kṛṣṇa conscious. Be a devotee of Lord Kṛṣṇa. Don't spoil your life in simply fulfilling your animal propensities. Human life is meant for self-realization, or Kṛṣṇa consciousness." These are the preachings of a *sādhu*. He is not satisfied with his own liberation. He always thinks about others. He is the most compassionate personality towards all the fallen souls. One of his qualifications, therefore, is *kāruṇika*, great mercy to the fallen souls. While engaged in preaching work, he has to meet with so many opposing elements, and therefore the *sādhu*, or devotee of the Lord, has to be very tolerant. Someone may ill-treat him because the conditioned souls are not prepared to receive the transcendental knowledge of devotional service. They do not like it; that is their disease. The *sādhu* has the thankless task of impressing upon them the importance of devotional service. Sometimes devotees are personally attacked with violence. Lord Jesus Christ was crucified, Haridāsa Ṭhākura was caned in twenty-two marketplaces, and Lord Caitanya's principal assistant, Nityānanda, was violently attacked by Jagāi and Mādhāi. But still they were tolerant because their mission was to deliver the fallen souls. One of the qualifications of a *sādhu* is that he is very tolerant and is merciful to all fallen souls. He is merciful because he is the well-wisher of all living entities. He is not only a well-wisher of human society, but a well-wisher of animal society as well. It is said here, *sarva-dehinām*, which indicates all living entities who have accepted material bodies. Not only does the human being have a material body, but other living entities, such as cats and dogs, also have material bodies. The devotee of the Lord is merciful to everyone-the cats, dogs, trees, etc. He treats all living entities in such a way that they can ultimately get salvation from this material entanglement. Śivānanda Sena, one of the disciples of Lord Caitanya, gave liberation to a dog by treating the dog transcendentally. There are many instances where a dog got salvation by association with a *sādhu*, because a *sādhu* engages in the highest philanthropic activities for the benediction of all living entities. Yet although a *sādhu* is not inimical towards anyone, the world is so ungrateful that even a *sādhu* has many enemies.

What is the difference between an enemy and a friend? It is a difference in behavior. A *sādhu* behaves with all conditioned souls for their ultimate relief from material entanglement. Therefore, no one can be more friendly than a *sādhu* in relieving a conditioned soul. A *sādhu* is calm, and he quietly and peacefully follows the principles of scripture. A *sādhu* means one who follows the principles of scripture and at the same time is a devotee of the Lord. One who actually follows the principles of scripture must be a devotee of God because all the *śāstras* instruct us to obey the orders of the Personality of Godhead. *Sādhu*, therefore, means a follower of the scriptural injunctions and a devotee of the Lord. All these characteristics are prominent in a devotee. A devotee develops all the good qualities of the demigods, whereas a nondevotee, even though academically qualified, has no actual good qualifications or good characteristics according to the standard of transcendental realization.

TEXT 22

मय्यनन्येन भावेन भक्तिं कुर्वन्ति ये दृढाम् ।
मत्कृते त्यक्तकर्माणस्त्यक्तस्वजनबान्धवाः ॥२२॥

mayy ananyena bhāvena
bhaktiṁ kurvanti ye dṛḍhām
mat-kṛte tyakta-karmāṇas
tyakta-svajana-bāndhavāḥ

mayi—unto Me; *ananyena bhāvena*—with undeviated mind; *bhaktim*—devotional service; *kurvanti*—perform; *ye*—those who; *dṛḍhām*—staunch; *mat-kṛte*—for My sake; *tyakta*—renounced; *karmāṇaḥ*—activities; *tyakta*—renounced; *sva-jana*—family relationships; *bāndhavāḥ*—friendly acquaintances.

TRANSLATION

Such a sādhu engages in staunch devotional service to the Lord without deviation. For the sake of the Lord he renounces all other connections, such as family relationships and friendly acquaintances within the world.

PURPORT

A person in the renounced order of life, a *sannyāsī,* is also called a *sādhu* because he renounces everything—his home, his comfort, his friends, his relatives, and his duties to friends and to family. He renounces everything for the sake of the Supreme Personality of Godhead. A *sannyāsī* is generally in the renounced order of life, but his renunciation will be successful only when his energy is employed in the service of the Lord with great austerity. It is said here, therefore, *bhaktiṁ kurvanti ye dṛḍhām.* A person who seriously engages in the service of the Lord and is in the renounced order of life is a *sādhu.* A *sādhu* is one who has given up all responsibility to society, family, and worldly humanitarianism, simply for the service of the Lord. As soon as he takes his birth in the world, a person has so many responsibilities and obligations—to the public, to the demigods, to the great sages, to the general living beings, to his parents, to the family forefathers and to many others. When he gives up all such obligations for the sake of the service of the Supreme Lord, he is not punished for such renunciation of obligation. But if for sense gratification a person renounces all such obligations, he is punished by the law of nature.

TEXT 23

मदाश्रयाः कथा मृष्टाः शृण्वन्ति कथयन्ति च ।
तपन्ति विविधास्तापा नैतान्मद्गतचेतसः ॥२३॥

mad-āśrayāḥ kathā mṛṣṭāḥ
śṛṇvanti kathayanti ca
tapanti vividhās tāpā
naitān mad-gata-cetasaḥ

mat-āśrayāḥ—about Me; *kathāḥ*—stories; *mṛṣṭāḥ*—delightful; *śṛṇvanti*—they hear; *kathayanti*—they chant; *ca*—and; *tapanti*—inflict suffering; *vividhāḥ*—various; *tāpāḥ*—the material miseries; *na*—do not; *etān*—unto them; *mat-gata*—fixed on Me; *cetasaḥ*—their thoughts.

TRANSLATION

Engaged constantly in chanting and hearing about Me, the Supreme Personality of Godhead, the sādhus do not suffer from material miseries because they are always filled with thoughts of My pastimes and activities.

PURPORT

There are multifarious miseries in material existence—those pertaining to the body and the mind, those imposed by other living entities and those imposed by natural disturbances. But a *sādhu* is not disturbed by such miserable conditions because his mind is always filled with Kṛṣṇa consciousness, and thus he does not like to talk about anything but the activities of the Lord. Mahārāja Ambarīṣa did not speak of anything but the pastimes of the Lord. *Vacāṁsi vaikuṇṭha-guṇānuvarṇane* (*Bhāg.* 9.4.18). He engaged his words only in glorification of the Supreme Personality of Godhead. *Sādhus* are always interested in hearing about the activities of the Lord or His devotees. Since they are filled with Kṛṣṇa consciousness, they are forgetful of the material miseries. Ordinary conditioned souls, being forgetful of the activities of the Lord, are always full of anxieties and material tribulations. On the other hand, since the devotees always engage in the topics of the Lord, they are forgetful of the miseries of material existence.

TEXT 24

त एते साधवः साध्वि सर्वसङ्गविवर्जिताः ।
सङ्गस्तेष्वथ ते प्रार्थ्यः सङ्गदोषहरा हि ते ॥२४॥

ta ete sādhavaḥ sādhvi
sarva-saṅga-vivarjitāḥ
saṅgas teṣv atha te prārthyaḥ
saṅga-doṣa-harā hi te

te ete—those very; *sādhavaḥ*—devotees; *sādhvi*—virtuous lady; *sarva*—all; *saṅga*—attachments; *vivarjitāḥ*—freed from; *saṅgaḥ*—attachment; *teṣu*—unto them; *atha*—hence; *te*—by you; *prārthyaḥ*—must be sought; *saṅga-doṣa*—the pernicious effects of material attachment; *harāḥ*—counteracters of; *hi*—indeed; *te*—they.

TRANSLATION

O My mother, O virtuous lady, these are the qualities of great devotees who are free from all attachment. You must seek attachment to such holy men, for this counteracts the pernicious effects of material attachment.

PURPORT

Kapila Muni herein advises His mother, Devahūti, that if she wants to be free from material attachment, she should increase her attachment for the *sādhus,* or devotees who are completely freed from all material attachment. In *Bhagavad-gītā,* Fifteenth Chapter, verse 5, it is stated who is qualified to enter into the kingdom of Godhead. It is said there, *nirmāna-mohā jita-saṅga-doṣāḥ.* This refers to one who is completely freed from the puffed-up condition of material possessiveness. A person may be materially very rich, opulent or respectable, but if he at all wants to transfer himself to the spiritual kingdom, back home, back to Godhead, then he has to be freed from the puffed-up condition of material possessiveness, because that is a false position.

The word *moha* used here means the false understanding that one is rich or poor. In this material world, the conception that one is very rich or very poor—or any such consciousness in connection with material existence—is false, because this body itself is false, or temporary. A pure soul who is prepared to be freed from this material entanglement must first of all be free from the association of the three modes of nature. Our consciousness at the present moment is polluted because of association with the three modes of nature; therefore in *Bhagavad-gītā* the same principle is stated. It is advised, *jita-saṅga-doṣāḥ:* one should be freed from the contaminated association of the three modes of material nature. Here also, in the *Śrīmad-Bhāgavatam*, this is confirmed: a pure devotee, who is preparing to transfer himself to the spiritual kingdom, is also freed from the association of the three modes of material nature. We have to seek the association of such devotees. For this reason we have begun the International Society for Krishna Consciousness. There are many mercantile, scientific and other associations in human society to develop a particular type of education or consciousness, but there is no association which helps one to get free from all material association. If anyone has reached the stage where he must become free from this material contamination, then he has to seek the association of devotees, wherein Kṛṣṇa consciousness is exclusively cultured. One can thereby become freed from all material association.

Because a devotee is freed from all contaminated material association, he is not affected by the miseries of material existence. Even though he appears to be in the material world, he is not affected by the miseries of the material world. How is it possible? There is a very good example in the activities of the cat. The cat carries her kittens in her mouth, and when she kills a rat she also carries the booty in her mouth. Thus both are carried in the mouth of the cat, but they are in different conditions. The kitten feels comfort in the mouth of the mother, whereas when the rat is carried in the mouth of the cat, the rat feels the blows of death. Similarly, those who are *sādhavaḥ*, or devotees engaged in Kṛṣṇa consciousness in the transcendental service of the Lord, do not feel the contamination of material miseries, whereas those who are not devotees in Kṛṣṇa consciousness actually feel the miseries of material existence. One should therefore give up the association of materialistic persons and seek the association of persons engaged in Kṛṣṇa consciousness, and by such association he will benefit in spiritual advancement. By their words and instructions, he will be able to cut off his attachment to material existence.

TEXT 25

सतां प्रसङ्गान्मम वीर्यसंविदो
भवन्ति हृत्कर्णरसायनाः कथाः ।
तज्जोषणादाश्वपवर्गवर्त्मनि
श्रद्धा रतिर्भक्तिरनुक्रमिष्यति ॥२५॥

satāṁ prasaṅgān mama vīrya-saṁvido
bhavanti hṛt-karṇa-rasāyanāḥ kathāḥ
taj-joṣaṇād āśv apavarga-vartmani
śraddhā ratir bhaktir anukramiṣyati

satām—of pure devotees; *prasaṅgāt*—through the association; *mama*—My; *vīrya*—wonderful activities; *saṁvidaḥ*—by discussion of; *bhavanti*—become; *hṛt*—to the heart; *karṇa*—to the ear; *rasa-ayanāḥ*—pleasing; *kathāḥ*—the stories; *tat*—of that; *joṣaṇāt*—by cultivation; *āśu*—quickly; *apavarga*—of liberation; *vartmani*—on the path; *śraddhā*—firm faith; *ratiḥ*—attraction; *bhaktiḥ*—devotion; *anukramiṣyati*—will follow in order.

TRANSLATION

In the association of pure devotees, discussion of the pastimes and activities of the Supreme Personality of Godhead is very pleasing and satisfying to the ear and the heart. By cultivating such knowledge one gradually becomes advanced on the path of liberation, and thereafter he is freed, and his attraction becomes fixed. Then real devotion and devotional service begin.

PURPORT

The process of advancing in Kṛṣṇa consciousness and devotional service is described here. The first point is that one must seek the association of persons who are Kṛṣṇa conscious and who engage in devotional service. Without such association one cannot make advancement. Simply by theoretical knowledge or study one cannot make any appreciable advancement. One must give up the association of materialistic persons and seek the association of devotees because without the association of devotees one cannot understand the activities of the Lord. Generally, people are convinced of the impersonal feature of the Absolute Truth. Because they do not associate with devotees, they cannot understand that the Absolute Truth can be a person and have personal activities. This is a very difficult subject matter, and unless one has personal understanding of the Absolute Truth, there is no meaning to devotion. Service or devotion cannot be offered to anything impersonal. Service must be offered to a person. Nondevotees cannot appreciate Kṛṣṇa consciousness by reading the *Śrīmad-Bhāgavatam* or any other Vedic literature wherein the activities of the Lord are described; they think that these activities are fictional, manufactured stories because spiritual life is not explained to them in the proper mood. To understand the personal activities of the Lord, one has to seek the association of devotees, and by such association, when one contemplates and tries to understand the transcendental activities of the Lord, the path to liberation is open, and he is freed. One who has firm faith in the Supreme Personality of Godhead becomes fixed, and his attraction for association with the Lord and the devotees increases. Association with devotees means association with the Lord. The devotee who makes this association develops the consciousness for rendering service to the Lord, and then, being situated in the transcendental position of devotional service, he gradually becomes perfect.

TEXT 26

भक्त्या पुमाञ्जातविराग ऐन्द्रियाद्
दृष्टश्रुतान्मद्रचनानुचिन्तया ।
चित्तस्य यत्तो ग्रहणे योगयुक्तो
यतिष्यते ऋजुभिर्योगमार्गैः ॥२६॥

bhaktyā pumāñ jāta-virāga aindriyād
dṛṣṭa-śrutān mad-racanānucintayā
cittasya yatto grahaṇe yoga-yukto
yatiṣyate ṛjubhir yoga-mārgaiḥ

bhaktyā—by devotional service; *pumān*—a person; *jāta-virāgaḥ*—having developed distaste; *aindriyāt*—for sense gratification; *dṛṣṭa*—seen (in this world); *śrutāt*—heard (in the next world); *mat-racana*—My activities of creation and so on; *anucintayā*—by constantly thinking about; *cittasya*—of the mind; *yattaḥ*—engaged; *grahaṇe*—in the control; *yoga-yuktaḥ*—situated in devotional service; *yatiṣyate*—will endeavor; *ṛjubhiḥ*—easy; *yoga-mārgaiḥ*—by the processes of mystic power.

TRANSLATION

Thus consciously engaged in devotional service in the association of devotees, a person gains distaste for sense gratification, both in this world and in the next, by constantly thinking about the activities of the Lord. This process of Kṛṣṇa consciousness is the easiest process of mystic power; when one is actually situated on that path of devotional service, he is able to control the mind.

PURPORT

In all scriptures people are encouraged to act in a pious way so that they can enjoy sense gratification not only in this life but also in the next. For example, one is promised promotion to the heavenly kingdom of higher planets by pious fruitive activities. But a devotee in the association of devotees prefers to contemplate the activities of the Lord—how He has created this universe, how He is maintaining it, how the creation dissolves, and how in the spiritual kingdom the Lord's pastimes are going on. There are full literatures describing these activities of the Lord, especially

Bhagavad-gītā, Brahma-saṁhitā and *Śrīmad-Bhāgavatam.* The sincere devotee who associates with devotees gets the opportunity to hear and contemplate this subject of the pastimes of the Lord, and the result is that he feels distaste for so-called happiness in this or that world, in heaven or on other planets. The devotees are simply interested in being transferred to the personal association of the Lord; they have no more attraction for temporary so-called happiness. That is the position of one who is *yoga-yukta.* One who is fixed in mystic power is not disturbed by the allurement of this world or that world; he is interested in the matters of spiritual understanding or the spiritual situation. This sublime situation is very easily attained by the easiest process, *bhakti-yoga. Ṛjubhir yoga-mārgaiḥ.* A very suitable word used here is *ṛjubhiḥ,* or "very easy." There are different processes of *yoga-mārga,* attaining *yoga* perfection, but this process, devotional service to the Lord, is the easiest. Not only is it the easiest process, but the result is sublime. Everyone, therefore, should try to take this process of Kṛṣṇa consciousness and reach the highest perfection of life.

TEXT 27

असेवयायं प्रकृतेर्गुणानां
ज्ञानेन वैराग्यविजृम्भितेन ।
योगेन मय्यर्पितया च भक्त्या
मां प्रत्यगात्मानमिहावरुन्धे ॥२७॥

asevayāyaṁ prakṛter guṇānāṁ
jñānena vairāgya-vijṛmbhitena
yogena mayy arpitayā ca bhaktyā
māṁ pratyag-ātmānam ihāvarundhe

asevayā—by not engaging in the service; *ayam*—this person; *prakṛteḥ guṇānām*—of the modes of material nature; *jñānena*—by Knowledge; *vairāgya*—with renunciation; *vijṛmbhitena*—developed; *yogena*—by practicing *yoga; mayi*—unto Me; *arpitayā*—fixed; *ca*—and; *bhaktyā*—with devotion; *mām*—unto Me; *pratyak-ātmānam*—the Absolute Truth; *iha*—in this very life; *avarundhe*—one attains.

TRANSLATION

Thus by not engaging in the service of the modes of material nature but by developing Kṛṣṇa consciousness, knowledge in renunciation, and by practicing yoga, in which the mind is always fixed in devotional service unto the Supreme

Personality of Godhead, one achieves My association in this very life, for I am the Supreme Personality, the Absolute Truth.

PURPORT

When one engages in devotional service to the Lord in the nine different kinds of *bhakti-yoga,* as enunciated in authoritative scriptures, such as hearing (*śravaṇam*), chanting (*kīrtanam*), remembering, offering worship, praying and offering personal service—either in one of them, or two or three or all of them—he naturally has no opportunity to engage in the service of the three modes of material nature. Unless one has good engagements in spiritual service, it is not possible to get out of the attachment to material service. Those who are not devotees, therefore, are interested in so-called humanitarian or philanthropic work, such as opening a hospital or charitable institution. These are undoubtedly good works in the sense that they are pious activities, and their result is that the performer may get some opportunities for sense gratification, either in this life or in the next. Devotional service, however, is beyond the boundary of sense gratification. It is completely spiritual activity. When one engages in the spiritual activities of devotional service, naturally he does not get any opportunity to engage in sense gratificatory activities. Kṛṣṇa conscious activities are performed not blindly but with perfect understanding of knowledge and renunciation. This kind of *yoga* practice, in which the mind is always fixed upon the Supreme Personality of Godhead in devotion, results in liberation in this very life. The person who performs such acts gets in touch with the Supreme Personality of Godhead. Lord Caitanya, therefore, approved the process of hearing from realized devotees about the pastimes of the Lord. It does not matter to what category of this world the audience belongs. If one meekly and submissively hears about the activities of the Lord from a realized soul, he will be able to conquer the Supreme Personality of Godhead, who is unconquerable by any other process. Hearing or associating with devotees is the most important function for self-realization.

TEXT 28

देवहूतिरुवाच

काचित्त्वय्युचिता भक्तिः कीदृशी मम गोचरा ।
यया पदं ते निर्वाणमञ्जसान्वाश्नवा अहम् ॥२८॥

devahūtir uvāca
kācit tvayy ucitā bhaktiḥ
kīdṛśī mama gocarā

yayā padaṁ te nirvāṇam
añjasānvāśnavā aham

devahūtiḥ uvāca—Devahūti said; *kācit*—what; *tvayi*—unto You; *ucitā*—proper; *bhaktiḥ*—devotional service; *kīdṛśī*—what kind; *mama*—by me; *go-carā*—fit to be practiced; *yayā*—by which; *padam*—feet; *te*—Your; *nirvāṇam*—liberation; *añjasā*—immediately; *anvāśnavai*—shall attain; *aham*—I.

TRANSLATION

On hearing this statement of the Lord, Devahūti inquired: What kind of devotional service is worth developing and practicing to help me easily and immediately attain the service of Your lotus feet?

PURPORT

It is stated in *Bhagavad-gītā* that no one is barred from rendering service to the Lord. Whether one is a woman or a laborer or a merchant, if he engages himself in the devotional service of the Lord he is promoted to the highest perfectional state and goes back home, back to Godhead. The devotional service most suitable for different types of devotees is determined and fixed by the mercy of the spiritual master.

TEXT 29

यो योगो भगवद्बाणो निर्वाणात्मंस्त्वयोदितः ।
कीदृशः कति चाङ्गानि यतस्तत्त्वावबोधनम् ॥२९॥

yo yogo bhagavad-bāṇo
nirvāṇātmaṁs tvayoditaḥ
kīdṛśaḥ kati cāṅgāni
yatas tattvāvabodhanam

yaḥ—which; *yogaḥ*—mystic yoga process; *bhagavat-bāṇaḥ*—aiming at the Supreme Personality of Godhead; *nirvāṇa-ātman*—O embodiment of *nirvāṇa; tvayā*—by You; *uditaḥ*—explained; *kīdṛśaḥ*—of what nature; *kati*—how many; *ca*—and; *aṅgāni*—branches; *yataḥ*—by which; *tattva*—of the truth; *avabodhanam*—understanding.

TRANSLATION

The mystic yoga system, as You have explained, aims at the Supreme Personality of Godhead and is meant for completely ending material existence. Please let me know the nature of that yoga system. How many ways are there by which one can understand in truth that sublime yoga?

PURPORT

There are different kinds of mystic *yoga* systems aiming for different phases of the Absolute Truth. The *jñāna-yoga* system aims at the impersonal Brahman effulgence, and the *haṭha-yoga* system aims at the localized personal aspect, the Paramātmā feature of the Absolute Truth, whereas *bhakti-yoga,* or devotional service, which is executed in nine different ways, headed by hearing and chanting, aims at complete realization of the Supreme Lord. There are different methods of self-realization. But here Devahūti especially refers to the *bhakti-yoga* system, which has already been primarily explained by the Lord. The different parts of the *bhakti-yoga* system are hearing, chanting, remembering, offering prayers, worshiping the Lord in the temple, accepting service to Him, carrying out His orders, making friendship with Him and ultimately surrendering everything for the service of the Lord. The word *nirvāṇātman* is very significant in this verse. Unless one accepts the process of devotional service, one cannot end the continuation of material existence. As far as *jñānīs* are concerned, they are interested in *jñāna-yoga,* but even if one elevates oneself, after a great performance of austerity, to the Brahman effulgence, there is a chance of falling down again to the material world. Therefore, *jñāna-yoga* does not actually end material existence. Similarly, regarding the *haṭha-yoga* system, which aims at the localized aspect of the Lord, Paramātmā, it has been experienced that many *yogīs,* such as Viśvāmitra, fall down. But *bhakti-yogīs,* once approaching the Supreme Personality of Godhead, never come back to this material world, as it is confirmed in the *Bhagavad-gītā. Yad gatvā na nivartante:* upon going, one never comes back. *Tyaktvā dehaṁ punar janma naiti:* after giving up this body, he never comes back again to accept a material body. *Nirvāṇa* does not finish the existence of the soul. The soul is ever existing. Therefore *nirvāṇa* means to end one's material existence, and to end material existence means to go back home, back to Godhead.

Sometimes it is asked how the living entity falls down from the spiritual world to the material world. Here is the answer. Unless one is elevated to the Vaikuṇṭha planets, directly in touch with the Supreme Personality of Godhead, he is prone to fall down, either from the impersonal Brahman realization or from an ecstatic trance of meditation. Another word in this verse, *bhagavad-bāṇaḥ,* is very significant. *Bāṇaḥ* means "arrow." The *bhakti-yoga* system is just like an arrow aiming up to the Supreme Personality of Godhead. The *bhakti-yoga* system never urges one towards the impersonal Brahman effulgence or to the point of Paramātmā realization. This *bāṇaḥ,* or arrow, is so sharp and swift that it goes directly to the Supreme Personality of Godhead, penetrating the regions of impersonal Brahman and localized Paramātmā.

TEXT 30

तदेतन्मे विजानीहि यथाहं मन्दधीर्हरे ।
सुखं बुद्ध्येय दुर्बोधं योषा भवदनुग्रहात् ॥३०॥

tad etan me vijānīhi
yathāhaṁ manda-dhīr hare
sukhaṁ buddhyeya durbodhaṁ
yoṣā bhavad-anugrahāt

tat etat—that same; *me*—to me; *vijānīhi*—please explain; *yathā*—so that; *aham*—I; *manda*—slow; *dhīḥ*—whose intelligence; *hare*—O my Lord; *sukham*—easily; *buddhyeya*—may understand; *durbodham*—very difficult to understand; *yoṣā*—a woman; *bhavat-anugrahāt*—by Your grace.

TRANSLATION

My dear son, Kapila, after all, I am a woman. It is very difficult for me to understand the Absolute Truth because my intelligence is not very great. But if You will kindly explain it to me, even though I am not very intelligent, I can understand it and thereby feel transcendental happiness.

PURPORT

Knowledge of the Absolute Truth is not very easily understood by ordinary, less intelligent men; but if the spiritual master is kind enough to the disciple, however unintelligent the disciple may be, then by the divine grace of the spiritual master everything is revealed. Viśvanātha Cakravartī Ṭhākura therefore says, *yasya prasādād,* by the mercy of the spiritual master, the mercy of the Supreme Personality of Godhead, *bhagavat-prasādaḥ,* is revealed. Devahūti requested her great son to be merciful towards her because she was a less intelligent woman and also His mother. By the grace of Kapiladeva it was quite possible for her to understand the Absolute Truth, even though the subject matter is very difficult for ordinary persons, especially women.

TEXT 31

मैत्रेय उवाच

विदित्वार्थं कपिलो मातुरित्थं
जातस्नेहो यत्र तन्वाभिजातः ।
तत्त्वाम्नायं यत्प्रवदन्ति सांख्यं
प्रोवाच वै भक्तिवितानयोगम् ॥३१॥

maitreya uvāca
viditvārthaṁ kapilo mātur itthaṁ
jāta-sneho yatra tanvābhijātaḥ
tattvāmnāyaṁ yat pravadanti sāṅkhyaṁ
provāca vai bhakti-vitāna-yogam

maitreyaḥ uvāca—Maitreya said; *viditvā*—having known; *artham*—purpose; *kapilaḥ*—Lord Kapila; *mātuḥ*—of His mother; *ittham*—thus; *jāta-snehaḥ*—became compassionate; *yatra*—upon her; *tanvā*—from her body; *abhijātaḥ*—born; *tattva-āmnāyam*—truths received by disciplic succession; *yat*—which; *pravadanti*—they call; *sāṅkhyam*—Sāṅkhya philosophy; *provāca*—He described; *vai*—in fact; *bhakti*—devotional service; *vitāna*—spreading; *yogam*—mystic *yoga.*

TRANSLATION

Śrī Maitreya said: After hearing the statement of His mother, Kapila could understand her purpose, and He became compassionate towards her because of being born of her body. He described the Sāṅkhya system of philosophy, which is a combination of devotional service and mystic realization, as received by disciplic succession.

TEXT 32

श्रीभगवानुवाच
देवानां गुणलिङ्गानामानुश्रविककर्मणाम् ।
सत्त्व एवैकमनसो वृत्तिः स्वाभाविकी तु या ।
अनिमित्ता भागवती भक्तिः सिद्धेर्गरीयसी ॥३२॥

śrī-bhagavān uvāca
devānāṁ guṇa-liṅgānām
ānuśravika-karmaṇām
sattva evaika-manaso
vṛttiḥ svābhāvikī tu yā
animittā bhāgavatī
bhaktiḥ siddher garīyasī

śrī-bhagavān uvāca—the Supreme Personality of Godhead said; *devānām*—of the senses or of the presiding deities of the senses; *guṇa-liṅgānām*—which detect sense objects; *ānuśravika*—according to scripture; *karmaṇām*—which work; *sattve*—unto the mind or unto the Lord; *eva*—only; *eka-manasaḥ*—of a man of undivided mind; *vṛttiḥ*—inclination; *svābhāvikī*—natural; *tu*—in fact; *yā*—which; *animittā*—without motive; *bhāgavatī*—to the

Personality of Godhead; *bhaktiḥ*—devotional service; *siddheḥ*—than salvation; *garīyasī*—better.

TRANSLATION

Lord Kapila said: The senses are symbolic representations of the demigods, and their natural inclination is to work under the direction of the Vedic injunctions. As the senses are representatives of the demigods, so the mind is the representative of the Supreme Personality of Godhead. The mind's natural duty is to serve. When that service spirit is engaged in devotional service to the Personality of Godhead, without any motive, that is far better even than salvation.

PURPORT

The senses of the living entity are always engaged in some occupation, either in activities prescribed in the injunctions of the *Vedas* or in material activities. The natural inclination of the senses is to work for something, and the mind is the center of the senses. The mind is actually the leader of the senses; therefore it is called *sattva.* Similarly, the leader of all the demigods who are engaged in the activities of this material world—the sun-god, moon-god, Indra and others—is the Supreme Personality of Godhead.

It is stated in the Vedic literature that the demigods are different limbs of the universal body of the Supreme Personality of Godhead. Our senses are also controlled by different demigods; our senses are representations of various demigods, and the mind is the representation of the Supreme Personality of Godhead. The senses, led by the mind, act under the influence of the demigods. When the service is ultimately aimed at the Supreme Personality of Godhead, the senses are in their natural position. The Lord is called Hṛṣīkeśa, for He is actually the proprietor and ultimate master of the senses. The senses and the mind are naturally inclined to work, but when they are materially contaminated they work for some material benefit or for the service of the demigods, although actually they are meant to serve the Supreme Personality of Godhead. The senses are called *hṛṣīka,* and the Supreme Personality of Godhead is called Hṛṣīkeśa. Indirectly, all the senses are naturally inclined to serve the Supreme Lord. That is called *bhakti.*

Kapiladeva said that when the senses, without desire for material profit or other selfish motives, are engaged in the service of the Supreme Personality of Godhead, one is situated in devotional service. That spirit of service is far better than *siddhi,* salvation. *Bhakti,* the inclination to serve the Supreme Personality of Godhead, is in a transcendental position far better than *mukti,* or liberation. Thus *bhakti* is the stage after liberation. Unless one is liberated one cannot engage the senses in the service of the Lord. When the senses are engaged either in material activities of sense gratification or in the activities of the Vedic injunctions, there is some motive, but when the same senses are engaged in the service of the Lord and there is no motive, that is called *animittā* and is the natural inclination of the mind. The conclusion is that when the mind, without being deviated either by Vedic injunctions or by material activities, is fully engaged in Kṛṣṇa consciousness, or devotional service to the Supreme Personality of Godhead, it is far better than the most aspired—for liberation from material entanglement.

TEXT 33

जरयत्याशु या कोशं निगीर्णमनलो यथा ॥३३॥

jarayaty āśu yā kośaṁ
nigīrṇam analo yathā

jarayati—dissolves; *āśu*—quickly; *yā*—which; *kośam*—the subtle body; *nigīrṇam*—things eaten; *analaḥ*—fire; *yathā*—as.

TRANSLATION

Bhakti, devotional service, dissolves the subtle body of the living entity without separate effort, just as fire in the stomach digests all that we eat.

PURPORT

Bhakti is in a far higher position than *mukti* because a person's endeavor to get liberation from the material encagement is automatically served in devotional service. The example is given here that the fire in the stomach can digest whatever we eat. If the digestive power is sufficient, then whatever we can eat will be digested by the fire in the stomach. Similarly, a devotee does not have to try separately to attain liberation. That very service to the Supreme Personality of Godhead is the process of his liberation because to engage oneself in the service of the Lord is to liberate oneself from material entanglement. Śrī Bilvamaṅgala Ṭhākura explained this position very nicely. He said, "If I have unflinching devotion unto the lotus feet of the Supreme Lord, then *mukti,* or liberation, serves me as my maidservant. *Mukti,* the maidservant, is always ready to do whatever I ask."

For a devotee, liberation is no problem at all. Liberation takes place without separate endeavor. *Bhakti,* therefore, is far better than *mukti* or the impersonalist position. The impersonalists undergo severe penances and austerities to attain *mukti,* but the *bhakta,* simply by engaging himself in the *bhakti* process, especially in chanting Hare Kṛṣṇa, Hare Kṛṣṇa, Kṛṣṇa Kṛṣṇa, Hare Hare/ Hare Rāma, Hare Rāma, Rāma Rāma, Hare Hare, immediately develops control over the tongue by engaging it in chanting, and accepting the remnants of foodstuff offered to the Personality of Godhead. As soon as the tongue is controlled, naturally all other senses are controlled automatically. Sense control is the perfection of the *yoga* principle, and one's liberation begins immediately as soon as he engages himself in the service of the Lord. It is confirmed by Kapiladeva that *bhakti,* or devotional service, is *garīyasī,* more glorious than *siddhi,* liberation.

TEXT 34

नैकात्मतां मे स्पृहयन्ति केचिन्
मत्पादसेवाभिरता मदीहाः ।
येऽन्योन्यतो भागवताः प्रसज्य
सभाजयन्ते मम पौरुषाणि ॥३४॥

naikātmatāṁ me spṛhayanti kecin
mat-pāda-sevābhiratā mad-īhāḥ
ye 'nyonyato bhāgavatāḥ prasajya
sabhājayante mama pauruṣāṇi

na—never; *eka-ātmatām*—merging into oneness; *me*—My; *spṛhayanti*—they desire; *kecit*—any; *mat-pāda-sevā*—the service of My lotus feet; *abhiratāḥ*—engaged in; *mat-īhāḥ*—endeavoring to attain Me; *ye*—those who; *anyonyataḥ*—mutually; *bhāgavatāḥ*—pure devotees; *prasajya*—assembling; *sabhājayante*—glorify; *mama*—My; *pauruṣāṇi*—glorious activities.

TRANSLATION

A pure devotee, who is attached to the activities of devotional service and who always engages in the service of My lotus feet, never desires to become one with Me. Such a devotee, who is unflinchingly engaged, always glorifies My pastimes and activities.

PURPORT

There are five kinds of liberation stated in the scriptures. One is to become one with the Supreme Personality of Godhead, or to forsake one's individuality and merge into the Supreme Spirit. This is called *ekātmatām.* A devotee never accepts this kind of liberation. The other four liberations are: to be promoted to the same planet as God (Vaikuṇṭha), to associate personally with the Supreme Lord, to achieve the same opulence as the Lord and to attain the same bodily features as the Supreme Lord. A pure devotee, as will be explained by Kapila Muni, does not aspire for any of the five liberations. He especially despises as hellish the idea of becoming one with the Supreme Personality of Godhead. Śrī Prabodhānanda Sarasvatī, a great devotee of Lord Caitanya, said, *kaivalyaṁ narakāyate:* "The happiness of becoming one with the Supreme Lord, which is aspired for by the Māyāvādīs, is considered hellish." That oneness is not for pure devotees.

There are many so-called devotees who think that in the conditioned state we may worship the Personality of Godhead but that ultimately there is no personality; they say that since the Absolute Truth is impersonal, one can imagine a personal form of the impersonal Absolute Truth for the time being, but as soon as one becomes liberated the worship stops. That is the theory put forward by the Māyāvāda philosophy. Actually the impersonalists do not merge into the existence of the Supreme Person but into His personal bodily luster, which is called the *brahma-jyotir.* Although that *brahmajyotir* is not different from His personal body, that sort of oneness (merging into the bodily luster of the Personality of Godhead) is not accepted by a pure devotee because the devotees engage in greater pleasure than the so-called pleasure of merging into His existence. The greatest pleasure is to serve the Lord. Devotees are always thinking about how to serve Him; they are always designing ways and means to serve the Supreme Lord, even in the midst of the greatest obstacles of material existence.

The Māyāvādīs accept the description of the pastimes of the Lord as stories, but actually they are not stories; they are historical facts. Pure devotees accept the narrations of the pastimes of the Lord not as stories but as Absolute Truth. The words *mama pauruṣāṇi* are significant. Devotees are very much attached to glorifying the activities of the Lord, whereas the Māyāvādīs cannot even think of these activities. According to them the Absolute Truth is impersonal. Without personal existence, how can there be activity? The impersonalists take the activities mentioned in the *Śrīmad-Bhāgavatam, Bhagavad-gītā* and other Vedic literatures as fictitious stories, and therefore they interpret them most mischievously. They have no idea of the Personality of Godhead. They unnecessarily poke their noses into the scripture and interpret it in a deceptive way in order to mislead the innocent public. The activities of Māyāvāda philosophy are very dangerous to the public, and therefore Lord Caitanya warned us never to hear from any Māyāvādī about any scripture. They will spoil the entire process, and the person hearing them will never be able to come to the path of devotional service to attain the highest perfection, or will be able to do so only after a very long time.

It is clearly stated by Kapila Muni that *bhakti* activities, or activities in devotional service, are transcendental to *mukti.* This is called *pañcama-puruṣārtha.* Generally, people engage in the activities of religion, economic development and sense gratification, and ultimately they work with an idea that they are going to become one with the Supreme Lord (*mukti*). But *bhakti* is transcendental to all these activities. The *Śrīmad-Bhāgavatam,* therefore, begins by stating that all kinds of pretentious religiosity is completely eradicated from the *Bhāgavatam.* Ritualistic activities for economic development and sense gratification and, after frustration in sense gratification, the desire to become one with the Supreme Lord, are all completely rejected in the *Bhāgavatam.* The *Bhāgavatam* is especially meant for the pure devotees, who always engage in Kṛṣṇa consciousness, in the activities of the Lord, and always glorify these transcendental activities. Pure devotees worship the transcendental activities of the Lord in Vṛndāvana, Dvārakā and Mathurā as they are narrated in the *Śrīmad-Bhāgavatam* and other *purāṇas.* The Māyāvādī philosophers completely reject them as stories, but actually they are great and worshipable subject matters and thus are relishable only for devotees. That is the difference between a Māyāvadī and a pure devotee.

TEXT 35

पश्यन्ति ते मे रुचिराण्यम्ब सन्तः
प्रसन्नवक्त्रारुणलोचनानि ।
रूपाणि दिव्यानि वरप्रदानि
साकं वाचं स्पृहणीयां वदन्ति ॥३५॥

paśyanti te me rucirāṇy amba santaḥ
prasanna-vaktrāruṇa-locanāni
rūpāṇi divyāni vara-pradāni
sākaṁ vācaṁ spṛhaṇīyāṁ vadanti

paśyanti—see; *te*—they; *me*—My; *rucirāṇi*—beautiful; *amba*—O mother; *santaḥ*—devotees; *prasanna*—smiling; *vaktra*—face; *aruṇa*—like the morning sun; *locanāni*—eyes; *rūpāṇi*—forms; *divyāni*—transcendental; *vara-pradāni*—benevolent; *sākam*—with Me; *vācam*—words; *spṛhaṇīyām*—favorable; *vadanti*—they speak.

TRANSLATION

O My mother, My devotees always see the smiling face of My form, with eyes like the rising morning sun. They like to see My various transcendental forms, which are all benevolent, and they also talk favorably with Me.

PURPORT

Māyāvādīs and atheists accept the forms of the Deities in the temple of the Lord as idols, but devotees do not worship idols. They directly worship the Personality of Godhead in His *arcā* incarnation. *Arcā* refers to the form which we can worship in our present condition. Actually, in our present state it is not possible to see God in His spiritual form because our material eyes and senses cannot conceive of a spiritual form. We cannot even see the spiritual form of the individual soul. When a man dies we cannot see how the spiritual form leaves the body. That is the defect of our material senses. In order to be seen by our material senses, the Supreme Personality of Godhead accepts a favorable form which is called *arcā-vigraha.* This *arcā-vigraha,* sometimes called the *arcā* incarnation, is not different from Him. Just as the Supreme Personality of Godhead accepts various incarnations, He takes on forms made out of matter—clay, wood, metal and jewels.

There are many śāstric injunctions which give instructions for carving forms of the Lord. These forms are not material. If God is all-pervading, then He is also in the material elements. There is no doubt about it. But the atheists think otherwise. Although they preach that everything is God, when they go to the temple and see the form of the Lord, they deny that He is God. According to their own theory, everything is God. Then why is the Deity not God? Actually, they have no conception of God. The devotees' vision, however, is different; their vision is smeared with love of God. As soon as they see the Lord in His different forms, the devotees become saturated with love, for they do not find any difference between the Lord and His form in the temple, as do the atheists. The smiling face of the Deity in the temple is beheld by the devotees as transcendental and spiritual, and the decoration of the body of the Lord is very much appreciated by the devotees. It is the duty of the spiritual master to teach how to decorate the Deity in the temple, how to cleanse the temple and how to worship the Deity. There are different procedures and rules and regulations which are followed in temples of Viṣṇu, and devotees go there and see the Deity, the *vigraha,* and spiritually enjoy the form because all of the Deities are benevolent. The devotees express their minds before the Deity, and in many instances the Deity also gives answers. But one must be a very elevated devotee in order to be able to speak with the Supreme Lord.

Sometimes the Lord informs the devotee through dreams. These exchanges of feelings between the Deity and the devotee are not understandable by atheists, but actually the devotee enjoys them. Kapila Muni is explaining how the devotees see the decorated body and face of the Deity and how they speak with Him in devotional service.

TEXT 36

तैर्दर्शनीयावयवैरुदार-
विलासहासेक्षितवामसूक्तैः ।
हृतात्मनो हृतप्राणांश्च भक्ति-
रनिच्छतो मे गतिमण्वीं प्रयुङ्क्ते ॥३६॥

tair darśanīyāvayavair udāra-
vilāsa-hāsekṣita-vāma-sūktaiḥ
hṛtātmano hṛta-prāṇāṁś ca bhaktir
anicchato me gatim aṇvīṁ prayuṅkte

taiḥ—by those forms; *darśanīya*—charming; *avayavaiḥ*—whose limbs; *udāra*—exalted; *vilāsa*—pastimes; *hāsa*—smiling; *īkṣita*—glances; *vāma*—pleasing; *sūktaiḥ*—whose delightful words; *hṛta*—captivated; *ātmanaḥ*—their minds; *hṛta*—captivated; *prāṇān*—their senses; *ca*—and; *bhaktiḥ*—devotional service; *anicchataḥ*—unwilling; *me*—My; *gatim*—abode; *aṇvīm*—subtle; *prayuṅkte*—secures.

TRANSLATION

Upon seeing the charming forms of the Lord, smiling and attractive, and hearing His very pleasing words, the pure devotee almost loses all other consciousness. His senses are freed from all other engagements, and he becomes absorbed in devotional service. Thus in spite of his unwillingness, he attains liberation without separate endeavor.

PURPORT

There are three divisions of devotees—first-class, second-class and third-class. Even the third-class devotees are liberated souls. It is explained in this verse that although they do not have knowledge, simply by seeing the beautiful decoration of the Deity in the temple, the devotee is absorbed in thought of Him and loses all other consciousness. Simply by fixing oneself in Kṛṣṇa consciousness, engaging the senses in the service of the Lord, one is imperceptibly liberated. This is also confirmed in *Bhagavad-gītā.* Simply by discharging uncontaminated devotional service as prescribed in the scriptures, one becomes equal to Brahman. In *Bhagavad-gītā* it is said, *brahma-bhūyāya kalpate.* This means that the living entity in his original state is Brahman because he is part and parcel of the Supreme Brahman. But simply because of his forgetfulness of his real nature as an eternal servitor of the Lord, he is overwhelmed and captured by *māyā.* His forgetfulness of his real constitutional position is *māyā.* Otherwise he is eternally Brahman.

When one is trained to become conscious of his position, he understands that he is the servitor of the Lord. "Brahman" refers to a state of self-realization. Even the third-class devotee—who is not advanced in knowledge of the Absolute Truth but simply offers obeisances with great devotion, thinks of the Lord, sees the Lord in the temple and brings forth flowers and fruits to offer to the Deity—becomes imperceptibly liberated. *Śraddhayānvitāḥ:* with great devotion the devotees offer worshipful respects and paraphernalia to the Deity. The Deities of Rādhā and Kṛṣṇa, Lakṣmī and Nārāyaṇa, and Rāma and Sītā are very attractive to devotees, so much so that when they see the statue decorated in the temple of the Lord they become fully absorbed in thought of the Lord. That is the state of liberation. In other words, it is confirmed herewith that even a third-class devotee is in the transcendental position, above those who are trying for liberation by speculation or by other methods. Even great impersonalists like Śukadeva Gosvāmī and the four Kumāras were attracted by the beauty of the Deities in the temple, by the decorations and by the aroma of *tulasī* offered to the Lord, and they became devotees. Even though they were in the liberated state, instead of remaining impersonalists they were attracted by the beauty of the Lord and became devotees.

Here the word *vilāsa* is very important. *Vilāsa* refers to the activities or pastimes of the Lord. It is a prescribed duty in temple worship that not only should one visit the temple to see the Deity nicely decorated, but at the same time he should hear the recitation of *Śrīmad-Bhāgavatam, Bhagavad-gītā* or some similar literature, which is regularly recited in the temple. It is the system in Vṛndāvana that in every temple there is recitation of the *śāstras.* Even third-class devotees who have no literary knowledge or no time to read *Śrīmad-Bhāgavatam* or *Bhagavad-gītā* get the opportunity to hear about the pastimes of the Lord. In this way their minds may remain always absorbed in the thought of the Lord—His form, His activities and His transcendental nature. This state of Kṛṣṇa consciousness is a liberated stage. Lord Caitanya, therefore, recommended five important processes in the discharge of devotional service: (1) to chant the holy names of the Lord, Hare Kṛṣṇa, Hare Kṛṣṇa, Kṛṣṇa Kṛṣṇa, Hare Hare/ Hare Rāma, Hare Rāma, Rāma Rāma, Hare Hare, (2) to associate with devotees and serve them as far as possible, (3) to hear *Śrīmad-Bhāgavatam,* (4) to see the decorated temple and the Deity and, if possible, (5) to live in a place like Vṛndāvana or Mathurā. These five items alone can help a devotee achieve the highest perfectional stage. This is confirmed in *Bhagavad-gītā* and here in the *Śrīmad-Bhāgavatam.* That third-class devotees can also imperceptibly achieve liberation is accepted in all Vedic literatures.

TEXT 37

अथो विभूतिं मम मायाविनस्ता-
मैश्वर्यमष्टाङ्गमनुप्रवृत्तम् ।
श्रियं भागवतीं वास्पृहयन्ति भद्रां
परस्य मे तेऽश्नुवते तु लोके ॥३७॥

atho vibhūtiṁ mama māyāvinas tām
aiśvaryam aṣṭāṅgam anupravṛttam
śriyaṁ bhāgavatīṁ vāspṛhayanti bhadrāṁ
parasya me te 'śnuvate tu loke

atho—then; *vibhūtim*—opulence; *mama*—of Me; *māyāvinaḥ*—of the Lord of *māyā; tām*—that; *aiśvaryam*—mystic perfection; *aṣṭa-aṅgam*—consisting of eight parts; *anupravṛttam*—following; *śriyam*—splendor; *bhāgavatīm*—of the kingdom of God; *vā*—or; *aspṛhayanti*—they do not desire; *bhadrām*—blissful; *parasya*—of the Supreme Lord; *me*—of Me; *te*—those devotees; *aśnuvate*—enjoy; *tu*—but; *loke*—in this life.

TRANSLATION

Thus because he is completely absorbed in thought of Me, the devotee does not desire even the highest benediction obtainable in the upper planetary systems, including Satyaloka. He does not desire the eight material perfections obtained from mystic yoga, nor does he desire to be elevated to the kingdom of God. Yet even without desiring them, the devotee enjoys, even in this life, all the offered benedictions.

PURPORT

The *vibhūti,* or opulences, offered by *māyā* are of many varieties. We have experience of different varieties of material enjoyment even on this planet, but if one is able to promote himself to higher planets like Candraloka, the sun or, still higher, Maharloka, Janaloka and Tapoloka, or even ultimately the highest planet, which is inhabited by

Brahmā and is called Satyaloka, there are immense possibilities for material enjoyment. For example, the duration of life on higher planets is far, far greater than on this planet. It is said that on the moon the duration of life is such that our six months are equal to one day. We cannot even imagine the duration of life on the highest planet. It is stated in *Bhagavad-gītā* that Brahmā's twelve hours are inconceivable even to our mathematicians. These are all descriptions of the external energy of the Lord, or *māyā*. Besides these, there are other opulences which the *yogīs* can achieve by their mystic power. They are also material. A devotee does not aspire for all these material pleasures, although they are available to him simply by wishing. By the grace of the Lord, a devotee can achieve wonderful success simply by willing, but a real devotee does not like that. Lord Caitanya Mahāprabhu has taught that one should not desire material opulence or material reputation, nor should one try to enjoy material beauty; one should simply aspire to be absorbed in the devotional service of the Lord, even if one does not get liberation but has to continue the process of birth and death unlimitedly. Actually, however, to one who engages in Kṛṣṇa consciousness, liberation is already guaranteed. Devotees enjoy all the benefits of the higher planets and the Vaikuṇṭha planets also. It is especially mentioned here, *bhāgavatīṁ bhadrām*. In the Vaikuṇṭha planets everything is eternally peaceful, yet a pure devotee does not even aspire to be promoted there. But still he gets that advantage; he enjoys all the facilities of the material and spiritual worlds, even during the present life-span.

TEXT 38

न कर्हिचिन्मत्पराः शान्तरूपे
नङ्क्ष्यन्ति नो मेऽनिमिषो लेढि हेतिः ।
येषामहं प्रिय आत्मा सुतश्च
सखा गुरुः सुहृदो दैवमिष्टम् ॥३८॥

na karhicin mat-parāḥ śānta-rūpe
naṅkṣyanti no me 'nimiṣo leḍhi hetiḥ
yeṣām ahaṁ priya ātmā sutaś ca
sakhā guruḥ suhṛdo daivam iṣṭam

na—not; *karhicit*—ever; *mat-parāḥ*—My devotees; *śānta-rūpe*—O mother; *naṅkṣyanti*—will lose; *no*—not; *me*—My; *animiṣaḥ*—time; *leḍhi*—destroys; *hetiḥ*—weapon; *yeṣām*—of whom; *aham*—I; *priyaḥ*—dear; *ātmā*—self; *sutaḥ*—son; *ca*—and; *sakhā*—friend; *guruḥ*—preceptor; *suhṛdaḥ*—benefactor; *daivam*—Deity; *iṣṭam*—chosen.

TRANSLATION

The Lord continued: My dear mother, devotees who receive such transcendental opulences are never bereft of them; neither weapons nor the change of time can destroy such opulences. Because the devotees accept Me as their friend, their relative, their son, preceptor, benefactor and Supreme Deity, they cannot be deprived of their possessions at any time.

PURPORT

It is stated in *Bhagavad-gītā* that one may elevate himself to the higher planetary systems, even up to Brahmaloka, by dint of pious activities, but when the effects of such pious activities are finished, one again comes back to this earth to begin a new life of activities. Thus even though one is promoted to the higher planetary system for enjoyment and a long duration of life, still that is not a permanent settlement. But as far as the devotees are concerned, their assets—the achievement of devotional service and the consequent opulence of Vaikuṇṭha, even on this planet—are never destroyed. In this verse Kapiladeva addresses His mother as *śānta-rūpā,* indicating that the opulences of devotees are fixed because devotees are eternally fixed in the Vaikuṇṭha atmosphere, which is called *śānta-rūpa* because it is in the mode of pure goodness, undisturbed by the modes of passion and ignorance. Once one is fixed in the devotional service of the Lord, his position of transcendental service cannot be destroyed, and the pleasure and service simply increase unlimitedly. For the devotees engaged in Kṛṣṇa consciousness, in the Vaikuṇṭha atmosphere, there is no influence of time. In the material world the influence of time destroys everything, but in the Vaikuṇṭha atmosphere there is no influence of time or of the demigods because there are no demigods in the Vaikuṇṭha planets. Here our activities are controlled by different demigods; even if we move our hand and leg, the action is controlled by the demigods. But in the Vaikuṇṭha atmosphere there is no influence of the demigods or of time; therefore there is no question of destruction. When the time element is present, there is the certainty of destruction, but when there is no time element—past, present or future—then everything is eternal. Therefore this verse uses the words *na naṅkṣyanti,* indicating that the transcendental opulences will never be destroyed.

The reason for freedom from destruction is also described. The devotees accept the Supreme Lord as the most dear personality and reciprocate with Him in different relationships. They accept the Supreme Personality of Godhead as the dearmost friend, the dearmost relative, the dearmost son, the dearmost preceptor, the dearmost well-wisher or the dearmost Deity. The Lord is eternal; therefore any relationship in which we accept Him is also eternal. It is clearly confirmed herein that the relationships cannot be destroyed, and therefore the opulences of those relationships are never destroyed. Every living entity has the propensity to love someone. We can see that if someone has no object of love, he generally directs his love to a pet animal like a cat or a dog. Thus the eternal propensity for love in all living entities is always searching for a place to reside. From this verse we can learn that we can love the Supreme Personality of Godhead as our dearmost object—as a friend, as a son, as a preceptor or as a well-wisher—and there will be no cheating and no end to such love. We shall eternally enjoy the relationship with the Supreme Lord in different aspects. A special feature of this verse is the acceptance of the Supreme Lord as the supreme preceptor. *Bhagavad-gītā* was spoken directly by the Supreme Lord, and Arjuna accepted Kṛṣṇa as *guru,* or spiritual master. Similarly, we should accept only Kṛṣṇa as the supreme spiritual master.

Kṛṣṇa, of course, means Kṛṣṇa and His confidential devotees; Kṛṣṇa is not alone. When we speak of Kṛṣṇa, "Kṛṣṇa" means Kṛṣṇa in His name, in His form, in His qualities, in His abode and in His associates. Kṛṣṇa is never alone, for the devotees of Kṛṣṇa are not impersonalists. For example, a king is always associated with his secretary, his commander, his servant and so much paraphernalia. As soon as we accept Kṛṣṇa and His associates as our preceptors, no ill effects can destroy our knowledge. In the material world the knowledge which we acquire may change because of the influence of time, but nevertheless the conclusions received from *Bhagavad-gītā,* directly from the speeches of the Supreme Lord, Kṛṣṇa, can never change. There is no use interpreting *Bhagavad-gītā;* it is eternal.

Kṛṣṇa, the Supreme Lord, should be accepted as one's best friend. He will never cheat. He will always give His friendly advice and friendly protection to the devotee. If Kṛṣṇa is accepted as a son, He will never die. Here we have a very loving son or child, but the father and mother, or those who are affectionate towards him, always hope, "May my son not die." But Kṛṣṇa actually never will die. Therefore those who accept Kṛṣṇa, or the Supreme Lord, as their son will never be bereft of their son. In many instances devotees have accepted the Deity as a son. In Bengal there are many such instances, and even after the death of the devotee, the Deity performs the *śrāddha* ceremony for the father. The relationship is never destroyed. People are accustomed to worship different forms of demigods, but in *Bhagavad-gītā* such a mentality is condemned; therefore one should be intelligent enough to worship only the Supreme Personality of Godhead in His different forms such as Lakṣmī-Nārāyaṇa, Sītā-Rāma and Rādhā-Kṛṣṇa. Thus one will never be cheated. By worshiping the demigods one may elevate himself to the higher planets, but during the dissolution of the material world, the deity and the abode of the deity will be destroyed. But one who worships the Supreme Personality of Godhead is promoted to the Vaikuṇṭha planets, where there is no influence of time, destruction or annihilation. The conclusion is that the time influence cannot act upon devotees who have accepted the Supreme Personality of Godhead as everything.

TEXTS 39-40

इमं लोकं तथैवामुमात्मानमुभयायिनम् ।
आत्मानमनु ये चेह ये रायः पशवो गृहाः ॥३९॥
विसृज्य सर्वानन्यांश्च मामेवं विश्वतोमुखम् ।
भजन्त्यनन्यया भक्त्या तान्मृत्योरतिपारये ॥४०॥

imaṁ lokaṁ tathaivāmum
ātmānam ubhayāyinam
ātmānam anu ye ceha
ye rāyaḥ paśavo gṛhāḥ

visṛjya sarvān anyāṁś ca
māṁ evaṁ viśvato-mukham
bhajanty ananyayā bhaktyā
tān mṛtyor atipāraye

imam—this; *lokam*—world; *tathā*—accordingly; *eva*—certainly; *amum*—that world; *ātmānam*—the subtle body; *ubhaya*—in both; *ayinam*—traveling; *ātmānam*—the body; *anu*—in relationship with; *ye*—those who; *ca*—also; *iha*—in this world; *ye*—that which; *rāyaḥ*—wealth; *paśavaḥ*—cattle; *gṛhāḥ*—houses; *visṛjya*—having given up; *sarvān*—all; *anyān*—other; *ca*—and; *mām*—Me; *evam*—thus; *viśvataḥ-mukham*—the all-pervading Lord of the universe; *bhajanti*—they worship; *ananyayā*—unflinching; *bhaktyā*—by devotional service; *tān*—them; *mṛtyoḥ*—of death; *atipāraye*—I take to the other side.

TRANSLATION

Thus the devotee who worships Me, the all-pervading Lord of the universe, in unflinching devotional service, gives up all aspirations to be promoted to heavenly planets or to become happy in this world with wealth, children, cattle, home or anything in relationship with the body. I take him to the other side of birth and death.

PURPORT

Unflinching devotional service, as described in these two verses, means engaging oneself in full Kṛṣṇa consciousness, or devotional service, accepting the Supreme Lord as all in all. Since the Supreme Lord is all-inclusive, if anyone worships Him with unflinching faith, he has automatically achieved all other opulences and performed all other duties. The Lord promises herein that He takes His devotee to the other side of birth and death. Lord Caitanya, therefore, recommended that one who aspires to go beyond birth and death should have no material possessions. This means that one should not try to be happy in this world or to be promoted to the heavenly world, nor should he try for material wealth, children, houses or cattle.

How liberation is imperceptibly achieved by a pure devotee and what the symptoms are have been explained. For the conditioned soul there are two statuses of living. One status is in this present life, and the other is our preparation for the next life. If I am in the mode of goodness then I may be preparing for promotion to the higher planets, if I am in the mode of passion then I shall remain here in a society where activity is very prominent, and if I am in the mode of ignorance I may be degraded to animal life or a lower grade of human life. But for a devotee there is no concern for this life or the next life because in any life he does not desire elevation in material prosperity or a high-grade or low-grade life. He prays to the Lord, "My dear Lord, it does not matter where I am born, but let me be born, even as an ant, in the house of a devotee." A pure devotee does not pray to the Lord for liberation from this material bondage. Actually, the pure devotee never thinks that he is fit for liberation. Considering his past life and his mischievous activities, he thinks that he is fit to be sent to the lowest region of hell. If in this life I am trying to become a devotee, this does not mean that in my many past lives I was one-hundred-percent pious. That is not possible. A devotee, therefore, is always conscious of his real position. Only by his full surrender to the Lord, by the Lord's grace, are his sufferings made shorter. As stated in *Bhagavad-gītā*, "Surrender unto Me, and I will give you protection from all kinds of sinful reaction." That is His mercy. But this does not mean that one who has surrendered to the lotus feet of the Lord has committed no misdeeds in his past life. A devotee always prays, "For my misdeeds, may I be born again and again, but my only prayer is that I may not forget Your service." The devotee has that much mental strength, and he prays to the Lord: "May I be born again and again, but let me be born in the home of Your pure devotee so that I may again get a chance to develop myself."

A pure devotee is not anxious to elevate himself in his next birth. He has already given up that sort of hope. In any life in which one is born, as a householder, or even as an animal, one must have some children, some resources or some possessions, but a devotee is not anxious to possess anything. He is satisfied with whatever is obtainable by God's grace. He is not at all attached to improving his social status or improving the status of education of his children. He is not neglectful—he is dutiful—but he does not spend too much time on the upliftment of temporary household or social life. He fully engages in the service of the Lord, and for other affairs he simply spares as much time as absolutely necessary (*yathārham upayuñjataḥ*). Such a pure devotee does not care for what is going to happen in the next life or in this life; he does not care even for family, children or society. He fully engages in the service of the Lord in Kṛṣṇa consciousness. It is stated in *Bhagavad-gītā* that without the knowledge of the devotee, the Lord arranges for His devotee to be immediately transferred to His transcendental abode just after leaving his body. After quitting his body he does not go into the womb of another mother. The ordinary common living entity, after death, is transferred to the womb of another mother, according to his *karma,* or activities, to take another type of body. But as far as the devotee is concerned, he is at once transferred to the spiritual world in the association of the Lord. That is the Lord's special mercy. How it is possible is explained in the following verses. Because He is all-powerful, the Lord can do anything and everything. He can excuse all sinful reactions. He can immediately transfer a person to Vaikuṇṭhaloka. That is the inconceivable power of the Supreme Personality of Godhead, who is favorably disposed to the pure devotees.

TEXT 41

नान्यत्र मद्भगवतः प्रधानपुरुषेश्वरात् ।
आत्मनः सर्वभूतानां भयं तीव्रं निवर्तते ॥४१॥

nānyatra mad bhagavataḥ
pradhāna-puruṣeśvarāt
ātmanaḥ sarva-bhūtānāṁ
bhayaṁ tīvraṁ nivartate

na—not; *anyatra*—otherwise; *mat*—than Myself; *bhagavataḥ*—the Supreme Personality of Godhead; *pradhāna-puruṣa-īśvarāt*—the Lord of both *prakṛti* and *puruṣa; ātmanaḥ*—the soul; *sarva-bhūtānām*—of all living beings; *bhayam*—fear; *tīvram*—terrible; *nivartate*—is forsaken.

TRANSLATION

The terrible fear of birth and death can never be forsaken by anyone who resorts to any shelter other than Myself, for I am the almighty Lord, the Supreme Personality of Godhead, the original source of all creation, and also the Supreme Soul of all souls.

PURPORT

It is indicated herein that the cycle of birth and death cannot be stopped unless one is a pure devotee of the Supreme Lord. It is said, *hariṁ vinā na mṛtim taranti.* One cannot surpass the cycle of birth and death unless one is favored by the Supreme Personality of Godhead. The same concept is confirmed herewith: one may take to the system of understanding the Absolute Truth by one's own imperfect sensory speculation, or one may try to realize the self by the mystic *yoga* process; but whatever one may do, unless he comes to the point of surrendering to the Supreme Personality of Godhead, no process can give him liberation. One may ask if this means that those who are undergoing so much penance and austerity by strictly following the rules and regulations are endeavoring in vain. The answer is given by *Śrīmad-Bhāgavatam* (10.2.32): *ye 'nye 'ravindākṣa vimukta-māninaḥ.* Lord Brahmā and other demigods prayed to the Lord when Kṛṣṇa was in the womb of Devakī: "My dear lotus-eyed Lord, there are persons who are puffed up with the thought that they have become liberated or one with God or have become God, but in spite of thinking in such a puffed-up way, their intelligence is not laudable. They are less intelligent." It is stated that their intelligence, whether high or low, is not even purified. In purified intelligence a living entity cannot think otherwise than to surrender. *Bhagavad-gītā,* therefore, confirms that purified intelligence arises in the person of a very wise man. *Bahūnāṁ janmanām ante jñānavān māṁ prapadyate.* After many, many births, one who is actually advanced in intelligence surrenders unto the Supreme Lord.

Without the surrendering process, one cannot achieve liberation. The *Bhāgavatam* says, "Those who are simply puffed up, thinking themselves liberated by some nondevotional process, are not polished or clear in intelligence, for they have not yet surrendered unto You. In spite of executing all kinds of austerities and penances or even arriving at the brink of spiritual realization in Brahman realization, they think that they are in the effulgence of Brahman, but actually, because they have no transcendental activities, they fall down to material activities." One should not be satisfied simply with knowing that one is Brahman. He must engage himself in the service of the Supreme Brahman; that is *bhakti.* The engagement of Brahman should be the service of Parabrahman. It is said that unless one becomes Brahman one cannot serve Brahman. The Supreme Brahman is the Supreme Personality of Godhead, and the living entity is also Brahman. Without realization that he is Brahman, spirit soul, an eternal servitor of the Lord, if one simply thinks that he is Brahman, his realization is only theoretical. He has to realize and at the same time engage himself in the devotional service of the Lord; then he can exist in the Brahman status. Otherwise he falls down.

The *Bhāgavatam* says that because nondevotees neglect the transcendental loving service of the lotus feet of the Personality of Godhead, their intelligence is not sufficient, and therefore these persons fall down. The living entity must have some activity. If he does not engage in the activity of transcendental service, he must fall down to material activity. As soon as one falls down to material activity, there is no rescue from the cycle of birth and death. It is stated here by Lord Kapila, "Without My mercy" (*nānyatra mad bhagavataḥ*). The Lord is stated here to be Bhagavān, the Supreme Personality of Godhead, indicating that He is full of all opulences and is therefore perfectly competent to deliver one from the cycle of birth and death. He is also called *pradhāna* because He is the Supreme. He is equal to everyone, but to one who surrenders to Him He is especially favorable. It is also confirmed in *Bhagavad-gītā* that the Lord is equal to everyone; no one is His enemy and no one is His friend. But to one who surrenders unto Him, He is especially inclined. By the grace of the Lord, simply by surrendering unto Him one can get out of this cycle of birth and death. Otherwise, one may go on in many, many lives and may many times attempt other processes for liberation.

TEXT 42

मद्भयाद्वाति वातोऽयं सूर्यस्तपति मद्भयात् ।
वर्षतीन्द्रो दहत्यग्निर्मृत्युश्चरति मद्भयात् ॥४२॥

mad-bhayād vāti vāto 'yaṁ
sūryas tapati mad-bhayāt
varṣatīndro dahaty agnir
mṛtyuś carati mad-bhayāt

mat-bhayāt—out of fear of Me; *vāti*—blows; *vātaḥ*—wind; *ayam*—this; *sūryaḥ*—the sun; *tapati*—shines; *mat-bhayāt*—out of fear of Me; *varṣati*—showers rain; *indraḥ*—Indra; *dahati*—burns; *agniḥ*—fire; *mṛtyuḥ*—death; *carati*—goes; *mat-bhayāt*—out of fear of Me.

TRANSLATION

It is because of My supremacy that the wind blows, out of fear of Me; the sun shines out of fear of Me, and the lord of the clouds, Indra, sends forth showers out of fear of Me. Fire burns out of fear of Me, and death goes about taking its toll out of fear of Me.

PURPORT

The Supreme Personality of Godhead, Kṛṣṇa, says in *Bhagavad-gītā* that the natural laws being enacted are correct in all activities because of His superintendence. No one should think that nature is working automatically, without superintendence. The Vedic literature says that the clouds are controlled by the demigod Indra, heat is distributed by the sun-god, the soothing moonlight is distributed by Candra, and the air is blowing under the arrangement of the demigod Vāyu. But above all these demigods, the Supreme Personality of Godhead is the chief living entity. *Nityo nityānāṁ cetanaś cetanānām.* The demigods are also ordinary living entities, but due to their faithfulness—their devotional service attitude—they have been promoted to such posts. These different demigods, or directors, such as Candra, Varuṇa and Vāyu, are called *adhikāri-devatā.* The demigods are departmental heads. The government of the Supreme Lord consists not only of one planet or two or three; there are millions of planets and millions of universes. The Supreme Personality of Godhead has a huge government, and He requires assistants. The demigods are considered His bodily limbs. These are the descriptions of Vedic literature. Under these circumstances, the sun-god, the moon-god, the fire-god and the air-god are working under the direction of the Supreme Lord. It is confirmed in the *Bhagavad-gītā, mayādhyakṣeṇa prakṛtiḥ sūyate sa-carācaram.* The natural laws are being conducted under His superintendence. Because He is in the background, everything is being performed punctually and regularly.

One who has taken shelter of the Supreme Personality of Godhead is completely protected from all other influences. He no longer serves or is obliged to anyone else. Of course he is not disobedient to anyone, but his full power of thought is absorbed in the service of the Lord. The statements by the Supreme Personality of Godhead Kapila that under His direction the air is blowing, the fire is burning and the sun is giving heat are not sentimental. The impersonalist may say that the *Bhāgavatam* devotees create and imagine someone as the Supreme Personality of Godhead and assign qualifications to Him; but actually it is neither imagination nor an imposition of artificial power in the name of Godhead. In the *Vedas* it is said, *bhīṣāsmād vātaḥ pavate/ bhīṣodeti sūryaḥ:* "By fear of the Supreme Lord the wind-god and the sun-god are acting." *Bhīṣāsmād agniś candraś ca/ mṛtyur dhāvati pañcamaḥ:* "Agni, Indra and Mṛtyu are also acting under His direction." These are the statements of the *Vedas.*

TEXT 43

ज्ञानवैराग्ययुक्तेन भक्तियोगेन योगिनः ।
क्षेमाय पादमूलं मे प्रविशन्त्यकुतोभयम् ॥४३॥

jñāna-vairāgya-yuktena
bhakti-yogena yoginaḥ
kṣemāya pāda-mūlaṁ me
praviśanty akuto-bhayam

jñāna—with knowledge; *vairāgya*—and renunciation; *yuktena*—equipped; *bhakti-yogena*—by devotional service; *yoginaḥ*—the *yogīs*; *kṣemāya*—for eternal benefit; *pāda-mūlam*—feet; *me*—My; *praviśanti*—take shelter of; *akutaḥ-bhayam*—without fear.

TRANSLATION

The yogīs, equipped with transcendental knowledge and renunciation and engaged in devotional service for their eternal benefit, take shelter of My lotus feet, and since I am the Lord, they are thus eligible to enter into the kingdom of Godhead without fear.

PURPORT

One who actually wants to be liberated from the entanglement of this material world and go back home, back to Godhead, is actually a mystic *yogī.* The words explicitly used here are *yuktena bhakti-yogena.* Those *yogīs,* or mystics, who engage in devotional service are the first-class *yogīs.* The first-class *yogīs,* as described in *Bhagavad-gītā,* are those who are constantly thinking of the Lord, the Supreme Personality of Godhead, Kṛṣṇa. These *yogīs* are not without knowledge and renunciation. To become a *bhakti-yogī* means to automatically attain knowledge and renunciation. That is the consequent result of *bhakti-yoga.* In the *Bhāgavatam,* First Canto, Second Chapter, it is also confirmed that one who engages in the devotional service of Vāsudeva, Kṛṣṇa, has complete transcendental knowledge and renunciation, and there is no explanation for these attainments. *Ahaitukī*—without reason, they come. Even if a person is completely illiterate, the transcendental knowledge of the scriptures is revealed unto him simply because of his engagement in devotional service. That is also stated in the Vedic literature. To anyone who has full faith in the Supreme Personality of Godhead and the spiritual master, all the import of the Vedic literatures is revealed. He does not have to seek separately; the *yogīs* who engage in devotional service are full in knowledge and renunciation. If there is a lack of knowledge and renunciation, it is to be understood that one is not in full devotional service. The conclusion is that one cannot be sure of entrance into the spiritual realm—in either the impersonal *brahmajyotir* effulgence of the Lord or the Vaikuṇṭha planets within that Brahman effulgence—unless he is surrendered unto the lotus feet of the Supreme Lord. The surrendered souls are called *akuto-bhaya.* They are doubtless and fearless, and their entrance into the spiritual kingdom is guaranteed.

TEXT 44

एतावानेव लोकेऽस्मिन् पुंसां निःश्रेयसोदयः ।
तीव्रेण भक्तियोगेन मनो मय्यर्पितं स्थिरम् ॥४४॥

etāvān eva loke 'smin
puṁsāṁ niḥśreyasodayaḥ
tīvreṇa bhakti-yogena
mano mayy arpitaṁ sthiram

etāvān eva—only so far; *loke asmin*—in this world; *puṁsām*—of men; *niḥśreyasa*—final perfection of life; *udayaḥ*—the attainment of; *tīvreṇa*—intense; *bhakti-yogena*—by practice of devotional service; *manaḥ*—mind; *mayi*—in Me; *arpitam*—fixed; *sthiram*—steady.

TRANSLATION

Therefore persons whose minds are fixed on the Lord engage in the intensive practice of devotional service. That is the only means for attainment of the final perfection of life.

PURPORT

Here the words *mano mayy arpitam,* which mean "the mind being fixed on Me," are significant. One should fix his mind on the lotus feet of Kṛṣṇa or His incarnation. To be fixed steadily in that freedom is the way of liberation. Ambarīṣa Mahārāja is an example. He fixed his mind on the lotus feet of the Lord, he spoke only on the pastimes of the Lord, he smelled only the flowers and *tulasī* offered to the Lord, he walked only to the temple of the Lord, he engaged his hands in cleansing the temple, he engaged his tongue in tasting the foodstuff offered to the Lord, and he engaged his ears for hearing the great pastimes of the Lord. In that way all his senses were engaged. First of all, the mind should be engaged at the lotus feet of the Lord, very steadily and naturally. Because the mind is the master of the senses, when the mind is engaged, all the senses become engaged. That is *bhakti-yoga. Yoga* means controlling the senses. The senses cannot be controlled in the proper sense of the term; they are always agitated. This is true also with a child—how long can he be forced to sit down silently? It is not possible. Even Arjuna said, *cañcalaṁ hi manaḥ kṛṣṇa:* "The mind is always agitated." The best course is to fix the mind on the lotus feet of the Lord. *Mano mayy arpitaṁ sthiram.* If one seriously engages in Kṛṣṇa consciousness, that is the highest perfectional stage. All Kṛṣṇa conscious activities are on the highest perfectional level of human life.

Thus end the Bhaktivedanta purports of the Third Canto, Twenty-fifth Chapter, of the Śrīmad-Bhāgavatam, *entitled "The Glories of Devotional Service."*

CHAPTER TWENTY-SIX

Fundamental Principles of Material Nature

TEXT 1

श्रीभगवानुवाच
अथ ते सम्प्रवक्ष्यामि तत्त्वानां लक्षणं पृथक् ।
यद्विदित्वा विमुच्येत पुरुषः प्राकृतैर्गुणैः ॥ १ ॥

śrī-bhagavān uvāca
atha te sampravakṣyāmi
tattvānāṁ lakṣaṇaṁ pṛthak
yad viditvā vimucyeta
puruṣaḥ prākṛtair guṇaiḥ

śrī-bhagavān uvāca—the Personality of Godhead said; *atha*—now; *te*—to you; *sampravakṣyāmi*—I shall describe; *tattvānām*—of the categories of the Absolute Truth; *lakṣaṇam*—the distinctive features; *pṛthak*—one by one; *yat*—which; *viditvā*—knowing; *vimucyeta*—one can be released; *puruṣaḥ*—any person; *prākṛtaiḥ*—of the material nature; *guṇaiḥ*—from the modes.

TRANSLATION

The Personality of Godhead, Kapila, continued: My dear mother, now I shall describe unto you the different categories of the Absolute Truth, knowing which any person can be released from the influence of the modes of material nature.

PURPORT

As stated in *Bhagavad-gītā,* one can understand the Supreme Personality of Godhead, the Absolute Truth, only through devotional service (*bhaktyā mām abhijānāti*). As stated in the *Bhāgavatam,* the object of devotional service is *mām,* Kṛṣṇa. And, as explained in the *Caitanya-caritāmṛta,* to understand Kṛṣṇa means to understand Kṛṣṇa in His personal form with His internal energy, His external energy, His expansions and His incarnations. There are many diverse departments of knowledge in understanding Kṛṣṇa. Sāṅkhya philosophy is especially meant for persons who are conditioned by this material world. It is generally understood by the *paramparā* system, or by disciplic succession, to be the science of devotional service. Preliminary studies of devotional service have already been explained. Now the analytical study of devotional service will be explained by the Lord, who says that by such an analytical study, one becomes freed from the modes of material nature. The same assertion is confirmed in *Bhagavad-gītā. Tato māṁ tattvato jñātvā:* by understanding the Lord according to various categories, one can become eligible to enter into the kingdom of God. This is also explained here. By understanding the science of devotional service in Sāṅkhya philosophy, one can become free from the modes of material nature. The eternal self, after becoming freed from the spell of material nature, becomes eligible to enter into the kingdom of God. As long as one has even a slight desire to enjoy or lord it over material nature, there is no chance of his being freed from the influence of nature's material modes. Therefore, one has to understand the Supreme Personality of Godhead analytically, as explained in the Sāṅkhya system of philosophy by Lord Kapiladeva.

TEXT 2

ज्ञानं निःश्रेयसार्थाय पुरुषस्यात्मदर्शनम् ।
यदाहुर्वर्णये तत्ते हृदयग्रन्थिभेदनम् ॥ २ ॥

jñānaṁ niḥśreyasārthāya
puruṣasyātma-darśanam
yad āhur varṇaye tat te
hṛdaya-granthi-bhedanam

jñānam—knowledge; *niḥśreyasa-arthāya*—for the ultimate perfection; *puruṣasya*—of a man; *ātma-darśanam*—self-realization; *yat*—which; *āhuḥ*—they said; *varṇaye*—I shall explain; *tat*—that; *te*—to you; *hṛdaya*—in the heart; *granthi*—the knots; *bhedanam*—cuts.

TRANSLATION

Knowledge is the ultimate perfection of self-realization. I shall explain that knowledge unto you by which the knots of attachment to the material world are cut.

PURPORT

It is said that by proper understanding of the pure self, or by self-realization, one can be freed from material attachment. Knowledge leads one to attain the ultimate perfection of life and to see oneself as he is. The *Śvetāśvatara Upaniṣad* (3.8) also confirms this. *Tam eva viditvāti-mṛtyum eti:* simply by understanding one's spiritual position, or by seeing oneself as he is, one can be freed from material entanglement. In various ways, the seeing of oneself is described in the Vedic literatures, and it is confirmed in the *Bhāgavatam* (*puruṣasya ātma-darśanam*) that one has to see oneself and know what he is. As Kapiladeva explains to His mother, this "seeing" can be done by hearing from the proper authoritative source. Kapiladeva is the greatest authority because He is the Personality of Godhead, and if someone accepts whatever is explained *as it is,* without interpretation, then he can see himself.

Lord Caitanya explained to Sanātana Gosvāmī the real constitutional position of the individual. He said directly that each and every individual soul is eternally a servitor of Kṛṣṇa. *Jīvera 'svarūpa' haya-kṛṣṇera 'nitya-dāsa':* every individual soul is eternally a servitor. When one is fixed in the understanding that he is part and parcel of the Supreme Soul and that his eternal position is to serve in association with the Supreme Lord, he becomes self-realized. This position of rightly understanding oneself cuts the knot of material attraction (*hṛdaya-granthi-bhedanam*). Due to false ego, or false identification of oneself with the body and the material world, one is entrapped by *māyā,* but as soon as one understands that he is qualitatively the same substance as the Supreme Lord because he belongs to the same category of spirit soul, and that his perpetual position is to serve, one attains *ātma-darśanam* and *hṛdaya-granthi-bhedanam,* self-realization. When one can cut the knot of attachment to the material world, his understanding is called knowledge. *Ātma-darśanam* means to see oneself by knowledge; therefore, when one is freed from the false ego by the cultivation of real knowledge, he sees himself, and that is the ultimate necessity of human life. The soul is thus isolated from the entanglement of the twenty-four categories of material nature. Pursuit of the systematic philosophic process called Sāṅkhya is called knowledge and self-revelation.

TEXT 3

अनादिरात्मा पुरुषो निर्गुणः प्रकृतेः परः ।
प्रत्यग्धामा स्वयंज्योतिर्विश्वं येन समन्वितम् ॥ ३ ॥

anādir ātmā puruṣo
nirguṇaḥ prakṛteḥ paraḥ
pratyag-dhāmā svayaṁ-jyotir
viśvaṁ yena samanvitam

anādiḥ—without a beginning; *ātmā*—the Supreme Soul; *puruṣaḥ*—the Personality of Godhead; *nirguṇaḥ*—transcendental to the material modes of nature; *prakṛteḥ paraḥ*—beyond this material world; *pratyak-dhāmā*—perceivable everywhere; *svayam-jyotiḥ*—self-effulgent; *viśvam*—the entire creation; *yena*—by whom; *samanvitam*—is maintained.

TRANSLATION

The Supreme Personality of Godhead is the Supreme Soul, and He has no beginning. He is transcendental to the material modes of nature and beyond the existence of this material world. He is perceivable everywhere because He is self-effulgent, and by His self-effulgent luster the entire creation is maintained.

PURPORT

The Supreme Personality of Godhead is described as being without beginning. He is *puruṣa,* the Supreme Spirit. *Puruṣa* means "person." When we think of a person in our present experience, that person has a beginning. This means that he has taken birth and that there is a history from the beginning of his life. But the Lord is particularly mentioned here as *anādi,* beginningless. If we examine all persons, we will find that everyone has a beginning, but when we approach a person who has no beginning, He is the Supreme Person. That is the definition given in the *Brahma-saṁhitā. Īśvaraḥ paramaḥ kṛṣṇaḥ:* the Supreme Personality of Godhead is Kṛṣṇa, the supreme controller; He is without beginning, and He is the beginning of everyone. This definition is found in all Vedic literatures.

The Lord is described as the soul, or spirit. What is the definition of spirit? Spirit is perceivable everywhere. Brahman means "great." His greatness is perceived everywhere. And what is that greatness? Consciousness. We have personal experience of consciousness, for it is spread all over the body; in every hair follicle of our body we can feel consciousness. This is individual consciousness. Similarly, there is superconsciousness. The example can be given of a small light and the sunlight. The sunlight is perceived everywhere, even within the room or in the sky, but the small light is experienced within a specific limit. Similarly, our consciousness is perceived within the limit of our particular body, but the superconsciousness, or the existence of God, is perceived everywhere. He is present everywhere by His energy. It is stated in the *Viṣṇu Purāṇa* that whatever we find, anywhere and everywhere, is the distribution of the energy of the Supreme Lord. In *Bhagavad-gītā* also it is confirmed that the Lord is all-pervading and exists everywhere by His two kinds of energy, one spiritual and the other material. Both the spiritual and material energies are spread everywhere, and that is the proof of the existence of the Supreme Personality of Godhead.

The existence of consciousness everywhere is not temporary. It is without beginning, and because it is without beginning, it is also without end. The theory that consciousness develops at a certain stage of material combination is not accepted herein, for the consciousness which exists everywhere is said to be without beginning. The materialistic or atheistic theory stating that there is no soul, that there is no God and that consciousness is the result of a combination of matter is not acceptable. Matter is not beginningless; it has a beginning. As this material body has a beginning, the universal body does also. And as our material body has begun on the basis of our soul, the entire gigantic universal body has begun on the basis of the Supreme Soul. The *Vedānta-sūtra* says, *janmādy asya.* This entire material exhibition—its creation, its growth, its maintenance and its dissolution—is an emanation from the Supreme Person. In *Bhagavad-gītā* also, the Lord says, "I am the beginning, the source of birth of everything."

The Supreme Personality of Godhead is described here. He is not a temporary person, nor does He have a beginning. He is without a cause, and He is the cause of all causes. *Paraḥ* means "transcendental," "beyond the creative energy." The Lord is the creator of the creative energy. We can see that there is a creative energy in the material world, but He is not under this energy. He is *prakṛti-paraḥ,* beyond this energy. He is not subjected to the threefold miseries created by the material energy because He is beyond it. The modes of material nature do not touch Him. It is explained here, *svayaṁ-jyotiḥ:* He is light Himself. We have experience in the material world of one light's being a reflection of another, just as moonlight is a reflection of the sunlight. Sunlight is also the reflection of the *brahmajyotir.* Similarly, *brahmajyotir,* the spiritual effulgence, is a reflection of the body of the Supreme Lord. This is confirmed in the *Brahma-saṁhitā: yasya prabhā prabhavataḥ.* The *brahmajyotir,* or Brahman effulgence, is due to His bodily luster. Therefore it is said here, *svayaṁ-jyotiḥ:* He Himself is light. His light is distributed in different ways, as the *brahmajyotir,* as sunlight and as moonlight. *Bhagavad-gītā* confirms that in the spiritual world there is no need of sunlight, moonlight or electricity. The *Upaniṣads* also confirm this; because the bodily luster of the Supreme Personality of Godhead is sufficient to illuminate the spiritual world, there is no need of sunlight, moonlight or any other light or electricity. This self-illumination also contradicts the theory that the spirit soul, or the spiritual consciousness, develops at a certain point in material combination. The term *svayaṁ-jyotiḥ* indicates that there is no tinge of anything material or any material reaction. It is confirmed here that the concept of the Lord's all-pervasiveness is due to His illumination everywhere. We have experience that the sun is situated in one place, but the sunlight is diffused all around for millions and millions of miles. That is our practical experience. Similarly, although the supreme light is situated in His personal abode, Vaikuṇṭha or Vṛndāvana, His light is diffused not only in the spiritual world but beyond that. In the material world also, that light is reflected by the sun globe, and the sunlight is reflected by the moon globe. Thus although He is situated in His own abode, His light is distributed all over the spiritual and material worlds. The *Brahma-saṁhitā* (5.37) confirms this. *Goloka eva nivasaty akhilātma-bhūtaḥ:* He is living in Goloka, but still He is present all over the creation. He is the Supersoul of everything, the Supreme Personality of Godhead, and He has innumerable transcendental qualities. It is also concluded that although He is undoubtedly a person, He is not a *puruṣa* of this material world. Māyāvādī philosophers cannot understand that beyond this material world there can be a person; therefore they are impersonalists. But it is explained very nicely here that the Personality of Godhead is beyond material existence.

TEXT 4

स एष प्रकृतिं सूक्ष्मां दैवीं गुणमयीं विभुः ।
यदृच्छयैवोपगतामभ्यपद्यत लीलया ॥ ४ ॥

sa eṣa prakṛtiṁ sūkṣmāṁ
daivīṁ guṇamayīṁ vibhuḥ
yadṛcchayaivopagatām
abhyapadyata līlayā

saḥ eṣaḥ—that same Supreme Personality of Godhead; *prakṛtim*—material energy; *sūkṣmām*—subtle; *daivīm*—related to Viṣṇu; *guṇamayīm*—invested with the three modes of material nature; *vibhuḥ*—the greatest of the great; *yadṛcchayā*—of His own will; *iva*—quite; *upagatām*—obtained; *abhyapadyata*—He accepted; *līlayā*—as His pastime.

TRANSLATION

As His pastime, that Supreme Personality of Godhead, the greatest of the great, accepted the subtle material energy, which is invested with three material modes of nature and which is related with Viṣṇu.

PURPORT

In this verse the word *guṇamayīm* is very significant. *Daivīm* means "the energy of the Supreme Personality of Godhead," and *guṇamayīm* means "invested with the three modes of material nature." When the material energy of the Supreme Personality of Godhead appears, this *guṇamayīm* energy acts as a manifestation of the energies of the three modes; it acts as a covering. The energy emanated from the Supreme Personality of Godhead manifests in two ways—as an emanation from the Supreme Lord and as a covering of the Lord's face. In *Bhagavad-gītā* it is said that because the whole world is illusioned by the three modes of material nature, the common conditioned soul, being covered by such energy, cannot see the Supreme Personality of Godhead. The example of a cloud is very nicely given. All of a sudden there may appear a big cloud in the sky. This cloud is perceived in two ways. To the sun the cloud is a creation of its energy, but to the ordinary common man in the conditioned state, it is a covering to the eyes; because of the cloud, the sun cannot be seen. It is not that the sun is actually covered by the cloud; only the vision of the ordinary being is covered. Similarly, although *māyā* cannot cover the Supreme Lord, who is beyond *māyā*, the material energy covers the ordinary living entities. Those conditioned souls who are covered are individual living entities, and He from whose energy *māyā* is created is the Supreme Personality of Godhead.

In another place in the *Śrīmad-Bhāgavatam*, in the First Canto, Seventh Chapter, it is stated that Vyāsadeva, by his spiritual vision, saw the Supreme Lord and the material energy standing behind Him. This indicates that material energy cannot cover the Lord, just as darkness cannot cover the sun. Darkness can cover a jurisdiction which is very insignificant in comparison to that of the sun. Darkness can cover a small cave, but not the open sky. Similarly, the covering capacity of the material energy is limited and cannot act on the Supreme Personality of Godhead, who is therefore called *vibhu*. As the appearance of a cloud is accepted by the sun, so the appearance of the material energy at a certain interval is accepted by the Lord. Although His material energy is utilized to create the material world, this does not mean that He is covered by that energy. Those who are covered by the material energy are called conditioned souls. The Lord accepts the material energy for His material pastimes in creation, maintenance and dissolution. But the conditioned soul is covered; he cannot understand that beyond this material energy there is the Supreme Personality of Godhead, who is the cause of all causes, just as a less intelligent person cannot understand that beyond the covering of the clouds there is bright sunshine.

TEXT 5

गुणैर्विचित्राः सृजतीं सरूपाः प्रकृतिं प्रजाः ।
विलोक्य मुमुहे सद्यः स इह ज्ञानगूहया ॥ ५ ॥

guṇair vicitrāḥ sṛjatīṁ
sa-rūpāḥ prakṛtiṁ prajāḥ
vilokya mumuhe sadyaḥ
sa iha jñāna-gūhayā

guṇaiḥ—by the threefold modes; *vicitrāḥ*—variegated; *sṛjatīm*—creating; *sa-rūpāḥ*—with forms; *prakṛtim*—material nature; *prajāḥ*—living entities; *vilokya*—having seen; *mumuhe*—was illusioned; *sadyaḥ*—at once; *saḥ*—the living entity; *iha*—in this world; *jñāna-gūhayā*—by the knowledge-covering feature.

TRANSLATION

Divided into varieties by her threefold modes, material nature creates the forms of the living entities, and the living entities, seeing this, are illusioned by the knowledge—covering feature of the illusory energy.

PURPORT

Material energy has the power to cover knowledge, but this covering cannot be applied to the Supreme Personality of Godhead. It is applicable only to the *prajāḥ*, or those who are born with material bodies, the conditioned souls. The different kinds of living entities vary according to the modes of material nature, as explained in *Bhagavad-gītā* and other Vedic literature. In *Bhagavad-gītā* (7.12) it is very nicely explained that although the modes of goodness, passion and ignorance are born of the Supreme Personality of Godhead, He is not subject to them. In other words, the energy emanating from the Supreme Personality of Godhead cannot act on Him; it acts on the conditioned souls, who are covered by the material energy. The Lord is the father of all living entities because He impregnates material energy with the conditioned souls. Therefore, the conditioned souls get bodies created by the material energy, whereas the father of the living entities is aloof from the three modes.

It is stated in the previous verse that the material energy was accepted by the Supreme Personality of Godhead in order that He might exhibit pastimes for the living entities who wanted to enjoy and lord it over the material energy. This world was created through the material energy of the Lord for the so-called enjoyment of such living entities. Why this material world was created for the sufferings of the conditioned souls is a very intricate question. There is a hint in the previous verse in the word *līlayā*, which means "for the pastimes of the Lord." The Lord wants to rectify the enjoying temperament of the conditioned souls. It is stated in *Bhagavad-gītā* that no one is the enjoyer but the Supreme Personality of Godhead. This material energy is created, therefore, for anyone who pretends to enjoy. An example can be cited here that there is no necessity for the government's creation of a separate police department, but because it is a fact that some of the citizens will not accept the state laws, a department to deal with criminals is necessary. There is no necessity, but at the same time there is a necessity. Similarly, there was no necessity to create this material world for the sufferings of the conditioned souls, but at the same time there are certain living entities, known as *nitya-baddha*, who are eternally conditioned. We say that they have been conditioned from time immemorial because no one can trace out when the living entity, the part and parcel of the Supreme Lord, became rebellious against the supremacy of the Lord.

It is a fact that there are two classes of men—those who are obedient to the laws of the Supreme Lord and those who are atheists or agnostics, who do not accept the existence of God and who want to create their own laws. They want to establish that everyone can create his own laws or his own religious path. Without tracing out the beginning of the existence of these two classes, we can take it for granted that some of the living entities revolted against the laws of the Lord. Such entities are called conditioned souls, for they are conditioned by the three modes of material nature. Therefore the words *guṇair vicitrāḥ* are used here.

In this material world there are 8,400,000 species of life. As spirit souls, they are all transcendental to this material world. Why, then, do they exhibit themselves in different stages of life? The answer is given here: they are under the spell of the three modes of material nature. Because they were created by the material energy, their bodies are made of the material elements. Covered by the material body, the spiritual identity is lost, and therefore the word *mumuhe* is used here, indicating that they have forgotten their own spiritual identity. This forgetfulness of spiritual identity is present in the *jīvas*, or souls, who are conditioned, being subject to be covered by the energy of material nature. *Jñāna-gūhayā* is another word used. *Gūhā* means "covering." Because the knowledge of the minute conditioned souls is covered, they are exhibited in so many species of life. It is said in the *Śrīmad-Bhāgavatam*, Seventh Chapter, First Canto, "The living entities are illusioned by the material energy." In the *Vedas* also it is stated that the eternal living entities are covered by different modes and that they are called tricolored—red, white and blue—living entities. Red is the representation of the mode of passion, white is the representation of the mode of goodness, and blue is the representation of the mode of ignorance. These modes of material nature belong to the material energy, and therefore the living entities under these different modes of material nature have different kinds of material bodies. Because they are forgetful of their spiritual identities, they think the material bodies to be themselves. To the conditioned soul, "me" means the material body. This is called *moha,* or bewilderment.

It is repeatedly said in the *Kaṭha Upaniṣad* that the Supreme Personality of Godhead is never affected by the influence of material nature. It is, rather, the conditioned souls, or the minute infinitesimal parts and parcels of the Supreme, who are affected by the influence of material nature and who appear in different bodies under the material modes.

TEXT 6

एवं पराभिध्यानेन कर्तृत्वं प्रकृतेः पुमान् ।
कर्मसु क्रियमाणेषु गुणैरात्मनि मन्यते ॥ ६ ॥

evaṁ parābhidhyānena
kartṛtvaṁ prakṛteḥ pumān
karmasu kriyamāṇeṣu
guṇair ātmani manyate

evam—in this way; *para*—other; *abhidhyānena*—by identification; *kartṛtvam*—the performance of activities; *prakṛteḥ*—of the material nature; *pumān*—the living entity; *karmasu kriyamāṇeṣu*—while the activities are being performed; *guṇaiḥ*—by the three modes; *ātmani*—to himself; *manyate*—he considers.

TRANSLATION

Because of his forgetfulness, the transcendental living entity accepts the influence of material energy as his field of activities, and thus actuated, he wrongly applies the activities to himself.

PURPORT

The forgetful living entity can be compared to a man who is under the influence of disease and has become mad or to a man haunted by ghosts, who acts without control and yet thinks himself to be in control. Under the influence of material nature, the conditioned soul becomes absorbed in material consciousness. In this consciousness, whatever is done under the influence of the material energy is accepted by the conditioned soul as self-actuated. Actually, the soul in his pure state of existence should be in Kṛṣṇa consciousness. When a person is not acting in Kṛṣṇa consciousness, he is understood to be acting in material consciousness. Consciousness cannot be killed, for the symptom of the living entity is consciousness. The material consciousness simply has to be purified. One becomes liberated by accepting Kṛṣṇa, or the Supreme Lord, as master and by changing the mode of consciousness from material consciousness to Kṛṣṇa consciousness.

TEXT 7

तदस्य संसृतिर्बन्धः पारतन्त्र्यं च तत्कृतम् ।
भवत्यकर्तुरीशस्य साक्षिणो निर्वृतात्मनः ॥ ७ ॥

tad asya saṁsṛtir bandhaḥ
pāra-tantryaṁ ca tat-kṛtam
bhavaty akartur īśasya
sākṣiṇo nirvṛtātmanaḥ

tat—from the misconception; *asya*—of the conditioned soul; *saṁsṛtiḥ*—conditioned life; *bandhaḥ*—bondage; *pāra-tantryam*—dependence; *ca*—and; *tat-kṛtam*—made by that; *bhavati*—is; *akartuḥ*—of the nondoer; *īśasya*—independent; *sākṣiṇaḥ*—the witness; *nirvṛta-ātmanaḥ*—joyful by nature.

TRANSLATION

Material consciousness is the cause of one's conditional life, in which conditions are enforced upon the living entity by the material energy. Although the spirit soul does not do anything and is transcendental to such activities, he is thus affected by conditional life.

PURPORT

The Māyāvādī philosopher, who does not differentiate between the Supreme Spirit and the individual spirit, says that the conditional existence of the living entity is his *līlā*, or pastime. But the word "pastime" implies employment in the activities of the Lord. The Māyāvādīs misuse the word and say that even if the living entity has become a stool-eating hog, he is also enjoying his pastimes. This is a most dangerous interpretation. Actually the Supreme Lord is the leader and maintainer of all living entities. His pastimes are transcendental to any material activity. Such pastimes of the Lord cannot be dragged to the level of the conditional activities of the living entities. In conditional life the living entity actually remains as if a captive in the hands of material energy. Whatever the material energy dictates, the conditioned soul does. He has no responsibility; he is simply the witness of the action, but he is forced to act in that way due to his offense in his eternal relationship with Kṛṣṇa. Lord Kṛṣṇa therefore says in *Bhagavad-gītā* that *māyā*, His material energy, is so forceful that it is insurmountable. But if a living entity simply understands that his constitutional position is to serve Kṛṣṇa and he tries to act on this principle, then however conditioned he may be, the influence of *māyā* immediately vanishes. This is clearly stated in *Bhagavad-gītā,* Seventh Chapter: Kṛṣṇa takes charge of anyone who surrenders to Him in helplessness, and thus the influence of *māyā*, or conditional life, is removed.

The spirit soul is actually *sac-cid-ānanda*—eternal, full of bliss and full of knowledge. Under the clutches of *māyā,* however, he suffers from continued birth, death, disease and old age. One has to be serious to cure this condition of material existence and transfer himself to Kṛṣṇa consciousness, for thus his long suffering may be mitigated without difficulty. In summary, the suffering of the conditioned soul is due to his attachment to material nature. This attachment should thus be transferred from matter to Kṛṣṇa.

TEXT 8

कार्यकारणकर्तृत्वे कारणं प्रकृतिं विदुः ।
भोक्तृत्वे सुखदुःखानां पुरुषं प्रकृतेः परम् ॥ ८ ॥

kārya-kāraṇa-kartṛtve
kāraṇaṁ prakṛtiṁ viduḥ
bhoktṛtve sukha-duḥkhānāṁ
puruṣaṁ prakṛteḥ param

kārya—the body; *kāraṇa*—the senses; *kartṛtve*—regarding the demigods; *kāraṇam*—the cause; *prakṛtim*—material nature; *viduḥ*—the learned understand; *bhoktṛtve*—regarding the perception; *sukha*—of happiness; *duḥkhānām*—and of distress; *puruṣam*—the spirit soul; *prakṛteḥ*—to material nature; *param*—transcendental.

TRANSLATION

The cause of the conditioned soul's material body and senses, and the senses' presiding deities, the demigods, is the material nature. This is understood by learned men. The feelings of happiness and distress of the soul, who is transcendental by nature, are caused by the spirit soul himself.

PURPORT

In *Bhagavad-gītā* it is said that when the Lord descends to this material world, He comes as a person by His own energy, *ātma-māyā*. He is not forced by any superior energy. He comes by His own will, and this can be called His pastime, or *līlā*. But here it is clearly stated that the conditioned soul is forced to take a certain type of body and senses under the three modes of material nature. That body is not received according to his own choice. In other words, a conditioned soul has no free choice; he has to accept a certain type of body according to his *karma.* But when there are bodily reactions as felt in happiness and distress, it is to be understood that the cause is the spirit soul himself. If he so desires, the spirit soul can change this conditional life of dualities by choosing to serve Kṛṣṇa. The living entity is the cause of his own suffering, but he can also be the cause of his eternal happiness. When he wants to engage in Kṛṣṇa consciousness, a suitable body is offered to him by the internal potency, the spiritual energy of the Lord, and when he wants to satisfy his senses, a material body is offered. Thus it is his free choice to accept a spiritual body or a material body, but once the body is accepted he has to enjoy or suffer the consequences. The Māyāvādī philosopher's presentation is that the living entity enjoys his pastimes by accepting the body of a hog. This theory is not acceptable, however, because the word "pastime" implies voluntary acceptance for enjoyment. Therefore this interpretation is most misleading. When there is enforced acceptance for suffering, it is not a pastime. The Lord's pastimes and the conditioned living entity's acceptance of karmic reaction are not on the same level.

TEXT 9

देवहूतिरुवाच
प्रकृतेः पुरुषस्यापि लक्षणं पुरुषोत्तम ।
ब्रूहि कारणयोरस्य सदसच्च यदात्मकम् ॥ ९ ॥

devahūtir uvāca
prakṛteḥ puruṣasyāpi
lakṣaṇaṁ puruṣottama
brūhi kāraṇayor asya
sad-asac ca yad-ātmakam

devahūtiḥ uvāca—Devahūti said; *prakṛteḥ*—of His energies; *puruṣasya*—of the Supreme Person; *api*—also; *lakṣaṇam*—characteristics; *puruṣa-uttama*—O Supreme Personality of Godhead; *brūhi*—kindly explain; *kāraṇayoḥ*—causes; *asya*—of this creation; *sat-asat*—manifest and unmanifest; *ca*—and; *yat-ātmakam*—consisting of which.

TRANSLATION

Devahūti said: O Supreme Personality of Godhead, kindly explain the characteristics of the Supreme Person and His energies, for both of these are the causes of this manifest and unmanifest creation.

PURPORT

Prakṛti, or material nature, is connected with both the Supreme Lord and the living entities, just as a woman is connected with her husband as a wife and with her children as a mother. In *Bhagavad-gītā* the Lord says that He impregnates mother nature with children, living entities, and thereafter all species of living entities become manifest. The relationship of all living entities with material nature has been explained. Now an understanding of the relationship between material nature and the Supreme Lord is sought by Devahūti. The product of that relationship is stated to be the manifest and unmanifest material world. The unmanifest material world is the subtle *mahat-tattva,* and from that *mahat-tattva* the material manifestation has emerged.

In the Vedic literatures it is said that by the glance of the Supreme Lord the total material energy is impregnated, and then everything is born of material nature. It is also confirmed in the Ninth Chapter of *Bhagavad-gītā* that under His glance, *adhyakṣeṇa*—under His direction and by His will—nature is working. It is not that nature works blindly. After understanding the position of the conditioned souls in relation to material nature, Devahūti wanted to know how nature works under the direction of the Lord and what the relationship is between the material nature and the Lord. In other words, she wanted to learn the characteristics of the Supreme Lord in relation to the material nature.

The relationship of the living entities with matter and that of the Supreme Lord with matter are certainly not on the same level, although the Māyāvādīs may interpret it in that way. When it is said that the living entities are bewildered, the Māyāvādī philosophers ascribe this bewilderment to the Supreme Lord. But that is not applicable. The Lord is never bewildered. That is the difference between personalists and impersonalists. Devahūti is not unintelligent. She has enough intelligence to understand that the living entities are not on the level of the Supreme Lord. Because the living entities are infinitesimal, they become bewildered or conditioned by material nature, but this does not mean that the Supreme Lord is also conditioned or bewildered. The difference between the conditioned soul and the Lord is that the Lord is the Lord, the master of material nature, and He is therefore not subject to its control. He is controlled neither by spiritual nature nor by material nature. He is the supreme controller Himself, and He cannot be compared to the ordinary living entities, who are controlled by the laws of material nature.

Two words used in this verse are *sat* and *asat.* The cosmic manifestation is *asat*—it does not exist—but the material energy of the Supreme Lord is *sat,* or ever existing.

Material nature is ever existing in its subtle form as the energy of the Lord, but it sometimes manifests this nonexistent or temporarily existent nature, the cosmos. An analogy may be made with the father and mother: the mother and the father exist, but sometimes the mother begets children. Similarly, this cosmic manifestation, which comes from the unmanifest material nature of the Supreme Lord, sometimes appears and again disappears. But the material nature is ever existing, and the Lord is the supreme cause for both the subtle and gross manifestations of this material world.

TEXT 10

श्रीभगवानुवाच
यत्तत्त्रिगुणमव्यक्तं नित्यं सदसदात्मकम् ।
प्रधानं प्रकृतिं प्राहुरविशेषं विशेषवत् ॥१०॥

śrī-bhagavān uvāca
yat tat tri-guṇam avyaktaṁ
nityaṁ sad-asad-ātmakam
pradhānaṁ prakṛtiṁ prāhur
aviśeṣaṁ viśeṣavat

śrī-bhagavān uvāca—the Supreme Personality of Godhead said; *yat*—now further; *tat*—that; *tri-guṇam*—combination of the three modes; *avyaktam*—unmanifested; *nityam*—eternal; *sat-asat-ātmakam*—consisting of cause and effect; *pradhānam*—the *pradhāna; prakṛtim-prakṛti; prāhuḥ*—they call; *aviśeṣam*—undifferentiated; *viśeṣa-vat*—possessing differentiation.

TRANSLATION

The Supreme Personality of Godhead said: The unmanifested eternal combination of the three modes is the cause of the manifest state and is called pradhāna. It is called prakṛti when in the manifested stage of existence.

PURPORT

The Lord points out material nature in its subtle stage, which is called *pradhāna,* and He analyzes this *pradhāna.* The explanation of *pradhāna* and *prakṛti* is that *pradhāna* is the subtle, undifferentiated sum total of all material elements. Although they are undifferentiated, one can understand that the total material elements are contained therein. When the total material elements are manifested by the interaction of the three modes of material nature, the manifestation is called *prakṛti.* Impersonalists say that Brahman is without variegatedness and without differentiation. One may say that *pradhāna* is the Brahman stage, but actually the Brahman stage is not *pradhāna. Pradhāna* is distinct from Brahman because in Brahman there is no existence of the material modes of nature. One may argue that the *mahat-tattva* is also different from *pradhāna* because in the *mahat-tattva* there are manifestations. The actual explanation of *pradhāna,* however, is given here: when the cause and effect are not clearly manifested (*avyakta*), the reaction of the total elements does not take place, and that stage of material nature is called *pradhāna. Pradhāna* is not the time element because in the time element there are actions and reactions, creation and annihilation. Nor is it the *jīva,* or marginal potency of living entities, or designated, conditioned living entities, because the designations of the living entities are not eternal. One adjective used in this connection is *nitya,* which indicates eternality. Therefore the condition of material nature immediately previous to its manifestation is called *pradhāna.*

TEXT 11

पञ्चभिः पञ्चभिर्ब्रह्म चतुर्भिर्दशभिस्तथा ।
एतच्चतुर्विंशतिकं गणं प्राधानिकं विदुः ॥११॥

pañcabhiḥ pañcabhir brahma
caturbhir daśabhis tathā
etac catur-viṁśatikaṁ
gaṇaṁ prādhānikaṁ viduḥ

pañcabhiḥ—with the five (gross elements); *pañcabhiḥ*—the five (subtle elements); *brahma*—Brahman; *caturbhiḥ*—the four (internal senses); *daśabhiḥ*—the ten (five senses for gathering knowledge and five organs of action); *tathā*—in that way; *etat*—this; *catuḥ-viṁśatikam*—consisting of twenty-four elements; *gaṇam*—aggregate; *prādhānikam*—comprising the *pradhāna; viduḥ*—they know.

TRANSLATION

The aggregate elements, namely the five gross elements, the five subtle elements, the four internal senses, the five senses for gathering knowledge and the five outward organs of action, are known as the pradhāna.

PURPORT

According to *Bhagavad-gītā,* the sum total of the twenty-four elements described herein is called the *yonir mahad brahma.* The sum total of the living entities is impregnated into this *yonir mahad brahma,* and they are born in different forms, beginning from Brahmā down to the insignificant ant. In the *Śrīmad-Bhāgavatam* and other Vedic literatures, the sum total of the twenty-four elements, *pradhāna,* is also described as *yonir mahad brahma;* it is the source of the birth and subsistence of all living entities.

TEXT 12

महाभूतानि पञ्चैव भूरापोऽग्निर्मरुन्नभः ।
तन्मात्राणि च तावन्ति गन्धादीनि मतानि मे ॥१२॥

mahā-bhūtāni pañcaiva
bhūr āpo 'gnir marun nabhaḥ
tan-mātrāṇi ca tāvanti
gandhādīni matāni me

mahā-bhūtāni—the gross elements; *pañca*—five; *eva*—exactly; *bhūḥ*—earth; *āpaḥ*—water; *agniḥ*—fire; *marut*—air; *nabhaḥ*—ether; *tat-mātrāṇi*—the subtle elements; *ca*—also; *tāvanti*—so many; *gandha-ādīni*—smell and so on (taste, color, touch and sound); *matāni*—considered; *me*—by Me.

TRANSLATION

There are five gross elements, namely earth, water, fire, air and ether. There are also five subtle elements: smell, taste, color, touch and sound.

TEXT 13

इन्द्रियाणि दश श्रोत्रं त्वग्दृग्रसननासिकाः ।
वाक्करौ चरणौ मेढ्रं पायुर्दशम उच्यते ॥१३॥

indriyāṇi daśa śrotraṁ
tvag dṛg rasana-nāsikāḥ
vāk karau caraṇau meḍhraṁ
pāyur daśama ucyate

indriyāṇi—the senses; *daśa*—ten; *śrotram*—the sense of hearing; *tvak*—the sense of touch; *dṛk*—the sense of sight; *rasana*—the sense of taste; *nāsikāḥ*—the sense of smell; *vāk*—the organ of speech; *karau*—two hands; *caraṇau*—the organs for traveling (legs); *meḍhram*—the generative organ; *pāyuḥ*—the evacuating organ; *daśamaḥ*—the tenth; *ucyate*—is called.

TRANSLATION

The senses for acquiring knowledge and the organs for action number ten, namely the auditory sense, the sense of taste, the tactile sense, the sense of

sight, the sense of smell, the active organ for speaking, the active organs for working, and those for traveling, generating and evacuating.

TEXT 14

मनो बुद्धिरहङ्कारश्चित्तमित्यन्तरात्मकम् ।
चतुर्धा लक्ष्यते भेदो वृत्त्या लक्षणरूपया ॥१४॥

mano buddhir ahaṅkāraś
cittam ity antar-ātmakam
caturdhā lakṣyate bhedo
vṛttyā lakṣaṇa-rūpayā

manaḥ—the mind; *buddhiḥ*—intelligence; *ahaṅkāraḥ*—ego; *cittam*—consciousness; *iti*—thus; *antaḥ-ātmakam*—the internal, subtle senses; *catuḥ-dhā*—having four aspects; *lakṣyate*—is observed; *bhedaḥ*—the distinction; *vṛttyā*—by their functions; *lakṣaṇa-rūpayā*—representing different characteristics.

TRANSLATION

The internal, subtle senses are experienced as having four aspects, in the shape of mind, intelligence, ego and contaminated consciousness. Distinctions between them can be made only by different functions, since they represent different characteristics.

PURPORT

The four internal senses, or subtle senses, described herein are defined by different characteristics. When pure consciousness is polluted by material contamination and when identification with the body becomes prominent, one is said to be situated under false ego. Consciousness is the function of the soul, and therefore behind consciousness there is soul. Consciousness polluted by material contamination is called *ahaṅkāra.*

TEXT 15

एतावानेव सङ्ख्यातो ब्रह्मणः सगुणस्य ह ।
सन्निवेशो मया प्रोक्तो यः कालः पञ्चविंशकः ॥१५॥

etāvān eva saṅkhyāto
brahmaṇaḥ sa-guṇasya ha

sanniveśo mayā prokto
yaḥ kālaḥ pañca-viṁśakaḥ

etāvān—so much; *eva*—just; *saṅkhyātaḥ*—enumerated; *brahmaṇaḥ*—of Brahman; *sa-guṇasya*—with material qualities; *ha*—indeed; *sanniveśaḥ*—arrangement; *mayā*—by Me; *proktaḥ*—spoken; *yaḥ*—which; *kālaḥ*—time; *pañca-viṁśakaḥ*—the twenty-fifth.

TRANSLATION

All these are considered the qualified Brahman. The mixing element, which is known as time, is counted as the twenty-fifth element.

PURPORT

According to the Vedic version there is no existence beyond Brahman. *Sarvaṁ khalv idaṁ brahma* (*Chāndogya Upaniṣad* 3.14.1). It is stated also in the *Viṣṇu Purāṇa* that whatever we see is *parasya brahmaṇaḥ śaktiḥ;* everything is an expansion of the energy of the Supreme Absolute Truth, Brahman. When Brahman is mixed with the three qualities goodness, passion and ignorance, there results the material expansion, which is sometimes called *saguṇa* Brahman and which consists of these twenty-five elements. In the *nirguṇa* Brahman, where there is no material contamination, or in the spiritual world, the three modes—goodness, passion and ignorance—are not present. Where *nirguṇa* Brahman is found, simple unalloyed goodness prevails. *Saguṇa* Brahman is described by the Sāṅkhya system of philosophy as consisting of twenty-five elements, including the time factor (past, present and future).

TEXT 16

प्रभावं पौरुषं प्राहुः कालमेके यतो भयम् ।
अहङ्कारविमूढस्य कर्तुः प्रकृतिमीयुषः ॥१६॥

prabhāvaṁ pauruṣaṁ prāhuḥ
kālam eke yato bhayam
ahaṅkāra-vimūḍhasya
kartuḥ prakṛtim īyuṣaḥ

prabhāvam—the influence; *pauruṣam*—of the Supreme Personality of Godhead; *prāhuḥ*—they have said; *kālam*—the time factor; *eke*—some; *yataḥ*—from which; *bhayam*—fear; *ahaṅkāra-vimūḍhasya*—deluded by false ego; *kartuḥ*—of the individual soul; *prakṛtim*—material nature; *īyuṣaḥ*—having contacted.

TRANSLATION

The influence of the Supreme Personality of Godhead is felt in the time factor, which causes fear of death due to the false ego of the deluded soul who has contacted material nature.

PURPORT

The living entity's fear of death is due to his false ego of identifying with the body. Everyone is afraid of death. Actually there is no death for the spirit soul, but due to our absorption in the identification of body as self, the fear of death develops. It is also stated in the *Śrīmad-Bhāgavatam* (11.2.37), *bhayaṁ dvitīyābhiniveśataḥ syāt. Dvitīya* refers to matter, which is beyond spirit. Matter is the secondary manifestation of spirit, for matter is produced from spirit. Just as the material elements described are caused by the Supreme Lord, or the Supreme Spirit, the body is also a product of the spirit soul. Therefore, the material body is called *dvitīya,* or "the second." One who is absorbed in this second element or second exhibition of the spirit is afraid of death. When one is fully convinced that he is not his body, there is no question of fearing death, since the spirit soul does not die.

If the spirit soul engages in the spiritual activities of devotional service, he is completely freed from the platform of birth and death. His next position is complete spiritual freedom from a material body. The fear of death is the action of the *kāla,* or the time factor, which represents the influence of the Supreme Personality of Godhead. In other words, time is destructive. Whatever is created is subject to destruction and dissolution, which is the action of time. Time is a representation of the Lord, and it reminds us also that we must surrender unto the Lord. The Lord speaks to every conditioned soul as time. He says in *Bhagavad-gītā* that if someone surrenders unto Him, then there is no longer any problem of birth and death. We should therefore accept the time factor as the Supreme Personality of Godhead standing before us. This is further explained in the following verse.

TEXT 17

प्रकृतेर्गुणसाम्यस्य निर्विशेषस्य मानवि ।
चेष्टा यतः स भगवान् काल इत्युपलक्षितः ॥१७॥

prakṛter guṇa-sāmyasya
nirviśeṣasya mānavi
ceṣṭā yataḥ sa bhagavān
kāla ity upalakṣitaḥ

prakṛteḥ—of material nature; *guṇa-sāmyasya*—without interaction of the three modes; *nirviśeṣasya*—without specific qualities; *mānavi*—O daughter of Manu; *ceṣṭā*—movement; *yataḥ*—from whom; *saḥ*—He; *bhagavān*—the Supreme Personality of Godhead; *kālaḥ*—time; *iti*—thus; *upalakṣitaḥ*—is designated.

TRANSLATION

My dear mother, O daughter of Svāyambhuva Manu, the time factor, as I have explained, is the Supreme Personality of Godhead, from whom the creation begins as a result of the agitation of the neutral, unmanifested nature.

PURPORT

The unmanifested state of material nature, *pradhāna,* is being explained. The Lord says that when the unmanifested material nature is agitated by the glance of the Supreme Personality of Godhead, it begins to manifest itself in different ways. Before this agitation, it remains in the neutral state, without interaction by the three modes of material nature. In other words, material nature cannot produce any variety of manifestations without the contact of the Supreme Personality of Godhead. This is very nicely explained in *Bhagavad-gītā.* The Supreme Personality of Godhead is the cause of the products of material nature. Without His contact, material nature cannot produce anything.

In the *Caitanya-caritāmṛta* also, a very suitable example is given in this connection. Although the nipples on a goat's neck appear to be breast nipples, they do not give milk. Similarly, material nature appears to the material scientist to act and react in a wonderful manner, but in reality it cannot act without the agitator, time, who is the representation of the Supreme Personality of Godhead. When time agitates the neutral state of material nature, material nature begins to produce varieties of manifestations. Ultimately it is said that the Supreme Personality of Godhead is the cause of creation. As a woman cannot produce children unless impregnated by a man, material nature cannot produce or manifest anything unless it is impregnated by the Supreme Personality of Godhead in the form of the time factor.

TEXT 18

अन्तः पुरुषरूपेण कालरूपेण यो बहिः ।
समन्वेत्येष सत्त्वानां भगवानात्ममायया ॥१८॥

antaḥ puruṣa-rūpeṇa
kāla-rūpeṇa yo bahiḥ

samanvety eṣa sattvānāṁ
bhagavān ātma-māyayā

antaḥ—within; *puruṣa-rūpeṇa*—in the form of Supersoul; *kāla-rūpeṇa*—in the form of time; *yaḥ*—He who; *bahiḥ*—without; *samanveti*—exists; *eṣaḥ*—He; *sattvānām*—of all living entities; *bhagavān*—the Supreme Personality of Godhead; *ātma-māyayā*—by His potencies.

TRANSLATION

By exhibiting His potencies, the Supreme Personality of Godhead adjusts all these different elements, keeping Himself within as the Supersoul and without as time.

PURPORT

Here it is stated that within the heart the Supreme Personality of Godhead resides as the Supersoul. This situation is also explained in *Bhagavad-gītā:* the Supersoul rests beside the individual soul and acts as a witness. This is also confirmed elsewhere in the Vedic literature: two birds are sitting on the same tree of the body; one is witnessing, and the other is eating the fruits of the tree. This *puruṣa,* or Paramātmā, who resides within the body of the individual soul, is described in *Bhagavad-gītā* (13.23) as the *upadraṣṭā,* witness, and the *anumantā,* sanctioning authority. The conditioned soul engages in the happiness and distress of the particular body given him by the arrangement of the external energy of the Supreme Lord. But the supreme living being, or the Paramātmā, is different from the conditioned soul. He is described in *Bhagavad-gītā* as *maheśvara,* or the Supreme Lord. He is Paramātmā, not *jīvātmā.* Paramātmā means the Supersoul, who is sitting by the side of the conditioned soul just to sanction his activities. The conditioned soul comes to this material world in order to lord it over material nature. Since one cannot do anything without the sanction of the Supreme Lord, He lives with the *jīva* soul as witness and sanction-giver. He is also *bhoktā;* He gives maintenance and sustenance to the conditioned soul.

Since the living entity is constitutionally part and parcel of the Supreme Personality of Godhead, the Lord is very affectionate to the living entities. Unfortunately, when the living entity is bewildered or illusioned by the external energy, he becomes forgetful of his eternal relationship with the Lord, but as soon as he becomes aware of his constitutional position, he is liberated. The minute independence of the conditioned soul is exhibited by his marginal position. If he likes, he can forget the Supreme Personality of Godhead and come into the material existence with a false ego to lord it over material nature, but if he likes he can turn his face to the service of the Lord. The individual living entity is given that independence. His conditional life is ended and his life becomes successful as soon as he turns his face to the Lord, but by misusing his independence he enters into material existence. Yet the Lord is so kind that, as Supersoul, He always remains with the conditioned soul. The concern of the Lord is neither to enjoy nor to suffer from the material body. He remains with the *jīva* simply as sanction-giver and witness so that the living entity can receive the results of his activities, good or bad.

Outside the body of the conditioned soul, the Supreme Personality of Godhead remains as the time factor. According to the Sāṅkhya system of philosophy, there are twenty-five elements. The twenty-four elements already described plus the time factor make twenty-five. According to some learned philosophers, the Supersoul is included to make a total of twenty-six elements.

TEXT 19

दैवात्क्षुभितधर्मिण्यां स्वस्यां योनौ परः पुमान् ।
आधत्त वीर्यं सासूत महत्तत्त्वं हिरण्मयम् ॥१९॥

daivāt kṣubhita-dharmiṇyāṁ
svasyāṁ yonau paraḥ pumān
ādhatta vīryaṁ sāsūta
mahat-tattvaṁ hiraṇmayam

daivāt—by the destiny of the conditioned souls; *kṣubhita*—agitated; *dharmiṇyām*—whose equilibrium of the modes; *svasyām*—His own; *yonau*—in the womb (material nature); *paraḥ pumān*—the Supreme Personality of Godhead; *ādhatta*—impregnated; *vīryam*—semen (His internal potency); *sā*—she (material nature); *asūta*—delivered; *mahat-tattvam*—the sum total of cosmic intelligence; *hiraṇmayam*—known as Hiraṇmaya.

TRANSLATION

After the Supreme Personality of Godhead impregnates material nature with His internal potency, material nature delivers the sum total of the cosmic intelligence, which is known as Hiraṇmaya. This takes place in material nature when she is agitated by the destinations of the conditioned souls.

PURPORT

This impregnation of material nature is described in *Bhagavad-gītā,* Fourteenth Chapter, verse 3. Material nature's primal factor is the *mahat-tattva,* or breeding source of all varieties. This part of material nature, which is called *pradhāna* as well as

Brahman, is impregnated by the Supreme Personality of Godhead and delivers varieties of living entities. Material nature in this connection is called Brahman because it is a perverted reflection of the spiritual nature.

It is described in the *Viṣṇu Purāṇa* that the living entities belong to the spiritual nature. The potency of the Supreme Lord is spiritual, and the living entities, although they are called marginal potency, are also spiritual. If the living entities were not spiritual, this description of impregnation by the Supreme Lord would not be applicable. The Supreme Lord does not put His semen into that which is not spiritual, but it is stated here that the Supreme Person puts His semen into material nature. This means that the living entities are spiritual by nature. After impregnation, material nature delivers all kinds of living entities, beginning from the greatest living creature, Lord Brahmā, down to the insignificant ant, in all varieties of form. In *Bhagavad-gītā* (14.4) material nature is clearly mentioned as *sarva-yoniṣu.* This means that of all varieties of species—demigods, human beings, animals, birds and beasts (whatever is manifested)—material nature is the mother, and the Supreme Personality of Godhead is the seed-giving father. Generally it is experienced that the father gives life to the child but the mother gives its body; although the seed of life is given by the father, the body develops within the womb of the mother. Similarly, the spiritual living entities are impregnated into the womb of material nature, but the body, being supplied by material nature, takes on many different species and forms of life. The theory that the symptoms of life are manifest by the interaction of the twenty-four material elements is not supported here. The living force comes directly from the Supreme Personality of Godhead and is completely spiritual. Therefore, no material scientific advancement can produce life. The living force comes from the spiritual world and has nothing to do with the interaction of the material elements.

TEXT 20

विश्वमात्मगतं व्यञ्जन् कूटस्थो जगदङ्कुरः ।
स्वतेजसापिबत्तीव्रमात्मप्रस्वापनं तमः ॥२०॥

viśvam ātma-gataṁ vyañjan
kūṭa-stho jagad-aṅkuraḥ
sva-tejasāpibat tīvram
ātma-prasvāpanaṁ tamaḥ

viśvam—the universe; *ātma-gatam*—contained within itself; *vyañjan*—manifesting; *kūṭa-sthaḥ*—unchangeable; *jagat-aṅkuraḥ*—the root of all cosmic manifestations; *sva-tejasā*—by its own effulgence; *apibat*—swallowed; *tīvram*—dense; *ātma-prasvāpanam*—which had covered the *mahat-tattva; tamaḥ*—darkness.

TRANSLATION

Thus, after manifesting variegatedness, the effulgent mahat-tattva, which contains all the universes within itself, which is the root of all cosmic manifestations and which is not destroyed at the time of annihilation, swallows the darkness that covered the effulgence at the time of dissolution.

PURPORT

Since the Supreme Personality of Godhead, is ever existing, all-blissful and full of knowledge, His different energies are also ever existing in the dormant stage. Thus when the *mahat-tattva* was created, it manifested the material ego and swallowed up the darkness which covered the cosmic manifestation at the time of dissolution. This idea can be further explained. A person at night remains inactive, covered by the darkness of night, but when he is awakened in the morning, the covering of night, or the forgetfulness of the sleeping state, disappears. Similarly, when the *mahat-tattva* appears after the night of dissolution, the effulgence is manifested to exhibit the variegatedness of this material world.

TEXT 21

यत्तत्सत्त्वगुणं स्वच्छं शान्तं भगवतः पदम् ।
यदाहुर्वासुदेवाख्यं चित्तं तन्महदात्मकम् ॥२१॥

yat tat sattva-guṇaṁ svacchaṁ
śāntaṁ bhagavataḥ padam
yad āhur vāsudevākhyaṁ
cittaṁ tan mahad-ātmakam

yat—which; *tat*—that; *sattva-guṇam*—the mode of goodness; *svaccham*—clear; *śāntam*—sober; *bhagavataḥ*—of the Personality of Godhead; *padam*—the status of understanding; *yat*—which; *āhuḥ*—is called; *vāsudeva-ākhyam*—by the name *vāsudeva; cittam*—consciousness; *tat*—that; *mahat-ātmakam*—manifest in the *mahat-tattva.*

TRANSLATION

The mode of goodness, which is the clear, sober status of understanding the Personality of Godhead and which is generally called vāsudeva, or consciousness, becomes manifest in the mahat-tattva.

PURPORT

The *vāsudeva* manifestation, or the status of understanding the Supreme Personality of Godhead, is called pure goodness, or *śuddha-sattva.* In the *śuddha-sattva* status there is no infringement of the other qualities, namely passion and ignorance. In the Vedic literature there is mention of the Lord's expansion as the four Personalities of Godhead—Vāsudeva, Saṅkarṣaṇa, Pradyumna and Aniruddha. Here in the reappearance of the *mahat-tattva* the four expansions of Godhead occur. He who is seated within as Supersoul expands first as Vāsudeva.

The *vāsudeva* stage is free from infringement by material desires and is the status in which one can understand the Supreme Personality of Godhead, or the objective which is described in the *Bhagavad-gītā* as *adbhuta.* This is another feature of the *mahat-tattva.* The *vāsudeva* expansion is also called Kṛṣṇa consciousness, for it is free from all tinges of material passion and ignorance. This clear state of understanding helps one to know the Supreme Personality of Godhead. The *vāsudeva* status is also explained in *Bhagavad-gītā* as *kṣetra-jña,* which refers to the knower of the field of activities as well as the Superknower. The living being who has occupied a particular type of body knows that body, but the Superknower, Vāsudeva, knows not only a particular type of body but also the field of activities in all the different varieties of bodies. In order to be situated in clear consciousness, or Kṛṣṇa consciousness, one must worship Vāsudeva. Vāsudeva is Kṛṣṇa alone. When Kṛṣṇa, or Viṣṇu, is alone, without the accompaniment of His internal energy, He is Vāsudeva. When He is accompanied by His internal potency, He is called Dvārakādhīśa. To have clear consciousness, or Kṛṣṇa consciousness, one has to worship Vāsudeva. It is also explained in *Bhagavad-gītā* that after many, many births one surrenders to Vāsudeva. Such a great soul is very rare.

In order to get release from the false ego, one has to worship Saṅkarṣaṇa. Saṅkarṣaṇa is also worshiped through Lord Śiva; the snakes which cover the body of Lord Śiva are representations of Saṅkarṣaṇa, and Lord Śiva is always absorbed in meditation upon Saṅkarṣaṇa. One who is actually a worshiper of Lord Śiva as a devotee of Saṅkarṣaṇa can be released from false, material ego. If one wants to get free from mental disturbances, one has to worship Aniruddha. For this purpose, worship of the moon planet is also recommended in the Vedic literature. Similarly, to be fixed in one's intelligence one has to worship Pradyumna, who is reached through the worship of Brahmā. These matters are explained in Vedic literature.

TEXT 22

स्वच्छत्वमविकारित्वं शान्तत्वमिति चेतसः ।
वृत्तिभिर्लक्षणं प्रोक्तं यथापां प्रकृतिः परा ॥२२॥

svacchatvam avikāritvaṁ
śāntatvam iti cetasaḥ
vṛttibhir lakṣaṇaṁ proktaṁ
yathāpāṁ prakṛtiḥ parā

svacchatvam—clarity; *avikāritvam*—freedom from all distraction; *śāntatvam*—serenity; *iti*—thus; *cetasaḥ*—of consciousness; *vṛttibhiḥ*—by characteristics; *lakṣaṇam*—traits; *proktam*—called; *yathā*—as; *apām*—of water; *prakṛtiḥ*—natural state; *parā*—pure.

TRANSLATION

After the manifestation of the mahat-tattva, these features appear simultaneously. As water in its natural state, before coming in contact with earth, is clear, sweet and unruffled, so the characteristic traits of pure consciousness are complete serenity, clarity, and freedom from distraction.

PURPORT

The pure status of consciousness, or Kṛṣṇa consciousness, exists in the beginning; just after creation, consciousness is not polluted. The more one becomes materially contaminated, however, the more consciousness becomes obscured. In pure consciousness one can perceive a slight reflection of the Supreme Personality of Godhead. As in clear, unagitated water, free from impurities, one can see everything clearly, so in pure consciousness, or Kṛṣṇa consciousness, one can see things as they are. One can see the reflection of the Supreme Personality of Godhead, and one can see his own existence as well. This state of consciousness is very pleasing, transparent and sober. In the beginning, consciousness is pure.

TEXTS 23-24

महत्तत्त्वाद्विकुर्वाणाद्भगवद्वीर्यसम्भवात् ।
क्रियाशक्तिरहङ्कारस्त्रिविधः समपद्यत ॥२३॥
वैकारिकस्तैजसश्च तामसश्च यतो भवः ।
मनसश्चेन्द्रियाणां च भूतानां महतामपि ॥२४॥

mahat-tattvād vikurvāṇād
bhagavad-vīrya-sambhavāt
kriyā-śaktir ahaṅkāras
tri-vidhaḥ samapadyata

vaikārikas taijasaś ca
tāmasaś ca yato bhavaḥ
manasaś cendriyāṇāṁ ca
bhūtānāṁ mahatām api

mahat-tattvāt—from the *mahat-tattva; vikurvāṇāt*—undergoing a change; *bhagavat-vīrya-sambhavāt*—evolved from the Lord's own energy; *kriyā-śaktiḥ*—endowed with active power; *ahaṅkāraḥ*—the material ego; *tri-vidhaḥ*—of the three kinds; *samapadyata*—sprang up; *vaikārikaḥ*—material ego in transformed goodness; *taijasaḥ*—material ego in passion; *ca*—and; *tāmasaḥ*—material ego in ignorance; *ca*—also; *yataḥ*—from which; *bhavaḥ*—the origin; *manasaḥ*—of the mind; *ca*—and; *indriyāṇām*—of the senses for perception and action; *ca*—and; *bhūtānām mahatām*—of the five gross elements; *api*—also.

TRANSLATION

The material ego springs up from the mahat-tattva, which evolved from the Lord's own energy. The material ego is endowed predominantly with active power of three kinds—good, passionate and ignorant. It is from these three types of material ego that the mind, the senses of perception, the organs of action, and the gross elements evolve.

PURPORT

In the beginning, from clear consciousness, or the pure state of Kṛṣṇa consciousness, the first contamination sprang up. This is called false ego, or identification of the body as self. The living entity exists in the natural state of Kṛṣṇa consciousness, but he has marginal independence, and this allows him to forget Kṛṣṇa. Originally, pure Kṛṣṇa consciousness exists, but because of misuse of marginal independence there is a chance of forgetting Kṛṣṇa. This is exhibited in actual life; there are many instances in which someone acting in Kṛṣṇa consciousness suddenly changes. In the *Upaniṣads* it is stated, therefore, that the path of spiritual realization is just like the sharp edge of a razor. The example is very appropriate. One shaves his cheeks with a sharp razor very nicely, but as soon as his attention is diverted from the activity, he immediately cuts his cheek because he mishandles the razor.

Not only must one come to the stage of pure Kṛṣṇa consciousness, but one must also be very careful. Any inattentiveness or carelessness may cause falldown. This falldown is due to false ego. From the status of pure consciousness, the false ego is born because of misuse of independence. We cannot argue about why false ego arises from pure consciousness. Factually, there is always the chance that this will happen, and therefore one has to be very careful. False ego is the basic principle for all material activities, which are executed in the modes of material nature. As soon as one deviates from pure Kṛṣṇa consciousness, he increases his entanglement in material reaction. The entanglement of materialism is the material mind, and from this material mind, the senses and material organs become manifest.

TEXT 25

सहस्रशिरसं साक्षाद्यमनन्तं प्रचक्षते ।
सङ्कर्षणाख्यं पुरुषं भूतेन्द्रियमनोमयम् ॥२५॥

sahasra-śirasaṁ sākṣād
yam anantaṁ pracakṣate
saṅkarṣaṇākhyaṁ puruṣaṁ
bhūtendriya-manomayam

sahasra-śirasam—with a thousand heads; *sākṣāt*—directly; *yam*—whom; *anantam*—Ananta; *pracakṣate*—they call; *saṅkarṣaṇa-ākhyam*—Saṅkarṣaṇa by name; *puruṣam*—the Supreme Personality of Godhead; *bhūta*—the gross elements; *indriya*—the senses; *manaḥ-mayam*—consisting of the mind.

TRANSLATION

The threefold ahaṅkāra, the source of the gross elements, the senses and the mind, is identical with them because it is their cause. It is known by the name of Saṅkarṣaṇa, who is directly Lord Ananta with a thousand heads.

TEXT 26

कर्तृत्वं करणत्वं च कार्यत्वं चेति लक्षणम् ।
शान्तघोरविमूढत्वमिति वा स्यादहङ्कृतेः ॥२६॥

kartṛtvaṁ karaṇatvaṁ ca
kāryatvaṁ ceti lakṣaṇam
śānta-ghora-vimūḍhatvam
iti vā syād ahaṅkṛteḥ

kartṛtvam—being the doer; *karaṇatvam*—being the instrument; *ca*—and; *kāryatvam*—being the effect; *ca*—also; *iti*—thus; *lakṣaṇam*—characteristic; *śānta*—serene; *ghora*—active; *vimūḍhatvam*—being dull; *iti*—thus; *vā*—or; *syāt*—may be; *ahaṅkṛteḥ*—of the false ego.

TRANSLATION

This false ego is characterized as the doer, as an instrument and as an effect. It is further characterized as serene, active or dull according to how it is influenced by the modes of goodness, passion and ignorance.

PURPORT

Ahaṅkāra, or false ego, is transformed into the demigods, the controlling directors of material affairs. As an instrument, the false ego is represented as different senses and sense organs, and as the result of the combination of the demigods and the senses, material objects are produced. In the material world we are producing so many things, and this is called advancement of civilization, but factually the advancement of civilization is a manifestation of the false ego. By false ego all material things are produced as objects of enjoyment. One has to cease increasing artificial necessities in the form of material objects. One great *ācārya*, Narottama dāsa Ṭhākura, has lamented that when one deviates from pure consciousness of Vāsudeva, or Kṛṣṇa consciousness, he becomes entangled in material activities. The exact words he uses are, *sat-saṅga chāḍi' kainu asate vilāsa/ te-kāraṇe lāgila ye karma-bandha-phāṅsa:* "I have given up the pure status of consciousness because I wanted to enjoy in the temporary, material manifestation; therefore I have been entangled in the network of actions and reactions."

TEXT 27

वैकारिकाद्विकुर्वाणान्मनस्तत्त्वमजायत ।
यत्सङ्कल्पविकल्पाभ्यां वर्तते कामसम्भवः ॥२७॥

vaikārikād vikurvāṇān
manas-tattvam ajāyata
yat-saṅkalpa-vikalpābhyāṁ
vartate kāma-sambhavaḥ

vaikārikāt—from the false ego of goodness; *vikurvāṇāt*—undergoing transformation; *manaḥ*—the mind; *tattvam*—principle; *ajāyata*—evolved; *yat*—whose; *saṅkalpa*—thoughts; *vikalpābhyām*—and by reflections; *vartate*—happens; *kāma-sambhavaḥ*—the rise of desire.

TRANSLATION

From the false ego of goodness, another transformation takes place. From this evolves the mind, whose thoughts and reflections give rise to desire.

PURPORT

The symptoms of the mind are determination and rejection, which are due to different kinds of desires. We desire that which is favorable to our sense gratification, and we reject that which is not favorable to sense gratification. The material mind is not fixed, but the very same mind can be fixed when engaged in the activities of Kṛṣṇa consciousness. Otherwise, as long as the mind is on the material platform, it is hovering, and all this rejection and acceptance is *asat*, temporary. It is stated that he whose mind is not fixed in Kṛṣṇa consciousness must hover between acceptance and rejection. However advanced a man is in academic qualifications, as long as he is not fixed in Kṛṣṇa consciousness he will simply accept and reject and will never be able to fix his mind on a particular subject matter.

TEXT 28

यद्विदुर्ह्यनिरुद्धाख्यं हृषीकाणामधीश्वरम् ।
शारदेन्दीवरश्यामं संराध्यं योगिभिः शनैः ॥२८॥

yad vidur hy aniruddhākhyaṁ
hṛṣīkāṇām adhīśvaram
śāradendīvara-śyāmaṁ
saṁrādhyaṁ yogibhiḥ śanaiḥ

yat—which mind; *viduḥ*—is known; *hi*—indeed; *aniruddha-ākhyam*—by the name Aniruddha; *hṛṣīkāṇām*—of the senses; *adhīśvaram*—the supreme ruler; *śārada*—autumnal; *indīvara*—like a blue lotus; *śyāmam*—bluish; *saṁrādhyam*—who is found; *yogibhiḥ*—by the *yogīs*; *śanaiḥ*—gradually.

TRANSLATION

The mind of the living entity is known by the name of Lord Aniruddha, the supreme ruler of the senses. He possesses a bluish-black form resembling a lotus flower growing in the autumn. He is found slowly by the yogīs.

PURPORT

The system of *yoga* entails controlling the mind, and the Lord of the mind is Aniruddha. It is stated that Aniruddha is four-handed, with Sudarśana *cakra*, conchshell, club and lotus flower. There are twenty-four forms of Viṣṇu, each differently named. Among these twenty-four forms, Saṅkarṣaṇa, Aniruddha, Pradyumna and Vāsudeva are depicted very nicely in the *Caitanya-caritāmṛta*, where it is stated that Aniruddha is worshiped by the *yogīs*. Meditation upon voidness is a modern invention of the fertile brain of some speculator. Actually the process of *yoga* meditation, as prescribed in this verse, should be fixed upon the form of Aniruddha. By meditating on Aniruddha one can become free from the agitation of acceptance and rejection. When one's mind is fixed upon Aniruddha, one gradually becomes God-realized; he approaches the pure status of Kṛṣṇa consciousness, which is the ultimate goal of *yoga*.

TEXT 29

तैजसात्तु विकुर्वाणाद् बुद्धितत्त्वमभूत्सति ।
द्रव्यस्फुरणविज्ञानमिन्द्रियाणामनुग्रहः ॥२९॥

taijasāt tu vikurvāṇād
buddhi-tattvam abhūt sati
dravya-sphuraṇa-vijñānam
indriyāṇām anugrahaḥ

taijasāt—from the false ego in passion; *tu*—then; *vikurvāṇāt*—undergoing transformation; *buddhi*—intelligence; *tattvam*—principle; *abhūt*—took birth; *sati*—O virtuous lady; *dravya*—objects; *sphuraṇa*—coming into view; *vijñānam*—ascertaining; *indriyāṇām*—to the senses; *anugrahaḥ*—giving assistance.

TRANSLATION

By transformation of the false ego in passion, intelligence takes birth, O virtuous lady. The functions of intelligence are to help in ascertaining the nature of objects when they come into view, and to help the senses.

PURPORT

Intelligence is the discriminating power to understand an object, and it helps the senses make choices. Therefore intelligence is supposed to be the master of the senses. The perfection of intelligence is attained when one becomes fixed in the activities of Kṛṣṇa consciousness. By the proper use of intelligence one's consciousness is expanded, and the ultimate expansion of consciousness is Kṛṣṇa consciousness.

TEXT 30

संशयोऽथ विपर्यासो निश्चयः स्मृतिरेव च ।
स्वाप इत्युच्यते बुद्धेर्लक्षणं वृत्तितः पृथक् ॥३०॥

saṁśayo 'tha viparyāso
niścayaḥ smṛtir eva ca
svāpa ity ucyate buddher
lakṣaṇaṁ vṛttitaḥ pṛthak

saṁśayaḥ—doubt; *atha*—then; *viparyāsaḥ*—misapprehension; *niścayaḥ*—correct apprehension; *smṛtiḥ*—memory; *eva*—also; *ca*—and; *svāpah*—sleep; *iti*—thus; *ucyate*—are said; *buddheḥ*—of intelligence; *lakṣaṇam*—characteristics; *vṛttitaḥ*—by their functions; *pṛthak*—different.

TRANSLATION

Doubt, misapprehension, correct apprehension, memory and sleep, as determined by their different functions, are said to be the distinct characteristics of intelligence.

PURPORT

Doubt is one of the important functions of intelligence; blind acceptance of something does not give evidence of intelligence. Therefore the word *saṁśaya* is very important; in order to cultivate intelligence, one should be doubtful in the beginning. But doubting is not very favorable when information is received from the proper source. In *Bhagavad-gītā* the Lord says that doubting the words of the authority is the cause of destruction.

As described in the Patañjali *yoga* system, *pramāṇa-viparyaya-vikalpa-nidra-smṛtyaḥ.* By intelligence only one can understand things as they are. By intelligence only can one understand whether or not he is the body. The study to determine whether one's identity is spiritual or material begins in doubt. When one is able to analyze his actual position, the false identification with the body is detected. This is *viparyāsa.* When false identification is detected, then real identification can be understood. Real understanding is described here as *niścayaḥ,* or proved experimental knowledge. This experimental knowledge can be achieved when one has understood the false knowledge. By experimental or proved knowledge, one can understand that he is not the body but spirit soul.

Smṛti means "memory," and *svāpa* means "sleep." Sleep is also necessary to keep the intelligence in working order. If there is no sleep, the brain cannot work nicely. In *Bhagavad-gītā* it is especially mentioned that persons who regulate eating, sleeping and other necessities of the body in the proper proportion become very successful in the *yoga* process. These are some of the aspects of the analytical study of intelligence as described in both the Patañjali *yoga* system and the Sāṅkhya philosophy system of Kapiladeva in *Śrīmad-Bhāgavatam.*

TEXT 31

तैजसानीन्द्रियाण्येव क्रियाज्ञानविभागशः ।
प्राणस्य हि क्रियाशक्तिर्बुद्धेर्विज्ञानशक्तिता ॥३१॥

taijasānīndriyāṇy eva
kriyā-jñāna-vibhāgaśaḥ
prāṇasya hi kriyā-śaktir
buddher vijñāna-śaktitā

taijasāni—produced from egoism in the mode of passion; *indriyāṇi*—the senses; *eva*—certainly; *kriyā*—action; *jñāna*—knowledge; *vibhāgaśaḥ*—according to; *prāṇasya*—of the vital energy; *hi*—indeed; *kriyā-śaktiḥ*—the senses of action; *buddheḥ*—of the intelligence; *vijñāna-śaktitā*—the senses for acquiring knowledge.

TRANSLATION

Egoism in the mode of passion produces two kinds of senses—the senses for acquiring knowledge and the senses of action. The senses of action depend on the vital energy, and the senses for acquiring knowledge depend on intelligence.

PURPORT

It has been explained in the previous verses that mind is the product of ego in goodness and that the function of the mind is acceptance and rejection according to desire. But here intelligence is said to be the product of ego in passion. That is the distinction between mind and intelligence; mind is a product of egoism in goodness, and intelligence is a product of egoism in passion. The desire to accept something and reject something is a very important factor of the mind. Since mind is a product of the mode of goodness, if it is fixed upon the Lord of the mind, Aniruddha, then the mind can be changed to Kṛṣṇa consciousness. It is stated by Narottama dāsa Ṭhākura that we always have desires. Desire cannot be stopped. But if we transfer our desires to please the Supreme Personality of Godhead, that is the perfection of life. As soon as the desire is transferred to lording it over material nature, it becomes contaminated by matter. Desire has to be purified. In the beginning, this purification process has to be carried out by the order of the spiritual master, since the spiritual master knows how the disciple's desires can be transformed into Kṛṣṇa consciousness. As far as intelligence is concerned, it is clearly stated here that it is a product of egoism in passion. By practice one comes to the point of the mode of goodness, and by surrendering or fixing the mind upon the Supreme Personality of Godhead, one becomes a very great personality, or *mahātmā.* In *Bhagavad-gītā* it is clearly said, *sa mahātmā sudurlabhaḥ:* "Such a great soul is very rare."

In this verse it is clear that both kinds of senses, the senses for acquiring knowledge and the senses for action, are products of egoism in the mode of passion. And because the sense organs for activity and for acquiring knowledge require energy, the vital energy, or life energy, is also produced by egoism in the mode of passion. We can actually see, therefore, that those who are very passionate can improve in material acquisition very quickly. It is recommended in the Vedic scriptures that if one wants to encourage a person in acquiring material possessions, one should also encourage him in sex life. We naturally find that those who are addicted to sex life are also materially advanced because sex life or passionate life is the impetus for the material advancement of civilization. For those who want to make spiritual advancement, there is almost no existence of the mode of passion. Only the mode of goodness is prominent. We find that those who engage in Kṛṣṇa consciousness are materially poor, but one who has eyes can see who is the greater. Although he appears to be materially poor, a person in Kṛṣṇa consciousness is not actually a poor man, but the person who has no taste for Kṛṣṇa consciousness and appears to be very happy with material possessions is actually poor. Persons infatuated by material consciousness are very intelligent in discovering things for material comforts, but they have no access to understanding the spirit soul and spiritual life. Therefore, if anyone wants to advance in spiritual life, he has to come back to the platform of purified desire, the purified desire for devotional service. As stated in the *Nārada Pañcarātra,* engagement in the service of the Lord when the senses are purified in Kṛṣṇa consciousness is called pure devotion.

TEXT 32

तामसाच्च विकुर्वाणाद्भगवद्वीर्यचोदितात् ।
शब्दमात्रमभूत्तस्मान्नभः श्रोत्रं तु शब्दगम् ॥३२॥

tāmasāc ca vikurvāṇād
bhagavad-vīrya-coditāt
śabda-mātram abhūt tasmān
nabhaḥ śrotraṁ tu śabdagam

tāmasāt—from egoism in ignorance; *ca*—and; *vikurvāṇāt*—undergoing transformation; *bhagavat-vīrya*—by the energy of the Supreme Personality of Godhead; *coditāt*—impelled; *śabda-mātram*—the subtle element sound; *abhūt*—was manifested; *tasmāt*—from that; *nabhaḥ*—ether; *śrotram*—the sense of hearing; *tu*—then; *śabda-gam*—which catches sound.

TRANSLATION

When egoism in ignorance is agitated by the sex energy of the Supreme Personality of Godhead, the subtle element sound is manifested, and from sound come the ethereal sky and the sense of hearing.

PURPORT

It appears from this verse that all the objects of our sense gratification are the products of egoism in ignorance. It is understood from this verse that by agitation of the element of egoism in ignorance, the first thing produced was sound, which is the subtle form of ether. It is stated also in the *Vedānta-sūtra* that sound is the origin of all objects of material possession and that by sound one can also dissolve this material existence. *Anāvṛttiḥ śabdāt* means "liberation by sound." The entire material manifestation began from sound, and sound can also end material entanglement, if it has a particular potency. The particular sound capable of doing this is the transcendental vibration Hare Kṛṣṇa. Our entanglement in material affairs has begun from material sound. Now we must purify that sound in spiritual understanding. There is sound in the spiritual world also. If we approach that sound, then our spiritual life begins, and the other requirements for spiritual advancement can be supplied. We have to understand very clearly that sound is the beginning of the creation of all material objects for our sense gratification. Similarly, if sound is purified, our spiritual necessities also are produced from sound.

Here it is said that from sound the ether became manifested and that the air became manifested from ether. How the ethereal sky comes from sound, how the air comes from sky and how fire comes from air will be explained later on. Sound is the cause of the sky, and sky is the cause of *śrotram,* the ear. The ear is the first sense for receiving knowledge. One must give aural reception to any knowledge one wants to receive, either material or spiritual. Therefore *śrotram* is very important. The Vedic knowledge is called *śruti;* knowledge has to be received by hearing. By hearing only can we have access to either material or spiritual enjoyment.

In the material world, we manufacture many things for our material comfort simply by hearing. They are already there, but just by hearing, one can transform them. If we want to build a very high skyscraper, this does not mean that we have to create it. The materials for the skyscraper—wood, metal, earth, etc.—are already there, but we make our intimate relationship with those already created material elements by hearing how to utilize them. Modern economic advancement for creation is also a product of hearing, and similarly one can create a favorable field of spiritual activities by hearing from the right source. Arjuna was a gross materialist in the bodily conception of life and was suffering from the bodily concept very acutely. But simply by hearing, Arjuna became a spiritualized, Kṛṣṇa conscious person. Hearing is very important, and that hearing is produced from the sky. By hearing only can we make proper use of that which already exists. The principle of hearing to properly utilize preconceived materials is applicable to spiritual paraphernalia as well. We must hear from the proper spiritual source.

TEXT 33

अर्थाश्रयत्वं शब्दस्य द्रष्टुर्लिङ्गत्वमेव च ।
तन्मात्रत्वं च नभसो लक्षणं कवयो विदुः ॥३३॥

arthāśrayatvaṁ śabdasya
draṣṭur liṅgatvam eva ca
tan-mātratvaṁ ca nabhaso
lakṣaṇaṁ kavayo viduḥ

artha-āśrayatvam—that which conveys the meaning of an object; *śabdasya*—of sound; *draṣṭuḥ*—of the speaker; *liṅgatvam*—that which indicates the presence; *eva*—also; *ca*—and; *tat-mātratvam*—the subtle element; *ca*—and; *nabhasaḥ*—of ether; *lakṣaṇam*—definition; *kavayaḥ*—learned persons; *viduḥ*—know.

TRANSLATION

Persons who are learned and who have true knowledge define sound as that which conveys the idea of an object, indicates the presence of a speaker screened from our view and constitutes the subtle form of ether.

PURPORT

It is very clear herein that as soon as we speak of hearing, there must be a speaker; without a speaker there is no question of hearing. Therefore the Vedic knowledge, which is known as *śruti*, or that which is received by hearing, is also called *apauruṣa.*

Apauruṣa means "not spoken by any person materially created." It is stated in the beginning of *Śrīmad-Bhāgavatam, tene brahma hṛdā.* The sound of Brahman, or *Veda,* was first impregnated into the heart of Brahmā, the original learned man (*ādi-kavaye*). How did he become learned? Whenever there is learning, there must be a speaker and the process of hearing. But Brahmā was the first created being. Who spoke to him? Since no one was there, who was the spiritual master to give knowledge? He was the only living creature; therefore the Vedic knowledge was imparted within his heart by the Supreme Personality of Godhead, who is seated within everyone as Paramātmā. Vedic knowledge is understood to be spoken by the Supreme Lord, and therefore it is free from the defects of material understanding. Material understanding is defective. If we hear something from a conditioned soul, it is full of defects. All material and mundane information is tainted by illusion, error, cheating and imperfection of the senses. Because Vedic knowledge was imparted by the Supreme Lord, who is transcendental to material creation, it is perfect. If we receive that Vedic knowledge from Brahmā in disciplic succession, then we receive perfect knowledge.

Every word we hear has a meaning behind it. As soon as we hear the word "water," there is a substance—water—behind the word. Similarly, as soon as we hear the word "God," there is a meaning to it. If we receive that meaning and explanation of "God" from God Himself, then it is perfect. But if we speculate about the meaning of "God," it is imperfect. *Bhagavad-gītā,* which is the science of God, is spoken by the Personality of Godhead Himself. This is perfect knowledge. Mental speculators or so-called philosophers who are researching what is actually God will never understand the nature of God. The science of God has to be understood in disciplic succession from Brahmā, who was first instructed about knowledge of God by God Himself. We can understand the knowledge of God by hearing *Bhagavad-gītā* from a person authorized in the disciplic succession.

When we speak of seeing, there must be form. By our sense perception, the beginning experience is the sky. Sky is the beginning of form. And from the sky, other forms emanate. The objects of knowledge and sense perception begin, therefore, from the sky.

TEXT 34

भूतानां छिद्रदातृत्वं बहिरन्तरमेव च ।
प्राणेन्द्रियात्मधिष्ण्यत्वं नभसो वृत्तिलक्षणम् ॥३४॥

bhūtānāṁ chidra-dātṛtvaṁ
bahir antaram eva ca

prāṇendriyātma-dhiṣṇyatvaṁ
nabhaso vṛtti-lakṣaṇam

bhūtānām—of all living entities; *chidra-dātṛtvam*—the accommodation of room; *bahiḥ*—external; *antaram*—internal; *eva*—also; *ca*—and; *prāṇa*—of the vital air; *indriya*—the senses; *ātma*—and the mind; *dhiṣṇyatvam*—being the field of activities; *nabhasaḥ*—of the ethereal element; *vṛtti*—activities; *lakṣaṇam*—characteristics.

TRANSLATION

The activities and characteristics of the ethereal element can be observed as accommodation for the room for the external and internal existences of all living entities, namely the field of activities of the vital air, the senses and the mind.

PURPORT

The mind, the senses and the vital force, or living entity, have forms, although they are not visible to the naked eye. Form rests in subtle existence in the sky, and internally it is perceived as the veins within the body and the circulation of the vital air. Externally there are invisible forms of sense objects. The production of the invisible sense objects is the external activity of the ethereal element, and the circulation of vital air and blood is its internal activity. That subtle forms exist in the ether has been proven by modern science by transmission of television, by which forms or photographs of one place are transmitted to another place by the action of the ethereal element. That is very nicely explained here. This verse is the potential basis of great scientific research work, for it explains how subtle forms are generated from the ethereal element, what their characteristics and actions are, and how the tangible elements, namely air, fire, water and earth, are manifested from the subtle form. Mental activities, or psychological actions of thinking, feeling and willing, are also activities on the platform of ethereal existence. The statement in *Bhagavad-gītā* that the mental situation at the time of death is the basis of the next birth is also corroborated in this verse. Mental existence transforms into tangible form as soon as there is an opportunity due to contamination or development of the gross elements from subtle form.

TEXT 35

नभसः शब्दतन्मात्रात्कालगत्या विकुर्वतः ।
स्पर्शोऽभवत्ततो वायुस्त्वक् स्पर्शस्य च सङ्ग्रहः ॥३५॥

nabhasaḥ śabda-tanmātrāt
kāla-gatyā vikurvataḥ
sparśo 'bhavat tato vāyus
tvak sparśasya ca saṅgrahaḥ

nabhasaḥ—from ether; *śabda-tanmātrāt*—which evolves from the subtle element sound; *kāla-gatyā*—under the impulse of time; *vikurvataḥ*—undergoing transformation; *sparśaḥ*—the subtle element touch; *abhavat*—evolved; *tataḥ*—thence; *vāyuḥ*—air; *tvak*—the sense of touch; *sparśasya*—of touch; *ca*—and; *saṅgrahaḥ*—perception.

TRANSLATION

From ethereal existence, which evolves from sound, the next transformation takes place under the impulse of time, and thus the subtle element touch and thence the air and sense of touch become prominent.

PURPORT

In the course of time, when the subtle forms are transformed into gross forms, they become the objects of touch. The objects of touch and the tactile sense also develop after this evolution in time. Sound is the first sense object to exhibit material existence, and from the perception of sound, touch perception evolves and from touch perception the perception of sight. That is the way of the gradual evolution of our perceptive objects.

TEXT 36

मृदुत्वं कठिनत्वं च शैत्यमुष्णत्वमेव च ।
एतत्स्पर्शस्य स्पर्शत्वं तन्मात्रत्वं नभस्वतः ॥३६॥

mṛdutvaṁ kaṭhinatvaṁ ca
śaityam uṣṇatvam eva ca
etat sparśasya sparśatvaṁ
tan-mātratvaṁ nabhasvataḥ

mṛdutvam—softness; *kaṭhinatvam*—hardness; *ca*—and; *śaityam*—cold; *uṣṇatvam*—heat; *eva*—also; *ca*—and; *etat*—this; *sparśasya*—of the subtle element touch; *sparśatvam*—the distinguishing attributes; *tat-mātratvam*—the subtle form; *nabhasvataḥ*—of air.

TRANSLATION

Softness and hardness and cold and heat are the distinguishing attributes of touch, which is characterized as the subtle form of air.

PURPORT

Tangibility is the proof of form. In actuality, objects are perceived in two different ways. They are either soft or hard, cold or hot, etc. This tangible action of the tactile sense is the result of the evolution of air, which is produced from the sky.

TEXT 37

चालनं व्यूहनं प्राप्तिर्नेतृत्वं द्रव्यशब्दयोः ।
सर्वेन्द्रियाणामात्मत्वं वायोः कर्माभिलक्षणम् ॥३७॥

cālanaṁ vyūhanaṁ prāptir
netṛtvaṁ dravya-śabdayoḥ
sarvendriyāṇām ātmatvaṁ
vāyoḥ karmābhilakṣaṇam

cālanam—moving; *vyūhanam*—mixing; *prāptiḥ*—allowing approach; *netṛtvam*—carrying; *dravya-śabdayoḥ*—particles of substances and sound; *sarva-indriyāṇām*—of all the senses; *ātmatvam*—providing for the proper functioning; *vāyoḥ*—of air; *karma*—by actions; *abhilakṣaṇam*—the distinct characteristics.

TRANSLATION

The action of the air is exhibited in movements, mixing, allowing approach to the objects of sound and other sense perceptions, and providing for the proper functioning of all other senses.

PURPORT

We can perceive the action of the air when the branches of a tree move or when dry leaves on the ground collect together. Similarly, it is only by the action of the air that a body moves, and when the air circulation is impeded, many diseases result. Paralysis, nervous breakdowns, madness and many other diseases are actually due to an insufficient circulation of air. In the Āyur-vedic system these diseases are treated on the basis of air circulation. If from the beginning one takes care of the process of air circulation, such diseases cannot take place. From the *Āyur-veda* as well as from the *Śrīmad-Bhāgavatam* it is clear that so many activities are going on internally and externally because of air alone, and as soon as there is some deficiency in the air circulation, these activities cannot take place. Here it is clearly stated, *netṛtvaṁ dravya-śabdayoḥ*. Our sense of proprietorship over action is also due to the activity of the air. If the air circulation is stifled, we cannot approach a place after hearing. If someone calls us, we hear the sound because of the air circulation, and we approach that sound or the place from which the sound comes. It is clearly said in this verse that these are all movements of the air. The ability to detect odors is also due to the action of the air.

TEXT 38

वायोश्च स्पर्शतन्मात्राद्रूपं दैवेरितादभूत् ।
समुत्थितं ततस्तेजश्चक्षू रूपोपलम्भनम् ॥३८॥

vāyoś ca sparśa-tanmātrād
rūpaṁ daiveritād abhūt
samutthitaṁ tatas tejaś
cakṣū rūpopalambhanam

vāyoḥ—from air; *ca*—and; *sparśa-tanmātrāt*—which evolves from the subtle element touch; *rūpam*—form; *daiva-īritāt*—according to destiny; *abhūt*—evolved; *samutthitam*—arose; *tataḥ*—from that; *tejaḥ*—fire; *cakṣuḥ*—sense of sight; *rūpa*—color and form; *upalambhanam*—perceiving.

TRANSLATION

By interactions of the air and the sensations of touch, one receives different forms according to destiny. By evolution of such forms, there is fire, and the eye sees different forms in color.

PURPORT

Because of destiny, the touch sensation, the interactions of air, and the situation of the mind, which is produced of the ethereal element, one receives a body according to his previous activities. Needless to say, a living entity transmigrates from one form to another. His form changes according to destiny and by the arrangement of a superior authority which controls the interaction of air and the mental situation. Form is the combination of different types of sense perception. Predestined activities are the plans of the mental situation and the interaction of air.

TEXT 39

द्रव्याकृतित्वं गुणता व्यक्तिसंस्थात्वमेव च ।
तेजस्त्वं तेजसः साध्वि रूपमात्रस्य वृत्तयः ॥३९॥

dravyākṛtitvaṁ guṇatā
vyakti-saṁsthātvam eva ca
tejastvaṁ tejasaḥ sādhvi
rūpa-mātrasya vṛttayaḥ

dravya—of an object; *ākṛtitvam*—dimension; *guṇatā*—quality; *vyakti-saṁsthātvam*—individuality; *eva*—also; *ca*—and; *tejastvam*—effulgence; *tejasaḥ*—of fire; *sādhvi*—O virtuous lady; *rūpa-mātrasya*—of the subtle element form; *vṛttayaḥ*—the characteristics.

TRANSLATION

My dear mother, the characteristics of form are understood by dimension, quality and individuality. The form of fire is appreciated by its effulgence.

PURPORT

Every form that we appreciate has its particular dimensions and characteristics. The quality of a particular object is appreciated by its utility. But the form of sound is independent. Forms which are invisible can be understood only by touch; that is the independent appreciation of invisible form. Visible forms are understood by analytical study of their constitution. The constitution of a certain object is appreciated by its internal action. For example, the form of salt is appreciated by the interaction of salty tastes, and the form of sugar is appreciated by the interaction of sweet tastes. Tastes and qualitative constitution are the basic principles in understanding the form of an object.

TEXT 40

द्योतनं पचनं पानमदनं हिममर्दनम् ।
तेजसो वृत्तयस्त्वेताः शोषणं क्षुत्तृडेव च ॥४०॥

dyotanaṁ pacanaṁ pānam
adanaṁ hima-mardanam
tejaso vṛttayas tv etāḥ
śoṣaṇaṁ kṣut tṛḍ eva ca

dyotanam—illumination; *pacanam*—cooking, digesting; *pānam*—drinking; *adanam*—eating; *hima-mardanam*—destroying cold; *tejasaḥ*—of fire; *vṛttayaḥ*—functions; *tu*—indeed; *etāḥ*—these; *śoṣaṇam*—evaporating; *kṣut*—hunger; *tṛṭ*—thirst; *eva*—also; *ca*—and.

TRANSLATION

Fire is appreciated by its light and by its ability to cook, to digest, to destroy cold, to evaporate, and to give rise to hunger, thirst, eating and drinking.

PURPORT

The first symptoms of fire are distribution of light and heat, and the existence of fire is also perceived in the stomach. Without fire we cannot digest what we eat. Without digestion there is no hunger and thirst or power to eat and drink. When there is insufficient hunger and thirst, it is understood that there is a shortage of fire within the stomach, and the Āyur-vedic treatment is performed in connection with the fire element, *agni-māndyam.* Since fire is increased by the secretion of bile, the treatment is to increase bile secretion. The Āyur-vedic treatment thus corroborates the statements in *Śrīmad-Bhāgavatam.* The characteristic of fire in subduing the influence of cold is known to everyone. Severe cold can always be counteracted by fire.

TEXT 41

रूपमात्राद्विकुर्वाणात्तेजसो दैवचोदितात् ।
रसमात्रमभूत्तस्मादम्भो जिह्वा रसग्रहः ॥४१॥

rūpa-mātrād vikurvāṇāt
tejaso daiva-coditāt
rasa-mātram abhūt tasmād
ambho jihvā rasa-grahaḥ

rūpa-mātrāt—which evolves from the subtle element form; *vikurvāṇāt*—undergoing transformation; *tejasaḥ*—from fire; *daiva-coditāt*—under a superior arrangement; *rasa-mātram*—the subtle element taste; *abhūt*—became manifested; *tasmāt*—from that; *ambhaḥ*—water; *jihvā*—the sense of taste; *rasa-grahaḥ*—which perceives taste.

TRANSLATION

By the interaction of fire and the visual sensation, the subtle element taste evolves under a superior arrangement. From taste, water is produced, and the tongue, which perceives taste, is also manifested.

PURPORT

The tongue is described here as the instrument for acquiring knowledge of taste. Because taste is a product of water, there is always saliva on the tongue.

TEXT 42

कषायो मधुरस्तिक्तः कट्वम्ल इति नैकधा ।
भौतिकानां विकारेण रस एको विभिद्यते ॥४२॥

kaṣāyo madhuras tiktaḥ
kaṭv amla iti naikadhā
bhautikānāṁ vikāreṇa
rasa eko vibhidyate

kaṣāyaḥ—astringent; *madhuraḥ*—sweet; *tiktaḥ*—bitter; *kaṭu*—pungent; *amlaḥ*—sour; *iti*—thus; *na-ekadhā*—manifoldly; *bhautikānām*—of other substances; *vikāreṇa*—by transformation; *rasaḥ*—the subtle element taste; *ekaḥ*—originally one; *vibhidyate*—is divided.

TRANSLATION

Although originally one, taste becomes manifold as astringent, sweet, bitter, pungent, sour and salty due to contact with other substances.

TEXT 43

क्लेदनं पिण्डनं तृप्तिः प्राणनाप्यायनोन्दनम् ।
तापापनोदो भूयस्त्वमम्भसो वृत्तयस्त्विमाः ॥४३॥

kledanaṁ piṇḍanaṁ tṛptiḥ
prāṇanāpyāyanondanam
tāpāpanodo bhūyastvam
ambhaso vṛttayas tv imāḥ

kledanam—moistening; *piṇḍanam*—coagulating; *tṛptiḥ*—causing satisfaction; *prāṇana*—maintaining life; *āpyāyana*—refreshing; *undanam*—softening; *tāpa*—heat; *apanodaḥ*—driving away; *bhūyastvam*—being in abundance; *ambhasaḥ*—of water; *vṛttayaḥ*—the characteristic functions; *tu*—in fact; *imāḥ*—these.

TRANSLATION

The characteristics of water are exhibited by its moistening other substances, coagulating various mixtures, causing satisfaction, maintaining life, softening things, driving away heat, incessantly supplying itself to reservoirs of water, and refreshing by slaking thirst.

PURPORT

Starvation can be mitigated by drinking water. It is sometimes found that if a person who has taken a vow to fast takes a little water at intervals, the exhaustion of fasting is at once mitigated. In the *Vedas* it is also stated, *āpomayaḥ prāṇaḥ:* "Life depends on water." With water, anything can be moistened or dampened. Flour dough can be prepared with a mixture of water. Mud is made by mixing earth with water. As stated in the beginning of *Śrīmad-Bhāgavatam,* water is the cementing ingredient of different material elements. If we build a house, water is actually the constituent in making the bricks. Fire, water and air are the exchanging elements for the entire material manifestation, but water is most prominent. Also, excessive heat can be reduced simply by pouring water on the heated field.

TEXT 44

रसमात्राद्विकुर्वाणादम्भसो दैवचोदितात् ।
गन्धमात्रमभूत्तस्मात्पृथ्वी घ्राणस्तु गन्धगः ॥४४॥

rasa-mātrād vikurvāṇād
ambhaso daiva-coditāt
gandha-mātram abhūt tasmāt
pṛthvī ghrāṇas tu gandhagaḥ

rasa-mātrāt—which evolves from the subtle element taste; *vikurvāṇāt*—undergoing transformation; *ambhasaḥ*—from water; *daiva-coditāt*—by a superior arrangement; *gandha-mātram*—the subtle element odor; *abhūt*—became manifest; *tasmāt*—from that; *pṛthvī*—earth; *ghrāṇaḥ*—the olfactory sense; *tu*—in fact; *gandha-gaḥ*—which perceives aromas.

TRANSLATION

Due to the interaction of water with the taste perception, the subtle element odor evolves under superior arrangement. Thence the earth and the olfactory sense, by which we can variously experience the aroma of the earth, become manifest.

TEXT 45

करम्भपूतिसौरभ्यशान्तोग्राम्लादिभिः पृथक् ।
द्रव्यावयववैषम्याद्गन्ध एको विभिद्यते ॥४५॥

karambha-pūti-saurabhya-
śāntogrāmlādibhiḥ pṛthak
dravyāvayava-vaiṣamyād
gandha eko vibhidyate

karambha—mixed; *pūti*—offensive; *saurabhya*—fragrant; *śānta*—mild; *ugra*—strong, pungent; *amla*—acid; *ādibhiḥ*—and so on; *pṛthak*—separately; *dravya*—of substance; *avayava*—of portions; *vaiṣamyāt*—according to diversity; *gandhaḥ*—odor; *ekaḥ*—one; *vibhidyate*—is divided.

TRANSLATION

Odor, although one, becomes many—as mixed, offensive, fragrant, mild, strong, acidic and so on—according to the proportions of associated substances.

PURPORT

Mixed smell is sometimes perceived in foodstuffs prepared from various ingredients, such as vegetables mixed with different kinds of spices and asafetida. Bad odors are perceived in filthy places, good smells are perceived from camphor, menthol and similar other products, pungent smells are perceived from garlic and onions, and acidic smells are perceived from turmeric and similar sour substances. The original aroma is the odor emanating from the earth, and when it is mixed with different substances, this odor appears in different ways.

TEXT 46

भावनं ब्रह्मणः स्थानं धारणं सद्विशेषणम् ।
सर्वसत्त्वगुणोद्भेदः पृथिवीवृत्तिलक्षणम् ॥४६॥

bhāvanaṁ brahmaṇaḥ sthānaṁ
dhāraṇaṁ sad-viśeṣaṇam
sarva-sattva-guṇodbhedaḥ
pṛthivī-vṛtti-lakṣaṇam

bhāvanam—modeling forms; *brahmaṇaḥ*—of the Supreme Brahman; *sthānam*—constructing places of residence; *dhāraṇam*—containing substances; *sat-viśeṣaṇam*—distinguishing the open space; *sarva*—all; *sattva*—of existence; *guṇa*—qualities; *udbhedaḥ*—the place for manifestation; *pṛthivī*—of earth; *vṛtti*—of the functions; *lakṣaṇam*—the characteristics.

TRANSLATION

The characteristics of the functions of earth can be perceived by modeling forms of the Supreme Brahman, by constructing places of residence, by preparing pots to contain water, etc. In other words, the earth is the place of sustenance for all elements.

PURPORT

Different elements, such as sound, sky, air, fire and water, can be perceived in the earth. Another feature of the earth especially mentioned here is that earth can manifest different forms of the Supreme Personality of Godhead. By this statement of Kapila's it is confirmed that the Supreme Personality of Godhead, Brahman, has innumerable forms, which are described in the scriptures. By manipulation of earth and its products, such as stone, wood and jewels, these forms of the Supreme Lord can be present before our eyes. When a form of Lord Kṛṣṇa or Lord Viṣṇu is manifested by presentation of a statue made of earth, it is not imaginary. The earth gives shape to the Lord's forms as described in the scriptures.

In the *Brahma-saṁhitā* there is description of Lord Kṛṣṇa's lands, the variegatedness of the spiritual abode, and the forms of the Lord playing a flute with His spiritual body. All these forms are described in the scriptures, and when they are thus presented they become worshipable. They are not imaginary as the Māyāvāda philosophy says. Sometimes the word *bhāvana* is misinterpreted as "imagination." But *bhāvana* does not mean "imagination;" it means giving actual shape to the description of Vedic literature. Earth is the ultimate transformation of all living entities and their respective modes of material nature.

TEXT 47

नभोगुणविशेषोऽर्थो यस्य तच्छ्रोत्रमुच्यते ।
वायोर्गुणविशेषोऽर्थो यस्य तत्स्पर्शनं विदुः ॥४७॥

nabho-guṇa-viśeṣo 'rtho
yasya tac chrotram ucyate
vāyor guṇa-viśeṣo 'rtho
yasya tat sparśanaṁ viduḥ

nabhaḥ-guṇa-viśeṣaḥ—the distinctive characteristic of sky (sound); *arthaḥ*—object of perception; *yasya*—whose; *tat*—that; *śrotram*—the auditory sense; *ucyate*—is called; *vāyoḥ guṇa-viśeṣaḥ*—the distinctive characteristic of air (touch); *arthaḥ*—object of perception; *yasya*—whose; *tat*—that; *sparśanam*—the tactile sense; *viduḥ*—they know.

TRANSLATION

The sense whose object of perception is sound is called the auditory sense, and that whose object of perception is touch is called the tactile sense.

PURPORT

Sound is one of the qualifications of the sky and is the subject matter for hearing. Similarly, touch is the qualification of the air and is the subject of the touch sensation.

TEXT 48

तेजोगुणविशेषोऽर्थो यस्य तच्चक्षुरुच्यते ।
अम्भोगुणविशेषोऽर्थो यस्य तद्रसनं विदुः ।
भूमेर्गुणविशेषोऽर्थो यस्य स घ्राण उच्यते ॥४८॥

tejo-guṇa-viśeṣo 'rtho
yasya tac cakṣur ucyate
ambho-guṇa-viśeṣo 'rtho
yasya tad rasanaṁ viduḥ
bhūmer guṇa-viśeṣo 'rtho
yasya sa ghrāṇa ucyate

tejaḥ-guṇa-viśeṣaḥ—the distinctive characteristic of fire (form); *arthaḥ*—object of perception; *yasya*—whose; *tat*—that; *cakṣuḥ*—the sense of sight; *ucyate*—is called; *ambhaḥ-guṇa-viśeṣaḥ*—the distinctive characteristic of water (taste); *arthaḥ*—object of perception; *yasya*—whose; *tat*—that; *rasanam*—the sense of taste; *viduḥ*—they know; *bhūmeḥ guṇa-viśeṣaḥ*—the distinctive characteristic of earth (odor); *arthaḥ*—object of perception; *yasya*—whose; *saḥ*—that; *ghrāṇaḥ*—the sense of smell; *ucyate*—is called.

TRANSLATION

The sense whose object of perception is form, the distinctive characteristic of fire, is the sense of sight. The sense whose object of perception is taste, the distinctive characteristic of water, is known as the sense of taste. Finally, the sense whose object of perception is odor, the distinctive characteristic of earth, is called the sense of smell.

TEXT 49

परस्य दृश्यते धर्मो ह्यपरस्मिन् समन्वयात् ।
अतो विशेषो भावानां भूमावेवोपलक्ष्यते ॥४९॥

parasya dṛśyate dharmo
hy aparasmin samanvayāt
ato viśeṣo bhāvānāṁ
bhūmāv evopalakṣyate

parasya—of the cause; *dṛśyate*—is observed; *dharmaḥ*—the characteristics; *hi*—indeed; *aparasmin*—in the effect; *samanvayāt*—in order; *ataḥ*—hence; *viśeṣaḥ*—the distinctive characteristic; *bhāvānām*—of all the elements; *bhūmau*—in earth; *eva*—alone; *upalakṣyate*—is observed.

TRANSLATION

Since the cause exists in its effect as well, the characteristics of the former are observed in the latter. That is why the peculiarities of all the elements exist in the earth alone.

PURPORT

Sound is the cause of the sky, sky is the cause of the air, air is the cause of fire, fire is the cause of water, and water is the cause of earth. In the sky there is only sound; in the air there are sound and touch; in the fire there are sound, touch and form; in water there are sound, touch, form and taste; and in the earth there are sound, touch, form, taste and smell. Therefore earth is the reservoir of all the qualities of the other elements. Earth is the sum total of all other elements. The earth has all five qualities of the elements, water has four qualities, fire has three, air has two, and the sky has only one quality, sound.

TEXT 50

एतान्यसंहत्य यदा महदादीनि सप्त वै ।
कालकर्मगुणोपेतो जगदादिरुपाविशत् ॥५०॥

etāny asaṁhatya yadā
mahad-ādīni sapta vai
kāla-karma-guṇopeto
jagad-ādir upāviśat

etāni—these; *asaṁhatya*—being unmixed; *yadā*—when; *mahat-ādīni*—the *mahat-tattva,* false ego and five gross elements; *sapta*—all together seven; *vai*—in fact; *kāla*—time; *karma*—work; *guṇa*—and the three modes of material nature; *upetaḥ*—accompanied by; *jagat-ādiḥ*—the origin of creation; *upāviśat*—entered.

TRANSLATION

When all these elements were unmixed, the Supreme Personality of Godhead, the origin of creation, along with time, work, and the qualities of the modes of material nature, entered into the universe with the total material energy in seven divisions.

PURPORT

After stating the generation of the causes, Kapiladeva speaks about the generation of the effects. At that time when the causes were unmixed, the Supreme Personality of

Godhead, in His feature of Garbhodakaśāyī Viṣṇu, entered within each universe. Accompanying Him were all of the seven primary elements—the five material elements, the total energy (*mahat-tattva*) and the false ego. This entrance of the Supreme Personality of Godhead involves His entering even the atoms of the material world. This is confirmed in the *Brahma-saṁhitā* (5.35): *aṇḍāntara-stha-paramāṇu-cayāntara-stham.* He is not only within the universe, but within the atoms also. He is within the heart of every living entity. Garbhodakaśāyī Viṣṇu, the Supreme Personality of Godhead, entered into everything.

TEXT 51

ततस्तेनानुविद्धेभ्यो युक्तेभ्योऽण्डमचेतनम् ।
उत्थितं पुरुषो यस्मादुदतिष्ठदसौ विराट् ॥५१॥

tatas tenānuviddhebhyo
yuktebhyo 'ṇḍam acetanam
utthitaṁ puruṣo yasmād
udatiṣṭhad asau virāṭ

tataḥ—then; *tena*—by the Lord; *anuviddhebhyaḥ*—from these seven principles, roused into activity; *yuktebhyaḥ*—united; *aṇḍam*—an egg; *acetanam*—unintelligent; *utthitam*—arose; *puruṣaḥ*—Cosmic Being; *yasmāt*—from which; *udatiṣṭhat*—appeared; *asau*—that; *virāṭ*—celebrated.

TRANSLATION

From these seven principles, roused into activity and united by the presence of the Lord, an unintelligent egg arose, from which appeared the celebrated Cosmic Being.

PURPORT

In sex life, the combination of matter from the parents, which involves emulsification and secretion, creates the situation whereby a soul is received within matter, and the combination of matter gradually develops into a complete body. The same principle exists in the universal creation: the ingredients were present, but only when the Lord entered into the material elements was matter actually agitated. That is the cause of creation. We can see this in our ordinary experience. Although we may have clay, water and fire, the elements take the shape of a brick only when we labor to combine them. Without the living energy, there is no possibility that matter can take shape. Similarly, this material world does not develop unless agitated by the Supreme

Lord as the *virāṭ-puruṣa. Yasmād udatiṣṭhad asau virāṭ:* by His agitation, space was created, and the universal form of the Lord also manifested therein.

TEXT 52

एतदण्डं विशेषाख्यं क्रमवृद्धैर्दशोत्तरैः ।
तोयादिभिः परिवृतं प्रधानेनावृतैर्बहिः ।
यत्र लोकवितानोऽयं रूपं भगवतो हरेः ॥५२॥

etad aṇḍaṁ viśeṣākhyaṁ
krama-vṛddhair daśottaraiḥ
toyādibhiḥ parivṛtaṁ
pradhānenāvṛtair bahiḥ
yatra loka-vitāno 'yaṁ
rūpaṁ bhagavato hareḥ

etat—this; *aṇḍam*—egg; *viśeṣa-ākhyam*—called *viśeṣa; krama*—one after another; *vṛddhaiḥ*—increased; *daśa*—ten times; *uttaraiḥ*—greater; *toya-ādibhiḥ*—by water and so on; *parivṛtam*—enveloped; *pradhānena*—by *pradhāna; āvṛtaiḥ*—covered; *bahiḥ*—on the outside; *yatra*—where; *loka-vitānaḥ*—the extension of the planetary systems; *ayam*—this; *rūpam*—form; *bhagavataḥ*—of the Supreme Personality of Godhead; *hareḥ*—of Lord Hari.

TRANSLATION

This universal egg, or the universe in the shape of an egg, is called the manifestation of material energy. Its layers of water, air, fire, sky, ego and mahat-tattva increase in thickness one after another. Each layer is ten times bigger than the previous one, and the final outside layer is covered by pradhāna. Within this egg is the universal form of Lord Hari, of whose body the fourteen planetary systems are parts.

PURPORT

This universe, or the universal sky which we can visualize with its innumerable planets, is shaped just like an egg. As an egg is covered by a shell, the universe is also covered by various layers. The first layer is water, the next is fire, then air, then sky, and the ultimate holding crust is *pradhāna.* Within this egglike universe is the universal form of the Lord as the *virāṭ-puruṣa.* All the different planetary situations are parts of His body. This is already explained in the beginning of *Śrīmad-Bhāgavatam,* Second Canto. The planetary systems are considered to form different bodily parts of that universal form of the Lord. Persons who cannot directly engage in the worship of the transcendental form of the Lord are advised to think of and worship this universal form. The lowest planetary system, Pātāla, is considered to be the sole of the Supreme Lord, and the earth is considered to be the belly of the Lord. Brahmaloka, or the highest planetary system, where Brahmā lives, is considered to be the head of the Lord.

This *virāṭ-puruṣa* is considered an incarnation of the Lord. The original form of the Lord is Kṛṣṇa, as confirmed in *Brahma-saṁhitā: ādi-puruṣa.* The *virāṭ-puruṣa* is also *puruṣa,* but He is not *ādi-puruṣa.* The *ādi-puruṣa* is Kṛṣṇa. *Īśvaraḥ paramaḥ kṛṣṇaḥ sac-cid-ānanda-vigrahaḥ/ anādir ādir govindaḥ.* In *Bhagavad-gītā* Kṛṣṇa is also accepted as the *ādi-puruṣa,* the original. Kṛṣṇa says, "No one is greater than I." There are innumerable expansions of the Lord, and all of them are *puruṣas,* or enjoyers, but neither the *virāṭ-puruṣa* nor the *puruṣa-avatāras*—Kāraṇodakaśāyī Viṣṇu, Garbhodakaśāyī Viṣṇu and Kṣīrodakaśāyī Viṣṇu—nor any of the many other expansions, is the original. In each universe there are Garbhodakaśāyī Viṣṇu, the *virāṭ-puruṣa* and Kṣīrodakaśāyī Viṣṇu. The active manifestation of the *virāṭ-puruṣa* is described here. Persons who are in the lower grade of understanding regarding the Supreme Personality of Godhead may think of the universal form of the Lord, for that is advised in the *Bhāgavatam.*

The dimensions of the universe are estimated here. The outer covering is made of layers of water, air, fire, sky, ego and *mahat-tattva,* and each layer is ten times greater than the one previous. The space within the hollow of the universe cannot be measured by any human scientist or anyone else, and beyond the hollow there are seven coverings, each one ten times greater than the one preceding it. The layer of water is ten times greater than the diameter of the universe, and the layer of fire is ten times greater than that of water. Similarly, the layer of air is ten times greater than that of fire. These dimensions are all inconceivable to the tiny brain of a human being.

It is also stated that this description is of only one egglike universe. There are innumerable universes besides this one, and some of them are many, many times greater. It is considered, in fact, that this universe is the smallest; therefore the predominating superintendent, or Brahmā, has only four heads for management. In other universes, which are far greater than this one, Brahmā has more heads. In the *Caitanya-caritāmṛta* it is stated that all these Brahmās were called one day by Lord Kṛṣṇa on the inquiry of the small Brahmā, who, after seeing all the larger Brahmās, was thunderstruck. That is the inconceivable potency of the Lord. No one can measure the length and breadth of God by speculation or by false identification with God. These attempts are symptoms of lunacy.

TEXT 53

हिरण्मयादण्डकोशादुत्थाय सलिलेशयात् ।
तमाविश्य महादेवो बहुधा निर्बिभेद खम् ॥५३॥

hiraṇmayād aṇḍa-kośād
utthāya salile śayāt
tam āviśya mahā-devo
bahudhā nirbibheda kham

hiraṇmayāt—golden; *aṇḍa-kośāt*—from the egg; *utthāya*—arising; *salile*—on the water; *śayāt*—lying; *tam*—in it; *āviśya*—having entered; *mahā-devaḥ*—the Supreme Personality of Godhead; *bahudhā*—in many ways; *nirbibheda*—divided; *kham*—apertures.

TRANSLATION

The Supreme Personality of Godhead, the virāṭ-puruṣa, situated Himself in that golden egg, which was lying on the water, and He divided it into many departments.

TEXT 54

निरभिद्यतास्य प्रथमं मुखं वाणी ततोऽभवत् ।
वाण्या वह्निरथो नासे प्राणोतो घ्राण एतयोः ॥५४॥

nirabhidyatāsya prathamaṁ
mukhaṁ vāṇī tato 'bhavat
vāṇyā vahnir atho nāse
prāṇoto ghrāṇa etayoḥ

nirabhidyata—appeared; *asya*—of Him; *prathamam*—first of all; *mukham*—a mouth; *vāṇī*—the organ of speech; *tataḥ*—then; *abhavat*—came forth; *vāṇyā*—with the organ of speech; *vahniḥ*—the god of fire; *athaḥ*—then; *nāse*—the two nostrils; *prāṇa*—the vital air; *utaḥ*—joined; *ghrāṇaḥ*—the olfactory sense; *etayoḥ*—in them.

TRANSLATION

First of all a mouth appeared in Him, and then came forth the organ of speech, and with it the god of fire, the deity who presides over that organ. Then a pair of nostrils appeared, and in them appeared the olfactory sense, as well as prāṇa, the vital air.

PURPORT

With the manifestation of speech, fire also became manifested, and with the manifestation of nostrils the vital air, the breathing process and the sense of smell also became manifested.

TEXT 55

घ्राणाद्वायुरभिद्येतामक्षिणी चक्षुरेतयोः ।
तस्मात्सूर्यो न्यभिद्येतां कर्णौ श्रोत्रं ततो दिशः ॥५५॥

ghrāṇād vāyur abhidyetām
akṣiṇī cakṣur etayoḥ
tasmāt sūryo nyabhidyetāṁ
karṇau śrotraṁ tato diśaḥ

ghrāṇāt—from the olfactory sense; *vāyuḥ*—the wind-god; *abhidyetām*—appeared; *akṣiṇī*—the two eyes; *cakṣuḥ*—the sense of sight; *etayoḥ*—in them; *tasmāt*—from that; *sūryaḥ*—the sun-god; *nyabhidyetām*—appeared; *karṇau*—the two ears; *śrotram*—the auditory sense; *tataḥ*—from that; *diśaḥ*—the deities presiding over the directions.

TRANSLATION

In the wake of the olfactory sense came the wind-god, who presides over that sense. Thereafter a pair of eyes appeared in the universal form, and in them the sense of sight. In the wake of this sense came the sun-god, who presides over it. Next there appeared in Him a pair of ears, and in them the auditory sense and in its wake the Dig-devatās, or the deities who preside over the directions.

PURPORT

The appearance of different bodily parts of the Lord's universal form and the appearance of the presiding deities of those bodily parts is being described. As in the womb of a mother a child gradually grows different bodily parts, so in the universal womb the universal form of the Lord gives rise to the creation of various paraphernalia. The senses appear, and over each of them there is a presiding deity. It is corroborated by this statement of *Śrīmad-Bhāgavatam*, and also by *Brahma-saṁhitā*, that the sun appeared after the appearance of the eyes of the universal form of the Lord. The sun is dependent on the eyes of the universal form. The *Brahma-saṁhitā* also says that the sun is the eye of the Supreme Personality of Godhead, Kṛṣṇa. *Yac-cakṣur eṣa savitā. Savitā* means "the sun." The sun is the eye of the Supreme Personality of Godhead. Actually, everything is created by the universal body of the Supreme Godhead. Material nature is simply the supplier of materials. The creation is actually done by the Supreme Lord, as confirmed in *Bhagavad-gītā* (9.10). *Mayādhyakṣeṇa prakṛtiḥ sūyate sa-carācaram:* "Under My direction does material nature create all moving and nonmoving objects in the cosmic creation."

TEXT 56

निर्बिभेद विराजस्त्वग्रोमश्मश्रवादयस्ततः ।
तत ओषधयश्चासन् शिश्नं निर्बिभिदे ततः ॥५६॥

nirbibheda virājas tvag-
roma-śmaśrv-ādayas tataḥ
tata oṣadhayaś cāsan
śiśnaṁ nirbibhide tataḥ

nirbibheda—appeared; *virājaḥ*—of the universal form; *tvak*—skin; *roma*—hair; *śmaśru*—beard, mustache; *ādayaḥ*—and so on; *tataḥ*—then; *tataḥ*—thereupon; *oṣadhayaḥ*—the herbs and drugs; *ca*—and; *āsan*—appeared; *śiśnam*—genitals; *nirbibhide*—appeared; *tataḥ*—after this.

TRANSLATION

Then the universal form of the Lord, the virāṭ-puruṣa, manifested His skin, and thereupon the hair, mustache and beard appeared. After this all the herbs and drugs became manifested, and then His genitals also appeared.

PURPORT

The skin is the site of the touch sensation. The demigods who control the production of herbs and medicinal drugs are the deities presiding over the tactile sense.

TEXT 57

रेतस्तस्मादाप आसन्निरभिद्यत वै गुदम् ।
गुदादपानोऽपानाच्च मृत्युर्लोकभयङ्करः ॥५७॥

retas tasmād āpa āsan
nirabhidyata vai gudam

gudād apāno 'pānāc ca
mṛtyur loka-bhayaṅkaraḥ

retaḥ—semen; *tasmāt*—from that; *āpaḥ*—the god who presides over the waters; *āsan*—appeared; *nirabhidyata*—was manifested; *vai*—indeed; *gudam*—an anus; *gudāt*—from the anus; *apānaḥ*—the organ of defecation; *apānāt*—from the organ of defecation; *ca*—and; *mṛtyuḥ*—death; *loka-bhayam-karaḥ*—causing fear throughout the universe.

TRANSLATION

After this, semen (the faculty of procreation) and the god who presides over the waters appeared. Next appeared an anus and then the organs of defecation and thereupon the god of death, who is feared throughout the universe.

PURPORT

It is understood herewith that the faculty to discharge semen is the cause of death. Therefore, *yogīs* and transcendentalists who want to live for greater spans of life voluntarily restrain themselves from discharging semen. The more one can restrain the discharge of semen, the more one can be aloof from the problem of death. There are many *yogīs* living up to three hundred or seven hundred years by this process, and in the *Bhāgavatam* it is clearly stated that discharging semen is the cause of horrible death. The more one is addicted to sexual enjoyment, the more susceptible he is to a quick death.

TEXT 58

हस्तौ च निरभिद्येतां बलं ताभ्यां ततः स्वराट् ।
पादौ च निरभिद्येतां गतिस्ताभ्यां ततो हरिः ॥५८॥

hastau ca nirabhidyetāṁ
balaṁ tābhyāṁ tataḥ svarāṭ
pādau ca nirabhidyetāṁ
gatis tābhyāṁ tato hariḥ

hastau—the two hands; *ca*—and; *nirabhidyetām*—were manifested; *balam*—power; *tābhyām*—from them; *tataḥ*—thereafter; *svarāṭ*—Lord Indra; *pādau*—the two feet; *ca*—and; *nirabhidyetām*—became manifested; *gatiḥ*—the process of movement; *tābhyām*—from them; *tataḥ*—then; *hariḥ*—Lord Viṣṇu.

TRANSLATION

Thereafter the two hands of the universal form of the Lord became manifested, and with them the power of grasping and dropping things, and

after that Lord Indra appeared. Next the legs became manifested, and with them the process of movement, and after that Lord Viṣṇu appeared.

PURPORT

The deity presiding over the hands is Indra, and the presiding deity of movement is the Supreme Personality of Godhead, Viṣṇu. Viṣṇu appeared on the appearance of the legs of the *virāṭ-puruṣa.*

TEXT 59

नाड्योऽस्य निरभिद्यन्त ताभ्यो लोहितमाभृतम् ।
नद्यस्ततः समभवन्नुदरं निरभिद्यत ॥५९॥

nāḍyo 'sya nirabhidyanta
tābhyo lohitam ābhṛtam
nadyas tataḥ samabhavann
udaraṁ nirabhidyata

nāḍyaḥ—the veins; *asya*—of the universal form; *nirabhidyanta*—became manifested; *tābhyaḥ*—from them; *lohitam*—blood; *ābhṛtam*—was produced; *nadyaḥ*—the rivers; *tataḥ*—from that; *samabhavan*—appeared; *udaram*—the stomach; *nirabhidyata*—became manifested.

TRANSLATION

The veins of the universal body became manifested and thereafter the red corpuscles, or blood. In their wake came the rivers (the deities presiding over the veins), and then appeared an abdomen.

PURPORT

Blood veins are compared to rivers; when the veins were manifested in the universal form, the rivers in the various planets were also manifested. The controlling deity of the rivers is also the controlling deity of the nervous system. In Āyur-vedic treatment, those who are suffering from the disease of nervous instability are recommended to take a bath by dipping into a flowing river.

TEXT 60

क्षुत्पिपासे ततः स्यातां समुद्रस्त्वेतयोरभूत् ।
अथास्य हृदयं भिन्नं हृदयान्मन उत्थितम् ॥६०॥

kṣut-pipāse tataḥ syātāṁ
samudras tv etayor abhūt
athāsya hṛdayaṁ bhinnaṁ
hṛdayān mana utthitam

kṣut-pipāse—hunger and thirst; *tataḥ*—then; *syātām*—appeared; *samudraḥ*—the ocean; *tu*—then; *etayoḥ*—in their wake; *abhūt*—appeared; *atha*—then; *asya*—of the universal form; *hṛdayam*—a heart; *bhinnam*—appeared; *hṛdayāt*—from the heart; *manaḥ*—the mind; *utthitam*—appeared.

TRANSLATION

Next grew feelings of hunger and thirst, and in their wake came the manifestation of the oceans. Then a heart became manifest, and in the wake of the heart the mind appeared.

PURPORT

The ocean is considered to be the presiding deity of the abdomen, where the feelings of hunger and thirst originate. When there is an irregularity in hunger and thirst, one is advised, according to Āyur-vedic treatment, to take a bath in the ocean.

TEXT 61

मनसश्चन्द्रमा जातो बुद्धिर्बुद्धेर्गिरां पतिः ।
अहङ्कारस्ततो रुद्रश्चित्तं चैत्यस्ततोऽभवत् ॥६१॥

manasaś candramā jāto
buddhir buddher girāṁ patiḥ
ahaṅkāras tato rudraś
cittaṁ caityas tato 'bhavat

manasaḥ—from the mind; *candramāḥ*—the moon; *jātaḥ*—appeared; *buddhiḥ*—intelligence; *buddheḥ*—from intelligence; *girām patiḥ*—the lord of speech (Brahmā); *ahaṅkāraḥ*—false ego; *tataḥ*—then; *rudraḥ*—Lord Śiva; *cittam*—consciousness; *caityaḥ*—the deity presiding over consciousness; *tataḥ*—then; *abhavat*—appeared.

TRANSLATION

After the mind, the moon appeared. Intelligence appeared next, and after intelligence, Lord Brahmā appeared. Then the false ego appeared and then Lord Śiva, and after the appearance of Lord Śiva came consciousness and the deity presiding over consciousness.

PURPORT

The moon appeared after the appearance of mind, and this indicates that the moon is the presiding deity of mind. Similarly, Lord Brahmā, appearing after intelligence, is the presiding deity of intelligence, and Lord Śiva, who appears after false ego, is the presiding deity of false ego. In other words, it is indicated that the moon-god is in the mode of goodness, whereas Lord Brahmā is in the mode of passion and Lord Śiva is in the mode of ignorance. The appearance of consciousness after the appearance of false ego indicates that, from the beginning, material consciousness is under the mode of ignorance and that one therefore has to purify himself by purifying his consciousness. This purificatory process is called Kṛṣṇa consciousness. As soon as the consciousness is purified, the false ego disappears. Identification of the body with the self is called false identification, or false ego. Lord Caitanya confirms this in His *Śikṣāṣṭaka.* He states that the first result of chanting the *mahā-mantra,* Hare Kṛṣṇa, is that dirt is cleared from the consciousness, or the mirror of the mind, and then at once the blazing fire of material existence is over. The blazing fire of material existence is due to false ego, but as soon as the false ego is removed, one can understand his real identity. At that point he is actually liberated from the clutches of *māyā.* As soon as one is freed from the clutches of false ego, his intelligence also becomes purified, and then his mind is always engaged upon the lotus feet of the Supreme Personality of Godhead.

The Supreme Personality of Godhead appeared on the full-moon day as Gauracandra, or the spotless transcendental moon. The material moon has spots on it, but on the transcendental moon, Gauracandra, there are no spots. In order to fix the purified mind in the service of the Supreme Lord, one has to worship the spotless moon, Gauracandra. Those who are materially passionate or those who want to exhibit their intelligence for material advancement in life are generally worshipers of Lord Brahmā, and persons who are in the gross ignorance of identifying with the body worship Lord Śiva. Materialists like Hiraṇyakaśipu and Rāvaṇa are worshipers of Lord Brahmā or Lord Śiva, but Prahlāda and other devotees in the service of Kṛṣṇa consciousness worship the Supreme Lord, the Personality of Godhead.

TEXT 62

एते ह्यभ्युत्थिता देवा नैवास्योत्थापनेऽशकन् ।
पुनराविविशुः खानि तमुत्थापयितुं क्रमात् ॥६२॥

ete hy abhyutthitā devā
naivāsyotthāpane 'śakan

punar āviviśuḥ khāni
tam utthāpayituṁ kramāt

ete—these; *hi*—indeed; *abhyutthitāḥ*—manifested; *devāḥ*—demigods; *na*—not; *eva*—at all; *asya*—of the *virāṭ-puruṣa; utthāpane*—in waking; *aśakan*—were able; *punaḥ*—again; *āviviśuḥ*—they entered; *khāni*—the apertures of the body; *tam*—Him; *utthāpayitum*—to awaken; *kramāt*—one after another.

TRANSLATION

When the demigods and presiding deities of the various senses were thus manifested, they wanted to wake their origin of appearance. But upon failing to do so, they reentered the body of the virāṭ-puruṣa one after another in order to wake Him.

PURPORT

In order to wake the sleeping Deity-controller within, one has to rechannel the sense activities from concentration on the outside to concentration inside. In the following verses, the sense activities which are required to wake the *virāṭ-puruṣa* will be explained very nicely.

TEXT 63

वह्निर्वाचा मुखं भेजे नोदतिष्ठत्तदा विराट् ।
घ्राणेन नासिके वायुर्नोदतिष्ठत्तदा विराट् ॥६३॥

vahnir vācā mukhaṁ bheje
nodatiṣṭhat tadā virāṭ
ghrāṇena nāsike vāyur
nodatiṣṭhat tadā virāṭ

vahniḥ—the god of fire; *vācā*—with the organ of speech; *mukham*—the mouth; *bheje*—entered; *na*—not; *udatiṣṭhat*—did arise; *tadā*—then; *virāṭ*—the *virāṭ-puruṣa; ghrāṇena*—with the olfactory sense; *nāsike*—into His two nostrils; *vāyuḥ*—the god of the winds; *na*—not; *udatiṣṭhat*—did arise; *tadā*—then; *virāṭ*—the *virāṭ-puruṣa.*

TRANSLATION

The god of fire entered His mouth with the organ of speech, but the virāṭ-puruṣa could not be aroused. Then the god of wind entered His nostrils with the sense of smell, but still the virāṭ-puruṣa refused to be awakened.

TEXT 64

अक्षिणी चक्षुषादित्यो नोदतिष्ठत्तदा विराट् ।
श्रोत्रेण कर्णौ च दिशो नोदतिष्ठत्तदा विराट् ॥६४॥

akṣiṇī cakṣuṣādityo
nodatiṣṭhat tadā virāṭ
śrotreṇa karṇau ca diśo
nodatiṣṭhat tadā virāṭ

akṣiṇī—His two eyes; *cakṣuṣā*—with the sense of sight; *ādityaḥ*—the sun-god; *na*—not; *udatiṣṭhat*—did arise; *tadā*—then; *virāṭ*—the *virāṭ-puruṣa; śrotreṇa*—with the sense of hearing; *karṇau*—His two ears; *ca*—and; *diśaḥ*—the deities presiding over the directions; *na*—not; *udatiṣṭhat*—did arise; *tadā*—then; *virāṭ*—the *virāṭ-puruṣa.*

TRANSLATION

The sun-god entered the eyes of the virāṭ-puruṣa with the sense of sight, but still the virāṭ-puruṣa did not get up. Similarly, the predominating deities of the directions entered through His ears with the sense of hearing, but still He did not get up.

TEXT 65

त्वचं रोमभिरोषध्यो नोदतिष्ठत्तदा विराट् ।
रेतसा शिश्नमापस्तु नोदतिष्ठत्तदा विराट् ॥६५॥

tvacaṁ romabhir oṣadhyo
nodatiṣṭhat tadā virāṭ
retasā śiśnam āpas tu
nodatiṣṭhat tadā virāṭ

tvacam—the skin of the *virāṭ-puruṣa; romabhiḥ*—with the hair on the body; *oṣadhyaḥ*—the deities presiding over the herbs and plants; *na*—not; *udatiṣṭhat*—did arise; *tadā*—then; *virāṭ*—the *virāṭ-puruṣa; retasā*—with the faculty of procreation; *śiśnam*—the organ of generation; *āpaḥ*—the water-god; *tu*—then; *na*—not; *udatiṣṭhat*—did arise; *tadā*—then; *virāṭ*—the *virāṭ-puruṣa.*

TRANSLATION

The predominating deities of the skin, herbs and seasoning plants entered the skin of the virāṭ-puruṣa with the hair of the body, but the Cosmic Being

refused to get up even then. The god predominating over water entered His organ of generation with the faculty of procreation, but the virāṭ-puruṣa still would not rise.

TEXT 66

गुदं मृत्युरपानेन नोदतिष्ठत्तदा विराट् ।
हस्ताविन्द्रो बलेनैव नोदतिष्ठत्तदा विराट् ॥६६॥

gudaṁ mṛtyur apānena
nodatiṣṭhat tadā virāṭ
hastāv indro balenaiva
nodatiṣṭhat tadā virāṭ

gudam—His anus; *mṛtyuḥ*—the god of death; *apānena*—with the organ of defecation; *na*—not; *udatiṣṭhat*—did arise; *tadā*—even then; *virāṭ*—the *virāṭ-puruṣa; hastau*—the two hands; *indraḥ*—Lord Indra; *balena*—with their power to grasp and drop things; *eva*—indeed; *na*—not; *udatiṣṭhat*—did arise; *tadā*—even then; *virāṭ*—the *virāṭ-puruṣa.*

TRANSLATION

The god of death entered His anus with the organ of defecation, but the virāṭ-puruṣa could not be spurred to activity. The god Indra entered the hands with their power of grasping and dropping things, but the virāṭ-puruṣa would not get up even then.

TEXT 67

विष्णुर्गत्यैव चरणौ नोदतिष्ठत्तदा विराट् ।
नाडीर्नद्यो लोहितेन नोदतिष्ठत्तदा विराट् ॥६७॥

viṣṇur gatyaiva caraṇau
nodatiṣṭhat tadā virāṭ
nāḍīr nadyo lohitena
nodatiṣṭhat tadā virāṭ

viṣṇuḥ—Lord Viṣṇu; *gatyā*—with the faculty of locomotion; *eva*—indeed; *caraṇau*—His two feet; *na*—not; *udatiṣṭhat*—did arise; *tadā*—even then; *virāṭ*—the *virāṭ-puruṣa; nāḍīḥ*—His blood vessels; *nadyaḥ*—the rivers or river-gods; *lohitena*—with the blood, with the power of circulation; *na*—not; *udatiṣṭhat*—did stir; *tadā*—even then; *virāṭ*—the *virāṭ-puruṣa.*

TRANSLATION

Lord Viṣṇu entered His feet with the faculty of locomotion, but the virāṭ-puruṣa refused to stand up even then. The rivers entered His blood vessels with the blood and the power of circulation, but still the Cosmic Being could not be made to stir.

TEXT 68

क्षुत्तृड्भ्यामुदरं सिन्धुर्नोदतिष्ठत्तदा विराट् ।
हृदयं मनसा चन्द्रो नोदतिष्ठत्तदा विराट् ॥६८॥

kṣut-tṛḍbhyām udaraṁ sindhur
nodatiṣṭhat tadā virāṭ
hṛdayaṁ manasā candro
nodatiṣṭhat tadā virāṭ

kṣut-tṛḍbhyām—with hunger and thirst; *udaram*—His abdomen; *sindhuḥ*—the ocean or ocean-god; *na*—not; *udatiṣṭhat*—did arise; *tadā*—even then; *virāṭ*—the *virāṭ-puruṣa*; *hṛdayam*—His heart; *manasā*—with the mind; *candraḥ*—the moon-god; *na*—not; *udatiṣṭhat*—did arise; *tadā*—even then; *virāṭ*—the *virāṭ-puruṣa.*

TRANSLATION

The ocean entered His abdomen with hunger and thirst, but the Cosmic Being refused to rise even then. The moon-god entered His heart with the mind, but the Cosmic Being would not be roused.

TEXT 69

बुद्ध्या ब्रह्मापि हृदयं नोदतिष्ठत्तदा विराट् ।
रुद्रोऽभिमत्या हृदयं नोदतिष्ठत्तदा विराट् ॥६९॥

buddhyā brahmāpi hṛdayaṁ
nodatiṣṭhat tadā virāṭ
rudro 'bhimatyā hṛdayaṁ
nodatiṣṭhat tadā virāṭ

buddhyā—with intelligence; *brahmā*—Lord Brahmā; *api*—also; *hṛdayam*—His heart; *na*—not; *udatiṣṭhat*—did arise; *tadā*—even then; *virāṭ*—the *virāṭ-puruṣa*; *rudraḥ*—Lord Śiva; *abhimatyā*—with the ego; *hṛdayam*—His heart; *na*—not; *udatiṣṭhat*—did arise; *tadā*—even then; *virāṭ*—the *virāṭ-puruṣa.*

TRANSLATION

Brahmā also entered His heart with intelligence, but even then the Cosmic Being could not be prevailed upon to get up. Lord Rudra also entered His heart with the ego, but even then the Cosmic Being did not stir.

TEXT 70

चित्तेन हृदयं चैत्यः क्षेत्रज्ञः प्राविशद्यदा ।
विराट् तदैव पुरुषः सलिलादुदतिष्ठत ॥७०॥

cittena hṛdayaṁ caityaḥ
kṣetra-jñaḥ prāviśad yadā
virāṭ tadaiva puruṣaḥ
salilād udatiṣṭhata

cittena—along with reason, consciousness; *hṛdayam*—the heart; *caityaḥ*—the deity presiding over consciousness; *kṣetra-jñaḥ*—the knower of the field; *prāviśat*—entered; *yadā*—when; *virāṭ*—the *virāṭ-puruṣa; tadā*—then; *eva*—just; *puruṣaḥ*—the Cosmic Being; *salilāt*—from the water; *udatiṣṭhata*—arose.

TRANSLATION

However, when the inner controller, the deity presiding over consciousness, entered the heart with reason, at that very moment the Cosmic Being arose from thc causal waters.

TEXT 71

यथा प्रसुप्तं पुरुषं प्राणेन्द्रियमनोधियः ।
प्रभवन्ति विना येन नोत्थापयितुमोजसा ॥७१॥

yathā prasuptaṁ puruṣaṁ
prāṇendriya-mano-dhiyaḥ
prabhavanti vinā yena
notthāpayitum ojasā

yathā—just as; *prasuptam*—sleeping; *puruṣam*—a man; *prāṇa*—the vital air; *indriya*—the senses for working and recording knowledge; *manaḥ*—the mind; *dhiyaḥ*—the intelligence; *prabhavanti*—are able; *vinā*—without; *yena*—whom (the Supersoul); *na*—not; *utthāpayitum*—to arouse; *ojasā*—by their own power.

TRANSLATION

When a man is sleeping, all his material assets—namely the vital energy, the senses for recording knowledge, the senses for working, the mind and the intelligence—cannot arouse him. He can be aroused only when the Supersoul helps him.

PURPORT

The explanation of Sāṅkhya philosophy is described here in detail in the sense that the *virāṭ-puruṣa,* or the universal form of the Supreme Personality of Godhead, is the original source of all the various sense organs and their presiding deities. The relationship between the *virāṭ-puruṣa* and the presiding deities or the living entities is so intricate that simply by exercising the sense organs, which are related to their presiding deities, the *virāṭ-puruṣa* cannot be aroused. It is not possible to arouse the *virāṭ-puruṣa* or to link with the Supreme Absolute Personality of Godhead by material activities. Only by devotional service and detachment can one perform the process of linking with the Absolute.

TEXT 72

तमस्मिन् प्रत्यगात्मानं धिया योगप्रवृत्तया ।
भक्त्या विरक्त्या ज्ञानेन विविच्यात्मनि चिन्तयेत् ॥७२॥

tam asmin pratyag-ātmānaṁ
dhiyā yoga-pravṛttayā
bhaktyā viraktyā jñānena
vivicyātmani cintayet

tam—upon Him; *asmin*—in this; *pratyak-ātmānam*—the Supersoul; *dhiyā*—with the mind; *yoga-pravṛttayā*—engaged in devotional service; *bhaktyā*—through devotion; *viraktyā*—through detachment; *jñānena*—through spiritual knowledge; *vivicya*—considering carefully; *ātmani*—in the body; *cintayet*—one should contemplate.

TRANSLATION

Therefore, through devotion, detachment and advancement in spiritual knowledge acquired through concentrated devotional service, one should contemplate that Supersoul as present in this very body although simultaneously apart from it.

PURPORT

One can realize the Supersoul within oneself. He is within one's body but apart from the body, or transcendental to the body. Although sitting in the same body as the individual soul, the Supersoul has no affection for the body, whereas the individual soul does. One has to detach himself, therefore, from this material body, by discharging devotional service. It is clearly mentioned here (*bhaktyā*) that one has to execute devotional service to the Supreme. As it is stated in the First Canto, Second Chapter, of *Śrīmad-Bhāgavatam* (1.2.7), *vāsudeve bhagavati bhakti-yogaḥ prayojitaḥ*. When Vāsudeva, the all-pervading Viṣṇu, the Supreme Personality of Godhead, is served in completely pure devotion, detachment from the material world immediately begins. The purpose of Sāṅkhya is to detach oneself from material contamination. This can be achieved simply by devotional service to the Supreme Personality of Godhead.

When one is detached from the attraction of material prosperity, one can actually concentrate his mind upon the Supersoul. As long as the mind is distracted towards the material, there is no possibility of concentrating one's mind and intelligence upon the Supreme Personality of Godhead or His partial representation, Supersoul. In other words, one cannot concentrate one's mind and energy upon the Supreme unless one is detached from the material world. Following detachment from the material world, one can actually attain transcendental knowledge of the Absolute Truth. As long as one is entangled in sense enjoyment, or material enjoyment, it is not possible to understand the Absolute Truth. This is also confirmed in *Bhagavad-gītā* (18.54). One who is freed from material contamination is joyful and can enter into devotional service, and by devotional service he can be liberated.

In the *Śrīmad-Bhāgavatam*, First Canto, it is stated that one becomes joyful by discharging devotional service. In that joyful attitude, one can understand the science of God, or Kṛṣṇa consciousness; otherwise it is not possible. The analytical study of the elements of material nature and the concentration of the mind upon the Supersoul are the sum and substance of the Sāṅkhya philosophical system. The perfection of this *sāṅkhya-yoga* culminates in devotional service unto the Absolute Truth.

Thus end the Bhaktivedanta purports of the Third Canto, Twenty-sixth Chapter, of the Śrīmad-Bhāgavatam, *entitled "Fundamental Principles of Material Nature."*

CHAPTER TWENTY-SEVEN

Understanding Material Nature

TEXT 1

श्रीभगवानुवाच
प्रकृतिस्थोऽपि पुरुषो नाज्यते प्राकृतैर्गुणैः ।
अविकारादकर्तृत्वान्निर्गुणत्वाज्जलार्कवत् ॥ १ ॥

śrī-bhagavān uvāca
prakṛti-stho 'pi puruṣo
nājyate prākṛtair guṇaiḥ
avikārād akartṛtvān
nirguṇatvāj jalārkavat

śrī-bhagavān uvāca—the Personality of Godhead said; *prakṛti-sthaḥ*—residing in the material body; *api*—although; *puruṣaḥ*—the living entity; *na*—not; *ajyate*—is affected; *prākṛtaiḥ*—of material nature; *guṇaiḥ*—by the modes; *avikārāt*—from being without change; *akartṛtvāt*—by freedom from proprietorship; *nirguṇatvāt*—from being unaffected by the qualities of material nature; *jala*—on water; *arkavat*—like the sun.

TRANSLATION

The Personality of Godhead Kapila continued: When the living entity is thus unaffected by the modes of material nature, because he is unchanging and does not claim proprietorship, he remains apart from the reactions of the modes, although abiding in a material body, just as the sun remains aloof from its reflection on water.

PURPORT

In the previous chapter Lord Kapiladeva has concluded that simply by beginning the discharge of devotional service one can attain detachment and transcendental knowledge for understanding the science of God. Here the same principle is confirmed. A person who is detached from the modes of material nature remains just like the sun reflected on water. When the sun is reflected on water, the movement of the water or the coolness or unsteadiness of the water cannot affect the sun. Similarly, *vāsudeve bhagavati bhakti-yogaḥ prayojitaḥ* (*Bhāg.* 1.2.7): when one engages fully in the activities of devotional service, *bhakti-yoga,* he becomes just like the sun reflected on water. Although a devotee appears to be in the material world, actually he is in the transcendental world. As the reflection of the sun appears to be on the water but is many millions of miles away from the water, so one engaged in the *bhakti-yoga* process is *nirguṇa,* or unaffected by the qualities of material nature.

Avikāra means "without change." It is confirmed in *Bhagavad-gītā* that each and every living entity is part and parcel of the Supreme Lord, and thus his eternal position is to cooperate or to dovetail his energy with the Supreme Lord. That is his unchanging position. As soon as he employs his energy and activities for sense gratification, this change of position is called *vikāra.* Similarly, even in this material body, when he practices devotional service under the direction of the spiritual master, he comes to the position which is without change because that is his natural duty. As stated in the *Śrīmad-Bhāgavatam,* liberation means reinstatement in one's original position. The original position is one of rendering service to the Lord (*bhakti-yogena, bhaktyā*). When one becomes detached from material attraction and engages fully in devotional service, that is changlessness. *Akartṛtvāt* means not doing anything for sense gratification. When one does something at his own risk, there is a sense of proprietorship and therefore a reaction, but when one does everything for Kṛṣṇa, there is no proprietorship over the activities. By changlessness and by not claiming the proprietorship of activities, one can immediately situate himself in the transcendental position in which one is not touched by the modes of material nature, just as the reflection of the sun is unaffected by the water.

TEXT 2

स एष यर्हि प्रकृतेर्गुणेष्वभिविषज्जते ।
अहङ्क्रियाविमूढात्मा कर्तास्मीत्यभिमन्यते ॥ २ ॥

sa eṣa yarhi prakṛter
guṇeṣv abhiviṣajjate
ahaṅkriyā-vimūḍhātmā
kartāsmīty abhimanyate

saḥ—that very living entity; *eṣaḥ*—this; *yarhi*—when; *prakṛteḥ*—of material nature; *guṇeṣu*—in the modes; *abhiviṣajjate*—is absorbed; *ahaṅkriyā*—by false ego; *vimūḍha*—bewildered; *ātmā*—the individual soul; *kartā*—the doer; *asmi*—I am; *iti*—thus; *abhimanyate*—he thinks.

TRANSLATION

When the soul is under the spell of material nature and false ego, identifying his body as the self, he becomes absorbed in material activities, and by the influence of false ego he thinks that he is the proprietor of everything.

PURPORT

Actually the conditioned soul is forced to act under the pressure of the modes of material nature. The living entity has no independence. When he is under the direction of the Supreme Personality of Godhead he is free, but when, under the impression that he is satisfying his senses, he engages in sense gratificatory activities, he is actually under the spell of material nature. In *Bhagavad-gītā* it is said, *prakṛteḥ kriyamāṇāni:* one acts according to the particular modes of nature he has acquired. *Guṇa* refers to the qualities of nature. He is under the qualities of nature, but he falsely thinks that he is the proprietor. This false sense of proprietorship can be avoided simply by engaging oneself in devotional service under the direction of the Supreme Lord or His bona fide representative. Arjuna, in *Bhagavad-gītā,* was trying to accept for himself the responsibility for killing his grandfather and teacher in the fight, but he became freed from that proprietorship of action when he acted under the direction of Kṛṣṇa. He fought, but he was actually freed from the reactions of fighting, although in the beginning, when he was nonviolent, unwilling to fight, the entire responsibility was upon him. That is the difference between liberation and conditioning. A conditioned soul may be very good and act in the mode of goodness, but still he is conditioned under the spell of material nature. A devotee, however, acts completely under the direction of the Supreme Lord. Thus his actions may not appear to be of a very high quality to the common man, but the devotee has no responsibility.

TEXT 3

तेन संसारपदवीमवशोऽभ्येत्यनिर्वृतः ।
प्रासङ्गिकैः कर्मदोषैः सदसन्मिश्रयोनिषु ॥ ३ ॥

tena saṁsāra-padavīm
avaśo 'bhyety anirvṛtaḥ
prāsaṅgikaiḥ karma-doṣaiḥ
sad-asan-miśra-yoniṣu

tena—by this; *saṁsāra*—of repeated birth and death; *padavīm*—the path; *avaśaḥ*—helplessly; *abhyeti*—he undergoes; *anirvṛtaḥ*—discontented; *prāsaṅgikaiḥ*—resulting from association with material nature; *karma-doṣaiḥ*—by faulty actions; *sat*—good; *asat*—bad; *miśra*—mixed; *yoniṣu*—in different species of life.

TRANSLATION

The conditioned soul therefore transmigrates into different species of life, higher and lower, because of his association with the modes of material nature. Unless he is relieved of material activities, he has to accept this position because of his faulty work.

PURPORT

Here the word *karma-doṣaiḥ* means "by faulty actions." This refers to any activity, good or bad, performed in this material world—they are all contaminated, faulty actions because of material association. The foolish conditioned soul may think that he is offering charity by opening hospitals for material benefit or by opening an educational institution for material education, but he does not know that all such work is also faulty because it will not give him relief from the process of transmigration from one body to another. It is clearly stated here, *sad-asan-miśra-yoniṣu.* This means that one may take birth in a very high family or he may take his birth in higher planets, among the demigods, for his so-called pious activities in the material world. But this work is also faulty because it does not give liberation. To take birth in a nice place or a high family does not mean that one avoids undergoing the material tribulations, the pangs of birth, death, old age and disease. A conditioned soul under the spell of material nature cannot understand that any action he performs for sense gratification is faulty and that only his activities in devotional service to the Lord can give him release from the reaction of faulty activities. Because he does not cease such faulty activities, he has to change to different bodies, some high and some low. That is called *saṁsāra-padavīm,* which means this material world, from which there is no release. One who desires material liberation has to turn his activities to devotional service. There is no alternative.

TEXT 4

अर्थे ह्यविद्यमानेऽपि संसृतिर्न निवर्तते ।
ध्यायतो विषयानस्य स्वप्नेऽनर्थागमो यथा ॥ ४ ॥

arthe hy avidyamāne 'pi
saṁsṛtir na nivartate

dhyāyato viṣayān asya
svapne 'narthāgamo yathā

arthe—real cause; *hi*—certainly; *avidyamāne*—not existing; *api*—although; *saṁsṛtiḥ*—the material existential condition; *na*—not; *nivartate*—does cease; *dhyāyataḥ*—contemplating; *viṣayān*—objects of the senses; *asya*—of the living entity; *svapne*—in a dream; *anartha*—of disadvantages; *āgamaḥ*—arrival; *yathā*—like.

TRANSLATION

Actually a living entity is transcendental to material existence, but because of his mentality of lording it over material nature, his material existential condition does not cease, and just as in a dream, he is affected by all sorts of disadvantages.

PURPORT

The example of a dream is very appropriate. Due to different mental conditions, in dreams we are put into advantageous and disadvantageous positions. Similarly, the spirit soul has nothing to do with this material nature, but because of his mentality of lording it over, he is put into the position of conditional existence.

Conditional existence is described here as *dhyāyato viṣayān asya. Viṣaya* means "an object of enjoyment." As long as one continues to think that he can enjoy material advantages, he is in conditioned life, but as soon as he comes to his senses, he develops the knowledge that he is not the enjoyer, for the only enjoyer is the Supreme Personality of Godhead. As confirmed in *Bhagavad-gītā* (5.29), He is the beneficiary for all the results of sacrifices and penances (*bhoktāraṁ yajña-tapasām*), and He is the proprietor of all the three worlds (*sarva-loka-maheśvaram*). He is the actual friend of all living entities. But instead of leaving proprietorship, enjoyment and the actual position as the friend of all living entities to the Supreme Personality of Godhead, we claim that we are the proprietors, the enjoyers and the friends. We perform philanthropic work, thinking that we are the friends of human society. Someone may proclaim himself to be a very good national worker, the best friend of the people and of the country, but actually he cannot be the greatest friend of everyone. The only friend is Kṛṣṇa. One should try to raise the consciousness of the conditioned soul to the platform of understanding that Kṛṣṇa is his actual friend. If one makes friendship with Kṛṣṇa, one will never be cheated, and he will get all help needed. Arousing this consciousness of the conditioned soul is the greatest service, not posing oneself as a great friend of another living entity. The power of friendship is limited. Although one claims to be a friend, he cannot be a friend unlimitedly. There are an unlimited number of living entities, and our resources are limited; therefore we cannot be of any real benefit to the people in general. The best service to the people in general is to awaken them to Kṛṣṇa consciousness so that they may know that the supreme enjoyer, the supreme proprietor and the supreme friend is Kṛṣṇa. Then this illusory dream of lording it over material nature will vanish.

TEXT 5

अत एव शनैश्चित्तं प्रसक्तमसतां पथि ।
भक्तियोगेन तीव्रेण विरक्त्या च नयेद्वशम् ॥ ५ ॥

ata eva śanaiś cittaṁ
prasaktam asatāṁ pathi
bhakti-yogena tīvreṇa
viraktyā ca nayed vaśam

ataḥ eva—therefore; *śanaiḥ*—gradually; *cittam*—mind, consciousness; *prasaktam*—attached; *asatām*—of material enjoyments; *pathi*—on the path; *bhakti-yogena*—by devotional service; *tīvreṇa*—very serious; *viraktyā*—without attachment; *ca*—and; *nayet*—he must bring; *vaśam*—under control.

TRANSLATION

It is the duty of every conditioned soul to engage his polluted consciousness, which is now attached to material enjoyment, in very serious devotional service with detachment. Thus his mind and consciousness will be under full control.

PURPORT

The process of liberation is very nicely explained in this verse. The cause of one's becoming conditioned by material nature is his thinking himself the enjoyer, the proprietor or the friend of all living entities. This false thinking is a result of contemplation on sense enjoyment. When one thinks that he is the best friend to his countrymen, to society or to humanity and he engages in various nationalistic, philanthropic and altruistic activities, all that is just so much concentration on sense gratification. The so-called national leader or humanist does not serve everyone; he serves his senses only. That is a fact. But the conditioned soul cannot understand this because he is bewildered by the spell of material nature. It is therefore recommended in this verse that one engage very seriously in the devotional service of the Lord. This means that one should not think that he is the proprietor, benefactor, friend or enjoyer. He should always be cognizant that the real enjoyer is Kṛṣṇa, the Supreme Personality of Godhead; that is the basic principle of *bhakti-yoga.* One must be firmly convinced of these three principles: one should always think that Kṛṣṇa is the proprietor, Kṛṣṇa is the enjoyer and Kṛṣṇa is the friend. Not only should he understand these principles himself, but he should try to convince others and propagate Kṛṣṇa consciousness.

As soon as one engages in such serious devotional service of the Lord, naturally the propensity to falsely claim lordship over material nature disappears. That detachment is called *vairāgya.* Instead of being absorbed in so-called material lordship, one engages in Kṛṣṇa consciousness; that is control of consciousness. The *yoga* process necessitates controlling the senses. *Yoga indriya-saṁyamaḥ.* Since the senses are always active, their activities should be engaged in devotional service—one cannot stop their activities. If one wants to artificially stop the activities of the senses, his attempt will be a failure. Even the great *yogī* Viśvāmitra, who was trying to control his senses by the *yoga* process, fell victim to the beauty of Menakā. There are many such instances. Unless one's mind and consciousness are fully engaged in devotional service, there is always the opportunity for the mind to become occupied with desires for sense gratification.

One particular point mentioned in this verse is very significant. It is said here, *prasaktam asatāṁ pathi:* the mind is always attracted by *asat,* the temporary, material existence. Because we have been associated with material nature since time immemorial, we have become accustomed to our attachment to this temporary material nature. The mind has to be fixed at the eternal lotus feet of the Supreme Lord. *Sa vai manaḥ kṛṣṇa-padaravindayoḥ.* One has to fix the mind at the lotus feet of Kṛṣṇa; then everything will be very nice. Thus the seriousness of *bhakti-yoga* is stressed in this verse.

TEXT 6

यमादिभिर्योगपथैरभ्यसञ् श्रद्धयान्वितः ।
मयि भावेन सत्येन मत्कथाश्रवणेन च ॥ ६ ॥

yamādibhir yoga-pathair
abhyasañ śraddhayānvitaḥ
mayi bhāvena satyena
mat-kathā-śravaṇena ca

yama-ādibhiḥ—beginning with *yama; yoga-pathaiḥ*—by the *yoga* system; *abhyasan*—practicing; *śraddhayā anvitaḥ*—with great faith; *mayi*—unto Me; *bhāvena*—with devotion; *satyena*—unalloyed; *mat-kathā*—stories about Me; *śravaṇena*—by hearing; *ca*—and.

TRANSLATION

One has to become faithful by practicing the controlling process of the yoga system and must elevate himself to the platform of unalloyed devotional service by chanting and hearing about Me.

PURPORT

Yoga is practiced in eight different stages: *yama, niyama, āsana, prāṇāyāma, pratyāhāra, dhāraṇā, dhyāna* and *samādhi. Yama* and *niyama* mean practicing the controlling process by following strict regulations, and *āsana* refers to the sitting postures. These help raise one to the standard of faithfulness in devotional service. The practice of *yoga* by physical exercise is not the ultimate goal; the real end is to concentrate and to control the mind and train oneself to be situated in faithful devotional service.

Bhāvena, or *bhāva,* is a very important factor in the practice of *yoga* or in any spiritual process. *Bhāva* is explained in *Bhagavad-gītā* (10.8). *Budhā bhāva-samanvitāḥ:* one should be absorbed in the thought of love of Kṛṣṇa. When one knows that Kṛṣṇa, the Supreme Personality of Godhead, is the source of everything and that everything emanates from Him (*ahaṁ sarvasya prabhavaḥ*), then one understands the *Vedānta* aphorism *janmādy asya yataḥ* ("the original source of everything"), and then he can become absorbed in *bhāva,* or the preliminary stage of love of Godhead.

Rūpa Gosvāmī explains very nicely in *Bhakti-rasāmṛta-sindhu* how this *bhāva,* or preliminary stage of love of God, is achieved. He states that one first of all has to become faithful (*śraddhayānvitaḥ*). Faith is attained by controlling the senses, either by *yoga* practice, following the rules and regulations and practicing the sitting postures, or by engaging directly in *bhakti-yoga,* as recommended in the previous verse. Of the nine different items of *bhakti-yoga,* the first and foremost is to chant and hear about the Lord. That is also mentioned here. *Mat-kathā-śravaṇena ca.* One may come to the standard of faithfulness by following the rules and regulations of the *yoga* system, and the same goal can be achieved simply by chanting and hearing about the transcendental activities of the Lord. The word *ca* is significant. *Bhakti-yoga* is direct, and the other process is indirect. But even if the indirect process is taken, there is no success unless one comes fully to the direct process of hearing and chanting the glories of the Lord. Therefore the word *satyena* is used here. In this connection Svāmī Śrīdhara comments that *satyena* means *niṣkapaṭena,* "without duplicity." The impersonalists are full of duplicity. Sometimes they pretend to execute devotional service, but their ultimate idea is to become one with the Supreme. This is duplicity, *kapaṭa*. The *Bhāgavatam* does not allow this duplicity. In the beginning of *Śrīmad-Bhāgavatam* it is clearly stated, *paramo nirmatsarāṇām:* "This treatise *Śrīmad-Bhāgavatam* is meant for those who are completely free from envy." The same point is again stressed here. Unless one is completely faithful to the Supreme Personality of Godhead and engages himself in the process of hearing and chanting the glories of the Lord, there is no possibility for liberation.

TEXT 7

सर्वभूतसमत्वेन निर्वैरेणाप्रसङ्गतः ।
ब्रह्मचर्येण मौनेन स्वधर्मेण बलीयसा ॥ ७ ॥

sarva-bhūta-samatvena
nirvaireṇāprasaṅgataḥ
brahmacaryeṇa maunena
sva-dharmeṇa balīyasā

sarva—all; *bhūta*—living entities; *samatvena*—by seeing equally; *nirvaireṇa*—without enmity; *aprasaṅgataḥ*—without intimate connections; *brahma-caryeṇa*—by celibacy; *maunena*—by silence; *sva-dharmeṇa*—by one's occupation; *balīyasā*—by offering the result.

TRANSLATION

In executing devotional service, one has to see every living entity equally, without enmity towards anyone yet without intimate connections with anyone. One has to observe celibacy, be grave and execute his eternal activities, offering the results to the Supreme Personality of Godhead.

PURPORT

A devotee of the Supreme Personality of Godhead who seriously engages in devotional service is equal to all living entities. There are various species of living entities, but a devotee does not see the outward covering; he sees the inner soul inhabiting the body. Because each and every soul is part and parcel of the Supreme Personality of Godhead, he does not see any difference. That is the vision of a learned devotee. As explained in *Bhagavad-gītā*, a devotee or a learned sage does not see any difference between a learned *brāhmaṇa*, a dog, an elephant or a cow because he knows that the body is the outer covering only and that the soul is actually part and parcel of the Supreme Lord. A devotee has no enmity towards any living entity, but that does not mean that he mixes with everyone. That is prohibited. *Aprasaṅgataḥ* means "not to be in intimate touch with everyone." A devotee is concerned with his execution of devotional service, and he should therefore mix with devotees only, in order to advance his objective. He has no business mixing with others, for although he does not see anyone as his enemy, his dealings are only with persons who engage in devotional service.

A devotee should observe the vow of celibacy. Celibacy does not necessitate that one be absolutely free from sex life; satisfaction with one's wife is permitted also under the vow of celibacy. The best policy is to avoid sex life altogether. That is preferable. Otherwise, a devotee can get married under religious principles and live peacefully with a wife.

A devotee should not speak needlessly. A serious devotee has no time to speak of nonsense. He is always busy in Kṛṣṇa consciousness. Whenever he speaks, he speaks about Kṛṣṇa. *Mauna* means "silence." Silence does not mean that one should not speak at all, but that he should not speak of nonsense. He should be very enthusiastic in speaking about Kṛṣṇa. Another important item described here is *sva-dharmeṇa,* or being exclusively occupied in one's eternal occupation, which is to act as the eternal servitor of the Lord, or to act in Kṛṣṇa consciousness. The next word, *balīyasā*, means "offering the results of all activities to the Supreme Personality of Godhead." A devotee does not act on his personal account for sense gratification. Whatever he earns, whatever he eats and whatever he does, he offers for the satisfaction of the Supreme Personality of Godhead.

TEXT 8

यदृच्छयोपलब्धेन सन्तुष्टो मितभुङ् मुनिः ।
विविक्तशरणः शान्तो मैत्रः करुण आत्मवान् ॥ ८ ॥

yadṛcchayopalabdhena
santuṣṭo mita-bhuṅ muniḥ
vivikta-śaraṇaḥ śānto
maitraḥ karuṇa ātmavān

yadṛcchayā—without difficulty; *upalabdhena*—with what is obtained; *santuṣṭaḥ*—satisfied; *mita*—little; *bhuk*—eating; *muniḥ*—thoughtful; *vivikta-śaraṇaḥ*—living in a secluded place; *śāntaḥ*—peaceful; *maitraḥ*—friendly; *karuṇaḥ*—compassionate; *ātma-vān*—self-possessed, self-realized.

TRANSLATION

For his income a devotee should be satisfied with what he earns without great difficulty. He should not eat more than what is necessary. He should live in a secluded place and always be thoughtful, peaceful, friendly, compassionate and self-realized.

PURPORT

Everyone who has accepted a material body must maintain the necessities of the body by acting or earning some livelihood. A devotee should only work for such income as is absolutely necessary. He should be satisfied always with such income and should not endeavor to earn more and more simply to accumulate the unnecessary. A person in the conditioned state who has no money is always found working very hard to earn some with the object of lording it over material nature. Kapiladeva instructs that we should not endeavor hard for things which may come automatically, without extraneous labor. The exact word used in this connection, *yadṛcchayā,* means that every living entity has a predestined happiness and distress in his present body; this is called the law of *karma.* It is not possible that simply by endeavors to accumulate more money a person will be able to do so, otherwise almost everyone would be on the same level of wealth. In reality everyone is earning and acquiring according to his predestined *karma.* According to the *Bhāgavatam* conclusion, we are sometimes faced with dangerous or miserable conditions without endeavoring for them, and similarly we may have prosperous conditions without endeavoring for them. We are advised to let these things come as predestined. We should engage our valuable time in prosecuting Kṛṣṇa consciousness. In other words, one should be satisfied by his natural condition. If by predestination one is put into a certain condition of life which is not very prosperous in comparison to another's position, one should not be disturbed. He should simply try to utilize his valuable time to advance in Kṛṣṇa consciousness. Advancement in Kṛṣṇa consciousness does not depend on any materially prosperous or distressed condition; it is free from the conditions imposed by material life. A very poor man can execute Kṛṣṇa consciousness as effectively as a very rich man. One should therefore be very satisfied with his position as offered by the Lord.

Another word here is *mita-bhuk.* This means that one should eat only as much as necessary to maintain the body and soul together. One should not be gluttonous to satisfy the tongue. Grains, fruits, milk and similar foods are allotted for human consumption. One should not be excessively eager to satisfy the tongue and eat that which is not meant for humanity. Particularly, a devotee should eat only *prasāda,* or food which is offered to the Personality of Godhead. His position is to accept the remnants of those foodstuffs. Innocent foods like grains, vegetables, fruits, flowers and milk preparations are offered to the Lord, and therefore there is no scope for offering foods which are in the modes of passion and ignorance. A devotee should not be greedy. It is also recommended that the devotee should be *muni,* or thoughtful; he should always think of Kṛṣṇa and how to render better service to the Supreme Personality of Godhead. That should be his only anxiety. As a materialist is always thoughtful about improving his material condition, a devotee's thoughts should always be engaged in improving his condition in Kṛṣṇa consciousness; therefore he should be a *muni.*

The next item recommended is that a devotee should live in a secluded place. Generally a common man is interested in pounds, shillings and pence, or materialistic advancement in life, which is unnecessary for a devotee. A devotee should select a place of residence where everyone is interested in devotional service. Generally, therefore, a devotee goes to a sacred place of pilgrimage where devotees live. It is recommended that he live in a place where there is no large number of ordinary men. It is very important to live in a secluded place (*vivikta-śaraṇa*). The next item is *śānta,* or peacefulness. The devotee should not be agitated. He should be satisfied with his natural income, eat only as much as he needs to keep his health, live in a secluded place and always remain peaceful. Peace of mind is necessary for prosecuting Kṛṣṇa consciousness.

The next item is *maitra,* friendliness. A devotee should be friendly to everyone, but his intimate friendship should be with devotees only. With others he should be official. He may say, "Yes, sir, what you say is all right," but he is not intimate with them. A devotee should, however, have compassion for persons who are innocent, who are neither atheistic nor very much advanced in spiritual realization. A devotee should be compassionate towards them and instruct them as far as possible in making advancement in Kṛṣṇa consciousness. A devotee should always remain *ātmavān,* or situated in his spiritual position. He should not forget that his main concern is to make advancement in spiritual consciousness, or Kṛṣṇa consciousness, and he should not ignorantly identify himself with the body or the mind. *Ātmā* means the body or the mind, but here the word *ātmavān* especially means that one should be self-possessed. He should always remain in the pure consciousness that he is spirit soul and not the material body or the mind. That will make him progress confidently in Kṛṣṇa consciousness.

TEXT 9

सानुबन्धे च देहेऽस्मिन्नकुर्वन्नसदाग्रहम् ।
ज्ञानेन दृष्टतत्त्वेन प्रकृतेः पुरुषस्य च ॥ ९ ॥

sānubandhe ca dehe 'sminn
akurvann asad-āgraham
jñānena dṛṣṭa-tattvena
prakṛteḥ puruṣasya ca

sa-anubandhe—with bodily relationships; *ca*—and; *dehe*—towards the body; *asmin*—this; *akurvan*—not doing; *asat-āgraham*—bodily concept of life; *jñānena*—through knowledge; *dṛṣṭa*—having seen; *tattvena*—the reality; *prakṛteḥ*—of matter; *puruṣasya*—of spirit; *ca*—and.

TRANSLATION

One's seeing power should be increased through knowledge of spirit and matter, and one should not unnecessarily identify himself with the body and thus become attracted by bodily relationships.

PURPORT

The conditioned souls are eager to identify with the body and consider that the body is "myself" and that anything in relationship with the body or possessions of the body is "mine." In Sanskrit this is called *aham-mamatā,* and it is the root cause of all conditional life. A person should see things as the combination of matter and spirit. He should distinguish between the nature of matter and the nature of spirit, and his real identification should be with spirit, not with matter. By this knowledge, one should avoid the false, bodily concept of life.

TEXT 10

निवृत्तबुद्ध्यवस्थानो दूरीभूतान्यदर्शनः ।
उपलभ्यात्मनात्मानं चक्षुषेवार्कमात्मदृक् ॥१०॥

nivṛtta-buddhy-avasthāno
dūrī-bhūtānya-darśanaḥ
upalabhyātmanātmānaṁ
cakṣuṣevārkam ātma-dṛk

nivṛtta—transcended; *buddhi-avasthānaḥ*—the stages of material consciousness; *dūrī-bhūta*—far off; *anya*—other; *darśanah*—conceptions of life; *upalabhya*—having realized; *ātmanā*—by his purified intellect; *ātmānam*—his own self; *cakṣuṣā*—with his eyes; *iva*—as; *arkam*—the sun; *ātma-dṛk*—the self-realized.

TRANSLATION

One should be situated in the transcendental position, beyond the stages of material consciousness, and should be aloof from all other conceptions of life. Thus realizing freedom from false ego, one should see his own self just as he sees the sun in the sky.

PURPORT

Consciousness acts in three stages under the material conception of life. When we are awake, consciousness acts in a particular way, when we are asleep it acts in a different way, and when we are in deep sleep, consciousness acts in still another way. To become Kṛṣṇa conscious, one has to become transcendental to these three stages of consciousness. Our present consciousness should be freed from all perceptions of life other than consciousness of Kṛṣṇa, the Supreme Personality of Godhead. This is called *dūrī-bhūtānya-darśanah,* which means that when one attains perfect Kṛṣṇa consciousness he does not see anything but Kṛṣṇa. In the *Caitanya-caritāmṛta* it is said that the perfect devotee may see many movable and immovable objects, but in everything he sees that the energy of Kṛṣṇa is acting. As soon as he remembers the energy of Kṛṣṇa, he immediately remembers Kṛṣṇa in His personal form. Therefore in all his observations he sees Kṛṣṇa only. In the *Brahma-saṁhitā* (5.38) it is stated that when one's eyes are smeared with love of Kṛṣṇa (*premāñjana-cchurita*), he always sees Kṛṣṇa, outside and inside. This is confirmed here; one should be freed from all other vision, and in that way he is freed from the false egoistic identification and sees himself as the eternal servitor of the Lord. *Cakṣuṣevārkam:* as we can see the sun without a doubt, one who is fully developed in Kṛṣṇa consciousness sees Kṛṣṇa and His energy. By this vision one becomes *ātma-dṛk,* or self-realized. When the false ego of identifying the body with the self is removed, actual vision of life is perceivable. The senses, therefore, also become purified. Real service of the Lord begins when the senses are purified. One does not have to stop the activities of the senses, but the false ego of identifying with the body has to be removed. Then the senses automatically become purified, and with purified senses one can actually discharge devotional service.

TEXT 11

मुक्तलिङ्गं सदाभासमसति प्रतिपद्यते ।
सतो बन्धुमसच्चक्षुः सर्वानुस्यूतमद्वयम् ॥११॥

mukta-liṅgaṁ sad-ābhāsam
asati pratipadyate
sato bandhum asac-cakṣuḥ
sarvānusyūtam advayam

mukta-liṅgam—transcendental; *sat-ābhāsam*—manifest as a reflection; *asati*—in the false ego; *pratipadyate*—he realizes; *sataḥ bandhum*—the support of the material cause; *asat-cakṣuḥ*—the eye (revealer) of the illusory energy; *sarva-anusyūtam*—entered into everything; *advayam*—without a second.

TRANSLATION

A liberated soul realizes the Absolute Personality of Godhead, who is transcendental and who is manifest as a reflection even in the false ego. He is the support of the material cause and He enters into everything. He is absolute, one without a second, and He is the eyes of the illusory energy.

PURPORT

A pure devotee can see the presence of the Supreme Personality of Godhead in everything materially manifested. He is present there only as a reflection, but a pure devotee can realize that in the darkness of material illusion the only light is the Supreme Lord, who is its support. It is confirmed in *Bhagavad-gītā* that the background of the material manifestation is Lord Kṛṣṇa. And, as confirmed in the *Brahma-saṁhitā*, Kṛṣṇa is the cause of all causes. In the *Brahma-saṁhitā* it is stated that the Supreme Lord, by His partial or plenary expansion, is present not only within this universe and each and every universe, but in every atom, although He is one without a second. The word *advayam*, "without a second," which is used in this verse, indicates that although the Supreme Personality of Godhead is represented in everything, including the atoms, He is not divided. His presence in everything is explained in the next verse.

TEXT 12

यथा जलस्थ आभासः स्थलस्थेनावदृश्यते ।
स्वाभासेन तथा सूर्यो जलस्थेन दिवि स्थितः ॥१२॥

yathā jala-stha ābhāsaḥ
sthala-sthenāvadṛśyate
svābhāsena tathā sūryo
jala-sthena divi sthitaḥ

yathā—as; *jala-sthaḥ*—situated on water; *ābhāsaḥ*—a reflection; *sthala-sthena*—situated on the wall; *avadṛśyate*—is perceived; *sva-ābhāsena*—by its reflection; *tathā*—in that way; *sūryaḥ*—the sun; *jala-sthena*—situated on the water; *divi*—in the sky; *sthitaḥ*—situated.

TRANSLATION

The presence of the Supreme Lord can be realized just as the sun is realized first as a reflection on water, and again as a second reflection on the wall of a room, although the sun itself is situated in the sky.

PURPORT

The example given herewith is perfect. The sun is situated in the sky, far, far away from the surface of the earth, but its reflection can be seen in a pot of water in the corner of a room. The room is dark, and the sun is far away in the sky, but the sun's reflection on the water illuminates the darkness of the room. A pure devotee can realize the presence of the Supreme Personality of Godhead in everything by the reflection of His energy. In the *Viṣṇu Purāṇa* it is stated that as the presence of fire is understood by heat and light, so the Supreme Personality of Godhead, although one without a second, is perceived everywhere by the diffusion of His different energies. It is confirmed in the *Īśopaniṣad* that the presence of the Lord is perceived everywhere by the liberated soul, just as the sunshine and the reflection can be perceived everywhere although the sun is situated far away from the surface of the globe.

TEXT 13

एवं त्रिवृदहङ्कारो भूतेन्द्रियमनोमयैः ।
स्वाभासैर्लक्षितोऽनेन सदाभासेन सत्यदृक् ॥१३॥

evaṁ trivṛd-ahaṅkāro
bhūtendriya-manomayaiḥ
svābhāsair lakṣito 'nena
sad-ābhāsena satya-dṛk

evam—thus; *tri-vṛt*—the threefold; *ahaṅkāraḥ*—false ego; *bhūta-indriya-manaḥ-mayaiḥ*—consisting of body, senses and mind; *sva-ābhāsaiḥ*—by its own reflections; *lakṣitaḥ*—is revealed; *anena*—by this; *sat-ābhāsena*—by a reflection of Brahman; *satya-dṛk*—the self-realized soul.

TRANSLATION

The self-realized soul is thus reflected first in the threefold ego and then in the body, senses and mind.

PURPORT

The conditioned soul thinks, "I am this body," but a liberated soul thinks, "I am not this body. I am spirit soul." This "I am" is called ego, or identification of the self. "I am this body" or "Everything in relationship to the body is mine" is called false ego, but when one is self-realized and thinks that he is an eternal servitor of the Supreme Lord, that identification is real ego. One conception is in the darkness of the threefold qualities of material nature—goodness, passion and ignorance—and the other is in the pure state of goodness, called *śuddha-sattva* or *vāsudeva*. When we say that we give up our ego, this means that we give up our false ego, but real ego is always present. When one is reflected through the material contamination of the body and mind in false identification, he is in the conditional state, but when he is reflected in the pure stage he is called liberated. The identification of oneself with one's material possessions in the conditional stage must be purified, and one must identify himself in relationship with the Supreme Lord. In the conditioned state one accepts everything as an object of sense gratification, and in the liberated state one accepts everything for the service of the Supreme Lord. Kṛṣṇa consciousness, devotional service, is the actual liberated stage of a living entity. Otherwise, both accepting and rejecting on the material platform or in voidness or impersonalism are imperfect conditions for the pure soul.

By the understanding of the pure soul, called *satya-dṛk*, one can see everything as a reflection of the Supreme Personality of Godhead. A concrete example can be given in this connection. A conditioned soul sees a very beautiful rose, and he thinks that the nice aromatic flower should be used for his own sense gratification. This is one kind of vision. A liberated soul, however, sees the same flower as a reflection of the Supreme Lord. He thinks, "This beautiful flower is made possible by the superior energy of the Supreme Lord; therefore it belongs to the Supreme Lord and should be utilized in His service." These are two kinds of vision. The conditioned soul sees the flower for his own enjoyment, and the devotee sees the flower as an object to be used in the service of the Lord. In the same way, one can see the reflection of the Supreme Lord in one's own senses, mind and body—in everything. With that correct vision, one can engage everything in the service of the Lord. It is stated in the *Bhakti-rasāmṛta-sindhu* that one who has engaged everything—his vital energy, his wealth, his intelligence and his words—in the service of the Lord, or who desires to engage all these in the service of the Lord, no matter how he is situated, is to be considered a liberated soul, or *satya-dṛk.* Such a man has understood things as they are.

TEXT 14

भूतसूक्ष्मेन्द्रियमनोबुद्ध्यादिष्विह निद्रया ।
लीनेष्वसति यस्तत्र विनिद्रो निरहङ्क्रियः ॥१४॥

bhūta-sūkṣmendriya-mano-
buddhy-ādiṣv iha nidrayā
līneṣv asati yas tatra
vinidro nirahaṅkriyaḥ

bhūta—the material elements; *sūkṣma*—the objects of enjoyment; *indriya*—the material senses; *manaḥ*—mind; *buddhi*—intelligence; *ādiṣu*—and so on; *iha*—here; *nidrayā*—by sleep; *līneṣu*—merged; *asati*—in the unmanifest; *yaḥ*—who; *tatra*—there; *vinidraḥ*—awake; *nirahaṅkriyaḥ*—freed from false ego.

TRANSLATION

Although a devotee appears to be merged in the five material elements, the objects of material enjoyment, the material senses and material mind and intelligence, he is understood to be awake and to be freed from the false ego.

PURPORT

The explanation by Rūpa Gosvāmī in the *Bhakti-rasāmṛta-sindhu* of how a person can be liberated even in this body is more elaborately explained in this verse. The living entity who has become *satya-dṛk,* who realizes his position in relationship with the Supreme Personality of Godhead, may remain apparently merged in the five elements of matter, the five material sense objects, the ten senses and the mind and intelligence, but still he is considered to be awake and to be freed from the reaction of false ego. Here the word *līna* is very significant. The Māyāvādī philosophers recommend merging in the impersonal effulgence of Brahman; that is their ultimate goal, or destination. That merging is also mentioned here. But in spite of merging, one can keep his individuality. The example given by Jīva Gosvāmī is that a green bird that enters a green tree appears to merge in the color of greenness, but actually the bird does not lose its individuality. Similarly, a living entity merged either in the material nature or in the spiritual nature does not give up his individuality. Real individuality is to understand oneself to be the eternal servitor of the Supreme Lord. This information is received from the mouth of Lord Caitanya. He said clearly, upon the inquiry of Sanātana Gosvāmī, that *a living entity is the servitor of Kṛṣṇa eternally.* Kṛṣṇa also confirms in *Bhagavad-gītā* that the living entity is eternally His part and parcel. The part and parcel is meant to serve the whole. This is individuality. It is so even in this material existence, when the living entity apparently merges in matter. His gross body is made up of five elements, his subtle body is made of mind, intelligence, false ego and contaminated consciousness, and he has five active senses and five knowledge-acquiring senses. In this way he merges in matter. But even while merged in the twenty-four elements of matter, he can keep his individuality as the eternal servitor of the Lord. Either in the spiritual nature or in the material nature, such a servitor is to be considered a liberated soul. That is the explanation of the authorities, and it is confirmed in this verse.

TEXT 15

मन्यमानस्तदात्मानमनष्टो नष्टवन्मृषा ।
नष्टेऽहङ्करणे द्रष्टा नष्टवित्त इवातुरः ॥१५॥

manyamānas tadātmānam
anaṣṭo naṣṭavan mṛṣā
naṣṭe 'haṅkaraṇe draṣṭā
naṣṭa-vitta ivāturaḥ

manyamānaḥ—thinking; *tadā*—then; *ātmānam*—himself; *anaṣṭaḥ*—although not lost; *naṣṭa-vat*—as lost; *mṛṣā*—falsely; *naṣṭe ahaṅkaraṇe*—because of the disappearance of the ego; *draṣṭā*—the seer; *naṣṭa-vittaḥ*—one who has lost his fortune; *iva*—like; *āturaḥ*—distressed.

TRANSLATION

The living entity can vividly feel his existence as the seer, but because of the disappearance of the ego during the state of deep sleep, he falsely takes himself to be lost, like a man who has lost his fortune and feels distressed, thinking himself to be lost.

PURPORT

Only in ignorance does a living entity think that he is lost. If by attainment of knowledge he comes to the real position of his eternal existence, he knows that he is not lost. An appropriate example is mentioned herein: *naṣṭa-vitta ivāturaḥ.* A person who has lost a great sum of money may think that he is lost, but actually he is not lost-only his money is lost. But due to his absorption in the money or identification with the money, he thinks that he is lost. Similarly, when we falsely identify with matter as our field of activities, we think that we are lost, although actually we are not. As soon as a person is awakened to the pure knowledge of understanding that he is an eternal servitor of the Lord, his own real position is revived. A living entity can never be lost. When one forgets his identity in deep sleep, he becomes absorbed in dreams, and he may think himself a different person or may think himself lost. But actually his identity is intact. This concept of being lost is due to false ego, and it continues as long as one is not awakened to the sense of his existence as an eternal servitor of the Lord. The Māyāvādī philosophers' concept of becoming one with the Supreme Lord is another symptom of being lost in false ego. One may falsely claim that he is the Supreme Lord, but actually he is not. This is the last snare of *māyā's* influence upon the living entity. To think oneself equal with the Supreme Lord or to think oneself to be the Supreme Lord Himself is also due to false ego.

TEXT 16

एवं प्रत्यवमृश्यासावात्मानं प्रतिपद्यते ।
साहङ्कारस्य द्रव्यस्य योऽवस्थानमनुग्रहः ॥१६॥

evaṁ pratyavamṛśyāsāv
ātmānaṁ pratipadyate
sāhaṅkārasya dravyasya
yo 'vasthānam anugrahaḥ

evam—thus; *pratyavamṛśya*—after understanding; *asau*—that person; *ātmānam*—his self; *pratipadyate*—realizes; *sa-ahaṅkārasya*—accepted under false ego; *dravyasya*—of the situation; *yaḥ*—who; *avasthānam*—resting place; *anugrahaḥ*—the manifester.

TRANSLATION

When, by mature understanding, one can realize his individuality, then the situation he accepts under false ego becomes manifest to him.

PURPORT

The Māyāvādī philosophers' position is that at the ultimate issue the individual is lost, everything becomes one, and there is no distinction between the knower, the knowable and knowledge. But by minute analysis we can see that this is not correct. Individuality is never lost, even when one thinks that the three different principles, namely the knower, the knowable and knowledge, are amalgamated or merged into one. The very concept that the three merge into one is another form of knowledge, and since the perceiver of the knowledge still exists, how can one say that the knower, knowledge and knowable have become one? The individual soul who is perceiving this knowledge still remains an individual. Both in material existence and in spiritual existence the individuality continues; the only difference is in the quality of the identity. In the material identity, the false ego acts, and because of false identification, one takes things to be different from what they actually are. That is the basic principle of conditional life. Similarly, when the false ego is purified, one takes everything in the right perspective. That is the state of liberation.

It is stated in the *Īśopaniṣad* that everything belongs to the Lord. *Īśāvāsyam idaṁ sarvam.* Everything exists on the energy of the Supreme Lord. This is also confirmed in *Bhagavad-gītā.* Because everything is produced of His energy and exists on His energy, the energy is not different from Him—but still the Lord declares, "I am not there." When one clearly understands one's constitutional position, everything becomes manifest. False egoistic acceptance of things conditions one, whereas acceptance of things as they are makes one liberated. The example given in the previous verse is applicable here: due to absorption of one's identity in his money, when the money is lost he thinks that he is also lost. But actually he is not identical with the money, nor does the money belong to him. When the actual situation is revealed, we understand that the money does not belong to any individual person or living entity, nor is it produced by man. Ultimately the money is the property of the Supreme Lord, and there is no question of its being lost. But as long as one falsely thinks, "I am the enjoyer," or "I am the Lord," this concept of life continues, and one remains conditioned. As soon as this false ego is eliminated, one is liberated. As confirmed in the *Bhāgavatam,* situation in one's real constitutional position is called *mukti,* or liberation.

TEXT 17

देवहूतिरुवाच

पुरुषं प्रकृतिर्ब्रह्मन्न विमुञ्चति कर्हिचित् ।
अन्योन्यापाश्रयत्वाच्च नित्यत्वादनयोः प्रभो ॥१७॥

devahūtir uvāca
puruṣaṁ prakṛtir brahman
na vimuñcati karhicit
anyonyāpāśrayatvāc ca
nityatvād anayoḥ prabho

devahūtiḥ uvāca—Devahūti said; *puruṣam*—the spirit soul; *prakṛtiḥ*—material nature; *brahman*—O *brāhmaṇa; na*—not; *vimuñcati*—does release; *karhicit*—at any time; *anyonya*—to one another; *apāśrayatvāt*—from attraction; *ca*—and; *nityatvāt*—from eternality; *anayoḥ*—of them both; *prabho*—O my Lord.

TRANSLATION

Śrī Devahūti inquired: My dear brāhmaṇa, does material nature ever give release to the spirit soul? Since one is attracted to the other eternally, how is their separation possible?

PURPORT

Devahūti, the mother of Kapiladeva, here makes her first inquiry. Although one may understand that spirit soul and matter are different, their actual separation is not possible, either by philosophical speculation or by proper understanding. The spirit soul is the marginal potency of the Supreme Lord, and matter is the external potency of the Lord. The two eternal potencies have somehow or other been combined, and since it is so difficult to separate one from the other, how is it possible for the individual soul to become liberated? By practical experience one can see that when the soul is separated from the body, the body has no real existence, and when the body is separated from the soul one cannot perceive the existence of the soul. As long as the soul and the body are combined, we can understand that there is life. But when they are separated, there is no manifested existence of the body or the soul. This question asked by Devahūti of Kapiladeva is more or less impelled by the philosophy of voidism. The voidists say that consciousness is a product of a combination of matter and that as soon as the consciousness is gone, the material combination dissolves, and therefore there is ultimately nothing but voidness. This absence of consciousness is called *nirvāṇa* in Māyāvāda philosophy.

TEXT 18

यथा गन्धस्य भूमेश्च न भावो व्यतिरेकतः ।
अपां रसस्य च यथा तथा बुद्धेः परस्य च ॥१८॥

yathā gandhasya bhūmeś ca
na bhāvo vyatirekataḥ
apāṁ rasasya ca yathā
tathā buddheḥ parasya ca

yathā—as; *gandhasya*—of aroma; *bhūmeḥ*—of earth; *ca*—and; *na*—no; *bhāvaḥ*—existence; *vyatirekataḥ*—separate; *apām*—of water; *rasasya*—of taste; *ca*—and; *yathā*—as; *tathā*—so; *buddheḥ*—of intelligence; *parasya*—of consciousness, spirit; *ca*—and.

TRANSLATION

As there is no separate existence of the earth and its aroma or of water and its taste, there cannot be any separate existence of intelligence and consciousness.

PURPORT

The example is given here that anything material has an aroma. The flower, the earth—everything—has an aroma. If the aroma is separated from the matter, the matter cannot be identified. If there is no taste to water, the water has no meaning; if there is no heat in the fire, the fire has no meaning. Similarly, when there is want of intelligence, spirit has no meaning.

TEXT 19

अकर्तुः कर्मबन्धोऽयं पुरुषस्य यदाश्रयः ।
गुणेषु सत्सु प्रकृतेः कैवल्यं तेष्वतः कथम् ॥१९॥

akartuḥ karma-bandho 'yaṁ
puruṣasya yad-āśrayaḥ
guṇeṣu satsu prakṛteḥ
kaivalyaṁ teṣv ataḥ katham

akartuḥ—of the passive performer, the nondoer; *karma-bandhaḥ*—bondage to fruitive activities; *ayam*—this; *puruṣasya*—of the soul; *yat-āśrayaḥ*—caused by attachment to the modes; *guṇeṣu*—while the modes; *satsu*—are existing; *prakṛteḥ*—of material nature; *kaivalyam*—freedom; *teṣu*—those; *ataḥ*—hence; *katham*—how.

TRANSLATION

Hence even though he is the passive performer of all activities, how can there be freedom for the soul as long as material nature acts on him and binds him?

PURPORT

Although the living entity desires freedom from the contamination of matter, he is not given release. Actually, as soon as a living entity puts himself under the control of the modes of material nature, his acts are influenced by the qualities of material nature, and he becomes passive. It is confirmed in *Bhagavad-gītā, prakṛteḥ kriyamāṇāni guṇaiḥ:* the living entity acts according to the qualities or modes of material nature. He falsely thinks that he is acting, but unfortunately he is passive. In other words, he has no opportunity to get out of the control of material nature because it has already conditioned him. In *Bhagavad-gītā* it is also stated that it is very difficult to get out of the clutches of material nature. One may try in different ways to think that everything is void in the ultimate issue, that there is no God and that even if the background of everything is spirit, it is impersonal. This speculation may go on, but actually it is very difficult to get out of the clutches of material nature. Devahūti poses the question that although one may speculate in many ways, where is liberation as long as one is under the spell of material nature? The answer is also found in *Bhagavad-gītā* (7.14): only one who has surrendered himself unto the lotus feet of the Supreme Lord Kṛṣṇa (*mām eva ye prapadyante*) can be freed from the clutches of *māyā.*

Since Devahūti is gradually coming to the point of surrender, her questions are very intelligent. How can one be liberated? How can one be in a pure state of spiritual existence as long as he is strongly held by the modes of material nature? This is also an indication to the false meditator. There are many so-called meditators who think, "I am the Supreme Spirit Soul. I am conducting the activities of material nature. Under my direction the sun is moving and the moon is rising." They think that by such contemplation or meditation they can become free, but it is seen that just three minutes after finishing such nonsensical meditation, they are immediately captured by the modes of material nature. Immediately after his high-sounding meditation, a "meditator" becomes thirsty and wants to smoke or drink. He is under the strong grip of material nature, yet he thinks that he is already free from the clutches of *māyā.* This question of Devahūti's is for such a person who falsely claims that he is everything, that ultimately everything is void, and that there are no sinful or pious activities. These are all atheistic inventions. Actually, unless a living entity surrenders unto the Supreme Personality of Godhead as instructed in *Bhagavad-gītā*, there is no liberation or freedom from the clutches of *māyā.*

TEXT 20

क्वचित् तत्त्वावमर्शेन निवृत्तं भयमुल्बणम् ।
अनिवृत्तनिमित्तत्वात्पुनः प्रत्यवतिष्ठते ॥२०॥

kvacit tattvāvamarśena
nivṛttaṁ bhayam ulbaṇam

anivṛtta-nimittatvāt
punaḥ pratyavatiṣṭhate

kvacit—in a certain case; *tattva*—the fundamental principles; *avamarśena*—by reflecting upon; *nivṛttam*—avoided; *bhayam*—fear; *ulbaṇam*—great; *anivṛtta*—not ceased; *nimittatvāt*—since the cause; *punaḥ*—again; *pratyavatiṣṭhate*—it appears.

TRANSLATION

Even if the great fear of bondage is avoided by mental speculation and inquiry into the fundamental principles, it may still appear again, since its cause has not ceased.

PURPORT

Material bondage is caused by putting oneself under the control of matter because of the false ego of lording it over material nature. *Bhagavad-gītā* (7.27) states, *icchā-dveṣa-samutthena.* Two kinds of propensities arise in the living entity. One propensity is *icchā,* which means desire to lord it over material nature or to be as great as the Supreme Lord. Everyone desires to be the greatest personality in this material world. *Dveṣa* means "envy." When one becomes envious of Kṛṣṇa, or the Supreme Personality of Godhead, one thinks, "Why should Kṛṣṇa be the all and all? I'm as good as Kṛṣṇa." These two items, desire to be the Lord and envy of the Lord, are the beginning cause of material bondage. As long as a philosopher, salvationist or voidist has some desire to be supreme, to be everything, or to deny the existence of God, the cause remains, and there is no question of his liberation.

Devahūti very intelligently says, "One may theoretically analyze and say that by knowledge he has become freed, but actually, as long as the cause exists, he is not free." *Bhagavad-gītā* confirms that after performing such speculative activities for many, many births, when one actually comes to his real consciousness and surrenders unto the Supreme Lord, Kṛṣṇa, then the fulfillment of his research in knowledge is actually achieved. There is a gulf of difference between theoretical freedom and actual freedom from material bondage. The *Bhāgavatam* (10.14.4) says that if one gives up the auspicious path of devotional service and simply tries to know things by speculation, one wastes his valuable time (*kliśyanti ye kevala-bodha-labdhaye*). The result of such a labor of love is simply labor; there is no other result. The labor of speculation is ended only by exhaustion. The example is given that there is no benefit in husking the skin of an empty paddy; the rice is already gone. Similarly, simply by the speculative process one cannot be freed from material bondage, for the cause still exists. One has to nullify the cause, and then the effect will be nullified. This is explained by the Supreme Personality of Godhead in the following verses.

TEXT 21

श्रीभगवानुवाच
अनिमित्तनिमित्तेन स्वधर्मेणामलात्मना ।
तीव्रया मयि भक्त्या च श्रुतसम्भृतया चिरम् ॥२१॥

śrī-bhagavān uvāca
animitta-nimittena
sva-dharmeṇāmalātmanā
tīvrayā mayi bhaktyā ca
śruta-sambhṛtayā ciram

śrī-bhagavān uvāca—the Supreme Personality of Godhead said; *animitta-nimittena*—without desiring the fruits of activities; *sva-dharmeṇa*—by executing one's prescribed duties; *amala-ātmanā*—with a pure mind; *tīvrayā*—serious; *mayi*—unto Me; *bhaktyā*—by devotional service; *ca*—and; *śruta*—hearing; *sambhṛtayā*—endowed with; *ciram*—for a long time.

TRANSLATION

The Supreme Personality of Godhead said: One can get liberation by seriously discharging devotional service unto Me and thereby hearing for a long time about Me or from Me. By thus executing one's prescribed duties, there will be no reaction, and one will be freed from the contamination of matter.

PURPORT

Śrīdhara Svāmī comments in this connection that by association with material nature alone one does not become conditioned. Conditional life begins only after one is infected by the modes of material nature. If someone is in contact with the police department, that does not mean that he is a criminal. As long as one does not commit criminal acts, even though there is a police department, he is not punished. Similarly, the liberated soul is not affected, although he is in the material nature. Even the Supreme Personality of Godhead is supposed to be in association with material nature when He descends, but He is not affected. One has to act in such a way that in spite of being in the material nature he is not affected by contamination. Although the lotus flower is in association with water, it does not mix with the water. That is how one has to live, as described here by the Personality of Godhead Kapiladeva (*animitta-nimittena sva-dharmeṇāmalātmanā*).

One can be liberated from all adverse circumstances simply by seriously engaging in devotional service. How this devotional service develops and becomes mature is explained here. In the beginning one has to perform his prescribed duties with a clean mind. Clean consciousness means Kṛṣṇa consciousness. One has to perform his prescribed duties in Kṛṣṇa consciousness. There is no necessity of changing one's prescribed duties; one simply has to act in Kṛṣṇa consciousness. In discharging Kṛṣṇa conscious duties, one should determine whether, by his professional or occupational duties, Kṛṣṇa, the Supreme Personality of Godhead, is satisfied. In another place in the *Bhāgavatam* it is said, *svanuṣṭhitasya dharmasya saṁsiddhir hari-toṣaṇam:* everyone has some prescribed duties to perform, but the perfection of such duties will be reached only if the Supreme Personality of Godhead, Hari, is satisfied by such actions. For example, Arjuna's prescribed duty was to fight, and the perfection of his fighting was tested by the satisfaction of Kṛṣṇa. Kṛṣṇa wanted him to fight, and when he fought for the satisfaction of the Lord, that was the perfection of his professional devotional duty. On the other hand, when, contrary to the wish of Kṛṣṇa, he was not willing to fight, that was imperfect.

If one wants to perfect his life, he should discharge his prescribed duties for the satisfaction of Kṛṣṇa. One must act in Kṛṣṇa consciousness, for such action will never produce any reaction (*animitta-nimittena*). This is also confirmed in *Bhagavad-gītā. Yajñārthāt karmaṇo 'nyatra:* all activities should be performed simply for Yajña, or the satisfaction of Viṣṇu. Anything done otherwise, without the satisfaction of Viṣṇu, or Yajña, produces bondage, so here it is also prescribed by Kapila Muni that one can transcend material entanglement by acting in Kṛṣṇa consciousness, which means seriously engaging in devotional service. This serious devotional service can develop by hearing for long periods of time. Chanting and hearing is the beginning of the process of devotional service. One should associate with devotees and hear from them about the Lord's transcendental appearance, activities, disappearance, instructions, etc.

There are two kinds of *śruti*, or scripture. One is spoken by the Lord, and the other is spoken about the Lord and His devotees. *Bhagavad-gītā* is the former and *Śrīmad-Bhāgavatam* the latter. One must hear these scriptures repeatedly from reliable sources in order to become fixed in serious devotional service. Through engagement in such devotional service, one becomes freed from the contamination of *māyā*. It is stated in the *Śrīmad-Bhāgavatam* that hearing about the Supreme Personality of Godhead cleanses the heart of all contamination caused by the influence of the three modes of material nature. By continuous, regular hearing, the effects of the contamination of lust and greed to enjoy or lord it over material nature diminish, and when lust and greed diminish, one then becomes situated in the mode of goodness. This is the stage of Brahman realization, or spiritual realization. In this way one becomes fixed on the transcendental platform. Remaining fixed on the transcendental platform is liberation from material entanglement.

TEXT 22

ज्ञानेन दृष्टतत्त्वेन वैराग्येण बलीयसा ।
तपोयुक्तेन योगेन तीव्रेणात्मसमाधिना ॥२२॥

jñānena dṛṣṭa-tattvena
vairāgyeṇa balīyasā
tapo-yuktena yogena
tīvreṇātma-samādhinā

jñānena—in knowledge; *dṛṣṭa-tattvena*—with vision of the Absolute Truth; *vairāgyeṇa*—with renunciation; *balīyasā*—very strong; *tapaḥ-yuktena*—by engagement in austerity; *yogena*—by mystic *yoga;* *tīvreṇa*—firmly fixed; *ātma-samādhinā*—by self-absorption.

TRANSLATION

This devotional service has to be performed strongly in perfect knowledge and with transcendental vision. One must be strongly renounced and must engage in austerity and perform mystic yoga in order to be firmly fixed in self-absorption.

PURPORT

Devotional service in Kṛṣṇa consciousness cannot be performed blindly due to material emotion or mental concoction. It is specifically mentioned here that one has to perform devotional service in full knowledge by visualizing the Absolute Truth. We can understand about the Absolute Truth by evolving transcendental knowledge, and the result of such transcendental knowledge will be manifested by renunciation. That renunciation is not temporary or artificial, but is very strong. It is said that development of Kṛṣṇa consciousness is exhibited by proportionate material detachment, or *vairāgya.* If one does not separate himself from material enjoyment, it is to be understood that he is not advancing in Kṛṣṇa consciousness. Renunciation in Kṛṣṇa consciousness is so strong that it cannot be deviated by any attractive illusion. One has to perform devotional service in full *tapasya,* austerity. One should fast on the two Ekādaśī days, which fall on the eleventh day of the waxing and waning moon, and on the birthdays of Lord Kṛṣṇa, Lord Rāma and Caitanya Mahāprabhu. There are many such fasting days. *Yogena* means "by controlling the senses and mind." *Yoga indriya-saṁyamaḥ. Yogena* implies that one is seriously absorbed in the self and is able, by development of knowledge, to understand his constitutional position in relationship with the Superself. In this way one becomes fixed in devotional service, and his faith cannot be shaken by any material allurement.

TEXT 23

प्रकृतिः पुरुषस्येह दह्यमाना त्वहर्निशम् ।
तिरोभवित्री शनकैरग्नेर्योनिरिवारणिः ॥२३॥

prakṛtiḥ puruṣasyeha
dahyamānā tv ahar-niśam
tiro-bhavitrī śanakair
agner yonir ivāraṇiḥ

prakṛtiḥ—the influence of material nature; *puruṣasya*—of the living entity; *iha*—here; *dahyamānā*—being consumed; *tu*—but; *ahaḥ-niśam*—day and night; *tiraḥ-bhavitrī*—disappearing; *śanakaiḥ*—gradually; *agneḥ*—of fire; *yoniḥ*—the cause of appearance; *iva*—as; *araṇiḥ*—wooden sticks.

TRANSLATION

The influence of material nature has covered the living entity, and thus it is as if the living entity were always in a blazing fire. But by the process of seriously discharging devotional service, this influence can be removed, just as wooden sticks which cause a fire are themselves consumed by it.

PURPORT

Fire is conserved in wooden sticks, and when circumstances are favorable, the fire is ignited. But the wooden sticks which are the cause of the fire are also consumed by the fire if it is properly dealt with. Similarly, the living entity's conditional life of material existence is due to his desire to lord it over material nature and due to his envy of the Supreme Lord. Thus his main diseases are that he wants to be one with the Supreme Lord or he wants to become the lord of material nature. The *karmīs* try to utilize the resources of material nature and thus become its lord and enjoy sense gratification, and the *jñānīs,* the salvationists, who have become frustrated in enjoying the material resources, want to become one with the Supreme Personality of Godhead or merge into the impersonal effulgence. These two diseases are due to material contamination. Material contamination can be consumed by devotional service because in devotional service these two diseases, namely the desire to lord it over material nature and the desire to become one with the Supreme Lord, are absent. Therefore the cause of material existence is at once consumed by the careful discharge of devotional service in Kṛṣṇa consciousness.

A devotee in full Kṛṣṇa consciousness appears superficially to be a great *karmī,* always working, but the inner significance of the devotee's activities is that they are meant for the satisfaction of the Supreme Lord. This is called *bhakti,* or devotional service. Arjuna was apparently a fighter but when by his fighting he satisfied the senses of Lord Kṛṣṇa, he became a devotee. Since a devotee also engages in philosophical research to understand the Supreme Person as He is, his activities may thus appear to be like those of a mental speculator, but actually he is trying to understand the spiritual nature and transcendental activities. Thus although the tendency for philosophical speculation exists, the material effects of fruitive activities and empiric speculation do not, because this activity is meant for the Supreme Personality of Godhead.

TEXT 24

भुक्तभोगा परित्यक्ता दृष्टदोषा च नित्यशः ।
नेश्वरस्याशुभं धत्ते स्वे महिम्नि स्थितस्य च ॥२४॥

bhukta-bhogā parityaktā
dṛṣta-doṣā ca nityaśaḥ
neśvarasyāśubhaṁ dhatte
sve mahimni sthitasya ca

bhukta—enjoyed; *bhogā*—enjoyment; *parityaktā*—given up; *dṛṣṭa*—discovered; *doṣā*—faultiness; *ca*—and; *nityaśaḥ*—always; *na*—not; *īśvarasya*—of the independent; *aśubham*—harm; *dhatte*—she inflicts; *sve mahimni*—in his own glory; *sthitasya*—situated; *ca*—and.

TRANSLATION

By discovering the faultiness of his desiring to lord it over material nature and by therefore giving it up, the living entity becomes independent and stands in his own glory.

PURPORT

Because the living entity is not actually the enjoyer of the material resources, his attempt to lord it over material nature is, at the ultimate issue, frustrated. As a result of frustration, he desires more power than the ordinary living entity and thus wants to merge into the existence of the supreme enjoyer. In this way he develops a plan for greater enjoyment.

When one is actually situated in devotional service, that is his independent position. Less intelligent men cannot understand the position of the eternal servant of the Lord. Because the word "servant" is used, they become confused; they cannot understand that this servitude is not the servitude of this material world. To be the servant of the Lord is the greatest position. If one can understand this and can thus revive one's original nature of eternal servitorship of the Lord, one stands fully independent. A living entity's independence is lost by material contact. In the spiritual field he has full independence, and therefore there is no question of becoming dependent upon the three modes of material nature. This position is attained by a devotee, and therefore he gives up the tendency for material enjoyment after seeing its faultiness.

The difference between a devotee and an impersonalist is that an impersonalist tries to become one with the Supreme so that he can enjoy without impediment, whereas a devotee gives up the entire mentality of enjoying and engages in the transcendental loving service of the Lord. That is his constitutional glorified position. At that time he is *īśvara,* fully independent. The real *īśvara* or *īśvaraḥ paramaḥ,* the supreme *īśvara,* or supreme independent, is Kṛṣṇa. The living entity is *īśvara* only when engaged in the service of the Lord. In other words, transcendental pleasure derived from loving service to the Lord is actual independence.

TEXT 25

यथा ह्यप्रतिबुद्धस्य प्रस्वापो बह्वनर्थभृत् ।
स एव प्रतिबुद्धस्य न वै मोहाय कल्पते ॥२५॥

yathā hy apratibuddhasya
prasvāpo bahv-anartha-bhṛt
sa eva pratibuddhasya
na vai mohāya kalpate

yathā—as; *hi*—indeed; *apratibuddhasya*—of one who is sleeping; *prasvāpaḥ*—the dream; *bahu-anartha-bhṛt*—bearing many inauspicious things; *saḥ eva*—that very dream;

pratibuddhasya—of one who is awake; *na*—not; *vai*—certainly; *mohāya*—for bewildering; *kalpate*—is capable.

TRANSLATION

In the dreaming state one's consciousness is almost covered, and one sees many inauspicious things, but when he is awakened and fully conscious, such inauspicious things cannot bewilder him.

PURPORT

In the condition of dreaming, when one's consciousness is almost covered, one may see many unfavorable things which cause disturbance or anxiety, but upon awakening, although he remembers what happened in the dream, he is not disturbed. Similarly the position of self-realization, or understanding of one's real relationship with the Supreme Lord, makes one completely satisfied, and the three modes of material nature, which are the cause of all disturbances, cannot affect him. In contaminated consciousness one sees everything to be for his own enjoyment, but in pure consciousness, or Kṛṣṇa consciousness, he sees that everything exists for the enjoyment of the supreme enjoyer. That is the difference between the dream state and wakefulness. The state of contaminated consciousness is compared to dream consciousness, and Kṛṣṇa consciousness is compared to the awakened stage of life. Actually, as stated in *Bhagavad-gītā*, the only absolute enjoyer is Kṛṣṇa. One who can understand that Kṛṣṇa is the proprietor of all the three worlds and that He is the friend of everyone is peaceful and independent. As long as a conditioned soul does not have this knowledge, he wants to be the enjoyer of everything; he wants to become a humanitarian or philanthropist and open hospitals and schools for his fellow human beings. This is all illusion, for one cannot benefit anyone by such material activities. If one wishes to benefit his fellow brother, he must awaken his dormant Kṛṣṇa consciousness. The Kṛṣṇa conscious position is that of *pratibuddha*, which means "pure consciousness."

TEXT 26

एवं विदिततत्त्वस्य प्रकृतिर्मयि मानसम् ।
युञ्जतो नापकुरुत आत्मारामस्य कर्हिचित् ॥२६॥

evaṁ vidita-tattvasya
prakṛtir mayi mānasam
yuñjato nāpakuruta
ātmārāmasya karhicit

evam—thus; *vidita-tattvasya*—to one who knows the Absolute Truth; *prakṛtiḥ*—material nature; *mayi*—on Me; *mānasam*—the mind; *yuñjataḥ*—fixing; *na*—not; *apakurute*—can do harm; *ātma-ārāmasya*—to one who rejoices in the self; *karhicit*—at any time.

TRANSLATION

The influence of material nature cannot harm an enlightened soul, even though he engages in material activities, because he knows the truth of the Absolute, and his mind is fixed on the Supreme Personality of Godhead.

PURPORT

Lord Kapila says that *mayi mānasam,* a devotee whose mind is always fixed upon the lotus feet of the Supreme Personality of Godhead, is called *ātmārāma* or *vidita-tattva. Ātmārāma* means "one who rejoices in the self," or "one who enjoys in the spiritual atmosphere." *Ātmā,* in the material sense, means the body or the mind, but when referring to one whose mind is fixed on the lotus feet of the Supreme Lord, *ātmārāma* means "one who is fixed in spiritual activities in relationship with the Supreme Soul." The Supreme Soul is the Personality of Godhead, and the individual soul is the living entity. When they engage in reciprocation of service and benediction, the living entity is said to be in the *ātmārāma* position. This *ātmārāma* position can be attained by one who knows the truth as it is. The truth is that the Supreme Personality of Godhead is the enjoyer and that the living entities are meant for His service and enjoyment. One who knows this truth, and who tries to engage all resources in the service of the Lord, escapes all material reactions and influences of the modes of material nature.

An example may be cited in this connection. Just as a materialist engages in constructing a big skyscraper, a devotee engages in constructing a big temple for Viṣṇu. Superficially, the skyscraper constructor and temple constructor are on the same level, for both are collecting wood, stone, iron and other building materials. But the person who constructs a skyscraper is a materialist, and the person who constructs a temple of Viṣṇu is *ātmārāma.* The materialist tries to satisfy himself in relation to his body by constructing a skyscraper, but the devotee tries to satisfy the Superself, the Supreme Personality of Godhead, by constructing the temple. Although both are engaged in the association of material activities, the devotee is liberated, and the materialist is conditioned. This is because the devotee, who is constructing the temple, has fixed his mind upon the Supreme Personality of Godhead, but the nondevotee, who is constructing the skyscraper, has his mind fixed in sense gratification. If, while performing any activity, even in material existence, one's mind is fixed upon the lotus feet of the Personality of Godhead, one will not be entangled or conditioned. The worker in devotional service, in full Kṛṣṇa consciousness, is always independent of the influence of material nature.

TEXT 27

यदैवमध्यात्मरतः कालेन बहुजन्मना ।
सर्वत्र जातवैराग्य आब्रह्मभुवनान्मुनिः ॥२७॥

yadaivam adhyātma-rataḥ
kālena bahu-janmanā
sarvatra jāta-vairāgya
ābrahma-bhuvanān munih

yadā—when; *evam*—thus; *adhyātma-rataḥ*—engaged in self-realization; *kālena*—for many years; *bahu-janmanā*—for many births; *sarvatra*—everywhere; *jāta-vairāgyaḥ*—detachment is born; *ā-brahma-bhuvanāt*—up to Brahmaloka; *muniḥ*—a thoughtful person.

TRANSLATION

When a person thus engages in devotional service and self-realization for many, many years and births, he becomes completely reluctant to enjoy any one of the material planets, even up to the highest planet, which is known as Brahmaloka; he becomes fully developed in consciousness.

PURPORT

Anyone engaged in devotional service to the Supreme Personality of Godhead is known as a devotee, but there is a distinction between pure devotees and mixed devotees. A mixed devotee engages in devotional service for the spiritual benefit of being eternally engaged in the transcendental abode of the Lord in full bliss and knowledge. In material existence, when a devotee is not completely purified, he expects material benefit from the Lord in the form of relief from material miseries, or he wants material gain, advancement in knowledge of the relationship between the Supreme Personality of Godhead and the living entity, or knowledge as to the real nature of the Supreme Lord. When a person is transcendental to these conditions, he is called a pure devotee. He does not engage himself in the service of the Lord for any material benefit or for understanding of the Supreme Lord. His one interest is that he loves the Supreme Personality of Godhead, and he spontaneously engages in satisfying Him.

The highest example of pure devotional service is that of the *gopīs* in Vṛndāvana. They are not interested in understanding Kṛṣṇa, but only in loving Him. That platform of love is the pure state of devotional service. Unless one is advanced to this pure state of devotional service, there is a tendency to desire elevation to a higher material position. A mixed devotee may desire to enjoy a comfortable life on another planet with a greater span of life, such as on Brahmaloka. These are material desires, but because a mixed devotee engages in the service of the Lord, ultimately, after many, many lives of material enjoyment, he undoubtedly develops Kṛṣṇa consciousness, and the symptom of this Kṛṣṇa consciousness is that he is no longer interested in any sort of materially elevated life. He does not even aspire to become a personality like Lord Brahmā.

TEXTS 28-29

मद्भक्तः प्रतिबुद्धार्थो मत्प्रसादेन भूयसा ।
निःश्रेयसं स्वसंस्थानं कैवल्याख्यं मदाश्रयम् ॥२८॥
प्राप्नोतीहाञ्जसा धीरः स्वदृशाच्छिन्नसंशयः ।
यद्गत्वा न निवर्तेत योगी लिङ्गाद्विनिर्गमे ॥२९॥

mad-bhaktaḥ pratibuddhārtho
mat-prasādena bhūyasā
niḥśreyasaṁ sva-saṁsthānaṁ
kaivalyākhyaṁ mad-āśrayam

prāpnotīhāñjasā dhīraḥ
sva-dṛśā cchinna-saṁśayaḥ
yad gatvā na nivarteta
yogī liṅgād vinirgame

mat-bhaktaḥ—My devotee; *pratibuddha-arthaḥ*—self-realized; *mat-prasādena*—by My causeless mercy; *bhūyasā*—unlimited; *niḥśreyasam*—the ultimate perfectional goal; *sva-saṁsthānam*—his abode; *kaivalya-ākhyam*—called *kaivalya;* *mat-āśrayam*—under My protection; *prāpnoti*—attains; *iha*—in this life; *añjasā*—truly; *dhīraḥ*—steady; *sva-dṛśā*—by knowledge of the self; *chinna-saṁśayaḥ*—freed from doubts; *yat*—to that abode; *gatvā*—having gone; *na*—never; *nivarteta*—comes back; *yogī*—the mystic devotee; *liṅgāt*—from the subtle and gross material bodies; *vinirgame*—after departing.

TRANSLATION

My devotee actually becomes self-realized by My unlimited causeless mercy, and thus, when freed from all doubts, he steadily progresses towards

his destined abode, which is directly under the protection of My spiritual energy of unadulterated bliss. That is the ultimate perfectional goal of the living entity. After giving up the present material body, the mystic devotee goes to that transcendental abode and never comes back.

PURPORT

Actual self-realization means becoming a pure devotee of the Lord. The existence of a devotee implies the function of devotion and the object of devotion. Self-realization ultimately means to understand the Personality of Godhead and the living entities; to know the individual self and the reciprocal exchanges of loving service between the Supreme Personality of Godhead and the living entity is real self-realization. This cannot be attained by the impersonalists or other transcendentalists; they cannot understand the science of devotional service. Devotional service is revealed to the pure devotee by the unlimited causeless mercy of the Lord. This is especially spoken of here by the Lord—*mat-prasādena,* "by My special grace." This is also confirmed in *Bhagavad-gītā.* Only those who engage in devotional service with love and faith receive the necessary intelligence from the Supreme Personality of Godhead so that gradually and progressively they can advance to the abode of the Personality of Godhead.

Niḥśreyasa means "the ultimate destination." *Sva-saṁsthāna* indicates that the impersonalists have no particular place to stay. The impersonalists sacrifice their individuality so that the living spark can merge into the impersonal effulgence emanating from the transcendental body of the Lord, but the devotee has a specific abode. The planets rest in the sunshine, but the sunshine itself has no particular resting place. When one reaches a particular planet, then he has a resting place. The spiritual sky, which is known as *kaivalya,* is simply blissful light on all sides, and it is under the protection of the Supreme Personality of Godhead. As stated in *Bhagavad-gītā* (14.27), *brahmaṇo hi pratiṣṭhāham:* the impersonal Brahman effulgence rests on the body of the Supreme Personality of Godhead. In other words, the bodily effulgence of the Supreme Personality of Godhead is *kaivalya,* or impersonal Brahman. In that impersonal effulgence there are spiritual planets, which are known as Vaikuṇṭhas, chief of which is Kṛṣṇaloka. Some devotees are elevated to the Vaikuṇṭha planets, and some are elevated to the planet Kṛṣṇaloka. According to the desire of the particular devotee, he is offered a particular abode, which is known as *sva-saṁsthāna,* his desired destination. By the grace of the Lord, the self-realized devotee engaged in devotional service understands his destination even while in the material body. He therefore performs his devotional activities steadily, without doubting, and after quitting his material body he at once reaches the destination for which he has prepared himself. After reaching that abode, he never comes back to this material world.

The words *liṅgād vinirgame,* which are used here, mean "after being freed from the two kinds of material bodies, subtle and gross." The subtle body is made of mind, intelligence, false ego and contaminated consciousness, and the gross body is made of five elements—earth, water, fire, air and ether. When one is transferred to the spiritual world, he gives up both the subtle and gross bodies of this material world. He enters the spiritual sky in his pure, spiritual body and is stationed in one of the spiritual planets. Although the impersonalists also reach that spiritual sky after giving up the subtle and gross material bodies, they are not placed in the spiritual planets; as they desire, they are allowed to merge in the spiritual effulgence emanating from the transcendental body of the Lord. The word *sva-saṁsthānam* is also very significant. As a living entity prepares himself, so he attains his abode. The impersonal Brahman effulgence is offered to the impersonalists, but those who want to associate with the Supreme Personality of Godhead in His transcendental form as Nārāyaṇa in the Vaikuṇṭhas, or with Kṛṣṇa in Kṛṣṇaloka, go to those abodes, wherefrom they never return.

TEXT 30

यदा न योगोपचितासु चेतो
मायासु सिद्धस्य विषज्जतेऽङ्ग ।
अनन्यहेतुष्वथ मे गतिः स्याद्
आत्यन्तिकी यत्र न मृत्युहासः ॥३०॥

yadā na yogopacitāsu ceto
māyāsu siddhasya viṣajjate 'ṅga
ananya-hetuṣv atha me gatiḥ syād
ātyantikī yatra na mṛtyu-hāsaḥ

yadā—when; *na*—not; *yoga-upacitāsu*—to powers developed by *yoga; cetaḥ*—the attention; *māyāsu*—manifestations of *māyā; siddhasya*—of a perfect *yogī; viṣajjate*—is attracted; *aṅga*—My dear mother; *ananya-hetuṣu*—having no other cause; *atha*—then; *me*—to Me; *gatiḥ*—his progress; *syāt*—becomes; *ātyantikī*—unlimited; *yatra*—where; *na*—not; *mṛtyu-hāsaḥ*—power of death.

TRANSLATION

When a perfect yogī's attention is no longer attracted to the by-products of mystic powers, which are manifestations of the external energy, his progress

towards Me becomes unlimited, and thus the power of death cannot overcome him.

PURPORT

Yogīs are generally attracted to the by-products of mystic yogic power, for they can become smaller than the smallest or greater than the greatest, achieve anything they desire, have power even to create a planet, or bring anyone they like under their subjection. *Yogīs* who have incomplete information of the result of devotional service are attracted by these powers, but these powers are material; they have nothing to do with spiritual progress. As other material powers are created by the material energy, mystic yogic powers are also material. A perfect *yogīs* mind is not attracted by any material power, but is simply attracted by unalloyed service to the Supreme Lord. For a devotee, the process of merging into the Brahman effulgence is considered to be hellish, and yogic power or the preliminary perfection of yogic power, to be able to control the senses, is automatically achieved. As for elevation to higher planets, a devotee considers this to be simply hallucinatory. A devotee's attention is concentrated only upon the eternal loving service of the Lord, and therefore the power of death has no influence over him. In such a devotional state, a perfect *yogī* can attain the status of immortal knowledge and bliss.

Thus end the Bhaktivedanta purports of the Third Canto, Twenty-seventh Chapter, of the Śrīmad-Bhāgavatam, *entitled "Understanding Material Nature."*

CHAPTER TWENTY-EIGHT

Kapila's Instructions on the Execution of Devotional Service

TEXT 1

श्रीभगवानुवाच
योगस्य लक्षणं वक्ष्ये सबीजस्य नृपात्मजे ।
मनो येनैव विधिना प्रसन्नं याति सत्पथम् ॥ १ ॥

śrī-bhagavān uvāca
yogasya lakṣaṇaṁ vakṣye
sabījasya nṛpātmaje
mano yenaiva vidhinā
prasannaṁ yāti sat-patham

śrī-bhagavān uvāca—the Personality of Godhead said; *yogasya*—of the *yoga* system; *lakṣaṇam*—description; *vakṣye*—I shall explain; *sabījasya*—authorized; *nṛpa-ātma-je*—O daughter of the King; *manaḥ*—the mind; *yena*—by which; *eva*—certainly; *vidhinā*—by practice; *prasannam*—joyful; *yāti*—attains; *sat-patham*—the path of the Absolute Truth.

TRANSLATION

The Personality of Godhead said: My dear mother, O daughter of the King, now I shall explain to you the system of yoga, the object of which is to concentrate the mind. By practicing this system one can become joyful and progressively advance towards the path of the Absolute Truth.

PURPORT

The *yoga* process explained by Lord Kapiladeva in this chapter is authorized and standard, and therefore these instructions should be followed very carefully. To begin, the Lord says that by *yoga* practice one can make progress towards understanding the Absolute Truth, the Supreme Personality of Godhead. In the previous chapter it has been clearly stated that the desired result of *yoga* is not to achieve some wonderful mystic power. One should not be at all attracted by such mystic power, but should attain progressive realization on the path of understanding the Supreme Personality of Godhead. This is also confirmed in *Bhagavad-gītā,* which states in the last verse of the Sixth Chapter that the greatest *yogī* is he who constantly thinks of Kṛṣṇa within himself, or he who is Kṛṣṇa conscious.

It is stated here that by following the system of *yoga* one can become joyful. Lord Kapila, the Personality of Godhead, who is the highest authority on *yoga,* here explains the *yoga* system known as *aṣṭāṅga-yoga,* which comprises eight different practices, namely *yama, niyama, āsana, prāṇāyāma, pratyāhāra, dhāraṇā, dhyāna* and *samādhi.* By all these stages of practice one must realize Lord Viṣṇu, who is the target of all *yoga.* There are so-called *yoga* practices in which one concentrates the mind on voidness or on the impersonal, but this is not approved by the authorized *yoga* system as explained by Kapiladeva. Even Patañjali explains that the target of all *yoga* is Viṣṇu. *Aṣṭāṅga-yoga* is therefore part of Vaiṣṇava practice because its ultimate goal is realization of Viṣṇu. The achievement of success in *yoga* is not acquisition of mystic power, which is condemned in the previous chapter, but, rather, freedom from all material designations and situation in one's constitutional position. That is the ultimate achievement in *yoga* practice.

TEXT 2

स्वधर्माचरणं शक्त्या विधर्माच्च निवर्तनम् ।
दैवाल्लब्धेन सन्तोष आत्मविच्चरणार्चनम् ॥ २ ॥

sva-dharmācaraṇaṁ śaktyā
vidharmāc ca nivartanam
daivāl labdhena santoṣa
ātmavic-caraṇārcanam

sva-dharma-ācaraṇam—executing one's prescribed duties; *śaktyā*—to the best of one's ability; *vidharmāt*—unauthorized duties; *ca*—and; *nivartanam*—avoiding; *daivāt*—by the grace of the Lord; *labdhena*—with what is achieved; *santoṣaḥ*—satisfied; *ātma-vit*—of the self-realized soul; *caraṇa*—the feet; *arcanam*—worshiping.

TRANSLATION

One should execute his prescribed duties to the best of his ability and avoid performing duties not allotted to him. One should be satisfied with as much gain as he achieves by the grace of the Lord, and one should worship the lotus feet of a spiritual master.

PURPORT

In this verse there are many important words which could be very elaborately explained, but we shall briefly discuss the important aspects of each. The final statement is *ātmavic-caraṇārcanam. Ātma-vit* means a self-realized soul or bona fide spiritual master. Unless one is self-realized and knows what his relationship with the Supersoul is, he cannot be a bona fide spiritual master. Here it is recommended that one should seek out a bona fide spiritual master and surrender unto him (*arcanam*), for by inquiring from and worshiping him one can learn spiritual activities.

The first recommendation is *sva-dharmācaraṇam.* As long as we have this material body there are various duties prescribed for us. Such duties are divided by a system of four social orders: *brāhmaṇa, kṣatriya, vaiśya* and *śūdra.* These particular duties are mentioned in the *śāstra,* and particularly in *Bhagavad-gītā. Sva-dharmācaraṇam* means that one must discharge the prescribed duties of his particular division of society faithfully and to the best of his ability. One should not accept another's duty. If one is born in a particular society or community, he should perform the prescribed duties for that particular division. If, however, one is fortunate enough to transcend the designation of birth in a particular society or community by being elevated to the standard of spiritual identity, then his *sva-dharma,* or duty, is solely that of serving the Supreme Personality of Godhead. The actual duty of one who is advanced in Kṛṣṇa consciousness is to serve the Lord. As long as one remains in the bodily concept of life, he may act according to the duties of social convention, but if one is elevated to the spiritual platform, he must simply serve the Supreme Lord; that is the real execution of *sva-dharma.*

TEXT 3

ग्राम्यधर्मनिवृत्तिश्च मोक्षधर्मरतिस्तथा ।
मितमेध्यादनं शश्वद्विविक्तक्षेमसेवनम् ॥ ३ ॥

grāmya-dharma-nivṛttiś ca
mokṣa-dharma-ratis tathā
mita-medhyādanaṁ śaśvad
vivikta-kṣema-sevanam

grāmya—conventional; *dharma*—religious practice; *nivṛttiḥ*—ceasing; *ca*—and; *mokṣa*—for salvation; *dharma*—religious practice; *ratiḥ*—being attracted to; *tathā*—in that way; *mita*—little; *medhya*—pure; *adanam*—eating; *śaśvat*—always; *vivikta*—secluded; *kṣema*—peaceful; *sevanam*—dwelling.

TRANSLATION

One should cease performing conventional religious practices and should be attracted to those which lead to salvation. One should eat very frugally and should always remain secluded so that he can achieve the highest perfection of life.

PURPORT

It is recommended herein that religious practice for economic development or the satisfaction of sense desires should be avoided. Religious practices should be executed only to gain freedom from the clutches of material nature. It is stated in the beginning of *Śrīmad-Bhāgavatam* that the topmost religious practice is that by which one can attain to the transcendental devotional service of the Lord, without reason or cause. Such religious practice is never hampered by any impediments, and by its performance one actually becomes satisfied. Here this is recommended as *mokṣa-dharma*, religious practice for salvation, or transcendence of the clutches of material contamination. Generally people execute religious practices for economic development or sense gratification, but that is not recommended for one who wants to advance in *yoga.*

The next important phrase is *mita-medhyādanam,* which means that one should eat very frugally. It is recommended in the Vedic literatures that a *yogī* eat only half what he desires according to his hunger. If one is so hungry that he could devour one pound of foodstuffs, then instead of eating one pound, he should consume only half a pound and supplement this with four ounces of water; one fourth of the stomach should be left empty for passage of air in the stomach. If one eats in this manner, he will avoid indigestion and disease. The *yogī* should eat in this way, as recommended in the *Śrīmad-Bhāgavatam* and all other standard scriptures. The *yogī* should live in a secluded place, where his *yoga* practice will not be disturbed.

TEXT 4

अहिंसा सत्यमस्तेयं यावदर्थपरिग्रहः ।
ब्रह्मचर्यं तपः शौचं स्वाध्यायः पुरुषार्चनम् ॥ ४ ॥

ahiṁsā satyam asteyaṁ
yāvad-artha-parigrahaḥ
brahmacaryaṁ tapaḥ śaucaṁ
svādhyāyaḥ puruṣārcanam

ahiṁsā—nonviolence; *satyam*—truthfulness; *asteyam*—refraining from theft; *yāvat-artha*—as much as necessary; *parigrahaḥ*—possessing; *brahmacaryam*—celibacy; *tapaḥ*—

austerity; *śaucam*—cleanliness; *sva-adhyāyaḥ*—study of the *Vedas; puruṣa-arcanam*—worship of the Supreme Personality of Godhead.

TRANSLATION

One should practice nonviolence and truthfulness, should avoid thieving and be satisfied with possessing as much as he needs for his maintenance. He should abstain from sex life, perform austerity, be clean, study the Vedas and worship the supreme form of the Supreme Personality of Godhead.

PURPORT

The word *puruṣārcanam* in this verse means worshiping the Supreme Personality of Godhead, especially the form of Lord Kṛṣṇa. In *Bhagavad-gītā* it is confirmed by Arjuna that Kṛṣṇa is the original *puruṣa,* or Personality of Godhead, *puruṣaṁ śāśvatam.* Therefore in *yoga* practice one not only must concentrate his mind on the person of Kṛṣṇa, but must also worship the form or Deity of Kṛṣṇa daily.

A *brahmacārī* practices celibacy, controlling his sex life. One cannot enjoy unrestricted sex life and practice *yoga;* this is rascaldom. So-called *yogīs* advertise that one can go on enjoying as one likes and simultaneously become a *yogī,* but this is totally unauthorized. It is very clearly explained here that one must observe celibacy. *Brahmacaryam* means that one leads his life simply in relationship with Brahman, or in full Kṛṣṇa consciousness. Those who are too addicted to sex life cannot observe the regulations which will lead them to Kṛṣṇa consciousness. Sex life should be restricted to persons who are married. A person whose sex life is restricted in marriage is also called a *brahmacārī.*

The word *asteyam* is also very important for a *yogī. Asteyam* means "to refrain from theft." In the broader sense, everyone who accumulates more than he needs is a thief. According to spiritual communism, one cannot possess more than he needs for his personal maintenance. That is the law of nature. Anyone who accumulates more money or more possessions than he needs is called a thief, and one who simply accumulates wealth without spending for sacrifice or for worship of the Personality of Godhead is a great thief.

Svādhyāyaḥ means "reading the authorized Vedic scriptures." Even if one is not Kṛṣṇa conscious and is practicing the *yoga* system, he must read standard Vedic literatures in order to understand. Performance of *yoga* alone is not sufficient. Narottama dāsa Ṭhākura, a great devotee and *ācārya* in the Gauḍīya Vaiṣṇava-sampradāya, says that all spiritual activities should be understood from three sources, namely saintly persons, standard scriptures and the spiritual master. These three guides are very important for progress in spiritual life. The spiritual master prescribes standard literature for the prosecution of the *yoga* of devotional service, and he himself speaks only from scriptural reference. Therefore reading standard scriptures is necessary for executing *yoga.* Practicing *yoga* without reading the standard literatures is simply a waste of time.

TEXT 5

मौनं सदासनजयः स्थैर्यं प्राणजयः शनैः ।
प्रत्याहारश्चेन्द्रियाणां विषयान्मनसा हृदि ॥ ५ ॥

maunaṁ sad-āsana-jayaḥ
sthairyaṁ prāṇa-jayaḥ śanaiḥ
pratyāhāraś cendriyāṇāṁ
viṣayān manasā hṛdi

maunam—silence; *sat*—good; *āsana*—yogic postures; *jayaḥ*—controlling; *sthairyam*—steadiness; *prāṇa-jayaḥ*—controlling the vital air; *śanaiḥ*—gradually; *pratyāhāraḥ*—withdrawal; *ca*—and; *indriyāṇām*—of the senses; *viṣayāt*—from the sense objects; *manasā*—with the mind; *hṛdi*—on the heart.

TRANSLATION

One must observe silence, acquire steadiness by practicing different yogic postures, control the breathing of the vital air, withdraw the senses from sense objects and thus concentrate the mind on the heart.

PURPORT

The yogic practices in general and *haṭha-yoga* in particular are not ends in themselves; they are means to the end of attaining steadiness. First one must be able to sit properly, and then the mind and attention will become steady enough for practicing *yoga.* Gradually, one must control the circulation of vital air, and with such control he will be able to withdraw the senses from sense objects. In the previous verse it is stated that one must observe celibacy. The most important aspect of sense control is controlling sex life. That is called *brahmacarya.* By practicing the different sitting postures and controlling the vital air, one can control and restrain the senses from unrestricted sense enjoyment.

TEXT 6

स्वधिष्ण्यानामेकदेशे मनसा प्राणधारणम् ।
वैकुण्ठलीलाभिध्यानं समाधानं तथात्मनः ॥ ६ ॥

sva-dhiṣṇyānām eka-deśe
manasā prāṇa-dhāraṇam
vaikuṇṭha-līlābhidhyānaṁ
samādhānaṁ tathātmanaḥ

sva-dhiṣṇyānām—within the vital air circles; *eka-deśe*—in one spot; *manasā*—with the mind; *prāṇa*—the vital air; *dhāraṇam*—fixing; *vaikuṇṭha-līlā*—on the pastimes of the Supreme Personality of Godhead; *abhidhyānam*—concentration; *samādhānam*—*samādhi*; *tathā*—thus; *ātmanaḥ*—of the mind.

TRANSLATION

Fixing the vital air and the mind in one of the six circles of vital air circulation within the body, thus concentrating one's mind on the transcendental pastimes of the Supreme Personality of Godhead, is called samādhi, or samādhāna, of the mind.

PURPORT

There are six circles of vital air circulation within the body. The first circle is within the belly, the second circle is in the area of the heart, the third is in the area of the lungs, the fourth is on the palate, the fifth is between the eyebrows, and the highest, the sixth circle, is above the brain. One has to fix his mind and the circulation of the vital air and thus think of the transcendental pastimes of the Supreme Lord. It is never mentioned that one should concentrate on the impersonal or void. It is clearly stated, *vaikuṇṭha-līlā. Līlā* means "pastimes." Unless the Absolute Truth, the Personality of Godhead, has transcendental activities, where is the scope for thinking of these pastimes? It is through the processes of devotional service, chanting and hearing of the pastimes of the Supreme Personality of Godhead, that one can achieve this concentration. As described in the *Śrīmad-Bhāgavatam*, the Lord appears and disappears according to His relationships with different devotees. The Vedic literatures contain many narrations of the Lord's pastimes, including the Battle of Kurukṣetra and historical facts relating to the life and precepts of devotees like Prahlāda Mahārāja, Dhruva Mahārāja and Ambarīṣa Mahārāja. One need only concentrate his mind on one such narration and become always absorbed in its thought. Then he will be in *samādhi. Samādhi* is not an artificial bodily state; it is the state achieved when the mind is virtually absorbed in thoughts of the Supreme Personality of Godhead.

TEXT 7

एतैरन्यैश्च पथिभिर्मनो दुष्टमसत्पथम् ।
बुद्ध्या युञ्जीत शनकैर्जितप्राणो ह्यतन्द्रितः ॥ ७ ॥

etair anyaiś ca pathibhir
mano duṣṭam asat-patham
buddhyā yuñjīta śanakair
jita-prāṇo hy atandritaḥ

etaiḥ—by these; *anyaiḥ*—by other; *ca*—and; *pathibhiḥ*—processes; *manaḥ*—the mind; *duṣṭam*—contaminated; *asat-patham*—on the path of material enjoyment; *buddhyā*—by the intelligence; *yuñjīta*—one must control; *śanakaiḥ*—gradually; *jita-prāṇaḥ*—the life air being fixed; *hi*—indeed; *atandritaḥ*—alert.

TRANSLATION

By these processes, or any other true process, one must control the contaminated, unbridled mind, which is always attracted by material enjoyment, and thus fix himself in thought of the Supreme Personality of Godhead.

PURPORT

Etair anyaiś ca. The general *yoga* process entails observing the rules and regulations, practicing the different sitting postures, concentrating the mind on the vital circulation of the air and then thinking of the Supreme Personality of Godhead in His Vaikuṇṭha pastimes. This is the general process of *yoga.* This same concentration can be achieved by other recommended processes, and therefore *anyaiś ca,* other methods, also can be applied. The essential point is that the mind, which is contaminated by material attraction, has to be bridled and concentrated on the Supreme Personality of Godhead. It cannot be fixed on something void or impersonal. For this reason, so-called *yoga* practices of voidism and impersonalism are not recommended in any standard *yoga-śāstra.* The real *yogī* is the devotee because his mind is always concentrated on the pastimes of Lord Kṛṣṇa. Therefore Kṛṣṇa consciousness is the topmost *yoga* system.

TEXT 8

शुचौ देशे प्रतिष्ठाप्य विजितासन आसनम् ।
तस्मिन् स्वस्ति समासीन ऋजुकायः समभ्यसेत् ॥ ८ ॥

śucau deśe pratiṣṭhāpya
vijitāsana āsanam
tasmin svasti samāsīna
ṛju-kāyaḥ samabhyaset

śucau deśe—in a sanctified place; *pratiṣṭhāpya*—after placing; *vijita-āsanaḥ*—controlling the sitting postures; *āsanam*—a seat; *tasmin*—in that place; *svasti samāsīnaḥ*—sitting in an easy posture; *ṛju-kāyaḥ*—keeping the body erect; *samabhyaset*—one should practice.

TRANSLATION

After controlling one's mind and sitting postures, one should spread a seat in a secluded and sanctified place, sit there in an easy posture, keeping the body erect, and practice breath control.

PURPORT

Sitting in an easy posture is called *svasti samāsīnaḥ*. It is recommended in the *yoga* scripture that one should put the soles of the feet between the two thighs and ankles and sit straight; that posture will help one to concentrate his mind on the Supreme Personality of Godhead. This very process is also recommended in *Bhagavad-gītā*, Sixth Chapter. It is further suggested that one sit in a secluded, sanctified spot. The seat should consist of deerskin and *kuśa* grass, topped with cotton.

TEXT 9

प्राणस्य शोधयेन्मार्गं पूरकुम्भकरेचकैः ।
प्रतिकूलेन वा चित्तं यथा स्थिरमचञ्चलम् ॥ ९ ॥

prāṇasya śodhayen mārgaṁ
pūra-kumbhaka-recakaiḥ
pratikūlena vā cittaṁ
yathā sthiram acañcalam

prāṇasya—of vital air; *śodhayet*—one should clear; *mārgam*—the passage; *pūra-kumbhaka-recakaiḥ*—by inhaling, retaining and exhaling; *pratikūlena*—by reversing; *vā*—or; *cittam*—the mind; *yathā*—so that; *sthiram*—steady; *acañcalam*—free from disturbances.

TRANSLATION

The yogī should clear the passage of vital air by breathing in the following manner: first he should inhale very deeply, then hold the breath in, and finally exhale. Or, reversing the process, the yogi can first exhale, then hold the breath outside, and finally inhale. This is done so that the mind may become steady and free from external disturbances.

PURPORT

These breathing exercises are performed to control the mind and fix it on the Supreme Personality of Godhead. *Sa vai manaḥ kṛṣṇa-padāravindayoḥ:* the devotee Ambarīṣa Mahārāja fixed his mind on the lotus feet of Kṛṣṇa twenty-four hours a day. The process of Kṛṣṇa consciousness is to chant Hare Kṛṣṇa and to hear the sound attentively so that the mind is fixed upon the transcendental vibration of Kṛṣṇa's name, which is nondifferent from Kṛṣṇa the personality. The real purpose of controlling the mind by the prescribed method of clearing the passage of the life air is achieved immediately if one fixes his mind directly on the lotus feet of Kṛṣṇa. The *haṭha-yoga* system, or breathing system, is especially recommended for those who are very absorbed in the concept of bodily existence, but one who can perform the simple process of chanting Hare Kṛṣṇa can fix the mind more easily.

Three different activities are recommended for clearing the passage of breath: *pūraka, kumbhaka* and *recaka.* Inhaling the breath is called *pūraka,* sustaining it within is called *kumbhaka,* and finally exhaling it is called *recaka.* These recommended processes can also be performed in the reverse order. After exhaling, one can keep the air outside for some time and then inhale. The nerves through which inhalation and exhalation are conducted are technically called *iḍā* and *piṅgalā.* The ultimate purpose of clearing the *iḍā* and *piṅgalā* passages is to divert the mind from material enjoyment. As stated in *Bhagavad-gītā,* one's mind is his enemy, and one's mind is also his friend; its position varies according to the different dealings of the living entity. If we divert our mind to thoughts of material enjoyment, then our mind becomes an enemy, and if we concentrate our mind on the lotus feet of Kṛṣṇa, then our mind is a friend. By the *yoga* system of *pūraka, kumbhaka* and *recaka* or by directly fixing the mind on the sound vibration of Kṛṣṇa or on the form of Kṛṣṇa, the same purpose is achieved. In *Bhagavad-gītā* it is said that one must practice the breathing exercise (*abhyāsa-yoga-yuktena*). by virtue of these processes of control, the mind cannot wander to external thoughts (*cetasā nānya-gāminā*). Thus one can fix his mind constantly on the Supreme Personality of Godhead and can attain (*yāti*) Him.

Practicing the *yoga* system of exercise and breath control is very difficult for a person in this age, and therefore Lord Caitanya recommended, *kīrtanīyaḥ sadā hariḥ:* one should always chant the holy name of the Supreme Lord, Kṛṣṇa, because Kṛṣṇa is the most suitable name of the Supreme Personality of Godhead. The name Kṛṣṇa and the Supreme Person Kṛṣṇa are nondifferent. Therefore, if one concentrates his mind on hearing and chanting Hare Kṛṣṇa, the same result is achieved.

TEXT 10

मनोऽचिरात्स्याद्विरजं जितश्वासस्य योगिनः ।
वाय्वग्निभ्यां यथा लोहं ध्मातं त्यजति वै मलम् ॥१०॥

mano 'cirāt syād virajaṁ
jita-śvāsasya yoginaḥ
vāyv-agnibhyāṁ yathā lohaṁ
dhmātaṁ tyajati vai malam

manaḥ—the mind; *acirāt*—soon; *syāt*—can be; *virajam*—free from disturbances; *jita-śvāsasya*—whose breathing is controlled; *yoginaḥ*—of the *yogī;* *vāyu agnibhyām*—by air and fire; *yathā*—just as; *loham*—gold; *dhmātam*—fanned; *tyajati*—becomes freed from; *vai*—certainly; *malam*—impurity.

TRANSLATION

The yogīs who practice such breathing exercises are very soon freed from all mental disturbances, just as gold, when put into fire and fanned with air, becomes free from all impurities.

PURPORT

This process of purifying the mind is also recommended by Lord Caitanya; He says that one should chant Hare Kṛṣṇa. He says further, *paraṁ vijayate:* "All glories to Śrī Kṛṣṇa *saṅkīrtana!*" All glories are given to the chanting of the holy names of Kṛṣṇa because as soon as one begins this process of chanting, the mind becomes purified. *Ceto-darpaṇa-mārjanam:* by chanting the holy name of Kṛṣṇa one is cleansed of the dirt that accumulates in the mind. One can purify the mind either by the breathing process or by the chanting process, just as one can purify gold by putting it in a fire and fanning it with a bellows.

TEXT 11

प्राणायामैर्दहेद्दोषान्धारणाभिश्च किल्बिषान् ।
प्रत्याहारेण संसर्गान्ध्यानेनानीश्वरान् गुणान् ॥११॥

prāṇāyāmair dahed doṣān
dhāraṇābhiś ca kilbiṣān
pratyāhāreṇa saṁsargān
dhyānenānīśvarān guṇān

prāṇāyāmaiḥ—by practice of *prāṇāyāma; dahet*—one can eradicate; *doṣān*—contaminations; *dhāraṇābhiḥ*—by concentrating the mind; *ca*—and; *kilbiṣān*—sinful activities; *pratyāhāreṇa*—by restraining the senses; *saṁsargān*—material association; *dhyānena*—by meditating; *anīśvarān guṇān*—the modes of material nature.

TRANSLATION

By practicing the process of prāṇāyāma, one can eradicate the contamination of his physiological condition, and by concentrating the mind one can become free from all sinful activities. By restraining the senses one can free himself from material association, and by meditating on the Supreme Personality of Godhead one can become free from the three modes of material attachment.

PURPORT

According to Āyur-vedic medical science the three items *kapha, pitta* and *vāyu* (phlegm, bile and air) maintain the physiological condition of the body. Modern medical science does not accept this physiological analysis as valid, but the ancient Āyur-vedic process of treatment is based upon these items. Āyur-vedic treatment concerns itself with the cause of these three elements, which are mentioned in many places in the *Bhāgavatam* as the basic conditions of the body. Here it is recommended that by practicing the breathing process of *prāṇāyāma* one can be released from contamination created by the principal physiological elements, by concentrating the mind one can become free from sinful activities, and by withdrawing the senses one can free himself from material association.

Ultimately, one has to meditate on the Supreme Personality of Godhead in order to be elevated to the transcendental position where he is no longer affected by the three modes of material nature. It is also confirmed in *Bhagavad-gītā* that one who engages himself in unalloyed devotional service at once becomes transcendental to the three modes of material nature and immediately realizes his identification with Brahman.

Sa guṇān samatītyaitān brahma-bhūyāya kalpate. For every item in the *yoga* system there is a parallel activity in *bhakti-yoga,* but the practice of *bhakti-yoga* is easier for this age. What was introduced by Lord Caitanya is not a new interpretation. *Bhakti-yoga* is a feasible process that begins with chanting and hearing. *Bhakti-yoga* and other *yogas* have as their ultimate goal the same Personality of Godhead, but one is practical, and the others are difficult. One has to purify his physiological condition by concentration and by restraint of the senses; then he can fix his mind upon the Supreme Personality of Godhead. That is called *samādhi.*

TEXT 12

यदा मनः स्वं विरजं योगेन सुसमाहितम् ।
काष्ठां भगवतो ध्यायेत्स्वनासाग्रावलोकनः ॥१२॥

yadā manaḥ svaṁ virajaṁ
yogena susamāhitam
kāṣṭhāṁ bhagavato dhyāyet
sva-nāsāgrāvalokanaḥ

yadā—when; *manaḥ*—the mind; *svam*—own; *virajam*—purified; *yogena*—by *yoga* practice; *su-samāhitam*—controlled; *kāṣṭhām*—the plenary expansion; *bhagavataḥ*—of the Supreme Personality of Godhead; *dhyāyet*—one should meditate upon; *sva-nāsā-agra*—the tip of one's nose; *avalokanaḥ*—looking at.

TRANSLATION

When the mind is perfectly purified by this practice of yoga, one should concentrate on the tip of the nose with half-closed eyes and see the form of the Supreme Personality of Godhead.

PURPORT

It is clearly mentioned here that one has to meditate upon the expansion of Viṣṇu. The word *kaṣṭhām* refers to Paramātmā, the expansion of the expansion of Viṣṇu. *Bhagavataḥ* refers to Lord Viṣṇu, the Supreme Personality of Godhead. The Supreme Godhead is Kṛṣṇa; from Him comes the first expansion, Baladeva, and from Baladeva come Saṅkarṣaṇa, Aniruddha and many other forms, followed by the *puruṣa-avatāras.* As mentioned in the previous verses (*puruṣārcanam*), this *puruṣa* is represented as the Paramātmā, or Supersoul. A description of the Supersoul, upon whom one must meditate, will be given in the following verses. In this verse it is clearly stated that one must meditate by fixing the vision on the tip of the nose and concentrating one's mind on the *kalā*, or the plenary expansion, of Viṣṇu.

TEXT 13

प्रसन्नवदनाम्भोजं पद्मगर्भारुणेक्षणम् ।
नीलोत्पलदलश्यामं शङ्खचक्रगदाधरम् ॥१३॥

prasanna-vadanāmbhojaṁ
padma-garbhāruṇekṣaṇam
nīlotpala-dala-śyāmaṁ
śaṅkha-cakra-gadā-dharam

prasanna—cheerful; *vadana*—countenance; *ambhojam*—lotuslike; *padma-garbha*—the interior of a lotus; *aruṇa*—ruddy; *īkṣaṇam*—with eyes; *nīla-utpala*—blue lotus; *dala*—petals; *śyāmam*—swarthy; *śaṅkha*—conch; *cakra*—discus; *gadā*—club; *dharam*—bearing.

TRANSLATION

The Supreme Personality of Godhead has a cheerful, lotuslike countenance with ruddy eyes like the interior of a lotus and a swarthy body like the petals of a blue lotus. He bears a conch, discus and mace in three of His hands.

PURPORT

It is definitely recommended herein that one concentrate his mind upon the form of Viṣṇu. There are twelve different forms of Viṣṇu, which are described in *Teachings of Lord Caitanya.* One cannot concentrate his mind on anything void or impersonal; the mind should be fixed on the personal form of the Lord, whose attitude is cheerful, as described in this verse. *Bhagavad-gītā* states that meditation on the impersonal or void features is very troublesome to the meditator. Those who are attached to the impersonal or void features of meditation have to undergo a difficult process because we are not accustomed to concentrating our minds upon anything impersonal. Actually such concentration is not even possible. *Bhagavad-gītā* also confirms that one should concentrate his mind on the Personality of Godhead.

The color of the Personality of Godhead, Kṛṣṇa, is described here as *nīlotpala-dala*, meaning that it is like that of a lotus flower with petals tinted blue and white. People always ask why Kṛṣṇa is blue. The color of the Lord has not been imagined by an artist. It is described in authoritative scripture. In the *Brahma-saṁhitā* also, the color of Kṛṣṇa's body is compared to that of a bluish cloud. The color of the Lord is not poetical imagination. There are authoritative descriptions in the *Brahma-saṁhitā, Śrīmad-Bhāgavatam, Bhagavad-gītā* and many of the *Purāṇas* of the Lord's body, His weapons and all other paraphernalia. The Lord's appearance is described here as *padma-garbhāruṇekṣaṇam.* His eyes resemble the inside of a lotus flower, and in His four hands He holds the four symbols: conchshell, discus, mace and lotus.

TEXT 14

लसत्पङ्कजकिञ्जल्कपीतकौशेयवाससम् ।
श्रीवत्सवक्षसं भ्राजत्कौस्तुभामुक्तकन्धरम् ॥१४॥

lasat-paṅkaja-kiñjalka-
pīta-kauśeya-vāsasam
śrīvatsa-vakṣasaṁ bhrājat
kaustubhāmukta-kandharam

lasat—shining; *paṅkaja*—of a lotus; *kiñjalka*—filaments; *pīta*—yellow; *kauśeya*—silk cloth; *vāsasam*—whose garment; *śrīvatsa*—bearing the mark of Śrīvatsa; *vakṣasam*—breast; *bhrājat*—brilliant; *kaustubha*—Kaustubha gem; *āmukta*—put on; *kandharam*—His neck.

TRANSLATION

His loins are covered by a shining cloth, yellowish like the filaments of a lotus. On His breast He bears the mark of Śrīvatsa, a curl of white hair. The brilliant Kaustubha gem is suspended from His neck.

PURPORT

The exact color of the garment of the Supreme Lord is described as saffron-yellow, just like the pollen of a lotus flower. The Kaustubha gem hanging on His chest is also described. His neck is beautifully decorated with jewels and pearls. The Lord is full in six opulences, one of which is wealth. He is very richly dressed with valuable jewels which are not visible within this material world.

TEXT 15

मत्तद्विरेफकलया परीतं वनमालया ।
परार्ध्यहारवलयकिरीटाङ्गदनूपुरम् ॥१५॥

matta-dvirepha-kalayā
parītaṁ vana-mālayā

parārdhya-hāra-valaya-
kirīṭāṅgada-nūpuram

matta—intoxicated; *dvi-repha*—with bees; *kalayā*—humming; *parītam*—garlanded; *vana-mālayā*—with a garland of forest flowers; *parārdhya*—priceless; *hāra*—pearl necklace; *valaya*—bracelets; *kirīṭa*—a crown; *aṅgada*—armlets; *nūpuram*—anklets.

TRANSLATION

He also wears around His neck a garland of attractive sylvan flowers, and a swarm of bees, intoxicated by its delicious fragrance, hums about the garland. He is further superbly adorned with a pearl necklace, a crown and pairs of armlets, bracelets and anklets.

PURPORT

From this description it appears that the flower garland of the Supreme Personality of Godhead is fresh. Actually, in Vaikuṇṭha, or the spiritual sky, there is nothing but freshness. Even the flowers picked from the trees and plants remain fresh, for everything in the spiritual sky retains its originality and does not fade. The fragrance of the flowers picked from the trees and made into garlands does not fade, for both the trees and the flowers are spiritual. When the flower is taken from the tree, it remains the same; it does not lose its aroma. The bees are equally attracted to the flowers whether they are on the garland or on the trees. The significance of spirituality is that everything is eternal and inexhaustible. Everything taken from everything remains everything, or, as has been stated, in the spiritual world one minus one equals one, and one plus one equals one. The bees hum around the fresh flowers, and their sweet sound is enjoyed by the Lord. The Lord's bangles, necklace, crown and anklets are all bedecked with invaluable jewels. Since the jewels and pearls are spiritual, there is no material calculation of their value.

TEXT 16

काञ्चीगुणोल्लसच्छ्रोणिं हृदयाम्भोजविष्टरम् ।
दर्शनीयतमं शान्तं मनोनयनवर्धनम् ॥१६॥

kāñcī-guṇollasac-chroṇiṁ
hṛdayāmbhoja-viṣṭaram
darśanīyatamaṁ śāntaṁ
mano-nayana-vardhanam

kāñcī—girdle; *guṇa*—quality; *ullasat*—brilliant; *śroṇim*—His loins and hips; *hṛdaya*—heart; *ambhoja*—lotus; *viṣṭaram*—whose seat; *darśanīya-tamam*—most charming to look at; *śāntam*—serene; *manaḥ*—minds, hearts; *nayana*—eyes; *vardhanam*—gladdening.

TRANSLATION

His loins and hips encircled by a girdle, He stands on the lotus of His devotee's heart. He is most charming to look at, and His serene aspect gladdens the eyes and souls of the devotees who behold Him.

PURPORT

The word *darśanīyatamam,* which is used in this verse, means that the Lord is so beautiful that the devotee-*yogī* does not wish to see anything else. His desire to see beautiful objects is completely satisfied by the sight of the Lord. In the material world we want to see beauty, but the desire is never satisfied. Because of material contamination, all the propensities we feel in the material world are ever unsatisfied. But when our desires to see, hear, touch, etc., are dovetailed for the satisfaction of the Supreme Personality of Godhead, they are on the level of the topmost perfection.

Although the Supreme Personality of Godhead in His eternal form is so beautiful and pleasing to the heart of the devotee, He does not attract the impersonalists, who want to meditate on His impersonal aspect. Such impersonal meditation is simply fruitless labor. The actual *yogīs,* with half-closed eyes, fix on the form of the Supreme Personality of Godhead, not upon anything void or impersonal.

TEXT 17

अपीच्यदर्शनं शश्वत्सर्वलोकनमस्कृतम् ।
सन्तं वयसि कैशोरे भृत्यानुग्रहकातरम् ॥१७॥

apīcya-darśanaṁ śaśvat
sarva-loka-namaskṛtam
santaṁ vayasi kaiśore
bhṛtyānugraha-kātaram

apīcya-darśanam—very beautiful to see; *śaśvat*—eternal; *sarva-loka*—by all the inhabitants of every planet; *namaḥ-kṛtam*—worshipable; *santam*—situated; *vayasi*—in youth; *kaiśore*—in boyhood; *bhṛtya*—upon His devotee; *anugraha*—to bestow blessings; *kātaram*—eager.

TRANSLATION

The Lord is eternally very beautiful, and He is worshipable by all the inhabitants of every planet. He is ever youthful and always eager to bestow His blessing upon His devotees.

PURPORT

The word *sarva-loka-namaskṛtam* means that He is worshipable by everyone on every planet. There are innumerable planets in the material world and innumerable planets in the spiritual world as well. On each planet there are innumerable inhabitants who worship the Lord, for the Lord is worshipable by all but the impersonalists. The Supreme Lord is very beautiful. The word *śaśvat* is significant. It is not that He appears beautiful to the devotees but is ultimately impersonal. *Śaśvat* means "ever existing." That beauty is not temporary. It is ever existing—He is always youthful. In the *Brahma-saṁhitā* (5.33) it is also stated: *advaitam acyutam anādim ananta-rūpam ādyaṁ purāṇa-puruṣaṁ nava-yauvanaṁ ca.* The original person is one without a second, yet He never appears old; He always appears as ever fresh as a blooming youth.

The Lord's facial expression always indicates that He is ready to show favor and benediction to the devotees; for the nondevotees, however, He is silent. As stated in *Bhagavad-gītā,* although He acts equally to everyone because He is the Supreme Personality of Godhead and because all living entities are His sons, He is especially inclined to those engaged in devotional service. The same fact is confirmed here: He is always anxious to show favor to the devotees. Just as the devotees are always eager to render service unto the Supreme Personality of Godhead, the Lord is also very eager to bestow benediction upon the pure devotees.

TEXT 18

कीर्तन्यतीर्थयशसं पुण्यश्लोकयशस्करम् ।
ध्यायेद्देवं समग्राङ्गं यावन्न च्यवते मनः ॥१८॥

kīrtanya-tīrtha-yaśasaṁ
puṇya-śloka-yaśaskaram
dhyāyed devaṁ samagrāṅgaṁ
yāvan na cyavate manaḥ

kīrtanya—worth singing; *tīrtha-yaśasam*—the glories of the Lord; *puṇya-śloka*—of the devotees; *yaśaḥ-karam*—enhancing the glory; *dhyāyet*—one should meditate; *devam*—upon the Lord; *samagra-aṅgam*—all the limbs; *yāvat*—as much as; *na*—not; *cyavate*—deviates; *manaḥ*—the mind.

TRANSLATION

The glory of the Lord is always worth singing, for His glories enhance the glories of His devotees. One should therefore meditate upon the Supreme Personality of Godhead and upon His devotees. One should meditate on the eternal form of the Lord until the mind becomes fixed.

PURPORT

One has to fix his mind on the Supreme Personality of Godhead constantly. When one is accustomed to thinking of one of the innumerable forms of the Lord—Kṛṣṇa, Viṣṇu, Rāma, Nārāyaṇa, etc.—he has reached the perfection of *yoga.* This is confirmed in the *Brahma-saṁhitā:* a person who has developed pure love for the Lord, and whose eyes are smeared with the ointment of transcendental loving exchange, always sees within his heart the Supreme Personality of Godhead. The devotees especially see the Lord in the beautiful blackish form of Śyāmasundara. That is the perfection of *yoga.* This *yoga* system should be continued until the mind does not vacillate for a moment. *Oṁ tad viṣṇoḥ paramaṁ padaṁ sadā paśyanti sūrayaḥ:* the form of Viṣṇu is the highest individuality and is always visible to sages and saintly persons.

The same purpose is served when a devotee worships the form of the Lord in the temple. There is no difference between devotional service in the temple and meditation on the form of the Lord, since the form of the Lord is the same whether He appears within the mind or in some concrete element. There are eight kinds of forms recommended for the devotees to see. The forms may be made out of sand, clay, wood or stone, they may be contemplated within the mind or made of jewels, metal or painted colors, but all the forms are of the same value. It is not that one who meditates on the form within the mind sees differently from one who worships the form in the temple. The Supreme Personality of Godhead is absolute, and there is therefore no difference between the two. The impersonalists, who desire to disregard the eternal form of the Lord, imagine some round figure. They especially prefer the *oṁkāra,* which also has form. In *Bhagavad-gītā* it is stated that *oṁkāra* is the letter form of the Lord. Similarly, there are statue forms and painting forms of the Lord.

Another significant word in this verse is *puṇya-śloka-yaśaskaram.* The devotee is called *puṇya-śloka.* As one becomes purified by chanting the holy name of the Lord, so one can become purified simply by chanting the name of a holy devotee. The pure devotee of the Lord and the Lord Himself are nondifferent. It is sometimes feasible to chant the name of a holy devotee. This is a very sanctified process. Lord Caitanya was once chanting the holy names of the *gopīs* when His students criticized Him: "Why are You chanting the names of the *gopīs*? Why not 'Kṛṣṇa'?" Lord Caitanya was irritated by the criticism, and so there was some misunderstanding between Him and His students. He wanted to chastise them for desiring to instruct Him on the transcendental process of chanting.

The beauty of the Lord is that the devotees who are connected with His activities are also glorified. Arjuna, Prahlāda, Janaka Mahārāja, Bali Mahārāja and many other devotees were not even in the renounced order of life, but were householders. Some of them, such as Prahlāda Mahārāja and Bali Mahārāja, were born of demoniac families. Prahlāda Mahārāja's father was a demon, and Bali Mahārāja was the grandson of Prahlāda Mahārāja, but still they have become famous because of their association with the Lord. Anyone who is eternally associated with the Lord is glorified with the Lord. The conclusion is that a perfect *yogī* should always be accustomed to seeing the form of the Lord, and unless the mind is fixed in that way, he should continue practicing *yoga*.

TEXT 19

स्थितं व्रजन्तमासीनं शयानं वा गुहाशयम् ।
प्रेक्षणीयेहितं ध्यायेच्छुद्धभावेन चेतसा ॥१९॥

sthitaṁ vrajantam āsīnaṁ
śayānaṁ vā guhāśayam
prekṣaṇīyehitaṁ dhyāyec
chuddha-bhāvena cetasā

sthitam—standing; *vrajantam*—moving; *āsīnam*—sitting; *śayānam*—lying down; *vā*—or; *guhā-āśayam*—the Lord dwelling in the heart; *prekṣaṇīya*—beautiful; *īhitam*—pastimes; *dhyāyet*—he should visualize; *śuddha-bhāvena*—pure; *cetasā*—by the mind.

TRANSLATION

Thus always merged in devotional service, the yogī visualizes the Lord standing, moving, lying down or sitting within him, for the pastimes of the Supreme Lord are always beautiful and attractive.

PURPORT

The process of meditating on the form of the Supreme Personality of Godhead within oneself and the process of chanting the glories and pastimes of the Lord are the same. The only difference is that hearing and fixing the mind on the pastimes of the Lord is easier than visualizing the form of the Lord within one's heart because as soon as one begins to think of the Lord, especially in this age, the mind becomes disturbed, and due to so much agitation, the process of seeing the Lord within the mind is interrupted. When there is sound vibrated praising the transcendental pastimes of the Lord, however, one is forced to hear. That hearing process enters into the mind, and the practice of *yoga* is automatically performed. For example, even a child can hear and derive the benefit of meditating on the pastimes of the Lord simply by listening to a reading from the *Bhāgavatam* that describes the Lord as He is going to the pasturing ground with His cows and friends. Hearing includes applying the mind. In this age of Kali-yuga, Lord Caitanya has recommended that one should always engage in chanting and hearing *Bhagavad-gītā*. The Lord also says that the *mahātmās*, or great souls, always engage in the process of chanting the glories of the Lord, and just by hearing, others derive the same benefit. *Yoga* necessitates meditation on the transcendental pastimes of the Lord, whether He is standing, moving, lying down, etc.

TEXT 20

तस्मिँल्लब्धपदं चित्तं सर्वावयवसंस्थितम् ।
विलक्ष्यैकत्र संयुज्यादङ्गे भगवतो मुनिः ॥२०॥

tasmil̐ labdha-padaṁ cittaṁ
sarvāvayava-saṁsthitam
vilakṣyaikatra saṁyujyād
aṅge bhagavato muniḥ

tasmin—on the form of the Lord; *labdha-padam*—fixed; *cittam*—the mind; *sarva*—all; *avayava*—limbs; *saṁsthitam*—fixed upon; *vilakṣya*—having distinguished; *ekatra*—in one place; *saṁyujyāt*—should fix the mind; *aṅge*—on each limb; *bhagavataḥ*—of the Lord; *muniḥ*—the sage.

TRANSLATION

In fixing his mind on the eternal form of the Lord, the yogī should not take a collective view of all His limbs, but should fix the mind on each individual limb of the Lord.

PURPORT

The word *muni* is very significant. *Muni* means one who is very expert in mental speculation or in thinking, feeling and willing. He is not mentioned here as a devotee or *yogī*. Those who try to meditate on the form of the Lord are called *munis*, or less intelligent, whereas those who render actual service to the Lord are called *bhakti-yogīs*. The thought process described below is for the education of the *muni*. In order to convince the *yogī* that the Absolute Truth, or Supreme Personality of Godhead, is never impersonal at any time, the following verses prescribe observing the Lord in His personal form, limb after limb. To think of the Lord as a whole may sometimes be impersonal; therefore, it is recommended here that one first think of His lotus feet, then His ankles, then the thighs, then the waist, then the chest, then the neck, then the face and so on. One should begin from the lotus feet and gradually rise to the upper limbs of the transcendental body of the Lord.

TEXT 21

सञ्चिन्तयेद्भगवतश्चरणारविन्दं
वज्राङ्कुशध्वजसरोरुहलाञ्छनाढ्यम् ।
उत्तुङ्गरक्तविलसन्नखचक्रवाल-
ज्योत्स्नाभिराहतमहद्धृदयान्धकारम् ॥२१॥

sañcintayed bhagavataś caraṇāravindaṁ
vajrāṅkuśa-dhvaja-saroruha-lāñchanāḍhyam
uttuṅga-rakta-vilasan-nakha-cakravāla-
jyotsnābhir āhata-mahad-dhṛdayāndhakāram

sañcintayet—he should concentrate; *bhagavataḥ*—of the Lord; *caraṇa-aravindam*—on the lotus feet; *vajra*—thunderbolt; *aṅkuśa*—goad (rod for driving elephants); *dhvaja*—banner; *saroruha*—lotus; *lāñchana*—marks; *āḍhyam*—adorned with; *uttuṅga*—prominent; *rakta*—red; *vilasat*—brilliant; *nakha*—nails; *cakravāla*—the circle of the moon; *jyotsnābhiḥ*—with splendor; *āhata*—dispelled; *mahat*—thick; *hṛdaya*—of the heart; *andhakāram*—darkness.

TRANSLATION

The devotee should first concentrate his mind on the Lord's lotus feet, which are adorned with the marks of a thunderbolt, a goad, a banner and a lotus. The splendor of their beautiful ruby nails resembles the orb of the moon and dispels the thick gloom of one's heart.

PURPORT

The Māyāvādī says that because one is unable to fix his mind on the impersonal existence of the Absolute Truth, one can imagine any form he likes and fix his mind on that imaginary form; but such a process is not recommended here. Imagination is always imagination and results only in further imagination.

A concrete description of the eternal form of the Lord is given here. The Lord's sole is depicted with distinctive lines resembling a thunderbolt, a flag, a lotus flower and a goad. The luster of His toenails, which are brilliantly prominent, resembles the light of the moon. If a *yogī* looks upon the marks of the Lord's sole and on the blazing brilliance of His nails, then he can be freed from the darkness of ignorance in material existence. This liberation is not achieved by mental speculation, but by seeing the light emanating from the lustrous toenails of the Lord. In other words, one has to fix his mind first on the lotus feet of the Lord if he wants to be freed from the darkness of ignorance in material existence.

TEXT 22

यच्छौचनिःसृतसरित्प्रवरोदकेन
तीर्थेन मूर्ध्न्यधिकृतेन शिवः शिवोऽभूत् ।
ध्यातुर्मनःशमलशैलनिसृष्टवज्रं
ध्यायेच्चिरं भगवतश्चरणारविन्दम् ॥२२॥

yac-chauca-niḥsṛta-sarit-pravarodakena
tīrthena mūrdhny adhikṛtena śivaḥ śivo 'bhūt
dhyātur manaḥ-śamala-śaila-nisṛṣṭa-vajraṁ
dhyāyec ciraṁ bhagavataś caraṇāravindam

yat—the Lord's lotus feet; *śauca*—washing; *niḥsṛta*—gone forth; *sarit-pravara*—of the Ganges; *udakena*—by the water; *tīrthena*—holy; *mūrdhni*—on his head; *adhikṛtena*—borne; *śivaḥ*—Lord Śiva; *śivaḥ*—auspicious; *abhūt*—became; *dhyātuḥ*—of the meditator; *manaḥ*—in the mind; *śamala-śaila*—the mountain of sin; *nisṛṣṭa*—hurled; *vajram*—thunderbolt; *dhyāyet*—one should meditate; *ciram*—for a long time; *bhagavataḥ*—of the Lord; *caraṇa-aravindam*—on the lotus feet.

TRANSLATION

The blessed Lord Śiva becomes all the more blessed by bearing on his head the holy waters of the Ganges, which has its source in the water that washed the Lord's lotus feet. The Lord's feet act like thunderbolts hurled to shatter the mountain of sin stored in the mind of the meditating devotee. One should therefore meditate on the lotus feet of the Lord for a long time.

PURPORT

In this verse the position of Lord Śiva is specifically mentioned. The impersonalist suggests that the Absolute Truth has no form and that one can therefore equally imagine the form of Viṣṇu or Lord Śiva or the goddess Durgā or their son Gaṇeśa. But actually the Supreme Personality of Godhead is the supreme master of everyone. In the *Caitanya-caritāmṛta* (*Ādi* 5.142) it is said, *ekale īśvara kṛṣṇa, ara saba bhṛtya:* the Supreme Lord is Kṛṣṇa, and everyone else, including Lord Śiva and Lord Brahmā—not to mention other demigods—is a servant of Kṛṣṇa. The same principle is described here. Lord Śiva is important because he is holding on his head the holy Ganges water, which has its origin in the foot-wash of Lord Viṣṇu. In the *Hari-bhakti-vilāsa,* by Sanātana Gosvāmī, it is said that anyone who puts the Supreme Lord and the demigods, including Lord Śiva and Lord Brahmā, on the same level, at once becomes a *pāṣaṇḍī,* or atheist. We should never consider that the Supreme Lord Viṣṇu and the demigods are on an equal footing.

Another significant point of this verse is that the mind of the conditioned soul, on account of its association with the material energy from time immemorial, contains heaps of dirt in the form of desires to lord it over material nature. This dirt is like a mountain, but a mountain can be shattered when hit by a thunderbolt. Meditating on the lotus feet of the Lord acts like a thunderbolt on the mountain of dirt in the mind of the *yogī.* If a *yogī* wants to shatter the mountain of dirt in his mind, he should concentrate on the lotus feet of the Lord and not imagine something void or impersonal. Because the dirt has accumulated like a solid mountain, one must meditate on the lotus feet of the Lord for quite a long time. For one who is accustomed to thinking of the lotus feet of the Lord constantly, however, it is a different matter. The devotees are so fixed on the lotus feet of the Lord that they do not think of anything else. Those who practice the *yoga* system must meditate on the lotus feet of the Lord for a long time after following the regulative principles and thereby controlling the senses.

It is specifically mentioned here, *bhagavataś caraṇāravindam:* one has to think of the lotus feet of the Lord. The Māyāvādīs imagine that one can think of the lotus feet of Lord Śiva or Lord Brahmā or the goddess Durgā to achieve liberation, but this is not so. *Bhagavataḥ* is specifically mentioned. *Bhagavataḥ* means "of the Supreme Personality of Godhead, Viṣṇu," and no one else. Another significant phrase in this verse is *śivaḥ śivo 'bhūt.* By his constitutional position, Lord Śiva is always great and auspicious, but since he has accepted on his head the Ganges water, which emanated from the lotus feet of the Lord, he has become even more auspicious and important. The stress is on the lotus feet of the Lord. A relationship with the lotus feet of the Lord can even enhance the importance of Lord Śiva, what to speak of other, ordinary living entities.

TEXT 23

जानुद्वयं जलजलोचनया जनन्या
लक्ष्म्याखिलस्य सुरवन्दितया विधातुः ।
ऊर्वोर्निधाय करपल्लवरोचिषा यत्
संलालितं हृदि विभोरभवस्य कुर्यात् ॥२३॥

jānu-dvayaṁ jalaja-locanayā jananyā
lakṣmyākhilasya sura-vanditayā vidhātuḥ
ūrvor nidhāya kara-pallava-rociṣā yat
saṁlālitaṁ hṛdi vibhor abhavasya kuryāt

jānu-dvayam—up to the knees; *jalaja-locanayā*—lotus-eyed; *jananyā*—mother; *lakṣmyā*—by Lakṣmī; *akhilasya*—of the entire universe; *sura-vanditayā*—worshiped by the demigods; *vidhātuḥ*—of Brahmā; *ūrvoḥ*—at the thighs; *nidhāya*—having placed; *kara-pallava-rociṣā*—with her lustrous fingers; *yat*—which; *saṁlālitam*—massaged; *hṛdi*—in the heart; *vibhoḥ*—of the Lord; *abhavasya*—transcendental to material existence; *kuryāt*—one should meditate.

TRANSLATION

The yogī should fix in his heart the activities of Lakṣmī, the goddess of fortune, who is worshiped by all demigods and is the mother of the supreme person, Brahmā. She can always be found massaging the legs and thighs of the transcendental Lord, very carefully serving Him in this way.

PURPORT

Brahmā is the appointed lord of the universe. Because his father is Garbhodakaśāyī Viṣṇu, Lakṣmī, the goddess of fortune, is automatically his mother. Lakṣmījī is worshiped by all demigods and by the inhabitants of other planets as well. Human beings are also eager to receive favor from the goddess of fortune. Lakṣmī is always engaged in massaging the legs and thighs of the Supreme Personality of Godhead Nārāyaṇa, who is lying on the ocean of Garbha within the universe. Brahmā is described here as the son of the goddess of fortune, but actually he was not born of her womb. Brahmā takes his birth from the abdomen of the Lord Himself. A lotus flower grows from the abdomen of Garbhodakaśāyī Viṣṇu, and Brahmā is born there. Therefore Lakṣmījī's massaging of the thighs of the Lord should not be taken as the behavior of an ordinary wife. The Lord is transcendental to the behavior of the ordinary male and female. The word *abhavasya* is very significant, for it indicates that He could produce Brahmā without the assistance of the goddess of fortune.

Since transcendental behavior is different from mundane behavior, it should not be taken that the Lord receives service from His wife just as a demigod or human being might receive service from his wife. It is advised here that the *yogī* always keep this picture in his heart. The devotee always thinks of this relationship between Lakṣmī and Nārāyaṇa; therefore he does not meditate on the mental plane as impersonalists and voidists do.

Bhava means "one who accepts a material body," and *abhava* means "one who does not accept a material body but descends in the original, spiritual body." Lord Nārāyaṇa is not born of anything material. Matter is generated from matter, but He is not born of matter. Brahmā is born after the creation, but since the Lord existed before the creation, the Lord has no material body.

TEXT 24

ऊरू सुपर्णभुजयोरधिशोभमाना-
वोजोनिधी अतसिकाकुसुमावभासौ ।
व्यालम्बिपीतवरवाससि वर्तमान-
काञ्चीकलापपरिरम्भि नितम्बबिम्बम् ॥२४॥

ūrū suparṇa-bhujayor adhi śobhamānāv
ojo-nidhī atasikā-kusumāvabhāsau
vyālambi-pīta-vara-vāsasi vartamāna-
kāñcī-kalāpa-parirambhi nitamba-bimbam

ūrū—the two thighs; *suparṇa*—of Garuḍa; *bhujayoḥ*—the two shoulders; *adhi*—on; *śobhamānau*—beautiful; *ojaḥ-nidhī*—the storehouse of all energy; *atasikā-kusuma*—of the linseed flower; *avabhāsau*—like the luster; *vyālambi*—extending down; *pīta*—yellow; *vara*—exquisite; *vāsasi*—on the cloth; *vartamāna*—being; *kāñcī-kalāpa*—by a girdle; *parirambhi*—encircled; *nitamba-bimbam*—His rounded hips.

TRANSLATION

Next, the yogi should fix his mind in meditation on the Personality of Godhead's thighs, the storehouse of all energy. The Lord's thighs are whitish blue, like the luster of the linseed flower, and appear most graceful when the Lord is carried on the shoulders of Garuḍa. Also the yogī should contemplate

His rounded hips, which are encircled by a girdle that rests on the exquisite yellow silk cloth that extends down to His ankles.

PURPORT

The Personality of Godhead is the reservoir of all strength, and His strength rests on the thighs of His transcendental body. His whole body is full of opulences: all riches, all strength, all fame, all beauty, all knowledge and all renunciation. The *yogī* is advised to meditate upon the transcendental form of the Lord, beginning from the soles of the feet and then gradually rising to the knees, to the thighs, and finally arriving at the face. The system of meditating on the Supreme Personality of Godhead begins from His feet.

The description of the transcendental form of the Lord is exactly represented in the *arcā-vigraha,* the statue in the temples. Generally, the lower part of the body of the statue of the Lord is covered with yellow silk. That is the Vaikuṇṭha dress, or the dress the Lord wears in the spiritual sky. This cloth extends down to the Lord's ankles. Thus, since the *yogī* has so many transcendental objectives on which to meditate, there is no reason for his meditating on something imaginary, as is the practice of the so-called *yogīs* whose objective is impersonal.

TEXT 25

नाभिह्रदं भुवनकोशगुहोदरस्थं
यत्रात्मयोनिधिषणाखिललोकपद्मम् ।
व्यूढं हरिन्मणिवृषस्तनयोरमुष्य
ध्यायेद् द्वयं विशदहारमयूखगौरम् ॥२५॥

nābhi-hradaṁ bhuvana-kośa-guhodara-sthaṁ
yatrātma-yoni-dhiṣaṇākhila-loka-padmam
vyūḍhaṁ harin-maṇi-vṛṣa-stanayor amuṣya
dhyāyed dvayaṁ viśada-hāra-mayūkha-gauram

nābhi-hradam—the navel lake; *bhuvana-kośa*—of all the worlds; *guhā*—the foundation; *udara*—on the abdomen; *stham*—situated; *yatra*—where; *ātma-yoni*—of Brahmā; *dhiṣaṇa*—residence; *akhila-loka*—containing all planetary systems; *padmam*—lotus; *vyūḍham*—sprang up; *harit-maṇi*—like emeralds; *vṛṣa*—most exquisite; *stanayoḥ*—of nipples; *amuṣya*—of the Lord; *dhyāyet*—he should meditate on; *dvayam*—the pair; *viśada*—white; *hāra*—of pearl necklaces; *mayūkha*—from the light; *gauram*—whitish.

TRANSLATION

The yogī should then meditate on His moonlike navel in the center of His abdomen. From His navel, which is the foundation of the entire universe, sprang the lotus stem containing all the different planetary systems. The lotus is the residence of Brahmā, the first created being. In the same way, the yogī should concentrate his mind on the Lord's nipples, which resemble a pair of most exquisite emeralds and which appear whitish because of the rays of the milk-white pearl necklaces adorning His chest.

PURPORT

The *yogī* is advised next to meditate upon the navel of the Lord, which is the foundation of all material creation. Just as a child is connected to his mother by the umbilical cord, so the first-born living creature, Brahmā, by the supreme will of the Lord, is connected to the Lord by a lotus stem. In the previous verse it was stated that the goddess of fortune, Lakṣmī, who engages in massaging the legs, ankles and thighs of the Lord, is called the mother of Brahmā, but actually Brahmā is born from the abdomen of the Lord, not from the abdomen of his mother. These are inconceivable conceptions of the Lord, and one should not think materially, "How can the father give birth to a child?"

It is explained in the *Brahma-saṁhitā* that each limb of the Lord has the potency of every other limb; because everything is spiritual, His parts are not conditioned. The Lord can see with His ears. The material ear can hear but cannot see, but we understand from the *Brahma-saṁhitā* that the Lord can also see with His ears and hear with His eyes. Any organ of His transcendental body can function as any other organ. His abdomen is the foundation of all the planetary systems. Brahmā holds the post of the creator of all planetary systems, but his engineering energy is generated from the abdomen of the Lord. Any creative function in the universe always has a direct connecting link with the Lord. The necklace of pearls which decorates the upper portion of the Lord's body is also spiritual, and therefore the *yogī* is advised to gaze at the whitish luster of the pearls decorating His chest.

TEXT 26

वक्षोऽधिवासमृषभस्य महाविभूतेः
पुंसां मनोनयननिर्वृतिमादधानम् ।
कण्ठं च कौस्तुभमणेरधिभूषणार्थं
कुर्यान्मनस्यखिललोकनमस्कृतस्य ॥२६॥

vakṣo 'dhivāsam ṛṣabhasya mahā-vibhūteḥ
puṁsāṁ mano-nayana-nirvṛtim ādadhānam
kaṇṭhaṁ ca kaustubha-maṇer adhibhūṣaṇārthaṁ
kuryān manasy akhila-loka-namaskṛtasya

vakṣaḥ—the chest; *adhivāsam*—the abode; *ṛṣabhasya*—of the Supreme Personality of Godhead; *mahā-vibhūteḥ*—of Mahā-Lakṣmī; *puṁsām*—of persons; *manaḥ*—to the mind; *nayana*—to the eyes; *nirvṛtim*—transcendental pleasure; *ādadhānam*—bestowing; *kaṇṭham*—the neck; *ca*—also; *kaustubha-maṇeḥ*—of the Kaustubha gem; *adhibhūṣaṇa-artham*—which enhances the beauty; *kuryāt*—he should meditate on; *manasi*—in the mind; *akhila-loka*—by the entire universe; *namaskṛtasya*—who is adored.

TRANSLATION

The yogī should then meditate on the chest of the Supreme Personality of Godhead, the abode of goddess Mahā-Lakṣmī. The Lord's chest is the source of all transcendental pleasure for the mind and full satisfaction for the eyes. The yogī should then imprint on his mind the neck of the Personality of Godhead, who is adored by the entire universe. The neck of the Lord serves to enhance the beauty of the Kaustubha gem, which hangs on His chest.

PURPORT

In the *Upaniṣads* it is said that the various energies of the Lord are working to create, destroy and maintain. These inconceivable varieties of energy are stored in the bosom of the Lord. As people generally say, God is all-powerful. That prowess is represented by Mahā-Lakṣmī, the reservoir of all energies, who is situated on the bosom of the transcendental form of the Lord. The *yogī* who can meditate perfectly on that spot on the transcendental form of the Lord can derive many material powers, which comprise the eight perfections of the *yoga* system.

It is stated herein that the beauty of the neck of the Lord enhances the beauty of the Kaustubha gem rather than vice versa. The gem itself becomes more beautiful because it is situated on the neck of the Lord. A *yogī* is therefore recommended to meditate upon the Lord's neck. The Lord's transcendental form can either be meditated upon in the mind or placed in a temple in the form of a statue and decorated in such a way that everyone can contemplate it. Temple worship, therefore, is meant for persons who are not so advanced that they can meditate upon the form of the Lord. There is no difference between constantly visiting the temple and directly seeing the transcendental form of the Lord; they are of equal value. The advantageous position of the *yogī* is that he can sit anywhere in a solitary place and meditate upon the form of the Lord. A less advanced person, however, has to go to the temple, and as long as he does not go to the temple he is unable to see the form of the Lord. Either by hearing, seeing or meditating, the objective is the transcendental form of the Lord; there is no question of voidness or impersonalism. The Lord can bestow the blessings of transcendental pleasure upon either the visitor of the temple, the meditator-*yogī* or one who hears about the Lord's transcendental form from scriptures like the *Śrīmad-Bhāgavatam* or *Bhagavad-gītā.* There are nine processes for executing devotional service, of which *smaraṇam,* or meditation, is one. *Yogīs* take advantage of the process of *smaraṇam,* whereas *bhakti-yogīs* take special advantage of the process of hearing and chanting.

TEXT 27

बाहूंश्च मन्दरगिरेः परिवर्तनेन
निर्णिक्तबाहुवलयानधिलोकपालान् ।
सञ्चिन्तयेद्दशशतारमसह्यतेजः
शङ्खं च तत्करसरोरुहराजहंसम् ॥२७॥

bāhūṁś ca mandara-gireḥ parivartanena
nirṇikta-bāhu-valayān adhiloka-pālān
sañcintayed daśa-śatāram asahya-tejaḥ
śaṅkhaṁ ca tat-kara-saroruha-rāja-haṁsam

bāhūn—the arms; *ca*—and; *mandara-gireḥ*—of Mount Mandara; *parivartanena*—by the revolving; *nirṇikta*—polished; *bāhu-valayān*—the arm ornaments; *adhiloka-pālān*—the source of the controllers of the universe; *sañcintayet*—one should meditate on; *daśa-śata-aram*—the Sudarśana disc (ten hundred spokes); *asahya-tejaḥ*—dazzling luster; *śaṅkham*—the conch; *ca*—also; *tat-kara*—in the hand of the Lord; *saroruha*—lotuslike; *rāja-haṁsam*—like a swan.

TRANSLATION

The yogī should further meditate upon the Lord's four arms, which are the source of all the powers of the demigods who control the various functions of material nature. Then the yogi should concentrate on the polished ornaments, which were burnished by Mount Mandara as it revolved. He should also duly contemplate the Lord's discus, the Sudarśana cakra, which contains one thousand spokes and a dazzling luster, as well as the conch, which looks like a swan in His lotuslike palm.

PURPORT

All departments of law and order emanate from the arms of the Supreme Personality of Godhead. The law and order of the universe is directed by different demigods, and it is here said to emanate from the Lord's arms. Mandara Hill is mentioned here because when the ocean was churned by the demons on one side and the demigods on the other, Mandara Hill was taken as the churning rod. The Lord in His tortoise incarnation became the pivot for the churning rod, and thus His ornaments were polished by the turning of Mandara Hill. In other words, the ornaments on the arms of the Lord are as brilliant and lustrous as if they had been polished very recently. The wheel in the hand of the Lord, called the Sudarśana *cakra*, has one thousand spokes. The *yogī* is advised to meditate upon each of the spokes. He should meditate upon each and every one of the component parts of the transcendental form of the Lord.

TEXT 28

कौमोदकीं भगवतो दयितां स्मरेत
दिग्धामरातिभटशोणितकर्दमेन ।
मालां मधुव्रतवरूथगिरोपघुष्टां
चैत्यस्य तत्त्वममलं मणिमस्य कण्ठे ॥२८॥

kaumodakīṁ bhagavato dayitāṁ smareta
digdhām arāti-bhaṭa-śoṇita-kardamena
mālāṁ madhuvrata-varūtha-giropaghuṣṭām
caityasya tattvam amalaṁ maṇim asya kaṇṭhe

kaumodakīm—the club named Kaumodakī; *bhagavataḥ*—of the Personality of Godhead; *dayitām*—very dear; *smareta*—one should remember; *digdhām*—smeared; *arāti*—of the enemies; *bhaṭa*—soldiers; *śoṇita-kardamena*—with the bloodstains; *mālām*—the garland; *madhuvrata*—of bumblebees; *varūtha*—of a swarm; *girā*—with the sound; *upaghuṣṭām*—surrounded; *caityasya*—of the living entity; *tattvam*—principle, truth; *amalam*—pure; *maṇim*—the pearl necklace; *asya*—of the Lord; *kaṇṭhe*—on the neck.

TRANSLATION

The yogī should meditate upon His club, which is named Kaumodakī and is very dear to Him. This club smashes the demons, who are always inimical soldiers, and is smeared with their blood. One should also concentrate on the nice garland on the neck of the Lord, which is always surrounded by bumblebees, with their nice buzzing sound, and one should meditate upon the

pearl necklace on the Lord's neck, which is considered to represent the pure living entities who are always engaged in His service.

PURPORT

The *yogī* must contemplate the different parts of the transcendental body of the Lord. Here it is stated that the constitutional position of the living entities should be understood. There are two kinds of living entities mentioned here. One is called the *arāti.* They are averse to understanding the pastimes of the Supreme Personality of Godhead. For them, the Lord appears with His hand clutching the terrible mace, which is always smeared with bloodstains from His killing of demons. Demons are also sons of the Supreme Personality of Godhead. As stated in *Bhagavad-gītā,* all the different species of living entities are sons of the Supreme Personality of Godhead. There are, however, two classes of living entities, who act in two different ways. The Supreme Lord keeps on His neck those living entities who are pure, as one protects the jewels and pearls on the bosom and neck of one's body. Those living entities in pure Kṛṣṇa consciousness are symbolized by the pearls on His neck. Those who are demons and are inimical towards the pastimes of the Supreme Personality of Godhead are punished by His mace, which is always smeared with the blood of such fallen living entities. The club of the Lord is very dear to Him because He uses this instrument to smash the bodies of the demons and mix their blood. As mud is kneaded with water and earth, so the earthly bodies of the enemies of the Lord, or the atheists, are smashed by the club of the Lord, which becomes muddied with the blood of such demons.

TEXT 29

भृत्यानुकम्पितधियेह गृहीतमूर्तेः
सञ्चिन्तयेद्भगवतो वदनारविन्दम् ।
यद्विस्फुरन्मकरकुण्डलवल्गितेन
विद्योतितामलकपोलमुदारनासम् ॥२९॥

bhṛtyānukampita-dhiyeha gṛhīta-mūrteḥ
sañcintayed bhagavato vadanāravindam
yad visphuran-makara-kuṇḍala-valgitena
vidyotitāmala-kapolam udāra-nāsam

bhṛtya—for the devotees; *anukampita-dhiyā*—out of compassion; *iha*—in this world; *gṛhīta-mūrteḥ*—who presents different forms; *sañcintayet*—one should meditate on; *bhagavataḥ*—of the Personality of Godhead; *vadana*—countenance; *aravindam*—lotuslike; *yat*—which;

visphuran—glittering; *makara*—alligator-shaped; *kuṇḍala*—of His earrings; *valgitena*—by the oscillation; *vidyotita*—illuminated; *amala*—crystal clear; *kapolam*—His cheeks; *udāra*—prominent; *nāsam*—His nose.

TRANSLATION

The yogī should then meditate on the lotuslike countenance of the Lord, who presents His different forms in this world out of compassion for the anxious devotees. His nose is prominent, and His crystal-clear cheeks are illuminated by the oscillation of His glittering alligator-shaped earrings.

PURPORT

The Lord descends to the material world out of His deep compassion for His devotees. There are two reasons for the Lord's appearance or incarnation in the material world. Whenever there is a discrepancy in the discharge of religious principles and there is prominence of irreligion, the Lord descends for the protection of the devotees and the destruction of the nondevotees. When He appears, His main purpose is to give solace to His devotees. He does not have to come Himself to destroy the demons, for He has many agents; even the external energy, *māyā,* has sufficient strength to kill them. But when He comes to show compassion to His devotees, He kills the nondevotees as a matter of course.

The Lord appears in the particular form loved by a particular type of devotee. There are millions of forms of the Lord, but they are one Absolute. As stated in the *Brahma-saṁhitā, advaitam acyutam anādim ananta-rūpam:* all the different forms of the Lord are one, but some devotees want to see Him in the form of Rādhā and Kṛṣṇa, others prefer Him as Sītā and Rāmacandra, others would see Him as Lakṣmī-Nārāyaṇa, and others want to see Him as four-handed Nārāyaṇa, Vāsudeva. The Lord has innumerable forms, and He appears in a particular form as preferred by a particular type of devotee. A *yogī* is advised to meditate upon the forms that are approved by devotees. A *yogī* cannot imagine a form for meditation. Those so-called *yogīs* who manufacture a circle or target are engaged in nonsense. Actually, a *yogī* must meditate upon the form of the Supreme Personality of Godhead that has been experienced by the Lord's pure devotees. *Yogī* means devotee. *Yogīs* who are not actually pure devotees should follow in the footsteps of devotees. It is especially mentioned here that the *yogī* should meditate upon the form which is thus approved; he cannot manufacture a form of the Lord.

TEXT 30

यच्छ्रीनिकेतमलिभिः परिसेव्यमानं
भूत्या स्वया कुटिलकुन्तलवृन्दजुष्टम् ।
मीनद्वयाश्रयमधिक्षिपदब्जनेत्रं
ध्यायेन्मनोमयमतन्द्रित उल्लसद्भ्रु ॥३०॥

yac chrī-niketam alibhiḥ parisevyamānaṁ
bhūtyā svayā kuṭila-kuntala-vṛnda-juṣṭam
mīna-dvayāśrayam adhikṣipad abja-netraṁ
dhyāyen manomayam atandrita ullasad-bhru

yat—which face of the Lord; *śrī-niketam*—a lotus; *alibhiḥ*—by bees; *parisevyamānam*—surrounded; *bhūtyā*—by elegance; *svayā*—its; *kuṭila*—curly; *kuntala*—of hair; *vṛnda*—by a multitude; *juṣṭam*—adorned; *mīna*—of fish; *dvaya*—a pair; *āśrayam*—dwelling; *adhikṣipat*—putting to shame; *abja*—a lotus; *netram*—having eyes; *dhyāyet*—one should meditate on; *manaḥ-mayam*—formed in the mind; *atandritaḥ*—attentive; *ullasat*—dancing; *bhru*—having eyebrows.

TRANSLATION

The yogi then meditates upon the beautiful face of the Lord, which is adorned with curly hair and decorated by lotuslike eyes and dancing eyebrows. A lotus surrounded by swarming bees and a pair of swimming fish would be put to shame by its elegance.

PURPORT

One important statement here is *dhyāyen manomayam. Manomayam* is not imagination. Impersonalists think that the *yogī* can imagine any form he likes, but, as stated here, the *yogī* must meditate upon the form of the Lord which is experienced by devotees. Devotees never imagine a form of the Lord. They are not satisfied by something imaginary. The Lord has different eternal forms; each devotee likes a particular form and thus engages himself in the service of the Lord by worshiping that form. The Lord's form is depicted in different ways according to scriptures. As already discussed, there are eight kinds of representations of the original form of the Lord. These representations can be produced by the use of clay, stone, wood, paint, sand, etc., depending upon the resources of the devotee.

Manomayam is a carving of the form of the Lord within the mind. This is included as one of the eight different carvings of the form of the Lord. It is not imagination.

Meditation on the actual form of the Lord may be manifested in different manners, but one should not conclude that one has to imagine a form. There are two comparisons in this verse: first the Lord's face is compared to a lotus, and then His black hair is compared to humming bees swarming around the lotus, and His two eyes are compared to two fish swimming about. A lotus flower on the water is very beautiful when surrounded by humming bees and fish. The Lord's face is self-sufficient and complete. His beauty defies the natural beauty of a lotus.

TEXT 31

तस्यावलोकमधिकं कृपयातिघोर-
तापत्रयोपशमनाय निसृष्टमक्ष्णोः ।
स्निग्धस्मितानुगुणितं विपुलप्रसादं
ध्यायेच्चिरं विपुलभावनया गुहायाम् ॥३१॥

tasyāvalokam adhikaṁ kṛpayātighora-
tāpa-trayopaśamanāya nisṛṣṭam akṣṇoḥ
snigdha-smitānuguṇitaṁ vipula-prasādaṁ
dhyāyec ciraṁ vipula-bhāvanayā guhāyām

tasya—of the Personality of Godhead; *avalokam*—glances; *adhikam*—frequent; *kṛpayā*—with compassion; *atighora*—most fearful; *tāpa-traya*—threefold agonies; *upaśamanāya*—soothing; *nisṛṣṭam*—cast; *akṣṇoḥ*—from His eyes; *snigdha*—loving; *smita*—smiles; *anuguṇitam*—accompanied by; *vipula*—abundant; *prasādam*—full of grace; *dhyāyet*—he should contemplate; *ciram*—for a long time; *vipula*—full; *bhāvanayā*—with devotion; *guhāyām*—in the heart.

TRANSLATION

The yogīs should contemplate with full devotion the compassionate glances frequently cast by the Lord's eyes, for they soothe the most fearful threefold agonies of His devotees. His glances, accompanied by loving smiles, are full of abundant grace.

PURPORT

As long as one is in conditional life, in the material body, it is natural that he will suffer from anxieties and agonies. One cannot avoid the influence of material energy, even when one is on the transcendental plane. Sometimes disturbances come, but the agonies and anxieties of the devotees are at once mitigated when they think of the

Supreme Personality of Godhead in His beautiful form or the smiling face of the Lord. The Lord bestows innumerable favors upon His devotee, and the greatest manifestation of His grace is His smiling face, which is full of compassion for His pure devotees.

TEXT 32

हासं हरेरवनताखिललोकतीव्र-
शोकाश्रुसागरविशोषणमत्युदारम् ।
सम्मोहनाय रचितं निजमाययास्य
भ्रूमण्डलं मुनिकृते मकरध्वजस्य ॥३२॥

hāsaṁ harer avanatākhila-loka-tīvra-
śokāśru-sāgara-viśoṣaṇam atyudāram
sammohanāya racitaṁ nija-māyayāsya
bhrū-maṇḍalaṁ muni-kṛte makara-dhvajasya

hāsam—the smile; *hareḥ*—of Lord Śrī Hari; *avanata*—bowed; *akhila*—all; *loka*—for persons; *tīvra-śoka*—caused by intense grief; *aśru-sāgara*—the ocean of tears; *viśoṣaṇam*—drying up; *ati-udāram*—most benevolent; *sammohanāya*—for charming; *racitam*—manifested; *nija-māyayā*—by His internal potency; *asya*—His; *bhrū-maṇḍalam*—arched eyebrows; *muni-kṛte*—for the good of the sages; *makara-dhvajasya*—of the sex-god.

TRANSLATION

A yogī should similarly meditate on the most benevolent smile of Lord Śrī Hari, a smile which, for all those who bow to Him, dries away the ocean of tears caused by intense grief. The yogī should also meditate on the Lord's arched eyebrows, which are manifested by His internal potency in order to charm the sex-god for the good of the sages.

PURPORT

The entire universe is full of miseries, and therefore the inhabitants of this material universe are always shedding tears out of intense grief. There is a great ocean of water made from such tears, but for one who surrenders unto the Supreme Personality of Godhead, the ocean of tears is at once dried up. One need only see the charming smile of the Supreme Lord. In other words, the bereavement of material existence immediately subsides when one sees the charming smile of the Lord.

It is stated in this verse that the charming eyebrows of the Lord are so fascinating that they cause one to forget the charms of sense attraction. The conditioned souls are shackled to material existence because they are captivated by the charms of sense gratification, especially sex life. The sex-god is called Makara-dhvaja. The charming brows of the Supreme Personality of Godhead protect the sages and devotees from being charmed by material lust and sex attraction. Yāmunācārya, a great *ācārya*, said that ever since he had seen the charming pastimes of the Lord, the charms of sex life had become abominable for him, and the mere thought of sex enjoyment would cause him to spit and turn his face. Thus if anyone wants to be aloof from sex attraction, he must see the charming smile and fascinating eyebrows of the Supreme Personality of Godhead.

TEXT 33

ध्यानायनं प्रहसितं बहुलाधरोष्ठ-
भासारुणायिततनुद्विजकुन्दपङ्क्ति ।
ध्यायेत्स्वदेहकुहरेऽवसितस्य विष्णो-
र्भक्त्यार्द्रयार्पितमना न पृथग्दिदृक्षेत् ॥३३॥

dhyānāyanaṁ prahasitaṁ bahulādharoṣṭha-
bhasaruṇāyita-tanu-dvija-kunda-paṅkti
dhyāyet svadeha-kuhare 'vasitasya viṣṇor
bhaktyārdrayārpita-manā na pṛthag didṛkṣet

dhyāna-ayanam—easily meditated upon; *prahasitam*—the laughter; *bahula*—abundant; *adhara-oṣṭha*—of His lips; *bhāsa*—by the splendor; *aruṇāyita*—rendered rosy; *tanu*—small; *dvija*—teeth; *kunda-paṅkti*—like a row of jasmine buds; *dhyāyet*—he should meditate upon; *sva-deha-kuhare*—in the core of his heart; *avasitasya*—who resides; *viṣṇoḥ*—of Viṣṇu; *bhaktyā*—with devotion; *ārdrayā*—steeped in love; *arpita-manāḥ*—his mind being fixed; *na*—not; *pṛthak*—anything else; *didṛkṣet*—he should desire to see.

TRANSLATION

With devotion steeped in love and affection, the yogī should meditate within the core of his heart upon the laughter of Lord Viṣṇu. The laughter of Viṣṇu is so captivating that it can be easily meditated upon. When the Supreme Lord is laughing, one can see His small teeth, which resemble jasmine buds rendered rosy by the splendor of His lips. Once devoting his mind to this, the yogī should no longer desire to see anything else.

PURPORT

It is recommended that the *yogī* visualize the laughter of the Lord after studying His smile very carefully. These particular descriptions of meditation on the smile, laughter, face, lips and teeth all indicate conclusively that God is not impersonal. It is described herein that one should meditate on the laughter or smiling of Viṣṇu. There is no other activity that can completely cleanse the heart of the devotee. The exceptional beauty of the laughter of Lord Viṣṇu is that when He smiles His small teeth, which resemble the buds of jasmine flowers, at once become reddish, reflecting His rosy lips. If the *yogī* is able to place the beautiful face of the Lord in the core of his heart, he will be completely satisfied. In other words, when one is absorbed in seeing the beauty of the Lord within himself, the material attraction can no longer disturb him.

TEXT 34

एवं हरौ भगवति प्रतिलब्धभावो
भक्त्या द्रवद्धृदय उत्पुलकः प्रमोदात् ।
औत्कण्ठ्यबाष्पकलया मुहुरर्द्यमान-
स्तच्चापि चित्तबडिशं शनकैर्वियुङ्क्ते ॥३४॥

evaṁ harau bhagavati pratilabdha-bhāvo
bhaktyā dravad-dhṛdaya utpulakaḥ pramodāt
autkaṇṭhya-bāṣpa-kalayā muhur ardyamānas
tac cāpi citta-baḍiśaṁ śanakair viyuṅkte

evam—thus; *harau*—towards Lord Hari; *bhagavati*—the Personality of Godhead; *pratilabdha*—developed; *bhāvaḥ*—pure love; *bhaktyā*—by devotional service; *dravat*—melting; *hṛdayaḥ*—his heart; *utpulakaḥ*—experiencing standing of the hairs of the body; *pramodāt*—from excessive joy; *autkaṇṭhya*—occasioned by intense love; *bāṣpa-kalayā*—by a stream of tears; *muhuḥ*—constantly; *ardyamānaḥ*—being afflicted; *tat*—that; *ca*—and; *api*—even; *citta*—the mind; *baḍiśam*—hook; *śanakaiḥ*—gradually; *viyuṅkte*—withdraws.

TRANSLATION

By following this course, the yogī gradually develops pure love for the Supreme Personality of Godhead, Hari. In the course of his progress in devotional service, the hairs on his body stand erect through excessive joy, and he is constantly bathed in a stream of tears occasioned by intense love. Gradually, even the mind, which he used as a means to attract the Lord, as one attracts a fish to a hook, withdraws from material activity.

PURPORT

Here it is clearly mentioned that meditation, which is an action of the mind, is not the perfect stage of *samādhi,* or absorption. In the beginning the mind is employed in attracting the form of the Supreme Personality of Godhead, but in the higher stages there is no question of using the mind. A devotee becomes accustomed to serving the Supreme Lord by purification of his senses. In other words, the *yoga* principles of meditation are required as long as one is not situated in pure devotional service. The mind is used to purify the senses, but when the senses are purified by meditation, there is no need to sit in a particular place and try to meditate upon the form of the Lord. One becomes so habituated that he automatically engages in the personal service of the Lord. When the mind forcibly is engaged upon the form of the Lord, this is called *nirbīja-yoga,* or lifeless *yoga,* for the *yogī* does not automatically engage in the personal service of the Lord. But when he is constantly thinking of the Lord, that is called *sabīja-yoga,* or living *yoga.* One has to be promoted to the platform of living *yoga.*

One should engage in the service of the Lord twenty-four hours a day, as confirmed in the *Brahma-saṁhitā.* The stage of *premāñjana-cchurita* can be attained by developing complete love. When one's love for the Supreme Personality of Godhead in devotional service is fully developed, one always sees the Lord, even without artificially meditating on His form. His vision is divine because he has no other engagement. At this stage of spiritual realization it is not necessary to engage the mind artificially. Since the meditation recommended in the lower stages is a means to come to the platform of devotional service, those already engaged in the transcendental loving service of the Lord are above such meditation. This stage of perfection is called Kṛṣṇa consciousness.

TEXT 35

मुक्ताश्रयं यर्हि निर्विषयं विरक्तं
निर्वाणमृच्छति मनः सहसा यथार्चिः ।
आत्मानमत्र पुरुषोऽव्यवधानमेक-
मन्वीक्षते प्रतिनिवृत्तगुणप्रवाहः ॥३५॥

muktāśrayaṁ yarhi nirviṣayaṁ viraktaṁ
nirvāṇam ṛcchati manaḥ sahasā yathārciḥ
ātmānam atra puruṣo 'vyavadhānam ekam
anvīkṣate pratinivṛtta-guṇa-pravāhaḥ

mukta-āśrayam—situated in liberation; *yarhi*—at which time; *nirviṣayam*—detached from sense objects; *viraktam*—indifferent; *nirvāṇam*—extinction; *ṛcchati*—obtains; *manaḥ*—the mind; *sahasā*—immediately; *yathā*—like; *arciḥ*—the flame; *ātmānam*—the mind; *atra*—at this time; *puruṣaḥ*—a person; *avyavadhānam*—without separation; *ekam*—one; *anvīkṣate*—experiences; *pratinivṛtta*—freed; *guṇa-pravāhaḥ*—from the flow of material qualities.

TRANSLATION

When the mind is thus completely freed from all material contamination and detached from material objectives, it is just like the flame of a lamp. At that time the mind is actually dovetailed with that of the Supreme Lord and is experienced as one with Him because it is freed from the interactive flow of the material qualities.

PURPORT

In the material world the activities of the mind are acceptance and rejection. As long as the mind is in material consciousness, it must be forcibly trained to accept meditation on the Supreme Personality of Godhead, but when one is actually elevated to loving the Supreme Lord, the mind is automatically absorbed in thought of the Lord. In such a position a *yogī* has no other thought than to serve the Lord. This dovetailing of the mind with the desires of the Supreme Personality of Godhead is called *nirvāṇa,* or making the mind one with the Supreme Lord.

The best example of *nirvāṇa* is cited in *Bhagavad-gītā.* In the beginning the mind of Arjuna deviated from Kṛṣṇa's. Kṛṣṇa wanted Arjuna to fight, but Arjuna did not want to, so there was disagreement. But after hearing *Bhagavad-gītā* from the Supreme Personality of Godhead, Arjuna dovetailed his mind with Kṛṣṇa's desire. This is called oneness. This oneness, however, did not cause Arjuna and Kṛṣṇa to lose their individualities. The Māyāvādī philosophers cannot understand this. They think that oneness necessitates loss of individuality. Actually, however, we find in *Bhagavad-gītā* that individuality is not lost. When the mind is completely purified in love of Godhead, the mind becomes the mind of the Supreme Personality of Godhead. The mind at that time does not act separately, nor does it act without inspiration to fulfill the desire of the Lord. The individual liberated soul has no other activity. *Pratinivṛtta-guṇa-pravāhaḥ.* In the conditioned state the mind is always engaged in activity impelled by the three modes of the material world, but in the transcendental stage, the material modes cannot disturb the mind of the devotee. The devotee has no other concern than to satisfy the desires of the Lord. That is the highest stage of perfection, called *nirvāṇa* or *nirvāṇa-mukti.* At this stage the mind becomes completely free from material desire.

Yathārciḥ. Arciḥ means "flame." When a lamp is broken or the oil is finished, we see that the flame of the lamp goes out. But according to scientific understanding, the flame is not extinguished; it is conserved. This is conservation of energy. Similarly, when the mind stops functioning on the material platform, it is conserved in the activities of the Supreme Lord. The Māyāvādī philosophers' conception of cessation of the functions of the mind is explained here: cessation of the mental functions means cessation of activities conducted under the influence of the three modes of material nature.

TEXT 36

सोऽप्येतया चरमया मनसो निवृत्त्या
तस्मिन्महिम्न्यवसितः सुखदुःखबाह्ये ।
हेतुत्वमप्यसति कर्तरि दुःखयोर्यत्
स्वात्मन् विधत्त उपलब्धपरात्मकाष्ठः ॥३६॥

so 'py etayā caramayā manaso nivṛttyā
tasmin mahimny avasitaḥ sukha-duḥkha-bāhye
hetutvam apy asati kartari duḥkhayor yat
svātman vidhatta upalabdha-parātma-kāṣṭhaḥ

saḥ—the *yogī*; *api*—moreover; *etayā*—by this; *caramayā*—ultimate; *manasaḥ*—of the mind; *nivṛttyā*—by cessation of material reaction; *tasmin*—in his; *mahimni*—ultimate glory; *avasitaḥ*—situated; *sukha-duḥkha-bāhye*—outside of happiness and distress; *hetutvam*—the cause; *api*—indeed; *asati*—a product of ignorance; *kartari*—in the false ego; *duḥkhayoḥ*—of pleasure and pain; *yat*—which; *sva-ātman*—to his own self; *vidhatte*—he attributes; *upalabdha*—realized; *para-ātma*—of the Personality of Godhead; *kāṣṭhaḥ*—the highest truth.

TRANSLATION

Thus situated in the highest transcendental stage, the mind ceases from all material reaction and becomes situated in its own glory, transcendental to all material conceptions of happiness and distress. At that time the yogī realizes the truth of his relationship with the Supreme Personality of Godhead. He discovers that pleasure and pain as well as their interactions, which he attributed to his own self, are actually due to the false ego, which is a product of ignorance.

PURPORT

Forgetfulness of one's relationship with the Supreme Personality of Godhead is a product of ignorance. By *yoga* practice one can eradicate this ignorance of thinking oneself independent of the Supreme Lord. One's actual relationship is eternally that of love. The living entity is meant to render transcendental loving service to the Lord. Forgetfulness of that sweet relationship is called ignorance, and in ignorance one is impelled by the three material modes of nature to think himself the enjoyer. When the devotee's mind is purified and he understands that his mind has to be dovetailed with the desires of the Supreme Personality of Godhead, he has attained the perfectional, transcendental stage, which is beyond the perception of material distress and happiness.

As long as one acts on his own account, he is subject to all the material perceptions of so-called happiness and distress. Actually there is no happiness. Just as there is no happiness in any of the activities of a madman, so in material activities the mental concoctions of happiness and distress are false. Actually everything is distress.

When the mind is dovetailed to act according to the desire of the Lord, one has attained the transcendental stage. The desire to lord it over material nature is the cause of ignorance, and when that desire is completely extinguished and the desires are dovetailed with those of the Supreme Lord, one has reached the perfectional stage. *Upalabdha-parātma-kāṣṭhaḥ. Upalabdha* means "realization." Realization necessarily indicates individuality. In the perfectional, liberated stage, there is actual realization. *Nivṛttyā* means that the living entity keeps his individuality; oneness means that he realizes happiness in the happiness of the Supreme Lord. In the Supreme Lord there is nothing but happiness. *Ānandamayo 'bhyāsāt:* the Lord is by nature full of transcendental happiness. In the liberated stage, oneness with the Supreme Lord means that one has no realization other than happiness. But the individual still exists, otherwise this word *upalabdha,* indicating individual realization of transcendental happiness, would not have been used.

TEXT 37

देहं च तं न चरमः स्थितमुत्थितं वा
सिद्धो विपश्यति यतोऽध्यगमत्स्वरूपम् ।
दैवादुपेतमथ दैववशादपेतं
वासो यथा परिकृतं मदिरामदान्धः ॥३७॥

dehaṁ ca taṁ na caramaḥ sthitam utthitaṁ vā
siddho vipaśyati yato 'dhyagamat svarūpam
daivād upetam atha daiva-vaśād apetaṁ
vāso yathā parikṛtaṁ madirā-madāndhaḥ

deham—material body; *ca*—and; *tam*—that; *na*—not; *caramaḥ*—last; *sthitam*—sitting; *utthitam*—rising; *vā*—or; *siddhaḥ*—the realized soul; *vipaśyati*—can conceive; *yataḥ*—because; *adhyagamat*—he has achieved; *sva-rūpam*—his real identity; *daivāt*—according to destiny;

upetam—arrived; *atha*—moreover; *daiva-vaśāt*—according to destiny; *apetam*—departed; *vāsaḥ*—clothing; *yathā*—as; *parikṛtam*—put on; *madirā-mada-andhaḥ*—one who is blinded by intoxication.

TRANSLATION

Because he has achieved his real identity, the perfectly realized soul has no conception of how the material body is moving or acting, just as an intoxicated person cannot understand whether or not he has clothing on his body.

PURPORT

This stage of life is explained by Rūpa Gosvāmī in his *Bhakti-rasāmṛta-sindhu.* A person whose mind is completely dovetailed with the desire of the Supreme Personality of Godhead, and who engages one hundred percent in the service of the Lord, forgets his material bodily demands.

TEXT 38

देहोऽपि दैववशगः खलु कर्म यावत्
स्वारम्भकं प्रतिसमीक्षत एव सासुः ।
तं सप्रपञ्चमधिरूढसमाधियोगः
स्वाप्नं पुनर्न भजते प्रतिबुद्धवस्तुः ॥३८॥

deho 'pi daiva-vaśagaḥ khalu karma yāvat
svārambhakaṁ pratisamīkṣata eva sāsuḥ
taṁ sa-prapañcam adhirūḍha-samādhi-yogaḥ
svāpnaṁ punar na bhajate pratibuddha-vastuḥ

dehaḥ—the body; *api*—moreover; *daiva-vaśa-gaḥ*—under the control of the Personality of Godhead; *khalu*—indeed; *karma*—activities; *yāvat*—as much as; *sva-ārambhakam*—begun by himself; *pratisamīkṣate*—continues to function; *eva*—certainly; *sa-asuḥ*—along with the senses; *tam*—the body; *sa-prapañcam*—with its expansions; *adhirūḍha-samādhi-yogaḥ*—being situated in *samādhi* by *yoga* practice; *svāpnam*—born in a dream; *punaḥ*—again; *na*—not; *bhajate*—he does accept as his own; *pratibuddha*—awake; *vastuḥ*—to his constitutional position.

TRANSLATION

The body of such a liberated yogī, along with the senses, is taken charge of by the Supreme Personality of Godhead, and it functions until its destined

activities are finished. The liberated devotee, being awake to his constitutional position and thus situated in samādhi, the highest perfectional stage of yoga, does not accept the by-products of the material body as his own. Thus he considers his bodily activities to be like the activities of a body in a dream.

PURPORT

The following questions may be posed. As long as the liberated soul is in contact with the body, why don't the bodily activities affect him? Doesn't he actually become contaminated by the action and reaction of material activities? In answer to such questions, this verse explains that the material body of a liberated soul is taken charge of by the Supreme Personality of Godhead. It is not acting due to the living force of the living entity; it is simply acting as a reaction to past activities. Even after being switched off, an electric fan moves for some time. That movement is not due to the electric current, but is a continuation of the last movement; similarly, although a liberated soul appears to be acting just like an ordinary man, his actions are to be accepted as the continuation of past activities. In a dream one may see himself expanded through many bodies, but when awake he can understand that those bodies were all false. Similarly, although a liberated soul has the by-products of the body-children, wife, house, etc.—he does not identify himself with those bodily expansions. He knows that they are all products of the material dream. The gross body is made of the gross elements of matter, and the subtle body is made of mind, intelligence, ego and contaminated consciousness. If one can accept the subtle body of a dream as false and not identify oneself with that body, then certainly an awake person need not identify with the gross body. As one who is awake has no connection with the activities of the body in a dream, an awakened, liberated soul has no connection with the activities of the present body. In other words, because he is acquainted with his constitutional position, he never accepts the bodily concept of life.

TEXT 39

यथा पुत्राच्च वित्ताच्च पृथङ्मर्त्यः प्रतीयते ।
अप्यात्मत्वेनाभिमताद्देहादेः पुरुषस्तथा ॥३९॥

yathā putrāc ca vittāc ca
pṛthaṅ martyaḥ pratīyate
apy ātmatvenābhimatād
dehādeḥ puruṣas tathā

yathā—as; *putrāt*—from a son; *ca*—and; *vittāt*—from wealth; *ca*—also; *pṛthak*—differently; *martyaḥ*—a mortal man; *pratīyate*—is understood; *api*—even; *ātmatvena*—by nature; *abhimatāt*—for which one has affection; *deha-ādeḥ*—from his material body, senses and mind; *puruṣaḥ*—the liberated soul; *tathā*—similarly.

TRANSLATION

Because of great affection for family and wealth, one accepts a son and some money as his own, and due to affection for the material body, one thinks that it is his. But actually, as one can understand that his family and wealth are different from him, the liberated soul can understand that he and his body are not the same.

PURPORT

The status of real knowledge is explained in this verse. There are many children, but we accept some children as our sons and daughters because of our affection for them, although we know very well that these children are different from us. Similarly, because of great affection for money, we accept some amount of wealth in the bank as ours. In the same way, we claim that the body is ours because of affection for it. I say that it is "my" body. I then extend that possessive concept and say, "It is my hand, my leg," and further, "It is my bank balance, my son, my daughter." But actually I know that the son and the money are separate from me. It is the same with the body; I am separate from my body. It is a question of understanding, and the proper understanding is called *pratibuddha.* By obtaining knowledge in devotional service, or Kṛṣṇa consciousness, one can become a liberated soul.

TEXT 40

यथोल्मुकाद्विस्फुलिङ्गाद्धूमाद्वापि स्वसम्भवात् ।
अप्यात्मत्वेनाभिमताद्यथाग्निः पृथगुल्मुकात् ॥४०॥

yatholmukād visphuliṅgād
dhūmād vāpi sva-sambhavāt
apy ātmatvenābhimatād
yathāgniḥ pṛthag ulmukāt

yathā—as; *ulmukāt*—from the flames; *visphuliṅgāt*—from the sparks; *dhūmāt*—from the smoke; *vā*—or; *api*—even; *sva-sambhavāt*—produced from itself; *api*—although; *ātmatvena*—by nature; *abhimatāt*—intimately connected; *yathā*—as; *agniḥ*—the fire; *pṛthak*—different; *ulmukāt*—from the flames.

TRANSLATION

The blazing fire is different from the flames, from the sparks and from the smoke, although all are intimately connected because they are born from the same blazing wood.

PURPORT

Although the blazing firewood, the sparks, the smoke and the flame cannot stay apart because each of them is part and parcel of the fire, still they are different from one another. A less intelligent person accepts the smoke as fire, although fire and smoke are completely different. The heat and light of the fire are separate, although one cannot differentiate fire from heat and light.

TEXT 41

भूतेन्द्रियान्तःकरणात्प्रधानाज्जीवसंज्ञितात् ।
आत्मा तथा पृथग्द्रष्टा भगवान् ब्रह्मसंज्ञितः ॥४१॥

bhūtendriyāntaḥ-karaṇāt
pradhānāj jīva-saṁjñitāt
ātmā tathā pṛthag draṣṭā
bhagavān brahma-saṁjñitaḥ

bhūta—the five elements; *indriya*—the senses; *antaḥ-karaṇāt*—from the mind; *pradhānāt*—from the *pradhāna; jīva-saṁjñitāt*—from the *jīva* soul; *ātmā*—the Paramātmā; *tathā*—so; *pṛthak*—different; *draṣṭā*—the seer; *bhagavān*—the Personality of Godhead; *brahma-saṁjñitaḥ*—called Brahman.

TRANSLATION

The Supreme Personality of Godhead, who is known as param brahma, is the seer. He is different from the jīva soul, or individual living entity, who is combined with the senses, the five elements and consciousness.

PURPORT

A clear conception of the complete whole is given herewith. The living entity is different from the material elements, and the supreme living entity, the Personality of Godhead, who is the creator of the material elements, is also different from the individual living entity. This philosophy is propounded by Lord Caitanya as *acintya-bhedābheda-tattva.* Everything is simultaneously one with and different from everything else. The cosmic manifestation created by the Supreme Lord by His material energy is also simultaneously different and nondifferent from Him. The material energy is nondifferent from the Supreme Lord, but at the same time, because that energy is acting in a different way, it is different from Him. Similarly, the individual living entity is one with and different from the Supreme Lord. This "simultaneously one and different" philosophy is the perfect conclusion of the *Bhāgavata* school, as confirmed here by Kapiladeva.

Living entities are compared to the sparks of a fire. As stated in the previous verse, fire, flame, smoke and firewood are combined together. Here the living entity, the material elements and the Supreme Personality of Godhead are combined together. The exact position of the living entities is just like that of the sparks of a fire; they are part and parcel. The material energy is compared to the smoke. The fire is also part and parcel of the Supreme Lord. In the *Viṣṇu Purāṇa* it is said that whatever we can see or experience, either in the material or spiritual world, is an expansion of the different energies of the Supreme Lord. As fire distributes its light and heat from one place, the Supreme Personality of Godhead distributes His different energies all over His creation.

The four principles of the Vaiṣṇava philosophic doctrine are *śuddha-advaita* (purified oneness), *dvaita-advaita* (simultaneous oneness and difference), *viśiṣṭa-advaita* and *dvaita.* All four principles of Vaiṣṇava philosophy are based on the thesis of *Śrīmad-Bhāgavatam* explained in these two verses.

TEXT 42

सवभूतेषु चात्मानं सर्वभूतानि चात्मनि ।
ईक्षेतानन्यभावेन भूतेष्विव तदात्मताम् ॥४२॥

sarva-bhūteṣu cātmānaṁ
sarva-bhūtāni cātmani
īkṣetānanya-bhāvena
bhūteṣv iva tad-ātmatām

sarva-bhūteṣu—in all manifestations; *ca*—and; *ātmānam*—the soul; *sarva-bhūtāni*—all manifestations; *ca*—also; *ātmani*—in the Supreme Spirit; *īkṣeta*—he should see; *ananya-bhāvena*—with equal vision; *bhūteṣu*—in all manifestations; *iva*—as; *tat-ātmatām*—the nature of itself.

TRANSLATION

A yogi should see the same soul in all manifestations, for all that exists is a manifestation of different energies of the Supreme. In this way the devotee

should see all living entities without distinction. That is realization of the Supreme Soul.

PURPORT

As stated in the *Brahma-saṁhitā*, not only does the Supreme Soul enter each and every universe, but He enters even the atoms. The Supreme Soul is present everywhere in the dormant stage, and when one can see the presence of the Supreme Soul everywhere, one is liberated from material designations.

The word *sarva-bhūteṣu* is to be understood as follows. There are four different divisions of species-living entities which sprout from the earth, living entities born of fermentation or germination, living entities which come from eggs and living entities which come from the embryo. These four divisions of living entities are expanded in 8,400,000 species of life. A person who is freed from material designations can see the same quality of spirit present everywhere or in every manifested living entity. Less intelligent men think that plants and grass grow out of the earth automatically, but one who is actually intelligent and has realized the self can see that this growth is not automatic; the cause is the soul, and the forms come out in material bodies under different conditions. By fermentation in the laboratory many germs are born, but this is due to the presence of the soul. The material scientist thinks that eggs are lifeless, but that is not a fact. From Vedic scripture we can understand that living entities in different forms are generated under different conditions. Birds evolve from eggs, and beasts and human beings are born from the embryo. The perfect vision of the *yogī* or devotee is that he sees the presence of the living entity everywhere.

TEXT 43

स्वयोनिषु यथा ज्योतिरेकं नाना प्रतीयते ।
योनीनां गुणवैषम्यात्तथात्मा प्रकृतौ स्थितः ॥४३॥

sva-yoniṣu yathā jyotir
ekaṁ nānā pratīyate
yonīnāṁ guṇa-vaiṣamyāt
tathātmā prakṛtau sthitaḥ

sva-yoniṣu—in forms of wood; *yathā*—as; *jyotiḥ*—fire; *ekam*—one; *nānā*—differently; *pratīyate*—is exhibited; *yonīnām*—of different wombs; *guṇa-vaiṣamyāt*—from the different conditions of the modes; *tathā*—so; *ātmā*—the spirit soul; *prakṛtau*—in the material nature; *sthitaḥ*—situated.

TRANSLATION

As fire is exhibited in different forms of wood, so, under different conditions of the modes of material nature, the pure spirit soul manifests itself in different bodies.

PURPORT

It is to be understood that the body is designated. *Prakṛti* is an interaction by the three modes of material nature, and according to these modes, someone has a small body, and someone has a very large body. For example, the fire in a big piece of wood appears very big, and in a stick the fire appears small. Actually, the quality of fire is the same everywhere, but the manifestation of material nature is such that according to the fuel, the fire appears bigger and smaller. Similarly, the soul in the universal body, although of the same quality, is different from the soul in the smaller body.

The small particles of soul are just like sparks of the larger soul. The greatest soul is the Supersoul, but the Supersoul is quantitatively different from the small soul. The Supersoul is described in the Vedic literature as the supplier of all necessities of the smaller soul (*nityo nityānām*). One who understands this distinction between the Supersoul and the individual soul is above lamentation and is in a peaceful position. When the smaller soul thinks himself quantitatively as big as the larger soul, he is under the spell of *māyā,* for that is not his constitutional position. No one can become the greater soul simply by mental speculation.

The smallness or greatness of different souls is described in the *Varāha Purāṇa* as *svāṁśa-vibhinnāṁśa.* The *svāṁśa* soul is the Supreme Personality of Godhead, and the *vibhinnāṁśa* souls, or small particles, are eternally small particles, as confirmed in *Bhagavad-gītā* (*mamaivāṁśo jīva-loke jīva-bhūtaḥ sanātanaḥ*). The small living entities are eternally part and parcel, and therefore it is not possible for them to be quantitatively as great as the Supersoul.

TEXT 44

तस्मादिमां स्वां प्रकृतिं दैवीं सदसदात्मिकाम् ।
दुर्विभाव्यां पराभाव्य स्वरूपेणावतिष्ठते ॥४४॥

tasmād imāṁ svāṁ prakṛtiṁ
daivīṁ sad-asad-ātmikām
durvibhāvyāṁ parābhāvya
svarūpeṇāvatiṣṭhate

tasmāt—thus; *imām*—this; *svām*—own; *prakṛtim*—material energy; *daivīm*—divine; *sat-asat-ātmikām*—consisting of cause and effect; *durvibhāvyām*—difficult to understand; *parābhāvya*—after conquering; *sva-rūpeṇa*—in the self-realized position; *avatiṣṭhate*—he remains.

TRANSLATION

Thus the yogī can be in the self-realized position after conquering the insurmountable spell of māyā, who presents herself as both the cause and effect of this material manifestation and is therefore very difficult to understand.

PURPORT

It is stated in *Bhagavad-gītā* that the spell of *māyā,* which covers the knowledge of the living entity, is insurmountable. However, one who surrenders unto Kṛṣṇa, the Supreme Personality of Godhead, can conquer this seemingly insurmountable spell of *māyā.* Here also it is stated that the *daivī prakṛti,* or the external energy of the Supreme Lord, is *durvibhāvyā,* very difficult to understand and very difficult to conquer. One must, however, conquer this insurmountable spell of *māyā,* and this is possible, by the grace of the Lord, when God reveals Himself to the surrendered soul. It is also stated here, *svarūpenāvatiṣṭhate. Svarūpa* means that one has to know that he is not the Supreme Soul, but rather, part and parcel of the Supreme Soul; that is self-realization. To think falsely that one is the Supreme Soul and that one is all-pervading is not *svarūpa.* This is not realization of his actual position. The real position is that one is part and parcel. It is recommended here that one remain in that position of actual self-realization. In *Bhagavad-gītā* this understanding is defined as Brahman realization.

After Brahman realization, one can engage in the activities of Brahman. As long as one is not self-realized, he engages in activities based on false identification with the body. When one is situated in his real self, then the activities of Brahman realization begin. The Māyāvādī philosophers say that after Brahman realization, all activities stop, but that is not actually so. If the soul is so active in its abnormal condition, existing under the covering of matter, how can one deny its activity when free? An example may be cited here. If a man in a diseased condition is very active, how can one imagine that when he is free from the disease he will be inactive? Naturally the conclusion is that when one is free from all disease his activities are pure. It may be said that the activities of Brahman realization are different from those of conditional life, but that does not stop activity. This is indicated in *Bhagavad-gītā* (18.54): after one realizes oneself to be Brahman, devotional service begins. *Mad-bhaktiṁ labhate parām:* after Brahman realization, one can engage in the devotional service of the Lord. Therefore devotional service of the Lord is activity in Brahman realization.

For those who engage in devotional service there is no spell of *māyā*, and their situation is all-perfect. The duty of the living entity, as a part and parcel of the whole, is to render devotional service to the whole. That is the ultimate perfection of life.

Thus end the Bhaktivedanta purports of the Third Canto, Twenty-eighth Chapter, of the Śrīmad-Bhāgavatam, *entitled "Lord Kapila's Instructions on the Execution of Devotional Service."*

CHAPTER TWENTY-NINE

Explanation of Devotional Service by Lord Kapila

TEXTS 1-2

देवहूतिरुवाच
लक्षणं महदादीनां प्रकृतेः पुरुषस्य च ।
स्वरूपं लक्ष्यतेऽमीषां येन तत्पारमार्थिकम् ॥ १ ॥
यथा सांख्येषु कथितं यन्मूलं तत्प्रचक्षते ।
भक्तियोगस्य मे मार्गं ब्रूहि विस्तरशः प्रभो ॥ २ ॥

devahūtir uvāca
lakṣaṇaṁ mahad-ādīnāṁ
prakṛteḥ puruṣasya ca
svarūpaṁ lakṣyate 'mīṣāṁ
yena tat-pāramārthikam

yathā sāṅkhyeṣu kathitaṁ
yan-mūlaṁ tat pracakṣate
bhakti-yogasya me mārgaṁ
brūhi vistaraśaḥ prabho

devahūtiḥ uvāca—Devahūti said; *lakṣaṇam*—symptoms; *mahat-ādīnām*—of the *mahat-tattva* and so on; *prakṛteḥ*—of material nature; *puruṣasya*—of the spirit; *ca*—and; *svarūpam*—the nature; *lakṣyate*—is described; *amīṣām*—of those; *yena*—by which; *tat-pārama-arthikam*—the true nature of them; *yathā*—as; *sāṅkhyeṣu*—in Sāṅkhya philosophy; *kathitam*—is explained; *yat*—of which; *mūlam*—ultimate end; *tat*—that; *pracakṣate*—they call; *bhakti-yogasya*—of devotional service; *me*—to me; *mārgam*—the path; *brūhi*—please explain; *vistaraśaḥ*—at length; *prabho*—my dear Lord Kapila.

TRANSLATION

Devahūti inquired: My dear Lord, You have already very scientifically described the symptoms of the total material nature and the characteristics of the spirit according to the Sāṅkhya system of philosophy. Now I shall request You to explain the path of devotional service, which is the ultimate end of all philosophical systems.

PURPORT

In this Twenty-ninth Chapter, the glories of devotional service are elaborately explained, and the influence of time on the conditioned soul is also described. The purpose of elaborately describing the influence of time is to detach the conditioned soul from his material activities, which are considered to be simply a waste of time. In the previous chapter, material nature, the spirit and the Supreme Lord, or Supersoul, are analytically studied, and in this chapter the principles of *bhakti-yoga,* or devotional service—the execution of activities in the eternal relationship between the living entities and the Personality of Godhead—are explained.

Bhakti-yoga, devotional service, is the basic principle of all systems of philosophy; all philosophy which does not aim for devotional service to the Lord is considered merely mental speculation. But of course *bhakti-yoga* with no philosophical basis is more or less sentiment. There are two classes of men. Some consider themselves intellectually advanced and simply speculate and meditate, and others are sentimental and have no philosophical basis for their propositions. Neither of these can achieve the highest goal of life—or, if they do, it will take them many, many years. Vedic literature therefore suggests that there are three elements—namely the Supreme Lord, the living entity and their eternal relationship—and the goal of life is to follow the principles of *bhakti,* or devotional service, and ultimately attain to the planet of the Supreme Lord in full devotion and love as an eternal servitor of the Lord.

Sāṅkhya philosophy is the analytical study of all existence. One has to understand everything by examining its nature and characteristics. This is called acquirement of knowledge. But one should not simply acquire knowledge without reaching the goal of life or the basic principle for acquiring knowledge—*bhakti-yoga.* If we give up *bhakti-yoga* and simply busy ourselves in the analytical study of the nature of things as they are, then the result will be practically nil. It is stated in the *Bhāgavatam* that such engagement is something like husking a paddy. There is no use beating the husk if the grain has already been removed. By the scientific study of material nature, the living entity and the Supersoul, one has to understand the basic principle of devotional service to the Lord.

TEXT 3

विरागो येन पुरुषो भगवन् सर्वतो भवेत् ।
आचक्ष्व जीवलोकस्य विविधा मम संसृतीः ॥ ३ ॥

virāgo yena puruṣo
bhagavan sarvato bhavet

ācakṣva jīva-lokasya
vividhā mama saṁsṛtīḥ

virāgaḥ—detached; *yena*—by which; *puruṣaḥ*—a person; *bhagavan*—my dear Lord; *sarvataḥ*—completely; *bhavet*—may become; *ācakṣva*—please describe; *jīva-lokasya*—for the people in general; *vividhāḥ*—manifold; *mama*—for myself; *saṁsṛtīḥ*—repetition of birth and death.

TRANSLATION

Devahūti continued: My dear Lord, please also describe in detail, both for me and for people in general, the continual process of birth and death, for by hearing of such calamities we may become detached from the activities of this material world.

PURPORT

In this verse the word *saṁsṛtīḥ* is very important. *Śreyaḥ-sṛti* means the prosperous path of advancement towards the Supreme Personality of Godhead, and *saṁsṛti* means the continued journey on the path of birth and death towards the darkest region of material existence. People who have no knowledge of this material world, God and their actual intimate relationship with Him are actually going to the darkest region of material existence in the name of progress in the material advancement of civilization. To enter the darkest region of material existence means to enter into a species of life other than the human species. Ignorant men do not know that after this life they are completely under the grip of material nature and will be offered a life which may not be very congenial. How a living entity gets different kinds of bodies will be explained in the next chapter. This continual change of bodies in birth and death is called *saṁsāra.* Devahūti requests her glorious son, Kapila Muni, to explain about this continued journey to impress upon the conditioned souls that they are undergoing a path of degradation by not understanding the path of *bhakti-yoga,* devotional service.

TEXT 4

कालस्येश्वररूपस्य परेषां च परस्य ते ।
स्वरूपं बत कुर्वन्ति यद्धेतोः कुशलं जनाः ॥ ४ ॥

kālasyeśvara-rūpasya
pareṣāṁ ca parasya te
svarūpaṁ bata kurvanti
yad-dhetoḥ kuśalaṁ janāḥ

kālasya—of time; *īśvara-rūpasya*—a representation of the Lord; *pareṣām*—of all others; *ca*—and; *parasya*—the chief; *te*—of You; *svarūpam*—the nature; *bata*—oh; *kurvanti*—perform; *yat-hetoḥ*—by whose influence; *kuśalam*—pious activities; *janāḥ*—people in general.

TRANSLATION

Please also describe eternal time, which is a representation of Your form and by whose influence people in general engage in the performance of pious activities.

PURPORT

However ignorant one may be regarding the path of good fortune and the path down to the darkest region of ignorance, everyone is aware of the influence of eternal time, which devours all the effects of our material activities. The body is born at a certain time, and immediately the influence of time acts upon it. From the date of the birth of the body, the influence of death is also acting; the advancement of age entails the influence of time on the body. If a man is thirty or fifty years old, then the influence of time has already devoured thirty or fifty years of the duration of his life.

Everyone is conscious of the last stage of life, when he will meet the cruel hands of death, but some consider their age and circumstances, concern themselves with the influence of time and thus engage in pious activities so that in the future they will not be put into a low family or an animal species. Generally, people are attached to sense enjoyment and so aspire for life on the heavenly planets. Therefore, they engage themselves in charitable or other pious activities, but actually, as stated in *Bhagavad-gītā*, one cannot get relief from the chain of birth and death even if he goes to the highest planet, Brahmaloka, because the influence of time is present everywhere within this material world. In the spiritual world, however, the time factor has no influence.

TEXT 5

लोकस्य मिथ्याभिमतेरचक्षुष-
श्चिरं प्रसुप्तस्य तमस्यनाश्रये ।
श्रान्तस्य कर्मस्वनुविद्धया धिया
त्वमाविरासीः किल योगभास्करः ॥ ५ ॥

lokasya mithyābhimater acakṣuṣaś
ciraṁ prasuptasya tamasy anāśraye

śrāntasya karmasv anuviddhayā dhiyā
tvam āvirāsīḥ kila yoga-bhāskaraḥ

lokasya—of the living entities; *mithyā-abhimateḥ*—deluded by false ego; *acakṣuṣaḥ*—blind; *ciram*—for a very long time; *prasuptasya*—sleeping; *tamasi*—in darkness; *anāśraye*—without shelter; *śrāntasya*—fatigued; *karmasu*—to material activities; *anuviddhayā*—attached; *dhiyā*—with the intelligence; *tvam*—You; *āvirāsīḥ*—have appeared; *kila*—indeed; *yoga*—of the *yoga* system; *bhāskaraḥ*—the sun.

TRANSLATION

My dear Lord, You are just like the sun, for You illuminate the darkness of the conditional life of the living entities. Because their eyes of knowledge are not open, they are sleeping eternally in that darkness without Your shelter, and therefore they are falsely engaged by the actions and reactions of their material activities, and they appear to be very fatigued.

PURPORT

It appears that Śrīmatī Devahūti, the glorious mother of Lord Kapiladeva, is very compassionate for the regrettable condition of people in general, who, not knowing the goal of life, are sleeping in the darkness of illusion. It is the general feeling of the Vaiṣṇava, or devotee of the Lord, that he should awaken them. Similarly, Devahūti is requesting her glorious son to illuminate the lives of the conditioned souls so that their most regrettable conditional life may be ended. The Lord is described herein as *yoga-bhāskara*, the sun of the system of all *yoga*. Devahūti has already requested her glorious son to describe *bhakti-yoga*, and the Lord has described *bhakti-yoga* as the ultimate *yoga* system.

Bhakti-yoga is the sunlike illumination for delivering the conditioned souls, whose general condition is described here. They have no eyes to see their own interests. They do not know that the goal of life is not to increase the material necessities of existence, because the body will not exist more than a few years. The living beings are eternal, and they have their eternal need. If one engages only in caring for the necessities of the body, not caring for the eternal necessities of life, then he is part of a civilization whose advancement puts the living entities in the darkest region of ignorance. Sleeping in that darkest region, one does not get any refreshment, but, rather, gradually becomes fatigued. He invents many processes to adjust this fatigued condition, but he fails and thus remains confused. The only path for mitigating his fatigue in the struggle for existence is the path of devotional service, or the path of Kṛṣṇa consciousness.

TEXT 6

मैत्रेय उवाच

इति मातुर्वचः श्लक्ष्णं प्रतिनन्द्य महामुनिः ।
आबभाषे कुरुश्रेष्ठ प्रीतस्तां करुणार्दितः ॥ ६ ॥

maitreya uvāca
iti mātur vacaḥ ślakṣṇaṁ
pratinandya mahā-muniḥ
ābabhāṣe kuru-śreṣṭha
prītas tāṁ karuṇārditaḥ

maitreyaḥ uvāca—Maitreya said; *iti*—thus; *mātuḥ*—of His mother; *vacaḥ*—the words; *ślakṣṇam*—gentle; *pratinandya*—welcoming; *mahā-muniḥ*—the great sage Kapila; *ābabhāṣe*—spoke; *kuru-śreṣṭha*—O best among the Kurus, Vidura; *prītaḥ*—pleased; *tām*—to her; *karuṇā*—with compassion; *arditaḥ*—moved.

TRANSLATION

Śrī Maitreya said: O best amongst the Kurus, the great sage Kapila, moved by great compassion and pleased by the words of His glorious mother, spoke as follows.

PURPORT

Lord Kapila was very satisfied by the request of His glorious mother because she was thinking not only in terms of her personal salvation but in terms of all the fallen conditioned souls. The Lord is always compassionate towards the fallen souls of this material world, and therefore He comes Himself or sends His confidential servants to deliver them. Since He is perpetually compassionate towards them, if some of His devotees also become compassionate towards them, He is very pleased with the devotees. In *Bhagavad-gītā* it is clearly stated that persons who are trying to elevate the condition of the fallen souls by preaching the conclusion of *Bhagavad-gītā*—namely, full surrender unto the Personality of Godhead—are very dear to Him. Thus when the Lord saw that His beloved mother was very compassionate towards the fallen souls, He was pleased, and He also became compassionate towards her.

TEXT 7

श्रीभगवानुवाच

भक्तियोगो बहुविधो मार्गैर्भामिनि भाव्यते ।
स्वभावगुणमार्गेण पुंसां भावो विभिद्यते ॥ ७ ॥

śrī-bhagavān uvāca
bhakti-yogo bahu-vidho
mārgair bhāmini bhāvyate
svabhāva-guṇa-mārgeṇa
puṁsāṁ bhāvo vibhidyate

śrī-bhagavān uvāca—the Personality of Godhead replied; *bhakti-yogaḥ*—devotional service; *bahu-vidhaḥ*—multifarious; *mārgaiḥ*—with paths; *bhāmini*—O noble lady; *bhāvyate*—is manifest; *svabhāva*—nature; *guṇa*—qualities; *mārgeṇa*—in terms of behavior; *puṁsām*—of the executors; *bhāvaḥ*—the appearance; *vibhidyate*—is divided.

TRANSLATION

Lord Kapila, the Personality of Godhead, replied: O noble lady, there are multifarious paths of devotional service in terms of the different qualities of the executor.

PURPORT

Pure devotional service in Kṛṣṇa consciousness is one because in pure devotional service there is no demand from the devotee to be fulfilled by the Lord. But generally people take to devotional service with a purpose. As stated in *Bhagavad-gītā*, people who are not purified take to devotional service with four purposes. A person who is distressed because of material conditions becomes a devotee of the Lord and approaches the Lord for mitigation of his distress. A person in need of money approaches the Lord to ask for some improvement in his monetary condition. Others, who are not in distress or in need of monetary assistance but are seeking knowledge in order to understand the Absolute Truth, also take to devotional service, and they inquire into the nature of the Supreme Lord. This is very nicely described in *Bhagavad-gītā* (7.16). Actually the path of devotional service is one without a second, but according to the devotees' condition, devotional service appears in multifarious varieties, as will be nicely explained in the following verses.

TEXT 8

अभिसन्धाय यो हिंसां दम्भं मात्सर्यमेव वा ।
संरम्भी भिन्नदृग्भावं मयि कुर्यात्स तामसः ॥ ८ ॥

abhisandhāya yo hiṁsāṁ
dambhaṁ mātsaryam eva vā

saṁrambhī bhinna-dṛg bhāvaṁ
mayi kuryāt sa tāmasaḥ

abhisandhāya—having in view; *yaḥ*—he who; *hiṁsām*—violence; *dambham*—pride; *mātsaryam*—envy; *eva*—indeed; *vā*—or; *saṁrambhī*—angry; *bhinna*—separate; *dṛk*—whose vision; *bhāvam*—devotional service; *mayi*—to Me; *kuryāt*—may do; *saḥ*—he; *tāmasaḥ*—in the mode of ignorance.

TRANSLATION

Devotional service executed by a person who is envious, proud, violent and angry, and who is a separatist, is considered to be in the mode of darkness.

PURPORT

It has already been stated in the *Śrīmad-Bhāgavatam,* First Canto, Second Chapter, that the highest, most glorious religion is the attainment of causeless, unmotivated devotional service. In pure devotional service, the only motive should be to please the Supreme Personality of Godhead. That is not actually a motive; that is the pure condition of the living entity. In the conditioned stage, when one engages in devotional service, he should follow the instruction of the bona fide spiritual master in full surrender. The spiritual master is the manifested representation of the Supreme Lord because he receives and presents the instructions of the Lord, as they are, by disciplic succession. It is described in *Bhagavad-gītā* that the teachings therein should be received by disciplic succession, otherwise there is adulteration. To act under the direction of a bona fide spiritual master with a motive to satisfy the Supreme Personality of Godhead is pure devotional service. But if one has a motive for personal sense gratification, his devotional service is manifested differently. Such a man may be violent, proud, envious and angry, and his interests are separate from the Lord's.

One who approaches the Supreme Lord to render devotional service, but who is proud of his personality, envious of others or vengeful, is in the mode of anger. He thinks that he is the best devotee. Devotional service executed in this way is not pure; it is mixed and is of the lowest grade, *tāmasaḥ.* Śrīla Viśvanātha Cakravartī Ṭhākura advises that a Vaiṣṇava who is not of good character should be avoided. A Vaiṣṇava is one who has taken the Supreme Personality of Godhead as the ultimate goal of life, but if one is not pure and still has motives, then he is not a Vaiṣṇava of the first order of good character. One may offer his respects to such a Vaiṣṇava because he has accepted the Supreme Lord as the ultimate goal of life, but one should not keep company with a Vaiṣṇava who is in the mode of ignorance.

TEXT 9

विषयानभिसन्धाय यश ऐश्वर्यमेव वा ।
अर्चादावर्चयेद्यो मां पृथग्भावः स राजसः ॥ ९ ॥

viṣayān abhisandhāya
yaśa aiśvaryam eva vā
arcādāv arcayed yo māṁ
pṛthag-bhāvaḥ sa rājasaḥ

viṣayān—sense objects; *abhisandhāya*—aiming at; *yaśaḥ*—fame; *aiśvaryam*—opulence; *eva*—indeed; *vā*—or; *arcā-ādau*—in worship of the Deity and so on; *arcayet*—may worship; *yaḥ*—he who; *mām*—Me; *pṛthak-bhāvaḥ*—a separatist; *saḥ*—he; *rājasaḥ*—in the mode of passion.

TRANSLATION

The worship of Deities in the temple by a separatist, with a motive for material enjoyment, fame and opulence, is devotion in the mode of passion.

PURPORT

The word "separatist" must be understood carefully. The Sanskrit words in this connection are *bhinna-dṛk* and *pṛthag-bhāvaḥ*. A separatist is one who sees his interest as separate from that of the Supreme Lord. Mixed devotees, or devotees in the modes of passion and ignorance, think that the interest of the Supreme Lord is supplying the orders of the devotee; the interest of such devotees is to draw from the Lord as much as possible for their sense gratification. This is the separatist mentality. Actually, pure devotion is explained in the previous chapter: the mind of the Supreme Lord and the mind of the devotee should be dovetailed. A devotee should not wish anything but to execute the desire of the Supreme. That is oneness. When the devotee has an interest or will different from the interest of the Supreme Lord, his mentality is that of a separatist. When the so-called devotee desires material enjoyment, without reference to the interest of the Supreme Lord, or he wants to become famous or opulent by utilizing the mercy or grace of the Supreme Lord, he is in the mode of passion.

Māyāvādīs, however, interpret this word "separatist" in a different way. They say that while worshiping the Lord, one should think himself one with the Supreme Lord. This is another adulterated form of devotion within the modes of material nature. The conception that the living entity is one with the Supreme is in the mode of ignorance. Oneness is actually based on oneness of interest. A pure devotee has no interest but to act on behalf of the Supreme Lord. When one has even a tinge of personal interest, his devotion is mixed with the three modes of material nature.

TEXT 10

कर्मनिर्हारमुद्दिश्य परस्मिन् वा तदर्पणम् ।
यजेद्यष्टव्यमिति वा पृथग्भावः स सात्त्विकः ॥१०॥

karma-nirhāram uddiśya
parasmin vā tad-arpaṇam
yajed yaṣṭavyam iti vā
pṛthag-bhāvaḥ sa sāttvikaḥ

karma—fruitive activities; *nirhāram*—freeing himself from; *uddiśya*—with the purpose of; *parasmin*—to the Supreme Personality of Godhead; *vā*—or; *tat-arpaṇam*—offering the result of activities; *yajet*—may worship; *yaṣṭavyam*—to be worshiped; *iti*—thus; *vā*—or; *pṛthak-bhāvaḥ*—separatist; *saḥ*—he; *sāttvikaḥ*—in the mode of goodness.

TRANSLATION

When a devotee worships the Supreme Personality of Godhead and offers the results of his activities in order to free himself from the inebrieties of fruitive activities, his devotion is in the mode of goodness.

PURPORT

The *brāhmaṇas, kṣatriyas, vaiśyas* and *śūdras,* along with the *brahmacārīs, gṛhasthas, vānaprasthas* and *sannyāsīs,* are the members of the eight divisions of *varṇas* and *āśramas,* and they have their respective duties to perform for the satisfaction of the Supreme Personality of Godhead. When such activities are performed and the results are offered to the Supreme Lord, they are called *karmārpaṇam,* duties performed for the satisfaction of the Lord. If there is any inebriety or fault, it is atoned for by this offering process. But if this offering process is in the mode of goodness rather than in pure devotion, then the interest is different. The four *āśramas* and the four *varṇas* act for some benefit in accordance with their personal interests. Therefore such activities are in the mode of goodness; they cannot be counted in the category of pure devotion. Pure devotional service as described by Rūpa Gosvāmī is free from all material desires. *Anyābhilāṣitā-śūnyam.* There can be no excuse for personal or material interest. Devotional activities should be transcendental to fruitive activities and empiric philosophical speculation. Pure devotional service is transcendental to all material qualities.

Devotional service in the modes of ignorance, passion and goodness can be divided into eighty-one categories. There are different devotional activities, such as hearing, chanting, remembering, worshiping, offering prayer, rendering service and surrendering everything, and each of them can be divided into three qualitative categories. There is hearing in the mode of passion, in the mode of ignorance and in the mode of goodness. Similarly, there is chanting in the mode of ignorance, passion and goodness, etc. Three multiplied by nine equals twenty-seven, and when again multiplied by three it becomes eighty-one. One has to transcend all such mixed materialistic devotional service in order to reach the standard of pure devotional service, as explained in the next verses.

TEXTS 11-12

मद्‌गुणश्रुतिमात्रेण मयि सर्वगुहाशये ।
मनोगतिरविच्छिन्ना यथा गङ्गाम्भसोऽम्बुधौ ॥११॥
लक्षणं भक्तियोगस्य निर्गुणस्य ह्युदाहृतम् ।
अहैतुक्यव्यवहिता या भक्तिः पुरुषोत्तमे ॥१२॥

mad-guṇa-śruti-mātreṇa
mayi sarva-guhāśaye
mano-gatir avicchinnā
yathā gaṅgāmbhaso 'mbudhau

lakṣaṇaṁ bhakti-yogasya
nirguṇasya hy udāhṛtam
ahaituky avyavahitā
yā bhaktiḥ puruṣottame

mat—of Me; *guṇa*—qualities; *śruti*—by hearing; *mātreṇa*—just; *mayi*—towards Me; *sarva-guhā-āśaye*—residing in everyone's heart; *manaḥ-gatiḥ*—the heart's course; *avicchinnā*—continuous; *yathā*—as; *gaṅgā*—of the Ganges; *ambhasaḥ*—of the water; *ambudhau*—towards the ocean; *lakṣaṇam*—the manifestation; *bhakti-yogasya*—of devotional service; *nirguṇasya*—unadulterated; *hi*—indeed; *udāhṛtam*—exhibited; *ahaitukī*—causeless; *avyavahitā*—not separated; *yā*—which; *bhaktiḥ*—devotional service; *puruṣa-uttame*—towards the Supreme Personality of Godhead.

TRANSLATION

The manifestation of unadulterated devotional service is exhibited when one's mind is at once attracted to hearing the transcendental name and

qualities of the Supreme Personality of Godhead, who is residing in everyone's heart. Just as the water of the Ganges flows naturally down towards the ocean, such devotional ecstasy, uninterrupted by any material condition, flows towards the Supreme Lord.

PURPORT

The basic principle of this unadulterated, pure devotional service is love of Godhead. *Mad-guṇa-śruti-mātreṇa* means "just after hearing about the transcendental qualities of the Supreme Personality of Godhead." These qualities are called *nirguṇa.* The Supreme Lord is uncontaminated by the modes of material nature; therefore He is attractive to the pure devotee. There is no need to practice meditation to attain such attraction; the pure devotee is already in the transcendental stage, and the affinity between him and the Supreme Personality of Godhead is natural and is compared to the Ganges water flowing towards the sea. The flow of the Ganges water cannot be stopped by any condition; similarly, a pure devotee's attraction for the transcendental name, form and pastimes of the Supreme Godhead cannot be stopped by any material condition. The word *avicchinnā,* "without interruptions," is very important in this connection. No material condition can stop the flow of the devotional service of a pure devotee.

The word *ahaitukī* means "without reason." A pure devotee does not render loving service to the Personality of Godhead for any cause or for any benefit, material or spiritual. This is the first symptom of unalloyed devotion. *Anyābhilāṣitā-śūnyam:* he has no desire to fulfill by rendering devotional service. Such devotional service is meant for the *puruṣottama,* the Supreme Personality, and not for anyone else. Sometimes pseudodevotees show devotion to many demigods, thinking the forms of the demigods to be the same as the Supreme Personality of Godhead's form. It is specifically mentioned herein, however, that *bhakti,* devotional service, is meant only for the Supreme Personality of Godhead, Nārāyaṇa, Viṣṇu, or Kṛṣṇa, not for anyone else.

Avyavahitā means "without cessation." A pure devotee must engage in the service of the Lord twenty-four hours a day, without cessation; his life is so molded that at every minute and every second he engages in some sort of devotional service to the Supreme Personality of Godhead. Another meaning of the word *avyavahitā* is that the interest of the devotee and the interest of the Supreme Lord are on the same level. The devotee has no interest but to fulfill the transcendental desire of the Supreme Lord. Such spontaneous service unto the Supreme Lord is transcendental and is never contaminated by the material modes of nature. These are the symptoms of pure devotional service, which is free from all contamination of material nature.

TEXT 13

सालोक्यसार्ष्टिसामीप्यसारूप्यैकत्वमप्युत ।
दीयमानं न गृह्णन्ति विना मत्सेवनं जनाः ॥१३॥

sālokya-sārṣṭi-sāmīpya-
sārūpyaikatvam apy uta
dīyamānaṁ na gṛhṇanti
vinā mat-sevanaṁ janāḥ

sālokya—living on the same planet; *sārṣṭi*—having the same opulence; *sāmīpya*—to be a personal associate; *sārūpya*—having the same bodily features; *ekatvam*—oneness; *api*—also; *uta*—even; *dīyamānam*—being offered; *na*—not; *gṛhṇanti*—do accept; *vinā*—without; *mat*—My; *sevanam*—devotional service; *janāḥ*—pure devotees.

TRANSLATION

A pure devotee does not accept any kind of liberation—sālokya, sārṣṭi, sāmīpya, sārūpya or ekatva—even though they are offered by the Supreme Personality of Godhead.

PURPORT

Lord Caitanya teaches us how to execute pure devotional service out of spontaneous love for the Supreme Personality of Godhead. In the *Śikṣāṣṭaka,* He prays to the Lord: "O Lord, I do not wish to gain from You any wealth, nor do I wish to have a beautiful wife, nor do I wish to have many followers. All I want from You is that in life after life I may remain a pure devotee at Your lotus feet." There is a similarity between the prayers of Lord Caitanya and the statements of *Śrīmad-Bhāgavatam.* Lord Caitanya prays, "in life after life," indicating that a devotee does not even desire the cessation of birth and death. The *yogīs* and empiric philosophers desire cessation of the process of birth and death, but a devotee is satisfied to remain even in this material world and execute devotional service.

It is clearly stated herein that a pure devotee does not desire *ekatva,* oneness with the Supreme Lord, as desired by the impersonalists, the mental speculators and the meditators. To become one with the Supreme Lord is beyond the dream of a pure devotee. Sometimes he may accept promotion to the Vaikuṇṭha planets to serve the

Lord there, but he will never accept merging into the Brahman effulgence, which he considers worse than hellish. Such *ekatva,* or merging into the effulgence of the Supreme Lord, is called *kaivalya,* but the happiness derived from *kaivalya* is considered by the pure devotee to be hellish. The devotee is so fond of rendering service to the Supreme Lord that the five kinds of liberation are not important to him. If one is engaged in pure transcendental loving service to the Lord, it is understood that he has already achieved the five kinds of liberation.

When a devotee is promoted to the spiritual world, Vaikuṇṭha, he receives four kinds of facilities. One of these is *sālokya,* living on the same planet as the Supreme Personality. The Supreme Person, in His different plenary expansions, lives on innumerable Vaikuṇṭha planets, and the chief planet is Kṛṣṇaloka. Just as within the material universe the chief planet is the sun, in the spiritual world the chief planet is Kṛṣṇaloka. From Kṛṣṇaloka, the bodily effulgence of Lord Kṛṣṇa is distributed not only to the spiritual world but to the material world as well; it is covered by matter, however, in the material world. In the spiritual world there are innumerable Vaikuṇṭha planets, and on each one the Lord is the predominating Deity. A devotee can be promoted to one such Vaikuṇṭha planet to live with the Supreme Personality of Godhead.

In *sārṣṭi* liberation the opulence of the devotee is equal to the opulence of the Supreme Lord. *Sāmīpya* means to be a personal associate of the Supreme Lord. In *sārūpya* liberation the bodily features of the devotee are exactly like those of the Supreme Person but for two or three symptoms found exclusively on the transcendental body of the Lord. Śrīvatsa, for example, the hair on the chest of the Lord, particularly distinguishes Him from His devotees.

A pure devotee does not accept these five kinds of spiritual existence, even if they are offered, and he certainly does not hanker after material benefits, which are all insignificant in comparison with spiritual benefits. When Prahlāda Mahārāja was offered some material benefit, he stated: "My Lord, I have seen that my father achieved all kinds of material benefits, and even the demigods were afraid of his opulence, but still, in a second, You have finished his life and all his material prosperity." For a devotee there is no question of desiring any material or spiritual prosperity. He simply aspires to serve the Lord. That is his highest happiness.

TEXT 14

स एव भक्तियोगाख्य आत्यन्तिक उदाहृतः ।
येनातिव्रज्य त्रिगुणं मद्भावायोपपद्यते ॥१४॥

sa eva bhakti-yogākhya
ātyantika udāhṛtaḥ
yenātivrajya tri-guṇaṁ
mad-bhāvāyopapadyate

saḥ—this; *eva*—indeed; *bhakti-yoga*—devotional service; *ākhyaḥ*—called; *ātyantikaḥ*—the highest platform; *udāhṛtaḥ*—explained; *yena*—by which; *ativrajya*—overcoming; *tri-guṇam*—the three modes of material nature; *mat-bhāvāya*—to My transcendental stage; *upapadyate*—one attains.

TRANSLATION

By attaining the highest platform of devotional service, as I have explained, one can overcome the influence of the three modes of material nature and be situated in the transcendental stage, as is the Lord.

PURPORT

Śrīpāda Śaṅkarācārya, who is supposed to be the leader of the impersonalist school of philosophers, has admitted in the beginning of his comments on *Bhagavad-gītā* that Nārāyaṇa, the Supreme Personality of Godhead, is beyond the material creation; except for Him, everything is within the material creation. It is also confirmed in the Vedic literature that before the creation there was only Nārāyaṇa; neither Lord Brahmā nor Lord Śiva existed. Only Nārāyaṇa, or the Supreme Personality of Godhead, Viṣṇu, or Kṛṣṇa, is always in the transcendental position, beyond the influence of material creation.

The material qualities of goodness, passion and ignorance cannot affect the position of the Supreme Personality of Godhead; therefore He is called *nirguṇa* (free from all tinges of material qualities). Here the same fact is confirmed by Lord Kapila: one who is situated in pure devotional service is transcendentally situated, as is the Lord. Just as the Lord is unaffected by the influence of the material modes, so too are His pure devotees. One who is not affected by the three modes of material nature is called a liberated soul, or *brahma-bhūta* soul. *Brahma-bhūtaḥ prasannātmā* is the stage of liberation. *Ahaṁ brahmāsmi:* "I am not this body." This is applicable only to the person who constantly engages in the devotional service of Kṛṣṇa and is thus in the transcendental stage; he is above the influence of the three modes of material nature.

It is the misconception of the impersonalists that one can worship any imaginary form of the Lord, or Brahman, and at the end merge in the Brahman effulgence. Of course, to merge into the bodily effulgence (Brahman) of the Supreme Lord is also liberation, as explained in the previous verse. *Ekatva* is also liberation, but that sort of liberation is never accepted by any devotee, for qualitative oneness is immediately attained as soon as one is situated in devotional service. For a devotee, that qualitative equality, which is the result of impersonal liberation, is already attained; he does not have to try for it separately. It is clearly stated here that simply by pure devotional service one becomes qualitatively as good as the Lord Himself.

TEXT 15

निषेवितेनानिमित्तेन स्वधर्मेण महीयसा ।
क्रियायोगेन शस्तेन नातिहिंस्रेण नित्यशः ॥१५॥

niṣevitenānimittena
sva-dharmeṇa mahīyasā
kriyā-yogena śastena
nātihiṁsreṇa nityaśaḥ

niṣevitena—executed; *animittena*—without attachment to the result; *sva-dharmeṇa*—by one's prescribed duties; *mahīyasā*—glorious; *kriyā-yogena*—by devotional activities; *śastena*—auspicious; *na*—without; *atihiṁsreṇa*—excessive violence; *nityaśaḥ*—regularly.

TRANSLATION

A devotee must execute his prescribed duties, which are glorious, without material profit. Without excessive violence, one should regularly perform one's devotional activities.

PURPORT

One has to execute his prescribed duties according to his social position as a *brāhmaṇa, kṣatriya, vaiśya* or *śūdra.* The prescribed duties of the four classes of men in human society are also described in *Bhagavad-gītā.* The activities of *brāhmaṇas* are to control the senses and to become simple, clean, learned devotees. The *kṣatriyas* have the spirit for ruling, they are not afraid on the battlefield, and they are charitable. The *vaiśyas,* or the mercantile class of men, trade in commodities, protect cows and develop agricultural produce. The *śūdras,* or laborer class, serve the higher classes because they themselves are not very intelligent.

From every position, as confirmed in *Bhagavad-gītā, sva-karmaṇā tam abhyarcya:* one can serve the Supreme Lord by performing one's prescribed duty. It is not that only the *brāhmaṇas* can serve the Supreme Lord and not the *śūdras.* Anyone can serve the Supreme Lord by performing his prescribed duties under the direction of a spiritual master, or representative of the Supreme Personality of Godhead. No one should think that his prescribed duties are inferior. A *brāhmaṇa* can serve the Lord by using his intelligence, and the *kṣatriya* can serve the Supreme Lord by using his military arts, just as Arjuna served Kṛṣṇa. Arjuna was a warrior; he had no time to study *Vedānta* or other highly intellectual books. The damsels in Vrajadhāma were girls born of the *vaiśya* class, and they engaged in protecting cows and producing agriculture. Kṛṣṇa's foster father, Nanda Mahārāja, and his associates were all *vaiśyas.* They were not at all educated, but they could serve Kṛṣṇa by loving Him and by offering everything to Him. Similarly, there are many instances in which *caṇḍālas,* or those lower than *śūdras,* have served Kṛṣṇa. Also, the sage Vidura was considered a *śūdra* because his mother happened to be *śūdra.* There are no distinctions, for it is declared by the Lord in *Bhagavad-gītā* that anyone engaged specifically in devotional service is elevated to the transcendental position without a doubt. Everyone's prescribed duty is glorious if it is performed in devotional service of the Lord, without desire for profit. Such loving service must be performed without reason, without impediment, and spontaneously. Kṛṣṇa is lovable, and one has to serve Him in whatever capacity one can. That is pure devotional service.

Another significant phrase in this verse is *nātihiṁsreṇa* ("with minimum violence or sacrifice of life"). Even if a devotee has to commit violence, it should not be done beyond what is necessary. Sometimes the question is put before us: "You ask us not to eat meat, but you are eating vegetables. Do you think that is not violence?" The answer is that eating vegetables is violence, and vegetarians are also committing violence against other living entities because vegetables also have life. Nondevotees are killing cows, goats and so many other animals for eating purposes, and a devotee, who is vegetarian, is also killing. But here, significantly, it is stated that every living entity has to live by killing another entity; that is the law of nature. *Jīvo jīvasya jīvanam:* one living entity is the life for another living entity. But for a human being, that violence should be committed only as much as necessary.

A human being is not to eat anything which is not offered to the Supreme Personality of Godhead. *Yajña-śiṣṭāśinaḥ santaḥ:* one becomes freed from all sinful reactions by eating foodstuffs which are offered to Yajña, the Supreme Personality of Godhead. A devotee therefore eats only *prasāda,* or foodstuffs offered to the Supreme Lord, and Kṛṣṇa says that when a devotee offers Him foodstuffs from the vegetable kingdom, with devotion, He eats that. A devotee is to offer to Kṛṣṇa foodstuffs prepared from vegetables. If the Supreme Lord wanted foodstuffs prepared from animal food, the devotee could offer this, but He does not order to do that.

We have to commit violence; that is a natural law. We should not, however, commit violence extravagantly, but only as much as ordered by the Lord. Arjuna engaged in the art of killing, and although killing is, of course, violence, he killed the enemy simply on Kṛṣṇa's order. In the same way, if we commit violence as it is necessary, by the order of the Lord, that is called *nātihiṁsā.* We cannot avoid violence, for we are put into a conditional life in which we have to commit violence, but we should not commit more violence than necessary or than ordered by the Supreme Personality of Godhead.

TEXT 16

मद्धिष्ण्यदर्शनस्पर्शपूजास्तुत्यभिवन्दनैः ।
भूतेषु मद्भावनया सत्त्वेनासङ्गमेन च ॥१६॥

mad-dhiṣṇya-darśana-sparśa-
pūjā-stuty-abhivandanaiḥ
bhūteṣu mad-bhāvanayā
sattvenāsaṅgamena ca

mat—My; *dhiṣṇya*—statue; *darśana*—seeing; *sparśa*—touching; *pūjā*—worshiping; *stuti*—praying to; *abhivandanaiḥ*—by offering obeisances; *bhūteṣu*—in all living entities; *mat*—of Me; *bhāvanayā*—with thought; *sattvena*—by the mode of goodness; *asaṅgamena*—with detachment; *ca*—and.

TRANSLATION

The devotee should regularly see My statues in the temple, touch My lotus feet and offer worshipable paraphernalia and prayer. He should see in the spirit of renunciation, from the mode of goodness, and see every living entity as spiritual.

PURPORT

Temple worship is one of the duties of a devotee. It is especially recommended for neophytes, but those who are advanced should not refrain from temple worship. There is a distinction in the manner a neophyte and an advanced devotee appreciate the Lord's presence in the temple. A neophyte considers the *arcā-vigraha* (the statue of the Lord) to be different from the original Personality of Godhead; he considers it a representation of the Supreme Lord in the form of a Deity. But an advanced devotee accepts the Deity in the temple as the Supreme Personality of Godhead. He does not see any difference between the original form of the Lord and the statue, or *arcā* form of the Lord, in the temple. This is the vision of a devotee whose devotional service is in the highest stage of *bhāva,* or love of Godhead, whereas a neophyte's worship in the temple is a matter of routine duty.

Temple Deity worship is one of the functions of a devotee. He goes regularly to see the Deity nicely decorated, and with veneration and respect he touches the lotus feet of the Lord and presents offerings of worship, such as fruits, flowers and prayers. At the same time, to advance in devotional service, a devotee should see other living entities as spiritual sparks, parts and parcels of the Supreme Lord. A devotee is to offer respect to every entity that has a relationship with the Lord. Because every living entity originally has a relationship with the Lord as part and parcel, a devotee should try to see all living entities on the same equal level of spiritual existence. As stated in *Bhagavad-gītā,* a *paṇḍita,* one who is learned, sees equally a very learned *brāhmaṇa,* a *śūdra,* a hog, a dog and a cow. He does not see the body, which is only an outward dress. He does not see the dress of a *brāhmaṇa,* or that of a cow or of a hog. He sees the spiritual spark, part and parcel of the Supreme Lord. If a devotee does not see every living entity as part and parcel of the Supreme Lord, he is considered *prākṛta-bhakta,* a materialistic devotee. He is not completely situated on the spiritual platform; rather, he is in the lowest stage of devotion. He does, however, show all respect to the Deity.

Although a devotee sees all living entities on the level of spiritual existence, he is not interested in associating with everyone. Simply because a tiger is part and parcel of the Supreme Lord does not mean that we embrace him because of his spiritual relationship with the Supreme Lord. We must associate only with persons who have developed Kṛṣṇa consciousness.

We should befriend and offer special respect to persons who are developed in Kṛṣṇa consciousness. Other living entities are undoubtedly part and parcel of the Supreme Lord, but because their consciousness is still covered and not developed in Kṛṣṇa consciousness, we should renounce their association. It is said by Viśvanātha Cakravartī Ṭhākura that even if one is a Vaiṣṇava, if he is not of good character his company should be avoided, although he may be offered the respect of a Vaiṣṇava. Anyone who accepts Viṣṇu as the Supreme Personality of Godhead is accepted as a Vaiṣṇava, but a Vaiṣṇava is expected to develop all the good qualities of the demigods.

The exact meaning of the word *sattvena* is given by Śrīdhara Svāmī as being synonymous with *dhairyeṇa,* or patience. One must perform devotional service with great patience. One should not give up the execution of devotional service because one or two attempts have not been successful. One must continue. Śrī Rūpa Gosvāmī also confirms that one should be very enthusiastic and execute devotional service with patience and confidence. Patience is necessary for developing the confidence that "Kṛṣṇa will certainly accept me because I am engaging in devotional service." One has only to execute service according to the rules and regulations to insure success.

TEXT 17

महतां बहुमानेन दीनानामनुकम्पया ।
मैत्र्या चैवात्मतुल्येषु यमेन नियमेन च ॥१७॥

mahatāṁ bahu-mānena
dīnānām anukampayā
maitryā caivātma-tulyeṣu
yamena niyamena ca

mahatām—to the great souls; *bahu-mānena*—with great respect; *dīnānām*—to the poor; *anukampayā*—with compassion; *maitryā*—with friendship; *ca*—also; *eva*—certainly; *ātma-tulyeṣu*—to persons who are equals; *yamena*—with control of the senses; *niyamena*—with regulation; *ca*—and.

TRANSLATION

The pure devotee should execute devotional service by giving the greatest respect to the spiritual master and the ācāryas. He should be compassionate to the poor and make friendship with persons who are his equals, but all his activities should be executed under regulation and with control of the senses.

PURPORT

In *Bhagavad-gītā*, Thirteenth Chapter, it is clearly stated that one should execute devotional service and advance on the path of spiritual knowledge by accepting the *ācārya. Ācāryopāsanam:* one should worship an *ācārya,* a spiritual master who knows things as they are. The spiritual master must be in the disciplic succession from Kṛṣṇa. The predecessors of the spiritual master are his spiritual master, his grand spiritual master, his great-grand spiritual master and so on, who form the disciplic succession of *ācāryas.*

It is recommended herewith that all the *ācāryas* be given the highest respect. It is stated, *guruṣu nara-matiḥ. Guruṣu* means "unto the *ācāryas*," and *nara-matiḥ* means "thinking like a common man." To think of the Vaiṣṇavas, the devotees, as belonging to a particular caste or community, to think of the *ācāryas* as ordinary men or to think of the Deity in the temple as being made of stone, wood or metal, is condemned. *Niyamena:* one should offer the greatest respect to the *ācāryas* according to the standard regulations. A devotee should also be compassionate to the poor. This does not refer to those who are poverty-stricken materially. According to devotional vision, a man is poor if he is not in Kṛṣṇa consciousness. A man may be very rich materially, but if he is not Kṛṣṇa conscious, he is considered poor. On the other hand, many *ācāryas,* such as Rūpa Gosvāmī and Sanātana Gosvāmī, used to live beneath trees every night. Superficially it appeared that they were poverty-stricken, but from their writings we can understand that in spiritual life they were the richest personalities.

A devotee shows compassion to those poor souls who are wanting in spiritual knowledge by enlightening them in order to elevate them to Kṛṣṇa consciousness. That is one of the duties of a devotee. He should also make friendship with persons who are on an equal level with himself or who have the same understanding that he does. For a devotee, there is no point in making friendships with ordinary persons; he should make friendship with other devotees so that by discussing among themselves, they may elevate one another on the path of spiritual understanding. This is called *iṣṭa-goṣṭhī.*

In *Bhagavad-gītā* there is reference to *bodhayantaḥ parasparam,* "discussing among themselves." Generally pure devotees utilize their valuable time in chanting and discussing various activities of Lord Kṛṣṇa or Lord Caitanya amongst themselves. There are innumerable books, such as the *Purāṇas, Mahābhārata, Bhāgavatam, Bhagavad-gītā* and *Upaniṣads,* which contain countless subjects for discussion among two devotees or more. Friendship should be cemented between persons with mutual interests and understanding. Such persons are said to be *sva jāti,* "of the same caste." The devotee should avoid a person whose character is not fixed in the standard understanding; even though he may be a Vaiṣṇava, or a devotee of Kṛṣṇa, if his character is not correctly representative, then he should be avoided. One should steadily control the senses and the mind and strictly follow the rules and regulations, and he should make friendship with persons of the same standard.

TEXT 18

आध्यात्मिकानुश्रवणान्नामसङ्कीर्तनाच्च मे ।
आर्जवेनार्यसङ्गेन निरहङ्क्रियया तथा ॥१८॥

ādhyātmikānuśravaṇān
nāma-saṅkīrtanāc ca me
ārjavenārya-saṅgena
nirahaṅkriyayā tathā

ādhyātmika—spiritual matters; *anuśravaṇāt*—from hearing; *nāma-saṅkīrtanāt*—from chanting the holy name; *ca*—and; *me*—My; *ārjavena*—with straightforward behavior; *ārya-saṅgena*—with association of saintly persons; *nirahaṅkriyayā*—without false ego; *tathā*—thus.

TRANSLATION

A devotee should always try to hear about spiritual matters and should always utilize his time in chanting the holy name of the Lord. His behavior should always be straightforward and simple, and although he is not envious but friendly to everyone, he should avoid the company of persons who are not spiritually advanced.

PURPORT

In order to advance in spiritual understanding, one has to hear from authentic sources about spiritual knowledge. One can understand the reality of spiritual life by following strict regulative principles and by controlling the senses. To have control it is necessary that one be nonviolent and truthful, refrain from stealing, abstain from sex life and possess only that which is absolutely necessary for keeping the body and soul together. One should not eat more than necessary, he should not collect more paraphernalia than necessary, he should not talk unnecessarily with common men, and he should not follow the rules and regulations without purpose. He should follow the rules and regulations so that he may actually make advancement.

There are eighteen qualifications mentioned in *Bhagavad-gītā*, among which is simplicity. One should be without pride; one should not demand unnecessary respect from others, and one should be nonviolent. *Amānitvam adambhitvam ahiṁsā.* One should be very tolerant and simple, one should accept the spiritual master, and one should control the senses. These are mentioned here and in *Bhagavad-gītā* as well. One should hear from authentic sources how to advance in spiritual life; such instructions should be taken from the *ācārya* and should be assimilated.

It is especially mentioned here, *nāma-saṅkīrtanāc ca:* one should chant the holy names of the Lord—Hare Kṛṣṇa, Hare Kṛṣṇa, Kṛṣṇa Kṛṣṇa, Hare Hare/ Hare Rāma, Hare Rāma, Rāma Rāma, Hare Hare—either individually or with others. Lord Caitanya has given special stress to chanting of these holy names of the Lord as the basic principle of spiritual advancement. Another word used here is *ārjavena*, meaning "without diplomacy." A devotee should not make plans out of self-interest. Of course, preachers sometimes have to make some plan to execute the mission of the Lord under proper guidance, but regarding personal self-interest, a devotee should always be without diplomacy, and he should avoid the company of persons who are not advancing in spiritual life. Another word is *ārya.* Āryans are persons who are advancing in knowledge of Kṛṣṇa consciousness as well as in material prosperity. The difference between the Āryan and non-Āryan, the *sura* and *asura,* is in their standards of spiritual advancement. Association with persons who are not spiritually advanced is forbidden. Lord Caitanya advised, *asat-saṅga-tyāga:* one should avoid persons who are attached to the temporary. *Asat* is one who is too materially attached, who is not a devotee of the Lord and who is too attached to women or enjoyable material things. Such a person, according to Vaiṣṇava philosophy, is a persona non grata.

A devotee should not be proud of his acquisitions. The symptoms of a devotee are meekness and humility. Although spiritually very advanced, he will always remain meek and humble, as Kavirāja Gosvāmī and all the other Vaiṣṇavas have taught us by personal example. Caitanya Mahāprabhu taught that one should be humbler than the grass on the street and more tolerant than the tree. One should not be proud or falsely puffed up. In this way one will surely advance in spiritual life.

TEXT 19

मद्धर्मणो गुणैरेतैः परिसंशुद्ध आशयः ।
पुरुषस्याञ्जसाभ्येति श्रुतमात्रगुणं हि माम् ॥१९॥

mad-dharmaṇo guṇair etaiḥ
parisaṁśuddha āśayaḥ
puruṣasyāñjasābhyeti
śruta-mātra-guṇaṁ hi mām

mat-dharmaṇaḥ—of My devotee; *guṇaiḥ*—with the attributes; *etaiḥ*—these; *parisaṁśuddhaḥ*—completely purified; *āśayaḥ*—consciousness; *puruṣasya*—of a person; *añjasā*—instantly; *abhyeti*—approaches; *śruta*—by hearing; *mātra*—simply; *guṇam*—quality; *hi*—certainly; *mām*—Me.

TRANSLATION

When one is fully qualified with all these transcendental attributes and his consciousness is thus completely purified, he is immediately attracted simply by hearing My name or hearing of My transcendental quality.

PURPORT

In the beginning of this instruction, the Lord explained to His mother that *mad-guṇa-śruti-mātreṇa,* simply by hearing of the name, quality, form, etc., of the Supreme Personality of Godhead, one is immediately attracted. A person becomes fully qualified with all transcendental qualities by following the rules and regulations, as recommended in different scriptures. We have developed certain unnecessary qualities by material association, and by following the above process we become free from that contamination. To develop transcendental qualities, as explained in the previous verse, one must become free from these contaminated qualities.

TEXT 20

यथा वातरथो घ्राणमावृङ्क्ते गन्ध आशयात् ।
एवं योगरतं चेत आत्मानमविकारि यत् ॥२०॥

yathā vāta-ratho ghrāṇam
āvṛṅkte gandha āśayāt
evaṁ yoga-rataṁ ceta
ātmānam avikāri yat

yathā—as; *vāta*—of air; *rathaḥ*—the chariot; *ghrāṇam*—sense of smell; *āvṛṅkte*—catches; *gandhaḥ*—aroma; *āśayāt*—from the source; *evam*—similarly; *yoga-ratam*—engaged in devotional service; *cetaḥ*—consciousness; *ātmānam*—the Supreme Soul; *avikāri*—unchanging; *yat*—which.

TRANSLATION

As the chariot of air carries an aroma from its source and immediately catches the sense of smell, similarly, one who constantly engages in devotional service, in Kṛṣṇa consciousness, can catch the Supreme Soul, who is equally present everywhere.

PURPORT

As a breeze carrying a pleasant fragrance from a garden of flowers at once captures the organ of smell, so one's consciousness, saturated with devotion, can at once capture the transcendental existence of the Supreme Personality of Godhead, who, in His Paramātmā feature, is present everywhere, even in the heart of every living being. It is stated in *Bhagavad-gītā* that the Supreme Personality of Godhead is *kṣetra jña,* present within this body, but He is also simultaneously present in every other body.

Since the individual soul is present only in a particular body, he is altered when another individual soul does not cooperate with him. The Supersoul, however, is equally present everywhere. Individual souls may disagree, but the Supersoul, being equally present in every body, is called unchanging, or *avikāri*. The individual soul, when fully saturated with Kṛṣṇa consciousness, can understand the presence of the Supersoul. It is confirmed in *Bhagavad-gītā* that (*bhaktyā mām abhijānāti*) a person saturated with devotional service in full Krsna consciousness can understand the Supreme Personality of Godhead, either as Supersoul or as the Supreme Person.

TEXT 21

अहं सर्वेषु भूतेषु भूतात्मावस्थितः सदा ।
तमवज्ञाय मां मर्त्यः कुरुतेऽर्चाविडम्बनम् ॥२१॥

ahaṁ sarveṣu bhūteṣu
bhūtātmāvasthitaḥ sadā
tam avajñāya māṁ martyaḥ
kurute 'rcā-viḍambanam

aham—I; *sarveṣu*—in all; *bhūteṣu*—living entities; *bhūta-ātmā*—the Supersoul in all beings; *avasthitaḥ*—situated; *sadā*—always; *tam*—that Supersoul; *avajñāya*—disregarding; *mām*—Me; *martyaḥ*—a mortal man; *kurute*—performs; *arcā*—of worship of the Deity; *viḍambanam*—imitation.

TRANSLATION

I am present in every living entity as the Supersoul. If someone neglects or disregards that Supersoul everywhere and engages himself in the worship of the Deity in the temple, that is simply imitation.

PURPORT

In purified consciousness, or Kṛṣṇa consciousness, one sees the presence of Kṛṣṇa everywhere. If, therefore, one only engages in Deity worship in the temple and does not consider other living entities, then he is in the lowest grade of devotional service. One who worships the Deity in the temple and does not show respect to others is a devotee on the material platform, in the lowest stage of devotional service. A devotee should try to understand everything in relationship with Kṛṣṇa and try to serve everything in that spirit. To serve everything means to engage everything in the service of Kṛṣṇa. If a person is innocent and does not know his relationship with

Kṛṣṇa, an advanced devotee should try to engage him in the service of Kṛṣṇa. One who is advanced in Kṛṣṇa consciousness can engage not only the living being but everything in the service of Kṛṣṇa.

TEXT 22

यो मां सर्वेषु भूतेषु सन्तमात्मानमीश्वरम् ।
हित्वार्चां भजते मौढ्याद्भस्मन्येव जुहोति सः ॥२२॥

yo māṁ sarveṣu bhūteṣu
santam ātmānam īśvaram
hitvārcāṁ bhajate mauḍhyād
bhasmany eva juhoti saḥ

yaḥ—one who; *mām*—Me; *sarveṣu*—in all; *bhūteṣu*—living entities; *santam*—being present; *ātmānam*—the Paramātmā; *īśvaram*—the Supreme Lord; *hitvā*—disregarding; *arcām*—the Deity; *bhajate*—worships; *mauḍhyāt*—because of ignorance; *bhasmani*—into ashes; *eva*—only; *juhoti*—offers oblations; *saḥ*—he.

TRANSLATION

One who worships the Deity of Godhead in the temples but does not know that the Supreme Lord, as Paramātmā, is situated in every living entity's heart, must be in ignorance and is compared to one who offers oblations into ashes.

PURPORT

It is stated clearly herein that the Supreme Personality of Godhead, in His plenary expansion of Supersoul, is present in all living entities. The living entities have 8,400,000 different kinds of bodies, and the Supreme Personality of Godhead is living in every body both as the individual soul and as the Supersoul. Since the individual soul is part and parcel of the Supreme Lord, in that sense the Lord is living in every body, and, as Supersoul, the Lord is also present as a witness. In both cases the presence of God in every living entity is essential. Therefore persons who profess to belong to some religious sect but who do not feel the presence of the Supreme Personality of Godhead in every living entity, and everywhere else, are in the mode of ignorance.

If, without this preliminary knowledge of the Lord's omnipresence, one simply attaches himself to the rituals in a temple, church or mosque, it is as if he were offering butter into ashes rather than into the fire. One offers sacrifices by pouring clarified butter into a fire and chanting Vedic *mantras,* but even if there are Vedic *mantras* and all conditions are favorable, if the clarified butter is poured on ashes, then such a sacrifice will be useless. In other words, a devotee should not ignore any living entity. The devotee must know that in every living entity, however insignificant he may be, even in an ant, God is present, and therefore every living entity should be kindly treated and should not be subjected to any violence. In modern civilized society, slaughterhouses are regularly maintained and supported by a certain type of religious principle. But without knowledge of the presence of God in every living entity, any so-called advancement of human civilization, either spiritual or material, is to be understood as being in the mode of ignorance.

TEXT 23

द्विषतः परकाये मां मानिनो भिन्नदर्शिनः ।
भूतेषु बद्धवैरस्य न मनः शान्तिमृच्छति ॥२३॥

dviṣataḥ para-kāye māṁ
mānino bhinna-darśinaḥ
bhūteṣu baddha-vairasya
na manaḥ śāntim ṛcchati

dviṣataḥ—of one who is envious; *para-kāye*—towards the body of another; *mām*—unto Me; *māninaḥ*—offering respect; *bhinna-darśinaḥ*—of a separatist; *bhūteṣu*—towards living entities; *baddha-vairasya*—of one who is inimical; *na*—not; *manaḥ*—the mind; *śāntim*—peace; *ṛcchati*—attains.

TRANSLATION

One who offers Me respect but is envious of the bodies of others and is therefore a separatist never attains peace of mind, because of his inimical behavior towards other living entities.

PURPORT

In this verse, two phrases, *bhūteṣu baddha-vairasya* ("inimical towards others") and *dviṣataḥ para-kāye* ("envious of another's body"), are significant. One who is envious of or inimical towards others never experiences any happiness. A devotee's vision, therefore, must be perfect. He should ignore bodily distinctions and should see only the presence of the part and parcel of the Supreme Lord, and the Lord Himself in His plenary expansion as Supersoul. That is the vision of a pure devotee. The bodily expression of a particular type of living entity is always ignored by the devotee.

It is expressed herein that the Lord is always eager to deliver the conditioned souls, who have been encaged within material bodies. Devotees are expected to carry the message or desire of the Lord to such conditioned souls and enlighten them with Kṛṣṇa consciousness. Thus they may be elevated to transcendental, spiritual life, and the mission of their lives will be successful. Of course this is not possible for living entities who are lower than human beings, but in human society it is feasible that all living entities can be enlightened with Kṛṣṇa consciousness. Even living entities who are lower than human can be raised to Kṛṣṇa consciousness by other methods. For example, Śivānanda Sena, a great devotee of Lord Caitanya, delivered a dog by feeding him *prasāda.* Distribution of *prasāda,* or remnants of foodstuffs offered to the Lord, even to the ignorant masses of people and to animals, gives such living entities the chance for elevation to Kṛṣṇa consciousness. Factually it happened that the same dog, when met by Lord Caitanya at Purī, was liberated from the material condition.

It is especially mentioned here that a devotee must be free from all violence (*jīvāhiṁsā*). Lord Caitanya has recommended that a devotee not commit violence to any living entity. Sometimes the question is raised that since vegetables also have life and devotees take vegetable foodstuffs, isn't that violence? Firstly, however, taking some leaves, twigs or fruit from a tree or plant does not kill the plant. Besides that, *jīvāhiṁsā* means that since every living entity has to pass through a particular type of body according to his past *karma,* although every living entity is eternal, he should not be disturbed in his gradual evolution. A devotee has to execute the principles of devotional service exactly as they are, and he must know that however insignificant a living entity may be, the Lord is present within him. A devotee must realize this universal presence of the Lord.

TEXT 24

अहमुच्चावचैर्द्रव्यैः क्रिययोत्पन्नयानघे ।
नैव तुष्येऽर्चितोऽर्चायां भूतग्रामावमानिनः ॥२४॥

aham uccāvacair dravyaiḥ
kriyayotpannayānaghe
naiva tuṣye 'rcito 'rcāyāṁ
bhūta-grāmāvamāninaḥ

aham—I; *ucca-avacaiḥ*—with various; *dravyaiḥ*—paraphernalia; *kriyayā*—by religious rituals; *utpannayā*—accomplished; *anaghe*—O sinless mother; *na*—not; *eva*—certainly; *tuṣye*—am pleased; *arcitaḥ*—worshiped; *arcāyām*—in the Deity form; *bhūta-grāma*—to other living entities; *avamāninaḥ*—with those who are disrespectful.

TRANSLATION

My dear Mother, even if he worships with proper rituals and paraphernalia, a person who is ignorant of My presence in all living entities never pleases Me by the worship of My Deities in the temple.

PURPORT

There are sixty-four different prescriptions for worship of the Deity in the temple. There are many items offered to the Deity, some valuable and some less valuable. It is prescribed in *Bhagavad-gītā:* "If a devotee offers Me a small flower, a leaf, some water or a little fruit, I will accept it." The real purpose is to exhibit one's loving devotion to the Lord; the offerings themselves are secondary. If one has not developed loving devotion to the Lord and simply offers many kinds of foodstuffs, fruits and flowers without real devotion, the offering will not be accepted by the Lord. We cannot bribe the Personality of Godhead. He is so great that our bribery has no value. Nor has He any scarcity; since He is full in Himself, what can we offer Him? Everything is produced by Him. We simply offer to show our love and gratitude to the Lord.

This gratitude and love for God is exhibited by a pure devotee, who knows that the Lord lives in every living entity. As such, temple worship necessarily includes distribution of *prasāda.* It is not that one should create a temple in his private apartment or private room, offer something to the Lord, and then eat. Of course, that is better than simply cooking foodstuffs and eating without understanding one's relationship with the Supreme Lord; people who act in this manner are just like animals. But the devotee who wants to elevate himself to the higher level of understanding must know that the Lord is present in every living entity, and, as stated in the previous verse, one should be compassionate to other living entities. A devotee should worship the Supreme Lord, be friendly to persons who are on the same level and be compassionate to the ignorant. One should exhibit his compassion for ignorant living entities by distributing *prasāda.* Distribution of *prasāda* to the ignorant masses of people is essential for persons who make offerings to the Personality of Godhead.

Real love and devotion is accepted by the Lord. Many valuable foodstuffs may be presented to a person, but if the person is not hungry, all such offerings are useless for him. Similarly, we may offer many valuable items to the Deity, but if we have no real sense of devotion and no real sense of the Lord's presence everywhere, then we are lacking in devotional service; in such a state of ignorance, we cannot offer anything acceptable to the Lord.

TEXT 25

अर्चादावर्चयेत्तावदीश्वरं मां स्वकर्मकृत् ।
यावन्न वेद स्वहृदि सर्वभूतेष्ववस्थितम् ॥२५॥

arcādāv arcayet tāvad
īśvaraṁ māṁ sva-karma-kṛt
yāvan na veda sva-hṛdi
sarva-bhūteṣv avasthitam

arcā-ādau—beginning with worship of the Deity; *arcayet*—one should worship; *tāvat*—so long; *īśvaram*—the Supreme Personality of Godhead; *mām*—Me; *sva*—his own; *karma*—prescribed duties; *kṛt*—performing; *yāvat*—as long as; *na*—not; *veda*—he realizes; *sva-hṛdi*—in his own heart; *sarva-bhūteṣu*—in all living entities; *avasthitam*—situated.

TRANSLATION

Performing his prescribed duties, one should worship the Deity of the Supreme Personality of Godhead until one realizes My presence in his own heart and in the hearts of other living entities as well.

PURPORT

Worship of the Deity of the Supreme Personality of Godhead is prescribed herewith even for persons who are simply discharging their prescribed duties. There are prescribed duties for the different social classes of men—the *brāhmaṇas,* the *vaiśyas,* the *kṣatriyas* and the *śūdras*—and for the different *āśramas-brahmacarya, gṛhastha, vānaprastha* and *sannyāsa.* One should worship the Deity of the Lord until one appreciates the presence of the Lord in every living entity. In other words, one should not be satisfied simply by discharging his duties properly; he must realize his relationship and the relationship of all other living entities with the Supreme Personality of Godhead. If he does not understand this, then even though he discharges his prescribed duties properly, it is to be understood that he is simply laboring without profit.

The word *sva-karma-kṛt* in this verse is very significant. *Sva-karma-kṛt* is one who engages in discharging his prescribed duties. It is not that one who has become a devotee of the Lord or who engages in devotional service should give up his prescribed duties. No one should be lazy under the plea of devotional service. One has to execute devotional service according to his prescribed duties. *Sva-karma-kṛt* means that one should discharge the duties prescribed for him without neglect.

TEXT 26

आत्मनश्च परस्यापि यः करोत्यन्तरोदरम् ।
तस्य भिन्नदृशो मृत्युर्विदधे भयमुल्बणम् ॥२६॥

ātmanaś ca parasyāpi
yaḥ karoty antarodaram
tasya bhinna-dṛśo mṛtyur
vidadhe bhayam ulbaṇam

ātmanaḥ—of himself; *ca*—and; *parasya*—of another; *api*—also; *yaḥ*—one who; *karoti*—discriminates; *antarā*—between; *udaram*—the body; *tasya*—of him; *bhinna-dṛśaḥ*—having a differential outlook; *mṛtyuḥ*—as death; *vidadhe*—I cause; *bhayam*—fear; *ulbaṇam*—great.

TRANSLATION

As the blazing fire of death, I cause great fear to whoever makes the least discrimination between himself and other living entities because of a differential outlook.

PURPORT

There are bodily differentiations among all varieties of living entities, but a devotee should not distinguish between one living entity and another on such a basis; a devotee's outlook should be that both the soul and Supersoul are equally present in all varieties of living entities.

TEXT 27

अथ मां सर्वभूतेषु भूतात्मानं कृतालयम् ।
अर्हयेद्दानमानाभ्यां मैत्र्याभिन्नेन चक्षुषा ॥२७॥

atha māṁ sarva-bhūteṣu
bhūtātmānaṁ kṛtālayam
arhayed dāna-mānābhyāṁ
maitryābhinnena cakṣuṣā

atha—therefore; *mām*—Me; *sarva-bhūteṣu*—in all creatures; *bhūta-ātmānam*—the Self in all beings; *kṛta-ālayam*—abiding; *arhayet*—one should propitiate; *dāna-mānābhyām*—through charity and respect; *maitryā*—through friendship; *abhinnena*—equal; *cakṣuṣā*—by viewing.

TRANSLATION

Therefore, through charitable gifts and attention, as well as through friendly behavior and by viewing all to be alike, one should propitiate Me, who abide in all creatures as their very Self.

PURPORT

It should not be misunderstood that because the Supersoul is dwelling within the heart of a living entity, the individual soul has become equal to Him. The equality of the Supersoul and the individual soul is misconceived by the impersonalist. Here it is distinctly mentioned that the individual soul should be recognized in relationship with the Supreme Personality of Godhead. The method of worshiping the individual soul is described here as either giving charitable gifts or behaving in a friendly manner, free from any separatist outlook. The impersonalist sometimes accepts a poor individual soul as being *daridra-nārāyaṇa,* meaning that Nārāyaṇa, the Supreme Personality of Godhead, has become poor. This is a contradiction. The Supreme Personality of Godhead is full in all opulences. He can agree to live with a poor soul or even with an animal, but this does not make Him poor.

There are two Sanskrit words used here, *māna* and *dāna. Māna* indicates a superior, and *dāna* indicates one who gives charitable gifts or is compassionate towards an inferior. We cannot treat the Supreme Personality of Godhead as an inferior who is dependent on our charitable gifts. When we give charity, it is to a person who is inferior in his material or economic condition. Charity is not given to a rich man. Similarly, it is explicitly stated here that *māna,* respect, is offered to a superior, and charity is offered to an inferior. The living entities, according to different results of fruitive activities, may become rich or poor, but the Supreme Personality of Godhead is unchangeable; He is always full in six opulences. Treating a living entity equally does not mean treating him as one would treat the Supreme Personality of Godhead. Compassion and friendliness do not necessitate falsely elevating someone to the exalted position of the Supreme Personality of Godhead. We should not, at the same time, misunderstand that the Supersoul situated in the heart of an animal like a hog and the Supersoul situated in the heart of a learned *brāhmaṇa* are different. The Supersoul in all living entities is the same Supreme Personality of Godhead. By His omnipotency, He can live anywhere, and He can create His Vaikuṇṭha situation everywhere. That is His inconceivable potency. Therefore, when Nārāyaṇa is living in the heart of a hog, He does not become a hog-Nārāyaṇa. He is always Nārāyaṇa and is unaffected by the body of the hog.

TEXT 28

जीवाःश्रेष्ठा ह्यजीवानां ततः प्राणभृतः शुभे ।
ततः सचित्ताः प्रवरास्ततश्चेन्द्रियवृत्तयः ॥२८॥

jīvāḥ śreṣṭhā hy ajīvānāṁ
tataḥ prāṇa-bhṛtaḥ śubhe
tataḥ sa-cittāḥ pravarās
tataś cendriya-vṛttayaḥ

jīvāḥ—living entities; *śreṣṭhāḥ*—better; *hi*—indeed; *ajīvānām*—than inanimate objects; *tataḥ*—than them; *prāṇa-bhṛtaḥ*—entities with life symptoms; *śubhe*—O blessed mother; *tataḥ*—than them; *sa-cittāḥ*—entities with developed consciousness; *pravarāḥ*—better; *tataḥ*—than them; *ca*—and; *indriya-vṛttayaḥ*—those with sense perception.

TRANSLATION

Living entities are superior to inanimate objects, O blessed mother, and among them, living entities who display life symptoms are better. Animals with developed consciousness are better than them, and better still are those who have developed sense perception.

PURPORT

In the previous verse it was explained that living entities should be honored by charitable gifts and friendly behavior, and in this verse and in the following verses, the description of different grades of living entities is given so that one can know when to behave friendly and when to give charity. For example, a tiger is a living entity, part and parcel of the Supreme Personality of Godhead, and the Supreme Lord is living in the heart of the tiger as Supersoul. But does this mean that we have to treat the tiger in a friendly manner? Certainly not. We have to treat him differently, giving him charity in the form of *prasāda*. The many saintly persons in the jungles do not treat the tigers in a friendly way, but they supply *prasāda* foodstuffs to them. The tigers come, take the food and go away, just as a dog does. According to the Vedic system, a dog is not allowed to enter the house. Because of their uncleanliness, cats and dogs are not allowed within the apartment of a gentleman, but are so trained that they stand outside. The compassionate householder will supply *prasāda* to the dogs and cats, who eat outside and then go away. We must treat the lower living entities compassionately, but this does not mean that we have to treat them in the same way we treat other human beings. The feeling of equality must be there, but the treatment should be discriminating. Just how discrimination should be maintained is given in the following six verses concerning the different grades of living conditions.

The first division is made between dead, stonelike matter and the living organism. A living organism is sometimes manifested even in stone. Experience shows that some hills and mountains grow. This is due to the presence of the soul within that stone. Above that, the next manifestation of the living condition is development of consciousness, and the next manifestation is the development of sense perception. In the *Mokṣa-dharma* section of the *Mahābhārata* it is stated that trees have developed sense perception; they can see and smell. We know by experience that trees can see. Sometimes in its growth a large tree changes its course of development to avoid some hindrances. This means that a tree can see, and according to *Mahābhārata*, a tree can also smell. This indicates the development of sense perception.

TEXT 29

तत्रापि स्पर्शवेदिभ्यः प्रवरा रसवेदिनः ।
तेभ्यो गन्धविदः श्रेष्ठास्ततः शब्दविदो वराः ॥२९॥

tatrāpi sparśa-vedibhyaḥ
pravarā rasa-vedinaḥ
tebhyo gandha-vidaḥ śreṣṭhās
tataḥ śabda-vido varāḥ

tatra—among them; *api*—moreover; *sparśa-vedibhyaḥ*—than those perceiving touch; *pravarāḥ*—better; *rasa-vedinaḥ*—those perceiving taste; *tebhyaḥ*—than them; *gandha-vidaḥ*—those perceiving smell; *śreṣṭhāḥ*—better; *tataḥ*—than them; *śabda-vidaḥ*—those perceiving sound; *varāḥ*—better.

TRANSLATION

Among the living entities who have developed sense perception, those who have developed the sense of taste are better than those who have developed only the sense of touch. Better than them are those who have developed the sense of smell, and better still are those who have developed the sense of hearing.

PURPORT

Although Westerners accept that Darwin first expounded the doctrine of evolution, the science of anthropology is not new. The development of the evolutionary process was known long before from the *Bhāgavatam*, which was written five thousand years ago. There are records of the statements of Kapila Muni, who was present almost in the beginning of the creation. This knowledge has existed since the Vedic time, and all these sequences are disclosed in Vedic literature; the theory of gradual evolution or anthropology is not new to the *Vedas*.

It is said here that amongst the trees there are also evolutionary processes; the different kinds of trees have touch perception. It is said that better than the trees are the fish because fish have developed the sense of taste. Better than the fish are the bees, who have developed the sense of smell, and better than them are the serpents because serpents have developed the sense of hearing. In the darkness of night a snake can find its eatables simply by hearing the frog's very pleasant cry. The snake can understand, "There is the frog," and he captures the frog simply because of its sound vibration. This example is sometimes given for persons who vibrate sounds simply for death. One may have a very nice tongue that can vibrate sound like the frogs, but that kind of vibration is simply calling death. The best use of the tongue and of sound vibration is to chant Hare Kṛṣṇa, Hare Kṛṣṇa, Kṛṣṇa Kṛṣṇa, Hare Hare/ Hare Rāma, Hare Rāma, Rāma Rāma, Hare Hare. That will protect one from the hands of cruel death.

TEXT 30

रूपभेदविदस्तत्र ततश्चोभयतोदतः ।
तेषां बहुपदाः श्रेष्ठाश्चतुष्पादस्ततो द्विपात् ॥३०॥

rūpa-bheda-vidas tatra
tataś cobhayato-datah
teṣāṁ bahu-padāḥ śreṣṭhāś
catuṣ-pādas tato dvi-pāt

rūpa-bheda—distinctions of form; *vidaḥ*—those who perceive; *tatra*—than them; *tataḥ*—than them; *ca*—and; *ubhayataḥ*—in both jaws; *dataḥ*—those with teeth; *teṣām*—of them; *bahu-padāḥ*—those who have many legs; *śreṣṭhāḥ*—better; *catuḥ-pādaḥ*—four-legged; *tataḥ*—than them; *dvi-pāt*—two-legged.

TRANSLATION

Better than those living entities who can perceive sound are those who can distinguish between one form and another. Better than them are those who have developed upper and lower sets of teeth, and better still are those who

have many legs. Better than them are the quadrupeds, and better still are the human beings.

PURPORT

It is said that certain birds, such as crows, can distinguish one form from another. Living entities that have many legs, like the wasp, are better than plants and grasses, which have no legs. Four-legged animals are better than many-legged living entities, and better than the animals is the human being, who has only two legs.

TEXT 31

ततो वर्णाश्च चत्वारस्तेषां ब्राह्मण उत्तमः ।
ब्राह्मणेष्वपि वेदज्ञो ह्यर्थज्ञोऽभ्यधिकस्ततः ॥३१॥

tato varṇāś ca catvāras
teṣāṁ brāhmaṇa uttamaḥ
brāhmaṇeṣv api veda-jño
hy artha-jño 'bhyadhikas tataḥ

tataḥ—among them; *varṇāḥ*—classes; *ca*—and; *catvāraḥ*—four; *teṣām*—of them; *brāhmaṇaḥ*—a *brāhmaṇa; uttamaḥ*—best; *brāhmaṇeṣu*—among the *brāhmaṇas; api*—moreover; *veda*—the *Vedas; jñaḥ*—one who knows; *hi*—certainly; *artha*—the purpose; *jñaḥ*—one who knows; *abhyadhikaḥ*—better; *tataḥ*—than him.

TRANSLATION

Among human beings, the society which is divided according to quality and work is best, and in that society, the intelligent men, who are designated as brāhmaṇas, are best. Among the brāhmaṇas, one who has studied the Vedas is the best, and among the brāhmaṇas who have studied the Vedas, one who knows the actual purport of Veda is the best.

PURPORT

The system of four classifications in human society according to quality and work is very scientific. This system of *brāhmaṇas, kṣatriyas, vaiśyas* and *śūdras* has now become vitiated as the present caste system in India, but it appears that this system has been current a very long time, since it is mentioned in *Śrīmad-Bhāgavatam* and *Bhagavad-gītā.* Unless there is such a division of the social orders in human society, including the intelligent class, the martial class, the mercantile class and the laborer class, there is always confusion as to who is to work for what purpose. A person trained to the stage of understanding the Absolute Truth is a *brāhmaṇa,* and when such a *brāhmaṇa* is *veda jña,* he understands the purpose of *Veda.* The purpose of *Veda* is to understand the Absolute. One who understands the Absolute Truth in three phases, namely Brahman, Paramātmā and Bhagavān, and who understands the term *Bhagavān* to mean the Supreme Personality of Godhead, is considered to be the best of the *brāhmaṇas,* or a Vaiṣṇava.

TEXT 32

अर्थज्ञात्संशयच्छेत्ता ततः श्रेयान् स्वकर्मकृत् ।
मुक्तसङ्गस्ततो भूयानदोग्धा धर्ममात्मनः ॥३२॥

artha-jñāt saṁśaya-cchettā
tataḥ śreyān sva-karma-kṛt
mukta-saṅgas tato bhūyān
adogdhā dharmam ātmanaḥ

artha-jñāt—than one who knows the purpose of the *Vedas; saṁśaya*—doubts; *chettā*—one who cuts off; *tataḥ*—than him; *śreyān*—better; *sva-karma*—his prescribed duties; *kṛt*—one who executes; *mukta-saṅgaḥ*—liberated from material association; *tataḥ*—than him; *bhūyān*—better; *adogdhā*—not executing; *dharmam*—devotional service; *ātmanaḥ*—for himself.

TRANSLATION

Better than the brāhmaṇa who knows the purpose of the Vedas is he who can dissipate all doubts, and better than him is one who strictly follows the brahminical principles. Better than him is one who is liberated from all material contamination, and better than him is a pure devotee, who executes devotional service without expectation of reward.

PURPORT

Artha jña brāhmaṇa refers to one who has made a thorough analytical study of the Absolute Truth and who knows that the Absolute Truth is realized in three different phases, namely Brahman, Paramātmā and Bhagavān. If someone not only has this knowledge but is able to clear all doubts if questioned about the Absolute Truth, he is considered better. Further, there may be a learned *brāhmaṇa*-Vaiṣṇava who can explain clearly and eradicate all doubts, but if he does not follow the Vaiṣṇava principles, then he is not situated on a higher level. One must be able to clear all doubts and simultaneously be situated in the brahminical characteristics. Such a person, who knows the purpose of the Vedic injunctions, who can employ the principles laid down in the Vedic literatures and who teaches his disciples in that way, is called an *ācārya.* The position of an *ācārya* is that he executes devotional service with no desire for elevation to a higher position of life.

The highest perfectional *brāhmaṇa* is the Vaiṣṇava. A Vaiṣṇava who knows the science of the Absolute Truth but is not able to preach such knowledge to others is described as being in the lower stage, one who not only understands the principles of the science of God but can also preach is in the second stage, and one who not only can preach but who also sees everything in the Absolute Truth and the Absolute Truth in everything is in the highest class of Vaiṣṇavas. It is mentioned here that a Vaiṣṇava is already a *brāhmaṇa;* in fact, the highest stage of brahminical perfection is reached when one becomes a Vaiṣṇava.

TEXT 33

तस्मान्मय्यर्पिताशेषक्रियार्थात्मा निरन्तरः ।
मय्यर्पितात्मनः पुंसो मयि संन्यस्तकर्मणः ।
न पश्यामि परं भूतमकर्तुः समदर्शनात् ॥३३॥

tasmān mayy arpitāśeṣa-
kriyārthātmā nirantaraḥ
mayy arpitātmanaḥ puṁso
mayi sannyasta-karmaṇaḥ
na paśyāmi paraṁ bhūtam
akartuḥ sama-darśanāt

tasmāt—than him; *mayi*—unto Me; *arpita*—offered; *aśeṣa*—all; *kriyā*—actions; *artha*—wealth; *ātmā*—life, soul; *nirantaraḥ*—without cessation; *mayi*—unto Me; *arpita*—offered; *ātmanaḥ*—whose mind; *puṁsaḥ*—than a person; *mayi*—unto Me; *sannyasta*—dedicated; *karmaṇaḥ*—whose activities; *na*—not; *paśyāmi*—I see; *param*—greater; *bhūtam*—living entity; *akartuḥ*—without proprietorship; *sama*—same; *darśanāt*—whose vision.

TRANSLATION

Therefore I do not find a greater person than he who has no interest outside of Mine and who therefore engages and dedicates all his activities and all his life—everything—unto Me without cessation.

PURPORT

In this verse the word *sama-darśanāt* means that he no longer has any separate interest; the devotee's interest and the Supreme Personality of Godhead's interest are one. For example, Lord Caitanya, in the role of a devotee, also preached the same philosophy. He preached that Kṛṣṇa is the worshipful Lord, the Supreme Personality of Godhead, and that the interest of His pure devotees is the same as His own.

Sometimes Māyāvādī philosophers, due to a poor fund of knowledge, define the word *sama-darśanāt* to mean that a devotee should see himself as one with the Supreme Personality of Godhead. This is foolishness. When one thinks himself one with the Supreme Personality of Godhead, there is no question of serving Him. When there is service, there must be a master. Three things must be present for there to be service: the master, the servant and the service. Here it is clearly stated that he who has dedicated his life, all his activities, his mind and his soul—everything—for the satisfaction of the Supreme Lord, is considered to be the greatest person.

The word *akartuḥ* means "without any sense of proprietorship." Everyone wants to act as the proprietor of his actions so that he can enjoy the result. A devotee, however, has no such desire; he acts because the Personality of Godhead wants him to act in a particular way. He has no personal motive. When Lord Caitanya preached Kṛṣṇa consciousness, it was not with the purpose that people would call Him Kṛṣṇa, the Supreme Personality of Godhead; rather, He preached that Kṛṣṇa is the Supreme Personality of Godhead and should be worshiped as such. A devotee who is a most confidential servant of the Lord never does anything for his personal account, but does everything for the satisfaction of the Supreme Lord. It is clearly stated, therefore, *mayi sannyasta-karmaṇaḥ:* the devotee works, but he works for the Supreme. It is also stated, *mayy arpitātmanaḥ:* "He gives his mind unto Me." These are the qualifications of a devotee, who, according to this verse, is accepted as the highest of all human beings.

TEXT 34

मनसैतानि भूतानि प्रणमेद्बहु मानयन् ।
ईश्वरो जीवकलया प्रविष्टो भगवानिति ॥३४॥

manasaitāni bhūtāni
praṇamed bahu-mānayan
īśvaro jīva-kalayā
praviṣṭo bhagavān iti

manasā—with the mind; *etāni*—to these; *bhūtāni*—living entities; *praṇamet*—he offers respects; *bahu-mānayan*—showing regard; *īśvaraḥ*—the controller; *jīva*—of the living entities; *kalayā*—by His expansion as the Supersoul; *praviṣṭah*—has entered; *bhagavān*—the Supreme Personality of Godhead; *iti*—thus.

TRANSLATION

Such a perfect devotee offers respects to every living entity because he is under the firm conviction that the Supreme Personality of Godhead has entered the body of every living entity as the Supersoul, or controller.

PURPORT

A perfect devotee, as described above, does not make the mistake of thinking that because the Supreme Personality of Godhead as Paramātmā has entered into the body of every living entity, every living entity has become the Supreme Personality of Godhead. This is foolishness. Suppose a person enters into a room; that does not mean that the room has become that person. Similarly, that the Supreme Lord has entered into each of the 8,400,000 particular types of material bodies does not mean that each of these bodies has become the Supreme Lord. Because the Supreme Lord is present, however, a pure devotee accepts each body as the temple of the Lord, and since the devotee offers respect to such temples in full knowledge, he gives respect to every living entity in relationship with the Lord. Māyāvādī philosophers wrongly think that because the Supreme Person has entered the body of a poor man, the Supreme Lord has become *daridra-nārāyaṇa*, or poor Nārāyaṇa. These are all blasphemous statements of atheists and nondevotees.

TEXT 35

भक्तियोगश्च योगश्च मया मानव्युदीरितः ।
ययोरेकतरेणैव पुरुषः पुरुषं व्रजेत् ॥३५॥

bhakti-yogaś ca yogaś ca
mayā mānavy udīritaḥ
yayor ekatareṇaiva
puruṣaḥ puruṣaṁ vrajet

bhakti-yogaḥ—devotional service; *ca*—and; *yogaḥ*—mystic *yoga; ca*—also; *mayā*—by Me; *mānavi*—O daughter of Manu; *udīritaḥ*—described; *yayoḥ*—of which two; *ekatareṇa*—by either one; *eva*—alone; *puruṣaḥ*—a person; *puruṣam*—the Supreme Person; *vrajet*—can achieve.

TRANSLATION

My dear mother, O daughter of Manu, a devotee who applies the science of devotional service and mystic yoga in this way can achieve the abode of the Supreme Person simply by that devotional service.

PURPORT

Herein the Supreme Personality of Godhead Kapiladeva perfectly explains that the mystic *yoga* system, consisting of eight different kinds of *yoga* activities, has to be performed with the aim of coming to the perfectional stage of *bhakti-yoga.* It is not acceptable for one to be satisfied simply by practicing the sitting postures and thinking himself complete. By meditation one must attain the stage of devotional service. As previously described, a *yogī* is advised to meditate on the form of Lord Viṣṇu from point to point, from the ankles to the legs to the knees to the thighs to the chest to the neck, and in this way gradually up to the face and then to the ornaments. There is no question of impersonal meditation.

When, by meditation on the Supreme Personality of Godhead in all detail, one comes to the point of love of God, that is the point of *bhakti-yoga,* and at that point he must actually render service to the Lord out of transcendental love. Anyone who practices *yoga* and comes to the point of devotional service can attain the Supreme Personality of Godhead in His transcendental abode. Here it is clearly stated, *puruṣaḥ puruṣaṁ vrajet:* the *puruṣa,* the living entity, goes to the Supreme Person. The Supreme Personality of Godhead and the living entity are qualitatively one; both are defined as *puruṣa.* The quality of *puruṣa* exists both in the Supreme Godhead and in the living entity. *Puruṣa* means "enjoyer," and the spirit of enjoyment is present both in the living entity and in the Supreme Lord. The difference is that the quantity of enjoyment is not equal. The living entity cannot experience the same quantity of enjoyment as the Supreme Personality of Godhead. An analogy may be made with a rich man and a poor man: the propensity for enjoyment is present in both, but the poor man cannot enjoy in the same quantity as the rich man. When the poor man dovetails his desires with those of the rich man, however, and when there is cooperation between the poor man and the rich man, or between the big and the small man, then the enjoyment is shared equally. That is like *bhakti-yoga. Puruṣaḥ puruṣaṁ vrajet:* when the living entity enters into the kingdom of God and cooperates with the Supreme Lord by giving Him enjoyment, he enjoys the same facility or the same amount of pleasure as the Supreme Personality of Godhead.

On the other hand, when the living entity wants to enjoy by imitating the Supreme Personality of Godhead, his desire is called *māyā,* and it puts him in the material atmosphere. A living entity who wants to enjoy on his personal account and not cooperate with the Supreme Lord is engaged in materialistic life. As soon as he dovetails his enjoyment with the Supreme Personality of Godhead, he is engaged in spiritual life. An example may be cited here: The different limbs of the body cannot enjoy life independently; they must cooperate with the whole body and supply food to the stomach. In so doing, all the different parts of the body enjoy equally in cooperation with the whole body. That is the philosophy of *acintya-bhedābheda,* simultaneous oneness and difference. The living entity cannot enjoy life in opposition to the Supreme Lord; he has to dovetail his activities with the Lord by practicing *bhakti-yoga.*

It is said herein that one can approach the Supreme Personality of Godhead by either the *yoga* process or the *bhakti-yoga* process. This indicates that factually there is no difference between *yoga* and *bhakti-yoga* because the target of both is Viṣṇu. In the modern age, however, a *yoga* process has been manufactured which aims at something void and impersonal. Actually, *yoga* means meditation on the form of Lord Viṣṇu. If the *yoga* practice is actually performed according to the standard direction, there is no difference between *yoga* and *bhakti-yoga.*

TEXT 36

एतद्भगवतो रूपं ब्रह्मणः परमात्मनः ।
परं प्रधानं पुरुषं दैवं कर्मविचेष्टितम् ॥३६॥

etad bhagavato rūpaṁ
brahmaṇaḥ paramātmanaḥ
paraṁ pradhānaṁ puruṣaṁ
daivaṁ karma-viceṣṭitam

etat—this; *bhagavataḥ*—of the Supreme Personality of Godhead; *rūpam*—form; *brahmaṇaḥ*—of Brahman; *parama-ātmanaḥ*—of Paramātmā; *param*—transcendental; *pradhānam*—chief; *puruṣam*—personality; *daivam*—spiritual; *karma-viceṣṭitam*—whose activities.

TRANSLATION

This puruṣa whom the individual soul must approach is the eternal form of the Supreme Personality of Godhead, who is known as Brahman and

Paramātmā. He is the transcendental chief personality, and His activities are all spiritual.

PURPORT

In order to distinguish the personality whom the individual soul must approach, it is described herein that this *puruṣa,* the Supreme Personality of Godhead, is the chief amongst all living entities and is the ultimate form of the impersonal Brahman effulgence and Paramātmā manifestation. Since He is the origin of the Brahman effulgence and Paramātmā manifestation, He is described herewith as the chief personality. It is confirmed in the *Kaṭha Upaniṣad, nityo nityānām:* there are many eternal living entities, but He is the chief maintainer. This is confirmed in *Bhagavad-gītā* also, where Lord Kṛṣṇa says, *ahaṁ sarvasya prabhavaḥ:* "I am the origin of everything, including the Brahman effulgence and Paramātmā manifestation." His activities are transcendental, as confirmed in *Bhagavad-gītā. Janma karma ca me divyam:* the activities and the appearance and disappearance of the Supreme Personality of Godhead are transcendental; they are not to be considered material. Anyone who knows this fact—that the appearance, disappearance and activities of the Lord are beyond material activities or material conception—is liberated. *Yo vetti tattvataḥ/ tyaktvā dehaṁ punar janma:* such a person, after quitting his body, does not come back again to this material world, but goes to the Supreme Person. It is confirmed here, *puruṣaḥ puruṣaṁ vrajet:* the living entity goes to the Supreme Personality simply by understanding His transcendental nature and activities.

TEXT 37

रूपभेदास्पदं दिव्यं काल इत्यभिधीयते ।
भूतानां महदादीनां यतो भिन्नदृशां भयम् ॥३७॥

rūpa-bhedāspadaṁ divyaṁ
kāla ity abhidhīyate
bhūtānāṁ mahad-ādīnāṁ
yato bhinna-dṛśāṁ bhayam

rūpa-bheda—of the transformation of forms; *āspadam*—the cause; *divyam*—divine; *kālaḥ*—time; *iti*—thus; *abhidhīyate*—is known; *bhūtānām*—of living entities; *mahat-ādīnām*—beginning with Lord Brahmā; *yataḥ*—because of which; *bhinna-dṛśām*—with separate vision; *bhayam*—fear.

TRANSLATION

The time factor, who causes the transformation of the various material manifestations, is another feature of the Supreme Personality of Godhead. Anyone who does not know that time is the same Supreme Personality is afraid of the time factor.

PURPORT

Everyone is afraid of the activities of time, but a devotee who knows that the time factor is another representation or manifestation of the Supreme Personality of Godhead has nothing to fear from the influence of time. The phrase *rūpa-bhedāspadam* is very significant. By the influence of time, so many forms are changing. For example, when a child is born his form is small, but in the course of time that form changes into a larger form, the body of a boy, and then the body of a young man. Similarly, everything is changed and transformed by the time factor, or by the indirect control of the Supreme Personality of Godhead. Usually, we do not see any difference between the body of a child and the body of a boy or young man because we know that these changes are due to the action of the time factor. There is cause for fear for a person who does not know how time acts.

TEXT 38

योऽन्तः प्रविश्य भूतानि भूतैरत्त्यखिलाश्रयः ।
स विष्ण्वाख्योऽधियज्ञोऽसौ कालः कलयतां प्रभुः ॥३८॥

yo 'ntaḥ praviśya bhūtāni
bhūtair atty akhilāśrayaḥ
sa viṣṇv-ākhyo 'dhiyajño 'sau
kālaḥ kalayatāṁ prabhuḥ

yaḥ—He who; *antaḥ*—within; *praviśya*—entering; *bhūtāni*—living entities; *bhūtaiḥ*—by living entities; *atti*—annihilates; *akhila*—of everyone; *āśrayaḥ*—the support; *saḥ*—He; *viṣṇu*—Viṣṇu; *ākhyaḥ*—named; *adhiyajñaḥ*—the enjoyer of all sacrifices; *asau*—that; *kālaḥ*—time factor; *kalayatām*—of all masters; *prabhuḥ*—the master.

TRANSLATION

Lord Viṣṇu, the Supreme Personality of Godhead, who is the enjoyer of all sacrifices, is the time factor and the master of all masters. He enters

everyone's heart, He is the support of everyone, and He causes every being to be annihilated by another.

PURPORT

Lord Viṣṇu, the Supreme Personality of Godhead, is clearly described in this passage. He is the supreme enjoyer, and all others are working as His servants. As stated in the *Caitanya caritāmṛta* (*Ādi* 5.14), *ekale īśvara kṛṣṇa:* the only Supreme Lord is Viṣṇu. *Āra saba bhṛtya:* all others are His servants. Lord Brahmā, Lord Śiva and other demigods are all servants. The same Viṣṇu enters everyone's heart as Paramātmā, and He causes the annihilation of every being through another being.

TEXT 39

न चास्य कश्चिद्दयितो न द्वेष्यो न च बान्धवः ।
आविशत्यप्रमत्तोऽसौ प्रमत्तं जनमन्तकृत् ॥३९॥

na cāsya kaścid dayito
na dveṣyo na ca bāndhavaḥ
āviśaty apramatto 'sau
pramattaṁ janam anta-kṛt

na—not; *ca*—and; *asya*—of the Supreme Personality of Godhead; *kaścit*—anyone; *dayitaḥ*—dear; *na*—not; *dveṣyaḥ*—enemy; *na*—not; *ca*—and; *bāndhavaḥ*—friend; *āviśati*—approaches; *apramattaḥ*—attentive; *asau*—He; *pramattam*—inattentive; *janam*—persons; *anta-kṛt*—the destroyer.

TRANSLATION

No one is dear to the Supreme Personality of Godhead, nor is anyone His enemy or friend. But He gives inspiration to those who have not forgotten Him and destroys those who have.

PURPORT

Forgetfulness of one's relationship with Lord Viṣṇu, the Supreme Personality of Godhead, is the cause of one's repeated birth and death. A living entity is as eternal as the Supreme Lord, but due to his forgetfulness he is put into this material nature and transmigrates from one body to another, and when the body is destroyed, he thinks that he is also destroyed. Actually, this forgetfulness of his relationship with Lord Viṣṇu is the cause of his destruction. Anyone who revives his consciousness of the original relationship receives inspiration from the Lord. This does not mean that the Lord is someone's enemy and someone else's friend. He helps everyone; one who is not bewildered by the influence of material energy is saved, and one who is bewildered is destroyed. It is said, therefore, *hariṁ vinā na mṛtim taranti:* no one can be saved from the repetition of birth and death without the help of the Supreme Lord. It is therefore the duty of all living entities to take shelter of the lotus feet of Viṣṇu and thus save themselves from the cycle of birth and death.

TEXT 40

यद्भयाद्वाति वातोऽयं सूर्यस्तपति यद्भयात् ।
यद्भयाद्वर्षते देवो भगणो भाति यद्भयात् ॥४०॥

yad-bhayād vāti vāto 'yaṁ
sūryas tapati yad-bhayāt
yad-bhayād varṣate devo
bha-gaṇo bhāti yad-bhayāt

yat—of whom (the Supreme Personality of Godhead); *bhayāt*—out of fear; *vāti*—blows; *vātaḥ*—the wind; *ayam*—this; *sūryaḥ*—sun; *tapati*—shines; *yat*—of whom; *bhayāt*—out of fear; *yat*—of whom; *bhayāt*—out of fear; *varṣate*—sends rains; *devaḥ*—the god of rain; *bha-gaṇaḥ*—the host of heavenly bodies; *bhāti*—shine; *yat*—of whom; *bhayāt*—out of fear.

TRANSLATION

Out of fear of the Supreme Personality of Godhead the wind blows, out of fear of Him the sun shines, out of fear of Him the rain pours forth showers, and out of fear of Him the host of heavenly bodies shed their luster.

PURPORT

The Lord states in *Bhagavad-gītā, mayādhyakṣeṇa prakṛtiḥ sūyate:* "Nature is working under My direction." The foolish person thinks that nature is working automatically, but such an atheistic theory is not supported in the Vedic literature. Nature is working under the superintendence of the Supreme Personality of Godhead. That is confirmed in *Bhagavad-gītā,* and we also find here that the sun shines under the direction of the Lord, and the cloud pours forth showers of rain under the direction of the Lord. All natural phenomena are under superintendence of the Supreme Personality of Godhead, Viṣṇu.

TEXT 41

यद्वनस्पतयो भीता लताश्चौषधिभिः सह ।
स्वे स्वे कालेऽभिगृह्णन्ति पुष्पाणि च फलानि च ॥४१॥

yad vanaspatayo bhītā
latāś cauṣadhibhiḥ saha
sve sve kāle 'bhigṛhṇanti
puṣpāṇi ca phalāni ca

yat—because of whom; *vanaḥ-patayaḥ*—the trees; *bhītāḥ*—fearful; *latāḥ*—creepers; *ca*—and; *oṣadhibhiḥ*—herbs; *saha*—with; *sve sve kāle*—each in its own season; *abhigṛhṇanti*—bear; *puṣpāṇi*—flowers; *ca*—and; *phalāni*—fruits; *ca*—also.

TRANSLATION

Out of fear of the Supreme Personality of Godhead the trees, creepers, herbs and seasonal plants and flowers blossom and fructify, each in its own season.

PURPORT

As the sun rises and sets and the seasonal changes ensue at their appointed times by the superintendence of the Supreme Personality of Godhead, so the seasonal plants, flowers, herbs and trees all grow under the direction of the Supreme Lord. It is not that plants grow automatically, without any cause, as the atheistic philosophers say. Rather, they grow in pursuance of the supreme order of the Supreme Personality of Godhead. It is confirmed in the Vedic literature that the Lord's diverse energies are working so nicely that it appears that everything is being done automatically.

TEXT 42

स्रवन्ति सरितो भीता नोत्सर्पत्युदधिर्यतः ।
अग्निरिन्धे सगिरिभिर्भूर्न मज्जति यद्भयात् ॥४२॥

sravanti sarito bhītā
notsarpaty udadhir yataḥ
agnir indhe sa-giribhir
bhūr na majjati yad-bhayāt

sravanti—flow; *saritaḥ*—rivers; *bhītāḥ*—fearful; *na*—not; *utsarpati*—overflows; *uda-dhiḥ*—the ocean; *yataḥ*—because of whom; *agniḥ*—fire; *indhe*—burns; *sa-giribhiḥ*—with its mountains; *bhūḥ*—the earth; *na*—not; *majjati*—sinks; *yat*—of whom; *bhayāt*—out of fear.

TRANSLATION

Out of fear of the Supreme Personality of Godhead the rivers flow, and the ocean never overflows. Out of fear of Him only does fire burn and does the earth, with its mountains, not sink in the water of the universe.

PURPORT

We can understand from the Vedic literature that this universe is half filled with water, on which Garbhodakaśāyī Viṣṇu is lying. From His abdomen a lotus flower has grown, and within the stem of that lotus flower all the different planets exist. The material scientist explains that all these different planets are floating because of the law of gravity or some other law; but the actual lawmaker is the Supreme Personality of Godhead. When we speak of law, we must understand that there must be a lawmaker. The material scientists can discover laws of nature, but they are unable to recognize the lawmaker. From *Śrīmad-Bhāgavatam* and *Bhagavad-gītā* we can know who the lawmaker is: the lawmaker is the Supreme Personality of Godhead.

It is said here that the planets do not sink. Since they are floating under the order or energy of the Supreme Godhead, they do not fall down into the water which covers half the universe. All the planets are heavy, with their various mountains, seas, oceans, cities, palaces and buildings, and yet they are floating. It is understood from this passage that all the other planets that are floating in the air have oceans and mountains similar to those on this planet.

TEXT 43

नभो ददाति श्वसतां पदं यन्नियमाददः ।
लोकं स्वदेहं तनुते महान् सप्तभिरावृतम् ॥४३॥

nabho dadāti śvasatāṁ
padaṁ yan-niyamād adaḥ
lokaṁ sva-dehaṁ tanute
mahān saptabhir āvṛtam

nabhaḥ—the sky; *dadāti*—gives; *śvasatām*—to the living entities; *padam*—abode; *yat*—of whom (the Supreme Personality of Godhead); *niyamāt*—under the control; *adaḥ*—that; *lokam*—the universe; *sva-deham*—own body; *tanute*—expands; *mahān*—the *mahat-tattva*; *saptabhiḥ*—with the seven (layers); *āvṛtam*—covered.

TRANSLATION

Subject to the control of the Supreme Personality of Godhead, the sky allows outer space to accommodate all the various planets, which hold innumerable living entities. The total universal body expands with its seven coverings under His supreme control.

PURPORT

It is understood from this verse that all the planets in outer space are floating, and they all hold living entities. The word *śvasatām* means "those who breathe," or the living entities. In order to accommodate them, there are innumerable planets. Every planet is a residence for innumerable living entities, and the necessary space is provided in the sky by the supreme order of the Lord. It is also stated here that the total universal body is increasing. It is covered by seven layers, and as there are five elements within the universe, so the total elements, in layers, cover the outside of the universal body. The first layer is of earth, and it is ten times greater in size than the space within the universe; the second layer is water, and that is ten times greater than the earthly layer; the third covering is fire, which is ten times greater than the water covering. In this way each layer is ten times greater than the previous one.

TEXT 44

गुणाभिमानिनो देवाः सर्गादिष्वस्य यद्भयात् ।
वर्तन्तेऽनुयुगं येषां वश एतच्चराचरम् ॥४४॥

guṇābhimānino devāḥ
sargādiṣv asya yad-bhayāt
vartante 'nuyugaṁ yeṣāṁ
vaśa etac carācaram

guṇa—the modes of material nature; *abhimāninaḥ*—in charge of; *devāḥ*—the demigods; *sarga-ādiṣu*—in the matter of creation and so on; *asya*—of this world; *yat-bhayāt*—out of fear of whom; *vartante*—carry out functions; *anuyugam*—according to the *yugas; yeṣām*—of whom; *vaśe*—under the control; *etat*—this; *cara-acaram*—everything animate and inanimate.

TRANSLATION

Out of fear of the Supreme Personality of Godhead, the directing demigods in charge of the modes of material nature carry out the functions of creation,

maintenance and destruction; everything animate and inanimate within this material world is under their control.

PURPORT

The three modes of material nature, namely goodness, passion and ignorance, are under the control of three deities—Brahmā, Viṣṇu and Lord Śiva. Lord Viṣṇu is in charge of the mode of goodness, Lord Brahmā is in charge of the mode of passion, and Lord Śiva is in charge of the mode of ignorance. Similarly, there are many other demigods in charge of the air department, the water department, the cloud department, etc. Just as the government has many different departments, so, within this material world, the government of the Supreme Lord has many departments, and all these departments function in proper order out of fear of the Supreme Personality of Godhead. Demigods are undoubtedly controlling all matter, animate and inanimate, within the universe, but above them the supreme controller is the Personality of Godhead. Therefore in the *Brahma-saṁhitā* it is said, *īśvaraḥ paramaḥ kṛṣṇaḥ.* Undoubtedly there are many controllers in the departmental management of this universe, but the supreme controller is Kṛṣṇa.

There are two kinds of dissolutions. One kind of dissolution takes place when Brahmā goes to sleep during his night, and the final dissolution takes place when Brahmā dies. As long as Brahmā does not die, creation, maintenance and destruction are actuated by different demigods under the superintendence of the Supreme Lord.

TEXT 45

सोऽनन्तोऽन्तकरः कालोऽनादिरादिकृदव्ययः ।
जनं जनेन जनयन्मारयन्मृत्युनान्तकम् ॥४५॥

so 'nanto 'nta-karaḥ kālo
'nādir ādi-kṛd avyayaḥ
janaṁ janena janayan
mārayan mṛtyunāntakam

saḥ—that; *anantaḥ*—endless; *anta-karaḥ*—destroyer; *kālaḥ*—time; *anādiḥ*—without beginning; *ādi-kṛt*—the creator; *avyayaḥ*—not liable to change; *janam*—persons; *janena*—by persons; *janayan*—creating; *mārayan*—destroying; *mṛtyunā*—by death; *antakam*—the lord of death.

TRANSLATION

The eternal time factor has no beginning and no end. It is the representative of the Supreme Personality of Godhead, the maker of the criminal world. It brings about the end of the phenomenal world, it carries on the work of creation by bringing one individual into existence from another, and likewise it dissolves the universe by destroying even the lord of death, Yamarāja.

PURPORT

By the influence of eternal time, which is a representative of the Supreme Personality of Godhead, the father begets a son, and the father dies by the influence of cruel death. But by time's influence, even the lord of cruel death is killed. In other words, all the demigods within the material world are temporary, like ourselves. Our lives last for one hundred years at the most, and similarly, although their lives may last for millions and billions of years, the demigods are not eternal. No one can live within this material world eternally. The phenomenal world is created, maintained and destroyed by the finger signal of the Supreme Personality of Godhead. Therefore a devotee does not desire anything in this material world. A devotee desires only to serve the Supreme Personality of Godhead. This servitude exists eternally; the Lord exists eternally, His servitor exists eternally, and the service exists eternally.

Thus end the Bhaktivedanta purports of the Third Canto, Twenty-ninth Chapter, of the Śrīmad-Bhāgavatam, *entitled "Explanation of Devotional Service by Lord Kapila."*

CHAPTER THIRTY

Description by Lord Kapila of Adverse Fruitive Activities

TEXT 1

कपिल उवाच
तस्यैतस्य जनो नूनं नायं वेदोरुविक्रमम् ।
काल्यमानोऽपि बलिनो वायोरिव घनावलिः ॥ १ ॥

kapila uvāca
tasyaitasya jano nūnaṁ
nāyaṁ vedoru-vikramam
kālyamāno 'pi balino
vāyor iva ghanāvaliḥ

kapilaḥ uvāca—Lord Kapila said; *tasya etasya*—of this very time factor; *janaḥ*—person; *nūnam*—certainly; *na*—not; *ayam*—this; *veda*—knows; *uru-vikramam*—the great strength; *kālyamānaḥ*—being carried off; *api*—although; *balinaḥ*—powerful; *vāyoḥ*—of the wind; *iva*—like; *ghana*—of clouds; *āvaliḥ*—a mass.

TRANSLATION

The Personality of Godhead said: As a mass of clouds does not know the powerful influence of the wind, a person engaged in material consciousness does not know the powerful strength of the time factor, by which he is being carried.

PURPORT

The great politician-*paṇḍita* named Cāṇakya said that even one moment of time cannot be returned even if one is prepared to pay millions of dollars. One cannot calculate the amount of loss there is in wasting valuable time. Either materially or spiritually, one should be very alert in utilizing the time which he has at his disposal. A conditioned soul lives in a particular body for a fixed measurement of time, and it is recommended in the scriptures that within that small measurement of time one has to finish Kṛṣṇa consciousness and thus gain release from the influence of the time factor.

But, unfortunately, those who are not in Kṛṣṇa consciousness are carried away by the strong power of time without their knowledge, as clouds are carried by the wind.

TEXT 2

यं यमर्थमुपादत्ते दुःखेन सुखहेतवे ।
तं तं धुनोति भगवान् पुमाञ्छोचति यत्कृते ॥ २ ॥

yaṁ yam artham upādatte
duḥkhena sukha-hetave
taṁ taṁ dhunoti bhagavān
pumāñ chocati yat-kṛte

yam yam—whatever; *artham*—object; *upādatte*—one acquires; *duḥkhena*—with difficulty; *sukha-hetave*—for happiness; *tam tam*—that; *dhunoti*—destroys; *bhagavān*—the Supreme Personality of Godhead; *pumān*—the person; *śocati*—laments; *yat-kṛte*—for which reason.

TRANSLATION

Whatever is produced by the materialist with great pain and labor for so-called happiness, the Supreme Personality, as the time factor, destroys, and for this reason the conditioned soul laments.

PURPORT

The main function of the time factor, which is a representative of the Supreme Personality of Godhead, is to destroy everything. The materialists, in material consciousness, are engaged in producing so many things in the name of economic development. They think that by advancing in satisfying the material needs of man they will be happy, but they forget that everything they have produced will be destroyed in due course of time. From history we can see that there were many powerful empires on the surface of the globe that were constructed with great pain and great perseverance, but in due course of time they have all been destroyed. Still the foolish materialists cannot understand that they are simply wasting time in producing material necessities, which are destined to be vanquished in due course of time. This waste of energy is due to the ignorance of the mass of people, who do not know that they are eternal and that they have an eternal engagement also. They do not know that this span of life in a particular type of body is but a flash in the eternal journey. Not knowing this fact, they take the small flash of life to be everything, and they waste time in improving economic conditions.

TEXT 3

यदध्रुवस्य देहस्य सानुबन्धस्य दुर्मतिः ।
ध्रुवाणि मन्यते मोहाद् गृहक्षेत्रवसूनि च ॥ ३ ॥

yad adhruvasya dehasya
sānubandhasya durmatiḥ
dhruvāṇi manyate mohād
gṛha-kṣetra-vasūni ca

yat—because; *adhruvasya*—temporary; *dehasya*—of the body; *sa-anubandhasya*—with that which is related; *durmatiḥ*—a misguided person; *dhruvāṇi*—permanent; *manyate*—thinks; *mohāt*—because of ignorance; *gṛha*—home; *kṣetra*—land; *vasūni*—wealth; *ca*—and.

TRANSLATION

The misguided materialist does not know that his very body is impermanent and that the attractions of home, land and wealth, which are in relationship to that body, are also temporary. Out of ignorance only, he thinks that everything is permanent.

PURPORT

The materialist thinks that persons engaged in Kṛṣṇa consciousness are crazy fellows wasting time by chanting Hare Kṛṣṇa, but actually he does not know that he himself is in the darkest region of craziness because of accepting his body as permanent. And, in relation to his body, he accepts his home, his country, his society and all other paraphernalia as permanent. This materialistic acceptance of the permanency of home, land, etc., is called the illusion of *māyā.* This is clearly mentioned here. *Mohād gṛha-kṣetra-vasūni:* out of illusion only does the materialist accept his home, his land and his money as permanent. Out of this illusion, the family life, national life and economic development, which are very important factors in modern civilization, have grown. A Kṛṣṇa conscious person knows that this economic development of human society is but temporary illusion.

In another part of *Śrīmad-Bhāgavatam,* the acceptance of the body as oneself, the acceptance of others as kinsmen in relationship to this body and the acceptance of the land of one's birth as worshipable are declared to be the products of an animal civilization. When, however, one is enlightened in Kṛṣṇa consciousness, he can use these for the service of the Lord. That is a very suitable proposition. Everything has a relationship with Kṛṣṇa. When all economic development and material advancement are utilized to advance the cause of Kṛṣṇa consciousness, a new phase of progressive life arises.

TEXT 4

जन्तुर्वै भव एतस्मिन् यां यां योनिमनुव्रजेत् ।
तस्यां तस्यां स लभते निर्वृतिं न विरज्यते ॥ ४ ॥

jantur vai bhava etasmin
yāṁ yāṁ yonim anuvrajet
tasyāṁ tasyāṁ sa labhate
nirvṛtiṁ na virajyate

jantuḥ—the living entity; *vai*—certainly; *bhave*—in worldly existence; *etasmin*—this; *yām yām*—whatever; *yonim*—species; *anuvrajet*—he may obtain; *tasyām tasyām*—in that; *saḥ*—he; *labhate*—achieves; *nirvṛtim*—satisfaction; *na*—not; *virajyate*—is averse.

TRANSLATION

The living entity, in whatever species of life he appears, finds a particular type of satisfaction in that species, and he is never averse to being situated in such a condition.

PURPORT

The satisfaction of the living entity in a particular type of body, even if it is most abominable, is called illusion. A man in a higher position may feel dissatisfaction with the standard of life of a lower-grade man, but the lower-grade man is satisfied in that position because of the spell of *māyā*, the external energy. *Māyā* has two phases of activities. One is called *prakṣepātmikā*, and the other is called *āvaraṇātmikā*. *Āvaraṇātmikā* means "covering," and *prakṣepātmikā* means "pulling down." In any condition of life, the materialistic person or animal will be satisfied because his knowledge is covered by the influence of *māyā*. In the lower grade or lower species of life, the development of consciousness is so poor that one cannot understand whether he is happy or distressed. This is called *āvaraṇātmikā*. Even a hog, who lives by eating stool, finds himself happy, although a person in a higher mode of life sees that the hog is eating stool. How abominable that life is!

TEXT 5

नरकस्थोऽपि देहं वै न पुमांस्त्यक्तुमिच्छति ।
नारक्यां निर्वृतौ सत्यां देवमायाविमोहितः ॥ ५ ॥

naraka-stho 'pi dehaṁ vai
na pumāṁs tyaktum icchati
nārakyāṁ nirvṛtau satyāṁ
deva-māyā-vimohitaḥ

naraka—in hell; *sthaḥ*—situated; *api*—even; *deham*—body; *vai*—indeed; *na*—not; *pumān*—person; *tyaktum*—to leave; *icchati*—wishes; *nārakyām*—hellish; *nirvṛtau*—enjoyment; *satyām*—when existing; *deva-māyā*—by the illusory energy of Viṣṇu; *vimohitaḥ*—deluded.

TRANSLATION

The conditioned living entity is satisfied in his own particular species of life; while deluded by the covering influence of the illusory energy, he feels little inclined to cast off his body, even when in hell, for he takes delight in hellish enjoyment.

PURPORT

It is said that once Indra, the King of heaven, was cursed by his spiritual master, Bṛhaspati, on account of his misbehavior, and he became a hog on this planet. After many days, when Brahmā wanted to recall him to his heavenly kingdom, Indra, in the form of a hog, forgot everything of his royal position in the heavenly kingdom, and he refused to go back. This is the spell of *māyā*. Even Indra forgets his heavenly standard of life and is satisfied with the standard of a hog's life. By the influence of *māyā* the conditioned soul becomes so affectionate towards his particular type of body that if he is offered, "Give up this body, and immediately you will have a king's body," he will not agree. This attachment strongly affects all conditioned living entities. Lord Kṛṣṇa is personally canvassing, "Give up everything in this material world. Come to Me, and I shall give you all protection," but we are not agreeable. We think, "We are quite all right. Why should we surrender unto Kṛṣṇa and go back to His kingdom?" This is called illusion, or *māyā*. Everyone is satisfied with his standard of living, however abominable it may be.

TEXT 6

आत्मजायासुतागारपशुद्रविणबन्धुषु ।
निरूढमूलहृदय आत्मानं बहु मन्यते ॥ ६ ॥

ātma-jāyā-sutāgāra-
paśu-draviṇa-bandhuṣu
nirūḍha-mūla-hṛdaya
ātmānaṁ bahu manyate

ātma—body; *jāyā*—wife; *suta*—children; *agāra*—home; *paśu*—animals; *draviṇa*—wealth; *bandhuṣu*—in friends; *nirūḍha-mūla*—deep-rooted; *hṛdayaḥ*—his heart; *ātmānam*—himself; *bahu*—highly; *manyate*—he thinks.

TRANSLATION

Such satisfaction with one's standard of living is due to deep-rooted attraction for body, wife, home, children, animals, wealth and friends. In such association, the conditioned soul thinks himself quite perfect.

PURPORT

This so-called perfection of human life is a concoction. Therefore, it is said that the materialist, however materially qualified he may be, is worthless because he is hovering on the mental plane, which will drag him again to the material existence of temporary life. One who acts on the mental plane cannot get promotion to the spiritual. Such a person is always sure to glide down again to material life. In the association of so-called society, friendship and love, the conditioned soul appears completely satisfied.

TEXT 7

सन्दह्यमानसर्वाङ्ग एषामुद्वहनाधिना ।
करोत्यविरतं मूढो दुरितानि दुराशयः ॥ ७ ॥

sandahyamāna-sarvāṅga
eṣām udvahanādhinā
karoty aviratam̐ mūḍho
duritāni durāśayaḥ

sandahyamāna—burning; *sarva*—all; *aṅgaḥ*—his limbs; *eṣām*—these family members; *udvahana*—for maintaining; *ādhinā*—with anxiety; *karoti*—he performs; *aviratam*—always; *mūḍhaḥ*—the fool; *duritāni*—sinful activities; *durāśayaḥ*—evil-minded.

TRANSLATION

Although he is always burning with anxiety, such a fool always performs all kinds of mischievous activities, with a hope which is never to be fulfilled, in order to maintain his so-called family and society.

PURPORT

It is said that it is easier to maintain a great empire than to maintain a small family, especially in these days, when the influence of Kali-yuga is so strong that everyone is harassed and full of anxieties because of accepting the false presentation of *māyā's* family. The family we maintain is created by *māyā*; it is the perverted reflection of the family in Kṛṣṇaloka. In Kṛṣṇaloka there are also family, friends, society, father and mother; everything is there, but they are eternal. Here, as we change bodies, our family relationships also change. Sometimes we are in a family of human beings, sometimes in a family of demigods, sometimes a family of cats, or sometimes a family of dogs. Family, society and friendship are flickering, and so they are called *asat*. It is said that as long as we are attached to this *asat*, temporary, nonexisting society and family, we are always full of anxieties. The materialists do not know that the family, society and friendship here in this material world are only shadows, and thus they become attached. Naturally their hearts are always burning, but in spite of all inconvenience, they still work to maintain such false families because they have no information of the real family association with Kṛṣṇa.

TEXT 8

आक्षिप्तात्मेन्द्रियः स्त्रीणामसतीनां च मायया ।
रहोरचितयालापैः शिशूनां कलभाषिणाम् ॥ ८ ॥

ākṣiptātmendriyaḥ strīṇām
asatīnāṁ ca māyayā
raho racitayālāpaiḥ
śiśūnāṁ kala-bhāṣiṇām

ākṣipta—charmed; *ātma*—heart; *indriyaḥ*—his senses; *strīṇām*—of women; *asatīnām*—false; *ca*—and; *māyayā*—by *māyā; rahaḥ*—in a solitary place; *racitayā*—displayed; *ālāpaiḥ*—by the talking; *śiśūnām*—of the children; *kala-bhāṣiṇām*—with sweet words.

TRANSLATION

He gives heart and senses to a woman, who falsely charms him with māyā. He enjoys solitary embraces and talking with her, and he is enchanted by the sweet words of the small children.

PURPORT

Family life within the kingdom of illusory energy, *māyā*, is just like a prison for the eternal living entity. In prison a prisoner is shackled by iron chains and iron bars. Similarly, a conditioned soul is shackled by the charming beauty of a woman, by her solitary embraces and talks of so-called love, and by the sweet words of his small children. Thus he forgets his real identity.

In this verse the words *strīṇām asatīnām* indicate that womanly love is just to agitate the mind of man. Actually, in the material world there is no love. Both the woman and the man are interested in their sense gratification. For sense gratification a woman creates an illusory love, and the man becomes enchanted by such false love and forgets his real duty. When there are children as the result of such a combination, the next attraction is to the sweet words of the children. The love of the woman at home and the talk of the children make one a secure prisoner, and thus he cannot leave his home. Such a person is termed, in Vedic language, a *gṛhamedhī,* which means "one whose center of attraction is home." *Gṛhastha* refers to one who lives with family, wife and children, but whose real purpose of living is to develop Kṛṣṇa consciousness. One is therefore advised to become a *gṛhastha* and not a *gṛhamedhī.* The *gṛhastha's* concern is to get out of the family life created by illusion and enter into real family life with Kṛṣṇa, whereas the *gṛhamedhi* s business is to repeatedly chain himself to so-called family life, in one life after another, and perpetually remain in the darkness of *māyā.*

TEXT 9

गृहेषु कूटधर्मेषु दुःखतन्त्रेष्वतन्द्रितः ।
कुर्वन्दुःखप्रतीकारं सुखवन्मन्यते गृही ॥ ९ ॥

gṛheṣu kūṭa-dharmeṣu
duḥkha-tantreṣv atandritaḥ
kurvan duḥkha-pratīkāraṁ
sukhavan manyate gṛhī

gṛheṣu—in family life; *kūṭa-dharmeṣu*—involving the practice of falsehood; *duḥkha-tantreṣu*—spreading miseries; *atandritaḥ*—attentive; *kurvan*—doing; *duḥkha-pratīkāram*—counteraction of miseries; *sukha-vat*—as happiness; *manyate*—thinks; *gṛhī*—the householder.

TRANSLATION

The attached householder remains in his family life, which is full of diplomacy and politics. Always spreading miseries and controlled by acts of sense gratification, he acts just to counteract the reactions of all his miseries, and if he can successfully counteract such miseries, he thinks that he is happy.

PURPORT

In *Bhagavad-gītā* the Personality of Godhead Himself certifies the material world as an impermanent place that is full of miseries. There is no question of happiness in this material world, either individually or in terms of family, society or country. If something is going on in the name of happiness, that is also illusion. Here in this material world, happiness means successful counteraction to the effects of distress. The material world is so made that unless one becomes a clever diplomat, his life will be a failure. Not to speak of human society, even the society of lower animals, the birds and bees, cleverly manages its bodily demands of eating, sleeping and mating. Human society competes nationally or individually, and in the attempt to be successful the entire human society becomes full of diplomacy. We should always remember that in spite of all diplomacy and all intelligence in the struggle for our existence, everything will end in a second by the supreme will. Therefore, all our attempts to become happy in this material world are simply a delusion offered by *māyā*.

TEXT 10

अर्थैरापादितैर्गुर्व्या हिंसयेतस्ततश्च तान् ।
पुष्णाति येषां पोषेण शेषभुग्यात्यधः स्वयम् ॥१०॥

arthair āpāditair gurvyā
hiṁsayetas-tataś ca tān
puṣṇāti yeṣāṁ poṣeṇa
śeṣa-bhug yāty adhaḥ svayam

arthaiḥ—by wealth; *āpāditaiḥ*—secured; *gurvyā*—great; *hiṁsayā*—by violence; *itaḥ-tataḥ*—here and there; *ca*—and; *tān*—them (family members); *puṣṇāti*—he maintains; *yeṣām*—of whom; *poṣeṇa*—because of the maintenance; *śeṣa*—remnants; *bhuk*—eating; *yāti*—he goes; *adhaḥ*—downwards; *svayam*—himself.

TRANSLATION

He secures money by committing violence here and there, and although he employs it in the service of his family, he himself eats only a little portion of the food thus purchased, and he goes to hell for those for whom he earned the money in such an irregular way.

PURPORT

There is a Bengali proverb, "The person for whom I have stolen accuses me of being a thief." The family members, for whom an attached person acts in so many criminal ways, are never satisfied. In illusion an attached person serves such family members, and by serving them he is destined to enter into a hellish condition of life. For example, a thief steals something to maintain his family, and he is caught and imprisoned. This is the sum and substance of material existence and attachment to material society, friendship and love. Although an attached family man is always engaged in getting money by hook or by crook for the maintenance of his family, he cannot enjoy more than what he could consume even without such criminal activities. A man who eats eight ounces of foodstuffs may have to maintain a big family and earn money by any means to support that family, but he himself is not offered more than what he can eat, and sometimes he eats the remnants that are left after his family members are fed. Even by earning money by unfair means, he cannot enjoy life for himself. That is called the covering illusion of *māyā.*

The process of illusory service to society, country and community is exactly the same everywhere; the same principle is applicable even to big national leaders. A national leader who is very great in serving his country is sometimes killed by his countrymen because of irregular service. In other words, one cannot satisfy his dependents by this illusory service, although one cannot get out of the service because servant is his constitutional position. A living entity is constitutionally part and parcel of the Supreme Being, but he forgets that he has to render service to the Supreme Being and diverts his attention to serving others; this is called *māyā.* By serving others he falsely thinks that he is master. The head of a family thinks of himself as the master of the family, or the leader of a nation thinks of himself as the master of the nation, whereas actually he is serving, and by serving *māyā* he is gradually going to hell. Therefore, a sane man should come to the point of Kṛṣṇa consciousness and engage in the service of the Supreme Lord, applying his whole life, all of his wealth, his entire intelligence and his full power of speaking.

TEXT 11

वार्तायां लुप्यमानायामारब्धायां पुनः पुनः ।
लोभाभिभूतो निःसत्त्वः परार्थे कुरुते स्पृहाम् ॥११॥

vārtāyāṁ lupyamānāyām
ārabdhāyāṁ punaḥ punaḥ
lobhābhibhūto niḥsattvaḥ
parārthe kurute spṛhām

vārtāyām—when his occupation; *lupyamānāyām*—is hampered; *ārabdhāyām*—undertaken; *punaḥ punaḥ*—again and again; *lobha*—by greed; *abhibhūtaḥ*—overwhelmed; *niḥsattvaḥ*—ruined; *para-arthe*—for the wealth of others; *kurute spṛhām*—he longs.

TRANSLATION

When he suffers reverses in his occupation, he tries again and again to improve himself, but when he is baffled in all attempts and is ruined, he accepts money from others because of excessive greed.

TEXT 12

कुटुम्बभरणाकल्पो मन्दभाग्यो वृथोद्यमः ।
श्रिया विहीनः कृपणो ध्यायञ्छ्वसिति मूढधीः ॥१२॥

kuṭumba-bharaṇākalpo
manda-bhāgyo vṛthodyamaḥ
śriyā vihīnaḥ kṛpaṇo
dhyāyañ chvasiti mūḍha-dhīḥ

kuṭumba—his family; *bharaṇa*—in maintaining; *akalpaḥ*—unable; *manda-bhāgyaḥ*—the unfortunate man; *vṛthā*—in vain; *udyamaḥ*—whose effort; *śriyā*—beauty, wealth; *vihīnaḥ*—bereft of; *kṛpaṇaḥ*—wretched; *dhyāyan*—grieving; *śvasiti*—he sighs; *mūḍha*—bewildered; *dhīḥ*—his intelligence.

TRANSLATION

Thus the unfortunate man, unsuccessful in maintaining his family members, is bereft of all beauty. He always thinks of his failure, grieving very deeply.

TEXT 13

एवं स्वभरणाकल्पं तत्कलत्रादयस्तथा ।
नाद्रियन्ते यथापूर्वं कीनाशा इव गोजरम् ॥१३॥

evaṁ sva-bharaṇākalpaṁ
tat-kalatrādayas tathā
nādriyante yathā pūrvaṁ
kīnāśā iva go-jaram

evam—thus; *sva-bharaṇa*—to maintain them; *akalpam*—unable; *tat*—his; *kalatra*—wife; *ādayaḥ*—and so on; *tathā*—so; *na*—not; *ādriyante*—do respect; *yathā*—as; *pūrvam*—before; *kīnāśāḥ*—farmers; *iva*—like; *go-jaram*—an old ox.

TRANSLATION

Seeing him unable to support them, his wife and others do not treat him with the same respect as before, even as miserly farmers do not accord the same treatment to their old and worn-out oxen.

PURPORT

Not only in the present age but from time immemorial, no one has liked an old man who is unable to earn in the family. Even in the modern age, in some communities or states, the old men are given poison so that they will die as soon as possible. In some cannibalistic communities, the old grandfather is sportingly killed, and a feast is held in which his body is eaten. The example is given that a farmer does not like an old bull who has ceased to work. Similarly, when an attached person in family life becomes old and is unable to earn, he is no longer liked by his wife, sons, daughters and other kinsmen, and he is consequently neglected, what to speak of not being given respect. It is judicious, therefore, to give up family attachment before one attains old age and take shelter of the Supreme Personality of Godhead. One should employ himself in the Lord's service so that the Supreme Lord can take charge of him, and he will not be neglected by his so-called kinsmen.

TEXT 14

तत्राप्यजातनिर्वेदो भ्रियमाणः स्वयम्भृतैः ।
जरयोपात्तवैरूप्यो मरणाभिमुखो गृहे ॥१४॥

tatrāpy ajāta-nirvedo
bhriyamāṇaḥ svayam bhṛtaiḥ
jarayopātta-vairūpyo
maraṇābhimukho gṛhe

tatra—there; *api*—although; *ajāta*—not arisen; *nirvedaḥ*—aversion; *bhriyamāṇaḥ*—being maintained; *svayam*—by himself; *bhṛtaiḥ*—by those who were maintained; *jarayā*—by old age; *upātta*—obtained; *vairūpyaḥ*—deformation; *maraṇa*—death; *abhimukhaḥ*—approaching; *gṛhe*—at home.

TRANSLATION

The foolish family man does not become averse to family life although he is maintained by those whom he once maintained. Deformed by the influence of old age, he prepares himself to meet ultimate death.

PURPORT

Family attraction is so strong that even if one is neglected by family members in his old age, he cannot give up family affection, and he remains at home just like a dog. In the Vedic way of life one has to give up family life when he is strong enough. It is advised that before getting too weak and being baffled in material activities, and before becoming diseased, one should give up family life and engage oneself completely in the service of the Lord for the remaining days of his life. It is enjoined, therefore, in the Vedic scriptures, that as soon as one passes fifty years of age, he must give up family life and live alone in the forest. After preparing himself fully, he should become a *sannyāsī* to distribute the knowledge of spiritual life to each and every home.

TEXT 15

आस्तेऽवमत्योपन्यस्तं गृहपाल इवाहरन् ।
आमयाव्यप्रदीप्ताग्निरल्पाहारोऽल्पचेष्टितः ॥१५॥

āste 'vamatyopanyastaṁ
gṛha-pāla ivāharan
āmayāvy apradīptāgnir
alpāhāro 'lpa-ceṣṭitaḥ

āste—he remains; *avamatyā*—negligently; *upanyastam*—what is placed; *gṛha-pālaḥ*—a dog; *iva*—like; *āharan*—eating; *āmayāvī*—diseased; *apradīpta-agniḥ*—having dyspepsia; *alpa*—little; *āhāraḥ*—eating; *alpa*—little; *ceṣṭitaḥ*—his activity.

TRANSLATION

Thus he remains at home just like a pet dog and eats whatever is so negligently given to him. Afflicted with many illnesses, such as dyspepsia and loss of appetite, he eats only very small morsels of food, and he becomes an invalid, who cannot work any more.

PURPORT

Before meeting death one is sure to become a diseased invalid, and when he is neglected by his family members, his life becomes less than a dog's because he is put into so many miserable conditions. Vedic literatures enjoin, therefore, that before the arrival of such miserable conditions, one should leave home and die without the knowledge of his family members. If a man leaves home and dies without his family's knowing, that is considered to be a glorious death. But an attached family man wants his family members to carry him in a great procession even after his death, and although he will not be able to see how the procession goes, he still desires that his body be taken gorgeously in procession. Thus he is happy without even knowing where he has to go when he leaves his body for the next life.

TEXT 16

वायुनोत्क्रमतोत्तारः कफसंरुद्धनाडिकः ।
कासश्वासकृतायासः कण्ठे घुरघुरायते ॥१६॥

vāyunotkramatottāraḥ
kapha-saṁruddha-nāḍikaḥ
kāsa-śvāsa-kṛtāyāsaḥ
kaṇṭhe ghura-ghurāyate

vāyunā—by air; *utkramatā*—bulging out; *uttāraḥ*—his eyes; *kapha*—with mucus; *saṁruddha*—congested; *nāḍikaḥ*—his windpipe; *kāsa*—coughing; *śvāsa*—breathing; *kṛta*—done; *āyāsaḥ*—difficulty; *kaṇṭhe*—in the throat; *ghura-ghurāyate*—he produces a sound like *ghura-ghura.*

TRANSLATION

In that diseased condition, one's eyes bulge due to the pressure of air from within, and his glands become congested with mucus. He has difficulty breathing, and upon exhaling and inhaling he produces a sound like "ghura-ghura," a rattling within the throat.

TEXT 17

शयानः परिशोचद्भिः परिवीतः स्वबन्धुभिः ।
वाच्यमानोऽपि न ब्रूते कालपाशवशं गतः ॥१७॥

śayānaḥ pariśocadbhiḥ
parivītaḥ sva-bandhubhiḥ
vācyamāno 'pi na brūte
kāla-pāśa-vaśaṁ gataḥ

śayānaḥ—lying down; *pariśocadbhiḥ*—lamenting; *parivītaḥ*—surrounded; *sva-bandhubhiḥ*—by his relatives and friends; *vācyamānaḥ*—being urged to speak; *api*—although; *na*—not; *brūte*—he speaks; *kāla*—of time; *pāśa*—the noose; *vaśam*—under the control of; *gataḥ*—gone.

TRANSLATION

In this way he comes under the clutches of death and lies down, surrounded by lamenting friends and relatives, and although he wants to speak with them, he no longer can because he is under the control of time.

PURPORT

For formality's sake, when a man is lying on his deathbed, his relatives come to him, and sometimes they cry very loudly, addressing the dying man: "Oh, my father!" "Oh, my friend!" or "Oh, my husband!" In that pitiable condition the dying man wants to speak with them and instruct them of his desires, but because he is fully under the control of the time factor, death, he cannot express himself, and that causes him inconceivable pain. He is already in a painful condition because of disease, and his glands and throat are choked up with mucus. He is already in a very difficult position, and when he is addressed by his relatives in that way, his grief increases.

TEXT 18

एवं कुटुम्बभरणे व्यापृतात्माजितेन्द्रियः ।
म्रियते रुदतां स्वानामुरुवेदनयास्तधीः ॥१८॥

evaṁ kuṭumba-bharaṇe
vyāpṛtātmājitendriyaḥ
mriyate rudatāṁ svānām
uru-vedanayāsta-dhīḥ

evam—thus; *kuṭumba-bharaṇe*—in maintaining a family; *vyāpṛta*—engrossed; *ātmā*—his mind; *ajita*—uncontrolled; *indriyaḥ*—his senses; *mriyate*—he dies; *rudatām*—while crying; *svānām*—his relatives; *uru*—great; *vedanayā*—with pain; *asta*—bereft of; *dhīḥ*—consciousness.

TRANSLATION

Thus the man, who engaged with uncontrolled senses in maintaining a family, dies in great grief, seeing his relatives crying. He dies most pathetically, in great pain and without consciousness.

PURPORT

In *Bhagavad-gītā* it is said that at the time of death one will be absorbed in the thoughts which he cultivated during his lifetime. A person who had no other idea than to properly maintain his family members must have family affairs in his last thoughts. That is the natural sequence for a common man. The common man does not know the destiny of his life; he is simply busy in his flash of life, maintaining his family. At the last stage, no one is satisfied with how he has improved the family economic condition; everyone thinks that he could not provide sufficiently. Because of his deep family affection, he forgets his main duty of controlling the senses and improving his spiritual consciousness. Sometimes a dying man entrusts the family affairs to either his son or some relative, saying, "I am going. Please look after the family." He does not know where he is going, but even at the time of death he is anxious about how his family will be maintained. Sometimes it is seen that a dying man requests the physician to increase his life at least for a few years so that the family maintenance plan which he has begun can be completed. These are the material diseases of the conditioned soul. He completely forgets his real engagement—to become Kṛṣṇa conscious—and is always serious about planning to maintain his family, although he changes families one after another.

TEXT 19

यमदूतौ तदा प्राप्तौ भीमौ सरभसेक्षणौ ।
स दृष्ट्वा त्रस्तहृदयः शकृन्मूत्रं विमुञ्चति ॥१९॥

yama-dūtau tadā prāptau
bhīmau sarabhasekṣaṇau
sa dṛṣṭvā trasta-hṛdayaḥ
śakṛn-mūtraṁ vimuñcati

yama-dūtau—two messengers of Yamarāja; *tadā*—at that time; *prāptau*—arrived; *bhīmau*—terrible; *sa-rabhasa*—full of wrath; *īkṣaṇau*—their eyes; *saḥ*—he; *dṛṣṭvā*—seeing; *trasta*—frightened; *hṛdayaḥ*—his heart; *śakṛt*—stool; *mūtram*—urine; *vimuñcati*—he passes.

TRANSLATION

At death, he sees the messengers of the lord of death come before him, their eyes full of wrath, and in great fear he passes stool and urine.

PURPORT

There are two kinds of transmigration of a living entity after passing away from the present body. One kind of transmigration is to go to the controller of sinful activities, who is known as Yamarāja, and the other is to go to the higher planets, up to

Vaikuṇṭha. Here Lord Kapila describes how persons engaged in activities of sense gratification to maintain a family are treated by the messengers of Yamarāja, called Yamadūtas. At the time of death the Yamadūtas become the custodians of those persons who have strongly gratified their senses. They take charge of the dying man and take him to the planet where Yamarāja resides. The conditions there are described in the following verses.

TEXT 20

यातनादेह आवृत्य पाशैर्बद्ध्वा गले बलात् ।
नयतो दीर्घमध्वानं दण्ड्यं राजभटा यथा ॥२०॥

yātanā-deha āvṛtya
pāśair baddhvā gale balāt
nayato dīrgham adhvānaṁ
daṇḍyaṁ rāja-bhaṭā yathā

yātanā—for punishment; *dehe*—his body; *āvṛtya*—covering; *pāśaiḥ*—with ropes; *baddhvā*—binding; *gale*—by the neck; *balāt*—by force; *nayataḥ*—they lead; *dīrgham*—long; *adhvānam*—distance; *daṇḍyam*—a criminal; *rāja-bhaṭāḥ*—the king's soldiers; *yathā*—as.

TRANSLATION

As a criminal is arrested for punishment by the constables of the state, a person engaged in criminal sense gratification is similarly arrested by the Yamadūtas, who bind him by the neck with strong rope and cover his subtle body so that he may undergo severe punishment.

PURPORT

Every living entity is covered by a subtle and gross body. The subtle body is the covering of mind, ego, intelligence and consciousness. It is said in the scriptures that the constables of Yamarāja cover the subtle body of the culprit and take him to the abode of Yamarāja to be punished in a way that he is able to tolerate. He does not die from this punishment because if he died, then who would suffer the punishment? It is not the business of the constables of Yamarāja to put one to death. In fact, it is not possible to kill a living entity because factually he is eternal; he simply has to suffer the consequences of his activities of sense gratification.

The process of punishment is explained in the *Caitanya-caritāmṛta.* Formerly the king's men would take a criminal in a boat in the middle of the river. They would dunk him by grasping a bunch of his hair and thrusting him completely underwater, and when he was almost suffocated, the king's constables would take him out of the water and allow him to breathe for some time, and then they would again dunk him in the water to suffocate. This sort of punishment is inflicted upon the forgotten soul by Yamarāja, as will be described in the following verses.

TEXT 21

तयोर्निर्भिन्नहृदयस्तर्जनैर्जातवेपथुः ।
पथि श्वभिर्भक्ष्यमाण आर्तोऽघं स्वमनुस्मरन् ॥२१॥

tayor nirbhinna-hṛdayas
tarjanair jāta-vepathuḥ
pathi śvabhir bhakṣyamāṇa
ārto 'ghaṁ svam anusmaran

tayoḥ—of the Yamadūtas; *nirbhinna*—broken; *hṛdayaḥ*—his heart; *tarjanaiḥ*—by the threatening; *jāta*—arisen; *vepathuḥ*—trembling; *pathi*—on the road; *śvabhiḥ*—by dogs; *bhakṣyamāṇaḥ*—being bitten; *ārtaḥ*—distressed; *agham*—sins; *svam*—his; *anusmaran*—remembering.

TRANSLATION

While carried by the constables of Yamarāja, he is overwhelmed and trembles in their hands. While passing on the road he is bitten by dogs, and he can remember the sinful activities of his life. He is thus terribly distressed.

PURPORT

It appears from this verse that while passing from this planet to the planet of Yamarāja, the culprit arrested by Yamarāja's constables meets many dogs, which bark and bite just to remind him of his criminal activities of sense gratification. It is said in *Bhagavad-gītā* that one becomes almost blind and is bereft of all sense when he is infuriated by the desire for sense gratification. He forgets everything. *Kāmais tais tair hṛta jñānāḥ.* One is bereft of all intelligence when he is too attracted by sense gratification, and he forgets that he has to suffer the consequences also. Here the chance for recounting his activities of sense gratification is given by the dogs engaged by Yamarāja. While we live in the gross body, such activities of sense gratification are encouraged even by modern government regulations. In every state all over the world, such activities are encouraged by the government in the form of birth control. Women are supplied pills, and they are allowed to go to a clinical laboratory to get assistance for abortions. This is going on as a result of sense gratification. Actually sex life is meant for begetting a good child, but because people have no control over the senses and there is no institution to train them to control the senses, the poor fellows fall victim to the criminal offenses of sense gratification, and they are punished after death as described in these pages of *Śrīmad-Bhāgavatam.*

TEXT 22

क्षुत्तृट्परीतोऽर्कदवानलानिलैः
सन्तप्यमानः पथि तप्तवालुके ।
कृच्छ्रेण पृष्ठे कशया च ताडित-
श्चलत्यशक्तोऽपि निराश्रमोदके ॥२२॥

kṣut-tṛṭ-parīto 'rka-davānalānilaiḥ
santapyamānaḥ pathi tapta-vāluke
kṛcchreṇa pṛṣṭhe kaśayā ca tāḍitaś
calaty aśakto 'pi nirāśramodake

kṣut-tṛṭ—by hunger and thirst; *parītaḥ*—afflicted; *arka*—sun; *dava-anala*—forest fires; *anilaiḥ*—by winds; *santapyamānaḥ*—being scorched; *pathi*—on a road; *tapta-vāluke*—of hot sand; *kṛcchreṇa*—painfully; *pṛṣṭhe*—on the back; *kaśayā*—with a whip; *ca*—and; *tāḍitaḥ*—beaten; *calati*—he moves; *aśaktaḥ*—unable; *api*—although; *nirāśrama-udake*—without shelter or water.

TRANSLATION

Under the scorching sun, the criminal has to pass through roads of hot sand with forest fires on both sides. He is whipped on the back by the constables because of his inability to walk, and he is afflicted by hunger and thirst, but unfortunately there is no drinking water, no shelter and no place for rest on the road.

TEXT 23

तत्र तत्र पतञ्छ्रान्तो मूर्च्छितः पुनरुत्थितः ।
पथा पापीयसा नीतस्तरसा यमसादनम् ॥२३॥

tatra tatra patañ chrānto
mūrcchitaḥ punar utthitaḥ
pathā pāpīyasā nītas
tarasā yama-sādanam

tatra tatra—here and there; *patan*—falling; *śrāntaḥ*—fatigued; *mūrcchitaḥ*—unconscious; *punaḥ*—again; *utthitaḥ*—risen; *pathā*—by the road; *pāpīyasā*—very inauspicious; *nītaḥ*—brought; *tarasā*—quickly; *yama-sādanam*—to the presence of Yamarāja.

TRANSLATION

While passing on that road to the abode of Yamarāja, he falls down in fatigue, and sometimes he becomes unconscious, but he is forced to rise again. In this way he is very quickly brought to the presence of Yamarāja.

TEXT 24

योजनानां सहस्राणि नवतिं नव चाध्वनः ।
त्रिभिर्मुहूर्तैर्द्वाभ्यां वा नीतः प्राप्नोति यातनाः ॥२४॥

yojanānāṁ sahasrāṇi
navatiṁ nava cādhvanaḥ
tribhir muhūrtair dvābhyāṁ vā
nītaḥ prāpnoti yātanāḥ

yojanānām—of *yojanas;* *sahasrāṇi*—thousands; *navatim*—ninety; *nava*—nine; *ca*—and; *adhvanaḥ*—from a distance; *tribhiḥ*—three; *muhūrtaiḥ*—within moments; *dvābhyām*—two; *vā*—or; *nītaḥ*—brought; *prāpnoti*—he receives; *yātanāḥ*—punishments.

TRANSLATION

Thus he has to pass ninety-nine thousand yojanas within two or three moments, and then he is at once engaged in the torturous punishment which he is destined to suffer.

PURPORT

One *yojana* is calculated to be eight miles, and he has to pass along a road which is therefore as much as 792,000 miles. Such a long distance is passed over within a few moments only. The subtle body is covered by the constables so that the living entity can pass such a long distance quickly and at the same time tolerate the suffering. This covering, although material, is of such fine elements that material scientists cannot discover what the coverings are made of. To pass 792,000 miles within a few moments seems wonderful to the modern space travelers. They have so far traveled at a speed of 18,000 miles per hour, but here we see that a criminal passes 792,000 miles within a few seconds only, although the process is not spiritual but material.

TEXT 25

आदीपनं स्वगात्राणां वेष्टयित्वोल्मुकादिभिः ।
आत्ममांसादनं क्वापि स्वकृत्तं परतोऽपि वा ॥२५॥

ādīpanaṁ sva-gātrāṇāṁ
veṣṭayitvolmukādibhiḥ
ātma-māṁsādanaṁ kvāpi
sva-kṛttaṁ parato 'pi vā

ādīpanam—setting on fire; *sva-gātrāṇām*—of his own limbs; *veṣṭayitvā*—having been surrounded; *ulmuka-ādibhiḥ*—by pieces of burning wood and so on; *ātma-māṁsa*—of his own flesh; *adanam*—eating; *kva api*—sometimes; *sva-kṛttam*—done by himself; *parataḥ*—by others; *api*—else; *vā*—or.

TRANSLATION

He is placed in the midst of burning pieces of wood, and his limbs are set on fire. In some cases he is made to eat his own flesh or have it eaten by others.

PURPORT

From this verse through the next three verses the description of punishment will be narrated. The first description is that the criminal has to eat his own flesh, burning with fire, or allow others like himself who are present there to eat. In the last great war, people in concentration camps sometimes ate their own stool, so there is no wonder that in the Yamasādana, the abode of Yamarāja, one who had a very enjoyable life eating others' flesh has to eat his own flesh.

TEXT 26

जीवतश्चान्त्राभ्युद्धारः श्वगृध्रैर्यमसादने ।
सर्पवृश्चिकदंशाद्यैर्दशद्भिश्चात्मवैशसम् ॥२६॥

jīvataś cāntrābhyuddhāraḥ
śva-gṛdhrair yama-sādane
sarpa-vṛścika-daṁśādyair
daśadbhiś cātma-vaiśasam

jīvataḥ—alive; *ca*—and; *antra*—of his entrails; *abhyuddhāraḥ*—pulling out; *śva-gṛdhraiḥ*—by dogs and vultures; *yama-sādane*—in the abode of Yamarāja; *sarpa*—by serpents; *vṛścika*—scorpions; *daṁśa*—gnats; *ādyaiḥ*—and so on; *daśadbhiḥ*—biting; *ca*—and; *ātma-vaiśasam*—torment of himself.

TRANSLATION

His entrails are pulled out by the hounds and vultures of hell, even though he is still alive to see it, and he is subjected to torment by serpents, scorpions, gnats and other creatures that bite him.

TEXT 27

कृन्तनं चावयवशो गजादिभ्यो भिदापनम् ।
पातनं गिरिशृङ्गेभ्यो रोधनं चाम्बुगर्तयोः ॥२७॥

kṛntanaṁ cāvayavaśo
gajādibhyo bhidāpanam
pātanaṁ giri-śṛṅgebhyo
rodhanaṁ cāmbu-gartayoḥ

kṛntanam—cutting off; *ca*—and; *avayavaśaḥ*—limb by limb; *gaja-ādibhyaḥ*—by elephants and so on; *bhidāpanam*—tearing; *pātanam*—hurling down; *giri*—of hills; *śṛṅgebhyaḥ*—from the tops; *rodhanam*—enclosing; *ca*—and; *ambu-gartayoḥ*—in water or in a cave.

TRANSLATION

Next his limbs are lopped off and torn asunder by elephants. He is hurled down from hilltops, and he is also held captive either in water or in a cave.

TEXT 28

यास्तामिस्रान्धतामिस्रा रौरवाद्याश्च यातनाः ।
भुङ्क्ते नरो वा नारी वा मिथः सङ्गेन निर्मिताः ॥२८॥

yās tāmisrāndha-tāmisrā
rauravādyāś ca yātanāḥ
bhuṅkte naro vā nārī vā
mithaḥ saṅgena nirmitāḥ

yāḥ—which; *tāmisra*—the name of a hell; *andha-tāmisrāḥ*—the name of a hell; *raurava*—the name of a hell; *ādyāḥ*—and so on; *ca*—and; *yātanāḥ*—punishments; *bhuṅkte*—undergoes; *naraḥ*—man; *vā*—or; *nārī*—woman; *vā*—or; *mithaḥ*—mutual; *saṅgena*—by association; *nirmitāḥ*—caused.

TRANSLATION

Men and women whose lives were built upon indulgence in illicit sex life are put into many kinds of miserable conditions in the hells known as Tāmisra, Andha-tāmisra and Raurava.

PURPORT

Materialistic life is based on sex life. The existence of all the materialistic people, who are undergoing severe tribulation in the struggle for existence, is based on sex. Therefore, in the Vedic civilization sex life is allowed only in a restricted way; it is for the married couple and only for begetting children. But when sex life is indulged in for sense gratification illegally and illicitly, both the man and the woman await severe punishment in this world or after death. In this world also they are punished by virulent diseases like syphilis and gonorrhea, and in the next life, as we see in this passage of *Śrīmad-Bhāgavatam,* they are put into different kinds of hellish conditions to suffer. In *Bhagavad-gītā,* First Chapter, illicit sex life is also very much condemned, and it is said that one who produces children by illicit sex life is sent to hell. It is confirmed here in the *Bhāgavatam* that such offenders are put into hellish conditions of life in Tāmisra, Andha-tāmisra and Raurava.

TEXT 29

अत्रैव नरकः स्वर्ग इति मातः प्रचक्षते ।
या यातना वै नारक्यस्ता इहाप्युपलक्षिताः ॥२९॥

atraiva narakaḥ svarga
iti mātaḥ pracakṣate
yā yātanā vai nārakyas
tā ihāpy upalakṣitāḥ

atra—in this world; *eva*—even; *narakaḥ*—hell; *svargaḥ*—heaven; *iti*—thus; *mātaḥ*—O mother; *pracakṣate*—they say; *yāḥ*—which; *yātanāḥ*—punishments; *vai*—certainly; *nārakyaḥ*—hellish; *tāḥ*—they; *iha*—here; *api*—also; *upalakṣitāḥ*—visible.

TRANSLATION

Lord Kapila continued: My dear mother, it is sometimes said that we experience hell or heaven on this planet, for hellish punishments are sometimes visible on this planet also.

PURPORT

Sometimes unbelievers do not accept these statements of scripture regarding hell. They disregard such authorized descriptions. Lord Kapila therefore confirms them by saying that these hellish conditions are also visible on this planet. It is not that they are only on the planet where Yamarāja lives. On the planet of Yamarāja, the sinful man is given the chance to practice living in the hellish conditions which he will have to endure in the next life, and then he is given a chance to take birth on another planet to continue his hellish life. For example, if a man is to be punished to remain in hell and eat stool and urine, then first of all he practices such habits on the planet of Yamarāja, and then he is given a particular type of body, that of a hog, so that he can eat stool and think that he is enjoying life. It is stated previously that in any hellish condition, the conditioned soul thinks he is happy. Otherwise, it would not be possible for him to suffer hellish life.

TEXT 30

एवं कुटुम्बं बिभ्राण उदरम्भर एव वा ।
विसृज्येहोभयं प्रेत्य भुङ्क्ते तत्फलमीदृशम् ॥३०॥

evaṁ kuṭumbaṁ bibhrāṇa
udaram bhara eva vā
visṛjyehobhayaṁ pretya
bhuṅkte tat-phalam īdṛśam

evam—in this way; *kuṭumbam*—family; *bibhrāṇaḥ*—he who maintained; *udaram*—stomach; *bharaḥ*—he who maintained; *eva*—only; *vā*—or; *visṛjya*—after giving up; *iha*—here; *ubhayam*—both of them; *pretya*—after death; *bhuṅkte*—he undergoes; *tat*—of that; *phalam*—result; *īdṛśam*—such.

TRANSLATION

After leaving this body, the man who maintained himself and his family members by sinful activities suffers a hellish life, and his relatives suffer also.

PURPORT

The mistake of modern civilization is that man does not believe in the next life. But whether he believes or not, the next life is there, and one has to suffer if one does not lead a responsible life in terms of the injunctions of authoritative scriptures like the *Vedas* and *Purāṇas.* Species lower than human beings are not responsible for their actions because they are made to act in a certain way, but in the developed life of human consciousness, if one is not responsible for his activities, then he is sure to get a hellish life, as described herein.

TEXT 31

एकः प्रपद्यते ध्वान्तं हित्वेदं स्वकलेवरम् ।
कुशलेतरपाथेयो भूतद्रोहेण यद् भृतम् ॥३१॥

ekaḥ prapadyate dhvāntaṁ
hitvedaṁ sva-kalevaram
kuśaletara-pātheyo
bhūta-droheṇa yad bhṛtam

ekaḥ—alone; *prapadyate*—he enters; *dhvāntam*—darkness; *hitvā*—after quitting; *idam*—this; *sva*—his; *kalevaram*—body; *kuśala-itara*—sin; *pātheyaḥ*—his passage money; *bhūta*—to other living entities; *droheṇa*—by injury; *yat*—which body; *bhṛtam*—was maintained.

TRANSLATION

He goes alone to the darkest regions of hell after quitting the present body, and the money he acquired by envying other living entities is the passage money with which he leaves this world.

PURPORT

When a man earns money by unfair means and maintains his family and himself with that money, the money is enjoyed by many members of the family, but he alone goes to hell. A person who enjoys life by earning money or by envying another's life, and who enjoys with family and friends, will have to enjoy alone the resultant sinful reactions accrued from such violent and illicit life. For example, if a man secures some money by killing someone and with that money maintains his family, those who enjoy the black money earned by him are also partially responsible and are also sent to hell, but he who is the leader is especially punished. The result of material enjoyment is that one takes with him the sinful reaction only, and not the money. The money he earned is left in this world, and he takes only the reaction.

In this world also, if a person acquires some money by murdering someone, the family is not hanged, although its members are sinfully contaminated. But the man who commits the murder and maintains his family is himself hanged as a murderer. The direct offender is more responsible for sinful activities than the indirect enjoyer. The great learned scholar Cāṇakya Paṇḍita says, therefore, that whatever one has in his possession had better be spent for the cause of *sat*, or the Supreme Personality of Godhead, because one cannot take his possessions with him. They remain here, and they will be lost. Either we leave the money or the money leaves us, but we will be separated. The best use of money as long as it is within our possession is to spend it to acquire Kṛṣṇa consciousness.

TEXT 32

दैवेनासादितं तस्य शमलं निरये पुमान् ।
भुङ्क्ते कुटुम्बपोषस्य हृतवित्त इवातुरः ॥३२॥

daivenāsāditaṁ tasya
śamalaṁ niraye pumān
bhuṅkte kuṭumba-poṣasya
hṛta-vitta ivāturaḥ

daivena—by the arrangement of the Supreme Personality of Godhead; *āsāditam*—obtained; *tasya*—his; *śamalam*—sinful reaction; *niraye*—in a hellish condition; *pumān*—the man; *bhuṅkte*—undergoes; *kuṭumba-poṣasya*—of maintaining a family; *hṛta-vittaḥ*—one whose wealth is lost; *iva*—like; *āturaḥ*—suffering.

TRANSLATION

Thus, by the arrangement of the Supreme Personality of Godhead, the maintainer of kinsmen is put into a hellish condition to suffer for his sinful activities, like a man who has lost his wealth.

PURPORT

The example set herein is that the sinful person suffers just like a man who has lost his wealth. The human form of body is achieved by the conditioned soul after many, many births and is a very valuable asset. Instead of utilizing this life to get liberation, if one uses it simply for the purpose of maintaining his so-called family and therefore performs foolish and unauthorized action, he is compared to a man who has lost his wealth and who, upon losing it, laments. When wealth is lost, there is no use lamenting, but as long as there is wealth, one has to utilize it properly and thereby gain eternal profit. It may be argued that when a man leaves his money earned by sinful activities, he also leaves his sinful activities here with his money. But it is especially mentioned herein that by superior arrangement (*daivenāsāditam*), although the man leaves behind him his sinfully earned money, he carries the effect of it. When a man steals some money, if he is caught and agrees to return it, he is not freed from the criminal punishment. By the law of the state, even though he returns the money, he has to undergo the punishment. Similarly, the money earned by a criminal process may be left by the man when dying, but by superior arrangement he carries with him the effect, and therefore he has to suffer hellish life.

TEXT 33

केवलेन ह्यधर्मेण कुटुम्बभरणोत्सुकः ।
याति जीवोऽन्धतामिस्रं चरमं तमसः पदम् ॥३३॥

kevalena hy adharmeṇa
kuṭumba-bharaṇotsukaḥ
yāti jīvo 'ndha-tāmisraṁ
caramaṁ tamasaḥ padam

kevalena—simply; *hi*—certainly; *adharmeṇa*—by irreligious activities; *kuṭumba*—family; *bharaṇa*—to maintain; *utsukaḥ*—eager; *yāti*—goes; *jīvaḥ*—a person; *andha-tāmisram*—to Andha-tāmisra; *caramam*—ultimate; *tamasaḥ*—of darkness; *padam*—region.

TRANSLATION

Therefore a person who is very eager to maintain his family and kinsmen simply by black methods certainly goes to the darkest region of hell, which is known as Andha-tāmisra.

PURPORT

Three words in this verse are very significant. *Kevalena* means "only by black methods," *adharmeṇa* means "unrighteous" or "irreligious," and *kuṭumba-bharaṇa* means "family maintenance." Maintaining one's family is certainly the duty of a householder, but one should be eager to earn his livelihood by the prescribed method, as stated in the scriptures. In *Bhagavad-gītā* it is described that the Lord has divided the social system into four classifications of castes, or *varṇas*, according to quality and work. Apart from *Bhagavad-gītā*, in every society a man is known according to his quality and work. For example, when a man is constructing wooden furniture, he is called a carpenter, and a man who works with an anvil and iron is called a blacksmith. Similarly, a man who is engaged in the medical or engineering fields has a particular duty and designation. All these human activities have been divided by the Supreme Lord into four *varṇas*, namely *brāhmaṇa, kṣatriya, vaiśya* and *śūdra*. In *Bhagavad-gītā* and in other Vedic literatures, the specific duties of the *brāhmaṇa, kṣatriya, vaiśya* and *śūdra* are mentioned.

One should work honestly according to his qualification. He should not earn his livelihood unfairly, by means for which he is not qualified. If a *brāhmaṇa* who works as a priest so that he may enlighten his followers with the spiritual way of life is not qualified as a priest, then he is cheating the public. One should not earn by such unfair means. The same is applicable to a *kṣatriya* or to a *vaiśya.* It is especially mentioned that the means of livelihood of those who are trying to advance in Kṛṣṇa consciousness must be very fair and uncomplicated. Here it is mentioned that he who earns his livelihood by unfair means (*kevalena*) is sent to the darkest hellish region. Otherwise, if one maintains his family by prescribed methods and honest means, there is no objection to one's being a family man.

TEXT 34

अधस्तान्नरलोकस्य यावतीर्यातनादयः ।
क्रमशः समनुक्रम्य पुनरत्राव्रजेच्छुचिः ॥३४॥

adhastān nara-lokasya
yāvatīr yātanādayaḥ
kramaśaḥ samanukramya
punar atrāvrajec chuciḥ

adhastāt—from below; *nara-lokasya*—human birth; *yāvatīḥ*—as many; *yātanā*—punishments; *ādayaḥ*—and so on; *kramaśaḥ*—in a regular order; *samanukramya*—having gone through; *punaḥ*—again; *atra*—here, on this earth; *āvrajet*—he may return; *śuciḥ*—pure.

TRANSLATION

Having gone through all the miserable, hellish conditions and having passed in a regular order through the lowest forms of animal life prior to human birth, and having thus been purged of his sins, one is reborn again as a human being on this earth.

PURPORT

Just as a prisoner, who has undergone troublesome prison life, is set free again, the person who has always engaged in impious and mischievous activities is put into hellish conditions, and when he has undergone different hellish lives, namely those of lower animals like cats, dogs and hogs, by the gradual process of evolution he again comes back as a human being. In *Bhagavad-gītā* it is stated that even though a person engaged in the practice of the *yoga* system may not finish perfectly and may fall down for some reason or other, his next life as a human being is guaranteed. It is stated that such a person, who has fallen from the path of *yoga* practice, is given a chance in his next life to take birth in a very rich family or in a very pious family. It is interpreted that "rich family" refers to a big mercantile family because generally people who engage in trades and mercantile business are very rich. One who engaged in the process of self-realization, or connecting with the Supreme Absolute Truth, but fell short is allowed to take birth in such a rich family, or he is allowed to take birth in the family of pious *brāhmaṇas;* either way, he is guaranteed to appear in human society in his next life. It can be concluded that if someone is not willing to enter into hellish life, as in Tāmisra or Andha-tāmisra, then he must take to the process of Kṛṣṇa consciousness, which is the first-class *yoga* system, because even if one is unable to attain complete Kṛṣṇa consciousness in this life, he is guaranteed at least to take his next birth in a human family. He cannot be sent into a hellish condition. Kṛṣṇa consciousness is the purest life, and it protects all human beings from gliding down to hell to take birth in a family of dogs or hogs.

Thus end the Bhaktivedanta purports of the Third Canto, Thirtieth Chapter, of the Śrīmad-Bhāgavatam, *entitled "Description by Lord Kapila of Adverse Fruitive Activities."*

CHAPTER THIRTY-ONE

Lord Kapila's Instructions on the Movements of the Living Entities

TEXT 1

श्रीभगवानुवाच
कर्मणा दैवनेत्रेण जन्तुर्देहोपपत्तये ।
स्त्रियाः प्रविष्ट उदरं पुंसो रेतःकणाश्रयः ॥ १ ॥

śrī-bhagavān uvāca
karmaṇā daiva-netreṇa
jantur dehopapattaye
striyāḥ praviṣṭa udaraṁ
puṁso retaḥ-kaṇāśrayaḥ

śrī-bhagavān uvāca—the Supreme Personality of Godhead said; *karmaṇā*—by the result of work; *daiva-netreṇa*—under the supervision of the Lord; *jantuḥ*—the living entity; *deha*—a body; *upapattaye*—for obtaining; *striyāḥ*—of a woman; *praviṣṭaḥ*—enters; *udaram*—the womb; *puṁsaḥ*—of a man; *retaḥ*—of semen; *kaṇa*—a particle; *āśrayaḥ*—dwelling in.

TRANSLATION

The Personality of Godhead said: Under the supervision of the Supreme Lord and according to the result of his work, the living entity, the soul, is made to enter into the womb of a woman through the particle of male semen to assume a particular type of body.

PURPORT

As stated in the last chapter, after suffering different kinds of hellish conditions, a man comes again to the human form of body. The same topic is continued in this chapter. In order to give a particular type of human form to a person who has already suffered hellish life, the soul is transferred to the semen of a man who is just suitable to become his father. During sexual intercourse, the soul is transferred through the semen of the father into the mother's womb in order to produce a particular type of body. This process is applicable to all embodied living entities, but it is especially mentioned for the man who was transferred to the Andha-tāmisra hell. After suffering there, when he who has had many types of hellish bodies, like those of dogs and hogs, is to come again to the human form, he is given the chance to take his birth in the same type of body from which he degraded himself to hell.

Everything is done by the supervision of the Supreme Personality of Godhead. Material nature supplies the body, but it does so under the direction of the Supersoul. It is said in *Bhagavad-gītā* that a living entity is wandering in this material world on a chariot made by material nature. The Supreme Lord, as Supersoul, is always present with the individual soul. He directs material nature to supply a particular type of body to the individual soul according to the result of his work, and the material nature supplies it. Here one word, *retaḥ-kaṇāśrayaḥ*, is very significant because it indicates that it is not the semen of the man that creates life within the womb of a woman; rather, the living entity, the soul, takes shelter in a particle of semen and is then pushed into the womb of a woman. Then the body develops. There is no possibility of creating a living entity without the presence of the soul simply by sexual intercourse. The materialistic theory that there is no soul and that a child is born simply by material combination of the sperm and ovum is not very feasible. It is unacceptable.

TEXT 2

कललं त्वेकरात्रेण पञ्चरात्रेण बुद्बुदम् ।
दशाहेन तु कर्कन्धूः पेश्यण्डं वा ततः परम् ॥ २ ॥

kalalaṁ tv eka-rātreṇa
pañca-rātreṇa budbudam
daśāhena tu karkandhūḥ
peśy aṇḍaṁ vā tataḥ param

kalalam—mixing of the sperm and ovum; *tu*—then; *eka-rātreṇa*—on the first night; *pañca-rātreṇa*—by the fifth night; *budbudam*—a bubble; *daśa-ahena*—in ten days; *tu*—then; *karkandhūḥ*—like a plum; *peśī*—a lump of flesh; *aṇḍam*—an egg; *vā*—or; *tataḥ*—thence; *param*—afterwards.

TRANSLATION

On the first night, the sperm and ovum mix, and on the fifth night the mixture ferments into a bubble. On the tenth night it develops into a form like a plum, and after that, it gradually turns into a lump of flesh or an egg, as the case may be.

PURPORT

The body of the soul develops in four different ways according to its different sources. One kind of body, that of the trees and plants, sprouts from the earth; the second kind of body grows from perspiration, as with flies, germs and bugs; the third kind of body develops from eggs; and the fourth develops from an embryo. This verse indicates that after emulsification of the ovum and sperm, the body gradually develops either into a lump of flesh or into an egg, as the case may be. In the case of birds it develops into an egg, and in the case of animals and human beings it develops into a lump of flesh.

TEXT 3

मासेन तु शिरो द्वाभ्यां बाह्वङ्घ्याद्यङ्गविग्रहः ।
नखलोमास्थिचर्माणि लिङ्गच्छिद्रोद्भवस्त्रिभिः ॥ ३ ॥

māsena tu śiro dvābhyāṁ
bāhv-aṅghry-ādy-aṅga-vigrahaḥ
nakha-lomāsthi-carmāṇi
liṅga-cchidrodbhavas tribhiḥ

māsena—within a month; *tu*—then; *śiraḥ*—a head; *dvābhyām*—in two months; *bāhu*—arms; *aṅghri*—feet; *ādi*—and so on; *aṅga*—limbs; *vigrahaḥ*—form; *nakha*—nails; *loma*—body hair; *asthi*—bones; *carmāṇi*—and skin; *liṅga*—organ of generation; *chidra*—apertures; *udbhavaḥ*—appearance; *tribhiḥ*—within three months.

TRANSLATION

In the course of a month, a head is formed, and at the end of two months the hands, feet and other limbs take shape. By the end of three months, the nails, fingers, toes, body hair, bones and skin appear, as do the organ of generation and the other apertures in the body, namely the eyes, nostrils, ears, mouth and anus.

TEXT 4

चतुर्भिर्धातवः सप्त पञ्चभिः क्षुत्तृडुद्भवः ।
षड्भिर्जरायुणा वीतः कुक्षौ भ्राम्यति दक्षिणे ॥ ४ ॥

caturbhir dhātavaḥ sapta
pañcabhiḥ kṣut-tṛḍ-udbhavaḥ
ṣaḍbhir jarāyuṇā vītaḥ
kukṣau bhrāmyati dakṣiṇe

caturbhiḥ—within four months; *dhātavaḥ*—ingredients; *sapta*—seven; *pañcabhiḥ*—within five months; *kṣut-tṛṭ*—of hunger and thirst; *udbhavaḥ*—appearance; *ṣaḍbhiḥ*—within six months; *jarāyuṇā*—by the amnion; *vītaḥ*—enclosed; *kukṣau*—in the abdomen; *bhrāmyati*—moves; *dakṣiṇe*—on the right side.

TRANSLATION

Within four months from the date of conception, the seven essential ingredients of the body, namely chyle, blood, flesh, fat, bone, marrow and semen, come into existence. At the end of five months, hunger and thirst make themselves felt, and at the end of six months, the fetus, enclosed by the amnion, begins to move on the right side of the abdomen.

PURPORT

When the body of the child is completely formed at the end of six months, the child, if he is male, begins to move on the right side, and if female, she tries to move on the left side.

TEXT 5

मातुर्जग्धान्नपानाद्यैरेधद्धातुरसम्मते ।
शेते विण्मूत्रयोर्गर्ते स जन्तुर्जन्तुसम्भवे ॥ ५ ॥

mātur jagdhānna-pānādyair
edhad-dhātur asammate
śete viṇ-mūtrayor garte
sa jantur jantu-sambhave

mātuḥ—of the mother; *jagdha*—taken; *anna-pāna*—by the food and drink; *ādyaiḥ*—and so on; *edhat*—increasing; *dhātuḥ*—the ingredients of his body; *asammate*—abominable; *śete*—remains; *viṭ-mūtrayoḥ*—of stools and urine; *garte*—in a hollow; *saḥ*—that; *jantuḥ*—fetus; *jantu*—of worms; *sambhave*—the breeding place.

TRANSLATION

Deriving its nutrition from the food and drink taken by the mother, the fetus grows and remains in that abominable residence of stools and urine, which is the breeding place of all kinds of worms.

PURPORT

In the *Mārkaṇḍeya Purāṇa* it is said that in the intestine of the mother the umbilical cord, which is known as *āpyāyanī,* joins the mother to the abdomen of the child, and through this passage the child within the womb accepts the mother's assimilated foodstuff. In this way the child is fed by the mother's intestine within the womb and grows from day to day. The statement of the *Mārkaṇḍeya Purāṇa* about the child's situation within the womb is exactly corroborated by modern medical science, and thus the authority of the *purāṇas* cannot be disproved, as is sometimes attempted by the Māyāvādī philosophers.

Since the child depends completely on the assimilated foodstuff of the mother, during pregnancy there are restrictions on the food taken by the mother. Too much salt, chili, onion and similar food is forbidden for the pregnant mother because the child's body is too delicate and new for him to tolerate such pungent food. Restrictions and precautions to be taken by the pregnant mother, as enunciated in the *smṛti* scriptures of Vedic literature, are very useful. We can understand from the Vedic literature how much care is taken to beget a nice child in society. The *garbhādhāna* ceremony before sexual intercourse was compulsory for persons in the higher grades of society, and it is very scientific. Other processes recommended in the Vedic literature during pregnancy are also very important. To take care of the child is the primary duty of the parents because if such care is taken, society will be filled with good population to maintain the peace and prosperity of the society, country and human race.

TEXT 6

कृमिभिः क्षतसर्वाङ्गः सौकुमार्यात्प्रतिक्षणम् ।
मूर्च्छामाप्नोत्युरुक्लेशस्तत्रत्यैः क्षुधितैर्मुहुः ॥ ६ ॥

kṛmibhiḥ kṣata-sarvāṅgaḥ
saukumāryāt pratikṣaṇam
mūrcchām āpnoty uru-kleśas
tatratyaiḥ kṣudhitair muhuḥ

kṛmibhiḥ—by worms; *kṣata*—bitten; *sarva-aṅgaḥ*—all over the body; *saukumāryāt*—because of tenderness; *prati-kṣaṇam*—moment after moment; *mūrcchām*—unconsciousness; *āpnoti*—he obtains; *uru-kleśaḥ*—whose suffering is great; *tatratyaiḥ*—being there (in the abdomen); *kṣudhitaiḥ*—hungry; *muhuḥ*—again and again.

TRANSLATION

Bitten again and again all over the body by the hungry worms in the abdomen itself, the child suffers terrible agony because of his tenderness. He thus becomes unconscious moment after moment because of the terrible condition.

PURPORT

The miserable condition of material existence is not only felt when we come out of the womb of the mother, but is also present within the womb. Miserable life begins from the moment the living entity begins to contact his material body. Unfortunately, we forget this experience and do not take the miseries of birth very seriously. In *Bhagavad-gītā,* therefore, it is specifically mentioned that one should be very alert to understand the specific difficulties of birth and death. Just as during the formation of this body we have to pass through so many difficulties within the womb of the mother, at the time of death there are also many difficulties. As described in the previous chapter, one has to transmigrate from one body to another, and the transmigration into the bodies of dogs and hogs is especially miserable. But despite such miserable conditions, due to the spell of *māyā* we forget everything and become enamored by the present so-called happiness, which is described as actually no more than a counteraction to distress.

TEXT 7

कटुतीक्ष्णोष्णलवणरूक्षाम्लादिभिरुल्बणैः ।
मातृभुक्तैरुपस्पृष्टः सर्वाङ्गोत्थितवेदनः ॥ ७ ॥

kaṭu-tīkṣṇoṣṇa-lavaṇa-
rūkṣāmlādibhir ulbaṇaiḥ
mātṛ-bhuktair upaspṛṣṭaḥ
sarvāṅgotthita-vedanaḥ

kaṭu—bitter; *tīkṣṇa*—pungent; *uṣṇa*—hot; *lavaṇa*—salty; *rūkṣa*—dry; *amla*—sour; *ādibhiḥ*—and so on; *ulbaṇaiḥ*—excessive; *mātṛ-bhuktaiḥ*—by foods eaten by the mother; *upaspṛṣṭaḥ*—affected; *sarva-aṅga*—all over the body; *utthita*—arisen; *vedanaḥ*—pain.

TRANSLATION

Owing to the mother's eating bitter, pungent foodstuffs, or food which is too salty or too sour, the body of the child incessantly suffers pains which are almost intolerable.

PURPORT

All descriptions of the child's bodily situation in the womb of the mother are beyond our conception. It is very difficult to remain in such a position, but still the child has to remain. Because his consciousness is not very developed, the child can tolerate it, otherwise he would die. That is the benediction of *māyā*, who endows the suffering body with the qualifications for tolerating such terrible tortures.

TEXT 8

उल्बेन संवृतस्तस्मिन्नन्त्रैश्च बहिरावृतः ।
आस्ते कृत्वा शिरः कुक्षौ भुग्नपृष्ठशिरोधरः ॥ ८ ॥

ulbena saṁvṛtas tasminn
antraiś ca bahir āvṛtaḥ
āste kṛtvā śiraḥ kukṣau
bhugna-pṛṣṭha-śirodharaḥ

ulbena—by the amnion; *saṁvṛtaḥ*—enclosed; *tasmin*—in that place; *antraiḥ*—by the intestines; *ca*—and; *bahiḥ*—outside; *āvṛtaḥ*—covered; *āste*—he lies; *kṛtvā*—having put; *śiraḥ*—the head; *kukṣau*—towards the belly; *bhugna*—bent; *pṛṣṭha*—back; *śiraḥ-dharaḥ*—neck.

TRANSLATION

Placed within the amnion and covered outside by the intestines, the child remains lying on one side of the abdomen, his head turned towards his belly and his back and neck arched like a bow.

PURPORT

If a grown man were put into such a condition as the child within the abdomen, completely entangled in all respects, it would be impossible for him to live even for a few seconds. Unfortunately, we forget all these sufferings and try to be happy in this life, not caring for the liberation of the soul from the entanglement of birth and death. It is an unfortunate civilization in which these matters are not plainly discussed to make people understand the precarious condition of material existence.

TEXT 9

अकल्पः स्वाङ्गचेष्टायां शकुन्त इव पञ्जरे ।
तत्र लब्धस्मृतिर्दैवात्कर्म जन्मशतोद्भवम् ।
स्मरन्दीर्घमनुच्छ्वासं शर्म किं नाम विन्दते ॥ ९ ॥

akalpaḥ svāṅga-ceṣṭāyāṁ
śakunta iva pañjare
tatra labdha-smṛtir daivāt
karma janma-śatodbhavam

smaran dīrgham anucchvāsaṁ
śarma kiṁ nāma vindate

akalpaḥ—unable; *sva-aṅga*—his limbs; *ceṣṭāyām*—to move; *śakuntaḥ*—a bird; *iva*—like; *pañjare*—in a cage; *tatra*—there; *labdha-smṛtiḥ*—having gained his memory; *daivāt*—by fortune; *karma*—activities; *janma-śata-udbhavam*—occurring during the last hundred births; *smaran*—remembering; *dīrgham*—for a long time; *anucchvāsam*—sighing; *śarma*—peace of mind; *kim*—what; *nāma*—then; *vindate*—can he achieve.

TRANSLATION

The child thus remains just like a bird in a cage, without freedom of movement. At that time, if the child is fortunate, he can remember all the troubles of his past one hundred births, and he grieves wretchedly. What is the possibility of peace of mind in that condition?

PURPORT

After birth the child may forget about the difficulties of his past lives, but when we are grown-up we can at least understand the grievous tortures undergone at birth and death by reading the authorized scriptures like *Śrīmad-Bhāgavatam.* If we do not believe in the scriptures, that is a different question, but if we have faith in the authority of such descriptions, then we must prepare for our freedom in the next life; that is possible in this human form of life. One who does not take heed of these indications of suffering in human existence is said to be undoubtedly committing suicide. It is said that this human form of life is the only means for crossing over the nescience of *māyā,* or material existence. We have a very efficient boat in this human form of body, and there is a very expert captain, the spiritual master; the scriptural injunctions are like favorable winds. If we do not cross over the ocean of the nescience of material existence in spite of all these facilities, then certainly we are all intentionally committing suicide.

TEXT 10

आरभ्य सप्तमान्मासाल्लब्धबोधोऽपि वेपितः ।
नैकत्रास्ते सूतिवातैर्विष्ठाभूरिव सोदरः ॥१०॥

ārabhya saptamān māsāl
labdha-bodho 'pi vepitaḥ

naikatrāste sūti-vātair
viṣṭhā-bhūr iva sodaraḥ

ārabhya—beginning; *saptamāt māsāt*—from the seventh month; *labdha-bodhaḥ*—endowed with consciousness; *api*—although; *vepitaḥ*—tossed; *na*—not; *ekatra*—in one place; *āste*—he remains; *sūti-vātaiḥ*—by the winds for childbirth; *viṣṭhā-bhūḥ*—the worm; *iva*—like; *sa-udaraḥ*—born of the same womb.

TRANSLATION

Thus endowed with the development of consciousness from the seventh month after his conception, the child is tossed downward by the airs that press the embryo during the weeks preceding delivery. Like the worms born of the same filthy abdominal cavity, he cannot remain in one place.

PURPORT

At the end of the seventh month the child is moved by the bodily air and does not remain in the same place, for the entire uterine system becomes slackened before delivery. The worms have been described here as *sodara. Sodara* means "born of the same mother." Since the child is born from the womb of the mother and the worms are also born of fermentation within the womb of the same mother, under the circumstances the child and the worms are actually brothers. We are very anxious to establish universal brotherhood among human beings, but we should take into consideration that even the worms are our brothers, what to speak of other living entities. Therefore, we should be concerned about all living entities.

TEXT 11

नाथमान ऋषिर्भीतः सप्तवध्रिः कृताञ्जलिः ।
स्तुवीत तं विक्लवया वाचा येनोदरेऽर्पितः ॥११॥

nāthamāna ṛṣir bhītaḥ
sapta-vadhriḥ kṛtāñjaliḥ
stuvīta taṁ viklavayā
vācā yenodare 'rpitaḥ

nāthamānaḥ—appealing; *ṛṣiḥ*—the living entity; *bhītaḥ*—frightened; *sapta-vadhriḥ*—bound by the seven layers; *kṛta-añjaliḥ*—with folded hands; *stuvīta*—prays; *tam*—to the Lord; *viklavayā*—faltering; *vācā*—with words; *yena*—by whom; *udare*—in the womb; *arpitaḥ*—he was placed.

TRANSLATION

The living entity in this frightful condition of life, bound by seven layers of material ingredients, prays with folded hands, appealing to the Lord, who has put him in that condition.

PURPORT

It is said that when a woman is having labor pains she promises that she will never again become pregnant and suffer from such a severely painful condition. Similarly, when one is undergoing some surgical operation he promises that he will never again act in such a way as to become diseased and have to undergo medical surgery, or when one falls into danger, he promises that he will never again make the same mistake. Similarly, the living entity, when put into a hellish condition of life, prays to the Lord that he will never again commit sinful activities and have to be put into the womb for repeated birth and death. In the hellish condition within the womb, the living entity is very much afraid of being born again, but when he is out of the womb, when he is in full life and good health, he forgets everything and commits again and again the same sins for which he was put into that horrible condition of existence.

TEXT 12

जन्तुरुवाच
तस्योपसन्नमवितुं जगदिच्छयात्त-
नानातनोर्भुवि चलच्चरणारविन्दम् ।
सोऽहं व्रजामि शरणं ह्यकुतोभयं मे
येनेदृशी गतिरदर्श्यसतोऽनुरूपा ॥१२॥

jantur uvāca
tasyopasannam avituṁ jagad icchayātta-
nānā-tanor bhuvi calac-caraṇāravindam
so 'haṁ vrajāmi śaraṇaṁ hy akuto-bhayaṁ me
yenedṛśī gatir adarśy asato'nurūpā

jantuḥ uvāca—the human soul says; *tasya*—of the Supreme Personality of Godhead; *upasannam*—having approached for protection; *avitum*—to protect; *jagat*—the universe; *icchayā*—by His own will; *ātta-nānā-tanoḥ*—who accepts various forms; *bhuvi*—on the earth; *calat*—walking; *caraṇa-aravindam*—the lotus feet; *saḥ aham*—I myself; *vrajāmi*—go; *śaraṇam*—unto the shelter; *hi*—indeed; *akutaḥ-bhayam*—giving relief from all fear; *me*—for me; *yena*—by whom; *īdṛśī*—such; *gatiḥ*—condition of life; *adarśi*—was considered; *asataḥ*—impious; *anurūpā*—befitting.

TRANSLATION

The human soul says: I take shelter of the lotus feet of the Supreme Personality of Godhead, who appears in His various eternal forms and walks on the surface of the world. I take shelter of Him only, because He can give me relief from all fear and from Him I have received this condition of life, which is just befitting my impious activities.

PURPORT

The word *calac-caraṇāravindam* refers to the Supreme Personality of Godhead, who actually walks or travels upon the surface of the world. For example, Lord Rāmacandra actually walked on the surface of the world, and Lord Kṛṣṇa also walked just like an ordinary man. The prayer is therefore offered to the Supreme Personality of Godhead, who descends to the surface of this earth, or any part of this universe, for the protection of the pious and the destruction of the impious. It is confirmed in *Bhagavad-gītā* that when there is an increase of irreligion and discrepancies arise in the real religious activities, the Supreme Lord comes to protect the pious and kill the impious. This verse indicates Lord Kṛṣṇa.

Another significant point in this verse is that the Lord comes, *icchayā,* by His own will. As Kṛṣṇa confirms in *Bhagavad-gītā, sambhavāmy ātma-māyayā:* "I appear at My will, by My internal potential power." He is not forced to come by the laws of material nature. It is stated here, *icchayā:* He does not *assume* any form, as the impersonalists think, because He comes at His own will, and the form in which He descends is His eternal form. As the Supreme Lord puts the living entity into the condition of horrible existence, He can also deliver him, and therefore one should seek shelter at the lotus feet of Kṛṣṇa. Kṛṣṇa demands, "Give up everything and surrender unto Me." And it is also said in *Bhagavad-gītā* that anyone who approaches Him does not come back again to accept a form in material existence, but goes back to Godhead, back home, never to return.

TEXT 13

यस्त्वत्र बद्ध इव कर्मभिरावृतात्मा
भूतेन्द्रियाशयमयीमवलम्ब्य मायाम् ।
आस्ते विशुद्धमविकारमखण्डबोध-
मातप्यमानहृदयेऽवसितं नमामि ॥१३॥

yas tv atra baddha iva karmabhir āvṛtātmā
bhūtendriyāśayamayīm avalambya māyām
āste viśuddham avikāram akhaṇḍa-bodham
ātapyamāna-hṛdaye 'vasitaṁ namāmi

yaḥ—who; *tu*—also; *atra*—here; *baddhaḥ*—bound; *iva*—as if; *karmabhiḥ*—by activities; *āvṛta*—covered; *ātmā*—the pure soul; *bhūta*—the gross elements; *indriya*—the senses; *āśaya*—the mind; *mayīm*—consisting of; *avalambya*—having fallen; *māyām*—into *māyā*; *āste*—remains; *viśuddham*—completely pure; *avikāram*—without change; *akhaṇḍa-bodham*—possessed of unlimited knowledge; *ātapyamāna*—repentant; *hṛdaye*—in the heart; *avasitam*—residing; *namāmi*—I offer my respectful obeisances.

TRANSLATION

I, the pure soul, appearing now bound by my activities, am lying in the womb of my mother by the arrangement of māyā. I offer my respectful obeisances unto Him who is also here with me but who is unaffected and changeless. He is unlimited, but He is perceived in the repentant heart. To Him I offer my respectful obeisances.

PURPORT

As stated in the previous verse, the *jīva* soul says, "I take shelter of the Supreme Lord." Therefore, constitutionally, the *jīva* soul is the subordinate servitor of the Supreme Soul, the Personality of Godhead. Both the Supreme Soul and the *jīva* soul are sitting in the same body, as confirmed in the *Upaniṣads*. They are sitting as friends, but one is suffering, and the other is aloof from suffering.

In this verse it is said, *viśuddham avikāram akhaṇḍa-bodham:* the Supersoul is always sitting apart from all contamination. The living entity is contaminated and suffering because he has a material body, but that does not mean that because the Lord is also with him, He also has a I material body. He is *avikāram*, changeless. He is always the same Supreme, but unfortunately the Māyāvādī philosophers, because of their impure hearts, cannot understand that the Supreme Soul, the Supersoul, is different from the individual soul. It is said here, *ātapyamāna-hṛdaye 'vasitam:* He is in the heart of every living entity, but He can be realized only by a soul who is repentant. The individual soul becomes repentant that he forgot his constitutional position, wanted to become one with the Supreme Soul and tried his best to lord it over material nature. He has been baffled, and therefore he is repentant. At that time, Supersoul, or the relationship between the Supersoul and the individual soul, is realized. As it is confirmed in

Bhagavad-gītā, after many, many births the knowledge comes to the conditioned soul that Vāsudeva is great, *He* is master, and *He* is Lord. The individual soul is the servant, and therefore he surrenders unto Him. At that time he becomes a *mahātmā*, a great soul. Therefore, a fortunate living being who comes to this understanding, even within the womb of his mother, has his liberation assured.

TEXT 14

यः पञ्चभूतरचिते रहितः शरीरे
च्छन्नोऽयथेन्द्रियगुणार्थचिदात्मकोऽहम् ।
तेनाविकुण्ठमहिमानमृषिं तमेनं
वन्दे परं प्रकृतिपूरुषयोः पुमांसम् ॥१४॥

yaḥ pañca-bhūta-racite rahitaḥ śarīre
cchanno 'yathendriya-guṇārtha-cid-ātmako 'ham
tenāvikuṇṭha-mahimānam ṛṣiṁ tam enaṁ
vande paraṁ prakṛti-pūruṣayoḥ pumāṁsam

yaḥ—who; *pañca-bhūta*—five gross elements; *racite*—made of; *rahitaḥ*—separated; *śarīre*—in the material body; *channaḥ*—covered; *ayathā*—unfitly; *indriya*—senses; *guṇa*—qualities; *artha*—objects of senses; *cit*—ego; *ātmakaḥ*—consisting of; *aham*—I; *tena*—by a material body; *avikuṇṭha-mahimānam*—whose glories are unobscured; *ṛṣim*—all-knowing; *tam*—that; *enam*—unto Him; *vande*—I offer obeisances; *param*—transcendental; *prakṛti*—to material nature; *pūruṣayoḥ*—to the living entities; *pumāṁsam*—unto the Supreme Personality of Godhead.

TRANSLATION

I am separated from the Supreme Lord because of my being in this material body, which is made of five elements, and therefore my qualities and senses are being misused, although I am essentially spiritual. Because the Supreme Personality of Godhead is transcendental to material nature and the living entities, because He is devoid of such a material body, and because He is always glorious in His spiritual qualities, I offer my obeisances unto Him.

PURPORT

The difference between the living entity and the Supreme Personality of Godhead is that the living entity is prone to be subjected to material nature, whereas the Supreme Godhead is always transcendental to material nature as well as to the living entities.

When the living entity is put into material nature, then his senses and qualities are polluted, or designated. There is no possibility for the Supreme Lord to become embodied by material qualities or material senses, for He is above the influence of material nature and cannot possibly be put in the darkness of ignorance like the living entities. Because of His full knowledge, He is never subjected to the influence of material nature. Material nature is always under His control, and it is therefore not possible that material nature can control the Supreme Personality of Godhead.

Since the identity of the living entity is very minute, he is prone to be subjected to material nature, but when he is freed from this material body, which is false, he attains the same, spiritual nature as the Supreme Lord. At that time there is no qualitative difference between him and the Supreme Lord, but because he is not so quantitatively powerful as to never be put under the influence of material nature, he is quantitatively different from the Lord.

The entire process of devotional service is to purify oneself of this contamination of material nature and put oneself on the spiritual platform, where he is qualitatively one with the Supreme Personality of Godhead. In the *Vedas* it is said that the living entity is always free. *Asaṅgo hy ayaṁ puruṣaḥ.* The living entity is liberated. His material contamination is temporary, and his actual position is that he is liberated. This liberation is achieved by Kṛṣṇa consciousness, which begins from the point of surrender. Therefore it is said here, "I offer my respectful obeisances unto the Supreme Person."

TEXT 15

यन्माययोरुगुणकर्मनिबन्धनेऽस्मिन्
सांसारिके पथि चरंस्तदभिश्रमेण ।
नष्टस्मृतिः पुनरयं प्रवृणीत लोकं
युक्त्या कया महदनुग्रहमन्तरेण ॥१५॥

yan-māyayoru-guṇa-karma-nibandhane 'smin
sāṁsārike pathi caraṁs tad-abhiśrameṇa
naṣṭa-smṛtiḥ punar ayaṁ pravṛṇīta lokaṁ
yuktyā kayā mahad-anugraham antareṇa

yat—of the Lord; *māyayā*—by the *māyā*; *uru-guṇa*—arising from the great modes; *karma*—activities; *nibandhane*—with bonds; *asmin*—this; *sāṁsārike*—of repeated birth and death; *pathi*—on the path; *caran*—wandering; *tat*—of him; *abhiśrameṇa*—with great pains; *naṣṭa*—lost; *smṛtiḥ*—memory; *punaḥ*—again; *ayam*—this living entity; *pravṛṇīta*—may realize;

lokam—his true nature; *yuktyā kayā*—by what means; *mahat-anugraham*—the mercy of the Lord; *antareṇa*—without.

TRANSLATION

The human soul further prays: The living entity is put under the influence of material nature and continues a hard struggle for existence on the path of repeated birth and death. This conditional life is due to his forgetfulness of his relationship with the Supreme Personality of Godhead. Therefore, without the Lord's mercy, how can he again engage in the transcendental loving service of the Lord?

PURPORT

The Māyāvādī philosophers say that simply by cultivation of knowledge by mental speculation, one can be liberated from the condition of material bondage. But here it is said one is liberated not by knowledge but by the mercy of the Supreme Lord. The knowledge the conditioned soul gains by mental speculation, however powerful it may be, is always too imperfect to approach the Absolute Truth. It is said that without the mercy of the Supreme Personality of Godhead one cannot understand Him or His actual form, quality and name. Those who are not in devotional service go on speculating for many, many thousands of years, but they are still unable to understand the nature of the Absolute Truth.

One can be liberated in the knowledge of the Absolute Truth simply by the mercy of the Supreme Personality of Godhead. It is clearly said herein that our memory is lost because we are now covered by His material energy. Arguments may be put forward as to why we have been put under the influence of this material energy by the supreme will of the Lord. This is explained in *Bhagavad-gītā*, where the Lord says, "I am sitting in everyone's heart, and due to Me one is forgetful or one is alive in knowledge." The forgetfulness of the conditioned soul is also due to the direction of the Supreme Lord. A living entity misuses his little independence when he wants to lord it over material nature. This misuse of independence, which is called *māyā,* is always available, otherwise there would be no independence. Independence implies that one can use it properly or improperly. It is not static; it is dynamic. Therefore, misuse of independence is the cause of being influenced by *māyā.*

Māyā is so strong that the Lord says that it is very difficult to surmount her influence. But one can do so very easily "if he surrenders unto Me." *Mām eva ye prapadyante:* anyone who surrenders unto Him can overcome the influence of the stringent laws of material nature. It is clearly said here that a living entity is put under the influence of *māyā* by His will, and if anyone wants to get out of this entanglement, this can be made possible simply by His mercy.

The activities of the conditioned souls under the influence of material nature are explained here. Every conditioned soul is engaged in different types of work under the influence of material nature. We can see in the material world that the conditioned soul acts so powerfully that he is playing wonderfully in creating the so-called advancements of material civilization for sense gratification. But actually his position is to know that he is an eternal servant of the Supreme Lord. When he is actually in perfect knowledge, he knows that the Lord is the supreme worshipful object and that the living entity is His eternal servant. Without this knowledge, he engages in material activities; that is called ignorance.

TEXT 16

ज्ञानं यदेतददधात्कतमः स देव-
स्त्रैकालिकं स्थिरचरेष्वनुवर्तितांशः ।
तं जीवकर्मपदवीमनुवर्तमाना-
स्तापत्रयोपशमनाय वयं भजेम ॥१६॥

jñānaṁ yad etad adadhāt katamaḥ sa devas
trai-kālikaṁ sthira-careṣv anuvartitāṁśaḥ
taṁ jīva-karma-padavīm anuvartamānās
tāpa-trayopaśamanāya vayaṁ bhajema

jñānam—knowledge; *yat*—which; *etat*—this; *adadhāt*—gave; *katamaḥ*—who other than; *saḥ*—that; *devaḥ*—the Personality of Godhead; *trai-kālikam*—of the three phases of time; *sthira-careṣu*—in the inanimate and animate objects; *anuvartita*—dwelling; *aṁśaḥ*—His partial representation; *tam*—unto Him; *jīva*—of the *jīva* souls; *karma-padavīm*—the path of fruitive activities; *anuvartamānāḥ*—who are pursuing; *tāpa-traya*—from the threefold miseries; *upaśamanāya*—for getting free; *vayam*—we; *bhajema*—must surrender.

TRANSLATION

No one other than the Supreme Personality of Godhead, as the localized Paramātmā, the partial representation of the Lord, is directing all inanimate and animate objects. He is present in the three phases of time-past, present and future. Therefore, the conditioned soul is engaged in different activities

by His direction, and in order to get free from the threefold miseries of this conditional life, we have to surrender unto Him only.

PURPORT

When a conditioned soul is seriously anxious to get out of the influence of the material clutches, the Supreme Personality of Godhead, who is situated within him as Paramātmā, gives him this knowledge: "Surrender unto Me." As the Lord says in *Bhagavad-gītā,* "Give up all other engagements. Just surrender unto Me." It is to be accepted that the source of knowledge is the Supreme Person. This is also confirmed in *Bhagavad-gītā. Mattaḥ smṛtir jñānam apohanaṁ ca.* The Lord says, "Through Me one gets real knowledge and memory, and one also forgets through Me." To one who wants to be materially satisfied or who wants to lord it over material nature, the Lord gives the opportunity to forget His service and engage in the so-called happiness of material activities. Similarly, when one is frustrated in lording it over material nature and is very serious about getting out of this material entanglement, the Lord, from within, gives him the knowledge that he has to surrender unto Him; then there is liberation.

This knowledge cannot be imparted by anyone other than the Supreme Lord or His representative. In the *Caitanya-caritāmṛta* Lord Caitanya instructs Rūpa Gosvāmī that the living entities wander in life after life, undergoing the miserable conditions of material existence. But when one is very anxious to get free from the material entanglement, he gets enlightenment through a spiritual master and Kṛṣṇa. This means that Kṛṣṇa as the Supersoul is seated within the heart of the living entity, and when the living entity is serious, the Lord directs him to take shelter of His representative, a bona fide spiritual master. Directed from within and guided externally by the spiritual master, one attains the path of Kṛṣṇa consciousness, which is the way out of the material clutches.

Therefore there is no possibility of one's being situated in his own position unless he is blessed by the Supreme Personality of Godhead. Unless he is enlightened with the supreme knowledge, one has to undergo the severe penalties of the hard struggle for existence in the material nature. The spiritual master is therefore the mercy manifestation of the Supreme Person. The conditioned soul has to take direct instruction from the spiritual master, and thus he gradually becomes enlightened to the path of Kṛṣṇa consciousness. The seed of Kṛṣṇa consciousness is sown within the heart of the conditioned soul, and when one hears instruction from the spiritual master, the seed fructifies, and one's life is blessed.

TEXT 17

देह्यन्यदेहविवरे जठराग्निनासृग्-
विण्मूत्रकूपपतितो भृशतप्तदेहः ।
इच्छन्नितो विवसितुं गणयन् स्वमासान्
निर्वास्यते कृपणधीर्भगवन् कदा नु ॥१७॥

dehy anya-deha-vivare jaṭharāgnināsṛg-
viṇ-mūtra-kūpa-patito bhṛśa-tapta-dehaḥ
icchann ito vivasituṁ gaṇayan sva-māsān
nirvāsyate kṛpaṇa-dhīr bhagavan kadā nu

dehī—the embodied soul; *anya-deha*—of another body; *vivare*—in the abdomen; *jaṭhara*—of the stomach; *agninā*—by the fire; *asṛk*—of blood; *viṭ*—stool; *mūtra*—and urine; *kūpa*—in a pool; *patitaḥ*—fallen; *bhṛśa*—strongly; *tapta*—scorched; *dehaḥ*—his body; *icchan*—desiring; *itaḥ*—from that place; *vivasitum*—to get out; *gaṇayan*—counting; *svamāsān*—his months; *nirvāsyate*—will be released; *kṛpaṇa-dhīḥ*—person of miserly intelligence; *bhagavan*—O Lord; *kadā*—when; *nu*—indeed.

TRANSLATION

Fallen into a pool of blood, stool and urine within the abdomen of his mother, his own body scorched by the mother's gastric fire, the embodied soul, anxious to get out, counts his months and prays, "O my Lord, when shall I, a wretched soul, be released from this confinement?"

PURPORT

The precarious condition of the living entity within the womb of his mother is described here. On one side of where the child is floating is the heat of gastric fire, and on the other side are urine, stool, blood and discharges. After seven months the child, who has regained his consciousness, feels the horrible condition of his existence and prays to the Lord. Counting the months until his release, he becomes greatly anxious to get out of the confinement. The so-called civilized man does not take account of this horrible condition of life, and sometimes, for the purpose of sense gratification, he tries to kill the child by methods of contraception or abortion. Unserious about the horrible condition in the womb, such persons continue in materialism, grossly misusing the chance of the human form of life.

The word *kṛpaṇa-dhīḥ* is significant in this verse. *Dhī* means "intelligence," and *kṛpaṇa* means "miserly." Conditional life is for persons who are of miserly intelligence or who do not properly utilize their intelligence. In the human form of life the intelligence is developed, and one has to utilize that developed intelligence to get out of the cycle of birth and death. One who does not do so is a miser, just like a person who has immense wealth but does not utilize it, keeping it simply to see. A person who does not actually utilize his human intelligence to get out of the clutches of *māyā*, the cycle of birth and death, is accepted as miserly. The exact opposite of miserly is *udāra*, "very magnanimous." A *brāhmaṇa* is called *udāra* because he utilizes his human intelligence for spiritual realization. He uses that intelligence to preach Kṛṣṇa consciousness for the benefit of the public, and therefore he is magnanimous.

TEXT 18

येनेदृशीं गतिमसौ दशमास्य ईश
सङ्ग्राहितः पुरुदयेन भवादृशेन ।
स्वेनैव तुष्यतु कृतेन स दीननाथः
को नाम तत्प्रति विनाञ्जलिमस्य कुर्यात् ॥१८॥

yenedṛśīṁ gatim asau daśa-māsya īśa
saṅgrāhitaḥ puru-dayena bhavādṛśena
svenaiva tuṣyatu kṛtena sa dīna-nāthaḥ
ko nāma tat-prati vināñjalim asya kuryāt

yena—by whom (the Lord); *īdṛśīm*—such; *gatim*—a condition; *asau*—that person (myself); *daśa-māsyaḥ*—ten months old; *īśa*—O Lord; *saṅgrāhitaḥ*—was made to accept; *puru-dayena*—very merciful; *bhavādṛśena*—incomparable; *svena*—own; *eva*—alone; *tuṣyatu*—may He be pleased; *kṛtena*—with His act; *saḥ*—that; *dīna-nāthaḥ*—refuge of the fallen souls; *kaḥ*—who; *nāma*—indeed; *tat*—that mercy; *prati*—in return; *vinā*—except with; *añjalim*—folded hands; *asya*—of the Lord; *kuryāt*—can repay.

TRANSLATION

My dear Lord, by Your causeless mercy I am awakened to consciousness, although I am only ten months old. For this causeless mercy of the Supreme Personality of Godhead, the friend of all fallen souls, there is no way to express my gratitude but to pray with folded hands.

PURPORT

As stated in *Bhagavad-gītā*, intelligence and forgetfulness are both supplied by the Supersoul sitting with the individual soul within the body. When He sees that a conditioned soul is very serious about getting out of the clutches of the material influence, the Supreme Lord gives intelligence internally as Supersoul and externally as the spiritual master, or, as an incarnation of the Personality of Godhead Himself, He helps by speaking instructions such as *Bhagavad-gītā.* The Lord is always seeking the opportunity to reclaim the fallen souls to His abode, the kingdom of God. We should always feel very much obliged to the Personality of Godhead, for He is always anxious to bring us into the happy condition of eternal life. There is no sufficient means to repay the Personality of Godhead for His act of benediction; therefore, we can simply feel gratitude and pray to the Lord with folded hands. This prayer of the child in the womb may be questioned by some atheistic people. How can a child pray in such a nice way in the womb of his mother? Everything is possible by the grace of the Lord. The child is put into such a precarious condition externally, but internally he is the same, and the Lord is there. By the transcendental energy of the Lord, everything is possible.

TEXT 19

पश्यत्ययं धिषणया ननु सप्तवध्रिः
शारीरके दमशरीर्यपरः स्वदेहे ।
यत्सृष्टयासं तमहं पुरुषं पुराणं
पश्ये बहिर्हृदि च चैत्यमिव प्रतीतम् ॥१९॥

paśyaty ayaṁ dhiṣaṇayā nanu sapta-vadhriḥ
śārīrake dama-śarīry aparaḥ sva-dehe
yat-sṛṣṭayāsaṁ tam ahaṁ puruṣaṁ purāṇaṁ
paśye bahir hṛdi ca caityam iva pratītam

paśyati—sees; *ayam*—this living entity; *dhiṣaṇayā*—with intelligence; *nanu*—only; *sapta-vadhriḥ*—bound by the seven layers of material coverings; *śārīrake*—agreeable and disagreeable sense perceptions; *dama-śarīrī*—having a body for self-control; *aparaḥ*—another; *sva-dehe*—in his body; *yat*—by the Supreme Lord; *sṛṣṭayā*—endowed; *āsam*—was; *tam*—Him; *aham*—I; *puruṣam*—person; *purāṇam*—oldest; *paśye*—see; *bahiḥ*—outside; *hṛdi*—in the heart; *ca*—and; *caityam*—the source of the ego; *iva*—indeed; *pratītam*—recognized.

TRANSLATION

The living entity in another type of body sees only by instinct; he knows only the agreeable and disagreeable sense perceptions of that particular body. But I have a body in which I can control my senses and can understand my

destination; therefore, I offer my respectful obeisances to the Supreme Personality of Godhead, by whom I have been blessed with this body and by whose grace I can see Him within and without.

PURPORT

The evolutionary process of different types of bodies is something like that of a fructifying flower. Just as there are different stages in the growth of a flower—the bud stage, the blooming stage and the full—fledged, grown-up stage of aroma and beauty—there are 8,400,000 species of bodies in gradual evolution, and there is systematic progress from the lower species of life to the higher. The human form of life is supposed to be the highest, for it offers consciousness for getting out of the clutches of birth and death. The fortunate child in the womb of his mother realizes his superior position and is thereby distinguished from other bodies. Animals in bodies lower than that of the human being are conscious only as far as their bodily distress and happiness are concerned; they cannot think of more than their bodily necessities of life-eating, sleeping, mating and defending. But in the human form of life, by the grace of God, the consciousness is so developed that a man can evaluate his exceptional position and thus realize the self and the Supreme Lord.

The word *dama-śarīrī* means that we have a body in which we can control the senses and the mind. The complication of materialistic life is due to an uncontrolled mind and uncontrolled senses. One should feel grateful to the Supreme Personality of Godhead for having obtained such a nice human form of body, and one should properly utilize it. The distinction between an animal and a man is that the animal cannot control himself and has no sense of decency, whereas the human being has the sense of decency and can control himself. If this controlling power is not exhibited by the human being, then he is no better than an animal. By controlling the senses, or by the process of *yoga* regulation, one can understand the position of his self, the Supersoul, the world and their interrelation; everything is possible by controlling the senses. Otherwise, we are no better than animals.

Real self-realization by means of controlling the senses is explained herein. One should try to see the Supreme Personality of Godhead and one's own self also. To think oneself the same as the Supreme is not self-realization. Here it is clearly explained that the Supreme Lord is *anādi,* or *purāṇa,* and He has no other cause. The living entity is born of the Supreme Godhead as part and parcel. It is confirmed in the *Brahma-saṁhitā, anādir ādir govindaḥ:* Govinda, the Supreme person, has no cause. He is unborn. But the living entity is born of Him. As confirmed in *Bhagavad-gītā, mamaivāṁśaḥ:* both the living entity and the Supreme Lord are unborn, but it has to be understood that the supreme cause of the part and parcel is the Supreme Personality of Godhead. *Brahma-saṁhitā* therefore says that everything has come from the Supreme Personality of Godhead (*sarva-kāraṇa-kāraṇam*). The *Vedānta-sūtra* confirms this also. *Janmādy asya yataḥ:* the Absolute Truth is the original source of everyone's birth. Kṛṣṇa also says in *Bhagavad-gītā, ahaṁ sarvasya prabhavaḥ:* "I am the source of birth of everything, including Brahmā and Lord Śiva and the living entities." This is self-realization. One should know that he is under the control of the Supreme Lord and not think that he is fully independent. Otherwise, why should he be put into conditional life?

TEXT 20

सोऽहं वसन्नपि विभो बहुदुःखवासं
गर्भान्न निर्जिगमिषे बहिरन्धकूपे ।
यत्रोपयातमुपसर्पति देवमाया
मिथ्यामतिर्यदनु संसृतिचक्रमेतत् ॥२०॥

so 'haṁ vasann api vibho bahu-duḥkha-vāsaṁ
garbhān na nirjigamiṣe bahir andha-kūpe
yatropayātam upasarpati deva-māyā
mithyā matir yad-anu saṁsṛti-cakram etat

saḥ aham—I myself; *vasan*—living; *api*—although; *vibho*—O Lord; *bahu-duḥkha*—with many miseries; *vāsam*—in a condition; *garbhāt*—from the abdomen; *na*—not; *nirjigamiṣe*—I wish to depart; *bahiḥ*—outside; *andha-kūpe*—in the blind well; *yatra*—where; *upayātam*—one who goes there; *upasarpati*—she captures; *deva-māyā*—the external energy of the Lord; *mithyā*—false; *matiḥ*—identification; *yat*—which *māyā*; *anu*—according to; *saṁsṛti*—of continual birth and death; *cakram*—cycle; *etat*—this.

TRANSLATION

Therefore, my Lord, although I am living in a terrible condition, I do not wish to depart from my mother's abdomen to fall again into the blind well of materialistic life. Your external energy, called deva-māyā, at once captures the newly born child, and immediately false identification, which is the beginning of the cycle of continual birth and death, begins.

PURPORT

As long as the child is within the womb of his mother, he is in a very precarious and horrible condition of life, but the benefit is that he revives pure consciousness of his relationship with the Supreme Lord and prays for deliverance. But once he is outside the abdomen, when a child is born, *māyā,* or the illusory energy, is so strong that he is immediately overpowered into considering his body to be his self. *Māyā* means "illusion," or that which is actually not. In the material world, everyone is identifying with his body. This false egoistic consciousness of "I am this body" at once develops after the child comes out of the womb. The mother and other relatives are awaiting the child, and as soon as he is born, the mother feeds him, and everyone takes care of him. The living entity soon forgets his position and becomes entangled in bodily relationships. The entire material existence is entanglement in this bodily conception of life. Real knowledge means to develop the consciousness of "I am not this body. I am spirit soul, an eternal part and parcel of the Supreme Lord." Real knowledge entails renunciation, or nonacceptance of this body as the self.

By the influence of *māyā,* the external energy, one forgets everything just after birth. Therefore the child is praying that he prefers to remain within the womb rather than come out. It is said that Śukadeva Gosvāmī, on this consideration, remained for sixteen years within the womb of his mother; he did not want to be entangled in false bodily identification. After cultivating such knowledge within the womb of his mother, he came out at the end of sixteen years and immediately left home so that he might not be captured by the influence of *māyā.* The influence of *māyā* is also explained in *Bhagavad-gītā* as insurmountable. But insurmountable *māyā* can be overcome simply by Kṛṣṇa consciousness. That is also confirmed in *Bhagavad-gītā* (7.14): *mām eva ye prapadyante māyām etāṁ taranti te.* Whoever surrenders unto the lotus feet of Kṛṣṇa can get out of this false conception of life. By the influence of *māyā* only, one forgets his eternal relationship with Kṛṣṇa and identifies himself with his body and the by-products of the body—namely wife, children, society, friendship and love. Thus he becomes a victim of the influence of *māyā,* and his materialistic life of continued birth and death becomes still more stringent.

TEXT 21

तस्मादहं विगतविक्लव उद्धरिष्य
आत्मानमाशु तमसः सुहृदात्मनैव ।
भूयो यथा व्यसनमेतदनेकरन्ध्रं
मा मे भविष्यदुपसादितविष्णुपादः ॥२१॥

tasmād ahaṁ vigata-viklava uddhariṣya
ātmānam āśu tamasaḥ suhṛdātmanaiva

bhūyo yathā vyasanam etad aneka-randhraṁ
mā me bhaviṣyad upasādita-viṣṇu-pādaḥ

tasmāt—therefore; *aham*—I; *vigata*—ceased; *viklavaḥ*—agitation; *uddhariṣye*—shall deliver; *ātmānam*—myself; *āśu*—quickly; *tamasaḥ*—from the darkness; *suhṛdā ātmanā*—with friendly intelligence; *eva*—indeed; *bhūyaḥ*—again; *yathā*—so that; *vyasanam*—plight; *etat*—this; *aneka-randhram*—entering many wombs; *mā*—not; *me*—my; *bhaviṣyat*—may occur; *upasādita*—placed (in my mind); *viṣṇu-pādaḥ*—the lotus feet of Lord Viṣṇu.

TRANSLATION

Therefore, without being agitated any more, I shall deliver myself from the darkness of nescience with the help of my friend, clear consciousness. Simply by keeping the lotus feet of Lord Viṣṇu in my mind, I shall be saved from entering into the wombs of many mothers for repeated birth and death.

PURPORT

The miseries of material existence begin from the very day when the spirit soul takes shelter in the ovum and sperm of the mother and father, they continue after he is born from the womb, and then they are further prolonged. We do not know where the suffering ends. It does not end, however, by one's changing his body. The change of body is taking place at every moment, but that does not mean that we are improving from the fetal condition of life to a more comfortable condition. The best thing is, therefore, to develop Kṛṣṇa consciousness. Here it is stated, *upasādita-viṣṇu-pādaḥ.* This means realization of Kṛṣṇa consciousness. One who is intelligent, by the grace of the Lord, and develops Kṛṣṇa consciousness, is successful in his life because simply by keeping himself in Kṛṣṇa consciousness, he will be saved from the repetition of birth and death.

The child prays that it is better to remain within the womb of darkness and be constantly absorbed in Kṛṣṇa consciousness than to get out and again fall a victim to the illusory energy. The illusory energy acts within the abdomen as well as outside the abdomen, but the trick is that one should remain Kṛṣṇa conscious, and then the effect of such a horrible condition cannot act unfavorably upon him. In *Bhagavad-gītā* it is said that one's intelligence is his friend, and the same intelligence can also be his enemy. Here also the same idea is repeated: *suhṛdātmanaiva,* friendly intelligence. Absorption of intelligence in the personal service of Kṛṣṇa and full consciousness of Kṛṣṇa always are the path of self-realization and liberation. Without being unnecessarily agitated, if we take to the process of Kṛṣṇa consciousness by constantly chanting Hare Kṛṣṇa, Hare Kṛṣṇa, Kṛṣṇa Kṛṣṇa, Hare Hare/ Hare Rāma, Hare Rāma, Rāma Rāma, Hare Hare, the cycle of birth and death can be stopped for good.

It may be questioned herein how the child can be fully Kṛṣṇa conscious within the womb of the mother without any paraphernalia with which to execute Kṛṣṇa consciousness. It is not necessary to arrange for paraphernalia to worship the Supreme Personality of Godhead, Viṣṇu. The child wants to remain within the abdomen of its mother and at the same time wants to become free from the clutches of *māyā*. One does not need any material arrangement to cultivate Kṛṣṇa consciousness. One can cultivate Kṛṣṇa consciousness anywhere and everywhere, provided he can always think of Kṛṣṇa. The *mahā-mantra*, Hare Kṛṣṇa, Hare Kṛṣṇa, Kṛṣṇa Kṛṣṇa, Hare Hare/ Hare Rāma, Hare Rāma, Rāma Rāma, Hare Hare, can be chanted even within the abdomen of one's mother. One can chant while sleeping, while working, while imprisoned in the womb or while outside. This Kṛṣṇa consciousness cannot be checked in any circumstance. The conclusion of the child's prayer is: "Let me remain in this condition; although it is very miserable, it is better not to fall a victim to *māyā* again by going outside."

TEXT 22

कपिल उवाच
एवं कृतमतिर्गर्भे दशमास्यः स्तुवन्नृषिः ।
सद्यः क्षिपत्यवाचीनं प्रसूत्यै सूतिमारुतः ॥२२॥

kapila uvāca
evaṁ kṛta-matir garbhe
daśa-māsyaḥ stuvann ṛṣiḥ
sadyaḥ kṣipaty avācīnaṁ
prasūtyai sūti-mārutaḥ

kapilaḥ uvāca—Lord Kapila said; *evam*—thus; *kṛta-matiḥ*—desiring; *garbhe*—in the womb; *daśa-māsyaḥ*—ten-month-old; *stuvan*—extolling; *ṛṣiḥ*—the living entity; *sadyaḥ*—at that very time; *kṣipati*—propels; *avācīnam*—turned downward; *prasūtyai*—for birth; *sūti-mārutaḥ*—the wind for childbirth.

TRANSLATION

Lord Kapila continued: The ten-month-old living entity has these desires even while in the womb. But while he thus extols the Lord, the wind that helps parturition propels him forth with his face turned downward so that he may be born.

TEXT 23

तेनावसृष्टः सहसा कृत्वावाक् शिर आतुरः ।
विनिष्क्रामति कृच्छ्रेण निरुच्छ्वासो हतस्मृतिः ॥२३॥

tenāvasṛṣṭaḥ sahasā
kṛtvāvāk śira āturaḥ
viniṣkrāmati kṛcchreṇa
nirucchvāso hata-smṛtiḥ

tena—by that wind; *avasṛṣṭaḥ*—pushed downward; *sahasā*—suddenly; *kṛtvā*—turned; *avāk*—downward; *śiraḥ*—his head; *āturaḥ*—suffering; *viniṣkrāmati*—he comes out; *kṛcchreṇa*—with great trouble; *nirucchvāsaḥ*—breathless; *hata*—deprived of; *smṛtiḥ*—memory.

TRANSLATION

Pushed downward all of a sudden by the wind, the child comes out with great trouble, head downward, breathless and deprived of memory due to severe agony.

PURPORT

The word *kṛcchreṇa* means "with great difficulty." When the child comes out of the abdomen through the narrow passage, due to pressure there the breathing system completely stops, and due to agony the child loses his memory. Sometimes the trouble is so severe that the child comes out dead or almost dead. One can imagine what the pangs of birth are like. The child remains for ten months in that horrible condition within the abdomen, and at the end of ten months he is forcibly pushed out. In *Bhagavad-gītā* the Lord points out that a person who is serious about advancement in spiritual consciousness should always consider the four pangs of birth, death, disease and old age. The materialist advances in many ways, but he is unable to stop these four principles of suffering inherent in material existence.

TEXT 24

पतितो भुव्यसृङ्मिश्रः विष्ठाभूरिव चेष्टते ।
रोरूयति गते ज्ञाने विपरीतां गतिं गतः ॥२४॥

patito bhuvy asṛṅ-miśraḥ
viṣṭhā-bhūr iva ceṣṭate
rorūyati gate jñāne
viparītāṁ gatiṁ gataḥ

patitaḥ—fallen; *bhuvi*—on the earth; *asṛk*—with blood; *miśraḥ*—smeared; *viṣṭhā-bhūḥ*—a worm; *iva*—like; *ceṣṭate*—he moves his limbs; *rorūyati*—cries loudly; *gate*—being lost; *jñāne*—his wisdom; *viparītām*—the opposite; *gatim*—state; *gataḥ*—gone to.

TRANSLATION

The child thus falls on the ground, smeared with stool and blood, and plays just like a worm germinated from the stool. He loses his superior knowledge and cries under the spell of māyā.

TEXT 25

परच्छन्दं न विदुषा पुष्यमाणो जनेन सः ।
अनभिप्रेतमापन्नः प्रत्याख्यातुमनीश्वरः ॥२५॥

para-cchandaṁ na viduṣā
puṣyamāṇo janena saḥ
anabhipretam āpannaḥ
pratyākhyātum anīśvaraḥ

para-chandam—the desire of another; *na*—not; *viduṣā*—understanding; *puṣyamāṇaḥ*—being maintained; *janena*—by persons; *saḥ*—he; *anabhipretam*—into undesirable circumstances; *āpannaḥ*—fallen; *pratyākhyātum*—to refuse; *anīśvaraḥ*—unable.

TRANSLATION

After coming out of the abdomen, the child is given to the care of persons who are unable to understand what he wants, and thus he is nursed by such persons. Unable to refuse whatever is given to him, he falls into undesirable circumstances.

PURPORT

Within the abdomen of the mother, the nourishment of the child was being carried on by nature's own arrangement. The atmosphere within the abdomen was not at all pleasing, but as far as the child's feeding was concerned, it was being properly done by the laws of nature. But upon coming out of the abdomen the child falls into a different atmosphere. He wants to eat one thing, but something else is given to him because no one knows his actual demand, and he cannot refuse the undesirables given to him. Sometimes the child cries for the mother's breast, but because the nurse thinks that it is due to pain within his stomach that he is crying, she supplies him some bitter medicine. The child does not want it, but he cannot refuse it. He is put in very awkward circumstances, and the suffering continues.

TEXT 26

शायितोऽशुचिपर्यङ्के जन्तुः स्वेदजदूषिते ।
नेशः कण्डूयनेऽङ्गानामासनोत्थानचेष्टने ॥२६॥

śāyito 'śuci-paryaṅke
jantuḥ svedaja-dūṣite
neśaḥ kaṇḍūyane 'ṅgānām
āsanotthāna-ceṣṭane

śāyitaḥ—laid down; *aśuci-paryaṅke*—on a foul bed; *jantuḥ*—the child; *sveda-ja*—with creatures born from sweat; *dūṣite*—infested; *na īśaḥ*—incapable of; *kaṇḍūyane*—scratching; *aṅgānām*—his limbs; *āsana*—sitting; *utthāna*—standing; *ceṣṭane*—or moving.

TRANSLATION

Laid down on a foul bed infested with sweat and germs, the poor child is incapable of scratching his body to get relief from his itching sensation to say nothing of sitting up, standing or even moving.

PURPORT

It should be noted that the child is born crying and suffering. After birth the same suffering continues, and he cries. Because he is disturbed by the germs in his foul bed, which is contaminated by his urine and stool, the poor child continues to cry. He is unable to take any remedial measure for his relief.

TEXT 27

तुदन्त्यामत्वचं दंशा मशका मत्कुणादयः ।
रुदन्तं विगतज्ञानं कृमयः कृमिकं यथा ॥२७॥

tudanty āma-tvacaṁ daṁśā
maśakā matkuṇādayaḥ
rudantaṁ vigata-jñānaṁ
kṛmayaḥ kṛmikaṁ yathā

tudanti—they bite; *āma-tvacam*—the baby, whose skin is soft; *daṁśāḥ*—gnats; *maśakāḥ*—mosquitoes; *matkuṇa*—bugs; *ādayaḥ*—and other creatures; *rudantam*—crying; *vigata*—deprived of; *jñānam*—wisdom; *kṛmayaḥ*—worms; *kṛmikam*—a worm; *yathā*—just as.

TRANSLATION

In his helpless condition, gnats, mosquitoes, bugs and other germs bite the baby, whose skin is tender, just as smaller worms bite a big worm. The child, deprived of his wisdom, cries bitterly.

PURPORT

The word *vigata-jñānam* means that the spiritual knowledge which the child developed in the abdomen is already lost to the spell of *māyā.* Owing to various kinds of disturbances and to being out of the abdomen, the child cannot remember what he was thinking of for his salvation. It is assumed that even if a person acquires some spiritually uplifting knowledge, circumstantially he is prone to forget it. Not only children but also elderly persons should be very careful to protect their sense of Kṛṣṇa consciousness and avoid unfavorable circumstances so that they may not forget their prime duty.

TEXT 28

इत्येवं शैशवं भुक्त्वा दुःखं पौगण्डमेव च ।
अलब्धाभीप्सितोऽज्ञानादिद्धमन्युः शुचार्पितः ॥२८॥

ity evaṁ śaiśavaṁ bhuktvā
duḥkhaṁ paugaṇḍam eva ca
alabdhābhīpsito 'jñānād
iddha-manyuḥ śucārpitaḥ

iti evam—in this way; *śaiśavam*—childhood; *bhuktvā*—having undergone; *duḥkham*—distress; *paugaṇḍam*—boyhood; *eva*—even; *ca*—and; *alabdha*—not achieved; *abhīpsitaḥ*—he whose desires; *ajñānāt*—due to ignorance; *iddha*—kindled; *manyuḥ*—his anger; *śucā*—by sorrow; *arpitaḥ*—overcome.

TRANSLATION

In this way, the child passes through his childhood, suffering different kinds of distress, and attains boyhood. In boyhood also he suffers pain over desires to get things he can never achieve. And thus, due to ignorance, he becomes angry and sorry.

PURPORT

From birth to the end of five years of age is called childhood. After five years up to the end of the fifteenth year is called *paugaṇḍa.* At sixteen years of age, youth begins.

The distresses of childhood are already explained, but when the child attains boyhood he is enrolled in a school which he does not like. He wants to play, but he is forced to go to school and study and take responsibility for passing examinations. Another kind of distress is that he wants to get some things with which to play, but circumstances may be such that he is not able to attain them, and he thus becomes aggrieved and feels pain. In one word, he is unhappy, even in his boyhood, just as he was unhappy in his childhood, what to speak of youth. Boys are apt to create so many artificial demands for playing, and when they do not attain satisfaction they become furious with anger, and the result is suffering.

TEXT 29

सह देहेन मानेन वर्धमानेन मन्युना ।
करोति विग्रहं कामी कामिष्वन्ताय चात्मनः ॥२९॥

saha dehena mānena
vardhamānena manyunā
karoti vigrahaṁ kāmī
kāmiṣv antāya cātmanaḥ

saha—with; *dehena*—the body; *mānena*—with false prestige; *vardhamānena*—increasing; *manyunā*—on account of anger; *karoti*—he creates; *vigraham*—enmity; *kāmī*—the lusty person; *kāmiṣu*—towards other lusty people; *antāya*—for destruction; *ca*—and; *ātmanaḥ*—of his soul.

TRANSLATION

With the growth of the body, the living entity, in order to vanquish his soul, increases his false prestige and anger and thereby creates enmity towards similarly lusty people.

PURPORT

In *Bhagavad-gītā*, Third Chapter, verse 36, Arjuna inquired from Kṛṣṇa about the cause of a living being's lust. It is said that a living entity is eternal and, as such, qualitatively one with the Supreme Lord. Then what is the reason he falls prey to the material and commits so many sinful activities by the influence of the material energy? In reply to this question, Lord Kṛṣṇa said that it is lust which causes a living entity to glide down from his exalted position to the abominable condition of material existence. This lust circumstantially changes into anger. Both lust and anger stand on the platform of the mode of passion. Lust is actually the product of the mode of passion, and in the absence of satisfaction of lust, the same desire transforms into anger on the platform of ignorance. When ignorance covers the soul, it is the source of his degradation to the most abominable condition of hellish life.

To raise oneself from hellish life to the highest position of spiritual understanding is to transform this lust into love of Kṛṣṇa. Śrī Narottama dāsa Ṭhākura, a great *ācārya* of the Vaiṣṇava *sampradāya,* said, *kāma kṛṣṇa-karmārpaṇe:* due to our lust, we want many things for our sense gratification, but the same lust can be transformed in a purified way so that *we want everything for the satisfaction of the Supreme Personality of Godhead.* Anger also can be utilized towards a person who is atheistic or who is envious of the Personality of Godhead. As we have fallen into this material existence because of our lust and anger, the same two qualities can be utilized for the purpose of advancing in Kṛṣṇa consciousness, and one can elevate himself again to his former pure, spiritual position. Śrīla Rūpa Gosvāmī has therefore recommended that because in material existence we have so many objects of sense gratification, which we need for the maintenance of the body, we should use all of them without attachment, for the purpose of satisfying the senses of Kṛṣṇa; that is actual renunciation.

TEXT 30

भूतैः पञ्चभिरारब्धे देहे देह्यबुधोऽसकृत् ।
अहंममेत्यसद्ग्राहः करोति कुमतिर्मतिम् ॥३०॥

bhūtaiḥ pañcabhir ārabdhe
dehe dehy abudho 'sakṛt
ahaṁ mamety asad-grāhaḥ
karoti kumatir matim

bhūtaiḥ—by material elements; *pañcabhiḥ*—five; *ārabdhe*—made; *dehe*—in the body; *dehī*—the living entity; *abudhaḥ*—ignorant; *asakṛt*—constantly; *aham*—I; *mama*—mine; *iti*—thus; *asat*—nonpermanent things; *grāhaḥ*—accepting; *karoti*—he does; *ku-matiḥ*—being foolish; *matim*—thought.

TRANSLATION

By such ignorance the living entity accepts the material body, which is made of five elements, as himself. With this misunderstanding, he accepts nonpermanent things as his own and increases his ignorance in the darkest region.

PURPORT

The expansion of ignorance is explained in this verse. The first ignorance is to identify one's material body, which is made of five elements, as the self, and the second is to accept something as one's own due to a bodily connection. In this way, ignorance expands. The living entity is eternal, but because of his accepting nonpermanent things, misidentifying his interest, he is put into ignorance, and therefore he suffers material pangs.

TEXT 31

तदर्थं कुरुते कर्म यद्बद्धो याति संसृतिम् ।
योऽनुयाति ददत्क्लेशमविद्याकर्मबन्धनः ॥३१॥

tad-arthaṁ kurute karma
yad-baddho yāti saṁsṛtim
yo 'nuyāti dadat kleśam
avidyā-karma-bandhanaḥ

tat-artham—for the sake of the body; *kurute*—he performs; *karma*—actions; *yat-baddhaḥ*—bound by which; *yāti*—he goes; *saṁsṛtim*—to repeated birth and death; *yaḥ*—which body; *anuyāti*—follows; *dadat*—giving; *kleśam*—misery; *avidyā*—by ignorance; *karma*—by fruitive activities; *bandhanaḥ*—the cause of bondage.

TRANSLATION

For the sake of the body, which is a source of constant trouble to him and which follows him because he is bound by ties of ignorance and fruitive activities, he performs various actions which cause him to be subjected to repeated birth and death.

PURPORT

In *Bhagavad-gītā* it is said that one has to work to satisfy Yajña, or Viṣṇu, for any work done without the purpose of satisfying the Supreme Personality of Godhead is a cause of bondage. In the conditioned state a living entity, accepting his body as himself, forgets his eternal relationship with the Supreme Personality of Godhead and acts on the interest of his body. He takes the body as himself, his bodily expansions as his kinsmen, and the land from which his body is born as worshipable. In this way he performs all sorts of misconceived activities, which lead to his perpetual bondage in repetition of birth and death in various species.

In modern civilization, the so-called social, national and government leaders mislead people more and more, under the bodily conception of life, with the result that all the leaders, with their followers, are gliding down to hellish conditions birth after birth. An example is given in *Śrīmad-Bhāgavatam. Andhā yathāndhair upanīyamānāḥ:* when a blind man leads several other blind men, the result is that all of them fall down in a ditch. This is actually happening. There are many leaders to lead the ignorant public, but because every one of them is bewildered by the bodily conception of life, there is no peace and prosperity in human society. So-called *yogīs* who perform various bodily feats are also in the same category as such ignorant people because the *haṭha-yoga* system is especially recommended for persons who are grossly implicated in the bodily conception. The conclusion is that as long as one is fixed in the bodily conception, he has to suffer birth and death.

TEXT 32

यद्यसद्भिः पथि पुनः शिश्नोदरकृतोद्यमैः ।
आस्थितो रमते जन्तुस्तमो विशति पूर्ववत् ॥३२॥

yady asadbhiḥ pathi punaḥ
śiśnodara-kṛtodyamaiḥ
āsthito ramate jantus
tamo viśati pūrvavat

yadi—if; *asadbhiḥ*—with the unrighteous; *pathi*—on the path; *punaḥ*—again; *śiśna*—for the genitals; *udara*—for the stomach; *kṛta*—done; *udyamaiḥ*—whose endeavors; *āsthitaḥ*—associating; *ramate*—enjoys; *jantuḥ*—the living entity; *tamaḥ*—darkness; *viśati*—enters; *pūrva-vat*—as before.

TRANSLATION

If, therefore, the living entity again associates with the path of unrighteousness, influenced by sensually minded people engaged in the pursuit of sexual enjoyment and the gratification of the palate, he again goes to hell as before.

PURPORT

It has been explained that the conditioned soul is put into the Andha-tāmisra and Tāmisra hellish conditions, and after suffering there he gets a hellish body like the dog's or hog's. After several such births, he again comes into the form of a human being. How the human being is born is also described by Kapiladeva. The human being develops in the mother's abdomen and suffers there and comes out again. After all these sufferings, if he gets another chance in a human body and wastes his valuable time in the association of persons who are concerned with sexual life and palatable dishes, then naturally he again glides down to the same Andha-tāmisra and Tāmisra hells.

Generally, people are concerned with the satisfaction of the tongue and the satisfaction of the genitals. That is material life. Material life means eat, drink, be merry and enjoy, with no concern for understanding one's spiritual identity and the process of spiritual advancement. Since materialistic people are concerned with the tongue, belly and genitals, if anyone wants to advance in spiritual life he must be very careful about associating with such people. To associate with such materialistic men is to commit purposeful suicide in the human form of life. It is said, therefore, that an intelligent man should give up such undesirable association and should always mix with saintly persons. When he is in association with saintly persons, all his doubts about the spiritual expansion of life are eradicated, and he makes tangible progress on the path of spiritual understanding. It is also sometimes found that people are very much addicted to a particular type of religious faith. Hindus, Muslims and Christians are faithful in their particular type of religion, and they go to the church, temple or mosque, but unfortunately they cannot give up the association of persons who are too much addicted to sex life and satisfaction of the palate. Here it is clearly said that one may officially be a very religious man, but if he associates with such persons, then he is sure to slide down to the darkest region of hell.

TEXT 33

सत्यं शौचं दया मौनं बुद्धिः श्रीर्ह्रीर्यशः क्षमा ।
शमो दमो भगश्चेति यत्सङ्गाद्याति सङ्क्षयम् ॥३३॥

satyaṁ śaucaṁ dayā maunaṁ
buddhiḥ śrīr hrīr yaśaḥ kṣamā
śamo damo bhagaś ceti
yat-saṅgād yāti saṅkṣayam

satyam—truthfulness; *śaucam*—cleanliness; *dayā*—mercy; *maunam*—gravity; *buddhiḥ*—intelligence; *śrīḥ*—prosperity; *hrīḥ*—shyness; *yaśaḥ*—fame; *kṣamā*—forgiveness; *śamaḥ*—control of the mind; *damaḥ*—control of the senses; *bhagaḥ*—fortune; *ca*—and; *iti*—thus; *yat-saṅgāt*—from association with whom; *yāti saṅkṣayam*—are destroyed.

TRANSLATION

He becomes devoid of truthfulness, cleanliness, mercy, gravity, spiritual intelligence, shyness, austerity, fame, forgiveness, control of the mind, control of the senses, fortune and all such opportunities.

PURPORT

Those who are too addicted to sex life cannot understand the purpose of the Absolute Truth, nor can they be clean in their habits, not to mention showing mercy to others. They cannot remain grave, and they have no interest in the ultimate goal of life. The ultimate goal of life is Kṛṣṇa, or Viṣṇu, but those who are addicted to sex life cannot understand that their ultimate interest is Kṛṣṇa consciousness. Such people have no sense of decency, and even in public streets or public parks they embrace each other just like cats and dogs and pass it off in the name of love-making. Such unfortunate creatures can never become materially prosperous. Behavior like that of cats and dogs keeps them in the position of cats and dogs. They cannot improve any material condition, not to speak of becoming famous. Such foolish persons may even make a show of so-called *yoga*, but they are unable to control the senses and mind, which is the real purpose of *yoga* practice. Such people can have no opulence in their lives. In a word, they are very unfortunate.

TEXT 34

तेष्वशान्तेषु मूढेषु खण्डितात्मस्वसाधुषु ।
सङ्गं न कुर्याच्छोच्येषु योषित्क्रीडामृगेषु च ॥३४॥

teṣv aśānteṣu mūḍheṣu
khaṇḍitātmasv asādhuṣu
saṅgaṁ na kuryāc chocyeṣu
yoṣit-krīḍā-mṛgeṣu ca

teṣu—with those; *aśānteṣu*—coarse; *mūḍheṣu*—fools; *khaṇḍita-ātmasu*—bereft of self-realization; *asādhuṣu*—wicked; *saṅgam*—association; *na*—not; *kuryāt*—one should make; *śocyeṣu*—pitiable; *yoṣit*—of women; *krīḍā-mṛgeṣu*—dancing dogs; *ca*—and.

TRANSLATION

One should not associate with a coarse fool who is bereft of the knowledge of self-realization and who is no more than a dancing dog in the hands of a woman.

PURPORT

The restriction of association with such foolish persons is especially meant for those who are in the line of advancement in Kṛṣṇa consciousness. Advancement in Kṛṣṇa consciousness involves developing the qualities of truthfulness, cleanliness, mercy, gravity, intelligence in spiritual knowledge, simplicity, material opulence, fame, forgiveness, and control of the mind and the senses. All these qualities are to be manifested with the progress of Kṛṣṇa consciousness, but if one associates with a *śūdra*, a foolish person who is like a dancing dog in the hands of a woman, then he cannot make any progress. Lord Caitanya has advised that any person who is engaged in Kṛṣṇa consciousness and who desires to pass beyond material nescience must not associate himself with women or with persons interested in material enjoyment. For a person seeking advancement in Kṛṣṇa consciousness, such association is more dangerous than suicide.

TEXT 35

न तथास्य भवेन्मोहो बन्धश्चान्यप्रसङ्गतः ।
योषित्सङ्गाद्यथा पुंसो यथा तत्सङ्गिसङ्गतः ॥३५॥

na tathāsya bhaven moho
bandhaś cānya-prasaṅgataḥ
yoṣit-saṅgād yathā puṁso
yathā tat-saṅgi-saṅgataḥ

na—not; *tathā*—in that manner; *asya*—of this man; *bhavet*—may arise; *mohaḥ*—infatuation; *bandhaḥ*—bondage; *ca*—and; *anya-prasaṅgataḥ*—from attachment to any other object; *yoṣit-saṅgāt*—from attachment to women; *yathā*—as; *puṁsaḥ*—of a man; *yathā*—as; *tat-saṅgi*—of men who are fond of women; *saṅgataḥ*—from the fellowship.

TRANSLATION

The infatuation and bondage which accrue to a man from attachment to any other object is not as complete as that resulting from attachment to a woman or to the fellowship of men who are fond of women.

PURPORT

Attachment to women is so contaminating that one becomes attached to the condition of material life not only by the association of women but by the contaminated association of persons who are too attached to them. There are many reasons for our conditional life in the material world, but the topmost of all such causes is the association of women, as will be confirmed in the following stanzas.

In Kali-yuga, association with women is very strong. In every step of life, there is association with women. If a person goes to purchase something, the advertisements are full of pictures of women. The physiological attraction for women is very great, and therefore people are very slack in spiritual understanding. The Vedic civilization, being based on spiritual understanding, arranges association with women very cautiously. Out of the four social divisions, the members of the first order (namely *brahmacarya*), the third order (*vānaprastha*) and the fourth order (*sannyāsa*) are strictly prohibited from female association. Only in one order, the householder, is there license to mix with women under restricted conditions. In other words, attraction for woman's association is the cause of the material conditional life, and anyone interested in being freed from this conditional life must detach himself from the association of women.

TEXT 36

प्रजापतिः स्वां दुहितरं दृष्ट्वा तद्रूपधर्षितः ।
रोहिद्भूतां सोऽन्वधावदृक्षरूपी हतत्रपः ॥३६॥

prajāpatiḥ svāṁ duhitaraṁ
dṛṣṭvā tad-rūpa-dharṣitaḥ
rohid-bhūtāṁ so 'nvadhāvad
ṛkṣa-rūpī hata-trapaḥ

prajā-patiḥ—Lord Brahmā; *svam*—his own; *duhitaram*—daughter; *dṛṣṭvā*—having seen; *tat-rūpa*—by her charms; *dharṣitaḥ*—bewildered; *rohit-bhūtām*—to her in the form of a deer; *saḥ*—he; *anvadhāvat*—ran; *ṛkṣa-rūpī*—in the form of a stag; *hata*—bereft of; *trapaḥ*—shame.

TRANSLATION

At the sight of his own daughter, Brahmā was bewildered by her charms and shamelessly ran up to her in the form of a stag when she took the form of a hind.

PURPORT

Lord Brahmā's being captivated by the charms of his daughter and Lord Śiva's being captivated by the Mohinī form of the Lord are specific instances which instruct us that even great demigods like Brahmā and Lord Śiva, what to speak of the ordinary conditioned soul, are captivated by the beauty of woman. Therefore, everyone is advised that one should not freely mix even with one's daughter or with one's mother or with one's sister, because the senses are so strong that when one becomes infatuated, the senses do not consider the relationship of daughter, mother or sister. It is best, therefore, to practice controlling the senses by performing *bhakti-yoga*, engaging in the service of Madana-mohana. Lord Kṛṣṇa's name is Madana-mohana, for He can subdue the god Cupid, or lust. Only by engaging in the service of Madana-mohana can one curb the dictates of Madana, Cupid. Otherwise, attempts to control the senses will fail.

TEXT 37

तत्सृष्टसृष्टसृष्टेषु को न्वखण्डितधीः पुमान् ।
ऋषिं नारायणमृते योषिन्मय्येह मायया ॥३७॥

tat-sṛṣṭa-sṛṣṭa-sṛṣṭeṣu
ko nv akhaṇḍita-dhīḥ pumān
ṛṣiṁ nārāyaṇam ṛte
yoṣin-mayyeha māyayā

tat—by Brahmā; *sṛṣṭa-sṛṣṭa-sṛṣṭeṣu*—amongst all living entities begotten; *kaḥ*—who; *nu*—indeed; *akhaṇḍita*—not distracted; *dhīḥ*—his intelligence; *pumān*—male; *ṛṣim*—the sage; *nārāyaṇam*—Nārāyaṇa; *ṛte*—except; *yoṣit-mayyā*—in the form of a woman; *iha*—here; *māyayā*—by *māyā*.

TRANSLATION

Amongst all kinds of living entities begotten by Brahmā, namely men, demigods and animals, none but the sage Nārāyaṇa is immune to the attraction of māyā in the form of woman.

PURPORT

The first living creature is Brahmā himself, and from him were created sages like Marīci, who in their turn created Kaśyapa Muni and others, and Kaśyapa Muni and the Manus created different demigods and human beings, etc. But there is none among them who is not attracted by the spell of *māyā* in the form of woman. Throughout the entire material world, beginning from Brahmā down to the small, insignificant creatures like the ant, everyone is attracted by sex life. That is the basic principle of this material world. Lord Brahmā's being attracted by his daughter is the vivid example that no one is exempt from sexual attraction to woman. Woman, therefore, is the wonderful creation of *māyā* to keep the conditioned soul in shackles.

TEXT 38

बलं मे पश्य मायायाः स्त्रीमय्या जयिनो दिशाम् ।
या करोति पदाक्रान्तान् भ्रूविजृम्भेण केवलम् ॥३८॥

balaṁ me paśya māyāyāḥ
strī-mayyā jayino diśām
yā karoti padākrāntān
bhrūvi-jṛmbheṇa kevalam

balam—the strength; *me*—My; *paśya*—behold; *māyāyāḥ*—of *māyā; strī-mayyāḥ*—in the shape of a woman; *jayinaḥ*—conquerors; *diśām*—of all directions; *yā*—who; *karoti*—makes; *pada-ākrāntān*—following at her heels; *bhrūvi*—of her eyebrows; *jṛmbheṇa*—by the movement; *kevalam*—merely.

TRANSLATION

Just try to understand the mighty strength of My māyā in the shape of woman, who by the mere movement of her eyebrows can keep even the greatest conquerors of the world under her grip.

PURPORT

There are many instances in the history of the world of a great conqueror's being captivated by the charms of a Cleopatra. One has to study the captivating potency of woman, and man's attraction for that potency. From what source was this generated? According to *Vedānta-sūtra*, we can understand that everything is generated from the Supreme Personality of Godhead. It is enunciated there, *janmādy asya yataḥ.* This means that the Supreme Personality of Godhead, or the Supreme Person, Brahman, the Absolute Truth, is the source from whom everything emanates. The captivating power of woman, and man's susceptibility to such attraction, must also exist in the Supreme Personality of Godhead in the spiritual world and must be represented in the transcendental pastimes of the Lord.

The Lord is the Supreme Person, the supreme male. As a common male wants to be attracted by a female, that propensity similarly exists in the Supreme Personality of Godhead. He also wants to be attracted by the beautiful features of a woman. Now the question is, if He wants to be captivated by such womanly attraction, would He be attracted by any material woman? It is not possible. Even persons who are in this material existence can give up womanly attraction if they are attracted by the Supreme Brahman. Such was the case with Haridāsa Ṭhākura. A beautiful prostitute tried to attract him in the dead of night, but since he was situated in devotional service, in transcendental love of Godhead, Haridāsa Ṭhākura was not captivated. Rather, he turned the prostitute into a great devotee by his transcendental association. This material attraction, therefore, certainly cannot attract the Supreme Lord. When He wants to be attracted by a woman, He has to create such a woman from His own energy. That woman is Rādhārāṇī. It is explained by the Gosvāmīs that Rādhārāṇī is the manifestation of the pleasure potency of the Supreme Personality of Godhead. When the Supreme Lord wants to derive transcendental pleasure, He has to create a woman from His internal potency. Thus the tendency to be attracted by womanly beauty is natural because it exists in the spiritual world. In the material world it is reflected pervertedly, and therefore there are so many inebrieties.

Instead of being attracted by material beauty, if one is accustomed to be attracted by the beauty of Rādhārāṇī and Kṛṣṇa, then the statement of *Bhagavad-gītā, paraṁ dṛṣṭvā nivartate,* holds true. When one is attracted by the transcendental beauty of Rādhā and Kṛṣṇa, he is no longer attracted by material feminine beauty. That is the special significance of Rādhā-Kṛṣṇa worship. That is testified to by Yāmunācārya. He says, "Since I have become attracted by the beauty of Rādhā and Kṛṣṇa, when there is attraction for a woman or a memory of sex life with a woman, I at once spit on it, and my face turns in disgust." When we are attracted by Madana-mohana and the beauty of Kṛṣṇa and His consorts, then the shackles of conditioned life, namely the beauty of a material woman, cannot attract us.

TEXT 39

सङ्गं न कुर्यात्प्रमदासु जातु
योगस्य पारं परमारुरुक्षुः ।
मत्सेवया प्रतिलब्धात्मलाभो
वदन्ति या निरयद्वारमस्य ॥३९॥

saṅgaṁ na kuryāt pramadāsu jātu
yogasya pāraṁ param ārurukṣuḥ
mat-sevayā pratilabdhātma-lābho
vadanti yā niraya-dvāram asya

saṅgam—association; *na*—not; *kuryāt*—one should make; *pramadāsu*—with women; *jātu*—ever; *yogasya*—of *yoga; pāram*—culmination; *param*—topmost; *ārurukṣuḥ*—one who aspires to reach; *mat-sevayā*—by rendering service unto Me; *pratilabdha*—obtained; *ātma-lābhaḥ*—self-realization; *vadanti*—they say; *yāḥ*—which women; *niraya*—to hell; *dvāram*—the gateway; *asya*—of the advancing devotee.

TRANSLATION

One who aspires to reach the culmination of yoga and has realized his self by rendering service unto Me should never associate with an attractive woman, for such a woman is declared in the scripture to be the gateway to hell for the advancing devotee.

PURPORT

The culmination of *yoga* is full Kṛṣṇa consciousness. This is affirmed in *Bhagavad-gītā:* a person who is always thinking of Kṛṣṇa in devotion is the topmost of all *yogīs.* And in the Second Chapter of the First Canto of *Śrīmad-Bhāgavatam,* it is also stated that when one becomes freed from material contamination by rendering devotional service unto the Supreme Personality of Godhead, he can at that time understand the science of God.

Here the word *pratilabdhātma-lābhaḥ* occurs. *Ātmā* means "self," and *lābha* means "gain." Generally, conditioned souls have lost their *ātmā,* or self, but those who are transcendentalists have realized the self. It is directed that such a self-realized soul who aspires to the topmost platform of yogic perfection should not associate with young women. In the modern age, however, there are so many rascals who recommend that while one has genitals he should enjoy women as much as he likes, and at the same time he can become a *yogī.* In no standard *yoga* system is the association of women accepted. It is clearly stated here that the association of women is the gateway to hellish life. The association of woman is very much restricted in the Vedic civilization. Out of the four social divisions, the *brahmacārī, vānaprastha* and the *sannyāsī*—three orders—are strictly prohibited from the association of women; only the *gṛhasthas,* or householders, are given license to have an intimate relationship with a woman, and that relationship is also restricted for begetting nice children. If, however, one wants to stick to continued existence in the material world, he may indulge in female association unrestrictedly.

TEXT 40

योपयाति शनैर्माया योषिद्देवविनिर्मिता ।
तामीक्षेतात्मनो मृत्युं तृणैः कूपमिवावृतम् ॥४०॥

yopayāti śanair māyā
yoṣid deva-vinirmitā
tām īkṣetātmano mṛtyuṁ
tṛṇaiḥ kūpam ivāvṛtam

yā—she who; *upayāti*—approaches; *śanaiḥ*—slowly; *māyā*—representation of *māyā; yoṣit*—woman; *deva*—by the Lord; *vinirmitā*—created; *tām*—her; *īkṣeta*—one must regard; *ātmanaḥ*—of the soul; *mṛtyum*—death; *tṛṇaiḥ*—with grass; *kūpam*—a well; *iva*—like; *āvṛtam*—covered.

TRANSLATION

The woman, created by the Lord, is the representation of māyā, and one who associates with such māyā by accepting services must certainly know that this is the way of death, just like a blind well covered with grass.

PURPORT

Sometimes it happens that a rejected well is covered by grass, and an unwary traveler who does not know of the existence of the well falls down, and his death is assured. Similarly, association with a woman begins when one accepts service from her, because woman is especially created by the Lord to give service to man. By accepting her service, a man is entrapped. If he is not intelligent enough to know that she is the gateway to hellish life, he may indulge in her association very liberally. This is restricted for those who aspire to ascend to the transcendental platform. Even fifty years ago in Hindu society, such association was restricted. A wife could not see her husband during the daytime. Householders even had different residential quarters. The internal quarters of a residential house were for the woman, and the external quarters were for the man. Acceptance of service rendered by a woman may appear very pleasing, but one should be very cautious in accepting such service because it is clearly said that woman is the gateway to death, or forgetfulness of one's self. She blocks the path of spiritual realization.

TEXT 41

यां मन्यते पतिं मोहान्मन्मायामृषभायतीम् ।
स्त्रीत्वं स्त्रीसङ्गतः प्राप्तो वित्तापत्यगृहप्रदम् ॥४१॥

yāṁ manyate patiṁ mohān
man-māyām ṛṣabhāyatīm
strītvaṁ strī-saṅgataḥ prāpto
vittāpatya-gṛha-pradam

yām—which; *manyate*—she thinks; *patim*—her husband; *mohāt*—due to illusion; *mat-māyām*—My *māyā; ṛṣabha*—in the form of a man; *āyatīm*—coming; *strītvam*—the state of being a woman; *strī-saṅgataḥ*—from attachment to a woman; *prāptaḥ*—obtained; *vitta*—wealth; *apatya*—progeny; *gṛha*—house; *pradam*—bestowing.

TRANSLATION

A living entity who, as a result of attachment to a woman in his previous life, has been endowed with the form of a woman, foolishly looks upon māyā in the form of a man, her husband, as the bestower of wealth, progeny, house and other material assets.

PURPORT

From this verse it appears that a woman is also supposed to have been a man in his (her) previous life, and due to his attachment to his wife, he now has the body of a woman. *Bhagavad-gītā* confirms this; a man gets his next life's birth according to what he thinks of at the time of death. If someone is too attached to his wife, naturally he thinks of his wife at the time of death, and in his next life he takes the body of a woman. Similarly, if a woman thinks of her husband at the time of death, naturally she gets the body of a man in the next life. In the Hindu scriptures, therefore, woman's chastity and devotion to man is greatly emphasized. A woman's attachment to her husband may elevate her to the body of a man in her next life, but a man's attachment to a woman will degrade him, and in his next life he will get the body of a woman. We should always remember, as it is stated in *Bhagavad-gītā*, that both the gross and subtle material bodies are dresses; they are the shirt and coat of the living entity. To be either a woman or a man only involves one's bodily dress. The soul in nature is actually the marginal energy of the Supreme Lord. Every living entity, being classified as energy, is supposed to be originally a woman, or one who is enjoyed. In the body of a man there is a greater opportunity to get out of the material clutches; there is less opportunity in the body of a woman. In this verse it is indicated that the body of a man should not be misused through forming an attachment to women and thus becoming too entangled in material enjoyment, which will result in getting the body of a woman in the next life. A woman is generally fond of household prosperity, ornaments, furniture and dresses. She is satisfied when the husband supplies all these things sufficiently. The relationship between man and woman is very complicated, but the substance is that one who aspires to ascend to the transcendental stage of spiritual realization should be very careful in accepting the association of a woman. In the stage of Kṛṣṇa consciousness, however, such restriction of association may be slackened because if a man's and woman's attachment is not to each other but to Kṛṣṇa, then both of them are equally eligible to get out of the material entanglement and reach the abode of Kṛṣṇa. As it is confirmed in *Bhagavad-gītā,* anyone who seriously takes to Kṛṣṇa consciousness—whether in the lowest species of life or a woman or of the less intelligent classes, such as the mercantile or laborer class—will go back home, back to Godhead, and reach the abode of Kṛṣṇa. A man should not be attached to a woman, nor should a woman be attached to a man. Both man and woman should be attached to the service of the Lord. Then there is the possibility of liberation from material entanglement for both of them.

TEXT 42

तामात्मनो विजानीयात्पत्यपत्यगृहात्मकम् ।
दैवोपसादितं मृत्युं मृगयोर्गायनं यथा ॥४२॥

tām ātmano vijānīyāt
paty-apatya-gṛhātmakam
daivopasāditaṁ mṛtyuṁ
mṛgayor gāyanaṁ yathā

tām—the Lord's *māyā; ātmanaḥ*—of herself; *vijānīyāt*—she should know; *pati*—husband; *apatya*—children; *gṛha*—house; *ātmakam*—consisting of; *daiva*—by the authority of the Lord; *upasāditam*—brought about; *mṛtyum*—death; *mṛgayoḥ*—of the hunter; *gāyanam*—the singing; *yathā*—as.

TRANSLATION

A woman, therefore, should consider her husband, her house and her children to be the arrangement of the external energy of the Lord for her death, just as the sweet singing of the hunter is death for the deer.

PURPORT

In these instructions of Lord Kapiladeva it is explained that not only is woman the gateway to hell for man, but man is also the gateway to hell for woman. It is a question of attachment. A man becomes attached to a woman because of her service, her beauty and many other assets, and similarly a woman becomes attached to a man for his giving her a nice place to live, ornaments, dress and children. It is a question of attachment for one another. As long as either is attached to the other for such material enjoyment, the woman is dangerous for the man, and the man is also dangerous for the woman. But if the attachment is transferred to Kṛṣṇa, both of them become Kṛṣṇa conscious, and then marriage is very nice. Śrīla Rūpa Gosvāmī therefore recommends:

anāsaktasya viṣayān
yathārham upayuñjataḥ
nirbandhaḥ kṛṣṇa-sambandhe
yuktaṁ vairāgyam ucyate
(*Bhakti-rasāmṛta-sindhu* 1.2.255)

Man and woman should live together as householders in relationship with Kṛṣṇa, only for the purpose of discharging duties in the service of Kṛṣṇa. Engage the children, engage the wife and engage the husband, all in Kṛṣṇa conscious duties, and then all these bodily or material attachments will disappear. Since the via medium is Kṛṣṇa, the consciousness is pure, and there is no possibility of degradation at any time.

TEXT 43

देहेन जीवभूतेन लोकाल्लोकमनुव्रजन् ।
भुञ्जान एव कर्माणि करोत्यविरतं पुमान् ॥४३॥

dehena jīva-bhūtena
lokāl lokam anuvrajan
bhuñjāna eva karmāṇi
karoty aviratam pumān

dehena—on account of the body; *jīva-bhūtena*—possessed by the living entity; *lokāt*—from one planet; *lokam*—to another planet; *anuvrajan*—wandering; *bhuñjānaḥ*—enjoying; *eva*—so; *karmāṇi*—fruitive activities; *karoti*—he does; *aviratam*—incessantly; *pumān*—the living entity.

TRANSLATION

Due to his particular type of body, the materialistic living entity wanders from one planet to another, following fruitive activities. In this way, he involves himself in fruitive activities and enjoys the result incessantly.

PURPORT

When the living entity is encaged in the material body, he is called *jīva-bhūta,* and when he is free from the material body he is called *brahma-bhūta.* By changing his material body birth after birth, he travels not only in the different species of life, but also from one planet to another. Lord Caitanya says that the living entities, bound up by fruitive activities, are wandering in this way throughout the whole universe, and if by some chance or by pious activities they get in touch with a bona fide spiritual master, by the grace of Kṛṣṇa, then they get the seed of devotional service. After getting this seed, if one sows it within his heart and pours water on it by hearing and chanting, the seed grows into a big plant, and there are fruits and flowers which the living entity can enjoy, even in this material world. That is called the *brahma-bhūta* stage. In his designated condition, a living entity is called materialistic, and upon being freed from all designations, when he is fully Kṛṣṇa conscious, engaged in devotional service, he is called liberated. Unless one gets the opportunity to associate with a bona fide spiritual master by the grace of the Lord, there is no possibility of one's liberation from the cycle of birth and death in the different species of life and through the different grades of planets.

TEXT 44

जीवो ह्यस्यानुगो देहो भूतेन्द्रियमनोमयः ।
तन्निरोधोऽस्य मरणमाविर्भावस्तु सम्भवः ॥४४॥

jīvo hy asyānugo deho
bhūtendriya-mano-mayaḥ
tan-nirodho 'sya maraṇam
āvirbhāvas tu sambhavaḥ

jīvaḥ—the living entity; *hi*—indeed; *asya*—of him; *anugaḥ*—suitable; *dehaḥ*—body; *bhūta*—gross material elements; *indriya*—senses; *manaḥ*—mind; *mayaḥ*—made of; *tat*—of the body; *nirodhaḥ*—destruction; *asya*—of the living entity; *maraṇam*—death; *āvirbhāvaḥ*—manifestation; *tu*—but; *sambhavaḥ*—birth.

TRANSLATION

In this way the living entity gets a suitable body with a material mind and senses, according to his fruitive activities. When the reaction of his particular activity comes to an end, that end is called death, and when a particular type of reaction begins, that beginning is called birth.

PURPORT

From time immemorial, the living entity travels in the different species of life and the different planets, almost perpetually. This process is explained in *Bhagavad-gītā*. *Bhrāmayan sarva-bhūtāni yantrārūḍhāni māyayā:* under the spell of *māyā*, everyone is wandering throughout the universe on the carriage of the body offered by the material energy. Materialistic life involves a series of actions and reactions. It is a long film spool of actions and reactions, and one life-span is just a flash in such a reactionary show. When a child is born, it is to be understood that his particular type of body is the beginning of another set of activities, and when an old man dies, it is to be understood that one set of reactionary activities is finished.

We can see that because of different reactionary activities, one man is born in a rich family, and another is born in a poor family, although both of them are born in the same place, at the same moment and in the same atmosphere. One who is carrying pious activity with him is given a chance to take his birth in a rich or pious family, and one who is carrying impious activity is given a chance to take birth in a lower, poor family. The change of body means a change to a different field of activities. Similarly, when the body of the boy changes into that of a youth, the boyish activities change into youthful activities.

It is clear that a particular body is given to the living entity for a particular type of activity. This process is going on perpetually, from a time which is impossible to trace out. Vaiṣṇava poets say, therefore, *anādi karama-phale,* which means that these actions and reactions of one's activity cannot be traced, for they may even continue from the last millennium of Brahmā's birth to the next millennium. We have seen the example in the life of Nārada Muni. In one millennium he was the son of a maidservant, and in the next millennium he became a great sage.

TEXTS 45-46

द्रव्योपलब्धिस्थानस्य द्रव्येक्षायोग्यता यदा ।
तत्पञ्चत्वमहंमानादुत्पत्तिर्द्रव्यदर्शनम् ॥४५॥
यथाक्ष्णोर्द्रव्यावयवदर्शनायोग्यता यदा ।
तदैव चक्षुषो द्रष्टुर्द्रष्टृत्वायोग्यतानयोः ॥४६॥

dravyopalabdhi-sthānasya
dravyekṣāyogyatā yadā
tat pañcatvam ahaṁ-mānād
utpattir dravya-darśanam

yathākṣṇor dravyāvayava-
darśanāyogyatā yadā
tadaiva cakṣuṣo draṣṭur
draṣṭṛtvāyogyatānayoḥ

dravya—of objects; *upalabdhi*—of perception; *sthānasya*—of the place; *dravya*—of objects; *īkṣā*—of perception; *ayogyatā*—incapability; *yadā*—when; *tat*—that; *pañcatvam*—death;

aham-mānāt—from the misconception of "I"; *utpattiḥ*—birth; *dravya*—the physical body; *darśanam*—viewing; *yathā*—just as; *akṣṇoḥ*—of the eyes; *dravya*—of objects; *avayava*—parts; *darśana*—of seeing; *ayogyatā*—incapability; *yadā*—when; *tadā*—then; *eva*—indeed; *cakṣuṣaḥ*—of the sense of sight; *draṣṭuḥ*—of the seer; *draṣṭṛtva*—of the faculty of seeing; *ayogyatā*—incapability; *anayoḥ*—of both of these.

TRANSLATION

When the eyes lose their power to see color or form due to morbid affliction of the optic nerve, the sense of sight becomes deadened. The living entity, who is the seer of both the eyes and the sight, loses his power of vision. In the same way, when the physical body, the place where perception of objects occurs, is rendered incapable of perceiving, that is known as death. When one begins to view the physical body as one's very self, that is called birth.

PURPORT

When one says, "I see," this means that he sees with his eyes or with his spectacles; he sees with the instrument of sight. If the instrument of sight is broken or becomes diseased or incapable of acting, then he, as the seer, also ceases to act. Similarly, in this material body, at the present moment the living soul is acting, and when the material body, due to its incapability to function, ceases, he also ceases to perform his reactionary activities. When one's instrument of action is broken and cannot function, that is called death. Again, when one gets a new instrument for action, that is called birth. This process of birth and death is going on at every moment, by constant bodily change. The final change is called death, and acceptance of a new body is called birth. That is the solution to the question of birth and death. Actually, the living entity has neither birth nor death, but is eternal. As confirmed in *Bhagavad-gītā, na hanyate hanyamāne śarīre:* the living entity never dies, even after the death or annihilation of this material body.

TEXT 47

तस्मान्न कार्यः सन्त्रासो न कार्पण्यं न सम्भ्रमः ।
बुद्‌ध्वा जीवगतिं धीरो मुक्तसङ्गश्चरेदिह ॥४७॥

tasmān na kāryaḥ santrāso
na kārpaṇyaṁ na sambhramaḥ
buddhvā jīva-gatiṁ dhīro
mukta-saṅgaś cared iha

tasmāt—on account of death; *na*—not; *kāryaḥ*—should be done; *santrāsaḥ*—horror; *na*—not; *kārpaṇyam*—miserliness; *na*—not; *sambhramaḥ*—eagerness for material gain; *buddhvā*—realizing; *jīva-gatim*—the true nature of the living entity; *dhīraḥ*—steadfast; *mukta-saṅgaḥ*—free from attachment; *caret*—one should move about; *iha*—in this world.

TRANSLATION

Therefore, one should not view death with horror, nor have recourse to defining the body as soul, nor give way to exaggeration in enjoying the bodily necessities of life. Realizing the true nature of the living entity, one should move about in the world free from attachment and steadfast in purpose.

PURPORT

A sane person who has understood the philosophy of life and death is very upset upon hearing of the horrible, hellish condition of life in the womb of the mother or outside of the mother. But one has to make a solution to the problems of life. A sane man should understand the miserable condition of this material body. Without being unnecessarily upset, he should try to find out if there is a remedy. The remedial measures can be understood when one associates with persons who are liberated. It must be understood who is actually liberated. The liberated person is described in *Bhagavad-gītā:* one who engages in uninterrupted devotional service to the Lord, having surpassed the stringent laws of material nature, is understood to be situated in Brahman.

The Supreme Personality of Godhead is beyond the material creation. It is admitted even by impersonalists like Śaṅkarācārya that Nārāyaṇa is transcendental to this material creation. As such, when one actually engages in the service of the Lord in various forms, either Nārāyaṇa or Rādhā-Kṛṣṇa or Sītā-Rāma, he is understood to be on the platform of liberation. The *Bhāgavatam* also confirms that liberation means to be situated in one's constitutional position. Since a living entity is eternally the servitor of the Supreme Lord, when one seriously and sincerely engages in the transcendental loving service of the Lord, he is situated in the position of liberation. One should try to associate with a liberated person, and then the problems of life, namely birth and death, can be solved.

While discharging devotional service in full Kṛṣṇa consciousness, one should not be miserly. He should not unnecessarily show that he has renounced this world. Actually, renunciation is not possible. If one renounces his palatial building and goes to a forest, there is actually no renunciation, for the palatial building is the property of the Supreme Personality of Godhead and the forest is also the property of the Supreme Personality of Godhead. If he changes from one property to another, that does not mean that he renounces; he was never the proprietor of either the palace or the forest. Renunciation necessitates renouncing the false understanding that one can lord it over material nature. When one renounces this false attitude and renounces the puffed-up position that he is also God, that is real renunciation. Otherwise, there is no meaning of renunciation. Rūpa Gosvāmī advises that if one renounces anything which could be applied in the service of the Lord and does not use it for that purpose, that is called *phalgu-vairāgya,* insufficient or false renunciation. Everything belongs to the Supreme Personality of Godhead; therefore everything can be engaged in the service of the Lord; nothing should be used for one's sense gratification. That is real renunciation. Nor should one unnecessarily increase the necessities of the body. We should be satisfied with whatever is offered and supplied by Kṛṣṇa without much personal endeavor. We should spend our time executing devotional service in Kṛṣṇa consciousness. That is the solution to the problem of life and death.

TEXT 48

सम्यग्दर्शनया बुद्ध्या योगवैराग्ययुक्तया ।
मायाविरचिते लोके चरेन्न्यस्य कलेवरम् ॥४८॥

samyag-darśanayā buddhyā
yoga-vairāgya-yuktayā
māyā-viracite loke
caren nyasya kalevaram

samyak-darśanayā—endowed with right vision; *buddhyā*—through reason; *yoga*—by devotional service; *vairāgya*—by detachment; *yuktayā*—strengthened; *māyā-viracite*—arranged by *māyā; loke*—to this world; *caret*—one should move about; *nyasya*—relegating; *kalevaram*—the body.

TRANSLATION

Endowed with right vision and strengthened by devotional service and a pessimistic attitude towards material identity, one should relegate his body to this illusory world through his reason. Thus one can be unconcerned with this material world.

PURPORT

It is sometimes misunderstood that if one has to associate with persons engaged in devotional service, he will not be able to solve the economic problem. To answer this argument, it is described here that one has to associate with liberated persons not directly, physically, but by understanding, through philosophy and logic, the problems of life. It is stated here, *samyag-darśanayā buddhyā:* one has to see perfectly, and by intelligence and yogic practice one has to renounce this world. That renunciation can be achieved by the process recommended in the Second Chapter of the First Canto of *Śrīmad-Bhāgavatam.*

The devotee's intelligence is always in touch with the Supreme Personality of Godhead. His attitude towards the material existence is one of detachment, for he knows perfectly well that this material world is a creation of illusory energy. Realizing himself to be part and parcel of the Supreme Soul, the devotee discharges his devotional service and is completely aloof from material action and reaction. Thus at the end he gives up his material body, or the material energy, and as pure soul he enters the kingdom of God.

Thus end the Bhaktivedanta purports of the Third Canto, Thirty-first Chapter, of the Śrīmad-Bhāgavatam, *entitled "Lord Kapila's Instructions on the Movements of the Living Entities."*

CHAPTER THIRTY-TWO

Entanglement in Fruitive Activities

TEXT 1

कपिल उवाच
अथ यो गृहमेधीयान्धर्मानेवावसन् गृहे ।
काममर्थं च धर्मान् स्वान् दोग्धि भूयः पिपर्ति तान् ॥ १ ॥

kapila uvāca
atha yo gṛha-medhīyān
dharmān evāvasan gṛhe
kāmam arthaṁ ca dharmān svān
dogdhi bhūyaḥ piparti tān

kapilaḥ uvāca—Lord Kapila said; *atha*—now; *yaḥ*—the person who; *gṛha-medhīyān*—of the householders; *dharmān*—duties; *eva*—certainly; *āvasan*—living; *gṛhe*—at home; *kāmam*—sense gratification; *artham*—economic development; *ca*—and; *dharmān*—religious rituals; *svān*—his; *dogdhi*—enjoys; *bhūyaḥ*—again and again; *piparti*—performs; *tān*—them.

TRANSLATION

The Personality of Godhead said: The person who lives in the center of household life derives material benefits by performing religious rituals, and thereby he fulfills his desire for economic development and sense gratification. Again and again he acts the same way.

PURPORT

There are two kinds of householders. One is called the *gṛhamedhī*, and the other is called the *gṛhastha*. The objective of the *gṛhamedhī* is sense gratification, and the objective of the *gṛhastha* is self-realization. Here the Lord is speaking about the *gṛhamedhī*, or the person who wants to remain in this material world. His activity is to enjoy material benefits by performing religious rituals for economic development and thereby ultimately satisfy the senses. He does not want anything more. Such a person works very hard throughout his life to become very rich and eat very nicely and drink. By giving some charity for pious activity he can go to a higher planetary atmosphere in the heavenly planets in his next life, but he does not want to stop the repetition of birth and death and finish with the concomitant miserable factors of material existence. Such a person is called a *gṛhamedhī*.

A *gṛhastha* is a person who lives with family, wife, children and relatives but has no attachment for them. He prefers to live in family life rather than as a mendicant or *sannyāsī*, but his chief aim is to achieve self-realization, or to come to the standard of Kṛṣṇa consciousness. Here, however, Lord Kapiladeva is speaking about the *gṛhamedhīs*, who have made their aim the materialistically prosperous life, which they achieve by sacrificial ceremonies, by charities and by good work. They are posted in good positions, and since they know that they are using up their assets of pious activities, they again and again perform activities of sense gratification. It is said by Prahlāda Mahārāja, *punaḥ punaś carvita-carvaṇānām*: they prefer to chew the already chewed. Again and again they experience the material pangs, even if they are rich and prosperous, but they do not want to give up this kind of life.

TEXT 2

स चापि भगवद्धर्मात्काममूढः पराङ्मुखः ।
यजते क्रतुभिर्देवान् पितॄंश्च श्रद्धयान्वितः ॥ २ ॥

sa cāpi bhagavad-dharmāt
kāma-mūḍhaḥ parāṅ-mukhaḥ
yajate kratubhir devān
pitṝṁś ca śraddhayānvitaḥ

saḥ—he; *ca api*—moreover; *bhagavat-dharmāt*—from devotional service; *kāma-mūḍhaḥ*—infatuated by lust; *parāk-mukhaḥ*—having the face turned away; *yajate*—worships; *kratubhiḥ*—with sacrificial ceremonies; *devān*—the demigods; *pitṝn*—the forefathers; *ca*—and; *śraddhayā*—with faith; *anvitaḥ*—endowed.

TRANSLATION

Such persons are ever bereft of devotional service due to being too attached to sense gratification, and therefore, although they perform various kinds of sacrifices and take great vows to satisfy the demigods and forefathers, they are not interested in Kṛṣṇa consciousness, devotional service.

PURPORT

In *Bhagavad-gītā* (7.20) it is said that persons who worship demigods have lost their intelligence: *kāmais tais tair hṛta jñānāḥ*. They are much attracted to sense gratification, and therefore they worship the demigods. It is, of course, recommended in the Vedic scriptures that if one wants money, health or education, then he should worship the various demigods. A materialistic person has manifold demands, and thus there are manifold demigods to satisfy his senses. The *gṛhamedhīs,* who want to continue a prosperous materialistic way of life, generally worship the demigods or the forefathers by offering *piṇḍa,* or respectful oblations. Such persons are bereft of Kṛṣṇa consciousness and are not interested in devotional service to the Lord. This kind of so-called pious and religious man is the result of impersonalism. The impersonalists maintain that the Supreme Absolute Truth has no form and that one can imagine any form he likes for his benefit and worship in that way. Therefore the *gṛhamedhīs* or materialistic men say that they can worship any form of a demigod as worship of the Supreme Lord. Especially amongst the Hindus, those who are meat-eaters prefer to worship goddess Kālī because it is prescribed that one can sacrifice a goat before that goddess. They maintain that whether one worships the goddess Kālī or the Supreme Personality of Godhead Viṣṇu or any demigod, the destination is the same. This is first-class rascaldom, and such people are misled. But they prefer this philosophy. *Bhagavad-gītā* does not accept such rascaldom, and it is clearly stated that such methods are meant for persons who have lost their intelligence. The same judgment is confirmed here, and the word *kāma-mūḍha,* meaning one who has lost his sense or is infatuated by the lust of attraction for sense gratification, is used. *Kāma-mūḍhas* are bereft of Kṛṣṇa consciousness and devotional service and are infatuated by a strong desire for sense gratification. The worshipers of demigods are condemned both in *Bhagavad-gītā* and in *Śrīmad-Bhāgavatam.*

TEXT 3

तच्छ्रद्धयाक्रान्तमतिः पितृदेवव्रतः पुमान् ।
गत्वा चान्द्रमसं लोकं सोमपाः पुनरेष्यति ॥ ३ ॥

tac-chraddhayākrānta-matiḥ
pitṛ-deva-vrataḥ pumān
gatvā cāndramasaṁ lokaṁ
soma-pāḥ punar eṣyati

tat—to the demigods and forefathers; *śraddhayā*—with reverence; *ākrānta*—overcome; *matiḥ*—his mind; *pitṛ*—to the forefathers; *deva*—to the demigods; *vrataḥ*—his vow; *pumān*—the person; *gatvā*—having gone; *cāndramasam*—to the moon; *lokam*—planet; *soma-pāḥ*—drinking *soma* juice; *punaḥ*—again; *eṣyati*—will return.

TRANSLATION

Such materialistic persons, attracted by sense gratification and devoted to the forefathers and demigods, can be elevated to the moon, where they drink an extract of the soma plant. They again return to this planet.

PURPORT

The moon is considered one of the planets of the heavenly kingdom. One can be promoted to this planet by executing different sacrifices recommended in the Vedic literature, such as pious activities in worshiping the demigods and forefathers with rigidity and vows. But one cannot remain there for a very long time. Life on the moon is said to last ten thousand years according to the calculation of the demigods. The demigods' time is calculated in such a way that one day (twelve hours) is equal to six months on this planet. It is not possible to reach the moon by any material vehicle like a sputnik, but persons who are attracted by material enjoyment can go to the moon by pious activities. In spite of being promoted to the moon, however, one has to come back to this earth again when the merits of his works in sacrifice are finished. This is also confirmed in *Bhagavad-gītā* (9.21): *te taṁ bhuktvā svarga-lokaṁ viśālaṁ kṣīṇe puṇye martya-lokaṁ viśanti.*

TEXT 4

यदा चाहीन्द्रशय्यायां शेतेऽनन्तासनो हरिः ।
तदा लोका लयं यान्ति त एते गृहमेधिनाम् ॥ ४ ॥

yadā cāhīndra-śayyāyāṁ
śete 'nantāsano hariḥ
tadā lokā layaṁ yānti
ta ete gṛha-medhinām

yadā—when; *ca*—and; *ahi-indra*—of the king of snakes; *śayyāyām*—on the bed; *śete*—lies; *ananta-āsanaḥ*—He whose seat is Ananta Śeṣa; *hariḥ*—Lord Hari; *tadā*—then; *lokāḥ*—the planets; *layam*—unto dissolution; *yānti*—go; *te ete*—those very; *gṛha-medhinām*—of the materialistic householders.

TRANSLATION

All the planets of the materialistic persons, including all the heavenly planets, such as the moon, are vanquished when the Supreme Personality of Godhead, Hari, goes to His bed of serpents, which is known as Ananta Śeṣa.

PURPORT

The materially attached are very eager to promote themselves to the heavenly planets such as the moon. There are many heavenly planets to which they aspire just to achieve more and more material happiness by getting a long duration of life and the paraphernalia for sense enjoyment. But the attached persons do not know that even if one goes to the highest planet, Brahmaloka, destruction exists there also. In *Bhagavad-gītā* the Lord says that one can even go to the Brahmaloka, but still he will find the pangs of birth, death, disease and old age. Only by approaching the Lord's abode, the Vaikuṇṭhaloka, does one not take birth again in this material world. The *gṛhamedhīs*, or materialistic persons, however, do not like to use this advantage. They would prefer to transmigrate perpetually from one body to another, or from one planet to another. They do not want the eternal, blissful life in knowledge in the kingdom of God.

There are two kinds of dissolutions. One dissolution takes place at the end of the life of Brahmā. At that time all the planetary systems, including the heavenly systems, are dissolved in water and enter into the body of Garbhodakaśāyī Viṣṇu, who lies on the Garbhodaka Ocean on the bed of serpents, called Śeṣa. In the other dissolution, which occurs at the end of Brahmā's day, all the lower planetary systems are destroyed. When Lord Brahmā rises after his night, these lower planetary systems are again created. The statement in *Bhagavad-gītā* that persons who worship the demigods have lost their intelligence is confirmed in this verse. These less intelligent persons do not know that even if they are promoted to the heavenly planets, at the time of dissolution they themselves, the demigods and all their planets will be annihilated. They have no information that eternal, blissful life can be attained.

TEXT 5

ये स्वधर्मान्न दुह्यन्ति धीराः कामार्थहेतवे ।
निःसङ्गा न्यस्तकर्माणः प्रशान्ताः शुद्धचेतसः ॥ ५ ॥

ye sva-dharmān na duhyanti
dhīrāḥ kāmārtha-hetave
niḥsaṅgā nyasta-karmāṇaḥ
praśāntāḥ śuddha-cetasaḥ

ye—those who; *sva-dharmān*—their own occupational duties; *na*—do not; *duhyanti*—take advantage of; *dhīrāḥ*—intelligent; *kāma*—sense gratification; *artha*—economic development; *hetave*—for the sake of; *niḥsaṅgāḥ*—free from material attachment; *nyasta*—given up; *karmāṇaḥ*—fruitive activities; *praśāntāḥ*—satisfied; *śuddha-cetasaḥ*—of purified consciousness.

TRANSLATION

Those who are intelligent and are of purified consciousness are completely satisfied in Kṛṣṇa consciousness. Freed from the modes of material nature, they do not act for sense gratification; rather, since they are situated in their own occupational duties, they act as one is expected to act.

PURPORT

The first-class example of this type of man is Arjuna. Arjuna was a *kṣatriya,* and his occupational duty was to fight. Generally, kings fight to extend their kingdoms, which they rule for sense gratification. But as far as Arjuna is concerned, he declined to fight for his own sense gratification. He said that although he could get a kingdom by fighting with his relatives, he did not want to fight with them. But when he was ordered by Kṛṣṇa and convinced by the teachings of *Bhagavad-gītā* that his duty was to satisfy Kṛṣṇa, then he fought. Thus he fought not for his sense gratification but for the satisfaction of the Supreme Personality of Godhead.

Persons who work at their prescribed duties, not for sense gratification but for gratification of the Supreme Lord, are called *niḥsaṅga,* freed from the influence of the modes of material nature. *Nyasta-karmāṇaḥ* indicates that the results of their activities are given to the Supreme Personality of Godhead. Such persons appear to be acting on the platform of their respective duties, but such activities are not performed for personal sense gratification; rather, they are performed for the Supreme Person. Such devotees are called *praśāntāḥ,* which means "completely satisfied." *Śuddha-cetasaḥ* means Kṛṣṇa conscious; their consciousness has become purified. In unpurified consciousness one thinks of himself as the Lord of the universe, but in purified consciousness one thinks himself the eternal servant of the Supreme Personality of Godhead. Putting oneself in that position of eternal servitorship to the Supreme Lord and working for Him perpetually, one actually becomes completely satisfied. As long as one works for his personal sense gratification, he will always be full of anxiety. That is the difference between ordinary consciousness and Kṛṣṇa consciousness.

TEXT 6

निवृत्तिधर्मनिरता निर्ममा निरहङ्कृताः ।
स्वधर्माप्तेन सत्त्वेन परिशुद्धेन चेतसा ॥ ६ ॥

nivṛtti-dharma-niratā
nirmamā nirahaṅkṛtāḥ

sva-dharmāptena sattvena
pariśuddhena cetasā

nivṛtti-dharma—in religious activities for detachment; *niratāḥ*—constantly engaged; *nirmamāḥ*—without a sense of proprietorship; *nirahaṅkṛtāḥ*—without false egoism; *sva-dharma*—by one's own occupational duties; *āptena*—executed; *sattvena*—by goodness; *pariśuddhena*—completely purified; *cetasā*—by consciousness.

TRANSLATION

By executing one's occupational duties, acting with detachment and without a sense of proprietorship or false egoism, one is posted in one's constitutional position by dint of complete purification of consciousness, and by thus executing so-called material duties he can easily enter into the kingdom of God.

PURPORT

Here the word *nivṛtti-dharma-niratāḥ* means "constantly engaging in executing religious activities for detachment." There are two kinds of religious performances. One is called *pravṛtti-dharma,* which means the religious activities performed by the *gṛhamedhīs* for elevation to higher planets or for economic prosperity, the final aim of which is sense gratification. Every one of us who has come to this material world has the sense of overlordship. This is called *pravṛtti.* But the opposite type of religious performance, which is called *nivṛtti,* is to act for the Supreme Personality of Godhead. Engaged in devotional service in Kṛṣṇa consciousness, one has no proprietorship claim, nor is one situated in the false egoism of thinking that he is God or the master. He always thinks himself the servant. That is the process of purifying consciousness. With pure consciousness only can one enter into the kingdom of God. Materialistic persons, in their elevated condition, can enter any one of the planets within this material world, but all are subjected to dissolution over and over again.

TEXT 7

सूर्यद्वारेण ते यान्ति पुरुषं विश्वतोमुखम् ।
परावरेशं प्रकृतिमस्योत्पत्त्यन्तभावनम् ॥ ७ ॥

sūrya-dvāreṇa te yānti
puruṣaṁ viśvato-mukham
parāvareśaṁ prakṛtim
asyotpatty-anta-bhāvanam

sūrya-dvāreṇa—through the path of illumination; *te*—they; *yānti*—approach; *puruṣam*—the Personality of Godhead; *viśvataḥ-mukham*—whose face is turned everywhere; *para-avara-īśam*—the proprietor of the spiritual and material worlds; *prakṛtim*—the material cause; *asya*—of the world; *utpatti*—of manifestation; *anta*—of dissolution; *bhāvanam*—the cause.

TRANSLATION

Through the path of illumination, such liberated persons approach the complete Personality of Godhead, who is the proprietor of the material and spiritual worlds and is the supreme cause of their manifestation and dissolution.

PURPORT

The word *sūrya-dvāreṇa* means "by the illuminated path," or through the sun planet. The illuminated path is devotional service. It is advised in the *Vedas* not to pass through the darkness, but to pass through the sun planet. It is also recommended here that by traversing the illuminated path one can be freed from the contamination of the material modes of nature; by that path one can enter into the kingdom where the completely perfect Personality of Godhead resides. The words *puruṣaṁ viśvato-mukham* mean the Supreme Personality of Godhead, who is all-perfect. All living entities other than the Supreme Personality of Godhead are very small, although they may be big by our calculation. Everyone is infinitesimal, and therefore in the *Vedas* the Supreme Lord is called the supreme eternal amongst all eternals. He is the proprietor of the material and spiritual worlds and the supreme cause of manifestation. Material nature is only the ingredient because actually the manifestation is caused by His energy. The material energy is also His energy; just as the combination of father and mother is the cause of childbirth, so the combination of the material energy and the glance of the Supreme Personality of Godhead is the cause of the manifestation of the material world. The efficient cause, therefore, is not matter, but the Lord Himself.

TEXT 8

द्विपरार्धावसाने यः प्रलयो ब्रह्मणस्तु ते ।
तावदध्यासते लोकं परस्य परचिन्तकाः ॥ ८ ॥

dvi-parārdhāvasāne yaḥ
pralayo brahmaṇas tu te
tāvad adhyāsate lokaṁ
parasya para-cintakāḥ

dvi-parārdha—two *parārdhas;* *avasāne*—at the end of; *yaḥ*—which; *pralayaḥ*—death; *brahmaṇaḥ*—of Lord Brahmā; *tu*—indeed; *te*—they; *tāvat*—so long; *adhyāsate*—dwell; *lokam*—on the planet; *parasya*—of the Supreme; *para-cintakāḥ*—thinking of the Supreme Personality of Godhead.

TRANSLATION

Worshipers of the Hiraṇyagarbha expansion of the Personality of Godhead remain within this material world until the end of two parārdhas, when Lord Brahmā also dies.

PURPORT

One dissolution is at the end of Brahmā's day, and one is at the end of Brahmā's life. Brahmā dies at the end of two *parārdhas,* at which time the entire material universe is dissolved. Persons who are worshipers of Hiraṇyagarbha, the plenary expansion of the Supreme Personality of Godhead Garbhodakaśāyī Viṣṇu, do not directly approach the Supreme Personality of Godhead in Vaikuṇṭha. They remain within this universe on Satyaloka or other higher planets until the end of the life of Brahmā. Then, with Brahmā, they are elevated to the spiritual kingdom.

The words *parasya para-cintakāḥ* mean "always thinking of the Supreme Personality of Godhead," or being always Kṛṣṇa conscious. When we speak of Kṛṣṇa, this refers to the complete category of *viṣṇu-tattva.* Kṛṣṇa includes the three *puruṣa* incarnations, namely Mahā-viṣṇu, Garbhodakaśāyī Viṣṇu and Kṣīrodakaśāyī Viṣṇu, as well as all the incarnations taken together. This is confirmed in the *Brahma-saṁhitā. Rāmādi-mūrtiṣu kalā-niyamena tiṣṭhan:* Lord Kṛṣṇa is perpetually situated with His many expansions, such as Rāma, Nṛsiṁha, Vāmana, Madhusūdana, Viṣṇu and Nārāyaṇa. He exists with all His plenary portions and the portions of His plenary portions, and each of them is as good as the Supreme Personality of Godhead. The words *parasya para-cintakāḥ* mean those who are fully Kṛṣṇa conscious. Such persons enter directly into the kingdom of God, the Vaikuṇṭha planets, or, if they are worshipers of the plenary portion Garbhodakaśāyī Viṣṇu, they remain within this universe until its dissolution, and after that they enter.

TEXT 9

क्ष्माम्भोऽनलानिलवियन्मनइन्द्रियार्थ-
भूतादिभिः परिवृतं प्रतिसञ्जिहीर्षुः ।
अव्याकृतं विशति यर्हि गुणत्रयात्मा
कालं पराख्यमनुभूय परः स्वयम्भूः ॥ ९ ॥

kṣmāmbho-'nalānila-viyan-mana-indriyārtha-
bhūtādibhiḥ parivṛtaṁ pratisañjihīrṣuḥ
avyākṛtaṁ viśati yarhi guṇa-trayātmā
kālaṁ parākhyam anubhūya paraḥ svayambhūḥ

kṣmā—earth; *ambhaḥ*—water; *anala*—fire; *anila*—air; *viyat*—ether; *manaḥ*—mind; *indriya*—the senses; *artha*—the objects of the senses; *bhūta*—ego; *ādibhiḥ*—and so on; *parivṛtam*—covered by; *pratisañjihīrṣuḥ*—desiring to dissolve; *avyākṛtam*—the changeless spiritual sky; *viśati*—he enters; *yarhi*—at which time; *guṇa-traya-ātmā*—consisting of the three modes; *kālam*—the time; *para-ākhyam*—two *parārdhas*; *anubhūya*—after experiencing; *paraḥ*—the chief; *svayambhūḥ*—Lord Brahmā.

TRANSLATION

After experiencing the inhabitable time of the three modes of material nature, known as two parārdhas, Lord Brahmā closes the material universe, which is covered by layers of earth, water, air, fire, ether, mind, ego, etc., and goes back to Godhead.

PURPORT

The word *avyākṛtam* is very significant in this verse. The same meaning is stated in *Bhagavad-gītā,* in the word *sanātana.* This material world is *vyākṛta,* or subject to changes, and it finally dissolves. But after the dissolution of this material world, the manifestation of the spiritual world, the *sanātana-dhāma,* remains. That spiritual sky is called *avyākṛta,* that which does not change, and there the Supreme Personality of Godhead resides. When, after ruling over the material universe under the influence of the time element, Lord Brahmā desires to dissolve it and enter into the kingdom of God, others then enter with him.

TEXT 10

एवं परेत्य भगवन्तमनुप्रविष्टा
ये योगिनो जितमरुन्मनसो विरागाः ।
तेनैव साकममृतं पुरुषं पुराणं
ब्रह्म प्रधानमुपयान्त्यगताभिमानाः ॥१०॥

evaṁ paretya bhagavantam anupraviṣṭā
ye yogino jita-marun-manaso virāgāḥ
tenaiva sākam amṛtaṁ puruṣaṁ purāṇaṁ
brahma pradhānam upayānty agatābhimānāḥ

evam—thus; *paretya*—having gone a long distance; *bhagavantam*—Lord Brahmā; *anupraviṣṭāḥ*—entered; *ye*—those who; *yoginaḥ*—*yogīs;* *jita*—controlled; *marut*—the breathing; *manasaḥ*—the mind; *virāgāḥ*—detached; *tena*—with Lord Brahmā; *eva*—indeed; *sākam*—together; *amṛtam*—the embodiment of bliss; *puruṣam*—unto the Personality of Godhead; *purāṇam*—the oldest; *brahma pradhānam*—the Supreme Brahman; *upayānti*—they go; *agata*—not gone; *abhimānāḥ*—whose false ego.

TRANSLATION

The yogīs who become detached from the material world by practice of breathing exercises and control of the mind reach the planet of Brahmā, which is far, far away. After giving up their bodies, they enter into the body of Lord Brahmā, and therefore when Brahmā is liberated and goes to the Supreme Personality of Godhead, who is the Supreme Brahman, such yogīs can also enter into the kingdom of God.

PURPORT

By perfecting their yogic practice, *yogīs* can reach the highest planet, Brahmaloka, or Satyaloka, and after giving up their material bodies, they can enter into the body of Lord Brahmā. Because they are not directly devotees of the Lord, they cannot get liberation directly. They have to wait until Brahmā is liberated, and only then, along with Brahmā, are they also liberated. It is clear that as long as a living entity is a worshiper of a particular demigod, his consciousness is absorbed in thoughts of that demigod, and therefore he cannot get direct liberation, or entrance into the kingdom of God, nor can he merge into the impersonal effulgence of the Supreme Personality of Godhead. Such *yogīs* or demigod worshipers are subjected to the chance of taking birth again when there is again creation.

TEXT 11

अथ तं सर्वभूतानां हृत्पद्मेषु कृतालयम् ।
श्रुतानुभावं शरणं व्रज भावेन भामिनि ॥११॥

atha taṁ sarva-bhūtānāṁ
hṛt-padmeṣu kṛtālayam
śrutānubhāvaṁ śaraṇaṁ
vraja bhāvena bhāmini

atha—therefore; *tam*—the Supreme Personality of Godhead; *sarva-bhūtānām*—of all living entities; *hṛt-padmeṣu*—in the lotus hearts; *kṛta-ālayam*—residing; *śruta-anubhāvam*—whose glories you have heard; *śaraṇam*—unto the shelter; *vraja*—go; *bhāvena*—by devotional service; *bhāmini*—My dear mother.

TRANSLATION

Therefore, My dear mother, by devotional service take direct shelter of the Supreme Personality of Godhead, who is seated in everyone's heart.

PURPORT

One can attain direct contact with the Supreme Personality of Godhead in full Kṛṣṇa consciousness and revive one's eternal relationship with Him as lover, as Supreme Soul, as son, as friend or as master. One can reestablish the transcendental loving relationship with the Supreme Lord in so many ways, and that feeling is true oneness. The oneness of the Māyāvādī philosophers and the oneness of Vaiṣṇava philosophers are different. The Māyāvādī and Vaiṣṇava philosophers both want to merge into the Supreme, but the Vaiṣṇavas do not lose their identities. They want to keep the identity of lover, parent, friend or servant.

In the transcendental world, the servant and master are one. That is the absolute platform. Although the relationship is servant and master, both the servant and the served stand on the same platform. That is oneness. Lord Kapila advised His mother that she did not need any indirect process. She was already situated in that direct process because the Supreme Lord had taken birth as her son. Actually, she did not need any further instruction because she was already in the perfectional stage. Kapiladeva advised her to continue in the same way. He therefore addressed His mother as *bhāmini* to indicate that she was already thinking of the Lord as her son. Devahūti is advised by Lord Kapila to take directly to devotional service, Kṛṣṇa consciousness, because without that consciousness one cannot become liberated from the clutches of *māyā*.

TEXTS 12-15

आद्यः स्थिरचराणां यो वेदगर्भः सहर्षिभिः ।
योगेश्वरैः कुमाराद्यैः सिद्धैर्योगप्रवर्तकैः ॥१२॥
भेददृष्ट्याभिमानेन निःसङ्गेनापि कर्मणा ।
कर्तृत्वात्सगुणं ब्रह्म पुरुषं पुरुषर्षभम् ॥१३॥
स संसृत्य पुनः काले कालेनेश्वरमूर्तिना ।
जाते गुणव्यतिकरे यथापूर्वं प्रजायते ॥१४॥

ऐश्वर्यं पारमेष्ठ्यं च तेऽपि धर्मविनिर्मितम् ।
निषेव्य पुनरायान्ति गुणव्यतिकरे सति ॥१५॥

ādyaḥ sthira-carāṇāṁ yo
veda-garbhaḥ saharṣibhiḥ
yogeśvaraiḥ kumārādyaiḥ
siddhair yoga-pravartakaiḥ

bheda-dṛṣṭyābhimānena
niḥsaṅgenāpi karmaṇā
kartṛtvāt saguṇaṁ brahma
puruṣaṁ puruṣarṣabham

sa saṁsṛtya punaḥ kāle
kāleneśvara-mūrtinā
jāte guṇa-vyatikare
yathā-pūrvaṁ prajāyate

aiśvaryaṁ pārameṣṭhyaṁ ca
te 'pi dharma-vinirmitam
niṣevya punar āyānti
guṇa-vyatikare sati

ādyaḥ—the creator, Lord Brahmā; *sthira-carāṇām*—of the immobile and mobile manifestations; *yaḥ*—he who; *veda-garbhaḥ*—the repository of the *Vedas; saha*—along with; *ṛsibhiḥ*—the sages; *yoga-īśvaraiḥ*—with great mystic *yogīs; kumāra-ādyaiḥ*—the Kumāras and others; *siddhaiḥ*—with the perfected living beings; *yoga-pravartakaiḥ*—the authors of the *yoga* system; *bheda-dṛṣṭyā*—because of independent vision; *abhimānena*—by misconception; *niḥsaṅgena*—nonfruitive; *api*—although; *karmaṇā*—by their activities; *kartṛtvāt*—from the sense of being a doer; *sa-guṇam*—possessing spiritual qualities; *brahma*—Brahman; *puruṣam*—the Personality of Godhead; *puruṣa-ṛsabham*—the first *puruṣa* incarnation; *saḥ*—he; *saṁsṛtya*—having attained; *punaḥ*—again; *kāle*—at the time; *kālena*—by time; *īśvara-mūrtinā*—the manifestation of the Lord; *jāte guṇa-vyatikare*—when the interaction of the modes arises; *yathā*—as; *pūrvam*—previously; *prajāyate*—is born; *aiśvaryam*—opulence; *pārameṣṭhyam*—royal; *ca*—and; *te*—the sages; *api*—also; *dharma*—by their pious activities; *vinirmitam*—produced; *niṣevya*—having enjoyed; *punaḥ*—again; *āyānti*—they return; *guṇa-vyatikare sati*—when the interaction of the modes takes place.

TRANSLATION

My dear mother, someone may worship the Supreme Personality of Godhead with a special self-interest, but even demigods such as Lord Brahmā, great

sages such as Sanat-kumāra and great munis such as Marīci have to come back to the material world again at the time of creation. When the interaction of the three modes of material nature begins, Brahmā, who is the creator of this cosmic manifestation and who is full of Vedic knowledge, and the great sages, who are the authors of the spiritual path and the yoga system, come back under the influence of the time factor. They are liberated by their nonfruitive activities and they attain the first incarnation of the puruṣa, but at the time of creation they come back in exactly the same forms and positions as they had previously.

PURPORT

That Brahmā becomes liberated is known to everyone, but he cannot liberate his devotees. Demigods like Brahmā and Lord Śiva cannot give liberation to any living entity. As it is confirmed in *Bhagavad-gītā,* only one who surrenders unto Kṛṣṇa, the Supreme Personality of Godhead, can be liberated from the clutches of *māyā.* Brahmā is called here *ādyaḥ sthira-carāṇām.* He is the original, first-created living entity, and after his own birth he creates the entire cosmic manifestation. He was fully instructed in the matter of creation by the Supreme Lord. Here he is called *veda-garbha,* which means that he knows the complete purpose of the *Vedas.* He is always accompanied by such great personalities as Marīci, Kaśyapa and the seven sages, as well as by great mystic *yogīs,* the Kumāras and many other spiritually advanced living entities, but he has his own interest, separate from the Lord's. *Bheda-dṛṣṭyā* means that Brahmā sometimes thinks that he is independent of the Supreme Lord, or he thinks of himself as one of the three equally independent incarnations. Brahmā is entrusted with creation, Viṣṇu maintains and Rudra, Lord Śiva, destroys. The three of them are understood to be incarnations of the Supreme Lord in charge of the three different material modes of nature, but none of them is independent of the Supreme Personality of Godhead. Here the word *bheda-dṛṣṭyā* occurs because Brahmā has a slight inclination to think that he is as independent as Rudra. Sometimes Brahmā thinks that he is independent of the Supreme Lord, and the worshiper also thinks that Brahmā is independent. For this reason, after the destruction of this material world, when there is again creation by the interaction of the material modes of nature, Brahmā comes back. Although Brahmā reaches the Supreme Personality of Godhead as the first *puruṣa* incarnation, Mahā-viṣṇu, who is full with transcendental qualities, he cannot stay in the spiritual world.

The specific significance of his coming back may be noted. Brahmā and the great *ṛṣis* and the great master of *yoga* (Śiva) are not ordinary living entities; they are very powerful and have all the perfections of mystic *yoga.* But still they have an inclination to try to become one with the Supreme, and therefore they have to come back. In the *Śrīmad-Bhāgavatam* it is accepted that as long as one thinks that he is equal with the Supreme Personality of Godhead, he is not completely purified or knowledgeable. In spite of going up to the first *puruṣa-avatāra,* Mahā-viṣṇu, after the dissolution of this material creation, such personalities again fall down or come back to the material creation.

It is a great falldown on the part of the impersonalists to think that the Supreme Lord appears within a material body and that one should therefore not meditate upon the form of the Supreme but should meditate instead on the formless. For this particular mistake, even the great mystic *yogīs* or great stalwart transcendentalists also come back again when there is creation. All living entities other than the impersonalists and monists can directly take to devotional service in full Kṛṣṇa consciousness and become liberated by developing transcendental loving service to the Supreme Personality of Godhead. Such devotional service develops in the degrees of thinking of the Supreme Lord as master, as friend, as son and, at last, as lover. These distinctions in transcendental variegatedness must always be present.

TEXT 16

ये त्विहासक्तमनसः कर्मसु श्रद्धयान्विताः ।
कुर्वन्त्यप्रतिषिद्धानि नित्यान्यपि च कृत्स्नशः ॥१६॥

ye tv ihāsakta-manasaḥ
karmasu śraddhayānvitāḥ
kurvanty apratiṣiddhāni
nityāny api ca kṛtsnaśaḥ

ye—those who; *tu*—but; *iha*—in this world; *āsakta*—addicted; *manasaḥ*—whose minds; *karmasu*—to fruitive activities; *śraddhayā*—with faith; *anvitāḥ*—endowed; *kurvanti*—perform; *apratiṣiddhāni*—with attachment to the result; *nityāni*—prescribed duties; *api*—certainly; *ca*—and; *kṛtsnaśaḥ*—repeatedly.

TRANSLATION

Persons who are too addicted to this material world execute their prescribed duties very nicely and with great faith. They daily perform all such prescribed duties with attachment to the fruitive result.

PURPORT

In this and the following six verses, the *Śrīmad-Bhāgavatam* criticizes persons who are too materially attached. It is enjoined in the Vedic scriptures that those who are attached to the enjoyment of material facilities have to sacrifice and undergo certain ritualistic performances. They have to observe certain rules and regulations in their daily lives to be elevated to the heavenly planets. It is stated in this verse that such persons cannot be liberated at any time. Those who worship demigods with the consciousness that each and every demigod is a separate God cannot be elevated to the spiritual world, what to speak of persons who are simply attached to duties for the upliftment of their material condition.

TEXT 17

रजसा कुण्ठमनसः कामात्मानोऽजितेन्द्रियाः ।
पितॄन् यजन्त्यनुदिनं गृहेष्वभिरताशयाः ॥१७॥

rajasā kuṇṭha-manasaḥ
kāmātmāno 'jitendriyāḥ
pitṝn yajanty anudinaṁ
gṛheṣv abhiratāśayāḥ

rajasā—by the mode of passion; *kuṇṭha*—full of anxieties; *manasaḥ*—their minds; *kāma-ātmānaḥ*—aspiring for sense gratification; *ajita*—uncontrolled; *indriyāḥ*—their senses; *pitṝn*—the forefathers; *yajanti*—they worship; *anudinam*—every day; *gṛheṣu*—in home life; *abhirata*—engaged; *āśayāḥ*—their minds.

TRANSLATION

Such persons, impelled by the mode of passion, are full of anxieties and always aspire for sense gratification due to uncontrolled senses. They worship the forefathers and are busy day and night improving the economic condition of their family, social or national life.

TEXT 18

त्रैवर्गिकास्ते पुरुषा विमुखा हरिमेधसः ।
कथायां कथनीयोरुविक्रमस्य मधुद्विषः ॥१८॥

trai-vargikās te puruṣā
vimukhā hari-medhasaḥ

kathāyāṁ kathanīyoru-
vikramasya madhudviṣaḥ

trai-vargikāḥ—interested in the three elevating processes; *te*—those; *puruṣāḥ*—persons; *vimukhāḥ*—not interested; *hari-medhasaḥ*—of Lord Hari; *kathāyām*—in the pastimes; *kathanīya*—worth chanting of; *uru-vikramasya*—whose excellent prowess; *madhu-dviṣaḥ*—the killer of the Madhu demon.

TRANSLATION

Such persons are called trai-vargika because they are interested in the three elevating processes. They are averse to the Supreme Personality of Godhead, who can give relief to the conditioned soul. They are not interested in the Supreme Personality's pastimes, which are worth hearing because of His transcendental prowess.

PURPORT

According to Vedic thought, there are four elevating principles, namely religiosity, economic development, sense gratification and liberation. Persons who are simply interested in material enjoyment make plans to execute prescribed duties. They are interested in the three elevating processes of religious rituals, economic elevation and sense enjoyment. By developing their economic condition, they can enjoy material life. Materialistic persons, therefore, are interested in those elevating processes, which are called *trai-vargika. Trai* means "three"; *vargika* means "elevating processes." Such materialistic persons are never attracted by the Supreme Personality of Godhead. Rather, they are antagonistic towards Him.

The Supreme Personality of Godhead is here described as *hari-medhaḥ,* or "He who can deliver one from the cycle of birth and death." Materialistic persons are never interested in hearing about the marvelous pastimes of the Lord. They think that they are fictions and stories and that the Supreme Godhead is also a man of material nature. They are not fit for advancing in devotional service, or Kṛṣṇa consciousness. Such materialistic persons are interested in newspaper stories, novels and imaginary dramas. The factual activities of the Lord, such as Lord Kṛṣṇa's acting in the Battle of Kurukṣetra, or the activities of the Pāṇḍavas, or the Lord's activities in Vṛndāvana or Dvārakā, are related in the *Bhagavad-gītā* and *Śrīmad-Bhāgavatam,* which are full of the activities of the Lord. But materialistic persons who engage in elevating their position in the material world are not interested in such activities of the Lord. They may be interested in the activities of a great politician or a great rich man of this world, but they are not interested in the transcendental activities of the Supreme Lord.

TEXT 19

नूनं दैवेन विहता ये चाच्युतकथासुधाम् ।
हित्वा शृण्वन्त्यसद्गाथाः पुरीषमिव विड्भुजः ॥१९॥

nūnaṁ daivena vihatā
ye cācyuta-kathā-sudhām
hitvā śṛṇvanty asad-gāthāḥ
purīṣam iva viḍ-bhujaḥ

nūnam—certainly; *daivena*—by the order of the Lord; *vihatāḥ*—condemned; *ye*—those who; *ca*—also; *acyuta*—of the infallible Lord; *kathā*—stories; *sudhām*—nectar; *hitvā*—having given up; *śṛṇvanti*—they hear; *asat-gāthāḥ*—stories about materialistic persons; *purīṣam*—stool; *iva*—like; *viṭ-bhujaḥ*—stool-eaters (hogs).

TRANSLATION

Such persons are condemned by the supreme order of the Lord. Because they are averse to the nectar of the activities of the Supreme Personality of Godhead, they are compared to stool-eating hogs. They give up hearing the transcendental activities of the Lord and indulge in hearing of the abominable activities of materialistic persons.

PURPORT

Everyone is addicted to hearing of the activities of another person, whether a politician or a rich man or an imaginary character whose activities are created in a novel. There are so many nonsensical literatures, stories and books of speculative philosophy. Materialistic persons are very interested in reading such literature, but when they are presented with genuine books of knowledge like *Śrīmad-Bhāgavatam*, *Bhagavad-gītā*, *Viṣṇu Purāṇa* or other scriptures of the world, such as the Bible and Koran, they are not interested. These persons are condemned by the supreme order as much as a hog is condemned. The hog is interested in eating stool. If the hog is offered some nice preparation made of condensed milk or ghee, he won't like it; he would prefer obnoxious, bad-smelling stool, which he finds very relishable. Materialistic persons are considered condemned because they are interested in hellish activities and not in transcendental activities. The message of the Lord's activities is nectar, and besides that message, any information in which we may be interested is actually hellish.

TEXT 20

दक्षिणेन पथार्यम्णः पितृलोकं व्रजन्ति ते ।
प्रजामनु प्रजायन्ते श्मशानान्तक्रियाकृतः ॥२०॥

dakṣiṇena pathāryamṇaḥ
pitṛ-lokaṁ vrajanti te
prajām anu prajāyante
śmaśānānta-kriyā-kṛtaḥ

dakṣiṇena—southern; *pathā*—by the path; *aryamṇaḥ*—of the sun; *pitṛ-lokam*—to Pitṛloka; *vrajanti*—go; *te*—they; *prajām*—their families; *anu*—along with; *prajāyante*—they take birth; *śmaśāna*—the crematorium; *anta*—to the end; *kriyā*—fruitive activities; *kṛtaḥ*—performing.

TRANSLATION

Such materialistic persons are allowed to go to the planet called Pitṛloka by the southern course of the sun, but they again come back to this planet and take birth in their own families, beginning again the same fruitive activities from birth to the end of life.

PURPORT

In *Bhagavad-gītā,* Ninth Chapter, verse 21, it is stated that such persons are elevated to the higher planetary systems. As soon as their lifetimes of fruitive activity are finished, they return to this planet, and thus they go up and come down. Those who are elevated to the higher planets again come back into the same family for which they had too much attachment; they are born, and the fruitive activities continue again until the end of life. There are different prescribed rituals from birth until the end of life, and they are very much attached to such activities.

TEXT 21

ततस्ते क्षीणसुकृताः पुनर्लोकमिमं सति ।
पतन्ति विवशा देवैः सद्यो विभ्रंशितोदयाः ॥२१॥

tatas te kṣīṇa-sukṛtāḥ
punar lokam imaṁ sati
patanti vivaśā devaiḥ
sadyo vibhraṁśitodayāḥ

tataḥ—then; *te*—they; *kṣīṇa*—exhausted; *su-kṛtāḥ*—results of their pious activities; *punaḥ*—again; *lokam imam*—to this planet; *sati*—O virtuous mother; *patanti*—fall; *vivaśāḥ*—

helpless; *devaiḥ*—by higher arrangement; *sadyaḥ*—suddenly; *vibhraṁśita*—caused to fall; *udayāḥ*—their prosperity.

TRANSLATION

When the results of their pious activities are exhausted, they fall down by higher arrangement and again come back to this planet, just as any person raised to a high position sometimes all of a sudden falls.

PURPORT

It is sometimes found that a person elevated to a very high position in government service falls down all of a sudden, and no one can check him. Similarly, after finishing their period of enjoyment, foolish persons who are very much interested in being elevated to the position of president in higher planets also fall down to this planet. The distinction between the elevated position of a devotee and that of an ordinary person attracted to fruitive activities is that when a devotee is elevated to the spiritual kingdom he never falls down, whereas an ordinary person falls, even if he is elevated to the highest planetary system, Brahmaloka. It is confirmed in *Bhagavad-gītā* (*ābrahma-bhuvanāl lokāḥ*) that even if one is elevated to a higher planet, he has to come down again. But Kṛṣṇa confirms in *Bhagavad-gītā* (8.16), *mām upetya tu kaunteya punar janma na vidyate*: "Anyone who attains My abode never comes back to this conditioned life of material existence."

TEXT 22

तस्मात्त्वं सर्वभावेन भजस्व परमेष्ठिनम् ।
तद्गुणाश्रयया भक्त्या भजनीयपदाम्बुजम् ॥२२॥

tasmāt tvaṁ sarva-bhāvena
bhajasva parameṣṭhinam
tad-guṇāśrayayā bhaktyā
bhajanīya-padāmbujam

tasmāt—therefore; *tvam*—you (Devahūti); *sarva-bhāvena*—with loving ecstasy; *bhajasva*—worship; *parameṣṭhinam*—the Supreme Personality of Godhead; *tat-guṇa*—the qualities of the Lord; *āśrayayā*—connected with; *bhaktyā*—by devotional service; *bhajanīya*—worshipable; *pada-ambujam*—whose lotus feet.

TRANSLATION

My dear mother, I therefore advise that you take shelter of the Supreme Personality of Godhead, for His lotus feet are worth worshiping. Accept this

with all devotion and love, for thus you can be situated in transcendental devotional service.

PURPORT

The word *parameṣṭhinam* is sometimes used in connection with Brahmā. *Parameṣṭhī* means "the supreme person." As Brahmā is the supreme person within this universe, Kṛṣṇa is the Supreme Personality in the spiritual world. Lord Kapiladeva advises His mother that she should take shelter of the lotus feet of the Supreme Personality of Godhead, Kṛṣṇa, because it is worthwhile. Taking shelter of demigods, even those in the highest positions, like Brahmā and Śiva, is not advised herein. One should take shelter of the Supreme Godhead.

Sarva-bhāvena means "in all-loving ecstasy." *Bhāva* is the preliminary stage of elevation before the attainment of pure love of Godhead. It is stated in *Bhagavad-gītā*, *budhā bhāva-samanvitāḥ:* one who has attained the stage of *bhāva* can accept the lotus feet of Lord Kṛṣṇa as worshipable. This is also advised here by Lord Kapila to His mother. Also significant in this verse is the phrase *tad-guṇāśrayayā bhaktyā.* This means that discharging devotional service unto Kṛṣṇa is transcendental; it is not material activity. This is confirmed in *Bhagavad-gītā:* those who engage in devotional service are accepted to be situated in the spiritual kingdom. *Brahma-bhuyāya kalpate:* they at once become situated in the transcendental kingdom.

Devotional service in full Kṛṣṇa consciousness is the only means for attaining the highest perfection of life for the human being. This is recommended herein by Lord Kapila to His mother. *Bhakti* is therefore *nirguṇa,* free from all tinges of material qualities. Although the discharge of devotional service appears to be like material activities, it is never *saguṇa,* or contaminated by material qualities. *Tad-guṇāśrayayā* means that Lord Kṛṣṇa's transcendental qualities are so sublime that there is no need to divert one's attention to any other activities. His behavior with the devotees is so exalted that a devotee need not try to divert his attention to any other worship. It is said that the demoniac Pūtanā came to kill Kṛṣṇa by poisoning Him, but because Kṛṣṇa was pleased to suck her breast, she was given the same position as His mother. Devotees pray, therefore, that if a demon who wanted to kill Kṛṣṇa gets such an exalted position, why should they go to anyone other than Kṛṣṇa for their worshipful attachment? There are two kinds of religious activities: one for material advancement and the other for spiritual advancement. By taking shelter under the lotus feet of Kṛṣṇa, one is endowed with both kinds of prosperity, material and spiritual. Why then should one go to any demigod?

TEXT 23

वासुदेवे भगवति भक्तियोगः प्रयोजितः ।
जनयत्याशु वैराग्यं ज्ञानं यद्ब्रह्मदर्शनम् ॥२३॥

vāsudeve bhagavati
bhakti-yogaḥ prayojitaḥ
janayaty āśu vairāgyaṁ
jñānaṁ yad brahma-darśanam

vāsudeve—unto Kṛṣṇa; *bhagavati*—the Personality of Godhead; *bhakti-yogaḥ*—devotional service; *prayojitaḥ*—discharged; *janayati*—produces; *āśu*—very soon; *vairāgyam*—detachment; *jñānam*—knowledge; *yat*—which; *brahma-darśanam*—self-realization.

TRANSLATION

Engagement in Kṛṣṇa consciousness and application of devotional service unto Kṛṣṇa make it possible to advance in knowledge and detachment, as well as in self-realization.

PURPORT

It is said by less intelligent men that *bhakti-yoga,* or devotional service, is meant for persons who are not advanced in transcendental knowledge and renunciation. But the fact is that if one engages in the devotional service of the Lord in full Kṛṣṇa consciousness, he does not have to attempt separately to practice detachment or to wait for an awakening of transcendental knowledge. It is said that one who engages unflinchingly in the devotional service of the Lord actually has all the good qualities of the demigods develop in him automatically. One cannot discover how such good qualities develop in the body of a devotee, but actually it happens. There is one instance where a hunter was taking pleasure in killing animals, but after becoming a devotee he was not prepared to kill even an ant. Such is the quality of a devotee.

Those who are very eager to advance in transcendental knowledge can engage themselves in pure devotional service, without wasting time in mental speculation. For arriving at the positive conclusions of knowledge in the Absolute Truth, the word *brahma-darśanam* is significant in this verse. *Brahma-darśanam* means to realize or to understand the Transcendence. One who engages in the service of Vāsudeva can actually realize what Brahman is. If Brahman is impersonal, then there is no question of *darśanam,* which means "seeing face to face." *Darśanam* refers to seeing the Supreme Personality of Godhead, Vāsudeva. Unless the seer and the seen are persons, there is no *darśanam. Brahma-darśanam* means that as soon as one sees the Supreme Personality of Godhead, he can at once realize what impersonal Brahman is. A devotee does not need to make separate investigations to understand the nature of Brahman. *Bhagavad-gītā* also confirms this. *Brahma-bhūyāya kalpate:* a devotee at once becomes a self-realized soul in the Absolute Truth.

TEXT 24

यदास्य चित्तमर्थेषु समेष्विन्द्रियवृत्तिभिः ।
न विगृह्णाति वैषम्यं प्रियमप्रियमित्युत ॥२४॥

yadāsya cittam artheṣu
sameṣv indriya-vṛttibhiḥ
na vigṛhṇāti vaiṣamyaṁ
priyam apriyam ity uta

yadā—when; *asya*—of the devotee; *cittam*—the mind; *artheṣu*—in the sense objects; *sameṣu*—same; *indriya-vṛttibhiḥ*—by the activities of the senses; *na*—not; *vigṛhṇāti*—does perceive; *vaiṣamyam*—difference; *priyam*—agreeable; *apriyam*—not agreeable; *iti*—thus; *uta*—certainly.

TRANSLATION

The exalted devotee's mind becomes equipoised in sensory activities, and he is transcendental to that which is agreeable and not agreeable.

PURPORT

The significance of advancement in transcendental knowledge and detachment from material attraction is exhibited in the personality of a highly advanced devotee. For him there is nothing agreeable or disagreeable because he does not act in any way for his personal sense gratification. Whatever he does, whatever he thinks, is for the satisfaction of the Personality of Godhead. Either in the material world or in the spiritual world, his equipoised mind is completely manifested. He can understand that in the material world there is nothing good; everything is bad due to its being contaminated by material nature. The materialists conclusions of good and bad, moral and immoral, etc., are simply mental concoction or sentiment. Actually there is nothing good in the material world. In the spiritual field everything is absolutely good. There is no inebriety in the spiritual varieties. Because a devotee accepts everything in spiritual vision, he is equipoised; that is the symptom of his being elevated to the transcendental position. He automatically attains detachment, *vairāgya,* then *jñāna,* knowledge, and then actual transcendental knowledge. The conclusion is that an advanced devotee dovetails himself in the transcendental qualities of the Lord, and in that sense he becomes qualitatively one with the Supreme Personality of Godhead.

TEXT 25

स तदैवात्मनात्मानं निःसङ्गं समदर्शनम् ।
हेयोपादेयरहितमारूढं पदमीक्षते ॥२५॥

sa tadaivātmanātmānaṁ
niḥsaṅgaṁ sama-darśanam
heyopādeya-rahitam
ārūḍhaṁ padam īkṣate

saḥ—the pure devotee; *tadā*—then; *eva*—certainly; *ātmanā*—by his transcendental intelligence; *ātmānam*—himself; *niḥsaṅgam*—without material attachment; *sama-darśanam*—equipoised in vision; *heya*—to be rejected; *upādeya*—acceptable; *rahitam*—devoid of; *ārūḍham*—elevated; *padam*—to the transcendental position; *īkṣate*—he sees.

TRANSLATION

Because of his transcendental intelligence, the pure devotee is equipoised in his vision and sees himself to be uncontaminated by matter. He does not see anything as superior or inferior, and he feels himself elevated to the transcendental platform of being equal in qualities with the Supreme Person.

PURPORT

Perception of the disagreeable arises from attachment. A devotee has no personal attachment to anything; therefore for him there is no question of agreeable or disagreeable. For the service of the Lord he can accept anything, even though it may be disagreeable to his personal interest. In fact, he is completely free from personal interest, and thus anything agreeable to the Lord is agreeable to him. For example, for Arjuna at first fighting was not agreeable, but when he understood that the fighting was agreeable to the Lord, he accepted the fighting as agreeable. That is the position of a pure devotee. For his personal interest there is nothing which is agreeable or disagreeable; everything is done for the Lord, and therefore he is free from attachment and detachment. That is the transcendental stage of neutrality. A pure devotee enjoys life in the pleasure of the Supreme Lord.

TEXT 26

ज्ञानमात्रं परं ब्रह्म परमात्मेश्वरः पुमान् ।
दृश्यादिभिः पृथग्भावैर्भगवानेक ईयते ॥२६॥

jñāna-mātraṁ paraṁ brahma
paramātmeśvaraḥ pumān
dṛśy-ādibhiḥ pṛthag bhāvair
bhagavān eka īyate

jñāna—knowledge; *mātram*—only; *param*—transcendental; *brahma*—Brahman; *parama-ātmā*—Paramātmā; *īśvaraḥ*—the controller; *pumān*—Supersoul; *dṛśi-ādibhiḥ*—by philosophical research and other processes; *pṛthak bhāvaiḥ*—according to different processes of understanding; *bhagavān*—the Supreme Personality of Godhead; *ekaḥ*—alone; *īyate*—is perceived.

TRANSLATION

The Supreme Personality of Godhead alone is complete transcendental knowledge, but according to the different processes of understanding He appears differently, either as impersonal Brahman, as Paramātmā, as the Supreme Personality of Godhead or as the puruṣa-avatāra.

PURPORT

The word *dṛśy-ādibhiḥ* is significant. According to Jīva Gosvāmī, *dṛśi* means *jñāna*, philosophical research. By different processes of philosophical research under different concepts, such as the process of *jñāna-yoga*, the same Bhagavān, or Supreme Personality of Godhead, is understood as impersonal Brahman. Similarly, by the eightfold *yoga* system He appears as the Paramātmā. But in pure Kṛṣṇa consciousness, or knowledge in purity, when one tries to understand the Absolute Truth, one realizes Him as the Supreme Person. The Transcendence is realized simply on the basis of knowledge. The words used here, *paramātmeśvaraḥ pumān*, are all transcendental, and they refer to Supersoul. Supersoul is also described as *puruṣa*, but the word *Bhagavān* directly refers to the Supreme Personality of Godhead, who is full of six opulences: wealth, fame, strength, beauty, knowledge and renunciation. He is the Personality of Godhead in different spiritual skies. The various descriptions of *paramātmā, īśvara* and *pumān* indicate that the expansions of the Supreme Godhead are unlimited.

Ultimately, to understand the Supreme Personality of Godhead one has to accept *bhakti-yoga*. By executing *jñāna-yoga* or *dhyāna-yoga* one has to eventually approach the *bhakti-yoga* platform, and then *Paramātmā, īśvara, pumān,* etc., are all clearly understood. It is recommended in the Second Canto of *Śrīmad-Bhāgavatam* that whether one is a devotee or fruitive actor or liberationist, if he is intelligent enough he should engage himself with all seriousness in the process of devotional service. It is also explained that whatever one desires which is obtainable by fruitive activities, even if one wants to be elevated to higher planets, can be achieved simply by execution of devotional service. Since the Supreme Lord is full in six opulences, He can bestow any one of them upon the worshiper.

The one Supreme Personality of Godhead reveals Himself to different thinkers as the Supreme person or impersonal Brahman or Paramātmā. Impersonalists merge into the impersonal Brahman, but that is not achieved by worshiping the impersonal Brahman. If one takes to devotional service and at the same time desires to merge into the existence of the Supreme Lord, he can achieve that. If someone desires at all to merge into the existence of the Supreme, he has to execute devotional service.

The devotee can see the Supreme Lord face to face, but the *jñānī,* the empiric philosopher or *yogī* cannot. They cannot be elevated to the positions of associates of the Lord. There is no evidence in the scriptures stating that by cultivating knowledge or worshiping the impersonal Brahman one can become a personal associate of the Supreme Personality of Godhead. Nor by executing the yogic principles can one become an associate of the Supreme Godhead. Impersonal Brahman, being formless, is described as *adṛśya* because the impersonal effulgence of *brahmajyotir* covers the face of the Supreme Lord. Some *yogīs* see the four-handed Viṣṇu sitting within the heart, and therefore in their case also the Supreme Lord is invisible. Only for the devotees is the Lord visible. Here the statement *dṛśy-ādibhiḥ* is significant. Since the Supreme Personality of Godhead is both invisible and visible, there are different features of the Lord. The Paramātmā feature and Brahman feature are invisible, but the Bhagavān feature is visible. In the *Viṣṇu Purāṇa* this fact is very nicely explained. The universal form of the Lord and the formless Brahman effulgence of the Lord, being invisible, are inferior features. The concept of the universal form is material, and the concept of impersonal Brahman is spiritual, but the highest spiritual understanding is the Personality of Godhead. The *Viṣṇu Purāṇa* states, *viṣṇur brahma-svarūpeṇa svayam eva vyavasthitaḥ:* Brahman's real feature is Viṣṇu, or the Supreme Brahman is Viṣṇu. *Svayam eva:* that is His personal feature. The supreme spiritual conception is the Supreme Personality of Godhead. It is also confirmed in *Bhagavad-gītā: yad gatvā na nivartante tad dhāma paramaṁ mama.* That specific abode called *paramaṁ mama* is the place from which, once one attains it, one does not return to this miserable, conditional life. Every place, every space and everything belongs to Viṣṇu, but where He personally lives is *tad dhāma paramam,* His supreme abode. One has to make one's destination the supreme abode of the Lord.

TEXT 27

एतावानेव योगेन समग्रेणेह योगिनः ।
युज्यतेऽभिमतो ह्यर्थो यदसङ्गस्तु कृत्स्नशः ॥२७॥

etāvān eva yogena
samagreṇeha yoginaḥ
yujyate 'bhimato hy artho
yad asaṅgas tu kṛtsnaśaḥ

etāvān—of such a measure; *eva*—just; *yogena*—by *yoga* practice; *samagreṇa*—all; *iha*—in this world; *yoginaḥ*—of the *yogī; yujyate*—is achieved; *abhimataḥ*—desired; *hi*—certainly; *arthaḥ*—purpose; *yat*—which; *asaṅgaḥ*—detachment; *tu*—indeed; *kṛtsnaśaḥ*—completely.

TRANSLATION

The greatest common understanding for all yogis is complete detachment from matter, which can be achieved by different kinds of yoga.

PURPORT

There are three kinds of *yoga,* namely *bhakti-yoga, jñāna-yoga* and *aṣṭāṅga-yoga.* Devotees, *jñānīs* and *yogīs* all try to get out of the material entanglement. The *jñānīs* try to detach their sensual activities from material engagement. The *jñāna-yogī* thinks that matter is false and that Brahman is truth; he tries, therefore, by cultivation of knowledge, to detach the senses from material enjoyment. The *aṣṭāṅga-yogīs* also try to control the senses. The devotees, however, try to engage the senses in the service of the Lord. Therefore it appears that the activities of the *bhaktas,* devotees, are better than those of the *jñānīs* and *yogīs.* The mystic *yogīs* simply try to control the senses by practicing the eight divisions of *yoga-yama, niyama, āsana, prāṇāyāma, pratyāhāra,* etc.—and the *jñānīs* try by mental reasoning to understand that sense enjoyment is false. But the easiest and most direct process is to engage the senses in the service of the Lord.

The purpose of all *yoga* is to detach one's sense activities from this material world. The final aims, however, are different. *Jñānīs* want to become one with the Brahman effulgence, *yogīs* want to realize Paramātmā, and devotees want to develop Kṛṣṇa consciousness and transcendental loving service to the Lord. That loving service is the perfect stage of sense control. The senses are actually active symptoms of life, and they cannot be stopped. They can be detached only if there is superior engagement. As it is confirmed in *Bhagavad-gītā, paraṁ dṛṣṭvā nivartate*: the activities of the senses can be stopped if they are given superior engagements. The supreme engagement is engagement of the senses in the service of the Lord. That is the purpose of all *yoga*.

TEXT 28

ज्ञानमेकं पराचीनैरिन्द्रियैर्ब्रह्म निर्गुणम् ।
अवभात्यर्थरूपेण भ्रान्त्या शब्दादिधर्मिणा ॥२८॥

jñānam ekaṁ parācīnair
indriyair brahma nirguṇam
avabhāty artha-rūpeṇa
bhrāntyā śabdādi-dharmiṇā

jñānam—knowledge; *ekam*—one; *parācīnaiḥ*—averse; *indriyaiḥ*—by the senses; *brahma*—the Supreme Absolute Truth; *nirguṇam*—beyond the material modes; *avabhāti*—appears; *artha-rūpeṇa*—in the form of various objects; *bhrāntyā*—mistakenly; *śabda-ādi*—sound and so on; *dharmiṇā*—endowed with.

TRANSLATION

Those who are averse to the Transcendence realize the Supreme Absolute Truth differently through speculative sense perception, and therefore, because of mistaken speculation, everything appears to them to be relative.

PURPORT

The Supreme Absolute Truth, the Personality of Godhead, is one, and He is spread everywhere by His impersonal feature. This is clearly expressed in *Bhagavad-gītā*. Lord Kṛṣṇa says, "Everything that is experienced is but an expansion of My energy." Everything is sustained by Him, but that does not mean that He is in everything. Sense perceptions, such as aural perception of the sound of a drum, visual perception of a beautiful woman, or perception of the delicious taste of a milk preparation by the tongue, all come through different senses and are therefore differently understood. Therefore sensory knowledge is divided in different categories, although actually everything is one as a manifestation of the energy of the Supreme Lord. Similarly, the energies of fire are heat and illumination, and by these two energies fire can display itself in many varieties, or in diversified sense perception. Māyāvādī philosophers declare this diversity to be false. But Vaiṣṇava philosophers do not accept the different manifestations as false; they accept them as nondifferent from the Supreme Personality of Godhead because they are a display of His diverse energies.

The philosophy that the Absolute is true and this creation is false (*brahma satyaṁ jagan mithyā*) is not accepted by Vaiṣṇava philosophers. The example is given that although all that glitters is not gold, this does not mean that a glittering object is false. For example, an oyster shell appears to be golden. This appearance of golden hue is due only to the perception of the eyes, but that does not mean that the oyster shell is false. Similarly, by seeing the form of Lord Kṛṣṇa one cannot understand what He actually is, but this does not mean that He is false. The form of Kṛṣṇa has to be understood as it is described in the books of knowledge such as *Brahma-saṁhitā. Īśvaraḥ paramaḥ kṛṣṇaḥ sac-cid-ānanda-vigrahaḥ:* Kṛṣṇa, the Supreme Personality of Godhead, has an eternal, blissful spiritual body. By our imperfect sense perception we cannot understand the form of the Lord. We have to acquire knowledge about Him. Therefore it is said here, *jñānam ekam. Bhagavad-gītā* confirms that they are fools who, simply upon seeing Kṛṣṇa, consider Him a common man. They do not know the unlimited knowledge, power and opulence of the Supreme Personality of Godhead. Material sense speculation leads to the conclusion that the Supreme is formless. It is because of such mental speculation that the conditioned soul remains in ignorance under the spell of illusory energy. The Supreme Person has to be understood by the transcendental sound vibrated by Him in *Bhagavad-gītā,* wherein He says that there is nothing superior to Himself; the impersonal Brahman effulgence is resting on His personality. The purified, absolute vision of *Bhagavad-gītā* is compared to the River Ganges. Ganges water is so pure that it can purify even the asses and cows. But anyone who, disregarding the pure Ganges, wishes to be purified instead by the filthy water flowing in a drain, cannot be successful. Similarly, one can successfully attain pure knowledge of the Absolute only by hearing from the pure Absolute Himself.

In this verse it is clearly said that those who are averse to the Supreme Personality of Godhead speculate with their imperfect senses about the nature of the Absolute Truth. The formless Brahman conception, however, can be received only by aural reception and not by personal experience. Knowledge is therefore acquired by aural reception. It is confirmed in the *Vedānta-sūtra, śāstra-yonitvāt:* one has to acquire pure knowledge from the authorized scriptures. So-called speculative arguments about the Absolute Truth are therefore useless. The actual identity of the living entity is his consciousness, which is always present while the living entity is awake, dreaming or in deep sleep.

Even in deep sleep, he can perceive by consciousness whether he is happy or distressed. Thus when consciousness is displayed through the medium of the subtle and gross material bodies, it is covered, but when the consciousness is purified, in Kṛṣṇa consciousness, one becomes free from the entanglement of repeated birth and death.

When uncontaminated pure knowledge is uncovered from the modes of material nature, the actual identity of the living entity is discovered: he is eternally a servitor of the Supreme Personality of Godhead. The process of uncovering is like this: the rays of sunshine are luminous, and the sun itself is also luminous. In the presence of the sun, the rays illuminate just like the sun, but when the sunshine is covered by the spell of a cloud, or by *māyā,* then darkness, the imperfection of perception, begins. Therefore, to get out of the entanglement of the spell of nescience, one has to awaken his spiritual consciousness, or Kṛṣṇa consciousness, in terms of the authorized scriptures.

TEXT 29

यथा महानहंरूपस्त्रिवृत्पञ्चविधः स्वराट् ।
एकादशविधस्तस्य वपुरण्डं जगद्यतः ॥२९॥

yathā mahān ahaṁ-rūpas
tri-vṛt pañca-vidhaḥ svarāṭ
ekādaśa-vidhas tasya
vapur aṇḍaṁ jagad yataḥ

yathā—as; *mahān*—the *mahat-tattva; aham-rūpaḥ*—the false ego; *tri-vṛt*—the three modes of material nature; *pañca-vidhaḥ*—the five material elements; *sva-rāṭ*—the individual consciousness; *ekādaśa-vidhaḥ*—the eleven senses; *tasya*—of the living entity; *vapuḥ*—the material body; *aṇḍam*—the *brahmāṇḍa; jagat*—the universe; *yataḥ*—from which or from whom.

TRANSLATION

From the total energy, the mahat-tattva, I have manifested the false ego, the three modes of material nature, the five material elements, the individual consciousness, the eleven senses and the material body. Similarly, the entire universe has come from the Supreme Personality of Godhead.

PURPORT

The Supreme Lord is described as *mahat-pada,* which means that the total material energy, known as the *mahat-tattva,* is lying at His lotus feet. The origin or the total energy of the cosmic manifestation is the *mahat-tattva.* From the *mahat-tattva* all the other twenty-four divisions have sprung, namely the eleven senses (including the mind), the five sense objects, the five material elements, and then consciousness, intelligence and false ego. The Supreme Personality of Godhead is the cause of the *mahat-tattva,* and therefore, in one sense, because everything is an emanation from the Supreme Lord, there is no difference between the Lord and the cosmic manifestation. But at the same time the cosmic manifestation is different from the Lord. The word *svarāṭ* is very significant here. *Svarāṭ* means "independent." The Supreme Lord is independent, and the individual soul is also independent. Although there is no comparison between the two qualities of independence, the living entity is minutely independent, and the Supreme Lord is fully independent. As the individual soul has a material body made of five elements and the senses, the supreme independent Lord similarly has the gigantic body of the universe. The individual body is temporary; similarly, the entire universe, which is considered to be the body of the Supreme Lord, is also temporary, and both the individual and universal bodies are products of the *mahat-tattva.* One has to understand the differences with intelligence. Everyone knows that his material body has developed from a spiritual spark, and similarly the universal body has developed from the supreme spark, Supersoul. As the individual body develops from the individual soul, the gigantic body of the universe develops from the Supreme Soul. Just as the individual soul has consciousness, the Supreme Soul is also conscious. But although there is a similarity between the consciousness of the Supreme Soul and the consciousness of the individual soul, the individual soul's consciousness is limited, whereas the consciousness of the Supreme Soul is unlimited. This is described in *Bhagavad-gītā* (13.3). *Kṣetrajñaṁ cāpi māṁ viddhi:* the Supersoul is present in every field of activity, just as the individual soul is present in the individual body. Both of them are conscious. The difference is that the individual soul is conscious of the individual body only, whereas the Supersoul is conscious of the total number of individual bodies.

TEXT 30

एतद्वै श्रद्धया भक्त्या योगाभ्यासेन नित्यशः ।
समाहितात्मा निःसङ्गो विरक्त्या परिपश्यति ॥३०॥

etad vai śraddhayā bhaktyā
yogābhyāsena nityaśaḥ
samāhitātmā niḥsaṅgo
viraktyā paripaśyati

etat—this; *vai*—certainly; *śraddhayā*—with faith; *bhaktyā*—by devotional service; *yoga-abhyāsena*—by practice of *yoga;* *nityaśaḥ*—always; *samāhita-ātmā*—he whose mind is fixed; *niḥsaṅgaḥ*—aloof from material association; *viraktyā*—by detachment; *paripaśyati*—understands.

TRANSLATION

This perfect knowledge can be achieved by a person who is already engaged in devotional service with faith, steadiness and full detachment, and who is always absorbed in thought of the Supreme. He is aloof from material association.

PURPORT

The atheistic mystic practitioner of *yoga* cannot understand this perfect knowledge. Only persons who engage in the practical activities of devotional service in full Kṛṣṇa consciousness can become absorbed in full *samādhi.* It is possible for them to see and understand the actual fact of the entire cosmic manifestation and its cause. It is clearly stated here that this is not possible to understand for one who has not developed devotional service in full faith. The words *samāhitātmā* and *samādhi* are synonymous.

TEXT 31

इत्येतत्कथितं गुर्वि ज्ञानं तद्ब्रह्मदर्शनम् ।
येनानुबुद्ध्यते तत्त्वं प्रकृतेः पुरुषस्य च ॥३१॥

ity etat kathitaṁ gurvi
jñānaṁ tad brahma-darśanam
yenānubuddhyate tattvaṁ
prakṛteḥ puruṣasya ca

iti—thus; *etat*—this; *kathitam*—described; *gurvi*—O respectful mother; *jñānam*—knowledge; *tat*—that; *brahma*—the Absolute Truth; *darśanam*—revealing; *yena*—by which; *anubuddhyate*—is understood; *tattvam*—the truth; *prakṛteḥ*—of matter; *puruṣasya*—of spirit; *ca*—and.

TRANSLATION

My dear respectful mother, I have already described the path of understanding the Absolute Truth, by which one can come to understand the real truth of matter and spirit and their relationship.

TEXT 32

ज्ञानयोगश्च मन्निष्ठो नैर्गुण्यो भक्तिलक्षणः ।
द्वयोरप्येक एवार्थो भगवच्छब्दलक्षणः ॥३२॥

jñāna-yogaś ca man-niṣṭho
nairguṇyo bhakti-lakṣaṇaḥ
dvayor apy eka evārtho
bhagavac-chabda-lakṣaṇaḥ

jñāna-yogaḥ—philosophical research; *ca*—and; *mat-niṣṭhaḥ*—directed towards Me; *nairguṇyaḥ*—free from the material modes of nature; *bhakti*—devotional service; *lakṣaṇaḥ*—named; *dvayoḥ*—of both; *api*—moreover; *ekaḥ*—one; *eva*—certainly; *arthaḥ*—purpose; *bhagavat*—the Supreme Personality of Godhead; *śabda*—by the word; *lakṣaṇaḥ*—signified.

TRANSLATION

Philosophical research culminates in understanding the Supreme Personality of Godhead. After achieving this understanding, when one becomes free from the material modes of nature, he attains the stage of devotional service. Either by devotional service directly or by philosophical research, one has to find the same destination, which is the Supreme Personality of Godhead.

PURPORT

It is said in *Bhagavad-gītā* that after many, many lives of philosophical research the wise man ultimately comes to the point of knowing that Vāsudeva, the Supreme Personality of Godhead, is everything, and therefore he surrenders unto Him. Such serious students in philosophical research are rare because they are very great souls. If by philosophical research one cannot come to the point of understanding the Supreme Person, then his task is not finished. His search in knowledge is still to be continued until he comes to the point of understanding the Supreme Lord in devotional service.

The opportunity for direct touch with the Personality of Godhead is given in *Bhagavad-gītā,* where it is also said that those who take to other processes, namely the processes of philosophical speculation and mystic *yoga* practice, have much trouble. After many, many years of much trouble, a *yogī* or wise philosopher may come to Him, but his path is very troublesome, whereas the path of devotional service is easy for everyone. One can achieve the result of wise philosophical speculation simply by discharging devotional service, and unless one reaches the point of understanding the Personality of Godhead by his mental speculation, all his research work is said to be simply a labor of love. The ultimate destination of the wise philosopher is to merge in the impersonal Brahman, but that Brahman is the effulgence of the Supreme Person. The Lord says in *Bhagavad-gītā* (14.27), *brahmaṇo hi pratiṣṭhāham amṛtasyāvyayasya ca:* "I am the basis of the impersonal Brahman, which is indestructible and is the supreme bliss." The Lord is the supreme reservoir of all pleasure, including Brahman pleasure; therefore, one who has unflinching faith in the Supreme Personality of Godhead is said to be already realized in impersonal Brahman and Paramātmā.

TEXT 33

यथेन्द्रियैः पृथग्द्वारैरर्थो बहुगुणाश्रयः ।
एको नानेयते तद्वद्भगवान् शास्त्रवर्त्मभिः ॥३३॥

yathendriyaiḥ pṛthag-dvārair
artho bahu-guṇāśrayaḥ
eko nāneyate tadvad
bhagavān śāstra-vartmabhiḥ

yathā—as; *indriyaiḥ*—by the senses; *pṛthak-dvāraiḥ*—in different ways; *arthaḥ*—an object; *bahu-guṇa*—many qualities; *āśrayaḥ*—endowed with; *ekaḥ*—one; *nānā*—differently; *īyate*—is perceived; *tadvat*—similarly; *bhagavān*—the Supreme Personality of Godhead; *śāstra-vartmabhiḥ*—according to different scriptural injunctions.

TRANSLATION

A single object is appreciated differently by different senses due to its having different qualities. Similarly, the Supreme Personality of Godhead is one, but according to different scriptural injunctions He appears to be different.

PURPORT

It appears that by following the path of *jñāna-yoga,* or empiric philosophical speculation, one reaches the impersonal Brahman, whereas by executing devotional service in Kṛṣṇa consciousness one enriches his faith in and devotion to the Personality of Godhead. But it is stated here that both *bhakti-yoga* and *jñāna-yoga* are meant for reaching the same destination—the Personality of Godhead. By the process of *jñāna-yoga* the same Personality of Godhead appears to be impersonal. As the same object appears to be different when perceived by different senses, the same Supreme Lord appears to be impersonal by mental speculation. A hill appears cloudy from a distance, and one who does not know may speculate that the hill is a cloud. Actually, it is not a cloud; it is a big hill. One has to learn from authority that the sight of a cloud is not actually a cloud but a hill. If one makes a little more progress, then instead of a cloud he sees the hill and something green. When one actually approaches the hill, he will see many varieties. Another example is in perceiving milk. When we see milk, we see that it is white; when we taste it, it appears that milk is very palatable. When we touch milk, it appears very cold; when we smell milk, it appears to have a very good flavor; and when we hear, we understand that it is called milk. Perceiving milk with different senses, we say that it is something white, something very delicious, something very aromatic, and so on. Actually, it is milk. Similarly, those who are trying to find the Supreme Godhead by mental speculation may approach the bodily effulgence, or the impersonal Brahman, and those who are trying to find the Supreme Godhead by *yoga* practice may find Him as the localized Supersoul, but those who are directly trying to approach the Supreme Truth by practice of *bhakti-yoga* can see Him face to face as the Supreme Person.

Ultimately, the Supreme Person is the destination of all different processes. The fortunate person who, by following the principles of scriptures, becomes completely purified of all material contamination, surrenders unto the Supreme Lord as everything. Just as one can appreciate the real taste of milk with the tongue and not with the eyes, nostrils or ears, one can similarly appreciate the Absolute Truth perfectly and with all relishable pleasure only through one path, devotional service. This is also confirmed in *Bhagavad-gītā. Bhaktyā mām abhijānāti:* if one wants to understand the Absolute Truth in perfection, he must take to devotional service. Of course, no one can understand the Absolute Truth in all perfection. That is not possible for the infinitesimal living entities. But the highest point of understanding by the living entity is reached by discharge of devotional service, not otherwise.

By following various scriptural paths, one may come to the impersonal effulgence of the Supreme Personality of Godhead. The transcendental pleasure derived from merging with or understanding the impersonal Brahman is very extensive because Brahman is *ananta. Tad brahma niṣkalaṁ anantam: brahmānanda* is unlimited. But that unlimited pleasure can also be surpassed. That is the nature of the Transcendence. The unlimited can be surpassed also, and that higher platform is Kṛṣṇa. When one deals directly with Kṛṣṇa, the mellow and the humor relished by reciprocation of devotional service is incomparable, even with the pleasure derived from transcendental Brahman. Prabodhānanda Sarasvatī therefore says that *kaivalya,* the Brahman pleasure, is undoubtedly very great and is appreciated by many philosophers, but to a devotee, who has understood how to derive pleasure from exchanging devotional service with the Lord, this unlimited Brahman appears to be hellish. One should try, therefore, to transcend even the Brahman pleasure in order to approach the position of dealing with Kṛṣṇa face to face. As the mind is the center of all the activities of the senses, Kṛṣṇa is called the master of the senses, Hṛṣīkeśa. The process is to fix the mind on Hṛṣīkeśa, or Kṛṣṇa, as Mahārāja Ambarīṣa did (*sa vai manaḥ kṛṣṇa-padāravindayoḥ*). *Bhakti* is the basic principle of all processes. Without *bhakti,* neither *jñāna-yoga* nor *aṣṭāṅga-yoga* can be successful, and unless one approaches Kṛṣṇa, the principles of self-realization have no ultimate destination.

TEXTS 34-36

क्रियया क्रतुभिर्दानैस्तपःस्वाध्यायमर्शनैः ।
आत्मेन्द्रियजयेनापि संन्यासेन च कर्मणाम् ॥३४॥
योगेन विविधाङ्गेन भक्तियोगेन चैव हि ।
धर्मेणोभयचिह्नेन यः प्रवृत्तिनिवृत्तिमान् ॥३५॥
आत्मतत्त्वावबोधेन वैराग्येण दृढेन च ।
ईयते भगवानेभिः सगुणो निर्गुणः स्वदृक् ॥३६॥

kriyayā kratubhir dānais
tapaḥ-svādhyāya-marśanaiḥ
ātmendriya-jayenāpi
sannyāsena ca karmaṇām

yogena vividhāṅgena
bhakti-yogena caiva hi
dharmeṇobhaya-cihnena
yaḥ pravṛtti-nivṛttimān

ātma-tattvāvabodhena
vairāgyeṇa dṛḍhena ca
īyate bhagavān ebhiḥ
saguṇo nirguṇaḥ sva-dṛk

kriyayā—by fruitive activities; *kratubhiḥ*—by sacrificial performances; *dānaiḥ*—by charity; *tapaḥ*—austerities; *svādhyāya*—study of Vedic literature; *marśanaiḥ*—and by philosophical research; *ātma-indriya-jayena*—by controlling the mind and senses; *api*—also; *sannyāsena*—by renunciation; *ca*—and; *karmaṇām*—of fruitive activities; *yogena*—by *yoga* practice; *vividha-aṅgena*—of different divisions; *bhakti-yogena*—by devotional service; *ca*—and; *eva*—certainly; *hi*—indeed; *dharmeṇa*—by prescribed duties; *ubhaya-cihnena*—having both symptoms; *yaḥ*—

which; *pravṛtti*—attachment; *nivṛtti-mān*—containing detachment; *ātma-tattva*—the science of self-realization; *avabodhena*—by understanding; *vairāgyeṇa*—by detachment; *dṛḍhena*—strong; *ca*—and; *īyate*—is perceived; *bhagavān*—the Supreme Personality of Godhead; *ebhiḥ*—by these; *sa-guṇaḥ*—in the material world; *nirguṇaḥ*—beyond the material modes; *sva-dṛk*—one who sees his constitutional position.

TRANSLATION

By performing fruitive activities and sacrifices, by distributing charity, by performing austerities, by studying various literatures, by conducting philosophical research, by controlling the mind, by subduing the senses, by accepting the renounced order of life and by performing the prescribed duties of one's social order; by performing the different divisions of yoga practice, by performing devotional service and by exhibiting the process of devotional service containing the symptoms of both attachment and detachment; by understanding the science of self-realization and by developing a strong sense of detachment, one who is expert in understanding the different processes of self-realization realizes the Supreme Personality of Godhead as He is represented in the material world as well as in transcendence.

PURPORT

As it is stated in the previous verse, one has to follow the principles of the scriptures. There are different prescribed duties for persons in the different social and spiritual orders. Here it is stated that performance of fruitive activities and sacrifices and distribution of charity are activities meant for persons who are in the householder order of society. There are four orders of the social system: *brahmacarya, gṛhastha, vānaprastha* and *sannyāsa.* For the *gṛhasthas,* or householders, performance of sacrifices, distribution of charity, and action according to prescribed duties are especially recommended. Similarly, austerity, study of Vedic literature, and philosophical research are meant for the *vānaprasthas,* or retired persons. Study of the Vedic literature from the bona fide spiritual master is meant for the *brahmacārī,* or student. *Ātmendriya-jaya,* control of the mind and taming of the senses, is meant for persons in the renounced order of life. All these different activities are prescribed for different persons so that they may be elevated to the platform of self-realization and from there to Kṛṣṇa consciousness, devotional service.

The words *bhakti-yogena caiva hi* mean that whatever is to be performed, as described in verse 34, whether *yoga* or sacrifice or fruitive activity or study of Vedic literature or philosophical research or acceptance of the renounced order of life, is to be executed in *bhakti-yoga*. The words *caiva hi,* according to Sanskrit grammar, indicate that one must perform all these activities mixed with devotional service, otherwise such activities will not produce any fruit. Any prescribed activity must be performed for the sake of the Supreme Personality of Godhead. It is confirmed in *Bhagavad-gītā* (9.27), *yat karoṣi yad aśnāsi:* "Whatever you do, whatever you eat, whatever you sacrifice, whatever austerities you undergo and whatever charities you give, the result should be given to the Supreme Lord." The word *eva* is added, indicating that one *must* execute activities in such a way. Unless one adds devotional service to all activities, he cannot achieve the desired result, but when *bhakti-yoga* is prominent in every activity, then the ultimate goal is sure.

One has to approach the Supreme Personality of Godhead, Kṛṣṇa, as it is stated in *Bhagavad-gītā:* "After many, many births, one approaches the Supreme Person, Kṛṣṇa, and surrenders unto Him, knowing that He is everything." Also in *Bhagavad-gītā,* the Lord says, *bhoktāraṁ yajña-tapasām:* "For anyone who is undergoing rigid austerity or for anyone performing different kinds of sacrifices, the beneficiary is the Supreme Personality of Godhead." He is the proprietor of all planets, and He is the friend of every living soul.

The words *dharmeṇobhaya-cihnena* mean that the *bhakti-yoga* process contains two symptoms, namely attachment for the Supreme Lord and detachment from all material affinities. There are two symptoms of advancement in the process of devotional service, just as there are two processes taking place while eating. A hungry man feels strength and satisfaction from eating, and at the same time he gradually becomes detached from eating any more. Similarly, with the execution of devotional service, real knowledge develops, and one becomes detached from all material activities. In no other activity but devotional service is there such detachment from matter and attachment for the Supreme. There are nine different processes to increase this attachment to the Supreme Lord: hearing, chanting, remembering, worshiping, serving the Lord, making friendship, praying, offering everything and serving the lotus feet of the Lord. The processes for increasing detachment from material affinities are explained in verse 36.

One can achieve elevation to the higher planetary systems like the heavenly kingdom by executing one's prescribed duties and by performing sacrifices. When one is transcendental to such desires because of accepting the renounced order of life, he can understand the Brahman feature of the Supreme, and when one is able to see his real constitutional position, he sees all other processes and becomes situated in the stage of pure devotional service. At that time he can understand the Supreme

Personality of Godhead, Bhagavān.

Understanding of the Supreme person is called *ātma-tattva-avabodhena,* which means "understanding of one's real constitutional position." If one actually understands one's constitutional position as an eternal servitor of the Supreme Lord, he becomes detached from the service of the material world. Everyone engages in some sort of service. If one does not know one's constitutional position, one engages in the service of his personal gross body or his family, society or country. But as soon as one is able to see his constitutional position (the word *sva-dṛk* means "one who is able to see"), he becomes detached from such material service and engages himself in devotional service.

As long as one is in the modes of material nature and is performing the duties prescribed in the scriptures, he can be elevated to higher planetary systems, where the predominating deities are material representations of the Supreme Personality of Godhead, like the sun-god, the moon-god, the air-god, Brahmā and Lord Śiva. All the different demigods are material representations of the Supreme Lord. By material activities one can approach only such demigods, as stated in *Bhagavad-gītā* (9.25). *Yānti deva-vratā devān:* those who are attached to the demigods and who perform the prescribed duties can approach the abodes of the demigods. In this way, one can go to the planet of the Pitās, or forefathers. Similarly, one who fully understands the real position of his life adopts devotional service and realizes the Supreme Personality of Godhead.

TEXT 37

प्रावोचं भक्तियोगस्य स्वरूपं ते चतुर्विधम् ।
कालस्य चाव्यक्तगतेर्योऽन्तर्धावति जन्तुषु ॥३७॥

pravocaṁ bhakti-yogasya
svarūpaṁ te catur-vidham
kālasya cāvyakta-gater
yo 'ntardhāvati jantuṣu

prāvocam—explained; *bhakti-yogasya*—of devotional service; *svarūpam*—the identity; *te*—to you; *catuḥ-vidham*—in four divisions; *kālasya*—of time; *ca*—also; *avyakta-gateḥ*—the movement of which is imperceptible; *yaḥ*—which; *antardhāvati*—chases; *jantuṣu*—the living entities.

TRANSLATION

My dear mother, I have explained to you the process of devotional service and its identity in four different social divisions. I have explained to you as

well how eternal time is chasing the living entities, although it is imperceptible to them.

PURPORT

The process of *bhakti-yoga,* devotional service, is the main river flowing down towards the sea of the Absolute Truth, and all other processes mentioned are just like tributaries. Lord Kapila is summarizing the importance of the process of devotional service. *Bhakti-yoga,* as described before, is divided into four divisions, three in the material modes of nature and one in transcendence, which is untinged by the modes of material nature. Devotional service mixed with the modes of material nature is a means for material existence, whereas devotional service without desires for fruitive result and without attempts for empirical philosophical research is pure, transcendental devotional service.

TEXT 38

जीवस्य संसृतीर्बह्वीरविद्याकर्मनिर्मिताः ।
यास्वङ्ग प्रविशन्नात्मा न वेद गतिमात्मनः ॥३८॥

jīvasya saṁsṛtīr bahvīr
avidyā-karma-nirmitāḥ
yāsv aṅga praviśann ātmā
na veda gatim ātmanaḥ

jīvasya—of the living entity; *saṁsṛtīḥ*—courses of material existence; *bahvīḥ*—many; *avidyā*—in ignorance; *karma*—by work; *nirmitāḥ*—produced; *yāsu*—into which; *aṅga*—My dear mother; *praviśan*—entering; *ātmā*—the living entity; *na*—not; *veda*—understands; *gatim*—the movement; *ātmanaḥ*—of himself.

TRANSLATION

There are varieties of material existence for the living entity according to the work he performs in ignorance or forgetfulness of his real identity. My dear mother, if anyone enters into that forgetfulness, he is unable to understand where his movements will end.

PURPORT

Once one enters into the continuation of material existence, it is very difficult to get out. Therefore the Supreme Personality of Godhead comes Himself or sends His bona fide representative, and He leaves behind scriptures like *Bhagavad-gītā* and *Śrīmad-Bhāgavatam*, so that the living entities hovering in the darkness of nescience may take advantage of the instructions, the saintly persons and the spiritual masters and thus be freed. Unless the living entity receives the mercy of the saintly persons, the spiritual master or Kṛṣṇa, it is not possible for him to get out of the darkness of material existence; by his own endeavor it is not possible.

TEXT 39

नैतत्खलायोपदिशेन्नाविनीताय कर्हिचित् ।
न स्तब्धाय न भिन्नाय नैव धर्मध्वजाय च ॥३९॥

naitat khalāyopadiśen
nāvinītāya karhicit
na stabdhāya na bhinnāya
naiva dharma-dhvajāya ca

na—not; *etat*—this instruction; *khalāya*—to the envious; *upadiśet*—one should teach; *na*—not; *avinītāya*—to the agnostic; *karhicit*—ever; *na*—not; *stabdhāya*—to the proud; *na*—not; *bhinnāya*—to the misbehaved; *na*—not; *eva*—certainly; *dharma-dhvajāya*—to the hypocrites; *ca*—also.

TRANSLATION

Lord Kapila continued: This instruction is not meant for the envious, for the agnostics or for persons who are unclean in their behavior. Nor is it for hypocrites or for persons who are proud of material possessions.

TEXT 40

न लोलुपायोपदिशेन्न गृहारूढचेतसे ।
नाभक्ताय च मे जातु न मद्भक्तद्विषामपि ॥४०॥

na lolupāyopadiśen
na gṛhārūḍha-cetase
nābhaktāya ca me jātu
na mad-bhakta-dviṣām api

na—not; *lolupāya*—to the greedy; *upadiśet*—one should instruct; *na*—not; *gṛha-ārūḍha-cetase*—to one who is too attached to family life; *na*—not; *abhaktāya*—to the nondevotee; *ca*—and; *me*—of Me; *jātu*—ever; *na*—not; *mat*—My; *bhakta*—devotees; *dviṣām*—to those who are envious of; *api*—also.

TRANSLATION

It is not to be instructed to persons who are too greedy and too attached to family life, nor to persons who are nondevotees and who are envious of the devotees and of the Personality of Godhead.

PURPORT

Persons who are always planning to do harm to other living entities are not eligible to understand Kṛṣṇa consciousness and cannot enter into the realm of transcendental loving service to the Lord. Also, there are so-called disciples who become submissive to a spiritual master most artificially, with an ulterior motive. They also cannot understand what Kṛṣṇa consciousness or devotional service is. Persons who, due to being initiated by another sect of religious faith, do not find devotional service as the common platform for approaching the Supreme Personality of Godhead, also cannot understand Kṛṣṇa consciousness. We have experience that some students come to join us, but because of being biased in some particular type of faith, they leave our camp and become lost in the wilderness. Actually, Kṛṣṇa consciousness is not a sectarian religious faith; it is a teaching process for understanding the Supreme Lord and our relationship with Him. Anyone can join this movement without prejudice, but unfortunately there are persons who feel differently. It is better, therefore, not to instruct the science of Kṛṣṇa consciousness to such persons.

Generally, materialistic persons are after some name, fame and material gain, so if someone takes to Kṛṣṇa consciousness for these reasons, he will never be able to understand this philosophy. Such persons take to religious principles as a social decoration. They admit themselves into some cultural institution for the sake of name only, especially in this age. Such persons also cannot understand the philosophy of Kṛṣṇa consciousness. Even if one is not greedy for material possessions but is too attached to family life, he also cannot understand Kṛṣṇa consciousness. Superficially, such persons are not very greedy for material possessions, but they are too attached to wife, children and family improvement. When a person is not contaminated by the above-mentioned faults yet at the ultimate issue is not interested in the service of the Supreme Personality of Godhead, or if he is a nondevotee, he also cannot understand the philosophy of Kṛṣṇa consciousness.

TEXT 41

श्रद्दधानाय भक्ताय विनीतायानसूयवे ।
भूतेषु कृतमैत्राय शुश्रूषाभिरताय च ॥४१॥

śraddadhānāya bhaktāya
vinītāyānasūyave
bhūteṣu kṛta-maitrāya
śuśrūṣābhiratāya ca

śraddadhānāya—faithful; *bhaktāya*—to the devotee; *vinītāya*—respectful; *anasūyave*—nonenvious; *bhūteṣu*—to all living entities; *kṛta-maitrāya*—friendly; *śuśrūṣā*—faithful service; *abhiratāya*—eager to render; *ca*—and.

TRANSLATION

Instruction should be given to the faithful devotee who is respectful to the spiritual master, nonenvious, friendly to all kinds of living entities and eager to render service with faith and sincerity.

TEXT 42

बहिर्जातविरागाय शान्तचित्ताय दीयताम् ।
निर्मत्सराय शुचये यस्याहं प्रेयसां प्रियः ॥४२॥

bahir-jāta-virāgāya
śānta-cittāya dīyatām
nirmatsarāya śucaye
yasyāhaṁ preyasāṁ priyaḥ

bahiḥ—for what is outside; *jāta-virāgāya*—to him who has developed detachment; *śānta-cittāya*—whose mind is peaceful; *dīyatām*—let this be instructed; *nirmatsarāya*—nonenvious; *śucaye*—perfectly cleansed; *yasya*—of whom; *aham*—I; *preyasām*—of all that is very dear; *priyaḥ*—the most dear.

TRANSLATION

This instruction should be imparted by the spiritual master to persons who have taken the Supreme Personality of Godhead to be more dear than anything, who are not envious of anyone, who are perfectly cleansed and who have developed detachment for that which is outside the purview of Kṛṣṇa consciousness.

PURPORT

In the beginning, no one can be elevated to the highest stage of devotional service. Here *bhakta* means one who does not hesitate to accept the reformatory processes for becoming a *bhakta.* In order to become a devotee of the Lord, one has to accept a spiritual master and inquire from him about how to progress in devotional service. To serve a devotee, to chant the holy name according to a certain counting method, to worship the Deity, to hear *Śrīmad-Bhāgavatam* or *Bhagavad-gītā* from a realized person and to live in a sacred place where devotional service is not disturbed are the first out of sixty-four devotional activities for making progress in devotional service. One who has accepted these five chief activities is called a devotee.

One must be prepared to offer the necessary respect and honor to the spiritual master. He should not be unnecessarily envious of his Godbrothers. Rather, if a Godbrother is more enlightened and advanced in Kṛṣṇa consciousness, one should accept him as almost equal to the spiritual master, and one should be happy to see such Godbrothers advance in Kṛṣṇa consciousness. A devotee should always be very kind to the general public in instructing Kṛṣṇa consciousness because that is the only solution for getting out of the clutches of *māyā*. That is really humanitarian work, for it is the way to show mercy to other people who need it very badly. The word *śuśrūṣābhiratāya* indicates a person who faithfully engages in serving the spiritual master. One should give personal service and all kinds of comforts to the spiritual master. A devotee who does so is also a bona fide candidate for taking this instruction. The word *bahir jāta-virāgāya* means a person who has developed detachment from external and internal material propensities. Not only is he detached from activities which are not connected to Kṛṣṇa consciousness, but he should be internally averse to the material way of life. Such a person must be nonenvious and should think of the welfare of all living entities, not only of the human beings, but living entities other than human beings. The word *śucaye* means one who is cleansed both externally and internally. To become actually cleansed externally and internally, one should chant the holy name of the Lord, Hare Kṛṣṇa, or Viṣṇu, constantly.

The word *dīyatām* means that knowledge of Kṛṣṇa consciousness should be offered by the spiritual master. The spiritual master must not accept a disciple who is not qualified; he should not be professional and should not accept disciples for monetary gains. The bona fide spiritual master must see the bona fide qualities of a person whom he is going to initiate. An unworthy person should not be initiated. The spiritual master should train his disciple in such a way so that in the future only the Supreme Personality of Godhead will be the dearmost goal of his life.

In these two verses the qualities of a devotee are fully explained. One who has actually developed all the qualities listed in these verses is already elevated to the post of a devotee. If one has not developed all these qualities, he still has to fulfill these conditions in order to become a perfect devotee.

TEXT 43

य इदं शृणुयादम्ब श्रद्धया पुरुषः सकृत् ।
यो वाभिधत्ते मच्चित्तः स ह्येति पदवीं च मे ॥४३॥

ya idaṁ śṛṇuyād amba
śraddhayā puruṣaḥ sakṛt
yo vābhidhatte mac-cittaḥ
sa hy eti padavīṁ ca me

yaḥ—he who; *idam*—this; *śṛṇuyāt*—may hear; *amba*—O mother; *śraddhayā*—with faith; *puruṣaḥ*—a person; *sakṛt*—once; *yaḥ*—he who; *vā*—or; *abhidhatte*—repeats; *mat-cittaḥ*—his mind fixed on Me; *saḥ*—he; *hi*—certainly; *eti*—attains; *padavīm*—abode; *ca*—and; *me*—My.

TRANSLATION

Anyone who once meditates upon Me with faith and affection, who hears and chants about Me, surely goes back home, back to Godhead.

Thus end the Bhaktivedanta purports of the Third Canto, Thirty-second Chapter, of the Śrīmad-Bhāgavatam, *entitled "Entanglement in Fruitive Activities."*

CHAPTER THIRTY-THREE

Activities of Kapila

TEXT 1

मैत्रेय उवाच
एवं निशम्य कपिलस्य वचो जनित्री
सा कर्दमस्य दयिता किल देवहूतिः ।
विस्रस्तमोहपटला तमभिप्रणम्य
तुष्टाव तत्त्वविषयाङ्कितसिद्धिभूमिम् ॥ १ ॥

maitreya uvāca
evaṁ niśamya kapilasya vaco janitrī
sā kardamasya dayitā kila devahūtiḥ
visrasta-moha-paṭalā tam abhipraṇamya
tuṣṭāva tattva-viṣayāṅkita-siddhi-bhūmim

maitreyaḥ uvāca—Maitreya said; *evam*—thus; *niśamya*—having heard; *kapilasya*—of Lord Kapila; *vacaḥ*—the words; *janitrī*—the mother; *sā*—she; *kardamasya*—of Kardama Muni; *dayitā*—the dear wife; *kila*—namely; *devahūtiḥ*—Devahūti; *visrasta*—freed from; *moha-paṭalā*—the covering of illusion; *tam*—unto Him; *abhipraṇamya*—having offered obeisances; *tuṣṭāva*—recited prayers; *tattva*—basic principles; *viṣaya*—in the matter of; *aṅkita*—the author; *siddhi*—of liberation; *bhūmim*—the background.

TRANSLATION

Śrī Maitreya said: Thus Devahūti, the mother of Lord Kapila and wife of Kardama Muni, became freed from all ignorance concerning devotional service and transcendental knowledge. She offered her obeisances unto the Lord, the author of the basic principles of the Sāṅkhya system of philosophy, which is the background of liberation, and she satisfied Him with the following verses of prayer.

PURPORT

The system of philosophy enunciated by Lord Kapila before His mother is the background for situation on the spiritual platform. The specific significance of this system of philosophy is stated herein as *siddhi-bhūmim*—it is the background of salvation. People who are suffering in this material world because they are conditioned by the material energy can easily get freedom from the clutches of matter by understanding the Sāṅkhya philosophy enunciated by Lord Kapila. By this system of philosophy, one can immediately become free, even though one is situated in this material world. That stage is called *jīvan-mukti.* This means that one is liberated even though one stays with his material body. That happened for Devahūti, the mother of Lord Kapila, and she therefore satisfied the Lord by offering her prayers. Anyone who understands the basic principle of Sāṅkhya philosophy is elevated in devotional service and becomes fully Kṛṣṇa conscious, or liberated, even within this material world.

TEXT 2

देवहूतिरुवाच
अथाप्यजोऽन्तःसलिले शयानं
भूतेन्द्रियार्थात्ममयं वपुस्ते ।
गुणप्रवाहं सदशेषबीजं
दध्यौ स्वयं यज्जठराब्जजातः ॥ २ ॥

devahūtir uvāca
athāpy ajo 'ntaḥ-salile śayānaṁ
bhūtendriyārthātma-mayaṁ vapus te
guṇa-pravāhaṁ sad-aśeṣa-bījaṁ
dadhyau svayaṁ yaj-jaṭharābja-jātaḥ

devahūtiḥ uvāca—Devahūti said; *atha api*—moreover; *ajaḥ*—Lord Brahmā; *antaḥ-salile*—in the water; *śayānam*—lying; *bhūta*—the material elements; *indriya*—the senses; *artha*—the sense objects; *ātma*—the mind; *mayam*—pervaded by; *vapuḥ*—body; *te*—Your; *guṇa-pravāham*—the source of the stream of the three modes of material nature; *sat*—manifest; *aśeṣa*—of all; *bījam*—the seed; *dadhyau*—meditated upon; *svayam*—himself; *yat*—of whom; *jaṭhara*—from the abdomen; *abja*—from the lotus flower; *jātaḥ*—born.

TRANSLATION

Devahūti said: Brahmā is said to be unborn because he takes birth from the lotus flower which grows from Your abdomen while You lie in the ocean at the bottom of the universe. But even Brahmā simply meditated upon You, whose body is the source of unlimited universes.

PURPORT

Brahmā is also named Aja, "he who is unborn." Whenever we think of someone's birth, there must be a material father and mother, for thus one is born. But Brahmā, being the first living creature within this universe, was born directly from the body of the Supreme Personality of Godhead who is known as Garbhodakaśāyī Viṣṇu, the Viṣṇu form lying down in the ocean at the bottom of the universe. Devahūti wanted to impress upon the Lord that when Brahmā wants to see Him, he has to meditate upon Him. "You are the seed of all creation," she said. "Although Brahmā was directly born from You, he still has to perform many years of meditation, and even then he cannot see You directly, face to face. Your body is lying within the vast water at the bottom of the universe, and thus You are known as Garbhodakaśāyī Viṣṇu."

The nature of the Lord's gigantic body is also explained in this verse. That body is transcendental, untouched by matter. Since the material manifestation has come from His body, His body therefore existed before the material creation. The conclusion is that the transcendental body of Viṣṇu is not made of material elements. The body of Viṣṇu is the source of all other living entities, as well as the material nature, which is also supposed to be the energy of that Supreme Personality of Godhead. Devahūti said, "You are the background of the material manifestation and all created energy; therefore Your delivering me from the clutches of *māyā* by explaining the system of Sāṅkhya philosophy is not so astonishing. But Your being born from my abdomen is certainly wonderful because although You are the source of all creation, You have so kindly taken birth as my child. That is most wonderful. Your body is the source of all the universe, and still You put Your body within the abdomen of a common woman like me. To me, that is most astonishing."

TEXT 3

स एव विश्वस्य भवान् विधत्ते
गुणप्रवाहेण विभक्तवीर्यः ।
सर्गाद्यनीहोऽवितथाभिसन्धि-
रात्मेश्वरोऽतर्क्यसहस्रशक्तिः ॥ ३ ॥

sa eva viśvasya bhavān vidhatte
guṇa-pravāheṇa vibhakta-vīryaḥ
sargādy anīho 'vitathābhisandhir
ātmeśvaro 'tarkya-sahasra-śaktiḥ

saḥ—that very person; *eva*—certainly; *viśvasya*—of the universe; *bhavān*—You; *vidhatte*—carry on; *guṇa-pravāheṇa*—by the interaction of the modes; *vibhakta*—divided; *vīryaḥ*—Your energies; *sarga-ādi*—the creation and so on; *anīhaḥ*—the nondoer; *avitatha*—not futile; *abhisandhiḥ*—Your determination; *ātma-īśvaraḥ*—the Lord of all living entities; *atarkya*—inconceivable; *sahasra*—thousands; *śaktiḥ*—possessing energies.

TRANSLATION

My dear Lord, although personally You have nothing to do, You have distributed Your energies in the interactions of the material modes of nature, and for that reason the creation, maintenance and dissolution of the cosmic manifestation take place. My dear Lord, You are self-determined and are the Supreme Personality of Godhead for all living entities. For them You created this material manifestation, and although You are one, Your diverse energies can act multifariously. This is inconceivable to us.

PURPORT

The statement made in this verse by Devahūti that the Absolute Truth has many diverse energies although He personally has nothing to do is confirmed in the *Upaniṣads.* There is no one greater than Him or on an equal level with Him, and everything is completely done by His energy, as if by nature. It is understood herein, therefore, that although the modes of material nature are entrusted to different manifestations like Brahmā, Viṣṇu and Śiva, each of whom is particularly invested with different kinds of power, the Supreme Lord is completely aloof from such activities. Devahūti is saying, "Although You personally are not doing anything, Your determination is absolute. There is no question of Your fulfilling Your will with the help of anyone else besides Yourself. You are, in the end, the Supreme Soul and the supreme controller. Your will, therefore, cannot be checked by anyone else." The Supreme Lord can check others' plans. As it is said, "Man proposes and God disposes." But when the Supreme Personality of Godhead proposes, that desire is under no one else's control. He is absolute. We are ultimately dependent on Him to fulfill our desires, but we cannot say that God's desires are also dependent. That is His inconceivable power. That which may be inconceivable for ordinary living entities is easily done by Him. And in spite of His being unlimited, He has subjected Himself to being known from the authoritative scriptures like the Vedic literatures. As it is said, *śabda-mūlatvāt:* He can be known through the *śabda-brahma,* or Vedic literature.

Why is the creation made? Since the Lord is the Supreme Personality of Godhead for all living entities, He created this material manifestation for those living entities who want to enjoy or lord it over material nature. As the Supreme Godhead, He arranges to fulfill their various desires. It is confirmed also in the *Vedas, eko bahūnāṁ yo vidadhāti kāmān:* the supreme one supplies the necessities of the many living entities. There is no limit to the demands of the different kinds of living entities, and the supreme one, the Supreme Personality of Godhead, alone maintains them and supplies them by His inconceivable energy.

TEXT 4

स त्वं भृतो मे जठरेण नाथ
कथं नु यस्योदर एतदासीत् ।
विश्वं युगान्ते वटपत्र एकः
शेते स्म मायाशिशुरङ्घ्रिपानः ॥ ४ ॥

sa tvaṁ bhṛto me jaṭhareṇa nātha
kathaṁ nu yasyodara etad āsīt
viśvaṁ yugānte vaṭa-patra ekaḥ
śete sma māyā-śiśur aṅghri-pānaḥ

saḥ—that very person; *tvam*—You; *bhṛtaḥ*—took birth; *me jaṭhareṇa*—by my abdomen; *nātha*—O my Lord; *katham*—how; *nu*—then; *yasya*—of whom; *udare*—in the belly; *etat*—this; *āsīt*—did rest; *viśvam*—universe; *yuga-ante*—at the end of the millennium; *vaṭa-patre*—on the leaf of a banyan tree; *ekaḥ*—alone; *śete sma*—You lay down; *māyā*—possessing inconceivable powers; *śiśuḥ*—a baby; *aṅghri*—Your toe; *pānaḥ*—licking.

TRANSLATION

As the Supreme Personality of Godhead, You have taken birth from my abdomen. O my Lord, how is that possible for the supreme one, who has in His belly all the cosmic manifestation? The answer is that it is possible, for at the end of the millennium You lie down on a leaf of a banyan tree, and just like a small baby, You lick the toe of Your lotus foot.

PURPORT

At the time of dissolution the Lord sometimes appears as a small baby lying on a leaf of a banyan tree, floating on the devastating water. Therefore Devahūti suggests, "Your lying down within the abdomen of a common woman like me is not so astonishing. You can lie down on the leaf of a banyan tree and float on the water of devastation as a small baby. It is not very wonderful, therefore, that You can lie down in the abdomen of my body. You teach us that those who are very fond of children within this material world and who therefore enter into marriage to enjoy family life with children can also have the Supreme Personality of Godhead as their child, and the most wonderful thing is that the Lord Himself licks His toe."

Since all the great sages and devotees apply all energy and all activities in the service of the lotus feet of the Lord, there must be some transcendental pleasure in the toes of His lotus feet. The Lord licks His toe to taste the nectar for which the devotees always aspire. Sometimes the Supreme Personality of Godhead Himself wonders how much transcendental pleasure is within Himself, and in order to taste His own potency, He sometimes takes the position of tasting Himself. Lord Caitanya is Kṛṣṇa Himself, but He appears as a devotee to taste the sweetness of the transcendental mellow in Himself which is tasted by Śrīmatī Rādhārāṇī, the greatest of all devotees.

TEXT 5

त्वं देहतन्त्रः प्रशमाय पाप्मनां
निदेशभाजां च विभो विभूतये ।
यथावतारास्तव सूकरादय-
स्तथायमप्यात्मपथोपलब्धये ॥ ५ ॥

tvaṁ deha-tantraḥ praśamāya pāpmanām
nideśa-bhājāṁ ca vibho vibhūtaye
yathāvatārās tava sūkarādayas
tathāyam apy ātma-pathopalabdhaye

tvam—You; *deha*—this body; *tantraḥ*—have assumed; *praśamāya*—for the diminution; *pāpmanām*—of sinful activities; *nideśa-bhājām*—of instructions in devotion; *ca*—and; *vibho*—O my Lord; *vibhūtaye*—for the expansion; *yathā*—as; *avatārāḥ*—incarnations; *tava*—Your; *sūkara-ādayaḥ*—the boar and other forms; *tathā*—so; *ayam*—this incarnation of Kapila; *api*—surely; *ātma-patha*—the path of self-realization; *upalabdhaye*—in order to reveal.

TRANSLATION

My dear Lord, You have assumed this body in order to diminish the sinful activities of the fallen and to enrich their knowledge in devotion and liberation. Since these sinful people are dependent on Your direction, by Your own will You assume incarnations as a boar and as other forms. Similarly, You have appeared in order to distribute transcendental knowledge to Your dependents.

PURPORT

In the previous verses, the general transcendental qualifications of the Supreme Personality of Godhead were described. Now the specific purpose of the Lord's appearance is also described. By His different energies He bestows different kinds of bodies upon the living entities, who are conditioned by their propensity to lord it over material nature, but in course of time these living entities become so degraded that they need enlightenment. It is stated in *Bhagavad-gītā* that whenever there are discrepancies in the discharge of the real purpose of this material existence, the Lord appears as an incarnation. The Lord's form as Kapila directs the fallen souls and enriches them with knowledge and devotion so that they may go back to Godhead. There are many incarnations of the Supreme Personality of Godhead, like those of the boar, the fish, the tortoise and the half-man half-lion. Lord Kapiladeva is also one of the incarnations of Godhead. It is accepted herein that Lord Kapiladeva appeared on the surface of the earth to give transcendental knowledge to the misguided conditioned souls.

TEXT 6

यन्नामधेयश्रवणानुकीर्तनाद्
यत्प्रह्वणाद्यत्स्मरणादपि क्वचित् ।
श्वादोऽपि सद्यः सवनाय कल्पते
कुतः पुनस्ते भगवन्नु दर्शनात् ॥ ६ ॥

yan-nāmadheya-śravaṇānukīrtanād
yat-prahvaṇād yat-smaraṇād api kvacit
śvādo 'pi sadyaḥ savanāya kalpate
kutaḥ punas te bhagavan nu darśanāt

yat—of whom (the Supreme Personality of Godhead); *nāmadheya*—the name; *śravaṇa*—hearing; *anukīrtanāt*—by chanting; *yat*—to whom; *prahvaṇāt*—by offering obeisances; *yat*—whom; *smaraṇāt*—by remembering; *api*—even; *kvacit*—at any time; *śva-adaḥ*—a dog-eater; *api*—even; *sadyaḥ*—immediately; *savanāya*—for performing Vedic sacrifices; *kalpate*—becomes eligible; *kutaḥ*—what to speak of; *punaḥ*—again; *te*—You; *bhagavan*—O Supreme Personality of Godhead; *nu*—then; *darśanāt*—by seeing face to face.

TRANSLATION

To say nothing of the spiritual advancement of persons who see the Supreme Person face to face, even a person born in a family of dog-eaters immediately becomes eligible to perform Vedic sacrifices if he once utters the

holy name of the Supreme Personality of Godhead or chants about Him, hears about His pastimes, offers Him obeisances or even remembers Him.

PURPORT

Herein the spiritual potency of chanting, hearing or remembering the holy name of the Supreme Lord is greatly stressed. Rūpa Gosvāmī has discussed the sequence of sinful activities of the conditioned soul, and he has established, in *Bhakti-rasāmṛta-sindhu,* that those who engage in devotional service become freed from the reactions of all sinful activities. This is also confirmed in *Bhagavad-gītā.* The Lord says that He takes charge of one who surrenders unto Him, and He makes him immune to all reactions to sinful activities. If by chanting the holy name of the Supreme Personality of Godhead one becomes so swiftly cleared of all reactions to sinful activities, then what is to be said of those persons who see Him face to face?

Another consideration here is that persons who are purified by the process of chanting and hearing become immediately eligible to perform Vedic sacrifices. Generally, only a person who is born in a family of *brāhmaṇas,* who has been reformed by the ten kinds of purificatory processes and who is learned in Vedic literature is allowed to perform the Vedic sacrifices. But here the word *sadyaḥ,* "immediately," is used, and Śrīdhara Svāmī also remarks that one can *immediately* become eligible to perform Vedic sacrifices. A person born in a family of the low caste which is accustomed to eat dogs is so positioned due to his past sinful activities, but by chanting or hearing once in pureness, or in an offenseless manner, he is immediately relieved of the sinful reaction. Not only is he relieved of the sinful reaction, but he immediately achieves the result of all purificatory processes. Taking birth in the family of a *brāhmaṇa* is certainly due to pious activities in one's past life. But still a child who is born in a family of a *brāhmaṇa* depends for his further reformation upon initiation into acceptance of a sacred thread and many other reformatory processes. But a person who chants the holy name of the Lord, even if born in a family of *caṇḍālas,* dog-eaters, does not need reformation. Simply by chanting Hare Kṛṣṇa, he immediately becomes purified and becomes as good as the most learned *brāhmaṇa.*

Śrīdhara Svāmī especially remarks in this connection, *anena pūjyatvaṁ lakṣyate.* Some caste *brāhmaṇas* remark that by chanting Hare Kṛṣṇa, purification *begins.* Of course, that depends on the individual process of chanting, but this remark of Śrīdhara Svāmī's is completely applicable if one chants the holy name of the Lord without offense, for he immediately becomes more than a *brāhmaṇa.* As Śrīdhara Svāmī says, *pūjyatvam:* he immediately becomes as respectable as a most learned *brāhmaṇa* and can be allowed to perform Vedic sacrifices. If simply by chanting the holy name of the Lord one becomes sanctified instantly, then what can be said of those persons who see the Supreme Lord face to face and who understand the descent of the Lord, as Devahūti understands Kapiladeva.

Usually, initiation depends on the bona fide spiritual master, who directs the disciple. If he sees that a disciple has become competent and purified by the process of chanting, he offers the sacred thread to the disciple just so that he will be recognized as one-hundred-percent equal with a *brāhmaṇa.* This is also confirmed in the *Hari-bhakti-vilāsa* by Śrī Sanātana Gosvāmī: "As a base metal like bell metal can be changed into gold by a chemical process, any person can similarly be changed into a *brāhmaṇa* by *dīkṣā-vidhāna*, the initiation process".

It is sometimes remarked that by the chanting process one begins to purify himself and can take birth in his next life in a *brāhmaṇa* family and then be reformed. But at this present moment, even those who are born in the best *brāhmaṇa* families are not reformed, nor is there any certainty that they are actually born of *brāhmaṇa* fathers. Formerly the *garbhādhāna* reformatory system was prevalent, but at the present moment there is no such *garbhādhāna,* or seed-giving ceremony. Under these circumstances, no one knows if a man is factually born of a *brāhmaṇa* father. Whether one has acquired the qualification of a *brāhmaṇa* depends on the judgment of the bona fide spiritual master. He bestows upon the disciple the position of a *brāhmaṇa* by his own judgment. When one is accepted as a *brāhmaṇa* in the sacred thread ceremony under the *pāñcarātrika* system, then he is *dvija,* twice-born. That is confirmed by Sanātana Gosvāmī: *dvijatvaṁ jāyate.* By the process of initiation by the spiritual master, a person is accepted as a *brāhmaṇa* in his purified state of chanting the holy name of the Lord. He then makes further progress to become a qualified Vaiṣṇava, which means that the brahminical qualification is already acquired.

TEXT 7

अहो बत श्वपचोऽतो गरीयान्
यज्जिह्वाग्रे वर्तते नाम तुभ्यम् ।
तेपुस्तपस्ते जुहुवुः सस्नुरार्या
ब्रह्मानूचुर्नाम गृणन्ति ये ते ॥ ७ ॥

aho bata śva-paco 'to garīyān
yaj-jihvāgre vartate nāma tubhyam
tepus tapas te juhuvuḥ sasnur āryā
brahmānūcur nāma gṛṇanti ye te

aho bata—oh, how glorious; *śva-pacaḥ*—a dog-eater; *ataḥ*—hence; *garīyān*—worshipable; *yat*—of whom; *jihvā-agre*—on the tip of the tongue; *vartate*—is; *nāma*—the holy name; *tubhyam*—unto You; *tepuḥ tapaḥ*—practiced austerities; *te*—they; *juhuvuḥ*—executed fire sacrifices; *sasnuḥ*—took bath in the sacred rivers; *āryāḥ*—Āryans; *brahma anūcuḥ*—studied the *Vedas; nāma*—the holy name; *gṛṇanti*—accept; *ye*—they who; *te*—Your.

TRANSLATION

Oh, how glorious are they whose tongues are chanting Your holy name! Even if born in the families of dog-eaters, such persons are worshipable. Persons who chant the holy name of Your Lordship must have executed all kinds of austerities and fire sacrifices and achieved all the good manners of the Āryans. To be chanting the holy name of Your Lordship, they must have bathed at holy places of pilgrimage, studied the Vedas and fulfilled everything required.

PURPORT

As it is stated in the previous verse, a person who has once offenselessly chanted the holy name of God becomes immediately eligible to perform Vedic sacrifices. One should not be astonished by this statement of *Śrīmad-Bhāgavatam.* One should not disbelieve or think, "How by chanting the holy name of the Lord can one become a holy man to be compared to the most elevated *brāhmaṇa?*" To eradicate such doubts in the minds of unbelievers, this verse affirms that the stage of chanting of the holy name of the Lord is not sudden, but that the chanters have already performed all kinds of Vedic rituals and sacrifices. It is not very astounding, for no one in this life can chant the holy name of the Lord unless he has passed all lower stages, such as performing the Vedic ritualistic sacrifices, studying the *Vedas* and practicing good behavior like that of the Āryans. All this must first have been done. Just as a student in a law class is to be understood to have already graduated from general education, anyone who is engaged in the chanting of the holy name of the Lord—Hare Kṛṣṇa, Hare Kṛṣṇa, Kṛṣṇa Kṛṣṇa, Hare Hare/ Hare Rāma, Hare Rāma, Rāma Rāma, Hare Hare—must have already passed all lower stages. It is said that those who simply chant the holy name with the tip of the tongue are glorious. One does not even have to chant the holy name and understand the whole procedure, namely the offensive stage, offenseless stage and pure stage; if the holy name is sounded on the tip of the tongue, that is also sufficient. It is said herein that *nāma,* a singular number, one name, Kṛṣṇa or Rāma, is sufficient. It is not that one has to chant all the holy names of the Lord. The holy names of the Lord are innumerable, and one does not have to chant all the names to prove that he has already undergone all the processes of Vedic ritualistic ceremonies. If one chants once only, it is to be understood that he has already passed all the examinations, not to speak of those who are chanting always, twenty-four hours a day. It is specifically said here, *tubhyam:* "unto You only." One must chant God's name, not, as the Māyāvādī philosophers say, any name, such as a demigod's name or the names of God's energies. Only the holy name of the Supreme Lord will be effective. Anyone who compares the holy name of the Supreme Lord to the names of the demigods is called *pāṣaṇḍī,* or an offender.

The holy name has to be chanted to please the Supreme Lord, and not for any sense gratification or professional purpose. If this pure mentality is there, then even though a person is born of a low family, such as a dog-eater's, he is so glorious that not only has he purified himself, but he is quite competent to deliver others. He is competent to speak on the importance of the transcendental name, just as Ṭhākura Haridāsa did. He was apparently born in a family of Muhammadans, but because he was chanting the holy name of the Supreme Lord offenselessly, Lord Caitanya empowered him to become the authority, or *ācārya,* of spreading the name. It did not matter that he was born in a family which was not following the Vedic rules and regulations. Caitanya Mahāprabhu and Advaita Prabhu accepted him as an authority because he was offenselessly chanting the name of the Lord. Authorities like Advaita Prabhu and Lord Caitanya immediately accepted that he had already performed all kinds of austerities, studied the *Vedas* and performed all sacrifices. That is automatically understood. There is a hereditary class of *brāhmaṇas* called the *smārta-brāhmaṇas,* however, who are of the opinion that even if such persons who are chanting the holy name of the Lord are accepted as purified, they still have to perform the Vedic rites or await their next birth in a family of *brāhmaṇas* so that they can perform the Vedic rituals. But actually that is not the case. Such a man does not need to wait for the next birth to become purified. He is at once purified. It is understood that he has already performed all sorts of rites. It is the so-called *brāhmaṇas* who actually have to undergo different kinds of austerities before reaching that point of purification. There are many other Vedic performances which are not described here. All such Vedic rituals have been already performed by the chanters of the holy name.

The word *juhuvuḥ* means that the chanters of the holy name have already performed all kinds of sacrifices. *Sasnuḥ* means that they have already traveled to all the holy places of pilgrimage and taken part in purificatory activities at those places. They are called *āryāḥ* because they have already finished all these requirements, and therefore they must be among the Āryans or those who have qualified themselves to become Āryans. "Āryan" refers to those who are civilized, whose manners are regulated according to the Vedic rituals. Any devotee who is chanting the holy name of the Lord is the best kind of Āryan. Unless one studies the *Vedas*, one cannot become an Āryan, but it is automatically understood that the chanters have already studied all the Vedic literature. The specific word used here is *anūcuḥ*, which means that because they have already completed all those recommended acts, they have become qualified to be spiritual masters.

The very word *gṛṇanti*, which is used in this verse, means to be already established in the perfectional stage of ritualistic performances. If one is seated on the bench of a high-court and is giving judgment on cases, it means that he has already passed all legal exams and is better than those who are engaged in the study of law or those expecting to study law in the future. In a similar way, persons who are chanting the holy name are transcendental to those who are factually performing the Vedic rituals and those who expect to be qualified (or, in other words, those who are born in families of *brāhmaṇas* but have not yet undergone the reformatory processes and who therefore expect to study the Vedic rituals and perform the sacrifices in the future).

There are many Vedic statements in different places saying that anyone who chants the holy name of the Lord becomes immediately freed from conditional life and that anyone who hears the holy name of the Lord, even though born of a family of dog-eaters, also becomes liberated from the clutches of material entanglement.

TEXT 8

तं त्वामहं ब्रह्म परं पुमांसं
प्रत्यक्स्रोतस्यात्मनि संविभाव्यम् ।
स्वतेजसा ध्वस्तगुणप्रवाहं
वन्दे विष्णुं कपिलं वेदगर्भम् ॥ ८ ॥

taṁ tvām ahaṁ brahma paraṁ pumāṁsaṁ
pratyak-srotasy ātmani saṁvibhāvyam
sva-tejasā dhvasta-guṇa-pravāhaṁ
vande viṣṇuṁ kapilaṁ veda-garbham

tam—unto Him; *tvām*—You; *aham*—I; *brahma*—Brahman; *param*—supreme; *pumāṁsam*—the Supreme Personality of Godhead; *pratyak-srotasi*—turned inwards; *ātmani*—in the mind; *saṁvibhāvyam*—meditated upon, perceived; *sva-tejasā*—by Your own potency; *dhvasta*—vanished; *guṇa-pravāham*—the influence of the modes of material nature; *vande*—I offer obeisances; *viṣṇum*—unto Lord Viṣṇu; *kapilam*—named Kapila; *veda-garbham*—the repository of the *Vedas.*

TRANSLATION

I believe, my Lord, that You are Lord Viṣṇu Himself under the name of Kapila, and You are the Supreme Personality of Godhead, the Supreme Brahman! The saints and sages, being freed from all the disturbances of the senses and mind, meditate upon You, for by Your mercy only can one become free from the clutches of the three modes of material nature. At the time of dissolution, all the Vedas are sustained in You only.

PURPORT

Devahūti, the mother of Kapila, instead of prolonging her prayers, summarized that Lord Kapila was none other than Viṣṇu and that since she was a woman it was not possible for her to worship Him properly simply by prayer. It was her intention that the Lord be satisfied. The word *pratyak* is significant. In yogic practice, the eight divisions are *yama, niyama, āsana, prāṇāyāma, pratyāhāra, dhāraṇā, dhyāna* and *samādhi. Pratyāhāra* means to wind up the activities of the senses. The level of realization of the Supreme Lord evidenced by Devahūti is possible when one is able to withdraw the senses from material activities. When one is engaged in devotional service, there is no scope for his senses to be engaged otherwise. In such full Kṛṣṇa consciousness, one can understand the Supreme Lord as He is.

TEXT 9

मैत्रेय उवाच

ईडितो भगवानेवं कपिलाख्यः परः पुमान् ।
वाचाविक्लवयेत्याह मातरं मातृवत्सलः ॥ ९ ॥

maitreya uvāca
īḍito bhagavān evaṁ
kapilākhyaḥ paraḥ pumān
vācāviklavayety āha
mātaraṁ mātṛ-vatsalaḥ

maitreyaḥ uvāca—Maitreya said; *īḍitaḥ*—praised; *bhagavān*—the Supreme Personality of Godhead; *evam*—thus; *kapila-ākhyaḥ*—named Kapila; *paraḥ*—supreme; *pumān*—person; *vācā*—with words; *aviklavayā*—grave; *iti*—thus; *āha*—replied; *mātaram*—to His mother; *mātṛ-vatsalaḥ*—very affectionate to His mother.

TRANSLATION

Thus the Supreme Personality of Godhead Kapila, satisfied by the words of His mother, towards whom He was very affectionate, replied with gravity.

PURPORT

Since the Lord is all-perfect, His exhibition of affection for His mother was also complete. After hearing the words of His mother, He most respectfully, with due gravity and good manners, replied.

TEXT 10

कपिल उवाच
मार्गेणानेन मातस्ते सुसेव्येनोदितेन मे ।
आस्थितेन परां काष्ठामचिरादवरोत्स्यसि ॥१०॥

kapila uvāca
mārgeṇānena mātas te
susevyenoditena me
āsthitena parāṁ kāṣṭhām
acirād avarotsyasi

kapilaḥ uvāca—Lord Kapila said; *mārgeṇa*—by the path; *anena*—this; *mātaḥ*—My dear mother; *te*—for you; *su-sevyena*—very easy to execute; *uditena*—instructed; *me*—by Me; *āsthitena*—being performed; *parām*—supreme; *kāṣṭhām*—goal; *acirāt*—very soon; *avarotsyasi*—you will attain.

TRANSLATION

The Personality of Godhead said: My dear mother, the path of self-realization which I have already instructed to you is very easy. You can execute this system without difficulty, and by following it you shall very soon be liberated, even within your present body.

PURPORT

Devotional service is so perfect that simply by following the rules and regulations and executing them under the direction of the spiritual master, one is liberated, as it is said herein, from the clutches of *māyā,* even in this body. In other yogic processes, or in empiric philosophical speculation, one is never certain whether or not he is at the perfectional stage. But in the discharge of devotional service, if one has unflinching faith in the instruction of the bona fide spiritual master and follows the rules and regulations, he is sure to be liberated, even within this present body. Śrīla Rūpa Gosvāmī, in the *Bhakti-rasāmṛta-sindhu,* has also confirmed this. *Īhā yasya harer dāsye:* regardless of where he is situated, anyone whose only aim is to serve the Supreme Lord under the direction of the spiritual master is called *jīvan-mukta,* or one who is liberated even with his material body. Sometimes doubts arise in the minds of neophytes about whether or not the spiritual master is liberated, and sometimes neophytes are doubtful about the bodily affairs of the spiritual master. The point of liberation, however, is not to see the bodily symptoms of the spiritual master. One has to see the spiritual symptoms of the spiritual master. *Jīvan-mukta* means that even though one is in the material body (there are still some material necessities, since the body is material), because one is fully situated in the service of the Lord, he should be understood to be liberated.

Liberation entails being situated in one's own position. That is the definition in the *Śrīmad-Bhāgavatam: muktir . . . svarūpeṇa vyavasthitiḥ.* The *svarūpa,* or actual identity of the living entity, is described by Lord Caitanya. *Jīvera 'svarūpa' haya—kṛṣṇera 'nitya-dāsa':* the real identity of the living entity is that he is eternally a servitor of the Supreme Lord. If someone is one-hundred-percent engaged in the service of the Lord, he is to be understood as liberated. One must understand whether or not he is liberated by his activities in devotional service, not by other symptoms.

TEXT 11

श्रद्धत्स्वैतन्मतं मह्यं जुष्टं यद्ब्रह्मवादिभिः ।
येन मामभयं याया मृत्युमृच्छन्त्यतद्विदः ॥११॥

śraddhatsvaitan mataṁ mahyaṁ
juṣṭaṁ yad brahma-vādibhiḥ
yena mām abhayaṁ yāyā
mṛtyum ṛcchanty atad-vidaḥ

śraddhatsva—you may rest assured; *etat*—about this; *matam*—instruction; *mahyam*—My; *juṣṭam*—followed; *yat*—which; *brahma-vādibhiḥ*—by transcendentalists; *yena*—by which; *mām*—unto Me; *abhayam*—without fear; *yāyāḥ*—you shall reach; *mṛtyum*—death; *ṛcchanti*—attain; *a-tat-vidaḥ*—persons who are not conversant with this.

TRANSLATION

My dear mother, those who are actually transcendentalists certainly follow My instructions, as I have given them to you. You may rest assured that if you traverse this path of self-realization perfectly, surely you shall be freed from fearful material contamination and shall ultimately reach Me. Mother, persons who are not conversant with this method of devotional service certainly cannot get out of the cycle of birth and death.

PURPORT

Material existence is full of anxiety, and therefore it is fearful. One who gets out of this material existence automatically becomes free from all anxieties and fear. One who follows the path of devotional service enunciated by Lord Kapila is very easily liberated.

TEXT 12

मैत्रेय उवाच
इति प्रदर्श्य भगवान् सतीं तामात्मनो गतिम् ।
स्वमात्रा ब्रह्मवादिन्या कपिलोऽनुमतो ययौ ॥१२॥

maitreya uvāca
iti pradarśya bhagavān
satīṁ tām ātmano gatim
sva-mātrā brahma-vādinyā
kapilo 'numato yayau

maitreyaḥ uvāca—Maitreya said; *iti*—thus; *pradarśya*—after instructing; *bhagavān*—the Supreme Personality of Godhead; *satīm*—venerable; *tām*—that; *ātmanaḥ*—of self-realization; *gatim*—path; *sva-mātrā*—from His mother; *brahma-vādinyā*—self-realized; *kapilaḥ*—Lord Kapila; *anumataḥ*—took permission; *yayau*—left.

TRANSLATION

Śrī Maitreya said: The Supreme Personality of Godhead Kapila, after instructing His beloved mother, took permission from her and left His home, His mission having been fulfilled.

PURPORT

The mission of the appearance of the Supreme Personality of Godhead in the form of Kapila was to distribute the transcendental knowledge of Sāṅkhya philosophy, which is full of devotional service. Having imparted that knowledge to His mother—and, through His mother, to the world—Kapiladeva had no more need to stay at home, so He took permission from His mother and left. Apparently He left home for spiritual realization, although He had nothing to realize spiritually because He Himself is the person to be spiritually realized. Therefore this is an example set by the Supreme Personality of Godhead while acting like an ordinary human being so that others might learn from Him. He could, of course, have stayed with His mother, but He indicated that there was no need to stay with the family. It is best to remain alone as a *brahmacārī, sannyāsī* or *vānaprastha* and cultivate Krsna consciousness throughout one's whole life. Those who are unable to remain alone are given license to live in household life with wife and children, not for sense gratification but for cultivation of Kṛṣṇa consciousness.

TEXT 13

सा चापि तनयोक्तेन योगादेशेन योगयुक् ।
तस्मिन्नाश्रम आपीडे सरस्वत्याः समाहिता ॥१३॥

sā cāpi tanayoktena
yogādeśena yoga-yuk
tasminn āśrama āpīḍe
sarasvatyāḥ samāhitā

sā—she; *ca*—and; *api*—also; *tanaya*—by her son; *uktena*—spoken; *yoga-ādeśena*—by the instruction on *yoga; yoga-yuk*—engaged in *bhakti-yoga; tasmin*—in that; *āśrame*—hermitage; *āpīḍe*—the flower crown; *sarasvatyāḥ*—of the Sarasvatī; *samāhitā*—fixed in *samādhi.*

TRANSLATION

As instructed by her son, Devahūti also began to practice bhakti-yoga in that very āśrama. She practiced samādhi in the house of Kardama Muni, which was so beautifully decorated with flowers that it was considered the flower crown of the River Sarasvatī.

PURPORT

Devahūti did not leave her house, because it is never recommended for a woman to leave her home. She is dependent. The very example of Devahūti was that when she was not married, she was under the care of her father, Svāyambhuva Manu, and then Svāyambhuva Manu gave her to Kardama Muni in charity. She was under the care of her husband in her youth, and then her son, Kapila Muni, was born. As soon as her son grew up, her husband left home, and similarly the son, after discharging His duty towards His mother, also left. She could also have left home, but she did not. Rather, she remained at home and began to practice *bhakti-yoga* as it was instructed by her great son, Kapila Muni, and because of her practice of *bhakti-yoga,* the entire home became just like a flower crown on the River Sarasvatī.

TEXT 14

अभीक्ष्णावगाहकपिशान् जटिलान् कुटिलालकान् ।
आत्मानं चोग्रतपसा बिभ्रती चीरिणं कृशम् ॥१४॥

abhīkṣṇāvagāha-kapiśān
jaṭilān kuṭilālakān
ātmānaṁ cogra-tapasā
bibhratī cīriṇaṁ kṛśam

abhīkṣṇa—again and again; *avagāha*—by bathing; *kapiśān*—gray; *jaṭilān*—matted; *kuṭila*—curled; *alakān*—hair; *ātmānam*—her body; *ca*—and; *ugra-tapasā*—by severe austerities; *bibhratī*—became; *cīriṇam*—clothed in rags; *kṛśam*—thin.

TRANSLATION

She began to bathe three times daily, and thus her curling black hair gradually became gray. Due to austerity, her body gradually became thin, and she wore old garments.

PURPORT

It is the practice of the *yogī, brahmacārī, vānaprastha* and *sannyāsī* to bathe at least three times daily—early in the morning, during noontime and in the evening. These principles are strictly followed even by some *gṛhasthas,* especially *brāhmaṇas,* who are elevated in spiritual consciousness. Devahūti was a king's daughter and almost a king's wife also. Although Kardama Muni was not a king, by his yogic mystic power he accommodated Devahūti very comfortably in a nice palace with maidservants and all opulence. But since she had learned austerity even in the presence of her husband, there was no difficulty for her to be austere. Still, because her body underwent severe austerity after the departure of her husband and son, she became thin. To be too fat is not very good for spiritually advanced life. Rather, one should reduce because if one becomes fat it is an impediment to progress in spiritual understanding. One should be careful not to eat too much, sleep too much or remain in a comfortable position. Voluntarily accepting some penances and difficulties, one should take less food and less sleep. These are the procedures for practicing any kind of *yoga,* whether *bhakti-yoga, jñāna-yoga* or *haṭha-yoga.*

TEXT 15

प्रजापतेः कर्दमस्य तपोयोगविजृम्भितम् ।
स्वगार्हस्थ्यमनौपम्यं प्रार्थ्यं वैमानिकैरपि ॥१५॥

prajāpateḥ kardamasya
tapo-yoga-vijṛmbhitam
sva-gārhasthyam anaupamyaṁ
prārthyaṁ vaimānikair api

prajā-pateḥ—of the progenitor of mankind; *kardamasya*—Kardama Muni; *tapaḥ*—by austerity; *yoga*—by *yoga; vijṛmbhitam*—developed; *sva-gārhasthyam*—his home and household paraphernalia; *anaupamyam*—unequaled; *prārthyam*—enviable; *vaimānikaiḥ*—by the denizens of heaven; *api*—even.

TRANSLATION

The home and household paraphernalia of Kardama, who was one of the Prajāpatis, was developed in such a way, by dint of his mystic powers of austerity and yoga, that his opulence was sometimes envied by those who travel in outer space in airplanes.

PURPORT

The statement in this verse that Kardama Muni's household affairs were envied even by persons who travel in outer space refers to the denizens of heaven. Their airships are not like those we have invented in the modern age, which fly only from one country to another; their airplanes were capable of going from one planet to another. There are many such statements in the *Śrīmad-Bhāgavatam* from which we can understand that there were facilities to travel from one planet to another, especially in the higher planetary system, and who can say that they are not still traveling? The speed of our airplanes and space vehicles is very limited, but, as we have already studied, Kardama Muni traveled in outer space in an airplane which was like a city, and he journeyed to see all the different heavenly planets. That was not an ordinary airplane, nor was it ordinary space travel. Because Kardama Muni was such a powerful mystic *yogī,* his opulence was envied by the denizens of heaven.

TEXT 16

पयःफेननिभाः शय्या दान्ता रुक्मपरिच्छदाः ।
आसनानि च हैमानि सुस्पर्शास्तरणानि च ॥१६॥

payaḥ-phena-nibhāḥ śayyā
dāntā rukma-paricchadāḥ
āsanāni ca haimāni
susparśāstaraṇāni ca

payaḥ—of milk; *phena*—the foam; *nibhāḥ*—resembling; *śayyāḥ*—beds; *dāntāḥ*—made of ivory; *rukma*—golden; *paricchadāḥ*—with covers; *āsanāni*—chairs and benches; *ca*—and; *haimāni*—made of gold; *su-sparśa*—soft to the touch; *āstaraṇāni*—cushions; *ca*—and.

TRANSLATION

The opulence of the household of Kardama Muni is described herein. The bedsheets and mattresses were all as white as the foam of milk, the chairs and benches were made of ivory and were covered by cloths of lace with golden filigree, and the couches were made of gold and had very soft pillows.

TEXT 17

स्वच्छस्फटिककुड्येषु महामारकतेषु च ।
रत्नप्रदीपा आभान्ति ललनारत्नसंयुताः ॥१७॥

svaccha-sphaṭika-kuḍyeṣu
mahā-mārakateṣu ca
ratna-pradīpā ābhānti
lalanā ratna-saṁyutāḥ

svaccha—pure; *sphaṭika*—marble; *kuḍyeṣu*—on the walls; *mahā-mārakateṣu*—decorated with valuable emeralds; *ca*—and; *ratna-pradīpāḥ*—jewel lamps; *ābhānti*—shine; *lalanāḥ*—women; *ratna*—with jewelry; *saṁyutāḥ*—decorated.

TRANSLATION

The walls of the house were made of first-class marble, decorated with valuable jewels. There was no need of light, for the household was illuminated

by the rays of these jewels. The female members of the household were all amply decorated with jewelry.

PURPORT

It is understood from this statement that the opulences of household life were exhibited in valuable jewels, ivory, first-class marble, and furniture made of gold and jewels. The clothes are also mentioned as being decorated with golden filigree. Everything actually had some value. It was not like the furniture of the present day, which is cast in valueless plastic or base metal. The way of Vedic civilization is that whatever was used in household affairs had to be valuable. In case of need, such items of value could be exchanged immediately. Thus one's broken and unwanted furniture and paraphernalia would never be without value. This system is still followed by Indians in household affairs. They keep metal utensils and golden ornaments or silver plates and valuable silk garments with gold embroidery, and in case of need, they can have some money in exchange immediately. There are exchanges for the moneylenders and the householders.

TEXT 18

गृहोद्यानं कुसुमितै रम्यं बह्वमरद्रुमैः ।
कूजद्विहङ्गमिथुनं गायन्मत्तमधुव्रतम् ॥१८॥

gṛhodyānaṁ kusumitai
ramyaṁ bahv-amara-drumaiḥ
kūjad-vihaṅga-mithunaṁ
gāyan-matta-madhuvratam

gṛha-udyānam—the household garden; *kusumitaiḥ*—with flowers and fruits; *ramyam*—beautiful; *bahu-amara-drumaiḥ*—with many celestial trees; *kūjat*—singing; *vihaṅga*—of birds; *mithunam*—with pairs; *gāyat*—humming; *matta*—intoxicated; *madhu-vratam*—with bees.

TRANSLATION

The compound of the main household was surrounded by beautiful gardens, with sweet, fragrant flowers and many trees which produced fresh fruit and were tall and beautiful. The attraction of such gardens was that singing birds would sit on the trees, and their chanting voices, as well as the humming sound of the bees, made the whole atmosphere as pleasing as possible.

TEXT 19

यत्र प्रविष्टमात्मानं विबुधानुचरा जगुः ।
वाप्यामुत्पलगन्धिन्यां कर्दमेनोपलालितम् ॥१९॥

yatra praviṣṭam ātmānaṁ
vibudhānucarā jaguḥ
vāpyām utpala-gandhinyāṁ
kardamenopalālitam

yatra—where; *praviṣṭam*—entered; *ātmānam*—unto her; *vibudha-anucarāḥ*—the associates of the denizens of heaven; *jaguḥ*—sang; *vāpyām*—in the pond; *utpala*—of lotuses; *gandhinyām*—with the fragrance; *kardamena*—by Kardama; *upalālitam*—treated with great care.

TRANSLATION

When Devahūti would enter that lovely garden to take her bath in the pond filled with lotus flowers, the associates of the denizens of heaven, the Gandharvas, would sing about Kardama's glorious household life. Her great husband, Kardama, gave her all protection at all times.

PURPORT

The ideal husband-and-wife relationship is very nicely described in this statement. Kardama Muni gave Devahūti all sorts of comforts in his duty as a husband, but he was not at all attached to his wife. As soon as his son, Kapiladeva, was grown up, Kardama at once left all family connection. Similarly, Devahūti was the daughter of a great king, Svāyambhuva Manu, and was qualified and beautiful, but she was completely dependent on the protection of her husband. According to Manu, women, the fair sex, should not have independence at any stage of life. In childhood a woman must be under the protection of the parents, in youth she must be under the protection of the husband, and in old age she must be under the protection of the grown children. Devahūti demonstrated all these statements of the *Manu-saṁhitā* in her life: as a child she was dependent on her father, later she was dependent on her husband, in spite of her opulence, and she was later on dependent on her son, Kapiladeva.

TEXT 20

हित्वा तदीप्सिततममप्याखण्डलयोषिताम् ।
किञ्चिच्चकार वदनं पुत्रविश्लेषणातुरा ॥२०॥

hitvā tad īpsitatamam
apy ākhaṇḍala-yoṣitām
kiñcic cakāra vadanaṁ
putra-viśleṣaṇāturā

hitvā—having given up; *tat*—that household; *īpsita-tamam*—most desirable; *api*—even; *ākhaṇḍala-yoṣitām*—by the wives of Lord Indra; *kiñcit cakāra vadanam*—she wore a sorry look on her face; *putra-viśleṣaṇa*—by separation from her son; *āturā*—afflicted.

TRANSLATION

Although her position was unique from all points of view, saintly Devahūti, in spite of all her possessions, which were envied even by the ladies of the heavenly planets, gave up all such comforts. She was only sorry that her great son was separated from her.

PURPORT

Devahūti was not at all sorry at giving up her material comforts, but she was very much aggrieved at the separation of her son. It may be questioned here that if Devahūti was not at all sorry to give up the material comforts of life, then why was she sorry about losing her son? Why was she so attached to her son? The answer is explained in the next verse. He was not an ordinary son. Her son was the Supreme Personality of Godhead. One can give up material attachment, therefore, only when one has attachment for the Supreme Person. This is explained in *Bhagavad-gītā. Paraṁ dṛṣṭvā nivartate.* Only when one actually has some taste for spiritual existence can he be reluctant to follow the materialistic way of life.

TEXT 21

वनं प्रव्रजिते पत्यावपत्यविरहातुरा ।
ज्ञाततत्त्वाप्यभून्नष्टे वत्से गौरिव वत्सला ॥२१॥

vanaṁ pravrajite patyāv
apatya-virahāturā
jñāta-tattvāpy abhūn naṣṭe
vatse gaur iva vatsalā

vanam—to the forest; *pravrajite patyau*—when her husband left home; *apatya-viraha*—by separation from her son; *āturā*—very sorry; *jñāta-tattvā*—knowing the truth; *api*—although; *abhūt*—she became; *naṣṭe vatse*—when her calf is lost; *gauḥ*—a cow; *iva*—like; *vatsalā*—affectionate.

TRANSLATION

Devahūti's husband had already left home and accepted the renounced order of life, and then her only son, Kapila, left home. Although she knew all the truths of life and death, and although her heart was cleansed of all dirt, she was very aggrieved at the loss of her son, just as a cow is affected when her calf dies.

PURPORT

A woman whose husband is away from home or has taken the renounced order of life should not be very sorry, because she still has the presence of her husband's representative, her son. It is said in the Vedic scriptures, *ātmaiva putro jāyate:* the husband's body is represented by the son. Strictly speaking, a woman is never widowed if she has a grown son. Devahūti was not very much affected while Kapila Muni was there, but upon His departure she was very afflicted. She grieved not because of her worldly relationship with Kardama Muni but because of her sincere love for the Personality of Godhead.

The example given here is that Devahūti became just like a cow who has lost her calf. A cow bereft of her calf cries day and night. Similarly, Devahūti was aggrieved, and she always cried and requested her friends and relatives, "Please bring my son home so that I may live. Otherwise, I shall die." This intense affection for the Supreme Personality of Godhead, although manifested as affection for one's son, is spiritually beneficial. Attachment for a material son obliges one to remain in material existence, but the same attachment, when transferred to the Supreme Lord, brings one elevation to the spiritual world in the association of the Lord.

Every woman can qualify herself as much as Devahūti and then can also have the Supreme Godhead as her son. If the Supreme Personality of Godhead can appear as the son of Devahūti, He can also appear as the son of any other woman, provided that woman is qualified. If one gets the Supreme Lord as a son, one can have the benefit of bringing up a nice son in this world and at the same time get promotion to the spiritual world to become the face-to-face associate of the Personality of Godhead.

TEXT 22

तमेव ध्यायती देवमपत्यं कपिलं हरिम् ।
बभूवाचिरतो वत्स निःस्पृहा तादृशे गृहे ॥२२॥

tam eva dhyāyatī devam
apatyaṁ kapilaṁ harim
babhūvācirato vatsa
niḥspṛhā tādṛśe gṛhe

tam—upon Him; *eva*—certainly; *dhyāyatī*—meditating; *devam*—divine; *apatyam*—son; *kapilam*—Lord Kapila; *harim*—the Supreme Personality of Godhead; *babhūva*—became; *aciratah*—very soon; *vatsa*—O dear Vidura; *niḥspṛhā*—unattached; *tādṛśe gṛhe*—to such a home.

TRANSLATION

O Vidura, thus always meditating upon her son, the Supreme Personality of Godhead Kapiladeva, she very soon became unattached to her nicely decorated home.

PURPORT

Here is a practical example of how one can elevate oneself in spiritual advancement by Kṛṣṇa consciousness. Kapiladeva is Kṛṣṇa, and He appeared as the son of Devahūti. After Kapiladeva left home, Devahūti was absorbed in thought of Him, and thus she was always Kṛṣṇa conscious. Her constant situation in Kṛṣṇa consciousness enabled her to be detached from hearth and home.

Unless we are able to transfer our attachment to the Supreme Personality of Godhead, there is no possibility of becoming freed from material attachment. The *Śrīmad-Bhāgavatam,* therefore, confirms that it is not possible for one to become liberated by cultivation of empiric philosophical speculation. Simply knowing that one is not matter but spirit soul, or Brahman, does not purify one's intelligence. Even if the impersonalist reaches the highest platform of spiritual realization, he falls down again to material attachment because of not being situated in the transcendental loving service of the Supreme Lord.

The devotees adopt the devotional process, hearing about the Supreme Lord's pastimes and glorifying His activities and thereby always remembering His beautiful eternal form. By rendering service, becoming His friend or His servant and offering Him everything that one possesses, one is able to enter into the kingdom of God. As it is said in *Bhagavad-gītā, tato māṁ tattvato jñātvā:* after discharging pure devotional service, one can understand the Supreme Personality of Godhead in fact, and thus one becomes eligible to enter into His association in one of the spiritual planets.

TEXT 23

ध्यायती भगवद्रूपं यदाह ध्यानगोचरम् ।
सुतः प्रसन्नवदनं समस्तव्यस्तचिन्तया ॥२३॥

dhyāyatī bhagavad-rūpaṁ
yad āha dhyāna-gocaram
sutaḥ prasanna-vadanaṁ
samasta-vyasta-cintayā

dhyāyatī—meditating; *bhagavat-rūpam*—upon the form of the Supreme Personality of Godhead; *yat*—which; *āha*—He instructed; *dhyāna-gocaram*—the object of meditation; *sutaḥ*—her son; *prasanna-vadanam*—with a smiling face; *samasta*—on the whole; *vyasta*—on the parts; *cintayā*—with her mind.

TRANSLATION

Thereafter, having heard with great eagerness and in all detail from her son, Kapiladeva, the eternally smiling Personality of Godhead, Devahūti began to meditate constantly upon the Viṣṇu form of the Supreme Lord.

TEXTS 24-25

भक्तिप्रवाहयोगेन वैराग्येण बलीयसा ।
युक्तानुष्ठानजातेन ज्ञानेन ब्रह्महेतुना ॥२४॥
विशुद्धेन तदात्मानमात्मना विश्वतोमुखम् ।
स्वानुभूत्या तिरोभूतमायागुणविशेषणम् ॥२५॥

bhakti-pravāha-yogena
vairāgyeṇa balīyasā
yuktānuṣṭhāna-jātena
jñānena brahma-hetunā

viśuddhena tadātmānam
ātmanā viśvato-mukham
svānubhūtyā tirobhūta-
māyā-guṇa-viśeṣaṇam

bhakti-pravāha-yogena—by continuous engagement in devotional service; *vairāgyeṇa*—by renunciation; *balīyasā*—very strong; *yukta-anuṣṭhāna*—by proper performance of duties; *jātena*—produced; *jñānena*—by knowledge; *brahma-hetunā*—due to realization of the Absolute Truth; *viśuddhena*—by purification; *tadā*—then; *ātmānam*—Supreme Personality of Godhead; *ātmanā*—with the mind; *viśvataḥ-mukham*—whose face is turned everywhere; *sva-anubhūtyā*—by self-realization; *tiraḥ-bhūta*—disappeared; *māyā-guṇa*—of the modes of material nature; *viśeṣaṇam*—distinctions.

TRANSLATION

She did so with serious engagement in devotional service. Because she was strong in renunciation, she accepted only the necessities of the body. She became situated in knowledge due to realization of the Absolute Truth, her heart became purified, she became fully absorbed in meditation upon the Supreme Personality of Godhead, and all misgivings due to the modes of material nature disappeared.

TEXT 26

ब्रह्मण्यवस्थितमतिर्भगवत्यात्मसंश्रये ।
निवृत्तजीवापत्तित्वात्क्षीणक्लेशाप्तनिर्वृतिः ॥२६॥

brahmaṇy avasthita-matir
bhagavaty ātma-saṁśraye
nivṛtta-jīvāpattitvāt
kṣīṇa-kleśāpta-nirvṛtiḥ

brahmaṇi—in Brahman; *avasthita*—situated; *matiḥ*—her mind; *bhagavati*—in the Supreme Personality of Godhead; *ātma-saṁśraye*—residing in all living entities; *nivṛtta*—freed; *jīva*—of the *jīva* soul; *āpattitvāt*—from the unfortunate condition; *kṣīṇa*—disappeared; *kleśa*—material pangs; *āpta*—attained; *nirvṛtiḥ*—transcendental bliss.

TRANSLATION

Her mind became completely engaged in the Supreme Lord, and she automatically realized the knowledge of the impersonal Brahman. As a Brahman-realized soul, she was freed from the designations of the materialistic concept of life. Thus all material pangs disappeared, and she attained transcendental bliss.

PURPORT

The previous verse states that Devahūti was already conversant with the Absolute Truth. It may be questioned why she was meditating. The explanation is that when one theoretically discusses the Absolute Truth, he becomes situated in the impersonal concept of the Absolute Truth. Similarly, when one seriously discusses the subject matter of the form, qualities, pastimes and entourage of the Supreme Personality of Godhead, he becomes situated in meditation on Him. If one has complete knowledge of the Supreme Lord, then knowledge of the impersonal Brahman is automatically realized. The Absolute Truth is realized by the knower according to three different angles of vision, namely impersonal Brahman, localized Supersoul and ultimately the Supreme Personality of Godhead. If one is situated, therefore, in knowledge of the Supreme Person, this implies that one is already situated in the concept of the Supersoul and impersonal Brahman.

In *Bhagavad-gītā* it is said, *brahma-bhūtaḥ prasannātmā.* This means that unless one is freed from the material entanglement and situated in Brahman, there is no question of entering into the understanding of devotional service or engaging in Kṛṣṇa consciousness. One who is engaged in devotional service to Kṛṣṇa is understood to be already realized in the Brahman concept of life because transcendental knowledge of the Supreme Personality of Godhead includes knowledge of Brahman. This is confirmed in *Bhagavad-gītā. Brahmaṇo hi pratiṣṭhāham:* the concept of the Personality of Godhead does not depend on Brahman. The *Viṣṇu Purāṇa* also confirms that one who has taken shelter of the all-auspicious Supreme Lord is already situated in the understanding of Brahman. In other words, one who is a Vaiṣṇava is already a *brāhmaṇa.*

Another significant point of this verse is that one has to observe the prescribed rules and regulations. As confirmed in *Bhagavad-gītā, yuktāhāra-vihārasya.* When one engages in devotional service in Kṛṣṇa consciousness, he still has to eat, sleep, defend and mate because these are necessities of the body. But he performs such activities in a regulated way. He has to eat *kṛṣṇa-prasāda.* He has to sleep according to regulated principles. The principle is to reduce the duration of sleep and to reduce eating, taking only what is needed to keep the body fit. In short, the goal is spiritual advancement, not sense gratification. Similarly, sex life must be reduced. Sex life is meant only for begetting Kṛṣṇa conscious children. Otherwise, there is no necessity for sex life. Nothing is prohibited, but everything is made *yukta,* regulated, with the higher purpose always in mind. By following all these rules and regulations of living, one becomes purified, and all misconceptions due to ignorance become nil. It is specifically mentioned here that the causes of material entanglement are completely vanquished.

The Sanskrit statement *anartha-nivṛtti* indicates that this body is unwanted. We are spirit soul, and there was never any need of this material body. But because we wanted to enjoy the material body, we have this body, through the material energy, under the direction of the Supreme Personality of Godhead. As soon as we are reestablished in our original position of servitorship to the Supreme Lord, we begin to forget the necessities of the body, and at last we forget the body.

Sometimes in a dream we get a particular type of body with which to work in the dream. I may dream that I am flying in the sky or that I have gone into the forest or some unknown place. But as soon as I am awake I forget all these bodies. Similarly, when one is Kṛṣṇa conscious, fully devoted, he forgets all his changes of body. We are always changing bodies, beginning at birth from the womb of our mother. But when we are awakened to Kṛṣṇa consciousness, we forget all these bodies. The bodily necessities become secondary, for the primary necessity is the engagement of the soul in real, spiritual life. The activities of devotional service in full Kṛṣṇa consciousness are the cause of our being situated in transcendence. The words *bhagavaty ātma-saṁśraye* denote the Personality of Godhead as the Supreme Soul, or the soul of everyone. In *Bhagavad-gītā* Kṛṣṇa says, *bījaṁ māṁ sarva-bhūtānām:* "I am the seed of all entities." By taking shelter of the Supreme Being by the process of devotional service, one becomes fully situated in the concept of the Personality of Godhead. As described by Kapila, *mad-guṇa-śruti-mātreṇa:* one who is fully Kṛṣṇa conscious, situated in the Personality of Godhead, is immediately saturated with love of God as soon as he hears about the transcendental qualities of the Lord.

Devahūti was fully instructed by her son, Kapiladeva, on how to concentrate her mind on the Viṣṇu form in full detail. Following the instructions of her son in the matter of devotional service, she contemplated the form of the Lord within herself with great devotional love. That is the perfection of Brahman realization or the mystic *yoga* system or devotional service. At the ultimate issue, when one is fully absorbed in thought of the Supreme Lord and meditates on Him constantly, that is the highest perfection. *Bhagavad-gītā* confirms that one who is always absorbed in such a way is to be considered the topmost *yogī*.

The real purpose of all processes of transcendental realization—*jñāna-yoga, dhyāna-yoga* or *bhakti-yoga*—is to arrive at the point of devotional service. If one endeavors simply to achieve knowledge of the Absolute Truth or the Supersoul but has no devotional service, he labors without gaining the real result. This is compared to beating the husks of wheat after the grains have already been removed. Unless one understands the Supreme Personality of Godhead to be the ultimate goal, it is valueless simply to speculate or perform mystic *yoga* practice. In the *aṣṭāṅga-yoga* system, the seventh stage of perfection is *dhyāna*. This *dhyāna* is the third stage in devotional service. There are nine stages of devotional service. The first is hearing, and then comes chanting and then contemplating. By executing devotional service, therefore, one automatically becomes an expert *jñānī* and an expert *yogī*. In other words, *jñāna* and *yoga* are different preliminary stages of devotional service.

Devahūti was expert in accepting the real substance; she contemplated the form of Viṣṇu in detail as advised by her smiling son, Kapiladeva. At the same time, she was thinking of Kapiladeva, who is the Supreme Personality of Godhead, and therefore she completely perfected her austerities, penances and transcendental realization.

TEXT 27

नित्यारूढसमाधित्वात्परावृत्तगुणभ्रमा ।
न सस्मार तदात्मानं स्वप्ने दृष्टमिवोत्थितः ॥२७॥

nityārūḍha-samādhitvāt
parāvṛtta-guṇa-bhramā
na sasmāra tadātmānaṁ
svapne dṛṣṭam ivotthitaḥ

nitya—eternal; *ārūḍha*—situated in; *samādhitvāt*—from trance; *parāvṛtta*—freed from; *guṇa*—of the modes of material nature; *bhramā*—illusion; *na sasmāra*—she did not remember; *tadā*—then; *ātmānam*—her material body; *svapne*—in a dream; *dṛṣṭam*—seen; *iva*—just as; *utthitaḥ*—one who has arisen.

TRANSLATION

Situated in eternal trance and freed from illusion impelled by the modes of material nature, she forgot her material body, just as one forgets his different bodies in a dream.

PURPORT

A great Vaiṣṇava said that he who has no remembrance of his body is not bound to material existence. As long as we are conscious of our bodily existence, it is to be understood that we are living conditionally, under the three modes of material nature. When one forgets his bodily existence, his conditional, material life is over. This forgetfulness is actually possible when we engage our senses in the transcendental loving service of the Lord. In the conditional state, one engages his senses as a member of a family or as a member of a society or country. But when one forgets all such membership in material circumstances and realizes that he is an eternal servant of the Supreme Lord, that is actual forgetfulness of material existence.

This forgetfulness actually occurs when one renders service unto the Lord. A devotee no longer works with the body for sense gratification with family, society, country, humanity and so on. He simply works for the Supreme Personality of Godhead, Kṛṣṇa. That is perfect Kṛṣṇa consciousness.

A devotee always merges in transcendental happiness, and therefore he has no experience of material distresses. This transcendental happiness is called eternal bliss. According to the opinion of devotees, constant remembrance of the Supreme Lord is called *samādhi,* or trance. If one is constantly in trance, there is no possibility of his being attacked or even touched by the modes of material nature. As soon as one is freed from the contamination of the three material modes, he no longer has to take birth to transmigrate from one form to another in this material world.

TEXT 28

तद्देहः परतःपोषोऽप्यकृशश्चाध्यसम्भवात् ।
बभौ मलैरवच्छन्नः सधूम इव पावकः ॥२८॥

tad-dehaḥ parataḥ poṣo
'py akṛśaś cādhy-asambhavāt
babhau malair avacchannaḥ
sadhūma iva pāvakaḥ

tat-dehaḥ—her body; *parataḥ*—by others (the damsels created by Kardama); *poṣaḥ*—maintained; *api*—although; *akṛśaḥ*—not thin; *ca*—and; *ādhi*—anxiety; *asambhavāt*—from not occurring; *babhau*—shone; *malaiḥ*—by dust; *avacchannaḥ*—covered; *sa-dhūmaḥ*—surrounded with smoke; *iva*—like; *pāvakaḥ*—a fire.

TRANSLATION

Her body was being taken care of by the spiritual damsels created by her husband, Kardama, and since she had no mental anxiety at that time, her body did not become thin. She appeared just like a fire surrounded by smoke.

PURPORT

Because she was always in trance in transcendental bliss, the thought of the Personality of Godhead was always carefully fixed in her mind. She did not become thin, for she was taken care of by the celestial maidservants created by her husband. It is said, according to the Āyur-vedic medical science, that if one is free from anxieties he generally becomes fat. Devahūti, being situated in Kṛṣṇa consciousness, had no mental anxieties, and therefore her body did not become thin. It is customary in the renounced order of life that one should not take any service from a servant or maid, but Devahūti was being served by the celestial maidservants. This may appear to be against the spiritual concept of life, but just as fire is still beautiful even when surrounded by smoke, she looked completely pure although it seemed that she was living in a luxurious way.

TEXT 29

स्वाङ्गं तपोयोगमयं मुक्तकेशं गताम्बरम् ।
दैवगुप्तं न बुबुधे वासुदेवप्रविष्टधीः ॥२९॥

svāṅgaṁ tapo-yogamayaṁ
mukta-keśaṁ gatāmbaram
daiva-guptaṁ na bubudhe
vāsudeva-praviṣṭa-dhīḥ

sva-aṅgam—her body; *tapaḥ*—austerity; *yoga*—*yoga* practice; *mayam*—fully engaged in; *mukta*—loosened; *keśam*—her hair; *gata*—disarrayed; *ambaram*—her garments; *daiva*—by the Lord; *guptam*—protected; *na*—not; *bubudhe*—she was aware of; *vāsudeva*—in the Supreme Personality of Godhead; *praviṣṭa*—absorbed; *dhīḥ*—her thoughts.

TRANSLATION

Because she was always absorbed in the thought of the Supreme Personality of Godhead, she was not aware that her hair was sometimes loosened or her garments were disarrayed.

PURPORT

In this verse the word *daiva-guptam*, "protected by the Supreme Personality of Godhead," is very significant. Once one surrenders unto the service of the Supreme Lord, the Lord takes charge of the maintenance of the devotee's body, and there is no need of anxiety for its protection. It is said in the Second Chapter, Second Canto, of *Śrīmad-Bhāgavatam* that a fully surrendered soul has no anxiety about the maintenance of his body. The Supreme Lord takes care of the maintenance of innumerable species of bodies; therefore, one who fully engages in His service will not go unprotected by the Supreme Lord. Devahūti was naturally unmindful of the protection of her body, which was being taken care of by the Supreme Person.

TEXT 30

एवं सा कपिलोक्तेन मार्गेणाचिरतः परम् ।
आत्मानं ब्रह्मनिर्वाणं भगवन्तमवाप ह ॥३०॥

evaṁ sā kapiloktena
mārgeṇāciratah param
ātmānaṁ brahma-nirvāṇaṁ
bhagavantam avāpa ha

evam—thus; *sā*—she (Devahūti); *kapila*—by Kapila; *uktena*—instructed; *mārgeṇa*—by the path; *aciratah*—soon; *param*—supreme; *ātmānam*—Supersoul; *brahma*—Brahman; *nirvāṇam*—cessation of materialistic existence; *bhagavantam*—the Supreme Personality of Godhead; *avāpa*—she achieved; *ha*—certainly.

TRANSLATION

My dear Vidura, by following the principles instructed by Kapila, Devahūti soon became liberated from material bondage, and she achieved the Supreme Personality of Godhead, as Supersoul, without difficulty.

PURPORT

Three words have been used in this connection to describe the achievement of Devahūti: *ātmānam, brahma-nirvāṇam* and *bhagavantam.* These refer to the gradual process of discovery of the Absolute Truth, mentioned herein as the *bhagavantam.* The Supreme Personality of Godhead resides in various Vaikuṇṭha planets. *Nirvāṇa* means to extinguish the pangs of material existence. When one is able to enter into the spiritual kingdom or into spiritual realization, one is automatically freed from material pangs. That is called *brahma-nirvāṇa.* According to Vedic scripture, *nirvāṇa* means cessation of the materialistic way of life. *Ātmānam* means realization of the Supersoul within the heart. Ultimately, the highest perfection is realization of the Supreme Personality of Godhead. It is to be understood that Devahūti entered the planet which is called Kapila Vaikuṇṭha. There are innumerable Vaikuṇṭha planets predominated by the expansions of Viṣṇu. All the Vaikuṇṭha planets are known by a particular name of Viṣṇu. As we understand from *Brahma-saṁhitā, advaitam acyutam anādim ananta-rūpam. Ananta* means "innumerable." The Lord has innumerable expansions of His transcendental form, and according to the different positions of the symbolical representations in His four hands, He is known as Nārāyaṇa, Pradyumna, Aniruddha, Vāsudeva, etc. There is also a Vaikuṇṭha planet known as Kapila Vaikuṇṭha, to which

Devahūti was promoted to meet Kapila and reside there eternally, enjoying the company of her transcendental son.

TEXT 31

तद्वीरासीत्पुण्यतमं क्षेत्रं त्रैलोक्यविश्रुतम् ।
नाम्ना सिद्धपदं यत्र सा संसिद्धिमुपेयुषी ॥३१॥

tad vīrāsīt puṇyatamaṁ
kṣetraṁ trailokya-viśrutam
nāmnā siddha-padaṁ yatra
sā saṁsiddhim upeyuṣī

tat—that; *vīra*—O brave Vidura; *āsīt*—was; *puṇya-tamam*—most sacred; *kṣetram*—place; *trai-lokya*—in the three worlds; *viśrutam*—known; *nāmnā*—by the name; *siddha-padam*—Siddhapada; *yatra*—where; *sā*—she (Devahūti); *saṁsiddhim*—perfection; *upeyuṣī*—achieved.

TRANSLATION

The place where Devahūti achieved her perfection, my dear Vidura, is understood to be a most sacred spot. It is known all over the three worlds as Siddhapada.

TEXT 32

तस्यास्तद्योगविधुतमार्त्यं मर्त्यमभूत्सरित् ।
स्रोतसां प्रवरा सौम्य सिद्धिदा सिद्धसेविता ॥३२॥

tasyās tad yoga-vidhuta-
mārtyaṁ martyam abhūt sarit
srotasāṁ pravarā saumya
siddhidā siddha-sevitā

tasyāḥ—of Devahūti; *tat*—that; *yoga*—by *yoga* practice; *vidhuta*—relinquished; *mārtyam*—material elements; *martyam*—her mortal body; *abhūt*—became; *sarit*—a river; *srotasām*—of all rivers; *pravarā*—the foremost; *saumya*—O gentle Vidura; *siddhi-dā*—conferring perfection; *siddha*—by persons desiring perfection; *sevitā*—resorted to.

TRANSLATION

Dear Vidura, the material elements of her body have melted into water and are now a flowing river, which is the most sacred of all rivers. Anyone who

bathes in that river also attains perfection, and therefore all persons who desire perfection go bathe there.

TEXT 33

कपिलोऽपि महायोगी भगवान् पितुराश्रमात् ।
मातरं समनुज्ञाप्य प्रागुदीचीं दिशं ययौ ॥३३॥

kapilo 'pi mahā-yogī
bhagavān pitur āśramāt
mātaraṁ samanujñāpya
prāg-udīcīṁ diśaṁ yayau

kapilaḥ—Lord Kapila; *api*—surely; *mahā-yogī*—the great sage; *bhagavān*—the Supreme Personality of Godhead; *pituḥ*—of His father; *āśramāt*—from the hermitage; *mātaram*—from His mother; *samanujñāpya*—having asked permission; *prāk-udīcīm*—northeast; *diśam*—direction; *yayau*—He went.

TRANSLATION

My dear Vidura, the great sage Kapila, the Personality of Godhead, left His father's hermitage with the permission of His mother and went towards the northeast.

TEXT 34

सिद्धचारणगन्धर्वैर्मुनिभिश्चाप्सरोगणैः ।
स्तूयमानः समुद्रेण दत्तार्हणनिकेतनः ॥३४॥

siddha-cāraṇa-gandharvair
munibhiś cāpsaro-gaṇaiḥ
stūyamānaḥ samudreṇa
dattārhaṇa-niketanaḥ

siddha—by the Siddhas; *cāraṇa*—by the Cāraṇas; *gandharvaiḥ*—by the Gandharvas; *munibhiḥ*—by the *munis; ca*—and; *apsaraḥ-gaṇaiḥ*—by the Apsarās (damsels of the heavenly planets); *stūyamānaḥ*—being extolled; *samudreṇa*—by the ocean; *datta*—given; *arhaṇa*—oblations; *niketanaḥ*—place of residence.

TRANSLATION

While He was passing in the northern direction, all the celestial denizens known as Cāraṇas and Gandharvas, as well as the munis and the damsels of

the heavenly planets, prayed and offered Him all respects. The ocean offered Him oblations and a place of residence.

PURPORT

It is understood that Kapila Muni first went towards the Himalayas and traced the course of the River Ganges, and He again came to the delta of the Ganges at the sea now known as the Bay of Bengal. The ocean gave Him residence at a place still known as Gaṅgā-sāgara, where the River Ganges meets the sea. That place is called Gaṅgā-sāgara-tīrtha, and even today people gather there to offer respects to Kapiladeva, the original author of the Sāṅkhya system of philosophy. Unfortunately, this Sāṅkhya system has been misrepresented by an imposter who is also named Kapila, but that other system of philosophy does not tally with anything described in the Sāṅkhya of Kapila in the *Śrīmad-Bhāgavatam.*

TEXT 35

आस्ते योगं समास्थाय सांख्याचार्यैरभिष्टुतः ।
त्रयाणामपि लोकानामुपशान्त्यै समाहितः ॥३५॥

āste yogaṁ samāsthāya
sāṅkhyācāryair abhiṣṭutaḥ
trayāṇām api lokānām
upaśāntyai samāhitaḥ

āste—He remains; *yogam*—yoga; *samāsthāya*—having practiced; *sāṅkhya*—of the Sāṅkhya philosophy; *ācāryaiḥ*—by the great teachers; *abhiṣṭutaḥ*—worshiped; *trayāṇām*—three; *api*—certainly; *lokānām*—of the worlds; *upaśāntyai*—for the deliverance; *samāhitaḥ*—fixed in trance.

TRANSLATION

Even now Kapila Muni is staying there in trance for the deliverance of the conditioned souls in the three worlds, and all the ācāryas, or great teachers, of the system of Sāṅkhya philosophy are worshiping Him.

TEXT 36

एतन्निगदितं तात यत्पृष्टोऽहं तवानघ ।
कपिलस्य च संवादो देवहूत्याश्च पावनः ॥३६॥

etan nigaditaṁ tāta
yat pṛṣṭo 'haṁ tavānagha
kapilasya ca saṁvādo
devahūtyāś ca pāvanaḥ

etat—this; *nigaditam*—spoken; *tāta*—O dear Vidura; *yat*—which; *pṛṣṭaḥ*—was asked; *aham*—I; *tava*—by you; *anagha*—O sinless Vidura; *kapilasya*—of Kapila; *ca*—and; *saṁvādaḥ*—conversation; *devahūtyāḥ*—of Devahūti; *ca*—and; *pāvanaḥ*—pure.

TRANSLATION

My dear son, since you have inquired from me, I have answered. O sinless one, the descriptions of Kapiladeva and His mother and their activities are the purest of all pure discourses.

TEXT 37

य इदमनुशृणोति योऽभिधत्ते
कपिलमुनेर्मतमात्मयोगगुह्यम् ।
भगवति कृतधीः सुपर्णकेता-
वुपलभते भगवत्पदारविन्दम् ॥३७॥

ya idam anuśṛṇoti yo 'bhidhatte
kapila-muner matam ātma-yoga-guhyam
bhagavati kṛta-dhīḥ suparṇa-ketāv
upalabhate bhagavat-padāravindam

yaḥ—whoever; *idam*—this; *anuśṛṇoti*—hears; *yaḥ*—whoever; *abhidhatte*—expounds; *kapila-muneḥ*—of the sage Kapila; *matam*—instructions; *ātma-yoga*—based on meditation on the Lord; *guhyam*—confidential; *bhagavati*—on the Supreme Personality of Godhead; *kṛta-dhīḥ*—having fixed his mind; *suparṇa-ketau*—who has a banner of Garuḍa; *upalabhate*—achieves; *bhagavat*—of the Supreme Lord; *pada-aravindam*—the lotus feet.

TRANSLATION

The description of the dealings of Kapiladeva and His mother is very confidential, and anyone who hears or reads this narration becomes a devotee of the Supreme Personality of Godhead, who is carried by Garuḍa, and he thereafter enters into the abode of the Supreme Lord to engage in the transcendental loving service of the Lord.

PURPORT

The narration of Kapiladeva and His mother, Devahūti, is so perfect and transcendental that even if one only hears or reads this description, he achieves the highest perfectional goal of life, for he engages in the loving service of the lotus feet of the Supreme Personality of Godhead. There is no doubt that Devahūti, who had the Supreme Lord as her son and who followed the instructions of Kapiladeva so nicely, attained the highest perfection of human life.

Thus end the Bhaktivedanta purports of the Third Canto, Thirty-third Chapter, of the Śrīmad-Bhāgavatam, *entitled "Activities of Kapila."*

END OF THE THIRD CANTO

Appendixes

The Author

His Divine Grace A. C. Bhaktivedanta Swami Prabhupāda appeared in this world in 1896 in Calcutta, India. He first met his spiritual master, Śrīla Bhaktisiddhānta Sarasvatī Gosvāmī, in Calcutta in 1922. Bhaktisiddhānta Sarasvatī, a prominent religious scholar and the founder of sixty-four Gauḍīya Maṭhas (Vedic institutes), liked this educated young man and convinced him to dedicate his life to teaching Vedic knowledge. Śrīla Prabhupāda became his student, and eleven years later (1933) at Allahabad he became his formally initiated disciple.

At their first meeting, in 1922, Śrīla Bhaktisiddhānta Sarasvatī Ṭhākura requested Śrīla Prabhupāda to broadcast Vedic knowledge through the English language. In the years that followed, Śrīla Prabhupāda wrote a commentary on the *Bhagavad-gītā*, assisted the Gauḍīya Maṭha in its work and, in 1944, without assistance, started an English fortnightly magazine, edited it, typed the manuscripts and checked the galley proofs. He even distributed the individual copies freely and struggled to maintain the publication. Once begun, the magazine never stopped; it is now being continued by his disciples in the West.

Recognizing Śrīla Prabhupāda's philosophical learning and devotion, the Gauḍīya Vaiṣṇava Society honored him in 1947 with the title "Bhaktivedanta." In 1950, at the age of fifty-four, Śrīla Prabhupāda retired from married life, and four years later he adopted the *vanaprastha* (retired) order to devote more time to his studies and writing. Śrīla Prabhupāda traveled to the holy city of Vṛndāvana, where he lived in very humble circumstances in the historic medieval temple of Rādhā-Dāmodara. There he engaged for several years in deep study and writing. He accepted the renounced order of life (*sannyāsa*) in 1959. At Rādhā-Dāmodara, Śrīla Prabhupāda began work on his life's masterpiece: a multivolume translation and commentary on the eighteen thousand verse *Śrīmad-Bhāgavatam* (*Bhāgavata Purāṇa*). He also wrote *Easy Journey to Other Planets*.

After publishing three volumes of the *Bhāgavatam*, Śrīla Prabhupāda came to the United States, in 1965, to fulfill the mission of his spiritual master. Since that time, His Divine Grace has written over forty volumes of authoritative translations, commentaries and summary studies of the philosophical and religious classics of India.

In 1965, when he first arrived by freighter in New York City, Śrīla Prabhupāda was practically penniless. It was after almost a year of great difficulty that he establish the

International Society for Krishna Consciousness in July of 1966. Under his careful guidance, the Society has grown within a decade to a worldwide confederation of almost one hundred *āśramas*, schools, temples, institutes and farm communities.

In 1968, Śrīla Prabhupāda created New Vṛndāvana, an experimental Vedic community in the hills of West Virginia. Inspired by the success of New Vṛndāvana, now a thriving farm community of more than one thousand acres, his students have since founded several similar communities in the United States and abroad.

In 1972, His Divine Grace introduced the Vedic system of primary and secondary education in the West by founding the *Gurukula* school in Dallas, Texas. The school began with 3 children in 1972, and by the beginning of 1975 the enrollment had grown to 150.

Śrīla Prabhupāda also inspired the construction of a large international center at Śrīdhāma Māyāpur in West Bengal, India, which is also the site for a planned institute of Vedic Studies. A similar project is the magnificent Kṛṣṇa-Balarāma Temple and International Guest House in Vṛndāvana, India. These are centers where Westerners can live to gain firsthand experience of Vedic culture.

Śrīla Prabhupāda's most significant contribution, however, is his books. Highly respected by the academic community for their authoritiveness, depth and clarity, they are used as standard textbooks in numerous college courses. His writings have been translated into eleven languages. The Bhaktivedanta Book Trust, established in 1972 exclusively to publish the works of His Divine Grace, has thus become the world's largest publisher of books in the field of Indian religion and philosophy. Its latest project is the publishing of Śrīla Prabhupāda's most recent work: a seventeen-volume translation and commentary—completed by Śrīla Prabhupāda in only eighteen months—on the Bengali religious classic *Śrī Caitanya-caritāmṛta.*

In the past ten years, in spite of his advanced age, Śrīla Prabhupāda has circled the globe twelve times on lecture tours that have taken him to six continents. In spite of such a vigorous schedule, Śrīla Prabhupāda continues to write prolifically. His writings constitute a veritable library of Vedic philosophy, religion, literature and culture.

References

The purports of *Śrīmad-Bhāgavatam* are all confirmed by standard Vedic authorities. The following authentic scriptures are specifically cited in this volume:

Amara-kośa, 144

Bhagavad-gītā, 3, 14-15, 16-17, 41, 42, 44, 48, 56, 58, 62, 66, 74, 77, 110, 115, 126, 131, 135, 146, 147, 152, 159, 181, 183, 184, 189, 193, 195, 198, 199, 209, 211, 213, 217, 220, 222, 223, 224, 236, 238, 240, 245, 246, 250, 253, 256, 258, 260, 264, 267, 270, 276, 287, 290, 292, 311, 313, 314, 324, 326, 328, 334, 338, 340, 342, 344, 345, 350, 361, 371, 384, 385, 429, 435, 460, 468, 496, 500, 503, 504, 509, 538, 543, 544, 545, 586, 591, 594, 604, 622, 644, 649, 650, 724, 747, 772, 780, 823, 945, 973-974, 975, 984, 991, 998, 1016, 1018, 1023, 1024, 1078, 1093, 1095, 1114, 1115, 1117, 1126, 1138, 1140, 1178-1179, 1196, 1200, 1201, 1202, 1205, 1223, 1226, 1250, 1273, 1279, 1285, 1302, 1310, 1318, 1333, 1334, 1335, 1340, 1345, 1349, 1352, 1353, 1383, 1385, 1388

Bhakti-rasāmṛta-sindhu, 148, 316, 1307, 1375

Brahma-saṁhitā, 24-25, 44, 82, 96, 107, 109, 151, 184, 216, 289, 313, 316, 326, 328, 406, 422-423, 426, 572, 597, 811, 903, 1026, 1027, 1028, 1073, 1077-1078, 1104, 1146, 1161, 1230, 1283, 1323, 1343, 1393

Bṛhan-nāradīya Purāṇa, 487

Caitanya-caritāmṛta, 18, 52-53, 579, 1152, 1225

Chāndogya Upaniṣad, 1041

Gopāla-tāpanī Upaniṣad, 316, 343

Hari-bhakti-vilāsa, 1369

Īśopaniṣad, 337, 1111

Kāśī-khaṇḍa, 289-290

Kaṭha Upaniṣad, 57, 1223

Nārada-pañcarātra, 981

Patañjali-yoga-sūtra, 1055-1056

Ṛg Veda, 620

Skanda Purāṇa, 108

Śrīmad-Bhāgavatam, 46, 131, 134, 135, 170, 178, 197, 265, 336, 347-348, 384, 431, 436, 447, 453, 560, 577, 578, 613, 649, 761, 957, 987, 990, 1016, 1042, 1060, 1089, 1092, 1115, 1117, 1294, 1375

Śvetāśvatara Upaniṣad, 683, 947, 1025

Varāha Purāṇa, 1177

Vedānta-sūtra, 66, 275, 724, 1027, 1058, 1284, 1301, 1343

Viṣṇu-dharma, 492

Viṣṇu Purāṇa, 477-478, 749, 1340

Glossary of Personal Names

A

Advaita Prabhu—an incarnation of Lord Viṣṇu who is a principal associate of another incarnation, Lord Śrī Caitanya Mahāprabhu.

Agni—the presiding demigod of fire.

Aja—a name of the Supreme Personality of Godhead, who is unborn.

Ambarīṣa Mahārāja—a great devotee king who perfectly executed all nine devotional practices (hearing, chanting, etc.).

Ananta—the thousand-headed serpent incarnation of the Lord, who sustains the planets on His hoods.

Aniruddha—one of the four original expansions of Lord Kṛṣṇa in the spiritual world.

Arjuna—one of the five Pāṇḍava brothers; Kṛṣṇa became his chariot driver and spoke to him the *Bhagavad-gītā.*

B

Bali Mahārāja—a king who became a great devotee by surrendering everything to Vāmanadeva, the Lord's dwarf-*brāhmaṇa* incarnation.

Bhaktisiddhānta Sarasvatī Ṭhākura—the spiritual master of His Divine Grace A. C. Bhaktivedanta Swami Prabhupāda.

Bhaktivinoda Ṭhākura—the spiritual master of Śrīla Bhaktisiddhānta Sarasvatī Ṭhākura.

Bharata—the son of Mahārāja Duṣyanta who renounced his kingdom and family at an early age. He became very advanced in spiritual practice, but later became attached to a pet deer and had to take two more births before achieving liberation.

Bilvamaṅgala Ṭhākura—a great devotee who wrote books describing the confidential pastimes of Lord Kṛṣṇa.

Brahmā—the first created living being and secondary creator of the material universe.

Bṛhaspati—the spiritual master of King Indra and chief priest of the heavenly planets.

C

Caitanya Mahāprabhu—the incarnation of the Lord who descended to teach love of God through the *saṅkīrtana* movement.

Cāṇakya Paṇḍita—the *brāhmaṇa* advisor of King Candragupta who was responsible for checking Alexander the Great's invasion of India.

Candra—the presiding demigod of the moon.

D

Devahūti—the mother of the Lord's incarnation Kapila.

Devakī—the mother of Lord Kṛṣṇa.

Dhṛtarāṣṭra—the uncle of the Pāṇḍavas whose attempt to usurp their kingdom for the sake of his own sons resulted in the Kurukṣetra war.

Dhruva Mahārāja—a great devotee who at the age of five performed severe austerities and realized the Supreme Personality of Godhead.

Diti—the wife of Kaśyapa Muni and mother of the demons Hiraṇyākṣa and Hiraṇyakaśipu.

Durgā—the personified material energy and wife of Lord Śiva.

Durvāsā Muni—a powerful mystic *yogī*, famous for his fearful curses.

Duryodhana—the eldest son of Dhṛtarāṣṭra and chief rival of the Pāṇḍavas.

Dvaipāyana—*See:* Vyāsadeva

Dvārakādhīśa—a name of the Supreme Personality of Godhead, the Lord of the city Dvārakā.

G

Gandhārī—the faithful wife of King Dhṛtarāṣṭra and mother of one hundred sons.

Gaṇeśa—the demigod in charge of material opulence and freedom from misfortune.

Garbhodakaśāyī Viṣṇu—the expansion of the Lord who enters into each universe.

Garuḍa—the great eagle who is the eternal carrier of Lord Viṣṇu.

Gauracandra—another name for Lord Śrī Caitanya Mahāprabhu.

Govinda—a name of the Supreme Personality of Godhead, who gives pleasure to the land, the cows and the senses.

H

Hanumān—the great monkey servitor of Lord Rāmacandra.

Harā— *See:* Rādhārāṇī

Hari—a name of the Supreme Personality of Godhead, who removes all obstacles to spiritual progress.

Haridāsa Ṭhākura—a great devotee and associate of Lord Śrī Caitanya Mahāprabhu who chanted three hundred thousand names of God a day.

Haryakṣa—*See:* Hiraṇyākṣa

Hiraṇyakaśipu—a demoniac king killed by the Lord's incarnation Nṛsiṁhadeva.

Hiraṇyākṣa—the demoniac son of Kaśyapa who was killed by Lord Varāha.

Hṛṣīkeśa—a name of the Supreme Personality of Godhead, the supreme master of everyone's senses.

I

Indra—the chief of the administrative demigods and king of the heavenly planets.

J

Jaḍa Bharata—Bharata Mahārāja in his final birth.

Jagāi and Mādhāi—two great debauchees whom Lord Nityānanda converted into Vaiṣṇavas.

Janaka Mahārāja—the father of Sītā-devī, consort of Lord Rāmacandra.

Jaya and Vijaya—two doorkeepers of Vaikuṇṭha who were cursed on account of offending the four Kumāra Ṛṣis, and who thus both had to take birth three times in the material world as great demons.

Jīva Gosvāmī—one of the six Vaiṣṇava spiritual masters who directly followed Lord Śrī Caitanya Mahāprabhu and systematically presented His teachings.

K

Kālī—*See:* Durgā

Kaṁsa—a demoniac king of the Bhoja dynasty and maternal uncle of Kṛṣṇa.

Kapila—the incarnation of the Lord who expounded *sāṅkhya-yoga,* the analysis of matter and spirit, as a means of cultivating devotional service to the Lord.

Kāraṇodakaśāyī Viṣṇu—the expansion of the Lord from whom all material universes emanate.

Kardama Muni—the father of Lord Kapila.

Kaśyapa Muni—a great saintly person who was the father of many demigods, including Lord Vāmanadeva, the Lord's dwarf-*brāhmaṇa* incarnation.

Keśī—a demon who attacked the inhabitants of Vṛndāvana in the form of a wild horse, but was killed by Lord Kṛṣṇa.

Kṛṣṇa—the Supreme Personality of Godhead appearing in His original, two-armed form.

Kṛṣṇadāsa Kavirāja—the great Vaiṣṇava spiritual master who recorded the biography and teachings of Lord Śrī Caitanya Mahāprabhu in the *Caitanya-caritāmṛta.*

Kṣīrodakaśāyī Viṣṇu—the expansion of the Lord who enters the heart of every created being as the Supersoul.

Kumāras—four learned ascetic sons of Lord Brahmā appearing eternally as children.

L

Lakṣmī—the goddess of fortune and eternal consort of the Supreme Personality of Godhead Nārāyaṇa.

M

Madana—Cupid, the demigod who incites lusty desires in the living beings.

Madana-mohana—a name of the Supreme Personality of Godhead, the enchanter of Cupid.

Mādhāi— *See:* Jagāi and Mādhāi

Madhusūdana—a name of the Supreme Personality of Godhead, the killer of the demon Madhu.

Mahā-lakṣmī—*See:* Lakṣmī

Mahā-Viṣṇu—*See:* Kāraṇodakaśāyī Viṣṇu

Maheśvara—*See:* Śiva

Maitreya Muni—the great sage who spoke *Śrīmad-Bhāgavatam* to Vidura.

Makara-dhvaja—a name of the demigod Cupid.

Manu—an original father and law-giver of the human race. There are fourteen Manus appearing in one day of Brahmā, namely (1) Svāyambhuva, (2) Svārociṣa, (3) Uttama, (4) Tāmasa, (5) Raivata, (6) Cākṣuṣa, (7) Vaivasvata, (8) Sāvarṇi, (9) Dakṣa-sāvarṇi, (10) Brahma-sāvarṇi, (11) Dharma-sāvarṇi, (12) Rudra-sāvarṇi, (13) Deva-sāvarṇi and (14) Indra-sāvarṇi.

Manu (Svāyambhuva)—the forefather of the human race and grandfather of Dhruva Mahārāja.

Marīci—one of the seven great sages who were born directly from Lord Brahmā.

Menakā—the famous society-girl of the heavenly planets who seduced the sage Viśvāmitra.

Mohinī—the Lord's incarnation as the most beautiful woman.

Mṛtyu—death personified.

Mukunda—a name of the Supreme Personality of Godhead, the giver of liberation.

N

Nanda Mahārāja—the King of Vraja and foster father of Lord Kṛṣṇa.

Nārada Muni—a pure devotee of the Lord who travels throughout the universes in his eternal body, glorifying devotional service. He is the spiritual master of Vyāsadeva and of many other great devotees.

Nārāyaṇa—a name of the Supreme Personality of Godhead, who is the source and goal of all living beings.

Narottama dāsa Thākura—a Vaiṣṇava spiritual master in the disciplic succession from Lord Śrī Caitanya Mahāprabhu; disciple of Kṛṣṇadāsa Kavirāja Gosvāmī and spiritual master of Viśvanātha Cakravartī Thākura.

Nityānanda—the incarnation of Lord Baladeva who is the principal associate of Lord Śrī Caitanya Mahāprabhu.

Nṛsiṁha—the incarnation of the Lord as half-man and half-lion who killed the demon Hiraṇyakaśipu.

P

Pāṇḍavas—Yudhiṣṭhira, Bhīma, Arjuna, Nakula and Sahadeva: the five warrior-brothers and intimate friends of Lord Kṛṣṇa, who were given rulership of the world by Him after their victory in the Battle of Kurukṣetra.

Parīkṣit Mahārāja—the emperor of the world who heard *Śrīmad-Bhāgavatam* from Śukadeva Gosvāmī and thus attained perfection.

Patañjali—the author of the original *yoga* system.

Prabodhānanda Sarasvatī—a great Vaiṣṇava poet and devotee of Lord Śri Caitanya Mahāprabhu.

Pradyumna—one of the four original expansions of Lord Kṛṣṇa in the spiritual world.

Prahlāda Mahārāja—a devotee persecuted by his demoniac father but protected and saved by the Lord.

Pūtanā—a witch who was sent by Kaṁsa to appear in the form of a beautiful woman to kill baby Kṛṣṇa but who was killed by Lord Kṛṣṇa and granted liberation.

R

Rādhārāṇī—the eternal consort and spiritual potency of Lord Kṛṣṇa.

Rādhā—the eternal consort and spiritual potency of Lord Kṛṣṇa.

Rahūgaṇa Mahārāja—the king who received spiritual instruction from Jaḍa Bharata.

Ramā—*See:* Lakṣmī

Rāmacandra—the incarnation of Lord Kṛṣṇa as the perfect king.

Rāvaṇa—a demoniac ruler who was killed by Lord Rāmacandra.

Romaharṣaṇa—the father of Sūta Gosvāmī. He was originally the speaker at the Naimiṣāraṇya assembly, but was killed by Lord Balarāma on account of his disrespect to the Lord.

Rudra—*See:* Śiva

Rukmiṇī—Lord Kṛṣṇa's principal queen in Dvārakā.

Rūpa Gosvāmī—the chief of the six Vaiṣṇava spiritual masters who directly followed Lord Śrī Caitanya Mahāprabhu and systematically presented His teachings.

S

Sanātana Gosvāmī—one of the six Vaiṣṇava spiritual masters who directly followed Lord Śrī Caitanya Mahāprabhu and systematically presented His teachings.

Sanat-kumāra—one of the four Kumāras. *See also:* Kumāras

Śaṅkarācārya—the incarnation of Lord Śiva who, ordered by the Supreme Lord, propagated the impersonal Māyāvāda philosophy, which maintains that there is no distinction between the Lord and the living entity.

Saṅkarṣaṇa—one of the four original expansions of Lord Kṛṣṇa in the spiritual world.

Śatarūpā—the wife of Svāyambhuva Manu and mother of Devahūti.

Saubhari Muni—a powerful mystic who became attracted to sex by accidently seeing a pair of mating fish.

Śaunaka Ṛṣi—the chief of the sages present at Naimiṣāraṇya when Sūta Gosvāmī spoke *Śrīmad-Bhāgavatam.*

Sītā—the eternal consort of Lord Rāmacandra.

Śiva—the presiding demigod of the mode of ignorance and the destruction of the material manifestation.

Śivānanda Sena—a great householder devotee of Lord Śrī Caitanya Mahāprabhu.

Śrīdhara Svāmī—the author of the oldest existing Vaiṣṇava commentaries on *Śrīmad-Bhāgavatam* and *Bhagavad-gītā.*

Śukadeva Gosvāmī—the sage who originally spoke *Śrīmad-Bhāgavatam* to King Parīkṣit just prior to the King's death.

Śukrācārya—the spiritual master of the demons.

Sūta Gosvāmī—the sage who recounted the discourses between Parīkṣit and Śukadeva to the sages assembled in the forest of Naimiṣāraṇya.

Svāyambhuva Manu—the original father of the human race.

Śyāmasundara—a name of the Supreme Personality of Godhead, who is blackish and very beautiful.

U

Uttānapāda—a son of Svāyambhuva Manu and father of Dhruva Mahārāja.

V

Vaivasvata Manu—*See:* Manu

Vāmana—the Lord's incarnation as a dwarf *brāhmaṇa* boy.

Varāha—the incarnation of the Supreme Personality of Godhead as a boar.

Varuṇa—the presiding demigod of the oceans.

Vasudeva—the father of Lord Kṛṣṇa.

Vāsudeva—a name of the Supreme Personality of Godhead, the proprietor of everything, material and spiritual.

Vāyu—the demigod in charge of the wind.

Vidura—a great devotee who heard *Śrīmad-Bhāgavatam* from Maitreya Muni.

Vijaya and Jaya—*See:* Jaya and Vijaya

Viṣṇu—a name of the Supreme Personality of Godhead, the creator and maintainer of the material universes.

Viśvanātha Cakravartī Ṭhākura—a Vaiṣṇava spiritual master and commentator on *Śrīmad-Bhāgavatam* in the disciplic succession from Lord Śrī Caitanya Mahāprabhu.

Vṛtra—a great demon killed by Indra. He was actually the devotee Citraketu who had been cursed by mother Durgā to take such a low birth.

Vyāsadeva—the original compiler of the *Vedas* and *Purāṇas* and author of the *Vedānta-sūtra* and *Mahābhārata.*

Y

Yadus—the descendants of Yadu, in which dynasty Lord Kṛṣṇa appeared.

Yajña—a name of the Supreme Personality of Godhead, the goal and enjoyer of all sacrifices.

Yamarāja—the demigod in charge of death and the punishment of sinful living entities.

Yāmunācārya—a great Vaiṣṇava spiritual master.

Yayāti—the king who, because of his lust, was cursed by Śukrācārya to prematurely accept old age.

General Glossary

A

Ācārya—a spiritual master who teaches by example.

Adbhuta—the *rasa* (devotional sentiment) of wonder or amazement.

Ahaṁ brahmāsmi—the Vedic aphorism "I am spirit."

Ārati—a ceremony for greeting the Lord with offerings of food, lamps, fans, flowers and incense.

Arcanā—the devotional process of Deity worship.

Āśramas—the four spiritual orders of life: celibate student, householder, retired life and renounced life.

Aṣṭāṅga-yoga—the mystic *yoga* system propounded by Patañjali in his *Yoga-sūtras.*

Asuras—atheistic demons.

Avatāra—a descent of the Supreme Lord.

Avidyā potency—the illusory energy of the Supreme Lord.

Āyur-veda—the section of the *Vedas* which expounds the Vedic science of medicine.

B

Bhagavad-gītā—the basic directions for spiritual life spoken by the Lord Himself. The discourse between the Supreme Lord, Kṛṣṇa, and His devotee Arjuna expounding devotional service as both the principal means and the ultimate end of spiritual perfection.

Bhagavān—a name of the Supreme Personality of Godhead, the possessor of all opulences.

Bhāgavata Purāṇa—*See: Śrīmad-Bhāgavatam*

Bhakta—a devotee.

Bhakti-rasāmṛta-sindhu—Rūpa Gosvāmī's definitive explanation of the science of devotional service.

Bhakti-yoga—linking with the Supreme Lord by devotional service.

Bhārata-varṣa—India, named after King Bharata.

Brahmacārī—a celibate student under the care of a bona fide spiritual master.

Brahmacarya—celibate student life; the first order of Vedic spiritual life.

Brahmajyoti—the bodily effulgence of the Supreme Lord, which constitutes the brilliant illumination of the spiritual sky.

Brahmaloka—the planet, ruled by Lord Brahmā, which is the highest planet in the material universe.

Brahman—the Absolute Truth; especially the impersonal aspect of the Absolute.

Brāhmaṇa—one wise in the *Vedas* who can guide society; the first Vedic social order.

Brāhmaṇas—those wise in the **Vedas** who can guide society; the first Vedic social order.

Brahma-saṁhitā—Lord Brahmā's prayers in glorification of the Supreme Lord.

Brahmāstra—a nuclear weapon produced by chanting *mantras.*

Bhāratavarṣa—India.

Buddhi-yoga—the engagement of one's intelligence in the service of the Lord.

C

Caitanya-caritāmṛta—Kṛṣṇadāsa Kavirāja's biography of the life and philosophy of Lord Śrī Caitanya Mahāprabhu.

Cāturmāsya—the four months of the Indian rainy season (from about the middle of July to the middle of October), during which time special vows for purification are recommended.

Causal Ocean—*See:* Kāraṇa Ocean

Cit-śakti—the knowledge potency of the Lord.

Cintāmaṇi—a mystically potent "touchstone" described in Vedic literatures.

D

Dharma—eternal occupational duty; religious principles.

Dhyāna—the practice of meditation upon the Supreme Lord residing within the heart as Supersoul.

Dvāpara-yuga—the third in the cycle of four ages. It lasts 864,000 years.

Dvārakā—the site of Lord Kṛṣṇa's city pastimes as an opulent prince.

E

Ekādaśī—a special fast day for increased remembrance of Kṛṣṇa, which comes on the eleventh day of both the waxing and waning moon.

G

Garbhādhāna-saṁskāra—Vedic purificatory ritual for obtaining good progeny; performed by husband and wife before child's conception.

Gauḍīya Vaiṣṇavas—devotees of Lord Kṛṣṇa coming in the disciplic succession begun by Lord Śrī Caitanya Mahāprabhu.

Goloka (Kṛṣṇaloka)—the highest spiritual planet, containing Kṛṣṇa's personal abodes, Dvārakā, Mathurā and Vṛndāvana.

Gopīs—Kṛṣṇa's cowherd girl friends, His most confidential servitors.

Gṛhastha—regulated householder life; the second order of Vedic spiritual life.

Guru—a spiritual master.

H

Hare Kṛṣṇa mantra—*See: Mahā-mantra*

Hari-bhakti-vilāsa—Sanātana Gosvāmī's book on the rules and regulations of Vaiṣṇava life.

Haṭha-yoga—the practice of postures and breathing exercises for achieving purification and sense control.

I

Ilāvṛta-varṣa—the original name of the earth, before it became known as Bhārata-varsa.

Iśopanisad—See: *Upaniṣads*

J

Jīva—the living entities, atomic parts of the Lord.

Jīva-tattva—the living entities, atomic parts of the Lord.

Jñāna—theoretical knowledge.

Jñāna-yoga—the process of approaching the Supreme by the cultivation of knowledge.

Jñāni—one who cultivates knowledge by empirical speculation.

K

Kalā—a form of the Lord that is an expansion of the Lord's original form.

Kali-yuga (Age of Kali)—the present age, characterized by quarrel; it is last in the cycle of four and began five thousand years ago.

Kalpa—daytime of Brahmā, 4,320,000,000 years.

Kāma—lust.

Kāraṇa Ocean—the corner of the spiritual universe in which Lord Mahā-Viṣṇu lies down to create the entirety of material universes.

Karatālas—hand cymbals used in *kīrtana.*

Karma—fruitive action, for which there is always reaction, good or bad.

Karmī—a person satisfied with working hard for flickering sense gratification.

Kaṭha Upaniṣad—*See: Upaniṣads*

Kīrtana—chanting the glories of the Supreme Lord.

Kṛṣṇa-kathā—topics concerning the Supreme Personality of Godhead.

Kṛṣṇaloka—the highest spiritual planet, containing Kṛṣṇa's personal abodes, Dvārakā, Mathurā and Vṛndāvana.

Kṣatriya—a warrior or administrator; the second Vedic social order.

Kuśa—auspicious grass used in Vedic rituals.

M

Mahābhārata—Vyāsadeva's epic history of the Kurukṣetra war.

Mahā-bhāva—the highest stage of love of God.

Mahā-mantra—the great chanting for deliverance:

Hare Kṛṣṇa, Hare Kṛṣṇa, Kṛṣṇa Kṛṣṇa, Hare Hare
Hare Rāma, Hare Rāma, Rāma Rāma, Hare Hare.

Mahāmāyā—the illusory material energy of the Lord.

Maṅgala-ārati—a predawn ceremony for greeting the Lord with offerings of food, lamps, fans, flowers and incense.

Mahātmā—a "great soul," who is advanced in realizing love of God.

Mahat-tattva—the total material energy in its original, undifferentiated form.

Mantra—a sound vibration that can deliver the mind from illusion.

Manu-saṁhitā—the original lawbook of human society.

Manvantaras—the lifetimes of each of the various Manus (original projectors of humankind).

Mārkaṇḍeya Purāṇa—*See: Purāṇas*

Mathurā—Lord Kṛṣṇa's abode, surrounding Vṛndāvana, where He took birth and later returned to after performing His Vṛndāvana pastimes.

Mauṣala-līlā—the self-destruction pastime of the Yadu dynasty.

Māyā—illusion; forgetfulness of one's relationship with Kṛṣṇa.

Māyāvāda—the monistic philosophy that there is no difference between the Lord and the living entities.

Māyāvādīs—impersonal philosophers who say that the Lord cannot have a transcendental body.

Mokṣa—liberation into the spiritual effulgence surrounding the Lord.

Mṛdaṅga—a clay drum used for congregational chanting.

Mukti—liberation from material existence.

N

Nārada-pañcarātra—Nārada Muni's book on the processes of Deity worship and *mantra* meditation.

Nirguṇa-brahma—the impersonal conception of the Supreme Truth as being without any qualities.

Nirvāṇa—the cessation of material activities and existence, which for Vaiṣṇavas does not deny spiritual activities and existence.

Nitya-baddhas—the imprisoned living entities who because of material desires reside in the temporary, material world.

Niyamas—restrictive regulations in the *yoga* system.

O

Oṁkāra—the sacred sound *om*, which is the beginning of many Vedic *mantras* and which represents the Supreme Lord.

P

Pāñcarātrikī formula—Pāñcarātra system of worshiping the Supreme Lord.

Paṇḍita—a scholar.

Paramahaṁsa—the highest stage of the *sannyāsa* order; a topmost devotee of the Lord.

Paramātmā—the Supreme Lord, dwelling within the heart of every living being.

Paramparā—the chain of spiritual masters in disciplic succession.

Parārdha—one half of Brahmā's lifetime of 4,320,000 × 2,000 × 30 × 12 × 100 years.

Pitās—departed ancestors who have been promoted to honorable positions on one of the higher planets.

Prajāpatis—the populators of the universe.

Prāṇāyāma—control of the breathing process as practiced in *aṣṭāṅga-yoga*.

Prasāda—food spiritualized by being offered to the Lord.

Pratyāhāra—withdrawal of the senses from all unnecessary activities.

Purāṇas—Vedic histories of the universe in relation to the Supreme Lord and His devotees.

Puruṣa—the enjoyer.

Puruṣa-avatāras—the three incarnations of the Supreme Lord who create and maintain the material universes.

R

Rajas—the material mode of passion.

Rājasūya—the great sacrifice performed by King Yudhiṣṭhira and attended by Lord Kṛṣṇa.

Rāmāyaṇa—the original epic of Lord Rāmacandra, written by Vālmīki Muni.

Ṛṣis—sages.

S

Sac-cid-ānanda-vigraha—the Lord's transcendental form, which is eternal, full of knowledge and bliss.

Saguṇa—having transcendental qualities.

Samādhi—complete absorption in meditation on the Supreme Lord.

Sāma Veda—one of the four original *Vedas.* It consists of musical settings of the sacrificial hymns.

Sampradāya—a disciplic succession of spiritual masters.

Sanātana—eternal.

Sāṅkhya—the philosophical analysis of matter and spirit and the controller of both.

Saṅkīrtana—public chanting of the names of God, the approved *yoga* process for this age.

Sannyāsa—renounced life; the fourth order of Vedic spiritual life.

Sarga—material creation.

Śāstras—revealed scriptures.

Sat—*See: Sanātana*

Satya-yuga—the first in the cycle of four ages. It lasts 1,728,000 years.

Siddhis—mystic powers acquired by the practice of *yoga.*

Śikṣāṣṭaka—eight verses by Lord Śrī Caitanya Mahāprabhu, glorifying the chanting of the Lord's holy name.

Smārtas—*brāhmaṇas* interested more in the external performance of Vedic rules and rituals than in attaining Lord Kṛṣṇa, the goal of the *Vedas.*

Smṛti—scriptures further explaining the original four *Vedas* and the *Upaniṣads.*

Smṛti-śāstra—supplementary explanations of the *Vedas.*

Śrāddha—a ritual performed for the benefit of one's departed ancestors.

Śravaṇaṁ kīrtanaṁ viṣṇoḥ—the devotional processes of hearing and chanting about Lord Viṣṇu.

Śuddha-sattva—the transcendental state of pure goodness, uncontaminated by the modes of material nature.

Śūdra—a laborer; the fourth of the Vedic social orders.

Sudarśana cakra—Lord Viṣṇu's disc weapon.

Svāmī—one who controls his mind and senses; title of one in the renounced order of life.

Śvetāśvatara Upaniṣad—*See: Upaniṣads*

T

Tapasya—austerity; accepting some voluntary inconvenience for a higher purpose.

Taṭastha-śakti—the living entities, the marginal potency of the Supreme Lord.

Tilaka—auspicious clay marks that sanctify a devotee's body as a temple of the Lord.

Tretā-yuga—the second in the cycle of four ages. It lasts 1,296,000 years.

Tulasī—a sacred plant dear to Lord Kṛṣṇa and worshiped by His devotees.

U

Upaniṣads—the philosophical section of the *Vedas*, meant for bringing the student closer to understanding the personal nature of the Absolute Truth.

V

Vaikuṇṭha—the spiritual world.

Vaiṣṇava—a devotee of Lord Viṣṇu, Kṛṣṇa.

Vaiśyas—farmers and merchants; the third Vedic social order.

Vānaprastha—one who has retired from family life; the third order of Vedic spiritual life.

Varṇas—the four occupational divisions of society; the intellectual class, the administrative class, the mercantile class, and the laborer class.

Varṇāśrama—the Vedic social system of four social and four spiritual orders.

Vedānta—the name for the philosophy presented in the *Vedānta-sūtra.*

Vedānta-sūtra—Vyāsadeva's philosophical summary of the conclusions of Vedic knowledge in the form of short aphorisms.

Vedas—the original revealed scriptures, first spoken by the Lord Himself.

Vedic literature—the original four *Vedas,* the *Upaniṣads, Purāṇas* and other supplements, and also all scriptures and commentaries written in pursuance of the Vedic conclusion.

Virāṭ-puruṣa—the "universal form" of the Lord as the totality of all material manifestations.

Viṣṇu, Lord—Kṛṣṇa's expansion for the creation and maintenance of the material universes.

Viṣṇu-tattva—the original Personality of Godhead's primary expansions, each of whom is equally God.

Vṛndāvana—Kṛṣṇa's personal abode, where He fully manifests His quality of sweetness.

Vyāsadeva—Kṛṣṇa's incarnation, at the end of Dvāpara-yuga, for compiling the *Vedas.*

Y

Yajña—an activity performed to satisfy either Lord Viṣṇu or the demigods.

Yajña-puruṣa—the supreme enjoyer of all sacrifices.

Yoga—various processes of spiritual realization, all ultimately meant for attaining the Supreme.

Yogamāyā—the internal, spiritual potency of the Lord.

Yoga-siddhis—material perfections achieved by practice of mystic meditation, such as the abilities to become lighter than air or smaller than the atom.

Yogī—a transcendentalist who, in one way or another, is striving for union with the Supreme.

Yojana—a Vedic unit of length, equal to about eight miles.

Yugas—ages in the life of a universe, occurring in a repeated cycle of four.

Sanskrit Pronunciation Guide

Vowels

अ a आ ā इ i ई ī उ u ऊ ū ऋ ṛ ॠ ṝ

ऌ ḷ ए e ऐ ai ओ o औ au

ं ṁ *(anusvāra)* ः ḥ *(visarga)*

Consonants

Gutturals:	क ka	ख kha	ग ga	घ gha	ङ ṅa
Palatals:	च ca	छ cha	ज ja	झ jha	ञ ña
Cerebrals:	ट ṭa	ठ ṭha	ड ḍa	ढ ḍha	ण ṇa
Dentals:	त ta	थ tha	द da	ध dha	न na
Labials:	प pa	फ pha	ब ba	भ bha	म ma
Semivowels:	य ya	र ra	ल la	व va	
Sibilants:	श śa	ष ṣa	स sa		
Aspirate:	ह ha	ऽ '*(avagraha)* – the apostrophe			

The numerals are: ०-0 १-1 २-2 ३-3 ४-4 ५-5 ६-6 ७-7 ८-8 ९-9

The vowels above should be pronounced as follows:

a – like the *a* in org*a*n or the *u* in b*u*t

ā – like the *a* in f*a*r but held twice as long as short *a*

i – like the *i* in p*i*n

ī – like the *i* in p*i*que but held twice as long as short *i*

u – like the *u* in p*u*sh

ū – like the *u* in r*u*le but held twice as long as short *u*

ṛ – like the *ri* in *ri*m

ṝ – like *ree* in *reed*

ḷ – like *l* followed by *r* (*lṛ*)

e – like the *e* in th*e*y

ai – like the *ai* in *ai*sle

o – like the *o* in g*o*

au – like the *ow* in h*ow*

ṁ *(anusvāra)* – a resonant nasal like the *n* in the French word *bon*

ḥ *(visarga)* – a final *h*-sound: *aḥ* is pronounced like *aha*; *iḥ* like *ihi*

The vowels are written as follows after a consonant:

ा ā ि i ी ī ु u ू ū ृ ṛ ॄ ṝ े e ै ai ो o ौ au

For example: क ka का kā कि ki की kī कु ku कू kū

कृ kṛ कॄ kṝ के ke कै kai को ko कौ kau

The vowel "a" is implied after a consonant with no vowel symbol.

The symbol virāma (्) indicates that there is no final vowel: क्

The consonants are pronounced as follows:

k – as in *k*ite

kh – as in Ec*kh*art

g – as in *g*ive

gh – as in di*g-h*ard

ṅ – as in si*ng*

c – as in *ch*air

ch – as in staun*ch-h*eart

j – as in *j*oy

jh – as in he*dgeh*og

ñ – as in can*y*on

ṭ – as in *t*ub

ṭh – as in ligh*t-h*eart

ḍ – as in *d*ove

ḍh – as in re*d-h*ot

ṇ – as r*na* (prepare to say the *r* and say *na*)

Cerebrals are pronounced with tongue to roof of mouth, but the following dentals are pronounced with tongue against teeth:

t – as in *t*ub but with tongue against teeth

th – as in ligh*t-h*eart but with tongue against teeth

d – as in *d*ove but with tongue against teeth

dh – as in re*d-h*ot but with tongue against teeth

n – as in *n*ut but with tongue between teeth

p – as in *p*ine

ph – as in u*ph*ill (not f)

b – as in *b*ird

bh – as in ru*b*-*h*ard

m – as in *m*other

y – as in *y*es

r – as in *r*un

l – as in *l*ight

v – as in *v*ine

ś *(palatal)* – as in the *s* in the German word *sprechen*

ṣ *(cerebral)* – as the *sh* in *sh*ine

s – as in *s*un

h – as in *h*ome

Generally two or more consonants in conjunction are written together in a special form, as for example: क्ष kṣa त्र tra

There is no strong accentuation of syllables in Sanskrit, or pausing between words in a line, only a flowing of short and long (twice as long as the short) syllables. A long syllable is one whose vowel is long (ā, ī, ū, e, ai, o, au), or whose short vowel is followed by more than one consonant (including anusvāra and visarga). Aspirated consonants (such as kha and gha) count as only single consonants.

Index of Sanskrit Verses

This index constitutes a complete listing of the first and third lines of each of the Sanskrit poetry verses and the first line of Sanskrit prose verse of this volume of *Śrīmad-Bhāgavatam*, arranged in English alphabetical order. In the first column the Sanskrit transliteration is given, and in the second and third columns respectively the chapter-verse references and page number for each verse are to be found.

A

ā smābhipṛcche 'dya patiṁ prajānāṁ 24.34 948
ābabhāṣe kuru-śreṣṭha 29.6 1186
ābhāty apārthaṁ nirmūlaṁ 7.16 273
abhīkṣṇāvagāha-kapiśān 33.14 1378
abhiplutya sva-gadayā 19.8 707

abhisambhāvya viśrambhāt 20.33 759
abhisandhāya yo hiṁsāṁ 29.8 1187
abhiṣṭuto viśva-sṛjā prasunair 18.8 686
abhūta-śatrur jagataḥ śoka-hartā 14.49 551
abhyadhād bhadrayā vācā 12.9 433

abhyadhāvad dhariḥ kruddhaḥ 18.16 693
abhyarcatī svalakam unnasam īkṣya 15.22 573
ācakṣva jīva-lokasya 29.3 1183
acīkḷpad yatra hi sarva-sattva- 5.8 164

adabhra-dayayā dṛṣṭyā 15.9 561
ādau gṛhītam avatara-śataika-bījaṁ 9.2 325
ādāyāntar adhād yas tu 2.11 59
ādeśe 'haṁ bhagavato 13.14 480

adharmaḥ pṛṣṭhato yasmān 12.25 444
adharmaś ca samedheta 21.55 827
adhastān nara-lokasya 30.34 1260
ādhatta vīryaṁ sāsūta 26.19 1045

ādhattāmbho rasa-mayaṁ 5.35 191
adhunaiṣo 'bhijin nāma 18.27 700
ādhyātmikānuśravaṇān 29.18 1202
ādi-daityo hiraṇyākṣo 14.2 514

ādideśāravindākṣa 4.19 133
ādīpanaṁ sva-gātrāṇāṁ 30.25 1253
adrākṣam ekam āsīnaṁ 4.6 121
ādyaḥ sthira-carāṇāṁ yo 32.12 1327
ādyas tu mahataḥ sargo 10.15 386
ādyo 'vatāro yatrāsau 6.8 222
āgas-kṛd bhaya-kṛd duṣkṛd 18.23 697

agnir indhe sa-giribhir 29.42 1227
āha cāyudham ādhatsva 19.10 708
āhainam ehy ajña mahīṁ vimuñca 18.3 681
ahaituky avyavahitā 29.12 1191
aham ātmātmanāṁ dhātaḥ 9.42 371

ahaṁ ca lokānugato vahāmi 21.16 791
ahaṁ cānya ime devās 6.40 252
ahaṁ cokto bhagavatā 4.4 120
ahaṁ mamābhimānotthaiḥ 25.16 980

ahaṁ mamety asad-grāhaḥ 31.30 1293
ahaṁ sarveṣu bhūteṣu 29.21 1205
ahaṁ tvāśṛṇavaṁ vidvan 22.14 842
aham uccāvacair dravyaiḥ 29.24 1208

ahaṁ-tattvād vikurvāṇān 5.30 188
ahaṅkāras tato rudraś 26.61 1081
ahaṅkāra-vimūḍhasya 26.16 1041
ahaṅkriyā-vimūḍhātmā 27.2 1092

ahanyamānā api tasya varcasā 17.25 673
ahiṁsā satyam asteyaṁ 28.4 1132
ahīndra-talpe 'dhiśayāna ekaḥ 8.10 303
ahny āpṛtārta-karaṇā niśi niḥśayānā 9.10 334

aho adbhutam etan me	12.51	465
aho bakī yaṁ stana-kāla-kūṭaṁ	2.23	74
aho bata śva-paco 'to garīyān	33.7	1369
aho batāścaryam idaṁ	13.21	484
aho etaj jagat-sraṣṭaḥ	20.51	771
aho me yakṣa-rakṣāṁsi	20.21	750
aho pāpacyamānānāṁ	24.27	940
aho pṛthāpi dhriyate 'rbhakārthe	1.40	38
aho rūpam aho dhairyam	20.32	759
āho svit saṁhatāḥ sarva	20.11	742
aiśvaryaṁ pārameṣṭhyaṁ ca	32.15	1327
aiśvarya-vairāgya-yaśo-'vabodha-	24.32	945
ajādayo vīkṣya śaśaṁsur āgatā	19.27	720
ājaghne sa tu tāṁ saumya	18.17	693
ājahārolbaṇaṁ krodhaṁ	18.13	691
ajānantyā paraṁ bhāvaṁ	23.54	911
ajasya janmotpatha-nāśanāya	1.44	43
ajāta-śatravaḥ śāntāḥ	25.21	987
ajāta-śatroḥ pratiyaccha dāyaṁ	1.11	9
ajīghanat svayaṁ divyaṁ	3.10	97
ājñā-karī yasya piśāca-caryā	14.29	535
akalpaḥ svāṅga-ceṣṭāyāṁ	31.9	1269
akāmāṁ cakame kṣattaḥ	12.28	447
ākarṇayan patra-rathendra-pakṣair	21.34	812
akartuḥ karma-bandho 'yaṁ	27.19	1113
ākrīḍa bālavad deva	18.24	698
akṣiṇī cakṣuṣādityo	26.64	1084
ākṣiptaṁ teja etarhi	16.36	653
ākṣiptātmendriyaḥ strīṇām	30.8	1239
ākūtiṁ rucaye prādāt	12.57	467
ākūtir devahūtiś ca	12.56	467
alabdhābhīpsito 'jñānād	31.28	1291
alakṣitaḥ svair avadhūta-veṣo	1.19	19
alakṣito yac-chara-kūṭa-gūḍho	1.38	36
alaṁ prajābhiḥ sṛṣṭābhir	12.17	439
alampaṭaḥ śīla-dharo guṇākaro	14.49	551
āliṅgya gāḍhaṁ praṇayena bhadraṁ	1.25	25
āmantritas tat-tanayāya śeṣaṁ	3.6	94
āmantrya taṁ muni-varam	22.26	855
āmayāvy apradīptāgnir	30.15	1245
ambho-guṇa-viśeṣo 'rtho	26.48	1071
aṁśena romabhiḥ kaṇḍūm	6.18	231
amuṣya durbhagatvaṁ vā	7.6	260
anabhipretam āpannaḥ	31.25	1289
anādir ātmā puruṣo	26.3	1025
ananta-liṅgaiḥ samalaṅkṛteṣu	1.18	18
ananya-dṛṣṭyā bhajatāṁ guhāśayaḥ	13.49	509
ananya-hetuṣv atha me gatiḥ syād	27.30	1127
anāpṛṣṭam api brūyur	7.36	287
āṇḍa-kośa uvāsāpsu	6.6	220
āṇḍakośo bahir ayaṁ	11.40	424
anena lokān prāg-līnān	10.7	379
aṅgaṁ ca mala-paṅkena	23.25	890
aṅgirā mukhato 'kṣṇo 'trir	12.24	444
anilenānvitaṁ jyotir	5.35	191
anilo 'pi vikurvāṇo	5.34	191
animittā bhāgavatī	25.32	1000
animitta-nimittena	27.21	1116
anivṛtta-nimittatvāt	27.20	1115
annaṁ coru-rasaṁ tebhyo	3.28	114
annaṁ sarva-guṇopetaṁ	23.29	892
antaḥ puruṣa-rūpeṇa	26.18	1043
antaḥ sa tasmin salila	11.32	417
antar bahiś cāmalam abja-netraṁ	14.50	552
antar-gataḥ sva-vivareṇa cakāra	15.43	601
antar-grāmeṣu mukhato	17.9	662
antarhite bhagavati	10.1	375
antar-jale 'hi-kaśipu-sparśānukūlāṁ	9.20	350
antar-jale 'nuvikasan-madhu-	15.17	568
anugrahāya bhaktānām	20.25	753
anugrahāyāstv api yarhi māyayā	21.20	796
anugrahāyeha caranti nūnaṁ	5.3	157

aṇur dvau paramāṇū syāt 11.5 400
anuvatsaro vatsaraś ca 11.14 405
anuvratānāṁ śiṣyāṇāṁ 7.36 287
anvākramat puṇya-cikīrṣayorvyām 1.17 16
anveṣann apratiratho 18.23 697

anvicchati patiṁ yuktaṁ 22.9 838
ānvīkṣikī trayī vārtā 12.44 460
anvīyamānas tarasā 20.24 752
anyāṁś ca dantavakrādīn 3.11 98
anyāni ceha dvija-deva-devaiḥ 1.23 22

anye punar bhagavato bhruva 23.8 876
anyeṣāṁ duṣkarataraṁ 4.34 152
anyeṣāṁ puṇya-ślokānām 19.34 728
anyonyāpāśrayatvāc ca 27.17 1111
anyonya-śleṣayottuṅga- 20.30 758

apakṣitam ivāsyāpi 11.33 418
apāṁ rasasya ca yathā 27.18 1112
apāśritarbhakāśvattham 4.8 122
apaśyat sarva-bhūtāni 24.46 962
apatya-kāmā cakame 14.8 518

apāvṛtaiḥ karṇa-randhrair 22.7 836
api kṣamaṁ no grahaṇāya bhartar 4.18 132
api nirmukta-saṅgasya 22.12 840
api sva-dorbhyāṁ vijayācyutābhyāṁ 1.36 35

api svid bhagavān eṣa 13.22 484
apīcya-darśanaṁ śaśvat 28.17 1145
apisvid anye ca nijātma-daivam 1.35 34
apisvid āste bhagavān sukhaṁ vo 1.34 33

āpīya karṇāñjalibhir bhavāpahām 13.50 510
āpo gāṅgā ivāgha-ghnīr 20.5 737
apramattodyatā nityaṁ 23.3 871
aprāyatyād ātmanas te 14.38 542

āptoryāmātirātrau ca 12.40 457
āpuḥ parāṁ mudam apūrvam upetya 15.26 580
apy ātmatvenābhimatād 28.39 1172
apy ātmatvenābhimatād 28.40 1173

apy āyuṣā vā kārtsnyena 14.21 527
ārabhya saptamān māsāl 31.10 1270
ārādhanaṁ bhagavatas tava sat- 9.13 341
ārādhayiṣyaty asurarṣabhehi taṁ 17.30 676
arcādāv arcayed yo māṁ 29.9 1189

arcādāv arcayet tāvad 29.25 1210
arhaty uddhava evāddhā 4.30 146
arhayed dāna-mānābhyāṁ 29.27 1211
ārjavenārya-saṅgena 29.18 1202
āropya svāṁ duhitaraṁ 21.36 814

arthābhāvaṁ viniścitya 7.18 275
arthair āpāditair gurvyā 30.10 1241
artha-jñāt saṁśaya-cchettā 29.32 1217
arthāśrayatvaṁ śabdasya 26.33 1059
arthāya jātasya yaduṣv ajasya 1.45 45

arthe hy avidyamāne 'pi 27.4 1094
ārtopasarpaṇaṁ bhūmann 14.15 522
arvāk-srotas tu navamaḥ 10.26 393
āsādya tarasā daityo 18.14 692
aśaknuvaṁs tad-virahaṁ 22.25 854

āsāṁ muhūrta ekasmin 3.8 95
āsanāni ca haimāni 33.16 1380
āsanna-śauṇḍīram upeta-sādhvasaṁ 18.21 696
āśāse putrayor mahyaṁ 14.42 546

āsāta urvyāḥ kuśalaṁ vidhāya 1.26 26
asat-kṛtaḥ sat-spṛhaṇīya-śīlaḥ 1.14 12
aśeṣa-saṅkleśa-śamaṁ vidhatte 7.14 271
asevayāyaṁ prakṛter guṇānāṁ 25.27 995

āsīnam urvyāṁ bhagavantam ādyaṁ 8.3 297
āsiñcad amba vatseti 22.25 854
asmāl lokād uparate 4.30 146
asmāsu vā ya ucito dhriyatāṁ sa 16.25 643

asrākṣīd bhagavān viśvaṁ 7.4 259
āśramāṁś ca yathā-saṅkhyam 12.41 458
aśṛṇon nāradād eṣā 22.10 839
āśṛṇvato māṁ anurāga-hāsa- 4.10 124

aṣṭādaśākṣauhiṇiko mad-aṁśair 3.14 100
astaud visargābhimukhas tam īḍyam 8.33 321
āste 'vamatyopanyastaṁ 30.15 1245
āste kṛtvā śiraḥ kukṣau 31.8 1269
āste sma bindusarasi 21.35 814

āste sva-puryāṁ yadu-deva-devo 1.12 10
āste viśuddham avikāram akhaṇḍa- 31.13 1274
āste yogaṁ samāsthāya 33.35 1396
āsthitena parāṁ kāṣṭhām 33.10 1374
āsthito ramate jantus 31.32 1295

asti hy adhastād iha kiñcanaitad 8.18 309
asūta yaṁ jāmbavatī vratāḍhyā 1.30 29
asyā uddharaṇe yatno 13.15 481
āsyād vāk sindhavo meḍhrān 12.26 445
ata eva śanaiś cittaṁ 27.5 1096

ataḥ paraṁ pravakṣyāmi 10.30 396
ataḥ sā suṣuve sadyo 23.48 906
atas tvam ṛṣi-mukhyebhyo 24.15 930
atas tvam upakurvāṇaḥ 22.14 842
ātatāyibhir utsṛṣṭā 19.21 715

atha māṁ sarva-bhūteṣu 29.27 1211
atha me deva sammoham 25.10 973
atha me kuru kalyāṇaṁ 14.15 522
atha samprasthite śukle 21.35 814

atha taṁ sarva-bhūtānāṁ 32.11 1325
atha tasyābhitaptasya 6.11 227
atha tasyośatīṁ devīm 16.13 630
atha te bhagaval-līlā 5.22 180

atha te bhrātṛ-putrāṇāṁ 3.12 98
atha te munayo dṛṣṭvā 16.27 645
atha te sampravakṣyāmi 26.1 1023
atha te tad-anujñātā 4.1 117

atha yo gṛha-medhīyān 32.1 1315
athābhidhyāyataḥ sargaṁ 12.21 442
athābhipretam anvīkṣya 9.27 358
athādarśe svam ātmānaṁ 23.30 892

athāha tan mantra-dṛśāṁ varīyān 1.10 8
athājani mayā tubhyaṁ 24.35 949
athāpi kāmam etaṁ te 14.22 528
athāpi me prapannāyā 23.51 908
athāpi pṛcche tvāṁ vīra 21.56 828

athāpy ajo 'ntaḥ-salile śayānaṁ 33.2 1362
atharvaṇe 'dadāc chāntiṁ 24.24 938
athāsya hṛdayaṁ bhinnaṁ 26.60 1081
athātra kim anuṣṭheyam 13.17 482
athātrāpītihāso 'yaṁ 14.7 517

atho na paśyanty urugāya nūnaṁ 5.45 203
atho vibhūtiṁ mama māyāvinas tām 25.37 1009
athopaspṛśya salilaṁ 14.32 537
athorudhāsṛjan māyāṁ 19.17 713
athoṭajam upāyātaṁ 21.48 821

aticerur vakra-gatyā 17.14 664
ātmā tathā pṛthag draṣṭā 28.41 1174
ātmajāḥ paridehy adya 24.15 930
ātmajām asitāpāṅgīṁ 21.27 803
ātma-jāyā-sutāgāra- 30.6 1237

ātma-māṁsādanaṁ kvāpi 30.25 1253
ātman labhante bhagavaṁs tavāṅghri- 5.40 197
ātmanaḥ sarva-bhūtānāṁ 25.41 1015
ātmānam anu ye ceha 25.39 1013

ātmānam atra puruṣo 'vyavadhānam 28.35 1167
ātmānaṁ brahma-nirvāṇaṁ 33.30 1393
ātmānaṁ ca kuru-śreṣṭha 4.35 153
ātmānaṁ cāsya nirbhinnam 6.25 234

ātmānaṁ cogra-tapasā 33.14 1378
ātmānaṁ sarva-bhūteṣu 24.46 962
ātmānaṁ vyakarod ātmā 5.28 186
ātmanaś ca parasyāpi 29.26 1211

ātmani prota-bhuvanaṁ 15.6 559
ātmano 'vasito vatsa 6.38 249
ātmano bibhratīṁ rūpaṁ 23.36 896
ātmānubhūtyānugata-prapañcaṁ 24.33 946

ātmany ātmānam āveśya 10.4 377
ātmany evātmanā vīkṣya 24.39 954
ātma-sthaṁ vyañjayām āsa 12.32 451
ātma-tattvāvabodhena 32.36 1350
ātmecchānugatāv ātmā 5.23 180

ātmendriya-jayenāpi 32.34 1350
ato bhagavato māyā 6.39 251
ato bhajiṣye samayena sādhvīṁ 22.19 847
ato dharmān pāramahaṁsya-mukhyān 22.19 847
ato hy anyonyam ātmānaṁ 22.4 831

ato mad-vayunaṁ lokaṁ 4.31 147
ato mayi ratiṁ kuryād 9.42 371
ato viśeṣo bhāvānāṁ 26.49 1071
atraiva narakaḥ svarga 30.29 1255
atropasṛṣṭam iti cotsmitam indirāyāḥ 15.42 600

atṛpnuma kṣulla-sukhāvahānāṁ 5.10 166
ātyantikena sattvena 6.28 236
atyantoparatir yatra 25.13 978
autkaṇṭhya-bāṣpa-kalayā muhur 28.34 1166
avabhāty artha-rupeṇa 32.28 1342

avādayaṁs tadā vyomni 24.7 922
avadhārya viriñcasya 19.1 703
avañcayat tiraścīno 18.15 692
āvayor anurūpo 'sāv 22.15 843

avido bhūri-tamaso 10.21 390
avidyā-saṁśaya-granthiṁ 24.18 933
avikārād akartṛtvān 27.1 1091
aviluptāvabodhātmā 7.5 259

āviśaty apramatto 'sau 29.39 1225
āviveśa sarasvatyāḥ 23.25 890
avyākṛtaṁ viśati yarhi guṇa-trayātmā 32.9 1324
avyākṛtasyānantasya 11.38 422

avyakta-mūlaṁ bhuvanāṅghripen- 8.29 318
ayajad yajña-puruṣaṁ 22.31 858
ayājayad dharma-sutam 3.18 104
ayājayad go-savena 2.32 84

ayaṁ siddha-gaṇādhīśaḥ 24.19 934
ayaṁ tu kathitaḥ kalpo 11.37 421
āyāmato vistarataḥ sva-māna- 8.25 315
ayane cāhanī prāhur 11.12 404
āyāsyati didṛkṣus tvāṁ 21.26 803

ayāta-yāmās tasyāsan 22.35 863
āyur-vedaṁ dhanur-vedaṁ 12.38 456

B

babhau malair avacchannaḥ 33.28 1391
babhrāja utkaca-kumud-gaṇavān 23.38 898
babhūvācirato vatsa 33.22 1385
babhūvithehājita-kīrti-mālāṁ 8.1 295
badarīṁ tvaṁ prayāhīti 4.4 120
badaryāśramam āsādya 4.32 149

bāḍham ity amum āmantrya 12.20 441
bāḍham ity anumanyeta 24.13 928
bāḍham udvoḍhu-kāmo 'ham 22.15 843
bahir-jāta-virāgāya 32.42 1357
bahubhir yakṣa-rakṣobhiḥ 19.21 715

bāhubhyo 'vartata kṣatraṁ 6.31 240
bahu-janma-vipakvena 24.28 940
bāhūṁś ca mandara-gireḥ 28.27 1158
bahv-āścaryaṁ mahā-yogī 23.43 902

balaṁ me paśya māyāyāḥ 31.38 1301
baliṁ haradbhiś cira-loka-pālaiḥ 2.21 72
baliṁ haranty ṛṣayo ye ca devāḥ 18.5 683
barhiṣmatī nāma purī 22.29 857

barhiṣmatīṁ nāma vibhur 22.32 859
bhagavac-chakti-yuktasya 12.21 442
bhagavad-bhakti-yogena 7.12 268
bhagavad-bhakti-yuktena 24.47 963

bhagavad-dhyāna-pūtena 12.3 428
bhagavad-racitā rājan 21.54 825
bhagavāṁs te 'kṣaro garbham 24.2 917
bhagavāṁs te prajā-bhartur 13.12 478

bhagavāṁs tu gadā-vegaṁ 18.15 692
bhagavān anugāv āha 16.29 647
bhagavān api viśvātmā 3.19 105
bhagavān eka āsedam 5.23 180
bhagavān eka evaiṣa 7.6 260

bhagavān svātma-māyāyā 4.3 118
bhagavān veda kālasya 11.17 408
bhagavān yajña-puruṣo 13.23 485
bhagavantaṁ paraṁ brahma 24.10 924
bhagavantaṁ parikramya 16.28 646

bhagavati kṛta-dhīḥ suparṇa-ketāv 33.37 1397
bhagavaty arpitādhyātmas 20.7 739
bhagavaty uru-mānāc ca 14.44 547
bhajanty ananyayā bhaktyā 25.40 1013
bhakti-pravāha-yogena 33.24 1386

bhakti-yogaś ca yogaś ca 29.35 1220
bhakti-yogasya me mārgaṁ 29.2 1181
bhakti-yogena tīvreṇa 27.5 1096
bhakti-yogo bahu-vidho 29.7 1187
bhaktyā gṛhīta-caraṇaḥ parayā ca 9.5 329

bhaktyā pumāñ jāta-virāga aindriyād 25.26 994
bhaktyā viraktyā jñānena 26.72 1088
bhartary āptorumānānāṁ 14.12 520
bhartuḥ purastād ātmānaṁ 23.35 896

bhartur mithaḥ suyaśasaḥ 15.25 577
bhasmāvaguṇṭhāmala-rukma-deho 14.25 531
bhautikānāṁ vikāreṇa 26.42 1067
bhautikāś ca kathaṁ kleśā 22.37 865

bhavad-vidheṣv atitarāṁ 21.24 801
bhavān bhagavato nityaṁ 5.21 179
bhāvanaṁ brahmaṇaḥ sthānaṁ 26.46 1069
bhavanti caiva yugapat 11.25 413

bhavaty akartur īśasya 26.7 1033
bhaviṣyatas tavābhadrāv 14.39 543
bheda-dṛṣṭyābhimānena 32.13 1327
bhinnaṁ saṁyojayām āsa 6.3 217

bhītā nililyire devās 17.22 671
bhittvā tri-pād vavṛdha eka uru- 9.16 345
bhoktṛtve sukha-duḥkhānāṁ 26.8 1034
bhrājiṣṇunā vimānena 23.41 900
bhrāmyate dhīr na tad-vākyair 2.10 57

bhrātuḥ kṣetre bhujiṣyāyāṁ 5.20 178
bhrātur yaviṣṭhasya sutān vibandhūn 1.6 5
bhṛgur vasiṣṭho dakṣaś ca 12.22 442
bhṛtyānukampita-dhiyeha gṛhīta- 28.29 1160
bhukta-bhogā parityaktā 27.24 1120

bhūmer guṇa-viśeṣo 'rtho 26.48 1071
bhuñjāna eva karmāṇi 31.43 1307
bhuṅkte kuṭumba-poṣasya 30.32 1258
bhuṅkte naro vā nārī vā 30.28 1254
bhūṣaṇāni parārdhyāni 23.29 892

bhūtaiḥ pañcabhir ārabdhe 31.30 1293
bhūtānāṁ chidra-dātṛtvaṁ 26.34 1060
bhūtānāṁ mahad-ādīnāṁ 29.37 1223
bhūtānāṁ nabha-ādīnāṁ 5.37 193
bhūtānāṁ śevadhiṁ dehaṁ 24.16 931

bhūta-preta-piśācāś ca 10.29 395
bhūta-sargas tṛtīyas tu 10.16 387
bhūta-sūkṣmendriya-mano- 27.14 1108
bhūtendriyāntaḥ-karaṇāt 28.41 1174

bhūteṣu baddha-vairasya 29.23 1207
bhūteṣu kṛta-maitrāya 32.41 1357
bhūteṣu mad-bhāvanayā 29.16 1198
bhūyād aghoni bhagavadbhir akāri 15.36 593

bhūyaḥ papraccha kauravyo 13.1 469
bhūyaḥ sakāśam upayāsyata āśu yo 16.26 644
bhūyas tvaṁ tapa ātiṣṭha 9.30 360
bhūyo mamāntikam itāṁ tad 16.12 629

bhūyo yathā vyasanam etad aneka- 31.21 1286
bodhenāṁśena boddhavyam 6.23 233
brahmacaryaṁ tapaḥ śaucaṁ 28.4 1132
brahmacaryeṇa maunena 27.7 1099

brahmādayo yat-kṛta-setu-pālā 14.29 535
brahman duhitṛbhis tubhyaṁ 23.52 909
brahman kathaṁ bhagavataś 7.2 255
brahmaṇā deva-devena 14.7 517
brahmāṇaṁ harṣayām āsa 13.24 486

brāhmaṇeṣv api veda-jño 29.31 1216
brahmaṇy avasthita-matir 33.26 1387
brahmaṇyasya paraṁ daivaṁ 16.17 633
brahma-putrān ṛte bhītā 17.15 665
brahma-śāpāpadeśena 4.29 144

brahmāsṛjat sva-mukhato 22.2 829
brahma-tejaḥ samartho 'pi 16.29 647
brahmāvabhāti vitato 12.48 463
brahmāvartaṁ yo 'dhivasan 21.25 802
brūhi kāraṇayor asya 26.9 1035

brūhi me 'jñasya mitratvād 7.40 292
brūhi me śraddadhānāya 13.3 470
buddhiṁ cāsya vinirbhinnāṁ 6.23 233
buddhvā jīva-gatiṁ dhīro 31.47 1310
buddhyā brahmāpi hṛdayaṁ 26.69 1086
buddhyā yuñjīta śanakair 28.7 1136

C

cacāla bhūḥ kurukṣetraṁ 3.12 98
cakāra karmāṇy atipūruṣāṇi 5.16 174
cakāsti śṛṅgoḍha-ghanena bhūyasā 13.41 502
cakre hiraṇyakaśipur 17.19 669
cakreṇa ciccheda niśāta-neminā 19.14 710

cakṣuṣāṁśena rūpāṇāṁ 6.15 229
cakṣuṣmat padmarāgāgryair 23.19 886
cālanaṁ vyūhanaṁ prāptir 26.37 1063
carācarauko bhagavan-mahīdhram 8.30 319
caramaḥ sad-viśeṣāṇām 11.1 397

caranti yasyāṁ bhūtāni 14.23 529
cārayann anugān gopān 2.29 81
caritaṁ tasya rājarṣer 13.3 470
caritreṇānavadyena 3.20 107
caturbhir dhātavaḥ sapta 31.4 1265

caturdhā lakṣyate bhedo 26.14 1040
cātur-hotraṁ karma-tantram 12.35 454
caturtha aindriyaḥ sargo 10.16 387
catur-yugānāṁ ca sahasram apsu 8.12 305
catvāri trīṇi dve caikaṁ 11.19 409

cerur vihāyasā lokāl 15.12 563
ceṣṭā yataḥ sa bhagavān 26.17 1042
cetaḥ khalv asya bandhāya 25.15 980
chandāṁsi yasya tvaci barhi-romasv 13.35 496
chandomayas tapo-vidyā- 22.2 829

chāyāyāḥ kardamo jajñe 12.27 446
chettā te hṛdaya-granthim 24.4 919
cikīrṣur bhagavān asyāḥ 2.25 77
cikīrṣur bhagavān jñānaṁ 24.30 943
citrā vāco 'tad-vidāṁ khe-carāṇāṁ 19.6 706

cittasya yatto grahaṇe yoga-yukto 25.26 994
cittena hṛdayaṁ caityaḥ 26.70 1087
cittenāṁśena yenāsau 6.26 235
cukrośa vimanā vārdhir 17.7 661
cukṣobhānyonyam āsādya 6.5 219

D

dadarśa devo jagato vidhātā 8.32 320
dadarśa gāṁ tatra suṣupsur agre 13.30 491
dadarśa munim āsīnaṁ 21.45 820
dadarśa tatrābhijitaṁ dharā-dharaṁ 18.2 680
dadhāra varṣāṇi śataṁ 15.1 555

daitya-rājasya ca brahman 14.3 514
daityasya yajñāvayavasya māyā- 18.20 695
daivād garīyasaḥ patyur 23.4 872
daivād upetam atha daiva-vaśād 28.37 1170
daivādhīneṣu kāmeṣu 3.23 109

daiva-guptaṁ na bubudhe 33.29 1392
daivāhatārtha-racanā ṛṣayo 'pi deva 9.10 334
daivāl labdhena santoṣa 28.2 1130
daivāt kṣubhita-dharmiṇyāṁ 26.19 1045
daivena durvitarkyeṇa 20.12 742

daivena te hata-dhiyo bhavataḥ	9.7	331
daivenāsāditaṁ tasya	30.32	1258
daivopasāditaṁ mṛtyuṁ	31.42	1306
dakṣāyādāt prasūtiṁ ca	12.57	467
dakṣiṇena pathāryamṇaḥ	32.20	1333
dakṣiṇī-kṛtya taṁ prīto	24.41	957
dampatyoḥ paryadāt prītyā	22.23	852
daṁṣṭrāgra-koṭyā bhagavaṁs tvayā	13.40	501
dānasya tapaso vāpi	7.34	286
darśanīyatamaṁ śāntaṁ	28.16	1144
darśayām āsa taṁ kṣattaḥ	21.8	782
daśāhena tu karkandhūḥ	31.2	1264
daśaite vidurākhyātāḥ	10.29	395
daśottarādhikair yatra	11.41	425
dayāluḥ śālinīm āha	24.1	917
dehaṁ ca taṁ na caramaḥ sthitam	28.37	1170
deha-nyāsaṁ ca tasyaivaṁ	4.34	152
dehena jīva-bhūtena	31.43	1307
dehena vai bhogavatā	20.47	769
deho 'pi daiva-vaśagaḥ khalu karma	28.38	1171
dehy anya-deha-vivare jaṭharā-	1.17	1280
deśataḥ kālato yo 'sāv	7.5	259
deva-deva jagad-dhātar	15.4	557
devahūty api sandeśaṁ	24.5	920
devānāṁ guṇa-liṅgānām	25.32	1000
devas tān āha saṁvigno	20.21	750
deva-sargaś cāṣṭa-vidho	10.28	394
devasya māyayā spṛṣṭā	2.10	57
devatāḥ prabhayā yā yā	20.22	751
devāv acakṣata gṛhīta-gadau parār-	15.27	581
devo 'devāñ jaghanataḥ	20.23	752
dhanyārpitāṅghri-tulasī-nava-dāma-	16.20	636
dharāṁ rajaḥ-svabhāvena	6.28	236
dharmaḥ stanād dakṣiṇato	12.25	444
dharmārtha-kāma-mokṣāṇāṁ	7.32	285
dharmaś catuṣ-pān manujān	11.21	411
dharmasya hy animittasya	10.9	381
dharmasya pādāś catvāras	12.35	454
dharmasya paramo guhyo	16.18	633
dharmasya te bhagavatas tri-yuga	16.22	638
dharmeṇobhaya-cihnena	32.35	1350
dhātar yad asmin bhava īśa jīvās	5.40	197
dhīr dhṛti-rasalomā ca	12.13	436
dhiyā nigṛhyamāṇo 'pi	12.7	432
dhiyābhinandyātmavatāṁ satāṁ gatir	25.12	977
dhiyopagṛhṇan smita-śobhitena	22.21	851
dhṛta-vratāsi bhadraṁ te	24.3	918
dhruvāṇi manyate mohād	30.3	1235
dhyānāyanaṁ prahasitaṁ bahulādha-	28.33	1165
dhyātur manaḥ-śamala-śaila-nisṛṣṭa-	28.22	1151
dhyāyan gate bhāgavate	4.35	153
dhyāyañ jajāpa virajaṁ	14.32	537
dhyāyatī bhagavad-rūpaṁ	33.23	1386
dhyāyato viṣayān asya	27.4	1095
dhyāyed devaṁ samagrāṅgaṁ	28.18	1146
dhyāyet svadeha-kuhare 'vasitasya	28.33	1165
digbhyo nipetur grāvāṇaḥ	19.18	714
dig-vāsaso mukta-keśān	20.40	764
dig-vāsaso yātudhānyaḥ	19.20	715
dīkṣānujanmopasadaḥ śirodharaṁ	13.37	498
diśas timirayan sarvā	15.10	562
diṣṭyā hato 'yaṁ jagatām aruntudas	19.30	722
diṣṭyā me bhagavān dṛṣṭo	22.6	834
diṣṭyā pāda-rajaḥ spṛṣṭaṁ	22.6	834
diṣṭyā tvāṁ vihitaṁ mṛtyum	18.28	701
diṣṭyā tvayānuśiṣṭo 'haṁ	22.7	835
diter jaṭhara-nirviṣṭaṁ	16.35	652
ditir dākṣāyaṇī kṣattar	14.8	518
ditis tu bhartur ādeśād	17.2	658
ditis tu vrīḍitā tena	14.33	538
divi bhuvy antarikṣe ca	17.3	658
divi-spṛśau hema-kirīṭa-koṭibhir	17.17	667

divyair dvādaśabhir varṣaiḥ 11.18 409
divyopakaraṇopetaṁ 23.14 883
dīyamānaṁ na gṛhṇanti 29.13 1193
dorbhiś caturbhir viditaṁ 4.7 121
dor-daṇḍa-ṣaṇḍa-vivare haratā 15.41 599

drakṣyanty agha-kṣata-dṛśo hy ahi- 16.10 626
draṣṭāsi māṁ tataṁ brahman 9.31 361
draṣṭuṁ yatante yatayaḥ 24.28 940
dravyākṛtitvaṁ guṇatā 26.39 1065
dravya-sphuraṇa-vijñānam 26.29 1054

dravyāvayava-vaiṣamyād 26.45 1068
dravyopalabdhi-sthānasya 31.45 1309
dṛṣṭā bhavadbhir nanu rājasūye 2.19 69
dṛṣṭo 'ṅguṣṭha-śiro-mātraḥ 13.22 484
dṛṣṭvā khe 'vasthitaṁ vakṣaḥ- 21.11 783

dṛṣṭvā pāpīyasīṁ sṛṣṭiṁ 12.3 428
dṛṣṭvā tat saukaraṁ rūpaṁ 13.20 484
dṛṣṭvānyāṁś ca mahotpātān 17.15 665
dṛśy-ādibhiḥ pṛthag bhāvair 32.26 1339
dṛśyate 'sann api draṣṭur 7.11 267

dukūla-kṣauma-kauśeyair 23.15 883
dukūle nirmale nūtne 23.28 891
dunoti cetaḥ smarato mamaitad 2.17 67
dunoti dīnāṁ vikramya 14.10 519

durāpā hy alpa-tapasaḥ 7.20 276
durbhago bata loko 'yaṁ 2.8 55
durvibhāvyāṁ parābhāvya 28.44 1177
duryodhano 'tapyata yat-sabhāyāṁ 1.36 35

dvādaśārdha-palonmānaṁ 11.9 402
dvāḥsthāv ādiśya bhagavān 16.32 650
dvāḥsu vidruma-dehalyā 23.18 885
dvaipāyanād anavaro 20.3 735

dvaipāyana-sakhas tv evaṁ 25.4 968
dvāri dyu-nadyā ṛṣabhaḥ kurūṇāṁ 5.1 155
dvāry etayor nivivisur miṣator apṛṣṭvā 15.29 583
dvau tāv ṛtuḥ ṣaḍ ayanaṁ 11.11 403

dvayor apy eka evārtho 32.32 1347
dvi-parārdhāvasāne yaḥ 32.8 1322
dvi-śaphāḥ paśavaś ceme 10.22 391
dviṣataḥ para-kāye māṁ 29.23 1207
dvitīyas tv ahamo yatra 10.15 386

dyaur naṣṭa-bhagaṇābhraughaiḥ 19.19 714
dyotanaṁ pacanaṁ pānam 26.40 1065
dyūte tv adharmeṇa jitasya sādhoḥ 1.8 6

E

ebhiḥ sṛja prajā bahvīḥ 12.14 437
ekādaśa samās tatra 2.26 78
ekādaśa-vidhas tasya 32.29 1344
ekaḥ prapadyate dhvāntaṁ 30.31 1257
ekaḥ svayaṁ sañ jagataḥ sisṛkṣayā- 21.19 795
ekaikasyāṁ daśa daśa 3.9 96

ekaṁ vyabhāṅkṣīd urudhā 10.8 380
ekānta-lābhaṁ vacaso nu puṁsāṁ 6.37 248
eko nāneyate tadvad 32.33 1348
eṣa ātma-patho 'vyakto 24.37 952
eṣa dainan-dinaḥ sargo 11.26 414

eṣa deva diter garbha 15.10 562
eṣā ghoratamā sandhyā 18.26 700
eṣā ghoratamā velā 14.23 529
eṣa hy aśeṣa-sattvānām 6.8 222

eṣa māṁ tvat-kṛte vidvan 14.10 519
eṣa mānavi te garbhaṁ 24.18 933
eṣa prapanna-varado ramayātma- 9.23 354
eṣa te 'haṁ vidhāsyāmi 14.17 524

eṣa te deva devānām 18.22 697
etac catur-viṁśatikaṁ 26.11 1038
etad aṇḍaṁ viśeṣākhyaṁ 26.52 1074
etad bhagavato rūpaṁ 29.36 1222

etad vai śraddhayā bhaktyā 32.30 1345
etair anyaiś ca pathibhir 28.7 1136
etan mahā-puṇyam alaṁ pavitraṁ 19.38 731
etan me janma loke 'smin 24.36 951

etān me pṛcchataḥ praśnān 7.40 292
etan nigaditaṁ tāta 33.36 1397
etāny asaṁhatya yadā 26.50 1072
etasmin me mano vidvan 7.7 261
etasyāṁ sādhvi sandhyāyām 14.24 530

etat kṣattar bhagavato 6.35 245
etat puraiva nirdiṣṭaṁ 16.30 648
etat sparśasya sparśatvaṁ 26.36 1062
etat ta ādi-rājasya 22.39 867
etau suretara-gatiṁ pratipadya sadyaḥ 16.26 644

etau tau pārṣadau mahyaṁ 16.2 617
etau tau pārṣadāv asya 19.29 722
etāvān eva loke 'smin 25.44 1020
etāvān eva saṅkhyāto 26.15 1040
etāvān eva yogena 32.27 1341

etāvāñ jīva-lokasya 10.9 381
etāvatālaṁ kālena 23.53 910
etāvaty ātmajair vīra 13.10 476
etāvaty eva śuśrūṣā 24.13 928
ete caika-śaphāḥ kṣattaḥ 10.23 392

ete devāḥ kalā viṣṇoḥ 5.38 194
ete hy abhyutthitā devā 26.62 1082
ete varṇāḥ sva-dharmeṇa 6.34 244
ete vayaṁ nyāsa-harā rasaukasāṁ 18.11 689

evam ātmabhuvādiṣṭaḥ 12.20 441
evam āviṣkṛtāśeṣa- 22.1 829
evaṁ bruvāṇam abalākhila- 23.9 878
evaṁ bruvāṇaṁ maitreyaṁ 7.1 255

evam etat purā pṛṣṭo 1.1 1
evaṁ gadābhyāṁ gurvībhyāṁ 18.18 694
evaṁ harau bhagavati pratilabdha- 28.34 1166
evaṁ hiraṇyākṣam asahya-vikramaṁ 19.31 724

evaṁ kālo 'py anumitaḥ 11.3 398
evaṁ kṛta-matir garbhe 31.22 1287
evaṁ kuṭumba-bharaṇe 30.18 1247
evaṁ kuṭumbaṁ bibhrāṇa 30.30 1256

evaṁ niśamya kapilasya vaco janitrī 33.1 1361
evaṁ parābhidhyānena 26.6 1032
evaṁ paretya bhagavantam 32.10 1324
evaṁ pratyavamṛśyāsāv 27.16 1110
evaṁ rajaḥ-plutaḥ sraṣṭā 10.30 396

evaṁ sā kapiloktena 33.30 1393
evaṁ samuditas tena 24.41 957
evaṁ sañcintya bhagavān 3.16 103
evaṁ sañcoditas tena 10.3 376
evaṁ sva-bharaṇākalpaṁ 30.13 1243

evaṁ tadaiva bhagavān aravinda- 15.37 594
evaṁ tam anubhāṣyātha 21.33 811
evaṁ tri-loka-guruṇā 4.32 149
evaṁ trivṛd-ahaṅkāro 27.13 1106
evam ugraśravāḥ pṛṣṭa 20.7 738

evaṁ vidita-tattvasya 27.26 1122
evaṁ vyāhṛtayaś cāsan 12.44 460
evaṁ yogānubhāvena 23.46 905
evaṁ yoga-rataṁ ceta 29.20 1204
evaṁ yukta-kṛtas tasya 12.52 465
evaṁ-vidhair aho-rātraiḥ 11.33 418

G

gaccha kāmaṁ mayāpṛṣṭo 24.38 953
gadā-pāṇir divaṁ yāto 17.20 670

gadāyām apaviddhāyām 19.5 705
gaja-mātraḥ pravavṛdhe 13.19 483
gāṁ kampayantau caraṇaiḥ pade pade 17.17 667
gāṁ paryaṭan medhya-vivikta-vṛttiḥ 1.19 19

gamiṣye dayitaṁ tasya 4.21 136
gandha-mātram abhūt tasmāt 26.44 1068
gandharvāpsarasaḥ siddhā 10.28 394
gāndharva-vṛttyā miṣatāṁ sva-bhāgaṁ 3.3 91

gandhe 'rcite tulasikābharaṇena tasyā 15.19 570
gāsyanti yad-yaśaḥ śuddhaṁ 14.45 547
gate śata-dhṛtau kṣattaḥ 24.21 936
gatvā cāndramasaṁ lokaṁ 32.3 1317

gatyā svāṁśena puruṣo 6.22 233
gaur ajo mahiṣaḥ kṛṣṇaḥ 10.22 391
gāvo 'trasann asṛg-dohās 17.13 664
gāyan kala-padaṁ reme 2.34 86

gāyanti taṁ sma gandharvā 24.7 922
ghoṣe 'raṇye ca paśavaḥ 17.12 663
ghrāṇād vāyur abhidyetām 26.55 1077
ghrāṇena nāsike vāyur 26.63 1083

ghrāṇena pṛthvyāḥ padavīṁ vijighran 13.28 490
ghrāṇenāṁśena gandhasya 6.14 229
girayaḥ pratyadṛśyanta 19.20 715
gīrbhis tv abhyagṛṇāt prīti- 21.12 784

gīta-saṁstuti-vāditraiḥ 22.28 856
gopucchair haribhir markair 21.44 819
gotra-līlātapatreṇa 2.33 86
go-viprārthāsavaḥ śūrāḥ 3.28 114

grahān puṇyatamān anye 17.14 664
graha-nakṣatra-tārāṇāṁ 7.33 285
graharkṣa-tārā-cakra-sthaḥ 11.13 404
grāmya-dharma-nivṛttiś ca 28.3 1131

gṛhamedheṣu yogeṣu 3.22 109
gṛhāṇaitāni nāmāni 12.14 437
gṛheṣu jāto grāmyāṇāṁ 24.29 941
gṛheṣu kūṭa-dharmeṣu 30.9 1240

gṛhīta-guṇa-bhedāya 15.5 558
gṛhītārhaṇam āsīnaṁ 21.49 822
gṛhīto 'nanya-bhāvena 5.19 177
gṛhodyānaṁ kusumitai 33.18 1381

gudād apāno 'pānāc ca 26.57 1079
gudaṁ mṛtyur apānena 26.66 1085
gudaṁ puṁso vinirbhinnaṁ 6.20 232
gūhantīṁ vrīḍayātmānaṁ 20.31 758

guṇābhimānino devāḥ 29.44 1229
guṇair vicitrāḥ sṛjatīṁ 26.5 1030
guṇānāṁ vṛttayo yeṣu 6.27 235

guṇa-pravāhaṁ sad-aśeṣa-bījaṁ 33.2 1362
guṇāvabhāse viguṇa 24.43 959
guṇāvatārair viśvasya 7.28 282
guṇa-vyatikarākāro 10.11 382

guṇena kālānugatena viddhaḥ 8.13 306
guṇeṣu saktaṁ bandhāya 25.15 980
guṇeṣu satsu prakṛteḥ 27.19 1113

H

hāhā-kāro mahān āsīd 16.34 651
haṁsa-pārāvata-vrātais 23.20 887
haṁsa-sārasa-cakrāhva- 10.25 393
haṁsa-śriyor vyajanayoḥ śiva-vāyu- 15.38 595

haṁso haṁsena yānena 24.20 935
haniṣyaty avatīryāsau 14.41 545
haranti balim āyattās 15.8 560
hareḥ padānusmṛti-nirvṛtasya 5.13 171

hāreṇu ca maharheṇa 23.32 894
hāreṇa cānanta-dhanena vatsa 8.28 318
harer dhṛta-kroḍa-tanoḥ sva-māyayā 20.8 739
harer viditvā gatim aṅga nāradād 18.1 679

hāsaṁ harer avanatākhila-loka-tīvra- 28.32 1164
hasanti yasyācaritam hi durbhagaḥ 14.28 534
hastau ca nirabhidyetāṁ 26.58 1079
hastāv asya vinirbhinnāv 6.21 232

hastāv indro balenaiva 26.66 1085
hata-śriyau brahma-śāpād 16.33 651
hetutvam apy asati kartari duḥkhayor 28.36 1169
heyopādeya-rahitam 32.25 1338

hiraṇmayād aṇḍa-kośād 26.53 1076
hiraṇmayaḥ sa puruṣaḥ 6.6 220
hiraṇya-keśaḥ padmākṣaḥ 24.17 932
hiraṇyākṣo 'nujas tasya 17.20 670

hiraṇyaṁ rajataṁ śayyāṁ 3.27 113
hitvā śṛṇvanty asad-gāthāḥ 32.19 1332
hitvā tad īpsitatamam 33.20 1383

hitvārcāṁ bhajate mauḍhyād 29.22 1206
hṛd indriyāṇy asur vyoma 12.11 434
hṛdayaṁ cāsya nirbhinnaṁ 6.24 234
hṛdayaṁ manasā candro 26.68 1086
hṛdayaṁ tasya hi brahma 22.3 830

hṛdi kāmo bhruvaḥ krodho 12.26 445
hṛdi sthito yacchati bhakti-pūte 5.4 158
hṛdīka-satyātmaja-cārudeṣṇa- 1.35 34
hṛtātmano hṛta-prāṇāṁś ca bhaktir 25.36 1007

I

icchā-dveṣa-vihīnena 24.47 963
icchann ito vivasituṁ gaṇayan sva- 31.17 1280
idaṁ śukla-kṛtaṁ tīrtham 23.23 889
īḍito bhagavān evaṁ 33.9 1373
īdṛg gṛhaṁ tat paśyantīṁ 23.22 888

īkṣetānanya-bhāvena 28.42 1175
imā duhitaraḥ satyas 24.14 929
imaṁ lokam amuṁ caiva 3.21 108
imaṁ lokaṁ tathaivāmum 25.39 1013
indriyāṇi daśa śrotraṁ 26.13 1039

indriyārtha-prasaṅgena 23.53 911
indriyārtheṣu sajjantyā 23.54 911
iṅgita-jñāḥ puru-prauḍhā 2.9 56
irāvatī svadhā dīkṣā 12.13 437

iṣṭvāgni-jihvaṁ payasā 14.9 518
īśvarasya vimuktasya 7.9 263
īśvareṇa paricchinnaṁ 10.12 384
īśvaro jīva-kalayā 29.34 1219

iti bhāgavataḥ pṛṣṭaḥ 2.1 47
iti bruvāṇaṁ viduraṁ vinītaṁ 13.5 472
iti kauṣāravākhyātām 19.33 726
iti mātur vacaḥ ślakṣṇaṁ 29.6 1186

iti mīmāṁsatas tasya 13.23 485
iti pradarśya bhagavān 33.12 1376
iti saha vidureṇa viśva-mūrter 4.27 142
iti sāyantanīṁ sandhyām 20.37 763

iti sva-mātur niravadyam īpsitaṁ 25.12 976
iti tad gṛṇatāṁ teṣāṁ 16.1 617
iti tāṁ vīra mārīcaḥ 14.16 523
iti tāsāṁ sva-śaktīnāṁ 6.1 215
iti tasya vacaḥ pādmo 12.9 433

iti te varṇitaḥ kṣattaḥ 12.1 427
itihāsa-purāṇāni 12.39 456
itthaṁ vrajan bhāratam eva varṣaṁ 1.20 20
ity abhidhyāyato nāsā- 13.18 483
ity ādiṣṭaḥ sva-guruṇā 12.15 438

ity ādṛtoktaḥ paramasya puṁsaḥ 4.14 128
ity āvedita-hārdāya 4.19 133
ity avyalīkaṁ praṇuto 'bja-nābhas 21.22 799
ity etat kathitaṁ gurvi 32.31 1346
ity evaṁ śaiśavaṁ bhuktvā 31.28 1291

ity ūcivāṁs tatra suyodhanena 1.14 12
ity uddhavād upākarṇya 4.23 137
ity uktaḥ sa tadā bhūyas 19.10 708
ity upasthīyamāno 'sau 13.46 507
īyate bhagavān ebhiḥ 32.36 1350

J

jagāda so 'smad-gurave 'nvitāya 8.8 301
jagāma bindusarasaḥ 21.33 811
jagāma lokaṁ svam akhaṇḍitotsavaṁ 19.31 724

jaghāna rundhānam asahya-vikramaṁ 13.32 493
jaghānotpatya gadayā 19.2 704
jagrāha līlayā prāptāṁ 19.11 709
jagrāha tri-śikhaṁ śūlaṁ 19.13 710

jagrāha vāso brahmarṣer 14.30 536
jagṛhur yakṣa-rakṣāṁsi 20.19 749
jagṛhus tad-visṛṣṭāṁ tāṁ 20.41 765
jālārka-raśmy-avagataḥ 11.5 400

janaṁ janena janayan 29.45 1230
janas-tapaḥ-satya-nivāsinas te 13.25 487
janasya kṛṣṇād vimukhasya daivād 5.3 157
janayaty āśu vairāgyaṁ 32.23 1336

jantur vai bhava etasmin 30.4 1236
jānu-dvayaṁ jalaja-locanayā jananyā 28.23 1153
jarayaty āśu yā kośaṁ 25.33 1002
jarayopātta-vairūpyo 30.14 1244
jāta-bhāvo vimānaṁ tad 23.37 897

jātaḥ sasarja bhūtādir 20.13 743
jātaḥ svayam ajaḥ sākṣād 25.1 965
jāta-harṣo 'patan mūrdhnā 21.12 784
jāta-kṣobhād bhagavato 20.12 742
jāte guṇa-vyatikare 32.14 1327

jigīṣayā susaṁrabdhāv 18.18 694
jihvā pravargyas tava śīrṣakaṁ kratoḥ 13.37 498
jihvayāṁśena ca rasaṁ 6.13 228
jijñāsayāhaṁ prakṛteḥ pūruṣasya 25.11 975
jitaṁ jitaṁ te 'jita yajña-bhāvana 13.34 495

jitvā sudurjayaṁ mṛtyum 24.38 953
jīvābhaya-pradānasya 7.41 293
jivaḥ śreṣṭha hy ajivanāṁ 29.28 1213
jīvasya gatayo yāś ca 7.31 284
jīvasya saṁsṛtīr bahvīr 32.38 1354

jīvataś cāntrābhyuddhāraḥ 30.26 1253
jīvo hy asyānugo deho 31.44 1308
jñānaṁ ca naigamaṁ yat tad 7.38 290
jñānam ekaṁ parācīnair 32.28 1342

jñānaṁ niḥśreyasārthāya 26.2 1024
jñānaṁ paraṁ man-mahimāvabhāsaṁ 4.13 127
jñānaṁ paraṁ svātma-rahaḥ- 4.18 132
jñānaṁ paraṁ svātma-rahaḥ- 4.25 139

jñānaṁ yad etad adadhāt katamaḥ sa 31.16 1278
jñāna-mātraṁ paraṁ brahma 32.26 1339
jñāna-vairāgya-yuktena 25.18 983
jñāna-vairāgya-yuktena 25.43 1019

jñāna-vijñāna-yogena 24.17 932
jñāna-yogaś ca man-niṣṭho 32.32 1347
jñānena dṛṣṭa-tattvena 27.9 1103
jñānena dṛṣṭa-tattvena 27.22 1118

jñānena vairāgya-balena dhīrā 5.42 199
jñānenāśamayat kṣattā 4.23 137
jñāta-tattvāpy abhūn naṣṭe 33.21 1383
jñāto 'haṁ bhavatā tv adya 9.36 366
jñāto 'si me 'dya sucirān nanu deha- 9.1 323

jñātvā tad dhṛdaye bhūyaś 12.50 464
juṣṭaṁ batādyākhila-sattva-rāśeḥ 21.13 786
juṣṭaṁ vicitra-vaitānair 23.19 886
jyotiṣāmbho 'nusaṁsṛṣṭaṁ 5.36 192

K

ka enam atropajuhāva jihmaṁ 1.15 13
ka eṣa yo 'sāv aham abja-pṛṣṭha 8.18 309
ka eva te tanayāṁ nādriyeta 22.16 844
kaccic chivaṁ devaka-bhoja-putryā 1.33 32
kaccid budhaḥ svasty anamīva āste 1.32 31

kaccid dhareḥ saumya sutaḥ sadṛkṣa 1.30 29
kaccid varūthādhipatir yadūnāṁ 1.28 28
kaccid yaśodhā ratha-yūthapānāṁ 1.38 36
kaccit kurūṇāṁ paramaḥ suhṛn no 1.27 27
kaccit purāṇau puruṣau svanābhya- 1.26 26

kaccit sukhaṁ sātvata-vṛṣṇi-bhoja- 1.29 29
kācit tvayy ucitā bhaktiḥ 25.28 996
kadā vā saha-saṁvāda 1.3 2
kadācid dhyāyataḥ sraṣṭur 12.34 453

kadamba-campakāśoka- 21.42 818
kadamba-kiñjalka-piśaṅga-vāsasā 8.28 318
kadarthī-kṛtya māṁ yad vo 16.2 618
kaḥ śraddadhītānyatamas tava prabho 13.43 504

kaḥ śraddadhyād upākartuṁ 6.35 245
kaivalyaṁ parama-mahān 11.2 398
kakudmino 'viddha-naso damitvā 3.4 92
kāla-dravya-guṇair asya 10.14 385

kāla-karma-guṇopeto 26.50 1072
kālākhyaṁ lakṣaṇaṁ brahman 10.10 382
kālākhyayā guṇamayaṁ kratubhir 11.15 406
kālākhyayāsādita-karma-tantro 8.12 305

kalalaṁ tv eka-rātreṇa	31.2	1264
kāla-māgadha-śālvādīn	3.10	97
kāla-māyāṁśa-yogena	5.33	190
kāla-sañjñāṁ tadā devīṁ	6.2	216
kālasya cāvyakta-gater	32.37	1353
kālasyeśvara-rūpasya	29.4	1183
kālātmano yat pramadā-yutāśramaḥ	4.16	130
kāla-vṛttyā tu māyāyāṁ	5.26	184
kālena bhūyasā kṣāmāṁ	23.5	872
kālena bhūyasā nūnaṁ	24.27	940
kālena so 'jaḥ puruṣāyuṣābhi-	8.22	312
kālena tāvad yamunām upetya	1.24	24
kālenānugatāśeṣa	11.28	415
kālindyāḥ katibhiḥ siddha	4.36	153
kālo 'yaṁ dvi-parārdhākhyo	11.38	422
kālo 'yaṁ paramāṇv-ādir	11.39	423
kalpo yatrābhavad brahmā	11.35	420
kālyamāno 'pi balino	30.1	1233
kaṁ vṛṇīta varaṁ vatsā	14.13	521
kāmāgninācyuta-ruṣā ca sudur-	9.8	332
kāmaḥ sa bhūyān naradeva te 'syāḥ	22.16	844
kāmam arthaṁ ca dharmān svān	32.1	1315
kāmaṁ bhavaḥ sva-vṛjinair nirayeṣu	15.49	612
kāmān siṣeve dvārvatyām	3.19	106
kāñcī-guṇollasac-chroṇiṁ	28.16	1144
kāñcī-kalāpa-vilasad-	20.29	757
kaṅka-gṛdhra-baka-śyena-	10.25	393
kaṇṭhaṁ ca kaustubha-maṇer	28.26	1157
kāntyā sasarja bhagavān	20.38	763
kāny anvatiṣṭhad dvārāṇi	20.1	733
kapilas tattva-saṅkhyātā	25.1	965
kapilasya ca saṁvādo	33.36	1397
kapilo 'pi mahā-yogī	33.33	1395
karāla-daṁṣṭraś cakṣurbhyāṁ	19.8	707
karāla-daṁṣṭro 'py akarāla-dṛgbhyām	13.28	490
karāla-daṁṣṭro 'śani-nisvano 'bravīd	18.7	686
karambha-pūti-saurabhya-	26.45	1068
kāraṇḍavaiḥ plavair haṁsaiḥ	21.43	818
kārdamaṁ vīryam āpanno	24.6	921
kareṇa karṇa-mūle 'han	19.25	718
karmaṇā daiva-netreṇa	31.1	1263
karmaṇāṁśena yenāsau	6.25	234
karma-nirhāram uddiśya	29.10	1190
karmāṇy anīhasya bhavo 'bhavasya te	4.16	129
karmasu kriyamāṇeṣu	26.6	1032
karṇāv asya vinirbhinnau	6.17	230
karoti karmāṇi kṛtāvatāro	5.5	160
karoti vigrahaṁ kāmī	31.29	1292
karoty avirataṁ mūḍho	30.7	1238
kartṛtvaṁ karaṇatvaṁ ca	26.26	1051
kartṛtvāt saguṇaṁ brahma	32.13	1327
kārtsnyena cādyeha gataṁ vidhātur	2.13	62
kārya-kāraṇa-kartrātmā	5.29	187
kārya-kāraṇa-kartṛtve	26.8	1034
kas tṛpnuyāt tīrtha-pado 'bhidhānāt	5.11	168
kāsa-śvāsa-kṛtāyāsaḥ	30.16	1246
kaṣāyo madhuras tiktaḥ	26.42	1067
kaścit syān me viśokāya	23.52	909
kāsi kasyāsi rambhoru	20.34	760
kāṣṭhāṁ bhagavato dhyāyet	28.12	1141
kasya rūpam abhūd dvedhā	12.52	465
katham enāṁ samunneṣya	13.16	481
kathaṁ srakṣyāmy ahaṁ lokān	12.34	453
kathāyāṁ kathanīyoru-	32.18	1331
kathyatāṁ bhagavan yatra	21.1	775
kaṭu-tīkṣṇoṣṇa-lavaṇa-	31.7	1268
kaumārīṁ darśayaṁś ceṣṭāṁ	2.28	80
kaumodakīṁ bhagavato dayitāṁ	28.28	1159
kauravya mahyāṁ dviṣator	18.20	695
kevalena hy adharmeṇa	30.33	1259
kharāś ca karkaśaiḥ kṣattaḥ	17.11	663
khārkāra-rabhasā mattāḥ	17.11	663

kharo 'śvo 'śvataro gauraḥ 10.23 392
khurāhatābhraḥ sita-daṁṣṭra īkṣā- 13.27 489
khuraiḥ kṣuraprair darayaṁs tad āpa 13.30 491
khyātiṁ ca bhṛgave 'yacchad 24.23 937
kīdṛśaḥ kati cāṅgāni 25.29 997

kim anvapṛcchan maitreyaṁ 20.4 735
kim ārabhata me brahman 20.9 740
kiṁ durāpādanaṁ teṣāṁ 23.42 901
kim etat sūkara-vyājaṁ 13.21 484
kiṁ nu naḥ kuśalaṁ brūyāṁ 2.7 53

kiṁ vā kṛtāgheṣv agham atyamarṣī 1.37 36
kiṁ vā punas tac-caraṇāravinda- 7.14 271
kiñcic cakāra vadanaṁ 33.20 1383
kirīṭa-sāhasra-hiraṇya-śṛṅgam 8.30 319
kirīṭa-sāhasra-maṇi-praveka- 8.6 300

kirīṭinaṁ kuṇḍalinaṁ 21.10 783
kīrtanya-tīrtha-yaśasaṁ 28.18 1146
kīrtiṁ hareḥ svāṁ sat-kartuṁ 6.36 247
kīrtiṁ vitanvatā loke 5.18 176
kiyān bhuvo 'yaṁ kṣapitoru-bhāro 3.14 100

kledanaṁ piṇḍanaṁ tṛptiḥ 26.43 1067
ko nāma loke puruṣārtha-sāravit 13.50 510
ko nv īśa te pāda-saroja-bhājāṁ 4.15 129
ko vā amuṣyāṅghri-saroja-reṇuṁ 2.18 68

ko vāṁ ihaitya bhagavat- 15.32 587
ko viśrambheta yogena 3.23 109
kolāhalo viramate 'cira-mātram uccair 15.18 569
kopitā munayaḥ śepur 3.24 111

kramaśaḥ samanukramya 30.34 1260
kṛcchreṇa pṛṣṭhe kaśayā ca tāḍitaś 30.22 1251
krīḍan vidhatte dvija-go-surāṇāṁ 5.7 162
krīḍāyām udyamo 'rbhasya 7.3 258

krīḍayopātta-dehasya 4.33 151
kriyā-śaktir ahaṅkāras 26.23 1050
kriyayā kratubhir dānais 32.34 1350
kriyā-yogena śastena 29.15 1196

kṛmibhiḥ kṣata-sarvāṅgaḥ 31.6 1267
kṛntanaṁ cāvayavaśo 30.27 1254
krodhaṁ durviṣahaṁ jātaṁ 12.6 432
krośantīnāṁ kareṇūnāṁ 19.35 728
kṛpayā samparītasya 21.38 815

kṛṣṇa-dyumaṇi nimloce 2.7 53
kṛtajñaḥ ko na seveta 19.36 729
kṛtaṁ tretā dvāparaṁ ca 11.18 409
kṛta-śokānutāpena 14.44 547
kṛto me 'nugrahaś ceti 16.16 632

kṛtrimān manyamānaiḥ svān 23.20 887
kṛtsna-prasāda-sumukhaṁ spṛhaṇīya- 15.39 596
kṛtvā dayāṁ ca jīveṣu 21.31 807
kṣaṇam iva puline yamasvasus tāṁ 4.27 142
kṣaṇān pañca viduḥ kāṣṭhāṁ 11.7 401

kṣattā mahā-bhāgavataḥ 20.2 734
kṣattānandaṁ paraṁ lebhe 19.33 726
kṣattopasṛtyācyuta-bhāva-siddhaḥ 5.1 155
kṣattrā vanaṁ praviṣṭena 1.1 1
kṣemaṁ sa kaccid yuyudhāna āste 1.31 30

kṣemaṁ vidhāsyati sa no bhagavāṁs 16.37 654
kṣemāya pāda-mūlaṁ me 25.43 1019
kṣiṇoti devo 'nimiṣas tu yeṣām 5.14 172
kṣiptaiḥ kaśipubhiḥ kāntaṁ 23.16 884

kṣitau śayānaṁ tam akuṇṭha- 19.27 720
kṣīyate tad-yaśaḥ sphītaṁ 22.13 841
kṣmāmbho-'nalānila-viyan-mana- 32.9 1324
kṣut-pipāse tataḥ syātāṁ 26.60 1081

kṣut-tṛḍbhyām udaraṁ sindhur 26.68 1086
kṣut-tṛḍbhyām upasṛṣṭās te 20.20 750
kṣut-tṛṭ-parīto 'rka-davānalānilaiḥ 30.22 1251
kṣut-tṛṭ-tridhātubhir imā muhur 9.8 332

kūjad-vihaṅga-mithunaṁ 33.18 1381
kunda-mandāra-kuṭajaiś 21.42 818
kurvan duḥkha-pratīkāraṁ 30.9 1240
kurvanti kāma-sukha-leśa-lavāya 9.7 331

kurvanty apratiṣiddhāni 32.16 1329
kuśāḥ kāśās ta evāsan 22.30 857
kuśa-kāśamayaṁ barhir 22.31 858
kuśaletara-pātheyo 30.31 1257

kutra kṣattur bhagavatā 1.3 2
kuṭumba-bharaṇākalpo 30.12 1243
kvacit tattvāvamarśena 27.20 1114

L

labdhāśiṣaḥ punar avekṣya tadīyam 15.44 602
labdha-yuṣmat-prasādānāṁ 15.7 559
laghūni vai samāmnātā 11.8 401
lakṣaṇaṁ bhakti-yogasya 29.12 1191
lakṣaṇaṁ mahad-ādīnāṁ 29.1 1181

lakṣyate 'ntar-gatāś cānye 11.41 425
lasat-paṅkaja-kiñjalka- 28.14 1143
lebhe 'ñjasādhokṣaja-sevayaiva 1.31 30
lebhe gatiṁ dhātry-ucitāṁ tato 'nyaṁ 2.23 74
likhanty adho-mukhī bhūmiṁ 23.50 908

līlāṁ hiraṇyākṣam avajñayā hataṁ 20.8 739
līlayā cāpi yujyeran 7.2 255
līlayā miṣataḥ śatroḥ 19.9 708
līlayā vyanudat tāṁs tān 2.30 83
līneṣv asati yas tatra 27.14 1108

lobhābhibhūto niḥsattvaḥ 30.11 1242
lokaṁ sva-dehaṁ tanute 29.43 1228
lokāṁś ca lokānugatān paśūṁś ca 21.17 792
lokān anucaran siddha 4.9 123
lokān ito vrajatam antara-bhāva- 15.34 591

lokān sa-pālāṁs trīṁś caṇḍi 14.39 543
loka-saṁsthāṁ yathā pūrvaṁ 20.17 746
loka-saṁsthāna-vijñāna 9.28 358
lokasya mithyābhimater acakṣuṣaś 29.5 1184

lokasya tamasāndhasya 25.9 972
loke kapila ity ākhyāṁ 24.19 935
loke tenāhatāloke 15.2 556
loko vikarma-nirataḥ kuśale 9.17 346

M

mā khido rāja-putrīttham 24.2 917
mā rakṣatainaṁ jakṣadhvam 20.20 750
mā veda-garbha gās tandrīṁ 9.29 359

mā vo 'nutāpa-kalayā bhagavat-smṛti- 15.36 593
mad-āśrayāḥ kathā mṛṣṭāḥ 25.23 990
mad-bhaktaḥ pratibuddhārtho 27.28 1125
mad-bhayād vāti vāto 'yaṁ 25.42 1017

mad-dharmaṇo guṇair etaiḥ 29.19 1203
mad-dhiṣṇya-darśana-sparśa- 29.16 1198
mad-guṇa-śruti-mātreṇa 29.11 1191
madhyaṁ viṣīdati bṛhat-stana-bhāra- 20.36 762
madhye kāmayamānānām 20.32 759

mahā-bhūtāni pañcaiva 26.12 1039
mahā-marakata-sthalyā 23.17 885
mahāmohaṁ ca mohaṁ ca 12.2 427
mahatāṁ bahu-mānena 29.17 1200
mahat-tattvād vikurvāṇād 5.29 187

mahat-tattvād vikurvāṇād 26.23 1050
mahīṁ gandha-guṇām ādhāt 5.36 192
mahīṁ pratiṣṭhām adhyasya 20.1 733
mahimā veda-garbho 'tha 12.1 427
mahyaṁ bhavasya bhavatāṁ ca 15.42 600

mainaṁ māyāvinaṁ dṛptaṁ 18.24 698
maitryā caivātma-tulyeṣu 29.17 1200
majjāyāḥ paṅktir utpannā 12.46 461
mālāṁ madhuvrata-varūtha- 28.28 1159
mām ātmānaṁ svayaṁ-jyotiḥ 24.39 954

māṁ khedayaty etad ajasya janma- 2.16 66
mānasā me sutā yuṣmat- 15.12 563
manasaitāni bhūtāni 29.34 1219
manasāṁśena yenāsau 6.24 234

manasaś candramā jāto 26.61 1081
manasaś cendriyāṇāṁ ca 26.24 1050
mānase caitrarathye ca 23.40 900
manaso dehataś cedaṁ 12.27 446

mānayām āsa tad-dharmaṁ	19.5	706
mānayan sa mṛdhe dharmaṁ	19.4	705
mānayann ātmanātmānam	20.45	768
mandāra-kunda-kurabotpala-	15.19	570
māṇḍavya-śāpād bhagavān	5.20	178
man-nideśāticāreṇa	14.38	542
mano 'cirāt syād virajaṁ	28.10	1139
mano brahmaṇi yuñjāno	24.43	959
mano buddhir ahaṅkāraś	26.14	1040
mano na tṛpyaty api śṛṇvatāṁ naḥ	5.7	162
mano yenaiva vidhinā	28.1	1129
mano-gatir avicchinnā	29.11	1191
mano-vīrya-varotsiktam	17.22	671
mantreṣu māṁ vā upahūya yat tvam	4.17	131
manuḥ syandanam āsthāya	21.36	814
manv-ādibhir idaṁ viśvam	11.27	414
manvantareṣu bhagavān	11.27	414
manvantareṣu manavas	11.25	413
manyamānas tadātmānam	27.15	1109
manye 'surān bhāgavatāṁs tryadhīśe	2.24	75
manyur manur mahinaso	12.12	436
mārganti yat te mukha-padma-nīḍaiś	5.41	198
mārgeṇānena mātas te	33.10	1374
marīcaye kalāṁ prādād	24.22	937
marīci-mukhyā munayo	12.29	448
marīci-pramukhair vipraiḥ	13.20	483
marīcir atry-aṅgirasau	12.22	442
marmāṇy abhīkṣṇaṁ pratudantaṁ	18.9	687
māsena tu śiro dvābhyāṁ	31.3	1265
mātaraṁ samanujñāpya	33.33	1395
mat-kṛte tyakta-karmāṇas	25.22	989
mātra ādhyātmikīṁ vidyāṁ	24.40	955
mātṛ-bhuktair upaspṛṣṭaḥ	31.7	1268
mat-sevayā pratilabdhātma-lābho	31.39	1302
matta-barhi-naṭāṭopam	21.41	817
matta-dvija-gaṇair ghuṣṭaṁ	21.41	817
matta-dvirepha-kalayā	28.15	1143
matta-dvirepha-vanamālikayā nivītau	15.28	582
mātur jagdhānna-pānādyair	31.5	1266
maunaṁ sad-āsana-jayaḥ	28.5	1134
maurvyābhijaghne gadayā vibhāvarīm	17.26	674
māyā nāma mahā-bhāga	5.25	183
mayā proktaṁ hi lokasya	24.35	949
mayā saha dahantībhir	12.17	439
mayā yathānūktam avādi te hareḥ	19.32	725
māyā-viracite loke	31.48	1312
mayi bhāvena satyena	27.6	1097
mayi saṁrambha-yogena	16.31	648
mayi tīrthī-kṛtāśeṣa-	21.30	806
mayy ananyena bhāvena	25.22	989
mayy arpitātmanaḥ puṁso	29.33	1218
mayy ātmānaṁ saha jagad	21.31	807
meḍhraṁ tasya vinirbhinnaṁ	6.19	231
mene 'santam ivātmānam	5.24	182
mīna-dvayāśrayam adhikṣipad abja-	28.30	1162
mita-medhyādanaṁ śaśvad	28.3	1131
mitho yadaiṣāṁ bhavitā vivādo	3.15	102
mithunī-bhūya gāyantas	20.46	769
mṛdu tīvraṁ tapo dīrghaṁ	4.22	136
mṛdutvaṁ kaṭhinatvaṁ ca	26.36	1062
mṛgayantīṁ patiṁ dāsyaty	21.27	803
mriyate rudatāṁ svānām	30.18	1247
mṛṇāla-gaurāyata-śeṣa-bhoga-	8.23	313
mṛtyoḥ kṛtvaiva mūrdhny aṅghrim	14.6	516
muhuḥ paridhayo 'bhūvan	17.8	661
muhur gṛṇanto vacasānurāga-	8.6	300
mukhato 'vartata brahma	6.30	238
mukhena lokārti-hara-smitena	8.27	317
mukta-liṅgaṁ sad-ābhāsam	27.11	1105
mukta-saṅgas tato bhūyān	29.32	1217
muktāśrayaṁ yarhi nirviṣayaṁ	28.35	1167
munir vivakṣur bhagavad-guṇānāṁ	5.12	169

mūrcchām āpnoty uru-kleśas 31.6 1267
muṣṇantam akṣṇā sva-ruco 'ruṇa- 18.2 680

N

na brahma-daṇḍa-dagdhasya 14.43 547
na cābudhyata taṁ kālaṁ 23.45 904
na cāsya kaścid dayito 29.39 1225
na hy alpārthodayas tasya 1.4 3
na hy antaraṁ bhagavatīha samasta- 15.33 588

na hy asya varṣmaṇaḥ puṁsāṁ 25.2 966
na hy avyaktaṁ bhagavataḥ 15.3 557
na hy edhante prajā nūnaṁ 12.51 465
na karhicin mat-parāḥ śānta-rūpe 25.38 1010
na lolupāyopadiśen 32.40 1355

na me garbham imaṁ brahman 14.34 539
na mṛtyu-pāśaiḥ pratimuktasya vīrā 18.10 688
na paśyāmi paraṁ bhūtam 29.33 1218
na sasmāra tadātmānaṁ 33.27 1390
na śrīr viraktam api māṁ vijahāti 16.7 623

na stabdhāya na bhinnāya 32.39 1355
na svasti yāsyasy anayā mamekṣataḥ 18.3 681
na tāni puṁsām amṛtāyanāni 1.9 7
na tathāsya bhaven moho 31.35 1298
na te 'jarākṣa-bhramir āyur eṣām 21.18 794

na tīrtha-pada-sevāyai 23.56 913
na tvaṁ dvijottama-kulaṁ yadi 16.23 639
na vai jātu mṛṣaiva syāt 21.24 801
na vārayām āsa nṛpaḥ snuṣāyāḥ 1.7 6
na vayaṁ bhagavan vidmas 16.16 632

na vayaṁ prabhavas tāṁ tvām 14.21 527
na vigṛhṇāti vaiṣamyaṁ 32.24 1337
na vismayo 'sau tvayi viśva-vismaye 13.43 504
na yācato 'dāt samayena dāyaṁ 1.8 6

na yadā ratham āsthāya 21.52 824
na yasya loke sva-janaḥ paro vā 14.26 532
na yāvad eṣa vardheta 18.25 699
na yujyamānayā bhaktyā 25.19 984

nābhaktāya ca me jātu 32.40 1355
nabhasaḥ śabda-tanmātrāt 26.35 1062
nabhaso 'nusṛtaṁ sparśaṁ 5.33 190

nābhi-hradād iha sato 'mbhasi yasya 9.24 355
nābhi-hradaṁ bhuvana-kośa- 28.25 1155
nabho dadāti śvasatāṁ 29.43 1228
nabho-guṇa-viśeṣo 'rtho 26.47 1070
nāḍīr nadyo lohitena 26.67 1085

nādriyante yathā pūrvaṁ 30.13 1243
nadyas tataḥ samabhavann 26.59 1080
nāḍyo 'sya nirabhidyanta 26.59 1080
nāhaṁ tathādmi yajamāna-havir 16.8 624
naicchad gadāṁ dīyamānāṁ 19.12 709

naikātmatāṁ me spṛhayanti kecin 25.34 1003
naikatra te jayati śālini pāda-padmaṁ 20.36 762
naikatrāste sūti-vātair 31.10 1271
naiṣāṁ vadhopāya iyān ato 'nyo 3.15 102
naiṣkarmyasya ca sāṅkhyasya 7.30 283

naitac citraṁ tvayi kṣattar 5.19 177
naitad batādhīśa padaṁ tavepsitaṁ 21.20 796
naitat khalāyopadiśen 32.39 1355
naitat pūrvaiḥ kṛtaṁ tvad ye 12.30 449
naitāvatā try-adhipater bata viśva- 16.24 641

naiva tuṣye 'rcito 'rcāyāṁ 29.24 1208
naiveśituṁ prabhur bhūmna 11.39 423
nākampata manāk kvāpi 19.16 712
nakha-lomāsthi-carmāṇi 31.3 1265
nālena salile mūlaṁ 9.37 367

namāma te deva padāravindaṁ 5.39 196
namāmy abhīkṣṇaṁ namanīya-pāda- 21.21 798
nāmāni kuru me dhātaḥ 12.8 433
nāmnā siddha-padaṁ yatra 33.31 1394

namo namas te 'khila-mantra-devatā- 13.39 499
namo namas te 'khila-yajña-tantave 19.30 722
namo rudrāya mahate 14.35 540
namo vijñāna-vīryāya 15.5 558

nānā-karma-vitānena 9.34 364
nānātvāt sva-kriyānīśāḥ 5.38 194
nandayām āsa suhṛdaḥ 3.16 103
nanu te tattva-saṁrādhya 4.26 140
nanv anyathā ko 'rhati deha-yogaṁ 1.44 43

nānyat tvad asti bhagavann api tan 9.1 323
nānyatra mad bhagavataḥ 25.41 1015
nānyopalakṣyaḥ padavīṁ prasādāc 1.42 40
nārādhanaṁ bhagavato vitaranty 15.24 576
nārakāś cānugṛhṇanti 14.43 547

naraka-stho 'pi dehaṁ vai 30.5 1237
nārakyāṁ nirvṛtau satyāṁ 30.5 1237
nārāyaṇo viśvasṛg ātma-yonir 5.9 165
nārvāg-gatas tat-khara-nāla-nāla- 8.19 310
naṣṭa-smṛtiḥ punar ayaṁ pravṛṇīta 31.15 1276

naṣṭe 'haṅkaraṇe draṣṭā 27.15 1109
nāsvādya manyu-daṣṭānāṁ 16.13 630
nātaḥ paraṁ parama yad bhavataḥ 9.3 326
nāthamāna ṛṣir bhītaḥ 31.11 1271
nātikṣāmaṁ bhagavataḥ 21.46 820

nātiprasīdati tathopacitopacārair 9.12 339
nātmāvasīdaty asmiṁs te 9.34 365
natvā diṣṭāya rahasi 14.31 537
nātyantikaṁ vigaṇayanty api te 15.48 611

nayato dīrgham adhvānaṁ 30.20 1249
neha yat karma dharmāya 23.56 913
neśaḥ kaṇḍūyane 'ṅgānām 31.26 1290
neśvarasyāśubhaṁ dhatte 27.24 1120

netraiḥ pibanto nayanābhirāmaṁ 2.20 70
nidhanam upagateṣu vṛṣṇi-bhojeṣv 4.28 143
nidrām indriya-vikledo 20.41 765
niḥsaṅgā nyasta-karmāṇaḥ 32.5 1319

niḥsaṅgo vyacarat kṣoṇīm 24.42 958
niḥśreyasaṁ sva-saṁsthānaṁ 27.28 1125
nīlotpala-dala-śyāmaṁ 28.13 1142
nimajjyāsmin hrade bhīru 23.23 888

nimeṣas tri-lavo jñeya 11.7 401
nimittāni ca tasyeha 7.39 291
nimlocati ravāv āsīd 4.2 118
nimlocaty arka āsīnam 14.9 518
nipātya tuṅgād ripu-yūtha-nāthaṁ 3.1 89

nirabhidyanta devānāṁ 6.11 227
nirabhidyatāsya prathamaṁ 26.54 1076
nirahaṅkṛtir nirmamaś ca 24.44 960
nirantaraṁ svayaṁ-jyotir 25.17 982
nirasta-sāmyātiśayo 'pi yat svayaṁ 14.27 533

nirbhinnaṁ tālu varuṇo 6.13 228
nirbhinnāny asya carmāṇi 6.16 229
nirbhinne akṣiṇī tvaṣṭā 6.15 229
nirbhinne aśvinau nāse 6.14 228
nirbibheda virājas tvag- 26.56 1078

nirghātā ratha-nirhrādā 17.8 661
nirīkṣatas tasya yayāv aśeṣa- 21.34 812
nirmatsarāya śucaye 32.42 1357
nirūḍha mūla-hṛdaya 30.6 1237
nirvairādibhir ātmānaṁ 14.46 548

nirveda-vādinīm evaṁ 24.1 917
nirviṇṇā nitarāṁ bhūmann 25.7 970
niryāpito yena suhṛt sva-purya 1.41 39
niśamya kauṣāraviṇopavarṇitāṁ 14.1 513

niśāmya tad-yoga-gatiṁ 23.35 896
niśamya te ghargharitaṁ sva-kheda- 13.25 486
niśamya vācaṁ vadato 13.1 469
niśāmyāsaṅkhyaśo yūthān 12.16 438

niśamyātma-bhuvā gītaṁ 17.1 657
niśāvasāna ārabdho 11.23 412
niśāyām anuvṛttāyāṁ 11.29 416
niṣevitenānimittena 29.15 1196

niṣevya punar āyānti 32.15 1327
niṣka-grīvaṁ valayinaṁ 23.31 893
niṣṇātaṁ yogamāyāsu 22.34 862
nityaṁ paryacarat prītyā 23.1 869

nityārūḍha-samādhitvāt 33.27 1390
nivītam āmnāya-madhu-vrata-śriyā 8.31 320
nivṛtta-buddhy-avasthāno 27.10 1103
nivṛtta-jīvāpattitvāt 33.26 1387
nivṛtta-sandhyā-niyamo 14.37 542

nivṛtti-dharma-niratā 32.6 1320
noddhavo 'ṇv api man-nyūno 4.31 147
nodhā vidhāya rūpaṁ svaṁ 23.47 906
nṛṇāṁ varṇāśramāṇāṁ ca 22.38 866
nūnaṁ bhṛtaṁ tad-abhighāti rajas 16.22 638
nūnaṁ caṅkramaṇaṁ deva 21.50 823
nūnaṁ daivena vihatā 32.19 1332
nūnaṁ nṛpāṇāṁ tri-madotpathānāṁ 1.43 42
nyapatan yatra romāṇi 22.29 857
nyāse kuṭīcakaḥ pūrvaṁ 12.43 460
nyavedayan viśva-sṛje 15.2 556

P

padā savyena tāṁ sādho 19.9 708
pādau ca nirabhidyetāṁ 26.58 1079
pādāv asya vinirbhinnau 6.22 233
padbhyāṁ bhagavato jajñe 6.33 243
padma-kośaṁ tadāviśya 10.8 380
padma-kośa-spṛdhā nīlair 23.33 894
padmam ambhaś ca tat-kāla- 10.5 378
padmaṁ yad arcanty ahi-rāja-kanyāḥ 8.5 298
pāhi māṁ paramātmaṁs te 20.26 754
pakṣaḥ pañca-daśāhāni 11.10 403
pañcabhiḥ pañcabhir brahma 26.11 1038
pānena te deva kathā-sudhāyāḥ 5.46 205
para-cchandaṁ na viduṣā 31.25 1289
paraṁ pradhānaṁ puruṣaṁ 29.36 1222
paraṁ pradhānaṁ puruṣaṁ 24.33 946

paraṁ śuśrūṣaṇaṁ mahyaṁ 13.12 478
paramāṇuḥ sa vijñeyo 11.1 397
parameṣṭhī tv apāṁ madhye 13.16 481
parānuṣaktaṁ tapanīyopakalpaṁ 18.9 687

parārdhya-hāra-valaya- 28.15 1144
parārdhya-keyūra-maṇi-praveka- 8.29 318
parasparaṁ tvad-guṇa-vāda-sīdhu- 21.17 792
parasya dṛśyate dharmo 26.49 1071
parāvareṣāṁ bhagavan vratāni 5.10 166

parāvareśaṁ prakṛtim 32.7 1321
parāvareśo mahad-aṁśa-yukto 2.15 64
pārāvatānyabhṛta-sārasa-cakravāka- 15.18 569
pareṇa bhakti-bhāvena 24.45 961
pareṇa viśatā svasmin 6.5 219
pareṣāṁ apareṣāṁ tvaṁ 15.4 557
pareṣāṁ gatim ācakṣva 11.16 407
parikraman vyomni vivṛtta-netraś 8.16 308
paripaśyaty udāsīnaṁ 25.18 983
parīto bhūta-parṣadbhir 14.24 530
parīto vatsapair vatsāṁś 2.27 79
parivrajat-padavīm āsthito 'haṁ 24.34 948
pārthāṁs tu devo bhagavān mukundo 1.12 10
pāṣaṇḍa-patha-vaiṣamyaṁ 7.31 284
paśyāmi nānyaṁ puruṣāt purātanād 17.30 676
paśyāmi viśva-sṛjam ekam aviśvam 9.3 326
paśyanti te me rucirāṇy amba santaḥ 25.35 1005
paśyanti yatra yuvayoḥ sura-liṅginoḥ 15.33 588
paśyaty ayaṁ dhiṣaṇayā nanu sapta- 31.19 1282
pātanaṁ giri-śṛṅgebhyo 30.27 1254
patanti vivaśā devaiḥ 32.21 1333
pathā pāpīyasā nītas 30.23 1251
pathi śvabhir bhakṣyamāṇa 30.21 1250
patiṁ sā pravrajiṣyantaṁ 23.49 907
patir bhavad-vidho yāsāṁ 14.12 520
patito bhuvy asṛṅ-miśraḥ 31.24 1288
patnī prajāpater uktā 21.3 776

paṭṭikābhiḥ patākābhir 23.14 883
pauṁsnaṁ vapur darśayānam 15.45 602
pauravendra-gṛhaṁ hitvā 1.2 1
pautras tava śrī-lalanā-lalāmaṁ 14.50 552

payaḥ-phena-nibhāḥ śayyā 33.16 1380
pāyunāṁśena yenāsau 6.20 232
petuḥ sumanaso divyāḥ 24.8 923
phaṇātapatrāyuta-mūrdha-ratna- 8.23 313
pītāṁśuke pṛthu-nitambini 15.40 598

pitari prasthite 'raṇyaṁ 25.5 969
pitṛbhyāṁ prasthite sādhvī 23.1 869
pitṛ-deva-manuṣyāṇām 11.16 407
pitṝn yajanty anudinaṁ 32.17 1330
plāvayanty utkaṭāṭopa- 11.31 417

prabhāvaṁ pauruṣaṁ prāhuḥ 26.16 1041
prabhavanti vinā yena 26.71 1087
prabuddha-karmā daivena 6.4 218
pradarśayantaṁ kṛpayā nakhendu- 8.26 316
pradarśyātapta-tapasām 2.11 58

pradhānaṁ prakṛtiṁ prāhur 26.10 1037
prāduścakartha yad idaṁ puruhūta 15.50 614
prāduṣkṛtānāṁ māyānām 19.22 715
prahasya bhāva-gambhīraṁ 20.38 763
prahasya prema-garbheṇa 19.1 703

prāhedaṁ viduraṁ prīta 25.4 968
prahṛṣṭa-romā bhagavat-kathāyāṁ 13.5 472
prahṛṣyamāṇair asubhiḥ 24.11 926
prajā vicitrākṛtaya 7.24 279

prajāḥ sasarja katidhā 10.1 375
prajāḥ sṛja yathā-pūrvaṁ 9.43 373
prajāḥ sṛjeti bhagavān 21.6 779
prajām anu prajāyante 32.20 1333

prajāpateḥ kardamasya 33.15 1379
prajāpates te vacasādhīśa tantyā 21.16 791
prajāpatiḥ svāṁ duhitaraṁ 31.36 1299
prajāpatīnāṁ patir eṣa mahyaṁ 22.20 849

prajāpatīnāṁ sa patiś 7.25 280
prajāpati-patiḥ sṛṣṭvā 20.9 740
prajāpati-patis tanvaṁ 12.33 452
prajāpatir nāma tayor akārṣīd 17.18 668

prajāpati-sutaḥ samrāṭ 21.25 802
prājāpatyaṁ tu tat tejaḥ 15.1 555
prajāvatīnāṁ bhadraṁ te 14.11 520
prajñāya baddhāñjalayo 'nuvākair 13.33 494
prakṛteḥ puruṣasyāpi 26.9 1035

prakṛter guṇa-sāmyasya 26.17 1042
prakṛtiḥ puruṣasyeha 27.23 1119
prakṛti-stho 'pi puruṣo 27.1 1091
pralobhayantīṁ jagṛhur 20.37 763
prāṁśuṁ padma-palāśākṣaṁ 21.47 820

prāṇād vasiṣṭhaḥ sañjāto 12.23 443
praṇamya pādau parivṛtya devam 4.20 134
prāṇasya hi kriyā-śaktir 26.31 1056
prāṇasya śodhayen mārgaṁ 28.9 1137
prāṇāyāmair dahed doṣān 28.11 1140

prāṇenāṁśena saṁsparśaṁ 6.16 229
prāṇendriyāṇāṁ yudhi śaurya- 19.38 731
prāṇendriyātma-dhiṣṇyatvaṁ 26.34 1061
prāṇināṁ hanyamānānāṁ 14.40 544
prāñjaliḥ praṇataś cedaṁ 13.6 473

prāpadyata svaḥ-saritaṁ 4.36 153
prāpnotīhāñjasā dhīraḥ 27.29 1125
prasaṅgam ajaraṁ pāśam 25.20 985
prāsaṅgikaiḥ karma-doṣaiḥ 27.3 1093

prasaṅkhyānāya tattvānāṁ 24.36 951
prasanna-vadanāmbhojaṁ 28.13 1142
praseduś ca diśaḥ sarvā 24.8 923
prāśitram āsye grasane grahās tu te 13.36 497

prasupta-loka-tantrāṇāṁ 6.1 215
pratasthe ratham āruhya 22.26 855
praticakṣīta māṁ loko 9.32 362
pratijagmuḥ pramuditāḥ 16.28 646

pratikūlena vā cittaṁ 28.9 1137
pratilabhya priyāṁ patnīṁ 13.2 470
pratinandya jagādedaṁ 16.1 617
prātiṣṭhan nandim āpannāḥ 24.25 938

pratiṣṭhitāḥ kriyā yasmin	20.51	771
prativaktuṁ na cotseha	2.1	47
pratīyata upadraṣṭuḥ	7.10	265
prattāṁ duhitaraṁ samrāṭ	22.24	853
praty āha taṁ subahu-vit	1.5	4
pratyācaṣṭātma-bhūr devān	15.11	563
pratyag-dhāmā svayaṁ-jyotir	26.3	1025
pratyag-dhṛtākṣāmbuja-kośam īṣad	8.4	298
pratyāha bhagavac-cittaḥ	7.8	262
pratyāhānunayan vācā	14.16	523
pratyāhāraś cendriyāṇāṁ	28.5	1134
pratyāhāreṇa saṁsargān	28.11	1140
pratyak-praśānta-dhīr dhīraḥ	24.44	960
pratyaṅga-mukhyāṅkita-mandirāṇi	1.23	22
pratyeṣyataṁ nikāśaṁ me	16.31	648
praty-ūṣeṣv anubaddhena	22.33	860
pravartaye bhāgavataṁ purāṇaṁ	8.2	296
pravāsa-sthasya yo dharmo	7.34	286
pravavur vāyavaś caṇḍās	19.18	714
praviśya tat tīrtha-varam	21.45	820
prāvocaṁ bhakti-yogasya	32.37	1353
pravṛddha-bhaktyā hy anubhāvitāśaye	14.48	550
pravṛddha-harṣo bhagavat-kathāyāṁ	7.42	293
pravṛddha-roṣaḥ sa kaṭhora-muṣṭinā	19.15	711
prayuktān bhoja-rājena	2.30	83
pṛccheḥ prabho mugdha ivāpramattas	4.17	131
prekṣāṁ kṣipantaṁ haritopalādreḥ	8.24	314
prekṣaṇīyehitaṁ dhyāyec	28.19	1148
prekṣayitvā bhuvo golaṁ	23.43	902
prema-gadgadayā vācā	23.5	872
prerito 'janayat svābhir	6.4	218
prīṇayann iva bhāratyā	7.1	255
prītaḥ pratyāha tān praśnān	10.3	376
prītas tubhyam ahaṁ tāta	13.9	475
prīto 'ham astu bhadraṁ te	9.39	368
priyaṁ prabhur grāmya iva priyāyā	3.5	93
priyavratottānapādau	12.56	467
priyavratottānapādau	21.2	776
priyavratottānapadoḥ	22.9	838
priyāyāḥ priyam anvicchan	23.12	882
procuḥ prāñjalayo viprāḥ	16.15	631
proktaṁ kilaitad bhagavattamena	8.7	300
provāca mahyaṁ sa dayālur ukto	8.9	302
pṛṣṭhato 'nvagamaṁ bhartuḥ	4.5	120
pṛṣṭo vārtāṁ pratibrūyād	2.3	49
pulahāya gatiṁ yuktāṁ	24.23	937
pulaho nābhito jajñe	12.24	444
pulakodbhinna-sarvāṅgo	2.5	50
puṁsām ato vividha-karmabhir	9.13	341
puṁsāṁ gatiṁ mṛgayatām iha yoga-	15.45	602
puṁsāṁ niḥśreyasārthena	5.17	175
puṁsāṁ sudūraṁ vasato 'pi puryāṁ	5.44	202
puṁsāṁ sva-kāmāya vivikta-mārgair	8.26	316
punaḥ katipayaiḥ sthānaṁ	19.29	722
punaḥ sa papraccha tam udyatāñjalir	14.1	513
punar āviviśuḥ khāni	26.62	1083
punar gadāṁ svām ādāya	18.16	693
puṇya-druma-latā-jālaiḥ	21.40	816
puṇyaṁ śivāmṛta-jalaṁ	21.39	815
purā mayā proktam ajāya nābhye	4.13	127
purā pitā no bhagavān	14.13	521
purāpavāritā dvāri	16.30	648
pureṣu puṇyopavanādri-kuñjeṣv	1.18	18
pūrṇārtho lakṣitas tena	2.5	51
pūrṇe varṣa-śate sādhvī	17.2	658
pūrtena tapasā yajñair	9.41	370
puruṣaṁ prakṛtir brahman	27.17	1111
puruṣas tad-upādānam	10.11	382
puruṣasya ca saṁsthānaṁ	7.38	290
puruṣasyāñjasābhyeti	29.19	1203
puruṣeṇātma-bhūtena	5.26	184
pūrvaḥ parārdho 'pakrānto	11.34	419

pūrvasyādau parārdhasya 11.35 420
puryāṁ kadācit krīḍadbhir 3.24 111
puṣṇāsi kṛṣṇād vimukho gata-śrīs 1.13 11
puṣṇāti yeṣāṁ poṣeṇa 30.10 1241
putrasyaiva ca putrāṇāṁ 14.45 547
putrayoś ca vadhaṁ kṛṣṇād 14.51 553

R

rāddhaṁ bata dvija-vṛṣaitad amogha- 23.10 879
rāddhaṁ niḥśreyasaṁ puṁsāṁ 9.41 370
raho racitayālāpaiḥ 30.8 1239
rajaḥ-pradhānān mahatas 20.13 743
rajasā kuṇṭha-manasaḥ 32.17 1330
rajo 'dhikāḥ karma-parā 10.26 393
rajo-bhājo bhagavato 10.18 389
rakṣati smāvyayo devaḥ 22.4 831
rāmāṁ niramayan reme 23.44 903
rasajñaḥ ko nu tṛpyeta 20.6 738
rasa-mātrād vikurvāṇād 26.44 1068
rasa-mātram abhūt tasmād 26.41 1066
rasāyā līlayonnītām 13.47 507
rati-rāso bhavet tīvraḥ 7.19 276
ratna-pradīpā ābhānti 33.17 1380
ratnodadhārauṣadhi-saumanasya 8.24 314
remāta uddāya mṛdhe sva-rikthaṁ 1.39 37
reme kṣaṇadayā datta- 3.21 108
reme nirasta-viṣayo 'py avaruddha- 9.19 349
retas tasmād āpa āsan 26.57 1078
retasā śiśnam āpas tu 26.65 1084
retasāṁśena yenāsāv 6.19 231
ṛg-yajuḥ-sāmātharvākhyān 12.37 455
rohid-bhūtāṁ so 'nvadhāvad 31.36 1299
rorūyati gate jñāne 31.24 1288
roṣaṁ samutthaṁ śamayan svayā 17.29 676
ṛṣayo yaiḥ parābhāvya 22.30 857
ṛṣe na tṛpyati manaḥ 14.4 515
ṛṣim ādyaṁ na badhnāti 9.35 365
ṛṣiṁ nārāyaṇam ṛte 31.37 1300
ṛṣīn ṛṣir hṛṣīkeśaḥ 20.52 772
ṛṣīṇāṁ bhūri-vīryāṇām 12.50 464
ṛṣīṇāṁ janma-karmāṇi 7.29 282
ṛṣīṇāṁ śrotu-kāmānāṁ 25.14 979
ṛṣīṇām upaśāntānāṁ 22.27 855
rucir yo bhagavān brahman 21.5 778
rudann iva hasan mugdha- 2.28 80
rudantaṁ vigata-jñānaṁ 31.27 1290
rudanto rāsabha-trastā 17.12 663
rudraḥ patir hi bhūtānāṁ 14.34 539
rudrāṇāṁ rudra-sṛṣṭānāṁ 12.16 438
rudro 'bhimatyā hṛdayaṁ 26.69 1086
rūpa-bhedāspadaṁ divyaṁ 29.37 1223
rūpa-bheda-vidas tatra 29.30 1215
rūpa-draviṇa-paṇyena 20.34 760
rūpaṁ tavaitan nanu duṣkṛtātmanāṁ 13.35 496
rūpaṁ vicitram idam asya vivṛṇvato 9.24 355
rūpaṁ yad etad avabodha-rasodayena 9.2 324
rūpa-mātrād vikurvāṇāt 26.41 1066
rūpāṇi divyāni vara-pradāni 25.35 1005
rūpāṇi sthāna ādhatse 21.51 824
ruṣopagūhamāno 'muṁ 19.24 717

S

sa āhato viśva-jitā hy avajñayā 19.26 719
sa ātmānaṁ manyamānaḥ 20.49 770
sa bhavān duhitṛ-sneha- 22.8 837
sa cāpi bhagavad-dharmāt 32.2 1316
sa cāpi śatarūpāyāṁ 12.56 467
sā cāpi tanayoktena 33.13 1377
sa cāvatīrṇaṁ tri-yugam 24.26 938
sa ceha vipra rājarṣir 21.26 803
sa dṛṣṭvā trasta-hṛdayaḥ 30.19 1248
sa eṣa doṣaḥ puruṣa-dviḍ āste 1.13 11
sa eṣa prakṛtiṁ sūkṣmāṁ 26.4 1028

sa eṣa sādho caramo bhavānām	4.12	126
sa eṣa yarhi prakṛter	27.2	1092
sa eva bhagavān adya	24.29	941
sa eva bhakti-yogākhya	29.14	1195
sa eva go-dhanaṁ lakṣmyā	2.29	81
sa eva pratibuddhasya	27.25	1121
sa eva sādhuṣu kṛto	23.55	912
sa eva sādhuṣu kṛto	25.20	985
sa eva viśvasya bhavān vidhatte	33.3	1363
sa evam ārādhita-pāda-tīrthād	4.20	134
sa evaṁ bhagavān pṛṣṭaḥ	5.17	175
sa evam ṛṣi-varyo 'yaṁ	1.5	4
sa evaṁ svāntaraṁ ninye	22.36	864
sa evam utsikta-madena vidviṣā	17.29	676
sa evānumato 'smābhir	16.3	619
sa evānyeṣv adharmeṇa	11.21	411
sa gām udastāt salilasya gocare	18.8	686
sā hatā tena gadayā	19.3	704
sa ittham āpṛṣṭa-purāṇa-kalpaḥ	7.42	293
sa ittham atyulbaṇa-karṇa-bāṇair	1.16	14
sa itthaṁ bhagavān urvīṁ	13.47	507
sa itthaṁ coditaḥ kṣattrā	7.8	262
sa itthaṁ gṛṇataḥ putrān	12.33	451
sa ittham udvīkṣya tad-abja-nāla-	8.19	310
sa kālaḥ paramāṇur vai	11.4	399
sa karma-bījaṁ rajasoparaktaḥ	8.33	321
sa karṇa-duḥśāsana-saubalānāṁ	3.13	99
sa kathaṁ sevayā tasya	2.3	49
sa kinnarān kimpuruṣān	20.45	768
sa muhūrtam abhūt tūṣṇīṁ	2.4	50
sa naḥ prasīdatāṁ bhāmo	14.36	541
sa nirgataḥ kaurava-puṇya-labdho	1.17	16
sa padma-kośaḥ sahasodatiṣṭhat	8.14	306
sa prahasya mahā-bāho	15.11	562
sa saṁsṛtya punaḥ kāle	32.14	1327
sā śraddadhānasya vivardhamānā	5.13	171
sa sva-dṛg bhagavān yasya	14.47	549
sā tad bhartuḥ samādāya	23.24	889
sa tadā labdha-tīrtho 'pi	19.4	705
sa tadaivātmanātmānaṁ	32.25	1338
sa tāṁ kṛta-mala-snānāṁ	23.36	896
sa taṁ mahā-bhāgavataṁ	4.24	138
sa taṁ niśāmyātta-rathāṅgam agrato	19.7	707
sa taṁ virajam arkābhaṁ	21.9	782
sa tu katham avaśiṣṭa uddhavo yad	4.28	143
sa tudyamāno 'ri-durukta-tomarair	18.6	685
sa tvam asyām apatyāni	13.11	477
sa tvaṁ bhṛto me jaṭhareṇa nātha	33.4	1365
sā tvāṁ brahman nṛpa-vadhūḥ	21.28	804
sa tvaṁ dvijānupatha-puṇya-rajaḥ-	16.21	636
sa tvaṁ vidhatsva śaṁ bhūmaṁs	15.9	561
sa tvayārādhitaḥ śuklo	24.4	919
sa ugra-dhanvann iyad evābabhāṣe	22.21	851
sa upavrajya varadaṁ	20.25	753
sa vā eṣa tadā draṣṭā	5.24	182
sā vā etasya saṁdraṣṭuḥ	5.25	183
sa vai bata bhraṣṭa-matis tavaiṣate	13.45	505
sa vai devarṣi-varyas tāṁ	23.4	872
sa vai drauṇy-astra-sampluṣṭaḥ	3.17	103
sa vai mahā-bhāgavato mahātmā	14.48	550
sa vai nivṛtti-dharmeṇa	7.12	268
sa vai ruroda devānāṁ	12.8	433
sa vai svāyambhuvaḥ samrāṭ	13.2	470
sa vai tirohitān dṛṣṭvā	17.23	672
sa vai viśva-sṛjāṁ garbho	6.7	221
sa vai viśva-sṛjām īśo	12.36	455
sa vajra-kūṭāṅga-nipāta-vega-	13.29	491
sa varṣa-pūgān udadhau mahā-balaś	17.26	673
sa vāsudevānucaraṁ praśāntaṁ	1.25	25
sa viditvātha bhāryāyās	14.31	537
sa viditvātmajānāṁ no	14.14	522
sa viṣṇv-ākhyo 'dhiyajño 'sau	29.38	1224

sa viśva-janma-sthiti-saṁyamārthe 5.16 174
śabda-brahmātmanas tasya 12.48 463
śabda-mātram abhūt tasmān 26.32 1058
sabhājayan viśuddhena 24.11 926
sabhāryaḥ saprajaḥ kāmān 22.33 860

sac-cakṣur janmanām ante 25.8 971
ṣaḍ ime prākṛtāḥ sargā 10.18 389
ṣaḍbhir jarāyuṇā vītaḥ 31.4 1265
sādhu pṛṣṭaṁ tvayā sādho 5.18 176
sādhu vīra tvayā pṛṣṭam 14.5 515

sādhv etad vyāhṛtaṁ vidvan 7.16 273
sādhyān gaṇān pitṛ-gaṇān 20.42 766
sādhyātmaḥ sādhidaivaś ca 6.9 223
sādhyebhyaś ca pitṛbhyaś ca 20.43 766
sadṛśo 'sti śivaḥ panthā 25.19 984

sa-dvitīyāḥ kim asṛjan 20.11 741
sadyaḥ kṣipaty avācīnaṁ 31.22 1287
sadyo 'jāyata tan-manyuḥ 12.7 432
sadyo harer anucarāv uru bibhyatas 15.35 592
sāgraṁ vai varṣa-sāhasram 20.15 745

saha dehena mānena 31.29 1292
sahācalā bhuvaś celur 17.4 659
sahāhaṁ svāṁśa-kalayā 21.32 810
sāhaṁ bhagavato nūnaṁ 23.57 914

sāhaṅkārasya dravyasya 27.16 1110
sahānujo yatra vṛkodarāhiḥ 1.11 9
sahasra-śirasaṁ sākṣād 26.25 1051
saivaṁ saṁvidite bhartrā 14.30 536

sākṣād bhagavatādiṣṭo 4.26 141
śaktyāpramattair gṛhyeta 13.10 476
salile sva-khurākrānta 13.46 507
sālokya-sārṣṭi-sāmīpya- 29.13 1193

samāhitaṁ te hṛdayaṁ 21.28 804
samāhitātmā niḥsaṅgo 32.30 1345
samāhutā bhīṣmaka-kanyayā ye 3.3 91
samanvety eṣa sattvānāṁ 26.18 1044

śambaraṁ dvividaṁ bāṇaṁ 3.11 98
saṁhatya daiva-yogena 20.14 744
saṁhṛtya sva-kulaṁ sphītaṁ 4.29 144
saṁlakṣyate sphaṭika-kuḍya upeta- 15.21 572
sammohanāya racitaṁ nija- 28.32 1164

śamo damo bhagaś ceti 31.33 1296
samprapede hariṁ bhaktyā 21.7 780
samprasīdati vā yeṣām 7.35 287
sampraśraya-praṇaya-vihvalayā 23.9 878
saṁrambhī bhinna-dṛg bhāvaṁ 29.8 1188

saṁśayo 'tha viparyāso 26.30 1055
saṁspardhayā dagdham athānuśocan 1.21 21
saṁsthāna-bhuktyā bhagavān 11.3 398
saṁsthāpayaināṁ jagatāṁ sa- 13.42 502
saṁsthāpya cāsmān pramṛjāśru 18.12 690

samutthitaṁ tatas tejaś 26.38 1064
saṁvatsaraḥ parivatsara 11.14 405
saṁvatsara-sahasrānte 6.38 249
saṁvatsara śataṁ nṛṇāṁ 11.12 404
saṁvatsarāvasānena 11.13 404

samyag-darśanayā buddhyā 31.48 1312
samyak śraddhāya puruṣaṁ 24.5 920
śanair jita-śvāsa-nivṛtta-citto 8.21 311
śanakair bhagaval-lokān 2.6 52

sanakaṁ ca sanandaṁ ca 12.4 430
sanat-kumāraṁ ca munīn 12.4 430
sanat-kumārāya sa cāha pṛṣṭaḥ 8.7 300
sañchinnaḥ saṁśayo mahyaṁ 7.15 272

sañcintayed bhagavataś caraṇāra- 28.21 1150
sañcintayed daśa-śatāram asahya- 28.27 1158
sandahyamāna-sarvāṅga 30.7 1238
sandhyā-sandhyāṁśayor antar 11.20 410

sāndīpaneḥ sakṛt proktaṁ 3.2 90
saṅgaṁ na kuryāc chocyeṣu 31.34 1297
saṅgaṁ na kuryāt pramadāsu jātu 31.39 1302
saṅgas teṣv atha te prārthyaḥ 25.24 991

saṅgītavad rodanavad	17.10	662
saṅgīyamāna-sat-kīrtiḥ	22.33	860
saṅgo yaḥ saṁsṛter hetur	23.55	912
saṅkarṣaṇākhyaṁ puruṣaṁ	26.25	1051
saṅkhyātāni sahasrāṇi	11.19	410
sāṅkhyāyanaḥ pāramahaṁsya-	8.8	301
ṣaṇ-nemy ananta-cchadi yat tri-ṇābhi	21.18	794
sanniveśo mayā prokto	26.15	1041
śānta-ghora-vimūḍhatvam	26.26	1051
sāntaḥ sarasi veśma-sthāḥ	23.26	890
santaṁ vayasi kaiśore	28.17	1145
sānubandhe ca dehe 'sminn	27.9	1103
saparyayā paryagṛhṇāt	21.48	822
saptamo mukhya-sargas tu	10.19	389
śarac-chaśi-karair mṛṣṭaṁ	2.34	86
śāradendīvara-śyāmaṁ	26.28	1053
sarajaṁ bibhratī vāso	23.24	889
sārasaiś cakravākaiś ca	21.43	818
sarasvatīm upaspṛśya	4.3	119
sarasvatyāṁ tapas tepe	21.6	779
sargādy anīho 'vitathābhisandhir	33.3	1363
sargam etaṁ prabhāvaiḥ svair	24.14	929
sargāṁś caivānusargāṁś ca	7.25	280
sarge 'nupacite krodhād	20.47	769
sargo nava-vidhas tasya	10.14	385
śārīrā mānasā divyā	22.37	865
sarpāḥ prasarpataḥ krūrā	20.48	770
sarpa-vṛścika-daṁśādyair	30.26	1253
sarva-bhūta-guhāvāsam	12.19	440
sarva-bhūta-samatvena	27.7	1099
sarva-bhūtāśayābhijñaḥ	23.22	888
sarva-bhūteṣu cātmānaṁ	28.42	1175
sarvāḥ kiśora-vayaso	23.26	890
sarva-jīvanikāyauko	20.16	745
sarva-kāma-dughaṁ divyaṁ	23.13	882
sarvaṁ tad bhagavān mahyam	23.51	908
sarvarddhy-upacayodarkaṁ	23.13	882
sarvartu-phala-puṣpāḍhyaṁ	21.40	816
sarvartu-śrībhir vibhrājat	15.16	567
sarvās tāś cāru-sarvāṅgyo	23.48	906
sarva-sattva-guṇodbhedaḥ	26.46	1069
sarvāśramān upādāya	14.18	524
sarvātiśayayā lakṣmyā	16.32	650
sarvātmanā śritaḥ kṛṣṇaṁ	20.3	735
sarvātmanānurūpāṁ te	22.11	840
sarvatra jāta-vairāgya	27.27	1124
sarvatra te 'viṣamayā munayaḥ sva-	15.29	583
sarva-veda-mayenedam	9.43	373
sarve vedāś ca yajñāś ca	7.41	293
sarve viyuktāḥ sva-vihāra-tantraṁ	5.48	207
sarvebhya eva vaktrebhyaḥ	12.39	457
sarvendriyāṇām ātmatvaṁ	26.37	1063
sasarja cchāyayāvidyāṁ	20.18	747
sasarja katidhā vīryaṁ	21.4	777
sasarja rūpa-tanmātraṁ	5.34	191
sasarjāgre 'ndha-tāmisram	12.2	427
ṣaṣṭhas tu tamasaḥ sargo	10.17	387
śāstram ijyāṁ stuti-stomaṁ	12.37	455
śaśvat svarūpa-mahasaiva nipīta-	9.14	342
sata eva padārthasya	11.2	398
śata-bhāgas tu vedhaḥ syāt	11.6	400
satāṁ prasaṅgān mama vīrya-saṁvido	25.25	992
śataṁ vyatīyuḥ śaradaḥ	23.46	905
śatarūpā mahā-rājñī	22.23	852
saṭā-śikhoddhūta-śivāmbu-bindubhir	13.44	505
satīṁ vyādāya śṛṇvanto	16.14	630
sato 'viśeṣa-bhug yas tu	11.4	399
sato bandhum asac-cakṣuḥ	27.11	1105
satrāṇi sarvāṇi śarīra-sandhis	13.38	499
satre purā viśva-sṛjāṁ vasūnāṁ	4.11	125
sat-sevanīyo bata pūru-vaṁśo	8.1	295
sattva evaika-manaso	25.32	1000

sattvākṛti-svabhāvena	12.15	438
sattvaṁ cāsya vinirbhinnaṁ	6.26	235
sattvaṁ viṣṭabhya virajaṁ	15.15	566
sātvatām ṛṣabhaṁ sarve	2.9	56
satyaṁ śaucaṁ dayā maunaṁ	31.33	1296
satyaṁ vayaṁ bho vana-gocarā mṛgā	18.10	688
saumyānuśoce tam adhaḥ-patantaṁ	1.41	39
sa-vidhaṁ jagṛhe pāṇīn	3.8	95
sāvitraṁ prājāpatyaṁ ca	12.42	459
savrīḍa iva taṁ samrāḍ	22.1	829
śayānaḥ pariśocadbhiḥ	30.17	1246
śayāne tvayi loko 'yaṁ	21.55	827
śāyito 'śuci-paryaṅke	31.26	1290
sendrān deva-gaṇān kṣībān	17.23	672
śete viṇ-mūtrayor garte	31.5	1266
seyaṁ bhagavato māyā	7.9	263
siddha-cāraṇa-gandharvair	33.34	1395
siddhair nuto dyudhuni-pāta-śiva-	23.39	899
siddhān vidyādharāṁś caiva	20.44	768
siddhāsi bhuṅkṣva vibhavān nija-	23.8	876
siddhyeta te kṛta-manobhava-	23.11	880
śikhareṣv indranīleṣu	23.18	885
siṁhaḥ kapir gajaḥ kūrmo	10.24	392
śīrṣṇo 'sya dyaur dharā padbhyāṁ	6.27	235
śivāya nas tvaṁ suhṛdām	18.27	700
śivāya nyasta-daṇḍāya	14.35	540
smaran bhagavad-ādeśam	21.49	822
smaran dīrgham anucchvāsaṁ	31.9	1270
smaran viśva-sṛjām īśo	6.10	225
smarantyā bhartur ādeśaṁ	19.23	716
śmaśāna-cakrānila-dhūli-dhūmra-	14.25	531
smayamānā viklavena	23.49	907
smayan pralabdhuṁ praṇipatya	17.27	674
snānena tāṁ mahārheṇa	23.28	891
snātaṁ kṛta-śiraḥ-snānaṁ	23.31	893
snehottha-romā skhalitākṣaras taṁ	4.14	128
snigdha-nīlālaka-vrāta-	21.9	782
snigdha-smitānuguṇitaṁ vipula-	28.31	1163
snigdha-smitāvalokena	3.20	107
so 'dhikṣipto bhagavatā	18.13	691
so 'haṁ bhavadbhya upalabdha-	16.6	621
so 'haṁ harer martya-viḍambanena	1.42	40
so 'haṁ nṛṇāṁ kṣulla-sukhāya	8.2	296
so 'haṁ tad-darśanāhlāda-	4.21	136
so 'haṁ tavaitat kathayāmi vatsa	8.9	302
so 'haṁ vasann api vibho bahu-	31.20	1284
so 'haṁ vrajāmi śaraṇaṁ hy akuto-	31.12	1272
so 'nanto 'nta-karaḥ kālo	29.45	1230
so 'ntaḥ śarīre 'rpita-bhūta-sūkṣmaḥ	8.11	304
so 'nu jñātvā vyavasitaṁ	22.22	851
so 'nupraviṣṭo bhagavāṁś	6.3	217
so 'nuviṣṭo bhagavatā	20.17	746
so 'pi kṣmām anujai rakṣan	3.18	105
so 'py aṁśa-guṇa-kālātmā	5.28	186
so 'py etayā caramayā manaso nivṛttyā	28.36	1169
so 'sādhu-vādas tat-kīrtiṁ	16.5	620
so 'sāv adabhra-karuṇo bhagavān	9.25	356
so 'śayiṣṭābdhi-salile	20.15	745
so 'vadhāryāsya kārpaṇyaṁ	20.28	755
so 'vadhyātaḥ sutair evaṁ	12.6	432
so 'yaṁ samasta-jagatāṁ suhṛd eka	9.22	353
sodapānāś ca saritaś	17.7	661
ṣoḍaśy-ukthau pūrva-vaktrāt	12.40	457
solkāś cāśanayaḥ petuḥ	17.4	659
somas tu retaḥ savanāny avasthitiḥ	13.38	499
śoṇāyitenādhara-bimba-bhāsā	8.27	317
sparśas tasyābhavaj jīvaḥ	12.47	462
sparśo 'bhavat tato vāyus	26.35	1062
śraddadhānāya bhaktāya	14.4	515
śraddadhānāya bhaktāya	32.41	1357
śraddhām aṅgirase 'yacchat	24.22	937
śrāddhasya ca vidhiṁ brahman	7.33	285

śraddhatsvaitan mataṁ mahyaṁ 33.11 1375
śraddhayātma-viśuddhy-arthaṁ 6.34 244
sragbhir vicitra-mālyābhir 23.15 883
srak tuṇḍa āsīt sruva īśa nāsayor 13.36 497
śrāntasya karmasv anuviddhayā dhiyā 29.5 1185

sravanti sarito bhītā 29.42 1227
sṛgālolūka-ṭaṅkāraiḥ 17.9 662
śrī rūpiṇī kvaṇayatī caraṇāravindaṁ 15.21 572
śrī-niketaṁ sarasvatyāṁ 4.6 121
śrīvatsa-vakṣasaṁ bhrājat 28.14 1143

śriyā vihīnaḥ kṛpaṇo 30.12 1243
śriyaṁ bhāgavatīṁ vāspṛhayanti 25.37 1009
sṛjann amarṣitaḥ śvāsān 18.14 692
sṛjasy adaḥ pāsi punar grasiṣyase 21.19 795
sṛjataḥ śrīnivāsasya 7.28 282

sṛjato me kṣitir vārbhiḥ 13.17 482
sṛjaty amogha-saṅkalpa 10.30 396
śṛṇoti gāyaty anumodate 'ñjasā 19.37 730
śṛṇvato dhyāyato viṣṇoḥ 22.35 863
śṛṇvīta bhaktyā śravayeta vośatīṁ 13.48 508

śroṇyor adhyastayā kāñcyā 23.32 894
srotasāṁ pravarā saumya 33.32 1394
śrotreṇa karṇau ca diśo 26.64 1084
śrotreṇāṁśena śabdasya 6.17 230

śrotum arhasi dīnasya 22.8 837
sṛṣṭvā bhūta-piśācāṁś ca 20.40 764
sṛṣṭvāgre mahad-ādīni 7.21 277
śrutānubhāvaṁ śaraṇaṁ 32.11 1325

śrutasya puṁsāṁ sucira-śramasya 13.4 471
śruteś ca vidvadbhir upākṛtāyāṁ 6.37 248
śrutvā bhāgavataṁ pautram 14.51 553
sthānaṁ tv ihānujānīhi 13.14 480

sthāpatyaṁ cāsṛjad vedaṁ 12.38 456
sthitaṁ vrajantam āsīnaṁ 28.19 1148
strī yāsīc chatarūpākhyā 12.54 466
strīṇāṁ nigṛhyamāṇānāṁ 14.40 544

strītvaṁ strī-saṅgataḥ prāpto 31.41 1304
striyāḥ praviṣṭa udaraṁ 31.1 1263
stuvīta taṁ viklavayā 31.11 1271
stūyamānaḥ samudreṇa 33.34 1395
śucau deśe pratiṣṭhāpya 28.8 1137

sudarśanāstraṁ bhagavān 19.22 715
sudatā subhruvā ślakṣṇa- 23.33 894
sukhaṁ buddhyeya durbodhaṁ 25.30 999
sukhāya karmāṇi karoti loko 5.2 156
sunāsāṁ sudvijāṁ snigdha- 20.30 758

suparṇa-pakṣopari rocamānaḥ 21.22 799
sūrya-dvāreṇa te yānti 32.7 1321
sūryaś candras tapaś caiva 12.11 434
sūryendu-vāyv-agny-agamaṁ tri- 8.31 320
śuśrūṣayā sauhṛdena 23.2 870

sutaḥ prasanna-vadanaṁ 33.23 1386
sutaṁ mṛdhe khaṁ vapuṣā grasantaṁ 3.6 94
suyodhanaṁ sānucaraṁ śayānaṁ 3.13 99
śvā sṛgālo vṛko vyāghro 10.24 392
svābhāsair lakṣito 'nena 27.13 1106

svābhāsena tathā sūryo 27.12 1106
svabhāva-guṇa-mārgeṇa 29.7 1187
svaccha-sphaṭika-kuḍyeṣu 33.17 1380
svacchatvam avikāritvaṁ 26.22 1049

sva-daṁṣṭrayoddhṛtya mahīṁ 13.31 492
sva-dharmācaraṇaṁ śaktyā 28.2 1130
sva-dharmāptena sattvena 32.6 1321
sva-dhiṣṇyānām eka-deśe 28.6 1135

svādo 'pi sadyaḥ savanāya kalpate 33.6 1367
sva-gārhasthyam anaupamyaṁ 33.15 1379
sva-garjitena kakubhaḥ 13.24 486
svāṁ deva māyām āsthāya 18.25 699

svam eva dhiṣṇyaṁ bahu mānayantaṁ 8.4 298
svaṁ svaṁ kālaṁ manur bhuṅkte 11.24 413
sva-mātrā brahma-vādinyā 33.12 1376
svāṅgaṁ tapo-yogamayaṁ 33.29 1392

svānubhūtyā tirobhūta- 33.25 1386
svāpa ity ucyate buddher 26.30 1055
sva-pauruṣe pratihate 19.12 709
svarāḥ sapta vihāreṇa 12.47 462
svardhuny-udārdraiḥ sva-jaṭā-kalāpair 8.5 298

svarṇa-māṣaiḥ kṛta-cchidraṁ 11.9 402
sva-rociṣā tat salilaṁ viśālaṁ 8.14 306
svarūpaṁ bata kurvanti 29.4 1183
svarūpaṁ lakṣyate 'mīṣāṁ 29.1 1181
svarūpeṇa mayopetaṁ 9.33 363

sva-sainya-caraṇa-kṣuṇṇaṁ 21.53 825
sva-sambhavaṁ niśāmyaivaṁ 9.26 357
sva-śānta-rūpeṣv itaraiḥ sva-rūpair 2.15 64
sva-sargasyāśiṣaṁ lokyām 14.37 541
sva-sutaṁ devahūty āha 25.6 970

svatas-tṛptasya ca kathaṁ 7.3 258
sva-tejasā dhvasta-guṇa-pravāhaṁ 33.8 1372
sva-tejasāpibat tīvram 26.20 1046
svato jñānaṁ kutaḥ puṁsāṁ 7.39 291
svayaṁ dhanur dvāri nidhāya māyāṁ 1.16 14

svayaṁ tad antar-hṛdaye 'vabhātam 8.22 312
svayaṁ tv asāmyātiśayas tryadhīśaḥ 2.21 72
svayambhūḥ sākam ṛṣibhir 24.9 924
svāyambhuvasya ca manor 21.1 775

sva-yoniṣu yathā jyotir 28.43 1176
sve sve kāle 'bhigṛhṇanti 29.41 1227
svenaiva tuṣyatu kṛtena sa dīna- 31.18 1281
śvetotpala-krīḍanakaṁ 21.10 783

svīyaṁ vākyam ṛtaṁ kartum 24.30 943
śyāmāvadātaṁ virajaṁ 4.7 121
śyāme pṛthāv urasi śobhitayā śriyā 15.39 596

T

ta ātma-sargaṁ taṁ kāyaṁ 20.43 766
ta ekadā bhagavato 15.13 564
ta enaṁ lolupatayā 20.23 752
ta ete sādhavaḥ sādhvi 25.24 991

ta eva cādaduḥ prītyā 20.39 764
tā imā yabhituṁ pāpā 20.26 754
tā naḥ kīrtaya bhadraṁ te 20.6 738
tābhyām antar-hṛdi brahman 9.30 360
tābhyāṁ miṣatsv animiṣeṣu 15.31 585

tābhyāṁ rūpa-vibhāgābhyāṁ 12.53 466
tac-chraddhayākrānta-matiḥ 32.3 1317
tad āhur akṣaraṁ brahma 11.42 425
tad asya kauṣārava śarma-dātur 5.15 173
tad asya saṁsṛtir bandhaḥ 26.7 1033

tad bhavān dahyamānāyāṁ 14.11 520
tad dhīty ātma-kṛtaṁ manye 16.4 619
tad etan me vijānīhi 25.30 999
tad evam ākarṇya jaleśa-bhāṣitaṁ 18.1 679
tad ojasā daitya-mahā-bhaṭārpitaṁ 19.14 710

tad vā idaṁ bhuvana-maṅgala 9.4 327
tad vaḥ prasādayāmy adya 16.4 619
tad vai bindusaro nāma 21.39 815
tad vām amuṣya paramasya vikuṇṭha- 15.34 591
tad vayaṁ nirvyalīkena 21.56 828

tad vidhehi namas tubhyaṁ 13.8 474
tad vilokya viyad-vyāpi 10.7 379
tad vilokyābja-sambhūto 10.5 378
tad vīrāsīt puṇyatamaṁ 33.31 1394

tad viśva-gurv-adhikṛtaṁ bhuvanaika- 15.26 580
tadā diteḥ samabhavat 19.23 716
tadā lokā layaṁ yānti 32.4 1318
tadā manūn sasarjānte 20.49 770

tadā mithuna-dharmeṇa 12.55 466
tadā puruṣa ātmānaṁ 25.17 982
tadā vikuṇṭha-dhiṣaṇāt 16.34 651
tadā viśveśvaraḥ kruddho 14.41 545

tadaiva cakṣuṣo draṣṭur 31.46 1309
tadaiva setavaḥ sarve 21.54 825
tad-arthaṁ kurute karma 31.31 1294
tad-bhagnamānān api gṛdhyato 'jñāñ 3.4 92

tad-dehaḥ parataḥ poṣo	33.28	1391
tad-guṇāśrayayā bhaktyā	32.22	1334
tad-rakta-paṅkāṅkita-gaṇḍa-tuṇḍo	13.32	493
tad-vyāhṛtāmṛta-kalā-	21.46	820
taijasānīndriyāṇy eva	5.31	189
taijasānīndriyāṇy eva	26.31	1056
taijasāt tu vikurvāṇād	26.29	1054
tair darśanīyāvayavair udāra-	25.36	1007
taj-joṣaṇād āśv apavarga-vartmani	25.25	992
tal loka-padmaṁ sa u eva viṣṇuḥ	8.15	307
tam adharme kṛta-matiṁ	12.29	448
tam āhāgādhayā vācā	9.28	358
tam āsīnam akarmāṇaṁ	25.6	970
tam asmin pratyag-ātmānaṁ	26.72	1088
tām ātmano vijānīyāt	31.42	1306
tam avajñāya māṁ martyaḥ	29.21	1205
tam āviśya mahā-devo	26.53	1076
tam āyāntam abhipretya	22.28	856
tāṁ cāpi yuṣmac-caraṇa-	7.18	275
tāṁ diśo jagṛhur ghorāṁ	12.33	452
tāṁ dṛṣṭvā sahasotthāya	23.27	891
tam eva dhyāyatī devam	33.22	1385
tam evāhur yugaṁ taj-jñā	11.20	410
tam evānv api dhīyante	11.29	416
tām īkṣetātmano mṛtyuṁ	31.40	1303
tam imaṁ te pravakṣyāmi	25.14	979
taṁ jīva-karma-padavīm anuvarta-	31.16	1278
tāṁ kvaṇac-caraṇāmbhojāṁ	20.29	757
taṁ muṣṭibhir vinighnantaṁ	19.25	718
taṁ niḥsarantaṁ salilād anudruto	18.7	686
tāṁ prārthayantīṁ lalanā-lalāmam	22.18	846
taṁ pravartayituṁ deham	24.37	952
tāṁ sa āpatatīṁ vīkṣya	19.11	709
taṁ sa-prapañcam adhirūḍha-	28.38	1171
taṁ sukhārādhyam ṛjubhir	19.36	729
taṁ taṁ dhunoti bhagavān	30.2	1234
taṁ tv āgataṁ pratihṛtaupayikaṁ sva-	15.38	595
taṁ tvā gatāhaṁ śaraṇaṁ śaraṇyaṁ	25.11	975
taṁ tvām ahaṁ brahma paraṁ	33.8	1372
taṁ tvāṁ vidāma bhagavan param	15.47	609
taṁ tvānubhūtyoparata-kriyārthaṁ	21.21	797
taṁ vai hiraṇyakaśipuṁ viduḥ prajā	17.18	668
taṁ vīkṣya duḥsaha-javaṁ	17.21	670
taṁ vīram ārād abhipadya vismayaḥ	17.31	677
taṁ vyagra-cakraṁ diti-putrādhamena	19.6	706
tama etad vibho vettha	15.3	557
tamāla-nīlaṁ sita-danta-koṭyā	13.33	494
tāmasāc ca vikurvāṇād	26.32	1058
tāmaso bhūta-sūkṣmādir	5.32	189
tamasy apāre vidurātma-sargaṁ	8.20	311
tāmisram andha-tāmisraṁ	20.18	747
tamo-mātrām upādāya	11.28	415
tān babhāṣe svabhūḥ putrān	12.5	431
tāñ chocya-śocyān avido 'nuśoce	5.14	172
tān dṛṣṭvā ye purā sṛṣṭāḥ	20.50	771
tān eva te mad-anusevanayāva-	3.7	875
tan mayāpāditaṁ hy agre	9.29	359
tan me sva-bhartur avasāyam	16.12	629
tan naḥ parāṇuda vibho	7.7	261
tan naicchad racayan yasya	2.2	47
tan naicchan mokṣa-dharmāṇo	12.5	431
tān vadasvānupūrvyeṇa	10.2	375
tān vai hy asad-vṛttibhir akṣibhir ye	5.45	203
tān vīkṣya vāta-raśanāṁś caturaḥ	15.30	584
tāni caikaikaśaḥ sraṣṭum	20.14	744
tāni me śraddadhānasya	25.3	967
tan-mātrāṇi ca tāvanti	26.12	1039
tan-mātratvaṁ ca nabhaso	26.33	1059
tan-nirodho 'sya maraṇam	31.44	1308
tāny eva te 'bhirūpāṇi	24.31	943
tapa ātiṣṭha bhadraṁ te	12.18	439
tapanti vividhās tāpā	25.23	990

tāpāpanodo bhūyastvam 26.43 1067
tapasā hy edhamānena 10.6 378
tapasā vidyayā yukto 20.52 772
tapasaiva paraṁ jyotir 12.19 440
tapasaiva yathā pūrvaṁ 12.18 440

tapo-draviṇa-dānaiś ca 24.3 918
tapo-yuktena yogena 27.22 1118
taranti hy añjasā mṛtyuṁ 16.19 635
tarhy eva naṅkṣyati śivas tava deva 16.23 639
tarhy eva tan-nābhi-saraḥ-sarojam 8.32 320

tarpayitvātha viprebhyo 3.26 112
tārtīyena svabhāvena 6.29 237
tasmā evaṁ jagat-sraṣṭre 9.44 373
tasmā idaṁ bhagavate nama id 15.50 614
tasmād ahaṁ vigata-viklava 31.21 1285

tasmād imāṁ svāṁ prakṛtiṁ 28.44 1177
tasmād yugānta-śvasanāvaghūrṇa- 8.17 308
tasmai guṇa-gaṇāḍhyāya 22.22 851
tasmai namas ta udara-stha-bhavāya 9.21 351
tasmai namo bhagavate 12.32 451

tasmai namo bhagavate 'nuvidhema 9.4 327
tasmai prādād varaṁ putraṁ 3.2 90
tasmān mayy arpitāśeṣa- 29.33 1218
tasmān na kāryaḥ santrāso 31.47 1310

tasmāt sūryo nyabhidyetāṁ 26.55 1077
tasmāt tvaṁ sarva-bhāvena 32.22 1334
tasmil̐ labdha-padaṁ cittaṁ 28.20 1149
tasmin bindusare 'vātsīd 25.5 969

tasmin mahā-bhāgavato 4.9 123
tasmin prasanne sakalāśiṣāṁ prabhau 13.49 509
tasmin praśānta-puruṣe gata-vigrahe 15.32 587
tasmin pratīpaḥ parakṛtya āste 1.15 13

tasmin praviṣṭe varuṇasya sainikā 17.25 673
tasmin sudhanvann ahani 21.37 815
tasmin svasti samāsīna 28.8 1137
tasmin sva-vikramam idaṁ sṛjato 9.23 354

tasmin svayaṁ vedamayo vidhātā 8.15 307
tasmin varīyasi praśnaḥ 1.4 3
tasmin vimāna utkṛṣṭāṁ 23.45 904
tasmin yayau paramahaṁsa-mahā- 15.37 594
tasminn alupta-mahimā 23.38 898

tasminn āśrama āpīḍe 33.13 1377
tasminn atītya munayaḥ ṣaḍ 15.27 581
tāsv apatyāny ajanayad 3.9 96
tasya bhinna-dṛśo mṛtyur 29.26 1211
tasya coddharataḥ kṣauṇīṁ 14.3 514

tasya nābher abhūt padmaṁ 20.16 745
tasya prapannākhila-lokapānām 1.45 45
tasya tvaṁ tamaso 'ndhasya 25.8 971
tasya vai duhitā brahman 21.3 776
tasyābhipaśyataḥ kha-sthaḥ 13.19 483

tasyāgnir āsyaṁ nirbhinnaṁ 6.12 227
tasyāḥ kāmaṁ na kaḥ kuryāt 14.17 524
tasyaiṣa daitya-ṛṣabhaḥ padāhato 19.28 721
tasyaitasya jano nūnaṁ 30.1 1233
tasyaiva cānte kalpo 'bhūd 11.36 421

tasyaivaṁ ramamāṇasya 3.22 109
tasyām ādhatta retas tāṁ 23.47 906
tasyāṁ bahu-tithe kāle 24.6 921
tasyāṁ jātaḥ purā śūdro 6.33 243

tasyāṁ praviṣṭo bhavanaṁ 22.32 859
tasyāṁ sa cāmbho-ruha-karṇikāyām 8.16 308
tasyāṁ sa vai mahā-yogī 21.4 777
tasyāṁ tasyāṁ sa labhate 30.4 1236

tasyāṁ tritasyośanaso manoś ca 1.22 22
tasyānuraktasya muner mukundaḥ 4.10 124
tasyāravinda-nayanasya padāravinda- 15.43 601
tasyārtha-sūkṣmābhiniviṣṭa-dṛṣṭer 8.13 306

tasyās tad yoga-vidhuta- 33.32 1394
tasyāśu samprasīdeyaṁ 9.40 369
tasyāvalokam adhikaṁ kṛpayātighora- 28.31 1163
tasyopasannam avituṁ jagad 31.12 1272

tasyoṣṇig āsīl lomabhyo	12.45	461
tat kardamāśrama-padaṁ	24.9	924
tat pañcatvam ahaṁ-mānād	31.45	1309
tat pratīccha dvijāgryemāṁ	22.11	840
tat sādhu-varyādiśa vartma śaṁ naḥ	5.4	158
tat tasya kaiṅkaryam alaṁ bhṛtān no	2.22	73
tat te 'nabhīṣṭam iva sattva-nidher	16.24	641
tat te vayaṁ loka-sisṛkṣayādya	5.48	207
tata ātmani loke ca	9.31	361
tata oṣadhayaś cāsan	26.56	1078
tataḥ katipayair māsair	3.25	111
tataḥ sa āgatya puraṁ sva-pitroś	3.1	89
tataḥ sa-cittāḥ pravarās	29.28	1213
tataḥ samādhi-yuktena	21.7	780
tataḥ sapatnaṁ mukhataś	19.2	704
tataḥ sarve nyavartanta	17.1	657
tātāmba kaṁsād uru-śaṅkitānāṁ	2.17	67
tataś ca gadayārātiṁ	18.17	693
tatas ta ṛṣayaḥ kṣattaḥ	24.25	938
tatas te kṣīṇa-sukṛtāḥ	32.21	1333
tatas tenānuviddhebhyo	26.51	1073
tatas tv ativrajya surāṣṭram ṛddhaṁ	1.24	24
tatas tvām abhidhāsyanti	12.10	434
tathā sa cāhaṁ parivoḍhu-kāmaḥ	21.15	789
tathaiva cānye nara-loka-vīrā	2.20	70
tathaiva hariṇaiḥ kroḍaiḥ	21.44	819
tathāpare cātma-samādhi-yoga-	5.47	206
tathāpi kīrtayāmy aṅga	6.36	247
tathāpi naḥ prajānāṁ te	13.7	473
tathāpi nāhaṁ pravṛṇomi bhūman	4.15	129
tathāpi tad-abhipretaṁ	4.5	120
tato 'bhavan mahat-tattvam	5.27	185
tato 'parām upādāya	12.49	464
tato hasan sa bhagavān	20.24	752
tato nanda-vrajam itaḥ	2.26	78
tato nivṛttaḥ krīḍiṣyan	17.24	672
tato nivṛtto 'pratilabdha-kāmaḥ	8.21	311
tato varṇāś ca catvāras	29.31	1216
tato vayaṁ mat-pramukhā yad-arthe	5.51	211
tatra cāste saha strībhir	23.34	895
tatra labdha-smṛtir daivāt	31.9	1269
tatra snātvā pitṝn devān	3.26	112
tatra tatra patañ chrānto	30.23	1251
tatra tatra vinikṣipta-	23.17	885
tatrāhṛtās tā nara-deva-kanyāḥ	3.7	95
tatrāpi daityaṁ gadayāpatantaṁ	13.31	492
tatrāpi sparśa-vedibhyaḥ	29.29	1214
tatrāpy ajāta-nirvedo	30.14	1244
tatrātha śuśrāva suhṛd-vinaṣṭiṁ	1.21	21
tatremaṁ ka upāsīran	7.37	288
tatreti-kṛtyam upaśikṣa yathopadeśaṁ	23.11	880
tatropalabhyāsura-loka-pālakaṁ	17.27	674
tat-sṛṣṭa-sṛṣṭa-sṛṣṭeṣu	31.37	1300
tat-tad-guṇānuśravaṇaṁ mukunda-	13.4	471
tat-trāṇāyāsṛjac cāsmān	22.3	830
tattvāmnāyaṁ yat pravadanti	25.31	1000
tattvānāṁ bhagavaṁs teṣāṁ	7.37	288
tattva-saṅkhyāna-vijñaptyai	24.10	924
tau tu gīrvāṇa-ṛṣabhau	16.33	651
tāv ādi-daityau sahasā	17.16	666
tāv āśvāsya jagat-sraṣṭā	24.20	935
tāv eva hy adhunā prāptau	16.35	652
tāv ubhau sukham edhete	7.17	274
tava kṣetre devahūtyāṁ	21.32	810
tava sandarśanād eva	22.5	833
tāvac chaśāsa kṣitim eka cakrām	1.20	20
tāvad adhyāsate lokaṁ	32.8	1322
tāvad bhayaṁ draviṇa-deha-suhṛn-	9.6	330
tāvan mamety asad-avagraha ārti-	9.6	330
tāvan na saṁsṛtir asau pratisaṅ-	9.9	333
tāvat prasanno bhagavān	21.8	781
tāvat tri-bhuvanaṁ sadyaḥ	11.31	417

tāvaty eva niśā tāta	11.22	411
tayā saṁsthāpayaty etad	7.4	259
tayā vibhraṁśita-jñānā	4.1	117
tayoḥ samuccayo māsaḥ	11.11	403
tayoḥ saṁvadatoḥ sūta	20.5	737
tayoḥ spṛdhos tigma-gadāhatāṅgayoḥ	18.19	694
tayor asurayor adya	16.36	653
tayor nirbhinna-hṛdayas	30.21	1250
te 'naika-janma-śamalaṁ sahasaiva	9.15	343
te ahārṣur devayanto	20.22	751
te dve muhūrtaḥ praharaḥ	11.8	402
te tu taj jagṛhū rūpaṁ	20.46	769
te vā amuṣya vadanāsita-padma-	15.44	602
te vai brahmaṇa ādeśāt	20.10	741
te yoga-māyayārabdha-	16.15	631
tebhyaḥ so 'sṛjat svīyaṁ	20.50	771
tebhyaś caikaikaśaḥ svasya	20.53	773
tebhyo 'dadāt tam ātmānam	20.44	768
tebhyo gandha-vidaḥ śreṣṭhās	29.29	1214
tebhyo virājam uddhṛtya	7.21	277
tejaso vṛttayas tv etāḥ	26.40	1065
tejastvaṁ tejasaḥ sādhvi	26.39	1065
tejīyasām api hy etan	12.31	450
tejo-guṇa-viśeṣo 'rtho	26.48	1071
tena saṁsāra-padavīm	27.3	1093
tenaiva me dṛśam anuspṛśatād	9.22	353
tenaiva sākam amṛtaṁ puruṣaṁ	32.10	1324
tenaiva tu muni-śreṣṭha	14.2	514
tenāṣṭa-lokapa-vihāra-kulācalendra-	23.39	899
tenāvasṛṣṭaḥ sahasā	31.23	1288
tenāvikuṇṭha-mahimānam ṛṣiṁ tam	31.14	1275
tenettham āhataḥ kṣattar	19.16	712
tepe tapo bahu-savo 'varurutsamānas	9.18	348
tepus tapas te juhuvuḥ sasnur āryā	33.7	1369
teṣāṁ bahu-padāḥ śreṣṭhāś	29.30	1215
teṣām itīritam ubhāv avadhārya	15.35	592
teṣāṁ maireya-doṣeṇa	4.2	118
teṣāṁ parānusaṁsargād	5.37	193
teṣāṁ saṁsthāṁ pramāṇaṁ ca	7.26	280
teṣāṁ satāṁ veda-vitāna-mūrtir	13.26	488
teṣāṁ śramo hy apārthāya	13.13	479
teṣāṁ supakva-yogānāṁ	15.7	559
teṣv aśānteṣu mūḍheṣu	31.34	1297
tiraścām aṣṭamaḥ sargaḥ	10.21	390
tiro-bhavitrī śanakair	27.23	1119
tīrthaṁ sudāsasya gavāṁ guhasya	1.22	22
tiryaṅ-mānuṣa-devānāṁ	7.27	281
tiryaṅ-manuṣya-vibudhādiṣu jīva-	9.19	349
tiryaṅ-nṛ-pitṛ-devānāṁ	11.26	414
tiṣṭhāmahe 'thāpi kathañcid ājau	18.11	689
tiṣṭhan niṣaṇṇaṁ parameṣṭhi-	2.22	73
titikṣavaḥ kāruṇikāḥ	25.21	987
tīvrayā mayi bhaktyā ca	27.21	1116
tīvreṇa bhakti-yogena	2.4	50
tīvreṇa bhakti-yogena	25.44	1020
todaṁ mṛṣan niragād ambu-madhyād	18.6	685
toyādibhiḥ parivṛtaṁ	26.52	1074
trai-vargikās te puruṣā	32.18	1330
trasareṇu-trikaṁ bhuṅkte	11.6	400
trayāṇām api lokānām	33.35	1396
trayīmayaṁ rūpam idaṁ ca saukaraṁ	13.41	502
trayodaśādadāt tāsāṁ	14.14	522
trayoviṁśati tattvānāṁ	6.2	216
tribhir muhūrtair dvābhyāṁ vā	30.24	1252
tri-lokyā yuga-sāhasraṁ	11.22	411
tri-lokyāṁ dahyamānāyāṁ	11.30	416
triṣṭum māṁsāt snuto 'nuṣṭub	12.45	461
tubhyaṁ mad-vicikitsāyām	9.37	367
tudanty āma-tvacaṁ daṁśā	31.27	1290
tuṣṭo 'ham adya tava mānavi	23.6	874
tvacam asya vinirbhinnāṁ	6.18	231
tvacaṁ romabhir oṣadhyo	26.65	1084

tvaṁ bhakti-yoga-paribhāvita-hṛt- 9.11 337
tvaṁ ca samyag anuṣṭhāya 21.30 806
tvaṁ deha-tantraḥ praśamāya 33.5 1366
tvaṁ deva śaktyāṁ guṇa-karma-yonau 5.50 210
tvam ekaḥ kila lokānāṁ 20.27 755

tvam ekaḥ kleśadas teṣām 20.27 755
tvam ekaḥ sarva-bhūtānāṁ 13.7 473
tvām eva dhīrāḥ puruṣaṁ viśanti 5.47 206
tvaṁ loka-pālo 'dhipatir bṛhac-chravā 17.28 675
tvaṁ naḥ sapatnair abhavāya kiṁ 18.4 682

tvaṁ naḥ surāṇām asi sānvayānāṁ 5.50 210
tvaṁ naḥ sva-cakṣuḥ paridehi śaktyā 5.51 211
tvaṁ pad-rathānāṁ kila yūthapādhipo 18.12 690
tvāṁ sūribhis tattva-bubhutsayāddhā 24.32 945
tvāṁ yogamāyā-balam alpa-pauruṣaṁ 18.4 682

tvattaḥ sanātano dharmo 16.18 633
tvayā me 'pacitis tāta 24.12 927
tvayerito yato varṇās 7.23 279
tvayi saṁsthite gadayā śīrṇa-śīrṣaṇy 18.5 683

U

ubhayatrāpi bhagavan 7.15 272
ubhayor antaraṁ vyoma 6.29 237
ubhayor ṛṣi-kulyāyāḥ 22.27 855
ūcuḥ suhṛttama-didṛkṣita-bhaṅga īṣat 15.31 585

udāplutaṁ viśvam idaṁ tadāsīd 8.10 303
uddhasat-taḍid-ambhoda- 17.6 660
uddhṛtya puṣpebhya ivārta-bandho 5.15 173
udyatasya hi kāmasya 22.12 840

ugraretā bhavaḥ kālo 12.12 436
ulbena saṁvṛtas tasminn 31.8 1269
unmūlayan naga-patīn 17.5 660
upagamya kuśāvarta 20.4 735

upaguhya ca bāhubhyām 22.24 853
upalabhyāsurā dharma 20.31 758
upalabhyātmanātmānaṁ 27.10 1103
upary adhaś ca ye lokā 7.26 280

upary upari vinyasta- 23.16 884
upāsaṁśritya malinaṁ 21.47 820
upasaṅgamya viprarṣim 14.33 538
upasarpati sarvātman 18.26 700
upāsate kāma-lavāya teṣāṁ 21.14 788

upāśritaḥ kañjam u loka-tattvaṁ 8.17 308
upaśrutya bhaven modaḥ 19.34 728
upāyād āśrama-padaṁ 21.37 815
upeyivān mūlam aśeṣa-mūlaṁ 21.15 789
ūrjasvantaṁ manyamāna 20.42 766

ūrū suparṇa-bhujayor adhi 28.24 1154
ūrvor nidhāya kara-pallava-rociṣā yat 28.23 1153
ūṣmāṇam indriyāṇy āhur 12.47 462
utkṣipta-vālaḥ kha-caraḥ kaṭhoraḥ 13.27 489
utpādya śāsa dharmeṇa 13.11 477

utpātā bahavas tatra 17.3 658
utsaṅgān nārado jajñe 12.23 443
utsrotasas tamaḥ-prāyā 10.20 390
utsṛṣṭa-dīrghormi-bhujair ivārtaś 13.29 491
utsunoṣīkṣamāṇānāṁ 20.35 761

uttarāyāṁ dhṛtaḥ pūror 3.17 103
utthāpyāpāyayad gāvas 2.31 84
utthāya sadyo jagṛhuḥ praharṣa- 3.7 95
utthāya viśva-vijayāya ca no viṣādaṁ 9.25 356

utthitaṁ puruṣo yasmād 26.51 1073
uttuṅga-rakta-vilasan-nakha- 28.21 1150
uvāca lalitāṁ vācaṁ 23.50 908
uvāsa tasmin salile pade sve 8.11 304

V

vācā svāṁśena vaktavyaṁ 6.12 227
vācaṁ duhitaraṁ tanvīṁ 12.28 447
vācaś ca nas tulasivad yadi te 'ṅghri- 15.49 612

vācāviklavayety āha 33.9 1373
vācyamāno 'pi na brūte 30.17 1246
vada naḥ sarga-saṁvyūhaṁ 7.27 281
vadhaṁ bhagavatā sākṣāt 14.42 546

vadhāt prapannārti-jihīrṣayeśo	1.43	42
vadhāya cāsatāṁ yas tvaṁ	21.50	823
vahnir vācā mukhaṁ bheje	26.63	1083
vaijayantyā srajā juṣṭam	17.21	671
vaikārikād vikurvāṇān	26.27	1052
vaikārikāś ca ye devā	5.30	188
vaikārikas taijasaś ca	5.29	187
vaikārikas taijasaś ca	26.24	1050
vaikarikas tu yaḥ proktaḥ	10.27	394
vaikāriko deva-sargaḥ	10.17	387
vaikhānasā vālakhilyau-	12.43	460
vaikṛtās traya evaite	10.27	394
vaikuṇṭha-līlābhidhyānaṁ	28.6	1135
vaikuṇṭhaṁ tad-adhiṣṭhānaṁ	16.27	645
vaimānikāḥ sa-lalanāś caritāni śaśvad	15.17	568
vaimānikān atyaśeta	23.41	900
vairāgya-bhaktyātmajayānubhāvita-	13.39	500
vairāgya-sāraṁ pratilabhya bodhaṁ	5.46	205
vaiśrambhake surasane	23.40	900
vaiśyas tad-udbhavo vārtāṁ	6.32	241
vajry ādravat taṁ sa-gaṇo ruṣāndhaḥ	3.5	93
vāk karau caraṇau meḍhraṁ	26.13	1039
vakṣo 'dhivāsam ṛṣabhasya mahā-	28.26	1157
vaktraṁ bhruvā kuṭilayā sphuṭa-	15.28	582
vaktuṁ bhavān no 'rhati yad	4.25	139
valgu-prakoṣṭha-valayaṁ vinatā-	15.40	598
vāma ūrāv adhiśritya	4.8	122
vanaṁ pravrajite patyāv	33.21	1383
vanaspaty-oṣadhi-latā-	10.19	389
vāṇyā vahnir atho nāse	26.54	1076
vāṇyānurāga-kalayātmajavad	16.11	627
vāpīṣu vidruma-taṭāsv amalāmṛtāpsu	15.22	573
vāpyām utpala-gandhinyāṁ	33.19	1382
vārāha iti vikhyāto	11.37	421
varāha-toko niragād	13.18	483
varṇāśrama-vibhāgāṁś ca	7.29	282
varṇitaṁ varṇanīyasya	22.39	867
varṣadbhiḥ pūya-keśāsṛg-	19.19	714
varṣatīndre vrajaḥ kopād	2.33	86
varṣatīndro dahaty agnir	25.42	1017
vārtā sañcaya-śālīna-	12.42	459
vartante 'nuyugaṁ yeṣāṁ	29.44	1229
vārtāyā daṇḍa-nīteś ca	7.32	285
vārtāyāṁ lupyamānāyām	30.11	1242
vārtayāṁśena puruṣo	6.21	232
vasanti yatra puruṣāḥ	15.14	565
vaśe sa-pālāl̐ lokāṁs trīn	17.19	669
vāsudeva-prasaṅgena	22.36	864
vasudevasya devakyāṁ	2.25	77
vāsudeve bhagavati	24.45	961
vāsudeve bhagavati	32.23	1336
vatsāṁ manor uccapadaḥ svasāraṁ	22.18	846
vavau vāyuḥ suduḥsparśaḥ	17.5	660
vavṛdhāte 'śma-sāreṇa	17.16	666
vayaṁ jayema helābhir	14.20	526
vayaṁ karma-karīs tubhyaṁ	23.27	891
vayaṁ vratair yac-caraṇāpaviddhām	14.26	532
vāyor guṇa-viśeṣo 'rtho	26.47	1070
vāyoś ca sparśa-tanmātrād	26.38	1064
vāyunotkramatottāraḥ	30.16	1246
vāyv-agnibhyāṁ yathā lohaṁ	28.10	1139
vedāham ādyaṁ puruṣam	24.16	931
vedāham antar manasīpsitaṁ te	4.11	125
vetreṇa cāskhalayatām atad-	15.30	584
vibabhājātmanātmānam	6.7	221
vibhajya navadhātmānaṁ	23.44	903
vicitra-divyābharaṇāṁśukānāṁ	8.25	315
vicitra-mārgāṁś carator jigīṣayā	18.19	694
vidhema cāsyai namasā saha tvayā	13.42	502
vidhunvatā vedamayaṁ nijaṁ vapur	13.44	505
viditvā tava caityaṁ me	21.23	800
viditvārthaṁ kapilo mātur itthaṁ	25.31	1000

viduro 'py uddhavāc chrutvā	4.33	151
vidyā dānaṁ tapaḥ satyaṁ	12.41	458
vidyādharī-sahasreṇa	23.37	897
vidyotamānaṁ vapuṣā	21.46	820
vidyut-kṣipan-makara-kuṇḍala-	15.41	599
vigāhyāgādha-gambhīrāṁ	16.14	630
vighūrṇitāpatad reje	19.3	704
vihāra-sthāna-viśrāma-	23.21	887
vijagāhe mahā-sattvo	17.24	672
vijitya loke 'khila-daitya-dānavān	17.28	675
vijñānātmātma-deha-sthaṁ	5.27	185
vikāraiḥ sahito yuktair	11.40	424
vikarṣan bṛhatīṁ senāṁ	21.53	825
vikramyainaṁ mṛdhe hatvā	18.28	701
vilakṣya daityaṁ bhagavān sahasra-	18.21	696
vilakṣyaikatra saṁyujyād	28.20	1149
vilīyante tadā kleśāḥ	7.13	270
vilokya cāmarṣa-pariplutendriyo	19.7	707
vilokya mumuhe sadyaḥ	26.5	1030
vimānaṁ kāma-gaṁ kṣattas	23.12	882
vimṛjya netre viduraṁ	2.6	52
vimuñcātma-tanuṁ ghorām	20.28	756
vinadya bhūyo vibudhodayāya	13.26	488
vinaṣṭāsu sva-māyāsu	19.24	717
vindeta bhūyas tata eva duḥkhaṁ	5.2	156
viniṣkrāmati kṛcchreṇa	31.23	1288
vinyasta-caraṇāmbhojam	21.11	783
vipannān viṣa-pānena	2.31	84
viprāṁs tu ko na viṣaheta yad-	16.9	625
viprāṇāṁ deva-devānāṁ	16.17	633
viprāṇāṁ saurabheyīṇāṁ	18.22	697
viprarṣabhān kṛtodvāhān	24.24	938
virāgo yena puruṣo	29.3	1182
virājam atapat svena	6.10	225
virajaṁ kṛta-svastyayanaṁ	23.30	892
virāṭ prāṇo daśa-vidha	6.9	223
virāṭ tadaiva puruṣaḥ	26.70	1087
viriñco 'pi tathā cakre	10.4	377
vīrye tvadīye ṛṣaya	21.29	805
viṣaṇṇa-cetasaṁ tena	9.27	358
visasarja tanuṁ tāṁ vai	20.39	764
visasarjātmanaḥ kāyaṁ	20.19	749
viṣayān abhisandhāya	29.9	1189
viśīrṇa-bāhv-aṅghri-śiroruho 'patad	19.26	719
vismāpanaṁ svasya ca	2.12	60
viṣṇor dhāma paraṁ sākṣāt	11.42	426
viṣṇur gatyaiva caraṇau	26.67	1085
viśo 'vartanta tasyorvor	6.32	241
visphūrjac-caṇḍa-kodaṇḍo	21.52	824
viśrambhād abhyadhattedaṁ	4.24	138
viśrambheṇātma-śaucena	23.2	870
visrasta-moha-paṭalā tam	33.1	1361
visṛjya kāmaṁ dambhaṁ ca	23.3	871
visṛjya sarvān anyāṁś ca	25.40	1013
visṛjyehobhayaṁ pretya	30.30	1256
viśrutau śruta-devasya	25.2	966
viśuddhena tadātmānam	33.25	1386
viśvam ātma-gataṁ vyañjan	26.20	1046
viśvaṁ vai brahma-tan-mātraṁ	10.12	384
viśvaṁ vicakṣate dhīrā	11.17	408
viśvaṁ yugānte vaṭa-patra ekaḥ	33.4	1365
viśva-sthity-udbhavāntārthā	5.22	180
viśvasya janma-sthiti-saṁyamārthe	5.43	201
viśvasya yaḥ sthiti-layodbhava-hetur	16.37	654
viśvāvasur nyapatat svād vimānād	22.17	845
viśvodbhava-sthiti-layeṣu nimitta-	9.14	342
vītaṁ yadā manaḥ śuddham	25.16	980
vitariṣye yayā cāsau	24.40	955
vitarkayanto bahudhā	20.33	759
vittasya coru-bhārasya	2.32	84
vivikta upasaṅgamya	24.26	939
vivikta-śaraṇaḥ śānto	27.8	1100

vivitsavas tattvam ataḥ parasya 8.3 297
vivṛddha-vijñāna-balo 10.6 378
vraja-striyo dṛgbhir anupravṛtta- 2.14 63
vraje ca vāso 'ri-bhayād iva svayaṁ 2.16 66
vrajema sarve śaraṇaṁ yad īśa 5.43 201

vrataṁ sa āsthito maunam 24.42 958
vṛkṇe sva-śūle bahudhāriṇā hareḥ 19.15 711
vṛttibhir lakṣaṇaṁ proktaṁ 26.22 1049
vyādhasyāpy anukampyānāṁ 14.36 541
vyajyedaṁ svena rūpeṇa 9.44 373

vyālambi-pīta-vara-vāsasi vartamāna- 28.24 1154
vyamuñcan vividhā vāco 17.10 662
vyarudan deva-liṅgāni 17.13 664
vyasanārṇavam atyeti 14.18 525
vyomni praviṣṭa-tamasā 17.6 660
vyūḍhaṁ harin-maṇi-vṛṣa-stanayor 28.25 1155

Y

ya ādyo bhagavān puṁsām 25.9 972
ya etena pumān nityaṁ 9.40 369

ya evam etāṁ hari-medhaso hareḥ 13.48 508
ya idam anuśṛṇoti yo 'bhidhatte 33.37 1397
ya idaṁ śṛṇuyād amba 32.43 1359
yā karoti padākrāntān 31.38 1301

yā ta ātma-bhṛtaṁ vīryaṁ 21.29 805
ya udyatam anādṛtya 22.13 841
yā vā kācit tvam abale 20.35 761
yā vai sva-garbheṇa dadhāra devaṁ 1.33 32

yā yātanā vai nārakyas 30.29 1255
yac ca vrajanty animiṣām 15.25 577
yac cakarthāṅga mat-stotraṁ 9.38 368
yac chraddhayā śrutavatyā ca bhaktyā 5.42 199

yac chrī-niketam alibhiḥ 28.30 1162
yac-chauca-niḥsṛta-sarit- 28.22 1151
yad ābhraṁśayituṁ bhogā 22.34 862
yad adhruvasya dehasya 30.3 1235

yad āhur varṇaye tat te 26.2 1024
yad āhur vāsudevākhyaṁ 26.21 1047
yad ardham āyuṣas tasya 11.34 419
yad arodīḥ sura-śreṣṭha 12.10 434
yad arthena vināmuṣya 7.10 265

yad astauṣīr guṇamayaṁ 9.39 368
yad brāhmaṇasya mukhataś carato 16.8 624
yad dharer nābhi-sarasa 11.36 421
yad dharma-sūnor bata rājasūye 2.13 62
yad gatvā na nivarteta 27.29 1125

yad okaḥ sarva-bhūtānāṁ 13.15 481
yad vā ayaṁ mantra-kṛd vo 1.2 1
yad vā tapasi te niṣṭhā 9.38 368
yad vanaspatayo bhītā 29.41 1227
yad viditvā vimucyeta 26.1 1023
yad vidur hy aniruddhākhyaṁ 26.28 1053
yad visphuran-makara-kuṇḍala- 28.29 1160
yad yad vidhatte bhagavān 25.3 967
yad yad yenāsṛjad devas 12.36 455

yadā ca pārtha-prahitaḥ sabhāyāṁ 1.9 7
yadā cāhīndra-śayyāyāṁ 32.4 1318
yadā manaḥ svaṁ virajaṁ 28.12 1141
yadā na yogopacitāsu ceto 27.30 1127
yadā rahitam ātmānaṁ 9.33 363

yadā sabhāyāṁ kuru-deva-devyāḥ 1.7 6
yadā sasmāra ṛṣabham 23.34 895
yadā sva-bhāryayā sārdhaṁ 13.6 473
yadā tu bhavataḥ śīla- 22.10 839

yadā tu rājā sva-sutān asādhūn 1.6 5
yadā tu sarva-bhūteṣu 9.32 362
yadaivam adhyātma-rataḥ 27.27 1124
yad-artham ātma-niyamais 21.23 800

yadāsya cittam artheṣu 32.24 1337
yad-bhayād varṣate devo 29.40 1226
yad-bhayād vāti vāto 'yaṁ 29.40 1226
yad-darśanaṁ janmabhir īḍya sadbhir 21.13 787

yadendriyoparāmo 'tha 7.13 269
yadopahūto bhavanaṁ praviṣṭo 1.10 8
yadṛcchayaivopagatām 26.4 1028
yadṛcchayopalabdhena 27.8 1100
yad-roma-garteṣu nililyur addhayas 13.34 495

yad-vṛttam anutiṣṭhan vai 12.31 450
yady asadbhiḥ pathi punaḥ 31.32 1295
yad-yad-dhiyā ta urugāya vibhāva- 9.11 337
yad-yogamāyā-guṇa-yoga-mohitaṁ 13.45 506
yaḥ karṇa-nāḍīṁ puruṣasya yāto 5.11 168

yaḥ kṛṣṇa-pādāṅkita-mārga-pāṁsuṣv 1.32 31
yaḥ pañca-bhūta-racite rahitaḥ śarīre 31.14 1275
yaḥ pañca-hāyano mātrā 2.2 47
yaḥ pṛṣṭo munibhiḥ prāha 22.38 866
yaḥ sṛjya-śaktim urudhocchvasayan 11.15 406

yair āśritas tīrtha-padaś 23.42 901
yair vastra-mālyābharaṇānulepanaiḥ 14.28 534
yais tattva-bhedair adhiloka-nātho 5.8 164
yajate kratubhir devān 32.2 1316
yajed yaṣṭavyam iti vā 29.10 1190

yajñasya ca vitānāni 7.30 283
yajñāya dhṛta-rūpāya 19.13 710
yam abhyaṣiñcac chata-patra-netro 1.29 29
yam āhur ādyaṁ puruṣaṁ 7.22 278

yām āhur ātmano hy ardhaṁ 14.19 525
yam āmananti sma hi śabda-yoniṁ 1.34 33
yām āśrityendriyārātīn 14.20 526
yāṁ harmya-pṛṣṭhe kvaṇad-aṅghri- 22.17 845

yāṁ manyate patiṁ mohān 31.41 1304
yaṁ rukmiṇī bhagavato 'bhilebhe 1.28 28
yaṁ vai vibhūtir upayāty anuvelam 16.20 636
yaṁ vānayor damam adhīśa bhavān 16.25 642

yāṁ vilokya prajās trastā 19.17 713
yaṁ yam artham upādatte 30.2 1234
yāṁ yoginaḥ saṁspṛhayanti samyag 2.19 69
yaṁ yogino yoga-samādhinā raho 19.28 721

yamādibhir yoga-pathair 27.6 1097
yama-dūtau tadā prāptau 30.19 1248
yāmāś catvāraś catvāro 11.10 403
yamāv utasvit tanayau pṛthāyāḥ 1.39 37
yamunopavane kūjad- 2.27 79

yan māṁ nṛlokān raha utsṛjantaṁ 4.12 126
yan māṁ tvaṁ manyase 'yuktaṁ 9.36 366
yan mano mayi nirbaddhaṁ 9.35 365
yan martya-līlaupayikaṁ sva-yoga- 2.12 60
yan me sañjagṛhe vākyaṁ 24.12 927

yan na vrajanty agha-bhido 15.23 574
yan nirvyalīkena hṛdā 13.9 475
yānaṁ rathān ibhān kanyā 3.27 113
yāni yāni ca rocante 24.31 943
yan-māyayoru-guṇa-karma- 31.15 1276

yan-mūla-ketā yatayo 'ñjasoru- 5.39 196
yan-nābhi-padma-bhavanād aham 9.21 351
yan-nāmadheya-śravaṇānukīrtanād 33.6 1367
yan-nāmāni ca gṛhṇāti 16.5 620
yānty ūṣmaṇā maharlokāj 11.30 416

yarhy eva karṇa-vivareṇa guhāṁ gato 15.46 608
yaś ca mūḍhatamo loke 7.17 274
yas tāṁ vivikta-caritair 16.21 636
yās tāmisrāndha-tāmisrā 30.28 1254

yas tatyājāgrajaṁ kṛṣṇe 20.2 734
yas tāvad asya balavān iha jīvitāśāṁ 9.17 346
yas te 'bhyadhāyi samayaḥ sakṛd 23.10 879
yās tu śrutā hata-bhagair nṛbhir ātta- 15.23 574

yas tu tatra pumān so 'bhūn 12.54 466
yas tūnmukhatvād varṇānāṁ 6.30 238
yas tv atra baddha iva karmabhir 31.13 1274
yas tv eka-vīro 'dhiratho vijigye 1.40 38

yas tv etayor dhṛto daṇḍo 16.3 619
yas tvad-vidhānām asatāṁ praśāntaye 17.31 677
yas tvaṁ duhitaraṁ gaccher 12.30 449
yasmād bibhemy aham api 9.18 348

yasmin bhagavato netrān	21.38	815
yasmin daśa-vidhaḥ prāṇaḥ	7.23	279
yasmin nṛṇāṁ grāmya-sukhānuvādair	5.12	169
yāsv aṅga praviśann ātmā	32.38	1354
yasya jñānopadeśāya	5.21	179
yasya vācā prajāḥ sarvā	15.8	560
yasyāgha-marṣoda-sarid-varāyāḥ	5.41	198
yasyāhaṁ hṛdayād āsaṁ	13.17	482
yasyāṁ sva-dhuram adhyasya	14.19	525
yasyāmṛtāmala-yaśaḥ-śravaṇāva-	16.6	621
yasyānavadyācaritaṁ manīṣiṇo	14.27	533
yasyāṅghri-pātaṁ raṇa-bhūr na sehe	1.37	36
yasyānurāga-pluta-hāsa-rāsa-	2.14	63
yasyāvatāra-guṇa-karma-viḍam-	9.15	343
yat kṛtveha yaśo viṣvag	13.8	474
yat saṅkulaṁ hari-padānati-mātra-	15.20	571
yat sānubandhe 'sati deha-gehe	5.44	202
yat sarva-bhūta-dayayāsad-alabhya-	9.12	339
yat svayaṁ bhagavān prītyā	22.5	833
yat svayaṁ cātma-vartmātmā	6.39	251
yat tat samādhi-yogarddhi-	20.53	773
yat tat sattva-guṇaṁ svacchaṁ	26.21	1047
yat tat tri-guṇam avyaktaṁ	26.10	1037
yat te 'nutāpa-viditair dṛḍha-bhakti-	15.47	609
yat tvaṁ pṛcchasi martyānāṁ	14.5	515
yat tvāṁ vimuktidaṁ prāpya	23.57	914
yātanā-deha āvṛtya	30.20	1249
yathā gandhasya bhūmeś ca	27.18	1112
yathā hiraṇyākṣa udāra-vikramo	19.32	725
yathā hy apratibuddhasya	27.25	1121
yathā jala-stha ābhāsaḥ	27.12	1106
yathā jale candramasaḥ	7.11	267
yathā mahān ahaṁ-rūpas	32.29	1344
yathā māṁ nātirocanti	14.22	528
yathā prasuptaṁ puruṣaṁ	26.71	1087
yathā punaḥ sve kha idaṁ niveśya	5.6	161
yathā putrāc ca vittāc ca	28.39	1172
yathā sāṅkhyeṣu kathitaṁ	29.2	1181
yathā sasarja bhūtāni	21.5	778
yathā sasarjāgra idaṁ nirīhaḥ	5.5	160
yathā vanān niḥsarato datā dhṛtā	13.40	501
yathā vāta-ratho ghrāṇam	29.20	1204
yathā-dharmaṁ jugupatuḥ	21.2	776
yathākṣṇor dravyāvayava-	31.46	1309
yathāttha bahu-rūpasya	10.10	382
yathāvatārās tava sūkarādayas	33.5	1366
yathedānīṁ tathāgre ca	10.13	385
yathendriyaiḥ pṛthag-dvārair	32.33	1348
yathobhayeṣāṁ ta ime hi lokā	5.49	208
yathoditaṁ sva-duhitṝḥ	24.21	936
yatholmukād visphuliṅgād	28.40	1173
yathopajoṣaṁ racitair	23.21	887
yāti jīvo 'ndha-tāmisraṁ	30.33	1259
yato 'bhavad viśvam idaṁ vicitraṁ	22.20	849
yato 'prāpya nyavartanta	6.40	252
yat-prasādād idaṁ viśvaṁ	14.47	549
yatra cādyaḥ pumān āste	15.15	566
yatra loka-vitāno 'yaṁ	26.52	1074
yatra naiḥśreyasaṁ nāma	15.16	567
yatra nārāyaṇo devo	4.22	136
yatra praviṣṭam ātmānaṁ	33.19	1382
yatra putraiś ca pautraiś ca	7.24	279
yatra viśva ime lokāḥ	7.22	278
yatropagīyate nityaṁ	7.20	276
yatropayātam upasarpati deva-māyā	31.20	1284
yat-saṅkalpa-vikalpābhyāṁ	26.27	1052
yat-sevayā bhagavataḥ	7.19	276
yat-sevayā caraṇa-padma-pavitra-	16.7	623
yat-sṛṣṭayāsaṁ tam ahaṁ puruṣaṁ	31.19	1282
yāvad baliṁ te 'ja harāma kāle	5.49	208
yāvad dinaṁ bhagavato	11.23	412
yāvan mano-vacaḥ stutvā	9.26	357

yāvan na veda sva-hṛdi	29.25	1210
yāvat pṛthaktvam idam ātmana	9.9	333
yayā padaṁ te nirvāṇam	25.28	997
yayor ekatareṇaiva	29.35	1220
yayottānapadaḥ putro	14.6	516
yayuḥ prabhāsaṁ saṁhṛṣṭā	3.25	111
yayur vaikuṇṭha-nilayaṁ	15.13	564
ye 'bhyarthitām api ca no nṛ-gatiṁ	15.24	576
ye 'hīyantāmutaḥ keśā	20.48	770
ye 'ṅga tvad-aṅghri-śaraṇā bhavataḥ	15.48	611
ye 'nimitta-nimittena	15.14	565
ye 'nyonyato bhāgavatāḥ prasajya	25.34	1003
ye brāhmaṇān mayi dhiyā kṣipato	16.11	627
ye ca me bhagavan pṛṣṭās	10.2	375
ye marīcy-ādayo viprā	20.10	741
ye māyayā te hata-medhasas tvat-	21.14	788
ye me sva-dharma-niratasya tapaḥ-	23.7	875
ye me tanūr dvija-varān duhatīr	16.10	626
ye saṁvasanto na vidur	2.8	55
ye saṁyuge 'cakṣata tārkṣya-putram	2.24	76
ye sva-dharmān na duhyanti	32.5	1319
ye tu tvadīya-caraṇāmbuja-kośa-	9.5	329
ye tv ihāsakta-manasaḥ	32.16	1329
ye tvānanyena bhāvena	15.6	559
yena mām abhayaṁ yāyā	33.11	1375
yena prajānām uta ātma-karma-	5.9	165
yena sambhāvyamānena	25.7	970
yena vā bhagavāṁs tuṣyed	7.35	287
yenānubuddhyate tattvaṁ	32.31	1346
yenātivrajya tri-guṇaṁ	29.14	1195
yenedṛśīṁ gatim asau daśa-māsya īśa	31.18	1281
yenocchiṣṭān dharṣayanti	20.41	765
yeṣām ahaṁ priya ātmā sutaś ca	25.38	1010
yeṣāṁ bibharmy aham akhaṇḍa-	16.9	625
yeṣāṁ bṛhat-kaṭi-taṭāḥ smita-śobhi-	15.20	571
yeṣāṁ na tuṣṭo bhagavān	13.13	479
yo 'ntaḥ praviśya bhūtāni	29.38	1224
yo 'ntarhito hṛdi gato 'pi durātmanāṁ	15.46	608
yo 'nuyāti dadat kleśam	31.31	1294
yo 'rkendv-agnīndra-vāyūnāṁ	21.51	824
yo 'vagraho 'haṁ mametīty	25.10	973
yo 'vidyayānupahato 'pi daśārdha-	9.20	350
yo deha-bhājāṁ bhayam īrayāṇaḥ	8.20	311
yo dehinām ayam atīva suhṛt sa deho	23.6	874
yo gajendraṁ jhaṣa-grastaṁ	19.35	728
yo jātas trāyate varṇān	6.31	240
yo māṁ sarveṣu bhūteṣu	29.22	1206
yo vā ahaṁ ca giriśaś ca vibhuḥ	9.16	345
yo vābhidhatte mac-cittaḥ	32.43	1359
yo vai hiraṇyākṣa-vadhaṁ	19.37	730
yo vai svasṝṇāṁ pitṛvad dadāti	1.27	27
yo visphurad-bhrū-viṭapena bhūmer	2.18	68
yo yogo bhagavad-bāṇo	25.29	997
yoga ādhyātmikaḥ puṁsāṁ	25.13	978
yogair hemeva durvarṇaṁ	14.46	548
yoga-nidrā-nimīlākṣaḥ	11.32	418
yogasya lakṣaṇaṁ vakṣye	28.1	1129
yogena mayy arpitayā ca bhaktyā	25.27	995
yogena vividhāṅgena	32.35	1350
yogeśvarādhīśvara eka etad	5.6	161
yogeśvaraiḥ kumārādyaiḥ	32.12	1327
yoginaḥ sa bhavān kiṁ svid	16.19	635
yojanānāṁ sahasrāṇi	30.24	1252
yonīnāṁ guṇa-vaiṣamyāt	28.43	1176
yopayāti śanair māyā	31.40	1303
yoṣit-saṅgād yathā puṁso	31.35	1298
yujyate 'bhimato hy artho	32.27	1341
yuktānuṣṭhāna-jātena	33.24	1386
yuñjato nāpakuruta	27.26	1122

General Index

Numerals in boldface type indicate references to translations of the verses of Śrīmad-Bhāgavatam.

A

Abhavāya defined, 682
Abhaya defined, 875
Abhayaṁ sattva-saṁśuddhiḥ
quoted, 41
Abhimanyu, 104
Abhyāsa-yoga-yuktena
quoted, 1138
Abortion, 1250-1251
Ābrahma-bhuvanāl-lokāḥ
quoted, 1334
Absolute Truth
impersonalists misunderstand, 807
inquiry into, 798
knowledge about. *See:* Knowledge, spiritual
Lord as, 171, 955
Lord killing miscreants as, 545, 553
Lord reveals, 945
Lord's mercy reveals, 610-611
Māyāvāda misconception about, 740
personal feature of, 149
process for knowing, 640
realization of, in stages, 608, 610
via Sāṇkhya philosophy, 951
three features of, 955
water from the Lord as, 505
See also: Kṛṣṇa, Lord; Supreme Lord, Reality vs. reflection; Disciplic succession; Spiritual master
Ācāryas, defined, 935
Ācāryas (saintly authorities)
in Brahma-sampradāya, 474-475
following, for success, 144
See also: Authority, spiritual: Disciplic succession: Spiritual master; *names of specific ācāryas*
Ācāryopāsanam, 1200
Acintya-bhedābheda, 1174, 1222
Acintya-bhedābheda-tattva (oneness & difference) philosophy, 2, 159
Activities
body needed for, 951
devotional service as goal of, 914
energy source for, 223-224
fruitive, devotional service dispels, 933
of God.*See:* Supreme Lord, activities of; Supreme Lord, pastimes of
in Kṛṣṇa consciousness, 737, 806-807, 836-837
Lord witnesses, 747
of lowborn devotees, 622
material, relief from, 15
material, 657, 785, 793, 794, 865
material vs. spiritual, 830
origin of, 185
pure & impure, 222, 248
reactions to, good & bad, 166, 209
sinful. *See:* Sinful activities
spiritual, in early morning, 769
symptomize consciousness, 247-248
transcendental, 270
See also: Fruitive activity; *Karma*; Duty; Pious activities; Sinful activity; Supreme Lord, pastimes of; Welfare activity
Acyuta-bhāva-siddha defined, 156
Adānta-gobhir viśatāṁ tamisraṁ
verse quoted, 347
Ādhāra-śaktim avalambya parāṁ sva-mūrtiṁ
verse quoted, 289
Adhikāri-devatā, 1018
Adhi-māsa defined, 795
Adhokṣaja defined, 176, 719

Ādhyātmika, ādhibhautika & ādhidaivika, 197, 222, 228
Ādi-purṣua, Kṛṣṇa as, 1075
Aditi, 93
Administrators
pride in, 360
of universe, 202
See also: Government; King(s); *Kṣatriyas;* Leaders, government
Advaita Ācārya, 1371
Advaitam acyutam anādim ananta-rūpam
quoted, 944, 1146, 1161, 1393
verse quoted, 96, 326
Advaita Prabhu offered *prasāda* to Haridāsa, 625
Advancement, spiritual. *See:* Knowledge, spiritual; Purification
good wife helps, 790, 840
health & luster as sign of, 821
instruction in, 792, 910
in Kṛṣṇa consciousness, 862-863
by saintly person's association, 912, 913
by self-control, 918
of society, 825
via spiritual master, 737, 876
Affection
of *gopīs* for Kṛṣṇa, 63
of Lord for His servitors, 623
real object of, 371-372
See also: Attachment; Emotions; Love; Supreme Lord, love for
Africa as island, 776
Age, current. *See:* Kali-yuga; Modern Age; Present Age
Age of Kali. *See:* Kali-yuga
Age (time of life)
for marriage, 842
for renouncing family life, 949
for son to deliver mother, 956
Ages, the four *(yuga* cycle), 733, 864, 939
See also: Dvāpara-yuga; Kali-yuga; Satya-yuga; Tretā-yuga
Age, present. *See:* Kali-yuga
Agelessness in spiritual world, 582
Agni, **824**, 899
Agni-hotra, 497
Agriculture
in society, 242
See also: Cows; *Vaiśyas*
Ahalyā, 211
Aham defined, 181, 253
Ahaṁ brahmāsmi
quoted, 966, 985, 1195
Aham evāsam evāgre
Quoted, 181, 289
Ahaṁ-mama defined, 203
Ahaṁ sarvasya prabhavaḥ, 66, 355, 650, 1098, 1223, 1284
Ahaṁ sarvasya prabhavo
quoted, 62
Ahaṅkāra defined, 435
Ahaṅkāra. See: False ego
Ahiṁsā defined, 959
Air element, 1062-1063, 1070
See also: Elements; Evolution
Air of life, 1063, **1134**, 1135, 1138-1139
Airplanes, spiritual, 517, 580
Airs in body, 222, 223
Air moving & Kardama traveling, analogy of, 901
Airplane
in ancient times, 846
of Brahmā, 936
See also: Space travel
Aja, Brahmā as, 1363
Ajña defined, 681
Ajñāta-sukṛti defined, 123
Akāma devotees, 801-802
Akṛtātmā defined, 835
Ākṛtim defined, 144
Akrūra, 32
Akṣaja defined, 812
Akuṇṭha-dhiṣṇya defined, 207
Ākūti, 467, **468**, 779
Akuto-bhaya defined, 1020
Alcohol in demoniac society, 544
Alphabet, Sanskrit, 462

Amānitvam adambhitvam
quoted, 959
Amara-kośa dictionary, quoted on *ākṛti*, 144
Ambarīṣa Mahārāja, 716, 959, 990, 1138, 1350
devotional service of, 1020
America as island, 776
Amṛta defined, 800
Aṁśa expansion, 925
Anādi defined, 1026
Anādi karama-phale
quoted, 1309
Anādir ādir govindaḥ
quoted, 1075, 1283
verse quoted, 426
Analogies
air moving & Kardama traveling, 901
angry father & *brāhmaṇas*, 628
of arrow & *bhakti-yoga*, 998
arrows & offenses, 14
of ax & Lord Kapila, 976
bamboo fire & Yadus' destruction, 21, 118
banyan's potency & Lord's potency, 252
of banyan tree & material existence, 975
big sky & Lord, 589
of bird in tree & Supersoul, 1044
birds, soul & Supersoul, 225
bird's nest & Lord's face, **198**, **199**
blind eyes & bad son, 12
of blind leading blind, 1295
blind men & modern leaders, 333
blind well & family life, 957
of blind well & female association, 1304
boat & human body, 576, 1270
body & society, 831, 832
of bodily limbs of Lord, & demigods, 1018
bodily parts & social body, 238-239
bullfight & Hiraṇyākṣa-Varāha battle, **695**, **696**
candles & Lord's expansions, 811, 925
captain & spiritual master, 576
of captain & spiritual master, 1270
of cat & material world, 992
of chewing chewed & sense gratification, 1316
Analogies
child's mischief & sense gratification, 270
clothing & material elements, 223
of cloud & illusory energy, 1029
of cloud & *māyā*, 1344
cobra & Bhīma, 36
cobra & demon, 691
of creation & birth, 1073
creeper & devotional service, 53
crows & materialists, 324
demons & play dolls, 83
disease & material life, 761
of diseased man & conditioned soul, 1178
doll's beauty & woman's beauty, 758-759
dramatic actor & Lord, 344
of dreaming & material life, 1095, 1122, 1172
of dreaming & transmigration, 1389
of dress & material body, 1305
of earth's aroma & soul's intelligence, 1113
of eating & devotional service, 1352
of electric fan & *karma*, 1172
electricity & consciousness, 260
electricity & Lord, 65
elephant & offense, 597
elephant dust & sins, 299
of embryo & universal form, 1077
eyelid & elder Pāṇḍavas, 37-38
father & Lord, 66
father "fighting" child & Lord "fighting" Hiraṇyākṣa, 712-713
of feeding stomach & service to Lord, 1222
of fire, flames and smoke, & Lord, living entities and material energy, 1174
of fire & living entities, 1177
fire & Lord, 258, 264-265, 1177
fire & material existence, 793-794, 940
of fire & material life, 1119
of fire's heat & *dharma*, 976
fire's sparks & living entities, 265
fire in wood & Lord's existence, 362
fire in wood & Lord's potency, 503
of firewood & bodies, 1177
firewood & *kṛṣṇa-kathā*, 168

Analogies (*continued*)
fire in wood & Lord in devotee's semen, 922
fish & foolish souls, 56, 59
flames & Kṛṣṇa's expansions, 328
flowers & Lord's face, 602
fortress & body, 527
frog & speculation, 226, 246, 250, 251-253
Ganges bath & hearing Lord's pastimes, 737
Ganges & Lord, 195
of Ganges River & *Bhagavad-gītā*, 1343
of Ganges River & devotee's attraction for Lord, 1106
Garuḍa's nectar & Kṛṣṇa's Rukmiṇī, 91
gem (unpolished) & Kardama, 821
of goat's neck nipples & material nature, 1043
of golden oyster shell & Lord and His creation, 1343
gold & identity, **548**
of green bird and tree & merging, 1108-1109
headless vision & illusory consciousness, 265-266
hog & fool, 274
of hog & materialist, 1332
honey & Kṛṣṇa's glories, 174
human body & universal form, 220
of husking paddy & speculation, 1115, 1182
of impregnation & creation's cause, 1043, 1046
impersonalist & lone spaceman, 76
islands & planets, 903
jaundice victims & nondevotees, 8
of king & Lord, 1012
king's soldiers & Lord's abode, 181
of knot of material attraction, 1023
Kṛṣṇa & covered flame, 78
of lamp flame & mind, 1168
leprosy & offense, 621
of Lord's wife and living entities' mother & material nature, 1036
of losing wealth & hellish punishment, 1258
of lotus & transcendentalist, 1116
machine parts & living entities, 589

Analogies
mad elephant & sex desire, 519
magician & Lord, 257
of maidservant & liberation, 1003
married man & devotee, 207
of material body & universal body, 1026
miser & loveless soul, 372
moon & Kardama, 898
moon & Lord, **55**, 268
moon on water & soul in matter, 267-268
nimba tree & envious soul, 195
nonpoisonous snake & devotee's wealth, 331
ocean & Lord's devotee, 961
of ocean of tears & grief of living entities, 1164
of ox & father, 1244
paddy tillers & speculators, 226
of police department & material world, 1030
postbox & Deity, 19
of prison life & family life, 1239
prison & material world, 257, 589
prison trustees & demigods, 213
of purifying gold & purifying mind, 1139
rain cloud & spiritual master's mercy, 794
of razor's edge & devotional service, 1051
razor's edge & spiritual path, 356
of rich and poor man & Lord and living entity, 1220
of river & devotional service, 1354
salt & sense gratification, 561
sandalwood tree & Lord's body, 318
of sensing an aroma & knowing Kṛṣṇa, 1204-1205
serpent & Hiraṇyākṣya, 699
serpents & negligent persons, 627
serpents & nondevotees, 727
sky & ear holes, 614
sky & Lord, 204
sleep & cosmic dissolution, 182, 218
of sleep & false ego, 1110
snake & fool, 12
of spark & soul, 1177
spider's web & Lord's Creation, 796

Analogies
of spiritual arithmetic, 1144
stage play & Lord's fighting pastime, 645
stars & Gandharva girls, 898
stomach & Lord, 589, 684
of stomach's fire & devotional service, 1002
of stool & material literatures, 1332
soul in body & Lord in nature, 183
sugar candy & Lord's speeches, 8
sun & Lord, 44, 54, 61, 65, 127-128, 264, 452, 808, 955, 973, 1028, 1185
sun & powerful beings, 450
of sun and reflection & detachment, 1092
sun & Supersoul, 605, 833
of sunlight & *brahmajyoti*, 1027
of sunlight & Lord's consciousness, 1026
sun rays & living entities, 264-265
of sun's rays & living entities, 982
sun's rays & Lord's mercy, 372
sun & *varṇāśrama* system, 826
tape recording & time, 384
of tasting milk & appreciating Lord, 1349
of television signals & subtle forms, 1061
tree's root & Lord, 684
tree upside down & material world, 626
of umbilical cord & lotus stem, 1156
upper body & twice-born, 640
Vedic law & bull's rope, 561
of waking & creation of *mahat-tattva*, 1047
of waking & self-realization, 1122
of water & consciousness, 1049
of watering seed of devotional service, 1308
of water's taste & soul's intelligence, 1113
wheel & time, 795
of wind & time, 1233
womb & material nature, 184
Ānanda-cinmaya-rasa-pratibhāvitābhiḥ
quoted, 107
Ānandamayo 'bhyāsāt
quoted, 1170
Ananta, annihilation by, 386, **418**
Ananta, Lord, 318, 810, 1051
Ananta defined, 761
Anāsaktasya viṣayān
verse quoted, 1307
Anātmanām defined, 615
Anasūyā, 937
Ancestors, oblations on behalf of, 767
Aṇḍāntara-stha-paramāṇu-cayāntara-stham
verse quoted, 216
Aṇḍāntarastha-paramāṇu-cayāntara-stham
quoted, 1073
Andha-tāmisra defined, 748, **1254**, 1254, **1259**, 1264, 1295
Andhaṁ tamaḥ praviśanti
verse quoted, 337
Andhatāmisra hell, 135
Andhā yathāndhair upanīyamānāḥ
quoted, 1295
verse quoted, 347
Aneka-bāhūdara-vaktra-netraṁ
verse quoted, 246
Anena pūjyatvaṁ lakṣyate
quoted, 1368
Aṅgāni yasya sakalendriya-vṛttimanti
quoted, 184
Anger
of Bhīma, 36
of Brahmā, result of, **432**, **433**
of *brāhmaṇas* & Vaiṣṇavas, 546, 628
cause of, **445**, **446**
conditioned soul covered by, 748
as criminal, 592
of Diti's demoniac sons, 668
of Duryodhana, 12
material & spiritual, 586
by Rudra principle, 435
of Śiva, 540
See also: Envy; Ignorance
Aṅgirā, 930, 937
Anila, 230
Animals
at Bindu-sarovara Lake, 817-819
birth as, 1256
bodily development of, 1265
consciousness of, 1283

Animals (*continued*)
devotees kind to, 988
disturbed at demons' birth, **662**, 663, **664**
foolish men compared to, 106, 274
forest-going not for becoming like, 957
Hiraṇyākṣa scared, 673
humans contrasted to, 393, 454, 511
vs. human beings, 966, 977, 1213, 1236, 1256, 1283
as ignorant, 391
in ignorance, 236, 237
ignorance mode degrades one to, 865
killing of, 1197
killing of, cause of, **544**
killing of, result of, 237
kṣatriyas killed, 823
levels of, **1214-1216**
liberation for, 989
once-born men compared to, 163-164
as pets, 1213
prasāda for, 1213
protection for, 241
satisfied with their life, 1236
senses for, 1214-1216
sense gratification for, 911
See also: Cows; Species of life; *names of other specific animals*
Animosity, cure for, 549
Aniruddha, **33**, **34**
Aniruddha, Lord
beauty of, 1053-1054
as Lord of mind, 1053, 1056
worship of, 1048, 1054, 1056
Annihilation
Lord as baby at, 1365-1366
two kinds of, 1230, 1319, 1323-1324
Anstakrdhāna form, 768
Antavanta ime dehāḥ
quoted, 951
Anthropomorphism, miscreants misunderstand God worship as, 496
Anubhāva defined, 550
Anukīrtaya defined, 968
Anxiety
knowledge dispels, 138
See also: Fear: Misery
Anyābhilāṣitā-śūnyam
quoted, 1190, 1192
Apāna air, 224
Apatya defined, 11
Apauruṣa defined, 1060
Appearance of the Lord. *See*: Supreme Lord, advent of; Supreme Lord, forms of
Āpomayaḥ prāṇaḥ
quoted, 1067
Apsarās, , **763-764**, **923**
Aprakaṭa defined, 61
Ārātrika ceremony, 861
Arcā-mūrti. *See*: Deity form
Arcanā process
for pleasing the Lord, 348
See also: Deity form; Supreme Lord, worship of; Worship
Arcā-vigraha defined, 1006, 1110
See also: Supreme Lord, Deity form of
Arjuna, 1148
addresses Lord as *ādyam*, 724
arrows of, 70, 71, 72
bow of, 37
cited on unwanted population, 666
detachment of, 1338
Kṛṣṇa and, 4, 71, 98
Kṛṣṇa &, 658, 837, 945, 952
Kṛṣṇa satisfied by, 1120, 1197-1198, 1320
mind dovetailed by, 1168
prescribed duty of, 1117
quoted on restless mind, 1020
quoted on universal form, 246
rejected *yoga* process, 604
satisfied the Lord, 340, 370
Śiva challenged, 37
spiritualized by hearing, 1059
surrender of, 1093
Āruhya kṛcchreṇa paraṁ padaṁ tataḥ
verse quoted, 335, 436
Arundhatī, **937**

Āryans, 454, 1370, 1372
civilization, 826
defined, 1202-1203
See also: *Varṇāśrama* system; Vedic culture
Asamprajñāta defined, 786
Asaṅgo hy ayaṁ puruṣaḥ
quoted, 1276
Asat defined, 977
Asat-saṅga- tyāga
quoted, 1203
Āsavam defined, 892
Asia as island, 776
Āśrama defined, 840
See also: *Brahmacārī*; Householders; Residences, Vedic vs. modern; Sannyāsa; Vānaprastha
Āśrama & *varṇa* system. *See:* *Varṇāśrama* system
Āśraya defined, 282
Asses at demons' birth, 663
Association
of devotees. *See:* Devotees of the Supreme Lord, association with
good & bad, 13, 94
with Kṛṣṇa, 913
with saintly person, 833, 834, 912, 913, 915
See also: Attachment, material
Association with devotees. *See:* Devotees, association with
Aṣṭāṅga-yoga, goal of, 581
Aṣṭāṅga-yoga, 786
divisions of, eight named, 1130, 1373
vs. other *yogas*, 1341
Astral travel. *See:* Space travel
Astrology, marriage by, 790, 930-931
Astronomy, Vedic
calendar according to, 795
See also: Planets; Universe
Asuras. *See:* Atheists; Demons; Nondevotee(s)
Āsurika-bhāva defined, 152
Aśvattha defined, 122
Aśvattha tree, 346
Aśvattha tree of material existence, 975
Aśvatthāmā, 104
Aśvinī-kumāras, 229
Ataḥ śrī-kṛṣṇa-nāmādi
quoted, 146
Atharvā, 930, **938**
Athāto brahma-jijñāsā
quoted, 170, 275, 798
Athavā bahunaitena
verse quoted, 217
Atheists
anthropomorphism charges by, 496
birth & death bind, 689
in bodily concept, 748
as contradictory, 284
daridra-nārāyaṇa philosophy of, 1220
defined, 195
Deity as idol to, 18-19
Deity of Lord unaccepted by, 1006
as demons, 94
devotees in role as, 645
God's laws not accepted by, 1031
Kṛṣṇa's departure enlivened, 54
Kṛṣṇa's instructions to, 68
Lord displeased by, 685
misinterpret Kṛṣṇa, 58, 74
quoted on *tulasī*, 570
temples discredited by, 23
temporary opulence for, 209
theory of consciousness of, 1027
think demigods equal to Supreme Lord, 1152
See also: Demons; Impersonalists; Māyāvādīs; Nondevotee(s); Philosophers, speculative; Scientists, material
Athetareṣāṁ paśūnāḥ aśanāpipāse
verse quoted, 391
Atikramam defined, 618
Ātmā defined, 605, 835
Ātmā. *See:* Soul
Ātmaiva putro jāyate
quoted, 1384
Ātmānandī defined, 948
Ātmārāma
defined, 1123
devotees as, 1123

Ato 'cyuto 'khile loke
verse quoted, 289
Atoms, Lord enters, 217
defined, 397
as living entities, 382
Lord within, 604-605
time measured by, 399, 400
universe likened to, 425
Atri, 930, 936, 937
Attachment
birth according to, 1305
to body, etc., 1235, 1239, 1294
bondage of, 986, 1165
compared to knot, 1025
to false love, 1239-1240
in family life, 1173, 1235, 1237-1239, 1294, 1305, 1356
freedom from. *See:* Detachment
to funeral ceremony, 1246
"good" and "bad" determined by, 1337-1339
illusion of, 974, 975
liberation from. *See:* Liberation
liberation hampered by, 991
to lording over, 1119, 1120
Lord transcendental to, 1301
lust, 1293
of Kṛṣṇa for devotees, 108
material, 60
material to bodily relations, 748-749
to man, 1306
of *prakṛti* & *puruṣa*, 976
removed by devotee's association, 991-992
removed by spiritual consciousness, 980
to results of prescribed duties, 1329-1334
rituals to purify, 1330
to sex life, detailed, 1295-1307
to sex life as binding, 1165
to sex life as universal, 1299-1301
vs. spiritual, 986
spiritual knowledge breaks, 920
transferred to Kṛṣṇa, 986
to wealth, 1111, 1173
for woman, reasons for, 1306-1307
Attachment
to women, dangers of, 1303-1305, 1306
to women as strongest attachment, 1299-1301
See also: Affection: Association; Bodily concept of life; Bondage; Desires; Fruitive activity; Desires, material
Auspicious substances before & after bathing, 894
Austerity
for *brahmacarya*, 821
four principles of, 774
See also: Sacrifices Australia as island, 776
Author, the (A.C. Bhaktivedanta Swami Prabhupāda), met Bhaktisiddhānta Sarasvatī, 833-834
Austerity
of Devahūti, 1377-1378
fasting, 1068
liberation unattainable by, 1016
needed for preaching, 301
origin of, 430
in sex life. *See:* Celibacy
as valuable, 1378
in spiritual culture, 639
See also: Acāryas; Disciplic succession; Spiritual master; Penance: Renunciation
Authorities, spiritual
benefit of approaching, 658
in Brahma-sampradāya, 474-475
following in footsteps of, 640
hearing from, 727, 839
knowledge via, 741
sex as approved by, 775
twelve listed, 336
Vedas as, 949-950
See also: *Ācāryas*; Devotees, pure devotees; Disciplic succession; Spiritual master
Avabodha-rasa defined, 325
Avajānanti māṁ mūḍhā
quoted, 41, 56, 350, 681, 947
verse quoted, 74
Avāṅ-mānasa-gocaraḥ
quoted, 226

Avatāra. See: Incarnation; Purusa-avatāras; Supreme Lord, advent of incarnations of; *names of individual avatāras*
defined, 508, 725
See also: Supreme Lord, incarnations of
Avidyā. See: Ignorance, mode of
devotees beyond, 388
defined, 934
Avidyā pañca-parvaiṣā
verse quoted, 749
Avyakta-mārga-vit defined, 741
Āyur Veda, 1063
Āyur-veda, cited on begetting male or female children, 881, 907
Āyur-vedic medicine, 1063, 1066, 1080-1081, 1391
bodily elements in, three named, 1140
Āyur-vedic medicine, *āsavam* as, 892
Ayur-vedic medicine for liver disease, 56

B

Badarikāśrama, 120, 137, 147
Bahūnām janmanām ante
quoted, 941, 1016
verse quoted, 245
Bahu-śākhā hy anantāś ca
verse quoted, 213, 222
Baladeva, Lord, 810
Baladeva. *See:* Balarāma, Lord
Balarāma, Lord, 26, 27, 1141
Bali Mahārāja, 1148
Ball-playing, princesses engaged in, 846
Balvala, 98
Balavān indriya-grāmo
quoted, 447
Bāna, 98
Banyan tree
Lord sat under, 122
potency of, 252
Barhiṣmatī, 856, 857, 859
Bathing, appropriate times for, 538
auspicious substances before & after, 894
ladies' directions for, 893
Bathing
medicinal, 1080-1081
in pilgrimage places, 889
principles of, 1378
See also: Cleanliness; Purification
Battle of Kurukṣetra. *See:* Kurukṣetra, Battle of
Beauty
of the Lord, 62, 82
of the Lord & nature, 314, 315
of Earth, 501
facial, 895
of Kardama's castle, 882-887, 888, 889
of Lord, 324, **596**, 597, 598-600, 600, 601, 602, 603, **1145**
of Lord & others compared, 324
material, 760, 761
material vs. spiritual, 758-759
of Rādhārānī & Kṛṣṇa, 600
spiritual, 1144-1145
of twilight woman, 757-763
of woman, 758, 897, 929
Beings, living. *See:* Living entities; Soul
Bee-king's favorite abode, 636
Beings. *See:* Living entities
Benediction from God, 875
See also: Supreme Lord, mercy of
Bengal, dacoits in, 704
Bhagavad-gītā
See also: Bhagavad-gītā, cited; *Bhagavad- gītā*, quotations from
absolute nature of, 171
Arjuna heard, 71
atheists misuse, 74
Bhāgavatam supplements, 135
compared to Ganges River, 1343
demigod worship condemned in, 703-704
discussion in, purpose of, 3-4
as elementary self-knowledge, 169, 170
establishes real religion, 445
as eternal, 1012
ever fresh, 164-165
Indian royalty hears, 861
insatiably interesting, 738

Bhagavad-gītā
knowledge from, 1060
as *kṛṣṇa-kathā*, 167, 168
Lord spoke, 737
misinterpretation of, 172
Śaṣkara's commentary on, 135
surrender as last word of, 605
Uddhava supplements, 149-150
Vaivasvata Manu in, 777
value of hearing from, 968
Viśvanātha Cakravartī cited on, 921
Bhagavad-gītā, cited
See also: Bhagavad-gītā, quotations from on
freedom from *māyā*, 1034
on birth in good family, 861-862
on bondage, 591
on demigod worshipers, 789
on destinations according to nature's modes, 864
on devotee as calm ocean, 961
on devotees, two types of, 788
on devotion, 159
on devotional service & greatest danger, 795
on devotional service surpassing nature's modes, 813 , 865
on duties of social orders, 827
on enjoyment, 761
on fool's consideration of Kṛṣṇa, 932
on fools, 496
on forgetfulness, 429
on higher taste, 270-271
on impersonalists, 328
on knowing Lord's transcendental nature, 689, 795, 926
on Lord as equal to all, 1017
on Lord as father, 503
on Lord's assistance, 509-510
on Lord's descent, 545
on Lord's instructions from within, 361
on Lord as original person, 724
on Lord as proprietor, 832-833
on Lord as sacrificial enjoyer, 716
on Lord as *Vedānta-sūtras* knower, 925
Bhagavad-gītā, cited
on Lord controlling *māyā*, 740
on Lord controlling *prakṛti*, 743
on Lord in everything but not everywhere, 963
on Lord known by devotional service, 964
on Lord's advent, 724, 740, 850
on Lord's grace destroying distress, 875-876
on lowborn person, 622
on lower species, 594
on lust & anger, 1292
on *mahātmās*, 879
on *mām*, 955
on material existence, tree of, 967
on material nature's impregnation, 1045
on materialists not achieving Kṛṣṇa consciousness, 773-774
on nondevotees, 152
on nature's laws under Lord's direction, 687
on nature as *sarva-yoniṣu*, 1046
on nature's stringent laws, 665
on offering God a fruit & flower, 853
on pious people, 287
on planetary systems, 236
on religion as surrender to God, 792
on sacrifices, 716, 772
on serving according to ability, 837
on sex life, 543
on social orders, 238, 240
on spirit soul, 220
on spiritual happiness, 786
on spiritual sky, 746
on Supersoul, 1044, 126
on surrender to Lord, 974
on topmost *yogī*, 780
on unwanted children, 544
on unwanted population, 666
on *Vedas* & God, 830
on working for Viṣṇu, 857
on *yoga's* perfection, 785
on *yogī* meditating on God, 721
on "*yogīs*", 781

Bhagavad-gītā, quotations from
on activities for Yajña, 1117
on affection for the Lord, 371
on *bhāva*, 1335
on becoming Kṛṣṇa's devotee, 934, 954
on body & soul, 951
on bondage to work, 914
on Brahman reached by devotional service, 1008, 1335
on conditioned souls, 222
on creation & annihilation, 385
on demigod worship, 1353
on devotee as best *yogī*, 902
on devotee as *mahātmā*, 1057
on devotee as eligible for kingdom of God, 1024, 1385
on devotee on level of Brahman, 1008
on devotional service, 147, 310-311, 326, 500, 607, 649
on devotional service from Brahman realization, 1178-1179
on "dovetailing" with the Supreme, 334
on discussion among devotees, 1201
on duties for worship of Lord, 1196
on eating & recreation, regulation of, 1388
on energy of Lord, 1343
on envious souls, 195
on fallen devotees, 48
on fools, 56, 74
on fools deriding Kṛṣṇa, 947
on great souls, 835
on heavenly enjoyment as temporary, 1318, 1334
on higher taste, 1302, 1342, 1383
on humility & pridelessness, 959
on knowing the Lord, 110, 253
on knowledge & remembrance from Kṛṣṇa, 1277
on Kṛṣṇa behind creation, 504
on Kṛṣṇa as beneficiary of sacrifices & penances, 1352
on Kṛṣṇa as Brahman's basis, 1126, 1348, 1388
on Kṛṣṇa as beyond *karma*, 58

Bhagavad-gītā, quotations from
on Kṛṣṇa as everything, 66
on Kṛṣṇa's advent, 77
on Kṛṣṇa as origin of all, 1098, 1223, 1284
on Kṛṣṇa as seed of all, 1389
on Kṛṣṇa known by devotional service, 1023, 1205, 1349
on Kṛṣṇa's abode, no return from, 998, 1334, 1340
on Kṛṣṇa's appearance as transcendental, 1223
on liberated stage for devotional service, 1195, 1388
on liberated souls, 813
on liberation by devotional service, 960
on liberation by Kṛṣṇa consciousness, 998, 1223
on liberation for one free of prestige, illusion, etc., 991, 992
on living entities as Lord's parts, 1177
on Lord appearing by His will, 1273
on Lord as all-pervading & aloof, 807-808
on Lord as one & different, 258
on Lord as great-grandfather, 468
on Lord creating cosmos, 184, 217
on Lord in heart, 224
on Lord's descent, 644
on Lord's inconceivability, 146
on Lord as origin of everything, 724
on Lord fulfilling our desires, 789, 798
on Lord in heart, 747, 756
on Lord knowing everything, 947
on Lord known by devotional service, 942
on Lord's advent, 823
on Lord's transcendental nature, 344
on love for Kṛṣṇa, 1098
on *mahātmās*, 250
on material desires, 1250, 1316
on materialists' association rejected, 991
on mind's restlessness, 1020
on modes' control, 1093, 1113-1114
on nature, 345
on nature controlled by Kṛṣṇa, 1018, 1078, 1226
on offering everything to God, 806

Bhagavad-gītā, quotations from (*continued*)
on offering results of all to Kṛṣṇa, 1385
on perfection, 245
on pleasing the Lord, 340
on real religion, 590
on remembrance & forgetfulness caused by Lord, 973-974, 1277
on sacrifices' & penances' beneficiary, 1095
on self-realization, happiness from, 984
on sense control, 538
on social orders, 460
on soul as eternal, 1310
on souls on bodily machine, 1308
on spiritual success, 837
on Supersoul as knower in all bodies, 1345
on surrender, 267, 1014, 1016, 1114, 1277, 1285
on surrender to God, 797, 941, 945
on time factor, 384
on thinking about Kṛṣṇa, 809
on time obscuring *yoga* system, 952
on transcendence, 131
on transcendence by devotional service, 1140
on universal form, 246
on *varṇāśrama* system, 826
on Vedic knowledge, 199
on worshiping God by one's work, 915
on *yogamāyā*, 338
on *yoga* practice, 1139
Bhagavad-racita defined, 826
Bhagavān. See: Kṛṣṇa, Lord; Supreme Lord
meaning of name, 969, 1339
Bhāgavatam. See: *Śrīmad-Bhāgavatam*
Bhagavat-prasāda defined, 875-876
See also: *Prasāda*; Supreme Lord, mercy of
Bhāgavata Purāna. See: *Śrīmad-Bhāgavatam*
Bhagavat-tattva-vijṣāna
quoted, 147
Bhajanty ananya-manaso
verse quoted, 250
Bhaktas. See: Devotees
Bhakti defined, 960, 1002
See also: Devotional service; Kṛṣṇa consciousness; Supreme Lord, love for
Bhakti-kārya defined, 828
Bhakti-rasāmrta-sindhu
cited on disciple & spiritual master, 836
cited on devotional service, 363
cited on love of God, 51
quoted on liberation, 148
quoted on renunciation, 1307
quoted on serving Lord, 1375
Bhaktisiddhānta Sarasvatī Gosvāmī
author met, 833-834
as Bhaktivinoda Ṭhākura's son, 849
Bhaktisiddhānta Gosvāmī Mahārāja as *naiṣṭhika-brahmacārī*, 459
Bhaktivedanta Swami Prabhupāda, A.C. (the author), met Bhaktisiddhānta Sarasvatī, 833-834
Bhaktivinoda Ṭhākura begot Bhaktisiddhānta Sarasvatī, 849
Bhakti-yoga, 787, 941, 942
defined, 443-444
as best *yoga*, 978, 998, 1019, 1339, 1341, 1348
in *Bhagavad-gītā*, 3-4
compared to arrow, 998
divisions of, 1353-1354
as transcendental, 1092
& *yoga* compared, 1221-1222
as *yoga's* basis, 1350
See also: Devotional service; Kṛṣṇa consciousness; Supreme Lord, love for
Bhaktyā mām abhijānāti
quoted, 110, 147, 253, 311, 326, 942, 1205, 1023, 1349
Bharata, King, 903
Bhāratavarṣa, 20, 695
See also: Earth planet; India
Bhāva, 1064, 1335
Bhāvana defined, 1070
Bhavānī (Pārvatī), 870, 921
Bhayaṁ dvitīyābhiniveśataḥ syāt
quoted, 1042
Bhīma
anger of, 9

Bhīma
in battle, 99
prowess of, 36
Bhiṣāsmād agniś cendraś ca
quoted, 1018
Bhiṣāsmād vātaḥ pavate
quoted, 1018
Bhīsma, **7**, 8, 178
Bhīsmaka, King, **91**
Bhojas, 117, 118, 119
Bhoktāraṁ yajña-tapasām
quoted, 1095, 1352
Bhrāmayan sarva-bhūtāni
quoted, 1308
Bhṛgu Muni, **416**, 418
Bhṛgu, 930, 937
Bhūḥ bhuvaḥ svaḥ hymns, **461**
Bhūḥ, Bhuvaḥ, Svaḥ worlds, 415
Bhūta-bhṛt defined, 209
Bhūtvā bhūtvā pralīyate
quoted, 256
Bhūta-grāmam imaṁ kṛtsnam, 385
Bhuvarloka, 237
Bible, 1332
Bījaṁ māṁ sarva-bhūtānām
quoted, 1389
Bilvamaṅgala Ṭhākura
quoted on devotional service surpassing liberation, 865
quoted on liberation as maidservant, 1002
Bindu-sarovara, **969**
Bindu-sarovara Lake, **811-812, 814,** 816-819, 889
Birds
at Bindu-sarovara Lake, 817, 818
at demons' birth, **663**
in Kardama's castle, 887
pious & impious, 817
Birth
in animal body, 1256
of bad sons, cause of, 543, 544
as beginning of bodily senses, 1310
as beginning of reaction to fruitive activity, 1309
in *brāhmaṇa* family, 1368-1369
Birth
causes of, 1064
conception process preceding, 104, 184
debts follow, 850
of demons, 659, 665-666
in devotee's association, 1013, 1014
devotee's status irrelevant to, 622
of Diti's demons, **658, 659,** 666, **667, 668,** 668-669
to dog-eaters, 1368
first & second, 928, 931
of God. *See:* Supreme Lord, advent of
in good family, 16, 48, 94, 861
for hellish life's continuance, 1256
high, no relief by, 1093-1100
as human, 1259-1261
of Lord & living entities contrasted, 210-211, 922
liberation from. *See:* Liberation
male vs. female, 881, 907
material activities—good or bad—cause, 1094
in material energy, 1038-1039
misery of, 1286-1288, 1291-1292
modes govern type of, 1014, 1093, 1177
process of, 652
purification for, 1369
sanctification before, 756
social status beyond, 114, 240-241, **282-283**
of twice-born, 163-164
of twins, 668-669
in Vedic culture, 177
works determine, 166
See also: Children: Transmigration
Birth & death, repeated
demons subject to, 689
devotional service surpasses, 954
Lord stops, 682
mundane war topics cause, 516
scientists can't challenge, 953
suffering of, 793
See also: Birth; Bondage, material; Death; Transmigration; Miseries;

Birth control, 177, 1250, 1280
Blasphemy
 toward Kṛṣṇa, 58
 as worst offense, 578-579
 See also: Offense(s)
Blindness, material & spiritual, 5
Blind well & family life, analogy of, 957
Bliss
 reciprocation of, 357
 of Brahman, 31
 of internal potency, 2
 See also: Ecstasy; Enjoyment; Happiness; Pleasure
Blood makes milk, 717
Boar incarnation. *See:* Varāha, Lord
Bodhayantaḥ parasparam
 quoted, 1201
Bodily concept of life, 974, 981, 984-985, 1025, 1031-1032, 1035, 1040, 1042, 1102-1103, 1107, 1112, 1171-1173, 1234-1237, 1285, 1293-1294
 atheists in, 748
 civilization in, 951
 conditioned souls in, 748-749
 demons in, 666-668
 soul in, 934
 See also: Attachment, material; Desires, material; Ignorance; Illusion; *Māyā*; Sense gratification
Body, material
 aging of, time causes, 1184, 1224
 airs in, 222, 223
 attachment to. *See:* Attachment
 atoms compose, 397
 of *brahmacārī*, 821
 Brahmā dropped, 756, 757, 770
 causes of, 1030-1031, 1061, 1064, 1177
 compared to boat, 576
 compared to dream body, 1172
 compared to dress, 1305
 compared to firewood, 1177
 compared to fort, 527
 consciousness beyond, 169
 consciousness not from, 1026
Body, material
 consciousness & superconsciousness in, 605
 at cosmic dissolution, 304
 crematorium for, 531
 as "dearmost object," 371
 at death, 720
 decorations for, 534
 as destructible, 951
 detachment from. *See:* Detachment
 development of, four ways of, 1265
 devotee transcendental to, 1171, 1208, 1388, 1390-1391
 as *dvitīya*, 1042
 elements of, 1127
 evolution of. *See:* Evolution extended, 1173
 fate of, 677
 formation of, 104
 four demands of, 454
 freedom from, , 957-958
 funeral for, 1245-1246
 of ghosts, 530
 gross, awarded to ancestors, 767
 gross & subtle conception of, 363
 gross & subtle coverings of, 223
 human, vs. others, 1283
 "I-and-mine" concept perpetuates, 203
 ingredients of, seven named, 1266
 by *karma*, 1035
 liberation from. *See:* Liberation
 living entity different from, 974, 981, 986, 1024, 1030, 1033-1034, 1042, 1102-1103, 1112, 1170-1174
 in Lord's service, 245, 248
 material activity requires, 951
 modes determine, 1030-1032, 1177
 modes of nature determine, 166
 necessities of, 793
 nature creates, 1030
 necessities of, for devotee, 1101-1102
 physiological elements of, three named, 1140
 purified by breathing exercise, 1140
 regulations for, 1388
 relationships pertaining to, 622

Body, material
senses of. *See:* Sense gratification; Senses
soul in. *See:* Soul, conditioned subtle
basis of, 1061
social body compared to, 238-239
society compared to, 831, 832
soul & Super soul in, 833
soul contrasted to, 951
spirit activates, 49, 220, 226
subtle, 756
as suffering, 951
as temple of Lord, 1220
as temporary, 1026, 1235
in womb, 652
yoga as freedom from, 721
See also: Birth; Death; Bodily concept of life; Ego, false; Intelligence; Mind; Living entities: Senses; Transmigration
Body of the Lord. *See:* Supreme Lord, body of
Body, spiritual
devotees acquire, 1126
ecstatic symptoms in, 50, 51
for Kṛṣṇa consciousness, 1035
See also: Soul
Body, subtle, **1002,** 1061
elements of, 1109, 1127
evolution of. *See:* Evolution
liberation from, 1127
punishment for, 1249
speeds possible for, 1252
Bondage
for all but devotees, 334
by *avidyā* potency, 260
by bodily conception, 296-297
by desire to be God, 273
from disharmony, 589
by false ego, 186, 188, 189
five causes of, 388
from foolishness, 347
by fruitive mentality, 305
in gross & subtle body, **363**
by "I-and-mine" mentality, 203
from independent mentality, 333-334
Bondage
original cause of, 212, 429
in psychic activities, 446
by sex attraction, 448
See also: Material world: *Māyā;* Misery; Modes of material nature
Bondage, material
freedom from, 792, 933, 934, 954, 957-958
to worldly work, 914
See also: Attachment, material; Desires, material; Ignorance; Illusion; Life, material; Material world; *Māyā;* Modes of nature; Suffering Boy
Books, spiritual. *See:* Vedic literature
Brahmā, **970**
attached to daughter, 1299, 1300
birth of, 1154, 1156, 1363
as creator, **1327-1328**
descendants of, 1300
knowledge from Lord to, 1060
Kṛṣṇa addressed by, 1016
liberation not given by, 1328
liberation of, **1324-1325**
liberation with, 1325
planet of, 1009-1010
qualities of, 1327-1328
quotations from. *See: Brahma-saṁhitā,* quotations from
as unborn, **1362,** 1363
universal annihilations at end of day & life of, 1230, 1319, 1323-1325
for universes, one each, 1075
worship of, 1082, 1325
Brahmā, Lord
anger of, 432, 433
as authority, 741
beyond time, 557
Bhāgavatam first spoken to, 128, 134, 135
birth of, 26, **308,** 559
boar appeared from, 483
body dropped by, 756, **757, 770**
Brahma-saṁhitā by, 316
creation by, 380, 381

Brahmā, Lord (*continued*)
as creator, 746, 747, **748**, 850, 927
of *brāhmaṇas*, 830
of demigods, 751
of demons, 751, **754**, 755, 756
of Gandharvas & Apsarās, **763**, 764
of ghosts & fiends, 765
of ignorance coverings, 748
of Kimpuruṣas & Kinnaras, **768**
of Manus, **771**
of Sādhyas & Pitās, 766
of sages, **772**, 773
of Siddhas & Vidyādharas, **768**
of snakes, **770**
day & night of, 412
day of, calculated, 286, 313
as demigods' chief, 696
demigods' fear allayed by, 657
demigods prayed to, 555-562
demons approached, for sex, **752, 754,** 755
demons born of, 751, **752**
desires human body, 576
disciplic succession from, 474-475, 609
disciplic succession of, 935
duty of, 359, 361
as enlightened from within, 358, 361
exalted status of, 346, 349, **449**, 450, 453
fears death, 419
first-born sons of, 585
as first created being, 746, 924, 925, 927
as first living being, 221
from Garbhodakaśāyī Viṣṇu, 924
as Haṁsa, 936
Hiranyakaśipu blessed by, 669
Hiraṇyākṣa condemned by, 698, 699
Hiraṇyākṣa misused boon from, 703
ignorance body relinquished by, **749**
independence of, **695**, 696, 746-748, 925
Kardama ordered by, to beget children, 779
Kardama praised by, 927
as Kardama's father, 927
knows hearts of all, 558
Kṛṣṇa above, 62

Brahmā, Lord
Kṛṣṇa summoned by, 77
Kṣīrodakaśāyī Viṣṇu relieves distress of, 754
Kumāras insubordinate to, 430, 431, 432
as liberated soul, 926
life-span of, **418-424**
Lord above, 724, 725
Lord Boar accepted prayer of, 703-704
Lord Boar advised by, to kill Hiraṇyākṣa, 700
Lord Boar "born" of, **704**
Lord Boar praised by, 687, 688
Lord empowers, to create cosmos, 747, 748
Lord inconceivable to, 250
Lord instructed, in heart, 925
Lord Kapila worshiped by, 925, 926
Lord's mercy on, 366
Lord ordered, to drop bad body, 756, 756, 757
in Lord's universal form, **233, 234**
Manus in day of, 733, 777, 864
meditation by, 312-313
moonlight form dropped by, **764**
origin of, 325
in passion, 201, 321, 756
passion mode supervised by, 747
penance by, 377
perplexity of, 309-311
prayed to the Lord, 323-328, 354-356
as Prajāpati, 778-779
quoted
on demons attacking him for sex, **754**, 755
on Hiraṇyākṣa as demon, 698-699
on Hiraṇyākṣa's death, 719, 720
on Kardama following his instructions, 927
on Kardama's daughters, 929
on Lord Boar & Hiraṇyākṣa, 699, 701
on Lord Kapila, 934, 935
returned to his planet, 936
sexually attracted to daughter, 448, 449
Siva excels, 531
sons of, 442, 443
space travel by, 936
as spiritual master, 927
as *sva-rāṭ*, 925

Brahmā, Lord
as Svayambhū, 924
transcendental status of, 463
universe re-created by, **746, 747**
Varāha from nostril of, 922
Vedas created by, 454-457
as *vidhātā*, 359
view by, atop lotus, **378-379**
witnessed Kṛṣṇa's pastimes, 362
Yakṣas & Rākṣasas attacked, 749, **750**, 751
yawning form dropped by, 765
Brahma-bandhus defined, 114
Brahma-bhāvana defined, 920
Brahma-bhūta defined, 1308
Brahma-bhūta persons, 813, 865
Brahma-bhūtaḥ prasannātmā
quoted, 984, 1195, 1388
Brahma-bhūyāya kalpate
quoted, 1008, 1335
Brahmacārī (Brahmacarya)
austerity for, 821
bodily feature of, 821
as cautioned about sex, 527
as celibate student, 778, 842-843
defined, 525
duties for, 1351
in Kṛṣṇa consciousness movement, 821
morning duty of, 821
naiṣṭhika-, 842-843, 936
restricted householder as, 1133
in Vedic society, 459
two types of, 842
yoga practice of, 604
See also: Varṇāśrama-dharma Disciple & spiritual master; *San- nyāsī*
Brahmacaryam defined, 1133
Brahma jānātīti brāhmaṇaḥ
quoted, 620
Brahmajyoti. See: Brahman effulgence
compared to sun's light, 1027
defined, 746
liberation to, 1004
Lord beyond, 985
Brahmajyoti
as Lord's bodily luster, 955
as Lord's effulgence, 1004, 1027
as sunlight's source, 1027
Brahmaloka, 802, **1124**, 1125, 1319
Brāhma marriage, 845
Brāhma-muhūrta defined, 769
Brahman (impersonal Absolute)
as Absolute Truth feature, 955
brāhmaṇa knows, 620
devotees realize, 1388
devotees respect, 343
everything as, 1041
happiness in, 31
as impersonal feature of Lord, 1339, 1340
living entity as, 966
Lord as basis of, 1348
as Lord's effulgence, 1004, 1026, 1027, 1126, 1188
personal and impersonal, 1336-1337
vs. *pradhāna*, 1037
as primary realization, 608, 610
realization of. *See:* Brahman realization
saguṇa, vs. *nirguṇa*, 1041
Supreme Brahman surpasses, 130
variety within, 346
time rotates about, 795
See also: Brahman effulgence; Soul; Spiritual world; Impersonalists; Māyāvādīs; Monists; Oneness, *appropriate entries*
Brahman (spirit). *See:* Soul
Brahman, Supreme. *See:* Absolute Truth: Supreme Lord
Māyāvāda misconception about, 740
Brahmānanda bliss, devotees beyond, 172
Brāhmaṇas
birth in family of, 1368-1369
caste, 1368
duties & service for, 1197
levels of, 1216
as magnanimous, 1281
purification for becoming, 1369
smārta-brāhmaṇas, 1371

Brāhmaṇas
spiritual master determines, 1369
Vaiṣṇava as highest, 1217
See also: Varṇāśrama system
Brāhmaṇas (priests & teachers)
cited on Nanda Mahārāja, 926
compared to head & heart, 831, 832
as created from Lord's face, 830
demons harass, 698
function of, 830, 831
killing of, absolution for, 730-731
kṣatriya's relationship to, 828, 831, 832
Lord protects, 831, 832
as Lord's heart, 831, 832
marrying *kṣatriya*, 805
perfection for, 727
present-day, 845
qualities of, 830, 831
sense gratification disinterests, 830
Brāhmaṇas (saintly intellectuals)
charity to, 112, 113, 114, 115-116, 242
defined, 458
falldown of, cause of, 356
as fed first, 117
fire ignited by, 503
Lord eats via, 624
Lord favors, 620
Lord's respect for, 624, 626, 627, 637
as material qualification, 148
Nārāyaṇa represented by, 628
pacifying the anger of, 595-596
protection for, 627
qualities of, 633
qualities and duties of, 7, 114, **238**, 239, 240, 242, 243, 245, 303
respect for, stressed by Kṛṣṇa, 640-641
as society's head, 640
true & false, 620
unqualified sons of, 543
wrath of, **546**, 547
See also: Varnāśrama-dharma
Brahman effulgence *(brahmajyoti)*
defined, 746
Brahman effulgence *(brahmajyoti)*
impersonalists aspire to, 76, 205, 207
as Lord's bodily luster, 955
spiritual & changeless, 327
via spiritual suicide, 530
as temporary abode, 335
worshipers of, 328
See also: Brahman (impersonal Absolute)
Brahmaṇo hi pratiṣṭhāham
quoted, 1126, 1348, 1388
Brahman realization, 985, 1002, 1179, 1339-1340, 1349-1350, 1388, 1393
falldown from, 998
as incomplete, 1016
by *yoga*, 998
Brahma-saṁhitā
cited on speculators, 250
on God, His incarnations & expansions, 718
on Lord & His abode, 784
on Lord as original person, 724
on Lord's innumerable expansions, 904
origin of, 313, 316
quoted
on Lord's expansions, 810-811
on Lord's innumerable forms, 753, 944
on planetary opulences, 903
Brahma-samhitā, as cited or quoted
on knowing the Lord, 326
on Kṛṣṇa, 426
on Lord's breathing, 423
on seeing the Lord, 615
on spiritual world, 572-573
on time, 406
Brahma-saṁhitā, quotations from
on form & abode of Lord, 1028
on forms of Lord, 1323
on internal energy, 107
on Kṛṣṇa as original, ever-youthful person, 1146, 1161
on Kṛṣṇa as original person, 1075, 1283, 1393
on Kṛṣṇa as supreme controller, 1026, 1075, 1230, 1343
on Lord's creation process, 216

Brahma-saṁhitā, quotations from
on Lord's effulgence, 1027
on Lord's expansions, 96
on Lord's flute, 82
on Lord's potency, 151, 184
on Mahā-Viṣṇu, 289
on seeing Kṛṣṇa with love, 1104
on seeing the Lord, 24-25
on sun as eye of Lord, 1078
on Supersoul, 1073
Brahma-sampradāya list, 474-475
Brahma-śāpa defined, 649
Brahma satyaṁ jagan mithyā
quoted, 1343
Brahma-saukhya defined, 761
Brahma-tejas defined, 356
Brahmāvarta, 802, 856
Brahmins. *See: Brāhmaṇas*
Brain, milk develops, 163
Brains. *See:* Intelligence; Mind
Breathing exercise, 1138-1140
Breathing process in *yoga,* 560, 606
Breasts of woman, 897
Bṛhan-nāradīya Purāṇa, Hare Kṛṣṇa *mantra* in, 487
Bṛhaspati, 25, 26
Budhā bhāva-samanvitāḥ
quoted, 1098, 1335
Buddha, Lord, preached atheism, 645
Buddhist philosophy, Śaṅkarācārya refuted, 135
Buddhi-yoga defined, 225
Bullfight, Hiraṇyākṣa-Varāha battle compared to, 695, 696
Bull(s)
in human society, 82, 163
Kṛṣṇa subdued, 92
Businessmen. *See: Vaiśyas*

C

Caitanya-caritāmṛta, cited on chanting the holy name, 579
Caitanya-caritāmṛta
cited on associating with saintly person, 912
cited on Kṛṣṇa conscious person as beyond rituals, 767
quoted on Deity form of the Lord, 18
quoted on mercy of spiritual master & Kṛṣṇa, 737
quoted on seed of devotional service, 52-53
Caitanya-caritāmṛta, quotations from
on Kṛṣṇa as master, others as servants, 1152, 1225
on soul as eternally Lord's servant, 1025, 1375
Caitanya Mahāprabhu
See also: Caitanya Mahāprabhu, cited; Caitanya Mahāprabhu, quotations from
appearance of, 1082
Bhaktisiddhānta Sarasvatī preaching message of, 849
in Brahma-sampradāya, 474-475
chanting of *gopīs'* names by, 1148
cited on disciplic succession, 140
cited on offending devotees, 597
cited
on associating with saintly person, 833, 912
on chanting God's holy name, 781, 821, 950
on five devotional activities, 732
on hearing from Māyāvādīs, 727
on human life's purpose, 848-849
on love of God, 877
contribution by, 543
glorified *gopīs,* 124
Haridāsa blessed by, 618
Haridāsa Ṭhākura accepted by, 1371
as Kṛṣṇa, 939
as Kṛṣṇa concealed, 639
Kṛṣṇa consciousness taught by, 1219
Lord comes as, 1366
love of God distributed by, 877
in love with God, 32, 51
mercy of, on dog, 1208
as missionary, 340
pleased by *saṅkīrtana,* 497-498
preaching movement of, 169

Caitanya Mahāprabhu (*continued*)
quoted on spiritual master, 239
Rūpa Gosvāmī praised, 877
with Rāmānanda Rāya, 612
as savior, 579
Vṛndāvana glorified by, 80
yoga process taught by, 606-607
Caitanya Mahāprabhu, cited
on chanting Hare Kṛṣṇa, 1082
on devotional service, five recommended kinds of, 1008-1009
on hearing, 996
on hearing from impersonalists, 1004-1005
on possessions, 1014
Caitanya Mahāprabhu, quotations from
on association, 986-987, 1203
on chanting Kṛṣṇa's names, 1139
on devotee as desireless, 1193
on soul as eternally Lord's servant, 1025, 1375
See also: Sikṣāṣṭaka, quotations from
Caitanya-sampradāya, misconception about Nityānanda in, 680-681
Caitya defined, 606
Cakra defined, 582
Cakra (wheel), 23
Cakra of Lord, 1159
Camarīs defined, 819
Cāṇakya Paṇḍit
cited on best use of wealth, 1257
cited on time, 383
cited on use of time, 1233
on enemies at home, 872
as good counselor, 9
quoted on bad son, 11-12
on rascal not speaking, 958-959
Cañcalā, 573
Cañcalaṁ hi manaḥ kṛṣṇa
quoted, 1020
Caṇḍāla can become devotee, 622
Caṇḍālas, 1197, 1368
Candles & Lord's expansions, analogy of, 811, 925
Candra, 1018
Cannibalism, 1244
Cāraṇas, 1395
"Caste system." *See*: Devotees, beyond bodily designation; *Varṇāśrama-dharma*
Caste system (*varnāśrama-dharma*), 114
Castle in sky, Kardama created, 883-887, 888
Catuḥ-ślokī Bhāgavatam, 134
Cātur-varṇyaṁ mayā sṛṣṭam
quoted, 460, 826
Catur-vyuha (quadruple expansion), 1048
Causal (Kāraṇa) Ocean universes in, 745, 746
See also: Garbha Ocean; *Mahat-tattva*
Cause and effect, 1072-1073
in cosmic manifestation, 226
See also: Karma
Cause, ultimate
of Creation, 742-743
See also: Absolute Truth; Creation (act of); Supreme Lord, as creator
Cedi, King of, 69
Celibacy
of brahmacārīs, 459
meaning of, 1100
necessity of, 1100
value of, 1079
in yoga practice, 604
yoga requires, 1133, 1134
See also: Sannyāsa; Sex life; *Varṇāśrama* system
Celibates. *See: Brahmacārī, Sannyāsīs*
Ceremonies. *See*: Sacrifice; Vedic rituals
Ceto-darpaṇa-mārjanam
quoted, 1139
Chaitanya. *See:* Caitanya Mahāprabhu
Chāndogya Upaniṣad, quoted on all as Brahman, 1041
Channa-avatāra defined, 638
Chanting and hearing, 301
See also: Hearing; Supreme Lord, hearing about
Chanting the holy names of the Lord
as *brahmacārī's* duty, 821
Caitanya cited on, 821

Chanting the holy names of the Lord
ecstatic symptoms from, 578, 579
ever fresh, 800
via Hare Kṛṣṇa *mantra*, 487
by Haridāsa Ṭhākura, 537
as highest thought, 649
for Kali-yuga, 780, 781, 950
in Kali-yuga, 550
liberation by, 863
as Lord Himself, 811
offenses in, effect of, 578-579
as only way, 607
progeny elevated by, 543
purifying power of, 639
two ways of, 538
in Vṛndāvana, 736
See also: Gāyatrī *mantra;* Hare Kṛṣṇa *mantra;* Supreme Lord, chanting about, name of
Chanting. *See:* Devotional service, of chanting...
Charity, 974, 996, 1351
to *brāhmaṇas*, 112, 113, 114, 114-115
highest form of, 293
at holy places, 112, 113
householders must give, 505
at pilgrimage places, 806
See also: Philanthropy: Sacrifice; Welfare activity work
Chastity in marriage, 39
Chastity of good wife, 524, 527
Cheaters
misinterpret *Bhagavad-gītā*, 172
mislead followers, 74
pseudo religionists as, 337
teaching "*yoga*", 603
Cheating
as conditioned defect, 927, 933
by material energy, 915
by "*yogīs*,", 761, 781
Child in womb. *See:* Human being, unborn
Children
begotten in sanctity, 756-757
born in good family, 861-862
desirable & undesirable, 665, 666
Children
innocence of, 584
Kṛṣṇa dolls for, 48
in modern Age, 931
parents begetting, 848, 931
as parents' expansions, 880
parents' responsibility to, 853-854
perfect persons begetting, 778
protection for, 627
purpose for having, 477-478, 521
qualification for conceiving, 652
sex for begetting, 881
via sexual intercourse, 520, 543, 544
transcendental, two types of, 848
twins, 668-669
See also: Daughter; Family life; Marriage: Son
Christ, Jesus, 654
Christ, Lord Jesus, 988
Cities
in ancient times, 856
See also: names of specific cities
Citizens
king welcomed back by, 856
See also: Population
C*in-mātra* defined, 207, 256
C*it-śakti* realization, 785-786
City-life "*yoga*," 604
Civilization, human. *See:* Society, human; *Varṇāśrama-dharma*; Vedic culture
Āryan, 826
basis of, 831
in bodily concept, 951
demoniac, 668
Cleanliness
mandatory times for, 538
in spiritual culture, 638-639
See also: Purification
Cloud (s)
demigod of, 1017
at demons' birth, 660, 661, 664
rain, spiritual master's mercy compared to, 793-794
Club, Viṣṇu holds, 23
Cobra and Bhīma, analogy of, 36

Cobra, demon compared to, 691
Comparisons. *See:* Analogies
Compassion
of devotees, 332, 333
for fallen souls, 158
of Lord for living beings, 182, 186
of Prahlāda, 549
of Vidura, 40
Conception, 1263-1264
Conchshell, Viṣṇu holds, 23
Concentration. *See:* Meditation
Conditioned souls. *See:* Souls, conditioned
Conditioning, material. *See:* Bondage; *Māyā*
Conjugal love, Kṛṣṇa enjoys, **108**
Consciousness, 1343-1344
atheistic theory of, 1027
of Brahmā, **558**
clear, worship of Vāsudeva for, 1048
compared to water, 1049
as eternal, 169, 247-248, **260,** 270
individual vs. supreme, 204, 221, 222
Lord's, as all-pervading, 1027
material, material life caused by, 1034
materialistic theory of, 1026, 1027
pure, 1040, 1049
pure condition of, **363**
pure vs. illusory, 266
purification of, 1082
shadow of, 185
of soul & Supersoul, 1345
as soul's symptom, 1026, 1040
from spirit, not matter, 1026
spiritual, vs. material, 1032
stages of, 1104
superconsciousness, Lord's, 1026
superconsciousness vs., 605-606
yogīs pursue, 204
See also: Ego, false, Knowledge; Kṛṣṇa consciousness, spiritual; Soul
Contraception, 1250-1251, 1280
Cosmic manifestation. *See:* Creation, the; Material world; Planets, material; Universe
Countries
demons & disturbances in, 660
materialist's consideration of, 668
See also: names of specific countries
Cowherd boy friends of Kṛṣṇa, 79
Cowherd girls. *See: Gopīs;* Rādhārāṇī
Cows
as defenseless, 627
at demons' birth, **664**
Earth compared to, 696
gavayas, 819
in human society, 81, 163-164, 242
Kṛṣṇa advised worshiping, 85
Kṛṣṇa favors, 620, 640
in Kṛṣṇa's childhood, 79
Lord protects, 831
milk of, 717
protection for, 115, 237
urine of, 56
Creation (act of)
by Brahmā
from body, 443-447
of entities, **389-396**
of universe, 427-468
cause of, 215, 216, 217
compared to birth, 1043, 1046
deities controlling, 201-202
dissolution of, 218
dormant within Lord, 181, 182
elements of, 216
by external & internal potencies, 256
of ignorance, purpose of, 428, 429
inquiry about, 310
of Kumāras, 430
of life, 1046
by Lord, 1035-1036, 1078
Lord entered, 216, 216-217, 217, **219,** 220
Lord gets credit for, 355
Lord impregnates, **210, 211**
as Lord's desire, 182
by Lord's energy, 743, 745-747, 797
on Lord's "heart," 162
from Lord's navel, **306, 307**

Creation (act of)
for Lord's pastimes, **1028,** 1030
of *mahat-tattva*, 1047
from Mahā-Viṣṇu, 289
ninefold process of, 386-395
of planetary divisions, 380, 381
process of, 162, 184-193, 307-308
purpose for, 1364-1365
purpose of, 182, 186, 212, 218
by *purusa-avatāras*, 160-161
sarga & *visarga*, 380
from seedling form, 380
sex life principle in, 1073
sound causes, 1058
time influences, 1043
universal form of, 215-245
of *Vedas*, 454-457
by *yogamāyā*, 180
See also: Absolute Truth; Cause, ultimate; Supreme Lord, as creato,: Material world; Universe; Evolution
Creation, the Material
for conditioned soul, 742-743
Manus in, 412-415
purpose of, 442, 478, 589
as shadow of reality, 346
See also: Mahat-tattva; Material world; Natur, Earth planet; Heavenly planets; Planets, material; Universe
Creeper of devotion, 52-53
Crematorium as Śiva's abode, 531
Crime's cause, 241
Culture. *See:* Civilization, human,: Society, human; *Varṇāśrama- dharma;* Vedic culture
Cupid, Diti attacked by, 519
Cupid (Kāmadeva), 28, 30
Curse
accepted without revenge, 628
bhakti-yoga dispels, 648-649
on gatekeepers of Vaikuṇṭha, 592-593, 613, 643-645, 653
on Yadus & Bhojas, 111, 115-116
Curse
on Yamarāja, 178
Cycle, *yuga*, 733, 864, 939
See also: Dvāpara-yuga; Kali-yuga; Satya-yuga; Tretā-yuga
Cycle of birth and death. *See:* Birth & death, repeated, Transmigration

D

Dadāmi buddhi-yogaṁ taṁ
verse quoted, 198
Daiva defined, 742
Daivī hy esā guṇamayī
verse quoted, 267
Daivī-māyā defined, 110
Dakṣa, **468, 518, 521, 522,** 778-779
Dāna, 1212
Dancing, material vs. spiritual, 764
Danger, the greatest, 795
Dantavakra, 98, 913
Daridra-nārāyaṇa, 578, 628
Daridra-nārāyaṇa concept, 1212
Daridra-nārāyana defined, 264
Darkness
universe covered by, at demons' birth, 657, **661**
See also: Ignorance
Darwin, 1214
Dāsī-putras defined, 13
Dāsīs defined, 13
Daughter & father, 853, 854
Daytime
demigods born from, 751
See also: Morning; Night; Twilight
Dead bodies, crematorium for, 531
Death
atheist's consideration of, 748
in blind-well analogy, 957
bodily luster fades at, 720
Brahmā fears, 419
caused by sex life, 1079
caused by time, 1231
controlled by Lord, 1017
Dhruva transcended, 516, 517

Death
as end of bodily senses, 1310
as end of reaction to fruitive activity, 1308
fear of, 1042, 1248, 1311
fear of, cause of, 428
freedom from, 516
frustration at, 1247-1248
liberation from. *See:* Liberation
Lord as, 1211
Lord causes, 1225
seeing Lord at, 720, 721
self beyond, 169
sorrow over, solution to, 138
suffering just before, 1246-1248
thoughts at time of, 1248
unconscious period after, 218
of wife after husband, 39
Yamarāja controls, 178, 179
Yamadūtas seen at, 1248-1249
yogī eludes, 692
See also: Birth & death, repeated: Killing: Transmigration
Debt to one's wife, 528
Debts, serving God liquidates, 850
Deer, musk, 819
Defects, the four, 927, 933
Deities of material nature. *See:* Demigods
Deity form of the Supreme Lord (*arcā-mūrti)*
as beyond wood & stone, 622
in children's dolls, 48
compared to postbox, 19
composition of, 219
circumambulation of, 646
in devotee's box, 718
devotees realize, 145
inspiration from, 147
as Lord Himself, 810-811
at *maṅgalārātrika* ceremony, 861
neophyte serves, 963
potency of, 18
purpose of, 17
sleeps, 352-353
as universally established, 17
Deity form of the Supreme Lord (*arcā-mūrti)*
whisk for fanning, 819
See also: Supreme Lord, worship of; Worship; *names of specific Deity forms*
Deity worship. *See:* Devotional service, of Deity worship
Delhi, 24, 856
Demigods, 1052
absent in Vaikuṇṭha, 1012
airplanes of, 1379-1380
authority of, 1017, 1018
born of daytime, 751
Brahmā allayed fear of, 657, 758
Brahmā chief among, 696
Brahmā created, 751
churning ocean, 1159
compared to Lord's bodily limbs, 1018
compared to prison managers, 213
as controllers, 1011, 1018, 1159, 1230
of death, 1079
defined, 164, 202
deities of, at demons' birth, 664
demons contrasted to, 667, 670, 751, 752, 758-759, 830
demons disturb, 555
demons exploit, 698, 704
demons overpowered, 653
as devotees of Lord, 1018
of directions, 1077
directions governed by, 899, 900
duties & qualifications of, 46, 84, 194-196, 213, 227
eight kinds of, 395
elevation to planets of, 1353
evolution of. *See:* Evolution
exalted status of, 209
of false ego, 1082
fear in, 658
of fire, 1076
function of, 383
in goodness, 236, 237, 751
good qualities of, 577-578
of hands, 1080

Demigods
Hiraṇyākṣa scared, 671, 673
humans contrasted to, 658
of intelligence, 1081-1082
Kardama surpassed, 901, 902
in knowledge, 758
Kṛṣṇa as appreciated by, 62
Kṛṣṇa attached to, 108
in Kṛṣṇa's family, 112, 119
liberation difficult by, 1325
Lord above, 578-579, 633, 634, 681
Lord Boar honored by, **687,** 688
Lord descends at request of, 940
Lord glorified by, 830
at Lord Kapila's advent, 922, 923
Lord protects, 688
as Lord's devotees, 685
Lord worshiped by, 813
as materialistic devotees, 340
of mind, 1081-1082
for modes, 1082
obedient to Lord, 1018
origin of, **188**
prayers by, **196-212**
prayers of, 703-704
pray to Brahmā, 555-562
priest of, 25
quoted on Lord Boar, 723
residence of. *See:* Heavenly planets sex desire doesn't dominate, 752
of rivers, 1080
of senses, 1088
senses as representatives of, 1001
as servants of Lord, 1152
source of, 463
as spiritually inclined, 660, 671
time measurement for, **404,** 410
of touch (& herbs & drugs), 1078
universal form reentered by, 1083-1087
universal form revealed to, 226
of waters, **1079**
of wind, **1077**
woman can't allure, 758-759

Demigods
worship of, 1082, 1317, 1330
worshipers of, 698, 704, 789
worship to, 85
See also: names of specific demigods
Democracy, 241
Demons
churning ocean, 1159
devotees in families of, 1148
killed by Lord, 1160
killed by *māyā,* 1161
Demons *(asuras)*
birth & death bind, 689
birth of, 659, 666
in bodily concept, 666-668
born of Brahmā, 750-751, 752
born of night, 751
Brahmā approached for sex by, 752, **752, 754,** 755
Brahmā created, 755, **756**
brāhmaṇas harassed by, 698
as cheaters & cheated, 781
compared to cobra, 692
defined, 94, 202
demigods contrasted to, 667, 670, 751, 752, 758-759, 830
demigods exploited by, 698, 704
devotees contrasted to, 758-759
devotees envied by, 684
Diti bore, **658, 659,** 665, 666
disturb devotees, 555
entered Diti's womb, 652
envy the Lord, 152
fate of, 677
gold amassed by, 688
in ignorance, 751, 758, 763
increasing nowadays, 659, 660, 666
intelligence lost by, 704
illicit sex creates, 543
Lord can liberate, 721
Lord challenged by, 679, 682, 683, 718
Lord envied by, 684, 689
Lord kills, 823, 922

Demons (*asuras*)
Lord overpowers, 690-692, 716, 719, 726
Lord punishes, 755-756
Lord roared at, 486
Lord's form misunderstood by, 680
Lord's mercy on, 69, 76, 545, 553
Lord vs., **44**, 45, 78, 79, 83
material world allures, 760
as "mighty" materialists, 666-668, 669-671, 673, 675, 688
miscreant scholars as, 287-288
Parāśara's mercy on, 302
prayers of, 703-704
seek sense gratification, 684, 698, 789, 830
seek sex life, 752, 757, 760, 762
as sinfully motivated, 703, 704
Śiva harassed by, 698
society of, 544
took twilight as woman, **757-763**
See also: Atheists; Impersonalists; Materialists; Nondevotees; Scientists, material; *names of specific demons*
Desire
anger follows, 586
fruitive, dispelled by devotional service, 933
Lord fulfills, 125, 788, 790, 792, 798, 799, 802, 805
material, wife satisfies, 524
material, transcendence of, 785
pure & impure, 446-446
selfless, in spiritual world, 565
for sense gratification, 331
sex
girl misled by, 804
of man & woman, 904
See also: Sex life
for wealth, 330
See also: Lust; Sense gratification; Sex life
Desire, material. *See:* Attachment
Desire, spiritual, vs. material, 1057
Desires
Lord beyond, **258**
Lord fulfills, 125
Desires
material, 218
See also: Affection; Attachment; Emotions; Love; Sense gratification; Sex life
Destiny. *See:* Fate; *Karma;* Supreme Lord, will of
of conditioned soul, 742
by modes of nature, 864
Detachment
of Arjuna, 1338
from body, **1168-1172**, 1388-1391
celibacy as primary, 1134
compared to sun unaffected by its reflection, 1092
of devotees, **1009**, 1013-1015, **1124-1125**, 1128, 1313, 1337-1339
by devotional service, 200, 269, 995, 1089, 1091-1092, 1096-1097, 1336-1338
by devotional service only, 1385
from eating, 1209
from external energy, 107
of Haridāsa Ṭhākura, 537
by higher taste, 270-271, 1383
from household, 109
by Kṛṣṇa conscious family life, 1307
Kṛṣṇa consciousness shown by, 1118
from liberation, 1004, **1193**, 1194
Lord's beauty causes, 314
Lord taught, 106
from mystic powers, **1127-1128**
needed for spiritual knowledge, **1088**, 1089
origin of, 430
from predestined distress, 1101
of pure devotees. *See:* Devotees, pure; Devotional service, pure
from results of work, 1320-1322
by self-realization, 1024
from sex life, 1165, 1302
of Śiva, 531-535
as *yogas* basic principle, 1341
See also: Attachment; Celibacy; Sense control: Austerity; Purification: Renunciation; Retirement

Devadatta air, 224
Devahūti, **467**
amazing appearance of, via Kardama's yogic power, 895, 896
austerities of, 1377-1378
beauty of, **844,** 846, 847, 895, 897, 898, 908
compared to moon, 898
compassion of, 1185, 1186
detachment of, 1390-1392
devotional service of, 1377-1393
as example of woman as dependent, 1377, 1382
family background of, 838, 847
in haggard condition, 881, 888, 889, 890
heard of Kardama from Nārada, 839
hearing of, benediction for, 1398
Kapila born from, 1363, 1365-1366
Kardama advised, to bathe in Lake Bindu-sarovara, 889
Kardama agreed to marry, 843-844, 847, 848
Kardama asked by, for fearlessness, 909
Kardama as spiritual master of, 920
Kardama attracted to, 897
Kardama blessed, 873-875, 877, 878
Kardama enjoyed with, 899, 900, **903-905**
Kardama impregnated, 906
Kardama informed, about Lord becoming her son, 918, 919, 920
Kardama loved by, 878
Kardama married, 853
Kardama's child desired by, **879,** 880
Kardama's departing disturbed, 907
Kardama served by, **869,** 870, 870-873, 874-876, 877, 897
Kardama's palace bewildered, 888
in Lake Bindu-sarovara, 890-896
laments to Kardama, 909, 910, 911, 913-915
liberation of, 1393
Lord Kapila in womb of, 922, 925, 935
as Lord Kapila's mother, 810, 935
Lord Kapila to enlighten, **934,** 956
Lord's prophecy about, 804-806, 810, 811
maidservants bathed & dressed, 891-894, 895
Devahūti
maintained by Lord, 1392
meditation of, **1386**
narration by, 971-976, 997-999, **1035, 1112-1115, 1181-1185,** 1364-1373
nine daughters born of, 906
pastimes of, as pure & confidential, **1397-1398**
prayers to Kapila by, 1364-1373
protected by family, 1382
qualifications of, 838, **844-845, 846-848, 869,** 870, 872
questions by
on birth & death, 1183
on devotional service for her, **997, 1181**
on liberation, 1112-1115
on Lord & His energies, **1035**
on mystic *yoga* system, 998
on *prakṛti* & *puruṣa*, 976
on spirit & matter, 975
on time, 1184
quoted on her desire for Kardama's child, 879, 881
renunciation by, 1383, **1387**
river of, 1394
seeking spiritual advancement, 910-915
served by maidservants, 1391
as Svāyambhuva's daughter, **1043**
Svāyambhuva Manu gave, to Kardama, **852-854**
Svāyambhuva Manu's affection for, 838, 853, 854
as Svāyambhuva Manu's daughter, 838, 847
Viśvāvasu bewildered by, 846, 847
yoga practiced by, 778
Devakī, 30, 77, 1016
Deva-patha defined, 641
Devarṣi-bhūtāpta-nṛṇāṁ pitṝṇām verse quoted, 431
Devas. See: Demigods
Devotees of the Supreme Lord (Vaiṣṇavas)
in advanced stage, 963
akāma, 801-802
ancestors of, liberated, 767
anger of, 628

Devotees (*continued*)
as Āryans, 1372
as assisted from within & without, 606
association with, 16, 158, 277, 296, 1199-1204
desire for, 1013, 1014
of good character only, 1188, 1199, 1201
importance of, 1102
in ISKCON, 992
knowledge by, 993
liberation by, 986-987, 1311-1312
only, 1100
by prostitute, 1302
for purification, 991-992
required, 993-994
value of, 1296
as *ātmārāma*, 1123
aware of Lord's presence, 471-472
Bhagavad-gītā for, 172
beyond *brahmānanda* bliss, 172
beyond bodily designation, 622
beyond emotionalism, 281
beyond falling down, 647
beyond hankering, 64
beyond *karmīs*, *jñānīs*, *yogīs*, 64, 195
beyond material activities, 793, 794
beyond material desires, 269
beyond reactions of work, 44
beyond speculators, 251-253
Bhagavad-gītā relished by, 738
birth as humans—at least—for, 1261
bodily necessities of, 1101, 1102
born in good families, 48
as *brāhmaṇa*, 620
Brahman realized by, 1388
Caitanya in role of, 639
cannot be counteracted, 653
celibacy for, 1099-1100
characteristics of, detailed, 986, 987-990
classes of, all liberated, 1007-1009
compared to calm ocean, 961
compared to gardeners, 53
compared to kittens, 992
compared to lotus, 1116

Devotees
compared to white ducks, 324
compassion for, 1101, 1102
compassion of, 1185, 1186, 1201, 1209
as compassionate, 158
compassionate, 331-333, 808-809
confidential service of, 150, 179-180
as courteous, 138-139
cry for the Lord, 153
curses by, 628
daily schedule of, 352
dealings with, caution in, 621
as dear to the Lord, 8, 46, 97-98, 108, 152, 270, 317
defined, 115, 239
Deity in box of, 718
Deity form pleases, 17
& Deities, relationships between, 1007
demigods as, 685, 1018
demigods' qualities develop in, 1336
demigods' relation to, 194, 195
demons contrasted to, 76, 758-759
demons disturb, 555
in demoniac families, 1148
demons envy, 683-684
dependence of, 330
descending to earth, 508
descend into world, 179
desires of, 330, 371, 446
desire devotional service, 790, 809
desirous & desireless, 802
desire service only, 64, 148-149, 200, 292-293, 316
desires of, as spiritual, 1170, 1192
detachment of, 995, 1005, 1009, 1013-1015, 1124-1125, 1128, 1219
devotional service satisfies, 698
difficulties don't disturb, 654-655
difficulties of, 14-15
diplomacy avoided by, 1202-1203
discussions among, 3
disagreements among, 629
distinction between, 1199-1200, 1201

Devotees
divisions of, 108
eat after the Lord, 624
in ecstasy, 31-32, 50, 51
enjoy all facilities, though desireless, 1011
equal vision of, 1099-1100, 1199, 1207, 1211-1213, 1220
eternal, 289
eternally related to Lord, 1011-1013
faithful, 515
faith of, 1126
false, 1356
in family life, 1316
faultless, 633
fearless, 41, 560, 809
as fed first, 117
feeding of, benefit from, 625
foods for, 1101, 1197-1198
foolish souls vs., 347
freedom for, 41
free from modes, 1195
free of worry, 330
as friend to all, 988, 1101, 1102
friendliness toward, inspired by Lord, 549
as friends of everyone, 40
full-time, 135-137
Gauḍīya, 2, 80
Godbrothers respected by, 1358
gopīs as best, 1125
as *gosvāmīs*, 149
gravity of, 1099-1100
happiness of, 249, 250-253, 1390
hearing about, 728
hearing & chanting satisfies, 130
hearing from. *See:* Devotees, association with; Devotional service, of hearing about Lord
hearts of, Lord's intimacy within, 329
heaven & hell same to, 614
householder, see Lord, 942
humility of, 1203
illusory energy vs., 378
immune to illusion, 362
impersonalists vs., 205, 206, 207

Devotees
vs. impersonalists, 1121
income for, 1101, 1102
increasing devotion of, 49-50
as independent, 1121
independence of, 693
influence innocent souls, 204
initiation of, 1369
as *īśvara*, 1121
in intermediate stage, 963
intelligence of, 58
internal potency known to, 30
intolerant of irreligion, 735
in knowledge, 261, 281
jñānīs vs., 364, 372-373
jñānīs contrasted to, 942
kinds of, 788, 802, 808-809, 948, 963
kind to all beings, 577, 578
as kind to animals, 989
as kings, 775
knowledgeable by Lord's grace, 409
know the "real brain," 504
Kṛṣṇa protects, 65
Kṛṣṇa known to, 41, 42, 73, 176
Kṛṣṇa's message nectarean to, 8, 167
labor of, reason for, 206, 207
lament Kṛṣṇa's departure, 54
levels of, 1217
as liberated souls, 813, 865
liberation for. *See:* Liberation & Lord, relationships between. *See:* Kṛṣṇa, relationships with; Supreme Lord, relationships with
life-span of, time can't touch, 794-795, 863
Lord anxious for return of, 628, 629
Lord appreciated by, 251-252
Lord arranges meetings with, 618
Lord as accepted by, 684
Lord assists, 367
Lord as child of, 1366
Lord favors, 1146-1158
Lord seen by, 1340
Lord as son of, 919, 922, 926

Devotees (*continued*)
Lord eats via, 624
Lord favors, 942
Lord forgives, 450, 453
Lord fulfills desires of, 780, 802, 805
Lord glorified, 97-98
Lord in guise of, 939
Lord instructs, 500
Lord known by, 942
Lord known to, 361
Lord known via, 325
Lord merciful to, 800, 801
Lord protects, 685, 755-756
Lord relieves, 545, 546
Lord relieves suffering of, 754
Lord respects, 626
Lord seen by, 942
as Lord's "enemy", 645, 653
Lord's forms as preferred by, 753, 754, 944
Lord's glance over, 596, 597
Lord's incarnations enliven, 486
Lord's pastimes benefit, 731-732
Lord's pastimes relished by, 738
Lord's relationship with, 546, 623
Lord's smile pacifies, 317
Lord's war topics for, 516
Lord's will done by, 102
Lord sympathetic to, 546
as *mahātmās*, 1057
maintained by Lord, 1392
vs. materialists, 1123-1124
materialistic, Lord's kindness on, 799
material needs minimized by, 786
material world forgotten by, 1390
material world not meant for, 797-798
meditation on, 1147
merciful to offenders, 204
mercy of, 1101, 1102, 1358
miseries unfelt by, 992
missionary work by, 333
mixed, 112, 124
mixed desires in, 340
mixed, vs. pure, 1124-1123

Devotees
in mode of goodness, 1190-1191
in mode of ignorance, 1188-1189
in mode of passion, 1189
in morning worship, 861
motive of, Lord knows, 510
as *muni*, 1102
vs. *munis*, 1150
names of, chanting of, 1148
neophyte, 48, 113, 1199, 1375
niṣkāma vs. *sakāma*, 340
nondevotees vs., 65
obliged to no one but Lord, 990, 1018
offenses avoided by, 578-579
offenses to, 597, 618
"one" with Lord, 809
one with Lord's desire, 1195, 1219
opulence comes easy to, 571
opulences of, as eternal, 1011-1012
pastimes of, 729
as peaceful, 64, 1101, 1103
as perplexed sometimes, 482
personality of, 577-578
pleasurable path for, 206, 207, 247, 250, 253
possessions of, 1057
as prayerful, 300
prayers by, 369
prayers of, 703-704
prayers by. *See:* Prayers
preachers & nonpreachers, 948
preachers. *See:* Devotional service, of preaching
previous qualifications for, 1370-1372
protected by Lord, 1160, 1392
punishment for, 593
pure devotees
as bewildered sometimes, 366
broadcast Lord's glories, 368
contrasted to demigods, 340
desire of, 329, 365, 612
glories of, 471-472
influence of, 471
Lord available to, 338

Devotees
pure devotees
Lord directs, 510
Lord lives with, 942
lotus feet of, dust of, 835
as only good people, 446
Prahlāda as, 548-552
qualities of, 551
see the Lord, 552, 595-596
as selfless, 340
smile of, 851-852
think of Kṛṣṇa, 851-852
See also: Ācāryas; Mahātmās; Saintly persons; Spiritual master
pure, as transcendental, 1195
pure, nature of, detailed, 1003-1014
pure, qualities of, 1219-1221
pure, vs. mixed, 1124-1125
pure. *See:* Pure devotees
qualifications for, twenty given, 1201-1203
qualities of, 577-578, 588, 620-621, 638-639, 1298
on razor-edge path, 356
as real religionists, 335
reject five liberations, 611
as respected by Lord Himself, 626
respect impersonal aspect of God, 343
see Lord everywhere, 362, 549
select specific forms of the Lord, 552
self-control in, 523
sex pleasure disinterests, 572
sincere vs. casual, 338
recommendations for, several described, 1099-1104
as renounced, 15
reside in spiritual world, 52, 53
rituals unnecessary for, 767
rules for, twenty given, 1201-1203
Rūpa Gosvāmī's books for, 292
as *sādhus*, 986, 987-990
sakāma, 801-802
sannyāsī, 248
as *sat*, 977
saved by Lord, 1226

Devotees
scripture followed by, 989
scriptures understood only by, 994
seclusion for, 1101, 1102
see all in relation to Kṛṣṇa, 1107
see Lord everywhere, 1205
self-realization for, 1101, 1102
as self-satisfied, 1123
self-realization of, 961
senses of, properly engaged, 270
separatist, 1188, 1189
serve society, 139-140
as servants eternally, 1326
serve Lord spontaneously, 1167, 1168
service to. *See:* Devotees, association with; Devotional service; Spiritual master
sincerity of, Lord knows, 510
Śiva as, 532, 535
Śiva best among, 870
society must respect, 640, 641
speech of, 1100
spiritual master chooses service of, 997
spiritual masters for. *See:* Spiritual master
spiritual masters must be, 239-240
spiritual variety for, 610
Śrīmad-Bhāgavatam relished by, 738
as straightforward, 1202
"superior" to Lord sometimes, 967
as surrendered souls, 103
surrender everything, 330
third-class, liberation for, 1007-1009
as thoughtful, 1101
as tolerant, 149, 988, 1014
as topmost transcendentalists, 173
as transcendental, 865, 1120, 1124, 1170, 1201, 1337-1338
*tulasī*plant important for, 570
two stages of, 272
unhappiness of, cause of, 332
Vedas known via, 149
in Vṛndāvana, 24, 80
wealth of, detachment for, 1101
wealth of, standards for earning, 1259-1260

Devotees (*continued*)
wives of, in Vaikuṇṭha, 572
worldly affairs of, 330
worship toward, 472
as *yogīs*, 967
yogīs contrasted to, 942
yogīs excelled by, 902
See also: Sages; Saints; Transcendentalists: *Brāhmaṇas;* Saintly persons; *names of specific devotees*
Devotional service to the Supreme Lord (bhakti-yoga)
accidental, 123-124
accumulative effect of, 342
activities of
by Ambarīṣa Mahārāja, 1020
listed, 1191, 1352
recommended five, 1358
activities saturated in, 219, 270-271
advantages of, 1336, 1354
detachment, 1089, 1097, 1125, 1341, 1352
advantages of
God realization, 1167, 1205, 1220, 1336-1337, 1340, 1347, 1349
happiness, 967, 1089
knowledge, 1126, 1345-1346, 1353
liberation, 1007-1009, 1092, 1116-1118, 1220, 1311-1312, 1375
perfection, 1020, 1117, 1335
purification, 1117-1118, 1120, 1368
self-realization, 984-985, 1178
in adverse conditions, 654-655
affectionate dealings in, 623
affectionate vs. opulent, 71
for all, 1197
in anger, 586, 649
appears mundane, 365
aṣṭānga-yoga in, 1130
attitude in, 206, 242, 244
basic principle of, 649
beginning & end of, 732
as benediction for hearing of Kapila, 1398
as best occupation, 1335

Devotional service
as best path, 206, 207, 246, 250, 253
as *best yoga*, 978, 1019, 1339-1342
as better than liberation, 1001-1002, 1002
beyond all other obligations, 431
beyond heaven-hell considerations, 613
beyond *karma, jñāna & yoga*, 159
beyond pilgrimages, 113
beyond *varṇāśrama-dharma*, 478
beyond Vedic *yajñas*, 499
bhāva in, 1098
birth-death process stopped by, 795, 953-954
bodily necessities in, 1388
body forgotten by, 1388-1391
by body, mind & speech, 248
body, mind & words in, 613
as *buddhi-yoga*, 225
candidates for, 287
of chanting, 1358
as best, 1098-1099
liberation by, 1003, 1116-1118
as meditation, 1148-1149
miseries relieved by, 990
necessity of, 1098-1099
offenselessly, 1371
potency of, 1368-1372
previous qualifications for, 1370-1372
purifies for performing sacrifices, 1368
purifies immediately, 1368-1372
value of, 990
of chanting devotee's name, 1148
of chanting Hare Kṛṣṇa, 1215
in all circumstances, 1287
for fixing mind on Kṛṣṇa, 1138
importance of, 1200
liberation by, 1286
Lord Caitanya praises, 1139
as purifying, 1082, 1139
value of, 1058
in childhood, 48
compared to arrow, 999
compared to eating, 1352
compared to feeding stomach, 1221

Devotional service
compared to fire in stomach, 1002
compared to growing seed, 52-53
compared to main river, 1354
compared to razor's edge, 356, 1051
complete vs. contaminated, 962
conceiving child in mood of, 652, 657
confidential, 134
constant, 1192
crying in, 153
curses overcome by, 648-649
daily schedule of, 353
danger of falling from, 356
debts liquidated by, 850
Deity form in, 17
of Deity worship
atheists & impersonalists reject, 1006
as authorized, 1070
with Deity as son, 1012
Deity dress in, 1155
Deity form for. See: Supreme Lord, Deity form of
as equal to meditation, 1147
as eternal relationship, 1011, 1012
kinds of, 1008, 1199
with knowledge of Supersoul, 1205, 1209-1210
as Kṛṣṇa, 1133
liberation by, 1007-1009
love required in, 1209
as meditation, 1158
in mind, 1162
philosophy of, 1108-1110
prasāda distribution to accompany, 1209
with prescribed duties, 1210
of Deity worship
required of all devotees, 1198-1199
spiritual master teaches, 1106
by demigods, 213
demigods qualified by, 1018
demons oppose, 684
desire centered around, 446

Devotional service
desires fulfilled by, 44
detachment by, 995, 1097, 1337-1338
devotee desires, 790
to devotees of Lord, liberation by, 986-987
devotee satisfied with, 698
as dictated from within & without, 606
as direct process, 1099
with dovetailed desires, 1168, 1170, 1220-1221
as duty of conditioned souls, 1096-1097
as dynamic, 50
early training in, 48
as easiest *yoga*, 995
ecstasies of, 1166
enthusiasm in, 1199
equal vision in, 1099, 1199, 1207, 1221
eternal nature of, 363
as eternal occupation, 1100
as eternal relationship, 1011-1012
everything meant for, 807-808
everything obtained by, 1335-1336, 1340
with everything used for Kṛṣṇa, 1107
examples of, 1385
falldown from, 1051
in family life, 1307
fasting in, 1119
as fearless, 1376
five activities in, 732
food offered in, 115
fruitive activity dispelled by, 933
as goal of spiritual life, 1182, 1347
as godly, 670
goodness perfected in, 787
as gradual process, 1124-1125
as grateful duty, 729
happiness by, 858, 1089
harmony by, 208
of hearing
for all, 996
by Arjuna, 1059
as attractive, 1203-1204
from authorized source, 968-969
benediction for, 1398

Devotional service (*continued*)
of hearing
as best, 1098-1099
& chanting, benediction for, 1359
& chanting, compared to watering seed, 1308
& chanting, as meditation, 1148-1149
& chanting, mind easily controlled by, 1149
in devotees' association, 1202
from devotees only, 1005
easier than meditation, 1148-1149
of first importance, 1389-1390
happiness from, 967-968
knowledge by, 1343
liberation by, 1058, 1116-1118
from Lord Himself, 1060
materialists reject, 1331-1333
miseries removed by, 990
necessity of, 1098, 1201
power of, 1058-1059
purification stages of, 1117-1118
as required, 1133
samādhi by, 1136
self-realization by, 1024
spontaneous desire for, 1192
in temple, 1008
value of, 967-969, 1058-1059
hearing & chanting in, 51, 53, 569
hearing Lord's war topics as, 516
as higher taste, 270-271
as highest charity, 293
as highest penance, 378
highest platform of, 364
human life for, 848
husband & wife share in, 868
as illuminated path, 1322
impersonalists require, 1339
incomplete, as still valuable, 1261
increases with age, 49, 50
independence in, 363
internal potency known by, 30
intimate result of, 329
Devotional service
jñāna-yoga vs., 271
as *karma-yoga*, 3
king must establish, 478
in knowledge, 1118-1119, 1182
knowledge & detachment by, 1336, 1337, 1351
in knowledge & renunciation, 996
knowledge by, 147, 197, 200, 1345-1346
kṛṣṇa-kathā in, 167, 168
of Lakṣmī, 1153, 1156
as liberation. *See:* Liberation
liberation by. *See:* Liberation Lord known only by, 1023-1024
liberation by, 148, 156, 794, 814 , 961-962
liberation surpassed by, 865
liberation via, 336
limitless, 809
Lord as approached by, 729
Lord identical to, 135-137
Lord known by, 110, 147, 265, 310, 312, 313
Lord obliged by, 317
Lord satisfied by, 159, 480, 813, 943, 961, 965
in love (*bhāva*), 1098, 1148, 1166-1167, 1170
love awakened by, 53, 71
lust & anger dispelled by, 446
materialists desireless of, 1317
material service eliminated by, 996
meditation in. *See:* Meditation
as mercy of Lord, 1126
mind controlled in, 1020
mind & senses controlled by, 560
mixed, 134, 287
in mode of goodness, 1190-1191
in mode of ignorance, 1188, 1191
in mode of passion, 1189, 1191
in modes, categories of, 1191
in modes of nature, 1354
motiveless, 317
motives for, four listed, 1187
nature's modes surpassed by, 865
necessity of. *See:* Devotional service, advantages of

Devotional service
neglected, material activity replaces, 1016
paths of, pure & motivated, 1187
patience in, 1200
perfection by, 780, 781
as perfection for *yogīs*, 984-985
as perfection of self-realization, 984-985
as personal, 985
pious people achieve, 59
via pious activities, 342
pleasure from, 568, 571, 1220-1221, 1350
power of, 942
processes of, 684
as practical, 1313
of preaching, 1358
assistance needed for, 1095
with compassion, 1102
door to door, 988
as duty, 1201
as higher, 1217
by Lord Caitanya, 1219
Lord pleased by, 1186
as merciful, 988
risks of, 988
teaching Kṛṣṇa is friend, 1095
with prescribed duties, 1116-1117
processes of. *See:* Devotional service, activities of
pure, 1187, 1188, 1256
Lord Caitanya's example of, 1193
vs. motivated, 1188-1191
Prahlāda Mahārāja's example of, 1194
as uninterrupted & unmotivated, 1192-1195
via pure devotees, 471
purifies even a *caṇḍāla*, 622
purification by, 1203-1204
with purified senses, 971
qualification for, 500
quick results by, 269
rasas in, 649
as reactionless, 1116, 1117
reactions in, freedom from, 1093-1094

Devotional service
relationships with Lord in. *See:* Kṛṣṇa, relationships with; Supreme Lord, relationships with
for real benefit, 347, 348
as real religion, 334, 335, 445
as real self-interest, 480
regulative, invokes love for Lord, 338
regulative vs. spontaneous, 272
of remembering, 1020
detachment by, 996
dhyāna-yoga as, 1390
miseries relieved by, 990
See also: Meditation
removes fear of death, 419
in renounced order, 989
renunciation as evidence of, 1118
renunciation by, 1019
required with every process, 1351-1353
results certain by, 1375
rules for, 1099-1104, 1196-1204
rules for, twenty given, 1201-1203
retirement absent in, 50
Sāṅkhya as, 1000, 1024
as Sāṅkhya philosophy's goal, 943
as satisfying, 1320
satisfying in itself, 129
scientific endeavors vs., 379
seed of, 1308
seed and creeper of, 52-53
self-realization followed by, 1179
self-realization from, 1125-1126
as self-surrender, 312
senses & mind meant for, 1001-1002
senses controlled by, 1097, 1300
senses engaged in, 270
senses perfected in, 787
with senses purified, 1021, 1167
sentimental, 1182
sincere endeavor in, 368
of *smaraṇam*. *See:* Devotional service, of remembering; Meditation
spiritual eyes opened by, 367

Devotional service (*continued*)
to spiritual master, 1200
via spiritual master, 200
via spiritual master & Kṛṣṇa, 736
spiritual realization by, 942, 962
spiritual vision of, 362
in spiritual world, 506, **565**
spontaneous, 272, 1167, 1192
as sublime, **607**
surpasses oneness with Lord, 601
superexcellence of, 878
stages of, 51
stages of development of, 983-984, **1116,** 1118
subtle body dissolved by, **1002**
symptoms of, two described, 1352
three stages of, 550
as topmost welfare work, 176
as topmost *yoga*, 159
as transcendental, 977-978, **1120,** 1335
tulasī plant in, 570
universal significance of, 443
wealth used in, 330
for women also, 997
of worship, 1082-1083, 1335
as Aniruddha, 1054, 1056
as Deity. *See:* Devotional service of Deity worship
as Hiraṇyagarbha, 1323
as Kṛṣṇa, 1133
as quadruple expansion, 1048
as Supersoul, **1088-1089**
work in, 761
as work's goal, 914
as *yoga,* best, 978, 1019, 1339-1341
& *yoga* compared, 1220-1221
as *yoga's* basis, 1350
as *yogī's* perfection, 984-985
See also: Devotees; Kṛṣṇa consciousness; Supreme Lord, love for; Supreme Lord, worship of
Dhāmas defined, 137
Dhanam defined, 143
Dhanaṣjaya air, 224
Dharitrī, 94
Dharma, 824
Dharma. See: Duty; Religion; Religious principles; *Varnāśrama-dharma*
Dharma defined, 953, 976
compared to fire's heat, 976
Dharma-glāni defined, 101
Dharmaṁ tu sākṣād bhagavat-praṇītaṁ
verse quoted, 336
Dharmarāja. *See:* Yamarāja
Dhīra defined, 200
Dhṛtarāṣṭra
Gāndhārī adopted blindness of, 873
King blindness of, 5
Kṛṣṇa's advice rejected by, **7,** 8
Vidura instructs, **8-11**
Vidura laments for, 40
Vidura left house of, 734
Yudhiṣṭhira cheated by, 7
Dhruva Mahārāja, **517**
Dhyāna-yoga, 1389-1390
Dig-devatās, **1077**
Digestion, 1066, 1133
Dīpārcir eva hi daśāntaram abhyupetya
quoted, 811
verse quoted, 328
Diplomacy, 1241
in palace life, 14
See also: Politics
Directions, demigods governing, 899, 900
Disciple & spiritual master, 836-838, 876, 910, 928
See also: *Brahmacārī*;Devotees
Disciples. *See: Brahmacārī:* Devotees; Spiritual master, kind to disciples
Disciplic succession, 1060, 1200
Disciplic succession *(paramparā)*
ācāryas guide, 144
Bhāgavatam via, 303
from Brahmā, 474-475, 609
hearing from, 301
knowledge via, 140
from Kumāras, 430
spiritual master in, 291
See also: Acāryas; Authorities: Spiritual master

Disciplic succession (*sampradāya*)
of Brahmā, 935
knowledge via, 726, 741, 933, 934
of Śiva, 868
for spiritual success, 835
See also: *Ācāryas;* Authority, spiritual; Spiritual master
Disease
material life compared to, 761, 876
waters curing, 816
See also: Suffering
Distress. *See*: Misery
caused by living entity himself, **1034-1035**
counteracting of, seen as happiness, 1241
material life as, 1170
as predestined by *karma*, 1101
Disturbance, marriage cures, 524
authority solves, 658
natural, at demons' birth, **659-666**
See also: Miseries: Suffering
Diti
blood from breasts of, 717
bore Kaśyapa's semen, 555
bore twin demons, **658, 659,** 666, 667, 668
condemned womb of, 544
Jaya & Vijaya in womb of, **652**
marriage of, **521, 522**
repentance of, 539-**541**
as sexually disturbed, **518-523, 536**
Divorce, cause of, 526, 790, 931
See also: Marriage
Divya years, 313
Dogs condemned, 547
Dogs at demons' birth, 662
Doll's beauty & woman's beauty, analogy of, 758
Dolls of Kṛṣṇa, 48
Doubt
proper & improper, 1055
freedom from, 935
See also: Ignorance
"Dovetailing" with the Supreme, 222
by pure devotees, 340
for superconsciousness, 606
Dowry in Vedic marriage, 852
Dramatic performances by the Lord, 344
Draupadī, offense to, **6,** 42
Dream
of severed head, 266
soul active in, 248
See also: *Māyā*
Drinking intoxicants, 117
Drooling in sleep, **765**
Duḥkha defined, 951
See also: Suffering
Duhitṛḥ defined, 627
Duḥśāsana, 6, **99**
Duplicity, 1099
Durātmā defined, 608
Duravabodha iva tavāyaṁ vihāra-yogo yad aśaraṇo śarīra idam
verse quoted, 265
Durgā as Śiva's wife, 532, 533, 535
Durgā (Kālī), goddess
cheats worshipers, 915
dacoits worshiped, 704
Durvāsā Muni, 716, 903
Durvāsā Muni, space travel by, 581
Duryodhana
daughter of, kidnapped by Kṛṣṇa's grandson, 845
fall of, 99-100
as offense personified, 11
Pāṇḍavas defeated, 38
Vidura insulted by, 12-13
Yudhiṣṭhira envied by, 35
Duties, prescribed, 1197
for Arjuna, 1320
Deity worship to accompany, 1210
for devotees in goodness, 1190
elevation by, 1351-1354
in Kṛṣṇa conscious way, **1116-1117**
material, vs. spiritual, 1131
results of, for Lord, 1320-1322
results of, materialists attached to, **1329-1334**
in *varṇāśrama* system, 1131, 1351

Duty
body according to, 166
of *brahmacārī*, 821
via Brahma-sampradāya, 474
devotional service transcends, 431
of disciple, 836-838
in enjoyment, 792
of father, 853, 855
of householder, 808
of husband, 840, 909-910
of *kṣatriya* kings, 823, 826
of ladies bathing, 893
Lord's assistance in, 360-361
in married life, 524-528
of parents, 521, 804
quality determines, 240-241
of *sannyāsīs*, 585, 808, 948
service attitude in, 244
in sex life, 520-521
of society's leaders, 640-641
of son to father, 474
of superior to subordinate, 909
of wife, 840, 870-874, 878
See also: Occupation: *Varṇāśrama-dharma*: *Karma*
Dvādaśaite vijānīmo
verse quoted, 336
Dvaita, 1175
Dvaitādvaita, 1175
Dvāpara-yuga, duration of, **409**, 410, 939
Dvāram āhur vimukteḥ
quoted, 987
Dvijatvaṁ jāyate
quoted, 1369
Dvārakā
as eternal place, 802-803
Kṛṣṇa as king of, 106
Kṛṣṇa returning to, 856
as spiritual kingdom, 137
Dvija-bandtius defined, 283
Dvija defined, 727, 928
Dvija-deva defined, 23
Dvijatvam defined, 828
Dvi-parārdha defined, 381
Dvivida, 98

E

Ear, proper use of, 614
spiritual master's instructions received via, 837
See also: Hearing
Earth
as Dharitrī, 94
as go, 55
living conditions vary on, 165
Lord maintains, 161
as middle planet, 209
Yadus "burdened", **100**, **101-102**
Yudhiṣṭhira ruled, 20, 105
Earth element
qualities of, 1070, 1072
See also: Elements; Evolution
Earth planet
as Bhārata-varṣa, 695, 903
compared to cow, 696
disturbed at demons' birth, 659, 660, 660, 661, 664, 666
flower-shower on, at Lord Kapila's advent, 923
as Ilāvṛta-varṣa, 695
inhabitants of. *See*: Human beings islands of, 776
Lord Boar rescued, 489-495
Lord Boar saved, 679, 680, 685, 686, 687, 688, 695
Lord Boar's tusks beautified, 501
passion mode binds one to, 865
planets inferior to, 492
upper planets excel, 395
See also: Material world
Earthquakes at demons' birth, 660
Eating
by animals, 391
in animal conditions, 209
austerity in, 1132, 1378
etiquette for, 117
killing for, 1197-1198

Eating
by the Lord, 110, 115, 623, 625
of meat, 1316
regulation of, 1101-1102, 1132, 1388
See: Meat-eating; *Prasāda*
See also: Food; *Prasāda*
Economic development
rituals for, 773
See also: Gold; Money; Opulence; Wealth
Economics, Vedic vs. modern, 81
Ecstasy
by crying for Kṛṣṇa, 153
forgetfulness in, 52
of Kṛṣṇa & *gopīs*, 63
in love of God, 128
from offenseless chanting, 578, 579
by seeing Kṛṣṇa's footprints, 32
Uddhava in, 50-51
See also: Bliss; Enjoyment; Happiness; Pleasure; Supreme Lord, love for
Education. *See:* Disciplic succession; Spiritual master
mundane, 446-447
in Vedic society, 458
Effulgence. *See:* Brahman effulgence
Eggs, life in, 1176
Egg, universe as, 745
Ego, false. *See:* False ego
evolution of, 744
foolishness of, 435
matter & spirit knotted by, 919
origin & by-products of, 387
See also: Bodily concept of life; Illusion; *Māyā*
Ego, real vs. false, 1107
Ekādaśī fasting, 1119
Ekadaṇḍi-sannyāsī, 248
Ekale īśvara kṛṣṇa, āra saba bhṛtya
quoted, 1152, 1225
Ekātmatām defined, 1004
Eko bahūnāṁ yo vidadhāti kāmān
quoted, 209, 967, 1365
Eko 'py asau racayituṁ jagad-aṇḍa-koṭiṁ
verse quoted, 216
Eko vai nārāyaṇa āsīn
quoted, 181
Electricity
consciousness compared to, 260
Lord compared to, 65
Elements
causes of. *See:* Evolution
classes of, named, 1038, 1044
earth, all qualities in, 1072
ether, qualities of, 1061
ether, subtle, sound as, 1059
evolution of, 1345
gross & subtle, five ea. listed, 1039
material nature entered by, 1073
mixing, time as, 1041
qualities of, 1072
in *saguṇa* Brahman, 1041
senses characteristic of, five given, 1070
as universal covering, 1074-1075
as *yonir mahad brahma*, 1038
See also: Evolution; *names of individual elements*
Elements, material
evolution of, 188-193
five listed, 744
listed, 216, 224, 424
See also: Fire; Energy, illusory (material); Nature, material; *names of specific elements*
Elephant dust and sins, analogy of, 299
Elephants, king of, Lord saved, 728
Embryo, human. *See:* Human being, unborn
Enemies at home, 872
Emotions
in love of God, 31-32
See also: Affection; Attachment; Love; Supreme Lord, love for
Energy, internal, *gopīs* as, 356
external, *māyā* as, 1009
of God. *See:* Supreme Lord, energies of; Supreme Lord, potency of, inconceivable
illusory (material), 915

Energy, internal (*continued*)
illusory, 1028-1032
of Lord
as all-pervading, 1026-1028
everything as, 1175
as His reflection, 1105-1106
internal, 968
Lord controls through, 1364
Lord one with & different from, 1111
marginal, 879
marginal, living entity as, 1044, 1051
material
as Lord's energy, 1322
compared to cloud, 1029
See also: Life; Nature, material; Power: Soul; Spiritual world; Supreme Lord, potencies of
Energy, material
beyond human comprehension, 504, 506
as cause and effect, 183
compared to tape recording, 384
controlling power of, 15
fructification of, 185
as gross & subtle coverings, 223
"I-and-mine" concept exploits, 203
as impregnated with living beings, 184, 185
as Kālī, 216
at Kṛṣṇa's back, 122
living entity overcome by, 264, 266
Lord impregnates, 503
as Lord's agent, 345
Lord's body beyond, 366-367
personified, 532, 535
as "quivering", 268, 269
as reflection of reality, 626
strength of, 453
three phases of, 388
time factor and, 383-384
See also: Elements, material; Material world; *Māyā;* Modes of material nature; Nature, material
Energy, spiritual
as central generating force, 224
Energy, spiritual
Yadus' destruction by, 118, 119
See also: Body, spiritual; Soul; Spiritual world
Enjoyment
action aims at, 3
by animals, 393
for devotees, 1009
hellish, 1237
Kṛṣṇa excels in, 63
in Lord's sleeping, 350-353
material
compared to smoke, 1174, 1175
as eternal, 1037
modes invested in, 1028-1029
in modes of nature, 966
regulated, 106
in Vaikuṇṭha, 572
See also: Bliss; Ecstasy; Happiness; Pleasure; Sense gratification Envy, 1356
Enjoyment, material
conditioned soul saved from, 734
conditioned soul seeks, 742, 748-749
degradation by, 861
disgust with, 798
for hogs & dogs, 789
in Kali-yuga, 749
Kṛṣṇa consciousness surpasses, 862
material world, 797
spiritual enjoyment vs., 761, 764
spiritual realization prevented by, 773
tasteless in the end, 863
Vedic process of, 791-792, 798
women seek, 912
"yogīs" encourage, 789
See also: Happiness; Pleasure; Sense gratification
Entanglement. *See:* Birth and death, repeated; Bondage, material; *Karma*; Transmigration
Entities, individual. *See:* Living entities
Envy
of God, 1115, 1120
in beastly persons, 152
in Duryodhana, 35

Envy
paramahaṁsa free of, 849
toward Kṛṣṇa, 69
See also: Anger: Atheists; Impersonalism; Ignorance
Equality of vision, 1099-1100
Etasmād ātmanaḥ ākāśaḥ sambhūtaḥ
quoted, 190
Ete cāṁśa-kalāḥ puṁsaḥ
verse quoted, 46
Eternal life
by Kṛṣṇa consciousness, 953
as materially impossible, 669, 670
See also: Spiritual world
Eternality
in conditional life only, 549
of consciousness, 169
by Lakṣmījī for *tulasī*, 637
of living entities, 259-260
of Lord & associates, 48, 290
of Lord's internal potency, 256
surrendered souls beyond, 476
in Vaikuṇṭha absent, 570
See also: Anger
Europe as island, 776
Evening. *See:* Night; Twilight
Ether element, **1059-1062**
See also: Elements; Evolution
Evolution
of false ego, 744
of material world, 184-193
See also: Species of life: Transmigration
Evolution (of material nature)
as old knowledge, 1214
detailed, **1058-1082**
from air, 1072
from air's interactions, 1064
from ether, 1061-1162, 1064
from false ego (*ahaṅkāra*), **1051, 1053, 1055, 1056-1058**
from fire, 1066, 1072
from form, 1064
from hearing, 1062
Evolution (of material nature)
from *mahat-tattva*, **1050,** 1344
from odor, 1068
from sight, 1066
from sky, 1060, 1061, 1072
from sound, 1062, 1072
from taste, 1066, 1068
from touch, 1062, 1064
from water, 1068, 1072
of air, 1063, 1072
of Brahmā, 1081-1082
of causes of material manifestation, 1036-1072
of earth, 1069, 1072
of effects within material manifestation, 1072-1089
of elements, **1051,** 1345
of ether, 1061
of fire, **1064,** 1072
of form, 1060, 1064
of god of death, **1079**
of gods of directions, **1077**
of god of fire, 1077
of god of hands, 1080
of God of movement, 1080
of god of sun, 1077-1078
of god of waters, **1079**
of god of wind, **1077**
of grasping, 1081
of hearing, 1058
of herbs & drugs, 1078
of intelligence, **1055, 1057**
of material energy, **1051**
of mind, **1051, 1053,** 1064
of moon, 1081-1082
of movement, **1080**
of oceans, 1081
of odor, 1069
of olfactory sense, **1077**
of organs of action, **1051**
of *prāṇa*, 1077
of rivers, 1080
of sense objects, 1061
of sense of hearing, 1077

Evolution (of material nature) (*continued*)
of senses, 1057
of senses' energy, 1057
of sight, 1062, 1064
of sight sense, **1077**
of Śiva, 1082
of sky, 1072
of smell, sense of, 1069
of sound, 1058
of speech organ, 1077
of taste, 1066
of tongue, 1067
of touch, 1062
of water, 1066, 1072
principle of, 1283
Evolution (of soul). *See:* Transmigration
Examples. *See:* Analogies
Existence. *See:* Life
Expansions of God. *See:* Supreme Lord, expansions of
"Eyes" in jeweled palaces, 886
Eyes, spiritual, 367

F

Factories as hellish, 334
Faith
as *Ahaṁ mamatā*, 1103
at birth, 1285
in *Bhagavad-gītā*, 172
caused by ignorance, 1169
compared to sleep & to losing wealth, 1109-1110
devotee free from, 1108
fear due to, 1042
freedom from, as liberation, 1111
freedom from, worship of Saṅkarṣaṇa for, **1049**
in God, 928
in goodness, **1053**
of identification with matter, 1111
in ignorance, 1058
kinds (modes) of, **1050**
in Lord's pastimes, 515
of lording over, 1115
Faith
material consciousness due to, 1082
material life due to, 1052
modes in, 1052
in one's husband, 39
in passion, **1054, 1057**
proprietorship as, 1093
qualities of, 1052
vs. real ego, 1107
in spiritual master, 921, 928-929
See also: Elements; Evolution; Illusion, of body as self: Knowledge
False ego
cause & effect of, 183-187
foolishness of, 435
as "I & mine," 203
illusion due to, 15
interactions of, 188, 189
origin & by-products of, 386
Śiva controls, 235
See: Ego, false
Family
affection for, 169
difficulty of maintaining, 1237
māyā, 1239
of Vasudeva, 27
See also: Children; Householders; Marriage; Parents; Son
Family life, 1377
association with women in, 1303
attachment in, **1173**, 1235, 1237-1239, 1294, 1305, 1356
children in, 1267
compared to blind well, 957
compared to prison, 1239
devotee desireless of, **1013-1015**
devotees in, examples of, 1148
duties in, 1015, 1267, 1351, 1353
elders rejected in, 1242-1244
father-son relationship in, 474-476
female association in, 1299
financial maintenance of, standard for, 1259-1260
gṛhamedhī, vs *gṛhastha*, 1240

Family life
illusion of, 1171-1173, 1239
of Indian royalty, 861
Kumāras rejected, 430-431
Kṛṣṇa conscious, 1148, 1306, 1316
Lord as child in, 1366, 1384-1385
miseries from, 330
old father in, compared to worn-out ox, 1243-1244
opulences in, 1380
purification for conception in, 1369
real, vs. illusory, 1238-1239
renunciation of, 948, 949, 957-958, 1244-1245
restrictions for, in Hindu society, 1304
sex life restricted to, 1133
sinful maintenance in, 1241
son represents husband in, 1384
in spiritual world, 1238
in Vedic society, 458
Vedic system of, 970
wealth in, 1380
work proper for maintaining, 1259-1260
See also: Gṛhamedhīs; Gṛhasthas: Children; Father; Householders; Mar- riage; Mother; Parents; Wife
Farming. *See:* Agriculture; *Vaiśyas*
Fasting
in devotional service, 1119
water eases, 1068
Fate
Lord controls, 15, 218
Fate
See also: Karma; Supreme Lord, will of
Father-son relationship, 474-476
Father
begetting children, 756
daughter & 853, 854
departed, oblations on behalf of, 767
dowry from, 852
as enemy, 872
first & second, 931
knowledge about, example of, 741
Lord compared to, 66
Father
obedience to, 928
son represents, 910
son saves soul of, 11
spiritual master as, 928-929, 931
of twice-born man, 163
See also: Children; Family life; Householders; Husband; Marriage: Parents
Fasting
in devotional service, 1119
water eases, 1068
Father "fighting" child & Lord "fighting" Hiraṇyākṣa, analogy of, 712
Fear, 1376
cause & cure for, 330
cause of, 311
of death, 428
in demigods, 658
devotees beyond, 41, 560, 613, 614
devotee free of, 809
freedom from, 686, 689, 876, 909
Kṛṣṇa exhibited, 66, 67, 68
in material world, 657, 875, 909
used in Lord's service, 649
"Feast," cannibalistic, 750
Females. *See:* Mother; Wife: Women
birth of, 881
male attracted to, 919-920
Fetus, human. *See:* Human being, unborn
Fighting pastime of the Lord, 644, 653
Fire
for cooking & ceremonies, 958
divine cause of, 118
mantra to ignite, 503
material existence compared to, 793-794, 940
in sacrifice to Viṣṇu, 519
widows entered, 39
Fire element
qualities of, 1065
See also: Elements; Evolution
Fire in wood & Lord in devotee's semen, analogy of, 922

Fire of digestion, 1066
Firewood and *kṛṣṇa-kathā*, analogy of, 168
Fish and foolish souls, analogy of, 55, 59
Flowers, spiritual, 569-570
 at Bindu-sarovara Lake, 818
 shower of, at Lord Kapila's advent, 923
 shower of, by demigods on Lord Boar, 687, 688
Flowers in spiritual world, 1144
Fog, Brahmā created, 452
Food
 for civilized men, 163
 digestion of, 1066, 1133
 earth supplies, 101
 for humans, 1101
 killing for, 1197-1198
 living entities as, 1197
 Lord supplies, 115
 "shortage" of, 161, 209
 soulful vs. sinful, 209
 types of, 115, 116
 See also: Meat-Eating; *Prasāda*
Fool
 counsel's effect on, 12
 happiness of, 274
Forefathers, liberation of, 767
Forest, retiring to, 957-958
Forest fire & material world, analogy of, 940
Forgetfulness
 by intoxication, 117
 Lord assists in, 224
Forgetfulness. *See:* Illusion; *Māyā*
Forgetting the Lord, 593
Form of God. *See:* Deity form; Supreme Lord, form of
Form, qualities of, 1065
Forms of the Lord. *See:* Supreme Lord, forms of
Freedom
 of conditioned souls restricted, 901
 from doubt, 934
 from fear, 876, 909
 by Kṛṣṇa consciousness, 793, 957
 from material bondage, 794, 933, 934, 954, 957-958
Freedom
 from material desires, 785
 for pilgrims, 41
 by serving Lord, 794, 960
 from work's reactions, 857
 See also: Independence; Liberation
Freedom from material world & desires. *See:* Liberation
Friend, devotee as, 988, 1101, 1102
Friendship
 with Kṛṣṇa, 79, 95
 with Vaiṣṇavas, 40
Friendships with devotees, 1201-1202
Frog-philosophers, 246, 250-253
Fruitive activity
 bondage by, 305
 devotional service dispels, 933
 as lotus bud of cosmic creation, 307
 misery from, 156
 origin of, 189
 See also: Activities, material; Bondage; *Karma*; *Karma;* Sense gratification; Sinful activities
Fruitive activities, entanglement of, detailed, 1315-1334
Fruitive workers. *See: Karmīs*; Materialists

G

Gadā defined, 582
Gambling, 774, 950
Gāndhārī, 873
Gandha-vanik defined, 242
Gāndīva bow, 37
Gandharva girls, Devahūti served by, 898
Gāndharva marriage, 844
Gandharvas, 1382
 Brahmā created, 763-764
 Devahūti attracted, 847
 at Lord Kapila's advent, 922
 moonlight form seized by, 764
Gandharva Viśvāvasu
 Devahūti bewildered, 846, 847
 moonlight form seized by, 764

Gaṅgā-sāgara-tīrtha, 1396
Ganges River, 1396
from Lord's lotus feet, 505, 626
bathing in, hearing Lord's pastimes compared to, 737
compared to the Lord, 195
cosmic course of, 298-299
material distress relieved by, 902
pilgrims bathe in, 889
purifying power of, 199, 299
Śiva holds, 1152
transcendental waters of, 816
Vidura-Maitreya meeting at, 155, 156
from Viṣṇu's toe, 902
Garbhādhāna defined, 543
Garbhādhāna ceremony, 666, 756
Garbhādhāna-saṁskāra, 1267, 1369
Garbhodaka Ocean, 724, 746, 1319, 1363
planets rest in, 492
size of, 482
Garbhodakaśāyī Viṣṇu, 220, 221, 303-307, 308, 743, 745, 745-746, 924, 1073, 1075, 1318, 1323, 1363
Brahmā dreams about, 412
Brahmā, Viṣṇu & Śiva from, 324
enjoys *rāsa* with external energy, 343
See also: Mahā-Viṣṇu; Supersoul; Supreme Lord
Gardens, Kardama & Devahūti visited, in mystic mansion, 900
Garuḍa, 38, 76, 91, 1154, 1398
Indra vs., 711
Sāma Veda vibrated by, 813
Gata-vyathah defined, 15
Gatekeepers of Vaikuṇṭha. *See:* Jaya & Vijaya
Gati, 937
Gauḍīya Vaiṣṇavas
Lord's forms as preferred by, 754
philosophy of, 2
worship Vṛndāvana, 80
See also: Devotees
Gauraveṇa defined, 870
Gauracandra
meaning of name, 1082
See also: Caitanya Mahāprabhu
Gaurī, 108
Gavayas defined, 819
See also: Cow Gayā temple, *śrāddha* ritual at, 767
Gayā, 11
Gāyatrī *mantra*
mahā-mantra vs., 538
origin of, 461
in Vedic hymns, 496
Gem, unpolished, Kardama compared to, 821
Ghosts, characteristics of, 530
Brahmā created, 765
conditioned soul harassed by, 765
impure people haunted by, 765
Girl
parents of, choose husband, 804
See also: Female; Woman
Gltā. See: Bhagavad-gītā
Glorifying the Lord. *See:* Supreme Lord, glorification of
Goal of life
See: Life, goal of
beyond bodily necessities, 140
creation facilitates, 182, 186, 187
as freedom from "I & mine," 203
spiritual blindness blocks, 5
Go-brāhmaṇa-hitāya ca
quoted, 620, 640, 831
God. *See:* Absolute Truth; Kṛṣṇa, Lord; Supreme Lord; Nārāyaṇa, Lord; Supersoul; Viṣṇu, Lord
God consciousness
See: Kṛṣṇa consciousness
of demigods & devotees, 209
See also: Devotional service
Go defined, 55, 696
See also: Cow
Goddess of fortune (Lakṣmī)
doorkeepers angered, 648
Lord's beauty surpasses, 599, 600

Goddess of fortune (*continued*)
in Lord's service, 623, 636
as Ramā, 354
rarely seen, 618
tulasī surpasses, 637
unsteady, 573
in Vaikuṇṭha, 572, 573
Goddess of learning, 446-447
Godhead, returning to
by knowing Lord's transcendental nature, 689
by meditating on Lord's form, 721
process of, 964
via Vedic principles, 860
See also: Goloka Vṛndāvana; Spiritual world; Transcendence
God realization
of devotees, 1105-1106, 1348
as *kaivalya*, 785
in Kṛṣṇa consciousness, 1104-1106
levels of, 1338-1340, 1349, 1393
pleasure from, 1349-1350
process of. *See:* Devotional service
real, vs. theoretical, 1016
of seeing Lord in His energy, 1106
as Supersoul, 1088-1089, 1274
See also: Brahman realization: Kṛṣṇa consciousness
"Gods." *See:* Demigods
Gokula (Kṛṣṇaloka), Rādhā & Kṛṣṇa in, 600
Gold
demons amass, 697
See also: Money; Opulence
Goloka eva nivasaty akhilātma-bhūtah quoted, 151, 1025
Goloka Vṛndāvana, 71, 683, 712, 725, 802
See also: Spiritual world; Supreme Lord, abode of: Vṛndāvana
Goodness
qualities of, 577-578
in spiritual world, 566, 610
Goodness, mode of
association with, 94
demigods born of, 752
Goodness, mode of
foods in, 115
heavenly planets in, 236, 237
higher planets via, 864-865
impersonalists in, 169, 173, 187
living entities in, 665
material vs. spiritual, 723, 925-926
mind produced by, 188
perfection of, 787
symptoms of, 169
transcending, 148
Viṣṇu worship in, 201
See also: Modes of material nature
Gopāla-tāpanī Upanisad, cited on Lord's lotus feet, 316
Gopāla-tāpanī Upaniṣad, quoted on Kṛṣṇa and gopīs, 343
Gopīs
as best devotees, 1125
born *vaiśyas*, 1197
names of, chanting of, 1148
Gopīs (cowherd damsels)
as internal potency, 357
Kṛṣṇa attracted, 913
Kṛṣṇa disturbed minds of, 908
Kṛṣṇa served by, 784
as Lord's internal potencies, 108, 109
as Lord's lovers, 63, 86, 124
lusty desires of, 649
in *rāsa* dance, 343
Goṣṭhy-ānandī defined, 948
Gosvāmī defined, 149
Gosvāmīs, Six, 1201
Govardhana Hill, Kṛṣṇa lifted, 86
Govardhana Hill, Lord lifted, 344
Government, Vedic system of. *See: Varṇāśrama* system
Government. *See:* Civilization, human; Leaders, government; Society, human; *Varṇāśrama* system
Government leaders
compared to blind men, 332, 1295
duty of, 479

Government leaders
enmity toward, 588
Kṛṣṇa exemplary for, 640
mundane interests of, 575-576
See also: Kṣatriyas; Varṇāśrama-dharma
Government
modern, 241
monarchical, 35, 105
worldwide, 20-21
See also: King(s); *Kṣatriyas;* Leaders, government; Society, human; *Varṇāśrama-dharma*; Vedic culture
Govinda, Lord, 810
Govinda, senses enlivened by, **967**
Govindam ādi-puruṣaṁ tam ahaṁ bhajāmi quoted, 313, 316
Grains
as society's livelihood, 242
wealth based on, 81
See also: Food
Grass, sages used, to worship God, 857
Gravitation, law of, 687
Gravity in speech, 1099-1100
Great souls. *See: Ācāryas;* Devotees, pure devotees; *Mahātmās;* Saintly persons; Spiritual master
Gṛhamedhl defined, 840
Gṛhamedhīs
demigods worshiped by, 1317
vs. *gṛhastha*, 1240, 1315
religiosity of, 1320
See also: Family life
Gṛhasthas. See: Householders; Varṇāśramadharma: Family life; Householders; Marriage
duties for, 1351
vs. *gṛhamedhī*, 1240, 1315
restricted, as *brahmacārīs*, 1133
Guhyaṁ viśuddhaṁ durbodhaṁ
verse quoted, 336
Guṇas. See: Modes of nature material nature
Guru. See: Spiritual master
Guruṣu nara-matiḥ
quoted, 1201
Gurv-aṣṭaka, quoted on mercy of Lord through spiritual master, **999**

H

Hair, bunches of, from *camarīs*, 819
Hallucination
material enjoyment compared to, 799
See also: Illusion; *Māyā*
Haṁsa-yāna defined, 936
Hanumān, 753, 754, 944
Happiness
beyond material world, 59
caused by living entity himself, **1035**
in devotional path, 206, 207
by devotional service, 1089, 1170, 1390
formula for, 197-198
good government brings, 105
by hearing about Lord, 967
by internal energy, 107
by Kṛṣṇa consciousness, 684, 772
by *kṛṣṇa-kathā*, 171
by Lord's grace, 26
by Lord's narrations, 249, 250, 253
by Lord's protection, 41
in marriage, 873
material vs. spiritual, 761, 764, 785-786, 786, 875-876
material, as temporary, 977-978
material, devotees don't care about, **995**
materialistic devotees seeking, 340
as predestined, 1101
qualifications for, 274
of self-realization, **984**, 1170
by religious life, 411
schemes for, frustrated, 157
in seeing Lord's form, 615
by serving Lord, 858
in spiritual life only, 185
in spiritual world, 581
See also: Chanting of the Supreme Lord's holy names: Bliss; Ecstasy; Enjoyment; Peace; Pleasure

Hardwar, 155
Hare Kṛṣṇa *mantra*
in *Bṛhan-nāradīya Purāṇa*, 487
happiness via, 614
hearing of, effect of, 167
offenses to, 578-579
power of, 538
quoted, 487, 538, 579, 607, 614, 649, 684, 817, 863
for success in yoga, 607
for thinking of Kṛṣṇa, 649
See also Devotional service: Chanting the holy names; Supreme Lord, name of Hare Kṛṣṇa
Hare Kṛṣṇa movement *See:* Kṛṣṇa consciousness movement, invitation into, 169
Hare Kṛṣṇa movement (ISKCON), healthy faces in, 821
Harer nāma defined, 625
Hari-bhakti-vilāsa
author of, 1152
quoted on initiation, 1368
Haridāsa Ṭhākura
Advaita and, 625
beaten, 654
beyond sex attraction, 537
chanting of, 1371
Caitanya's mercy on, 618
persecuted, **988**
as transcendental, 1301
Harmony with the Lord, 589-591
Hariṁ vinā na mṛtim taranti
quoted, 795, 1226
Haryakṣa. *See:* Hiraṇyākṣa
Hata-medhasaḥ defined, 789
Haṭha-yoga, 1134, 1138, 1295
"*Haṭha-yoga*" vs. real *yoga* system, 603-604
Havirbhū, 937
Health
āsavam aids, 892
of Hare Kṛṣṇa people, 821
Hearing from & about Lord. *See:* Devotional service, of hearing
Hearing
from authorities, 301, 839
importance of, 950
kṛṣṇa-kathā, 167-168, 169
of Lord. *See:* Supreme Lord, hearing about
of Lord's devotees, 728
from spiritual master, 837
spiritual world known by, 566
value of, 230
worthwhile subject for, 509, 511
See also: Sound, transcendental; Supreme Lord, hearing about
Hearing sense, 1063-1064, 1070
Heart
brāhmaṇas compared to, 831, 832
enlightenment from, 358, 361
generating force from, 224
importance of, 445
"knot" of affection in, 920
Kṛṣṇa in, 25
Lord in, 747, 756-757, 801, 921, 922, 962
seed of devotion in, 52, 53
Heavenly planets
devotees curious about, 144
fear in, 658
via goodness mode, 864
inhabitants of, 505, 506
king of. *See:* Indra
musicians & dancers in, 763
pārijāta tree in, 93
pleasure on, rejected by devotees, 611, 612
residents of. *See:* Demigods
See also: Creation, the material; Earth planet; Planets, material: Demigods; Spiritual world; Universe
Hell for *Bhāgavatam's* offenders, 135
Andha-tāmisra, 1255, **1259,** 1264, 1295
devotee's attitude toward, 613, 614
devotees avoid, 1261
factories as, 335
householders saved from, 428
Raurava, 1255
release from, 1260, 1263, 1296

Hell for *Bhāgavatam's* offenders
satisfaction in, 1237
sense gratification leads to, 1296
for sinful maintenance of family, 1259
sufferings of, **1253-1260**
sufferings similar to, 1256
Tāmiṣra, 1254
three named, 1255
See also: Demons; Miseries
Hetunānena kaunteya
verse quoted, 183, 384
Himalayas, holy place in, **136-137**
Himalayas, king of, daughter of, 869
Hindu culture. *See*: Āryan civilization; *Varṇāśrama-dharma;* Vedic culture
Hinduism
demigod worship in, 1316
householders in, restrictions for, 1304
Hindustan, 695
Hindu temples, Haridāsa didn't enter, 618
Hiranyagarbha defined, 746
Hiraṇyagarbha, Lord, 1323
Hiraṇyakaśipu, 652, 653
birth of, 658, 659, 668, 669
body of, 666, 667
Brahmā blessed, 669-670
Hiraṇyākṣa assisted, 670
Lord Nrsiṁha and, 922
pride & power of, 669, 671
Hiraṇyākṣa, 493, 514, 652, 653
birth of, 658, 659, 668, 669
body of, 666, 667
Brahmā advised Lord Boar to kill, 699-701
Brahmā condemned, 698, 699
Brahmā's blessing misused by, 703
compared to snake, 699
death of, 719-720, 726
as Haryaksa, 694
hearing about, benefit of, 730, 732
Hiraṇyakaśipu assisted by, 671
Lord Boar challenged, 689-691
Lord Boar challenged by, 679, 680, 682
Lord Boar chased by, 686, 688
Hiraṇyākṣa
Lord Boar endured insults of, 685, 686, 688, 689
Lord Boar fought, 690-695, 696, **704**-719, 720, 726
mystic display by, 713-716
ocean harassed by, 672-674
pride & power of, 670-674
quoted on Lord Boar "fleeing,", 686
Varuṇa advised, **676-678**
Varuṇa "challenged" by, **675, 676**
History
in *Śrīmad-Bhāgavatam*, 776-77
of Lord worth hearing, 509, 511
in *Purāṇas*, 457
in Vedic literatures, 167, 170
of Viṣṇu temples, 23
in Yudhiṣṭhira's era, 20
Hitvātma-pātaṁ gṛham andha-kūpam
quoted, 957
Hlādinī potency, 30
Hobgoblins. *See*: Ghosts
Hog, material enjoyment of, 789
Hog incarnation. *See*: Varāha, Lord
Holy men. *See*: *Ācāryas*: Devotees, pure devotees; *Mahātmās*; Saintly persons; Spiritual master; Sages; Saints; Transcendentalists
Holy names of God. *See*: Chanting of the Supreme Lord's the holy names; Hare Kṛṣṇa *mantra*; Supreme Lord, name of
Holy places. *See*: Pilgrimage places
Homes for different living entities, **164,** 165
Homosexuality, 755
Household life. *See*: Family life; *Gṛhamedhīs*; *Gṛhasthas*
Householders (*gṛhasthas*)
begetting children, **667**
devotee, see Lord, 942
duty of, 809
fire used by, 958
gṛhamedhī contrasted to, 840
of Indian royalty, 861

Householders *(continued)*
in Kṛṣṇa consciousness, 907
in Kṛṣṇa consciousness movement, 821
Kṛṣṇa's example for, 109
in *māyā*, 808
money-managing by, 808
responsibility of, 458, 525-527
retiring from family life, 910, 949
in safest *āśrama*, 527
sannyāsīs enlighten, 808
sannyāsīs honored by, 586
sex life for, 843
See also: Children: Family life; Father; Husband; Mother; Parents; Wife; Marriage; Sex life
Hṛdaya-granthi defined, 919
Hṛṣīkeśa
defined, **1001**
Lord as, 1350
Human beings
animals contrasted to, 393, 454, 511
animal killing by, 237
animallike, 1297
between demigods & demons, 209
birth as, **1260,** 1261
black & white, 166
classes of. *See: Varṇāśrama* system
compared to crows & white ducks, 324
criterion for, 106, 163-164
death for. *See:* Death
demigods contrasted to, 658
as devotees or demons, **1030**
for devotional service, 848
duty of, 323
foods for, 1101
goal of, 48, 115
indebted to others, 113
Kṛṣṇa consciousness for all, 1208
Kṛṣṇa in role as, 73
levels of, detailed, **1216**-1219
as limited, 309
limited brain of, 506, 507
Lord in form of, 932
Human beings
Lord's relations with, 173
as Manu's descendants, 858
materialistic. *See:* Materialists
mental speculation degrades, 173
milk essential for, 163
newborn, frustration of, **1289, 1290**
newborn, misery of, **1286-1291**
in *paramahaṁsa* stage, 849
in passion, 237, 237-238
population of, 101, 177
purpose of, 953
responsibility necessary for, 419
sense gratification not for, 911
sex (gender) of, determination of, **1265**
sexual inclination of, 393, 448, 450
three principles for, 115
time for, vs. demigods' time, 404, 410
as twice-born, 931
two types of, 556
unborn, 1263-1288
"brothers" of, 1271
development of, 1265
misery of, **1266-1272,** 1280
nourishment for, **1266**
prayers by, 1272-1286
remembrance for, **1270**
See also: Civilization, human: Life; Living entities; Society, human; Souls, conditioned Hunger. *See:* Starvation
Human life
vs. animal life, 1213, 1236, 1256, 1283
as child, misery of, **1288-1289**
compared to good boat, 1270
evolution to. *See:* Transmigration
intelligence in, 1281
as man, advantage of, 1305
as opportunity to end suffering, 1270
as regulated life, **966**
sense & mind control in, 1283
as valuable, 1258
See also: Human beings
Humility, 1203

Hunter
in Kṛṣṇa's disappearance pastime, 58
Nārada's mercy on, 204
Husband. *See:* Father; Householders: Marriage; Parents
duty of, 520-521
duty of, 840, 909-910
girl's parents choose, 804
qualification of, 840
as spiritual master, 921
taking *sannyāsa,* 956
wife as property of, 854, 856
wife attracting, 881
wife's duty to, 840, 870-874, 877
Huta-hutāśana defined, 821
Hymns, Vedic. *See:* Vedic *mantras*

I

"I-and-mine" conception, 203
Idaṁ hi viśvaṁ bhagavān ivetaraḥ
quoted, 384
Identity
forgetfulness of, 260
self-control purifies, 549
spiritual suicide destroys, 530
three types of, 221, 222
See also: Consciousness; Living entities: Self-realization; Soul
Idol worship, 18
Ignorance
Brahmā created coverings of, 747, 748
Brahmā relinquished body of, 749, 751
compared to fog, 452
demons in, 758, 763
kinds of, two given, 1293-1294
material world in, 748-749
night as body of, 749, 751
of real self-interest, 1185
of transmigration, 1183
See also: Bodily concept of life; Darkness; Ignorance, mode of; Illusion: *Māyā*
Ignorance, mode of
See: Modes of material nature
Ignorance, mode of
bodily identification from, 187
degradation by, 865
demons born of, 752
as predominant, 169
Śiva worshipers in, 201-202, 235
See also: Māyā
Ihā yasya harer dāsye
quoted, 1375
verse quoted, 148-149
Illicit sex. *See:* Sex life
Illusion. *See:* Bodily concept of life; Ego, false; Hallucination; Ignorance; Insanity: *Māyā*
of becoming one with Lord, 1328
begins at birth, 1284
bodily concept as, 749
of bodily identification, lust & greed from, 981, 1060
of body as self, 973, 1031, 1042, 1102, 1286, 1293-1294
covering energy of, 1028-1029
of demigod worship, 1082, 1317, 1330
of envy of God, 1115
of equality with Lord, 1177-1178
in family life, 1171-1173
of forgetfulness, 1354-1355
of forgetfulness of identity, 1008
of forgetfulness of relationship with Lord, 1169, 1225-1226
of forgetfulness of spiritual knowledge, 1291
of forgetting one's self to be servant of Lord, 1169, 1277
freedom from, by surrender, 1033, 1114-1115
of freedom from control of material energy, 1032
of ignorance of transmigration, 1183
of impersonal God. *See:* Impersonalism; Impersonalists of independence, 1114
Lord not covered by, 1029
Lord removes, 973, 974
of Lord seen as formless, 1328-1329
of Lord seen as illusioned, 1036
of Lord seen as material, 1343

Illusion (*continued*)
of Lord unseen by conditioned soul, **1029**
lost, of thinking one's self as, 1009-1110
of love in material world, 1239-1240
of male or female identity, **976**
of material happiness, **978**
of material life as permanent, 1233-1235
of material world as soul's field of activities, 1032
materialists in, 915
"māyā consciousness," **980**
modes cause, **1030-1032**
of nationalism, 1241-1242
philanthropy as, 1096
of possessing wealth, 1257, 1258
of proprietorship, 1093, 1173
removed by chanting, 1082
of satisfaction in any condition, 1236-1237
of self as enjoyer, 1095, 1096
of self as friend to all, 1095
of speculative knowledge, **1342**, 1343
of spiritual identity forgotten, **1031**, **1044**, 1170, 1225
of tree's reflection, 346
of wealth, **1111**
in womb also, **1286**
See also: Atheists; False ego; *Māyā*
Immortality. *See:* Eternal life: Eternality
Impersonal Absolute Brahman. *See:* Brahman (impersonal Absolute)
Impersonalism
dangers of, **1005**
devotees reject, **1003-1005**
devotional service vs., **994**
as inferior, **1002**
as *māyā* s last snare, **1110**
"oneness" idea of, **1110-1111**, 1326
voidism, **1112**
yoga misunderstood as, 1130, 1136, 1150, 1155, 1161-1162, 1168, 1178
Impersonalists (Māyāvādīs)
Absolute Truth misunderstood by, 807
Bhāgavatam misinterpreted by, 128, 181
Impersonalists (Māyāvādīs)
Brahmā condemns, 327-328
compared to Lord's enemies, 76
consciousness misinterpreted by, 204
as defeated, 346
deny essential topics, 173-174
Deity of Lord unaccepted by, **1006**
demigods worshiped by, 1316
deny service attitude, 364
devotees contrasted to, 123, 173, 206-207
vs. devotees of Lord, **1003-1005**, 1121
devotees surpass, 329
devotional service difficult for, 1329
devotional service required for, 1339
as duplicitous, 1099
falldown of, 335, 435
fear spiritual variety, 575
in goodness, 169, 173
happiness of, 249
hearing from, forbidden, **1005**
imaginary meditation of, 782
Kumāras as, 601, 608, 615
as less intelligent, 268
leader of, 1195
liberation for, 1126-1127, 1195
Lord misunderstood by, 725, 807-808
Lord not seen by, 615
Lord's features convert, 601, 602
Lord's kindness toward, 597
Lord thought formless by, **1328-1329**
loveless, 372
meditation of, 603, 1142, 1144-1145, 1147, 1150, 1152, 1154-1155, 1161-1162
merging desired by, 1108, 1126, 1195
mistake Lord (Supersoul) & living entity, 1220
oṁkāra worshiped by, 1147
"oneness" concept of, 1219
oneness misunderstood by, 1168
personalists stronger than, 538
"poor Nārāyaṇa" concept of, 1212
prayers of, 368
Śaṅkarācārya, 1195

Impersonalists (Māyāvādīs)
scriptures misunderstood by, 1005
see diverse creation as false, 1341-1343
see Lord as illusioned, 1036
see material life as pastime, 1034, 1035
see soul as inactive, 1178
senses "stopped" by, 270
separatist misunderstood by, 1189
silent, 958
spiritual master's position beyond, 239
spiritual suicide by, 530
Śrīmad-Bhāgavatam refutes, 423
struggle for realization, 205, 207
theory of, refuted, 589-590, 796
think themselves one with Lord, 1189
thought process of, 353
universal form for, 219, 226
worship by, 1195
worship Śiva, 530, 534
yoga polluted by, 785
See also: Atheists; Philosophers, speculative: *Jñānīs;* Māyāvādīs; Monists
Impious persons. *See:* Atheists; Demons; Impersonalists; Materialists; Māyāvādīs; Nondevotees
Impious species, 817
Incarnations of God. *See:* Supreme Lord, incarnations of
Incarnations of Godhead
demons misunderstand, 680
innumerable, 753-754
Kṛṣṇa as origin of, 718
purpose of, 678, 953
See also: Avatāra; Supreme Lord, advent of; Supreme Lord, forms of; *names of specific incarnations*
Incarnations. *See:* Supreme Lord, incarnations of; *names of individual incarnations*
Incarnation of the Supreme Lord
as Kṛṣṇa, 61
as Nara-Nārāyaṇa, 137
purpose of, 42-43, 45, 163, 164
See also: Supreme Lord, advent of
Independence
of Brahmā, 694, 695, 746-748, 925
of conditioned soul illusory, 15
conditioned soul misuses, 748
of living entity subordinate, 126
of Lord & living entities, 696
mentality of, 333
misuse of, 429
proper use of, 102, 475-476
See also: Freedom; Liberation
India
as Bhāratavarsa, 20, 696
caste system in, 1216
children worship Kṛṣṇa in, 48
civilization of, decline of, 826
dowry-custom in, 853
gypsy-trading in, 819
holy places in, 24
hospitality toward saintly persons in, 584
marriage in, 39, 789, 930
most popular *yoga* in, 607
pilgrimage places in, 735
royalty of, Kṛṣṇa conscious life of, 861
social orders degraded in, 845
son's sacrifice for father in, 11
spiritual residences in, 855-856
śrāddha ritual in, 767
temple construction in, 23
See also: Vedic culture
Indra, 1017, 1018
Indra, King, 824
direction governed by, 899
Garuḍa deferred to, 711
impudence of, 93
Kṛṣṇa defamed, 85
power of, 545
prowess of, 38
as temporary post, 612
in universal form, 232
vs. Vṛtra, 718
Indrāri-vyākularh lokam
verse quoted, 46
Industry, big, condemned, 242

Industry, big, as hellish, 335
Injunctions, Vedic. *See:* Vedic injunctions
Insanity
  ghosts induce, 766
  See also: Hallucination; Illusion; *Māyā*
Insomnia, cause of, 334
Instinct for devotional service, 48
Intellectuals. *See: Brāhmaṇas;* Philosophers, speculative
Intelligence
  in *buddhi-yoga,* 225
  compared to taste & aroma, 1113
  of demons lost, 704
  for doubting, **1055**
  fixed on Kṛṣṇa, 58
  as friend or enemy, 1285
  functions of, 1055
  for Kṛṣṇa consciousness, **1055**
  Lord as basis of, 747
  beyond mind & senses, 480
  vs. mind, 1056
  miserly, 1281
  for self-realization, 343, **1057**
  of sense enjoyer spoiled, 789
  sleep broken by, in nondevotees, 334
  soul known by, 1113
  source of, 185
  for spiritual knowledge, **999**
  for women, **999**
  of woman, 912, 921
  worship of Lord Pradyumna for, **1049**
  See also: Elements; Evolution: Knowledge; Mind
International Society for Krishna Consciousness (ISKCON), healthy faces in, 821
International Society for Krishna Consciousness (ISKCON) . *See:* Kṛṣṇa consciousness movement, invitation into, 169
Intoxication, 774, 950
  effect of, 117
  imitating Śiva by, 534
  of Yadus, 102, 103
  "*yogīs*" advocate, 604
Irreligion defined, 952
  See also: Atheists; Demons; Sinful ac- tivities
Īśāvāsyam idaṁ sarvam
  quoted, 1111
ISKCON, for association with devotees, **992**
Islands
  Earth's continents as, 776
  planets compared to, 903
Iśopaniṣad
cited on Lord's proprietorship & living entity's share, 791-792
  cited on Lord's effulgence covering His face, 488, 608
  quoted on religious principles, 336
Īśopaniṣad. See: Śrī Īśopaniṣad
Iṣṭa-goṣṭhī, 1201
Īśvara, Lord & devotee as, 1121
Īśvaraḥ paramaḥ kṛṣṇaḥ
  quoted, 44, 371, 1230, 1343
  verse quoted, 426
Īśvaraḥ sarva-bhūtānāṁ
  quoted, 604
Itara defined, 64
Iti māṁ yo 'bhijānāti
  verse quoted, 44

J

Jackals at demons' birth, 662
Jaḍa Bharata, cited on spiritual success, 835
Jagāi and Mādhāi, 988
Jagannātha, Lord, Caitanya as, 618
Jagannātha Purl, 17, 137
Jagannātha Purī, Haridāsa in, 618
Jagatera adharma nāśi' dharma sthāpite
  verse quoted, 17
Jaipur temple, 861
Jāmbavatī, 29
Janaka Mahārāja, 1148
Janayaty āśu vairāgyaṁ
  verse quoted, 197
Janmādy asya yataḥ
  quoted, 66, 396, **1026**, 1098, 1284, 1301

Janma karma ca me divyam
quoted, 1223
Japa defined, 538
Jarāsandha, 97
Jaundice victims and nondevotees, analogy of, 8
Jaya & Vijaya (gatekeepers of Vaikuṇṭha), 666, 667
angered goddess of fortune, 648
entered Diti's womb, 651
as Lord's "enemies,"645, 653
sages' confrontation with, 582-593
submissive to Kumāras' curse, 628
Jayadeva, quoted on Lord Varāha, 489-490
Jealousy. *See:* Envy
Jesus Christ, Lord, 988
Jewels
in Kardama Muni's castle, 882, 885
See also: Gold; Money; Opulence
Jīva. See: Living entities; Souls, conditioned: Soul
defined, 982
nature of, 982
Jīva Gosvāmī, cited
on Cupid, 28
on Kṛṣṇa conscious liberation, 1108
on Lord's abode, 144
on time, 384
on topics drawn from different millenniums, 482
on Uddhava & Vidura, 25
on Yadu dynasty, 102
Jīvan-mukta defined, 148
Jīvan-mukti, 1362
Jīvera 'svarūpa' haya-kṛṣṇera 'nitya-dāsa'
quoted, 1375
Jīvo jīvasya jīvanam
quoted, 1197
Jña defined, 681
Jñāna. See: Knowledge *Jñānīs. See:* Philosophers, speculative; Knowledge, spiritual
Jñāna-bhakta defined, 124
Jñāna defined, 933
Jñāna-yoga
bhakti superior to, 1339-1340
Jñāna-yoga
goal & value of, 998
goal of, Lord as, 1348
vs. other *yogas*, 1341
Jñāna-yogūy, 915
Jñāna-karmādy-anāvṛtam
quoted, 316
Jñānis
defined, 207, 942
desire oneness with Supreme, 69
devotees contrasted to, 942
as materialists, 1120
See also: Brāhmaṇas; Impersonalists: Māyāvādīs; Monists; Philosophers, speculative
Jupiter planet, 665

K

Kadrū, 711
Kaiṭabha demon, 934
Kaivalya, 1126
Kaivalya defined, 785
See also: Oneness
Kaivalyaṁ narakāyate
quoted, 1004
Kalā, 937
defined, 1042
See also: Time
Kala-cakra defined, 405, 408
Kāla defined, 382, 406
Kalā expansion, 810, 925
Kāla-śakti, 304, 305
See also: Energy, material; *Māyā*
Kalau nāsty eva nāsty eva
quoted, 780, 821, 950
Kalau śūdra-sambhavaḥ
quoted, 845
Kālayavana, 97
Kālī, goddess, 216, 1316
cheats worshipers, 915
dacoits worshiped, 704
Kāliya, 84

Kali-yuga (age of Kali)
kṛṣṇa-kathā for, 203
marriage degraded in, 39
personification of, 241
Kali-yuga (present Age)
Caitanya appears in, 638
degraded progeny in, 543
duration of, 410
meditation in, by chanting, 550
religion diminished in, 411
sacrifice for, 497
yoga process for, 607
"yogīs" in, 603
Kali-yuga (Age of Quarrel)
chanting Lord's name for, 779, 781, 950
demons & disturbances in, 666
Lord's advent in, 939
marriage in, 790, 845, 931
material enjoyment pursued in, 749
miracle waters in, 816
sannyāsa in, 950
society in, 845, 848, 950
yoga meditation impractical in, 781
See also: Modern Age; Present Age
Kāmadeva, 28, 30
Kāmais tais tair hṛta jñānāḥ
quoted, 1250, 1316
Kāma kṛṣṇa-karmārpaṇe
quoted, 1293
Kāmaṁ krodhaṁ bhayam
quoted, 649
Kāma-śāstra, cited on sex life, 881
Kaṁsa, 913
Kṛṣṇa "feared", 67, 68
Kṛṣṇa killed, 89, 90
plotted against Kṛṣṇa, 78, 83
Kaṁsa, King, 649
Kaṇāda, 397
Kandarpa-koṭi-kamanīya
verse quoted, 82
Kapila, Lord
advent of, purpose of, 943, 949, **951**
as *aṁśa* expansion, 925
Kapila, Lord
atheist imitator of, 1396
benediction from, 1359
bodily features of, 933
born from Devahūti, 1364, 1365-1366
Brahmā worshiped, 925-926, 926
compared to ax, 976
demigods at advent of, 922, 923
as Devahūti's son, 935
Devahūti's attachment to, **1383-1385**
in Devahūti's womb, 934
Devahūti to be enlightened by, 934, 956
example set by, 1376-1377
as Garbhodakaśāyī Viṣṇu, 1363
hearing of, benediction for, **1397**
incarnates for giving knowledge, 1367
as incarnation, **965,** 973
as incarnation of God, 932, 946
Kardama addresses, 943-948
Kardama instructed by, 953, **955,** 956
from Kardama's semen, 922
as Kardama's son, 848, 926, 942, 943, 945, 948
mission of, **966,** 976, 1377
narration by, 977-996, 1036-1110, **1116-1177, 1187-1359, 1375**
pastimes of, as pure & confidential, 1397-1398
planet of, 1393
praised by Devahūti, 1185, 1363-1367, 1373
praised by Śaunaka, **966**
qualities of, 1374
quoted on Devahūti, 956
quoted on His advent, 948, **951**
quoted on Kardama, 953-954, **955**
renunciation by, 1376-1377, 1396
residence of today, 1396
Sāṅkhya philosophy explained by, 810, 848, 925, 933-35, 943, **951**
as *śaraṇya*, 976
as Supreme Lord, **1016**-1019, **1373, 1383,** 1396
surrender to. *See:* Surrender to Lord
travels of, 1396
Kapila, the other, 810, 925, 934

Kāraṇa (Causal) Ocean universes in, 745, 746
See also: Garbha Ocean; Mahat-tattva
Kāraṇodakaśāyī Viṣṇu, 1075
Kāraṇodakaśāyī Viṣṇu (Mahā-Viṣṇu), 743, 746
Kardama Muni, 447-448, **969**
agreed to marry Svāyambhuva Manu's daughter, 843, **844**-845, 847, 848
appeared lustrous after austerity, 821
airplane of, 1379
as *brahmacārī*, 848, 853
Brahmā ordered, to beget children, 779
Brahmā praised, 927
as Brahmā's son, 927
compared to air moving, **901**
compared to moon, 898
compared to unpolished gem, 821
created castle in sky, 882-887, 888
as cultured, 842
daughters of, Brahmā
quoted on, 929
daughters of, marriage of, **937-938**
demigods surpassed by, 901, 902
Devahūti advised by, to bathe in Lake Bindu-sarovara, 889
Devahūti asked, for fearlessness, 909
Devahūti attracted, 897
Devahūti bewildered by palace of, 888
Devahūti blessed by, 873-875, 877, 878
Devahūti desired child by, 879, 880
Devahūti disturbed at departure of, 907
Devahūti heard about, from Nārada, 839
Devahūti impregnated by, 906
Devahūti informed by, about Lord becoming her son, 918, **919**, 920
Devahūti laments to, 909, 911
Devahūti loved by, 873
Devahūti married by, 853
Devahūti served, 869, **870**, 870-873, 874-876, 877, 897
as Devahūti's spiritual master, 920
enjoyed with Devahūti, 899, 900, 903-905
expanded into nine forms, 903-904, 906
expresses desires to Lord, 789, 790
Kardama Muni
gone back to Godhead, 964
house of, 1377, 1380-1382
leaving home, 948-949
as liberated soul, 813
Lord as realized by, 960, 963
Lord fulfilled desires of, 801
Lord in semen of, 922
Lord Kapila addressed by, 943-948
Lord Kapila instructs, 953, 955, 956
as Lord Kapila's father, 810, 848, 926, 942, 943, 945, 948
Lord moved to tears by, 816
Lord pleased by, 780, 781
as Lord's devotee, 902, 903
Lord seen by, 782-785, 786, 813, 821
Lord's prophecy to, 804-807, 809
as Lord's servant, 849, 851
meditation of, 779, 781
in mystic mansion, 898-901, 905
as mystic *yogī*, 778, 882, 895, 896, 901-**904**, 906, 907
opulences of, 1378-1382
as Prajāpati, 927
quoted on demigods, 940-941
quoted on Devahūti & transcendence, 874, 875, 877
quoted on Lord becoming Devahūti's son, 918, **919**
quoted on Lord Kapila's advent, 943
renunciation of, 957, 960-962, **963**, 964
sages married daughters of, 937-938
as *sannyāsī*, 958
spiritually powerful, 872, 879-881
Svāyambhuva Manu approached, 820
Svāyambhuva Manu gave Devahūti to, 852-854
Svāyambhuva Manu glorified by 823-827, **828**
Svāyambhuva Manu grateful to, 833-836, 836
Svāyambhuva Manu implored, to marry his daughter, 837-843
Svāyambhuva Manu offered obeisances by, 824

Kardama Muni (*continued*)
Svāyambhuva Manu received by, 821, 822
as transcendentalist, 878, 879-880, 902
Karma
See: Laws of God
compared to electric fan, 1172
defined, 3
of devotees, 44
duality due to, 195
intelligence according to, 746
karma-yoga vs., 3
Lord beyond, 45
Lord awards, 962
prosperity due to, 1101
yajñārtha-, 857
See also: Activities, material; Birth and death, repeated; Destiny; Sinful activities; Bondage; Cause and effect; Fate; Fruitive activity; Supreme Lord, will of; Transmigration
Karmīs
as materialists, 1119
See also: Materialists
Karmārpaṇam, 1190
Karmāṇi nirdahati kintu ca bhakti-bhājām
quoted, 44
Karma-yoga, 915
Karma-yoga defined, 3
Karma-yogī defined, 760
Karmīs (fruitive workers), 64
goal of, 635
See also: Materialists; Nondevotees
Karṇa, 12, 99
Karṇa-randhraiḥ defined, 836
Kārttikeya, 30
Kāśa grass, 857
Kāśī-khaṇḍa, quoted on eternality, 289
Kastūrī defined, 819
Kaśyapa, 76, 976, 1026
appeasing wife, 524-532
Diti seduced, 518-523, 518-23, 536
frailty of, 523
as impersonalist, 538
Kaśyapa
as Śiva's older brother, 531-532
sons of, 652
Kaṭha Upaniṣad, cited on Lord as leading living entity, 791
cited on Lord as transcendental, 1032
quoted on Lord as chief eternal, 1223
quoted on Lord as maintainer, 1364
Kauravas (Kurus), 7, 16, 21, 734
Kṛṣṇa's instructions ignored by, 735
Yadus vs., 845
Kaustubha gem, 1143, 1157
Kāyam defined, 465-466
Keśava dhṛta-śūkara-rūpa
verse quoted, 489
Keśī demon, 718
Kibā vipra, kibā nyāsī, śūdra kene naya
verse quoted, 239
Killing of cows condemned, 81, 115, 237
King(s)
false pride of, 42
Kṛṣṇa as king of, 10
as Lord's representative, 105
See also: Government; *Kṣatriyas*; Leaders, government; *Varṇāśrama-dharma*; *names of specific kings*
Kingdom of God. *See:* Spiritual world; Vṛndāvana
Khyāti, 937
Kidnapping, marriage by, 844, 845, 846
Killing
of *brāhmaṇa*, absolution for, 730, 731
by *kṣatriya* kings, 823
by Lord liberates, 682
See also: Death; War
Kimpuruṣas, 769
King(s)
citizens welcoming back, 856
devotees as, 775
duty of, 826
killing by, 823
as Lord's representative, 824
protection by, 823, 826

King(s)
sage's relationship to, 828
in *Śrīmad-Bhāgavatam*, 776-77
See also: *Kṣatriyas*; Leaders, government; *names of specific kings*
Kinnaras, 769
Kīrtana defined, 538
Kīrtana. See: Devotional service, of chanting...
Kīrtanīyaḥ sadā hariḥ
quoted, 1139
Kliśyanti ye kevala-bodha-labdhaye
quoted, 1115
Knowledge
about Absolute Truth, levels of, 1217
animal's level of, 391
via authority, 741
in Brahmā, 429-430, 557
to Brahmā from within, 1060
of *brāhmaṇas* & Vaiṣṇavas, 1217
demigods in, 758
by devotional service, 1204-1205, 1336-1337, 1346, 1351, 1352
devotional service as goal of, 1182
devotional service requires, 1118-1119
in disciplic succession, 1060
via disciplic succession, 726, 933
by hearing, 1343
Kṛṣṇa consciousness as, 934
of Kṛṣṇa as proprietor, enjoyer & friend 1096
about Lord
compared to tasting milk, 1349
by devotional service only, 1204-1205, 1349
levels of, 1217
liberation by, 1223
by scriptures, 1341-1343
as Supersoul, 1205-1207
as *Vedas'* purpose, 1217
liberation by, 798
material affection destroyed by, 919-920
material, as defective, 1060
by modes of nature, 966
from senses, as imperfect, 1341
of spirit & matter, 1103
Knowledge
spiritual
advantages of, 1058-1059, 1060, 1344
advantages of, for detachment, 983-984, 1118-1119
advantages of, for devotional service, 1118-1119
advantages of, for liberation, 977, 1223, 1279-1280
advantages of, for self-realization, 983-984, 1025
detachment needed for, 1088-1089
by devotees' association, 993-994
by devotional service, 985, 1019
as eternal, 1012
from faith, 1019
intelligence helpful for, 999
vs. material, 1060
necessity of. *See:* Knowledge, spiritual, advantages of
of real identity, 1168-1173
sādhus give, 987
Sāṅkhya as, 1024-1026
sources of, three named, 1133
from spiritual master, 972, 999
from spiritual master, 974, 999, 1060, 1133, 1359
via spiritual master, 927
time covers, 952
of transmigration, 1183
of true identity, 1110-1111
by worshiping Lord, 773
See also: Absolute Truth
Knowledge, speculative
bondage by, 446
devotion surpasses, 197, 269
frustration in, 206
as hellish path, 327-328
illusory energy causes, 323
Lord beyond, 189, 226, 309, 506, 640
love of God beyond, 124
origin of, 189
pure devotees beyond, 130

Knowledge, speculative (*continued*)
result of, 69
service attitude surpasses, 242-244
sleeplessness by, 334
transcendental knowledge beyond, 140
See also: Māyāvādīs; Monists; Impersonalists; Philosophers, speculative; Scientists, material
Knowledge, spiritual (about God)
advancement of, 315
based on affection for God, 372
bewilderment inspires, in pure devotees, 366
beyond erudition, 56
beyond goodness, 148
beyond material conceptions, 366, 506, 507
beyond material qualifications, 368
beyond material senses, 367
blindness no hindrance to, 5
competent teacher for, 376
as complex, 273
defined, 106
via Deity, 147
for devotees only, 361
devotees impart, 139-140
by devotional service, 147, 158, 159, 310, 312, 313, 326
as dictated from within & without, 358, 606
difficulties as favorable to, 2
via disciplic succession, 140
from effulgence to personal feature, 609, 610
by eyes tinged with love, 367
via faith & devotion, 608
by following authorities, 640
by hearing, 206, 230
via husband-wife team, 524
literature for reviving, 167, 170
via Lord's lotus feet, 199-200
by Lord's mercy, 610-611
by love & devotion, 145
milk needed for, 163
by penance, 324
perfected by chanting holy names, 579
by pilgrimage, 19-20, 137
Knowledge, spiritual (about God)
via pure devotees, 443
qualification for, 134, 157
by Sāṅkhya philosophy, 284
as seeing Lord everywhere, 362
by sincerity, 338, 510
by speculative process, 69
via spiritual master, 288, 290, 291
as spiritual society's goal, 525
by submissiveness, 189, 226
three types of, 147
in *Vedas*, 456
via Vedic literature, 199
See also: Absolute Truth; Vedic knowledge
Koran, 1333
Krishna. *See:* Kṛṣṇa *Kṛpaṇa* defined, 1280-1281
Krishna. *See:* Kṛṣṇa, Lord Kriyā, 937
Kṛkara air, 224
Krodha defined, 435
Kṛsaṇa defined, 242
Kṛṣṇa, Lord
abode of. See: Spiritual world; Vaikuṇṭha
as absolute, 1012
as *ādi-puruṣa*, 1075
chanting about. See: Devotional service, of chanting
color of, 1142
compared to king, 1012
desire of, Arjuna accepted, 1168
devotees of. *See:* Devotees
disciplic succession from, 1060, 1201
See also: Spiritual master
as equal to all, 1017
everywhere as reflection, 1105-1106
expansions of, examples of, 1323
eye of, sun as, 1078
food offered to. *See: Prasāda* foods offerable to, 1197-1198
form of, 1070
form of, known from scriptures, 1343
as friend of all, 1096
knowledge about. *See:* Knowledge, about Lord; Knowledge, spiritual

Kṛṣṇa, Lord
love for. *See:* Love for God
as Madana-mohana, 1300
as original form of Lord, 1133
pastimes of, as worshipable, 1005
pastimes of, examples of, 1135
prescribed duties for satisfying, 1116-1117
as proprietor, enjoyer & friend, 1122
quotations from. *See: Bhagavad-gītā,* quotations from
reflected in material world, 1105, 1106
relationships with
as eternal, 1011-1013
as friend, 1011, 1012
kinds of, 1012
in Lord's family, 1238-1239
as son, 1011, 1012
seen everywhere by devotee, 1104
service to. *See:* Devotional service
as spiritual master, 1012
as supreme controller, 1230
as Supreme Personality of Godhead, 1027
surrender to. *See:* Surrender
as transcendental, 1195
viṣṇu-tattva included in, 1323
See also: Supreme Lord
Kṛṣṇa, Lord (*specific references only*)
See also: Supreme Lord
absolute nature of, 171
acted in exemplary way, 640
activities of. *See:* Kṛṣṇa, pastimes of
advent of
compared to sunrise, 54
by devotee's request, 77
eternal, 151
purpose of, 59
superexcellence of, 61
transcendental, 152
See also: Incarnation; Supreme Lord, advent of
in *arcā* (Deity) form, 18, 220
appearances of, purpose of, 622
Arjuna and, 7, 8, 837, 945, 952
Kṛṣṇa, Lord (*specific references only*)
association with, 16-17, 913
atheist's opinion of, 58
Balarāma expands from, 26
beauty of, 61, 62, 71, 82, 107
beyond reactions to work, 58
beyond Superself, 480
as blissful, 24, 107
body of, nonmaterial, 932
Brahmā's realization of, 316
bulls subdued by, 92
Caitanya as, 639, 939
as *cakrī,* 23
castles constructed by, 884
as child, 75, 78, 80-81
children of, 97
compared to covered flame, 78
compared to dramatic actor, 344
compared to lion cub, 80, 81
compared to moon, 109
compared to playful father, 66
as cowherd boy, 79, 81
Cupid and, 28
demigods under, 85
demons killed by, 81, 83
as detached, 107, 109
disappearance of, 54, 58, 60, 77
dolls of, children worship, 48
Dvārakā's citizens welcoming back, 856
Draupadī protected by, 42
in Dvārakā, 34, 106
enemies of, 69
envy toward, 10, 11
eternity, bliss & knowledge in, 426
expansions of, 101-102
expansions of, in Vaikuṇṭha, 581
family of, 100, 101-102, 117-118
"fearful," 66, 67, 69
female consorts of, 108
flute sound of, 81
fool's consideration of, 932
footprints of, 32
forgetting about, as worst misery, 551

Kṛṣṇa, Lord (*specific references only*) (*continued*)
form(s) of, **59**, 60, 75, 83
as friend of distressed, 95
as God, 54-57, 65, 72-75
gopīs attracted to, **86**
gopīs' minds disturbed by, 908
gopīs lusty for, 649
grandson of, kidnapped Duryodhana's daughter, 845
as grateful master, 90
in Hare Kṛṣṇa *mantra*, 487
hearing about, 167, 169, 170
as highest object of meditation, 603-604
as householder, 109
in human role, 61, 74
incarnations come from, 718
Indra attacked, 93
internal potencies of, 108-109
Kaṁsa vs., 68, 83, 89
Kauravas ignored instructions of, 735
as Keśava, 489
kindness of, 75, 76
as king of kings, 10
knowledge about. *See:* Knowledge, spiritual
in Kurukṣetra war, fools criticize, 516
Kurus as tolerated by, 42
land traversed by, 24
as Lord of threes, 72-73
lotus feet of, **69**
love for
eyes smeared with, 615
in *gopīs*, 63, 124
Kṛṣṇa's beauty awakens, 70-72
in separation, **134**, 135, 136
in Vasudeva, 67-68
in Vṛndāvana, 56, 81
See: Devotional service; Kṛṣṇa consciousness; Supreme Lord, love for
as Madana-mohana & Madana-dāha, 600
married Nāgnajitī, 92
married princesses, 95, 96
meditation on. *See:* Meditation on Kṛṣṇa
mercy of, 61, 69, 75, 76

Kṛṣṇa, Lord (*specific references only*)
merging with, 69
mission of, on earth, 43, 345
as misunderstood, 41, 55, 65
mother of, Devakī as, 33
mother of, Pūtanā as, 75
name of, as Kṛṣṇa Himself, 950
name of, chanting of. *See:* Chanting of the Supreme Lord's holy names
as Nanda's son, 926
Narakāsura killed by, 94
Nārāyaṇa surpassed by, 61
omniscient, 131, 132
opulences of, 61, 73
as original cause, 426
as original form of God, 944
Pāṇḍavas and, 2, 10
"parents" of, 68, 81
pastime (s) of
Brahmā witnessed, 362
bewildering, **130**, **131**, **132**
"contradictory," 66-68, 73, 130
eternal, 54, 122-123
at Govardhana Hill, **85**, **86**
in human role, 74
with Kāliya, **84**
perfect, 66
purpose of, 59
summarized, 77-86
transcendental, 110
in two-handed form, 61
as Vasudeva's son, 67-68
as peace messenger, 8
playful, 66, 68
protecting cows & *brāhmaṇas*, 641
protecting surrendered souls, 622
prowess of, 10, 70, 83
purusas accompany, 65
quoted on surrender to Himself, 634
Rādhārāṇī's beauty vs., 600
as Ranchor, 97
in *rāsa* dance, 343
relating everything to. *See:* Kṛṣṇa consciousness

Kṛṣṇa, Lord (*specific references only*)
relationship with, as friend, 79
relationship with, as parent, 78, 81
remembrance of, 24
Rukmṇī kidnapped by, 845
Rukminī rescued by, 91
as Sāndipani Muni's student, **90,** 291
Saṣkarācārya accepted, 135
search for, 24, 151
seeing, face to face, 24-25
senses of, 110
separation from, 55
service for satisfying, 480
as shelter, 75-76, 121
sincere soul helped by, 736
Śiśupāla killed by, 70
Śiva worships, 534
as Soul of self, **34**
speeches by, **7,** 8
spiritual dictation from, 606
spiritual form of, 410
spiritual master knows, 239-240
in submissive role, 622
subordinate role of, 73
superexcellence of, 61, 62
as Supreme Lord, 696, 718, 925-926
as Supersoul, 57
surrender to, 73
surrender to, salvation by, 666
as Syāmasundara, 41
as teacher, 84
as tolerant, **42**
topics about. *See: Kṛṣṇa-kathā*
Uddhava and, 25, 48-51
Vasudeva and, 27, 78
Vidura devoted to, 734, 735
Viṣṇu forms amalgamate in, 146
Vṛndāvana and, 2, 34, 56, 78, 80
wheel symbol of, 23
wives of, 93, 95
worshipable by all, **72,** 73
Yadus misunderstood, 54, 55, **56**
See also: Rādhā-Kṛṣṇa: Supreme Lord

Kṛṣṇa consciousness. *See:* Devotional service; Knowledge, spiritual; God consciousness
activities in, 738, 806-807
advantages of, **1020, 1261,** 1297, 1336, 1389
detachment, 1097, 1341
God realization, **995-996,** 1104, **1166-1167, 1204-1205,** 1326, **1336-1337,** 1340
liberation, 977, 979, 987, 1305, 1323, 1335, 1385
purification, 1117-1118, 1120, 1321, 1388
relief from suffering, 977, **993,** 1286
for all, 1306
children trained in, 848
as clear consciousness, **1049**
compared to sensing an aroma, **1204-1205**
conditioned souls advancing in, 862
consciousness purified by, 1082
different duties in, 836-837
defined, 603, 605-606
detachment in, 1118
dovetailing in, 737
duty to spread, 809
eligible and ineligible candidates for, **1355-1358**
eternal life by, 953
ever fresh, 863
falldown from, 1051
freedom by, 958, 959
as greatest gift, 878
happiness by, 684, 772
as hearing Kṛṣṇa's name, 1138
householder in, 907
of Indian royalty, 861
as independent of material position, 1101, **1286**
intelligence for, 1055
as knowledge, 934
liberation by. See: Liberation
vs. māyā consciousness, 980
Lord's form revealed in, 784
material enjoyment surpassed by, 862
materialists can't achieve, 773
mind controlled by, 1020, 1053, 1097

Kṛṣṇa consciousness
misery stopped by, 858, 866
mission of, 858
as mystic power, 995
nature's modes surpassed by, 864, 960
necessity of. See: Kṛṣṇa consciousness, advantages of as nonsectarian, 1356
oneness in, 1326
as panacea, 551
perfection of, 537, 860-862
perfection in one life by, 996
persons in. *See:* Devotees
preachers of. See: Devotional service, of preaching
protects from hellish birth, 1260
as pure & original consciousness, 1032
qualities gained in, 1298
in renounced orders, 1377
sacrifices in, 723
salvation by, 666
as self-realization, 1104
self-realization by, 1344
science of, 810-812
in society832, 860
Society for, 992
as spontaneous service platform, 1169
super excellence of, 878
as transcendental, 979-983
time transcended by, 793
as universal, 1356
as *vāsudeva* expansion, 1048
wealth to be used for, 1257
as welfare work for all, 767
for women, 1305-1306
worship of Vāsudeva for, 1047
as *yoga's* perfection, 1303
yogī in, 780
See also: Devotional service
Kṛṣṇa consciousness movement (ISKCON), healthy faces in, 821
Kṛṣṇa consciousness movement, invitation into, 169
harmony in, formula for, 590-591
prohibitions in, 639
society's progeny saved by, 542-543
Kṛṣṇa-dvaipāyana Vyāsa. *See:* Vyāsadeva
Kṛṣṇa-kathā (topics about Kṛṣṇa)
as absolute and transcendental, 167, 171
as essential, 174
"I-and-mine" concept dispelled by, 203
purifying power of, 167-168
See also: Supreme Lord, glories of; Supreme Lord, hearing about
Kṛṣṇaloka, 1194
devotees elevated to, 1126-1127
family life in, 1238
Kṛṣṇaloka, Rādhā & Kṛṣṇa in, 600, 602
Kṛṣṇaloka (Goloka Vṛndāvana), 683, 712, 725, 803
See also: Spiritual world; Supreme Lord, abode of; Vṛndāvana
Kṛṣṇa-prema defined, 877
See also: Supreme Lord, love for
Kṛṣṇa Society, 992
Kṣatram defined, 828
Kṛṣṇa-sandarbha, cited
on Cupid, 28
on Lord's disappearance, 145
Kṛṣṇas tu bhagavān svayam quoted, 65
Kṣatriyas (soldiers & statesmen)
brāhmaṇa's relationship to, 828, 831, 832
chivalry of, 10
compared to whole body, 832
as created from Lord's arms, 830, 831
defined, 458
duties & service for, 1197
duty of, 823
kidnap-marriage by, 845
killing by, 823
marriage of, 13
marrying *brāhmaṇa*, 805
present-day, 845
quality & duty of, 7, 240, 241, 242
as twice-born, 640
See also: Government; King(s); Leaders, government; *Varṇāśrama-dharma*
Kṣetra-jña defined, 832, 1048
Ksetrajña-śakti defined, 260

Ksetrī defined, 242
Kṣetra jñaṁ cāpi māṁ viddhi
quoted, 1345
Kṣīrodakaśāyī Viṣṇu, 743, 746, 754
See also: Supersoul
Ksipāmy ajasram aśubhān
verse quoted, 195
Kṣīrodakaśāyī Visnu, 1075
Kṣīrodakaśāyī Viṣṇu. *See:* Supersoul
Kumāras, 300
Kumāras, the four, 936
Deities attracted, 1008
anger of, 585-586
Brahmā's narration about, 563, 580-596
childlike innocence of, 584
converted to personalists, 609
disobedient, 476
as impersonalists, 601, 609
Lord petitioning, 628
Lord seen by, 595
Lord's mercy on, 618
Lord's speech bewildered, 631, 633
mystic travel by, 580, 581
as oldest beings, 584-585
origin of, 430
rejected family life, 430-431
repentance by, 612-613, 633
at Vaikuṇṭha's entrance, 650
Kuntī, Queen (Pṛthā)
sons of, 10, 38, 39
as Vasudeva's sister, 27
Kūrma air, 224
Kurukṣetra, 802
Kurukṣetra, Battle of, 7, 35
cause of, 622
devotee as glorified by, 43, 97
history of, purpose of, 167
soldiers at, 70, 72
spiritual effect of, 516
Kurukṣetra war
Arjuna disturbed during, 658
Kauravas lost, 735
Kṛṣṇa returning to Dvārakā after, 856
Kurus (Kauravas), 7, 16, 42
Kṛṣṇa's instructions ignored by, 735
Yadus vs., 845
Kuryāt defined, 372
Kuśa grass, 857
Kuśāvarta (Hardwar), 734, 735, 736
Kuvera, 899

L

Ladies. *See:* Women
Lake Bindu-sarovara, 812, **814**, **816-819**, **889**
Laksmīdevī, 250
Lakṣmī, 944
as Brahmā's "mother", 1153, 1156
meditation on, 1153
with Visnu, 1157
Lakṣmī. *See:* Goddess of fortune
Lakṣmī-Nārāyaṇa, 753, 754
Lakṣmī-sahasra-śata-sambhrama-sevyamānam
quoted, 109, 572-573, 597
Lava-mātra sādhu-saṅge sarva-siddhi haya
quoted, 986
Lawbook for human beings, 479
Laws
of God, 99
of nature, 105, 157
See also: Fate; *Karma;* Supreme Lord, will of
Laws of God
harmony with, as religion, 590
living beings under, 333
unbreakable, 561
Laws of nature. *See:* Nature, material, laws of
Leaders, government
food shortage due to, 161
godless, 42
in present Age, 823, 827
rise & fall of, 670
See also: Government; King(s); *Kṣatriyas;* Politics
Leprosy, offense compared to, 621
Liberation
anger after, 586-587
for animals, 1094

Liberation (*continued*)
austerity & penance don't give, 1016
beyond modes of nature, 148-149
by *bhakti-yoga* only, 998
from bodily identification, detailed, 1168-1172
of Brahmā, 1324, 1325
Brahman bliss follows, 30
to *brahmajyoti*, 1004
by Brahmā's liberation, 1325
by chanting Hare Kṛṣṇa, 1003
chaste wife facilitates, 524
by chanting Lord's holy names, 863
children trained for, 848
compared to maidservant, 1002-1003
of conditioned souls, 734
as constitutional position, 1375
creation facilitates, 101, 105, 218
by Deity worship, **1007-1009**
of demons killed by Lord, 553
demigod worship can't give, 1330
desire for, value of, 977
detachment required for, 991
Devahūti's questions on, 1112-1115
of devotees, 207
of devotee's ancestors, 767
of devotees & demons compared, 76
for devotees, vs. for impersonalists, 1126-1127
for devotees as eternal, 1126-1127
devotees desireless of, **1013-1015**, **1191-1194**
by devotional service, 156, 207, 269, 364, 813, 960, 1019-1020, 1092, 1095, 1097, 1116-1118, 1311-1312, 1375-1377, 1385
devotional service as, 1092, 1107, **1116-1118**, 1311-1312
devotional service includes, 1002
by devotional service only, 998, 1016-1018, 1099, 1114, 1185, 1308, 1321, 1335, 1376
devotional service surpasses, 865, **1003-1005**
by devotional service to Lord's devotees, 986-987
as difficult, 1114
for enemies of Kṛṣṇa, 70-72
exclusive path toward, 337

Liberation
as freedom from false ego, 1111
of forefathers, 767
from false ego, 189
by hearing & chanting, **1116-1118**
by hearing from Lord, **1007-1009**
by hearing of Kapila & Devahūti, 1398
highest, 998
imperceptibly attained, 1007-1009
imperceptibly attained by devotee, 1013-1015
impersonal, devotional service required for, 1339
for impersonalists, vs. devotees, 1195
Kapila's benediction for, **1359**
five kinds of, 611
kinds of, five described, **1193-1194**
kinds of, five listed, 1003
by hearing Lord's war pastimes, 516
of *jñānīs* & devotees compared, 364
by knowing Kṛṣṇa, 70-72, 251-252
by knowledge from spiritual master, 971
by knowing Lord's activities, 926
by knowing soul & Supersoul, 224
by knowledge & devotion, 127, 269
by Kṛṣṇa consciousness, 986, 1223
by *kṛṣṇa-kathā*, 168, 169
by Kṛṣṇa only, 1328
Lord arranges, 1015
Lord desires for all, 1282
by Lord's association, 913
Lord's grace needed for, 635
by Lord's mercy, 1278, 1354-1355
materialists desire, 612
from material bondage, 792
for materially disgusted, 798
by meditating on Lord's form, 720, 721
by merging with the Lord, 69
from modes of nature, 1091, 1092, 1140
as natural condition, 1275-1276
nirvāṇa, 1393
in one life through Kṛṣṇa consciousness, 996
of oneness in identity with Lord, 1004
as parent's duty to children, 521

Liberation
personal vs. impersonal, 71, 129
presumption of, by nondevotees, 1016
qualifications for, 578
real, vs. false, 1114
via saintly person, 834, 913
by *samādhi*, 1391
by Sāṅkhya philosophy, 1023-1024, 1362
by seeing Lord's lotus feet, 1151
by serving Lord, 187
by serving *mahātmās*, 277
son facilitates, 11
to spiritual planet of devotee's desire, 1126
to spiritual world as eternal, 1334
by surrender, 1016, 1017, 1019
symptoms of, **1166-1172**
true & false, 196
via Vṛndāvana, 80
by *yoga*, 430
See also: Freedom; Independence; Purification; Oneness
Life
airs of, 222, 223
animal vs. human, 106
creation of, 1046
debts in, 850
duration of, **418**, 419
early training in, 459
essence of, 174
eternal. See: Eternal life
everywhere, 1176
goal of. *See*: Goal of life
by going back to Godhead, 964
via good marriage, 524-526
human body facilitates, 576
as love of God, 877
via saintly person, 833, 834
seeing Lord's form as, 785, 786
spiritual society oriented toward, 458
as surrender to God, 792, 793
See also: Perfection: Spiritual world
human. *See*: Human beings
from life, not matter, 1073
Life
purpose of, 520, 723
soul causes, 1176
span of
as destined, 669
of devotees timeless, 795, 863-864
of Manu, 863, 865
in Satya-yuga, 782
for *yoga* perfection, 779-781
species of. *See*: Species of life
spiritual master's order as, 928
in Vedic culture, 848-879, 860-861
See also: Life, material; Living entities; Soul
for spiritual life, 576
See also: Consciousness: Human beings; Human beings; Living entities; Material life; Soul; Spiritual life
Life, material
activities of, 658, 793, 794
compared to disease, 761
compared to forest fire, 793-794
demons promote, 666-668, 671
as fearful, 909
freedom from, 793, 794
laws of, 670
as sense gratification, 841
as sex life, 748, 752
spiritual life vs., 761
transmigration perpetuates, 793
See also: Birth and death, repeated; Bondage, material; Materialists; Material world
Life-span on heavenly planets, 1010
Light, Lord as source of, 1027
Light, origin of, **191**
Light of the universe, 556
See also: Brahman effulgence
Līlā defined, 1033, 1034-1035
Literature
material & spiritual, 509, 511
glorifying the Lord, 249
mundane & spiritual, 164-165, 167, 170-171
for pure devotees, 292

Literature (*continued*)
See also: Vedic literatures; *names of specific Vedic literatures*
Living entities
ability of, material & spiritual, 368
anger of, cause of, 435
animosity among, 549
annihilation of, through others by Supersoul, 1225
atomic to universal, 382
attachment natural to, 986-987
awakening of, by Supersoul, 1088
birth of, 177, 184-185, 211, 221
birth of, from semen, 652
birth of, vs. Lord's advent, 922
bondage of, 261
as Brahman, 966, 1016
Brahmā as chief of, 349
as brothers, 1271
changeless position for, 1091-1092
classes of, 166
classes of, demons & devotees, 1160
compared to mango & *nimba* trees, 195
compared to moon's reflections, 267-268
compared to poor man, 1220
compared to sparks of fire, 1174-1175
compared to sun's rays, 982
compared to sparks & sunrays, 265
composition of, 223
consciousness in, 204, 221-222
consciousness of. *See:* Consciousness
controlled by demigods, 1011
constitutional position of, 158, 187, 189, 209, 218, 266, 333-334, 338, 364, 428
covered by illusory energy, 1029
creation of, 1046
crossbreeding of, 284
defenseless, five listed, 627
defects of, four named, 1060
defined, 223
demigods control, 194, 195
dependence of, 41, 110
as dependent, 791
Living entities
dependent on the Lord, 333-334, 360
discrimination between, condemned, 1211
discrimination between, proper, 1214
desires of, 218, 219
desires of. *See:* Desire at dissolution of universe, 415
at dissolution of universe, 304
divine vs. demoniac, 698
divisions of species of, four named, 1176
as dormant devotees, 48
dormant within Lord, 181, 182
duty of, 73
enemies of, 591-592
as enjoyer falsely, 1095
equality of, 362
equality with, 1199
equal treatment for, 1211-1214
eternal, 563, 1310
eternal engagement of, 953
as eternally active, 247-248
eternal necessities of, 1185
as everywhere, 1176
fall of, plan behind, 645
false ego of, 186, 188, 189
as false *purusas*, 241
fate of, cause of, 218
fear death, 428
as food, 1197
food supply for, 115
forgetfulness in, 224, 260
forget their identity, 428, 429
form of, subtle, 1061
as friend limitedly, 1096
frustration of, 266
good qualities attainable by, 577-578
greatest misery of, 551
happiness of, 59
in harmony or disharmony, 589, 591
on higher planets, 505
human form of, value of, 576
ignorant of self-interest, 1184
illusioned. *See:* Illusion

Living entities
independence of, 126, 186, 212, 213, 341, 429, 475-476, 696, 748, 1278, 1344
as individual, 1108, 1170
as individual eternally, 1110-1111
kindness toward, 577, 578
Kṛṣṇa conscious. *See:* Devotees levels of, detailed, 1212-1218
levels of, related to senses, 1212-1216
levels of, satisfaction in any of, 1236
as liberated normally, 1276
liberation for. *See:* Liberation
vs. Lord, 967, 976, 1012, 1025, 1035, 1036, 1044, 1089, 1095, 1121, 1174-1175, 1177, 1205, 1220, 1274, 1275-1276, 1283, 1322, 1345
life durations of, 407, 418-419
livelihood of, 242
Lord affectionate to, 353-354
Lord appears within species of, 350
Lord as leader of, 791, 932
Lord assists, from within, 368
Lord contrasted to, 903, 922, 932, 960
Lord contrasted to. *See:* Supreme Lord, living entities contrasted to
Lord empowers, 213
Lord encompasses, 361
Lord in heart of, 746, 756-757
Lord maintains, 946
and Lord, oneness of, 982, 1025
Lord equal to, 1226
Lord present in each, 1207
Lord provides for & preaches to, 797
Lord's compassion on, 182
Lord sees, 271
Lord's expansions, 162, 212
as Lord's parts, 371-372
as Lord's parts & parcels, 181, 723, 746, 748, 809
as Lord's potency, 260, 264, 265
Lord's qualities shared by, 622
Lord sustains, 161
Lord within, 126
Lord within hearts of, 472

Living entities
maintained by Lord, 1365
as marginal energy, 879
in material world, 212-213, 866
memory source for, 126
marginal nature of, 1044, 1051, 1275-1276
merged in matter, 1108
milk essential for, 163
miseries of, 197
by modes of nature, 166
mountains as, 486
nature maintains, 101
oldest among, **584**
as one with & different from Lord, 1174
original attachment of, 339
as part & parcel of Lord, 1284
pious, 665
pious, serve the Lord, 59
planets for, 1229
planetary accomodations for, 359
planetary systems for, 236, 237
pleasure of, 110
population of, 161, 177
as predominated, 273, 357
procreation of, 468
as *puruṣa*, 1220
rebellious, 266
reflect Lord's qualities, 381
relationships among, 622
respected by devotees, 1220
residences of, 52, 165
satisfied anywhere, 1256, 1236
scriptures guiding, 99
in seedling form, 380
self-interest of, 480
as servants, 211, 242-245, 290
as servant of Lord, 1107-1108, 1110, 1219, 1274-1275, 1320-1322, 1353-1354
as servant of Lord eternally, 1109, 1375
service attitude in, 364
sinful, punishments for, 1253, 1254
as sleeping, 1185
soul & Supersoul in all, 1205-1206, 1211

Living entities (*continued*)
as soul combined with matter, 1112
soul of. *See:* Soul, conditioned
as soul or not body, 973-974, 977, 982, 985, 1031, 1034, 1042, 1046, 1112, 1170-1173, 1177, 1388
soul within, as affection's object, 371
speak in Lord's service, 613
species of, cause of, 381
species & divisions of, 1176
as spirit souls, 509
as spiritual, 184, 185, 268, 1046
spiritual forms of, 567
spiritual literature for, 509, 511
spiritual revival of, 772
stonelike, 1213
struggle for existence, 379
subtle bodies of, 304
success secret for, 371
sufferings of. *See:* Suffering vs. Supersoul, 1220
sun's effect on, **407**
temporary life for, 1231
as transcendental, **1095**
as tricolored, 1032
types of, **281**
unconscious stage of, 218
vision in, 204
universe arranged for, 428
Vedas regulate, 561
witnessed by Supersoul, 1044
worship of them, 1212, 1213
Yamarāja judges, 178, 179
See also: Material life; Soul, conditioned; *names of individual kinds and groups of* Lord, Supreme: Animals; Human beings; Soul; Souls, conditioned
Lord Caitanya. *See:* Caitanya Mahāprabhu
Lord in the heart. *See:* Supersoul
Lord, the. *See:* Kṛṣṇa, Lord; Supreme Lord
Lotus feet of the Lord. *See:* Supreme Lord, lotus feet of
Lotus flower from Garbhodakaśāyī Viṣṇu, 746
Lotus flower(s)
beauty of, 199
Brahmā's view from, 378-380
earth planet compared to, 501
Kṛṣṇa's beauty vs., 62
from Lord's abdomen, **306,** 307
Viṣṇu holds, 23
"Love feast," cannibalistic, 750, 751
Love
for God. *See:* Supreme Lord, love for
between Lord & living beings, 353
eternal, vs. temporary, 1012
vs. lust, 1293
material, as false, 1239-1240
in material world absent, 526
as pleasurable burden, 101
service based on, 364
true & false, 371-372
in Vṛndāvana, 63
See also: Affection; Devotional service; Supreme Lord, love for; Supreme Lord, relationships with
Love for God, 1125, 1148, 1166
in *bhakti-yoga,* 1220
in Deity worship required, 1209
elevation by, 1335
as Kṛṣṇa, 1098, 1104
See also: *Bhakti-yoga;* Devotional service
Lust. *See:* Attachment, material; Desires, material; Sense gratification; Sex life
causes anger, 435
as enemy, 592
immunity from, 450
vs. love, 1293
in mode of passion, 1293
origin of, 446
purification of, 1293
See also: Attachment

M

Madana-mohana, 1300
Mad-bhaktiṁ labhate parām quoted, 1178-1179

Madhu demon, 922
Mādhurya-rasa defined, 364
Mādrī, 38
Magic. *See:* Mystic power
Mahābhārata, purpose of, 167, 170, 283
cited on Gāndhārī & Dhṛtarāṣṭra, 873
sacred, 729
Mahābhāva defined, 550
Mahājano yena gataḥ sa panthāḥ
quoted, 640, 950
Mahā-mantra. See: Devotional service, of chanting Hare Kṛṣṇa; Supreme Lord, names of: Hare Kṛṣṇa *mantra*
Mahāntaṁ vibhum ātmānam
quoted, 65
Mahā-moha defined, 749
Mahā-mohas tu vijñeyo
verse quoted, 749
Mahā-prasāda defined, 532
Mahārāja Parīkṣit. *See:* Parīkṣit Mahārāja
Mahārājas. *See: individual names*
Mahārāja Yudhiṣṭhira. *See:* Yudhiṣṭhira Mahārāja
Mahat defined, 835
Mahātmānas tu māṁ pārtha
verse quoted, 250
Mahātmās defined, 251, 277, 608
Kṛṣṇa consciousness makes one, 1057
material energy can't control, 879
spiritual success via, 835
See also: Ācāryas; Devotees, pure devotees; Saintly persons; Spiritual master
Mahat-pāda-rajo-'bhiṣekam
quoted, 835
Mahat-sevāṁ dvāram āhur vimuktes
quoted, 987
Mahat-tattva, 744, 1036, 1047-1049, 1051, 1344
Mahat-tattva, creation of, 386
material nature entered by, 1073
See also: *Pradhāna*
Mahat-tattva defined, 186, 187
Mahā-Viṣṇu (Kāranārnavaśāyī Viṣṇu), 34, 184, 289, 743, 746
breathing of, 422, 426
Mahā-Viṣṇu (Kāranārnavaśāyī Viṣṇu)
See also: Purusa-avatāras: Garbhodakaśāyī Viṣṇu; Supersoul
Mahā-yogī defined, 778
Maheśvara. *See:* Śiva, Lord
Maitreya Muni
as *bhagavān*, 969
narration by, 970-1398
Maitreya Ṛṣi
as authority, 741
Bhāgavatam narrated by, 303
met the Lord accidentally, 123, 124
as mixed devotee, 124
Hiraṇyākṣa-Lord Boar narration by, via spiritual master, 726
qualification of, 141, 175
Quoted
on Brahmā, 935
on Brahmā allaying demigods' fear, 657
on Brahmā & Lord, 703
on Brahmā & Lord Kapila, 925
on Creation's cause, 743
on Devahūti & Kardama, 869
on Devahūti worshiping Lord, 920
on God, Garuḍa, & sage Kardama, 799
on Hiraṇyākṣa & Lord, 679, 691
on Kardama & Kapila, 957
on Kardama & Lord, 802-803
on Kardama & Svāyambhuva Manu, 829
on Kardama's creating aerial mansion, 882
on Kardama's meditation, 779
on Lord Boar & Hiraṇyākṣa, 724, 726
Vidura heard from, about Lord, 727
Vidura met, at Hardwar, 734, 736
Vidura's meeting with, cause for, 2
Vidura's questions to, 155-174
Mahīdhraḥ defined, 489
Mahīyasāṁ pāda-rajo-'bhiṣekaṁ
verse quoted, 347
Mala-māsa defined, 795
Mala-snāna defined, 893
Male
birth of, 881

Male (*continued*)
discharge of, during sex, 907
female attracted to, 919-920
See also: Father; Husband; Man; Son
Mamaivāṁśo jīva-loke
quoted, 1177
Mām defined, 955
Mamaivāṁśo jīva-loke
quoted, 371
Mama yonir mahad-brahma
quoted, 184
Mām eva ye prapadyante
quoted, 1114, 1277, 1285
verse quoted, 267
Mām upetya tu kaunteya
quoted, 1334
Man
woman combined with, 930, 931
woman contrasted to, 871
woman's sex desire exceeds, 904
See also: Father; Husband; Male; Son
Man comes from *Manu*, 858
Mandara Hill, 1159
Man-eaters (Rākṣasas), 749-750, 751
Maṅgala defined, 803
Maṅgalārātrika ceremony, 861
Man & woman, origin of, 466
Mankind. *See:* Human beings; Society, human
Māndavya Muni, 178
Manigrīva, 204
Man-manā bhava mad-bhakto
quoted, 607, 649, 809, 945, 954
Manomayam, 1162
"Man proposes, God disposes," 126, 805
Mansion, aerial
Kardama & Devahūti in, 897-901, 905
Kardama created, 882-887, 888
Mantras, two types of, 538
for "becoming God," 761, 837
Hare Kṛṣṇa. *See:* Hare Kṛṣṇa *mantra*
See also: Chanting the holy names; Gāyatrī *mantra;* Hare Kṛṣṇa *mantra;* Sound, transcendental
Manu, 73, 221
Brahmā created, 771
in Brahmā's day, 777
duty & duration of, 733
humans descend from, 858
life-span of, 863, 864
as Lord's representative, 824
man comes from, 858
Svāyambhuva. *See:* Svāyambhuva Manu
Vaivasvata, 733, 777
Manu, Svāyambhuva
birth of, 466
genealogical succession from, 475
glories of, 471
as surrendered soul, 475, 476
Manu-saṁhitā, 479
cited on woman, 854, 856
cited on woman's dependence, 1382
Manu-smṛti, cited on marriage, 845
Manus in creation, 412-415
Mānuṣya defined, 221
Manuṣya-sare defined, 280
Maraṇaṁ hy andha-tāmisraṁ
verse quoted, 749
Marīci, 448, 742, 924, 930, 936, 937, 1328-1329
Mārkaṇḍeya Purāṇa, cited on human embryo, 1266-1267
Marriage
ancient process for, 521, 522
by astrology, 930-931
cooperation in, result of, 524-526
different kinds of, 843-845
duty in, 478, 526
father arranges, 437
happiness in, 873
intercaste, 805
in Kali-yuga, 790, 845, 846, 931
of *kṣatriyas*, 10, 13
parents arranged, 930
recommended for disturbed souls, 524
of Rukmiṇī, 91
sex as basis of, 931
sexual principles in, 543

Marriage
unhappiness in, 931
in Vedic culture, 95, 804-806, 842, 844-845, 853, 930, 931
Vedic vs. modern, 790
wife faithful in, 39
woman's position in, 854, 856
See also: Children; Family life; Householders; Husband; Sex life; Wife; Parents; Sex life; Wife
Mars planet, 665
Maruts, 718
Maryādā-vyatikrama defined, 141
Material attachment. *See:* Attachment
Material body. *See:* Body, material; Body, subtle
Material desires. *See:* Attachment, material; Desires; Enjoyment, material; Sense gratification; Sex life
Material energy. *See:* Elements, material: Energy, material
Material existence compared to banyan tree, 975
Material world; *Māyā;* Nature, material
Material enjoyment. *See:* Enjoyment, material Materialism. *See:* Bodily concept of life; Fruitive activity;
Materialism
blinds internal vision, 204
bondage of, 1094
conditioned soul's two diseases of, 1119
in ignorance & passion, 169
illusion of. *See:* Illusion
See also: Attachment, material; Bondage; Desires, material; Sense gratification
Materialists
association with, 987
association with, degradation by, 987, 1296
association with, to be avoided, 1099-1100, 1102, 1202-1203, 1297-1298
as bewildered, 41
characteristics of, 1233-1245, 1297
"chewing the chewed," 348
compared to hogs, 1332-1333
as condemned, 1332-1333
Materialists
demigods worshiped by, 1317
detailed description of, 1233-1245
devotees vs., 330
vs. devotees, 1123-1124
devotees may appear to be, 1120
in family life, 1305-1306, 1315-1316
frustration of, result of, 612
literatures for, 170
literature of, compared to stool, 1332
Lord rejected by, 1331-1333
minds of, disturbed, 200
poverty of, 1057
processes of elevation for, 1331
religionists as, 1296
scriptures rejected by, 1331-1333
subjects for hearing by, 1331-1333
troublesome life of, 334
types of, ineligible for Kṛṣṇa consciousness, 1355-1357
worship demigods, 1082
worship Śiva, 534
See also: Atheists; Demons; *Karmīs;* Nondevotees; Scientists, material; Soul(s), conditioned
Materialists; Sense gratification Materialists
activities of, 785
in illusion, 915
lack love of God, 877-878
Lord punishes, 677
seek sex life, 905
spiritual realization not achieved by, 773
as warmongers, 676, 677, 679
See also: Atheists; Demons; Nondevotees; Souls, conditioned
Material life. *See:* Life, material; Material world
attachment causes, 986-987
basis of, as sex life, 1254-1255
bondage of, 1094, 1354-1355
compared to dreaming, 1095, 1122
compared to fire, 1119
cow-keeping example of, 978
devotee desireless of, 1013-1015

Materialists (*continued*)
devotional service eliminates, 996
diplomacy required in, 1241
as distressful, 1170
disturbance unavoidable in, 1164
false ego causes, 1052, 1082
as fearful, 1376
vs. liberated life, 981
liberation from. *See:* Liberation
material consciousness causes, 1033
as miserable. *See:* Misery; Suffering
miseries of, detailed, 1262-1294
modes govern, 980
necessities of, *Vedas* provide for, 965
as pastime, impersonalists claim, 1033, 1029
philosophy of, 1296
satisfaction with, illusion of, 1236-1237
sex life as impetus for, 1057
as waste of time, 1233-1234
See also: Attachment; Materialists; Material world
Material nature. *See:* Nature, material
Material nature, modes of. *See:* Modes of material nature
Material world
as *asat*, 1036-1037
beauty of, source of, 314, 315
compared to cat, 992
compared to criminal department, 589
compared to forest fire, 940
compared to ocean of nescience, 576
compared to police department, 1030
creation of. *See:* Creation; Evolution good & bad in, 1337-1338
demons allured by, 760
devotees not meant for, 797-798
disharmony in, 208
false ego in, 186-189
fear in, 657-658, 876
first fall into, 429
forced service in, 364
as frustrating, 157
goodness in, 925
Material world
happiness mixed with distress in, 977-978
hearing about, as useless, 509, 511
historical lesson of, 671
identity forgotten in, 428
in ignorance, 748-749
illumination of, 268
as illusion, 463
illusion in. *See:* Illusion
immunity from, 363
ingredients of, 216
knowledge in, as defective, 1060
liberation from. *See:* Liberation lighted by Lord's effulgence, indirectly, 1028
literatures of, 164
living entities in, 866
lording propensity in, 243-245
Lord creates, 797
Lord maintains, 160, 161
Lord's appearance in, 42, 43, 45
as Lord's energy, 932, 946, 1028-1029
Lord's relationship to, 807, 808
as male-female attraction, 919-920
manifest, vs. unmanifest, 1036
as *māya's* kingdom, 626
as miserable, 1240-1241
miseries of. *See:* Miseries: Suffering: Death
purpose for, 1030
misers of, four given, 564
misery in, 859, 866, 940
modes of nature in, 723
peace formula in, 373
prosperity in, by hard labor, 571
purpose of, 101, 105, 161, 182, 184-185, 186, 212, 259
real but temporary, 385
for rebellious souls, 187-188, 273, 589, 591
as reflection of Kṛṣṇa, 1105-1106
relativity in, 1342
renunciation of, 793, 794
for sense enjoyers, 797
spiritual world contrasted to, 346, 565, 575, 588
spiritual world vs., 723, 800, 925, 932

Material world
  Supreme Spirit evolves, 220, 226
  as temporary, 1037
  time in, 952
  violence necessary in, 1197-1198
  See also: Bondage; Creation, the; Earth; Energy, material; Heavenly planets; Modes of nature; *Māyā*; Nature, material; Universe
Mathematics, time factor in, 383
Mathurā, 736, 802-803
  Deity of, 18
  as holy place, 24
  Kṛṣṇa entered, 89-90
Matir na kṛṣṇe parataḥ svato vā
  verse quoted, 347
Mat-sthāni sarva-bhūtāni
  quoted, 258
Mattaḥ sarvaṁ pravartate
  quoted, 724
Mattaḥ smṛtir jñānam apohanaṁ ca
  quoted, 213, 1279
Matter. *See:* Elements, material; Energy, material; Nature, material
  as *aparā* inferior, 976
  from life, 1042, 1073
  living entity merged in, 1108
  & soul combined, living entity as, 1112
  & spirit, knowledge of, 1103
Mauna defined, 958
Māyā
  activities of, two described, 1236
  all attracted by, 1300
  compared to cloud, 1344
  defined, 973
  demons killed by, 1161
  as external energy, 1010
  family in, 1238-1240
  Lord controls, 1277
  Lord creates & is beyond, 1029
  as Lord's agent, 974
  man's form as, 1305
  removed by devotional service, 1033
  strength of, 1178, 1285
Māyā
  woman's form as, 1300-1304
  See also: Illusion
Māyā (illusion energy)
  Brahmā creates, 428
  compared to dream, 266, 268
  conditioned soul in, 767, 962
  conditioned souls under, 324
  defined, 15, 183, 417, 487, 589, 590, 626, 951
  Durgā as, 532, 535
  everyone in, 836
  freedom from, 189, 960
  householder in, 808
  last snare of, 189, 235, 243-245, 266-267, 273, 962
  Lord above, 245, 256, 257, 261, 265
  Lord & living entity in relation to, 960
  Lord controls, 740
  love hindered by, 372
  material vision as, 462
  Mayāvāda misconceptions about, 731, 740
  nondevotees harassed by, 756
  as powerful opponent, 379
  sense enjoyment as, 743
  suffering as, 275
  in Vidura-Duryodhana encounter, 15
  woman's beauty as, 758
  "yogīs" see Lord's form as, 615
  See also: Bodily concept of life; Ego, false; Hallucination; Ignorance; Illusion: Energy, material; Material world; Modes of material nature; Nature, material
Māyā consciousness, 980
Mayādhyakṣeṇa prakṛtiḥ
  quoted, 345, 504, 1018, 1078, 1226
  verse quoted, 183, 384
Mayā tatam idaṁ sarvaṁ
  verse quoted, 258
Māyā (Durgā, Kālī), goddess
  cheats worshipers, 915
  dacoits worshiped, 704
Māyāvāda philosophy. *See:* Impersonalism
Māyāvādi-bhāṣya śunile haya sarva nāśa
  quoted, 727

Māyāvādīs
  hearing from, condemned, 727, 731
  Lord misunderstood by, 685 , 731, 753, 944
  name of, meaning of, 731
  offend *Bhāgavatam*, 135
  Supreme Brahman misunderstood by, 740
  See also: Impersonalists; *Jñānīs*; Monists; Philosophers, speculative
Meat-eating, 774, 950, 1317
Meat-eating. *See:* Cows
Medicine, Ayur-vedic, 1063, 1066, 1080-1081, 1140, 1391
Medicine, Ayur-vedic, *āsavam* as, 892
Medicine for liver disease, 55
Meditation
  artificial (not spontaneous), 1167, 1168
  authorized process of, 603-605
  for "becoming God," 761, 779, 903
  on Brahmā, 559
  chanting holy names surpasses, 578, 579
  & Deity worship equal, 1157
  on demigods, by impersonalists, 1152
  on devotees of Lord, 1147
  false, 1114
  on Govinda, 736
  hearing & chanting as, 1148-1149
  on heart, 1134
  imaginary, 1150
  impersonal, as difficult, 1142, 1150
  as impersonal never, 1142, 1145, 1150, 1154-1156, 1158, 1161-1163
  in Kali-yuga impractical, 781
  on Kṛṣṇa, 649
  on Lakṣmī, 1153
  on Lord, 1136, 1389
  on Lord's form, 1147-1150
  on Lord's pastimes, 1135-1137
  on Lord's personal feature, 602, 609
  mind for, 1166-1167
  perfection in, 781
  as personal, 1220
  personal vs. impersonal, 327-328, 1387
  for present Age, 550
Meditation
  progressive order of, 1150, 1155
  Rudra in, 441
  as *smaranam*, 1158
  sense gratification precludes, 778
  on Supersoul, 773, 1141
  two types of, 446
  "*yogīs*" in, 608
  of *yogī* on Lord, 721, 1142-1166
  See also: Devotional service, of remembering: Knowledge, speculative; Kṛṣṇa consciousness; *Yoga*
Meditation on Kṛṣṇa
  antiseptic effect of, 31
  by cowherd boys, 79
  as devotional service, 312
  in enmity, 76
  at Lord's lotus feet, 200
  See also: Supreme Lord, love for; Trance
Menakā, 1097
Mental speculation. *See:* Knowledge, speculative; Philosophers, speculative
Mental speculators. *See:* Atheists; Impersonalists; *Jñānīs* Māyāvādīs; Scientists, material
Mercury planet, 664
Mercy in spiritual culture, 639
  See also: Supreme Lord, mercy of
Mercy of God. *See:* Supreme Lord, mercy of
Mercy of *sādhus*, devotees, 988
Merging with the Supreme. *See:* Brahman (impersonal Absolute); Impersonalists; *Jñānīs*; Liberation; Māyāvādīs; Monists; Oneness
Meru, Mount, 899, 900
Metaphysical calculation of time, 383
Military, the, necessary, 456
Milk
  blood makes, 717
  in serpent-nondevotee analogy, 727
  in snake-fool analogy, 12
  value of, 81, 164
  See also: Cows
Milk ocean
  moon born from, 55

Milk ocean
  Viṣṇu in, 202
Millenniums
  religious principles in, 638
  of Varāha's appearances, 482, 514
  See also: Dvāpara-yuga; Kali-yuga; Satya-yuga; Tretā-yuga
Mind
  activities of, on ethereal platform, 1061
  as Aniruddha, 1053-1054
  Aniruddha as Lord of, 1053, 1056
  of child reflects parents' mind, 756
  compared to lamp flame, 1168
  contamination in, 1152
  control of, 446, 560, 1020
    by hearing & chanting, 1149
    human life affords, 1283
    by Kṛṣṇa consciousness, 1021, 1053, 1097
    by worship of Lord Aniruddha, 1048, 1054, 1056
    See also: Detachment
  dovetailed with Lord, 1168, 1170, 1189
  ecstasy unbalances, 32
  as friend or enemy, 1138
  hearing Hare Kṛṣṇa focuses, 950
  vs. intelligence, 1057
  Lord beyond, 226
  Lord represented by, 1001
  in Lord's service, 248
  for lower meditation stage, 1166-1167
  moon controls, 388
  material, vs. spiritualized, 1168
  nature of, 1053
  origin of, 33, 188
  pure, for God realization, 500
  purified, nature of, 1166-1170
  purified by breath exercise, 1139
  purified by chanting Hare Kṛṣṇa, 1139
  semen influenced by, 652
  as senses' leader, 1001
  speculators agitate, 952
  as subtle body, 756
Mind
  See also: Elements; Evolution: Knowledge, speculative; Intelligence; Meditation
Miseries
  causes of, 332
  cures for, 330-331, 551
  of devotees temporary, 629
  from independent conception, 333-334
  Lord's narrations destroy, 509, 511
  material advancement causes, 393-394
  in material world, 565
  miscreants cause, 545
  See also: Bondage; Hell
Misery
  by aversion to Lord's supremacy, 158
  Bhāgavatam dispels, 297
  of birth, 1288-1290, 1291
  birth begins, 1286
  body after body, 1267-1270
  care for, 171, 172, 272
  devotional service dispels, 293
  devotees free from, 992
  from fruitive action, 157
  "I & mine" causes, 203
  from illusory identification, 265-266
  in impersonal path, 206, 207
  Lord's lotus feet remove, 196, 197, 198
  of material life, detailed, 1263-1294
  of newborn human, 1288-1290
  ocean of tears from, 1164
  removed by hearing about Lord, 990
  removed by Lord, 1164
  solution for, 1311-1312
  soul beyond, 268, 275
  three types of, 197, 198
  types of, three named, 990
  Vidura's question on, 261
  See also: Hell; Suffering
Misery. *See:* Suffering
Missionary activity satisfies the Lord, 340, 341
  See also: Welfare activity
Mitra, 232

Modern Age. *See:* Kali-yuga; Present Age
children in, 931
interplanetary travel in, 901
mental speculation in, 933-934
Modes of material nature
association of, as contaminating, 992
attachment to, conditional life as, 980
birth according to, 1013, 1094, 1177
body according to, 166
colors representing, 1031
control conditioned souls, 1030-1032, 1093, 1114
controlled by demigods, 1230
deities dominating, 201-202
demigods for, 1082
devotee free from, 1195
devotional service in, 1354
disharmony due to, 208
destinations according to, 864
elevation through, 965-966
false ego in, 187-189, 1052-1053, 1055, 1058
false ego in, manifestations from, 1058
freedom from. *See:* Liberation of goodness, creation of, 1048
function of, 259
of goodness, pure. *See: Śuddha-sattva* material energy invested with, 1028-1029
Kṛṣṇa consciousness surpasses, 865, 960
living entities according to, 165, 237, 238, 284
Lord beyond, 960
Lord's activities beyond, 257
in material world, 723
relations with Lord according to, 173
in *saguṇa* Brahman, 1041
transcendence beyond, 148-149, 169
unmanifested, as *pradhāna*, 1037, 1038
See also: Māyā; Nature, material; *names of specific modes:* Goodness; Ignorance; Nature, material; Passion
Modes of nature
chanting Hare Kṛṣṇa dispels, 639
freedom from, 363
Modes of nature
as mixed together, 447, 610
planets accommodate, 359
primary interaction of, 387
Rudra's birth caused by, 435
in spiritual world, 566
three predominates of, 324, 345
time's influence as, 383, 384
See also: Energy, material; Goodness; Ignorance; *Māyā;* Passion
Mogul emperors, palaces of, 886
Moha defined, 749, 1032
Mohiṇī, 1299
Mokṣa. See: Liberation
Money. *See:* Economic development; Gold; Jewels; Opulence: Wealth
fear of losing, 875
householder managing, 809
Monism. *See:* Impersonalism
Monists *See:* Brahman effulgence; Impersonalists
Bhāgavatam forbidden for, 135
cited on merging with Supreme, 785
devotional service beyond, 124
See also: Impersonalists; *Jñānīs;* Māyāvādīs; Philosophers, speculative
Months in Vedic calendar, 795
Moon
demigod of, 1018
at demons' birth, 662
at dissolution of universe, 415-416
elevation to, 1318-1319
Kardama & Devahūti compared to, 898
Kṛṣṇa's beauty vs., 62, 108
life-span on, 1010
in Lord's universal form, 234
milk ocean produced, 55-56
mind controlled by, 388
Moon and the Lord, analogy of, 55, 56, 268
reflects sunlight, 556
Moonlight, Brahmā dropped form of, 764
Moon on water & soul in matter, analogy of, 267-268
Morality, goal of, 336

Morning
brahmacārīs duty in, 821
early, for spiritual cultivation, 757, 769
See also: Daytime; Night; Twilight
Mother
begetting children, 756
as enemy, 872
first & second, 931
knowledge from, example of, 741
son delivers, in old age, 956
of twins, 668
See also: Children; Family life; Householders; Marriage; Parents; Wife
Mṛgaḥ defined, 681
Mucukunda, 97
Mūḍha-dhiyaḥ defined, 763
Mūḍhas defined, 305, 932, 947
Muhammadan, Haridāsa as, 618
Mukti defined, 611-612
Mukti. See: Liberation
Muktir...svarūpeṇa vyavasthitiḥ
quoted, 1375
Muni
vs. bhakti-yogī, 1150
defined, 959, 1149
devotee as, 1102
Mūrtimat defined, 567
Mūla-prakṛtir avikṛtir
quoted, 216
Mura, 98
Music
at Lord Kapila's advent, 922
material vs. spiritual, 764
necessary in society, 456
seven notes of, 462
in Svāyambhuva Manu's palace, 860-861
Musk deer, 819
Mystic power
devotee desireless of, 1010
examples of, 1128
of Hiraṇyākṣa, 712-715
of Kardama, 777, 882, 896, 896, 901-904, 906, 907
Mystic power
Kṛṣṇa consciousness as, 995
as material, 1128
requirement for attaining, 778
of Supreme Lord, 716, 719
yoga's goal not, 1130
See also: Power; *Yogīs*, perfections attainable by; *Yogīs*, power of
Mystics. *See:* Devotees; Sages; Saints; Transcendentalists; *Yogis*
Mystic *yoga*
goal of, 560
travel by, 581
See also: Kṛṣṇa consciousness; Meditation; *Yoga*
Mystic *yogīs*
goal of, 635
past, present & future seen by, 408-409
See also: Devotees; Transcendentalists; *Yogīs*

N

Na cyavante hi yad-bhaktā
verse quoted, 289
Na hanyate hanyamāne śarīre
quoted, 1310
Nāga air, 224
Nāgas, 770
Nāgnajitī, Princess, 92
Nāhaṁ prakāśah sarvasya
quoted, 146, 338-339
Na hy asya karhicid rājan
verse quoted, 131
Naimiṣāraṇya, sages at, 727
Naiṣāṁ matis tāvad urukramāṅghriṁ
verse quoted, 347
Naiṣṭhika-brahmacārī defined, 459, 842, 843, 936
Nakula, 38
Nalakūvara, 204
Na māṁ karmāṇi limpanti
quoted, 58, 344
verse quoted, 44
Namasyantaś ca māṁ bhaktyā
verse quoted, 250

Names of the Lord. *See:* Chanting the holy names; Hare Kṛṣṇa *mantra;* Supreme Lord, name of
of husband not called by wife, 871
Namo brahmaṇya-devāya
quoted, 831
Namo namas te 'stu sahasra-kṛtvaḥ
verse quoted, 468
Nanda Mahārāja, 926, 1197
Kṛṣṇa instructed, 85
as *vaiśya*, 79
Nāntaṁ na madhyaṁ na punas tavādiṁ
verse quoted, 246
Nārada Muni, 1309
Nārada Muni reformed hunter, 204
as authority, 740
birth of, 442, 443
Brahmā returned home with, 936
in Brahma-sampradāya, 474
Devahūti heard about Kardama from, 839
elevation of, 876
exalted position of, 443
as *naiṣṭhika-brahmacārī*, 936
potency of, 517
quoted on time, 384, 385
Yudhiṣṭhira welcoming, 806
Nārada-pañcarātra, cited on serving Lord with one's purified senses, 984
Nārada-paṇcarātra, arcanā regulations in, 347
Narakāsura demon, 94, 95
Nara-Nārāyaṇa sages
at Badarikāśrama, 120, 137
confidential message to, 150
Deity of, 147
Nārāyaṇa
as supreme, 1195
See also: Supreme Lord
Nārāyaṇa, Lord, 810, 944
beauty of, 598-599, 600, 601, 602, 603
as Deity of Vaikuṇṭha, 565
as Kṛṣṇa's expansion, 603
Kṛṣṇa surpasses, 61
symbols decorating, 582
Nārāyaṇa, Lord
wife of, 573
as yoga's goal, 603
See also: Absolute Truth; Kṛṣṇa, Lord; Supersoul: Supreme Lord; Viṣṇu, Lord
Nārāyaṇa-para defined, 41, 560
Nārāyaṇa-parāḥ sarve
quoted, 560
Narottama dāsa Ṭhākura, cited on pilgrimage places, 736
cited on three sources of spiritual knowledge, 1133-1134
quoted on changing lust to Kṛṣṇa's satisfaction, 1293
quoted on entanglement of material life, 1052
Narottama dāsa Ṭhākura, quoted on devotional service, 113
Na siddha-mukhyā asurā manuṣyāḥ
verse quoted, 336
Na te viduḥ svārtha-gatiṁ hi Viṣṇuṁ
verse quoted, 347
Nations. *See:* Countries; *names of specific countries*
Nationalism as illusory service, 1242
Nature
Rudra principle in, 435, 436
See also: Creation, the material; Energy, material; Material world
Nature, material, 1033-1089
agitated by Lord, 1043-1045
association with, conditioning due to more than, 1116
as automatic-appearing, 1226-1227
beauty of, vs. Lord's beauty, 314, 315
birth into. *See:* Birth
bodies created by, 1030
compared to mother of living entities, 1036
compared to wife of Lord, 1036
for conditioned soul's sense enjoyment, 742-743
constitution of, 744
controlled by demigods, 1230
controlled by Lord, 1017-1018, 1036, 1226-1231

Nature, material
controls living entities, 1032
creation of, purpose for, 1364
departments of, 1230
disturbed at demons' birth, 659-666
elements of. *See:* Elements
entered by Lord, elements & *mahat-tattva*, 1073
as eternal, 1037
evolution in. *See:* Evolution
impregnated by Lord, 1046
influence of, freedom from, 1113-1115
laws of, 105, 157
conditioned souls under, 792
laws of
Nature *(continued)* laws of
on interplanetary travel, 901
as stringent, 666, 667, 748
transcendentalists surpass, 692
laws of, Lord makes, 1228
liberation from. *See:* Liberation
Lord controls, 687, 743
Lord directs, 101, 105
lording it over, 670
as Lord's energy, 1322
as mother, 1046
pilgrimage through, 18
as *prakṛti*, 976
principles of, 1033-1089
as *saguṇa* Brahman, 1041
spirit activates, 220
& Supreme Lord, relationship between, 1036
time agitates, 1043
unmanifest, as *pradhāna*, 1037
See also: Body, material; Creation (act of); Creation, the material; Elements, material; Energy, material; *Māyā;* Modes of material nature; Planets; Universe(s)
Nāyam ātmā pravacanena labhyo
quoted, 57
Nectar of Devotion, The, 51
Neti neti defined, 353
New Delhi, Mogul castles in, 886
Ni defined, 143
Night
as body of ignorance, 749, 751
demons born of, 752
See also: Daytime; Morning; Twilight
Nikhilāsv apy avasthāsu
verse quoted, 148
Nimbārka-sampradāya, 430
Nimba tree and envious soul, analogy of, 195
Nimitta-mātraṁ bhava savyasācin
verse quoted, 98
Nirbandhaḥ kṛṣṇa-sambandhe
verse quoted, 1307
Nirbīja-yoga, 1167
Nirguṇa defined, 256
Nirguṇa vs. *saguṇa* Brahman, 1041
Nirmāna-mohā jita-saṅga-doṣāḥ
quoted, 991-992
Nirṛti, 899
Nirvāṇa, 998, 1112, 1168, 1393
See also: Liberation
Nirvyalīka defined, 703
Niṣkāma defined, 340
Nitya-baddhas defined, 212
Nitya-muktas defined, 187
Nityānanda Prabhu, misconception about, 680-681
Nitya-baddha, 1031
Nitya-siddhas defined, 48, 112
Nityasyoktāḥ śarīriṇaḥ
quoted, 951
Nityānanda, 988
Nityo nityānām
quoted, 1223
Nityo nityānāṁ cetanaś cetanānām
quoted, 1018, 1137
Nivṛtti vs. *pravṛtti,* 1321
Nondevotee(s)
associating with, 11
destiny of, 341
hearing from, condemned, 727
Lord's form beyond, 145, 146
Lord's message bitter to, 8
māyā harasses, 755

Nondevotee(s) (*continued*)
as son, 8
See also: Atheists; Demons; Impersonalists; Philosophers, speculative; Scientists, material; *Karmīs;* Materialists; Māyāvādīs
Nonviolence
goal of, 336
improper application of, 642
North Pole as island, 776
Nṛsiṁha, Lord
appeared from pillar, 922
Prahlāda and, 767

O

Obedience to father, 476
Obeisances to the Lord, 349
Obligations, worldly, devotional service transcends, 431
Occupations. *See:* Duty; *Varṇāśrama-dharma*
of eternal living entity, 953
material vs. spiritual, 830
Ocean feared Varāha, 491
Oceans, salt and milk, 56
at demons' birth, 661
devotee compared to, 961
Garbha (Garbhodaka), 724, 746
Hiraṇyākṣa harassed, 672-674
Odor, kinds of, 1069
Offense(s)
to *Bhāgavatam,* 135
to brāhmaṇa, 649
to devotees, 340, 592, 597
by devotees reflect on the Lord, 621
by gatekeepers, 584, 585
to Lord, 152, 204
punishment for, 593
to pure devotee, 111
to Śiva, 540
to superiors, 141, 142
in spiritual world possible, 618
ten listed, 578-579
to Vidura, 15
See also: Sin(s) ful activity
Old age, material vs. spiritual, 49
son delivers mother in, 956
See also: Age (time of life); Life, span of; Time
Old men, protection for, 627
Omens
at demons' birth, 659-666
planetary, 665
Oṁkāra, impersonalists worship, 1147
Oṁ tad viṣṇoḥ paramaṁ padaṁ
quoted, 253, 620, 650, 1147
Oneness
by agreement, 222
desire for, 266-267, 273
by glorifying the Lord, 248
as illusory snare, 189
for impersonalists, 205, 207
of Lord and His pleasure, 2
of Lord and His service, 135-137
personal vs. impersonal, 785, 807-808, 809
Śiśupāla merged in, 69
See also: Brahman (impersonal Absolute); Impersonalists; *Jñānīs;* Liberation; Māyāvādīs; Monists; Philosophers, speculative; Supreme Lord, love for
Oneness & difference of Lord & living entity (*acintya-bhedābheda-tattva*), 2, 159-160
Oneness with the Supreme, serving the Lord surpasses, 601
See also: Brahman effulgence; Imper- sonalists; Liberation; Philosophers, speculative
Opportunities, intelligent person uses, 914
Opulence
of Kardama's castle, 882-887, 888
of Kṛṣṇa and others compared, 61
as Lord's mercy, 858
of planets, 903
of Supreme Lord, 939, 945-946
of Yudhiṣṭhira's kingdom, 35
See also: Economic developments; Jewels; Money; Mystic power; Perfection: Possessions; Wealth

Orders of life. *See: Varṇāśrama-dharma*
Orders, social. See: Brāhmaṇas; Kṣatriyas; Vaiśyas; Sūdras
Organs for action, five listed, 1039-1040
Oṣadhya, 231
Oversoul. *See:* Supersoul

P

Padma defined, 582
Padma Purāṇa, cited on Brahmā, 420
Padma Purāṇa, quoted on Lord's inconceivability, 146
Pain. *See:* Misery
Pain. *See:* Suffering
Pakistan, India included, 695
Palace (s)
  of Mogul emperors, 886
  in sky, Kardama created, 882-887, 888
Pañcāśordhvaṁ vanaṁ vrajet
  quoted, 949
Pañca-yajña, purpose of, 526
Pāṇḍavas, 654-655, 728
  Dhṛtarāṣṭra vs., 5
  family history of, 38
  Kṛṣṇa's relation to, 2, 10
  as Pṛthā's sons, 10
Pāṇḍu Mahārāja, 38, 39
Pantheism, 807
  See also: Brahman (impersonal Absolute); Oneness; Supreme Lord, all-pervading; Supreme Lord, all-pervading & aloof
Parā-bhakti defined, 329, 962
Para defined, 962
Paraḥ defined, 1027
Paradise. *See:* Heavenly planets; Spiritual world
Paramahaṁsas, 199, 274-275
Paramahaṁsa defined, 849
Parama-sammataḥ defined, 775
Paramāṁ sthitim defined, 140
Paramāṇu-vāda, cited on atomism, 397
Paramātmā. *See:* Supreme Lord: Supersoul
Paraṁ dṛṣṭvā nivartate
  quoted, 1302, 1342, 1383
Paramo nirmatsarāṇām
  quoted, 1099
Paramparā defined, 726
  See also: Disciplic succession
Paramātmanaḥ defined, 151
Paraṁ bhavam ajānanto
  verse quoted, 74
Param defined, 314
Paraṁ dṛṣṭvā nivartate
  quoted, 324, 538
Pārameṣṭhya defined, 631-632
Paramparā. See: Disciplic succession
Parā prakṛti defined, 107, 250
Parārdha defined, 420
Parārdhānte so 'budhyata gopa-veśo
  quoted, 343
Parā śakti defined, 241
Paraṁ vijayate śrī-kṛṣṇa-saṅkīrtanam
  quoted, 1139
Parasya brahmaṇaḥ śaktis
  quoted, 946
Parāśara, 123, 302
Parārdhas, 1322-1324
Parasya brahmaṇaḥ śaktiḥ
  quoted, 1041
Parāsya śaktir vividhaiva śrūyate
  quoted, 264, 683, 901, 947
Parents
  begetting children, 931
  children as expansions of, 880
  children's marriage arranged by, 804, 852-853, 855, 930
  obligation to, 68
  See also: Children: Family; Father; Householders; Husband; Mother; Wife; Marriage
Pārijāta tree, 93
Parīkṣit Mahārāja, 695
  as embryo, 104
  inquired about Vidura-Maitreya meeting, 3
  prowess of, 241
Paritrāṇāya sādhūnāṁ
  quoted, 823
  verse quoted, 77

Pārthas. *See:* Pāṇḍavas
Pārvatī, 533
Pāṣaṇḍī defined, 195, 325
Parivrāja defined, 948
Pārvatl (Bhavānī), 869-870, 921
Passion, mode of
altruism in, 169, 187-188
in begetting children, 881
Brahmā immune to, 365, 366
Brahmā in, 756
Brahmā represents, 557, 559
Brahmā supervises, 747
Brahmā's anger in, 432
Brahmā worshipers in, 201
charity in, 974
creation by, 185, 306, 321
destiny according to, 864-865
humans in, 393
lust & anger in, 1292
senses produced by, 189
twilight time for, 757
war caused by, 21
See also: Modes of material nature
Pastime defined, 1034, 1035, 1135
Pastimes of the Lord. *See:* Supreme Lord, pastimes of Patasjali, 1130
Pāśupati weapon, 37
Pātāla-mūleśvara-bhoga'saṁhatau
verse quoted, 492
Patañjali, 428, 603
Patañjali *yoga* system, 1056
Patañjali, *yoga* system of, 785, 786
Patañjali-sūtras, 785
Paugaṇḍa defined, 1291-1292
Pauravī, 27
Patient in disease-material life analogy, 761
Peace
by begetting nice children, 666
beyond material desires, 64
beyond "quivering matter,"268, 269
for *dhīras*, 200
formula, 590, 640-641
in good government, 105
Peace
harmony and, 208
Kṛṣṇa as messenger of, 8
by *kṛṣṇa-kathā*, 169
by Lord's glance, 270
in Vedic society, 242, 243
See also: Happiness
Peacefulness for devotee, 1101, 1102
Penance, 1016, 1378
for enlightenment, 358, 361
highest form of, 377
Lord known by, 324
in retirement, 458
by Rudra, 440
See also: Austerity
Perception, sense
knowledge beyond, 741
See also: Speculation, mental
Perfection
by acting according to ability, 837
by devotional service, 780, 781
by hearing Lord's pastimes, 728
of Kṛṣṇa consciousness, 860-862
love of God as, 876-878
in meditation, 781
rāsa-līlā as, 182
by saintly person's association, 833, 834
of senses in Lord's service, 787
in spiritual life, 781
via spiritual master, 835-837, 928-929
three principles for, 115
in *yoga,* 779-781, 784-786, 883, 903, 941
See also: Goal of life; Success; Supreme Lord, love for
Personalists flourish in Vaikuṇṭha, 567
Personalists. *See:* Devotees
Personality of Godhead. *See:* Kṛṣṇa, Lord; Supreme Lord, personal feature of
Persons. *See:* Animals; Human beings; Living entities; Soul; Souls, conditioned; Supreme Lord
Philanthropy, 996, 1094, 1096, 1122, 1184, 1316

Philanthropy. *See:* Welfare activity
Philosophers. *See: Ācāryas; Brāhmaṇas; Jñānīs; Māyāvādīs;* Sages
Philosophers, speculative *(jñānīs)*
Bhāgavatam misinterpreted by, 135
Brahmā's example to, 309, 310, 313
buddhi-yoga beyond, 225
devotees "agree" with, 364
folly of, 246, 250-253
goal of, 635
as godless, 158
on hankering platform, 64
inactivity theory of, 247
lack love of God, 372
"Ph.D," 226
should surrender to God, 506
See also: Impersonalists; *Jñānīs;* Knowledge, speculative; Māyāvādīs; Monists; Scientists, material
Philosophy of Māyāvādīs, 353
Philosophy. *See:* Absolute Truth; *Acintya-bhedābheda-tattva;* Knowledge; *names of specific philosophies*, spiritual
Physician in disease-material life analogy, 761
Piety, 996, 1184, 1316
devotional service beyond, 16, 59
Dhṛtarāṣṭra & Duryodhana bereft of, 7, 8
See also: Religious principles
Pig incarnation. *See:* Varāha, Lord
Pilgrimage places
bathing in, 889
charity at, 806
devotional service excels, 113
Himalayas, 137
journey to, 19
listed, 22, 137
Lord's lotus feet as, 16
Mathurā, 46
at present, 736
purpose of, 16, 17, 46
for purification, 736
topmost, 24
Vṛndāvana, 46, 80
Piṇḍa, 1317
Piṇḍa-siddhi, cited on pregnancy, 668
Pious activities, accumulative result of, 342
See also: Missionary activity; Welfare activity
Pious persons. *See:* Devotees; Saintly persons
Pious species, 665, 817
Pitās, 766
Pitā planets, time on, 404
Pīṭha-sthāna defined, 857
Pitṛloka, 1333
Planets
compared to islands, 903
differences among, 903
disturbed at demons' birth, 659, 665
Earth. *See:* Earth planet
as floating, 1228, 1229
heavenly, devotee desireless of, 1013, 1015
heavenly, elevation to & falldown from, 1318, 1333-1335
heavenly, life-spans on, 1010
heavenly, temporary abodes only, 1011, 1319, 1321
heavenly. *See:* Heavenly planets
for living entities, 1229
living entities vary according to, 165, 236, 237
Lord floats, 687
lower, via ignorance mode, 864-865
pious & impious, 665
as round, 903
spiritual, 1011-1013, 1126-1127, 1193-1194
in spiritual sky, 746
three systems of, 936
time on, 286
travel between, 1379
travel to, 901
in universal form, 1074
See also: Creation, the; Earth; Heavenly planets; Material world; Universe; *names of specific planets*
Planets, material
accommodate varieties of beings, 381
at annihilation of universe, 408, 412

Planets, material (*continued*)
"gravitation" supports, 503
in seed form, 380
sun illuminates, 556
systems of
design of, 359
listed, 492
threefold, 412, **414**, 415
time measured by, 399
travel between, 395
types of, 381
See also: Creation, the material; Earth planet; Heavenly planets; Universe
Pleasure
burden of love as, 101-102
of devotees & impersonalists compared, 206-207
by devotional service, 1221
of four Kumāras, 631
from God realization, 1349-1350
in goodness, 787
by hearing devotee's pastimes, 728
by hearing Lord's pastimes, 727
literature giving, 164
by loving Kṛṣṇa, 24, 81
temporary, rejected by devotees, 612
under supernatural control, 110
by visiting Vṛndāvana, 80
See also: Enjoyment, material; Happiness; Sense gratification: Bliss; Ecstasy; Enjoyment; Happiness; Love; Sense gratification; Peace
Poison in Pūtanā, 75
Poison in serpent-nondevotee analogy, 727
Poison, Śiva swallowed, 535
Politics
Cānakya expert in, 9
in Vedic society, 242
See also: Government; King(s); *Kṣatriyas;* Leaders, government; *Varnāśrama-dharma*
Politicians. *See:* Government leaders
Population "problem,"101, 161, 177
demoniac, increasing nowadays, 659, 666
Population "problem"
in Kali-yuga, 845, 848, 950
Prajāpatis increased, 778-779
by sanctified sex life, 756-757, 775
Vedic culture regulates, 666
See also: Citizens; Society, human
Possessions
attachment to, 64
See also: Attachment: Wealth
Postbox and Deity, analogy of, 19
Potencies of the Lord. *See:* Supreme Lord, potencies of
Poverty of materialists, 1057
Power, 450
of devotional service, 942
of Lord & living entity contrasted, 903
material, 670
mystic. *See:* Mystic power spiritual, 785
of yogī, 888, 896
See also: Energy
Prabhāsa, 112, 113
Prabhava defined, 96
Prabodhānanda Sarasvatī, cited on divine view of heavenly elevation, monism & sense control, 876
quoted on liberation, 1004
quoted on oneness as hellish, 1004
Pradhāna
agitated by time, 1043
vs. Brahman, 1037
defined & detailed, 1038
vs. *prakṛti*, 1037
as universal crust, 1074
as *yonir mahad brahma*, 1038
See also: Mahat-tattva
Pradhānam defined, 946
Pradyumna, 28
Pradyumna, Lord, 810
Pradyumna, Lord, worship of, 1048
Prahlāda Mahārāja, 1148
cited on Lord's advent in Kali-yuga, 939
in difficulty, 654
glories of, 548-552

Prahlāda Mahārāja
Nṛsiṁhadeva and, 767
quoted on chewing chewed, 1316
quoted on family life as blind well, 957, 957-958
quoted on material wealth as worthless, 1194
quoted on taking shelter of God, 957
Prahlādo janako bhīṣmo
verse quoted, 336
Prajahāti yadā kāmān
quoted, 334
Prajāpati, 231
Prajāpatis, 741, 778-779, 850, 927
Prajās defined, 241
Prakata defined, 61
Prākṛta-bhakta, 1199
Prakṛteḥ kriyamāṇāni
quoted, 1093, 1114
Prakṛti
defined, 1037
defined & detailed, 976
living entities as, 976
nature as, 976
vs. *pradhāna*, 1038
as supernatural, 110
See also: Energy, material; *Māyā;* Modes of material nature; Nature, material
Pramāṇa-viparyaya-vikalpa-nidrā-smṛtayaḥ
quoted, 1055
Prāna air, 221, 224
Praṇava, 461, 463
Prāṇāyāma, 1140
Prasāda, 1197-1198, 1388
for animals, 1213
distribution of, required, 1209
elevation by, 1208
tongue controlled by, 1003
Prasāda (food offered to the Lord), 115, 209, 270
devotees accept, 625
eating of, 787
mahā-, 533
in *śrāddha* ritual, 767
See also: Supreme Lord, mercy of
Prasūti, 467, 468, 779
Pratibimba defined, 381
Pratyāhāra, 1373
Pratyag-akṣaja defined, 812
Pravṛtti vs. *nivṛtti*, 1320
Prayāga, 17, 735, 889
Prayer(s)
by child in womb, 1272-1286
composition of, 300
by demigods, 196-212
of demigods & demons contrasted, 703-704
by Devahūti to Lord Kapila, 972-976, 1363-1372
inspiration for, 300, 368
Preaching Kṛṣṇa consciousness authorization for, 152, 150, 301
beyond mundane missionary work, 169
by Lord's servants, 140
offenses in, 141, 142
as protection from falldown, 356
by sages to Varāha, 494-507
sincerity for, 369
to Śiva, 540, 541
See also: Supreme Lord, praying to, benefit of; Supreme Lord, worship of, glorification of: Devotional service, of preaching
Preachers
cannot be counteracted, 653
difficulties of, plan behind, 654-655
as missionaries, 948
sannyāsīs as, 458, 586
true & false,337
See also: Ācāryas; Brāhmaṇas; Devotees; *Sannyāsīs;* Spiritual master
Pregnancy with twins, 668-669
See also: Birth
Premāñjana-cchurita
quoted, 1104
Premāṣjana-cchurita-bhakti-vilocanena
verse quoted, 25
Premā pumartho mahān
quoted, 877
Present Age. *See:* Kali-yuga; Modern Age
demons & disturbances in, 659, 660, 666
heads of state in, 823, 827

Present Age (*continued*)
pilgrimage places in, 736
in Vaivasvata Manu, 733, 777
Pride, 360
types & effects of, 42
wife must give up, 872
See also: False ego Priests, Vedic.
See: Brāhmaṇas
Priests, Vedic. *See: Brāhmaṇas;* Devotees
Princesses
Kṛṣṇa married, 95, 96
ksatriyas married, 10
played sports, 846
Priyavrata, 467
Priyavrata, King, 776, 838
Problem, authority solves, 658
Prostitute, Diti acted like, 536
Protection
for defenseless beings, 627
of father's soul by son, 11
by God. *See:* Supreme Lord, protection by
by king, 823, 826
for Pāṇḍava twins, 38
for upper social classes, 640, 641
in Vedic society, 79, 241, 242
See also; Supreme Lord, protection by
Pṛthā. *See:* Kuntī, Queen
Psychology
of husband & wife contrasted, 871
of virgin woman in love, 843
Pulakāśru defined, 579
Pulaha, 930, 937
Pulastya, 302, 930, 937
Punaḥ punaś carvita-carvaṇānām
quoted, 1316
Punishment by the Lord, 99
Punishment for neglect of dependents, 627
compared to losing wealth, 1258
Punishment for neglect of dependents
diseases as, 1255
in hell, 1255-1258
for illicit sex life, 1254
for meat-eating, 1253
Punishment for neglect of dependents
for misuse of wealth, 1257-1258
for sinful, after death, 1253, 1254
for sinful use of wealth, 1257
Purānas
as beginningless, 303
defined, 457
purpose of, 167
Vaikuṇṭha known via, 566
Pure devotee(s) of the Supreme Lord
See: Devotees, pure devotees
association with, 16, 71, 269
beyond confusion, 66-67
beyond difficulties, 14-15
beyond heavenly attraction, 144
beyond philosophical speculation, 124, 130
beyond pilgrimages, 112-113
desire service only, 71, 129
Lord attached to, 108
Lord known to, 32, 110
Lord present among, 46
mission of, 158
offenses to, 111
service to, 277
suffers in Lord's absence, 55, 133
symptoms of, 173
Purification
in begetting children, 666
by chanting Hare Kṛṣṇa, 639
by devotional service, 51, 158, 159
by "dovetailing" with the Supreme, 222
fearlessness by, 41
by glorifying the Lord, 247
by hearing Lord's pastimes, 737
by Kṛṣṇa consciousness, 622
by *kṛṣṇa-kathā*, 168
mantras for, 538
by pilgrimage, 736
by pilgrim's journey, 19
by pure devotee's association, 71
receiving Lord's mercy requires, 610-611
by self-control, 548-549
of senses, 607, 813

Purification
by thinking of the Lord, 32
by transcendental water, 505
by worshiping the Lord, 245
See also: Austerity; Bathing; Devotional service; Sacrifices; Self-realization: Cleanliness; Liberation
Pūru Mahārāja, 104, 295, 295-296
Puruṣa
defined, 1026
defined & detailed, 976
living entity as, 976, 1220
Lord as, 976, 1221
Purusa-avatāras, 1141, 1323, 1329
as creative incarnations, 160
listed, 278
Lord as basis of, 73, 175, 181
three named, 1075
See also: Garbhodakaśāyī Viṣṇu; Mahā-Viṣṇu; Supersoul; Viṣṇu, Lord: *names of individual avatāras*
Puruṣa defined, 932
Purusa-śakti defined, 241
Pūtanā, 1335
Pūtanā, Kṛṣṇa mercy on, 75

Q

Qualifications of a devotee of God, 578
Qualities, material. *See:* Modes of material nature
Questions
to qualified teacher, 376
by Vidura to Maitreya, 155-174, 256-291
by Vidura to Uddhava, 25-46
Questions & answers, material vs. spiritual, 3-4

R

Rādha-Kṛṣṇa
beauty of, 758-759
chanting names of, 736
Gauḍīya Vaisnava prefers, 754
See also: Kṛṣṇa, Lord
Rādhārāṇī, 1302, 1366
Rādhārāṇī, beauty of, 600
Rādhārāṇī, Śrīmatī, 250
Rāga-bhakti defined, 159, 272
Rahūgaṇa Mahārāja & Jaḍa Bharata, 835
Rain cloud & spiritual master's mercy, analogy of, 793
Rain, demigod of, 1017
Rājasūya sacrifice, 62, 70
Rājasika marriage, 844-845
Rāja-vidyā defined, 607
Rajo-guṇa. See: Passion, mode of
Rākṣasas defined, 543
Rākṣasas (man-eaters), 749-750, 751
Ramā, 354
Rāma, Lord, 34
Hanumān worships, 753, 754, 944
Rāvaṇa overpowered by, 691
Śiva meditates on, 870
Rāmādi-mūrtiṣu kalā-niyamena tiṣṭhan quoted, 753, 1323
Rāmānanda Rāya, 612
Rāmāyaṇa, quoted on Hanumān's love for Sītā-Rāma, 754
Rameśvara, 137
Rāmeśvaram, 736
Rāsa-līlā
dance, 343, 357
as perfection of life, 182
in Vṛndāvana, 87
See also: Gopīs
Rasas. See: Kṛṣṇa, relationships with; Supreme Lord, relationships with
Rasa-varjaṁ raso 'py asya paraṁ dṛṣṭvā nivartate quoted, 276
Rāvaṇa, 543, 573, 683, 691
Reactions, sinful. *See: Karma;* Sinful ac- tivities
Reading, material vs. spiritual, 164
Reality vs. reflection, 346
Reality. See: Absolute Truth; Spiritual world
Realization, God. *See:* Knowledge, spiritual
Realization, spiritual
by devotional service, 942

Realization, spiritual (*continued*)
process of, 921
See also: God realization; Knowledge; Kṛṣṇa consciousness; Self- realization; Spiritual life
Reflection
in moon-on-water analogy, 267-268
in theory of Supreme, 204
Regulative principles
in daily worship, 352
for human beings, 106
purpose of, 17, 159
See also: Laws of God: Religious principles; Vedic injunctions
Reincarnation. *See:* Birth & death, repeated; Body, material; Consciousness; Transmigration
Relationships, bodily vs. spiritual, 622
See also: Supreme Lord, relationships with
of *brāhmaṇas & kṣatriyas*, 828, 831, 832
of disciple & spiritual master, 836-838, 876, 910, 928
to God. *See:* Supreme Lord, love for of kings & sages, 828
Relief, material vs. spiritual, 910
Religion
defined, 335
devotional service as essence of, 334-336
enforcement of, 642
false, 953
goal of, 287
as harmony with God's laws, 590
for humans, 445
as Lord's laws, 791, 792
in Satya-yuga, 411
service attitude in, 243
as surrender to God, 792
Yudhiṣṭhira established, 35
See also: Devotional service; Kṛṣṇa consciousness; Sacrifice; Worship; Religious principles
Religiosity, material, 1005, 1132, 1206, 1356
Religious principles
authorities on, 336
confidential conclusion of, 634
Deity form establishes, 17
four listed, 454, 458
good progeny by, 542-543
Lord protects, 350
purpose of, 48
three listed, 639
See also: Devotional service; Kṛṣṇa consciousness; Purification; Sacrifices; Supreme Lord, worship of: Regulative principles; Religion; Vedic injunctions
Renounced orders. *See: Varṇāśrama* system
Renunciants. *See: Sannyāsīs*
Renunciation
cause for, 15
by devotional service, 985, 1019-1020
devotional service requires, 996
for devotional service, 431, 500
as evidence of devotional service, 1118-1119
of family life, 949, 957-958
of family life required, 1245
four principles of, 774
by Kapila and Kardama, 1384
by knowledge, 1313
by *kṛṣṇa-kathā*, 171-172
by Lord, 637
of material life, 793, 794
on pilgrimage, 19
real, vs. false, 990, 1312
self-realization aided by, 983
of sex life, 1079
by Śiva, 535
in *varṇāśrama* system, 1351
See also: Austerity: Detachment; Retirement; *Sannyāsa*
Repentance by Diti, 539-541
See also: Austerity; Penance
Residences, Vedic vs. modern, 855-856
Respect toward *brāhmaṇas*, 628
Retirement
from mundane service, 49

Retirement
value of, 287
See also: Sannyāsa; Vānaprastha; Pilgrimage places; Renunciation; *Sannyāsīs*
Ṛg Veda from Mahā-Viṣṇu, 34
Rg Veda, quoted on brāhmaṇas, 620
Ritualistic ceremonies. *See:* Sacrifices; Vedic injunctions
devotees don't need, 767
for economic development, 773
See also: Sacrifices; Supreme Lord, worship of; *names of specific ceremonies*
Rituals, Vedic, seven listed, 499
See also: Sacrifice; Worship
Rivers, sacred, 199
Rohiṇī, 27
Ṛṣabhadeva, cited on children, 521
Ṛṣabha, Lord, cited on material world, 919-920
Ṛṣi-kulas defined, 855
Ṛṣis defined, 930
See also: Sages
Ṛtus defined, 795
Ruci, 779
Rudra, 235
Rudra, Lord, 1328
Rudra. *See:* Siva, Lord
Rukminī, 28, 91, 109, 250
Rukmiṇī, Kṛṣṇa kidnapped, 845
Rukmiṇī-Kṛṣṇa, Gauḍīya Vaiṣṇava worships, 754
Rules and regulations. *See:* Austerity; Purification; Sacrifices
Rūpa Gosvāmī
as author, 51
Caitanya praised by, 877
cited on disciple & spiritual master, 836
cited on relating everything with Kṛṣṇa, 737-738
money-managing shown by, 809
quoted on Caitanya as Kṛṣṇa, 939
quoted on devotional service, 316
teachings of, 292
Rūpa Gosvāmī, quotations from
on pure devotional service, 1190, 1192
Rūpa Gosvāmī, quotations from
on renunciation, 1306-1307
on serving Lord, 1375
Rudra principle, effect of, 435

S

Śabda-brahma defined, 462
Śabda-mūlatvāt
quoted, 1364
Sabīja-yoga, 1167
Śacī, 93
Sac-cid-ānanda-vigraha defined, 796
Sacred places. *See:* Pilgrimage places
Sacrifice, 1351-1353
chanting makes one eligible for, 1368
in ignorance, 1206
Sacrifice (*yajña*)
by family men, 526
feeding *brāhmaṇas* vs., 625
food offered to Lord in, 115, 209, 270
to Indra, 85
into fire, 518
in Kṛṣṇa consciousness, 723
to Lord, 342
Lord as enjoyer of, 716, 723, 806
for Lord's pleasure, 772, 859
by Parāśara, 302
plates in, 498
for present Age, 497
for protection of fallen father, 11
purpose of, 115
types of, 499, 716
Vedic *mantras* in, 503
by widows, 39
See also: Austerity; Purification; Ritualistic ceremonies; Supreme Lord, worship of: Charity; Vedic rituals; Welfare activity; Worship
Sādhana-bhakti defined, 272
Sādhu-saṅga defined, 912
Sādhana-siddhas defined, 112
Sādhvī defined, 870

Sādhu defined, 643
defined, 988
as devotee of Lord, 987
as friend, 989
knowledge from, 987
nature of, detailed, 987-990
See also: Devotees
Sādhur eva sa mantavyaḥ
quoted, 986
Sādhus. See: Devotees; Sages; Saints; Transcendentalists
Sādhyas, 766
Sages
Brahmā created, 773
as *dvija-devas*, 23
Kardama's daughters married by, 937-938
king's relationship to, 828
at Naimiṣāraṇya meeting, 727
nine named, 930
as perfect persons, 778
worshiping God, 857
See also: *Brāhmaṇas; Jñānīs; Ṛṣis;* Saintly persons: Devotees; Pure devotees; Saints; Transcendentalists
Sa guṇān samatītyaitān
quoted, 1140-1141
Saguṇa vs. *nirguṇa* Brahman, 1041
Sahadeva, 38
Sahasra-yuga-paryantam
quoted, 313
Sa guṇān samatītyaitān
quoted, 960
Saintly persons, qualities of, 578
association with, 833, 834, 912, 913, 915
function of, 836
as perfect persons, 778
residences of, 855-856
See also: Ācāryas; Brāhmaṇas; Devotees, pure devotees; *Mahātmās;* Sages; Spiritual master
Saints
mercy of, 21
see good in others, 75
Saints
See also: Devotees; *Sādhus*; Pure devotees; Sages; Transcendentalists
Sa kāleneha mahatā
quoted, 952
Sakāma defined, 340
Sakāma devotees, 801-802
Sakti-tattvas defined, 212
Saktyāveśa-avatāras defined, 179
Śakuni, 12
Śālva, 97
Salvation. *See:* Devotional service; Freedom; Oneness: Liberation
Samādhi, 1172, 1391
by remembering Lord, 1136
Samādhi defined, 446, 604, 785
Samādhi. See: Trance
Sa mahātmā sudurlabhaḥ
quoted, 1057
Samajāyata defined, 109
Samāna air, 224
Sāma Veda, Garuda vibrating, 813
Sāmba, 30
Śambara, 98
Sambhavāmy ātma-māyayā
quoted, 1273
Sampradāya defined, 430
Sampradāya. See: Disciplic succession
Samprajñāta defined, 786
Saṁsāra defined, 793, 975
See also: Birth and death, repeated; Bondage, material; Transmigration
Saṁśaya defined, 934
Saṁvatsara defined, 405
Sanātana Gosvāmī, cited on hearing from nondevotees, 727
Sanātana Gosvāmī, 1025, 1152
quoted on initiation, 1369
Sarhsāra. See: Transmigration
Sanat-kumāra, 301, 1328
Sāndīpani Muni, 90, 291
Sanaka, Sanātana, Sanandana & Sanat- kumara. *See:* Kumāras, the four

Sanātana defined, 634
Śaṅkara. *See:* Śiva (Śaṅkara), Lord
Saṅkarācārya as Śiva, 530
Śaṅkarācārya, cited
on Nārāyana as supreme, 1195
on beauty, true & false, 759
on Nārāyaṇa, 784
on woman's breasts, 897
Saṅkarṣaṇa, 1051
worship of, 1048
Saṅkarṣaṇa, Lord, 810-811
Śaṅkarācārya, Śrīpāda
avoided *Bhāgavatam*, 135
cited on Ganges, 199
Kṛṣṇa accepted by, 57
Saṅkarṣaṇa, cosmic dissolution by, 416, 417
Saṅkarṣaṇa, Lord, 301
Śaṅkha defined, 582
Sāṅkhya philosophy, 1089, 1181, 1376
defined, 1000
as devotional service, 1024
devotional service as goal of, 976
liberation by, 1023-1024, 1361
prakṛti & *puruṣa* as subjects of, 976
as self-realization, 1025
as spiritual knowledge, 1025
See also: Devotional service
Sāṅkhya philosophy, purpose of, 106, 284
Brahmā created, 429-430
devotional service as goal of, 943
Kapiladeva explained, 810, 848, 925, 933-935, 943, 951
mental speculation vs., 951-952
purpose of, 953
for self-realization, 951
subject of, 424
two types of, 810
Sāṅkhyāyana Muni, 301, 302
Saṅkīrtana. See: Preaching Kṛṣṇa consciousness; Supreme Lord, glorification of
Saṅkīrtana movement
Indian royalty relishes, 861
Saṅkīrtana movement
See also: Chanting of the Supreme Lord's holy names; Kṛṣṇa consciousness movement; Supreme Lord, glorification of
Saṅkīrtana-yajña for Kali-yuga, 498
See also: Chanting the holy names; Hare Kṛṣṇa *mantra;* Preachers; Supreme Lord, glorification of
Sannyāsa, necessity of, 1244-1246
Sannyāsa (renounced life)
bogus vs. bona fide, 948
danger in, 528
defined, 458
divisions of, 460
in Kali-yuga, 950
perfectional stage of, 849
purpose of, 950
women not allowed in, 956
See also: Renunciation
Sannyāsīs (renunciants)
bogus, 950
bogus vs. bona fide, 948
detachment of, 958
duty of, 809, 948
goal of, 31
gṛhasthas support, 525, 527
preaching of, 586
qualification for, 41
as traveler, 948, 958
trees shelter, 121
two types of, 248
wife forbidden for, 956
See also: Renunciation
Saraṇya, Lord as, 976
Sanskrit alphabet, 462
Śānti, 938
Sarasvatī, goddess, 446
Sarasvatī River, 779, 812, 816, 855, 890, 924, 1377
holy places on, 19
Kṛṣṇa at, 118, 121
Sarva-kāraṇa-kāranam
quoted, 946

Sarvātmanā yaḥ śaraṇaṁ śaraṇyaṁ
verse quoted, 431
Sārūpya-mukti defined, 129
Sarva-dharmān parityajya
quoted, 222
Sarva-gata defined, 165
Sarvaṁ khalv idaṁ brahma
quoted, 162, 1041
Sarvasya cāhaṁ hṛdi sanniviṣṭo
quoted, 756
verse quoted, 126, 224
Sarvatra prakāśa tāṅra-bhakta sukhe dite
verse quoted, 18
Śāstras (scriptures). *See: Bhagavad-gītā; Śrīmad-Bhāgavatam; Vedas; names of other specific scriptures*
Śāstras (Vedic scriptures). See: Literature; Vedas; Vedic literature; names of specific literatures
Śāstra-yonitvāt
quoted, 1343
Śatarūpā, 466
Śatarūpā, Queen, **803, 852**
Satataṁ kīrtayanto māṁ
verse quoted, 250
Sat defined, 977
Satī, 541
Satisfaction in worst condition of life, 1256
Satisfaction. See: Happiness; Peace
Ṣaṭ-karma-nipuṇo vipro
quoted, 239
Sat-saṅga chāḍi kainu asate vilāsa
quoted, 1052
Sattva-saṁśuddhiḥ defined, 41
Sātvatas defined, 222
Saturn planet, 660, 665
Satyabhāmā, 93
Satyaloka, 1010
Satya-yuga
duration of, 410
Kardama saw Lord in, 782
life-span in, 782
Lord appears in, 939
Satya-yuga
meditation meant for, 607
religiosity in, 411
Saubala, 99
Saubhari Muni, 904
Suvarna-vaṇik defined, 242
Śaunaka
quoted on narrations of Lord's pastimes, 737
quoted on Svāyambhuva Manu, 733
as sages' chief, 727
Śaunaka Ṛṣi, narration by, **965,** 966
Sa vai manaḥ kṛṣṇa-padāravindayoḥ
quoted, 1097, 1350
Sāyujya-mukti defined, 207
"Scholars" deny surrender to Kṛṣṇa, 954
Scientific research on subtle forms, 1061
Scientists
birth-death process baffles, 953-954
Lord's laws control, 747, 748
Scientists, material
atom as considered by, 397
cannot make food, 115
cannot produce life, 184
destiny of, 335
fools impressed by, 504
in illusion, 324
Lord unseen to, 192-193
nature vs., 379-380
planets misunderstood by, 165
puzzled by the Supreme, 251
space travel and, 566, 581
See also: Atheists: Philosophers, speculative
Scripture
as authority on Kṛṣṇa, 1142-1143
as authority on *yoga*, 979
detachment by hearing from, 996
devotees follow, 988
devotees only can understand, 994
discussed among devotees, 1201
evolution told in, 1215
impersonalists misunderstand, 1005
Lord known by, 1341-1343
materialists reject, 1331, 1332

Scripture
as mercy of Lord, 1355
piety taught in, 994
temple recitations of, 1008
yogīs must read, 1133
See also: Bhagavad-gītā; Śrīmad- Bhāgavatam; Vedas; and others by name
Scriptures
See: Bhagavad-gītā; Śrīmad- Bhāgavatam; Vedas; names of other specific scriptures
beginning & advanced, 170
compared to favorable breeze, 576
"contradiction" in, 66-67
as God's laws, 100
sex life according to, 536
See also: Vedas; Vedic literature; names of specific Vedic literatures
Seclusion, 1101, 1102
Sectarianism, bodily concept causes, 749
Seed
of banyan tree, 252
of devotional service, 52-53
Self. *See:* Soul
Self-control, animosity cured by, 548-549
Self-interest, devotional service as, 480
Selfishness displeases the Lord, 340
Self-realization
authorized process for, 603-605
in *Bhagavad-gītā*, 169
brahma-bhūta stage of, 865
by *buddhi-yoga*, 225
by chanting Hare Kṛṣṇa, 950
characteristics & symptoms of, detailed, 984, 1023, 1168-1172
as clear consciousness, 1049
compared to waking from dream, 1122
conclusion of, 266-267
consciousness realized by, 204
defined, 586
detachment by, 1025
of devotee, 961, 1101, 1102
by devotional service, 984-985, 1126
devotional service follows, 983-984, 1179
Self-realization
by goodness, 169
happiness of, 1170
by hearing from authority, 1025
of identity as part & parcel of Lord, 1177-1178
intelligence for, 1056
via intelligence, 343
knowledge & detachment in, 200
by Kṛṣṇa consciousness, 1344
Kṛṣṇa consciousness as, 1104
life arranged for, 428
lower modes block, 169
man meant for, 164
in moon-on-water analogy, 267-268
prerequisite for, 363
process of, 807-809
process of. *See:* Devotional service
real, vs. false, 1283
requirement for, 778
Sāṅkhya philosophy for, 951
by serving Lord, 962
Sāṅkhya as, 1025
sex attraction hinders, 448, 449
society needs, 139, 140
spiritual master needed for, 291
in Vedic culture, 458
vision from, 409
See also: Devotional service; God realization; Meditation; Spiritual life; *Yoga:* Knowledge, spiritual; Kṛṣṇa consciousness; Soul
Self-realized souls. *See: Ācāryas;* Devotees, pure devotees; *Mahātmās;* Saintly persons; Spiritual master
Sense gratification
for animals, 911
brāhmaṇas averse to, 830-831
conditioned soul seeks, 767
demons pursue, 670, 684, 698, 764, 789, 830
for fools, 789
householder not meant for, 840
humans not meant for, 911
material life as, 797, 841
material vs. spiritual, 787

Self-realized souls (*continued*)
meditation precluded by, 778
See also: Attachment, material; Bodily concept of life; Desires; Enjoyment, material; Happiness; Pleasure; Sex life
Semen, impregnation by, 104, 177, 184
Sense control, 1020
artificial, 1097
by chanting Hare Kṛṣṇa, 1003
by devotional service, 1097, 1301-1302
human life affords, 1283
by *prasāda*, 1003
See also: Austerity; Celibacy; Detachment; Renunciation
Sense gratification
adverse effect of, 370
compared to chewing chewed, 1316
as criminal, 592
degradation by, 1297
demigods desire, 340
detachment from, 270
devotees don't care about, 995
devotees reject, 611, 612
vs. devotional service, 971
in family life, 1315-1317
higher force controls, 110
inauspicious result of, 331
intelligence lost by, 1250
for the Lord, 212
marriage for, condemned, 526
material & spiritual, 587
philanthropy as, 1096
religion not for, 1132
secondary in Vaikuṇṭha, 568
Vedas regulate, 561
wealth used for, 330
world encourages, 1250
See also: Bliss; Desire; Ecstasy; Enjoyment; Happiness; Lust: Attachment, material; Desires, material; Sex life
Sense objects, five listed, 744
Senses
for animals, 1214-1216
Senses
bodily airs power, 224
control of
caution in, 447-448
by demigods, 388
via good wife, 527
by personalists, 538
purpose of, 560
sense purification vs., 607
in *yoga*, 603-604
See also: Sense control: Meditation; *Yoga*
as demigods' representatives, 1001
for devotional service, 1020
as elements' distinctive characteristics, five given, 1070
embryonic development of, 1265
evolution of, 190, 192
evolution of. *See:* Evolution
gratification of. *See:* Sense gratification
higher engagement for, 270
imperfect, 609
internal (subtle), four aspects of, 1040
knowledge-acquiring, five listed, 1039
levels of, 1212-1216
living entity separate from, 1310
Lord beyond, 226
material & spiritual, 367
mind & intelligence above, 480
mind leads, 1001
origin of, 189, 228-230
owner of, 479
proper use of, 1083
purified in devotional service, 1104
servants of, 363
soul disturbed by, 270
spiritual, vs. material, 971
time factor on, 383
transcendental, 110
of trees, 1214
universal form entered by, 1083-1086
Vedas regulate, 561
working (organs for action), five listed, 1039-1040

Senses
  See also: Body, material; *names of individual senses;* False ego; Intelligence; Mind
Senses, material
  happiness beyond, 761, 786
  knowledge-acquiring, 744
  Lord beyond range of, 719, 812
  purification of, 812
  for working, 744
  See also: Body, material; Intelligence; Mind
Separatism, 1187-1189, 1208
Serpent (s)
  Brahmā created, 770
  Hiraṇyākṣa compared to, 699
  nondevotees compared to, 727
Servants of God. *See:* Devotees
Service
material vs. spiritual, 364
  illusory vs. eternal, 243, 244-245, 266
  See also: Devotional service
Service to God. *See:* Devotional service
Service to Lord. *See:* Devotional service; Living entity, as servant of Lord
Śeṣa, 1319
Śeṣa, Lord, 73, 314
Sex desire
  girl misled by, 804
  of man & woman, 904
  See also: Attachment, material; Desires; Enjoyment, material; Sense gratification; Sex life
Sex (gender), determination of, 1266
Sex life
  animal vs. human, 393
  animallike, 1297
  attachment to
    degradation by, 1297
    detailed, 1296-1306
    freedom from, 1165
    as universal, 1299-1301
  for begetting children, 666, 848, 881
  as binding, 1164-1165
  Brahmā attracted to, 448, 449, 452
Sex life
  brahmacārīs abstain from, 459
  cleanliness after, 538
  conditioned souls seek, 748-749
  as creation principle, 1073
  dangers in, 448-449, 450-453
  death caused by, 1079
  demigods free of, 752, 758
  demons pursue752, 761, 762
  discharges during, determine child's gender, 907
  Diti desired, 518-523, 536
  of hogs & humans, 274
  homosexual, 755
  for householders, 843, 881
  illicit, 774, 950
  illicit, invites ghosts, 530
  illicit, punishment for, 1255
  illicit, safeguard against, 527
  impregnation from, 104, 184
  inauspicious time for, 529, 531
  irregular, as prostitution, 536, 539
  Kali-yuga marriage based on, 790, 931
  kāma-śāstra cited on, 881
  knowledge & detachment vs., 200
  of Lord transcendental, 109, 110
  lust for, 523
  material life based on, 1057, 1255
  materialists indulge in, 905
  as material life's basis, 748-749, 752
  mentality during, importance of, 652
  misidentification with matter by, 919
  origin of, 231, 466, 1301
  perfect devotee beyond, 537
  permissible, 1100
  as pleasurable duty, 528, 529
  preparation for, 543
  for procreation, 520
  for procreation, purification of, 1267
  purified, population by, 775
  purpose of, 476-477
  by religious principles, 543
  by renunciant condemned, 527
  restrictions for, 1133, 1255, 1388

Sex life (*continued*)
spiritual pleasure surpasses, 571
spiritual enjoyment vs., 761
soul comes during, 1263
time forgotten during, 905
Yāmunācārya cited on, 1165
Yāmunācārya quoted on, 1302
"*yoga*" and, 604
"*yogīs*" encourage, 761
See also: Children; Lust; Marriage: Attachment, material; Desires, material; Sense gratification
Siddhaloka, 936
Siddhaloka planet, life on, 395
Siddhas
Brahmā created, 768
Kardama praised by, 900
Kuvera praised by, 899
space travel by, 923
Siddhas defined, 813
Siddhi as goal of *yoga*, 581
Siddhapada, 1394
Sight, 1071
Signs. *See:* Omens Silence vow, 959
Śikṣāṣṭaka, cited on purification by chanting Hare Kṛṣṇa, 1082
Śikṣāṣṭaka, quotations from
on chanting Kṛṣṇa's names, 1139
on cleansing heart by chanting, 1139
on devotee as desireless, 1193
on *saṅkīrtana*, 1139
Sincerity to serve God, 368, 510
Sin
excused by Lord, 1015
in forgetfulness of Lord, 974
for maintaining family, 1241
punishments for, detailed, 1248-1260
reactions of, devotional service doesn't produce, 1116-1117
reactions of, devotional service removes, 1367-1368
witnessed by Supersoul, 1044
See also: Materialism
Sinful activity
atheists flaunt, 748
of devotees forgiven by the Lord, 453
demigods & devotees free of, 703, 704
demons indulge in, 703, 704
four listed, 950
freedom from, 736
by ghosts, 530
hearing Hiraṇyākṣa-Varāha pastimes absolves, 730
in mind given up, 756
neglecting dependents as, 627
natural disturbance indicates, 660
as offense in chanting holy name, 579
spiritual culture vs., 639
surrender to God absolves, 797
thinking of Kṛṣṇa cleanses, 649
of wayward wife, 872
worst type of, 452
See also: Karma
Sin(s)
eating without sacrifice as, 115, 209
Ganges destroys, 199, 299
holy places absolve, 16, 17
pitiable result of, 173
spiritual blindness from, 5, 17
See also: Offense(s)
Siraḥ-snāna defined, 893-894
Śiśupāla, 69, 70-72, 91, 913
Sītādevī, 250
Sītā-Rāma, Hanumān devoted to, 754, 944
Sitting postures
described, 1137
in *yoga*, 1134
Śiva, Lord (Rudra), 1328
as annihilator, 850
as Āśutoṣa, 540
born of Brahmā's anger, 433
cosmic dissolution by, 415
devotees of, 534
disciplic succession from, 870
food remnants of, 532-533
Ganges held by, 1152

Śiva, Lord (Rudra)
ghosts worship, 529
headhunter harassed, 698
Kaśyapa heeded, 529-535
kind to women, 541
Lord above, 345
& Mohinī, 1299
as Mahādeva, 533-534
in meditation, 441
names of, 436
offense to, 539
offspring of, 438
Pārvatī served, 869-870
as Pārvatī's spiritual master, 920-921
as Rāvaṇa's lord, 691
residences of, 435
Saṅkarṣaṇa worshiped by, 1048
as servant of Supreme Lord, 1152
as topmost Vaiṣṇava, 870
unmarried women worship, 870
wives of, 437
worship of, 1082
Śiva defined, 816
Śivānanda Sena, 1208
Śiva(Śaṅkara), Lord
Arjuna tested by, 37
false ego rules by, 235
as ignorance mode deity, 201-202
Kārttikeya born of, 30
Lord's creation preceded, 181
Six Gosvāmīs, 1201
Sky, 1070
Skyscrapers in ancient times, 846, 884
Sky symbolizes Supreme Soul, 190
Sleep
brahmacārī minimizes, 821
drooling in, 765
of living beings after dissolution, 218
Lord creates during, 289
of Lord, 351-353, 418, 423
necessity of, 1055-1056
of nondevotees fitful, 334
regulation of, 1388
Smara, 28
Smārta-brāhmaṇas, 1371
Smile, Kṛṣṇa conscious, 851
Smell, sense of, 1064, 1071
Smells, kinds of, 1069
Smṛti-śāstra, cited
on ladies bathing, 893
on male-female discharges during sex, 907
Snake and fool, analogy of, 12
Snakes. *See:* Serpents
Snakes as untamable, 391
Snake-king, 84
Society, divisions in. *See: Varaṇāśrama* system
Society, human
agrarian, 81, 242
Bhāgavatam helps, 297
birth control in, 177
bodily designations in, 166
in chaos, 827
compared to blind leading blind, 333
compared to body, 831, 832
criterion for, 370, 454
defenseless beings in, 627
devotees serve, 139-140
"food shortage" in, 161
good progeny in, formula for, 542-543
householders support, 525
ideal leaders needed in, 640
industry degrades, 242
irresponsibility in, 419
in Kali-yuga, 845, 848
Kṛṣṇa consciousness for, 832, 860
Kṛṣṇa consciousness purifies, 622
kṣatriyas protect, 240, 242
lawbook for, 479
laws governing, 561
leaders of, 114
literature for, 509, 511
literature in, 164, 167, 170-171
orders of, purpose of, 525, 527
passion causes war in, 21
peace formula for, 242
pilgrims beyond customs of, 19

Society, human (*continued*)
protection lacking in, 241
of purified people, 757
reformation of, 544
religious leaders of, 336
sacrifice meant for, 209
sages uplift, 23
See: Human beings; Human life
sexual degradation in, 448, 527, 544
spiritual life for, 859
as spiritually advanced, 825-826
suicide in, 530
upper classes respected in, 640, 641
Vedic knowledge for, 456
See also: Civilization, human; Human beings; Population: Human beings; *Varnāśrama- dharma;* Vedic culture
Soma plant, 1318
Son-father relationship, 474-476
Son
as enemy, 872
as father's representative, 910
as father's servant, 928
mother delivered by, in old age, 956
obliged to parents, 68
saves father's soul, 11
See also: Children
Soul
See also: Soul, conditioned; Soul, liberated
as active always, 1178
beyond fatigue, 49
beyond material qualities, 268
beyond miseries, 333
beyond senses, mind & intelligence, 480
beyond suffering, 275
in bodily concept, 934
body contrasted to, 951
body develops from, 226
body energized by, 720
Buddhists deny, 135
as central generating force, 223-224
compared to bird, 225, 1044
compared to spark of fire, 1177
Soul
at conception, 1263
consciousness as symptom of, 1026, 1040
as consciousness, 221, 222, 259-260
departed, oblations to, 767
elements covering, 223
equality of, 363
as eternal, 977, 1042
eternal, 951
forgetting himself, 260
goodness reveals, 169
ignorance about, 748
as individual eternally, 1110-1111
intelligence as symptom of, 1113
as life's cause, 1176
limited consciousness of, 605-606
as Lord's separated expansion, 357
living entity as, 77, 982, 985, 1017, 1024, 1034, 1042, 1046, 1102, 1112, 1177, 1388-1389
Lord impregnates nature with, 1030
as Lord's part & parcel, 982, 1178, 1179, 1206
in matter, cause of, 591
& matter combined, living entity as, 1112
as misidentified, 387
nature of, 1034
nature of, detailed, 982
nondevotees misunderstand, 159
senses of, 971
as servant of Lord eternally, 1024, 1092, 1109
of Śiśupāla merged with Kṛṣṇa, 70
size of, 982
vs. Supersoul, 1178, 1205, 1212
svāṁśa, vs. vibhinnāṁśa, 1177
as transcendental, 1034
Supersoul contrasted to, 605-606, 832-833, 962
Supersoul realized by, 785, 786
symptoms of, 169, 204, 226, 247
transmigration of
devotional service stops, 795
material life caused by, 793
See also: Birth and death, repeated; Bondage, material; Destiny; *Karma*

Soul
in womb of mother, 104
See also: Identity; Living entities; Self-realization; Souls, conditioned; Transmigration
Souls, conditioned
in bodily concept, 748-749
compared to diseased man, 1178
compared to fire, 1177
compared to fish out of water, 59
compared to haunted or mad man, 1032
controlled by material nature, 1032-1034, 1014
controlled by modes, 1030, 1031, 1093
covered by illusory energy, 1030-1032
creation made for, 1364
Creation provided for, 742-743
defects of, four named, 1060
deny essential topics, 174
devotees compassionate toward, 332
devotional service essential for, 443
duty of, devotional service as, 1097
"eternally," 1031
as false doers, 15
four defects of, 927
ghosts harass, 765
good wife helps, 524, 527
history of, 1030
ignorance-coverings of, 748-749
illusory enjoyment of, 161
in illusion, 428
illusions of. *See:* Illusion
as impregnated into world, 503
independence of, 1044
vs. liberated soul, 1107
liberation for. *See:* Liberation
Kṛṣṇa conscious advancement by, 862
Lord comes to redeem, 622
Lord contrasted to, 740, 960
Lord gives memory to, 224
Lord's kindness to, 734
lording propensity of, 243-245
in lotus-flower reservoir, 746
Souls, conditioned
material creation meant for, 182, 186, 212, 259
material diseases of, two, 1120
in *māyā*, 962
misdirected interests of, 575
misidentify with matter, 919
misplaced affection of, 371-372
modes of nature control, 257
movement of, restricted, 901
nature's laws control, 792
as *puruṣa* or *prakṛti*, 975
reincarnation of. *See:* Transmigration as servant & subordinate to Lord, 1274-1275
seek sense enjoyment, 743, 748-749, 767
seek sex life, 748-749
sense gratification and, 331, 561
spiritual life necessary for all, 1207
vs. Supersoul, 1089, 1220, 1274-1275, 1345
& Supersoul, relationship between, 1044, 1274-1275
Supersoul for. *See:* Supreme Lord, as Supersoul transmigration of. *See:* Transmigration *See also:* Illusion; Living entities; Material life
suffering of, 940
See also: Animals; Human beings; Living entities; Materialists; Soul
Souls, liberated
vs. conditioned soul, 1107
detailed, 1168-1173
devotees as, 813
See also: Ācāryas; Devotees, pure devotees; *Mahātmās;* Spiritual master
Sound
importance of, 230
material vs. spiritual, 800
as subtle form of ether, 1058, 1059
transcendental, 169
See also: Mantra South Pole as island, 776
Sound, transcendental
of Lord Boar's voice, 486-487

Sound, transcendental (*continued*)
  origin of, 462
  result of hearing, 329, 957
  See also: Chanting the holy names; Gāyatrī *mantra;* Hare Kṛṣṇa *mantra;* Supreme Lord, hearing about
Spaceman floating and impersonalist merging, analogy of, 76
Space travel, 1379
  by Brahmā, 936
  of humans & Siddhas contrasted, 923
  by mystic *yogis*, 581
  to other planets, 901
  by Siddhas, 395
  by *yogī*, 903
Species of life
  impious, 817
  Lord creates, 724
  number of, 724, 753
  pious, 665, 817
  See also: Animals; Human beings; Living entities
Speculation, mental. *See:* Knowledge, speculative; Philosophers, speculative
  as defective, 933
  as doubtful, 934
  Sāṅkhya philosophy vs., 951-952
Speculation, material
  compared to husking paddy, 1115, 1182
  as difficult process, 1347
  examples of, 1349
  faults of, 1342-1344
  as faulty process, 1348-1349
  vs. philosophical speculation, 1120
  as valueless, 1113-1115, 1182
Speculation, philosophical, 1120
Speech
  gravity in, 1100
  of Lord, 631
  proper use of, 613-614
Spider's web & Lord's Creation, analogy of, 796
Spirit
  advantages of, 977, 1123
Spirit
  as basis of affection, 372
  compared to razor's edge, 1050
  develops matter, 220
  devotees seen on basis of, 622
  everything as, 462
  impersonalists misconceive, 352
  necessity of, 977, 1123
  See: Soul; Supreme Lord Spiritual life
  See also: Body, spiritual; Brahman (impersonal Absolute); Soul; Spiritual world: Devotional service; Kṛṣṇa consciousness
Spiritualists. *See:* Devotees; Transcendentalists; *Yogis*
Spiritual knowledge. *See:* Knowledge, spiritual
Spiritual life. *See:* Devotional service; God consciousness
  advancement in. *See:* Advancement, spiritual
  compared to razor's edge, 356
  demigods promote, 667, 671
  early morning best for, 757, 769
  formula for achieving, 625
  human society meant for, 859
  materialists ineligible for, 773
  material life vs., 761
  offenses to avoid in, 578-579
  perfection in, 781, 835-837
  principles of, 638-639
  qualification for, 368
  sense enjoyment precludes, 773
  Vṛndāvana conducive to, 736
  See also: Devotional service; Knowledge, spiritual; Kṛṣṇa consciousness; Spiritual world
Spiritual light. *See:* Brahman effulgence
Spiritual master
  association with, 972
  of author, 459
  bogus vs. bona fide, 836
  in Brahmā's succession, 474-475
  compared to captain, 1270
  compared to ship's captain, 576

Spiritual master
confidence in, 376
Deity worship taught by, 1006
of demigods, 25
devotee's service chosen by, 997
devotional service via, 213
disciple asking favor from, 838
disciples of, duty of, 471, 836-838
in disciplic succession, 1200
disciple serving, 876
as eternal father, 163
faith in, 921, 928-929, 1375
as father, 928, 931
hearing from, 200, 248, 726, 836
husband as, 920
initiation by, 1358, 1368, 1369
instructions of, execution of, 836, 921, 928
kind to disciples, 288
knowledge by mercy of, 999
knowledge from, 972, 1060, 1131, 1133-1134
knowledge via, 927
Kṛṣṇa accepted, 90-91
as liberated, 1375-1376
Lord as, 1011, 1012, 1060
Lord known via, 876
as Lord's representative, 1188
Lord within as, 159
mercy of, 793, 999, 1355
as necessary, 245, 290, 291
necessity of, 972
offense to, 579
perfection via, 835-837
purification taught by, 1057
qualifications of, 140-142, 239-240, 1131, 1218, 1358
reciprocates disciple's service, 910
respect for, 1356-1358
spiritual advancement via, 736
for spiritual seekers, 3
success via, 276
as transparent medium to Kṛṣṇa, 606
trains by one's tendency, 837
of twice-born men, 163

Spiritual master
as within & without, 358
worship of, 1200
See also: Acāryas; Devotees, pure devotees; Disciplic succession

Spiritual planets. *See:* Planets, spiritual; Vaikuṇṭha planets

Spiritual sky
impersonalists attain, 1127
See also: Planets, spiritual; Spiritual world; Vaikuṇṭha planets

Spiritual world
attaining to. *See:* Liberation
devotees attain, 1127
elevation to, as eternal, 1335
as eternal & changeless, 1324
as eternal & supreme, 1340
falldown from, 998
flowers in, 1144
Kapila Vaikuṇṭha, 1393
lighted by Lord's luster, 1027
See also: Planets, spiritual; Vaikuṇṭha planets

Spiritual world (Vaikuṇṭha)
airplanes in, 568, 571, 580-581
as animate, 569, 582
attractive features of, 571
beyond material contact, 325, 326
blissful, 59, 107
composition of, 573
devotional creeper enters, 53
devotional service predominates in, 565
discussions about, value of, 575-576
earthly representatives of, 137
eligibility for entering, 127
enemies absent in, 644
entrance qualifications for, 577-578, 584, 588
eternal, 256
everything personal in, 567, 569
fragrances in, 568, 569-570
general description of, 565-589, 589, 590
goddesses of fortune in, 572, 573, 597-598
goodness in, 566

Spiritual world (Vaikuṇṭha) (*continued*)
harmony in, 589, 589-591
impersonalist's conception of, refuted, 575
inhabitants of, 712
inhabitants of as ageless, 582
as "bewildered," 506
good qualities of, 588
resemble Nārāyaṇa, 565
sole desire of, 568
Kṛṣṇa's expansions rule, 581
Kurukṣetra warriors went to, 72
landscape of, 567, 568, 569-570
location of, 598
Lord & devotees qualitatively equal in, 471
as Lord's internal potency, 932
material world vs., 723, 800, 925, 932
mystic *yogīs* enter, 581
Nārāyaṇa predominates, 565
opulence in, 626
path to, 813
planets in, 71, 746
in pure goodness, 723, 925
residences in, 564
respect for leaders in, 588
self-effulgent, 746
self-illuminating, 646
sense gratification absent in, 568
service attitude in, 364
sex desire absent in, 572
time in, 327, 423
variety in, 610
as visited via *Vedas*, 566
for worship in opulence, 71
See also: Goloka Vṛndāvana: Vṛndāvana
Sports
princesses played, 846
with women, demons arrange, 761
Śraddadhāna defined, 172
Śrāddha, 937
Śravaṇaṁ kīrtanam defined, 612
Śrāddha ritual, 767
Śrīdhara Svāmī, cited on monists and *Śrīmad-Bhāgavatam*, 135
Śrīdhara Svāmī
cited on *brāhmaṇas*, 1368
quoted on purification by chanting, 1368
Śrīdhara Svāmī, cited on *tri-yuga*, 638
on Brahmā dropping his body, 756
on Hiraṇyākṣa addressing Lord Boar, 681, 682, 684
on Lord's form, 944
on Lord's opulences, 939
Srī Caitanya-caritāmṛta. See: Caitanya-caritāmṛta Śrī Īśopaniṣad
cited on Lord's effulgence, 985
quoted on Lord as controller of all, 1111
Śrīmad-Bhāgavatam
ancient history of, 303
atomic theory in, 397
cited on chanting offensively, 578
cited on good qualities, 577, 578
essence of, 471
establishes real religion, 445
ever fresh, 164-165
four key verses in, 134-135
for *Gītā* graduates, 135
happiness from hearing, 967
hearing of, 249-250
hearing from, benefit of, 732
as history, 776-777
Indian royalty hears, 861
insatiably interesting, 738
as *kṛṣṇa-kathā*, 168
as Lord's personality, 128
Lord spoke, to Brahmā, 128
Lord's pastimes given in, 1005
materialistic religion rejected by, 1005
Māyāvādīs interpret, 135, 181
quoted on devotional service, 265
as *Paramahaṁsa-saṁhitā*, 849
sages heard, from Sūta Gosvāmī, 727
Śaṣkarācārya avoided, 135
society benefits by, 297
speaker of, 297, 298, 301
students of, advice to, 144
Vyāsa compiled, 170

Śrīmad-Bhāgavatam
See also: Vedic literature; Śrīmad-Bhāgavatam, cited; Śrīmad-Bhāgavatam, quotations from
Śrīmad-Bhāgavatam cited
on Absolute Truth, 955
on devotees & material world, 797-798
on devotional service, 1019
on hearing from authority, 727
on Kali-yuga marriage, 790, 931
on knowledge & renunciation by devotional service, 985
on Lord & His material energy, 1029
on Lord's innumerable incarnations, 753-754
on pure goodness, 723
on Siddhas, 923
on spiritual happiness, 761
on superior's responsibility to subordinate, 909
on Supreme Lord, 946
on Viṣṇu, 850
on worshiping Lord to fulfill desires, 790
Śrīmad-Bhāgavatam, quotations from
on Ambarīṣa Mahārāja, 990, 1097, 1349
on bhakti-yoga, 613
on blind leading blind, 1295
on Brahmā taught through heart, 1060
on chewing chewed, 1316
on devotional service to Vāsudeva, 1089, 1092
on dust of great devotee's feet, 835
on duties' perfection as pleasing Lord, 1117
on fear of death, 1042
on foolish man, 347-348
on glorification of Kṛṣṇa by Ambarīṣa Mahārāja, 990, 1097, 1350
on impersonalists, 436
on illusion, 1031
on liberation, 1375
on liberation, presumption of, by non-devotees, 1016
on Lord as forgiving, 453
on Lord's energies, 396
Śrīmad-Bhāgavatam, quotations from
on pure religion, 1099
on religious principles, 336
on service to devotees & to materialists, 987
on speculation as waste of time, 1115
on taking shelter of God, 957
on time, 383
Śrīvatsa, 1143, 1194
Śrīvatsa jewel, 318
Śrīvatsa mark, 712
Śruti defined, 1058-1059, 1059-1060
Stars reflect sunlight, 556
Gandharva girls compared to, 898
See also: Astrology; Astronomy: Planets, material; Universe
Starvation
cause of, 161, 209
solution to, 81
Sthāyi-bhāva defined, 550
Stomach, Lord compared to, 684
Strī defined, 880, 921
See also: Woman
Strī-śūdra-dvijabandhus defined, 170
Students
training of, 498
in Vedic society, 458, 459
See also: Spiritual master
Substances, auspicious, before & after bathing, 894
Subtle body. *See:* Body, material, subtle; Ego, false; Intelligence; Mind
Subtle body, elements of, 1172
Subtle bodies
at partial cosmic dissolution, 304
See also: False ego; Intelligence; Mind
Śucaḥ defined, 682
Success
by pleasing the Lord, 85
See also: Goal of life; Perfection
Śucīnām śrīmatām gehe
quoted, 48
Sudarśana *cakra*, 716, 1158
Śuddhādvaita, 1175
Śuddha-sattva, 1048, 1107

Śuddha-sattva defined, 148, 566-567, 610, 925
Śūdra
as created from Lord's legs, 830
defined, 178
duty of, 242, 243-244
Kali-yuga society as, 845, 950
Śūdras
association with, 1298
duties & service for, 1197
Suffering
birth after birth, 1287
of birth & death, 793
body as, 951
in childhood, 1292
of child in womb, 1266-1272, 1280
of conditioned souls, 940
devotee's view of, 1014
while dying, 1247-1249
Ganges relieves, 902
of hell, 1253-1260
hellish, on Earth, 1255
Kṛṣṇa consciousness stops, 859, 866
Lord relieves, 756, 876
in material world, 859, 866, 940
in old age, 1245
See: Misery
See also: Distress; Hell; Misery; Punishment
Sugar candy and Lord's speeches, analogy of, 8
Suhṛdaṁ sarva-bhūtānām
quoted, 586
Suhṛttama defined, 586
Suicide
by ignoring human life, 576
material & spiritual, 530
Śukrācārya, 805
Śukadeva Gosvāmī, 968
birth undesired by, 1286
Deities attracted, 1008
Sun as eye of Lord, 1078
Sun
brahmacārī rises before, 821
at demons' birth, 660
Lord compared to, 808, 955
Sun
rising & setting of, devotee's life undiminished by, 863
Supersoul compared to, 833
varṇāśrama system compared to, 826
Sunlight from *brahmajyoti*, 1027
Sun, Lord compared to, 44, 53, 54, 61, 65, 127, 264
at dissolution of universe, 415-416
duty of, 407
lights the universe, 556
as Lord's eye, 405
purifying power of, 450
Supersoul compared to, 605
time measured by, 399, 404
Sun-god
cow as daughter of, 627
qualification for seeing, 372
Superconsciousness, Lord's, 1027
Superconsciousness defined, 159, 605-606
Superior, responsibility of, to subordinate, 909
Supersoul. *See:* Supreme Lord, as Supersoul
Supreme Lord
See also: Kapila, Lord; Kṛṣṇa, Lord
as absolute, 1161
as Absolute Truth, 995-996
as all-pervading Lord of the universe, 1013
appearance days of, fasting on, 1119
association with. *See:* Supreme Lord, relationships with attachment for, 1383
as baby on banyan leaf, 1365-1366
beauty of, 1142-1166
benedictions of, to devotees, 1146
bodies possible for, 968
bodily luster of. *See:* Supreme Lord, effulgence of
bodily parts of, as omnipotent, 1156
body of, as transcendental, 1154, 1156, 1363
body of, universe as, 1345
as Brahman, Supreme, 1017
Brahman feature of. *See:* Brahman; Supreme Lord, impersonal feature of
Caitanya. *See:* Caitanya Mahāprabhu

Supreme Lord
carrier of, 1154-1155
as *catur-vyūha* (quadruple expansion), 1048, 1054
as cause of all, 1283, 1322, 1363
of creation, 1177
of creation, maintenance & destruction, 1231
of death, 1225
of remembrance & forgetfulness, 1277
chanting about. *See:* Devotional service, of chanting ... ; Devotional service, of preaching
as child of devotees, 1366
color of, scriptures give, 1142
compared to fire, 1174, 1177
compared to rich man, 1221
compared to sun, 973, 982, 1029, 1185
compassion of, 1186
consciousness of His, 1026
as controller
of demigods, 1230
by His energies, 1364
of nature, 1018, 1226-1231
by time factor, 1041-1045
ultimately, 1229, 1230
covering energy of, 1029, 1030
as creator, 1077, 1231
as death, 1211
decorations of, 1142-1144, **1156-1158**, 1160
defined, 1026
Deity form of, 1012
materials for forming, 1070, 1147, 1162
as transcendental, **1203**
Deity worship to. *See:* Devotional service, of Deity worship
vs. demigods, 1152
devotees of. *See:* Devotees
devotional service to. *See:* Devotional service
disciplic succession from. *See:* Disciplic succession
dress of, 1143, **1145**, 1154-1155
effulgence of. *See:* Brahman; *Brahmajyoti*

Supreme Lord
energies of. *See:* Energy
as enjoyer alone, 1096
as enjoyer of all sacrifices, 1224
envy of, 1119
as equal to all, 1226
as eternal, 1026-1028
as eternally related to His devotee, 1011-1013
excuses surrendered devotee, 1014
expansions of, 1141
eye of, sun as, 1078
face of, compared to lotus, **1162**
faith in. *See:* Faith in God
as father, 1030, 1046
features of, compared, 1339-1341
food offerable to if love included, 1209
food offered to. *See: Prasāda*
foods offerable to, 1101, 1197-1198
forgetfulness & remembrance from, 974
form of
Deity, 1012, 1070, 1147, 1162, 1201
Supreme Lord form of
described in detail, 1142-1166
by devotees' desires, 1161
as eternal, 1273
meditation on, 1147
as pleasing to devotees, 1006, 1007-1008
as Śyāmasundara, 1147
as friend of all, 1096
garland of, 1144
as goal
of all activities, 1351-1353
of spiritual life, 1347
of *yoga*, 1129-1130, 1157-1158, 1161, 1389
as greatest of the great, 1028
as greatest transcendentalist, 975
hearing about & from. *See:* Devotional service, of
hearing as Hṛṣīkeśa, 1001
illusory energy of. *See:* Energy, illusory; *Māyā*
impersonal & personal features of, 1339-1340

Supreme Lord (*continued*)
as goal
impersonal feature of, 1337, 1342-1343, 1387-1388
impersonal philosophy on. *See:* Impersonalism
impregnates material nature, **1045-1046**
incarnations of
for conditioned souls' benefit, 1367
examples of, 1367
Kapiladeva as, 966, 973
purposes for, 1161, 1273, 1367
puruṣas, 1323
as son, 1384-1385
as tortoise, **1158**
as universal form. *See:* Universal form
voluntarily come, 1034
Vyāsadeva as, 969
See also: names of individual incarnations
as inconceivable, 1075
as independent, 1273, 1345, 1363, 1364
internal energy of, 968
Kapila. *See:* Kapila, Lord Kapila as, 966, **1017, 1018, 1373,** 1383, 1129
Kaustubha gem of, 1143, **1157**
knowledge about. *See:* Knowledge, about Lord; Knowledge, spiritual
knowledge from, 966
Kṛṣṇa as, 1026
as lawmaker, 1228
laws of, atheists ignore, 1031
liberation arranged by, 1014
as light, 1028
light from, *brahmajyoti* as, 1027
limb-by-limb meditation on, 1149
vs. living entities, 967, 976, 982, 1012, 1029, 1030, 1032, 1033-1035, 1044, 1089, 1096, 1123, 1153, **1174,** 1177, 1205, 1220, 1274-1276, 1283, 1322, 1345
and living entity, oneness of, 982, 1025, 1175
lotus feet of, 1150-1152
lotus toes of, 1366
love for. *See:* Love for God

Supreme Lord
as maintainer of all, 1223, 1264
as master
of all masters, **1224-1225**
of death's activities, **1017**
of demigods, 1018
of the senses, 1001, 1350
& material nature, relationship between, 1036
material nature agitated by, 1043-1046
material nature entered by, 1073
māyā of. *See: Māyā*
meditation on. *See:* Devotional service, of remembering; Meditation
mercy of, 1044, 1161, **1281,** 1354-1355
merging with, compared to green bird & tree, 1108
mind as representative of, 1001
names of
potency of, 1366-1372
chanting of. *See:* Devotional service, of chanting Hare Kṛṣṇa
See also: individual names of Lord
as Nārāyaṇa, 1195
as *nirguṇa*, 1195
as *oṁkāra*, 1147
as omnipotent, 1156
as one with & different from His energy, 1111
as one with His devotees, 1012
opulences of, 967, **1143,** 1155, 1340
as origin
of all, 1026-1028
of creation, 1015
of Brahman & Paramātmā, 1223
of sex attraction, 1301
of universes, 1363
original form of, Kṛṣṇa as, 1133
as Paramātmā. *See:* Supreme Lord, as Supersoul
part & parcel of, souls as, 1177-1179, 1206
pastimes of
materialists reject, 1331-1333
material world created for, 1028, 1030-1031

Supreme Lord
pastimes of
meditation on, 1149
as pleasing to hear, 993
for reclaiming conditioned souls, 1030
as transcendental, 1033
as voluntary, 1035
See also: Kṛṣṇa, relationships with; Supreme Lord, relationships with
as person, 985, 1018, 1026, 1028, 1146, 1162, 1166, 1336-1337, 1340, 1343, 1388
personal & impersonal features of, 1339-1341
personal form of. *See:* Supreme Lord, form of
pleasure in, 1365
pleasure potency of, 1302
preaching about. *See:* Devotional service, of preaching
as proprietor of all, 1096, 1312, 1322
protection by, 1392
as *puruṣa*, 975, 1220
quadruple expansion of, 1048
realizing Him. *See:* God realization; Knowledge, about Lord
relationships with, 1326, 1329
in Deity form, 1006, 1011-1012
of demons, 1160
of Devahūti, 1326
of devotees, vs. demons, 1160
as eternal, 1011-1013
as His mother, 1384-1385
kinds of, 1011-1012
of Lakṣmī, 1154, **1156**
as loving servant, 1169-1170
pleasure from, 1349
of Pūtanā, 1335
of service & benediction, 1123
as a superior, 967
in Supersoul form, 1274-1275
remembrance & forgetfulness from, 974
as savior of devotees, 1226
seen by devotees only, 1340
seen everywhere by devotee, 1107

Supreme Lord
as self-effulgent, **1026,** 1028
service to. *See:* Devotional service as son of Devahūti, 1363, **1365-1384**
as soul & Supersoul, 1206
as spiritual master (preceptor), 1011, 1012, 1060
Śrīvatsa of, **1143,** 1194
Sudarśana *cakra* of, 1159
as Supersoul, 1062
for all, 1204-1208
annihilation of living entities by, 1225
compared to bird, 1044
devotee understands, 1220
as element, 1045
everywhere, 1176, 1204-1208
form of, described in detail, 1142-1166
Garbhodakaśāyī Viṣṇu, 1073
impersonalists misunderstand, 1221
as independent, 1212
vs. living entity, 1220
meditation on, 1088-1089, **1141**
mercy of, 1044, 1281-1282
philosophy of, 1045
realization of, 985, 998, 1338-1340, 1393
vs. soul, 1177, 1205, 1212, 1220, 1274-1275, 1345
& soul, relationship between, 1044
as transcendental, 1212, 1274
wakens living entity, 1088
as witness, 1044
supremacy of, 967, 972-973, 975, 982, 1011, 1014, 1018, 1025-1029, 1031, 1034, 1036, 1043, 1072, 1096, 1105, 1146, 1154-1158, 1226-1231, 1272-1275, 1278, 1321, 1338-1340, 1342, 1345, 1364, **1373**
as supreme controller, 1364
as supreme shelter, 976, 1335-1336
as supreme soul of souls, **1015**
surrender to. *See:* Surrender
as *svāṁśa* soul, 1177
symbols of, 1142, 1159
as time, **1224-1225,** 1231, 1233

Supreme Lord (*continued*)
as time factor, 1044, 1225
as transcendental, 1025-1028, 1030-1031, 1136, 1154, 1156, 1223, 1275-1276
transcendental to illusory energy, 1029-1030, 1031
as transcendental to material attachment, 1302
as unborn, 965
universal form of. *See:* Universal form
universe entered by, 1076
Vedas from, 1060
visible & invisible features of, 1340
weapons of, 1143
as worshipable, 1146
worship of. *See:* Devotional service, of worship
youthfulness of, 1146
See also: names of individual forms of Lord

Supersoul (Paramātmā)
as Absolute Truth feature, 955
as aspect of Absolute Truth, 610
compared to sun, 833
devotional service pleases, 158, 159-160
dictation from, 549, 606
fate caused by, 218
incarnations from, 325
knows everything, 962
Kṛṣṇa beyond, 480
Lord as, 743, 747, 747-748, 756-757, 785, 801, 832, 833, 962
meditation on, 773
mystic *yogīs* misunderstand, 223
resides in milk ocean, 55-56
soul contrasted to, 605-606, 962
soul realizing, 785, 786
as Superconsciousness, 125, 159
universal form as entered by, 307
as witness within, 218, 224, 261
Yadus saw Kṛṣṇa as, 57
yoga meditation seeks, 604
See also: Kṣīrodakaśāyī Viṣṇu; Supreme Lord

Supreme Brahman
Māyāvāda misconception about, 740
See also: Absolute Truth; Supreme Lord

Supreme Lord (Personality of Godhead)
abode of, 683, 724, 725, 784, 942
devotional creeper reaches, 53
as highest opulence, 144
temples as, 23
See also: Spiritual world; Vṛndāvaṇa
above all, 83, 85, 580-581
as absolute, 730, 737, 811, 816
absolute nature of, 46, 51, 71
as Absolute Truth, 945, 955
accidental meeting with, 123
activities of. *See:* Supreme Lord, pastimes of
inconceivable, 682
liberation by knowing, 926
acts by His energies, 832
acts wonderfully, 504
as *adhokṣaja*, 226, 719
as *ādi*, 724
as Ādi-keśava, 17
advent of
chanting Lord's glories invokes, 46
at demigods' request, 940
demons deride, 680
for devotee's sake, 26, 45-46, 65
as devotee's son, 919-920, 921, 922, 926
via Garuḍa, 813
by internal potency, 740, 921, 932, 946-947, 955
in Kali-yuga, 939
living entity's birth vs., 922
to protect pious & kill demons, 823
purpose of, 26, 43, 70, 101, 544-546, 645, 952
for religion's revival & irreligion's removal, 850
as transcendental, 43, 45, 925
See also: Avatāra: Incarnation; Kṛṣṇa, Lord, advent of
affectionate, 353-354, 623-624
aham indicates, 181

Supreme Lord (Personality of Godhead)
as Ajita, 680, 812
all-pervading, 690, 922
all-pervading & aloof, 690, 725, 743, 808
all-pervasive, 549, 724-725
as *ananta*, 944
anger in, 644
Arjuna addressed, as original, 724
Arjuna satisfied, 340
as *asamaurdhva*, 945
association with, 126, 135-136, 913
atheists displease, 685
atheists envy, 689
in atoms, 606
attachment to, 338, 649
attained by sense & mind control, 560
as *avatāra*, 508, 725
aversion to, cause of, 335
awakens living beings, 218
at banyan tree, 122
benedictions from, 798, 805, 875-876
as beyond
envious souls, 152
estimation, 246, 257, 250, 252, 253
froglike Ph.D's, 226
His energies, 264, 265
illusion, 245
improvement, 44
material activities, 130
material qualities, 43, 44, 45, 256-257, 263-264
material senses, 146, 176-177, 226
speculators, 189
beyond measurement, 718, 719
beyond sense perception, 812
Bhagavad-gītā spoken by, 737
as *bhakta-vatsala*, 942
"birth" of. *See:* Supreme Lord, advent of
beauty of, **122**, 199, 314, 324, **596**, 597, 598-**599**, 600, 601, **602**, **603**
beyond being offended, 597
beyond being order supplier, 339
beyond demigods, 633, 634

Supreme Lord (Personality of Godhead)
beyond material eyes, 552
beyond speculation, **334**, 367, 506, 507
beyond *Vedas* & penances, 443
Bhagavad-gītā according to, 74, 172
as Bhagavān, 353-354
as Bhakta-vatsala, 624
as *bhūta-bhṛt*, 209
as Bindu-Mādhava, 17
blissful, 31
boar incarnation of. *See:* Varāha, Lord
body & soul of, identical, 366-367
body of, 121-122, 144, 145, 314-315
demons misunderstand, 680
as nonmaterial, 932
as transcendental, 947
as worshipful, 696
See also: Supreme Lord, form of
Brahmā compared to, 557, 558
Brahmā empowered by, to create cosmos, 747-748
Brahmā instructed by, in heart, 925
brāhmaṇa's relation to, 620, 628
Brahmā ordered by, to drop bad body, 756
in Brahmā's post, 463
Brahmā's prayers to, 323-328
Brahmā under, 724
as cause of all causes, 946
chanting about
freedom by, 794
See also: Chanting of the Supreme Lord's holy names
as Caitanya Mahāprabhu, 340-341
as *caitya-guru*, 159, 368, 606
captivated by respectful souls, **628**
as cause of all causes, 183, 184, 217, 317
changeless, 211, 256, 257
chanting about, 53
circumambulation around, 646
cited
on His living where pure devotees glorify Him, 942
compared to spider, 796

Supreme Lord (Personality of Godhead) (*continued*)
cited
compared to stomach, 684
compared to sun, 808, 955
compared to tree's root, 684
conditioned soul contrasted to, 740, 960
conditioned soul helped by, 733
as creator, 743, 745-747, 748, 797, 883
as creator & controller, 796
as creator, maintainer, annihilator, 850
See also: Bhagavad-gītā, cited
compared to big sky, 589
compared to dramatic actor, 344
compared to
electricity, 65
fire, 258, 265
Ganges, 195
king, 257
moon, 267-268
post office, 19
sky, 204
sun, 44, 54, 127, 264, 168
compared to fire in wood, 362
compared to sun, 452
compassionate, 86, 182, 186
competitive reciprocation with, 317
complete cosmic arrangement by, 160, 161
concentration on, 312, 313
confidential associates of, 179
as controller, 355, 406
cosmos dormant within, 181, 182
creation by, 181-182, 184, 192, 321
as creativity's source, 321
credit due to, 355, 360
Deity form of. *See:* Deity form
demigods under, 681
demigods worship, 813
demigods dissatisfy, 339-340
demigods under, 194, 195, 202, 213
demons liberated by, 76
dependence on, 41, 330, 360

Supreme Lord (Personality of Godhead)
as desire fulfiller, 316
desires creation, 101, 182, 186
as detached, 257, 258
devotees of. *See:* Devotees dexterity of, 251-252
devotional service to. *See:* Devotional service
demons challenge, 679-680, 682, 683, 718
demons envy, 684, 689
demons killed by, 823, 922
demons liberated by, 721
demons overpowered by, 690-692, 716, 719, 726
demons punished by, 755-756
desires fulfilled by, 788, 789, 790, 791, 798, 799, 805
in Devahūti's womb, 922, 925
devotees of. *See:* Devotees devotional service to. *See:* Devotional service
disappearance of, 144, 145, 146, 151
doorkeepers' fall arranged by, 647
dress of, 314-315
eats via *brāhmaṇas*, 624, 625
effulgence of, 608, 955
enemies of, 76, 649
elephant king saved by, 729
energies of bewilder both worlds, 506
creation by, 180
creation, maintenance & annihilation by, 796
distinctions between, 264
everything a product of, 808
illusory, 914
inconceivable, 919
internal, 30, 682
Kālī among, 216
Lord acts by, 832
material vs. spiritual, 879-880, 932
material world as, 946
for protection, 823
real & shadow, 108
superior & inferior, 162, 224
See *also:* Supreme Lord, potency of
enlightens from within, 358, 361, 549
envy toward, 152

Supreme Lord (Personality of Godhead)
as equally disposed, 268
exemplary behavior of, 106
existed before creation, 374
expansions of equally potent, 328
expansions of
as *Ādi-caturbhuja*, 34
creation entered by, 217
eight named, 23
function of, 30
innumerable, 904
Lord one with, 258
as nondifferent, 810, 925
plenary, 30
purpose of, 212
two types of, 810
twofold, 357
types of, 96, 223
See also: Supreme Lord, forms of
faith in, 929
as father of all, 210-211, 919
as father, 503
fearless, 686
fights for fun, 712, 713
fighting spirit in, 644, 653
food offered to, 115, 209, 270
food supplied by, 161
fool's consideration of, 932, 947
forgetting about, cause of, 224
as forgiving, 451, 453, 618
as forgotten, 506, 593
form of
all-pervading, 142
in Deity, 145
as devotees prefer, 753, 754, 944
eleven named, 552
as eternal, 696, 754
identical, 328, 956
innumerable, 753-754, 904, 944
Kṛṣṇa as origin of, 944
impersonalist's conception of, 615
manifest by devotee's desire, 338
Māyāvādīs misunderstand, 753
Supreme Lord (Personality of Godhead)
form of
meditation on, 720, 721
as nondifferent, 810-811
in pure goodness, 610
qualities of, 43, 45
realization of, 785, 786
as spiritual, 723, 740, 946-947, 955
as transcendental, 328, 784, 944, 947
in varied species, 350
Vedas reveal, 488
in Vedic literature, 782, 784
as *virāt-rūpa*, 146
yogīs want to see, 787
See also: Incarnations; Supreme Lord, body of;: Deity form; Kṛṣṇa, expansions of; Supreme Lord, expansions of
freedom by serving, 431
as friend to all, 586
Garuḍa carries, 813
glance of, 489, 596, 597
glories of
essential, 174
ever fresh, 164
hearing about, 249, 250
inconceivable, 250, 251-253
glorification of
as devotee's desire, 612
in devotee's morning worship, 861
freedom by, 756, 793
Indian royalty hears, 861
Lord present at, 942
for *mahātmās*, 277
by Maitreya, 472
pilgrimage places for, 46
in prayer, 300
as prime necessity, 248
as spiritual activity, 830
as transcendental enjoyment, 764
by Vaikuṇṭha's residents, 568
with Vedic hymns, 487, 488

Supreme Lord (Personality of Godhead) (*continued*)
glorification of
See also: Chanting of the Supreme Lord's holy names; *Saṅkīrtana* movement: Preachers; *Saṇkīrtana-yajña*
as goal of all, 780, 781
as goal of endeavor, 370
as goal of religion, 634
goddess of fortune serves, 572, 573
as goodness reservoir, 787
as Govinda, 289
gratitude toward, 209
as great-grandfather, 468
grateful & ungrateful feelings toward, 729-730
greatness of, 623, 713, 718-720, 945, 946
as Hari, 17
harmony in serving, 589-591
hearing about
bogus vs. bona fide, 725-736, 731
for cleansing heart, 337-338
compared to Ganges bath, 737
compared to watering seed, 53
detachment by, 200
devotees, 732
devotees relish, 611, 612
ear's capacity for, 613-614
effect of, 189
freedom by, 793, 794
glorification follows, 247
impersonalists fearful of, 249
importance of, 950
by Indian royalty, 861
love develops by, 329, 957
from pure devotees, 471
perfection by, 959
purifying power of, 737
qualification for, 515
in Vaikuṇṭha, 568
in heart of all, 472, 596, 737, 746-747, 756-57, 801, 921
in heart, 158, 159-160, 204

Supreme Lord (Personality of Godhead)
in heart of pure devotee, 329, 338, 958
householder forgets, 808-809
as Hṛṣīkeśa, 479
in human form, 932
in human role, 350
humility pleases, 354-355
impartial, 344, 429
impersonal feature of, 258
impregnates matter, 183, 184, 185
impersonalists misunderstand, 726, 807-808
incarnation of. *See:* Incarnation inspiration from, 159
as actors, 344
origin of, 325
purpose of, 508
in species, 350
in *yugas*, 638
See also: *Avatāra;* Supreme Lord, ad- vent of
incarnations of. *See:* Incarnations independent, 696, 922, 946
inconceivable, 506, 507
inspires from the heart, 549-550
invisible, 682
as Jagannātha, 17
as Janārdana, 480
Kardama as servant of, 849, 851
Kardama expresses desires to, 790
Kardama moved, to tears, 816
Kardama pleased, 780, 781
Kardama realized, 960, 962
Kardama receives prophecy from, 804-807, 809, 810
Kardama saw, 782-785, 786, 813, 821
Kardama's desires fulfilled by, 801
in Kardama's semen, 922
karma awarded by, 962
as Keśava, 717, 718
killing by, 545, 553
king represents, 105, 775
kisses by, 574
as knower in all bodies, 832-833

Supreme Lord (Personality of Godhead)
knowing advent & activities of, 795
knowledge about, 134, 147
knowledge about. *See:* Knowledge, spiritual
knows everything, 682, 801, 945, 946-947, 962
Kṛṣṇa as, **56,** 696, 718, 925
Kumāras addressed by, 618-**621,** **623,** **625,** 628
laws of. *See:* Laws of God
as leading living entity, 791, 932
liberation given by, 682
limitless, 506, 809
literature about, 167, 170-171
living entity accommodated & advised by, 797
living entity contrasted to, 903, 922, 932, 960
living entity contrasted to in birth process, 211
living entity maintained by, 946
living entity part & parcel of, 723, 746, 748-749, 809
infallibility, 155-156
living entity contrasted to, 343, 381
in opulences, 61
in power, 75, 83
in transcendence, 43-45, 256-257, 264-265
living entities helped by, 429
lotus feet of
as shelter, 902, 945
yogī sees, 941
beyond offenders, 204, 205
demigods worship, 196-204
detachment via, 199-200
devotional creeper seeks, 53
dust of, 272
Ganges as, 299
Ganges flows from, 626
glories of, 602
as *kṛṣṇa-kathā,* 171-172
Lord's kindness reveals, 618
tulasī leaves at, **613,** **637**
pure devotees cherish, 471
toenails of, 316
Vidura received, **472**

Supreme Lord (Personality of Godhead)
love for
in affection or opulence, 71
by associating with devotees, 71
Caitanya distributed, 877
Caitanya personified, 51
crying due to, 153
dormant, 71, 72
eyes opened by, 367
forgetfulness in, 100
gradual development of, 51
individual preferences in, 443
Lord controlled by, 272
materialists lack, 877
as perfection, 876-878
qualification for, 372
seeing the Lord with, 25
in service attitude, 364
spontaneous, 329
stages of, 550
"suffering" from, 55
symptoms of, 31, 124
via Vedic sound, **329**
See also: Supreme Lord, relationships with as: Devotional service; Kṛṣṇa consciousness as.
Madhusūdana, 922
as Madhusūdana, 17-18
maintains everyone, **946**
as maintainer, 160, 161, 209, **353**
Manu represents, 824
Manu worshiped, 857, 858
materialists punished by, 677
māyā controlled by, 740
Māyāvādī misunderstands, 685, 731, 944
"meditation" for becoming, 761, 780, 903
mercy of
activities for achieving, 919
birth-death cycle stopped by, 795
Brahmā prayed for, **353**
compared to sun's rays, 372
for crossing nescience, 635
on demons & devotees compared, 76

Supreme Lord (Personality of Godhead) (*continued*)
mercy of
on devotee, 800, 801
on fallen souls, 357
food as, 115
for knowing Kṛṣṇa, 57
Lord's narrations as, 509
love of God as, 876-878
on miscreants, 545
prerequisite for receiving, 610-611
via pure devotees, 340
via spiritual master, 876
for success, 310-311, 313
for surrendered souls, 506
understanding by, 954
wealth as, 858
modes of nature under, 960
mortality lesson taught by, 670
as mystic master, 716, 719
name of
as Lord Himself, 950
as nondifferent, 810
offenses to, 578-579
potency of, 537
for present Age, 550
See also: Chanting the holy names; Hare Kṛṣṇa *mantra;* Supreme Lord, *specific names*
via Nārada we can know, 443
narrations about, purpose of, 509, 511
nature controlled by, 687, 743
nature's beauty reflects, 314, 315
as *nirguṇa*, 256
as *nirvikāra*, 832
obedience to, 46, 136
offenses to, 578-579
offering everything to, 806
offering fruit & flower to, 853
offering fruitive results to, 342
omnipotency of, 344, 362-363
omnipresent, 127
as one & different, 2, 257, 264, 808
one & many, 810-811, 832-834
Supreme Lord (Personality of Godhead)
oneness with, 148, 222, 807-810, 809
as one without second, 26, 181, 258
opulence as mercy of, 858
opulences of, 44, 257, 637, 939, 945-946
order of, execution of, 144
orders from, 653
as "order supplier," 173
as original person, 724
as origin of all, 724, 850
as origin of species, 724
as Padmanābha, 594
Pāṇḍavas' house dear to, 2
as Parabrahman, 371
parts & parcels of. *See:* Living entities
pastimes of
as boar, 490
chivalrous, 516
for devotees, 44
devotees benefit by, 732
devotee's pastimes related to, 728
devotees relish, 738
dramatic, 344
enthusiasm over, 294
as eternal, 151
fools disbelieve in, 352
hearing of, 726, 727, 730, 731, 737
Indian royalty hears, 861
as Lord Himself, 730
meaningful, 508-509, 511
purpose of, 44, 163, 164
talking & thinking of, 959
as transcendental, 256-257, 738
See also: Supreme Lord, activities of as person, 944, 947
perseverance in pursuing, 151
personal feature of, 149, 250, 253
as highest feature, 608, 610
impersonal feature vs., 334
meditation on, 602, 609
qualification for seeing, 615
plan of, submission to, 654-655
planets floated by, 687

Supreme Lord (Personality of Godhead)
pleased by brahminical qualities, 633
pleased by fruit-&-flower offering, 853
pleased by social cooperation, 832
pleased by *varṇāśrama* system, 478
as pleasure reservoir, 787
pleasure of
devotion for, 269
pilgrimage for, 19
as success standard, 85
potencies of
banyan seeds exhibit, 252
beyond human brain, 506, 507
compared to fire in wood, 503
eternal & temporary, 256
parā prakṛti among, 250
potencies of
for pleasure, 550, **596**
sleeping & awake, 182
See also: Energy, internal; Energy, material
potency of, inconceivable, 682-683, 718, **740,** 743, 903
prayers to, for assistance, **356, 360**
praying to, benefit of, 805
as predominator, 273, 626
as proprietor, 290, 690, 791, 807-808, 832-833
protection by
active-but-aloof, 832
for *brāhmaṇas* & cows, 831-832
for demigods, 688
for devotees, 44, 546, 594, 685
from falldown, 356
via His names, 537
for Kṛṣṇa conscious society, 832
kṣatriyas represent, 240
Lord's lotus feet for, 196, 197
for Parīkṣit's embryo, 104
for pious people, 823
from sex attraction, 450
for surrendered souls, 41, 755-756
for twice-born, cows & demigods, 163, 164
punishes wrongdoer, 99-100
pure devotees of. *See:* Pure devotees

Supreme Lord (Personality of Godhead)
as *puruṣa*, 932, 944, 946-947
as Puruṣottama, 17-18
qualities of, living beings reflect, 381
quoted on blessing Brahmā, 360-361
quoted
on Brahmā's impure body, 756
on His fulfilling Kardama's desires, 801
See also: Bhagavad-gītā, quotations from
realization of. *See:* Knowledge, spiritual
rebellion against, 347-348
rebellion toward, 158, 187, 189
reciprocating bliss with, 357
relationships with, 173, 276
intimate basis of, 329
qualifications for, 443
in *rāsa-līlā*, 357
in reciprocal service, 623
See also: Supreme Lord, love for
religion as laws of, 35, 136, **791,** 792 (assuming137)
as religion's goal, 287
religion as service to, 335
remembrance of, 344, 747
devotees saved by, 134
ecstasy from, 51
Lord identical with, 51
pilgrimage for, 46
tall temples for, 23
Uddhava enlivened by, 48-51
remembrance of, as meditation's goal, 781
renunciation by, 637
representatives of, 148-149, 158
respect due to, 349
respect for, 68
as revealed to submissive souls, 226
as root of creation, 345
as root of everything, 684
as *sac-cid-ānanda-vigraha*, 622, 796
sac-cid-ānanda form of, 44, 45, 145, 182
sacrifices for satisfying, 772, 858
as sacrificial enjoyer, 715, 716, 722, 723, 806
satisfaction from seeing, 615

Supreme Lord (Personality of Godhead) (*continued*)
satisfaction of, 370, 479-480
scientists subordinate to, 504, 747
seeing the, 17, 24-25, 142
as seen
as Absolute Truth, 955
by *bhakti-yoga*, 787
at death, 720, 721
by devotees, 942
by purified senses, 812
by *yogī*, 941
seen by love, 367, 372-373
seen face to face, 595-596
seen within & without, 552
as seer, 270
senses of, 2, 184
sentient, 685, 796
separation from, 134, 135-136
serpent of, 313-314
servants of. *See:* Devotees
service to. *See:* Devotional service
via serving spiritual master, 876
as shelter, 957
sincere souls helped by, 368, 510
sinless souls approach, 17
sky represents, 190
sleep of, 350, 352
smile of, effect of, 317
as Soul of universe, 220, 226
in species of life, 350
speech of, 631, 632, 800
speculation on, useless, 246, 250-253
Śrīvatsa mark on, 712
subordination to, 588
Sudarśana weapon of, 716
suffering relieved by, 756, 876
as *śukla*, 792
supports Himself, 319
supremacy of, 495
as Supreme Brahman, 130
as Supersoul (Paramātmā), 743, 747, 756-757, 785, 801, 832, 833, 962

Supreme Lord (Personality of Godhead)
surrendered souls dear to, **353, 354**
surrender to
as best choice, 506
defined, 103
as devotional service, 312
direction by, 756
fearlessness by, 330
fools deny, 954
as *Gita's* conclusion, 605
as harmonious life, 590, 590-591
illusion dispelled by, 266-267
as life's goal, 792
Lord quoted on, 945
Lord wants, 797
protection by, 41, 755
as real religion, 336
religion as, 792
as starting point, 159
success by, 780, 781
as *yoga's* completion, 941
as Śyāmasundara, 25, 596
thinking about, 330, 649, 809
as time (*kāla*), 383, 399, 405, 406
tīrtha-kīrti, 46
topics of, effects of, 469
transcendental, 784, 800, 925
as *tri-yuga*, 638, 939
unconquerable, 680, 812
universal form of, social orders from, 830, 831
universal form of. *See:* Universal form
varṇāśrama system from, 826
as *uttamaśloka*, 300
as Varāha. *See:* Varāha, Lord
as Vāsudeva, 961-962
as *Vedānta-sūtra* s knower, 925
Vedas identical with, 33
Vedas for knowing, 830
as *Vedas* personified, 496, 497
veda-vādis deny, 496
as *vīryavān*, 185
as *viśva-mūrti*, 142

Supreme Lord (Personality of Godhead)
voice of, 486-487
wealth as mercy of, 858
will of, 344
will of, caused Yadus' destruction, 117-119
will of, creation by, 181
as within & without, 361
working to satisfy, 857
world's relationship to, 807, 808
worshipable by all, 824
worship of
benefit of, 858
daily schedule in, 353
by demigods, 813
desires fulfilled by, 790, 798, 802
as devotee prefers, 754
fools deny, 954
knowledge by, 773
as necessity, 945
by one's ability, 915
in raising children, 476-477
result of, 634
by sages, 857
in temple, 861
worshiping devotees excels, 472
See *also:* Deity form; Devotional service: Supreme Lord, glorification of; Worship
as Yajñeśvara, 498
yogamāyā potency of, 581
"yoga" for becoming, 934, 941
yogīs contrasted to, 904
yogīs meditate on, 721
yogīs overpowered by, 716
See also: Absolute Truth; Kṛṣṇa, Lord; Nārāyaṇa, Lord; Supersoul; Varāha, Lord; Viṣṇu, Lord
Sura defined, 698
Sura-janas defined, 645
Suras. See: Demigods; Devotees
Surādhama defined, 682
Surrender. *See:* Supreme Lord, surrender to
Surrender to the Lord. *See:* Supreme Lord, surrender to
after many births, 1352
of Arjuna, 1093
attitude of, 1219
freedom attained by, 1113-1115
of intelligent, 1016
Kṛṣṇa advises, 1014
Kṛṣṇa asks, 974
Kṛṣṇa demands, 1273
liberation by, 1016-1018, 1019
Lord alone worthy of, 976
māyā overcome by, 1287
protection by, 974, 1034, 1277, 1368, 1392
time reminds us to, 1042
Susammata defined, 935
Sūta Gosvāmī at Parīkṣit-Śukadeva meeting, 376
Sūta Gosvāmī, 968
narration by, 969-1398
quoted on Vidura & Maitreya, 727
quoted on Vidura hearing boar incarnation pastime, 739
sages heard *Śrīmad-Bhāgavatam* from, 727
Sva-dharma, 1131
Sva-karmaṇā tam abhyarcya
quoted, 915, 1196
Sva-pāda-mūlaṁ bhajataḥ priyasya
verse quoted, 453
Svanuṣṭhitasya dharmasya
quoted, 1117
"Svāmīs", 950, 959
Svāṁśa expansion, 810
Svarāṭ defined, 364
Svarūpa defined, 364, 426, 1375
Svarūpa-siddhi defined, 338
Svāśrayāśraya defined, 319
Svayambhū defined, 307-308
Svayam-prakāśa defined, 96
Svayambhūr nāradaḥ śambhuḥ
verse quoted, 336
Svāyambhuva devastation, Varāha appeared in, 493
Svāyambhuva Manu. *See:* Manu, Svāyambhuva

Svāyambhuva Manu, 1377, 1382
affectionate to Devahūti, 838, **853**, 854
boar incarnation contemporary with, 733
in Brahmāvarta, 802
daughters of, 778-779, 1043
as Devahūti's father, 838, 847
gave Devahūti to Kardama, 852-854
grateful to Kardama, 833-836, 836
implored Kardama to marry his daughter, 837-843
Kardama agreed to marry daughter of, **843**, 847, 848
Kardama approached by, 822
Kardama glorifies, 823-826, 828
Kardama offered obeisances to, 824
Kardama received, 821, 822
Kṛṣṇa conscious life of, 860, 861-865
Svāyambhuva Manu life-span of, 864, 865
as Lord's representative, 824
as Prajāpati, **741**, 778-779
progeny of, 775
quoted on Brahmā & *brāhmaṇas*, 830
returned to Barhiṣmatī, 856, 859
as righteous ruler, 802
sages' residences pleased, 855-856
sons of, 775
traveled with wife & daughter, 814
Vaivasvata Manu contrasted to, 777
worshiped Lord, 857, 858
Śveta-varāha millennium, 482
Śvetāśvatara Upaniṣad, quoted on liberation, 1025
Śvetāśvatara Upaniṣad, quoted on Lord's energies, 683, 1024-1025
Swan airplane, Brahmā travels in, 936
Śyāmasundara, 1147
Syān mahat-sevayā viprāḥ
quoted, 17

T

Tad brahma niṣkalaṁ anantam
quoted, 1349
Tā enam abruvann āyatanaṁ
verse quoted, 209
Tam eva viditvāti-mṛtyum eti
quoted, 1025
Tamas defined, 748
See also: Ignorance
Tāmisra, 1295
Tamasaḥ defined, 325, 1188
Tamo-guṇa. See: Ignorance, mode of
Tamo 'viveko mohaḥ syād
verse quoted, 749
Tān ahaṁ dviṣataḥ krūrān
verse quoted, 195
Tan-mātra defined, 744
Tantram defined, 283-284
Tapas defined, 430
See also: Austerity; Penance
Tapasya defined, 774
Taste, 1066, 1071
See also: Austerity
Tape recording and time, analogy of, 384-385
Tārkṣya (Kaśyapa), 76
Tattva-vit defined, 736
Tato bhūya iva te tamo
verse quoted, 337
Tato māṁ tattvato jñātvā
quoted, 1024, 1385
Taxes, *brāhmaṇas* exempt from, 242
Teachers, spiritual. *See: Ācāryas; Brāhmaṇas;* Spiritual master
true & false, 335-336
See also: Ācāryas; Brāhmaṇas; Spiritual master
Teachings of Lord Caitanya, cited on Viṣṇu forms, 1142
Teeth, white, 895
Te dvandva-moha-nirmuktā
verse quoted, 17
Temples, circumambulation of, 646
See also: Deity form; Supreme Lord, worship of; Worship
Temple of the Supreme Lord
worship in, 861

Temple of the Supreme Lord
See also: Deity form; Supreme Lord, worship of
Temples, purpose of, 23, 147
Tene brahma hṛdā ya ādi-kavaye
quoted, 1060
Tennis with women, demons arrange, 761
Teṣāṁ satata-yuktānām
quoted, 159
verse quoted, 198, 500
Te taṁ bhuktvā svarga-lokaṁ viśālaṁ
quoted, 1318
Ṭhākura Haridāsa. *See:* Haridāsa Ṭhākura
Theism as *Bhāgavatam*'s essence, 135
Theft, *yogi* should avoid, 1133
Thinking about Kṛṣṇa, 649
Three, Lord of, 72-73
Tila-vaṇik defined, 242
Time, 1353
atomic to universal, 382
atoms calculate, 397, 399-401
as cause of death, 1231
compared to tape recording, 384
compared to wheel, 795
compared to wind, 1233
creation depends on, 1043
defined, 383-384
demigods' vs. human, 404, 410
as destroyer, 1042, 1234
devotees beyond, 795
devotees unaffected by, 1011-1013
divisions of, 399-405, 406
effects of, 1062, 1184, 1224, 1231
as element, 1041
eternal, 385
ether stimulated by, 1062
forgotten during sex life, 905
four millenniums of, 410
fructifies the creation, 185
as goddess Kālī, 216
great souls beyond, 557
Kṛṣṇa beyond, 131, 132
Kṛṣṇa consciousness transcends, 793
Time
Kṛṣṇa's form of, 43
as Lord, 1043, 1234
Lord as, 1044
of Lord's one second, 422
as Lord's influence, 1042-1044
as Lord's representative, 1231
lunar calculation of, 1318
material nature agitated by, 1043
in material world, 952
mystic's awareness of, 409
nature of, detailed, 1041-1043
parārdhas, 1323, 1324
pot for measuring, 402
priceless, 383
as reminder to surrender, 1042
Śiva's awareness of, 531
soul beyond, 260
space and, 399
in spiritual world, 327, 423
strength of, 1233-1234
systematic schedule of, 384, 386
in universe, 286
Vaikuṇṭha planets free from, 1011-1012
value of, 1233-1234
Vedic divisions of, 795
yoga system obscured by, 952
See also: Kali-yuga (present Age)
Tīrtha defined, 806
Tīrtha
See also: Pilgrimage places
Tongue as controlled in *yoga*, 604
Touch, 1070
qualities of, 1062
as subtle form of air, 1063
Touch sense, 230-231
Trai-vargika, 1331
Trance *(samādhi)*
defined, 312
ecstatic symptoms of, 51
two types of, 786
See also: Kṛṣṇa consciousness: Meditation on Kṛṣṇa

Transcendence
See: Kṛṣṇa consciousness: Liberation; Spiritual world
beyond goodness, 148
as freedom, 876
Lord revealed in, 176
of material desires, 785
See also: Godhead, returning to; Kṛṣṇa consciousness; Liberation; Spiritual world
Transcendentalists
See: Devotees; Imper- sonalists; *Yogīs*
beyond disturbance, 2, 200
fixed position of, 268
leader of, 443
nature's laws surpassed by, 692
as *paramhaṁsas*, 275
pure devotees best among, 160
satisfaction for, 615
service to, 275
true & false, 603, 604
two types of, 131
See also: Devotees; *Jñānīs*; Sages; Saints; *Yogis*
Transmigration, 971
as beginningless, 1309
caused by fruitive reactions, 1307-1309
caused by modes, 1014, 1093, 1176
causes of, 1064
compared to dreaming, 1390
as cycle, 1011
directed by Lord as Supersoul, 1264
downward, 1248
from hell to humanity, 1264
to higher planets & back, 1318, 1333-1335
knowledge of, necessary, 1183
liberation from. *See:* Liberation
to man's body, 1305
of materialists, 1307
miseries accompany, 1267-1268
modes determine, 1014, 1093, 1177
to moon, 1318
by reactions of fruitive activities, 1307-1309
remembrance of, in womb, 1270
Transmigration
subtle body determines, 1061
suffering continues in, 1286
system for elevation by, 1260
to woman's form, 1305
See also: Birth; Death
Transmigration of the soul
devotional service stops, 795
by family affection, 168
via father's semen, 652
material life caused by, 793
work determines, 177
See also: Birth & death, repeated; Body, material: Bondage; Death, material; Destiny; *Karma*
Trasareṇu defined, 400
Travel, space. *See:* Space travel
Tree
at Bindu-sarovara Lake, 816, 818
at demons' birth, 664
feels pain, 390
pious, 818
pious & impious, 817
root of, Lord compared to, 684
with roots upward, 346
senses of, 1214
as shelter, 121
in Vṛndāvana, 79-80
Tretā-yuga, 939
Tretā-yuga, duration of, 410
Tridaṇḍi-sannyāsī defined, 248
Tri-kāla-jñas defined, 408, 557
Tri-pāda-bhūti-gati defined, 964
Tri-yuga defined, 638, 938
Truth. *See:* Absolute Truth
Twice-born man, 163
See also: Brāhmaṇas; Kṣatriyas; Vaiśyas
Truth. *See:* Absolute Truth; Reality vs. reflection; Spiritual world
Tulasī, 1008, 1019
Tulasī leaves
fragrance of, power of, 601
Lakṣmī excelled by, 637

Tulasī leaves
at Lord's feet, 636-637
in Vaikuṇṭha, 570, 574
value of, 613
Twice-born *brāhmaṇas*, 640
Twilight
demons took, as woman, 757-763
as passion period, 757
See also: Daytime; Morning; Night
Tyaktvā deham punar janma
quoted, 998, 1223

U

Udāna air, 224
Uddhava
beyond modes of nature, 148-149
doubts of, 130, 132
ecstasy of, 50-51, 128
expanded as Vasu, 126
as faithful, 144
forgot material world, 52
Lord instructed, 134
Lord's activities bewildered, 66, 67, 68
in Lord's family, 25
Lord's mercy on, 126
as Lord's representative, 147
mourning Lord's disappearance, 54
as pure devotee, 47-51, 124, 129
quoted on Kṛṣṇa's pastimes, 89
in separation from the Lord, 134, 135-137
Vidura questions,, 25-46
Vidura's relation to, 138-142
Ugrasena, 29, 73
Umā, worship to, for good wife, 790
United Nations, 20
United States, Kṛṣṇa conscious *yoga* in, 607
Universal form of the Supreme Lord (*virāṭ-rūpa)* , 1340
appearance of bodily parts of, 1076-1082
Arjuna quoted on, 246
awakening of, 1087, 1088
compared to developing embryo, 1176
Universal form of the Supreme Lord (*virāṭ-rūpa)*
creation of, 215-245, 307-308
defined, 162
demigods reenter, 1083
immeasurable, 246
as incarnation, 1075
manifestation of, detailed, 1073-1088
planetary systems in, 1074
social orders in, 238, 240, 242, 245
Supreme Soul causes, 226
as temporary exhibition, 145-146, 219
Universe
administrators of, 202
annihilation of, 408, 415-417, 493, 1319
annihilation of, Lord as baby at, 1365-1366
annihilation of, two kinds of, 1230, 1319, 1323
atoms compose, 397
beyond comprehension, 226
Brahmā re-created, 746-747, 747-748
in Causal Ocean, 745
cause of, 183
compared to tree, 345
covering layers of, 1324
coverings of, detailed, 1075
darkness covered, at demons' birth, 657, 661
devotees preach throughout, 140
devotional creeper penetrates, 53
directions of, demigods governing, 899, 900
disturbed at demons' birth, 659-666
dissolution of, 289, 304
divisions of, 936
Diti's pregnancy darkened, 555, 556
as egg, 745
entered by Lord, 1076
entered by Lord, elements, & *mahat-tattva*, 1073
evolution of, 190
as expanding, 1229
Kāraṇodakaśāyī Viṣṇu breathes, 746
as living entity, 382
Lord as Soul of, 217, 220, 226

Universe (*continued*)
Lord creates, 796
Lord illuminates, 54
Lord maintains, 161
as Lord's body, 1345
from Lord's breathing, 289
Lord's Deity form throughout, 17
Prajāpatis populated, 779, 850
Purāṇas as history of, 457
root cause of, 345-346
single sun in, 556
size & structure of, 424, 425
structure of, 220-221
time in, 399
traveling beyond, 581
Viṣṇu as source of, 1364
See also: Creation, the; Energy, material; Heavenly planets; Planets, material; Spiritual world; Material world
Upapurāṇa defined, 456
Upakurvāṇa-brahmacārī defined, 842
Upaniṣads, cited on Vedic scriptural revelation by faith in God & spiritual master, 928
Utsava defined, 725
Uttānapāda, King, 467, 517, 776, 838, 847
Uttarā, 104

V

Vacāṁsi vaikuṇṭha-guṇānuvarṇane quoted, 990
Vacasāmṛtena discussed, 800
Vaibhava-vilāsa defined, 96
Vaidhi-bhakti defined, 159
Vaikuṇṭha planets, 1393
demigods not in, 1011
devotees elevated to, 1127
devotee's facilities in, 1194
as eternal abodes, 1011-1013
See also: Planets, spiritual; Spiritual world
Vaikuṇṭha. *See:* Spiritual world
Vairāgya defined, 430, 500
See also: Detachment; Renunciation Vaiṣṇava
Vairāgya defined
defined, 1097, 1118
as highest *brāhmaṇa*, 1217
levels of, 1217
See also: Devotees
Vaiṣṇavānāṁ yathā śambhuḥ quoted, 870
Vaiṣṇavas. *See:* Devotees
Vaiṣṇava philosophy principles of, four, 1174
See also: Devotional service; Kṛṣṇa consciousness
Vaiśyas, duties & service for, 1197
Vaiśyas (farmers, merchants),
as created from Lord's waist, 830
defined, 458
duty of, 79, 85, 242
present-day, 845
as twice-born, 640
See also: Varṇāśrama-dharma
Vaivasvata Manu, 733, 777
Vajrāṅgajī (Hanumān), 753, 754, 944
Vāk, 447
Vālmīki Muni, meditation of, 779
Vāmana, Lord, 810
Vana-gocaraḥ defined, 681
Vānaprasthas, duties for, 1351
Vānaprastha (retired life)
defined, 458
divisions of, 460
for forest-going, 957-958
pilgrimage purifies, 736
wife allowed in, 956
See also: Varṇāśrama-dharma
Varāha, Lord (boar incarnation)
as *ādi-sūkara*, 724
advent of, 421, 483-487, 493
advent of, time of, 733
body of, 489, 494
Brahmā advised, to kill Hiraṇyākṣa, 699-703
Brahmā praised, 687
from Brahmā's nostril, 704, 922
Brahmā's prayer accepted by, 703-704
demigods honored, 687, 688, 704-705

Varāha, Lord (boar incarnation)
Earth rescued by, 489-495
hearing about, value of, 509, 511
Hiraṇyākṣa killed by, 492, 493
Jayadeva quoted on, 489-490
pure water from, 505
sages glorifying, 494-507
as transcendental hog, 490
two incarnations of, 514
as *Vedas* personified, 488
Varāha, Lord
Earth saved by, 679, 680, 685, 686, 687, 688, 696
existing eternally, 754
form of, potency of, 740
form of, pure, 722, 723
form of, transcendental, 696
hair of, fell at Barhiṣmatī, 857
hearing about, benefit of, 730, 732
Hiraṇyākṣa challenged, 679, 680, 681-683
Hiraṇyakṣa challenged by, 689-691
Hiraṇyākṣa chased, 686, 688
Hiraṇyākṣa fought, 690-695, 696, 704-719, 719, 726
Hiraṇyākṣa's insults endured by, 685, 686, 687, 688, 689
as original boar, 724
quoted on Hiraṇyākṣa, 689
Svāyambhuva Manu contemporary with, 777
Varṇāśramācāravatā
verse quoted, 477-478
Varṇa-saṣkara defined, 666
Varṇāśrama-dharma (caste system)
brāhmaṇas in, 114
divisions & purpose of, 458-460, 478, 478-479, 525, 527
origin of, 460
See also: Brāhmaṇas; Kṣatriyas; Vaiśyas; Vānaprastha; Sūdras; Sannyāsīs; Vedic culture
compared to covered sun, 825-826
divine vs. degraded forms of, 825-827
divisions in, eight named, 1190, 1210
duties according to, 1130, 1197, 1259-1260, 1351
Varṇāśrama-dharma (caste system)
female association restricted in, 1299, 1303
as human necessity, 1216-1217
renounced orders in, 1377
social orders in, 1351
as spiritual society, 832
Vāsudeva, worship of, 1048
See also: Āryan civilization; *Brahmacārī; Brāhmaṇas;* Householders; *Kṣatriyas; Sannyāsī; Śūdras; Vaiśyas; Vānaprastha;* Vedic culture
Vāsudeva manifestation as *śuddha-sattva*, 1048
Vāsudeva state, 1107
Vāsudeve bhagavati
quoted, 1089, 1092
Varuṇa, 228, 824
capital city of, 674
Hiraṇyākṣa advised by, 676-678
Hiraṇyākṣa "challenged,", 675, 676
responsibilities of, 899
Vasati daśana-śikhare dharaṇī tava lagnā
verse quoted, 489
Vasiṣṭha, 930, 937
Vasiṣṭha Muni, 302
Vāsudeva, Lord, 810
Vāsudeva defined, 925
Vasudeva
family of, 27
feared Kaṁsa, 78
Kṛṣṇa carried to safety by, 68
as Kṛṣṇa's father, 77
Vāsudeva, Kṛṣṇa in Dvārakā as, 34
Vasudeva defined, 148
Vāsudeva-parāyaṇaḥ defined, 431
Vāsudevaḥ sarvam iti
quoted, 716
verse quoted, 245
Vāsudeve bhagavati
verse quoted, 197
Vāsudevo vā idaṁ agra āsīt
verse quoted, 181
Vasus, 125, 126
Vāyu, 824, 899

Vāyur yamo 'gnir varuṇaḥ śaṅāṅkaḥ
verse quoted, 468
Vedaiś ca sarvair aham eva vedyo
quoted, 199, 253
verse quoted, 224
Vedānta defined, 239
Vedānta-sūtra
cited on Lord as origin of everything, 724
Lord as knower of, 925
quoted on Brahman, 274-275
quoted on inquiry into Absolute Truth, 798
quoted on Lord as source of everyone's birth, 1027, 1098, 1284
quoted on scriptures, 1343
subject of, 170
Vedas
as authority, 949, 950
gradual elevation given by, 966
from Lord, 1060
Lord identical with, 33
Lord known beyond, 149-150
Lord "learned," 90
as Lord's directions, 792
material enjoyment provided in, 798
paths given in, four named, 1331
as perfect, 1060
purpose of, 830, 1216-1217
as second mother, 931
Vedic literature. *See: Bhagavad-gītā; Śrīmad-Bhāgavatam; Vedas; and others by name*
See also: Vedic literature; *names of specific Vedic literatures*
Veda-vādī defined, 496
Vedeṣu durlabham adurlabham ātma-bhaktau
verse quoted, 96, 326
Vedic culture
basis of, 832
begetting children in, 756
economics of, 82
exemplary woman in, 870
husband & wife in, 871
marriage in, 95, 804, 841-842, 845, 853, 930-931
Vedic culture
population control in, 666
retiring from family in, 910
sannyāsīs respected in, 586
science in, 403
spiritual life-style of, 848-849, 860, 861
time calculations in, 795
white teeth in, 895
See also: Aryan civilization; India: *Varṇāśrama-dharma*
Vedic injunctions
for dining at festivals, 117
Kṛṣṇa followed, 106
purpose of, 59
See also: Regulative principles; Religious principles
Vedic knowledge
in Brahmā's succession, 475
brāhmaṇas inclined to, 238, 239, 240
by hearing, 230
perfection of, 239
See also: Knowledge, spiritual; *Vedas*; Vedic literature
Vedic literature (*Vedas*)
author of, 170
child-conceiving process in, 652
devotional processes in, 684
foolish followers of, 496, 497
as laws of God, 561
as Lord's breath, 488
Lord's form in, 782, 784
material & spiritual instruction in, 881
offense to, 579
origin of, 420, 455-457, 559
purpose of, 199
sense control in, 272
simplified version of, 283
supplements to, 456
teacher required for, 90
as transcendental sound, 462
Vaikuṇṭha via, 566
See also: Literature; *Vedas; names of specific Vedic literatures*

Vedic *mantras* (hymns)
by devotee-sages for Lord Boar, 487, 488
fire ignited by, 503
Gāyatrī among, 496
two types of, 538
See also: Chanting the holy names; Gāyatrī *mantra;* Hare Kṛṣṇa *mantra;* Sound, transcendental; Vedic literature
Vedic rituals, seven listed, 497-498
See also: Sacrifice; Worship
Vegetarianism, 1197-1198
Venuṁ kvanaṇtam aravinda-dalāyatākṣaṁ
verse quoted, 82
Venus planet, **664**
Vibhāvarī, 674
Vibhramaḥ defined, 502
Vibhinnāṁśa expansions, 810
Vicitravīrya, 178
Viditātma-tattva defined, 586
Vidura, **968**
chivalrous, 516
compassionate, 40
Dhṛtarāṣṭra instructed by, 8-11
Dhṛtarāstra's house left by, 734
Duryodhana insulted, 12-13
eagerness of, 469
in ecstatic love of God, 153
family heritage of, 13, 16, 177
heard from Maitreya about Lord, 727
kṛṣṇa-kathā sought by, 167-168
as Kṛṣṇa's devotee, 734, 735
Kṛṣṇa with, **472**
met Maitreya at Hardwar, 734, 735
pilgrimage purified, 736
on pilgrimage, 18, 24
psychological inquiry by, 26
as pure devotee, 3
questions Maitreya, 155-174, 256-291
questions Uddhava, 25-46
quoted on Brahmā, 741
quoted on Prajāpatis, 742
quoted on Svāyambhuva Manu's progeny, 775
Vidura
renouncing home, 1
in transcendence, 155-156, **176**
traveling incognito, 41
Uddhava's relation to, 139-142
as Vyāsa's son, 735
as Yamarāja, 178, 179
Vidyādharas, 768
Vijñāna defined, 933
Vikarma yac cotpatitaṁ kathañcid
verse quoted, 453
Vikhyāta defined, 803
Vilāsa defined, 1008
Vinatā, 711
Violence
ordered for Arjuna, 1197-1198
restrictions in, 1197-1198
Viraha defined, 55-56
Viraktimat defined, 773
Virāṭ-puruṣa. See: Universal form of Lord
Virāṭ-rūpa. See: Universal form
Vīryavān defined, 185
Viṣa defined, 242
Visarga defined, 380
Vision, two types of, 5, 204, 205
Viśiṣṭādvaita, 1175
Viṣṇu, Lord
above Brahmā & Siva, 325, 345-346
amalgamates in Kṛṣṇa, 145, 146
Brahmā born from, alone, 1154, 1156
carrier of, 38
as central Deity, 850
as creator, 743
form of, described in detail, 1142-1166
expands into the creation, 217
forms of, 1053-1054, 1142
as goodness Deity, 201
maintains everyone, 850
meditation on, order of, 1221
names of, eight given, 23
puruṣa-avatāras, 1075
sacrifice meant for, 115
symbols of, 23

Viṣṇu, Lord (*continued*)
temples of, origin of, 23
Vaikuṇṭha planets named for, 1393
worship of, 650
worship of form of, 1147
See also: Garbhodakaśāyī Viṣṇu; Kṛṣṇa, Lord; Nārāyaṇa, Lord; Supreme Lord; MahāViṣṇu; *Purusa-avatāras;* Supersoul
Viṣṇu-bhaktaḥ smṛto daiva
quoted, 388, 649
Viṣṇu demigod, 233
Viṣṇu-dharma, quoted on planets, 492
Viṣṇu Purāṇa, quoted on *varṇāśrama* system, 477-478
Viṣṇu Purāṇa
quoted on Brahman, 1041
quoted on Viṣṇu feature of Brahman, 1340
Viṣṇu Purāṇa, quotations from
on coverings of ignorance, 749
on Lord's energy, 947
Viṣṇusvāmi-sampradāya, 870
Viṣṇur ārādhyate panthā
verse quoted, 477-478
Viṣṇur brahma-svarūpeṇa svayam eva vyavasthitaḥ
quoted, 1340
Viśrambheṇa defined, 870-871
Viśuddham defined, 723
Viṣṇur mahān sa iha yasya kalā-viśeṣo, 289
verse quoted, 423
Viṣṇu-tattvas, 1323
Ādi-caturbhuja is, 34
defined, 212, 223
Lord expands as, 181
Viṣṭabhyāham idaṁ kṛtsnam
verse quoted, 217
Viśvāmitra, 527, 998, 1097
Viśvanātha Cakravartī Ṭhākura, quoted on mercy of Lord by mercy of spiritual master, 999
Viśvanātha Cakravartī Ṭhākura
cited on Brahmā's birth, 420
Viśvanātha Cakravartī Ṭhākura
as authority, 144
cited on burden of love, 101
cited on Kṛṣṇa's disappearance, 54
cited on *saṁsāra*, 793
cited on spiritual master's instruction, 921, 928-929
cited on success via spiritual master, 835, 836-37
cited on Supreme Lord via spiritual master, 876
Viśvāvasu, 764, 846, 847
Voidism
philosophy of, 1112
See also: Impersonalism
Vow of celibacy, 459
Vow of silence, 958
Vṛndāvana, 1008-1009
Vṛndāvana (Vraja)
cows in, 81
devotees ecstatic in, 24
as eternal place, 802-803
forest of, 79-80
Gauḍīya Vaiṣṇavas worship, 80
Goloka, 71
Kṛṣṇa as loved in, 81
Kṛṣṇa identical with, 2, 80
Kṛṣṇa never leaves, 34
Kṛṣṇa's identity in, 57
Kṛṣṇa's pastimes in, 63, 77-86
as pilgrimage place, 736, 889
See also: Goloka Vṛndāvana: Spiritual world
Vṛṣṇi, descendants of, intoxicated, 117
Vṛtra, 718
Vyāna air, 224
Vyāsadeva, 735, 797, 968
cited on Lord & His material energy, 1029
literatures by, 167, 170-171
parents of, 123, 178
Vyavasāyātmikā buddhir
quoted, 837
verse quoted, 213

W

War
 cause of, 21, 100, 101
 compared to bamboo fire, 21
 Kurukṣetra. *See:* Kurukṣetra, Battle of
 war materialists start, 676, 677, 679
 See also: Death; Killing; *Kṣatriyas*
Warfare, two types of, 516
Water, 1068
 See also: Elements; Evolution
Waters, spiritual. *See: names of specific lakes, oceans & rivers*
Wealth
 attachment for, 1173
 available to devotees, 129
 desire for, 330
 for devotee, 1101-1102
 false identification with, 1111
 for family maintenance, standard for obtaining, 1260
 in grains & cows, 82
 for householders, 1243, 1380
 in Kṛṣṇa's service, 1235, 1312
 as Lord's mercy, 858
 misuse of, as punishable, 1257-1258
 as predestined by *karma*, 1101
 proper & improper use of, 1257
 of pure devotee, 510
 sacrifice of, required, 1133
 satisfaction with, 1130, 1133
 sinfully acquired, as punishable, 1256-1260
 in spiritual world, 571
 suffering from lack of, 1244
 as temporary, 1235
 unsteady, 573
 See also: Economic development; Gold; Jewels; Money: Opulence; Possessions
Weather, 1018
Weather, bad, demoniac population causes, 660
Welfare work
 by *brāhmaṇas*, 114
 by devotees, 333
Welfare work
 devotional service as, 176
 by *gṛhasthas* (householders), 525, 586
 material & spiritual, 169
 by Nara-Nārāyaṇa, 137
 perfection of, 371
Well, blind, family life compared to, 957, 957-958
Wheel, time compared to, 795
Wife
 duty of, 524, 527, 840, 870-874, 877
 as enemy, 872
 faithless, 872
 good, lucky man has, 790
 husband as spiritual master of, 920
 husband attracted by, 881
 husband's debt to, 528
 husband's duty to, 909-910
 as jokingly glorified, 528, 529
 as man's better half, 526
 prostitute contrasted to, 536
 for *sannyāsī* forbidden, 956
 for sense gratification condemned, 526
 vānaprastha can keep, 956
 See also: Children; Family life; Householders; Mother; Parents; Woman; Marriage
Wind, demigod of, 1018
Winds at demons' birth, 659, 660
Women
 association with
  compared to blind well, 1304
  dangers of, 1302-1305
  in family life, 1303
  in Kṛṣṇa consciousness, 1306
  restricted, 1298-1300, 1302-1306
 attachments of, 1305
 attachment to, 1240, 1299-1302, 1306
 bathing directions for, 893
 beauty of, 758, 897, 929
 birth control needless for, 177
 corruption of, 527, 544
 demigods not allured by, 758-759
 demons pursue, 758, 761, 762
 as dependent, 854, 956

Women
devotional service open to, 997
discharge of, during sex, 907
in disturbed mind, 908
faithful to husbands, 39
form of, as *māyā*, 1304
impregnation of, 1264
intelligence of, 912, 921, 999
in Kṛṣṇa consciousness, 1306
Lord as son for, 1384-1385
man combined with, 930, 931
man contrasted to, 871
marriage of, 521, 522
material enjoyment sought by, 912
men mixing with, 448-449
origin of, **466**
pregnant, 1266-1267, 1272
protection for, 627, 969, 1377, 1382
as *puruṣa* or *prakṛti*, 975
sannyāsa forbids, 956
"sannyāsīs" seeking, 950
service from, dangers of, 1304
sex desire of, 804, 904
Śiva's mercy on, 541
son as husband's representative for, 1384
twilight taken as, 757-763
unmarried, worship Śiva, 870
in Vaikuṇṭha, 572
virgin, psychology of, 843
as widow, 1384
See also: Female; Girl; Wife: *Gopīs;* Marriage; Sex life
Work for devotee householders, 1259-1260
Work. *See:* Activities; Devotional service; Energy; Sacrifices; *Yoga*; Duty; *Karma: Śūdras*
World, material. *See:* Material world
World. *See:* Creation, the; Earth; Material world; Planets, material; Universe
Worship
by brāhmaṇas, 620
to cows, 84, 85
to demigods, 85, 698, 704, 789
Worship
to God & demigods compared, 195
God vs. demigod, 634
to God. *See:* Supreme Lord, worship of
to goddess Kālī, 216
highest form of, 533
to Kālī, 704
to material energy, 915
to Śiva for good husband, 870
to sun, 407
to Umā for good wife, 790
to Viṣṇu, **657**
See also: Deity form; Devotional service; Sacrifice; Supreme Lord, worship of; Vedic rituals
Worship of demigods. *See:* Demigods, worship of
Worship of Supreme Lord. *See:* Devotional service, of worship

Y

Yac-cakṣur eṣa savitā
quoted, 1078
Yac-cakṣur eṣa savitā sakala-grahāṇāṁ
verse quoted, 406
Yad gatvā na nivartante
quoted, 998, 1340
Yadā yadā hi dharmasya
quoted, 953
Yajñārthāt karmaṇo 'nyatra
quoted, 1117
Yajña-śiṣṭāśinah santaḥ
quoted, 1197
Yadus vs. Kurus, 845
Yadu dynasty
as burden of love, 101, 102
commander of, 28
conquests of, **9**, 10
disappearance of, 58, 102
intoxication destroyed, 117
Kṛṣṇa as Lord of, 8
Kṛṣṇa misunderstood by, 54, 55, 60
as spiritually cultured, 115

Yad-vijijñāsayā yuktā
verse quoted, 131
Yaḥ kāraṇārṇava-jale bhajati sma yoga-
verse quoted, 289
Yajña defined, 696, 857
See also: Sacrifices
Yajña. See: Sacrifice
Yajñārthāt karmaṇo 'nyatra
quoted, 914
Yakṣas, 749, 750-751, 751
Yama, 824, 899
Yam defined, 721
Yamarāja
punishes negligent guardians, 627
quoted on religion, 336
region of, 90
as Vidura, 178, 179
Yaṁ śyāmasundaram acintya-guṇa-svarūpaṁ
verse quoted, 25
Yamunā River
Kāliya poisoned, 84
Kṛṣṇa and Vasudeva crossing, 68
pilgrims bathe in, 889
scenery along, 79
Uddhava-Vidura meeting at, 24, 25
Yasmin vijñāte sarvam evaṁ vijñātaṁ bhavati
quoted, 281
Yas tādṛg eva hi ca Viṣṇutayā vibhāti
verse quoted, 328
Yasya prasādād bhagavat-prasādaḥ
quoted, 876
Yasyaika-niśvasita-kālam athāvalambya
verse quoted, 289, 423
Yasyājñayā bhramati saṁbhṛta-kāla-cakro
verse quoted, 406
Yasyopamāno na babhūva so 'cyuto
verse quoted, 492
Yatatām api siddhānām
quoted, 813
Yawning, Brahmā dropped form of, 765
Yayāti Mahārāja, 805
Yei kṛṣṇa-tattva-vettā, sei 'guru' haya
quoted, 239
Ye 'nye 'ravindākṣa vimukta-māninas
verse quoted, 335, 436
Yeṣām tv anta-gataṁ pāpaṁ
verse quoted, 17
Ye yathā māṁ prapadyante
quoted, 126, 338, 340
Yama & *niyama*, 1098
Yamadūtas, 1248-1249
Yamarāja, punishments of, 1249
Yamasādana, 1253
Yāmunācārya
cited on sex life, 1165
quoted on sex life, 1302
Yānti deva-vratā devān
quoted, 1353
Yasya prabhā prabhavataḥ
quoted, 1027
Yasya prasādād bhagavat prasādaḥ
quoted, 999
Yathārham upayañjataḥ
quoted, 1015
Yat karoṣi yad aśnāsi
quoted, 1352
"Yes," saying, to order of father or spiritual master, 928
Ye 'nye 'ravindākṣa vimukta-māninaḥ
quoted, 1016
Ye yathā māṁ prapadyante
quoted, 798
Yoga
aṣṭāñga-, 785, 786
authentic method of, 603-605
austerity valuable in, 1378
basis of, 549
bhakti, 787, 941
best, *bhakti* as, 978, 995, 998, 1019, 1098, 1339-1341
bhakti as basis of, 1350
bhakti-yoga. See: Devotional service
& bhakti-yoga compared, 1220-1221
bodily postures in, 773
bogus vs. bona fide, 721, 779, 786, 789, 934, 941-942

Yoga (*continued*)
bogus, vs. real, 979, 1130, 1161-1162
Brahmā created, 430
cheaters & cheated in, 781
defined, 760
detachment as basic principle of, 1341
direct, *bhakti* as, 1098
divisions of, eight named, 1373
eight divisions of, 778
eightfold process of, 31
exercise in, 1098
goal of, Lord as, 1389-1390
highest form of, 603
impersonalist's faulty view of, 1130, 1136, 1150, 1155, 1161-1162, 1168, 1178
jñāna-, 915
in Kali-yuga impractical, 781
karma-, 915
kinds & goals of, 998
kinds of, three compared, 1341-1342
Kṛṣṇa consciousness as perfection of, 1303
Lord as goal of, 1129, 1158, 1161
Lord only originates, 979
meditation in, 1221
as meditation on Lord Aniruddha, 1053-1054
for merging with the Lord, 70
perfections in, 581, 606, 780, 784-786, 882, 903, 941
real purpose of, 560
real, vs. bogus, 979, 1130, 1161, 1303
requirements in, 1130-1141
breath exercise, 1138-1139
celibacy, 1132-1134
duties, prescribed, 1130
eating frugally, 1132
fixing vision, 1141
hearing pastimes of Lord, 1135
honesty, 1133
life-air control, 1134-1135
meditation on Lord, 1140
meditation on Lord's form, 1142-1166
prāṇāyāma, 1140
religion for, 1132
Yoga
requirements in
satisfaction, 1131, 1133
scriptural reading, 1133
secluded & sanctified place, 1137
sense restraint, 1140
sitting postures, 1134, 1137
worship of Lord, 1133
worship of spiritual master, 1131
rebellious systems of, 348
sāṅkhya-, 925
sabīja, vs. *nirbīja*, 1167
as sense control, 1020
sense enjoyers ineligible for, 789, 821
sex life restricted in, 1303
smaraṇam in, 1158
stages of, eight listed, 1098
time obscured, 952
See also: Devotional service; Kṛṣṇa consciousness; Mystic *yoga*; Meditation on Kṛṣṇa Transcendence
Yoga indriya-saṁyamaḥ
quoted, 1097, 1119
Yoga-lakṣaṇa defined, 778
Yogamāyā
creation by, 180
for devotees, 388
Kṛṣṇa appeared by, 60
energy, 682, 796
Lord as curtained by, 615
Lord expands by, 96
opulence created by, 631-632
spiritual happiness via, 581
virāṭ form exhibited by, 246
Yoga-nidrā defined, 289, 418, 423, 426
Yoga-samādhi defined, 773
Yoga-siddhi defined, 408-409
Yogīs
best, *bhaktas* as, 1019
bogus vs. bona fide, 786, 789, 941-942
Brahmā worshiped by, 1325
death eluded by, 692
desire oneness, 70, 223

Yogīs
devotees contrasted to, 942
devotees as, 967
devotional service as perfection for, 984-985
devotees excel, 780, 902
expansive power of, 904
false, 1294, 1297
four kinds of, 635
longevity of, through celibacy, 1079
look for Lord's form, 787
Lord contrasted to, 904
Lord overpowers, 716
Lord seen by, 941
meditate on Lord, 721
perfections attainable by, 882
perfect vs. pretentious, 903
power of, 888, 895, 896
requirements for, detailed. *See: Yoga*, requirements in
see Lord in heart, 596
sex life victimizes, 527
as skinny, 821
so-called, encourage sex life, 761
space travel by, 903
travel via Ganges, 299
true & false, 608
visit Vaikuṇṭha, 650
See also: Devotees; Mystic powers; *Yoga yogis*; Transcendentalists
Yojana defined, 1252
Yonir mahad-brahma pradhāna as, 1038
as total elements, 1038
Yuktāhāra-vihārasya
quoted, 1388
Yudhiṣṭhira Mahārāja, 776, 806
Dhṛtarāṣṭra cheated, 7
as ideal king, 104, 105
Kṛṣṇa's reign under, 106
as religious, 35
tolerance of, 9
wife of, 6
as world emperor, 20
Yuga cycle, 733, 864, 939
See also: Dvāpara-yuga; Kali-yuga; Satya-yuga; Tretā-yuga
Yugas, duration of, 410
See also: Dvāpara-yuga; Kali-yuga; Satya-yuga; Tretā-yuga
Yuga-sandhyās defined, 410
Yuyudhāna, 30

Notes

Notes

Notes

Notes

Notes

Notes

Notes

Notes